Peterson's Scholarships, Grants & Prizes 2012

PETERSON'S
Publishing

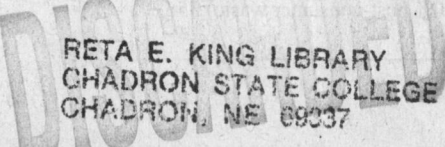

About Peterson's Publishing

Peterson's Publishing provides the accurate, dependable, high-quality education content and guidance you need to succeed. No matter where you are on your academic or professional path, you can rely on Peterson's print and digital publications for the most up-to-date education exploration data, expert test-prep tools, and top-notch career success resources—everything you need to achieve your goals.

Visit us online at **www.petersonspublishing.com** and let Peterson's help you achieve your goals.

For more information, contact Peterson's Publishing, 2000 Lenox Drive, Lawrenceville, NJ 08648; 800-338-3282 Ext. 54229; or find us online at www.petersonspublishing.com.

© 2011 Peterson's, a Nelnet company

Bernadette Webster, Director of Publishing; Mark D. Snider, Editor; John Wells, Research Project Manager; Jim Bonar, Research Associate; Phyllis Johnson, Programmer; Ray Golaszewski, Publishing Operations Manager; Linda M. Williams, Composition Manager

ISBN-13: 978-0-7689-3293-5
ISBN-10: 0-7689-3293-9

Printed in the United States of America

10 9 8 7 6 5 4 3 2 1   13 12 11

Sixteenth Edition

OTHER RECOMMENDED TITLES

Peterson's The Best Scholarships for the Best Sudents

Peterson's How to Get Money for College: Financing Your Future Beyond Federal Aid

Peterson's Paying for College: Answers to All Your Questions About Financial Aid, Scholarships, Tuition Payment Plans, and Everything Else You Need to Know

Contents

A Note from the Peterson's Editors

Billions of dollars are given to students and their families every year to help pay for college. Last year, private donors and governmental agencies made available billions of dollars in financial aid to help undergraduate students pay for college. Yet, to the average person, the task of finding financial aid awards in this huge network of scholarships, grants, and prizes appears to be nearly impossible.

For nearly forty years, Peterson's has given students and parents the most comprehensive, up-to-date information on how to get their fair share of the financial aid pie. *Peterson's Scholarships, Grants & Prizes* was created to help students and their families pinpoint those specific private financial aid programs that best match students' backgrounds, interests, talents, or abilities.

In *Peterson's Scholarships, Grants & Prizes*, you will find more than 4,000 award programs and resources that are providing financial awards to undergraduates in the 2011–12 academic year. Foundations, fraternal and ethnic organizations, community service clubs, churches and religious groups, philanthropies, companies and industry groups, labor unions and public employees' associations, veterans' groups, and trusts and bequests are all possible sources.

For those seeking to enter college, *Peterson's Scholarships, Grants & Prizes* includes information needed to make financing a college education as seamless as possible.

The **How to Find an Award That's Right for You** section paints a complete picture of the financial aid landscape, discusses strategies for finding financial awards, provides important tips on how to avoid scholarship scams, and offers insight into how to make scholarship management organizations work for you.

Also found in **How to Find an Award That's Right for You** is the "How To Use This Guide" article, which describes how the more than 4,000 awards in the guide are profiled, along with information on how to search for an award in one of eleven categories.

If you would like to compare awards quickly, refer to the **Quick-Reference Chart.** Here you can search through "Scholarships, Grants & Prizes At-a-Glance" and select awards by the highest dollar amount.

In the **Profiles of Scholarships, Grants & Prizes** section you'll find updated award programs, along with information about award sponsors. The profile section is divided into three categories: *Academic Fields/Career Goals, Nonacademic/Noncareer Criteria,* and *Miscellaneous Criteria.* Each profile provides all of the need-to-know information about available scholarships, grants, and prizes.

Finally, the back of the book features thirteen **Indexes** listing scholarships, grants, and prizes based on award name; sponsor; academic fields/career goals; civic, professional, social, or union affiliation; corporate affiliation; employment/volunteer experience; impairment; military service; nationality or ethnic background; religious affiliation; residence; location of study; and talent/interest area.

At the end of this book, don't miss the special section of ads placed by Peterson's preferred clients. Their financial support helps make it possible for Peterson's Publishing to continue to provide you with the highest-quality test-prep, educational exploration, and career-preparation resources you need to succeed on your educational journey.

Join the financial aid conversation on Facebook® and Twitter™ at www.facebook.com/pay4undergrad and www.twitter.com/pay4undergrad and receive additional scholarship and award advice. Peterson's resources are available to help you do your best on these important exams—and others in your future.

Peterson's publishes a full line of books—financial aid, career preparation, test prep, and education exploration. Peterson's publications can be found at high school guidance offices, college libraries and career centers, and your local bookstore and library. Peterson's books are now also available as eBooks.

We welcome any comments or suggestions you may have about this publication. Your feedback will help us make educational dreams possible for you—and others like you.

HOW TO FIND AN AWARD THAT'S RIGHT FOR YOU

All About Scholarships

Dr. Gary M. Bell
Academic Dean, Honors College, Texas Tech University

During the next four (or more) years you will spend earning your college baccalaureate degree, think of the learning task as your primary employment. It is helpful to think of a scholarship as part of the salary for undertaking your job of learning. One of your first inquiries as you examine a potential college setting is about the type of assistance it might provide given your interests, academic record, and personal history. Talk to a financial aid officer or a scholarship coordinator at the school. At most schools, these are special officers—people specifically employed to assist you in your quest for financial assistance. Virtually all schools also have brochures or publications that list scholarship opportunities at their institution. Get this literature and read it carefully.

Also, visit your local bookstore or public library for books that have several hundred scholarships listed in different categories. These books are inexpensive and can be found in the reference section. Excellent information is also available on the Web at http://www.petersons.com/ finaid.

Last, high school counselors often have keen insight into resources available at colleges, especially for the schools in your area. These people are the key points of contact between institutions of higher education and you.

In general, it is not a good idea to use a private company that promises to provide you with a list of scholarships for which you might be eligible. Such lists are often very broad, and you can secure the same results by using available high school, university, Web-based, and published information. The scholarship search you perform online will probably be more fruitful than what any private company can do for you.

What do we mean by the word "scholarship," anyway? In the very broadest sense, scholarships consist of outright grants of monetary assistance to eligible students to help them attend college. The money is applied to tuition or the cost of living while in school. Scholarships do not need to be repaid. They do, however, often carry stringent criteria for maintaining them, such as the achievement of a certain grade point average, the carrying of a given number of class hours, matriculation in a specific program, or membership in a designated group. Scholarships at many schools may be combined with college work-study programs, in which some work is also required. Often, scholarships are combined with other forms of financial aid so that collectively they provide you with a truly attractive financial aid package. This may include low-interest loan programs to make the school of your choice financially feasible.

Scholarships generally fall into three major categories: *need-based scholarships*, predicated on income; *merit-based scholarships*, based on your academic and sometimes extracurricular achievements; and *association-based scholarships*, which are dependent on as many different associations as you can imagine (for instance, your home county, your identification with a particular group, fraternal and religious organizations, or the company for which a parent may work). The range of reasons for which scholarships are given is almost infinite.

Most schools accommodate students who have financial need. The largest and best grant programs are the U.S. government-sponsored Federal Pell Grants and the Federal Supplemental Educational Opportunity Grants, which you might want to explore with your financial aid counselor. There is also the Academic Competitiveness Grant (ACG) that is open to Pell Grant recipients who have attended a "rigorous" high school program. Also inquire about state-sponsored scholarship and grant programs.

Merit-based scholarships come from a variety of sources—the university, individual departments or colleges within the university, state scholarship programs, or special donors who want to assist worthy students. Remember this as you meet with your financial aid officer, because he or she knows that different opportunities may be available for you as a petroleum engineering, agriculture, accounting, pre-veterinary, or performing arts major. Merit-based scholarships are typically designed to reward the highest performers on such precollege measures as standardized tests (the SAT or ACT) and high school grades.Because repeated performance on standardized tests often leads to higher scores, it may be financially advantageous for you to take these college admission tests several times.

Inquire about each of the three categories of scholarships. The association-based scholarships can sometimes be particularly helpful and quite surprising.

Employers of parents, people from specific geographic locations, or organizations (churches, civic groups, unions, special interest clubs, and even family name associations) may provide assistance for college students. Campus scholarship literature is the key to unlocking the mysteries of association-based financial assistance (and the other two categories as well), but personal interviews with financial officers are also crucial.

There are several issues to keep in mind as you seek scholarship assistance. Probably the most important is to determine deadlines that apply to a scholarship for which you may be eligible. It's wise to begin your search early, so that your eligibility is not nullified by missing a published deadline. Most scholarship opportunities require that you complete an application form, and it is time well spent to make sure your answers are neat, grammatically correct, and logical. Correct spelling is essential. Have someone proofread your application. Keep in mind that if applications require essays, fewer students typically take the time to complete these essays, and this gives those students who do so a better chance of winning that particular scholarship. Always be truthful in these applications, but at the same time provide the most positive self-portrayal to enhance your chances of being considered. Most merit-based and association-based scholarships are awarded competitively.

Finally, let the people who offer you assistance know whether you will accept their offer. Too many students simply assume that a scholarship offer means automatic acceptance. This is not the case! In most instances, you must send a letter of acknowledgement and acceptance. Virtually all schools have agreed that students must make up their minds about scholarship acceptance no later than May 1, but earlier deadlines may apply.

As you probably know, tuition at private schools is typically higher than tuition at state colleges and universities. Scholarships can narrow this gap. Many private institutions have a great deal of money to spend on scholarship assistance, so you may find that with a scholarship, going to a private college will cost no more than attending a state-supported college or university. **Note:** A substantial scholarship from a private school may still leave you with a very large annual bill to cover the difference between the scholarship amount and the actual cost of tuition, fees, and living expenses.

When you evaluate a scholarship, take into account your final out-of-pocket costs. Also consider the length of time for which the school extends scholarship support. Be cautious about schools that promise substantial assistance for the first year to get you there, but then provide little or nothing in subsequent years. The most attractive and meaningful scholarships are offered for four to five years. Do not abandon the scholarship search once you are enrolled at the school of your choice. Often, a number of additional scholarship opportunities are available for you once you're enrolled, especially as you prove your ability and interest in a given field.

A Strategy for Finding Awards

Private scholarships and awards can be characterized by unpredictable, sometimes seemingly bizarre, criteria. Before you begin your award search, write a personal profile of yourself to help establish as many criteria as possible that might form a basis for your scholarship award. Here is a basic checklist of fifteen questions you should consider:

1. What are your career goals?

Be both narrow and broad in your designations. If, for example, you aim to be a TV news reporter, you will find many awards specific to this field in the *TV/Radio Broadcasting* section. However, collegiate broadcasting courses are offered in departments or schools of communication. So, be sure that you consider *Communications* as a relevant section for your search. Consider *Journalism,* too, for the same reasons. Then look under other broadly inclusive but possibly relevant areas, such as *Trade/Technical Specialties.* Or check a related but different field, such as *Performing Arts.* Finally, look under marginally related basic academic fields, such as *Humanities, Social Sciences,* or *Political Science.* We make every attempt to provide the best cross-reference aids, but the nuances of specific awards can be difficult to capture even with the most flexible cross-referencing systems. You will need to be broadly associative in your thinking to get the most out of this wealth of information.

If you have no clear career goal, browsing the huge variety of academic/career awards may well spark new interest in a career path. Be open to imagining yourself filling different career roles that you previously may not have considered.

2. In what academic fields might you major?

Your educational experiences or your sense about your personal talents or interests may have given you a good idea of what academic discipline you wish to pursue. Again, use both broad and narrow focuses in designing your search, and look at related subject fields. For example, if you want to major in history, check the *History* section, but be sure to check out *Social Sciences* and *Humanities* as well, and maybe *Area/Ethnic Studies. Education,* for example, could suggest the perfect scholarship for a future historian.

3. In which jobs, industries, or occupations have your parents or other members of your immediate family been employed? What employment experiences do you have?

Individual companies, employee organizations, trade unions, government agencies, and industry associations frequently establish scholarships for workers, children of workers, or other relatives of workers from specific companies or industries. These awards might require that you stay in the same career field, but most are offered regardless of the field of study you wish to undertake. Also, if one of your parents is a public service employee, especially a firefighter or police officer, you have many relevant awards from which to choose.

4. Do you have any hobbies or special interests? Have you ever been an officer or leader of a group? Do you possess special skills or talents? Have you won any competitions? Are you a good writer?

From bowling to clarinet playing, from caddying to ham radio operating, your special interests can win awards for you from groups that wish to promote and/or reward these pursuits. Many scholarships are targeted to "student leaders," including sports team captains; yearbook or newspaper editors; student government officers; and club, organization, and community activists.

5. Where do you live? Where have you lived? Where will you go to college?

Residence criteria are among the most common qualifications for scholarship aid. Local clubs and companies provide millions of dollars in scholarship aid to students who live in a particular state, province, region, or section of a state. This means that your residential identity puts you at the head of the line for these grants. State of residence can—depending on the sponsor's criteria—include the place of your official residence, the place you attend college, the place you were born, or anywhere you have lived for more than a year.

6. What is your family's ethnic heritage?

Hundreds of scholarships have been endowed for students who can claim a particular nationality or racial or ethnic descent. Partial ethnic descent frequently qualifies, so don't be put off if you do not think of your identity as a specific "ethnic" entity. Awards are available for Colonial American,

English, Welsh, Scottish, European, and other backgrounds that students may not consider especially "ethnic." One is even available for descendants of signers of the Declaration of Independence, whatever ethnicity that might have turned out to be some ten generations later.

7. **Do you have a physical disability?**
Many awards are available to individuals with physical disabilities. Of course, commonly recognized impairments of mobility, sight, communication, and hearing are recognized, but learning disabilities and chronic diseases, such as asthma and epilepsy, are also criteria for some awards.

8. **Do you currently or have you ever served in the Armed Forces? Did one of your parents serve? In a war? Was one of your parents lost or disabled while serving in the Armed Forces?**
Hundreds of awards use these qualifications.

9. **Do you belong to a civic association, union, or religious organization? Do your parents belong to such a group?**
Hundreds of clubs and religious groups provide scholarship assistance to members or children of members.

10. **Are you male or female?**

11. **What is your age?**

12. **Do you qualify for need-based aid?**

13. **Did you graduate in the upper one-half, upper one-third, or upper one-quarter of your class?**

14. **Do you plan to attend a two-year college, a four-year college, or a trade/technical school?**

15. **In what academic year will you be entering?**

Be expansive when considering your possible qualifications. Although some awards may be small, you may

Scholarship Management Organizations

Richard Woodland
Former Director of Financial Aid, Rutgers University–Camden

The search for private scholarships can be confusing and frustrating for parents and students. Many families feel that they just don't know how to go about the process, so they either hire a private scholarship search company or simply give up. The success rate of many scholarship search firms is not good, and college financial aid professionals always warn parents to be skeptical of exaggerated claims.

The process also confuses many donors. A corporation may want to help its employees or the children of its employees, or may want to offer a national scholarship program to its customers or the general public. Unfortunately, the corporation may not want to devote valuable administrative time to managing a scholarship program. Similarly, many donors sat to target their funds to a particular group of students but simply do not know how.

Stepping in to help are scholarship management organizations. Although many have been around for a long time, most people know very little about them because scholarship management organizations often do not administer scholarship funds directly to students. Rather, they serve as a clearinghouse for their member donor organizations. Today, savvy parents and students can go online to find these organizations and the scholarship programs they administer.

Two of the largest scholarship management programs are the National Merit Scholarship Corporation and Scholarship America. The National Merit Scholarship Corporation sponsors a competitive scholarship program that seeks to identify and reward the top students in the nation. High school students who meet published entry/participation requirements enter these competitions by taking the Preliminary SAT/National Merit Scholarship Qualifying Test (PSAT/NMSQT®), usually as juniors. A particular year's test is the entry vehicle to a specific annual competition. For example, the 2011 PSAT/NMSQT was the qualifying test for entry into competitions for scholarships to be awarded in 2013. For more information, visit http://www.nationalmerit.org.

Another major player is Scholarship America, which has distributed more than $2.5 billion dollars to more than 1.7 million students since its founding more than fifty years ago. Scholarship America has become the nation's largest private-sector scholarship and educational support organization by involving communities, corporations, organizations, and individuals in the support of students through its major programs, Dollars for Scholars and Scholarship Management Services. Working with national leaders in response to the September 11th tragedy and with corporations such as Kohl's and Best Buy, Scholarship America is an important organization that helps thousands of students every year. For more information, go to http://scholarshipamerica.org.

In addition to the National Merit Scholarship Fund and Scholarship America, other organizations raise funds and administer scholarships for specific groups of students. These organizations include:

- American Indian College Fund
  www.collegefund.org
- Hispanic Scholarship Fund
  www.hsf.net
- United Negro College Fund
  www.uncf.org
- Organization of Chinese Americans
  www.ocanational.org
- National FFA Organization (Future Farmers of America) **www.ffa.org**
- Gates Millennium Scholars
  www.gmsp.org

In addition to using scholarship search engines, think broadly about your background, your interests, your family connections (work, religious, fraternal organizations), and your future career plans. Then spend some time browsing the Web. We hope that some of the sources mentioned here will help. Remember, the key is to start early (junior year in high school is best) and be persistent.

Winning the Scholarship with a Winning Essay

Who knew it was going to be this hard? You've already dealt with SO much: the SAT, doing community service, excelling in your AP class, etc. Convincing your parents that you will be fine 1,500 miles from home and that each and every one of those college application fees are, yes, absolutely necessary! Learning calculus for goodness sake!

And now in front of you—yet, for right now, somehow out of reach—the golden ticket to make it all come true. Just 500 words (more or less) separate you from those hallowed halls: It's the scholarship essay.

IS IT REALLY THAT EASY?

Much as you may feel like, c'mon, I'm worth it, just give me the scholarship money, we all know it just doesn't work like that. Because you know what—lots of students are worth it! And lots of students are special, just like you! And where does that leave a scholarship selection committee in deciding to whom their money should be awarded? Yes, now you are catching on—they will pour over *everyone's* scholarship essay.

So, first and foremost, write your scholarship essay in a way that makes it EASY for the scholarship-awarding committees to do their job! It's almost like a partnership—you show them (in 500 words, more or less) why YOU ARE THE MOST WORTHY RECIPIENT and they say, thank you, you are right, here is a scholarship for you and everyone wins! Easy, right?

SORRY, IT REALLY ISN'T THAT EASY

What? You are still sitting there in front of a blank computer screen with nary a thought or sentence? Understood. It's really not that easy. That, too, is part of the point.

No doubt that your GPA, SAT scores, volunteer efforts, leadership roles, and community service are immensely important, but again, you must remember that, during the process of selecting an award recipient, pretty much all the applicants are going to be stellar on some level. And so the scholarship-awarding committee uses your essay to see what sets you apart from the crowd. They are looking for a reason to select you over everyone else.

Your scholarship essay serves many purposes. You have to convince the scholarship-awarding committee you are able to:

- Effectively communicate through the written word
- Substantiate your merit and unique qualities
- Follow directions and adhere to guidelines

A winning scholarship essay can mean up to tens of thousands of dollars for your college education, so let's get started on putting that money in YOUR hands!

EFFECTIVE WRITTEN COMMUNICATION

Be Passionate

Let's face it—you have already written lots of essays. And, we won't tell, but most were probably about topics that were as interesting to you as watching paint dry, right? But you plowed through them and even managed to get some good grades along the way. You may think about just "plowing through" your scholarship essay the same way—mustering up the same amount of excitement you feel when you have to watch old home movies of your Aunt Monica on her summer camping trips. But that would be a huge mistake!

An important feature of all winning essays is that they are written on subjects about which the author is truly passionate. Think about it—it actually takes a good bit of effort to fake passion for a subject. But when you are genuinely enthusiastic about something, the words and thoughts flow much more easily and your passion and energy naturally shine through in your writing. Therefore, when you are choosing your scholarship essay topic, be sure it is something you truly care about and can show your affinity for—keeping both you and your reader interested and intrigued!

Be Positive

You've probably heard the expression: "If you don't have anything nice to say, don't say anything at all." Try to steer clear of essays that are too critical, pessimistic, or antagonistic. This doesn't mean that your essay shouldn't acknowledge a serious problem or that everything has to have a happy ending. But it does mean that you should not just write about the negative. If you are writing about a problem, present solutions. If your story doesn't have a happy ending, write about what you learned from the experience and how you would do things differently if faced with a similar situation in the future. Your optimism is what makes the scholarship-awarding committee excited about giving you money to pursue your dreams. Use positive language and be proud to share yourself and your accomplishments. Everyone likes an uplifting story and even scholarship judges want to feel your enthusiasm and zest for life.

Be Clear and Concise

Don't fall into the common essay-writing trap of using general statements instead of specific ones. All scholarship judges read at least one essay that starts with "Education is the key to success." And that means nothing to them. What does mean something is writing about how your 10th grade English teacher opened your eyes to the understated beauty and simplicity of haiku—how less can be more—and how that then translated into you donating some of your old video games to a homeless shelter, where you now volunteer once a month. That's powerful stuff! It's a very real story, clearly correlating education to a successful outcome. Focusing on a specific and concise example from your life helps readers relate to you and your experiences. It also guarantees you bonus points for originality!

Edit and Proofread and Then Edit and Proofread

There is an old saying: "Behind every good writer is an even better editor." Find people (friends, siblings, coaches, teachers, guidance counselors) to read your essay, to provide feedback on how to make it better, and to edit it for silly, sloppy mistakes. Some people will read your essay and find issues with your grammar. Others will read your essay and point out how one paragraph doesn't make sense in relation to another paragraph. Some people will tell you how to give more examples to better make your point. All of those people are giving you great information, and you need to take it all in and use it to your advantage! However, don't be overwhelmed by it, and don't let it become all about what everyone else thinks. It's your essay and your thoughts—the goal of editing and proofreading is to clean up the rough edges and make the entire essay shine!

And when you do get to that magical point where you think "DONE!"—instead, just put the essay aside for a few days. Come back to it with an open mind and read, edit, and proofread it one last time. Check it one last time for spelling and grammar fumbles. Check it one last time for clarity and readability (reading it out loud helps!). Check it one last time to ensure it effectively communicates why you are absolutely the winning scholarship candidate!

YOUR UNIQUE QUALITIES

It's one thing to help out at the local library a few hours a week; it's a completely different thing if you took it upon yourself to suggest, recruit, organize, and lead a fundraising campaign to buy 10 new laptops for kids to use at the library!

And don't simply rattle off all your different group memberships. Write about things you did that demonstrate leadership and initiative within those groups—did you recruit new members or offer to head up a committee or find a way for the local news station to cover your event or reach out to another organization and collaborate on an activity? Think about your unique qualities and how you use them to bring about change.

A SLICE OF YOUR LIFE

While one goal of your essay is surely to explain why you should win the scholarship money, an equally important goal is to reveal something about you, something that makes it easy to see why you should win. Notice we said to reveal "something" about you and not "everything" about you. Most likely, the rest of the scholarship application gathers quite a bit of information about you. The essay is where you need to hone in on just one aspect of your unique talents, one aspect of an experience, one aspect of reaching a goal. It's not about listing all your accomplishments in your essay (again, you probably did that on the application). It's about sharing a slice of your life—telling your story and giving your details about what makes YOU memorable.

YOUR ACCOMPLISHMENTS, LOUD AND PROUD

Your extracurricular activities illustrate your personal priorities and let the scholarship selection committee know what's important to you. Being able to elaborate on your accomplishments and awards within those activities certainly bolsters your chances of winning the scholarship. Again, though, be careful to not just repeat what is already on the application itself. Use your essay to focus on a specific accomplishment (or activity or talent or award) of which you are most proud.

Did your community suffer through severe flooding last spring? And did you organize a clothing drive for neighbors who were in need? How did that make you feel? What feedback did you get? How did it inspire your desire to become a climatologist?

Were school budget cuts going to mean the disbanding of some afterschool clubs? Did you work with teachers and parents to write a proposal to present to the school board, addressing how new funds could be raised in order to save the clubs? How did that make you feel? What feedback did you get? How did it inspire you to start a writing lab for junior high kids?

You have done great things—think about that one special accomplishment and paint the picture of how it has made you wiser, stronger, or more compassionate to the world around you. Share the details!

But Don't Go Overboard

A five hanky story may translate into an Oscar-worthy movie, but rarely does it translate into winning a scholarship. If your main reason for applying for the scholarship is that you feel you deserve the money because of how much suffering you have been through, you need a better reason. Scholarship selection committees are not really interested in awarding money to people with problems; they want to award money to people who solve problems. While it's just fine to write about why you need the scholarship money to continue your education, it's not fine for your essay to simply be a laundry list of family tragedies and hardships.

So, instead of presenting a sob story, present how you have succeeded and what you have accomplished despite the hardships and challenges you faced. Remember that everyone has faced difficulties. What's unique about you is how YOU faced your difficulties and overcame them. That is what makes your essay significant and memorable.

FOLLOWING DIRECTIONS

Does Your Essay Really Answer the Question?

Have you ever been asked one question but felt like there was another question that was really being asked? Maybe your dad said something like, "Tell me about your new friend Logan." But what he really meant to ask you was, "Tell me about your new friend Logan. Do his lip rings and tattoos mean he's involved in things I don't want you involved in?"

The goal of every scholarship judge is to determine the best applicant out of a pool of applicants who are all rather similar. Pay attention and you'll find that the essay question is an alternate way for you to answer the real question the scholarship-awarding committee wants to ask. For instance, an organization giving an award to students who plan to study business might ask, "Why do you want to study business?" But their real underlying question is, "Why are you the best future business person to whom we should give our money?" If there is a scholarship for students who want to become doctors, you can bet that 99 percent of the students applying want to become doctors. And if you apply for that scholarship with an essay simply delving into your lifelong desire to be a potter, well, that doesn't make you unique, it makes you pretty much unqualified for that opportunity. Be sure to connect your personal skills, characteristics, and experiences with the objectives of the scholarship and its awarding organization.

Does Your Essay Theme Tie In?

Let's say that you are applying for a community service-based award and, on the application, you go ahead and list all the community service groups you belong to and all the awards you have won. But in your essay, you write about how homeless people should find a job instead of sitting on street corners begging for money. Hey—everyone is entitled to their opinion, but would you agree that there is some sort of disconnect between your application and your essay? And no doubt you have made the scholarship-awarding committee wonder the same thing.

So how do you ensure your essay doesn't create a conflicting message? You need to examine the theme of your essay and how it relates both to your application and the reason the scholarship exists in the first place. If the scholarship-funding organization seeks to give money to someone who wants a career in public relations and your essay focuses on how you are not really a "people person," well, you can see how that sends a mixed message to your reader.

Think about it this way: The theme of your essay should naturally flow around the overarching purpose or goal of the organization awarding the scholarship money. Once you have clarified this nugget, you can easily see if and how your words tie in to the organization's vision of whom their scholarship winner is.

Three More Pieces of Advice

1. Follow the essay length guidelines closely. You certainly don't want your essay disqualified simply because it was too long or too short!

2. The deadline is the deadline. A day late and you could certainly be more than a dollar short in terms of the award money that isn't going to be awarded to you if your application is not received by the due date. Begin the essay writing process well in advance of the scholarship deadline. Writing and editing and rewriting takes time so you should probably allow yourself at least 2 weeks to write your scholarship essay.

3. Tell the truth. No need to say anything further on that, right? Right.

Getting in the Minority Scholarship Mix

Did you know that a great duck call can win you scholarship money in the Chick and Sophie Major Memorial Duck Calling Contest?

Web site: http://www.stuttgartarkansas.org/index.php?
fuseaction= p0004.&mod=45

Perhaps duck calling is not your calling but creativity with Duck brand duct tape is. If so, the "Stuck at Prom" scholarship may be just for you—design promware for you and your date and win some moola!

Web site: http://www.duckbrand.com/Promotions/
stuck-at-prom/Rules.aspx

How about this tall order? Tall Clubs International awards scholarships to men who are taller than 6'2" or women who are taller than 5'10".

Web site: http://www.tall.org/scholarships.cfm

Oh, not necessarily the minority group you had in mind? That's OK because guess what? In this day and age, just about everyone is a minority of some sort. It all depends on a scholarship benefactor's definition of minority.

In the college realm, the word "minority" takes on myriad meanings. One definition of a minority which often springs to mind is of someone of an underrepresented ethnicity, such as Native Americans, African Americans, or Hispanic Americans. No question there. Similarly though, a minority can be someone pursuing an underrepresented college major, such as paranormal research. Think that all scholarships for minorities target United States–specific groups? Think again. For example, Canadian students, whether they plan to study at home or abroad, can qualify for scholarships for aboriginals. Getting the picture? The key is to use your own unique qualities as you search for scholarships. Think about your gender, your family's economic status, your religious background and your geographic locale just to start the ball rolling. Once you broadly frame your search

along those lines you'll quickly see how easily you can qualify for a scholarship!

AM I REALLY A MINORITY?

No matter the source—federal, state, professional organization, private endowment, corporate donor, college, or university—they all offer minority scholarships, looking to create diversity and inclusion in an increasingly global marketplace.

It's more than probable that you fit into at least one of the ever-expanding minority scholarship categories—nearly everyone does—by some broadly based definition of minority. Some of the niche scholarship "minorities" have already been mentioned. Now let's take a look at some of the broader categories—one of which likely fits you!

African American Students

While African Americans make up a large U.S. minority group, they are still met with one of the biggest barriers to college enrollment—money. To combat that challenge, scholarships for African American students have grown over the years, with some of the best sources of funding found within partnerships between minority organizations and corporate sponsors.

As the nation's largest minority education organization, the United Negro College Fund (UNCF) provides operating funds for 39-member historically black colleges and universities (HBCUs), along with scholarships and internships for students at about 900 institutions. The UNCF has helped more than 350,000 students attend and graduate college with the more than $3.2 billion it has raised—more funds helping minorities attend college than any other entity outside of the U.S. government.

United Negro College Fund
8260 Willow Oaks Corporate Drive
P.O. Box 10444
Fairfax, VA 22031-8044
Phone: 800-331-2244
Web site: www.uncf.org

Hispanic American Students

Fortunately, over the years, the U.S. government has contributed $15 million dollars toward startup costs for the development of Hispanic universities and colleges and $70 million toward already established Hispanic universities and colleges. The effort has been paying off with dramatic increases in college enrollment by Hispanic American students. Scholarship programs for Hispanic American students look to increase the number of Hispanic students studying in subject areas most underrepresented by them, for instance, the sciences, engineering, math, and technology.

As the nation's leading Hispanic higher-education fund, the Hispanic Scholarship Fund (HSF) works to remove the barriers keeping many Hispanic American students from earning a college degree. Over the past 35 years, HSF has awarded more than $300 million in scholarships and supported a wide range of outreach and education programs for both college students and their families.

Hispanic Scholarship Fund
55 Second Street, Suite 1500
San Francisco, CA 94105
Phone: 877-HSF-INFO (877-473-4636)
E-mail: scholar1@hsf.net
Web site: www.hsf.net

Asian American Students

Identifying yourself as Asian American means you probably consider yourself Cambodian, Hmong, Laotian, Malaysian, Okinawan, Tahitian, or Thai—just to name a few possibilities. As a somewhat smaller, yet growing, minority group, Asian Americans attend college more than any other minority group and tend to stay in college once they have enrolled. Excellent merit-based aid sources for Asian American students include cultural organizations, university departments such as law and journalism, and professional organizations.

The Asian & Pacific Islander American Scholarship Fund (APIASF), founded in 2003, is the nation's largest 501(c)(3) nonprofit organization providing scholarships to Asian and Pacific Islander Americans with financial need.

The Asian & Pacific Islander American Scholarship Fund
1900 L Street NW, Suite 210
Washington, DC 20036

Phone: 202-986-6892
Phone (toll-free): 877-808-7032
Fax: 202-530-0643
E-mail: info@apiasf.org
Web site: http://apiasf.org/

Native American Students

Native American (inclusive of American Indians and Native Alaskans) students make up the smallest minority population on college campuses. As you explore scholarship opportunities for Native Americans, you may find that you'll need proof of your Native American status, which means your Certificate of Indian Blood (CIB), as well as belonging to a well-recognized tribe. If you are like most Native American descendants, though, you will probably not have this proof, as many tribes change names and have nonexistent documentation records. If somehow you do have a CIB and belong to a tribe, you may have an upper hand in qualifying for some more esoteric scholarship and grant programs.

The American Indian College Fund puts its mark on Indian higher education through its funding and creation of awareness of the unique, community-based accredited Tribal Colleges and Universities. The Fund awards about 6,000 annual scholarships to American Indian students seeking to better their lives through education.

The American Indian College Fund
8333 Greenwood Boulevard
Denver, CO 80221
Phone: 303-426-8900
Phone (toll-free): 800-776-3863
Web site: www.collegefund.org/

Interracial Students

There is an interesting trend in minority scholarships where scholarship-funding organizations seek to include students of mixed heritage, blended cultures, and students whose ethnic backgrounds don't fit neatly into one particular category. Search for prizes tagged as "interracial scholarships," "multicultural scholarships," or "multiethnic scholarships."

Gay, Lesbian, Bisexual, and Transgender Students

Gay, lesbian, bisexual, and transgender (GLBT) students are recognized as a legitimate minority and many colleges and organizations offer scholarships to this group.

As a GLBT student, also be on the lookout for scholarship opportunities for sons and daughters of gay and lesbian parents, as well as friends and allies of the GLBT community.

Since its inception in 2001, the Point Foundation has invested more than $3 million in outstanding gay, lesbian, bisexual, and transgender students. An average Point Scholarship is about $13,600 and covers tuition, books, supplies, room and board, transportation, and living expenses.

Point Foundation
5757 Wilshire Boulevard, Suite 370
Los Angeles, CA 90036
Phone: 323-933-1234
Fax: 866-397-6468
E-mail: info@pointfoundation.org
Web site: www.pointfoundation.org

EVERYONE NEEDS A GOOD RESOURCE

From specialized databases to award programs serving as umbrella organizations for numerous other organizations and awards, many resources are out there, all with one goal—to help you find the money you need to get you on your college path.

Minority On-Line Information Service (MOLIS)

MOLIS, a service of the Federal Information Exchange (FEDIX), provides information about minority institutions and also includes a database of scholarship and fellowship opportunities for minority students.

Web site: www.molis.org/

CHCI

CHCI provides a free, comprehensive list of scholarships, internships, and fellowships for Hispanic students.

Web site: www.chci.org/doclib/20112141737204152-CHCIDirectory6thEdition.pdf?trail=201142719432

Gates Millennium Scholars

The Gates Millennium Scholars program was founded by a grant from the Bill and Melinda Gates Foundation with the intention of increasing the number of African Americans, Native Americans, Asian Americans, and Hispanic Americans enrolling in and completing undergraduate and graduate degree programs.

Gates Millennium Scholars
P.O. Box 10500
Fairfax, VA 22031-8044
Phone (toll-free): 877-690-4677
Web site: www.gmsp.org

GETTING CREATIVE WITH MINORITY SCHOLARSHIPS

Now that you are really thinking outside of the box, you may consider one or more of your outstanding features as the conduit to classifying yourself as a minority.

And if you still need some more inspiration:

- Juniata College in Pennsylvania offers a scholarship for left-handed students.
- Little People of America offers a scholarship to adult students who are 4'10" or shorter.
- There are even scholarships for white males offered by a non-profit group in Texas—as controversial as that sounds!

Be creative and get in the mix! To which minority groups do *you* belong?

Scholarship Scams: What They Are and What to Watch Out For

Several hundred thousand students seek and find scholarships every year. Most students' families require some outside help to pay for tuition costs. Although most of this outside help, in the form of grants, scholarships, low-interest loans, and work-study programs, comes either from the state and federal government or the colleges themselves, scholarships from private sources are an extremely important component of this network. An award from a private source can tilt the scales weighing whether a student can afford to attend a specific college during a particular year. Unfortunately for prospective scholarship seekers, the private-aid sector is virtually without patterns or rules. It has, over many years, become a patchwork of individual programs, each with its own award criteria, timetables, application procedures, and decision-making processes. It requires considerable effort to understand and effectively benefit from private scholarships.

Regrettably, the combination of an urgency to locate money, limited time, and the complex and bewildering scholarship system has created opportunities for fraud. It has been estimated that for every 10 students who receive a legitimate scholarship, one is victimized by a fraudulent scheme or scam that poses as a legitimate foundation, scholarship sponsor, or scholarship search service. Every year, hundreds of thousands of families are cheated out of millions of dollars in various scholarship scams.

These fraudulent businesses advertise in campus newspapers, distribute flyers, mail letters and postcards, provide toll-free phone numbers, and have Web sites. The most obvious frauds operate as scholarship search services or scholarship clearinghouses. Another segment sets up as a scholarship sponsor, pockets the money from the fees that are paid by thousands of hopeful scholarship seekers, and returns little, if anything, in proportion to the amount it collects. A few of these scams inflict even greater harm by gaining access to individual credit or checking accounts with the intent to extort funds.

A typical mode of operation is for a fraudulent firm to send out an extensive mailing to college and high school students, claiming that the company has either a scholarship or a scholarship list for the students. These companies often provide toll-free numbers. When recipients call, they are told by high-pressure telemarketers that the company has unclaimed scholarships and that for fees ranging from $10 to $400 the callers get back at least $1000 in scholarship money or the fee will be refunded. Customers who pay, if they receive anything at all, are mailed a list of sources of financial aid that are no better than, and are in many cases inferior to, what can be found in *Peterson's Scholarships, Grants & Prizes* or any of the other major scholarship guides available in bookstores and libraries or on the Web. The "lucky" recipients have to apply on their own for the scholarships. Many of the programs are contests, loans, or work-study programs rather than gift aid. Some are no longer in existence, have expired deadlines, or set eligibility requirements that students cannot meet. Customers who seek refunds have to demonstrate that they have applied in writing to each source on the list and received a rejection letter from each of them. Frequently, even when customers can provide this almost impossible-to-obtain proof, they do not receive refunds. In the worst cases, the companies ask for consumers' checking account or credit card numbers and take funds without authorization.

The Federal Trade Commission (FTC) warns students and their parents to be wary of fraudulent search services that promise to do all the work for you.

"Bogus scholarship search services are just a variation of the 'you have won' prize-promotion scam, targeted to a particular audience—students and parents who are anxious about paying for college," says Jodie Bernstein, former director of the FTC's Bureau of Consumer Protection. "They guarantee students and their families free scholarship money... all they have to do to claim it is pay an up-front fee."

Legitimate scholarship search services do exist. However, a scholarship search service cannot truthfully guarantee that a student will receive a scholarship, and students almost always fare as well or better by doing their own homework using a reliable scholarship information source, such as *Peterson's Scholarships, Grants & Prizes*, than by wasting money—and more important, time— with a search service that promises a scholarship.

The FTC warns scholarship seekers to be alert for these seven warning signs of a scam:

1. **"This scholarship is guaranteed or your money back."**

   No service can guarantee that it will obtain a grant or scholarship for you. Refund guarantees often have impossible conditions attached. Review a service's refund policies in writing before you pay a fee. Typically, fraudulent scholarship search services require that applicants show rejection letters from each of the sponsors on the list they provide. If a sponsor no longer exists, if it really does not provide scholarships, or if it has a rolling application deadline, letters of rejection are almost impossible to obtain.

2. **"The scholarship service will do all the work."**

   Unfortunately, nobody else can fill out the personal information forms, write the essays, and supply the references that many scholarship applications require.

3. **"The scholarship will cost some money."**

   Be wary of any charges related to scholarship information services or individual scholarship applications, especially in significant amounts. Some legitimate scholarship sponsors charge fees to defray their processing expenses. True scholarship sponsors, however, should distribute money, not make it from application fees. Before you send money to apply for a scholarship, investigate the sponsor.

4. **"You can't get this information anywhere else."**

   In addition to Peterson's, scholarship directories from other publishers are available in any large bookstore, public library, or high school guidance office.

   Additional information on private scholarship programs can be found at www.petersons.com/finaid.

5. **"You are a finalist" in a contest you never entered, or "You have been selected by a national foundation to receive a scholarship."**
   Most legitimate scholarship programs almost never seek out particular applicants. Most scholarship sponsors will only contact you in response to your inquiry. Most lack the budget and mandate to do anything more than this. If you think that any real possibility exists that you may have been selected to receive a scholarship, investigate before you send any money. Make sure the sponsor or program is legitimate.

6. **"The scholarship service needs your credit card or checking account number in advance."**
   Never provide your credit card or bank account number over the phone to the representative of an organization that you do not know. A legitimate need-based scholarship program will not ask for your personal account numbers. Get information in writing first. Note: An unscrupulous operation does not need your signature on a check. Some schemes can drain a victim's account with unauthorized withdrawals without the account holder's signature.

7. **"You are invited to a free seminar (or interview) with a trained financial aid consultant who will unlock the secrets of how to make yourself eligible for more financial aid."**
   Sometimes these consultants offer good tips on preparing for college, but often they are trying to get you to sign a long-term contract for services you don't need. Often, these "consultants" are trying to sell you other financial products, such as annuities, life insurance, or other services that have little to do with college aid. By doing your own research using books from Peterson's or other respected organizations, using the Web, and working with your high school guidance office and the college financial aid office, you will get all the help you need to a thoroughly research the financing of your college education.

In addition to the FTC's seven signs of a scam, keep these points in mind when considering a scholarship program:

- Fraudulent scholarship operations often use official-sounding names containing words such as "federal," "national," "administration," "division," "federation," and "foundation." Their names are often a slight variation on a name of a legitimate government or private organization. Do not be fooled by a name that seems reputable or official, by an official-looking seal, or by a Washington, D.C., address.

- If you win a scholarship, you will receive official written notification by mail, not over the phone. If the sponsor calls to inform you of your award, it will follow up with a letter in the mail. If you receive a request for money via phone, the operation is probably fraudulent.
- Be wary if an organization's address is a post office box number or a residential address. If a bona fide scholarship program uses a post office box number, it will usually include a street address and phone number on its stationery.
- Beware of phone numbers with a 900 area code. These may charge you a fee of several dollars a minute for a call that could be a long recording providing only a list of addresses or names.
- A dishonest operation may pressure an applicant by claiming that awards are given on a first-come, first-served basis. Some scholarship programs give preference to early applicants; however, if you are told—especially over the phone—that you must respond quickly, but that you will not hear about the results for several months, you should be suspicious.
- Be wary of endorsements. Fraudulent operations claim endorsements by groups with names similar to well-known private or government organizations. The Better Business Bureau (BBB) and other government agencies do not endorse businesses.

If an organization requires that you pay a fee for a scholarship, and you have never heard of the organization before and cannot verify that it is a legitimate operation, the best advice is to pay nothing. If you have already paid money to such an organization and now have reason to doubt its legitimacy, call your bank to stop payment on your check if possible, or call your credit card company and explain that you think you are the victim of consumer fraud.

To find out how to recognize, report, and stop a scholarship scam, contact:

Federal Trade Commission
Consumer Response Center
600 Pennsylvania Avenue, N.W.
Washington, D.C. 20580
Web site: www.ftc.gov

The Better Business Bureau (BBB) maintains files of businesses about which it has received complaints. Call your local BBB office and the BBB office where the organization in question is located; each local BBB has different records. Call 703-276-0100 to get the phone number of your local BBB, or log on to www.bbb.org for a directory of local BBBs and downloadable BBB complaint forms. The national address is:

The Council of Better Business Bureaus
4200 Wilson Boulevard, Suite 800
Arlington, VA 22203-1838

Many wonderful and legitimate scholarships are available to qualified students who spend the time and effort to locate and apply for them. However, exercise caution in using scholarship search service, and when you must pay money, always use careful judgment when considering a scholarship program's sponsor.

How to Use This Guide

The more than 4,000 award programs described in this book are organized into eleven broad categories that represent the major factors used to determine eligibility for scholarships, awards, and prizes. To build a basic list of awards available to you, look under the broad category or categories that fit your particular academic goals, skills, personal characteristics, or background. The categories are:

- Academic Fields/Career Goals
- Civic, Professional, Social, or Union Affiliation
- Corporate Affiliation
- Employment/Volunteer Experience
- Impairment
- Military Service
- Nationality or Ethnic Heritage
- Religious Affiliation
- Residence/Location of Study
- Talent/Interest Area
- Miscellaneous Criteria

The **Academic Fields/Career Goals** category is subdivided into 131 subject areas that are organized alphabetically by award sponsor. The *Military Service* category is subdivided alphabetically by branch of service. All other categories are organized A to Z by the name of the award sponsor.

Full descriptive profiles appear in only one location in the book. Cross-references to the name and page number of the full descriptive profile appear at other locations under the other relevant categories for the award. The full description appears in the first relevant location in the book and cross-references later locations, so you will always be redirected toward the front of the book.

Your major field of study and career goals have central importance in college planning. As a result, we have combined these into a single category and have given this category precedence over the others. The **Academic Fields/Career Goals** section appears first in the book. If an academic major or career area is a criterion for a scholarship, the description of this award will appear in this section.

Within the **Academic Fields/Career Goals** section, cross-references are only from and to other academic fields or career areas. They are not provided to this section from the other ten categories. You will be able to locate relevant awards from nonacademic or noncareer criteria through the indexes in the back of this book.

For example, the full descriptive profile of a scholarship for any type of engineering student who resides in Ohio, Pennsylvania, or West Virginia might appear under *Aviation/Aerospace*, which happens to be the first engineering category heading in the **Academic Fields/Career Goals** section. Cross-references to this first listing may occur from any other relevant engineering or technological academic field subject area, such as *Chemical Engineering, Civil Engineering, Electrical Engineering/Electronics, Engineering-Related Technologies, Engineering/Technology, Mechanical Engineering,* or *Nuclear Science.* There would not be a cross-reference from the *Residence* category. However, the name of the award will appear in the Residence index under Ohio, Pennsylvania, and West Virginia. Check each of the indexes relevant to your search to get the most out of the guide's listings.

Within the major category sections, descriptive profiles are organized alphabetically by the name of the sponsoring organization. If more than one award from the same organization appears in a particular section, the awards are listed alphabetically under the sponsor name, which appears only once, by the name of the first award.

HOW THE PROFILES ARE ORGANIZED

Here are the elements of a full profile:

Name of Sponsoring Organization

These appear alphabetically under the appropriate category. In most instances, acronyms are given as full names. However, occasionally a sponsor will refer to itself by an acronym. In these instances, we present the sponsor's name as an acronym.

World Wide Web Address

Award Name

Brief Textual Description of the Award

Academic Fields/Career Goals (only in the Academic Fields/Career Goals section of the book)

This is a list of all academic or career subject terms that are assigned to this award.

Award

Is it a scholarship? A prize for winning a competition? A forgivable loan? For what type and for what years of college can it be used? Is it renewable or is it for only one year?

Eligibility Requirements

Application Requirements

What information do you need to supply to be considered? What are the deadlines?

Contact

If provided by the sponsor, this element includes the name, mailing address, phone and fax numbers, and e-mail address of the person to contact for information about a specific award.

USING THE INDEXES

The alphabetical indexes in the back of the book are designed to aid your search. Two are name indexes. One lists scholarships alphabetically by academic fields and career goals. The other ten indexes supply access by nonacademic and noncareer criteria. The indexes give you the page number of the descriptions of relevant awards regardless of the part of the book in which they appear.

These are the indexes:

> Award Name
> Sponsor
> Academic Fields/Career Goals
> > [131 subject areas, from Academic Advising to Women's Studies]
> Civic, Professional, Social, or Union Affiliation
> Corporate Affiliation
> Employment/Volunteer Experience
> Impairment
> Military Service

> Nationality or Ethnic Heritage
> Religious Affiliation
> Residence
> Location of Study
> Talent/Interest Area

In general, when using the indexes, writing down the names and page numbers of the awards that you are interested in is an effective technique.

DATA COLLECTION PROCEDURES

Peterson's takes its responsibility to its readers as a provider of trustworthy information very seriously. Peterson's administered an electronic survey between January and May 2011 in order to update information from all programs listed within this guide. All collected data was updated between January and May 2011. Additional award program data was obtained between January 2008 and May 2011. Peterson's research staff makes every effort to verify unusual figures and resolve discrepancies. Nonetheless, errors and omissions are possible in a data collection endeavor of this scope. Also, facts and figures, such as number and amount of awards, can suddenly change, or awards can be discontinued by a sponsoring organization. Therefore, readers should verify data with the specific sponsoring agency responsible for administering these awards before applying.

CRITERIA FOR INCLUSION IN THIS BOOK

The programs listed in this book have the primary characteristics of legitimate scholarships: verifiable sponsor addresses and phone numbers, appropriate descriptive materials, and fees that, if required, are not exorbitant. Peterson's assumes that these fees are used to defray administrative expenses and are not major sources of income.

QUICK REFERENCE CHART

Scholarships, Grants & Prizes At-a-Glance

This chart lists award programs that indicate that their largest award provides more than $2000. The awards are ranked in descending order on the basis of the dollar amount of the largest award. Because the award criteria in the "Academic Fields/Career Goals and Nonacademic/Noncareer Criteria" column may represent only some of the criteria or limitations that affect eligibility for the award, you should refer to the full description in the award profiles to ascertain all relevant details.

Award Name	Page Number	Highest Dollar Amount	Lowest Dollar Amount	Number of Awards	Academic Fields/Career Goals and Nonacademic/Noncareer Criteria
Army ROTC Green to Gold Scholarship Program for Two-Year, Three-Year and Four-Year Scholarships, Active Duty Enlisted Personnel	622	$130,000	$10,000	300–400	Military Service: Army.
Intel Science Talent Search	864	$100,000	$7500	40	Must be in high school.
Careers Through Culinary Arts Program Cooking Competition for Scholarships	209	$90,000	$1000	50–70	Culinary Arts; Hospitality Management. Residence: Arizona; California; Illinois; Maryland; New York; Pennsylvania; Virginia.
SME Family Scholarship	298	$80,000	$5000	1–10	Engineering/Technology.
Terry Foundation Scholarship	793	$76,000	$19,000	208–650	Residence: Texas. Studying in Texas. Talent/Interest Area: leadership.
UNCF/Merck Science Initiative	145	$70,000	$25,000		Biology; Chemical Engineering; Environmental Science; Health and Medical Sciences; Natural Sciences; Neurobiology; Physical Sciences. Limited to Black (non-Hispanic) students.
Elks National Foundation Most Valuable Student Scholarship Contest	816	$60,000	$4000	500	Talent/Interest Area: leadership.
Davidson Fellows Scholarship Program	398	$50,000	$10,000	15–20	Literature/English/Writing; Mathematics; Music; Philosophy; Science, Technology, and Society.
Intel International Science and Engineering Fair	864	$50,000	$500	1	Must be in high school.
Miss America Organization Competition Scholarships	820	$50,000	$2000	70	Talent/Interest Area: beauty pageant.
National Security Agency Stokes Educational Scholarship Program	198	$50,000	$1000	15–20	Computer Science/Data Processing; Electrical Engineering/Electronics; Foreign Language; Mathematics.
U.S. Army ROTC Four-Year Nursing Scholarship	444	$50,000	$5000	250	Nursing. Military Service: Army; Army National Guard.
Young Epidemiology Scholars Competition	304	$50,000	$1000	120	Environmental Health; Health and Medical Sciences; Public Health.
Kentucky Transportation Cabinet Civil Engineering Scholarship Program	177	$44,000	$10,600	15–25	Civil Engineering. Residence: Kentucky. Studying in Kentucky.
Tuition Exchange Scholarships	597	$41,000	$4000	5,000–7,000	Employment/Volunteer Experience: teaching.
Boettcher Foundation Scholarships	719	$40,000	$13,000	40	Residence: Colorado. Studying in Colorado. Talent/Interest Area: leadership.
Mas Family Scholarship Award	152	$40,000	$8000	5–10	Business/Consumer Services; Chemical Engineering; Civil Engineering; Communications; Economics; Electrical Engineering/Electronics; Engineering-Related Technologies; International Studies; Journalism; Materials Science, Engineering, and Metallurgy; Mechanical Engineering. Nationality: Latin American/Caribbean. Limited to Hispanic students.

Award Name	Page Number	Highest Dollar Amount	Lowest Dollar Amount	Number of Awards	Academic Fields/Career Goals and Nonacademic/Noncareer Criteria
National Academy of Television Arts and Sciences John Cannon Memorial Scholarship	187	$40,000	$1000	1–10	Communications; TV/Radio Broadcasting.
Ron Brown Scholar Program	678	$40,000	$10,000	10–20	Talent/Interest Area: leadership. Limited to Black (non-Hispanic) students.
U.S. Army ROTC Four-Year College Scholarship	623	$40,000	$9000	1,000–2,000	Military Service: Army; Army National Guard.
U.S. Army ROTC Four-Year Historically Black College/University Scholarship	602	$40,000	$9000	20–200	Disability: physically disabled. Military Service: Army; Army National Guard.
Science, Mathematics, and Research for Transformation Defense Scholarship for Service Program	93	$39,000	$22,000	200	Applied Sciences; Engineering-Related Technologies; Engineering/Technology; Mathematics; Physical Sciences.
Undergraduate Research STEM Scholarships	96	$35,000	$8500	1–35	Applied Sciences; Aviation/Aerospace; Biology; Chemical Engineering; Computer Science/Data Processing; Electrical Engineering/Electronics; Engineering-Related Technologies; Materials Science, Engineering, and Metallurgy; Mathematics; Mechanical Engineering; Physical Sciences; Science, Technology, and Society. Studying in Virginia.
Master's Scholarship Program	169	$32,000	$25,000	1–15	Chemical Engineering; Computer Science/Data Processing; Electrical Engineering/Electronics; Engineering/Technology; Materials Science, Engineering, and Metallurgy. Limited to American Indian/Alaska Native; Black (non-Hispanic); Hispanic students.
Environmental Protection Scholarship	141	$30,000	$15,000	1–2	Biology; Chemical Engineering; Civil Engineering; Earth Science; Environmental Science; Hydrology; Mechanical Engineering; Natural Sciences. Studying in Kentucky.
Florida Association of Post-secondary Schools and Colleges Scholarship Program	736	$30,000	$1000	1–400	Residence: Florida. Studying in Florida.
The Frank M. and Gertrude R. Doyle Foundation, Inc.	849	$30,000	$500	varies	
Los Alamos Employees' Scholarship	754	$30,000	$1000	50	Residence: New Mexico.
South Carolina Police Corps Scholarship	390	$30,000	$7500	20	Law Enforcement/Police Administration.
Voice of Democracy Program	832	$30,000	$1000	54	Talent/Interest Area: public speaking; writing.
Queen Elisabeth Competition	426	$26,749	$1337	varies	Music. Talent/Interest Area: music; music/singing.
Princess Grace Awards in Dance, Theater, and Film	314	$25,000	$5000	15–25	Filmmaking/Video; Performing Arts.
Sons of Italy National Leadership Grants Competition General Scholarships	680	$25,000	$5000	8–14	Nationality: Italian.
U.S. Army ROTC Military Junior College (MJC) Scholarship	418	$25,000	$2705	110–150	Military and Defense Studies. Disability: physically disabled. Military Service: Army; Army National Guard.
Illinois Restaurant Association Educational Foundation Scholarships	210	$24,000	$750	50–70	Culinary Arts; Food Science/Nutrition; Food Service/Hospitality; Hospitality Management. Employment/Volunteer Experience: food service; hospitality. Residence: Illinois.
National FFA Collegiate Scholarship Program	552	$22,000	$1000	1,500–1,600	Civic Affiliation: Future Farmers of America.
American Academy of Chefs Chaine des Rotisseurs Scholarship	207	$21,000	$1000	10	Culinary Arts; Food Service/Hospitality.
Accenture American Indian Scholarship	654	$20,000	$2000	10	Limited to American Indian/Alaska Native students.
Coca-Cola Scholars Program	842	$20,000	$10,000	250	Must be in high school.
Gates Millennium Scholars Program	654	$20,000	$500	150	Talent/Interest Area: leadership. Limited to American Indian/Alaska Native students.

Award Name	Page Number	Highest Dollar Amount	Lowest Dollar Amount	Number of Awards	Academic Fields/Career Goals and Nonacademic/Noncareer Criteria
GlaxoSmithKline Opportunity Scholarship	795	$20,000	$5000	1–10	Residence: North Carolina. Studying in North Carolina.
Greenhouse Scholars	743	$20,000	$500	8–20	Residence: Colorado. Talent/Interest Area: leadership.
Horatio Alger Scholarship Programs	851	$20,000	$2500	784	Must be in high school.
Kermit B. Nash, Jr. Academic Scholarship	613	$20,000	$5000	1	Disability: physically disabled.
Milton Fisher Scholarship for Innovation and Creativity	862	$20,000	$1000	5–8	
Primary Care Resource Initiative for Missouri Loan Program	136	$20,000	$5000	100	Behavioral Science; Dental Health/Services; Food Science/Nutrition; Health and Medical Sciences; Nursing; Psychology. Residence: Missouri. Studying in Missouri.
Samsung American Legion Scholarship	634	$20,000	$1000	98	Military Service: General.
Society of Women Engineers Scholarships	299	$20,000	$1000	1–130	Engineering/Technology.
Verizon Foundation Scholarship	581	$20,000	$5000	250	Corporate Affiliation.
Washington Crossing Foundation Scholarship	482	$20,000	$1000	5–10	Political Science; Public Policy and Administration.
Maryland Association of Private Colleges and Career Schools Scholarship	153	$19,950	$500	50	Business/Consumer Services; Computer Science/Data Processing; Dental Health/Services; Engineering/Technology; Food Science/Nutrition; Home Economics; TV/Radio Broadcasting; Trade/Technical Specialties. Residence: Maryland. Studying in Maryland.
American Legion Department of Kansas High School Oratorical Contest	806	$18,000	$150	4	Talent/Interest Area: public speaking.
American Legion National High School Oratorical Contest	808	$18,000	$1500	54	Talent/Interest Area: public speaking.
Critical Needs Teacher Loan/Scholarship	241	$15,506	$5514	varies	Education; Foreign Language; Mathematics; Special Education. Studying in Mississippi.
Air Force ROTC College Scholarship	616	$15,000	$9000	2,000–4,000	Military Service: Air Force.
Armenian Relief Society Undergraduate Scholarship	655	$15,000	$13,000	varies	Nationality: Armenian.
Blade Your Ride Scholarship Program	862	$15,000	$5000	3–5	
Community Foundation Scholarship Program	729	$15,000	$1000	100–150	Residence: Florida.
First in Family Scholarship	750	$15,000	$12,500	10	Residence: Alabama. Studying in Alabama.
GuildScholar Award	606	$15,000	$10,000	16	Disability: visually impaired.
Jesse Brown Memorial Youth Scholarship Program	586	$15,000	$5000	12	Employment/Volunteer Experience: community service; helping handicapped.
Lowe's Educational Scholarship	590	$15,000	$1000	375	Employment/Volunteer Experience: community service. Talent/Interest Area: leadership.
McFarland Charitable Nursing Scholarship	448	$15,000	$1000	3–5	Nursing.
National Beta Club Scholarship	552	$15,000	$1000	213	Civic Affiliation: National Beta Club.
National Black MBA Association Graduate Scholarship Program	856	$15,000	$2500	10–25	
National Black MBA Association PhD Scholarship Program	672	$15,000	$5000	1–2	Limited to Black (non-Hispanic) students.
Pennsylvania Institute of Certified Public Accountants Sophomore Scholarship	70	$15,000	$1000	60–85	Accounting. Residence: Pennsylvania. Studying in Pennsylvania.
Pride Foundation Scholarship Program	783	$15,000	$1000	90–130	Residence: Alaska; Idaho; Montana; Oregon; Washington. Talent/Interest Area: LGBT issues.
Texas 4-H Opportunity Scholarship	793	$15,000	$1500	225	Residence: Texas. Studying in Texas. Talent/Interest Area: animal/agricultural competition.

Award Name	Page Number	Highest Dollar Amount	Lowest Dollar Amount	Number of Awards	Academic Fields/Career Goals and Nonacademic/Noncareer Criteria
Tribal Priority Award	666	$15,000	$2500	1–5	Limited to American Indian/Alaska Native students.
Howard P. Rawlings Educational Excellence Awards Guaranteed Access Grant	757	$14,800	$400	1,000	Residence: Maryland. Studying in Maryland.
American Angus Auxiliary Scholarship	856	$14,000	$1000	10	Must be in high school.
DeVry Dean's Scholarships	845	$13,500	$1500	varies	Must be in high school.
National Space Grant College and Fellowship Program	97	$13,333	$1250	1–50	Applied Sciences; Aviation/Aerospace; Chemical Engineering; Civil Engineering; Computer Science/Data Processing; Earth Science; Engineering/Technology; Mathematics; Mechanical Engineering; Natural Sciences; Physical Sciences. Residence: Nevada. Studying in Nevada.
National Honor Society Scholarships	552	$13,000	$1000	200	Civic Affiliation: National Honor Society.
Legislative Scholarship	776	$12,995	$2000	275	Residence: Ohio. Studying in Ohio.
Airline Pilots Association Scholarship Program	523	$12,000	$1000	1–3	Civic Affiliation: Airline Pilots Association.
Humane Studies Fellowships	185	$12,000	$2000	140–180	Communications; Economics; History; Humanities; Law/Legal Services; Literature/English/Writing; Political Science; Social Sciences.
Kappa Alpha Theta Foundation Merit Based Scholarship Program	547	$12,000	$1000	200–230	Civic Affiliation: Greek Organization.
Massachusetts AFL-CIO Scholarship	758	$12,000	$250	100–150	Residence: Massachusetts. Studying in Massachusetts.
National Italian American Foundation Category I Scholarship	673	$12,000	$2500	varies	Nationality: Italian.
National Italian American Foundation Category II Scholarship	107	$12,000	$2500	varies	Area/Ethnic Studies. Talent/Interest Area: Italian language.
Principal's Leadership Award	824	$12,000	$1000	100	Talent/Interest Area: leadership.
U.S. Army ROTC Guaranteed Reserve Forces Duty (GRFD), (ARNG/USAR) and Dedicated ARNG Scholarships	602	$12,000	$10,000	800–1,000	Disability: physically disabled. Military Service: Army National Guard.
U.S. Department of Education Fulbright-Hays Project Abroad Scholarship for Programs in China	117	$12,000	$1000	1–20	Asian Studies; Education. Talent/Interest Area: foreign language.
Entitlement Cal Grant B	721	$11,853	$700	56,200	Residence: California. Studying in California.
Law Enforcement Personnel Dependents Scholarship	584	$11,853	$100	varies	Employment/Volunteer Experience: police/firefighting. Residence: California. Studying in California.
Seneca Nation Higher Education Program	680	$11,000	$6000	varies	Limited to American Indian/Alaska Native students.
SPIE Educational Scholarships in Optical Science and Engineering	96	$11,000	$2000	100–150	Applied Sciences; Chemical Engineering; Electrical Engineering/Electronics; Engineering-Related Technologies; Engineering/Technology; Materials Science, Engineering, and Metallurgy; Mechanical Engineering.
Frank O'Bannon Grant Program	790	$10,992	$200	48,408–70,239	Residence: Indiana. Studying in Indiana.
Vermont Incentive Grants	798	$10,800	$500	varies	Residence: Vermont.
Competitive Cal Grant A	721	$10,302	$4370	1,000–2,000	Residence: California. Studying in California.
AG Bell College Scholarship Program	599	$10,000	$1000	10–25	Disability: hearing impaired.
A Legacy of Hope Scholarships for Survivors of Childhood Cancer	791	$10,000	$500	1–6	Residence: Colorado; Montana.
Alton Higgins, MD and Dorothy Higgins Scholarship	349	$10,000	$5000	varies	Health and Medical Sciences. Limited to Black (non-Hispanic) students.
American Dental Hygienists' Association Institute Research Grant	216	$10,000	$1000	1	Dental Health/Services. Civic Affiliation: American Dental Hygienist's Association.

Award Name	Page Number	Highest Dollar Amount	Lowest Dollar Amount	Number of Awards	Academic Fields/Career Goals and Nonacademic/Noncareer Criteria
American Legion National Headquarters Eagle Scout of the Year	583	$10,000	$2500	4	Employment/Volunteer Experience: community service.
Arkansas Governor's Scholars Program	715	$10,000	$4000	375	Residence: Arkansas. Studying in Arkansas.
"Atlas Shrugged" Essay Contest	840	$10,000	$50	84	
California Junior Miss Scholarship Program	720	$10,000	$500	25	Residence: California. Talent/Interest Area: beauty pageant; leadership; public speaking.
California Masonic Foundation Scholarship Awards	720	$10,000	$1000	50–60	Residence: California.
Carmen V. D'Anna Memorial Scholarship of the Mars Supermarket Educational Fund	724	$10,000		1	Residence: Maryland. Studying in Maryland.
Christianson Grant	852	$10,000	$2500	8	
Cystic Fibrosis Scholarship	602	$10,000	$1000	40–50	Disability: physically disabled.
DC Tuition Assistance Grant Program	733	$10,000	$2500	7,000	Residence: District of Columbia.
Director's Scholarship Award	296	$10,000	$1000	1–5	Engineering/Technology. Talent/Interest Area: leadership.
Doc Hurley Scholarship	734	$10,000	$2000	varies	Residence: Connecticut.
Eagle Scout of the Year Scholarship	532	$10,000	$1000	1	Civic Affiliation: Boy Scouts. Residence: Nebraska.
E. Wayne Kay Community College Scholarship Award	297	$10,000	$1000	1–20	Engineering/Technology; Trade/Technical Specialties.
Executive Women International Scholarship Program	846	$10,000	$1000	75–100	Must be in high school.
ExploraVision Science Competition	830	$10,000	$5000	varies	Talent/Interest Area: science.
Federation of American Consumers and Travelers Graduating High School Senior Scholarship	541	$10,000	$2500	2	Civic Affiliation: Federation of American Consumers and Travelers.
Federation of American Consumers and Travelers In-School Scholarship	847	$10,000	$2500	2	
Federation of American Consumers and Travelers Second Chance Scholarship	847	$10,000	$2500	2	
Fisher Broadcasting Inc. Scholarship for Minorities	150	$10,000	$1000	5	Business/Consumer Services; Journalism; TV/Radio Broadcasting. Limited to ethnic minority students.
Girls Going Places Entrepreneurship Award Program	819	$10,000	$1000	15	Talent/Interest Area: entrepreneurship; leadership.
Hellenic Times Scholarship Fund	664	$10,000	$500	30–40	Nationality: Greek.
Herman O. West Foundation Scholarship Program	576	$10,000	$2500	1–7	Corporate Affiliation.
The Hirsch Family Scholarship	844	$10,000	$2000		
Hispanic College Fund Scholarship Program	665	$10,000	$500	500–600	Limited to Hispanic students.
Holocaust Remembrance Project Essay Contest	819	$10,000	$300	30	Talent/Interest Area: writing.
HORIZONS Scholarship	419	$10,000	$500	5–6	Military and Defense Studies.
HSF/General College Scholarship Program	665	$10,000	$1000	2,900–3,500	Nationality: Hispanic; Latin American/Caribbean; Mexican; Spanish. Limited to Hispanic students.
Illinois Future Teachers Corps Program	238	$10,000	$5000		Education. Residence: Illinois. Studying in Illinois.
James R. Hoffa Memorial Scholarship Fund	544	$10,000	$1000	1–100	Civic Affiliation: International Brotherhood of Teamsters.

Award Name	Page Number	Highest Dollar Amount	Lowest Dollar Amount	Number of Awards	Academic Fields/Career Goals and Nonacademic/Noncareer Criteria
Janet L. Hoffmann Loan Assistance Repayment Program	241	$10,000	$1500	700	Education; Law/Legal Services; Nursing; Social Services; Therapy/Rehabilitation. Residence: Maryland. Studying in Maryland.
John Lennon Scholarship Program	420	$10,000	$5000	3	Music. Talent/Interest Area: music.
Lee-Jackson Educational Foundation Scholarship Competition	752	$10,000	$1000	27	Residence: Virginia. Talent/Interest Area: writing.
Legislative Essay Scholarship	732	$10,000	$1000	62	Residence: Delaware.
Les Dames d'Escoffier Scholarship	212	$10,000	$2500	3	Culinary Arts; Food Science/Nutrition; Food Service/Hospitality.
LIFE Lessons Scholarships Program	854	$10,000	$1000	51	
Marine Corps Scholarship Foundation	570	$10,000	$500	1,000–1,500	Civic Affiliation: American Legion or Auxiliary; Boy Scouts. Military Service: Marine Corps.
Medicus Student Exchange	681	$10,000	$2000	1–10	Nationality: Swiss. Talent/Interest Area: foreign language.
Miller Electric International World Skills Competition Scholarship	264	$10,000	$1000	1	Engineering-Related Technologies; Engineering/Technology; Materials Science, Engineering, and Metallurgy; Trade/Technical Specialties.
Minnie Pearl Scholarship	604	$10,000		1	Disability: hearing impaired.
NAAS Awards	550	$10,000	$200	10–14	Civic Affiliation: National Academy of American Scholars.
Nancy Lorraine Jensen Memorial Scholarship	170	$10,000	$2500	1–6	Chemical Engineering; Electrical Engineering/Electronics; Mechanical Engineering. Nationality: Norwegian. Talent/Interest Area: science.
National Aviation Explorer Scholarships	123	$10,000	$3000	5	Aviation/Aerospace. Talent/Interest Area: aviation; leadership.
National Peace Essay Contest	373	$10,000	$1000	50–53	International Studies; Peace and Conflict Studies. Talent/Interest Area: writing.
National Society of Women Engineers Scholarships	200	$10,000	$1000	varies	Computer Science/Data Processing; Engineering/Technology.
NBFAA Youth Scholarship Program	593	$10,000	$500	varies	Employment/Volunteer Experience: police/firefighting. Residence: California; Connecticut; Georgia; Indiana; Kentucky; Louisiana; Maryland; Minnesota; New Jersey; New York; North Carolina; Pennsylvania; Tennessee; Virginia; Washington.
Needham and Company September 11th Scholarship Fund	857	$10,000	$7000	8–15	
Nightingale Awards of Pennsylvania Nursing Scholarship	456	$10,000	$6000	6	Nursing. Studying in Pennsylvania.
NRA Youth Educational Summit (YES) Scholarships	856	$10,000	$1000	1–6	Must be in high school.
Oracle Community Impact Scholarship	691	$10,000	$5000		Residence: California. Limited to Black (non-Hispanic) students.
Patriot's Pen	831	$10,000	$1000	46	Talent/Interest Area: writing.
Phelan Art Award in Filmmaking	314	$10,000	$5000	3	Filmmaking/Video.
Phelan Art Award in Video	314	$10,000	$5000	3	Filmmaking/Video.
Ronald Reagan College Leaders Scholarship Program	826	$10,000	$1000	100	Talent/Interest Area: leadership.
San Diego Pathways to College Scholarship	596	$10,000	$1000	25	Employment/Volunteer Experience: community service. Residence: California. Studying in California.
Sir John M. Templeton Fellowships Essay Contest	852	$10,000	$1000	6	
Soroptimist Women's Opportunity Award	865	$10,000	$500	varies	
Spencer Scholarship	370	$10,000	$5000	10–20	Insurance and Actuarial Science.

Award Name	Page Number	Highest Dollar Amount	Lowest Dollar Amount	Number of Awards	Academic Fields/Career Goals and Nonacademic/Noncareer Criteria
Stephen Phillips Memorial Scholarship Fund	791	$10,000	$3000	150–200	Residence: Connecticut; Maine; Massachusetts; New Hampshire; Rhode Island; Vermont.
Swanson Scholarship	800	$10,000	$1000	1–10	Residence: Nebraska.
Tailhook Educational Foundation Scholarship	626	$10,000	$2000	50	Military Service: Coast Guard; Marine Corps; Navy.
Talbots Women's Scholarship Fund	866	$10,000	$1000	5–50	
Technical Minority Scholarship	171	$10,000	$1000	122	Chemical Engineering; Computer Science/Data Processing; Electrical Engineering/Electronics; Engineering-Related Technologies; Engineering/Technology; Materials Science, Engineering, and Metallurgy; Mechanical Engineering; Physical Sciences. Limited to ethnic minority students.
Teletoon Animation Scholarship	115	$10,000	$5000	9	Arts; Filmmaking/Video. Residence: Alberta; British Columbia; Manitoba; New Brunswick; Newfoundland; North West Territories; Nova Scotia; Ontario; Prince Edward Island; Quebec; Saskatchewan.
"The Fountainhead" Essay Contest	840	$10,000	$50	236	Must be in high school.
Theodore R. and Vivian M. Johnson Scholarship Program for Children of UPS Employees or UPS Retirees	580	$10,000	$1000	1–50	Corporate Affiliation. Residence: Florida. Studying in Florida.
Toshiba/NSTA ExploraVision Awards Program	198	$10,000	$5000	16–32	Computer Science/Data Processing; Engineering/Technology; Nuclear Science; Physical Sciences.
Washington State Achievers Program Scholarship	726	$10,000	$5000	600	Residence: Washington. Studying in Washington.
Win Free College Tuition Giveaway	857	$10,000	$500	1	
Worldfest Student Film Award	315	$10,000	$1000	10	Filmmaking/Video.
Young American Creative Patriotic Art Awards Program	821	$10,000	$500	8	Talent/Interest Area: art.
YoungArts, National Foundation for Advancement in the Arts	835	$10,000	$100	15	Talent/Interest Area: art; music/singing; photography/photogrammetry/filmmaking.
Minnesota State Grant Program	762	$9444	$100	71,000–105,000	Residence: Minnesota. Studying in Minnesota.
DeVry High School Scholarship	845	$9000	$2000	varies	Must be in high school.
DeVry University First Scholar Award	815	$9000	$3000		Talent/Interest Area: science.
Edward T. Conroy Memorial Scholarship Program	591	$9000	$7200	121	Employment/Volunteer Experience: police/firefighting. Military Service: General. Residence: Maryland. Studying in Maryland.
Connecticut Independent College Student Grants	730	$8700	$250	varies	Residence: Connecticut. Studying in Connecticut.
Delegate Scholarship Program-Maryland	757	$8650	$200	3,500	Residence: Maryland. Studying in Maryland.
Washington Award for Vocational Excellence (WAVE)	801	$8592	$1	147	Residence: Washington. Studying in Washington.
Critical Languages Scholarships for Intensive Summer Institute in Turkish Language	326	$8500	$8000	50–60	Foreign Language. Talent/Interest Area: Turkish language.
New Jersey Society of Certified Public Accountants High School Scholarship Program	68	$8500	$6500	15–20	Accounting. Residence: New Jersey.
North Carolina Student Loan Program for Health, Science, and Mathematics	221	$8500	$3000	1	Dental Health/Services; Health Administration; Health and Medical Sciences; Nursing; Physical Sciences; Therapy/Rehabilitation. Residence: North Carolina.
Vermont Part-Time Student Grants	799	$8100	$250	varies	Residence: Vermont.

Award Name	Page Number	Highest Dollar Amount	Lowest Dollar Amount	Number of Awards	Academic Fields/Career Goals and Nonacademic/Noncareer Criteria
AACE International Competitive Scholarship	99	$8000	$2000	15–25	Architecture; Aviation/Aerospace; Business/Consumer Services; Chemical Engineering; Civil Engineering; Construction Engineering/Management; Electrical Engineering/Electronics; Engineering-Related Technologies; Engineering/Technology; Mechanical Engineering.
AIFS-HACU Scholarships	654	$8000	$6000	varies	Talent/Interest Area: international exchange. Limited to Hispanic students.
Kapadia Scholarships	302	$8000	$1500	varies	Engineering/Technology.
Liederkranz Foundation Scholarship Award for Voice	822	$8000	$1000	14–18	Talent/Interest Area: music/singing.
Pat and Jim Host Scholarship	363	$8000	$2000	1	Hospitality Management; Travel/Tourism.
Vocational Nurse Scholarship Program	449	$8000	$4000	varies	Nursing. Residence: California.
Washington Scholars Program	801	$7733	$1	147	Residence: Washington. Studying in Washington.
Washington State Need Grant Program	801	$7717	$103	71,233	Residence: Washington. Studying in Washington.
AGC Education and Research Foundation Undergraduate Scholarships	176	$7500	$2500	100	Civil Engineering; Construction Engineering/Management; Engineering/Technology.
American Legion Department of Pennsylvania High School Oratorical Contest	712	$7500	$4000	3	Residence: Pennsylvania. Talent/Interest Area: public speaking.
Civil Air Patrol Academic Scholarships	539	$7500	$1000	40	Civic Affiliation: Civil Air Patrol.
Epsilon Sigma Alpha Foundation Scholarships	662	$7500	$350	125–175	Limited to ethnic minority students.
E. Wayne Kay Scholarship	297	$7500	$2500	10–30	Engineering/Technology; Trade/Technical Specialties.
International Violoncello Competition	832	$7500	$2500	3	Talent/Interest Area: music.
Leveraged Incentive Grant Program	768	$7500	$250	varies	Residence: New Hampshire. Studying in New Hampshire.
NJ Student Tuition Assistance Reward Scholarship	770	$7500	$2500	varies	Residence: New Jersey. Studying in New Jersey.
Outstanding Scholar Recruitment Program	770	$7500	$2500	varies	Residence: New Jersey. Studying in New Jersey.
Palmetto Fellows Scholarship Program	788	$7500	$6700	4,846	Residence: South Carolina. Studying in South Carolina.
Paraprofessional Teacher Preparation Grant	241	$7500	$250	varies	Education. Residence: Massachusetts.
Soozie Courter "Sharing a Brighter Tomorrow" Hemophilia Scholarship Program	612	$7500	$2500	20	Disability: physically disabled.
South Dakota Space Grant Consortium Undergraduate and Graduate Student Scholarships	129	$7500	$1000	45–50	Aviation/Aerospace; Earth Science; Energy and Power Engineering; Engineering-Related Technologies; Engineering/Technology; Environmental Science; Materials Science, Engineering, and Metallurgy; Mathematics; Natural Sciences; Physical Sciences; Science, Technology, and Society. Studying in South Dakota.
TELACU Education Foundation	735	$7500	$500	350–600	Residence: California; Illinois; New York; Texas.
William Faulkner-William Wisdom Creative Writing Competition	827	$7500	$250	7	Talent/Interest Area: English language; writing.
Tuition Aid Grant	770	$7272	$868	varies	Residence: New Jersey. Studying in New Jersey.
Indiana National Guard Supplemental Grant	621	$7110	$20	503–925	Military Service: Air Force National Guard; Army National Guard. Residence: Indiana. Studying in Indiana.
Charles and Lucille King Family Foundation Scholarships	184	$7000	$3500	10–20	Communications; Filmmaking/Video; TV/Radio Broadcasting.
GEAR UP Alaska Scholarship	701	$7000	$3500	varies	Residence: Alaska.

Award Name	Page Number	Highest Dollar Amount	Lowest Dollar Amount	Number of Awards	Academic Fields/Career Goals and Nonacademic/Noncareer Criteria
Myrtle and Earl Walker Scholarship Fund	272	$7000	$1000	1–25	Engineering-Related Technologies; Engineering/Technology; Mechanical Engineering.
Senatorial Scholarships-Maryland	758	$7000	$400	7,000	Residence: Maryland. Studying in Maryland.
Society of Hispanic Professional Engineers Foundation	169	$7000	$500	varies	Chemical Engineering; Civil Engineering; Electrical Engineering/Electronics; Engineering-Related Technologies; Engineering/Technology; Materials Science, Engineering, and Metallurgy; Mechanical Engineering; Natural Sciences; Physical Sciences; Science, Technology, and Society. Limited to Hispanic students.
Society of Women Engineers–Freshmen Scholarships	299	$7000	$1000	1–36	Engineering/Technology.
Twin Towers Orphan Fund	868	$7000	$5000	varies	
Pennsylvania Burglar and Fire Alarm Association Youth Scholarship Program	594	$6500	$500	6–8	Employment/Volunteer Experience: police/firefighting. Residence: Pennsylvania.
Toward EXcellence Access and Success (TEXAS Grant)	794	$6080	$2680		Residence: Texas. Studying in Texas.
Adeline Rosenberg Memorial Prize	817	$6000	$4000	2	Talent/Interest Area: music.
Adult Vocational Training Competitive Scholarship	660	$6000	$3000	5	Limited to American Indian/Alaska Native students.
American Legion Department of New York High School Oratorical Contest	711	$6000	$2000	varies	Residence: New York. Talent/Interest Area: public speaking.
Archbold Scholarship Program	344	$6000	$600	50	Health and Medical Sciences; Nursing. Residence: Florida; Georgia.
Contemporary Record Society National Competition for Performing Artists	814	$6000	$2000	1	Talent/Interest Area: music/singing.
Friends of 440 Scholarship Fund, Inc.	739	$6000	$500	1–60	Residence: Florida.
GCSAA Scholars Competition	358	$6000	$500	varies	Horticulture/Floriculture. Civic Affiliation: Golf Course Superintendents Association of America.
Gilbane Scholarship Program	103	$6000	$5000	1	Architecture; Engineering/Technology; Mathematics. Residence: Delaware; New Jersey; Pennsylvania. Limited to Black (non-Hispanic) students.
Golden Gate Restaurant Association Scholarship Foundation	322	$6000	$1000	9–15	Food Service/Hospitality; Hospitality Management. Residence: California.
Higher Education Scholarship Program	675	$6000	$50	72	Limited to American Indian/Alaska Native students.
Marion Huber Learning Through Listening Awards	560	$6000	$2000	6	Civic Affiliation: Recording for the Blind and Dyslexic. Employment/Volunteer Experience: community service. Disability: learning disabled. Talent/Interest Area: leadership.
Mary P. Oenslager Scholastic Achievement Awards	560	$6000	$1000	9	Civic Affiliation: Recording for the Blind and Dyslexic. Employment/Volunteer Experience: community service. Disability: visually impaired. Talent/Interest Area: leadership.
Minnesota Indian Scholarship	671	$6000		500–600	Residence: Minnesota. Studying in Minnesota. Limited to American Indian/Alaska Native students.
Minority Scholarship Award for Academic Excellence in Physical Therapy	338	$6000	$5000	8–10	Health and Medical Sciences. Limited to ethnic minority students.
Montana University System Honor Scholarship	765	$6000	$4000	200	Residence: Montana. Studying in Montana.
National Competition for Composers' Recordings	815	$6000	$2000	1	Talent/Interest Area: music/singing.
Office and Professional Employees International Union Howard Coughlin memorial scholarship fund	556	$6000	$2400	18	Civic Affiliation: Office and Professional Employees International Union.
Undergraduate Competitive Scholarship	660	$6000	$3000	17	Limited to American Indian/Alaska Native students.

Award Name	Page Number	Highest Dollar Amount	Lowest Dollar Amount	Number of Awards	Academic Fields/Career Goals and Nonacademic/Noncareer Criteria
Tuition Equalization Grant (TEG) Program	794	$5712	$3808		Residence: Texas. Studying in Texas.
Nissan Scholarship	763	$5652	$5596	varies	Residence: Mississippi. Studying in Mississippi.
Academic Scholars Program	777	$5500	$1800	varies	Studying in Oklahoma.
MOAA American Patriot Scholarship	640	$5500	$2500	65	Military Service: General.
North Dakota Scholars Program	775	$5461	$4160	45–50	Residence: North Dakota. Studying in North Dakota.
Oregon Veterans' Education Aid	643	$5400	$3600	1–200	Military Service: General. Residence: Oregon. Studying in Oregon.
Kansas Teacher Service Scholarship	239	$5374	$2150	varies	Education.
ASSE-United Parcel Service Scholarship	463	$5300	$4000	varies	Occupational Safety and Health. Civic Affiliation: American Society of Safety Engineers.
United Parcel Service Diversity Scholarship Program	464	$5250	$4000	varies	Occupational Safety and Health. Civic Affiliation: American Society of Safety Engineers. Limited to ethnic minority students.
Higher Education Legislative Plan (HELP)	763	$5151	$830	varies	Residence: Mississippi. Studying in Mississippi.
Taylor Opportunity Program for Students–Honors Level	754	$5106	$680	7,522	Residence: Louisiana. Studying in Louisiana.
Academy of Motion Picture Arts and Sciences Student Academy Awards	313	$5000	$2000	3–12	Filmmaking/Video.
AHETEMS Scholarships	293	$5000	$1000	100	Engineering/Technology; Mathematics; Science, Technology, and Society.
AIA New Jersey Scholarship Program	99	$5000	$2500	4–6	Architecture. Residence: New Jersey. Studying in New Jersey.
Alabama Student Assistance Program	701	$5000	$300	varies	Residence: Alabama. Studying in Alabama.
Albert E. Wischmeyer Memorial Scholarship Award	294	$5000	$1000	1–10	Engineering/Technology. Residence: New York. Studying in New York.
All-Ink.com College Scholarship Program	837	$5000	$1000	5–10	
American Academy of Chefs Chair's Scholarship	207	$5000	$1000	5	Culinary Arts; Food Service/Hospitality.
American Association of Family & Consumer Sciences National Undergraduate Scholarship	355	$5000		1	Home Economics.
American Chemical Society Scholars Program	160	$5000	$1000	100–200	Chemical Engineering; Environmental Science; Materials Science, Engineering, and Metallurgy; Natural Sciences; Paper and Pulp Engineering. Limited to American Indian/Alaska Native; Black (non-Hispanic); Hispanic students.
American Legion Legacy Scholarship	634	$5000	$2000	varies	Military Service: General.
American Occupational Therapy Foundation State Association Scholarships	338	$5000	$150	varies	Health and Medical Sciences; Therapy/Rehabilitation. Civic Affiliation: American Occupational Therapy Association.
Angus Foundation Scholarships	553	$5000	$250	75–90	Civic Affiliation: American Angus Association.
Arkansas Academic Challenge Scholarship Program	715	$5000	$1250	25,000–30,000	Residence: Arkansas. Studying in Arkansas.
ARTBA-TDF Lanford Family Highway Workers Memorial Scholarship Program	583	$5000	$1000	varies	Employment/Volunteer Experience: construction; roadway workers.
Arthur and Gladys Cervenka Scholarship Award	294	$5000	$1000	1–10	Engineering/Technology.
Arthur J. Packard Memorial Scholarship	208	$5000	$2000	3	Culinary Arts; Food Service/Hospitality; Hospitality Management; Recreation, Parks, Leisure Studies; Travel/Tourism.
Ashby B. Carter Memorial Scholarship Fund Founders Award	550	$5000	$2000	3	Civic Affiliation: National Alliance of Postal and Federal Employees.

Award Name	Page Number	Highest Dollar Amount	Lowest Dollar Amount	Number of Awards	Academic Fields/Career Goals and Nonacademic/Noncareer Criteria
BMI Student Composer Awards	109	$5000	$500	10	Arts; Music. Talent/Interest Area: music/singing.
Boys and Girls Clubs of Chicago Scholarships	537	$5000	$3000	varies	Civic Affiliation: Boys or Girls Club. Residence: Illinois.
Brickfish Scholarships	841	$5000	$50	5–30	
Caterpillar Scholars Award Fund	294	$5000	$1000	1–15	Engineering/Technology.
Central Scholarship Bureau Grants	722	$5000	$1000	20–30	Residence: Maryland.
Chapter 3-Peoria Endowed Scholarship	294	$5000	$1000	5	Engineering/Technology. Residence: Illinois. Studying in Illinois.
Chapter 4-Lawrence A. Wacker Memorial Scholarship	294	$5000	$1000	1–10	Engineering/Technology; Mechanical Engineering. Studying in Wisconsin.
Chapter 6-Fairfield County Scholarship	294	$5000	$1000	4	Engineering/Technology.
Chapter 23-Quad Cities Iowa/Illinois Scholarship	295	$5000	$1000	5	Engineering/Technology. Studying in Illinois; Iowa.
Chapter 31-Tri City Scholarship	295	$5000	$1000	5	Engineering/Technology. Studying in Michigan.
Chapter 63-Portland James E. Morrow Scholarship	295	$5000	$1000	5	Engineering/Technology. Residence: Oregon; Washington. Studying in Oregon; Washington.
Chapter 63-Portland Uncle Bud Smith Scholarship	295	$5000	$1000	5	Engineering/Technology. Residence: Oregon; Washington. Studying in Oregon; Washington.
Chapter 67-Phoenix Scholarship	295	$5000	$1000	1–5	Engineering/Technology; Industrial Design; Mechanical Engineering; Trade/Technical Specialties. Studying in Arizona.
Chapter 93-Albuquerque Scholarship	295	$5000	$1000	1–5	Engineering/Technology. Studying in New Mexico.
Chapter 198-Downriver Detroit Scholarship	295	$5000	$1000	1–5	Engineering/Technology; Industrial Design; Mechanical Engineering; Trade/Technical Specialties. Studying in Michigan.
Chesapeake Urology Associates Scholarship	342	$5000	$1500	3	Health and Medical Sciences; Nursing. Residence: Maryland.
Christa McAuliffe Teacher Scholarship Loan-Delaware	235	$5000	$1000	1–60	Education. Residence: Delaware. Studying in Delaware.
Clan MacBean Foundation Grant Program	105	$5000	$500	1–5	Area/Ethnic Studies; Child and Family Studies.
Clarence and Josephine Myers Scholarship	296	$5000	$1000	5	Engineering/Technology. Studying in Indiana.
Clinton J. Helton Manufacturing Scholarship Award Fund	296	$5000	$1000	1–5	Engineering/Technology; Trade/Technical Specialties. Studying in Colorado.
College Scholarship Assistance Program	800	$5000	$400	varies	Residence: Virginia. Studying in Virginia.
Colorado Student Grant	727	$5000	$850	60,307	Residence: Colorado. Studying in Colorado.
Congressional Black Caucus Spouses Education Scholarship	844	$5000	$500	250–400	
Congressional Hispanic Caucus Institute Scholarship Awards	660	$5000	$1000	100–150	Limited to Hispanic students.
Connie and Robert T. Gunter Scholarship	296	$5000	$1000	1–5	Engineering/Technology. Studying in Georgia.
Constant Memorial Scholarship for Aquidneck Island Residents	114	$5000	$2000	1–2	Arts; Music. Residence: Rhode Island. Talent/Interest Area: art; music.
Continental Society, Daughters of Indian Wars Scholarship	235	$5000	$2500	3	Education; Social Services. Limited to American Indian/Alaska Native students.
CSP Finalist Scholarships for High School Seniors	723	$5000	$500	300–400	Residence: Ohio.
Culinary Trust Scholarship Program for Culinary Study and Research	209	$5000	$1000	21	Culinary Arts; Food Science/Nutrition; Food Service/Hospitality.
Daughters of the Cincinnati Scholarship	617	$5000	$3000	4–5	Military Service: Air Force; Army; Coast Guard; Marine Corps; Navy.

Award Name	Page Number	Highest Dollar Amount	Lowest Dollar Amount	Number of Awards	Academic Fields/Career Goals and Nonacademic/Noncareer Criteria
Delaware Nursing Incentive Scholarship Loan	444	$5000	$1000	1–40	Nursing. Residence: Delaware.
Donaldson D. Frizzell Scholarship	848	$5000	$2500	6	
Doris and John Carpenter Scholarship	687	$5000	$2000		Limited to Black (non-Hispanic) students.
Duke Energy Scholars Program	575	$5000	$1000	15	Corporate Affiliation.
Edelman Nursing Excellence Scholarship Program	450	$5000	$2000	20–30	Nursing; Corporate Affiliation.
Education Exchange College Grant Program	818	$5000	$1000	34	Talent/Interest Area: leadership.
Edward M. Nagel Foundation Scholarship	73	$5000	$2000	varies	Accounting; Business/Consumer Services; Economics. Residence: California. Limited to Black (non-Hispanic) students.
Edward S. Roth Manufacturing Engineering Scholarship	296	$5000	$1000	1–10	Engineering/Technology. Studying in California; Florida; Illinois; Massachusetts; Minnesota; Ohio; Texas; Utah.
Electronic Document Systems Foundation Scholarship Awards	197	$5000	$250	40	Computer Science/Data Processing; Graphics/Graphic Arts/Printing; Marketing.
Elie Wiesel Prize in Ethics Essay Contest	816	$5000	$500	5	Talent/Interest Area: writing.
Emerging Texas Artist Scholarship	115	$5000	$500	8–12	Arts. Studying in Texas. Talent/Interest Area: art.
E. Wayne Kay Co-op Scholarship	297	$5000	$1000	1–10	Engineering/Technology.
Federated Garden Clubs of Connecticut Inc. Scholarships	140	$5000	$1000	2–5	Biology; Horticulture/Floriculture; Landscape Architecture. Residence: Connecticut. Studying in Connecticut.
Federation of American Consumers and Travelers Trade/Technical School Scholarship	541	$5000	$1000	1–3	Civic Affiliation: Federation of American Consumers and Travelers.
Fleet Reserve Association Education Foundation Scholarships	625	$5000	$1000	1–25	Military Service: Coast Guard; Marine Corps; Navy.
Florida Bankers Educational Foundation (FBEF) Scholarship/Loan	150	$5000	$750	5–10	Business/Consumer Services. Residence: Florida. Studying in Florida.
Foreclosure.com Scholarship Program	848	$5000	$1000	5	
Fort Wayne Chapter 56 Scholarship	297	$5000	$1000	1–10	Engineering/Technology; Industrial Design; Mechanical Engineering; Trade/Technical Specialties. Studying in Indiana.
Franz Stenzel M.D. and Kathryn Stenzel Scholarship Fund	347	$5000	$2000	70	Health and Medical Sciences; Nursing. Residence: Oregon.
Gene and John Athletic Scholarship	829	$5000	$2500	1–3	Talent/Interest Area: LGBT issues; athletics/sports.
General John Ratay Educational Fund Grants	639	$5000	$4000	1–5	Military Service: General.
Georgia Engineering Foundation Scholarship Program	284	$5000	$1000	45	Engineering/Technology. Employment/Volunteer Experience: community service. Residence: Georgia.
Geraldo Rivera Scholarship	380	$5000	$1000	varies	Journalism; TV/Radio Broadcasting.
Governors Scholarship Program	726	$5000	$1000	30	Residence: Washington. Studying in Washington.
Graco Inc. Scholarship Program	576	$5000	$3500	varies	Corporate Affiliation.
Graduate and Professional Scholarship Program-Maryland	220	$5000	$1000	584	Dental Health/Services; Health and Medical Sciences; Law/Legal Services; Nursing; Social Services. Residence: Maryland. Studying in Maryland.
Great Falls Broadcasters Association Scholarship	518	$5000	$2000	1	TV/Radio Broadcasting. Residence: Montana. Studying in Montana.
Guiliano Mazzetti Scholarship Award	297	$5000	$1000	1–10	Engineering/Technology.
Harry C. Jaecker Scholarship	349	$5000	$2000	varies	Health and Medical Sciences. Limited to Black (non-Hispanic) students.

Award Name	Page Number	Highest Dollar Amount	Lowest Dollar Amount	Number of Awards	Academic Fields/Career Goals and Nonacademic/Noncareer Criteria
Harry Ludwig Scholarship Fund	611	$5000	$500	1–3	Disability: visually impaired.
HENAAC Scholars Program	199	$5000	$500	87	Computer Science/Data Processing; Engineering-Related Technologies; Materials Science, Engineering, and Metallurgy; Mathematics. Talent/Interest Area: leadership. Limited to Hispanic students.
Herbert Hoover Uncommon Student Award	744	$5000	$1000	15	Residence: Iowa.
Hispanic Engineer National Achievement Awards Corporation Scholarship Program	125	$5000	$500	12–20	Aviation/Aerospace; Biology; Chemical Engineering; Civil Engineering; Computer Science/Data Processing; Electrical Engineering/Electronics; Engineering/Technology; Materials Science, Engineering, and Metallurgy; Mechanical Engineering; Nuclear Science. Limited to Hispanic students.
Hispanic Metropolitan Chamber Scholarships	665	$5000	$1000	40	Nationality: Hispanic. Residence: Oregon; Washington. Limited to Hispanic students.
Houston Symphony Ima Hogg Competition	423	$5000	$300	5	Music. Talent/Interest Area: music.
Howard Rock Foundation Scholarship Program	659	$5000	$2500	3	Limited to American Indian/Alaska Native students.
IFMA Foundation Scholarships	102	$5000	$1500	25–35	Architecture; Construction Engineering/Management; Engineering-Related Technologies; Engineering/Technology; Interior Design; Urban and Regional Planning.
Indiana Health Care Policy Institute Nursing Scholarship	449	$5000	$750	1–5	Nursing. Residence: Indiana. Studying in Illinois; Indiana; Kentucky; Michigan; Ohio.
Indian American Scholarship Fund	666	$5000	$500	3	Nationality: Indian. Residence: Georgia. Limited to Asian/Pacific Islander students.
Indiana Nursing Scholarship Fund	459	$5000	$200	490–690	Nursing. Residence: Indiana. Studying in Indiana.
International Society of Automation Education Foundation Scholarships	125	$5000	$500	5–15	Aviation/Aerospace; Chemical Engineering; Electrical Engineering/Electronics; Energy and Power Engineering; Engineering-Related Technologies; Engineering/Technology; Heating, Air-Conditioning, and Refrigeration Mechanics; Materials Science, Engineering, and Metallurgy; Mechanical Engineering; Paper and Pulp Engineering; Pharmacy.
ISA Educational Foundation Scholarships	267	$5000	$500	10	Engineering-Related Technologies.
James L. and Genevieve H. Goodwin Memorial Scholarship	429	$5000	$1000	10	Natural Resources. Residence: Connecticut.
Jane M. Klausman Women in Business Scholarships	159	$5000	$4000	12	Business/Consumer Services.
Jerry McDowell Fund	267	$5000	$1000	1–3	Engineering-Related Technologies; Engineering/Technology.
Jesse Jones Jr. Scholarship	158	$5000	$2000		Business/Consumer Services. Limited to Black (non-Hispanic) students.
Jewish Vocational Service Scholarship Fund	667	$5000	$1000	125–200	Nationality: Jewish. Residence: California. Religion: Jewish.
Jimi Hendrix Endowment Fund Scholarship	428	$5000	$2000	varies	Music. Limited to Black (non-Hispanic) students.
John Kimball Memorial Trust Scholarship Program for the Study of History	354	$5000	$300	3–10	History. Residence: Massachusetts.
Joseph Shinoda Memorial Scholarship	360	$5000	$1000	8–15	Horticulture/Floriculture.
Judith McManus Price Scholarship	521	$5000	$2000	varies	Urban and Regional Planning. Limited to American Indian/Alaska Native; Black (non-Hispanic); Hispanic students.
Kansas City Initiative Scholarship	690	$5000	$2500	varies	Residence: Kansas. Limited to Black (non-Hispanic) students.

Award Name	Page Number	Highest Dollar Amount	Lowest Dollar Amount	Number of Awards	Academic Fields/Career Goals and Nonacademic/Noncareer Criteria
Kappa Alpha Theta Foundation Named Endowment Grant Program	547	$5000	$100	1–50	Civic Affiliation: Greek Organization.
Keck Foundation Scholarship	690	$5000	$2000	varies	Limited to Black (non-Hispanic) students.
Kentucky Minority Educator Recruitment and Retention (KMERR) Scholarship	239	$5000	$2500	400	Education. Residence: Kentucky. Studying in Kentucky. Limited to ethnic minority students.
Kentucky Teacher Scholarship Program	239	$5000	$325	100–300	Education. Residence: Kentucky. Studying in Kentucky.
Kosciuszko Foundation Chopin Piano Competition	424	$5000	$1500	3	Music; Performing Arts. Talent/Interest Area: music/singing.
Leveraging Educational Assistance State Partnership Program (LEAP)	745	$5000	$400	varies	Studying in Idaho.
Lilly Reintegration Scholarship	607	$5000	$2500	70–100	Disability: physically disabled.
L. Ron Hubbard's Illustrators of the Future Contest	812	$5000	$500	12	Talent/Interest Area: art.
L. Ron Hubbard's Writers of the Future Contest	812	$5000	$500	12	Talent/Interest Area: writing.
Lucile B. Kaufman Women's Scholarship	297	$5000	$1000	1–5	Engineering/Technology.
Mae Maxey Memorial Scholarship	116	$5000	$1000	varies	Arts; Literature/English/Writing. Limited to Black (non-Hispanic) students.
Maine Community Foundation Scholarship Programs	756	$5000	$500	150–700	Residence: Maine.
Math, Engineering, Science, Business, Education, Computers Scholarships	147	$5000	$500	180	Business/Consumer Services; Computer Science/Data Processing; Education; Engineering/Technology; Humanities; Physical Sciences; Science, Technology, and Society; Social Sciences. Limited to American Indian/Alaska Native students.
Minority Teacher Incentive Grant Program	234	$5000	$2500	82	Education. Studying in Connecticut. Limited to ethnic minority students.
Missouri Professional and Practical Nursing Student Loan Program	452	$5000	$2500	60–70	Nursing. Residence: Missouri. Studying in Missouri.
"My Turn" Essay Competition	398	$5000	$1000	10	Literature/English/Writing. Talent/Interest Area: writing.
National Asian-American Journalists Association Newhouse Scholarship	374	$5000	$1000	5	Journalism.
National High School Journalist of the Year/Sister Rita Jeanne Scholarships	186	$5000	$2000	1–7	Communications; Journalism; Photojournalism/Photography; TV/Radio Broadcasting.
National Leadership Development Grant	663	$5000	$1000	5–10	Religion: Methodist. Limited to ethnic minority students.
National Scholarship Program	600	$5000	$1000	10–20	Disability: hearing impaired; physically disabled; visually impaired.
Native American Journalists Association Scholarships	381	$5000	$500	10	Journalism. Civic Affiliation: Native American Journalists Association. Talent/Interest Area: writing. Limited to American Indian/Alaska Native students.
Native American Leadership in Education (NALE)	147	$5000	$500	30	Business/Consumer Services; Education; Humanities; Physical Sciences; Science, Technology, and Society. Limited to American Indian/Alaska Native students.
Naval Reserve Association Scholarship Program	649	$5000	$1000	varies	Military Service: Navy.
New England Employee Benefits Council Scholarship Program	68	$5000	$1000	1–3	Accounting; Business/Consumer Services; Economics; Health Administration; Human Resources; Insurance and Actuarial Science; Law/Legal Services; Public Health; Public Policy and Administration. Residence: Connecticut; Maine; Massachusetts; New Hampshire; Rhode Island; Vermont. Studying in Connecticut; Maine; Massachusetts; New Hampshire; Rhode Island; Vermont.

Award Name	Page Number	Highest Dollar Amount	Lowest Dollar Amount	Number of Awards	Academic Fields/Career Goals and Nonacademic/Noncareer Criteria
New York State Tuition Assistance Program	772	$5000	$500	350,000–360,000	Residence: New York. Studying in New York.
Norm Manly—YMTA Maritime Educational Scholarships	871	$5000	$1000		
North Carolina Association of CPAs Foundation Scholarships	67	$5000	$1000	50–60	Accounting. Residence: North Carolina. Studying in North Carolina.
North Central Region 9 Scholarship	298	$5000	$1000	1–10	Engineering/Technology; Industrial Design; Mechanical Engineering; Trade/Technical Specialties. Studying in Iowa; Michigan; Minnesota; Nebraska; North Dakota; South Dakota; Wisconsin.
NSCS Scholar Abroad Scholarship	554	$5000	$2500	3	Civic Affiliation: National Society of Collegiate Scholars.
Nurse Education Assistance Loan Program	457	$5000	$1500		Nursing. Residence: Ohio. Studying in Ohio.
Nurse Education Scholarship Loan Program (NESLP)	456	$5000	$400	varies	Nursing. Residence: North Carolina. Studying in North Carolina.
Nurse Scholars Program-Undergraduate (North Carolina)	456	$5000	$3000	450	Nursing. Residence: North Carolina. Studying in North Carolina.
Outdoor Writers Association of America Bodie McDowell Scholarship Award	189	$5000	$1000	2–5	Communications; Filmmaking/Video; Journalism; Literature/English/Writing; Photojournalism/Photography; TV/Radio Broadcasting. Talent/Interest Area: amateur radio; photography/photogrammetry/filmmaking; writing.
Patrick Kerr Skateboard Scholarship	860	$5000	$1000	4	Must be in high school.
Pellegrini Scholarship Grants	681	$5000	$500	50	Nationality: Swiss. Residence: Connecticut; Delaware; New Jersey; New York; Pennsylvania.
PFund Foundation Scholarship Program	783	$5000	$2000	18–20	Residence: Minnesota. Studying in Minnesota. Talent/Interest Area: LGBT issues.
PHCC Educational Foundation Scholarship Program	155	$5000	$2500	1–4	Business/Consumer Services; Engineering-Related Technologies; Engineering/Technology; Heating, Air-Conditioning, and Refrigeration Mechanics; Mechanical Engineering; Trade/Technical Specialties.
Police Officers and Firefighters Survivors Education Assistance Program-Alabama	701	$5000	$2000	15–30	Residence: Alabama. Studying in Alabama.
Print and Graphics Scholarships Foundation	189	$5000	$1500	200–220	Communications; Graphics/Graphic Arts/Printing.
Promise of Nursing Scholarship	447	$5000	$1000	varies	Nursing. Studying in California; Florida; Georgia; Illinois; Massachusetts; Michigan; New Jersey; Tennessee; Texas.
Raise the Nation Child of a Single Parent Scholarship	861	$5000	$100	1–50	
Raise the Nation Continuing Education Scholarship	861	$5000	$100	1–50	
Raise the Nation Student Loan Grant	595	$5000	$100	1–50	Employment/Volunteer Experience: community service.
Raymond W. Cannon Memorial Scholarship Program	394	$5000	$2000	varies	Law/Legal Services; Pharmacy. Limited to Black (non-Hispanic) students.
Regents Professional Opportunity Scholarships	772	$5000	$1000		Residence: New York. Studying in New York.
Regional and Restricted Scholarship Award Program	729	$5000	$250	200–300	Residence: Connecticut.
Samuel Robinson Award	699	$5000	$250	16	Religion: Presbyterian.
Screen Actors Guild Foundation/John L. Dales Scholarship Fund (Standard)	562	$5000	$3000	100–125	Civic Affiliation: Screen Actors' Guild.
Sergeant Major Douglas R. Drum Memorial Scholarship	634	$5000	$1000	1–24	Military Service: General.

Award Name	Page Number	Highest Dollar Amount	Lowest Dollar Amount	Number of Awards	Academic Fields/Career Goals and Nonacademic/Noncareer Criteria
SHRM Foundation Student Scholarships	364	$5000	$200	40	Human Resources. Civic Affiliation: Society for Human Resource Management.
Siemens Awards for Advanced Placement	864	$5000	$2000	102	Must be in high school.
Sigma Xi Grants-In-Aid of Research	87	$5000	$1000	400	Agriculture; Animal/Veterinary Sciences; Biology; Chemical Engineering; Earth Science; Engineering/Technology; Health and Medical Sciences; Mechanical Engineering; Meteorology/Atmospheric Science; Physical Sciences; Science, Technology, and Society; Social Sciences.
Society of Physics Students Leadership Scholarships	479	$5000	$2000	17–22	Physical Sciences. Civic Affiliation: Society of Physics Students.
Society of Plastics Engineers Scholarship Program	170	$5000	$1000	25–30	Chemical Engineering; Electrical Engineering/Electronics; Engineering/Technology; Industrial Design; Materials Science, Engineering, and Metallurgy; Trade/Technical Specialties.
South Carolina Teacher Loan Program	247	$5000	$2500	1,121	Education; Special Education. Residence: South Carolina. Studying in South Carolina.
SPENDonLIFE College Scholarship	865	$5000	$500	2–10	
Stanley A. Doran Memorial Scholarship	542	$5000	$2000	1	Civic Affiliation: Fleet Reserve Association/Auxiliary. Military Service: Coast Guard; Marine Corps; Navy.
Stan Scott Scholarship	193	$5000	$1500		Communications; Journalism.
Sun Student College Scholarship Program	594	$5000	$2000	1–16	Employment/Volunteer Experience: community service. Residence: Arizona.
Taylor Michaels Scholarship Fund	590	$5000	$1000	varies	Employment/Volunteer Experience: community service. Limited to ethnic minority students.
TCU Texas Youth Entrepreneur of the Year Awards	794	$5000	$1000	6	Residence: Texas. Talent/Interest Area: entrepreneurship.
Theta Delta Chi Educational Foundation Inc. Scholarship	867	$5000	$1000	15	
Tribal Business Management Program (TBM)	57	$5000	$500	35	Accounting; Business/Consumer Services; Computer Science/Data Processing; Economics; Electrical Engineering/Electronics; Engineering-Related Technologies. Limited to American Indian/Alaska Native students.
Truckload Carriers Association Scholarship Fund	156	$5000	$1500	18	Business/Consumer Services; Transportation.
The Udall Scholarship	868	$5000		80	
Underwood-Smith Teacher Scholarship Program	250	$5000	$1620	53–60	Education. Residence: West Virginia. Studying in West Virginia.
Utah Centennial Opportunity Program for Education	798	$5000	$300	2,988	Residence: Utah. Studying in Utah.
Vincent L. Hawkinson Scholarship for Peace and Justice	799	$5000	$1000	1–10	Residence: Iowa; Minnesota; North Dakota; South Dakota; Wisconsin. Studying in Iowa; Minnesota; North Dakota; South Dakota; Wisconsin. Talent/Interest Area: leadership.
Warner Norcross and Judd LLP Scholarship for Minority Students	391	$5000	$1000	3	Law/Legal Services. Residence: Michigan. Studying in Michigan. Limited to ethnic minority students.
Watson-Brown Foundation Scholarship	801	$5000	$3000	200–200	Residence: Georgia; South Carolina.
William and Lucille Ash Scholarship	787	$5000	$1000	3	Residence: California. Studying in California.
William E. Weisel Scholarship Fund	258	$5000	$1000	1–10	Electrical Engineering/Electronics; Engineering/Technology; Mechanical Engineering; Trade/Technical Specialties.
WJA Scholarship Program	117	$5000	$500	1	Arts; Trade/Technical Specialties. Talent/Interest Area: art.
Women's Independence Scholarship Program	870	$5000	$250	500–600	

Award Name	Page Number	Highest Dollar Amount	Lowest Dollar Amount	Number of Awards	Academic Fields/Career Goals and Nonacademic/Noncareer Criteria
Worldstudio AIGA Scholarships	117	$5000	$1000	10–25	Arts; Graphics/Graphic Arts/Printing.
W. Price Jr. Memorial Scholarship	597	$5000	$2000	4	Employment/Volunteer Experience: food service.
Young Artist Competition	470	$5000	$500	8	Performing Arts. Residence: Illinois; Indiana; Iowa; Kansas; Manitoba; Michigan; Minnesota; Missouri; Nebraska; North Dakota; Ontario; South Dakota; Wisconsin. Talent/Interest Area: music.
Youth Activity Fund	432	$5000	$500	10–30	Natural Sciences; Science, Technology, and Society.
Taylor Opportunity Program for Students–Performance Level	755	$4706	$480	9,621	Residence: Louisiana. Studying in Louisiana.
Brook Hollow Golf Club Scholarship	844	$4500	$2000		Must be in high school.
DeVry/Keller Military Service Grant	636	$4500	$1000	varies	Military Service: General.
Ernest Alan and Barbara Park Meyer Scholarship Fund	778	$4500	$1000	5	Residence: Oregon.
Glenn Miller Instrumental Scholarship	818	$4500	$1000	3	Talent/Interest Area: music/singing.
Greater Washington Society of CPAs Scholarship	63	$4500	$2000	3–5	Accounting. Residence: District of Columbia. Studying in District of Columbia.
Hawaii Association of Broadcasters Scholarship	517	$4500	$500	20–30	TV/Radio Broadcasting.
New Jersey Society of Certified Public Accountants College Scholarship Program	68	$4500	$4000	40–50	Accounting. Residence: New Jersey. Studying in New Jersey.
Federal Supplemental Educational Opportunity Grant Program	726	$4400	$100	varies	Residence: North Carolina.
Charley Wootan Grant Program	867	$4394	$1000	varies	
Taylor Opportunity Program for Students–Opportunity Level	755	$4306	$280	23,645	Residence: Louisiana. Studying in Louisiana.
ASCSA Summer Sessions Scholarships	92	$4250	$500	10–11	Anthropology; Archaeology; Architecture; Art History; Arts; Classics; Historic Preservation and Conservation; History; Humanities; Museum Studies; Philosophy; Religion/Theology. Talent/Interest Area: international exchange.
American Legion Department of Indiana High School Oratorical Contest	708	$4200	$200	4–8	Residence: Indiana. Talent/Interest Area: public speaking.
Pennsylvania State Grant	782	$4120	$200	varies	Residence: Pennsylvania.
Academy of Television Arts and Sciences College Television Awards	836	$4000	$500	25	
Alexander and Maude Hadden Scholarship	598	$4000	$2500	varies	Employment/Volunteer Experience: community service.
American Legion Auxiliary Spirit of Youth Scholarship	629	$4000	$1000	5–5	Military Service: General.
American Legion Department of New Jersey High School Oratorical Contest	807	$4000	$1000	5	Talent/Interest Area: public speaking.
American Legion Department of Tennessee High School Oratorical Contest	712	$4000	$1000	1–3	Residence: Tennessee. Talent/Interest Area: public speaking.
American Society for Enology and Viticulture Scholarships	82	$4000	$500	30	Agriculture; Chemical Engineering; Food Science/Nutrition; Horticulture/Floriculture.
Armed Forces Communications and Electronics Association ROTC Scholarship Program	122	$4000	$2000	35–45	Aviation/Aerospace; Communications; Computer Science/Data Processing; Electrical Engineering/Electronics; Engineering-Related Technologies; Engineering/Technology; Foreign Language; International Studies; Mathematics; Physical Sciences. Military Service: Air Force; Army; Marine Corps; Navy.

Award Name	Page Number	Highest Dollar Amount	Lowest Dollar Amount	Number of Awards	Academic Fields/Career Goals and Nonacademic/Noncareer Criteria
BCIC Young Innovator Scholarship Competition (Idea Mash Up)	95	$4000	$2000		Applied Sciences; Biology; Business/Consumer Services; Earth Science; Engineering-Related Technologies; Engineering/Technology; Environmental Science; Graphics/Graphic Arts/Printing; Mathematics; Natural Sciences; Physical Sciences.
Bridging Scholarship for Study Abroad in Japan	104	$4000	$2500	40–80	Area/Ethnic Studies; Asian Studies; Foreign Language.
California Wine Grape Growers Foundation Scholarship	721	$4000	$1000	1–6	Residence: California. Studying in California.
C.A.R. Scholarship Foundation Award	486	$4000	$2000	varies	Real Estate. Residence: California. Studying in California.
Church's Chicken Opportunity Scholarship	580	$4000	$2000		Corporate Affiliation. Limited to Black (non-Hispanic) students.
CIA Undergraduate Scholarships	89	$4000	$1000	15–30	American Studies; Aviation/Aerospace; Computer Science/Data Processing; Criminal Justice/Criminology; Foreign Language; History; Law Enforcement/Police Administration; Military and Defense Studies; Natural Sciences; Near and Middle East Studies; Peace and Conflict Studies; Political Science.
Community Banker Association of Illinois Annual Scholarship Program	728	$4000	$1000	13	Residence: Illinois.
Community Banker Association of Illinois Children of Community Banking Scholarship William C. Harris Memorial Scholarship	539	$4000	$1000	1	Civic Affiliation: Community Banker Association of Illinois. Employment/Volunteer Experience: banking. Residence: Illinois.
Elks Emergency Educational Grants	541	$4000	$1000	varies	Civic Affiliation: Elks Club.
Engineering Scholarship	161	$4000	$1000	1–5	Chemical Engineering; Civil Engineering; Electrical Engineering/Electronics; Engineering-Related Technologies; Engineering/Technology; Materials Science, Engineering, and Metallurgy; Mechanical Engineering. Residence: Pennsylvania.
Federal Junior Duck Stamp Conservation and Design Competition	116	$4000	$1000	3	Arts. Talent/Interest Area: art.
Gerald W. & Jean Purmal Endowed Scholarship	690	$4000	$1000		Limited to Black (non-Hispanic) students.
GMP Memorial Scholarship Program	542	$4000	$2000	10	Civic Affiliation: Glass, Molders, Pottery, Plastics and Allied Workers International Union.
International Foodservice Editorial Council Communications Scholarship	77	$4000	$1000	1–8	Advertising/Public Relations; Communications; Food Science/Nutrition; Food Service/Hospitality; Graphics/Graphic Arts/Printing; Journalism; Literature/English/Writing; Photojournalism/Photography. Talent/Interest Area: photography/photogrammetry/filmmaking; writing.
Iowa Tuition Grant Program	749	$4000	$100	16,000–17,500	Residence: Iowa. Studying in Iowa.
John F. and Anna Lee Stacey Scholarship Fund	112	$4000	$1000	3–5	Arts. Talent/Interest Area: art.
John L. Dales Scholarship Program	562	$4000	$3000	1–16	Civic Affiliation: Screen Actors' Guild.
Kaiser Permanente Allied Healthcare Scholarship	344	$4000	$3000	40	Health and Medical Sciences; Social Services; Therapy/Rehabilitation. Residence: California. Studying in California.
Lois McMillen Memorial Scholarship Fund	110	$4000	$500	1–5	Arts. Residence: Connecticut. Talent/Interest Area: art.
Luterman Scholarship	532	$4000	$1000	7	Civic Affiliation: American Legion or Auxiliary. Military Service: Army.
Malcolm Baldrige Scholarship	148	$4000	$2000	1–3	Business/Consumer Services; International Studies. Residence: Connecticut. Studying in Connecticut.

Award Name	Page Number	Highest Dollar Amount	Lowest Dollar Amount	Number of Awards	Academic Fields/Career Goals and Nonacademic/Noncareer Criteria
Mississippi Press Association Education Foundation Scholarship	379	$4000	$1000	1	Journalism. Residence: Mississippi.
New Mexico Vietnam Veteran Scholarship	642	$4000	$3500	100	Military Service: General. Residence: New Mexico. Studying in New Mexico.
NGPA Education Fund, Inc.	131	$4000	$3000	3–4	Aviation/Aerospace. Employment/Volunteer Experience: community service. Talent/Interest Area: LGBT issues; aviation.
Part-Time Grant Program	790	$4000	$20	4,680–6,700	Residence: Indiana. Studying in Indiana.
Remington Club Scholarship	580	$4000	$1000	varies	Corporate Affiliation. Residence: California.
South Florida Fair College Scholarship	790	$4000	$1000	10	Residence: Florida.
Specialty Equipment Market Association Memorial Scholarship Fund	301	$4000	$1000	90	Engineering/Technology; Trade/Technical Specialties. Talent/Interest Area: automotive.
SSPI International Scholarships	133	$4000	$2500	1–4	Aviation/Aerospace; Communications; Law/Legal Services; Meteorology/Atmospheric Science; Military and Defense Studies.
Student-View Scholarship program	866	$4000	$500	11	Must be in high school.
Tennessee Education Lottery Scholarship Program Tennessee HOPE Scholarship	793	$4000	$2000	varies	Residence: Tennessee. Studying in Tennessee.
Tennessee Student Assistance Award	793	$4000	$100	25,000–35,000	Residence: Tennessee. Studying in Tennessee.
Union Plus Credit Card Scholarship Program	524	$4000	$500	varies	Civic Affiliation: American Federation of State, County, and Municipal Employees.
Union Plus Education Foundation Scholarship Program	568	$4000	$500	100–120	Civic Affiliation: AFL-CIO.
Union Plus Scholarship Program	551	$4000	$500	3	Civic Affiliation: National Association of Letter Carriers.
University Film and Video Association Carole Fielding Student Grants	314	$4000	$1000	5	Filmmaking/Video.
Vertical Flight Foundation Scholarship	118	$4000	$1500	10–17	Aviation/Aerospace; Electrical Engineering/Electronics; Engineering-Related Technologies; Mechanical Engineering.
Wenderoth Undergraduate Scholarship	559	$4000	$1750	1–4	Civic Affiliation: Phi Sigma Kappa.
Weyerhaeuser Company Foundation Scholarships	581	$4000	$1000	50	Corporate Affiliation.
William L. Cullison Scholarship	431	$4000	$2000	1	Natural Resources; Paper and Pulp Engineering.
William Winter Teacher Scholar Loan	242	$4000	$1333	varies	Education. Residence: Mississippi. Studying in Mississippi.
Working Abroad Grant	852	$4000	$2000	5–8	
WRI College Scholarship Program	180	$4000	$1500	varies	Civil Engineering; Construction Engineering/Management.
Young Women in Public Affairs Award	871	$4000	$1000	5	Must be in high school.
Sallie Mae Fund Unmet Need Scholarship Program	862	$3800	$1000	varies	
Kaiser Permanente Forgivable Student Loan Program	451	$3750	$2500	varies	Nursing; Corporate Affiliation. Residence: California. Studying in California.
Early Childhood Educators Scholarship Program	241	$3600	$150	varies	Education.
Teacher Assistant Scholarship Fund	243	$3600	$600	varies	Education. Employment/Volunteer Experience: teaching. Residence: North Carolina. Studying in North Carolina.
American Foreign Service Association (AFSA) Financial Aid Award Program	524	$3500	$1000	50–60	Civic Affiliation: American Foreign Service Association.
American Legion Department of Arkansas High School Oratorical Contest	707	$3500	$1250	4	Residence: Arkansas. Talent/Interest Area: public speaking.

Award Name	Page Number	Highest Dollar Amount	Lowest Dollar Amount	Number of Awards	Academic Fields/Career Goals and Nonacademic/Noncareer Criteria
American Society of Naval Engineers Scholarship	93	$3500	$2500	8–14	Applied Sciences; Aviation/Aerospace; Civil Engineering; Electrical Engineering/Electronics; Energy and Power Engineering; Engineering/Technology; Marine/Ocean Engineering; Materials Science, Engineering, and Metallurgy; Mechanical Engineering; Physical Sciences.
American Welding Society District Scholarship Program	263	$3500	$100	150–200	Engineering-Related Technologies; Trade/Technical Specialties.
Anchor Scholarship Foundation Program	648	$3500	$1000	35–43	Military Service: Navy.
Armenian Students Association of America Inc. Scholarships	655	$3500	$1000	30	Nationality: Armenian.
BDSA Scholarships	812	$3500	$1000	varies	Talent/Interest Area: golf.
International Order Of The Golden Rule Awards of Excellence Scholarship	329	$3500	$2000	2	Funeral Services/Mortuary Science.
Kansas Nursing Service Scholarship Program	451	$3500	$2500	varies	Nursing.
National Defense Transportation Association, Scott Air Force Base-St. Louis Area Chapter Scholarship	766	$3500	$2000	6	Residence: Illinois; Missouri. Studying in Colorado; Illinois; Indiana; Iowa; Kansas; Michigan; Minnesota; Missouri; Montana; Nebraska; North Dakota; South Dakota; Wisconsin; Wyoming.
OAB Foundation Scholarship	188	$3500	$2500	4	Communications; Journalism; TV/Radio Broadcasting. Residence: Oregon. Studying in Oregon.
Robert Guthrie PKU Scholarship and Awards	610	$3500	$500	4–8	Disability: physically disabled.
Unmet NEED Grant Program	674	$3500	$1000	10–500	Residence: Pennsylvania. Limited to Black (non-Hispanic) students.
Nebraska Opportunity Grant	767	$3400	$100	varies	Residence: Nebraska. Studying in Nebraska.
American Cancer Society, Florida Division R.O.C.K. College Scholarship Program	599	$3300	$300	200–225	Disability: physically disabled. Residence: Florida. Studying in Florida. Talent/Interest Area: leadership.
Cal Grant C	721	$3168	$576	7,761	Residence: California. Studying in California.
Sussman-Miller Educational Assistance Fund	703	$3100	$500	29	Residence: New Mexico.
Taylor Opportunity Program for Students–Tech Level	755	$3021	$280	1,785	Residence: Louisiana. Studying in Louisiana.
Actuarial Diversity Scholarship	370	$3000	$1000		Insurance and Actuarial Science; Mathematics. Limited to American Indian/Alaska Native; Black (non-Hispanic); Hispanic students.
Adelante Fund Scholarships	650	$3000	$1000	30–45	Nationality: Hispanic. Studying in Arizona; California; Florida; Illinois; New Mexico; New York; Texas. Talent/Interest Area: leadership. Limited to Hispanic students.
Admiral Mike Boorda Loan Program	646	$3000	$500	1–100	Military Service: Marine Corps; Navy.
Air Force Sergeants Association Scholarship	616	$3000	$500	30	Military Service: Air Force; Air Force National Guard.
AKA Educational Advancement Foundation Youth Partners Accessing Capital Scholarship	523	$3000	$1000	varies	Civic Affiliation: Alpha Kappa Alpha.
The Alexander Foundation Scholarship Program	703	$3000	$300	6–35	Residence: Colorado. Studying in Colorado. Talent/Interest Area: LGBT issues.
AMBUCS Scholars-Scholarships for Therapists	118	$3000	$500	275	Audiology; Therapy/Rehabilitation.
American Dietetic Association Foundation Scholarship Program	317	$3000	$500	200–225	Food Science/Nutrition. Civic Affiliation: American Dietetic Association.
American Geological Institute Minority Scholarship	222	$3000	$250	20–30	Earth Science; Hydrology; Meteorology/Atmospheric Science; Oceanography. Limited to ethnic minority students.

Award Name	Page Number	Highest Dollar Amount	Lowest Dollar Amount	Number of Awards	Academic Fields/Career Goals and Nonacademic/Noncareer Criteria
American Hotel & Lodging Educational Foundation Pepsi Scholarship	207	$3000	$500	varies	Culinary Arts; Food Service/Hospitality; Hospitality Management; Recreation, Parks, Leisure Studies; Travel/Tourism. Residence: District of Columbia.
American Montessori Society Teacher Education Scholarship Fund	230	$3000	$1000	10–20	Education.
American Philological Association/ Archaeological Institute of America Minority Scholarship	98	$3000	$500	1–2	Archaeology; Classics. Limited to ethnic minority students.
American Physical Society Corporate-Sponsored Scholarship for Minority Undergraduate Students Who Major in Physics	477	$3000	$2000	varies	Physical Sciences. Limited to ethnic minority students.
American Physical Society Scholarship for Minority Undergraduate Physics Majors	475	$3000	$2000	25–30	Physical Sciences. Limited to American Indian/ Alaska Native; Black (non-Hispanic); Hispanic students.
American Savings Foundation Scholarships	713	$3000	$500	varies	Residence: Connecticut.
American Water Ski Educational Foundation Scholarship	536	$3000	$1500	5	Civic Affiliation: USA Water Ski. Talent/Interest Area: leadership.
Annual Award Program	697	$3000	$800	20–45	Religion: Muslim faith.
Annual Scholarship Grant Program	208	$3000	$500		Culinary Arts; Food Service/Hospitality; Hospitality Management; Recreation, Parks, Leisure Studies; Travel/Tourism.
Arizona Nursery Association Foundation Scholarship	356	$3000	$500	12–16	Horticulture/Floriculture.
Arthur Ross Foundation Scholarship	683	$3000	$1000		Limited to Black (non-Hispanic) students.
Associated General Contractors NYS Scholarship	176	$3000	$1500	10–20	Civil Engineering; Construction Engineering/ Management; Surveying, Surveying Technology, Cartography, or Geographic Information Science; Trade/Technical Specialties; Transportation. Residence: New York.
Astrid G. Cates and Myrtle Beinhauer Scholarship Funds	564	$3000	$1000	2–7	Civic Affiliation: Mutual Benefit Society. Residence: Yukon.
A.T. Cross Scholarship	580	$3000	$1000	varies	Corporate Affiliation. Residence: Rhode Island.
Blackfeet Nation Higher Education Grant	656	$3000	$2800	180	Limited to American Indian/Alaska Native students.
Capitol Scholarship Program	729	$3000	$500	4,500–5,500	Residence: Connecticut. Studying in Connecticut; District of Columbia; Maine; Massachusetts; New Hampshire; Pennsylvania; Rhode Island; Vermont.
Chief Master Sergeants of the Air Force Scholarship Program	616	$3000	$500	30	Military Service: Air Force; Air Force National Guard.
CollegeBound Foundation Last Dollar Grant	724	$3000	$500	45–60	Residence: Maryland. Studying in Maryland.
College Tuition Assistance Program	670	$3000	$2000	25–30	Residence: New Jersey; New York. Limited to Hispanic students.
Deerfield Plastics/Barker Family Scholarship	574	$3000	$1500	1	Corporate Affiliation. Residence: Kentucky; Massachusetts.
Delta Sigma Pi Undergraduate Scholarship	149	$3000	$250	1–40	Business/Consumer Services. Civic Affiliation: Greek Organization.
Distinguished Raven FAC Memorial Scholarship	662	$3000	$500	5–10	Nationality: Lao/Hmong. Limited to Asian/ Pacific Islander students.
Donaldson Company Inc. Scholarship Program	575	$3000	$1000	varies	Corporate Affiliation.
Don't Mess With Texas Scholarship Program	734	$3000	$1000	2–3	Residence: Texas. Studying in Texas.
Duck Brand Duct Tape "Stuck at Prom" Scholarship Contest	851	$3000	$1000	3	

Award Name	Page Number	Highest Dollar Amount	Lowest Dollar Amount	Number of Awards	Academic Fields/Career Goals and Nonacademic/Noncareer Criteria
DuPont Challenge Science Essay Awards Program	816	$3000	$100	100	Talent/Interest Area: writing.
Edna F. Blum Foundation Scholarship	687	$3000	$1000		Residence: New York. Limited to Black (non-Hispanic) students.
Educators for Maine Forgivable Loan Program	235	$3000	$2000	500	Education. Residence: Maine.
Edward & Hazel Stephenson Scholarship	687	$3000	$1000		Limited to Black (non-Hispanic) students.
Edward J. and Virginia M. Routhier Nursing Scholarship	459	$3000	$500		Nursing. Studying in Rhode Island.
Florida Society of Newspaper Editors Minority Scholarship Program	185	$3000	$1500	1	Communications; Journalism. Studying in Florida. Limited to ethnic minority students.
Florida Society of Newspaper Editors Multimedia Scholarship	185	$3000	$1500	varies	Communications; Journalism. Studying in Florida.
Hubertus W.V. Wellems Scholarship for Male Students	167	$3000	$2000	1	Chemical Engineering; Engineering-Related Technologies; Engineering/Technology; Physical Sciences. Civic Affiliation: National Association for the Advancement of Colored People. Limited to ethnic minority students.
Humana Foundation Scholarship Program	852	$3000	$1500	75	
Illinois Education Foundation Signature Fund Scholarship	746	$3000	$800	30	Residence: Illinois. Studying in Illinois.
International Airlines Travel Agent Network Foundation Scholarship	362	$3000	$500	10–15	Hospitality Management; Travel/Tourism.
James Duval Phelan Literary Award	828	$3000	$2000	3	Talent/Interest Area: writing.
Jo Anne J. Trow Scholarships	837	$3000	$1000	35	
John M. Azarian Memorial Armenian Youth Scholarship Fund	152	$3000	$500	1–5	Business/Consumer Services. Nationality: Armenian.
Joseph A. McAlinden Divers Scholarship	647	$3000	$500		Military Service: Marine Corps; Navy.
Joseph H. Bearns Prize in Music	814	$3000	$2000	2	Talent/Interest Area: music.
Joseph Henry Jackson Literary Award	787	$3000	$2000	3	Residence: California; Nevada. Talent/Interest Area: writing.
Joseph S. Rumbaugh Historical Oration Contest	825	$3000	$1000	1–3	Talent/Interest Area: public speaking.
Kentucky Tuition Grant (KTG)	752	$3000	$200	12,000–13,000	Residence: Kentucky. Studying in Kentucky.
Kildee Scholarships	85	$3000	$2000	3	Agriculture; Animal/Veterinary Sciences.
Landscape Architecture Foundation/California Landscape Architectural Student Fund Scholarships Program	360	$3000	$1000	15	Horticulture/Floriculture; Landscape Architecture. Studying in California.
Marion A. and Eva S. Peeples Scholarships	240	$3000	$1000	30–35	Education; Engineering/Technology; Food Science/Nutrition; Nursing; Trade/Technical Specialties. Residence: Indiana. Studying in Indiana.
MasterCard Worldwide Special Support Program	691	$3000	$2000	1	Limited to Black (non-Hispanic) students.
Minority Nurse Magazine Scholarship Program	452	$3000	$1000	3	Nursing. Limited to ethnic minority students.
Miss American Coed Pageant	823	$3000	$150	52	Talent/Interest Area: beauty pageant.
Mississippi Health Care Professions Loan/Scholarship Program	346	$3000	$1500	varies	Health and Medical Sciences; Psychology; Therapy/Rehabilitation. Residence: Mississippi. Studying in Mississippi.
Missouri Higher Education Academic Scholarship (Bright Flight)	764	$3000	$1000	varies	Residence: Missouri. Studying in Missouri.

Award Name	Page Number	Highest Dollar Amount	Lowest Dollar Amount	Number of Awards	Academic Fields/Career Goals and Nonacademic/Noncareer Criteria
MRCA Foundation Scholarship Program	102	$3000	$500	25	Architecture; Civil Engineering; Construction Engineering/Management; Drafting; Engineering/Technology; Industrial Design; Materials Science, Engineering, and Metallurgy; Trade/Technical Specialties. Employment/Volunteer Experience: construction.
NAAS II National Awards	855	$3000	$500	1–5	
National Asphalt Pavement Association Research and Education Foundation Scholarship Program	178	$3000	$500	50–150	Civil Engineering; Construction Engineering/Management.
National Federation of Paralegal Associates Inc. Thomson Reuters Scholarship	393	$3000	$2000	2	Law/Legal Services.
National High School Essay Contest	831	$3000	$750	3	Talent/Interest Area: writing.
National Multiple Sclerosis Society Mid America Chapter Scholarship	610	$3000	$1000	100	Disability: physically disabled.
New Economy Technology and SciTech Scholarships	270	$3000	$1000	varies	Engineering-Related Technologies; Engineering/Technology; Natural Sciences; Physical Sciences. Residence: Pennsylvania. Studying in Pennsylvania.
Ohio American Legion Scholarships	533	$3000	$2000	15–18	Civic Affiliation: American Legion or Auxiliary. Military Service: General.
OSCPA Educational Foundation Scholarship Program	69	$3000	$500	50–100	Accounting. Residence: Oregon. Studying in Oregon.
Passport to College Promise Scholarship	800	$3000	$1	1–400	Residence: Washington. Studying in Washington.
Pennsylvania Masonic Youth Foundation Educational Endowment Fund Scholarships	558	$3000	$1000	varies	Civic Affiliation: Freemasons.
PFLAG Scholarship Awards Program	782	$3000	$500	5–10	Residence: Georgia. Studying in Georgia. Talent/Interest Area: LGBT issues.
Plastics Pioneers Scholarships	168	$3000	$1500	30–40	Chemical Engineering; Engineering-Related Technologies; Engineering/Technology; Materials Science, Engineering, and Metallurgy; Trade/Technical Specialties.
Profile in Courage Essay Contest	398	$3000	$500	7	Literature/English/Writing. Talent/Interest Area: writing.
Rama Scholarship for the American Dream	208	$3000	$1000		Culinary Arts; Food Service/Hospitality; Hospitality Management; Recreation, Parks, Leisure Studies; Travel/Tourism. Limited to ethnic minority students.
Roadway Worker Memorial Scholarship Program	838	$3000	$2000	2–5	
Rockefeller State Wildlife Scholarship	141	$3000	$2000	20–30	Biology; Marine Biology; Marine/Ocean Engineering; Natural Resources; Oceanography. Residence: Louisiana. Studying in Louisiana.
Roothbert Fund Inc. Scholarship	785	$3000	$2000	20	Studying in Connecticut; Delaware; District of Columbia; Maryland; Massachusetts; New Hampshire; New Jersey; New York; Ohio; Pennsylvania; Rhode Island; Vermont; Virginia; West Virginia.
Scholarships for Education, Business and Religion	149	$3000	$500	varies	Business/Consumer Services; Education; Religion/Theology. Residence: California.
Seaspace Scholarship Program	402	$3000	$500	10–15	Marine Biology; Oceanography.
Seol Bong Scholarship	678	$3000	$2000	23	Nationality: Korean. Residence: Connecticut; Delaware; Maine; Massachusetts; New Hampshire; New Jersey; New York; Pennsylvania; Rhode Island; Vermont. Studying in Connecticut; Delaware; Maine; Massachusetts; New Hampshire; New Jersey; New York; Pennsylvania; Rhode Island; Vermont. Limited to Asian/Pacific Islander students.

SCHOLARSHIPS, GRANTS & PRIZES AT-A-GLANCE

Award Name	Page Number	Highest Dollar Amount	Lowest Dollar Amount	Number of Awards	Academic Fields/Career Goals and Nonacademic/Noncareer Criteria
Siemens Competition in Math, Science and Technology	493	$3000	$1000	varies	Science, Technology, and Society.
Society of Louisiana CPAs Scholarships	70	$3000	$500	varies	Accounting. Residence: Louisiana. Studying in Louisiana.
Society of Sponsors of the United States Navy Centennial Scholarship Program	647	$3000	$500	1–5	Military Service: Marine Corps; Navy.
SOLE—The International Society of Logistics Scholarship/Doctoral Dissertation Awards	272	$3000	$500	1–3	Engineering-Related Technologies.
Sonne Scholarship	449	$3000	$1000	2–4	Nursing. Residence: Illinois. Studying in Illinois.
Sorantin Young Artist Award	426	$3000	$1000	5–12	Music; Performing Arts. Talent/Interest Area: music.
Texas History Essay Contest	90	$3000	$1000	3	American Studies; History. Talent/Interest Area: writing.
Two Ten Footwear Foundation Scholarship	597	$3000	$500	200–300	Employment/Volunteer Experience: leather/footwear.
USA Freestyle Martial Arts Scholarship	596	$3000	$1000	2	Employment/Volunteer Experience: community service. Residence: California. Talent/Interest Area: athletics/sports.
Video Contest for College Students	813	$3000	$100	8	Talent/Interest Area: art.
Wal-Mart Higher Reach Scholarship	581	$3000	$250	varies	Corporate Affiliation.
West Virginia Engineering, Science and Technology Scholarship Program	259	$3000	$1500	200–300	Electrical Engineering/Electronics; Engineering-Related Technologies; Engineering/Technology; Science, Technology, and Society. Residence: West Virginia. Studying in West Virginia.
William P. Willis Scholarship	777	$3000	$2000		Residence: Oklahoma. Studying in Oklahoma.
Wings Over America Scholarship	650	$3000	$1000	40	Military Service: Navy.
Wisconsin Higher Education Grants (WHEG)	803	$3000	$250	varies	Residence: Wisconsin. Studying in Wisconsin.
Writer's Digest Annual Writing Competition	833	$3000	$25	100	Talent/Interest Area: writing.
Writer's Digest Self-Published Book Awards	834	$3000	$1000	10	Talent/Interest Area: writing.
WSTLA American Justice Essay Scholarship Contest	394	$3000	$2000	3	Law/Legal Services. Studying in Washington.
California Farm Bureau Scholarship	78	$2750	$1800	30	Agribusiness; Agriculture. Residence: California. Studying in California.
Howard P. Rawlings Educational Excellence Awards Educational Assistance Grant	757	$2700	$400	15,000–30,000	Residence: Maryland. Studying in Maryland.
New Century Scholarship	790	$2682	$457	1	Residence: Utah. Studying in Utah.
Virginia Tuition Assistance Grant Program (Private Institutions)	800	$2650		22,000	Residence: Virginia. Studying in Virginia.
Postsecondary Child Care Grant Program-Minnesota	762	$2600	$100	varies	Residence: Minnesota. Studying in Minnesota.
South Carolina Tuition Grants Program	789	$2600	$100		Residence: South Carolina. Studying in South Carolina.
ACES Copy Editing Scholarship	373	$2500	$1000	varies	Journalism. Talent/Interest Area: writing.
Adult Students in Scholastic Transition	846	$2500	$250	100–150	
Agnes Jones Jackson Scholarship	550	$2500	$1500	1	Civic Affiliation: National Association for the Advancement of Colored People. Limited to ethnic minority students.
AIA/AAF Minority/Disadvantaged Scholarship	99	$2500	$500	20	Architecture. Limited to ethnic minority students.

Award Name	Page Number	Highest Dollar Amount	Lowest Dollar Amount	Number of Awards	Academic Fields/Career Goals and Nonacademic/Noncareer Criteria
AIAA Foundation Undergraduate Scholarship	93	$2500	$2000	30	Applied Sciences; Aviation/Aerospace; Electrical Engineering/Electronics; Engineering-Related Technologies; Engineering/Technology; Materials Science, Engineering, and Metallurgy; Mechanical Engineering; Physical Sciences; Science, Technology, and Society. Civic Affiliation: American Institute of Aeronautics and Astronautics.
Air Traffic Control Association Scholarship	121	$2500	$600	7–12	Aviation/Aerospace; Engineering/Technology. Employment/Volunteer Experience: air traffic controller field. Talent/Interest Area: aviation.
Allen and Joan Bildner Scholarship	683	$2500	$2000	varies	Residence: New Jersey. Limited to Black (non-Hispanic) students.
American Board of Funeral Service Education Scholarships	329	$2500	$500	5–15	Funeral Services/Mortuary Science.
American Council of the Blind Scholarships	599	$2500	$1000	16–20	Disability: visually impaired.
American Legion Auxiliary Department of Florida National Presidents' Scholarship	627	$2500	$500	3–15	Military Service: General.
American Legion Auxiliary Department of Maine National President's Scholarship	582	$2500	$1000	3	Employment/Volunteer Experience: community service. Military Service: General. Residence: Maine.
American Legion Auxiliary Department of North Dakota National President's Scholarship	582	$2500	$1000	3	Employment/Volunteer Experience: community service. Military Service: General. Residence: North Dakota. Studying in North Dakota.
American Legion Auxiliary Department of Oregon National President's Scholarship	630	$2500	$1000	3	Military Service: General. Residence: Oregon.
American Legion Auxiliary Department of Utah National President's Scholarship	527	$2500	$1000	15	Civic Affiliation: American Legion or Auxiliary. Military Service: General. Residence: Utah.
American Legion Auxiliary National President's Scholarship	629	$2500	$1500	10–15	Military Service: General.
American Legion Auxiliary National President's Scholarships	632	$2500	$1000	15	Military Service: General.
American Legion Department of Washington Children and Youth Scholarships	534	$2500	$1500	2	Civic Affiliation: American Legion or Auxiliary. Military Service: General. Residence: Washington. Studying in Washington.
BIA Higher Education Grant	665	$2500	$50	1–150	Limited to American Indian/Alaska Native students.
Breakthrough to Nursing Scholarships for Racial/Ethnic Minorities	446	$2500	$1000	varies	Nursing. Limited to ethnic minority students.
Buckingham Memorial Scholarship	582	$2500	$1000	2–4	Employment/Volunteer Experience: air traffic controller field.
California Council of the Blind Scholarships	600	$2500	$375	20	Disability: visually impaired. Residence: California. Studying in California.
Carpe Diem Foundation of Illinois Scholarship Competition	841	$2500	$1500	10–20	
Claricode Medical Software Scholarship Essay	842	$2500	$500	3	
Clem Judd, Jr. Memorial Scholarship	362	$2500	$1000	2	Hospitality Management. Residence: Hawaii. Limited to Asian/Pacific Islander students.
CrossLites Scholarship Award	815	$2500	$100	33	Talent/Interest Area: writing.
Deloras Jones RN Nursing as a Second Career Scholarship	450	$2500	$1000	varies	Nursing. Residence: California. Studying in California.
Deloras Jones RN Scholarship Program	450	$2500	$1000	varies	Nursing. Residence: California. Studying in California.
Deloras Jones RN Underrepresented Groups in Nursing Scholarship	450	$2500	$1000	varies	Nursing. Residence: California. Studying in California. Limited to ethnic minority students.

Award Name	Page Number	Highest Dollar Amount	Lowest Dollar Amount	Number of Awards	Academic Fields/Career Goals and Nonacademic/Noncareer Criteria
Donna Jamison Lago Memorial Scholarship	674	$2500	$500	9	Talent/Interest Area: writing. Limited to Black (non-Hispanic) students.
Education Foundation, Inc. National Guard Association of Colorado Scholarships	619	$2500	$500	20–30	Military Service: Air Force National Guard; Army National Guard. Residence: Colorado.
E. Wayne Kay High School Scholarship	297	$2500	$1000	1–20	Engineering/Technology.
Explosive Ordnance Disposal Memorial Scholarship	586	$2500	$1900	25–75	Employment/Volunteer Experience: explosive ordinance disposal. Military Service: General.
Foundation for Accounting Education Scholarship	69	$2500	$200	1–200	Accounting. Residence: New York. Studying in New York.
Foundation for Surgical Technology Scholarship Fund	343	$2500	$500	10–20	Health and Medical Sciences.
Foundation of the National Student Nurses' Association Career Mobility Scholarship	446	$2500	$1000	varies	Nursing.
Foundation of the National Student Nurses' Association General Scholarships	447	$2500	$1000	varies	Nursing.
Foundation of the National Student Nurses' Association Specialty Scholarship	447	$2500	$1000	varies	Nursing.
Friends of Bill Rutherford Education Fund	778	$2500	$1000	1–2	Residence: Oregon.
Fulfilling Our Dreams Scholarship Fund	679	$2500	$500	50–60	Nationality: Hispanic; Latin American/Caribbean. Residence: California. Studying in California. Limited to Hispanic students.
HANA Scholarship	663	$2500	$1500	varies	Religion: Methodist. Talent/Interest Area: leadership. Limited to American Indian/Alaska Native; Asian/Pacific Islander; Hispanic students.
Harry and Rose Howell Scholarship	570	$2500	$2000	3	Civic Affiliation: Naval Sea Cadet Corps.
HBCUConnect.com Minority Scholarship Program	663	$2500	$1000	1–12	Limited to ethnic minority students.
High School Scholarship	284	$2500	$1500	6	Engineering/Technology. Residence: Florida.
Hopi Education Award	666	$2500	$50	1–400	Limited to American Indian/Alaska Native students.
Institute of Management Accountants Memorial Education Fund Scholarships	65	$2500	$1000	6–15	Accounting; Business/Consumer Services.
Jackson-Stricks Scholarship	607	$2500	$1500	1–7	Disability: physically disabled. Residence: New York. Studying in New York.
Jennifer Curtis Byler Scholarship for the Study of Public Affairs	188	$2500	$1000	1	Communications; Public Policy and Administration.
Joseph S. Garske Collegiate Grant Program	543	$2500	$1500	1–4	Civic Affiliation: Golf Course Superintendents Association of America.
Kentucky Educational Excellence Scholarship (KEES)	752	$2500	$125	65,000–68,000	Residence: Kentucky. Studying in Kentucky.
Kentucky Society of Certified Public Accountants College Scholarship	65	$2500	$1000	23	Accounting. Residence: Kentucky. Studying in Kentucky.
Koniag Education Foundation Academic/Graduate Scholarship	668	$2500	$500	130–170	Limited to American Indian/Alaska Native students.
Korean-American Scholarship Foundation Northeastern Region Scholarships	669	$2500	$1000	60	Nationality: Korean. Studying in Connecticut; Maine; Massachusetts; New Hampshire; New Jersey; New York; Rhode Island; Vermont. Limited to Asian/Pacific Islander students.
Larry Fullerton Photojournalism Scholarship	472	$2500	$500	1–2	Photojournalism/Photography. Residence: Ohio. Studying in Ohio. Talent/Interest Area: photography/photogrammetry/filmmaking.
LEAGUE Foundation Academic Scholarship	822	$2500	$1500	4–8	Talent/Interest Area: LGBT issues.

Award Name	Page Number	Highest Dollar Amount	Lowest Dollar Amount	Number of Awards	Academic Fields/Career Goals and Nonacademic/Noncareer Criteria
Legislative Endowment Scholarships	771	$2500	$1000	1	Residence: New Mexico. Studying in New Mexico.
Lessans Family Scholarship	657	$2500	$1000	12–20	Nationality: Jewish. Residence: Maryland. Religion: Jewish.
Leveraging Educational Assistance Partnership	714	$2500	$100	varies	Residence: Arizona. Studying in Arizona.
Library Research Grants	108	$2500	$500	varies	Art History; Arts. Studying in California. Talent/Interest Area: art.
Literacy Grant Competition	544	$2500	$300	18	Civic Affiliation: Phi Kappa Phi.
Lyndon Baines Johnson Foundation Grants-in-Aid Research	353	$2500	$500	10–20	History; Political Science. Studying in Texas.
Maine State Society Foundation Scholarship	756	$2500	$1000	5–10	Residence: Maine. Studying in Maine.
Marshall E. McCullough-National Dairy Shrine Scholarships	85	$2500	$1000	2	Agriculture; Animal/Veterinary Sciences; Journalism.
Mary Rubin and Benjamin M. Rubin Scholarship Fund	722	$2500	$1000	20–35	Residence: Maryland.
Massachusetts Gilbert Matching Student Grant Program	759	$2500	$200	varies	Residence: Massachusetts. Studying in Massachusetts.
Minnesota Space Grant Consortium Scholarship Program	127	$2500	$500	30–80	Aviation/Aerospace; Earth Science; Engineering/Technology; Mathematics; Physical Sciences. Studying in Minnesota.
Minority Scholarship Award for Academic Excellence-Physical Therapist Assistant	339	$2500	$2000	1	Health and Medical Sciences; Therapy/Rehabilitation. Limited to ethnic minority students.
Minority Undergraduate Retention Grant-Wisconsin	695	$2500	$250	varies	Residence: Wisconsin. Studying in Wisconsin. Limited to ethnic minority students.
Missouri Broadcasters Association Scholarship	518	$2500	$1000	3	TV/Radio Broadcasting. Residence: Missouri. Studying in Missouri.
Missouri Insurance Education Foundation Scholarship	370	$2500	$2000	6	Insurance and Actuarial Science. Residence: Missouri. Studying in Missouri.
NASA Idaho Space Grant Consortium Scholarship Program	141	$2500	$1000	1–15	Biology; Chemical Engineering; Civil Engineering; Computer Science/Data Processing; Earth Science; Electrical Engineering/Electronics; Geography; Materials Science, Engineering, and Metallurgy; Mathematics; Mechanical Engineering; Natural Sciences; Physical Sciences. Studying in Idaho.
National Ground Water Research and Educational Foundation's Len Assante Scholarship	226	$2500	$1000	5–10	Earth Science; Environmental Science; Hydrology.
New Jersey Association of Realtors Educational Foundation Scholarship Program	487	$2500	$1000	20–32	Real Estate. Civic Affiliation: New Jersey Association of Realtors. Residence: New Jersey.
New Mexico Student Incentive Grant	771	$2500	$200	1	Residence: New Mexico. Studying in New Mexico.
NMCRS Gold Star Scholarships for Children of Deceased Service Members	647	$2500	$500	1–100	Military Service: Marine Corps; Navy.
North Carolina 4-H Development Fund Scholarships	773	$2500	$500	varies	Residence: North Carolina. Studying in North Carolina.
North Carolina Hispanic College Fund Scholarship	674	$2500	$500	varies	Residence: North Carolina. Limited to Hispanic students.
Northwest Journalists of Color Scholarship	375	$2500	$500	1–4	Journalism. Residence: Washington. Limited to ethnic minority students.
Ohio Environmental Science & Engineering Scholarships	311	$2500	$1250	18	Environmental Science. Studying in Ohio.
Optimist International Oratorical Contest	825	$2500	$1000	90–115	Talent/Interest Area: public speaking.

Award Name	Page Number	Highest Dollar Amount	Lowest Dollar Amount	Number of Awards	Academic Fields/Career Goals and Nonacademic/Noncareer Criteria
Raymond W. Miller, PE Scholarship	284	$2500	$1500	1	Engineering/Technology. Residence: Florida. Studying in Florida.
RDW Group Inc. Minority Scholarship for Communications	190	$2500	$1000		Communications. Residence: Rhode Island. Limited to ethnic minority students.
Richard B. Gassett, PE Scholarship	284	$2500	$1500	1	Engineering/Technology. Residence: Florida. Studying in Florida.
San Diego Fire Victims Scholarship-General Fund	787	$2500	$500	5	Residence: California.
San Diego Fire Victims Scholarship-Latino Fund	679	$2500	$500	5	Residence: California. Studying in California. Limited to Hispanic students.
Scotts Company Scholars Program	358	$2500	$500	5	Horticulture/Floriculture.
Seventeen Magazine Fiction Contest	828	$2500	$100	8	Talent/Interest Area: writing.
Sidney B. Meadows Scholarship	361	$2500	$1500	10–15	Horticulture/Floriculture. Residence: Arkansas; Florida; Georgia; Kentucky; Louisiana; Maryland; Mississippi; Missouri; North Carolina; Oklahoma; South Carolina; Tennessee; Texas; Virginia.
Simon Youth Foundation Community Scholarship Program	864	$2500	$1400	100–200	Must be in high school.
Society of Physics Students Outstanding Student in Research	479	$2500	$500	1–2	Physical Sciences. Civic Affiliation: Society of Physics Students.
South Carolina Need-Based Grants Program	788	$2500	$1250	1–26,730	Residence: South Carolina. Studying in South Carolina.
Stockholm Scholarship Program	571	$2500	$2000	1	Civic Affiliation: Naval Sea Cadet Corps.
Swiss Benevolent Society of Chicago Scholarships	681	$2500	$750	30	Nationality: Swiss. Residence: Illinois; Wisconsin.
Tennessee Society of CPA Scholarship	71	$2500	$250	120–130	Accounting. Residence: Tennessee.
Undergraduate Marketing Education Merit Scholarships	147	$2500	$500	3	Business/Consumer Services; Marketing.
Utah Leveraging Educational Assistance Partnership	798	$2500	$300	3,252	Residence: Utah. Studying in Utah.
WIFLE Scholarship Program	202	$2500	$500	1–5	Computer Science/Data Processing; Law Enforcement/Police Administration; Physical Sciences; Public Policy and Administration; Social Sciences. Employment/Volunteer Experience: community service.
Writer's Digest Popular Fiction Awards	833	$2500	$500	6	Talent/Interest Area: writing.
Y.C. Yang Civil Engineering Scholarship	175	$2500	$2000	2	Civil Engineering.
Datatel Scholars Foundation Scholarship	844	$2400	$1000	270	
Massachusetts Assistance for Student Success Program	759	$2400	$300	25,000–30,000	Residence: Massachusetts. Studying in Connecticut; District of Columbia; Maine; Massachusetts; New Hampshire; Pennsylvania; Rhode Island; Vermont.
Peter and Alice Koomruian Armenian Education Fund	676	$2300	$1000	5–20	Nationality: Armenian.
Florida Postsecondary Student Assistance Grant	738	$2235	$200	varies	Residence: Florida. Studying in Florida.
Florida Private Student Assistance Grant	738	$2235	$200	varies	Residence: Florida. Studying in Florida.
Florida Public Student Assistance Grant	738	$2235	$200	varies	Residence: Florida. Studying in Florida.
Florida Student Assistance Grant-Career Education	738	$2235	$200		Residence: Florida. Studying in Florida.
Menominee Indian Tribe Adult Vocational Training Program	670	$2200	$100	50–70	Limited to American Indian/Alaska Native students.
Menominee Indian Tribe of Wisconsin Higher Education Grants	671	$2200	$100	136	Limited to American Indian/Alaska Native students.

Award Name	Page Number	Highest Dollar Amount	Lowest Dollar Amount	Number of Awards	Academic Fields/Career Goals and Nonacademic/Noncareer Criteria
Scholarship Incentive Program (ScIP)	733	$2200	$700	1,000–1,253	Residence: Delaware. Studying in Delaware; Pennsylvania.
Osage Higher Education Scholarship	676	$2100	$1200	1,000	Limited to American Indian/Alaska Native students.
West Virginia Higher Education Grant Program	802	$2100	$375	20,000–21,152	Residence: West Virginia. Studying in Pennsylvania; West Virginia.

PROFILES OF SCHOLARSHIPS, GRANTS & PRIZES

Academic Fields/Career Goals

ACADEMIC ADVISING

WHOMENTORS.COM, INC.

http://www.WHOmentors.com/

ACCREDITED REPRESENTATIVE (FULL)

Prize Awards available for women of Good Moral Character who are successfully approved by the Board of Immigration Appeals to practice immigration law with a recognized nonprofit organization to represent an alien before an immigration court or the United States Citizenship and Immigration Service (USCIS).

Academic Fields/Career Goals: Academic Advising; Area/Ethnic Studies; Asian Studies; Communications; Criminal Justice/Criminology; Foreign Language; Law/Legal Services; Public Policy and Administration; Women's Studies.

Award: Prize for use in freshman, sophomore, junior, senior, graduate, or postgraduate years; not renewable. *Number:* 1–20. *Amount:* $500–$1000.

Eligibility Requirements: Applicant must be of Chinese, Japanese, Korean, or Latin American/Caribbean heritage; Asian/Pacific Islander or Hispanic; age 17-35; enrolled or expecting to enroll full- or part-time at a two-year or four-year or technical institution or university; single female and must have an interest in beauty pageant, entrepreneurship, foreign language, international exchange, or public speaking. Applicant must have 3.5 GPA or higher. Available to U.S. and non-U.S. citizens.

Application Requirements: Application, driver's license, essay, financial need analysis, interview, photo, portfolio, resume, references, self-addressed stamped envelope, test scores, transcript, complete 10 week, 300 internship. *Deadline:* May 15.

Contact: Rauhmel Fox, CEO
WHOmentors.com, Inc.
110 Pacific Avenue, Suite 250
San Francisco, CA 94111
Phone: 415-373-6767
E-mail: rauhmel@whomentors.com

ACCOUNTING

ALABAMA SOCIETY OF CERTIFIED PUBLIC ACCOUNTANTS

http://www.ascpa.org/

ASCPA EDUCATIONAL FOUNDATION SCHOLARSHIP

Scholarships available for students with a declared major in accounting. Must have completed intermediate accounting courses with a "B" average in all accounting courses, and a "B" average overall. Available for fourth or fifth year of study.

Academic Fields/Career Goals: Accounting.

Award: Scholarship for use in senior or graduate years; not renewable. *Number:* up to 24. *Amount:* up to $1500.

Eligibility Requirements: Applicant must be enrolled or expecting to enroll full- or part-time at a four-year institution or university; resident of Alabama and studying in Alabama. Applicant must have 3.0 GPA or higher. Available to U.S. citizens.

Application Requirements: Application, essay, photo, transcript. *Deadline:* March 15.

Contact: Diane Christy, Communications Director
Alabama Society of Certified Public Accountants
1103 South Perry Street
PO Box 5000
Montgomery, AL 36104
Phone: 334-834-7650
E-mail: dchristy@ascpa.org

ALASKA SOCIETY OF CERTIFIED PUBLIC ACCOUNTANTS

http://www.akcpa.org/

PAUL HAGELBARGER MEMORIAL FUND SCHOLARSHIP

Scholarships open to all junior, senior, and graduate students who are majoring in accounting and attending institutions in Alaska.

Academic Fields/Career Goals: Accounting.

Award: Scholarship for use in junior, senior, or graduate years; not renewable. *Number:* 2–3. *Amount:* $2000.

Eligibility Requirements: Applicant must be enrolled or expecting to enroll full-time at a four-year institution or university and studying in Alaska. Available to U.S. citizens.

Application Requirements: Application, resume, references, transcript. *Deadline:* November 15.

Contact: Linda Plimpton, Executive Director
Alaska Society of Certified Public Accountants
341 West Tudor Road, Suite 105
Anchorage, AK 99503
Phone: 907-562-4334
Fax: 907-562-4025
E-mail: akcpa@ak.net

AMERICAN ASSOCIATION OF HISPANIC CERTIFIED PUBLIC ACCOUNTANTS (AAHCPA)

http://www.alpfa.org/

ALPFA ANNUAL SCHOLARSHIP PROGRAM

One-time award to undergraduate and graduate Hispanic/Latino students pursuing degrees in accounting, finance, and related majors. Awarded based on financial need and academic performance. Must be enrolled full-time at a U.S. college or university. Minimum 3.0 GPA required. Must be U.S. citizens or legal permanent residents.

Academic Fields/Career Goals: Accounting; Business/Consumer Services.

Award: Scholarship for use in freshman, sophomore, junior, or senior years; not renewable. *Number:* varies. *Amount:* $1250–$1500.

Eligibility Requirements: Applicant must be of Hispanic heritage and enrolled or expecting to enroll full-time at a two-year or four-year institution or university. Applicant must have 3.0 GPA or higher. Available to U.S. citizens.

Application Requirements: Application, essay, financial need analysis, references, transcript. *Deadline:* March 15.

Contact: Geraldine Contreras, Director of Student Affairs
American Association of Hispanic Certified Public Accountants (AAHCPA)
801 South Grand Ave, Suite 650
Los Angeles, CA 90017
E-mail: geraldine.contreras@national.alpfa.org

AMERICAN INSTITUTE OF CERTIFIED PUBLIC ACCOUNTANTS

http://www.aicpa.org/

AICPA/ACCOUNTEMPS STUDENT SCHOLARSHIP

The AICPA/Accountemps Student Scholarship program provides financial assistance to outstanding accounting students who demonstrate the potential to become leaders in the CPA profession. Students must have maintained a minimum GPA of 3.0 and have completed at least 30 semester credit hours (or equivalent) with at least 6 semester hours (or equivalent) in accounting coursework. Students must be enrolled full-time for the upcoming academic year. Additionally, award recipients are required to perform 16 community service hours to advocate on behalf of the CPA profession. More details and information is available on the program web site: http://ThisWayToCPA.com/aicpascholarships.

Academic Fields/Career Goals: Accounting.

Award: Scholarship for use in sophomore, junior, senior, or graduate years; not renewable. *Number:* up to 5. *Amount:* up to $2500.

Eligibility Requirements: Applicant must be enrolled or expecting to enroll full-time at a four-year institution or university. Applicant must have 3.0 GPA or higher. Available to U.S. citizens.

Application Requirements: Application, essay, references, test scores, transcript. *Deadline:* April 1.

Contact: Elizabeth DeBragga, Scholarship Programs Coordinator
American Institute of Certified Public Accountants
American Institute of CPAs, 220 Leigh Farm Road
Durham, NC 27707
Phone: 919-402-4931
Fax: 919-419-4705
E-mail: scholarships@aicpa.org

SCHOLARSHIP FOR MINORITY ACCOUNTING STUDENTS

The AICPA Minority Scholarship awards outstanding minority students to encourage their selection of accounting as a major and their ultimate entry into the profession. Funding is provided by the AICPA Foundation, with contributions from the New Jersey Society of CPAs and Robert Half International. For four decades, this program has provided over $14.6 million in scholarships to approximately 8,000 accounting scholars. Additionally, award recipients are required to perform 16 community service hours to advocate on behalf of the CPA profession. More details and information is available on the program web site: http://ThisWay-ToCPA.com/aicpascholarships.

Academic Fields/Career Goals: Accounting.

Award: Scholarship for use in sophomore, junior, senior, or graduate years; not renewable. *Number:* 67–110. *Amount:* up to $3000.

Eligibility Requirements: Applicant must be American Indian/Alaska Native, Asian/Pacific Islander, Black (non-Hispanic), or Hispanic and enrolled or expecting to enroll full-time at a four-year institution or university. Applicant must have 3.0 GPA or higher. Available to U.S. citizens.

Application Requirements: Application, essay, references, test scores, transcript, copy of acceptance letter. *Deadline:* April 1.

Contact: Elizabeth DeBragga, Scholarship Programs Coordinator
American Institute of Certified Public Accountants
220 Leigh Farm Road
Durham, NC 27707
Phone: 919-402-4931
Fax: 919-419-4705
E-mail: scholarships@aicpa.org

AMERICAN SOCIETY OF WOMEN ACCOUNTANTS

http://www.aswa.org/

AMERICAN SOCIETY OF WOMEN ACCOUNTANTS TWO-YEAR COLLEGE SCHOLARSHIP

Scholarship for students pursuing an accounting or finance degree in community, state, or two-year colleges. Must have a minimum cumulative college GPA of 3.0 and be a member of ASWA.

Academic Fields/Career Goals: Accounting.

Award: Scholarship for use in sophomore year; not renewable. *Number:* varies. *Amount:* varies.

Eligibility Requirements: Applicant must be enrolled or expecting to enroll full-time at a two-year institution. Applicant or parent of applicant must be member of American Society of Women Accountants. Applicant must have 3.0 GPA or higher. Available to U.S. citizens.

Application Requirements: Application, essay, financial need analysis, references, transcript. *Deadline:* varies.

Contact: Kristin Edwards, Administrator
American Society of Women Accountants
8405 Greensboro Drive, Suite 800
McLean, VA 22102
Phone: 703-506-3265
Fax: 703-506-3266
E-mail: kedwards@aswa.org

AMERICAN SOCIETY OF WOMEN ACCOUNTANTS UNDERGRADUATE SCHOLARSHIP

Scholarship awards are presented to students who have completed their sophomore year of college and are majoring in accounting or finance. Candidates will be reviewed on leadership, character, communication skills, scholastic average, and financial need.

Academic Fields/Career Goals: Accounting.

Award: Scholarship for use in junior, senior, or graduate years; not renewable. *Number:* varies. *Amount:* varies.

Eligibility Requirements: Applicant must be enrolled or expecting to enroll full- or part-time at a four-year institution or university and must have an interest in leadership. Available to U.S. and non-U.S. citizens.

Application Requirements: Application, essay, financial need analysis, references, transcript. *Deadline:* varies.

Contact: Kristin Edwards, Administrator
American Society of Women Accountants
8405 Greensboro Drive, Suite 800
McLean, VA 22102
Phone: 703-506-3265
Fax: 703-506-3266
E-mail: kedwards@aswa.org

ASSOCIATION OF CERTIFIED FRAUD EXAMINERS

http://www.acfe.com/

RITCHIE-JENNINGS MEMORIAL SCHOLARSHIP

Applicant must be an undergraduate or graduate student, currently enrolled full-time (12 semester hours undergraduate; 9 semester hours graduate, or equivalent) at an accredited four-year college or university (or equivalent) with a declared major or minor in accounting or criminal justice.

Academic Fields/Career Goals: Accounting; Criminal Justice/Criminology.

Award: Scholarship for use in freshman, sophomore, junior, or senior years; not renewable. *Number:* up to 30. *Amount:* $1000.

Eligibility Requirements: Applicant must be enrolled or expecting to enroll full-time at a four-year institution or university. Available to U.S. and non-U.S. citizens.

Application Requirements: Application, essay, references, transcript. *Deadline:* April 16.

Contact: Keely Miers, Scholarship Coordinator
Association of Certified Fraud Examiners
The Gregor Building, 716 West Avenue
Austin, TX 78701
Phone: 800-245-3321
Fax: 512-478-9297
E-mail: scholarships@acfe.com

CATCHING THE DREAM

http://www.catchingthedream.org/

TRIBAL BUSINESS MANAGEMENT PROGRAM (TBM)

Renewable scholarships available for Native American and Alaska Native students to study business administration, economic development, and related subjects, with the goal to provide experts in business management to Native American tribes in the U.S. Must be at least one-quarter Native American from a federally recognized, state recognized, or terminated tribe. Must demonstrate high academic achievement, depth of character, leadership, seriousness of purpose, and service orientation.

Academic Fields/Career Goals: Accounting; Business/Consumer Services; Computer Science/Data Processing; Economics; Electrical Engineering/Electronics; Engineering-Related Technologies.

Award: Scholarship for use in freshman, sophomore, junior, senior, graduate, or postgraduate years; renewable. *Number:* up to 35. *Amount:* $500–$5000.

Eligibility Requirements: Applicant must be American Indian/Alaska Native and enrolled or expecting to enroll full-time at a four-year institution or university. Applicant must have 3.0 GPA or higher. Available to U.S. citizens.

Application Requirements: Application, essay, financial need analysis, photo, references, test scores, transcript, certificate of Indian blood. *Deadline:* varies.

Contact: Mary Frost, Recruiter
Catching the Dream
8200 Mountain Road, NE, Suite 203
Albuquerque, NM 87110
Phone: 505-262-2351
Fax: 505-262-0534
E-mail: nscholarsh@aol.com

CENTRAL INTELLIGENCE AGENCY

http://www.cia.gov/

CENTRAL INTELLIGENCE AGENCY UNDERGRADUATE SCHOLARSHIP PROGRAM

Need and merit-based award for students with minimum 3.0 GPA, who are interested in working for the Central Intelligence Agency upon graduation. Renewable for four years of undergraduate study. Must apply in senior year of high school or sophomore year in college. For further information refer to web site http://www.cia.gov.

Academic Fields/Career Goals: Accounting; Business/Consumer Services; Computer Science/Data Processing; Economics; Electrical Engineering/Electronics; Foreign Language; Geography; Graphics/Graphic Arts/Printing; International Studies; Political Science; Surveying, Surveying Technology, Cartography, or Geographic Information Science.

Award: Scholarship for use in freshman, sophomore, junior, or senior years; renewable. *Number:* varies. *Amount:* up to $18,000.

Eligibility Requirements: Applicant must be age 18 and over and enrolled or expecting to enroll full-time at a four-year institution or university. Applicant must have 3.0 GPA or higher. Available to U.S. citizens.

Application Requirements: Application, financial need analysis, resume, references, test scores, transcript. *Deadline:* November 1.

Contact: Van Patrick, Chief, College Relations
Central Intelligence Agency
Recruitment Center, L 100 LF7
Washington, DC 20505
Phone: 703-613-8388
Fax: 703-613-7676
E-mail: ivanilp0@ucia.gov

CIRI FOUNDATION (TCF)

http://www.thecirifoundation.org/

CARL H. MARRS SCHOLARSHIP FUND

Merit-based scholarship for exceptional academic and community service experience. Awards students seeking an undergraduate or graduate degree in business administration, economics, finance, organizational management, accounting, or similar field. Applicant must be Alaska Native original enrollee to CIRI or descendant. Minimum 3.7 cumulative GPA required.

Academic Fields/Career Goals: Accounting; Business/Consumer Services; Economics.

Award: Scholarship for use in freshman, sophomore, junior, senior, or graduate years; not renewable. *Number:* varies. *Amount:* $20,000.

Eligibility Requirements: Applicant must be American Indian/Alaska Native and enrolled or expecting to enroll full-time at a two-year or four-year institution or university. Available to U.S. and non-U.S. citizens.

Application Requirements: Application, essay, references, transcript, proof of eligibility, birth certificate or adoption decree. *Deadline:* June 1.

Contact: Susan Anderson, President and Chief Executive Officer
CIRI Foundation (TCF)
3600 San Jeronimo Drive, Suite 256
Anchorage, AK 99508-2870
Phone: 907-793-3575
E-mail: tcf@thecirifoundation.org

CLEVELAND SCHOLARSHIP PROGRAMS

http://www.cspohio.org/

CSP MANAGED FUNDS-CLEVELAND BROWNS MARION MOTLEY SCHOLARSHIP

Renewable scholarship of $2500 to students enrolled in a high school located in Northeast Ohio, on track to graduate from high school at the end of the current academic year and planning to enroll in college in the next academic year.

Academic Fields/Career Goals: Accounting; Business/Consumer Services; Journalism; Marketing; Sports-Related/Exercise Science; Therapy/Rehabilitation.

Award: Scholarship for use in freshman year; renewable. *Number:* 2. *Amount:* $2500.

Eligibility Requirements: Applicant must be high school student; planning to enroll or expecting to enroll full-time at a four-year institution or university; resident of Ohio and studying in Ohio. Applicant must have 2.5 GPA or higher. Available to U.S. citizens.

Application Requirements: Application, essay, financial need analysis, interview, resume, references, test scores, transcript, tax form, FAFSA. *Deadline:* October 24.

Contact: Bridget Vaughn, Scholarship Committee
Cleveland Scholarship Programs
200 Public Square, Suite 3820
Cleveland, OH 44114
Phone: 216-241-5587 Ext. 113
Fax: 216-241-6184
E-mail: bvaughn@cspohio.org

COHEN & COMPANY CPAS

http://www.cohencpa.com/

COHEN AND COMPANY CPAS SCHOLARSHIP

Renewable scholarships for outstanding sophomores and juniors enrolled full-time at accredited Ohio colleges or universities. Must be majoring in accounting. Deadline varies.

Academic Fields/Career Goals: Accounting.

Award: Scholarship for use in sophomore or junior years; renewable. *Number:* varies. *Amount:* $500–$1000.

Eligibility Requirements: Applicant must be enrolled or expecting to enroll full-time at a four-year institution or university and studying in Ohio. Available to U.S. citizens.

Application Requirements: Application, essay, references. *Deadline:* varies.

Contact: Angela Ferenchka, Scholarship Coordinator
Cohen & Company CPAs
1350 Euclid Avenue, Suite 800
Cleveland, OH 44115
Phone: 216-579-1040
Fax: 216-579-0111

COLORADO SOCIETY OF CERTIFIED PUBLIC ACCOUNTANTS EDUCATIONAL FOUNDATION

http://www.cocpa.org/

COLORADO COLLEGE AND UNIVERSITY SCHOLARSHIPS

Award available to declared accounting majors at Colorado colleges and universities with accredited accounting programs. Must have completed at least 8 semester hours of accounting courses. Overall GPA and accounting GPA must be at least 3.0. Must be Colorado resident.

Academic Fields/Career Goals: Accounting.

Award: Scholarship for use in junior, senior, graduate, or postgraduate years; not renewable. *Number:* 15–20. *Amount:* $2500.

Eligibility Requirements: Applicant must be enrolled or expecting to enroll full- or part-time at a four-year institution or university; resident of Colorado and studying in Colorado. Applicant must have 3.0 GPA or higher. Available to U.S. citizens.

Application Requirements: Application, references, transcript. *Deadline:* varies.

Contact: Gena Mantz, Membership Coordinator
Colorado Society of Certified Public Accountants Educational Foundation
7979 East Tufts Avenue, Suite 1000
Denver, CO 80237-2845
Phone: 303-741-8613
Fax: 303-773-6344
E-mail: gmantz@cocpa.org

COLORADO HIGH SCHOOL SCHOLARSHIPS

Scholarships awarded in the spring of each year to outstanding high school seniors who plan to major in accounting.

Academic Fields/Career Goals: Accounting.

Award: Scholarship for use in freshman year; not renewable. *Number:* up to 10. *Amount:* $1000.

Eligibility Requirements: Applicant must be high school student; planning to enroll or expecting to enroll full- or part-time at a four-year institution or university; resident of Colorado and studying in Colorado. Applicant must have 3.0 GPA or higher. Available to U.S. citizens.

Application Requirements: Application, test scores, transcript. *Deadline:* March 1.

Contact: Gena Mantz, Membership Coordinator
Colorado Society of Certified Public Accountants Educational Foundation
7979 East Tufts Avenue, Suite 1000
Denver, CO 80237-2845
Phone: 303-741-8613
Fax: 303-773-6344
E-mail: gmantz@cocpa.org

COMMUNITY FOUNDATION OF WESTERN MASSACHUSETTS

http://www.communityfoundation.org/

GREATER SPRINGFIELD ACCOUNTANTS SCHOLARSHIP

MA and Hartford County, CT residents who have completed their college sophomore year, pursuing accounting or finance.

Academic Fields/Career Goals: Accounting; Finance.

Award: Scholarship for use in junior or senior years; not renewable. *Number:* 3. *Amount:* $1000.

Eligibility Requirements: Applicant must be enrolled or expecting to enroll full-time at a two-year or four-year institution and resident of Connecticut or Massachusetts. Available to U.S. citizens.

Application Requirements: Application, financial need analysis, transcript, Student Aid Report (SAR). *Deadline:* March 31.

Contact: Dorothy Theriaque, Education Associate
Community Foundation of Western Massachusetts
1500 Main Street, PO Box 15769
Springfield, MA 01115
Phone: 413-732-2858
Fax: 413-733-8565
E-mail: scholar@communityfoundation.org

CONNECTICUT SOCIETY OF CERTIFIED PUBLIC ACCOUNTANTS

http://www.cscpa.org/

CSCPA CANDIDATE'S AWARD

Scholarship of $3000 that assists students in complying with the 150-hour requirement of the Connecticut State Board of Accountancy to sit for the Uniform Certified Public Accountant Examination. An overall GPA of 3.0.

Academic Fields/Career Goals: Accounting.

Award: Scholarship for use in senior year; not renewable. *Number:* 8–10. *Amount:* $3000.

Eligibility Requirements: Applicant must be enrolled or expecting to enroll full- or part-time at a four-year institution or university; resident of Connecticut and studying in Connecticut. Applicant must have 3.0 GPA or higher. Available to U.S. citizens.

Application Requirements: Application, essay, transcript. *Deadline:* August 31.

Contact: Ms. Jill A. Wise, Program Coordinator
Connecticut Society of Certified Public Accountants
845 Brook Street, Building Two
Rocky Hill, CT 06067

EDUCATIONAL FOUNDATION FOR WOMEN IN ACCOUNTING (EFWA)

http://www.efwa.org/

MICHELE L. MCDONALD SCHOLARSHIP

Individuals eligible for this award will be women who are returning to college from the workforce or after raising children. Scholarship recipients will be awarded $1000 to begin their studies in pursuit of a college degree in accounting.

Academic Fields/Career Goals: Accounting.

Award: Scholarship for use in freshman, sophomore, junior, or senior years; not renewable. *Number:* varies. *Amount:* $1000.

Eligibility Requirements: Applicant must be enrolled or expecting to enroll full- or part-time at a four-year institution or university and married female. Available to U.S. citizens.

Application Requirements: Application, financial need analysis, transcript. *Deadline:* April 15.

Contact: Cynthia Hires, Foundation Administrator
Educational Foundation for Women in Accounting (EFWA)
PO Box 1925
Southeastern, PA 19399-1925
Phone: 610-407-9229
Fax: 610-644-3713
E-mail: info@efwa.org

ROWLING, DOLD & ASSOCIATES LLP SCHOLARSHIP

One year $1000 scholarship award for minority women enrolled in an accounting program at an accredited college or university. Women returning to school with undergraduate status; incoming, current, or reentry juniors or seniors; or minority women are all eligible.

Academic Fields/Career Goals: Accounting.

Award: Scholarship for use in junior, senior, or graduate years; not renewable. *Number:* varies. *Amount:* $1000.

Eligibility Requirements: Applicant must be American Indian/Alaska Native, Asian/Pacific Islander, Black (non-Hispanic), or Hispanic; enrolled or expecting to enroll full- or part-time at a four-year institution or university and female. Available to U.S. citizens.

Application Requirements: Application, financial need analysis, transcript. *Deadline:* April 15.

Contact: Cynthia Hires, Foundation Administrator
Educational Foundation for Women in Accounting (EFWA)
PO Box 1925
Southeastern, PA 19399-1925
Phone: 610-407-9229
Fax: 610-644-3713
E-mail: info@efwa.org

SEATTLE AMERICAN SOCIETY OF WOMEN ACCOUNTANTS CHAPTER SCHOLARSHIP

Scholarship for an amount up to $2000 to be awarded to a women attending an accredited school within the State of Washington. The scholarship will be renewable for one additional year upon satisfactory completion of course requirements. Must pursue a degree in accounting.

Academic Fields/Career Goals: Accounting.

Award: Scholarship for use in freshman, sophomore, junior, or senior years; renewable. *Number:* varies. *Amount:* up to $2000.

Eligibility Requirements: Applicant must be enrolled or expecting to enroll full- or part-time at a four-year institution or university; female and studying in Washington. Available to U.S. citizens.

Application Requirements: Application, financial need analysis, transcript. *Deadline:* April 15.

Contact: Cynthia Hires, Foundation Administrator
Educational Foundation for Women in Accounting (EFWA)
PO Box 1925
Southeastern, PA 19399-1925
Phone: 610-407-9229
Fax: 610-644-3713
E-mail: info@efwa.org

WOMEN IN NEED SCHOLARSHIP

Scholarship provides financial assistance to female reentry students who wish to pursue a degree in accounting. Scholarship is available to incoming, current, or reentry juniors.

Academic Fields/Career Goals: Accounting.

Award: Scholarship for use in junior year; renewable. *Number:* 1. *Amount:* $2000.

Eligibility Requirements: Applicant must be enrolled or expecting to enroll full- or part-time at a four-year institution or university and female. Available to U.S. citizens.

Application Requirements: Application, financial need analysis, transcript. *Deadline:* April 15.

Contact: Cynthia Hires, Foundation Administrator
Educational Foundation for Women in Accounting (EFWA)
PO Box 1925
Southeastern, PA 19399-1925
Phone: 610-407-9229
Fax: 610-644-3713
E-mail: info@efwa.org

WOMEN IN TRANSITION SCHOLARSHIP

Renewable award available to incoming or current freshmen and women returning to school with a freshman status. Scholarship value may be up to $16,000 over four years.

Academic Fields/Career Goals: Accounting.

Award: Scholarship for use in freshman year; renewable. *Number:* 1. *Amount:* up to $4000.

Eligibility Requirements: Applicant must be enrolled or expecting to enroll full- or part-time at a four-year institution or university and female. Available to U.S. citizens.

Application Requirements: Application, financial need analysis, transcript. *Deadline:* April 15.

Contact: Cynthia Hires, Foundation Administrator
Educational Foundation for Women in Accounting (EFWA)
PO Box 1925
Southeastern, PA 19399-1925
Phone: 610-407-9229
Fax: 610-644-3713
E-mail: info@efwa.org

EDUCATIONAL FOUNDATION OF THE MASSACHUSETTS SOCIETY OF CERTIFIED PUBLIC ACCOUNTANTS

http://www.CPATrack.com/

F. GRANT WAITE, CPA, MEMORIAL SCHOLARSHIP

Scholarship available to undergraduate accounting major who has completed sophomore year. Must demonstrate financial need and superior academic standing. Preference given to married students with children. Information available on web site at http://www.cpatrack.com.

Academic Fields/Career Goals: Accounting.

Award: Scholarship for use in junior or senior years; not renewable. *Number:* 1. *Amount:* $1000.

Eligibility Requirements: Applicant must be enrolled or expecting to enroll full-time at a four-year institution or university. Available to U.S. citizens.

Application Requirements: Application, financial need analysis, references, transcript. *Deadline:* March 17.

Contact: Barbara Iannoni, Academic Coordinator
Educational Foundation of the Massachusetts Society of
Certified Public Accountants
105 Chauncy Street
Boston, MA 02111
Phone: 617-556-4000
Fax: 617-556-4126
E-mail: biannoni@mscpaonline.org

KATHLEEN M. PEABODY, CPA, MEMORIAL SCHOLARSHIP

Scholarship available for Massachusetts resident who has completed sophomore year. Must be accounting major with plans to seek an accounting career in Massachusetts. Must demonstrate academic excellence and financial need. Information on web site at http://www.cpatrack.com.

Academic Fields/Career Goals: Accounting.

Award: Scholarship for use in junior or senior years; not renewable. *Number:* 1. *Amount:* $2500.

Eligibility Requirements: Applicant must be enrolled or expecting to enroll full-time at a four-year institution or university and resident of Massachusetts. Available to U.S. citizens.

Application Requirements: Application, financial need analysis, references, transcript. *Deadline:* March 17.

Contact: Barbara Iannoni, Academic Coordinator
Educational Foundation of the Massachusetts Society of
Certified Public Accountants
105 Chauncy Street
Boston, MA 02111
Phone: 617-556-4000
Fax: 617-556-4126
E-mail: biannoni@mscpaonline.org

MSCPA FIRM SCHOLARSHIP

Scholarship to encourage individuals who have demonstrated academic excellence and financial need to pursue a career in public accounting in Massachusetts.

Academic Fields/Career Goals: Accounting.

Award: Scholarship for use in junior, senior, graduate, or postgraduate years; not renewable. *Number:* 12–16. *Amount:* $2500.

Eligibility Requirements: Applicant must be enrolled or expecting to enroll full-time at a four-year institution or university and resident of Massachusetts. Available to U.S. citizens.

Application Requirements: Application, essay, financial need analysis, references, transcript. *Deadline:* March 17.

Contact: Barbara Iannoni, Academic Coordinator
Educational Foundation of the Massachusetts Society of
Certified Public Accountants
105 Chauncy Street
Boston, MA 02111
Phone: 617-556-4000
Fax: 617-556-4126
E-mail: biannoni@mscpaonline.org

PAYCHEX INC. ENTREPRENEUR SCHOLARSHIP

Scholarships available to students who are residents of Massachusetts and attending a Massachusetts college or university. Must be an accounting major entering their junior year, have a minimum 3.0 GPA, and demonstrate financial need. Application and information on web site at http://www.cpatrack.com.

Academic Fields/Career Goals: Accounting.

Award: Scholarship for use in junior year; not renewable. *Number:* 1. *Amount:* $1000.

Eligibility Requirements: Applicant must be enrolled or expecting to enroll full-time at a four-year institution or university; resident of Massachusetts and studying in Massachusetts. Applicant must have 3.0 GPA or higher. Available to U.S. citizens.

Application Requirements: Application, financial need analysis, transcript. *Deadline:* March 17.

Contact: Barbara Iannoni, Academic Coordinator
Educational Foundation of the Massachusetts Society of
Certified Public Accountants
105 Chauncy Street
Boston, MA 02111
Phone: 617-556-4000
Fax: 617-556-4126
E-mail: biannoni@mscpaonline.org

FLORIDA INSTITUTE OF CERTIFIED PUBLIC ACCOUNTANTS EDUCATIONAL FOUNDATION, INC.

http://www.ficpa.org/

1040K RUN/WALK SCHOLARSHIPS

Scholarship for African American permanent resident of Miami-Dade, Broward, Monroe or Palm Beach Counties. Applicants must be full-time, 4th- or 5th-year accounting majors at one of the following Florida institutions: Barry University, Florida Atlantic University, Florida International University, Nova Southeastern University, St. Thomas University, or University of Miami. See web site for details http://www1.ficpa.org/ficpa/Visitors/Careers/EdFoundation/Scholar.ships/Availa.

Academic Fields/Career Goals: Accounting.

Award: Scholarship for use in senior year; not renewable. *Number:* up to 3. *Amount:* up to $3000.

Eligibility Requirements: Applicant must be Black (non-Hispanic); enrolled or expecting to enroll full-time at a four-year institution or university; resident of Florida and studying in Florida. Applicant must have 3.0 GPA or higher. Available to U.S. citizens.

Application Requirements: Application, references, transcript, must be recommended by accounting faculty committee at Florida college or university attended. *Deadline:* February 15.

Contact: Mrs. Betsy Wilson, Educational Foundation Assistant
Florida Institute of Certified Public Accountants Educational Foundation, Inc.
325 West College Avenue, PO Box 5437
Tallahassee, FL 32314
Phone: 850-224-2727 Ext. 0
Fax: 850-222-8190
E-mail: wilsonb@ficpa.org

FICPA EDUCATIONAL FOUNDATION SCHOLARSHIPS

Scholarship for full-time or part-time (minimum of six credit hours), fourth- or fifth-year accounting major at participating Florida colleges or universities. Must be a Florida resident and plan to practice accounting in Florida. See web site for list of institutions http://www1.ficpa.org/ficpa/Visitors/Careers/EdFoundation/Scholarships.

Academic Fields/Career Goals: Accounting.

Award: Scholarship for use in senior year; not renewable. *Number:* up to 81. *Amount:* $1000–$2000.

Eligibility Requirements: Applicant must be enrolled or expecting to enroll full- or part-time at a four-year institution or university; resident of Florida and studying in Florida. Applicant must have 3.0 GPA or higher. Available to U.S. citizens.

Application Requirements: Application, references, transcript, must be recommended by faculty committee at school attended. *Deadline:* March 15.

Contact: Mrs. Betsy Wilson, Educational Foundation Assistant
Florida Institute of Certified Public Accountants Educational Foundation, Inc.
325 West College Avenue, PO Box 5437
Tallahassee, FL 32314
Phone: 850-224-2727 Ext. 0
Fax: 850-222-8190
E-mail: wilsonb@ficpa.org

GEORGIA GOVERNMENT FINANCE OFFICERS ASSOCIATION

http://www.ggfoa.org/

GGFOA SCHOLARSHIP

The scholarship recognizes outstanding performance in the study of public finance at the undergraduate and graduate level and encourages careers in state and local government. The GGFOA Scholarship is awarded to undergraduate or graduate students who meet the eligibility requirements and are preparing for a career in public finance. Must have nomination by the head of the applicable program (e.g., public administration, accounting, finance). Preference will be given to GGFOA members and employees of GGFOA governmental entities who are eligible for in-state tuition.

Academic Fields/Career Goals: Accounting; Business/Consumer Services; Finance.

Award: Scholarship for use in freshman, sophomore, junior, senior, or graduate years; not renewable. *Number:* 1–2. *Amount:* $3000.

Eligibility Requirements: Applicant must be enrolled or expecting to enroll full- or part-time at a four-year institution or university and studying in Georgia. Applicant must have 3.0 GPA or higher. Available to U.S. citizens.

Application Requirements: Application, essay, resume, references, test scores, transcript. *Deadline:* September 10.

Contact: Scholarship Selection Committee–GGFOA
Georgia Government Finance Officers Association
GEFA/Attn: Arlene Durrah, 233 Peachtree Street, NE/Harris Tower Suite 900
Atlanta, GA 30303

GEORGIA SOCIETY OF CERTIFIED PUBLIC ACCOUNTANTS

http://www.gscpa.org/

BEN W. BRANNON MEMORIAL SCHOLARSHIP FUND

Scholarship for a rising junior or senior undergraduate accounting major or a graduate student enrolled in a master's level accounting or business administration program at a college or university accredited by the Southern Association of Colleges and Schools. Applicant must demonstrate a commitment to pursuing a career in accounting, be a resident of Georgia and maintain an overall GPA of 3.0.

Academic Fields/Career Goals: Accounting; Business/Consumer Services.

Award: Scholarship for use in junior, senior, or graduate years; not renewable. *Number:* 1. *Amount:* varies.

Eligibility Requirements: Applicant must be enrolled or expecting to enroll full- or part-time at a four-year institution or university and resident of Georgia. Applicant must have 3.0 GPA or higher. Available to U.S. citizens.

Application Requirements: Application, essay, financial need analysis, resume, transcript, residence proof. *Deadline:* March 15.

Contact: Shannon Cannon, Educational Foundation Staff Liaison
Georgia Society of Certified Public Accountants
3353 Peachtree Road, NE, Suite 400
Atlanta, GA 30326-1414
Phone: 404-231-8676 Ext. 2937
E-mail: scannon@gscpa.org

CHAPTER AWARDED SCHOLARSHIPS

Scholarship for a rising junior or senior undergraduate accounting major or a graduate student enrolled in a master's level accounting or business administration program at a college or university accredited by the Southern Association of Colleges and Schools. Applicant must demonstrate a commitment to pursuing a career in accounting, be a resident of Georgia and maintain an overall GPA of 3.0. Must contact the local GSCPA chapter for more information.

Academic Fields/Career Goals: Accounting; Business/Consumer Services.

Award: Scholarship for use in junior, senior, or graduate years; not renewable. *Number:* 1. *Amount:* varies.

Eligibility Requirements: Applicant must be enrolled or expecting to enroll full- or part-time at a four-year institution or university and resident of Georgia. Applicant must have 3.0 GPA or higher. Available to U.S. citizens.

Application Requirements: Application, essay, financial need analysis, resume, test scores, residence proof. *Deadline:* September 1.

Contact: Mrs. Shannon Cannon, Educational Foundation Staff Liaison
  Georgia Society of Certified Public Accountants
  3353 Peachtree Road, NE, Suite 400
  Atlanta, GA 30326-1414
  Phone: 404-231-8676 Ext. 2937
  Fax: 404-237-1291
  E-mail: scannon@gscpa.org

CHERRY, BEKAERT AND HOLLAND LLP ACCOUNTING SCHOLARSHIP

Scholarship for a rising junior or senior undergraduate accounting major or a graduate student enrolled in a master's level accounting or business administration program at a college or university accredited by the Southern Association of Colleges and Schools. Applicant must demonstrate a commitment to pursuing a career in accounting, be a resident of Georgia and maintain an overall GPA of 3.0.

Academic Fields/Career Goals: Accounting; Business/Consumer Services.

Award: Scholarship for use in junior, senior, or graduate years; not renewable. *Number:* 1. *Amount:* varies.

Eligibility Requirements: Applicant must be enrolled or expecting to enroll full- or part-time at a four-year institution or university and resident of Georgia. Applicant must have 3.0 GPA or higher. Available to U.S. citizens.

Application Requirements: Application, essay, financial need analysis, resume, transcript, residence proof. *Deadline:* March 15.

Contact: Shannon Cannon, Educational Foundation Staff Liaison
  Georgia Society of Certified Public Accountants
  3353 Peachtree Road, NE, Suite 400
  Atlanta, GA 30326-1414
  Phone: 404-231-8676 Ext. 2937
  E-mail: scannon@gscpa.org

COLLINS/MOODY-COMPANY SCHOLARSHIP

Scholarship for a rising junior or senior undergraduate accounting major or a graduate student enrolled in a master's level accounting or business administration program at a college or university accredited by the Southern Association of Colleges and Schools. Applicant must demonstrate a commitment to pursuing a career in accounting, be a resident of Georgia and maintain an overall GPA of 3.0.

Academic Fields/Career Goals: Accounting; Business/Consumer Services.

Award: Scholarship for use in junior, senior, or graduate years; not renewable. *Number:* 1. *Amount:* varies.

Eligibility Requirements: Applicant must be enrolled or expecting to enroll full- or part-time at a four-year institution or university and resident of Georgia. Applicant must have 3.0 GPA or higher. Available to U.S. citizens.

Application Requirements: Application, essay, financial need analysis, resume, transcript, residence proof. *Deadline:* March 15.

Contact: Shannon Cannon, Educational Foundation Staff Liaison
  Georgia Society of Certified Public Accountants
  3353 Peachtree Road, NE, Suite 400
  Atlanta, GA 30326-1414
  Phone: 404-231-8676 Ext. 2937
  E-mail: scannon@gscpa.org

EDUCATIONAL FOUNDATION DIRECT SCHOLARSHIPS

Scholarship for a rising junior or senior undergraduate accounting major or a graduate student enrolled in a master's level accounting or business administration program at a college or university accredited by the Southern Association of Colleges and Schools. Applicant must demonstrate a commitment to pursuing a career in accounting, be a resident of Georgia and maintain an overall GPA of 3.0.

Academic Fields/Career Goals: Accounting; Business/Consumer Services.

Award: Scholarship for use in junior, senior, or graduate years; not renewable. *Number:* 1. *Amount:* varies.

Eligibility Requirements: Applicant must be enrolled or expecting to enroll full- or part-time at a four-year institution or university and res-

ident of Georgia. Applicant must have 3.0 GPA or higher. Available to U.S. citizens.

Application Requirements: Application, essay, financial need analysis, resume, transcript, residence proof. *Deadline:* March 15.

Contact: Shannon Cannon, Educational Foundation Staff Liaison
  Georgia Society of Certified Public Accountants
  3353 Peachtree Road, NE, Suite 400
  Atlanta, GA 30326-1414
  Phone: 404-231-8676 Ext. 2937
  E-mail: scannon@gscpa.org

JULIUS M. JOHNSON MEMORIAL SCHOLARSHIP

Scholarship for a rising junior or senior undergraduate accounting major or a graduate student enrolled in a master's level accounting or business administration program at a college or university accredited by the Southern Association of Colleges and Schools. Applicant must demonstrate a commitment to pursuing a career in accounting, be a resident of Georgia and maintain an overall GPA of 3.0.

Academic Fields/Career Goals: Accounting; Business/Consumer Services.

Award: Scholarship for use in junior, senior, or graduate years; not renewable. *Number:* 1. *Amount:* varies.

Eligibility Requirements: Applicant must be enrolled or expecting to enroll full- or part-time at a four-year institution or university and resident of Georgia. Applicant must have 3.0 GPA or higher. Available to U.S. citizens.

Application Requirements: Application, essay, financial need analysis, resume, transcript, residence proof. *Deadline:* March 15.

Contact: Shannon Cannon, Educational Foundation Staff Liaison
  Georgia Society of Certified Public Accountants
  3353 Peachtree Road, NE, Suite 400
  Atlanta, GA 30326-1414
  Phone: 404-231-8676 Ext. 2937
  E-mail: scannon@gscpa.org

PAYCHEX ENTREPRENEUR SCHOLARSHIP

Scholarship for a rising junior or senior undergraduate accounting major or a graduate student enrolled in a master's level accounting or business administration program at a college or university accredited by the Southern Association of Colleges and Schools. Applicant must demonstrate a commitment to pursuing a career in accounting, be a resident of Georgia and maintain an overall GPA of 3.0.

Academic Fields/Career Goals: Accounting; Business/Consumer Services.

Award: Scholarship for use in junior, senior, or graduate years; not renewable. *Number:* 1. *Amount:* varies.

Eligibility Requirements: Applicant must be enrolled or expecting to enroll full- or part-time at a four-year institution or university and resident of Georgia. Applicant must have 3.0 GPA or higher. Available to U.S. citizens.

Application Requirements: Application, essay, financial need analysis, resume, transcript, residence proof. *Deadline:* March 15.

Contact: Shannon Cannon, Educational Foundation Staff Liaison
  Georgia Society of Certified Public Accountants
  3353 Peachtree Road, NE, Suite 400
  Atlanta, GA 30326-1414
  Phone: 404-231-8676 Ext. 2937
  E-mail: scannon@gscpa.org

ROBERT H. LANGE MEMORIAL SCHOLARSHIP

Scholarship for a rising junior or senior undergraduate accounting major or a graduate student enrolled in a master's level accounting or business administration program at a college or university accredited by the Southern Association of Colleges and Schools. Applicant must demonstrate a commitment to pursuing a career in accounting, be a resident of Georgia and maintain an overall GPA of 3.0.

Academic Fields/Career Goals: Accounting; Business/Consumer Services.

Award: Scholarship for use in junior, senior, or graduate years; not renewable. *Number:* 1. *Amount:* varies.

Eligibility Requirements: Applicant must be enrolled or expecting to enroll full- or part-time at a four-year institution or university and resident of Georgia. Applicant must have 3.0 GPA or higher. Available to U.S. citizens.

Application Requirements: Application, essay, financial need analysis, resume, transcript, residence proof. *Deadline:* March 15.

Contact: Shannon Cannon, Educational Foundation Staff Liaison
Georgia Society of Certified Public Accountants
3353 Peachtree Road, NE, Suite 400
Atlanta, GA 30326-1414
Phone: 404-231-8676 Ext. 2937
E-mail: scannon@gscpa.org

GOVERNMENT FINANCE OFFICERS ASSOCIATION

http://www.gfoa.org/

MINORITIES IN GOVERNMENT FINANCE SCHOLARSHIP

Awards upper-division undergraduate or graduate students of public administration, governmental accounting, finance, political science, economics, or business administration to recognize outstanding performance by minority students preparing for a career in state and local government finance.

Academic Fields/Career Goals: Accounting; Business/Consumer Services; Economics; Political Science; Public Policy and Administration.

Award: Scholarship for use in freshman, sophomore, junior, senior, or graduate years; not renewable. *Number:* 1. *Amount:* $5000.

Eligibility Requirements: Applicant must be American Indian/Alaska Native, Asian/Pacific Islander, Black (non-Hispanic), or Hispanic and enrolled or expecting to enroll full- or part-time at a two-year or four-year institution or university. Available to U.S. and Canadian citizens.

Application Requirements: Application, essay, resume, references, transcript. *Deadline:* February 29.

Contact: Jake Lorentz, Assistant Director
Government Finance Officers Association
203 North LaSalle Street, Suite 2700
Chicago, IL 60601-1210
Phone: 312-977-9700 Ext. 267
E-mail: jlorentz@gfoa.org

GREATER KANAWHA VALLEY FOUNDATION

http://www.tgkvf.org/

CHARLESTON CHAPTER OF WEST VIRGINIA SOCIETY OF CERTIFIED PUBLIC ACCOUNTANTS SCHOLARSHIP

Award for a graduating high school senior who is a resident of Kanawha or Putnam county, West Virginia, and enrolling in a program in accounting in any accredited U.S. college or university. For information and application visit http://www.tgkvf.org.

Academic Fields/Career Goals: Accounting.

Award: Scholarship for use in freshman year; renewable. *Number:* 2. *Amount:* $1000.

Eligibility Requirements: Applicant must be high school student; planning to enroll or expecting to enroll full-time at a four-year institution or university and resident of West Virginia. Available to U.S. citizens.

Application Requirements: Application, test scores, transcript. *Deadline:* January 15.

Contact: Susan Hoover, Scholarship Program Officer
Greater Kanawha Valley Foundation
1600 Huntington Square, 900 Lee Street, East
PO Box 3041
Charleston, WV 25301
Phone: 304-346-3620
E-mail: shoover@tgkvf.org

CHARLESTON ROTARY CLUB SCHOLARSHIP

Award available for student resident of the Charleston, West Virginia area who is enrolled or will be enrolled in a program of business or a related field at a two-year or four-year college/university in West Virginia. Preference is given to students having prior business or entrepreneurial experience who have demonstrated service to their schools and communities and high academic performance.

Academic Fields/Career Goals: Accounting; Advertising/Public Relations; Business/Consumer Services; Finance; Marketing.

Award: Scholarship for use in freshman, sophomore, junior, or senior years; renewable. *Number:* 2. *Amount:* $1000.

Eligibility Requirements: Applicant must be enrolled or expecting to enroll full-time at a two-year or four-year institution or university; resident of West Virginia and studying in West Virginia. Available to U.S. citizens.

Application Requirements: Application, test scores, transcript. *Deadline:* January 15.

Contact: Susan Hoover, Scholarship Program Officer
Greater Kanawha Valley Foundation
1600 Huntington Square, 900 Lee Street, East
PO Box 3041
Charleston, WV 25301
Phone: 304-346-3620
E-mail: shoover@tgkvf.org

GREATER WASHINGTON SOCIETY OF CERTIFIED PUBLIC ACCOUNTANTS

http://www.gwscpa.org/

GREATER WASHINGTON SOCIETY OF CPAS SCHOLARSHIP

Scholarship available to accounting students. School must offer an accounting degree that qualifies graduates to sit for the CPA exam (must meet the 150-hour rule). Minimum 3.0 GPA in major courses required. Application details on our web site http://www.gwscpa.org.

Academic Fields/Career Goals: Accounting.

Award: Scholarship for use in junior, senior, or graduate years; not renewable. *Number:* 3–5. *Amount:* $2000–$4500.

Eligibility Requirements: Applicant must be enrolled or expecting to enroll full-time at a four-year institution or university; resident of District of Columbia and studying in District of Columbia. Applicant must have 3.0 GPA or higher. Available to U.S. citizens.

Application Requirements: Application, essay, financial need analysis, resume, references, transcript. *Deadline:* February 15.

Contact: Kari Bedell, Executive Director
Greater Washington Society of Certified Public Accountants
1111 19th St. NW
#1200
Washington, DC 20036
Phone: 202-464-6001
E-mail: info@gwscpa.org

HAWAII SOCIETY OF CERTIFIED PUBLIC ACCOUNTANTS

http://www.hscpa.org/

HSCPA SCHOLARSHIP PROGRAM FOR ACCOUNTING STUDENTS

Scholarship for Hawaii resident currently attending an accredited Hawaii college or university. Minimum 3.0 GPA required. Must be majoring, or concentrating, in accounting with the intention to sit for the CPA exam, and have completed an intermediate accounting course. Number of awards vary from year to year.

Academic Fields/Career Goals: Accounting.

Award: Scholarship for use in freshman, sophomore, junior, or senior years; not renewable. *Number:* varies. *Amount:* $500–$1500.

Eligibility Requirements: Applicant must be enrolled or expecting to enroll full-time at a four-year institution or university; resident of Hawaii and studying in Hawaii. Applicant must have 3.0 GPA or higher. Available to U.S. citizens.

Application Requirements: Application, references, test scores, transcript. *Deadline:* January 31.

Contact: Kathy Castillo, Executive Director
Hawaii Society of Certified Public Accountants
900 Fort Street Mall, Suite 850
Honolulu, HI 96813
Phone: 808-537-9475
Fax: 808-537-3520
E-mail: info@hscpa.org

ILLINOIS CPA SOCIETY

http://www.icpas.org/

HERMAN J. NEAL SCHOLARSHIP

Scholarships of $4000 available to African-American students who demonstrate strong academic performance in their goal to become a CPA and would benefit from scholarship support. College seniors as well as individuals that have graduated and wish to return to school to complete the coursework needed to become a CPA are encouraged to apply.

Academic Fields/Career Goals: Accounting.

Award: Scholarship for use in junior, senior, or graduate years; renewable. *Number:* 4. *Amount:* up to $4000.

Eligibility Requirements: Applicant must be Black (non-Hispanic); enrolled or expecting to enroll full-time at a four-year institution or university; resident of Illinois and studying in Illinois. Applicant must have 3.0 GPA or higher. Available to U.S. citizens.

Application Requirements: Application, transcript. *Deadline:* November 30.

Contact: Katie Miller, Scholarship Coordinator
Illinois CPA Society
550 West Jackson, Suite 900
Chicago, IL 60661-5716
Phone: 312-993-0407 Ext. 216
Fax: 312-993-9954
E-mail: millerk@icpas.org

ILLINOIS CPA SOCIETY ACCOUNTING SCHOLARSHIP

Awarded to high achieving Illinois college and university students who are completing their fifth year of education and planning to sit for the CPA Examination. The program is designed to help students who have CPA potential but need financial assistance for tuition and fees for their fifth year of education.

Academic Fields/Career Goals: Accounting.

Award: Scholarship for use in senior, graduate, or postgraduate years; not renewable. *Number:* 12. *Amount:* up to $4000.

Eligibility Requirements: Applicant must be enrolled or expecting to enroll full-time at a four-year institution or university; resident of Illinois and studying in Illinois. Applicant must have 3.0 GPA or higher. Available to U.S. citizens.

Application Requirements: Application, transcript. *Deadline:* November 30.

Contact: Katie Miller, Scholarship Coordinator
Illinois CPA Society
550 West Jackson, Suite 900
Chicago, IL 60661-5716
Phone: 312-993-0407 Ext. 216
Fax: 312-993-9954
E-mail: millerk@icpas.org

INDEPENDENT COLLEGE FUND OF MARYLAND (I-FUND)

http://www.i-fundinfo.org/

BRANCH BANKING & TRUST COMPANY SCHOLARSHIPS

Scholarship to a student pursuing a degree in a business-related major or have a demonstrated interest in a business career or should have six credit hours of accounting plus a demonstrated interest in financial accounting. Student must be a rising junior or senior in one of Maryland's independent colleges. Must have a minimum of 3.0 GPA.

Academic Fields/Career Goals: Accounting; Business/Consumer Services.

Award: Scholarship for use in junior or senior years; not renewable. *Number:* 1. *Amount:* $2500.

Eligibility Requirements: Applicant must be enrolled or expecting to enroll full-time at a four-year institution or university. Applicant must have 3.0 GPA or higher. Available to U.S. citizens.

Application Requirements: Application. *Deadline:* varies.

Contact: Lori Subotich, Director of Programs and Scholarships
Independent College Fund of Maryland (I-Fund)
3225 Ellerslie Avenue, Suite C160
Baltimore, MD 21218-3519
Phone: 443-997-5700
Fax: 443-997-2740
E-mail: lsubot@jhmi.edu

CHEVY CHASE BANK SCHOLARSHIP

Student must be majoring in or have a demonstrated interest in business management, finance, accounting, sales or marketing. Must be a rising sophomore, junior, or senior in one of Maryland's independent colleges. Must have a minimum at least 3.0 GPA.

Academic Fields/Career Goals: Accounting; Business/Consumer Services.

Award: Scholarship for use in sophomore, junior, or senior years; not renewable. *Number:* 1. *Amount:* $2500.

Eligibility Requirements: Applicant must be enrolled or expecting to enroll full-time at a four-year institution or university and studying in Maryland. Applicant must have 3.0 GPA or higher. Available to U.S. citizens.

Application Requirements: Application, thank you letters. *Deadline:* varies.

Contact: Lori Subotich, Director of Programs and Scholarships
Independent College Fund of Maryland (I-Fund)
3225 Ellerslie Avenue, Suite C160
Baltimore, MD 21218-3519
Phone: 443-997-5700
Fax: 443-997-2740
E-mail: lsubot@jhmi.edu

LEGG MASON SCHOLARSHIPS

Award to students majoring in business or have a demonstrated interested in financial services. Must be a rising junior or senior in one of Maryland's independent colleges. Must have at least 3.0 GPA.

Academic Fields/Career Goals: Accounting; Business/Consumer Services.

Award: Scholarship for use in junior or senior years; not renewable. *Number:* 1. *Amount:* $2500.

Eligibility Requirements: Applicant must be enrolled or expecting to enroll full- or part-time at a four-year institution or university and studying in Maryland. Applicant must have 3.0 GPA or higher. Available to U.S. citizens.

Application Requirements: Application, thank you letters. *Deadline:* varies.

Contact: Lori Subotich, Director of Programs and Scholarships
Independent College Fund of Maryland (I-Fund)
3225 Ellerslie Avenue, Suite C160
Baltimore, MD 21218-3519
Phone: 443-997-5700
Fax: 443-997-2740
E-mail: lsubot@jhmi.edu

INSTITUTE OF INTERNAL AUDITORS RESEARCH FOUNDATION

http://www.theiia.org/

ESTHER R. SAWYER RESEARCH AWARD

Awarded to a student entering or currently enrolled in an internal auditing program at an IIA-affiliated school. Awarded based on submission of an original manuscript on a specific topic related to modern internal auditing.

Academic Fields/Career Goals: Accounting.

Award: Prize for use in freshman, sophomore, junior, senior, or graduate years; not renewable. *Number:* 1. *Amount:* $5000.

Eligibility Requirements: Applicant must be enrolled or expecting to enroll full-time at a four-year institution or university. Available to U.S. and non-U.S. citizens.

Application Requirements: Application, applicant must enter a contest, essay, references. *Deadline:* March 1.

Contact: Susan Dworkis, Research Foundation Administrator
Institute of Internal Auditors Research Foundation
247 Maitland Avenue
Altamonte Springs, FL 32701-4201
Phone: 407-937-1357
E-mail: research@theiia.org

INSTITUTE OF MANAGEMENT ACCOUNTANTS

http://www.imanet.org/

INSTITUTE OF MANAGEMENT ACCOUNTANTS MEMORIAL EDUCATION FUND SCHOLARSHIPS

Scholarships for IMA undergraduate or graduate student members studying at accredited institutions in the U.S. and Puerto Rico. Must be pursuing a career in management accounting, financial management, or information technology, and have a minimum GPA of 3.0. Awards based on academic merit, IMA participation, strength of recommendations, and quality of written statements.

Academic Fields/Career Goals: Accounting; Business/Consumer Services.

Award: Scholarship for use in sophomore, junior, senior, or graduate years; not renewable. *Number:* 6–15. *Amount:* $1000–$2500.

Eligibility Requirements: Applicant must be enrolled or expecting to enroll full- or part-time at a two-year or four-year institution or university. Applicant must have 3.0 GPA or higher. Available to U.S. citizens.

Application Requirements: Application, essay, resume, references, transcript. *Deadline:* February 15.

Contact: Jodi Ryan, Director, Alliances & Student/Academic
Communities
Institute of Management Accountants
10 Paragon Drive
Montvale, NJ 07645-1760
Phone: 800-638-4427 Ext. 1556
E-mail: jryan@imanet.org

STUART CAMERON AND MARGARET MCLEOD MEMORIAL SCHOLARSHIP

Scholarships for IMA undergraduate or graduate student members studying at accredited institutions in the U.S. and Puerto Rico and carrying 12 credits per semester. Must be pursuing a career in management accounting, financial management, or information technology, and have a minimum GPA of 3.0. Awards based on academic merit, IMA participation, strength of recommendations, and quality of written statements.

Academic Fields/Career Goals: Accounting; Business/Consumer Services.

Award: Scholarship for use in junior, senior, or graduate years; not renewable. *Number:* 1. *Amount:* $5000.

Eligibility Requirements: Applicant must be enrolled or expecting to enroll full- or part-time at a two-year or four-year institution or university. Applicant must have 3.0 GPA or higher. Available to U.S. citizens.

Application Requirements: Application, essay, resume, transcript. *Deadline:* February 15.

Contact: Jodi Ryan, Director, Alliances & Student/Academic
Communities
Institute of Management Accountants
10 Paragon Drive
Montvale, NJ 07645-1760
Phone: 800-638-4427 Ext. 1556
E-mail: jryan@imanet.org

KENTUCKY SOCIETY OF CERTIFIED PUBLIC ACCOUNTANTS

http://www.kycpa.org/

KENTUCKY SOCIETY OF CERTIFIED PUBLIC ACCOUNTANTS COLLEGE SCHOLARSHIP

Nonrenewable award for accounting majors at a Kentucky college or university. Must rank in upper third of class or have a minimum 3.0 GPA. Must be a Kentucky resident.

Academic Fields/Career Goals: Accounting.

Award: Scholarship for use in sophomore, junior, or senior years; not renewable. *Number:* up to 23. *Amount:* $1000–$2500.

Eligibility Requirements: Applicant must be enrolled or expecting to enroll full-time at a two-year or four-year institution or university; resident of Kentucky and studying in Kentucky. Applicant must have 3.0 GPA or higher. Available to U.S. and non-U.S. citizens.

Application Requirements: Application, essay, references, transcript. *Deadline:* January 31.

Contact: Becky Ackerman, Foundation Administrator
Kentucky Society of Certified Public Accountants
1735 Alliant Avenue
Louisville, KY 40299
Phone: 502-266-5272
Fax: 502-261-9512
E-mail: backerman@kycpa.org

LATINO BUSINESS PROFESSIONALS (LBP) OF NORTHERN CALIFORNIA

http://www.lbpbayarea.org/

LBP MONETARY SCHOLARSHIP

$500 to $1500 scholarships for minority students pursuing careers in accounting, finance, and business-related fields.

Academic Fields/Career Goals: Accounting; Finance.

Award: Scholarship for use in freshman, sophomore, junior, or senior years; not renewable. *Number:* 5–20. *Amount:* $500–$1500.

Eligibility Requirements: Applicant must be of Hispanic heritage; enrolled or expecting to enroll full-time at a two-year or four-year institution or university; resident of California and studying in California. Applicant must have 2.5 GPA or higher. Available to U.S. and non-U.S. citizens.

Application Requirements: Application, essay, transcript, tax return. *Deadline:* February 28.

Contact: Ms. Veronica Sosa, Scholarship Committee Chair
Latino Business Professionals (LBP) of Northern California
1346 The Alameda, No. A-210
San Jose, CA 95126
E-mail: scholarships@lbpbayarea.org

LAWRENCE P. DOSS SCHOLARSHIP FOUNDATION

http://www.lawrencepdossfnd.org/

LAWRENCE P. DOSS SCHOLARSHIP FOUNDATION

Renewable scholarships are available to residents of Michigan who are seniors graduating from a high school in the greater Detroit area. Must be pursuing a degree in accounting, finance, management or business. Financial need considered.

Academic Fields/Career Goals: Accounting; Business/Consumer Services.

Award: Scholarship for use in freshman year; renewable. *Number:* 5. *Amount:* $20,000.

Eligibility Requirements: Applicant must be high school student; planning to enroll or expecting to enroll full-time at a four-year institution or university; single and resident of Michigan. Applicant must have 2.5 GPA or higher. Available to U.S. citizens.

Application Requirements: Application, essay, financial need analysis, interview, references, test scores, transcript. *Deadline:* March 15.

Contact: Judith Doss, President and Chief Executive Officer
Lawrence P. Doss Scholarship Foundation
PO Box 351037
Detroit, MI 48235-9998
Phone: 313-891-5834
Fax: 313-891-4520
E-mail: lpdsfoundation@aol.com

MARYLAND ASSOCIATION OF CERTIFIED PUBLIC ACCOUNTANTS EDUCATIONAL FOUNDATION

http://www.tomorrowscpa.org/

STUDENT SCHOLARSHIP IN ACCOUNTING MD ASSOCIATION OF CPAS

Award for Maryland residents who will have completed at least 60 credit hours at a Maryland college or university by the time of the award. Must have 3.0 GPA, demonstrate commitment to 150 semester hours of education, and intend to pursue a career as a certified public accountant. Number of awards varies. Must submit accounting department chairman's signature on required statement. Must be a member of the Tomorrow's CPA program. U.S. citizenship required. See web site at http://www.tomorrowscpa.org for further details.

Academic Fields/Career Goals: Accounting.

Award: Scholarship for use in junior or senior years; renewable. *Number:* 10–20. *Amount:* $500–$1000.

Eligibility Requirements: Applicant must be enrolled or expecting to enroll full-time at a four-year institution or university; resident of Maryland and studying in Maryland. Applicant must have 3.0 GPA or higher. Available to U.S. citizens.

Application Requirements: Application, financial need analysis, references, transcript. *Deadline:* April 15.

Contact: Career Initiatives Specialist
Maryland Association of Certified Public Accountants
Educational Foundation
901 Dulaney Road, Suite 710
Towson, MD 21204
Phone: 410-296-8713
E-mail: TCPA@macpa.org

MICHIGAN ASSOCIATION OF CPAS

http://www.michcpa.org/

FIFTH/GRADUATE YEAR STUDENT SCHOLARSHIP

Scholarship for a full-time student in senior year, or a student with a combination of education and employment (defined as a minimum of two classes per term and 20 hours per week of employment). Must be majoring in accounting, and a U.S. citizen.

Academic Fields/Career Goals: Accounting.

Award: Scholarship for use in senior year; not renewable. *Number:* 16–25. *Amount:* up to $4000.

Eligibility Requirements: Applicant must be enrolled or expecting to enroll full-time at a four-year institution or university and studying in Michigan. Available to U.S. citizens.

Application Requirements: Application, essay, financial need analysis, references, transcript. *Deadline:* January 31.

Contact: MACPA Academic Services Specialist
Michigan Association of CPAs
5480 Corporate Drive, Suite 200
Troy, MI 48007-5068
Phone: 248-267-3700
Fax: 248-267-3737
E-mail: macpa@michcpa.org

MINNESOTA SOCIETY OF CERTIFIED PUBLIC ACCOUNTANTS

http://www.mncpa.org/

MNCPA SCHOLARSHIP PROGRAM

Scholarships given for graduate study in accounting to students from a Minnesota college or university who passed the CPA exam during the previous year. Must be a sophomore, junior or senior (going on to graduate school). At least a 3.0 GPA in accounting.

Academic Fields/Career Goals: Accounting.

Award: Scholarship for use in sophomore, junior, or senior years; not renewable. *Number:* up to 25. *Amount:* up to $1000.

Eligibility Requirements: Applicant must be enrolled or expecting to enroll full-time at a four-year institution or university and studying in Minnesota. Applicant must have 3.0 GPA or higher. Available to U.S. citizens.

Application Requirements: Application. *Deadline:* varies.

Contact: Membership Committee
Minnesota Society of Certified Public Accountants
1650 West 82nd Street, Suite 600
Bloomington, MN 55431
Phone: 952-885-5517
Fax: 952-831-7875

MONTANA SOCIETY OF CERTIFIED PUBLIC ACCOUNTANTS

http://www.mscpa.org/

MONTANA SOCIETY OF CERTIFIED PUBLIC ACCOUNTANTS SCHOLARSHIP

Scholarship available to one student in each of the following four schools: Montana State University Billings, MSU Bozeman, Carroll College, and University of Montana. Must be: 1. Accounting Major 2. At least a junior standing with at least one semester of coursework remaining 3. Minimum GPA of 3.0 4. Graduate students eligible 5. Preference will be given to student members of the MSCPA 6. Graduate of a Montana high school and currently a Montana residen. Additional scholarships are awarded through our Endowment Fund and may be applied for through the Montana Community Foundation.

Academic Fields/Career Goals: Accounting.

Award: Scholarship for use in junior, senior, or graduate years; not renewable. *Number:* 4–6. *Amount:* $1000.

Eligibility Requirements: Applicant must be enrolled or expecting to enroll full-time at a four-year institution or university; resident of Montana and studying in Montana. Applicant must have 3.0 GPA or higher. Available to U.S. citizens.

Application Requirements: Application, essay, resume, transcript. *Deadline:* varies.

Contact: Mrs. Margaret Herriges, Communications Director
Montana Society of Certified Public Accountants
PO Box 138
Helena, MT 59624-0138
Phone: 406-442-7301
E-mail: mscpa@mscpa.org

NATIONAL BLACK MBA ASSOCIATION-TWIN CITIES CHAPTER

http://www.nbmbaatc.org/

TWIN CITIES CHAPTER UNDERGRADUATE SCHOLARSHIP

Award for minority students in first, second, third or fourth year full-time in an accredited undergraduate business or management program during the fall semester working towards a bachelor's degree. Get application from web site at http://www.nbmbaatc.org.

Academic Fields/Career Goals: Accounting; Business/Consumer Services.

Award: Scholarship for use in freshman, sophomore, junior, or senior years; not renewable. *Number:* 5. *Amount:* up to $3500.

Eligibility Requirements: Applicant must be Black (non-Hispanic); enrolled or expecting to enroll full-time at a four-year institution or university; resident of Minnesota and studying in Minnesota. Available to U.S. citizens.

Application Requirements: Application, essay, transcript. *Deadline:* April 7.

Contact: Victor Patterson, President
National Black MBA Association-Twin Cities Chapter
PO Box 2709
Minneapolis, MN 55402
Phone: 651-223-7373

NATIONAL SOCIETY OF ACCOUNTANTS

http://www.nsacct.org/

CHARLES EARP MEMORIAL SCHOLARSHIP

Annual award for the student designated as most outstanding of all National Society of Accountants scholarship recipients receive an additional stipend of approximately $200.

Academic Fields/Career Goals: Accounting.

Award: Scholarship for use in freshman, sophomore, junior, or senior years; not renewable. *Number:* 1. *Amount:* $200.

Eligibility Requirements: Applicant must be enrolled or expecting to enroll full- or part-time at a four-year institution or university. Available to U.S. and Canadian citizens.

Application Requirements: Application, financial need analysis, transcript, appraisal form. *Deadline:* March 10.

Contact: Sally Brasse, Director of Education Programs
National Society of Accountants
1010 North Fairfax Street
Alexandria, VA 22314-1574
Phone: 703-549-6400 Ext. 1307
E-mail: sbrasse@nsacct.org

NATIONAL SOCIETY OF ACCOUNTANTS SCHOLARSHIP

One-time award of $500 to $1000 available to undergraduate students. Applicants must maintain a 3.0 GPA and have declared a major in accounting. Must submit an appraisal form and transcripts in addition to application. Must be U.S. or Canadian citizen attending an accredited U.S. school.

Academic Fields/Career Goals: Accounting.

Award: Scholarship for use in freshman, sophomore, junior, or senior years; not renewable. *Number:* up to 40. *Amount:* $500–$1000.

Eligibility Requirements: Applicant must be enrolled or expecting to enroll full- or part-time at a two-year or four-year institution or university. Applicant must have 3.0 GPA or higher. Available to U.S. and Canadian citizens.

Application Requirements: Application, financial need analysis, transcript, appraisal form. *Deadline:* March 10.

Contact: Susan E. Noell, Director of Education Programs
National Society of Accountants
1010 North Fairfax Street
Alexandria, VA 22314-1574
Phone: 703-549-6400 Ext. 1312
Fax: 703-549-2984 Ext. 1312
E-mail: snoell@nsacct.org

NSA LOUIS AND FANNIE SAGER MEMORIAL SCHOLARSHIP AWARD

Up to $1000 will be awarded annually to a graduate of a Virginia public high school who is enrolled as an undergraduate at a Virginia college or university. Applicant must major in accounting. Must submit proof of graduation from a Virginia public school.

Academic Fields/Career Goals: Accounting.

Award: Scholarship for use in freshman, sophomore, junior, or senior years; not renewable. *Number:* 1. *Amount:* $500–$1000.

Eligibility Requirements: Applicant must be enrolled or expecting to enroll full- or part-time at a two-year or four-year institution or university; resident of Virginia and studying in Virginia. Applicant must have 3.0 GPA or higher. Available to U.S. and Canadian citizens.

Application Requirements: Application, financial need analysis, transcript, appraisal form. *Deadline:* March 10.

Contact: Sally Brasse, Director
National Society of Accountants
1010 North Fairfax Street
Alexandria, VA 22314-1574
Phone: 703-549-6400 Ext. 1307
E-mail: sbrasse@nsacct.org

STANLEY H. STEARMAN SCHOLARSHIP

One award for accounting major who is a relative of an active, retired, or deceased member of National Society of Accountants. Must be citizen of the United States or Canada and attend school in the United States. Minimum GPA of 3.0 required. Not available for freshman year. Submit application, appraisal form, and letter of intent.

Academic Fields/Career Goals: Accounting.

Award: Scholarship for use in freshman, sophomore, junior, senior, or graduate years; renewable. *Number:* 1. *Amount:* up to $2000.

Eligibility Requirements: Applicant must be enrolled or expecting to enroll full- or part-time at a two-year or four-year institution or university. Applicant or parent of applicant must be member of National Society of Accountants. Applicant must have 3.0 GPA or higher. Available to U.S. and Canadian citizens.

Application Requirements: Application, essay, financial need analysis, transcript, appraisal form. *Deadline:* March 10.

Contact: Sally Brasse, Director of Education Programs
National Society of Accountants
1010 North Fairfax Street
Alexandria, VA 22314-1574
Phone: 703-549-6400 Ext. 1307
Fax: 703-549-2984
E-mail: sbrasse@nsacct.org

NC CPA FOUNDATION INC.

*http://www.ncacpa.org/Member_Connections/
NC_CPA_Foundation_Inc.aspx*

NORTH CAROLINA ASSOCIATION OF CPAS FOUNDATION SCHOLARSHIPS

Scholarship available for North Carolina residents enrolled in a program leading to a degree in accounting or its equivalent in a North Carolina college or university. Must have completed at least one college or university level accounting course and have completed at least 36 semester hours (or equivalent) by the start of the spring semester of the year of application. The applicant must be sponsored by one accounting faculty members. Application and information at http://csbapp.csb.uncw.edu/nccpa.

Academic Fields/Career Goals: Accounting.

Award: Scholarship for use in sophomore, junior, senior, or graduate years; not renewable. *Number:* 50–60. *Amount:* $1000–$5000.

Eligibility Requirements: Applicant must be enrolled or expecting to enroll full- or part-time at a two-year or four-year institution or university; resident of North Carolina and studying in North Carolina. Applicant must have 3.0 GPA or higher. Available to U.S. citizens.

Application Requirements: Application, essay, transcript. *Deadline:* February 10.

Contact: NC CPA Foundation Inc.
PO Box 80188
Raleigh, NC 27623
Phone: 800-722-2836

NEBRASKA SOCIETY OF CERTIFIED PUBLIC ACCOUNTANTS

http://www.nescpa.com/

NEBRASKA SOCIETY OF CPAS SCHOLARSHIP

Scholarship awards are presented to accounting students who have completed their junior year; accounting majors who plan to sit for the CPA exam; students who have the interest and capabilities of becoming a successful accountant and who are considering an accounting career in Nebraska are to be considered. Recipients need not necessarily have the highest scholastic average.

Academic Fields/Career Goals: Accounting.

Award: Scholarship for use in senior year; not renewable. *Number:* varies. *Amount:* varies.

Eligibility Requirements: Applicant must be enrolled or expecting to enroll full-time at a four-year institution or university. Available to U.S. citizens.

Application Requirements: Application, nomination letter. *Deadline:* August 1.

Contact: Sheila Burroughs, Vice President
Nebraska Society of Certified Public Accountants
635 South 14th Street, Suite 330
Lincoln, NE 68508
Phone: 402-476-8482
Fax: 402-476-8731
E-mail: society@nescpa.org

NEVADA SOCIETY OF CERTIFIED PUBLIC ACCOUNTANTS

http://www.nevadacpa.org/

NEVADA SOCIETY OF CPAS SCHOLARSHIP

Scholarships available for accounting students in one of Nevada's four community colleges, or for juniors or seniors attending either University of Nevada, Las Vegas, or University of Nevada, Reno. Must be planning a career in accounting.

Academic Fields/Career Goals: Accounting.

Award: Scholarship for use in freshman, sophomore, junior, or senior years; not renewable. *Number:* 6. *Amount:* up to $1500.

Eligibility Requirements: Applicant must be enrolled or expecting to enroll full-time at a two-year or four-year institution or university; resident of Nevada and studying in Nevada. Available to U.S. citizens.

Application Requirements: Application. *Deadline:* varies.

Contact: Sharon Uithoven, Executive Director
Nevada Society of Certified Public Accountants
5250 Neil Road, Suite 205
Reno, NV 89502
Phone: 775-826-6800 Ext. 104
Fax: 775-826-7942
E-mail: uithoven@nevadacpa.org

NEW ENGLAND EMPLOYEE BENEFITS COUNCIL

http://www.neebc.org/

NEW ENGLAND EMPLOYEE BENEFITS COUNCIL SCHOLARSHIP PROGRAM

Renewable award designed to encourage undergraduate or graduate students to pursue a course of study leading to a bachelor's degree or higher in the employee benefits field. Must be a resident of/or studying in Maine, Massachusetts, New Hampshire, Rhode Island, Connecticut or Vermont. Must have demonstrated interest in the fields of employee benefits, human resources, business law.

Academic Fields/Career Goals: Accounting; Business/Consumer Services; Economics; Health Administration; Human Resources; Insurance and Actuarial Science; Law/Legal Services; Public Health; Public Policy and Administration.

Award: Scholarship for use in freshman, sophomore, junior, or senior years; renewable. *Number:* 1–3. *Amount:* $1000–$5000.

Eligibility Requirements: Applicant must be enrolled or expecting to enroll full- or part-time at a four-year institution or university; resident of Connecticut, Maine, Massachusetts, New Hampshire, Rhode Island, or Vermont and studying in Connecticut, Maine, Massachusetts, New Hampshire, Rhode Island, or Vermont. Available to U.S. citizens.

Application Requirements: Application, essay, references, transcript. *Deadline:* April 1.

Contact: Linda Viens, Manager of Operations and Member Services
New England Employee Benefits Council
240 Bear Hill Road, Suite 102
Waltham, MA 02451
Phone: 781-684-8700
E-mail: linda@neebc.org

NEW HAMPSHIRE SOCIETY OF CERTIFIED PUBLIC ACCOUNTANTS

http://www.nhscpa.org/

NEW HAMPSHIRE SOCIETY OF CERTIFIED PUBLIC ACCOUNTANTS SCHOLARSHIP FUND

One-time award for New Hampshire resident majoring full-time in accounting. Must be entering senior year at a four-year college or university or pursuing a master's degree. Maximum of seven awards of up to $1000 are granted.

Academic Fields/Career Goals: Accounting.

Award: Scholarship for use in senior year; not renewable. *Number:* 1–7. *Amount:* $500–$1000.

Eligibility Requirements: Applicant must be enrolled or expecting to enroll full-time at a four-year institution or university and resident of New Hampshire. Available to U.S. citizens.

Application Requirements: Application, references, transcript. *Deadline:* November 1.

Contact: Debra Bolduc
E-mail: dbolduc@nhscpa.org

NEW JERSEY SOCIETY OF CERTIFIED PUBLIC ACCOUNTANTS

http://www.njscpa.org/

NEW JERSEY SOCIETY OF CERTIFIED PUBLIC ACCOUNTANTS COLLEGE SCHOLARSHIP PROGRAM

Award for college juniors or those entering an accounting-related graduate program. Must be a New Jersey resident attending a four-year New Jersey institution. Must be nominated by accounting department chair or submit application directly. Minimum 3.0 GPA required. Award values from $4000 to $4500.

Academic Fields/Career Goals: Accounting.

Award: Scholarship for use in junior or senior years; not renewable. *Number:* 40–50. *Amount:* $4000–$4500.

Eligibility Requirements: Applicant must be enrolled or expecting to enroll full- or part-time at a four-year institution or university; resident of New Jersey and studying in New Jersey. Applicant must have 3.0 GPA or higher. Available to U.S. citizens.

Application Requirements: Application, interview, resume, references, transcript. *Deadline:* January 16.

Contact: Janice Amatucci, Membership Mgr., NextGen Outreach
New Jersey Society of Certified Public Accountants
425 Eagle Rock Avenue, Suite 100
Roseland, NJ 07068-1723
Phone: 973-226-4494
Fax: 973-226-7425
E-mail: jamatucci@njscpa.org

NEW JERSEY SOCIETY OF CERTIFIED PUBLIC ACCOUNTANTS HIGH SCHOOL SCHOLARSHIP PROGRAM

Renewable scholarship for New Jersey high school seniors who wish to pursue a degree in accounting. Must be resident of New Jersey. Scholarship value is from $6500 to $8500. Deadline: December.

Academic Fields/Career Goals: Accounting.

Award: Scholarship for use in freshman year; renewable. *Number:* 15–20. *Amount:* $6500–$8500.

Eligibility Requirements: Applicant must be high school student; planning to enroll or expecting to enroll full-time at a four-year institution or university and resident of New Jersey. Available to U.S. citizens.

Application Requirements: Application, essay, interview, test scores, transcript.

Contact: Janice Amatucci, Membership Mgr., NextGen Outreach
New Jersey Society of Certified Public Accountants
425 Eagle Rock Avenue, Suite 100
Roseland, NJ 07068-1723
Phone: 973-226-4494
Fax: 973-226-7425
E-mail: jamatucci@njscpa.org

NEW YORK STATE EDUCATION DEPARTMENT

http://www.highered.nysed.gov/

REGENTS PROFESSIONAL OPPORTUNITY SCHOLARSHIP

Scholarship for New York residents beginning or already enrolled in an approved degree-granting program of study in New York that leads to licensure in a particular profession. See the web site for the list of eligible professions. Must be U.S. citizen or permanent resident. Award recipients must agree to practice upon licensure in their profession in New York for 12 months for each annual payment received. Priority given to economically disadvantaged members of minority groups underrepresented in the professions.

Academic Fields/Career Goals: Accounting; Architecture; Dental Health/Services; Engineering/Technology; Health and Medical Sciences; Interior Design; Landscape Architecture; Law/Legal Services; Nursing; Pharmacy; Psychology; Social Services.

Award: Scholarship for use in freshman, sophomore, junior, senior, or graduate years; renewable. *Number:* 220. *Amount:* up to $5000.

Eligibility Requirements: Applicant must be enrolled or expecting to enroll full-time at a two-year or four-year institution or university; resident of New York and studying in New York. Available to U.S. citizens.

Application Requirements: Application. *Deadline:* May 31.

Contact: Lewis Hall, Supervisor
New York State Education Department
89 Washington Avenue, Room 1078 EBA
Albany, NY 12234
Phone: 518-486-1319
Fax: 518-486-5346
E-mail: scholar@mail.nysed.gov

NEW YORK STATE SOCIETY OF CERTIFIED PUBLIC ACCOUNTANTS FOUNDATION FOR ACCOUNTING EDUCATION

http://www.nysscpa.org/page/future-cpas/college-students

FOUNDATION FOR ACCOUNTING EDUCATION SCHOLARSHIP

Awards up to $200 to $2500 scholarships to college students to encourage them to pursue a career in accounting. Must be a New York resident studying in New York and maintaining a 3.0 GPA.

Academic Fields/Career Goals: Accounting.

Award: Scholarship for use in junior, senior, or graduate years; not renewable. *Number:* 1–200. *Amount:* $200–$2500.

Eligibility Requirements: Applicant must be enrolled or expecting to enroll full- or part-time at a four-year institution or university; resident of New York and studying in New York. Applicant must have 3.0 GPA or higher. Available to U.S. citizens.

Application Requirements: Application, essay, financial need analysis, references, transcript. *Deadline:* March 1.

Contact: Ms. Christine James, Membership Marketing Specialist
New York State Society of Certified Public Accountants
Foundation for Accounting Education
3 Park Ave, 18th Floor
New York, NY 10016
Phone: 212-719-8363
E-mail: cjames@nysspca.org

OREGON ASSOCIATION OF PUBLIC ACCOUNTANTS SCHOLARSHIP FOUNDATION

http://www.oaia.net/

OAIA SCHOLARSHIP

Scholarships of $1000 to $2000 are awarded to full-time students. Must be a resident of the state of Oregon and major in accounting studies at an accredited school in the state of Oregon. The scholarship may be used for tuition, fees, books or other academic expenses incurred during the term.

Academic Fields/Career Goals: Accounting.

Award: Scholarship for use in freshman, sophomore, junior, or senior years; not renewable. *Number:* 5. *Amount:* $1000–$2000.

Eligibility Requirements: Applicant must be enrolled or expecting to enroll full-time at a two-year or four-year institution or university; resident of Oregon and studying in Oregon. Available to U.S. citizens.

Application Requirements: Application, financial need analysis, references, transcript. *Deadline:* April 1.

Contact: Susan Robertson, Treasurer
Oregon Association of Public Accountants Scholarship Foundation
1804 43rd Avenue, NE
Portland, OR 97213
Phone: 503-282-7247
Fax: 503-282-7406
E-mail: srobertson4oaia@aol.com

OREGON STUDENT ASSISTANCE COMMISSION

http://www.GetCollegeFunds.org/

NICHOLAS DIERMANN MEMORIAL SCHOLARSHIP

Scholarship available for Oregon high school graduates who are enrolled or planning to enroll in a four-year public college or university in the U.S. and major in music, performing arts, accounting, or sales (computer, software) operations. Must submit an additional essay and reapply annually for renewal of award.

Academic Fields/Career Goals: Accounting; Business/Consumer Services; Music; Performing Arts.

Award: Scholarship for use in freshman, sophomore, junior, or senior years; not renewable.

Eligibility Requirements: Applicant must be enrolled or expecting to enroll full-time at a four-year institution or university and resident of Oregon. Available to U.S. citizens.

Application Requirements: Application, essay, financial need analysis, transcript, activities chart. *Deadline:* March 1.

Contact: Director of Grant Programs
Oregon Student Assistance Commission
1500 Valley River Drive, Suite 100
Eugene, OR 97401-7020
Phone: 800-452-8807

OSCPA EDUCATIONAL FOUNDATION

http://www.orcpa.org/

OSCPA EDUCATIONAL FOUNDATION SCHOLARSHIP PROGRAM

One-time award for students majoring in accounting. Must attend an accredited Oregon college/university or community college on full-time basis. High school seniors must have a minimum 3.5 GPA. College students must have a minimum 3.2 GPA. Must be a U.S. citizen and Oregon resident.

Academic Fields/Career Goals: Accounting.

Award: Scholarship for use in freshman, sophomore, junior, senior, or graduate years; not renewable. *Number:* 50–100. *Amount:* $500–$3000.

Eligibility Requirements: Applicant must be enrolled or expecting to enroll full-time at a two-year or four-year or technical institution or university; resident of Oregon and studying in Oregon. Available to U.S. citizens.

Application Requirements: Application, test scores, transcript. *Deadline:* February 17.

Contact: Tonna Hollis, Member Services and Manager
OSCPA Educational Foundation
PO Box 4555
Beaverton, OR 97076-4555
Phone: 503-641-7200 Ext. 29
Fax: 503-626-2942
E-mail: thollis@orcpa.org

PENNSYLVANIA INSTITUTE OF CERTIFIED PUBLIC ACCOUNTANTS

http://www.cpazone.org/

PENNSYLVANIA INSTITUTE OF CERTIFIED PUBLIC ACCOUNTANTS SOPHOMORE SCHOLARSHIP

To promote the accounting profession and CPA credential as an exciting and rewarding career path. Scholarship amounts range from $1,000–$15,000 and can be renewed annually until you graduate. Candidates must have completed a 36 credit hours and have a minimum 3.0 GPA.

Academic Fields/Career Goals: Accounting.

Award: Scholarship for use in sophomore, junior, senior, graduate, or postgraduate years; renewable. *Number:* 60–85. *Amount:* $1000–$15,000.

Eligibility Requirements: Applicant must be enrolled or expecting to enroll full-time at a four-year institution or university; resident of Pennsylvania and studying in Pennsylvania. Applicant must have 3.0 GPA or higher. Available to U.S. and non-U.S. citizens.

Application Requirements: Application, essay, resume, references, transcript. *Deadline:* March 10.

> **Contact:** Scholarship Committee
> Pennsylvania Institute of Certified Public Accountants
> 1650 Arch Street, 17th Floor
> Philadelphia, PA 19103
> *E-mail:* schools@picpa.org

RHODE ISLAND FOUNDATION

http://www.rifoundation.org/

CARL W. CHRISTIANSEN SCHOLARSHIP

Award for Rhode Island residents pursuing full-time study in accounting or related fields. Must maintain a minimum 3.0 GPA, and for full-time study only.

Academic Fields/Career Goals: Accounting.

Award: Scholarship for use in freshman, sophomore, junior, senior, or graduate years; not renewable. *Amount:* $1000.

Eligibility Requirements: Applicant must be enrolled or expecting to enroll full-time at a two-year or four-year institution or university and resident of Rhode Island. Applicant must have 3.0 GPA or higher. Available to U.S. citizens.

Application Requirements: Application. *Deadline:* January 15.

> **Contact:** Denise Jacobson
> *E-mail:* djacobson@riscpa.org

RHODE ISLAND SOCIETY OF CERTIFIED PUBLIC ACCOUNTANTS

http://www.riscpa.org/

RHODE ISLAND SOCIETY OF CERTIFIED PUBLIC ACCOUNTANTS SCHOLARSHIP

Annual scholarship for graduates and undergraduates majoring in accounting, who are legal residents of Rhode Island and U.S. citizens. Must have interest in a career in public accounting, and submit one-page memo outlining that interest. Minimum GPA of 3.0 required. For more information, see web site http://www.riscpa.org.

Academic Fields/Career Goals: Accounting.

Award: Scholarship for use in freshman, sophomore, junior, senior, or graduate years; not renewable. *Number:* varies. *Amount:* varies.

Eligibility Requirements: Applicant must be enrolled or expecting to enroll full-time at a four-year institution or university and resident of Rhode Island. Applicant must have 3.0 GPA or higher. Available to U.S. citizens.

Application Requirements: Application, resume, references, test scores, transcript. *Deadline:* January 15.

> **Contact:** Robert Mancini, Executive Director
> Rhode Island Society of Certified Public Accountants
> 45 Royal Little Drive
> Providence, RI 02904
> *Phone:* 401-331-5720
> *Fax:* 401-454-5780
> *E-mail:* rmancini@riscpa.org

SAN DIEGO FOUNDATION

http://www.sdfoundation.org/

FRANK H. AULT SCHOLARSHIP

Scholarship to provide financial assistance for the next academic year to current students in their sophomore, junior, or senior year who have declared a major in finance or accounting. Applicants must have a demonstrated financial need and a minimum 3.0 GPA. Students must have participated in extracurricular or community service activities. Preference will be given to students who are active members of or have taken leadership in their school's accounting society.

Academic Fields/Career Goals: Accounting.

Award: Scholarship for use in sophomore, junior, or senior years; not renewable. *Number:* 6. *Amount:* $2500.

Eligibility Requirements: Applicant must be enrolled or expecting to enroll full-time at a four-year institution or university and resident of California. Applicant must have 3.0 GPA or higher. Available to U.S. citizens.

Application Requirements: Application, financial need analysis, references, transcript, personal statement, copy of tax return. *Deadline:* January 26.

> **Contact:** Shryl Helvie, Scholarship Coordinator
> San Diego Foundation
> 2508 Historic Decatur Road, Suite 200
> San Diego, CA 92106
> *Phone:* 619-814-1307
> *Fax:* 619-239-1710
> *E-mail:* shryl@sdfoundation.org

SOCIETY OF AUTOMOTIVE ANALYSTS

http://www.cybersaa.org/

SOCIETY OF AUTOMOTIVE ANALYSTS SCHOLARSHIP

A scholarship of $1500 awarded to students in economics, finance, business administration or marketing management. Minimum 3.0 GPA required. Must submit two letters of recommendation.

Academic Fields/Career Goals: Accounting; Business/Consumer Services; Economics.

Award: Scholarship for use in freshman, sophomore, junior, or senior years; not renewable. *Number:* 2. *Amount:* $1500.

Eligibility Requirements: Applicant must be enrolled or expecting to enroll full-time at a two-year or four-year or technical institution or university. Applicant must have 3.0 GPA or higher. Available to U.S. and non-U.S. citizens.

Application Requirements: Application, references, transcript. *Deadline:* June 1.

> **Contact:** Lynne Hall, Awards and Scholarships
> Society of Automotive Analysts
> 21400 Oakwood Boulevard
> Dearborn, MI 48124
> *Phone:* 313-240-4000
> *Fax:* 313-240-8641

SOCIETY OF LOUISIANA CERTIFIED PUBLIC ACCOUNTANTS

http://www.lcpa.org/

SOCIETY OF LOUISIANA CPAS SCHOLARSHIPS

One-time award for accounting majors. Applicant must be a Louisiana resident attending a four-year college or university in Louisiana. For full-time undergraduates entering their junior or senior year, or full-time graduate students. Minimum 2.5 GPA required. Deadline varies. Must be U.S. citizen.

Academic Fields/Career Goals: Accounting.

Award: Scholarship for use in junior, senior, or graduate years; not renewable. *Number:* varies. *Amount:* $500–$3000.

Eligibility Requirements: Applicant must be enrolled or expecting to enroll full-time at a four-year institution or university; resident of Louisiana and studying in Louisiana. Applicant must have 2.5 GPA or higher. Available to U.S. citizens.

Application Requirements: Application, essay, references, transcript. *Deadline:* varies.

Contact: Lisa Richardson, Member Services Manager
Society of Louisiana Certified Public Accountants
2400 Veterans Boulevard, Suite 500
Kenner, LA 70062-4739
Phone: 504-904-1139
Fax: 504-469-7930
E-mail: lrichardson@lcpa.org

SOUTH DAKOTA CPA SOCIETY

http://www.sdcpa.org/

5TH YEAR FULL TUITION SCHOLARSHIP

Scholarship pays for the full tuition for a South Dakota student to attend an accredited South Dakota college or university. If awarded the scholarship, the student must become a member of the SD CPA Society, work for or be supervised by a member of the SD CPA Society for 2 years, and upon eligibility, must sit for a minimum of 4 parts of the CPA exam per year for two years or until completed.

Academic Fields/Career Goals: Accounting.

Award: Scholarship for use in senior year; not renewable. *Number:* up to 2. *Amount:* $6800.

Eligibility Requirements: Applicant must be enrolled or expecting to enroll full-time at a four-year institution or university and studying in South Dakota. Applicant must have 3.0 GPA or higher. Available to U.S. citizens.

Application Requirements: Application, essay, transcript. *Deadline:* December 1.

Contact: Laura Coome, Executive Director
South Dakota CPA Society
PO Box 2080
Sioux Falls, SD 57101-2080
Phone: 605-334-3848
E-mail: lcoome@iw.net

EXCELLENCE IN ACCOUNTING SCHOLARSHIP

Scholarships available for senior undergraduate and graduate students majoring in accounting. Must have completed 90 credit hours, demonstrated excellence in academics and leadership potential. Application available online at http://www.sdcpa.org.

Academic Fields/Career Goals: Accounting.

Award: Scholarship for use in senior or graduate years; renewable. *Number:* 4–10. *Amount:* $500–$1500.

Eligibility Requirements: Applicant must be enrolled or expecting to enroll full-time at a four-year institution or university and studying in South Dakota. Available to U.S. citizens.

Application Requirements: Application, transcript. *Deadline:* December 1.

Contact: Laura Coome, Executive Director
South Dakota CPA Society
PO Box 2080
Sioux Falls, SD 57101
Phone: 605-334-3848

SOUTH DAKOTA RETAILERS ASSOCIATION

http://www.sdra.org/

SOUTH DAKOTA RETAILERS ASSOCIATION SCHOLARSHIP PROGRAM

One-time award to assist full-time students studying for a career in retailing. Applicants must have graduated from a South Dakota high school or be enrolled in postsecondary school in South Dakota. The award value and the number of awards granted varies annually.

Academic Fields/Career Goals: Accounting; Business/Consumer Services; Computer Science/Data Processing; Electrical Engineering/Electronics; Food Service/Hospitality; Graphics/Graphic Arts/Printing; Interior Design.

Award: Scholarship for use in freshman, sophomore, junior, senior, graduate, or postgraduate years; not renewable. *Number:* varies. *Amount:* $250–$1000.

Eligibility Requirements: Applicant must be enrolled or expecting to enroll full-time at a two-year or four-year or technical institution or university and studying in South Dakota. Available to U.S. and non-U.S. citizens.

Application Requirements: Application, essay, resume, references, transcript. *Deadline:* April 11.

Contact: Donna Leslie, Communications Director
South Dakota Retailers Association
PO Box 638
Pierre, SD 57501
Phone: 800-658-5545
Fax: 605-224-2059
E-mail: dleslie@sdra.org

TENNESSEE SOCIETY OF CPAS

http://www.tncpa.org/

TENNESSEE SOCIETY OF CPA SCHOLARSHIP

Scholarships are available only to full-time students who have completed introductory courses in accounting and/or students majoring in accounting. Applicants must be legal residents of Tennessee.

Academic Fields/Career Goals: Accounting.

Award: Scholarship for use in freshman, sophomore, junior, senior, or graduate years; not renewable. *Number:* 120–130. *Amount:* $250–$2500.

Eligibility Requirements: Applicant must be enrolled or expecting to enroll full-time at a four-year institution or university and resident of Tennessee. Available to U.S. citizens.

Application Requirements: Application, financial need analysis, references, transcript. *Deadline:* June 1.

Contact: Wendy Garvin, Member Services Manager
Tennessee Society of CPAs
201 Powell Place
Brentwood, TN 37027
Phone: 615-377-3825
Fax: 390-377-3904
E-mail: wgarvin@tscpa.com

TKE EDUCATIONAL FOUNDATION

http://www.tke.org/

HARRY J. DONNELLY MEMORIAL SCHOLARSHIP

One-time award of $900 given to a member of Tau Kappa Epsilon pursuing an undergraduate degree in accounting or a graduate degree in law. Applicant should have demonstrated leadership ability within his chapter, campus, or community.

Academic Fields/Career Goals: Accounting; Law/Legal Services.

Award: Scholarship for use in freshman, sophomore, junior, senior, or graduate years; not renewable. *Number:* 1. *Amount:* $900.

Eligibility Requirements: Applicant must be enrolled or expecting to enroll full-time at a four-year institution or university and must have an interest in leadership. Applicant or parent of applicant must be member of Tau Kappa Epsilon. Applicant must have 3.0 GPA or higher. Available to U.S. and non-U.S. citizens.

Application Requirements: Application, essay, photo, transcript, narrative summary of how TKE membership has benefited applicant. *Deadline:* February 29.

Contact: Gary A. Reed, President and Chief Executive Officer
TKE Educational Foundation
8645 Founders Road
Indianapolis, IN 46268-1393
Phone: 317-872-6533
Fax: 317-875-8353
E-mail: reedga@tke.org

W. ALLAN HERZOG SCHOLARSHIP

One $3000 award for an undergraduate member of TKE who is a full-time student pursuing a finance or accounting degree. Minimum 2.75 GPA required. Preference given to members of Nu Chapter. Applicant should have record of leadership within chapter and campus organizations.

Academic Fields/Career Goals: Accounting; Business/Consumer Services.

Award: Scholarship for use in freshman, sophomore, junior, or senior years; not renewable. *Number:* 1. *Amount:* $3000.

Eligibility Requirements: Applicant must be enrolled or expecting to enroll full-time at a four-year institution or university; male and must have an interest in leadership. Applicant or parent of applicant must be member of Tau Kappa Epsilon. Available to U.S. and non-U.S. citizens.

Application Requirements: Application, essay, photo, transcript, narrative summary of how TKE membership has benefited applicant. *Deadline:* February 29.

Contact: Gary A. Reed, President and Chief Executive Officer
TKE Educational Foundation
8645 Founders Road
Indianapolis, IN 46268-1393
Phone: 317-872-6533
Fax: 317-875-8353
E-mail: reedga@tke.org

UNITED NEGRO COLLEGE FUND

http://www.uncf.org/

ALFRED CHISHOLM/BASF MEMORIAL SCHOLARSHIP FUND

Scholarship for a student who has a relative employed by the BASF Corporation. Must attend an historically black college or university and have minimum GPA of 2.7 to apply. Eligible majors include engineering, accounting, mathematics, chemistry, biology, computer science, law, electrical engineering, chemical engineering, environmental engineering, mechanical engineering, petroleum engineering, pulp and paper engineering, systems engineering, and construction engineering.

Academic Fields/Career Goals: Accounting; Biology; Computer Science/Data Processing; Construction Engineering/Management; Electrical Engineering/Electronics; Engineering/Technology; Law/Legal Services; Mathematics; Mechanical Engineering; Paper and Pulp Engineering.

Award: Scholarship for use in freshman, sophomore, junior, or senior years; not renewable. *Amount:* $5000.

Eligibility Requirements: Applicant must be Black (non-Hispanic) and enrolled or expecting to enroll full- or part-time at a four-year institution or university.

Application Requirements: *Deadline:* May 31.

Contact: Director, Program Services
United Negro College Fund
8260 Willow Oaks Corporate Drive
PO Box 10444
Fairfax, VA 22031-8044
Phone: 800-331-2244
E-mail: rebecca.bennett@uncf.org

AVIS BUDGET GROUP SCHOLARSHIP

$5000 scholarship for second-semester sophomore majoring in business, finance, economics, or accounting. Minimum 3.0 GPA required.

Academic Fields/Career Goals: Accounting; Business/Consumer Services; Economics; Finance.

Award: Scholarship for use in sophomore or junior years; not renewable. *Amount:* $5000.

Eligibility Requirements: Applicant must be Black (non-Hispanic) and enrolled or expecting to enroll at a four-year institution. Applicant must have 3.0 GPA or higher. Available to U.S. citizens.

Application Requirements: *Deadline:* continuous.

Contact: Director, Program Services
United Negro College Fund
8260 Willow Oaks Corporate Drive
PO Box 10444
Fairfax, VA 22031-8044
Phone: 800-331-2244
E-mail: rebecca.bennett@uncf.org

AVON WOMEN IN SEARCH OF EXCELLENCE SCHOLARSHIP

$2500 scholarships for traditional and non-traditional female students attending UNCF member colleges and universities. At least half of the awards will be directed to women in the non-traditional age category. Must have 2.5 GPA and major in business, finance, economics, accounting, or marketing.

Academic Fields/Career Goals: Accounting; Business/Consumer Services; Economics; Finance; Marketing.

Award: Scholarship for use in freshman year; not renewable. *Amount:* $2500.

Eligibility Requirements: Applicant must be Black (non-Hispanic); enrolled or expecting to enroll at a four-year institution or university and female. Applicant must have 2.5 GPA or higher. Available to U.S. citizens.

Application Requirements: *Deadline:* continuous.

Contact: Director, Program Services
United Negro College Fund
8260 Willow Oaks Corporate Drive
PO Box 10444
Fairfax, VA 22031-8044
Phone: 800-331-2244
E-mail: rebecca.bennett@uncf.org

CARDINAL HEALTH SCHOLARSHIP

Scholarship available to African American undergraduates at all four-year accredited institutions. Students must be a rising sophomore or junior, majoring in accounting/finance, IS, marketing purchasing/operations, engineering or chemistry, or in their first or second year of pursuing a degree in pharmacy. Applicants must demonstrate non-collegiate leadership experience. Minimum 3.0 GPA required. Apply online http://www.uncf.org.

Academic Fields/Career Goals: Accounting; Business/Consumer Services; Chemical Engineering; Civil Engineering; Computer Science/Data Processing; Engineering/Technology; Mechanical Engineering; Pharmacy.

Award: Scholarship for use in freshman, sophomore, junior, or senior years; renewable. *Number:* varies. *Amount:* $5000.

Eligibility Requirements: Applicant must be Black (non-Hispanic); enrolled or expecting to enroll full-time at a four-year institution or university and must have an interest in leadership. Applicant must have 3.0 GPA or higher. Available to U.S. and non-U.S. citizens.

Application Requirements: Application, financial need analysis, FAFSA, Student Aid Report (SAR). *Deadline:* October 30.

Contact: Director, Program Services
United Negro College Fund
8260 Willow Oaks Corporate Drive
PO Box 10444
Fairfax, VA 22031-8044
Phone: 800-331-2244
E-mail: rebecca.bennett@uncf.org

CARGILL SCHOLARSHIP PROGRAM

Scholarship awarded to undergraduate freshman, sophomore, or junior enrolled in a UNCF member college or university or in one of the following institutions: Kansas State University, University of Illinois, University of Minnesota, Iowa State University, North Carolina A & T State University and University of Wisconsin-Madison. Eligible majors include finance, accounting, computer science, MIS, chemistry, biochemistry, agricultural and animal sciences, microbiology, information technology, chemical engineering, mechanical engineering. Minimum GPA of 3.0 required. See web site for additional information http://www.uncf.org.

Academic Fields/Career Goals: Accounting; Agriculture; Animal/Veterinary Sciences; Biology; Chemical Engineering; Computer Science/Data Processing; Finance; Food Science/Nutrition; Mechanical Engineering.

Award: Scholarship for use in freshman, sophomore, or junior years; renewable. *Number:* varies. *Amount:* $5000.

Eligibility Requirements: Applicant must be Black (non-Hispanic) and enrolled or expecting to enroll full-time at a four-year institution or university. Applicant must have 3.0 GPA or higher. Available to U.S. and non-U.S. citizens.

Application Requirements: Application, financial need analysis, FAFSA, Student Aid Report (SAR).

Contact: Director, Program Services
United Negro College Fund
8260 Willow Oaks Corporate Drive
PO Box 10444
Fairfax, VA 22031-8044
Phone: 800-331-2244
E-mail: rebecca.bennett@uncf.org

EDWARD M. NAGEL FOUNDATION SCHOLARSHIP

Applicants must be African American residents of California within the top 25 percent of their high school graduating class. Must be enrolled in a UNCF member college or university and pursue a degree in business, economics, or accounting. The scholarship value ranges from $2000 to $5000. For additional information and general scholarship application, visit web site: http://www.uncf.org.

Academic Fields/Career Goals: Accounting; Business/Consumer Services; Economics.

Award: Scholarship for use in freshman, sophomore, junior, or senior years; not renewable. *Number:* varies. *Amount:* $2000–$5000.

Eligibility Requirements: Applicant must be Black (non-Hispanic); enrolled or expecting to enroll full-time at a four-year institution or university and resident of California. Applicant must have 3.0 GPA or higher. Available to U.S. citizens.

Application Requirements: Application, financial need analysis, FAFSA.

Contact: Director, Program Services
United Negro College Fund
8260 Willow Oaks Corporate Drive
PO Box 10444
Fairfax, VA 22031-8044
Phone: 800-331-2244
E-mail: rebecca.bennett@uncf.org

FORD/UNCF CORPORATE SCHOLARS PROGRAM

Annual scholarship and networking opportunities with Ford Motor Company available to selected African-American college students. Must be undergraduate sophomores majoring in engineering, finance, accounting, information systems, marketing, or operations management at a UNCF member college or university or at a selected historically black college or university. Minimum 3.0 GPA required. Online application and additional information available at web site http://www.uncf.org.

Academic Fields/Career Goals: Accounting; Business/Consumer Services; Computer Science/Data Processing; Electrical Engineering/Electronics; Engineering/Technology; Finance; Marketing; Mechanical Engineering.

Award: Scholarship for use in sophomore year; not renewable. *Number:* 1. *Amount:* up to $5000.

Eligibility Requirements: Applicant must be Black (non-Hispanic) and enrolled or expecting to enroll full-time at a four-year institution. Applicant must have 3.0 GPA or higher. Available to U.S. citizens.

Application Requirements: Application, essay, financial need analysis, resume, references, transcript. *Deadline:* May 22.

Contact: Director, Program Services
United Negro College Fund
8260 Willow Oaks Corporate Drive
PO Box 10444
Fairfax, VA 22031-8044
Phone: 800-331-2244
E-mail: rebecca.bennett@uncf.org

GENERAL MILLS CORPORATE SCHOLARS AWARD

$5,000 scholarship for accounting, business, economics, finance, human resources, logistics, marketing, marketing research, operations management, or supply chain management majors, based on academic performance, career aspirations, demonstrated leadership, and achievement. Preference given to eligible students either attending college or with permanent addresses in Minnesota, Wisconsin, Iowa, Nebraska, North Dakota or South Dakota. Minimum 3.25 GPA required.

Academic Fields/Career Goals: Accounting; Asian Studies; Business/Consumer Services; Economics; Finance; Human Resources; Marketing.

Award: Scholarship for use in freshman, sophomore, or junior years; not renewable. *Amount:* up to $5000.

Eligibility Requirements: Applicant must be Black (non-Hispanic) and enrolled or expecting to enroll at a four-year institution or university.

Application Requirements: *Deadline:* April 30.

Contact: Director, Program Services
United Negro College Fund
8260 Willow Oaks Corporate Drive
PO Box 10444
Fairfax, VA 22031-8044
Phone: 800-331-2244
E-mail: rebecca.bennett@uncf.org

LOCKHEED MARTIN/UNCF SCHOLARSHIP

Scholarship available to African American undergraduate freshman and sophomore students at participating colleges and universities. Eligible majors include business, finance, accounting, computer science, supply chain management, electrical engineering, computer engineering, industrial engineering, mechanical engineering, systems engineering, aerospace engineering, and nuclear engineering. For a list of eligible institutions and to apply online, visit web site http://www.uncf.org.

Academic Fields/Career Goals: Accounting; Business/Consumer Services; Computer Science/Data Processing; Electrical Engineering/Electronics; Engineering/Technology; Finance; Mechanical Engineering.

Award: Scholarship for use in freshman or sophomore years; not renewable. *Amount:* $5000.

Eligibility Requirements: Applicant must be Black (non-Hispanic) and enrolled or expecting to enroll full-time at a four-year institution or university. Applicant must have 3.0 GPA or higher. Available to U.S. citizens.

Application Requirements: Application, transcript. *Deadline:* April 28.

Contact: Director, Program Services
United Negro College Fund
8260 Willow Oaks Corporate Drive
PO Box 10444
Fairfax, VA 22031-8044
Phone: 800-331-2244
E-mail: rebecca.bennett@uncf.org

MBIA/WILLIAM O. BAILEY SCHOLARS PROGRAM

Two full-tuition awards given to qualified juniors from New York, New Jersey, or Connecticut with at least a 3.0 GPA and majoring in business or finance. Must attend a UNCF member college or university. For more details visit web site http://www.uncf.org.

Academic Fields/Career Goals: Accounting; Business/Consumer Services; Finance.

Award: Scholarship for use in junior year; not renewable. *Number:* 2. *Amount:* varies.

Eligibility Requirements: Applicant must be Black (non-Hispanic); enrolled or expecting to enroll full-time at a four-year institution or university and resident of Connecticut, New Jersey, or New York. Applicant must have 3.0 GPA or higher. Available to U.S. citizens.

Application Requirements: Application, financial need analysis. *Deadline:* continuous.

Contact: Director, Program Services
United Negro College Fund
8260 Willow Oaks Corporate Drive
PO Box 10444
Fairfax, VA 22031-8044
Phone: 800-331-2244
E-mail: rebecca.bennett@uncf.org

NASCAR/WENDELL SCOTT, SR. SCHOLARSHIP

Award for African American junior or senior undergraduates or graduate students. Undergraduates must have a 3.0 GPA and graduate students must have a 3.2 GPA. Please visit web site for eligible majors and a list of eligible colleges and universities and to apply online http://www.uncf.org.

Academic Fields/Career Goals: Accounting; Business/Consumer Services; Communications; Computer Science/Data Processing; Engineering/Technology; Finance; Marketing; Mechanical Engineering.

Award: Scholarship for use in junior or senior years; renewable. *Number:* varies. *Amount:* $1500–$2000.

Eligibility Requirements: Applicant must be Black (non-Hispanic) and enrolled or expecting to enroll full- or part-time at a four-year institution or university. Available to U.S. citizens.

Application Requirements: Application, financial need analysis, photo, resume, references, transcript, FAFSA, Student Aid Report (SAR).

Contact: Director, Program Services
United Negro College Fund
8260 Willow Oaks Corporate Drive
PO Box 10444
Fairfax, VA 22031-8044
Phone: 800-331-2244
E-mail: rebecca.bennett@uncf.org

PRINCIPAL FINANCIAL GROUP SCHOLARSHIPS

Scholarships available to African American students who are residents of Iowa and majoring in business, finance, information systems, or liberal arts who are attending a UNCF member college or university. Minimum 3.0 GPA required. For additional information please go to web site http://www.uncf.com.

Academic Fields/Career Goals: Accounting; Business/Consumer Services; Computer Science/Data Processing; Finance; Humanities; Social Sciences.

Award: Scholarship for use in freshman, sophomore, junior, or senior years; not renewable. *Number:* varies. *Amount:* up to $12,000.

Eligibility Requirements: Applicant must be Black (non-Hispanic); enrolled or expecting to enroll full- or part-time at a four-year institution or university and resident of Iowa. Applicant must have 3.0 GPA or higher. Available to U.S. citizens.

Application Requirements: Application, financial need analysis. *Deadline:* March 1.

Contact: Director, Program Services
United Negro College Fund
8260 Willow Oaks Corporate Drive
PO Box 10444
Fairfax, VA 22031-8044
Phone: 800-331-2244
E-mail: rebecca.bennett@uncf.org

TOYOTA/UNCF SCHOLARSHIP

Scholarship to undergraduate freshman with at least a 3.0 GPA majoring in engineering, finance, economics, accounting, information systems, education, marketing, communications, computer science, liberal arts, political science, English, business, architecture, history, psychology, supply chain management, electrical engineering, information technology, business sales, computer engineering, industrial engineering, civil engineering, environmental engineering, management, mechanical engineering, management information systems, construction engineering, biomedical engineering, international business, manufacturing engineering, network administration, or public administration. Must attend one of the following UNCF member colleges or universities: Bethune-Cookman College, Clark Atlanta University, Morehouse College, Spelman College, Tuskegee University, or Xavier University. For additional information, visit http://www.uncf.org.

Academic Fields/Career Goals: Accounting; Business/Consumer Services; Communications; Computer Science/Data Processing; Economics; Electrical Engineering/Electronics; History; Literature/English/Writing; Mechanical Engineering; Political Science; Psychology; Public Policy and Administration.

Award: Scholarship for use in freshman year; not renewable. *Number:* varies. *Amount:* $7500.

Eligibility Requirements: Applicant must be Black (non-Hispanic) and enrolled or expecting to enroll full-time at a four-year institution or university. Applicant must have 3.0 GPA or higher. Available to U.S. and non-U.S. citizens.

Application Requirements: Application, financial need analysis. *Deadline:* January 30.

Contact: Director, Program Services
United Negro College Fund
8260 Willow Oaks Corporate Drive
PO Box 10444
Fairfax, VA 22031-8044
Phone: 800-331-2244
E-mail: rebecca.bennett@uncf.org

UBS/PAINEWEBBER SCHOLARSHIP

Applicant must be a sophomore or junior at one of UNCF member institutions and have a GPA of 3.0 or above. Preferred majors include: accounting, business administration, economics, finance, marketing, banking, or any other business-related field. Must be able to document an unmet financial need. For more information and to apply, go to http://www.uncf.org.

Academic Fields/Career Goals: Accounting; Business/Consumer Services; Economics; Finance; Marketing.

Award: Scholarship for use in sophomore or junior years; not renewable. *Amount:* $8000.

Eligibility Requirements: Applicant must be Black (non-Hispanic) and enrolled or expecting to enroll full- or part-time at a four-year institution or university. Applicant must have 3.0 GPA or higher. Available to U.S. citizens.

Application Requirements: Application, essay, financial need analysis, resume, references, transcript. *Deadline:* November 27.

Contact: Scholarship Committee
United Negro College Fund
8260 Willow Oaks Corporate Drive, PO Box 10444
Fairfax, VA 22031
Phone: 800-331-2244

UNITED WATER CORPORATE SCHOLARS PROGRAM

The UNCF Scholars program will provide selected candidates a 10-week paid internship at one of United Water's for profit facilities and UNCF will provide $5,000 scholarships for the 2011–2012 academic year paid for by the United Water Foundation. The internships will be offered at the following locations: Oradell and Hackensack, New Jersey; Harrisburg, Pennsylvania; Indianapolis, Indiana; Perry, Georgia; and Springfield, Massachusetts. Each candidate will need to go through the United Water for-profit hiring process. Must be a student at a four-year college and have minimum 3.0 GPA.

Academic Fields/Career Goals: Accounting; Chemical Engineering; Civil Engineering; Communications; Electrical Engineering/Electronics; Environmental Science; Human Resources; Marketing; Mechanical Engineering.

Award: Scholarship for use in sophomore year; not renewable. *Amount:* up to $5000.

Eligibility Requirements: Applicant must be Black (non-Hispanic) and enrolled or expecting to enroll full-time at a four-year institution or university. Applicant must have 3.0 GPA or higher.

Application Requirements: *Deadline:* May 31.

Contact: Director, Program Services
United Negro College Fund
8260 Willow Oaks Corporate Drive
PO Box 10444
Fairfax, VA 22031-8044
Phone: 800-331-2244
E-mail: rebecca.bennett@uncf.org

VERIZON FOUNDATION SCHOLARSHIP

Scholarships for students who reside within one of twenty states and attend Morehouse College, Paul Quinn College, Saint Paul's College, Virginia Union University, or Howard University. Must be majoring in business, engineering, information technology, human resources, or related field and have a minimum 3.0 GPA. Prospective applicants should complete the student profile found at web site http://www.uncf.org.

Academic Fields/Career Goals: Accounting; Business/Consumer Services; Computer Science/Data Processing; Engineering/Technology; Engineering-Related Technologies; Human Resources; Marketing.

Award: Scholarship for use in freshman, sophomore, junior, or senior years; not renewable. *Number:* 1. *Amount:* $5097.

Eligibility Requirements: Applicant must be Black (non-Hispanic) and enrolled or expecting to enroll full-time at a four-year institution or university. Applicant must have 3.0 GPA or higher. Available to U.S. citizens.

Application Requirements: Application, financial need analysis.

Contact: Director, Program Services
United Negro College Fund
8260 Willow Oaks Corporate Drive
PO Box 10444
Fairfax, VA 22031-8044
Phone: 800-331-2244
E-mail: rebecca.bennett@uncf.org

WELLS FARGO/UNCF SCHOLARSHIP FUND

Award for African American sophomores, juniors, and MBA students enrolled in a UNCF member college or university. Eligible majors include business, finance, accounting, architecture, computer engineering, electrical engineering, and systems engineering. Must be a resident of California, Minnesota, Indiana, Arizona, Illinois, Ohio, Washington, Oregon, Wisconsin, Michigan, Alaska, Iowa, Texas,

Nebraska, Colorado, Idaho, Montana, Nevada, New Mexico, North Dakota, South Dakota, Utah or Wyoming. Apply online at http://www.uncf.org.

Academic Fields/Career Goals: Accounting; Architecture; Business/Consumer Services; Computer Science/Data Processing; Electrical Engineering/Electronics; Finance.

Award: Scholarship for use in sophomore or junior years; renewable. *Number:* varies. *Amount:* up to $2000.

Eligibility Requirements: Applicant must be Black (non-Hispanic) and enrolled or expecting to enroll full-time at a four-year institution or university. Applicant must have 2.5 GPA or higher. Available to U.S. citizens.

Application Requirements: Application, financial need analysis, FAFSA, Student Aid Report (SAR). *Deadline:* October 31.

Contact: Director, Program Services
United Negro College Fund
8260 Willow Oaks Corporate Drive
PO Box 10444
Fairfax, VA 22031-8044
Phone: 800-331-2244
E-mail: rebecca.bennett@uncf.org

VIRCHOW, KRAUSE & COMPANY, LLP

http://www.virchowkrause.com/

VIRCHOW, KRAUSE AND COMPANY SCHOLARSHIP

One-time scholarship for students enrolled either full-time or part-time in accredited colleges or universities of Wisconsin, majoring in accounting.

Academic Fields/Career Goals: Accounting.

Award: Scholarship for use in freshman, sophomore, junior, or senior years; not renewable. *Number:* up to 3. *Amount:* up to $1000.

Eligibility Requirements: Applicant must be enrolled or expecting to enroll full- or part-time at a two-year or four-year institution or university and studying in Wisconsin. Available to U.S. citizens.

Application Requirements: Application, transcript. *Deadline:* varies.

Contact: Darbie Miller, Human Resources Coordinator
Virchow, Krause & Company, LLP
4600 American Parkway, PO Box 7398
Madison, WI 53707-7398
Phone: 608-240-2474
Fax: 608-249-1411
E-mail: dmiller@virchowkrause.com

VIRGINIA SOCIETY OF CERTIFIED PUBLIC ACCOUNTANTS EDUCATIONAL FOUNDATION

http://www.vscpa.com/

H. BURTON BATES JR. ANNUAL SCHOLARSHIP

Award to a junior or senior accounting major currently enrolled in an accredited Virginia college or university, or to a student who has earned their undergraduate degree and is taking additional coursework in order to sit for the CPA exam. Must demonstrate academic excellence and financial need.

Academic Fields/Career Goals: Accounting.

Award: Scholarship for use in junior or senior years; not renewable. *Number:* 1.

Eligibility Requirements: Applicant must be enrolled or expecting to enroll full-time at a four-year institution or university; resident of Virginia and studying in Virginia. Applicant must have 3.0 GPA or higher. Available to U.S. citizens.

Application Requirements: Application, essay, resume, references, transcript. *Deadline:* April 1.

Contact: Ms. Molly Wash, Career and Academic Relations Director
Virginia Society of Certified Public Accountants Educational Foundation
4309 Cox Road
Glen Allen, VA 23060
E-mail: mwash@vscpa.com

THOMAS M. BERRY JR. ANNUAL SCHOLARSHIP

Awarded to a student who has demonstrated academic excellence, financial need, and exemplary leadership skills. Applicant must have completed three credit hours of accounting and be currently registered for at least three more accounting credit hours.

Academic Fields/Career Goals: Accounting.

Award: Scholarship for use in sophomore, junior, senior, or graduate years; not renewable. *Number:* 1. *Amount:* $2500.

Eligibility Requirements: Applicant must be enrolled or expecting to enroll full- or part-time at a two-year or four-year institution or university and studying in Virginia. Applicant must have 3.0 GPA or higher. Available to U.S. citizens.

Application Requirements: Application, essay, resume, references, transcript. *Deadline:* April 1.

Contact: Ms. Molly Wash, Career and Academic Relations Director
Virginia Society of Certified Public Accountants Educational Foundation
4309 Cox Road
Glen Allen, VA 23060

VIRGINIA SOCIETY OF CPAS EDUCATIONAL FOUNDATION MINORITY SCHOLARSHIP

One-time award for a student currently enrolled in a Virginia college or university undergraduate program with the intent to pursue accounting or a business related field of study. Applicant must have at least six hours of accounting and be currently registered for at least 3 more accounting credit hours. Applicant must be a member of one of the VSCPA-defined minority groups (African-American, Hispanic-American, Native American or Asian Pacific American). Minimum overall and accounting GPA of 3.0 is required.

Academic Fields/Career Goals: Accounting; Business/Consumer Services.

Award: Scholarship for use in freshman, sophomore, junior, or senior years; not renewable. *Number:* 3–5. *Amount:* $1000.

Eligibility Requirements: Applicant must be American Indian/Alaska Native, Asian/Pacific Islander, Black (non-Hispanic), or Hispanic; enrolled or expecting to enroll full- or part-time at a two-year or four-year institution or university and studying in Virginia. Applicant must have 3.0 GPA or higher. Available to U.S. citizens.

Application Requirements: Application, essay, resume, references, transcript. *Deadline:* April 1.

Contact: Tracey Zink, Community Relations Coordinator
Virginia Society of Certified Public Accountants Educational Foundation
4309 Cox Road
Glen Allen, VA 23060
Phone: 800-612-9427
E-mail: tzink@vscpa.com

VIRGINIA SOCIETY OF CPAS EDUCATIONAL FOUNDATION UNDERGRADUATE SCHOLARSHIP

One-time award for a student currently enrolled in a Virginia college or university undergraduate program with the intent to pursue accounting or a business-related field of study. Applicant must have at least six hours of accounting and be currently registered for at least 3 more accounting credit hours. Minimum overall and accounting GPA of 3.0 is required.

Academic Fields/Career Goals: Accounting; Business/Consumer Services.

Award: Scholarship for use in freshman, sophomore, junior, or senior years; not renewable. *Number:* 3–5. *Amount:* $1000.

Eligibility Requirements: Applicant must be enrolled or expecting to enroll full- or part-time at a two-year or four-year institution or university and studying in Virginia. Applicant must have 3.0 GPA or higher. Available to U.S. citizens.

Application Requirements: Application, essay, resume, references, transcript. *Deadline:* April 1.

Contact: Tracey Zink, Community Relations Coordinator
Virginia Society of Certified Public Accountants Educational Foundation
4309 Cox Road
Glen Allen, VA 23060
Phone: 800-612-9427
E-mail: tzink@vscpa.com

WOMEN'S INDEPENDENCE SCHOLARSHIP PROGRAM, INC.

http://www.wispinc.org/

COUNSELOR, ADVOCATE, AND SUPPORT STAFF SCHOLARSHIP PROGRAM

Scholarship for workers in the field of domestic violence. Minimum one year working in the field of domestic violence and employer recommendation required. Scholarship value up to $3000.

Academic Fields/Career Goals: Accounting; Business/Consumer Services; Child and Family Studies; Psychology; Social Sciences; Social Services; Therapy/Rehabilitation; Women's Studies.

Award: Scholarship for use in freshman, sophomore, junior, senior, or graduate years; renewable. *Number:* up to 50. *Amount:* up to $3000.

Eligibility Requirements: Applicant must be enrolled or expecting to enroll full- or part-time at a two-year or four-year or technical institution or university. Applicant or parent of applicant must have employment or volunteer experience in human services. Applicant must have 3.0 GPA or higher. Available to U.S. citizens.

Application Requirements: Application, essay, financial need analysis, references. *Deadline:* August 1.

Contact: Nancy Soward, Executive Director

Women's Independence Scholarship Program, Inc.

4900 Randall Parkway, Suite H

Wilmington, NC 28403

Phone: 910-397-7742 Ext. 101

Fax: 910-397-0023

E-mail: nancy@wispinc.org

WYOMING TRUCKING ASSOCIATION SCHOLARSHIP FUND TRUST

http://www.wytruck.org/

WYOMING TRUCKING ASSOCIATION SCHOLARSHIP TRUST FUND

To qualify, students must (1) be a graduate of a Wyoming high school; (2) plan to pursue a course of study which will lead to a career in the Highway Transportation Industry with the following approved courses of study: business management, computer skills, accounting, office procedures and management, safety, diesel mechanics and truck driving; (3) attend a Wyoming school (University, Community College or trade school) approved by the WTA Scholarship Committee.

Academic Fields/Career Goals: Accounting; Business/Consumer Services; Communications; Computer Science/Data Processing; Marketing; Trade/Technical Specialties; Transportation.

Award: Scholarship for use in freshman, sophomore, junior, or senior years; not renewable. *Number:* 4–8. *Amount:* $500–$1000.

Eligibility Requirements: Applicant must be enrolled or expecting to enroll full-time at a two-year or four-year or technical institution or university; resident of Wyoming and studying in Wyoming. Available to U.S. citizens.

Application Requirements: Application, essay, financial need analysis, references, test scores, transcript. *Deadline:* March 10.

Contact: Kathy Cundall, Administrative Assistant

Wyoming Trucking Association Scholarship Fund Trust

PO Box 1909

Casper, WY 82602

Phone: 307-234-1579

E-mail: wytruck@aol.com

ADVERTISING/PUBLIC RELATIONS

GREATER KANAWHA VALLEY FOUNDATION

http://www.tgkvf.org/

CHARLESTON ROTARY CLUB SCHOLARSHIP

• See page 63

GREAT FALLS ADVERTISING FEDERATION

http://www.gfaf.com/

GREAT FALLS ADVERTISING FEDERATION COLLEGE SCHOLARSHIP

Scholarship of $2000 for college juniors who are residents of Montana. Must intend to pursue a career in communications, marketing, advertising, fine arts, or other related field. The number of awards vary. Must maintain a minimum 3.0 GPA.

Academic Fields/Career Goals: Advertising/Public Relations; Arts; Business/Consumer Services; Communications; Marketing.

Award: Scholarship for use in junior year; renewable. *Number:* varies. *Amount:* $2000.

Eligibility Requirements: Applicant must be enrolled or expecting to enroll full-time at a four-year institution or university and resident of Montana. Applicant must have 3.0 GPA or higher. Available to U.S. citizens.

Application Requirements: Application, essay, resume, references, transcript, work samples. *Deadline:* February 2.

Contact: Christine Depa, Administrative Assistant

Great Falls Advertising Federation

609 Tenth Avenue South, Suite B

Great Falls, MT 59405

Phone: 406-761-6453

Fax: 406-453-1128

E-mail: gfaf@gfaf.com

HIGH SCHOOL MARKETING/COMMUNICATIONS SCHOLARSHIP

Two scholarships of $2000 for high school seniors who are residents of Montana. Must intend to pursue a career in communications, marketing, advertising, or other related field.

Academic Fields/Career Goals: Advertising/Public Relations; Business/Consumer Services; Communications; Marketing.

Award: Scholarship for use in freshman year; not renewable. *Number:* 2. *Amount:* $2000.

Eligibility Requirements: Applicant must be high school student; planning to enroll or expecting to enroll full-time at a four-year institution or university and resident of Montana. Available to U.S. citizens.

Application Requirements: Application, essay, resume, references, self-addressed stamped envelope, cover letter describing how the scholarship money will be used. *Deadline:* February 29.

Contact: Christine Depa, Administrative Assistant

Great Falls Advertising Federation

609 Tenth Avenue South, Suite B

Great Falls, MT 59405

Phone: 406-761-6453

Fax: 406-453-1128

E-mail: gfaf@gfaf.com

INTERNATIONAL FOODSERVICE EDITORIAL COUNCIL

http://www.ifeconline.com/

INTERNATIONAL FOODSERVICE EDITORIAL COUNCIL COMMUNICATIONS SCHOLARSHIP

Applicant must be a full-time student enrolled in an accredited postsecondary educational institution working toward an associate, bachelor's, or master's degree. Must demonstrate financial need, academic achievement, service orientation, and writing ability. Must have background, education, and interests indicating preparedness for entering careers in editorial or public relations within the foodservice industry.

Academic Fields/Career Goals: Advertising/Public Relations; Communications; Food Science/Nutrition; Food Service/Hospitality; Graphics/Graphic Arts/Printing; Journalism; Literature/English/Writing; Photojournalism/Photography.

Award: Scholarship for use in freshman, sophomore, junior, senior, or graduate years; not renewable. *Number:* 1–8. *Amount:* $1000–$4000.

Eligibility Requirements: Applicant must be enrolled or expecting to enroll full-time at a two-year or four-year or technical institution or university and must have an interest in photography/photogrammetry/filmmaking or writing. Available to U.S. and non-U.S. citizens.

Application Requirements: Application, essay, resume, references, transcript. *Deadline:* March 15.

Contact: Carol Lally, Executive Director
International Foodservice Editorial Council
PO Box 491
Hyde Park, NY 12538-0491
Phone: 845-229-6973
Fax: 845-229-6993
E-mail: ifec@aol.com

PUBLIC RELATIONS STUDENT SOCIETY OF AMERICA

http://www.prssa.org/

PUBLIC RELATIONS SOCIETY OF AMERICA MULTICULTURAL AFFAIRS SCHOLARSHIP

Two, one-time $1500 awards for members of a principal minority group who are in their junior or senior year at an accredited four-year college or university. Must have at least a 3.0 GPA and be preparing for career in public relations or communications. Must be a full-time student and U.S. citizen.

Academic Fields/Career Goals: Advertising/Public Relations; Communications.

Award: Scholarship for use in freshman, sophomore, junior, or senior years; not renewable. *Number:* 2. *Amount:* $1500.

Eligibility Requirements: Applicant must be American Indian/Alaska Native, Asian/Pacific Islander, Black (non-Hispanic), or Hispanic and enrolled or expecting to enroll full-time at a four-year institution or university. Applicant must have 3.0 GPA or higher. Available to U.S. citizens.

Application Requirements: Application, essay, financial need analysis, references, transcript. *Deadline:* April 18.

Contact: Dora Tovar, Chair, Multicultural Communications Section
Public Relations Student Society of America
33 Maiden Lane, 11th Floor
New York, NY 10038-5150
Phone: 212-460-1476
Fax: 212-995-0757
E-mail: jeneen.garcia@prsa.org

RHODE ISLAND FOUNDATION

http://www.rifoundation.org/

J. D. EDSAL ADVERTISING SCHOLARSHIP

Award to benefit Rhode Island residents studying advertising (ex: public relations, marketing, graphic design, film, video, television, or broadcast production) with the expectation of pursuing a career in one of more of these fields. Applicants must be college undergraduates, sophomore or above.

Academic Fields/Career Goals: Advertising/Public Relations; Communications; Filmmaking/Video; Graphics/Graphic Arts/Printing; Marketing; TV/Radio Broadcasting.

Award: Scholarship for use in sophomore, junior, or senior years; renewable. *Amount:* $500–$1000.

Eligibility Requirements: Applicant must be enrolled or expecting to enroll full-time at a four-year institution or university and resident of Rhode Island. Available to U.S. citizens.

Application Requirements: Application, essay, financial need analysis, references, self-addressed stamped envelope, transcript. *Deadline:* April 30.

Contact: Libby Monahan, Funds Administrator
Rhode Island Foundation
One Union Station
Providence, RI 02903
Phone: 401-274-4564 Ext. 3117
E-mail: libbym@rifoundation.org

STRAIGHTFORWARD MEDIA

http://www.straightforwardmedia.com/

STRAIGHTFORWARD MEDIA BUSINESS SCHOOL SCHOLARSHIP

Scholarship of $500 for undergraduate and graduate students pursuing a business-related degree, including but not limited to economics, finance, marketing, and management. Students pursuing an online business degree are also eligible. Awarded four times per year. Deadlines: March 31, June 30, September 30, and December 31.

Academic Fields/Career Goals: Advertising/Public Relations; Business/Consumer Services; Economics; Finance; Marketing.

Award: Scholarship for use in freshman, sophomore, junior, senior, or graduate years; not renewable. *Number:* 4. *Amount:* $500.

Eligibility Requirements: Applicant must be enrolled or expecting to enroll full- or part-time at a two-year or four-year or technical institution or university. Available to U.S. and non-U.S. citizens.

Application Requirements: Essay. *Deadline:* varies.

Contact: Scholarship Committee
StraightForward Media
508 7th Street
Suite 202
Rapid City, SD 57701
Phone: 605-348-3042

STRAIGHTFORWARD MEDIA MEDIA & COMMUNICATIONS SCHOLARSHIP

Scholarship of $500 available to students of media and communications. Must be majoring in programs such as journalism, broadcasting, advertising, speech, mass communications, or marketing. Awarded four times per year. Deadlines: March 31, June 30, September 30, and December 31. For more information, visit web site http://www.straightforward-media.com/media/form.php.

Academic Fields/Career Goals: Advertising/Public Relations; Communications; Journalism; Marketing; Photojournalism/Photography; TV/Radio Broadcasting.

Award: Scholarship for use in freshman, sophomore, junior, or senior years; not renewable. *Number:* 4. *Amount:* $500.

Eligibility Requirements: Applicant must be enrolled or expecting to enroll full- or part-time at a two-year or four-year or technical institution or university. Available to U.S. and non-U.S. citizens.

Application Requirements: Essay. *Deadline:* varies.

Contact: Scholarship Committee
StraightForward Media
508 7th Street
Suite 202
Rapid City, SD 57701
Phone: 605-348-3042

AGRIBUSINESS

CALIFORNIA FARM BUREAU SCHOLARSHIP FOUNDATION

http://www.cfbf.com/

CALIFORNIA FARM BUREAU SCHOLARSHIP

Renewable award given to students attending a four-year college in California. Applicants must be California residents preparing for a career in the agricultural industry.

Academic Fields/Career Goals: Agribusiness; Agriculture.

Award: Scholarship for use in freshman, sophomore, junior, or senior years; renewable. *Number:* up to 30. *Amount:* $1800–$2750.

Eligibility Requirements: Applicant must be enrolled or expecting to enroll full-time at a four-year institution; resident of California and studying in California. Available to U.S. citizens.

Application Requirements: Application, essay, interview, references, transcript. *Deadline:* March 1.

Contact: Darlene Licciardo, Scholarship Coordinator
California Farm Bureau Scholarship Foundation
2300 River Plaza Drive
Sacramento, CA 95833
Phone: 916-561-5500
Fax: 916-561-5690
E-mail: dlicciardo@cfbf.com

CHS FOUNDATION

http://www.chsfoundation.org/

CHS FOUNDATION HIGH SCHOOL SCHOLARSHIPS

Scholarships available to graduating high school seniors who plan to enroll in an agricultural-related program of study in a two-year or four-year college or university. Student must be a U.S. citizen. For additional information and an application, see web site http://www.chsfoundation.org.

Academic Fields/Career Goals: Agribusiness; Agriculture; Horticulture/Floriculture.

Award: Scholarship for use in freshman year; not renewable. *Number:* 50. *Amount:* $1000.

Eligibility Requirements: Applicant must be high school student and planning to enroll or expecting to enroll full- or part-time at a two-year or four-year or technical institution or university. Available to U.S. citizens.

Application Requirements: Application, essay, references, transcript. *Deadline:* April 1.

Contact: Scholarship Committee
Phone: 800-814-0506
E-mail: info@chsfoundation.org

CHS FOUNDATION TWO-YEAR COLLEGE SCHOLARSHIPS

Non-renewable scholarship available to first-year agricultural students at a two-year college. Must be studying an agricultural-related major; scholarship is intended for the second year of study. Must be a U.S. citizen. For additional information and application, see web site http://www.chsfoundation.org.

Academic Fields/Career Goals: Agribusiness; Agriculture; Horticulture/Floriculture.

Award: Scholarship for use in sophomore year; not renewable. *Number:* 25. *Amount:* $1000.

Eligibility Requirements: Applicant must be enrolled or expecting to enroll full- or part-time at a two-year or technical institution. Available to U.S. citizens.

Application Requirements: Application, essay, references, transcript. *Deadline:* April 1.

Contact: Scholarship Committee
Phone: 800-814-0506
E-mail: info@chsfoundation.org

CHS FOUNDATION UNIVERSITY SCHOLARSHIPS

Renewable scholarship available for students in sophomore, junior, or senior year currently studying agriculture at select universities around the nation. Preference given to students interested in a career in or studying agricultural-based cooperatives and working towards a degree in agribusiness or production agriculture. Students apply to the School of Agriculture or Financial Aid Office at one of the participating universities and follow individual procedures and deadlines for that institution. For additional information and a list of participating universities, see web site http://www.chsfoundation.org.

Academic Fields/Career Goals: Agribusiness; Agriculture.

Award: Scholarship for use in sophomore, junior, or senior years; not renewable. *Number:* up to 150. *Amount:* $1000.

Eligibility Requirements: Applicant must be enrolled or expecting to enroll full- or part-time at a four-year institution or university. Available to U.S. citizens.

Application Requirements: Application, essay, references, transcript.

Contact: Scholarship Committee
Phone: 800-814-0506
E-mail: info@chsfoundation.org

GOLF COURSE SUPERINTENDENTS ASSOCIATION OF AMERICA

http://www.eifg.org/

GOLF COURSE SUPERINTENDENTS ASSOCIATION OF AMERICA STUDENT ESSAY CONTEST

Up to three awards for essays focusing on the golf course management profession. Undergraduates and graduate students pursuing turf grass science, agronomy, or any field related to golf course management may apply. Applicant must be a member of GCSAA. In addition to cash prizes, winning entries may be published or excerpted in News-line or Golf Course Management magazine.

Academic Fields/Career Goals: Agribusiness; Horticulture/Floriculture; Recreation, Parks, Leisure Studies.

Award: Prize for use in freshman, sophomore, junior, or senior years; not renewable. *Number:* up to 3. *Amount:* $1000–$2000.

Eligibility Requirements: Applicant must be enrolled or expecting to enroll full-time at a two-year or four-year institution or university. Applicant or parent of applicant must be member of Golf Course Superintendents Association of America. Available to U.S. and non-U.S. citizens.

Application Requirements: Application, applicant must enter a contest, essay. *Deadline:* March 31.

Contact: Mischia Wright, Senior Manager, Development
Golf Course Superintendents Association of America
1421 Research Park Drive
Lawrence, KS 66049-3859
Phone: 800-472-7878 Ext. 4445
E-mail: mwright@gcsaa.org

HOLSTEIN ASSOCIATION USA INC.

http://www.holsteinusa.com/

ROBERT H. RUMLER SCHOLARSHIP

Awards to encourage deserving and qualified persons with an established interest in the dairy field, who have demonstrated leadership qualities and managerial abilities to pursue a master's degree in business administration.

Academic Fields/Career Goals: Agribusiness; Business/Consumer Services.

Award: Scholarship for use in freshman, sophomore, junior, senior, or graduate years; not renewable. *Number:* 1. *Amount:* $3000.

Eligibility Requirements: Applicant must be enrolled or expecting to enroll full-time at an institution or university and must have an interest in leadership. Applicant must have 3.0 GPA or higher. Available to U.S. and non-U.S. citizens.

Application Requirements: Application, essay, photo, references, transcript. *Deadline:* April 15.

Contact: John Meyer, Chief Executive Officer
Holstein Association USA Inc.
One Holstein Place, PO Box 808
Brattleboro, VT 05302-0808
Phone: 802-254-4551
Fax: 802-254-8251
E-mail: jmeyer@holstein.com

INTERTRIBAL TIMBER COUNCIL

http://www.itcnet.org/

TRUMAN D. PICARD SCHOLARSHIP

The program is dedicated to assisting Native American/Native-Alaskan youth seeking careers in natural resources. Graduating senior high school students and those currently attending institutions of higher education are encouraged to apply. A valid tribal/Alaska native corporation's enrollment card is required.

Academic Fields/Career Goals: Agribusiness; Agriculture; Environmental Science; Natural Resources.

Award: Scholarship for use in freshman, sophomore, junior, senior, or graduate years; not renewable. *Number:* 15–20. *Amount:* $1500–$2000.

Eligibility Requirements: Applicant must be American Indian/Alaska Native and enrolled or expecting to enroll full-time at a two-year or four-year institution or university. Available to U.S. citizens.

Application Requirements: Application, essay, resume, references, transcript, enrollment card. *Deadline:* March 18.

Contact: Joann Reynolds, Education Committee
Intertribal Timber Council
1112 NE 21st Avenue, Suite 4
Portland, OR 97232-2114
Phone: 503-282-4296
Fax: 503-282-1274
E-mail: itc1@teleport.com

MAINE DEPARTMENT OF AGRICULTURE, FOOD AND RURAL RESOURCES

http://www.maine.gov/agriculture

MAINE RURAL REHABILITATION FUND SCHOLARSHIP PROGRAM

One-time scholarship open to Maine residents enrolled in or accepted by any school, college, or university. Must be full time and demonstrate financial need. Those opting for a Maine institution given preference. Major must lead to an agricultural career. Minimum 3.0 GPA required.

Academic Fields/Career Goals: Agribusiness; Agriculture; Animal/Veterinary Sciences.

Award: Scholarship for use in freshman, sophomore, junior, senior, graduate, or postgraduate years; not renewable. *Number:* 10–20. *Amount:* $800–$2000.

Eligibility Requirements: Applicant must be enrolled or expecting to enroll full-time at a two-year or four-year or technical institution or university and resident of Maine. Applicant must have 3.0 GPA or higher. Available to U.S. citizens.

Application Requirements: Application, driver's license, financial need analysis, transcript. *Deadline:* June 15.

Contact: Jane Aiudi, Director of Marketing
Maine Department of Agriculture, Food and Rural Resources
28 State House Station
Augusta, ME 04333-0028
Phone: 207-287-7628
Fax: 207-287-5576
E-mail: jane.aiudi@maine.gov

MINNESOTA SOYBEAN RESEARCH AND PROMOTION COUNCIL

http://www.mnsoybean.org/

MINNESOTA SOYBEAN RESEARCH AND PROMOTION COUNCIL YOUTH SOYBEAN SCHOLARSHIP

Up to six $1000 awards available to high school seniors who are residents of Minnesota. Must demonstrate activity in agriculture with plans to study in an agricultural related program. For more details see web site http://www.mnsoybean.org.

Academic Fields/Career Goals: Agribusiness; Agriculture; Food Science/Nutrition.

Award: Scholarship for use in freshman year; not renewable. *Number:* 10. *Amount:* up to $1000.

Eligibility Requirements: Applicant must be Hispanic; high school student; planning to enroll or expecting to enroll full-time at a two-year or four-year or technical institution or university and resident of Minnesota. Applicant or parent of applicant must have employment or volunteer experience in agriculture or farming. Available to U.S. citizens.

Application Requirements: Application, resume, references, self-addressed stamped envelope, transcript. *Deadline:* February 28.

Contact: Vicki Trudeau, Scholarship Coordinator
Minnesota Soybean Research and Promotion Council
151 Saint Andrews Court, Suite 710
Mankato, MN 56001
Phone: 888-896-9678
E-mail: vicki@mnsoybean.com

MONSANTO AGRIBUSINESS SCHOLARSHIP

http://www.monsanto.ca/

MONSANTO CANADA OPPORTUNITY SCHOLARSHIP PROGRAM

Scholarship available to a first year postsecondary student who is a Canadian citizen. Must be majoring in the agriculture, forestry, business, or biotechnology at a Canadian institution.

Academic Fields/Career Goals: Agribusiness; Agriculture; Science, Technology, and Society.

Award: Scholarship for use in freshman year; not renewable. *Number:* 50–60. *Amount:* $1500.

Eligibility Requirements: Applicant must be of Canadian heritage; high school student and planning to enroll or expecting to enroll full-time at a four-year or technical institution or university. Available to Canadian citizens.

Application Requirements: Application, essay, references, transcript, university/college acceptance letter. *Deadline:* May 16.

Contact: Scholarship Coordinator
Monsanto Agribusiness Scholarship
900-One Research Road
Winnipeg, MB R3T 6E3
Phone: 204-985-1000
Fax: 888-667-4944

NATIONAL CATTLEMEN'S FOUNDATION

http://www.nationalcattlemensfoundation.org/

CME BEEF INDUSTRY SCHOLARSHIP

Ten $1500 scholarships will be awarded to students who intend to pursue a career in the beef industry, including areas such as agricultural education, communications, production, or research. Must be enrolled as an undergraduate student in a four-year institution.

Academic Fields/Career Goals: Agribusiness; Agriculture; Communications.

Award: Scholarship for use in freshman, sophomore, junior, or senior years; not renewable. *Number:* 10. *Amount:* $1500.

Eligibility Requirements: Applicant must be enrolled or expecting to enroll full-time at a four-year institution or university. Available to U.S. citizens.

Application Requirements: Application, essay, references, transcript. *Deadline:* varies.

Contact: RoxAnn Johnson, Executive Director
National Cattlemen's Foundation
9110 East Nichols Avenue, Suite 300
Centennial, CO 80112
Phone: 303-850-3388
Fax: 303-694-7372
E-mail: mcf@beef.org

NATIONAL DAIRY SHRINE

http://www.dairyshrine.org/

NDS STUDENT RECOGNITION CONTEST

Awards available to college seniors enrolled in dairy science courses. Applicants must be nominated by their college or university professor and must intend to continue in the dairy field. A college or university may nominate up to 2 applicants.

Academic Fields/Career Goals: Agribusiness; Agriculture; Animal/Veterinary Sciences; Food Science/Nutrition.

Award: Prize for use in senior year; not renewable. *Number:* 2–10. *Amount:* $1000–$2000.

Eligibility Requirements: Applicant must be enrolled or expecting to enroll full-time at a four-year institution or university. Applicant must have 2.5 GPA or higher. Available to U.S. and Canadian citizens.

Application Requirements: Application, photo, references, transcript, nomination. *Deadline:* April 15.

Contact: Executive Director
　　　E-mail: info@dairyshrine.org

NATIONAL POTATO COUNCIL WOMEN'S AUXILIARY

http://www.nationalpotatocouncil.org/

POTATO INDUSTRY SCHOLARSHIP

The auxiliary scholarship is for full-time students studying in a potato-related field, who desire to work in the potato industry after graduation. Minimum 3.0 GPA required.

Academic Fields/Career Goals: Agribusiness; Agriculture; Food Science/Nutrition; Horticulture/Floriculture.

Award: Scholarship for use in senior year; not renewable. *Number:* 1. *Amount:* $5000.

Eligibility Requirements: Applicant must be enrolled or expecting to enroll full-time at a four-year institution or university. Available to U.S. citizens.

Application Requirements: Application, essay, resume, references, transcript. *Deadline:* June 15.

Contact: John Keeling, Executive Vice President and Chief Executive Officer
　　　National Potato Council Women's Auxiliary
　　　1300 L Street, NW, Suite 910
　　　Washington, DC 20005
　　　Phone: 202-682-9456 Ext. 203
　　　Fax: 202-682-0333
　　　E-mail: johnkeeling@nationalpotatocouncil.org

NATIONAL POULTRY AND FOOD DISTRIBUTORS ASSOCIATION

http://www.npfda.org/

NATIONAL POULTRY AND FOOD DISTRIBUTORS ASSOCIATION SCHOLARSHIP FOUNDATION

The scholarships are awarded to full-time students in their junior or senior years at a U.S. college pursuing degrees in poultry science, food science, agricultural business, or other related areas of study pertaining to the poultry and food industries.

Academic Fields/Career Goals: Agribusiness; Agriculture; Animal/Veterinary Sciences; Food Science/Nutrition; Food Service/Hospitality.

Award: Scholarship for use in junior or senior years; not renewable. *Number:* 4. *Amount:* $1500–$2000.

Eligibility Requirements: Applicant must be enrolled or expecting to enroll full-time at a four-year institution or university. Available to U.S. and non-U.S. citizens.

Application Requirements: Application, essay, references, transcript. *Deadline:* May 31.

Contact: Kristin McWhorter, Executive Director
　　　National Poultry and Food Distributors Association
　　　3150 Highway 34 East, Suite 209
　　　Newnan, GA 30265
　　　Phone: 877-845-1545
　　　Fax: 770-535-7385
　　　E-mail: kkm@npfda.org

NEW YORK STATE ASSOCIATION OF AGRICULTURAL FAIRS

http://www.nyfairs.org/

NEW YORK STATE ASSOCIATION OF AGRICULTURAL FAIRS AND NEW YORK STATE SHOWPEOPLE'S ASSOCIATION ANNUAL SCHOLARSHIP

Scholarship of $1000 given to New York high school seniors and students attending college and planning to pursue, or already pursuing a degree in an agricultural field, a fair management related field or an outdoor amusement related field.

Academic Fields/Career Goals: Agribusiness; Agriculture.

Award: Scholarship for use in freshman, sophomore, junior, senior, or graduate years; not renewable. *Number:* 6. *Amount:* $1000.

Eligibility Requirements: Applicant must be enrolled or expecting to enroll full-time at a two-year or four-year institution or university and resident of New York. Available to U.S. citizens.

Application Requirements: Application, essay, references, transcript. *Deadline:* April 9.

Contact: Mark St. Jacques, President
　　　New York State Association of Agricultural Fairs
　　　392 Old Schuylerville Road
　　　Greenwich, NY 12834
　　　Phone: 518-692-2464
　　　E-mail: markwashfair@aol.com

OHIO FARMERS UNION

http://www.ohfarmersunion.org/

VIRGIL THOMPSON MEMORIAL SCHOLARSHIP CONTEST

Award available to members of Ohio Farmers Union who are enrolled as full-time college sophomores, juniors or seniors. Awards of $1000 to winner and $500 each to two runners-up.

Academic Fields/Career Goals: Agribusiness; Agriculture.

Award: Scholarship for use in sophomore, junior, or senior years; not renewable. *Number:* 1–3. *Amount:* $500–$1000.

Eligibility Requirements: Applicant must be enrolled or expecting to enroll full-time at a four-year institution or university and resident of Ohio. Applicant or parent of applicant must be member of Ohio Farmers Union. Available to U.S. citizens.

Application Requirements: Application, applicant must enter a contest, essay. *Deadline:* December 31.

Contact: Maria Miller, Public Relations Director
　　　Ohio Farmers Union
　　　PO Box 363
　　　Ottawa, OH 45875
　　　Phone: 419-523-5300
　　　Fax: 419-523-5913
　　　E-mail: m-miller@ohfarmersunion.org

SOCIETY FOR RANGE MANAGEMENT

http://www.rangelands.org/

MASONIC RANGE SCIENCE SCHOLARSHIP

Renewable award for undergraduate students pursuing degree in agribusiness, agriculture, animal/veterinary sciences, earth science, natural resources and range science.

Academic Fields/Career Goals: Agribusiness; Agriculture; Animal/Veterinary Sciences; Environmental Science; Natural Resources.

Award: Scholarship for use in freshman or sophomore years; renewable. *Number:* 1. *Amount:* $1000.

Eligibility Requirements: Applicant must be enrolled or expecting to enroll full-time at a four-year institution or university. Available to U.S. citizens.

Application Requirements: Application, essay, references, test scores, transcript. *Deadline:* January 15.

Contact: Vicky Trujillo, Executive Assistant
Society for Range Management
10030 West 27th Avenue
Wheat Ridge, CO 80215-6601
Phone: 303-986-3309
Fax: 303-986-3892
E-mail: vtrujillo@rangelands.org

SOIL AND WATER CONSERVATION SOCIETY-NEW JERSEY CHAPTER

http://www.geocities.com/njswcs

EDWARD R. HALL SCHOLARSHIP

Two $500 scholarships awarded annually to students attending a New Jersey accredited college or New Jersey residents attending any out-of-state college. Undergraduate students, with the exception of freshmen, are eligible. Must be enrolled in a curriculum related to natural resources. Other areas related to conservation may qualify.

Academic Fields/Career Goals: Agribusiness; Agriculture; Animal/Veterinary Sciences; Biology; Earth Science; Environmental Science; Horticulture/Floriculture; Natural Resources; Natural Sciences.

Award: Scholarship for use in sophomore, junior, or senior years; not renewable. *Number:* 2. *Amount:* $500.

Eligibility Requirements: Applicant must be enrolled or expecting to enroll full-time at a two-year or four-year institution or university and resident of New Jersey. Available to U.S. and non-U.S. citizens.

Application Requirements: Application, essay, financial need analysis, references, transcript, list of clubs and organizations related to natural resources of which applicant is a member. *Deadline:* April 15.

Contact: Fireman E. Bear Chapter, c/o USDA-NRCS
Soil and Water Conservation Society-New Jersey Chapter
220 Davidson Avenue, Fourth Floor
Somerset, NJ 08873
Phone: 732-932-9295
E-mail: njswcs@yahoo.com

SOUTH DAKOTA BOARD OF REGENTS

http://www.sdbor.edu/

SOUTH DAKOTA BOARD OF REGENTS BJUGSTAD SCHOLARSHIP

Scholarship for graduating North or South Dakota high school senior who is a Native American. Must demonstrate academic achievement, character and leadership abilities. Must submit proof of tribal enrollment. One-time award of $500. Must rank in upper half of class or have a minimum 2.5 GPA. Must be pursuing studies in agriculture, agribusiness, or natural resources.

Academic Fields/Career Goals: Agribusiness; Agriculture; Natural Resources.

Award: Scholarship for use in freshman year; not renewable. *Number:* 1. *Amount:* $500.

Eligibility Requirements: Applicant must be American Indian/Alaska Native; high school student; planning to enroll or expecting to enroll full-time at a four-year institution or university; resident of North Dakota or South Dakota and must have an interest in leadership. Applicant must have 2.5 GPA or higher. Available to U.S. citizens.

Application Requirements: Application, references, transcript, proof of tribal enrollment. *Deadline:* February 15.

Contact: Dr. Paul Turman, Director of Academic Assessment
South Dakota Board of Regents
306 East Capitol Avenue, Suite 200
Pierre, SD 57501-2545
Phone: 605-773-3455
E-mail: pault@sdbor.edu

AGRICULTURE

AGRILIANCE, LAND O' LAKES, AND CROPLAN GENETICS

http://www.agriliance.com/

CAREERS IN AGRICULTURE SCHOLARSHIP PROGRAM

Awards $1000 to 20 high school seniors interested in agriculture-related studies. Must be planning to enroll in a two- or four-year agriculture-related curriculum.

Academic Fields/Career Goals: Agriculture.

Award: Scholarship for use in freshman year; not renewable. *Number:* 20. *Amount:* $1000.

Eligibility Requirements: Applicant must be high school student and planning to enroll or expecting to enroll full-time at a two-year or four-year institution or university. Available to U.S. citizens.

Application Requirements: Application, essay. *Deadline:* March 1.

Contact: Annette Degnan, Director, Advertising and Communications
Agriliance, Land O' Lakes, and Croplan Genetics
PO Box 64089
St. Paul, MN 55164-0089
Phone: 651-355-5126
E-mail: adegnan@mbrservices.com

ALABAMA GOLF COURSE SUPERINTENDENTS ASSOCIATION

http://www.agcsa.org/

ALABAMA GOLF COURSE SUPERINTENDENT'S ASSOCIATION'S DONNIE ARTHUR MEMORIAL SCHOLARSHIP

One-time award for students majoring in agriculture with an emphasis on turf-grass management. Must have a minimum 2.0 GPA. Applicant must be a full-time student. High school students not considered. Award available to U.S. citizens.

Academic Fields/Career Goals: Agriculture; Horticulture/Floriculture.

Award: Scholarship for use in freshman, sophomore, junior, or senior years; not renewable. *Number:* 1. *Amount:* $2000.

Eligibility Requirements: Applicant must be enrolled or expecting to enroll full-time at a two-year or four-year institution or university. Applicant must have 2.5 GPA or higher. Available to U.S. citizens.

Application Requirements: Application, essay, references, transcript. *Deadline:* October 15.

Contact: Melanie Bonds, Secretary
Alabama Golf Course Superintendents Association
PO Box 661214
Birmingham, AL 35266-1214
Phone: 205-967-0397
E-mail: agcsa@charter.net

ALBERTA HERITAGE SCHOLARSHIP FUND

http://www.alis.alberta.ca/

ALBERTA BARLEY COMMISSION-EUGENE BOYKO MEMORIAL SCHOLARSHIP

Award of CAN$500 to recognize and encourage students entering the field of crop production and/or crop processing technology studies. Must be a Canadian citizen or landed immigrant attending an Alberta postsecondary institution. Students must be enrolled in the second or subsequent year of postsecondary study and taking courses that have an emphasis on crop production and/or crop processing technology. Awarded on basis of academic achievement. For additional information, see web site http://alis.alberta.ca.

Academic Fields/Career Goals: Agriculture.

Award: Scholarship for use in sophomore, junior, or senior years; not renewable. *Number:* 1.

Eligibility Requirements: Applicant must be enrolled or expecting to enroll full-time at a four-year institution or university and resident of Alberta. Available to Canadian citizens.

Application Requirements: Application, transcript. *Deadline:* August 1.

Contact: Scholarship Committee
Alberta Heritage Scholarship Fund
9940 106th Street, Fourth Floor, Sterling Place
PO Box 28000, Station Main
Edmonton, AB T5J 4R4
Canada
Phone: 780-427-8640
E-mail: scholarships@gov.ab.ca

AMERICAN OIL CHEMISTS' SOCIETY

http://www.aocs.org/

AOCS BIOTECHNOLOGY STUDENT EXCELLENCE AWARD

Award to recognize an outstanding paper in the field of biotechnology presented by a student at the AOCS annual meeting and Expo. Graduate students presenting within the Biotechnology Division technical program are eligible for the award.

Academic Fields/Career Goals: Agriculture; Chemical Engineering; Food Science/Nutrition.

Award: Prize for use in senior or graduate years; not renewable. *Number:* 1–3. *Amount:* $100–$300.

Eligibility Requirements: Applicant must be enrolled or expecting to enroll full-time at a four-year institution or university. Available to U.S. and non-U.S. citizens.

Application Requirements: Application, references, abstract. *Deadline:* varies.

Contact: Barbara A. Semeraro, Area Manager, Membership
American Oil Chemists' Society
AOCS, P.O. Box 17190
Urbana, IL 61803
Phone: 217-693-4804
Fax: 217-693-4849
E-mail: awards@aocs.org

AMERICAN SOCIETY FOR ENOLOGY AND VITICULTURE

http://www.asev.org/

AMERICAN SOCIETY FOR ENOLOGY AND VITICULTURE SCHOLARSHIPS

One-time award for college juniors, seniors, and graduate students residing in North America and enrolled in a program studying viticulture, enology, or any field related to the wine and grape industry. Minimum 3.0 GPA for undergraduates; minimum 3.2 GPA for graduate students. Must be a resident of the United States, Canada, or Mexico.

Academic Fields/Career Goals: Agriculture; Chemical Engineering; Food Science/Nutrition; Horticulture/Floriculture.

Award: Scholarship for use in junior, senior, or graduate years; not renewable. *Number:* up to 30. *Amount:* $500–$4000.

Eligibility Requirements: Applicant must be enrolled or expecting to enroll full-time at a four-year institution or university. Applicant must have 3.0 GPA or higher. Available to U.S. and non-U.S. citizens.

Application Requirements: Application, essay, financial need analysis, references, transcript. *Deadline:* March 1.

Contact: Laurie Radcliff, Office Coordinator
American Society for Enology and Viticulture
PO Box 1855
Davis, CA 95617-1855
Phone: 530-753-3142
Fax: 530-753-3318
E-mail: society@asev.org

AMERICAN SOCIETY OF AGRICULTURAL AND BIOLOGICAL ENGINEERS

http://www.asabe.org/

AMERICAN SOCIETY OF AGRICULTURAL AND BIOLOGICAL ENGINEERS FOUNDATION SCHOLARSHIP

One scholarship will be awarded to an undergraduate student member of ASABE who has completed at least one year of undergraduate study. Must be majoring in agriculture or biological engineering. Must have a minimum of 2.5 GPA. For more details see web site http://www.asabe.org.

Academic Fields/Career Goals: Agriculture.

Award: Scholarship for use in sophomore, junior, or senior years; not renewable. *Number:* 1. *Amount:* $1000.

Eligibility Requirements: Applicant must be enrolled or expecting to enroll full-time at a four-year institution or university. Applicant must have 2.5 GPA or higher. Available to U.S. and Canadian citizens.

Application Requirements: Application, essay, financial need analysis, resume, references. *Deadline:* March 17.

Contact: Carol Flautt, Scholarship Program
American Society of Agricultural and Biological Engineers
2950 Niles Road
St. Joseph, MI 49085
Phone: 269-932-7036
Fax: 269-429-3852
E-mail: flautt@asabe.org

WILLIAM J. ADAMS, JR. AND MARIJANE E. ADAMS SCHOLARSHIP

One-time award for a full-time U.S. or Canadian undergraduate who is a student member of the American Society of Agricultural Engineers and a declared major in biological or agricultural engineering. Must be at least a sophomore and have minimum 2.5 GPA. Must be interested in agricultural machinery product design or development. Application procedures can be found on http://www.asabe.org web site.

Academic Fields/Career Goals: Agriculture; Biology.

Award: Scholarship for use in sophomore, junior, or senior years; not renewable. *Number:* 1. *Amount:* $1000.

Eligibility Requirements: Applicant must be enrolled or expecting to enroll full-time at a four-year institution or university. Applicant must have 2.5 GPA or higher. Available to U.S. and Canadian citizens.

Application Requirements: Application, essay, financial need analysis, resume, references. *Deadline:* March 17.

Contact: Carol Flautt, Scholarship Program
American Society of Agricultural and Biological Engineers
2950 Niles Road
St. Joseph, MI 49085-9659
Phone: 269-932-7036
Fax: 269-429-3852
E-mail: flautt@asabe.org

AMERICAN SOCIETY OF AGRONOMY, CROP SCIENCE SOCIETY OF AMERICA, SOIL SCIENCE SOCIETY OF AMERICA

http://www.asa-cssa-sssa.org/

HANK BEACHELL FUTURE LEADER SCHOLARSHIP

Scholarship for undergraduate students for $3500 and negotiated travel expenses to the scholarship experience site. Must have completed the sophomore year, and must be majoring in agronomy, crop science, soil science, or other related disciplines. For more information on eligibility criteria and nominee qualifications visit web site https://www.agronomy.org/awards/award/detail/?a=5.

Academic Fields/Career Goals: Agriculture.

Award: Scholarship for use in junior or senior years; not renewable. *Number:* up to 4. *Amount:* up to $3500.

Eligibility Requirements: Applicant must be enrolled or expecting to enroll full-time at a two-year or four-year institution or university. Available to U.S. and non-U.S. citizens.

Application Requirements: Application, resume, references, letter of interest, nomination letter. *Deadline:* February 26.

Contact: Leann Malison, Program Manager
American Society of Agronomy, Crop Science Society of
America, Soil Science Society of America
677 South Segoe Road
Madison, WI 53711
Phone: 608-268-4949
Fax: 608-273-2021
E-mail: lmalison@agronomy.org

J. FIELDING REED SCHOLARSHIP

Scholarship of $1000 to honor an outstanding undergraduate senior pursuing a career in soil or plant sciences. Must have GPA of 3.0, or above, and nominations should contain a history of community and campus leadership activities, specifically in agriculture. For more information on nomination and eligibility criteria, visit web site https://www.agronomy.org/awards/award/detail/?a=6.

Academic Fields/Career Goals: Agriculture.

Award: Scholarship for use in senior year; not renewable. *Number:* 1. *Amount:* up to $1000.

Eligibility Requirements: Applicant must be enrolled or expecting to enroll full-time at a four-year institution or university and must have an interest in leadership. Applicant or parent of applicant must have employment or volunteer experience in community service. Applicant must have 3.0 GPA or higher. Available to U.S. and non-U.S. citizens.

Application Requirements: Application, resume, references, letter of interest. *Deadline:* February 26.

Contact: Leann Malison, Program Manager
American Society of Agronomy, Crop Science Society of
America, Soil Science Society of America
677 South Segoe Road
Madison, WI 53711
Phone: 608-268-4949
Fax: 608-273-2021
E-mail: lmalison@agronomy.org

ARRL FOUNDATION INC.

http://www.arrl.org/

FRANCIS WALTON MEMORIAL SCHOLARSHIP

Award given to individual with any active Amateur Radio license class, with preference to applicant that provide documentation of CW proficiency of more than 5 wpm. Must demonstrate financial need, academic merit and interest in promoting Amateur Radio.

Academic Fields/Career Goals: Agriculture; Communications; Electrical Engineering/Electronics; History; Journalism; Law/Legal Services; TV/Radio Broadcasting.

Award: Scholarship for use in freshman, sophomore, junior, senior, or graduate years; not renewable. *Number:* 1. *Amount:* $500.

Eligibility Requirements: Applicant must be enrolled or expecting to enroll full-time at a four-year institution or university; resident of Illinois, Indiana, or Wisconsin and must have an interest in amateur radio. Applicant must have 3.0 GPA or higher. Available to U.S. citizens.

Application Requirements: Application, financial need analysis, transcript. *Deadline:* February 1.

Contact: Ms. Mary Hobart, Secretary
ARRL Foundation Inc.
225 Main Street
Newington, CT 06111-1494
Phone: 860-594-0397
E-mail: k1mmh@arrl.org

ASSOCIATION ON AMERICAN INDIAN AFFAIRS, INC.

http://www.indian-affairs.org/

ELIZABETH AND SHERMAN ASCHE MEMORIAL SCHOLARSHIP FUND

Scholarship of up to $1500 available for undergraduate and graduate students seeking a bachelor's or master's degree in science or public health. Students must apply each year. Must be a Native American. See web site for details http://www.indian-affairs.org.

Academic Fields/Career Goals: Agriculture; Animal/Veterinary Sciences; Biology; Chemical Engineering; Dental Health/Services; Earth Science; Health and Medical Sciences; Marine Biology; Natural Sciences; Nursing; Physical Sciences; Public Health.

Award: Scholarship for use in freshman, sophomore, junior, senior, or graduate years; not renewable. *Number:* 8. *Amount:* up to $1500.

Eligibility Requirements: Applicant must be American Indian/Alaska Native and enrolled or expecting to enroll full-time at a two-year or four-year institution or university. Available to U.S. citizens.

Application Requirements: Application, essay, financial need analysis, references, transcript. *Deadline:* June 13.

Contact: Lisa Wyzlic, Director of Scholarship Programs
Association on American Indian Affairs, Inc.
966 Hungerford Drive, Suite 12-B
Rockville, MD 20850
Phone: 240-314-7155
Fax: 240-314-7159
E-mail: lw.aaia@verizon.net

CALCOT-SEITZ FOUNDATION

http://www.calcot.com/

CALCOT-SEITZ SCHOLARSHIP

Scholarship for young students from Arizona, New Mexico, Texas and California who plan to attend a college or are attending a college offering at least a four-year degree in agriculture.

Academic Fields/Career Goals: Agriculture.

Award: Scholarship for use in freshman, sophomore, junior, or senior years; not renewable. *Number:* 1–20. *Amount:* up to $3000.

Eligibility Requirements: Applicant must be enrolled or expecting to enroll full-time at a four-year institution and resident of Arizona, California, New Mexico, or Texas. Available to U.S. and non-U.S. citizens.

Application Requirements: Application, photo, references, test scores, transcript. *Deadline:* March 31.

Contact: Marci S. Cunningham, Scholarship Committee
Calcot-Seitz Foundation
PO Box 259
Bakersfield, CA 93302
Phone: 661-327-5961
Fax: 661-861-9870
E-mail: info@calcot.com

CALIFORNIA CATTLEMEN'S ASSOCIATION

http://www.calcattlemen.org/

CALIFORNIA CATTLEMEN'S ASSOCIATION SCHOLARSHIP

Scholarship is available for YCC members pursuing careers within the industry. Applications are available on the web site or through the CCA office. Applicant must be an U.S. citizen.

Academic Fields/Career Goals: Agriculture.

Award: Scholarship for use in freshman year; not renewable. *Number:* up to 5. *Amount:* varies.

Eligibility Requirements: Applicant must be high school student and planning to enroll or expecting to enroll full-time at a two-year or four-year or technical institution or university. Available to U.S. citizens.

Application Requirements: Application, essay, references, transcript. *Deadline:* July 20.

Contact: Megan Huber, Director of Finance
California Cattlemen's Association
1221 H Street
Sacramento, CA 95814-1910
Phone: 916-444-0845
Fax: 916-444-2194
E-mail: megan@calcattlemen.org

CALIFORNIA FARM BUREAU SCHOLARSHIP FOUNDATION

http://www.cfbf.com/

CALIFORNIA FARM BUREAU SCHOLARSHIP
• *See page 78*

CHS FOUNDATION

http://www.chsfoundation.org/

CHS FOUNDATION HIGH SCHOOL SCHOLARSHIPS
• *See page 78*

CHS FOUNDATION TWO-YEAR COLLEGE SCHOLARSHIPS
• *See page 78*

CHS FOUNDATION UNIVERSITY SCHOLARSHIPS
• *See page 78*

DAIRY MANAGEMENT

http://www.dairyinfo.com/

NATIONAL DAIRY PROMOTION AND RESEARCH BOARD SCHOLARSHIP

One-time scholarship of $1500 given to sophomores, juniors and seniors in college/university programs that emphasize dairy. Majors include communications/public relations, journalism, marketing, business, economics, nutrition, food science and agricultural education.

Academic Fields/Career Goals: Agriculture; Business/Consumer Services; Communications; Economics; Food Science/Nutrition; Journalism.

Award: Scholarship for use in sophomore, junior, or senior years; not renewable. *Number:* 19. *Amount:* $1500.

Eligibility Requirements: Applicant must be enrolled or expecting to enroll full-time at a two-year or four-year institution or university. Available to U.S. citizens.

Application Requirements: Application, references, transcript. *Deadline:* May 31.

Contact: Jolene Griffin, Manager of Industry Communications
Dairy Management
10255 West Higgins Road
Rosemont, IL 60018
Phone: 847-627-9920
Fax: 847-803-2077
E-mail: jgriffin@rosedmi.com

GARDEN CLUB OF AMERICA

http://www.gcamerica.org/

THE ELIZABETH GARDNER NORWEB SUMMER ENVIRONMENTAL STUDIES SCHOLARSHIP

Award for college students who wish to pursue summer studies doing field work, research, or classroom work in the environmental field following their freshman, sophomore, or junior years.

Academic Fields/Career Goals: Agriculture; Earth Science; Environmental Science; Natural Resources.

Award: Scholarship for use in freshman, sophomore, or junior years; not renewable. *Number:* 4. *Amount:* $2000.

Eligibility Requirements: Applicant must be enrolled or expecting to enroll full-time at a four-year institution or university. Available to U.S. and non-U.S. citizens.

Application Requirements: Application, essay, references, self-addressed stamped envelope, transcript. *Deadline:* February 10.

Contact: Connie Yates, Scholarship Committee Administrator
Garden Club of America
14 East 60th Street, Third Floor
New York, NY 10022-1002
Phone: 212-753-8287
E-mail: cyates@gcamerica.org

GEORGE T. WELCH TRUST

http://www.bakerboyer.com/

BERNICE AND PAT MURPHY SCHOLARSHIP FUND

Grants for students majoring in agriculture. Must be enrolled full-time and maintain a minimum GPA of 2.0. Must reapply. The budget form must be completed and cover the entire school year.

Academic Fields/Career Goals: Agriculture.

Award: Scholarship for use in freshman, sophomore, junior, or senior years; not renewable. *Number:* varies. *Amount:* varies.

Eligibility Requirements: Applicant must be enrolled or expecting to enroll full-time at a four-year institution or university. Available to U.S. citizens.

Application Requirements: Application. *Deadline:* April 13.

Contact: Ted Cohan, Trust Portfolio Manager
George T. Welch Trust
Baker Boyer Bank, Investment Management & Trust Services
7 West Main, PO Box 1796
Walla Walla, WA 99362
Phone: 509-526-1204
Fax: 509-522-3136
E-mail: cohant@bakerboyer.com

G.B. PESCIALLO MEMORIAL SCHOLARSHIP FUND

Grants for students majoring in agriculture. Must be enrolled full-time and maintain a minimum GPA of 2.0. Must reapply. The budget form must be completed and cover the entire school year.

Academic Fields/Career Goals: Agriculture.

Award: Scholarship for use in freshman, sophomore, junior, or senior years; not renewable. *Number:* varies. *Amount:* varies.

Eligibility Requirements: Applicant must be enrolled or expecting to enroll full-time at a four-year institution or university. Available to U.S. citizens.

Application Requirements: Application, responsibility shown in one or more of the following areas: community, school, home, church. *Deadline:* April 13.

Contact: Ted Cohan, Trust Portfolio Manager
George T. Welch Trust
Baker Boyer Bank, Investment Management & Trust Services
7 West Main, PO Box 1796
Walla Walla, WA 99362
Phone: 509-526-1204
Fax: 509-522-3136
E-mail: cohant@bakerboyer.com

INTERTRIBAL TIMBER COUNCIL

http://www.itcnet.org/

TRUMAN D. PICARD SCHOLARSHIP
• *See page 79*

JAPANESE AMERICAN CITIZENS LEAGUE (JACL)

http://www.jacl.org/

NATIONAL JACL HEADQUARTERS SCHOLARSHIP

Scholarship offers over 30 awards to qualified students nationwide. Scholarships are provided to students at the entering freshman, undergraduate, graduate, law, financial need and creative & performing arts. All scholarships are one-time awards. Every applicant must be an active National JACL member at either an Individual or Student/Youth Level.

Academic Fields/Career Goals: Agriculture; Journalism; Law/Legal Services; Literature/English/Writing; Public Policy and Administration.

Award: Scholarship for use in freshman, sophomore, junior, senior, or graduate years; not renewable. *Number:* 30. *Amount:* varies.

Eligibility Requirements: Applicant must be of Japanese heritage; Asian/Pacific Islander and enrolled or expecting to enroll full-time at a two-year or four-year institution or university. Available to U.S. and non-U.S. citizens.

Application Requirements: Application, financial need analysis, references, transcript. *Deadline:* varies.

Contact: Scholarship Committee
Japanese American Citizens League (JACL)
1765 Sutter Street
San Francisco, CA 94115
Phone: 415-921-5225
E-mail: jacl@jacl.org

MAINE DEPARTMENT OF AGRICULTURE, FOOD AND RURAL RESOURCES

http://www.maine.gov/agriculture

MAINE RURAL REHABILITATION FUND SCHOLARSHIP PROGRAM

• *See page 79*

MINNESOTA SOYBEAN RESEARCH AND PROMOTION COUNCIL

http://www.mnsoybean.org/

COLLEGE SOYBEAN SCHOLARSHIP

Scholarship available for undergraduate junior or senior who is a resident of Minnesota and pursuing an education in soybean agronomy, soil science, or soybean genetics. Must be active in ag-related and/or campus/community activities and maintain a minimum GPA of 2.0. Application must include a paragraph to indicate how student's education will relate back to the soybean farmer or soybean industry.

Academic Fields/Career Goals: Agriculture.

Award: Scholarship for use in junior or senior years; not renewable. *Number:* up to 3. *Amount:* $2000.

Eligibility Requirements: Applicant must be enrolled or expecting to enroll full-time at a four-year institution or university and resident of Minnesota. Available to U.S. citizens.

Application Requirements: Application, resume, references, transcript. *Deadline:* February 28.

Contact: Vicki Trudeau, Scholarship Coordinator
Minnesota Soybean Research and Promotion Council
151 Saint Andrews Court, Suite 710
Mankato, MN 56001
Phone: 888-896-9678
E-mail: vicki@mnsoybean.com

MINNESOTA SOYBEAN RESEARCH AND PROMOTION COUNCIL YOUTH SOYBEAN SCHOLARSHIP

• *See page 79*

MONSANTO AGRIBUSINESS SCHOLARSHIP

http://www.monsanto.ca/

MONSANTO CANADA OPPORTUNITY SCHOLARSHIP PROGRAM

• *See page 79*

NATIONAL CATTLEMEN'S FOUNDATION

http://www.nationalcattlemensfoundation.org/

CME BEEF INDUSTRY SCHOLARSHIP

• *See page 79*

NATIONAL COUNCIL OF STATE GARDEN CLUBS INC. SCHOLARSHIP

http://www.gardenclub.org/

NATIONAL COUNCIL OF STATE GARDEN CLUBS INC. SCHOLARSHIP

Scholarship to students for study in agriculture education, horticulture, floriculture, landscape design, botany, biology, plant pathology/science, forestry, agronomy, environmental concerns.

Academic Fields/Career Goals: Agriculture; Biology; Environmental Science; Horticulture/Floriculture.

Award: Scholarship for use in sophomore, junior, senior, or graduate years; not renewable. *Number:* 34. *Amount:* $3500.

Eligibility Requirements: Applicant must be enrolled or expecting to enroll full-time at a two-year or four-year institution or university. Applicant must have 3.0 GPA or higher. Available to U.S. citizens.

Application Requirements: Application, financial need analysis, references, transcript. *Deadline:* March 1.

Contact: Kathy Romine, National Headquarters
National Council of State Garden Clubs Inc. Scholarship
4401 Magnolia Avenue
St. Louis, MO 63110-3492
Phone: 314-776-7574 Ext. 15
Fax: 314-776-5108
E-mail: headquarters@gardenclub.org

NATIONAL DAIRY SHRINE

http://www.dairyshrine.org/

KILDEE SCHOLARSHIPS

Top 25 contestants in the three most recent national intercollegiate dairy cattle judging contests are eligible to apply for two $3000 one-time scholarships for graduate study in the field related to dairy cattle production or vet school at the university of their choice. Also the top 25 contestants in the most recent National 4-H & National FFA Dairy Judging contests are eligible to apply for one $2000 scholarship for undergraduate study in the field related to dairy cattle production at the university of their choice.

Academic Fields/Career Goals: Agriculture; Animal/Veterinary Sciences.

Award: Scholarship for use in sophomore, junior, or senior years; not renewable. *Number:* 3. *Amount:* $2000–$3000.

Eligibility Requirements: Applicant must be enrolled or expecting to enroll full-time at a four-year institution or university. Applicant must have 2.5 GPA or higher. Available to U.S. and Canadian citizens.

Application Requirements: Application, photo, references, transcript. *Deadline:* April 15.

Contact: Executive Director
E-mail: info@dairyshrine.org

MARSHALL E. MCCULLOUGH-NATIONAL DAIRY SHRINE SCHOLARSHIPS

Scholarship for high school seniors planning to enter a four-year college or university with an intent to major in dairy/animal science with a communications emphasis, or agricultural journalism with a dairy/animal science emphasis.

Academic Fields/Career Goals: Agriculture; Animal/Veterinary Sciences; Journalism.

Award: Scholarship for use in freshman year; not renewable. *Number:* 2. *Amount:* $1000–$2500.

Eligibility Requirements: Applicant must be high school student and planning to enroll or expecting to enroll full-time at a four-year institution or university. Available to U.S. citizens.

Application Requirements: Application, photo, references, transcript, video. *Deadline:* April 15.

Contact: Executive Director
E-mail: info@dairyshrine.org

NATIONAL DAIRY SHRINE/DAIRY MARKETING INC. MILK MARKETING SCHOLARSHIPS

One-time awards for undergraduate students pursuing careers in marketing of dairy products. Major areas can include: dairy science, animal science, agricultural economics, agricultural communications, agricultural education, general education, food and nutrition, home economics and journalism. For more information, visit web site http://www.dairyshrine.org.

Academic Fields/Career Goals: Agriculture; Animal/Veterinary Sciences; Food Science/Nutrition; Marketing.

Award: Scholarship for use in sophomore or junior years; not renewable. *Number:* 7–10. *Amount:* $1000–$1500.

Eligibility Requirements: Applicant must be enrolled or expecting to enroll full-time at a four-year institution or university. Applicant must have 2.5 GPA or higher. Available to U.S. citizens.

Application Requirements: Application, photo, references, transcript. *Deadline:* April 15.

Contact: Executive Director
E-mail: info@dairyshrine.org

NATIONAL DAIRY SHRINE/IAGER DAIRY SCHOLARSHIP

$1000 annual scholarship to encourage qualified second-year dairy students in a two-year agricultural school to pursue careers in the dairy industry. Scholarships will be awarded based on academic standing, leadership ability, interest in the dairy industry, and plans for the future. Cumulative 2.5 GPA required.

Academic Fields/Career Goals: Agriculture.

Award: Scholarship for use in sophomore year; not renewable. *Number:* 1. *Amount:* up to $1000.

Eligibility Requirements: Applicant must be enrolled or expecting to enroll full-time at a two-year or technical institution. Available to U.S. citizens.

Application Requirements: Application, photo, references, transcript. *Deadline:* April 15.

Contact: Dr. David Selner, Executive Director
National Dairy Shrine
PO Box 725
Denmark, WI 54208
Phone: 920-863-6333
E-mail: info@dairyshrine.org

NATIONAL DAIRY SHRINE/KLUSSENDORF SCHOLARSHIP

The scholarship will be granted to a student successfully completing the first, second or third years at a two-year or four-year college or university. To be eligible, students must major in a dairy science (animal science) curriculum with plans to enter the dairy cattle field as a breeder, owner, herdsperson, or fitter.

Academic Fields/Career Goals: Agriculture; Animal/Veterinary Sciences.

Award: Scholarship for use in freshman, sophomore, or junior years; not renewable. *Number:* 1–6. *Amount:* $2000.

Eligibility Requirements: Applicant must be enrolled or expecting to enroll full-time at a two-year or four-year institution or university. Available to U.S. and Canadian citizens.

Application Requirements: Application, references, transcript. *Deadline:* April 15.

Contact: Executive Director
E-mail: info@dairyshrine.org

NDS STUDENT RECOGNITION CONTEST
• See page 80

NATIONAL GARDEN CLUBS INC.

http://www.gardenclub.org/

NATIONAL GARDEN CLUBS INC. SCHOLARSHIP PROGRAM

One-time award for full-time students in plant sciences, agriculture and related or allied subjects. Applicants must have at least a 3.25 GPA.

Academic Fields/Career Goals: Agriculture; Biology; Earth Science; Environmental Science; Horticulture/Floriculture; Landscape Architecture.

Award: Scholarship for use in junior, senior, or graduate years; not renewable. *Number:* 34. *Amount:* $3500.

Eligibility Requirements: Applicant must be enrolled or expecting to enroll full-time at a four-year institution or university. Available to U.S. citizens.

Application Requirements: Application, financial need analysis, photo, resume, references, transcript. *Deadline:* March 1.

Contact: Sandra Robinson, Vice President for Scholarship
National Garden Clubs Inc.
4401 Magnolia Avenue
St. Louis, MO 63110
Phone: 606-878-7281
E-mail: sandyr@kayandkay.com

NATIONAL POTATO COUNCIL WOMEN'S AUXILIARY

http://www.nationalpotatocouncil.org/

POTATO INDUSTRY SCHOLARSHIP
• See page 80

NATIONAL POULTRY AND FOOD DISTRIBUTORS ASSOCIATION

http://www.npfda.org/

NATIONAL POULTRY AND FOOD DISTRIBUTORS ASSOCIATION SCHOLARSHIP FOUNDATION
• See page 80

NEW YORK STATE ASSOCIATION OF AGRICULTURAL FAIRS

http://www.nyfairs.org/

NEW YORK STATE ASSOCIATION OF AGRICULTURAL FAIRS AND NEW YORK STATE SHOWPEOPLE'S ASSOCIATION ANNUAL SCHOLARSHIP
• See page 80

NEW YORK STATE GRANGE

http://www.nysgrange.com/

HOWARD F. DENISE SCHOLARSHIP

Awards for undergraduates under 21 years old to pursue studies in agriculture. Must be a New York resident with a minimum 3.0 GPA. One-time award of $1000.

Academic Fields/Career Goals: Agriculture.

Award: Scholarship for use in freshman, sophomore, junior, or senior years; not renewable. *Number:* 1–6. *Amount:* $1000.

Eligibility Requirements: Applicant must be age 21 or under; enrolled or expecting to enroll full-time at a two-year or four-year institution and resident of New York. Applicant must have 3.0 GPA or higher. Available to U.S. citizens.

Application Requirements: Application, financial need analysis, references, transcript. *Deadline:* April 15.

Contact: Scholarship Committee
New York State Grange
100 Grange Place
Cortland, NY 13045
Phone: 607-756-7553
Fax: 607-756-7757
E-mail: nysgrange@nysgrange.com

OHIO FARMERS UNION

http://www.ohfarmersunion.org/

JOSEPH FITCHER SCHOLARSHIP CONTEST

Scholarship available to member of Ohio Farmers Union who is a high school junior or senior, or enrolled as a college freshman. Participants are to submit an application obtained from OFU and a typed essay on "Agricultural Opportunities in the Future". Award of $1000 to winner and $250 to two runners-up.

Academic Fields/Career Goals: Agriculture.

Award: Scholarship for use in freshman year; not renewable. *Number:* 1–3. *Amount:* $250–$1000.

Eligibility Requirements: Applicant must be high school student; planning to enroll or expecting to enroll full-time at a four-year institution or university and resident of Ohio. Applicant or parent of applicant must be member of Ohio Farmers Union. Available to U.S. citizens.

Application Requirements: Application, applicant must enter a contest, essay. *Deadline:* December 31.

Contact: Maria Miller, Public Relations Director
Ohio Farmers Union
PO Box 363
Ottawa, OH 45875
Phone: 419-523-5300
Fax: 419-523-5913
E-mail: m-miller@ohfarmersunion.org

VIRGIL THOMPSON MEMORIAL SCHOLARSHIP CONTEST
• *See page 80*

OREGON STUDENT ASSISTANCE COMMISSION

http://www.GetCollegeFunds.org/

OREGON HORTICULTURE SOCIETY SCHOLARSHIP

Award for college sophomore or above for fall term/semester in undergraduate study, with a preference to those students majoring in horticulture. To be used at Oregon public and nonprofit colleges and universities only. 2.5 GPA or above required.

Academic Fields/Career Goals: Agriculture.

Award: Scholarship for use in sophomore, junior, or senior years; not renewable.

Eligibility Requirements: Applicant must be enrolled or expecting to enroll at a four-year institution or university and studying in Oregon. Applicant must have 2.5 GPA or higher.

Application Requirements: Application. *Deadline:* March 1.

Contact: Director of Grant Programs
Oregon Student Assistance Commission
1500 Valley River Drive, Suite 100
Eugene, OR 97401-7020
Phone: 800-452-8807

PENNSYLVANIA ASSOCIATION OF CONSERVATION DISTRICTS AUXILIARY

http://www.pacd.org/

PACD AUXILIARY SCHOLARSHIPS

Award for residents of Pennsylvania who are upperclassmen pursuing a degree program in agricultural and/or environmental science, and/or environmental education. Must be studying at a two- or four-year Pennsylvania institution. Must be U.S. citizens. Submit resume. One-time award of $500.

Academic Fields/Career Goals: Agriculture; Biology; Environmental Science; Horticulture/Floriculture.

Award: Scholarship for use in junior or senior years; not renewable. *Number:* 1. *Amount:* $500.

Eligibility Requirements: Applicant must be enrolled or expecting to enroll full- or part-time at a four-year institution or university; resident of Pennsylvania and studying in Pennsylvania. Available to U.S. citizens.

Application Requirements: Application, driver's license, essay, financial need analysis, resume, transcript, GPA verification. *Deadline:* June 15.

Contact: District Clerk
Pennsylvania Association of Conservation Districts Auxiliary
1407 Blair Street
Hollidaysburg, PA 16648-2468
Phone: 814-696-0877 Ext. 5
Fax: 814-696-9981
E-mail: bcd@blairconsevationdistrict.org

PROFESSIONAL GROUNDS MANAGEMENT SOCIETY

http://www.pgms.org/

ANNE SEAMAN PROFESSIONAL GROUNDS MANAGEMENT SOCIETY MEMORIAL SCHOLARSHIP

One-time award for citizens of the United States and Canada who are studying to enter the field of grounds management or a closely related field such as agronomy, horticulture, landscape contracting, and irrigation on a full-time basis. Write for further information. Must be sponsored by a PGMS member. The member must write a letter of recommendation for the applicant.

Academic Fields/Career Goals: Agriculture; Civil Engineering; Horticulture/Floriculture; Landscape Architecture.

Award: Scholarship for use in freshman, sophomore, junior, or senior years; not renewable. *Number:* 3. *Amount:* $250–$1500.

Eligibility Requirements: Applicant must be enrolled or expecting to enroll full-time at a two-year or four-year institution or university. Available to U.S. and Canadian citizens.

Application Requirements: Application, driver's license, financial need analysis, resume, references, self-addressed stamped envelope, transcript. *Deadline:* September 15.

Contact: Jenny Smith, Association Coordinator
Professional Grounds Management Society
720 Light Street
Baltimore, MD 21230-3816
Phone: 410-223-2861
Fax: 410-752-8295
E-mail: pgms@assnhqtrs.com

SIGMA XI, THE SCIENTIFIC RESEARCH SOCIETY

http://www.sigmaxi.org/

SIGMA XI GRANTS-IN-AID OF RESEARCH

Award to undergraduate and graduate students currently enrolled in degree seeking programs. Applications are accepted through an online form only. Deadlines for all application material are March 15 and October 15 annually and are available online two months prior to the deadline (January 15 and August 14 respectively).

Academic Fields/Career Goals: Agriculture; Animal/Veterinary Sciences; Biology; Chemical Engineering; Earth Science; Engineering/Technology; Health and Medical Sciences; Mechanical Engineering; Meteorology/Atmospheric Science; Physical Sciences; Science, Technology, and Society; Social Sciences.

Award: Grant for use in freshman, sophomore, junior, senior, or graduate years; not renewable. *Number:* 400. *Amount:* $1000–$5000.

Eligibility Requirements: Applicant must be enrolled or expecting to enroll full-time at a four-year institution or university. Available to U.S. and non-U.S. citizens.

Application Requirements: Application, references. *Deadline:* varies.

Contact: Kevin Bowen JD, Program Manager, Grants and Society Awards
Sigma Xi, The Scientific Research Society
3106 East NC Highway 54
Research Triangle Park, NC 27709
Phone: 800-243-6534 Ext. 206
E-mail: giar@sigmaxi.org

AGRICULTURE

SOCIETY FOR RANGE MANAGEMENT

http://www.rangelands.org/

MASONIC RANGE SCIENCE SCHOLARSHIP
• *See page 80*

SOIL AND WATER CONSERVATION SOCIETY-NEW JERSEY CHAPTER

http://www.geocities.com/njswcs

EDWARD R. HALL SCHOLARSHIP
• *See page 81*

SOUTH DAKOTA BOARD OF REGENTS

http://www.sdbor.edu/

SOUTH DAKOTA BOARD OF REGENTS BJUGSTAD SCHOLARSHIP
• *See page 81*

SOUTH FLORIDA FAIR AND PALM BEACH COUNTY EXPOSITIONS INC.

http://www.southfloridafair.com/

SOUTH FLORIDA FAIR AGRICULTURAL COLLEGE SCHOLARSHIP

Renewable award of $2000 for students pursuing a degree in agriculture. Must be a permanent resident of Florida.

Academic Fields/Career Goals: Agriculture.

Award: Scholarship for use in freshman, sophomore, junior, or senior years; renewable. *Number:* 2. *Amount:* $2000.

Eligibility Requirements: Applicant must be enrolled or expecting to enroll full- or part-time at a four-year institution or university and resident of Florida. Available to U.S. and non-U.S. citizens.

Application Requirements: Application, essay, references, test scores, transcript. *Deadline:* October 15.

Contact: Agriculture Committee
South Florida Fair and Palm Beach County Expositions Inc.
PO Box 210367
West Palm Beach, FL 33421-0367
Phone: 561-790-5245

TURF AND ORNAMENTAL COMMUNICATORS ASSOCIATION

http://www.toca.org/

TURF AND ORNAMENTAL COMMUNICATORS ASSOCIATION SCHOLARSHIP PROGRAM

One-time award for undergraduate students majoring or minoring in technical communications or in a green industry field such as horticulture, plant sciences, botany, or agronomy. The applicant must demonstrate an interest in using this course of study in the field of communications. An overall GPA of 3.0 is required in major area of study.

Academic Fields/Career Goals: Agriculture; Communications; Horticulture/Floriculture.

Award: Scholarship for use in freshman, sophomore, junior, or senior years; not renewable. *Number:* 1. *Amount:* $2500.

Eligibility Requirements: Applicant must be enrolled or expecting to enroll full-time at a two-year or four-year institution or university. Applicant must have 3.0 GPA or higher. Available to U.S. and non-U.S. citizens.

Application Requirements: Application, essay, portfolio, resume, references, transcript. *Deadline:* March 1.

Contact: Den Gardner, Executive Director
Turf and Ornamental Communicators Association
120 West Main Street, Suite 200
PO Box 156
New Prague, MN 56071
Phone: 952-758-6340
E-mail: toca@gardnerandgardnercommunications.com

UNITED NEGRO COLLEGE FUND

http://www.uncf.org/

CARGILL SCHOLARSHIP PROGRAM
• *See page 72*

WASHINGTON ASSOCIATION OF WINE GRAPE GROWERS

http://www.wawgg.org/

WALTER J. CLORE SCHOLARSHIP

A scholarship of minimum $500 to a maximum $2000 is awarded to undergraduate and graduate students enrolled in areas of study pertaining to the wine industry. Scholarships will be given to students who are residents of the state of Washington. The number of awards vary each year.

Academic Fields/Career Goals: Agriculture; Food Science/Nutrition.

Award: Scholarship for use in freshman, sophomore, junior, senior, or graduate years; not renewable. *Number:* 6. *Amount:* $500–$2000.

Eligibility Requirements: Applicant must be enrolled or expecting to enroll full-time at a two-year or four-year institution or university and resident of Washington. Available to U.S. and non-U.S. citizens.

Application Requirements: Application, essay, resume, references, transcript. *Deadline:* November 30.

Contact: Vicky Scharlau, Executive Director
Washington Association of Wine Grape Growers
PO Box 716
Cashmere, WA 98815
Phone: 509-782-8234
E-mail: vicky@501consultants.com

WOMEN GROCERS OF AMERICA

http://www.nationalgrocers.org/

MARY MACEY SCHOLARSHIP

Award for students intending to pursue a career in the independent sector of the grocery industry. One-time award for students who have completed freshman year. Submit statement and recommendation from sponsor in the grocery industry. Applicant should have a minimum 2.0 GPA.

Academic Fields/Career Goals: Agriculture; Business/Consumer Services; Food Service/Hospitality.

Award: Scholarship for use in sophomore, junior, senior, graduate, or postgraduate years; not renewable. *Number:* 2–7. *Amount:* $1000.

Eligibility Requirements: Applicant must be enrolled or expecting to enroll full-time at a two-year or four-year institution or university. Available to U.S. citizens.

Application Requirements: Application, references, transcript, personal statement. *Deadline:* May 15.

Contact: Kristen Comley, Director of Administration
Women Grocers of America
1005 North Glebe Road, Suite 250
Arlington, VA 22201-5758
Phone: 703-516-0700
Fax: 703-516-0115
E-mail: kcomley@nationalgrocers.org

AMERICAN STUDIES

AMERICAN FEDERATION OF STATE, COUNTY, AND MUNICIPAL EMPLOYEES

http://www.afscme.org/

AFSCME/UNCF UNION SCHOLARS PROGRAM

One-time award for a sophomore or junior majoring in ethnic studies, women's studies, labor studies, American studies, sociology, anthropology, history, political science, psychology, social work or economics. Must be African-American, Hispanic-American, Asian Pacific Islander, or American-Indian/Alaska Native. Minimum 2.5 GPA.

Academic Fields/Career Goals: American Studies; Anthropology; History; Political Science; Psychology; Social Sciences; Social Services; Women's Studies.

Award: Scholarship for use in sophomore or junior years; not renewable. *Number:* 10. *Amount:* up to $5000.

Eligibility Requirements: Applicant must be American Indian/Alaska Native, Asian/Pacific Islander, Black (non-Hispanic), or Hispanic and enrolled or expecting to enroll full-time at a four-year institution or university. Applicant must have 2.5 GPA or higher. Available to U.S. citizens.

Application Requirements: Application, essay, references, transcript. *Deadline:* February 28.

Contact: Philip Allen, Scholarship Coordinator
American Federation of State, County, and Municipal Employees
1625 L Street, NW
Washington, DC 20036-5687
Phone: 202-429-1250
Fax: 202-429-1293
E-mail: pallen@asscme.org

ASSOCIATION OF FORMER INTELLIGENCE OFFICERS

http://www.afio.com/13_scholarships.htm

CIA UNDERGRADUATE SCHOLARSHIPS

The type of institution attended is less important than the clarity that the course of study being undertaken leads to a career in the U.S. Intelligence Community. So this covers law enforcement, foreign policy, intelligence analysis, counterterrorism, homeland security, foreign language mastery (Farsi, Tagalog, Pashto, Urdu, Mandarin, Arabic, Hindi, etc.—not Spanish or French), and related disciplines. Applicants seeking funding for law or medical school are placed in a third tier as less appropriate to current needs of the I.C. which already suffers from too many lawyers. Applicants must be a U.S. citizen studying at a U.S. Institution. Advanced knowledge and near-native performance in one of the mission-critical languages mentioned above puts applicants at top of consideration.

Academic Fields/Career Goals: American Studies; Aviation/Aerospace; Computer Science/Data Processing; Criminal Justice/Criminology; Foreign Language; History; Law Enforcement/Police Administration; Military and Defense Studies; Natural Sciences; Near and Middle East Studies; Peace and Conflict Studies; Political Science.

Award: Scholarship for use in freshman, sophomore, junior, senior, graduate, or postgraduate years; not renewable. *Number:* 15–30. *Amount:* $1000–$4000.

Eligibility Requirements: Applicant must be enrolled or expecting to enroll full- or part-time at a two-year or four-year or technical institution or university. Applicant must have 3.0 GPA or higher. Available to U.S. and Canadian citizens.

Application Requirements: Application, autobiography, photo, references, transcript, letter explaining intent and goals. *Deadline:* July 31.

Contact: Mrs. Priscilla ADAMS, Director, AFIO Scholarship Programs
Association of Former Intelligence Officers
6723 Whittier Ave Suite 200
McLean, VA 22101
Phone: 703-790-0320
Fax: 703-991-1278
E-mail: afio@afio.com

THE GEORGIA TRUST FOR HISTORIC PRESERVATION

http://www.georgiatrust.org/

B. PHINIZY SPALDING, HUBERT B. OWENS, AND THE NATIONAL SOCIETY OF THE COLONIAL DAMES OF AMERICA IN THE STATE OF GEORGIA ACADEMIC SCHOLARSHIPS

The Georgia Trust annually awards two $1000 and two $1,500 scholarships to encourage the study of historic preservation and related fields. Recipients are chosen on the basis of leadership and academic achievement. Applicants must be residents of Georgia enrolled in an accredited Georgia institution.

Academic Fields/Career Goals: American Studies; Historic Preservation and Conservation; History; Landscape Architecture.

Award: Scholarship for use in freshman, sophomore, junior, senior, or graduate years; not renewable. *Number:* 4. *Amount:* $1000–$1500.

Eligibility Requirements: Applicant must be enrolled or expecting to enroll full-time at a four-year institution or university; resident of Georgia and studying in Georgia. Applicant must have 3.0 GPA or higher. Available to U.S. citizens.

Application Requirements: Application, essay, resume, references, transcript. *Deadline:* February 13.

Contact: *Phone:* 404-885-7817
Fax: 404-875-2205
E-mail: kryan@georgiatrust.org

ORGANIZATION OF AMERICAN HISTORIANS

http://www.oah.org/

BINKLEY-STEPHENSON AWARD

One-time award of $500 for the best scholarly article published in the Journal of American History during the preceding calendar year. For more information, go to: http://www.oah.org/awards/awards.binkleystephenson.index.html.

Academic Fields/Career Goals: American Studies; History.

Award: Prize for use in freshman, sophomore, junior, senior, graduate, or postgraduate years; not renewable. *Number:* 1. *Amount:* $500.

Eligibility Requirements: Applicant must be enrolled or expecting to enroll full- or part-time at a two-year or four-year or technical institution or university and must have an interest in writing. Available to U.S. and non-U.S. citizens.

Application Requirements: Application, applicant must enter a contest. *Deadline:* continuous.

Contact: Award and Prize Committee Coordinator
Organization of American Historians
112 North Bryan Avenue
PO Box 5457
Bloomington, IN 47407-5457
Phone: 812-855-7311
Fax: 812-855-0696

SONS OF THE REPUBLIC OF TEXAS

http://www.srttexas.org/

PRESIDIO LA BAHIA AWARD

Award of $2000 is available annually for winning participants in the competition, with a minimum first place prize of $1200 for the best published book. Competition is open to any person interested in the Spanish Colonial influence on Texas culture. Refer to web site http://www.srttexas.org/labahia.html for details.

Academic Fields/Career Goals: American Studies; History.

Award: Prize for use in freshman, sophomore, junior, senior, graduate, or postgraduate years; not renewable. *Number:* 1. *Amount:* $1200–$2000.

Eligibility Requirements: Applicant must be enrolled or expecting to enroll full- or part-time at a four-year institution or university and must have an interest in writing. Available to U.S. and non-U.S. citizens.

Application Requirements: Applicant must enter a contest, 4 copies of published writings. *Deadline:* September 30.

Contact: Janet Knox, Administrative Assistant
Sons of the Republic of Texas
1717 Eighth Street
Bay City, TX 77414
Phone: 979-245-6644
E-mail: srttexas@srttexas.org

TEXAS HISTORY ESSAY CONTEST

Contest for best essay on the history of Texas written by graduating seniors in any high school in the United States. History, government and English students are particularly encouraged to participate. Prizes will be scholarships to the college of each winner's choice or will be given to the student directly if he or she does not intend to attend a college or university. First prize $3000, second prize $2000, third prize $1000.

Academic Fields/Career Goals: American Studies; History.

Award: Prize for use in freshman year; not renewable. *Number:* 3. *Amount:* $1000–$3000.

Eligibility Requirements: Applicant must be high school student; planning to enroll or expecting to enroll full- or part-time at a two-year or four-year or technical institution or university and must have an interest in writing. Available to U.S. citizens.

Application Requirements: Applicant must enter a contest, essay. *Deadline:* January 31.

Contact: Janet Knox, Administrative Assistant
Sons of the Republic of Texas
1717 Eighth Street
Bay City, TX 77414
Phone: 979-245-6644
E-mail: srttexas@srttexas.org

UNITED NEGRO COLLEGE FUND

http://www.uncf.org/

AFSCME/UNCF/HARVARD UNIVERSITY LWP UNION SCHOLARS PROGRAM

Scholarship available to undergraduate sophomores and juniors who become members of AFSCME and get involved in outreach work for the union. Eligible majors include: American studies, anthropology, economics, English, ethnic studies, history, labor studies, political science, psychology, social work, sociology, Spanish and women's studies. Minimum 2.5 GPA required. For additional information visit web site http://www.uncf.org.

Academic Fields/Career Goals: American Studies; Anthropology; Area/Ethnic Studies; Economics; History; Literature/English/Writing; Political Science; Public Policy and Administration; Social Sciences; Social Services; Women's Studies.

Award: Scholarship for use in sophomore or junior years; renewable. *Number:* 1. *Amount:* up to $5000.

Eligibility Requirements: Applicant must be Black (non-Hispanic) and enrolled or expecting to enroll full- or part-time at a four-year institution. Applicant or parent of applicant must be member of American Federation of State, County, and Municipal Employees. Applicant must have 2.5 GPA or higher. Available to U.S. citizens.

Application Requirements: Application. *Deadline:* March 4.

Contact: Director, Program Services
United Negro College Fund
8260 Willow Oaks Corporate Drive
PO Box 10444
Fairfax, VA 22031-8044
Phone: 800-331-2244
E-mail: rebecca.bennett@uncf.org

ANIMAL/VETERINARY SCIENCES

AMERICAN QUARTER HORSE FOUNDATION (AQHF)

http://www.aqha.com/foundation

AQHF RACING SCHOLARSHIPS

Scholarships for members of AQHA/AQHYA who have experience within the racing industry or are seeking a career in the industry. Applicants seeking a career in the racing industry may specialize in veterinary medicine, racetrack management or other related fields. Members may apply during their senior year of high school or while enrolled at an accredited college, university or vocational school. Renewable up to four years. Minimum 2.5 GPA required.

Academic Fields/Career Goals: Animal/Veterinary Sciences.

Award: Scholarship for use in freshman, sophomore, junior, or senior years; renewable. *Number:* 5. *Amount:* $8000.

Eligibility Requirements: Applicant must be enrolled or expecting to enroll full-time at a two-year or four-year or technical institution or university and must have an interest in animal/agricultural competition. Applicant or parent of applicant must be member of American Quarter Horse Association. Applicant must have 2.5 GPA or higher. Available to U.S. and Canadian citizens.

Application Requirements: Application, essay, financial need analysis, photo, references, transcript. *Deadline:* January 2.

Contact: Laura Owens, Scholarship Office
American Quarter Horse Foundation (AQHF)
2601 East Interstate 40
Amarillo, TX 79104
Phone: 806-378-5029
Fax: 806-376-1005
E-mail: foundation@aqha.org

AQHF TELEPHONY EQUINE VETERINARY SCHOLARSHIP

Scholarship to an AQHA member in an equine veterinary medicine or surgery program who wishes to pursue an equine-focused veterinary practice. Applicants must be enrolled as a third year student when applying. Funding will be applied to students last year of the veterinary program. Minimum GPA 3.0 required.

Academic Fields/Career Goals: Animal/Veterinary Sciences.

Award: Scholarship for use in junior year; not renewable. *Number:* 1. *Amount:* $10,000.

Eligibility Requirements: Applicant must be enrolled or expecting to enroll full-time at a four-year institution or university. Applicant or parent of applicant must be member of American Quarter Horse Association. Applicant must have 3.0 GPA or higher. Available to U.S. and Canadian citizens.

Application Requirements: Application, financial need analysis, photo, references, transcript. *Deadline:* January 2.

Contact: Scholarship Office
American Quarter Horse Foundation (AQHF)
2601 East Interstate 40
Amarillo, TX 79104
Phone: 806-378-5029
Fax: 806-376-1005
E-mail: foundation@aqha.org

ARIZONA QUARTER HORSE YOUTH RACING SCHOLARSHIP

Scholarship to an AQHA/AQHYA member from Arizona who has experience within the racing industry or is seeking a career in the industry. Applicants seeking a career in the racing industry may specialize in veterinary medicine, racetrack management or other related fields. Members may apply during their senior year of high school or while enrolled at an accredited college, university or vocational school. Minimum GPA 2.5 required.

Academic Fields/Career Goals: Animal/Veterinary Sciences; Recreation, Parks, Leisure Studies.

Award: Scholarship for use in freshman, sophomore, junior, or senior years; not renewable. *Number:* 1. *Amount:* $500.

Eligibility Requirements: Applicant must be enrolled or expecting to enroll full-time at a two-year or four-year or technical institution or university and resident of Arizona. Applicant or parent of applicant must be member of American Quarter Horse Association. Applicant must have 2.5 GPA or higher. Available to U.S. and Canadian citizens.

Application Requirements: Application, financial need analysis, photo, references, transcript, proof of residency. *Deadline:* January 2.

Contact: Scholarship Office
American Quarter Horse Foundation (AQHF)
2601 East Interstate 40
Amarillo, TX 79104
Phone: 806-378-5029
Fax: 806-376-1005
E-mail: foundation@aqha.org

APPALOOSA HORSE CLUB-APPALOOSA YOUTH PROGRAM

http://www.appaloosayouth.com/

LEW AND JOANN EKLUND EDUCATIONAL SCHOLARSHIP

One-time award for college juniors and seniors and graduate students studying a field related to the equine industry. Must be member or dependent of member of the Appaloosa Horse Club.

Academic Fields/Career Goals: Animal/Veterinary Sciences.

Award: Scholarship for use in junior, senior, or graduate years; not renewable. *Number:* 1. *Amount:* $2000.

Eligibility Requirements: Applicant must be enrolled or expecting to enroll full-time at a four-year institution or university. Applicant or parent of applicant must be member of Appaloosa Horse Club/Appaloosa Youth Association. Applicant must have 2.5 GPA or higher. Available to U.S. and non-U.S. citizens.

Application Requirements: Application, applicant must enter a contest, essay, photo, references, transcript. *Deadline:* June 1.

Contact: Anna Brown, AYF Coordinator
Appaloosa Horse Club-Appaloosa Youth Program
2720 West Pullman Road
Moscow, ID 83843
Phone: 208-882-5578 Ext. 264
Fax: 208-882-8150
E-mail: youth@appaloosa.com

ASSOCIATION ON AMERICAN INDIAN AFFAIRS, INC.

http://www.indian-affairs.org/

ELIZABETH AND SHERMAN ASCHE MEMORIAL SCHOLARSHIP FUND
• *See page 83*

MAINE DEPARTMENT OF AGRICULTURE, FOOD AND RURAL RESOURCES

http://www.maine.gov/agriculture

MAINE RURAL REHABILITATION FUND SCHOLARSHIP PROGRAM
• *See page 79*

NATIONAL DAIRY SHRINE

http://www.dairyshrine.org/

KILDEE SCHOLARSHIPS
• *See page 85*

MARSHALL E. MCCULLOUGH-NATIONAL DAIRY SHRINE SCHOLARSHIPS
• *See page 85*

NATIONAL DAIRY SHRINE/DAIRY MARKETING INC. MILK MARKETING SCHOLARSHIPS
• *See page 85*

NATIONAL DAIRY SHRINE/KLUSSENDORF SCHOLARSHIP
• *See page 86*

NDS STUDENT RECOGNITION CONTEST
• *See page 80*

NATIONAL POULTRY AND FOOD DISTRIBUTORS ASSOCIATION

http://www.npfda.org/

NATIONAL POULTRY AND FOOD DISTRIBUTORS ASSOCIATION SCHOLARSHIP FOUNDATION
• *See page 80*

SIGMA XI, THE SCIENTIFIC RESEARCH SOCIETY

http://www.sigmaxi.org/

SIGMA XI GRANTS-IN-AID OF RESEARCH
• *See page 87*

SOCIETY FOR RANGE MANAGEMENT

http://www.rangelands.org/

MASONIC RANGE SCIENCE SCHOLARSHIP
• *See page 80*

SOIL AND WATER CONSERVATION SOCIETY-NEW JERSEY CHAPTER

http://www.geocities.com/njswcs

EDWARD R. HALL SCHOLARSHIP
• *See page 81*

STRAIGHTFORWARD MEDIA

http://www.straightforwardmedia.com/

STRAIGHTFORWARD MEDIA VOCATIONAL-TECHNICAL SCHOOL SCHOLARSHIP

Scholarship of $500 available to students enrolled in vocational and technical education programs. Awarded four times per year. Deadlines: November 30, February 28, May 31, and August 31. To apply, visit http://www.straightforwardmedia.com/votech/form.php.

Academic Fields/Career Goals: Animal/Veterinary Sciences; Cosmetology; Culinary Arts; Dental Health/Services; Fire Sciences; Heating, Air-Conditioning, and Refrigeration Mechanics; Pharmacy; Real Estate; Sports-Related/Exercise Science; Trade/Technical Specialties.

Award: Scholarship for use in freshman, sophomore, junior, or senior years; not renewable. *Number:* 4. *Amount:* $500.

Eligibility Requirements: Applicant must be enrolled or expecting to enroll full- or part-time at a two-year or four-year or technical institution or university. Available to U.S. and non-U.S. citizens.

Application Requirements: Essay. *Deadline:* varies.

Contact: Scholarship Committee
StraightForward Media
508 7th Street
Suite 202
Rapid City, SD 57701
Phone: 605-348-3042

UNITED NEGRO COLLEGE FUND

http://www.uncf.org/

CARGILL SCHOLARSHIP PROGRAM
• *See page 72*

WILSON ORNITHOLOGICAL SOCIETY

http://www.wilsonsociety.org/

GEORGE A. HALL/HAROLD F. MAYFIELD AWARD

One-time award for scientific research on birds. Available to independent researchers without access to funds or facilities at a college or university. Must be a nonprofessional to apply. Submit research proposal.

Academic Fields/Career Goals: Animal/Veterinary Sciences; Biology; Natural Resources.

Award: Grant for use in freshman, sophomore, junior, or senior years; not renewable. *Number:* 1. *Amount:* $1000.

Eligibility Requirements: Applicant must be enrolled or expecting to enroll full- or part-time at a four-year institution or university. Available to U.S. and non-U.S. citizens.

Application Requirements: Application, references, proposal. *Deadline:* February 1.

Contact: Dr. Carla Dove, Research Grants Coordinator
Wilson Ornithological Society
Museum of Zoology, University of Michigan
1109 Geddes Avenue
Ann Arbor, MI 48109-1079
Phone: 202-633-0787
E-mail: dove@si.edu

PAUL A. STEWART AWARDS

One-time award for studies of bird movements based on banding, analysis of recoveries, and returns of banded birds, or research with an emphasis on economic ornithology. Submit research proposal.

Academic Fields/Career Goals: Animal/Veterinary Sciences; Biology; Natural Resources.

Award: Grant for use in freshman, sophomore, junior, or senior years; not renewable. *Number:* 1–4. *Amount:* up to $500.

Eligibility Requirements: Applicant must be enrolled or expecting to enroll full- or part-time at a four-year institution or university. Available to U.S. and non-U.S. citizens.

Application Requirements: Application, references, proposal. *Deadline:* February 1.

Contact: Dr. Carla Dove, Research Grants Coordinator
Wilson Ornithological Society
Museum of Zoology, University of Michigan
1109 Geddes Avenue
Ann Arbor, MI 48109-1079
Phone: 202-633-0787
E-mail: dove@si.edu

ANTHROPOLOGY

AMERICAN FEDERATION OF STATE, COUNTY, AND MUNICIPAL EMPLOYEES

http://www.afscme.org/

AFSCME/UNCF UNION SCHOLARS PROGRAM
• *See page 89*

AMERICAN SCHOOL OF CLASSICAL STUDIES AT ATHENS

http://www.ascsa.edu.gr/

ASCSA SUMMER SESSIONS SCHOLARSHIPS

Funding for ASCSA Summer Sessions participants only. Awards for graduate students, high school teachers, and college teachers. One award (Charles Edwards for $500) at undergraduate level used only for participation in the ASCSA Summer Sessions. Six-week sessions in Greece are conducted to become acquainted with Greece and its antiquities. Funding cannot be used for home institution in U.S.

Academic Fields/Career Goals: Anthropology; Archaeology; Architecture; Art History; Arts; Classics; Historic Preservation and Conservation; History; Humanities; Museum Studies; Philosophy; Religion/Theology.

Award: Scholarship for use in senior or graduate years; not renewable. *Number:* 10–11. *Amount:* $500–$4250.

Eligibility Requirements: Applicant must be enrolled or expecting to enroll part-time at a four-year institution or university and must have an interest in international exchange. Available to U.S. and non-U.S. citizens.

Application Requirements: Application, references, transcript. *Deadline:* January 15.

Contact: Chairman, Committee on the Summer Sessions
American School of Classical Studies at Athens
ASCSA, 6-8 Charlton Street
Princeton, NJ 08540
Phone: 609-683-0800
Fax: 609-924-0578
E-mail: ascsa@ascsa.org

POLISH HERITAGE ASSOCIATION OF MARYLAND

http://www.pha-md.org/

DR. JOSEPHINE WTULICH MEMORIAL SCHOLARSHIP

Scholarship will be awarded to a student whose major is in the humanities, sociology, or anthropology. Must be of Polish descent (at least two Polish grandparents), resident of Maryland, and a U.S. citizen. Scholarship value is $1500.

Academic Fields/Career Goals: Anthropology; Humanities; Social Sciences.

Award: Scholarship for use in freshman, sophomore, junior, or senior years; not renewable. *Number:* 1. *Amount:* up to $1500.

Eligibility Requirements: Applicant must be of Polish heritage; enrolled or expecting to enroll full-time at a two-year or four-year institution or university and resident of Maryland. Available to U.S. citizens.

Application Requirements: Application, essay, interview, photo, references, test scores, transcript. *Deadline:* March 31.

Contact: Thomas Hollowak, Scholarship Committee
Polish Heritage Association of Maryland
Seven Dendron Court
Baltimore, MD 21234
Phone: 410-837-4268
E-mail: thollowak@ubalt.edu

UNITED NEGRO COLLEGE FUND

http://www.uncf.org/

AFSCME/UNCF/HARVARD UNIVERSITY LWP UNION SCHOLARS PROGRAM
• *See page 90*

APPLIED SCIENCES

AMERICAN INDIAN SCIENCE AND ENGINEERING SOCIETY

http://www.aises.org/

A.T. ANDERSON MEMORIAL SCHOLARSHIP PROGRAM

Award for full-time students majoring in math, engineering, science, technology, medicine or natural resources. Must be at least one quarter American-Indian/Alaska Native or have tribal recognition, and be member of AISES. Must have minimum 3.0 GPA.

Academic Fields/Career Goals: Applied Sciences; Biology; Business/Consumer Services; Earth Science; Health and Medical Sciences; Materials Science, Engineering, and Metallurgy; Meteorology/Atmospheric Science; Natural Resources; Natural Sciences; Nuclear Science; Physical Sciences.

Award: Scholarship for use in freshman, sophomore, junior, or senior years; not renewable. *Number:* varies. *Amount:* $1000–$2000.

Eligibility Requirements: Applicant must be American Indian/Alaska Native and enrolled or expecting to enroll full-time at a two-year or four-year institution or university. Applicant must have 3.0 GPA or higher. Available to U.S. citizens.

Application Requirements: Application, essay, resume, references, transcript, tribal enrollment document. *Deadline:* June 15.

Contact: Scholarship Information
American Indian Science and Engineering Society
PO Box 9828
Albuquerque, NM 87119-9828
Phone: 505-765-1052
Fax: 505-765-5608
E-mail: info@aises.org

BURLINGTON NORTHERN SANTA FE FOUNDATION SCHOLARSHIP

Award for high school senior for study of science, business, education, and health administration. Must reside in Arizona, Colorado, Kansas, Minnesota, Montana, North Dakota, New Mexico, Oklahoma, Oregon, South Dakota, Washington, or California. Must be at least one quarter American-Indian or Alaska Native and/or member of federally recognized tribe. Minimum 2.0 GPA required.

Academic Fields/Career Goals: Applied Sciences; Biology; Business/Consumer Services; Education; Engineering/Technology; Health Administration; Meteorology/Atmospheric Science; Natural Sciences; Nuclear Science; Physical Sciences.

Award: Scholarship for use in freshman, sophomore, junior, or senior years; renewable. *Number:* up to 5. *Amount:* up to $2500.

Eligibility Requirements: Applicant must be American Indian/Alaska Native; high school student; planning to enroll or expecting to enroll full-time at a two-year or four-year or technical institution or university and resident of Arizona, California, Colorado, Kansas, Minnesota, Montana, New Mexico, North Dakota, Oklahoma, Oregon, South Dakota, or Washington. Available to U.S. citizens.

Application Requirements: Application, essay, resume, references, transcript, tribal identification; certificate of Indian blood (CIB). *Deadline:* April 15.

Contact: Scholarship Information
American Indian Science and Engineering Society
PO Box 9828
Albuquerque, NM 87119-9828
Phone: 505-765-1052
Fax: 505-765-5608
E-mail: info@aises.org

AMERICAN INSTITUTE OF AERONAUTICS AND ASTRONAUTICS

http://www.aiaa.org/

AIAA FOUNDATION UNDERGRADUATE SCHOLARSHIP

Available to college students that will be sophomores, juniors and seniors enrolled full-time in an accredited college/university. Must be AIAA student member to apply. Course of study must provide entry into some field of science or engineering encompassed by AIAA. Minimum 3.300 GPA required.

Academic Fields/Career Goals: Applied Sciences; Aviation/Aerospace; Electrical Engineering/Electronics; Engineering/Technology; Engineering-Related Technologies; Materials Science, Engineering, and Metallurgy; Mechanical Engineering; Physical Sciences; Science, Technology, and Society.

Award: Scholarship for use in sophomore, junior, or senior years; not renewable. *Number:* 30. *Amount:* $2000–$2500.

Eligibility Requirements: Applicant must be enrolled or expecting to enroll full-time at a two-year or four-year institution or university. Applicant or parent of applicant must be member of American Institute of Aeronautics and Astronautics. Applicant must have 3.5 GPA or higher. Available to U.S. and non-U.S. citizens.

Application Requirements: Application, essay, references, transcript. *Deadline:* January 31.

Contact: Stephen Brock, Student Programs Team Leader
American Institute of Aeronautics and Astronautics
Suite 500, 1801 Alexander Bell Drive
Reston, VA 20191
Phone: 703-264-7500

AMERICAN SOCIETY FOR ENGINEERING EDUCATION

http://www.asee.org/

SCIENCE, MATHEMATICS, AND RESEARCH FOR TRANSFORMATION DEFENSE SCHOLARSHIP FOR SERVICE PROGRAM

Award established by the Department of Defense to support the education, recruitment, and retention of undergraduate and graduate students in the fields of science, technology, engineering, and mathematics. Available only to full-time undergraduate or graduate students with 3.0 GPA or above.

Academic Fields/Career Goals: Applied Sciences; Engineering/Technology; Engineering-Related Technologies; Mathematics; Physical Sciences.

Award: Scholarship for use in sophomore, junior, or senior years; renewable. *Number:* 200. *Amount:* $22,000–$39,000.

Eligibility Requirements: Applicant must be age 18 and over and enrolled or expecting to enroll full-time at a two-year or four-year institution or university. Applicant must have 3.0 GPA or higher. Available to U.S. citizens.

Application Requirements: Application, essay, references, transcript. *Deadline:* December 14.

Contact: Evan Gaines, Project Coordinator
American Society for Engineering Education
1818 N Street, NW, Suite 600
Washington, DC 20036
Phone: 202-331-3544
Fax: 202-265-8504
E-mail: smart@asee.org

AMERICAN SOCIETY OF NAVAL ENGINEERS

http://www.navalengineers.org/

AMERICAN SOCIETY OF NAVAL ENGINEERS SCHOLARSHIP

Award for naval engineering students in the final year of an undergraduate program or after one year of graduate study at an accredited institution. Must be full-time student and a U.S. citizen. Minimum 2.5

GPA required. Award of $2500 for undergraduates and $3500 for graduate students. Graduate student applicants are required to be member of the American Society of Naval Engineers.

Academic Fields/Career Goals: Applied Sciences; Aviation/Aerospace; Civil Engineering; Electrical Engineering/Electronics; Energy and Power Engineering; Engineering/Technology; Marine/Ocean Engineering; Materials Science, Engineering, and Metallurgy; Mechanical Engineering; Physical Sciences.

Award: Scholarship for use in senior or graduate years; renewable. *Number:* 8–14. *Amount:* $2500–$3500.

Eligibility Requirements: Applicant must be enrolled or expecting to enroll full-time at a four-year institution or university. Applicant must have 2.5 GPA or higher. Available to U.S. citizens.

Application Requirements: Application, photo, references, self-addressed stamped envelope, test scores, transcript. *Deadline:* February 15.

Contact: David Woodbury, Director of Business & Operations
American Society of Naval Engineers
1452 Duke Street
Alexandria, VA 22314-3458
Phone: 703-836-6727
Fax: 703-836-7491
E-mail: dwoodbury@navalengineers.org

ARRL FOUNDATION INC.

http://www.arrl.org/

CHARLES N. FISHER MEMORIAL SCHOLARSHIP

One-time award available to amateur radio operators in any class. Applicant must be majoring in electronics, communications, or a related field. Preference is given to residents of Arizona and Los Angeles, Orange County, San Diego, or Santa Barbara, California. Must attend a regionally accredited institution.

Academic Fields/Career Goals: Applied Sciences; Communications; Electrical Engineering/Electronics; Engineering/Technology.

Award: Scholarship for use in freshman, sophomore, junior, or senior years; not renewable. *Number:* 1. *Amount:* $1000.

Eligibility Requirements: Applicant must be enrolled or expecting to enroll full-time at a four-year institution or university; resident of Arizona or California and must have an interest in amateur radio. Available to U.S. citizens.

Application Requirements: Application, transcript. *Deadline:* February 1.

Contact: Ms. Mary Hobart, Secretary
ARRL Foundation Inc.
225 Main Street
Newington, CT 06111-1494
Phone: 860-594-0397
E-mail: k1mmh@arrl.org

MISSISSIPPI SCHOLARSHIP

Available to students pursuing a degree in electronics, communications, or related fields. Must be licensed in any class of amateur radio operators.

Academic Fields/Career Goals: Applied Sciences; Communications; Electrical Engineering/Electronics; Engineering/Technology.

Award: Scholarship for use in freshman, sophomore, junior, or senior years; not renewable. *Number:* 1. *Amount:* $500.

Eligibility Requirements: Applicant must be age 30 or under; enrolled or expecting to enroll full-time at a four-year institution or university; resident of Mississippi; studying in Mississippi and must have an interest in amateur radio. Applicant or parent of applicant must be member of American Radio Relay League. Available to U.S. citizens.

Application Requirements: Application, transcript. *Deadline:* February 1.

Contact: Ms. Mary Hobart, Secretary
ARRL Foundation Inc.
225 Main Street
Newington, CT 06111-1494
Phone: 860-594-0397
E-mail: k1mmh@arrl.org

PAUL AND HELEN L. GRAUER SCHOLARSHIP

Available to students licensed as novice amateur radio operators. Applicant must be majoring in electronics, communications, or a related field. Preference given to residents of Iowa, Kansas, Missouri, and Nebraska. Pursuit of a baccalaureate or higher degree preferred at an institution in Iowa, Kansas, Missouri, or Nebraska.

Academic Fields/Career Goals: Applied Sciences; Communications; Electrical Engineering/Electronics; Engineering/Technology.

Award: Scholarship for use in freshman, sophomore, junior, senior, or graduate years; not renewable. *Number:* 1. *Amount:* $1000.

Eligibility Requirements: Applicant must be enrolled or expecting to enroll full-time at a four-year institution or university; resident of Iowa, Kansas, Missouri, or Nebraska; studying in Iowa, Kansas, Missouri, or Nebraska and must have an interest in amateur radio. Available to U.S. citizens.

Application Requirements: Application, transcript. *Deadline:* February 1.

Contact: Ms. Mary Hobart, Secretary
ARRL Foundation Inc.
225 Main Street
Newington, CT 06111-1494
Phone: 860-594-0397
E-mail: k1mmh@arrl.org

ASSOCIATION OF CALIFORNIA WATER AGENCIES

http://www.acwa.com/

ASSOCIATION OF CALIFORNIA WATER AGENCIES SCHOLARSHIPS

Three $3000 awards available to juniors and seniors who are California residents attending California universities. Must be in a water-related field of study. Community college transfers are also eligible as long as they will hold junior class standing as of the fall.

Academic Fields/Career Goals: Applied Sciences; Biology; Civil Engineering; Environmental Science; Hydrology; Natural Resources; Natural Sciences; Surveying, Surveying Technology, Cartography, or Geographic Information Science.

Award: Scholarship for use in junior or senior years; not renewable. *Number:* 3. *Amount:* $3000.

Eligibility Requirements: Applicant must be enrolled or expecting to enroll full-time at a four-year institution or university; resident of California and studying in California. Available to U.S. citizens.

Application Requirements: Application, essay, references, transcript. *Deadline:* April 1.

Contact: Sheri Van Wert, Communications Coordinator
Association of California Water Agencies
901 K Street, Suite 100
Sacramento, CA 95814
Phone: 916-441-4545
Fax: 916-325-2316
E-mail: lavonnew@acwanet.com

CLAIR A. HILL SCHOLARSHIP

Scholarship is administered by a different member agency each year and guidelines vary based on the administrator. Contact ACWA for current information. Applicants must be in a water-related field of study and must be a resident of California enrolled in a California four-year college or university.

Academic Fields/Career Goals: Applied Sciences; Biology; Civil Engineering; Environmental Science; Hydrology; Natural Resources; Natural Sciences; Surveying, Surveying Technology, Cartography, or Geographic Information Science.

Award: Scholarship for use in junior or senior years; not renewable. *Number:* 1. *Amount:* $5000.

Eligibility Requirements: Applicant must be enrolled or expecting to enroll full-time at a four-year institution or university; resident of California and studying in California. Available to U.S. citizens.

Application Requirements: Application, essay, references, transcript. *Deadline:* February 1.

Contact: Sheri Van Wert, Communications Coordinator
Association of California Water Agencies
910 K Street, Suite 100
Sacramento, CA 95814
Phone: 916-441-4545
Fax: 916-325-2316
E-mail: sheriv@acwa.com

ASTRONAUT SCHOLARSHIP FOUNDATION

http://www.astronautscholarship.org/

ASTRONAUT SCHOLARSHIP FOUNDATION

Scholarship candidates must be nominated by the faculty members. Students may not apply directly for the scholarship. Must be U.S. citizens. Scholarship nominees must be engineering or natural or applied science students.

Academic Fields/Career Goals: Applied Sciences; Aviation/Aerospace; Biology; Chemical Engineering; Computer Science/Data Processing; Earth Science; Electrical Engineering/Electronics; Engineering-Related Technologies; Materials Science, Engineering, and Metallurgy; Mechanical Engineering; Meteorology/Atmospheric Science.

Award: Scholarship for use in sophomore, junior, senior, or graduate years; renewable. *Number:* 19. *Amount:* $10,000.

Eligibility Requirements: Applicant must be enrolled or expecting to enroll full-time at a four-year institution or university. Available to U.S. citizens.

Application Requirements: Financial need analysis, references, transcript. *Deadline:* varies.

Contact: Linn LeBlanc, Executive Director
Astronaut Scholarship Foundation
6225 Vectorspace Boulevard
Titusville, FL 32780
Phone: 321-269-6101 Ext. 6176
Fax: 321-264-9176
E-mail: linnleblanc@astronautscholarship.org

BARRY M. GOLDWATER SCHOLARSHIP AND EXCELLENCE IN EDUCATION FOUNDATION

http://www.act.org/goldwater

BARRY M. GOLDWATER SCHOLARSHIP AND EXCELLENCE IN EDUCATION PROGRAM

One-time award to college juniors and seniors who will pursue advanced degrees in mathematics, natural sciences, or engineering. Students planning to study medicine are eligible if they plan a career in research. Candidates must be nominated by their college or university. Minimum 3.0 GPA required. Nomination deadline: February 1.

Academic Fields/Career Goals: Applied Sciences; Biology; Chemical Engineering; Civil Engineering; Computer Science/Data Processing; Earth Science; Engineering/Technology; Materials Science, Engineering, and Metallurgy; Mechanical Engineering; Natural Sciences; Nuclear Science; Physical Sciences.

Award: Scholarship for use in junior or senior years; renewable. *Number:* up to 300. *Amount:* up to $7500.

Eligibility Requirements: Applicant must be enrolled or expecting to enroll full-time at a two-year or four-year institution or university. Applicant must have 3.0 GPA or higher. Available to U.S. citizens.

Application Requirements: Application, essay, references, transcript, school nomination. *Deadline:* February 1.

Contact: Ms. Lucy Decher, Administrative Officer
Barry M. Goldwater Scholarship and Excellence in Education Foundation
6225 Brandon Avenue, Suite 315
Springfield, VA 22150-2519
Phone: 703-756-6012
Fax: 703-756-6015
E-mail: goldh2o@vacoxmail.com

BRITISH COLUMBIA INNOVATION COUNCIL

http://www.bcic.ca/

BCIC YOUNG INNOVATOR SCHOLARSHIP COMPETITION (IDEA MASH UP)

Awards offered by each secondary school in British Columbia to innovative students who enroll full time in a British Columbia post-secondary institution in the year following graduation from grade 12. Must be enrolled in a program in science, technology, engineering, mathematics, digital arts/media design, or business entrepreneurship. Applicants must describe in detail a new technology that is derived from combining two or more current technologies (mechanisms, methods, objects, tools, processes) that can be used to benefit the community or the world. Must not have any negative impact on humans, any other living thing, or the environment, and must have a practical and positive purpose. See web site for additional information http://www.bcic.ca.

Academic Fields/Career Goals: Applied Sciences; Biology; Business/Consumer Services; Earth Science; Engineering/Technology; Engineering-Related Technologies; Environmental Science; Graphics/Graphic Arts/Printing; Mathematics; Natural Sciences; Physical Sciences.

Award: Scholarship for use in freshman year; not renewable. *Amount:* $2000–$4000.

Eligibility Requirements: Applicant must be Canadian citizen; high school student and planning to enroll or expecting to enroll full-time at a four-year institution or university.

Application Requirements: Application, applicant must enter a contest. *Deadline:* June 30.

Contact: Tera Moon, Programs Specialist
British Columbia Innovation Council
1188 West Georgia Street, 9th Floor
Vancouver, BC V6E 4A2
Phone: 604-602-5253
Fax: 604-683-6567
E-mail: programs@bcic.ca

PAUL AND HELEN TRUSSELL SCIENCE AND TECHNOLOGY SCHOLARSHIP

CAN $5000 to $20000 award to a new recipient each year over a 4-year period. Student must be enrolled in the sciences and have graduated high school in the Kootenay/Boundary region of British Columbia. Student must be entering 3rd year of studies at a BC or AB post secondary institution. Available to Canadian citizens and landed immigrants.

Academic Fields/Career Goals: Applied Sciences; Biology; Chemical Engineering; Computer Science/Data Processing; Earth Science; Geography; Meteorology/Atmospheric Science; Natural Resources; Natural Sciences; Nuclear Science; Physical Sciences; Science, Technology, and Society.

Award: Scholarship for use in junior or senior years; renewable. *Number:* 1.

Eligibility Requirements: Applicant must be Canadian citizen; enrolled or expecting to enroll full-time at a two-year or four-year institution or university; resident of British Columbia and studying in Alberta or British Columbia. Applicant must have 3.0 GPA or higher.

Application Requirements: Application, resume, references, transcript, proof of citizenship. *Deadline:* May 31.

Contact: BC Innovation Council
British Columbia Innovation Council
1188 West Georgia Street, Ninth Floor
Vancouver, BC V6E 4A2
Phone: 604-602-5253
Fax: 604-683-6567
E-mail: info@bcic.ca

FOUNDATION FOR SCIENCE AND DISABILITY

http://stemd.org/

GRANTS FOR DISABLED STUDENTS IN THE SCIENCES

Available to graduate students who are disabled. Awards are given for an assistive device or as financial support for scientific research. Undergraduate seniors may apply. One-time award. Electronic application is available.

Academic Fields/Career Goals: Applied Sciences; Biology; Chemical Engineering; Civil Engineering; Computer Science/Data Processing; Electrical Engineering/Electronics; Engineering/Technology; Health and Medical Sciences; Mechanical Engineering; Physical Sciences.

Award: Grant for use in senior or graduate years; not renewable. *Number:* 1–3. *Amount:* $1000.

Eligibility Requirements: Applicant must be enrolled or expecting to enroll full-time at an institution or university. Applicant must be hearing impaired, learning disabled, physically disabled, or visually impaired. Available to U.S. citizens.

Application Requirements: Application, essay, references, transcript. *Deadline:* December 1.

Contact: Richard Mankin, Grants Committee Chair
Foundation for Science and Disability
503 89th Street NW
Gainesville, FL 32607
Phone: 352-374-5774
Fax: 352-374-5781
E-mail: rmankin@nersp.nerdc.ufl.edu

INTERNATIONAL SOCIETY FOR OPTICAL ENGINEERING-SPIE

http://www.spie.org/scholarships

SPIE EDUCATIONAL SCHOLARSHIPS IN OPTICAL SCIENCE AND ENGINEERING

Scholarships for high school seniors, undergraduate and graduate students who are SPIE student member. High school students will receive a one-year complimentary student membership. Undergraduate and graduate students must be enrolled in an optics, photonics, imaging, optoelectronics program or related discipline for the full year. More details on eligibility and application requirements/forms can be found at http://spie.org/scholarships.

Academic Fields/Career Goals: Applied Sciences; Chemical Engineering; Electrical Engineering/Electronics; Engineering/Technology; Engineering-Related Technologies; Materials Science, Engineering, and Metallurgy; Mechanical Engineering.

Award: Scholarship for use in freshman, sophomore, junior, senior, or graduate years; not renewable. *Number:* 100–150. *Amount:* $2000–$11,000.

Eligibility Requirements: Applicant must be enrolled or expecting to enroll full- or part-time at a two-year or four-year or technical institution or university. Available to U.S. and non-U.S. citizens.

Application Requirements: Application, essay, references. *Deadline:* January 15.

Contact: Scholarship Committee
International Society for Optical Engineering-SPIE
PO Box 10
Bellingham, WA 98227-0010
Phone: 360-676-3290 Ext. 5452
Fax: 360-647-1445
E-mail: scholarships@spie.org

NASA'S VIRGINIA SPACE GRANT CONSORTIUM

http://www.vsgc.odu.edu/

TEACHER EDUCATION STEM SCHOLARSHIP PROGRAM

Scholarships designated for students enrolled at a Virginia Space Grant college or university in a program that will lead to teacher certification in a STEM (science, technology, engineering and math) pre-college setting. Students may apply as a graduating high school senior, a sophomore community college student with plans to transfer to a STEM education program at a VSGC member institution or any undergraduate or graduate STEM major at a VSGC member university.

Academic Fields/Career Goals: Applied Sciences; Biology; Earth Science; Education; Engineering/Technology; Environmental Science; Marine Biology; Natural Sciences; Oceanography; Physical Sciences; Science, Technology, and Society; Trade/Technical Specialties.

Award: Scholarship for use in freshman, sophomore, junior, senior, graduate, or postgraduate years; not renewable. *Number:* 1–10. *Amount:* $1000.

Eligibility Requirements: Applicant must be enrolled or expecting to enroll full-time at a two-year or four-year institution or university and studying in Virginia. Applicant must have 3.0 GPA or higher. Available to U.S. citizens.

Application Requirements: Application, essay, resume, references, transcript. *Deadline:* March 22.

Contact: Mr. Chris Carter, Deputy Director
NASA's Virginia Space Grant Consortium
VSGC ODU - PHEC 600 Butler Farm Road
Hampton, VA 23666
Phone: 757-766-5210
Fax: 757-766-5205

UNDERGRADUATE RESEARCH STEM SCHOLARSHIPS

Scholarships designated for undergraduate students pursuing any field of study with aerospace relevance. Must attend one of the five Virginia Space Grant colleges and universities. Must have minimum 3.0 GPA. Please refer to web site for further details http://www.vsgc.odu.edu.

Academic Fields/Career Goals: Applied Sciences; Aviation/Aerospace; Biology; Chemical Engineering; Computer Science/Data Processing; Electrical Engineering/Electronics; Engineering-Related Technologies; Materials Science, Engineering, and Metallurgy; Mathematics; Mechanical Engineering; Physical Sciences; Science, Technology, and Society.

Award: Scholarship for use in junior or senior years; not renewable. *Number:* 1–35. *Amount:* $8500–$35,000.

Eligibility Requirements: Applicant must be enrolled or expecting to enroll full-time at a four-year institution or university and studying in Virginia. Applicant must have 3.0 GPA or higher. Available to U.S. citizens.

Application Requirements: Application, essay, resume, references, transcript. *Deadline:* February 11.

Contact: Mr. Chris Carter, Deputy Director
NASA's Virginia Space Grant Consortium
VSGC PHEC 600 Butler Farm Road
Hampton, VA 23666
Phone: 757-766-5210
Fax: 757-766-5205

VIRGINIA STEM COMMUNITY COLLEGE SCHOLARSHIPS

This scholarship is designated for Virginia community college students studying STEM fields involving science, technology, engineering and math with aerospace relevance. Applicant must be U.S. citizen with a minimum GPA of 3.0 currently enrolled full time with at least one semester of coursework (minimum of 12 credit hours) completed.

Academic Fields/Career Goals: Applied Sciences; Biology; Computer Science/Data Processing; Construction Engineering/Management; Drafting; Electrical Engineering/Electronics; Engineering/Technology; Environmental Science; Industrial Design; Materials Science, Engineering, and Metallurgy; Mathematics; Mechanical Engineering.

Award: Scholarship for use in sophomore year; not renewable. *Number:* 1–12. *Amount:* $1500.

Eligibility Requirements: Applicant must be enrolled or expecting to enroll full-time at a two-year institution and studying in Virginia. Applicant must have 3.0 GPA or higher. Available to U.S. citizens.

Application Requirements: Application, essay, resume, references, transcript. *Deadline:* March 22.

Contact: Mr. Chris Carter, Deputy Director
NASA's Virginia Space Grant Consortium
VSGC ODU - PHEC 600 Butler Farm Road
Hampton, VA 23666
Phone: 757-766-5210
Fax: 757-766-5205
E-mail: cxcarter@odu.edu

NATIONAL INVENTORS HALL OF FAME

http://www.invent.org/

COLLEGIATE INVENTORS COMPETITION FOR UNDERGRADUATE STUDENTS

National competition to encourage college students to be active in science, engineering, mathematics, technology, and creative invention, while stimulating their problem solving abilities. This prestigious challenge recognizes the working relationship between student and advisor who are involved in projects that can be patented. The prize winning undergraduate student or student-team receives a $10,000 cash prize.

Academic Fields/Career Goals: Applied Sciences; Biology; Chemical Engineering; Computer Science/Data Processing; Engineering/Technology; Engineering-Related Technologies; Environmental Science;

Health and Medical Sciences; Materials Science, Engineering, and Metallurgy; Physical Sciences.

Award: Prize for use in freshman, sophomore, junior, or senior years; not renewable. *Number:* up to 1. *Amount:* up to $10,000.

Eligibility Requirements: Applicant must be enrolled or expecting to enroll full-time at a four-year institution or university. Available to U.S. and non-U.S. citizens.

Application Requirements: Application, applicant must enter a contest. *Deadline:* May 16.

Contact: Program Coordinator
National Inventors Hall of Fame
221 South Broadway Street
Akron, OH 44308-1505
Phone: 703-706-0081

COLLEGIATE INVENTORS COMPETITION-GRAND PRIZE

The competition was designed to encourage college students to be active in science, engineering, mathematics, technology and creative invention, while stimulating their problem-solving abilities. This prestigious challenge recognizes the working relationship between a student and his or her advisor who are involved in projects leading to inventions that can be patented. The winning student or student team receives a $25,000 cash prize. The advisers of the winning entries will receive $3000.

Academic Fields/Career Goals: Applied Sciences; Biology; Chemical Engineering; Computer Science/Data Processing; Engineering/Technology; Engineering-Related Technologies; Environmental Science; Health and Medical Sciences; Materials Science, Engineering, and Metallurgy; Physical Sciences.

Award: Prize for use in freshman, sophomore, junior, senior, graduate, or postgraduate years; not renewable. *Number:* up to 1. *Amount:* up to $25,000.

Eligibility Requirements: Applicant must be enrolled or expecting to enroll full-time at a two-year or four-year institution or university. Available to U.S. and non-U.S. citizens.

Application Requirements: Application, applicant must enter a contest. *Deadline:* May 16.

Contact: Program Coordinator
National Inventors Hall of Fame
221 South Broadway Street
Akron, OH 44308-1505
Phone: 703-706-0081

NEVADA NASA SPACE GRANT CONSORTIUM

http://www.nvspacegrant.org/

NATIONAL SPACE GRANT COLLEGE AND FELLOWSHIP PROGRAM

The grant provides graduate fellowships and undergraduate scholarship to qualified students majoring in science, technology, engineering, mathematics and science education. Must be a U.S. citizen (permanent residence status, green card or student visa is not accepted) and enrolled full-time in an accredited educational institution in the state of Nevada. Minimum 3.0 GPA required. Awardees cannot receive other federal training grants during the time they are receiving a Nevada NASA Space Grant award.

Academic Fields/Career Goals: Applied Sciences; Aviation/Aerospace; Chemical Engineering; Civil Engineering; Computer Science/Data Processing; Earth Science; Engineering/Technology; Mathematics; Mechanical Engineering; Natural Sciences; Physical Sciences.

Award: Scholarship for use in freshman, sophomore, junior, senior, or graduate years; not renewable. *Number:* 1–50. *Amount:* $1250–$13,333.

Eligibility Requirements: Applicant must be enrolled or expecting to enroll full-time at a two-year or four-year institution or university; resident of Nevada and studying in Nevada. Applicant must have 3.0 GPA or higher. Available to U.S. citizens.

Application Requirements: Application, essay, resume, references, transcript, research proposal. *Deadline:* April 28.

Contact: Leone Thierman, Program Coordinator
Nevada NASA Space Grant Consortium
2601 Enterprise Road
Reno, NV 89512
Phone: 775-784-3476
Fax: 775-784-1127
E-mail: nvspacegrant@nshe.nevada.edu

TKE EDUCATIONAL FOUNDATION

http://www.tke.org/

CARROL C. HALL MEMORIAL SCHOLARSHIP

One-time award of $700 given to a full-time undergraduate member of Tau Kappa Epsilon, who is earning a degree in education or science and has plans to become a teacher or pursue a profession in science. Applicant should have a demonstrated record of leadership within his chapter, on campus and the community.

Academic Fields/Career Goals: Applied Sciences; Biology; Earth Science; Education; Meteorology/Atmospheric Science; Physical Sciences.

Award: Scholarship for use in freshman, sophomore, junior, or senior years; not renewable. *Number:* 1. *Amount:* $700.

Eligibility Requirements: Applicant must be enrolled or expecting to enroll full-time at a four-year institution or university and must have an interest in leadership. Applicant or parent of applicant must be member of Tau Kappa Epsilon. Applicant must have 3.0 GPA or higher. Available to U.S. and non-U.S. citizens.

Application Requirements: Application, essay, photo, transcript. *Deadline:* February 29.

Contact: Gary A. Reed, President and Chief Executive Officer
TKE Educational Foundation
8645 Founders Road
Indianapolis, IN 46268-1393
Phone: 317-872-6533
Fax: 317-875-8353
E-mail: reedga@tke.org

UNIVERSITIES SPACE RESEARCH ASSOCIATION

http://www.usra.edu/

UNIVERSITIES SPACE RESEARCH ASSOCIATION SCHOLARSHIP PROGRAM

Award for full-time undergraduate students who have completed at least two years of college credit by the time the award is received. Must be majoring in the physical sciences or engineering; which include, but are not limited to, aerospace engineering, astronomy, biophysics, chemistry, chemical engineering, computer science, electrical engineering, geophysics, geology, mathematics, mechanical engineering, physics, and space science education. Must be U.S. citizen. Minimum 3.5 GPA required.

Academic Fields/Career Goals: Applied Sciences; Aviation/Aerospace; Chemical Engineering; Civil Engineering; Earth Science; Electrical Engineering/Electronics; Engineering/Technology; Materials Science, Engineering, and Metallurgy; Mechanical Engineering; Nuclear Science; Physical Sciences; Science, Technology, and Society.

Award: Scholarship for use in junior or senior years; not renewable. *Number:* 4. *Amount:* $1000.

Eligibility Requirements: Applicant must be enrolled or expecting to enroll full-time at a four-year institution or university. Applicant must have 3.5 GPA or higher. Available to U.S. citizens.

Application Requirements: Application, essay, references, transcript. *Deadline:* May 1.

Contact: Dr. Hussein Jirdeh, Director of University Relations
Universities Space Research Association
10211 Wincopin Circle, Suite 500
Columbia, MD 21044-3432
Phone: 410-730-2656
Fax: 410-730-3496
E-mail: hjirdeh@usra.edu

VERMONT SPACE GRANT CONSORTIUM

http://www.cems.uvm.edu/vsgc

VERMONT SPACE GRANT CONSORTIUM SCHOLARSHIP PROGRAM

Applicant must be a U.S. citizen, Vermont resident, graduating senior in a Vermont high school, or current undergraduate with a minimum 3.0 GPA enrolled full-time for the following academic year in a degree program in a Vermont institution of higher education. Must plan to pursue a professional career which has direct relevance to the U.S. aerospace industry and the goals of NASA. Three awards will be given to Burlington Technical College Aviation Technology Program.

Academic Fields/Career Goals: Applied Sciences; Aviation/Aerospace; Biology; Computer Science/Data Processing; Earth Science; Engineering/Technology; Engineering-Related Technologies; Materials Science, Engineering, and Metallurgy; Meteorology/Atmospheric Science; Physical Sciences.

Award: Scholarship for use in freshman, sophomore, junior, or senior years; not renewable. *Number:* up to 15. *Amount:* up to $2500.

Eligibility Requirements: Applicant must be enrolled or expecting to enroll full-time at a two-year or four-year or technical institution or university; resident of Vermont and studying in Vermont. Applicant must have 3.0 GPA or higher. Available to U.S. citizens.

Application Requirements: Application, essay, references, test scores, transcript. *Deadline:* April 13.

Contact: Laurel Zeno, Program Coordinator
Vermont Space Grant Consortium
University of Vermont, College of Engineering and Math, Votey Hall
Burlington, VT 05405-0156
Phone: 802-656-1429
Fax: 802-656-1102
E-mail: zeno@cems.uvm.edu

ARCHAEOLOGY

AMERICAN PHILOLOGICAL ASSOCIATION

http://www.apaclassics.org/

MINORITY STUDENT SUMMER SCHOLARSHIP

Award to minority undergraduate students for a scholarship to further an undergraduate's preparation for graduate work in classics or archaeology. Eligible proposals might include (but are not limited to) participation in summer programs or field schools in Italy, Greece, Egypt, or language training at institutions in the U.S, Canada, or Europe. Amount of the award will be $3000. Application must be supported by a member of the APA or the AIA.

Academic Fields/Career Goals: Archaeology; Arts; Classics; Foreign Language; History.

Award: Scholarship for use in freshman, sophomore, junior, or senior years; not renewable. *Number:* 1. *Amount:* $3000.

Eligibility Requirements: Applicant must be American Indian/Alaska Native, Asian/Pacific Islander, Black (non-Hispanic), or Hispanic and enrolled or expecting to enroll full-time at a four-year institution or university. Available to U.S. and non-U.S. citizens.

Application Requirements: Application, essay, financial need analysis, references, transcript. *Deadline:* December 11.

Contact: Adam Blistein, Executive Director
American Philological Association
University of Pennsylvania, 249 South 36th Street, 292 Logan Hall
Philadelphia, PA 19104-6304
Phone: 215-898-4975
Fax: 210-542-8503
E-mail: apaclassics@sas.upenn.edu

AMERICAN SCHOOL OF CLASSICAL STUDIES AT ATHENS

http://www.ascsa.edu.gr/

ASCSA SUMMER SESSIONS SCHOLARSHIPS
• See page 92

ARCHAEOLOGICAL INSTITUTE OF AMERICA

http://www.archaeological.org/

AMERICAN PHILOLOGICAL ASSOCIATION/ ARCHAEOLOGICAL INSTITUTE OF AMERICA MINORITY SCHOLARSHIP

Award available to support a minority undergraduate's preparation for graduate work in classics or classical archaeology. Minority designation includes African-American, Hispanic-American, Asian-American, or Native American. All applications must be sent to the American Philological Association by mail, faxes and emails are not accepted.

Academic Fields/Career Goals: Archaeology; Classics.

Award: Scholarship for use in freshman, sophomore, junior, or senior years; not renewable. *Number:* 1–2. *Amount:* $500–$3000.

Eligibility Requirements: Applicant must be American Indian/Alaska Native, Asian/Pacific Islander, Black (non-Hispanic), or Hispanic and enrolled or expecting to enroll full- or part-time at a two-year or four-year institution or university. Available to U.S. and non-U.S. citizens.

Application Requirements: Application, references, transcript, application letter. *Deadline:* December 15.

Contact: Prof. Helen Nagy
E-mail: inagy@ups.edu

JANE C. WALDBAUM ARCHAEOLOGICAL FIELD SCHOOL SCHOLARSHIP

Scholarship available to support participation in an archaeological excavation or survey project. Open to junior and senior undergraduates and first-year graduate students who are currently enrolled in a U.S. or Canadian college or university. Applicants cannot have previously participated in an archaeological excavation, and must be at least a junior at time of application. Applicants must be at least 18 years of age. The annual deadline is the Sunday after March 1st.

Academic Fields/Career Goals: Archaeology.

Award: Scholarship for use in junior, senior, or graduate years; not renewable. *Number:* 7. *Amount:* $1000.

Eligibility Requirements: Applicant must be age 18 and over and enrolled or expecting to enroll full- or part-time at a four-year institution or university. Available to U.S. and non-U.S. citizens.

Application Requirements: Application, references, transcript. *Deadline:* March 6.

Contact: Laurel Sparks, Coordinator, Lecture and Fellowship
Archaeological Institute of America
656 Beacon Street
Boston, MA 02215-2006
Phone: 617-358-4184
Fax: 617-353-6550
E-mail: lsparks@aia.bu.edu

HARVARD TRAVELLERS CLUB

http://www.harvardtravellersclub.org/

HARVARD TRAVELLERS CLUB GRANTS

Approximately three grants made each year to persons with projects that involve intelligent travel and exploration. The travel must be intimately involved with research and/or exploration. Prefer applications from persons working on advanced degrees.

Academic Fields/Career Goals: Archaeology; Area/Ethnic Studies; Geography; History; Humanities; Natural Sciences.

Award: Grant for use in freshman, sophomore, junior, senior, graduate, or postgraduate years; not renewable. *Number:* 3–4. *Amount:* $500–$1000.

Eligibility Requirements: Applicant must be enrolled or expecting to enroll full- or part-time at a four-year institution or university. Available to U.S. and non-U.S. citizens.

Application Requirements: Autobiography, financial need analysis, resume, references. *Deadline:* February 28.

Contact: Mr. Jesse R. Page, Trustee
Harvard Travellers Club
PO Box 162
Lincoln, MA 01773
Phone: 781-259-8665
E-mail: jessepage@comcast.net

ARCHITECTURE

AACE INTERNATIONAL

http://www.aacei.org/

AACE INTERNATIONAL COMPETITIVE SCHOLARSHIP

One-time awards to full-time students pursuing a degree in engineering, construction management, quantity surveying, and related fields. Applications accepted between January 1 and February 15. For more information, visit web site http://www.aacei.org/awards/scholarships/.

Academic Fields/Career Goals: Architecture; Aviation/Aerospace; Business/Consumer Services; Chemical Engineering; Civil Engineering; Construction Engineering/Management; Electrical Engineering/Electronics; Engineering/Technology; Engineering-Related Technologies; Mechanical Engineering.

Award: Scholarship for use in freshman, sophomore, junior, senior, or graduate years; not renewable. *Number:* 15–25. *Amount:* $2000–$8000.

Eligibility Requirements: Applicant must be enrolled or expecting to enroll full-time at a two-year or four-year institution or university. Available to U.S. and non-U.S. citizens.

Application Requirements: Application, applicant must enter a contest, essay, references, transcript. *Deadline:* February 15.

Contact: Ms. Ashley Alexander, Administrator-Education
AACE International
209 Prairie Avenue, Suite 100
Morgantown, WV 26501
Phone: 304-296-8444 Ext. 115
Fax: 304-291-5728
E-mail: aalexander@aacei.org

AIA NEW JERSEY SCHOLARSHIP FOUNDATION, INC.

http://www.aia-nj.org/

AIA NEW JERSEY SCHOLARSHIP PROGRAM

Scholarship available to New Jersey residents or residents from other states attending school in New Jersey. Must be full-time student in an accredited architectural program at a School of Architecture and have completed one full year of study toward a first professional degree. Applicant must indicate interest in and commitment to pursuing an architectural career in New Jersey after graduation. See web site for more information and application http://www.aia-nj.org/about/scholarship.shtml.

Academic Fields/Career Goals: Architecture.

Award: Scholarship for use in freshman, sophomore, junior, or senior years; renewable. *Number:* 4–6. *Amount:* $2500–$5000.

Eligibility Requirements: Applicant must be enrolled or expecting to enroll full-time at a four-year institution or university; resident of New Jersey and studying in New Jersey. Available to U.S. and non-U.S. citizens.

Application Requirements: Application, essay, financial need analysis, portfolio, references, transcript. *Fee:* $5. *Deadline:* June 9.

Contact: Robert Zaccone, President
AIA New Jersey Scholarship Foundation, Inc.
414 River View Plaza
Trenton, NJ 08611-3420
Phone: 201-767-9575
E-mail: rzaarchitect@earthlink.net

AMERICAN INSTITUTE OF ARCHITECTS

http://www.aia.org/

AIA/AAF MINORITY/DISADVANTAGED SCHOLARSHIP

Award to aid high school seniors and college freshmen from minority or disadvantaged backgrounds who are planning to study architecture in an NAAB accredited program. Twenty awards per year, renewable for two additional years. Amounts based on financial need. Must include one letter of recommendation from a high school guidance counselor, AIA component, architect, or other individual who is aware of the student's interest and aptitude. Applications are due in March.

Academic Fields/Career Goals: Architecture.

Award: Scholarship for use in freshman year; renewable. *Number:* 20. *Amount:* $500–$2500.

Eligibility Requirements: Applicant must be American Indian/Alaska Native, Asian/Pacific Islander, Black (non-Hispanic), or Hispanic and enrolled or expecting to enroll full-time at a two-year or four-year or technical institution or university. Available to U.S. citizens.

Application Requirements: Application, essay, references, transcript, statement of disadvantaged circumstances, drawing. *Deadline:* varies.

Contact: Jamie Yeung, AIA Scholarships
American Institute of Architects
1735 New York Avenue, NW
Washington, DC 20006-5292
Phone: 202-626-7529
Fax: 202-626-7509
E-mail: scholarships@aia.org

AMERICAN INSTITUTE OF ARCHITECTS, NEW YORK CHAPTER

http://www.aiany.org/

DOUGLAS HASKELL AWARD FOR STUDENT JOURNALISM

One-time award for architectural students to encourage excellence in writing on architecture and related design fields. Submit ten copies of published article, essay, or journal with 100-word statement of purpose.

Academic Fields/Career Goals: Architecture; Art History; Engineering/Technology; Landscape Architecture.

Award: Prize for use in freshman, sophomore, junior, or senior years; not renewable. *Number:* 1–3. *Amount:* $5000.

Eligibility Requirements: Applicant must be enrolled or expecting to enroll full- or part-time at a two-year or four-year or technical institution or university and must have an interest in writing. Available to U.S. citizens.

Application Requirements: Application, essay. *Fee:* $15. *Deadline:* April 18.

Contact: Marcus Bleyer, Scholarship Committee
American Institute of Architects, New York Chapter
536 LaGuardia Place
New York, NY 10012
Phone: 212-358-6117
E-mail: mbleyer@aiany.org

WOMEN'S ARCHITECTURAL AUXILIARY ELEANOR ALLWORK SCHOLARSHIP GRANTS

Award available to students seeking first professional degree in architecture from an accredited New York school. Must demonstrate financial need. Must be a resident of New York metropolitan area. Must be nominated by Dean of architectural school.

Academic Fields/Career Goals: Architecture.

Award: Scholarship for use in freshman, sophomore, junior, senior, or graduate years; not renewable. *Number:* 3. *Amount:* $10,000.

Eligibility Requirements: Applicant must be enrolled or expecting to enroll full-time at a four-year institution or university; resident of New York and studying in New York. Available to U.S. citizens.

Application Requirements: Application, resume, references, self-addressed stamped envelope, student project in an 8.5 x 11 binder (flat artwork only), letter from an architect. *Deadline:* April 18.

Contact: Marcus Bleyer, Coordinator
American Institute of Architects, New York Chapter
536 LaGuardia Place
New York, NY 10012
Phone: 212-358-6117
E-mail: mbleyer@aiany.org

AMERICAN INSTITUTE OF ARCHITECTS WEST VIRGINIA CHAPTER

http://www.aiawv.org/

AIA WEST VIRGINIA SCHOLARSHIP PROGRAM

Applicant must have completed junior year of an accredited undergraduate architectural program or enrolled in an accredited Master of Architecture program. Applicant must present a portfolio of work to judging committee. The number of scholarships awarded varies based on the number of applicants. Award will be sent to recipient's school for disbursement for the following semester fees. For additional information, go to web site http://www.aiawv.org.

Academic Fields/Career Goals: Architecture.

Award: Scholarship for use in senior year; not renewable. *Number:* varies. *Amount:* up to $12,500.

Eligibility Requirements: Applicant must be enrolled or expecting to enroll full-time at a four-year institution or university and resident of West Virginia. Available to U.S. citizens.

Application Requirements: Application, resume, references, transcript, personal letter, examples of work. *Deadline:* May 30.

Contact: Roberta Guffey, Executive Director
American Institute of Architects West Virginia Chapter
223 Hale Street
Charleston, WV 25301
Phone: 304-344-9872
Fax: 304-343-0205
E-mail: roberta.guffey@aiawv.org

AMERICAN SCHOOL OF CLASSICAL STUDIES AT ATHENS

http://www.ascsa.edu.gr/

ASCSA SUMMER SESSIONS SCHOLARSHIPS
• See page 92

AMERICAN SOCIETY OF HEATING, REFRIGERATING, AND AIR CONDITIONING ENGINEERS, INC.

http://www.ashrae.org/

ASHRAE REGION IV BENNY BOOTLE SCHOLARSHIP

One-year scholarship available to an undergraduate engineering or architecture student enrolled full-time in a program accredited by ABET or NAAB and attending a school located within the geographic boundaries of ASHRAE Region IV. See web site for application and additional information http://www.ashrae.org.

Academic Fields/Career Goals: Architecture; Engineering/Technology.

Award: Scholarship for use in freshman, sophomore, junior, or senior years; not renewable. *Number:* 1. *Amount:* $3000.

Eligibility Requirements: Applicant must be enrolled or expecting to enroll full-time at a four-year institution or university and studying in Georgia, North Carolina, or South Carolina. Applicant must have 3.0 GPA or higher. Available to U.S. and non-U.S. citizens.

Application Requirements: Application, financial need analysis, references, transcript. *Deadline:* December 1.

Contact: Lois Benedict, Scholarship Administrator
American Society of Heating, Refrigerating, and Air
Conditioning Engineers, Inc.
1791 Tullie Circle, NE
Atlanta, GA 30329-1683
Phone: 404-636-8400 Ext. 1120
E-mail: lbenedict@ashrae.org

ASSOCIATION FOR WOMEN IN ARCHITECTURE FOUNDATION

http://www.awa-la.org/

ASSOCIATION FOR WOMEN IN ARCHITECTURE SCHOLARSHIP

Must be a California resident or nonresident attending school in California. Must major in architecture or a related field and have completed one year (18 units) of schooling. Recipients may reapply. Open to women only. Interview in Los Angeles required. Applications available the beginning of February.

Academic Fields/Career Goals: Architecture; Interior Design; Landscape Architecture.

Award: Scholarship for use in sophomore, junior, senior, or graduate years; not renewable. *Number:* 5. *Amount:* $1000.

Eligibility Requirements: Applicant must be enrolled or expecting to enroll full-time at a two-year or four-year or technical institution or university; female and studying in California. Available to U.S. and non-U.S. citizens.

Application Requirements: Application, portfolio, references, self-addressed stamped envelope, transcript, personal statement. *Deadline:* April 15.

Contact: Mary Werk, Scholarship Chair
Association for Women in Architecture Foundation
22815 Frampton Avenue
Torrance, CA 90501-5034
Phone: 310-534-8466
Fax: 310-257-6885
E-mail: scholarship@awa-la.org

THE DALLAS FOUNDATION

http://www.dallasfoundation.org/

DALLAS CENTER FOR ARCHITECTURE FOUNDATION—HKS/JOHN HUMPHRIES SCHOLARSHIP

The scholarship must be used in the year it is awarded. If the funds are not used in this time period, they will be forfeited. The funds are intended to be used for college tuition towards a degree in architecture, and as such, will be routed directly to the appropriate college office for credit towards tuition. Must be a Dallas city resident.

Academic Fields/Career Goals: Architecture.

Award: Scholarship for use in freshman year; not renewable. *Amount:* $2000.

Eligibility Requirements: Applicant must be high school student; planning to enroll or expecting to enroll full-time at a four-year institution or university and resident of Texas.

Application Requirements: Application, essay, portfolio, references, transcript. *Deadline:* March 31.

Contact: Rachel Lasseter, Program Associate
The Dallas Foundation
900 Jackson Street, Suite 705
Dallas, TX 75202
Phone: 214-741-9898
E-mail: scholarships@dallasfoundation.org

WHITLEY PLACE SCHOLARSHIP

Established in 2009, the Whitley Place Scholarship seeks to provide aid to graduating seniors in Prosper ISD who plan to study civil engineering, construction science, construction management, architecture, landscape architecture, planning, public administration, mechanical engineering or other math/science related fields.

Academic Fields/Career Goals: Architecture; Civil Engineering; Engineering/Technology; Landscape Architecture; Mathematics; Mechanical Engineering; Physical Sciences; Public Policy and Administration.

Award: Scholarship for use in freshman, sophomore, junior, or senior years; renewable. *Amount:* $2500.

Eligibility Requirements: Applicant must be high school student; planning to enroll or expecting to enroll full-time at a two-year or four-year institution or university and resident of Texas. Applicant must have 3.0 GPA or higher.

Application Requirements: Application, driver's license, financial need analysis, resume, references, transcript. *Deadline:* March 31.

Contact: Rachel Lasseter, Program Associate
The Dallas Foundation
900 Jackson Street, Suite 705
Dallas, TX 75202
Phone: 214-741-9898
E-mail: scholarships@dallasfoundation.org

FLORIDA EDUCATIONAL FACILITIES PLANNERS' ASSOCIATION

http://www.fefpa.org/

FEFPA ASSISTANTSHIP

Renewable scholarship for full-time sophomores, juniors, seniors and graduate students enrolled in an accredited four-year Florida university or community college, majoring in facilities planning or a field related to facilities planning. Must be a resident of Florida with a 3.0 GPA.

Academic Fields/Career Goals: Architecture; Construction Engineering/Management.

Award: Scholarship for use in sophomore, junior, senior, or graduate years; renewable. *Number:* 2. *Amount:* $3000.

Eligibility Requirements: Applicant must be enrolled or expecting to enroll full-time at a four-year institution or university; resident of Florida and studying in Florida. Applicant must have 3.0 GPA or higher. Available to U.S. and non-U.S. citizens.

Application Requirements: Application, essay, financial need analysis, references, test scores, transcript. *Deadline:* June 1.

Contact: Robert Griffith, Selection Committee Chair
Florida Educational Facilities Planners' Association
Florida International University, University Park, CSC 142A
Miami, FL 33199
Phone: 305-348-4070 Ext. 4002
Fax: 305-341-3377
E-mail: griffith@fiu.edu

GARDEN CLUB OF AMERICA

http://www.gcamerica.org/

GCA AWARD IN DESERT STUDIES

Students must be enrolled at an accredited U.S. university. Scholarship intended to have a wide scope pertaining to the arid environment, with preference given to projects that generate scientifically sound water and plant management. Selection is by a panel appointed by the Desert Botanical Garden.

Academic Fields/Career Goals: Architecture; Environmental Science; Horticulture/Floriculture; Landscape Architecture; Natural Sciences.

Award: Prize for use in sophomore, junior, senior, or graduate years; not renewable. *Number:* 1. *Amount:* $4000.

Eligibility Requirements: Applicant must be enrolled or expecting to enroll full-time at a four-year institution or university.

Application Requirements: Application, resume, references, transcript. *Deadline:* January 15.

Contact: Cathy Babcock, Director of Horticulture
Garden Club of America
Desert Botanical Garden, 1201 N. Galvin Parkway
Phoenix, AZ 85008
E-mail: cbabcock@dbg.org

THE GEORGIA TRUST FOR HISTORIC PRESERVATION

http://www.georgiatrust.org/

J. NEEL REID PRIZE

A $4000 fellowship is given to an architecture student, architecture intern or a recently-registered architect residing, studying or working in Georgia. Proposed projects should involve the study of an aspect of classic architecture.

Academic Fields/Career Goals: Architecture; Historic Preservation and Conservation; Landscape Architecture.

Award: Prize for use in sophomore, junior, senior, graduate, or postgraduate years; not renewable. *Number:* 1. *Amount:* $4000.

Eligibility Requirements: Applicant must be enrolled or expecting to enroll full- or part-time at a four-year institution or university and resident of Georgia. Available to U.S. citizens.

Application Requirements: Application, essay, references, samples of architectural drawing and itinerary budget. *Deadline:* February 16.

Contact: *Phone:* 404-885-7817
Fax: 404-875-2205
E-mail: kryan@georgiatrust.org

HELLENIC UNIVERSITY CLUB OF PHILADELPHIA

http://www.hucphila.org/

DIMITRI J. VERVERELLI MEMORIAL SCHOLARSHIP FOR ARCHITECTURE AND/OR ENGINEERING

$2000 award for full-time student enrolled in an architecture or engineering degree program at an accredited four-year college or university. High school seniors accepted for enrollment in such a degree program may also apply. Must be a U.S. citizen of Greek descent and a resident of particular counties in NJ or PA.

Academic Fields/Career Goals: Architecture; Engineering/Technology.

Award: Scholarship for use in freshman, sophomore, junior, or senior years; not renewable. *Number:* varies. *Amount:* up to $2000.

Eligibility Requirements: Applicant must be of Greek heritage; enrolled or expecting to enroll full-time at a four-year institution or university and resident of New Jersey or Pennsylvania. Available to U.S. citizens.

Application Requirements: Application, financial need analysis, transcript. *Deadline:* April 21.

Contact: Anna Hadgis, Scholarship Chairman
Hellenic University Club of Philadelphia
PO Box 42199
Philadelphia, PA 19101-2199
Phone: 610-613-4310
E-mail: hucphila@yahoo.com

ILLUMINATING ENGINEERING SOCIETY OF NORTH AMERICA

http://www.iesna.org/

ROBERT W. THUNEN MEMORIAL SCHOLARSHIPS

One-time award for juniors, seniors, or graduate students enrolled at four-year colleges and universities in northern California, Nevada, Oregon, or Washington pursuing lighting career. Must submit statement describing proposed lighting course work or project and three recommendations, at least one from someone involved professionally or academically with lighting. Curriculum must be accredited by ABET, ACSA, or FIDER.

Academic Fields/Career Goals: Architecture; Engineering/Technology; Engineering-Related Technologies; Interior Design; Performing Arts; TV/Radio Broadcasting.

Award: Scholarship for use in junior, senior, or graduate years; not renewable. *Number:* 2. *Amount:* $2500.

Eligibility Requirements: Applicant must be enrolled or expecting to enroll full-time at a four-year institution or university and studying in California, Nevada, Oregon, or Washington. Available to U.S. and non-U.S. citizens.

Application Requirements: Application, references, transcript. *Deadline:* April 1.

Contact: Phil Hall, Chairman
Illuminating Engineering Society of North America
120 Wall Street
New York, NY 10005-4001
Phone: 510-864-0204
Fax: 510-248-5017
E-mail: mrcatisbac@aol.com

ILLUMINATING ENGINEERING SOCIETY OF NORTH AMERICA–GOLDEN GATE SECTION

http://www.iesgg.org/

ALAN LUCAS MEMORIAL EDUCATIONAL SCHOLARSHIP

Scholarship available to full-time student for pursuit of lighting education or research as part of undergraduate, graduate, or doctoral studies. Scholarships may be made by those who will be a junior, senior, or graduate student in an accredited four-year college or university located in Northern California. The scholarships to be awarded will be at least $1500.

Academic Fields/Career Goals: Architecture; Electrical Engineering/Electronics; Filmmaking/Video; Interior Design.

Award: Scholarship for use in junior, senior, or graduate years; not renewable. *Number:* 1. *Amount:* $1500.

Eligibility Requirements: Applicant must be enrolled or expecting to enroll full-time at a four-year institution or university and studying in California. Available to U.S. citizens.

Application Requirements: Application, references, transcript, statement of purpose, description of work in progress, scholar agreement form. *Deadline:* April 1.

Contact: Phil Hall, Scholarship Committee
Illuminating Engineering Society of North America–Golden Gate Section
1514 Gibbons Drive
Alameda, CA 94501
Phone: 510-864-0204
Fax: 510-864-8511
E-mail: iesggthunenfund@aol.com

INTERNATIONAL FACILITY MANAGEMENT ASSOCIATION FOUNDATION

http://www.ifmafoundation.org/

IFMA FOUNDATION SCHOLARSHIPS

One-time scholarships of up to $5000 awarded to students currently enrolled in full-time facility management programs or related programs. Minimum 3.2 GPA required for undergraduates and 3.5 for graduate students.

Academic Fields/Career Goals: Architecture; Construction Engineering/Management; Engineering/Technology; Engineering-Related Technologies; Interior Design; Urban and Regional Planning.

Award: Scholarship for use in junior, senior, graduate, or postgraduate years; not renewable. *Number:* 25–35. *Amount:* $1500–$5000.

Eligibility Requirements: Applicant must be enrolled or expecting to enroll full-time at a four-year institution or university. Available to U.S. and non-U.S. citizens.

Application Requirements: Application, resume, references, transcript, letter of professional intent. *Deadline:* May 31.

Contact: William Rub, Executive Director
International Facility Management Association Foundation
One East Greenway Plaza, Suite 1100
Houston, TX 77046
Phone: 713-623-4362 Ext. 158
E-mail: william.rub@ifma.org

MIDWEST ROOFING CONTRACTORS ASSOCIATION

http://www.mrca.org/

MRCA FOUNDATION SCHOLARSHIP PROGRAM

Renewable scholarships for full-time students enrolled or intending to enroll in an accredited university, college, community college, or trade school. Applicant must be pursuing a curriculum leading to a career in the construction industry or related. Award amount ranges from $500 to $3000.

Academic Fields/Career Goals: Architecture; Civil Engineering; Construction Engineering/Management; Drafting; Engineering/Technology; Industrial Design; Materials Science, Engineering, and Metallurgy; Trade/Technical Specialties.

Award: Scholarship for use in freshman, sophomore, junior, or senior years; not renewable. *Number:* up to 25. *Amount:* $500–$3000.

Eligibility Requirements: Applicant must be enrolled or expecting to enroll full-time at a two-year or four-year or technical institution or university. Applicant or parent of applicant must have employment or volunteer experience in construction. Applicant must have 3.0 GPA or higher. Available to U.S. citizens.

Application Requirements: Application, essay, financial need analysis, photo, resume, references, test scores, transcript. *Deadline:* June 20.

Contact: Ms. Peggy Doherty, Operations Manager
Midwest Roofing Contractors Association
4700 West Lake Avenue
Glenview, IL 60025
Phone: 847-375-6378
Fax: 847-375-6473

NATIONAL ASSOCIATION OF WOMEN IN CONSTRUCTION

http://www.nawic.org/

NAWIC UNDERGRADUATE SCHOLARSHIPS

One-time award for any student having at least one year of study remaining in a construction-related program leading to an associate or higher degree. Awards range from $500 to $2000. Submit application and transcript of grades.

Academic Fields/Career Goals: Architecture; Civil Engineering; Drafting; Electrical Engineering/Electronics; Engineering/Technology; Engineering-Related Technologies; Interior Design; Landscape Architecture; Mechanical Engineering; Trade/Technical Specialties.

Award: Scholarship for use in sophomore or junior years; not renewable. *Number:* 40–50. *Amount:* $500–$2000.

Eligibility Requirements: Applicant must be enrolled or expecting to enroll full-time at a two-year or four-year or technical institution or university. Applicant must have 3.0 GPA or higher. Available to U.S. and Canadian citizens.

Application Requirements: Application, essay, financial need analysis, interview, transcript. *Deadline:* March 15.

Contact: Scholarship Committee
National Association of Women in Construction
327 South Adams Street
Fort Worth, TX 76104
Phone: 817-877-5551
Fax: 817-877-0324

NEW YORK STATE EDUCATION DEPARTMENT

http://www.highered.nysed.gov/

REGENTS PROFESSIONAL OPPORTUNITY SCHOLARSHIP
• *See page 69*

OREGON STUDENT ASSISTANCE COMMISSION

http://www.GetCollegeFunds.org/

SOUTHERN OREGON ARCHITECTS SCHOLARSHIP

Award available to graduating seniors (including home-schooled seniors) residing in and attending Curry, Harney, Jackson, Josephine, Klamath, Lake, or Malheur County high schools. Must attend a four-year nonprofit college or university in the United States, major in architecture, and be a U.S. citizen.

Academic Fields/Career Goals: Architecture.

Award: Scholarship for use in freshman year; not renewable.

Eligibility Requirements: Applicant must be high school student; planning to enroll or expecting to enroll at a four-year institution or university and resident of Oregon. Available to U.S. citizens.

Application Requirements: Application. *Deadline:* March 1.

Contact: Director of Grant Programs
Oregon Student Assistance Commission
1500 Valley River Drive, Suite 100
Eugene, OR 97401-7020
Phone: 800-452-8807

PLUMBING-HEATING-COOLING CONTRACTORS EDUCATION FOUNDATION

http://www.foundation.phccweb.org/

DELTA FAUCET COMPANY SCHOLARSHIP PROGRAM

Applicants must be sponsored by a member of the National Association of Plumbing-Heating-Cooling Contractors. Must pursue studies in a major related to the plumbing-heating-cooling industry. Visit web site for additional information.

Academic Fields/Career Goals: Architecture; Business/Consumer Services; Engineering/Technology; Engineering-Related Technologies; Heating, Air-Conditioning, and Refrigeration Mechanics; Mechanical Engineering; Trade/Technical Specialties.

Award: Scholarship for use in freshman, sophomore, junior, or senior years; renewable. *Number:* 6. *Amount:* $2500.

Eligibility Requirements: Applicant must be enrolled or expecting to enroll full- or part-time at a two-year or four-year or technical institution or university. Available to U.S. and Canadian citizens.

Application Requirements: Application, essay, interview, references, test scores, transcript. *Deadline:* May 1.

Contact: John Zink, Scholarship Coordinator
Plumbing-Heating-Cooling Contractors Education Foundation
PO Box 6808
Falls Church, VA 22046
Phone: 800-533-7694
E-mail: naphcc@naphcc.org

TURNER CONSTRUCTION COMPANY

http://www.turnerconstruction.com/

YOUTHFORCE 2020 SCHOLARSHIP PROGRAM

Award for five graduating high school seniors from New York City schools of $2000 each year, a total of $8000 after completing four years of college. As a scholarship recipient, students must maintain a 2.80 GPA and complete a four-year summer internship at Turner that begins immediately following the first full year of college.

Academic Fields/Career Goals: Architecture; Civil Engineering; Electrical Engineering/Electronics; Engineering/Technology; Interior Design; Landscape Architecture; Mechanical Engineering.

Award: Scholarship for use in freshman, sophomore, junior, or senior years; renewable. *Number:* 5. *Amount:* $2000.

Eligibility Requirements: Applicant must be American Indian/Alaska Native, Asian/Pacific Islander, Black (non-Hispanic), or Hispanic; high school student; planning to enroll or expecting to enroll full-time at a four-year institution or university and resident of New York. Applicant must have 3.0 GPA or higher. Available to U.S. citizens.

Application Requirements: Application, autobiography, essay, financial need analysis, interview, photo, resume, references, test scores, transcript. *Deadline:* May 2.

Contact: Stephanie V. Burns, Director of Community Affairs
Turner Construction Company
375 Hudson Street, 6th Floor
New York, NY 10014
Phone: 212-229-6000 Ext. 6480
Fax: 212-229-6083
E-mail: sburns@tcco.com

UNICO NATIONAL INC.

http://www.unico.org/

THEODORE MAZZA SCHOLARSHIP

Scholarship available to a graduating high school senior. Must reside and attend high school within the corporate limits or adjoining suburbs of a city wherein an active chapter of UNICO National is located. Application must be signed by student's principal and properly certified by sponsoring chapter president and chapter secretary. Must have letter of endorsement from president or scholarship chairperson of sponsoring chapter.

Academic Fields/Career Goals: Architecture; Art History; Arts; Music.

Award: Scholarship for use in freshman year; not renewable. *Number:* up to 1. *Amount:* $1500.

Eligibility Requirements: Applicant must be high school student and planning to enroll or expecting to enroll full-time at a four-year institution or university. Available to U.S. citizens.

Application Requirements: Application, financial need analysis, references, transcript. *Deadline:* varies.

Contact: Ann Tichenor, Secretary
UNICO National Inc.
271 U.S. Highway 46 West, Suite A-108
Fairfield, NJ 07004
Phone: 973-808-0035
Fax: 973-808-0043

UNITED NEGRO COLLEGE FUND

http://www.uncf.org/

GILBANE SCHOLARSHIP PROGRAM

Scholarship provides financial assistance for African American undergraduate sophomores or juniors who are residents of New Jersey, Pennsylvania, and Delaware, and have completed a paid summer internship program with Gilbane. Applicants must major in engineering, mathematics, or architecture at a participating UNCF member, HBCU, or majority institution. Minimum 2.5 GPA required. Information and online application at web site http://www.uncf.org.

Academic Fields/Career Goals: Architecture; Engineering/Technology; Mathematics.

Award: Scholarship for use in sophomore or junior years; not renewable. *Number:* 1. *Amount:* $5000–$6000.

Eligibility Requirements: Applicant must be Black (non-Hispanic); enrolled or expecting to enroll full-time at a four-year institution or university and resident of Delaware, New Jersey, or Pennsylvania. Applicant must have 2.5 GPA or higher. Available to U.S. citizens.

Application Requirements: Application. *Deadline:* November 20.

Contact: Director, Program Services
United Negro College Fund
8260 Willow Oaks Corporate Drive
PO Box 10444
Fairfax, VA 22031-8044
Phone: 800-331-2244
E-mail: rebecca.bennett@uncf.org

WELLS FARGO/UNCF SCHOLARSHIP FUND
• *See page 74*

WEST VIRGINIA SOCIETY OF ARCHITECTS/AIA

http://www.aiawv.org/

WEST VIRGINIA SOCIETY OF ARCHITECTS/AIA SCHOLARSHIP

Award for a West Virginia resident who has completed at least their sixth semester of an NAAB-accredited architectural program by application deadline. Must submit resume and letter stating need, qualifications, and desire.

Academic Fields/Career Goals: Architecture.

Award: Scholarship for use in junior, senior, graduate, or postgraduate years; not renewable. *Number:* varies. *Amount:* up to $11,000.

Eligibility Requirements: Applicant must be enrolled or expecting to enroll full-time at an institution or university and resident of West Virginia. Available to U.S. citizens.

Application Requirements: Application, resume, references, transcript. *Deadline:* May 30.

Contact: Ms. Roberta Guffey, Executive Director
West Virginia Society of Architects/AIA
223 Hale Street
Charleston, WV 25323
Phone: 304-344-9872
Fax: 304-343-0205
E-mail: roberta.guffey@aiawv.org

AREA/ETHNIC STUDIES

AMERICAN COUNCIL FOR POLISH CULTURE

http://www.polishcultureacpc.org/

ACPC SUMMER STUDIES IN POLAND SCHOLARSHIP

Scholarship enables American students of Polish descent to participate in summer study offered by many of Poland's universities. Must be entering junior or senior year at a college or university.

Academic Fields/Career Goals: Area/Ethnic Studies; Foreign Language.

Award: Scholarship for use in junior or senior years; not renewable. *Number:* 2. *Amount:* $2000.

Eligibility Requirements: Applicant must be of Polish heritage and enrolled or expecting to enroll full-time at a four-year institution or university. Available to U.S. citizens.

Application Requirements: Application, resume, references, transcript. *Deadline:* April 1.

Contact: Ms. Camille Kopielski, Chair, ACPC Scholarship Committee
American Council for Polish Culture
1015 Cypress Drive
Arlington Heights, IL 60005
Phone: 847-394-2520

SKALNY SCHOLARSHIP FOR POLISH STUDIES

Scholarships are intended for U.S. citizen students pursuing some Polish studies (major may be in other fields) at universities in the United States who have completed at least two years of college or university work at an accredited institution.

Academic Fields/Career Goals: Area/Ethnic Studies; Foreign Language.

Award: Scholarship for use in junior, senior, graduate, or postgraduate years; not renewable. *Number:* 2. *Amount:* $3000.

Eligibility Requirements: Applicant must be of Polish heritage and enrolled or expecting to enroll full-time at a four-year institution or university. Available to U.S. citizens.

Application Requirements: Application, resume, references, transcript, copy of an academic project on a Polish topic in English. *Deadline:* May 3.

Contact: Ms. Ursula Brodowicz, Chair, Scholarships Committee
American Council for Polish Culture
11 Brinley Way
Newington, CT 06111
Phone: 860-521-0201
E-mail: ubrodowicz@earthlink.net

ASSOCIATION OF TEACHERS OF JAPANESE BRIDGING CLEARINGHOUSE FOR STUDY ABROAD IN JAPAN

http://www.colorado.edu/ealc/atj

BRIDGING SCHOLARSHIP FOR STUDY ABROAD IN JAPAN

Scholarships for U.S. students studying in Japan on semester or year-long programs. Deadlines: April 6 and October 6.

Academic Fields/Career Goals: Area/Ethnic Studies; Asian Studies; Foreign Language.

Award: Scholarship for use in junior or senior years; not renewable. *Number:* 40–80. *Amount:* $2500–$4000.

Eligibility Requirements: Applicant must be enrolled or expecting to enroll full-time at a four-year institution or university. Available to U.S. citizens.

Application Requirements: Application, essay, financial need analysis, references, transcript. *Deadline:* April 6.

Contact: Ms. Susan Schmidt, Executive Director, Bridging Project
Association of Teachers of Japanese Bridging Clearinghouse for Study Abroad in Japan
University of Colorado, 240 Humanities Building
Campus Box 279
Boulder, CO 80309-0279
Phone: 303-492-5487
E-mail: atj@colorado.edu

CANADIAN INSTITUTE OF UKRAINIAN STUDIES

http://www.cius.ca/

CANADIAN INSTITUTE OF UKRAINIAN STUDIES RESEARCH GRANTS

Grants for students who pursue Ukrainian and Ukrainian-Canadian studies in history, literature, language, education, social sciences, women's studies, law, and library sciences.

Academic Fields/Career Goals: Area/Ethnic Studies; Canadian Studies; European Studies.

Award: Grant for use in freshman, sophomore, junior, or senior years; renewable. *Number:* 1. *Amount:* varies.

Eligibility Requirements: Applicant must be enrolled or expecting to enroll full-time at a four-year institution or university. Available to U.S. and non-U.S. citizens.

Application Requirements: Application. *Deadline:* March 1.

Contact: Iryna Fedoriw, Administrative Assistant
Canadian Institute of Ukrainian Studies
University of Alberta, 430 Pembina Hall
Edmonton, AB T6G 2H8
Canada
Phone: 780-492-2972
E-mail: cius@ualberta.ca

LEO J. KRYSA UNDERGRADUATE SCHOLARSHIP

One-time award for a Canadian citizen or a landed immigrant to enter their final year of undergraduate study in pursuit of a degree with emphasis on Ukrainian and/or Ukrainian-Canadian studies in the disciplines of education, history, humanities, or social sciences. To be used at any Canadian university for an eight-month period of study. Dollar amount CAN$3500.

Academic Fields/Career Goals: Area/Ethnic Studies; Education; History; Humanities; Social Sciences.

Award: Scholarship for use in senior year; not renewable. *Number:* 1.

Eligibility Requirements: Applicant must be Canadian citizen; enrolled or expecting to enroll full-time at a four-year institution or university; resident of Alberta, British Columbia, Manitoba, New Brunswick, Newfoundland, North West Territories, Nova Scotia, Ontario, Prince Edward Island, Quebec, Saskatchewan, or Yukon and studying in Alberta, British Columbia, Manitoba, New Brunswick, Newfoundland, Nova Scotia, Ontario, Prince Edward Island, Quebec, or Saskatchewan.

Application Requirements: Application, references, transcript. *Deadline:* March 1.

Contact: Iryna Fedoriw, Administrative Assistant
Canadian Institute of Ukrainian Studies
University of Alberta, 430 Pembina Hall
Edmonton, AB T6G 2H8
Canada
Phone: 780-492-2972
E-mail: cius@ualberta.ca

CLAN MACBEAN FOUNDATION

http://www.clanmacbean.net/

CLAN MACBEAN FOUNDATION GRANT PROGRAM

Award is open to men and women of any race, color, creed or nationality. Grant is for course of study or project which reflects direct involvement in the preservation or enhancement of Scottish culture, or an effort that would contribute directly to the improvement of the human family.

Academic Fields/Career Goals: Area/Ethnic Studies; Child and Family Studies.

Award: Grant for use in freshman, sophomore, junior, senior, graduate, or postgraduate years; not renewable. *Number:* 1–5. *Amount:* $500–$5000.

Eligibility Requirements: Applicant must be enrolled or expecting to enroll full-time at a two-year or four-year institution or university. Available to U.S. and non-U.S. citizens.

Application Requirements: Application, references, transcript. *Deadline:* May 1.

Contact: Kenneth E. Bean, Chairman
Clan MacBean Foundation
7475 West 5th Avenue, Suite 201A
Lakewood, CO 80226
Phone: 303-233-6002
Fax: 303-233-6002
E-mail: macbean@ecentral.com

CONNECTICUT COMMUNITY FOUNDATION

http://www.conncf.org/

TADEUSZ SENDZIMIR SCHOLARSHIPS-ACADEMIC YEAR SCHOLARSHIPS

Scholarship of $5000 for graduate and undergraduate students of Polish descent, residing in Connecticut, who are studying Polish language, history or culture during the academic year at a college or university in the United States or Poland.

Academic Fields/Career Goals: Area/Ethnic Studies.

Award: Scholarship for use in freshman, sophomore, junior, senior, or graduate years; not renewable. *Number:* 1–3. *Amount:* up to $5000.

Eligibility Requirements: Applicant must be of Polish heritage; enrolled or expecting to enroll full- or part-time at a two-year or four-year institution or university and resident of Connecticut. Available to U.S. and non-Canadian citizens.

Application Requirements: Application, essay, references, transcript. *Deadline:* March 15.

Contact: Josh Carey, Program Officer
Connecticut Community Foundation
43 Field Street
Waterbury, CT 06702-1216
Phone: 203-753-1315
E-mail: jcarey@conncf.org

TADEUSZ SENDZIMIR SCHOLARSHIPS-SUMMER SCHOOL PROGRAMS

Scholarship of $3000 for graduate and undergraduate students of Polish descent, residing in Connecticut, who are studying Polish language, history or culture during the academic year at a college or university in the United States or Poland.

Academic Fields/Career Goals: Area/Ethnic Studies.

Award: Scholarship for use in freshman, sophomore, junior, senior, or graduate years; not renewable. *Number:* 1. *Amount:* up to $3000.

Eligibility Requirements: Applicant must be of Polish heritage; age 18 and over; enrolled or expecting to enroll full- or part-time at a two-year or four-year institution or university and resident of Connecticut. Available to U.S. and non-Canadian citizens.

Application Requirements: Application, essay, financial need analysis, references, transcript, physician's certificate. *Deadline:* March 15.

Contact: Josh Carey, Program Officer
Connecticut Community Foundation
43 Field Street
Waterbury, CT 06702-1216
Phone: 203-753-1315
E-mail: jcarey@conncf.org

COSTUME SOCIETY OF AMERICA

http://www.costumesocietyamerica.com/

ADELE FILENE TRAVEL AWARD

One-time award available to society members to assist with travel expenses to attend the Costume Society of America national symposium. Must be currently enrolled students. Recipient will present either a juried paper or a poster.

Academic Fields/Career Goals: Area/Ethnic Studies; Art History; Arts; Historic Preservation and Conservation; History; Home Economics; Museum Studies; Performing Arts.

Award: Prize for use in freshman, sophomore, junior, senior, or graduate years; not renewable. *Number:* 1. *Amount:* $150–$500.

Eligibility Requirements: Applicant must be enrolled or expecting to enroll full- or part-time at a two-year or four-year or technical institution or university. Applicant or parent of applicant must be member of Costume Society of America. Available to U.S. and non-U.S. citizens.

Application Requirements: Application, applicant must enter a contest, references. *Deadline:* March 1.

Contact: Noel Liccardi, Program Contact
Costume Society of America
203 Towne Center Drive
Hillsborough, NJ 08844
Phone: 800-272-9447
Fax: 908-450-1118
E-mail: national.office@costumesocietyamerica.com

STELLA BLUM RESEARCH GRANT

One-time award to support a CSA undergraduate or graduate student member in good standing working on a research project in the field of North American costume. Must be enrolled at an accredited institution. Must submit faculty recommendation. Merit-based award of $3000.

Academic Fields/Career Goals: Area/Ethnic Studies; Art History; Arts; Historic Preservation and Conservation; History; Home Economics; Museum Studies; Performing Arts.

Award: Grant for use in freshman, sophomore, junior, senior, or graduate years; not renewable. *Number:* 1. *Amount:* $3000.

Eligibility Requirements: Applicant must be enrolled or expecting to enroll full-time at a two-year or four-year or technical institution or university. Applicant or parent of applicant must be member of Costume Society of America. Available to U.S. and non-U.S. citizens.

Application Requirements: Application, essay, references, transcript, proposal of the research project (with budget analysis if necessary). *Deadline:* May 1.

Contact: Noel Liccardi, Program Contact
Costume Society of America
203 Towne Center Drive
Hillsborough, NJ 08844
Phone: 800-272-9447
Fax: 908-450-1118
E-mail: national.office@costumesocietyamerica.com

HARVARD TRAVELLERS CLUB

http://www.harvardtravellersclub.org/

HARVARD TRAVELLERS CLUB GRANTS
• *See page 98*

HAWAIIAN LODGE, F&AM

http://www.glhawaii.org/

HAWAIIAN LODGE SCHOLARSHIPS

Scholarship dedicated to worthy students in the areas of engineering, sciences, Hawaiian studies, and education, who would otherwise not be able to attend college.

Academic Fields/Career Goals: Area/Ethnic Studies; Biology; Chemical Engineering; Civil Engineering; Computer Science/Data Processing; Education; Electrical Engineering/Electronics; Energy and Power Engineering; Engineering/Technology; Engineering-Related Technologies; Health and Medical Sciences.

Award: Scholarship for use in freshman, sophomore, junior, or senior years; renewable. *Number:* 4–16. *Amount:* $1000.

Eligibility Requirements: Applicant must be enrolled or expecting to enroll full-time at a four-year institution or university; resident of Hawaii and must have an interest in Hawaiian language/culture. Applicant must have 3.0 GPA or higher. Available to U.S. citizens.

Application Requirements: Application, driver's license, essay, financial need analysis, interview, references, test scores, transcript. *Deadline:* June 1.

Contact: Chairman, Scholarship Committee
Hawaiian Lodge, F&AM
1227 Makiki Street
Honolulu, HI 96814
Phone: 808-979-7809
E-mail: secretary@hawaiianlodge.org

JAPANESE GOVERNMENT/THE MONBUSHO SCHOLARSHIP PROGRAM

http://www.la.us.emb-japan.go.jp/

JAPANESE STUDIES SCHOLARSHIP

One-time award of 134,000 yen (subject to change for budgetary reasons) per month will be given to each grantee which is open to undergraduate college/university students (university must be outside Japan). One-year course designed to develop Japanese language aptitude and knowledge of the country's culture, areas which the applicant must currently be studying. Scholarship comprises transportation, accommodations, medical expenses, and monthly and arrival allowances.

Academic Fields/Career Goals: Area/Ethnic Studies; Asian Studies; Foreign Language.

Award: Scholarship for use in freshman, sophomore, junior, or senior years; not renewable. *Number:* varies.

Eligibility Requirements: Applicant must be age 35 or under; enrolled or expecting to enroll full-time at a two-year or four-year institution or university and must have an interest in Japanese language. Available to U.S. citizens.

Application Requirements: Application, driver's license, interview, photo, references, test scores, transcript, medical certificate, certificate of enrollment. *Deadline:* March 4.

Contact: Jean Do, Scholarship Program Coordinator
Japanese Government/The Monbusho Scholarship Program
350 South Grand Avenue, Suite 1700
Los Angeles, CA 90071
Phone: 213-617-6700 Ext. 338
Fax: 213-617-6728
E-mail: info@la-cgjapan.org

KE ALI'I PAUAHI FOUNDATION

http://www.pauahi.org/

CHARLES COCKETT 'OHANA SCHOLARSHIP

Applicant must be majoring in Hawaiian Studies/Language/Culture and/or Education. Part-time students are acceptable.

Academic Fields/Career Goals: Area/Ethnic Studies; Education.

Award: Scholarship for use in freshman, sophomore, junior, or graduate years; not renewable. *Number:* 2. *Amount:* $500.

Eligibility Requirements: Applicant must be enrolled or expecting to enroll full- or part-time at a four-year institution or university. Available to U.S. citizens.

Application Requirements: Application, transcript, Student Aid Report (SAR), college acceptance letter. *Deadline:* April 1.

Contact: Mavis Shiraishi-Nagao, Scholarship Administrator
Phone: 808-534-3966
E-mail: scholarships@pauahi.org

JOHNNY PINEAPPLE SCHOLARSHIP

Scholarship is for full-time students pursuing a degree in Hawaiian language or Hawaiian studies at an accredited institution of higher learning with minimum GPA of 3.5. Submit two letters of recommendation from school, community organization or religious leaders. Submit essay describing involvement in community service including organizations, number of hours/length of volunteer service and how you intend to continue to benefit the Hawaiian community.

Academic Fields/Career Goals: Area/Ethnic Studies; Foreign Language.

Award: Scholarship for use in freshman, sophomore, junior, senior, or graduate years; not renewable. *Number:* up to 1. *Amount:* up to $1100.

Eligibility Requirements: Applicant must be enrolled or expecting to enroll full-time at a two-year or four-year institution or university and must have an interest in Hawaiian language/culture. Applicant must have 3.5 GPA or higher. Available to U.S. citizens.

Application Requirements: Application, essay, financial need analysis, references, transcript, college acceptance letter, completed SAR. *Deadline:* April 1.

Contact: Mavis Shiraishi-Nagao, Scholarship Administrator
Phone: 808-534-3966
E-mail: scholarships@pauahi.org

KOSCIUSZKO FOUNDATION

http://www.kosciuszkofoundation.org/

YEAR ABROAD PROGRAM IN POLAND

Grants for upper division and graduate students who wish to study language and culture at the Center for Polish Language and Culture in the World, Jagiellonian University in Cracow, Poland. US citizens who are undergraduate sophomores, juniors, seniors and graduate students may apply. Must have letters of recommendation, personal statement, and transcript. Covers tuition fees and provides stipend for housing. Application fee: $50. Minimum 3.0 GPA required. Restricted to U.S. citizens.

Academic Fields/Career Goals: Area/Ethnic Studies; Foreign Language.

Award: Scholarship for use in junior, senior, or graduate years; not renewable. *Number:* varies. *Amount:* $675–$1350.

Eligibility Requirements: Applicant must be enrolled or expecting to enroll full-time at a four-year institution or university and must have an interest in Polish language. Applicant must have 3.0 GPA or higher. Available to U.S. citizens.

Application Requirements: Application, essay, interview, photo, references, transcript, personal statement. *Fee:* $50. *Deadline:* January 5.

Contact: Ms. Addy Tymczyszyn, Scholarship and Grant Officer for Americans
Kosciuszko Foundation
15 East 65th Street
New York, NY 10065
Phone: 212-734-2130 Ext. 210
Fax: 212-628-4552
E-mail: addy@thekf.org

MEMORIAL FOUNDATION FOR JEWISH CULTURE

http://www.mfjc.org/

MEMORIAL FOUNDATION FOR JEWISH CULTURE INTERNATIONAL SCHOLARSHIP PROGRAM FOR COMMUNITY SERVICE

The purpose of the International Community Service Scholarship Program is to assist well qualified individuals to train for careers in the rabbinate, Jewish education, social work, and as religious functionaries in Diaspora Jewish communities in need of such personnel.

Academic Fields/Career Goals: Area/Ethnic Studies; Religion/Theology; Social Services.

Award: Scholarship for use in freshman, sophomore, junior, or senior years; renewable. *Number:* varies. *Amount:* up to $3000.

Eligibility Requirements: Applicant must be Jewish; enrolled or expecting to enroll full- or part-time at a two-year or four-year or technical institution or university and must have an interest in Jewish culture. Available to U.S. and non-U.S. citizens.

Application Requirements: Application, interview, references. *Deadline:* November 30.

Contact: Dr. Marc G. Brandriss, Assistant Director
Memorial Foundation for Jewish Culture
50 Broadway, 34th Floor
New York, NY 10004
Phone: 212-425-6606
Fax: 212-425-6602
E-mail: office@mfjc.org

NATIONAL ITALIAN AMERICAN FOUNDATION

http://www.niaf.org/

NATIONAL ITALIAN AMERICAN FOUNDATION CATEGORY II SCHOLARSHIP

Award available to students majoring or minoring in Italian language, Italian Studies, Italian-American Studies or a related field who have outstanding potential and high academic achievements. Minimum 3.5 GPA required. Must be a U.S. citizen and be enrolled in an accredited institution of higher education. Application can only be submitted online. For further information, deadlines, and online application visit web site http://www.niaf.org/scholarships/index.asp.

Academic Fields/Career Goals: Area/Ethnic Studies.

Award: Scholarship for use in freshman, sophomore, junior, senior, or graduate years; not renewable. *Number:* varies. *Amount:* $2500–$12,000.

Eligibility Requirements: Applicant must be enrolled or expecting to enroll full-time at a two-year or four-year institution or university and must have an interest in Italian language. Applicant must have 3.5 GPA or higher. Available to U.S. citizens.

Application Requirements: Application, essay, references, transcript. *Deadline:* March 6.

Contact: Serena Cantoni, Director, Culture and Education
The National Italian American Foundation, 1860 19th Street NW
Washington, DC 20009
Phone: 202-939-3107
E-mail: serena@niaf.org

SONS OF NORWAY FOUNDATION

http://www.sonsofnorway.com/

KING OLAV V NORWEGIAN-AMERICAN HERITAGE FUND

Scholarship available to American students interested in studying Norwegian heritage or modern Norway, or Norwegian students 18 or older interested in studying North American culture. Selection of applicants is based on a 500-word essay, educational and career goals, community service, work experience, and GPA. Must have minimum 3.0 GPA.

Academic Fields/Career Goals: Area/Ethnic Studies.

Award: Scholarship for use in freshman, sophomore, junior, or senior years; not renewable. *Number:* 4–8. *Amount:* $1000–$1500.

Eligibility Requirements: Applicant must be of Norwegian heritage and Norwegian citizen; age 18-30 and enrolled or expecting to enroll full-time at a four-year institution or university. Applicant must have 3.0 GPA or higher. Available to U.S. and non-Canadian citizens.

Application Requirements: Application, essay, references, transcript. *Deadline:* March 1.

Contact: Scholarship Coordinator
Sons of Norway Foundation
1455 West Lake Street
Minneapolis, MN 55408-2666
Phone: 612-827-3611
Fax: 612-827-0658

STRAIGHTFORWARD MEDIA

http://www.straightforwardmedia.com/

STRAIGHTFORWARD MEDIA LIBERAL ARTS SCHOLARSHIP

Scholarship of $500 available exclusively to liberal arts students. Awarded four times per year. For more information, see Web http://www.straightforwardmedia.com/liberal-arts/form.php.

Academic Fields/Career Goals: Area/Ethnic Studies; Art History; Classics; Economics; Foreign Language; History; Humanities; Literature/English/Writing; Philosophy; Political Science; Psychology; Social Sciences.

Award: Scholarship for use in freshman, sophomore, junior, or senior years; not renewable. *Number:* 4. *Amount:* $500.

Eligibility Requirements: Applicant must be enrolled or expecting to enroll full- or part-time at a two-year or four-year or technical institution or university. Available to U.S. and non-U.S. citizens.

Application Requirements: Essay. *Deadline:* varies.

Contact: Scholarship Committee
StraightForward Media
508 7th Street
Suite 202
Rapid City, SD 57701
Phone: 605-348-3042

UNITED NEGRO COLLEGE FUND

http://www.uncf.org/

AFSCME/UNCF/HARVARD UNIVERSITY LWP UNION SCHOLARS PROGRAM
• *See page 90*

WHOMENTORS.COM, INC.

http://www.WHOmentors.com/

ACCREDITED REPRESENTATIVE (FULL)
• *See page 56*

ART HISTORY

AMERICAN INSTITUTE OF ARCHITECTS, NEW YORK CHAPTER

http://www.aiany.org/

DOUGLAS HASKELL AWARD FOR STUDENT JOURNALISM
• *See page 99*

AMERICAN LEGION AUXILIARY DEPARTMENT OF WASHINGTON

http://www.walegion-aux.org/

FLORENCE LEMCKE MEMORIAL SCHOLARSHIP IN FINE ARTS

One-time award for the child of a deceased or living veteran. Must be senior in high school in Washington and planning to pursue an education in the fine arts. Must submit statement of veteran's military service. Must be a resident of Washington state.

Academic Fields/Career Goals: Art History; Arts; Literature/English/Writing.

Award: Scholarship for use in freshman year; not renewable. *Number:* 1. *Amount:* $300.

Eligibility Requirements: Applicant must be high school student; age 20 or under; planning to enroll or expecting to enroll full- or part-time at a two-year or four-year institution or university; resident of Washington; studying in Washington and must have an interest in art or writing. Available to U.S. citizens. Applicant or parent must meet one or more of the following requirements: general military experience; retired from active duty; disabled or killed as a result of military service; prisoner of war; or missing in action.

Application Requirements: Application, essay, references, transcript. *Deadline:* March 1.

Contact: Nicole Ross, Department Secretary
American Legion Auxiliary Department of Washington
3600 Ruddell Road
Lacey, WA 98503
Phone: 360-456-5995
Fax: 360-491-7442
E-mail: secretary@walegion-aux.org

AMERICAN SCHOOL OF CLASSICAL STUDIES AT ATHENS

http://www.ascsa.edu.gr/

ASCSA SUMMER SESSIONS SCHOLARSHIPS
• See page 92

COSTUME SOCIETY OF AMERICA

http://www.costumesocietyamerica.com/

ADELE FILENE TRAVEL AWARD
• See page 105

STELLA BLUM RESEARCH GRANT
• See page 105

THE GETTY FOUNDATION

http://www.getty.edu/foundation/

LIBRARY RESEARCH GRANTS

Library Research Grants are intended for scholars of all nationalities and at any level who demonstrate a compelling need to use materials housed in the Getty Research Library, and whose place of residence is more than eighty miles from the Getty Center. Projects must relate to specific items in the library collection. Research period may last several days to a maximum of three months.

Academic Fields/Career Goals: Art History; Arts.

Award: Grant for use in freshman, sophomore, junior, senior, graduate, or postgraduate years; renewable. *Number:* varies. *Amount:* $500–$2500.

Eligibility Requirements: Applicant must be enrolled or expecting to enroll full- or part-time at a four-year institution or university; studying in California and must have an interest in art. Available to U.S. and non-U.S. citizens.

Application Requirements: Application, financial need analysis, resume, references, project proposal. *Deadline:* November 1.

Contact: The Getty Foundation
Library Research Grants, 1200 Getty Center Drive, Suite 800
Los Angeles, CA 90049-1685
Phone: 310-440-7320
Fax: 310-440-7703
E-mail: researchgrants@getty.edu

OREGON STUDENT ASSISTANCE COMMISSION

http://www.GetCollegeFunds.org/

KIRCHHOFF FAMILY FINE ARTS SCHOLARSHIP

Award available to students studying fine art, graphic design, or art history at an Oregon four-year nonprofit college or university. Preference will be given to upper-level undergraduates and MFA students. Semifinalists may be asked to submit non-returnable slides or photos of art samples. Recipients may apply for one additional year of funding.

Academic Fields/Career Goals: Art History; Arts; Graphics/Graphic Arts/Printing.

Award: Scholarship for use in freshman, sophomore, junior, senior, or graduate years; not renewable.

Eligibility Requirements: Applicant must be enrolled or expecting to enroll at a four-year institution or university.

Application Requirements: Application, portfolio. *Deadline:* March 1.

Contact: Director of Grant Programs
Oregon Student Assistance Commission
1500 Valley River Drive, Suite 100
Eugene, OR 97401-7020
Phone: 800-452-8807

ROBERT H. MOLLOHAN FAMILY CHARITABLE FOUNDATION, INC.

http://www.mollohanfoundation.org/

MARY OLIVE EDDY JONES ART SCHOLARSHIP

Scholarship awarded to a rising sophomore or junior seriously interested in pursuing an art-related degree. Applicant must be a West Virginia resident attending a West Virginia college or university.

Academic Fields/Career Goals: Art History; Arts; Graphics/Graphic Arts/Printing.

Award: Scholarship for use in sophomore or junior years; not renewable. *Number:* 1–3. *Amount:* up to $1000.

Eligibility Requirements: Applicant must be enrolled or expecting to enroll full- or part-time at a four-year institution or university; resident of West Virginia and studying in West Virginia. Available to U.S. citizens.

Application Requirements: Application, essay, portfolio, resume, references, transcript. *Deadline:* February 9.

Contact: Aime L. Shaffer, Program Manager
Robert H. Mollohan Family Charitable Foundation, Inc.
1000 Technology Drive, Suite 2000
Fairmont, WV 26554
Phone: 304-333-6783
Fax: 304-333-3900
E-mail: ashaffer@wvhtf.org

STRAIGHTFORWARD MEDIA

http://www.straightforwardmedia.com/

STRAIGHTFORWARD MEDIA LIBERAL ARTS SCHOLARSHIP
• See page 107

UNICO NATIONAL INC.

http://www.unico.org/

THEODORE MAZZA SCHOLARSHIP
• See page 103

ARTS

ALLIANCE FOR YOUNG ARTISTS AND WRITERS INC.

http://www.artandwriting.org/

SCHOLASTIC ART AND WRITING AWARDS-ART SECTION

Awards only graduating students currently enrolled in grades 7 to 12 who attend a public, private, parochial, or home school in the United States, U.S. territories, or U.S. sponsored schools abroad. May submit an art and/or a photography portfolio.

Academic Fields/Career Goals: Arts; Literature/English/Writing.

Award: Scholarship for use in freshman year; not renewable. *Number:* varies. *Amount:* varies.

Eligibility Requirements: Applicant must be high school student; planning to enroll or expecting to enroll full- or part-time at a four-year institution or university and must have an interest in art or photography/photogrammetry/filmmaking. Available to U.S. and non-U.S. citizens.

Application Requirements: Application, applicant must enter a contest, essay, portfolio, references, original works, electronic files for regional judging. *Deadline:* varies.

Contact: Scholarship Committee
Alliance for Young Artists and Writers Inc.
557 Broadway
New York, NY 10012
Phone: 212-343-6493
E-mail: a&wgeneralinfo@scholastic.com

SCHOLASTIC ART AND WRITING AWARDS-WRITING SECTION SCHOLARSHIP

Students currently enrolled in grades 7 to 12 who attend a public, private, parochial, or home school in the United States, U.S. territories, or U.S. sponsored schools abroad may apply.

Academic Fields/Career Goals: Arts; Literature/English/Writing.

Award: Scholarship for use in freshman year; not renewable. *Number:* varies. *Amount:* varies.

Eligibility Requirements: Applicant must be high school student; planning to enroll or expecting to enroll full- or part-time at a four-year institution or university and must have an interest in writing. Available to U.S. and non-U.S. citizens.

Application Requirements: Application, applicant must enter a contest, essay, portfolio, references, manuscript. *Deadline:* varies.

Contact: General Information
Alliance for Young Artists and Writers Inc.
557 Broadway
New York, NY 10012-1396
Phone: 212-343-7791
Fax: 212-389-3939
E-mail: a&wgeneralinfo@scholastic.com

AMERICAN INSTITUTE OF POLISH CULTURE INC.

http://www.ampolinstitute.org/

HARRIET IRSAY SCHOLARSHIP GRANT

Merit-based $1000 scholarships for students studying communications, public relations, and/or journalism. All U.S. citizens may apply, but preference will be given to U.S. citizens of Polish heritage. Must submit three letters of recommendation on appropriate letterhead with application mailed directly to AIPC. For study in the United States only. Non-refundable fee of $10 will be collected.

Academic Fields/Career Goals: Arts; Communications; Education; Foreign Language; Journalism; Public Policy and Administration.

Award: Scholarship for use in freshman, sophomore, junior, senior, or graduate years; not renewable. *Number:* 10–15. *Amount:* $1000.

Eligibility Requirements: Applicant must be enrolled or expecting to enroll full-time at a two-year or four-year institution or university. Available to U.S. citizens.

Application Requirements: Application, resume, references, self-addressed stamped envelope, transcript. *Fee:* $10. *Deadline:* April 20.

Contact: Scholarship Committee
American Institute of Polish Culture Inc.
1440 79th Street Causeway, Suite 117
Miami, FL 33141-3555
Phone: 305-864-2349
Fax: 305-865-5150
E-mail: info@ampolinstitute.org

AMERICAN LEGION AUXILIARY DEPARTMENT OF WASHINGTON

http://www.walegion-aux.org/

FLORENCE LEMCKE MEMORIAL SCHOLARSHIP IN FINE ARTS
• *See page 107*

AMERICAN PHILOLOGICAL ASSOCIATION

http://www.apaclassics.org/

MINORITY STUDENT SUMMER SCHOLARSHIP
• *See page 98*

AMERICAN SCHOOL OF CLASSICAL STUDIES AT ATHENS

http://www.ascsa.edu.gr/

ASCSA SUMMER SESSIONS SCHOLARSHIPS
• *See page 92*

ART DIRECTORS CLUB

http://www.adcglobal.org/

ART DIRECTORS CLUB NATIONAL SCHOLARSHIPS

Six $2500 scholarships for sophomores and juniors enrolled in accredited art schools and colleges around the country. Must have successfully completed the first year of an accredited undergraduate or portfolio program.

Academic Fields/Career Goals: Arts.

Award: Scholarship for use in sophomore or junior years; not renewable. *Number:* 6. *Amount:* $2500.

Eligibility Requirements: Applicant must be enrolled or expecting to enroll full-time at a four-year institution or university. Available to U.S. and non-U.S. citizens.

Application Requirements: Application, essay, portfolio, resume, references, transcript, 5 images of recent work on CD. *Deadline:* April 30.

Contact: Education Coordinator
Art Directors Club
106 West 29th Street
New York, NY 10009
Phone: 212-643-1440 Ext. 16
Fax: 212-643-4293
E-mail: isabel@adcglobal.org

BMI FOUNDATION INC.

http://www.bmifoundation.org/

BMI STUDENT COMPOSER AWARDS

One-time awards for original compositions in the classical genre for young student composers who are under age 26 and citizens of the Western Hemisphere. Must submit application and original musical score. Application available at web site http://www.bmifoundation.org.

Academic Fields/Career Goals: Arts; Music.

Award: Prize for use in freshman, sophomore, junior, senior, graduate, or postgraduate years; not renewable. *Number:* up to 10. *Amount:* $500–$5000.

Eligibility Requirements: Applicant must be age 26 or under; enrolled or expecting to enroll full-time at a two-year or four-year institution or university and must have an interest in music/singing. Available to U.S. and non-U.S. citizens.

Application Requirements: Application, self-addressed stamped envelope, original musical score. *Deadline:* February 1.

Contact: Mr. Ralph N. Jackson, Director
BMI Foundation Inc.
320 West 57th Street
New York, NY 10019
Phone: 212-586-2000
Fax: 212-245-8986
E-mail: classical@bmi.com

CHRISTOPHER PETTIET SCHOLARSHIP FUND

http://www.theactorscircle.com/chris.html

CHRISTOPHER PETTIET MEMORIAL FUND

Provides scholarships for young actors to study. Total number of available awards and dollar value of each award varies. Award for both full-time and part-time study. Deadline varies.

Academic Fields/Career Goals: Arts.

Award: Scholarship for use in freshman, sophomore, junior, senior, or graduate years; not renewable. *Number:* varies. *Amount:* varies.

Eligibility Requirements: Applicant must be enrolled or expecting to enroll full- or part-time at a two-year or four-year or technical institution or university and must have an interest in theater. Available to U.S. and non-U.S. citizens.

Application Requirements: Application. *Deadline:* varies.

Contact: Scholarship Committee
Christopher Pettiet Scholarship Fund
The Actors Circle, 4475 Sepulveda Boulevard
Culver City, CA 90230
Phone: 310-837-4536
E-mail: workshops@theactorscircle.com

CIRI FOUNDATION (TCF)

http://www.thecirifoundation.org/

CIRI FOUNDATION SUSIE QIMMIQSAK BEVINS ENDOWMENT SCHOLARSHIP FUND

Award of $2000 maximum based on stated need is offered to Alaska Native original enrollee or descendants of Cook Inlet Region Inc., who are studying the literary, performing, or visual arts. Must be accepted or enrolled in a two- or four-year undergraduate degree or graduate degree program. Deadlines: June 1 and December 1.

Academic Fields/Career Goals: Arts; Literature/English/Writing; Performing Arts.

Award: Scholarship for use in freshman, sophomore, junior, senior, or graduate years; not renewable. *Number:* varies. *Amount:* up to $2000.

Eligibility Requirements: Applicant must be American Indian/Alaska Native and enrolled or expecting to enroll full-time at a two-year or four-year institution or university. Available to U.S. and non-U.S. citizens.

Application Requirements: Application, essay, references, transcript, proof of eligibility, birth certificate or adoption decree. *Deadline:* varies.

Contact: Susan Anderson, President and Chief Executive Officer
CIRI Foundation (TCF)
3600 San Jeronimo Drive, Suite 256
Anchorage, AK 99508-2870
Phone: 907-793-3575
E-mail: tcf@thecirifoundation.org

COLLEGEBOUND FOUNDATION

http://www.collegeboundfoundation.org/

JANET B. SONDHEIM SCHOLARSHIP

You must: major in: (a) fine arts (dance, music, art, drama, photography), or (b) any field of study, but you must plan to teach; have a cumulative 3.0 GPA or better; and submit a one-page essay describing your accomplishments to date and your personal and professional goals, focusing on why you are interested in a career in the arts or teaching.

Academic Fields/Career Goals: Arts; Education; Music; Special Education.

Award: Scholarship for use in freshman, sophomore, junior, or senior years; renewable. *Number:* 1. *Amount:* $500.

Eligibility Requirements: Applicant must be high school student; planning to enroll or expecting to enroll full-time at a two-year or four-year institution or university and resident of Maryland. Applicant must have 3.0 GPA or higher. Available to U.S. citizens.

Application Requirements: Application, essay, resume, references, transcript. *Deadline:* March 1.

Contact: Deana Carr-Davis, Associate Program Director, Scholarship Programs
CollegeBound Foundation
300 Water Street, Suite 300
Baltimore, MD 21202
Phone: 410-783-2905 Ext. 207
Fax: 410-727-5786
E-mail: dcarr-davis@collegeboundfoundation.org

THE COMMUNITY FOUNDATION FOR GREATER ATLANTA, INC.

http://www.cfgreateratlanta.org/

JAMES M. AND VIRGINIA M. SMYTH SCHOLARSHIP

Scholarship of $2000 annually for up to four years to students enrolled at an accredited college pursuing an undergraduate degree. Applicant should pursue a degree in the arts and sciences, human services, music or ministry.

Academic Fields/Career Goals: Arts; Humanities; Music; Natural Sciences; Physical Sciences; Religion/Theology.

Award: Scholarship for use in freshman, sophomore, junior, or senior years; renewable. *Number:* 12–15. *Amount:* $2000.

Eligibility Requirements: Applicant must be enrolled or expecting to enroll full-time at a four-year institution or university. Applicant must have 3.0 GPA or higher. Available to U.S. citizens.

Application Requirements: Application, driver's license, essay, financial need analysis, references, transcript. *Deadline:* March 15.

Contact: Kristina Morris, Program Associate
The Community Foundation for Greater Atlanta, Inc.
50 Hurt Plaza, Suite 449
Atlanta, GA 30303
Phone: 404-688-5525
E-mail: scholarships@cfgreateratlanta.org

CONGRESSIONAL BLACK CAUCUS FOUNDATION, INC.

http://www.cbcfinc.org/

CBC SPOUSES VISUAL ARTS SCHOLARSHIP

Provides financial assistance to undergraduate students pursuing a career in the visual arts.

Academic Fields/Career Goals: Arts.

Award: Scholarship for use in freshman, sophomore, junior, or senior years; not renewable. *Number:* 10. *Amount:* $3000.

Eligibility Requirements: Applicant must be enrolled or expecting to enroll full-time at a two-year or four-year institution. Applicant must have 2.5 GPA or higher. Available to U.S. citizens.

Application Requirements: Application, essay, financial need analysis, photo, portfolio, resume, transcript, photograph of 5 original pieces of artwork. *Deadline:* April 29.

Contact: Ms. Janet J. Carter, Scholarships Coordinator
Congressional Black Caucus Foundation, Inc.
1720 Massachusetts Ave, NW
Washington, DC 20036
Phone: 202-263-2800
E-mail: scholarships@cbcfinc.org

CONNECTICUT COMMUNITY FOUNDATION

http://www.conncf.org/

LOIS MCMILLEN MEMORIAL SCHOLARSHIP FUND

One-time scholarship to a woman who is actively pursuing or who would like to pursue an artistic career. Must reside in Connecticut. Preference will be given to artists in the visual arts of painting and design.

Academic Fields/Career Goals: Arts.

Award: Scholarship for use in freshman, sophomore, junior, or senior years; not renewable. *Number:* 1–5. *Amount:* $500–$4000.

Eligibility Requirements: Applicant must be enrolled or expecting to enroll full- or part-time at a two-year or four-year institution or university; female; resident of Connecticut and must have an interest in art. Available to U.S. citizens.

Application Requirements: Application, essay, financial need analysis, portfolio, references, transcript. *Deadline:* March 15.

Contact: Josh Carey, Program Officer
Connecticut Community Foundation
43 Field Street
Waterbury, CT 06702-1216
Phone: 203-753-1315
E-mail: jcarey@conncf.org

COSTUME SOCIETY OF AMERICA

http://www.costumesocietyamerica.com/

ADELE FILENE TRAVEL AWARD
• *See page 105*

STELLA BLUM RESEARCH GRANT
• *See page 105*

ELIZABETH GREENSHIELDS FOUNDATION

http://www.elizabethgreenshieldsfoundation.org/

ELIZABE━━━━━━━━━━━━RANT
Award of $━━━━━━━━━━━━in painting, drawing, printmaking━━━━━━━━━━ational or figurative. Must subm━━━━━━━━━━rks. Must reapply to renew. App━━━━━━━━━━also accepted.

Academic ━━━━━━

Award: Gra━━━━━━━━━━, or senior years; not renewable.

Eligibility ━━━━━━━━━━lled or expecting to enroll full-━━━━━━━━━━technical institution or universit━━━━━━━━━━ble to U.S. and non-U.S. citizen━━

Application ━━━━━━━━━━must enter a contest. *Deadline:* c━━

Contact: Diane Pitcher, Applications Coordinator
Elizabeth Greenshields Foundation
1814 Sherbrooke Street, W, Suite 1
Montreal, QC H3H IE4
Phone: 514-937-9225
E-mail: greenshields@bellnet.ca

FLORIDA PTA/PTSA

http://www.floridapta.org/

FLORIDA PTA/PTSA FINE ARTS SCHOLARSHIP
Renewable award of $1000 to a graduating Florida high school senior who plans to attend a fine arts program within the State of Florida. Must have a least a two-year attendance in a Florida PTA/PTSA high school. Minimum 3.0 GPA.

Academic Fields/Career Goals: Arts.

Award: Scholarship for use in freshman year; renewable. *Number:* 3. *Amount:* $1000.

Eligibility Requirements: Applicant must be high school student; planning to enroll or expecting to enroll full-time at a four-year institution or university; resident of Florida and studying in Florida. Applicant must have 3.0 GPA or higher. Available to U.S. citizens.

Application Requirements: Application, essay, references. *Deadline:* March 1.

Contact: Janice Bailey, Executive Director
Florida PTA/PTSA
1747 Orlando Central Parkway
Orlando, FL 32809
Phone: 407-855-7604
Fax: 407-240-9577
E-mail: janice@floridapta.org

GENERAL FEDERATION OF WOMEN'S CLUBS OF MASSACHUSETTS

http://www.gfwcma.org/

GENERAL FEDERATION OF WOMEN'S CLUBS OF MASSACHUSETTS PENNIES FOR ART SCHOLARSHIP
Scholarship in art for graduating high school seniors who are residents of Massachusetts. The award is for tuition only and will be sent directly to the recipient's college. Must submit letter of recommendation from high school art instructor.

Academic Fields/Career Goals: Arts.

Award: Scholarship for use in freshman year; not renewable. *Number:* varies. *Amount:* up to $800.

Eligibility Requirements: Applicant must be high school student; planning to enroll or expecting to enroll full-time at a four-year institution or university; resident of Massachusetts and must have an interest in art. Available to U.S. citizens.

Application Requirements: Application, driver's license, essay, portfolio, references, self-addressed stamped envelope. *Deadline:* March 1.

Contact: Joan Shanahan, Arts Chairman
General Federation of Women's Clubs of Massachusetts
PO Box 703
Upton, MA 01568-0703
E-mail: cmje@aol.com

THE GETTY FOUNDATION

http://www.getty.edu/foundation/

LIBRARY RESEARCH GRANTS
• *See page 108*

GOLDEN KEY INTERNATIONAL HONOUR SOCIETY

http://www.goldenkey.org/

VISUAL AND PERFORMING ARTS ACHIEVEMENT AWARDS
Award of $500 will be given to winners in each of the following nine categories: painting, drawing, photography, sculpture, computer-generated art/graphic design/illustration, mixed media, instrumental performance, vocal performance, and dance.

Academic Fields/Career Goals: Arts; Graphics/Graphic Arts/Printing.

Award: Prize for use in freshman, sophomore, junior, senior, graduate, or postgraduate years; not renewable. *Number:* 9. *Amount:* $500.

Eligibility Requirements: Applicant must be enrolled or expecting to enroll full- or part-time at a four-year institution or university and must have an interest in art. Available to U.S. and non-U.S. citizens.

Application Requirements: Application, applicant must enter a contest, artwork, cover letter. *Deadline:* April 1.

Contact: Scholarship Program Administrators
Golden Key International Honour Society
PO Box 23737
Nashville, TN 37202
Phone: 800-377-2401

GREAT FALLS ADVERTISING FEDERATION

http://www.gfaf.com/

GREAT FALLS ADVERTISING FEDERATION COLLEGE SCHOLARSHIP
• *See page 76*

HIGH SCHOOL ART SCHOLARSHIP
Two scholarships of $2000 for high school seniors who are residents of Montana. Must intend to pursue a career in art or other related field.

Academic Fields/Career Goals: Arts.

Award: Scholarship for use in freshman year; not renewable. *Number:* 2. *Amount:* $2000.

Eligibility Requirements: Applicant must be high school student; planning to enroll or expecting to enroll full-time at a two-year or four-year institution or university and resident of Montana. Available to U.S. citizens.

Application Requirements: Application, essay, portfolio, resume, references, self-addressed stamped envelope, cover letter describing how the scholarship money will be used. *Deadline:* February 29.

Contact: Christine Depa, Administrative Assistant
Great Falls Advertising Federation
609 Tenth Avenue South, Suite B
Great Falls, MT 59405
Phone: 406-761-6453
Fax: 406-453-1128
E-mail: gfaf@gfaf.com

IFDA EDUCATIONAL FOUNDATION

http://www.ifdaef.org/

RUTH CLARK FURNITURE DESIGN SCHOLARSHIP

Scholarship available to students studying design at an accredited college or design school with a focus on residential furniture design. Applicant must submit five examples of original designs, three of which must be residential furniture examples. May be CD-ROM (pdf format only), slides, photographs, or copies of drawings no larger than 8 1/2" x 11". Include five sets of each design example with a short description of each illustration.

Academic Fields/Career Goals: Arts; Industrial Design.

Award: Scholarship for use in sophomore, junior, senior, or graduate years; not renewable. *Number:* 1. *Amount:* $3000.

Eligibility Requirements: Applicant must be enrolled or expecting to enroll full-time at a four-year institution or university. Available to U.S. and non-U.S. citizens.

Application Requirements: Application, essay, references, transcript, 2 digital copies of the design work done in class. *Deadline:* March 31.

Contact: Merry Mabbett Dean, Director of Scholarships & Grants
IFDA Educational Foundation
10765 SW Canterbury Lane, #101
Tigard, OR 97224
Phone: 503-367-0151
Fax: 866-362-9107
E-mail: merrymabbettinc@comcast.net

JACK J. ISGUR FOUNDATION

JACK J. ISGUR FOUNDATION SCHOLARSHIP

Awards scholarships to juniors, seniors, and graduate students with intentions of teaching the humanities in Missouri schools, preferably within grades kindergarten through 8th grade. Applicants interested in teaching in rural schools will take precedence.

Academic Fields/Career Goals: Arts; Education; Humanities; Literature/English/Writing; Music; Performing Arts.

Award: Scholarship for use in junior, senior, graduate, or postgraduate years; not renewable. *Number:* 5–40. *Amount:* $750.

Eligibility Requirements: Applicant must be enrolled or expecting to enroll full- or part-time at a four-year institution or university. Available to U.S. and non-U.S. citizens.

Application Requirements: Application, interview, references, transcript. *Deadline:* May 1.

Contact: Mr. Charles F. Jensen, Administrator–Jack J. Isgur Foundation
Jack J. Isgur Foundation
Stinson Morrison Hecker Law Firm, 1201 Walnut Street, 29th floor
Kansas City, MO 64106
Phone: 816-691-2760
Fax: 816-691-3495
E-mail: cjensen@stinson.com

JOHN F. AND ANNA LEE STACEY SCHOLARSHIP FUND

http://www.nationalcowboymuseum.org/

JOHN F. AND ANNA LEE STACEY SCHOLARSHIP FUND

Scholarships for artists who are high school graduates between the ages of 18 and 35, who are U.S. citizens, and whose work is devoted to the classical or conservative tradition of Western culture. Awards are for drawing or painting only. Must submit no more than ten color digital images of work.

Academic Fields/Career Goals: Arts.

Award: Scholarship for use in freshman, sophomore, junior, senior, graduate, or postgraduate years; renewable. *Number:* 3–5. *Amount:* $1000–$4000.

Eligibility Requirements: Applicant must be age 18-35; enrolled or expecting to enroll full- or part-time at a four-year institution or university and must have an interest in art. Available to U.S. citizens.

Application Requirements: Application, autobiography, photo, portfolio, references, digital images. *Deadline:* February 1.

Contact: Ms. Anne Morand, Curator of Art
John F. and Anna Lee Stacey Scholarship Fund
National Cowboy and Western Heritage Museum
1700 63rd Street, NE
Oklahoma City, OK 73111
Phone: 405-478-2250 Ext. 236
Fax: 405-478-4714
E-mail: amorand@nationalcowboymuseum.org

KE ALI'I PAUAHI FOUNDATION

http://www.pauahi.org/

BRUCE T. AND JACKIE MAHI ERICKSON GRANT

Grant to support an undergraduate or graduate student pursuing studies in the creation of crafts, art and photography, and/or independent research relating to historical Hawaiian crafts and arts. Must be in good academic standing, demonstrate financial need, and be pursuing a post-secondary degree.

Academic Fields/Career Goals: Arts; Photojournalism/Photography.

Award: Grant for use in freshman, sophomore, junior, senior, or graduate years; not renewable. *Number:* 1. *Amount:* up to $800.

Eligibility Requirements: Applicant must be enrolled or expecting to enroll full-time at a two-year or four-year institution or university and must have an interest in Hawaiian language/culture. Available to U.S. citizens.

Application Requirements: Application, financial need analysis, references, transcript, college acceptance letter, copy of SAR. *Deadline:* April 1.

Contact: Mavis Shiraishi-Nagao, Scholarship Administrator
Ke Ali'i Pauahi Foundation
567 South King Street, Suite 160
Honolulu, HI 96813
Phone: 808-534-3966
E-mail: scholarships@pauahi.org

NATIVE HAWAIIAN VISUAL ARTS SCHOLARSHIP

Scholarship open to University of Hawaii undergraduate or graduate student majoring in art, to encourage studies in the area of visual arts. This includes, but is not limited to, drawing, painting, printmaking, graphic design, fiber arts, sculpture, ceramics, digital art (computer), photography, and film-making or video production. Selection based on artistic merit as demonstrated by an artistic portfolio and academic achievements. Minimum GPA of 3.2 required. Submit hard-copy photos of artistic works created (CD's and DVD's will not be accepted).

Academic Fields/Career Goals: Arts.

Award: Scholarship for use in freshman, sophomore, junior, senior, or graduate years; not renewable. *Number:* 1. *Amount:* $1500.

Eligibility Requirements: Applicant must be enrolled or expecting to enroll full-time at an institution or university; resident of Hawaii; studying in Hawaii and must have an interest in art or photography/photogrammetry/filmmaking. Available to U.S. citizens.

Application Requirements: Application, financial need analysis, portfolio, transcript, Student Aid Report (SAR), Transcripts & Art Portfolio. *Deadline:* April 1.

Contact: Mavis Shiraishi-Nagao, Scholarship Administrator
Phone: 808-534-3966
E-mail: scholarships@pauahi.org

MEDIA ACTION NETWORK FOR ASIAN AMERICANS

http://www.manaa.org/

MANAA MEDIA SCHOLARSHIPS FOR ASIAN AMERICAN STUDENTS

One-time award to students pursuing careers in film and television production as writers, directors, producers, and studio executives. Students must have a strong desire to advance a positive and enlightened understanding of the Asian-American experience in mainstream media. See web site http://www.manaa.org for application deadline and additional information.

Academic Fields/Career Goals: Arts; Filmmaking/Video; TV/Radio Broadcasting.

Award: Scholarship for use in freshman, sophomore, junior, senior, or graduate years; not renewable. *Number:* 1. *Amount:* $1000.

Eligibility Requirements: Applicant must be Asian/Pacific Islander and enrolled or expecting to enroll full-time at a two-year or four-year or technical institution or university. Available to U.S. citizens.

Application Requirements: Essay, financial need analysis, references, transcript, work sample. *Deadline:* varies.

Contact: Scholarship Coordinator
Media Action Network for Asian Americans
PO Box 11105
Burbank, CA 91510
E-mail: manaaletters@yahoo.com.

METAVUE CORPORATION

http://www.metavue.com/

FW RAUSCH ARTS AND HUMANITIES PAPER CONTEST

Eight to eleven awards given a year to undergraduate students enrolled at an accredited college or university in the U.S. Scholarships are granted for exemplary work in one of a variety of arts- and humanities-related areas the contestant may choose from. Work may focus on research, biography or critical essay.

Academic Fields/Career Goals: Arts; Humanities.

Award: Prize for use in freshman, sophomore, junior, or senior years; not renewable. *Number:* 8–11. *Amount:* $15–$500.

Eligibility Requirements: Applicant must be enrolled or expecting to enroll full-time at a two-year or four-year institution or university. Applicant must have 3.0 GPA or higher. Available to U.S. citizens.

Application Requirements: Applicant must enter a contest, essay. *Deadline:* May 1.

Contact: Teresa Rufflo
Phone: 608-577-0642
E-mail: scholarships@metavue.com

MINNESOTA COMMUNITY FOUNDATION

http://www.mncommunityfoundation.org/

FRANK CHANEY MEMORIAL SCHOLARSHIP

Scholarship to legal dependents of employees of the Andersen Corporation, who demonstrate artistic ability and wish to enroll in an art-related degree program in a postsecondary educational institution.

Academic Fields/Career Goals: Arts.

Award: Scholarship for use in freshman year; renewable. *Number:* varies. *Amount:* up to $3000.

Eligibility Requirements: Applicant must be high school student; planning to enroll or expecting to enroll full-time at a four-year institution or university and must have an interest in art. Applicant or parent of applicant must be affiliated with Andersen Corporation. Applicant must have 2.5 GPA or higher. Available to U.S. citizens.

Application Requirements: Application, portfolio, references. *Deadline:* April 4.

Contact: Donna Paulson, Administrative Assistant
Minnesota Community Foundation
55 Fifth Street East, Suite 600
St. Paul, MN 55101-1797
Phone: 651-325-4212
Fax: 651-224-9502
E-mail: dkp@mncommunityfoundation.org

THE NAMTA FOUNDATION

http://www.namtafoundation.org/

NAMTA FOUNDATION VISUAL ARTS MAJOR SCHOLARSHIP

The NAMTA Foundation Visual Arts Scholarship is open to high school seniors, undergraduate and graduate students. Student must be majoring or planning to major in the field of visual arts, such as painting, drawing, sketching, sculpture and other creative arts—excluding music or the performing arts—as an art major or an art educator. Must submit a minimum of 2, with a maximum of 3 examples of work specifying the type of medium that was used for each. Examples will be accepted by electronic means only (CD or email). Do not submit original pieces, as they will not be accepted. Must graduate from high school or its equivalent before July 1 of the year in which they will receive the scholarship, if awarded. Must submit a high school or equivalent transcript. Applicants will be judged primarily on artistic talent/potential, and their degree of interest and enthusiasm for the fine arts. Some consideration will be given to GPA, extracurricular activities, and financial need.

Academic Fields/Career Goals: Arts.

Award: Scholarship for use in freshman, sophomore, junior, senior, or graduate years; not renewable. *Number:* 2–6. *Amount:* $2000.

Eligibility Requirements: Applicant must be enrolled or expecting to enroll full- or part-time at a two-year or four-year institution or university. Available to U.S. and non-U.S. citizens.

Application Requirements: Application, essay, test scores, transcript, 3 electronic examples of applicant's artwork. *Deadline:* March 1.

Contact: Leah Siffringer, NAMTA Foundation Staff Liaison
The NAMTA Foundation
20200 Zion Avenue
Cornelius, NC 28031
Phone: 704-892-6244
Fax: 704-892-6247
E-mail: lsiffringer@namta.org

NATIONAL OPERA ASSOCIATION

http://www.noa.org/

NOA VOCAL COMPETITION/LEGACY AWARD PROGRAM

Awards granted based on competitive audition to support study and career development. Singers compete in Scholarship and Artist Division. Legacy Awards are granted for study and career development in any opera-related career to those who further NOA's goal of increased minority participation in the profession.

Academic Fields/Career Goals: Arts; Performing Arts.

Award: Prize for use in freshman, sophomore, junior, senior, graduate, or postgraduate years; not renewable. *Number:* 3–8. *Amount:* $500–$2000.

Eligibility Requirements: Applicant must be age 18-24; enrolled or expecting to enroll full- or part-time at a two-year or four-year or technical institution or university and must have an interest in music or music/singing. Available to U.S. and non-U.S. citizens.

Application Requirements: Application, applicant must enter a contest, driver's license, photo, references, audition tape/proposal. *Fee:* $25. *Deadline:* October 15.

Contact: Robert Hansen, Executive Secretary
National Opera Association
2403 Russell Long Boulevard, PO Box 60869
Canyon, TX 79016-0001
Phone: 806-651-2857
Fax: 806-651-2958
E-mail: hansen@mail.wtamu.edu

NATIONAL SCULPTURE SOCIETY

http://www.nationalsculpture.org/

NSS EDUCATIONAL SCHOLARSHIPS

Scholarships of $2,000 each are available for students of figurative or representational sculpture. Scholarships are paid directly to the academic institution through which the student applies. The educational institution the student attends must be an accredited U.S. institution. Please note that work that is inspired by nature—or figurative or realist sculpture—is preferred.

Academic Fields/Career Goals: Arts.

Award: Scholarship for use in freshman, sophomore, junior, senior, or graduate years; not renewable. *Number:* 4. *Amount:* $2000.

Eligibility Requirements: Applicant must be enrolled or expecting to enroll full- or part-time at a two-year or four-year or technical institution or university and must have an interest in art. Available to U.S. and non-U.S. citizens.

Application Requirements: Application, financial need analysis, references, transcript, images of works of sculpture created by applicant. *Deadline:* May 30.

Contact: Elizabeth Helm, Awards Administrator
National Sculpture Society
75 Varick Street, 11th Floor
New York, NY 10013
Phone: 212-764-5645 Ext. 10
Fax: 212-764-5651
E-mail: elizabeth@nationalsculpture.org

OREGON STUDENT ASSISTANCE COMMISSION

http://www.GetCollegeFunds.org/

KIRCHHOFF FAMILY FINE ARTS SCHOLARSHIP
• *See page 108*

P. BUCKLEY MOSS FOUNDATION

http://www.mossfoundation.org/

P. BUCKLEY MOSS ENDOWED SCHOLARSHIP

Scholarship of up to $1500 to one or more high school seniors with financial need, a certified language-related learning disability, and artistic talent who plan a career in visual arts.

Academic Fields/Career Goals: Arts.

Award: Scholarship for use in freshman, sophomore, junior, or senior years; not renewable. *Number:* 1. *Amount:* up to $1500.

Eligibility Requirements: Applicant must be high school student; planning to enroll or expecting to enroll full-time at a two-year or four-year institution or university and must have an interest in art. Applicant must be learning disabled. Applicant must have 2.5 GPA or higher. Available to U.S. citizens.

Application Requirements: Application, essay, financial need analysis, portfolio, transcript. *Deadline:* March 1.

Contact: Brenda Simmons
P. Buckley Moss Foundation
152 P. Buckley Moss Drive
Waynesboro, VA 22980
Phone: 540-932-1728
Fax: 540-941-8865
E-mail: foundation@mossfoundation.org

POLISH ARTS CLUB OF BUFFALO SCHOLARSHIP FOUNDATION

http://www.pacb.bfn.org/

POLISH ARTS CLUB OF BUFFALO SCHOLARSHIP FOUNDATION TRUST

Provides educational scholarships to students of Polish background who are legal residents of New York. Must be enrolled at the junior level or above in an accredited college or university in NY. Must be a U.S. citizen. For application and additional information, visit web site http://www.pacb.bfn.org.

Academic Fields/Career Goals: Arts; Filmmaking/Video; Humanities; Music; Performing Arts.

Award: Scholarship for use in junior, senior, graduate, or postgraduate years; not renewable. *Number:* 1–3. *Amount:* $1000.

Eligibility Requirements: Applicant must be of Polish heritage; enrolled or expecting to enroll full- or part-time at a four-year institution or university and resident of New York. Available to U.S. citizens.

Application Requirements: Application, essay, interview, portfolio, resume, references, self-addressed stamped envelope. *Deadline:* June 15.

Contact: Anne Flansburg, Selection Chair
Polish Arts Club of Buffalo Scholarship Foundation
24 Amherston Drive
Williamsville, NY 14221-7002
Phone: 716-863-3631
E-mail: anneflanswz@aol.com

RHODE ISLAND FOUNDATION

http://www.rifoundation.org/

CONSTANT MEMORIAL SCHOLARSHIP FOR AQUIDNECK ISLAND RESIDENTS

Award to individuals who have been residents of Aquidneck Island for at least three years, are enrolled as a visual art or music majors (sophomore, junior, or senior) in an accredited four-year post-secondary institution, and are able to demonstrate financial need.

Academic Fields/Career Goals: Arts; Music.

Award: Scholarship for use in sophomore, junior, or senior years; not renewable. *Number:* 1–2. *Amount:* $2000–$5000.

Eligibility Requirements: Applicant must be enrolled or expecting to enroll full-time at a four-year institution or university; resident of Rhode Island and must have an interest in art or music. Available to U.S. citizens.

Application Requirements: Application, essay, financial need analysis, references, transcript, samples of work done within the last 12 months. *Deadline:* June 1.

Contact: Libby Monahan, Funds Administrator
Rhode Island Foundation
One Union Station
Providence, RI 02903
Phone: 401-274-4564 Ext. 3117
E-mail: libbym@rifoundation.org

MJSA EDUCATION FOUNDATION JEWELRY SCHOLARSHIP

Scholarships ranging from $500 to $2000 are available for students enrolled in tool making, design, metals fabrication or other jewelry-related courses of study at colleges, universities or non-profit technical schools on the post-secondary level in the United States. Renewable up to four years if the student maintains good academic standing.

Academic Fields/Career Goals: Arts.

Award: Scholarship for use in freshman year; renewable. *Number:* varies. *Amount:* $500–$2000.

Eligibility Requirements: Applicant must be enrolled or expecting to enroll full-time at a two-year or four-year or technical institution or university and must have an interest in art. Available to U.S. citizens.

Application Requirements: Application, essay, financial need analysis, self-addressed stamped envelope, transcript. *Deadline:* May 14.

Contact: Libby Monahan, Funds Administrator
Rhode Island Foundation
One Union Station
Providence, RI 02903
Phone: 401-274-4564 Ext. 3117
E-mail: libbym@rifoundation.org

ROBERT H. MOLLOHAN FAMILY CHARITABLE FOUNDATION, INC.

http://www.mollohanfoundation.org/

MARY OLIVE EDDY JONES ART SCHOLARSHIP
• *See page 108*

SERVICE EMPLOYEES INTERNATIONAL UNION (SEIU)

http://www.seiu.org/

SEIU MOE FONER SCHOLARSHIP PROGRAM FOR VISUAL AND PERFORMING ARTS

Scholarship for students pursuing a degree or training full time in the visual or performing arts. Scholarship funding must be applied to tuition at a two- or four-year college, university, or an accredited community college, technical or trade school in an arts-related field.

Academic Fields/Career Goals: Arts; Performing Arts.

Award: Scholarship for use in freshman, sophomore, junior, or senior years; not renewable. *Number:* 1. *Amount:* $5000.

Eligibility Requirements: Applicant must be enrolled or expecting to enroll full-time at a two-year or four-year or technical institution or university. Applicant or parent of applicant must be member of Service Employees International Union. Available to U.S. citizens.

Application Requirements: Application, essay, transcript, 6 copies of a single original creative work. *Deadline:* March 1.

Contact: c/o Scholarship Program Administrators, Inc.
Service Employees International Union (SEIU)
PO Box 23737
Nashville, TN 37202-3737
Phone: 615-320-3149
Fax: 615-320-3151
E-mail: info@spaprog.com

STRAIGHTFORWARD MEDIA

http://www.straightforwardmedia.com/

STRAIGHTFORWARD MEDIA ART SCHOOL SCHOLARSHIP

Award of $500 for students pursuing a degree in any art-related field. May be used for full- or part-time study. Scholarship is awarded four times per year. Deadlines: November 30, February 28, May 31, and August 31. For more information, visit web site http://www.straightforwardmedia.com/art/form.php.

Academic Fields/Career Goals: Arts.

Award: Scholarship for use in freshman, sophomore, junior, or senior years; not renewable. *Number:* 4. *Amount:* $500.

Eligibility Requirements: Applicant must be enrolled or expecting to enroll full- or part-time at a two-year or four-year or technical institution or university. Available to U.S. and non-U.S. citizens.

Application Requirements: Essay. *Deadline:* varies.

Contact: Scholarship Committee
StraightForward Media
508 7th Street
Suite 202
Rapid City, SD 57701
Phone: 605-348-3042

TELETOON

http://www.teletoon.com/

TELETOON ANIMATION SCHOLARSHIP

Scholarship competition created by TELETOON to encourage creative, original, and imaginative animation by supporting Canadians studying in the animation field or intending to pursue studies in animation. One-time award. Must submit portfolio.

Academic Fields/Career Goals: Arts; Filmmaking/Video.

Award: Scholarship for use in freshman, sophomore, junior, senior, graduate, or postgraduate years; not renewable. *Number:* 9. *Amount:* $5000–$10,000.

Eligibility Requirements: Applicant must be enrolled or expecting to enroll full-time at a two-year or four-year or technical institution or university and resident of Alberta, British Columbia, Manitoba, New Brunswick, Newfoundland, North West Territories, Nova Scotia, Ontario, Prince Edward Island, Quebec, or Saskatchewan. Available to Canadian citizens.

Application Requirements: Application, driver's license, essay, portfolio, transcript, 5-minute film. *Deadline:* June 15.

Contact: Denise Vaughan, Senior Coordinator, Public Relations
Teletoon
BCE Place, 181 Bay Street
PO Box 787
Toronto, ON M5J 2T3
Canada
Phone: 416-956-2060
Fax: 416-956-2070
E-mail: denisev@teletoon.com

TEXAS ARTS AND CRAFTS EDUCATIONAL FOUNDATION

http://www.tacef.org/

EMERGING TEXAS ARTIST SCHOLARSHIP

Scholarships for art work offered to students attending colleges or universities in Texas either part-time or full-time. Scholarships are awarded as prizes in a juried art exhibit at the Texas State Arts and Crafts Fair. From 8 to 12 awards are granted annually.

Academic Fields/Career Goals: Arts.

Award: Scholarship for use in freshman, sophomore, junior, senior, graduate, or postgraduate years; not renewable. *Number:* 8–12. *Amount:* $500–$5000.

Eligibility Requirements: Applicant must be enrolled or expecting to enroll full- or part-time at a two-year or four-year or technical institution or university; studying in Texas and must have an interest in art. Available to U.S. citizens.

Application Requirements: Application, applicant must enter a contest, references, 4 color slides of work. *Deadline:* March 15.

Contact: Debbie Luce, Assistant Director
Texas Arts and Crafts Educational Foundation
4000 River Side Drive East
Kerrville, TX 78028
Phone: 830-896-5711
Fax: 830-896-5569
E-mail: info@tacef.org

UNICO NATIONAL INC.

http://www.unico.org/

THEODORE MAZZA SCHOLARSHIP
• *See page 103*

UNITARIAN UNIVERSALIST ASSOCIATION

http://www.uua.org/

MARION BARR STANFIELD ART SCHOLARSHIP

Scholarship for graduate or undergraduate Unitarian Universalist students preparing for a career in fine arts. Eligibility is limited to those in the study of painting, drawing, photography, and/or sculpture. Performing arts majors are not eligible.

Academic Fields/Career Goals: Arts; Photojournalism/Photography.

Award: Scholarship for use in freshman, sophomore, junior, senior, or graduate years; not renewable. *Number:* varies. *Amount:* varies.

Eligibility Requirements: Applicant must be Unitarian Universalist and enrolled or expecting to enroll full-time at a four-year institution or university. Available to U.S. citizens.

Application Requirements: Application, essay, financial need analysis, portfolio, references, list of works, personal tax information. *Deadline:* varies.

Contact: Ms. Hillary Goodridge, Program Director
Unitarian Universalist Association
PO Box 301149
Boston, MA 02130
Phone: 617-971-9600
Fax: 617-971-0029
E-mail: uufp@aol.com

PAULY D'ORLANDO MEMORIAL ART SCHOLARSHIP

Scholarship for graduate or undergraduate students preparing for a career in fine arts. Student must be studying painting, drawing, photography, and/or sculpture. Performing arts majors are not eligible.

Academic Fields/Career Goals: Arts; Photojournalism/Photography.

Award: Scholarship for use in freshman, sophomore, junior, senior, or graduate years; not renewable. *Number:* varies. *Amount:* varies.

Eligibility Requirements: Applicant must be Unitarian Universalist and enrolled or expecting to enroll full-time at a four-year institution or university. Available to U.S. citizens.

Application Requirements: Application, essay, financial need analysis, references, list of works, personal tax information. *Deadline:* varies.

Contact: Ms. Hillary Goodridge, Program Director
Unitarian Universalist Association
PO Box 301149
Boston, MA 02130
Phone: 617-971-9600
Fax: 617-971-0029
E-mail: uufp@aol.com

STANFIELD AND D'ORLANDO ART SCHOLARSHIP

Scholarships for both master's and undergraduate Unitarian Universalist students studying the fields of art and law.

Academic Fields/Career Goals: Arts; Law/Legal Services.

Award: Scholarship for use in freshman, sophomore, junior, senior, or graduate years; not renewable. *Number:* varies. *Amount:* varies.

Eligibility Requirements: Applicant must be Unitarian Universalist and enrolled or expecting to enroll full- or part-time at a four-year institution or university. Available to U.S. citizens.

Application Requirements: Application. *Deadline:* February 15.

Contact: Ms. Hillary Goodridge, Program Director
Unitarian Universalist Association
PO Box 301149
Boston, MA 02130
Phone: 617-971-9600
Fax: 617-971-0029
E-mail: uufp@aol.com

UNITED NEGRO COLLEGE FUND

http://www.uncf.org/

HOUSTON SYMPHONY/TOP LADIES SCHOLARSHIP

Scholarship awarded to Iowa residents attending a UNCF member college or university and majoring in art. Minimum 2.5 GPA required. Prospective applicants should complete the general application found at web site http://www.uncf.org.

Academic Fields/Career Goals: Arts.

Award: Scholarship for use in freshman, sophomore, junior, or senior years; not renewable. *Number:* 1. *Amount:* varies.

Eligibility Requirements: Applicant must be Black (non-Hispanic); enrolled or expecting to enroll full- or part-time at a four-year institution or university and resident of Iowa. Applicant must have 2.5 GPA or higher. Available to U.S. citizens.

Application Requirements: Application, financial need analysis.

Contact: Director, Program Services
United Negro College Fund
8260 Willow Oaks Corporate Drive
PO Box 10444
Fairfax, VA 22031-8044
Phone: 800-331-2244
E-mail: rebecca.bennett@uncf.org

MAE MAXEY MEMORIAL SCHOLARSHIP

Award for students with an interest in poetry attending a UNCF member college or university. Minimum 2.5 GPA required. The scholarship value ranges from $1000 to $5000.

Academic Fields/Career Goals: Arts; Literature/English/Writing.

Award: Scholarship for use in freshman, sophomore, junior, or senior years; not renewable. *Number:* varies. *Amount:* $1000–$5000.

Eligibility Requirements: Applicant must be Black (non-Hispanic) and enrolled or expecting to enroll full- or part-time at a four-year institution or university. Applicant must have 2.5 GPA or higher. Available to U.S. and non-U.S. citizens.

Application Requirements: Application, financial need analysis.

Contact: Director, Program Services
United Negro College Fund
8260 Willow Oaks Corporate Drive
PO Box 10444
Fairfax, VA 22031-8044
Phone: 800-331-2244
E-mail: rebecca.bennett@uncf.org

OSSIE DAVIS ENDOWMENT SCHOLARSHIP

Scholarship designed for African American incoming freshman attending a four-year historically black college or university. The student must also be willing to use artistic activism to proactively address the concerns of humanity. Eligible majors include African American studies, communications, fine arts, humanities, performing arts, political science, social sciences, theater arts/drama. Minimum 3.0 GPA required.

Academic Fields/Career Goals: Arts; Communications; Humanities; Performing Arts; Political Science; Social Sciences.

Award: Scholarship for use in freshman year; not renewable. *Amount:* up to $6800.

Eligibility Requirements: Applicant must be Black (non-Hispanic); high school student and planning to enroll or expecting to enroll full-time at a four-year institution or university. Applicant must have 3.0 GPA or higher.

Application Requirements: *Deadline:* May 31.

Contact: Director, Program Services
United Negro College Fund
8260 Willow Oaks Corporate Drive
PO Box 10444
Fairfax, VA 22031-8044
Phone: 800-331-2244
E-mail: rebecca.bennett@uncf.org

WILLIAM & NORA LICTENBURG SCHOLARSHIP

Scholarship for students attending UNCF member colleges and universities and majoring in Art. Minimum 2.5 GPA required. For more information see Website: http://www.uncf.org/forstudents/scholarship.asp.

Academic Fields/Career Goals: Arts.

Award: Scholarship for use in senior year.

Eligibility Requirements: Applicant must be Black (non-Hispanic) and enrolled or expecting to enroll at a four-year institution. Applicant must have 2.5 GPA or higher.

Application Requirements: Application.

Contact: Director, Program Services
United Negro College Fund
8260 Willow Oaks Corporate Drive
PO Box 10444
Fairfax, VA 22031-8044
Phone: 800-331-2244
E-mail: rebecca.bennett@uncf.org

U.S. FISH AND WILDLIFE SERVICE

http://www.fws.gov/duckstamps

FEDERAL JUNIOR DUCK STAMP CONSERVATION AND DESIGN COMPETITION

Any student in grades K–12, public, private, or home schooled, may enter this competiti... all 50 ... ia, and U.S. Territories. Teache... ...ided to teach conservation issue... ...c rendering of one of the North... ...nters it into their state's Junior... ...e Best of Show to be sent to the... ...dlines: South Carolina, January... ...tes and territories March 15. Fu... ...kstamps.fws.gov.

Academic Fie...

Award: Prize... ...ble. *Number:* 3. *Amount:* $100...

Eligibility R... ... school student; planning to en... ...e at a two-year or four-year inst... ...Available to U.S. citizens.

Application F... ...st enter a contest. *Deadline:* varies.

Contact: Elizabeth Jackson, Program Coordinator
U.S. Fish and Wildlife Service
4401 North Fairfax Drive, Suite 4073
Arlington, VA 22203-1622
Phone: 703-358-2073
E-mail: elizabeth_jackson@fws.gov

VARIAZIONE MIXED MEDIA ARTISTS' COLLECTIVE

http://www.zneart.com/

LEARNING SCHOLARSHIP

Scholarship available to all high school seniors, undergraduate and graduate students, as well as artists who are not enrolled full-time, but enrolled in art classes in order to expand their skills.

Academic Fields/Career Goals: Arts.

Award: Scholarship for use in freshman, sophomore, junior, senior, or graduate years; not renewable. *Number:* varies. *Amount:* $100.

Eligibility Requirements: Applicant must be enrolled or expecting to enroll full- or part-time at a two-year or four-year or technical institution or university and must have an interest in art. Available to U.S. citizens.

Application Requirements: Application, applicant must enter a contest, driver's license, financial need analysis, collage work. *Deadline:* April 15.

Contact: Scholarship Coordinator
VariaZioNE Mixed Media Artists' Collective
1152 Crellin Road
Pleasanton, CA 94566

WOMEN'S JEWELRY ASSOCIATION

http://www.womensjewelry.org/

WJA SCHOLARSHIP PROGRAM

Program is designed to encourage talented female students and help support their studies in the jewelry field. Applicants required to submit original drawings of their jewelry designs. Visit http://www.womensjewelry.org for current information.

Academic Fields/Career Goals: Arts; Trade/Technical Specialties.

Award: Scholarship for use in freshman, sophomore, junior, senior, graduate, or postgraduate years; not renewable. *Number:* 1. *Amount:* $500–$5000.

Eligibility Requirements: Applicant must be enrolled or expecting to enroll full- or part-time at a two-year or four-year or technical institution or university; female and must have an interest in art. Available to U.S. and non-U.S. citizens.

Application Requirements: Application, essay, portfolio. *Deadline:* May 1.

Contact: Scholarship Committee
Women's Jewelry Association
7000 West Southwest Highway, Suite 202
Chicago Ridge, IL 60415
Phone: 708-361-6266
Fax: 708-361-6166
E-mail: info@womensjewelry.org

WORLDSTUDIO FOUNDATION

http://www.aiga.org/

WORLDSTUDIO AIGA SCHOLARSHIPS

Scholarships available for minority and economically disadvantaged students who are pursuing degrees in the design/arts disciplines in colleges and universities in the United States.

Academic Fields/Career Goals: Arts; Graphics/Graphic Arts/Printing.

Award: Scholarship for use in freshman, sophomore, junior, senior, or graduate years; not renewable. *Number:* 10–25. *Amount:* $1000–$5000.

Eligibility Requirements: Applicant must be enrolled or expecting to enroll full-time at a two-year or four-year or technical institution or university. Available to U.S. citizens.

Application Requirements: Application, essay, portfolio, references, transcript. *Deadline:* April 1.

Contact: Tiia Schurig, Web production manager
Worldstudio Foundation
164 Fifth Avenue
New York, NY 10010
Phone: 212-807-1990
Fax: 212-807-1799
E-mail: scholarship@aiga.org

ASIAN STUDIES

ASSOCIATION OF TEACHERS OF JAPANESE BRIDGING CLEARINGHOUSE FOR STUDY ABROAD IN JAPAN

http://www.colorado.edu/ealc/atj

BRIDGING SCHOLARSHIP FOR STUDY ABROAD IN JAPAN
• See page 104

CIEE: COUNCIL ON INTERNATIONAL EDUCATIONAL EXCHANGE

http://www.ciee.org/

U.S. DEPARTMENT OF EDUCATION FULBRIGHT-HAYS PROJECT ABROAD SCHOLARSHIP FOR PROGRAMS IN CHINA

Scholarships offered to students who are participating in a CIEE Chinese language programs in China or Taiwan. Must be a U.S. citizen enrolled in a CIEE program. Students must have completed the equivalent of two years study in Chinese language (documented). Deadlines: April 1 and November 1. There is also a return requirement for scholarship awardees to submit a program report and evaluation.

Academic Fields/Career Goals: Asian Studies; Education.

Award: Scholarship for use in junior or senior years; not renewable. *Number:* 1–20. *Amount:* $1000–$12,000.

Eligibility Requirements: Applicant must be enrolled or expecting to enroll full-time at a four-year institution or university and must have an interest in foreign language. Applicant must have 3.0 GPA or higher. Available to U.S. citizens.

Application Requirements: Application, essay, financial need analysis, references, transcript, copy of passport or birth certificate. *Deadline:* varies.

Contact: CIEE Scholarship Committee
CIEE: Council on International Educational Exchange
300 Fore Street
Portland, ME 04101
Phone: 800-407-8839
E-mail: studyinfo@ciee.org

JAPANESE GOVERNMENT/THE MONBUSHO SCHOLARSHIP PROGRAM

http://www.la.us.emb-japan.go.jp/

JAPANESE STUDIES SCHOLARSHIP
• See page 106

UNITED NEGRO COLLEGE FUND

http://www.uncf.org/

GENERAL MILLS CORPORATE SCHOLARS AWARD
• See page 73

WHOMENTORS.COM, INC.

http://www.WHOmentors.com/

ACCREDITED REPRESENTATIVE (FULL)
• See page 56

AUDIOLOGY

NATIONAL AMBUCS INC.

http://www.ambucs.org/

AMBUCS SCHOLARS-SCHOLARSHIPS FOR THERAPISTS

Scholarships are open to students who are U.S. citizens at a junior level or above in college. Must be enrolled in an accredited program by the appropriate health therapy profession authority in physical therapy, occupational therapy, speech-language pathology, or audiology and must demonstrate a financial need. Application available on web site at http://www.ambucs.com. Paper applications are not accepted.

Academic Fields/Career Goals: Audiology; Therapy/Rehabilitation.

Award: Scholarship for use in junior, senior, graduate, or postgraduate years; not renewable. *Number:* 275. *Amount:* $500–$3000.

Eligibility Requirements: Applicant must be enrolled or expecting to enroll full-time at a four-year institution or university. Available to U.S. citizens.

Application Requirements: Application, essay, financial need analysis, enrollment certification form. *Deadline:* April 15.

Contact: Janice Blankenship, Scholarship Coordinator
National AMBUCS Inc.
PO Box 5127
High Point, NC 27262
Phone: 336-852-0052 Ext. 10
Fax: 336-852-6830
E-mail: janiceb@ambucs.org

AVIATION/AEROSPACE

AACE INTERNATIONAL

http://www.aacei.org/

AACE INTERNATIONAL COMPETITIVE SCHOLARSHIP
• See page 99

AHS INTERNATIONAL—THE VERTICAL FLIGHT SOCIETY

http://www.vtol.org/

VERTICAL FLIGHT FOUNDATION SCHOLARSHIP

This award is available for undergraduate, graduate, or doctoral study in aerospace, electrical, or mechanical engineering. Applicants must have an interest in vertical flight technology.

Academic Fields/Career Goals: Aviation/Aerospace; Electrical Engineering/Electronics; Engineering-Related Technologies; Mechanical Engineering.

Award: Scholarship for use in sophomore, junior, senior, graduate, or postgraduate years; not renewable. *Number:* 10–17. *Amount:* $1500–$4000.

Eligibility Requirements: Applicant must be enrolled or expecting to enroll full-time at a four-year institution or university. Applicant must have 3.5 GPA or higher. Available to U.S. and non-U.S. citizens.

Application Requirements: Application, essay, resume, references, transcript. *Deadline:* February 1.

Contact: Ms. Kay Yosua Brackins, Deputy Director
AHS International—The Vertical Flight Society
217 North Washington Street
Alexandria, VA 22314
Phone: 703-684-6777
Fax: 703-739-9279
E-mail: kbrackins@vtol.org

AIRCRAFT ELECTRONICS ASSOCIATION EDUCATIONAL FOUNDATION

http://www.aea.net/

BENDIX/KING AVIONICS SCHOLARSHIP

Scholarship of $1000 available to high school, college, vocational, or technical school students who plan to or are attending an avionics or aircraft repair program in an accredited school.

Academic Fields/Career Goals: Aviation/Aerospace.

Award: Scholarship for use in freshman, sophomore, junior, or senior years; not renewable. *Number:* 1. *Amount:* $1000.

Eligibility Requirements: Applicant must be enrolled or expecting to enroll full- or part-time at a two-year or four-year or technical institution or university. Applicant must have 2.5 GPA or higher. Available to U.S. citizens.

Application Requirements: Application, essay, transcript. *Deadline:* February 15.

Contact: Mike Adamson, Executive Director
Aircraft Electronics Association Educational Foundation
4217 South Hocker Drive
Independence, MO 64055-0963
Phone: 816-373-6565
E-mail: info@aea.net

BUD GLOVER MEMORIAL SCHOLARSHIP

Scholarship available to high school seniors and college students who plan to attend or are attending an avionics or aircraft repair program in an accredited school.

Academic Fields/Career Goals: Aviation/Aerospace; Trade/Technical Specialties.

Award: Scholarship for use in freshman, sophomore, junior, or senior years; not renewable. *Number:* 1. *Amount:* $1000.

Eligibility Requirements: Applicant must be enrolled or expecting to enroll full- or part-time at a two-year or four-year or technical institution or university. Applicant must have 2.5 GPA or higher. Available to U.S. and Canadian citizens.

Application Requirements: Application, essay, references, test scores, transcript. *Deadline:* February 15.

Contact: Mike Adamson, Executive Director
Aircraft Electronics Association Educational Foundation
4217 South Hocker Drive
Independence, MO 64055-0963
Phone: 816-373-6565
E-mail: info@aea.net

CHUCK PEACOCK MEMORIAL SCHOLARSHIP

Scholarship of $1000 for high school seniors or college students who plan to attend or are attending an aviation management program in an accredited school.

Academic Fields/Career Goals: Aviation/Aerospace.

Award: Scholarship for use in freshman, sophomore, junior, or senior years; not renewable. *Number:* 1. *Amount:* $1000.

Eligibility Requirements: Applicant must be enrolled or expecting to enroll full- or part-time at a two-year or four-year or technical institution or university. Applicant must have 2.5 GPA or higher. Available to U.S. citizens.

Application Requirements: Application, essay, transcript. *Deadline:* February 15.

Contact: Mike Adamson, Executive Director
Aircraft Electronics Association Educational Foundation
4217 South Hocker Drive
Independence, MO 64055-0963
Phone: 816-373-6565
E-mail: info@aea.net

DAVID ARVER MEMORIAL SCHOLARSHIP

Scholarship of $1000 available to high school seniors and college students who plan to or are attending an avionics or aircraft repair program in an accredited school. Restricted to use for study in the following states: Iowa, Illinois, Indiana, Kansas, Michigan, Minnesota, Mississippi, North Dakota, Nebraska, South Dakota, and Wisconsin. See web site for details http://www.aea.net/scholarship.

Academic Fields/Career Goals: Aviation/Aerospace.

Award: Scholarship for use in freshman, sophomore, junior, or senior years; not renewable. *Number:* 1. *Amount:* $1000.

Eligibility Requirements: Applicant must be enrolled or expecting to enroll full- or part-time at a two-year or four-year or technical institution or university. Applicant must have 2.5 GPA or higher. Available to U.S. and non-U.S. citizens.

Application Requirements: Application, essay, references, test scores, transcript. *Deadline:* February 15.

Contact: Mike Adamson, Executive Director
Aircraft Electronics Association Educational Foundation
4217 South Hocker Drive
Independence, MO 64055-0963
Phone: 816-373-6565
E-mail: info@aea.net

DUTCH AND GINGER ARVER SCHOLARSHIP

Scholarship available to high school seniors or college students who plan to attend or are attending an avionics or aircraft repair program in an accredited school.

Academic Fields/Career Goals: Aviation/Aerospace; Trade/Technical Specialties.

Award: Scholarship for use in freshman, sophomore, junior, or senior years; not renewable. *Number:* 1. *Amount:* $1000.

Eligibility Requirements: Applicant must be enrolled or expecting to enroll full- or part-time at a two-year or four-year or technical institution or university. Applicant must have 2.5 GPA or higher. Available to U.S. citizens.

Application Requirements: Application, essay, references, test scores, transcript. *Deadline:* February 15.

Contact: Mike Adamson, Executive Director
Aircraft Electronics Association Educational Foundation
4217 South Hocker Drive
Independence, MO 64055-0963
Phone: 816-373-6565
E-mail: info@aea.net

FIELD AVIATION COMPANY INC. SCHOLARSHIP

Scholarship for high school seniors and college students who plan to or are attending an avionics or aircraft repair program in an accredited college/university. The educational institution must be located in Canada.

Academic Fields/Career Goals: Aviation/Aerospace.

Award: Scholarship for use in freshman, sophomore, junior, or senior years; not renewable. *Number:* 1. *Amount:* $1000.

Eligibility Requirements: Applicant must be enrolled or expecting to enroll full-time at a two-year or four-year or technical institution or university. Applicant must have 2.5 GPA or higher. Available to Canadian citizens.

Application Requirements: Application, essay, references, test scores, transcript. *Deadline:* February 15.

Contact: Mike Adamson, Executive Director
Aircraft Electronics Association Educational Foundation
4217 South Hocker Drive
Independence, MO 64055-0963
Phone: 816-373-6565
E-mail: info@aea.net

GARMIN-JERRY SMITH MEMORIAL SCHOLARSHIP

Scholarship available for high school, college, or vocational or technical school students who plan to attend or are attending an avionics or aircraft repair program in an accredited vocational or technical school.

Academic Fields/Career Goals: Aviation/Aerospace; Trade/Technical Specialties.

Award: Scholarship for use in freshman, sophomore, junior, or senior years; not renewable. *Number:* 1. *Amount:* $1000.

Eligibility Requirements: Applicant must be enrolled or expecting to enroll full-time at a two-year or four-year or technical institution or university. Applicant must have 2.5 GPA or higher. Available to U.S. and non-U.S. citizens.

Application Requirements: Application, essay, transcript. *Deadline:* February 15.

Contact: Mike Adamson, Executive Director
Aircraft Electronics Association Educational Foundation
4217 South Hocker Drive
Independence, MO 64055-0963
Phone: 816-373-6565
E-mail: info@aea.net

GARMIN SCHOLARSHIP

Scholarship available to high school seniors and college students who plan to attend or are attending an avionics or aircraft repair program in an accredited school.

Academic Fields/Career Goals: Aviation/Aerospace; Trade/Technical Specialties.

Award: Scholarship for use in freshman, sophomore, junior, or senior years; not renewable. *Number:* 1. *Amount:* $2000.

Eligibility Requirements: Applicant must be enrolled or expecting to enroll full- or part-time at a two-year or four-year or technical institution or university. Applicant must have 2.5 GPA or higher. Available to U.S. citizens.

Application Requirements: Application, essay, references, test scores, transcript. *Deadline:* February 15.

Contact: Mike Adamson, Executive Director
Aircraft Electronics Association Educational Foundation
4217 South Hocker Drive
Independence, MO 64055-0963
Phone: 816-373-6565
E-mail: info@aea.net

JOHNNY DAVIS MEMORIAL SCHOLARSHIP

Scholarship of $1000 available to high school seniors and college students who plan to or are attending an avionics or aircraft repair program in an accredited school.

Academic Fields/Career Goals: Aviation/Aerospace.

Award: Scholarship for use in freshman, sophomore, junior, or senior years; not renewable. *Number:* 1. *Amount:* $1000.

Eligibility Requirements: Applicant must be enrolled or expecting to enroll full- or part-time at a two-year or four-year or technical institution or university. Applicant must have 2.5 GPA or higher. Available to U.S. citizens.

Application Requirements: Application, essay, transcript. *Deadline:* February 15.

Contact: Mike Adamson, Executive Director
Aircraft Electronics Association Educational Foundation
4217 South Hocker Drive
Independence, MO 64055-0963
Phone: 816-373-6565
E-mail: info@aea.net

L-3 AVIONICS SYSTEMS SCHOLARSHIP

Scholarship of $2500 available to high school seniors and college students who plan to attend or are attending an avionics or aircraft repair program in an accredited school.

Academic Fields/Career Goals: Aviation/Aerospace.

Award: Scholarship for use in freshman, sophomore, junior, or senior years; not renewable. *Number:* 1. *Amount:* $2500.

Eligibility Requirements: Applicant must be enrolled or expecting to enroll full- or part-time at a two-year or four-year or technical institution or university. Applicant must have 2.5 GPA or higher. Available to U.S. citizens.

Application Requirements: Application, essay, transcript. *Deadline:* February 15.

Contact: Mike Adamson, Executive Director
Aircraft Electronics Association Educational Foundation
4217 South Hocker Drive
Independence, MO 64055-0963
Phone: 816-373-6565
E-mail: info@aea.net

LEE TARBOX MEMORIAL SCHOLARSHIP

Scholarship available to high school seniors or college students who plan to attend or are attending an avionics or aircraft repair program in an accredited school.

Academic Fields/Career Goals: Aviation/Aerospace; Trade/Technical Specialties.

Award: Scholarship for use in freshman, sophomore, junior, or senior years; not renewable. *Number:* 1. *Amount:* $2500.

Eligibility Requirements: Applicant must be enrolled or expecting to enroll full- or part-time at a two-year or four-year or technical institution or university. Applicant must have 2.5 GPA or higher. Available to U.S. citizens.

Application Requirements: Application, essay, references, test scores, transcript. *Deadline:* February 15.

Contact: Mike Adamson, Executive Director
Aircraft Electronics Association Educational Foundation
4217 South Hocker Drive
Independence, MO 64055-0963
Phone: 816-373-6565
E-mail: info@aea.net

LOWELL GAYLOR MEMORIAL SCHOLARSHIP

Scholarship for high school seniors and college students who plan to attend or are attending an avionics or aircraft repair program in an accredited school. Minimum 2.5 GPA required.

Academic Fields/Career Goals: Aviation/Aerospace; Trade/Technical Specialties.

Award: Scholarship for use in freshman, sophomore, junior, or senior years; not renewable. *Number:* 1. *Amount:* $1000.

Eligibility Requirements: Applicant must be enrolled or expecting to enroll full- or part-time at a two-year or four-year or technical institution or university. Applicant must have 2.5 GPA or higher. Available to U.S. and non-U.S. citizens.

Application Requirements: Application, essay, references, test scores, transcript. *Deadline:* February 15.

Contact: Mike Adamson, Executive Director
Aircraft Electronics Association Educational Foundation
4217 South Hocker Drive
Independence, MO 64055-0963
Phone: 816-373-6565
E-mail: info@aea.net

MID-CONTINENT INSTRUMENT SCHOLARSHIP

Scholarship available to high school seniors or college students who plan to attend or are attending an avionics or aircraft repair program in an accredited school.

Academic Fields/Career Goals: Aviation/Aerospace; Trade/Technical Specialties.

Award: Scholarship for use in freshman, sophomore, junior, or senior years; not renewable. *Number:* 1. *Amount:* $1000.

Eligibility Requirements: Applicant must be enrolled or expecting to enroll full- or part-time at a two-year or four-year or technical institution or university. Applicant must have 2.5 GPA or higher. Available to U.S. citizens.

Application Requirements: Application, essay, references, test scores, transcript. *Deadline:* February 15.

Contact: Mike Adamson, Executive Director
Aircraft Electronics Association Educational Foundation
4217 South Hocker Drive
Independence, MO 64055-0963
Phone: 816-373-6565
E-mail: info@aea.net

MONTE R. MITCHELL GLOBAL SCHOLARSHIP

Scholarship of $1000 available to European students pursuing a degree in aviation maintenance technology, avionics, or aircraft repair at an accredited school located in Europe or the United States.

Academic Fields/Career Goals: Aviation/Aerospace.

Award: Scholarship for use in freshman, sophomore, junior, or senior years; not renewable. *Number:* 1. *Amount:* $1000.

Eligibility Requirements: Applicant must be enrolled or expecting to enroll full- or part-time at a two-year or four-year or technical institution or university. Applicant must have 2.5 GPA or higher. Available to citizens of countries other than the U.S. or Canada.

Application Requirements: Application, essay, references, transcript. *Deadline:* February 15.

Contact: Mike Adamson, Executive Director
Aircraft Electronics Association Educational Foundation
4217 South Hocker Drive
Independence, MO 64055-0963
Phone: 816-373-6565
E-mail: info@aea.net

SPORTY'S PILOT SHOP/CINCINNATI AVIONICS

Scholarship of $2000 available to high school seniors and college students who plan to attend or are attending an avionics or aircraft repair program in an accredited school.

Academic Fields/Career Goals: Aviation/Aerospace.

Award: Scholarship for use in freshman, sophomore, junior, or senior years; not renewable. *Number:* 1. *Amount:* $2000.

Eligibility Requirements: Applicant must be enrolled or expecting to enroll full- or part-time at a two-year or four-year or technical institution or university. Applicant must have 2.5 GPA or higher. Available to U.S. citizens.

Application Requirements: Application, essay, references, test scores, transcript. *Deadline:* February 15.

Contact: Mike Adamson, Executive Director
Aircraft Electronics Association Educational Foundation
4217 South Hocker Drive
Independence, MO 64055-0963
Phone: 816-373-6565
E-mail: info@aea.net

AIRPORT MINORITY ADVISORY COUNCIL EDUCATIONAL AND SCHOLARSHIP PROGRAM

http://www.amac-org.com/

AMACESP STUDENT SCHOLARSHIPS

Applicant must be seeking a BS or BA with interest and desire to pursue a career in the aviation/airport industry and seeking a degree in Aviation, Business Administration, Accounting, Architecture, Engineering or Finance and admitted by an accredited school or university for the current school term in which you are applying for a scholarship. Demonstration of a cumulative 3.0 GPA and involvement in community activities and extracurricular activities. Applicants must be a U.S. Citizen. A commitment to involvement in furthering the mission of the Airport Minority Advisory Council (AMAC) by participating in the AMAC Student Program. AMAC Member Scholarship Awards are offered to Airport Minority Advisory Council (AMAC) members, their spouses, and their children. The AMAC Aviation & Professional Development Committee grant four $2,000 scholarships each year to a number of students who are enrolled in an aviation related program and have a grade point average 3.0 or higher.

Academic Fields/Career Goals: Aviation/Aerospace.

Award: Scholarship for use in sophomore, junior, or senior years; not renewable. *Number:* 1–3. *Amount:* $2000.

Eligibility Requirements: Applicant must be enrolled or expecting to enroll full-time at a four-year institution or university. Applicant must have 3.0 GPA or higher. Available to U.S. citizens.

Application Requirements: Application, essay, references, transcript. *Deadline:* continuous.

Contact: Mr. Gene Roth, Executive Director
Airport Minority Advisory Council Educational and
Scholarship Program
2345 Crystal Drive, Suite 902
Arlington, VA 22202
Phone: 703-414-2622 Ext. 1
Fax: 703-414-2686
E-mail: gene.roth@amac-org.com

AIRPORTS COUNCIL INTERNATIONAL-NORTH AMERICA

http://www.aci-na.org/

ACI-NA AIRPORT COMMISSIONER'S SCHOLARSHIP

Up to 3 scholarships per fall and spring semesters may be awarded in amounts up to $2500 per recipient to an undergraduate or graduate student. Applicant must be majoring in airport management or airport administration. Deadlines: December 15 and April 15.

Academic Fields/Career Goals: Aviation/Aerospace.

Award: Scholarship for use in freshman, sophomore, junior, senior, or graduate years; not renewable. *Number:* up to 3. *Amount:* up to $2500.

Eligibility Requirements: Applicant must be enrolled or expecting to enroll full-time at a four-year institution or university. Applicant must have 3.0 GPA or higher. Available to U.S. and Canadian citizens.

Application Requirements: Application, essay, resume, references, transcript. *Deadline:* varies.

Contact: Scholarship Committee
Airports Council International-North America
1775 K Street NW, Suite 500
Washington, DC 20006
Phone: 202-293-8500
Fax: 202-331-1362

AIR TRAFFIC CONTROL ASSOCIATION INC.

http://www.atca.org/

AIR TRAFFIC CONTROL ASSOCIATION SCHOLARSHIP

Scholarships for students in programs leading to a bachelor's degree or higher in aviation-related courses of study, and for full-time employees engaged in advanced study to improve their skills in air traffic control or aviation. Visit web site for additional information http://www.atca.org.

Academic Fields/Career Goals: Aviation/Aerospace; Engineering/Technology.

Award: Scholarship for use in freshman, sophomore, junior, senior, or graduate years; not renewable. *Number:* 7–12. *Amount:* $600–$2500.

Eligibility Requirements: Applicant must be enrolled or expecting to enroll full- or part-time at a four-year institution or university and must have an interest in aviation. Applicant or parent of applicant must have employment or volunteer experience in air traffic control. Available to U.S. citizens.

Application Requirements: Application, driver's license, essay, financial need analysis, resume, references, transcript. *Deadline:* May 1.

Contact: Miguel Vazquez, Director
Air Traffic Control Association Inc.
1101 King Street, Suite 300
Alexandria, VA 22201-2302
Phone: 703-522-5717
Fax: 703-527-7251
E-mail: info@atca.org

ALASKAN AVIATION SAFETY FOUNDATION

http://www.aasfonline.com/

ALASKAN AVIATION SAFETY FOUNDATION MEMORIAL SCHOLARSHIP FUND

Scholarships for undergraduate or graduate study in aviation. Must be a resident of Alaska and a U.S. citizen. Write for deadlines and details.

Academic Fields/Career Goals: Aviation/Aerospace.

Award: Scholarship for use in freshman, sophomore, junior, senior, or graduate years; not renewable. *Number:* 1–3. *Amount:* $500–$750.

Eligibility Requirements: Applicant must be enrolled or expecting to enroll full- or part-time at a two-year or four-year or technical institution or university; resident of Alaska and must have an interest in aviation. Available to U.S. citizens.

Application Requirements: Application, driver's license, financial need analysis, references, test scores, transcript. *Deadline:* May 30.

Contact: Scholarship Committee
Alaskan Aviation Safety Foundation
c/o Aviation Technology Division UAA, 2811 Merril Field Drive
Anchorage, AK 99501
Phone: 907-243-7237

AMERICAN ASSOCIATION OF AIRPORT EXECUTIVES-SOUTHWEST CHAPTER

http://www.swaaae.org/

SWAAAE ACADEMIC SCHOLARSHIPS

A scholarship of $1500 for students pursuing an undergraduate or graduate degree in airport management may apply annually for an academic scholarship. Applicant must attend a college in Arizona, California, Nevada, Utah, or Hawaii.

Academic Fields/Career Goals: Aviation/Aerospace.

Award: Scholarship for use in sophomore, junior, senior, or graduate years; not renewable. *Number:* 5. *Amount:* $500–$1500.

Eligibility Requirements: Applicant must be enrolled or expecting to enroll full- or part-time at a four-year institution or university and studying in Arizona, California, Hawaii, Nevada, or Utah. Available to U.S. and non-U.S. citizens.

Application Requirements: Application. *Deadline:* September 29.

Contact: Charles Mangum, Scholarship Committee
American Association of Airport Executives-Southwest Chapter
8565 North Sand Dune Place
Tucson, AZ 85743
Phone: 520-682-9565
E-mail: cman2122@comcast.net

AMERICAN INSTITUTE OF AERONAUTICS AND ASTRONAUTICS

http://www.aiaa.org/

AIAA FOUNDATION UNDERGRADUATE SCHOLARSHIP

• *See page 93*

AMERICAN SOCIETY OF NAVAL ENGINEERS

http://www.navalengineers.org/

AMERICAN SOCIETY OF NAVAL ENGINEERS SCHOLARSHIP

• *See page 93*

AOPA AIR SAFETY FOUNDATION

http://www.asf.org/

AOPA AIR SAFETY FOUNDATION/DONALD BURNSIDE MEMORIAL SCHOLARSHIP

Scholarship of $1000 given to a U.S. citizen who, without assistance, would find it difficult to obtain a college education. The recipient must be enrolled in and plan to continue a college curriculum leading to a degree in the field of aviation. Must maintain a 3.25 GPA.

Academic Fields/Career Goals: Aviation/Aerospace.

Award: Scholarship for use in junior or senior years; not renewable. *Number:* 1. *Amount:* $1000.

Eligibility Requirements: Applicant must be enrolled or expecting to enroll full- or part-time at a four-year institution or university. Available to U.S. citizens.

Application Requirements: Essay, self-addressed stamped envelope, transcript, original and 7 copies of entire application package. *Deadline:* March 31.

Contact: Dr. Mark Sherman, Scholarship Committee
AOPA Air Safety Foundation
Farmingdale State College, 107 Lupton Hall, 2350
Broadhollow Road
Farmingdale, NY 11735
Phone: 631-420-2308

AOPA AIR SAFETY FOUNDATION/MCALLISTER MEMORIAL SCHOLARSHIP

One-time scholarship of $1000 to U.S. citizens who would find it difficult to obtain a college education without assistance. The recipient must be enrolled in and plan to continue a college curriculum leading to a degree in the field of aviation. Must maintain a 3.25 GPA.

Academic Fields/Career Goals: Aviation/Aerospace.

Award: Scholarship for use in junior or senior years; not renewable. *Number:* 1. *Amount:* $1000.

Eligibility Requirements: Applicant must be enrolled or expecting to enroll full- or part-time at a four-year institution or university and must have an interest in aviation. Available to U.S. citizens.

Application Requirements: Essay, self-addressed stamped envelope, transcript, original and 7 copies of entire application packet. *Deadline:* March 31.

Contact: Dr. Mark Sherman, Scholarship Committee
AOPA Air Safety Foundation
Farmingdale State College, 107 Lupton Hall, 2350
Broadhollow Road
Farmingdale, NY 11735
Phone: 631-420-2308

ARMED FORCES COMMUNICATIONS AND ELECTRONICS ASSOCIATION, EDUCATIONAL FOUNDATION

http://www.afcea.org/education/scholarships

ARMED FORCES COMMUNICATIONS AND ELECTRONICS ASSOCIATION GENERAL EMMETT PAIGE SCHOLARSHIP

Scholarships of $2000 each will be awarded to persons on active duty in the uniformed military services, to veterans, and to their spouses or dependents, who are currently enrolled full-time in an eligible degree program at an accredited four-year college or university in the United States. Candidate must be a U.S. citizen, majoring in the C4I-related fields. Veterans attending college as freshmen are eligible to apply; all others must be at least sophomores.

Academic Fields/Career Goals: Aviation/Aerospace; Chemical Engineering; Communications; Computer Science/Data Processing; Electrical Engineering/Electronics; Engineering/Technology; Engineering-Related Technologies; International Studies; Mathematics; Physical Sciences.

Award: Scholarship for use in freshman, sophomore, or junior years; not renewable. *Number:* 8–12. *Amount:* $2000.

Eligibility Requirements: Applicant must be enrolled or expecting to enroll full-time at a four-year institution or university. Applicant must have 3.0 GPA or higher. Available to U.S. citizens. Applicant must have general military experience.

Application Requirements: Application, references, transcript. *Deadline:* March 1.

Contact: Ms. Norma Corrales, Director, Scholarships & Awards
Program
Armed Forces Communications and Electronics Association,
Educational Foundation
4400 Fair Lakes Court
Fairfax, VA 22015
Phone: 703-631-6149
E-mail: scholarship@afcea.org

ARMED FORCES COMMUNICATIONS AND ELECTRONICS ASSOCIATION ROTC SCHOLARSHIP PROGRAM

Award for ROTC students in their sophomore or junior years enrolled in four-year accredited colleges or universities in the United States. Eligible fields of study are electronics or electrical, communications, or aerospace engineering; physics; mathematics; and computer science. Must exhibit academic excellence and potential to serve as an officer in the armed forces of the United States. Nominations are submitted by professors of military science, naval science, or aerospace studies.

Academic Fields/Career Goals: Aviation/Aerospace; Communications; Computer Science/Data Processing; Electrical Engineering/Electronics; Engineering/Technology; Engineering-Related Technologies; Foreign Language; International Studies; Mathematics; Physical Sciences.

Award: Scholarship for use in sophomore or junior years; not renewable. *Number:* 35–45. *Amount:* $2000–$4000.

Eligibility Requirements: Applicant must be enrolled or expecting to enroll full-time at a four-year institution or university. Available to U.S. citizens. Applicant must have served in the Air Force, Army, Marine Corps, or Navy.

Application Requirements: Application, references, transcript. *Deadline:* March 1.

Contact: Ms. Norma Corrales, Director, Scholarships & Awards
Program
Armed Forces Communications and Electronics Association,
Educational Foundation
4400 Fair Lakes Court
Fairfax, VA 22015
Phone: 703-631-6149
E-mail: scholarship@afcea.org

DISABLED WAR VETERANS SCHOLARSHIP

Scholarships are offered to active-duty service personnel, honorably discharged U.S. military veterans, reservists, and National Guard personnel who are disabled because of wounds received during active-duty combat service in Enduring Freedom-Afghanistan or Iraqi Freedom Operations. Candidates must be majoring in fields related to C4I, the support of U.S. intelligence, national security enterprises, or with relevance to the mission of AFCEA.

Academic Fields/Career Goals: Aviation/Aerospace; Computer Science/Data Processing; Education; Electrical Engineering/Electronics; Engineering/Technology; Mathematics; Physical Sciences.

Award: Scholarship for use in freshman, sophomore, junior, or senior years; not renewable. *Number:* 2. *Amount:* $2500.

Eligibility Requirements: Applicant must be enrolled or expecting to enroll full- or part-time at a two-year or four-year institution or university. Applicant must be hearing impaired, physically disabled, or visually impaired. Available to U.S. citizens. Applicant must have general military experience.

Application Requirements: Application, references, transcript. *Deadline:* April 1.

Contact: Miss. Norma Corrales, Director of AFCEA Educational
Foundation Scholarship Program
Armed Forces Communications and Electronics Association,
Educational Foundation
4400 Fair Lakes Parkway
Fairfax, VA 22033
Phone: 703-631-6149
E-mail: ncorrales@afcea.org

LTG DOUGLAS D. BUCHHOLZ MEMORIAL SCHOLARSHIP

Candidates must be current active enlisted soldiers assigned to Fort Gordon, Georgia, and be majoring in the following or related fields of electrical, chemical, systems or aerospace engineering, mathematics, physics, science or mathematics education, or computer science. Majors directly related to the support of U.S. Intelligence enterprises or national security with relevance to the mission of AFCEA will also be eligible.

Academic Fields/Career Goals: Aviation/Aerospace; Chemical Engineering; Computer Science/Data Processing; Electrical Engineering/Electronics; Mathematics; Physical Sciences.

Award: Scholarship for use in freshman, sophomore, junior, or senior years; not renewable. *Number:* 1. *Amount:* $2000.

Eligibility Requirements: Applicant must be enrolled or expecting to enroll full- or part-time at a two-year or four-year institution or university and resident of Georgia. Applicant must have 2.5 GPA or higher. Available to U.S. citizens. Applicant must have general military experience.

Application Requirements: Application, essay. *Deadline:* varies.

Contact: Mr. Joseph S. Yavorsky, President, AFCEA Augusta-Fort
Gordon Chapter
E-mail: president@afcea-augusta.org

WILLIAM E. "BUCK" BRAGUNIER SCHOLARSHIP FOR OUTSTANDING LEADERSHIP

Scholarships of $2,000 each will be awarded annually to one competitively selected and deserving undergraduate student attending an accredited four-year college or university in the San Diego, California geographical community.

Academic Fields/Career Goals: Aviation/Aerospace; Chemical Engineering; Communications; Computer Science/Data Processing; Electrical Engineering/Electronics; Engineering-Related Technologies; Mathematics; Physical Sciences.

Award: Scholarship for use in sophomore or junior years; not renewable. *Number:* 1. *Amount:* $2000.

Eligibility Requirements: Applicant must be enrolled or expecting to enroll full-time at a four-year institution or university and studying in California.

Application Requirements: Application, references, transcript. *Deadline:* May 1.

Contact: Ms. Norma Corrales, Director, Scholarships & Awards
Program
Armed Forces Communications and Electronics Association,
Educational Foundation
AFCEA Educational Foundation, 4400 Fair Lakes Court
Fairfax, VA 22033
Phone: 703-631-6149
E-mail: scholarship@afcea.org

ASSOCIATION OF FORMER INTELLIGENCE OFFICERS

http://www.afio.com/13_scholarships.htm

CIA UNDERGRADUATE SCHOLARSHIPS
• See page 89

ASTRONAUT SCHOLARSHIP FOUNDATION

http://www.astronautscholarship.org/

ASTRONAUT SCHOLARSHIP FOUNDATION
• See page 95

AVIATION COUNCIL OF PENNSYLVANIA

http://www.acpfly.com/

AVIATION COUNCIL OF PENNSYLVANIA SCHOLARSHIP PROGRAM

Awards for Pennsylvania residents to pursue studies at Pennsylvania institutions leading to career as professional pilot or in the fields of aviation technology or aviation management. Awards at discretion of Aviation Council of Pennsylvania. Three to four scholarships ranging from $500 to $1000. Applicants for the aviation management scholarship may attend institutions outside of Pennsylvania.

Academic Fields/Career Goals: Aviation/Aerospace.

Award: Scholarship for use in freshman, sophomore, junior, or senior years; not renewable. *Number:* 3–4. *Amount:* $500–$1000.

Eligibility Requirements: Applicant must be enrolled or expecting to enroll full- or part-time at a two-year or four-year or technical institution or university; resident of Pennsylvania; studying in Pennsylvania and must have an interest in aviation. Available to U.S. citizens.

Application Requirements: Application, financial need analysis, references, transcript. *Deadline:* varies.

Contact: Robert Rockmaker, Coordinator
Aviation Council of Pennsylvania
3111 Arcadia Avenue
Allentown, PA 18103-6903
Phone: 610-797-6911
Fax: 610-797-8238
E-mail: info@acpfly.com

AVIATION DISTRIBUTORS AND MANUFACTURERS ASSOCIATION INTERNATIONAL

http://www.adma.org/

ADMA SCHOLARSHIP

Scholarship to provide assistance to students pursuing careers in the aviation field. Those enrolled in an accredited Aviation program may be eligible.

Academic Fields/Career Goals: Aviation/Aerospace.

Award: Scholarship for use in junior or senior years; not renewable. *Number:* 1. *Amount:* up to $2000.

Eligibility Requirements: Applicant must be enrolled or expecting to enroll full-time at a two-year or four-year institution or university and must have an interest in aviation. Applicant must have 3.0 GPA or higher. Available to U.S. citizens.

Application Requirements: Application, essay, financial need analysis, references, transcript. *Deadline:* March 28.

Contact: Scholarship Committee
Aviation Distributors and Manufacturers Association
International
100 North 20th Street, Fourth Floor
Philadelphia, PA 19103-1443
Phone: 215-564-3484
Fax: 215-963-9785
E-mail: adma@fernley.com

BOY SCOUTS OF AMERICA-MUSKINGUM VALLEY COUNCIL

http://www.learning-for-life.org/

NATIONAL AVIATION EXPLORER SCHOLARSHIPS

$3000-$10,000 scholarships for aviation Explorers pursuing a career in the aviation industry. The intent of these scholarships is to identify and reward those individuals who best exemplify the qualities that lead to success in the aviation industry. Must be participant of the Learning for Life Exploring program.

Academic Fields/Career Goals: Aviation/Aerospace.

Award: Scholarship for use in freshman, sophomore, junior, or senior years; not renewable. *Number:* 5. *Amount:* $3000–$10,000.

Eligibility Requirements: Applicant must be age 18 and over; enrolled or expecting to enroll full- or part-time at a technical institution and must have an interest in aviation or leadership. Available to U.S. and non-U.S. citizens.

Application Requirements: Application, essay, references. *Deadline:* March 31.

Contact: Bill Rogers, Associate Director
Boy Scouts of America-Muskingum Valley Council
1325 West Walnut Hill Lane
PO Box 152079
Irving, TX 75015-2079
Phone: 972-580-2433
Fax: 972-580-2137
E-mail: brogers@lflmail.org

CHARLIE WELLS MEMORIAL SCHOLARSHIP FUND

http://www.wellsscholarship.com/

CHARLIE WELLS MEMORIAL AVIATION GRANT

Applicant must be enrolled in and attending school regularly, or already have a high school diploma or GED. Must be a resident of the United States or one of its territories.

Academic Fields/Career Goals: Aviation/Aerospace.

Award: Grant for use in freshman, sophomore, junior, senior, or graduate years; not renewable. *Number:* varies. *Amount:* varies.

Eligibility Requirements: Applicant must be enrolled or expecting to enroll full- or part-time at a four-year institution or university. Available to U.S. citizens.

Application Requirements: Application, references, transcript. *Deadline:* April 30.

Contact: Roger Thompson, Manager
Charlie Wells Memorial Scholarship Fund
PO Box 262
Springfield, IL 62705-0262
Phone: 217-899-3263
E-mail: rog@wellsscholarship.com

CHARLIE WELLS MEMORIAL AVIATION SCHOLARSHIP

Scholarship(s) of varying amounts will be awarded each year when funds are available. The applicant must be a resident of the United States or one of its territories. Must be a full-time student majoring in an aviation-oriented curriculum.

Academic Fields/Career Goals: Aviation/Aerospace.

Award: Scholarship for use in freshman, sophomore, junior, senior, or graduate years; not renewable. *Number:* varies. *Amount:* varies.

Eligibility Requirements: Applicant must be enrolled or expecting to enroll full-time at a four-year institution or university. Available to U.S. citizens.

Application Requirements: Application, references, transcript. *Deadline:* April 30.

Contact: Roger Thompson, Manager
Charlie Wells Memorial Scholarship Fund
PO Box 262
Springfield, IL 62705-0262
Phone: 217-899-3263
E-mail: rog@wellsscholarship.com

CIVIL AIR PATROL, USAF AUXILIARY

http://www.capnhq.gov/

MAJOR GENERAL LUCAS V. BEAU FLIGHT SCHOLARSHIPS SPONSORED BY THE ORDER OF DAEDALIANS

One-time scholarships for active cadets of the Civil Air Patrol who desire a career in military aviation. Award is to be used toward flight training for a private pilot license. Must be 15 1/2 to 18 1/2 years of age on April 1st of the year for which applying. Must be an active CAP cadet officer. Not open to the general public.

Academic Fields/Career Goals: Aviation/Aerospace.

Award: Scholarship for use in freshman year; not renewable. *Number:* 5. *Amount:* $2100.

Eligibility Requirements: Applicant must be high school student; planning to enroll or expecting to enroll full- or part-time at a four-year institution or university; single and must have an interest in aviation. Applicant or parent of applicant must be member of Civil Air Patrol. Available to U.S. citizens.

Application Requirements: Application, essay, interview, photo, references, test scores, transcript. *Deadline:* March 1.

Contact: Kelly Easterly, Assistant Program Manager
Civil Air Patrol, USAF Auxiliary
105 South Hansell Street, Building 714
Maxwell Air Force Base, AL 36112-6332
Phone: 334-953-8640
Fax: 334-953-6699
E-mail: cpr@capnhq.gov

DAEDALIAN FOUNDATION

http://www.daedalians.org/

DAEDALIAN FOUNDATION MATCHING SCHOLARSHIP PROGRAM

Scholarship program, wherein the foundation matches amounts given by flights, or chapters of the Order of Daedalians, to deserving college and university students who are pursuing a career as a military aviator.

Academic Fields/Career Goals: Aviation/Aerospace.

Award: Scholarship for use in freshman, sophomore, junior, senior, or graduate years; not renewable. *Number:* 75–80. *Amount:* up to $2000.

Eligibility Requirements: Applicant must be enrolled or expecting to enroll full-time at a four-year institution or university. Available to U.S. citizens.

Application Requirements: Application, photo, test scores, flight/ROTC/CAP recommendation. *Deadline:* December 31.

Contact: Carole Thomson, Program Executive Secretary
Daedalian Foundation
55 Main Circle, Building 676
Randolph AFB, TX 78148
Phone: 210-945-2113
Fax: 210-945-2112
E-mail: icarus@texas.net

EAA AVIATION FOUNDATION, INC.

http://www.eaa.org/

HANSEN SCHOLARSHIP

Renewable scholarship of $1000 for a student enrolled in an accredited institution and pursuing a degree in aerospace engineering or aeronautical engineering. Student must be in good standing; financial need not a requirement. Must be an EAA member. Applications may be downloaded from the web site http://www.youngeagles.org.

Academic Fields/Career Goals: Aviation/Aerospace.

Award: Scholarship for use in freshman, sophomore, junior, or senior years; not renewable. *Number:* up to 1. *Amount:* up to $1000.

Eligibility Requirements: Applicant must be enrolled or expecting to enroll full-time at a two-year or four-year or technical institution or university. Applicant or parent of applicant must be member of Experimental Aircraft Association. Available to U.S. and non-U.S. citizens.

Application Requirements: Application. *Deadline:* February 29.

Contact: Jane Smith, Scholarship Coordinator
EAA Aviation Foundation, Inc.
P.O. Box 3086
Oshkosh, WI 54903-3086
Phone: 920-426-6823
Fax: 920-426-4873
E-mail: jsmith@eaa.org

PAYZER SCHOLARSHIP

Scholarship for a student accepted or enrolled in an accredited college, university, or postsecondary school with an emphasis on technical information. Awarded to an individual who is seeking a major and declares an intention to pursue a professional career in engineering, mathematics, or the physical/biological sciences. Visit http://www.youngeagles.org for criteria and to download official application. Must be an EAA member or recommended by an EAA member.

Academic Fields/Career Goals: Aviation/Aerospace; Biology; Engineering/Technology; Physical Sciences.

Award: Scholarship for use in freshman, sophomore, junior, or senior years; not renewable. *Number:* up to 1. *Amount:* up to $5000.

Eligibility Requirements: Applicant must be enrolled or expecting to enroll full-time at a two-year or four-year or technical institution or university. Applicant or parent of applicant must be member of Experimental Aircraft Association. Available to U.S. and non-U.S. citizens.

Application Requirements: Application. *Deadline:* February 29.

Contact: Jane Smith, Scholarship Coordinator
EAA Aviation Foundation, Inc.
PO Box 3086
Oshkosh, WI 54903-3086
Phone: 920-426-6823
Fax: 920-426-4873
E-mail: jsmith@eaa.org

GENERAL AVIATION MANUFACTURERS ASSOCIATION

http://www.gama.aero/

EDWARD W. STIMPSON "AVIATION EXCELLENCE" AWARD

One-time scholarship award for students who are graduating from high school and have been accepted to attend aviation college or university in the upcoming year. See web site at http://www.gama.aero for more details.

Academic Fields/Career Goals: Aviation/Aerospace.

Award: Scholarship for use in freshman year; not renewable. *Number:* 1. *Amount:* $500.

Eligibility Requirements: Applicant must be high school student; planning to enroll or expecting to enroll full-time at a four-year institution or university and must have an interest in aviation. Applicant must have 3.0 GPA or higher. Available to U.S. citizens.

Application Requirements: Application, essay, references, transcript. *Deadline:* April 28.

Contact: Katie Pribyl, Director, Communications
General Aviation Manufacturers Association
1400 K Street, NW, Suite 801
Washington, DC 20005-2485
Phone: 202-393-1500
Fax: 202-842-4063
E-mail: kpribyl@gama.aero

HAROLD S. WOOD AWARD FOR EXCELLENCE

One-time scholarship award for an university student who is attending a National Intercollegiate Flying Association (NIFA) school. Must have completed at least one semester of coursework. See web site at http://www.gama.aero for additional details.

Academic Fields/Career Goals: Aviation/Aerospace.

Award: Scholarship for use in freshman, sophomore, junior, or senior years; not renewable. *Number:* 1. *Amount:* $1000.

Eligibility Requirements: Applicant must be enrolled or expecting to enroll full-time at a four-year institution or university. Applicant must have 3.0 GPA or higher. Available to U.S. citizens.

Application Requirements: Application, references, transcript, nomination. *Deadline:* February 24.

Contact: Katie Pribyl, Director, Communications
General Aviation Manufacturers Association
1400 K Street, NW, Suite 801
Washington, DC 20005-2485
Phone: 202-393-1500
Fax: 202-842-4063
E-mail: kpribyl@gama.aero

GRAND RAPIDS COMMUNITY FOUNDATION

http://www.grfoundation.org/

JOSHUA ESCH MITCHELL AVIATION SCHOLARSHIP

For students pursuing studies in the field of professional pilot with an emphasis on general aviation, flight engineer, or airway science. Applicant must be a U.S. citizens enrolled in a full- or part-time program at a college or university in the United States providing an accredited flight science curriculum. Applicant should have a minimum GPA of 2.75.

Academic Fields/Career Goals: Aviation/Aerospace.

Award: Scholarship for use in sophomore, junior, or senior years; not renewable. *Number:* 1. *Amount:* $1000.

Eligibility Requirements: Applicant must be enrolled or expecting to enroll full-time at a four-year institution and must have an interest in aviation. Applicant must have 2.5 GPA or higher. Available to U.S. citizens.

Application Requirements: Application, financial need analysis, references, transcript. *Deadline:* April 1.

Contact: Ruth Bishop, Education Program Officer
Grand Rapids Community Foundation
161 Ottawa Avenue, NW, 209 C
Grand Rapids, MI 49503-2757
Phone: 616-454-1751 Ext. 103
Fax: 616-454-6455
E-mail: rbishop@grfoundation.org

HISPANIC ENGINEER NATIONAL ACHIEVEMENT AWARDS CORPORATION (HENAAC)

http://www.henaac.org/

HISPANIC ENGINEER NATIONAL ACHIEVEMENT AWARDS CORPORATION SCHOLARSHIP PROGRAM

Scholarships available to Hispanic students maintaining a 3.0 GPA. Must be studying an engineering or science-related field.

Academic Fields/Career Goals: Aviation/Aerospace; Biology; Chemical Engineering; Civil Engineering; Computer Science/Data Processing; Electrical Engineering/Electronics; Engineering/Technology; Materials Science, Engineering, and Metallurgy; Mechanical Engineering; Nuclear Science.

Award: Scholarship for use in freshman, sophomore, junior, or senior years; renewable. *Number:* 12–20. *Amount:* $500–$5000.

Eligibility Requirements: Applicant must be Hispanic and enrolled or expecting to enroll full-time at a four-year institution or university. Applicant must have 3.0 GPA or higher. Available to U.S. and non-U.S. citizens.

Application Requirements: Application, essay, resume, references, transcript. *Deadline:* April 30.

Contact: Kathy Barrera, Scholarship Selection Committee
Hispanic Engineer National Achievement Awards Corporation (HENAAC)
3900 Whiteside Street
Los Angeles, CA 90063
Phone: 323-262-0997
E-mail: kathy@henaac.org

ILLINOIS PILOTS ASSOCIATION

http://www.illinoispilots.com/

ILLINOIS PILOTS ASSOCIATION MEMORIAL SCHOLARSHIP

Recipient must be a resident of Illinois established in an Illinois postsecondary institution in a full-time aviation-related program. Applicants will be judged by the scholarship committee, and the award (usually $500 annually) will be sent directly to the recipient's school. For further details visit web site http://www.illinoispilots.com.

Academic Fields/Career Goals: Aviation/Aerospace.

Award: Scholarship for use in sophomore, junior, or senior years; not renewable. *Number:* 1. *Amount:* $500–$1000.

Eligibility Requirements: Applicant must be enrolled or expecting to enroll full-time at a two-year or four-year or technical institution or university; resident of Illinois; studying in Illinois and must have an interest in aviation. Available to U.S. citizens.

Application Requirements: Application, essay, photo, references, transcript. *Deadline:* March 1.

Contact: Ruth Frantz, Scholarship Committee Chairman
Illinois Pilots Association
40W297 Apache Lane
Huntley, IL 60142
Phone: 847-669-3821
E-mail: landings8e@aol.com

INTERNATIONAL SOCIETY OF AUTOMATION (ISA)

http://www.isa.org/

INTERNATIONAL SOCIETY OF AUTOMATION EDUCATION FOUNDATION SCHOLARSHIPS

One-time scholarship for students enrolled full-time study majoring in one of the following: heating, air-conditioning, refrigeration mechanics, chemical engineering, mechanical engineering, electrical engineering/electronics or automation curriculum. Must have a minimum GPA of 3.0. The scholarship value is $500 to $5000. Deadline is February 15.

Academic Fields/Career Goals: Aviation/Aerospace; Chemical Engineering; Electrical Engineering/Electronics; Energy and Power Engineering; Engineering/Technology; Engineering-Related Technologies; Heating, Air-Conditioning, and Refrigeration Mechanics; Materials Science, Engineering, and Metallurgy; Mechanical Engineering; Paper and Pulp Engineering; Pharmacy.

Award: Scholarship for use in sophomore, junior, or graduate years; not renewable. *Number:* 5–15. *Amount:* $500–$5000.

Eligibility Requirements: Applicant must be enrolled or expecting to enroll full-time at a two-year or four-year or technical institution or university. Applicant must have 3.0 GPA or higher. Available to U.S. and non-U.S. citizens.

Application Requirements: Application, essay, references, self-addressed stamped envelope, transcript, 2 reference letters, 1 of which must be signed by faculty advisor. *Deadline:* February 15.

Contact: Dianna L. Noyes, Scholarship Committee
International Society of Automation (ISA)
67 Alexander Drive, PO Box 1277
Research Triangle Park, NC 27709

INTERNATIONAL SOCIETY OF WOMEN AIRLINE PILOTS (ISA+21)

http://www.iswap.org/

INTERNATIONAL SOCIETY OF WOMEN AIRLINE PILOTS AIRLINE SCHOLARSHIPS

Scholarships are available to women who are pursuing careers as airline pilots. Applicants must demonstrate financial need. Must have an U.S. FAA Commercial Pilot Certificate with an Instrument Rating and First Class Medical Certificate. Must have flight time in a fixed wing aircraft commensurate with the rating sought.

Academic Fields/Career Goals: Aviation/Aerospace.

Award: Scholarship for use in freshman, sophomore, junior, or senior years; not renewable. *Number:* up to 5. *Amount:* varies.

Eligibility Requirements: Applicant must be age 21 and over; enrolled or expecting to enroll full-time at a four-year institution or university and female. Available to U.S. and non-U.S. citizens.

Application Requirements: Application, driver's license, financial need analysis, interview, photo, resume, references, transcript, income tax forms, logbook pages, pilot licenses, medical certificates. *Deadline:* December 10.

Contact: Cheryl Konter, Scholarship Chairwoman
International Society of Women Airline Pilots (ISA+21)
2250 East Tropicana Avenue, Suite 19-395
Las Vegas, NV 89119-6594
Phone: 630-234-4199
E-mail: ckonter@yahoo.com

INTERNATIONAL SOCIETY OF WOMEN AIRLINE PILOTS FINANCIAL SCHOLARSHIP

Scholarships are available to women who are pursuing careers as airline pilots. Must have flight time in a fixed wing aircraft commensurate with the rating sought. Must have flight time in a fixed wing aircraft commensurate with the rating sought.

Academic Fields/Career Goals: Aviation/Aerospace.

Award: Scholarship for use in freshman, sophomore, junior, or senior years; not renewable. *Number:* 1. *Amount:* varies.

Eligibility Requirements: Applicant must be age 21 and over; enrolled or expecting to enroll full-time at a four-year institution or university and female. Available to U.S. and non-U.S. citizens.

Application Requirements: Application, driver's license, financial need analysis, interview, photo, resume, references, transcript, copies of income tax forms, logbook pages, pilot licenses, medical certificates. *Deadline:* December 10.

Contact: Cheryl Konter, Scholarship Chairwoman
International Society of Women Airline Pilots (ISA+21)
2250 East Tropicana Avenue, Suite 19-395
Las Vegas, NV 89119-6594
Phone: 630-234-4199
E-mail: ckonter@yahoo.com

INTERNATIONAL SOCIETY OF WOMEN AIRLINE PILOTS FIORENZA DE BERNARDI MERIT SCHOLARSHIP

Financial award will aid those pilots endeavoring to fill some of the basic squares, i.e. a CFI, CFII, MEI or any international equivalents. Must have flight time in a fixed wing aircraft commensurate with the rating sought. Must have flight time in a fixed wing aircraft commensurate with the rating sought.

Academic Fields/Career Goals: Aviation/Aerospace.

Award: Scholarship for use in freshman, sophomore, junior, or senior years; not renewable. *Number:* 1. *Amount:* varies.

Eligibility Requirements: Applicant must be age 21 and over; enrolled or expecting to enroll full- or part-time at a four-year institution or university and female. Available to U.S. and non-U.S. citizens.

Application Requirements: Application, driver's license, financial need analysis, interview, photo, resume, references, transcript, copies of income tax forms, logbook pages, pilot licenses, medical certificates. *Deadline:* December 10.

Contact: Cheryl Konter, Scholarship Chairwoman
International Society of Women Airline Pilots (ISA+21)
2250 East Tropicana Avenue, Suite 19-395
Las Vegas, NV 89119-6594
Phone: 630-234-4199
E-mail: ckonter@yahoo.com

INTERNATIONAL SOCIETY OF WOMEN AIRLINE PILOTS GRACE MCADAMS HARRIS SCHOLARSHIP

Scholarship may fund any ISA scholarship if the applicant has demonstrated an exceptionally spirited and ingenious attitude under difficult circumstances in the field of aviation. Applicants must have an U.S. FAA Commercial Pilot Certificate with an Instrument Rating and First Class Medical Certificate. Visit web site http://www.iswap.org for more details.

Academic Fields/Career Goals: Aviation/Aerospace.

Award: Scholarship for use in freshman, sophomore, junior, or senior years; not renewable. *Number:* 1. *Amount:* varies.

Eligibility Requirements: Applicant must be age 21 and over; enrolled or expecting to enroll full-time at a four-year institution or university; female and must have an interest in aviation. Available to U.S. and non-U.S. citizens.

Application Requirements: Application, driver's license, financial need analysis, interview, photo, references, transcript, copies of income tax forms, logbook pages, pilot licenses, medical certificates. *Deadline:* December 10.

Contact: Cheryl Konter, Scholarship Chairwoman
International Society of Women Airline Pilots (ISA+21)
2250 East Tropicana Avenue, Suite 19-395
Las Vegas, NV 89119-6594
Phone: 630-234-4199
E-mail: ckonter@yahoo.com

INTERNATIONAL SOCIETY OF WOMEN AIRLINE PILOTS HOLLY MULLENS MEMORIAL SCHOLARSHIP

Financial award is reserved for that applicant who is a single mother. Applicants must have an U.S. FAA Commercial Pilot Certificate with an Instrument Rating and First Class Medical Certificate. Visit web site http://www.iswap.org for more details.

Academic Fields/Career Goals: Aviation/Aerospace.

Award: Scholarship for use in freshman, sophomore, junior, or senior years; not renewable. *Number:* 1. *Amount:* varies.

Eligibility Requirements: Applicant must be age 21 and over; enrolled or expecting to enroll full-time at a four-year institution or university and single female. Available to U.S. and non-U.S. citizens.

Application Requirements: Application, driver's license, financial need analysis, interview, references, transcript, copies of income tax forms, logbook pages, pilot licenses, medical certificates. *Deadline:* December 10.

Contact: Cheryl Konter, Scholarship Chairwoman
International Society of Women Airline Pilots (ISA+21)
2250 East Tropicana Avenue, Suite 19-395
Las Vegas, NV 89119-6594
Phone: 630-234-4199
E-mail: ckonter@yahoo.com

INTERNATIONAL SOCIETY OF WOMEN AIRLINE PILOTS NORTH CAROLINA FINANCIAL SCHOLARSHIP

Scholarships for a woman pilot from North Carolina interested in a career in the airline world. Must have flight time in a fixed wing aircraft commensurate with the rating sought. Must have flight time in a fixed wing aircraft commensurate with the rating sought.

Academic Fields/Career Goals: Aviation/Aerospace.

Award: Scholarship for use in freshman, sophomore, junior, or senior years; not renewable. *Number:* 1. *Amount:* varies.

Eligibility Requirements: Applicant must be age 21 and over; enrolled or expecting to enroll full-time at a four-year institution or university; female and resident of North Carolina. Available to U.S. and non-U.S. citizens.

Application Requirements: Application, driver's license, financial need analysis, interview, photo, resume, references, transcript, copies of income tax forms, logbook pages, pilot licenses, medical certificates. *Deadline:* December 10.

Contact: Cheryl Konter, Scholarship Chairwoman
International Society of Women Airline Pilots (ISA+21)
2250 East Tropicana Avenue, Suite 19-395
Las Vegas, NV 89119-6594
Phone: 630-234-4199
E-mail: ckonter@yahoo.com

LINCOLN COMMUNITY FOUNDATION

http://www.lcf.org/

LAWRENCE "LARRY" FRAZIER MEMORIAL SCHOLARSHIP

Scholarship for graduating seniors and former graduates of a high school in Nebraska who, upon graduation, intend to pursue a career in the fields of aviation, insurance, or law. Applicants must attend a two- or four-year college or university in Nebraska. Preferred applicants will have experience in debate and will have participated in Girl Scouts or Boy Scouts during her/his youth.

Academic Fields/Career Goals: Aviation/Aerospace; Business/Consumer Services; Law/Legal Services.

Award: Scholarship for use in freshman year; not renewable. *Number:* 1. *Amount:* $500–$1000.

Eligibility Requirements: Applicant must be high school student; planning to enroll or expecting to enroll full-time at a two-year or four-year institution or university; resident of Nebraska and studying in Nebraska. Applicant or parent of applicant must be member of Boy Scouts or Girl Scouts. Applicant must have 2.5 GPA or higher. Available to U.S. citizens.

Application Requirements: Application, essay, financial need analysis, test scores, transcript. *Deadline:* April 15.

Contact: Sonya Brakeman, Grants/Scholarships Coordinator
Lincoln Community Foundation
215 Centennial Mall South, Suite 100
Lincoln, NE 68508
Phone: 402-474-2345
Fax: 402-476-8532
E-mail: sonyab@lcf.org

MANUFACTURERS ASSOCIATION OF MAINE

http://www.mainemfg.com/

MAINE METAL PRODUCTS EDUCATION FUND SCHOLARSHIP PROGRAM

Manufacturers Education Fund offers scholarship awards to individuals seeking education in the metal trades/precision manufacturing field of study. Any Maine student or worker can apply for tuition assistance at any Maine institute of higher learning. All applicants must be full-time students and maintain a minimum of a C average.

Academic Fields/Career Goals: Aviation/Aerospace; Engineering/Technology; Engineering-Related Technologies; Industrial Design; Marine/Ocean Engineering; Materials Science, Engineering, and Metallurgy; Mechanical Engineering; Trade/Technical Specialties.

Award: Scholarship for use in freshman, sophomore, junior, senior, graduate, or postgraduate years; not renewable. *Number:* 5–25. *Amount:* $250–$1000.

Eligibility Requirements: Applicant must be enrolled or expecting to enroll full- or part-time at a two-year or four-year or technical institution or university; resident of Maine and studying in Maine. Available to U.S. citizens.

Application Requirements: Application, essay, references, transcript. *Deadline:* May 1.

Contact: Angel Kimball, Office and Finance Administrator
Manufacturers Association of Maine
386 Bridgton Road, Attn: Scholarship Committee
Westbrook, ME 04092
Phone: 207-854-2153
Fax: 207-854-3865
E-mail: info@mainemfg.com

NASA/MARYLAND SPACE GRANT CONSORTIUM

http://www.mdspacegrant.org/

NASA MARYLAND SPACE GRANT CONSORTIUM UNDERGRADUATE SCHOLARSHIPS

Scholarship for full-time student majoring in the biological and life sciences, chemistry, geological sciences, physics, astronomy, engineering, computer science, or other related fields. Must be a U.S. citizen and a Maryland resident. Enrollment in an affiliate institution of the Maryland Space Grant Consortium is necessary.

Academic Fields/Career Goals: Aviation/Aerospace; Biology; Chemical Engineering; Computer Science/Data Processing; Earth Science; Engineering/Technology; Environmental Science; Materials Science, Engineering, and Metallurgy; Mathematics; Physical Sciences.

Award: Scholarship for use in freshman, sophomore, junior, or senior years; not renewable. *Number:* varies. *Amount:* up to $1000.

Eligibility Requirements: Applicant must be enrolled or expecting to enroll full-time at a four-year institution or university; resident of Maryland and studying in Maryland. Applicant must have 3.0 GPA or higher. Available to U.S. citizens.

Application Requirements: Application, essay, references. *Deadline:* May 15.

Contact: Richard Henry, Director
NASA/Maryland Space Grant Consortium
Johns Hopkins University, 203 Bloomberg Center for Physics
and Astronomy, 3400 N
Baltimore, MD 21218-2686
Phone: 410-516-7350
Fax: 410-516-4109
E-mail: henry@jhu.edu

NASA MINNESOTA SPACE GRANT CONSORTIUM

http://www.aem.umn.edu/mnsgc

MINNESOTA SPACE GRANT CONSORTIUM SCHOLARSHIP PROGRAM

Scholarships for full-time undergraduates attending institutions belonging to the Minnesota Space Grant Consortium—institution list on the web site. Preference given to students studying aerospace engineering, space science, and NASA-related math, science, or engineering fields. Minimum 3.0 GPA required. Must be U.S. citizen. For more details go to http://www.aem.umn.edu/mnsgc.

Academic Fields/Career Goals: Aviation/Aerospace; Earth Science; Engineering/Technology; Mathematics; Physical Sciences.

Award: Scholarship for use in sophomore, junior, or senior years; not renewable. *Number:* 30–80. *Amount:* $500–$2500.

Eligibility Requirements: Applicant must be enrolled or expecting to enroll full-time at a two-year or four-year institution or university and studying in Minnesota. Applicant must have 3.0 GPA or higher. Available to U.S. citizens.

Application Requirements: Application, references, transcript. *Deadline:* continuous.

Contact: Minnesota Space Grant, Department of Aerospace Engineering
NASA Minnesota Space Grant Consortium
107 Akerman Hall, 110 Union Street, SE
Minneapolis, MN 55455
Phone: 612-626-9295
E-mail: mnsgc@aem.umn.edu

NASA MISSISSIPPI SPACE GRANT CONSORTIUM

http://www.olemiss.edu/programs/nasa

MISSISSIPPI SPACE GRANT CONSORTIUM SCHOLARSHIP

Scholarship of $3000 awarded to undergraduate students in the fields of science, technology, engineering, and math. Must be U.S. citizens, community college graduates, and enrolled in a program of full-time study at one of the MSSGC universities. Minimum 3.0 GPA. Underrepresented minorities, females, and students with disabilities are encouraged to apply.

Academic Fields/Career Goals: Aviation/Aerospace; Engineering/Technology; Engineering-Related Technologies; Mathematics; Physical Sciences.

Award: Scholarship for use in freshman, sophomore, junior, or senior years; not renewable. *Number:* 10. *Amount:* $3000.

Eligibility Requirements: Applicant must be enrolled or expecting to enroll full-time at a four-year institution or university. Applicant must have 3.0 GPA or higher. Available to U.S. citizens.

Application Requirements: Application, references, transcript, statement of goals and plan of study. *Deadline:* March 21.

Contact: Margaret Schaff, Project Coordinator
NASA Mississippi Space Grant Consortium
c/o University of Mississippi, 308 Vardaman Hall
PO Box 1848
University, MS 38677-1848
Phone: 662-915-1187
Fax: 662-915-3927
E-mail: mschaff@olemiss.edu

NASA MONTANA SPACE GRANT CONSORTIUM

http://www.spacegrant.montana.edu/

MONTANA SPACE GRANT SCHOLARSHIP PROGRAM

Awards are made on a competitive basis to students enrolled in fields of study relevant to the aerospace sciences and engineering. Must be U.S. citizen enrolled as full-time student at a Montana Consortium campus.

Academic Fields/Career Goals: Aviation/Aerospace; Biology; Chemical Engineering; Civil Engineering; Computer Science/Data Processing; Electrical Engineering/Electronics; Engineering/Technology; Mathematics; Mechanical Engineering.

Award: Scholarship for use in freshman, sophomore, junior, or senior years; not renewable. *Number:* 15–20. *Amount:* up to $1000.

Eligibility Requirements: Applicant must be enrolled or expecting to enroll full-time at a four-year institution or university and studying in Montana. Available to U.S. citizens.

Application Requirements: Application, essay, references, transcript. *Deadline:* April 2.

Contact: Glenda Winslow, Program Coordinator
NASA Montana Space Grant Consortium
416 Cobleigh Hall
Bozeman, MT 59717-3835
Phone: 406-994-4223
Fax: 406-994-4452
E-mail: winslow@spacegrant.montana.edu

NASA RHODE ISLAND SPACE GRANT CONSORTIUM

http://ri.spacegrant.org/

NASA RHODE ISLAND SPACE GRANT CONSORTIUM UNDERGRADUATE RESEARCH SCHOLARSHIP

Scholarship for undergraduate students for study and/or outreach related to NASA and space sciences, engineering and/or technology. Must attend a Rhode Island Space Grant Consortium participating school. Recipients are expected to devote a maximum of 4 hours per week in science education for K–12 children and teachers. See web site for additional information http://www.spacegrant.brown.edu.

Academic Fields/Career Goals: Aviation/Aerospace; Engineering/Technology; Meteorology/Atmospheric Science.

Award: Scholarship for use in sophomore, junior, or senior years; not renewable. *Number:* up to 2. *Amount:* up to $4000.

Eligibility Requirements: Applicant must be enrolled or expecting to enroll full-time at a four-year institution or university and studying in Rhode Island. Applicant must have 3.0 GPA or higher. Available to U.S. citizens.

Application Requirements: Application, essay, resume, references, transcript. *Deadline:* varies.

Contact: Juliet Duyster, Program Manager
NASA Rhode Island Space Grant Consortium
Brown University
PO Box 1846
Providence, RI 02912
Phone: 401-863-1151
E-mail: juliet_duyster@brown.edu

NASA RISGC SCIENCE EN ESPANOL SCHOLARSHIP FOR UNDERGRADUATE STUDENTS

Award for undergraduate students attending a Rhode Island Space Grant Consortium participating school and studying in any space-related field of science, math, engineering, or other field with applications in space study. Recipients are expected to devote a maximum of 8 hours per week in outreach activities, supporting ESL teachers with science instruction.

Academic Fields/Career Goals: Aviation/Aerospace; Engineering/Technology; Mathematics.

Award: Scholarship for use in sophomore, junior, or senior years; not renewable. *Number:* 2. *Amount:* up to $4000.

Eligibility Requirements: Applicant must be enrolled or expecting to enroll full-time at a four-year institution or university and studying in Rhode Island. Applicant must have 3.0 GPA or higher. Available to U.S. citizens.

Application Requirements: Application, essay, resume, transcript. *Deadline:* varies.

Contact: Juliet Duyster, Program Manager
NASA Rhode Island Space Grant Consortium
Brown University
PO Box 1846
Providence, RI 02912
Phone: 401-863-1151
E-mail: juliet_duyster@brown.edu

NASA RISGC SUMMER SCHOLARSHIP FOR UNDERGRADUATE STUDENTS

Scholarship for full-time summer study. Students are expected to devote 75 percent of their time to a research project with a faculty adviser and 25 percent to outreach activities in science education for K–12 students and teachers. Must attend a Rhode Island Space Grant Consortium participating school. See web site for additional information http://www.spacegrant.brown.edu.

Academic Fields/Career Goals: Aviation/Aerospace; Education.

Award: Scholarship for use in sophomore, junior, or senior years; not renewable. *Number:* up to 2. *Amount:* up to $4000.

Eligibility Requirements: Applicant must be enrolled or expecting to enroll full-time at a four-year institution or university and studying in Rhode Island. Applicant must have 3.0 GPA or higher. Available to U.S. citizens.

Application Requirements: Application, resume, references, letter of interest. *Deadline:* varies.

Contact: Juliet Duyster, Program Manager
NASA Rhode Island Space Grant Consortium
Brown University
PO Box 1846
Providence, RI 02912
Phone: 401-863-1151
E-mail: juliet_duyster@brown.edu

NASA SOUTH CAROLINA SPACE GRANT CONSORTIUM

http://www.cofc.edu/~scsgrant

KATHRYN SULLIVAN SCIENCE AND ENGINEERING FELLOWSHIP

Fellowship awarded to a rising senior by the beginning of the fall semester. All applicants must be citizens of the United States. Each application must be sponsored by a faculty advisor. Awards will be for the senior academic year. Visit web site http://spinner.cofc.edu/~scsgrant/scholar/kathysullivan.html.

Academic Fields/Career Goals: Aviation/Aerospace; Biology; Earth Science; Engineering/Technology; Engineering-Related Technologies.

Award: Scholarship for use in senior year; not renewable. *Number:* 1. *Amount:* up to $7000.

Eligibility Requirements: Applicant must be enrolled or expecting to enroll full-time at a four-year institution or university and studying in South Carolina. Available to U.S. citizens.

Application Requirements: Application, applicant must enter a contest, essay, resume, references, transcript. *Deadline:* February 9.

Contact: Tara B. Scozzaro, MPA Program Manager
NASA South Carolina Space Grant Consortium
66 George Street
Charleston, SC 29424
Phone: 843-953-5463
Fax: 843-953-5446
E-mail: scozzarot@cofc.edu

PRE-SERVICE TEACHER SCHOLARSHIP

SC Space Grant Consortium now offers a $3000 scholarship for students interested in becoming a middle or high school science, technology, engineering or mathematics teacher. The goal of the program is to increase the number of quality teachers pursuing degrees in science, technology, engineering and mathematics (STEM) education. Application Requirements: in two pages or less provide a brief lesson plan related to one of NASA's areas of research in STEM. Include: (a) a general outline of how you would use the lesson, including intended age level, (b) goals/results envisioned for students, (c) suggested modifications or additions to the activity and (d) ideas for evaluation, a brief description of your proposed use of the scholarship funds (1 page max). Include one recent copy of your college transcript(s) and two letters of recommendation, including one from your faculty advisor. See web site for more information: http://spinner.cofc.edu/~scsgrant/scholar/preservice.html.

Academic Fields/Career Goals: Aviation/Aerospace; Biology; Education; Electrical Engineering/Electronics; Engineering/Technology; Materials Science, Engineering, and Metallurgy; Mechanical Engineering; Physical Sciences.

Award: Scholarship for use in sophomore, junior, senior, or graduate years; not renewable. *Number:* 2–5. *Amount:* $3000.

Eligibility Requirements: Applicant must be enrolled or expecting to enroll full-time at a four-year institution or university and studying in South Carolina. Available to U.S. citizens.

Application Requirements: Application, applicant must enter a contest, resume, references, transcript, be working towards teaching certificate. *Deadline:* February 9.

Contact: Tara B. Scozzaro, Program Manager
NASA South Carolina Space Grant Consortium
66 George Street
Charleston, SC 29424
Phone: 843-953-5463
Fax: 843-953-3411
E-mail: scozzarot@cocf.edu

UNDERGRADUATE RESEARCH AWARD PROGRAM

The undergraduate research program is designed to increase the number of highly trained scientists and engineers and enable undergraduate students to conduct NASA-related research. Awards: Research money awarded by the SC Space Grant Consortium will be administered as a stipend through the Financial Aid office on whose campus the Scholar is working. The full research stipend amount is $5,000. Two types of Undergraduate Research stipends are available, each $5,000. Up to $500 of the $5,000 will be available for research related expenses, not including any application fees. The applicant may select which one they wish to apply for: (a) An academic year award given to students interested in conducting research on an aerospace- or space science-related topic during the academic calendar year or (b) A student may conduct aerospace or space science related research for 10 weeks in the summer. For details refer to web site: http://spinner.cofc.edu/~scsgrant/scholar/undergraduate.html

Academic Fields/Career Goals: Aviation/Aerospace; Biology; Earth Science; Engineering/Technology; Engineering-Related Technologies.

Award: Grant for use in freshman, sophomore, junior, or senior years; not renewable. *Number:* 5–10. *Amount:* up to $5000.

Eligibility Requirements: Applicant must be enrolled or expecting to enroll full-time at a four-year institution or university and studying in South Carolina. Available to U.S. citizens.

Application Requirements: Application, applicant must enter a contest, essay, resume, references, transcript, research proposal. *Deadline:* February 9.

Contact: Mrs. Tara B. Scozzaro, Program Manager
NASA South Carolina Space Grant Consortium
College of Charleston, 66 George Street
Charleston, SC 29424
Phone: 843-953-5463
Fax: 843-953-5446
E-mail: scozzarot@cofc.edu

NASA SOUTH DAKOTA SPACE GRANT CONSORTIUM

http://www.sdspacegrant.sdsmt.edu/

SOUTH DAKOTA SPACE GRANT CONSORTIUM UNDERGRADUATE AND GRADUATE STUDENT SCHOLARSHIPS

Scholarship for undergraduate graduate students pursuing studies in science, technology, engineering, math, aerospace, or related fields at South Dakota institutions. Women and minorities are encouraged to apply. For more information, see web site http://sdspacegrant.sdsmt.edu/.

Academic Fields/Career Goals: Aviation/Aerospace; Earth Science; Energy and Power Engineering; Engineering/Technology; Engineering-Related Technologies; Environmental Science; Materials Science, Engineering, and Metallurgy; Mathematics; Natural Sciences; Physical Sciences; Science, Technology, and Society.

Award: Scholarship for use in freshman, sophomore, junior, senior, or graduate years; renewable. *Number:* 45–50. *Amount:* $1000–$7500.

Eligibility Requirements: Applicant must be enrolled or expecting to enroll full- or part-time at a four-year institution or university and studying in South Dakota. Applicant must have 3.0 GPA or higher. Available to U.S. citizens.

Application Requirements: Application, resume, references, transcript. *Deadline:* varies.

Contact: Mr. Thomas Durkin, Deputy Director
NASA South Dakota Space Grant Consortium
SD Space Grant Consortium, 501 East Saint Joseph Street
Rapid City, SD 57701
Phone: 605-394-1975
Fax: 605-394-5360
E-mail: thomas.durkin@sdsmt.edu

NASA'S VIRGINIA SPACE GRANT CONSORTIUM

http://www.vsgc.odu.edu/

UNDERGRADUATE RESEARCH STEM SCHOLARSHIPS
• *See page 96*

NASA WEST VIRGINIA SPACE GRANT CONSORTIUM

http://www.nasa.wvu.edu/

WEST VIRGINIA SPACE GRANT CONSORTIUM UNDERGRADUATE FELLOWSHIP PROGRAM

Scholarships intended to support undergraduate students pursuing a degree in science, technology, engineering, or math. Students are given opportunities to work with faculty members within their major department on research projects, or students may participate in the Consortium Challenge Program. Must be U.S. citizen. Refer to web site for further details http://www.nasa.wvu.edu.

Academic Fields/Career Goals: Aviation/Aerospace; Computer Science/Data Processing; Energy and Power Engineering; Engineering/Technology; Engineering-Related Technologies; Environmental Science; Meteorology/Atmospheric Science; Natural Sciences; Nuclear Science; Physical Sciences.

Award: Scholarship for use in freshman, sophomore, junior, or senior years; not renewable. *Number:* varies. *Amount:* $1000–$2000.

Eligibility Requirements: Applicant must be enrolled or expecting to enroll full-time at a four-year institution or university. Available to U.S. citizens.

Application Requirements: Application. *Deadline:* March 7.

Contact: Candy Cordwell, Program Manager
NASA West Virginia Space Grant Consortium
West Virginia University, G-68 Engineering Sciences Building
PO Box 6070
Morgantown, WV 26506-6070
Phone: 304-293-4099 Ext. 3738
Fax: 304-293-4970
E-mail: cordwell@nasa.wvu.edu

NASA WISCONSIN SPACE GRANT CONSORTIUM

http://www.uwgb.edu/WSGC

WISCONSIN SPACE GRANT CONSORTIUM UNDERGRADUATE RESEARCH PROGRAM

One-time award of up to $3500 for a U.S. citizen enrolled full-time, admitted to, or applying to any undergraduate program at a Wisconsin Space Grant Consortium college or university. Award goes to a student to create and implement their own small research study. Minimum 3.0 GPA required. Submit proposal with budget. Refer to web site for more information http://www.uwgb.edu/wsgc.

Academic Fields/Career Goals: Aviation/Aerospace.

Award: Grant for use in freshman, sophomore, junior, or senior years; not renewable. *Number:* 15. *Amount:* up to $3500.

Eligibility Requirements: Applicant must be enrolled or expecting to enroll full-time at a four-year institution or university; resident of Wisconsin and studying in Wisconsin. Applicant must have 3.0 GPA or higher. Available to U.S. citizens.

Application Requirements: Application, references, transcript, proposal with budget. *Deadline:* February 4.

Contact: Sue Weiler, Office Coordinator
NASA Wisconsin Space Grant Consortium
University of Wisconsin-Green Bay
Natural and Applied Sciences, 2420 Nicolet Drive
Green Bay, WI 54311-7001
Phone: 920-465-2108
Fax: 920-465-2376
E-mail: weilers@uwgb.edu

WISCONSIN SPACE GRANT CONSORTIUM UNDERGRADUATE SCHOLARSHIP PROGRAM

Scholarship of up to $1500 for a U.S. citizen enrolled full-time in, admitted to, or applying to any undergraduate program at a Wisconsin Space Grant Consortium college or university. Awards will be given to students with outstanding potential in programs of aerospace, space science, or other interdisciplinary space-related studies. Minimum 3.0 GPA required. Refer to web site for more information http://www.uwgb.edu/wsgc.

Academic Fields/Career Goals: Aviation/Aerospace.

Award: Scholarship for use in freshman, sophomore, junior, or senior years; not renewable. *Number:* 15–20. *Amount:* up to $1500.

Eligibility Requirements: Applicant must be enrolled or expecting to enroll full-time at a four-year institution or university; resident of Wisconsin and studying in Wisconsin. Applicant must have 3.0 GPA or higher. Available to U.S. citizens.

Application Requirements: Application, essay, references, transcript. *Deadline:* February 4.

Contact: Sue Weiler, Office Coordinator
NASA Wisconsin Space Grant Consortium
University of Wisconsin-Green Bay
Natural and Applied Sciences, 2420 Nicolet Drive
Green Bay, WI 54311-7001
Phone: 920-465-2108
Fax: 920-465-2376
E-mail: weilers@uwgb.edu

NATIONAL AIR TRANSPORTATION ASSOCIATION FOUNDATION

http://www.nata.aero/

DAN L. MEISINGER, SR. MEMORIAL LEARN TO FLY SCHOLARSHIP

Scholarship established in the honor and memory of Dan L. Meisinger Sr., whose career in aviation spanned 63 years. He was founder of Executive Beechcraft, headquartered in Kansas City, Mo., and was twice named Beech Aircraft's Man of the Year. Purpose of fund is to provide an annual flight training scholarship to a qualified individual. For more information, visit web site http://www.nata.aero/web/page/952/sectionid/554/pagelevel/3/tertiary.asp.

Academic Fields/Career Goals: Aviation/Aerospace.

Award: Scholarship for use in freshman, sophomore, junior, or senior years; not renewable. *Number:* 1. *Amount:* $2500.

Eligibility Requirements: Applicant must be age 18 and over and enrolled or expecting to enroll full-time at a two-year or four-year institution or university. Available to U.S. citizens.

Application Requirements: Application, interview, references, test scores, transcript. *Deadline:* November 28.

Contact: Mr. Adam Coulby, Manager, Education & Training
National Air Transportation Association Foundation
National Air Transportation Association, 4226 King Street
Alexandria, VA 22302

NATA BUSINESS SCHOLARSHIP

Scholarship available for education or training to establish a career in the business aviation industry. Applicable education includes any aviation-related two-year, four-year or graduate degree program at an accredited college or university. Must be 18 years of age or older, be nominated and endorsed by a representative of a regular or associate member company of the NATA. Applicable training includes any aviation maintenance program under the aegis of Part 147 or 65, any pilot certificate or rating under Part 61 or 141, and any aviation-related two-year, four-year or graduate degree program at an accredited college or university. In addition, the NATA Strategic Management for Aviation Service Firms, held yearly at the Transportation Center/Northwestern University, qualifies for applicable training. Visit web site for more information http://www.nata.aero/web/page/1097/sectionid/554/pagelevel/3/tertiary.aspx.

Academic Fields/Career Goals: Aviation/Aerospace.

Award: Scholarship for use in freshman, sophomore, junior, or senior years; not renewable. *Number:* 1. *Amount:* up to $2500.

Eligibility Requirements: Applicant must be age 18 and over and enrolled or expecting to enroll full-time at a two-year or four-year or technical institution or university. Available to U.S. citizens.

Application Requirements: Application, essay, resume, transcript. *Deadline:* December 1.

Contact: Mr. Adam Coulby, Manager, Education & Training
National Air Transportation Association Foundation
National Air Transportation Association, 4226 King Street
Alexandria, VA 22302

PIONEERS OF FLIGHT SCHOLARSHIP PROGRAM

Scholarship awards will be announced each year during NATA's annual spring convention. Interested students must complete the attached application and submit it along with a complete transcript of grades, a letter of recommendation, an essay on general aviation and a paper indicating career goals in general aviation postmarked no later than the last Friday in December. For more information, visit web site http://www.nata.aero/web/page/1098/sectionid/554/pagelevel/3/tertiary.aspx.

Academic Fields/Career Goals: Aviation/Aerospace.

Award: Scholarship for use in sophomore or junior years; not renewable. *Number:* 2. *Amount:* $1000.

Eligibility Requirements: Applicant must be age 18 and over and enrolled or expecting to enroll full- or part-time at a four-year institution or university. Applicant must have 3.0 GPA or higher. Available to U.S. citizens.

Application Requirements: Application, driver's license, references, test scores, transcript. *Deadline:* December 26.

Contact: Dr. Gregory Schwab, Chair, Department of Aerospace
Technology
National Air Transportation Association Foundation
Indiana State University, Department of Aerospace
Technology, TC 216
Terre Haute, IN 47809
E-mail: aeschwab@isugw.indstate.edu

NATIONAL BUSINESS AVIATION ASSOCIATION INC.

http://www.nbaa.org/

NBAA INTERNATIONAL OPERATORS SCHOLARSHIP

One-time $5000 scholarship offered to one or more recipients. Include with application: 500-word essay explaining how this scholarship will help the applicant achieve their international aviation career goals, statement of the funds required to achieve these goals, and at least one professional letter of recommendation, preferably from an NBAA member company employee.

Academic Fields/Career Goals: Aviation/Aerospace.

Award: Scholarship for use in freshman, sophomore, junior, or senior years; not renewable. *Number:* 1. *Amount:* $5000.

Eligibility Requirements: Applicant must be enrolled or expecting to enroll full- or part-time at a two-year or four-year or technical institution or university. Applicant must have 3.0 GPA or higher. Available to U.S. and non-U.S. citizens.

Application Requirements: Application, essay, references. *Deadline:* January 31.

Contact: Jay Evans, Director, Operations
National Business Aviation Association Inc.
1200 18th Street North West, Suite 400
Washington, DC 20036-2527
Phone: 202-783-9353
Fax: 202-331-8364
E-mail: jevans@nbaa.org

NBAA JANICE K. BARDEN SCHOLARSHIP

One-time $1000 scholarship for students officially enrolled in NBAA/UAA programs. Must be U.S. citizen, officially enrolled in an aviation-related program with 3.0 minimum GPA. Include with application: 250-word essay describing the applicant's interest and goals for a career in the business aviation industry; letter of recommendation from member of aviation department faculty at institution where applicant is enrolled.

Academic Fields/Career Goals: Aviation/Aerospace.

Award: Scholarship for use in sophomore, junior, senior, graduate, or postgraduate years; not renewable. *Number:* 5. *Amount:* $1000.

Eligibility Requirements: Applicant must be enrolled or expecting to enroll full-time at a two-year or four-year institution or university. Applicant must have 3.0 GPA or higher. Available to U.S. citizens.

Application Requirements: Application, essay, resume, references, transcript. *Deadline:* November 1.

Contact: Jay Evans, Director, Operations
National Business Aviation Association Inc.
1200 18th Street North West, Suite 400
Washington, DC 20036-2527
Phone: 202-783-9353
Fax: 202-331-8364
E-mail: jevans@nbaa.org

NBAA LAWRENCE GINOCCHIO AVIATION SCHOLARSHIP

One-time $5000 scholarship for students officially enrolled in NBAA/UAA programs. Must be officially enrolled in aviation-related program with 3.0 minimum GPA. Include with application: a 500- to 1000-word essay describing interest in and goals for a career in the business aviation industry while demonstrating strength of character. Must also have two letters of recommendation, including one from member of aviation department faculty at institution where applicant is enrolled.

Academic Fields/Career Goals: Aviation/Aerospace.

Award: Scholarship for use in sophomore, junior, senior, or graduate years; not renewable. *Number:* 5. *Amount:* $5000.

Eligibility Requirements: Applicant must be enrolled or expecting to enroll full-time at a four-year institution or university. Applicant must have 3.0 GPA or higher. Available to U.S. and Canadian citizens.

Application Requirements: Application, essay, resume, references, transcript, proof of enrollment. *Deadline:* August 1.

Contact: Jay Evans, Director, Operations
National Business Aviation Association Inc.
1200 18th Street North West, Suite 400
Washington, DC 20036-2527
Phone: 202-783-9353
Fax: 202-331-8364
E-mail: jevans@nbaa.org

NBAA WILLIAM M. FANNING MAINTENANCE SCHOLARSHIP

One-time award given to two students pursuing careers as maintenance technicians. One award will benefit a student who is currently enrolled in an accredited Airframe and Power-plant (A&P) program at an approved FAR Part 147 school. The second award will benefit an individual who is not currently enrolled but has been accepted into an A&P program. Include with application: a 250-word essay describing applicant's interest in and goals for a career in the aviation maintenance field. A letter of recommendation from an NBAA Member Company representative is encouraged.

Academic Fields/Career Goals: Aviation/Aerospace.

Award: Scholarship for use in freshman, sophomore, junior, senior, or graduate years; not renewable. *Number:* 2. *Amount:* $2500.

Eligibility Requirements: Applicant must be enrolled or expecting to enroll full-time at a two-year or four-year or technical institution or university. Available to U.S. citizens.

Application Requirements: Application, essay, resume, references, transcript. *Deadline:* August 1.

Contact: Jay Evans, Director, Operations
National Business Aviation Association Inc.
1200 18th Street North West, Suite 400
Washington, DC 20036-2527
Phone: 202-783-9353
Fax: 202-331-8364
E-mail: jevans@nbaa.org

U.S. AIRCRAFT INSURANCE GROUP PDP SCHOLARSHIP

One-time $1000 scholarship for applicants enrolled full-time in a college or university offering the NBAA (National Business Aviation Association) Professional Development Program (PDP). Must be U.S. citizen, officially enrolled in aviation-related program with 3.0 minimum GPA. Include with application: 250 word essay describing goals for a career in the business aviation flight department. A letter of recommendation from an NBAAA Member Company representative is encouraged.

Academic Fields/Career Goals: Aviation/Aerospace.

Award: Scholarship for use in sophomore, junior, senior, graduate, or postgraduate years; not renewable. *Number:* 1. *Amount:* $1000.

Eligibility Requirements: Applicant must be enrolled or expecting to enroll full-time at a two-year or four-year institution or university. Applicant must have 3.0 GPA or higher. Available to U.S. citizens.

Application Requirements: Application, essay, resume, references, transcript, proof of enrollment. *Deadline:* August 1.

Contact: Jay Evans, Director, Operations
National Business Aviation Association Inc.
1200 18th Street North West, Suite 400
Washington, DC 20036-2527
Phone: 202-783-9353
Fax: 202-331-8364
E-mail: jevans@nbaa.org

NATIONAL GAY PILOTS ASSOCIATION

http://www.ngpa.org/

NGPA EDUCATION FUND, INC.

Scholarship for candidates pursuing a career as a professional pilot. Funds cannot be used to pay for the basic private certificate; they must be applied towards advanced fight training at a government certified flight school or to college tuition if enrolled in an accredited aviation degree program. Applicants must provide evidence of their contribution to the gay and lesbian community.

Academic Fields/Career Goals: Aviation/Aerospace.

Award: Scholarship for use in freshman, sophomore, junior, or senior years; not renewable. *Number:* 3–4. *Amount:* $3000–$4000.

Eligibility Requirements: Applicant must be age 18 and over; enrolled or expecting to enroll full- or part-time at a two-year or four-year or technical institution or university and must have an interest in aviation or LGBT issues. Applicant or parent of applicant must have employment or volunteer experience in community service. Available to U.S. and non-U.S. citizens.

Application Requirements: Application, essay, references, transcript, copies of the applicant's pilot certificate, medical certificate, recent logbook page. *Deadline:* March 31.

Contact: Capt. Steve Walker, Executive Director
National Gay Pilots Association
PO Box 1652
San Jose, CA 95109
Phone: 214-336-0873
Fax: 214-350-0447
E-mail: ExecDir@ngpa.org

NEVADA NASA SPACE GRANT CONSORTIUM

http://www.nvspacegrant.org/

NATIONAL SPACE GRANT COLLEGE AND FELLOWSHIP PROGRAM
• *See page 97*

PALWAUKEE AIRPORT PILOTS ASSOCIATION

http://www.pwkpilots.org/

PALWAUKEE AIRPORT PILOTS ASSOCIATION SCHOLARSHIP PROGRAM

Scholarship offered to Illinois residents who are attending accredited programs at Illinois institutions. Must be pursuing a course of study in an aviation-related program. Minimum GPA of 2.0. Applications available on web site http://www.pwkpilots.org.

Academic Fields/Career Goals: Aviation/Aerospace.

Award: Scholarship for use in freshman, sophomore, junior, or senior years; not renewable. *Number:* 2. *Amount:* $500–$1000.

Eligibility Requirements: Applicant must be age 18 and over; enrolled or expecting to enroll full-time at a two-year or four-year or technical institution or university; resident of Illinois; studying in Illinois and must have an interest in aviation. Available to U.S. citizens.

Application Requirements: Application, driver's license, references, transcript, copy of FAA medical certificate, pilot certificate. *Deadline:* May 1.

Contact: Raymond Chou, Chairman, Scholarship Committee
Palwaukee Airport Pilots Association
1020 South Plant Road
Wheeling, IL 60090
Phone: 847-537-2580
Fax: 847-537-8183
E-mail: scholarship@pwkpilots.org

PROFESSIONAL AVIATION MAINTENANCE FOUNDATION

http://www.pama.org/

PROFESSIONAL AVIATION MAINTENANCE FOUNDATION STUDENT SCHOLARSHIP PROGRAM

For students enrolled in an airframe and power plant licensing program. Must have a B average and have completed 25 percent of the program. Must reapply each year.

Academic Fields/Career Goals: Aviation/Aerospace; Trade/Technical Specialties.

Award: Scholarship for use in freshman, sophomore, junior, or senior years; not renewable. *Number:* 10–30. *Amount:* $1000.

Eligibility Requirements: Applicant must be enrolled or expecting to enroll full-time at a two-year or four-year or technical institution or university and must have an interest in aviation. Applicant must have 3.0 GPA or higher. Available to U.S. and non-U.S. citizens.

Application Requirements: Application, financial need analysis, references, self-addressed stamped envelope, transcript. *Deadline:* October 31.

Contact: Marge Milligan, Marketing Assistant
Professional Aviation Maintenance Foundation
717 Princess Street
Alexandria, VA 22314
Phone: 724-772-4092
Fax: 724-776-3049
E-mail: milligan@sae.org

RHODE ISLAND PILOTS ASSOCIATION

http://www.ripilots.com/

RHODE ISLAND PILOTS ASSOCIATION SCHOLARSHIP

A scholarship open to Rhode Island residents to begin or advance a career in aviation. Must be age 16 or above.

Academic Fields/Career Goals: Aviation/Aerospace.

Award: Scholarship for use in freshman, sophomore, junior, or senior years; not renewable. *Number:* 2–4. *Amount:* $500–$1000.

Eligibility Requirements: Applicant must be age 16 and over; enrolled or expecting to enroll full- or part-time at a two-year or four-year or technical institution; resident of Rhode Island and must have an interest in aviation. Available to U.S. citizens.

Application Requirements: Application, essay, financial need analysis, references, test scores, transcript. *Deadline:* February 28.

Contact: Marilyn Biagetti, Scholarship Chair
Rhode Island Pilots Association
Hangar One, 644 Airport Road
Warwick, RI 02886
Phone: 401-568-3497
Fax: 401-568-5392
E-mail: biagettim@cox.net

SOCIETY OF AUTOMOTIVE ENGINEERS

http://www.sae.org/

BMW/SAE ENGINEERING SCHOLARSHIP

Scholarship is provided by BMW AG in recognition of its commitment to excellence in engineering. This scholarship is in support of the SAE Foundation to ensure an adequate supply of well-trained engineers for the future. One scholarship will be awarded at $1500 per year, renewable for four years. Must have a 3.75 GPA, rank in the 90th percentile in both math and critical reading on SAT or composite ACT scores. A 3.0 GPA must be maintained to renew the scholarship.

Academic Fields/Career Goals: Aviation/Aerospace; Chemical Engineering; Electrical Engineering/Electronics; Engineering/Technology; Engineering-Related Technologies; Mechanical Engineering.

Award: Scholarship for use in freshman year; renewable. *Number:* 1. *Amount:* $1500.

Eligibility Requirements: Applicant must be high school student and planning to enroll or expecting to enroll full-time at a four-year institution or university. Available to U.S. citizens.

Application Requirements: Application, essay, test scores, transcript. *Deadline:* December 15.

Contact: Marguerite Milligan, Marketing Assistant
Society of Automotive Engineers
400 Commonwealth Drive
Warrendale, PA 15096-0001
Phone: 724-772-7158
Fax: 724-776-3049
E-mail: customerservice@sae.org

EDWARD D. HENDRICKSON/SAE ENGINEERING SCHOLARSHIP

Scholarship of $4000 awarded at $1000 per year for four years. A 3.0 GPA and continued engineering enrollment must be maintained to renew the scholarship. Applicants must have a 3.75 GPA, rank in the 90th percentile in both math and critical reading on SAT or composite ACT scores, and pursue an engineering degree accredited by ABET.

Academic Fields/Career Goals: Aviation/Aerospace; Chemical Engineering; Electrical Engineering/Electronics; Engineering/Technology; Engineering-Related Technologies; Mechanical Engineering.

Award: Scholarship for use in freshman year; renewable. *Number:* 1. *Amount:* $1000.

Eligibility Requirements: Applicant must be high school student and planning to enroll or expecting to enroll full-time at a four-year institution or university. Available to U.S. citizens.

Application Requirements: Application, essay, test scores, transcript. *Deadline:* December 15.

Contact: Connie Harnish, SAE Educational Relations
Society of Automotive Engineers
400 Commonwealth Drive
Warrendale, PA 15096-0001
Phone: 724-772-4047
Fax: 724-776-0890
E-mail: connie@sae.org

TMC/SAE DONALD D. DAWSON TECHNICAL SCHOLARSHIP

One scholarship of $1500 a year for up to four years as long as a 3.0 GPA and continuing engineering enrollment is maintained. High school seniors must have a 3.25 or higher GPA, SAT math 600 or above and critical reading 550 or above and/or an ACT composite score 27 or above. Transfer students from accredited four-year colleges/universities must have a 3.0 GPA. Students from postsecondary technical/vocational schools must have a 3.5 GPA.

Academic Fields/Career Goals: Aviation/Aerospace; Chemical Engineering; Electrical Engineering/Electronics; Engineering/Technology; Engineering-Related Technologies; Materials Science, Engineering, and Metallurgy; Mechanical Engineering.

Award: Scholarship for use in freshman, sophomore, junior, or senior years; renewable. *Number:* 1. *Amount:* $1500.

Eligibility Requirements: Applicant must be enrolled or expecting to enroll full-time at a two-year or four-year or technical institution or university. Available to U.S. citizens.

Application Requirements: Application, essay, test scores, transcript. *Deadline:* December 15.

Contact: Connie Harnish, SAE Educational Relations
Society of Automotive Engineers
400 Commonwealth Drive
Warrendale, PA 15096-0001
Phone: 724-772-4047
Fax: 724-776-0890
E-mail: connie@sae.org

SOCIETY OF SATELLITE PROFESSIONALS INTERNATIONAL

http://www.sspi.org/

SSPI INTERNATIONAL SCHOLARSHIPS

Scholarship open to students majoring or planning to major in fields related to satellite communications. Selection is based on academic and leadership achievement, commitment to pursue education and career opportunities in the satellite industry or a field making direct use of satellite technology. Available to members of SSPI.

Academic Fields/Career Goals: Aviation/Aerospace; Communications; Law/Legal Services; Meteorology/Atmospheric Science; Military and Defense Studies.

Award: Scholarship for use in freshman, sophomore, junior, senior, or graduate years; not renewable. *Number:* 1–4. *Amount:* $2500–$4000.

Eligibility Requirements: Applicant must be enrolled or expecting to enroll full-time at a two-year or four-year institution or university. Available to U.S. and non-U.S. citizens.

Application Requirements: Essay, financial need analysis, references, transcript, sample of work. *Deadline:* May 15.

Contact: Ms. Tamara Bond, Director of Membership
Society of Satellite Professionals International
The New York Information Technology Center, 55 Broad Street, 14th Floor
New York, NY 10004
Phone: 212-809-5199 Ext. 103
Fax: 212-825-0075
E-mail: tbond@sspi.org

STUDENT PILOT NETWORK

STUDENT PILOT NETWORK-FLIGHT DREAM AWARD

Award is for General Aviation Pilot Flight Training. Open to all persons actively engaged in flight training at a registered SPN flight school. Must be a U.S. or Canadian citizen.

Academic Fields/Career Goals: Aviation/Aerospace.

Award: Grant for use in freshman, sophomore, junior, senior, graduate, or postgraduate years; renewable. *Number:* 1–3. *Amount:* $300–$750.

Eligibility Requirements: Applicant must be enrolled or expecting to enroll full- or part-time at a two-year or four-year or technical institution and must have an interest in aviation. Available to U.S. and Canadian citizens.

Application Requirements: Application, essay. *Deadline:* November 15.

Contact: William Terry, President
Student Pilot Network
1830 Wallace Avenue, Suite 208
St. Charles, IL 60174
Phone: 480-419-7927
E-mail: info@studentpilot.net

UNIVERSITIES SPACE RESEARCH ASSOCIATION

http://www.usra.edu/

UNIVERSITIES SPACE RESEARCH ASSOCIATION SCHOLARSHIP PROGRAM
• *See page 97*

UNIVERSITY AVIATION ASSOCIATION

http://www.uaa.aero/

CAE SIMUFLITE CITATION TYPE RATING SCHOLARSHIP

Scholarship open to undergraduate seniors and post-baccalaureate graduates of aviation degree programs up to two years after graduation. Must have a minimum 3.25 GPA.

Academic Fields/Career Goals: Aviation/Aerospace.

Award: Scholarship for use in senior year; not renewable. *Number:* 4. *Amount:* $10,500.

Eligibility Requirements: Applicant must be enrolled or expecting to enroll full-time at a four-year institution or university and must have an interest in aviation. Available to U.S. citizens.

Application Requirements: Application, essay, resume, references, transcript, FAA first class medical certificate. *Deadline:* March 31.

Contact: Dr. David Newmyer, Professor and Department Chair, Aviation Management and Flight
University Aviation Association
1365 Douglas Drive
Carbondale, IL 62901
Phone: 616-453-8898
Fax: 618-453-7286
E-mail: newmyer@siu.edu

JOSEPH FRASCA EXCELLENCE IN AVIATION SCHOLARSHIP

Established to encourage those who demonstrate the highest level of commitment to and achievement in aviation studies. Applicant must be a junior or senior currently enrolled in a UAA member institution. Must be FAA certified/qualified in either aviation maintenance or flight, have membership in at least one aviation organization, and be involved in aviation activities, projects, and events. Minimum 3.0 GPA required.

AVIATION/AEROSPACE

Academic Fields/Career Goals: Aviation/Aerospace.

Award: Scholarship for use in junior or senior years; not renewable. *Number:* 2. *Amount:* $2000.

Eligibility Requirements: Applicant must be enrolled or expecting to enroll full- or part-time at a four-year institution or university and must have an interest in aviation. Applicant must have 3.0 GPA or higher. Available to U.S. and non-U.S. citizens.

Application Requirements: Application, essay, financial need analysis, references, transcript, FAA certification. *Deadline:* April 10.

Contact: Dr. David A. Newmyer, Department Chair, Aviation
      Management and Flight
  University Aviation Association
  1365 Douglas Drive
  Carbondale, IL 62901-6623
  Phone: 618-453-8898
  Fax: 618-453-4850
  E-mail: newmyer@siu.edu

PAUL A. WHELAN AVIATION SCHOLARSHIP

One-time award of $2000 given to sophomore, junior, senior or graduate. Must be a U.S. citizen. Must be enrolled in University Aviation Association member institution. 2.5 GPA required. FAA certification, membership in aviation-related association preferred.

Academic Fields/Career Goals: Aviation/Aerospace.

Award: Scholarship for use in sophomore, junior, senior, or graduate years; not renewable. *Number:* 1. *Amount:* $2000.

Eligibility Requirements: Applicant must be enrolled or expecting to enroll full-time at a two-year or four-year institution or university and must have an interest in aviation. Applicant must have 2.5 GPA or higher. Available to U.S. citizens.

Application Requirements: Application, essay, references, transcript, FAA certification. *Deadline:* May 15.

Contact: David A. Newmyer, Department Chair, Aviation Management
      and Flight
  University Aviation Association
  Southern Illinois University at Carbondale, College of Applied
      Sciences and Arts
  Carbondale, IL 62901-6623
  Phone: 618-453-8898
  Fax: 618-453-7268
  E-mail: newmyer@siu.edu

VERMONT SPACE GRANT CONSORTIUM

http://www.cems.uvm.edu/vsgc

VERMONT SPACE GRANT CONSORTIUM SCHOLARSHIP PROGRAM

• See page 98

VIRGINIA AVIATION AND SPACE EDUCATION FORUM

http://www.doav.virginia.gov/

JOHN R. LILLARD VIRGINIA AIRPORT OPERATORS COUNCIL SCHOLARSHIP PROGRAM

Scholarship of $3000 offered to high school seniors planning a career in the field of aviation. Must be enrolled or accepted into an aviation-related program at an accredited college. Minimum 3.75 unweighted GPA.

Academic Fields/Career Goals: Aviation/Aerospace.

Award: Scholarship for use in freshman year; not renewable. *Number:* 1. *Amount:* $3000.

Eligibility Requirements: Applicant must be high school student; planning to enroll or expecting to enroll full-time at a four-year institution or university and must have an interest in aviation. Available to U.S. and non-U.S. citizens.

Application Requirements: Application, essay, financial need analysis, references, transcript. *Deadline:* February 20.

Contact: Betty Wilson, Program Coordinator
  Virginia Aviation and Space Education Forum
  c/o Virginia Department of Aviation, 5702 Gulfstream
  Richmond, VA 23250-2422
  Phone: 804-236-3624
  Fax: 804-236-3636
  E-mail: betty.wilson@doav.virginia.gov

WILLARD G. PLENTL AVIATION SCHOLARSHIP PROGRAM

Scholarship of $1000 awarded to a high school senior who is planning an aviation career in a non-engineering area.

Academic Fields/Career Goals: Aviation/Aerospace.

Award: Scholarship for use in freshman year; not renewable. *Number:* 1. *Amount:* $1000.

Eligibility Requirements: Applicant must be high school student; planning to enroll or expecting to enroll full-time at a four-year institution or university and must have an interest in aviation. Applicant must have 3.5 GPA or higher. Available to U.S. and non-U.S. citizens.

Application Requirements: Application, essay, financial need analysis, references, transcript. *Deadline:* February 20.

Contact: Betty Wilson, Program Coordinator
  Virginia Aviation and Space Education Forum
  5702 Gulfstream Road
  Richmond, VA 23250-2422
  E-mail: betty.wilson@doav.virginia.gov

WOMEN IN AVIATION, INTERNATIONAL

http://www.wai.org/

AIRBUS LEADERSHIP GRANT

One scholarship to a college sophomore or higher level student who is pursuing a degree in an aviation-related field. Must have a minimum GPA of 3.0 and must exhibit leadership potential. Must be a WAI member.

Academic Fields/Career Goals: Aviation/Aerospace.

Award: Scholarship for use in sophomore, junior, or senior years; not renewable. *Number:* 1. *Amount:* $5000.

Eligibility Requirements: Applicant must be enrolled or expecting to enroll full- or part-time at a four-year institution or university and must have an interest in leadership. Applicant or parent of applicant must be member of Women in Aviation, International. Applicant must have 3.0 GPA or higher. Available to U.S. and non-U.S. citizens.

Application Requirements: Application, essay, resume, references. *Deadline:* November 15.

Contact: Donna Wallace, Scholarships Committee
  Women in Aviation, International
  Morningstar Airport, 3647 State Route 503 South
  West Alexandria, OH 45381
  Phone: 937-839-4647
  Fax: 937-839-4645
  E-mail: dwallace@wai.org

BOEING COMPANY CAREER ENHANCEMENT SCHOLARSHIP

Scholarship available for a woman who wishes to advance her career in aerospace technology or a related management field. Open to full-time or part-time employees currently in the aerospace industry or related field. Students pursuing aviation-related degrees that are at the junior level with a minimum GPA of 2.5 are also eligible.

Academic Fields/Career Goals: Aviation/Aerospace.

Award: Scholarship for use in junior or senior years; not renewable. *Number:* 1. *Amount:* $2500.

Eligibility Requirements: Applicant must be enrolled or expecting to enroll full- or part-time at a four-year institution or university and female. Applicant or parent of applicant must be member of Women in Aviation, International. Available to U.S. and non-U.S. citizens.

Application Requirements: Application, essay, resume, references. *Deadline:* November 15.

Contact: Donna Wallace, Scholarships Committee
Women in Aviation, International
Morningstar Airport, 3647 State Route 503 South
West Alexandria, OH 45381
Phone: 937-839-4647
Fax: 937-839-4645
E-mail: dwallace@wai.org

DASSAULT FALCON JET CORPORATION SCHOLARSHIP

Scholarship of $1000 available for a woman pursuing an undergraduate or graduate degree in an aviation-related field. Applicant must be a U.S. citizen with fluency in English. Must have minimum 3.0 GPA or better (on a 4.0 scale) in her most recent year of schooling. Must be a member of WAI.

Academic Fields/Career Goals: Aviation/Aerospace.

Award: Scholarship for use in freshman, sophomore, junior, or senior years; not renewable. *Number:* 1. *Amount:* $1000.

Eligibility Requirements: Applicant must be enrolled or expecting to enroll full- or part-time at a four-year institution or university and female. Applicant or parent of applicant must be member of Women in Aviation, International. Applicant must have 3.0 GPA or higher. Available to U.S. citizens.

Application Requirements: Application, essay, resume, references. *Deadline:* November 15.

Contact: Donna Wallace, Scholarships Committee
Women in Aviation, International
Morningstar Airport, 3647 State Route 503 South
West Alexandria, OH 45381
Phone: 937-839-4647
Fax: 937-839-4645
E-mail: dwallace@wai.org

DELTA AIR LINES AIRCRAFT MAINTENANCE TECHNOLOGY SCHOLARSHIP

Scholarship of $5000 available to a student currently enrolled in an aviation maintenance technology program, or pursuing a degree in aviation maintenance technology. Applicant must be a full-time student with a minimum of two semesters left in the program or degree. Must have minimum GPA of 3.0 or better (on a 4.0 scale). Must be a member of WAI. Must be an U.S. citizen or an eligible non-citizen.

Academic Fields/Career Goals: Aviation/Aerospace.

Award: Scholarship for use in freshman, sophomore, or junior years; not renewable. *Number:* 1. *Amount:* $5000.

Eligibility Requirements: Applicant must be enrolled or expecting to enroll full-time at a two-year or four-year or technical institution or university. Applicant or parent of applicant must be member of Women in Aviation, International. Applicant must have 3.0 GPA or higher. Available to U.S. and non-U.S. citizens.

Application Requirements: Application, essay, resume, references. *Deadline:* November 15.

Contact: Donna Wallace, Scholarships Committee
Women in Aviation, International
Morningstar Airport, 3647 State Route 503 South
West Alexandria, OH 45381
Phone: 937-839-4647
Fax: 937-839-4645
E-mail: dwallace@wai.org

DELTA AIR LINES ENGINEERING SCHOLARSHIP

Scholarship to a student currently enrolled in a baccalaureate degree in aerospace/ aeronautical, electrical, or mechanical engineering. Applicants must be full-time students at the junior or senior level with a minimum of two semesters left. Must have minimum GPA of 3.0. Must be a member of WAI. Must be U.S. citizens or eligible non-citizens.

Academic Fields/Career Goals: Aviation/Aerospace; Electrical Engineering/Electronics; Mechanical Engineering.

Award: Scholarship for use in junior or senior years; not renewable. *Number:* 1. *Amount:* $5000.

Eligibility Requirements: Applicant must be enrolled or expecting to enroll full-time at a four-year institution or university. Applicant or parent of applicant must be member of Women in Aviation, International. Applicant must have 3.0 GPA or higher. Available to U.S. and non-U.S. citizens.

Application Requirements: Application, essay, resume, references. *Deadline:* November 15.

Contact: Donna Wallace, Scholarships Committee
Women in Aviation, International
Morningstar Airport, 3647 State Route 503 South
West Alexandria, OH 45381
Phone: 937-839-4647
Fax: 937-839-4645
E-mail: dwallace@wai.org

DELTA AIR LINES MAINTENANCE MANAGEMENT/ AVIATION BUSINESS MANAGEMENT SCHOLARSHIP

Scholarship to a student currently enrolled in an associate or baccalaureate degree in aviation maintenance management or aviation business management. Applicant must be a full-time college student, with a minimum of two semesters left. Must have a minimum GPA of 3.0. Must be a member of WAI and be a U.S. citizen or an eligible non-citizen.

Academic Fields/Career Goals: Aviation/Aerospace.

Award: Scholarship for use in freshman, sophomore, or junior years; not renewable. *Number:* 1. *Amount:* $5000.

Eligibility Requirements: Applicant must be enrolled or expecting to enroll full-time at a two-year or four-year institution or university. Applicant or parent of applicant must be member of Women in Aviation, International. Applicant must have 3.0 GPA or higher. Available to U.S. and non-U.S. citizens.

Application Requirements: Application, essay, resume, references. *Deadline:* November 15.

Contact: Donna Wallace, Scholarships Committee
Women in Aviation, International
Morningstar Airport, 3647 State Route 503 South
West Alexandria, OH 45381
Phone: 937-839-4647
Fax: 937-839-4645
E-mail: dwallace@wai.org

GAT WINGS TO THE FUTURE MANAGEMENT SCHOLARSHIP

Scholarship of $2500 to a female student in an aviation management or aviation business program at an accredited college or university. Applicant must be full-time student with a minimum 3.0 GPA. Must be a member of WAI. Refer to web site for further details http://www.wai.org.

Academic Fields/Career Goals: Aviation/Aerospace.

Award: Scholarship for use in freshman, sophomore, junior, or senior years; not renewable. *Number:* 1. *Amount:* $2500.

Eligibility Requirements: Applicant must be enrolled or expecting to enroll full-time at a two-year or four-year institution or university and female. Applicant or parent of applicant must be member of Women in Aviation, International. Applicant must have 3.0 GPA or higher. Available to U.S. and non-U.S. citizens.

Application Requirements: Application, essay, resume, references. *Deadline:* November 15.

Contact: Donna Wallace, Scholarships Committee
Women in Aviation, International
Morningstar Airport, 3647 State Route 503 South
West Alexandria, OH 45381
Phone: 937-839-4647
Fax: 937-839-4645
E-mail: dwallace@wai.org

KEEP FLYING SCHOLARSHIP

One scholarship of up to $3000 will be awarded to an individual working on an instrument or multi engine rating, commercial or initial flight instructor certificate. Flight training must be completed within one year. Minimum requirements: private pilot certificate, 100 hours of flight time, and a copy of a current written test (with passing grade) for the certificate/rating sought. Must be a member of WAI. Finalist will only be interviewed at the annual Women in Aviation Conference.

Academic Fields/Career Goals: Aviation/Aerospace.

Award: Scholarship for use in freshman year; not renewable. *Number:* 1. *Amount:* $3000.

Eligibility Requirements: Applicant must be enrolled or expecting to enroll full- or part-time at a technical institution. Applicant or parent of applicant must be member of Women in Aviation, International. Available to U.S. and non-U.S. citizens.

Application Requirements: Application, essay, resume, references. *Deadline:* November 15.

Contact: Donna Wallace, Scholarships Committee
Women in Aviation, International
Morningstar Airport, 3647 State Route 503 South
West Alexandria, OH 45381
Phone: 937-839-4647
Fax: 937-839-4645
E-mail: dwallace@wai.org

WOMEN IN AVIATION, INTERNATIONAL ACHIEVEMENT AWARDS

Two scholarships will be awarded to a full-time college or university student, and one to an individual, not necessarily a student, pursuing an aviation-related career goal. Must be a member of WAI.

Academic Fields/Career Goals: Aviation/Aerospace.

Award: Scholarship for use in freshman, sophomore, junior, or senior years; not renewable. *Number:* 2. *Amount:* $1000.

Eligibility Requirements: Applicant must be enrolled or expecting to enroll full-time at a two-year or four-year institution or university. Applicant or parent of applicant must be member of Women in Aviation, International. Available to U.S. and non-U.S. citizens.

Application Requirements: Application. *Deadline:* November 15.

Contact: Donna Wallace, Scholarships Committee
Women in Aviation, International
Morningstar Airport, 3647 State Route 503 South
West Alexandria, OH 45381
Phone: 937-839-4647
Fax: 937-839-4645
E-mail: dwallace@wai.org

WOMEN IN AVIATION, INTERNATIONAL MANAGEMENT SCHOLARSHIPS

Scholarship available to a female in an aviation management field who has demonstrated traits of leadership, community spirit, and volunteerism. Must be a member of WAI. Scholarship to be used to attend a leadership-related course or seminar or work towards an advanced degree, that raises the individual's level of management.

Academic Fields/Career Goals: Aviation/Aerospace.

Award: Scholarship for use in freshman, sophomore, junior, or senior years; not renewable. *Number:* 1. *Amount:* $1250.

Eligibility Requirements: Applicant must be enrolled or expecting to enroll full- or part-time at a two-year or four-year or technical institution or university; female and must have an interest in leadership. Applicant or parent of applicant must be member of Women in Aviation, International. Available to U.S. and non-U.S. citizens.

Application Requirements: Application. *Deadline:* November 15.

Contact: Donna Wallace, Scholarships Committee
Women in Aviation, International
Morningstar Airport, 3647 State Route 503 South
West Alexandria, OH 45381
Phone: 937-839-4647
Fax: 937-839-4645
E-mail: dwallace@wai.org

WOMEN IN CORPORATE AVIATION CAREER SCHOLARSHIPS

Scholarship to a person who is interested in continued pursuit of a career in any job classification in corporate/business aviation. Applicants should be actively working toward their goal and show financial need. Award can be used toward the NBAA professional development program courses, flight training, dispatcher training, or upgrades in aviation education, and so forth, but cannot include general business course work. Must be a member of WAI.

Academic Fields/Career Goals: Aviation/Aerospace.

Award: Scholarship for use in freshman, sophomore, junior, or senior years; not renewable. *Number:* 1. *Amount:* $2000.

Eligibility Requirements: Applicant must be enrolled or expecting to enroll full- or part-time at a two-year or four-year or technical institution or university and female. Applicant or parent of applicant must be member of Women in Aviation, International. Available to U.S. and non-U.S. citizens.

Application Requirements: Application, essay, financial need analysis, resume, references, transcript. *Deadline:* November 15.

Contact: Donna Wallace, Scholarships Committee
Women in Aviation, International
Morningstar Airport, 3647 State Route 503 South
West Alexandria, OH 45381
Phone: 937-839-4647
Fax: 937-839-4645
E-mail: dwallace@wai.org

WOMEN MILITARY AVIATORS INC. DREAM OF FLIGHT SCHOLARSHIP

An annual $2500 scholarship for tuition or flight training for a FAA private pilot rating or advanced rating at an accredited institution or school. Applicant must be an academic student or a flight student. Must be able to complete training within one year of the award. Must be a member of WAI.

Academic Fields/Career Goals: Aviation/Aerospace.

Award: Scholarship for use in freshman, sophomore, junior, or senior years; not renewable. *Number:* 1. *Amount:* $2500.

Eligibility Requirements: Applicant must be enrolled or expecting to enroll full- or part-time at a two-year or four-year or technical institution or university. Applicant or parent of applicant must be member of Women in Aviation, International. Available to U.S. and non-U.S. citizens.

Application Requirements: Application, financial need analysis, resume, references. *Deadline:* November 15.

Contact: Donna Wallace, Scholarships Committee
Women in Aviation, International
Morningstar Airport, 3647 State Route 503 South
West Alexandria, OH 45381
Phone: 937-839-4647
Fax: 937-839-4645
E-mail: dwallace@wai.org

WRIGHT CHAPTER, WOMEN IN AVIATION, INTERNATIONAL, ELISHA HALL MEMORIAL SCHOLARSHIP

Scholarship offered to a woman seeking to further the aviation career in flight training, aircraft scheduling or dispatch, aviation management, aviation maintenance, or avionics. Preference will be given to applicants from Cincinnati Ohio area. Must be a member of WAI, but does not have to be member of Cincinnati Chapter.

Academic Fields/Career Goals: Aviation/Aerospace.

Award: Scholarship for use in freshman, sophomore, junior, or senior years; not renewable. *Number:* 1. *Amount:* $1000.

Eligibility Requirements: Applicant must be enrolled or expecting to enroll full- or part-time at a two-year or four-year or technical institution or university and female. Applicant or parent of applicant must be member of Women in Aviation, International. Available to U.S. and non-U.S. citizens.

Application Requirements: Application, essay, resume, references. *Deadline:* November 15.

Contact: Donna Wallace, Scholarships Committee
Women in Aviation, International
Morningstar Airport, 3647 State Route 503 South
West Alexandria, OH 45381
Phone: 937-839-4647
Fax: 937-839-4645
E-mail: dwallace@wai.org

BEHAVIORAL SCIENCE

MISSOURI DEPARTMENT OF HEALTH AND SENIOR SERVICES

http://www.dhss.mo.gov/

PRIMARY CARE RESOURCE INITIATIVE FOR MISSOURI LOAN PROGRAM

Forgivable loans for Missouri residents attending Missouri institutions pursuing a degree as a primary care physician or dentist, dental hygienist, psychiatrist, psychologist, licensed professional counselor, licensed clinical social worker or dietitian/nutritionist. To be forgiven participant must work in a Missouri health professional shortage area.

Academic Fields/Career Goals: Behavioral Science; Dental Health/Services; Food Science/Nutrition; Health and Medical Sciences; Nursing; Psychology.

Award: Forgivable loan for use in freshman, sophomore, junior, senior, graduate, or postgraduate years; not renewable. *Number:* 100. *Amount:* $5000–$20,000.

Eligibility Requirements: Applicant must be enrolled or expecting to enroll full-time at a four-year institution or university; resident of Missouri and studying in Missouri. Available to U.S. citizens.

Application Requirements: Application, proof of Missouri residency. *Deadline:* June 30.

Contact: Cheryl Thomas, Health and Senior Services Manager
Missouri Department of Health and Senior Services
PO Box 570
Jefferson City, MO 65102-0570
Phone: 800-891-7415
Fax: 573-522-8146
E-mail: cheryl.thomas@dhss.mo.gov

SOCIETY FOR APPLIED ANTHROPOLOGY

http://www.sfaa.net/

PETER KONG-MING NEW STUDENT PRIZE

Prize awarded for SFAA's annual student research competition in the applied social and behavioral sciences. The issue of research question should be in the domain of health care or human services (broadly construed). The winner of the competition will receive a cash prize of $2000, a crystal trophy, and travel funds to attend the annual meeting of the SFAA. For more details, see web site at http://www.sfaa.net.

Academic Fields/Career Goals: Behavioral Science; Health and Medical Sciences; Social Sciences.

Award: Prize for use in freshman, sophomore, junior, or senior years; not renewable. *Number:* 1–1. *Amount:* up to $2000.

Eligibility Requirements: Applicant must be enrolled or expecting to enroll full- or part-time at a two-year or four-year or technical institution or university. Available to U.S. and non-U.S. citizens.

Application Requirements: Application, applicant must enter a contest, manuscript. *Deadline:* December 31.

Contact: Dr. J. May, Executive Director
Society for Applied Anthropology
PO Box 2436
Oklahoma City, OK 73101-2436
Phone: 405-843-5113
E-mail: tom@sfaa.net

SOCIETY FOR THE SCIENTIFIC STUDY OF SEXUALITY

http://www.sexscience.org/

SOCIETY FOR THE SCIENTIFIC STUDY OF SEXUALITY STUDENT RESEARCH GRANT

Award to support students doing scientific research related to sexuality. Purpose of research can be master's thesis or doctoral dissertation, but this is not a requirement. Must be enrolled in degree-granting program. Deadlines: February 1 and September 1. One-time award of $1000.

Academic Fields/Career Goals: Behavioral Science; Biology; Education; Health and Medical Sciences; Nursing; Psychology; Public Health; Religion/Theology; Social Sciences; Women's Studies.

Award: Grant for use in freshman, sophomore, junior, senior, or graduate years; not renewable. *Number:* 2. *Amount:* $1000.

Eligibility Requirements: Applicant must be enrolled or expecting to enroll full- or part-time at a four-year institution or university. Available to U.S. and non-U.S. citizens.

Application Requirements: Application, driver's license, resume. *Deadline:* varies.

Contact: David Fleming, Executive Director
Society for the Scientific Study of Sexuality
PO Box 416
Allentown, PA 18105
Phone: 610-530-2483
Fax: 610-530-2485
E-mail: thesociety@inetmail.att.net

BIOLOGY

AIST FOUNDATION

http://www.aistfoundation.org/

ASSOCIATION FOR IRON AND STEEL TECHNOLOGY OHIO VALLEY CHAPTER SCHOLARSHIP

Scholarship of $1000 per year for up to four years provided that applicant continues to meet requirements and reapplies for scholarship. Applicant must be a dependent of Ohio Valley Chapter member, or student or Young Professional member. Must attend or plan to attend an accredited school full-time and pursue a degree in any technological field, including engineering, physics, computer sciences, chemistry or other fields approved by the scholarship committee.

Academic Fields/Career Goals: Biology; Computer Science/Data Processing; Electrical Engineering/Electronics; Engineering/Technology; Engineering-Related Technologies; Materials Science, Engineering, and Metallurgy; Physical Sciences.

Award: Scholarship for use in freshman, sophomore, junior, or senior years; not renewable. *Number:* 1–2. *Amount:* $1000.

Eligibility Requirements: Applicant must be enrolled or expecting to enroll full-time at a four-year institution or university. Applicant or parent of applicant must be member of Association for Iron and Steel Technology. Applicant must have 3.0 GPA or higher. Available to U.S. and non-U.S. citizens.

Application Requirements: Application, essay, resume, references, test scores, transcript. *Deadline:* March 31.

Contact: Jeff McKain, Scholarship Chairman
AIST Foundation
11451 Reading Road
Cincinnati, OH 45241
Phone: 724-776-6040
E-mail: jeff.mckain@xtek.com

ALBERTA HERITAGE SCHOLARSHIP FUND

http://www.alis.alberta.ca/

ALBERTA HERITAGE SCHOLARSHIP FUND ABORIGINAL HEALTH CAREERS BURSARY

Award for aboriginal students in Alberta, entering their second or subsequent year of postsecondary education in a health field. Must be Indian, Inuit, or Metis students who have been living in Alberta for at least the last three years, and are enrolled full-time at the technical, college, or university level. Students are selected on the basis of financial need, previous academic record, program of study, involvement in the aboriginal community, and experience in the healthcare field. For additional information and an application, visit web site http://alis.alberta.ca.

Academic Fields/Career Goals: Biology; Dental Health/Services; Health Administration; Health and Medical Sciences; Nursing; Therapy/Rehabilitation.

Award: Scholarship for use in sophomore, junior, or senior years; not renewable.

Eligibility Requirements: Applicant must be Canadian citizen; American Indian/Alaska Native; enrolled or expecting to enroll full-time at a two-year or four-year or technical institution or university and resident of Alberta.

Application Requirements: Application, essay, financial need analysis, references, transcript, proof of Aboriginal status. *Deadline:* May 1.

Contact: Scholarship Committee
Alberta Heritage Scholarship Fund
9940 106th Street, Fourth Floor, Sterling Place
PO Box 28000, Station Main
Edmonton, AB T5J 4R4
Canada
Phone: 780-427-8640
E-mail: scholarships@gov.ab.ca

AMERICAN ASSOCIATION OF BLOOD BANKS-SBB SCHOLARSHIP AWARDS

http://www.aabb.org/

AABB-FENWAL SCHOLARSHIP AWARD

Scholarship for an individual enrolled, accepted for enrollment in, or having recently completed a program leading to Specialist in Blood Banking certification in an AABB-accredited institution.

Academic Fields/Career Goals: Biology.

Award: Scholarship for use in freshman, sophomore, junior, senior, or graduate years; not renewable. *Number:* 2. *Amount:* varies.

Eligibility Requirements: Applicant must be enrolled or expecting to enroll full- or part-time at an institution or university. Available to U.S. citizens.

Application Requirements: Application. *Deadline:* June 1.

Contact: Scholarship Coordinator
E-mail: rsinger@aabb.org

AMERICAN INDIAN SCIENCE AND ENGINEERING SOCIETY

http://www.aises.org/

A.T. ANDERSON MEMORIAL SCHOLARSHIP PROGRAM
• *See page 93*

BURLINGTON NORTHERN SANTA FE FOUNDATION SCHOLARSHIP
• *See page 93*

AMERICAN PHYSIOLOGICAL SOCIETY

http://www.the-aps.org/

DAVID S. BRUCE AWARDS FOR EXCELLENCE IN UNDERGRADUATE RESEARCH

Award available for research in physiology. The student must be enrolled as an undergraduate student at the time of the application. The applicant must be the first author on a submitted abstract for the EB meeting and must be working with an APS member who attests that the student is deserving of the first authorship.

Academic Fields/Career Goals: Biology; Health and Medical Sciences; Neurobiology.

Award: Prize for use in freshman, sophomore, junior, or senior years; not renewable. *Number:* 6–20. *Amount:* up to $500.

Eligibility Requirements: Applicant must be enrolled or expecting to enroll full-time at a four-year institution or university. Available to U.S. and non-U.S. citizens.

Application Requirements: Application, essay, references, first author abstract. *Deadline:* January 10.

Contact: Dr. Marsha Lakes Matyas, Director of Education Programs
American Physiological Society
9650 Rockville Pike
Bethesda, MD 20814
Phone: 301-634-7132
Fax: 301-634-7098
E-mail: mmatyas@the-aps.org

AMERICAN SOCIETY OF AGRICULTURAL AND BIOLOGICAL ENGINEERS

http://www.asabe.org/

WILLIAM J. ADAMS, JR. AND MARIJANE E. ADAMS SCHOLARSHIP
• *See page 82*

AMERICAN SOCIETY OF ICHTHYOLOGISTS AND HERPETOLOGISTS

http://www.asih.org/

GAIGE FUND AWARD

Funds are used to provide support to young herpetologists for museum or laboratory study, travel, fieldwork, or any other activity that will effectively enhance their professional careers and their contributions to the science of herpetology. Applicants must be members of ASIH and be enrolled for an advanced degree. Visit web site at http://www.asih.org for additional information.

Academic Fields/Career Goals: Biology.

Award: Grant for use in freshman, sophomore, junior, senior, or graduate years; not renewable. *Number:* 5–10. *Amount:* $400–$1000.

Eligibility Requirements: Applicant must be enrolled or expecting to enroll full-time at a four-year institution or university. Applicant or parent of applicant must be member of American Society of Ichthyologists and Herpetologists. Available to U.S. and non-U.S. citizens.

Application Requirements: Application, financial need analysis, references. *Deadline:* March 1.

Contact: Maureen Donnelly, Secretary
American Society of Ichthyologists and Herpetologists
11200 SW Eighth Street
Miami, FL 33199
Phone: 305-348-1235
Fax: 305-348-1986
E-mail: asih@fiu.edu

RANEY FUND AWARD

Applications are solicited for grants awarded from the Raney Fund for ichthyology. Funds are used to provide support for young ichthyologists for museums or laboratory study, travel, fieldwork, or any activity that will effectively enhance their professional careers and their contributions to the sciences of ichthyology. Must be a member of ASIH and be enrolled for an advanced degree. Visit web site at http://www.asih.org for additional information.

Academic Fields/Career Goals: Biology.

Award: Grant for use in freshman, sophomore, junior, senior, or graduate years; not renewable. *Number:* 5–10. *Amount:* $400–$1000.

Eligibility Requirements: Applicant must be enrolled or expecting to enroll full-time at a four-year institution or university. Applicant or parent of applicant must be member of American Society of Ichthyologists and Herpetologists. Available to U.S. and non-U.S. citizens.

Application Requirements: Application, financial need analysis, references. *Deadline:* March 1.

Contact: Maureen Donnelly, Secretary
American Society of Ichthyologists and Herpetologists
11200 SW Eighth Street
Miami, FL 33199
Phone: 305-348-1235
Fax: 305-348-1986
E-mail: asih@fiu.edu

ARNOLD AND MABEL BECKMAN FOUNDATION

http://www.beckman-foundation.com/

BECKMAN SCHOLARS PROGRAM

Scholarship for four-year college undergraduate students in chemistry, biochemistry, and the biological and medical sciences. Provides undergraduate research experiences and comprehensive faculty mentoring.

Academic Fields/Career Goals: Biology; Health and Medical Sciences; Neurobiology; Physical Sciences.

Award: Scholarship for use in freshman, sophomore, junior, or senior years; not renewable. *Number:* varies. *Amount:* $19,300.

Eligibility Requirements: Applicant must be enrolled or expecting to enroll full-time at a four-year institution or university. Available to U.S. citizens.

Application Requirements: Application. *Deadline:* varies.

Contact: Program Administrator
Arnold and Mabel Beckman Foundation
100 Academy
PO Box 13219
Irvine, CA 92617
Phone: 949-721-2222
Fax: 949-721-2225
E-mail: beckmanscholars@beckman-foundation.com

ARRL FOUNDATION INC.

http://www.arrl.org/

YASME FOUNDATION SCHOLARSHIP

Multiple awards are available to students who possess an active amateur radio license. Preference given to high school applicants ranked in top 5% of class and college students ranked in top 10% of class. Participation in local Amateur Radio club and community service is important. Two awards are renewable up to three years based on transcript review.

Academic Fields/Career Goals: Biology; Engineering/Technology; Engineering-Related Technologies; Natural Sciences; Science, Technology, and Society.

Award: Scholarship for use in freshman, sophomore, junior, or senior years; renewable. *Amount:* $2000.

Eligibility Requirements: Applicant must be enrolled or expecting to enroll at a four-year institution or university and must have an interest in amateur radio. Applicant must have 3.5 GPA or higher.

Application Requirements: Application, transcript. *Deadline:* February 1.

Contact: Ms. Mary Hobart, Secretary
ARRL Foundation Inc.
225 Main Street
Newington, CT 06111-1494
Phone: 860-594-0397
E-mail: k1mmh@arrl.org

ASSOCIATION OF CALIFORNIA WATER AGENCIES

http://www.acwa.com/

ASSOCIATION OF CALIFORNIA WATER AGENCIES SCHOLARSHIPS
• *See page 94*

CLAIR A. HILL SCHOLARSHIP
• *See page 94*

ASSOCIATION ON AMERICAN INDIAN AFFAIRS, INC.

http://www.indian-affairs.org/

ELIZABETH AND SHERMAN ASCHE MEMORIAL SCHOLARSHIP FUND
• *See page 83*

ASTRONAUT SCHOLARSHIP FOUNDATION

http://www.astronautscholarship.org/

ASTRONAUT SCHOLARSHIP FOUNDATION
• *See page 95*

BARRY M. GOLDWATER SCHOLARSHIP AND EXCELLENCE IN EDUCATION FOUNDATION

http://www.act.org/goldwater

BARRY M. GOLDWATER SCHOLARSHIP AND EXCELLENCE IN EDUCATION PROGRAM
• *See page 95*

BRITISH COLUMBIA INNOVATION COUNCIL

http://www.bcic.ca/

BCIC YOUNG INNOVATOR SCHOLARSHIP COMPETITION (IDEA MASH UP)
• *See page 95*

PAUL AND HELEN TRUSSELL SCIENCE AND TECHNOLOGY SCHOLARSHIP
• *See page 95*

CHEMICAL INSTITUTE OF CANADA

http://www.cheminst.ca/

ALFRED BADER SCHOLARSHIP

Scholarships available to undergraduate seniors who are members of the Canadian Society for Chemistry and who have achieved excellence in organic chemistry or biochemistry. Students must be nominated and submit a project report. U.S. citizens must be enrolled in a Canadian university.

Academic Fields/Career Goals: Biology; Physical Sciences.

Award: Scholarship for use in senior year; not renewable. *Number:* 1–3. *Amount:* $1000.

Eligibility Requirements: Applicant must be enrolled or expecting to enroll full-time at an institution or university. Applicant or parent of applicant must be member of Canadian Society for Chemistry. Available to U.S. and non-U.S. citizens.

Application Requirements: References, transcript, honours research project report. *Deadline:* May 30.

Contact: Gale Thirlwall, Awards Manager
Chemical Institute of Canada
130 Slater Street, Suite 550
Ottawa, ON K1P 6E2
Canada
Phone: 613-232-6252 Ext. 223
E-mail: awards@cheminst.ca

CONGRESSIONAL BLACK CAUCUS FOUNDATION, INC.

http://www.cbcfinc.org/

CONGRESSIONAL BLACK CAUCUS SPOUSES CHEERIOS BRAND HEALTH INITIATIVE

Scholarship to increase the number of minority students pursuing degrees in the fields of medicine, engineering, technology, nutrition and other health-related professions. Minimum 2.5 GPA required. Preference is given to students who reside or attend school in a congressional district represented by a member of the Congressional Black Caucus.

Academic Fields/Career Goals: Biology; Chemical Engineering; Health Administration; Health and Medical Sciences; Health Information Management/Technology; Science, Technology, and Society.

Award: Scholarship for use in freshman, sophomore, junior, senior, or graduate years; not renewable. *Number:* 200. *Amount:* $500–$1800.

Eligibility Requirements: Applicant must be enrolled or expecting to enroll full-time at a two-year or four-year institution or university. Applicant must have 2.5 GPA or higher. Available to U.S. citizens.

Application Requirements: Application, essay, financial need analysis, photo, resume, references, transcript. *Deadline:* June 1.

Contact: Ms. Janet J. Carter, Scholarships Coordinator
Congressional Black Caucus Foundation, Inc.
1720 Massachusetts Avenue, NW
Washington, DC 20036
Phone: 202-263-2800
Fax: 202-263-0845
E-mail: scholarships@cbcfinc.org

CUSHMAN FOUNDATION FOR FORAMINIFERAL RESEARCH

http://www.cushmanfoundation.org/

LOEBLICH AND TAPPAN STUDENT RESEARCH AWARD

Research award given to both graduate and undergraduates interested in foraminiferal research. The maximum dollar value for the award is $2000.

Academic Fields/Career Goals: Biology; Marine Biology.

Award: Grant for use in freshman, sophomore, junior, senior, or graduate years; not renewable. *Number:* 1–57. *Amount:* $100–$2000.

Eligibility Requirements: Applicant must be enrolled or expecting to enroll full- or part-time at a four-year institution or university. Available to U.S. and non-U.S. citizens.

Application Requirements: Resume, references, proposal for research. *Deadline:* September 15.

Contact: Jennifer Jett, Secretary and Treasurer
Cushman Foundation for Foraminiferal Research
MRC 121 Department of Paleobiology, PO Box 37012
Washington, DC 20013-7012
E-mail: jettje@si.edu

EAA AVIATION FOUNDATION, INC.

http://www.eaa.org/

PAYZER SCHOLARSHIP
• See page 124

FEDERATED GARDEN CLUBS OF CONNECTICUT

http://www.ctgardenclubs.org/

FEDERATED GARDEN CLUBS OF CONNECTICUT INC. SCHOLARSHIPS

One-time award for Connecticut residents entering his or her junior, senior, or graduate year at a Connecticut college or university and pursuing studies in gardening, landscaping, or biology. Minimum 3.0 GPA. PhD candidates are not eligible.

Academic Fields/Career Goals: Biology; Horticulture/Floriculture; Landscape Architecture.

Award: Scholarship for use in junior, senior, or graduate years; not renewable. *Number:* 2–5. *Amount:* $1000–$5000.

Eligibility Requirements: Applicant must be enrolled or expecting to enroll full-time at a four-year institution or university; resident of Connecticut and studying in Connecticut. Applicant must have 3.0 GPA or higher. Available to U.S. citizens.

Application Requirements: Application, driver's license, financial need analysis, references, self-addressed stamped envelope, test scores, transcript. *Deadline:* July 1.

Contact: Barbara Bomblad, Office Manager
Federated Garden Clubs of Connecticut
14 Business Park Drive
PO Box 854
Branford, CT 06405-0854
Phone: 203-488-5528
Fax: 203-488-5528 Ext. 51
E-mail: fgcctoff@hotmail.com

FOUNDATION FOR SCIENCE AND DISABILITY

http://stemd.org/

GRANTS FOR DISABLED STUDENTS IN THE SCIENCES
• See page 95

GREATER KANAWHA VALLEY FOUNDATION

http://www.tgkvf.org/

MATH AND SCIENCE SCHOLARSHIP

Awarded to students pursuing a degree in math, science or engineering at any accredited college or university. For purposes of this fund, science shall include chemistry, physics, biology and other scientific fields. Scholarships are awarded for one or more years. Must be a resident of West Virginia.

Academic Fields/Career Goals: Biology; Engineering/Technology; Mathematics; Physical Sciences.

Award: Scholarship for use in freshman, sophomore, junior, or senior years; renewable. *Number:* 1. *Amount:* $1000.

Eligibility Requirements: Applicant must be enrolled or expecting to enroll full-time at a four-year institution or university and resident of West Virginia. Available to U.S. citizens.

Application Requirements: Application, essay, references, transcript. *Deadline:* January 15.

Contact: Susan Hoover, Scholarship Coordinator
Greater Kanawha Valley Foundation
PO Box 3041
Charleston, WV 25331
Phone: 304-346-3620
Fax: 304-346-3640

HAWAIIAN LODGE, F&AM

http://www.glhawaii.org/

HAWAIIAN LODGE SCHOLARSHIPS
• See page 106

HISPANIC ENGINEER NATIONAL ACHIEVEMENT AWARDS CORPORATION (HENAAC)

http://www.henaac.org/

HISPANIC ENGINEER NATIONAL ACHIEVEMENT AWARDS CORPORATION SCHOLARSHIP PROGRAM
• See page 125

INDEPENDENT COLLEGE FUND OF MARYLAND (I-FUND)

http://www.i-fundinfo.org/

HEALTH AND LIFE SCIENCES PROGRAM SCHOLARSHIPS

Program includes $5000 scholarships for students majoring in or demonstrating a career interest in the biological sciences, biochemistry, biophysics, microbiology and related scientific fields including chemistry, computer science, physics and environmental health. Must enroll at an independent college in Maryland.

Academic Fields/Career Goals: Biology; Chemical Engineering; Environmental Health; Health and Medical Sciences.

Award: Scholarship for use in sophomore, junior, or senior years; not renewable. *Number:* 1. *Amount:* $5000.

Eligibility Requirements: Applicant must be enrolled or expecting to enroll full-time at a four-year institution or university and studying in Maryland. Available to U.S. citizens.

Application Requirements: Application. *Deadline:* varies.

Contact: Lori Subotich, Director of Programs and Scholarships
Independent College Fund of Maryland (I-Fund)
3225 Ellerslie Avenue, Suite C160
Baltimore, MD 21218-3519
Phone: 443-997-5700
Fax: 443-997-2740
E-mail: lsubot@jhmi.edu

INDEPENDENT LABORATORIES INSTITUTE SCHOLARSHIP ALLIANCE

http://www.acil.org/

INDEPENDENT LABORATORIES INSTITUTE SCHOLARSHIP ALLIANCE

Scholarships are given to full-time undergraduate juniors or seniors, or graduate students majoring in the physical sciences: physics, chemistry, geology, engineering, biology or environmental science.

Academic Fields/Career Goals: Biology; Chemical Engineering; Civil Engineering; Earth Science; Electrical Engineering/Electronics; Engineering/Technology; Engineering-Related Technologies; Environmental Science; Fire Sciences; Materials Science, Engineering, and Metallurgy; Mechanical Engineering; Physical Sciences.

Award: Scholarship for use in freshman, sophomore, junior, senior, or graduate years; not renewable. *Number:* 1–2. *Amount:* $1000–$2000.

Eligibility Requirements: Applicant must be enrolled or expecting to enroll full-time at a four-year institution or university. Available to U.S. citizens.

Application Requirements: Application, resume, references, transcript. *Deadline:* April 7.

Contact: Janet Allen, Senior Administrator
Independent Laboratories Institute Scholarship Alliance
1629 K Street, NW, Suite 400
Washington, DC 20006-1633
Phone: 202-887-5872 Ext. 204
Fax: 202-887-0021
E-mail: jallen@acil.org

KENTUCKY ENERGY AND ENVIRONMENT CABINET

http://www.eec.ky.gov/

ENVIRONMENTAL PROTECTION SCHOLARSHIP

Renewable awards for college juniors, seniors, and graduate students for in-state tuition, fees, room and board, and a book allowance at a Kentucky public university. Minimum 3.0 GPA required. Must work full-time for the Kentucky Department for Environmental Protection upon graduation (six months for each semester of scholarship support received). Interview required.

Academic Fields/Career Goals: Biology; Chemical Engineering; Civil Engineering; Earth Science; Environmental Science; Hydrology; Mechanical Engineering; Natural Sciences.

Award: Scholarship for use in junior, senior, or graduate years; renewable. *Number:* 1–2. *Amount:* $15,000–$30,000.

Eligibility Requirements: Applicant must be enrolled or expecting to enroll full-time at a four-year institution or university and studying in Kentucky. Applicant must have 3.0 GPA or higher. Available to U.S. and non-U.S. citizens.

Application Requirements: Application, essay, interview, references, transcript, valid work permit for non-citizens. *Deadline:* February 15.

Contact: James Kipp, Scholarship Program Coordinator
Kentucky Energy and Environment Cabinet
233 Mining/Mineral Resources Building
Lexington, KY 40506-0107
Phone: 859-257-1299
Fax: 859-323-1049
E-mail: kipp@uky.edu

LOUISIANA OFFICE OF STUDENT FINANCIAL ASSISTANCE

http://www.osfa.la.gov/

ROCKEFELLER STATE WILDLIFE SCHOLARSHIP

For college undergraduates with a minimum of 60 credit hours who are majoring in Forestry, Wildlife, or Marine Science, and for college graduate students who are majoring in Forestry, Wildlife, or Marine Science. College undergraduates must have a grade point average of at least 2.50 to apply. College graduate students must have a grade point average of at least 3.00 in order to apply. Renewable up to three years as an undergraduate and two years as a graduate student.

Academic Fields/Career Goals: Biology; Marine Biology; Marine/Ocean Engineering; Natural Resources; Oceanography.

Award: Scholarship for use in freshman, sophomore, junior, senior, graduate, or postgraduate years; renewable. *Number:* 20–30. *Amount:* $2000–$3000.

Eligibility Requirements: Applicant must be enrolled or expecting to enroll full-time at a four-year institution or university; resident of Louisiana and studying in Louisiana. Applicant must have 2.5 GPA or higher. Available to U.S. citizens.

Application Requirements: Application, test scores, transcript, FAFSA. *Deadline:* July 1.

Contact: Bonnie Lavergne, Public Information
Louisiana Office of Student Financial Assistance
PO Box 91202
Baton Rouge, LA 70821-9202
Phone: 800-259-5626 Ext. 1012
Fax: 225-612-6508
E-mail: custserv@osfa.la.gov

NASA IDAHO SPACE GRANT CONSORTIUM

http://www.id.spacegrant.org/

NASA IDAHO SPACE GRANT CONSORTIUM SCHOLARSHIP PROGRAM

Applicants must attend an Idaho accredited institution and maintain a 3.0 GPA. Major/career interest in engineering, mathematics, science or secondary education in math or science. Applicants must be a US citizen.

Academic Fields/Career Goals: Biology; Chemical Engineering; Civil Engineering; Computer Science/Data Processing; Earth Science; Electrical Engineering/Electronics; Geography; Materials Science, Engineering, and Metallurgy; Mathematics; Mechanical Engineering; Natural Sciences; Physical Sciences.

Award: Scholarship for use in freshman, sophomore, junior, or senior years; renewable. *Number:* 1–15. *Amount:* $1000–$2500.

Eligibility Requirements: Applicant must be enrolled or expecting to enroll full-time at a two-year or four-year institution or university and studying in Idaho. Applicant must have 3.0 GPA or higher. Available to U.S. citizens.

Application Requirements: Application, essay, resume, references, test scores, transcript. *Deadline:* March 1.

Contact: Becky Highfill, Program Manager
NASA Idaho Space Grant Consortium
PO Box 441011
Moscow, ID 83844-1011
Phone: 208-885-6438
Fax: 208-885-1339
E-mail: bhighfill@uidaho.edu

NASA/MARYLAND SPACE GRANT CONSORTIUM

http://www.mdspacegrant.org/

NASA MARYLAND SPACE GRANT CONSORTIUM UNDERGRADUATE SCHOLARSHIPS
• *See page 127*

NASA MONTANA SPACE GRANT CONSORTIUM

http://www.spacegrant.montana.edu/

MONTANA SPACE GRANT SCHOLARSHIP PROGRAM
• *See page 128*

NASA SOUTH CAROLINA SPACE GRANT CONSORTIUM

http://www.cofc.edu/~scsgrant

KATHRYN SULLIVAN SCIENCE AND ENGINEERING FELLOWSHIP
• *See page 128*

PRE-SERVICE TEACHER SCHOLARSHIP
• *See page 129*

UNDERGRADUATE RESEARCH AWARD PROGRAM
• *See page 129*

NASA'S VIRGINIA SPACE GRANT CONSORTIUM

http://www.vsgc.odu.edu/

TEACHER EDUCATION STEM SCHOLARSHIP PROGRAM
• *See page 96*

UNDERGRADUATE RESEARCH STEM SCHOLARSHIPS
• *See page 96*

VIRGINIA STEM COMMUNITY COLLEGE SCHOLARSHIPS
• *See page 96*

NATIONAL ASSOCIATION OF WATER COMPANIES-NEW JERSEY CHAPTER

http://www.nawc.org/

NATIONAL ASSOCIATION OF WATER COMPANIES-NEW JERSEY CHAPTER SCHOLARSHIP

For college students interested in a career in the water utility industry or any related field. Must be U.S. citizen, five-year resident of New Jersey, high school senior or enrolled in a New Jersey college or university. Must maintain a 3.0 GPA.

Academic Fields/Career Goals: Biology; Business/Consumer Services; Communications; Computer Science/Data Processing; Earth Science; Economics; Engineering/Technology; Law/Legal Services; Natural Resources; Physical Sciences; Trade/Technical Specialties.

Award: Scholarship for use in freshman, sophomore, junior, senior, or graduate years; not renewable. *Number:* 1. *Amount:* $2500.

Eligibility Requirements: Applicant must be enrolled or expecting to enroll full- or part-time at a two-year or four-year institution or university; resident of New Jersey and studying in New Jersey. Applicant must have 3.0 GPA or higher. Available to U.S. citizens.

Application Requirements: Application, essay, references, transcript. *Deadline:* April 1.

Contact: Gail P. Brady, Scholarship Committee Chairperson
National Association of Water Companies-New Jersey Chapter
49 Howell Drive
Verona, NJ 07044
Phone: 973-669-5807
E-mail: gbradygbconsult@verizon.net

NATIONAL COUNCIL OF STATE GARDEN CLUBS INC. SCHOLARSHIP

http://www.gardenclub.org/

NATIONAL COUNCIL OF STATE GARDEN CLUBS INC. SCHOLARSHIP
• *See page 85*

NATIONAL GARDEN CLUBS INC.

http://www.gardenclub.org/

NATIONAL GARDEN CLUBS INC. SCHOLARSHIP PROGRAM
• *See page 86*

NATIONAL INSTITUTES OF HEALTH

https://ugsp.nih.gov/

NIH UNDERGRADUATE SCHOLARSHIP PROGRAM FOR STUDENTS FROM DISADVANTAGED BACKGROUNDS

Award to student from a disadvantaged background is one who comes from a family with an annual income below a level based on low-income thresholds according to family size, as published by the U.S. Bureau of the Census. Must be enrolled full-time at a postsecondary institution and have a GPA of 3.5 or higher. Visit web site http://www.ugsp.nih.gov for more details.

Academic Fields/Career Goals: Biology; Health and Medical Sciences; Social Sciences.

Award: Scholarship for use in freshman, sophomore, junior, or senior years; renewable. *Number:* 7–10. *Amount:* $20,000.

Eligibility Requirements: Applicant must be enrolled or expecting to enroll full-time at a two-year or four-year institution or university. Applicant must have 3.5 GPA or higher. Available to U.S. citizens.

Application Requirements: Application, essay, financial need analysis, references, transcript. *Deadline:* February 28.

Contact: Executive Assistant
National Institutes of Health
Two Center Drive, Room 2W11A, MSC 0230
Bethesda, MD 20892-0230
Phone: 888-352-3001
Fax: 301-496-2555
E-mail: wardron@mail.nih.gov

NATIONAL INVENTORS HALL OF FAME

http://www.invent.org/

COLLEGIATE INVENTORS COMPETITION FOR UNDERGRADUATE STUDENTS
• *See page 96*

COLLEGIATE INVENTORS COMPETITION-GRAND PRIZE
• *See page 97*

OREGON STUDENT ASSISTANCE COMMISSION

http://www.GetCollegeFunds.org/

OREGON FOUNDATION FOR BLACKTAIL DEER SCHOLARSHIP

One-time award for Oregon high school graduate enrolled in forestry, biology, wildlife science, or related majors in an Oregon college or university. Must demonstrate a serious commitment to career in wildlife management. Must submit 250-word essay on wildlife management. More information is available at web site: https://secure.osac.state.or.us.

Academic Fields/Career Goals: Biology; Environmental Science; Natural Resources.

Award: Scholarship for use in freshman, sophomore, junior, or senior years; not renewable. *Number:* varies. *Amount:* varies.

Eligibility Requirements: Applicant must be enrolled or expecting to enroll full-time at a four-year institution; resident of Oregon and studying in Oregon. Available to U.S. citizens.

Application Requirements: Application, essay, financial need analysis, references, transcript, activity chart, previous year's hunting license. *Deadline:* March 1.

Contact: Director of Grant Programs
Oregon Student Assistance Commission
1500 Valley River Drive, Suite 100
Eugene, OR 97401-7020
Phone: 800-452-8807 Ext. 7395

PEARSON BENJAMIN CUMMINGS

http://www.pearsonhighered.com/

PEARSON BENJAMIN CUMMINGS ALLIED HEALTH STUDENT SCHOLARSHIP

Two scholarships of $1,250 awarded to students currently enrolled in an anatomy, physiology or microbiology course. Students are also eligible if they have successfully completed one of these courses within the past two years.

Academic Fields/Career Goals: Biology; Health and Medical Sciences.

Award: Scholarship for use in freshman, sophomore, junior, or senior years; not renewable. *Number:* 2. *Amount:* $1250.

Eligibility Requirements: Applicant must be enrolled or expecting to enroll full-time at a four-year institution or university. Available to U.S. citizens.

Application Requirements: Application, essay. *Deadline:* November 1.

Contact: Scholarship Committee
Pearson Benjamin Cummings
1301 Sansome Street
San Francisco, CA 94111
Phone: 415-402-2500

PEARSON BENJAMIN CUMMINGS BIOLOGY PRIZE SCHOLARSHIP

Five scholarships of $500 each to biology majors who are currently enrolled in a general biology course or who have successfully completed a general biology course within the past two years.

Academic Fields/Career Goals: Biology.

Award: Scholarship for use in freshman, sophomore, junior, or senior years; not renewable. *Number:* 5. *Amount:* $500.

Eligibility Requirements: Applicant must be enrolled or expecting to enroll full-time at a four-year institution or university. Available to U.S. citizens.

Application Requirements: Application. *Deadline:* November 6.

Contact: Scholarship Committee
Pearson Benjamin Cummings
1301 Sansome Street
San Francisco, CA 94111
Phone: 415-402-2500

PENNSYLVANIA ASSOCIATION OF CONSERVATION DISTRICTS AUXILIARY

http://www.pacd.org/

PACD AUXILIARY SCHOLARSHIPS
• *See page 87*

ROBERT H. MOLLOHAN FAMILY CHARITABLE FOUNDATION, INC.

http://www.mollohanfoundation.org/

HIGH TECHNOLOGY SCHOLARS PROGRAM

Scholarship for West Virginia students pursuing a technology-related career and residing in one of the following counties: Barbour, Brooke, Calhoun, Doddridge, Gilmer, Grant, Hancock, Harrison, Marion, Marshall, Mineral, Monongalia, Ohio, Pleasants, Preston, Ritchie, Taylor, Tucker, Tyler, Wetzel, Wood. Scholarship recipients become eligible for a paid internship with a West Virginia business. Students may also apply for debt-forgiveness loans up to $2000 per year.

Academic Fields/Career Goals: Biology; Chemical Engineering; Computer Science/Data Processing; Electrical Engineering/Electronics; Energy and Power Engineering; Engineering/Technology; Engineering-Related Technologies; Mechanical Engineering; Physical Sciences.

Award: Scholarship for use in freshman year; not renewable. *Number:* 1–60. *Amount:* $500–$2000.

Eligibility Requirements: Applicant must be high school student; planning to enroll or expecting to enroll full-time at a four-year institution or university and resident of West Virginia. Applicant must have 3.0 GPA or higher. Available to U.S. citizens.

Application Requirements: Application, essay, resume, references, test scores, transcript. *Deadline:* February 9.

Contact: Aime L. Shaffer, Program Manager
Robert H. Mollohan Family Charitable Foundation, Inc.
1000 Technology Drive, Suite 2000
Fairmont, WV 26554
Phone: 304-333-6783
Fax: 304-333-3900
E-mail: ashaffer@wvhtf.org

SAN DIEGO FOUNDATION

http://www.sdfoundation.org/

BIOCOM SCHOLARSHIP

Scholarship open to graduating high school seniors with a minimum 3.5 GPA, who plan to attend an accredited two-year college or four-year university in the United States. Applicants must demonstrate a likelihood of achieving academic success with primary emphasis in biology, chemistry, physical and computational bio-sciences or biomedical engineering. Scholarship may be renewable for four years provided the recipient maintains a positive academic and citizenship record.

Academic Fields/Career Goals: Biology; Physical Sciences; Science, Technology, and Society.

Award: Scholarship for use in freshman year; renewable. *Number:* 5. *Amount:* $1500.

Eligibility Requirements: Applicant must be high school student; planning to enroll or expecting to enroll full-time at a two-year or four-year institution or university and resident of California. Applicant must have 3.5 GPA or higher. Available to U.S. citizens.

Application Requirements: Application, references, transcript, personal statement, copy of tax return. *Deadline:* January 26.

Contact: Shryl Helvie, Scholarship Coordinator
San Diego Foundation
2508 Historic Decatur Road, Suite 200
San Diego, CA 92106
Phone: 619-814-1307
Fax: 619-239-1710
E-mail: shryl@sdfoundation.org

SIGMA XI, THE SCIENTIFIC RESEARCH SOCIETY

http://www.sigmaxi.org/

SIGMA XI GRANTS-IN-AID OF RESEARCH
• *See page 87*

SOCIETY FOR INTEGRATIVE AND COMPARATIVE BIOLOGY

http://www.sicb.org/

LIBBIE H. HYMAN MEMORIAL SCHOLARSHIP

Scholarship provides assistance to students to take courses or to carry on research on invertebrates at a marine freshwater or terrestrial field station. For more information and/or an application, go to web site http://www.sicb.org.

Academic Fields/Career Goals: Biology; Marine Biology.

Award: Scholarship for use in senior year; not renewable. *Number:* 1. *Amount:* $750–$1200.

Eligibility Requirements: Applicant must be enrolled or expecting to enroll full- or part-time at a four-year institution or university. Available to U.S. and non-U.S. citizens.

Application Requirements: Application, essay, financial need analysis, references, transcript. *Deadline:* March 6.

Contact: Bruno Pernet, Chair, Scholarship Committee
Society for Integrative and Comparative Biology
California State University
Long Beach, CA 90840
Phone: 562-985-5378
Fax: 562-985-8878
E-mail: bpernet@csulb.edu

SOCIETY FOR THE SCIENTIFIC STUDY OF SEXUALITY

http://www.sexscience.org/

SOCIETY FOR THE SCIENTIFIC STUDY OF SEXUALITY STUDENT RESEARCH GRANT
• *See page 137*

SOIL AND WATER CONSERVATION SOCIETY-NEW JERSEY CHAPTER

http://www.geocities.com/njswcs

EDWARD R. HALL SCHOLARSHIP
• *See page 81*

TKE EDUCATIONAL FOUNDATION

http://www.tke.org/

CARROL C. HALL MEMORIAL SCHOLARSHIP
• *See page 97*

TIMOTHY L. TASCHWER SCHOLARSHIP

Scholarship available to an undergraduate member of Tau Kappa Epsilon. Must be a full-time student with at least sophomore year standing and a minimum GPA of 2.75. Applicant must be pursuing a degree in natural resources, earth sciences or related subjects and have a record of active TKE chapter leadership involvement. Preference shall be given to qualified graduates of the TKE Leadership Academy.

Academic Fields/Career Goals: Biology; Earth Science; Environmental Science; Natural Resources.

Award: Scholarship for use in sophomore, junior, or senior years; not renewable. *Number:* varies. *Amount:* $500.

Eligibility Requirements: Applicant must be enrolled or expecting to enroll full-time at a four-year institution or university; male and must have an interest in leadership. Applicant or parent of applicant must be member of Tau Kappa Epsilon. Available to U.S. and non-U.S. citizens.

Application Requirements: Application, photo, transcript, narrative summary of how TKE membership has benefited applicant. *Deadline:* February 29.

Contact: Scholarship Committee
TKE Educational Foundation
8645 Founders Road
Indianapolis, IN 46268-1336
Phone: 317-872-6533
Fax: 317-875-8353
E-mail: tef@tke.org

UNITED NEGRO COLLEGE FUND

http://www.uncf.org/

ALFRED CHISHOLM/BASF MEMORIAL SCHOLARSHIP FUND
• *See page 72*

ARLENE BENTON NOLAN AND JOHN NOLAN SCHOLARSHIP

One-time award for African American students who have a permanent residence in Prince George's County, Maryland. Must be graduating high senior or high school graduate; plan to major in biology, chemistry, engineering, mathematics, nursing, physical sciences, physics, pre-medicine, pre-nursing, or science; and attend a UNCF member college or university. Minimum GPA of 3.0 required.

Academic Fields/Career Goals: Biology; Engineering/Technology; Mathematics; Nursing; Physical Sciences.

Award: Scholarship for use in freshman year; not renewable. *Amount:* up to $1500.

Eligibility Requirements: Applicant must be Black (non-Hispanic); enrolled or expecting to enroll at a four-year institution and resident of Maryland. Applicant must have 3.0 GPA or higher. Available to U.S. citizens.

Application Requirements: *Deadline:* May 31.

Contact: Director, Program Services
United Negro College Fund
8260 Willow Oaks Corporate Drive
PO Box 10444
Fairfax, VA 22031-8044
Phone: 800-331-2244
E-mail: rebecca.bennett@uncf.org

CARGILL SCHOLARSHIP PROGRAM
• *See page 72*

CATHOLIC HEALTHCARE WEST CORPORATE SCHOLARS PROGRAM

Award for paid summer internship opportunity with Catholic Healthcare West (CHW) at one of its California or Arizona locations. Successful completion of the internship will result in the intern receiving a need-based scholarship of $10,000. Must be college sophomore, have a minimum 3.0 GPA, and majoring in biology, chemistry, health, hospital administration, microbiology, nursing, pharmacy, physics, or pre-medicine.

Academic Fields/Career Goals: Biology; Health and Medical Sciences; Nursing; Pharmacy; Physical Sciences.

Award: Scholarship for use in sophomore year; not renewable. *Amount:* up to $10,000.

Eligibility Requirements: Applicant must be enrolled or expecting to enroll at a four-year institution. Applicant must have 3.0 GPA or higher. Available to U.S. citizens.

Application Requirements: *Deadline:* April 25.

Contact: Director, Program Services
United Negro College Fund
8260 Willow Oaks Corporate Drive
PO Box 10444
Fairfax, VA 22031-8044
Phone: 800-331-2244
E-mail: rebecca.bennett@uncf.org

CHARLES E. CULPEPPER SCHOLARSHIP

Scholarship of $1000 available for African American students attending UNCF member colleges and universities and completing the Fisk Pre-Medicine program. Should have minimum GPA of 3.0 with majors in science and technology. For additional information and an online general application, visit http://www.uncf.org.

Academic Fields/Career Goals: Biology; Health and Medical Sciences; Natural Sciences.

Award: Scholarship for use in freshman, sophomore, junior, or senior years; not renewable. *Number:* varies. *Amount:* $1000.

Eligibility Requirements: Applicant must be Black (non-Hispanic) and enrolled or expecting to enroll full- or part-time at a four-year institution or university. Applicant must have 3.0 GPA or higher. Available to U.S. and non-U.S. citizens.

Application Requirements: Application, financial need analysis, FAFSA, Student Aid Report (SAR).

Contact: Director, Program Services
United Negro College Fund
8260 Willow Oaks Corporate Drive
PO Box 10444
Fairfax, VA 22031-8044
Phone: 800-331-2244
E-mail: rebecca.bennett@uncf.org

EARL & PATRICIA ARMSTRONG SCHOLARSHIP

Scholarship up to $3000 for students at UNCF member colleges and universities studying pre-medicine, biology, or health. Minimum 3.0 GPA required.

Academic Fields/Career Goals: Biology.

Award: Scholarship for use in freshman year; not renewable. *Amount:* up to $3000.

Eligibility Requirements: Applicant must be Black (non-Hispanic) and enrolled or expecting to enroll at a four-year institution or university. Applicant must have 3.0 GPA or higher. Available to U.S. citizens.

Application Requirements: *Deadline:* continuous.

Contact: Director, Program Services
United Negro College Fund
8260 Willow Oaks Corporate Drive
PO Box 10444
Fairfax, VA 22031-8044
Phone: 800-331-2244
E-mail: rebecca.bennett@uncf.org

MEDTRONIC FOUNDATION SCHOLARSHIP

Scholarship for undergraduate sophomores and juniors majoring in engineering or science related subjects and attending a UNCF member college or university. A paid summer internship is included in the award. Minimum 3.3 GPA required. Prospective applicants should complete the student profile found at web site http://www.uncf.org.

Academic Fields/Career Goals: Biology; Chemical Engineering; Civil Engineering; Electrical Engineering/Electronics; Engineering/Technology; Engineering-Related Technologies; Health and Medical Sciences; Mechanical Engineering; Physical Sciences.

Award: Scholarship for use in sophomore or junior years; not renewable. *Number:* 1–5. *Amount:* $5000.

Eligibility Requirements: Applicant must be Black (non-Hispanic) and enrolled or expecting to enroll full- or part-time at a four-year institution or university. Available to U.S. citizens.

Application Requirements: Application, financial need analysis, resume, references. *Deadline:* April 15.

Contact: Director, Program Services
United Negro College Fund
8260 Willow Oaks Corporate Drive
PO Box 10444
Fairfax, VA 22031-8044
Phone: 800-331-2244
E-mail: rebecca.bennett@uncf.org

UNCF/MERCK SCIENCE INITIATIVE

Students must be undergraduate juniors (3.3 GPA), graduate students, or postdoctoral fellows majoring in the life or physical sciences. Eligible majors include pre-medicine, science, chemistry, biochemistry, biology, microbiology, biotechnical, biomedical research, health, medicine, comp biology, animal science, and chemical engineering. Application and additional information at http://www.uncf.org.

Academic Fields/Career Goals: Biology; Chemical Engineering; Environmental Science; Health and Medical Sciences; Natural Sciences; Neurobiology; Physical Sciences.

Award: Scholarship for use in junior, senior, graduate, or postgraduate years; not renewable. *Amount:* $25,000–$70,000.

Eligibility Requirements: Applicant must be Black (non-Hispanic) and enrolled or expecting to enroll full-time at an institution or university. Available to U.S. and non-U.S. citizens.

Application Requirements: Application, resume, references, transcript. *Deadline:* December 15.

Contact: Dr. Jerry Bryant, UNCF
United Negro College Fund
8260 Willow Oaks Corporate Drive
Fairfax, VA 22031
E-mail: uncfmerck@uncf.org

VERMONT SPACE GRANT CONSORTIUM

http://www.cems.uvm.edu/vsgc

VERMONT SPACE GRANT CONSORTIUM SCHOLARSHIP PROGRAM
• See page 98

WILSON ORNITHOLOGICAL SOCIETY

http://www.wilsonsociety.org/

GEORGE A. HALL/HAROLD F. MAYFIELD AWARD
• See page 92

PAUL A. STEWART AWARDS
• See page 92

BUSINESS/CONSUMER SERVICES

AACE INTERNATIONAL

http://www.aacei.org/

AACE INTERNATIONAL COMPETITIVE SCHOLARSHIP
• See page 99

AMERICAN ASSOCIATION OF HISPANIC CERTIFIED PUBLIC ACCOUNTANTS (AAHCPA)

http://www.alpfa.org/

ALPFA ANNUAL SCHOLARSHIP PROGRAM
• See page 56

AMERICAN CONGRESS ON SURVEYING AND MAPPING

http://www.acsm.net/

TRI-STATE SURVEYING AND PHOTOGRAMMETRY KRIS M. KUNZE MEMORIAL SCHOLARSHIP

One-time award of $1000 for students pursuing college-level courses in business administration or business management. Candidates, in order of priority, include professional land surveyors and certified photogrammetrists, land survey interns and students enrolled in a two- or four-year program in surveying and mapping. Must be ACSM member.

Academic Fields/Career Goals: Business/Consumer Services; Surveying, Surveying Technology, Cartography, or Geographic Information Science.

Award: Scholarship for use in freshman, sophomore, junior, or senior years; not renewable. *Number:* 1. *Amount:* $1000.

Eligibility Requirements: Applicant must be enrolled or expecting to enroll full- or part-time at a two-year or four-year institution or university. Applicant or parent of applicant must be member of American Congress on Surveying and Mapping. Available to U.S. citizens.

Application Requirements: Application, essay, references, transcript, membership proof. *Deadline:* October 1.

Contact: Dawn James, ACSM Member Organizations Administrator
American Congress on Surveying and Mapping
6 Montgomery Village Avenue, Suite 403
Gaithersburg, MD 20879
Phone: 240-632-9716 Ext. 113
Fax: 240-632-1321
E-mail: dawn.james@acsm.net

AMERICAN INDIAN SCIENCE AND ENGINEERING SOCIETY

http://www.aises.org/

A.T. ANDERSON MEMORIAL SCHOLARSHIP PROGRAM
• *See page 93*

BURLINGTON NORTHERN SANTA FE FOUNDATION SCHOLARSHIP
• *See page 93*

AMERICAN PUBLIC TRANSPORTATION FOUNDATION

http://www.apta.com/

DAN REICHARD JR. SCHOLARSHIP

Scholarship for study towards a career in the business administration/management area of the transit industry. Must be sponsored by APTA member organization and complete internship with APTA member organization. Minimum GPA of 3.0 required.

Academic Fields/Career Goals: Business/Consumer Services; Transportation.

Award: Scholarship for use in sophomore, junior, senior, or graduate years; renewable. *Number:* 1. *Amount:* $2500.

Eligibility Requirements: Applicant must be enrolled or expecting to enroll full-time at a two-year or four-year institution or university. Applicant must have 3.0 GPA or higher. Available to U.S. and Canadian citizens.

Application Requirements: Application, essay, financial need analysis, references, transcript, verification of enrollment for the current semester, copy of fee schedule from the college/university. *Deadline:* June 16.

Contact: Pamela Boswell, Vice President of Program Management
American Public Transportation Foundation
1666 K Street, NW
Washington, DC 20006-1215
Phone: 202-496-4803
Fax: 202-496-2323
E-mail: pboswell@apta.com

AMERICAN WELDING SOCIETY

http://www.aws.org/

JAMES A. TURNER, JR. MEMORIAL SCHOLARSHIP

Award for a full-time student pursuing minimum four-year bachelor's degree in business that will lead to a management career in welding store operations or a welding distributorship. Applicant must be working in this field at least 10 hours per week. Submit verification of employment, a copy of proposed curriculum, and acceptance letter.

Academic Fields/Career Goals: Business/Consumer Services.

Award: Scholarship for use in freshman, sophomore, junior, or senior years; renewable. *Number:* 1. *Amount:* $3500.

Eligibility Requirements: Applicant must be age 18 and over and enrolled or expecting to enroll full-time at a four-year institution or university. Available to U.S. citizens.

Application Requirements: Application, financial need analysis, references, transcript. *Deadline:* February 15.

Contact: Vicki Pinsky, Manager, Foundation
American Welding Society
550 Le Jeune Road, NW
Miami, FL 33126
Phone: 800-443-9353 Ext. 212
Fax: 305-443-7559
E-mail: vpinsky@aws.org

AMERICAN WHOLESALE MARKETERS ASSOCIATION

http://www.awmanet.org/

RAY FOLEY MEMORIAL YOUTH EDUCATION FOUNDATION SCHOLARSHIP

Scholarship program annually offers two $5000 scholarships to deserving students. Awards are based on academic merit and a career interest in the candy/tobacco/ convenience-products wholesale industry. Must be employed by an AWMA wholesaler distributor member or be an immediate family member. Must be enrolled full-time in an undergraduate or graduate program. For details visit web site http://www.awmanet.org/.

Academic Fields/Career Goals: Business/Consumer Services.

Award: Scholarship for use in freshman, sophomore, junior, senior, or graduate years; not renewable. *Number:* 2. *Amount:* $5000.

Eligibility Requirements: Applicant must be enrolled or expecting to enroll full-time at a four-year institution or university. Available to U.S. citizens.

Application Requirements: Application, essay, references. *Deadline:* May 21.

Contact: Kathy Trost, Manager of Education
American Wholesale Marketers Association
2750 Prosperity Avenue, Suite 530
Fairfax, VA 22031
Phone: 800-482-2962 Ext. 648
Fax: 703-573-5738
E-mail: kathyt@awmanet.org

ARRL FOUNDATION INC.

http://www.arrl.org/

WILLIAM R. GOLDFARB MEMORIAL SCHOLARSHIP

Award for baccalaureate study in business, computers, medical or nursing, engineering, or sciences. Must be a licensed amateur radio operator. Must demonstrate financial need. Must be a high school senior.

Academic Fields/Career Goals: Business/Consumer Services; Computer Science/Data Processing; Engineering/Technology; Health and Medical Sciences; Natural Sciences; Nursing; Physical Sciences.

Award: Scholarship for use in freshman, sophomore, junior, or senior years; not renewable. *Number:* 1. *Amount:* $10,000.

Eligibility Requirements: Applicant must be high school student; planning to enroll or expecting to enroll full-time at a four-year institution or university and must have an interest in amateur radio. Available to U.S. citizens.

Application Requirements: Application, financial need analysis, transcript, FAFSA, Student Aid Report (SAR). *Deadline:* February 1.

Contact: Ms. Mary Hobart, Secretary
ARRL Foundation Inc.
225 Main Street
Newington, CT 06111-1494
Phone: 860-594-0397
E-mail: k1mmh@arrl.org

ASSOCIATION FOR FOOD AND DRUG OFFICIALS

http://www.afdo.org/

ASSOCIATION FOR FOOD AND DRUG OFFICIALS SCHOLARSHIP FUND

A $1500 scholarship for students in their third or fourth year of college/university who have demonstrated a desire for a career in research, regulatory work, quality control, or teaching in an area related to some aspect of food, drugs, or consumer products safety. Minimum 3.0 GPA required in first two years of undergraduate study. For further information visit web site http://www.afdo.org.

Academic Fields/Career Goals: Business/Consumer Services; Food Science/Nutrition.

Award: Scholarship for use in junior or senior years; not renewable. *Number:* 2. *Amount:* $1500.

Eligibility Requirements: Applicant must be enrolled or expecting to enroll full-time at a four-year institution or university. Applicant must have 3.0 GPA or higher. Available to U.S. and non-U.S. citizens.

Application Requirements: Application, essay, references, transcript. *Deadline:* February 1.

Contact: Leigh Stamdaugh, Administrative/Special Projects Assistant
Association for Food and Drug Officials
2550 Kingston Road, Suite 311
York, PA 17402
Phone: 717-757-2888
Fax: 717-755-8089
E-mail: afdo@afdo.org

BALTIMORE CHAPTER OF THE AMERICAN MARKETING ASSOCIATION

http://www.amabaltimore.org/

UNDERGRADUATE MARKETING EDUCATION MERIT SCHOLARSHIPS

Scholarship of $2500 awarded for first place and two $500 runner-up awards for full-time students in marketing. Must be attending a 4-year college or university in Maryland with credits equivalent to the status of a junior or senior as of September.

Academic Fields/Career Goals: Business/Consumer Services; Marketing.

Award: Scholarship for use in sophomore or junior years; not renewable. *Number:* 3. *Amount:* $500–$2500.

Eligibility Requirements: Applicant must be enrolled or expecting to enroll full-time at a four-year institution or university. Applicant must have 3.0 GPA or higher. Available to U.S. and non-U.S. citizens.

Application Requirements: Application, test scores. *Deadline:* February 16.

Contact: Marisa O'Brien, Scholarship Committee
Baltimore Chapter of the American Marketing Association
22 West Road, Suite 301
Towson, MD 21204
Phone: 410-467-2529
E-mail: scholarship@amabaltimore.org

BRITISH COLUMBIA INNOVATION COUNCIL

http://www.bcic.ca/

BCIC YOUNG INNOVATOR SCHOLARSHIP COMPETITION (IDEA MASH UP)
• See page 95

CATCHING THE DREAM

http://www.catchingthedream.org/

MATH, ENGINEERING, SCIENCE, BUSINESS, EDUCATION, COMPUTERS SCHOLARSHIPS

Renewable scholarships for Native American students planning to study math, engineering, science, business, education, and computers, or presently studying in these fields. Study of social science, humanities and liberal arts also funded. Scholarships are awarded on merit and on the basis of likelihood of recipient improving the lives of Native American people. Scholarships are available nationwide.

Academic Fields/Career Goals: Business/Consumer Services; Computer Science/Data Processing; Education; Engineering/Technology; Humanities; Physical Sciences; Science, Technology, and Society; Social Sciences.

Award: Scholarship for use in freshman, sophomore, junior, senior, graduate, or postgraduate years; renewable. *Number:* 180. *Amount:* $500–$5000.

Eligibility Requirements: Applicant must be American Indian/Alaska Native and enrolled or expecting to enroll full-time at a two-year or four-year institution or university. Applicant must have 3.0 GPA or higher. Available to U.S. citizens.

Application Requirements: Application, essay, financial need analysis, photo, references, test scores, transcript, certificate of Indian blood. *Deadline:* varies.

Contact: Mary Frost, Recruiter
Catching the Dream
8200 Mountain Road, NE, Suite 203
Albuquerque, NM 87110
Phone: 505-262-2351
Fax: 505-262-0534
E-mail: nscholarsh@aol.com

NATIVE AMERICAN LEADERSHIP IN EDUCATION (NALE)

Renewable scholarships available for Native American and Alaska Native students. Must be at least one-quarter Native American from a federally recognized, state recognized, or terminated tribe. Must be U.S. citizen. Must demonstrate high academic achievement, depth of character, leadership, seriousness of purpose, and service orientation.

Academic Fields/Career Goals: Business/Consumer Services; Education; Humanities; Physical Sciences; Science, Technology, and Society.

Award: Scholarship for use in freshman, sophomore, junior, senior, graduate, or postgraduate years; renewable. *Number:* up to 30. *Amount:* $500–$5000.

Eligibility Requirements: Applicant must be American Indian/Alaska Native and enrolled or expecting to enroll full-time at a four-year institution or university. Applicant must have 3.0 GPA or higher. Available to U.S. citizens.

Application Requirements: Application, essay, financial need analysis, photo, references, test scores, transcript, certificate of Indian blood. *Deadline:* varies.

Contact: Mary Frost, Recruiter
Catching the Dream
8200 Mountain Road, NE, Suite 203
Albuquerque, NM 87110
Phone: 505-262-2351
Fax: 505-262-0534
E-mail: nscholarsh@aol.com

TRIBAL BUSINESS MANAGEMENT PROGRAM (TBM)
• See page 57

CENTRAL INTELLIGENCE AGENCY

http://www.cia.gov/

CENTRAL INTELLIGENCE AGENCY UNDERGRADUATE SCHOLARSHIP PROGRAM
• See page 58

CIRI FOUNDATION (TCF)

http://www.thecirifoundation.org/

CAP LATHROP SCHOLARSHIP PROGRAM

Award for an Alaska Native enrollee or descendant of original enrollee to an ANCSA regional or village corporation. Must be enrolled or accepted into an accredited or authorized college or university as a full-time student and have a minimum 3.0 GPA. An applicant must be a declared major in broadcast, telecommunications, business, engineering, journalism, or other media related degree programs to be considered.

Academic Fields/Career Goals: Business/Consumer Services; Journalism; TV/Radio Broadcasting.

Award: Scholarship for use in freshman, sophomore, junior, senior, or graduate years; not renewable. *Number:* varies. *Amount:* up to $4000.

Eligibility Requirements: Applicant must be American Indian/Alaska Native and enrolled or expecting to enroll full-time at a two-year or four-year institution or university. Applicant must have 3.0 GPA or higher. Available to U.S. and Canadian citizens.

Application Requirements: Application, essay, financial need analysis, photo, references, transcript, proof of eligibility, statement of purpose. *Deadline:* June 1.

Contact: Susan Anderson, President and Chief Executive Officer
CIRI Foundation (TCF)
3600 San Jeronimo Drive, Suite 256
Anchorage, AK 99508-2870
Phone: 907-793-3575
E-mail: tcf@thecirifoundation.org

CARL H. MARRS SCHOLARSHIP FUND
• *See page 58*

CLEVELAND SCHOLARSHIP PROGRAMS

http://www.cspohio.org/

CSP MANAGED FUNDS-CLEVELAND BROWNS MARION MOTLEY SCHOLARSHIP
• *See page 58*

CONNECTICUT COMMUNITY FOUNDATION

http://www.conncf.org/

MALCOLM BALDRIGE SCHOLARSHIP

One-time award for undergraduates studying in accredited colleges or universities of Connecticut majoring in international business or trade. Must be a Connecticut resident. The award value is in the range of $2000 to $4000 and up to two scholarships are granted annually.

Academic Fields/Career Goals: Business/Consumer Services; International Studies.

Award: Scholarship for use in freshman, sophomore, junior, or senior years; not renewable. *Number:* 1–3. *Amount:* $2000–$4000.

Eligibility Requirements: Applicant must be enrolled or expecting to enroll full- or part-time at a two-year or four-year institution or university; resident of Connecticut and studying in Connecticut. Available to U.S. citizens.

Application Requirements: Application, essay, financial need analysis, references, transcript. *Deadline:* March 15.

Contact: Josh Carey, Program Officer
Connecticut Community Foundation
43 Field Street
Waterbury, CT 06702-1216
Phone: 203-753-1315
E-mail: jcarey@conncf.org

CUBAN AMERICAN NATIONAL FOUNDATION

http://www.masscholarships.org/

MAS FAMILY SCHOLARSHIPS

Graduate and undergraduate scholarships in the fields of engineering, business, international relations, economics, communications, and journalism. Applicants must be Cuban-American and have graduated in the top 10 percent of high school class or have minimum 3.5 college GPA. Selection based on need, academic performance, leadership. Those who have already received awards and maintained high level of performance are given preference over new applicants.

Academic Fields/Career Goals: Business/Consumer Services; Chemical Engineering; Communications; Economics; Electrical Engineering/Electronics; Engineering/Technology; Engineering-Related Technologies; Journalism; Mechanical Engineering; Political Science.

Award: Scholarship for use in freshman, sophomore, junior, senior, or graduate years; renewable. *Number:* 10–15. *Amount:* up to $10,000.

Eligibility Requirements: Applicant must be of Latin American/Caribbean heritage; Hispanic; enrolled or expecting to enroll full-time at a two-year or four-year institution or university and must have an interest in leadership. Applicant must have 3.5 GPA or higher. Available to U.S. citizens.

Application Requirements: Application, driver's license, essay, financial need analysis, references, test scores, transcript, proof of Cuban descent, proof of admission. *Deadline:* March 31.

Contact: Melanie Martinez, Director of Community Relations
Cuban American National Foundation
PO Box 14-1898
Miami, FL 33114
Phone: 305-592-0075
E-mail: mmartinez@jmcffmasscholarships.org

DADE COMMUNITY FOUNDATION

http://www.jackituckfield.org/

DR. FELIX H. REYLER (FIBA) SCHOLARSHIP

Award for an undergraduate junior or senior enrolled full time in a program of business/finance at a Florida college or university. Must be a resident of Florida. Students graduating from the Academy for International Business and Finance at Miami Jackson Senior High and children of Florida International Bankers Association members may also apply. May reapply for a second year of the award if a 3.0 GPA is maintained. For additional information and application, visit web site http://www.dadecommunityfoundation.org.

Academic Fields/Career Goals: Business/Consumer Services; Finance.

Award: Scholarship for use in junior or senior years; not renewable. *Number:* 2. *Amount:* $2500.

Eligibility Requirements: Applicant must be enrolled or expecting to enroll full-time at a four-year institution or university; resident of Florida and studying in Florida. Applicant must have 3.0 GPA or higher. Available to U.S. citizens.

Application Requirements: Application, financial need analysis, resume, transcript, personal statement. *Deadline:* April 24.

Contact: Ted Seijo, Scholarship Coordinator
Dade Community Foundation
1160 Northwest 87 Street
Miami, FL 33150-2544
Phone: 305-371-2711
E-mail: ted.seijo@dadecommunityfoundation.org

SEITLIN FRANKLIN E. WHEELER SCHOLARSHIP

Award available for South Florida high school seniors who are planning to enroll in a two- or four-year college or university studying business or insurance. Applicant must demonstrate the highest ethical standards, commitment to excellence, and involvement in the community. Minimum GPA of 3.0 and a one-page essay on "Ethics" are required. For additional information and application, see web site http://www.dadecommunity-foundation.org.

Academic Fields/Career Goals: Business/Consumer Services; Insurance and Actuarial Science.

Award: Scholarship for use in freshman year; not renewable. *Number:* 2. *Amount:* $1500.

Eligibility Requirements: Applicant must be high school student; planning to enroll or expecting to enroll full-time at a two-year or four-year institution or university and resident of Florida. Applicant must have 3.0 GPA or higher. Available to U.S. citizens.

Application Requirements: Application, essay, resume, references, transcript. *Deadline:* May 8.

Contact: Ted Seijo, Scholarship Coordinator
Dade Community Foundation
1160 Northwest 87 Street
Miami, FL 33150-2544
Phone: 305-371-2711
E-mail: ted.seijo@dadecommunityfoundation.org

DAIRY MANAGEMENT

http://www.dairyinfo.com/

NATIONAL DAIRY PROMOTION AND RESEARCH BOARD SCHOLARSHIP
• *See page 84*

DECA (DISTRIBUTIVE EDUCATION CLUBS OF AMERICA)

http://www.deca.org/

HARRY A. APPLEGATE SCHOLARSHIP

Scholarship available to current DECA or Collegiate DECA members for undergraduate study. Must major in marketing education, merchandising, and/or management. Nonrenewable award for high school students based on DECA activities, grades, and need.

Academic Fields/Career Goals: Business/Consumer Services; Education; Fashion Design; Finance; Marketing.

Award: Scholarship for use in freshman, sophomore, junior, or senior years; not renewable. *Number:* 20–25. *Amount:* $1000.

Eligibility Requirements: Applicant must be enrolled or expecting to enroll full-time at a two-year or four-year institution or university. Applicant or parent of applicant must be member of Distribution Ed Club or Future Business Leaders of America. Available to U.S. and non-U.S. citizens.

Application Requirements: Application, references, test scores, transcript, copy of DECA chapter roster. *Deadline:* January 21.

Contact: Kathy Onion, Marketing Assistant
DECA (Distributive Education Clubs of America)
1908 Association Drive
Reston, VA 20191-1594
Phone: 703-860-5000 Ext. 248
E-mail: kathy_onion@deca.org

DELTA SIGMA PI LEADERSHIP FOUNDATION

http://www.dspnet.org/

DELTA SIGMA PI UNDERGRADUATE SCHOLARSHIP

Applicant must be a member of Delta Sigma Pi in good standing with at least one full semester or quarter of college remaining in the fall following application.

Academic Fields/Career Goals: Business/Consumer Services.

Award: Scholarship for use in sophomore, junior, or senior years; not renewable. *Number:* 1–40. *Amount:* $250–$3000.

Eligibility Requirements: Applicant must be enrolled or expecting to enroll full-time at a four-year institution or university. Available to U.S. and non-U.S. citizens.

Application Requirements: Application, essay, financial need analysis, references, transcript, description of fraternity, campus, community involvement. *Deadline:* June 15.

Contact: Shanda Gray, Executive Vice President
Delta Sigma Pi Leadership Foundation
330 South Campus Avenue
Oxford, OH 45056
Phone: 513-523-1907
Fax: 513-523-7292
E-mail: foundation@dspnet.org

EASTERN STAR-GRAND CHAPTER OF CALIFORNIA

http://www.oescal.org/

SCHOLARSHIPS FOR EDUCATION, BUSINESS AND RELIGION

Scholarship of $500 to $3000 awarded to students residing in California for post-secondary study. These scholarships are awarded for the study of business, education or religion.

Academic Fields/Career Goals: Business/Consumer Services; Education; Religion/Theology.

Award: Scholarship for use in freshman, sophomore, junior, or senior years; renewable. *Number:* varies. *Amount:* $500–$3000.

Eligibility Requirements: Applicant must be enrolled or expecting to enroll full-time at a two-year or four-year or technical institution or university and resident of California. Applicant must have 3.0 GPA or higher. Available to U.S. citizens.

Application Requirements: Application, financial need analysis, photo, references, self-addressed stamped envelope, transcript, proof of acceptance to college or university. *Deadline:* March 8.

Contact: Maryann Barrios, Grand Secretary
Eastern Star-Grand Chapter of California
16960 Bastanchury Road, Suite E
Yorba Linda, CA 92886-1711
Phone: 714-986-2380
Fax: 714-986-2385
E-mail: gsecretary@oescal.org

FAMILY, CAREER AND COMMUNITY LEADERS OF AMERICA-TEXAS ASSOCIATION

http://www.texasfccla.org/

FCCLA HOUSTON LIVESTOCK SHOW AND RODEO SCHOLARSHIP

Renewable scholarship for graduating high school seniors enrolled in full-time program in family and consumer sciences. Must be Texas resident and should study in Texas. Must have minimum GPA of 3.5.

Academic Fields/Career Goals: Business/Consumer Services; Home Economics.

Award: Scholarship for use in freshman year; renewable. *Number:* up to 10. *Amount:* $12,000.

Eligibility Requirements: Applicant must be high school student; planning to enroll or expecting to enroll full-time at a four-year institution or university; single; resident of Texas and studying in Texas. Applicant or parent of applicant must be member of Family, Career and Community Leaders of America. Applicant must have 3.5 GPA or higher. Available to U.S. citizens.

Application Requirements: Application, essay, photo, references, test scores, transcript. *Deadline:* March 1.

Contact: Staff
Family, Career and Community Leaders of America-Texas
Association
3530 Bee Caves Road, Suite 101
Austin, TX 78746-9616
Phone: 512-306-0099
Fax: 512-306-0041
E-mail: fccla@texasfccla.org

FCCLA REGIONAL SCHOLARSHIPS

One-time award for graduating high school seniors enrolled in full-time program in family and consumer sciences. Must be Texas resident and should study in Texas. Must have minimum GPA of 2.5.

Academic Fields/Career Goals: Business/Consumer Services; Home Economics.

Award: Scholarship for use in freshman year; not renewable. *Number:* up to 5. *Amount:* $1000.

Eligibility Requirements: Applicant must be high school student; planning to enroll or expecting to enroll full-time at a four-year institution or university; single; resident of Texas and studying in Texas. Applicant or parent of applicant must be member of Family, Career and Community Leaders of America. Applicant must have 2.5 GPA or higher. Available to U.S. citizens.

Application Requirements: Application, essay, references, test scores, transcript. *Deadline:* March 1.

Contact: Staff
Family, Career and Community Leaders of America-Texas
Association
3530 Bee Caves Road, Suite 101
Austin, TX 78746-9616
Phone: 512-306-0099
Fax: 512-306-0041
E-mail: fccla@texasfccla.org

FCCLA TEXAS FARM BUREAU SCHOLARSHIP

One-time award for a graduating high school senior enrolled in full-time program in family and consumer sciences. Must be a Texas resident and must study in Texas. Must have minimum GPA of 2.5. The award value is $1000.

Academic Fields/Career Goals: Business/Consumer Services; Home Economics.

Award: Scholarship for use in freshman year; not renewable. *Number:* 1. *Amount:* $1000.

Eligibility Requirements: Applicant must be high school student; planning to enroll or expecting to enroll full-time at a four-year institution or university; single; resident of Texas and studying in Texas. Applicant or parent of applicant must be member of Family, Career and Community Leaders of America. Applicant must have 2.5 GPA or higher. Available to U.S. citizens.

Application Requirements: Application, driver's license, essay, references, test scores, transcript. *Deadline:* March 1.

Contact: Staff
Family, Career and Community Leaders of America-Texas Association
3530 Bee Caves Road, Suite 101
Austin, TX 78746-9616
Phone: 512-306-0099
Fax: 512-306-0041
E-mail: fccla@texasfccla.org

FISHER BROADCASTING COMPANY

http://www.fsci.com/

FISHER BROADCASTING INC. SCHOLARSHIP FOR MINORITIES

Applicant must be of non-white origin, must be at least a sophomore, must be a U.S. citizen and must be in broadcast, marketing or journalism courses. If the applicant is permanent resident of the states of Washington, Oregon, Idaho or Montana, tuition may be applied to an out-of-state school. If the applicant is not a permanent resident of the above-mentioned states, tuition must be applied to a school in Washington, Oregon, Idaho or Montana. Require a minimum of 2.5 GPA.

Academic Fields/Career Goals: Business/Consumer Services; Journalism; TV/Radio Broadcasting.

Award: Scholarship for use in sophomore, junior, or senior years; not renewable. *Number:* up to 5. *Amount:* $1000–$10,000.

Eligibility Requirements: Applicant must be American Indian/Alaska Native, Asian/Pacific Islander, Black (non-Hispanic), or Hispanic and enrolled or expecting to enroll full-time at a two-year or four-year or technical institution or university. Applicant must have 2.5 GPA or higher. Available to U.S. citizens.

Application Requirements: Application, essay, financial need analysis, interview, references, transcript, citizenship proof. *Deadline:* April 30.

Contact: Annnarie Hitchcock, Human Resources Administrator
Fisher Broadcasting Company
100 Fourth Avenue North, Suite 510
Seattle, WA 98109
Phone: 206-404-6050
Fax: 206-404-6760
E-mail: ahitchcock@fsci.com

FLORIDA BANKERS EDUCATIONAL FOUNDATION

http://www.floridabankers.com/

FLORIDA BANKERS EDUCATIONAL FOUNDATION (FBEF) SCHOLARSHIP/LOAN

Program designed to support the education of future and/or current Florida bankers. Must be a Florida resident enrolled for at least 12 credit hours per year at FBEF participating Florida university and maintain a minimum 2.5 GPA. Loan to be paid back if program requirements are not met, including successfully completing degree and working for one year, full-time at a Florida bank after graduation.

Academic Fields/Career Goals: Business/Consumer Services.

Award: Forgivable loan for use in freshman, sophomore, junior, senior, or graduate years; not renewable. *Number:* 5–10. *Amount:* $750–$5000.

Eligibility Requirements: Applicant must be enrolled or expecting to enroll full- or part-time at a four-year institution or university; resident of Florida and studying in Florida. Applicant must have 2.5 GPA or higher. Available to U.S. citizens.

Application Requirements: Application, essay, interview, resume, references, transcript, authorization to pull credit history. *Deadline:* varies.

Contact: Ms. Letty Newton, Director
Florida Bankers Educational Foundation
PO Box 1360
Tallahassee, FL 32302-1360
Phone: 850-224-2265 Ext. 139
Fax: 850-222-6338
E-mail: lnewton@floridabankers.com

FUKUNAGA SCHOLARSHIP FOUNDATION

http://www.servco.com/

FUKUNAGA SCHOLARSHIP FOUNDATION

Renewable scholarships available only to Hawaii residents pursuing a business degree at the undergraduate level at an accredited institution. Minimum 3.0 GPA required.

Academic Fields/Career Goals: Business/Consumer Services.

Award: Scholarship for use in freshman, sophomore, junior, or senior years; renewable. *Number:* 10–15. *Amount:* $4000.

Eligibility Requirements: Applicant must be enrolled or expecting to enroll full-time at a four-year institution or university and resident of Hawaii. Applicant must have 3.0 GPA or higher. Available to U.S. citizens.

Application Requirements: Application, essay, financial need analysis, interview, references, test scores, transcript, FAFSA, Student Aid Report (SAR). *Deadline:* March 1.

Contact: Mrs. Sandy Wong, Program Administrator
Fukunaga Scholarship Foundation
PO Box 2788
Honolulu, HI 96803-2788
Phone: 808-564-1386
Fax: 808-523-3937
E-mail: sandyw@servco.com

GEORGIA GOVERNMENT FINANCE OFFICERS ASSOCIATION

http://www.ggfoa.org/

GGFOA SCHOLARSHIP
• See page 61

GEORGIA SOCIETY OF CERTIFIED PUBLIC ACCOUNTANTS

http://www.gscpa.org/

BEN W. BRANNON MEMORIAL SCHOLARSHIP FUND
• See page 61

CHAPTER AWARDED SCHOLARSHIPS
• See page 61

CHERRY, BEKAERT AND HOLLAND LLP ACCOUNTING SCHOLARSHIP
• See page 62

COLLINS/MOODY-COMPANY SCHOLARSHIP
• See page 62

EDUCATIONAL FOUNDATION DIRECT SCHOLARSHIPS
• See page 62

JULIUS M. JOHNSON MEMORIAL SCHOLARSHIP
• See page 62

PAYCHEX ENTREPRENEUR SCHOLARSHIP
• See page 62

ROBERT H. LANGE MEMORIAL SCHOLARSHIP
• See page 62

GOLDEN KEY INTERNATIONAL HONOUR SOCIETY

http://www.goldenkey.org/

BUSINESS ACHIEVEMENT AWARD

Award to members who excel in the study of business. Applicants will be asked to respond to a problem posed by an honorary member within the discipline. The response will be in the form of a professional business report. One winner will receive a $1000 award. The second place winner will receive $750 and the third place winner will receive $500.

Academic Fields/Career Goals: Business/Consumer Services.

Award: Prize for use in freshman, sophomore, junior, senior, graduate, or postgraduate years; not renewable. *Number:* 3. *Amount:* $500–$1000.

Eligibility Requirements: Applicant must be enrolled or expecting to enroll full- or part-time at a four-year institution or university. Available to U.S. and non-U.S. citizens.

Application Requirements: Application, applicant must enter a contest, essay, references, transcript, business-related report. *Deadline:* March 3.

Contact: Scholarship Program Administrators
Golden Key International Honour Society
PO Box 23737
Nashville, TN 37202-3737
Phone: 800-377-2401
E-mail: scholarships@goldenkey.org

GOVERNMENT FINANCE OFFICERS ASSOCIATION

http://www.gfoa.org/

FRANK L. GREATHOUSE GOVERNMENT ACCOUNTING SCHOLARSHIP

One to two scholarships awarded to undergraduate or graduate students enrolled full-time, preparing for a career in state or local government finance. Submit resume. One-time award of $3500.

Academic Fields/Career Goals: Business/Consumer Services; Public Policy and Administration.

Award: Scholarship for use in freshman, sophomore, junior, senior, or graduate years; not renewable. *Number:* 1–2. *Amount:* $3500.

Eligibility Requirements: Applicant must be enrolled or expecting to enroll full-time at a two-year or four-year or technical institution or university. Available to U.S. and Canadian citizens.

Application Requirements: Application, essay, resume, references, transcript. *Deadline:* February 29.

Contact: Jake Lorentz, Assistant Director
Government Finance Officers Association
203 North LaSalle Street, Suite 2700
Chicago, IL 60601-1210
Phone: 312-977-9700 Ext. 267
E-mail: jlorentz@gfoa.org

MINORITIES IN GOVERNMENT FINANCE SCHOLARSHIP
• *See page 63*

GREATER KANAWHA VALLEY FOUNDATION

http://www.tgkvf.org/

CHARLESTON ROTARY CLUB SCHOLARSHIP
• *See page 63*

WILLARD H. ERWIN JR. MEMORIAL SCHOLARSHIP FUND

Award of $1000 for West Virginia residents who are starting their junior or senior year of undergraduate or graduate studies in a business or health-care finance degree program. Must be enrolled at a college in West Virginia. Scholarships are awarded on the basis of financial need and scholastic ability.

Academic Fields/Career Goals: Business/Consumer Services; Health Administration.

Award: Scholarship for use in junior, senior, or graduate years; renewable. *Number:* 1. *Amount:* $1000.

Eligibility Requirements: Applicant must be enrolled or expecting to enroll full- or part-time at a four-year institution or university; resident of West Virginia and studying in West Virginia. Available to U.S. citizens.

Application Requirements: Application, essay, financial need analysis, references, self-addressed stamped envelope, test scores, transcript. *Deadline:* January 15.

Contact: Susan Hoover, Scholarship Coordinator
Greater Kanawha Valley Foundation
PO Box 3041
Charleston, WV 25331
Phone: 304-346-3620
Fax: 304-346-3640

GREAT FALLS ADVERTISING FEDERATION

http://www.gfaf.com/

GREAT FALLS ADVERTISING FEDERATION COLLEGE SCHOLARSHIP
• *See page 76*

HIGH SCHOOL MARKETING/COMMUNICATIONS SCHOLARSHIP
• *See page 76*

HOLSTEIN ASSOCIATION USA INC.

http://www.holsteinusa.com/

ROBERT H. RUMLER SCHOLARSHIP
• *See page 78*

IDAHO STATE BROADCASTERS ASSOCIATION

http://www.idahobroadcasters.org/

WAYNE C. CORNILS MEMORIAL SCHOLARSHIP

Scholarship for students enrolled in an Idaho school on a full-time basis. Must be majoring in a broadcasting related field. Must have minimum GPA of 2.0 if in the first two years of school or 2.5 in the last two years of school.

Academic Fields/Career Goals: Business/Consumer Services; Engineering/Technology; Journalism; TV/Radio Broadcasting.

Award: Scholarship for use in sophomore, junior, or senior years; not renewable. *Number:* 3. *Amount:* $1000.

Eligibility Requirements: Applicant must be enrolled or expecting to enroll full-time at a four-year institution or university; resident of Idaho and studying in Idaho. Applicant must have 2.5 GPA or higher. Available to U.S. citizens.

Application Requirements: Application, essay, references, transcript. *Deadline:* March 15.

Contact: Connie Searles, President & CEO
Idaho State Broadcasters Association
1674 Hill Rd., Ste. 3
Boise, ID 83702
Phone: 208-345-3072
Fax: 208-343-8046
E-mail: isba@qwestoffice.net

INDEPENDENT COLLEGE FUND OF MARYLAND (I-FUND)

http://www.i-fundinfo.org/

BRANCH BANKING & TRUST COMPANY SCHOLARSHIPS
• *See page 64*

CHEVY CHASE BANK SCHOLARSHIP
• See page 64

LEGG MASON SCHOLARSHIPS
• See page 64

INSTITUTE FOR OPERATIONS RESEARCH AND THE MANAGEMENT SCIENCES

http://www.informs.org/

GEORGE NICHOLSON STUDENT PAPER COMPETITION

Honors outstanding papers in the field of operations research and the management sciences. Entrant must be student on or after the year of application. Research papers present original results and be written by student. Electronic submission of paper required.

Academic Fields/Career Goals: Business/Consumer Services.

Award: Prize for use in junior, senior, graduate, or postgraduate years; not renewable. *Number:* up to 6. *Amount:* $100–$600.

Eligibility Requirements: Applicant must be enrolled or expecting to enroll full- or part-time at a four-year institution or university. Available to U.S. and non-U.S. citizens.

Application Requirements: Application, applicant must enter a contest, references. *Deadline:* June 30.

Contact: Mark Doherty, Executive Director
Institute for Operations Research and the Management Sciences
7240 Parkway Drive, Suite 310
Hanover, MD 21076-1310
Phone: 410-850-0300
Fax: 410-684-2963
E-mail: mark.doherty@informs.org

INSTITUTE OF MANAGEMENT ACCOUNTANTS

http://www.imanet.org/

INSTITUTE OF MANAGEMENT ACCOUNTANTS MEMORIAL EDUCATION FUND SCHOLARSHIPS
• See page 65

STUART CAMERON AND MARGARET MCLEOD MEMORIAL SCHOLARSHIP
• See page 65

JOHN M. AZARIAN MEMORIAL ARMENIAN YOUTH SCHOLARSHIP FUND

http://www.azariangroup.com/

JOHN M. AZARIAN MEMORIAL ARMENIAN YOUTH SCHOLARSHIP FUND

Grants awarded to undergraduate students of Armenian descent, attending a full-time four-year college or university within the United States. Compelling financial need is the main criteria. Minimum 2.5 GPA required. Preference to business majors given. Applicant must be a member of Armenian Church.

Academic Fields/Career Goals: Business/Consumer Services.

Award: Grant for use in freshman, sophomore, junior, or senior years; renewable. *Number:* 1–5. *Amount:* $500–$3000.

Eligibility Requirements: Applicant must be of Armenian heritage and enrolled or expecting to enroll full-time at a four-year institution or university. Applicant must have 2.5 GPA or higher. Available to U.S. citizens.

Application Requirements: Application, essay, financial need analysis, resume, references, test scores, transcript. *Deadline:* May 31.

Contact: Mr. John M. Azarian Jr., President
John M. Azarian Memorial Armenian Youth Scholarship Fund
The Azarian Group, L.L.C., The Azarian Building, 6 Prospect Street, Suite 1B
Midland Park, NJ 07432
Phone: 201-444-7111
Fax: 201-444-6655
E-mail: jazarian@azariangroup.com

JORGE MAS CANOSA FREEDOM FOUNDATION

http://www.jorgemascanosa.org/

MAS FAMILY SCHOLARSHIP AWARD

Scholarship for Cuban American student who is a direct descendant of those who left Cuba or was born in Cuba. Minimum 3.5 GPA in college. Scholarships available only in the fields of engineering, business, international relations, economics, communications and journalism.

Academic Fields/Career Goals: Business/Consumer Services; Chemical Engineering; Civil Engineering; Communications; Economics; Electrical Engineering/Electronics; Engineering-Related Technologies; International Studies; Journalism; Materials Science, Engineering, and Metallurgy; Mechanical Engineering.

Award: Scholarship for use in freshman, sophomore, junior, senior, or graduate years; renewable. *Number:* 5–10. *Amount:* $8000–$40,000.

Eligibility Requirements: Applicant must be of Latin American/Caribbean heritage; Hispanic and enrolled or expecting to enroll full-time at a two-year or four-year institution or university. Applicant must have 3.5 GPA or higher. Available to U.S. and non-U.S. citizens.

Application Requirements: Application, essay, financial need analysis, references, test scores, transcript, proof of Cuban descent. *Deadline:* April 15.

Contact: Mr. Daniel Lafuente, Mas Scholarship Coordinator
Jorge Mas Canosa Freedom Foundation
1312 SW 27th Avenue
Miami, FL 33145
Phone: 305-592-7768
E-mail: dlafuente@canf.org

KE ALI'I PAUAHI FOUNDATION

http://www.pauahi.org/

NATIVE HAWAIIAN CHAMBER OF COMMERCE SCHOLARSHIP

Scholarship for students enrolled in an undergraduate or graduate degree-seeking program from an accredited post-secondary educational institution majoring in business administration. Minimum 3.0 GPA.

Academic Fields/Career Goals: Business/Consumer Services.

Award: Scholarship for use in freshman, sophomore, junior, senior, or graduate years; not renewable. *Number:* 9. *Amount:* $500–$1000.

Eligibility Requirements: Applicant must be enrolled or expecting to enroll full-time at a four-year institution or university. Applicant must have 3.0 GPA or higher. Available to U.S. citizens.

Application Requirements: Application, financial need analysis, references, transcript, Student Aid Report (SAR), college acceptance letter. *Deadline:* April 1.

Contact: Mavis Shiraishi-Ngao, Scholarship Administrator
Phone: 808-534-3966
E-mail: scholarships@pauahi.org

LAGRANT FOUNDATION

http://www.lagrantfoundation.org/

LAGRANT FOUNDATION SCHOLARSHIP FOR GRADUATES

Awards are for undergraduate and graduate minority students who are attending accredited four-year institutions and are pursuing careers in the fields of advertising, marketing, and public relations. Minimum 3.2 GPA required.

Academic Fields/Career Goals: Business/Consumer Services; Communications.

Award: Scholarship for use in freshman, sophomore, junior, senior, graduate, or postgraduate years; renewable. *Number:* 12. *Amount:* up to $10,000.

Eligibility Requirements: Applicant must be American Indian/Alaska Native, Asian/Pacific Islander, Black (non-Hispanic), or Hispanic and enrolled or expecting to enroll full-time at a four-year institution or university. Available to U.S. citizens.

Application Requirements: Application, essay, resume, references, transcript. *Deadline:* February 28.

Contact: Program Manager
Lagrant Foundation
626 Wilshire Boulevard, Suite 700
Los Angeles, CA 90017-2920
Phone: 323-469-8680
Fax: 323-469-8683

LAGRANT FOUNDATION SCHOLARSHIP FOR UNDERGRADUATES

Awards are for undergraduate and graduate minority students who are attending accredited four-year institutions and are pursuing careers in the fields of advertising, marketing, and public relations. Minimum 2.75 GPA required.

Academic Fields/Career Goals: Business/Consumer Services; Communications.

Award: Scholarship for use in freshman, sophomore, junior, senior, or graduate years; renewable. *Number:* 22. *Amount:* up to $5000.

Eligibility Requirements: Applicant must be American Indian/Alaska Native, Asian/Pacific Islander, Black (non-Hispanic), or Hispanic and enrolled or expecting to enroll full-time at a four-year institution or university. Available to U.S. citizens.

Application Requirements: Application, essay, resume, references, transcript. *Deadline:* February 28.

Contact: Program Manager
Lagrant Foundation
626 Wilshire Boulevard, Suite 700
Los Angeles, CA 90017-2920
Phone: 323-469-8680
Fax: 323-469-8683

LAWRENCE P. DOSS SCHOLARSHIP FOUNDATION

http://www.lawrencepdossfnd.org/

LAWRENCE P. DOSS SCHOLARSHIP FOUNDATION
• See page 65

LEAGUE OF UNITED LATIN AMERICAN CITIZENS NATIONAL EDUCATIONAL SERVICE CENTERS INC.

http://www.lnesc.org/

GE/LULAC SCHOLARSHIP

The scholarship for business and engineering students offers outstanding minority or low-income students entering their sophomore year in pursuit of an undergraduate degree a renewable scholarship up to 3 years.

Academic Fields/Career Goals: Business/Consumer Services; Engineering/Technology.

Award: Scholarship for use in sophomore, junior, or senior years; renewable. *Number:* up to 9. *Amount:* up to $5000.

Eligibility Requirements: Applicant must be American Indian/Alaska Native, Asian/Pacific Islander, Black (non-Hispanic), or Hispanic and enrolled or expecting to enroll full-time at a four-year institution or university. Applicant must have 3.0 GPA or higher. Available to U.S. citizens.

Application Requirements: Application, references, transcript, personal statement with career goals. *Deadline:* July 15.

Contact: Scholarship Administrator
League of United Latin American Citizens National
Educational Service Centers Inc.
2000 L Street NW, Suite 610
Washington, DC 20036
Phone: 202-835-9646 Ext. 10
Fax: 202-835-9685

LINCOLN COMMUNITY FOUNDATION

http://www.lcf.org/

LAWRENCE "LARRY" FRAZIER MEMORIAL SCHOLARSHIP
• See page 127

MAINE EDUCATION SERVICES

http://www.mesfoundation.com/

MAINE STATE CHAMBER OF COMMERCE SCHOLARSHIP-HIGH SCHOOL SENIOR

Two scholarships available for graduating high school seniors, one who is planning to pursue an associate degree in a technical program, and one who is planning to pursue a bachelor's degree in a business-related area. Preference may be given to students attending Maine colleges. Awards are based on academic excellence, student activities, financial need, letters of recommendation, and a required essay.

Academic Fields/Career Goals: Business/Consumer Services; Engineering/Technology.

Award: Scholarship for use in freshman year; not renewable. *Number:* up to 2. *Amount:* up to $1500.

Eligibility Requirements: Applicant must be high school student; planning to enroll or expecting to enroll full-time at a two-year or four-year or technical institution or university and resident of Maine. Available to U.S. citizens.

Application Requirements: Application, essay, financial need analysis, references, transcript. *Deadline:* April 18.

Contact: Kim Benjamin, Vice President of Operations
Maine Education Services
131 Presumpscot Street
Portland, ME 04103
Phone: 207-791-3600

MARYLAND ASSOCIATION OF PRIVATE COLLEGES AND CAREER SCHOOLS

http://www.mapccs.org/

MARYLAND ASSOCIATION OF PRIVATE COLLEGES AND CAREER SCHOOLS SCHOLARSHIP

Awards for study at trade schools only. Must enter school same year high school is completed. For use only in Maryland and by Maryland residents.

Academic Fields/Career Goals: Business/Consumer Services; Computer Science/Data Processing; Dental Health/Services; Engineering/Technology; Food Science/Nutrition; Home Economics; Trade/Technical Specialties; TV/Radio Broadcasting.

Award: Scholarship for use in freshman year; not renewable. *Number:* 50. *Amount:* $500–$19,950.

Eligibility Requirements: Applicant must be high school student; planning to enroll or expecting to enroll full-time at a technical institution; resident of Maryland and studying in Maryland. Available to U.S. citizens.

Application Requirements: Application, references, transcript, letter of eligibility from the MAPCCS career school. *Deadline:* April 11.

Contact: Jeannie Schwartz, Director of Placements
Maryland Association of Private Colleges and Career Schools
1539 Merriet Boulevard, PO Box 206
Baltimore, MD 21222
Phone: 410-282-4012
Fax: 410-282-4133
E-mail: jeannie.schwartz@computertraining.com

NATIONAL ASSOCIATION FOR THE ADVANCEMENT OF COLORED PEOPLE

http://www.naacp.org/

EARL G. GRAVES NAACP SCHOLARSHIP

One-time award of $5000 to a full-time minority student. Must be an enrolled sophomore, junior or senior at an accredited college or university in the United States as a declared business major, or a graduate student enrolled or accepted in a master's or doctoral program within a business school at an accredited university. Applicant must be in the top 20% of his/her class.

Academic Fields/Career Goals: Business/Consumer Services.

Award: Scholarship for use in sophomore, junior, senior, or graduate years; not renewable. *Number:* 1. *Amount:* $5000.

Eligibility Requirements: Applicant must be American Indian/Alaska Native, Asian/Pacific Islander, Black (non-Hispanic), or Hispanic and enrolled or expecting to enroll full-time at a four-year institution or university. Available to U.S. citizens.

Application Requirements: Application, financial need analysis, references, transcript. *Deadline:* March 16.

Contact: Victor Goode, Attorney
National Association for the Advancement of Colored People
4805 Mount Hope Drive
Baltimore, MD 21215-3297
Phone: 410-580-5760
E-mail: info@naacp.org

NATIONAL ASSOCIATION OF WATER COMPANIES-NEW JERSEY CHAPTER

http://www.nawc.org/

NATIONAL ASSOCIATION OF WATER COMPANIES-NEW JERSEY CHAPTER SCHOLARSHIP
• See page 142

NATIONAL BLACK MBA ASSOCIATION-TWIN CITIES CHAPTER

http://www.nbmbaatc.org/

TWIN CITIES CHAPTER UNDERGRADUATE SCHOLARSHIP
• See page 66

NATIONAL SECURITY EDUCATION PROGRAM

http://www.iie.org/

NATIONAL SECURITY EDUCATION PROGRAM (NSEP) DAVID L. BOREN UNDERGRADUATE SCHOLARSHIPS

The Boren Scholarships provide funding to American undergraduate students for study abroad in regions critical to U.S. national interests. Emphasized world areas include Africa, Asia, Central and Eastern Europe, the NIS, Latin America and the Caribbean, and the Middle East. NSEP scholarship recipients incur a service agreement. Must be a U.S. citizen. Program must have a foreign language component.

Academic Fields/Career Goals: Business/Consumer Services; Economics; Engineering-Related Technologies; Environmental Science; Foreign Language; International Studies.

Award: Scholarship for use in freshman, sophomore, junior, or senior years; not renewable. *Number:* 130–150. *Amount:* up to $20,000.

Eligibility Requirements: Applicant must be enrolled or expecting to enroll full- or part-time at a two-year or four-year institution or university. Available to U.S. citizens.

Application Requirements: Application, essay, financial need analysis, references, transcript, campus review. *Deadline:* February 10.

Contact: National Security Education Program
1400 K Street, NW, Suite 650
Washington, DC 20005-2403
Phone: 800-618-6737
Fax: 202-326-7672
E-mail: boren@iie.org

NATIONAL URBAN LEAGUE

http://www.nulbeep.org/

BLACK EXECUTIVE EXCHANGE PROGRAM JERRY BARTOW SCHOLARSHIP FUND

Scholarships for undergraduate students at participating Historically Black Colleges and Universities. Must be sophomore, junior, or senior, majoring in business, management, technology, or education. Must be available to receive award at BEEP's annual conference.

Academic Fields/Career Goals: Business/Consumer Services; Education; Engineering/Technology.

Award: Scholarship for use in sophomore, junior, or senior years; not renewable. *Number:* 2. *Amount:* $5000.

Eligibility Requirements: Applicant must be Black (non-Hispanic) and enrolled or expecting to enroll full-time at a four-year institution or university. Applicant must have 2.5 GPA or higher. Available to U.S. citizens.

Application Requirements: Application. *Deadline:* February 1.

Contact: William Dawson, Scholarship Committee
National Urban League
120 Wall Street
New York, NY 10005
Phone: 212-558-5300
Fax: 212-344-5332
E-mail: beep2005@nul.org

NEBRASKA DECA

http://www.nedeca.org/

NEBRASKA DECA LEADERSHIP SCHOLARSHIP

Awards applicants who intend to pursue a full-time two- or four-year course of study in a marketing or business-related field. Applicant must be active in DECA and involved in community service activities.

Academic Fields/Career Goals: Business/Consumer Services.

Award: Scholarship for use in freshman year; not renewable. *Number:* 2–9. *Amount:* $250–$1000.

Eligibility Requirements: Applicant must be high school student; planning to enroll or expecting to enroll full-time at a two-year or four-year or technical institution or university and resident of Nebraska. Applicant or parent of applicant must be member of Distribution Ed Club or Future Business Leaders of America. Applicant must have 2.5 GPA or higher. Available to U.S. citizens.

Application Requirements: Application, essay, resume, references, test scores, transcript, DECA participation and accomplishment documents. *Deadline:* February 1.

Contact: Scholarship Review Committee
Nebraska DECA
301 Centennial Mall South, PO Box 94987
Lincoln, NE 68509-4987
Phone: 402-471-4803
Fax: 402-471-0117
E-mail: nedeca@nedeca.org

NEW ENGLAND EMPLOYEE BENEFITS COUNCIL

http://www.neebc.org/

NEW ENGLAND EMPLOYEE BENEFITS COUNCIL SCHOLARSHIP PROGRAM
• See page 68

NEW ENGLAND WATER WORKS ASSOCIATION

http://www.newwa.org/

FRANCIS X. CROWLEY SCHOLARSHIP

Scholarships are awarded to eligible civil engineering, environmental and business management students on the basis of merit, character, and need. Preference given to those students whose programs are considered by a committee as beneficial to water works practice in New England. NEWWA student membership is required to receive a scholarship award. Applicants for scholarships should be residents or attend school in New England. (Maine, New Hampshire, Vermont, Massachusetts, Rhode Island and Connecticut).

Academic Fields/Career Goals: Business/Consumer Services; Civil Engineering; Environmental Science.

Award: Scholarship for use in freshman, sophomore, junior, senior, or graduate years; not renewable. *Number:* 1. *Amount:* up to $3000.

Eligibility Requirements: Applicant must be enrolled or expecting to enroll full-time at a four-year institution or university. Applicant or parent of applicant must be member of New England Water Works Association. Available to U.S. citizens.

Application Requirements: Application, essay, references, transcript. *Fee:* $25. *Deadline:* July 1.

Contact: Thomas MacElhaney, Chair, Scholarship Committee
New England Water Works Association
c/o PRELOAD Inc., 60 Commerce Drive
Hauppauge, NY 11788
Phone: 631-231-8100
Fax: 978-418-9156
E-mail: tmacelhaney@preloadinc.com

OREGON STUDENT ASSISTANCE COMMISSION

http://www.GetCollegeFunds.org/

NICHOLAS DIERMANN MEMORIAL SCHOLARSHIP
• *See page 69*

PLUMBING-HEATING-COOLING CONTRACTORS EDUCATION FOUNDATION

http://www.foundation.phccweb.org/

DELTA FAUCET COMPANY SCHOLARSHIP PROGRAM
• *See page 103*

PHCC EDUCATIONAL FOUNDATION NEED-BASED SCHOLARSHIP

Need-based scholarship worth $2500 to a student enrolled in an approved four-year PHCC apprenticeship program, or at an accredited two-year technical college, community college, or an accredited four-year college or university.

Academic Fields/Career Goals: Business/Consumer Services; Engineering/Technology; Engineering-Related Technologies; Heating, Air-Conditioning, and Refrigeration Mechanics; Mechanical Engineering; Trade/Technical Specialties.

Award: Scholarship for use in freshman, sophomore, junior, or senior years; not renewable. *Number:* 1. *Amount:* $2500.

Eligibility Requirements: Applicant must be enrolled or expecting to enroll full-time at a two-year or four-year or technical institution or university. Available to U.S. and Canadian citizens.

Application Requirements: Application, essay, financial need analysis, interview, references, test scores, transcript. *Deadline:* May 1.

Contact: John Zink, Scholarship Coordinator
Plumbing-Heating-Cooling Contractors Education Foundation
PO Box 6808
Falls Church, VA 22046
Phone: 800-533-7694
E-mail: naphcc@naphcc.org

PHCC EDUCATIONAL FOUNDATION SCHOLARSHIP PROGRAM

Applicants must be sponsored by a member of the National Association of Plumbing-Heating-Cooling Contractors. Must pursue studies in a major related to the plumbing-heating-cooling industry. Visit web site for additional information.

Academic Fields/Career Goals: Business/Consumer Services; Engineering/Technology; Engineering-Related Technologies; Heating, Air-Conditioning, and Refrigeration Mechanics; Mechanical Engineering; Trade/Technical Specialties.

Award: Scholarship for use in freshman, sophomore, junior, or senior years; not renewable. *Number:* 1–4. *Amount:* $2500–$5000.

Eligibility Requirements: Applicant must be enrolled or expecting to enroll full-time at a two-year or four-year or technical institution or university. Applicant must have 2.5 GPA or higher. Available to U.S. and Canadian citizens.

Application Requirements: Application, essay, interview, references, test scores, transcript. *Deadline:* May 1.

Contact: John Zink, Scholarship Coordinator
Plumbing-Heating-Cooling Contractors Education Foundation
PO Box 6808
Falls Church, VA 22046
Phone: 800-533-7694
E-mail: naphcc@naphcc.org

RHODE ISLAND FOUNDATION

http://www.rifoundation.org/

RAYMOND H. TROTT SCHOLARSHIP FOR BANKING

Scholarship for needy Rhode Island residents attending Rhode Island College whose studies are focused on banking and business. Must demonstrate financial need.

Academic Fields/Career Goals: Business/Consumer Services.

Award: Scholarship for use in senior year; not renewable. *Number:* 1. *Amount:* $1000.

Eligibility Requirements: Applicant must be American Indian/Alaska Native, Asian/Pacific Islander, Black (non-Hispanic), or Hispanic; enrolled or expecting to enroll full-time at a four-year institution or university and resident of Rhode Island. Available to U.S. citizens.

Application Requirements: Application, essay, financial need analysis, references, transcript. *Deadline:* varies.

Contact: Libby Monahan, Funds Administrator
Rhode Island Foundation
One Union Station
Providence, RI 02903
Phone: 401-274-4564 Ext. 3117
E-mail: libbym@rifoundation.org

ROBERT H. MOLLOHAN FAMILY CHARITABLE FOUNDATION, INC.

http://www.mollohanfoundation.org/

TEAMING TO WIN BUSINESS SCHOLARSHIP

Scholarship for a rising college sophomore or junior pursuing a degree in business administration at a West Virginia college or university.

Academic Fields/Career Goals: Business/Consumer Services.

Award: Scholarship for use in sophomore or junior years; not renewable. *Number:* 2. *Amount:* up to $1000.

Eligibility Requirements: Applicant must be enrolled or expecting to enroll full- or part-time at a four-year institution or university; resident of West Virginia; studying in West Virginia and must have an interest in leadership. Applicant must have 3.0 GPA or higher. Available to U.S. citizens.

Application Requirements: Application, essay, interview, resume, references, test scores, transcript. *Deadline:* February 9.

Contact: Aime L. Shaffer, Program Manager
Robert H. Mollohan Family Charitable Foundation, Inc.
1000 Technology Drive, Suite 2000
Fairmont, WV 26554
Phone: 304-333-6783
Fax: 304-333-3900
E-mail: ashaffer@wvhtf.org

SALES PROFESSIONALS-USA

http://www.salesprofessionals-usa.com/

SALES PROFESSIONALS-USA SCHOLARSHIP

Scholarships are awarded to students furthering their degree or obtaining a degree in business or marketing. The scholarships are initiated and awarded by the individual Sales Pros Clubs (located in Colorado, Kansas and Missouri) and are not nationally awarded. A listing of local clubs can be found at http://www.salesprofessionals-usa.com.

Academic Fields/Career Goals: Business/Consumer Services.

Award: Scholarship for use in freshman, sophomore, junior, or senior years; not renewable. *Number:* 3–5. *Amount:* $600–$1000.

Eligibility Requirements: Applicant must be enrolled or expecting to enroll full- or part-time at a two-year or four-year institution or university; resident of Colorado, Indiana, or Kansas and studying in Colorado, Kansas, or Missouri. Applicant must have 3.0 GPA or higher. Available to U.S. citizens.

Application Requirements: Application, essay. *Deadline:* varies.

Contact: Jay Berg, National President
Sales Professionals-USA
2870 North Speer Boulevard
Denver, CO 80001
Phone: 303-433-1051
E-mail: jberg@spacelogic.net

SAN DIEGO FOUNDATION

http://www.sdfoundation.org/

ENERGY OF ACHIEVEMENT SDG&E SCHOLARSHIP

Scholarship to provide financial assistance to graduating high school seniors who are attending an accredited two-year college or four-year university in the United States. Applicants must have a minimum 2.5 GPA and be majoring in business related areas, computer science, or engineering. Students must have a demonstrated financial need and be actively involved in extracurricular activities, community service, work experience, or athletics.

Academic Fields/Career Goals: Business/Consumer Services; Computer Science/Data Processing; Engineering/Technology.

Award: Scholarship for use in freshman year; not renewable. *Number:* 10. *Amount:* $2500.

Eligibility Requirements: Applicant must be high school student; planning to enroll or expecting to enroll full-time at a two-year or four-year institution or university and resident of California. Applicant or parent of applicant must have employment or volunteer experience in community service. Applicant must have 2.5 GPA or higher. Available to U.S. citizens.

Application Requirements: Application, references, transcript, personal statement, copy of tax return. *Deadline:* January 26.

Contact: Shryl Helvie, Scholarship Coordinator
San Diego Foundation
2508 Historic Decatur Road, Suite 200
San Diego, CA 92106
Phone: 619-814-1307
Fax: 619-239-1710
E-mail: shryl@sdfoundation.org

SOCIETY OF AUTOMOTIVE ANALYSTS

http://www.cybersaa.org/

SOCIETY OF AUTOMOTIVE ANALYSTS SCHOLARSHIP
• *See page 70*

SOUTH DAKOTA RETAILERS ASSOCIATION

http://www.sdra.org/

SOUTH DAKOTA RETAILERS ASSOCIATION SCHOLARSHIP PROGRAM
• *See page 71*

STRAIGHTFORWARD MEDIA

http://www.straightforwardmedia.com/

STRAIGHTFORWARD MEDIA BUSINESS SCHOOL SCHOLARSHIP
• *See page 77*

TEXAS FAMILY BUSINESS ASSOCIATION AND SCHOLARSHIP FOUNDATION

http://www.texasfamilybusiness.org/

TEXAS FAMILY BUSINESS ASSOCIATION SCHOLARSHIP

Scholarships awarded to eligible Texas family business members to help them obtain an education in business. Applicants must be planning to return to or stay with their family business.

Academic Fields/Career Goals: Business/Consumer Services.

Award: Scholarship for use in freshman, sophomore, junior, or senior years; not renewable. *Number:* 1. *Amount:* varies.

Eligibility Requirements: Applicant must be enrolled or expecting to enroll full- or part-time at a four-year institution or university; resident of Texas; studying in Texas and must have an interest in entrepreneurship. Available to U.S. citizens.

Application Requirements: Application, essay, transcript. *Deadline:* varies.

Contact: William Kirshner, President
Texas Family Business Association and Scholarship Foundation
2301 Rodd Field Road
Corpus Christi, TX 78414
Phone: 361-882-1686
Fax: 361-888-6602
E-mail: info@texasfamilybusiness.org

TKE EDUCATIONAL FOUNDATION

http://www.tke.org/

W. ALLAN HERZOG SCHOLARSHIP
• *See page 71*

TRUCKLOAD CARRIERS ASSOCIATION

http://www.truckload.org/

TRUCKLOAD CARRIERS ASSOCIATION SCHOLARSHIP FUND

This scholarship fund is for persons affiliated with the trucking industry and their families to pursue higher education. Special consideration will be given to applicants pursuing transportation or business degrees. Minimum 3.3 GPA required. For junior and senior undergraduate students at four-year college or university. Further information and application deadlines available at web site http://www.truckload.org.

Academic Fields/Career Goals: Business/Consumer Services; Transportation.

Award: Scholarship for use in junior or senior years; not renewable. *Number:* 18. *Amount:* $1500–$5000.

Eligibility Requirements: Applicant must be enrolled or expecting to enroll full-time at a four-year institution or university. Applicant or parent of applicant must have employment or volunteer experience in transportation industry. Available to U.S. and Canadian citizens.

Application Requirements: Application, essay, financial need analysis, transcript, course schedule including tuition and fees. *Deadline:* May 23.

Contact: Debbie Sparks, Vice President of Development
Truckload Carriers Association
555 East Braddock Road
Alexandria, VA 22314
Phone: 703-838-1950
Fax: 703-836-6610
E-mail: tca@truckload.org

UNITED DAUGHTERS OF THE CONFEDERACY

http://www.hqudc.org/

WALTER REED SMITH SCHOLARSHIP

Award for full-time female undergraduate students who are descendant of a Confederate soldier, studying nutrition, home economics, nursing, business administration, or computer science in accredited college or university. Minimum 3.0 GPA required. Submit application and letter of endorsement from sponsoring chapter of the United Daughters of the Confederacy.

Academic Fields/Career Goals: Business/Consumer Services; Computer Science/Data Processing; Food Science/Nutrition; Home Economics; Nursing.

Award: Scholarship for use in freshman, sophomore, junior, or senior years; renewable. *Number:* 1–2. *Amount:* $800–$1000.

Eligibility Requirements: Applicant must be enrolled or expecting to enroll full-time at a four-year institution or university and female. Applicant or parent of applicant must be member of United Daughters of the Confederacy. Applicant must have 3.0 GPA or higher. Available to U.S. citizens.

Application Requirements: Application, essay, financial need analysis, photo, references, self-addressed stamped envelope, transcript, copy of applicant's birth certificate, copy of confederate ancestor's proof of service. *Deadline:* March 15.

Contact: United Daughters of the Confederacy
328 North Boulevard
Richmond, VA 23220-4009
Phone: 804-355-1636
E-mail: hqudc@rcn.com

UNITED NEGRO COLLEGE FUND

http://www.uncf.org/

AVIS BUDGET GROUP SCHOLARSHIP

• *See page 72*

AVON WOMEN IN SEARCH OF EXCELLENCE SCHOLARSHIP

• *See page 72*

BANK OF AMERICA SCHOLARSHIP

Scholarship supports UNCF students attending a UNCF college or university located in any of the Bank of America core states and majoring in business, finance, education, marketing, computer science, or information technology. Minimum 3.0 GPA required. List of eligible institutions and additional information at web site http://www.uncf.org.

Academic Fields/Career Goals: Business/Consumer Services; Computer Science/Data Processing; Education; Finance; Marketing.

Award: Scholarship for use in freshman, sophomore, junior, or senior years; not renewable. *Number:* 1. *Amount:* $1000.

Eligibility Requirements: Applicant must be Black (non-Hispanic); enrolled or expecting to enroll full-time at a four-year institution or university and studying in Florida, Georgia, North Carolina, South Carolina, or Texas. Applicant must have 3.0 GPA or higher. Available to U.S. and non-U.S. citizens.

Application Requirements: Application, essay, references, transcript. *Deadline:* November 25.

Contact: Director, Program Services
United Negro College Fund
8260 Willow Oaks Corporate Drive
PO Box 10444
Fairfax, VA 22031-8044
Phone: 800-331-2244
E-mail: rebecca.bennett@uncf.org

CARDINAL HEALTH SCHOLARSHIP

• *See page 72*

CASTLE ROCK FOUNDATION SCHOLARSHIP

$3,600 scholarship awarded to students majoring in business or engineering attending the following institutions: Bethune-Cookman College, LeMoyne-Owen College, Morehouse College, Shaw University, Spelman College, Tuskegee University, or Xavier University. Minimum GPA of 2.5 required.

Academic Fields/Career Goals: Business/Consumer Services; Engineering/Technology.

Award: Scholarship for use in freshman, sophomore, junior, or senior years; renewable. *Number:* 10. *Amount:* $3600.

Eligibility Requirements: Applicant must be Black (non-Hispanic) and enrolled or expecting to enroll full-time at a four-year institution or university. Applicant must have 2.5 GPA or higher. Available to U.S. and non-U.S. citizens.

Application Requirements: Application, financial need analysis, FAFSA, Student Aid Report (SAR).

Contact: Director, Program Services
United Negro College Fund
8260 Willow Oaks Corporate Drive
PO Box 10444
Fairfax, VA 22031-8044
Phone: 800-331-2244
E-mail: rebecca.bennett@uncf.org

COY G. EKLUND SCHOLARSHIP

Scholarship available to students at UNCF member colleges and universities majoring in business. Must have minimum 2.5 GPA.

Academic Fields/Career Goals: Business/Consumer Services.

Award: Scholarship for use in freshman year; not renewable.

Eligibility Requirements: Applicant must be Black (non-Hispanic) and enrolled or expecting to enroll at a two-year or four-year institution. Applicant must have 2.5 GPA or higher. Available to U.S. citizens.

Application Requirements: *Deadline:* continuous.

Contact: Director, Program Services
United Negro College Fund
8260 Willow Oaks Corporate Drive
PO Box 10444
Fairfax, VA 22031-8044
Phone: 800-331-2244
E-mail: rebecca.bennett@uncf.org

EDWARD M. NAGEL FOUNDATION SCHOLARSHIP

• *See page 73*

FLOWERS INDUSTRIES SCHOLARSHIP

Awards given to students majoring in business, marketing, computer science, or food service at one of the following colleges or universities: Bethune-Cookman, Clark Atlanta, Stillman or Virginia Union. Minimum 2.5 GPA required. Apply online at web site http://www.uncf.org.

Academic Fields/Career Goals: Business/Consumer Services; Computer Science/Data Processing; Food Service/Hospitality; Marketing.

Award: Scholarship for use in freshman, sophomore, junior, or senior years; not renewable. *Number:* 1. *Amount:* $2500.

Eligibility Requirements: Applicant must be Black (non-Hispanic) and enrolled or expecting to enroll full-time at a four-year institution or university. Applicant must have 2.5 GPA or higher. Available to U.S. citizens.

Application Requirements: Application, financial need analysis. *Deadline:* continuous.

Contact: Director, Program Services
United Negro College Fund
8260 Willow Oaks Corporate Drive
PO Box 10444
Fairfax, VA 22031-8044
Phone: 800-331-2244
E-mail: rebecca.bennett@uncf.org

FORD/UNCF CORPORATE SCHOLARS PROGRAM
• *See page 73*

GENERAL MILLS CORPORATE SCHOLARS AWARD
• *See page 73*

GEORGE REID WILLIAMS SCHOLARSHIP

Scholarship available to one male and one female student majoring in math, engineering, or business administration with a GPA of 2.5 or better who attends a UNCF member college or university.

Academic Fields/Career Goals: Business/Consumer Services; Engineering/Technology; Mathematics.

Award: Scholarship for use in freshman year; not renewable. *Number:* 2.

Eligibility Requirements: Applicant must be Black (non-Hispanic) and enrolled or expecting to enroll at a four-year institution or university. Applicant must have 2.5 GPA or higher. Available to U.S. citizens.

Contact: Director, Program Services
United Negro College Fund
8260 Willow Oaks Corporate Drive
PO Box 10444
Fairfax, VA 22031-8044
Phone: 800-331-2244
E-mail: rebecca.bennett@uncf.org

JESSE JONES JR. SCHOLARSHIP

Scholarship is funded through the Chrysler Minority Dealership Association for business students attending a UNCF member college or university. Minimum 2.5 GPA required. Scholarship value ranges from $2000 to $5000.

Academic Fields/Career Goals: Business/Consumer Services.

Award: Scholarship for use in freshman, sophomore, junior, or senior years; not renewable. *Amount:* $2000–$5000.

Eligibility Requirements: Applicant must be Black (non-Hispanic) and enrolled or expecting to enroll full- or part-time at a four-year institution or university. Applicant must have 2.5 GPA or higher. Available to U.S. and non-U.S. citizens.

Application Requirements: Application, financial need analysis. *Deadline:* continuous.

Contact: Director, Program Services
United Negro College Fund
8260 Willow Oaks Corporate Drive
PO Box 10444
Fairfax, VA 22031-8044
Phone: 800-331-2244
E-mail: rebecca.bennett@uncf.org

JOHN WALTER BRIDGEMAN SCHOLARSHIP PROGRAM

Scholarships for students from Harlem, New York attending historically black colleges and universities and with business or business-related majors. Minimum 3.0 GPA required. For a list of eligible schools and to apply online please visit web site http:www.uncf.org.

Academic Fields/Career Goals: Business/Consumer Services.

Award: Scholarship for use in freshman year; renewable. *Amount:* up to $2000.

Eligibility Requirements: Applicant must be Black (non-Hispanic); enrolled or expecting to enroll full-time at a four-year institution or university and resident of New York. Applicant must have 3.0 GPA or higher.

Application Requirements: Essay, financial need analysis, references, transcript. *Deadline:* May 31.

Contact: Director, Program Services
United Negro College Fund
8260 Willow Oaks Corporate Drive
PO Box 10444
Fairfax, VA 22031-8044
Phone: 800-331-2244
E-mail: rebecca.bennett@uncf.org

LOCKHEED MARTIN/UNCF SCHOLARSHIP
• *See page 73*

MBIA/WILLIAM O. BAILEY SCHOLARS PROGRAM
• *See page 73*

NASCAR/WENDELL SCOTT, SR. SCHOLARSHIP
• *See page 73*

PRINCIPAL FINANCIAL GROUP SCHOLARSHIPS
• *See page 74*

SBC-PACIFIC BELL SCHOLARSHIP

Scholarship for students who are residents of California and attending UNCF member colleges and universities. Open to majors in Engineering, Business, Finance, Economics, Computer Science, Information Technology with a minimum GPA 3.0. For more information see Website: http://www.uncf.org/forstudents/scholarship.asp.

Academic Fields/Career Goals: Business/Consumer Services; Computer Science/Data Processing; Economics; Engineering/Technology; Finance.

Award: Scholarship for use in junior year. *Amount:* $5000.

Eligibility Requirements: Applicant must be Black (non-Hispanic); enrolled or expecting to enroll at a four-year institution or university and resident of California. Applicant must have 3.0 GPA or higher.

Contact: Director, Program Services
United Negro College Fund
8260 Willow Oaks Corporate Drive
PO Box 10444
Fairfax, VA 22031-8044
Phone: 800-331-2244
E-mail: rebecca.bennett@uncf.org

SONY CORPORATION SCHOLARSHIP

Scholarship for students who are residents of New York or New Jersey and attending UNCF member colleges and universities or Howard University. Student must be a Business major with a minimum GPA of 2.5. For more information see Website: http://www.uncf.org/forstudents/scholarship.asp.

Academic Fields/Career Goals: Business/Consumer Services.

Award: Scholarship for use in freshman, sophomore, junior, or senior years. *Amount:* up to $5000.

Eligibility Requirements: Applicant must be Black (non-Hispanic); enrolled or expecting to enroll at a four-year institution or university and resident of New Jersey or New York. Applicant must have 2.5 GPA or higher.

Contact: Director, Program Services
United Negro College Fund
8260 Willow Oaks Corporate Drive
PO Box 10444
Fairfax, VA 22031-8044
Phone: 800-331-2244
E-mail: rebecca.bennett@uncf.org

TOYOTA/UNCF SCHOLARSHIP
• *See page 74*

UBS/PAINEWEBBER SCHOLARSHIP
• *See page 74*

VERIZON FOUNDATION SCHOLARSHIP
• *See page 74*

WELLS FARGO/UNCF SCHOLARSHIP FUND
• *See page 74*

VIRGINIA SOCIETY OF CERTIFIED PUBLIC ACCOUNTANTS EDUCATIONAL FOUNDATION

http://www.vscpa.com/

VIRGINIA SOCIETY OF CPAS EDUCATIONAL FOUNDATION MINORITY SCHOLARSHIP
• *See page 75*

VIRGINIA SOCIETY OF CPAS EDUCATIONAL FOUNDATION UNDERGRADUATE SCHOLARSHIP
• *See page 75*

WOMEN GROCERS OF AMERICA

http://www.nationalgrocers.org/

MARY MACEY SCHOLARSHIP
• *See page 88*

WOMEN IN LOGISTICS, NORTHERN CALIFORNIA

http://www.womeninlogistics.org/

WOMEN IN LOGISTICS SCHOLARSHIP

Award for students (undergraduate and graduate, male or female) who are studying (and eventually plan to pursue a career in) logistics/supply chain management. Applicants must be enrolled in a degree program at a San Francisco Bay Area institution and have at least one semester left, as this award goes for tuition and fees- it is NOT a cash prize that is handed directly to the winner. The deadline varies, but typically it falls on November 1st. While student need *may* be taken into account, awards are based primarily on merit, relevant work background and demonstrated interest in the field.

Academic Fields/Career Goals: Business/Consumer Services; Trade/Technical Specialties; Transportation.

Award: Scholarship for use in freshman, sophomore, junior, senior, or graduate years; not renewable. *Number:* 1–3. *Amount:* $1000–$2000.

Eligibility Requirements: Applicant must be enrolled or expecting to enroll full- or part-time at a two-year or four-year institution or university; resident of California and studying in California. Applicant or parent of applicant must be member of Women in Logistics. Available to U.S. and non-U.S. citizens.

Application Requirements: Application, applicant must enter a contest, essay, resume, references. *Deadline:* November 1.

Contact: Susan Cholette, Scholarship Director
Women in Logistics, Northern California
PO Box 194681
San Francisco, CA 94119-4681
Phone: 415-405-2173
E-mail: cholette@sfsu.edu

WOMEN'S INDEPENDENCE SCHOLARSHIP PROGRAM, INC.

http://www.wispinc.org/

COUNSELOR, ADVOCATE, AND SUPPORT STAFF SCHOLARSHIP PROGRAM
• *See page 76*

WYOMING TRUCKING ASSOCIATION SCHOLARSHIP FUND TRUST

http://www.wytruck.org/

WYOMING TRUCKING ASSOCIATION SCHOLARSHIP TRUST FUND
• *See page 76*

Y'S MEN INTERNATIONAL

http://www.ysmenusa.com/

ALEXANDER SCHOLARSHIP LOAN FUND

The purpose of the fund is to promote the training of staff of the YMCA and/or those seeking to become members or staff of the YMCA. Deadlines: May 30 for fall semester, and October 30 for spring semester.

Academic Fields/Career Goals: Business/Consumer Services; Child and Family Studies; Education; Human Resources; Social Sciences; Social Services; Sports-Related/Exercise Science.

Award: Scholarship for use in freshman, sophomore, junior, or senior years; renewable. *Number:* varies. *Amount:* varies.

Eligibility Requirements: Applicant must be enrolled or expecting to enroll full- or part-time at a two-year or four-year institution or university. Available to U.S. citizens.

Application Requirements: Application. *Fee:* $1. *Deadline:* varies.

Contact: Dean Currie, Area Service Director
Y's Men International
629 Lantana Lane
Imperial, CA 92251
Phone: 908-753-9493
Fax: 602-935-6322
E-mail: kidcurrie@adelphia.net

ZONTA INTERNATIONAL FOUNDATION

http://www.zonta.org/

JANE M. KLAUSMAN WOMEN IN BUSINESS SCHOLARSHIPS

Awards for female students entering their third or fourth year in an undergraduate business degree. Application available at web site http://www.zonta.org.

Academic Fields/Career Goals: Business/Consumer Services.

Award: Scholarship for use in junior or senior years; not renewable. *Number:* up to 12. *Amount:* $4000–$5000.

Eligibility Requirements: Applicant must be enrolled or expecting to enroll full-time at a four-year institution or university and female. Available to U.S. and non-U.S. citizens.

Application Requirements: Application, essay, references. *Deadline:* varies.

Contact: Ana Ubides, Programs Manager
Zonta International Foundation
1211 West 22nd Street, Suite 900
Oak Brook, IL 60523
Fax: 630-928-1559
E-mail: progrmas@zonta.org

CAMPUS ACTIVITIES

NATIONAL ASSOCIATION FOR CAMPUS ACTIVITIES

http://www.naca.org/

MARKLEY SCHOLARSHIP

Scholarship available to students who are strongly involved in the field of student activities and/or student activities employment, and who have made significant contributions to NACA Central. Must be classified as a junior, senior or graduate student at a four-year school located in the former NACA South Central region, or a sophomore in the former NACA South Central region. Must have minimum 2.5 GPA.

Academic Fields/Career Goals: Campus Activities.

Award: Scholarship for use in junior, senior, or graduate years; not renewable. *Number:* up to 2. *Amount:* $250–$300.

Eligibility Requirements: Applicant must be enrolled or expecting to enroll full- or part-time at a four-year institution and studying in Arkansas, Louisiana, New Mexico, Oklahoma, or Texas. Applicant or parent of applicant must have employment or volunteer experience in community service. Applicant must have 2.5 GPA or higher. Available to U.S. citizens.

Application Requirements: Application, resume. *Deadline:* September 1.

Contact: Dionne Ellison, Administrative Assistant
National Association for Campus Activities
13 Harbison Way
Columbia, SC 29212-3401
Phone: 803-732-6222 Ext. 131
Fax: 803-749-1047
E-mail: dionnee@naca.org

CANADIAN STUDIES

CANADIAN INSTITUTE OF UKRAINIAN STUDIES

http://www.cius.ca/

CANADIAN INSTITUTE OF UKRAINIAN STUDIES RESEARCH GRANTS
• *See page 104*

CHEMICAL ENGINEERING

AACE INTERNATIONAL

http://www.aacei.org/

AACE INTERNATIONAL COMPETITIVE SCHOLARSHIP
• *See page 99*

AIST FOUNDATION

http://www.aistfoundation.org/

ASSOCIATION FOR IRON AND STEEL TECHNOLOGY BENJAMIN F. FAIRLESS SCHOLARSHIP (AIME)

Scholarships for students of metallurgy, metallurgical engineering, or materials science and engineering, mechanical engineering, electrical engineering, interested in a career in ferrous related industries as demonstrated by an internship or related experience, or who have plans to pursue such experiences during college. Student may apply after first term of freshman year of college. Applications are accepted December 1 through March 1 each year.

Academic Fields/Career Goals: Chemical Engineering; Electrical Engineering/Electronics; Engineering-Related Technologies; Materials Science, Engineering, and Metallurgy; Mechanical Engineering.

Award: Scholarship for use in sophomore, junior, senior, graduate, or postgraduate years; not renewable. *Number:* 3. *Amount:* $2000.

Eligibility Requirements: Applicant must be enrolled or expecting to enroll full-time at a four-year institution or university. Applicant must have 3.0 GPA or higher. Available to U.S. and non-U.S. citizens.

Application Requirements: Application, essay, resume, references, transcript. *Deadline:* March 2.

Contact: Lori Wharrey, Board Administrator
AIST Foundation
186 Thorn Hill Road
Warrendale, PA 15086-7528
Phone: 724-814-3044
E-mail: lwharrey@aist.org

ASSOCIATION FOR IRON AND STEEL TECHNOLOGY DAVID H. SAMSON CANADIAN SCHOLARSHIP

Scholarship of $2000 available for children of AIST members who are Canadian citizens. Renewable for up to four years. Student must be studying engineering at a Canadian institution or, in the absence of engineering applicants, the award may be made to an eligible student studying chemistry, geology, mathematics, or physics.

Academic Fields/Career Goals: Chemical Engineering; Civil Engineering; Electrical Engineering/Electronics; Engineering/Technology; Materials Science, Engineering, and Metallurgy.

Award: Scholarship for use in freshman, sophomore, junior, or senior years; renewable. *Number:* 1. *Amount:* $2000.

Eligibility Requirements: Applicant must be Canadian citizen and enrolled or expecting to enroll full-time at a four-year institution or university. Applicant or parent of applicant must be member of Association for Iron and Steel Technology. Applicant must have 3.0 GPA or higher.

Application Requirements: Application, essay, resume, references, test scores, transcript. *Deadline:* June 30.

Contact: Robert Kneale, AIST Northern Member Chapter Scholarship Chair
AIST Foundation
PO Box 1734
Cambridge, ON N1R 7G8

AMERICAN CHEMICAL SOCIETY

http://www.acs.org/

AMERICAN CHEMICAL SOCIETY SCHOLARS PROGRAM

Renewable award for minority students pursuing studies in chemistry, biochemistry, chemical technology, chemical engineering, or any chemical science. Must be U.S. citizen or permanent resident and have minimum 3.0 GPA. Must be Native American, African-American, or Hispanic.

Academic Fields/Career Goals: Chemical Engineering; Environmental Science; Materials Science, Engineering, and Metallurgy; Natural Sciences; Paper and Pulp Engineering.

Award: Scholarship for use in freshman, sophomore, junior, or senior years; renewable. *Number:* 100–200. *Amount:* $1000–$5000.

Eligibility Requirements: Applicant must be American Indian/Alaska Native, Black (non-Hispanic), or Hispanic and enrolled or expecting to enroll full-time at a two-year or four-year or technical institution or university. Applicant must have 3.0 GPA or higher. Available to U.S. citizens.

Application Requirements: Application, financial need analysis, references, test scores, transcript. *Deadline:* March 1.

Contact: Mr. Robert J. Hughes, Manager, ACS Scholars Program
American Chemical Society
1155 16th Street NW
Washington, DC 20036
Phone: 202-872-6048
Fax: 202-872-4361

AMERICAN CHEMICAL SOCIETY, RUBBER DIVISION

http://www.rubber.org/

AMERICAN CHEMICAL SOCIETY, RUBBER DIVISION UNDERGRADUATE SCHOLARSHIP

Candidate must be majoring in a technical discipline relevant to the rubber industry with a "B" or better overall academic average. Two scholarships are awarded to juniors and seniors enrolled in an accredited college or university in the United States, Canada, Mexico, India or Brazil.

Academic Fields/Career Goals: Chemical Engineering; Engineering/Technology; Materials Science, Engineering, and Metallurgy; Mechanical Engineering; Science, Technology, and Society.

Award: Scholarship for use in junior or senior years; not renewable. *Number:* 3. *Amount:* $5000.

Eligibility Requirements: Applicant must be enrolled or expecting to enroll full-time at a four-year institution or university. Applicant must have 3.0 GPA or higher. Available to U.S. and non-U.S. citizens.

Application Requirements: Application, essay, interview, references, test scores, transcript. *Deadline:* March 1.

Contact: Christie Robinson, Education and Publications Manager
American Chemical Society, Rubber Division
250 South Forge Road, PO Box 499
Akron, OH 44325
Phone: 330-972-7814
Fax: 330-972-5269
E-mail: education@rubber.org

AMERICAN COUNCIL OF ENGINEERING COMPANIES OF PENNSYLVANIA (ACEC/PA)

http://www.acecpa.org/

ENGINEERING SCHOLARSHIP

Scholarship for full-time engineering students enrolled in accredited colleges or universities. Must be U.S. citizen. Up to five awards are granted annually.

Academic Fields/Career Goals: Chemical Engineering; Civil Engineering; Electrical Engineering/Electronics; Engineering/Technology; Engineering-Related Technologies; Materials Science, Engineering, and Metallurgy; Mechanical Engineering.

Award: Scholarship for use in freshman, sophomore, junior, or senior years; not renewable. *Number:* 1–5. *Amount:* $1000–$4000.

Eligibility Requirements: Applicant must be enrolled or expecting to enroll full-time at a four-year institution or university and resident of Pennsylvania. Available to U.S. citizens.

Application Requirements: Application, essay, resume, references, transcript. *Deadline:* December 1.

Contact: Laurie Troutman, Administrative Assistant
American Council of Engineering Companies of Pennsylvania (ACEC/PA)
2040 Linglestown Road, Suite 200
Harrisburg, PA 17110
Phone: 717-540-6811
Fax: 717-540-6815
E-mail: laurie@acecpa.org

AMERICAN INSTITUTE OF CHEMICAL ENGINEERS

http://www.aiche.org/

CHEME-CAR NATIONAL LEVEL COMPETITION

Each student chapter region may send their first and second place winners to the design competition. Multiple entries from a single school may be permitted at the regional competitions, but only one entry per school is allowed at the national competition. Students majoring in chemical engineering can participate.

Academic Fields/Career Goals: Chemical Engineering.

Award: Prize for use in freshman, sophomore, junior, or senior years; not renewable. *Number:* up to 3. *Amount:* $200–$2000.

Eligibility Requirements: Applicant must be enrolled or expecting to enroll full-time at a four-year institution or university. Available to U.S. and non-U.S. citizens.

Application Requirements: Application, applicant must enter a contest, student chapter name, team contact, list of team members, title of entry, description of chemical reaction/drive system, list of chemicals to be used and estimated quantity needed. *Fee:* $100. *Deadline:* June 30.

Contact: Prof. David Dixon, Department of Chemistry and Chemical Engineering
American Institute of Chemical Engineers
South Dakota School of Mines and Technology, 501 East Saint Joseph Street
Rapid City, SD 57701
Phone: 605-394-1235
Fax: 605-394-1232
E-mail: david.dixon@sdsmt.edu

DONALD F. AND MILDRED TOPP OTHMER FOUNDATION-NATIONAL SCHOLARSHIP AWARDS

Awards for 15 national AICHE student members, a scholarship of $1000. Awards are presented on the basis of academic achievement and involvement in student chapter activities. The student chapter advisor must make nominations. Only one nomination will be accepted from each AICHE student chapter or chemical engineering club.

Academic Fields/Career Goals: Chemical Engineering.

Award: Scholarship for use in freshman, sophomore, junior, senior, or graduate years; not renewable. *Number:* 15. *Amount:* $1000.

Eligibility Requirements: Applicant must be enrolled or expecting to enroll full-time at a four-year institution or university. Available to U.S. and non-U.S. citizens.

Application Requirements: Application, essay, references, transcript, statement of long-range career plans. *Deadline:* May 11.

Contact: AIChE Awards Administrator
American Institute of Chemical Engineers
Three Park Avenue
New York, NY 10016-5901
Phone: 212-591-7107
Fax: 212-591-8882
E-mail: awards@aiche.org

ENVIRONMENTAL DIVISION UNDERGRADUATE STUDENT PAPER AWARD

Cash prizes awarded to full-time undergraduate students who prepare the best original papers based on the results of research or an investigation related to the environment. The work must be performed during the student's undergraduate enrollment, and the paper must be submitted prior to or within six months of graduation. Student must be the sole author of the paper, but faculty guidance is encouraged. Student must be a member of the American Institute of Chemical Engineers Student Chapter.

Academic Fields/Career Goals: Chemical Engineering; Environmental Science.

Award: Prize for use in freshman, sophomore, junior, or senior years; not renewable. *Number:* 3. *Amount:* $100–$300.

Eligibility Requirements: Applicant must be enrolled or expecting to enroll full-time at a four-year institution or university. Available to U.S. and non-U.S. citizens.

Application Requirements: Applicant must enter a contest, essay, references, 5 copies of the nomination package. *Deadline:* May 15.

Contact: Tapas Das, Environmental Division Awards Committee
American Institute of Chemical Engineers
125 Mandy Place, NE
Olympia, WA 98516
Phone: 360-456-0573
E-mail: shivaniki@comcast.net

JOHN J. MCKETTA UNDERGRADUATE SCHOLARSHIP

A $5000 scholarship will be awarded to a junior or senior student member of AICHE who is planning a career in the chemical engineering process industries. Must maintain a 3.0 GPA. Applicant should show leadership or activity in either the school's AICHE student chapter or other university sponsored campus activities. Must attend ABET-accredited school in the United States, Canada, or Mexico.

Academic Fields/Career Goals: Chemical Engineering.

Award: Scholarship for use in junior or senior years; not renewable. *Number:* 1. *Amount:* $5000.

Eligibility Requirements: Applicant must be enrolled or expecting to enroll full-time at a four-year institution or university and must have an interest in leadership. Applicant must have 3.0 GPA or higher. Available to U.S. and non-U.S. citizens.

Application Requirements: Application, essay, references. *Deadline:* May 25.

Contact: AIChE Awards Administrator
American Institute of Chemical Engineers
Three Park Avenue
New York, NY 10016
Phone: 212-591-7107
Fax: 212-591-8882
E-mail: awards@aiche.org

MINORITY AFFAIRS COMMITTEE AWARD FOR OUTSTANDING SCHOLASTIC ACHIEVEMENT

Award recognizing the outstanding achievements of a chemical engineering student who serves as a role model for minority students. Offers $1000 award and $500 travel allowance to attend AICHE meeting. Must be nominated.

Academic Fields/Career Goals: Chemical Engineering.

Award: Scholarship for use in freshman, sophomore, junior, senior, or graduate years; not renewable. *Number:* 1. *Amount:* $1500.

Eligibility Requirements: Applicant must be American Indian/Alaska Native, Asian/Pacific Islander, Black (non-Hispanic), or Hispanic and enrolled or expecting to enroll full-time at a four-year institution or university. Applicant must have 3.0 GPA or higher. Available to U.S. and non-U.S. citizens.

Application Requirements: Application. *Deadline:* May 15.

Contact: Dr. Emmanuel Dada, Scholarship Administrator
American Institute of Chemical Engineers
PO Box 8
Princeton, NJ 08543
Phone: 212-591-7107
E-mail: emmanuel_dada@fmc.com

MINORITY SCHOLARSHIP AWARDS FOR COLLEGE STUDENTS

Award for college undergraduates who are studying chemical engineering. Must be a member of a minority group that is underrepresented in chemical engineering. Must be an AICHE national student member at the time of application. Recipients of this scholarship are eligible to reapply.

Academic Fields/Career Goals: Chemical Engineering.

Award: Scholarship for use in freshman, sophomore, junior, or senior years; renewable. *Number:* up to 10. *Amount:* $1000.

Eligibility Requirements: Applicant must be American Indian/Alaska Native, Asian/Pacific Islander, Black (non-Hispanic), or Hispanic and enrolled or expecting to enroll full-time at a two-year or four-year institution or university. Applicant must have 3.0 GPA or higher. Available to U.S. and non-U.S. citizens.

Application Requirements: Application, essay, financial need analysis, references, transcript, career objective. *Deadline:* May 15.

Contact: Dr. Emmanuel Dada, FMC Corporation
American Institute of Chemical Engineers
PO Box 8
Princeton, NJ 08543
Phone: 212-591-7107
E-mail: emmanuel_dada@fmc.com

MINORITY SCHOLARSHIP AWARDS FOR INCOMING COLLEGE FRESHMEN

Up to ten awards of $1000 for high school graduates who are members of a minority group that is underrepresented in chemical engineering. Students must be high school seniors planning to enroll during the next academic year in a four-year college or university offering a science/engineering degree.

Academic Fields/Career Goals: Chemical Engineering.

Award: Scholarship for use in freshman year; not renewable. *Number:* up to 10. *Amount:* $1000.

Eligibility Requirements: Applicant must be American Indian/Alaska Native, Asian/Pacific Islander, Black (non-Hispanic), or Hispanic; high school student and planning to enroll or expecting to enroll full-time at a four-year institution or university. Applicant must have 3.0 GPA or higher. Available to U.S. and non-U.S. citizens.

Application Requirements: Application, essay, financial need analysis, references, transcript, confirmation of minority status. *Deadline:* May 15.

Contact: Dr. Emmanuel Dada, Minority Affairs Committee
American Institute of Chemical Engineers
PO Box 8
Princeton, NJ 08543
Phone: 212-591-7107
E-mail: emmanuel_dada@fmc.com

NATIONAL STUDENT DESIGN COMPETITION-INDIVIDUAL

Three cash prizes for student contest problem that typifies a real, working, chemical engineering design situation. Competition statements are distributed online to student chapter advisors and department heads.

Academic Fields/Career Goals: Chemical Engineering.

Award: Prize for use in freshman, sophomore, junior, senior, or graduate years; not renewable. *Number:* 3. *Amount:* $200–$500.

Eligibility Requirements: Applicant must be enrolled or expecting to enroll full-time at a four-year institution or university. Available to U.S. and non-U.S. citizens.

Application Requirements: Applicant must enter a contest, essay. *Deadline:* June 6.

Contact: AIChE Awards Administrator
American Institute of Chemical Engineers
Three Park Avenue
New York, NY 10016
Phone: 212-591-7107
Fax: 212-591-8882
E-mail: awards@aiche.org

NATIONAL STUDENT DESIGN COMPETITION-TEAM (WILLIAM CUNNINGHAM AWARD)

Design contest for chemical engineering students.

Academic Fields/Career Goals: Chemical Engineering.

Award: Prize for use in freshman, sophomore, junior, senior, or graduate years; not renewable. *Number:* 1. *Amount:* up to $600.

Eligibility Requirements: Applicant must be enrolled or expecting to enroll full-time at a four-year institution or university. Available to U.S. and non-U.S. citizens.

Application Requirements: Application, applicant must enter a contest, essay. *Deadline:* June 6.

Contact: AIChE Awards Administrator
American Institute of Chemical Engineers
Three Park Avenue
New York, NY 10016
Phone: 212-591-7107
Fax: 212-591-8882
E-mail: awards@aiche.org

NATIONAL STUDENT PAPER COMPETITION

First place winners from each of the nine regional student paper competitions present their prize-winning papers during the American Institute of Chemical Engineers meeting held in the current calendar year. First prize is $500, second prize is $300, and third prize is $200.

Academic Fields/Career Goals: Chemical Engineering.

Award: Prize for use in freshman, sophomore, junior, senior, or graduate years; not renewable. *Number:* 3. *Amount:* $200–$500.

Eligibility Requirements: Applicant must be enrolled or expecting to enroll full-time at a four-year institution or university. Available to U.S. and non-U.S. citizens.

Application Requirements: Applicant must enter a contest, student paper. *Deadline:* varies.

Contact: AIChE Awards Administrator
American Institute of Chemical Engineers
Three Park Avenue
New York, NY 10016-5901
Phone: 212-591-7107
Fax: 212-591-8882
E-mail: awards@aiche.org

NORTH AMERICAN MIXING FORUM (NAMF) STUDENT AWARD

Award to encourage, recognize, and reward students for quality research in the area of mixing. Any graduate or undergraduate student doing research in the field of fluid mixing at an accredited university in North America is eligible.

Academic Fields/Career Goals: Chemical Engineering.

Award: Prize for use in freshman, sophomore, junior, senior, or graduate years; not renewable. *Number:* 1. *Amount:* up to $500.

Eligibility Requirements: Applicant must be enrolled or expecting to enroll full-time at a four-year institution or university. Available to U.S. and non-U.S. citizens.

Application Requirements: Applicant must enter a contest, essay, references, cover letter including title of work, name and address of author, abstract, theory or model development, experimental setup/procedures, results and discussion. *Deadline:* March 15.

Contact: Dr. Ricahrd K. Grenville, Student Award Committee
American Institute of Chemical Engineers
1007 Market Street, B8214
Wilmington, DE 19898
Phone: 302-774-2256
Fax: 302-774-2457
E-mail: richard.k.grenville@usa.dupont.com

OUTSTANDING STUDENT CHAPTER ADVISOR AWARD

Award for service and leadership in guiding the activities of an AIChE student chapter in accordance with AIChE principles. Must be advisor of a chartered AIChE student chapter for at least the last three years. Award winners cannot be renominated.

Academic Fields/Career Goals: Chemical Engineering.

Award: Prize for use in freshman, sophomore, junior, or senior years; not renewable. *Number:* 1. *Amount:* up to $1000.

Eligibility Requirements: Applicant must be enrolled or expecting to enroll full-time at a four-year institution or university. Available to U.S. and non-U.S. citizens.

Application Requirements: Application, references, 4 copies of the nomination. *Deadline:* June 1.

Contact: Marvin Borgmeyer, Scholarship Committee
American Institute of Chemical Engineers
PO Box 1607
Baton Rouge, LA 70821-1607
Phone: 225-977-6206
Fax: 225-977-6396

PROCESS DEVELOPMENT DIVISION STUDENT PAPER AWARD

Award presented to a full-time graduate or undergraduate student who prepares the best technical paper to describe the results of process development related studies within chemical engineering. Must be carried out while the student is enrolled at a university with an accredited chemical engineering program. Student must be the primary author. Paper must be suitable for publication in a refereed journal. Must be a member of AIChE.

Academic Fields/Career Goals: Chemical Engineering.

Award: Prize for use in freshman, sophomore, junior, senior, or graduate years; not renewable. *Number:* 1. *Amount:* $200.

Eligibility Requirements: Applicant must be enrolled or expecting to enroll full-time at a four-year institution or university. Available to U.S. and non-U.S. citizens.

Application Requirements: References, original and five copies of the nomination form. *Deadline:* June 15.

Contact: A R. Cartolano, Awards Committee Chair
American Institute of Chemical Engineers
7201 Hamilton Boulevard
Allentown, PA 18195-1501
Phone: 610-481-4262
E-mail: cartolar@airproducts.com

REGIONAL STUDENT PAPER COMPETITION

Students present technical papers at the student regional conferences which are held during spring. Deadlines for regional conferences vary. First prize is $200, second prize is $100, and third prize is $50. First place winner from each region present their paper at the regional competition.

Academic Fields/Career Goals: Chemical Engineering.

Award: Prize for use in freshman, sophomore, junior, or senior years; not renewable. *Number:* 3. *Amount:* $50–$200.

Eligibility Requirements: Applicant must be enrolled or expecting to enroll full-time at a four-year institution or university. Available to U.S. and non-U.S. citizens.

Application Requirements: Applicant must enter a contest, student paper. *Deadline:* varies.

Contact: AIChE Awards Administrator
American Institute of Chemical Engineers
Three Park Avenue
New York, NY 10016-5901
Phone: 212-591-7107
Fax: 212-591-8882
E-mail: awards@aiche.org

SAFETY AND CHEMICAL ENGINEERING EDUCATION (SACHE) STUDENT ESSAY AWARD FOR SAFETY

Awards individuals or a team submitting the best essays on the topic of chemical process safety. Essays may focus on process safety in education, relevance of safety in undergraduate education, or integrating safety principles into the undergraduate chemical engineering curriculum.

Academic Fields/Career Goals: Chemical Engineering.

Award: Prize for use in freshman, sophomore, junior, or senior years; not renewable. *Number:* up to 4. *Amount:* $500.

Eligibility Requirements: Applicant must be enrolled or expecting to enroll full-time at a four-year institution or university. Available to U.S. and non-U.S. citizens.

Application Requirements: Applicant must enter a contest, essay. *Deadline:* June 5.

Contact: AIChE Awards Administrator
American Institute of Chemical Engineers
Three Park Avenue
New York, NY 10016
Phone: 212-591-7107
Fax: 212-591-8880
E-mail: awards@aiche.org

SAFETY AND HEALTH NATIONAL STUDENT DESIGN COMPETITION AWARD FOR SAFETY

Four $600 awards available for each of the teams or individuals who apply one or more of the following concepts of inherent safety in their designs: design the plant for easier and effective maintainability; design the plant with less waste; design the plant with special features that demonstrate inherent safety; include design concepts regarding the entire life cycle. The school must have a student chapter of AIChE.

Academic Fields/Career Goals: Chemical Engineering; Industrial Design.

Award: Prize for use in freshman, sophomore, junior, senior, or graduate years; not renewable. *Number:* 4. *Amount:* $600.

Eligibility Requirements: Applicant must be enrolled or expecting to enroll full- or part-time at a four-year institution or university. Available to U.S. and non-U.S. citizens.

Application Requirements: Application, design. *Deadline:* June 6.

Contact: AIChE Awards Administrator
American Institute of Chemical Engineers
Three Park Avenue
New York, NY 10016
Phone: 212-591-7478
Fax: 212-591-8882
E-mail: awards@aiche.org

AMERICAN OIL CHEMISTS' SOCIETY

http://www.aocs.org/

AOCS BIOTECHNOLOGY STUDENT EXCELLENCE AWARD
• *See page 82*

AMERICAN SOCIETY FOR ENOLOGY AND VITICULTURE

http://www.asev.org/

AMERICAN SOCIETY FOR ENOLOGY AND VITICULTURE SCHOLARSHIPS
• *See page 82*

ARMED FORCES COMMUNICATIONS AND ELECTRONICS ASSOCIATION, EDUCATIONAL FOUNDATION

http://www.afcea.org/education/scholarships

AFCEA YOUNG ENTREPRENEUR SCHOLARSHIP

The scholarship is intended for students attending school on a part-time basis, whether at a two-year community college or accredited university institution. Part-time status will be defined as enrollment in at least two classes (semester-equivalent) with a declared major in a science or technology degree program or a declared major in a business field with a science or technology minor.

Academic Fields/Career Goals: Chemical Engineering; Computer Science/Data Processing; Electrical Engineering/Electronics; Engineering/Technology; Engineering-Related Technologies; Mathematics; Physical Sciences.

Award: Scholarship for use in junior, senior, or postgraduate years; not renewable. *Number:* 1–5. *Amount:* $2000.

Eligibility Requirements: Applicant must be age 40 or under and enrolled or expecting to enroll part-time at a two-year or four-year institution or university. Applicant must have 3.0 GPA or higher. Available to U.S. citizens.

Application Requirements: Application, references. *Deadline:* March 1.

Contact: Miss. Tammy Goehring
Armed Forces Communications and Electronics Association, Educational Foundation
4400 Fair Lakes Court
Fairfax, VA 22033
Phone: 703-631-6119
E-mail: smallbusiness@afcea.org

ARMED FORCES COMMUNICATIONS AND ELECTRONICS ASSOCIATION GENERAL EMMETT PAIGE SCHOLARSHIP
• *See page 122*

ARMED FORCES COMMUNICATIONS AND ELECTRONICS ASSOCIATION GENERAL JOHN A. WICKHAM SCHOLARSHIP

Scholarships of $2000 for U.S. citizens enrolled full-time in four-year, accredited colleges or universities in the United States and majoring in C4I-related fields. Applicant must be a sophomore or junior with minimum GPA of 3.5.

Academic Fields/Career Goals: Chemical Engineering; Communications; Computer Science/Data Processing; Electrical Engineering/Electronics; Engineering/Technology; Engineering-Related Technologies; International Studies; Mathematics; Physical Sciences.

Award: Scholarship for use in sophomore or junior years; not renewable. *Number:* 8–12. *Amount:* $2000.

Eligibility Requirements: Applicant must be enrolled or expecting to enroll full-time at a four-year institution or university. Applicant must have 3.5 GPA or higher. Available to U.S. citizens.

Application Requirements: Application, references, transcript. *Deadline:* May 1.

Contact: Ms. Norma Corrales, Director, Scholarships & Awards Program
Armed Forces Communications and Electronics Association, Educational Foundation
4400 Fair Lakes Court
Fairfax, VA 22015
Phone: 703-631-6149
E-mail: scholarship@afcea.org

LTG DOUGLAS D. BUCHHOLZ MEMORIAL SCHOLARSHIP
• *See page 122*

WILLIAM E. "BUCK" BRAGUNIER SCHOLARSHIP FOR OUTSTANDING LEADERSHIP
• *See page 123*

ARRL FOUNDATION INC.

http://www.arrl.org/

GARY WAGNER, K3OMI SCHOLARSHIP

One $1000 award available to student who possesses a Novice class or higher amateur radio license and who is or will be attending a four-year college. Applicant must be majoring in or intend to major in a field of engineering. Financial need must be demonstrated.

Academic Fields/Career Goals: Chemical Engineering; Civil Engineering; Construction Engineering/Management; Electrical Engineering/Electronics; Energy and Power Engineering; Engineering/Technology; Engineering-Related Technologies; Materials Science, Engineering, and Metallurgy; Mechanical Engineering.

Award: Scholarship for use in freshman, sophomore, junior, or senior years; not renewable. *Number:* 1. *Amount:* $1000.

Eligibility Requirements: Applicant must be enrolled or expecting to enroll at a four-year institution or university; resident of Maryland, North Carolina, Tennessee, Virginia, or West Virginia and must have an interest in amateur radio.

Application Requirements: Application, financial need analysis, transcript. *Deadline:* February 1.

Contact: Ms. Mary Hobart, Secretary
ARRL Foundation Inc.
225 Main Street
Newington, CT 06111-1494
Phone: 860-594-0397
E-mail: k1mmh@arrl.org

ASSOCIATION ON AMERICAN INDIAN AFFAIRS, INC.

http://www.indian-affairs.org/

ELIZABETH AND SHERMAN ASCHE MEMORIAL SCHOLARSHIP FUND
• *See page 83*

ASTRONAUT SCHOLARSHIP FOUNDATION

http://www.astronautscholarship.org/

ASTRONAUT SCHOLARSHIP FOUNDATION
• *See page 95*

AUTOMOTIVE HALL OF FAME

http://www.automotivehalloffame.org/

AUTOMOTIVE HALL OF FAME EDUCATIONAL FUNDS

Award for full-time undergraduate and graduate students pursuing studies in automotive and related technologies. Must submit two letters of recommendation supporting automotive interests. Minimum 3.0 cumulative GPA required. Student must study in the United States and either be a United States Citizen or on a Student Visa.

Academic Fields/Career Goals: Chemical Engineering; Electrical Engineering/Electronics; Engineering/Technology; Engineering-Related Technologies; Industrial Design; Marketing; Mechanical Engineering; Trade/Technical Specialties; Transportation.

Award: Scholarship for use in freshman, sophomore, junior, senior, or graduate years; renewable. *Number:* 20. *Amount:* $500–$2000.

Eligibility Requirements: Applicant must be enrolled or expecting to enroll full-time at a two-year or four-year or technical institution or university and must have an interest in automotive. Applicant must have 3.0 GPA or higher. Available to U.S. and non-U.S. citizens.

Application Requirements: Application, financial need analysis, references, self-addressed stamped envelope, transcript. *Deadline:* June 1.

Contact: Lynne Hall, Scholarship Coordinator
Automotive Hall of Fame
21400 Oakwood Boulevard
Dearborn, MI 48124-4078
Phone: 313-240-4000 Ext. 229
Fax: 313-240-8641

BARRY M. GOLDWATER SCHOLARSHIP AND EXCELLENCE IN EDUCATION FOUNDATION

http://www.act.org/goldwater

BARRY M. GOLDWATER SCHOLARSHIP AND EXCELLENCE IN EDUCATION PROGRAM
• *See page 95*

BRITISH COLUMBIA INNOVATION COUNCIL

http://www.bcic.ca/

PAUL AND HELEN TRUSSELL SCIENCE AND TECHNOLOGY SCHOLARSHIP
• *See page 95*

CHEMICAL INSTITUTE OF CANADA

http://www.cheminst.ca/

CSCHE CHEMICAL ENGINEERING LOCAL SECTION SCHOLARSHIPS

Scholarships for undergraduate students in chemical engineering who are entering their final year of studies at a Canadian university. Applicants must be paid undergraduate student members of Canadian Society for Chemical Engineering. Leadership qualities, demonstrated contributions to the Society such as participation in student chapters, and academic performance will be considered.

Academic Fields/Career Goals: Chemical Engineering.

Award: Scholarship for use in senior year; not renewable. *Number:* 2. *Amount:* $2000.

Eligibility Requirements: Applicant must be enrolled or expecting to enroll full-time at an institution or university and studying in Alberta, British Columbia, Manitoba, New Brunswick, Newfoundland, Nova Scotia, Ontario, Prince Edward Island, Quebec, or Saskatchewan. Applicant or parent of applicant must be member of Canadian Society for Chemical Engineering. Available to U.S. and non-U.S. citizens.

Application Requirements: Resume, references, transcript. *Deadline:* April 30.

Contact: Gale Thirlwall, Awards Manager
Chemical Institute of Canada
130 Slater Street, Suite 550
Ottawa, ON K1P 6E2
Canada
Phone: 613-232-6252 Ext. 223
E-mail: awards@cheminst.ca

CONGRESSIONAL BLACK CAUCUS FOUNDATION, INC.

http://www.cbcfinc.org/

CONGRESSIONAL BLACK CAUCUS SPOUSES CHEERIOS BRAND HEALTH INITIATIVE
• *See page 139*

CUBAN AMERICAN NATIONAL FOUNDATION

http://www.masscholarships.org/

MAS FAMILY SCHOLARSHIPS
• *See page 148*

ENGINEERS' SOCIETY OF WESTERN PENNSYLVANIA

http://www.eswp.com/

JOSEPH A. LEVENDUSKY MEMORIAL SCHOLARSHIP

Scholarship of up to $7000 awarded to an undergraduate student in mechanical or chemical engineering. Must be accepted or enrolled in good standing as a student at an accredited institution.

Academic Fields/Career Goals: Chemical Engineering; Mechanical Engineering.

Award: Scholarship for use in freshman, sophomore, junior, or senior years; not renewable. *Number:* 1. *Amount:* $7000.

Eligibility Requirements: Applicant must be enrolled or expecting to enroll full-time at a four-year institution or university. Available to U.S. and non-U.S. citizens.

Application Requirements: Application, essay, financial need analysis, references, transcript. *Deadline:* September 1.

Contact: Conor McGarvey, Conference Manager
Engineers' Society of Western Pennsylvania
337 Fourth Avenue
Pittsburgh, PA 15222
Phone: 412-261-0710
Fax: 412-261-1606
E-mail: c.mcgarvey@eswp.com

FOUNDATION FOR SCIENCE AND DISABILITY

http://stemd.org/

GRANTS FOR DISABLED STUDENTS IN THE SCIENCES
• *See page 95*

HAWAIIAN LODGE, F&AM

http://www.glhawaii.org/

HAWAIIAN LODGE SCHOLARSHIPS
• *See page 106*

HISPANIC ENGINEER NATIONAL ACHIEVEMENT AWARDS CORPORATION (HENAAC)

http://www.henaac.org/

HISPANIC ENGINEER NATIONAL ACHIEVEMENT AWARDS CORPORATION SCHOLARSHIP PROGRAM
• *See page 125*

INDEPENDENT COLLEGE FUND OF MARYLAND (I-FUND)

http://www.i-fundinfo.org/

HEALTH AND LIFE SCIENCES PROGRAM SCHOLARSHIPS
• *See page 140*

INDEPENDENT LABORATORIES INSTITUTE SCHOLARSHIP ALLIANCE

http://www.acil.org/

INDEPENDENT LABORATORIES INSTITUTE SCHOLARSHIP ALLIANCE
• *See page 141*

INTERNATIONAL SOCIETY FOR OPTICAL ENGINEERING-SPIE

http://www.spie.org/scholarships

SPIE EDUCATIONAL SCHOLARSHIPS IN OPTICAL SCIENCE AND ENGINEERING
• *See page 96*

INTERNATIONAL SOCIETY OF AUTOMATION (ISA)

http://www.isa.org/

INTERNATIONAL SOCIETY OF AUTOMATION EDUCATION FOUNDATION SCHOLARSHIPS
• *See page 125*

JORGE MAS CANOSA FREEDOM FOUNDATION

http://www.jorgemascanosa.org/

MAS FAMILY SCHOLARSHIP AWARD
• *See page 152*

KENTUCKY ENERGY AND ENVIRONMENT CABINET

http://www.eec.ky.gov/

ENVIRONMENTAL PROTECTION SCHOLARSHIP
• *See page 141*

LOS ANGELES COUNCIL OF BLACK PROFESSIONAL ENGINEERS

http://www.lablackengineers.org/

AL-BEN SCHOLARSHIP FOR ACADEMIC INCENTIVE

One-time scholarship for students enrolled full-time with scholastic achievements in the academic pursuits of engineering, math, computer or scientific studies. Must be from a minority group. Scholarship value is $500 to $1000. Two scholarships are granted annually. Preference given to residents of Southern California.

Academic Fields/Career Goals: Chemical Engineering; Civil Engineering; Computer Science/Data Processing; Electrical Engineering/Electronics; Engineering/Technology; Engineering-Related Technologies; Materials Science, Engineering, and Metallurgy; Mechanical Engineering; Physical Sciences.

Award: Scholarship for use in freshman, sophomore, junior, or senior years; not renewable. *Number:* 2. *Amount:* $500–$1000.

Eligibility Requirements: Applicant must be American Indian/Alaska Native, Asian/Pacific Islander, Black (non-Hispanic), or Hispanic and enrolled or expecting to enroll full-time at a four-year institution or university. Available to U.S. citizens.

Application Requirements: Application, essay, references, transcript. *Deadline:* April 2.

Contact: Leroy Freelon, President
Los Angeles Council of Black Professional Engineers
PO Box 881029
Los Angeles, CA 90009
Phone: 310-635-7734
E-mail: lfreelonjr@aol.com

AL-BEN SCHOLARSHIP FOR PROFESSIONAL MERIT

One-time scholarship for students enrolled full-time with scholastic achievements in the academic pursuits of engineering, math, computer or scientific studies. Must be from a minority group. Scholarship value is $500 to $1000. Two scholarships are granted annually. Preference given to residents of Southern California.

Academic Fields/Career Goals: Chemical Engineering; Civil Engineering; Computer Science/Data Processing; Electrical Engineering/Electronics; Engineering/Technology; Engineering-Related Technologies; Materials Science, Engineering, and Metallurgy; Mechanical Engineering; Physical Sciences.

Award: Scholarship for use in freshman, sophomore, junior, or senior years; not renewable. *Number:* 2. *Amount:* $500–$1000.

Eligibility Requirements: Applicant must be American Indian/Alaska Native, Asian/Pacific Islander, Black (non-Hispanic), or Hispanic and enrolled or expecting to enroll full-time at a four-year institution or university. Available to U.S. citizens.

Application Requirements: Application, essay, references, transcript. *Deadline:* April 2.

Contact: Leroy Freelon, President
Los Angeles Council of Black Professional Engineers
PO Box 881029
Los Angeles, CA 90009
Phone: 310-635-7734
E-mail: lfreelonjr@aol.com

AL-BEN SCHOLARSHIP FOR SCHOLASTIC ACHIEVEMENT

Scholarships for students enrolled full-time with scholastic achievements in the academic pursuits of engineering, math, computer or scientific studies. Must be from a minority group.

Academic Fields/Career Goals: Chemical Engineering; Civil Engineering; Computer Science/Data Processing; Electrical Engineering/

Electronics; Engineering/Technology; Engineering-Related Technologies; Materials Science, Engineering, and Metallurgy; Mechanical Engineering; Physical Sciences.

Award: Scholarship for use in freshman, sophomore, junior, or senior years; not renewable. *Number:* 2. *Amount:* $500–$1000.

Eligibility Requirements: Applicant must be American Indian/Alaska Native, Asian/Pacific Islander, Black (non-Hispanic), or Hispanic and enrolled or expecting to enroll full-time at a four-year institution or university. Available to U.S. citizens.

Application Requirements: Application, essay, references, transcript. *Deadline:* April 2.

Contact: Leroy Freelon, President
Los Angeles Council of Black Professional Engineers
PO Box 881029
Los Angeles, CA 90009
Phone: 310-635-7734
E-mail: lfreelonjr@aol.com

MICHIGAN SOCIETY OF PROFESSIONAL ENGINEERS

http://www.michiganspe.org/

MICHIGAN SOCIETY OF PROFESSIONAL ENGINEERS HARRY R. BALL, P.E. GRANT

One $1000 grant for a Michigan high school student to study engineering at an ABET-accredited college or university in Michigan. Minimum 3.0 GPA required in grades eleven and twelve.

Academic Fields/Career Goals: Chemical Engineering; Civil Engineering; Construction Engineering/Management; Electrical Engineering/Electronics; Engineering/Technology; Mechanical Engineering.

Award: Grant for use in freshman year; not renewable. *Number:* 1. *Amount:* $1000.

Eligibility Requirements: Applicant must be high school student; planning to enroll or expecting to enroll full-time at a four-year institution or university; resident of Michigan and studying in Michigan. Applicant must have 3.0 GPA or higher. Available to U.S. citizens.

Application Requirements: Application, test scores, transcript. *Deadline:* February 15.

Contact: Maura Nessan, Executive Director
Michigan Society of Professional Engineers
215 North Walnut Street
PO Box 15276
Lansing, MI 48901-5276
Phone: 517-487-9388
E-mail: mspe@michiganspe.org

MICHIGAN SOCIETY OF PROFESSIONAL ENGINEERS KENNETH B. FISHBECK, P.E. MEMORIAL GRANT

One $1000 grant for a Michigan high school student to study engineering at an ABET-accredited college or university in Michigan. Submit application to local MSPE chapter chair. Applicants should demonstrate qualifications of high merit and professional ethics.

Academic Fields/Career Goals: Chemical Engineering; Civil Engineering; Construction Engineering/Management; Electrical Engineering/Electronics; Engineering/Technology; Mechanical Engineering.

Award: Grant for use in freshman year; not renewable. *Number:* 1. *Amount:* $1000.

Eligibility Requirements: Applicant must be high school student; planning to enroll or expecting to enroll full-time at a four-year institution or university; resident of Michigan and studying in Michigan. Applicant must have 3.0 GPA or higher. Available to U.S. citizens.

Application Requirements: Application, test scores, transcript. *Deadline:* February 15.

Contact: Maura Nessan, Executive Director
Michigan Society of Professional Engineers
215 North Walnut Street
PO Box 15276
Lansing, MI 48901-5276
Phone: 517-487-9388
E-mail: mspe@michiganspe.org

NASA IDAHO SPACE GRANT CONSORTIUM

http://www.id.spacegrant.org/

NASA IDAHO SPACE GRANT CONSORTIUM SCHOLARSHIP PROGRAM
• *See page 141*

NASA/MARYLAND SPACE GRANT CONSORTIUM

http://www.mdspacegrant.org/

NASA MARYLAND SPACE GRANT CONSORTIUM UNDERGRADUATE SCHOLARSHIPS
• *See page 127*

NASA MONTANA SPACE GRANT CONSORTIUM

http://www.spacegrant.montana.edu/

MONTANA SPACE GRANT SCHOLARSHIP PROGRAM
• *See page 128*

NASA'S VIRGINIA SPACE GRANT CONSORTIUM

http://www.vsgc.odu.edu/

UNDERGRADUATE RESEARCH STEM SCHOLARSHIPS
• *See page 96*

NATIONAL ASSOCIATION FOR THE ADVANCEMENT OF COLORED PEOPLE

http://www.naacp.org/

HUBERTUS W.V. WELLEMS SCHOLARSHIP FOR MALE STUDENTS

Scholarship for a male, full-time student, majoring in one of the following: engineering, chemistry, physics, or mathematical sciences. Graduate student may be full- or part-time and have 2.5 minimum GPA. Graduating high school seniors and undergraduates must have 3.0 minimum GPA. Must demonstrate financial need. Undergraduate scholarship is $2000; and graduate scholarship is $3000.

Academic Fields/Career Goals: Chemical Engineering; Engineering/Technology; Engineering-Related Technologies; Physical Sciences.

Award: Scholarship for use in freshman, sophomore, junior, senior, or graduate years; not renewable. *Number:* 1. *Amount:* $2000–$3000.

Eligibility Requirements: Applicant must be American Indian/Alaska Native, Asian/Pacific Islander, Black (non-Hispanic), or Hispanic; enrolled or expecting to enroll full- or part-time at a two-year or four-year institution or university and male. Applicant or parent of applicant must be member of National Association for the Advancement of Colored People. Applicant must have 3.0 GPA or higher. Available to U.S. citizens.

Application Requirements: Application, financial need analysis, references, transcript. *Deadline:* March 7.

Contact: Victor Goode, Attorney
National Association for the Advancement of Colored People
4805 Mount Hope Drive
Baltimore, MD 21215-3297
Phone: 410-580-5760
E-mail: info@naacp.org

NATIONAL BOARD OF BOILER AND PRESSURE VESSEL INSPECTORS

http://www.nationalboard.org/

NATIONAL BOARD TECHNICAL SCHOLARSHIP

Two $6000 scholarships to selected students meeting eligibility standards, who are pursuing a bachelor's degree in certain engineering or related studies. Must be a child, step-child, grandchild, or great-grandchild of a past or present National Board member (living or deceased), or of a past or present Commissioned Inspector (living or deceased), employed by a member jurisdiction, or of a past or present National Board employee (living or deceased).

Academic Fields/Career Goals: Chemical Engineering; Electrical Engineering/Electronics; Mechanical Engineering.

Award: Scholarship for use in freshman, sophomore, junior, or senior years; not renewable. *Number:* 2. *Amount:* $6000.

Eligibility Requirements: Applicant must be enrolled or expecting to enroll full-time at a four-year or technical institution or university. Applicant or parent of applicant must be member of National Board of Boiler and Pressure Vessel Inspectors. Applicant must have 3.0 GPA or higher. Available to U.S. and Canadian citizens.

Application Requirements: Application, essay, references, transcript. *Deadline:* February 29.

Contact: Donald Tanner, Executive Director
National Board of Boiler and Pressure Vessel Inspectors
1055 Crupper Avenue
Columbus, OH 43229-1183
Phone: 614-888-8320
Fax: 614-888-0750
E-mail: dtanner@nationalboard.org

NATIONAL INVENTORS HALL OF FAME

http://www.invent.org/

COLLEGIATE INVENTORS COMPETITION FOR UNDERGRADUATE STUDENTS
• *See page 96*

COLLEGIATE INVENTORS COMPETITION-GRAND PRIZE
• *See page 97*

NATIONAL SOCIETY OF PROFESSIONAL ENGINEERS

http://www.nspe.org/

MAUREEN L. AND HOWARD N. BLITMAN, PE SCHOLARSHIP TO PROMOTE DIVERSITY IN ENGINEERING

Award of $5000 in two disbursements of $2,500 to a high school senior from an ethnic minority who has been accepted into an ABET-accredited engineering program at a four-year college or university.

Academic Fields/Career Goals: Chemical Engineering; Civil Engineering; Electrical Engineering/Electronics; Engineering/Technology; Engineering-Related Technologies; Materials Science, Engineering, and Metallurgy; Mechanical Engineering.

Award: Scholarship for use in freshman year; not renewable. *Number:* 1. *Amount:* $5000.

Eligibility Requirements: Applicant must be American Indian/Alaska Native, Black (non-Hispanic), or Hispanic; high school student and planning to enroll or expecting to enroll full-time at a four-year institution or university. Applicant must have 2.5 GPA or higher. Available to U.S. citizens.

Application Requirements: Application, essay, references, test scores, transcript. *Deadline:* March 1.

Contact: Cindy Simpson, Director of Education
National Society of Professional Engineers
1420 King Street
Alexandria, VA 22314-2794
Phone: 703-684-2833
E-mail: csimpson@nspe.org

PAUL H. ROBBINS HONORARY SCHOLARSHIP

Awarded annually to a current engineering undergraduate student entering the junior year in an ABET-accredited engineering program and attending a college/university that participates in the NSPE Professional Engineers in Higher Education (PEHE) Sustaining University Program(SUP).

Academic Fields/Career Goals: Chemical Engineering; Civil Engineering; Electrical Engineering/Electronics; Engineering/Technology; Engineering-Related Technologies; Materials Science, Engineering, and Metallurgy; Mechanical Engineering.

Award: Scholarship for use in junior year; renewable. *Number:* 1. *Amount:* $5000.

Eligibility Requirements: Applicant must be enrolled or expecting to enroll full-time at a four-year institution or university. Applicant or parent of applicant must be member of National Society of Professional Engineers. Available to U.S. citizens.

Application Requirements: Application, essay, references, test scores, transcript. *Deadline:* March 1.

Contact: Cindy Simpson, Director of Education
National Society of Professional Engineers
1420 King Street
Alexandria, VA 22314-2794
Phone: 703-684-2833
E-mail: csimpson@nspe.org

PROFESSIONAL ENGINEERS IN INDUSTRY SCHOLARSHIP

Applicants must be sponsored by an NSPE/PEI member. Students must have completed a minimum of two semesters or three quarters of undergraduate engineering studies (or be enrolled in graduate study) accredited by ABET.

Academic Fields/Career Goals: Chemical Engineering; Civil Engineering; Electrical Engineering/Electronics; Engineering/Technology; Engineering-Related Technologies; Materials Science, Engineering, and Metallurgy; Mechanical Engineering.

Award: Scholarship for use in sophomore, junior, or senior years; not renewable. *Number:* 1. *Amount:* $2500.

Eligibility Requirements: Applicant must be enrolled or expecting to enroll full-time at a four-year institution or university. Applicant must have 3.5 GPA or higher. Available to U.S. citizens.

Application Requirements: Application, essay, resume, references, transcript, work experience certificates. *Deadline:* April 1.

Contact: Erin Garcia Reyes, Practice Division Manager
National Society of Professional Engineers
1420 King Street
Alexandria, VA 22314
Phone: 703-684-2884
E-mail: egarcia@nspe.org

NEVADA NASA SPACE GRANT CONSORTIUM

http://www.nvspacegrant.org/

NATIONAL SPACE GRANT COLLEGE AND FELLOWSHIP PROGRAM
• *See page 97*

NEW MEXICO COMMISSION ON HIGHER EDUCATION

http://www.hed.state.nm.us/

MINORITY DOCTORAL ASSISTANCE LOAN-FOR-SERVICE PROGRAM

Award program enacted to increase the number of ethnic minorities and women available to teach engineering, physical or life sciences, mathematics, and other academic disciplines in which ethnic minorities or women are demonstrably underrepresented in New Mexico colleges and universities. Award may be renewable for up to four years.

Academic Fields/Career Goals: Chemical Engineering; Engineering/Technology; Mathematics; Mechanical Engineering; Natural Sciences; Physical Sciences.

Award: Forgivable loan for use in freshman, sophomore, junior, senior, or graduate years; renewable. *Number:* varies. *Amount:* $15,000.

Eligibility Requirements: Applicant must be American Indian/Alaska Native, Asian/Pacific Islander, Black (non-Hispanic), or Hispanic; enrolled or expecting to enroll full-time at a four-year institution or university; resident of New Mexico and studying in New Mexico. Available to U.S. citizens.

Application Requirements: Application, essay, references, transcript. *Deadline:* March 15.

Contact: Theresa Acker, Financial Aid Division
New Mexico Commission on Higher Education
1068 Cerrillos Road
Santa Fe, NM 87505-1650
Phone: 505-476-6506
Fax: 505-476-6511
E-mail: tashina.banks-moore@state.nm.us

OREGON STUDENT ASSISTANCE COMMISSION

http://www.GetCollegeFunds.org/

AMERICAN COUNCIL OF ENGINEERING COMPANIES OF OREGON SCHOLARSHIP

Renewable award for graduating high school seniors or those who have had no previous college education. For use at any Oregon four-year college that offers accredited programs in chemical, civil, electrical, industrial, or mechanical engineering. Preference for applicants interested in the consulting engineering profession.

Academic Fields/Career Goals: Chemical Engineering; Civil Engineering; Electrical Engineering/Electronics; Engineering-Related Technologies; Mechanical Engineering.

Award: Scholarship for use in freshman, sophomore, junior, or senior years; renewable. *Number:* varies. *Amount:* varies.

Eligibility Requirements: Applicant must be enrolled or expecting to enroll full-time at a four-year institution; resident of Oregon and studying in Oregon. Available to U.S. citizens.

Application Requirements: Application, essay, transcript, activities chart. *Deadline:* March 1.

Contact: Scholarship Coordinator
Oregon Student Assistance Commission
1500 Valley River Drive, Suite 100
Eugene, OR 97401-7020
Phone: 800-452-8807

PLASTICS INSTITUTE OF AMERICA

http://www.plasticsinstitute.org/

PLASTICS PIONEERS SCHOLARSHIPS

Financial grants awarded to undergraduate students needing help in their education expenses to enter into a full-time career in any and all segments of the plastics industry, with emphasis on "hands on" participation in the many fields where members of the Plastics Pioneers Association have spent their professional years. Applicants must be U.S. citizens.

Academic Fields/Career Goals: Chemical Engineering; Engineering/Technology; Engineering-Related Technologies; Materials Science, Engineering, and Metallurgy; Trade/Technical Specialties.

Award: Scholarship for use in freshman, sophomore, junior, or senior years; renewable. *Number:* 30–40. *Amount:* $1500–$3000.

Eligibility Requirements: Applicant must be enrolled or expecting to enroll full- or part-time at a two-year or four-year or technical institution. Available to U.S. citizens.

Application Requirements: Application, essay, resume, references, transcript. *Deadline:* April 1.

Contact: Aldo Crugnola, Executive Director
Plastics Institute of America
333 Aiken Street
Lowell, MA 01854
Phone: 978-934-2575
Fax: 978-459-9420
E-mail: pia@uml.edu

ROBERT H. MOLLOHAN FAMILY CHARITABLE FOUNDATION, INC.

http://www.mollohanfoundation.org/

HIGH TECHNOLOGY SCHOLARS PROGRAM
• *See page 143*

SEMICONDUCTOR RESEARCH CORPORATION (SRC)

http://www.src.org/

MASTER'S SCHOLARSHIP PROGRAM

Scholarship given to women or members of an under represented minority category (African-American, Hispanic, Native American). Scholarships are for study in disciplines related to microelectronics at US-based universities having research funded by the Semiconductor Research Corporation and require US citizenship or permanent resident status.

Academic Fields/Career Goals: Chemical Engineering; Computer Science/Data Processing; Electrical Engineering/Electronics; Engineering/Technology; Materials Science, Engineering, and Metallurgy.

Award: Scholarship for use in senior or graduate years; renewable. *Number:* 1–15. *Amount:* $25,000–$32,000.

Eligibility Requirements: Applicant must be American Indian/Alaska Native, Black (non-Hispanic), or Hispanic and enrolled or expecting to enroll full-time at a four-year institution or university. Applicant must have 3.0 GPA or higher. Available to U.S. citizens.

Application Requirements: Application, resume, references, test scores, transcript. *Deadline:* February 15.

Contact: Virginia Wiggins, Student Relations Manager
Semiconductor Research Corporation (SRC)
PO Box 12053
Research Triangle Park, NC 27709-2053
Phone: 919-941-9453
E-mail: students@src.org

SIGMA XI, THE SCIENTIFIC RESEARCH SOCIETY

http://www.sigmaxi.org/

SIGMA XI·GRANTS-IN-AID OF RESEARCH
• *See page 87*

SOCIETY OF AUTOMOTIVE ENGINEERS

http://www.sae.org/

BMW/SAE ENGINEERING SCHOLARSHIP
• *See page 132*

EDWARD D. HENDRICKSON/SAE ENGINEERING SCHOLARSHIP
• *See page 132*

TMC/SAE DONALD D. DAWSON TECHNICAL SCHOLARSHIP
• *See page 133*

SOCIETY OF HISPANIC PROFESSIONAL ENGINEERS FOUNDATION

http://www.henaac.org/

SOCIETY OF HISPANIC PROFESSIONAL ENGINEERS FOUNDATION

Scholarships awarded to Hispanic engineering and science students throughout the United States. Scholarships are awarded at the beginning of every academic year based upon academic achievement, financial need, involvement in campus and community activities, career goals and counselor recommendations.

Academic Fields/Career Goals: Chemical Engineering; Civil Engineering; Electrical Engineering/Electronics; Engineering/Technology; Engineering-Related Technologies; Materials Science, Engineering, and Metallurgy; Mechanical Engineering; Natural Sciences; Physical Sciences; Science, Technology, and Society.

Award: Scholarship for use in freshman, sophomore, junior, senior, or graduate years; not renewable. *Number:* varies. *Amount:* $500–$7000.

Eligibility Requirements: Applicant must be Hispanic and enrolled or expecting to enroll full-time at a four-year institution or university. Available to U.S. citizens.

Application Requirements: Application, financial need analysis, resume, references. *Deadline:* May 15.

Contact: Kathy Borunda Barrera, Manager, Scholars Program
Society of Hispanic Professional Engineers Foundation
3900 Whiteside Street
Los Angeles, CA 90063
Phone: 323-415-9600
Fax: 323-415-7038
E-mail: kathy@henaac.org

SOCIETY OF PLASTICS ENGINEERS (SPE) FOUNDATION

http://www.4spe.org/

FLEMING/BASZCAK SCHOLARSHIP

Award available for a full-time undergraduate student, with a demonstrated interest in the plastics industry. Must be a U.S. citizen and provide documentation of Mexican heritage.

Academic Fields/Career Goals: Chemical Engineering; Electrical Engineering/Electronics; Engineering/Technology; Industrial Design; Materials Science, Engineering, and Metallurgy; Trade/Technical Specialties.

Award: Scholarship for use in freshman, sophomore, junior, or senior years; not renewable. *Number:* 1. *Amount:* $2000.

Eligibility Requirements: Applicant must be of Mexican heritage; Hispanic and enrolled or expecting to enroll full-time at a two-year or four-year institution or university. Available to U.S. citizens.

Application Requirements: Application, essay, financial need analysis, references, transcript. *Deadline:* February 15.

Contact: Gail R. Bristol, Managing Director
Society of Plastics Engineers (SPE) Foundation
13 Church Hill Road
Newtown, CT 06470
Phone: 203-740-5447
Fax: 203-775-8490
E-mail: foundation@4spe.org

PLASTICS PIONEERS ASSOCIATION SCHOLARSHIPS

Scholarships available to undergraduate students who are committed to becoming "hands-on" workers in the plastics industry, such as plastics technicians or engineers.

Academic Fields/Career Goals: Chemical Engineering; Engineering/Technology.

Award: Scholarship for use in freshman, sophomore, junior, or senior years; renewable. *Number:* up to 10. *Amount:* $3000.

Eligibility Requirements: Applicant must be enrolled or expecting to enroll full-time at a two-year or four-year or technical institution or university. Available to U.S. and Canadian citizens.

Application Requirements: Application, essay, financial need analysis, resume, references, transcript. *Deadline:* January 15.

Contact: Ms. Gail Bristol, Managing Director
Society of Plastics Engineers (SPE) Foundation
13 Church Hill Road
Newtown, CT 06470
Phone: 203-740-5447
Fax: 203-775-8490
E-mail: foundation@4spe.org

SOCIETY OF PLASTICS ENGINEERS SCHOLARSHIP PROGRAM

Scholarships awarded to full-time students who have demonstrated or expressed an interest in the plastics industry. Major or course of study must be beneficial to a career in the plastics industry.

Academic Fields/Career Goals: Chemical Engineering; Electrical Engineering/Electronics; Engineering/Technology; Industrial Design; Materials Science, Engineering, and Metallurgy; Trade/Technical Specialties.

Award: Scholarship for use in freshman, sophomore, junior, senior, or graduate years; not renewable. *Number:* 25–30. *Amount:* $1000–$5000.

Eligibility Requirements: Applicant must be enrolled or expecting to enroll full-time at a two-year or four-year or technical institution or university. Available to U.S. and non-U.S. citizens.

Application Requirements: Application, essay, financial need analysis, references, transcript. *Deadline:* February 15.

Contact: Gail R. Bristol, Managing Director
Society of Plastics Engineers (SPE) Foundation
13 Church Hill Road
Newtown, CT 06470
Phone: 203-740-5447
Fax: 203-775-8490
E-mail: foundation@4spe.org

SOCIETY OF WOMEN ENGINEERS-ROCKY MOUNTAIN SECTION

http://www.swe-rms.org/

SOCIETY OF WOMEN ENGINEERS-ROCKY MOUNTAIN SECTION SCHOLARSHIP PROGRAM

One-time award for female high school seniors in Colorado and Wyoming (except zip codes 80800 and 81599), who intend to enroll in engineering or computer science at an ABET-accredited college or university in those states. Female college students who have already enrolled in those programs may also apply. For more information visit web site http://www.swe-rms.org and look for local scholarships.

Academic Fields/Career Goals: Chemical Engineering; Computer Science/Data Processing; Engineering/Technology; Mechanical Engineering.

Award: Scholarship for use in freshman, sophomore, junior, senior, or graduate years; not renewable. *Number:* 3–5. *Amount:* $500–$1000.

Eligibility Requirements: Applicant must be enrolled or expecting to enroll full-time at a two-year or four-year or technical institution or university; female; resident of Colorado or Wyoming and studying in Colorado or Wyoming. Applicant must have 3.5 GPA or higher. Available to U.S. citizens.

Application Requirements: Application, essay, resume, references, test scores, transcript. *Deadline:* February 1.

Contact: Barbara Kontogiannis, Scholarship Chair
Society of Women Engineers-Rocky Mountain Section
PO Box 260692
Lakewood, CO 80226-0692
Phone: 303-971-5213
E-mail: barbekon@stanfordalumni.org

SONS OF NORWAY FOUNDATION

http://www.sonsofnorway.com/

NANCY LORRAINE JENSEN MEMORIAL SCHOLARSHIP

Scholarship available for full-time undergraduate study in chemistry, physics or in chemical, electrical, or mechanical engineering by a female student who is a U.S. citizen, and a current member, daughter, or granddaughter of a current member of Sons of Norway. The annual award will be at least 50 percent of the tuition for one semester and no more than 100 percent of the tuition for one year. Must have attained a SAT score of at least 1800, a math score of 600 or better, or an ACT score of at least 26. Applicant must have completed at least one term of studies in the above fields. The award will be made jointly payable to the student and her institution. The award is renewable two times during undergraduate study.

Academic Fields/Career Goals: Chemical Engineering; Electrical Engineering/Electronics; Mechanical Engineering.

Award: Scholarship for use in sophomore, junior, or senior years; not renewable. *Number:* 1–6. *Amount:* $2500–$10,000.

Eligibility Requirements: Applicant must be of Norwegian heritage; age 17-35; enrolled or expecting to enroll full-time at a four-year institution or university; female and must have an interest in science. Applicant must have 3.5 GPA or higher. Available to U.S. citizens.

Application Requirements: Application, essay, photo, references, test scores, transcript. *Deadline:* April 1.

Contact: Scholarship Coordinator
Sons of Norway Foundation
1455 West Lake Street
Minneapolis, MN 55408-2666
Phone: 612-827-3611
Fax: 612-827-0658
E-mail: foundation@sofn.com

STRAIGHTFORWARD MEDIA

http://www.straightforwardmedia.com/

STRAIGHTFORWARD MEDIA ENGINEERING SCHOLARSHIP

Scholarship of $500 to students attending or planning to enroll in a post-secondary engineering program in the United States or abroad. Scholarship is awarded four times per year. Deadlines: March 31, June 30, September 30, and December 31. For more information, see Web http://www.straightforwardmedia.com/engineering/form.php.

Academic Fields/Career Goals: Chemical Engineering; Civil Engineering; Electrical Engineering/Electronics; Energy and Power Engineering; Engineering/Technology; Engineering-Related Technologies; Materials Science, Engineering, and Metallurgy; Mechanical Engineering; Paper and Pulp Engineering.

Award: Scholarship for use in freshman, sophomore, junior, or senior years; not renewable. *Number:* 4. *Amount:* $500.

Eligibility Requirements: Applicant must be enrolled or expecting to enroll full- or part-time at a two-year or four-year or technical institution or university. Available to U.S. and non-U.S. citizens.

Application Requirements: Essay. *Deadline:* varies.

Contact: Scholarship Committee
StraightForward Media
508 7th Street
Suite 202
Rapid City, SD 57701
Phone: 605-348-3042

UNITED NEGRO COLLEGE FUND

http://www.uncf.org/

CARDINAL HEALTH SCHOLARSHIP
• *See page 72*

CARGILL SCHOLARSHIP PROGRAM
• *See page 72*

EMERSON PROCESS MANAGEMENT SCHOLARSHIP

Awards of up to $6975 for undergraduate students at UNCF member colleges and universities studying selective engineering fields. Minimum 2.5 GPA required. For additional information, go to Web site http://www.uncf.org/forstudents/scholarship.asp.

Academic Fields/Career Goals: Chemical Engineering; Civil Engineering; Electrical Engineering/Electronics; Engineering/Technology; Mechanical Engineering.

Award: Scholarship for use in freshman, sophomore, junior, or senior years; not renewable. *Amount:* up to $6975.

Eligibility Requirements: Applicant must be Black (non-Hispanic) and enrolled or expecting to enroll at a four-year institution. Applicant must have 2.5 GPA or higher. Available to U.S. citizens.

Application Requirements: *Deadline:* continuous.

Contact: Director, Program Services
United Negro College Fund
8260 Willow Oaks Corporate Drive
PO Box 10444
Fairfax, VA 22031-8044
Phone: 800-331-2244
E-mail: rebecca.bennett@uncf.org

GENERAL MILLS TECHNOLOGY SCHOLARS AWARD

$5,000 scholarship based on academic performance, career aspirations, demonstrated leadership, and achievement. Must be college freshman, sophomore, or junior, have a minimum GPA of 3.0, and major in engineering-related, food science or computer science field.

Academic Fields/Career Goals: Chemical Engineering; Computer Science/Data Processing; Electrical Engineering/Electronics; Engineering/Technology; Food Science/Nutrition; Mechanical Engineering.

Award: Scholarship for use in freshman, sophomore, or junior years; not renewable. *Amount:* up to $5000.

Eligibility Requirements: Applicant must be Black (non-Hispanic) and enrolled or expecting to enroll at a four-year institution or university. Applicant must have 3.0 GPA or higher.

Application Requirements: *Deadline:* April 30.

Contact: Director, Program Services
United Negro College Fund
8260 Willow Oaks Corporate Drive
PO Box 10444
Fairfax, VA 22031-8044
Phone: 800-331-2244
E-mail: rebecca.bennett@uncf.org

MALCOLM PIRNIE CORPORATE SCHOLARS PROGRAM

Scholarship and 8–10 week internship available to African American undergraduate sophomores, juniors, and first year graduate students in information technology, environmental science, civil, chemical, or environmental engineering, or construction management. Must be a U.S. citizen or permanent resident attending any accredited U.S. college or university and have a minimum 2.8 GPA. Apply online at web site http://www.uncf.org.

Academic Fields/Career Goals: Chemical Engineering; Civil Engineering; Computer Science/Data Processing; Construction Engineering/Management; Engineering/Technology; Environmental Science.

Award: Scholarship for use in sophomore, junior, or graduate years; not renewable. *Amount:* $3000.

Eligibility Requirements: Applicant must be Black (non-Hispanic) and enrolled or expecting to enroll full-time at a four-year institution or university. Available to U.S. and non-U.S. citizens.

Application Requirements: Application, resume, references, transcript. *Deadline:* April 12.

Contact: Director, Program Services
United Negro College Fund
8260 Willow Oaks Corporate Drive
PO Box 10444
Fairfax, VA 22031-8044
Phone: 800-331-2244
E-mail: rebecca.bennett@uncf.org

MEDTRONIC FOUNDATION SCHOLARSHIP
• *See page 145*

UNCF/MERCK SCIENCE INITIATIVE
• *See page 145*

UNITED WATER CORPORATE SCHOLARS PROGRAM
• *See page 74*

UNIVERSITIES SPACE RESEARCH ASSOCIATION

http://www.usra.edu/

UNIVERSITIES SPACE RESEARCH ASSOCIATION SCHOLARSHIP PROGRAM
• *See page 97*

UTAH SOCIETY OF PROFESSIONAL ENGINEERS

http://www.uspeonline.com/

UTAH SOCIETY OF PROFESSIONAL ENGINEERS JOE RHOADS SCHOLARSHIP

One-time award for entering freshman pursuing studies in the field of engineering (civil, chemical, electrical, or engineering related technologies.) Minimum 3.5 GPA required. Must be a U.S. citizen and Utah resident attending school in Utah.

Academic Fields/Career Goals: Chemical Engineering; Civil Engineering; Construction Engineering/Management; Electrical Engineering/Electronics; Energy and Power Engineering; Engineering/Technology; Marine/Ocean Engineering; Mechanical Engineering.

Award: Scholarship for use in freshman year; not renewable. *Number:* 1. *Amount:* $1000.

Eligibility Requirements: Applicant must be high school student; planning to enroll or expecting to enroll full-time at a four-year institution or university; resident of Utah and studying in Utah. Applicant must have 3.5 GPA or higher. Available to U.S. citizens.

Application Requirements: Application, essay, resume, references, test scores, transcript. *Deadline:* March 23.

Contact: Dan Church, Joe Rhoads Scholarship Chair
Utah Society of Professional Engineers
488 East Winchester Street, Suite 400
Murray, UT 84107
E-mail: churchd@pbworld.com

XEROX

http://www.xerox.com//

TECHNICAL MINORITY SCHOLARSHIP

Scholarships are made available to minority students enrolled in technical degree programs at the bachelor's degree level or above. Eligible students must have a GPA of 3.0 or higher and show financial need. Refer to web site http://www.studentcareers-xerox-com.tmpqa.com/ for details.

Academic Fields/Career Goals: Chemical Engineering; Computer Science/Data Processing; Electrical Engineering/Electronics; Engineering/Technology; Engineering-Related Technologies; Materials Science, Engineering, and Metallurgy; Mechanical Engineering; Physical Sciences.

Award: Scholarship for use in freshman, sophomore, junior, senior, graduate, or postgraduate years; not renewable. *Number:* up to 122. *Amount:* $1000–$10,000.

Eligibility Requirements: Applicant must be American Indian/Alaska Native, Asian/Pacific Islander, Black (non-Hispanic), or Hispanic and enrolled or expecting to enroll full-time at a four-year institution or university. Applicant must have 3.0 GPA or higher. Available to U.S. citizens.

Application Requirements: Application, financial need analysis, resume. *Deadline:* September 30.

Contact: Stephanie Michalowski
Xerox
150 State Street
Rochester, NY 14614
Fax: 585-482-3095
E-mail: xtmsp@rballiance.com

CHILD AND FAMILY STUDIES

CALIFORNIA STUDENT AID COMMISSION

http://www.csac.ca.gov/

CHILD DEVELOPMENT TEACHER AND SUPERVISOR GRANT PROGRAM

Award is for those students pursuing an approved course of study leading to a Child Development Permit issued by the California Commission on Teacher Credentialing. In exchange for each year funding is received, recipients agree to provide one year of service in a licensed childcare center.

Academic Fields/Career Goals: Child and Family Studies; Education.

Award: Grant for use in freshman, sophomore, junior, senior, or graduate years; renewable. *Number:* up to 300. *Amount:* $1000–$2000.

Eligibility Requirements: Applicant must be enrolled or expecting to enroll full- or part-time at a two-year or four-year institution or university; resident of California and studying in California. Applicant or parent of applicant must have employment or volunteer experience in teaching/education. Available to U.S. citizens.

Application Requirements: Application, financial need analysis, references, GPA verification. *Deadline:* April 16.

Contact: Catalina Mistler, Chief, Program Administration & Services Division
California Student Aid Commission
PO Box 419026
Rancho Cordova, CA 95741-9026
Phone: 916-526-7268
Fax: 916-526-8002
E-mail: studentsupport@csac.ca.gov

CLAN MACBEAN FOUNDATION

http://www.clanmacbean.net/

CLAN MACBEAN FOUNDATION GRANT PROGRAM
• *See page 105*

COLLEGEBOUND FOUNDATION

http://www.collegeboundfoundation.org/

JEANETTE R. WOLMAN SCHOLARSHIP

Renewable scholarship of $500 available for students specializing in pre-law, social work, or a field that focuses on child advocacy. Minimum cumulative GPA of 3.0 required.

Academic Fields/Career Goals: Child and Family Studies; Law/Legal Services; Social Services.

Award: Scholarship for use in freshman, sophomore, junior, or senior years; renewable. *Number:* 1. *Amount:* $500.

Eligibility Requirements: Applicant must be high school student; planning to enroll or expecting to enroll full-time at a two-year or four-year institution or university and resident of Maryland. Applicant must have 3.0 GPA or higher. Available to U.S. citizens.

Application Requirements: Application, financial need analysis, resume, references, transcript. *Deadline:* March 1.

Contact: Deana Carr-Davis, Associate Program Director, Scholarship Programs
CollegeBound Foundation
300 Water Street, Suite 300
Baltimore, MD 21202
Phone: 410-783-2905 Ext. 207
Fax: 410-727-5786
E-mail: dcarr-davis@collegeboundfoundation.org

KE ALI'I PAUAHI FOUNDATION

http://www.pauahi.org/

MYRON & LAURA THOMPSON SCHOLARSHIP

Scholarships for students pursuing a degree in the field of early childhood education. Preference will be given to students who demonstrate an interest in working with Hawaiian children in Hawaii after completion of their education. Applicants must demonstrate financial need. Submit two letters of recommendation from teachers, counselors or community organization.

Academic Fields/Career Goals: Child and Family Studies; Education.

Award: Scholarship for use in freshman, sophomore, junior, senior, or graduate years; not renewable. *Number:* 2. *Amount:* $1300.

Eligibility Requirements: Applicant must be enrolled or expecting to enroll full-time at a four-year institution or university. Available to U.S. citizens.

Application Requirements: Application, financial need analysis, references, transcript, Student Aid Report (SAR), college acceptance letter. *Deadline:* April 1.

Contact: Mavis Shiraishi-Nagao, Scholarship Administrator
Phone: 808-534-3966
E-mail: scholarships@pauahi.org

KENTUCKY HIGHER EDUCATION ASSISTANCE AUTHORITY (KHEAA)

http://www.kheaa.com/

EARLY CHILDHOOD DEVELOPMENT SCHOLARSHIP

Awards scholarship with conditional service commitment for part-time students currently employed by participating ECD facility or providing training in ECD for an approved organization. For more information, visit web site http://www.kheaa.com.

Academic Fields/Career Goals: Child and Family Studies; Education.

Award: Scholarship for use in freshman, sophomore, junior, or senior years; not renewable. *Number:* 1000–1300. *Amount:* up to $1800.

Eligibility Requirements: Applicant must be enrolled or expecting to enroll part-time at a two-year or four-year institution or university; resident of Kentucky and studying in Kentucky. Available to U.S. citizens.

Application Requirements: Application, financial need analysis, FAFSA. *Deadline:* continuous.

Contact: David Lawhorn, Program Coordinator
Kentucky Higher Education Assistance Authority (KHEAA)
PO Box 798
Frankfort, KY 40602-0798
Phone: 800-928-8926 Ext. 67383
Fax: 502-696-7373
E-mail: dlawhorn@kheaa.com

MARGARET MCNAMARA MEMORIAL FUND

http://www.wbfn.org/

MARGARET MCNAMARA MEMORIAL FUND FELLOWSHIPS

One-time award for female students from developing countries enrolled in accredited graduate programs relating to women and children. Must be attending an accredited institution in the United States. Candidates must plan to return to their countries within two years. Must be over 25 years of age. U.S. citizens are not eligible.

Academic Fields/Career Goals: Child and Family Studies; Social Services; Women's Studies.

Award: Grant for use in freshman, sophomore, junior, senior, graduate, or postgraduate years; not renewable. *Number:* 5–6. *Amount:* up to $11,000.

Eligibility Requirements: Applicant must be age 25 and over; enrolled or expecting to enroll full-time at a four-year institution or university and female. Available to citizens of countries other than the U.S. or Canada.

Application Requirements: Application, essay, financial need analysis, photo, references, transcript, copy of visa, I20 and DS2019. *Deadline:* February 28.

Contact: Chairman, Selection Committee
        Margaret McNamara Memorial Fund
        MSN-H2-204, 1818 H Street, NW
        Washington, DC 20433
        Phone: 202-473-8751
        Fax: 202-522-3142
        E-mail: mmmf@worldbank.org

OHIO CHILD CARE RESOURCE & REFERRAL ASSOCIATION

http://www.occrra.org/

T.E.A.C.H. EARLY CHILDHOOD OHIO SCHOLARSHIPS

For Early Childhood Professionals working in Ohio. AAS Scholarships available. Must earn under $15/hr and work 30 hours per week with children.

Academic Fields/Career Goals: Child and Family Studies; Education.

Award: Scholarship for use in freshman, sophomore, junior, or senior years; renewable.

Eligibility Requirements: Applicant must be enrolled or expecting to enroll full- or part-time at a two-year or four-year institution; resident of Ohio and studying in Ohio. Available to U.S. citizens.

Application Requirements: Application.

Contact: Greg Yorker, Director
        E-mail: teach@occrra.org

SAN DIEGO FOUNDATION

http://www.sdfoundation.org/

CALIFORNIA ASSOCIATION OF FAMILY AND CONSUMER SCIENCES-SAN DIEGO CHAPTER

Scholarships to graduating high school seniors, current college students, or graduate students majoring in food sciences, dietetics, nutrition, food services, hospitality, human development or child and family development, apparel, fashion and textile services, housing and interiors, consumer economics, management and resources, or family and consumer science education. For more details visit http://www.sdfoundation.org/scholarships/cafsc.shtml.

Academic Fields/Career Goals: Child and Family Studies; Fashion Design; Food Science/Nutrition; Food Service/Hospitality; Home Economics.

Award: Scholarship for use in freshman, sophomore, junior, senior, or graduate years; not renewable. *Number:* varies. *Amount:* varies.

Eligibility Requirements: Applicant must be enrolled or expecting to enroll full- or part-time at a two-year or four-year or technical institution or university and resident of California. Applicant must have 2.5 GPA or higher. Available to U.S. citizens.

Application Requirements: Application, references, transcript, personal statement, copy of tax return. *Deadline:* January 26.

Contact: Shryl Helvie, Scholarship Coordinator
        San Diego Foundation
        2508 Historic Decatur Road, Suite 200
        San Diego, CA 92106
        Phone: 619-814-1307
        Fax: 619-239-1710
        E-mail: shryl@sdfoundation.org

SOCIETY OF PEDIATRIC NURSES

http://www.pedsnurses.org/

SOCIETY OF PEDIATRIC NURSES EDUCATIONAL SCHOLARSHIP

Award to a member engaged in a BSN completion program or a graduate program that will advance the health of children. Nominee must be a current Society of Pediatric Nurses member.

Academic Fields/Career Goals: Child and Family Studies; Health and Medical Sciences; Nursing.

Award: Scholarship for use in freshman, sophomore, junior, senior, or graduate years; not renewable. *Number:* 1. *Amount:* $500.

Eligibility Requirements: Applicant must be enrolled or expecting to enroll full-time at a four-year institution or university. Applicant or parent of applicant must be member of Society of Pediatric Nurses. Applicant or parent of applicant must have employment or volunteer experience in nursing. Available to U.S. citizens.

Application Requirements: Application, essay, resume, references. *Deadline:* November 14.

Contact: Scholarship Committee
        Society of Pediatric Nurses
        7794 Grow Drive
        Pensacola, FL 32514
        Phone: 800-723-2902
        Fax: 850-484-8762
        E-mail: spn@puetzamc.com

WOMEN'S INDEPENDENCE SCHOLARSHIP PROGRAM, INC.

http://www.wispinc.org/

COUNSELOR, ADVOCATE, AND SUPPORT STAFF SCHOLARSHIP PROGRAM
• See page 76

Y'S MEN INTERNATIONAL

http://www.ysmenusa.com/

ALEXANDER SCHOLARSHIP LOAN FUND
• See page 159

ZETA PHI BETA SORORITY INC. NATIONAL EDUCATIONAL FOUNDATION

http://www.zphib1920.org/

LULLELIA W. HARRISON SCHOLARSHIP IN COUNSELING

Scholarships available for students enrolled in a graduate or undergraduate degree program in counseling. Awarded for full-time study for one academic year. See web site for additional information and application http://www.zphib1920.org.

Academic Fields/Career Goals: Child and Family Studies; Psychology; Social Sciences; Social Services.

Award: Scholarship for use in freshman, sophomore, junior, senior, or graduate years; not renewable. *Number:* 1. *Amount:* $500–$1000.

Eligibility Requirements: Applicant must be enrolled or expecting to enroll full-time at a four-year institution or university. Applicant or parent of applicant must be member of Zeta Phi Beta. Available to U.S. citizens.

Application Requirements: Application, essay, references, transcript, enrollment proof. *Deadline:* February 1.

Contact: Cheryl Williams, National Second Vice President
        Zeta Phi Beta Sorority Inc. National Educational Foundation
        1734 New Hampshire Avenue, NW
        Washington, DC 20009-2595
        Fax: 318-232-4593
        E-mail: 2ndanti@zphib1920.org

CIVIL ENGINEERING

AACE INTERNATIONAL

http://www.aacei.org/

AACE INTERNATIONAL COMPETITIVE SCHOLARSHIP
• See page 99

AIST FOUNDATION

http://www.aistfoundation.org/

ASSOCIATION FOR IRON AND STEEL TECHNOLOGY DAVID H. SAMSON CANADIAN SCHOLARSHIP
• *See page 160*

AMERICAN COUNCIL OF ENGINEERING COMPANIES OF PENNSYLVANIA (ACEC/PA)

http://www.acecpa.org/

ENGINEERING SCHOLARSHIP
• *See page 161*

AMERICAN GROUND WATER TRUST

http://www.agwt.org/

AMERICAN GROUND WATER TRUST-THOMAS STETSON SCHOLARSHIP

For students entering their freshman year in a full-time program of study at a four-year accredited university or college located west of the Mississippi River and intending to pursue a career in ground water-related field. Must be U.S. citizen or legal resident with 3.0 GPA or higher. For more information see web site http://www.agwt.org.

Academic Fields/Career Goals: Civil Engineering; Hydrology; Natural Resources.

Award: Scholarship for use in freshman year; not renewable. *Number:* 1. *Amount:* up to $1500.

Eligibility Requirements: Applicant must be enrolled or expecting to enroll full-time at a four-year institution or university. Applicant must have 3.0 GPA or higher. Available to U.S. citizens.

Application Requirements: Application, essay, references, transcript. *Deadline:* June 1.

Contact: Garret Graaskamp, Ground Water Specialist
American Ground Water Trust
50 Pleasant Street, Suite 2
Concord, NH 03301-4073
Phone: 603-228-5444
Fax: 603-228-6557
E-mail: trustinfo@agwt.org

AMERICAN PUBLIC TRANSPORTATION FOUNDATION

http://www.apta.com/

TRANSIT HALL OF FAME SCHOLARSHIP AWARD PROGRAM

Renewable award for sophomores, juniors, seniors or graduate students studying transportation or rail transit engineering. Must be sponsored by APTA member organization and complete an internship program with a member organization. Must have a minimum 3.0 GPA and be a U.S. or Canadian citizen.

Academic Fields/Career Goals: Civil Engineering; Electrical Engineering/Electronics; Engineering/Technology; Engineering-Related Technologies; Mechanical Engineering; Transportation.

Award: Scholarship for use in sophomore, junior, senior, or graduate years; renewable. *Number:* 1. *Amount:* $2500.

Eligibility Requirements: Applicant must be enrolled or expecting to enroll full-time at a two-year or four-year institution or university. Applicant must have 3.0 GPA or higher. Available to U.S. and Canadian citizens.

Application Requirements: Application, essay, financial need analysis, references, transcript, nomination by APTA member, verification of enrollment, copy of fee schedule from the college/university for the academic year. *Deadline:* June 16.

Contact: Pamela Boswell, Vice President of Program Management
American Public Transportation Foundation
1666 K Street, NW
Washington, DC 20006-1215
Phone: 202-496-4803
Fax: 202-496-4323

AMERICAN RAILWAY ENGINEERING AND MAINTENANCE OF WAY ASSOCIATION

http://www.arema.org/

AREMA MICHAEL R. GARCIA SCHOLARSHIP

Award for students enrolled in a four- or five-year program leading to a bachelor's degree in engineering or engineering technology. This scholarship is for students who are married and/or are supporting a family while enrolled as a student.

Academic Fields/Career Goals: Civil Engineering; Construction Engineering/Management; Electrical Engineering/Electronics; Engineering/Technology; Engineering-Related Technologies.

Award: Scholarship for use in freshman, sophomore, junior, or senior years; not renewable. *Number:* 1. *Amount:* $2000.

Eligibility Requirements: Applicant must be enrolled or expecting to enroll full-time at a four-year institution or university and married. Available to U.S. citizens.

Application Requirements: Application, resume, references, transcript, cover letter. *Deadline:* March 11.

Contact: Lisa Hall, Director of Marketing
American Railway Engineering and Maintenance of Way Association
10003 Derekwood Lane, Suite 210
Lanham, MD 20706
Phone: 301-459-3200 Ext. 705
E-mail: lhall@arema.org

AREMA PRESIDENTIAL SPOUSE SCHOLARSHIP

Scholarship is awarded to an enrolled female student who has completed at least one quarter or semester in an accredited four- or five-year engineering or engineering technology undergraduate degree program.

Academic Fields/Career Goals: Civil Engineering; Construction Engineering/Management; Electrical Engineering/Electronics; Engineering/Technology; Engineering-Related Technologies.

Award: Scholarship for use in freshman, sophomore, junior, or senior years; not renewable. *Number:* varies. *Amount:* $1000.

Eligibility Requirements: Applicant must be enrolled or expecting to enroll full-time at a four-year institution or university and female. Available to U.S. citizens.

Application Requirements: Application, references, transcript, cover letter. *Deadline:* March 11.

Contact: Lisa Hall, Director of Marketing
American Railway Engineering and Maintenance of Way Association
10003 Derekwood Lane, Suite 210
Lanham, MD 20706
Phone: 301-459-3200 Ext. 705
E-mail: lhall@arema.org

AREMA UNDERGRADUATE SCHOLARSHIPS

Scholarships are awarded to engineering students who have a potential interest in railway engineering careers. Minimum 2.0 GPA required.

Academic Fields/Career Goals: Civil Engineering; Construction Engineering/Management; Electrical Engineering/Electronics; Engineering/Technology; Engineering-Related Technologies.

Award: Scholarship for use in freshman, sophomore, junior, or senior years; not renewable. *Amount:* $1000.

Eligibility Requirements: Applicant must be enrolled or expecting to enroll full-time at a four-year institution or university. Available to U.S. and Canadian citizens.

Application Requirements: Application, resume, references, transcript, cover letter. *Deadline:* March 11.

Contact: Lisa Hall, Director of Marketing
American Railway Engineering and Maintenance of Way Association
10003 Derekwood Lane, Suite 210
Lanham, MD 20706
Phone: 301-459-3200 Ext. 705
E-mail: lhall@arema.org

AMERICAN SOCIETY OF CIVIL ENGINEERS

http://www.asce.org/

EUGENE C. FIGG JR. CIVIL ENGINEERING SCHOLARSHIP

Applicant must be currently enrolled junior or senior civil engineering student at an ABET-accredited institution and an ASCE National Student Member in good standing.

Academic Fields/Career Goals: Civil Engineering.

Award: Scholarship for use in junior or senior years; not renewable. *Number:* 1. *Amount:* $3000.

Eligibility Requirements: Applicant must be enrolled or expecting to enroll full- or part-time at a four-year institution or university. Applicant or parent of applicant must be member of American Society of Civil Engineers. Available to U.S. citizens.

Application Requirements: Application, financial need analysis, resume, references, transcript, personal statement. *Deadline:* February 9.

Contact: Ting Wei, Scholarship Coordinator
American Society of Civil Engineers
1801 Alexander Bell Drive
Reston, VA 20191-4400
Phone: 703-295-6300 Ext. 6106
Fax: 703-295-6222

SAMUEL FLETCHER TAPMAN ASCE STUDENT CHAPTER/CLUB SCHOLARSHIP

Awards available to currently enrolled undergraduates. Must be a member of local ASCE Student Chapter/Club and an ASCE National Student Member in good standing. Selection is based on the applicant's justification of award, educational plan, academic performance and standing, potential for development, leadership capacity, ASCE activities, and financial need.

Academic Fields/Career Goals: Civil Engineering; Construction Engineering/Management.

Award: Scholarship for use in freshman, sophomore, junior, or senior years; not renewable. *Number:* 12. *Amount:* up to $2000.

Eligibility Requirements: Applicant must be enrolled or expecting to enroll full- or part-time at a four-year institution or university. Applicant or parent of applicant must be member of American Society of Civil Engineers. Available to U.S. citizens.

Application Requirements: Application, essay, financial need analysis, resume, references, transcript, annual budget. *Deadline:* February 9.

Contact: Ting Wei, Scholarship Coordinator
American Society of Civil Engineers
1801 Alexander Bell Drive
Reston, VA 20191-4400
Phone: 703-295-6300 Ext. 6106
Fax: 703-295-6222

Y.C. YANG CIVIL ENGINEERING SCHOLARSHIP

Applicants must be student members in good standing of the Society. Currently enrolled junior or senior civil engineering students at an institution with an ABET-accredited program and an interest in structural engineering may apply.

Academic Fields/Career Goals: Civil Engineering.

Award: Scholarship for use in junior or senior years; not renewable. *Number:* 2. *Amount:* $2000–$2500.

Eligibility Requirements: Applicant must be enrolled or expecting to enroll full- or part-time at a four-year institution or university. Available to U.S. and non-U.S. citizens.

Application Requirements: Application, financial need analysis, resume, references, test scores, transcript, personal statement. *Deadline:* February 9.

Contact: Ting Wei, Scholarship Coordinator
American Society of Civil Engineers
1801 Alexander Bell Drive
Reston, VA 20191-4400
Phone: 703-295-6300 Ext. 6106
Fax: 703-295-6222

AMERICAN SOCIETY OF CIVIL ENGINEERS-MAINE SECTION

http://www.maineasce.org/

AMERICAN SOCIETY OF CIVIL ENGINEERS-MAINE HIGH SCHOOL SCHOLARSHIP

One-time award available to high school student in senior year, pursuing a course of study in civil engineering. Must be enrolled in a four year ABET accredited Civil Engineering program at the time of award. Must be a resident of Maine. Essay, references and transcript required with application.

Academic Fields/Career Goals: Civil Engineering.

Award: Scholarship for use in freshman year; not renewable. *Number:* 2. *Amount:* $2000.

Eligibility Requirements: Applicant must be high school student; planning to enroll or expecting to enroll full-time at a four-year institution or university and resident of Maine. Available to U.S. citizens.

Application Requirements: Application, essay, references, transcript. *Deadline:* January 31.

Contact: Ms. Leslie L. Corrow, Senior Engineer P.E.
American Society of Civil Engineers-Maine Section
141 Main Street, PO Box 650
Pittsfield, ME 04967
Phone: 207-487-3328 Ext. 243
Fax: 207-487-3124
E-mail: leslie.corrow@kleinschmidtusa.com

AMERICAN SOCIETY OF NAVAL ENGINEERS

http://www.navalengineers.org/

AMERICAN SOCIETY OF NAVAL ENGINEERS SCHOLARSHIP

• *See page 93*

AMERICAN WELDING SOCIETY

http://www.aws.org/

ARSHAM AMIRIKIAN ENGINEERING SCHOLARSHIP

Awarded to an undergraduate pursuing a minimum four-year degree in civil engineering or welding-related program at an accredited university. Applicant must be a minimum of 18 years of age, have a minimum 3.0 GPA and be a citizen of the United States.

Academic Fields/Career Goals: Civil Engineering; Materials Science, Engineering, and Metallurgy; Trade/Technical Specialties.

Award: Scholarship for use in freshman, sophomore, junior, or senior years; not renewable. *Number:* 1. *Amount:* $2500.

Eligibility Requirements: Applicant must be age 18 and over and enrolled or expecting to enroll full- or part-time at a four-year institution or university. Applicant must have 3.0 GPA or higher. Available to U.S. citizens.

Application Requirements: Application, financial need analysis, references, transcript. *Deadline:* February 15.

Contact: Vicki Pinsky, Manager, Foundation
American Welding Society
550 Le Jeune Road, NW
Miami, FL 33126
Phone: 800-443-9353 Ext. 212
Fax: 305-443-7559
E-mail: vpinsky@aws.org

MATSUO BRIDGE COMPANY LTD. OF JAPAN SCHOLARSHIP

Awarded to a college junior or senior, or graduate student pursuing a minimum four-year degree in civil engineering, welding engineering, welding engineering technology, or related discipline. Applicant must have a minimum 3.0 overall GPA. Financial need is not required to apply. Must be U.S. citizen.

Academic Fields/Career Goals: Civil Engineering; Engineering/Technology; Engineering-Related Technologies; Materials Science, Engineering, and Metallurgy.

Award: Scholarship for use in junior or senior years; not renewable. *Number:* 1. *Amount:* $2500.

Eligibility Requirements: Applicant must be age 18 and over and enrolled or expecting to enroll full- or part-time at a two-year or four-year institution or university. Applicant must have 3.0 GPA or higher. Available to U.S. citizens.

Application Requirements: Application, financial need analysis, references, transcript. *Deadline:* January 15.

Contact: Vicki Pinsky, Manager, Foundation
American Welding Society
550 Le Jeune Road, NW
Miami, FL 33126
Phone: 800-443-9353 Ext. 212
Fax: 305-443-7559
E-mail: vpinsky@aws.org

ARRL FOUNDATION INC.

http://www.arrl.org/

GARY WAGNER, K3OMI SCHOLARSHIP
• *See page 164*

ASSOCIATED GENERAL CONTRACTORS EDUCATION AND RESEARCH FOUNDATION

http://www.agcfoundation.org/

AGC EDUCATION AND RESEARCH FOUNDATION UNDERGRADUATE SCHOLARSHIPS

College sophomores and juniors enrolled or planning to enroll in a full-time, four or five-year ABET or ACCE-accredited construction management or construction-related engineering program are eligible to apply. High school seniors and college freshmen are not eligible.

Academic Fields/Career Goals: Civil Engineering; Construction Engineering/Management; Engineering/Technology.

Award: Scholarship for use in sophomore, junior, or senior years; renewable. *Number:* 100. *Amount:* $2500–$7500.

Eligibility Requirements: Applicant must be enrolled or expecting to enroll full-time at a four-year institution or university. Available to U.S. citizens.

Application Requirements: Application, essay, financial need analysis, references, transcript. *Deadline:* November 1.

Contact: Floretta Slade, Director of Programs
Associated General Contractors Education and Research Foundation
2300 Wilson Boulevard, Suite 400
Arlington, VA 22201
Phone: 703-837-5342
Fax: 703-837-5451
E-mail: sladef@agc.org

ASSOCIATED GENERAL CONTRACTORS OF NEW YORK STATE, LLC

http://www.agcnys.org/

ASSOCIATED GENERAL CONTRACTORS NYS SCHOLARSHIP

One-time scholarship for students enrolled full-time study in civil engineering, construction management and construction technology and diesel technology. Must have minimum GPA of 2.5. Scholarship value is from $1500 to $3000. Must be resident of New York.

Academic Fields/Career Goals: Civil Engineering; Construction Engineering/Management; Surveying, Surveying Technology, Cartography, or Geographic Information Science; Trade/Technical Specialties; Transportation.

Award: Scholarship for use in sophomore, junior, senior, or graduate years; not renewable. *Number:* 10–20. *Amount:* $1500–$3000.

Eligibility Requirements: Applicant must be enrolled or expecting to enroll full-time at a two-year or four-year or technical institution or university and resident of New York. Applicant must have 2.5 GPA or higher. Available to U.S. citizens.

Application Requirements: Application, financial need analysis, references, transcript. *Deadline:* May 15.

Contact: Brendan Manning, Education and Environmental Director
Associated General Contractors of New York State, LLC
10 Airline Drive, Suite 203
Albany, NY 12205
Phone: 518-456-1134
E-mail: bmanning@agcnys.org

ASSOCIATION OF CALIFORNIA WATER AGENCIES

http://www.acwa.com/

ASSOCIATION OF CALIFORNIA WATER AGENCIES SCHOLARSHIPS
• *See page 94*

CLAIR A. HILL SCHOLARSHIP
• *See page 94*

BARRY M. GOLDWATER SCHOLARSHIP AND EXCELLENCE IN EDUCATION FOUNDATION

http://www.act.org/goldwater

BARRY M. GOLDWATER SCHOLARSHIP AND EXCELLENCE IN EDUCATION PROGRAM
• *See page 95*

THE DALLAS FOUNDATION

http://www.dallasfoundation.org/

JERE W. THOMPSON, JR, SCHOLARSHIP FUND

Renewable scholarships awarded to full-time undergraduate juniors or seniors with disadvantaged backgrounds, who are pursuing a degree in civil engineering and closely related disciplines at Texas colleges and universities. Up to $2000 awarded each semester, beginning with junior year. Must maintain 2.5 GPA. Special consideration given to students from Collin, Dallas, Denton, and Tarrant Counties, Texas.

Academic Fields/Career Goals: Civil Engineering.

Award: Scholarship for use in junior or senior years; renewable. *Number:* 1–2. *Amount:* up to $4000.

Eligibility Requirements: Applicant must be enrolled or expecting to enroll full-time at a four-year institution or university; resident of Texas and studying in Texas. Available to U.S. citizens.

Application Requirements: Application, essay, financial need analysis, references, test scores, transcript. *Deadline:* April 1.

Contact: Rachel Lasseter, Program Associate
The Dallas Foundation
900 Jackson Street, Suite 705
Dallas, TX 75202
Phone: 214-741-9898
Fax: 214-741-9848
E-mail: scholarships@dallasfoundation.org

WHITLEY PLACE SCHOLARSHIP
• *See page 100*

ENGINEERS' SOCIETY OF WESTERN PENNSYLVANIA

http://www.eswp.com/

JAMES D. COOPER STUDENT PAPER COMPETITION

Prize of $1000 given to undergraduate and graduate students in civil engineering. The lead author of the winning paper in each category (undergraduate and graduate) will receive a $1000 IBC fellowship, complimentary conference registration, and hotel and travel allowances to attend the International Bridge Conference in Pittsburgh, Pennsylvania. Entry form is available at http://www.eswp.com/PDF/IBCStudent-Paper.pdf.

Academic Fields/Career Goals: Civil Engineering.

Award: Prize for use in freshman, sophomore, junior, senior, or graduate years; not renewable. *Number:* 2. *Amount:* up to $1000.

Eligibility Requirements: Applicant must be enrolled or expecting to enroll full- or part-time at a two-year or four-year institution or university. Available to U.S. and non-U.S. citizens.

Application Requirements: Application, applicant must enter a contest, self-addressed stamped envelope, 10-page manuscript. *Deadline:* March 1.

Contact: Conor McGarvey, Conference Manager
Engineers' Society of Western Pennsylvania
337 Fourth Avenue
Pittsburgh, PA 15222
Phone: 412-261-0710
Fax: 412-261-1606

FLORIDA ENGINEERING SOCIETY

http://www.fleng.org/

DAVID F. LUDOVICI SCHOLARSHIP

One-time scholarship of $1000 given to students in their junior or senior year in any Florida university engineering program, with at least 3.0 GPA. Applicants must be interested in civil, structural, or consulting engineering.

Academic Fields/Career Goals: Civil Engineering; Construction Engineering/Management; Engineering/Technology.

Award: Scholarship for use in junior or senior years; not renewable. *Number:* 1. *Amount:* $1000.

Eligibility Requirements: Applicant must be enrolled or expecting to enroll full-time at an institution or university; resident of Florida and studying in Florida. Applicant must have 3.0 GPA or higher. Available to U.S. citizens.

Application Requirements: Application, references, self-addressed stamped envelope, transcript. *Deadline:* February 1.

Contact: Dana D. Dixon-Smith, Scholarship Committee Staff Liaison
Florida Engineering Society
125 South Gadsden Street
Tallahassee, FL 32301
Phone: 850-224-7121
Fax: 850-222-4349
E-mail: dsmith@fleng.org

FECON SCHOLARSHIP

One-time scholarship of $1000 given to Florida citizens in their junior or senior year, who are enrolled or accepted into a Florida university engineering program. Minimum 3.0 GPA required. Applicant must be interested in pursuing a career in the field of construction.

Academic Fields/Career Goals: Civil Engineering; Construction Engineering/Management.

Award: Scholarship for use in junior or senior years; not renewable. *Number:* 1. *Amount:* $1000.

Eligibility Requirements: Applicant must be enrolled or expecting to enroll full-time at an institution or university; resident of Florida and studying in Florida. Applicant must have 3.0 GPA or higher. Available to U.S. citizens.

Application Requirements: Application, essay, references, self-addressed stamped envelope, transcript. *Deadline:* February 15.

Contact: Dana D. Dixon-Smith, Scholarship Committee Staff Liaison
Florida Engineering Society
125 South Gadsden Street
Tallahassee, FL 32301
Phone: 850-224-7121
Fax: 850-222-4349
E-mail: dsmith@fleng.org

FOUNDATION FOR SCIENCE AND DISABILITY

http://stemd.org/

GRANTS FOR DISABLED STUDENTS IN THE SCIENCES
• *See page 95*

HAWAIIAN LODGE, F&AM

http://www.glhawaii.org/

HAWAIIAN LODGE SCHOLARSHIPS
• *See page 106*

HISPANIC ENGINEER NATIONAL ACHIEVEMENT AWARDS CORPORATION (HENAAC)

http://www.henaac.org/

HISPANIC ENGINEER NATIONAL ACHIEVEMENT AWARDS CORPORATION SCHOLARSHIP PROGRAM
• *See page 125*

INDEPENDENT LABORATORIES INSTITUTE SCHOLARSHIP ALLIANCE

http://www.acil.org/

INDEPENDENT LABORATORIES INSTITUTE SCHOLARSHIP ALLIANCE
• *See page 141*

JORGE MAS CANOSA FREEDOM FOUNDATION

http://www.jorgemascanosa.org/

MAS FAMILY SCHOLARSHIP AWARD
• *See page 152*

KENTUCKY ENERGY AND ENVIRONMENT CABINET

http://www.eec.ky.gov/

ENVIRONMENTAL PROTECTION SCHOLARSHIP
• *See page 141*

KENTUCKY TRANSPORTATION CABINET

http://www.transportation.ky.gov/scholarship

KENTUCKY TRANSPORTATION CABINET CIVIL ENGINEERING SCHOLARSHIP PROGRAM

Scholarships awarded to qualified Kentucky residents who wish to study civil engineering at University of Kentucky, Western Kentucky University, University of Louisville or Kentucky State University. Applicant should be a graduate of an accredited Kentucky high school or a Kentucky resident. Scholarship recipients are given opportunities to work for the Cabinet during summers and job opportunities upon graduation within the state of KY.

Academic Fields/Career Goals: Civil Engineering.

Award: Scholarship for use in freshman, sophomore, junior, or senior years; renewable. *Number:* 15–25. *Amount:* $10,600–$44,000.

Eligibility Requirements: Applicant must be enrolled or expecting to enroll full-time at a four-year institution or university; resident of Kentucky and studying in Kentucky. Applicant must have 3.0 GPA or higher. Available to U.S. and non-U.S. citizens.

Application Requirements: Application, essay, interview, references, test scores, transcript. *Deadline:* March 1.

Contact: Jamie Bewley Byrd, Scholarship Program Administrator
Kentucky Transportation Cabinet
200 Mero Street
Frankfort, KY 40622
E-mail: jamie.bewleybyrd@ky.gov

LOS ANGELES COUNCIL OF BLACK PROFESSIONAL ENGINEERS

http://www.lablackengineers.org/

AL-BEN SCHOLARSHIP FOR ACADEMIC INCENTIVE
• *See page 166*

AL-BEN SCHOLARSHIP FOR PROFESSIONAL MERIT
• *See page 166*

AL-BEN SCHOLARSHIP FOR SCHOLASTIC ACHIEVEMENT
• *See page 166*

MICHIGAN SOCIETY OF PROFESSIONAL ENGINEERS

http://www.michiganspe.org/

MICHIGAN SOCIETY OF PROFESSIONAL ENGINEERS HARRY R. BALL, P.E. GRANT
• *See page 166*

MICHIGAN SOCIETY OF PROFESSIONAL ENGINEERS KENNETH B. FISHBECK, P.E. MEMORIAL GRANT
• *See page 166*

MIDWEST ROOFING CONTRACTORS ASSOCIATION

http://www.mrca.org/

MRCA FOUNDATION SCHOLARSHIP PROGRAM
• *See page 102*

NASA IDAHO SPACE GRANT CONSORTIUM

http://www.id.spacegrant.org/

NASA IDAHO SPACE GRANT CONSORTIUM SCHOLARSHIP PROGRAM
• *See page 141*

NASA MONTANA SPACE GRANT CONSORTIUM

http://www.spacegrant.montana.edu/

MONTANA SPACE GRANT SCHOLARSHIP PROGRAM
• *See page 128*

NATIONAL ASPHALT PAVEMENT ASSOCIATION RESEARCH AND EDUCATION FOUNDATION

http://www.hotmix.org/

NATIONAL ASPHALT PAVEMENT ASSOCIATION RESEARCH AND EDUCATION FOUNDATION SCHOLARSHIP PROGRAM

Our Scholarship program provides funding for undergraduate and graduate students who are U.S. citizens enrolled in a full time civil engineering, construction management, or construction engineering curriculum at an accredited four year college/university or two-year technical institution. The student must take at least one course on Hot Mix Asphalt (HMA) Technology. Refer to web site for more details at http://www.hotmix.org/index.php?option=com_content&task=view&id=97&Itemid=410.

Academic Fields/Career Goals: Civil Engineering; Construction Engineering/Management.

Award: Scholarship for use in freshman, sophomore, junior, senior, graduate, or postgraduate years; not renewable. *Number:* 50–150. *Amount:* $500–$3000.

Eligibility Requirements: Applicant must be enrolled or expecting to enroll full-time at a two-year or four-year or technical institution or university. Available to U.S. citizens.

Application Requirements: Application, essay, references, transcript. *Deadline:* varies.

Contact: Mrs. Carolyn Wilson, Vice President, Finance and Operations
National Asphalt Pavement Association Research and
Education Foundation
NAPA Research & Education Foundation
5100 Forbes Boulevard
Lanham, MD 20706-4413
Phone: 301-731-4748 Ext. 127
Fax: 301-731-4621
E-mail: cwilson@hotmix.org

NATIONAL ASSOCIATION OF WOMEN IN CONSTRUCTION

http://www.nawic.org/

NAWIC UNDERGRADUATE SCHOLARSHIPS
• *See page 102*

NATIONAL SOCIETY OF PROFESSIONAL ENGINEERS

http://www.nspe.org/

MAUREEN L. AND HOWARD N. BLITMAN, PE SCHOLARSHIP TO PROMOTE DIVERSITY IN ENGINEERING
• *See page 167*

PAUL H. ROBBINS HONORARY SCHOLARSHIP
• *See page 168*

PROFESSIONAL ENGINEERS IN INDUSTRY SCHOLARSHIP
• *See page 168*

NEVADA NASA SPACE GRANT CONSORTIUM

http://www.nvspacegrant.org/

NATIONAL SPACE GRANT COLLEGE AND FELLOWSHIP PROGRAM
• *See page 97*

NEW ENGLAND WATER WORKS ASSOCIATION

http://www.newwa.org/

ELSON T. KILLAM MEMORIAL SCHOLARSHIP

Scholarships are awarded to eligible civil and environmental engineering students on the basis of merit, character, and need. Preference given to those students whose programs are considered by a committee as beneficial to water works practice in New England. NEWWA student membership is required to receive a scholarship award. Applicants for scholarships should be residents or attend school in New England. (Maine, New Hampshire, Vermont, Massachusetts, Rhode Island and Connecticut).

Academic Fields/Career Goals: Civil Engineering; Environmental Science.

Award: Scholarship for use in freshman, sophomore, junior, senior, or graduate years; not renewable. *Number:* 1. *Amount:* up to $1500.

Eligibility Requirements: Applicant must be enrolled or expecting to enroll full-time at a four-year institution or university. Applicant or parent of applicant must be member of New England Water Works Association. Available to U.S. citizens.

Application Requirements: Application, essay, references, transcript. *Fee:* $25. *Deadline:* July 1.

Contact: Thomas MacElhaney, Chair, Scholarship Committee
New England Water Works Association
c/o PRELOAD Inc., 60 Commerce Drive
Hauppauge, NY 11788
Phone: 631-231-8100
Fax: 978-418-9156
E-mail: tmacelhaney@preloadinc.com

FRANCIS X. CROWLEY SCHOLARSHIP
• *See page 155*

JOSEPH MURPHY SCHOLARSHIP

Scholarships are awarded to eligible civil or environmental engineering students on the basis of merit, character, and need. Preference given to those students whose programs are considered by a committee as beneficial to water works practice in New England. NEWWA student membership is required to receive a scholarship award.

Academic Fields/Career Goals: Civil Engineering; Environmental Science.

Award: Scholarship for use in freshman, sophomore, junior, senior, or graduate years; not renewable. *Number:* 1. *Amount:* up to $1500.

Eligibility Requirements: Applicant must be enrolled or expecting to enroll full-time at a four-year institution or university. Applicant or parent of applicant must be member of New England Water Works Association. Available to U.S. citizens.

Application Requirements: Application, essay, references, transcript. *Fee:* $25. *Deadline:* July 1.

Contact: Thomas MacElhaney, Chair, Scholarship Committee
New England Water Works Association
c/o PRELOAD Inc., 60 Commerce Drive
Hauppauge, NY 11788
Phone: 631-231-8100
Fax: 978-418-9156
E-mail: tmacelhaney@preloadinc.com

WORKS GEORGE E. WATTERS MEMORIAL SCHOLARSHIP.

Scholarships are awarded to eligible Civil Engineering students on the basis of merit, character, and need. Preference given to those students whose programs are considered by a committee as beneficial to water works practice in New England. NEWWA student membership is required to receive a scholarship award. Applicants for scholarships should be residents or attend school in New England. (Maine, New Hampshire, Vermont, Massachusetts, Rhode Island and Connecticut).

Academic Fields/Career Goals: Civil Engineering.

Award: Scholarship for use in freshman, sophomore, junior, senior, or graduate years; not renewable. *Number:* 1. *Amount:* up to $5000.

Eligibility Requirements: Applicant must be enrolled or expecting to enroll full-time at a four-year institution or university. Available to U.S. citizens.

Application Requirements: Application, essay, references, transcript. *Fee:* $25. *Deadline:* July 1.

Contact: Thomas MacElhaney, Chair, Scholarship Committee
New England Water Works Association
c/o PRELOAD Inc., 60 Commerce Drive
Hauppauge, NY 11788
Phone: 631-231-8100
Fax: 978-418-9156
E-mail: tmacelhaney@preloadinc.com

OREGON STUDENT ASSISTANCE COMMISSION

http://www.GetCollegeFunds.org/

AMERICAN COUNCIL OF ENGINEERING COMPANIES OF OREGON SCHOLARSHIP
• *See page 168*

PROFESSIONAL CONSTRUCTION ESTIMATORS ASSOCIATION

http://www.pcea.org/

TED WILSON MEMORIAL SCHOLARSHIP FOUNDATION

Amount up to $1500 to a deserving student (high school senior, college freshman, sophomore, or junior) based on their academic ability, need, and desire to enter the construction industry.

Academic Fields/Career Goals: Civil Engineering; Construction Engineering/Management; Drafting; Electrical Engineering/Electronics; Engineering/Technology; Heating, Air-Conditioning, and Refrigeration Mechanics; Landscape Architecture; Mechanical Engineering; Surveying, Surveying Technology, Cartography, or Geographic Information Science; Trade/Technical Specialties.

Award: Scholarship for use in freshman, sophomore, junior, or senior years; not renewable. *Number:* 5. *Amount:* up to $1500.

Eligibility Requirements: Applicant must be enrolled or expecting to enroll full-time at a two-year or four-year or technical institution or university; resident of Florida, Georgia, North Carolina, South Carolina, or Virginia and studying in Florida, Georgia, North Carolina, South Carolina, or Virginia. Available to U.S. and non-U.S. citizens.

Application Requirements: Application, financial need analysis, interview, references, transcript. *Deadline:* March 15.

Contact: Kim Lybrand, National Office Manager
Professional Construction Estimators Association
PO Box 680336
Charlotte, NC 28216-0336
Phone: 704-987-9978
Fax: 704-987-9979
E-mail: pcea@pcea.org

PROFESSIONAL GROUNDS MANAGEMENT SOCIETY

http://www.pgms.org/

ANNE SEAMAN PROFESSIONAL GROUNDS MANAGEMENT SOCIETY MEMORIAL SCHOLARSHIP
• *See page 87*

ROCKY MOUNTAIN COAL MINING INSTITUTE

http://www.rmcmi.org/

ROCKY MOUNTAIN COAL MINING INSTITUTE SCHOLARSHIP

Must be full-time college sophomore or junior at time of application, pursuing a degree in mining-related fields or engineering disciplines such as mining, geology, mineral processing, or metallurgy. For residents of Arizona, Colorado, Montana, New Mexico, North Dakota, Texas, Utah, and Wyoming. Scholarship value is $2500 per year for two-years sent directly to school for tuition.

Academic Fields/Career Goals: Civil Engineering; Earth Science; Engineering/Technology; Engineering-Related Technologies; Materials Science, Engineering, and Metallurgy.

Award: Scholarship for use in junior or senior years; renewable. *Number:* 8. *Amount:* $2500.

Eligibility Requirements: Applicant must be enrolled or expecting to enroll full-time at a four-year institution or university and resident of Arizona, Colorado, Montana, New Mexico, North Dakota, Texas, Utah, or Wyoming. Available to U.S. citizens.

Application Requirements: Application, interview, references. *Deadline:* February 1.

Contact: Karen Inzano, Executive Director
Rocky Mountain Coal Mining Institute
8057 South Yukon Way
Littleton, CO 80128-5510
Phone: 303-948-3300
E-mail: mail@rmcmi.org

SOCIETY OF HISPANIC PROFESSIONAL ENGINEERS FOUNDATION

http://www.henaac.org/

SOCIETY OF HISPANIC PROFESSIONAL ENGINEERS FOUNDATION
• *See page 169*

STRAIGHTFORWARD MEDIA

http://www.straightforwardmedia.com/

STRAIGHTFORWARD MEDIA ENGINEERING SCHOLARSHIP
• *See page 170*

TEXAS DEPARTMENT OF TRANSPORTATION

http://www.txdot.gov/

CONDITIONAL GRANT PROGRAM

Renewable award to students who are considered economically disadvantaged based on federal guidelines. The maximum amount awarded per semester is $3,000 not to exceed $6000 per academic year. Students already enrolled in an undergraduate program should have minimum GPA 2.5 and students newly enrolling should have minimum GPA 3.0.

Academic Fields/Career Goals: Civil Engineering; Computer Science/Data Processing; Occupational Safety and Health.

Award: Grant for use in freshman, sophomore, junior, or senior years; renewable. *Number:* varies. *Amount:* up to $6000.

Eligibility Requirements: Applicant must be enrolled or expecting to enroll full-time at a four-year institution or university; resident of Texas and studying in Texas. Available to U.S. citizens.

Application Requirements: Application, essay, interview, references, test scores, transcript. *Deadline:* March 1.

Contact: Minnie Brown, Program Coordinator
Texas Department of Transportation
125 East 11th Street
Austin, TX 78701-2483
Phone: 512-416-4979
Fax: 512-416-4980
E-mail: mbrown2@dot.state.tx.us

TURNER CONSTRUCTION COMPANY

http://www.turnerconstruction.com/

YOUTHFORCE 2020 SCHOLARSHIP PROGRAM
• *See page 103*

UNITED NEGRO COLLEGE FUND

http://www.uncf.org/

CARDINAL HEALTH SCHOLARSHIP
• *See page 72*

EMERSON PROCESS MANAGEMENT SCHOLARSHIP
• *See page 170*

MALCOLM PIRNIE CORPORATE SCHOLARS PROGRAM
• *See page 171*

MEDTRONIC FOUNDATION SCHOLARSHIP
• *See page 145*

UNITED WATER CORPORATE SCHOLARS PROGRAM
• *See page 74*

UNIVERSITIES SPACE RESEARCH ASSOCIATION

http://www.usra.edu/

UNIVERSITIES SPACE RESEARCH ASSOCIATION SCHOLARSHIP PROGRAM
• *See page 97*

UTAH SOCIETY OF PROFESSIONAL ENGINEERS

http://www.uspeonline.com/

UTAH SOCIETY OF PROFESSIONAL ENGINEERS JOE RHOADS SCHOLARSHIP
• *See page 171*

WIRE REINFORCEMENT INSTITUTE EDUCATION FOUNDATION

http://www.wirereinforcementinstitute.org/

WRI COLLEGE SCHOLARSHIP PROGRAM

Academic scholarships for qualified high school seniors and current undergraduate and graduate level students intending to or presently pursuing four-year or graduate-level degrees in structural and/or civil engineering at accredited four-year universities or colleges in the U.S. or Canada.

Academic Fields/Career Goals: Civil Engineering; Construction Engineering/Management.

Award: Scholarship for use in freshman, sophomore, junior, senior, or graduate years; not renewable. *Number:* varies. *Amount:* $1500–$4000.

Eligibility Requirements: Applicant must be enrolled or expecting to enroll full-time at a four-year institution or university. Available to U.S. and non-U.S. citizens.

Application Requirements: Application, essay, references, test scores, transcript. *Deadline:* April 15.

Contact: Scholarship Selection Committee
Wire Reinforcement Institute Education Foundation
942 Main Street, Suite 300
Hartford, CT 06103

CLASSICS

ACL/NJCL NATIONAL LATIN EXAM

http://www.nle.org/

NATIONAL LATIN EXAM SCHOLARSHIP

Scholarships to high school seniors who are gold medal winners in Latin III, III-IV Prose, III-IV Poetry, or Latin V-VI. Applicants must agree to take at least one year of Latin or classical Greek in college.

Academic Fields/Career Goals: Classics; Foreign Language.

Award: Scholarship for use in freshman, sophomore, junior, or senior years; renewable. *Number:* 21. *Amount:* $1000.

Eligibility Requirements: Applicant must be high school student; planning to enroll or expecting to enroll full-time at a four-year institution or university and must have an interest in Greek language or Latin language. Available to U.S. and non-U.S. citizens.

Application Requirements: Application, essay, references, test scores, transcript. *Deadline:* May 11.

Contact: Mrs. Ephy Howard, Scholarship Chairperson
Phone: 888-378-7721

AMERICAN CLASSICAL LEAGUE/ NATIONAL JUNIOR CLASSICAL LEAGUE

http://www.aclclassics.org/

NATIONAL JUNIOR CLASSICAL LEAGUE SCHOLARSHIP

A one-time award available to graduating high school seniors, who are members of the Junior Classical League. Preference is given to students who plan to major in the classics.

Academic Fields/Career Goals: Classics; Foreign Language; Humanities.

Award: Scholarship for use in freshman year; not renewable. *Number:* 7. *Amount:* $1000–$2000.

Eligibility Requirements: Applicant must be high school student; planning to enroll or expecting to enroll full-time at a two-year or four-year institution or university and must have an interest in foreign language. Applicant or parent of applicant must be member of Junior Classical League. Available to U.S. and non-U.S. citizens.

Application Requirements: Application, essay, references, transcript, list of 5 extracurricular activities and 5 community activities. *Deadline:* May 1.

Contact: Geri Dutra, Administrator
American Classical League/National Junior Classical League
Miami University, 422 Wells Mill Drive
Oxford, OH 45066
Phone: 513-529-7741
Fax: 513-529-7742
E-mail: info@aclclassics.org

AMERICAN PHILOLOGICAL ASSOCIATION

http://www.apaclassics.org/

MINORITY STUDENT SUMMER SCHOLARSHIP
• *See page 98*

AMERICAN SCHOOL OF CLASSICAL STUDIES AT ATHENS

http://www.ascsa.edu.gr/

ASCSA SUMMER SESSIONS SCHOLARSHIPS
• *See page 92*

ARCHAEOLOGICAL INSTITUTE OF AMERICA

http://www.archaeological.org/

AMERICAN PHILOLOGICAL ASSOCIATION/ ARCHAEOLOGICAL INSTITUTE OF AMERICA MINORITY SCHOLARSHIP
• *See page 98*

STRAIGHTFORWARD MEDIA

http://www.straightforwardmedia.com/

STRAIGHTFORWARD MEDIA LIBERAL ARTS SCHOLARSHIP
• *See page 107*

COMMUNICATIONS

ADC RESEARCH INSTITUTE

http://www.adc.org/

JACK SHAHEEN MASS COMMUNICATIONS SCHOLARSHIP AWARD

Awarded to Arab-American students who excel in the mass communications field (journalism, radio, television or film). Must be a junior or senior undergraduate or graduate student. Must be U.S. citizen. Minimum 3.0 GPA required.

Academic Fields/Career Goals: Communications; Filmmaking/Video; Journalism; TV/Radio Broadcasting.

Award: Scholarship for use in junior, senior, or graduate years; not renewable. *Number:* 1–6. *Amount:* $500–$1000.

Eligibility Requirements: Applicant must be of Arab heritage and enrolled or expecting to enroll full- or part-time at a four-year institution or university. Applicant must have 3.0 GPA or higher. Available to U.S. citizens.

Application Requirements: Application, essay, references, transcript, copies of original articles, videos, films. *Deadline:* April 12.

Contact: Mr. Nawar Shora, Director of Diversity and Law Enforcement Outreach
ADC Research Institute
1732 Wisconsin Avenue, NW
Washington, DC 20007
Phone: 202-244-2990
Fax: 202-244-3196
E-mail: nshora@adc.org

AMERICAN INSTITUTE OF POLISH CULTURE INC.

http://www.ampolinstitute.org/

HARRIET IRSAY SCHOLARSHIP GRANT
• *See page 109*

AMERICAN LEGION DEPARTMENT OF NEW YORK

http://www.ny.legion.org/

AMERICAN LEGION DEPARTMENT OF NEW YORK PRESS ASSOCIATION SCHOLARSHIP

A $1000 scholarship for children of NY American Legion or American Legion Auxiliary members, members of SAL or ALA Juniors or graduates of NY AL Boys State or Girls State. Must be entering or attending accredited four-year college pursuing communications degree.

Academic Fields/Career Goals: Communications.

Award: Scholarship for use in freshman, sophomore, junior, or senior years; not renewable. *Number:* 1. *Amount:* $1000.

Eligibility Requirements: Applicant must be enrolled or expecting to enroll full-time at a four-year institution or university and resident of New York. Applicant or parent of applicant must be member of American Legion or Auxiliary. Available to U.S. citizens. Applicant or parent must meet one or more of the following requirements: general military experience; retired from active duty; disabled or killed as a result of military service; prisoner of war; or missing in action.

Application Requirements: Application. *Deadline:* April 15.

Contact: NYAL Press Association
American Legion Department of New York
PO Box 650
East Aurora, NY 14502

AMERICAN LEGION PRESS CLUB OF NEW JERSEY

http://www.alpcnj.org/

AMERICAN LEGION PRESS CLUB OF NEW JERSEY AND POST 170 ARTHUR DEHARDT MEMORIAL SCHOLARSHIP

Merit-based scholarship awarded to two students entering their freshman year. Eligible applicants will be the son, daughter, grandson, or granddaughter of a current card-holding member of the American Legion. Any student who has graduated from either American Legion Boys' State or Girls' State program shall be eligible. Must go into communication field.

Academic Fields/Career Goals: Communications; Journalism; Photojournalism/Photography; TV/Radio Broadcasting.

Award: Scholarship for use in freshman year; not renewable. *Number:* 2. *Amount:* $500.

Eligibility Requirements: Applicant must be high school student; planning to enroll or expecting to enroll full-time at a four-year institution or university; single and resident of New Jersey. Applicant or parent of applicant must be member of American Legion or Auxiliary. Available to U.S. citizens. Applicant or parent must meet one or more of the following requirements: general military experience; retired from active duty; disabled or killed as a result of military service; prisoner of war; or missing in action.

Application Requirements: Application, essay, transcript, copy of graduation certificates, DD-214. *Deadline:* July 1.

Contact: Dorothy Saunders, Scholarship Chairman
American Legion Press Club of New Jersey
Three Lewis Street
Wayne, NJ 07470-4716

AMERICAN QUARTER HORSE FOUNDATION (AQHF)

http://www.aqha.com/foundation

AQHF JOURNALISM OR COMMUNICATIONS SCHOLARSHIP

Scholarship of $8000 for AQHA/AQHYA members who hold the membership one year or more year, pursuing a degree in journalism or communications. Recipient must intend to pursue career in news, editorial or print journalism and/or photojournalism. Members may apply during their senior year of high school or while enrolled as a freshman at an accredited college, university or vocational school. Minimum 2.5 GPA required.

Academic Fields/Career Goals: Communications; Journalism.

Award: Scholarship for use in freshman, sophomore, junior, or senior years; renewable. *Number:* 1. *Amount:* $8000.

Eligibility Requirements: Applicant must be enrolled or expecting to enroll full-time at a two-year or four-year or technical institution or university and must have an interest in animal/agricultural competition. Applicant or parent of applicant must be member of American Quarter Horse Association. Applicant must have 2.5 GPA or higher. Available to U.S. and Canadian citizens.

Application Requirements: Application, essay, financial need analysis, photo, references, transcript. *Deadline:* January 2.

Contact: Laura Owens, Scholarship Office
American Quarter Horse Foundation (AQHF)
2601 East Interstate 40
Amarillo, TX 79104
Phone: 806-378-5029
Fax: 806-376-1005
E-mail: foundation@aqha.org

ARAB AMERICAN SCHOLARSHIP FOUNDATION

http://www.lahc.org/

LEBANESE AMERICAN HERITAGE CLUB'S SCHOLARSHIP FUND

Scholarship for high school, undergraduate, or graduate students who are of Arab descent. Minimum 3.0 GPA required for high school and undergraduate applicants, 3.5 GPA for graduate student applicants. Must be U.S. citizens.

Academic Fields/Career Goals: Communications; Political Science.

Award: Scholarship for use in freshman, sophomore, junior, senior, or graduate years; not renewable. *Number:* 1. *Amount:* $1000.

Eligibility Requirements: Applicant must be of Arab heritage; enrolled or expecting to enroll full-time at a four-year institution or university and resident of Michigan. Applicant must have 3.0 GPA or higher. Available to U.S. citizens.

Application Requirements: Application, essay, financial need analysis, references, transcript, Student Aid Report (SAR). *Deadline:* April 6.

Contact: Suehalia Amen, Communications-Chair
Arab American Scholarship Foundation
The Lebanese American Heritage Club, 4337 Maple Road
Dearborn, MI 48126
Phone: 313-846-8480
Fax: 313-846-2710
E-mail: sueamen@lahc.org

ARMED FORCES COMMUNICATIONS AND ELECTRONICS ASSOCIATION, EDUCATIONAL FOUNDATION

http://www.afcea.org/education/scholarships

ARMED FORCES COMMUNICATIONS AND ELECTRONICS ASSOCIATION GENERAL EMMETT PAIGE SCHOLARSHIP
• *See page 122*

ARMED FORCES COMMUNICATIONS AND ELECTRONICS ASSOCIATION GENERAL JOHN A. WICKHAM SCHOLARSHIP
• *See page 164*

ARMED FORCES COMMUNICATIONS AND ELECTRONICS ASSOCIATION ROTC SCHOLARSHIP PROGRAM
• *See page 122*

WILLIAM E. "BUCK" BRAGUNIER SCHOLARSHIP FOR OUTSTANDING LEADERSHIP
• *See page 123*

ARRL FOUNDATION INC.

http://www.arrl.org/

CHARLES N. FISHER MEMORIAL SCHOLARSHIP
• *See page 94*

DR. JAMES L. LAWSON MEMORIAL SCHOLARSHIP

One-time award of $500 available to general amateur radio operators. For baccalaureate or higher course of study in electronics, communications or a related field.

Academic Fields/Career Goals: Communications; Electrical Engineering/Electronics.

Award: Scholarship for use in freshman, sophomore, junior, senior, or graduate years; not renewable. *Number:* 1. *Amount:* $500.

Eligibility Requirements: Applicant must be enrolled or expecting to enroll full-time at a four-year institution or university; resident of Connecticut, Maine, Massachusetts, New Hampshire, New York, Rhode Island, or Vermont; studying in Connecticut, Maine, Massachusetts, New Hampshire, New York, Rhode Island, or Vermont and must have an interest in amateur radio. Available to U.S. citizens.

Application Requirements: Application, transcript. *Deadline:* February 1.

Contact: Ms. Mary Hobart, Secretary
ARRL Foundation Inc.
225 Main Street
Newington, CT 06111-1494
Phone: 860-594-0397
E-mail: k1mmh@arrl.org

EUGENE GENE SALLEE, W4YFR MEMORIAL SCHOLARSHIP

One $500 award is available to a student who is a Georgia resident and who has a Technician class or higher amateur radio license.

Academic Fields/Career Goals: Communications; Electrical Engineering/Electronics.

Award: Scholarship for use in freshman, sophomore, junior, or senior years; not renewable. *Number:* 1. *Amount:* $500.

Eligibility Requirements: Applicant must be enrolled or expecting to enroll full- or part-time at a two-year or four-year institution or university; resident of Georgia and must have an interest in amateur radio. Applicant must have 3.0 GPA or higher.

Application Requirements: Application, transcript. *Deadline:* February 1.

Contact: Ms. Mary Hobart, Secretary
ARRL Foundation Inc.
225 Main Street
Newington, CT 06111-1494
Phone: 860-594-0397
E-mail: k1mmh@arrl.org

FRANCIS WALTON MEMORIAL SCHOLARSHIP
• See page 83

FRED R. MCDANIEL MEMORIAL SCHOLARSHIP

One $500 award is available to students who possess a General class or higher amateur radio license. Applicants must be studying electronics, communications or related fields at a four-year college or university. Preference will be given to applicants with a 3.0 GPA or higher on a 4.0 scale.

Academic Fields/Career Goals: Communications; Electrical Engineering/Electronics.

Award: Scholarship for use in freshman, sophomore, junior, or senior years; not renewable. *Number:* 1. *Amount:* $500.

Eligibility Requirements: Applicant must be enrolled or expecting to enroll full- or part-time at a four-year institution or university; resident of Arkansas, Louisiana, Mississippi, New Mexico, Oklahoma, or Texas and must have an interest in amateur radio. Applicant must have 3.0 GPA or higher.

Application Requirements: Application, transcript. *Deadline:* February 1.

Contact: Ms. Mary Hobart, Secretary
ARRL Foundation Inc.
225 Main Street
Newington, CT 06111-1494
Phone: 860-594-0397
E-mail: k1mmh@arrl.org

IRVINE W. COOK WA0CGS SCHOLARSHIP

One-time award of $1000 to students pursuing a baccalaureate or higher degree in communications, electronics, or related fields. Must be a amateur radio operator. Preference to Kansas resident but may attend school in any state.

Academic Fields/Career Goals: Communications; Electrical Engineering/Electronics.

Award: Scholarship for use in freshman, sophomore, junior, or senior years; not renewable. *Number:* 1. *Amount:* $1000.

Eligibility Requirements: Applicant must be enrolled or expecting to enroll full-time at a four-year institution or university; resident of Kansas and must have an interest in amateur radio. Available to U.S. citizens.

Application Requirements: Application, transcript. *Deadline:* February 1.

Contact: Ms. Mary Hobart, Secretary
ARRL Foundation Inc.
225 Main Street
Newington, CT 06111-1494
Phone: 860-594-0397
E-mail: k1mmh@arrl.org

L. PHIL WICKER SCHOLARSHIP

One-time award available to electronics or communications students pursuing a baccalaureate or higher degree. Must be a licensed general amateur radio operator.

Academic Fields/Career Goals: Communications; Electrical Engineering/Electronics.

Award: Scholarship for use in freshman, sophomore, junior, senior, or graduate years; not renewable. *Number:* 1. *Amount:* $500.

Eligibility Requirements: Applicant must be enrolled or expecting to enroll full-time at a four-year institution or university; resident of North Carolina, South Dakota, Virginia, or West Virginia; studying in North Carolina, South Carolina, Virginia, or West Virginia and must have an interest in amateur radio. Available to U.S. citizens.

Application Requirements: Application, transcript. *Deadline:* February 1.

Contact: Ms. Mary Hobart, Secretary
ARRL Foundation Inc.
225 Main Street
Newington, CT 06111-1494
Phone: 860-594-0397
E-mail: k1mmh@arrl.org

MAGNOLIA DX ASSOCIATION SCHOLARSHIP

One $500 award is available to a student majoring in electronics, communications, computer science, engineering or a related field. Preference is given to graduating high school seniors. Residents of Mississippi or students studying in Mississippi are given first priority.

Academic Fields/Career Goals: Communications; Computer Science/Data Processing; Electrical Engineering/Electronics; Engineering/Technology.

Award: Scholarship for use in freshman, sophomore, junior, or senior years; not renewable. *Number:* 1. *Amount:* $500.

Eligibility Requirements: Applicant must be enrolled or expecting to enroll at a two-year or four-year or technical institution or university; resident of Mississippi; studying in Mississippi and must have an interest in amateur radio.

Application Requirements: Application, transcript. *Deadline:* February 1.

Contact: Ms. Mary Hobart, Secretary
ARRL Foundation Inc.
225 Main Street
Newington, CT 06111-1494
Phone: 860-594-0397
E-mail: k1mmh@arrl.org

MISSISSIPPI SCHOLARSHIP
• See page 94

PAUL AND HELEN L. GRAUER SCHOLARSHIP
• See page 94

ASIAN AMERICAN JOURNALISTS ASSOCIATION

http://www.aaja.org/

ASIAN-AMERICAN JOURNALISTS ASSOCIATION SCHOLARSHIP

Award of $5000 for high school seniors and college students pursuing careers in the news media. Asian heritage is not required. Minimum 2.5 GPA required. Based on scholarship, goals, journalistic ability, financial need, and commitment to the Asian-American community. Visit web site http://www.aaja.org for application and details.

Academic Fields/Career Goals: Communications; Journalism; Photojournalism/Photography; TV/Radio Broadcasting.

Award: Scholarship for use in freshman, sophomore, junior, senior, or graduate years; renewable. *Number:* 10. *Amount:* $5000.

Eligibility Requirements: Applicant must be enrolled or expecting to enroll full-time at a two-year or four-year institution or university. Applicant or parent of applicant must have employment or volunteer experience in journalism/broadcasting. Applicant must have 2.5 GPA or higher. Available to U.S. and non-U.S. citizens.

Application Requirements: Application, essay, financial need analysis, resume, references, transcript. *Deadline:* March 28.

Contact: Kim Mizuhara, Programs Coordinator
Asian American Journalists Association
1182 Market Street, Suite 320
San Francisco, CA 94102
Phone: 415-346-2051 Ext. 102
Fax: 415-346-6343
E-mail: programs@aaja.org

CHARLES AND LUCILLE KING FAMILY FOUNDATION, INC.

http://www.kingfoundation.org/

CHARLES AND LUCILLE KING FAMILY FOUNDATION SCHOLARSHIPS

Renewable award for college undergraduates at junior or senior level pursuing television, film, or communication studies to further their education. Must attend a four-year undergraduate institution. Minimum 3.0 GPA required to renew scholarship. Must have completed at least two years of study and be currently enrolled in a U.S. college or university. Application may be downloaded on web site.

Academic Fields/Career Goals: Communications; Filmmaking/Video; TV/Radio Broadcasting.

Award: Scholarship for use in junior or senior years; renewable. *Number:* 10–20. *Amount:* $3500–$7000.

Eligibility Requirements: Applicant must be enrolled or expecting to enroll full-time at a four-year institution or university. Applicant must have 3.0 GPA or higher. Available to U.S. and non-U.S. citizens.

Application Requirements: Application, essay, financial need analysis, references, transcript. *Deadline:* March 15.

Contact: Michael Donovan, Educational Director
Charles and Lucille King Family Foundation, Inc.
366 Madison Avenue, Tenth Floor
New York, NY 10017
Phone: 212-682-2913
Fax: 212-949-0728
E-mail: info@kingfoundation.org

CINCINNATI LITHO CLUB

http://www.cincylithoclub.org/

BILL STAUDT/AL HARTNETT SCHOLARSHIP

Scholarship awarded to high school graduates who plan to attend, or are currently enrolled in, college or vocational school. Applicant must be pursuing a career in the areas of printing or publishing.

Academic Fields/Career Goals: Communications; Graphics/Graphic Arts/Printing.

Award: Scholarship for use in freshman year; not renewable. *Number:* varies. *Amount:* varies.

Eligibility Requirements: Applicant must be high school student and planning to enroll or expecting to enroll full-time at a two-year or four-year or technical institution or university. Available to U.S. citizens.

Application Requirements: Application, resume, transcript. *Deadline:* varies.

Contact: Scholarship Administrator
Cincinnati Litho Club
6550 Donjoy Drive
Cincinnati, OH 45242
Phone: 910-575-0399

DAY INTERNATIONAL SCHOLARSHIP

Scholarship awarded to high school graduates who plan to attend, or are currently enrolled in, college or vocational school. Applicant must be pursuing a career in the areas of printing or publishing.

Academic Fields/Career Goals: Communications; Graphics/Graphic Arts/Printing.

Award: Scholarship for use in freshman year; not renewable. *Number:* varies. *Amount:* varies.

Eligibility Requirements: Applicant must be high school student and planning to enroll or expecting to enroll full-time at a two-year or four-year or technical institution or university. Available to U.S. citizens.

Application Requirements: Application, resume, transcript. *Deadline:* varies.

Contact: Scholarship Administrator
Cincinnati Litho Club
6550 Donjoy Drive
Cincinnati, OH 45242
Phone: 910-575-0399

CONNECTICUT CHAPTER OF SOCIETY OF PROFESSIONAL JOURNALISTS

http://www.ctspj.org/

CONNECTICUT SPJ BOB EDDY SCHOLARSHIP PROGRAM

One-time awards of $250 to $2000 for college juniors or seniors planning a career in journalism. Must be a Connecticut resident attending a four year college or any student attending a four year college in Connecticut.

Academic Fields/Career Goals: Communications; Journalism; Photojournalism/Photography.

Award: Scholarship for use in junior or senior years; not renewable. *Number:* 5. *Amount:* $250–$2000.

Eligibility Requirements: Applicant must be enrolled or expecting to enroll full-time at a four-year institution or university; resident of Connecticut; studying in Connecticut and must have an interest in writing. Available to U.S. and non-U.S. citizens.

Application Requirements: Application, applicant must enter a contest, essay, financial need analysis, transcript. *Deadline:* April 4.

Contact: Debra A. Estock, Scholarship Committee Chairman
Connecticut Chapter of Society of Professional Journalists
71 Kenwood Avenue
Fairfield, CT 06824
Phone: 203-255-2127
E-mail: debae@optonline.net

CUBAN AMERICAN NATIONAL FOUNDATION

http://www.masscholarships.org/

MAS FAMILY SCHOLARSHIPS
• *See page 148*

DADE COMMUNITY FOUNDATION

http://www.jackituckfield.org/

LEO SUAREZ SCHOLARSHIP

Award available to a public high school senior in the Miami, Dade, and Broward county area who is planning to enroll in a two- or four-year college or university and study journalism, broadcasting, mass communications or related fields. Must be a resident of South Florida, have a 3.0 GPA, and attach writing samples of published work to scholarship application. For additional information, visit web site http://www.dadecommunityfoundation.org.

Academic Fields/Career Goals: Communications; Journalism; TV/Radio Broadcasting.

Award: Scholarship for use in freshman year; not renewable. *Number:* 1. *Amount:* $1000.

Eligibility Requirements: Applicant must be high school student; planning to enroll or expecting to enroll full-time at a two-year or four-

year institution or university and resident of Florida. Applicant must have 3.0 GPA or higher. Available to U.S. citizens.

Application Requirements: Application, references, transcript, published examples of writing. *Deadline:* March 21.

Contact: Ted Seijo, Scholarship Coordinator
Dade Community Foundation
1160 Northwest 87 Street
Miami, FL 33150-2544
Phone: 305-371-2711
E-mail: ted.seijo@dadecommunityfoundation.org

DAIRY MANAGEMENT

http://www.dairyinfo.com/

NATIONAL DAIRY PROMOTION AND RESEARCH BOARD SCHOLARSHIP
• *See page 84*

FLORIDA SOCIETY OF NEWSPAPER EDITORS-SCHOLARSHIP COMMITTEE

http://www.fsne.org/minorityscholar.html

FLORIDA SOCIETY OF NEWSPAPER EDITORS MINORITY SCHOLARSHIP PROGRAM

Awards full-time students in their junior year, majoring in journalism or mass communications at an accredited program in Florida. Must maintain a GPA of 3.0. Must be a member of an ethnic minority. In order to maintain eligibility, the applicant must successfully complete a paid summer internship at a Florida newspaper between the junior and senior year.

Academic Fields/Career Goals: Communications; Journalism.

Award: Scholarship for use in senior year; not renewable. *Number:* 1. *Amount:* $1500–$3000.

Eligibility Requirements: Applicant must be American Indian/Alaska Native, Asian/Pacific Islander, Black (non-Hispanic), or Hispanic; enrolled or expecting to enroll full-time at a four-year institution or university and studying in Florida. Applicant must have 3.0 GPA or higher. Available to U.S. citizens.

Application Requirements: Application, driver's license, resume. *Deadline:* March 15.

Contact: Rosemary Armao, Scholarship Committee
Florida Society of Newspaper Editors-Scholarship Committee
c/o Sarasota Herald Tribune, 801 South Tamiami Trial
Sarasota, FL 34230

FLORIDA SOCIETY OF NEWSPAPER EDITORS MULTIMEDIA SCHOLARSHIP

Scholarships for multicultural, full-time students, majoring in journalism or mass communications at an accredited program at a four-year college or university in Florida, and pursuing careers in the field of multimedia or multi-platform journalism. Must successfully complete a paid multimedia internship at a Florida newspaper. Must maintain a minimum GPA of 2.5.

Academic Fields/Career Goals: Communications; Journalism.

Award: Scholarship for use in freshman, sophomore, junior, or senior years; not renewable. *Number:* varies. *Amount:* $1500–$3000.

Eligibility Requirements: Applicant must be enrolled or expecting to enroll full-time at a four-year institution or university and studying in Florida. Applicant must have 2.5 GPA or higher. Available to U.S. citizens.

Application Requirements: Application, driver's license, resume, references, clips or examples of relevant classroom work. *Deadline:* May 1.

Contact: Pat Yack, Editor
Florida Society of Newspaper Editors-Scholarship Committee
The Florida Times-Union, One Riverside Avenue
Jacksonville, FL 32202
Phone: 904-359-4111
E-mail: pat.yack@jacksonville.com

GREAT FALLS ADVERTISING FEDERATION

http://www.gfaf.com/

GREAT FALLS ADVERTISING FEDERATION COLLEGE SCHOLARSHIP
• *See page 76*

HIGH SCHOOL MARKETING/COMMUNICATIONS SCHOLARSHIP
• *See page 76*

GREAT LAKES COMMISSION

http://www.glc.org/

CAROL A. RATZA MEMORIAL SCHOLARSHIP

One-time award to full-time students at a college or university in the Great Lake states (IL, IN, MI, MN, NY, OH, PA, WI) or Canadian provinces of Ontario or Quebec. Must have a demonstrated interest in the environmental or economic applications of electronic communications technology, exhibit academic excellence, and have a sincere appreciation for the Great Lakes and their protection.

Academic Fields/Career Goals: Communications; Computer Science/Data Processing; Environmental Science; Graphics/Graphic Arts/Printing; Journalism; Natural Resources; Natural Sciences; Science, Technology, and Society; TV/Radio Broadcasting.

Award: Scholarship for use in freshman, sophomore, junior, or senior years; not renewable. *Number:* 1. *Amount:* $1000.

Eligibility Requirements: Applicant must be enrolled or expecting to enroll full-time at a two-year or four-year or technical institution or university; resident of Illinois, Indiana, Michigan, Minnesota, New York, Ohio, Ontario, Pennsylvania, Quebec, or Wisconsin and studying in Illinois, Indiana, Michigan, Minnesota, New York, Ohio, Ontario, Pennsylvania, Quebec, or Wisconsin. Available to U.S. and Canadian citizens.

Application Requirements: Application, essay, resume, references, transcript, letter of intent explaining career goals. *Deadline:* March 31.

Contact: Christine Manninen, Program Manager
Great Lakes Commission
Eisenhower Corporate Park, 2805 South Industrial Highway, Suite 100
Ann Arbor, MI 48104-6791
Phone: 734-971-9135
Fax: 734-971-9150
E-mail: manninen@glc.org

INSTITUTE FOR HUMANE STUDIES

http://www.theihs.org/

HUMANE STUDIES FELLOWSHIPS

Renewable award for undergraduate and graduate students in selected disciplines. Applicants should have demonstrated interest in classical liberal or libertarian ideas and must intend to pursue a scholarly career. Minimum 3.5 GPA required. Application fee: $25.

Academic Fields/Career Goals: Communications; Economics; History; Humanities; Law/Legal Services; Literature/English/Writing; Political Science; Social Sciences.

Award: Scholarship for use in junior or senior years; not renewable. *Number:* 140–180. *Amount:* $2000–$12,000.

Eligibility Requirements: Applicant must be enrolled or expecting to enroll full-time at a two-year or four-year institution or university. Applicant must have 3.5 GPA or higher. Available to U.S. and Canadian citizens.

Application Requirements: Application, essay, resume, references, test scores, transcript. *Fee:* $25. *Deadline:* December 31.

Contact: Director, Humane Studies Fellowship
E-mail: HSF@TheIHS.org

INTERNATIONAL COMMUNICATIONS INDUSTRIES FOUNDATION

http://www.infocomm.org/scholarships

ICIF SCHOLARSHIP FOR EMPLOYEES AND DEPENDENTS OF MEMBER ORGANIZATIONS

Scholarship for a spouse, child, stepchild or grandchild of an employee of an InfoComm International member organization or for an employee of an InfoComm International member organization. Must be majoring in audiovisual related fields, such as audio, video, audiovisual, electronics, telecommunications, technical theatre, data networking, software development, and information technology. Minimum of 2.75 GPA required. Must show evidence of AV experience (completed course, job, internship, etc).

Academic Fields/Career Goals: Communications; Computer Science/Data Processing; Electrical Engineering/Electronics; Filmmaking/Video.

Award: Scholarship for use in freshman, sophomore, junior, senior, or graduate years; not renewable. *Number:* 1–50. *Amount:* $1500.

Eligibility Requirements: Applicant must be enrolled or expecting to enroll full-time at a two-year or four-year or technical institution or university. Applicant must have 3.0 GPA or higher. Available to U.S. and non-U.S. citizens.

Application Requirements: Application, essay, references, transcript. *Deadline:* May 10.

Contact: Ms. Shana R. Rieger, Membership & Social Media Program
    Manager
    International Communications Industries Foundation
    11242 Waples Mill Road, Suite 200
    Fairfax, VA 22030
    Phone: 703-273-7200 Ext. 3690
    Fax: 703-278-8082
    E-mail: srieger@infocomm.org

INTERNATIONAL COMMUNICATIONS INDUSTRIES FOUNDATION AV SCHOLARSHIP

Scholarship for students majoring in audiovisual related fields such as audio, video, audiovisual, electronics, telecommunications, technical theatre, data networking, software development, information and technology. Minimum 2.75 GPA required. Must provide evidence of audiovisual knowledge (completed course, job, internship, etc.).

Academic Fields/Career Goals: Communications; Computer Science/Data Processing; Electrical Engineering/Electronics; Filmmaking/Video.

Award: Scholarship for use in freshman, sophomore, junior, senior, or graduate years; not renewable. *Number:* 1–50. *Amount:* $1200.

Eligibility Requirements: Applicant must be enrolled or expecting to enroll full-time at a two-year or four-year or technical institution or university. Applicant must have 3.0 GPA or higher. Available to U.S. and Canadian citizens.

Application Requirements: Application, essay, references, transcript. *Deadline:* May 10.

Contact: Ms. Shana R. Rieger, Membership & Social Media Program
    Manager
    International Communications Industries Foundation
    11242 Waples Mill Road, Suite 200
    Fairfax, VA 22030
    Phone: 703-273-7200 Ext. 3690
    Fax: 703-278-8082
    E-mail: srieger@infocomm.org

INTERNATIONAL FOODSERVICE EDITORIAL COUNCIL

http://www.ifeconline.com/

INTERNATIONAL FOODSERVICE EDITORIAL COUNCIL COMMUNICATIONS SCHOLARSHIP

• See page 77

JOHN BAYLISS BROADCAST FOUNDATION

http://www.baylissfoundation.org/

JOHN BAYLISS BROADCAST RADIO SCHOLARSHIP

One-time award for college juniors or seniors majoring in broadcast communications with a concentration in radio broadcasting. Must have history of radio-related activities and a GPA of at least 3.0.

Academic Fields/Career Goals: Communications; Journalism; TV/Radio Broadcasting.

Award: Scholarship for use in junior or senior years; not renewable. *Number:* 2–6. *Amount:* $5000.

Eligibility Requirements: Applicant must be enrolled or expecting to enroll full-time at a four-year institution or university. Applicant must have 3.0 GPA or higher. Available to U.S. citizens.

Application Requirements: Application, essay, resume, references, self-addressed stamped envelope, transcript. *Deadline:* April 30.

Contact: Chairperson
    John Bayliss Broadcast Foundation
    171 17th Street
    Pacific Grove, CA 93950
    E-mail: info@baylissfoundation.org

JORGE MAS CANOSA FREEDOM FOUNDATION

http://www.jorgemascanosa.org/

MAS FAMILY SCHOLARSHIP AWARD

• See page 152

JOURNALISM EDUCATION ASSOCIATION

http://www.jea.org/

NATIONAL HIGH SCHOOL JOURNALIST OF THE YEAR/ SISTER RITA JEANNE SCHOLARSHIPS

One-time award recognizes the nation's top high school journalists. Open to graduating high school seniors planning to study journalism and/or mass communications in college and pursue a career in the field. Applicants must have JEA member as adviser. Minimum 3.0 GPA required. Submit portfolio to state contest coordinator by February 15.

Academic Fields/Career Goals: Communications; Journalism; Photojournalism/Photography; TV/Radio Broadcasting.

Award: Scholarship for use in freshman year; not renewable. *Number:* 1–7. *Amount:* $2000–$5000.

Eligibility Requirements: Applicant must be high school student; age 17-19 and planning to enroll or expecting to enroll full-time at a four-year institution or university. Applicant must have 3.0 GPA or higher. Available to U.S. citizens.

Application Requirements: Application, applicant must enter a contest, essay, photo, portfolio, references, self-addressed stamped envelope, transcript, samples of work. *Deadline:* February 15.

Contact: Connie Fulkerson, Administrative Assistant
    Journalism Education Association
    Kansas State University, 103 Kedzie Hall
    Manhattan, KS 66506-1505
    Phone: 785-532-5532
    Fax: 785-532-5563
    E-mail: jea@spub.ksu.edu

KATU THOMAS R. DARGAN MINORITY SCHOLARSHIP

http://www.katu.com/

THOMAS R. DARGAN MINORITY SCHOLARSHIP

Up to four awards for minority students who are citizens of the United States pursuing broadcast or communications studies. Must be a resident of Oregon or Washington attending an out-of-state institution or be enrolled at a four-year college or university in Oregon or Washington. Minimum 3.0 GPA required.

Academic Fields/Career Goals: Communications; Journalism; TV/Radio Broadcasting.

Award: Scholarship for use in freshman, sophomore, junior, or senior years; renewable. *Number:* 1–4. *Amount:* $6000.

Eligibility Requirements: Applicant must be American Indian/Alaska Native, Asian/Pacific Islander, Black (non-Hispanic), or Hispanic; enrolled or expecting to enroll full-time at a four-year institution or university and resident of Oregon or Washington. Applicant must have 3.0 GPA or higher. Available to U.S. citizens.

Application Requirements: Application, essay, financial need analysis, interview, references, transcript. *Deadline:* April 30.

Contact: Human Resources
KATU Thomas R. Dargan Minority Scholarship
PO Box 2
Portland, OR 97207-0002

KE ALI'I PAUAHI FOUNDATION

http://www.pauahi.org/

JOSEPH A. SOWA SCHOLARSHIP

Award for study in the field of communications. Requires a minimum GPA of 3.0. Must demonstrate financial need. Submit two letters recommendation from a teacher, counselor, employer or community organization. Submit essay demonstrating how to engage young people through communication and describe your leadership potential in the community.

Academic Fields/Career Goals: Communications.

Award: Scholarship for use in freshman, sophomore, junior, senior, or graduate years; not renewable. *Number:* 1. *Amount:* $1500.

Eligibility Requirements: Applicant must be enrolled or expecting to enroll full-time at a four-year institution or university. Applicant must have 3.0 GPA or higher. Available to U.S. citizens.

Application Requirements: Application, essay, references, transcript, Student Aid Report (SAR), college acceptance letter. *Deadline:* April 1.

Contact: Mavis Shiraishi-Nagao, Scholarship Administrator
Phone: 808-534-3966
E-mail: scholarships@pauahi.org

LAGRANT FOUNDATION

http://www.lagrantfoundation.org/

LAGRANT FOUNDATION SCHOLARSHIP FOR GRADUATES
• *See page 152*

LAGRANT FOUNDATION SCHOLARSHIP FOR UNDERGRADUATES
• *See page 153*

NATIONAL ACADEMY OF TELEVISION ARTS AND SCIENCES

http://www.emmyonline.tv/

NATIONAL ACADEMY OF TELEVISION ARTS AND SCIENCES JOHN CANNON MEMORIAL SCHOLARSHIP

Scholarships are distributed over a four-year period up to $40,000 awarded prior to the first year of study and three additional awards of $1000 granted in subsequent years if the recipient demonstrates satisfactory progress towards a degree in a communications-oriented program. Must submit SAT or ACT scores. Must be child or grandchild of NATAS member. Application available on the Web at http://www.emmyonline.org/emmy/scholr.html.

Academic Fields/Career Goals: Communications; TV/Radio Broadcasting.

Award: Scholarship for use in freshman, sophomore, junior, or senior years; renewable. *Number:* 1–10. *Amount:* $1000–$40,000.

Eligibility Requirements: Applicant must be high school student and planning to enroll or expecting to enroll full-time at a four-year insti-

tution or university. Applicant must have 3.0 GPA or higher. Available to U.S. and non-U.S. citizens.

Application Requirements: Application, essay, references, test scores, transcript. *Deadline:* varies.

Contact: Ms. Pamela Kotch, Scholarship Manager
National Academy of Television Arts and Sciences
111 West 57th Street, Suite 600
New York, NY 10019
Phone: 212-586-8424
Fax: 212-246-8129
E-mail: pkotch@emmyonline.tv

NATIONAL ASSOCIATION OF BLACK JOURNALISTS

http://www.nabj.org/

NABJ SCHOLARSHIP

Scholarship for a student who is currently attending an accredited four-year college or university. Must be enrolled as an undergraduate or graduate student majoring in journalism (print, radio, online, or television). Minimum 2.5 GPA. Must be a member of NABJ. Scholarship value and the number of awards granted varies annually.

Academic Fields/Career Goals: Communications; Journalism; TV/Radio Broadcasting.

Award: Scholarship for use in freshman, sophomore, junior, senior, or graduate years; not renewable. *Number:* varies. *Amount:* varies.

Eligibility Requirements: Applicant must be enrolled or expecting to enroll full-time at a four-year institution or university. Applicant must have 2.5 GPA or higher. Available to U.S. and non-U.S. citizens.

Application Requirements: Application, driver's license, essay, interview, references, transcript. *Deadline:* March 17.

Contact: Irving Washington, Manager
National Association of Black Journalists
8701-A Adelphi Road
Adelphi, MD 20783-1716
Phone: 301-445-7100
Fax: 301-445-7101
E-mail: iwashington@nabj.org

NATIONAL ASSOCIATION OF BROADCASTERS

http://www.nab.org/

NATIONAL ASSOCIATION OF BROADCASTERS GRANTS FOR RESEARCH IN BROADCASTING

Award program is intended to fund research on economic, business, social, and policy issues important to station managers and other decision-makers in the United States commercial broadcast industry. Competition is open to all academic personnel. Graduate students and senior undergraduates are invited to submit proposals. For details refer to web site http://www.nab.org.

Academic Fields/Career Goals: Communications; Journalism; TV/Radio Broadcasting.

Award: Grant for use in senior, graduate, or postgraduate years; not renewable. *Number:* 2. *Amount:* $5000.

Eligibility Requirements: Applicant must be enrolled or expecting to enroll full-time at a four-year institution or university. Available to U.S. and non-U.S. citizens.

Application Requirements: Application, references, research proposal, budget. *Deadline:* February 1.

Contact: Debbie Milman, Research Director
National Association of Broadcasters
1771 N Street NW
Washington, DC 20036
Phone: 202-429-5383
Fax: 202-429-4199
E-mail: dmilman@nab.org

NATIONAL ASSOCIATION OF HISPANIC JOURNALISTS (NAHJ)

http://www.nahj.org/

NATIONAL ASSOCIATION OF HISPANIC JOURNALISTS SCHOLARSHIP

One-time award for high school seniors, college undergraduates, and first-year graduate students who are pursuing careers in English- or Spanish-language print, photo, broadcast, or online journalism. Students may major or plan to major in any subject, but must demonstrate a sincere desire to pursue a career in journalism. Must submit resume and work samples. Applications available only on web site http://www.nahj.org.

Academic Fields/Career Goals: Communications; Journalism; Photojournalism/Photography; TV/Radio Broadcasting.

Award: Scholarship for use in freshman, sophomore, junior, senior, or graduate years; not renewable. *Number:* varies. *Amount:* $1000–$2000.

Eligibility Requirements: Applicant must be enrolled or expecting to enroll full-time at a four-year institution or university and must have an interest in photography/photogrammetry/filmmaking or writing. Available to U.S. citizens.

Application Requirements: Application, essay, financial need analysis, resume, references, transcript, work samples. *Deadline:* March 31.

Contact: Virginia Galindo, Program Assistant
National Association of Hispanic Journalists (NAHJ)
1000 National Press Building, 529 14th Street, NW, Suite 1000
Washington, DC 20045-2001
Phone: 202-662-7145
E-mail: vgalindo@nahj.org

NATIONAL ASSOCIATION OF WATER COMPANIES-NEW JERSEY CHAPTER

http://www.nawc.org/

NATIONAL ASSOCIATION OF WATER COMPANIES-NEW JERSEY CHAPTER SCHOLARSHIP
• *See page 142*

NATIONAL CATTLEMEN'S FOUNDATION

http://www.nationalcattlemensfoundation.org/

CME BEEF INDUSTRY SCHOLARSHIP
• *See page 79*

NATIONAL INSTITUTE FOR LABOR RELATIONS RESEARCH

http://www.nilrr.org/

NATIONAL INSTITUTE FOR LABOR RELATIONS RESEARCH WILLIAM B. RUGGLES JOURNALISM SCHOLARSHIP

One-time award for undergraduate or graduate study in journalism or mass communications. Submit 500-word essay on the right-to-work principle. High school seniors accepted into certified journalism school may apply. Specify "Journalism" or "Ruggles" scholarship on any correspondence.

Academic Fields/Career Goals: Communications; Journalism.

Award: Scholarship for use in freshman, sophomore, junior, senior, graduate, or postgraduate years; not renewable. *Number:* 1. *Amount:* $2000.

Eligibility Requirements: Applicant must be enrolled or expecting to enroll full-time at a four-year institution or university and must have an interest in writing. Available to U.S. citizens.

Application Requirements: Application, essay, transcript. *Deadline:* December 31.

Contact: Cathy Jones, Scholarship Coordinator
National Institute for Labor Relations Research
5211 Port Royal Road, Suite 510
Springfield, VA 22151
Phone: 703-321-9606 Ext. 2231
Fax: 703-321-7143
E-mail: research@nilrr.org

NATIONAL STONE, SAND AND GRAVEL ASSOCIATION (NSSGA)

http://www.nssga.org/

JENNIFER CURTIS BYLER SCHOLARSHIP FOR THE STUDY OF PUBLIC AFFAIRS

One-time award open to graduating high school seniors or students already enrolled in a public affairs major in college, who are sons or daughters of an aggregates company employee.

Academic Fields/Career Goals: Communications; Public Policy and Administration.

Award: Scholarship for use in freshman, sophomore, junior, or senior years; not renewable. *Number:* 1. *Amount:* $1000–$2500.

Eligibility Requirements: Applicant must be enrolled or expecting to enroll full-time at a four-year institution or university. Available to U.S. and non-U.S. citizens.

Application Requirements: Application, applicant must enter a contest, essay, references, transcript, 300- to 500-word statement of plans for career in public affairs. *Deadline:* May 31.

Contact: Scholarship Coordinator
National Stone, Sand and Gravel Association (NSSGA)
1605 King Street
Arlington, VA 22314
Phone: 703-525-8788
Fax: 703-525-7782
E-mail: info@nssga.org

NEW JERSEY BROADCASTERS ASSOCIATION

http://www.njba.com/

MICHAEL S. LIBRETTI SCHOLARSHIP

Scholarships for undergraduate students in broadcasting, communication and journalism. Must be a New Jersey resident.

Academic Fields/Career Goals: Communications; Journalism; TV/Radio Broadcasting.

Award: Scholarship for use in freshman, sophomore, junior, or senior years; not renewable. *Number:* 1. *Amount:* up to $5000.

Eligibility Requirements: Applicant must be enrolled or expecting to enroll full-time at a four-year institution or university and resident of New Jersey. Available to U.S. citizens.

Application Requirements: Application. *Deadline:* varies.

Contact: Phil Roberts, Scholarships Coordinator
New Jersey Broadcasters Association
Broadcast House, 348 Applegarth Road
Monroe Township, NJ 08831
Phone: 888-652-2366
Fax: 609-860-0110
E-mail: njba@njba.com

OREGON ASSOCIATION OF BROADCASTERS

http://www.theoab.org/

OAB FOUNDATION SCHOLARSHIP

Award for students to begin or continue their education in broadcast and related studies. Must have a minimum GPA of 3.25. Must be a resident of Oregon studying in Oregon. For more details, refer to web site at http//www.TheOAB.org.

Academic Fields/Career Goals: Communications; Journalism; TV/Radio Broadcasting.

Award: Scholarship for use in freshman, sophomore, junior, senior, graduate, or postgraduate years; renewable. *Number:* 4. *Amount:* $2500–$3500.

Eligibility Requirements: Applicant must be enrolled or expecting to enroll full-time at a two-year or four-year institution or university; resident of Oregon and studying in Oregon. Available to U.S. citizens.

Application Requirements: Application, essay, financial need analysis, resume, references, transcript. *Deadline:* May 27.

Contact: Bill Johnstone, President and Chief Executive Officer
Oregon Association of Broadcasters
7150 Hampton Street, SW, Suite 240
Portland, OR 97223-8366
Phone: 503-443-2299
Fax: 503-443-2488
E-mail: theoab@theoab.org

OUTDOOR WRITERS ASSOCIATION OF AMERICA

http://www.owaa.org/

OUTDOOR WRITERS ASSOCIATION OF AMERICA BODIE MCDOWELL SCHOLARSHIP AWARD

One-time award for college level candidates who demonstrate outdoor communication talent and intend to make a career in this field. Applicants are nominated by their institution and must submit examples of outdoor communications work.

Academic Fields/Career Goals: Communications; Filmmaking/Video; Journalism; Literature/English/Writing; Photojournalism/Photography; TV/Radio Broadcasting.

Award: Scholarship for use in junior, senior, graduate, or postgraduate years; not renewable. *Number:* 2–5. *Amount:* $1000–$5000.

Eligibility Requirements: Applicant must be enrolled or expecting to enroll full- or part-time at a four-year institution or university and must have an interest in amateur radio, photography/photogrammetry/filmmaking, or writing. Available to U.S. and non-U.S. citizens.

Application Requirements: Application, essay, references, transcript. *Deadline:* March 1.

Contact: Ms. Robin Giner, Executive Director
Outdoor Writers Association of America
615 Oak Street, Suite 201
Missoula, MT 59801
Phone: 406-728-7434
Fax: 406-728-7445
E-mail: info@owaa.org

PRINT AND GRAPHIC SCHOLARSHIP FOUNDATION

http://www.printing.org/

PRINT AND GRAPHICS SCHOLARSHIPS FOUNDATION

Applicant must be interested in a career in graphic communications, printing technology or management, or publishing. Selection is based on academic record, class rank, recommendations, biographical information, and extracurricular activities. Deadlines are March 1 for high school students, April 1 for enrolled college students. Award available to applicants outside United States, as long as they are attending a U.S. institution.

Academic Fields/Career Goals: Communications; Graphics/Graphic Arts/Printing.

Award: Scholarship for use in freshman, sophomore, junior, senior, or graduate years; renewable. *Number:* 200–220. *Amount:* $1500–$5000.

Eligibility Requirements: Applicant must be enrolled or expecting to enroll full-time at a two-year or four-year or technical institution or university. Applicant must have 3.0 GPA or higher. Available to U.S. and non-U.S. citizens.

Application Requirements: Application, essay, references, self-addressed stamped envelope, test scores, transcript. *Deadline:* varies.

Contact: Bernie Eckert, Administrator
Print and Graphic Scholarship Foundation
200 Deer Run Road
Sewickley, PA 15143
Phone: 412-259-1740
Fax: 412-741-2311
E-mail: pgsf@printing.org

PUBLIC RELATIONS STUDENT SOCIETY OF AMERICA

http://www.prssa.org/

PUBLIC RELATIONS SOCIETY OF AMERICA MULTICULTURAL AFFAIRS SCHOLARSHIP
• See page 77

RADIO & TELEVISION NEWS DIRECTORS FOUNDATION

http://www.rtndf.org/

CAROLE SIMPSON SCHOLARSHIP

Award of $2000 for minority sophomore, junior, or senior undergraduate student enrolled in an electronic journalism program. Submit one to three examples of reporting or producing skills on audio cassette tape or videotape, totaling 15 minutes or less, with scripts.

Academic Fields/Career Goals: Communications; Journalism; TV/Radio Broadcasting.

Award: Scholarship for use in sophomore, junior, or senior years; not renewable. *Number:* 1. *Amount:* $2000.

Eligibility Requirements: Applicant must be American Indian/Alaska Native, Asian/Pacific Islander, Black (non-Hispanic), or Hispanic; enrolled or expecting to enroll full-time at a four-year institution or university and must have an interest in photography/photogrammetry/filmmaking or writing. Available to U.S. and non-U.S. citizens.

Application Requirements: Application, essay, resume, references, video or audio tape of work. *Deadline:* May 12.

Contact: Melanie Lo, Project Coordinator
Radio & Television News Directors Foundation
1600 K Street, NW, Suite 700
Washington, DC 20006
Phone: 202-467-5218
Fax: 202-223-4007
E-mail: irvingw@rtndf.org

KEN KASHIWAHARA SCHOLARSHIP

One-time award of $2500 for minority sophomore, junior, or senior whose career objective is electronic journalism. Submit examples showing reporting or producing skills on CD or DVD, with scripts.

Academic Fields/Career Goals: Communications; Journalism; TV/Radio Broadcasting.

Award: Scholarship for use in sophomore, junior, or senior years; not renewable. *Number:* 1. *Amount:* $2500.

Eligibility Requirements: Applicant must be American Indian/Alaska Native, Asian/Pacific Islander, Black (non-Hispanic), or Hispanic and enrolled or expecting to enroll full-time at a four-year institution or university. Available to U.S. and non-U.S. citizens.

Application Requirements: Application, essay, resume, references, video or audio tape of work, statement explaining career in electronic journalism. *Deadline:* May 12.

Contact: Melanie Lo, Program Coordinator
Radio & Television News Directors Foundation
1600 K Street, NW, Suite 700
Washington, DC 20006
Phone: 202-467-5218
E-mail: melaniel@rtnda.org

LOU AND CAROLE PRATO SPORTS REPORTING SCHOLARSHIP

One-time tuition grant of $1000 is given to a deserving student with strong writing skills and planning a career as a sports reporter in television or radio.

Academic Fields/Career Goals: Communications; Journalism; TV/Radio Broadcasting.

Award: Grant for use in sophomore, junior, or senior years; not renewable. *Number:* 1. *Amount:* $1000.

Eligibility Requirements: Applicant must be enrolled or expecting to enroll full-time at a four-year institution or university and must have an interest in writing. Available to U.S. and non-U.S. citizens.

Application Requirements: Application, essay, resume, references, video or audio tape of work, cover letter with reasons for seeking scholarship. *Deadline:* May 11.

Contact: Stacey Staniak, Project Manager
Radio & Television News Directors Foundation
4121 Plank Road 512
Fredericksburg, VA 22407-2838
Phone: 202-467-5214
E-mail: staceys@rtnda.org

PRESIDENTS SCHOLARSHIP

Two Presidents Scholarships available to full-time college sophomore, junior, or senior year whose career objective is electronic journalism. Must have at least one full year of college remaining.

Academic Fields/Career Goals: Communications; Journalism; TV/Radio Broadcasting.

Award: Scholarship for use in sophomore, junior, or senior years; not renewable. *Number:* 2. *Amount:* $2500.

Eligibility Requirements: Applicant must be enrolled or expecting to enroll full-time at a four-year institution or university. Available to U.S. and non-U.S. citizens.

Application Requirements: Application, essay, resume, references, CD or DVD of work. *Deadline:* May 11.

Contact: Stacey Staniak, Project Manager
Radio & Television News Directors Foundation
4121 Plank Road 512
Fredericksburg, VA 22407-2838
Phone: 202-467-5214
E-mail: staceys@rtnda.org

RHODE ISLAND FOUNDATION

http://www.rifoundation.org/

J. D. EDSAL ADVERTISING SCHOLARSHIP

• *See page 77*

RDW GROUP INC. MINORITY SCHOLARSHIP FOR COMMUNICATIONS

One-time award to provide support for minority students who wish to pursue a course of study in communications at the undergraduate or graduate level. Must be a Rhode Island resident and must demonstrate financial need.

Academic Fields/Career Goals: Communications.

Award: Scholarship for use in freshman, sophomore, junior, senior, or graduate years; not renewable. *Amount:* $1000–$2500.

Eligibility Requirements: Applicant must be American Indian/Alaska Native, Asian/Pacific Islander, Black (non-Hispanic), or Hispanic; enrolled or expecting to enroll full-time at a four-year institution or university and resident of Rhode Island. Available to U.S. citizens.

Application Requirements: Application, essay, self-addressed stamped envelope, transcript. *Deadline:* April 30.

Contact: Libby Monahan, Funds Administrator
Rhode Island Foundation
One Union Station
Providence, RI 02903
Phone: 401-274-4564 Ext. 3117
E-mail: libbym@rifoundation.org

SOCIETY FOR TECHNICAL COMMUNICATION

http://www.stc.org/

SOCIETY FOR TECHNICAL COMMUNICATION SCHOLARSHIP PROGRAM

Award for study relating to communication of information about technical subjects. Applicants must be full-time graduate students working toward a master's or doctoral degree, or undergraduate students working toward a bachelor's degree. Must have completed at least one year of postsecondary education and have at least one full year of academic work remaining. Two awards available for undergraduate students, two available for graduate students.

Academic Fields/Career Goals: Communications; Science, Technology, and Society.

Award: Scholarship for use in sophomore, junior, senior, or graduate years; not renewable. *Number:* up to 4. *Amount:* up to $1500.

Eligibility Requirements: Applicant must be enrolled or expecting to enroll full-time at a four-year institution or university. Available to U.S. and non-U.S. citizens.

Application Requirements: Application, essay, references, transcript. *Deadline:* February 15.

Contact: Scott DeLoach, Manager, Scholarship Selection Committee
Society for Technical Communication
834 C Dekalb Avenue, NE
Atlanta, GA 30307

SOCIETY FOR TECHNICAL COMMUNICATION–LONE STAR CHAPTER

http://www.stc-dfw.org/

LONE STAR COMMUNITY SCHOLARSHIPS

Scholarship for graduate or undergraduate student working toward a degree or certificate in the technical communication field. We also provide a scholarship for those returning to school to either further their studies in technical communication through approved training courses or career advancement classes. For further information see web site http://www.stc-dfw.org.

Academic Fields/Career Goals: Communications.

Award: Scholarship for use in freshman, sophomore, junior, senior, or graduate years; not renewable. *Number:* 1–4. *Amount:* varies.

Eligibility Requirements: Applicant must be Hispanic; enrolled or expecting to enroll full- or part-time at a four-year institution or university and resident of Oklahoma or Texas. Available to U.S. and non-U.S. citizens.

Application Requirements: Application, references, transcript. *Deadline:* March 28.

Contact: Rob Harris, Scholarship Committee Manager
Society for Technical Communication–Lone Star Chapter
PO Box 515065
Dallas, TX 75251-5065
Phone: 940-391-0167
E-mail: scholarship@stc-dfw.org

SOCIETY OF PROFESSIONAL JOURNALISTS-SOUTH FLORIDA CHAPTER

http://www.spjsofla.net/

GARTH REEVES, JR. MEMORIAL SCHOLARSHIPS

Scholarships for senior high school students, undergraduate, and graduate minority students preparing for a news career. Must be a South Florida resident. Amount is determined by need; minimum award is $500. One-time award, renewable upon application. Academic performance and quality of work for student or professional news media is considered.

Academic Fields/Career Goals: Communications; Journalism.

Award: Scholarship for use in freshman, sophomore, junior, senior, or graduate years; not renewable. *Number:* 1–12. *Amount:* $500–$1500.

Eligibility Requirements: Applicant must be American Indian/Alaska Native, Asian/Pacific Islander, Black (non-Hispanic), or Hispanic; enrolled or expecting to enroll full- or part-time at a two-year or four-year institution or university and resident of Florida. Applicant must have 3.0 GPA or higher. Available to U.S. citizens.

Application Requirements: Application, financial need analysis, resume, references, self-addressed stamped envelope, transcript, examples of applicant's journalism, three clips and photographs for print journalists, one tape for broadcast journalists. *Deadline:* April 15.

Contact: Oline Cogdill, Chair, Scholarship Committee
Society of Professional Journalists-South Florida Chapter
200 East Las Olas Boulevard
Fort Lauderdale, FL 33301
Phone: 954-356-4886
E-mail: ocogdill@sun-sentinel.com

SOCIETY OF SATELLITE PROFESSIONALS INTERNATIONAL

http://www.sspi.org/

SSPI INTERNATIONAL SCHOLARSHIPS
• *See page 133*

STRAIGHTFORWARD MEDIA

http://www.straightforwardmedia.com/

STRAIGHTFORWARD MEDIA MEDIA & COMMUNICATIONS SCHOLARSHIP
• *See page 77*

TEXAS ASSOCIATION OF BROADCASTERS

http://www.tab.org/

BELO TEXAS BROADCAST EDUCATION FOUNDATION SCHOLARSHIP

Scholarship of $2000 to undergraduate and graduate students enrolled in a fully accredited program of instruction that emphasizes radio or television broadcasting or communications at a four-year college or university in Texas. Student must be a member of the Texas Association of Broadcasters. Must have a GPA of 3.0 minimum.

Academic Fields/Career Goals: Communications; TV/Radio Broadcasting.

Award: Scholarship for use in freshman, sophomore, junior, senior, or graduate years; not renewable. *Number:* 1. *Amount:* $2000.

Eligibility Requirements: Applicant must be enrolled or expecting to enroll full-time at a four-year institution or university and studying in Texas. Applicant or parent of applicant must be member of Texas Association of Broadcasters. Applicant must have 3.0 GPA or higher. Available to U.S. and non-U.S. citizens.

Application Requirements: Application, essay, financial need analysis, references. *Deadline:* May 3.

Contact: Craig Bean, Public Service Manager
Texas Association of Broadcasters
502 East 11th Street, Suite 200
Austin, TX 78701
Phone: 512-322-9944
Fax: 512-322-0522
E-mail: craig@tab.org

BONNER MCLANE TEXAS BROADCAST EDUCATION FOUNDATION SCHOLARSHIP

Scholarship of $2000 to a undergraduate and students enrolled in a fully accredited program of instruction that emphasizes radio or television broadcasting or communications at a four-year college or university in Texas. Student must be a member of the Texas Association of Broadcasters. Must have a GPA of 3.0 minimum.

Academic Fields/Career Goals: Communications; TV/Radio Broadcasting.

Award: Scholarship for use in freshman, sophomore, junior, senior, or graduate years; not renewable. *Number:* 1. *Amount:* $2000.

Eligibility Requirements: Applicant must be enrolled or expecting to enroll full-time at a four-year institution or university and studying in Texas. Applicant or parent of applicant must be member of Texas Associ-

ation of Broadcasters. Applicant must have 3.0 GPA or higher. Available to U.S. and non-U.S. citizens.

Application Requirements: Application, essay, financial need analysis, references. *Deadline:* May 3.

Contact: Craig Bean, Public Service Manager
Texas Association of Broadcasters
502 East 11th Street, Suite 200
Austin, TX 78701
Phone: 512-322-9944
Fax: 512-322-0522
E-mail: craig@tab.org

STUDENT TEXAS BROADCAST EDUCATION FOUNDATION SCHOLARSHIP

Scholarship of $2000 to a undergraduate or a graduate student enrolled in a program of instruction that emphasizes radio or television broadcasting or communications at a two-year or technical school in Texas. Student must be a member of the Texas Association of Broadcasters. Must have a GPA of 3.0 minimum.

Academic Fields/Career Goals: Communications; TV/Radio Broadcasting.

Award: Scholarship for use in freshman, sophomore, junior, or senior years; not renewable. *Number:* 1. *Amount:* $2000.

Eligibility Requirements: Applicant must be enrolled or expecting to enroll full-time at a two-year or technical institution and studying in Texas. Applicant or parent of applicant must be member of Texas Association of Broadcasters. Applicant must have 3.0 GPA or higher. Available to U.S. and non-U.S. citizens.

Application Requirements: Application, essay, financial need analysis, references. *Deadline:* May 3.

Contact: Craig Bean, Public Service Manager
Texas Association of Broadcasters
502 East 11th Street, Suite 200
Austin, TX 78701
Phone: 512-322-9944
Fax: 512-322-0522
E-mail: craig@tab.org

TOM REIFF TEXAS BROADCAST EDUCATION FOUNDATION SCHOLARSHIP

Scholarship of $2000 to undergraduate and graduate students enrolled in a fully accredited program of instruction that emphasizes radio or television broadcasting or communications at a four-year college or university in Texas. Student must be a member of the Texas Association of Broadcasters. Must have a GPA of 3.0 minimum.

Academic Fields/Career Goals: Communications; TV/Radio Broadcasting.

Award: Scholarship for use in freshman, sophomore, junior, senior, or graduate years; not renewable. *Number:* 1. *Amount:* $2000.

Eligibility Requirements: Applicant must be enrolled or expecting to enroll full-time at a four-year institution or university and studying in Texas. Applicant or parent of applicant must be member of Texas Association of Broadcasters. Applicant must have 3.0 GPA or higher. Available to U.S. and non-U.S. citizens.

Application Requirements: Application, essay, financial need analysis, references. *Deadline:* May 3.

Contact: Craig Bean, Public Service Manager
Texas Association of Broadcasters
502 East 11th Street, Suite 200
Austin, TX 78701
Phone: 512-322-9944
Fax: 512-322-0522
E-mail: craig@tab.org

UNDERGRADUATE TEXAS BROADCAST EDUCATION FOUNDATION SCHOLARSHIP

Scholarship of $2000 to a undergraduate student enrolled in a fully accredited program of instruction that emphasizes radio or television broadcasting or communications at a four-year college or university in Texas. Student must be a member of the Texas Association of Broadcasters. Must have a GPA of 3.0 minimum.

Academic Fields/Career Goals: Communications; TV/Radio Broadcasting.

Award: Scholarship for use in freshman, sophomore, junior, or senior years; not renewable. *Number:* 1. *Amount:* $2000.

Eligibility Requirements: Applicant must be enrolled or expecting to enroll full-time at a four-year institution or university and studying in Texas. Applicant or parent of applicant must be member of Texas Association of Broadcasters. Applicant must have 3.0 GPA or higher. Available to U.S. and non-U.S. citizens.

Application Requirements: Application, essay, financial need analysis, references. *Deadline:* May 3.

Contact: Craig Bean, Public Service Manager
Texas Association of Broadcasters
502 East 11th Street, Suite 200
Austin, TX 78701
Phone: 512-322-9944
Fax: 512-322-0522
E-mail: craig@tab.org

VANN KENNEDY TEXAS BROADCAST EDUCATION FOUNDATION SCHOLARSHIP

Scholarship of $2000 to a undergraduate or graduate student enrolled in a fully accredited program of instruction that emphasizes radio or television broadcasting or communications at college or university in Texas. Student must be a member of the Texas Association of Broadcasters. Must have a GPA of 3.0 minimum.

Academic Fields/Career Goals: Communications; TV/Radio Broadcasting.

Award: Scholarship for use in freshman, sophomore, junior, or senior years; not renewable. *Number:* 1. *Amount:* $2000.

Eligibility Requirements: Applicant must be enrolled or expecting to enroll full-time at a two-year or four-year institution or university and studying in Texas. Applicant or parent of applicant must be member of Texas Association of Broadcasters. Applicant must have 3.0 GPA or higher. Available to U.S. and non-U.S. citizens.

Application Requirements: Application, essay, financial need analysis, references. *Deadline:* May 3.

Contact: Craig Bean, Public Service Manager
Texas Association of Broadcasters
502 East 11th Street, Suite 200
Austin, TX 78701
Phone: 512-322-9944
Fax: 512-322-0522
E-mail: craig@tab.org

TEXAS GRIDIRON CLUB INC.

http://www.spjfw.org/

TEXAS GRIDIRON CLUB SCHOLARSHIPS

$500 to $1000 scholarships for full-time or part-time college juniors, seniors, or graduate students majoring in newspaper, photojournalism, or broadcast fields. Must be Texas resident or going to school in Texas.

Academic Fields/Career Goals: Communications; Journalism; Photojournalism/Photography; TV/Radio Broadcasting.

Award: Scholarship for use in junior, senior, or graduate years; not renewable. *Number:* 10–15. *Amount:* $500–$1000.

Eligibility Requirements: Applicant must be enrolled or expecting to enroll full- or part-time at a four-year institution or university and resident of Texas. Available to U.S. citizens.

Application Requirements: Application, essay, financial need analysis, references, transcript, work samples. *Deadline:* March 3.

Contact: Angie Summers, Scholarships Coordinator
Texas Gridiron Club Inc.
709 Houston Street
Arlington, TX 76012
E-mail: asummers@star-telegram.com

TEXAS OUTDOOR WRITERS ASSOCIATION

http://www.towa.org/

TEXAS OUTDOOR WRITERS ASSOCIATION SCHOLARSHIP

Annual merit award available to students attending an accredited Texas college or university preparing for a career which would incorporate communications skills about the outdoors, environmental conservation, or resource management. Minimum 2.5 GPA required. Submit writing/photo samples.

Academic Fields/Career Goals: Communications; Environmental Science; Natural Resources.

Award: Scholarship for use in freshman, sophomore, junior, senior, graduate, or postgraduate years; not renewable. *Number:* 2. *Amount:* $1000–$1500.

Eligibility Requirements: Applicant must be enrolled or expecting to enroll full- or part-time at a four-year institution or university; resident of Texas; studying in Texas and must have an interest in writing. Applicant must have 2.5 GPA or higher. Available to U.S. citizens.

Application Requirements: Application, references, transcript, writing/photo samples. *Deadline:* February 15.

Contact: Chester Moore, Jr., Scholarship Chair
Texas Outdoor Writers Association
101 Broad Street
Orange, TX 77630
Phone: 409-882-0945
Fax: 409-882-0945
E-mail: saltwater@fishgame.com

TKE EDUCATIONAL FOUNDATION

http://www.tke.org/

GEORGE W. WOOLERY MEMORIAL SCHOLARSHIP

Scholarship available to initiated undergraduate members of Tau Kappa Epsilon who are full-time students in good standing, and pursuing a degree in communications or marketing with a cumulative GPA of 2.5 or higher. Record of leadership within the TKE chapter and on campus should be submitted. Preference will be given to members of Beta-Sigma Chapter, but if no qualified candidate applies, the award will be open to any member of TKE.

Academic Fields/Career Goals: Communications.

Award: Scholarship for use in freshman, sophomore, junior, or senior years; not renewable. *Number:* 1. *Amount:* $600.

Eligibility Requirements: Applicant must be enrolled or expecting to enroll full-time at a four-year institution or university; male and must have an interest in leadership. Applicant or parent of applicant must be member of Tau Kappa Epsilon. Applicant must have 2.5 GPA or higher. Available to U.S. and non-U.S. citizens.

Application Requirements: Application, essay, photo, transcript, narrative summary of how TKE membership has benefited applicant. *Deadline:* February 29.

Contact: Scholarship Committee
TKE Educational Foundation
8645 Founders Road
Indianapolis, IN 46268-1336
Phone: 317-872-6533
Fax: 317-875-8353
E-mail: tef@tke.org

TURF AND ORNAMENTAL COMMUNICATORS ASSOCIATION

http://www.toca.org/

TURF AND ORNAMENTAL COMMUNICATORS ASSOCIATION SCHOLARSHIP PROGRAM
• *See page 88*

UNITED METHODIST COMMUNICATIONS

http://www.umcom.org/

LEONARD M. PERRYMAN COMMUNICATIONS SCHOLARSHIP FOR ETHNIC MINORITY STUDENTS

One-time award to assist United Methodist ethnic minority students who are college students intending to pursue careers in religious communications.

Academic Fields/Career Goals: Communications; Journalism; Photojournalism/Photography; Religion/Theology; TV/Radio Broadcasting.

Award: Scholarship for use in junior or senior years; not renewable. *Number:* 1. *Amount:* $2500.

Eligibility Requirements: Applicant must be Methodist; American Indian/Alaska Native, Asian/Pacific Islander, Black (non-Hispanic), or

Hispanic and enrolled or expecting to enroll full-time at a two-year or four-year institution or university. Available to U.S. citizens.

Application Requirements: Application, essay, photo, references, transcript. *Deadline:* March 15.

Contact: Communications Resourcing Team
United Methodist Communications
810 12th Avenue, South
PO Box 320
Nashville, TN 37202-0320
Phone: 888-278-4862
Fax: 615-742-5485
E-mail: scholarships@umcom.org

UNITED NEGRO COLLEGE FUND

http://www.uncf.org/

C-SPAN SCHOLARSHIP PROGRAM

Scholarship and paid summer internship for students majoring in communications, journalism, political science, English, history, or radio/TV/film. Applicant must be African American undergraduate sophomore or junior attending a UNCF member college or university and have a minimum GPA of 3.0. Please visit web site for more information and online application http://www.uncf.org.

Academic Fields/Career Goals: Communications; History; Journalism; Literature/English/Writing; Political Science; TV/Radio Broadcasting.

Award: Scholarship for use in sophomore or junior years; not renewable. *Number:* 1. *Amount:* $2000.

Eligibility Requirements: Applicant must be Black (non-Hispanic) and enrolled or expecting to enroll full- or part-time at a four-year institution or university. Applicant must have 3.0 GPA or higher. Available to U.S. citizens.

Application Requirements: Application, financial need analysis, transcript, FAFSA, Student Aid Report (SAR).

Contact: Program Services
United Negro College Fund
8260 Willow Oaks Corporate Drive
Fairfax, VA 22031
Phone: 703-205-3486

FLYTE TYME PRODUCTIONS SCHOLARSHIP

Scholarship up to $5,000 for students attending UNCF member colleges and universities and majoring in engineering or communications. Must be Minnesota resident and have minimum 2.5 GPA. Scholarship is coupled with a paid summer internship at Flyte Tyme.

Academic Fields/Career Goals: Communications; Engineering/Technology.

Award: Scholarship for use in freshman year; not renewable. *Amount:* up to $5000.

Eligibility Requirements: Applicant must be Black (non-Hispanic); enrolled or expecting to enroll at a four-year institution or university and resident of Minnesota. Applicant must have 2.5 GPA or higher. Available to U.S. citizens.

Application Requirements: *Deadline:* continuous.

Contact: Director, Program Services
United Negro College Fund
8260 Willow Oaks Corporate Drive
PO Box 10444
Fairfax, VA 22031-8044
Phone: 800-331-2244
E-mail: rebecca.bennett@uncf.org

JOHN LENNON SCHOLARSHIP

Scholarships for students at UNCF member institutes majoring in performing arts, music, mass communications and communications. Must have at least 3.0 GPA. Prospective applicants should complete the Student Profile found at web site http://www.uncf.org.

Academic Fields/Career Goals: Communications; Music; Performing Arts.

Award: Scholarship for use in freshman year; not renewable. *Number:* 1. *Amount:* up to $5000.

Eligibility Requirements: Applicant must be Black (non-Hispanic); high school student and planning to enroll or expecting to enroll full- or part-time at a four-year institution or university. Applicant must have 3.0 GPA or higher. Available to U.S. citizens.

Application Requirements: Application, essay, financial need analysis, photo, references, transcript. *Deadline:* April 15.

Contact: Program Services Department
United Negro College Fund
8260 Willow Oaks Corporate Drive, PO Box 10444
Fairfax, VA 22031
Phone: 703-205-3486

NASCAR/WENDELL SCOTT, SR. SCHOLARSHIP
• *See page 73*

OSSIE DAVIS ENDOWMENT SCHOLARSHIP
• *See page 116*

READER'S DIGEST FOUNDATION SCHOLARSHIP

Scholarship for encouraging academically superior students, who write well, to enter the field of print journalism. Students attending UNCF member colleges and universities and majoring in communications, journalism, or English are eligible to apply. Students must be in their junior or senior year and have a GPA of 3.0 or better. Applicants must submit a published writing sample with their application.

Academic Fields/Career Goals: Communications; Journalism; Literature/English/Writing.

Award: Scholarship for use in junior or senior years; not renewable. *Amount:* up to $5000.

Eligibility Requirements: Applicant must be Black (non-Hispanic) and enrolled or expecting to enroll full- or part-time at a four-year institution or university. Applicant must have 3.0 GPA or higher. Available to U.S. citizens.

Application Requirements: Application, financial need analysis, photo, resume, references, transcript, published writing sample. *Deadline:* February 15.

Contact: Program Services
United Negro College Fund
8260 Willow Oaks Corporate Drive
Fairfax, VA 22031
Phone: 703-205-3486

STAN SCOTT SCHOLARSHIP

Scholarship for students who are attending UNCF member colleges and universities, majoring in Communications or Journalism and focused on writing and print media. Minimum GPA 3.0. For more information see Website: http://www.uncf.org/forstudents/scholarship.asp.

Academic Fields/Career Goals: Communications; Journalism.

Award: Scholarship for use in sophomore year; renewable. *Amount:* $1500–$5000.

Eligibility Requirements: Applicant must be enrolled or expecting to enroll at a four-year institution or university. Applicant must have 3.0 GPA or higher.

Contact: Director, Program Services
United Negro College Fund
8260 Willow Oaks Corporate Drive
PO Box 10444
Fairfax, VA 22031-8044
Phone: 800-331-2244
E-mail: rebecca.bennett@uncf.org

TOYOTA/UNCF SCHOLARSHIP
• *See page 74*

UNITED WATER CORPORATE SCHOLARS PROGRAM
• *See page 74*

VALLEY PRESS CLUB, SPRINGFIELD NEWSPAPERS

http://www.valleypressclub.com/

VALLEY PRESS CLUB SCHOLARSHIPS, THE REPUBLICAN SCHOLARSHIP, CHANNEL 22 SCHOLARSHIP

Nonrenewable award for graduating high school seniors from Connecticut and Massachusetts, who are interested in television journalism, photojournalism, broadcast journalism, or print journalism.

Academic Fields/Career Goals: Communications; Journalism; Photojournalism/Photography; TV/Radio Broadcasting.

Award: Scholarship for use in freshman year; not renewable. *Number:* 5. *Amount:* $1000.

Eligibility Requirements: Applicant must be high school student; planning to enroll or expecting to enroll full-time at a four-year institution or university; resident of Connecticut or Massachusetts and must have an interest in writing. Available to U.S. citizens.

Application Requirements: Application, financial need analysis, interview, references, test scores, transcript. *Deadline:* April 1.

Contact: Robert McClellan, Scholarship Committee Chair
Valley Press Club, Springfield Newspapers
PO Box 5475
Springfield, MA 01101
Phone: 413-783-3355

VIRGINIA ASSOCIATION OF BROADCASTERS

http://www.vabonline.com/

VIRGINIA ASSOCIATION OF BROADCASTERS SCHOLARSHIP AWARD

Scholarships are available to entering juniors and seniors majoring in mass communications-related courses. Must either be a resident of Virginia or be enrolled at a Virginia college or university. Must be U.S. citizen and enrolled full-time.

Academic Fields/Career Goals: Communications.

Award: Scholarship for use in junior or senior years; renewable. *Number:* 4. *Amount:* $500–$1000.

Eligibility Requirements: Applicant must be enrolled or expecting to enroll full-time at a four-year institution or university; resident of Virginia and studying in Virginia. Available to U.S. and non-U.S. citizens.

Application Requirements: Application, essay, financial need analysis, transcript. *Deadline:* February 15.

Contact: Ruby Seal, Director of Administration
Virginia Association of Broadcasters
600 Peter Jefferson Parkway, Suite 300
Charlottesville, VA 22911
Phone: 434-977-3716
Fax: 434-979-2439
E-mail: ruby.seal@easterassociates.com

WASHINGTON NEWS COUNCIL

http://www.wanewscouncil.org/

DICK LARSEN SCHOLARSHIP PROGRAM

One-time award for a student at a Washington state four-year public or private college with a serious interest in a career in communications-journalism, public relations, politics, or a related field. Must be resident of Washington state and U.S. citizen. See web site for more information.

Academic Fields/Career Goals: Communications; Journalism; Political Science.

Award: Scholarship for use in freshman, sophomore, junior, senior, or graduate years; not renewable. *Number:* 1. *Amount:* $2000.

Eligibility Requirements: Applicant must be enrolled or expecting to enroll full-time at a four-year institution; resident of Washington and studying in Washington. Available to U.S. citizens.

Application Requirements: Application, essay, financial need analysis, references, transcript, 3 samples of work. *Deadline:* April 15.

Contact: Washington News Council Scholarship Committee
Washington News Council
PO Box 3672
Seattle, WA 98124-3672

HERB ROBINSON SCHOLARSHIP PROGRAM

One-time award to a graduating Washington state high school senior who is entering a four-year public or private college or university in Washington. Must have a serious interest in a career in communications-journalism, public relations, politics or a related field. Must be resident of Washington state and a U.S. citizen. See web site for more information.

Academic Fields/Career Goals: Communications; Journalism; Political Science.

Award: Scholarship for use in freshman year; not renewable. *Number:* 1. *Amount:* $2000.

Eligibility Requirements: Applicant must be high school student; planning to enroll or expecting to enroll full-time at a four-year institution or university; resident of Washington and studying in Washington. Available to U.S. citizens.

Application Requirements: Application, essay, financial need analysis, references, transcript. *Deadline:* April 15.

Contact: John Hamer, Executive Director
Washington News Council
PO Box 3672
Seattle, WA 98124-3672
Phone: 206-262-9793
E-mail: info@wanewscouncil.org

WHOMENTORS.COM, INC.

http://www.WHOmentors.com/

ACCREDITED REPRESENTATIVE (FULL)

• *See page 56*

WISCONSIN BROADCASTERS ASSOCIATION FOUNDATION

http://www.wi-broadcasters.org/

WISCONSIN BROADCASTERS ASSOCIATION FOUNDATION SCHOLARSHIP

Four $2000 scholarships offered to assist students enrolled in broadcasting-related educational programs at four-year public or private institutions. Applicants must either have graduated from a Wisconsin high school, or be attending a Wisconsin college or university, must have completed at least 60 credits, and must be planning a career in radio or television broadcasting.

Academic Fields/Career Goals: Communications; TV/Radio Broadcasting.

Award: Scholarship for use in freshman, sophomore, junior, or senior years; not renewable. *Number:* 4. *Amount:* $2000.

Eligibility Requirements: Applicant must be enrolled or expecting to enroll full-time at a four-year institution or university and studying in Wisconsin. Available to U.S. citizens.

Application Requirements: Application, essay, references, transcript. *Deadline:* October 20.

Contact: John Laabs, President
Wisconsin Broadcasters Association Foundation
44 East Mifflin Street, Suite 900
Madison, WI 53703
Phone: 608-255-2600
Fax: 608-256-3986
E-mail: jlaabs@aol.com

WMTW-TV 8-AUBURN, MAINE

http://www.wmtw.com/

BOB ELLIOT-WMTW-TV 8 JOURNALISM SCHOLARSHIP

Awards $1500 to one graduating high school senior who plans to major in journalism, communications or a related area of study. This scholarship is one-time-only. Application available at http://www.wmtw.com.

Academic Fields/Career Goals: Communications; Journalism; TV/Radio Broadcasting.

Award: Scholarship for use in freshman year; not renewable. *Number:* 1. *Amount:* $1500.

Eligibility Requirements: Applicant must be high school student; planning to enroll or expecting to enroll full-time at a four-year institution or university and resident of Maine. Available to U.S. citizens.

Application Requirements: Application, essay, references, transcript. *Deadline:* March 24.

Contact: David Butta, Scholarship Coordinator
WMTW-TV 8-Auburn, Maine
PO Box 8
Auburn, ME 04211-0008
Phone: 207-514-1317
E-mail: wmtw@wmtw.com

WOMEN'S BASKETBALL COACHES ASSOCIATION

http://www.wbca.org/

ROBIN ROBERTS/WBCA SPORTS COMMUNICATIONS SCHOLARSHIP AWARD

One-time award for female student athletes who have completed their eligibility and plan to go to graduate school. Must major in communications. Must be nominated by the head coach of women's basketball who is a member of the WBCA.

Academic Fields/Career Goals: Communications; Journalism.

Award: Scholarship for use in senior, graduate, or postgraduate years; not renewable. *Number:* 1. *Amount:* $4000.

Eligibility Requirements: Applicant must be enrolled or expecting to enroll full- or part-time at a four-year institution or university; female and must have an interest in athletics/sports. Available to U.S. and non-U.S. citizens.

Application Requirements: Application, references, statistics. *Deadline:* February 15.

Contact: Betty Jaynes, Consultant
Women's Basketball Coaches Association
4646 Lawrenceville Highway
Lilburn, GA 30047-3620
Phone: 770-279-8027 Ext. 102
Fax: 770-279-6290
E-mail: bettyj@wbca.org

WYOMING TRUCKING ASSOCIATION SCHOLARSHIP FUND TRUST

http://www.wytruck.org/

WYOMING TRUCKING ASSOCIATION SCHOLARSHIP TRUST FUND

• *See page 76*

COMPUTER SCIENCE/ DATA PROCESSING

AIST FOUNDATION

http://www.aistfoundation.org/

ASSOCIATION FOR IRON AND STEEL TECHNOLOGY OHIO VALLEY CHAPTER SCHOLARSHIP

• *See page 137*

AMERICAN FOUNDATION FOR THE BLIND

http://www.afb.org/

PAUL W. RUCKES SCHOLARSHIP

Scholarship of $1000 to an undergraduate or graduate student studying in the field of engineering or in computer, physical, or life sciences. For more information and application requirements, please visit http://www.afb.org/scholarships.asp.

Academic Fields/Career Goals: Computer Science/Data Processing; Electrical Engineering/Electronics; Engineering/Technology; Natural Sciences; Physical Sciences.

Award: Scholarship for use in freshman, sophomore, junior, or senior years; not renewable. *Number:* 1. *Amount:* $1000.

Eligibility Requirements: Applicant must be enrolled or expecting to enroll full-time at a two-year or four-year institution or university. Applicant must be visually impaired. Available to U.S. citizens.

Application Requirements: Application, essay, references, transcript, proof of post-secondary acceptance and legal blindness, proof of citizenship, FAFSA. *Deadline:* April 30.

Contact: Dawn Bodrogi, Information Center
American Foundation for the Blind
11 Penn Plaza, Suite 300
New York, NY 10001
Phone: 212-502-7661
Fax: 212-502-7771
E-mail: afbinfo@afb.net

AMERICAN SOCIETY FOR INFORMATION SCIENCE AND TECHNOLOGY

http://www.asis.org/

JOHN WILEY & SONS BEST JASIST PAPER AWARD

Award of $1500 to recognize the best refereed paper published in the volume year of the JASIT preceding the ASIST annual meeting. John Wiley & Sons Inc., shall contribute $500 towards travel expenses to attend the ASIST annual meeting. No nomination procedure is used for this award. All eligible papers are considered.

Academic Fields/Career Goals: Computer Science/Data Processing; Library and Information Sciences.

Award: Prize for use in freshman, sophomore, junior, senior, graduate, or postgraduate years; not renewable. *Number:* 1. *Amount:* $2000.

Eligibility Requirements: Applicant must be enrolled or expecting to enroll full-time at a four-year institution or university. Available to U.S. and non-U.S. citizens.

Application Requirements: Application, essay. *Deadline:* varies.

Contact: Awards Coordinator
American Society for Information Science and Technology
1320 Fenwick Lane, Suite 510
Silver Spring, MD 20910-3602
Phone: 301-495-0900
Fax: 301-495-0810
E-mail: asis@asis.org

ARMED FORCES COMMUNICATIONS AND ELECTRONICS ASSOCIATION, EDUCATIONAL FOUNDATION

http://www.afcea.org/education/scholarships

AFCEA YOUNG ENTREPRENEUR SCHOLARSHIP

• *See page 163*

ARMED FORCES COMMUNICATIONS AND ELECTRONICS ASSOCIATION GENERAL EMMETT PAIGE SCHOLARSHIP

• *See page 122*

ARMED FORCES COMMUNICATIONS AND ELECTRONICS ASSOCIATION GENERAL JOHN A. WICKHAM SCHOLARSHIP

• *See page 164*

ARMED FORCES COMMUNICATIONS AND ELECTRONICS ASSOCIATION ROTC SCHOLARSHIP PROGRAM
• See page 122

DISABLED WAR VETERANS SCHOLARSHIP
• See page 122

LTG DOUGLAS D. BUCHHOLZ MEMORIAL SCHOLARSHIP
• See page 122

WILLIAM E. "BUCK" BRAGUNIER SCHOLARSHIP FOR OUTSTANDING LEADERSHIP
• See page 123

ARRL FOUNDATION INC.

http://www.arrl.org/

MAGNOLIA DX ASSOCIATION SCHOLARSHIP
• See page 183

PHD ARA SCHOLARSHIP

Award for journalism, computer science, or electronic engineering students. Must be a amateur radio operator and preference given to students who are children of deceased amateur radio operators. One award of $1000 per year.

Academic Fields/Career Goals: Computer Science/Data Processing; Electrical Engineering/Electronics; Journalism.

Award: Scholarship for use in freshman, sophomore, junior, or senior years; not renewable. Number: 1. Amount: $1000.

Eligibility Requirements: Applicant must be enrolled or expecting to enroll full-time at a four-year institution or university; resident of Iowa, Kansas, Missouri, or Nebraska and must have an interest in amateur radio. Applicant or parent of applicant must be member of American Radio Relay League. Available to U.S. citizens.

Application Requirements: Application, transcript. Deadline: February 1.

Contact: Ms. Mary Hobart, Secretary
ARRL Foundation Inc.
225 Main Street
Newington, CT 06111-1494
Phone: 860-594-0397
E-mail: k1mmh@arrl.org

RAY, NORP & KATIE, WOKTE PAUTZ SCHOLARSHIP

One $500–1000 award is available to a resident of the ARRL Midwest Division studying electronics or computer science at a four-year college or university. Applicant should possess a General class or higher amateur radio license and be a member of the ARRL.

Academic Fields/Career Goals: Computer Science/Data Processing; Electrical Engineering/Electronics.

Award: Scholarship for use in freshman, sophomore, junior, or senior years; not renewable. Number: 1. Amount: $500–$1000.

Eligibility Requirements: Applicant must be enrolled or expecting to enroll at a four-year institution or university; resident of Iowa, Kansas, Missouri, or Nevada and must have an interest in amateur radio. Applicant or parent of applicant must be member of American Radio Relay League.

Application Requirements: Application, transcript. Deadline: February 1.

Contact: Ms. Mary Hobart, Secretary
ARRL Foundation Inc.
225 Main Street
Newington, CT 06111-1494
Phone: 860-594-0397
E-mail: k1mmh@arrl.org

WILLIAM R. GOLDFARB MEMORIAL SCHOLARSHIP
• See page 146

ASSOCIATION OF FORMER INTELLIGENCE OFFICERS

http://www.afio.com/13_scholarships.htm

CIA UNDERGRADUATE SCHOLARSHIPS
• See page 89

ASTRONAUT SCHOLARSHIP FOUNDATION

http://www.astronautscholarship.org/

ASTRONAUT SCHOLARSHIP FOUNDATION
• See page 95

BARRY M. GOLDWATER SCHOLARSHIP AND EXCELLENCE IN EDUCATION FOUNDATION

http://www.act.org/goldwater

BARRY M. GOLDWATER SCHOLARSHIP AND EXCELLENCE IN EDUCATION PROGRAM
• See page 95

BRITISH COLUMBIA INNOVATION COUNCIL

http://www.bcic.ca/

PAUL AND HELEN TRUSSELL SCIENCE AND TECHNOLOGY SCHOLARSHIP
• See page 95

CATCHING THE DREAM

http://www.catchingthedream.org/

MATH, ENGINEERING, SCIENCE, BUSINESS, EDUCATION, COMPUTERS SCHOLARSHIPS
• See page 147

TRIBAL BUSINESS MANAGEMENT PROGRAM (TBM)
• See page 57

CENTRAL INTELLIGENCE AGENCY

http://www.cia.gov/

CENTRAL INTELLIGENCE AGENCY UNDERGRADUATE SCHOLARSHIP PROGRAM
• See page 58

DEVRY, INC.

http://www.devry.edu/

CISCO/COMPTIA SCHOLARSHIP

Award to high school graduates and GED recipients who successfully completed IT essentials I or CCNA the semester prior to entering college. Amount of $1200 per semester, valued up to $7,200 over the life of the award. Must apply and start with DeVry within one year of college graduation date.

Academic Fields/Career Goals: Computer Science/Data Processing; Electrical Engineering/Electronics; Engineering/Technology; Engineering-Related Technologies.

Award: Scholarship for use in freshman year; renewable. Number: varies. Amount: up to $2400.

Eligibility Requirements: Applicant must be high school student and planning to enroll or expecting to enroll full-time at an institution or university. Available to U.S. and Canadian citizens.

Application Requirements: Application.

Contact: Thonie Simpson, National High School Program Manager
DeVry, Inc.
One Tower Lane
Oak Brook Terrace, IL 60181-4624
Phone: 630-706-3122
E-mail: scholarships@devry.edu

ELECTRONIC DOCUMENT SYSTEMS FOUNDATION

http://www.edsf.org/

ELECTRONIC DOCUMENT SYSTEMS FOUNDATION SCHOLARSHIP AWARDS

Scholarships are awarded to full-time students with a 3.0 minimum average who are preparing for careers in the document management and graphic communications industry including document preparation; production or distribution; one-to-one marketing; graphic arts and communication; e-commerce; imaging science; printing; web authoring; electronic publishing; computer science; telecommunications, sales and/or marketing or related fields.

Academic Fields/Career Goals: Computer Science/Data Processing; Graphics/Graphic Arts/Printing; Marketing.

Award: Scholarship for use in freshman, sophomore, junior, senior, or graduate years; not renewable. *Number:* 40. *Amount:* $250–$5000.

Eligibility Requirements: Applicant must be enrolled or expecting to enroll full-time at a two-year or four-year or technical institution or university. Applicant must have 3.0 GPA or higher. Available to U.S. and non-U.S. citizens.

Application Requirements: Application, essay, references, transcript, description of activities and work experience. *Deadline:* May 1.

Contact: Gina Lacy, Program Manager
E-mail: gina.lacy@edsf.org

FOUNDATION FOR SCIENCE AND DISABILITY

http://stemd.org/

GRANTS FOR DISABLED STUDENTS IN THE SCIENCES
• *See page 95*

GREAT LAKES COMMISSION

http://www.glc.org/

CAROL A. RATZA MEMORIAL SCHOLARSHIP
• *See page 185*

HAWAIIAN LODGE, F&AM

http://www.glhawaii.org/

HAWAIIAN LODGE SCHOLARSHIPS
• *See page 106*

HEMOPHILIA HEALTH SERVICES

http://www.hemophiliahealth.com/

SCOTT TARBELL SCHOLARSHIP

Award to U.S. citizens with hemophilia A or B severe and related bleeding disorders. Students must be majoring or seeking a degree or certification in computer science and/or math. Applicants must be high school seniors, high school graduates (or equivalent/GED), college freshmen, sophomores, or juniors.

Academic Fields/Career Goals: Computer Science/Data Processing; Mathematics.

Award: Scholarship for use in freshman, sophomore, junior, or senior years; not renewable. *Number:* 1–2. *Amount:* $1500–$2000.

Eligibility Requirements: Applicant must be enrolled or expecting to enroll full-time at a four-year institution or university. Applicant must be physically disabled. Available to U.S. citizens.

Application Requirements: Application, essay, financial need analysis, references, test scores, transcript, doctor certification form. *Deadline:* May 1.

Contact: Sally Johnson, Manager Operations Support
Hemophilia Health Services
c/o Scholarship Program Administrators, Inc.
PO Box 23737
Nashville, TN 37202-3737
Phone: 615-850-5175
Fax: 615-352-2588
E-mail: scholarship@hemophiliahealth.com

HISPANIC ENGINEER NATIONAL ACHIEVEMENT AWARDS CORPORATION (HENAAC)

http://www.henaac.org/

HISPANIC ENGINEER NATIONAL ACHIEVEMENT AWARDS CORPORATION SCHOLARSHIP PROGRAM
• *See page 125*

INTERNATIONAL COMMUNICATIONS INDUSTRIES FOUNDATION

http://www.infocomm.org/scholarships

ICIF SCHOLARSHIP FOR EMPLOYEES AND DEPENDENTS OF MEMBER ORGANIZATIONS
• *See page 186*

INTERNATIONAL COMMUNICATIONS INDUSTRIES FOUNDATION AV SCHOLARSHIP
• *See page 186*

LOS ANGELES COUNCIL OF BLACK PROFESSIONAL ENGINEERS

http://www.lablackengineers.org/

AL-BEN SCHOLARSHIP FOR ACADEMIC INCENTIVE
• *See page 166*

AL-BEN SCHOLARSHIP FOR PROFESSIONAL MERIT
• *See page 166*

AL-BEN SCHOLARSHIP FOR SCHOLASTIC ACHIEVEMENT
• *See page 166*

MARYLAND ASSOCIATION OF PRIVATE COLLEGES AND CAREER SCHOOLS

http://www.mapccs.org/

MARYLAND ASSOCIATION OF PRIVATE COLLEGES AND CAREER SCHOOLS SCHOLARSHIP
• *See page 153*

MICROSOFT CORPORATION

http://www.microsoft.com/

YOU CAN MAKE A DIFFERENCE SCHOLARSHIP

Scholarship for high school students who want make an impact with technology. All students who submit proposals will receive a free copy of Microsoft Visual Studio NET Academic Edition.

Academic Fields/Career Goals: Computer Science/Data Processing.

Award: Scholarship for use in freshman year; not renewable. *Number:* 10. *Amount:* $5000.

Eligibility Requirements: Applicant must be high school student and planning to enroll or expecting to enroll full- or part-time at a four-year institution or university. Available to U.S. citizens.

Application Requirements: Application, transcript. *Deadline:* April 30.

Contact: Scholarship Committee
Microsoft Corporation
One Microsoft Way
Redmond, WA 98052-6399
Phone: 800-642-7676
Fax: 425-936-7329
E-mail: award-info@microsoft.com

NASA IDAHO SPACE GRANT CONSORTIUM

http://www.id.spacegrant.org/

NASA IDAHO SPACE GRANT CONSORTIUM SCHOLARSHIP PROGRAM
• *See page 141*

NASA/MARYLAND SPACE GRANT CONSORTIUM

http://www.mdspacegrant.org/

NASA MARYLAND SPACE GRANT CONSORTIUM UNDERGRADUATE SCHOLARSHIPS
• *See page 127*

NASA MONTANA SPACE GRANT CONSORTIUM

http://www.spacegrant.montana.edu/

MONTANA SPACE GRANT SCHOLARSHIP PROGRAM
• *See page 128*

NASA'S VIRGINIA SPACE GRANT CONSORTIUM

http://www.vsgc.odu.edu/

UNDERGRADUATE RESEARCH STEM SCHOLARSHIPS
• *See page 96*

VIRGINIA STEM COMMUNITY COLLEGE SCHOLARSHIPS
• *See page 96*

NASA WEST VIRGINIA SPACE GRANT CONSORTIUM

http://www.nasa.wvu.edu/

WEST VIRGINIA SPACE GRANT CONSORTIUM UNDERGRADUATE FELLOWSHIP PROGRAM
• *See page 129*

NATIONAL ASSOCIATION OF WATER COMPANIES-NEW JERSEY CHAPTER

http://www.nawc.org/

NATIONAL ASSOCIATION OF WATER COMPANIES-NEW JERSEY CHAPTER SCHOLARSHIP
• *See page 142*

NATIONAL INVENTORS HALL OF FAME

http://www.invent.org/

COLLEGIATE INVENTORS COMPETITION FOR UNDERGRADUATE STUDENTS
• *See page 96*

COLLEGIATE INVENTORS COMPETITION-GRAND PRIZE
• *See page 97*

NATIONAL SCIENCE TEACHERS ASSOCIATION

http://www.nsta.org/

TOSHIBA/NSTA EXPLORAVISION AWARDS PROGRAM

A competition for all students in grades K–12 attending a public, private or home school in the United States, Canada, or U.S. Territories. It is designed to encourage students to combine their imagination with their knowledge of science and technology to explore visions of the future.

Academic Fields/Career Goals: Computer Science/Data Processing; Engineering/Technology; Nuclear Science; Physical Sciences.

Award: Prize for use in freshman year; not renewable. *Number:* 16–32. *Amount:* $5000–$10,000.

Eligibility Requirements: Applicant must be high school student; age 21 or under and planning to enroll or expecting to enroll full-time at a two-year or four-year or technical institution or university. Available to U.S. and Canadian citizens.

Application Requirements: Application, applicant must enter a contest, essay, project description, bibliography, 5 Web page graphics, abstract. *Deadline:* January 29.

Contact: Award Program Coordinator
National Science Teachers Association
1840 Wilson Boulevard
Arlington, VA 22201
Phone: 800-397-5679
Fax: 703-243-7177
E-mail: exploravision@nsta.org

NATIONAL SECURITY AGENCY

http://www.nsa.gov/

NATIONAL SECURITY AGENCY STOKES EDUCATIONAL SCHOLARSHIP PROGRAM

Renewable awards for high school students planning to attend a four-year undergraduate institution to study foreign languages, computer science, math, electrical engineering, or computer engineering, or a field of study leading to a career in Intelligence Analysis. Must be at least 16 to apply. Must be a U.S. citizen. Minimum 3.0 GPA required, and minimum SAT score of 1100. For application visit web site http://www.nsa.gov/programs/employ/index.html.

Academic Fields/Career Goals: Computer Science/Data Processing; Electrical Engineering/Electronics; Foreign Language; Mathematics.

Award: Scholarship for use in freshman, sophomore, junior, or senior years; renewable. *Number:* 15–20. *Amount:* $1000–$50,000.

Eligibility Requirements: Applicant must be high school student; age 16 and over and planning to enroll or expecting to enroll full-time at a four-year institution or university. Applicant must have 3.0 GPA or higher. Available to U.S. citizens.

Application Requirements: Application, essay, interview, resume, references, test scores, transcript. *Deadline:* November 30.

Contact: Anne Clark, Program Manager
National Security Agency
9800 Savage Road, Suite 6779
Fort Meade, MD 20755-6779
Phone: 866-672-4473
Fax: 410-854-3002
E-mail: amclark@nsa.gov

NEVADA NASA SPACE GRANT CONSORTIUM

http://www.nvspacegrant.org/

NATIONAL SPACE GRANT COLLEGE AND FELLOWSHIP PROGRAM
• *See page 97*

ROBERT H. MOLLOHAN FAMILY CHARITABLE FOUNDATION, INC.

http://www.mollohanfoundation.org/

HIGH TECHNOLOGY SCHOLARS PROGRAM
• *See page 143*

RURAL TECHNOLOGY FUND

http://ruraltechfund.org/

SOCIAL ENTREPRENEURSHIP SCHOLARSHIP

This scholarship is open to students from schools in Kentucky who have a passion for using technology skills to make a positive social change in the world or at home in their communities. Applicants must be an active member of the Student Technology Leadership Program at his or her respective high school.

Academic Fields/Career Goals: Computer Science/Data Processing.

Award: Scholarship for use in freshman year; not renewable. *Number:* 1. *Amount:* $500.

Eligibility Requirements: Applicant must be high school student; planning to enroll or expecting to enroll at a four-year institution and studying in Kentucky. Available to U.S. citizens.

Application Requirements: Application, essay. *Deadline:* April 15.

Contact: Bowling Green, KY 42101
    E-mail: info@ruraltechfund.com

SAN DIEGO FOUNDATION

http://www.sdfoundation.org/

ENERGY OF ACHIEVEMENT SDG&E SCHOLARSHIP
• *See page 156*

SEMICONDUCTOR RESEARCH CORPORATION (SRC)

http://www.src.org/

MASTER'S SCHOLARSHIP PROGRAM
• *See page 169*

SOCIETY OF HISPANIC PROFESSIONAL ENGINEERS FOUNDATION

http://www.henaac.org/

HENAAC SCHOLARS PROGRAM

Applicants must be student leaders majoring in engineering, math, computer science, or material science. Must be of Hispanic origin and/or significantly participate in and promote organizations and activates in the Hispanic Community.

Academic Fields/Career Goals: Computer Science/Data Processing; Engineering-Related Technologies; Materials Science, Engineering, and Metallurgy; Mathematics.

Award: Scholarship for use in freshman, sophomore, junior, senior, or graduate years; renewable. *Number:* up to 87. *Amount:* $500–$5000.

Eligibility Requirements: Applicant must be Hispanic; enrolled or expecting to enroll full-time at a four-year institution or university and must have an interest in leadership. Applicant must have 3.0 GPA or higher. Available to U.S. and non-U.S. citizens.

Application Requirements: Application, essay, resume, references, transcript. *Deadline:* April 30.

Contact: Kathy Borunda Barrera, Manager, Scholars Program
    Society of Hispanic Professional Engineers Foundation
    3900 Whiteside Street
    Los Angeles, CA 90063
    Phone: 323-262-0997
    Fax: 323-262-0947
    E-mail: kathy@henaac.org

SOCIETY OF WOMEN ENGINEERS

http://www.swe.org/

SWE BATON ROUGE SECTION SCHOLARSHIPS

Scholarship of $1000 available to female applicants who plan to attend the college in fall semester engineering or computer science. Only for full-time study.

Academic Fields/Career Goals: Computer Science/Data Processing; Engineering/Technology.

Award: Scholarship for use in freshman year; not renewable. *Number:* 6–7. *Amount:* $1000.

Eligibility Requirements: Applicant must be enrolled or expecting to enroll full-time at a four-year institution or university; female and resident of Louisiana. Available to U.S. citizens.

Application Requirements: Application, test scores, transcript. *Deadline:* April 21.

Contact: Scholarship Committee
    Society of Women Engineers
    120 South La Salle Street, Suite 1515
    Chicago, IL 60603
    Phone: 312-596-5223
    E-mail: scholarshipapplication@swe.org

SWE CALIFORNIA GOLDEN GATE SECTION SCHOLARSHIPS

Scholarships awarded to female entering freshmen pursuing degrees in engineering, computer science, physical science, or mathematics. Applicants must be attending high school, or living within the boundaries of the Golden Gate Section.

Academic Fields/Career Goals: Computer Science/Data Processing; Engineering/Technology; Physical Sciences.

Award: Scholarship for use in freshman year; not renewable. *Number:* 10–15. *Amount:* $1000.

Eligibility Requirements: Applicant must be enrolled or expecting to enroll full-time at a four-year institution or university; female and resident of California. Available to U.S. citizens.

Application Requirements: Application, essay, references, transcript. *Deadline:* April 15.

Contact: Amy Len, Scholarship Chair
    Society of Women Engineers
    2625 Alcatraz Avenue, PO Box 356
    Berkeley, CA 94705
    Phone: 650-225-8756

SWE CONNECTICUT SECTION JEAN R. BEERS SCHOLARSHIP

Tuition-based annual scholarship program for qualified female students attending school in/or living within the boundaries of the Connecticut Section. Amount of $1500 for entering sophomore, junior, or senior student. The number of scholarships offered depends upon the amount of donations received and the number of qualified applicants.

Academic Fields/Career Goals: Computer Science/Data Processing; Engineering/Technology; Physical Sciences.

Award: Scholarship for use in sophomore, junior, or senior years; not renewable. *Number:* varies. *Amount:* $1500.

Eligibility Requirements: Applicant must be enrolled or expecting to enroll full- or part-time at a four-year institution or university; female and resident of Connecticut. Available to U.S. citizens.

Application Requirements: Application, essay, financial need analysis. *Deadline:* January 31.

Contact: Scholarship Committee
Society of Women Engineers
120 South La Salle Street, Suite 1515
Chicago, IL 60603
Phone: 312-596-5223
E-mail: scholarshipapplication@swe.org

SWE GREATER NEW ORLEANS SECTION SCHOLARSHIP

Scholarships available to women pursuing baccalaureate or graduate degree in an ABET-accredited or SWE-approved schools for engineering, or CSAB/ABET accredited schools, or SWE approved schools for computer science. Available to students from the following parishes: Jefferson, Lafourche, Orleans, Plaquemines, St. Bernard, St. Charles, St. James, St. John, St. Tammany, Tangipahoa, or Terrebonne.

Academic Fields/Career Goals: Computer Science/Data Processing; Engineering/Technology.

Award: Scholarship for use in freshman, sophomore, junior, senior, or graduate years; not renewable. *Amount:* varies.

Eligibility Requirements: Applicant must be enrolled or expecting to enroll full-time at a four-year institution or university; female and resident of Louisiana. Available to U.S. citizens.

Application Requirements: Application. *Deadline:* March 31.

Contact: Scholarship Committee
Society of Women Engineers
120 South La Salle Street, Suite 1515
Chicago, IL 60603
Phone: 312-596-5223
E-mail: scholarshipapplication@swe.org

SOCIETY OF WOMEN ENGINEERS-DALLAS SECTION

http://www.dallaswe.org/

NATIONAL SOCIETY OF WOMEN ENGINEERS SCHOLARSHIPS

Provides financial assistance to women admitted to accredited baccalaureate or graduate programs, in preparation for careers in engineering, engineering technology, and computer science. Minimum GPA of 3.5 for freshman applicants and 3.0 for sophomore, junior, senior, and graduate applicants.

Academic Fields/Career Goals: Computer Science/Data Processing; Engineering/Technology.

Award: Scholarship for use in freshman, sophomore, junior, senior, or graduate years; not renewable. *Number:* varies. *Amount:* $1000–$10,000.

Eligibility Requirements: Applicant must be enrolled or expecting to enroll full-time at a four-year institution or university and female. Applicant must have 3.5 GPA or higher. Available to U.S. and non-U.S. citizens.

Application Requirements: Application, essay, references, transcript, letter of acceptance from the accredited college or university. *Deadline:* May 15.

Contact: Scholarship Selection Committee
Society of Women Engineers-Dallas Section
230 East Ohio Street, Suite 400
Chicago, IL 60611-3265
Phone: 312-596-5223
E-mail: scholarshipapplication@swe.org

SOCIETY OF WOMEN ENGINEERS-ROCKY MOUNTAIN SECTION

http://www.swe-rms.org/

SOCIETY OF WOMEN ENGINEERS-ROCKY MOUNTAIN SECTION SCHOLARSHIP PROGRAM
• *See page 170*

SOCIETY OF WOMEN ENGINEERS-TWIN TIERS SECTION

http://www.swetwintiers.org/

SOCIETY OF WOMEN ENGINEERS-TWIN TIERS SECTION SCHOLARSHIP

Scholarship available to female students who reside or attend school in the Twin Tiers SWE section of New York. This is limited to zip codes that begin with 148, 149, 169 and residents of Bradford County, Pennsylvania. Applicant must be accepted or enrolled in an undergraduate degree program in engineering or computer science at an ABET-, CSAB- or SWE-accredited school.

Academic Fields/Career Goals: Computer Science/Data Processing; Engineering/Technology.

Award: Scholarship for use in freshman year; not renewable. *Number:* 4–6. *Amount:* $2000.

Eligibility Requirements: Applicant must be high school student; planning to enroll or expecting to enroll full-time at a four-year institution or university; female and resident of New York or Pennsylvania. Applicant must have 3.0 GPA or higher. Available to U.S. citizens.

Application Requirements: Application, essay, resume, references, self-addressed stamped envelope, transcript, letter of acceptance, personal information, and achievements. *Deadline:* March 25.

Contact: Amy Litwiler, Scholarship Chair
Society of Women Engineers-Twin Tiers Section
PO Box 798
Corning, NY 14830
Phone: 607-974-6261
E-mail: litwilerak@corning.com

SOUTH DAKOTA RETAILERS ASSOCIATION

http://www.sdra.org/

SOUTH DAKOTA RETAILERS ASSOCIATION SCHOLARSHIP PROGRAM
• *See page 71*

TEXAS DEPARTMENT OF TRANSPORTATION

http://www.txdot.gov/

CONDITIONAL GRANT PROGRAM
• *See page 180*

UNITED DAUGHTERS OF THE CONFEDERACY

http://www.hqudc.org/

WALTER REED SMITH SCHOLARSHIP
• *See page 157*

UNITED NEGRO COLLEGE FUND

http://www.uncf.org/

ACCENTURE SCHOLARSHIP

Scholarships of $2000 to undergraduate sophomores and juniors with 3.0 GPA or higher. Applicants must be majoring in engineering or computer science and enrolled at either Morehouse College or Spelman College. Visit web site for more information http://www.uncf.org.

Academic Fields/Career Goals: Computer Science/Data Processing; Engineering/Technology.

Award: Scholarship for use in sophomore or junior years; not renewable. *Number:* 5. *Amount:* $2000.

Eligibility Requirements: Applicant must be Black (non-Hispanic); enrolled or expecting to enroll full-time at a four-year institution or university and studying in Georgia. Applicant must have 3.0 GPA or higher. Available to U.S. citizens.

Application Requirements: Application, financial need analysis, FAFSA, Student Aid Report (SAR).

Contact: Program Services
United Negro College Fund
8260 Willow Oaks Corporate Drive
Fairfax, VA 22031
Phone: 703-205-3486

ALFRED CHISHOLM/BASF MEMORIAL SCHOLARSHIP FUND
• *See page 72*

BANK OF AMERICA SCHOLARSHIP
• *See page 157*

CARDINAL HEALTH SCHOLARSHIP
• *See page 72*

CARGILL SCHOLARSHIP PROGRAM
• *See page 72*

CISCO/UNCF SCHOLARS PROGRAM
Scholarship provides financial support for African-American electrical engineering or computer science majors, attending specific UNCF member college or university, with a special focus on women and students who demonstrate community service. Minimum 3.2 GPA required. List of participating institutions and online application are available at web site http://www.uncf.org.

Academic Fields/Career Goals: Computer Science/Data Processing; Electrical Engineering/Electronics.

Award: Scholarship for use in sophomore year; not renewable. *Number:* 1. *Amount:* $4000.

Eligibility Requirements: Applicant must be Black (non-Hispanic) and enrolled or expecting to enroll full-time at a four-year institution or university. Available to U.S. and non-U.S. citizens.

Application Requirements: Application, financial need analysis. *Deadline:* April 15.

Contact: Director, Program Services
United Negro College Fund
8260 Willow Oaks Corporate Drive
PO Box 10444
Fairfax, VA 22031-8044
Phone: 800-331-2244
E-mail: rebecca.bennett@uncf.org

COMPUWARE ACADEMIC SCHOLARSHIP
Award available to a resident of Southeast Michigan or student living within a Compuware service area. Must major in the fields of computer science, information technology and software development. Must be African-American student attending a four year institution in Michigan or a Historically Black College or University. Minimum 3.0 GPA required.

Academic Fields/Career Goals: Computer Science/Data Processing.

Award: Scholarship for use in sophomore or junior years; not renewable. *Amount:* $5000.

Eligibility Requirements: Applicant must be Black (non-Hispanic); enrolled or expecting to enroll at a four-year institution and resident of Michigan. Applicant must have 3.0 GPA or higher. Available to U.S. citizens.

Application Requirements: *Deadline:* continuous.

Contact: Director, Program Services
United Negro College Fund
8260 Willow Oaks Corporate Drive
PO Box 10444
Fairfax, VA 22031-8044
Phone: 800-331-2244
E-mail: rebecca.bennett@uncf.org

EDS CORPORATE SCHOLARS PROGRAM
UNCF?s Corporate Scholars Programs provide eligible students with both scholarships college and paid internship opportunities at America's leading Fortune 500 corporations and national organizations. The goal of the program is to ensure that successful corporations have a ready pool of well-trained, ethnically diverse young professionals who can create the products and efficiencies companies need to compete in the dynamic, globally integrated marketplace.

Academic Fields/Career Goals: Computer Science/Data Processing.

Award: Scholarship for use in junior year. *Amount:* $7500.

Eligibility Requirements: Applicant must be Black (non-Hispanic) and enrolled or expecting to enroll at a four-year institution or university. Applicant must have 3.0 GPA or higher. Available to U.S. citizens.

Application Requirements: *Deadline:* continuous.

Contact: Director, Program Services
United Negro College Fund
8260 Willow Oaks Corporate Drive
PO Box 10444
Fairfax, VA 22031-8044
Phone: 800-331-2244
E-mail: rebecca.bennett@uncf.org

FLOWERS INDUSTRIES SCHOLARSHIP
• *See page 157*

FORD/UNCF CORPORATE SCHOLARS PROGRAM
• *See page 73*

GENERAL MILLS TECHNOLOGY SCHOLARS AWARD
• *See page 171*

GOOGLE SCHOLARSHIP
Scholarships available for African American undergraduate juniors, seniors, graduate students, and postgraduates who are studying computer science, computer engineering, and electrical engineering. Selected students will receive $10,000 for an academic year of study and will be invited to attend the all-expenses-paid Annual Google Scholars Retreat. Minimum GPA of 2.5 required. Apply online at web site http://www.uncf.org.

Academic Fields/Career Goals: Computer Science/Data Processing; Electrical Engineering/Electronics.

Award: Scholarship for use in sophomore, junior, or senior years; not renewable. *Amount:* up to $10,000.

Eligibility Requirements: Applicant must be Black (non-Hispanic) and enrolled or expecting to enroll full-time at a four-year institution or university. Applicant must have 2.5 GPA or higher. Available to U.S. citizens.

Application Requirements: Application, transcript. *Deadline:* May 31.

Contact: Director, Program Services
United Negro College Fund
8260 Willow Oaks Corporate Drive
PO Box 10444
Fairfax, VA 22031-8044
Phone: 800-331-2244
E-mail: rebecca.bennett@uncf.org

LOCKHEED MARTIN/UNCF SCHOLARSHIP
• *See page 73*

MALCOLM PIRNIE CORPORATE SCHOLARS PROGRAM
• *See page 171*

NASCAR/WENDELL SCOTT, SR. SCHOLARSHIP
• *See page 73*

PRINCIPAL FINANCIAL GROUP SCHOLARSHIPS
• *See page 74*

SBC-PACIFIC BELL SCHOLARSHIP
• *See page 158*

TOYOTA/UNCF SCHOLARSHIP
• *See page 74*

TRW INFORMATION TECHNOLOGY MINORITY SCHOLARSHIP
Scholarship for students who are attending Howard University, George Mason University, Morgan State, Virginia Polytechnic Institute, or Pennsylvania State and majoring in Computer Science/MIS or Computer

Science. Minimum GPA of 3.0. For more information see Website: http://www.uncf.org/forstudents/scholarship.asp.

Academic Fields/Career Goals: Computer Science/Data Processing.

Award: Scholarship for use in sophomore or junior years. *Amount:* $3000.

Eligibility Requirements: Applicant must be Black (non-Hispanic) and enrolled or expecting to enroll at a four-year institution. Applicant must have 3.0 GPA or higher.

Contact: Director, Program Services
United Negro College Fund
8260 Willow Oaks Corporate Drive
PO Box 10444
Fairfax, VA 22031-8044
Phone: 800-331-2244
E-mail: rebecca.bennett@uncf.org

UPS/UNCF CORPORATE SCHOLARS PROGRAM

Award consists of both a scholarship and internship. Applicant must be an African American sophomore or junior undergraduate majoring in finance, marketing, computer science, human resources, electrical engineering, information technology, industrial engineering, mechanical engineering. Must be enrolled at selected historically black colleges and universities, and majority institutions and have a minimum 3.0 GPA. See web site for more information and online application http://www.uncf.org.

Academic Fields/Career Goals: Computer Science/Data Processing; Electrical Engineering/Electronics; Finance; Human Resources; Marketing; Mechanical Engineering.

Award: Scholarship for use in sophomore or junior years; renewable. *Number:* varies. *Amount:* up to $10,000.

Eligibility Requirements: Applicant must be Black (non-Hispanic) and enrolled or expecting to enroll full- or part-time at a four-year institution or university. Applicant must have 3.0 GPA or higher. Available to U.S. citizens.

Application Requirements: Application, financial need analysis. *Deadline:* February 10.

Contact: Director, Program Services
United Negro College Fund
8260 Willow Oaks Corporate Drive
PO Box 10444
Fairfax, VA 22031-8044
Phone: 800-331-2244
E-mail: rebecca.bennett@uncf.org

USENIX ASSOCIATION SCHOLARSHIP

Scholarship for students attending UNCF member colleges and universities and majoring in Information Systems, Computer Science/MIS, or Computer Science. Minimum 3.5 GPA required. Funds may be used for tuition, room and board, books, or to repay federal student loans. For more information see Website: http://www.uncf.org/forstudents/scholarship.asp.

Academic Fields/Career Goals: Computer Science/Data Processing.

Award: Scholarship for use in freshman, sophomore, junior, or senior years. *Amount:* up to $10,000.

Eligibility Requirements: Applicant must be enrolled or expecting to enroll at a four-year institution. Applicant must have 3.5 GPA or higher.

Contact: Director, Program Services
United Negro College Fund
8260 Willow Oaks Corporate Drive
PO Box 10444
Fairfax, VA 22031-8044
Phone: 800-331-2244
E-mail: rebecca.bennett@uncf.org

USENIX ASSOCIATION SCHOLARSHIP

Scholarship for computer science or information systems majors. Must have 3.5 GPA to qualify. Funds may be used for tuition, room/board, books, or to repay federal student loans. For use in UNCF member colleges and universities only.

Academic Fields/Career Goals: Computer Science/Data Processing.

Award: Scholarship for use in freshman, sophomore, junior, or senior years; not renewable. *Number:* varies. *Amount:* up to $10,000.

Eligibility Requirements: Applicant must be Black (non-Hispanic) and enrolled or expecting to enroll full- or part-time at a four-year institution

or university. Applicant must have 3.5 GPA or higher. Available to U.S. and non-U.S. citizens.

Application Requirements: Application, financial need analysis. *Deadline:* continuous.

Contact: Director, Program Services
United Negro College Fund
8260 Willow Oaks Corporate Drive
PO Box 10444
Fairfax, VA 22031-8044
Phone: 800-331-2244
E-mail: rebecca.bennett@uncf.org

VERIZON FOUNDATION SCHOLARSHIP
• See page 74

WELLS FARGO/UNCF SCHOLARSHIP FUND
• See page 74

VERMONT SPACE GRANT CONSORTIUM

http://www.cems.uvm.edu/vsgc

VERMONT SPACE GRANT CONSORTIUM SCHOLARSHIP PROGRAM
• See page 98

WIFLE FOUNDATION, INC.

http://www.wifle.org/

WIFLE SCHOLARSHIP PROGRAM

Scholarship to encourage women to pursue a career in federal law enforcement. Applicant must be enrolled in, or be transferring to, a four-year program in criminal justice, social sciences, public administration, chemistry, physics, computer science, or related studies and have a minimum GPA of 3.0. May also be in a graduate program. Must demonstrate commitment to the community through volunteer community service or an internship in a law enforcement agency. Must be a United States citizen.

Academic Fields/Career Goals: Computer Science/Data Processing; Law Enforcement/Police Administration; Physical Sciences; Public Policy and Administration; Social Sciences.

Award: Scholarship for use in sophomore, junior, or senior years; not renewable. *Number:* 1–5. *Amount:* $500–$2500.

Eligibility Requirements: Applicant must be enrolled or expecting to enroll full-time at a four-year institution or university and female. Applicant or parent of applicant must have employment or volunteer experience in community service. Applicant must have 3.0 GPA or higher. Available to U.S. citizens.

Application Requirements: Application, essay, references, transcript. *Deadline:* May 1.

Contact: Ms. Monica Rocchio, Vice President
WIFLE Foundation, Inc.
2200 Wilson Boulevard, Suite 102, PMB-204
Arlington, VA 22201-3324
Phone: 703-548-9211
Fax: 410-451-7373
E-mail: wifle@comcast.net

WYOMING TRUCKING ASSOCIATION SCHOLARSHIP FUND TRUST

http://www.wytruck.org/

WYOMING TRUCKING ASSOCIATION SCHOLARSHIP TRUST FUND
• See page 76

XEROX

http://www.xerox.com//

TECHNICAL MINORITY SCHOLARSHIP
• See page 171

CONSTRUCTION ENGINEERING/ MANAGEMENT

AACE INTERNATIONAL

http://www.aacei.org/

AACE INTERNATIONAL COMPETITIVE SCHOLARSHIP
• *See page 99*

AMERICAN RAILWAY ENGINEERING AND MAINTENANCE OF WAY ASSOCIATION

http://www.arema.org/

AREMA MICHAEL R. GARCIA SCHOLARSHIP
• *See page 174*

AREMA PRESIDENTIAL SPOUSE SCHOLARSHIP
• *See page 174*

AREMA UNDERGRADUATE SCHOLARSHIPS
• *See page 174*

AMERICAN SOCIETY OF CIVIL ENGINEERS

http://www.asce.org/

CONSTRUCTION ENGINEERING SCHOLARSHIP

Scholarship for freshman, sophomore, junior, or first-year senior who is a Construction Institute (CI) student member and/or ASCE National Student Member in good standing at the time of application and award.

Academic Fields/Career Goals: Construction Engineering/Management.

Award: Scholarship for use in freshman, sophomore, junior, or senior years; renewable. *Number:* varies. *Amount:* varies.

Eligibility Requirements: Applicant must be enrolled or expecting to enroll full- or part-time at a four-year institution or university. Applicant or parent of applicant must be member of American Society of Civil Engineers. Available to U.S. citizens.

Application Requirements: Application, financial need analysis, resume, references, transcript, annual budget. *Deadline:* April 1.

Contact: Construction Scholarship
American Society of Civil Engineers
1801 Alexander Bell Drive
Reston, VA 20191-4400

SAMUEL FLETCHER TAPMAN ASCE STUDENT CHAPTER/CLUB SCHOLARSHIP
• *See page 175*

ARRL FOUNDATION INC.

http://www.arrl.org/

GARY WAGNER, K3OMI SCHOLARSHIP
• *See page 164*

ASSOCIATED GENERAL CONTRACTORS EDUCATION AND RESEARCH FOUNDATION

http://www.agcfoundation.org/

AGC EDUCATION AND RESEARCH FOUNDATION GRADUATE SCHOLARSHIPS

College seniors enrolled in, or others possessing a degree in, an undergraduate construction management or construction-related engineering program, are eligible to apply. Applicant must be enrolled or planning to enroll in a graduate level construction management or construction-related engineering degree program as a full-time student.

Academic Fields/Career Goals: Construction Engineering/Management.

Award: Scholarship for use in senior or graduate years; not renewable. *Number:* 2. *Amount:* $7500.

Eligibility Requirements: Applicant must be enrolled or expecting to enroll full-time at a four-year institution or university. Available to U.S. citizens.

Application Requirements: Application, essay, financial need analysis, transcript. *Deadline:* November 1.

Contact: Floretta Slade, Director of Programs
Associated General Contractors Education and Research
Foundation
2300 Wilson Boulevard, Suite 400
Arlington, VA 22201
Phone: 703-837-5342
Fax: 703-837-5451
E-mail: sladef@agc.org

AGC EDUCATION AND RESEARCH FOUNDATION UNDERGRADUATE SCHOLARSHIPS
• *See page 176*

ASSOCIATED GENERAL CONTRACTORS OF NEW YORK STATE, LLC

http://www.agcnys.org/

ASSOCIATED GENERAL CONTRACTORS NYS SCHOLARSHIP
• *See page 176*

COLORADO CONTRACTORS ASSOCIATION INC.

http://www.coloradocontractors.org/

COLORADO CONTRACTORS ASSOCIATION SCHOLARSHIP PROGRAM

Scholarships of $2500 for junior and senior students who are interested in pursuing a career in heavy-highway-municipal-utility construction. Scholarships are only awarded to students who attend the following institutions: Colorado School of Mines, Colorado State University-Fort Collins, Colorado State University-Pueblo.

Academic Fields/Career Goals: Construction Engineering/Management.

Award: Scholarship for use in junior or senior years; not renewable. *Number:* varies. *Amount:* $2500.

Eligibility Requirements: Applicant must be enrolled or expecting to enroll full- or part-time at a four-year institution or university. Available to U.S. citizens.

Application Requirements: Application. *Deadline:* varies.

Contact: Scholarship Program Coordinator
Colorado Contractors Association Inc.
6880 South Yosemite Court, Suite 200
Centennial, CO 80112-1421
Phone: 290-290-6611
Fax: 290-290-9141
E-mail: info@coloradocontractors.org

FLORIDA EDUCATIONAL FACILITIES PLANNERS' ASSOCIATION

http://www.fefpa.org/

FEFPA ASSISTANTSHIP
• *See page 101*

FLORIDA ENGINEERING SOCIETY

http://www.fleng.org/

DAVID F. LUDOVICI SCHOLARSHIP
• *See page 177*

FECON SCHOLARSHIP
• *See page 177*

INTERNATIONAL FACILITY MANAGEMENT ASSOCIATION FOUNDATION

http://www.ifmafoundation.org/

IFMA FOUNDATION SCHOLARSHIPS
• *See page 102*

MICHIGAN SOCIETY OF PROFESSIONAL ENGINEERS

http://www.michiganspe.org/

MICHIGAN SOCIETY OF PROFESSIONAL ENGINEERS HARRY R. BALL, P.E. GRANT
• *See page 166*

MICHIGAN SOCIETY OF PROFESSIONAL ENGINEERS KENNETH B. FISHBECK, P.E. MEMORIAL GRANT
• *See page 166*

MIDWEST ROOFING CONTRACTORS ASSOCIATION

http://www.mrca.org/

MRCA FOUNDATION SCHOLARSHIP PROGRAM
• *See page 102*

NASA'S VIRGINIA SPACE GRANT CONSORTIUM

http://www.vsgc.odu.edu/

VIRGINIA STEM COMMUNITY COLLEGE SCHOLARSHIPS
• *See page 96*

NATIONAL ASPHALT PAVEMENT ASSOCIATION RESEARCH AND EDUCATION FOUNDATION

http://www.hotmix.org/

NATIONAL ASPHALT PAVEMENT ASSOCIATION RESEARCH AND EDUCATION FOUNDATION SCHOLARSHIP PROGRAM
• *See page 178*

NATIONAL CONSTRUCTION EDUCATION FOUNDATION

http://www.abc.org/

TRIMMER EDUCATION FOUNDATION SCHOLARSHIPS FOR CONSTRUCTION MANAGEMENT

Scholarships are available to students in a major related to the construction industry. Applicants must be enrolled at an educational institution with an ABC student chapter, and be current, active members or employed by an ABC member firm. Architecture and most engineering programs are excluded. Applicants must have a minimum overall GPA of 2.85 and 3.0 in the major. If no courses have been taken in the major, a minimum overall GPA of 3.0 is required. Visit web site http://www.abc.org.

Academic Fields/Career Goals: Construction Engineering/Management.

Award: Scholarship for use in sophomore, junior, or senior years; not renewable. *Number:* 10–15. *Amount:* up to $5000.

Eligibility Requirements: Applicant must be enrolled or expecting to enroll full-time at a two-year or four-year institution or university. Available to U.S. citizens.

Application Requirements: Application, essay, financial need analysis, references, transcript, Student Aid Report (SAR). *Deadline:* May 22.

Contact: John Strock, Director, Career and Constructions
National Construction Education Foundation
4250 North Fairfax Drive, Ninth Floor
Arlington, VA 22203-1607
Phone: 703-812-2008
E-mail: strock@abc.org

PROFESSIONAL CONSTRUCTION ESTIMATORS ASSOCIATION

http://www.pcea.org/

TED WILSON MEMORIAL SCHOLARSHIP FOUNDATION
• *See page 179*

UNITED NEGRO COLLEGE FUND

http://www.uncf.org/

ALFRED CHISHOLM/BASF MEMORIAL SCHOLARSHIP FUND
• *See page 72*

MALCOLM PIRNIE CORPORATE SCHOLARS PROGRAM
• *See page 171*

UTAH SOCIETY OF PROFESSIONAL ENGINEERS

http://www.uspeonline.com/

UTAH SOCIETY OF PROFESSIONAL ENGINEERS JOE RHOADS SCHOLARSHIP
• *See page 171*

WIRE REINFORCEMENT INSTITUTE EDUCATION FOUNDATION

http://www.wirereinforcementinstitute.org/

WRI COLLEGE SCHOLARSHIP PROGRAM
• *See page 180*

COSMETOLOGY

AMERICAN HEALTH AND BEAUTY AIDS INSTITUTE

http://www.ahbai.org/

FRED LUSTER, SR. EDUCATION FOUNDATION SCHOLARSHIP FUND

Scholarship of $250 awarded to cosmetology students currently enrolled in, or accepted by, a state-approved cosmetic art training facility prior to applying for scholarship. Student must have completed initial 300 hours before funds are approved or disbursed to the facility.

Academic Fields/Career Goals: Cosmetology.

Award: Scholarship for use in senior year; not renewable. *Number:* varies. *Amount:* $250.

Eligibility Requirements: Applicant must be enrolled or expecting to enroll full-time at a four-year institution or university. Available to U.S. and non-U.S. citizens.

Application Requirements: Application, photo, references, transcript. *Deadline:* April 15.

Contact: Geri Jones, Executive Director
American Health and Beauty Aids Institute
PO Box 19510
Chicago, IL 60619-0510
Phone: 708-633-6328
Fax: 708-633-6329
E-mail: ahbai1@sbcglobal.net

JOE FRANCIS HAIRCARE SCHOLARSHIP FOUNDATION

http://www.joefrancis.com/

JOE FRANCIS HAIRCARE SCHOLARSHIP PROGRAM

Scholarships are awarded for $1000 each, with 20 scholarships awarded annually. Applicants are evaluated for their potential to successfully complete school, their financial need, and their commitment to a long-term career in cosmetology. Must be enrolled in school by fall of award year.

Academic Fields/Career Goals: Cosmetology.

Award: Scholarship for use in freshman or sophomore years; not renewable. *Number:* 20. *Amount:* $1000.

Eligibility Requirements: Applicant must be enrolled or expecting to enroll full- or part-time at a technical institution. Available to U.S. citizens.

Application Requirements: Application, essay, financial need analysis, references. *Deadline:* June 1.

Contact: Kim Larson, Administrator
Joe Francis Haircare Scholarship Foundation
PO Box 50625
Minneapolis, MN 55405
Phone: 651-769-1757
Fax: 651-459-8371
E-mail: kimlarsonmn@gmail.com

STRAIGHTFORWARD MEDIA

http://www.straightforwardmedia.com/

STRAIGHTFORWARD MEDIA VOCATIONAL-TECHNICAL SCHOOL SCHOLARSHIP

• *See page 91*

CRIMINAL JUSTICE/ CRIMINOLOGY

ALBERTA HERITAGE SCHOLARSHIP FUND

http://www.alis.alberta.ca/

ROBERT C. CARSON MEMORIAL BURSARY

Award of CAN$500 to provide financial assistance to aboriginal students who are Alberta residents and full-time students enrolled in the second year of law enforcement or criminal justice program. Must be attending and nominated by one of the following qualifying Alberta institutions: Lethbridge College, Mount Royal College, Grant MacEwan College, the University of Calgary, or the University of Alberta. For additional information, see web site http://alis.alberta.ca.

Academic Fields/Career Goals: Criminal Justice/Criminology; Law Enforcement/Police Administration; Law/Legal Services.

Award: Scholarship for use in sophomore year; not renewable.

Eligibility Requirements: Applicant must be Canadian citizen; American Indian/Alaska Native; enrolled or expecting to enroll full-time at a two-year or four-year institution or university; resident of Alberta and studying in Alberta.

Application Requirements: Application, transcript, nomination from educational institution. *Deadline:* October 1.

Contact: Scholarship Committee
Alberta Heritage Scholarship Fund
9940 106th Street, Fourth Floor, Sterling Place
PO Box 28000, Station Main
Edmonton, AB T5J 4R4
Canada
Phone: 780-427-8640
E-mail: scholarships@gov.ab.ca

AMERICAN CRIMINAL JUSTICE ASSOCIATION-LAMBDA ALPHA EPSILON

http://www.acjalae.org/

AMERICAN CRIMINAL JUSTICE ASSOCIATION-LAMBDA ALPHA EPSILON NATIONAL SCHOLARSHIP

Awarded only to members of the American Criminal Justice Association. One-time award of $100 to $400. Members may reapply each year. Must have minimum 3.0 GPA. Must pursue studies in law/legal services, criminal justice/law, or the social sciences.

Academic Fields/Career Goals: Criminal Justice/Criminology; Law/ Legal Services; Social Sciences.

Award: Scholarship for use in freshman, sophomore, junior, senior, or graduate years; not renewable. *Number:* 9. *Amount:* $100–$400.

Eligibility Requirements: Applicant must be enrolled or expecting to enroll full- or part-time at a two-year or four-year institution or university. Applicant or parent of applicant must be member of American Criminal Justice Association. Applicant must have 3.0 GPA or higher. Available to U.S. citizens.

Application Requirements: Application, applicant must enter a contest, references, transcript. *Deadline:* December 31.

Contact: Karen Campbell, Executive Secretary
American Criminal Justice Association-Lambda Alpha Epsilon
PO Box 601047
Sacramento, CA 95860-1047
Phone: 916-484-6553
Fax: 916-488-2227
E-mail: acjalae@aol.com

AMERICAN SOCIETY OF CRIMINOLOGY

http://www.asc41.com/

AMERICAN SOCIETY OF CRIMINOLOGY GENE CARTE STUDENT PAPER COMPETITION

Award for full-time undergraduate or graduate students. Must submit a conceptual or empirical paper on a subject directly relating to criminology. Papers must be 7500 words or less.

Academic Fields/Career Goals: Criminal Justice/Criminology; Law Enforcement/Police Administration; Law/Legal Services; Social Sciences.

Award: Prize for use in freshman, sophomore, junior, senior, or graduate years; not renewable. *Number:* 3. *Amount:* $200–$500.

Eligibility Requirements: Applicant must be enrolled or expecting to enroll full-time at a four-year institution or university and must have an interest in writing. Available to U.S. and non-U.S. citizens.

Application Requirements: Applicant must enter a contest, conceptual or empirical paper on a subject directly relating to criminology. *Deadline:* April 15.

Contact: Andrew Hochstetlet, Scholarship Committee
American Society of Criminology
Iowa State University, 203D East Hall
Ames, IA 50011-4504
Phone: 515-294-2841
E-mail: hochstet@iastate.edu

ASSOCIATION OF CERTIFIED FRAUD EXAMINERS

http://www.acfe.com/

RITCHIE-JENNINGS MEMORIAL SCHOLARSHIP
• *See page 57*

ASSOCIATION OF FORMER INTELLIGENCE OFFICERS

http://www.afio.com/13_scholarships.htm

CIA UNDERGRADUATE SCHOLARSHIPS
• *See page 89*

CONNECTICUT ASSOCIATION OF WOMEN POLICE

http://www.cawp.net/

CONNECTICUT ASSOCIATION OF WOMEN POLICE SCHOLARSHIP

Available to Connecticut residents graduating from an accredited high school, and entering a college or university in Connecticut as a criminal justice major.

Academic Fields/Career Goals: Criminal Justice/Criminology; Law Enforcement/Police Administration.

Award: Scholarship for use in freshman year; not renewable. *Number:* 1–3. *Amount:* $200–$500.

Eligibility Requirements: Applicant must be high school student; planning to enroll or expecting to enroll full-time at a two-year or four-year institution or university; resident of Connecticut and studying in Connecticut. Available to U.S. citizens.

Application Requirements: Application, essay, financial need analysis, references, transcript. *Deadline:* April 30.

Contact: Gail McDonnell, Scholarship Committee
Connecticut Association of Women Police
PO Box 1653
Hartford, CT 06144
Phone: 860-527-7300

INDIANA SHERIFFS' ASSOCIATION

http://www.indianasheriffs.org/

INDIANA SHERIFFS' ASSOCIATION SCHOLARSHIP PROGRAM

Applicant must be an Indiana resident majoring in a criminal justice/law enforcement field at an Indiana college or university. Must be a member or dependent child or grandchild of a member of the association. Must be a full-time student with at least 12 credit hours.

Academic Fields/Career Goals: Criminal Justice/Criminology; Law Enforcement/Police Administration.

Award: Scholarship for use in freshman, sophomore, junior, or senior years; not renewable. *Number:* up to 40. *Amount:* up to $500.

Eligibility Requirements: Applicant must be enrolled or expecting to enroll full-time at a two-year or four-year institution or university; resident of Indiana and studying in Indiana. Applicant or parent of applicant must be member of Indiana Sheriffs' Association. Available to U.S. citizens.

Application Requirements: Application, essay, transcript, SAT scores. *Deadline:* April 1.

Contact: Laura Vest, Administrative Director
Indiana Sheriffs' Association
7215 E 21st St, Ste E
Indianapolis, IN 46219
Phone: 317-356-3633
Fax: 317-356-3996
E-mail: lvest@indianasheriffs.org

MISSOURI SHERIFFS' ASSOCIATION

http://www.mosheriffs.com/

JOHN DENNIS SCHOLARSHIP

Awards for Missouri high school seniors planning to attend a Missouri college or university and pursuing a career in criminal justice. Award is based on financial need. Students must be in upper one-third of their graduating class and participate in extracurricular activities. Minimum 2.0 GPA required.

Academic Fields/Career Goals: Criminal Justice/Criminology.

Award: Scholarship for use in freshman year; not renewable. *Number:* 16. *Amount:* $1000.

Eligibility Requirements: Applicant must be high school student; planning to enroll or expecting to enroll full-time at a two-year or four-year institution or university; resident of Missouri and studying in Missouri. Available to U.S. citizens.

Application Requirements: Application, essay, financial need analysis, test scores. *Deadline:* January 31.

Contact: Ms. Karen Logan, Administrative Assistant
Missouri Sheriffs' Association
6605 Business Highway 50 West
Jefferson City, MO 65109-6307
Phone: 573-635-5925 Ext. 100
E-mail: karen@mosheriffs.com

NATIONAL BLACK POLICE ASSOCIATION

http://www.blackpolice.org/

ALPHONSO DEAL SCHOLARSHIP AWARD

$500 scholarship for high school senior and U.S. citizen to attend a two-year college or university. Must study law enforcement or other related criminal justice field. Minimum 2.5 GPA required.

Academic Fields/Career Goals: Criminal Justice/Criminology; Law Enforcement/Police Administration; Law/Legal Services; Social Sciences; Social Services.

Award: Scholarship for use in freshman year; not renewable. *Number:* 4. *Amount:* $500.

Eligibility Requirements: Applicant must be high school student and planning to enroll or expecting to enroll full-time at a two-year or four-year institution or university. Available to U.S. citizens.

Application Requirements: Application, photo, references, transcript, letter of acceptance. *Deadline:* June 1.

Contact: Ronald Hampton, Executive Director
National Black Police Association
30 Kennedy Street NW, Suite 101
Washington, DC 20011
Phone: 202-986-2070
Fax: 202-986-0410
E-mail: nbpanatofc@worldnet.att.net

NORTH CAROLINA STATE EDUCATION ASSISTANCE AUTHORITY

http://www.ncseaa.edu/

NORTH CAROLINA SHERIFFS' ASSOCIATION UNDERGRADUATE CRIMINAL JUSTICE SCHOLARSHIPS

One-time award for full-time North Carolina resident undergraduate students majoring in criminal justice at a University of North Carolina school. Priority given to child of any North Carolina law enforcement officer. Letter of recommendation from county sheriff required.

Academic Fields/Career Goals: Criminal Justice/Criminology; Law Enforcement/Police Administration.

Award: Scholarship for use in freshman, sophomore, junior, or senior years; not renewable. *Number:* up to 10. *Amount:* $1000–$2000.

Eligibility Requirements: Applicant must be enrolled or expecting to enroll full-time at a four-year institution or university; resident of North Carolina and studying in North Carolina. Applicant or parent of applicant must have employment or volunteer experience in police/firefighting. Available to U.S. citizens.

Application Requirements: Application, financial need analysis, references, transcript, statement of career goals. *Deadline:* continuous.

Contact: Nolita Goldston, Assistant, Scholarship and Grant Division
North Carolina State Education Assistance Authority
PO Box 13663
Research Triangle Park, NC 27709
Phone: 919-549-8614
Fax: 919-248-4687
E-mail: ngoldston@ncseaa.edu

WHOMENTORS.COM, INC.

http://www.WHOmentors.com/

ACCREDITED REPRESENTATIVE (FULL)

• *See page 56*

CULINARY ARTS

AMERICAN ACADEMY OF CHEFS

http://www.acfchefs.org/

CHAINE DES ROTISSEURS SCHOLARSHIPS

Applicant must be an exemplary student, or be currently enrolled in an accredited, postsecondary school of culinary arts, or other postsecondary culinary training program, or should have completed a grading or marking period (trimester, semester or quarter). Must submit two letters of recommendation from industry and/or culinary professionals; financial aid release form; official transcript showing current GPA.

Academic Fields/Career Goals: Culinary Arts.

Award: Scholarship for use in freshman, sophomore, junior, or senior years; not renewable. *Number:* varies. *Amount:* up to $1000.

Eligibility Requirements: Applicant must be enrolled or expecting to enroll full-time at a two-year or four-year institution or university. Available to U.S. citizens.

Application Requirements: Application, financial need analysis, references, transcript. *Deadline:* December 1.

Contact: Jennifer DiMayo, Executive Coordinator
American Academy of Chefs
180 Center Place Way
St. Augustine, FL 32095
Phone: 800-624-9458
Fax: 904-825-4758
E-mail: jdimayo@acfchefs.net

AMERICAN CULINARY FEDERATION

http://www.acfchefs.org/

AMERICAN ACADEMY OF CHEFS CHAINE DES ROTISSEURS SCHOLARSHIP

One-time award to exemplary students currently enrolled in a full-time two-year culinary program. Must have completed a grading or marking period.

Academic Fields/Career Goals: Culinary Arts; Food Service/Hospitality.

Award: Scholarship for use in freshman year; not renewable. *Number:* 10. *Amount:* $1000–$21,000.

Eligibility Requirements: Applicant must be enrolled or expecting to enroll full- or part-time at a two-year institution. Available to U.S. and non-U.S. citizens.

Application Requirements: Application, references, transcript. *Deadline:* December 1.

Contact: Debra Moore, Academic Administrator
American Culinary Federation
180 Center Place Way
St. Augustine, FL 32095
Phone: 800-624-9458
Fax: 904-825-4758
E-mail: academy@acfchefs.net

AMERICAN ACADEMY OF CHEFS CHAIR'S SCHOLARSHIP

One-time award to exemplary students currently enrolled in a full-time two- or four-year culinary program. Must have a career goal of becoming a chef or pastry chef.

Academic Fields/Career Goals: Culinary Arts; Food Service/Hospitality.

Award: Scholarship for use in freshman, sophomore, junior, or senior years; not renewable. *Number:* 5. *Amount:* $1000–$5000.

Eligibility Requirements: Applicant must be enrolled or expecting to enroll full- or part-time at a two-year or four-year or technical institution or university. Available to U.S. and non-U.S. citizens.

Application Requirements: Application, references, transcript. *Deadline:* July 1.

Contact: Scholarship Committee
American Culinary Federation
180 Center Place Way
St. Augustine, FL 32095

AMERICAN HOTEL AND LODGING EDUCATIONAL FOUNDATION

http://www.ahlef.org/

AMERICAN HOTEL & LODGING EDUCATIONAL FOUNDATION PEPSI SCHOLARSHIP

Scholarships of $500 to $3000 awarded to graduates of Hospitality High School in Washington, DC. The scholarship recipients are selected by Hospitality High based upon a set of minimum eligibility criteria which includes graduate of Hospitality High, a minimum 2.5 GPA, and at least 250 hours in the hotel/hospitality industry.

Academic Fields/Career Goals: Culinary Arts; Food Service/Hospitality; Hospitality Management; Recreation, Parks, Leisure Studies; Travel/Tourism.

Award: Scholarship for use in freshman, sophomore, junior, or senior years; not renewable. *Number:* varies. *Amount:* $500–$3000.

Eligibility Requirements: Applicant must be enrolled or expecting to enroll full-time at a two-year or four-year institution or university and resident of District of Columbia. Applicant must have 2.5 GPA or higher. Available to U.S. and non-U.S. citizens.

Application Requirements: Application, essay, financial need analysis, resume, transcript, nomination from Hospitality High School. *Deadline:* May 1.

Contact: Christa Boatman, Foundation Manager
American Hotel and Lodging Educational Foundation
1201 New York Avenue NW, Suite 600
Washington, DC 20005
Phone: 202-289-3139
E-mail: cboatman@ahlef.org

ANNUAL SCHOLARSHIP GRANT PROGRAM

Students are selected for this award by their school which must be an AH&LEF affiliated program. Available to full-time students who have completed at least one or two years of a hospitality-related degree, are U.S. citizens or have permanent U.S. resident status. Minimum GPA of 3.0. A list of affiliated schools and designated contacts at the schools is available on http://www.ahlef.org.

Academic Fields/Career Goals: Culinary Arts; Food Service/Hospitality; Hospitality Management; Recreation, Parks, Leisure Studies; Travel/Tourism.

Award: Scholarship for use in sophomore, junior, or senior years; not renewable. *Amount:* $500–$3000.

Eligibility Requirements: Applicant must be enrolled or expecting to enroll full-time at a two-year or four-year institution or university. Applicant must have 3.0 GPA or higher. Available to U.S. citizens.

Application Requirements: Application, essay, financial need analysis, references, transcript, nomination from school. *Deadline:* May 1.

Contact: Christa Boatman, Foundation Manager
American Hotel and Lodging Educational Foundation
1201 New York Avenue NW, Suite 600
Washington, DC 20005-3931
Phone: 202-289-3139
Fax: 202-289-3199
E-mail: cboatman@ahlef.org

ARTHUR J. PACKARD MEMORIAL SCHOLARSHIP

Each AH&LEF affiliated university nominates its best qualified student to compete in the national competition. First-place winner receives a $5000 scholarship, second-place receives $3000 and third-place receives $2000. List of affiliated schools and their designated contacts can be found on http://www.ahlef.org.

Academic Fields/Career Goals: Culinary Arts; Food Service/Hospitality; Hospitality Management; Recreation, Parks, Leisure Studies; Travel/Tourism.

Award: Scholarship for use in junior or senior years; not renewable. *Number:* 3. *Amount:* $2000–$5000.

Eligibility Requirements: Applicant must be enrolled or expecting to enroll full-time at a two-year or four-year institution or university. Applicant must have 3.5 GPA or higher. Available to U.S. citizens.

Application Requirements: Application, essay, financial need analysis, resume, references, transcript, nomination from AH&LEF affiliated school. *Deadline:* May 1.

Contact: Ms. Christa Boatman, Foundation Manager
American Hotel and Lodging Educational Foundation
1201 New York Ave NW, Suite 600
Washington, DC 20005
Phone: 202-289-3139
Fax: 202-289-3110

ECOLAB SCHOLARSHIP PROGRAM

Award for students enrolled full-time in United States baccalaureate or associate program leading to degree in hospitality management.

Academic Fields/Career Goals: Culinary Arts; Food Service/Hospitality; Hospitality Management; Recreation, Parks, Leisure Studies; Travel/Tourism.

Award: Scholarship for use in freshman, sophomore, junior, or senior years; not renewable. *Number:* varies. *Amount:* $1000–$2000.

Eligibility Requirements: Applicant must be enrolled or expecting to enroll full-time at a two-year or four-year institution or university. Available to U.S. and non-U.S. citizens.

Application Requirements: Application, essay, financial need analysis, resume, transcript. *Deadline:* May 1.

Contact: Ms. Christa Boatman, Foundation Manager
American Hotel and Lodging Educational Foundation
1201 New York Avenue SW, Suite 600
Washington, DC 20005-3931
Phone: 202-289-3139
Fax: 202-289-3199
E-mail: cboatman@ahlef.org

HYATT HOTELS FUND FOR MINORITY LODGING MANAGEMENT

Scholarship available for African-American, Hispanic, American Indian, Alaskan Native, Asian, or Pacific Islander in a baccalaureate hospitality management program. Must be at least a sophomore in a four-year program.

Academic Fields/Career Goals: Culinary Arts; Food Service/Hospitality; Hospitality Management; Recreation, Parks, Leisure Studies; Travel/Tourism.

Award: Scholarship for use in sophomore, junior, or senior years; not renewable. *Number:* varies. *Amount:* $2000.

Eligibility Requirements: Applicant must be American Indian/Alaska Native, Asian/Pacific Islander, Black (non-Hispanic), or Hispanic and enrolled or expecting to enroll full-time at a two-year or four-year institution or university. Available to U.S. citizens.

Application Requirements: Application, essay, financial need analysis, resume, references, transcript. *Deadline:* May 1.

Contact: Ms. Christa Boatman, Foundation Manager
American Hotel and Lodging Educational Foundation
1201 New York Avenue, Suite 600
Washington, DC 20005
Phone: 202-289-3139
Fax: 202-289-3199
E-mail: cboatman@ahlef.org

INCOMING FRESHMAN SCHOLARSHIPS

This program is exclusively for incoming freshman interested in pursuing hospitality-related undergraduate programs. Preference will be given to any applicant who is a graduate of the Educational Institute's Lodging Management Program (LMP, which is a two-year high school program). Must have a minimum 2.0 GPA.

Academic Fields/Career Goals: Culinary Arts; Food Service/Hospitality; Hospitality Management; Recreation, Parks, Leisure Studies; Travel/Tourism.

Award: Scholarship for use in freshman year; not renewable. *Amount:* $1000–$2000.

Eligibility Requirements: Applicant must be high school student and planning to enroll or expecting to enroll full-time at a two-year or four-year institution or university. Available to U.S. citizens.

Application Requirements: Application, essay, financial need analysis, resume, transcript. *Deadline:* May 1.

Contact: Christa Boatman, Foundation Manager
American Hotel and Lodging Educational Foundation
1201 New York Avenue NW, Suite 600
Washington, DC 20005-3197
Phone: 202-289-3139
Fax: 202-289-3199
E-mail: cboatman@ahlef.org

RAMA SCHOLARSHIP FOR THE AMERICAN DREAM

Schools participating in this program include Bethune-Cookman College, California State Polytechnic University, Cornell University, Florida International University, Georgia State university, Greenville Technical College, Howard University, Johnson & Wales University, New York University, University of Central Florida, University of Houston, University of South Carolina, and Virginia Tech. The participating schools select the student nominees based upon a set of minimum eligibility criteria which include: enrolled in at least 9 credit hours for the fall and spring semesters, majoring in an undergraduate or graduate hospitality management program, minimum GPA of 2.5, US citizenship or permanent resident, and schools must give preference to students of Asian-Indian descent or other minority groups, as well as JHM employees and their dependents.

Academic Fields/Career Goals: Culinary Arts; Food Service/Hospitality; Hospitality Management; Recreation, Parks, Leisure Studies; Travel/Tourism.

Award: Scholarship for use in sophomore, junior, senior, or graduate years; not renewable. *Amount:* $1000–$3000.

Eligibility Requirements: Applicant must be American Indian/Alaska Native, Asian/Pacific Islander, Black (non-Hispanic), or Hispanic and enrolled or expecting to enroll full- or part-time at a two-year or four-year institution or university. Applicant must have 2.5 GPA or higher. Available to U.S. citizens.

Application Requirements: Application, essay, financial need analysis, references, transcript, nomination from school. *Deadline:* May 1.

Contact: Ms. Christa Boatman, Foundation Manager
American Hotel and Lodging Educational Foundation
1201 New York Avenue, NW, Suite 600
Washington, DC 20005
Phone: 202-289-3139
Fax: 202-289-3199
E-mail: cboatman@ahlef.org

STEVEN HYMANS EXTENDED STAY SCHOLARSHIP

Each year the AH&LA Extended Stay Council selects one AH&LEF affiliated school to receive the fund monies and the selected school designates the winning students. In 2011, Michigan State University has been designated. The minimum eligibility for the student nominees include: full-time enrollment, minimum GPA of 3.0, US citizenship or permanent residency, some experience either working or interning (paid or unpaid) at a lodging property, and preference will be given to those with experience at an extended stay property.

Academic Fields/Career Goals: Culinary Arts; Food Service/Hospitality; Hospitality Management; Recreation, Parks, Leisure Studies; Travel/Tourism.

Award: Scholarship for use in freshman, sophomore, junior, or senior years; not renewable. *Number:* 1000–3000. *Amount:* $500–$2000.

Eligibility Requirements: Applicant must be enrolled or expecting to enroll full-time at an institution or university. Applicant must have 3.0 GPA or higher. Available to U.S. citizens.

Application Requirements: Application, essay, financial need analysis, resume, transcript, nominees selected by school. *Deadline:* May 1.

Contact: Ms. Christa Boatman, Foundation Manager
American Hotel and Lodging Educational Foundation
1201 New York Avenue NW, Suite 600
Washington, DC 20005
Phone: 202-289-3139
Fax: 202-289-3199
E-mail: cboatman@ahlef.org

CANFIT

http://www.canfit.org/

CANFIT NUTRITION, PHYSICAL EDUCATION AND CULINARY ARTS SCHOLARSHIP

Awards undergraduate and graduate African-American, American-Indian/Alaska Native, Asian-American, Pacific Islander or Latino/Hispanic students who express financial need and are studying nutrition, physical education, or culinary arts in California. GPA of minimum 2.5 for undergraduates and 3.0 for graduates. See web site for essay topic http://www.canfit.org.

Academic Fields/Career Goals: Culinary Arts; Food Science/Nutrition; Food Service/Hospitality; Health and Medical Sciences; Sports-Related/Exercise Science.

Award: Scholarship for use in junior, senior, or graduate years; not renewable. *Number:* 5–10. *Amount:* $500–$1500.

Eligibility Requirements: Applicant must be of African, Chinese, Hispanic, Indian, or Japanese heritage; American Indian/Alaska Native, Asian/Pacific Islander, or Black (non-Hispanic); enrolled or expecting to enroll full-time at a four-year or technical institution or university; resident of California and studying in California. Applicant must have 2.5 GPA or higher. Available to U.S. citizens.

Application Requirements: Application, essay, financial need analysis, photo, references, transcript. *Deadline:* March 31.

Contact: Ms. Arnell J. Hinkle, Executive Director
CANFIT
2140 Shattuck Avenue, Suite 610
Berkeley, CA 94704
Phone: 510-644-1533 Ext. 12
Fax: 510-644-1535
E-mail: info@canfit.org

CAREERS THROUGH CULINARY ARTS PROGRAM INC.

http://www.ccapinc.org/

CAREERS THROUGH CULINARY ARTS PROGRAM COOKING COMPETITION FOR SCHOLARSHIPS

Applicants MUST be a senior in a C-CAP designated partner high school in Arizona; Prince George's County, Maryland; Tidewater, Virginia; or the cities of Boston, Chicago, Los Angeles, New York, Philadelphia or Washington, DC. Applicants MUST be accepted into the cooking competition for scholarships.

Academic Fields/Career Goals: Culinary Arts; Hospitality Management.

Award: Scholarship for use in freshman, sophomore, junior, or senior years; not renewable. *Number:* 50–70. *Amount:* $1000–$90,000.

Eligibility Requirements: Applicant must be high school student; age 21 or under; planning to enroll or expecting to enroll full- or part-time at a two-year or four-year or technical institution and resident of Arizona, California, Illinois, Maryland, New York, Pennsylvania, or Virginia. Available to U.S. and non-U.S. citizens.

Application Requirements: Application, applicant must enter a contest, essay, financial need analysis, interview, references, test scores, transcript. *Deadline:* varies.

Contact: Check website for local coordinator's contact information.

CHEF2CHEF SCHOLARSHIP FUND

http://www.chefs4students.org/

CHEF4STUDENTS CULINARY GRANT PROGRAM

Awards to students attending an accredited culinary school or institute. Based on demonstrated financial need, participation in online culinary forum, essay. Deadline varies.

Academic Fields/Career Goals: Culinary Arts.

Award: Grant for use in freshman, sophomore, junior, or senior years; renewable. *Number:* up to 30. *Amount:* up to $1000.

Eligibility Requirements: Applicant must be enrolled or expecting to enroll full- or part-time at a four-year institution or university. Available to U.S. and non-U.S. citizens.

Application Requirements: Application, essay, financial need analysis, references, transcript. *Deadline:* varies.

Contact: David Nelson, Program Manager
Chef2Chef Scholarship Fund
1360 Indian Trail Number 13
Steamboat Springs, CO 80487
Phone: 970-846-0059
Fax: 970-871-6115
E-mail: dnelson@chefs4students.org

THE CULINARY TRUST

http://www.theculinarytrust.org/

CULINARY TRUST SCHOLARSHIP PROGRAM FOR CULINARY STUDY AND RESEARCH

Scholarships provides funds to qualified applicants for beginning, continuing, and specialty education courses at accredited culinary schools worldwide, as well as, independent study for research projects. Applicants must have at least, a minimum 3.0 GPA, must write an essay, submit two letters of recommendation. Application fee: $35.

Academic Fields/Career Goals: Culinary Arts; Food Science/Nutrition; Food Service/Hospitality.

Award: Scholarship for use in freshman, sophomore, junior, senior, graduate, or postgraduate years; not renewable. *Number:* 21. *Amount:* $1000–$5000.

Eligibility Requirements: Applicant must be age 18 and over and enrolled or expecting to enroll full- or part-time at a two-year or four-year or technical institution or university. Applicant must have 3.0 GPA or higher. Available to U.S. and non-U.S. citizens.

Application Requirements: Application, essay, interview, references, transcript. *Fee:* $35. *Deadline:* March 1.

Contact: Amy Blackburn, Administrator
The Culinary Trust
PO Box 273
New York, NY 10013
Phone: 888-345-4666
Fax: 888-345-4666
E-mail: culinarytrust@mac.com

ILLINOIS RESTAURANT ASSOCIATION EDUCATIONAL FOUNDATION

http://www.illinoisrestaurants.org/

ILLINOIS RESTAURANT ASSOCIATION EDUCATIONAL FOUNDATION SCHOLARSHIPS

Scholarship available to Illinois residents enrolled in a food service management, culinary arts, or hospitality management concentration in an accredited program of a two- or four-year college or university. Must be a U.S. citizen.

Academic Fields/Career Goals: Culinary Arts; Food Science/Nutrition; Food Service/Hospitality; Hospitality Management.

Award: Scholarship for use in freshman, sophomore, junior, senior, graduate, or postgraduate years; not renewable. *Number:* 50–70. *Amount:* $750–$24,000.

Eligibility Requirements: Applicant must be enrolled or expecting to enroll full- or part-time at a two-year or four-year or technical institution or university and resident of Illinois. Applicant or parent of applicant must have employment or volunteer experience in food service or hospitality/hotel administration/operations. Available to U.S. citizens.

Application Requirements: Application, essay, photo, references, transcript. *Deadline:* May 15.

Contact: Blue Ribbon Scholarship Committee
Illinois Restaurant Association Educational Foundation
200 North LaSalle, Suite 880
Chicago, IL 60601-1014
Phone: 312-787-4000
Fax: 312-787-4792

JAMES BEARD FOUNDATION INC.

http://www.jamesbeard.org/

AMERICAN RESTAURANT SCHOLARSHIP

Scholarships available for students who plan to enroll or are already enrolled at a licensed or accredited culinary school. Up to one award of $4000 available.

Academic Fields/Career Goals: Culinary Arts.

Award: Scholarship for use in freshman, sophomore, junior, senior, or graduate years; not renewable. *Number:* up to 1. *Amount:* up to $4000.

Eligibility Requirements: Applicant must be enrolled or expecting to enroll full-time at a four-year institution or university. Available to U.S. and non-U.S. citizens.

Application Requirements: Application, essay, financial need analysis, references, transcript. *Deadline:* May 15.

Contact: Caroline Stuart, Scholarship Director
James Beard Foundation Inc.
54 Comstock Hill Road
New Canaan, CT 06840
Phone: 212-675-4984 Ext. 311
Fax: 212-645-1438
E-mail: jamesbeardfound@hotmail.com

BERN LAXER MEMORIAL SCHOLARSHIP

Scholarship for students seeking careers in food service and hospitality management. One scholarship given in one of three programs: culinary, hospitality management, and viticulture/oenology. Program and school must be accredited in accordance with the James Beard Foundation scholarship criteria. Must be resident of Florida and substantiate residency; have a high school diploma or the equivalent; and have a minimum of one-year culinary experience either as a student or employee. Applicants may reapply each year for a maximum of four years. See web site at http://www.jamesbeard.org for further details.

Academic Fields/Career Goals: Culinary Arts; Food Science/Nutrition; Hospitality Management.

Award: Scholarship for use in freshman, sophomore, junior, or senior years; not renewable. *Number:* 1. *Amount:* $5000.

Eligibility Requirements: Applicant must be enrolled or expecting to enroll full- or part-time at a four-year institution or university and resident of Florida. Available to U.S. and non-U.S. citizens.

Application Requirements: Application, essay, financial need analysis, references, transcript. *Deadline:* May 15.

Contact: Diane Brown, Director, Educational and Community
Programming
James Beard Foundation Inc.
167 West 12th Street
New York, NY 10011
Phone: 212-627-1128
E-mail: dhbrown@jamesbeard.org

BLACKBERRY FARM SCHOLARSHIP

One $2525 award available to applicants who are high school seniors or graduates who plan to enroll or students who are already enrolled at least part-time in a course of study at a licensed or accredited culinary school.

Academic Fields/Career Goals: Culinary Arts.

Award: Scholarship for use in freshman, sophomore, junior, or senior years; not renewable. *Number:* 1. *Amount:* $2525.

Eligibility Requirements: Applicant must be enrolled or expecting to enroll full- or part-time at a two-year or four-year institution or university.

Application Requirements: Proof of residency. *Deadline:* May 15.

Contact: Diane Brown, Director, Educational and Community
Programming
James Beard Foundation Inc.
167 West 12th Street
New York, NY 10011
Phone: 212-627-1128
E-mail: dhbrown@jamesbeard.org

BOB ZAPPATELLI MEMORIAL SCHOLARSHIP

One $3000 award is available to applicants who are planning to enroll or currently enrolled in an accredited program of culinary studies or food and beverage studies. Applicant must have work experience in food and beverage and must demonstrate strong leadership skills and passion for the culinary arts. Preference will be given to an employee or relative of a Benchmark employee.

Academic Fields/Career Goals: Culinary Arts.

Award: Scholarship for use in freshman, sophomore, junior, or senior years; not renewable. *Number:* 1. *Amount:* $3000.

Eligibility Requirements: Applicant must be enrolled or expecting to enroll full- or part-time at a two-year or four-year institution or university.

Application Requirements: Proof of residency. *Deadline:* May 15.

Contact: Diane Brown, Director, Educational and Community
Programming
James Beard Foundation Inc.
167 West 12th Street
New York, NY 10011
Phone: 212-627-1128
E-mail: dhbrown@jamesbeard.org

THE CHEFS FOR LOUISIANA COOKERY SCHOLARSHIP

Up to two $2000 awards are available to residents of Louisiana who are pursuing a career in the culinary field at an accredited culinary college/university located in the state of Louisiana.

Academic Fields/Career Goals: Culinary Arts.

Award: Scholarship for use in freshman, sophomore, junior, or senior years; not renewable. *Number:* up to 2. *Amount:* $2000.

Eligibility Requirements: Applicant must be enrolled or expecting to enroll full- or part-time at a two-year or four-year institution or university; resident of Louisiana and studying in Louisiana.

Application Requirements: Proof of residency. *Deadline:* May 15.

Contact: Diane Brown, Director, Educational and Community
Programming
James Beard Foundation Inc.
167 West 12th Street
New York, NY 10011
Phone: 212-627-1128
E-mail: dhbrown@jamesbeard.org

CHRISTIAN WOLFFER SCHOLARSHIP

One $2000 award is available to New York residents planning to enroll or currently enrolled at a licensed or accredited culinary school or wine studies program. Minimum GPA of 3.0 required.

Academic Fields/Career Goals: Culinary Arts.

Award: Scholarship for use in freshman, sophomore, junior, or senior years; not renewable. *Number:* 1. *Amount:* $2000.

Eligibility Requirements: Applicant must be enrolled or expecting to enroll full- or part-time at a two-year or four-year institution or university and resident of New York. Applicant must have 3.0 GPA or higher.

Application Requirements: Proof of residency. *Deadline:* May 15.

Contact: Diane Brown, Director, Educational and Community
Programming
James Beard Foundation Inc.
167 West 12th Street
New York, NY 10011
Phone: 212-627-1128
E-mail: dhbrown@jamesbeard.org

CLAY TRIPLETTE SCHOLARSHIP

Scholarship for deserving students who want to pursue a baking and pastry degree. Up to two awards of $5000. Applicants must plan to enroll or already be enrolled in an accredited baking or pastry studies program at a licensed or accredited culinary school. Must submit a 250 word essay on James Beard.

Academic Fields/Career Goals: Culinary Arts.

Award: Scholarship for use in freshman, sophomore, junior, or senior years; not renewable. *Number:* up to 2. *Amount:* $5000.

Eligibility Requirements: Applicant must be enrolled or expecting to enroll full-time at a four-year institution or university. Available to U.S. citizens.

Application Requirements: Application, essay, financial need analysis, references, transcript. *Deadline:* May 15.

Contact: Caroline Stuart, Scholarship Director
James Beard Foundation Inc.
167 West 12th Street
New York, NY 10011
Phone: 212-675-4984 Ext. 311
Fax: 212-645-1438
E-mail: jamesbeardfound@hotmail.com

JAMES BEARD FOUNDATION GENERAL SCHOLARSHIPS

One-time scholarships valued $2000 towards tuition at an accredited culinary school of student's choice. The amount of each scholarship will be at the discretion of the James Beard Foundation scholarship committee. Candidates must demonstrate a strong commitment to the culinary arts, an exceptional academic or work record, and financial need.

Academic Fields/Career Goals: Culinary Arts.

Award: Scholarship for use in freshman, sophomore, junior, senior, or graduate years; not renewable. *Amount:* $2000.

Eligibility Requirements: Applicant must be enrolled or expecting to enroll full- or part-time at a four-year institution or university. Available to U.S. and non-U.S. citizens.

Application Requirements: Application, essay, financial need analysis, references, transcript. *Deadline:* May 15.

Contact: Caroline Stuart, Scholarship Director
James Beard Foundation Inc.
167 West 12th Street
New York, NY 10011
Phone: 212-675-4984 Ext. 311
Fax: 212-645-1438
E-mail: jamesbeardfound@hotmail.com

LA TOQUE SCHOLARSHIP IN WINE STUDIES

Scholarship for $3000 toward tuition in an accredited Wine Studies program of the student's choice. For both full-time and part-time study. See web site at http://www.jamesbeard.org for further details.

Academic Fields/Career Goals: Culinary Arts.

Award: Scholarship for use in freshman, sophomore, junior, senior, or graduate years; not renewable. *Number:* 1. *Amount:* $3000.

Eligibility Requirements: Applicant must be enrolled or expecting to enroll full- or part-time at a four-year institution or university. Available to U.S. and non-U.S. citizens.

Application Requirements: Application, essay, financial need analysis, references, transcript. *Deadline:* May 15.

Contact: Caroline Stuart, Scholarship Director
James Beard Foundation Inc.
167 West 12th Street
New York, NY 10011
Phone: 212-675-4984 Ext. 311
Fax: 212-645-1438
E-mail: jamesbeardfound@hotmail.com

PETER CAMERON/HOUSEWARES CHARITY FOUNDATION SCHOLARSHIP

Nonrenewable scholarships for high school seniors planning to enroll at a licensed or accredited culinary school who have a minimum GPA of 3.0. For more information, see web site http://www.jamesbeard.org.

Academic Fields/Career Goals: Culinary Arts.

Award: Scholarship for use in freshman year; not renewable. *Number:* 1. *Amount:* $4000.

Eligibility Requirements: Applicant must be high school student and planning to enroll or expecting to enroll full-time at a four-year institution or university. Applicant must have 3.0 GPA or higher. Available to U.S. and non-U.S. citizens.

Application Requirements: Application, essay, financial need analysis, references, transcript. *Deadline:* May 15.

Contact: Caroline Stuart, Scholarship Director
James Beard Foundation Inc.
167 West 12th Street
New York, NY 10011
Phone: 212-675-4984 Ext. 311
Fax: 212-645-1438
E-mail: jamesbeardfound@hotmail.com

PETER KUMP MEMORIAL SCHOLARSHIP

One-time award towards tuition at an accredited or licensed culinary school of student's choice. Candidates must have a minimum of one year of experience in the culinary field, demonstrate financial need, and have at least a 3.0 GPA on a 4.0 scale.

Academic Fields/Career Goals: Culinary Arts.

Award: Scholarship for use in freshman year; not renewable. *Number:* up to 3. *Amount:* $4000.

Eligibility Requirements: Applicant must be high school student and planning to enroll or expecting to enroll full- or part-time at a four-year institution or university. Applicant must have 3.0 GPA or higher. Available to U.S. and non-U.S. citizens.

Application Requirements: Application, essay, financial need analysis, references, transcript. *Deadline:* May 15.

Contact: Caroline Stuart, Scholarship Director
James Beard Foundation Inc.
167 West 12th Street
New York, NY 10011
Phone: 212-675-4984 Ext. 311
Fax: 212-645-1438
E-mail: jamesbeardfound@hotmail.com

SPENCER'S RESTAURANT SCHOLARSHIP

One $5000 award is available to applicants who are high school seniors or graduates who plan to enroll or students who are already enrolled at least part-time in a course of study at a licensed or accredited culinary school.

Academic Fields/Career Goals: Culinary Arts.

Award: Scholarship for use in freshman, sophomore, junior, or senior years; not renewable. *Number:* 1. *Amount:* $5000.

Eligibility Requirements: Applicant must be enrolled or expecting to enroll full- or part-time at a two-year or four-year institution or university.

Application Requirements: Proof of residency. *Deadline:* May 15.

Contact: Diane Brown, Director, Educational and Community
Programming
James Beard Foundation Inc.
167 West 12th Street
New York, NY 10011
Phone: 212-627-1128
E-mail: dhbrown@jamesbeard.org

STEVEN SCHER MEMORIAL SCHOLARSHIP FOR ASPIRING RESTAURANTEURS

Two $5000 awards are available to applicants enrolled or accepted in a culinary or hospitality management program at an accredited institution. Applicants must detail their work experience, submit essay, and include a list of their top three favorite restaurants (noting their location) and explain why they have earned that ranking. One award is for use at an institution of the recipient's choice and the second is for use only at the French Culinary Institute in New York City. Special consideration will be given to career changers.

Academic Fields/Career Goals: Culinary Arts.

Award: Scholarship for use in freshman, sophomore, junior, or senior years; not renewable. *Number:* 2. *Amount:* $5000.

Eligibility Requirements: Applicant must be enrolled or expecting to enroll full- or part-time at a two-year or four-year institution or university.

Application Requirements: Essay, proof of residency. *Deadline:* May 15.

Contact: Diane Brown, Director, Educational and Community
Programming
James Beard Foundation Inc.
167 West 12th Street
New York, NY 10011
Phone: 212-627-1128
E-mail: dhbrown@jamesbeard.org

STUDIO AT THE MONTAGE RESORT & SPA SCHOLARSHIP

Up to two $2500 awards are available to applicants who are high school seniors or graduates who plan to enroll or students who are already enrolled at least part-time in a course of study at a licensed or accredited culinary school.

Academic Fields/Career Goals: Culinary Arts.

Award: Scholarship for use in freshman, sophomore, junior, or senior years; not renewable. *Number:* up to 2. *Amount:* $2500.

Eligibility Requirements: Applicant must be enrolled or expecting to enroll full- or part-time at a two-year or four-year institution or university.

Application Requirements: Proof of residency. *Deadline:* May 15.

Contact: Diane Brown, Director, Educational and Community
Programming
James Beard Foundation Inc.
167 West 12th Street
New York, NY 10011
Phone: 212-627-1128
E-mail: dhbrown@jamesbeard.org

T. J. BARTOLOTTA SCHOLARSHIP

Scholarship for students who are high school seniors or graduates who plan to enroll or students who are already enrolled at least part-time in a course of study at a licensed or accredited culinary school. Preference will be given to residents of Wisconsin or to those studying in a Wisconsin culinary arts program.

Academic Fields/Career Goals: Culinary Arts.

Award: Scholarship for use in freshman, sophomore, junior, or senior years; not renewable. *Number:* 1. *Amount:* $3750.

Eligibility Requirements: Applicant must be enrolled or expecting to enroll full- or part-time at a two-year or four-year institution or university.

Application Requirements: Proof of residency. *Deadline:* May 15.

Contact: Diane Brown, Director, Educational and Community
Programming
James Beard Foundation Inc.
167 West 12th Street
New York, NY 10011
Phone: 212-627-1128
E-mail: dhbrown@jamesbeard.org

ZOV'S BISTRO SCHOLARSHIP

Up to two $4000 awards available to applicants who are high school seniors or graduates who plan to enroll or students who are already enrolled at least part-time in a course of study at a licensed or accredited culinary school.

Academic Fields/Career Goals: Culinary Arts.

Award: Scholarship for use in freshman, sophomore, junior, or senior years; not renewable. *Number:* up to 2. *Amount:* $4000.

Eligibility Requirements: Applicant must be enrolled or expecting to enroll full- or part-time at a two-year or four-year institution or university.

Application Requirements: Proof of residency. *Deadline:* May 15.

Contact: Diane Brown, Director, Educational and Community
Programming
James Beard Foundation Inc.
167 West 12th Street
New York, NY 10011
Phone: 212-627-1128
E-mail: dhbrown@jamesbeard.org

LES DAMES D'ESCOFFIER INTERNATIONAL

http://www.ldei.org/

LES DAMES D'ESCOFFIER SCHOLARSHIP

One-time scholarship for women of all ages seeking training in the areas of food, wine, hospitality, nutrition, food technology, the arts of the table, and other fields. Scholarship valued at $2500 to $10,000. Deadline varies.

Academic Fields/Career Goals: Culinary Arts; Food Science/Nutrition; Food Service/Hospitality.

Award: Scholarship for use in freshman, sophomore, junior, senior, graduate, or postgraduate years; not renewable. *Number:* 3. *Amount:* $2500–$10,000.

Eligibility Requirements: Applicant must be enrolled or expecting to enroll full- or part-time at a two-year or four-year or technical institution or university and female. Available to U.S. and Canadian citizens.

Application Requirements: Application, essay, references, self-addressed stamped envelope, transcript. *Deadline:* varies.

Contact: Greg Jewell, Executive Director
Les Dames d'Escoffier International
KBC MPI Headquarters, PO Box 4961
Louisville, KY 40204
Phone: 502-456-1851
Fax: 502-456-1821
E-mail: gjewell@aecmanagement.com

MAINE RESTAURANT ASSOCIATION

http://www.mainerestaurant.com/

MAINE RESTAURANT ASSOCIATION EDUCATION FOUNDATION SCHOLARSHIP FUND

Scholarship available to students (Maine Residents Only) who wish to pursue higher education in culinary arts, restaurant, and hotel or hospitality management. Preference will be given to those in Maine-based institutions and those who intend to pursue a career in food service.

Academic Fields/Career Goals: Culinary Arts; Hospitality Management.

Award: Scholarship for use in freshman, sophomore, junior, or senior years; not renewable. *Number:* 1–8. *Amount:* $500–$2000.

Eligibility Requirements: Applicant must be enrolled or expecting to enroll full- or part-time at a two-year or four-year or technical institution or university and resident of Maine. Available to U.S. citizens.

Application Requirements: Application, essay, transcript. *Deadline:* May 1.

Contact: Becky Jacobson, Operations Manager
Maine Restaurant Association
Five Wade Street
PO Box 5060
Augusta, ME 04332-5060
Phone: 207-623-2178
E-mail: info@mainerestaurant.com

MAINE SCHOOL FOOD SERVICE ASSOCIATION (MSFSA) CONTINUING EDUCATION SCHOLARSHIP

http://www.mainesfsa.org/

MAINE SCHOOL FOOD SERVICE ASSOCIATION CONTINUING EDUCATION SCHOLARSHIP

Awarded to students from Maine enrolling in nutrition or culinary arts. It is also available to employees of school nutrition programs wishing to continue their education. Applicant can be a high school senior, college student, or member of MSFSA. Applicant must be attending an institution in Maine.

Academic Fields/Career Goals: Culinary Arts; Food Science/Nutrition; Food Service/Hospitality; Home Economics.

Award: Scholarship for use in freshman, sophomore, junior, senior, graduate, or postgraduate years; not renewable. *Number:* 1–4. *Amount:* $250–$1200.

Eligibility Requirements: Applicant must be enrolled or expecting to enroll full- or part-time at a two-year or four-year or technical institution or university; resident of Maine and studying in Maine. Available to U.S. citizens.

Application Requirements: Application, essay, resume, references, transcript, acceptance letter. *Deadline:* April 1.

Contact: Judith D. Campbell RD, Education Committee Chair
Maine School Food Service Association (MSFSA) Continuing Education Scholarship
9 Wentworth Drive
Scarborough, ME 04074
Phone: 207-730-4701
Fax: 207-730-4702

OREGON STUDENT ASSISTANCE COMMISSION

http://www.GetCollegeFunds.org/

OREGON WINE BROTHERHOOD SCHOLARSHIP

Award for residents of Oregon or Washington majoring in enology, viticulture, or culinary arts with an emphasis on wine. Must attend Chemeketa, Central Oregon, Lane, Mt. Hood, Southwestern Oregon, Umpqua, or Walla Walla Community Colleges, Southern Oregon and Oregon State Universities, or University of California at Davis. Must reapply annually for renewal.

Academic Fields/Career Goals: Culinary Arts; Food Science/Nutrition.

Award: Scholarship for use in freshman, sophomore, junior, or senior years; not renewable. *Number:* varies. *Amount:* varies.

Eligibility Requirements: Applicant must be enrolled or expecting to enroll full-time at a two-year or four-year institution or university and resident of Oregon or Washington. Available to U.S. citizens.

Application Requirements: Application, essay, financial need analysis, transcript, activities chart. *Deadline:* March 1.

Contact: Scholarship Coordinator
Oregon Student Assistance Commission
1500 Valley River Drive, Suite 100
Eugene, OR 97401-7020
Phone: 800-452-8807

STRAIGHTFORWARD MEDIA

http://www.straightforwardmedia.com/

STRAIGHTFORWARD MEDIA VOCATIONAL-TECHNICAL SCHOOL SCHOLARSHIP

• *See page 91*

WISCONSIN BAKERS ASSOCIATION (WBA)

http://www.umwba.org/

ROBERT W. HILLER SCHOLARSHIP FUND

Scholarship of $1000 awarded for students at all levels in a baking/pastry arts-related program that prepares candidates for a retail baking profession. Minimum 2.85 GPA required.

Academic Fields/Career Goals: Culinary Arts.

Award: Scholarship for use in freshman, sophomore, junior, senior, graduate, or postgraduate years; not renewable. *Number:* varies. *Amount:* $1000.

Eligibility Requirements: Applicant must be enrolled or expecting to enroll full-time at a four-year institution or university. Available to U.S. citizens.

Application Requirements: Application, essay, resume, references. *Deadline:* June 2.

Contact: Rebeca Borrero-Hoover, Scholarship Committee
Wisconsin Bakers Association (WBA)
8112 West Bluemound Road, Suite 71
Milwaukee, WI 53213
Phone: 414-258-5552
Fax: 414-258-5582
E-mail: information@umwba.org

WOMEN CHEFS AND RESTAURATEURS

http://www.womenchefs.org/

FRENCH CULINARY INSTITUTE/ITALIAN CULINARY EXPERIENCE SCHOLARSHIP

Scholarship intended for a culinary student wishing to specialize in Italian cuisine. Recipient must be a new enrollment and satisfy all entrance requirements of the FCI. Scholarship award is applied to total program fee.

Academic Fields/Career Goals: Culinary Arts; Food Service/Hospitality.

Award: Scholarship for use in freshman, sophomore, junior, senior, graduate, or postgraduate years; not renewable. *Number:* 1. *Amount:* $5000.

Eligibility Requirements: Applicant must be enrolled or expecting to enroll full-time at a four-year institution or university. Available to U.S. and non-U.S. citizens.

Application Requirements: Application, essay. *Fee:* $25. *Deadline:* March 31.

Contact: Dori Sacksteder, Director of Programs
Women Chefs and Restaurateurs
455 South Fourth Street, Suite 650
Louisville, KY 40202
Phone: 502-581-0300 Ext. 219
Fax: 502-589-3602
E-mail: dsacksteder@hqtrs.com

DENTAL HEALTH/ SERVICES

ALBERTA HERITAGE SCHOLARSHIP FUND

http://www.alis.alberta.ca/

ALBERTA HERITAGE SCHOLARSHIP FUND ABORIGINAL HEALTH CAREERS BURSARY

• *See page 137*

JASON LANG SCHOLARSHIP

Award of CAN$1000 to reward the outstanding academic achievement of Alberta postsecondary students who are studying full-time in Alberta. Must be a Canadian citizen or permanent resident and Alberta resident. Must be enrolled full-time in an undergraduate or professional program, such as law, medicine, pharmacy, or dentistry at an eligible Alberta post-secondary institution. Nominated by Awards Office at institution on the basis of achieving a minimum GPA of 3.2 in the previous academic year. May be awarded up to three times to one student. For additional information, see web site http://alis.alberta.ca.

Academic Fields/Career Goals: Dental Health/Services; Health and Medical Sciences; Law/Legal Services; Pharmacy.

Award: Scholarship for use in sophomore, junior, or senior years; not renewable.

Eligibility Requirements: Applicant must be Canadian citizen; enrolled or expecting to enroll full-time at a two-year or four-year or technical institution or university; resident of Alberta and studying in Alberta.

Application Requirements: Application, test scores, transcript. *Deadline:* varies.

Contact: Scholarship Committee
Alberta Heritage Scholarship Fund
9940 106th Street, Fourth Floor, Sterling Place
PO Box 28000, Station Main
Edmonton, AB T5J 4R4
Canada
Phone: 780-427-8640
E-mail: scholarships@gov.ab.ca

NORTHERN ALBERTA DEVELOPMENT COUNCIL BURSARY

Return service bursary awards CAN$6000 per year for up to two years to increase the number of trained professionals in Northern Alberta and to encourage students from Northern Alberta to obtain a postsecondary education. Must be residents of Alberta, and planning to enroll in a full-time postsecondary program in a field in demand in Northern Alberta. Fields in demand include: education, healthcare and medical, engineering and technical fields, social work. Applicants must also be within two years of completion of their postsecondary program. Students must live and work for one year in Northern Alberta for each year of assistance awarded. For additional information, go to web site http://alis.alberta.ca.

Academic Fields/Career Goals: Dental Health/Services; Education; Engineering/Technology; Health and Medical Sciences; Social Services.

Award: Scholarship for use in freshman, sophomore, junior, or senior years; not renewable.

Eligibility Requirements: Applicant must be Canadian citizen; enrolled or expecting to enroll full-time at a two-year or four-year or technical institution or university; resident of Alberta and studying in Alberta.

Application Requirements: Application, essay, financial need analysis, transcript. *Deadline:* May 15.

Contact: Scholarship Committee
Alberta Heritage Scholarship Fund
9940 106th Street, Fourth Floor, Sterling Place
PO Box 28000, Station Main
Edmonton, AB T5J 4R4
Canada
Phone: 780-427-8640
E-mail: scholarships@gov.ab.ca

AMERICAN ACADEMY OF ORAL AND MAXILLOFACIAL RADIOLOGY

http://www.aaomr.org/

CHARLES R. MORRIS STUDENT RESEARCH AWARD

Award to applicants from accredited programs performing research in oral and maxillofacial radiology. Applicant must be a full-time undergraduate or predoctoral student at the time of research, be nominated by the institution where research was carried out, and submit a manuscript detailing the research project.

Academic Fields/Career Goals: Dental Health/Services.

Award: Grant for use in junior, senior, or graduate years; not renewable. *Number:* 1. *Amount:* $1000.

Eligibility Requirements: Applicant must be enrolled or expecting to enroll full-time at a four-year institution or university. Available to U.S. and non-U.S. citizens.

Application Requirements: Application, references, manuscript. *Deadline:* June 16.

Contact: Dr. Michael K. Shrout, Executive Director
American Academy of Oral and Maxillofacial Radiology
Box 1010
Evans, GA 30809-1010
Phone: 706-271-2881
E-mail: mshrout@mcg.edu

AMERICAN DENTAL ASSISTANTS ASSOCIATION

http://www.dentalassistant.org/

JULIETTE A. SOUTHARD/ORAL B LABORATORIES SCHOLARSHIP

Leadership-based award available to students enrolled in an ADAA dental assistant's program. Proof of acceptance into ADAA program and two letters of reference are required.

Academic Fields/Career Goals: Dental Health/Services.

Award: Scholarship for use in freshman, sophomore, junior, senior, graduate, or postgraduate years; not renewable. *Number:* up to 10. *Amount:* varies.

Eligibility Requirements: Applicant must be enrolled or expecting to enroll full- or part-time at a two-year or four-year institution or university and must have an interest in leadership. Applicant or parent of applicant must be member of American Dental Assistants Association. Available to U.S. citizens.

Application Requirements: Application, essay, financial need analysis, references, transcript. *Deadline:* March 1.

Contact: Erek Armentrout, Membership Development Manager
American Dental Assistants Association
35 East Wacker Drive, Suite 1730
Chicago, IL 60601-2211
Phone: 312-541-1550
Fax: 312-541-1496
E-mail: earmentrout@adaa1.com

AMERICAN DENTAL ASSOCIATION (ADA) FOUNDATION

http://www.adafoundation.org/

AMERICAN DENTAL ASSOCIATION FOUNDATION DENTAL ASSISTING SCHOLARSHIP PROGRAM

Applicant must be enrolled as a full-time student with a minimum of 12 credit hours in a dental assistant program accredited by the Commission on Dental Accreditation of the American Dental Association. Must be a U.S. citizen, permanent resident is ineligible to apply. Must have an accumulative 3.5 GPA based on a 4.0 scale. Applicants must be recommended by the dental assisting program director at the school where accepted into the dental assisting program. Applicants must demonstrate a minimum financial need of $1000.

Academic Fields/Career Goals: Dental Health/Services.

Award: Scholarship for use in freshman year; not renewable. *Number:* up to 10. *Amount:* up to $1000.

Eligibility Requirements: Applicant must be enrolled or expecting to enroll full-time at a two-year or four-year institution. Applicant must have 3.5 GPA or higher. Available to U.S. citizens.

Application Requirements: Application, essay, financial need analysis, references. *Deadline:* April 23.

Contact: Rose Famularo, Coordinator
American Dental Association (ADA) Foundation
211 East Chicago Avenue
Chicago, IL 60611
Phone: 312-440-2763
E-mail: famularor@ada.org

AMERICAN DENTAL ASSOCIATION FOUNDATION DENTAL HYGIENE SCHOLARSHIP PROGRAM

Applicant must be enrolled full-time with a minimum of 12 Credit hours as a student in an accredited dental hygiene program accredited by the Commission of Dental Accreditation of the American Dental Association. Must be U.S. citizen, permanent resident is ineligible to apply. Must have a minimum 3.5 GPA on a 4.0 scale. Applicants must be recommended by the dental hygiene program director and may request application materials from that same individual at the school where they are currently enrolled as an entering final year student in a dental hygiene program. Applicants must demonstrate a minimum financial need of $1000.

Academic Fields/Career Goals: Dental Health/Services.

Award: Scholarship for use in senior year; not renewable. *Number:* up to 15. *Amount:* up to $1000.

Eligibility Requirements: Applicant must be enrolled or expecting to enroll full-time at a four-year institution or university. Applicant must have 3.5 GPA or higher. Available to U.S. citizens.

Application Requirements: Application, essay, financial need analysis, references. *Deadline:* April 23.

Contact: Rose Famularo, Coordinator
American Dental Association (ADA) Foundation
211 East Chicago Avenue
Chicago, IL 60611
Phone: 312-440-2763
E-mail: famularor@ada.org

AMERICAN DENTAL ASSOCIATION FOUNDATION DENTAL LAB TECHNOLOGY SCHOLARSHIP

Applicant must be enrolled as a full-time student with a minimum of 12 credit hours as a last-year student in a dental laboratory technology program accredited by the Commission on Dental Accreditation of the American Dental Association. Must be a U.S. citizen, permanent resident is ineligible to apply. Must have an accumulative minimum 3.5 GPA based on a 4.0 scale. Applicants must be recommended by the dental laboratory technology program director at the school where attending. Applicant must demonstrate a $1,000 financial need.

Academic Fields/Career Goals: Dental Health/Services.

Award: Scholarship for use in senior year; not renewable. *Number:* up to 5. *Amount:* up to $1000.

Eligibility Requirements: Applicant must be enrolled or expecting to enroll full-time at a four-year institution or university. Applicant must have 3.5 GPA or higher. Available to U.S. citizens.

Application Requirements: Application, essay, financial need analysis, references. *Deadline:* April 23.

Contact: Rose Famularo, Coordinator
American Dental Association (ADA) Foundation
211 East Chicago Avenue
Chicago, IL 60611
Phone: 312-440-2763
E-mail: famularor@ada.org

AMERICAN DENTAL ASSOCIATION FOUNDATION DENTAL STUDENT SCHOLARSHIP PROGRAM

One-time award for entering second-year students at a dental school accredited by the American Dental Association Commission on Dental Accreditation. Must have 3.0 GPA, and be enrolled full-time (minimum of 12 hours). Must show financial need and be a U.S. citizen, a permanent resident is ineligible to apply. Applicants may request application materials from associate dean for student affairs at the dental school where they are currently enrolled. An applicant must be recommended to the ADA Foundation by the school official.

Academic Fields/Career Goals: Dental Health/Services.

Award: Scholarship for use in sophomore year; not renewable. *Number:* up to 25. *Amount:* up to $2500.

Eligibility Requirements: Applicant must be enrolled or expecting to enroll full-time at a four-year institution or university. Applicant must have 3.0 GPA or higher. Available to U.S. citizens.

Application Requirements: Application, essay, financial need analysis, references. *Deadline:* October 4.

Contact: Rose Famularo, Coordinator
American Dental Association (ADA) Foundation
211 East Chicago Avenue
Chicago, IL 60611
Phone: 312-440-2763
E-mail: famularor@ada.org

AMERICAN DENTAL ASSOCIATION FOUNDATION UNDERREPRESENTED MINORITY DENTAL STUDENT SCHOLARSHIP PROGRAM

One-time scholarship award for entering second-year students at a dental school accredited by the American Dental Association Commission on Dental Accreditation of a minority group that is underrepresented in dental school enrollment. Based on financial need and academic achievement. Must be U.S. citizen, a permanent resident is ineligible to apply. Must be a full-time students (minimum 12 hours). Must have minimum 3.0 GPA. Applicants may request application materials from associate dean for student affairs at the school where they are currently enrolled and must be recommended by the school official. Applicants must demonstrate a minimum financial need of $2500.

Academic Fields/Career Goals: Dental Health/Services.

Award: Scholarship for use in sophomore year; not renewable. *Number:* up to 25. *Amount:* up to $2500.

Eligibility Requirements: Applicant must be American Indian/Alaska Native, Black (non-Hispanic), or Hispanic and enrolled or expecting to enroll full-time at a four-year institution or university. Applicant must have 3.0 GPA or higher. Available to U.S. citizens.

Application Requirements: Application, essay, financial need analysis, references. *Deadline:* October 4.

Contact: Rose Famularo, Coordinator
American Dental Association (ADA) Foundation
211 East Chicago Avenue
Chicago, IL 60611
Phone: 312-440-2763
E-mail: famularor@ada.org

AMERICAN DENTAL HYGIENISTS' ASSOCIATION (ADHA) INSTITUTE

http://www.adha.org/institute

ADHA INSTITUTE GENERAL SCHOLARSHIPS

One-time award to students enrolled in an accredited dental hygiene program in the United States. Must be a full-time student pursuing a certificate, associate, baccalaureate degree. Applicant must demonstrate a minimum GPA of 3.0 and completed one year in a dental hygiene curriculum. Must be an active ADHA member or student member of ADHA.

Academic Fields/Career Goals: Dental Health/Services.

Award: Scholarship for use in sophomore, junior, or senior years; not renewable. *Number:* 1. *Amount:* $1000.

Eligibility Requirements: Applicant must be enrolled or expecting to enroll full-time at a two-year or four-year or technical institution or university. Applicant or parent of applicant must be member of American Dental Hygienist's Association. Applicant must have 3.0 GPA or higher. Available to U.S. citizens.

Application Requirements: Application, essay, financial need analysis, references. *Deadline:* February 1.

Contact: Star Jackson, Executive Administrator
American Dental Hygienists' Association (ADHA) Institute
444 North Michigan Avenue
Suie 3400
Chicago, IL 60611
Phone: 312-440-8944
Fax: 312-440-6764
E-mail: starj@adha.net

AMERICAN DENTAL HYGIENISTS' ASSOCIATION INSTITUTE MINORITY SCHOLARSHIP

Nonrenewable awards for members of minority groups currently underrepresented in dental hygiene, including males. Must have minimum 3.0 GPA. Must have completed one year of a dental hygiene curriculum, and show financial need of at least $1500. ADHA of SADHA membership required. Refer to web site http://www.adha.org for more details.

Academic Fields/Career Goals: Dental Health/Services.

Award: Scholarship for use in sophomore, junior, or senior years; not renewable. *Number:* 2. *Amount:* $1500–$2000.

Eligibility Requirements: Applicant must be American Indian/Alaska Native, Asian/Pacific Islander, Black (non-Hispanic), or Hispanic and enrolled or expecting to enroll full-time at a two-year or four-year institution or university. Applicant or parent of applicant must be member of American Dental Hygienist's Association. Applicant must have 3.0 GPA or higher. Available to U.S. citizens.

Application Requirements: Application, financial need analysis, references. *Deadline:* May 1.

Contact: Star Jackson, Executive Administrator
American Dental Hygienists' Association (ADHA) Institute
444 North Michigan Avenue
Suie 3400
Chicago, IL 60611
Phone: 312-440-8944
Fax: 312-440-6764
E-mail: starj@adha.net

AMERICAN DENTAL HYGIENISTS' ASSOCIATION INSTITUTE RESEARCH GRANT

The purpose of this program is to promote the oral health of the public by providing funding to research projects specializing in dental hygiene: improving dental hygiene and practice, advance dental hygiene through the discovery and application of knowledge which includes original research, developmental prospects and qualitative and quantitative research, develop and expand upon the dental hygiene body of knowledge and promote the delivery of quality oral healthcare. Applicants must be a licensed dental hygienist or a student pursuing a dental hygiene degree and member of ADHA. Priority will be given to proposals addressing the ADHA National Research Agenda. Please refer to web site for further details http://www.adha.org/institute.

Academic Fields/Career Goals: Dental Health/Services.

Award: Grant for use in freshman, sophomore, junior, senior, or graduate years; not renewable. *Number:* 1. *Amount:* $1000–$10,000.

Eligibility Requirements: Applicant must be enrolled or expecting to enroll full-time at a four-year institution or university. Applicant or parent of applicant must be member of American Dental Hygienist's Association. Available to U.S. citizens.

Application Requirements: Application, grant proposal. *Deadline:* February 28.

Contact: Star Jackson, Executive Administrator
American Dental Hygienists' Association (ADHA) Institute
444 North Michigan Avenue
Suie 3400
Chicago, IL 60611
Phone: 312-440-8944
Fax: 312-440-6764
E-mail: starj@adha.net

AMERICAN DENTAL HYGIENISTS' ASSOCIATION PART-TIME SCHOLARSHIP

Awarded to a dental student pursuing a certificate, associate, baccalaureate, or graduate degree on a part-time basis. Must be an active ADHA member or student member of ADHA. Must have completed one year of dental hygiene curricula at an accredited dental hygiene program in United States. Must demonstrate GPA of at least 3.0, and financial need of $1500 or more.

Academic Fields/Career Goals: Dental Health/Services.

Award: Scholarship for use in sophomore, junior, senior, or graduate years; not renewable. *Number:* 1–1. *Amount:* $1500.

Eligibility Requirements: Applicant must be enrolled or expecting to enroll part-time at a two-year or four-year institution or university. Applicant or parent of applicant must be member of American Dental Hygienist's Association. Applicant must have 3.0 GPA or higher. Available to U.S. citizens.

Application Requirements: Application, essay, financial need analysis, references. *Deadline:* February 1.

Contact: Star Jackson, Executive Administrator
American Dental Hygienists' Association (ADHA) Institute
444 North Michigan Avenue
Suie 3400
Chicago, IL 60611
Phone: 312-440-8944
Fax: 312-440-6764
E-mail: starj@adha.net

COLGATE "BRIGHT SMILES, BRIGHT FUTURES" MINORITY SCHOLARSHIP

One time award for members of minority groups currently underrepresented in dental hygiene programs at the certificate educational level. Must be an active student member of ADHA. Applicant must have completed one year of dental hygiene curricula at an accredited dental hygiene program in United States. Applicant must demonstrate GPA of at least 3.0, and financial need of $1500 or more.

Academic Fields/Career Goals: Dental Health/Services.

Award: Scholarship for use in sophomore year; not renewable. *Number:* 1–2. *Amount:* $1250.

Eligibility Requirements: Applicant must be American Indian/Alaska Native, Asian/Pacific Islander, Black (non-Hispanic), or Hispanic and enrolled or expecting to enroll full-time at a two-year or technical institution. Applicant or parent of applicant must be member of American Dental Hygienist's Association. Applicant must have 3.0 GPA or higher. Available to U.S. citizens.

Application Requirements: Application, essay, financial need analysis, references. *Deadline:* February 1.

Contact: Star Jackson, Executive Administrator
American Dental Hygienists' Association (ADHA) Institute
444 North Michigan Avenue
Suie 3400
Chicago, IL 60611
Phone: 312-440-8944
Fax: 312-440-6764
E-mail: starj@adha.net

CREST ORAL-B LABORATORIES DENTAL HYGIENE SCHOLARSHIP

Scholarships to baccalaureate degree students who demonstrate intent to encourage professional excellence, promote quality research, and support dental hygiene through public and private education. Must be an active SADHA or ADHA member. Must have completed one year of dental hygiene curricula at an accredited dental hygiene program in United States. Must demonstrate GPA of at least 3.5, and financial need of $1500 or more.

Academic Fields/Career Goals: Dental Health/Services.

Award: Scholarship for use in sophomore, junior, or senior years; not renewable. *Number:* 1–2. *Amount:* $1000.

Eligibility Requirements: Applicant must be enrolled or expecting to enroll full-time at a four-year institution or university. Applicant or parent of applicant must be member of American Dental Hygienist's Association. Applicant must have 3.5 GPA or higher. Available to U.S. citizens.

Application Requirements: Application, essay, financial need analysis, references. *Deadline:* May 1.

Contact: Star Jackson, Executive Administrator
American Dental Hygienists' Association (ADHA) Institute
444 North Michigan Avenue
Suie 3400
Chicago, IL 60611
Phone: 312-440-8944
Fax: 312-440-6764
E-mail: starj@adha.net

DR. ALFRED C. FONES SCHOLARSHIP

One-time award to an applicant in the baccalaureate or graduate degree categories who intends to become a dental hygiene teacher/educator. Must have a minimum 3.0 GPA. Must have completed one year of dental hygiene curriculum at an accredited dental hygiene program in United States. Must demonstrate a financial need of $1500 or more. Must be an active ADHA member or student member of ADHA.

Academic Fields/Career Goals: Dental Health/Services.

Award: Scholarship for use in sophomore, junior, senior, or graduate years; not renewable. *Number:* 1–1. *Amount:* $1500.

Eligibility Requirements: Applicant must be enrolled or expecting to enroll full-time at a four-year institution or university. Applicant or parent of applicant must be member of American Dental Hygienist's Association. Applicant must have 3.0 GPA or higher. Available to U.S. citizens.

Application Requirements: Application, essay, financial need analysis, references. *Deadline:* February 1.

Contact: Star Jackson, Executive Administrator
American Dental Hygienists' Association (ADHA) Institute
444 North Michigan Avenue
Suie 3400
Chicago, IL 60611
Phone: 312-440-8944
Fax: 312-440-6764
E-mail: starj@adha.net

DR. HAROLD HILLENBRAND SCHOLARSHIP

One time award to an applicant who demonstrates specific academic excellence and outstanding clinical performance. Must have completed one year of dental hygiene curricula at an accredited dental hygiene program in United States. Must demonstrate a financial need of $1500 or more. Must be an active ADHA member or student member of ADHA. Must demonstrate GPA of at least 3.5.

Academic Fields/Career Goals: Dental Health/Services.

Award: Scholarship for use in sophomore, junior, senior, or graduate years; not renewable. *Number:* 1–1. *Amount:* $1500.

Eligibility Requirements: Applicant must be enrolled or expecting to enroll full-time at a four-year institution. Applicant or parent of applicant must be member of American Dental Hygienist's Association. Applicant must have 3.5 GPA or higher. Available to U.S. citizens.

Application Requirements: Application, essay, financial need analysis, references. *Deadline:* February 1.

Contact: Star Jackson, Executive Administrator
American Dental Hygienists' Association (ADHA) Institute
444 North Michigan Avenue
Suie 3400
Chicago, IL 60611
Phone: 312-440-8944
Fax: 312-440-6764
E-mail: starj@adha.net

IRENE E. NEWMAN SCHOLARSHIP

One time award to an applicant at the baccalaureate or graduate degree level who demonstrates strong potential in public health or community dental health. Must be an active ADHA member or student member of ADHA. Must have completed one year of dental hygiene curricula at an accredited dental hygiene program in United States. Applicant must demonstrate a GPA of at least 3.0. Must demonstrate a financial need of $1500 or more.

Academic Fields/Career Goals: Dental Health/Services; Public Health.

Award: Scholarship for use in sophomore, junior, senior, or graduate years; not renewable. *Number:* 1–1. *Amount:* $1500.

Eligibility Requirements: Applicant must be enrolled or expecting to enroll full-time at a four-year institution or university. Applicant or parent of applicant must be member of American Dental Hygienist's Association. Applicant must have 3.0 GPA or higher. Available to U.S. citizens.

Application Requirements: Application, essay, financial need analysis, references. *Deadline:* February 1.

Contact: Star Jackson, Executive Administrator
American Dental Hygienists' Association (ADHA) Institute
444 North Michigan Avenue
Suie 3400
Chicago, IL 60611
Phone: 312-440-8944
Fax: 312-440-6764
E-mail: starj@adha.net

MARGARET E. SWANSON SCHOLARSHIP

One time award to an applicant enrolled in a certificate/associate-level dental hygiene program who demonstrates exceptional organizational leadership potential. Must be an active student member of ADHA. Must have completed one year of dental hygiene curricula at an accredited dental hygiene program in United States. Must demonstrate GPA of at least 3.0, and financial need of $1500 or more.

Academic Fields/Career Goals: Dental Health/Services.

Award: Scholarship for use in sophomore year; not renewable. *Number:* 1–1. *Amount:* $1500.

Eligibility Requirements: Applicant must be enrolled or expecting to enroll full-time at a two-year or technical institution and must have an interest in leadership. Applicant or parent of applicant must be member of American Dental Hygienist's Association. Applicant must have 3.0 GPA or higher. Available to U.S. citizens.

Application Requirements: Application, essay, financial need analysis, references. *Deadline:* February 1.

Contact: Star Jackson, Executive Administrator
American Dental Hygienists' Association (ADHA) Institute
444 North Michigan Avenue
Suie 3400
Chicago, IL 60611
Phone: 312-440-8944
Fax: 312-440-6764
E-mail: starj@adha.net

MARSH AFFINITY GROUP SERVICES SCHOLARSHIP

Scholarships to applicants pursuing baccalaureate degrees in dental hygiene. Must be an active SADHA or ADHA member. Must have completed one year of dental hygiene curricula at an accredited dental hygiene program in United States. Must demonstrate GPA between 3.0 and 3.5, and financial need of $1500 or more.

Academic Fields/Career Goals: Dental Health/Services.

Award: Scholarship for use in sophomore, junior, or senior years; not renewable. *Number:* 1. *Amount:* $1000.

Eligibility Requirements: Applicant must be enrolled or expecting to enroll full-time at a four-year institution or university. Applicant or parent of applicant must be member of American Dental Hygienist's Association. Available to U.S. citizens.

Application Requirements: Application, essay, financial need analysis, references. *Deadline:* May 1.

Contact: Star Jackson, Executive Administrator
American Dental Hygienists' Association (ADHA) Institute
444 North Michigan Avenue
Suie 3400
Chicago, IL 60611
Phone: 312-440-8944
Fax: 312-440-6764
E-mail: starj@adha.net

SIGMA PHI ALPHA UNDERGRADUATE SCHOLARSHIP

Awarded to an outstanding Sigma Phi Alpha member pursuing a certificate/associate or baccalaureate degree at a school with an active chapter of the Sigma Phi Alpha Dental Hygiene Honor Society. Applicant must demonstrate GPA of at least 3.5. Must have completed one year of dental hygiene curricula at an accredited dental hygiene program in United States. Must demonstrate a financial need of $1500 or more. Must be an active SADHA or ADHA member.

Academic Fields/Career Goals: Dental Health/Services.

Award: Scholarship for use in sophomore, junior, or senior years; not renewable. *Number:* 1–1. *Amount:* $1000.

Eligibility Requirements: Applicant must be enrolled or expecting to enroll full-time at a two-year or four-year or technical institution or university. Applicant or parent of applicant must be member of American Dental Hygienist's Association. Applicant must have 3.5 GPA or higher. Available to U.S. citizens.

Application Requirements: Application, essay, financial need analysis, references. *Deadline:* February 1.

Contact: Star Jackson, Executive Administrator
American Dental Hygienists' Association (ADHA) Institute
444 North Michigan Avenue
Suie 3400
Chicago, IL 60611
Phone: 312-440-8944
Fax: 312-440-6764
E-mail: starj@adha.net

WILMA MOTLEY CALIFORNIA MERIT SCHOLARSHIP

Three scholarships available annually to individuals pursuing an certificate/associate, baccalaureate, degree completion in dental hygiene, Registered Dental Hygienist in Alternative Practice (RDHAP) or masters's or doctorate degree in dental hygiene or related field. Applicants must be attend a dental hygiene program in California. Must demonstrate leadership experience and a minim GPA of 3.5. Awarded solely on merit: no financial need requirement.

Academic Fields/Career Goals: Dental Health/Services.

Award: Scholarship for use in sophomore, junior, senior, or graduate years; not renewable. *Number:* 1–3. *Amount:* $2000.

Eligibility Requirements: Applicant must be enrolled or expecting to enroll full-time at a two-year or four-year institution or university; studying in California and must have an interest in leadership. Applicant or parent of applicant must be member of American Dental Hygienist's Association. Applicant must have 3.5 GPA or higher. Available to U.S. citizens.

Application Requirements: Application, essay, references. *Deadline:* February 1.

Contact: Star Jackson, Executive Administrator
American Dental Hygienists' Association (ADHA) Institute
444 North Michigan Avenue
Suie 3400
Chicago, IL 60611
Phone: 312-440-8944
Fax: 312-440-6764
E-mail: starj@adha.net

AMERICAN LEGION AUXILIARY DEPARTMENT OF WYOMING

AMERICAN LEGION AUXILIARY DEPARTMENT OF WYOMING PAST PRESIDENTS' PARLEY HEALTH CARE SCHOLARSHIP

Scholarship of $300 is available for a student in the human healthcare field. Must be a resident of Wyoming, a U.S. citizen, and attend a school in Wyoming. Minimum 3.5 GPA required.

Academic Fields/Career Goals: Dental Health/Services; Health and Medical Sciences; Nursing; Therapy/Rehabilitation.

Award: Scholarship for use in sophomore year; not renewable. *Number:* up to 2. *Amount:* $300.

Eligibility Requirements: Applicant must be enrolled or expecting to enroll full-time at a two-year or four-year or technical institution or university; resident of Wyoming and studying in Wyoming. Applicant must have 3.5 GPA or higher. Available to U.S. citizens.

Application Requirements: Application, financial need analysis, transcript. *Deadline:* June 1.

Contact: Sonja Wright, Department Secretary
American Legion Auxiliary Department of Wyoming
PO Box 2198
Gillette, WY 82717
Phone: 307-686-7137
Fax: 307-686-7137
E-mail: deptwy@collinscom.net

AMERICAN MEDICAL TECHNOLOGISTS

http://www.amt1.com/

AMERICAN MEDICAL TECHNOLOGISTS STUDENT SCHOLARSHIP

One-time award for the undergraduate study of medical technology, medical laboratory technician, office laboratory technician, phlebotomy, or medical, dental assisting. Include SASE.

Academic Fields/Career Goals: Dental Health/Services; Health and Medical Sciences.

Award: Scholarship for use in freshman, sophomore, junior, or senior years; not renewable. *Number:* 5. *Amount:* $500.

Eligibility Requirements: Applicant must be enrolled or expecting to enroll full- or part-time at a two-year or four-year institution or university. Available to U.S. citizens.

Application Requirements: Application, essay, financial need analysis, references, self-addressed stamped envelope, transcript. *Deadline:* April 1.

Contact: Linda Kujbida, Scholarship Coordinator
American Medical Technologists
10700 West Higgins Road, Suite 150
Rosemont, IL 60018
Phone: 847-823-5169
Fax: 847-823-0458
E-mail: amtmail@aol.com

ARRL FOUNDATION INC.

http://www.arrl.org/

CAROLE J. STREETER, KB9JBR SCHOLARSHIP

One $750 award is available to a student with a Technician class or higher radio license. Preference for students studying in the health and healing arts fields. Applicants with basic Morse Code proficiency are preferred.

Academic Fields/Career Goals: Dental Health/Services; Health and Medical Sciences; Nursing; Oncology; Optometry; Osteopathy; Therapy/Rehabilitation.

Award: Scholarship for use in freshman, sophomore, junior, senior, or graduate years; not renewable. *Number:* 1. *Amount:* $750.

Eligibility Requirements: Applicant must be enrolled or expecting to enroll full- or part-time at a two-year or four-year institution or university and must have an interest in amateur radio. Available to U.S. citizens.

Application Requirements: Application, transcript. *Deadline:* February 1.

Contact: Ms. Mary Hobart, Secretary
ARRL Foundation Inc.
225 Main Street
Newington, CT 06111-1494
Phone: 860-594-0397
E-mail: k1mmh@arrl.org

ASSOCIATION ON AMERICAN INDIAN AFFAIRS, INC.

http://www.indian-affairs.org/

ELIZABETH AND SHERMAN ASCHE MEMORIAL SCHOLARSHIP FUND

• *See page 83*

BETHESDA LUTHERAN COMMUNITIES

http://www.bethesdalutherancommunities.org/

DEVELOPMENTAL DISABILITIES SCHOLASTIC ACHIEVEMENT SCHOLARSHIP FOR COLLEGE STUDENTS WHO ARE LUTHERAN

One-time award for Lutheran students who have completed sophomore year in studies related to developmental disabilities. Awards of up to $3000. 3.0 GPA required.

Academic Fields/Career Goals: Dental Health/Services; Education; Health Administration; Health and Medical Sciences; Health Information Management/Technology; Humanities; Religion/Theology; Social Services; Special Education; Therapy/Rehabilitation.

Award: Scholarship for use in junior or senior years; not renewable. *Number:* 1–2. *Amount:* up to $3000.

Eligibility Requirements: Applicant must be Lutheran and enrolled or expecting to enroll full-time at a four-year institution or university. Applicant must have 3.0 GPA or higher. Available to U.S. and Canadian citizens.

Application Requirements: Application, essay, resume, references, transcript. *Deadline:* April 15.

Contact: Pam Bergen, Executive Assistant for Mission Advancement
Bethesda Lutheran Communities
600 Hoffmann Drive
Watertown, WI 53094-6294
Phone: 920-206-4410
Fax: 920-206-7706
E-mail: pam.bergen@mailblc.org

DELAWARE STATE DENTAL SOCIETY

http://www.delawarestatedentalsociety.org/

G. LAYTON GRIER SCHOLARSHIP

One-time award for Delaware residents to study dentistry. Freshmen are not eligible. Must be a U.S. citizen. Student must have financial need and good academic standing.

Academic Fields/Career Goals: Dental Health/Services.

Award: Scholarship for use in sophomore, junior, or senior years; not renewable. *Number:* 3. *Amount:* $1000.

Eligibility Requirements: Applicant must be enrolled or expecting to enroll full-time at a four-year institution or university and resident of Delaware. Available to U.S. citizens.

Application Requirements: Application, financial need analysis, interview, references, transcript, proof of residency, biographical sketch. *Deadline:* March 1.

Contact: Delaware State Dental Society
200 Continental Drive, Suite 111
Wilmington, DE 19713
Phone: 302-368-7634
Fax: 302-368-7669
E-mail: dedentalsociety@gmail.com

HELLENIC UNIVERSITY CLUB OF PHILADELPHIA

http://www.hucphila.org/

NICHOLAS S. HETOS, DDS MEMORIAL GRADUATE SCHOLARSHIP

$2000 scholarships for a senior undergraduate or graduate student with financial need pursuing studies leading to a Doctor of Dental Medicine or Doctor of Dental Surgery degree. Must be a U.S. citizen of Greek descent and a resident of particular counties in NJ or PA.

Academic Fields/Career Goals: Dental Health/Services.

Award: Scholarship for use in senior or graduate years; not renewable. *Number:* up to 1. *Amount:* $2000.

Eligibility Requirements: Applicant must be of Greek heritage; enrolled or expecting to enroll full-time at a four-year institution or university and resident of New Jersey or Pennsylvania. Available to U.S. citizens.

Application Requirements: Application, financial need analysis, transcript. *Deadline:* April 21.

Contact: Anna Hadgis, Scholarship Chairman
Hellenic University Club of Philadelphia
PO Box 42199
Philadelphia, PA 19101-2199
Phone: 610-613-4310
E-mail: hucphila@yahoo.com

HISPANIC DENTAL ASSOCIATION FOUNDATION

http://www.hdassoc.org/

DR. JUAN D. VILLARREAL/HISPANIC DENTAL ASSOCIATION FOUNDATION

Scholarship offered to Hispanic U.S. students who have been accepted into or are currently enrolled in an accredited dental or dental hygiene program in the state of Texas. Scholarship will obligate the grantees to complete the current year of their dental or dental hygiene program. Scholastic achievement, leadership skills, community service and commitment to improving the health of the Hispanic community will all be considered. Must be a current member of the Hispanic Dental Association.

Academic Fields/Career Goals: Dental Health/Services.

Award: Scholarship for use in freshman, sophomore, junior, or senior years; not renewable. *Number:* up to 3. *Amount:* $500–$1000.

Eligibility Requirements: Applicant must be of Hispanic heritage; enrolled or expecting to enroll full-time at a two-year or four-year institution or university; resident of Texas and studying in Texas. Available to U.S. citizens.

Application Requirements: Application, essay, references, transcript. *Deadline:* June 1.

Contact: Rita Brummett, Scholarship Committee
Hispanic Dental Association Foundation
3085 Stevenson Drive, Suite 200
Springfield, IL 62703
Phone: 217-529-6517
Fax: 217-529-9120

PROCTOR AND GAMBLE ORAL CARE AND HDA FOUNDATION SCHOLARSHIP

Scholarships available to Hispanic students entering into their first year of an accredited dental, dental hygiene, dental assisting, or dental technician program. Scholastic achievement, community service, leadership, and commitment to improving health of the Hispanic community will all be considered. Must be member of the Hispanic Dental Association.

Academic Fields/Career Goals: Dental Health/Services.

Award: Scholarship for use in freshman year; not renewable. *Number:* up to 15. *Amount:* up to $1000.

Eligibility Requirements: Applicant must be high school student and planning to enroll or expecting to enroll full-time at a two-year or technical institution. Available to U.S. citizens.

Application Requirements: Application, essay, references, transcript. *Deadline:* June 1.

Contact: Rita Brummett, Associate Director
Hispanic Dental Association Foundation
3085 Stevenson Drive, Suite 200
Springfield, IL 62703
Phone: 217-529-6517
Fax: 217-529-9120
E-mail: rbrummett@hdassoc.org

INDIAN HEALTH SERVICES, UNITED STATES DEPARTMENT OF HEALTH AND HUMAN SERVICES

http://www.ihs.gov/

INDIAN HEALTH SERVICE HEALTH PROFESSIONS PRE-GRADUATE SCHOLARSHIPS

Renewable scholarship for Native American students who are enrolled either part- or full-time in courses leading to a bachelor degree in the areas of pre-medicine or pre-dentistry. Must intend to serve Indian people upon completion of professional healthcare education. Minimum 2.0 GPA required.

Academic Fields/Career Goals: Dental Health/Services; Health and Medical Sciences.

Award: Scholarship for use in freshman, sophomore, junior, or senior years; renewable. *Number:* varies. *Amount:* varies.

Eligibility Requirements: Applicant must be American Indian/Alaska Native and enrolled or expecting to enroll full- or part-time at a two-year or four-year or technical institution or university. Available to U.S. citizens.

Application Requirements: Application, applicant must enter a contest, essay, references, transcript, proof of descent. *Deadline:* February 28.

Contact: Dawn Kelly, Branch Chief
Indian Health Services, United States Department of Health and Human Services
801 Thompson Avenue, Suite 120
Rockville, MD 20852
Phone: 301-443-6197
Fax: 301-443-6048
E-mail: dawn.kelly@ihs.gov

INTERNATIONAL ORDER OF THE KING'S DAUGHTERS AND SONS

http://www.iokds.org/

HEALTH CAREERS SCHOLARSHIP

Award for students preparing for careers in medicine, dentistry, pharmacy, physical or occupational therapy, and medical technologies. Must be a U.S. or Canadian citizen, enrolled full-time in a school accredited in the field involved and located in the U.S. or Canada. For all students, except those preparing for an RN degree, application must be for at least the third year of college. RN students must have completed the first year of schooling. Premedicine students are not eligible to apply. For those students seeking degrees of MD or DDS application must be for at least the second year of medical or dental school. Each applicant must supply proof of acceptance in the school involved.

Academic Fields/Career Goals: Dental Health/Services; Health and Medical Sciences; Nursing; Therapy/Rehabilitation.

Award: Scholarship for use in sophomore, junior, senior, or graduate years; not renewable. *Number:* 40–50. *Amount:* $500–$1000.

Eligibility Requirements: Applicant must be enrolled or expecting to enroll full-time at a four-year institution or university. Available to U.S. and Canadian citizens.

Application Requirements: Application, photo, resume, references, self-addressed stamped envelope, transcript, itemized budget. *Deadline:* varies.

Contact: Director, Health Careers Department
International Order of the King's Daughters and Sons
PO Box 1017
Chautauqua, NY 14722-1017
Phone: 716-357-4951

MARYLAND ASSOCIATION OF PRIVATE COLLEGES AND CAREER SCHOOLS

http://www.mapccs.org/

MARYLAND ASSOCIATION OF PRIVATE COLLEGES AND CAREER SCHOOLS SCHOLARSHIP
• *See page 153*

MARYLAND STATE HIGHER EDUCATION COMMISSION

http://www.mhec.state.md.us/

GRADUATE AND PROFESSIONAL SCHOLARSHIP PROGRAM-MARYLAND

Graduate and professional scholarships provide need-based financial assistance to students attending a Maryland school of medicine, dentistry, law, pharmacy, social work, or nursing. Funds are provided to specific Maryland colleges and universities. Students must demonstrate financial need and be Maryland residents. Contact institution financial aid office for more information.

Academic Fields/Career Goals: Dental Health/Services; Health and Medical Sciences; Law/Legal Services; Nursing; Social Services.

Award: Scholarship for use in freshman, sophomore, junior, or senior years; renewable. *Number:* up to 584. *Amount:* $1000–$5000.

Eligibility Requirements: Applicant must be enrolled or expecting to enroll full- or part-time at a four-year institution or university; resident of Maryland and studying in Maryland. Available to U.S. citizens.

Application Requirements: Application, financial need analysis, contact institution financial aid office. *Deadline:* March 1.

Contact: Monica Wheatley, Program Manager
Maryland State Higher Education Commission
839 Bestgate Road, Suite 400
Annapolis, MD 21401
Phone: 410-260-4560
Fax: 410-260-3202
E-mail: mwheatle@mhec.state.md.us

MISSOURI DEPARTMENT OF HEALTH AND SENIOR SERVICES

http://www.dhss.mo.gov/

PRIMARY CARE RESOURCE INITIATIVE FOR MISSOURI LOAN PROGRAM
• *See page 136*

NATIONAL ARAB AMERICAN MEDICAL ASSOCIATION

http://www.naama.com/

FOUNDATION SCHOLARSHIP

Scholarship of $1000 each to qualified students of Arabic extraction enrolled in a U.S. or Canadian medical, osteopathic, or dental school.

Academic Fields/Career Goals: Dental Health/Services; Health and Medical Sciences; Osteopathy.

Award: Scholarship for use in freshman, sophomore, junior, senior, or graduate years; not renewable. *Number:* 2. *Amount:* $1000.

Eligibility Requirements: Applicant must be of Arab heritage and enrolled or expecting to enroll full-time at a four-year institution or university. Applicant must have 3.0 GPA or higher. Available to U.S. and Canadian citizens.

Application Requirements: Application, essay, financial need analysis, transcript. *Deadline:* July 1.

Contact: Mouhanad Hammami, Executive Director
National Arab American Medical Association
801 South Adams Road, Suite 208
Birmingham, MI 48009
Phone: 248-646-3661
Fax: 248-646-0617
E-mail: naama@naama.com

NATIONAL DENTAL ASSOCIATION FOUNDATION

http://www.ndaonline.org/

NATIONAL DENTAL ASSOCIATION FOUNDATION COLGATE-PALMOLIVE SCHOLARSHIP PROGRAM (UNDERGRADUATES)

A scholarship of up to $1000 is given to sophomores through juniors in a dental school who are under-represented minority students. Applicants should be a member of NDA. Number of scholarships granted varies.

Academic Fields/Career Goals: Dental Health/Services.

Award: Scholarship for use in sophomore, junior, or senior years; not renewable. *Number:* up to 100. *Amount:* $700–$1000.

Eligibility Requirements: Applicant must be American Indian/Alaska Native, Asian/Pacific Islander, Black (non-Hispanic), or Hispanic and enrolled or expecting to enroll full-time at a four-year institution or university. Available to U.S. citizens.

Application Requirements: Application, financial need analysis, resume, references, transcript, letter of request. *Deadline:* May 15.

Contact: Roosevelt Brown, President
National Dental Association Foundation
3517 16th Street, NW
Washington, DC 20010
Phone: 501-681-6110
Fax: 541-376-4008
E-mail: rbndaf1@comcast.net

NEW MEXICO COMMISSION ON HIGHER EDUCATION

http://www.hed.state.nm.us/

ALLIED HEALTH STUDENT LOAN PROGRAM-NEW MEXICO

Award to New Mexico residents studying in New Mexico to increase the number of physician assistants in areas of the state which have experienced shortages of health practitioners. Provides educational loans to students seeking certification/licensers in an eligible health field. As a condition of each loan, the student must declare intent to practice as a health professional in a designated shortage area. For every year of service, a portion of the loan will be forgiven.

Academic Fields/Career Goals: Dental Health/Services; Health and Medical Sciences; Nursing; Therapy/Rehabilitation.

Award: Forgivable loan for use in freshman, sophomore, junior, or senior years; renewable. *Number:* 1–40. *Amount:* up to $12,000.

Eligibility Requirements: Applicant must be enrolled or expecting to enroll full- or part-time at a four-year institution or university; resident of New Mexico and studying in New Mexico. Available to U.S. citizens.

Application Requirements: Application, financial need analysis, transcript, FAFSA. *Deadline:* July 1.

Contact: Theresa Acker, Financial Aid Division
New Mexico Commission on Higher Education
1068 Cerrillos Road
Santa Fe, NM 87505-1650
Phone: 505-476-6506
Fax: 505-476-6511
E-mail: theresa.acker@state.nm.us

NEW YORK STATE EDUCATION DEPARTMENT

http://www.highered.nysed.gov/

REGENTS PROFESSIONAL OPPORTUNITY SCHOLARSHIP
• *See page 69*

NORTH CAROLINA STATE EDUCATION ASSISTANCE AUTHORITY

http://www.ncseaa.edu/

NORTH CAROLINA STUDENT LOAN PROGRAM FOR HEALTH, SCIENCE, AND MATHEMATICS

Renewable award for North Carolina residents studying health-related fields, or science or math education. Based on merit, need, and promise of service as a health professional or educator in an under-served area of North Carolina. Need two co-signers. Submit surety statement.

Academic Fields/Career Goals: Dental Health/Services; Health Administration; Health and Medical Sciences; Nursing; Physical Sciences; Therapy/Rehabilitation.

Award: Forgivable loan for use in freshman, sophomore, junior, senior, or graduate years; renewable. *Number:* 1. *Amount:* $3000–$8500.

Eligibility Requirements: Applicant must be enrolled or expecting to enroll full-time at a two-year or four-year institution or university and resident of North Carolina. Available to U.S. citizens.

Application Requirements: Application, financial need analysis, transcript. *Deadline:* June 1.

Contact: Edna Williams, Manager, Selection and Origination
North Carolina State Education Assistance Authority
PO Box 14223
Research Triangle Park, NC 27709
Phone: 800-700-1775 Ext. 4658
E-mail: eew@ncseaa.edu

OREGON STUDENT ASSISTANCE COMMISSION

http://www.GetCollegeFunds.org/

CLARK-PHELPS SCHOLARSHIP

Award for high school graduates who are residents of Oregon or Alaska and are studying nursing (undergraduate or graduate), dentistry, or medicine. Must be enrolled in a public institution in Oregon, with preference for Oregon Health & Science University, and working toward a 4-year degree or graduate degree. Must reapply annually for award renewal.

Academic Fields/Career Goals: Dental Health/Services; Health and Medical Sciences; Nursing.

Award: Scholarship for use in freshman, sophomore, junior, senior, or graduate years; not renewable.

Eligibility Requirements: Applicant must be enrolled or expecting to enroll full-time at a four-year institution or university; resident of Alaska or Oregon and studying in Oregon. Available to U.S. citizens.

Application Requirements: Application, essay, financial need analysis, transcript, activities chart. *Deadline:* March 1.

Contact: Director of Grant Programs
Oregon Student Assistance Commission
1500 Valley River Drive, Suite 100
Eugene, OR 97401-7020
Phone: 800-452-8807

STRAIGHTFORWARD MEDIA

http://www.straightforwardmedia.com/

STRAIGHTFORWARD MEDIA MEDICAL PROFESSIONS SCHOLARSHIP

Scholarship of $500 available to full-time students in any health-related field. Awarded four times per year. Deadlines: March 31, June 30, September 30, and December 31.

Academic Fields/Career Goals: Dental Health/Services; Environmental Health; Health Administration; Health and Medical Sciences; Health Information Management/Technology; Nursing; Occupational Safety and Health; Oncology; Optometry; Osteopathy; Pharmacy; Therapy/Rehabilitation.

Award: Scholarship for use in freshman, sophomore, junior, or senior years; not renewable. *Number:* 4. *Amount:* $500.

Eligibility Requirements: Applicant must be enrolled or expecting to enroll full- or part-time at a two-year or four-year or technical institution or university. Available to U.S. and non-U.S. citizens.

Application Requirements: Essay. *Deadline:* varies.

Contact: Scholarship Committee
StraightForward Media
508 7th Street
Suite 202
Rapid City, SD 57701
Phone: 605-348-3042

STRAIGHTFORWARD MEDIA VOCATIONAL-TECHNICAL SCHOOL SCHOLARSHIP
• See page 91

SUPREME GUARDIAN COUNCIL, INTERNATIONAL ORDER OF JOB'S DAUGHTERS

http://www.iojd.org/

GROTTO SCHOLARSHIP

Scholarships of $1500 to aid Job's Daughters students of outstanding ability whom have a sincerity of purpose. High school seniors, or graduates, junior college, technical school, or college students who are in early graduation programs, and pursuing an education in dentistry, preferably with some training in the handicapped field are eligible to apply.

Academic Fields/Career Goals: Dental Health/Services.

Award: Scholarship for use in freshman, sophomore, junior, senior, graduate, or postgraduate years; not renewable. *Number:* 1. *Amount:* $1500.

Eligibility Requirements: Applicant must be age 18-30; enrolled or expecting to enroll full- or part-time at a two-year or four-year or technical institution or university and single female. Applicant or parent of applicant must be member of Jobs Daughters. Available to U.S. and non-U.S. citizens.

Application Requirements: Application, essay, references, transcript. *Deadline:* April 30.

Contact: Christal Bindrich, Scholarship Committee Chairman
Supreme Guardian Council, International Order of Job's Daughters
5351 South Butterfield Way
Greenfield, WI 53221
Phone: 414-423-0016
E-mail: christalbindrich@wi.rr.com

U. S. DEPARTMENT OF HEALTH AND HUMAN SERVICES

http://www.hhs.gov/about/whatwedo.html/

U. S. PUBLIC HEALTH SERVICE-HEALTH RESOURCES AND SERVICES ADMINISTRATION, BUREAU OF HEALTH PROFESSIONS SCHOLARSHIPS FOR DISADVANTAGED STUDENTS

One-time award for full-time students from disadvantaged backgrounds enrolled in health professions and nursing programs. Institution must apply for funding and must be eligible to receive SDS funds. Students must contact financial aid office to apply.

Academic Fields/Career Goals: Dental Health/Services; Health and Medical Sciences; Nursing; Therapy/Rehabilitation.

Award: Scholarship for use in freshman, sophomore, junior, senior, or graduate years; not renewable. *Number:* up to 400. *Amount:* varies.

Eligibility Requirements: Applicant must be enrolled or expecting to enroll full-time at a two-year or four-year institution or university. Available to U.S. citizens.

Application Requirements: Application, financial need analysis. *Deadline:* varies.

Contact: Andrea Stampone, Scholarship Coordinator
U. S. Department of Health and Human Services
Division of Health Careers Diversity Development, 5600 Fishers Lane, Parklawn Bu
Rockville, MD 20857
Phone: 301-443-4776
Fax: 301-446-0846
E-mail: callcenter@hrsa.gov

DRAFTING

MIDWEST ROOFING CONTRACTORS ASSOCIATION

http://www.mrca.org/

MRCA FOUNDATION SCHOLARSHIP PROGRAM
• *See page 102*

NASA'S VIRGINIA SPACE GRANT CONSORTIUM

http://www.vsgc.odu.edu/

VIRGINIA STEM COMMUNITY COLLEGE SCHOLARSHIPS
• *See page 96*

NATIONAL ASSOCIATION OF WOMEN IN CONSTRUCTION

http://www.nawic.org/

NAWIC UNDERGRADUATE SCHOLARSHIPS
• *See page 102*

PROFESSIONAL CONSTRUCTION ESTIMATORS ASSOCIATION

http://www.pcea.org/

TED WILSON MEMORIAL SCHOLARSHIP FOUNDATION
• *See page 179*

EARTH SCIENCE

ALASKA GEOLOGICAL SOCIETY INC.

http://www.alaskageology.org/

ALASKA GEOLOGICAL SOCIETY SCHOLARSHIP

Scholarship available for a full-time junior or senior undergraduate or graduate student enrolled at any Alaska university with academic emphasis in earth sciences.

Academic Fields/Career Goals: Earth Science.

Award: Scholarship for use in junior, senior, or graduate years; not renewable. *Number:* 3–6. *Amount:* $500–$1500.

Eligibility Requirements: Applicant must be enrolled or expecting to enroll full-time at a four-year institution or university and studying in Alaska. Available to U.S. and non-U.S. citizens.

Application Requirements: Financial need analysis, references, transcript, cover letter, thesis proposal (for graduate students). *Deadline:* March 20.

Contact: Micaela Weeks, Scholarship Committee Chair
Alaska Geological Society Inc.
PO Box 101288
Anchorage, AK 99510-1288
Phone: 907-564-5635
E-mail: micaela.weeks@bp.com

AMERICAN GEOLOGICAL INSTITUTE

http://www.agiweb.org/

AMERICAN GEOLOGICAL INSTITUTE MINORITY SCHOLARSHIP

Scholarship available only to students currently enrolled in an accredited institution as an undergraduate or graduate student majoring in geoscience, including the geoscience sub-disciplines of geology, geophysics, geochemistry, hydrology, meteorology, physical oceanography, planetary geology, or earth-science education. Verifiable ethnic minority status as Black, Hispanic, or Native American is required. For more information, visit web site http://www.agiweb.org/mpp.

Academic Fields/Career Goals: Earth Science; Hydrology; Meteorology/Atmospheric Science; Oceanography.

Award: Scholarship for use in sophomore, junior, or senior years; not renewable. *Number:* 20–30. *Amount:* $250–$3000.

Eligibility Requirements: Applicant must be American Indian/Alaska Native, Asian/Pacific Islander, Black (non-Hispanic), or Hispanic and enrolled or expecting to enroll full-time at a two-year or four-year institution or university. Available to U.S. citizens.

Application Requirements: Application, essay, references, test scores, transcript. *Deadline:* March 13.

Contact: Cindy Martinez, Geo-Science Workforce Specialist
American Geological Institute
4220 King Street
Alexandria, VA 22302-1507
Phone: 703-379-2480 Ext. 244
E-mail: cmm@agiweb.org

AMERICAN INDIAN SCIENCE AND ENGINEERING SOCIETY

http://www.aises.org/

A.T. ANDERSON MEMORIAL SCHOLARSHIP PROGRAM
• *See page 93*

ARIZONA HYDROLOGICAL SOCIETY

http://www.azhydrosoc.org/

ARIZONA HYDROLOGICAL SOCIETY SCHOLARSHIP

One-time award to outstanding undergraduate or graduate students who have demonstrated academic excellence in water resources related fields as a means of encouraging them to continue to develop as water resources professionals. Must be a resident of Arizona and be enrolled in a postsecondary Arizona institution.

Academic Fields/Career Goals: Earth Science; Hydrology; Natural Resources; Nuclear Science; Science, Technology, and Society.

Award: Scholarship for use in sophomore, junior, senior, or graduate years; not renewable. *Number:* 3. *Amount:* $3000.

Eligibility Requirements: Applicant must be enrolled or expecting to enroll full-time at a two-year or four-year or technical institution or university; resident of Arizona and studying in Arizona. Available to U.S. citizens.

Application Requirements: Application, essay, financial need analysis, references, transcript. *Deadline:* April 30.

Contact: Aregai Tecle, Professor
Arizona Hydrological Society
PO Box 15018
Flagstaff, AZ 86011
Phone: 928-523-6642
Fax: 928-556-7112
E-mail: aregai.tecle@nau.edu

ASSOCIATION FOR WOMEN GEOSCIENTISTS, PUGET SOUND CHAPTER

http://www.awg.org/

AWG CRAWFORD FIELD CAMP SCHOLARSHIP

Two $500 scholarships will be awarded to promising undergraduate women students who will be attending field camp during the summer.

Academic Fields/Career Goals: Earth Science.

Award: Scholarship for use in freshman, sophomore, junior, or senior years; not renewable. *Number:* 2. *Amount:* $500.

Eligibility Requirements: Applicant must be enrolled or expecting to enroll full-time at a four-year institution or university and female. Applicant must have 3.0 GPA or higher. Available to U.S. citizens.

Application Requirements: Application, essay, references, transcript. *Deadline:* February 16.

Contact: Richard Yuretich, Department of Geosciences, University of
        Massachusetts-Amherst
        Association for Women Geoscientists, Puget Sound Chapter
        611 North Pleasant Street, 233 Morrill Science Center
        Amherst, MA 01003-9297

AWG MINORITY SCHOLARSHIP

Scholarship available for an African American, Hispanic, or Native American full-time student who is pursuing an undergraduate degree in the geosciences at an accredited college or university.

Academic Fields/Career Goals: Earth Science.

Award: Scholarship for use in freshman, sophomore, junior, or senior years; not renewable. *Number:* 1. *Amount:* up to $5000.

Eligibility Requirements: Applicant must be American Indian/Alaska Native, Black (non-Hispanic), or Hispanic; enrolled or expecting to enroll full-time at a four-year institution or university and female. Available to U.S. citizens.

Application Requirements: Application, references, transcript, SAT or ACT scores. *Deadline:* June 30.

Contact: Kim Begay Jackson, Minority Scholarship Coordinator
        Association for Women Geoscientists, Puget Sound Chapter
        PO Box 30645
        Lincoln, NE 68503-0645
        E-mail: awgscholarship@yahoo.com

OSAGE CHAPTER SCHOLARSHIP

Scholarship for undergraduate women pursuing independent research in geosciences. Amount varies based on merit up to $500.

Academic Fields/Career Goals: Earth Science.

Award: Scholarship for use in freshman, sophomore, junior, or senior years; not renewable. *Number:* 1. *Amount:* up to $500.

Eligibility Requirements: Applicant must be enrolled or expecting to enroll full-time at a four-year institution or university and female. Available to U.S. citizens.

Application Requirements: Application, transcript, one-page description of research project, budget, letter of support from research supervisor. *Deadline:* April 1.

Contact: Jessica Finnearty, AWG Osage Chapter President
        Association for Women Geoscientists, Puget Sound Chapter
        University of Kansas, 1475 Jayhawk Boulevard, Room 120
        Lawrence, KS 66045
        E-mail: jfinne@ku.edu

PENELOPE HANSHAW SCHOLARSHIP

Scholarship available for women who are currently enrolled as full-time, graduate or undergraduate geoscience majors in an accredited, degree-granting college or university in Delaware, the District of Columbia, Maryland, Virginia, or West Virginia. The candidate must demonstrate academic excellence by a GPA not lower than 3.0 and awareness of the importance of community outreach by participation in geoscience or Earth science education activities.

Academic Fields/Career Goals: Earth Science; Education.

Award: Scholarship for use in freshman, sophomore, junior, senior, or graduate years; not renewable. *Number:* 1. *Amount:* $500.

Eligibility Requirements: Applicant must be enrolled or expecting to enroll full-time at a four-year institution or university; female and studying in Delaware, District of Columbia, Maryland, Virginia, or West Virginia. Applicant or parent of applicant must have employment or volunteer experience in teaching/education. Applicant must have 3.0 GPA or higher. Available to U.S. citizens.

Application Requirements: Application, references, transcript. *Deadline:* April 30.

Contact: Laurel M. Bybell, U.S. Geological Survey
        Association for Women Geoscientists, Puget Sound Chapter
        926 National Center
        Reston, VA 20192

PUGET SOUND CHAPTER SCHOLARSHIP

Scholarship for undergraduate women committed to completing a bachelor's degree and pursuing a career or graduate work in the geosciences, including geology, environmental/engineering geology, geochemistry, geophysics, and hydrology. Must be sophomore, junior, or senior woman enrolled in a university or two-year college in western Washington State, west of the Columbia and Okanogan Rivers. Must have minimum 3.2 GPA. Must be a U.S. citizen or permanent resident.

Academic Fields/Career Goals: Earth Science; Environmental Science; Hydrology; Physical Sciences.

Award: Scholarship for use in freshman, sophomore, junior, or senior years; not renewable. *Number:* 1. *Amount:* $1000.

Eligibility Requirements: Applicant must be enrolled or expecting to enroll full-time at a two-year or four-year institution or university; female and studying in Washington. Available to U.S. citizens.

Application Requirements: Essay, financial need analysis, references, transcript. *Deadline:* November 3.

Contact: Anne Udaloy, Scholarship Committee Chair
        Association for Women Geoscientists, Puget Sound Chapter
        1910 East Fourth Avenue, PO Box 65
        Olympia, WA 98506
        Phone: 206-543-9024
        E-mail: scholarship@awg-ps.org

SUSAN EKDALE MEMORIAL SCHOLARSHIP

A single $1500 scholarship will be awarded to a female student in the geosciences to help defray field camp expenses. Applicant must be attending a Utah institution of higher learning, or be a Utah resident attending college elsewhere.

Academic Fields/Career Goals: Earth Science.

Award: Scholarship for use in freshman, sophomore, junior, senior, or graduate years; not renewable. *Number:* 1. *Amount:* $1500.

Eligibility Requirements: Applicant must be enrolled or expecting to enroll full-time at a four-year institution or university; female and resident of Utah. Available to U.S. citizens.

Application Requirements: Application, essay, references, self-addressed stamped envelope, letter of eligibility from the department verifying field of study. *Deadline:* March 28.

Contact: Janae Wallace, Scholarship Committee
        Association for Women Geoscientists, Puget Sound Chapter
        PO Box 146100
        Salt Lake City, UT 84114

WILLIAM RUCKER GREENWOOD SCHOLARSHIP

Scholarship available for minority women who are currently enrolled as full-time, graduate or undergraduate geoscience majors in an accredited, degree-granting college or university in Delaware, the District of Columbia, Maryland, Virginia, or West Virginia. The candidate must demonstrate awareness of the importance of community outreach by participation in geoscience or Earth science education activities that reflect AWG's goals and potential for leadership as a future geoscience professional.

Academic Fields/Career Goals: Earth Science; Education.

Award: Scholarship for use in freshman, sophomore, junior, senior, or graduate years; not renewable. *Number:* 1. *Amount:* $1000.

Eligibility Requirements: Applicant must be American Indian/Alaska Native, Asian/Pacific Islander, Black (non-Hispanic), or Hispanic; enrolled or expecting to enroll full-time at a four-year institution or university; female and studying in Delaware, District of Columbia, Maryland, Virginia, or West Virginia. Applicant or parent of applicant must have employment or volunteer experience in teaching/education. Available to U.S. citizens.

Application Requirements: Application, references. *Deadline:* April 30.

Contact: Laurel M. Bybell, U.S. Geological Survey
        Association for Women Geoscientists, Puget Sound Chapter
        926 National Center
        Reston, VA 20192

ASSOCIATION OF ENGINEERING GEOLOGISTS

http://www.aegfoundation.org/

MARLIAVE FUND

One-time award to support undergraduate and graduate students studying engineering geology and geological engineering.

Academic Fields/Career Goals: Earth Science; Engineering/Technology; Engineering-Related Technologies.

Award: Scholarship for use in senior or graduate years; not renewable. *Number:* 1. *Amount:* $1000.

Eligibility Requirements: Applicant must be enrolled or expecting to enroll full-time at a four-year institution or university. Available to U.S. citizens.

Application Requirements: Application, essay, resume, references, transcript. *Deadline:* April 15.

Contact: Paul M. Santi, Scholarship Committee
 Association of Engineering Geologists
 Department of Geology and Geological Engineering, Berthoud Hall
 Golden, CO 80401
 Phone: 303-757-2926

TILFORD FUND

Scholarship of $1000 for student members of AEG. Three to four awards are granted annually. For undergraduate students, the scholarship goes toward the cost of a geology field camp course or senior thesis field research. For graduate students, the scholarship would apply to field research.

Academic Fields/Career Goals: Earth Science.

Award: Scholarship for use in freshman, sophomore, junior, senior, or graduate years; not renewable. *Number:* 3–4. *Amount:* $1000.

Eligibility Requirements: Applicant must be enrolled or expecting to enroll full-time at a four-year institution or university. Applicant or parent of applicant must be member of Association of Engineering Geologists. Available to U.S. citizens.

Application Requirements: Application, essay, resume, references, transcript. *Deadline:* February 1.

Contact: Deb Green Tilford, Chairman, Scholarship Committee
 Association of Engineering Geologists
 79 Forest Lane
 Placitas, NM 87043
 E-mail: tilgreen@aol.com

ASSOCIATION ON AMERICAN INDIAN AFFAIRS, INC.

http://www.indian-affairs.org/

ELIZABETH AND SHERMAN ASCHE MEMORIAL SCHOLARSHIP FUND

• *See page 83*

ASTRONAUT SCHOLARSHIP FOUNDATION

http://www.astronautscholarship.org/

ASTRONAUT SCHOLARSHIP FOUNDATION

• *See page 95*

BARRY M. GOLDWATER SCHOLARSHIP AND EXCELLENCE IN EDUCATION FOUNDATION

http://www.act.org/goldwater

BARRY M. GOLDWATER SCHOLARSHIP AND EXCELLENCE IN EDUCATION PROGRAM

• *See page 95*

BRITISH COLUMBIA INNOVATION COUNCIL

http://www.bcic.ca/

BCIC YOUNG INNOVATOR SCHOLARSHIP COMPETITION (IDEA MASH UP)

• *See page 95*

PAUL AND HELEN TRUSSELL SCIENCE AND TECHNOLOGY SCHOLARSHIP

• *See page 95*

GARDEN CLUB OF AMERICA

http://www.gcamerica.org/

THE ELIZABETH GARDNER NORWEB SUMMER ENVIRONMENTAL STUDIES SCHOLARSHIP

• *See page 84*

INDEPENDENT LABORATORIES INSTITUTE SCHOLARSHIP ALLIANCE

http://www.acil.org/

INDEPENDENT LABORATORIES INSTITUTE SCHOLARSHIP ALLIANCE

• *See page 141*

INTERNATIONAL ASSOCIATION OF GREAT LAKES RESEARCH

http://www.iaglr.org/

PAUL W. RODGERS SCHOLARSHIP

Award given to any senior undergraduate, master's or doctoral student who wishes to pursue a future in research, conservation, education, communication, management, or other knowledge-based activity pertaining to the Great Lakes.

Academic Fields/Career Goals: Earth Science; Education; Environmental Science; Hydrology; Marine Biology; Natural Resources; Natural Sciences.

Award: Scholarship for use in senior or graduate years; not renewable. *Number:* 1. *Amount:* $2000.

Eligibility Requirements: Applicant must be enrolled or expecting to enroll full-time at a four-year institution or university. Available to U.S. and non-U.S. citizens.

Application Requirements: Application, essay, references, transcript. *Deadline:* March 1.

Contact: Wendy Foster, Business Manager
 International Association of Great Lakes Research
 Business Office, 4840 South State Road
 Ann Arbor, MI 48108
 Phone: 734-665-5303
 E-mail: office@iaglr.org

KENTUCKY ENERGY AND ENVIRONMENT CABINET

http://www.eec.ky.gov/

ENVIRONMENTAL PROTECTION SCHOLARSHIP

• *See page 141*

MINERALOGICAL SOCIETY OF AMERICA

http://www.minsocam.org/

MINERALOGICAL SOCIETY OF AMERICA-GRANT FOR STUDENT RESEARCH IN MINERALOGY AND PETROLOGY

Grant for research in mineralogy and petrology. Selection based on qualifications of applicant; quality, innovativeness, and scientific significance of the research; and likelihood of project success. May not be used for tuition, living expenses, travel, or researcher salary. Application available on web site at http://www.minsocam.org.

Academic Fields/Career Goals: Earth Science; Gemology; Natural Resources; Natural Sciences; Physical Sciences.

Award: Grant for use in freshman, sophomore, junior, senior, or graduate years; not renewable. *Number:* 2.

Eligibility Requirements: Applicant must be enrolled or expecting to enroll full- or part-time at a four-year institution or university. Available to U.S. and non-U.S. citizens.

Application Requirements: Application, resume. *Deadline:* June 1.

Contact: Dr. J. Alexander Speer, Executive Director
Mineralogical Society of America
3635 Concorde Parkway, Suite 500
Chantilly, VA 20151-1110
Phone: 703-652-9950
E-mail: jaspeer@minsocam.org

MONTANA FEDERATION OF GARDEN CLUBS

http://www.mtfgc.org/

LIFE MEMBER MONTANA FEDERATION OF GARDEN CLUBS SCHOLARSHIP

Applicant must be at least a sophomore, majoring in conservation, horticulture, park or forestry, floriculture, greenhouse management, land management, or related subjects. Must be in need of assistance. Must have a potential for a successful future. Must be ranked in upper half of class or have a minimum 2.7 GPA. Must be a Montana resident and all study must be done in Montana.

Academic Fields/Career Goals: Earth Science; Horticulture/Floriculture; Landscape Architecture; Natural Resources.

Award: Scholarship for use in sophomore, junior, or senior years; not renewable. *Number:* 1. *Amount:* $1000.

Eligibility Requirements: Applicant must be enrolled or expecting to enroll full-time at a four-year institution or university; resident of Montana and studying in Montana. Applicant must have 2.5 GPA or higher. Available to U.S. citizens.

Application Requirements: Driver's license, references, transcript. *Deadline:* May 1.

Contact: Joyce Backa, Life Members Scholarship Chairman
Montana Federation of Garden Clubs
513 Skyline Drive
Craig, MT 59404-8712
Phone: 406-235-4229
E-mail: rjback@bresnan.net

NASA IDAHO SPACE GRANT CONSORTIUM

http://www.id.spacegrant.org/

NASA IDAHO SPACE GRANT CONSORTIUM SCHOLARSHIP PROGRAM
• *See page 141*

NASA/MARYLAND SPACE GRANT CONSORTIUM

http://www.mdspacegrant.org/

NASA MARYLAND SPACE GRANT CONSORTIUM UNDERGRADUATE SCHOLARSHIPS
• *See page 127*

NASA MINNESOTA SPACE GRANT CONSORTIUM

http://www.aem.umn.edu/mnsgc

MINNESOTA SPACE GRANT CONSORTIUM SCHOLARSHIP PROGRAM
• *See page 127*

NASA SOUTH CAROLINA SPACE GRANT CONSORTIUM

http://www.cofc.edu/~scsgrant

KATHRYN SULLIVAN SCIENCE AND ENGINEERING FELLOWSHIP
• *See page 128*

UNDERGRADUATE RESEARCH AWARD PROGRAM
• *See page 129*

NASA SOUTH DAKOTA SPACE GRANT CONSORTIUM

http://www.sdspacegrant.sdsmt.edu/

SOUTH DAKOTA SPACE GRANT CONSORTIUM UNDERGRADUATE AND GRADUATE STUDENT SCHOLARSHIPS
• *See page 129*

NASA'S VIRGINIA SPACE GRANT CONSORTIUM

http://www.vsgc.odu.edu/

TEACHER EDUCATION STEM SCHOLARSHIP PROGRAM
• *See page 96*

NATIONAL ASSOCIATION OF GEOSCIENCE TEACHERS & FAR WESTERN SECTION

http://www.mlkwolves.org/

NATIONAL ASSOCIATION OF GEOSCIENCE TEACHERS-FAR WESTERN SECTION SCHOLARSHIP

Academically superior students currently enrolled in school in Hawaii, Nevada, or California are eligible to apply for one of three $500 scholarships to the school of their choice. Must be a high school senior or community college student enrolling full time (12 quarter units) in a bachelor's degree program in geology at a four-year institution or an undergraduate geology major enrolling in an upper division field geology course of approximately 30 field mapping days.

Academic Fields/Career Goals: Earth Science.

Award: Scholarship for use in sophomore, junior, or senior years; not renewable. *Number:* 3. *Amount:* $500.

Eligibility Requirements: Applicant must be enrolled or expecting to enroll full- or part-time at a four-year institution or university and studying in California, Hawaii, or Nevada. Available to U.S. citizens.

Application Requirements: Application, references, transcript, endorsement signature of a regular member of NAGT-FWS in the reference letter. *Deadline:* April 1.

Contact: Mike Martin, Geology Scholarship Coordinator
National Association of Geoscience Teachers & Far Western Section
c/o Martin Luther King High School, 9301 Wood Road
Riverside, CA 92508
Phone: 951-789-5690
E-mail: mmartin@rusd.k12.ca.us

NATIONAL ASSOCIATION OF WATER COMPANIES-NEW JERSEY CHAPTER

http://www.nawc.org/

NATIONAL ASSOCIATION OF WATER COMPANIES-NEW JERSEY CHAPTER SCHOLARSHIP
• See page 142

NATIONAL GARDEN CLUBS INC.

http://www.gardenclub.org/

NATIONAL GARDEN CLUBS INC. SCHOLARSHIP PROGRAM
• See page 86

NATIONAL GROUND WATER RESEARCH AND EDUCATIONAL FOUNDATION

http://www.ngwa.org/

NATIONAL GROUND WATER RESEARCH AND EDUCATIONAL FOUNDATION'S LEN ASSANTE SCHOLARSHIP

Scholarships granted to full-time students only, including high school graduates and currently enrolled undergraduates. Previous scholarship recipients are ineligible. Applicant must be entering a field of study that serves, supports, or promotes the ground water industry. Qualifying majors: geology, hydrology, hydrogeology, environmental sciences, microbiology, and well-drilling two-year associate degree programs. Minimum 2.5 GPA required.

Academic Fields/Career Goals: Earth Science; Environmental Science; Hydrology.

Award: Scholarship for use in freshman, sophomore, junior, or senior years; not renewable. *Number:* 5–10. *Amount:* $1000–$2500.

Eligibility Requirements: Applicant must be enrolled or expecting to enroll full-time at a two-year or four-year or technical institution or university. Applicant must have 2.5 GPA or higher. Available to U.S. and non-U.S. citizens.

Application Requirements: Application, essay, transcript. *Deadline:* January 15.

Contact: Ms. Rachel Jones, Scholarship Coordinator
National Ground Water Research and Educational Foundation
601 Dempsey Road
Westerville, OH 43081
Phone: 614-898-7791 Ext. 504
Fax: 614-897-7786
E-mail: rjones@ngwa.org

NEVADA NASA SPACE GRANT CONSORTIUM

http://www.nvspacegrant.org/

NATIONAL SPACE GRANT COLLEGE AND FELLOWSHIP PROGRAM
• See page 97

OZARKA NATURAL SPRING WATER

http://www.ozarkawater.com/

EARTH SCIENCE SCHOLARSHIP

Scholarships offered to qualified students who are currently enrolled or planning to enroll in an earth/environmental sciences program at a public or private, not-for-profit, four-year college or university. Must be Texas resident with a minimum 3.0 GPA.

Academic Fields/Career Goals: Earth Science; Environmental Science.

Award: Scholarship for use in freshman, sophomore, junior, or senior years; not renewable. *Number:* 2. *Amount:* $10,000.

Eligibility Requirements: Applicant must be enrolled or expecting to enroll full-time at a four-year institution or university and resident of Texas. Applicant must have 3.0 GPA or higher. Available to U.S. citizens.

Application Requirements: Application, essay, transcript. *Deadline:* March 31.

Contact: David Feckley, Scholarship Committee
Ozarka Natural Spring Water
3265 FM 2869
Hawkins, TX 75765
Phone: 800-678-4448
E-mail: edcfund@texas.net

ROCKY MOUNTAIN COAL MINING INSTITUTE

http://www.rmcmi.org/

ROCKY MOUNTAIN COAL MINING INSTITUTE SCHOLARSHIP
• See page 179

SIGMA XI, THE SCIENTIFIC RESEARCH SOCIETY

http://www.sigmaxi.org/

SIGMA XI GRANTS-IN-AID OF RESEARCH
• See page 87

SOIL AND WATER CONSERVATION SOCIETY

http://www.swcs.org/

DONALD A. WILLIAMS SCHOLARSHIP SOIL CONSERVATION SCHOLARSHIP

Scholarship provides financial assistance to members of SWCS, who are currently employed but who wish to improve their technical or administrative competence in a conservation-related field through course work at an accredited college or through a program of special study. Download the application form from the SWCS homepage at http://www.swcs.org.

Academic Fields/Career Goals: Earth Science; Natural Resources; Natural Sciences.

Award: Scholarship for use in freshman, sophomore, junior, or senior years; renewable. *Number:* up to 3. *Amount:* $1500.

Eligibility Requirements: Applicant must be enrolled or expecting to enroll full- or part-time at a four-year institution or university. Applicant or parent of applicant must be affiliated with Swanson Brothers Lumber Company. Applicant or parent of applicant must be member of Soil and Water Conservation Society. Applicant or parent of applicant must have employment or volunteer experience in environmental-related field. Available to U.S. and non-U.S. citizens.

Application Requirements: Application, financial need analysis, budget. *Deadline:* February 13.

Contact: Sue Lynes, Executive Assistant
Soil and Water Conservation Society
945 Ankeny Road, SW
Ankeny, IA 50023-9723
Phone: 515-289-2331 Ext. 112
Fax: 515-289-1227
E-mail: sueann.lynes@swcs.org

SOIL AND WATER CONSERVATION SOCIETY-NEW JERSEY CHAPTER

http://www.geocities.com/njswcs

EDWARD R. HALL SCHOLARSHIP
• See page 81

TKE EDUCATIONAL FOUNDATION

http://www.tke.org/

CARROL C. HALL MEMORIAL SCHOLARSHIP
• *See page 97*

TIMOTHY L. TASCHWER SCHOLARSHIP
• *See page 144*

UNIVERSITIES SPACE RESEARCH ASSOCIATION

http://www.usra.edu/

UNIVERSITIES SPACE RESEARCH ASSOCIATION SCHOLARSHIP PROGRAM
• *See page 97*

VERMONT SPACE GRANT CONSORTIUM

http://www.cems.uvm.edu/vsgc

VERMONT SPACE GRANT CONSORTIUM SCHOLARSHIP PROGRAM
• *See page 98*

ECONOMICS

CATCHING THE DREAM

http://www.catchingthedream.org/

TRIBAL BUSINESS MANAGEMENT PROGRAM (TBM)
• *See page 57*

CENTRAL INTELLIGENCE AGENCY

http://www.cia.gov/

CENTRAL INTELLIGENCE AGENCY UNDERGRADUATE SCHOLARSHIP PROGRAM
• *See page 58*

CIRI FOUNDATION (TCF)

http://www.thecirifoundation.org/

CARL H. MARRS SCHOLARSHIP FUND
• *See page 58*

CUBAN AMERICAN NATIONAL FOUNDATION

http://www.masscholarships.org/

MAS FAMILY SCHOLARSHIPS
• *See page 148*

DAIRY MANAGEMENT

http://www.dairyinfo.com/

NATIONAL DAIRY PROMOTION AND RESEARCH BOARD SCHOLARSHIP
• *See page 84*

GOVERNMENT FINANCE OFFICERS ASSOCIATION

http://www.gfoa.org/

MINORITIES IN GOVERNMENT FINANCE SCHOLARSHIP
• *See page 63*

INSTITUTE FOR HUMANE STUDIES

http://www.theihs.org/

HUMANE STUDIES FELLOWSHIPS
• *See page 185*

JORGE MAS CANOSA FREEDOM FOUNDATION

http://www.jorgemascanosa.org/

MAS FAMILY SCHOLARSHIP AWARD
• *See page 152*

NATIONAL ASSOCIATION OF NEGRO BUSINESS AND PROFESSIONAL WOMEN'S CLUBS INC.

http://www.nanbpwc.org/

JULIANNE MALVEAUX SCHOLARSHIP

Scholarship for African-American women who are college sophomores or juniors enrolled in an accredited college or university. Applicants must be majoring in journalism, economics, or a related field. Minimum 3.0 GPA required. Must be a U.S. citizen.

Academic Fields/Career Goals: Economics; Journalism.

Award: Scholarship for use in sophomore or junior years; not renewable. *Number:* 1. *Amount:* $1000.

Eligibility Requirements: Applicant must be Black (non-Hispanic); enrolled or expecting to enroll full-time at a four-year institution or university and female. Applicant must have 3.0 GPA or higher. Available to U.S. citizens.

Application Requirements: Application, essay, references, transcript. *Deadline:* April 30.

Contact: Scholarship Program Director
National Association of Negro Business and Professional
Women's Clubs Inc.
1806 New Hampshire Avenue, NW
Washington, DC 20009-3298
Phone: 202-483-4206
E-mail: info@nanbpwc.org

NATIONAL ASSOCIATION OF WATER COMPANIES-NEW JERSEY CHAPTER

http://www.nawc.org/

NATIONAL ASSOCIATION OF WATER COMPANIES-NEW JERSEY CHAPTER SCHOLARSHIP
• *See page 142*

NATIONAL SECURITY EDUCATION PROGRAM

http://www.iie.org/

NATIONAL SECURITY EDUCATION PROGRAM (NSEP) DAVID L. BOREN UNDERGRADUATE SCHOLARSHIPS
• *See page 154*

NATIONAL SOCIETY DAUGHTERS OF THE AMERICAN REVOLUTION

http://www.dar.org/

NATIONAL SOCIETY DAUGHTERS OF THE AMERICAN REVOLUTION ENID HALL GRISWOLD MEMORIAL SCHOLARSHIP

Scholarship of $1000 awarded to a deserving junior or senior enrolled in an accredited college or university in the United States who is majoring in political science, history, government, or economics.

Academic Fields/Career Goals: Economics; History; Political Science.

Award: Scholarship for use in junior or senior years; not renewable. *Number:* 1. *Amount:* $1000.

Eligibility Requirements: Applicant must be enrolled or expecting to enroll full-time at a four-year institution or university. Available to U.S. citizens.

Application Requirements: Application, financial need analysis, references, self-addressed stamped envelope, transcript, letter of sponsorship. *Deadline:* February 15.

Contact: Eric Weisz, Manager, Office of the Reporter General
National Society Daughters of the American Revolution
1776 D Street, NW
Washington, DC 20006-5303
Phone: 202-628-1776
Fax: 202-879-3348
E-mail: nsdarscholarships@dar.org

NEW ENGLAND EMPLOYEE BENEFITS COUNCIL

http://www.neebc.org/

NEW ENGLAND EMPLOYEE BENEFITS COUNCIL SCHOLARSHIP PROGRAM
• *See page 68*

OFFICE AND PROFESSIONAL EMPLOYEES INTERNATIONAL UNION

http://www.opeiu.org/

JOHN KELLY LABOR STUDIES SCHOLARSHIP FUND

Scholarship of up to $3000 given to graduate or undergraduate students who have labor studies, social sciences, industrial relation as their major. Ten scholarships are granted. Applicants should be a member or associate member of the union.

Academic Fields/Career Goals: Economics; Social Sciences.

Award: Scholarship for use in freshman, sophomore, junior, senior, or graduate years; not renewable. *Number:* 10. *Amount:* up to $3000.

Eligibility Requirements: Applicant must be enrolled or expecting to enroll full-time at a four-year institution or university. Available to U.S. citizens.

Application Requirements: Application, essay, transcript. *Deadline:* March 31.

Contact: Mary Mahoney, Secretary-Treasurer
Office and Professional Employees International Union
80 Eighth Avenue, 6th Floor
New York, NY 10011
Phone: 202-393-4464
Fax: 202-887-0910
E-mail: mmahoney@opeiudc.org

SOCIETY OF AUTOMOTIVE ANALYSTS

http://www.cybersaa.org/

SOCIETY OF AUTOMOTIVE ANALYSTS SCHOLARSHIP
• *See page 70*

STRAIGHTFORWARD MEDIA

http://www.straightforwardmedia.com/

STRAIGHTFORWARD MEDIA BUSINESS SCHOOL SCHOLARSHIP
• *See page 77*

STRAIGHTFORWARD MEDIA LIBERAL ARTS SCHOLARSHIP
• *See page 107*

UNITED NEGRO COLLEGE FUND

http://www.uncf.org/

AFSCME/UNCF/HARVARD UNIVERSITY LWP UNION SCHOLARS PROGRAM
• *See page 90*

AVIS BUDGET GROUP SCHOLARSHIP
• *See page 72*

AVON WOMEN IN SEARCH OF EXCELLENCE SCHOLARSHIP
• *See page 72*

EDWARD M. NAGEL FOUNDATION SCHOLARSHIP
• *See page 73*

GENERAL MILLS CORPORATE SCHOLARS AWARD
• *See page 73*

SBC-PACIFIC BELL SCHOLARSHIP
• *See page 158*

TOYOTA/UNCF SCHOLARSHIP
• *See page 74*

UBS/PAINEWEBBER SCHOLARSHIP
• *See page 74*

EDUCATION

ALBERTA HERITAGE SCHOLARSHIP FUND

http://www.alis.alberta.ca/

ANNA AND JOHN KOLESAR MEMORIAL SCHOLARSHIPS

Award of CAN$1500 to recognize and reward the academic excellence of a high school student entering a Faculty of Education. Must be resident of Alberta and plan to enroll full-time in the first year of an education program. Must be from a family where neither parent obtained a university degree. Selection based on the highest average obtained on three grade 12 subjects. Must be a Canadian citizen or permanent resident. For additional information and application, visit web site http://alis.alberta.ca.

Academic Fields/Career Goals: Education; Special Education.

Award: Scholarship for use in freshman year; not renewable. *Number:* 1.

Eligibility Requirements: Applicant must be Canadian citizen; high school student; planning to enroll or expecting to enroll full-time at a two-year or four-year institution or university and resident of Alberta. Applicant must have 3.0 GPA or higher.

Application Requirements: Application, test scores, transcript. *Deadline:* July 1.

Contact: Scholarship Committee
Alberta Heritage Scholarship Fund
9940 106th Street, Fourth Floor, Sterling Place
PO Box 28000, Station Main
Edmonton, AB T5J 4R4
Canada
Phone: 780-427-8640
E-mail: scholarships@gov.ab.ca

LANGUAGES IN TEACHER EDUCATION SCHOLARSHIPS

Awards of CAN$2500 to Alberta students enrolled full-time in the final two years of a recognized teacher preparation program in Alberta, taking courses that will allow them to teach languages other than English in Alberta schools. Must be Canadian citizen or permanent resident and a resident of Alberta. Must intend to teach in Alberta after graduation. Nominations by faculty of education. For additional information, visit web site http://alis.alberta.ca.

Academic Fields/Career Goals: Education; Foreign Language.

Award: Scholarship for use in junior or senior years; not renewable. *Number:* 13.

Eligibility Requirements: Applicant must be enrolled or expecting to enroll full-time at a four-year institution or university; resident of Alberta and studying in Alberta. Available to Canadian citizens.

Application Requirements: Nomination by institution. *Deadline:* varies.

Contact: Scholarship Committee
Alberta Heritage Scholarship Fund
9940 106th Street, Fourth Floor, Sterling Place
PO Box 28000, Station Main
Edmonton, AB T5J 4R4
Canada
Phone: 780-427-8640
E-mail: scholarships@gov.ab.ca

NORTHERN ALBERTA DEVELOPMENT COUNCIL BURSARY

• *See page 214*

ALPHA KAPPA ALPHA

http://www.akaeaf.org/

AKA EDUCATIONAL ADVANCEMENT FOUNDATION MERIT SCHOLARSHIP

Scholarships for students demonstrating exceptional academic achievements. Applicant must have completed a minimum of one year in a degree-granting institution and be continuing their program in that institution. Must have GPA of 3.0 or higher and show evidence of leadership by participating in community or campus activities.

Academic Fields/Career Goals: Education.

Award: Scholarship for use in sophomore, junior, senior, or graduate years; not renewable. *Number:* varies. *Amount:* $1000–$2000.

Eligibility Requirements: Applicant must be enrolled or expecting to enroll full-time at a four-year institution or university and must have an interest in leadership. Applicant must have 3.0 GPA or higher. Available to U.S. and non-U.S. citizens.

Application Requirements: Application, references. *Deadline:* varies.

Contact: Andrea Kerr, Program Coordinator
Alpha Kappa Alpha
5656 South Stony Island Avenue
Chicago, IL 60637
Phone: 773-947-0026 Ext. 8
E-mail: akaeaf@akaeaf.net

AMERICAN ASSOCIATION FOR HEALTH EDUCATION

http://www.aahperd.org/aahe

BILL KANE SCHOLARSHIP

Scholarship available to any undergraduate student officially enrolled as a health education major at an accredited college or university in the United States or a U.S. territory.

Academic Fields/Career Goals: Education.

Award: Scholarship for use in freshman, sophomore, junior, or senior years; not renewable. *Number:* 1. *Amount:* $1000.

Eligibility Requirements: Applicant must be enrolled or expecting to enroll full-time at a four-year institution or university. Applicant must have 3.0 GPA or higher. Available to U.S. citizens.

Application Requirements: Application, essay, resume, references, transcript. *Deadline:* November 15.

Contact: Ms. Linda Moore, Program Manager
American Association for Health Education
1900 Association Drive
Reston, VA 20191-1599
Phone: 703-476-3837
Fax: 703-476-6638
E-mail: aahe@aahperd.org

AMERICAN FEDERATION OF TEACHERS

http://www.aft.org/

ROBERT G. PORTER SCHOLARS PROGRAM-AFT MEMBERS

Nonrenewable grant provides continuing education for school teachers, paraprofessionals and school-related personnel, higher education faculty and professionals, employees of state and local governments, nurses and other health professionals. Must be member of the American Federation of Teachers for at least one year.

Academic Fields/Career Goals: Education.

Award: Grant for use in freshman, sophomore, junior, or senior years; not renewable. *Number:* up to 10. *Amount:* $1000.

Eligibility Requirements: Applicant must be enrolled or expecting to enroll full- or part-time at a four-year institution or university. Applicant or parent of applicant must have employment or volunteer experience in nursing or teaching/education. Available to U.S. citizens.

Application Requirements: Application, essay, references, statement of need. *Deadline:* March 31.

Contact: Bernadette Bailey, Scholarship Coordinator
American Federation of Teachers
555 New Jersey Avenue, NW
Washington, DC 20001
Phone: 202-879-4481
Fax: 202-879-4406
E-mail: bbailey@aft.org

AMERICAN FOUNDATION FOR THE BLIND

http://www.afb.org/

DELTA GAMMA FOUNDATION FLORENCE MARGARET HARVEY MEMORIAL SCHOLARSHIP

The scholarship provides one scholarship of $1000 to an undergraduate or graduate student who has exhibited academic excellence, and is studying in the field of rehabilitation and/or education of persons who are blind or visually impaired. Must submit proof of legal blindness. For additional information and application requirements, refer to web site http://www.afb.org/scholarships.asp.

Academic Fields/Career Goals: Education; Therapy/Rehabilitation.

Award: Scholarship for use in freshman, sophomore, junior, or senior years; not renewable. *Number:* 1. *Amount:* $1000.

Eligibility Requirements: Applicant must be enrolled or expecting to enroll full- or part-time at a two-year or four-year institution or university. Applicant must be visually impaired. Available to U.S. citizens.

Application Requirements: Application, essay, references, transcript, proof of post-secondary acceptance and legal blindness. *Deadline:* April 30.

Contact: Dawn Bodrogi, Information Center and Library Coordinator
American Foundation for the Blind
11 Penn Plaza, Suite 300
New York, NY 10001
Phone: 212-502-7661
Fax: 212-502-7771
E-mail: afbinfo@afb.net

RUDOLPH DILLMAN MEMORIAL SCHOLARSHIP

One-time award not open to previous recipients. Four scholarships of $2500 each to undergraduate or graduate students who are studying in the field of rehabilitation and/or education of persons who are blind or visually impaired. One of these grants is specifically for a student who meets all requirements and submits evidence of economic need. Must submit proof of legal blindness. For additional information and application requirements, visit web site http://www.afb.org/scholarships.asp.

Academic Fields/Career Goals: Education; Therapy/Rehabilitation.

Award: Scholarship for use in freshman, sophomore, junior, or senior years; not renewable. *Number:* up to 4. *Amount:* $2500.

Eligibility Requirements: Applicant must be enrolled or expecting to enroll full- or part-time at a two-year or four-year institution or university. Applicant must be visually impaired. Available to U.S. citizens.

Application Requirements: Application, essay, financial need analysis, references, transcript, proof of legal blindness, acceptance letter. *Deadline:* April 30.

Contact: Dawn Bodrogi, Information Center and Library Coordinator
American Foundation for the Blind
11 Penn Plaza, Suite 300
New York, NY 10001
Phone: 212-502-7661
Fax: 212-502-7771
E-mail: afbinfo@afb.net

AMERICAN INDIAN SCIENCE AND ENGINEERING SOCIETY

http://www.aises.org/

BURLINGTON NORTHERN SANTA FE FOUNDATION SCHOLARSHIP
• See page 93

AMERICAN INSTITUTE OF POLISH CULTURE INC.

http://www.ampolinstitute.org/

HARRIET IRSAY SCHOLARSHIP GRANT
• See page 109

AMERICAN LEGION AUXILIARY DEPARTMENT OF IOWA

http://www.ialegion.org/ala

AMERICAN LEGION AUXILIARY DEPARTMENT OF IOWA HARRIET HOFFMAN MEMORIAL MERIT AWARD FOR TEACHER TRAINING

One-time award for Iowa residents attending Iowa institutions who are the children, grandchildren, or great-grandchildren of veterans. Preference given to descendants of deceased veterans.

Academic Fields/Career Goals: Education.

Award: Scholarship for use in freshman, sophomore, junior, or senior years; not renewable. *Number:* 1. *Amount:* $400.

Eligibility Requirements: Applicant must be enrolled or expecting to enroll full-time at a four-year institution or university; resident of Iowa and studying in Iowa. Available to U.S. citizens. Applicant or parent must meet one or more of the following requirements: general military experience; retired from active duty; disabled or killed as a result of military service; prisoner of war; or missing in action.

Application Requirements: Application, essay, financial need analysis, photo, references, self-addressed stamped envelope, test scores, transcript. *Deadline:* June 1.

Contact: Marlene Valentine, Secretary and Treasurer
American Legion Auxiliary Department of Iowa
720 Lyon Street
Des Moines, IA 50309
Phone: 515-282-7987
Fax: 515-282-7583
E-mail: alasectreas@ialegion.org

AMERICAN LEGION DEPARTMENT OF MISSOURI

http://www.missourilegion.org/

ERMAN W. TAYLOR MEMORIAL SCHOLARSHIP

Two $500 awards are given annually to a student planning on obtaining a degree in education. Applicants must be unmarried Missouri resident below age 21, and must use the scholarship as a full-time student in an accredited college or university. Must be an unmarried descendant of a veteran having served 90 days on active duty in the Army, Air Force, Navy, Marine Corps or Coast Guard of the United States, and having an honorable discharge.

Academic Fields/Career Goals: Education.

Award: Scholarship for use in freshman year; not renewable. *Number:* 2. *Amount:* $500.

Eligibility Requirements: Applicant must be high school student; age 21 or under; planning to enroll or expecting to enroll full-time at a two-year or four-year institution or university; single and resident of Missouri. Available to U.S. citizens. Applicant or parent must meet one or more of the following requirements: general military experience; retired from active duty; disabled or killed as a result of military service; prisoner of war; or missing in action.

Application Requirements: Application, essay, test scores, discharge certificate. *Deadline:* April 20.

Contact: John Doane, Chairman
American Legion Department of Missouri
PO Box 179
Jefferson City, MO 65102
Phone: 417-924-8596
Fax: 573-225-1406
E-mail: info@missourilegion.org

AMERICAN MONTESSORI SOCIETY

http://www.amshq.org/

AMERICAN MONTESSORI SOCIETY TEACHER EDUCATION SCHOLARSHIP FUND

One-time award for aspiring Montessori teacher candidates. Requires verification that applicant has been accepted into the AMS Montessori Teacher Education program.

Academic Fields/Career Goals: Education.

Award: Scholarship for use in freshman, sophomore, junior, senior, or graduate years; not renewable. *Number:* 10–20. *Amount:* $1000–$3000.

Eligibility Requirements: Applicant must be enrolled or expecting to enroll full-time at a two-year or four-year or technical institution or university. Available to U.S. and non-U.S. citizens.

Application Requirements: Application, essay, financial need analysis, references. *Deadline:* May 1.

Contact: Abbie Kelly, Manager of Teacher Education Services
American Montessori Society
281 Park Avenue South
New York, NY 10010
Phone: 212-358-1250 Ext. 315
Fax: 212-358-1256
E-mail: abbie@amshq.org

ARCTIC INSTITUTE OF NORTH AMERICA

http://www.arctic.ucalgary.ca/

JIM BOURQUE SCHOLARSHIP

One-time award of CAN$1000 to Canadian aboriginal student enrolled in postsecondary training in education, environmental studies, traditional knowledge or telecommunications. Must submit, in 500 words or less, a description of their intended program of study and reasons for their choice of program. Must include most recent high school or college/university transcript; a signed letter of recommendation from a community leader, a statement of financial need which indicates funding already received or expected; and proof of enrollment in, or application to, a post secondary institution. Applicants must also provide proof of Canadian Aboriginal descent. Applicants are evaluated based on need, relevance of study, achievements, return of investment and overall presentation of the application.

Academic Fields/Career Goals: Education; Environmental Science; Natural Resources; Natural Sciences.

Award: Scholarship for use in freshman, sophomore, junior, or senior years; not renewable. *Number:* 1.

Eligibility Requirements: Applicant must be of Canadian heritage and Canadian citizen; American Indian/Alaska Native; enrolled or expecting to enroll full-time at a four-year institution or university and resident of Alberta, British Columbia, Manitoba, New Brunswick, Newfoundland, North West Territories, Nova Scotia, Ontario, Prince Edward Island, Quebec, Saskatchewan, or Yukon.

Application Requirements: Essay, financial need analysis, references, transcript, proof of enrollment in or application to a post-secondary institution. *Deadline:* July 16.

Contact: Trisha Carleton, Administrative Assistant
Arctic Institute of North America
University of Calgary, 2500 University Drive, NW
Calgary, AB T2N 1N4
Phone: 403-220-7515
Fax: 403-282-4609
E-mail: pdcarlet@ucalgary.ca

ARIZONA BUSINESS EDUCATION ASSOCIATION

http://www.azbea.org/

ABEA STUDENT TEACHER SCHOLARSHIPS

Scholarships awarded to future business education teachers. Must be member of ABEA. Must be a student in last semester or two of an undergraduate Arizona business education teacher program at an accredited university or four-year college or in a post-baccalaureate Arizona business education teacher certification program at an accredited university or four-year college.

Academic Fields/Career Goals: Education.

Award: Scholarship for use in junior or senior years; not renewable. *Number:* up to 3. *Amount:* $500.

Eligibility Requirements: Applicant must be enrolled or expecting to enroll full-time at a four-year institution or university and resident of Arizona. Applicant or parent of applicant must be member of Arizona Business Education Association. Available to U.S. citizens.

Application Requirements: Application, resume, references, transcript. *Deadline:* April 1.

Contact: Shirley Eittreim, Scholarships Committee Chair
Arizona Business Education Association
Northland Pioneer College, PO Box 610
Holbrook, AZ 86025
Phone: 928-532-6151
E-mail: sjeittreim@cybertrails.com

ARMED FORCES COMMUNICATIONS AND ELECTRONICS ASSOCIATION, EDUCATIONAL FOUNDATION

http://www.afcea.org/education/scholarships

DISABLED WAR VETERANS SCHOLARSHIP

• See page 122

ASRT EDUCATION AND RESEARCH FOUNDATION

http://www.asrtfoundation.org/

ELEKTA RADIATION THERAPY EDUCATORS SCHOLARSHIP

Open to ASRT members only who are therapist-educators and completing a bachelor's, master's, or doctoral degree to enhance their position as a program director, faculty member, clinical coordinator or clinical instructor. One of the following must also be true: applicant holds an unrestricted state license, is registered by the American Registry of Radiologic Technologists, or registered with an equivalent certifying body.

Academic Fields/Career Goals: Education; Health and Medical Sciences; Oncology.

Award: Scholarship for use in freshman, sophomore, junior, senior, or graduate years; not renewable. *Number:* 4. *Amount:* $5000.

Eligibility Requirements: Applicant must be enrolled or expecting to enroll full- or part-time at a four-year institution or university. Applicant or parent of applicant must be member of American Society of Radiologic Technologists. Available to U.S. and Canadian citizens.

Application Requirements: Application, essay, financial need analysis, resume, references. *Deadline:* February 1.

Contact: Debbie Freeman, Community and Program Manager
ASRT Education and Research Foundation
15000 Central Avenue, SE
Albuquerque, NM 87123-3909
Phone: 505-298-4500 Ext. 1307
E-mail: foundation@asrt.org

MEDICAL IMAGING EDUCATORS SCHOLARSHIP

Open to ASRT members only who are completing a bachelor's, master's, or doctoral degree to enhance their position as a medical imaging program director, faculty member, clinical coordinator or clinical instructor. One of the following must also be true: applicant holds an unrestricted state license, is registered by the American Registry of Radiologic Technologists, or registered with an equivalent certifying body.

Academic Fields/Career Goals: Education; Health and Medical Sciences; Radiology.

Award: Scholarship for use in freshman, sophomore, junior, senior, or graduate years; not renewable. *Number:* 4. *Amount:* $5000.

Eligibility Requirements: Applicant must be enrolled or expecting to enroll full- or part-time at a four-year institution or university. Applicant or parent of applicant must be member of American Society of Radiologic Technologists. Available to U.S. and Canadian citizens.

Application Requirements: Application, essay, financial need analysis, resume, references. *Deadline:* February 1.

Contact: Debbie Freeman, Community and Program Manager
ASRT Education and Research Foundation
15000 Central Avenue, SE
Albuquerque, NM 87123-3909
Phone: 505-298-4500 Ext. 1307
E-mail: foundation@asrt.org

ASSOCIATION FOR WOMEN GEOSCIENTISTS, PUGET SOUND CHAPTER

http://www.awg.org/

PENELOPE HANSHAW SCHOLARSHIP

• See page 223

WILLIAM RUCKER GREENWOOD SCHOLARSHIP

• See page 223

ASSOCIATION OF RETIRED TEACHERS OF CONNECTICUT

http://www.ctretiredteachers.org/

ARTC GLEN MOON SCHOLARSHIP

Renewable scholarship to Connecticut high school seniors, who intend to pursue a career in teaching. Must demonstrate a positive financial need.

Academic Fields/Career Goals: Education.

Award: Scholarship for use in freshman year; renewable. *Number:* 2–3. *Amount:* $1500–$2000.

Eligibility Requirements: Applicant must be high school student; planning to enroll or expecting to enroll full- or part-time at a four-year institution or university and resident of Connecticut. Available to U.S. citizens.

Application Requirements: Application, driver's license, financial need analysis, references, test scores, transcript. *Deadline:* March 31.

Contact: Teresa Barton, Scholarship Committee
Association of Retired Teachers of Connecticut
111 South Road
Farmington, CT 06032
Phone: 866-343-2782
E-mail: info@ctretiredteachers.org

ASSOCIATION ON AMERICAN INDIAN AFFAIRS, INC.

http://www.indian-affairs.org/

EMILIE HESEMEYER MEMORIAL SCHOLARSHIP

Scholarship is open to undergraduate students who are Native American. Preference is given, but not limited to, students in the education curriculum. Students in a 2-year college must be on track to transfer to a 4-year college. Scholarship is renewable up to four years pending satisfactory progress toward any single degree. See our web site at http://www.indian-affairs.org for details.

Academic Fields/Career Goals: Education.

Award: Scholarship for use in freshman, sophomore, junior, or senior years; renewable. *Number:* 6. *Amount:* $1500.

Eligibility Requirements: Applicant must be American Indian/Alaska Native and enrolled or expecting to enroll full-time at a two-year or four-year institution or university. Available to U.S. citizens.

Application Requirements: Application, essay, financial need analysis, references, transcript. *Deadline:* June 13.

Contact: Lisa Wyzlic, Director of Scholarship Programs
Association on American Indian Affairs, Inc.
966 Hungerford Drive, Suite 12-B
Rockville, MD 20850
Phone: 240-314-7155
Fax: 240-314-7159
E-mail: lw.aaia@verizon.net

BETHESDA LUTHERAN COMMUNITIES

http://www.bethesdalutherancommunities.org/

DEVELOPMENTAL DISABILITIES SCHOLASTIC ACHIEVEMENT SCHOLARSHIP FOR COLLEGE STUDENTS WHO ARE LUTHERAN
• *See page 218*

BNY MELLON, N.A.

http://www.bnymellon.com/

JOHN L. BATES SCHOLARSHIP

Scholarship only for students who are pursuing a career in education. Not for graduate study programs. Must be resident of Massachusetts. Eligible applicant must be recommended by educational institution.

Academic Fields/Career Goals: Education.

Award: Scholarship for use in freshman, sophomore, junior, or senior years; not renewable. *Number:* varies. *Amount:* $300–$2000.

Eligibility Requirements: Applicant must be enrolled or expecting to enroll full-time at a four-year institution or university and resident of Massachusetts. Available to U.S. citizens.

Application Requirements: Application, essay, transcript. *Deadline:* April 15.

Contact: June Kfoury McNeil, Vice President
BNY Mellon, N.A.
201 Washington Street, 024-0092
Boston, MA 02108
Phone: 617-722-3891

CALIFORNIA STUDENT AID COMMISSION

http://www.csac.ca.gov/

CHILD DEVELOPMENT TEACHER AND SUPERVISOR GRANT PROGRAM
• *See page 172*

CALIFORNIA TEACHERS ASSOCIATION (CTA)

http://www.cta.org/

L. GORDON BITTLE MEMORIAL SCHOLARSHIP

Awards scholarships annually to active SCTA members for study in a teacher preparatory program. Students may reapply each year. Not available to those who are currently working in public schools as members of CTA. Minimum 3.5 GPA.

Academic Fields/Career Goals: Education.

Award: Scholarship for use in freshman, sophomore, junior, senior, or graduate years; not renewable. *Number:* up to 3. *Amount:* $2500.

Eligibility Requirements: Applicant must be enrolled or expecting to enroll full-time at a two-year or four-year institution or university and resident of California. Applicant or parent of applicant must be member of California Teachers Association. Applicant must have 3.5 GPA or higher. Available to U.S. citizens.

Application Requirements: Application, essay, references, transcript. *Deadline:* February 8.

Contact: Janeya Collins, Scholarship Coordinator
California Teachers Association (CTA)
PO Box 921
Burlingame, CA 94011-0921
Phone: 650-552-5468
Fax: 650-552-5001
E-mail: scholarships@cta.org

MARTIN LUTHER KING, JR. MEMORIAL SCHOLARSHIP

Awards for ethnic minority members of the California Teachers Association, their dependent children, and ethnic minority members of Student California Teachers Association who want to pursue degrees or credentials in public education. Minimum 3.5 GPA.

Academic Fields/Career Goals: Education.

Award: Scholarship for use in freshman, sophomore, junior, senior, or graduate years; not renewable. *Number:* varies. *Amount:* $1000–$2000.

Eligibility Requirements: Applicant must be American Indian/Alaska Native, Asian/Pacific Islander, Black (non-Hispanic), or Hispanic; enrolled or expecting to enroll full-time at a two-year or four-year institution or university and resident of California. Applicant or parent of applicant must be member of California Teachers Association. Applicant must have 3.5 GPA or higher. Available to U.S. citizens.

Application Requirements: Application, essay, financial need analysis, references. *Deadline:* March 14.

Contact: Janeya Collins, Scholarship Coordinator
California Teachers Association (CTA)
PO Box 921
Burlingame, CA 94011-0921
Phone: 650-552-5468
Fax: 650-552-5001
E-mail: scholarships@cta.org

CANADIAN INSTITUTE OF UKRAINIAN STUDIES

http://www.cius.ca/

LEO J. KRYSA UNDERGRADUATE SCHOLARSHIP
• *See page 104*

CANADIAN RECREATIONAL CANOEING ASSOCIATION

http://www.paddlingcanada.com/

BILL MASON MEMORIAL SCHOLARSHIP FUND

The Bill Mason Memorial Scholarship Fund is a tribute to the late Bill Mason, a Canadian recognized both nationally and internationally as an avid canoeist, environmentalist, filmmaker, photographer, artist and public speaker. The scholarship is intended to incorporate some of the characteristics that made Bill Mason unique and to help ensure that the memory, spirit and ideals that he represented are kept fresh in the minds of Canadians. Applicants must demonstrate experience and competency in any or all of the following: canoeing and kayaking skills, wilderness travel experience, wilderness leadership and guiding, environmental issues, communication skills.

Academic Fields/Career Goals: Education; Environmental Science; Natural Resources; Natural Sciences; Recreation, Parks, Leisure Studies; Sports-Related/Exercise Science.

Award: Scholarship for use in sophomore, senior, graduate, or post-graduate years; not renewable. *Number:* 1–1. *Amount:* $943.

Eligibility Requirements: Applicant must be Canadian citizen; enrolled or expecting to enroll full-time at a two-year or four-year or technical institution or university; resident of Alberta, British Columbia, Manitoba, New Brunswick, Newfoundland, North West Territories, Nova Scotia, Ontario, Prince Edward Island, Quebec, Saskatchewan, or Yukon and studying in Alberta, British Columbia, Manitoba, New Brunswick, Newfoundland, North West Territories, Nova Scotia, Ontario, Prince Edward Island, Quebec, Saskatchewan, or Yukon. Applicant must have 3.0 GPA or higher.

Application Requirements: Application, applicant must enter a contest, driver's license, financial need analysis, resume, test scores, transcript. *Deadline:* August 30.

Contact: Sue Burns, Business Manager
Canadian Recreational Canoeing Association
PO Box 20069
RPO Taylor Kidd
Kingston, ON K7P 2T6
Canada
Phone: 613-547-3196
E-mail: info@paddlingcanada.com

CATCHING THE DREAM

http://www.catchingthedream.org/

MATH, ENGINEERING, SCIENCE, BUSINESS, EDUCATION, COMPUTERS SCHOLARSHIPS
• *See page 147*

NATIVE AMERICAN LEADERSHIP IN EDUCATION (NALE)
• *See page 147*

CIEE: COUNCIL ON INTERNATIONAL EDUCATIONAL EXCHANGE

http://www.ciee.org/

U.S. DEPARTMENT OF EDUCATION FULBRIGHT-HAYS PROJECT ABROAD SCHOLARSHIP FOR PROGRAMS IN CHINA
• *See page 117*

COLLEGEBOUND FOUNDATION

http://www.collegeboundfoundation.org/

ALICE G. PINDERHUGHES SCHOLARSHIP

You must: major in the field of education and plan to teach in grades K–12; have a cumulative 3.0 GPA or better; demonstrate financial need; and submit a one-page typed essay describing a teacher who has made an impact on you and the reasons why you want to become a teacher.

Academic Fields/Career Goals: Education.

Award: Scholarship for use in freshman, sophomore, junior, or senior years; renewable. *Number:* 1. *Amount:* $500.

Eligibility Requirements: Applicant must be high school student; planning to enroll or expecting to enroll full-time at a two-year or four-year institution or university and resident of Maryland. Applicant must have 3.0 GPA or higher. Available to U.S. citizens.

Application Requirements: Application, essay, financial need analysis, resume, references, transcript. *Deadline:* March 1.

Contact: Deana Carr-Davis, Associate Program Director, Scholarship Programs
CollegeBound Foundation
300 Water Street, Suite 300
Baltimore, MD 21202
Phone: 410-783-2905 Ext. 207
Fax: 410-727-5786
E-mail: dcarr-davis@collegeboundfoundation.org

JANET B. SONDHEIM SCHOLARSHIP
• *See page 110*

SHEILA Z. KOLMAN MEMORIAL SCHOLARSHIP

You must: major in the field of education or a related field and aspire to become a teacher; have a cumulative 2.5 GPA or better; demonstrate financial need; and submit an essay (500–1,000 words) describing how a teacher affected your life in a positive way.

Academic Fields/Career Goals: Education.

Award: Scholarship for use in freshman, sophomore, junior, or senior years; renewable. *Number:* 1. *Amount:* $1000.

Eligibility Requirements: Applicant must be high school student; planning to enroll or expecting to enroll full-time at a two-year or four-year institution or university and resident of Maryland. Applicant must have 2.5 GPA or higher. Available to U.S. citizens.

Application Requirements: Application, essay, financial need analysis, resume, references, transcript. *Deadline:* March 1.

Contact: Deana Carr-Davis, Associate Program Director, Scholarship Programs
CollegeBound Foundation
300 Water Street, Suite 300
Baltimore, MD 21202
Phone: 410-783-2905 Ext. 207
Fax: 410-727-5786
E-mail: dcarr-davis@collegeboundfoundation.org

COLLEGE FOUNDATION OF NORTH CAROLINA

http://www.cfnc.org/

DOTTIE MARTIN TEACHERS SCHOLARSHIP

Awards annual scholarship of $500. Must be currently enrolled in an education program with an established career plan for teaching in North Carolina. Recent high school graduates are not eligible to apply. Applications may be downloaded from http://www.ncfrw.com/programs/dmtsf.html.

Academic Fields/Career Goals: Education.

Award: Scholarship for use in freshman, sophomore, junior, or senior years; not renewable. *Number:* 2–3. *Amount:* $500.

Eligibility Requirements: Applicant must be enrolled or expecting to enroll full-time at a two-year or four-year institution or university. Available to U.S. citizens.

Application Requirements: Application, transcript. *Deadline:* June 1.

Contact: Joyce Glass, Scholarship Committee
College Foundation of North Carolina
4413 Driftwood Drive
Clemmons, NC 27012
Phone: 336-766-0067
E-mail: fwglass@earthlink.net

CONFEDERATED TRIBES OF GRAND RONDE

http://www.grandronde.org/

EULA PETITE MEMORIAL COMPETITIVE SCHOLARSHIP

Available to any enrolled member of the Confederated Tribes of Grand Ronde. Available to education majors only. Renewable for six terms/four semesters of continuous study. Intended for last two years of undergraduate study or any two years of graduate study.

Academic Fields/Career Goals: Education.

Award: Scholarship for use in junior, senior, or graduate years; renewable. *Number:* 1. *Amount:* $7000.

Eligibility Requirements: Applicant must be American Indian/Alaska Native and enrolled or expecting to enroll full-time at a four-year institution or university. Applicant must have 3.0 GPA or higher. Available to U.S. and non-U.S. citizens.

Application Requirements: Application, essay, references, transcript, verification of tribal enrollment. *Deadline:* April 30.

Contact: Tribal Scholarship Coordinator
Confederated Tribes of Grand Ronde
9615 Grand Ronde Road
Grand Ronde, OR 97347
Phone: 800-422-0232 Ext. 2275
Fax: 503-879-2286
E-mail: education@grandronde.org

CONNECTICUT ASSOCIATION FOR HEALTH, PHYSICAL EDUCATION, RECREATION & DANCE

http://www.ctahperd.org/

GIBSON-LAEMEL CTAHPERD SCHOLARSHIP

Awarded to a college junior or senior accepted into a program of professional studies of health, physical education, recreation or dance. Post baccalaureate students are also eligible. Must be a Connecticut resident and attend a university or four-year college in Connecticut. Minimum 2.5 GPA required.

Academic Fields/Career Goals: Education; Sports-Related/Exercise Science.

Award: Scholarship for use in junior or senior years; not renewable. *Number:* 1–2. *Amount:* $1000.

Eligibility Requirements: Applicant must be enrolled or expecting to enroll full-time at a four-year institution or university; resident of Connecticut and studying in Connecticut. Applicant must have 2.5 GPA or higher. Available to U.S. citizens.

Application Requirements: Application, essay, references, transcript. *Deadline:* May 1.

Contact: Ms. Janice Skene, Scholarship Chair
Connecticut Association for Health, Physical Education, Recreation & Dance
Eastbury School, Neipsic Road
Glastonbury, CT 06033
Phone: 860-652-7858
E-mail: skenej@glastonburyus.org

MARY BENEVENTO CTAHPERD SCHOLARSHIP

Scholarship awarded to a graduating high school senior who plans to engage in professional studies in the fields of health education, physical education, recreation, or dance. Must be resident of Connecticut and plan to attend a university or four-year college in Connecticut.

Academic Fields/Career Goals: Education; Sports-Related/Exercise Science.

Award: Scholarship for use in freshman year; not renewable. *Number:* 1–2. *Amount:* $1000.

Eligibility Requirements: Applicant must be high school student; planning to enroll or expecting to enroll full-time at a four-year institution or university; resident of Connecticut and studying in Connecticut. Applicant must have 3.0 GPA or higher. Available to U.S. citizens.

Application Requirements: Application, essay, references, test scores, transcript. *Deadline:* April 1.

Contact: Janice Skene, Scholarship Chair
Connecticut Association for Health, Physical Education, Recreation & Dance
Eastbury School, Neipsic Road
Glastonbury, CT 06033
Phone: 860-652-7858
E-mail: skenej@glastonburyus.org

CONNECTICUT ASSOCIATION OF LATINOS IN HIGHER EDUCATION (CALAHE)

http://www.calahe.org/

CONNECTICUT ASSOCIATION OF LATINOS IN HIGHER EDUCATION SCHOLARSHIPS

Must demonstrate involvement with, and commitment to, activities that promote Latino pursuit of education. Must have a 3.0 GPA, be a U.S. citizen or permanent resident, be a resident of Connecticut, and attend a Connecticut higher education institution.

Academic Fields/Career Goals: Education.

Award: Scholarship for use in freshman, sophomore, junior, or senior years; not renewable. *Number:* 17–17. *Amount:* $1000.

Eligibility Requirements: Applicant must be Hispanic; enrolled or expecting to enroll full-time at a two-year or four-year or technical institution or university; resident of Connecticut and studying in Connecticut. Applicant must have 3.0 GPA or higher. Available to U.S. citizens.

Application Requirements: Application, essay, financial need analysis, transcript, Student Aid Report (SAR). *Deadline:* April 15.

Contact: Dr. Wilson Luna, Gateway Community-Technical College
Connecticut Association of Latinos in Higher Education (CALAHE)
60 Sargent Drive
New Haven, CT 06511
Phone: 203-285-2210
Fax: 203-285-2211
E-mail: wluna@gwcc.commnet.edu

CONNECTICUT DEPARTMENT OF HIGHER EDUCATION

http://www.ctdhe.org/

MINORITY TEACHER INCENTIVE GRANT PROGRAM

Program provides up to $5,000 a year for two years of full-time study in a teacher preparation program for the junior or senior year at a Connecticut college or university. Applicant must be African-American, Hispanic/Latino, Asian American or Native American heritage and be nominated by the Education Dean. Program graduates who teach in Connecticut public schools may be eligible for loan reimbursement stipends up to $2,500 per year for up to four years.

Academic Fields/Career Goals: Education.

Award: Grant for use in junior or senior years; renewable. *Number:* 82. *Amount:* $2500–$5000.

Eligibility Requirements: Applicant must be American Indian/Alaska Native, Asian/Pacific Islander, Black (non-Hispanic), or Hispanic; enrolled or expecting to enroll full-time at a four-year institution or university and studying in Connecticut. Available to U.S. citizens.

Application Requirements: Application. *Deadline:* October 1.

Contact: Ms. Judy-Ann Staple, Associate
Connecticut Department of Higher Education
61 Woodland Street
Hartford, CT 06105
Phone: 860-947-1855
Fax: 860-947-1838
E-mail: mtip@ctdhe.org

CONNECTICUT EDUCATION FOUNDATION INC.

http://www.cea.org/

SCHOLARSHIP FOR MINORITY COLLEGE STUDENTS

An award for qualified minority candidates who have been accepted into a teacher preparation program at an accredited Connecticut college or university. Must have a 2.75 GPA.

Academic Fields/Career Goals: Education.

Award: Scholarship for use in freshman, sophomore, junior, or senior years; not renewable. *Number:* 2. *Amount:* up to $1000.

Eligibility Requirements: Applicant must be American Indian/Alaska Native, Asian/Pacific Islander, Black (non-Hispanic), or Hispanic;

enrolled or expecting to enroll full-time at a two-year or four-year institution or university and studying in Connecticut. Available to U.S. citizens.

Application Requirements: Application, essay, references, transcript, income verification, letter of acceptance, copy of SAR. *Deadline:* May 1.

Contact: Sheila Cohen, President
Connecticut Education Foundation Inc.
Connecticut Education Foundation, 21 Oak Street, Suite 500
Hartford, CT 06106
Phone: 860-525-5641

SCHOLARSHIP FOR MINORITY HIGH SCHOOL STUDENTS

Award for qualified minority candidates who have been accepted into an accredited two or four-year Connecticut college or university and intend to enter the teaching profession. Must have 2.75 GPA.

Academic Fields/Career Goals: Education.

Award: Scholarship for use in freshman year; not renewable. *Number:* 1. *Amount:* up to $500.

Eligibility Requirements: Applicant must be American Indian/Alaska Native, Asian/Pacific Islander, Black (non-Hispanic), or Hispanic; high school student; planning to enroll or expecting to enroll full-time at a four-year institution or university and studying in Connecticut. Available to U.S. citizens.

Application Requirements: Application, essay, references, transcript, letter of acceptance, income verification, copy of SAR. *Deadline:* May 1.

Contact: President
Connecticut Education Foundation Inc.
21 Oak Street, Suite 500
Hartford, CT 06106
Phone: 860-525-5641

CONTINENTAL SOCIETY, DAUGHTERS OF INDIAN WARS

http://www.csdiw.org/

CONTINENTAL SOCIETY, DAUGHTERS OF INDIAN WARS SCHOLARSHIP

Award for a certified Indian tribal member enrolled in an undergraduate degree program in education or social service. Must maintain minimum 3.0 GPA and work with Native Americans in a social service or educational role after graduation. Preference given to those in or entering junior year.

Academic Fields/Career Goals: Education; Social Services.

Award: Scholarship for use in freshman, sophomore, junior, or senior years; not renewable. *Number:* 3. *Amount:* $2500–$5000.

Eligibility Requirements: Applicant must be American Indian/Alaska Native and enrolled or expecting to enroll full-time at a two-year or four-year institution or university. Applicant must have 3.0 GPA or higher. Available to U.S. citizens.

Application Requirements: Application, essay, financial need analysis, references, transcript, tribal membership proof. *Deadline:* June 15.

Contact: Mrs. Leslie V Canavan, National Scholarship Chairman
Continental Society, Daughters of Indian Wars
P O Box 6695
Chesterfield, MO 63006-6695
Phone: 314-647-7986
E-mail: Leslie@khs65.com

CULTURAL SERVICES OF THE FRENCH EMBASSY

http://www.frenchculture.org/

TEACHING ASSISTANT PROGRAM IN FRANCE

Grants support American students as they teach English for 6–9 months in the French school system. Monthly stipend of about 780 euros (net) supports recipient in the life-style of a typical French student. Must be U.S. citizen or a permanent resident (not a French citizen). Proficiency in French is required. and may not have received a similar grant from the French government for the last three years. For additional information and application, visit web site http://www.frenchculture.org.

Academic Fields/Career Goals: Education; Foreign Language.

Award: Grant for use in junior, senior, graduate, or postgraduate years; not renewable. *Number:* 1480. *Amount:* $1050.

Eligibility Requirements: Applicant must be age 20-29; enrolled or expecting to enroll full- or part-time at a four-year institution or university and must have an interest in French language. Available to U.S. citizens.

Application Requirements: Application, photo, references, self-addressed stamped envelope, transcript. *Fee:* $35.

Contact: Carolyn Collins, Educational Affairs Program Officer
Cultural Services of the French Embassy
4101 Reservoir Road, NW
Washington, DC 20007
Phone: 202-944-6294
E-mail: assistant.washington-amba@diplomatie.gouv.fr

DECA (DISTRIBUTIVE EDUCATION CLUBS OF AMERICA)

http://www.deca.org/

HARRY A. APPLEGATE SCHOLARSHIP
• See page 149

DELAWARE HIGHER EDUCATION OFFICE

http://www.doe.k12.de.us

CHRISTA MCAULIFFE TEACHER SCHOLARSHIP LOAN-DELAWARE

Award for legal residents of Delaware who are U.S. citizens or eligible non-citizens. Must be full-time student enrolled at a Delaware college in an undergraduate program leading to teacher certification. High school seniors must rank in upper half of class and have a combined score of 1570 on the SAT. Undergraduates must have at least a 2.75 cumulative GPA. For details visit web site http://www.doe.k12.de.us.

Academic Fields/Career Goals: Education.

Award: Forgivable loan for use in freshman, sophomore, junior, or senior years; renewable. *Number:* 1–60. *Amount:* $1000–$5000.

Eligibility Requirements: Applicant must be enrolled or expecting to enroll full-time at a four-year institution or university; resident of Delaware and studying in Delaware. Available to U.S. citizens.

Application Requirements: Application, essay, test scores, transcript. *Deadline:* March 28.

Contact: Carylin Brinkley, Program Administrator
Delaware Higher Education Office
Carvel State Office Building, 820 North French Street, Fifth Floor
Wilmington, DE 19801-3509
Phone: 302-577-5240
Fax: 302-577-6765
E-mail: cbrinkley@doe.k12.de.us

EASTERN STAR-GRAND CHAPTER OF CALIFORNIA

http://www.oescal.org/

SCHOLARSHIPS FOR EDUCATION, BUSINESS AND RELIGION
• See page 149

FINANCE AUTHORITY OF MAINE

http://www.famemaine.com/

EDUCATORS FOR MAINE FORGIVABLE LOAN PROGRAM

Forgivable loan for residents of Maine who are high school seniors, college students, or college graduates with a minimum 3.0 GPA, studying or preparing to study teacher education. Must teach in Maine upon graduation. Award based on merit. For application information see web site http://www.famemaine.com.

Academic Fields/Career Goals: Education.

Award: Forgivable loan for use in freshman, sophomore, junior, or senior years; renewable. *Number:* up to 500. *Amount:* $2000–$3000.

Eligibility Requirements: Applicant must be enrolled or expecting to enroll full-time at a two-year or four-year institution or university and resident of Maine. Applicant must have 3.0 GPA or higher. Available to U.S. citizens.

Application Requirements: Application, essay, test scores, transcript. *Deadline:* May 15.

Contact: Claude Roy, Manager, Operations
Finance Authority of Maine
Five Community Drive
PO Box 949
Augusta, ME 04332-0949
Phone: 207-620-3507
E-mail: education@famemaine.com

QUALITY CHILD CARE EDUCATION SCHOLARSHIP PROGRAM

Open to residents of Maine who are taking a minimum of one childhood education course or are pursuing a child development associate certificate, associate degree, baccalaureate degree, or post-baccalaureate teacher certification in child-care related fields. Scholarships of up to $500 per course or $2000 per year available. See web site for information http://www.famemaine.com.

Academic Fields/Career Goals: Education.

Award: Scholarship for use in freshman, sophomore, junior, or senior years; not renewable. *Number:* 70–300. *Amount:* $500–$2000.

Eligibility Requirements: Applicant must be enrolled or expecting to enroll full- or part-time at a two-year or four-year institution and resident of Maine. Available to U.S. citizens.

Application Requirements: Application, financial need analysis, tax return. *Deadline:* continuous.

Contact: Claude Roy, Manager, Operations
Finance Authority of Maine
Five Community Drive
PO Box 949
Augusta, ME 04332-0949
Phone: 207-620-3507
E-mail: education@famemaine.com

GENERAL BOARD OF HIGHER EDUCATION AND MINISTRY

http://www.gbhem.org/

EDITH M. ALLEN SCHOLARSHIP

Scholarship for outstanding African-American graduate or undergraduate students pursuing a degree in education, social work, medicine, and/or other health professions. Must be enrolled at a United Methodist college or university and be an active, full member of the United Methodist Church for at least three years.

Academic Fields/Career Goals: Education; Health and Medical Sciences; Social Services.

Award: Scholarship for use in freshman, sophomore, junior, or senior years; not renewable. *Number:* varies. *Amount:* varies.

Eligibility Requirements: Applicant must be Methodist; Black (non-Hispanic) and enrolled or expecting to enroll full-time at a four-year institution or university. Available to U.S. citizens.

Application Requirements: Application, essay, references, transcript. *Deadline:* March 1.

Contact: Scholarship Committee
General Board of Higher Education and Ministry
The United Methodist Church, 1001 19th Avenue South
PO Box 340007
Nashville, TN 37202
Phone: 615-340-7344
E-mail: umscholar@gbhem.org

GENERAL FEDERATION OF WOMEN'S CLUBS OF MASSACHUSETTS

http://www.gfwcma.org/

NEWTONVILLE WOMAN'S CLUB SCHOLARSHIPS

Applicant must be a senior in a Massachusetts high school in who will enroll in a four-year accredited college or university in a teacher-training program that leads to certification to teach.

Academic Fields/Career Goals: Education.

Award: Scholarship for use in freshman year; not renewable. *Number:* 1. *Amount:* $600.

Eligibility Requirements: Applicant must be high school student; planning to enroll or expecting to enroll full-time at a four-year institution or university and resident of Massachusetts. Available to U.S. citizens.

Application Requirements: Application, driver's license, essay, interview, references, self-addressed stamped envelope, transcript. *Deadline:* March 1.

Contact: Marta DiBenedetto, Scholarship Chairman
General Federation of Women's Clubs of Massachusetts
245 Dutton Road, PO Box 679
Sudbury, MA 01776-0679
Phone: 978-444-9105
E-mail: marta_dibenedetto@nylim.com

GEORGE T. WELCH TRUST

http://www.bakerboyer.com/

SARA CARLSON MEMORIAL FUND

Grants for students majoring in education. Must be enrolled full-time and maintain a minimum GPA of 2.0. Must reapply. The budget form must be completed and cover the entire school year.

Academic Fields/Career Goals: Education.

Award: Scholarship for use in freshman, sophomore, junior, or senior years; not renewable. *Number:* varies. *Amount:* up to $300.

Eligibility Requirements: Applicant must be enrolled or expecting to enroll full-time at a four-year institution or university. Available to U.S. citizens.

Application Requirements: Application. *Deadline:* April 13.

Contact: Ted Cohan, Trust Portfolio Manager
George T. Welch Trust
Baker Boyer Bank, Investment Management & Trust Services
7 West Main, PO Box 1796
Walla Walla, WA 99362
Phone: 509-526-1204
Fax: 509-522-3136
E-mail: cohant@bakerboyer.com

GEORGIA ASSOCIATION OF EDUCATORS

http://www.gae.org/

GAE GFIE SCHOLARSHIP FOR ASPIRING TEACHERS

Scholarships will be awarded to graduating seniors who currently attend a fully accredited public Georgia high school and will attend a fully accredited Georgia college or university within the next twelve months. Must have a 3.0 GPA. Must submit three letters of recommendation. Must have plans to enter the teaching profession.

Academic Fields/Career Goals: Education.

Award: Scholarship for use in freshman year; not renewable. *Number:* up to 20. *Amount:* $1000.

Eligibility Requirements: Applicant must be enrolled or expecting to enroll full-time at a two-year or four-year institution or university; resident of Georgia and studying in Georgia. Applicant must have 3.0 GPA or higher. Available to U.S. citizens.

Application Requirements: Application, references, transcript. *Deadline:* February 1.

Contact: Sharon Henderson, Staff Associate
Georgia Association of Educators
100 Crescent Centre Parkway, Suite 500
Tucker, GA 30084-7049
Phone: 678-837-1114
Fax: 678-837-1150
E-mail: sharon.henderson@gae.org

GOLDEN APPLE FOUNDATION

http://www.goldenapple.org/

GOLDEN APPLE SCHOLARS OF ILLINOIS

Applicants must be between the ages of 16 and 21 and maintain a GPA of 2.5. Eligible applicants must be residents of Illinois studying in Illinois. Recipients must agree to teach in high-need Illinois schools.

Academic Fields/Career Goals: Education.

Award: Scholarship for use in freshman, sophomore, junior, or senior years; renewable. *Number:* 100–150. *Amount:* $23,000.

Eligibility Requirements: Applicant must be age 16-21; enrolled or expecting to enroll full-time at a four-year institution or university; resident of Illinois and studying in Illinois. Available to U.S. citizens.

Application Requirements: Application, essay, interview, photo, references, test scores, transcript, social security card. *Deadline:* November 15.

Contact: Ms. Patricia Kilduff, Director of Recruitment and Placement
Golden Apple Foundation
8 South Michigan Avenue, Suite 700
Chicago, IL 60603-3318
Phone: 312-407-0006 Ext. 105
E-mail: kilduff@goldenapple.org

GOLDEN KEY INTERNATIONAL HONOUR SOCIETY

http://www.goldenkey.org/

EDUCATION ACHIEVEMENT AWARDS

Awards members who excel in the study of education. Eligible applicants are undergraduate, graduate and postgraduate members who are currently enrolled in classes at a degree-granting program. One winner will receive a $1000 award. The second place winner will receive $750 and the third place winner will receive $500.

Academic Fields/Career Goals: Education.

Award: Prize for use in freshman, sophomore, junior, senior, graduate, or postgraduate years; not renewable. *Number:* 3. *Amount:* $500–$1000.

Eligibility Requirements: Applicant must be enrolled or expecting to enroll full- or part-time at a four-year institution or university. Available to U.S. and non-U.S. citizens.

Application Requirements: Application, applicant must enter a contest, essay, references, transcript, education related paper or report. *Deadline:* March 3.

Contact: Scholarship Program Administrators
Golden Key International Honour Society
PO Box 23737
Nashville, TN 37202-3737
Phone: 800-377-2401
E-mail: scholarships@goldenkey.org

GREATER KANAWHA VALLEY FOUNDATION

http://www.tgkvf.org/

JOSEPH C. BASILE, II MEMORIAL SCHOLARSHIP FUND

Award for residents of West Virginia who are majoring in education. Must be an undergraduate at a college or university in West Virginia. Award based on financial need.

Academic Fields/Career Goals: Education.

Award: Scholarship for use in freshman, sophomore, junior, or senior years; not renewable. *Number:* 1–2. *Amount:* $750.

Eligibility Requirements: Applicant must be enrolled or expecting to enroll full-time at a four-year institution or university; resident of West Virginia and studying in West Virginia. Available to U.S. citizens.

Application Requirements: Application, essay, financial need analysis, references, self-addressed stamped envelope, test scores, transcript. *Deadline:* January 15.

Contact: Susan Hoover, Scholarship Coordinator
Greater Kanawha Valley Foundation
PO Box 3041
Charleston, WV 25331
Phone: 304-346-3620
Fax: 304-346-3640
E-mail: tgkvf@tgkvf.org

HAWAIIAN LODGE, F&AM

http://www.glhawaii.org/

HAWAIIAN LODGE SCHOLARSHIPS
• *See page 106*

HAWAII EDUCATION ASSOCIATION

http://www.heaed.com/

HAWAII EDUCATION ASSOCIATION STUDENT TEACHER SCHOLARSHIP

Scholarship available to children or grandchildren of HEA members. Intent is to minimize the need for employment during student teaching semester. Must be enrolled full-time in an undergraduate or post-baccalaureate program in accredited institution of higher learning.

Academic Fields/Career Goals: Education.

Award: Scholarship for use in senior, graduate, or postgraduate years; not renewable. *Number:* up to 2. *Amount:* up to $3000.

Eligibility Requirements: Applicant must be enrolled or expecting to enroll full-time at a four-year institution or university. Applicant or parent of applicant must be member of Hawaii Education Association. Available to U.S. citizens.

Application Requirements: Application, driver's license, financial need analysis, photo, references, transcript. *Deadline:* April 1.

Contact: Scholarship Committee
Hawaii Education Association
1953 South Beretania Street, Suite 3C
Honolulu, HI 96826-1304
Phone: 808-949-6657
Fax: 808-944-2032
E-mail: hea.office@heaed.com

HIROSHI BARBARA KIM YAMASHITA HEA SCHOLARSHIP

Two $2000 scholarships awarded to full-time undergraduate education majors currently attending an accredited institution of higher learning and intending to teach in a Hawaii public school. Minimum 3.2 GPA required.

Academic Fields/Career Goals: Education.

Award: Scholarship for use in freshman, sophomore, junior, or senior years; not renewable. *Number:* 2. *Amount:* $2000.

Eligibility Requirements: Applicant must be enrolled or expecting to enroll full-time at a two-year or four-year or technical institution or university. Available to U.S. citizens.

Application Requirements: Application, financial need analysis, references, test scores. *Deadline:* April 1.

Contact: Carol Yoneshige, Executive Director
Hawaii Education Association
1953 South Beretania Street, Suite 3C
Honolulu, HI 96826-1340
Phone: 808-949-6657
Fax: 808-944-2032
E-mail: hea.office@heaed.com

ILLINOIS PTA

http://www.illinoispta.org/

ILLINOIS PTA LILLIAN E. GLOVER SCHOLARSHIP

Scholarship has evolved to encourage Illinois college-bound high school seniors entering the field of education or an education-related field at the college/university of their choice.

Academic Fields/Career Goals: Education.

Award: Scholarship for use in freshman year; not renewable. *Amount:* $500–$1000.

Eligibility Requirements: Applicant must be high school student; planning to enroll or expecting to enroll full-time at a four-year institution or university and resident of Illinois. Available to U.S. citizens.

Application Requirements: Application, essay, resume, references, test scores, transcript. *Deadline:* March 5.

Contact: Toni Bugay, Scholarship Chairman
Illinois PTA
901 South Spring Street
Springfield, IL 62704
Phone: 217-528-9617
Fax: 217-528-9490
E-mail: il_office@pta.org

ILLINOIS STUDENT ASSISTANCE COMMISSION (ISAC)

http://www.collegezone.org/

ILLINOIS FUTURE TEACHERS CORPS PROGRAM

Scholarships are available for students planning to become teachers in Illinois. Students must be Illinois residents, enrolled or accepted as a junior or above in a Teacher Education Program at an Illinois college or university. By receiving the award, students agree to teach for five years at either a public, private, or parochial Illinois preschool, or at a public elementary or secondary school.

Academic Fields/Career Goals: Education.

Award: Scholarship for use in junior, senior, or graduate years; renewable. *Amount:* $5000–$10,000.

Eligibility Requirements: Applicant must be enrolled or expecting to enroll full- or part-time at a four-year institution or university; resident of Illinois and studying in Illinois. Available to U.S. citizens.

Application Requirements: Application, financial need analysis, FAFSA. *Deadline:* March 1.

Contact: College Zone Counselor
Illinois Student Assistance Commission (ISAC)
1755 Lake Cook Road
Deerfield, IL 60015-5209
Phone: 800-899-4722
Fax: 847-831-8549
E-mail: collegezone@isac.org

MINORITY TEACHERS OF ILLINOIS SCHOLARSHIP PROGRAM

Award for minority students intending to become school teachers; teaching commitment attached to receipt. Number of scholarships and the individual dollar amounts vary.

Academic Fields/Career Goals: Education; Special Education.

Award: Scholarship for use in freshman, sophomore, junior, senior, graduate, or postgraduate years; renewable. *Amount:* up to $5000.

Eligibility Requirements: Applicant must be American Indian/Alaska Native, Asian/Pacific Islander, Black (non-Hispanic), or Hispanic; enrolled or expecting to enroll full- or part-time at a two-year or four-year institution or university; resident of Illinois and studying in Illinois. Available to U.S. citizens.

Application Requirements: Application, transcript. *Deadline:* March 1.

Contact: College Zone Counselor
Illinois Student Assistance Commission (ISAC)
1755 Lake Cook Road
Deerfield, IL 60015-5209
Phone: 800-899-4722
Fax: 847-831-8549
E-mail: collegezone@isac.org

INDIANA RETIRED TEACHER'S ASSOCIATION (IRTA)

http://www.retiredteachers.org/

INDIANA RETIRED TEACHERS ASSOCIATION FOUNDATION SCHOLARSHIP

Scholarship available to college sophomores or juniors who are enrolled full-time in an education program at an Indiana college or university for a baccalaureate degree. The applicant must be the child, grandchild, legal dependant or spouse of an active, retired or deceased member of the Indiana State Teachers Retirement Fund.

Academic Fields/Career Goals: Education.

Award: Scholarship for use in sophomore or junior years; not renewable. *Number:* 8. *Amount:* $1500.

Eligibility Requirements: Applicant must be enrolled or expecting to enroll full-time at a four-year institution or university; resident of Indiana and studying in Indiana. Applicant or parent of applicant must have employment or volunteer experience in teaching/education. Available to U.S. and non-U.S. citizens.

Application Requirements: Application, essay, financial need analysis, references, transcript. *Deadline:* February 22.

Contact: Executive Director
Indiana Retired Teacher's Association (IRTA)
150 West Market Street, Suite 610
Indianapolis, IN 46204-2812
Phone: 888-454-9333
Fax: 317-637-9671

INTERNATIONAL ASSOCIATION OF GREAT LAKES RESEARCH

http://www.iaglr.org/

PAUL W. RODGERS SCHOLARSHIP
• See page 224

INTERNATIONAL TECHNOLOGY EDUCATION ASSOCIATION

http://www.iteaconnect.org/

INTERNATIONAL TECHNOLOGY EDUCATION ASSOCIATION UNDERGRADUATE SCHOLARSHIP IN TECHNOLOGY EDUCATION

A scholarship for undergraduate students pursuing a degree in technology education and technological studies. Applicants must be members of the association.

Academic Fields/Career Goals: Education; Engineering/Technology; Science, Technology, and Society.

Award: Scholarship for use in freshman, sophomore, junior, or senior years; not renewable. *Number:* 3. *Amount:* $1000.

Eligibility Requirements: Applicant must be enrolled or expecting to enroll full-time at a four-year institution or university. Applicant or parent of applicant must be member of International Technology Education Association. Applicant must have 2.5 GPA or higher. Available to U.S. and non-U.S. citizens.

Application Requirements: Application, resume, references, transcript. *Deadline:* December 1.

Contact: Scholarship Committee
International Technology Education Association
1914 Association Drive, Suite 201
Reston, VA 20191
Phone: 703-860-2100
Fax: 703-860-0353
E-mail: iteaordr@iris.org

JACK J. ISGUR FOUNDATION

JACK J. ISGUR FOUNDATION SCHOLARSHIP
• See page 112

KANSAS BOARD OF REGENTS

http://www.kansasregents.org/

KANSAS TEACHER SERVICE SCHOLARSHIP

Scholarship to encourage talented students to enter the teaching profession and teach in Kansas in specific curriculum areas or in underserved areas of Kansas. Students must be Kansas residents attending a postsecondary institution in Kansas. For more details, refer to web site http://www.kansasregents.org.

Academic Fields/Career Goals: Education.

Award: Scholarship for use in junior, senior, or graduate years; renewable. *Number:* varies. *Amount:* $2150–$5374.

Eligibility Requirements: Applicant must be enrolled or expecting to enroll full- or part-time at a four-year institution or university. Applicant must have 3.0 GPA or higher. Available to U.S. citizens.

Application Requirements: Application, essay, financial need analysis, resume, references, test scores, transcript. *Fee:* $12. *Deadline:* May 1.

Contact: Diane Lindeman, Director of Student Financial Assistance
Kansas Board of Regents
1000 Jackson, SW, Suite 520
Topeka, KS 66612-1368
Phone: 785-296-3517
Fax: 785-296-0983
E-mail: dlindeman@ksbor.org

KE ALI'I PAUAHI FOUNDATION

http://www.pauahi.org/

CHARLES COCKETT 'OHANA SCHOLARSHIP
• See page 106

DAN AND RACHEL MAHI EDUCATIONAL SCHOLARSHIP

Scholarship provides support to undergraduate or graduate students. Must demonstrate financial need. Minimum GPA of 2.0 required. Submit two letters of recommendation; one from a teacher or counselor and one from and employer or community or organization.

Academic Fields/Career Goals: Education.

Award: Scholarship for use in freshman, sophomore, junior, senior, or graduate years; not renewable. *Number:* 1–2. *Amount:* $800–$1000.

Eligibility Requirements: Applicant must be enrolled or expecting to enroll full-time at a two-year or four-year institution or university. Available to U.S. citizens.

Application Requirements: Application, financial need analysis, references, transcript, college acceptance letter, copy of SAR. *Deadline:* April 1.

Contact: Mrs. Mavis Shiraishi-Nagao, Scholarship Administrator
Ke Ali'i Pauahi Foundation
567 S. King Street, Suite 160
Honolulu, HI 96813
Phone: 808-534-3966
E-mail: scholarships@pauahi.org

GLADYS KAMAKAKUOKALANI AINOA BRANDT SCHOLARSHIP

Provides scholarships for full-time junior, senior or graduate students at an accredited university aspiring to enter the educational profession. Applicants must demonstrate financial need, a GPA of 2.5 or higher is required, and priority will be given to current or former residents of Kauai. Submit two letters of recommendation from a teacher, counselor or community organization.

Academic Fields/Career Goals: Education.

Award: Scholarship for use in junior, senior, or graduate years; not renewable. *Number:* up to 4. *Amount:* up to $3000.

Eligibility Requirements: Applicant must be enrolled or expecting to enroll full-time at a four-year institution or university and resident of Hawaii. Applicant must have 2.5 GPA or higher. Available to U.S. citizens.

Application Requirements: Application, essay, financial need analysis, references, transcript, signed application confirmation page, copy of completed Student Aid Report (SAR). *Deadline:* April 1.

Contact: Mavis Shiraishi-Nagao, Scholarship Administrator
Phone: 808-534-3966
E-mail: scholarships@pauahi.org

INSPIRATIONAL EDUCATOR SCHOLARSHIP

In recognition of inspirational educators who have made a difference in the lives of students, this endowment provides educational scholarships for full- or part-time college students pursuing a career in the field of education. Submit two letters or recommendation from teachers, counselors, employers, coaches or other citing examples of how applicant has already worked in and will continue to work with Hawaiian community. Submit essay on applicant's commitment to education and how you would use scholarship funds for educational costs.

Academic Fields/Career Goals: Education.

Award: Scholarship for use in freshman, sophomore, junior, senior, or graduate years; not renewable. *Number:* up to 2. *Amount:* up to $1200.

Eligibility Requirements: Applicant must be enrolled or expecting to enroll full- or part-time at a two-year or four-year institution or university. Available to U.S. citizens.

Application Requirements: Application, essay, financial need analysis, references, transcript, college acceptance letter, copy of signed online application confirmation page, copy of completed SAR. *Deadline:* April 1.

Contact: Mavis Shiraishi-Nagao, Scholarship Administrator
Phone: 808-534-3966
E-mail: scholarships@pauahi.org

MYRON & LAURA THOMPSON SCHOLARSHIP
• See page 172

KENTUCKY DEPARTMENT OF EDUCATION

http://www.education.ky.gov/

KENTUCKY MINORITY EDUCATOR RECRUITMENT AND RETENTION (KMERR) SCHOLARSHIP

Scholarship for minority teacher candidates who rank in the upper half of their class or have a minimum 2.5 GPA. Must be a U.S. citizen and Kentucky resident enrolled in one of Kentucky's eight public institutions. Must teach one semester in Kentucky for each semester the scholarship is received.

Academic Fields/Career Goals: Education.

Award: Forgivable loan for use in freshman, sophomore, junior, or senior years; renewable. *Number:* 400. *Amount:* $2500–$5000.

Eligibility Requirements: Applicant must be American Indian/Alaska Native, Asian/Pacific Islander, Black (non-Hispanic), or Hispanic; enrolled or expecting to enroll full-time at a two-year or four-year institution or university; resident of Kentucky and studying in Kentucky. Applicant must have 2.5 GPA or higher. Available to U.S. citizens.

Application Requirements: Application, references, test scores, transcript. *Deadline:* continuous.

Contact: Natasha Murray, State Program Coordinator
Kentucky Department of Education
500 Mero Street, 17th Floor
Frankfort, KY 40601
Phone: 502-564-1479
Fax: 502-564-6952
E-mail: michael.dailey@education.ky.gov

KENTUCKY HIGHER EDUCATION ASSISTANCE AUTHORITY (KHEAA)

http://www.kheaa.com/

EARLY CHILDHOOD DEVELOPMENT SCHOLARSHIP
• See page 172

KENTUCKY TEACHER SCHOLARSHIP PROGRAM

Awards Kentucky residents attending Kentucky institutions and pursuing initial teacher certification programs. Must teach one semester for each semester of award received. In critical shortage areas, must teach one semester for every two semesters of award received. If teaching service is not rendered, the scholarship converts to a loan that must be repaid with interest. For more information, see Web http://www.kheaa.com.

Academic Fields/Career Goals: Education.

Award: Forgivable loan for use in freshman, sophomore, junior, or senior years; renewable. *Number:* 100–300. *Amount:* $325–$5000.

Eligibility Requirements: Applicant must be enrolled or expecting to enroll full-time at a two-year or four-year institution or university; resident of Kentucky and studying in Kentucky. Available to U.S. citizens.

Application Requirements: Application, financial need analysis, FAFSA. *Deadline:* May 1.

Contact: Jennifer Toth, Scholarship Coordinator
Kentucky Higher Education Assistance Authority (KHEAA)
PO Box 798
Frankfort, KY 40602
Phone: 800-928-8926 Ext. 67392
Fax: 502-696-7473
E-mail: jtoth@kheaa.com

MINORITY EDUCATOR RECRUITMENT AND RETENTION SCHOLARSHIP

Conversion loan or scholarship for Kentucky residents. Provides up to $5000 per academic year to minority students majoring in teacher education and pursuing initial teacher certification. Must be repaid with interest if scholarship requirements are not met.

Academic Fields/Career Goals: Education; Special Education.

Award: Forgivable loan for use in freshman, sophomore, junior, or senior years; not renewable. *Number:* 200–300. *Amount:* up to $5000.

Eligibility Requirements: Applicant must be American Indian/Alaska Native, Asian/Pacific Islander, Black (non-Hispanic), or Hispanic; enrolled or expecting to enroll full-time at a two-year or four-year institution or university; resident of Kentucky and studying in Kentucky. Available to U.S. citizens.

Application Requirements: Application. *Deadline:* continuous.

Contact: Natasha Murray, Program Director, Kentucky Department of Education
Kentucky Higher Education Assistance Authority (KHEAA)
500 Metro Street
Frankfort, KY 40601
Phone: 502-564-1479
E-mail: natasha.murray@education.ky.gov

LINCOLN COMMUNITY FOUNDATION

http://www.lcf.org/

DALE E. SIEFKES MEMORIAL SCHOLARSHIP

One scholarship available to a college student currently pursuing a career in education. Applicant should be a junior or senior level Nebraska college or university student with a GPA of 3.8 or higher. See web site for application http://www.lcf.org.

Academic Fields/Career Goals: Education.

Award: Scholarship for use in junior or senior years; not renewable. *Number:* 1. *Amount:* $500–$1000.

Eligibility Requirements: Applicant must be enrolled or expecting to enroll full-time at a four-year institution or university and studying in Nebraska. Applicant must have 3.5 GPA or higher. Available to U.S. citizens.

Application Requirements: Application, essay, financial need analysis, test scores, transcript. *Deadline:* April 15.

Contact: Sonya Brakeman, Grants/Scholarships Coordinator
Lincoln Community Foundation
215 Centennial Mall South, Suite 100
Lincoln, NE 68508
Phone: 402-474-2345
Fax: 402-476-8532
E-mail: sonyab@lcf.org

FLORENCE TURNER KARLIN SCHOLARSHIP FOR UNDERGRADUATES

Scholarship for former graduate of any high school in Nebraska who is pursuing a degree in education in a college or university in Nebraska. Applicants must have completed at least their sophomore year in college and have a GPA of 3.0 or better.

Academic Fields/Career Goals: Education.

Award: Scholarship for use in junior or senior years; not renewable. *Number:* 1–10. *Amount:* $500–$1000.

Eligibility Requirements: Applicant must be enrolled or expecting to enroll full-time at a two-year or four-year institution or university; resident of Nebraska and studying in Nebraska. Applicant must have 3.0 GPA or higher. Available to U.S. citizens.

Application Requirements: Application, essay, references, test scores, transcript. *Deadline:* March 15.

Contact: Sonya Brakeman, Grants/Scholarships Coordinator
Lincoln Community Foundation
215 Centennial Mall South, Suite 100
Lincoln, NE 68508
Phone: 402-474-2345
Fax: 402-476-8532
E-mail: sonyab@lcf.org

GEORGE AND LYNNA GENE COOK SCHOLARSHIP

Applicants must be a current graduating senior or a former graduate of any high school in Nebraska with a GPA of 3.0 or better. Must be members of First Church of God congregations that are affiliated with the church body located in Anderson, Indiana. Must be pursuing a degree in ministry or education and demonstrate financial need.

Academic Fields/Career Goals: Education; Religion/Theology.

Award: Scholarship for use in freshman, sophomore, junior, or senior years; renewable. *Number:* 1. *Amount:* $500.

Eligibility Requirements: Applicant must be enrolled or expecting to enroll full-time at a two-year or four-year institution or university. Applicant must have 3.0 GPA or higher. Available to U.S. citizens.

Application Requirements: Application, financial need analysis, test scores, transcript, letter of recommendation from the pastor or other current congregation leader. *Deadline:* March 15.

Contact: Sonya Brakeman, Grants/Scholarships Coordinator
Lincoln Community Foundation
215 Centennial Mall South, Suite 100
Lincoln, NE 68508
Phone: 402-474-2345
Fax: 402-476-8532
E-mail: sonyab@lcf.org

NEBRASKA RURAL COMMUNITY SCHOOLS ASSOCIATION SCHOLARSHIP

Scholarships for students attending schools in Nebraska and holding current memberships in NRCSA. Must major in education and demonstrate financial need. Applicants should also demonstrate academic achievement, leadership, character, and initiative. Preferred students will be involved in extracurricular activities. Minimum GPA of 3.5 is required.

Academic Fields/Career Goals: Education.

Award: Scholarship for use in freshman year; not renewable. *Number:* 6. *Amount:* $500–$1000.

Eligibility Requirements: Applicant must be high school student; planning to enroll or expecting to enroll full-time at a four-year institution or university; resident of Nebraska and studying in Nebraska. Applicant must have 3.5 GPA or higher. Available to U.S. citizens.

Application Requirements: Application, essay, financial need analysis, references. *Deadline:* February 9.

Contact: Sonya Brakeman, Grants/Scholarships Coordinator
Lincoln Community Foundation
215 Centennial Mall South, Suite 100
Lincoln, NE 68508
Phone: 402-474-2345
Fax: 402-476-8532
E-mail: sonyab@lcf.org

MARION D. AND EVA S. PEEPLES FOUNDATION TRUST SCHOLARSHIP PROGRAM

http://www.jccf.org/

MARION A. AND EVA S. PEEPLES SCHOLARSHIPS

Award for undergraduate study in nursing, dietetics, and teaching in industrial arts. Applicant must reapply each year for renewal. Recipient must maintain 2.5 GPA. Must be Indiana resident and attending an Indiana school.

Academic Fields/Career Goals: Education; Engineering/Technology; Food Science/Nutrition; Nursing; Trade/Technical Specialties.

Award: Scholarship for use in freshman, sophomore, junior, or senior years; not renewable. *Number:* 30–35. *Amount:* $1000–$3000.

Eligibility Requirements: Applicant must be enrolled or expecting to enroll full-time at a two-year or four-year or technical institution or university; resident of Indiana and studying in Indiana. Applicant must have 2.5 GPA or higher. Available to U.S. citizens.

Application Requirements: Application, driver's license, financial need analysis, interview, references, self-addressed stamped envelope, test scores, transcript. *Deadline:* March 1.

Contact: Kim Kastings, Scholarship Director
Marion D. and Eva S. Peeples Foundation Trust Scholarship Program
PO Box 217
Franklin, IN 46131-2311
Phone: 317-738-2213
Fax: 317-738-9113
E-mail: kimk@jccf.org

MARYLAND STATE HIGHER EDUCATION COMMISSION

http://www.mhec.state.md.us/

JANET L. HOFFMANN LOAN ASSISTANCE REPAYMENT PROGRAM

Provides assistance for repayment of loan debt to Maryland residents working full-time in nonprofit organizations and state or local governments. Must submit Employment Verification Form and Lender Verification Form.

Academic Fields/Career Goals: Education; Law/Legal Services; Nursing; Social Services; Therapy/Rehabilitation.

Award: Grant for use in freshman, sophomore, junior, or senior years; not renewable. *Number:* up to 700. *Amount:* $1500–$10,000.

Eligibility Requirements: Applicant must be enrolled or expecting to enroll full-time at a four-year institution or university; resident of Maryland and studying in Maryland. Applicant or parent of applicant must have employment or volunteer experience in government/politics. Available to U.S. citizens.

Application Requirements: Application, transcript, IRS 1040 form. *Deadline:* September 30.

Contact: Tamika McKelvin, Office of Student Financial Assistance
Maryland State Higher Education Commission
839 Bestgate Road, Suite 400
Annapolis, MD 21401
Phone: 410-260-4546
Fax: 410-260-3203
E-mail: tmckelvil@mhec.state.md.us

MASSACHUSETTS OFFICE OF STUDENT FINANCIAL ASSISTANCE

http://www.osfa.mass.edu/

EARLY CHILDHOOD EDUCATORS SCHOLARSHIP PROGRAM

Scholarship to provide financial assistance for currently employed early childhood educators and providers who enroll in an associate or bachelor degree program in Early Childhood Education or related programs. Awards are not based on financial need. Individuals taking their first college-level ECE course are eligible for 100 percent tuition, while subsequent ECE courses are awarded at 50 percent tuition. Can be used for one class each semester.

Academic Fields/Career Goals: Education.

Award: Scholarship for use in freshman, sophomore, junior, or senior years; not renewable. *Number:* varies. *Amount:* $150–$3600.

Eligibility Requirements: Applicant must be enrolled or expecting to enroll full- or part-time at a four-year institution or university. Available to U.S. citizens.

Application Requirements: Application. *Deadline:* July 1.

Contact: Robert Brun, Director of Scholarships and Grants
Massachusetts Office of Student Financial Assistance
454 Broadway, Suite 200
Revere, MA 02151
Phone: 617-727-9420
Fax: 617-727-0667
E-mail: osfa@osfa.mass.edu

PARAPROFESSIONAL TEACHER PREPARATION GRANT

Grant providing financial aid assistance to Massachusetts residents, who are currently employed as paraprofessionals in Massachusetts public schools and wish to obtain higher education and become certified as full-time teachers.

Academic Fields/Career Goals: Education.

Award: Grant for use in freshman, sophomore, junior, or senior years; not renewable. *Number:* varies. *Amount:* $250–$7500.

Eligibility Requirements: Applicant must be enrolled or expecting to enroll full- or part-time at a two-year or four-year institution or university and resident of Massachusetts. Available to U.S. citizens.

Application Requirements: Application, FAFSA. *Deadline:* August 1.

Contact: Robert Brun, Director of Scholarships and Grants
Massachusetts Office of Student Financial Assistance
454 Broadway, Suite 200
Revere, MA 02151
Phone: 617-727-9420
Fax: 617-727-0667
E-mail: osfa@osfa.mass.edu

MEMORIAL FOUNDATION FOR JEWISH CULTURE

http://www.mfjc.org/

MEMORIAL FOUNDATION FOR JEWISH CULTURE, SCHOLARSHIPS FOR POST-RABBINICAL STUDENTS

Scholarship program is to assist well-qualified individuals to train for careers in the rabbinate, Jewish education, social work, and as religious functionaries in Diaspora Jewish communities in need of such personnel. Open to any individual, regardless of country of origin, who is presently receiving, or plans to undertake, training in a recognized yeshiva, teacher training seminary, school of social work, university or other educational institution.

Academic Fields/Career Goals: Education; Religion/Theology; Social Services.

Award: Scholarship for use in freshman, sophomore, junior, or senior years; renewable. *Number:* varies. *Amount:* varies.

Eligibility Requirements: Applicant must be Jewish; enrolled or expecting to enroll full- or part-time at a two-year or four-year or technical institution or university and must have an interest in Jewish culture. Available to U.S. and non-U.S. citizens.

Application Requirements: Application, photo, references. *Deadline:* November 30.

Contact: Dr. Jerry Hochbaum, Executive Vice President
Memorial Foundation for Jewish Culture
50 Broadway, 34th Floor
New York, NY 10004
Phone: 212-425-6606
Fax: 212-425-6602
E-mail: office@mfjc.org

MISSISSIPPI OFFICE OF STUDENT FINANCIAL AID

http://www.mississippi.edu/

CRITICAL NEEDS TEACHER LOAN/SCHOLARSHIP

Eligible applicants will agree to employment immediately upon degree completion as a full-time classroom teacher in a public school located in a critical teacher shortage area in the state of Mississippi. Must verify the intention to pursue a first bachelor's degree in teacher education. Award covers tuition and required fees, average cost of room and meals plus allowance for books. Must be enrolled at a Mississippi college or university.

Academic Fields/Career Goals: Education; Foreign Language; Mathematics; Special Education.

Award: Forgivable loan for use in junior or senior years; not renewable. *Number:* varies. *Amount:* $5514–$15,506.

Eligibility Requirements: Applicant must be enrolled or expecting to enroll full- or part-time at a four-year institution or university and studying in Mississippi. Applicant must have 2.5 GPA or higher. Available to U.S. and non-U.S. citizens.

Application Requirements: Application, test scores, transcript. *Deadline:* March 31.

Contact: Mrs. Jennifer Rogers, Director of Student Financial Aid
Mississippi Office of Student Financial Aid
3825 Ridgewood Road
Jackson, MS 39211-6453
Phone: 601-432-6997
E-mail: sfa@mississippi.edu

WILLIAM WINTER TEACHER SCHOLAR LOAN

Scholarship available to a junior or senior student at a four-year Mississippi college or university. Applicants must enroll in a program of study leading to a Class A teacher educator license.

Academic Fields/Career Goals: Education.

Award: Forgivable loan for use in junior or senior years; not renewable. *Number:* varies. *Amount:* $1333–$4000.

Eligibility Requirements: Applicant must be enrolled or expecting to enroll full-time at a four-year institution or university; resident of Mississippi and studying in Mississippi. Applicant must have 2.5 GPA or higher. Available to U.S. citizens.

Application Requirements: Application, test scores, letter of acceptance. *Deadline:* March 31.

Contact: Mrs. Jennifer Rogers, Director of Student Financial Aid
Mississippi Office of Student Financial Aid
3825 Ridgewood Road
Jackson, MS 39211-6453
Phone: 601-432-6997
E-mail: sfa@mississippi.edu

NASA RHODE ISLAND SPACE GRANT CONSORTIUM

http://ri.spacegrant.org/

NASA RISGC SUMMER SCHOLARSHIP FOR UNDERGRADUATE STUDENTS
• See page 128

NASA SOUTH CAROLINA SPACE GRANT CONSORTIUM

http://www.cofc.edu/~scsgrant

PRE-SERVICE TEACHER SCHOLARSHIP
• See page 129

NASA'S VIRGINIA SPACE GRANT CONSORTIUM

http://www.vsgc.odu.edu/

TEACHER EDUCATION STEM SCHOLARSHIP PROGRAM
• See page 96

NATIONAL ASSOCIATION FOR THE ADVANCEMENT OF COLORED PEOPLE

http://www.naacp.org/

NAACP LILLIAN AND SAMUEL SUTTON EDUCATION SCHOLARSHIP

Scholarship for a full-time student who is enrolled in an accredited college in the United States. Graduating high school seniors and undergraduate students must have 2.5 minimum GPA. Graduate students must have 3.0 minimum GPA. Undergraduate scholarship is for $1000; and graduate scholarship is $2000.

Academic Fields/Career Goals: Education.

Award: Scholarship for use in freshman, sophomore, junior, senior, or graduate years; not renewable. *Number:* 1. *Amount:* $1000–$2000.

Eligibility Requirements: Applicant must be American Indian/Alaska Native, Asian/Pacific Islander, Black (non-Hispanic), or Hispanic and enrolled or expecting to enroll full- or part-time at a four-year institution or university. Applicant or parent of applicant must be member of National Association for the Advancement of Colored People. Available to U.S. citizens.

Application Requirements: Application, financial need analysis, references, transcript. *Deadline:* March 7.

Contact: Victor Goode, Attorney
National Association for the Advancement of Colored People
4805 Mount Hope Drive
Baltimore, MD 21215-3297
Phone: 410-580-5760
E-mail: info@naacp.org

NATIONAL COUNCIL OF TEACHERS OF MATHEMATICS

http://www.nctm.org/

PROSPECTIVE SECONDARY TEACHER COURSE WORK SCHOLARSHIPS

Grant provides financial support to college students preparing for teaching secondary school mathematics. Award of $10,000 will be granted in two phases, with $5000 for the recipient's third year of full-time study, and $5000 for fourth year. Must be student members of NCTM and cannot reapply. Must submit proposal, essay, letters of recommendation, and transcripts.

Academic Fields/Career Goals: Education; Mathematics.

Award: Scholarship for use in junior or senior years; not renewable. *Number:* 2. *Amount:* up to $5000.

Eligibility Requirements: Applicant must be enrolled or expecting to enroll full-time at a four-year institution or university. Available to U.S. and non-U.S. citizens.

Application Requirements: Application, essay, references, transcript, written proposal. *Deadline:* May 9.

Contact: Mathematics Education Trust
National Council of Teachers of Mathematics
1906 Association Drive
Reston, VA 20191-1502
Phone: 703-620-9840 Ext. 2112
Fax: 703-476-2970
E-mail: exec@nctm.org

NATIONAL FEDERATION OF THE BLIND OF CONNECTICUT

http://www.nfbct.org/

BRIAN CUMMINS MEMORIAL SCHOLARSHIP

Scholarship of $5000 awarded to college or graduate student enrolled in a full-time program to teach blind and visually impaired students in Connecticut.

Academic Fields/Career Goals: Education; Special Education.

Award: Scholarship for use in freshman, sophomore, junior, senior, or graduate years; not renewable. *Number:* 1. *Amount:* $5000.

Eligibility Requirements: Applicant must be enrolled or expecting to enroll full-time at a four-year institution or university and resident of Connecticut. Available to U.S. citizens.

Application Requirements: Application, references, transcript. *Deadline:* October 15.

Contact: Scholarship Committee
National Federation of the Blind of Connecticut
477 Connecticut Boulevard, Suite 217
East Hartford, CT 06108
Phone: 860-289-1971
Fax: 860-291-2795
E-mail: info@nfbct.org

NATIONAL INSTITUTE FOR LABOR RELATIONS RESEARCH

http://www.nilrr.org/

APPLEGATE/JACKSON/PARKS FUTURE TEACHER SCHOLARSHIP

Scholarship available to all education majors currently attending school. High school seniors accepted into a teacher education program may also apply. Award is based on an essay demonstrating knowledge of and interest in compulsory unionism in education. Specify "Education" or "Future Teacher Scholarship" on any correspondence.

Academic Fields/Career Goals: Education; Special Education.

Award: Scholarship for use in freshman, sophomore, junior, senior, graduate, or postgraduate years; not renewable. *Number:* 1. *Amount:* $1000.

Eligibility Requirements: Applicant must be enrolled or expecting to enroll full-time at a four-year institution or university. Available to U.S. citizens.

Application Requirements: Application, essay, transcript. *Deadline:* December 31.

Contact: Cathy Jones, Scholarship Coordinator
National Institute for Labor Relations Research
5211 Port Royal Road
Springfield, VA 22151
Phone: 703-321-9606 Ext. 2231
Fax: 703-321-7143
E-mail: research@nilrr.org

NATIONAL URBAN LEAGUE

http://www.nulbeep.org/

BLACK EXECUTIVE EXCHANGE PROGRAM JERRY BARTOW SCHOLARSHIP FUND

• *See page 154*

NEW HAMPSHIRE POSTSECONDARY EDUCATION COMMISSION

http://www.nh.gov/postsecondary

WORKFORCE INCENTIVE PROGRAM

The program provides incentive for students to pursue careers in critical workforce shortage areas at appropriate New Hampshire institutions and to encourage students to then seek employment in New Hampshire after completion of their career program. May be a part- or full-time student in an approved program, and should demonstrate financial need as determined by the institution.

Academic Fields/Career Goals: Education; Foreign Language; Nursing; Special Education.

Award: Forgivable loan for use in freshman, sophomore, junior, senior, graduate, or postgraduate years; not renewable. *Number:* varies. *Amount:* varies.

Eligibility Requirements: Applicant must be enrolled or expecting to enroll full- or part-time at a four-year institution or university; resident of New Hampshire and studying in New Hampshire. Available to U.S. citizens.

Application Requirements: Application. *Deadline:* varies.

Contact: Ms. Cynthia Capodestria, Student Financial Aid Administrator
New Hampshire Postsecondary Education Commission
Three Barrell Court, Suite 300
Concord, NH 03301-8543
Phone: 603-271-2555 Ext. 360
E-mail: cynthia.capodestria@pec.state.nh.us

NEW MEXICO COMMISSION ON HIGHER EDUCATION

http://www.hed.state.nm.us/

TEACHER LOAN-FOR-SERVICE

Purpose is to proactively address New Mexico's teacher shortage by providing students with the financial resources to complete or enhance their post-secondary teacher preparation education.

Academic Fields/Career Goals: Education.

Award: Forgivable loan for use in freshman, sophomore, junior, or senior years; renewable. *Number:* 1. *Amount:* up to $4000.

Eligibility Requirements: Applicant must be enrolled or expecting to enroll full- or part-time at a four-year institution or university; resident of New Mexico and studying in New Mexico. Available to U.S. citizens.

Application Requirements: Application, financial need analysis, FAFSA. *Deadline:* July 1.

Contact: Theresa Acker, Financial Aid Division
New Mexico Commission on Higher Education
1068 Cerrillos Road
Santa Fe, NM 87505-1650
Phone: 505-476-6506
Fax: 505-476-6511
E-mail: theresa.acker@state.nm.us

NORTH CAROLINA ASSOCIATION OF EDUCATORS

http://www.ncae.org/

MARY MORROW-EDNA RICHARDS SCHOLARSHIP

One-time award for junior year of study in four-year education degree program. Preference given to members of the student branch of the North Carolina Association of Educators. Must be North Carolina resident attending a North Carolina institution. Must agree to teach in North Carolina for two years after graduation. Must be a junior in college when application is filed.

Academic Fields/Career Goals: Education.

Award: Scholarship for use in junior or senior years; not renewable. *Number:* 3. *Amount:* up to $1000.

Eligibility Requirements: Applicant must be enrolled or expecting to enroll full-time at a four-year institution or university; resident of North Carolina and studying in North Carolina. Available to U.S. citizens.

Application Requirements: Application, essay, financial need analysis, references, transcript. *Deadline:* January 14.

Contact: Annette Montgomery, Communications Secretary
North Carolina Association of Educators
PO Box 27347
Raleigh, NC 27611
Phone: 800-662-7924
Fax: 919-839-8229
E-mail: annette.montgomery@ncae.org

NORTH CAROLINA STATE EDUCATION ASSISTANCE AUTHORITY

http://www.ncseaa.edu/

TEACHER ASSISTANT SCHOLARSHIP FUND

Funding to attend a public or private four-year college or university in North Carolina with an approved teacher education program. Applicant must be employed full-time as a teacher assistant in an instructional area while pursuing licensure and maintain employment to remain eligible. Must have at least 3.0 cumulative GPA. Refer to web site for further details http://www.ncseaa.edu/tas.htm.

Academic Fields/Career Goals: Education.

Award: Scholarship for use in freshman, sophomore, junior, or senior years; renewable. *Number:* varies. *Amount:* $600–$3600.

Eligibility Requirements: Applicant must be enrolled or expecting to enroll full- or part-time at a four-year institution or university; resident of North Carolina and studying in North Carolina. Applicant or parent of applicant must have employment or volunteer experience in teaching/

education. Applicant must have 3.0 GPA or higher. Available to U.S. citizens.

Application Requirements: Application, financial need analysis, transcript, FAFSA. *Deadline:* March 31.

Contact: Rashonn Albritton, Processing Assistant
North Carolina State Education Assistance Authority
PO Box 13663
Research Triangle Park, NC 27709
Phone: 919-549-8614
Fax: 919-248-4687
E-mail: ralbritton@ncseaa.edu

NORTH CAROLINA TEACHING FELLOWS COMMISSION

http://www.teachingfellows.org/

NORTH CAROLINA TEACHING FELLOWS SCHOLARSHIP PROGRAM

Award for North Carolina high school seniors planning to pursue teacher training studies. Must agree to teach in a North Carolina public or government school for four years or repay award. For more details visit web site http://www.teachingfellows.org.

Academic Fields/Career Goals: Education.

Award: Forgivable loan for use in freshman year; renewable. *Number:* 500. *Amount:* $6500.

Eligibility Requirements: Applicant must be high school student; planning to enroll or expecting to enroll full-time at a four-year institution or university; resident of North Carolina and studying in North Carolina. Applicant must have 3.5 GPA or higher. Available to U.S. citizens.

Application Requirements: Application, essay, interview, references, test scores, transcript. *Deadline:* varies.

Contact: Lynne Stewart, Program Officer
North Carolina Teaching Fellows Commission
3739 National Drive, Suite 100
Raleigh, NC 27612
Phone: 919-781-6833 Ext. 103
Fax: 919-781-6527
E-mail: tfellows@ncforum.org

OHIO CHILD CARE RESOURCE & REFERRAL ASSOCIATION

http://www.occrra.org/

T.E.A.C.H. EARLY CHILDHOOD OHIO SCHOLARSHIPS
• *See page 173*

OKLAHOMA STATE REGENTS FOR HIGHER EDUCATION

http://www.okhighered.org/

FUTURE TEACHER SCHOLARSHIP-OKLAHOMA

Open to outstanding Oklahoma high school graduates who agree to teach in shortage areas. Must rank in top 15 percent of graduating class or score above 85th percentile on ACT or similar test, or be accepted in an educational program. Students nominated by institution. Reapply to renew. Must attend college/university in Oklahoma.

Academic Fields/Career Goals: Education.

Award: Scholarship for use in freshman, sophomore, junior, senior, or graduate years; renewable. *Amount:* $500–$1500.

Eligibility Requirements: Applicant must be enrolled or expecting to enroll full- or part-time at a two-year or four-year institution or university; resident of Oklahoma and studying in Oklahoma. Available to U.S. citizens.

Application Requirements: Application, essay, test scores, transcript. *Deadline:* varies.

Contact: Scholarship Programs Coordinator
Oklahoma State Regents for Higher Education
PO Box 108850
Oklahoma City, OK 73101-8850
Phone: 800-858-1840
Fax: 405-225-9230
E-mail: studentinfo@osrhe.edu

OREGON PTA

http://www.oregonpta.org/

TEACHER EDUCATION SCHOLARSHIP

Nonrenewable scholarships to high school seniors or college students who are Oregon residents who want to teach in Oregon at an elementary or secondary school. The scholarship may be used at any Oregon public college or university that trains teachers or that transfers credits in education.

Academic Fields/Career Goals: Education.

Award: Scholarship for use in freshman, sophomore, junior, or senior years; not renewable. *Number:* varies. *Amount:* $500.

Eligibility Requirements: Applicant must be enrolled or expecting to enroll full-time at a two-year or four-year institution or university; resident of Oregon and studying in Oregon. Available to U.S. citizens.

Application Requirements: Application, essay, references, self-addressed stamped envelope, test scores, transcript. *Deadline:* March 21.

Contact: Scholarship Committee
Oregon PTA
4506 Southeast Belmont Street, Suite 108-B
Portland, OR 97215
Fax: 503-234-6024
E-mail: or_office@pta.org

OREGON STUDENT ASSISTANCE COMMISSION

http://www.GetCollegeFunds.org/

FRIENDS OF OREGON STUDENTS SCHOLARSHIP

Renewable award for 5th-year senior or graduate student for fall term/ semester pursuing a masters degree in education or education-related field. Preference given to nontraditional students or those who are the first generation in their families to attend college. Must be working and continue to work while attending school at least half time. Essay and references required.

Academic Fields/Career Goals: Education.

Award: Scholarship for use in senior or graduate years; renewable. *Number:* varies. *Amount:* varies.

Eligibility Requirements: Applicant must be enrolled or expecting to enroll full-time at a four-year institution or university and resident of Oregon. Available to U.S. citizens.

Application Requirements: Application, essay, financial need analysis, interview, references, transcript, activity chart, additional documents to donor. *Deadline:* March 1.

Contact: Director of Grant Programs
Oregon Student Assistance Commission
1500 Valley River Drive, Suite 100
Eugene, OR 97401-7020
Phone: 800-452-8807 Ext. 7395

HARRIET A. SIMMONS SCHOLARSHIP

One-time award available to Oregon residents who are enrolled in an elementary or secondary education program in an Oregon college or university, entering senior or fifth-year, or graduate students in a fifth year for elementary or secondary teaching certificate. Apply at http://www.getcollegefunds.org.

Academic Fields/Career Goals: Education.

Award: Scholarship for use in senior or graduate years; not renewable. *Amount:* varies.

Eligibility Requirements: Applicant must be enrolled or expecting to enroll full-time at a four-year institution or university; resident of Oregon and studying in Oregon. Available to U.S. citizens.

Application Requirements: Application, essay, financial need analysis, transcript. *Deadline:* March 1.

Contact: Director of Grant Programs
Oregon Student Assistance Commission
1500 Valley River Drive, Suite 100
Eugene, OR 97401-7020
Phone: 800-452-8807 Ext. 7395

JAMES CARLSON MEMORIAL SCHOLARSHIP

One-time award for elementary or secondary education majors entering the final year of their program, or graduate students in fifth year for elementary or secondary certificate. Applicants may qualify according to one of the following: (1) "Diverse environments" essay, (2) dependents of Oregon Education Association members (no essay); or (3) students committed to teaching autistic children.

Academic Fields/Career Goals: Education; Special Education.

Award: Scholarship for use in senior or graduate years; not renewable. *Amount:* varies.

Eligibility Requirements: Applicant must be enrolled or expecting to enroll full-time at a four-year institution or university and resident of Oregon. Applicant or parent of applicant must be member of Oregon Education Association. Available to U.S. citizens.

Application Requirements: Application, essay, financial need analysis, transcript, activity chart. *Deadline:* March 1.

Contact: Scholarship Programs Coordinator
Oregon Student Assistance Commission
1500 Valley River Drive, Suite 100
Eugene, OR 97401-7020
Phone: 800-452-8807 Ext. 7466

NETTIE HANSELMAN JAYNES SCHOLARSHIP

One-time award for students majoring in elementary and secondary education entering their senior or fifth year or graduate students in their fifth year for elementary or secondary certificate. To be used at any four-year college in Oregon.

Academic Fields/Career Goals: Education.

Award: Scholarship for use in senior or graduate years; not renewable. *Number:* varies. *Amount:* varies.

Eligibility Requirements: Applicant must be enrolled or expecting to enroll full-time at a four-year institution; resident of Oregon and studying in Oregon. Available to U.S. citizens.

Application Requirements: Application, essay, financial need analysis, transcript, activities chart. *Deadline:* March 1.

Contact: Director of Grant Programs
Oregon Student Assistance Commission
1500 Valley River Drive, Suite 100
Eugene, OR 97401-7020
Phone: 800-452-8807 Ext. 7395

TEACH FOR OREGON SCHOLARSHIP

Award is available to college juniors and seniors studying to become a teacher at a four-year college or university in the United States. Applicant must be working (and continue to work) while attending school (exceptions granted during required practicum periods). Preference will be given to non-traditional students or students who are the first in their families to attend college. Finalists will be interviewed.

Academic Fields/Career Goals: Education.

Award: Scholarship for use in junior or senior years; not renewable.

Eligibility Requirements: Applicant must be enrolled or expecting to enroll full- or part-time at a four-year institution or university. Applicant must have 2.5 GPA or higher.

Application Requirements: Application, essay, references. *Deadline:* March 1.

Contact: Director of Grant Programs
Oregon Student Assistance Commission
1500 Valley River Drive, Suite 100
Eugene, OR 97401-7020
Phone: 800-452-8807

PI LAMBDA THETA INC.

http://www.pilambda.org/

DISTINGUISHED STUDENT SCHOLAR AWARD

The award is presented in recognition of an education major who has displayed leadership potential and a strong dedication to education. Award given out in odd years. Minimum 3.5 GPA required.

Academic Fields/Career Goals: Education.

Award: Prize for use in freshman, sophomore, junior, or senior years; not renewable. *Number:* 1. *Amount:* $500.

Eligibility Requirements: Applicant must be enrolled or expecting to enroll full- or part-time at a four-year institution or university and must have an interest in leadership. Applicant or parent of applicant must have employment or volunteer experience in community service. Applicant must have 3.5 GPA or higher. Available to U.S. and non-U.S. citizens.

Application Requirements: Application, resume, references, transcript, 2 letters of support from faculty members other than the nominator, letter of endorsement from the nominee's chapter. *Deadline:* February 10.

Contact: Pam Todd, Manager, Member Services
Pi Lambda Theta Inc.
4101 East Third Street, PO Box 6626
Bloomington, IN 47407-6626
Phone: 812-339-3411
Fax: 812-339-3462
E-mail: office@pilambda.org

GRADUATE STUDENT SCHOLAR AWARD

The award is presented in recognition of an outstanding graduate student who is an education major. Award given out in odd years. Minimum 3.5 GPA required.

Academic Fields/Career Goals: Education.

Award: Prize for use in senior or graduate years; not renewable. *Number:* 1. *Amount:* $1000.

Eligibility Requirements: Applicant must be enrolled or expecting to enroll full- or part-time at a four-year institution or university and must have an interest in leadership. Applicant or parent of applicant must have employment or volunteer experience in community service. Applicant must have 3.5 GPA or higher. Available to U.S. and non-U.S. citizens.

Application Requirements: Application, essay, resume, references, transcript, letter of endorsement from nominee's chapter. *Deadline:* February 10.

Contact: Pam Todd, Manager, Member Services
Pi Lambda Theta Inc.
4101 East Third Street, PO Box 6626
Bloomington, IN 47407-6626
Phone: 812-339-3411
Fax: 812-339-3462
E-mail: office@pilambda.org

NADEEN BURKEHOLDER WILLIAMS MUSIC SCHOLARSHIP

The scholarship provides $1000 to an outstanding K–12 teacher who is pursuing a graduate degree at an accredited college or university and who is either a music education teacher or applies music systematically in teaching another subject. Minimum 3.5 GPA required.

Academic Fields/Career Goals: Education; Music.

Award: Scholarship for use in freshman, sophomore, junior, senior, or graduate years; not renewable. *Number:* 1–5. *Amount:* $1000.

Eligibility Requirements: Applicant must be enrolled or expecting to enroll full- or part-time at a four-year institution or university and must have an interest in music. Applicant or parent of applicant must have employment or volunteer experience in teaching/education. Applicant must have 3.5 GPA or higher. Available to U.S. and non-U.S. citizens.

Application Requirements: Application, essay, portfolio, resume, references. *Deadline:* February 10.

Contact: Pam Todd, Manager, Member Services
Pi Lambda Theta Inc.
4101 East Third Street, PO Box 6626
Bloomington, IN 47407-6626
Phone: 812-339-3411
Fax: 812-339-3462
E-mail: office@pilambda.org

STUDENT SUPPORT SCHOLARSHIP

The scholarship is available to current members of Pi Lambda Theta who will be a full-time or part-time student enrolled in a minimum of three semester hours at a regionally accredited institution during the year following the award. Minimum 3.5 GPA required.

Academic Fields/Career Goals: Education.

Award: Scholarship for use in sophomore, junior, senior, graduate, or postgraduate years; not renewable. *Number:* 1–6. *Amount:* $750.

Eligibility Requirements: Applicant must be enrolled or expecting to enroll full- or part-time at a two-year or four-year or technical institution or university. Applicant must have 3.5 GPA or higher. Available to U.S. and non-U.S. citizens.

Application Requirements: Application, essay, transcript. *Deadline:* February 10.

Contact: Pam Todd, Manager, Member Services
Pi Lambda Theta Inc.
4101 East Third Street, PO Box 6626
Bloomington, IN 47407-6626
Phone: 812-339-3411
Fax: 812-339-3462
E-mail: office@pilambda.org

TOBIN SORENSON PHYSICAL EDUCATION SCHOLARSHIP

The scholarship provides $1000 for tuition to an outstanding student who intends to pursue a career at the K–12 level as a physical education teacher, adaptive physical education teacher, coach, recreational therapist, dance therapist, or similar professional focusing on teaching the knowledge and use of the human body. Awarded in odd years only. Minimum 3.5 GPA required.

Academic Fields/Career Goals: Education; Sports-Related/Exercise Science; Therapy/Rehabilitation.

Award: Scholarship for use in sophomore, junior, senior, or graduate years; not renewable. *Number:* 1. *Amount:* $1000.

Eligibility Requirements: Applicant must be enrolled or expecting to enroll full- or part-time at a two-year or four-year institution or university. Applicant must have 3.5 GPA or higher. Available to U.S. and non-U.S. citizens.

Application Requirements: Application, resume, references, transcript. *Deadline:* February 10.

Contact: Pam Todd, Controller
Pi Lambda Theta Inc.
4101 East Third Street, PO Box 6626
Bloomington, IN 47407-6626
Phone: 812-339-3411
Fax: 812-339-3462
E-mail: office@pilambda.org

PRESBYTERIAN CHURCH (USA)

http://www.pcusa.org/financialaid

STUDENT OPPORTUNITY SCHOLARSHIP

Designed to assist undergraduate students with their junior and senior year of college. Restricted to members of the Presbyterian Church (USA).

Academic Fields/Career Goals: Education; Health and Medical Sciences; Religion/Theology; Social Sciences; Social Services.

Award: Scholarship for use in junior or senior years; renewable. *Number:* 68. *Amount:* up to $3000.

Eligibility Requirements: Applicant must be Presbyterian and enrolled or expecting to enroll full-time at a four-year institution or university. Applicant must have 2.5 GPA or higher. Available to U.S. citizens.

Application Requirements: Application, essay, financial need analysis, resume, references, transcript. *Deadline:* June 1.

Contact: Laura Bryan, Associate, Financial Aid for Studies
Presbyterian Church (USA)
Financial Aid for Studies
100 Witherspoon Street
Louisville, KY 40202-1396
Phone: 888-728-7228 Ext. 5735
E-mail: finaid@pcusa.org

SARAH KLENKE MEMORIAL TEACHING SCHOLARSHIP

http://www.sarahklenkescholarship.org/

SARAH ELIZABETH KLENKE MEMORIAL TEACHING SCHOLARSHIP

Scholarship for graduating senior or high school graduate enrolling in secondary schooling. Should have a desire to major in education. Minimum 2.0 GPA required. Participation in JROTC or team sport is required.

Academic Fields/Career Goals: Education.

Award: Scholarship for use in freshman or senior years; not renewable. *Number:* 1. *Amount:* $1000.

Eligibility Requirements: Applicant must be enrolled or expecting to enroll full-time at a two-year or four-year institution or university. Available to U.S. and non-U.S. citizens.

Application Requirements: Application, essay, references, letter from coach or teacher confirming participation in ROTC or team sport. *Deadline:* April 15.

Contact: Aaron Klenke, Scholarship Committee
Sarah Klenke Memorial Teaching Scholarship
3131 Glade Springs
Kingwood, TX 77339
Phone: 281-358-7933
E-mail: aaron.klenke@gmail.com

SIEMENS FOUNDATION/SIEMENS-WESTINGHOUSE SCHOLARSHIP

http://www.siemens-foundation.org/

SIEMENS TEACHER SCHOLARSHIP

Scholarships for undergraduate and graduate students majoring in education, and enrolled at historically black colleges and universities that are members of the Thurgood Marshall Scholarship Fund and the United Negro College Fund. The scholarship value and the number of scholarships granted varies annually.

Academic Fields/Career Goals: Education.

Award: Scholarship for use in freshman, sophomore, junior, senior, or graduate years; not renewable. *Number:* varies. *Amount:* varies.

Eligibility Requirements: Applicant must be Black (non-Hispanic) and enrolled or expecting to enroll full- or part-time at a four-year institution or university. Available to U.S. and non-U.S. citizens.

Application Requirements: Application. *Deadline:* varies.

Contact: Scholarship Committee
Siemens Foundation/Siemens-Westinghouse Scholarship
170 Wood Avenue South
Iselin, NJ 08830
Phone: 877-822-5233
Fax: 732-603-5890
E-mail: foundation.us@siemens.com

SIGMA ALPHA IOTA PHILANTHROPIES, INC.

http://www.sai-national.org/

SIGMA ALPHA IOTA MUSICIANS WITH SPECIAL NEEDS SCHOLARSHIP

One-time award of $1500 offered yearly for female member of SAI who is visually impaired, and a member of a college or alumnae chapter. Submit fifteen-minute tape or evidence of work in composition, musicology, or research.

Academic Fields/Career Goals: Education; Music; Performing Arts.

Award: Scholarship for use in freshman, sophomore, junior, or senior years; not renewable. *Number:* 1. *Amount:* $1500.

Eligibility Requirements: Applicant must be enrolled or expecting to enroll full- or part-time at a four-year institution or university; female and must have an interest in music/singing. Applicant or parent of applicant must be member of Sigma Alpha Iota. Applicant must be visually impaired. Available to U.S. and non-U.S. citizens.

Application Requirements: Application, essay, resume, references, transcript, videotape or DVD. *Deadline:* March 15.

Contact: Karen Louise Gearreald, Director
Sigma Alpha Iota Philanthropies, Inc.
One Tunnel Road
Asheville, NC 28805
Phone: 828-251-0606
Fax: 828-251-0644
E-mail: karen118@cox.net

SIGMA ALPHA IOTA UNDERGRADUATE SCHOLARSHIPS

One-time awards of $1500 to $2000 to female undergraduate members of SAI who are freshman, sophomores or juniors. For use in sophomore, junior, or senior year. Must be over 18 years of age and studying performing arts or performing arts education. Contact local chapter for further details.

Academic Fields/Career Goals: Education; Performing Arts.

Award: Scholarship for use in sophomore, junior, or senior years; not renewable. *Number:* 15. *Amount:* $1500–$2000.

Eligibility Requirements: Applicant must be age 18 and over; enrolled or expecting to enroll full-time at a four-year institution or university; female and must have an interest in music/singing. Applicant or parent of applicant must be member of Sigma Alpha Iota. Applicant must have 2.5 GPA or higher. Available to U.S. and non-U.S. citizens.

Application Requirements: Application, essay, financial need analysis, references, transcript. *Deadline:* March 15.

Contact: Kathi Bower Peterson, Project Director
Sigma Alpha Iota Philanthropies, Inc.
One Tunnel Road
Asheville, NC 28805
Phone: 828-251-0606
Fax: 828-251-0644
E-mail: jkpete@cox.net

SOCIETY FOR THE SCIENTIFIC STUDY OF SEXUALITY

http://www.sexscience.org/

SOCIETY FOR THE SCIENTIFIC STUDY OF SEXUALITY STUDENT RESEARCH GRANT
• See page 137

SOUTH CAROLINA STUDENT LOAN CORPORATION

http://www.scstudentloan.org/

SOUTH CAROLINA TEACHER LOAN PROGRAM

One-time awards for South Carolina residents attending four-year postsecondary institutions in South Carolina. Recipients must teach in the South Carolina public school system in a critical-need area after graduation. Twenty percent of loan forgiven for each year of service. Write for additional requirements.

Academic Fields/Career Goals: Education; Special Education.

Award: Forgivable loan for use in freshman, sophomore, junior, senior, or graduate years; not renewable. *Number:* up to 1121. *Amount:* $2500–$5000.

Eligibility Requirements: Applicant must be enrolled or expecting to enroll full- or part-time at a four-year institution or university; resident of South Carolina and studying in South Carolina. Applicant must have 3.0 GPA or higher. Available to U.S. citizens.

Application Requirements: Application, references, test scores, promissory note. *Deadline:* June 1.

Contact: Jennifer Jones-Gaddy, Vice President
South Carolina Student Loan Corporation
PO Box 21487
Columbia, SC 29221
Phone: 803-798-0916
Fax: 803-772-9410
E-mail: jgaddy@slc.sc.edu

SOUTH DAKOTA BOARD OF REGENTS

http://www.sdbor.edu/

HAINES MEMORIAL SCHOLARSHIP

One-time scholarship for South Dakota public university students who are sophomores, juniors, or seniors having at least a 2.5 GPA and majoring in a teacher education program. Must include resume with application. Must be South Dakota resident.

Academic Fields/Career Goals: Education.

Award: Scholarship for use in sophomore, junior, or senior years; not renewable. *Number:* 1. *Amount:* $2150.

Eligibility Requirements: Applicant must be enrolled or expecting to enroll full-time at an institution or university; resident of South Dakota and studying in South Dakota. Applicant must have 3.5 GPA or higher. Available to U.S. citizens.

Application Requirements: Application, essay, resume, typed statement describing personal philosophy and philosophy of education. *Deadline:* February 8.

Contact: Dr. Paul Turman, Director of Academic Assessment
South Dakota Board of Regents
306 East Capitol Avenue, Suite 200
Pierre, SD 57501-2545
Phone: 605-773-3455
E-mail: pault@sdbor.edu

SOUTH DAKOTA BOARD OF REGENTS ANNIS I. FOWLER/KADEN SCHOLARSHIP

Scholarship for graduating South Dakota high school seniors to pursue a career in elementary education at a South Dakota public university. University must be one of the following: BHSU, BSU, NSU or USD. Applicants must have a cumulative GPA of 3.0 after three years of high school. One-time award.

Academic Fields/Career Goals: Education.

Award: Scholarship for use in freshman year; not renewable. *Number:* 2. *Amount:* $1000.

Eligibility Requirements: Applicant must be high school student; planning to enroll or expecting to enroll full-time at a four-year institution or university; resident of South Dakota and studying in South Dakota. Applicant must have 3.0 GPA or higher. Available to U.S. citizens.

Application Requirements: Application, essay, references, test scores, transcript, ACT scores. *Deadline:* February 15.

Contact: Dr. Paul Turman, Director of Academic Assessment
South Dakota Board of Regents
306 East Capitol Avenue, Suite 200
Pierre, SD 57501-2545
Phone: 605-773-3455
E-mail: pault@sdbor.edu

STATE OF WYOMING, ADMINISTERED BY UNIVERSITY OF WYOMING

http://www.uwyo.edu/scholarships

SUPERIOR STUDENT IN EDUCATION SCHOLARSHIP-WYOMING

Scholarship available each year to sixteen new Wyoming high school graduates who plan to teach in Wyoming. The award covers costs of undergraduate tuition at the University of Wyoming or any Wyoming community college.

Academic Fields/Career Goals: Education.

Award: Scholarship for use in freshman, sophomore, junior, or senior years; renewable. *Number:* 16–16. *Amount:* $1000.

Eligibility Requirements: Applicant must be high school student; planning to enroll or expecting to enroll full-time at a two-year or four-year institution or university; resident of Wyoming and studying in Wyoming. Applicant must have 3.0 GPA or higher. Available to U.S. citizens.

Application Requirements: Application, references, test scores, transcript. *Deadline:* October 31.

Contact: Tammy Mack, Assistant Director, Scholarships
State of Wyoming, Administered by University of Wyoming
Student Financial Aid Department 3335, 1000 East University Avenue
Laramie, WY 82071-3335
Phone: 307-766-2412
E-mail: westmack@uwyo.edu

STRAIGHTFORWARD MEDIA

http://www.straightforwardmedia.com/

STRAIGHTFORWARD MEDIA TEACHER SCHOLARSHIP

Scholarship of $500 for students planning to be teachers of any kind and at any level. Must be U.S. citizen. Awarded four times per year. Deadlines: January 14, April 14, July 14, and October 14. For more information, see web site http://www.straightforwardmedia.com/education/form.php.

Academic Fields/Career Goals: Education; Special Education.

Award: Scholarship for use in freshman, sophomore, junior, or senior years; not renewable. *Number:* 4. *Amount:* $500.

Eligibility Requirements: Applicant must be enrolled or expecting to enroll full- or part-time at a two-year or four-year or technical institution or university. Available to U.S. citizens.

Application Requirements: Essay. *Deadline:* varies.

Contact: Scholarship Committee
StraightForward Media
508 7th Street
Suite 202
Rapid City, SD 57701
Phone: 605-348-3042

TENNESSEE EDUCATION ASSOCIATION

http://www.teateachers.org/

TEA DON SAHLI-KATHY WOODALL FUTURE TEACHERS OF AMERICA SCHOLARSHIP

Scholarship is available to a high school senior planning to major in education, attending a high school which has an FTA Chapter affiliated with TEA, and planning to enroll in a Tennessee college.

Academic Fields/Career Goals: Education.

Award: Scholarship for use in freshman year; not renewable. *Number:* 1. *Amount:* $1000.

Eligibility Requirements: Applicant must be high school student; planning to enroll or expecting to enroll full-time at a four-year institution or university; resident of Tennessee and studying in Tennessee. Applicant must have 3.0 GPA or higher. Available to U.S. citizens.

Application Requirements: Application, applicant must enter a contest, essay, financial need analysis, references, transcript, statement of income. *Deadline:* March 1.

Contact: Stephanie Faulkner, Manager of Business Affairs
Tennessee Education Association
801 Second Avenue North
Nashville, TN 37201-1099
Phone: 615-242-8392
Fax: 615-259-4581
E-mail: sfaulkner@tea.nea.org

TEA DON SAHLI-KATHY WOODALL MINORITY SCHOLARSHIP

Scholarship is available to a minority high school senior planning to major in education and planning to enroll in a Tennessee college. Application must be made by an FTA Chapter, or by the student with the recommendation of an active TEA member.

Academic Fields/Career Goals: Education.

Award: Scholarship for use in freshman year; not renewable. *Number:* 1. *Amount:* $1000.

Eligibility Requirements: Applicant must be American Indian/Alaska Native, Asian/Pacific Islander, Black (non-Hispanic), or Hispanic; high school student; planning to enroll or expecting to enroll full-time at a four-year institution or university; resident of Tennessee and studying in Tennessee. Applicant must have 3.0 GPA or higher. Available to U.S. citizens.

Application Requirements: Application, applicant must enter a contest, essay, financial need analysis, references, transcript, statement of income. *Deadline:* March 1.

Contact: Stephanie Faulkner, Manager of Business Affairs
Tennessee Education Association
801 Second Avenue North
Nashville, TN 37201-1099
Phone: 615-242-8392
Fax: 615-259-4581
E-mail: sfaulkner@tea.nea.org

TEA DON SAHLI-KATHY WOODALL UNDERGRADUATE SCHOLARSHIP

Scholarship is available to undergraduate students who are student TEA members. Application must be made through the local STEA Chapter. Amount varies form $500 to $1000.

Academic Fields/Career Goals: Education.

Award: Scholarship for use in freshman, sophomore, junior, or senior years; not renewable. *Number:* 4. *Amount:* $500–$1000.

Eligibility Requirements: Applicant must be enrolled or expecting to enroll full- or part-time at a four-year institution or university; resident of Tennessee and studying in Tennessee. Applicant or parent of applicant must be member of Tennessee Education Association. Applicant must have 3.0 GPA or higher. Available to U.S. citizens.

Application Requirements: Application, essay, financial need analysis, references, transcript, statement of income. *Deadline:* March 1.

Contact: Stephanie Faulkner, Manager of Business Affairs
Tennessee Education Association
801 Second Avenue North
Nashville, TN 37201-1099
Phone: 615-242-8392
Fax: 615-259-4581
E-mail: sfaulkner@tea.nea.org

TENNESSEE STUDENT ASSISTANCE CORPORATION

http://www.tn.gov/collegepays

CHRISTA MCAULIFFE SCHOLARSHIP PROGRAM

Scholarship to assist and support Tennessee students who have demonstrated a commitment to a career in educating the youth of Tennessee. Offered to college seniors for a period of one academic year. Must have a minimum college GPA of 3.5. Must have attained scores on either the ACT or SAT which meet or exceed the national norms. Award is made on a periodic basis as funding becomes available.

Academic Fields/Career Goals: Education.

Award: Scholarship for use in senior year; not renewable. *Number:* up to 1. *Amount:* up to $500.

Eligibility Requirements: Applicant must be enrolled or expecting to enroll full-time at a four-year institution or university; resident of Tennessee and studying in Tennessee. Applicant must have 3.5 GPA or higher. Available to U.S. citizens.

Application Requirements: Application, essay. *Deadline:* April 1.

Contact: Ms. Kathy Stripling, Scholarship Administrator
Tennessee Student Assistance Corporation
Parkway Towers, 404 James Robertson Parkway, Suite 1510
Nashville, TN 37243-0820
Phone: 866-291-2675 Ext. 155
Fax: 615-741-6101
E-mail: kathy.stripling@tn.gov

MINORITY TEACHING FELLOWS PROGRAM/ TENNESSEE

Forgivable loan for minority Tennessee residents pursuing teaching careers. Minimum 2.75 GPA required for high school applicant, minimum 2.5 GPA required for college applicant. Must be in the top quarter of the class or score an 18 on ACT. Must teach one year for each year the award is received, or repay loan.

Academic Fields/Career Goals: Education; Special Education.

Award: Forgivable loan for use in freshman, sophomore, junior, or senior years; renewable. *Number:* 19–116. *Amount:* up to $5000.

Eligibility Requirements: Applicant must be American Indian/Alaska Native, Asian/Pacific Islander, Black (non-Hispanic), or Hispanic; enrolled or expecting to enroll full-time at a two-year or four-year institution or university; resident of Tennessee and studying in Tennessee. Available to U.S. citizens.

Application Requirements: Application, essay, references, test scores, transcript, statement of Intent. *Deadline:* April 15.

Contact: Mr. Mike McCormack, Scholarship Administrator
Tennessee Student Assistance Corporation
Parkway Towers, 404 James Robertson Parkway, Suite 1510
Nashville, TN 37243-0820
Phone: 866-291-2675 Ext. 140
Fax: 615-741-6101
E-mail: mike.mccormack@tn.gov

TENNESSEE TEACHING SCHOLARS PROGRAM

Forgivable loan for college juniors, seniors, and college graduates admitted to a teacher education program in Tennessee with a minimum GPA of 2.75. Students must commit to teach in a Tennessee public school one year for each year of the award. Must be a U.S. citizen and resident of Tennessee.

Academic Fields/Career Goals: Education.

Award: Forgivable loan for use in junior, senior, or graduate years; renewable. *Number:* up to 180. *Amount:* up to $4500.

Eligibility Requirements: Applicant must be enrolled or expecting to enroll full- or part-time at a four-year institution or university; resident of Tennessee and studying in Tennessee. Available to U.S. citizens.

Application Requirements: Application, references, test scores, transcript. *Deadline:* April 15.

Contact: Mr. Mike McCormack, Scholarship Administrator
Tennessee Student Assistance Corporation
404 James Robertson Parkway, Suite 1510, Parkway Towers
Nashville, TN 37243-0820
Phone: 866-291-2675 Ext. 140
Fax: 615-741-6101
E-mail: mike.mccormack@tn.gov

TKE EDUCATIONAL FOUNDATION

http://www.tke.org/

CARROL C. HALL MEMORIAL SCHOLARSHIP
• *See page 97*

FRANCIS J. FLYNN MEMORIAL SCHOLARSHIP

Award of $1300 for an undergraduate member of TKE who is a full-time student pursuing a degree in mathematics or education. Minimum 2.75 GPA required. Leadership within chapter or campus organizations recognized. Preference will be given to members of Theta-Sigma Chapter.

Academic Fields/Career Goals: Education; Mathematics.

Award: Scholarship for use in freshman, sophomore, junior, or senior years; not renewable. *Number:* 1. *Amount:* $1300.

Eligibility Requirements: Applicant must be enrolled or expecting to enroll full-time at a four-year institution or university; male and must have an interest in leadership. Applicant or parent of applicant must be member of Tau Kappa Epsilon. Available to U.S. and non-U.S. citizens.

Application Requirements: Application, essay, photo, transcript, narrative summary of how TKE membership has benefited applicant. *Deadline:* February 29.

Contact: Gary A. Reed, President and Chief Executive Officer
TKE Educational Foundation
8645 Founders Road
Indianapolis, IN 46268-1393
Phone: 317-872-6533
Fax: 317-875-8353
E-mail: reedga@tke.org

UNITED NEGRO COLLEGE FUND

http://www.uncf.org/

BANK OF AMERICA SCHOLARSHIP
• *See page 157*

EARL C. SAMS FOUNDATION SCHOLARSHIP

Award of up to $3000 is available for African American students who are residents of Texas. Must be elementary or secondary education majors

attending Jarvis Christian College, Paul Quinn College, or Wiley College. Must have a minimum GPA of 2.5. For additional information and general scholarship application, visit web site http://www.uncf.org.

Academic Fields/Career Goals: Education.

Award: Scholarship for use in freshman, sophomore, junior, or senior years; not renewable. *Number:* varies. *Amount:* up to $3000.

Eligibility Requirements: Applicant must be Black (non-Hispanic); enrolled or expecting to enroll full-time at a two-year or four-year institution or university and resident of Texas. Applicant must have 2.5 GPA or higher. Available to U.S. citizens.

Application Requirements: Application, financial need analysis, FAFSA, Student Aid Report (SAR).

Contact: Director, Program Services
United Negro College Fund
8260 Willow Oaks Corporate Drive
PO Box 10444
Fairfax, VA 22031-8044
Phone: 800-331-2244
E-mail: rebecca.bennett@uncf.org

UTAH STATE OFFICE OF EDUCATION

http://www.schools.utah.gov/cert

T.H. BELL TEACHING INCENTIVE LOAN-UTAH

Renewable awards for Utah residents who are high school seniors wishing to pursue teaching careers. The award value varies depending upon tuition and fees at a Utah institution. Must agree to teach in a Utah public school or pay back loan through monthly installments.

Academic Fields/Career Goals: Education.

Award: Forgivable loan for use in freshman, sophomore, junior, or senior years; renewable. *Number:* 25–50. *Amount:* varies.

Eligibility Requirements: Applicant must be enrolled or expecting to enroll full-time at a four-year institution or university; resident of Utah and studying in Utah. Available to U.S. citizens.

Application Requirements: Application, essay, test scores, transcript. *Deadline:* March 26.

Contact: Linda Alder, Education Specialist
Utah State Office of Education
250 East 500 South, PO Box 144200
Salt Lake City, UT 84114-4200
Phone: 801-538-7923
Fax: 801-538-7973
E-mail: linda.alder@schools.utah.gov

VERMONT-NEA

http://www.vtnea.org/

VERMONT-NEA/MAIDA F. TOWNSEND SCHOLARSHIP

Scholarship of $1000 to sons and daughters of Vermont-NEA members in their last year of high school, undergraduates, and graduate students. Students majoring in any discipline are eligible to apply, but preference may be given to those majoring in education, or having that intention.

Academic Fields/Career Goals: Education.

Award: Scholarship for use in freshman, sophomore, junior, senior, or graduate years; not renewable. *Number:* 5. *Amount:* $1000.

Eligibility Requirements: Applicant must be enrolled or expecting to enroll full- or part-time at a two-year or four-year or technical institution or university. Applicant or parent of applicant must be member of Vermont-NEA. Applicant or parent of applicant must have employment or volunteer experience in teaching/education. Available to U.S. and non-U.S. citizens.

Application Requirements: Application, essay, references, test scores, transcript, cover letter. *Deadline:* February 1.

Contact: Sandy Perkins, Administrative Assistant
Vermont-NEA
10 Wheelock Street
Montpelier, VT 05602-3737
Phone: 802-223-6375
E-mail: sperkins@vtnea.org

VIRGINIA CONGRESS OF PARENTS AND TEACHERS

http://www.vapta.org/

FRIEDA L. KOONTZ SCHOLARSHIP

Scholarship of $1200 to graduating high school students planning to enter teaching or other youth-serving professions in Virginia. Must be Virginia residents graduating from a Virginia public high school with a Parent-Teacher-Student Association (PTSA) and attending a Virginia college or university. Minimum 2.5 GPA required.

Academic Fields/Career Goals: Education.

Award: Scholarship for use in freshman year; not renewable. *Number:* 1. *Amount:* $1200.

Eligibility Requirements: Applicant must be high school student; planning to enroll or expecting to enroll full-time at a four-year institution or university; resident of Virginia and studying in Virginia. Applicant or parent of applicant must be member of Parent-Teacher Association/Organization. Applicant must have 2.5 GPA or higher. Available to U.S. citizens.

Application Requirements: Application, essay, references, test scores, transcript. *Deadline:* March 1.

Contact: Daniel Phillips, Scholarship Chair
Virginia Congress of Parents and Teachers
1027 Wilmer Avenue
Richmond, VA 23227-2419
Phone: 804-264-1234
E-mail: info@vapta.org

GENERAL (UNNAMED) SCHOLARSHIPS

General scholarships in addition to the Freida L. Koontz and John S. Davis Scholarships. Only graduating students enrolled in a Virginia school that is a PTA or PTSA school may apply. See web site for application details.

Academic Fields/Career Goals: Education.

Award: Scholarship for use in freshman year; not renewable. *Number:* 10–20. *Amount:* $1000.

Eligibility Requirements: Applicant must be high school student; planning to enroll or expecting to enroll full-time at a four-year institution or university and resident of Virginia. Applicant or parent of applicant must be member of Parent-Teacher Association/Organization. Applicant must have 2.5 GPA or higher. Available to U.S. citizens.

Application Requirements: Application, essay, references, test scores, transcript. *Deadline:* March 1.

Contact: Daniel Phillips, Scholarship Chair
Virginia Congress of Parents and Teachers
1027 Wilmer Avenue
Richmond, VA 23227-2419
Phone: 804-264-1234
E-mail: info@vapta.org

S. JOHN DAVIS SCHOLARSHIP

Scholarship of $1200 to Virginia residents graduating from a Virginia public school that has a Parent-Teacher-Student Association (PTSA) or PTA. Must be planning to attend a Virginia college or university and pursuing a career in teaching or qualifying for service with a youth-serving agency in Virginia. Minimum 2.5 GPA required.

Academic Fields/Career Goals: Education.

Award: Scholarship for use in freshman year; not renewable. *Number:* 1. *Amount:* $1200.

Eligibility Requirements: Applicant must be high school student; planning to enroll or expecting to enroll full-time at a four-year institution or university; resident of Virginia and studying in Virginia. Applicant or parent of applicant must be member of Parent-Teacher Association/Organization. Applicant must have 2.5 GPA or higher. Available to U.S. citizens.

Application Requirements: Application, essay. *Deadline:* March 1.

Contact: Daniel Phillips, Scholarship Chair
Virginia Congress of Parents and Teachers
1027 Wilmer Avenue
Richmond, VA 23227-2419
Phone: 804-264-1234
E-mail: info@vapta.org

WEST VIRGINIA HIGHER EDUCATION POLICY COMMISSION-STUDENT SERVICES

http://www.wvhepcnew.wvnet.edu/

UNDERWOOD-SMITH TEACHER SCHOLARSHIP PROGRAM

Award for West Virginia residents at West Virginia institutions pursuing teaching careers. Must have a 3.5 GPA after completion of two years of course work. Must teach two years in West Virginia public schools for each year the award is received. Recipients will be required to sign an agreement acknowledging an understanding of the program's requirements and their willingness to repay the award if appropriate teaching service is not rendered.

Academic Fields/Career Goals: Education.

Award: Scholarship for use in junior, senior, graduate, or postgraduate years; renewable. *Number:* 53–60. *Amount:* $1620–$5000.

Eligibility Requirements: Applicant must be enrolled or expecting to enroll full-time at a four-year institution or university; resident of West Virginia and studying in West Virginia. Applicant must have 3.0 GPA or higher. Available to U.S. citizens.

Application Requirements: Application, essay, references. *Deadline:* March 1.

Contact: Darlene Elmore, Scholarship Coordinator
West Virginia Higher Education Policy Commission-Student Services
1018 Kanawha Boulevard East, Suite 700
Charleston, WV 25301
Phone: 304-558-4618 Ext. 278
Fax: 304-558-4622
E-mail: elmore@hepc.wvnet.edu

WISCONSIN CONGRESS OF PARENTS AND TEACHERS INC.

http://www.wisconsinpta.org/

BROOKMIRE-HASTINGS SCHOLARSHIPS

One-time award to graduating high school seniors from Wisconsin public schools. Must pursue a degree in education. High school must have an active PTA in good standing of the Wisconsin PTA.

Academic Fields/Career Goals: Education; Special Education.

Award: Scholarship for use in freshman year; not renewable. *Number:* up to 2. *Amount:* $1000.

Eligibility Requirements: Applicant must be high school student; planning to enroll or expecting to enroll full-time at a four-year institution or university and resident of Wisconsin. Available to U.S. citizens.

Application Requirements: Application, essay, interview, references, transcript. *Deadline:* March 1.

Contact: Kim Schwantes, Executive Administrator
Wisconsin Congress of Parents and Teachers Inc.
4797 Hayes Road, Suite 2
Madison, WI 53704-3256
Phone: 608-244-1455

WISCONSIN MATHEMATICS COUNCIL, INC.

http://www.wismath.org/

ARNE ENGEBRETSEN WISCONSIN MATHEMATICS COUNCIL SCHOLARSHIP

Scholarship for Wisconsin high school senior who is planning to study mathematics education and teach mathematics at K–12 level.

Academic Fields/Career Goals: Education; Mathematics.

Award: Scholarship for use in freshman year; not renewable. *Number:* 1. *Amount:* $2000.

Eligibility Requirements: Applicant must be high school student; planning to enroll or expecting to enroll full-time at a four-year institution or university and resident of Wisconsin. Available to U.S. citizens.

Application Requirements: Application, essay, resume, references, transcript. *Deadline:* March 1.

Contact: Debra Pass, Scholarship Committee
Wisconsin Mathematics Council, Inc.
W175 N11117 Stonewood Drive, Suite 204
Germantown, WI 53022
Phone: 262-437-0174
E-mail: wmc@wismath.org

ETHEL A. NEIJAHR WISCONSIN MATHEMATICS COUNCIL SCHOLARSHIP

Scholarship for a Wisconsin resident who is currently enrolled in teacher education programs in a Wisconsin institution studying mathematics education. Minimum GPA of 3.0 required.

Academic Fields/Career Goals: Education; Mathematics.

Award: Scholarship for use in junior or senior years; not renewable. *Number:* 1. *Amount:* $2000.

Eligibility Requirements: Applicant must be enrolled or expecting to enroll full-time at a four-year institution or university; resident of Wisconsin and studying in Wisconsin. Applicant must have 3.0 GPA or higher. Available to U.S. citizens.

Application Requirements: Application, essay, resume, references, transcript. *Deadline:* March 1.

Contact: Debra Pass, Scholarship Committee
Wisconsin Mathematics Council, Inc.
W175 N11117 Stonewood Drive, Suite 204
Germantown, WI 53022
Phone: 262-437-0174
E-mail: wmc@wismath.org

SISTER MARY PETRONIA VAN STRATEN WISCONSIN MATHEMATICS COUNCIL SCHOLARSHIP

Scholarship for a Wisconsin resident who is currently enrolled in teacher education programs in Wisconsin institution studying mathematics education. Minimum GPA of 3.0 required.

Academic Fields/Career Goals: Education; Mathematics.

Award: Scholarship for use in junior or senior years; not renewable. *Number:* 1. *Amount:* $2000.

Eligibility Requirements: Applicant must be enrolled or expecting to enroll full-time at a four-year institution or university; resident of Wisconsin and studying in Wisconsin. Applicant must have 3.0 GPA or higher. Available to U.S. citizens.

Application Requirements: Application, essay, resume, references, transcript. *Deadline:* March 1.

Contact: Debra Pass, Scholarship Committee
Wisconsin Mathematics Council, Inc.
W175 N11117 Stonewood Drive, Suite 204
Germantown, WI 53022
Phone: 262-437-0174
E-mail: wmc@wismath.org

WOMEN BAND DIRECTORS INTERNATIONAL

http://www.womenbanddirectors.org/

CHARLOTTE PLUMMER OWEN MEMORIAL SCHOLARSHIP

One-time award for women instrumental music majors enrolled in a four-year institution. Applicants must be working toward a degree in music education with the intention of becoming a band director. See web site for application http://www.womenbanddirectors.org/.

Academic Fields/Career Goals: Education; Music; Performing Arts.

Award: Scholarship for use in freshman, sophomore, junior, or senior years; not renewable. *Number:* 4. *Amount:* $300.

Eligibility Requirements: Applicant must be enrolled or expecting to enroll full-time at a four-year institution or university; female and must have an interest in music/singing. Available to U.S. and non-U.S. citizens.

Application Requirements: Application, essay, photo, references, transcript. *Deadline:* December 1.

Contact: Nicole Aakre-Rubis, Scholarship Chair
Women Band Directors International
16085 Excel Way
Rosemount, MN 55068

MARTHA ANN STARK MEMORIAL SCHOLARSHIP

One-time award for women instrumental music majors enrolled in a four-year institution. Applicants must be working toward a degree in music education with the intention of becoming a band director. Three of the scholarships are designated for college upperclassmen, and one is open to all levels. See web site for application http://www.womenbanddirectors.org/.

Academic Fields/Career Goals: Education; Music; Performing Arts.

Award: Scholarship for use in freshman, sophomore, junior, or senior years; not renewable. *Number:* 1. *Amount:* $300.

Eligibility Requirements: Applicant must be enrolled or expecting to enroll full-time at a four-year institution or university; female and must have an interest in music/singing. Available to U.S. and non-U.S. citizens.

Application Requirements: Application, essay, photo, references, transcript. *Deadline:* December 1.

Contact: Nicole Aakre-Rubis, Scholarship Chair
Women Band Directors International
16085 Excel Way
Rosemount, MN 55068

VOLKWEIN MEMORIAL SCHOLARSHIP

One-time award for female instrumental music majors enrolled in a four-year institution. Applicants must be working toward a degree in music education with the intention of becoming a band director. Three of the scholarships are designated for college upperclassmen, and one is open to all levels. See web site for application http://www.womenbanddirectors.org/.

Academic Fields/Career Goals: Education; Music; Performing Arts.

Award: Scholarship for use in freshman, sophomore, junior, senior, or graduate years; not renewable. *Number:* 4. *Amount:* $300–$500.

Eligibility Requirements: Applicant must be enrolled or expecting to enroll full-time at a four-year institution or university; female and must have an interest in music/singing. Available to U.S. and non-U.S. citizens.

Application Requirements: Application, essay, photo, references, self-addressed stamped envelope, transcript. *Deadline:* December 1.

Contact: Nicole Aakre-Rubis, Scholarship Chair
Women Band Directors International
16085 Excel Way
Rosemount, MN 55068

Y'S MEN INTERNATIONAL

http://www.ysmenusa.com/

ALEXANDER SCHOLARSHIP LOAN FUND
• *See page 159*

ZETA PHI BETA SORORITY INC. NATIONAL EDUCATIONAL FOUNDATION

http://www.zphib1920.org/

ISABEL M. HERSON SCHOLARSHIP IN EDUCATION

Scholarships available for graduate or undergraduate students enrolled in a degree program in either elementary or secondary education. Award for full-time study for one academic year. See web site for additional information and application http://www.zphib1920.org.

Academic Fields/Career Goals: Education.

Award: Scholarship for use in freshman, sophomore, junior, senior, or graduate years; not renewable. *Number:* 1. *Amount:* $500–$1000.

Eligibility Requirements: Applicant must be enrolled or expecting to enroll full-time at a four-year institution or university. Available to U.S. citizens.

Application Requirements: Application, essay, references, transcript, enrollment proof. *Deadline:* February 1.

Contact: Cheryl Williams, National Second Vice President
Zeta Phi Beta Sorority Inc. National Educational Foundation
1734 New Hampshire Avenue, NW
Washington, DC 20009-2595
Fax: 318-232-4593
E-mail: 2ndanti@zphib1920.org

ELECTRICAL ENGINEERING/ ELECTRONICS

AACE INTERNATIONAL
http://www.aacei.org/

AACE INTERNATIONAL COMPETITIVE SCHOLARSHIP
• See page 99

AHS INTERNATIONAL—THE VERTICAL FLIGHT SOCIETY
http://www.vtol.org/

VERTICAL FLIGHT FOUNDATION SCHOLARSHIP
• See page 118

AIST FOUNDATION
http://www.aistfoundation.org/

AISI/AIST FOUNDATION PREMIER SCHOLARSHIPS
This award is granted to the highest scoring FeMET at StEEL scholarship applicants. It is similar to the FeMET Scholarship but awards $10,000 per year.

Academic Fields/Career Goals: Electrical Engineering/Electronics; Materials Science, Engineering, and Metallurgy; Mechanical Engineering.

Award: Scholarship for use in junior or senior years; renewable. *Number:* 1. *Amount:* $10,000.

Eligibility Requirements: Applicant must be enrolled or expecting to enroll full-time at a four-year institution or university. Applicant must have 3.0 GPA or higher. Available to U.S. and non-U.S. citizens.

Application Requirements: Application, essay, interview, resume, references, transcript.

Contact: Lori Wharrey, Board Administrator
AIST Foundation
186 Thorn Hill Road
Warrendale, PA 15086-7528
Phone: 724-814-3044
E-mail: lwharrey@aist.org

AIST WILLIAM E. SCHWABE MEMORIAL SCHOLARSHIP
One-time $3000 scholarship awarded to a full-time undergraduate student in engineering, metallurgy, or materials science and engineering, mechanical engineering, electrical engineering program at an accredited North American university.

Academic Fields/Career Goals: Electrical Engineering/Electronics; Engineering/Technology; Materials Science, Engineering, and Metallurgy; Mechanical Engineering.

Award: Scholarship for use in sophomore, junior, or senior years; not renewable. *Number:* 1. *Amount:* $3000.

Eligibility Requirements: Applicant must be enrolled or expecting to enroll full-time at a four-year institution or university. Applicant must have 3.0 GPA or higher. Available to U.S. and non-U.S. citizens.

Application Requirements: Application, essay, resume, references, transcript. *Deadline:* March 2.

Contact: Lori Wharrey, Board Administrator
AIST Foundation
186 Thorn Hill Road
Warrendale, PA 15086-7528
Phone: 724-814-3044
E-mail: lwharrey@aist.org

ASSOCIATION FOR IRON AND STEEL TECHNOLOGY BENJAMIN F. FAIRLESS SCHOLARSHIP (AIME)
• See page 160

ASSOCIATION FOR IRON AND STEEL TECHNOLOGY DAVID H. SAMSON CANADIAN SCHOLARSHIP
• See page 160

ASSOCIATION FOR IRON AND STEEL TECHNOLOGY OHIO VALLEY CHAPTER SCHOLARSHIP
• See page 137

ASSOCIATION FOR IRON AND STEEL TECHNOLOGY RONALD E. LINCOLN SCHOLARSHIP
Scholarship for students of metallurgy, metallurgical engineering, or materials science and engineering, mechanical engineering, electrical engineering, interested in a career in ferrous related industries as demonstrated by an internship or related experience, or who have plans to pursue such experiences during college. Student may apply after first term of freshman year of college. Applications are accepted from December 1 through March 1 each year.

Academic Fields/Career Goals: Electrical Engineering/Electronics; Materials Science, Engineering, and Metallurgy; Mechanical Engineering.

Award: Scholarship for use in sophomore, junior, or senior years; not renewable. *Number:* 2. *Amount:* $3000.

Eligibility Requirements: Applicant must be enrolled or expecting to enroll full-time at a four-year institution or university. Applicant must have 3.0 GPA or higher. Available to U.S. and non-U.S. citizens.

Application Requirements: Application, essay, resume, references, transcript. *Deadline:* March 2.

Contact: Lori Wharrey, Board Administrator
AIST Foundation
186 Thorn Hill Road
Warrendale, PA 15086-7528
Phone: 724-814-3044
E-mail: lwharrey@aist.org

ASSOCIATION FOR IRON AND STEEL TECHNOLOGY WILLY KORF MEMORIAL SCHOLARSHIP
Scholarships for students of metallurgy, metallurgical engineering, or materials science and engineering, mechanical engineering, and electrical engineering who have a genuine demonstrated interest in a career in ferrous related industries as demonstrated by an internship or related experience, or who have plans to pursue such experiences during college. Student may apply first during the freshman year of college. Applications are accepted December 1 through March 1 each year.

Academic Fields/Career Goals: Electrical Engineering/Electronics; Materials Science, Engineering, and Metallurgy; Mechanical Engineering.

Award: Scholarship for use in sophomore, junior, or senior years; not renewable. *Number:* 2. *Amount:* $3000.

Eligibility Requirements: Applicant must be enrolled or expecting to enroll full-time at a four-year institution or university. Applicant must have 3.0 GPA or higher. Available to U.S. and non-U.S. citizens.

Application Requirements: Application, essay, resume, references, transcript. *Deadline:* March 2.

Contact: Lori Wharrey, AIST Board Administrator
AIST Foundation
186 Thorn Hill Road
Warrendale, PA 15086
Phone: 724-776-6040 Ext. 621
E-mail: lwharrey@aist.org

STEEL ENGINEERING EDUCATION LINK (STEEL) SCHOLARSHIPS
Available to all technical engineering disciplines. Apply in Sophomore year. Recipient, following confirmation of a corporate sponsor, receives $5000 toward tuition for their Junior year, a paid Summer internship at a North American steel producing company, and an additional $5000 toward tuition on their Senior year, provided they maintain a 3.0 GPA or higher and receive a satisfactory internship report.

Academic Fields/Career Goals: Electrical Engineering/Electronics; Materials Science, Engineering, and Metallurgy; Mechanical Engineering.

Award: Scholarship for use in junior or senior years; renewable. *Number:* 1–10. *Amount:* $5000.

Eligibility Requirements: Applicant must be enrolled or expecting to enroll full-time at a four-year institution or university. Applicant must have 3.0 GPA or higher. Available to U.S. and non-U.S. citizens.

Application Requirements: Application, essay, resume, references, transcript. *Deadline:* March 2.

Contact: Lori Wharrey, Board Administrator
AIST Foundation
186 Thorn Hill Road
Warrendale, PA 15086-7528
Phone: 724-814-3044
E-mail: lwharrey@aist.org

AMERICAN COUNCIL OF ENGINEERING COMPANIES OF PENNSYLVANIA (ACEC/PA)

http://www.acecpa.org/

ENGINEERING SCHOLARSHIP
• *See page 161*

AMERICAN FOUNDATION FOR THE BLIND

http://www.afb.org/

PAUL W. RUCKES SCHOLARSHIP
• *See page 195*

AMERICAN INSTITUTE OF AERONAUTICS AND ASTRONAUTICS

http://www.aiaa.org/

AIAA FOUNDATION UNDERGRADUATE SCHOLARSHIP
• *See page 93*

AMERICAN PUBLIC TRANSPORTATION FOUNDATION

http://www.apta.com/

LOUIS T. KLAUDER SCHOLARSHIP

Scholarships for study towards a career in the rail transit industry as an electrical or mechanical engineer. Must be sponsored by APTA member organization and complete internship with APTA member organization. Minimum GPA of 3.0 required.

Academic Fields/Career Goals: Electrical Engineering/Electronics; Mechanical Engineering.

Award: Scholarship for use in sophomore, junior, senior, or graduate years; renewable. *Number:* 1. *Amount:* $2500.

Eligibility Requirements: Applicant must be enrolled or expecting to enroll full-time at a two-year or four-year institution or university. Applicant must have 3.0 GPA or higher. Available to U.S. and Canadian citizens.

Application Requirements: Application, essay, financial need analysis, references, transcript, verification of enrollment for the current semester, copy of fee schedule from the college/university. *Deadline:* June 16.

Contact: Pamela Boswell, Vice President of Program Management
American Public Transportation Foundation
1666 K Street, NW
Washington, DC 20006-1215
Phone: 202-496-4803
Fax: 202-496-2323
E-mail: pboswell@apta.com

TRANSIT HALL OF FAME SCHOLARSHIP AWARD PROGRAM
• *See page 174*

AMERICAN RAILWAY ENGINEERING AND MAINTENANCE OF WAY ASSOCIATION

http://www.arema.org/

AREMA MICHAEL R. GARCIA SCHOLARSHIP
• *See page 174*

AREMA PRESIDENTIAL SPOUSE SCHOLARSHIP
• *See page 174*

AREMA UNDERGRADUATE SCHOLARSHIPS
• *See page 174*

AMERICAN SOCIETY OF HEATING, REFRIGERATING, AND AIR CONDITIONING ENGINEERS, INC.

http://www.ashrae.org/

ALWIN B. NEWTON SCHOLARSHIP FUND

Scholarship available to undergraduate students pursuing a bachelor of science or engineering degree, who are enrolled full-time in a program accredited by the Accreditation Board for Engineering and Technology. Application and additional information on web site http://www.ashrae.org.

Academic Fields/Career Goals: Electrical Engineering/Electronics; Engineering/Technology; Engineering-Related Technologies; Heating, Air-Conditioning, and Refrigeration Mechanics; Mechanical Engineering; Trade/Technical Specialties.

Award: Scholarship for use in sophomore, junior, or senior years; not renewable. *Number:* 1. *Amount:* $3000.

Eligibility Requirements: Applicant must be enrolled or expecting to enroll full-time at a four-year institution or university and must have an interest in leadership. Applicant must have 3.0 GPA or higher. Available to U.S. and non-U.S. citizens.

Application Requirements: Application, financial need analysis, references, transcript. *Deadline:* December 1.

Contact: Lois Benedict, Scholarship Administrator
American Society of Heating, Refrigerating, and Air
Conditioning Engineers, Inc.
1791 Tullie Circle, NE
Atlanta, GA 30329-1683
Phone: 404-636-8400 Ext. 1120
E-mail: lbenedict@ashrae.org

ASHRAE MEMORIAL SCHOLARSHIP

One-time $3000 award for full-time study in heating, ventilating, refrigeration, and air conditioning in an ABET-accredited program at an accredited school. See web site for application and additional information http://www.ashrae.org.

Academic Fields/Career Goals: Electrical Engineering/Electronics; Engineering/Technology; Engineering-Related Technologies; Heating, Air-Conditioning, and Refrigeration Mechanics; Trade/Technical Specialties.

Award: Scholarship for use in freshman, sophomore, junior, or senior years; not renewable. *Number:* 1. *Amount:* $3000.

Eligibility Requirements: Applicant must be enrolled or expecting to enroll full-time at a four-year institution or university. Applicant must have 3.0 GPA or higher. Available to U.S. and non-U.S. citizens.

Application Requirements: Application, financial need analysis, references, transcript. *Deadline:* December 1.

Contact: Lois Benedict, Scholarship Administrator
American Society of Heating, Refrigerating, and Air
Conditioning Engineers, Inc.
1791 Tullie Circle, NE
Atlanta, GA 30329-1683
Phone: 404-636-8400 Ext. 1120
E-mail: lbenedict@ashrae.org

DUANE HANSON SCHOLARSHIP

Scholarship available to undergraduate students pursuing a bachelor of science or engineering degree, who are enrolled full-time in a program.

ELECTRICAL ENGINEERING/ELECTRONICS

One-time $3000 award for study in heating, ventilating, refrigeration, and air conditioning in an ABET-accredited program at an accredited school. See web site for application and additional information http://www.ashrae.org.

Academic Fields/Career Goals: Electrical Engineering/Electronics; Engineering/Technology; Engineering-Related Technologies; Heating, Air-Conditioning, and Refrigeration Mechanics; Trade/Technical Specialties.

Award: Scholarship for use in freshman, sophomore, junior, or senior years; not renewable. *Number:* 1. *Amount:* $3000.

Eligibility Requirements: Applicant must be enrolled or expecting to enroll full-time at a four-year institution or university. Applicant must have 3.0 GPA or higher. Available to U.S. and non-U.S. citizens.

Application Requirements: Application, financial need analysis, references, transcript. *Deadline:* December 1.

Contact: Lois Benedict, Scholarship Administrator
American Society of Heating, Refrigerating, and Air
Conditioning Engineers, Inc.
1791 Tullie Circle, NE
Atlanta, GA 30329-1683
Phone: 404-636-8400 Ext. 1120
E-mail: lbenedict@ashrae.org

ENGINEERING TECHNOLOGY SCHOLARSHIP

Three one-year $3,000 scholarships available annually to full-time Engineering Technology students enrolled in or accepted to a post-secondary educational institution for a bachelor degree or an associate degree and pursuing a course of study which is a preparatory curriculum for the HVAC&R profession.

Academic Fields/Career Goals: Electrical Engineering/Electronics; Energy and Power Engineering; Engineering/Technology; Heating, Air-Conditioning, and Refrigeration Mechanics.

Award: Scholarship for use in freshman year; not renewable. *Number:* 3. *Amount:* $3000.

Eligibility Requirements: Applicant must be enrolled or expecting to enroll full-time at a two-year or four-year institution or university. Applicant must have 3.0 GPA or higher.

Application Requirements: Application, references, transcript. *Deadline:* May 1.

Contact: Lois Benedict, Scholarship Administrator
American Society of Heating, Refrigerating, and Air
Conditioning Engineers, Inc.
1791 Tullie Circle, NE
Atlanta, GA 30329-1683
Phone: 404-636-8400 Ext. 1120
E-mail: lbenedict@ashrae.org

FRANK M. CODA SCHOLARSHIP

Available to undergraduate students enrolled full time in an ABET-accredited program leading to bachelor of science or engineering degree. Applicants are also judged on future service to the HVAC&R profession, character and leadership ability. For application and additional information, see web site http://www.ashrae.org.

Academic Fields/Career Goals: Electrical Engineering/Electronics; Engineering/Technology; Engineering-Related Technologies; Heating, Air-Conditioning, and Refrigeration Mechanics; Mechanical Engineering; Trade/Technical Specialties.

Award: Scholarship for use in sophomore, junior, or senior years; not renewable. *Number:* 1. *Amount:* $5000.

Eligibility Requirements: Applicant must be enrolled or expecting to enroll full-time at a four-year institution or university and must have an interest in leadership. Applicant must have 3.0 GPA or higher. Available to U.S. and non-U.S. citizens.

Application Requirements: Application, financial need analysis, references, transcript. *Deadline:* December 1.

Contact: Lois Benedict, Scholarship Administrator
American Society of Heating, Refrigerating, and Air
Conditioning Engineers, Inc.
1791 Tullie Circle, NE
Atlanta, GA 30329-1683
Phone: 404-636-8400 Ext. 1120
E-mail: lbenedict@ashrae.org

HENRY ADAMS SCHOLARSHIP

One-time $3000 award for full-time study in heating, ventilating, refrigeration, and air conditioning in an ABET-accredited program at an accredited school. Must be pursuing a bachelor of science or engineering degree. See web site for application and additional information http://www.ashrae.org.

Academic Fields/Career Goals: Electrical Engineering/Electronics; Engineering/Technology; Engineering-Related Technologies; Heating, Air-Conditioning, and Refrigeration Mechanics; Trade/Technical Specialties.

Award: Scholarship for use in freshman, sophomore, junior, or senior years; not renewable. *Number:* 1. *Amount:* $3000.

Eligibility Requirements: Applicant must be enrolled or expecting to enroll full-time at a four-year institution or university and must have an interest in leadership. Applicant must have 3.0 GPA or higher. Available to U.S. and non-U.S. citizens.

Application Requirements: Application, financial need analysis, references, transcript. *Deadline:* December 1.

Contact: Lois Benedict, Scholarship Administrator
American Society of Heating, Refrigerating, and Air
Conditioning Engineers, Inc.
1791 Tullie Circle, NE
Atlanta, GA 30329-1683
Phone: 404-636-8400 Ext. 1120
E-mail: lbenedict@ashrae.org

REUBEN TRANE SCHOLARSHIP

Undergraduate engineering scholarships awarded in two disbursements of $5000 each at the beginning of the student's junior and senior year. Must be a full-time student enrolled in a bachelor of science or engineering degree accredited by the Accreditation Board for Engineering and Technology. See web site for application package and additional information http://www.ashrae.org.

Academic Fields/Career Goals: Electrical Engineering/Electronics; Engineering/Technology; Heating, Air-Conditioning, and Refrigeration Mechanics; Mechanical Engineering; Trade/Technical Specialties.

Award: Scholarship for use in junior or senior years; renewable. *Number:* 2. *Amount:* $10,000.

Eligibility Requirements: Applicant must be enrolled or expecting to enroll full-time at a four-year institution or university. Applicant must have 3.0 GPA or higher. Available to U.S. and non-U.S. citizens.

Application Requirements: Application, financial need analysis, references, transcript. *Deadline:* December 1.

Contact: Lois Benedict, Scholarship Administrator
American Society of Heating, Refrigerating, and Air
Conditioning Engineers, Inc.
1791 Tullie Circle, NE
Atlanta, GA 30329-1683
Phone: 404-636-8400 Ext. 1120
E-mail: lbenedict@ashrae.org

WILLIS H. CARRIER SCHOLARSHIP

One-year scholarship of $10,000 available to undergraduate students enrolled full time in an ABET-accredited program leading to a bachelor of science or engineering degree. See web site for application and further details http://www.ashrae.org.

Academic Fields/Career Goals: Electrical Engineering/Electronics; Engineering/Technology; Engineering-Related Technologies; Heating, Air-Conditioning, and Refrigeration Mechanics.

Award: Scholarship for use in sophomore, junior, or senior years; not renewable. *Number:* 2. *Amount:* $10,000.

Eligibility Requirements: Applicant must be enrolled or expecting to enroll full-time at a four-year institution or university. Applicant must have 3.0 GPA or higher. Available to U.S. citizens.

Application Requirements: Application, financial need analysis, references, transcript. *Deadline:* December 1.

Contact: Lois Benedict, Scholarship Administrator
American Society of Heating, Refrigerating, and Air
Conditioning Engineers, Inc.
1791 Tullie Circle, NE
Atlanta, GA 30329-1683
Phone: 404-636-8400 Ext. 1120
E-mail: lbenedict@ashrae.org

AMERICAN SOCIETY OF NAVAL ENGINEERS

http://www.navalengineers.org/

AMERICAN SOCIETY OF NAVAL ENGINEERS SCHOLARSHIP
• *See page 93*

ARMED FORCES COMMUNICATIONS AND ELECTRONICS ASSOCIATION, EDUCATIONAL FOUNDATION

http://www.afcea.org/education/scholarships

AFCEA YOUNG ENTREPRENEUR SCHOLARSHIP
• *See page 163*

ARMED FORCES COMMUNICATIONS AND ELECTRONICS ASSOCIATION GENERAL EMMETT PAIGE SCHOLARSHIP
• *See page 122*

ARMED FORCES COMMUNICATIONS AND ELECTRONICS ASSOCIATION GENERAL JOHN A. WICKHAM SCHOLARSHIP
• *See page 164*

ARMED FORCES COMMUNICATIONS AND ELECTRONICS ASSOCIATION ROTC SCHOLARSHIP PROGRAM
• *See page 122*

DISABLED WAR VETERANS SCHOLARSHIP
• *See page 122*

LTG DOUGLAS D. BUCHHOLZ MEMORIAL SCHOLARSHIP
• *See page 122*

WILLIAM E. "BUCK" BRAGUNIER SCHOLARSHIP FOR OUTSTANDING LEADERSHIP
• *See page 123*

ARRL FOUNDATION INC.

http://www.arrl.org/

CHARLES N. FISHER MEMORIAL SCHOLARSHIP
• *See page 94*

DR. JAMES L. LAWSON MEMORIAL SCHOLARSHIP
• *See page 182*

EARL I. ANDERSON SCHOLARSHIP

Award for students in electronic engineering or related technical field. Student must be an amateur radio operator and member of the American Radio Relay League. Preference given to students who reside and attend classes in Illinois, Indiana, Michigan, or Florida.

Academic Fields/Career Goals: Electrical Engineering/Electronics.

Award: Scholarship for use in freshman, sophomore, junior, or senior years; not renewable. *Number:* 3. *Amount:* $1250.

Eligibility Requirements: Applicant must be enrolled or expecting to enroll full-time at a four-year institution or university; resident of Florida, Illinois, Indiana, or Michigan; studying in Florida, Illinois, Indiana, or Michigan and must have an interest in amateur radio. Applicant or parent of applicant must be member of American Radio Relay League. Available to U.S. citizens.

Application Requirements: Application, transcript. *Deadline:* February 1.

Contact: Ms. Mary Hobart, Secretary
ARRL Foundation Inc.
225 Main Street
Newington, CT 06111-1494
Phone: 860-594-0397
E-mail: k1mmh@arrl.org

EDMOND A. METZGER SCHOLARSHIP

Scholarship for licensed amateur radio operators, at the novice class or above. Applicants must be undergraduate or graduate electrical engineering students and members of the Amateur Radio Relay League.

Academic Fields/Career Goals: Electrical Engineering/Electronics.

Award: Scholarship for use in freshman, sophomore, junior, senior, or graduate years; not renewable. *Number:* 1. *Amount:* $500.

Eligibility Requirements: Applicant must be enrolled or expecting to enroll full-time at a four-year institution or university; resident of Illinois, Indiana, or Wisconsin; studying in Illinois, Indiana, or Wisconsin and must have an interest in amateur radio. Applicant or parent of applicant must be member of American Radio Relay League. Available to U.S. citizens.

Application Requirements: Application, transcript. *Deadline:* February 1.

Contact: Ms. Mary Hobart, Secretary
ARRL Foundation Inc.
225 Main Street
Newington, CT 06111-1494
Phone: 860-594-0397
E-mail: k1mmh@arrl.org

EUGENE GENE SALLEE, W4YFR MEMORIAL SCHOLARSHIP
• *See page 183*

FRANCIS WALTON MEMORIAL SCHOLARSHIP
• *See page 83*

FRED R. MCDANIEL MEMORIAL SCHOLARSHIP
• *See page 183*

GARY WAGNER, K3OMI SCHOLARSHIP
• *See page 164*

IRARC MEMORIAL JOSEPH P. RUBINO WA4MMD SCHOLARSHIP

Need-based award available to licensed amateur radio operators. Preference is given to Brevard County residents or, secondarily, to all Florida residents. Must maintain 2.5 GPA and pursue an undergraduate degree or electronic technician certification.

Academic Fields/Career Goals: Electrical Engineering/Electronics.

Award: Scholarship for use in freshman, sophomore, junior, or senior years; not renewable. *Number:* varies. *Amount:* $750.

Eligibility Requirements: Applicant must be enrolled or expecting to enroll full-time at a four-year or technical institution or university; resident of Florida and must have an interest in amateur radio. Applicant or parent of applicant must be member of American Radio Relay League. Applicant must have 2.5 GPA or higher. Available to U.S. citizens.

Application Requirements: Application, financial need analysis, transcript. *Deadline:* February 1.

Contact: Ms. Mary Hobart, Secretary
ARRL Foundation Inc.
225 Main Street
Newington, CT 06111-1494
Phone: 860-594-0397
E-mail: k1mmh@arrl.org

IRVINE W. COOK WA0CGS SCHOLARSHIP
• *See page 183*

L. PHIL WICKER SCHOLARSHIP
• *See page 183*

MAGNOLIA DX ASSOCIATION SCHOLARSHIP
• *See page 183*

MISSISSIPPI SCHOLARSHIP
• *See page 94*

PAUL AND HELEN L. GRAUER SCHOLARSHIP
• *See page 94*

PERRY F. HADLOCK MEMORIAL SCHOLARSHIP

For students licensed as technicians. Preference given to students attending Clarkson University, Potsdam, New York. If no Clarkson applicants, open to all Atlantic and Hudson Divisions. Applicants must pursue a bachelor's degree or higher. Preference given to electrical and electronics engineering majors.

Academic Fields/Career Goals: Electrical Engineering/Electronics.

Award: Scholarship for use in freshman, sophomore, junior, senior, or graduate years; not renewable. *Number:* 1. *Amount:* $2000.

Eligibility Requirements: Applicant must be enrolled or expecting to enroll full-time at a four-year institution or university and must have an interest in amateur radio. Available to U.S. citizens.

Application Requirements: Application, transcript. *Deadline:* February 1.

Contact: Ms. Mary Hobart, Secretary
ARRL Foundation Inc.
225 Main Street
Newington, CT 06111-1494
Phone: 860-594-0397
E-mail: k1mmh@arrl.org

PHD ARA SCHOLARSHIP
• *See page 196*

RAY, NORP & KATIE, WOKTE PAUTZ SCHOLARSHIP
• *See page 196*

ASTRONAUT SCHOLARSHIP FOUNDATION

http://www.astronautscholarship.org/

ASTRONAUT SCHOLARSHIP FOUNDATION
• *See page 95*

AUTOMOTIVE HALL OF FAME

http://www.automotivehalloffame.org/

AUTOMOTIVE HALL OF FAME EDUCATIONAL FUNDS
• *See page 164*

CATCHING THE DREAM

http://www.catchingthedream.org/

TRIBAL BUSINESS MANAGEMENT PROGRAM (TBM)
• *See page 57*

CENTRAL INTELLIGENCE AGENCY

http://www.cia.gov/

CENTRAL INTELLIGENCE AGENCY UNDERGRADUATE SCHOLARSHIP PROGRAM
• *See page 58*

CUBAN AMERICAN NATIONAL FOUNDATION

http://www.masscholarships.org/

MAS FAMILY SCHOLARSHIPS
• *See page 148*

DEVRY, INC.

http://www.devry.edu/

CISCO/COMPTIA SCHOLARSHIP
• *See page 196*

FOUNDATION FOR SCIENCE AND DISABILITY

http://stemd.org/

GRANTS FOR DISABLED STUDENTS IN THE SCIENCES
• *See page 95*

HAWAIIAN LODGE, F&AM

http://www.glhawaii.org/

HAWAIIAN LODGE SCHOLARSHIPS
• *See page 106*

HISPANIC ENGINEER NATIONAL ACHIEVEMENT AWARDS CORPORATION (HENAAC)

http://www.henaac.org/

HISPANIC ENGINEER NATIONAL ACHIEVEMENT AWARDS CORPORATION SCHOLARSHIP PROGRAM
• *See page 125*

ILLUMINATING ENGINEERING SOCIETY OF NORTH AMERICA–GOLDEN GATE SECTION

http://www.iesgg.org/

ALAN LUCAS MEMORIAL EDUCATIONAL SCHOLARSHIP
• *See page 102*

INDEPENDENT LABORATORIES INSTITUTE SCHOLARSHIP ALLIANCE

http://www.acil.org/

INDEPENDENT LABORATORIES INSTITUTE SCHOLARSHIP ALLIANCE
• *See page 141*

INTERNATIONAL COMMUNICATIONS INDUSTRIES FOUNDATION

http://www.infocomm.org/scholarships

ICIF SCHOLARSHIP FOR EMPLOYEES AND DEPENDENTS OF MEMBER ORGANIZATIONS
• *See page 186*

INTERNATIONAL COMMUNICATIONS INDUSTRIES FOUNDATION AV SCHOLARSHIP
• *See page 186*

INTERNATIONAL SOCIETY FOR OPTICAL ENGINEERING-SPIE

http://www.spie.org/scholarships

SPIE EDUCATIONAL SCHOLARSHIPS IN OPTICAL SCIENCE AND ENGINEERING
• *See page 96*

INTERNATIONAL SOCIETY OF AUTOMATION (ISA)

http://www.isa.org/

INTERNATIONAL SOCIETY OF AUTOMATION EDUCATION FOUNDATION SCHOLARSHIPS
• *See page 125*

JORGE MAS CANOSA FREEDOM FOUNDATION

http://www.jorgemascanosa.org/

MAS FAMILY SCHOLARSHIP AWARD
• *See page 152*

KOREAN-AMERICAN SCIENTISTS AND ENGINEERS ASSOCIATION

http://www.ksea.org/

KSEA SCHOLARSHIPS

Scholarship for undergraduate or graduate students in the United States with Korean heritage. Applicant should major in science, engineering, or related fields and should be a KSEA member.

Academic Fields/Career Goals: Electrical Engineering/Electronics; Engineering/Technology; Engineering-Related Technologies; Science, Technology, and Society.

Award: Scholarship for use in freshman, sophomore, junior, senior, or graduate years; not renewable. *Number:* 1–35. *Amount:* $1000–$1500.

Eligibility Requirements: Applicant must be of Korean heritage; Asian/Pacific Islander and enrolled or expecting to enroll full-time at a two-year or four-year institution or university. Applicant or parent of applicant must be member of Korean-American Scientists and Engineers Association. Available to U.S. citizens.

Application Requirements: Application, essay, resume, references, transcript. *Deadline:* February 15.

Contact: Scholarships Coordinator
Korean-American Scientists and Engineers Association
1952 Gallows Road, Suite 300
Vienna, VA 22182
Phone: 703-748-1221
Fax: 703-748-1331
E-mail: sejong@ksea.org

LOS ANGELES COUNCIL OF BLACK PROFESSIONAL ENGINEERS

http://www.lablackengineers.org/

AL-BEN SCHOLARSHIP FOR ACADEMIC INCENTIVE
• *See page 166*

AL-BEN SCHOLARSHIP FOR PROFESSIONAL MERIT
• *See page 166*

AL-BEN SCHOLARSHIP FOR SCHOLASTIC ACHIEVEMENT
• *See page 166*

MICHIGAN SOCIETY OF PROFESSIONAL ENGINEERS

http://www.michiganspe.org/

MICHIGAN SOCIETY OF PROFESSIONAL ENGINEERS HARRY R. BALL, P.E. GRANT
• *See page 166*

MICHIGAN SOCIETY OF PROFESSIONAL ENGINEERS KENNETH B. FISHBECK, P.E. MEMORIAL GRANT
• *See page 166*

NASA IDAHO SPACE GRANT CONSORTIUM

http://www.id.spacegrant.org/

NASA IDAHO SPACE GRANT CONSORTIUM SCHOLARSHIP PROGRAM
• *See page 141*

NASA MONTANA SPACE GRANT CONSORTIUM

http://www.spacegrant.montana.edu/

MONTANA SPACE GRANT SCHOLARSHIP PROGRAM
• *See page 128*

NASA SOUTH CAROLINA SPACE GRANT CONSORTIUM

http://www.cofc.edu/~scsgrant

PRE-SERVICE TEACHER SCHOLARSHIP
• *See page 129*

NASA'S VIRGINIA SPACE GRANT CONSORTIUM

http://www.vsgc.odu.edu/

UNDERGRADUATE RESEARCH STEM SCHOLARSHIPS
• *See page 96*

VIRGINIA STEM COMMUNITY COLLEGE SCHOLARSHIPS
• *See page 96*

NATIONAL ASSOCIATION OF WOMEN IN CONSTRUCTION

http://www.nawic.org/

NAWIC UNDERGRADUATE SCHOLARSHIPS
• *See page 102*

NATIONAL BOARD OF BOILER AND PRESSURE VESSEL INSPECTORS

http://www.nationalboard.org/

NATIONAL BOARD TECHNICAL SCHOLARSHIP
• *See page 167*

NATIONAL SECURITY AGENCY

http://www.nsa.gov/

NATIONAL SECURITY AGENCY STOKES EDUCATIONAL SCHOLARSHIP PROGRAM
• *See page 198*

NATIONAL SOCIETY OF PROFESSIONAL ENGINEERS

http://www.nspe.org/

MAUREEN L. AND HOWARD N. BLITMAN, PE SCHOLARSHIP TO PROMOTE DIVERSITY IN ENGINEERING
• *See page 167*

PAUL H. ROBBINS HONORARY SCHOLARSHIP
• *See page 168*

PROFESSIONAL ENGINEERS IN INDUSTRY SCHOLARSHIP
• *See page 168*

OREGON STUDENT ASSISTANCE COMMISSION

http://www.GetCollegeFunds.org/

AMERICAN COUNCIL OF ENGINEERING COMPANIES OF OREGON SCHOLARSHIP
• *See page 168*

PROFESSIONAL CONSTRUCTION ESTIMATORS ASSOCIATION

http://www.pcea.org/

TED WILSON MEMORIAL SCHOLARSHIP FOUNDATION
• *See page 179*

ROBERT H. MOLLOHAN FAMILY CHARITABLE FOUNDATION, INC.

http://www.mollohanfoundation.org/

HIGH TECHNOLOGY SCHOLARS PROGRAM
• *See page 143*

SEMICONDUCTOR RESEARCH CORPORATION (SRC)

http://www.src.org/

MASTER'S SCHOLARSHIP PROGRAM
• *See page 169*

SOCIETY OF AUTOMOTIVE ENGINEERS

http://www.sae.org/

BMW/SAE ENGINEERING SCHOLARSHIP
• *See page 132*

EDWARD D. HENDRICKSON/SAE ENGINEERING SCHOLARSHIP
• *See page 132*

TMC/SAE DONALD D. DAWSON TECHNICAL SCHOLARSHIP
• *See page 133*

SOCIETY OF BROADCAST ENGINEERS INC.

http://www.sbe.org/

ROBERT GREENBERG/HAROLD E. ENNES SCHOLARSHIP FUND AND ENNES EDUCATIONAL FOUNDATION BROADCAST TECHNOLOGY SCHOLARSHIP

Merit-based awards for undergraduate students to study the technical aspects of broadcast engineering. Students should apply as high school senior or college freshman and may use the award for a two- or four-year college or university program. One-time award of $1000–$1500.

Academic Fields/Career Goals: Electrical Engineering/Electronics; Engineering-Related Technologies; TV/Radio Broadcasting.

Award: Scholarship for use in freshman, sophomore, junior, or senior years; renewable. *Number:* 3. *Amount:* $1000–$1500.

Eligibility Requirements: Applicant must be enrolled or expecting to enroll full-time at a two-year or four-year institution or university. Applicant must have 3.0 GPA or higher. Available to U.S. citizens.

Application Requirements: Application, essay, references, self-addressed stamped envelope, transcript. *Deadline:* July 1.

Contact: Executive Secretary
Society of Broadcast Engineers Inc.
9102 North Meridian Street, Suite 150
Indianapolis, IN 46260
Phone: 317-846-9000
Fax: 317-846-9120

SOCIETY OF HISPANIC PROFESSIONAL ENGINEERS FOUNDATION

http://www.henaac.org/

SOCIETY OF HISPANIC PROFESSIONAL ENGINEERS FOUNDATION
• *See page 169*

SOCIETY OF MANUFACTURING ENGINEERS EDUCATION FOUNDATION

http://www.smeef.org/

WILLIAM E. WEISEL SCHOLARSHIP FUND

Scholarship will be given to a full-time undergraduate student enrolled in an engineering or technology degree program in the U.S. or Canada, seeking a career in manufacturing. Consideration will be given to students who intend to apply their knowledge in the sub-specialty of medical robotics. Minimum of 3.0 GPA is required. Scholarships will be limited to United States and Canadian citizens.

Academic Fields/Career Goals: Electrical Engineering/Electronics; Engineering/Technology; Mechanical Engineering; Trade/Technical Specialties.

Award: Scholarship for use in sophomore, junior, or senior years; not renewable. *Number:* 1–10. *Amount:* $1000–$5000.

Eligibility Requirements: Applicant must be enrolled or expecting to enroll full-time at a four-year institution or university. Applicant must have 3.0 GPA or higher. Available to U.S. and Canadian citizens.

Application Requirements: Application, essay, resume, references, transcript. *Deadline:* February 1.

Contact: Society of Manufacturing Engineers Education Foundation
One SME Drive
PO Box 930
Dearborn, MI 48121-0930
Phone: 313-425-3300
E-mail: foundation@sme.org

SOCIETY OF MOTION PICTURE AND TELEVISION ENGINEERS

http://www.smpte.org/

LOU WOLF MEMORIAL SCHOLARSHIP

Award for students enrolled in an accredited high school, two-year or four-year college or university. Must be members of Society of Motion Picture and Television Engineers.

Academic Fields/Career Goals: Electrical Engineering/Electronics; Engineering/Technology; Engineering-Related Technologies; Filmmaking/Video; TV/Radio Broadcasting.

Award: Scholarship for use in freshman, sophomore, junior, senior, graduate, or postgraduate years; not renewable. *Number:* 1–3. *Amount:* $100–$2000.

Eligibility Requirements: Applicant must be enrolled or expecting to enroll full-time at a two-year or four-year institution or university and must have an interest in photography/photogrammetry/filmmaking. Applicant or parent of applicant must be member of Society of Motion Picture and Television Engineers. Available to U.S. and non-U.S. citizens.

Application Requirements: Application, essay, references, transcript. *Deadline:* June 1.

Contact: Sally-Ann D'Amato, Director of Operations
Society of Motion Picture and Television Engineers
SMPTE, 3 Barker Avenue
White Plains, NY 10601
Phone: 914-761-1100 Ext. 4965
E-mail: sdamato@smpte.org

SOCIETY OF PLASTICS ENGINEERS (SPE) FOUNDATION

http://www.4spe.org/

FLEMING/BASZCAK SCHOLARSHIP
• *See page 169*

SOCIETY OF PLASTICS ENGINEERS SCHOLARSHIP PROGRAM
• *See page 170*

SONS OF NORWAY FOUNDATION

http://www.sonsofnorway.com/

NANCY LORRAINE JENSEN MEMORIAL SCHOLARSHIP
• *See page 170*

SOUTH DAKOTA RETAILERS ASSOCIATION

http://www.sdra.org/

SOUTH DAKOTA RETAILERS ASSOCIATION SCHOLARSHIP PROGRAM
• *See page 71*

STRAIGHTFORWARD MEDIA

http://www.straightforwardmedia.com/

STRAIGHTFORWARD MEDIA ENGINEERING SCHOLARSHIP
• *See page 170*

TURNER CONSTRUCTION COMPANY

http://www.turnerconstruction.com/

YOUTHFORCE 2020 SCHOLARSHIP PROGRAM
• *See page 103*

UNITED NEGRO COLLEGE FUND

http://www.uncf.org/

ALFRED CHISHOLM/BASF MEMORIAL SCHOLARSHIP FUND
• *See page 72*

CISCO/UNCF SCHOLARS PROGRAM
• *See page 201*

EMERSON PROCESS MANAGEMENT SCHOLARSHIP
• *See page 170*

FORD/UNCF CORPORATE SCHOLARS PROGRAM
• *See page 73*

GENERAL MILLS TECHNOLOGY SCHOLARS AWARD
• *See page 171*

GOOGLE SCHOLARSHIP
• *See page 201*

LOCKHEED MARTIN/UNCF SCHOLARSHIP
• *See page 73*

MEDTRONIC FOUNDATION SCHOLARSHIP
• *See page 145*

TOYOTA/UNCF SCHOLARSHIP
• *See page 74*

UNITED WATER CORPORATE SCHOLARS PROGRAM
• *See page 74*

UPS/UNCF CORPORATE SCHOLARS PROGRAM
• *See page 202*

WELLS FARGO/UNCF SCHOLARSHIP FUND
• *See page 74*

UNIVERSITIES SPACE RESEARCH ASSOCIATION

http://www.usra.edu/

UNIVERSITIES SPACE RESEARCH ASSOCIATION SCHOLARSHIP PROGRAM
• *See page 97*

UTAH SOCIETY OF PROFESSIONAL ENGINEERS

http://www.uspeonline.com/

UTAH SOCIETY OF PROFESSIONAL ENGINEERS JOE RHOADS SCHOLARSHIP
• *See page 171*

WEST VIRGINIA HIGHER EDUCATION POLICY COMMISSION-STUDENT SERVICES

http://www.wvhepcnew.wvnet.edu/

WEST VIRGINIA ENGINEERING, SCIENCE AND TECHNOLOGY SCHOLARSHIP PROGRAM

Award for full-time students attending West Virginia institutions, pursuing a degree in engineering, science, or technology. Must be a resident of West Virginia. Must have a 3.0 GPA, and after graduation, must work in the fields of engineering, science, or technology in West Virginia one year for each year the award was received.

Academic Fields/Career Goals: Electrical Engineering/Electronics; Engineering/Technology; Engineering-Related Technologies; Science, Technology, and Society.

Award: Scholarship for use in freshman, sophomore, junior, or senior years; renewable. *Number:* 200–300. *Amount:* $1500–$3000.

Eligibility Requirements: Applicant must be enrolled or expecting to enroll full-time at a two-year or four-year or technical institution or university; resident of West Virginia and studying in West Virginia. Applicant must have 3.0 GPA or higher. Available to U.S. citizens.

Application Requirements: Application, essay, test scores, transcript. *Deadline:* March 1.

Contact: Darlene Elmore, Scholarship Coordinator
West Virginia Higher Education Policy Commission-Student Services
1018 Kanawha Boulevard East, Suite 700
Charleston, WV 25301
Phone: 304-558-4618
E-mail: elmore@hepc.wvnet.edu

WOMEN IN AVIATION, INTERNATIONAL

http://www.wai.org/

DELTA AIR LINES ENGINEERING SCHOLARSHIP
• *See page 135*

XEROX

http://www.xerox.com//

TECHNICAL MINORITY SCHOLARSHIP
• *See page 171*

ENERGY AND POWER ENGINEERING

AMERICAN NUCLEAR SOCIETY

http://www.ans.org/

DECOMMISSIONING, DECONTAMINATION, AND REUTILIZATION UNDERGRADUATE SCHOLARSHIP

Undergraduate scholarship for students who have completed two or more years in a course of study leading to a degree in nuclear science, nuclear engineering, or a nuclear-related field.

Academic Fields/Career Goals: Energy and Power Engineering; Nuclear Science.

Award: Scholarship for use in junior or senior years; not renewable. *Number:* 1. *Amount:* $2000.

Eligibility Requirements: Applicant must be enrolled or expecting to enroll full-time at a four-year institution or university. Available to U.S. citizens.

Application Requirements: Application, essay, references, transcript. *Deadline:* February 1.

Contact: Scholarship Coordinator
American Nuclear Society
555 North Kensington Avenue
La Grange Park, IL 60526
Phone: 708-352-6611
Fax: 708-352-0499
E-mail: outreach@ans.org

AMERICAN SOCIETY OF HEATING, REFRIGERATING, AND AIR CONDITIONING ENGINEERS, INC.

http://www.ashrae.org/

ENGINEERING TECHNOLOGY SCHOLARSHIP
• *See page 254*

AMERICAN SOCIETY OF NAVAL ENGINEERS

http://www.navalengineers.org/

AMERICAN SOCIETY OF NAVAL ENGINEERS SCHOLARSHIP
• *See page 93*

ARRL FOUNDATION INC.

http://www.arrl.org/

GARY WAGNER, K3OMI SCHOLARSHIP
• *See page 164*

HAWAIIAN LODGE, F&AM

http://www.glhawaii.org/

HAWAIIAN LODGE SCHOLARSHIPS
• *See page 106*

INTERNATIONAL SOCIETY OF AUTOMATION (ISA)

http://www.isa.org/

INTERNATIONAL SOCIETY OF AUTOMATION EDUCATION FOUNDATION SCHOLARSHIPS
• *See page 125*

NASA SOUTH DAKOTA SPACE GRANT CONSORTIUM

http://www.sdspacegrant.sdsmt.edu/

SOUTH DAKOTA SPACE GRANT CONSORTIUM UNDERGRADUATE AND GRADUATE STUDENT SCHOLARSHIPS
• *See page 129*

NASA WEST VIRGINIA SPACE GRANT CONSORTIUM

http://www.nasa.wvu.edu/

WEST VIRGINIA SPACE GRANT CONSORTIUM UNDERGRADUATE FELLOWSHIP PROGRAM
• *See page 129*

ROBERT H. MOLLOHAN FAMILY CHARITABLE FOUNDATION, INC.

http://www.mollohanfoundation.org/

HIGH TECHNOLOGY SCHOLARS PROGRAM
• *See page 143*

STRAIGHTFORWARD MEDIA

http://www.straightforwardmedia.com/

STRAIGHTFORWARD MEDIA ENGINEERING SCHOLARSHIP
• *See page 170*

UTAH SOCIETY OF PROFESSIONAL ENGINEERS

http://www.uspeonline.com/

UTAH SOCIETY OF PROFESSIONAL ENGINEERS JOE RHOADS SCHOLARSHIP
• *See page 171*

ENGINEERING-RELATED TECHNOLOGIES

AACE INTERNATIONAL

http://www.aacei.org/

AACE INTERNATIONAL COMPETITIVE SCHOLARSHIP
• *See page 99*

AHS INTERNATIONAL—THE VERTICAL FLIGHT SOCIETY

http://www.vtol.org/

VERTICAL FLIGHT FOUNDATION SCHOLARSHIP
• *See page 118*

AIST FOUNDATION

http://www.aistfoundation.org/

ASSOCIATION FOR IRON AND STEEL TECHNOLOGY BALTIMORE CHAPTER SCHOLARSHIP
Scholarship for child, grandchild, or spouse of a member of the Baltimore Chapter of AIST. Must be high school seniors who are currently enrolled undergraduate students pursuing a career in engineering or metallurgy. Student may reapply each year for the term of their college education.

Academic Fields/Career Goals: Engineering/Technology; Engineering-Related Technologies; Materials Science, Engineering, and Metallurgy.

Award: Scholarship for use in freshman, sophomore, junior, or senior years; not renewable. *Number:* 1. *Amount:* $1500.

Eligibility Requirements: Applicant must be enrolled or expecting to enroll full-time at a four-year institution or university. Applicant or parent of applicant must be member of Association for Iron and Steel Technology. Available to U.S. citizens.

Application Requirements: Application, essay, test scores, transcript. *Deadline:* April 30.

Contact: Thomas J. Russo, Program Coordinator
AIST Foundation
1430 Sparrows Point Boulevard
Sparrows Point, MD 21219-1014

ASSOCIATION FOR IRON AND STEEL TECHNOLOGY BENJAMIN F. FAIRLESS SCHOLARSHIP (AIME)
• *See page 160*

ASSOCIATION FOR IRON AND STEEL TECHNOLOGY OHIO VALLEY CHAPTER SCHOLARSHIP
• *See page 137*

AMERICAN COUNCIL OF ENGINEERING COMPANIES OF PENNSYLVANIA (ACEC/PA)

http://www.acecpa.org/

ENGINEERING SCHOLARSHIP
• *See page 161*

AMERICAN INSTITUTE OF AERONAUTICS AND ASTRONAUTICS

http://www.aiaa.org/

AIAA FOUNDATION UNDERGRADUATE SCHOLARSHIP
• *See page 93*

AMERICAN PUBLIC TRANSPORTATION FOUNDATION

http://www.apta.com/

TRANSIT HALL OF FAME SCHOLARSHIP AWARD PROGRAM
• *See page 174*

AMERICAN RAILWAY ENGINEERING AND MAINTENANCE OF WAY ASSOCIATION

http://www.arema.org/

AREMA MICHAEL R. GARCIA SCHOLARSHIP
• *See page 174*

AREMA PRESIDENTIAL SPOUSE SCHOLARSHIP
• *See page 174*

AREMA UNDERGRADUATE SCHOLARSHIPS
• *See page 174*

COMMITTEE 12-RAIL TRANSIT UNDERGRADUATE SCHOLARSHIP
Applicants must be enrolled as full-time students, or as part-time students working full time in the railway industry, in an accredited four- or five-year program leading to a bachelor's degree in engineering or engineering technology. Must have completed at least one quarter or semester in college prior to submitting an application and have a minimum 2.00 GPA.

Academic Fields/Career Goals: Engineering/Technology; Engineering-Related Technologies.

Award: Scholarship for use in freshman, sophomore, junior, or senior years; not renewable. *Number:* varies. *Amount:* $1000.

Eligibility Requirements: Applicant must be enrolled or expecting to enroll full- or part-time at a four-year institution or university. Available to U.S. citizens.

Application Requirements: Application, resume, references, transcript, cover letter. *Deadline:* March 11.

Contact: Lisa Hall, Director of Marketing
American Railway Engineering and Maintenance of Way
Association
10003 Derekwood Lane, Suite 210
Lanham, MD 20706
Phone: 301-459-3200 Ext. 705
E-mail: lhall@arema.org

CSX SCHOLARSHIP
Applicants must be enrolled as full-time students in a four- or five-year program leading to a bachelor's degree in engineering or engineering technology in a curriculum which has been accredited by the Accreditation Board of Engineering and Technology (or comparable accreditation in Canada and Mexico). Must have completed at least one quarter

or semester in college prior to submitting an application and have a minimum 2.00 GPA.

Academic Fields/Career Goals: Engineering/Technology; Engineering-Related Technologies.

Award: Scholarship for use in freshman, sophomore, junior, or senior years; not renewable. *Number:* varies. *Amount:* $2500.

Eligibility Requirements: Applicant must be enrolled or expecting to enroll full-time at a four-year institution or university. Available to U.S. citizens.

Application Requirements: Application, resume, references, self-addressed stamped envelope, transcript, cover letter. *Deadline:* March 11.

Contact: Lisa Hall, Director of Marketing
American Railway Engineering and Maintenance of Way
Association
10003 Derekwood Lane, Suite 210
Lanham, MD 20706
Phone: 301-459-3200 Ext. 705
E-mail: lhall@arema.org

NORFOLK SOUTHERN FOUNDATION SCHOLARSHIP

Applicants must be enrolled as full-time students in a four- or five-year undergraduate program in engineering or engineering technology. Institution must be located in Norfolk Southern's service area (22 states, the District of Columbia, and Ontario, Canada). Must have completed at least one quarter or semester in college prior to submitting an application and have a minimum 2.00 GPA.

Academic Fields/Career Goals: Engineering/Technology; Engineering-Related Technologies.

Award: Scholarship for use in freshman, sophomore, junior, or senior years; not renewable. *Number:* varies. *Amount:* $1000.

Eligibility Requirements: Applicant must be enrolled or expecting to enroll full-time at a four-year institution or university and resident of Alabama, Delaware, Florida, Georgia, Illinois, Indiana, Iowa, Kentucky, Louisiana, Maryland, Minnesota, Missouri, Montana, New Jersey, or North Carolina. Available to U.S. citizens.

Application Requirements: Application, resume, references, transcript, cover letter. *Deadline:* March 11.

Contact: Lisa Hall, Director of Marketing
American Railway Engineering and Maintenance of Way
Association
10003 Derekwood Lane, Suite 210
Lanham, MD 20706
Phone: 301-459-3200 Ext. 705
E-mail: lhall@arema.org

PB RAIL ENGINEERING SCHOLARSHIP

Applicants must be enrolled as full-time students in a four- or five-year program leading to a bachelor's degree in engineering or engineering technology in a curriculum which has been accredited by the Accreditation Board of Engineering and Technology (or comparable accreditation in Canada and Mexico). Must have completed at least one quarter or semester in college prior to submitting an application and have a minimum 2.00 GPA.

Academic Fields/Career Goals: Engineering/Technology; Engineering-Related Technologies.

Award: Scholarship for use in freshman, sophomore, junior, or senior years; not renewable. *Number:* varies. *Amount:* $2000.

Eligibility Requirements: Applicant must be enrolled or expecting to enroll full-time at a four-year institution or university. Available to U.S. citizens.

Application Requirements: Application, resume, references, self-addressed stamped envelope, transcript, cover letter. *Deadline:* March 11.

Contact: Lisa Hall, Director of Marketing
American Railway Engineering and Maintenance of Way
Association
10003 Derekwood Lane, Suite 210
Lanham, MD 20706
Phone: 301-459-3200 Ext. 705
E-mail: lhall@arema.org

REMSA SCHOLARSHIP

Applicants must be enrolled as full-time students in a four- or five-year program leading to a bachelor's degree in engineering or engineering technology in a curriculum which has been accredited by the Accreditation Board of Engineering and Technology (or comparable accredi-

tation in Canada and Mexico). Must have completed at least one quarter or semester in college prior to submitting an application and have a minimum 2.0 GPA.

Academic Fields/Career Goals: Engineering/Technology; Engineering-Related Technologies.

Award: Scholarship for use in freshman, sophomore, junior, or senior years; not renewable. *Number:* varies. *Amount:* $1000.

Eligibility Requirements: Applicant must be enrolled or expecting to enroll full-time at a four-year institution or university. Available to U.S. citizens.

Application Requirements: Application, resume, references, self-addressed stamped envelope, transcript, cover letter. *Deadline:* March 11.

Contact: Lisa Hall, Director of Marketing
American Railway Engineering and Maintenance of Way
Association
10003 Derekwood Lane, Suite 210
Lanham, MD 20706
Phone: 301-459-3200 Ext. 705
E-mail: lhall@arema.org

AMERICAN SOCIETY FOR ENGINEERING EDUCATION

http://www.asee.org/

SCIENCE, MATHEMATICS, AND RESEARCH FOR TRANSFORMATION DEFENSE SCHOLARSHIP FOR SERVICE PROGRAM
• See page 93

AMERICAN SOCIETY OF HEATING, REFRIGERATING, AND AIR CONDITIONING ENGINEERS, INC.

http://www.ashrae.org/

ALWIN B. NEWTON SCHOLARSHIP FUND
• See page 253

ASHRAE GENERAL SCHOLARSHIP

One-time award of $3000 for full-time study in heating, ventilating, refrigeration, and air conditioning in an ABET-accredited program at an accredited school. Must be pursuing a bachelor of science or engineering degree with a GPA of minimum 3.0. See web site for application and additional information http://www.ashrae.org.

Academic Fields/Career Goals: Engineering/Technology; Engineering-Related Technologies; Heating, Air-Conditioning, and Refrigeration Mechanics; Trade/Technical Specialties.

Award: Scholarship for use in freshman, sophomore, junior, or senior years; not renewable. *Number:* 2. *Amount:* $3000.

Eligibility Requirements: Applicant must be enrolled or expecting to enroll full-time at a four-year institution or university and must have an interest in leadership. Applicant must have 3.0 GPA or higher. Available to U.S. and non-U.S. citizens.

Application Requirements: Application, financial need analysis, references, transcript. *Deadline:* December 1.

Contact: Lois Benedict, Scholarship Administrator
American Society of Heating, Refrigerating, and Air
Conditioning Engineers, Inc.
1791 Tullie Circle, NE
Atlanta, GA 30329-1683
Phone: 404-636-8400 Ext. 1120
E-mail: lbenedict@ashrae.org

ASHRAE MEMORIAL SCHOLARSHIP
• See page 253

ASHRAE REGION VIII SCHOLARSHIP

One-year scholarship available to undergraduate engineering student enrolled full time in an ABET-accredited program at a school located within the geographic boundaries of ASHRAE'S Region VIII or accredited by the Consejo de Acreditacion de la Ensenanza de la Ingenieria in Mexico. See web site for application and additional information http://www.ashrae.org.

Academic Fields/Career Goals: Engineering/Technology; Engineering-Related Technologies.

Award: Scholarship for use in freshman, sophomore, junior, or senior years; not renewable. *Number:* 1. *Amount:* $3000.

Eligibility Requirements: Applicant must be enrolled or expecting to enroll full-time at a four-year institution or university and studying in Arkansas, Louisiana, Oklahoma, or Texas. Applicant must have 3.0 GPA or higher. Available to U.S. and non-U.S. citizens.

Application Requirements: Application, financial need analysis, references, transcript. *Deadline:* December 1.

Contact: Lois Benedict, Scholarship Administrator
American Society of Heating, Refrigerating, and Air
    Conditioning Engineers, Inc.
1791 Tullie Circle, NE
Atlanta, GA 30329-1683
Phone: 404-636-8400 Ext. 1120
E-mail: lbenedict@ashrae.org

DUANE HANSON SCHOLARSHIP
• *See page 253*

FRANK M. CODA SCHOLARSHIP
• *See page 254*

HENRY ADAMS SCHOLARSHIP
• *See page 254*

WILLIS H. CARRIER SCHOLARSHIP
• *See page 254*

AMERICAN WELDING SOCIETY

http://www.aws.org/

AIRGAS-JERRY BAKER SCHOLARSHIP

Awarded to full-time undergraduate pursuing a minimum four-year degree in welding engineering or welding engineering technology. Applicant must be a minimum of 18 years of age and have a 3.0 GPA. Priority will be given to those individuals residing or attending school in the states of Alabama, Georgia or Florida.

Academic Fields/Career Goals: Engineering-Related Technologies; Materials Science, Engineering, and Metallurgy.

Award: Scholarship for use in freshman, sophomore, junior, or senior years; not renewable. *Number:* 1. *Amount:* $2500.

Eligibility Requirements: Applicant must be age 18 and over and enrolled or expecting to enroll full-time at a four-year institution or university. Applicant must have 3.0 GPA or higher. Available to U.S. and Canadian citizens.

Application Requirements: Application, essay, financial need analysis, references, transcript. *Deadline:* January 15.

Contact: Vicki Pinsky, Manager, Foundation
American Welding Society
550 Le Jeune Road, NW
Miami, FL 33126
Phone: 800-443-9353 Ext. 212
Fax: 305-443-7559
E-mail: vpinsky@aws.org

AIRGAS-TERRY JARVIS MEMORIAL SCHOLARSHIP

Award for a full-time undergraduate pursuing a minimum four-year degree in welding engineering or welding engineering technology. Must have a minimum 2.8 overall GPA with a 3.0 GPA in engineering courses. Priority given to applicants residing or attending school in Florida, Georgia, or Alabama.

Academic Fields/Career Goals: Engineering/Technology; Engineering-Related Technologies; Materials Science, Engineering, and Metallurgy.

Award: Scholarship for use in freshman, sophomore, junior, or senior years; not renewable. *Number:* 1. *Amount:* $2500.

Eligibility Requirements: Applicant must be age 18 and over and enrolled or expecting to enroll full-time at a four-year institution or university. Applicant must have 3.0 GPA or higher. Available to U.S. and Canadian citizens.

Application Requirements: Application, essay, financial need analysis, references, transcript. *Deadline:* February 15.

Contact: Vicki Pinsky, Manager, Foundation
American Welding Society
550 Le Jeune Road, NW
Miami, FL 33126
Phone: 800-443-9353 Ext. 212
Fax: 305-443-7559
E-mail: vpinsky@aws.org

AMERICAN WELDING SOCIETY DISTRICT SCHOLARSHIP PROGRAM

Award for students in vocational training, community college, or a degree program in welding or a related field of study. Applicants must be high school graduates or equivalent. Must reside in the United States and attend a U.S. institution. Recipients may reapply. Must include personal statement of career goals.

Academic Fields/Career Goals: Engineering-Related Technologies; Trade/Technical Specialties.

Award: Scholarship for use in freshman, sophomore, junior, or senior years; not renewable. *Number:* 150–200. *Amount:* $100–$3500.

Eligibility Requirements: Applicant must be age 18 and over and enrolled or expecting to enroll full- or part-time at a two-year or four-year or technical institution or university. Available to U.S. citizens.

Application Requirements: Application, financial need analysis, transcript. *Deadline:* March 1.

Contact: Nazdhia Prado-Pulido, Assistant, Foundation
American Welding Society
550 Le Jeune Road, NW
Miami, FL 33126
Phone: 800-443-9353 Ext. 250
Fax: 305-443-7559
E-mail: nprado-pulido@aws.org

AMERICAN WELDING SOCIETY INTERNATIONAL SCHOLARSHIP

Award for full-time international students pursuing a bachelor's or graduate degree in joining technologies. Scholarship not available to students residing in North America. Applicants must have completed at least one year of welding or related field of study at a baccalaureate degree-granting institution and be in the top 20 percent of that institution's grading system. For more information see web site http://www.aws.org/foundation/intl_scholarships.html.

Academic Fields/Career Goals: Engineering/Technology; Engineering-Related Technologies; Materials Science, Engineering, and Metallurgy; Trade/Technical Specialties.

Award: Scholarship for use in freshman, sophomore, junior, senior, or graduate years; not renewable. *Number:* 1. *Amount:* up to $2500.

Eligibility Requirements: Applicant must be enrolled or expecting to enroll full-time at a four-year institution or university. Available to citizens of countries other than the U.S. or Canada.

Application Requirements: Application, essay, financial need analysis, resume, references, transcript, proof of citizenship, proof of acceptance. *Deadline:* April 1.

Contact: Vicki Pinsky, Manager, Foundation
American Welding Society
550 Le Jeune Road, NW
Miami, FL 33126
Phone: 800-443-9353 Ext. 212
Fax: 305-443-7559
E-mail: vpinsky@aws.org

DONALD F. HASTINGS SCHOLARSHIP

Award for undergraduate pursuing a four-year degree either full-time or part-time in welding engineering or welding engineering technology. Preference given to students residing or attending school in California or Ohio. Submit copy of proposed curriculum. Must rank in upper half of class or have a minimum GPA of 2.5. Must also include acceptance letter.

Academic Fields/Career Goals: Engineering/Technology; Engineering-Related Technologies; Trade/Technical Specialties.

Award: Scholarship for use in freshman, sophomore, junior, or senior years; renewable. *Number:* 1. *Amount:* $2500.

Eligibility Requirements: Applicant must be age 18 and over and enrolled or expecting to enroll full- or part-time at a four-year institution or university. Applicant must have 2.5 GPA or higher. Available to U.S. citizens.

Application Requirements: Application, financial need analysis, references, transcript. *Deadline:* February 15.

Contact: Vicki Pinsky, Manager, Foundation
American Welding Society
550 Le Jeune Road, NW
Miami, FL 33126
Phone: 800-443-9353 Ext. 212
Fax: 305-443-7559
E-mail: vpinsky@aws.org

EDWARD J. BRADY MEMORIAL SCHOLARSHIP

Award for an undergraduate student pursuing a four-year degree either full- or part-time in welding engineering or welding engineering technology.

Academic Fields/Career Goals: Engineering/Technology; Engineering-Related Technologies; Trade/Technical Specialties.

Award: Scholarship for use in freshman, sophomore, junior, or senior years; not renewable. *Number:* 1. *Amount:* $2500.

Eligibility Requirements: Applicant must be age 18 and over and enrolled or expecting to enroll full- or part-time at a four-year institution or university. Available to U.S. citizens.

Application Requirements: Application, essay, financial need analysis, references, transcript, copy of proposed curriculum, acceptance letter. *Deadline:* February 15.

Contact: Vicki Pinsky, Manager, Foundation
American Welding Society
550 LeJeune Road, NW
Miami, FL 33126
Phone: 800-443-9353 Ext. 212
E-mail: vpinsky@aws.org

HOWARD E. AND WILMA J. ADKINS MEMORIAL SCHOLARSHIP

Award for a full-time junior or senior in welding engineering or welding engineering technology. Preference to welding engineering students and those residing or attending school in Wisconsin or Kentucky. Must have at least 3.2 GPA in engineering, scientific, and technical subjects and a 2.8 GPA overall. No financial need is required to apply. Award may be granted a maximum of two years. Reapply each year. Submit copy of proposed curriculum and an acceptance letter.

Academic Fields/Career Goals: Engineering/Technology; Engineering-Related Technologies; Trade/Technical Specialties.

Award: Scholarship for use in junior or senior years; not renewable. *Number:* 1. *Amount:* $2500.

Eligibility Requirements: Applicant must be age 18 and over and enrolled or expecting to enroll full-time at a four-year institution. Available to U.S. citizens.

Application Requirements: Application, essay, references, transcript. *Deadline:* February 15.

Contact: Vicki Pinsky, Manager, Foundation
American Welding Society
550 Le Jeune Road, NW
Miami, FL 33126
Phone: 800-443-9353 Ext. 212
Fax: 305-443-7559
E-mail: vpinsky@aws.org

JOHN C. LINCOLN MEMORIAL SCHOLARSHIP

Award for an undergraduate pursuing a four-year degree either full time or part time in engineering or welding engineering technology. Priority given to welding engineering students residing or attending school in the states of Ohio or Arizona. Applicant must have a minimum 2.5 overall GPA. Proof of financial need is required to qualify.

Academic Fields/Career Goals: Engineering/Technology; Engineering-Related Technologies; Materials Science, Engineering, and Metallurgy.

Award: Scholarship for use in freshman, sophomore, junior, or senior years; not renewable. *Number:* 1. *Amount:* $3500.

Eligibility Requirements: Applicant must be age 18 and over and enrolled or expecting to enroll full- or part-time at a four-year institution. Applicant must have 2.5 GPA or higher. Available to U.S. citizens.

Application Requirements: Application, financial need analysis, references, transcript. *Deadline:* February 15.

Contact: Vicki Pinsky, Manager, Foundation
American Welding Society
550 Le Jeune Road, NW
Miami, FL 33126
Phone: 800-443-9353 Ext. 212
Fax: 305-443-7559
E-mail: vpinsky@aws.org

MATSUO BRIDGE COMPANY LTD. OF JAPAN SCHOLARSHIP

• *See page 176*

MILLER ELECTRIC INTERNATIONAL WORLD SKILLS COMPETITION SCHOLARSHIP

Applicant must compete in the National Skills USA-VICA Competition for Welding, and advance to the AWS Weld Trials at the AWS International Welding and Fabricating Exposition and Convention, which is held on a bi-annual basis. The winner of the U.S. Weld Trial Competition will receive the scholarship for $10,000 and runner up will receive $1000. For additional information, see web site http://www.aws.org/foundation/national_scholarships.html.

Academic Fields/Career Goals: Engineering/Technology; Engineering-Related Technologies; Materials Science, Engineering, and Metallurgy; Trade/Technical Specialties.

Award: Scholarship for use in freshman, sophomore, junior, or senior years; renewable. *Number:* 1. *Amount:* $1000–$10,000.

Eligibility Requirements: Applicant must be enrolled or expecting to enroll full- or part-time at a four-year institution or university. Available to U.S. citizens.

Application Requirements: Applicant must enter a contest.

Contact: Vicki Pinsky, Manager, Foundation
American Welding Society
550 Le Jeune Road, NW
Miami, FL 33126
Phone: 800-443-9353 Ext. 212
Fax: 305-443-7559
E-mail: vpinsky@aws.org

MILLER ELECTRIC MFG. CO. SCHOLARSHIP

Two awards of $3000 each are available for undergraduate students who will be seniors in a four-year bachelor's degree in welding engineering technology or welding engineering. Applicant must be U.S. citizen planning to attend a U.S. institution and have a minimum 3.0 GPA. Priority given to students attending Ferris State University. Must exhibit a strong interest in welding equipment and have prior work experience in the welding equipment field.

Academic Fields/Career Goals: Engineering/Technology; Engineering-Related Technologies; Materials Science, Engineering, and Metallurgy; Trade/Technical Specialties.

Award: Scholarship for use in senior year; not renewable. *Number:* 2. *Amount:* $3000.

Eligibility Requirements: Applicant must be age 18 and over and enrolled or expecting to enroll full- or part-time at a four-year institution or university. Applicant must have 3.0 GPA or higher. Available to U.S. citizens.

Application Requirements: Application, transcript. *Deadline:* February 15.

Contact: Vicki Pinsky, Manager, Foundation
American Welding Society
550 Le Jeune Road, NW
Miami, FL 33126
Phone: 800-443-9353 Ext. 212
Fax: 305-443-7559
E-mail: vpinsky@aws.org

PRAXAIR INTERNATIONAL SCHOLARSHIP

Award for a full-time student demonstrating leadership and pursuing a four-year degree in welding engineering or welding engineering technology. Priority given to welding engineering students. Must be a U.S. or Canadian citizen. Financial need is not required. Must have minimum 2.5 GPA.

Academic Fields/Career Goals: Engineering/Technology; Engineering-Related Technologies; Materials Science, Engineering, and Metallurgy.

Award: Scholarship for use in freshman, sophomore, junior, or senior years; not renewable. *Number:* 1. *Amount:* $2500.

Eligibility Requirements: Applicant must be age 18 and over and enrolled or expecting to enroll full-time at a four-year institution or university. Applicant must have 2.5 GPA or higher. Available to U.S. and Canadian citizens.

Application Requirements: Application, financial need analysis, references, transcript. *Deadline:* February 15.

Contact: Vicki Pinsky, Manager, Foundation
American Welding Society
550 Le Jeune Road, NW
Miami, FL 33126
Phone: 800-443-9353 Ext. 212
Fax: 305-443-7559
E-mail: vpinsky@aws.org

WILLIAM A. AND ANN M. BROTHERS SCHOLARSHIP

Awarded to a full-time undergraduate pursuing a bachelor's degree in welding or welding-related program at an accredited university. Applicant must have a minimum 2.5 overall GPA. Proof of financial need is required.

Academic Fields/Career Goals: Engineering-Related Technologies; Materials Science, Engineering, and Metallurgy.

Award: Scholarship for use in freshman, sophomore, junior, or senior years; not renewable. *Number:* 1. *Amount:* $3500.

Eligibility Requirements: Applicant must be age 18 and over and enrolled or expecting to enroll full-time at a four-year institution or university. Applicant must have 2.5 GPA or higher. Available to U.S. citizens.

Application Requirements: Application, financial need analysis, references, transcript. *Deadline:* February 15.

Contact: Vicki Pinsky, Manager, Foundation
American Welding Society
550 Le Jeune Road, NW
Miami, FL 33126
Phone: 800-443-9353 Ext. 212
Fax: 305-443-7559
E-mail: vpinsky@aws.org

WILLIAM B. HOWELL MEMORIAL SCHOLARSHIP

Awarded to a full-time undergraduate student pursuing a minimum four-year degree in a welding program at an accredited university. Priority will be given to those individuals residing or attending schools in the state of Florida, Michigan, and Ohio. Minimum 2.5 GPA required.

Academic Fields/Career Goals: Engineering/Technology; Engineering-Related Technologies; Materials Science, Engineering, and Metallurgy.

Award: Scholarship for use in freshman, sophomore, junior, or senior years; not renewable. *Number:* 1. *Amount:* $2500.

Eligibility Requirements: Applicant must be age 18 and over; enrolled or expecting to enroll full-time at a four-year institution; resident of Florida, Michigan, or Ohio and studying in Florida, Michigan, or Ohio. Applicant must have 2.5 GPA or higher. Available to U.S. citizens.

Application Requirements: Application, essay, financial need analysis, references, transcript. *Deadline:* February 15.

Contact: Vicki Pinsky, Manager, Foundation
American Welding Society
550 Le Jeune Road, NW
Miami, FL 33126
Phone: 305-443-9353 Ext. 212
Fax: 305-443-7559
E-mail: vpinsky@aws.org

ARMED FORCES COMMUNICATIONS AND ELECTRONICS ASSOCIATION, EDUCATIONAL FOUNDATION

http://www.afcea.org/education/scholarships

AFCEA YOUNG ENTREPRENEUR SCHOLARSHIP
• *See page 163*

ARMED FORCES COMMUNICATIONS AND ELECTRONICS ASSOCIATION GENERAL EMMETT PAIGE SCHOLARSHIP
• *See page 122*

ARMED FORCES COMMUNICATIONS AND ELECTRONICS ASSOCIATION GENERAL JOHN A. WICKHAM SCHOLARSHIP
• *See page 164*

ARMED FORCES COMMUNICATIONS AND ELECTRONICS ASSOCIATION ROTC SCHOLARSHIP PROGRAM
• *See page 122*

VICE ADMIRAL JERRY O. TUTTLE, USN (RET.) AND MRS. BARBARA A. TUTTLE SCIENCE AND TECHNOLOGY SCHOLARSHIP

Scholarships of $2000 for students working full-time toward an undergraduate bachelor of science technology degree. Candidate must be a U.S. citizen enrolled in a technology-related field and be a sophomore or junior at the time of application. Primary consideration will be given to military enlisted candidates.

Academic Fields/Career Goals: Engineering/Technology; Engineering-Related Technologies; Science, Technology, and Society.

Award: Scholarship for use in sophomore or junior years; not renewable.

Eligibility Requirements: Applicant must be enrolled or expecting to enroll full-time at a four-year institution or university. Available to U.S. citizens. Applicant must have general military experience.

Application Requirements: Application, references, transcript. *Deadline:* November 1.

Contact: Norma Corrales, Director of Scholarships and Awards
Armed Forces Communications and Electronics Association, Educational Foundation
4400 Fair Lakes Court
Fairfax, VA 22033
Phone: 703-631-6149
E-mail: scholarship@afcea.org

WILLIAM E. "BUCK" BRAGUNIER SCHOLARSHIP FOR OUTSTANDING LEADERSHIP
• *See page 123*

ARRL FOUNDATION INC.

http://www.arrl.org/

GARY WAGNER, K3OMI SCHOLARSHIP
• *See page 164*

HENRY BROUGHTON, K2AE MEMORIAL SCHOLARSHIP

At least one $1000 award is available to students located within 70 miles of Schenectady, NY. Applicant must possess a General class amateur radio license and major in engineering or a science related field.

Academic Fields/Career Goals: Engineering/Technology; Engineering-Related Technologies.

Award: Scholarship for use in freshman, sophomore, junior, senior, or graduate years; not renewable. *Number:* 1. *Amount:* $1000.

Eligibility Requirements: Applicant must be enrolled or expecting to enroll at a four-year institution or university and resident of New York.

Application Requirements: Application, transcript. *Deadline:* February 1.

Contact: Ms. Mary Hobart, Secretary
ARRL Foundation Inc.
225 Main Street
Newington, CT 06111-1494
Phone: 860-594-0397
E-mail: k1mmh@arrl.org

YASME FOUNDATION SCHOLARSHIP
• *See page 139*

ASSOCIATION OF ENGINEERING GEOLOGISTS

http://www.aegfoundation.org/

MARLIAVE FUND
• *See page 224*

ASTRONAUT SCHOLARSHIP FOUNDATION

http://www.astronautscholarship.org/

ASTRONAUT SCHOLARSHIP FOUNDATION
• *See page 95*

AUTOMOTIVE HALL OF FAME

http://www.automotivehalloffame.org/

AUTOMOTIVE HALL OF FAME EDUCATIONAL FUNDS
• *See page 164*

BRITISH COLUMBIA INNOVATION COUNCIL

http://www.bcic.ca/

BCIC YOUNG INNOVATOR SCHOLARSHIP COMPETITION (IDEA MASH UP)
• *See page 95*

CATCHING THE DREAM

http://www.catchingthedream.org/

TRIBAL BUSINESS MANAGEMENT PROGRAM (TBM)
• *See page 57*

CUBAN AMERICAN NATIONAL FOUNDATION

http://www.masscholarships.org/

MAS FAMILY SCHOLARSHIPS
• *See page 148*

DELAWARE HIGHER EDUCATION OFFICE

http://www.doe.k12.de.us

DELAWARE SOLID WASTE AUTHORITY JOHN P. "PAT" HEALY SCHOLARSHIP

Award for legal residents of Delaware who are U.S. citizens or eligible non-citizens. Must be high school seniors or full-time college students in their freshman or sophomore years. Must major in either environmental engineering or environmental sciences at a Delaware college. Selection based on financial need, academic performance, community and school involvement, and leadership ability.

Academic Fields/Career Goals: Engineering-Related Technologies; Environmental Science.

Award: Scholarship for use in freshman or sophomore years; renewable. *Number:* 1. *Amount:* $2000.

Eligibility Requirements: Applicant must be enrolled or expecting to enroll full-time at a two-year or four-year institution or university; resident of Delaware; studying in Delaware and must have an interest in leadership. Applicant or parent of applicant must have employment or volunteer experience in community service. Applicant must have 3.0 GPA or higher. Available to U.S. citizens.

Application Requirements: Application, financial need analysis, FAFSA, Student Aid Report (SAR). *Deadline:* March 14.

Contact: Carylin Brinkley, Program Administrator
Delaware Higher Education Office
Carvel State Office Building, 820 North French Street, Fifth Floor
Wilmington, DE 19801-3509
Phone: 302-577-5240
Fax: 302-577-6765
E-mail: cbrinkley@doe.k12.de.us

DEVRY, INC.

http://www.devry.edu/

CISCO/COMPTIA SCHOLARSHIP
• *See page 196*

GLOBAL AUTOMOTIVE AFTERMARKET SYMPOSIUM

http://www.automotivescholarships.com/

GAAS SCHOLARSHIP

To receive a scholarship, applicants must be a high school graduate enrolled in a college-level program or an ASE/NATEF certified postsecondary automotive technical program.

Academic Fields/Career Goals: Engineering-Related Technologies; Trade/Technical Specialties.

Award: Scholarship for use in freshman year; not renewable. *Number:* up to 150. *Amount:* $1000.

Eligibility Requirements: Applicant must be enrolled or expecting to enroll full-time at a four-year or technical institution or university. Available to U.S. and Canadian citizens.

Application Requirements: Application, essay, photo, references, transcript. *Deadline:* March 31.

Contact: Emily McConnell, Scholarship Committee
Global Automotive Aftermarket Symposium
Research Triangle Park
PO Box 13966, NC 27709-3966
Phone: 919-406-8802
E-mail: emcconnell@mema.org

HAWAIIAN LODGE, F&AM

http://www.glhawaii.org/

HAWAIIAN LODGE SCHOLARSHIPS
• *See page 106*

ILLUMINATING ENGINEERING SOCIETY OF NORTH AMERICA

http://www.iesna.org/

ROBERT W. THUNEN MEMORIAL SCHOLARSHIPS
• *See page 101*

INDEPENDENT LABORATORIES INSTITUTE SCHOLARSHIP ALLIANCE

http://www.acil.org/

INDEPENDENT LABORATORIES INSTITUTE SCHOLARSHIP ALLIANCE
• *See page 141*

INTERNATIONAL FACILITY MANAGEMENT ASSOCIATION FOUNDATION

http://www.ifmafoundation.org/

IFMA FOUNDATION SCHOLARSHIPS
• *See page 102*

INTERNATIONAL SOCIETY FOR OPTICAL ENGINEERING-SPIE

http://www.spie.org/scholarships

SPIE EDUCATIONAL SCHOLARSHIPS IN OPTICAL SCIENCE AND ENGINEERING
• *See page 96*

INTERNATIONAL SOCIETY OF AUTOMATION

http://www.isa.org/

ISA EDUCATIONAL FOUNDATION SCHOLARSHIPS

Scholarships to graduate and undergraduate students who demonstrate outstanding potential for long-range contribution to the fields of automation and control.

Academic Fields/Career Goals: Engineering-Related Technologies.

Award: Scholarship for use in sophomore, junior, or graduate years; renewable. *Number:* up to 10. *Amount:* $500–$5000.

Eligibility Requirements: Applicant must be enrolled or expecting to enroll full-time at a two-year or four-year institution or university. Applicant must have 3.0 GPA or higher. Available to U.S. and non-U.S. citizens.

Application Requirements: Application, essay, references, transcript. *Deadline:* February 15.

Contact: Scholarship Committee
International Society of Automation
67 Alexander Drive
Research Triangle Park, NC 27709

INTERNATIONAL SOCIETY OF AUTOMATION (ISA)

http://www.isa.org/

INTERNATIONAL SOCIETY OF AUTOMATION EDUCATION FOUNDATION SCHOLARSHIPS
• *See page 125*

INTERNATIONAL SOCIETY OF EXPLOSIVES ENGINEERS

http://www.isee.org/

JERRY MCDOWELL FUND

Scholarship of $1000 to $5000 to students whose field of education is related to the commercial explosives industry.

Academic Fields/Career Goals: Engineering/Technology; Engineering-Related Technologies.

Award: Scholarship for use in freshman, sophomore, junior, or senior years; not renewable. *Number:* 1–3. *Amount:* $1000–$5000.

Eligibility Requirements: Applicant must be enrolled or expecting to enroll full-time at a two-year or four-year institution or university. Available to U.S. and non-U.S. citizens.

Application Requirements: Application, financial need analysis, references, transcript, statement of goal. *Deadline:* May 1.

Contact: Arlene Chafe, Assistant to the Executive Director
International Society of Explosives Engineers
30325 Bainbridge Road
Cleveland, OH 44139
Phone: 440-349-4400
Fax: 440-349-3788
E-mail: foundation@isee.org

JORGE MAS CANOSA FREEDOM FOUNDATION

http://www.jorgemascanosa.org/

MAS FAMILY SCHOLARSHIP AWARD
• *See page 152*

KOREAN-AMERICAN SCIENTISTS AND ENGINEERS ASSOCIATION

http://www.ksea.org/

KSEA SCHOLARSHIPS
• *See page 257*

LOS ANGELES COUNCIL OF BLACK PROFESSIONAL ENGINEERS

http://www.lablackengineers.org/

AL-BEN SCHOLARSHIP FOR ACADEMIC INCENTIVE
• *See page 166*

AL-BEN SCHOLARSHIP FOR PROFESSIONAL MERIT
• *See page 166*

AL-BEN SCHOLARSHIP FOR SCHOLASTIC ACHIEVEMENT
• *See page 166*

MAINE SOCIETY OF PROFESSIONAL ENGINEERS

http://www.mespe.org/

MAINE SOCIETY OF PROFESSIONAL ENGINEERS VERNON T. SWAINE-ROBERT E. CHUTE SCHOLARSHIP

Nonrenewable scholarship for full-time study for freshmen only. Must be a Maine resident. Application can also be obtained by sending e-mail to rgmglads@twi.net.

Academic Fields/Career Goals: Engineering/Technology; Engineering-Related Technologies.

Award: Scholarship for use in freshman year; not renewable. *Number:* 1–2. *Amount:* $1500.

Eligibility Requirements: Applicant must be high school student; planning to enroll or expecting to enroll full-time at a four-year institution or university; resident of Maine and studying in Maine. Applicant must have 2.5 GPA or higher. Available to U.S. citizens.

Application Requirements: Application, essay, interview, references, self-addressed stamped envelope, test scores, transcript. *Deadline:* March 1.

Contact: Robert G. Martin, Scholarship Committee Chairman
Maine Society of Professional Engineers
1387 Augusta Road
Belgrade, ME 04917
Phone: 207-495-2244
E-mail: rgmglads@twi.net

MANUFACTURERS ASSOCIATION OF MAINE

http://www.mainemfg.com/

MAINE METAL PRODUCTS EDUCATION FUND SCHOLARSHIP PROGRAM
• *See page 127*

MINERALS, METALS, AND MATERIALS SOCIETY (TMS)

http://www.tms.org/

TMS/EMPMD GILBERT CHIN SCHOLARSHIP

One $2,000 scholarship is available to an undergraduate students in their sophomore and junior years, who are studying subjects in relation to synthesis and processing, structure, properties, and performance of electronic, photonic, magnetic, and superconducting materials as well as materials used in packaging, and interconnecting such materials in device structures. An additional $500 for travel expenses is available to the recipient in order to personally accept the award at the TMS Annual Meeting and Exhibition. The scholarship recipient is known as the EMPMD Gilbert Chin Scholar.

Academic Fields/Career Goals: Engineering/Technology; Engineering-Related Technologies; Materials Science, Engineering, and Metallurgy.

Award: Scholarship for use in sophomore or junior years; not renewable. *Number:* 1. *Amount:* $2000.

Eligibility Requirements: Applicant must be enrolled or expecting to enroll full-time at a four-year institution or university. Available to U.S. and non-U.S. citizens.

Application Requirements: Application, essay, resume, references, transcript. *Deadline:* March 15.

Contact: TMS Student Awards Program
Minerals, Metals, and Materials Society (TMS)
184 Thorn Hill Road
Warrendale, PA 15086
Phone: 724-776-9000 Ext. 232
Fax: 724-776-3770
E-mail: students@tms.org

TMS/EPD SCHOLARSHIP

Four $2,000 scholarships are available to full-time undergraduate applicants in their sophomore or junior years, who are majoring in the extraction and processing of minerals, metals and materials. Each scholarship recipient is also given the opportunity to select up to five Extraction & Processing Division-sponsored conference proceedings or textbooks to be donated in the recipient's name to his/her college or university library. Awards are presented during the Extraction & Processing Division luncheon at the TMS Annual Meeting and Exhibition. Up to $500 for travel expenses is available to each recipient in order to accept the award at the luncheon. Scholarship recipients are known as EPD Scholars.

Academic Fields/Career Goals: Engineering/Technology; Engineering-Related Technologies; Materials Science, Engineering, and Metallurgy.

Award: Scholarship for use in sophomore or junior years; not renewable. *Number:* 4. *Amount:* $2000.

Eligibility Requirements: Applicant must be enrolled or expecting to enroll full-time at a four-year institution or university. Available to U.S. and non-U.S. citizens.

Application Requirements: Application, essay, resume, references, transcript. *Deadline:* March 15.

Contact: TMS Student Awards Program
Minerals, Metals, and Materials Society (TMS)
184 Thorn Hill Road
Warrendale, PA 15086
Phone: 724-776-9000 Ext. 232
Fax: 724-776-3770
E-mail: awards@tms.org

TMS/INTERNATIONAL SYMPOSIUM ON SUPERALLOYS SCHOLARSHIP PROGRAM

Scholarships with up to $500 in travel reimbursements are available to undergraduate and graduate students majoring in metallurgical and/or materials science and engineering with an emphasis on all aspects of the high-temperature, high-performance materials used in the gas turbine industry and all other applications. Awards are presented in conjunction with the Materials Science and Technology Conference.

Academic Fields/Career Goals: Engineering/Technology; Engineering-Related Technologies; Materials Science, Engineering, and Metallurgy.

Award: Scholarship for use in sophomore, junior, or graduate years; not renewable. *Number:* 2. *Amount:* $2000.

Eligibility Requirements: Applicant must be enrolled or expecting to enroll full-time at a four-year institution or university. Available to U.S. and non-U.S. citizens.

Application Requirements: Application, essay, resume, references, transcript. *Deadline:* March 15.

Contact: TMS Student Awards Program
Minerals, Metals, and Materials Society (TMS)
184 Thorn Hill Road
Warrendale, PA 15086
Phone: 724-776-9000 Ext. 232
Fax: 724-776-3770
E-mail: awards@tms.org

TMS J. KEITH BRIMACOMBE PRESIDENTIAL SCHOLARSHIP

One $5,000 cash award scholarship is made to an undergraduate student majoring in metallurgical engineering, materials science and engineering, or minerals processing/extraction programs. In addition, a travel stipend of $1,000 is available for the recipient to attend the TMS Annual Meeting, to formally receive the scholarship.

Academic Fields/Career Goals: Engineering/Technology; Engineering-Related Technologies; Materials Science, Engineering, and Metallurgy.

Award: Scholarship for use in sophomore or junior years; not renewable. *Number:* 1. *Amount:* $5000.

Eligibility Requirements: Applicant must be enrolled or expecting to enroll full-time at a four-year institution or university. Available to U.S. and non-U.S. citizens.

Application Requirements: Application, essay, resume, references, transcript. *Deadline:* March 15.

Contact: TMS Student Awards Program
Minerals, Metals, and Materials Society (TMS)
184 Thorn Hill Road
Warrendale, PA 15086
Phone: 724-776-9000 Ext. 232
Fax: 724-776-3770
E-mail: awards@tms.org

TMS/LMD SCHOLARSHIP PROGRAM

Scholarships are available to full-time undergraduate applicants who are majoring in metallurgical and/or materials science and engineering with an emphasis on both traditional (aluminum, magnesium, beryllium, titanium, lithium and other reactive metals) and emerging (composites, laminates, etc.) light metals. Additionally, recipients may select up to $300 worth of Light Metals Division-sponsored conference proceedings or textbooks to be donated in the recipient's name to his/her college or university library. Each recipient may also choose up to $400 worth of books for his/her personal use. As the awards are presented during the Light Metals Division luncheon at the TMS Annual Meeting and Exhibition, up to $600 for travel expenses is available to each recipient.

Academic Fields/Career Goals: Engineering/Technology; Engineering-Related Technologies; Materials Science, Engineering, and Metallurgy.

Award: Scholarship for use in sophomore or junior years; not renewable. *Number:* 3. *Amount:* $4000.

Eligibility Requirements: Applicant must be enrolled or expecting to enroll full-time at a four-year institution or university. Available to U.S. and non-U.S. citizens.

Application Requirements: Application, essay, resume, references, transcript. *Deadline:* March 15.

Contact: TMS Student Awards Program
Minerals, Metals, and Materials Society (TMS)
184 Thorn Hill Road
Warrendale, PA 15086
Phone: 724-776-9000 Ext. 232
Fax: 724-776-3770
E-mail: awards@tms.org

TMS OUTSTANDING STUDENT PAPER CONTEST-UNDERGRADUATE

This contest is open all student members of TMS and offers an undergraduate and graduate division. Students are encouraged to submit essays on global or national issues as well as technical research papers, relating to any field of metallurgy or materials science. Students should display original thought and creativity in the development of the essays, which should include a comprehensive bibliography on which the paper is based.

Academic Fields/Career Goals: Engineering/Technology; Engineering-Related Technologies; Materials Science, Engineering, and Metallurgy.

Award: Prize for use in freshman, sophomore, junior, or senior years; not renewable. *Number:* 2. *Amount:* $500–$1000.

Eligibility Requirements: Applicant must be enrolled or expecting to enroll full-time at a four-year institution or university. Available to U.S. and non-U.S. citizens.

Application Requirements: Application, applicant must enter a contest, essay. *Deadline:* May 1.

Contact: TMS Student Awards Program
Minerals, Metals, and Materials Society (TMS)
184 Thorn Hill Road
Warrendale, PA 15086
Phone: 724-776-9000 Ext. 232
Fax: 724-776-3770
E-mail: awards@tms.org

TMS/STRUCTURAL MATERIALS DIVISION SCHOLARSHIP

Scholarships are available to full-time undergraduate applicants who are majoring in metallurgical and/or materials science and engineering with an emphasis on the science and engineering of load-bearing materials, including studies into the nature of a material's physical properties based upon its microstructure and operating environment. Awards are presented at the TMS Annual Meeting and Exhibition, and up to $500 is available for each recipient's travel expenses.

Academic Fields/Career Goals: Engineering/Technology; Engineering-Related Technologies; Materials Science, Engineering, and Metallurgy.

Award: Scholarship for use in sophomore or junior years; not renewable. *Number:* 2. *Amount:* $2500.

Eligibility Requirements: Applicant must be enrolled or expecting to enroll full-time at a four-year institution or university. Available to U.S. and non-U.S. citizens.

Application Requirements: Application, essay, resume, references, transcript. *Deadline:* March 15.

Contact: TMS Student Awards Program
Minerals, Metals, and Materials Society (TMS)
184 Thorn Hill Road
Warrendale, PA 15086
Phone: 724-776-9000 Ext. 232
Fax: 724-776-3770
E-mail: awards@tms.org

NASA MISSISSIPPI SPACE GRANT CONSORTIUM

http://www.olemiss.edu/programs/nasa

MISSISSIPPI SPACE GRANT CONSORTIUM SCHOLARSHIP
• See page 127

NASA RHODE ISLAND SPACE GRANT CONSORTIUM

http://ri.spacegrant.org/

NASA RHODE ISLAND SPACE GRANT CONSORTIUM OUTREACH SCHOLARSHIP FOR UNDERGRADUATE STUDENTS

Scholarship for undergraduate students attending a Rhode Island Space Grant Consortium participating institution and studying in any space-related field of science, math, engineering, or other field with applications in space study. Recipients are expected to devote a maximum of 8 hours per week to outreach activities in science education for K–12 children and teachers.

Academic Fields/Career Goals: Engineering-Related Technologies; Mathematics; Science, Technology, and Society.

Award: Scholarship for use in sophomore, junior, or senior years; not renewable. *Number:* up to 2. *Amount:* up to $4000.

Eligibility Requirements: Applicant must be enrolled or expecting to enroll full-time at a four-year institution or university and studying in Rhode Island. Applicant must have 3.0 GPA or higher. Available to U.S. citizens.

Application Requirements: Application, essay, resume, references, transcript, letter of interest. *Deadline:* varies.

Contact: Juliet Duyster, Program Manager
NASA Rhode Island Space Grant Consortium
Brown University
PO Box 1846
Providence, RI 02912
Phone: 401-863-1151
E-mail: juliet_duyster@brown.edu

NASA SOUTH CAROLINA SPACE GRANT CONSORTIUM

http://www.cofc.edu/~scsgrant

KATHRYN SULLIVAN SCIENCE AND ENGINEERING FELLOWSHIP
• See page 128

UNDERGRADUATE RESEARCH AWARD PROGRAM
• See page 129

NASA SOUTH DAKOTA SPACE GRANT CONSORTIUM

http://www.sdspacegrant.sdsmt.edu/

SOUTH DAKOTA SPACE GRANT CONSORTIUM UNDERGRADUATE AND GRADUATE STUDENT SCHOLARSHIPS
• See page 129

NASA'S VIRGINIA SPACE GRANT CONSORTIUM

http://www.vsgc.odu.edu/

UNDERGRADUATE RESEARCH STEM SCHOLARSHIPS
• See page 96

NASA WEST VIRGINIA SPACE GRANT CONSORTIUM

http://www.nasa.wvu.edu/

WEST VIRGINIA SPACE GRANT CONSORTIUM UNDERGRADUATE FELLOWSHIP PROGRAM
• See page 129

NATIONAL ASSOCIATION FOR THE ADVANCEMENT OF COLORED PEOPLE

http://www.naacp.org/

HUBERTUS W.V. WELLEMS SCHOLARSHIP FOR MALE STUDENTS
• See page 167

NATIONAL ASSOCIATION OF WOMEN IN CONSTRUCTION

http://www.nawic.org/

NAWIC UNDERGRADUATE SCHOLARSHIPS
• *See page 102*

NATIONAL INVENTORS HALL OF FAME

http://www.invent.org/

COLLEGIATE INVENTORS COMPETITION FOR UNDERGRADUATE STUDENTS
• *See page 96*

COLLEGIATE INVENTORS COMPETITION-GRAND PRIZE
• *See page 97*

NATIONAL SECURITY EDUCATION PROGRAM

http://www.iie.org/

NATIONAL SECURITY EDUCATION PROGRAM (NSEP) DAVID L. BOREN UNDERGRADUATE SCHOLARSHIPS
• *See page 154*

NATIONAL SOCIETY OF PROFESSIONAL ENGINEERS

http://www.nspe.org/

MAUREEN L. AND HOWARD N. BLITMAN, PE SCHOLARSHIP TO PROMOTE DIVERSITY IN ENGINEERING
• *See page 167*

PAUL H. ROBBINS HONORARY SCHOLARSHIP
• *See page 168*

PROFESSIONAL ENGINEERS IN INDUSTRY SCHOLARSHIP
• *See page 168*

NATIONAL STONE, SAND AND GRAVEL ASSOCIATION (NSSGA)

http://www.nssga.org/

BARRY K. WENDT MEMORIAL SCHOLARSHIP

Scholarship is restricted to a student in an engineering school who plans to pursue a career in the aggregates industry. One-time award for full-time students attending a four-year college or university.

Academic Fields/Career Goals: Engineering-Related Technologies; Materials Science, Engineering, and Metallurgy.

Award: Scholarship for use in freshman, sophomore, junior, or senior years; not renewable. *Number:* 1. *Amount:* up to $2500.

Eligibility Requirements: Applicant must be enrolled or expecting to enroll full-time at a four-year institution or university. Available to U.S. and non-U.S. citizens.

Application Requirements: Application, essay, references, transcript, 300- to 500-word statement of plans for career in the aggregates industry. *Deadline:* June 2.

Contact: Scholarship Committee
National Stone, Sand and Gravel Association (NSSGA)
1605 King Street
Arlington, VA 22314
Phone: 703-525-8788
Fax: 703-525-7782
E-mail: info@nssga.org

OREGON STUDENT ASSISTANCE COMMISSION

http://www.GetCollegeFunds.org/

AMERICAN COUNCIL OF ENGINEERING COMPANIES OF OREGON SCHOLARSHIP
• *See page 168*

PENNSYLVANIA HIGHER EDUCATION ASSISTANCE AGENCY

http://www.pheaa.org/

NEW ECONOMY TECHNOLOGY AND SCITECH SCHOLARSHIPS

Renewable award for Pennsylvania residents pursuing a degree in science or technology at a PHEAA-approved two- or four-year Pennsylvania college or university. Must maintain minimum GPA of 3.0. Must commence employment in Pennsylvania in a field related to degree within one year after graduation, and work one year for each year the scholarship was awarded.

Academic Fields/Career Goals: Engineering/Technology; Engineering-Related Technologies; Natural Sciences; Physical Sciences.

Award: Scholarship for use in freshman, sophomore, junior, or senior years; renewable. *Number:* varies. *Amount:* $1000–$3000.

Eligibility Requirements: Applicant must be age 18 and over; enrolled or expecting to enroll full-time at a two-year or four-year or technical institution or university; resident of Pennsylvania and studying in Pennsylvania. Applicant must have 3.0 GPA or higher. Available to U.S. citizens.

Application Requirements: Application, FAFSA. *Deadline:* December 31.

Contact: State Grant and Special Programs Division
Pennsylvania Higher Education Assistance Agency
1200 North Seventh Street
Harrisburg, PA 17102-1444
Phone: 800-692-7392

PLASTICS INSTITUTE OF AMERICA

http://www.plasticsinstitute.org/

PLASTICS PIONEERS SCHOLARSHIPS
• *See page 168*

PLUMBING-HEATING-COOLING CONTRACTORS EDUCATION FOUNDATION

http://www.foundation.phccweb.org/

DELTA FAUCET COMPANY SCHOLARSHIP PROGRAM
• *See page 103*

PHCC EDUCATIONAL FOUNDATION NEED-BASED SCHOLARSHIP
• *See page 155*

PHCC EDUCATIONAL FOUNDATION SCHOLARSHIP PROGRAM
• *See page 155*

ROBERT H. MOLLOHAN FAMILY CHARITABLE FOUNDATION, INC.

http://www.mollohanfoundation.org/

HIGH TECHNOLOGY SCHOLARS PROGRAM
• *See page 143*

ROCKY MOUNTAIN COAL MINING INSTITUTE

http://www.rmcmi.org/

ROCKY MOUNTAIN COAL MINING INSTITUTE SCHOLARSHIP
• *See page 179*

SIMPLEHUMAN

http://www.simplehuman.com/

SIMPLE SOLUTIONS DESIGN COMPETITION

IDSA-endorsed competition to promote creative problem-solving through product design and increase public awareness of industrial design. Applicants must be enrolled in an Industrial Design program or a closely related program at a design school or university and must design a new, innovative product/technology/concept for making household chores easier. Entries evaluated on utility, efficiency, innovation, research, and aesthetics. See web site for details http://www.simple-human.com/design.

Academic Fields/Career Goals: Engineering/Technology; Engineering-Related Technologies; Industrial Design.

Award: Prize for use in freshman, sophomore, junior, or senior years; not renewable. *Number:* 1. *Amount:* $5000.

Eligibility Requirements: Applicant must be enrolled or expecting to enroll full- or part-time at a two-year or four-year or technical institution or university. Available to U.S. and non-U.S. citizens.

Application Requirements: Application, applicant must enter a contest, one PDF or JPEG of design, specs, materials, explanation. *Deadline:* February 27.

Contact: Sarah Beachler, Marketing & Communications Associate
Phone: 310-436-2278
Fax: 310-538-9196
E-mail: sbeachler@simplehuman.com

SOCIETY OF AUTOMOTIVE ENGINEERS

http://www.sae.org/

BMW/SAE ENGINEERING SCHOLARSHIP
• *See page 132*

DETROIT SECTION SAE TECHNICAL SCHOLARSHIP

Two $3500 renewable freshman scholarships will be awarded. Applicants must be a child or grandchild of a current SAE Detroit Section member. Student must maintain a 2.5 GPA and remain in good standing at the college or university in order to qualify for scholarship renewal. A student having completed a two-year program may continue for an additional consecutive two years at a second school offering a complete engineering or science baccalaureate degree program.

Academic Fields/Career Goals: Engineering/Technology; Engineering-Related Technologies; Mechanical Engineering.

Award: Scholarship for use in freshman or junior years; renewable. *Number:* 2. *Amount:* $3500.

Eligibility Requirements: Applicant must be enrolled or expecting to enroll full-time at a two-year or four-year institution or university. Applicant or parent of applicant must be member of Society of Automotive Engineers. Applicant must have 2.5 GPA or higher. Available to U.S. citizens.

Application Requirements: Application, financial need analysis, test scores, transcript, FAFSA. *Deadline:* December 1.

Contact: Connie Harnish, SAE Educational Relations
Society of Automotive Engineers
400 Commonwealth Drive
Warrendale, PA 15096-0001
Phone: 724-772-4047
E-mail: connie@sae.org

EDWARD D. HENDRICKSON/SAE ENGINEERING SCHOLARSHIP
• *See page 132*

RALPH K. HILLQUIST HONORARY SAE SCHOLARSHIP

A $1000 nonrenewable scholarship awarded every other year at the SAE Noise and Vibration Conference. Applicants must be U.S. citizens enrolled full-time as a junior in a U.S. university. A minimum 3.0 GPA with significant academic and leadership achievements is required. The student must also have a declared major in mechanical engineering or an automotive-related engineering discipline, with preference given to those with studies in the areas of expertise related to noise and vibration.

Academic Fields/Career Goals: Engineering/Technology; Engineering-Related Technologies; Mechanical Engineering.

Award: Scholarship for use in junior year; not renewable. *Number:* 1. *Amount:* $1000.

Eligibility Requirements: Applicant must be enrolled or expecting to enroll full-time at a four-year institution or university. Applicant or parent of applicant must be member of Society of Automotive Engineers. Applicant must have 3.0 GPA or higher. Available to U.S. citizens.

Application Requirements: Application, essay, transcript. *Deadline:* February 1.

Contact: Connie Harnish, SAE Educational Relations
Society of Automotive Engineers
400 Commonwealth Drive
Warrendale, PA 15096-0001
Phone: 724-772-4047
E-mail: connie@sae.org

SAE WILLIAM G. BELFREY MEMORIAL GRANT

Two $1000 grants awarded annually. One grant will be awarded to a Canadian citizen enrolled at any Canadian university, and one grant will be specific to the University of Toronto. Applicants must be citizens of Canada.

Academic Fields/Career Goals: Engineering/Technology; Engineering-Related Technologies.

Award: Grant for use in junior year; not renewable. *Number:* 2. *Amount:* $1000.

Eligibility Requirements: Applicant must be Canadian citizen and enrolled or expecting to enroll full-time at a four-year institution or university.

Application Requirements: Application, essay, resume, references, transcript. *Deadline:* April 1.

Contact: Connie Harnish, SAE Educational Relations
Society of Automotive Engineers
400 Commonwealth Drive
Warrendale, PA 15096-0001
Phone: 724-772-4047
E-mail: connie@sae.org

TMC/SAE DONALD D. DAWSON TECHNICAL SCHOLARSHIP
• *See page 133*

YANMAR/SAE SCHOLARSHIP

Eligible applicants will be citizens of North America (U.S., Canada, Mexico) and will be entering their junior year of undergraduate engineering or enrolled in a postgraduate engineering or related science program. Applicants must be pursuing a course of study or research related to the conservation of energy in transportation, agriculture, construction, and power generation. Emphasis will be placed on research or study related to the internal combustion engine.

Academic Fields/Career Goals: Engineering/Technology; Engineering-Related Technologies; Materials Science, Engineering, and Metallurgy; Mechanical Engineering.

Award: Scholarship for use in junior, senior, or graduate years; renewable. *Number:* 1. *Amount:* $1000.

Eligibility Requirements: Applicant must be enrolled or expecting to enroll full-time at a four-year institution or university. Available to U.S. and non-U.S. citizens.

Application Requirements: Application, essay, self-addressed stamped envelope, test scores, transcript. *Deadline:* April 1.

Contact: Connie Harnish, SAE Educational Relations
Society of Automotive Engineers
400 Commonwealth Drive
Warrendale, PA 15096
Phone: 724-772-4047
E-mail: connie@sae.org

SOCIETY OF BROADCAST ENGINEERS INC.

http://www.sbe.org/

ROBERT GREENBERG/HAROLD E. ENNES SCHOLARSHIP FUND AND ENNES EDUCATIONAL FOUNDATION BROADCAST TECHNOLOGY SCHOLARSHIP
• *See page 258*

SOCIETY OF HISPANIC PROFESSIONAL ENGINEERS FOUNDATION

http://www.henaac.org/

HENAAC SCHOLARS PROGRAM
• *See page 199*

SOCIETY OF HISPANIC PROFESSIONAL ENGINEERS FOUNDATION
• *See page 169*

SOCIETY OF MANUFACTURING ENGINEERS EDUCATION FOUNDATION

http://www.smeef.org/

MYRTLE AND EARL WALKER SCHOLARSHIP FUND

Scholarship available to full-time undergraduate students enrolled in a degree program in manufacturing engineering or technology in the United States or Canada. Minimum GPA of 3.0. Scholarship value and number of awards granted varies.

Academic Fields/Career Goals: Engineering/Technology; Engineering-Related Technologies; Mechanical Engineering.

Award: Scholarship for use in freshman, sophomore, junior, or senior years; not renewable. *Number:* 1–25. *Amount:* $1000–$7000.

Eligibility Requirements: Applicant must be enrolled or expecting to enroll full-time at a two-year or four-year or technical institution or university. Applicant must have 3.0 GPA or higher. Available to U.S. and Canadian citizens.

Application Requirements: Application, essay, resume, references, test scores, transcript. *Deadline:* February 1.

Contact: SME Education Foundation
Society of Manufacturing Engineers Education Foundation
One SME Drive, PO Box 930
Dearborn, MI 48121
Phone: 313-425-3300
Fax: 313-425-3411
E-mail: foundation@sme.org

SOCIETY OF MOTION PICTURE AND TELEVISION ENGINEERS

http://www.smpte.org/

LOU WOLF MEMORIAL SCHOLARSHIP
• *See page 259*

STUDENT PAPER AWARD

Contest for best paper by a current Student Member of SMPTE. Paper must deal with some technical phase of motion pictures, television, photographic instrumentation, or their closely allied arts and sciences. For more information see web site http://www.smpte.org.

Academic Fields/Career Goals: Engineering/Technology; Engineering-Related Technologies; Filmmaking/Video; TV/Radio Broadcasting.

Award: Prize for use in freshman, sophomore, junior, senior, graduate, or postgraduate years; not renewable. *Number:* 1. *Amount:* up to $1500.

Eligibility Requirements: Applicant must be enrolled or expecting to enroll full- or part-time at a four-year or technical institution or university and must have an interest in photography/photogrammetry/filmmaking. Applicant or parent of applicant must be member of Society of Motion Picture and Television Engineers. Available to U.S. and non-U.S. citizens.

Application Requirements: Application, applicant must enter a contest, essay, student ID card. *Deadline:* July 1.

Contact: Sally-Ann D'Amato, Director of Operations
Society of Motion Picture and Television Engineers
SMPTE, 3 Barker Avenue
White Plains, NY 10601
Phone: 914-761-1100 Ext. 4965
E-mail: sdamato@smpte.org

SOCIETY OF WOMEN ENGINEERS

http://www.swe.org/

SWE SOUTH OHIO SCIENCE FAIR SCHOLARSHIP

Two $300 scholarships awarded to graduating high school senior females for outstanding achievement in engineering or the related sciences. One scholarship is awarded at both the West District Science Fair for the Dayton area at Central State University and the Southwest District Science Fair for the Cincinnati area at Miami University for a total of two grants.

Academic Fields/Career Goals: Engineering/Technology; Engineering-Related Technologies.

Award: Scholarship for use in freshman year; not renewable. *Number:* 2. *Amount:* $300.

Eligibility Requirements: Applicant must be high school student; planning to enroll or expecting to enroll full-time at a four-year institution or university; female; resident of Ohio and must have an interest in science. Available to U.S. citizens.

Application Requirements: Application, references, test scores, transcript. *Deadline:* varies.

Contact: Scholarship Committee
Society of Women Engineers
120 South La Salle Street, Suite 1515
Chicago, IL 60603
Phone: 312-596-5223
E-mail: scholarshipapplication@swe.org

SOLE—THE INTERNATIONAL SOCIETY OF LOGISTICS

http://www.sole.org/

SOLE—THE INTERNATIONAL SOCIETY OF LOGISTICS SCHOLARSHIP/DOCTORAL DISSERTATION AWARDS

One-time award for students enrolled in a program of study in logistics. Must have a minimum 3.5 GPA. Must submit transcript and references with application. Scholarship application form is at http://sole.org/downloads/ScholarshipApplicationFormJan2009.doc.

Academic Fields/Career Goals: Engineering-Related Technologies.

Award: Scholarship for use in freshman, sophomore, junior, senior, or graduate years; not renewable. *Number:* 1–3. *Amount:* $500–$3000.

Eligibility Requirements: Applicant must be enrolled or expecting to enroll full-time at a four-year institution or university. Applicant must have 3.5 GPA or higher. Available to U.S. and non-U.S. citizens.

Application Requirements: Application, references, transcript. *Deadline:* May 15.

Contact: Sarah James, Executive Director
SOLE—The International Society of Logistics
8100 Professional Place, Suite 111
Hyattsville, MD 20785-2229
Phone: 301-459-8446
Fax: 301-459-1522
E-mail: solehq@erols.com

STRAIGHTFORWARD MEDIA

http://www.straightforwardmedia.com/

STRAIGHTFORWARD MEDIA ENGINEERING SCHOLARSHIP
• *See page 170*

TAG AND LABEL MANUFACTURERS INSTITUTE INC.

http://www.tlmi.com/

TLMI FOUR-YEAR COLLEGES/FULL-TIME STUDENTS SCHOLARSHIP

A $5000 scholarship awarded to a sophomore or junior attending a four-year accredited college or university on a full-time basis. Must demonstrate interest in entering the tag and label industry during their junior or senior year.

Academic Fields/Career Goals: Engineering-Related Technologies; Flexography; Graphics/Graphic Arts/Printing.

Award: Scholarship for use in junior or senior years; renewable. *Number:* up to 6. *Amount:* $5000.

Eligibility Requirements: Applicant must be enrolled or expecting to enroll full-time at a four-year institution or university. Applicant must have 3.0 GPA or higher. Available to U.S. and Canadian citizens.

Application Requirements: Application, interview, portfolio, resume, references, transcript. *Deadline:* March 31.

Contact: Scholarship Committee
Tag and Label Manufacturers Institute Inc.
One Blackburn Center
Gloucester, MA 01930
Phone: 978-282-1400
E-mail: office@tlmi.com

TECHNICAL ASSOCIATION OF THE PULP & PAPER INDUSTRY (TAPPI)

http://www.tappi.org/

CORRUGATED PACKAGING DIVISION SCHOLARSHIPS

Award to applicants working full time or part time in the box business and attending day/night school for a graduate or undergraduate degree or to a full-time student in a two- or four-year college, university or technical school. Information can be found at http://www.tappi.org/s_tappi/sec.asp?CID=6101&DID=546695.

Academic Fields/Career Goals: Engineering-Related Technologies; Paper and Pulp Engineering.

Award: Scholarship for use in freshman, sophomore, junior, senior, or graduate years; not renewable. *Number:* 1–5. *Amount:* $1000–$2000.

Eligibility Requirements: Applicant must be enrolled or expecting to enroll full- or part-time at a four-year or technical institution or university. Applicant must have 3.0 GPA or higher. Available to U.S. and non-U.S. citizens.

Application Requirements: Application, references, transcript.

Contact: Mr. Charles Bohanan, Director of Standards and Awards
Technical Association of the Pulp & Paper Industry (TAPPI)
15 Technology Parkway South
Norcross, GA 30092
Phone: 770-209-7276
Fax: 770-446-6947
E-mail: standards@tappi.org

TRANSPORTATION CLUBS INTERNATIONAL

http://www.transportationclubsinternational.com/

TRANSPORTATION CLUBS INTERNATIONAL FRED A. HOOPER MEMORIAL SCHOLARSHIP

Merit-based award available to currently enrolled college students majoring in traffic management, transportation, physical distribution, logistics, or a related field. Must have completed at least one year of post-high school education. One-time award of $1500. Must submit three references. Available to citizens of the United States, Canada, and Mexico.

Academic Fields/Career Goals: Engineering-Related Technologies; Transportation.

Award: Scholarship for use in freshman, sophomore, junior, or senior years; not renewable. *Number:* 1. *Amount:* $1500.

Eligibility Requirements: Applicant must be enrolled or expecting to enroll full- or part-time at a two-year or four-year or technical institution or university. Available to U.S. and non-U.S. citizens.

Application Requirements: Application, essay, photo, references, transcript. *Deadline:* April 30.

Contact: Bill Blair, Scholarships Trustee
Transportation Clubs International
c/o Zimmer Worldwide Logistics
15710 JFK Boulevard, Suite 575
Houston, TX 77032
Phone: 832-300-5905
E-mail: bblair@zimmerworldwide.com

UNITED NEGRO COLLEGE FUND

http://www.uncf.org/

MEDTRONIC FOUNDATION SCHOLARSHIP
• *See page 145*

VERIZON FOUNDATION SCHOLARSHIP
• *See page 74*

VERMONT SPACE GRANT CONSORTIUM

http://www.cems.uvm.edu/vsgc

VERMONT SPACE GRANT CONSORTIUM SCHOLARSHIP PROGRAM
• *See page 98*

WEST VIRGINIA HIGHER EDUCATION POLICY COMMISSION-STUDENT SERVICES

http://www.wvhepcnew.wvnet.edu/

WEST VIRGINIA ENGINEERING, SCIENCE AND TECHNOLOGY SCHOLARSHIP PROGRAM
• *See page 259*

XEROX

http://www.xerox.com//

TECHNICAL MINORITY SCHOLARSHIP
• *See page 171*

ENGINEERING/ TECHNOLOGY

AACE INTERNATIONAL

http://www.aacei.org/

AACE INTERNATIONAL COMPETITIVE SCHOLARSHIP
• *See page 99*

AIR TRAFFIC CONTROL ASSOCIATION INC.

http://www.atca.org/

AIR TRAFFIC CONTROL ASSOCIATION SCHOLARSHIP
• *See page 121*

AIST FOUNDATION

http://www.aistfoundation.org/

AIST ALFRED B. GLOSSBRENNER AND JOHN KLUSCH SCHOLARSHIPS

Scholarship intended to award high school senior who plans on pursuing a degree in metallurgy or engineering. Student must have previous academic excellence in science courses. Applicant must be a dependent of a AIST Northeastern Ohio chapter member.

Academic Fields/Career Goals: Engineering/Technology; Materials Science, Engineering, and Metallurgy.

Award: Scholarship for use in freshman year; not renewable. *Number:* 2. *Amount:* $1000.

Eligibility Requirements: Applicant must be high school student and planning to enroll or expecting to enroll full-time at a four-year institution or university. Applicant or parent of applicant must be member of Association for Iron and Steel Technology. Available to U.S. and non-U.S. citizens.

Application Requirements: Application, essay, resume, references, test scores, transcript. *Deadline:* April 30.

Contact: Richard J. Kurz, Chapter Secretary
 AIST Foundation
 22831 East State Street, Route 62
 Alliance, OH 44601

AIST WILLIAM E. SCHWABE MEMORIAL SCHOLARSHIP

• See page 252

ASSOCIATION FOR IRON AND STEEL TECHNOLOGY BALTIMORE CHAPTER SCHOLARSHIP

• See page 261

ASSOCIATION FOR IRON AND STEEL TECHNOLOGY DAVID H. SAMSON CANADIAN SCHOLARSHIP

• See page 160

ASSOCIATION FOR IRON AND STEEL TECHNOLOGY MIDWEST CHAPTER BETTY MCKERN SCHOLARSHIP

Scholarship awarded to a graduating female high school senior, or to an undergraduate freshman, sophomore, or junior enrolled in a fully AIST-accredited college or university. Applicant must be in good academic standing. Must be a dependant of an AIST Midwest chapter member.

Academic Fields/Career Goals: Engineering/Technology.

Award: Scholarship for use in freshman, sophomore, junior, or senior years; not renewable. *Number:* 1. *Amount:* $3000.

Eligibility Requirements: Applicant must be enrolled or expecting to enroll full-time at a four-year institution or university and female. Applicant or parent of applicant must be member of Association for Iron and Steel Technology. Available to U.S. and non-U.S. citizens.

Application Requirements: Application, essay, resume, references, test scores, transcript. *Deadline:* March 15.

Contact: AIST Midwest Member Chapter Scholarships Chair
 AIST Foundation
 c/o Barry Felton, 250 West US Highway 12
 Burns Harbor, IN 46304

ASSOCIATION FOR IRON AND STEEL TECHNOLOGY MIDWEST CHAPTER DON NELSON SCHOLARSHIP

One scholarship for a graduating high school senior, or undergraduate freshman, sophomore or junior enrolled in a fully AIST-accredited college or university. Applicant must be in good academic standing. Must be a dependent of an AIST Midwest chapter member. May reapply each year for the duration of college education.

Academic Fields/Career Goals: Engineering/Technology.

Award: Scholarship for use in freshman, sophomore, junior, or senior years; not renewable. *Number:* 1. *Amount:* up to $1000.

Eligibility Requirements: Applicant must be enrolled or expecting to enroll full-time at a four-year institution or university. Applicant or parent of applicant must be member of Association for Iron and Steel Technology. Available to U.S. and non-U.S. citizens.

Application Requirements: Application, essay, resume, references, test scores, transcript. *Deadline:* March 15.

Contact: AIST Midwest Member Chapter Scholarships Chair
 AIST Foundation
 c/o Barry Felton, 250 West US Highway 12
 Burns Harbor, IN 46304

ASSOCIATION FOR IRON AND STEEL TECHNOLOGY MIDWEST CHAPTER ENGINEERING SCHOLARSHIP

Two four-year scholarships awarded to graduating high school senior or undergraduate freshman, sophomore or junior enrolled in a fully AIST-accredited college or university majoring engineering. Applicant must be in good academic standing. Must be a dependent of an AIST Midwest chapter member. May reapply each year for the duration of college education.

Academic Fields/Career Goals: Engineering/Technology.

Award: Scholarship for use in freshman, sophomore, or junior years; renewable. *Number:* 2. *Amount:* $1500.

Eligibility Requirements: Applicant must be enrolled or expecting to enroll full-time at a four-year institution or university. Applicant or parent of applicant must be member of Association for Iron and Steel Technology. Available to U.S. and non-U.S. citizens.

Application Requirements: Application, essay, resume, references, test scores, transcript. *Deadline:* March 15.

Contact: AIST Midwest Member Chapter Scholarships Chair
 AIST Foundation
 c/o Barry Felton, 250 West US Highway 12
 Burns Harbor, IN 46304

ASSOCIATION FOR IRON AND STEEL TECHNOLOGY MIDWEST CHAPTER JACK GILL SCHOLARSHIP

Scholarship for a graduating high school senior, or undergraduate freshman, sophomore, or junior enrolled in a fully AIST-accredited college or university majoring engineering. Applicant must be in good academic standing. Must be a dependent of an AIST Midwest chapter member. May reapply each year for the duration of college education.

Academic Fields/Career Goals: Engineering/Technology.

Award: Scholarship for use in freshman, sophomore, junior, or senior years; not renewable. *Number:* 1. *Amount:* $3000.

Eligibility Requirements: Applicant must be enrolled or expecting to enroll full-time at a four-year institution or university. Applicant or parent of applicant must be member of Association for Iron and Steel Technology. Available to U.S. and non-U.S. citizens.

Application Requirements: Application, essay, resume, references, test scores, transcript. *Deadline:* March 15.

Contact: AIST Midwest Member Chapter Scholarships Chair
 AIST Foundation
 c/o Barry Felton, 250 West US Highway 12
 Burns Harbor, IN 46304

ASSOCIATION FOR IRON AND STEEL TECHNOLOGY MIDWEST CHAPTER MEL NICKEL SCHOLARSHIP

Scholarship awarded to a graduating high school senior, or undergraduate freshman, sophomore or junior enrolled in a fully AIST-accredited college or university majoring engineering. Applicant must be in good academic standing. Must be a dependent of an AIST Midwest chapter member. May reapply each year for the term of their college education.

Academic Fields/Career Goals: Engineering/Technology.

Award: Scholarship for use in freshman, sophomore, junior, or senior years; not renewable. *Number:* 1. *Amount:* $3000.

Eligibility Requirements: Applicant must be enrolled or expecting to enroll full-time at a four-year institution or university. Applicant or parent of applicant must be member of Association for Iron and Steel Technology. Available to U.S. and non-U.S. citizens.

Application Requirements: Application, essay, resume, references, test scores, transcript. *Deadline:* March 15.

Contact: AIST Midwest Member Chapter Scholarships Chair
 AIST Foundation
 c/o Barry Felton, 250 West US Highway 12
 Burns Harbor, IN 46304

ASSOCIATION FOR IRON AND STEEL TECHNOLOGY MIDWEST CHAPTER NON-ENGINEERING SCHOLARSHIP

Scholarship for graduating high school senior, or undergraduate freshman, sophomore, or junior enrolled in a fully AIST-accredited college or university. Applicant must be in good academic standing and dependent of an AIST Midwest chapter member. Recipients may reapply each year for the term of their college education.

Academic Fields/Career Goals: Engineering/Technology.

Award: Scholarship for use in freshman, sophomore, junior, or senior years; not renewable. *Number:* 3. *Amount:* $1500.

Eligibility Requirements: Applicant must be enrolled or expecting to enroll full-time at a four-year institution or university. Applicant or parent of applicant must be member of Association for Iron and Steel Technology. Available to U.S. and non-U.S. citizens.

Application Requirements: Application, essay, resume, references, test scores, transcript. *Deadline:* March 15.

Contact: AIST Midwest Member Chapter Scholarships Chair
AIST Foundation
c/o Barry Felton, 250 West US Highway 12
Burns Harbor, IN 46304

ASSOCIATION FOR IRON AND STEEL TECHNOLOGY MIDWEST CHAPTER WESTERN STATES SCHOLARSHIP

Scholarship of $3000 awarded to a graduating high school senior, or undergraduate freshman, sophomore, junior, or senior enrolled in a fully AIST-accredited college or university. Applicant must be in good academic standing and a dependant of an AIST Midwest chapter member. Recipients may reapply each year for the term of their college education.

Academic Fields/Career Goals: Engineering/Technology.

Award: Scholarship for use in freshman, sophomore, junior, or senior years; not renewable. *Number:* 1. *Amount:* $3000.

Eligibility Requirements: Applicant must be enrolled or expecting to enroll full-time at a four-year institution or university. Applicant or parent of applicant must be member of Association for Iron and Steel Technology. Available to U.S. and non-U.S. citizens.

Application Requirements: Application, essay, resume, references, test scores, transcript. *Deadline:* March 15.

Contact: AIST Midwest Member Chapter Scholarships Chair
AIST Foundation
c/o Barry Felton, 250 West US Highway 12
Burns Harbor, IN 46304

ASSOCIATION FOR IRON AND STEEL TECHNOLOGY NORTHWEST MEMBER CHAPTER SCHOLARSHIP

Scholarships of $1000 available to encourage a Pacific Northwest area student to prepare for a career in engineering. Must be the child, grandchild, spouse, or niece/nephew of a member in good standing of the AIST Northwest Chapter. Award based on academic achievements in chemistry, mathematics, and physics.

Academic Fields/Career Goals: Engineering/Technology; Materials Science, Engineering, and Metallurgy.

Award: Scholarship for use in freshman, sophomore, junior, or senior years; not renewable. *Number:* 2. *Amount:* $1000.

Eligibility Requirements: Applicant must be enrolled or expecting to enroll full- or part-time at a four-year institution or university. Applicant or parent of applicant must be member of Association for Iron and Steel Technology. Available to U.S. citizens.

Application Requirements: Application, essay, resume, references, test scores, transcript. *Deadline:* April 30.

Contact: Gerardo L. Giraldo, AIST Northwest Chapter Secretary
AIST Foundation
2434 Eyres Place West
Seattle, WA 98199
Phone: 206-285-7897
E-mail: acero9938@comcast.net

ASSOCIATION FOR IRON AND STEEL TECHNOLOGY OHIO VALLEY CHAPTER SCHOLARSHIP
• See page 137

ASSOCIATION FOR IRON AND STEEL TECHNOLOGY PITTSBURGH CHAPTER SCHOLARSHIP

Scholarships of $2500 for children, stepchildren, grandchildren, or spouse of a member in good standing of the Pittsburgh Chapter. Applicant must be a high school senior or currently enrolled undergraduate preparing for a career in engineering or metallurgy.

Academic Fields/Career Goals: Engineering/Technology; Materials Science, Engineering, and Metallurgy.

Award: Scholarship for use in freshman, sophomore, junior, or senior years; not renewable. *Number:* 2–3. *Amount:* $2500.

Eligibility Requirements: Applicant must be enrolled or expecting to enroll full-time at a four-year institution or university. Applicant or parent of applicant must be member of Association for Iron and Steel Technology. Available to U.S. citizens.

Application Requirements: Application, essay, resume, references, test scores, transcript. *Deadline:* April 30.

Contact: Daniel J. Kos, Program Coordinator
AIST Foundation
375 Saxonburg Boulevard
Saxonburg, PA 16056
E-mail: dkos@ii-vi.com

ASSOCIATION FOR IRON AND STEEL TECHNOLOGY SOUTHEAST MEMBER CHAPTER SCHOLARSHIP

Scholarship of $3000 for children, stepchildren, grandchildren, or spouse of active Southeast Chapter members who are pursuing a career in engineering, the sciences, or other majors relating to iron and steel production. Students may reapply for the scholarship each year for their term of college.

Academic Fields/Career Goals: Engineering/Technology; Materials Science, Engineering, and Metallurgy.

Award: Scholarship for use in freshman, sophomore, junior, or senior years; renewable. *Number:* 1. *Amount:* $3000.

Eligibility Requirements: Applicant must be enrolled or expecting to enroll full- or part-time at a four-year institution or university. Applicant or parent of applicant must be member of Association for Iron and Steel Technology. Available to U.S. citizens.

Application Requirements: Application, essay, resume, references, test scores, transcript. *Deadline:* April 30.

Contact: Mike Hutson, AIST Southeast Chapter Secretary
AIST Foundation
803 Floyd Street
Kings Mountain, NC 29086
Phone: 704-730-8320
Fax: 704-730-8321
E-mail: mike@johnhutsoncompany.com

ALBERTA HERITAGE SCHOLARSHIP FUND

http://www.alis.alberta.ca/

NORTHERN ALBERTA DEVELOPMENT COUNCIL BURSARY
• See page 214

AMERICAN CHEMICAL SOCIETY, RUBBER DIVISION

http://www.rubber.org/

AMERICAN CHEMICAL SOCIETY, RUBBER DIVISION UNDERGRADUATE SCHOLARSHIP
• See page 160

AMERICAN COUNCIL OF ENGINEERING COMPANIES OF PENNSYLVANIA (ACEC/PA)

http://www.acecpa.org/

ENGINEERING SCHOLARSHIP
• See page 161

AMERICAN FOUNDATION FOR THE BLIND

http://www.afb.org/

PAUL W. RUCKES SCHOLARSHIP
• See page 195

AMERICAN INDIAN SCIENCE AND ENGINEERING SOCIETY

http://www.aises.org/

BURLINGTON NORTHERN SANTA FE FOUNDATION SCHOLARSHIP
• *See page 93*

AMERICAN INSTITUTE OF AERONAUTICS AND ASTRONAUTICS

http://www.aiaa.org/

AIAA FOUNDATION UNDERGRADUATE SCHOLARSHIP
• *See page 93*

AMERICAN INSTITUTE OF ARCHITECTS, NEW YORK CHAPTER

http://www.aiany.org/

DOUGLAS HASKELL AWARD FOR STUDENT JOURNALISM
• *See page 99*

AMERICAN NUCLEAR SOCIETY

http://www.ans.org/

AMERICAN NUCLEAR SOCIETY VOGT RADIOCHEMISTRY SCHOLARSHIP

One-time award for juniors, seniors, and first-year graduate students enrolled or proposing research in radio-analytical or analytical application of nuclear science. Must be U.S. citizen or permanent resident.

Academic Fields/Career Goals: Engineering/Technology; Nuclear Science.

Award: Scholarship for use in junior, senior, or graduate years; not renewable. *Number:* 1. *Amount:* $3000.

Eligibility Requirements: Applicant must be enrolled or expecting to enroll full-time at a four-year institution or university. Available to U.S. citizens.

Application Requirements: Application, references, transcript, sponsorship letter from ANS organization. *Deadline:* February 1.

Contact: Scholarship Coordinator
American Nuclear Society
555 North Kensington Avenue
La Grange Park, IL 60526
Phone: 708-352-6611
Fax: 708-352-0499
E-mail: outreach@ans.org

AMERICAN PUBLIC TRANSPORTATION FOUNDATION

http://www.apta.com/

JACK GILSTRAP SCHOLARSHIP

Awarded the APTF scholarship to the applicant with the highest score. Must be in public transportation industry-related fields of study. Must be sponsored by AFTA member organization and complete an internship program with a member organization. Minimum 3.0 GPA required.

Academic Fields/Career Goals: Engineering/Technology; Transportation.

Award: Scholarship for use in sophomore, junior, senior, or graduate years; renewable. *Number:* 1. *Amount:* $2500.

Eligibility Requirements: Applicant must be enrolled or expecting to enroll full-time at a two-year or four-year institution or university. Applicant must have 3.0 GPA or higher. Available to U.S. and Canadian citizens.

Application Requirements: Application, essay, financial need analysis, references, transcript, verification of enrollment for the current semester and copy of fee schedule from the college/university. *Deadline:* June 16.

Contact: Pamela Boswell, Vice President of Program Management
American Public Transportation Foundation
1666 K Street, NW
Washington, DC 20006-1215
Phone: 202-496-4803
Fax: 202-496-2323
E-mail: pboswell@apta.com

TRANSIT HALL OF FAME SCHOLARSHIP AWARD PROGRAM
• *See page 174*

AMERICAN RAILWAY ENGINEERING AND MAINTENANCE OF WAY ASSOCIATION

http://www.arema.org/

AREMA MICHAEL R. GARCIA SCHOLARSHIP
• *See page 174*

AREMA PRESIDENTIAL SPOUSE SCHOLARSHIP
• *See page 174*

AREMA UNDERGRADUATE SCHOLARSHIPS
• *See page 174*

COMMITTEE 12-RAIL TRANSIT UNDERGRADUATE SCHOLARSHIP
• *See page 261*

CSX SCHOLARSHIP
• *See page 261*

JOHN J. CUNNINGHAM MEMORIAL SCHOLARSHIP (SPONSORED JOINTLY BY COMMITTEES 11 AND 17)

Scholarship awarded to a junior or senior college student pursuing an undergraduate degree in a professional field that has direct applications in the passenger rail sector. Minimum 2.00 GPA required.

Academic Fields/Career Goals: Engineering/Technology; Transportation.

Award: Scholarship for use in junior or senior years; not renewable. *Number:* varies. *Amount:* $1000.

Eligibility Requirements: Applicant must be enrolled or expecting to enroll full-time at a four-year institution or university. Available to U.S. citizens.

Application Requirements: Application, resume, references, transcript, cover letter. *Deadline:* March 11.

Contact: Lisa Hall, Director of Marketing
American Railway Engineering and Maintenance of Way Association
10003 Derekwood Lane, Suite 210
Lanham, MD 20706
Phone: 301-459-3200 Ext. 705
E-mail: lhall@arema.org

NORFOLK SOUTHERN FOUNDATION SCHOLARSHIP
• *See page 262*

PB RAIL ENGINEERING SCHOLARSHIP
• *See page 262*

REMSA SCHOLARSHIP
• *See page 262*

AMERICAN SOCIETY FOR ENGINEERING EDUCATION

http://www.asee.org/

SCIENCE, MATHEMATICS, AND RESEARCH FOR TRANSFORMATION DEFENSE SCHOLARSHIP FOR SERVICE PROGRAM
• *See page 93*

AMERICAN SOCIETY OF AGRICULTURAL AND BIOLOGICAL ENGINEERS

http://www.asabe.org/

ASABE FOUNDATION SCHOLARSHIP

Award for full-time engineering undergraduate student in the U.S. or Canada. Must be active student member of the American Society of Agricultural Engineers. Must have a minimum of 3.0 GPA. Write for more information and special application procedures. One-time award of $1000. Must have completed one year of school, and must submit paper titled "My Goals in the Engineering Profession".

Academic Fields/Career Goals: Engineering/Technology.

Award: Scholarship for use in sophomore, junior, or senior years; not renewable. *Number:* 1. *Amount:* $1000.

Eligibility Requirements: Applicant must be enrolled or expecting to enroll full-time at a four-year institution or university. Applicant must have 3.0 GPA or higher. Available to U.S. and Canadian citizens.

Application Requirements: Application, essay, financial need analysis, resume, references. *Deadline:* March 17.

Contact: Carol Flautt, Scholarship Program
American Society of Agricultural and Biological Engineers
2950 Niles Road
St. Joseph, MI 49085
Phone: 269-932-7036
Fax: 269-429-3852
E-mail: flautt@asabe.org

AMERICAN SOCIETY OF CERTIFIED ENGINEERING TECHNICIANS

http://www.ascet.org/

JOSEPH C. JOHNSON MEMORIAL GRANT

Grant for $750 given to qualified applicants in order to offset the cost of tuition, books and lab fees. Applicant must be a U.S. citizen or a legal resident of the country in which the applicant is currently living, as well as be either a student, certified, regular, registered or associate member of ASCET. Student must be enrolled in an engineering technology program. For further information, visit http://www.ascet.org.

Academic Fields/Career Goals: Engineering/Technology.

Award: Grant for use in freshman, sophomore, junior, or senior years; not renewable. *Number:* 1. *Amount:* $750.

Eligibility Requirements: Applicant must be enrolled or expecting to enroll full- or part-time at a two-year or four-year or technical institution or university. Applicant must have 3.0 GPA or higher. Available to U.S. citizens.

Application Requirements: Application, financial need analysis, photo, references, transcript. *Deadline:* April 1.

Contact: Mr. Tim Latham, General Manager
American Society of Certified Engineering Technicians
PO Box 1536
Brandon, MS 39043
Phone: 601-824-8991
E-mail: tim-latham@ascet.org

JOSEPH M. PARISH MEMORIAL GRANT

Grant of $500 will be awarded to a student to be used to offset the cost of tuition, books and lab fees. Applicant must be a student member of

ASCET and be a U.S. citizen or a legal resident of the country in which the applicant is currently living. The award will be given to full time students enrolled in an engineering technology program; students pursuing a BS degree in engineering are not eligible for this grant. For more information, visit http://www.ascet.org.

Academic Fields/Career Goals: Engineering/Technology.

Award: Grant for use in freshman, sophomore, junior, or senior years; not renewable. *Number:* 1. *Amount:* $500.

Eligibility Requirements: Applicant must be enrolled or expecting to enroll full- or part-time at a two-year or four-year or technical institution or university. Applicant must have 3.0 GPA or higher. Available to U.S. citizens.

Application Requirements: Application, financial need analysis, photo, references, transcript. *Deadline:* April 1.

Contact: Mr. Tim Latham, General Manager
American Society of Certified Engineering Technicians
PO Box 1536
Brandon, MS 39043
Phone: 601-824-8991
E-mail: tim-latham@ascet.org

AMERICAN SOCIETY OF HEATING, REFRIGERATING, AND AIR CONDITIONING ENGINEERS, INC.

http://www.ashrae.org/

ALWIN B. NEWTON SCHOLARSHIP FUND
• *See page 253*

ASHRAE GENERAL SCHOLARSHIP
• *See page 262*

ASHRAE MEMORIAL SCHOLARSHIP
• *See page 253*

ASHRAE REGION IV BENNY BOOTLE SCHOLARSHIP
• *See page 100*

ASHRAE REGION VIII SCHOLARSHIP
• *See page 262*

DUANE HANSON SCHOLARSHIP
• *See page 253*

ENGINEERING TECHNOLOGY SCHOLARSHIP
• *See page 254*

FRANK M. CODA SCHOLARSHIP
• *See page 254*

HENRY ADAMS SCHOLARSHIP
• *See page 254*

REUBEN TRANE SCHOLARSHIP
• *See page 254*

WILLIS H. CARRIER SCHOLARSHIP
• *See page 254*

AMERICAN SOCIETY OF NAVAL ENGINEERS

http://www.navalengineers.org/

AMERICAN SOCIETY OF NAVAL ENGINEERS SCHOLARSHIP
• *See page 93*

AMERICAN SOCIETY OF PLUMBING ENGINEERS

http://www.aspe.org/

ALFRED STEELE ENGINEERING SCHOLARSHIP

Scholarships of $1000 are awarded for the members of American society of plumbing engineers towards education and professional development on plumbing engineering and designing.

Academic Fields/Career Goals: Engineering/Technology; Industrial Design.

Award: Scholarship for use in freshman, sophomore, junior, or senior years; not renewable. *Number:* 5. *Amount:* $1000.

Eligibility Requirements: Applicant must be enrolled or expecting to enroll full-time at a two-year or four-year or technical institution or university. Applicant must have 3.0 GPA or higher. Available to U.S. and non-U.S. citizens.

Application Requirements: Application, essay, references, transcript, statement of personal achievement. *Deadline:* September 1.

Contact: Stacey Kidd, Membership Director
American Society of Plumbing Engineers
8614 Catalpa Avenue, Suite 1007
Chicago, IL 60656-1116
Phone: 773-693-2773
Fax: 773-695-9007
E-mail: skidd@aspe.org

AMERICAN WELDING SOCIETY

http://www.aws.org/

AIRGAS-TERRY JARVIS MEMORIAL SCHOLARSHIP
• *See page 263*

AMERICAN WELDING SOCIETY INTERNATIONAL SCHOLARSHIP
• *See page 263*

D. FRED AND MARIAN L. BOVIE NATIONAL SCHOLARSHIP

Scholarship for welding engineering at The Ohio State University.

Academic Fields/Career Goals: Engineering/Technology.

Award: Scholarship for use in freshman, sophomore, junior, or senior years; not renewable. *Number:* 1–1. *Amount:* up to $3000.

Eligibility Requirements: Applicant must be enrolled or expecting to enroll full-time at an institution or university and studying in Ohio. Applicant must have 3.0 GPA or higher. Available to U.S. citizens.

Application Requirements: Application, financial need analysis, references, transcript. *Deadline:* February 15.

Contact: Vicki Pinsky, Manager, AWS Foundation
American Welding Society
AWS Foundation, 550 Le Jeune Road, NW
Miami, FL 33126
Phone: 305-443-9353 Ext. 212
Fax: 305-443-7559
E-mail: vpinsky@aws.org

DONALD AND SHIRLEY HASTINGS SCHOLARSHIP

Award for U.S. citizen at least 18 years of age pursuing a four-year undergraduate degree in welding engineering or welding engineering technology. Priority given to welding engineering students. Preference is given to students residing or attending school in California or Ohio. Submit copy of proposed curriculum. Minimum GPA of 2.5 required.

Academic Fields/Career Goals: Engineering/Technology; Materials Science, Engineering, and Metallurgy.

Award: Scholarship for use in freshman, sophomore, junior, or senior years; not renewable. *Number:* 1. *Amount:* $2500.

Eligibility Requirements: Applicant must be age 18 and over and enrolled or expecting to enroll full- or part-time at a four-year institution or university. Available to U.S. citizens.

Application Requirements: Application, financial need analysis, references, transcript, FAFSA. *Deadline:* February 15.

Contact: Vicki Pinsky, Manager, Foundation
American Welding Society
550 Le Jeune Road, NW
Miami, FL 33126
Phone: 800-443-9353 Ext. 212
Fax: 305-443-7559
E-mail: vpinsky@aws.org

DONALD F. HASTINGS SCHOLARSHIP
• *See page 263*

EDWARD J. BRADY MEMORIAL SCHOLARSHIP
• *See page 264*

HOWARD E. AND WILMA J. ADKINS MEMORIAL SCHOLARSHIP
• *See page 264*

JACK R. BARCKHOFF WELDING MANAGEMENT SCHOLARSHIP

Scholarship for a college junior at The Ohio State University. Must complete course in Total Welding Management. Essay required on improving the world of welding and the welding industry in the US.

Academic Fields/Career Goals: Engineering/Technology.

Award: Scholarship for use in junior year; not renewable. *Number:* 2. *Amount:* up to $2500.

Eligibility Requirements: Applicant must be enrolled or expecting to enroll full- or part-time at an institution or university and studying in Ohio. Available to U.S. citizens.

Application Requirements: Application, essay, financial need analysis, references, transcript. *Deadline:* February 15.

Contact: Vicki Pinsky, Manager
American Welding Society
AWS Foundation, 550 Le Jeune Road, NW
Miami, FL 33126
Phone: 305-443-9353 Ext. 212
Fax: 305-443-7559
E-mail: vpinsky@aws.org

JOHN C. LINCOLN MEMORIAL SCHOLARSHIP
• *See page 264*

MATSUO BRIDGE COMPANY LTD. OF JAPAN SCHOLARSHIP
• *See page 176*

MILLER ELECTRIC INTERNATIONAL WORLD SKILLS COMPETITION SCHOLARSHIP
• *See page 264*

MILLER ELECTRIC MFG. CO. SCHOLARSHIP
• *See page 264*

PAST PRESIDENTS' SCHOLARSHIP

Scholarship available to students pursuing a bachelor's degree in welding engineering, welding engineering technology, or an engineering program with emphasis on welding. Also open to graduate students pursuing a master's or doctorate in engineering or management.

Academic Fields/Career Goals: Engineering/Technology; Mechanical Engineering.

Award: Scholarship for use in junior or senior years; not renewable. *Number:* 1. *Amount:* $2500.

Eligibility Requirements: Applicant must be enrolled or expecting to enroll full- or part-time at a four-year institution. Available to U.S. citizens.

Application Requirements: Application, financial need analysis, references, transcript. *Deadline:* February 15.

Contact: Ms. Vicki Pinsky, Manager
American Welding Society
550 LeJeune Road, NW
Miami, FL 33126

PRAXAIR INTERNATIONAL SCHOLARSHIP
• *See page 264*

RESISTANCE WELDER MANUFACTURERS' ASSOCIATION SCHOLARSHIP

$2500 award to students who express an interest in the resistance welding process while pursuing a career in welding engineering. Available to U.S. and Canadian citizens. Must be a junior in a four-year program only and maintain a minimum 3.0 GPA.

Academic Fields/Career Goals: Engineering/Technology; Materials Science, Engineering, and Metallurgy.

Award: Scholarship for use in junior year; not renewable. *Number:* 1. *Amount:* $2500.

Eligibility Requirements: Applicant must be enrolled or expecting to enroll full- or part-time at a four-year institution or university. Applicant must have 3.0 GPA or higher. Available to U.S. and Canadian citizens.

Application Requirements: Application, essay, resume, transcript. *Deadline:* February 15.

Contact: Vicki Pinsky, Manager, Foundation
American Welding Society
550 Le Jeune Road, NW
Miami, FL 33126
Phone: 800-443-9353 Ext. 212
Fax: 305-443-7559
E-mail: vpinsky@aws.org

ROBERT L. PEASLEE DETROIT BRAZING AND SOLDERING DIVISION SCHOLARSHIP

$2500 award for students pursuing a minimum four-year bachelor's degree in welding engineering or welding engineering technology with an emphasis on brazing and soldering applications. Must be minimum 18 years of age and at least a college junior. 3.0 GPA required.

Academic Fields/Career Goals: Engineering/Technology; Materials Science, Engineering, and Metallurgy.

Award: Scholarship for use in junior or senior years; not renewable. *Number:* 1. *Amount:* $2500.

Eligibility Requirements: Applicant must be age 18 and over and enrolled or expecting to enroll full- or part-time at a four-year institution or university. Applicant must have 3.0 GPA or higher. Available to U.S. and Canadian citizens.

Application Requirements: Application, financial need analysis, resume, references, transcript, statement of unmet financial need. *Deadline:* February 15.

Contact: Vicki Pinsky, Manager, Foundation
American Welding Society
550 Le Jeune Road, NW
Miami, FL 33126
Phone: 800-443-9353 Ext. 212
Fax: 305-443-7559
E-mail: vpinsky@aws.org

WILLIAM B. HOWELL MEMORIAL SCHOLARSHIP
• *See page 265*

ARIZONA PROFESSIONAL CHAPTER OF AISES

http://www.azpcofaises.org/

ARIZONA PROFESSIONAL CHAPTER OF AISES SCHOLARSHIP

Scholarship awarded to American Indian/Alaska Natives attending Arizona schools of higher education pursuing degrees in the sciences, engineering, medicine, natural resources, math, and technology. Student must be a full-time undergraduate student (at least 12 hours per semester) at an accredited two-year or four-year college or university.

Academic Fields/Career Goals: Engineering/Technology; Health and Medical Sciences; Natural Resources; Physical Sciences.

Award: Scholarship for use in freshman, sophomore, junior, or senior years; not renewable. *Number:* varies. *Amount:* varies.

Eligibility Requirements: Applicant must be American Indian/Alaska Native; enrolled or expecting to enroll full-time at a two-year or four-year institution or university and studying in Arizona. Applicant must have 2.5 GPA or higher. Available to U.S. citizens.

Application Requirements: Application, essay, portfolio, resume, references, transcript, proof of tribal enrollment, copy of AISES membership card. *Deadline:* August 17.

Contact: Jaime Ashike, Scholarship Committee
Arizona Professional Chapter of AISES
PO Box 2528
Phoenix, AZ 85002
Phone: 480-326-0958
E-mail: amazing_butterfly@hotmail.com

ARMED FORCES COMMUNICATIONS AND ELECTRONICS ASSOCIATION, EDUCATIONAL FOUNDATION

http://www.afcea.org/education/scholarships

AFCEA YOUNG ENTREPRENEUR SCHOLARSHIP
• *See page 163*

ARMED FORCES COMMUNICATIONS AND ELECTRONICS ASSOCIATION GENERAL EMMETT PAIGE SCHOLARSHIP
• *See page 122*

ARMED FORCES COMMUNICATIONS AND ELECTRONICS ASSOCIATION GENERAL JOHN A. WICKHAM SCHOLARSHIP
• *See page 164*

ARMED FORCES COMMUNICATIONS AND ELECTRONICS ASSOCIATION ROTC SCHOLARSHIP PROGRAM
• *See page 122*

DISABLED WAR VETERANS SCHOLARSHIP
• *See page 122*

VICE ADMIRAL JERRY O. TUTTLE, USN (RET.) AND MRS. BARBARA A. TUTTLE SCIENCE AND TECHNOLOGY SCHOLARSHIP
• *See page 265*

ARRL FOUNDATION INC.

http://www.arrl.org/

CHARLES N. FISHER MEMORIAL SCHOLARSHIP
• *See page 94*

GARY WAGNER, K3OMI SCHOLARSHIP
• *See page 164*

HENRY BROUGHTON, K2AE MEMORIAL SCHOLARSHIP
• *See page 265*

MAGNOLIA DX ASSOCIATION SCHOLARSHIP
• *See page 183*

MISSISSIPPI SCHOLARSHIP
• *See page 94*

PAUL AND HELEN L. GRAUER SCHOLARSHIP
• *See page 94*

WILLIAM R. GOLDFARB MEMORIAL SCHOLARSHIP
• *See page 146*

YASME FOUNDATION SCHOLARSHIP
• *See page 139*

ASM MATERIALS EDUCATION FOUNDATION

http://www.asmfoundation.org/

ASM OUTSTANDING SCHOLARS AWARDS

Awards for student members of ASM International studying metallurgy or materials science and engineering. Must have completed at least one year of college to apply. Awards are merit-based; financial need is not considered.

Academic Fields/Career Goals: Engineering/Technology; Materials Science, Engineering, and Metallurgy.

Award: Scholarship for use in sophomore, junior, or senior years; not renewable. *Number:* 3. *Amount:* $2000.

Eligibility Requirements: Applicant must be enrolled or expecting to enroll full-time at a four-year institution or university. Applicant or parent of applicant must be member of ASM International. Available to U.S. and non-U.S. citizens.

Application Requirements: Application, essay, photo, references, transcript. *Deadline:* May 1.

Contact: Pergentina Deatherage, Administrator, Foundation Programs
ASM Materials Education Foundation
9639 Kinsman Road
Materials Park, OH 44073-0002
Phone: 440-338-5151
Fax: 440-338-4634

EDWARD J. DULIS SCHOLARSHIP

Award of $1500 for student members of ASM International studying metallurgy or materials science and engineering. Award is merit based; financial need is not considered.

Academic Fields/Career Goals: Engineering/Technology; Materials Science, Engineering, and Metallurgy.

Award: Scholarship for use in freshman, sophomore, junior, or senior years; not renewable. *Number:* 1. *Amount:* $1500.

Eligibility Requirements: Applicant must be enrolled or expecting to enroll full-time at a four-year institution or university. Applicant or parent of applicant must be member of ASM International. Available to U.S. and Canadian citizens.

Application Requirements: Application, photo, references, transcript. *Deadline:* May 1.

Contact: Pergentina Deatherage, Administrator, Foundation Programs
ASM Materials Education Foundation
9639 Kinsman Road
Materials Park, OH 44073-0002
Phone: 440-338-5151
Fax: 440-338-4634

GEORGE A. ROBERTS SCHOLARSHIP

Awards for college juniors or seniors studying metallurgy or materials engineering in North America. Applicants must be student members of ASM International. Awards based on need, interest in field, academics, and character.

Academic Fields/Career Goals: Engineering/Technology; Materials Science, Engineering, and Metallurgy.

Award: Scholarship for use in junior or senior years; not renewable. *Number:* 7. *Amount:* $6000.

Eligibility Requirements: Applicant must be enrolled or expecting to enroll full-time at an institution or university. Applicant or parent of applicant must be member of ASM International. Available to U.S. and Canadian citizens.

Application Requirements: Application, essay, financial need analysis, photo, references, transcript. *Deadline:* May 1.

Contact: Pergentina Deatherage, Administrator, Foundation Programs
ASM Materials Education Foundation
9639 Kinsman Road
Materials Park, OH 44073-0002
Phone: 440-338-5151
Fax: 440-338-4634

JOHN M. HANIAK SCHOLARSHIP

Award for student members of ASM International studying metallurgy or materials science and engineering. Must have completed at least one year of college to apply. Award is merit based; financial need is not considered.

Academic Fields/Career Goals: Engineering/Technology; Materials Science, Engineering, and Metallurgy.

Award: Scholarship for use in freshman, sophomore, junior, or senior years; not renewable. *Number:* 1. *Amount:* $1500.

Eligibility Requirements: Applicant must be enrolled or expecting to enroll full-time at a four-year institution or university. Applicant or parent of applicant must be member of ASM International. Available to U.S. and Canadian citizens.

Application Requirements: Application, essay, references, self-addressed stamped envelope, transcript. *Deadline:* May 1.

Contact: Pergentina Deatherage, Administrator, Foundation Programs
ASM Materials Education Foundation
9639 Kinsman Road
Materials Park, OH 44073-0002
Phone: 440-338-5151
Fax: 440-338-4634

WILLIAM P. WOODSIDE FOUNDER'S SCHOLARSHIP

$10,000 scholarship for college junior or senior studying metallurgy or materials engineering in North America. Must be a student member of ASM International. Award based on need, interest in field, academics, and character.

Academic Fields/Career Goals: Engineering/Technology; Materials Science, Engineering, and Metallurgy.

Award: Scholarship for use in junior or senior years; not renewable. *Number:* 1. *Amount:* up to $10,000.

Eligibility Requirements: Applicant must be enrolled or expecting to enroll full-time at an institution or university. Applicant or parent of applicant must be member of ASM International. Available to U.S. and Canadian citizens.

Application Requirements: Application, essay, financial need analysis, photo, references, transcript. *Deadline:* May 1.

Contact: Pergentina Deatherage, Administrator, Foundation Programs
ASM Materials Education Foundation
9639 Kinsman Road
Materials Park, OH 44073-0002
Phone: 440-338-5151
Fax: 440-338-4634

ASPRS, THE IMAGING AND GEOSPATIAL INFORMATION SOCIETY

http://www.asprs.org/

ABRAHAM ANSON MEMORIAL SCHOLARSHIP

Award to encourage students to pursue education in geospatial science or technology related to photogrammetry, remote sensing, surveying and mapping. Must be enrolled or intending to enroll in a U.S. college or university in geospatial science, surveying and mapping and related fields. Must submit with application a list of all applicable courses taken, a statement of work experience including internships, special projects, technical papers, and courses taught that may support the student's capabilities in this field. For additional information and online application, see web site http://www.asprs.org/membership/scholar.html.

Academic Fields/Career Goals: Engineering/Technology; Surveying, Surveying Technology, Cartography, or Geographic Information Science.

Award: Scholarship for use in freshman, sophomore, junior, or senior years; not renewable. *Number:* 1. *Amount:* $1000.

Eligibility Requirements: Applicant must be enrolled or expecting to enroll full-time at a four-year institution or university. Available to U.S. citizens.

Application Requirements: Application, essay, resume, references, transcript. *Deadline:* December 1.

Contact: Jesse Winch, Scholarship Administrator
Phone: 301-493-0290 Ext. 101

FRANCIS H. MOFFITT MEMORIAL SCHOLARSHIP

Award to encourage upper-division undergraduate and graduate-level students to pursue a course of study in surveying and photogrammetry leading to a career in the mapping profession. Must be enrolled or intending to enroll in a college or university in the U.S. in the field of surveying or photogrammetry. Application must include listing of all courses taken in the field, internships, special projects, courses taught, technical papers that demonstrate applicant's capabilities in the field, two letters of recommendation, and a short statement detailing contributions to the field and future career plans. For additional information, see web site http://www.asprs.org.

Academic Fields/Career Goals: Engineering/Technology; Surveying, Surveying Technology, Cartography, or Geographic Information Science.

Award: Scholarship for use in junior or senior years; not renewable. *Number:* 1. *Amount:* $3000.

Eligibility Requirements: Applicant must be enrolled or expecting to enroll at a four-year institution or university. Available to U.S. citizens.

Application Requirements: Application, essay, references, transcript. *Deadline:* December 1.

Contact: Jesse Winch, Scholarship Administrator
    Phone: 301-493-0290 Ext. 101

JOHN O. BEHRENS INSTITUTE FOR LAND INFORMATION MEMORIAL SCHOLARSHIP

Award to encourage study in geospatial science or technology or land information systems/records. Must be an undergraduate student enrolled or intending to enroll in a U.S. college or university in the designated field. Application must be submitted electronically and must include a list of completed courses in the field, papers, research reports, or other items produced by the applicant that demonstrate capability in the field, and internships, work experience, special projects or courses taught that support potential excellence in the field. Additional information and application on web site http://www.asprs.org/membership/scholar.html.

Academic Fields/Career Goals: Engineering/Technology; Surveying, Surveying Technology, Cartography, or Geographic Information Science.

Award: Scholarship for use in freshman, sophomore, junior, or senior years; not renewable. *Number:* 1. *Amount:* $1000.

Eligibility Requirements: Applicant must be enrolled or expecting to enroll full-time at a four-year institution or university. Available to U.S. citizens.

Application Requirements: Application, essay, resume, references, transcript. *Deadline:* December 1.

Contact: Jesse Winch, Scholarship Administrator
    Phone: 301-493-0290 Ext. 101

KENNETH J. OSBORN MEMORIAL SCHOLARSHIP

Award to encourage students who display the interest and aptitude to enter the profession of surveying, mapping, geospatial information and technology, and photogrammetry. Student must be enrolled or intending to enroll in a college or university in the U.S. in a program of study to prepare for the profession. Application must be submitted electronically. For additional requirements that must accompany electronic application, visit web site http://www.asprs.org/membership/scholar.html.

Academic Fields/Career Goals: Engineering/Technology; Surveying, Surveying Technology, Cartography, or Geographic Information Science.

Award: Scholarship for use in freshman, sophomore, junior, or senior years; not renewable. *Number:* 1. *Amount:* $2000.

Eligibility Requirements: Applicant must be enrolled or expecting to enroll full-time at a four-year institution or university. Available to U.S. citizens.

Application Requirements: Application, essay, resume, references, transcript. *Deadline:* December 1.

Contact: Jesse Winch, Scholarship Administrator
    Phone: 301-493-0290 Ext. 101

ROBERT E. ALTENHOFEN MEMORIAL SCHOLARSHIP

One-time award of $2000 available for undergraduate or graduate study in theoretical photogrammetry. Applicant must supply a sample of work in photogrammetry and a statement of plans for future study in the field. Must be a member of ASPRS.

Academic Fields/Career Goals: Engineering/Technology; Surveying, Surveying Technology, Cartography, or Geographic Information Science.

Award: Scholarship for use in junior, senior, or graduate years; not renewable. *Number:* 1. *Amount:* $2000.

Eligibility Requirements: Applicant must be enrolled or expecting to enroll full-time at a four-year institution or university and must have an interest in photography/photogrammetry/filmmaking. Applicant or parent of applicant must be member of American Society for Photogrammetry and Remote Sensing. Available to U.S. and non-U.S. citizens.

Application Requirements: Application, essay, references, transcript, work sample. *Deadline:* December 1.

Contact: Jesse Winch, Program Manager
    ASPRS, The Imaging and Geospatial Information Society
    5410 Grosvenor Lane, Suite 210
    Bethesda, MD 20814-2160
    Phone: 301-493-0290 Ext. 101
    Fax: 301-493-0208
    E-mail: scholarships@asprs.org

ASSOCIATED GENERAL CONTRACTORS EDUCATION AND RESEARCH FOUNDATION

http://www.agcfoundation.org/

AGC EDUCATION AND RESEARCH FOUNDATION UNDERGRADUATE SCHOLARSHIPS
• See page 176

ASSOCIATION OF ENGINEERING GEOLOGISTS

http://www.aegfoundation.org/

MARLIAVE FUND
• See page 224

AUTOMOTIVE HALL OF FAME

http://www.automotivehalloffame.org/

AUTOMOTIVE HALL OF FAME EDUCATIONAL FUNDS
• See page 164

BARRY M. GOLDWATER SCHOLARSHIP AND EXCELLENCE IN EDUCATION FOUNDATION

http://www.act.org/goldwater

BARRY M. GOLDWATER SCHOLARSHIP AND EXCELLENCE IN EDUCATION PROGRAM
• See page 95

BOYS AND GIRLS CLUBS OF SAN DIEGO

http://www.sdyouth.org/

SPENCE REESE SCHOLARSHIP

Renewable scholarship for graduating male high school seniors in the United States for study of law, medicine, engineering, and political science. Awarded based on academic standing, academic ability, financial need, and character.

Academic Fields/Career Goals: Engineering/Technology; Health and Medical Sciences; Law/Legal Services; Political Science.

Award: Scholarship for use in freshman, sophomore, junior, or senior years; renewable. *Number:* up to 8. *Amount:* $2000.

Eligibility Requirements: Applicant must be high school student; planning to enroll or expecting to enroll full-time at a four-year institution or university and male. Applicant must have 3.5 GPA or higher. Available to U.S. citizens.

Application Requirements: Application, essay, financial need analysis, interview, references, self-addressed stamped envelope, test scores, transcript. *Deadline:* April 1.

Contact: Boys & Girls Clubs of Greater San Diego, Spence Reese
    Scholarship Administrator
    Boys and Girls Clubs of San Diego
    4635 Clairemont Mesa Blvd.
    San Diego, CA 92117
    E-mail: mahazzard@sdyouth.org

BRITISH COLUMBIA INNOVATION COUNCIL

http://www.bcic.ca/

BCIC YOUNG INNOVATOR SCHOLARSHIP COMPETITION (IDEA MASH UP)
• *See page 95*

CATCHING THE DREAM

http://www.catchingthedream.org/

MATH, ENGINEERING, SCIENCE, BUSINESS, EDUCATION, COMPUTERS SCHOLARSHIPS
• *See page 147*

COLLEGEBOUND FOUNDATION

http://www.collegeboundfoundation.org/

DR. FREEMAN A. HRABOWSKI, III SCHOLARSHIP
You must: be accepted to and attend UMBC; major in the field of engineering or science or technology; have a cumulative 3.0 GPA or better; and an SAT (CR+M) score of at least 1000.

Academic Fields/Career Goals: Engineering/Technology; Mathematics; Science, Technology, and Society.

Award: Scholarship for use in freshman, sophomore, junior, or senior years; renewable. *Number:* 1. *Amount:* $1500.

Eligibility Requirements: Applicant must be high school student; planning to enroll or expecting to enroll full-time at a four-year institution or university; resident of Maryland and studying in Maryland. Applicant must have 3.0 GPA or higher. Available to U.S. citizens.

Application Requirements: Application, financial need analysis, resume, references, test scores, transcript. *Deadline:* March 1.

Contact: Deana Carr-Davis, Associate Program Director, Scholarship
   Programs
   CollegeBound Foundation
   300 Water Street, Suite 300
   Baltimore, MD 21202
   Phone: 410-783-2905 Ext. 207
   Fax: 410-727-5786
   E-mail: dcarr-davis@collegeboundfoundation.org

GEORGE V. MCGOWAN SCHOLARSHIP
You must: major in the field of engineering; have a cumulative 3.0 GPA or better and an SAT (CR+M) score of at least 1000.

Academic Fields/Career Goals: Engineering/Technology.

Award: Scholarship for use in freshman year; renewable. *Number:* 1–1. *Amount:* $1500.

Eligibility Requirements: Applicant must be high school student; planning to enroll or expecting to enroll full-time at a four-year institution or university; resident of Maryland and studying in Maryland. Applicant must have 3.0 GPA or higher. Available to U.S. citizens.

Application Requirements: Application, financial need analysis, resume, references, test scores, transcript. *Deadline:* March 1.

Contact: Deana Carr-Davis, Associate Program Director, Scholarship
   Programs
   CollegeBound Foundation
   300 Water Street, Suite 300
   Baltimore, MD 21202
   Phone: 410-783-2905 Ext. 207
   Fax: 410-727-5786
   E-mail: dcarr-davis@collegeboundfoundation.org

THE COMMUNITY FOUNDATION FOR GREATER ATLANTA, INC.

http://www.cfgreateratlanta.org/

TECH HIGH SCHOOL ALUMNI ASSOCIATION/W.O. CHENEY MERIT SCHOLARSHIP FUND
Scholarship for students pursuing degrees in mathematics, engineering, or one of the physical sciences. Cumulative high school GPA of 3.7 or higher or in upper 10 percent of graduating class. SAT (math and critical reading) of at least 1300. For complete eligibility requirements and application, visit http://www.cfgreateratlanta.org.

Academic Fields/Career Goals: Engineering/Technology; Mathematics; Physical Sciences.

Award: Scholarship for use in freshman, sophomore, junior, or senior years; renewable. *Number:* 1–4. *Amount:* up to $5000.

Eligibility Requirements: Applicant must be high school student; planning to enroll or expecting to enroll full-time at a four-year institution or university and resident of Georgia. Applicant must have 3.5 GPA or higher. Available to U.S. citizens.

Application Requirements: Application, driver's license, essay, financial need analysis, references, test scores, transcript. *Deadline:* March 15.

Contact: Kristina Morris, Program Associate
   The Community Foundation for Greater Atlanta, Inc.
   50 Hurt Plaza, Suite 449
   Atlanta, GA 30303
   Phone: 404-688-5525
   E-mail: scholarships@cfgreateratlanta.org

CUBAN AMERICAN NATIONAL FOUNDATION

http://www.masscholarships.org/

MAS FAMILY SCHOLARSHIPS
• *See page 148*

THE DALLAS FOUNDATION

http://www.dallasfoundation.org/

WHITLEY PLACE SCHOLARSHIP
• *See page 100*

DAYTON FOUNDATION

http://www.daytonfoundation.org/

R.C. APPENZELLER FAMILY ENDOWMENT FUND
One-time award to students from the Greater Miami Valley, Ohio pursuing a career in engineering at an accredited college or university.

Academic Fields/Career Goals: Engineering/Technology.

Award: Scholarship for use in freshman year; not renewable. *Number:* 10–12. *Amount:* up to $1000.

Eligibility Requirements: Applicant must be high school student; planning to enroll or expecting to enroll full-time at a two-year or four-year institution or university and resident of Ohio. Applicant must have 3.0 GPA or higher. Available to U.S. citizens.

Application Requirements: Application, essay, financial need analysis, references, transcript. *Deadline:* March 26.

Contact: Elizabeth Horner, Scholarship Program Officer
   Dayton Foundation
   500 Kettering Tower
   Dayton, OH 45423
   Phone: 937-225-9955
   E-mail: ehorner@daytonfoundation.org

DENVER FOUNDATION

http://www.denverfoundation.org/

RBC DAIN RAUSCHER COLORADO SCHOLARSHIP FUND
Scholarships for undergraduate education to outstanding Colorado high school seniors. Five $5000 scholarships will be awarded to students intending to pursue a degree in science or engineering. Must have at least a 3.75 cumulative GPA. Students who have a parent, step-parent, grandparent, aunt, or uncle who is employed by RBC Dain Rauscher are not eligible to apply.

Academic Fields/Career Goals: Engineering/Technology; Science, Technology, and Society.

Award: Scholarship for use in freshman year; not renewable. *Number:* 5. *Amount:* $5000.

Eligibility Requirements: Applicant must be high school student; planning to enroll or expecting to enroll full-time at a four-year institution or university and studying in Colorado. Available to U.S. citizens.

Application Requirements: Application, test scores, transcript. *Deadline:* April 4.

Contact: Karla Bieniulis, Scholarship Committee
Denver Foundation
55 Madison Street, Eighth Floor
Denver, CO 80206
Phone: 303-300-1790 Ext. 103
Fax: 303-300-6547
E-mail: info@denverfoundation.org

DEVRY, INC.

http://www.devry.edu/

CISCO/COMPTIA SCHOLARSHIP
• See page 196

EAA AVIATION FOUNDATION, INC.

http://www.eaa.org/

PAYZER SCHOLARSHIP
• See page 124

ENGINEERS FOUNDATION OF OHIO

http://www.ohioengineer.com/

ENGINEERS FOUNDATION OF OHIO GENERAL FUND SCHOLARSHIP

Applicant must be a college junior or senior at the end of the academic year in which the application is submitted. Must be enrolled full-time at an Ohio college or university in a curriculum leading to a BS degree in engineering or its equivalent. Minimum GPA of 3.0 required. Must be a U.S. citizen and permanent resident of Ohio.

Academic Fields/Career Goals: Engineering/Technology.

Award: Scholarship for use in junior or senior years; not renewable. *Number:* 1. *Amount:* $1000.

Eligibility Requirements: Applicant must be enrolled or expecting to enroll full-time at a four-year institution or university; resident of Ohio and studying in Ohio. Applicant must have 3.0 GPA or higher. Available to U.S. citizens.

Application Requirements: Application, essay, financial need analysis, test scores, transcript. *Deadline:* December 15.

Contact: Pam McClure, Manager of Administration
Engineers Foundation of Ohio
400 South Fifth Street, Suite 300
Columbus, OH 43215
Phone: 614-223-1177
E-mail: efo@ohioengineer.com

LLOYD A. CHACEY, PE-OHIO SOCIETY OF PROFESSIONAL ENGINEERS MEMORIAL SCHOLARSHIP

Scholarship available for a son, daughter, brother, sister, niece, nephew, spouse or grandchild of a current member of the Ohio Society of Professional Engineers, or of a deceased member who was in good standing at the time of his or her death. Must be enrolled full-time at an Ohio college or university in a curriculum leading to a degree in engineering or its equivalent. Must have a minimum of 3.0 GPA. Must be a U.S. citizen and permanent resident of Ohio.

Academic Fields/Career Goals: Engineering/Technology.

Award: Scholarship for use in junior or senior years; renewable. *Number:* 1–2. *Amount:* $2000.

Eligibility Requirements: Applicant must be enrolled or expecting to enroll full-time at a four-year institution or university; resident of Ohio and studying in Ohio. Applicant must have 3.0 GPA or higher. Available to U.S. citizens.

Application Requirements: Application, essay, financial need analysis, test scores, transcript. *Deadline:* December 15.

Contact: Pam McClure, Manager of Administration
Engineers Foundation of Ohio
400 South Fifth Street, Suite 300
Columbus, OH 43215
Phone: 614-223-1177
E-mail: efo@ohioengineer.com

RAYMOND H. FULLER, PE MEMORIAL SCHOLARSHIP

Scholarship of $1000 to graduating high school seniors who will enter their freshman year in college the next fall. Recipients must be accepted for enrollment in an engineering program at an Ohio college or university. Must have a minimum of 3.0 GPA. Must be a U.S. citizen and permanent resident of Ohio. Consideration will be given to the prospective recipient's academic achievement, interest in a career in engineering and financial need as determined by interviews and from references.

Academic Fields/Career Goals: Engineering/Technology.

Award: Scholarship for use in freshman year; not renewable. *Number:* 1. *Amount:* $1000.

Eligibility Requirements: Applicant must be high school student; planning to enroll or expecting to enroll full-time at a four-year institution or university; resident of Ohio and studying in Ohio. Applicant must have 3.0 GPA or higher. Available to U.S. citizens.

Application Requirements: Application, essay, financial need analysis, interview, references, test scores, transcript. *Deadline:* December 15.

Contact: Pam McClure, Manager of Administration
Engineers Foundation of Ohio
400 South Fifth Street, Suite 300
Columbus, OH 43215
Phone: 614-223-1177
E-mail: efo@ohioengineer.com

FLORIDA ENGINEERING SOCIETY

http://www.fleng.org/

ACEC/FLORIDA SCHOLARSHIP

One-time scholarship of $5000 given to Florida citizen pursuing a bachelor's, master's or doctoral degree in an ABET-approved engineering program or in an accredited land surveying program. Students must be entering their junior, senior, or fifth year of college.

Academic Fields/Career Goals: Engineering/Technology; Surveying, Surveying Technology, Cartography, or Geographic Information Science.

Award: Scholarship for use in junior or senior years; not renewable. *Number:* 1. *Amount:* $5000.

Eligibility Requirements: Applicant must be enrolled or expecting to enroll full-time at a four-year institution or university and resident of Florida. Available to U.S. citizens.

Application Requirements: Application, essay, references, test scores, transcript. *Deadline:* February 15.

Contact: Dana D. Dixon-Smith, Scholarship Committee Staff Liaison
Florida Engineering Society
125 South Gadsden Street
Tallahassee, FL 32301
Phone: 850-224-7121
Fax: 850-222-4349
E-mail: dsmith@fleng.org

DAVID F. LUDOVICI SCHOLARSHIP
• See page 177

ERIC PRIMAVERA MEMORIAL SCHOLARSHIP

One-time scholarship of $1000 given to students in their junior or senior year in a Florida university engineering program. Minimum 3.0 GPA required.

Academic Fields/Career Goals: Engineering/Technology.

Award: Scholarship for use in junior or senior years; not renewable. *Number:* 1. *Amount:* $1000.

Eligibility Requirements: Applicant must be enrolled or expecting to enroll full-time at an institution or university; resident of Florida and studying in Florida. Applicant must have 3.0 GPA or higher. Available to U.S. citizens.

Application Requirements: Application, references, self-addressed stamped envelope, transcript. *Deadline:* February 1.

Contact: Dana D. Dixon-Smith, Scholarship Committee Staff Liaison
Florida Engineering Society
125 South Gadsden Street
Tallahassee, FL 32301
Phone: 850-224-7121
Fax: 850-222-4349

HIGH SCHOOL SCHOLARSHIP

One-time scholarship given to high school seniors who are residents of Florida. Minimum 3.5 GPA required. Applicant must have genuine interest in engineering.

Academic Fields/Career Goals: Engineering/Technology.

Award: Scholarship for use in freshman year; not renewable. *Number:* 6. *Amount:* $1500–$2500.

Eligibility Requirements: Applicant must be high school student; planning to enroll or expecting to enroll full-time at a four-year institution or university and resident of Florida. Applicant must have 3.5 GPA or higher. Available to U.S. citizens.

Application Requirements: Application, interview, test scores, transcript, IB and AP exam results. *Deadline:* February 1.

Contact: Dana D. Dixon-Smith, Scholarship Committee Staff Liaison
Florida Engineering Society
125 South Gadsden Street
Tallahassee, FL 32301
Phone: 850-224-7121
Fax: 850-222-4349
E-mail: dsmith@fleng.org

RAYMOND W. MILLER, PE SCHOLARSHIP

One-time scholarship given to students in their junior or senior year in a Florida university engineering program. Minimum 3.0 GPA required.

Academic Fields/Career Goals: Engineering/Technology.

Award: Scholarship for use in junior or senior years; not renewable. *Number:* 1. *Amount:* $1500–$2500.

Eligibility Requirements: Applicant must be enrolled or expecting to enroll full-time at an institution or university; resident of Florida and studying in Florida. Applicant must have 3.0 GPA or higher. Available to U.S. citizens.

Application Requirements: Application, references, self-addressed stamped envelope, transcript. *Deadline:* February 1.

Contact: Dana D. Dixon-Smith, Scholarship Committee Staff Liaison
Florida Engineering Society
125 South Gadsden Street
Tallahassee, FL 32301
Phone: 850-224-7121
Fax: 850-222-4349
E-mail: dsmith@fleng.org

RICHARD B. GASSETT, PE SCHOLARSHIP

One-time scholarship given to students in their junior or senior year in a Florida university engineering program. Minimum 3.0 GPA required.

Academic Fields/Career Goals: Engineering/Technology.

Award: Scholarship for use in junior or senior years; not renewable. *Number:* 1. *Amount:* $1500–$2500.

Eligibility Requirements: Applicant must be enrolled or expecting to enroll full-time at an institution or university; resident of Florida and studying in Florida. Applicant must have 3.0 GPA or higher. Available to U.S. citizens.

Application Requirements: Application, references, self-addressed stamped envelope, transcript. *Deadline:* February 1.

Contact: Dana D. Dixon-Smith, Scholarship Committee Staff Liaison
Florida Engineering Society
125 South Gadsden Street
Tallahassee, FL 32301
Phone: 850-224-7121
Fax: 850-222-4349
E-mail: dsmith@fleng.org

FOUNDATION FOR SCIENCE AND DISABILITY

http://stemd.org/

GRANTS FOR DISABLED STUDENTS IN THE SCIENCES
• See page 95

GEORGIA SOCIETY OF PROFESSIONAL ENGINEERS/GEORGIA ENGINEERING FOUNDATION

http://www.gefinc.org/

GEORGIA ENGINEERING FOUNDATION SCHOLARSHIP PROGRAM

Awards scholarships to students who are preparing for a career in engineering or engineering technology. Must be U.S. citizens and legal residents of Georgia. Must be attending or accepted in an ABET-accredited program. Separate applications are available: one for use by high school seniors and new college freshmen and one for use by college upperclassmen.

Academic Fields/Career Goals: Engineering/Technology.

Award: Scholarship for use in freshman, sophomore, junior, or senior years; not renewable. *Number:* 45. *Amount:* $1000–$5000.

Eligibility Requirements: Applicant must be enrolled or expecting to enroll full-time at a four-year institution or university and resident of Georgia. Applicant or parent of applicant must have employment or volunteer experience in community service. Available to U.S. citizens.

Application Requirements: Application, photo, references, test scores, transcript. *Deadline:* August 31.

Contact: Roseana Richards, Scholarship Committee Chairman
Georgia Society of Professional Engineers/Georgia
Engineering Foundation
233 Peachtree Street, Suite 700, Harris Tower
Atlanta, GA 30303
Phone: 404-521-2324
E-mail: richardsr@pondco.com

GOLDEN KEY INTERNATIONAL HONOUR SOCIETY

http://www.goldenkey.org/

ENGINEERING/TECHNOLOGY ACHIEVEMENT AWARD

Award to members who excel in the study of engineering or technology. Applicants will be asked to respond to a problem posed by an honorary member within the discipline. One winner will receive a $1000 award. The second place winner will receive $750 and the third place winner will receive $500.

Academic Fields/Career Goals: Engineering/Technology.

Award: Prize for use in freshman, sophomore, junior, senior, graduate, or postgraduate years; not renewable. *Number:* 3. *Amount:* $500–$1000.

Eligibility Requirements: Applicant must be enrolled or expecting to enroll full- or part-time at a four-year institution or university. Available to U.S. and non-U.S. citizens.

Application Requirements: Application, applicant must enter a contest, essay, references, transcript, engineering-related report, cover page from the online registration. *Deadline:* March 3.

Contact: Scholarship Program Administrators
Golden Key International Honour Society
PO Box 23737
Nashville, TN 37202-3737
Phone: 800-377-2401
E-mail: scholarships@goldenkey.org

GREATER KANAWHA VALLEY FOUNDATION

http://www.tgkvf.org/

MATH AND SCIENCE SCHOLARSHIP
• See page 140

HAWAIIAN LODGE, F&AM

http://www.glhawaii.org/

HAWAIIAN LODGE SCHOLARSHIPS
• *See page 106*

HELLENIC UNIVERSITY CLUB OF PHILADELPHIA

http://www.hucphila.org/

DIMITRI J. VERVERELLI MEMORIAL SCHOLARSHIP FOR ARCHITECTURE AND/OR ENGINEERING
• *See page 101*

HISPANIC ENGINEER NATIONAL ACHIEVEMENT AWARDS CORPORATION (HENAAC)

http://www.henaac.org/

HISPANIC ENGINEER NATIONAL ACHIEVEMENT AWARDS CORPORATION SCHOLARSHIP PROGRAM
• *See page 125*

IDAHO STATE BROADCASTERS ASSOCIATION

http://www.idahobroadcasters.org/

WAYNE C. CORNILS MEMORIAL SCHOLARSHIP
• *See page 151*

ILLINOIS SOCIETY OF PROFESSIONAL ENGINEERS

http://www.illinoisengineer.com/

ILLINOIS SOCIETY OF PROFESSIONAL ENGINEERS ADVANTAGE AWARD/FOUNDATION SCHOLARSHIP

Applicant must be a member or son or daughter of ISPE member in good standing and attend an Illinois university approved by the Accreditation Board of Engineering. Applicant must be at least a junior at the approved university. Required essay must address why applicant wishes to become a professional engineer. Must have a B average.

Academic Fields/Career Goals: Engineering/Technology.

Award: Scholarship for use in junior or senior years; not renewable. *Number:* 1. *Amount:* $1000.

Eligibility Requirements: Applicant must be enrolled or expecting to enroll full-time at a four-year institution and studying in Illinois. Applicant must have 3.0 GPA or higher. Available to U.S. and non-U.S. citizens.

Application Requirements: Application, essay, references, transcript. *Deadline:* March 31.

Contact: Nicole Palmisano, Scholarship Coordinator
Illinois Society of Professional Engineers
100 East Washington Street
Springfield, IL 62701
Phone: 217-544-7424 Ext. 238
E-mail: NicolePalmisano@illinoisengineer.com

ILLINOIS SOCIETY OF PROFESSIONAL ENGINEERS/ MELVIN E. AMSTUTZ MEMORIAL AWARD

Applicant must attend an Illinois university approved by the Accreditation Board of Engineering. Applicant must be at least a junior in university he or she attends, and must prove financial need. Essay must address why applicant wishes to become a professional engineer. Must have a B average.

Academic Fields/Career Goals: Engineering/Technology.

Award: Scholarship for use in junior or senior years; not renewable. *Number:* 1. *Amount:* $1500.

Eligibility Requirements: Applicant must be enrolled or expecting to enroll full-time at a four-year institution and studying in Illinois. Available to U.S. and non-U.S. citizens.

Application Requirements: Application, essay, financial need analysis, references. *Deadline:* March 31.

Contact: Nicole Palmisano, Scholarship Coordinator
Illinois Society of Professional Engineers
100 East Washington Street
Springfield, IL 62701
Phone: 217-544-7424 Ext. 238
E-mail: NicolePalmisano@illinoisengineer.com

ILLUMINATING ENGINEERING SOCIETY OF NORTH AMERICA

http://www.iesna.org/

ROBERT W. THUNEN MEMORIAL SCHOLARSHIPS
• *See page 101*

INDEPENDENT LABORATORIES INSTITUTE SCHOLARSHIP ALLIANCE

http://www.acil.org/

INDEPENDENT LABORATORIES INSTITUTE SCHOLARSHIP ALLIANCE
• *See page 141*

INDIANA SOCIETY OF PROFESSIONAL ENGINEERS

http://www.indspe.org/

INDIANA ENGINEERING SCHOLARSHIP

Award for Indiana resident who attends an Indiana educational institution, or commutes daily to a school outside Indiana. Applicant must have accrued the minimum of one-half the credits required for an undergraduate ABET-accredited engineering degree. For details and an application visit web site http://indspe.org.

Academic Fields/Career Goals: Engineering/Technology.

Award: Scholarship for use in junior or senior years; not renewable. *Number:* 3. *Amount:* $750.

Eligibility Requirements: Applicant must be enrolled or expecting to enroll full- or part-time at a four-year institution or university and resident of Indiana. Available to U.S. citizens.

Application Requirements: Application, resume, references, transcript. *Deadline:* May 1.

Contact: Mr. Harold E. Dungan, Scholarship Coordinator
Indiana Society of Professional Engineers
HNTB, 111 Monument Circle, Suite 1200
Indianapolis, IN 46204
Phone: 317-636-4682 Ext. 75245
Fax: 317-917-5211
E-mail: hdungan@hntb.com

INSTITUTE OF INDUSTRIAL ENGINEERS

http://www.iienet.org/

A.O. PUTNAM MEMORIAL SCHOLARSHIP

Available to undergraduate students enrolled in any school in the United States and its territories, Canada, and Mexico, provided: (1) the school's industrial engineering program or equivalent is accredited by an agency or organization recognized by IIE; and (2) the student is pursuing a course of study in industrial engineering. Priority is given to students who have demonstrated an interest in management consulting. The endowment provided for one scholarship of $700 for the past academic year.

Academic Fields/Career Goals: Engineering/Technology.

Award: Scholarship for use in freshman, sophomore, junior, or senior years; not renewable. *Number:* 1. *Amount:* up to $700.

Eligibility Requirements: Applicant must be enrolled or expecting to enroll full-time at a four-year institution or university. Applicant or parent of applicant must be member of Institute of Industrial Engineers. Available to U.S. and non-U.S. citizens.

Application Requirements: Application, references, transcript, nomination. *Deadline:* November 15.

Contact: Bonnie Cameron, Operations Administrator
Institute of Industrial Engineers
3577 Parkway Lane, Suite 200
Norcross, GA 30092-2988
Phone: 770-449-0461 Ext. 105
E-mail: bcameron@iienet.org

BENJAMIN WILLARD NIEBEL SCHOLARSHIP

Scholarship available to undergraduate students enrolled in any school in the United States and its territories, Canada, and Mexico, provided the school's engineering program or equivalent is accredited by an agency recognized by IIE and the student is pursuing a course of study in industrial engineering with interest in methods, standards, and work design. Applicant should have a 3.4 GPA on a 4.0 scale.

Academic Fields/Career Goals: Engineering/Technology.

Award: Scholarship for use in freshman, sophomore, junior, or senior years; not renewable. *Amount:* up to $4000.

Eligibility Requirements: Applicant must be enrolled or expecting to enroll full-time at a two-year or four-year institution or university. Available to U.S. and non-U.S. citizens.

Application Requirements: *Deadline:* November 15.

Contact: Bonnie Cameron, Operations Administrator
Institute of Industrial Engineers
3577 Parkway Lane, Suite 200
Norcross, GA 30092-2988
Phone: 770-449-0461 Ext. 105
E-mail: bcameron@iienet.org

C.B. GAMBRELL UNDERGRADUATE SCHOLARSHIP

One-time award for undergraduate industrial engineering students who are U.S. citizens graduated from a U.S. high school with a class standing above freshman level in an ABET-accredited IE program. Must be a member of Industrial Engineers, have a minimum GPA of 3.4, and be nominated by a department head.

Academic Fields/Career Goals: Engineering/Technology.

Award: Scholarship for use in sophomore, junior, or senior years; not renewable. *Number:* up to 1. *Amount:* up to $4000.

Eligibility Requirements: Applicant must be enrolled or expecting to enroll full-time at a four-year institution or university. Applicant or parent of applicant must be member of Institute of Industrial Engineers. Available to U.S. citizens.

Application Requirements: Application, references, nomination. *Deadline:* November 15.

Contact: Bonnie Cameron, Operations Administrator
Institute of Industrial Engineers
3577 Parkway Lane, Suite 200
Norcross, GA 30092-2988
Phone: 770-449-0461 Ext. 105
E-mail: bcameron@iienet.org

CIE UNDERGRADUATE SCHOLARSHIP

$1,000 scholarship will be awarded to an undergraduate industrial engineering student for the best application of corporate social responsibility, resilience, or sustainability principals aligned with classic industrial engineering techniques to a project for an enterprise. Interested candidates must complete an application form, as well as submit a complete description of the project, including provision of a financial analysis using the triple-bottom line definitions of sustainability, showing a positive cash flow or return on investment to the enterprise over the project life. Applicants should have at least a 3.4 GPA.

Academic Fields/Career Goals: Engineering/Technology.

Award: Scholarship for use in freshman, sophomore, junior, or senior years; not renewable. *Number:* 1. *Amount:* $1000.

Eligibility Requirements: Applicant must be enrolled or expecting to enroll full-time at a four-year institution or university.

Application Requirements: Application, references, project description. *Deadline:* February 1.

Contact: Bonnie Cameron, Operations Administrator
Institute of Industrial Engineers
3577 Parkway Lane, Suite 200
Norcross, GA 30092-2988
Phone: 770-449-0461 Ext. 105
E-mail: bcameron@iienet.org

DWIGHT D. GARDNER SCHOLARSHIP

Scholarship available to undergraduate students enrolled in an industrial engineering program in any school in the United States and its territories, Canada, and Mexico, provided the school's engineering program or equivalent is accredited by an agency recognized by IIE. Must be an IIE member. Minimum 3.4 GPA required. Must be nominated by department head.

Academic Fields/Career Goals: Engineering/Technology.

Award: Scholarship for use in freshman, sophomore, junior, or senior years; not renewable. *Number:* 3. *Amount:* up to $3000.

Eligibility Requirements: Applicant must be enrolled or expecting to enroll full-time at a four-year institution or university. Applicant or parent of applicant must be member of Institute of Industrial Engineers. Available to U.S. and non-U.S. citizens.

Application Requirements: Application, essay, financial need analysis, references, transcript, nomination. *Deadline:* November 15.

Contact: Bonnie Cameron, Operations Administrator
Institute of Industrial Engineers
3577 Parkway Lane, Suite 200
Norcross, GA 30092-2988
Phone: 770-449-0461 Ext. 105
E-mail: bcameron@iienet.org

HAROLD AND INGE MARCUS SCHOLARSHIP

Available to undergraduate students enrolled in any school in the United States provided the school's engineering program is accredited by an agency recognized by IIE and the student is pursuing a course of study in industrial engineering. This award is intended to recognize academic excellence and noteworthy contribution to the development of the industrial engineering profession. Applicants should have at least a 3.4 GPA on a 4.0 scale.

Academic Fields/Career Goals: Engineering/Technology.

Award: Scholarship for use in freshman, sophomore, junior, or senior years; not renewable. *Amount:* up to $4000.

Eligibility Requirements: Applicant must be enrolled or expecting to enroll full-time at a two-year or four-year institution or university. Available to U.S. citizens.

Application Requirements: *Deadline:* November 15.

Contact: Bonnie Cameron, Operations Administrator
Institute of Industrial Engineers
3577 Parkway Lane, Suite 200
Norcross, GA 30092-2988
Phone: 770-449-0461 Ext. 105
E-mail: bcameron@iienet.org

IIE COUNCIL OF FELLOWS UNDERGRADUATE SCHOLARSHIP

Awards to undergraduate students enrolled in any school in the United States and its territories, Canada and Mexico, provided the school's engineering program or equivalent is accredited by an agency recognized by IIE and the student is pursuing a course of study in industrial engineering. Must be IIE member and have minimum 3.4 GPA. Write to IIE Headquarters to obtain application form.

Academic Fields/Career Goals: Engineering/Technology.

Award: Scholarship for use in freshman, sophomore, junior, or senior years; not renewable. *Number:* varies.

Eligibility Requirements: Applicant must be enrolled or expecting to enroll full-time at a four-year institution or university. Applicant or parent of applicant must be member of Institute of Industrial Engineers. Available to U.S. and non-U.S. citizens.

Application Requirements: Application. *Deadline:* November 15.

Contact: Bonnie Cameron, Operations Administrator
Institute of Industrial Engineers
3577 Parkway Lane, Suite 200
Norcross, GA 30092-2988
Phone: 770-449-0461 Ext. 105
E-mail: bcameron@iienet.org

JOHN L. IMHOFF SCHOLARSHIP

Available to a student pursuing an industrial engineering degree who, by academic, employment and/or professional achievements, has made noteworthy contributions to the development of the industrial engineering profession through international understanding. At least one scholarship of $1,000 will be awarded in the spring. Note that IIE membership is not required. Applicant should have at least a 3.4 GPA.

Academic Fields/Career Goals: Engineering/Technology.

Award: Scholarship for use in freshman, sophomore, junior, or senior years; not renewable. *Amount:* $1000.

Eligibility Requirements: Applicant must be enrolled or expecting to enroll full-time at a four-year institution or university.

Application Requirements: Essay, references. *Deadline:* November 15.

Contact: Bonnie Cameron, Operations Administrator
Institute of Industrial Engineers
3577 Parkway Lane, Suite 200
Norcross, GA 30092-2988
Phone: 770-449-0461 Ext. 105
E-mail: bcameron@iienet.org

LISA ZAKEN AWARD FOR EXCELLENCE

Award for undergraduate and graduate students enrolled in any school, and pursuing a course of study in industrial engineering. Award is intended to recognize excellence in scholarly activities and leadership related to the industrial engineering profession on campus. Must maintain at least a 3.0 GPA.

Academic Fields/Career Goals: Engineering/Technology.

Award: Prize for use in freshman, sophomore, junior, senior, or graduate years; not renewable. *Number:* up to 1. *Amount:* up to $4000.

Eligibility Requirements: Applicant must be enrolled or expecting to enroll full-time at a four-year institution or university. Applicant or parent of applicant must be member of Institute of Industrial Engineers. Applicant must have 3.0 GPA or higher. Available to U.S. and non-U.S. citizens.

Application Requirements: Application, essay, references, nomination form. *Deadline:* November 15.

Contact: Bonnie Cameron, Operations Administrator
Institute of Industrial Engineers
3577 Parkway Lane, Suite 200
Norcross, GA 30092-2988
Phone: 770-449-0461 Ext. 105
E-mail: bcameron@iienet.org

MARVIN MUNDEL MEMORIAL SCHOLARSHIP

Scholarship awarded to undergraduate students enrolled in any school in the United States, Canada, or Mexico with an accredited industrial engineering program. Priority given to students who have demonstrated an interest in work measurement and methods engineering. Must be active Institute members with 3.4 GPA or above. Must be nominated by department head or faculty adviser.

Academic Fields/Career Goals: Engineering/Technology.

Award: Scholarship for use in freshman, sophomore, junior, or senior years; not renewable. *Amount:* $4000.

Eligibility Requirements: Applicant must be enrolled or expecting to enroll full-time at a four-year institution or university. Applicant or parent of applicant must be member of Institute of Industrial Engineers. Available to U.S. and non-U.S. citizens.

Application Requirements: Application, nomination. *Deadline:* November 15.

Contact: Bonnie Cameron, Operations Administrator
Institute of Industrial Engineers
3577 Parkway Lane, Suite 200
Norcross, GA 30092-2988
Phone: 770-449-0461 Ext. 105
E-mail: bcameron@iienet.org

PRESIDENTS SCHOLARSHIP

Scholarship available to undergraduate students pursuing a course of study in industrial engineering. This award is intended to recognize excellence in scholarly activities and leadership of the industrial engineering profession. A candidate must be active in a student chapter and must have demonstrated leadership and promoted IIE involvement on campus. Applicants should have at least a 3.4 GPA.

Academic Fields/Career Goals: Engineering/Technology.

Award: Scholarship for use in freshman, sophomore, junior, or senior years; not renewable.

Eligibility Requirements: Applicant must be enrolled or expecting to enroll full-time at a four-year institution or university.

Application Requirements: *Deadline:* November 15.

Contact: Bonnie Cameron, Operations Administrator
Institute of Industrial Engineers
3577 Parkway Lane, Suite 200
Norcross, GA 30092-2988
Phone: 770-449-0461 Ext. 105
E-mail: bcameron@iienet.org

UNITED PARCEL SERVICE SCHOLARSHIP FOR FEMALE STUDENTS

One-time award for female undergraduate students enrolled at any school in the United States, Canada, or Mexico in an industrial engineering program. Must be a member of Institute of Industrial Engineers, have a minimum GPA of 3.4, and be nominated by a department head.

Academic Fields/Career Goals: Engineering/Technology.

Award: Scholarship for use in freshman, sophomore, junior, or senior years; not renewable. *Number:* 1. *Amount:* up to $4000.

Eligibility Requirements: Applicant must be enrolled or expecting to enroll full-time at a four-year or technical institution or university and female. Applicant or parent of applicant must be member of Institute of Industrial Engineers. Available to U.S. and non-U.S. citizens.

Application Requirements: Application, references, transcript, nomination. *Deadline:* November 15.

Contact: Bonnie Cameron, Operations Administrator
Institute of Industrial Engineers
3577 Parkway Lane, Suite 200
Norcross, GA 30092-2988
Phone: 770-449-0461 Ext. 105
E-mail: bcameron@iienet.org

UPS SCHOLARSHIP FOR MINORITY STUDENTS

One-time award for minority undergraduate students enrolled at any school in the United States, Canada, or Mexico in an industrial engineering program. Must be a member of Institute of Industrial Engineers. Nominated students by IE department heads will be sent an application package to complete and return before November 15.

Academic Fields/Career Goals: Engineering/Technology.

Award: Scholarship for use in freshman, sophomore, junior, or senior years; not renewable. *Number:* 1. *Amount:* up to $4000.

Eligibility Requirements: Applicant must be American Indian/Alaska Native, Asian/Pacific Islander, Black (non-Hispanic), or Hispanic and enrolled or expecting to enroll full-time at a four-year institution or university. Applicant or parent of applicant must be member of Institute of Industrial Engineers. Applicant must have 3.0 GPA or higher. Available to U.S. and non-U.S. citizens.

Application Requirements: Application, references, transcript, nomination. *Deadline:* November 15.

Contact: Bonnie Cameron, Operations Administrator
Institute of Industrial Engineers
3577 Parkway Lane, Suite 200
Norcross, GA 30092-2988
Phone: 770-449-0461 Ext. 105
E-mail: bcameron@iienet.org

INTERNATIONAL FACILITY MANAGEMENT ASSOCIATION FOUNDATION

http://www.ifmafoundation.org/

IFMA FOUNDATION SCHOLARSHIPS
• See page 102

INTERNATIONAL SOCIETY FOR OPTICAL ENGINEERING-SPIE

http://www.spie.org/scholarships

SPIE EDUCATIONAL SCHOLARSHIPS IN OPTICAL SCIENCE AND ENGINEERING
• *See page 96*

INTERNATIONAL SOCIETY OF AUTOMATION (ISA)

http://www.isa.org/

INTERNATIONAL SOCIETY OF AUTOMATION EDUCATION FOUNDATION SCHOLARSHIPS
• *See page 125*

INTERNATIONAL SOCIETY OF EXPLOSIVES ENGINEERS

http://www.isee.org/

JERRY MCDOWELL FUND
• *See page 267*

INTERNATIONAL TECHNOLOGY EDUCATION ASSOCIATION

http://www.iteaconnect.org/

INTERNATIONAL TECHNOLOGY EDUCATION ASSOCIATION UNDERGRADUATE SCHOLARSHIP IN TECHNOLOGY EDUCATION
• *See page 238*

INTERNATIONAL UNION OF ELECTRONIC, ELECTRICAL, SALARIED, MACHINE, AND FURNITURE WORKERS-CWA

http://www.iue-cwa.org/

DAVID J. FITZMAURICE ENGINEERING SCHOLARSHIP
One-time award of $2000 for a student whose parent or grandparent is a member of the IUE-CWA. Applicant must be pursuing undergraduate engineering degree. Submit family financial status form with application.

Academic Fields/Career Goals: Engineering/Technology.

Award: Scholarship for use in freshman, sophomore, junior, or senior years; not renewable. *Number:* 1. *Amount:* $2000.

Eligibility Requirements: Applicant must be enrolled or expecting to enroll full-time at a four-year institution or university. Applicant or parent of applicant must be member of International Union of Electronic, Electrical, Salaries, Machine and Furniture Workers. Available to U.S. and Canadian citizens.

Application Requirements: Application, essay, financial need analysis, references, test scores, transcript. *Deadline:* March 31.

Contact: Sue McElroy, Scholarship Committee
International Union of Electronic, Electrical, Salaried, Machine, and Furniture Workers-CWA
501 Third Street, NW
Washington, DC 20001
Phone: 202-434-0676
Fax: 202-434-1250

KOREAN-AMERICAN SCIENTISTS AND ENGINEERS ASSOCIATION

http://www.ksea.org/

INYONG HAM SCHOLARSHIP
Scholarship of $1000 awarded to undergraduate and graduate students of Korean heritage majoring in science, engineering or related fields. Must be KSEA members or apply for membership at the time of scholarship application.

Academic Fields/Career Goals: Engineering/Technology.

Award: Scholarship for use in freshman, sophomore, junior, senior, or graduate years; not renewable. *Number:* 1. *Amount:* $1000.

Eligibility Requirements: Applicant must be of Korean heritage; Asian/Pacific Islander and enrolled or expecting to enroll full-time at a two-year or four-year institution or university. Applicant or parent of applicant must be member of Korean-American Scientists and Engineers Association. Available to U.S. citizens.

Application Requirements: Application, essay, resume, references, test scores, transcript. *Deadline:* February 15.

Contact: Scholarship Committee
Korean-American Scientists and Engineers Association
1952 Gallows Road, Suite 300
Vienna, VA 22182
Phone: 703-748-1221

KSEA SCHOLARSHIPS
• *See page 257*

LEAGUE OF UNITED LATIN AMERICAN CITIZENS NATIONAL EDUCATIONAL SERVICE CENTERS INC.

http://www.lnesc.org/

GE/LULAC SCHOLARSHIP
• *See page 153*

GM/LULAC SCHOLARSHIP
Renewable award for minority students who are pursuing an undergraduate degree in engineering at an accredited college or university. Must maintain a minimum 3.0 GPA. Selection is based in part on the likelihood of pursuing a successful career in engineering.

Academic Fields/Career Goals: Engineering/Technology.

Award: Scholarship for use in freshman, sophomore, junior, or senior years; renewable. *Number:* up to 20. *Amount:* up to $2000.

Eligibility Requirements: Applicant must be American Indian/Alaska Native, Asian/Pacific Islander, Black (non-Hispanic), or Hispanic and enrolled or expecting to enroll full-time at a four-year institution or university. Applicant must have 3.0 GPA or higher. Available to U.S. citizens.

Application Requirements: Application, essay, references, transcript. *Deadline:* July 15.

Contact: Scholarship Administrator
League of United Latin American Citizens National
Educational Service Centers Inc.
2000 L Street NW, Suite 610
Washington, DC 20036
Phone: 202-835-9646 Ext. 10
Fax: 202-835-9685

LOS ANGELES COUNCIL OF BLACK PROFESSIONAL ENGINEERS

http://www.lablackengineers.org/

AL-BEN SCHOLARSHIP FOR ACADEMIC INCENTIVE
• *See page 166*

AL-BEN SCHOLARSHIP FOR PROFESSIONAL MERIT
• *See page 166*

AL-BEN SCHOLARSHIP FOR SCHOLASTIC ACHIEVEMENT
• *See page 166*

MAINE EDUCATION SERVICES

http://www.mesfoundation.com/

MAINE STATE CHAMBER OF COMMERCE SCHOLARSHIP-HIGH SCHOOL SENIOR
• *See page 153*

MAINE SOCIETY OF PROFESSIONAL ENGINEERS

http://www.mespe.org/

MAINE SOCIETY OF PROFESSIONAL ENGINEERS VERNON T. SWAINE-ROBERT E. CHUTE SCHOLARSHIP
• *See page 267*

MANUFACTURERS ASSOCIATION OF MAINE

http://www.mainemfg.com/

MAINE METAL PRODUCTS EDUCATION FUND SCHOLARSHIP PROGRAM
• *See page 127*

MARINE TECHNOLOGY SOCIETY

http://www.mtsociety.org/

MTS STUDENT SCHOLARSHIP FOR GRADUATING HIGH SCHOOL SENIORS

Scholarship of $2000 available to high school seniors who have been accepted into a full-time undergraduate program and have an interest in marine technology.

Academic Fields/Career Goals: Engineering/Technology; Marine/Ocean Engineering.

Award: Scholarship for use in freshman year; not renewable. *Number:* varies. *Amount:* $2000.

Eligibility Requirements: Applicant must be high school student and planning to enroll or expecting to enroll full-time at a four-year institution or university. Available to U.S. and non-U.S. citizens.

Application Requirements: Application, essay, references, transcript, college acceptance letter. *Deadline:* April 15.

Contact: Suzanne Voelker, Operations Administrator
Marine Technology Society
5565 Sterrett Place, Suite 108
Columbia, MD 21044
Phone: 410-884-5330
E-mail: suzanne.voelker@mtsociety.org

MARION D. AND EVA S. PEEPLES FOUNDATION TRUST SCHOLARSHIP PROGRAM

http://www.jccf.org/

MARION A. AND EVA S. PEEPLES SCHOLARSHIPS
• *See page 240*

MARYLAND ASSOCIATION OF PRIVATE COLLEGES AND CAREER SCHOOLS

http://www.mapccs.org/

MARYLAND ASSOCIATION OF PRIVATE COLLEGES AND CAREER SCHOOLS SCHOLARSHIP
• *See page 153*

MICHIGAN SOCIETY OF PROFESSIONAL ENGINEERS

http://www.michiganspe.org/

MICHIGAN SOCIETY OF PROFESSIONAL ENGINEERS HARRY R. BALL, P.E. GRANT
• *See page 166*

MICHIGAN SOCIETY OF PROFESSIONAL ENGINEERS KENNETH B. FISHBECK, P.E. MEMORIAL GRANT
• *See page 166*

MIDWEST ROOFING CONTRACTORS ASSOCIATION

http://www.mrca.org/

MRCA FOUNDATION SCHOLARSHIP PROGRAM
• *See page 102*

MINERALS, METALS, AND MATERIALS SOCIETY (TMS)

http://www.tms.org/

TMS/EMPMD GILBERT CHIN SCHOLARSHIP
• *See page 268*

TMS/EPD SCHOLARSHIP
• *See page 268*

TMS/INTERNATIONAL SYMPOSIUM ON SUPERALLOYS SCHOLARSHIP PROGRAM
• *See page 268*

TMS J. KEITH BRIMACOMBE PRESIDENTIAL SCHOLARSHIP
• *See page 268*

TMS/LMD SCHOLARSHIP PROGRAM
• *See page 268*

TMS OUTSTANDING STUDENT PAPER CONTEST-UNDERGRADUATE
• *See page 269*

TMS/STRUCTURAL MATERIALS DIVISION SCHOLARSHIP
• *See page 269*

MINNESOTA COMMUNITY FOUNDATION

http://www.mncommunityfoundation.org/

HANS O. NYMAN ENGINEERING SCHOLARSHIP

One renewable scholarship of $1500 to students with at least two years of undergraduate study, currently participating in Co-Op Learning Internship at District Energy.

Academic Fields/Career Goals: Engineering/Technology.

Award: Scholarship for use in junior or senior years; renewable. *Number:* 1. *Amount:* $1500.

Eligibility Requirements: Applicant must be enrolled or expecting to enroll full- or part-time at a four-year institution or university. Available to U.S. citizens.

Application Requirements: Application, transcript. *Deadline:* varies.

Contact: Donna Paulson, Administrative Assistant
Minnesota Community Foundation
55 Fifth Street East, Suite 600
St. Paul, MN 55101-1797
Phone: 651-325-4212
Fax: 651-224-9502
E-mail: dkp@mncommunityfoundation.org

NASA/MARYLAND SPACE GRANT CONSORTIUM

http://www.mdspacegrant.org/

NASA MARYLAND SPACE GRANT CONSORTIUM UNDERGRADUATE SCHOLARSHIPS
• *See page 127*

NASA MINNESOTA SPACE GRANT CONSORTIUM

http://www.aem.umn.edu/mnsgc

MINNESOTA SPACE GRANT CONSORTIUM SCHOLARSHIP PROGRAM
• *See page 127*

NASA MISSISSIPPI SPACE GRANT CONSORTIUM

http://www.olemiss.edu/programs/nasa

MISSISSIPPI SPACE GRANT CONSORTIUM SCHOLARSHIP
• *See page 127*

NASA MONTANA SPACE GRANT CONSORTIUM

http://www.spacegrant.montana.edu/

MONTANA SPACE GRANT SCHOLARSHIP PROGRAM
• *See page 128*

NASA RHODE ISLAND SPACE GRANT CONSORTIUM

http://ri.spacegrant.org/

NASA RHODE ISLAND SPACE GRANT CONSORTIUM UNDERGRADUATE RESEARCH SCHOLARSHIP
• *See page 128*

NASA RISGC SCIENCE EN ESPANOL SCHOLARSHIP FOR UNDERGRADUATE STUDENTS
• *See page 128*

NASA SOUTH CAROLINA SPACE GRANT CONSORTIUM

http://www.cofc.edu/~scsgrant

KATHRYN SULLIVAN SCIENCE AND ENGINEERING FELLOWSHIP
• *See page 128*

PRE-SERVICE TEACHER SCHOLARSHIP
• *See page 129*

UNDERGRADUATE RESEARCH AWARD PROGRAM
• *See page 129*

NASA SOUTH DAKOTA SPACE GRANT CONSORTIUM

http://www.sdspacegrant.sdsmt.edu/

SOUTH DAKOTA SPACE GRANT CONSORTIUM UNDERGRADUATE AND GRADUATE STUDENT SCHOLARSHIPS
• *See page 129*

NASA'S VIRGINIA SPACE GRANT CONSORTIUM

http://www.vsgc.odu.edu/

TEACHER EDUCATION STEM SCHOLARSHIP PROGRAM
• *See page 96*

VIRGINIA STEM COMMUNITY COLLEGE SCHOLARSHIPS
• *See page 96*

NASA WEST VIRGINIA SPACE GRANT CONSORTIUM

http://www.nasa.wvu.edu/

WEST VIRGINIA SPACE GRANT CONSORTIUM UNDERGRADUATE FELLOWSHIP PROGRAM
• *See page 129*

NATIONAL ACTION COUNCIL FOR MINORITIES IN ENGINEERING-NACME INC.

http://www.nacme.org/

NACME SCHOLARS PROGRAM

Renewable award for African-American, American-Indian, or Latino student enrolled in a baccalaureate engineering program. Must attend an ABET-accredited institution full-time and complete one semester with a minimum 2.7 GPA. Must be a U.S. citizen. Award money is given to participating institutions who select applicants and disperse funds. Check web site for details http://www.nacme.org.

Academic Fields/Career Goals: Engineering/Technology.

Award: Scholarship for use in freshman, sophomore, junior, or senior years; renewable. *Number:* varies. *Amount:* up to $5000.

Eligibility Requirements: Applicant must be American Indian/Alaska Native, Black (non-Hispanic), or Hispanic and enrolled or expecting to enroll full-time at a four-year institution or university. Available to U.S. citizens.

Application Requirements: Application, financial need analysis, references. *Deadline:* continuous.

Contact: Aileen M. Walter, Director, Scholar Management
National Action Council for Minorities in Engineering-NACME Inc.
440 Hamilton Avenue, Suite 302
White Plains, NY 10601
Phone: 914-539-4010

NATIONAL ASSOCIATION FOR THE ADVANCEMENT OF COLORED PEOPLE

http://www.naacp.org/

HUBERTUS W.V. WELLEMS SCHOLARSHIP FOR MALE STUDENTS
• *See page 167*

NATIONAL ASSOCIATION OF WATER COMPANIES-NEW JERSEY CHAPTER

http://www.nawc.org/

NATIONAL ASSOCIATION OF WATER COMPANIES-NEW JERSEY CHAPTER SCHOLARSHIP
• See page 142

NATIONAL ASSOCIATION OF WOMEN IN CONSTRUCTION

http://www.nawic.org/

NAWIC UNDERGRADUATE SCHOLARSHIPS
• See page 102

NATIONAL INVENTORS HALL OF FAME

http://www.invent.org/

COLLEGIATE INVENTORS COMPETITION FOR UNDERGRADUATE STUDENTS
• See page 96

COLLEGIATE INVENTORS COMPETITION-GRAND PRIZE
• See page 97

NATIONAL SCIENCE TEACHERS ASSOCIATION

http://www.nsta.org/

TOSHIBA/NSTA EXPLORAVISION AWARDS PROGRAM
• See page 198

NATIONAL SOCIETY OF PROFESSIONAL ENGINEERS

http://www.nspe.org/

MAUREEN L. AND HOWARD N. BLITMAN, PE SCHOLARSHIP TO PROMOTE DIVERSITY IN ENGINEERING
• See page 167

PAUL H. ROBBINS HONORARY SCHOLARSHIP
• See page 168

PROFESSIONAL ENGINEERS IN INDUSTRY SCHOLARSHIP
• See page 168

NATIONAL URBAN LEAGUE

http://www.nulbeep.org/

BLACK EXECUTIVE EXCHANGE PROGRAM JERRY BARTOW SCHOLARSHIP FUND
• See page 154

NEVADA NASA SPACE GRANT CONSORTIUM

http://www.nvspacegrant.org/

NATIONAL SPACE GRANT COLLEGE AND FELLOWSHIP PROGRAM
• See page 97

NEW MEXICO COMMISSION ON HIGHER EDUCATION

http://www.hed.state.nm.us/

MINORITY DOCTORAL ASSISTANCE LOAN-FOR-SERVICE PROGRAM
• See page 168

NEW YORK STATE EDUCATION DEPARTMENT

http://www.highered.nysed.gov/

REGENTS PROFESSIONAL OPPORTUNITY SCHOLARSHIP
• See page 69

OREGON STUDENT ASSISTANCE COMMISSION

http://www.GetCollegeFunds.org/

JEFFREY ALAN SCOGGINS MEMORIAL SCHOLARSHIP

Award for college junior or above for fall term/semester in undergraduate study at an Oregon four-year nonprofit college or university. Membership in the Sigma Chi fraternity is preferred. Recipients can reapply for additional year of funding, which may be used towards graduate study.

Academic Fields/Career Goals: Engineering/Technology.

Award: Scholarship for use in junior, senior, or graduate years; not renewable.

Eligibility Requirements: Applicant must be enrolled or expecting to enroll at a four-year institution or university and studying in Oregon. Applicant must have 3.0 GPA or higher.

Application Requirements: Application. *Deadline:* March 1.

Contact: Director of Grant Programs
Oregon Student Assistance Commission
1500 Valley River Drive, Suite 100
Eugene, OR 97401-7020
Phone: 800-452-8807

WILLIAM D. AND RUTH D. ROY SCHOLARSHIP

Scholarships available for Oregon high school graduates, home scholars, and GED recipients. Preference given to older, nontraditional students or students who are the first generation in their family to attend college. Must major in engineering and attend Portland State University or Oregon State University. Minimum 2.75 GPA required. Must enroll at least half-time. Must compete annually for renewal.

Academic Fields/Career Goals: Engineering/Technology.

Award: Scholarship for use in freshman, sophomore, junior, or senior years; not renewable. *Amount:* varies.

Eligibility Requirements: Applicant must be enrolled or expecting to enroll full- or part-time at a four-year institution or university; resident of Oregon and studying in Oregon. Available to U.S. citizens.

Application Requirements: Application, essay, financial need analysis, transcript, activities chart. *Deadline:* March 1.

Contact: Director of Grant Programs
Oregon Student Assistance Commission
1500 Valley River Drive, Suite 100
Eugene, OR 97401-7020
Phone: 800-452-8807 Ext. 7395

PENNSYLVANIA HIGHER EDUCATION ASSISTANCE AGENCY

http://www.pheaa.org/

NEW ECONOMY TECHNOLOGY AND SCITECH SCHOLARSHIPS
• See page 270

PLASTICS INSTITUTE OF AMERICA

http://www.plasticsinstitute.org/

PLASTICS PIONEERS SCHOLARSHIPS
• *See page 168*

PLUMBING-HEATING-COOLING CONTRACTORS EDUCATION FOUNDATION

http://www.foundation.phccweb.org/

DELTA FAUCET COMPANY SCHOLARSHIP PROGRAM
• *See page 103*

PHCC EDUCATIONAL FOUNDATION NEED-BASED SCHOLARSHIP
• *See page 155*

PHCC EDUCATIONAL FOUNDATION SCHOLARSHIP PROGRAM
• *See page 155*

PROFESSIONAL CONSTRUCTION ESTIMATORS ASSOCIATION

http://www.pcea.org/

TED WILSON MEMORIAL SCHOLARSHIP FOUNDATION
• *See page 179*

ROBERT H. MOLLOHAN FAMILY CHARITABLE FOUNDATION, INC.

http://www.mollohanfoundation.org/

HIGH TECHNOLOGY SCHOLARS PROGRAM
• *See page 143*

ROCKY MOUNTAIN COAL MINING INSTITUTE

http://www.rmcmi.org/

ROCKY MOUNTAIN COAL MINING INSTITUTE SCHOLARSHIP
• *See page 179*

SAN DIEGO FOUNDATION

http://www.sdfoundation.org/

ENERGY OF ACHIEVEMENT SDG&E SCHOLARSHIP
• *See page 156*

QUALCOMM SAN DIEGO SCIENCE, TECHNOLOGY, ENGINEERING, AND MATHEMATICS SCHOLARSHIP
Scholarship to provide financial assistance to students majoring in science, technology, engineering, or mathematics, and attending the University of California, San Diego, San Diego State University or California State University, San Marcos. Consideration will be given to students who have participated in extracurricular activities, community service or work experience. Scholarship may be renewable for up to four years provided students adhere to the terms and conditions.

Academic Fields/Career Goals: Engineering/Technology; Mathematics; Science, Technology, and Society.

Award: Scholarship for use in freshman, sophomore, junior, or senior years; renewable. *Number:* 5. *Amount:* $2500.

Eligibility Requirements: Applicant must be enrolled or expecting to enroll full-time at an institution or university; resident of California and studying in California. Applicant or parent of applicant must have employment or volunteer experience in community service. Applicant must have 3.5 GPA or higher. Available to U.S. citizens.

Application Requirements: Application, financial need analysis, references, transcript, personal statement, copy of tax return. *Deadline:* January 26.

Contact: Shryl Helvie, Scholarship Coordinator
San Diego Foundation
2508 Historic Decatur Road, Suite 200.
San Diego, CA 92106
Phone: 619-814-1307
Fax: 619-239-1710
E-mail: shryl@sdfoundation.org

SEMICONDUCTOR RESEARCH CORPORATION (SRC)

http://www.src.org/

MASTER'S SCHOLARSHIP PROGRAM
• *See page 169*

SIGMA XI, THE SCIENTIFIC RESEARCH SOCIETY

http://www.sigmaxi.org/

SIGMA XI GRANTS-IN-AID OF RESEARCH
• *See page 87*

SIMPLEHUMAN

http://www.simplehuman.com/

SIMPLE SOLUTIONS DESIGN COMPETITION
• *See page 271*

SOCIETY FOR IMAGING SCIENCE AND TECHNOLOGY

http://www.imaging.org/

RAYMOND DAVIS SCHOLARSHIP
Award available to an undergraduate junior or senior or graduate student enrolled full-time in an accredited program of photographic, imaging science or engineering. Minimum award is $1000. Applications processed between October 15 and December 15 only.

Academic Fields/Career Goals: Engineering/Technology; Physical Sciences.

Award: Scholarship for use in junior, senior, or graduate years; renewable. *Number:* 1–2. *Amount:* $1000.

Eligibility Requirements: Applicant must be enrolled or expecting to enroll full-time at a four-year institution or university. Available to U.S. and non-U.S. citizens.

Application Requirements: Application, references, transcript. *Deadline:* October 1.

Contact: Donna Smith, Executive Assistant
Society for Imaging Science and Technology
7003 Kilworth Lane
Springfield, VA 22151
Phone: 703-642-9090 Ext. 17
Fax: 703-642-9094
E-mail: info@imaging.org

SOCIETY OF AUTOMOTIVE ENGINEERS

http://www.sae.org/

BMW/SAE ENGINEERING SCHOLARSHIP
• *See page 132*

DETROIT SECTION SAE TECHNICAL SCHOLARSHIP
• *See page 271*

EDWARD D. HENDRICKSON/SAE ENGINEERING SCHOLARSHIP
• *See page 132*

FRED M. YOUNG SR./SAE ENGINEERING SCHOLARSHIP

Scholarship of $4000 awarded at $1000 per year for four years. Applicants must have a 3.75 GPA, rank in the 90th percentile in both math and critical reading on SAT or composite ACT scores, and pursue an engineering degree accredited by ABET. A 3.0 GPA and continued engineering enrollment must be maintained to renew the scholarship.

Academic Fields/Career Goals: Engineering/Technology.

Award: Scholarship for use in freshman year; renewable. *Number:* 1. *Amount:* $1000.

Eligibility Requirements: Applicant must be high school student and planning to enroll or expecting to enroll full-time at a four-year institution or university. Available to U.S. citizens.

Application Requirements: Application, essay, test scores, transcript. *Deadline:* December 15.

Contact: Connie Harnish, SAE Educational Relations
Society of Automotive Engineers
400 Commonwealth Drive
Warrendale, PA 15096
Phone: 724-772-4047
E-mail: connie@sae.org

RALPH K. HILLQUIST HONORARY SAE SCHOLARSHIP
• *See page 271*

SAE BALTIMORE SECTION BILL BRUBAKER SCHOLARSHIP

Nonrenewable scholarship for any family member of a Baltimore SAE member, or any high school senior accepted to an engineering program at a Maryland university.

Academic Fields/Career Goals: Engineering/Technology.

Award: Scholarship for use in freshman year; not renewable. *Number:* 1. *Amount:* up to $1000.

Eligibility Requirements: Applicant must be high school student; planning to enroll or expecting to enroll full-time at an institution or university and studying in Maryland. Applicant or parent of applicant must be member of Society of Automotive Engineers. Available to U.S. citizens.

Application Requirements: Application, essay, resume, transcript. *Deadline:* May 10.

Contact: Marguerite Milligan, Marketing Assistant
Society of Automotive Engineers
400 Commonwealth Drive
Warrendale, PA 15096-0001
Phone: 724-772-7158
Fax: 724-776-3049
E-mail: customerservice@sae.org

SAE LONG TERM MEMBER SPONSORED SCHOLARSHIP

The scholarship recognizes outstanding SAE student members who actively support SAE and its activities. Applications may be submitted by the student or by the SAE faculty advisor, an SAE Section officer or a community leader. The student must be a junior who will be entering the senior year of undergraduate engineering studies. Number of award varies.

Academic Fields/Career Goals: Engineering/Technology.

Award: Scholarship for use in senior year; not renewable. *Number:* varies. *Amount:* $1000.

Eligibility Requirements: Applicant must be enrolled or expecting to enroll full-time at a four-year institution or university. Applicant or parent of applicant must be member of Society of Automotive Engineers. Available to U.S. citizens.

Application Requirements: Application, references. *Deadline:* April 1.

Contact: Connie Harnish, SAE Educational Relations
Society of Automotive Engineers
400 Commonwealth Drive
Warrendale, PA 15096
Phone: 724-772-4047
E-mail: connie@sae.org

SAE WILLIAM G. BELFREY MEMORIAL GRANT
• *See page 271*

TAU BETA PI/SAE ENGINEERING SCHOLARSHIP

Six scholarships valued at $1000 each will be awarded for the freshman year only. Applicants must have a 3.75 GPA, rank in the 90th percentile in both math and critical reading for SAT scores or for composite ACT scores, and pursue an engineering program accredited by the engineering accreditation commission of the Accreditation Board for Engineering and Technology.

Academic Fields/Career Goals: Engineering/Technology.

Award: Scholarship for use in freshman year; not renewable. *Number:* 6. *Amount:* $1000.

Eligibility Requirements: Applicant must be high school student and planning to enroll or expecting to enroll full- or part-time at a four-year institution or university. Available to U.S. citizens.

Application Requirements: Application, essay, test scores, transcript. *Deadline:* December 15.

Contact: Connie Harnish, SAE Educational Relations
Society of Automotive Engineers
400 Commonwealth Drive
Warrendale, PA 15096
Phone: 724-772-4047
E-mail: connie@sae.org

TMC/SAE DONALD D. DAWSON TECHNICAL SCHOLARSHIP
• *See page 133*

YANMAR/SAE SCHOLARSHIP
• *See page 271*

SOCIETY OF HISPANIC PROFESSIONAL ENGINEERS

http://www.shpe.org/

AHETEMS SCHOLARSHIPS

Merit-based and need-based scholarships are awarded, in the amount of $1000 to $5000 to high school graduating seniors, undergraduate students, and graduate students who demonstrate both significant motivation and aptitude for a career in science, technology, engineering or mathematics. Must have a minimum GPA of 3.0 (for high school seniors and undergraduates) and 3.25 for graduate students.

Academic Fields/Career Goals: Engineering/Technology; Mathematics; Science, Technology, and Society.

Award: Scholarship for use in freshman, sophomore, junior, senior, or graduate years; not renewable. *Number:* up to 100. *Amount:* $1000–$5000.

Eligibility Requirements: Applicant must be enrolled or expecting to enroll full-time at a two-year or four-year or technical institution or university. Applicant must have 3.0 GPA or higher. Available to U.S. and non-U.S. citizens.

Application Requirements: Application, references, transcript, personal statement. *Deadline:* April 1.

Contact: Rafaela Schwan, AHETEMS Office
Society of Hispanic Professional Engineers
The University of Texas at Arlington, College of Engineering,
PO Box 19019
Arlington, TX 76019-0019
Phone: 817-272-0776
Fax: 817-272-2548
E-mail: rschwan@shpe.org

SOCIETY OF HISPANIC PROFESSIONAL ENGINEERS FOUNDATION

http://www.henaac.org/

SOCIETY OF HISPANIC PROFESSIONAL ENGINEERS FOUNDATION
• *See page 169*

SOCIETY OF MANUFACTURING ENGINEERS EDUCATION FOUNDATION

http://www.smeef.org/

ALBERT E. WISCHMEYER MEMORIAL SCHOLARSHIP AWARD

Applicants must be residents of Western New York State, graduating high school seniors or current undergraduate students enrolled in an accredited degree program in manufacturing engineering, manufacturing engineering technology or mechanical technology in New York. Must have an GPA of 3.0.

Academic Fields/Career Goals: Engineering/Technology.

Award: Scholarship for use in freshman, sophomore, junior, or senior years; not renewable. *Number:* 1–10. *Amount:* $1000–$5000.

Eligibility Requirements: Applicant must be enrolled or expecting to enroll full-time at a four-year institution or university; resident of New York and studying in New York. Applicant must have 3.0 GPA or higher. Available to U.S. citizens.

Application Requirements: Application, essay, resume, references, transcript. *Deadline:* February 1.

Contact: Society of Manufacturing Engineers Education Foundation
One SME Drive
PO Box 930
Dearborn, MI 48121-0930
Phone: 313-425-3300
E-mail: foundation@sme.org

ARTHUR AND GLADYS CERVENKA SCHOLARSHIP AWARD

One-time award to full-time students enrolled in a degree program in manufacturing engineering or technology. Preference given to students attending a Florida institution. Minimum 3.0 GPA required.

Academic Fields/Career Goals: Engineering/Technology.

Award: Scholarship for use in freshman, sophomore, junior, or senior years; not renewable. *Number:* 1–10. *Amount:* $1000–$5000.

Eligibility Requirements: Applicant must be enrolled or expecting to enroll full-time at a four-year institution or university. Applicant must have 3.0 GPA or higher. Available to U.S. citizens.

Application Requirements: Application, essay, resume, references, transcript. *Deadline:* February 1.

Contact: Society of Manufacturing Engineers Education Foundation
One SME Drive
PO Box 930
Dearborn, MI 48121-0930
Phone: 313-425-3300
E-mail: foundation@sme.org

CATERPILLAR SCHOLARS AWARD FUND

Supports five one-time scholarships for full-time students enrolled in a manufacturing engineering program. Minority applicants may apply as incoming freshmen. Applicants must have an overall minimum GPA of 3.0.

Academic Fields/Career Goals: Engineering/Technology.

Award: Scholarship for use in freshman, sophomore, junior, or senior years; not renewable. *Number:* 1–15. *Amount:* $1000–$5000.

Eligibility Requirements: Applicant must be enrolled or expecting to enroll full-time at a four-year institution or university. Applicant must have 3.0 GPA or higher. Available to U.S. and Canadian citizens.

Application Requirements: Application, essay, resume, references, transcript. *Deadline:* February 1.

Contact: Society of Manufacturing Engineers Education Foundation
One SME Drive
PO Box 930
Dearborn, MI 48121-0930
Phone: 313-425-3300
E-mail: foundation@sme.org

CHAPTER 3-PEORIA ENDOWED SCHOLARSHIP

Applicants must be seeking a bachelor's degree in manufacturing engineering, industrial engineering, manufacturing technology, or a manufacturing-related degree program at either Bradley University (Peoria, Illinois) or Illinois State University (Normal, Illinois).

Academic Fields/Career Goals: Engineering/Technology.

Award: Scholarship for use in freshman, sophomore, or junior years; not renewable. *Number:* up to 5. *Amount:* $1000–$5000.

Eligibility Requirements: Applicant must be enrolled or expecting to enroll full-time at a two-year or four-year or technical institution or university; resident of Illinois and studying in Illinois. Applicant must have 3.0 GPA or higher. Available to U.S. and Canadian citizens.

Application Requirements: Application, essay, resume, references, test scores, transcript. *Deadline:* February 1.

Contact: Society of Manufacturing Engineers Education Foundation
One SME Drive
PO Box 930
Dearborn, MI 48121-0930
Phone: 313-425-3300
E-mail: foundation@sme.org

CHAPTER 4-LAWRENCE A. WACKER MEMORIAL SCHOLARSHIP

Awards available to full-time students enrolled in or accepted to a degree program in manufacturing, mechanical or industrial engineering at a college or university in the state of Wisconsin. One scholarship will be granted to a graduating high school senior and the other will be granted to a current undergraduate student. Minimum GPA of 3.0 required.

Academic Fields/Career Goals: Engineering/Technology; Mechanical Engineering.

Award: Scholarship for use in freshman, sophomore, junior, or senior years; not renewable. *Number:* 1–10. *Amount:* $1000–$5000.

Eligibility Requirements: Applicant must be enrolled or expecting to enroll full-time at a four-year institution or university and studying in Wisconsin. Applicant must have 3.0 GPA or higher. Available to U.S. citizens.

Application Requirements: Application, essay, resume, references, transcript. *Deadline:* February 1.

Contact: Society of Manufacturing Engineers Education Foundation
One SME Drive
PO Box 930
Dearborn, MI 48121-0930
Phone: 313-425-3300
E-mail: foundation@sme.org

CHAPTER 6-FAIRFIELD COUNTY SCHOLARSHIP

Scholarship applicants must be full-time undergraduate students enrolled in a degree program in manufacturing engineering, technology, or a closely related field in the United States or Canada. Preference is given to residents of, or students studying in, the eastern part of the United States.

Academic Fields/Career Goals: Engineering/Technology.

Award: Scholarship for use in freshman, sophomore, or junior years; not renewable. *Number:* up to 4. *Amount:* $1000–$5000.

Eligibility Requirements: Applicant must be enrolled or expecting to enroll full-time at a two-year or four-year or technical institution. Applicant must have 3.0 GPA or higher. Available to U.S. and Canadian citizens.

Application Requirements: Application, essay, resume, references, test scores, transcript. *Deadline:* February 1.

Contact: Society of Manufacturing Engineers Education Foundation
One SME Drive
PO Box 930
Dearborn, MI 48121-0930
Phone: 313-425-3300
E-mail: foundation@sme.org

CHAPTER 17-ST. LOUIS SCHOLARSHIP

Scholarship will be given to full-time or part-time students enrolled in a manufacturing engineering, industrial technology, or other related program. Must study in Missouri or Illinois. Minimum of 2.5 GPA is required.

Academic Fields/Career Goals: Engineering/Technology.

Award: Scholarship for use in freshman, sophomore, junior, or senior years; not renewable. *Number:* varies. *Amount:* varies.

Eligibility Requirements: Applicant must be enrolled or expecting to enroll full-time at a four-year institution or university and studying in Illinois or Missouri. Applicant must have 2.5 GPA or higher. Available to U.S. and Canadian citizens.

Application Requirements: Application, essay, resume, references, transcript. *Deadline:* February 1.

Contact: Society of Manufacturing Engineers Education Foundation
One SME Drive
PO Box 930
Dearborn, MI 48121-0930
Phone: 313-425-3300
E-mail: foundation@sme.org

CHAPTER 23-QUAD CITIES IOWA/ILLINOIS SCHOLARSHIP

Scholarship applicant must be entering freshman or current undergraduate student pursuing a bachelor's degree in manufacturing engineering or a related field at an accredited college or university in Iowa or Illinois.

Academic Fields/Career Goals: Engineering/Technology.

Award: Scholarship for use in freshman, sophomore, or junior years; not renewable. *Number:* up to 5. *Amount:* $1000–$5000.

Eligibility Requirements: Applicant must be enrolled or expecting to enroll full-time at a four-year institution or university and studying in Illinois or Iowa. Available to U.S. and Canadian citizens.

Application Requirements: Application, essay, resume, references, test scores, transcript. *Deadline:* February 1.

Contact: Society of Manufacturing Engineers Education Foundation
One SME Drive
PO Box 930
Dearborn, MI 48121-0930
Phone: 313-425-3300
E-mail: foundation@sme.org

CHAPTER 31-TRI CITY SCHOLARSHIP

Applicants must be seeking a bachelor's degree in manufacturing, mechanical, or industrial engineering, engineering technology, industrial technology or closely related field of study. Must be enrolled in or plan to attend an accredited college or university in the state of Michigan.

Academic Fields/Career Goals: Engineering/Technology.

Award: Scholarship for use in freshman, sophomore, junior, or senior years; not renewable. *Number:* up to 5. *Amount:* $1000–$5000.

Eligibility Requirements: Applicant must be enrolled or expecting to enroll full-time at a two-year or four-year or technical institution or university and studying in Michigan. Applicant must have 3.0 GPA or higher. Available to U.S. and Canadian citizens.

Application Requirements: Application, essay, resume, test scores, transcript. *Deadline:* February 1.

Contact: Society of Manufacturing Engineers Education Foundation
One SME Drive
PO Box 930
Dearborn, MI 48121-0930
Phone: 313-425-3300
E-mail: foundation@sme.org

CHAPTER 63-PORTLAND JAMES E. MORROW SCHOLARSHIP

Applicants must be pursuing a career in manufacturing or a related field. Preference will be given to students planning to attend Oregon or southwest Washington schools. Preference will also be given to applicants who reside within the states of Oregon or southwest Washington.

Academic Fields/Career Goals: Engineering/Technology.

Award: Scholarship for use in freshman, sophomore, or junior years; not renewable. *Number:* up to 5. *Amount:* $1000–$5000.

Eligibility Requirements: Applicant must be enrolled or expecting to enroll full-time at a two-year or four-year or technical institution or university; resident of Oregon or Washington and studying in Oregon or Washington. Available to U.S. and Canadian citizens.

Application Requirements: Application, essay, resume, references, test scores, transcript. *Deadline:* February 1.

Contact: Society of Manufacturing Engineers Education Foundation
One SME Drive
PO Box 930
Dearborn, MI 48121-0930
Phone: 313-425-3300
E-mail: foundation@sme.org

CHAPTER 63-PORTLAND UNCLE BUD SMITH SCHOLARSHIP

Applicants must be pursuing a career in manufacturing or a related field. Preference will be given to students planning to attend Oregon or southwest Washington schools. Preference will also be given to applicants who reside within the states of Oregon or southwest Washington.

Academic Fields/Career Goals: Engineering/Technology.

Award: Scholarship for use in freshman, sophomore, or junior years; not renewable. *Number:* up to 5. *Amount:* $1000–$5000.

Eligibility Requirements: Applicant must be enrolled or expecting to enroll full-time at a two-year or four-year or technical institution or university; resident of Oregon or Washington and studying in Oregon or Washington. Available to U.S. and Canadian citizens.

Application Requirements: Application, essay, resume, references, test scores, transcript. *Deadline:* February 1.

Contact: Society of Manufacturing Engineers Education Foundation
One SME Drive
PO Box 930
Dearborn, MI 48121-0930
Phone: 313-425-3300
E-mail: foundation@sme.org

CHAPTER 67-PHOENIX SCHOLARSHIP

Award for a high school senior who plans on enrolling in a manufacturing program technology or manufacturing technology program or an undergraduate student enrolled in a manufacturing engineering technology, manufacturing technology, industrial technology, or closely related program at an accredited college or university in Arizona. Applicants must have an overall GPA of 2.5. Scholarship ranges from $1000 to $5000.

Academic Fields/Career Goals: Engineering/Technology; Industrial Design; Mechanical Engineering; Trade/Technical Specialties.

Award: Scholarship for use in freshman, sophomore, junior, or senior years; not renewable. *Number:* 1–5. *Amount:* $1000–$5000.

Eligibility Requirements: Applicant must be enrolled or expecting to enroll full-time at a two-year or four-year institution or university and studying in Arizona. Applicant must have 2.5 GPA or higher. Available to U.S. citizens.

Application Requirements: Application, essay, resume, references, test scores, transcript. *Deadline:* February 1.

Contact: Society of Manufacturing Engineers Education Foundation
One SME Drive
PO Box 930
Dearborn, MI 48121-0930
Phone: 313-425-3300
E-mail: foundation@sme.org

CHAPTER 93-ALBUQUERQUE SCHOLARSHIP

Scholarship to students entering freshmen or current undergraduate students pursuing a bachelor's degree in manufacturing engineering or a related field who plan to or are attending an accredited college or university in New Mexico.

Academic Fields/Career Goals: Engineering/Technology.

Award: Scholarship for use in freshman, sophomore, junior, or senior years; not renewable. *Number:* 1–5. *Amount:* $1000–$5000.

Eligibility Requirements: Applicant must be enrolled or expecting to enroll full-time at a four-year institution or university and studying in New Mexico. Available to U.S. citizens.

Application Requirements: Application, essay, resume, references, test scores, transcript. *Deadline:* February 1.

Contact: Society of Manufacturing Engineers Education Foundation
One SME Drive
PO Box 930
Dearborn, MI 48121-0930
Phone: 313-425-3300
E-mail: foundation@sme.org

CHAPTER 198-DOWNRIVER DETROIT SCHOLARSHIP

One-time award for an individual seeking an associates degree, bachelor's degree, or graduate degree in manufacturing, mechanical or industrial engineering, engineering technology, or industrial technology at an accredited public or private college or university in Michigan. Must have a minimum GPA of 2.5. Preference is given to applicants who are a child or grandchild of a current SME Downriver Chapter No. 198 member, a member of its student chapter, or a Michigan resident.

Academic Fields/Career Goals: Engineering/Technology; Industrial Design; Mechanical Engineering; Trade/Technical Specialties.

Award: Scholarship for use in freshman, sophomore, junior, senior, or graduate years; not renewable. *Number:* 1–5. *Amount:* $1000–$5000.

Eligibility Requirements: Applicant must be enrolled or expecting to enroll full-time at a two-year or four-year institution or university and studying in Michigan. Applicant must have 2.5 GPA or higher. Available to U.S. citizens.

Application Requirements: Application, essay, resume, references, test scores, transcript, student statement letter. *Deadline:* February 1.

Contact: Society of Manufacturing Engineers Education Foundation
One SME Drive
PO Box 930
Dearborn, MI 48121-0930
Phone: 313-425-3300
E-mail: foundation@sme.org

CLARENCE AND JOSEPHINE MYERS SCHOLARSHIP

Applicants must be an undergraduate or graduate student pursuing a degree in engineering or a manufacturing-related field at a college within the state of Indiana.

Academic Fields/Career Goals: Engineering/Technology.

Award: Scholarship for use in freshman, sophomore, junior, or senior years; not renewable. *Number:* up to 5. *Amount:* $1000–$5000.

Eligibility Requirements: Applicant must be enrolled or expecting to enroll full-time at a two-year or four-year or technical institution or university and studying in Indiana. Available to U.S. and Canadian citizens.

Application Requirements: Application, essay, references, test scores, transcript. *Deadline:* February 1.

Contact: Society of Manufacturing Engineers Education Foundation
One SME Drive
PO Box 930
Dearborn, MI 48121-0930
Phone: 313-425-3300
E-mail: foundation@sme.org

CLINTON J. HELTON MANUFACTURING SCHOLARSHIP AWARD FUND

One-time award to full-time students enrolled in a degree program in manufacturing engineering or technology at one of the following institutions: Colorado State University, University of Colorado–all campuses. Applicants must possess an overall minimum GPA of 3.3.

Academic Fields/Career Goals: Engineering/Technology; Trade/Technical Specialties.

Award: Scholarship for use in freshman, sophomore, junior, or senior years; not renewable. *Number:* 1–5. *Amount:* $1000–$5000.

Eligibility Requirements: Applicant must be enrolled or expecting to enroll full-time at a four-year institution or university and studying in Colorado. Available to U.S. citizens.

Application Requirements: Application, essay, references, test scores, transcript. *Deadline:* February 1.

Contact: Society of Manufacturing Engineers Education Foundation
One SME Drive
PO Box 930
Dearborn, MI 48121-0930
Phone: 313-425-3300
E-mail: foundation@sme.org

CONNIE AND ROBERT T. GUNTER SCHOLARSHIP

One-time award will be given for full-time undergraduate students enrolled in a degree program in manufacturing engineering or technology. Minimum 3.5 GPA is required. Must study in Georgia.

Academic Fields/Career Goals: Engineering/Technology.

Award: Scholarship for use in freshman, sophomore, junior, or senior years; not renewable. *Number:* 1–5. *Amount:* $1000–$5000.

Eligibility Requirements: Applicant must be enrolled or expecting to enroll full-time at a four-year institution or university and studying in Georgia. Applicant must have 3.5 GPA or higher. Available to U.S. citizens.

Application Requirements: Application, essay, resume, references, transcript. *Deadline:* February 1.

Contact: Society of Manufacturing Engineers Education Foundation
One SME Drive
PO Box 930
Dearborn, MI 48121-0930
Phone: 313-425-3300
E-mail: foundation@sme.org

DETROIT CHAPTER ONE-FOUNDING CHAPTER SCHOLARSHIP

Several awards will be available in each of the following: associate degree and equivalent, baccalaureate degree and graduate degree programs. Minimum GPA of 3.5 is required. Preference given to undergraduate or graduate student enrolled in a manufacturing engineering or technology program at one of the sponsored institutions.

Academic Fields/Career Goals: Engineering/Technology.

Award: Scholarship for use in freshman, sophomore, junior, senior, or graduate years; not renewable. *Number:* 3. *Amount:* $1000.

Eligibility Requirements: Applicant must be enrolled or expecting to enroll full- or part-time at a two-year or four-year institution or university and studying in Michigan. Applicant must have 3.5 GPA or higher. Available to U.S. citizens.

Application Requirements: Application, references. *Deadline:* February 1.

Contact: Society of Manufacturing Engineers Education Foundation
One SME Drive
PO Box 930
Dearborn, MI 48121-0930
Phone: 313-425-3300
E-mail: foundation@sme.org

DIRECTOR'S SCHOLARSHIP AWARD

Scholarship award for full-time undergraduate students enrolled in a manufacturing or related degree program in the United States or Canada. Preference will be given to students who demonstrate leadership skills in a community, academic, or professional environment. Average GPA of 3.5 required.

Academic Fields/Career Goals: Engineering/Technology.

Award: Scholarship for use in freshman, sophomore, junior, or senior years; not renewable. *Number:* 1–5. *Amount:* $1000–$10,000.

Eligibility Requirements: Applicant must be enrolled or expecting to enroll full-time at a four-year institution or university and must have an interest in leadership. Applicant must have 3.5 GPA or higher. Available to U.S. and Canadian citizens.

Application Requirements: Application, essay, resume, references, transcript. *Deadline:* February 1.

Contact: Society of Manufacturing Engineers Education Foundation
One SME Drive
PO Box 930
Dearborn, MI 48121-0930
Phone: 313-425-3300
E-mail: foundation@sme.org

EDWARD S. ROTH MANUFACTURING ENGINEERING SCHOLARSHIP

Award to a graduating high school senior, a current full-time undergraduate or graduate student enrolled in an accredited four-year degree program in manufacturing engineering at a sponsored ABET-accredited school. Minimum GPA of 3.0 and be a U.S. citizen.

Academic Fields/Career Goals: Engineering/Technology.

Award: Scholarship for use in freshman, sophomore, junior, senior, or graduate years; not renewable. *Number:* 1–10. *Amount:* $1000–$5000.

Eligibility Requirements: Applicant must be enrolled or expecting to enroll full-time at a four-year institution or university and studying in California, Florida, Illinois, Massachusetts, Minnesota, Ohio, Texas, or Utah. Applicant must have 3.0 GPA or higher. Available to U.S. citizens.

Application Requirements: Application, interview, resume, references, transcript. *Deadline:* February 1.

Contact: Society of Manufacturing Engineers Education Foundation
One SME Drive
PO Box 930
Dearborn, MI 48121-0930
Phone: 313-425-3300
E-mail: foundation@sme.org

E. WAYNE KAY COMMUNITY COLLEGE SCHOLARSHIP AWARD

One-time award to full-time students enrolled at an accredited community college or trade school which offers programs in manufacturing or closely related field in the United States or Canada. Minimum GPA of 3.0 required. Scholarship applicants may be entering freshmen or sophomore students with less than 60 college credit hours completed and be seeking a career in manufacturing engineering or technology.

Academic Fields/Career Goals: Engineering/Technology; Trade/Technical Specialties.

Award: Scholarship for use in freshman or sophomore years; not renewable. *Number:* 1–20. *Amount:* $1000–$10,000.

Eligibility Requirements: Applicant must be enrolled or expecting to enroll full-time at a two-year or four-year or technical institution or university. Applicant must have 3.0 GPA or higher. Available to U.S. and Canadian citizens.

Application Requirements: Application, essay, resume, references, transcript. *Deadline:* February 1.

Contact: Society of Manufacturing Engineers Education Foundation
One SME Drive
PO Box 930
Dearborn, MI 48121-0930
Phone: 313-425-3300
E-mail: foundation@sme.org

E. WAYNE KAY CO-OP SCHOLARSHIP

Scholarship will be awarded for graduating high school senior or full-time undergraduate student enrolled in a degree program in manufacturing or a closely related field at a two year Community College or trade school in the United States or Canada. Average of 3.0 GPA is required.

Academic Fields/Career Goals: Engineering/Technology.

Award: Scholarship for use in freshman, sophomore, junior, or senior years; not renewable. *Number:* 1–10. *Amount:* $1000–$5000.

Eligibility Requirements: Applicant must be enrolled or expecting to enroll full-time at a two-year or four-year or technical institution or university. Applicant must have 3.0 GPA or higher. Available to U.S. and non-U.S. citizens.

Application Requirements: Application, essay, resume, references, transcript. *Deadline:* February 1.

Contact: Society of Manufacturing Engineers Education Foundation
One SME Drive
PO Box 930
Dearborn, MI 48121-0930
Phone: 313-425-3300
E-mail: foundation@sme.org

E. WAYNE KAY HIGH SCHOOL SCHOLARSHIP

Scholarship available for student enrolled full-time in manufacturing engineering or technology program at an accredited college or university. Minimum 3.0 GPA required.

Academic Fields/Career Goals: Engineering/Technology.

Award: Scholarship for use in freshman, sophomore, junior, or senior years; renewable. *Number:* 1–20. *Amount:* $1000–$2500.

Eligibility Requirements: Applicant must be enrolled or expecting to enroll full-time at a four-year institution or university. Applicant must have 3.0 GPA or higher. Available to U.S. and Canadian citizens.

Application Requirements: Application, essay, references, test scores, transcript. *Deadline:* February 1.

Contact: Society of Manufacturing Engineers Education Foundation
One SME Drive
PO Box 930
Dearborn, MI 48121-0930
Phone: 313-425-3300
E-mail: foundation@sme.org

E. WAYNE KAY SCHOLARSHIP

Scholarship for full-time undergraduate students enrolled in a degree program in manufacturing engineering, technology, or a closely related field in the United States or Canada. Minimum of 3.0 GPA is required.

Academic Fields/Career Goals: Engineering/Technology; Trade/Technical Specialties.

Award: Scholarship for use in freshman, sophomore, junior, or senior years; not renewable. *Number:* 10–30. *Amount:* $2500–$7500.

Eligibility Requirements: Applicant must be enrolled or expecting to enroll full-time at a four-year institution or university. Applicant must have 3.0 GPA or higher. Available to U.S. and Canadian citizens.

Application Requirements: Application, essay, resume, references, test scores, transcript. *Deadline:* February 1.

Contact: Society of Manufacturing Engineers Education Foundation
One SME Drive
PO Box 930
Dearborn, MI 48121-0930
Phone: 313-425-3300
E-mail: foundation@sme.org

FORT WAYNE CHAPTER 56 SCHOLARSHIP

One-time award for an individual seeking an associates degree, bachelor's degree, or graduate degree in manufacturing, mechanical or industrial engineering, engineering technology, or industrial technology at an accredited public or private college or university in Indiana. Must have a minimum GPA of 2.5. Preference given to applicants who are a child or grandchild of a current SME Fort Wayne Chapter No. 56 member, a member of its student chapter, or an Indiana resident.

Academic Fields/Career Goals: Engineering/Technology; Industrial Design; Mechanical Engineering; Trade/Technical Specialties.

Award: Scholarship for use in freshman, sophomore, junior, senior, or graduate years; not renewable. *Number:* 1–10. *Amount:* $1000–$5000.

Eligibility Requirements: Applicant must be enrolled or expecting to enroll full-time at a two-year or four-year institution or university and studying in Indiana. Applicant must have 2.5 GPA or higher. Available to U.S. citizens.

Application Requirements: Application, essay, resume, references, transcript. *Deadline:* February 1.

Contact: Society of Manufacturing Engineers Education Foundation
One SME Drive
PO Box 930
Dearborn, MI 48121-0930
Phone: 313-425-3300
E-mail: foundation@sme.org

GUILIANO MAZZETTI SCHOLARSHIP AWARD

One-time award available to full-time students enrolled in a degree program in manufacturing engineering or technology in the United States or Canada. Minimum GPA of 3.0 required.

Academic Fields/Career Goals: Engineering/Technology.

Award: Scholarship for use in freshman, sophomore, junior, or senior years; not renewable. *Number:* 1–10. *Amount:* $1000–$5000.

Eligibility Requirements: Applicant must be enrolled or expecting to enroll full-time at a four-year institution or university. Applicant must have 3.0 GPA or higher. Available to U.S. and Canadian citizens.

Application Requirements: Application, essay, resume, references, transcript. *Deadline:* February 1.

Contact: Society of Manufacturing Engineers Education Foundation
One SME Drive
PO Box 930
Dearborn, MI 48121-0930
Phone: 313-425-3300
E-mail: foundation@sme.org

LUCILE B. KAUFMAN WOMEN'S SCHOLARSHIP

Scholarships available for female full-time undergraduate students enrolled in a degree program in manufacturing engineering, technology or a closely related field in the United States or Canada. Minimum of 3.0 GPA is required. Scholarship value and the number of awards granted varies.

Academic Fields/Career Goals: Engineering/Technology.

Award: Scholarship for use in freshman, sophomore, junior, or senior years; not renewable. *Number:* 1–5. *Amount:* $1000–$5000.

Eligibility Requirements: Applicant must be enrolled or expecting to enroll full-time at a four-year institution or university and female. Applicant must have 3.0 GPA or higher. Available to U.S. and Canadian citizens.

Application Requirements: Application, essay, resume, references, transcript. *Deadline:* February 1.

Contact: Society of Manufacturing Engineers Education Foundation
One SME Drive
PO Box 930
Dearborn, MI 48121-0930
Phone: 313-425-3300
E-mail: foundation@sme.org

MYRTLE AND EARL WALKER SCHOLARSHIP FUND
• *See page 272*

NORTH CENTRAL REGION 9 SCHOLARSHIP

Award to a full-time student enrolled in a manufacturing, mechanical, or industrial engineering degree program in North Central Region 9 (Iowa, Minnesota, Nebraska, North Dakota, South Dakota, Wisconsin, and the upper peninsula of Michigan). Applicants must have a 3.0 GPA.

Academic Fields/Career Goals: Engineering/Technology; Industrial Design; Mechanical Engineering; Trade/Technical Specialties.

Award: Scholarship for use in freshman, sophomore, junior, or senior years; not renewable. *Number:* 1–10. *Amount:* $1000–$5000.

Eligibility Requirements: Applicant must be enrolled or expecting to enroll full-time at a four-year institution or university and studying in Iowa, Michigan, Minnesota, Nebraska, North Dakota, South Dakota, or Wisconsin. Applicant must have 3.0 GPA or higher. Available to U.S. citizens.

Application Requirements: Application, essay, resume, references, transcript. *Deadline:* February 1.

Contact: Society of Manufacturing Engineers Education Foundation
One SME Drive
PO Box 930
Dearborn, MI 48121-0930
Phone: 313-425-3300
E-mail: foundation@sme.org

SME FAMILY SCHOLARSHIP

Scholarships awarded to children or grandchildren of Society of Manufacturing Engineers members. Must be graduating high school senior planning to pursue full-time studies for an undergraduate degree in manufacturing engineering, manufacturing engineering technology, or a closely related engineering study at an accredited college or university. Minimum GPA of 3.0 required. Scholarship value and the number of awards granted varies annually.

Academic Fields/Career Goals: Engineering/Technology.

Award: Scholarship for use in freshman, sophomore, junior, or senior years; renewable. *Number:* 1–10. *Amount:* $5000–$80,000.

Eligibility Requirements: Applicant must be enrolled or expecting to enroll full-time at a four-year institution or university. Applicant must have 3.0 GPA or higher. Available to U.S. and non-U.S. citizens.

Application Requirements: Application, essay, interview, photo, resume, references, test scores, transcript. *Deadline:* February 1.

Contact: Society of Manufacturing Engineers Education Foundation
One SME Drive
PO Box 930
Dearborn, MI 48121-0930
Phone: 313-425-3300
E-mail: foundation@sme.org

WALT BARTRAM MEMORIAL EDUCATION AWARD

Scholarship available for graduating high school seniors who commit to enroll in, or full-time college or university students pursuing a degree in, manufacturing engineering or a closely related field within the areas of New Mexico, Arizona or Southern California.

Academic Fields/Career Goals: Engineering/Technology.

Award: Scholarship for use in freshman, sophomore, junior, or senior years; not renewable. *Number:* 1. *Amount:* $1500.

Eligibility Requirements: Applicant must be enrolled or expecting to enroll full-time at a four-year institution or university; resident of Arizona, California, or New Mexico and studying in Arizona, California, or New Mexico. Applicant or parent of applicant must be member of Soil and Water Conservation Society. Available to U.S. and Canadian citizens.

Application Requirements: Application, resume, references, transcript, 2 copies of student statement letter. *Deadline:* February 1.

Contact: Society of Manufacturing Engineers Education Foundation
One SME Drive
PO Box 930
Dearborn, MI 48121-0930
Phone: 313-425-3300
E-mail: foundation@sme.org

WICHITA CHAPTER 52 SCHOLARSHIP

Award for an individual seeking an associates degree, bachelor's degree, or graduate degree in manufacturing, mechanical or industrial engineering, engineering technology, or industrial technology at an accredited public or private college or university in Kansas, Oklahoma or Missouri. Applicants must have a minimum GPA of 2.5. Preference given to applicants who are a relative of a current SME Wichita Chapter No. 52 member or a Kansas resident.

Academic Fields/Career Goals: Engineering/Technology; Industrial Design; Mechanical Engineering; Trade/Technical Specialties.

Award: Scholarship for use in freshman, sophomore, junior, senior, or graduate years; not renewable. *Number:* 1. *Amount:* up to $1500.

Eligibility Requirements: Applicant must be enrolled or expecting to enroll full-time at a two-year or four-year institution or university and studying in Kansas, Missouri, or Oklahoma. Applicant must have 2.5 GPA or higher. Available to U.S. citizens.

Application Requirements: Application, resume, references, transcript, student statement letter. *Deadline:* February 1.

Contact: Society of Manufacturing Engineers Education Foundation
One SME Drive
PO Box 930
Dearborn, MI 48121-0930
Phone: 313-425-3300
E-mail: foundation@sme.org

WILLIAM E. WEISEL SCHOLARSHIP FUND
• *See page 258*

SOCIETY OF MOTION PICTURE AND TELEVISION ENGINEERS

http://www.smpte.org/

LOU WOLF MEMORIAL SCHOLARSHIP
• *See page 259*

STUDENT PAPER AWARD
• *See page 272*

SOCIETY OF PETROLEUM ENGINEERS

http://www.spe.org/

GUS ARCHIE MEMORIAL SCHOLARSHIPS

Renewable award for students who have not attended college or university before and are planning to enroll in a petroleum engineering degree program at a four-year institution. Must have minimum 3.0 GPA.

Academic Fields/Career Goals: Engineering/Technology.

Award: Scholarship for use in freshman, sophomore, junior, or senior years; renewable. *Number:* 1–2. *Amount:* $6000.

Eligibility Requirements: Applicant must be enrolled or expecting to enroll full-time at a four-year institution or university. Applicant must have 3.0 GPA or higher. Available to U.S. and non-U.S. citizens.

Application Requirements: Application, financial need analysis, photo, references, test scores, transcript. *Deadline:* April 30.

Contact: Young Member Program
Society of Petroleum Engineers
PO Box 833836
Richardson, TX 75083
Phone: 972-952-9452
Fax: 972-952-9435
E-mail: studentactivities@spe.org

SOCIETY OF PLASTICS ENGINEERS (SPE) FOUNDATION

http://www.4spe.org/

FLEMING/BASZCAK SCHOLARSHIP
• *See page 169*

PLASTICS PIONEERS ASSOCIATION SCHOLARSHIPS
• *See page 169*

SOCIETY OF PLASTICS ENGINEERS SCHOLARSHIP PROGRAM
• *See page 170*

SOCIETY OF WOMEN ENGINEERS

http://www.swe.org/

COLUMBIA RIVER SECTION SCHOLARSHIPS

Scholarships available to students attending University of Portland, Portland State University, or Oregon Institute of Technology or a transfer student from an Oregon or Southwest Washington Community College planning or pursuing an engineering degree at one of those schools. 1 award $750 award for SWE Student Members at Oregon universities and 1 $300 award for community college transfer students to Oregon university engineering programs.

Academic Fields/Career Goals: Engineering/Technology.

Award: Scholarship for use in freshman, sophomore, junior, or senior years; not renewable. *Number:* 2. *Amount:* $300–$750.

Eligibility Requirements: Applicant must be enrolled or expecting to enroll full-time at a four-year institution or university; female and studying in Oregon or Washington. Applicant must have 2.5 GPA or higher. Available to U.S. citizens.

Application Requirements: Application, essay, references, transcript. *Deadline:* March 1.

Contact: Scholarship Committee
Society of Women Engineers
120 South La Salle Street, Suite 1515
Chicago, IL 60603
Phone: 312-596-5223
E-mail: scholarshipapplication@swe.org

MINNESOTA SWE SECTION SCHOLARSHIP

Scholarship of $1500 for qualified women students with junior or senior standing in an accredited engineering program at schools in Minnesota, North Dakota and South Dakota. Applicants are judged on the basis of potential to succeed as an engineers, communication skills, extracurricular or community involvement and leadership skills, demonstration of work experience and successes and academic success.

Academic Fields/Career Goals: Engineering/Technology.

Award: Scholarship for use in junior or senior years; not renewable. *Number:* 1. *Amount:* $1500.

Eligibility Requirements: Applicant must be enrolled or expecting to enroll full-time at a four-year institution or university; female and studying in Minnesota, North Dakota, or South Dakota. Available to U.S. citizens.

Application Requirements: Application, references, transcript. *Deadline:* March 15.

Contact: Scholarship Committee
Society of Women Engineers
120 South La Salle Street, Suite 1515
Chicago, IL 60603
Phone: 312-596-5223
E-mail: scholarshipapplication@swe.org

NEW JERSEY SCHOLARSHIP

Scholarship granted to female New Jersey resident majoring in engineering. Available to incoming freshman. Minimum 3.5 GPA required.

Academic Fields/Career Goals: Engineering/Technology.

Award: Scholarship for use in freshman year; not renewable. *Number:* 1. *Amount:* $5000.

Eligibility Requirements: Applicant must be enrolled or expecting to enroll full-time at a four-year institution or university; female and resident of New Jersey. Applicant must have 3.5 GPA or higher. Available to U.S. citizens.

Application Requirements: Application, essay, references, self-addressed stamped envelope, test scores, transcript. *Deadline:* May 14.

Contact: Scholarship Committee
Society of Women Engineers
120 South La Salle Street, Suite 1515
Chicago, IL 60603
Phone: 312-596-5223
E-mail: scholarshipapplication@swe.org

SOCIETY OF WOMEN ENGINEERS–FRESHMEN SCHOLARSHIPS

Scholarships for female engineering (including computer science) students studying ABET-accredited programs in the U.S. or 4 schools in Mexico. Applicants complete one application and are considered for all scholarships for which they are eligible. Other criteria: class level, major, location of school or home, financial need, under-represented, leadership, activities, SWE membership, etc. Some are renewable. List of scholarships at http//www.swe.org/scholarships.

Academic Fields/Career Goals: Engineering/Technology.

Award: Scholarship for use in freshman year; not renewable. *Number:* 1–36. *Amount:* $1000–$7000.

Eligibility Requirements: Applicant must be enrolled or expecting to enroll full-time at a four-year institution or university and female. Applicant must have 3.5 GPA or higher. Available to U.S. and non-U.S. citizens.

Application Requirements: Application, essay, resume, references, self-addressed stamped envelope, transcript, leadership, activities. *Deadline:* May 15.

Contact: Scholarship Committee
Society of Women Engineers
120 South La Salle Street, Suite 1515
Chicago, IL 60603
Phone: 312-596-5223
E-mail: scholarshipapplication@swe.org

SOCIETY OF WOMEN ENGINEERS–REENTRY/ NONTRADITIONAL SCHOLARSHIPS

Applicants complete one SWE application and are considered for all scholarships for which they are eligible. Re-entry applicants must have been out of the engineering job market and technical work as well as out of school for a minimum of two years prior to the current course of study. List of scholarships at http//www.swe.org/scholarships. Deadline for freshmen 5/15. Deadline for sophomores and above 2/15.

Academic Fields/Career Goals: Engineering/Technology.

Award: Scholarship for use in freshman, sophomore, junior, senior, or graduate years; not renewable. *Number:* 4. *Amount:* $1250–$2000.

Eligibility Requirements: Applicant must be enrolled or expecting to enroll full- or part-time at a four-year institution or university and female. Available to U.S. and non-U.S. citizens.

Application Requirements: Application, essay, resume, references, transcript, leadership, activities, work experience. *Deadline:* February 15.

Contact: Scholarship Committee
Society of Women Engineers
120 South La Salle Street, Suite 1515
Chicago, IL 60603
Phone: 312-596-5223
E-mail: scholarshipapplication@swe.org

SOCIETY OF WOMEN ENGINEERS SCHOLARSHIPS

Scholarships for female engineering (including computer science) students studying ABET-accredited programs in the U.S. or 4 schools in Mexico. Applicants complete one application and are considered for all scholarships for which they are eligible. Other criteria: class level, major, location of school or home, financial need, under-represented, leadership, activities, SWE membership, etc. Some are renewable. List of scholarships at http//www.swe.org/scholarships.

Academic Fields/Career Goals: Engineering/Technology.

Award: Scholarship for use in sophomore, junior, senior, graduate, or postgraduate years; not renewable. *Number:* 1–130. *Amount:* $1000–$20,000.

Eligibility Requirements: Applicant must be enrolled or expecting to enroll full-time at a four-year institution or university and female. Applicant must have 3.0 GPA or higher. Available to U.S. and non-U.S. citizens.

Application Requirements: Application, essay, resume, references, transcript, activities, leadership, work experience. *Deadline:* February 15.

Contact: Scholarship Committee
Society of Women Engineers
120 South La Salle Street, Suite 1515
Chicago, IL 60603
Phone: 312-596-5223
E-mail: scholarshipapplication@swe.org

SWE BATON ROUGE SECTION SCHOLARSHIPS
• *See page 199*

SWE CALIFORNIA GOLDEN GATE SECTION SCHOLARSHIPS
• *See page 199*

SWE CALIFORNIA SANTA CLARA VALLEY SECTION SCHOLARSHIP

Scholarship of $1000 for entering freshman, sophomore, junior, senior, and graduate students. Applicants meeting the following requirements are eligible to apply: (1) plan to attend school full-time in the fall next year in an ABET-accredited engineering program (2) are permanent residents or attend school in the South San Francisco Bay area.

Academic Fields/Career Goals: Engineering/Technology.

Award: Scholarship for use in freshman, sophomore, junior, senior, or graduate years; not renewable. *Number:* 15. *Amount:* $1000.

Eligibility Requirements: Applicant must be enrolled or expecting to enroll full-time at a four-year institution or university; female; resident of California and studying in California. Available to U.S. citizens.

Application Requirements: Application, references, transcript. *Deadline:* March 31.

Contact: Scholarship Committee
Society of Women Engineers
120 South La Salle Street, Suite 1515
Chicago, IL 60603
Phone: 312-596-5223
E-mail: scholarshipapplication@swe.org

SWE CHICAGO REGIONAL SECTION SCHOLARSHIPS

Scholarships are available for female high school seniors, continuing college students, transfer college students, graduate students and re-entry students who will be attending an ABET-accredited engineering school to pursue a BS or higher degree full-time or studying an ABET-accredited program. Applicant must have at least a 3.0 GPA. Must submit an essay on the topic "Why I want to be an engineer."

Academic Fields/Career Goals: Engineering/Technology.

Award: Scholarship for use in freshman, sophomore, junior, or senior years; not renewable. *Number:* 1. *Amount:* $1000.

Eligibility Requirements: Applicant must be enrolled or expecting to enroll full-time at a four-year institution or university; female and resident of Illinois. Applicant must have 3.0 GPA or higher. Available to U.S. citizens.

Application Requirements: Application, essay, transcript, acceptance letter. *Deadline:* April 15.

Contact: Scholarship Committee
Society of Women Engineers
120 South La Salle Street, Suite 1515
Chicago, IL 60603
Phone: 312-596-5223
E-mail: scholarshipapplication@swe.org

SWE CONNECTICUT SECTION JEAN R. BEERS SCHOLARSHIP
• *See page 199*

SWE GREATER NEW ORLEANS SECTION SCHOLARSHIP
• *See page 200*

SWE LEHIGH VALLEY SECTION SCHOLARSHIP

Applicants must be female graduating high school seniors, within the Lehigh Valley Section, planning on attending an ABET-accredited college or university in the following fall semester.

Academic Fields/Career Goals: Engineering/Technology.

Award: Scholarship for use in freshman year; not renewable. *Number:* 6–10. *Amount:* $1000.

Eligibility Requirements: Applicant must be high school student; planning to enroll or expecting to enroll full-time at a four-year institution or university; female; resident of Pennsylvania and must have an interest in leadership. Available to U.S. citizens.

Application Requirements: Application, acceptance letter, survey form and supplemental form. *Deadline:* February 15.

Contact: Scholarship Committee
Society of Women Engineers
120 South La Salle Street, Suite 1515
Chicago, IL 60603
Phone: 312-596-5223
E-mail: scholarshipapplication@swe.org

SWE ST. LOUIS SCHOLARSHIP

One $500 scholarship will be awarded to an entering sophomore, junior, or senior undergraduate student, or a graduate student attending one of the following colleges or universities: Southern Illinois University, Parks College of Engineering and Aviation/St. Louis University, Missouri University of Science and Technology or Washington University.

Academic Fields/Career Goals: Engineering/Technology.

Award: Scholarship for use in sophomore, junior, senior, or graduate years; not renewable. *Number:* 1. *Amount:* $500.

Eligibility Requirements: Applicant must be enrolled or expecting to enroll full-time at a four-year institution or university; female and studying in Illinois or Missouri. Applicant or parent of applicant must be member of Society of Women Engineers. Available to U.S. citizens.

Application Requirements: Application, references, test scores, transcript. *Deadline:* varies.

Contact: Scholarship Committee
Society of Women Engineers
120 South La Salle Street, Suite 1515
Chicago, IL 60603
Phone: 312-596-5223
E-mail: scholarshipapplication@swe.org

SWE SOUTH OHIO SCIENCE FAIR SCHOLARSHIP
• *See page 272*

SOCIETY OF WOMEN ENGINEERS-DALLAS SECTION

http://www.dallaswe.org/

FRESHMAN ENGINEERING SCHOLARSHIP FOR DALLAS WOMEN

Scholarship for freshman women pursuing a degree in engineering. Applicant must be a Texas resident. Please refer to web site for further details http://www.dallaswe.org.

Academic Fields/Career Goals: Engineering/Technology.

Award: Scholarship for use in freshman year; not renewable. *Number:* 2. *Amount:* $500.

Eligibility Requirements: Applicant must be high school student; planning to enroll or expecting to enroll full-time at a four-year institution or university; female and resident of Texas. Available to U.S. citizens.

Application Requirements: Application, financial need analysis, references, transcript, confirmation of enrollment. *Deadline:* May 15.

Contact: Luanne Beckley, Scholarship Coordinator
Society of Women Engineers-Dallas Section
PO Box 852022
Richardson, TX 75085-2022
Phone: 214-670-9273

NATIONAL SOCIETY OF WOMEN ENGINEERS SCHOLARSHIPS
• *See page 200*

SOCIETY OF WOMEN ENGINEERS-ROCKY MOUNTAIN SECTION

http://www.swe-rms.org/

SOCIETY OF WOMEN ENGINEERS-ROCKY MOUNTAIN SECTION SCHOLARSHIP PROGRAM
• See page 170

SOCIETY OF WOMEN ENGINEERS-TWIN TIERS SECTION

http://www.swetwintiers.org/

SOCIETY OF WOMEN ENGINEERS-TWIN TIERS SECTION SCHOLARSHIP
• See page 200

SPECIALTY EQUIPMENT MARKET ASSOCIATION

http://www.sema.org/

SPECIALTY EQUIPMENT MARKET ASSOCIATION MEMORIAL SCHOLARSHIP FUND

Scholarship for higher education in the automotive field. All applicants must be attending a U.S. institution. For further details visit web site http://www.sema.org.

Academic Fields/Career Goals: Engineering/Technology; Trade/Technical Specialties.

Award: Scholarship for use in freshman, sophomore, junior, senior, or graduate years; not renewable. *Number:* up to 90. *Amount:* $1000–$4000.

Eligibility Requirements: Applicant must be enrolled or expecting to enroll full-time at a two-year or four-year or technical institution or university and must have an interest in automotive. Applicant must have 2.5 GPA or higher. Available to U.S. and non-U.S. citizens.

Application Requirements: Application, essay, photo, references, self-addressed stamped envelope, transcript. *Deadline:* April 20.

Contact: Pat Talaska-Benson, Director, Educational Services
Specialty Equipment Market Association
1575 South Valley Vista Drive
PO Box 4910
Diamond Bar, CA 91765
Phone: 909-396-0289 Ext. 137
Fax: 909-860-0184
E-mail: patt@sema.org

STRAIGHTFORWARD MEDIA

http://www.straightforwardmedia.com/

STRAIGHTFORWARD MEDIA ENGINEERING SCHOLARSHIP
• See page 170

TAU BETA PI ASSOCIATION

http://www.tbp.org/

TAU BETA PI SCHOLARSHIP PROGRAM

One-time award for initiated members of Tau Beta Pi in their senior year of full-time undergraduate engineering study.

Academic Fields/Career Goals: Engineering/Technology.

Award: Scholarship for use in senior year; not renewable. *Number:* 80–150. *Amount:* $2000.

Eligibility Requirements: Applicant must be enrolled or expecting to enroll full-time at a four-year institution or university. Applicant or parent of applicant must be member of Tau Beta Pi Association. Available to U.S. and non-U.S. citizens.

Application Requirements: Application, essay, references. *Deadline:* March 1.

Contact: Dylan Lane, Communications Specialist
Phone: 865-546-4578
E-mail: dylan@tbp.org

TECHNICAL ASSOCIATION OF THE PULP & PAPER INDUSTRY (TAPPI)

http://www.tappi.org/

NONWOVENS DIVISION SCHOLARSHIP

Award to applicants enrolled as full-time students in a state accredited undergraduate program. Must be in a program preparatory to a career in the nonwovens industry or demonstrate an interest in the areas, be recommended and endorsed by an instructor or faculty member and maintain a 3.0 GPA. Information can be found at http://www.tappi.org/s_tappi/sec.asp?CID=6101&DID=546695.

Academic Fields/Career Goals: Engineering/Technology; Paper and Pulp Engineering.

Award: Scholarship for use in freshman, sophomore, junior, or senior years; not renewable. *Number:* 1. *Amount:* $1000.

Eligibility Requirements: Applicant must be enrolled or expecting to enroll full-time at a four-year institution or university. Applicant must have 3.0 GPA or higher. Available to U.S. and non-U.S. citizens.

Application Requirements: Application, references, transcript. *Deadline:* February 15.

Contact: Mr. Charles Bohanan, Director of Standards and Awards
Technical Association of the Pulp & Paper Industry (TAPPI)
15 Technology Parkway South
Norcross, GA 30092
Phone: 770-209-7276
Fax: 770-446-6947
E-mail: standards@tappi.org

PAPER AND BOARD DIVISION SCHOLARSHIPS

Award to TAPPI student member or an undergraduate member of a TAPPI Student Chapter enrolled as a college or university undergraduate in an engineering or science program. Must be sophomore, junior, or senior and able to show a significant interest in the paper industry. Information can be found at http://www.tappi.org/s_tappi/sec.asp?CID=6101&DID=546695.

Academic Fields/Career Goals: Engineering/Technology; Paper and Pulp Engineering.

Award: Scholarship for use in sophomore, junior, or senior years; not renewable. *Number:* 1–4. *Amount:* $1000.

Eligibility Requirements: Applicant must be enrolled or expecting to enroll full-time at a four-year institution or university. Available to U.S. and non-U.S. citizens.

Application Requirements: Application, references, transcript. *Deadline:* February 15.

Contact: Mr. Charles Bohanan, Director of Standards and Awards
Technical Association of the Pulp & Paper Industry (TAPPI)
15 Technology Parkway South
Norcross, GA 30092
Phone: 770-209-7276
Fax: 770-446-6947
E-mail: standards@tappi.org

TAPPI PROCESS AND PRODUCT QUALITY DIVISION SCHOLARSHIP

The TAPPI Process and Product Quality Scholarship is awarded to TAPPI student members or student chapter members to encourage them to pursue careers in the pulp and paper industry and to develop awareness of quality management.

Academic Fields/Career Goals: Engineering/Technology.

Award: Scholarship for use in sophomore, junior, or senior years; not renewable. *Number:* 1. *Amount:* $500.

Eligibility Requirements: Applicant must be enrolled or expecting to enroll full-time at a four-year institution or university. Available to U.S. and non-U.S. citizens.

Application Requirements: Application, references, transcript. *Deadline:* February 15.

Contact: Mr. Charles Bohanan, Director of Standards and Awards
Technical Association of the Pulp & Paper Industry (TAPPI)
15 Technology Parkway South
Norcross, GA 30092
Phone: 770-209-7276
Fax: 770-446-6947
E-mail: standards@tappi.org

TRIANGLE EDUCATION FOUNDATION

http://www.triangle.org/

KAPADIA SCHOLARSHIPS

Award ranges from $1500 to $8000 to an undergraduate or graduate Triangle members in good standing, with preference to engineering majors, non-US citizens, members of the Zoroastrian religion and Michigan State student.

Academic Fields/Career Goals: Engineering/Technology.

Award: Scholarship for use in freshman, sophomore, junior, senior, or graduate years; not renewable. *Number:* varies. *Amount:* $1500–$8000.

Eligibility Requirements: Applicant must be enrolled or expecting to enroll full-time at a four-year institution or university and male. Applicant must have 3.0 GPA or higher. Available to U.S. and non-U.S. citizens.

Application Requirements: Application, essay, financial need analysis, references, self-addressed stamped envelope, transcript. *Deadline:* February 15.

Contact: Scott Bova, President
Triangle Education Foundation
120 South Center Street
Plainfield, IN 46168-1214
Phone: 317-705-9803
Fax: 317-837-9642
E-mail: sbova@triangle.org

RUST SCHOLARSHIP

Awards $5500 annually based on a combination of need, grades and participation in campus and Triangle Activities. All other things being equal, preference is given to applicants in the core engineering disciplines or hard sciences.

Academic Fields/Career Goals: Engineering/Technology.

Award: Scholarship for use in freshman, sophomore, junior, or senior years; not renewable. *Number:* 1. *Amount:* up to $5500.

Eligibility Requirements: Applicant must be enrolled or expecting to enroll full-time at a four-year institution or university and male. Applicant must have 3.0 GPA or higher. Available to U.S. and non-U.S. citizens.

Application Requirements: Application, essay, financial need analysis, references, self-addressed stamped envelope, transcript. *Deadline:* February 15.

Contact: Scott Bova, President
Triangle Education Foundation
120 South Center Street
Plainfield, IN 46168-1214
Phone: 317-705-9803
Fax: 317-837-9642
E-mail: sbova@triangle.org

SEVCIK SCHOLARSHIP

One-time award up to $1000 annually for active member of the Triangle Fraternity based on need, preference to an Ohio State student, preference to an Engineering student. Refer to web site http://www.triangle.org/programs/scholarshipsloans/ for details.

Academic Fields/Career Goals: Engineering/Technology.

Award: Scholarship for use in freshman, sophomore, junior, or senior years; not renewable. *Number:* 1. *Amount:* up to $1000.

Eligibility Requirements: Applicant must be American Indian/Alaska Native, Asian/Pacific Islander, Black (non-Hispanic), or Hispanic; enrolled or expecting to enroll full-time at a four-year institution or university and male. Applicant must have 3.0 GPA or higher. Available to U.S. and non-U.S. citizens.

Application Requirements: Application, essay, financial need analysis, references, self-addressed stamped envelope, transcript. *Deadline:* February 15.

Contact: Scott Bova, President
Triangle Education Foundation
120 South Center Street
Plainfield, IN 46168-1214
Phone: 317-705-9803
Fax: 317-837-9642
E-mail: sbova@triangle.org

TURNER CONSTRUCTION COMPANY

http://www.turnerconstruction.com/

YOUTHFORCE 2020 SCHOLARSHIP PROGRAM
• *See page 103*

UNITED NEGRO COLLEGE FUND

http://www.uncf.org/

ACCENTURE SCHOLARSHIP
• *See page 200*

ALFRED CHISHOLM/BASF MEMORIAL SCHOLARSHIP FUND
• *See page 72*

ARLENE BENTON NOLAN AND JOHN NOLAN SCHOLARSHIP
• *See page 144*

ASEA BROWN BOVERI SCHOLARSHIP

Award for students majoring in electrical, mechanical, industrial, or nuclear engineering and attending a UNCF member college or university. Minimum 2.5 GPA required.

Academic Fields/Career Goals: Engineering/Technology.

Award: Scholarship for use in freshman year; not renewable.

Eligibility Requirements: Applicant must be Black (non-Hispanic) and enrolled or expecting to enroll at a four-year institution or university. Applicant must have 2.5 GPA or higher. Available to U.S. citizens.

Application Requirements: *Deadline:* continuous.

Contact: Director, Program Services
United Negro College Fund
8260 Willow Oaks Corporate Drive
PO Box 10444
Fairfax, VA 22031-8044
Phone: 800-331-2244
E-mail: rebecca.bennett@uncf.org

BATTELLE SCHOLARS PROGRAM

Scholarship of $10,000 for paid summer internship to African American residents of central Ohio who are undergraduate juniors majoring in engineering at a UNCF member college or university. Must have a minimum GPA of 3.0. Visit web site for more information and online application http://www.uncf.org.

Academic Fields/Career Goals: Engineering/Technology.

Award: Scholarship for use in junior year; not renewable. *Number:* varies. *Amount:* $10,000.

Eligibility Requirements: Applicant must be Black (non-Hispanic); enrolled or expecting to enroll full- or part-time at a four-year institution or university and resident of Ohio. Applicant must have 3.0 GPA or higher. Available to U.S. citizens.

Application Requirements: Application, financial need analysis.

Contact: Program Services
United Negro College Fund
8260 Willow Oaks Corporate Drive
Fairfax, VA 22031
Phone: 703-205-3486

CARDINAL HEALTH SCHOLARSHIP
• *See page 72*

CARTER AND BURGESS SCHOLARSHIP

Need-based scholarship for students from Ft. Worth, Texas. If there aren't enough engineering students in Ft. Worth, the scholarship pool may extend to the entire state of Texas and HBCUs. Students studying engineering with minimum GPA of 2.5 are eligible. The scholarship value varies, based on need.

Academic Fields/Career Goals: Engineering/Technology.

Award: Scholarship for use in freshman, sophomore, junior, or senior years; renewable. *Number:* 1. *Amount:* varies.

Eligibility Requirements: Applicant must be Black (non-Hispanic); enrolled or expecting to enroll full-time at a four-year institution or university and resident of Texas. Applicant must have 2.5 GPA or higher. Available to U.S. citizens.

Application Requirements: Application, financial need analysis, FAFSA, Student Aid Report (SAR).

Contact: Director, Program Services
        United Negro College Fund
        8260 Willow Oaks Corporate Drive
        PO Box 10444
        Fairfax, VA 22031-8044
        Phone: 800-331-2244
        E-mail: rebecca.bennett@uncf.org

CASTLE ROCK FOUNDATION SCHOLARSHIP
• *See page 157*

CHEVRONTEXACO SCHOLARS PROGRAM

Scholarships for college juniors or seniors majoring in engineering and enrolled full-time in one of the following institutions: Clark Atlanta University, Morehouse College, Spelman College, or Tuskegee University. Minimum 2.5 GPA required. Preference given to students who are permanent residents of Texas, Florida, or California; however, students from other states are eligible to apply. Apply online at http://www.uncf.org.

Academic Fields/Career Goals: Engineering/Technology.

Award: Scholarship for use in junior or senior years; not renewable. *Number:* 1. *Amount:* up to $3000.

Eligibility Requirements: Applicant must be Black (non-Hispanic) and enrolled or expecting to enroll full-time at a four-year institution or university. Applicant must have 2.5 GPA or higher. Available to U.S. citizens.

Application Requirements: Application, financial need analysis. *Deadline:* February 18.

Contact: Director, Program Services
        United Negro College Fund
        8260 Willow Oaks Corporate Drive
        PO Box 10444
        Fairfax, VA 22031-8044
        Phone: 800-331-2244
        E-mail: rebecca.bennett@uncf.org

EMERSON PROCESS MANAGEMENT SCHOLARSHIP
• *See page 170*

FLYTE TYME PRODUCTIONS SCHOLARSHIP
• *See page 193*

FORD/UNCF CORPORATE SCHOLARS PROGRAM
• *See page 73*

GENERAL MILLS TECHNOLOGY SCHOLARS AWARD
• *See page 171*

GEORGE REID WILLIAMS SCHOLARSHIP
• *See page 158*

GILBANE SCHOLARSHIP PROGRAM
• *See page 103*

LOCKHEED MARTIN/UNCF SCHOLARSHIP
• *See page 73*

MALCOLM PIRNIE CORPORATE SCHOLARS PROGRAM
• *See page 171*

MEDTRONIC FOUNDATION SCHOLARSHIP
• *See page 145*

NASCAR/WENDELL SCOTT, SR. SCHOLARSHIP
• *See page 73*

SBC-PACIFIC BELL SCHOLARSHIP
• *See page 158*

VERIZON FOUNDATION SCHOLARSHIP
• *See page 74*

UNIVERSITIES SPACE RESEARCH ASSOCIATION

http://www.usra.edu/

UNIVERSITIES SPACE RESEARCH ASSOCIATION SCHOLARSHIP PROGRAM
• *See page 97*

UTAH SOCIETY OF PROFESSIONAL ENGINEERS

http://www.uspeonline.com/

UTAH SOCIETY OF PROFESSIONAL ENGINEERS JOE RHOADS SCHOLARSHIP
• *See page 171*

VERMONT SPACE GRANT CONSORTIUM

http://www.cems.uvm.edu/vsgc

VERMONT SPACE GRANT CONSORTIUM SCHOLARSHIP PROGRAM
• *See page 98*

WEST VIRGINIA HIGHER EDUCATION POLICY COMMISSION-STUDENT SERVICES

http://www.wvhepcnew.wvnet.edu/

WEST VIRGINIA ENGINEERING, SCIENCE AND TECHNOLOGY SCHOLARSHIP PROGRAM
• *See page 259*

WISCONSIN SOCIETY OF PROFESSIONAL ENGINEERS

http://www.wspe.org/

WISCONSIN SOCIETY OF PROFESSIONAL ENGINEERS SCHOLARSHIPS

Scholarships are awarded each year to high school seniors having qualifications for success in engineering education. Must be a U.S. citizen and Wisconsin resident and have a minimum GPA of 3.0.

Academic Fields/Career Goals: Engineering/Technology.

Award: Scholarship for use in freshman year; not renewable. *Number:* 3. *Amount:* $1000.

Eligibility Requirements: Applicant must be high school student; planning to enroll or expecting to enroll full-time at a four-year institution or university and resident of Wisconsin. Applicant must have 3.0 GPA or higher. Available to U.S. citizens.

Application Requirements: Application, essay, interview, references, self-addressed stamped envelope, test scores, transcript. *Deadline:* December 28.

Contact: Mr. Christopher Roper, Executive Director
        Wisconsin Society of Professional Engineers
        7044 South 13th Street
        Oak Creek, WI 53154
        Phone: 414-908-4950 Ext. 107
        E-mail: c.roper@wspe.org

XEROX

http://www.xerox.com//

TECHNICAL MINORITY SCHOLARSHIP
• *See page 171*

ENTOMOLOGY

ENTOMOLOGICAL FOUNDATION

http://www.entfdn.org/

BIOQUIP UNDERGRADUATE SCHOLARSHIP

Award to assist students in obtaining a degree in entomology or pursuing a career as an entomologist. Must have minimum of 90 college credit hours by September 1 following the application deadline, and either completed two junior-level entomology courses or a research project in entomology. Preference will be given to students with demonstrated financial need.

Academic Fields/Career Goals: Entomology.

Award: Scholarship for use in freshman, sophomore, junior, or senior years; renewable. *Number:* up to 1. *Amount:* $2000.

Eligibility Requirements: Applicant must be enrolled or expecting to enroll full- or part-time at a four-year institution or university. Available to U.S. and non-U.S. citizens.

Application Requirements: Application, resume, references, transcript. *Deadline:* July 1.

Contact: Melodie Dziduch, Awards Coordinator
E-mail: melodie@entfdn.org

ENVIRONMENTAL HEALTH

ASSOCIATION OF ENVIRONMENTAL HEALTH ACADEMIC PROGRAMS (AEHAP)

http://www.aehap.org/

NSF INTERNATIONAL SCHOLAR PROGRAM

Award available for college junior or senior in an AEHAP Environmental Health Academic Program. Student will spend summer on an independent research project in conjunction with their home university and NSF International and the AEHAP Office. Must have consent and commitment from advisor to help develop and oversee research project. Stipend will be paid in two sums, and advisor will receive $500 stipend. Project results may also be submitted to AEHAP Student Research Competition for $500 award.

Academic Fields/Career Goals: Environmental Health.

Award: Scholarship for use in junior or senior years; not renewable. *Number:* 1. *Amount:* $3500.

Eligibility Requirements: Applicant must be enrolled or expecting to enroll full-time at a four-year institution or university and must have an interest in writing. Available to U.S. citizens.

Application Requirements: Application, essay, resume, references, cover letter, letter of adviser support. *Deadline:* April 16.

Contact: Yalonda Sinde, AEHAP Scholarship Committee
Association of Environmental Health Academic Programs (AEHAP)
8620 Roosevelt Way NE Suite A
Seattle, WA 98115
Phone: 206-522-5272
E-mail: info@aehap.org

COLLEGE BOARD/ROBERT WOOD JOHNSON FOUNDATION YES PROGRAM

http://www.collegeboard.com/

YOUNG EPIDEMIOLOGY SCHOLARS COMPETITION

Two $50,000 scholarships awarded to students who present outstanding research projects in the field of epidemiology. A select number of national finalists receive $15,000, $20,000, and $35,000 scholarships. YES Competition is open to high school juniors and seniors who are U.S. citizens or permanent residents.

Academic Fields/Career Goals: Environmental Health; Health and Medical Sciences; Public Health.

Award: Prize for use in freshman year; not renewable. *Number:* up to 120. *Amount:* $1000–$50,000.

Eligibility Requirements: Applicant must be high school student and planning to enroll or expecting to enroll full- or part-time at a four-year institution or university. Available to U.S. citizens.

Application Requirements: Application, applicant must enter a contest, research project report. *Deadline:* February 2.

Contact: The College Board
College Board/Robert Wood Johnson Foundation YES Program
11911 Freedom Drive, Suite 300
Reston, VA 20190
Phone: 800-626-9795 Ext. 5849
Fax: 703-707-5599
E-mail: yes@collegeboard.org

CYNTHIA E. MORGAN SCHOLARSHIP FUND (CEMS)

http://www.cemsfund.com/

CYNTHIA E. MORGAN MEMORIAL SCHOLARSHIP FUND, INC.

Award for a high school junior or senior, or a current college student, who is a Maryland resident and first generation college student. No previous generation (parents or grandparents) may have attended any college/university. Scholarship for use only at a Maryland post-secondary school or medical school. Must be majoring in, or plan to enter, a medical-related field (for example: doctor, nurse, radiologist).

Academic Fields/Career Goals: Environmental Health; Health and Medical Sciences; Health Information Management/Technology; Neurobiology; Nursing; Occupational Safety and Health; Oncology; Osteopathy; Pharmacy; Psychology; Radiology; Therapy/Rehabilitation.

Award: Scholarship for use in freshman, sophomore, junior, senior, graduate, or postgraduate years; not renewable. *Number:* 1. *Amount:* $1000.

Eligibility Requirements: Applicant must be enrolled or expecting to enroll full- or part-time at a two-year or four-year or technical institution or university; resident of Maryland and studying in Maryland. Available to U.S. citizens.

Application Requirements: Application, essay. *Deadline:* February 25.

Contact: Mr. John C. Kantorski Jr., Founder and President
Cynthia E. Morgan Scholarship Fund (CEMS)
5516 Maudes Way
White Marsh, MD 21162-3417
Phone: 410-458-6312
Fax: 443-927-7321
E-mail: administrator@cemsfund.com

FLORIDA ENVIRONMENTAL HEALTH ASSOCIATION

http://www.feha.org/

FLORIDA ENVIRONMENTAL HEALTH ASSOCIATION EDUCATIONAL SCHOLARSHIP AWARDS

Scholarships offered to students interested in pursuing a career in the field of environmental health, or to enhance an existing career in environmental health. Applicant must be a member of FEHA in good standing.

Academic Fields/Career Goals: Environmental Health; Public Health.

Award: Scholarship for use in junior or senior years; not renewable. *Number:* 1–10. *Amount:* $500–$1000.

Eligibility Requirements: Applicant must be enrolled or expecting to enroll full- or part-time at a four-year institution or university. Applicant or parent of applicant must be member of Florida Environmental Health Association. Applicant must have 2.5 GPA or higher. Available to U.S. and non-U.S. citizens.

Application Requirements: Application, references, transcript. *Deadline:* varies.

Contact: Michelle Kearney, Scholarship Committee Chair
Florida Environmental Health Association
5101 Ortega Boulevard
Jacksonville, FL 32210-8305
Phone: 850-245-4444 Ext. 2716
E-mail: michelle_kearney@doh.state.fl.us

INDEPENDENT COLLEGE FUND OF MARYLAND (I-FUND)

http://www.i-fundinfo.org/

HEALTH AND LIFE SCIENCES PROGRAM SCHOLARSHIPS
• *See page 140*

NATIONAL ENVIRONMENTAL HEALTH ASSOCIATION/AMERICAN ACADEMY OF SANITARIANS

http://www.neha.org/

NATIONAL ENVIRONMENTAL HEALTH ASSOCIATION/AMERICAN ACADEMY OF SANITARIANS SCHOLARSHIP

One-time award for college juniors, seniors, and graduate students pursuing studies in environmental health sciences or public health. Undergraduates must be enrolled full-time in an approved program that is accredited by the Environmental Health Accreditation Council (EHAC) or a NEHA institutional/educational or sustaining member school.

Academic Fields/Career Goals: Environmental Health; Public Health.

Award: Scholarship for use in junior or senior years; renewable. *Number:* 3–4. *Amount:* $1000–$2000.

Eligibility Requirements: Applicant must be enrolled or expecting to enroll full-time at a two-year or four-year institution or university. Available to U.S. citizens.

Application Requirements: Application, references, transcript. *Deadline:* February 1.

Contact: Cindy Dimmitt, Scholarship Coordinator
National Environmental Health Association/American
Academy of Sanitarians
720 South Colorado Boulevard, Suite 1000-N
Denver, CO 80246-1926
Phone: 303-756-9090
Fax: 303-691-9490
E-mail: cdimmitt@neha.org

SAEMS-SOUTHERN ARIZONA ENVIRONMENTAL MANAGEMENT SOCIETY

http://www.saems.org/

ENVIRONMENTAL SCHOLARSHIPS

Applicant must be a student in any accredited Southern Arizona college or university. Student must have a minimum GPA of 2.5 or be a full- or part-time student and plan on pursuing a career in the environmental arena.

Academic Fields/Career Goals: Environmental Health; Environmental Science; Natural Resources.

Award: Scholarship for use in freshman, sophomore, junior, senior, or graduate years; not renewable. *Number:* 2. *Amount:* $3000.

Eligibility Requirements: Applicant must be enrolled or expecting to enroll full- or part-time at a two-year or four-year institution or university and studying in Arizona. Applicant must have 2.5 GPA or higher. Available to U.S. and non-U.S. citizens.

Application Requirements: Application, essay, interview. *Deadline:* March 15.

Contact: Dan Uthe, Scholarship Committee Chair
SAEMS-Southern Arizona Environmental Management
Society
PO Box 41433
Tucson, AZ 85717
Phone: 520-791-5630
Fax: 520-791-5346
E-mail: dan.uthe@tucsonaz.com

STRAIGHTFORWARD MEDIA

http://www.straightforwardmedia.com/

STRAIGHTFORWARD MEDIA MEDICAL PROFESSIONS SCHOLARSHIP
• *See page 221*

WASHINGTON STATE ENVIRONMENTAL HEALTH ASSOCIATION

http://www.wseha.org/

CIND M. TRESER MEMORIAL SCHOLARSHIP PROGRAM

Scholarships are available for undergraduate students pursuing a major in environmental health or related science and intending to practice environmental health. Must be a resident of Washington. For more details see web site http://www.wseha.org.

Academic Fields/Career Goals: Environmental Health.

Award: Scholarship for use in freshman, sophomore, junior, or senior years; not renewable. *Number:* 1–2. *Amount:* $500–$1000.

Eligibility Requirements: Applicant must be enrolled or expecting to enroll full-time at a four-year institution or university and resident of Washington. Applicant must have 3.0 GPA or higher. Available to U.S. citizens.

Application Requirements: Application, references, transcript. *Deadline:* March 15.

Contact: Mr. Charles Treser, Scholarship Committee Chair
Washington State Environmental Health Association
3045 57th Street, NW
Seattle, WA 98107
Phone: 206-616-2097
E-mail: ctreser@u.washington.edu

WINDSTAR FOUNDATION

http://www.wstar.org/

WINDSTAR ENVIRONMENTAL STUDIES SCHOLARSHIPS

Two $500 scholarships for qualified undergraduates entering their junior or senior year of college, and one $1000 scholarship for graduate students entering their second year of graduate school.

Academic Fields/Career Goals: Environmental Health; Environmental Science.

Award: Scholarship for use in junior, senior, or graduate years; renewable. *Number:* up to 3. *Amount:* $500–$1000.

Eligibility Requirements: Applicant must be enrolled or expecting to enroll full-time at a four-year institution or university. Applicant must have 3.0 GPA or higher. Available to U.S. citizens.

Application Requirements: Application, essay, transcript. *Deadline:* June 1.

Contact: Executive Director
Windstar Foundation
PO Box 656
Snowmass, CO 81654
E-mail: windstarco@wstar.org

WISCONSIN ASSOCIATION FOR FOOD PROTECTION

http://www.wafp-wi.org/

E.H. MARTH FOOD AND ENVIRONMENTAL SCHOLARSHIP

Scholarship awarded to promote and sustain interest in the fields of study that may lead to a career in dairy, food, or environmental sanitation. One scholarship is awarded per year and previous applicants and recipients may reapply.

Academic Fields/Career Goals: Environmental Health.

Award: Scholarship for use in freshman, sophomore, junior, or senior years; not renewable. *Number:* 1. *Amount:* $1500.

Eligibility Requirements: Applicant must be enrolled or expecting to enroll full-time at a four-year institution or university; resident of Wisconsin and studying in Wisconsin. Available to U.S. and non-U.S. citizens.

Application Requirements: Application, references, transcript. *Deadline:* July 1.

Contact: Mr. Jim Wickert, Chairman, Scholarship Committee
Wisconsin Association for Food Protection
3834 Ridgeway Ave.
Madison, WI 53704
Phone: 608-241-2438
E-mail: jwick16060@tds.net

ENVIRONMENTAL SCIENCE

AIR & WASTE MANAGEMENT ASSOCIATION–ALLEGHENY MOUNTAIN SECTION

http://www.ams-awma.org/

ALLEGHENY MOUNTAIN SECTION AIR & WASTE MANAGEMENT ASSOCIATION SCHOLARSHIP

Scholarships for qualified students enrolled in an undergraduate program leading to a career in a field related directly to the environment. Open to current undergraduate students or high school students accepted full-time in a four-year college or university program in Western Pennsylvania or West Virginia. Applicants must have a minimum B average or a 3.0 GPA.

Academic Fields/Career Goals: Environmental Science.

Award: Scholarship for use in freshman, sophomore, junior, or senior years; not renewable. *Number:* up to 2. *Amount:* up to $1500.

Eligibility Requirements: Applicant must be enrolled or expecting to enroll full-time at a four-year institution or university; resident of Pennsylvania or West Virginia and studying in Pennsylvania or West Virginia. Applicant must have 3.0 GPA or higher. Available to U.S. citizens.

Application Requirements: Application, essay, resume, references, transcript, plan of study. *Deadline:* March 31.

Contact: David Testa, Scholarship Chair
Air & Waste Management Association–Allegheny Mountain Section
c/o Equitable Resources Inc., 225 North Shore Drive
Pittsburgh, PA 15212
Phone: 412-787-6803
Fax: 412-787-6717
E-mail: dtesta@calgoncarbon-us.com

AIR & WASTE MANAGEMENT ASSOCIATION–COASTAL PLAINS CHAPTER

http://www.awmacoastalplains.org/

COASTAL PLAINS CHAPTER OF THE AIR AND WASTE MANAGEMENT ASSOCIATION ENVIRONMENTAL STEWARD SCHOLARSHIP

Scholarships awarded to first- or second-year students pursuing a career in environmental science or physical science. Minimum high school and college GPA of 2.5 required. A 500-word paper on personal and professional goals must be submitted.

Academic Fields/Career Goals: Environmental Science; Physical Sciences.

Award: Scholarship for use in freshman or sophomore years; not renewable. *Number:* 5. *Amount:* $800.

Eligibility Requirements: Applicant must be enrolled or expecting to enroll full-time at a two-year or four-year institution or university. Applicant must have 2.5 GPA or higher. Available to U.S. citizens.

Application Requirements: Application, references, test scores, 500-word paper on personal and professional goals. *Deadline:* varies.

Contact: Dwain G. Waters, Treasurer
Air & Waste Management Association–Coastal Plains Chapter
One Energy Place
Pensacola, FL 32520-0328
Phone: 850-444-6527
Fax: 850-444-6217
E-mail: gdwaters@southernco.com

AMERICAN CHEMICAL SOCIETY

http://www.acs.org/

AMERICAN CHEMICAL SOCIETY SCHOLARS PROGRAM
• *See page 160*

AMERICAN INSTITUTE OF CHEMICAL ENGINEERS

http://www.aiche.org/

ENVIRONMENTAL DIVISION UNDERGRADUATE STUDENT PAPER AWARD
• *See page 161*

AMERICAN METEOROLOGICAL SOCIETY

http://www.ametsoc.org/

AMS FRESHMAN UNDERGRADUATE SCHOLARSHIP

Scholarships will be awarded, based on academic excellence, to high school seniors entering their freshman year of study in the atmospheric, oceanic, or hydrologic sciences. For use in freshman and sophomore years, with second-year funding dependent on successful completion of first year.

Academic Fields/Career Goals: Environmental Science; Hydrology; Marine/Ocean Engineering; Meteorology/Atmospheric Science.

Award: Scholarship for use in freshman year; not renewable. *Number:* 14. *Amount:* $5000.

Eligibility Requirements: Applicant must be high school student and planning to enroll or expecting to enroll full-time at a two-year or four-year or technical institution or university. Applicant must have 3.0 GPA or higher. Available to U.S. and non-U.S. citizens.

Application Requirements: Application, essay, references, test scores, transcript. *Deadline:* February 22.

Contact: Mrs. Donna Sampson, Development and Student Program
Manager
American Meteorological Society
45 Beacon Street
Boston, MA 02108
Phone: 617-227-2426 Ext. 246
Fax: 617-742-8718
E-mail: dfernand@ametsoc.org

ARCTIC INSTITUTE OF NORTH AMERICA

http://www.arctic.ucalgary.ca/

JIM BOURQUE SCHOLARSHIP
• *See page 230*

ASSOCIATION FOR WOMEN GEOSCIENTISTS, PUGET SOUND CHAPTER

http://www.awg.org/

PUGET SOUND CHAPTER SCHOLARSHIP
• *See page 223*

ASSOCIATION OF CALIFORNIA WATER AGENCIES

http://www.acwa.com/

ASSOCIATION OF CALIFORNIA WATER AGENCIES SCHOLARSHIPS
• *See page 94*

CLAIR A. HILL SCHOLARSHIP
• *See page 94*

ASSOCIATION OF NEW JERSEY ENVIRONMENTAL COMMISSIONS

http://www.anjec.org/

LECHNER SCHOLARSHIP
Award of $1000 scholarship for a student entering his/her junior or senior year at an accredited New Jersey college or university. Must be a New Jersey resident and have a minimum GPA of 3.0.

Academic Fields/Career Goals: Environmental Science.

Award: Scholarship for use in junior or senior years; not renewable. *Number:* 1. *Amount:* $1000.

Eligibility Requirements: Applicant must be enrolled or expecting to enroll full-time at a four-year institution or university; resident of New Jersey and studying in New Jersey. Applicant must have 3.0 GPA or higher. Available to U.S. citizens.

Application Requirements: Application, essay, references, transcript.

Contact: Sandy Batty, Executive Director
Association of New Jersey Environmental Commissions
PO Box 157
Mendham, NJ 07945
Phone: 973-539-7547
Fax: 973-539-7713
E-mail: sbatty@anjec.org

AUDUBON SOCIETY OF WESTERN PENNSYLVANIA

http://www.aswp.org/

BEULAH FREY ENVIRONMENTAL SCHOLARSHIP
Scholarship available to high school seniors pursuing studies in the environmental and natural sciences. Students who are applying to a two- or four-year college to further their studies in an environmentally-related field are eligible to apply. Scholarship is restricted to the residents of the seven counties around Pittsburgh.

Academic Fields/Career Goals: Environmental Science; Natural Sciences.

Award: Scholarship for use in freshman year; not renewable. *Number:* 1–2. *Amount:* $1000.

Eligibility Requirements: Applicant must be high school student; planning to enroll or expecting to enroll full-time at a two-year or four-year institution or university and resident of Pennsylvania. Available to U.S. citizens.

Application Requirements: Application, essay, references, test scores, transcript. *Deadline:* March 31.

Contact: Patricia O'Neill, Director of Education
Audubon Society of Western Pennsylvania
614 Dorseyville Road
Pittsburgh, PA 15238
Phone: 412-963-6100
Fax: 412-963-6761
E-mail: toneill@aswp.org

BRITISH COLUMBIA INNOVATION COUNCIL

http://www.bcic.ca/

BCIC YOUNG INNOVATOR SCHOLARSHIP COMPETITION (IDEA MASH UP)
• *See page 95*

CANADIAN RECREATIONAL CANOEING ASSOCIATION

http://www.paddlingcanada.com/

BILL MASON MEMORIAL SCHOLARSHIP FUND
• *See page 232*

CONSERVATION FEDERATION OF MISSOURI

http://www.confedmo.org/

CHARLES P. BELL CONSERVATION SCHOLARSHIP
Eight scholarships of $250 to $600 for Missouri students and/or teachers whose studies or projects are related to natural science, resource conservation, earth resources, or environmental protection. Must be used for study in Missouri. See application for eligibility details.

Academic Fields/Career Goals: Environmental Science; Natural Resources; Natural Sciences.

Award: Scholarship for use in freshman, sophomore, junior, senior, or graduate years; not renewable. *Number:* 8. *Amount:* $250–$600.

Eligibility Requirements: Applicant must be enrolled or expecting to enroll full- or part-time at a four-year institution or university; resident of Missouri and studying in Missouri. Available to U.S. citizens.

Application Requirements: Application, financial need analysis, references, transcript, work experience certificate. *Deadline:* January 15.

Contact: Administrative Associate
Conservation Federation of Missouri
728 West Main Street
Jefferson City, MO 65101-1559
Phone: 573-634-2322
Fax: 573-634-8205
E-mail: confedmo@sockets.net

DELAWARE HIGHER EDUCATION OFFICE

http://www.doe.k12.de.us

DELAWARE SOLID WASTE AUTHORITY JOHN P. "PAT" HEALY SCHOLARSHIP
• *See page 266*

EARTH ISLAND INSTITUTE

http://www.earthisland.org/

BROWER YOUTH AWARDS

Annual national award that recognizes six young people for outstanding activism and achievements in the fields of environmental and social justice advocacy. The winners of the award receive $3000 in cash, a trip to California for the award ceremony and Yosemite camping trip, and ongoing access to resources and opportunities to further their work at Earth Island Institute. Applicant's age must be between 13 and 22.

Academic Fields/Career Goals: Environmental Science; Peace and Conflict Studies.

Award: Prize for use in freshman, sophomore, junior, or senior years; not renewable. *Number:* 6. *Amount:* $3000.

Eligibility Requirements: Applicant must be age 13-22 and enrolled or expecting to enroll full- or part-time at a two-year or four-year or technical institution or university. Available to U.S. and non-U.S. citizens.

Application Requirements: Application, essay, photo, references. *Deadline:* May 15.

Contact: Ms. Anisha Desai, Program Director
Earth Island Institute
300 Broadway, Suite 28
San Francisco, CA 94133
Phone: 510-859-9144 Ext. 144
E-mail: bya@earthisland.org

ENVIRONMENTAL PROFESSIONALS' ORGANIZATION OF CONNECTICUT

http://www.epoc.org/

EPOC ENVIRONMENTAL SCHOLARSHIP FUND

Scholarships awarded annually to junior, senior, and graduate level students (full- or part-time) enrolled in accepted programs of study leading the student to become an environmental professional in Connecticut.

Academic Fields/Career Goals: Environmental Science.

Award: Scholarship for use in junior, senior, or graduate years; not renewable. *Number:* 2–3. *Amount:* varies.

Eligibility Requirements: Applicant must be enrolled or expecting to enroll full- or part-time at a four-year institution or university. Available to U.S. citizens.

Application Requirements: Application, essay, financial need analysis, references, transcript. *Deadline:* May 7.

Contact: John Figurelli, Scholarship Fund Coordinator
Environmental Professionals' Organization of Connecticut
PO Box 176
Amston, CT 06231-0176
Phone: 860-513-1473
Fax: 860-228-4902
E-mail: figurelj@wseinc.com

FRIENDS OF THE FRELINGHUYSEN ARBORETUM

http://www.arboretumfriends.org/

BENJAMIN C. BLACKBURN SCHOLARSHIP

One-time award for undergraduate and graduate students who are pursuing degrees in horticulture, landscape architecture, or environmental studies. Must be a New Jersey resident. Minimum 3.0 GPA required.

Academic Fields/Career Goals: Environmental Science; Horticulture/Floriculture; Landscape Architecture; Natural Resources.

Award: Scholarship for use in sophomore, junior, senior, or graduate years; not renewable. *Number:* 1. *Amount:* $5000.

Eligibility Requirements: Applicant must be enrolled or expecting to enroll full- or part-time at a four-year institution or university and resident of New Jersey. Applicant must have 3.0 GPA or higher. Available to U.S. citizens.

Application Requirements: Application, essay, references, transcript. *Deadline:* April 14.

Contact: Ann Abrams, Scholarship Committee
Friends of the Frelinghuysen Arboretum
53 East Hanover Avenue, PO Box 1295
Morristown, NJ 07962-1295
Phone: 973-326-7603
E-mail: aabrams@morrisparks.net

GARDEN CLUB OF AMERICA

http://www.gcamerica.org/

CAROLINE THORN KISSEL SUMMER ENVIRONMENTAL STUDIES SCHOLARSHIP

Scholarship for students to promote environmental studies by students who are either residents of the state of New Jersey or non-residents pursuing study in New Jersey or its surrounding waters.

Academic Fields/Career Goals: Environmental Science.

Award: Scholarship for use in freshman, sophomore, junior, or senior years; not renewable. *Number:* 1. *Amount:* $2000.

Eligibility Requirements: Applicant must be enrolled or expecting to enroll full- or part-time at a two-year or four-year or technical institution or university; resident of New Jersey and studying in New Jersey. Available to U.S. citizens.

Application Requirements: Application, essay, references. *Deadline:* February 10.

Contact: Connie Yates, Scholarship Committee Administrator
Garden Club of America
14 East 60th Street, Third Floor
New York, NY 10022-1002
Phone: 212-753-8287
E-mail: cyates@gcamerica.org

THE ELIZABETH GARDNER NORWEB SUMMER ENVIRONMENTAL STUDIES SCHOLARSHIP
• *See page 84*

GCA AWARD IN DESERT STUDIES
• *See page 101*

GREAT LAKES COMMISSION

http://www.glc.org/

CAROL A. RATZA MEMORIAL SCHOLARSHIP
• *See page 185*

INDEPENDENT LABORATORIES INSTITUTE SCHOLARSHIP ALLIANCE

http://www.acil.org/

INDEPENDENT LABORATORIES INSTITUTE SCHOLARSHIP ALLIANCE
• *See page 141*

INDIANA WILDLIFE FEDERATION ENDOWMENT

http://www.indianawildlife.org/

CHARLES A. HOLT INDIANA WILDLIFE FEDERATION ENDOWMENT SCHOLARSHIP

A $1000 scholarship will be awarded to an Indiana resident enrolled in or planning to enroll in a course of study related to resource conservation or environmental education at the undergraduate level. A 6–12 month internship with the Indiana Wildlife Federation is offered in conjunction with the scholarship.

Academic Fields/Career Goals: Environmental Science; Natural Resources.

Award: Scholarship for use in sophomore, junior, or senior years; not renewable. *Number:* 1. *Amount:* $1000.

Eligibility Requirements: Applicant must be enrolled or expecting to enroll full-time at a four-year institution or university; resident of Indiana and studying in Indiana. Available to U.S. citizens.

Application Requirements: Application, essay, references. *Deadline:* May 1.

Contact: Debbie Twardy, Office Manager
Indiana Wildlife Federation Endowment
4715 West 106th Street
Zionsville, IN 46077
Phone: 317-875-9453
E-mail: info@indianawildlife.org

INTERNATIONAL ASSOCIATION OF GREAT LAKES RESEARCH

http://www.iaglr.org/

PAUL W. RODGERS SCHOLARSHIP
• *See page 224*

INTERTRIBAL TIMBER COUNCIL

http://www.itcnet.org/

TRUMAN D. PICARD SCHOLARSHIP
• *See page 79*

JUST WITHIN REACH FOUNDATION

ENVIRONMENTAL SCIENCES AND MARINE STUDIES SCHOLARSHIP

Three scholarships of $2000 are given to environmental science scholars and three of $2000 are given to marine studies scholars. Must be U.S. citizens and must be either undergraduate students currently enrolled in a postsecondary institution or high school seniors accepted as full-time students of an accredited, public or private four-year college or university in the United States. Minimum 3.0 GPA required.

Academic Fields/Career Goals: Environmental Science; Marine Biology.

Award: Scholarship for use in freshman, sophomore, junior, or senior years; not renewable. *Number:* 6. *Amount:* $2000.

Eligibility Requirements: Applicant must be enrolled or expecting to enroll full-time at a four-year institution or university. Applicant must have 3.0 GPA or higher. Available to U.S. citizens.

Application Requirements: Application, essay, financial need analysis, resume, references, transcript. *Deadline:* March 12.

Contact: Scholarship Committee
Just Within Reach Foundation
3940 Laurel Canyon Boulevard, PO Box 256
Studio City, CA 91604

KENTUCKY ENERGY AND ENVIRONMENT CABINET

http://www.eec.ky.gov/

ENVIRONMENTAL PROTECTION SCHOLARSHIP
• *See page 141*

LAND CONSERVANCY OF NEW JERSEY

http://www.tlc-nj.org/

ROGERS FAMILY SCHOLARSHIP

Scholarship to deserving individuals who plan careers in environmental science, natural resource management, conservation, horticulture, park administration, or a related field. Must be a resident of New Jersey and considering a career in New Jersey. Payment is made directly to the institution that the successful candidate attends.

Academic Fields/Career Goals: Environmental Science; Horticulture/Floriculture; Natural Resources; Recreation, Parks, Leisure Studies.

Award: Scholarship for use in freshman, sophomore, junior, or senior years; not renewable. *Number:* varies. *Amount:* up to $7000.

Eligibility Requirements: Applicant must be enrolled or expecting to enroll full- or part-time at a four-year institution or university and resident of New Jersey. Applicant must have 3.0 GPA or higher. Available to U.S. citizens.

Application Requirements: Application, essay, resume, references, transcript. *Deadline:* April 1.

Contact: Scholarship Program
Land Conservancy of New Jersey
19 Boonton Avenue
Boonton, NJ 07005
Phone: 973-541-1010
E-mail: info@tlc-nj.org

RUSSELL W. MYERS SCHOLARSHIP

Scholarship to deserving individuals who plan careers in environmental science, natural resource management, conservation, horticulture, park administration, or a related field. Must be a resident of New Jersey and considering a career in New Jersey. Payment is made directly to the institution that the successful candidate attends.

Academic Fields/Career Goals: Environmental Science; Horticulture/Floriculture; Natural Resources; Recreation, Parks, Leisure Studies.

Award: Scholarship for use in freshman, sophomore, junior, or senior years; not renewable. *Number:* varies. *Amount:* up to $7000.

Eligibility Requirements: Applicant must be enrolled or expecting to enroll full-time at a four-year institution or university and resident of New Jersey. Applicant must have 3.0 GPA or higher. Available to U.S. citizens.

Application Requirements: Application, essay, references, transcript. *Deadline:* April 1.

Contact: The Scholarship Program
Land Conservancy of New Jersey
19 Boonton Avenue
Boonton, NJ 07005
Phone: 973-541-1010

MANITOBA FORESTRY ASSOCIATION

http://www.thinktrees.org/

DR. ALAN BEAVEN FORESTRY SCHOLARSHIP

Awarded annually to a Manitoba resident selected by a committee of association members. Must be a recent high school graduate entering first year forestry program at a Canadian university or technical school. Scholarship of $500 (Canadian Dollars) will be paid in the student's name to the university or school as part of the tuition.

Academic Fields/Career Goals: Environmental Science; Natural Resources.

Award: Scholarship for use in freshman year; not renewable. *Number:* 1. *Amount:* $300–$475.

Eligibility Requirements: Applicant must be Canadian citizen; high school student; planning to enroll or expecting to enroll full-time at a two-year or four-year or technical institution or university and resident of Manitoba.

Application Requirements: Application, references, transcript. *Deadline:* July 31.

Contact: Executive Director
Manitoba Forestry Association
900 Corydon Avenue
Winnipeg, MB R3M 0Y4
Canada
Phone: 204-453-3182
E-mail: info@thinktrees.org

MISSOURI DEPARTMENT OF NATURAL RESOURCES

http://www.dnr.mo.gov/

ENVIRONMENTAL EDUCATION SCHOLARSHIP PROGRAM (EESP)

Scholarship to minority and other underrepresented students pursuing a bachelor's or master's degree in an environmental course of study. Must be a Missouri resident having a cumulative high school GPA of 3.0 or if enrolled in college, must have cumulative GPA of 2.5.

Academic Fields/Career Goals: Environmental Science.

Award: Scholarship for use in freshman, sophomore, junior, senior, or graduate years; renewable. *Number:* 16. *Amount:* $2000.

Eligibility Requirements: Applicant must be American Indian/Alaska Native, Asian/Pacific Islander, Black (non-Hispanic), or Hispanic; enrolled or expecting to enroll full-time at a four-year institution or university and resident of Missouri. Applicant must have 3.0 GPA or higher. Available to U.S. citizens.

Application Requirements: Application, essay, references, transcript. *Deadline:* June 1.

Contact: Dana Muessig, Executive
Missouri Department of Natural Resources
PO Box 176
Jefferson City, MO 65102
Phone: 800-361-4827
Fax: 573-526-3878
E-mail: danamuessig@dnr.mo.gov

NASA/MARYLAND SPACE GRANT CONSORTIUM

http://www.mdspacegrant.org/

NASA MARYLAND SPACE GRANT CONSORTIUM UNDERGRADUATE SCHOLARSHIPS
• *See page 127*

NASA SOUTH DAKOTA SPACE GRANT CONSORTIUM

http://www.sdspacegrant.sdsmt.edu/

SOUTH DAKOTA SPACE GRANT CONSORTIUM UNDERGRADUATE AND GRADUATE STUDENT SCHOLARSHIPS
• *See page 129*

NASA'S VIRGINIA SPACE GRANT CONSORTIUM

http://www.vsgc.odu.edu/

TEACHER EDUCATION STEM SCHOLARSHIP PROGRAM
• *See page 96*

VIRGINIA STEM COMMUNITY COLLEGE SCHOLARSHIPS
• *See page 96*

NASA WEST VIRGINIA SPACE GRANT CONSORTIUM

http://www.nasa.wvu.edu/

WEST VIRGINIA SPACE GRANT CONSORTIUM UNDERGRADUATE FELLOWSHIP PROGRAM
• *See page 129*

NATIONAL COUNCIL OF STATE GARDEN CLUBS INC. SCHOLARSHIP

http://www.gardenclub.org/

NATIONAL COUNCIL OF STATE GARDEN CLUBS INC. SCHOLARSHIP
• *See page 85*

NATIONAL GARDEN CLUBS INC.

http://www.gardenclub.org/

NATIONAL GARDEN CLUBS INC. SCHOLARSHIP PROGRAM
• *See page 86*

NATIONAL GROUND WATER RESEARCH AND EDUCATIONAL FOUNDATION

http://www.ngwa.org/

NATIONAL GROUND WATER RESEARCH AND EDUCATIONAL FOUNDATION'S LEN ASSANTE SCHOLARSHIP
• *See page 226*

NATIONAL INVENTORS HALL OF FAME

http://www.invent.org/

COLLEGIATE INVENTORS COMPETITION FOR UNDERGRADUATE STUDENTS
• *See page 96*

COLLEGIATE INVENTORS COMPETITION-GRAND PRIZE
• *See page 97*

NATIONAL SAFETY COUNCIL

http://www.cshema.org/

CAMPUS SAFETY, HEALTH AND ENVIRONMENTAL MANAGEMENT ASSOCIATION SCHOLARSHIP AWARD PROGRAM

One $2000 scholarship available to full-time undergraduate or graduate students in all majors to encourage the study of safety and environmental management.

Academic Fields/Career Goals: Environmental Science; Occupational Safety and Health.

Award: Scholarship for use in freshman, sophomore, junior, senior, or graduate years; not renewable. *Number:* 1. *Amount:* $2000.

Eligibility Requirements: Applicant must be enrolled or expecting to enroll full-time at a four-year institution or university. Available to U.S. and Canadian citizens.

Application Requirements: Application, essay, transcript. *Deadline:* March 31.

Contact: Scholarship Committee
National Safety Council
12100 Sunset Hills Road, Suite 130
Reston, VA 20190-3221
Phone: 703-234-4141
Fax: 703-435-4390

NATIONAL SECURITY EDUCATION PROGRAM

http://www.iie.org/

NATIONAL SECURITY EDUCATION PROGRAM (NSEP) DAVID L. BOREN UNDERGRADUATE SCHOLARSHIPS
• *See page 154*

NEW ENGLAND WATER WORKS ASSOCIATION

http://www.newwa.org/

ELSON T. KILLAM MEMORIAL SCHOLARSHIP
• *See page 179*

FRANCIS X. CROWLEY SCHOLARSHIP
• *See page 155*

JOSEPH MURPHY SCHOLARSHIP
• *See page 179*

OHIO ACADEMY OF SCIENCE/OHIO ENVIRONMENTAL EDUCATION FUND

http://www.ohiosci.org/

OHIO ENVIRONMENTAL SCIENCE & ENGINEERING SCHOLARSHIPS

Merit-based, non-renewable, tuition-only scholarships awarded to undergraduate students admitted to Ohio state or private colleges and universities. Must be able to demonstrate knowledge of, and commitment to, careers in environmental sciences or environmental engineering.

Academic Fields/Career Goals: Environmental Science.

Award: Scholarship for use in senior year; not renewable. *Number:* 18. *Amount:* $1250–$2500.

Eligibility Requirements: Applicant must be enrolled or expecting to enroll full- or part-time at a two-year or four-year institution or university and studying in Ohio. Applicant must have 3.0 GPA or higher. Available to U.S. citizens.

Application Requirements: Application, essay, resume, references, self-addressed stamped envelope, transcript. *Deadline:* June 1.

Contact: Mr. Lynn E. Elfner, Chief Executive Officer
Ohio Academy of Science/Ohio Environmental Education Fund
1500 West Third Avenue, Suite 228
Columbus, OH 43212-2817
Phone: 614-488-2228
Fax: 614-488-7629
E-mail: oas@iwaynet.net

OREGON STUDENT ASSISTANCE COMMISSION

http://www.GetCollegeFunds.org/

OREGON FOUNDATION FOR BLACKTAIL DEER SCHOLARSHIP
• *See page 142*

ROYDEN M. BODLEY SCHOLARSHIP

One-time award open to Oregon high school graduates who earned their Eagle rank in Boy Scouts of America Cascade Pacific Council. Must be enrolled, or planning to enroll, in an Oregon college or university in an undergraduate program in forestry, wildlife conservation, environmental studies, or related fields that continue interest in the outdoors. Must reapply annually to renew award.

Academic Fields/Career Goals: Environmental Science; Natural Resources; Natural Sciences.

Award: Scholarship for use in freshman year; not renewable. *Number:* varies. *Amount:* varies.

Eligibility Requirements: Applicant must be enrolled or expecting to enroll full-time at a four-year institution or university; male; resident of Oregon and studying in Oregon. Applicant or parent of applicant must be member of Boy Scouts. Available to U.S. citizens.

Application Requirements: Application, essay, financial need analysis, transcript, activity chart. *Deadline:* March 1.

Contact: Director of Grant Programs
Oregon Student Assistance Commission
1500 Valley River Drive, Suite 100
Eugene, OR 97401-7020
Phone: 800-452-8807 Ext. 7395

OZARKA NATURAL SPRING WATER

http://www.ozarkawater.com/

EARTH SCIENCE SCHOLARSHIP
• *See page 226*

PENNSYLVANIA ASSOCIATION OF CONSERVATION DISTRICTS AUXILIARY

http://www.pacd.org/

PACD AUXILIARY SCHOLARSHIPS
• *See page 87*

SAEMS-SOUTHERN ARIZONA ENVIRONMENTAL MANAGEMENT SOCIETY

http://www.saems.org/

ENVIRONMENTAL SCHOLARSHIPS
• *See page 305*

SOCIETY FOR RANGE MANAGEMENT

http://www.rangelands.org/

MASONIC RANGE SCIENCE SCHOLARSHIP
• *See page 80*

SOIL AND WATER CONSERVATION SOCIETY-NEW JERSEY CHAPTER

http://www.geocities.com/njswcs

EDWARD R. HALL SCHOLARSHIP
• *See page 81*

TECHNICAL ASSOCIATION OF THE PULP & PAPER INDUSTRY (TAPPI)

http://www.tappi.org/

ENVIRONMENTAL WORKING GROUP SCHOLARSHIP

Annual awards for SME student members who are undergraduate students at or above the level of a sophomore and enrolled at an ABET-accredited or equivalent college. Minimum of one $2500 scholarship. Information can be found at http://www.tappi.org/s_tappi/sec.asp?CID=6101&DID=546695.

Academic Fields/Career Goals: Environmental Science; Paper and Pulp Engineering.

Award: Scholarship for use in sophomore, junior, or senior years; not renewable. *Number:* 1. *Amount:* $2500.

Eligibility Requirements: Applicant must be enrolled or expecting to enroll full-time at a four-year institution or university. Applicant must have 3.0 GPA or higher. Available to U.S. and non-U.S. citizens.

Application Requirements: Application, interview, references, transcript. *Deadline:* February 15.

Contact: Mr. Charles Bohanan, Director of Standards and Awards
Technical Association of the Pulp & Paper Industry (TAPPI)
15 Technology Parkway South
Norcross, GA 30033
Phone: 770-209-7276
Fax: 770-446-6947
E-mail: standards@tappi.org

TEXAS OUTDOOR WRITERS ASSOCIATION

http://www.towa.org/

TEXAS OUTDOOR WRITERS ASSOCIATION SCHOLARSHIP
• *See page 192*

TKE EDUCATIONAL FOUNDATION

http://www.tke.org/

TIMOTHY L. TASCHWER SCHOLARSHIP
• *See page 144*

UNITED NEGRO COLLEGE FUND

http://www.uncf.org/

MALCOLM PIRNIE CORPORATE SCHOLARS PROGRAM
• *See page 171*

UNCF/MERCK SCIENCE INITIATIVE
• *See page 145*

UNITED WATER CORPORATE SCHOLARS PROGRAM
• *See page 74*

UNITED STATES ENVIRONMENTAL PROTECTION AGENCY

http://www.epa.gov/enviroed

NATIONAL NETWORK FOR ENVIRONMENTAL MANAGEMENT STUDIES FELLOWSHIP

Fellowship program designed to provide undergraduate and graduate students with research opportunities at one of EPA's facilities nationwide. EPA awards approximately 40 NNEMS fellowships per year. Selected students receive a stipend for performing their research project. EPA develops an annual catalog of research projects available for student application. Submit a complete application package as described in the annual catalog. Minimum 3.0 GPA required.

Academic Fields/Career Goals: Environmental Science; Natural Resources.

Award: Grant for use in freshman, sophomore, junior, senior, graduate, or postgraduate years; not renewable. *Number:* 20–25. *Amount:* varies.

Eligibility Requirements: Applicant must be enrolled or expecting to enroll full- or part-time at a two-year or four-year institution or university. Applicant must have 3.0 GPA or higher. Available to U.S. citizens.

Application Requirements: Application, resume, references, transcript. *Deadline:* January 22.

Contact: Michael Baker, Acting Director
United States Environmental Protection Agency
Environmental Education Division, 1200 Pennsylvania
  Avenue, NW, MC 1704A
Washington, DC 20460
Phone: 202-564-0446
Fax: 202-564-2754
E-mail: baker.michael@epa.gov

VIRGINIA ASSOCIATION OF SOIL AND WATER CONSERVATION DISTRICTS EDUCATIONAL FOUNDATION INC.

http://www.vaswcd.org/

VASWCD EDUCATIONAL FOUNDATION INC. SCHOLARSHIP AWARDS PROGRAM

Scholarship to provide financial support to Virginia residents majoring in, or showing a strong desire to major in, a course curriculum related to natural resource conservation and/or environmental studies. Applicants must be full-time students who have applied to an undergraduate freshman-level curriculum. Must rank in the top 20 percent of graduating class or have a 3.0 or greater GPA, and demonstrate an active interest in conservation. Recipients may reapply to their individual SWCD for scholarship consideration in ensuing years.

Academic Fields/Career Goals: Environmental Science; Natural Resources.

Award: Scholarship for use in freshman year; not renewable. *Number:* 4. *Amount:* $1000.

Eligibility Requirements: Applicant must be high school student; planning to enroll or expecting to enroll full-time at a four-year institution or university and resident of Virginia. Applicant must have 3.0 GPA or higher. Available to U.S. citizens.

Application Requirements: Application, essay, financial need analysis, references, transcript. *Deadline:* March 1.

Contact: Jennifer Krick, District Manager
Virginia Association of Soil and Water Conservation Districts
  Educational Foundation Inc.
John Marshall Soil and Water
98 Alexandria Pike, Suite 31
Warrenton, VA 20186
Phone: 540-347-3120 Ext. 116
Fax: 540-349-0878
E-mail: jennifer.krick@va.nacdnet.net

WINDSTAR FOUNDATION

http://www.wstar.org/

WINDSTAR ENVIRONMENTAL STUDIES SCHOLARSHIPS
• *See page 305*

EUROPEAN STUDIES

CANADIAN INSTITUTE OF UKRAINIAN STUDIES

http://www.cius.ca/

CANADIAN INSTITUTE OF UKRAINIAN STUDIES RESEARCH GRANTS
• *See page 104*

GERMAN ACADEMIC EXCHANGE SERVICE (DAAD)

http://www.daad.org/

GERMAN ACADEMIC EXCHANGE INFORMATION VISITS

Grants are available for an information visit of seven to twelve days to groups of 10 to 15 students, accompanied by a faculty member. The purpose of this program is to increase the knowledge of specific German subjects and institutions within the framework of an academic study tour. Preference will be given to groups with a homogeneous academic background. Application should reach DAAD, New York at least six months before the beginning date of the planned visit. Participants may be drawn from more than one institution. DAAD offers up to around 9,600 euros to subsidize room and board, depending on size of group and length of stay. (50 euros per participant per day) Participants will have to supplement the funding provided by DAAD with resources of their own. Groups will not be eligible for funding in successive years.

Academic Fields/Career Goals: European Studies; German Studies.

Award: Grant for use in junior, senior, or graduate years; not renewable. *Number:* varies. *Amount:* varies.

Eligibility Requirements: Applicant must be enrolled or expecting to enroll full-time at a four-year institution or university. Available to U.S. and non-U.S. citizens.

Application Requirements: Application, applicant must enter a contest. *Deadline:* varies.

Contact: Jane Fu, Information Officer
German Academic Exchange Service (DAAD)
871 United Nations Plaza
New York, NY 10017
Phone: 212-758-3223 Ext. 201
E-mail: daadny@daad.org

FASHION DESIGN

DECA (DISTRIBUTIVE EDUCATION CLUBS OF AMERICA)

http://www.deca.org/

HARRY A. APPLEGATE SCHOLARSHIP
• *See page 149*

SAN DIEGO FOUNDATION

http://www.sdfoundation.org/

CALIFORNIA ASSOCIATION OF FAMILY AND CONSUMER SCIENCES-SAN DIEGO CHAPTER
• *See page 173*

FILMMAKING/VIDEO

ACADEMY FOUNDATION OF THE ACADEMY OF MOTION PICTURE ARTS AND SCIENCES

http://www.oscars.org/saa

ACADEMY OF MOTION PICTURE ARTS AND SCIENCES STUDENT ACADEMY AWARDS

Award available to students who have made a narrative, documentary, alternative, or animated film of up to 60 minutes within the curricular structure of an accredited college or university. Initial entry must be on 1/ 2 inch VHS tape. 16mm or larger format print or digital beta-cam tape required for further rounds. Prizes awarded in four categories. Each category awards gold ($5000), silver ($3000), and bronze ($2000). Visit web site for details and application http://www.oscars.org/saa.

Academic Fields/Career Goals: Filmmaking/Video.

Award: Prize for use in freshman, sophomore, junior, senior, or graduate years; not renewable. *Number:* 3–12. *Amount:* $2000–$5000.

Eligibility Requirements: Applicant must be enrolled or expecting to enroll full-time at a two-year or four-year institution or university. Available to U.S. and non-U.S. citizens.

Application Requirements: Application, applicant must enter a contest, 16mm or larger format film print or NTSC digital betacam version of the entry (BetaSP format is not acceptable), DVD. *Deadline:* April 2.

Contact: Richard Miller, Awards Administration Director
Academy Foundation of the Academy of Motion Picture Arts and Sciences
8949 Wilshire Boulevard
Beverly Hills, CA 90211-1972
Phone: 310-247-3000 Ext. 129
Fax: 310-859-9619
E-mail: rmiller@oscars.org

ACADEMY OF MOTION PICTURE STUDENT ACADEMY AWARD-HONORARY FOREIGN FILM

One award is given to an applicant from an institution outside the U.S. and a member of CILECT. Visit web site for applications http://www.oscars.org/saa.

Academic Fields/Career Goals: Filmmaking/Video.

Award: Prize for use in freshman, sophomore, junior, senior, or graduate years; not renewable. *Number:* 1. *Amount:* $1000.

Eligibility Requirements: Applicant must be enrolled or expecting to enroll full-time at a four-year institution or university. Available to Canadian and non-U.S. citizens.

Application Requirements: Application, applicant must enter a contest, self-addressed stamped envelope, 16mm, 35mm, 70mm, or digital betacam version. *Deadline:* March 23.

Contact: Richard Miller, Awards Administration Director
Academy Foundation of the Academy of Motion Picture Arts and Sciences
8949 Wilshire Boulevard
Beverly Hills, CA 90211-1972
Phone: 310-247-3000
Fax: 310-859-9619
E-mail: rmiller@oscars.org

ADC RESEARCH INSTITUTE

http://www.adc.org/

JACK SHAHEEN MASS COMMUNICATIONS SCHOLARSHIP AWARD
• *See page 181*

CHARLES AND LUCILLE KING FAMILY FOUNDATION, INC.

http://www.kingfoundation.org/

CHARLES AND LUCILLE KING FAMILY FOUNDATION SCHOLARSHIPS
• *See page 184*

ILLUMINATING ENGINEERING SOCIETY OF NORTH AMERICA–GOLDEN GATE SECTION

http://www.iesgg.org/

ALAN LUCAS MEMORIAL EDUCATIONAL SCHOLARSHIP
• *See page 102*

INTERNATIONAL COMMUNICATIONS INDUSTRIES FOUNDATION

http://www.infocomm.org/scholarships

ICIF SCHOLARSHIP FOR EMPLOYEES AND DEPENDENTS OF MEMBER ORGANIZATIONS
• *See page 186*

INTERNATIONAL COMMUNICATIONS INDUSTRIES FOUNDATION AV SCHOLARSHIP
• *See page 186*

MEDIA ACTION NETWORK FOR ASIAN AMERICANS

http://www.manaa.org/

MANAA MEDIA SCHOLARSHIPS FOR ASIAN AMERICAN STUDENTS
• *See page 113*

OUTDOOR WRITERS ASSOCIATION OF AMERICA

http://www.owaa.org/

OUTDOOR WRITERS ASSOCIATION OF AMERICA BODIE MCDOWELL SCHOLARSHIP AWARD
• *See page 189*

PHI DELTA THETA FOUNDATION

http://www.phideltatheta.org/

FRANCIS D. LYON SCHOLARSHIPS FOR STUDENTS OF FILM

Two scholarships of up to $3000 each for undergraduate and graduate students of filmmaking. Must have completed two full years of college and be enrolled in an institution in the U.S. or Canada. Award based on talent, academic excellence, and financial need. Application deadline is March 15.

Academic Fields/Career Goals: Filmmaking/Video.

Award: Scholarship for use in junior or senior years; not renewable. *Number:* 2. *Amount:* up to $3000.

Eligibility Requirements: Applicant must be enrolled or expecting to enroll full-time at a four-year institution or university. Available to U.S. and non-U.S. citizens.

Application Requirements: Application, essay, photo, references, transcript, sample of work. *Deadline:* March 15.

Contact: Linda R. Brattain, Administrative Assistant
Phi Delta Theta Foundation
2 South Campus Avenue
Oxford, OH 45056
Phone: 513-523-6345
Fax: 513-523-9200
E-mail: linda@phideltatheta.org

POLISH ARTS CLUB OF BUFFALO SCHOLARSHIP FOUNDATION

http://www.pacb.bfn.org/

POLISH ARTS CLUB OF BUFFALO SCHOLARSHIP FOUNDATION TRUST

• *See page 114*

PRINCESS GRACE FOUNDATION-USA

http://www.pgfusa.org/

PRINCESS GRACE AWARDS IN DANCE, THEATER, AND FILM

One-time scholarship for students enrolled full-time in film or video, dance, or theater program. For dance, applicant must have completed at least one year of undergraduate study; for theater, final year of study in either undergraduate or graduate level; and for film, must be in thesis program. The number of scholarships varies from ten to twelve annually.

Academic Fields/Career Goals: Filmmaking/Video; Performing Arts.

Award: Grant for use in sophomore, junior, senior, or graduate years; not renewable. *Number:* 15–25. *Amount:* $5000–$25,000.

Eligibility Requirements: Applicant must be enrolled or expecting to enroll full-time at a four-year institution or university. Available to U.S. citizens.

Application Requirements: Application, applicant must enter a contest, essay, photo, portfolio, resume, references, self-addressed stamped envelope, nomination.

Contact: Ms. Jelena Tadic, Program Manager
Princess Grace Foundation-USA
150 East 58th Street, 25th Floor
New York, NY 10155
Phone: 212-317-1470
E-mail: grants@pgfusa.org

RHODE ISLAND FOUNDATION

http://www.rifoundation.org/

J. D. EDSAL ADVERTISING SCHOLARSHIP

• *See page 77*

SAN FRANCISCO FOUNDATION

http://www.sff.org/

PHELAN ART AWARD IN FILMMAKING

Award presented in every even-numbered year to recognize achievement in film making. Must have been born in California, but need not be a current resident. Applicants must provide a copy of their birth certificate with their application. Scholarship values from $5000 to $10,000. Deadline varies.

Academic Fields/Career Goals: Filmmaking/Video.

Award: Prize for use in freshman, sophomore, junior, senior, graduate, or postgraduate years; not renewable. *Number:* 3. *Amount:* $5000–$10,000.

Eligibility Requirements: Applicant must be enrolled or expecting to enroll full- or part-time at a two-year or four-year institution or university. Available to U.S. citizens.

Application Requirements: Application, applicant must enter a contest, self-addressed stamped envelope. *Deadline:* varies.

Contact: Art Awards Coordinator
San Francisco Foundation
225 Bush Street, Suite 500
San Francisco, CA 94104
Phone: 415-733-8500

PHELAN ART AWARD IN VIDEO

Award presented in every even-numbered year to recognize achievement in video. Must have been born in California, but need not be a current resident. Applicants must provide a copy of their birth certificates with their application. Scholarship value is $5000 to $10,000. Deadline varies.

Academic Fields/Career Goals: Filmmaking/Video.

Award: Prize for use in freshman, sophomore, junior, senior, graduate, or postgraduate years; not renewable. *Number:* 3. *Amount:* $5000–$10,000.

Eligibility Requirements: Applicant must be enrolled or expecting to enroll full- or part-time at a two-year or four-year institution or university. Available to U.S. citizens.

Application Requirements: Application, applicant must enter a contest, self-addressed stamped envelope. *Deadline:* varies.

Contact: Art Awards Coordinator
San Francisco Foundation
225 Bush Street, Suite 500
San Francisco, CA 94104
Phone: 415-733-8500

SOCIETY OF MOTION PICTURE AND TELEVISION ENGINEERS

http://www.smpte.org/

LOU WOLF MEMORIAL SCHOLARSHIP
• *See page 259*

STUDENT PAPER AWARD
• *See page 272*

TELETOON

http://www.teletoon.com/

TELETOON ANIMATION SCHOLARSHIP
• *See page 115*

UNIVERSITY FILM AND VIDEO ASSOCIATION

http://www.ufva.org/

UNIVERSITY FILM AND VIDEO ASSOCIATION CAROLE FIELDING STUDENT GRANTS

Up to $4000 is available for production grants in narrative, documentary, experimental, new-media/installation, or animation. Up to $1000 is available for grants in research. Applicant must be sponsored by a faculty person who is an active member of the University Film and Video Association. Fifty percent of award distributed upon completion of project.

Academic Fields/Career Goals: Filmmaking/Video.

Award: Grant for use in freshman, sophomore, junior, senior, or graduate years; not renewable. *Number:* up to 5. *Amount:* $1000–$4000.

Eligibility Requirements: Applicant must be enrolled or expecting to enroll full- or part-time at a two-year or four-year institution or university. Available to U.S. and non-U.S. citizens.

Application Requirements: Application, essay, resume, references, project description, budget. *Deadline:* December 15.

Contact: Prof. Robert Johnson Jr., Chair
University Film and Video Association
Framingham State College, 100 State Street
Framingham, MA 01701-9101
Phone: 508-626-4684
Fax: 508-626-4847
E-mail: rjohnso@frc.mass.edu

WOMEN IN FILM AND TELEVISION (WIFT)

http://www.wif.org/

WIF FOUNDATION SCHOLARSHIP

Scholarships for female students based on their academic standing, artistic talents and commitment to a film-based curriculum with special consideration for financial need, regardless of age, ethnicity or religious affiliation. Scholarships to such schools as University of California, Los Angles, University of Southern California, Chapman University and AFI are available to female students who are already enrolled and have been nominated by instructors and faculty at respective schools.

Academic Fields/Career Goals: Filmmaking/Video.

Award: Scholarship for use in freshman, sophomore, junior, or senior years; not renewable. *Number:* up to 3. *Amount:* up to $1000.

Eligibility Requirements: Applicant must be enrolled or expecting to enroll part-time at a two-year or four-year or technical institution or university and female. Available to U.S. citizens.

Application Requirements: Application, essay, financial need analysis, references, transcript. *Deadline:* varies.

Contact: Gayle Nachlis, Executive Director
Women in Film and Television (WIFT)
8857 West Olympic Boulevard, Suite 201
Beverly Hills, CA 90211
Phone: 310-657-5144 Ext. 28
Fax: 310-657-5154
E-mail: gnachlis@wif.org

WORLDFEST INTERNATIONAL FILM AND VIDEO FESTIVAL

http://www.worldfest.org/

WORLDFEST STUDENT FILM AWARD

Award for students enrolled full-time or part-time in accredited colleges or universities majoring filmmaking.

Academic Fields/Career Goals: Filmmaking/Video.

Award: Prize for use in freshman, sophomore, junior, senior, or graduate years; not renewable. *Number:* 10. *Amount:* $1000–$10,000.

Eligibility Requirements: Applicant must be enrolled or expecting to enroll full- or part-time at a two-year or four-year or technical institution or university. Available to U.S. and non-U.S. citizens.

Application Requirements: Application, applicant must enter a contest, references, film/tape entry, student ID. *Fee:* $45. *Deadline:* December 15.

Contact: Hunter Todd, Executive Director
Worldfest International Film and Video Festival
9898 BIssonnet Street, Suite 650
PO Box 56566
Houston, TX 77256-6566
Phone: 713-965-9955
Fax: 713-965-9960
E-mail: hunter@worldfest.org

FINANCE

COMMUNITY FOUNDATION OF WESTERN MASSACHUSETTS

http://www.communityfoundation.org/

GREATER SPRINGFIELD ACCOUNTANTS SCHOLARSHIP
• *See page 59*

DADE COMMUNITY FOUNDATION

http://www.jackituckfield.org/

DR. FELIX H. REYLER (FIBA) SCHOLARSHIP
• *See page 148*

DECA (DISTRIBUTIVE EDUCATION CLUBS OF AMERICA)

http://www.deca.org/

HARRY A. APPLEGATE SCHOLARSHIP
• *See page 149*

GEORGIA GOVERNMENT FINANCE OFFICERS ASSOCIATION

http://www.ggfoa.org/

GGFOA SCHOLARSHIP
• *See page 61*

GREATER KANAWHA VALLEY FOUNDATION

http://www.tgkvf.org/

CHARLESTON ROTARY CLUB SCHOLARSHIP
• *See page 63*

LATINO BUSINESS PROFESSIONALS (LBP) OF NORTHERN CALIFORNIA

http://www.lbpbayarea.org/

LBP MONETARY SCHOLARSHIP
• *See page 65*

STRAIGHTFORWARD MEDIA

http://www.straightforwardmedia.com/

STRAIGHTFORWARD MEDIA BUSINESS SCHOOL SCHOLARSHIP
• *See page 77*

UNITED NEGRO COLLEGE FUND

http://www.uncf.org/

AVIS BUDGET GROUP SCHOLARSHIP
• *See page 72*

AVON WOMEN IN SEARCH OF EXCELLENCE SCHOLARSHIP
• *See page 72*

BANK OF AMERICA SCHOLARSHIP
• *See page 157*

CARGILL SCHOLARSHIP PROGRAM
• *See page 72*

FORD/UNCF CORPORATE SCHOLARS PROGRAM
• *See page 73*

GENERAL MILLS CORPORATE SCHOLARS AWARD
• *See page 73*

LOCKHEED MARTIN/UNCF SCHOLARSHIP
• *See page 73*

MBIA/WILLIAM O. BAILEY SCHOLARS PROGRAM
• *See page 73*

NASCAR/WENDELL SCOTT, SR. SCHOLARSHIP
• *See page 73*

PRINCIPAL FINANCIAL GROUP SCHOLARSHIPS
• *See page 74*

SBC-PACIFIC BELL SCHOLARSHIP
• *See page 158*

UBS/PAINEWEBBER SCHOLARSHIP
• *See page 74*

UPS/UNCF CORPORATE SCHOLARS PROGRAM
• *See page 202*

WELLS FARGO/UNCF SCHOLARSHIP FUND
• *See page 74*

FIRE SCIENCES

BOY SCOUTS OF AMERICA-MUSKINGUM VALLEY COUNCIL

http://www.learning-for-life.org/

INTERNATIONAL ASSOCIATION OF FIRE CHIEFS FOUNDATION SCHOLARSHIP

Two $500 scholarships for Explorers who are pursuing a full-time career in the fire sciences. Must be high school senior and participant of the Learning for Life Exploring program.

Academic Fields/Career Goals: Fire Sciences.

Award: Scholarship for use in freshman year; not renewable. *Number:* 2. *Amount:* $500.

Eligibility Requirements: Applicant must be high school student and planning to enroll or expecting to enroll full-time at a four-year institution or university. Available to U.S. and non-U.S. citizens.

Application Requirements: Application, essay, photo, references, test scores, transcript. *Deadline:* July 1.

Contact: Scholarship Committee
Boy Scouts of America-Muskingum Valley Council
S210, PO Box 152079
Irving, TX 75015

INDEPENDENT LABORATORIES INSTITUTE SCHOLARSHIP ALLIANCE

http://www.acil.org/

INDEPENDENT LABORATORIES INSTITUTE SCHOLARSHIP ALLIANCE
• *See page 141*

INTERNATIONAL ASSOCIATION OF ARSON INVESTIGATORS EDUCATIONAL FOUNDATION INC.

http://www.firearson.com/

JOHN CHARLES WILSON SCHOLARSHIP & ROBERT DORAN SCHOLARSHIP

One-time award to members in good standing of IAAI or the immediate family of a member or must be sponsored by an IAAI member. Must enroll or plan to enroll full-time in an accredited college or university that offers courses in police, fire sciences, or any arson investigation-related field. Application available at web site.

Academic Fields/Career Goals: Fire Sciences; Law Enforcement/Police Administration.

Award: Scholarship for use in freshman, sophomore, junior, senior, or graduate years; not renewable. *Number:* up to 4. *Amount:* $500–$1000.

Eligibility Requirements: Applicant must be enrolled or expecting to enroll full-time at a two-year or four-year institution or university. Available to U.S. and non-U.S. citizens.

Application Requirements: Application, driver's license, essay, resume, references, test scores, transcript. *Deadline:* February 15.

Contact: Gloria Guernsey Ryan, Office Manager
International Association of Arson Investigators Educational
Foundation Inc.
2111 Baldwin Avenue Suite 203
Crofton, MD 21114
Phone: 410-451-FIRE Ext. 3473
Fax: 410-451-9049
E-mail: iaai@firearson.com

LEARNING FOR LIFE

http://www.learning-for-life.org/

INTERNATIONAL ASSOCIATIONS OF FIRE CHIEFS FOUNDATION SCHOLARSHIP

Applicant must be a graduating high school senior in May or June of the year the application is issued and a Fire Service Explorer. The school selected by the applicant must be an accredited public or proprietary institution.

Academic Fields/Career Goals: Fire Sciences.

Award: Scholarship for use in freshman year; not renewable. *Number:* 2. *Amount:* $500.

Eligibility Requirements: Applicant must be high school student and planning to enroll or expecting to enroll full- or part-time at a two-year or four-year institution or university. Applicant or parent of applicant must be member of Explorer Program/Learning for Life. Available to U.S. citizens.

Application Requirements: Application, essay, photo, references, transcript. *Deadline:* July 1.

Contact: William Taylor, Scholarships and Awards Coordinator
E-mail: btaylor@lflmail.org

MARYLAND STATE HIGHER EDUCATION COMMISSION

http://www.mhec.state.md.us/

CHARLES W. RILEY FIRE AND EMERGENCY MEDICAL SERVICES TUITION REIMBURSEMENT PROGRAM

Award intended to reimburse members of rescue organizations serving Maryland communities for tuition costs of course work towards a degree or certificate in fire service or medical technology. Must attend a two- or four-year school in Maryland. Minimum 2.0 GPA. The scholarship is worth up to $6500.

Academic Fields/Career Goals: Fire Sciences; Health and Medical Sciences; Trade/Technical Specialties.

Award: Scholarship for use in freshman, sophomore, junior, or senior years; not renewable. *Number:* up to 150. *Amount:* up to $6500.

Eligibility Requirements: Applicant must be enrolled or expecting to enroll full- or part-time at a two-year or four-year institution or university; resident of Maryland and studying in Maryland. Applicant or parent of applicant must have employment or volunteer experience in police/firefighting. Available to U.S. citizens.

Application Requirements: Application, transcript, tuition receipt, proof of enrollment. *Deadline:* July 1.

Contact: Maura Sappington, Office of Student Financial Assistance
Maryland State Higher Education Commission
839 Bestgate Road, Suite 400
Annapolis, MD 21401-3013
Phone: 410-260-4569
Fax: 410-260-3203
E-mail: msapping@mhec.state.md.us

OREGON STUDENT ASSISTANCE COMMISSION

http://www.GetCollegeFunds.org/

NEIL HAMILTON MEMORIAL SCHOLARSHIP

One-time award for graduating seniors who will be studying fire science or fire suppression/protection at an Oregon community college. Recipients must attend college at least half-time.

Academic Fields/Career Goals: Fire Sciences.

Award: Scholarship for use in freshman year; not renewable.

Eligibility Requirements: Applicant must be high school student; planning to enroll or expecting to enroll full- or part-time at a two-year institution and studying in Oregon. Applicant must have 2.5 GPA or higher.

Application Requirements: Application. *Deadline:* March 1.

Contact: Director of Grant Programs
Oregon Student Assistance Commission
1500 Valley River Drive, Suite 100
Eugene, OR 97401-7020
Phone: 800-452-8807

STRAIGHTFORWARD MEDIA

http://www.straightforwardmedia.com/

STRAIGHTFORWARD MEDIA VOCATIONAL-TECHNICAL SCHOOL SCHOLARSHIP
• See page 91

FLEXOGRAPHY

FOUNDATION OF FLEXOGRAPHIC TECHNICAL ASSOCIATION

http://www.flexography.org/

FOUNDATION OF FLEXOGRAPHIC TECHNICAL ASSOCIATION SCHOLARSHIP COMPETITION

Awards students enrolled in a FFTA Flexo in Education Program with plans to attend a postsecondary institution, or be currently enrolled in a postsecondary institution offering a course of study in flexography. Must demonstrate an interest in a career in flexography, and maintain an overall GPA of at least 3.0. Must reapply.

Academic Fields/Career Goals: Flexography.

Award: Scholarship for use in freshman, sophomore, junior, or senior years; not renewable. *Number:* 10–15. *Amount:* up to $2000.

Eligibility Requirements: Applicant must be enrolled or expecting to enroll full-time at a four-year or technical institution or university. Applicant must have 3.0 GPA or higher. Available to U.S. citizens.

Application Requirements: Application, essay, references, transcript. *Deadline:* March 14.

Contact: Shelley Rubin, Educational Program Coordinator
Foundation of Flexographic Technical Association
900 Marconi Avenue
Ronkonkoma, NY 11779-7212
Phone: 631-737-6020 Ext. 36
Fax: 631-737-6813
E-mail: srubin@flexography.org

TAG AND LABEL MANUFACTURERS INSTITUTE INC.

http://www.tlmi.com/

TLMI FOUR-YEAR COLLEGES/FULL-TIME STUDENTS SCHOLARSHIP
• See page 273

FOOD SCIENCE/ NUTRITION

AMERICAN DIETETIC ASSOCIATION

http://www.eatright.org/

AMERICAN DIETETIC ASSOCIATION FOUNDATION SCHOLARSHIP PROGRAM

ADAF scholarships are available for undergraduate and graduate students enrolled in programs, including dietetic internships, preparing for entry to dietetics practice as well as dietetics professionals engaged in continuing education at the graduate level. Scholarship funds are provided by many state dietetic associations, dietetic practice groups, past ADA leaders and corporate donors. Scholarships require ADA membership. Details available on web site http://www.eatright.org/CADE/content.aspx?id=7934.

Academic Fields/Career Goals: Food Science/Nutrition.

Award: Scholarship for use in sophomore, junior, or senior years; not renewable. *Number:* 200–225. *Amount:* $500–$3000.

Eligibility Requirements: Applicant must be enrolled or expecting to enroll full- or part-time at a two-year or four-year institution or university. Applicant or parent of applicant must be member of American Dietetic Association. Available to U.S. citizens.

Application Requirements: Application, essay, financial need analysis, references, transcript. *Deadline:* February 15.

Contact: Eva Donovan, Education Coordinator
American Dietetic Association
120 South Riverside Plaza, Suite 2000
Chicago, IL 60606-6695
Phone: 312-899-0040 Ext. 4876
E-mail: education@eatright.org

AMERICAN INSTITUTE OF WINE AND FOOD-PACIFIC NORTHWEST CHAPTER

http://www.aiwf.org/

CULINARY, VINIFERA, AND HOSPITALITY SCHOLARSHIP

One-time award available to residents of Washington State. Must be enrolled full-time in an accredited culinary, vinifera, or hospitality program in Washington State. Must have completed two years. Minimum 3.0 GPA required. Deadline: continuous.

Academic Fields/Career Goals: Food Science/Nutrition; Food Service/Hospitality; Hospitality Management.

Award: Scholarship for use in junior or senior years; not renewable. *Number:* 4. *Amount:* $1500.

Eligibility Requirements: Applicant must be enrolled or expecting to enroll full-time at a four-year or two-year or technical institution or university; resident of Washington and studying in Washington. Applicant must have 3.0 GPA or higher. Available to U.S. and non-U.S. citizens.

Application Requirements: Application, resume, references. *Deadline:* continuous.

Contact: Brad Sturman, Scholarship Coordinator
American Institute of Wine and Food-Pacific Northwest
Chapter
224 18th Avenue
Kirkland, WA 98033
Phone: 206-679-6228

AMERICAN OIL CHEMISTS' SOCIETY

http://www.aocs.org/

AOCS BIOTECHNOLOGY STUDENT EXCELLENCE AWARD
• *See page 82*

AOCS HEALTH AND NUTRITION DIVISION STUDENT EXCELLENCE AWARD

$500 award and certificate to recognize the outstanding merit and performance of a student in the health and nutrition field. Student will present a paper at the Annual Meeting of the Society.

Academic Fields/Career Goals: Food Science/Nutrition.

Award: Prize for use in senior year; not renewable. *Number:* 1–1. *Amount:* $500.

Eligibility Requirements: Applicant must be enrolled or expecting to enroll full-time at a four-year institution or university. Available to U.S. and non-U.S. citizens.

Application Requirements: Application, references, abstract. *Deadline:* October 15.

Contact: Barbara A. Semeraro, Area Manager, Membership
American Oil Chemists' Society
AOCS, P.O. Box 17190
Urbana, IL 61803
Phone: 217-693-4804
Fax: 217-693-4849
E-mail: awards@aocs.org

AMERICAN SOCIETY FOR ENOLOGY AND VITICULTURE

http://www.asev.org/

AMERICAN SOCIETY FOR ENOLOGY AND VITICULTURE SCHOLARSHIPS
• *See page 82*

ASSOCIATION FOR FOOD AND DRUG OFFICIALS

http://www.afdo.org/

ASSOCIATION FOR FOOD AND DRUG OFFICIALS SCHOLARSHIP FUND
• *See page 146*

CANFIT

http://www.canfit.org/

CANFIT NUTRITION, PHYSICAL EDUCATION AND CULINARY ARTS SCHOLARSHIP
• *See page 209*

CHILD NUTRITION FOUNDATION

http://www.schoolnutrition.org/

NANCY CURRY SCHOLARSHIP

Scholarship assists members of the American School Food Service Association and their dependents to pursue educational and career advancement in school food-service or child nutrition.

Academic Fields/Career Goals: Food Science/Nutrition; Food Service/Hospitality.

Award: Scholarship for use in freshman, sophomore, junior, senior, graduate, or postgraduate years; not renewable. *Number:* varies. *Amount:* varies.

Eligibility Requirements: Applicant must be enrolled or expecting to enroll full- or part-time at a two-year or four-year or technical institution or university. Applicant or parent of applicant must have employment or volunteer experience in food service. Applicant must have 3.0 GPA or higher. Available to U.S. citizens.

Application Requirements: Application, essay, resume, references, test scores, transcript, proof of enrollment. *Deadline:* April 15.

Contact: Ruth O'Brien, Scholarship Manager
Child Nutrition Foundation
700 South Washington Street, Suite 300
Alexandria, VA 22314
Phone: 703-739-3900 Ext. 150
E-mail: robrien@asfsa.org

PROFESSIONAL GROWTH SCHOLARSHIP

Scholarships for child nutrition professionals who are pursuing graduate education in a food science management or nutrition-related field of study.

Academic Fields/Career Goals: Food Science/Nutrition; Food Service/Hospitality.

Award: Scholarship for use in freshman, sophomore, junior, senior, graduate, or postgraduate years; not renewable. *Number:* varies. *Amount:* varies.

Eligibility Requirements: Applicant must be enrolled or expecting to enroll full- or part-time at a two-year or four-year or technical institution or university. Applicant or parent of applicant must have employment or volunteer experience in food service. Applicant must have 3.5 GPA or higher. Available to U.S. citizens.

Application Requirements: Application, essay, resume, references, transcript, proof of enrollment, official program requirement. *Deadline:* April 15.

Contact: Scholarship Manager
Child Nutrition Foundation
700 South Washington Street, Suite 300
Alexandria, VA 22314
Phone: 703-739-3900 Ext. 150
Fax: 703-739-3915
E-mail: robrien@asfsa.org

SCHWAN'S FOOD SERVICE SCHOLARSHIP

Program is designed to assist members of the American School Food Service Association and their dependents as they pursue educational advancement in the field of child nutrition.

Academic Fields/Career Goals: Food Science/Nutrition; Food Service/Hospitality.

Award: Scholarship for use in freshman, sophomore, junior, senior, graduate, or postgraduate years; not renewable. *Number:* varies. *Amount:* varies.

Eligibility Requirements: Applicant must be enrolled or expecting to enroll full- or part-time at a two-year or four-year or technical institution or university. Applicant or parent of applicant must have employment or volunteer experience in food service. Applicant must have 2.5 GPA or higher. Available to U.S. citizens.

Application Requirements: Application, essay, resume, references, transcript, proof of enrollment, official program requirements. *Deadline:* April 15.

Contact: Ruth O'Brien, Scholarship Manager
Child Nutrition Foundation
700 South Washington Street, Suite 300
Alexandria, VA 22314
Phone: 703-739-3900 Ext. 150
E-mail: robrien@asfsa.org

THE CULINARY TRUST

http://www.theculinarytrust.org/

CULINARY TRUST SCHOLARSHIP PROGRAM FOR CULINARY STUDY AND RESEARCH
• *See page 209*

DAIRY MANAGEMENT

http://www.dairyinfo.com/

NATIONAL DAIRY PROMOTION AND RESEARCH BOARD SCHOLARSHIP
• *See page 84*

ILLINOIS RESTAURANT ASSOCIATION EDUCATIONAL FOUNDATION

http://www.illinoisrestaurants.org/

ILLINOIS RESTAURANT ASSOCIATION EDUCATIONAL FOUNDATION SCHOLARSHIPS
• *See page 210*

INSTITUTE OF FOOD TECHNOLOGISTS

http://www.ift.org/

FOOD MICROBIOLOGY DIVISION SCHOLARSHIP

Two awards are available to students interested in food microbiology. Student must be, or apply to become, a member of the IFT Food Microbiology Division at the time of the application. Student must submit a statement of interest in food microbiology, including a description of career objectives and professional aspirations.

Academic Fields/Career Goals: Food Science/Nutrition.

Award: Scholarship for use in junior or senior years; not renewable. *Number:* 2. *Amount:* $500.

Eligibility Requirements: Applicant must be enrolled or expecting to enroll full- or part-time at a four-year institution or university. Applicant or parent of applicant must be member of Institute of Food Technologists.

Application Requirements: Application, essay, references, transcript. *Deadline:* February 19.

Contact: Anna Proctor, IFT Foundation Coordinator
Institute of Food Technologists
525 West Van Buren Street, Suite 1000
Chicago, IL 60607
Phone: 312-782-8424
E-mail: akproctor@ift.org

GEORGE R. FOSTER MEMORIAL SCHOLARSHIP

One $1000 award for scholastically outstanding high school graduates or seniors expecting to graduate from high school entering college for the first time in an approved program in food science/technology.

Academic Fields/Career Goals: Food Science/Nutrition.

Award: Scholarship for use in freshman or sophomore years; not renewable. *Number:* 1. *Amount:* $1000.

Eligibility Requirements: Applicant must be enrolled or expecting to enroll full- or part-time at a four-year institution or university.

Application Requirements: Application, essay, transcript. *Deadline:* March 15.

Contact: Anna Proctor, IFT Foundation Coordinator
Institute of Food Technologists
525 West Van Buren Street, Suite 1000
Chicago, IL 60607
Phone: 312-782-8424
E-mail: akproctor@ift.org

INSTITUTE OF FOOD TECHNOLOGISTS FRESHMAN SCHOLARSHIPS

Awards for scholastically outstanding high school graduates or seniors entering college in an approved four-year program in food sciences or technology. Program must be approved by the Institute of Food Technologists Education Committee.

Academic Fields/Career Goals: Food Science/Nutrition.

Award: Scholarship for use in freshman year; not renewable. *Number:* 15. *Amount:* $1000.

Eligibility Requirements: Applicant must be enrolled or expecting to enroll full-time at a four-year institution or university. Applicant must have 3.0 GPA or higher. Available to U.S. and non-U.S. citizens.

Application Requirements: Application, references, transcript. *Deadline:* March 15.

Contact: Anna Proctor, IFT Foundation Coordinator
Institute of Food Technologists
525 West Van Buren Street, Suite 1000
Chicago, IL 60607
Phone: 312-782-8424
E-mail: akproctor@ift.org

INSTITUTE OF FOOD TECHNOLOGISTS QUALITY ASSURANCE DIVISION JUNIOR/SENIOR SCHOLARSHIPS

One-time award for college juniors and seniors who are taking or have taken a course in quality assurance and have demonstrated an interest in the quality assurance area.

Academic Fields/Career Goals: Food Science/Nutrition.

Award: Scholarship for use in junior or senior years; not renewable. *Number:* 2. *Amount:* $2000.

Eligibility Requirements: Applicant must be enrolled or expecting to enroll full-time at a four-year institution. Available to U.S. and non-U.S. citizens.

Application Requirements: Application, references, transcript. *Deadline:* February 19.

Contact: Anna Proctor, IFT Foundation Coordinator
Institute of Food Technologists
525 West Van Buren Street, Suite 1000
Chicago, IL 60607
Phone: 312-782-8424
E-mail: akproctor@ift.org

INSTITUTE OF FOOD TECHNOLOGISTS SOPHOMORE SCHOLARSHIPS

Awards available to college freshmen for use in sophomore year. Applicants must major in food science or food technology in a four-year Institute of Food Technologists Education Committee-approved program and must have a 2.5 GPA.

Academic Fields/Career Goals: Food Science/Nutrition.

Award: Scholarship for use in sophomore year; not renewable. *Number:* 15. *Amount:* $1000.

Eligibility Requirements: Applicant must be enrolled or expecting to enroll full-time at a four-year institution or university. Applicant must have 2.5 GPA or higher. Available to U.S. and non-U.S. citizens.

Application Requirements: Application, references, transcript. *Deadline:* March 1.

Contact: Anna Proctor, IFT Foundation Coordinator
Institute of Food Technologists
525 West Van Buren Street, Suite 1000
Chicago, IL 60607
Phone: 312-782-8424
E-mail: akproctor@ift.org

INTERNATIONAL FOODSERVICE EDITORIAL COUNCIL

http://www.ifeconline.com/

INTERNATIONAL FOODSERVICE EDITORIAL COUNCIL COMMUNICATIONS SCHOLARSHIP
• *See page 77*

JAMES BEARD FOUNDATION INC.

http://www.jamesbeard.org/

BERN LAXER MEMORIAL SCHOLARSHIP
• *See page 210*

LES DAMES D'ESCOFFIER INTERNATIONAL

http://www.ldei.org/

LES DAMES D'ESCOFFIER SCHOLARSHIP

• *See page 212*

MAINE SCHOOL FOOD SERVICE ASSOCIATION (MSFSA) CONTINUING EDUCATION SCHOLARSHIP

http://www.mainesfsa.org/

MAINE SCHOOL FOOD SERVICE ASSOCIATION CONTINUING EDUCATION SCHOLARSHIP

• *See page 213*

MARION D. AND EVA S. PEEPLES FOUNDATION TRUST SCHOLARSHIP PROGRAM

http://www.jccf.org/

MARION A. AND EVA S. PEEPLES SCHOLARSHIPS

• *See page 240*

MARYLAND ASSOCIATION OF PRIVATE COLLEGES AND CAREER SCHOOLS

http://www.mapccs.org/

MARYLAND ASSOCIATION OF PRIVATE COLLEGES AND CAREER SCHOOLS SCHOLARSHIP

• *See page 153*

MINNESOTA SOYBEAN RESEARCH AND PROMOTION COUNCIL

http://www.mnsoybean.org/

MINNESOTA SOYBEAN RESEARCH AND PROMOTION COUNCIL YOUTH SOYBEAN SCHOLARSHIP

• *See page 79*

MISSOURI DEPARTMENT OF HEALTH AND SENIOR SERVICES

http://www.dhss.mo.gov/

PRIMARY CARE RESOURCE INITIATIVE FOR MISSOURI LOAN PROGRAM

• *See page 136*

NATIONAL DAIRY SHRINE

http://www.dairyshrine.org/

NATIONAL DAIRY SHRINE/DAIRY MARKETING INC. MILK MARKETING SCHOLARSHIPS

• *See page 85*

NDS STUDENT RECOGNITION CONTEST

• *See page 80*

NATIONAL POTATO COUNCIL WOMEN'S AUXILIARY

http://www.nationalpotatocouncil.org/

POTATO INDUSTRY SCHOLARSHIP

• *See page 80*

NATIONAL POULTRY AND FOOD DISTRIBUTORS ASSOCIATION

http://www.npfda.org/

NATIONAL POULTRY AND FOOD DISTRIBUTORS ASSOCIATION SCHOLARSHIP FOUNDATION

• *See page 80*

OREGON STUDENT ASSISTANCE COMMISSION

http://www.GetCollegeFunds.org/

OREGON WINE BROTHERHOOD SCHOLARSHIP

• *See page 213*

SAN DIEGO FOUNDATION

http://www.sdfoundation.org/

CALIFORNIA ASSOCIATION OF FAMILY AND CONSUMER SCIENCES-SAN DIEGO CHAPTER

• *See page 173*

UNITED DAUGHTERS OF THE CONFEDERACY

http://www.hqudc.org/

WALTER REED SMITH SCHOLARSHIP

• *See page 157*

UNITED NEGRO COLLEGE FUND

http://www.uncf.org/

CARGILL SCHOLARSHIP PROGRAM

• *See page 72*

GENERAL MILLS TECHNOLOGY SCHOLARS AWARD

• *See page 171*

WASHINGTON ASSOCIATION OF WINE GRAPE GROWERS

http://www.wawgg.org/

WALTER J. CLORE SCHOLARSHIP

• *See page 88*

FOOD SERVICE/ HOSPITALITY

AMERICAN CULINARY FEDERATION

http://www.acfchefs.org/

AMERICAN ACADEMY OF CHEFS CHAINE DES ROTISSEURS SCHOLARSHIP
• *See page 207*

AMERICAN ACADEMY OF CHEFS CHAIR'S SCHOLARSHIP
• *See page 207*

AMERICAN HOTEL AND LODGING EDUCATIONAL FOUNDATION

http://www.ahlef.org/

AMERICAN HOTEL & LODGING EDUCATIONAL FOUNDATION PEPSI SCHOLARSHIP
• *See page 207*

ANNUAL SCHOLARSHIP GRANT PROGRAM
• *See page 208*

ARTHUR J. PACKARD MEMORIAL SCHOLARSHIP
• *See page 208*

ECOLAB SCHOLARSHIP PROGRAM
• *See page 208*

HYATT HOTELS FUND FOR MINORITY LODGING MANAGEMENT
• *See page 208*

INCOMING FRESHMAN SCHOLARSHIPS
• *See page 208*

RAMA SCHOLARSHIP FOR THE AMERICAN DREAM
• *See page 208*

STEVEN HYMANS EXTENDED STAY SCHOLARSHIP
• *See page 209*

AMERICAN INSTITUTE OF WINE AND FOOD-PACIFIC NORTHWEST CHAPTER

http://www.aiwf.org/

CULINARY, VINIFERA, AND HOSPITALITY SCHOLARSHIP
• *See page 317*

CALIFORNIA RESTAURANT ASSOCIATION EDUCATIONAL FOUNDATION

http://www.calrest.org/

ACADEMIC SCHOLARSHIP FOR HIGH SCHOOL SENIORS

One-time scholarship awarded to high school seniors to support their education in the restaurant and/or food service industry. Applicants must be citizens of the United States or its territories (American Samoa, Guam, Puerto Rico, and U.S. Virgin Islands).

Academic Fields/Career Goals: Food Service/Hospitality.

Award: Scholarship for use in freshman year; not renewable. *Number:* varies. *Amount:* up to $2000.

Eligibility Requirements: Applicant must be high school student; planning to enroll or expecting to enroll full-time at a two-year or four-year or technical institution or university and resident of California. Applicant must have 2.5 GPA or higher. Available to U.S. and non-U.S. citizens.

Application Requirements: Application, essay, interview, resume, references, transcript. *Deadline:* April 15.

Contact: Mrs. Kathie Griley, Director, Industry Education
California Restaurant Association Educational Foundation
621 Capitol Mall, Suite 2000
Sacramento, CA 95814
Phone: 800-765-4842 Ext. 2756
E-mail: kgriley@calrest.org

ACADEMIC SCHOLARSHIP FOR UNDERGRADUATE STUDENTS

Scholarships awarded to college students to support their education in the restaurant and food service industry. Minimum 2.75 GPA required. Individuals must be citizens of the United States or its territories (American Samoa, Guam, Puerto Rico, and U.S. Virgin Islands).

Academic Fields/Career Goals: Food Service/Hospitality.

Award: Scholarship for use in freshman, sophomore, junior, or senior years; not renewable. *Number:* varies. *Amount:* varies.

Eligibility Requirements: Applicant must be enrolled or expecting to enroll full-time at a four-year institution or university and resident of California. Applicant must have 2.5 GPA or higher. Available to U.S. and non-U.S. citizens.

Application Requirements: Application, essay, interview, references, transcript. *Deadline:* March 31.

Contact: Mrs. Kathie Griley, Director, Industry Education
California Restaurant Association Educational Foundation
621 Capitol Mall, Suite 2000
Sacramento, CA 95814
Phone: 800-765-4842 Ext. 2756
E-mail: kgriley@calrest.org

CANFIT

http://www.canfit.org/

CANFIT NUTRITION, PHYSICAL EDUCATION AND CULINARY ARTS SCHOLARSHIP
• *See page 209*

CHILD NUTRITION FOUNDATION

http://www.schoolnutrition.org/

NANCY CURRY SCHOLARSHIP
• *See page 318*

PROFESSIONAL GROWTH SCHOLARSHIP
• *See page 318*

SCHWAN'S FOOD SERVICE SCHOLARSHIP
• *See page 318*

COLORADO RESTAURANT ASSOCIATION

http://www.coloradorestaurant.com/

CRA UNDERGRADUATE SCHOLARSHIPS

Scholarship of $1000 to $2000 for applicants intending to pursue education in the undergraduate level in the field of food service or hospitality and have a GPA of at least 2.75.

Academic Fields/Career Goals: Food Service/Hospitality.

Award: Scholarship for use in freshman, sophomore, junior, or senior years; not renewable. *Number:* 15. *Amount:* $1000–$2000.

Eligibility Requirements: Applicant must be enrolled or expecting to enroll full- or part-time at a four-year institution or university. Available to U.S. and non-U.S. citizens.

Application Requirements: Application, resume, references, transcript. *Deadline:* April 6.

Contact: Mary Mino, President
Colorado Restaurant Association
730 East Seventh Avenue
Denver, CO 80203
Phone: 800-522-2972
Fax: 303-830-2973
E-mail: info@coloradorestaurant.com

PROSTART SCHOLARSHIPS

Scholarship of $500 to $1000 for applicants currently in high school and intending to pursue education in the field of food service or hospitality and have a GPA of at least 3.0.

Academic Fields/Career Goals: Food Service/Hospitality.

Award: Scholarship for use in freshman year; not renewable. *Number:* 15. *Amount:* $500–$1000.

Eligibility Requirements: Applicant must be high school student and planning to enroll or expecting to enroll full- or part-time at a four-year institution or university. Applicant must have 3.0 GPA or higher. Available to U.S. and non-U.S. citizens.

Application Requirements: Application, resume, references, transcript. *Deadline:* April 6.

Contact: Mary Mino, President
Colorado Restaurant Association
730 East Seventh Avenue
Denver, CO 80203
Phone: 800-522-2972
Fax: 303-830-2973
E-mail: info@coloradorestaurant.com

THE CULINARY TRUST

http://www.theculinarytrust.org/

CULINARY TRUST SCHOLARSHIP PROGRAM FOR CULINARY STUDY AND RESEARCH
• See page 209

GOLDEN GATE RESTAURANT ASSOCIATION

http://www.ggra.org/

GOLDEN GATE RESTAURANT ASSOCIATION SCHOLARSHIP FOUNDATION

One-time award for any student pursuing a food service degree at a 501(c)(3) institution, or institutions approved by the Board of Trustees. California residency and personal interview in San Francisco is required. Minimum GPA of 2.75 required. For further information email donnalyn@ggra.org, or visit ggra.org/scholarships.aspx.

Academic Fields/Career Goals: Food Service/Hospitality; Hospitality Management.

Award: Scholarship for use in freshman, sophomore, junior, or senior years; not renewable. *Number:* 9–15. *Amount:* $1000–$6000.

Eligibility Requirements: Applicant must be enrolled or expecting to enroll full- or part-time at a two-year or four-year or technical institution or university and resident of California. Available to U.S. citizens.

Application Requirements: Application, essay, financial need analysis, interview, references, transcript. *Deadline:* April 30.

Contact: Donnalyn Murphy, Trustee and Secretary
Golden Gate Restaurant Association
120 Montgomery Street, Suite 1280
San Francisco, CA 94104
Phone: 415-781-5348 Ext. 2
Fax: 415-781-3925
E-mail: education@ggra.org

ILLINOIS RESTAURANT ASSOCIATION EDUCATIONAL FOUNDATION

http://www.illinoisrestaurants.org/

ILLINOIS RESTAURANT ASSOCIATION EDUCATIONAL FOUNDATION SCHOLARSHIPS
• See page 210

INTERNATIONAL EXECUTIVE HOUSEKEEPERS ASSOCIATION

http://www.ieha.org/

INTERNATIONAL EXECUTIVE HOUSEKEEPERS EDUCATIONAL FOUNDATION

One-time award of up to $800 for students planning careers in the area of facilities management. Must be enrolled in IEHA-approved courses at a participating college or university. Must be a member of IEHA.

Academic Fields/Career Goals: Food Service/Hospitality; Home Economics; Trade/Technical Specialties.

Award: Scholarship for use in freshman, sophomore, junior, or senior years; not renewable. *Number:* 10. *Amount:* $800.

Eligibility Requirements: Applicant must be enrolled or expecting to enroll full- or part-time at a two-year or four-year or technical institution or university. Applicant or parent of applicant must be member of International Executive Housekeepers Association. Available to U.S. and non-U.S. citizens.

Application Requirements: Application, essay, transcript. *Deadline:* January 10.

Contact: Beth Risinger, Chief Executive Officer and Executive Director
International Executive Housekeepers Association
Education Department, 1001 Eastwind Drive, Suite 301
Westerville, OH 43081-3361
Phone: 800-200-6342
Fax: 614-895-7166
E-mail: excel@ieha.org

INTERNATIONAL FOODSERVICE EDITORIAL COUNCIL

http://www.ifeconline.com/

INTERNATIONAL FOODSERVICE EDITORIAL COUNCIL COMMUNICATIONS SCHOLARSHIP
• See page 77

INTERNATIONAL FOOD SERVICE EXECUTIVES ASSOCIATION

http://www.ifsea.com/

WORTHY GOAL SCHOLARSHIP FUND

Scholarships to assist individuals in receiving food service management or vocational training beyond high school. Applicant must be enrolled or accepted as full-time student in a food service related major for the fall term following the award.

Academic Fields/Career Goals: Food Service/Hospitality.

Award: Scholarship for use in freshman, sophomore, junior, or senior years; not renewable. *Number:* 15. *Amount:* $1000–$1500.

Eligibility Requirements: Applicant must be enrolled or expecting to enroll full-time at a two-year or four-year or technical institution or university. Available to U.S. citizens.

Application Requirements: Essay, financial need analysis, references, transcript, financial statement summary, work experience documentation. *Deadline:* March 1.

Contact: Steve Schroeder, IFSEA President
International Food Service Executives Association
500 Ryland Street Suite 200
Reno, NV 89502
Phone: 775-825-2665
Fax: 775-825-6411
E-mail: steve@IFSEA.com

KENTUCKY RESTAURANT ASSOCIATION EDUCATIONAL FOUNDATION

http://www.kyra.org/

KENTUCKY RESTAURANT ASSOCIATION EDUCATIONAL FOUNDATION SCHOLARSHIP

Scholarship available for high school graduate or equivalent accepted to an associate or bachelor's degree program in food service, or student already enrolled in an associate, bachelor's, or master's degree food service program. Applicant must be a resident of Kentucky or within 25 miles of Kentucky's borders for previous 18 months.

Academic Fields/Career Goals: Food Service/Hospitality.

Award: Scholarship for use in freshman, sophomore, junior, or senior years; renewable. *Number:* varies. *Amount:* varies.

Eligibility Requirements: Applicant must be enrolled or expecting to enroll full-time at a four-year institution or university and resident of Kentucky. Available to U.S. citizens.

Application Requirements: Application, references, transcript, proof of acceptance. *Deadline:* varies.

Contact: Scholarship Committee
Kentucky Restaurant Association Educational Foundation
133 Evergreen Road, Suite 201
Louisville, KY 40243
Phone: 800-896-0414
Fax: 502-896-0465
E-mail: info@kyra.org

LES DAMES D'ESCOFFIER INTERNATIONAL

http://www.ldei.org/

LES DAMES D'ESCOFFIER SCHOLARSHIP
• *See page 212*

MAINE SCHOOL FOOD SERVICE ASSOCIATION (MSFSA) CONTINUING EDUCATION SCHOLARSHIP

http://www.mainesfsa.org/

MAINE SCHOOL FOOD SERVICE ASSOCIATION CONTINUING EDUCATION SCHOLARSHIP
• *See page 213*

MISSOURI TRAVEL COUNCIL

http://www.missouritravel.com/

MISSOURI TRAVEL COUNCIL TOURISM SCHOLARSHIP

One-time award for Missouri resident pursuing hospitality-related major such as hotel/restaurant management or parks and recreation. Applicant must be currently enrolled in an accredited college or university in the state of Missouri. Selection is based on essay, GPA, community involvement, academic activities, and hospitality-related experience.

Academic Fields/Career Goals: Food Service/Hospitality; Hospitality Management; Travel/Tourism.

Award: Scholarship for use in sophomore, junior, or senior years; not renewable. *Number:* 2. *Amount:* $1000.

Eligibility Requirements: Applicant must be enrolled or expecting to enroll full-time at a four-year institution or university; resident of Missouri and studying in Missouri. Applicant must have 3.0 GPA or higher. Available to U.S. citizens.

Application Requirements: Application, essay, references, transcript. *Deadline:* March 1.

Contact: Pat Amick, Executive Director
Missouri Travel Council
204 East High Street
Jefferson City, MO 65101-3287
Phone: 573-636-2814
Fax: 573-636-5783
E-mail: pamick@sockets.net

NATIONAL POULTRY AND FOOD DISTRIBUTORS ASSOCIATION

http://www.npfda.org/

NATIONAL POULTRY AND FOOD DISTRIBUTORS ASSOCIATION SCHOLARSHIP FOUNDATION
• *See page 80*

NATIONAL RESTAURANT ASSOCIATION EDUCATIONAL FOUNDATION

http://www.nraef.org/

COCA-COLA SALUTE TO EXCELLENCE SCHOLARSHIP AWARD

Scholarship for a student currently enrolled in college who has completed at least one semester in a restaurant and/or foodservice-related program.

Academic Fields/Career Goals: Food Service/Hospitality.

Award: Scholarship for use in sophomore, junior, senior, graduate, or postgraduate years; not renewable. *Number:* 2. *Amount:* $5000.

Eligibility Requirements: Applicant must be enrolled or expecting to enroll full-time at a two-year or four-year or technical institution or university. Applicant or parent of applicant must have employment or volunteer experience in food service. Available to U.S. citizens.

Application Requirements: Application, essay, transcript, proof of total hours worked. *Deadline:* March 21.

Contact: Shanna Young, Manager
National Restaurant Association Educational Foundation
175 West Jackson Boulevard, Suite 1500
Chicago, IL 60604-2702
Phone: 800-765-2122 Ext. 744
Fax: 312-566-9733
E-mail: syoung@nraef.org

NATIONAL RESTAURANT ASSOCIATION EDUCATIONAL FOUNDATION UNDERGRADUATE SCHOLARSHIPS FOR COLLEGE STUDENTS

Awarded to college students who have demonstrated a commitment to both postsecondary hospitality education and to a career in the industry with 750 hours of industry work experience. Minimum 2.75 GPA required. Application deadlines: March 31, July 31 and October 31.

Academic Fields/Career Goals: Food Service/Hospitality; Hospitality Management.

Award: Scholarship for use in sophomore, junior, or senior years; not renewable. *Number:* varies. *Amount:* $2000.

Eligibility Requirements: Applicant must be enrolled or expecting to enroll full- or part-time at a four-year institution or university. Applicant or parent of applicant must have employment or volunteer experience in food service. Available to U.S. citizens.

Application Requirements: Application, essay, resume, references, transcript, copies of paycheck stubs or a letter from employers verifying total work hours. *Deadline:* varies.

Contact: Shanna Young, Manager
National Restaurant Association Educational Foundation
175 West Jackson Boulevard, Suite 1500
Chicago, IL 60604-2702
Phone: 800-765-2122 Ext. 744
Fax: 312-566-9733
E-mail: syoung@nraef.org

NATIONAL RESTAURANT ASSOCIATION EDUCATIONAL FOUNDATION UNDERGRADUATE SCHOLARSHIPS FOR HIGH SCHOOL SENIORS AND GENERAL EDUCATION DIPLOMA (GED) GRADUATE S

Scholarship awarded to high school students who have demonstrated a commitment to both postsecondary hospitality education and to a career in the industry. Must have 250 hours of industry experience, be between ages of 17 and 19, and have minimum 2.75 GPA.

Academic Fields/Career Goals: Food Service/Hospitality; Hospitality Management.

Award: Scholarship for use in freshman year; not renewable. *Number:* varies. *Amount:* $2000.

Eligibility Requirements: Applicant must be age 17-19 and enrolled or expecting to enroll full-time at a four-year institution or university. Applicant or parent of applicant must have employment or volunteer experience in food service. Available to U.S. citizens.

Application Requirements: Application, essay, references, transcript, letter of acceptance, industrial experience letter. *Deadline:* May 16.

Contact: Shanna Young, Manager
National Restaurant Association Educational Foundation
175 West Jackson Boulevard, Suite 1500
Chicago, IL 60604-2702
Phone: 800-765-2122 Ext. 744
Fax: 312-566-9733
E-mail: syoung@nraef.org

PROSTART® NATIONAL CERTIFICATE OF ACHIEVEMENT SCHOLARSHIP

For high school junior and senior students who have earned Pro Start National Certificate of Achievement and are continuing their education in a restaurant or foodservice program. For application and details visit web site http://nraef.org.

Academic Fields/Career Goals: Food Service/Hospitality.

Award: Scholarship for use in freshman year; not renewable. *Number:* varies. *Amount:* $2000.

Eligibility Requirements: Applicant must be high school student and planning to enroll or expecting to enroll full- or part-time at a four-year institution or university. Available to U.S. citizens.

Application Requirements: Application. *Deadline:* August 15.

Contact: Shanna Young, Manager
National Restaurant Association Educational Foundation
175 West Jackson Boulevard, Suite 1500
Chicago, IL 60604-2702
Phone: 800-765-2122 Ext. 744
Fax: 312-566-9733
E-mail: syoung@nraef.org

NATIONAL TOURISM FOUNDATION

http://www.ntfonline.com/

CLEVELAND LEGACY I AND II SCHOLARSHIP AWARDS

Award for Ohio residents pursuing travel and tourism studies. Must be enrolled full-time in two- or four-year institution and a resident of Ohio. Minimum 3.0 GPA required. Submit resume.

Academic Fields/Career Goals: Food Service/Hospitality; Hospitality Management; Travel/Tourism.

Award: Scholarship for use in freshman, sophomore, junior, or senior years; not renewable. *Number:* 1. *Amount:* $1000.

Eligibility Requirements: Applicant must be enrolled or expecting to enroll full-time at a two-year or four-year institution or university and resident of Ohio. Applicant must have 3.0 GPA or higher. Available to U.S. citizens.

Application Requirements: Application, essay, resume, references, transcript. *Deadline:* May 10.

Contact: Michelle Gorin, Projects Coordinator
National Tourism Foundation
546 East Main Street
Lexington, KY 40508-3071
Phone: 800-682-8886
Fax: 859-226-4437

NEW HORIZONS KATHY LETARTE SCHOLARSHIP

One $1000 scholarship awarded to an undergraduate student entering his or her junior year of study. Applicant must be enrolled in a tourism-related program at an accredited four-year college or university. Must have minimum 3.0 GPA. Applicant must be Michigan resident. Refer to web site for further details http://www.ntfonline.com/scholarships/index.php.

Academic Fields/Career Goals: Food Service/Hospitality; Hospitality Management; Travel/Tourism.

Award: Scholarship for use in freshman, sophomore, junior, or senior years; not renewable. *Number:* 1. *Amount:* $1000.

Eligibility Requirements: Applicant must be enrolled or expecting to enroll full-time at a two-year or four-year institution or university and resident of Michigan. Applicant must have 3.0 GPA or higher. Available to U.S. citizens.

Application Requirements: Application, essay, resume, references, transcript. *Deadline:* May 10.

Contact: Michelle Gorin, Projects Coordinator
National Tourism Foundation
546 East Main Street
Lexington, KY 40508-3071
Phone: 800-682-8886
Fax: 859-226-4437

SOCIETIE DES CASINOS DU QUEBEC SCHOLARSHIP

Award for resident of Quebec who is pursuing travel and tourism studies. May attend a four-year college or university. Minimum 3.0 GPA required.

Academic Fields/Career Goals: Food Service/Hospitality; Hospitality Management; Travel/Tourism.

Award: Scholarship for use in freshman, sophomore, junior, or senior years; not renewable. *Number:* 1. *Amount:* $1000.

Eligibility Requirements: Applicant must be enrolled or expecting to enroll full-time at a two-year or four-year institution and resident of Quebec. Applicant must have 3.0 GPA or higher. Available to Canadian citizens.

Application Requirements: Application, essay, resume, references, transcript. *Deadline:* May 10.

Contact: Michelle Gorin, Projects Coordinator
National Tourism Foundation
546 East Main Street
Lexington, KY 40508-3071
Phone: 800-682-8886
Fax: 859-226-4437

TAMPA, HILLSBOROUGH LEGACY SCHOLARSHIP

One-time award for Florida resident who is pursuing studies in travel and tourism. Must attend a Florida college or university. Minimum 3.0 GPA required.

Academic Fields/Career Goals: Food Service/Hospitality; Hospitality Management; Travel/Tourism.

Award: Scholarship for use in freshman, sophomore, junior, or senior years; not renewable. *Number:* 1. *Amount:* $1000.

Eligibility Requirements: Applicant must be enrolled or expecting to enroll full-time at a two-year or four-year institution or university; resident of Florida and studying in Florida. Applicant must have 3.0 GPA or higher. Available to U.S. citizens.

Application Requirements: Application, essay, resume, references, transcript. *Deadline:* May 10.

Contact: Michelle Gorin, Projects Coordinator
National Tourism Foundation
546 East Main Street
Lexington, KY 40508-3071
Phone: 800-682-8886
Fax: 859-226-4437

TAUCK SCHOLARS SCHOLARSHIPS

Four undergraduate scholarships awarded to students entering their sophomore or junior years of study in travel and tourism-related degrees. Applicants will receive $3000 over two years; $1500 awarded first year and $1500 awarded the following year. Must have minimum 3.0 GPA. Please refer to web site for further details http://www.ntfonline.org.

Academic Fields/Career Goals: Food Service/Hospitality; Hospitality Management; Travel/Tourism.

Award: Scholarship for use in sophomore or junior years; renewable. *Number:* 4. *Amount:* $1500.

Eligibility Requirements: Applicant must be enrolled or expecting to enroll full-time at a two-year or four-year institution or university. Applicant must have 3.0 GPA or higher. Available to U.S. citizens.

Application Requirements: Application, essay, resume, references, transcript. *Deadline:* May 10.

Contact: Michelle Gorin, Projects Coordinator
National Tourism Foundation
546 East Main Street
Lexington, KY 40508-3071
Phone: 800-682-8886
Fax: 859-226-4437

TULSA SCHOLARSHIP AWARDS

Scholarship available for Oklahoma residents pursuing travel and tourism studies. Must be enrolled in an Oklahoma four-year institution. Minimum 3.0 GPA required. Submit resume.

Academic Fields/Career Goals: Food Service/Hospitality; Hospitality Management; Travel/Tourism.

Award: Scholarship for use in freshman, sophomore, junior, or senior years; not renewable. *Number:* 1. *Amount:* $500.

Eligibility Requirements: Applicant must be enrolled or expecting to enroll full-time at a four-year institution or university; resident of Oklahoma and studying in Oklahoma. Applicant must have 3.0 GPA or higher. Available to U.S. citizens.

Application Requirements: Application, essay, resume, references, transcript. *Deadline:* May 10.

Contact: Michelle Gorin, Projects Coordinator
National Tourism Foundation
546 East Main Street
Lexington, KY 40508-3071
Phone: 800-682-8886
Fax: 859-226-4437

YELLOW RIBBON SCHOLARSHIP

One-time scholarship for residents of North America with physical or sensory disabilities who are pursuing travel and tourism studies at a North American institution. Must be entering postsecondary education with a minimum 3.0 GPA or must be maintaining at least a 2.5 GPA at college level. Must submit resume and essay explaining plans to utilize his or her education in travel and tourism career.

Academic Fields/Career Goals: Food Service/Hospitality; Hospitality Management; Travel/Tourism.

Award: Scholarship for use in freshman, sophomore, junior, or senior years; not renewable. *Number:* 1. *Amount:* $2500.

Eligibility Requirements: Applicant must be enrolled or expecting to enroll full-time at a two-year or four-year institution or university. Applicant must be hearing impaired, physically disabled, or visually impaired. Available to U.S. and Canadian citizens.

Application Requirements: Application, essay, resume, references, transcript. *Deadline:* May 10.

Contact: Michelle Gorin, Projects Coordinator
National Tourism Foundation
546 East Main Street
Lexington, KY 40508-3071
Phone: 800-682-8886
Fax: 859-226-4437

SAN DIEGO FOUNDATION

http://www.sdfoundation.org/

CALIFORNIA ASSOCIATION OF FAMILY AND CONSUMER SCIENCES-SAN DIEGO CHAPTER
• *See page 173*

SOUTH DAKOTA RETAILERS ASSOCIATION

http://www.sdra.org/

SOUTH DAKOTA RETAILERS ASSOCIATION SCHOLARSHIP PROGRAM
• *See page 71*

UNITED NEGRO COLLEGE FUND

http://www.uncf.org/

FLOWERS INDUSTRIES SCHOLARSHIP
• *See page 157*

WOMEN CHEFS AND RESTAURATEURS

http://www.womenchefs.org/

FRENCH CULINARY INSTITUTE/ITALIAN CULINARY EXPERIENCE SCHOLARSHIP
• *See page 213*

WOMEN GROCERS OF AMERICA

http://www.nationalgrocers.org/

MARY MACEY SCHOLARSHIP
• *See page 88*

FOREIGN·LANGUAGE

ACL/NJCL NATIONAL LATIN EXAM

http://www.nle.org/

NATIONAL LATIN EXAM SCHOLARSHIP
• *See page 181*

ALBERTA HERITAGE SCHOLARSHIP FUND

http://www.alis.alberta.ca/

FELLOWSHIPS FOR FULL-TIME STUDIES IN FRENCH

Awards of between CAN$500 and CAN$1000 to assist Albertans in pursuing postsecondary studies taught in French. Must be Alberta resident, Canadian citizen, or landed immigrant, and plan to register full-time in a postsecondary program in Alberta of at least one semester in length. Must be enrolled in a minimum of three courses per semester which have French as the language of instruction. For additional information and application, see web site http://alis.alberta.ca.

Academic Fields/Career Goals: Foreign Language.

Award: Scholarship for use in freshman, sophomore, junior, or senior years; not renewable. *Number:* varies.

Eligibility Requirements: Applicant must be Canadian citizen; enrolled or expecting to enroll full-time at a two-year or four-year or technical institution or university; resident of Alberta and must have an interest in French language.

Application Requirements: Application, transcript. *Deadline:* November 15.

Contact: Scholarship Committee
Alberta Heritage Scholarship Fund
9940 106th Street, Fourth Floor, Sterling Place
PO Box 28000, Station Main
Edmonton, AB T5J 4R4
Canada
Phone: 780-427-8640
E-mail: scholarships@gov.ab.ca

LANGUAGES IN TEACHER EDUCATION SCHOLARSHIPS
• *See page 229*

ALPHA MU GAMMA, THE NATIONAL COLLEGIATE FOREIGN LANGUAGE SOCIETY

http://www.lacitycollege.edu/

NATIONAL ALPHA MU GAMMA SCHOLARSHIPS

One-time award to student members of Alpha Mu Gamma with a minimum 3.5 GPA, who plan to continue study of a foreign language. Must participate in a national scholarship competition. Apply through local chapter advisers. Freshmen are not eligible. Must submit a copy of

Alpha Mu Gamma membership certificate. Can study overseas if part of his/her school program.

Academic Fields/Career Goals: Foreign Language.

Award: Scholarship for use in sophomore, junior, senior, graduate, or postgraduate years; not renewable. *Number:* 3. *Amount:* up to $750.

Eligibility Requirements: Applicant must be enrolled or expecting to enroll full- or part-time at a two-year or four-year institution or university. Applicant or parent of applicant must be member of Alpha Mu Gamma. Applicant must have 3.5 GPA or higher. Available to U.S. and non-U.S. citizens.

Application Requirements: Application, applicant must enter a contest, essay, references, transcript, photocopy of Alpha Mud Gamma membership. *Deadline:* February 1.

Contact: Hisham Malek, Scholarship Coordinator
Alpha Mu Gamma, The National Collegiate Foreign Language Society
855 North Vermont Avenue
Los Angeles, CA 90029
Phone: 323-644-9752
Fax: 323-644-9752
E-mail: amgnat@lacitycollege.edu

AMERICAN CLASSICAL LEAGUE/ NATIONAL JUNIOR CLASSICAL LEAGUE

http://www.aclclassics.org/

NATIONAL JUNIOR CLASSICAL LEAGUE SCHOLARSHIP
• *See page 181*

AMERICAN COUNCIL FOR POLISH CULTURE

http://www.polishcultureacpc.org/

ACPC SUMMER STUDIES IN POLAND SCHOLARSHIP
• *See page 104*

SKALNY SCHOLARSHIP FOR POLISH STUDIES
• *See page 104*

AMERICAN FOUNDATION FOR TRANSLATION AND INTERPRETATION

http://www.afti.org/

AFTI SCHOLARSHIPS IN SCIENTIFIC AND TECHNICAL TRANSLATION, LITERARY TRANSLATION, AND INTERPRETATION

Scholarships for full-time students enrolled or planning to enroll in a degree program in scientific and technical translation, literary translation, or interpreter training. Must have a 3.0 GPA.

Academic Fields/Career Goals: Foreign Language.

Award: Scholarship for use in sophomore, junior, or senior years; not renewable. *Number:* 1–2. *Amount:* $2500.

Eligibility Requirements: Applicant must be enrolled or expecting to enroll full-time at a four-year institution or university. Applicant must have 3.0 GPA or higher. Available to U.S. citizens.

Application Requirements: Application, essay, references, transcript, proof of admission to T/I program. *Deadline:* June 1.

Contact: Eleanor Krawutschke, Executive Director, AFTI
American Foundation for Translation and Interpretation
350 East Michigan Avenue, Columbia Plaza, Suite 101
Kalamazoo, MI 49007
Phone: 269-383-6893
E-mail: aftiorg@aol.com

AMERICAN INSTITUTE OF POLISH CULTURE INC.

http://www.ampolinstitute.org/

HARRIET IRSAY SCHOLARSHIP GRANT
• *See page 109*

AMERICAN PHILOLOGICAL ASSOCIATION

http://www.apaclassics.org/

MINORITY STUDENT SUMMER SCHOLARSHIP
• *See page 98*

AMERICAN RESEARCH INSTITUTE IN TURKEY (ARIT)

http://www.ccat.sas.upenn.edu/ARIT

CRITICAL LANGUAGES SCHOLARSHIPS FOR INTENSIVE SUMMER INSTITUTE IN TURKISH LANGUAGE

Scholarships available for Intensive Summer Institute in Turkish Language. The program places students in intensive, eight-week summer courses in Turkish at all levels held at institutions in five locations in Turkey. See web site for additional information and application http://www.caorc.org/centers/arit.htm.

Academic Fields/Career Goals: Foreign Language.

Award: Scholarship for use in freshman, sophomore, junior, or senior years; not renewable. *Number:* 50–60. *Amount:* $8000–$8500.

Eligibility Requirements: Applicant must be enrolled or expecting to enroll full-time at a four-year institution or university and must have an interest in Turkish language. Applicant must have 3.0 GPA or higher. Available to U.S. citizens.

Application Requirements: Application, essay, references, test scores, transcript, language test. *Deadline:* November 1.

Contact: For further information refer to Web page in description above.

ARMED FORCES COMMUNICATIONS AND ELECTRONICS ASSOCIATION, EDUCATIONAL FOUNDATION

http://www.afcea.org/education/scholarships

ARMED FORCES COMMUNICATIONS AND ELECTRONICS ASSOCIATION ROTC SCHOLARSHIP PROGRAM
• *See page 122*

ASSOCIATION OF FORMER INTELLIGENCE OFFICERS

http://www.afio.com/13_scholarships.htm

CIA UNDERGRADUATE SCHOLARSHIPS
• *See page 89*

ASSOCIATION OF TEACHERS OF JAPANESE BRIDGING CLEARINGHOUSE FOR STUDY ABROAD IN JAPAN

http://www.colorado.edu/ealc/atj

BRIDGING SCHOLARSHIP FOR STUDY ABROAD IN JAPAN
• *See page 104*

CENTRAL INTELLIGENCE AGENCY

http://www.cia.gov/

CENTRAL INTELLIGENCE AGENCY UNDERGRADUATE SCHOLARSHIP PROGRAM
• *See page 58*

CULTURAL SERVICES OF THE FRENCH EMBASSY

http://www.frenchculture.org/

TEACHING ASSISTANT PROGRAM IN FRANCE
• *See page 235*

DONALD KEENE CENTER OF JAPANESE CULTURE

http://www.donaldkeenecenter.org/

JAPAN-U.S. FRIENDSHIP COMMISSION PRIZE FOR THE TRANSLATION OF JAPANESE LITERATURE

Annual prize for the best translation into English of a modern work of literature or for the best classical literary translation, or the prize is divided between a classical and a modern work. To qualify, works must be book-length translations of Japanese literary works: novels, collections of short stories, literary essays, memoirs, drama or poetry.

Academic Fields/Career Goals: Foreign Language.

Award: Prize for use in freshman, sophomore, junior, or senior years; not renewable. *Number:* 2. *Amount:* $3000.

Eligibility Requirements: Applicant must be enrolled or expecting to enroll full- or part-time at a two-year or four-year or technical institution or university. Available to U.S. citizens.

Application Requirements: Application, applicant must enter a contest, resume, unpublished manuscripts. *Deadline:* February 29.

Contact: Kia Cheleen, Assistant Director
Donald Keene Center of Japanese Culture
507 Kent Hall, MC 3920
1140 Amsterdam Avenue, Columbia University
New York, NY 10027
Phone: 212-854-5036
E-mail: donald-keene-center@columbia.edu

GERMAN ACADEMIC EXCHANGE SERVICE (DAAD)

http://www.daad.org/

DAAD UNIVERSITY SUMMER COURSE GRANT

Scholarships are awarded to students pursuing full-time study at Canadian or US colleges or universities. There are no restrictions as to field of study, but applicants must have attained at least Sophomore standing (second-year standing in Canada) at the time of application. Scholarships are available for courses lasting a minimum of three weeks. The scholarship is approximately 850 Euro, which covers tuition, room and board in whole or in part. Accommodations are arranged by the host institution. In addition, DAAD will provide an international travel subsidy of 300–450 Euro. Scholarship recipients are expected to devote their full attention to the course and may not concurrently undertake individual research. A written report is requested within four weeks of the end of the course.

Academic Fields/Career Goals: Foreign Language.

Award: Grant for use in sophomore, junior, senior, or graduate years; not renewable. *Number:* varies. *Amount:* varies.

Eligibility Requirements: Applicant must be enrolled or expecting to enroll full-time at a four-year institution or university and must have an interest in German language/culture. Available to U.S. and non-U.S. citizens.

Application Requirements: Application, applicant must enter a contest, essay, resume, references, transcript. *Deadline:* December 15.

Contact: Jane Fu, Information Officer
German Academic Exchange Service (DAAD)
871 United Nations Plaza
New York, NY 10017
Phone: 212-758-3223 Ext. 201
E-mail: daadny@daad.org

JAPANESE GOVERNMENT/THE MONBUSHO SCHOLARSHIP PROGRAM

http://www.la.us.emb-japan.go.jp/

JAPANESE STUDIES SCHOLARSHIP
• *See page 106*

KE ALI'I PAUAHI FOUNDATION

http://www.pauahi.org/

JOHNNY PINEAPPLE SCHOLARSHIP
• *See page 106*

SARAH KELI'ILOLENA LUM KONIA NAKOA SCHOLARSHIP

Award to recognize the academic achievements of students pursuing the study and perpetuation of the Hawaiian language, including Hawaiian culture and history. Must be a Hawaii resident, and demonstrate a financial need. Submit essay demonstrating applicant's achievements in studying Hawaiian Language, culture and history; propose a realistic plan to complete college level Hawaiian language studies; and plan to share this knowledge with others in the Hawaiian community.

Academic Fields/Career Goals: Foreign Language; History.

Award: Scholarship for use in freshman, sophomore, junior, senior, or graduate years; not renewable. *Number:* 1. *Amount:* $600.

Eligibility Requirements: Applicant must be enrolled or expecting to enroll full-time at a four-year institution or university; resident of Hawaii; studying in Hawaii and must have an interest in Hawaiian language/culture. Available to U.S. citizens.

Application Requirements: Application, essay, financial need analysis, transcript, Student Aid Report (SAR), college acceptance letter. *Deadline:* April 1.

Contact: Mavis Shiraishi-Nagao, Scholarship Administrator
Phone: 808-534-3966
E-mail: scholarships@pauahi.org

KLINGON LANGUAGE INSTITUTE

http://www.kli.org/

KOR MEMORIAL SCHOLARSHIP

Scholarship for undergraduate or graduate student in a program leading to a degree in a field related to language studies. Must send application materials by mail.

Academic Fields/Career Goals: Foreign Language.

Award: Scholarship for use in freshman, sophomore, junior, senior, or graduate years; not renewable. *Number:* 1. *Amount:* $500.

Eligibility Requirements: Applicant must be enrolled or expecting to enroll full-time at a four-year institution or university and must have an interest in foreign language. Available to U.S. citizens.

Application Requirements: Application, resume, references, nominating letter from chair, head, or dean, a brief statement of goals. *Deadline:* June 1.

Contact: Dr. Lawrence Schoen, Director
Klingon Language Institute
PO Box 634
Flourtown, PA 19031
E-mail: lawrence@kli.org

KOSCIUSZKO FOUNDATION

http://www.kosciuszkofoundation.org/

YEAR ABROAD PROGRAM IN POLAND
• *See page 106*

MISSISSIPPI OFFICE OF STUDENT FINANCIAL AID

http://www.mississippi.edu/

CRITICAL NEEDS TEACHER LOAN/SCHOLARSHIP
• *See page 241*

NATIONAL ASSOCIATION OF HISPANIC JOURNALISTS (NAHJ)

http://www.nahj.org/

MARIA ELENA SALINAS SCHOLARSHIP

One-time scholarship for high school seniors, college undergraduates, and first-year graduate students who are pursuing careers in Spanish-language broadcast (radio or TV) journalism. Students may major or plan to major in any subject, but must demonstrate a sincere desire to pursue a career in this field. Must submit essays and demo tapes (audio or video) in Spanish. Scholarship includes the opportunity to serve an internship with Univision Spanish-language television news network.

Academic Fields/Career Goals: Foreign Language; Journalism; TV/Radio Broadcasting.

Award: Scholarship for use in freshman, sophomore, junior, senior, or graduate years; not renewable. *Number:* 2. *Amount:* $5000.

Eligibility Requirements: Applicant must be enrolled or expecting to enroll full-time at a four-year institution or university and must have an interest in Spanish language. Available to U.S. citizens.

Application Requirements: Application, driver's license, essay, financial need analysis, resume, references, transcript. *Deadline:* March 31.

Contact: Virginia Galindo, Program Assistant
National Association of Hispanic Journalists (NAHJ)
1000 National Press Building, 529 14th Street, NW, Suite 1000
Washington, DC 20045-2001
Phone: 202-662-7145
E-mail: vgalindo@nahj.org

NATIONAL SECURITY AGENCY

http://www.nsa.gov/

NATIONAL SECURITY AGENCY STOKES EDUCATIONAL SCHOLARSHIP PROGRAM
• *See page 198*

NATIONAL SECURITY EDUCATION PROGRAM

http://www.iie.org/

NATIONAL SECURITY EDUCATION PROGRAM (NSEP) DAVID L. BOREN UNDERGRADUATE SCHOLARSHIPS
• *See page 154*

NEW HAMPSHIRE POSTSECONDARY EDUCATION COMMISSION

http://www.nh.gov/postsecondary

WORKFORCE INCENTIVE PROGRAM
• *See page 243*

NORWICH JUBILEE ESPERANTO FOUNDATION

http://www.esperanto-gb.org/

NOJEF TRAVEL GRANTS

Grants to help young Esperanto-speakers to use and improve their knowledge of the language, by traveling to congresses, and summer courses. Applicant must already speak Esperanto sufficiently well enough to take part in planned activity, and should be under 26 years old. For more information, refer to web site http://www.esperanto-gb.org/nojef/nojef-en.htm.

Academic Fields/Career Goals: Foreign Language.

Award: Grant for use in freshman, sophomore, junior, senior, or graduate years; not renewable. *Number:* 1–20. *Amount:* $64–$1600.

Eligibility Requirements: Applicant must be age 26 or under; enrolled or expecting to enroll full- or part-time at a two-year or four-year or technical institution or university and must have an interest in Spanish language. Available to U.S. and non-U.S. citizens.

Application Requirements: Application, essay, references. *Deadline:* continuous.

Contact: Dr. Kathleen M. Hall, Scholarship Committee
Norwich Jubilee Esperanto Foundation
37 Granville Court, Cheney Lane
Oxford OX3 0HS
Phone: 44--865-245-509

SONS OF ITALY FOUNDATION

http://www.osia.org/

SONS OF ITALY NATIONAL LEADERSHIP GRANTS COMPETITION LANGUAGE SCHOLARSHIP

Scholarships for undergraduate students in their junior or senior year of study who are majoring in Italian language studies. Must be a U.S. citizen of Italian descent. For more details see web site http://www.osia.org.

Academic Fields/Career Goals: Foreign Language.

Award: Scholarship for use in junior or senior years; not renewable. *Number:* up to 1. *Amount:* up to $10,000.

Eligibility Requirements: Applicant must be of Italian heritage and enrolled or expecting to enroll full-time at a four-year institution or university. Available to U.S. citizens.

Application Requirements: Application, driver's license, essay, resume, references, self-addressed stamped envelope, test scores, transcript. *Fee:* $30. *Deadline:* February 28.

Contact: Ms. Amy Petrine, Scholarship Coordinator
Sons of Italy Foundation
219 E Street, NE
Washington, DC 20002
Phone: 202-547-2900
E-mail: scholarships@osia.org

STRAIGHTFORWARD MEDIA

http://www.straightforwardmedia.com/

STRAIGHTFORWARD MEDIA LIBERAL ARTS SCHOLARSHIP
• *See page 107*

UNITED NEGRO COLLEGE FUND

http://www.uncf.org/

CARMEN ROSARIO BATTLE SCHOLARSHIP

Awards for students attending UNCF member colleges and universities. Must have minimum 2.5 GPA and major in mathematics or Spanish.

Academic Fields/Career Goals: Foreign Language; Mathematics.

Award: Scholarship for use in freshman year; not renewable.

Eligibility Requirements: Applicant must be Black (non-Hispanic) and enrolled or expecting to enroll at a four-year institution or university. Applicant must have 2.5 GPA or higher. Available to U.S. citizens.

Application Requirements: *Deadline:* continuous.

Contact: Director, Program Services
United Negro College Fund
8260 Willow Oaks Corporate Drive
PO Box 10444
Fairfax, VA 22031-8044
Phone: 800-331-2244
E-mail: rebecca.bennett@uncf.org

WHOMENTORS.COM, INC.

http://www.WHOmentors.com/

ACCREDITED REPRESENTATIVE (FULL)
• *See page 56*

FUNERAL SERVICES/ MORTUARY SCIENCE

ALABAMA FUNERAL DIRECTORS ASSOCIATION INC.

http://www.alabamafda.org/

ALABAMA FUNERAL DIRECTORS ASSOCIATION SCHOLARSHIP

Two $1000 scholarships available to Alabama residents. Applicant must have been accepted by an accredited mortuary science school and be sponsored by a member of the AFDA. Must maintain a minimum 2.5 GPA. Deadline: no later than 30 days prior to the AFDA mid winter meeting and annual convention.

Academic Fields/Career Goals: Funeral Services/Mortuary Science.

Award: Scholarship for use in freshman, sophomore, junior, or senior years; not renewable. *Number:* 2. *Amount:* $1000.

Eligibility Requirements: Applicant must be enrolled or expecting to enroll full- or part-time at a four-year institution or university and resident of Alabama. Applicant must have 2.5 GPA or higher. Available to U.S. citizens.

Application Requirements: Application, essay, photo, references, transcript, two proofs of residency (such as voter registration, drivers license, or tax returns). *Deadline:* varies.

Contact: Denise Edmisten, Executive Director
Alabama Funeral Directors Association Inc.
7956 Vaughn Road, PO Box 380
Montgomery, AL 36116
Phone: 334-956-8000
Fax: 334-956-8001

AMERICAN BOARD OF FUNERAL SERVICE EDUCATION

http://www.abfse.org/

AMERICAN BOARD OF FUNERAL SERVICE EDUCATION SCHOLARSHIPS

One-time award for students who are enrolled in an accredited funeral science education program and have completed at least one term/ semester. Deadlines: March 1 and September 1. For more details see web site http//www.abfse.org.

Academic Fields/Career Goals: Funeral Services/Mortuary Science.

Award: Scholarship for use in freshman, sophomore, junior, or senior years; not renewable. *Number:* 5–15. *Amount:* $500–$2500.

Eligibility Requirements: Applicant must be enrolled or expecting to enroll full-time at a two-year or four-year institution or university. Available to U.S. and non-U.S. citizens.

Application Requirements: Application, essay, financial need analysis, references, transcript. *Deadline:* varies.

Contact: Dr. Michael Smith, Executive Director
American Board of Funeral Service Education
3414 Ashland Avenue, Suite G
St. Joseph, MO 64506
Phone: 816-233-3747
E-mail: exdir@abfse.org

INTERNATIONAL ORDER OF THE GOLDEN RULE

http://www.ogr.org/

INTERNATIONAL ORDER OF THE GOLDEN RULE AWARDS OF EXCELLENCE SCHOLARSHIP

One-time scholarship for mortuary science students to prepare for a career in funeral service. Must: be enrolled in a mortuary science degree program at an accredited mortuary school, have a minimum 3.0 GPA, commit to working at an independently owned funeral home, and be scheduled to graduate within this calendar year.

Academic Fields/Career Goals: Funeral Services/Mortuary Science.

Award: Scholarship for use in freshman, sophomore, junior, or senior years; not renewable. *Number:* 2. *Amount:* $2000–$3500.

Eligibility Requirements: Applicant must be enrolled or expecting to enroll full- or part-time at a two-year or four-year or technical institution or university. Applicant must have 3.0 GPA or higher. Available to U.S. and non-U.S. citizens.

Application Requirements: Application, essay, transcript. *Deadline:* January 31.

Contact: Lisa Krabbenhoft, Director of Education
International Order of the Golden Rule
3520 Executive Center Drive #300
Austin, TX 78731
Phone: 800-637-8030
Fax: 512-334-5514
E-mail: lkrabbenhoft@ogr.org

MISSOURI FUNERAL DIRECTORS & EMBLAMERS ASSOCIATION

http://www.mofuneral.org/

MISSOURI FUNERAL DIRECTORS ASSOCIATION SCHOLARSHIPS

Scholarship to Missouri residents pursuing a career in funeral services or mortuary science.

Academic Fields/Career Goals: Funeral Services/Mortuary Science.

Award: Scholarship for use in freshman, sophomore, junior, or senior years; not renewable. *Number:* up to 5. *Amount:* $300–$600.

Eligibility Requirements: Applicant must be enrolled or expecting to enroll full- or part-time at a technical institution and resident of Missouri. Available to U.S. citizens.

Application Requirements: Application, resume, references. *Deadline:* April 15.

Contact: Don Otto, Jr., JD, Executive Director
Missouri Funeral Directors & Emblamers Association
1105 Southwest Blvd, Suite A
Jefferson City, MO 65109
Phone: 573-635-1661
Fax: 573-635-9494
E-mail: info@mofuneral.org

NATIONAL FUNERAL DIRECTORS AND MORTICIANS ASSOCIATION

http://www.nfdma.com/

NATIONAL FUNERAL DIRECTORS AND MORTICIANS ASSOCIATION SCHOLARSHIP

Awards for high school graduates who have preferably worked in or had one year of apprenticeship in the funeral home business.

Academic Fields/Career Goals: Funeral Services/Mortuary Science.

Award: Scholarship for use in freshman year; not renewable. *Number:* 1. *Amount:* $1500.

Eligibility Requirements: Applicant must be high school student and planning to enroll or expecting to enroll full- or part-time at a four-year institution or university. Available to U.S. citizens.

Application Requirements: Application, resume, references, test scores. *Deadline:* April 15.

Contact: Eva Cranford, Scholarship Coordinator
National Funeral Directors and Morticians Association
Omega World Center, 3951 Snapfinger Parkway, Suite 570
Decatur, GA 30035
Phone: 718-625-4656
E-mail: lladyc23@aol.com

GEMOLOGY

MINERALOGICAL SOCIETY OF AMERICA

http://www.minsocam.org/

MINERALOGICAL SOCIETY OF AMERICA-GRANT FOR STUDENT RESEARCH IN MINERALOGY AND PETROLOGY
• *See page 225*

GEOGRAPHY

ASSOCIATION OF AMERICAN GEOGRAPHERS

http://www.aag.org/

DARREL HESS COMMUNITY COLLEGE GEOGRAPHY SCHOLARSHIPS

Two $1,000 scholarships will be awarded to students from community colleges, junior colleges, city colleges, or similar two-year educational institutions who will be transferring as geography majors to four year colleges and universities.

Academic Fields/Career Goals: Geography.

Award: Grant for use in junior year; not renewable. *Number:* 2–4. *Amount:* $1000.

Eligibility Requirements: Applicant must be enrolled or expecting to enroll at a two-year institution.

Application Requirements: Applications consist of a form, unofficial transcripts and two letters of reference to be submitted ONLINE.

Contact: Dr. Patricia Solis, Director of Outreach and Strategic Initiatives
Association of American Geographers
1710 Sixteenth Street NW
Washington, DC 20009
Phone: 202-234-1450
E-mail: grantsawards@aag.org

BRITISH COLUMBIA INNOVATION COUNCIL

http://www.bcic.ca/

PAUL AND HELEN TRUSSELL SCIENCE AND TECHNOLOGY SCHOLARSHIP
• *See page 95*

CENTRAL INTELLIGENCE AGENCY

http://www.cia.gov/

CENTRAL INTELLIGENCE AGENCY UNDERGRADUATE SCHOLARSHIP PROGRAM
• *See page 58*

GAMMA THETA UPSILON-INTERNATIONAL GEOGRAPHIC HONOR SOCIETY

http://www.gtuhonors.org/

BUZZARD-MAXFIELD-RICHASON AND RECHLIN SCHOLARSHIP

Award is granted to a student who is a Gamma Theta Upsilon member, majoring in geography, will be a senior undergraduate and who has been accepted into a graduate program in geography.

Academic Fields/Career Goals: Geography.

Award: Scholarship for use in senior or graduate years; not renewable. *Number:* 5. *Amount:* $1000.

Eligibility Requirements: Applicant must be enrolled or expecting to enroll full-time at a four-year institution or university. Applicant or parent of applicant must be member of Gamma Theta Upsilon. Applicant must have 3.0 GPA or higher. Available to U.S. and non-U.S. citizens.

Application Requirements: Application, references, transcript. *Deadline:* May 31.

Contact: Dr. Donald Zeigler, Scholarship Committee
Gamma Theta Upsilon-International Geographic Honor Society
Old Dominion University, 1881 University Drive
Virginia Beach, VA 23453
E-mail: dzeigler@odu.edu

HARVARD TRAVELLERS CLUB

http://www.harvardtravellersclub.org/

HARVARD TRAVELLERS CLUB GRANTS
• *See page 98*

NASA IDAHO SPACE GRANT CONSORTIUM

http://www.id.spacegrant.org/

NASA IDAHO SPACE GRANT CONSORTIUM SCHOLARSHIP PROGRAM
• *See page 141*

GERMAN STUDIES

GERMAN ACADEMIC EXCHANGE SERVICE (DAAD)

http://www.daad.org/

GERMAN ACADEMIC EXCHANGE INFORMATION VISITS
• *See page 312*

GRAPHICS/GRAPHIC ARTS/ PRINTING

BRITISH COLUMBIA INNOVATION COUNCIL

http://www.bcic.ca/

BCIC YOUNG INNOVATOR SCHOLARSHIP COMPETITION (IDEA MASH UP)
• *See page 95*

CENTRAL INTELLIGENCE AGENCY

http://www.cia.gov/

CENTRAL INTELLIGENCE AGENCY UNDERGRADUATE SCHOLARSHIP PROGRAM
• *See page 58*

CINCINNATI LITHO CLUB

http://www.cincylithoclub.org/

BILL STAUDT/AL HARTNETT SCHOLARSHIP
• *See page 184*

DAY INTERNATIONAL SCHOLARSHIP
• *See page 184*

ELECTRONIC DOCUMENT SYSTEMS FOUNDATION

http://www.edsf.org/

ELECTRONIC DOCUMENT SYSTEMS FOUNDATION SCHOLARSHIP AWARDS
• *See page 197*

GOLDEN KEY INTERNATIONAL HONOUR SOCIETY

http://www.goldenkey.org/

VISUAL AND PERFORMING ARTS ACHIEVEMENT AWARDS
• *See page 111*

GRAVURE EDUCATION FOUNDATION

http://www.gaa.org/

GEF RESOURCE CENTER SCHOLARSHIPS

Scholarships are awarded annually to students enrolled full-time at one of the designated GEF gravure printing resource centers: Arizona State University, California Polytechnic State University, Clemson University, Murray State University, Rochester Institute of Technology, University of Wisconsin-Stout, and Western Michigan University.

Academic Fields/Career Goals: Graphics/Graphic Arts/Printing.

Award: Scholarship for use in sophomore, junior, senior, or graduate years; not renewable. *Number:* varies. *Amount:* varies.

Eligibility Requirements: Applicant must be enrolled or expecting to enroll full-time at a four-year institution or university. Applicant must have 3.0 GPA or higher. Available to U.S. citizens.

Application Requirements: Application. *Deadline:* May 31.

Contact: Robert Sheridan, Director of Development
Gravure Education Foundation
1200 A Scottsville Road
Rochester, NY 14624
Phone: 518-589-5153
Fax: 585-436-7689
E-mail: rbsheridan@gaa.org

GRAVURE CATALOG AND INSERT COUNCIL SCHOLARSHIP

Scholarship of up to $1000 for a student enrolled full-time at a college or university designated by GEF as a gravure printing resource center. Must be at least a junior and have a minimum GPA of 3.0.

Academic Fields/Career Goals: Graphics/Graphic Arts/Printing.

Award: Scholarship for use in junior or senior years; not renewable. *Number:* 1. *Amount:* up to $1000.

Eligibility Requirements: Applicant must be enrolled or expecting to enroll full-time at a four-year institution or university. Applicant must have 3.0 GPA or higher. Available to U.S. and non-U.S. citizens.

Application Requirements: Application, essay, transcript. *Deadline:* May 31.

Contact: Robert Sheridan, Director of Development
Gravure Education Foundation
1200 A Scottsville Road
Rochester, NY 14624
Phone: 518-589-5153
Fax: 585-436-7689
E-mail: rbsheridan@gaa.org

GRAVURE EDUCATION FOUNDATION CORPORATE LEADERSHIP SCHOLARSHIPS

Scholarships for full-time sophomore, junior, senior, or graduate students enrolled at any of the GEF-funded colleges or universities. Must demonstrate a declared major in printing, graphic arts, or graphic communications. Minimum 3.0 GPA required.

Academic Fields/Career Goals: Graphics/Graphic Arts/Printing.

Award: Scholarship for use in sophomore, junior, senior, or graduate years; not renewable. *Number:* 3–6. *Amount:* up to $2000.

Eligibility Requirements: Applicant must be enrolled or expecting to enroll full-time at a four-year institution or university. Applicant must have 3.0 GPA or higher. Available to U.S. and non-U.S. citizens.

Application Requirements: Application, essay, transcript. *Deadline:* May 31.

Contact: Robert Sheridan, Director of Development
Gravure Education Foundation
GEF, 1200-A Scottsville Road
Rochester, NY 14624
E-mail: rbsheridan@gaa.org

HALLMARK GRAPHIC ARTS SCHOLARSHIP

One scholarship award of up to $1500 for a student enrolled full-time at a college or university designated by GEF as a gravure resource center. Must be at least a junior and maintain a minimum GPA of 3.0. Must demonstrate interest in gravure printing and graphic arts.

Academic Fields/Career Goals: Graphics/Graphic Arts/Printing.

Award: Scholarship for use in junior or senior years; not renewable. *Number:* 1. *Amount:* up to $1500.

Eligibility Requirements: Applicant must be enrolled or expecting to enroll full-time at a four-year institution or university and must have an interest in leadership. Applicant must have 3.0 GPA or higher. Available to U.S. citizens.

Application Requirements: Application, essay, transcript. *Deadline:* March 31.

Contact: Robert Sheridan, Director of Development
Gravure Education Foundation
1200 A Scottsville Road
Rochester, NY 14624
Phone: 518-589-5153
Fax: 585-436-7689
E-mail: rbsheridan@gaa.org

LEON C. HART MEMORIAL SCHOLARSHIP

One scholarship of up to $1000 awarded to a student enrolled full-time at a college or university designated by GEF as a gravure printing resource center. Must maintain a minimum GPA of 3.0. Preference given to students who show an interest in printing education as a career path.

Academic Fields/Career Goals: Graphics/Graphic Arts/Printing.

Award: Scholarship for use in freshman, sophomore, junior, senior, graduate, or postgraduate years; not renewable. *Number:* 1. *Amount:* up to $1000.

Eligibility Requirements: Applicant must be enrolled or expecting to enroll full-time at a two-year or four-year or technical institution or university. Applicant or parent of applicant must have employment or volunteer experience in community service. Applicant must have 3.0 GPA or higher. Available to U.S. citizens.

Application Requirements: Application, essay, financial need analysis, transcript. *Deadline:* May 31.

Contact: Robert Sheridan, Director of Development
Gravure Education Foundation
1200 A Scottsville Road
Rochester, NY 14624
Phone: 518-589-5153
Fax: 585-436-7689
E-mail: rbsheridan@gaa.org

WERNER B. THIELE MEMORIAL SCHOLARSHIP

Two scholarships of up to $1250 each are awarded to students enrolled full-time at a college or university designated by GEF as a gravure printing resource center: Arizona State University, California Polytechnic State University, Clemson University, Murray State University, Rochester Institute of Technology, University of Wisconsin-Stout, and Western Michigan University. Minimum GPA of 3.0 required.

Academic Fields/Career Goals: Graphics/Graphic Arts/Printing.

Award: Scholarship for use in junior or senior years; not renewable. *Number:* up to 2. *Amount:* up to $1250.

Eligibility Requirements: Applicant must be enrolled or expecting to enroll full-time at a four-year institution or university. Applicant must have 3.0 GPA or higher. Available to U.S. citizens.

Application Requirements: Application, essay, transcript. *Deadline:* May 31.

Contact: Robert Sheridan, Director of Development
Gravure Education Foundation
1200 A Scottsville Road
Rochester, NY 14624
Phone: 518-589-5153
Fax: 585-436-7689
E-mail: rbsheridan@gaa.org

GREAT LAKES COMMISSION

http://www.glc.org/

CAROL A. RATZA MEMORIAL SCHOLARSHIP
• See page 185

INTERNATIONAL FOODSERVICE EDITORIAL COUNCIL

http://www.ifeconline.com/

INTERNATIONAL FOODSERVICE EDITORIAL COUNCIL COMMUNICATIONS SCHOLARSHIP
• See page 77

MAINE GRAPHICS ARTS ASSOCIATION

http://www.megaa.org/

MAINE GRAPHICS ART ASSOCIATION

One-time award for Maine high school students majoring in graphic arts at any university. Must submit transcript and references with application.

Academic Fields/Career Goals: Graphics/Graphic Arts/Printing.

Award: Scholarship for use in freshman year; not renewable. *Number:* up to 20. *Amount:* $100–$500.

Eligibility Requirements: Applicant must be high school student; planning to enroll or expecting to enroll full- or part-time at a four-year institution or university and resident of Maine. Available to U.S. citizens.

Application Requirements: Application, references, transcript. *Deadline:* May 15.

Contact: Angie Dougherty, Director
Maine Graphics Arts Association
PO Box 874
Auburn, ME 04212-0874
Phone: 207-883-9525
Fax: 207-883-3158
E-mail: edpougher@maine.rr.com

NATIONAL ASSOCIATION OF HISPANIC JOURNALISTS (NAHJ)

http://www.nahj.org/

NEWHOUSE SCHOLARSHIP PROGRAM

Two-year $5000 annually award for students who are pursuing careers in the newspaper industry as reporters, editors, graphic artists, or photojournalists. Recipient is expected to participate in summer internship at a Newhouse newspaper following their junior year. Students must submit resume and writing samples.

Academic Fields/Career Goals: Graphics/Graphic Arts/Printing; Journalism; Photojournalism/Photography.

Award: Scholarship for use in junior or senior years; not renewable. *Number:* varies. *Amount:* $5000.

Eligibility Requirements: Applicant must be enrolled or expecting to enroll full-time at a four-year institution or university. Available to U.S. citizens.

Application Requirements: Application, essay, financial need analysis, resume, references, transcript, work samples. *Deadline:* March 31.

Contact: Virginia Galindo, Program Assistant
National Association of Hispanic Journalists (NAHJ)
1000 National Press Building, 529 14th Street, NW, Suite 1000
Washington, DC 20045-2001
Phone: 202-662-7145
E-mail: vgalindo@nahj.org

NEW ENGLAND PRINTING AND PUBLISHING COUNCIL

http://www.ppcne.org/

NEW ENGLAND GRAPHIC ARTS SCHOLARSHIP

Applicants must be residents of New England who have admission to an accredited two-year vocational or technical college or a four-year college or university that offers a degree program related to printing or graphic arts. Renewable for up to four years if student maintains 2.5 GPA.

Academic Fields/Career Goals: Graphics/Graphic Arts/Printing.

Award: Scholarship for use in freshman, sophomore, junior, or senior years; renewable. *Number:* varies. *Amount:* up to $2500.

Eligibility Requirements: Applicant must be enrolled or expecting to enroll full-time at a two-year or four-year or technical institution or university and resident of Connecticut, Maine, Massachusetts, New Hampshire, Rhode Island, or Vermont. Applicant must have 2.5 GPA or higher. Available to U.S. citizens.

Application Requirements: Application, financial need analysis, test scores, transcript. *Deadline:* May 15.

Contact: Jay Smith, Scholarship Chair
New England Printing and Publishing Council
166 New Boston Street
Woburn, MA 01801
Phone: 781-944-1116
Fax: 781-944-3905
E-mail: jay@mhcp.com

OREGON STUDENT ASSISTANCE COMMISSION

http://www.GetCollegeFunds.org/

KIRCHHOFF FAMILY FINE ARTS SCHOLARSHIP
• See page 108

PRINT AND GRAPHIC SCHOLARSHIP FOUNDATION

http://www.printing.org/

PRINT AND GRAPHICS SCHOLARSHIPS FOUNDATION
• See page 189

PRINTING INDUSTRY OF MINNESOTA EDUCATION FOUNDATION

http://www.pimn.org/

PRINTING INDUSTRY OF MINNESOTA EDUCATION FOUNDATION SCHOLARSHIP FUND

The fund offers $1000 renewable scholarships to full-time students enrolled in two- or four-year institutions and technical colleges offering degrees in the print communications discipline. Applicant must be a Minnesota resident and be committed to a career in the print communications industry. Minimum 3.0 GPA required. Priority given to children of PIM member company employees.

Academic Fields/Career Goals: Graphics/Graphic Arts/Printing; Journalism.

Award: Scholarship for use in freshman, sophomore, junior, or senior years; renewable. *Number:* 10–15. *Amount:* $1000.

Eligibility Requirements: Applicant must be enrolled or expecting to enroll full-time at a two-year or four-year or technical institution or university; resident of Minnesota and studying in Minnesota, New York, or Wisconsin. Applicant must have 3.0 GPA or higher. Available to U.S. citizens.

Application Requirements: Application, essay, references, test scores, transcript, copy of college admission form, proof of admission. *Deadline:* April 1.

Contact: Kristin Davis, Director of Education Services
Printing Industry of Minnesota Education Foundation
2829 University Avenue, SE, Suite 750
Minneapolis, MN 55414-3248
Phone: 651-789-5508
E-mail: kristinp@pimn.org

RHODE ISLAND FOUNDATION

http://www.rifoundation.org/

J. D. EDSAL ADVERTISING SCHOLARSHIP
• See page 77

ROBERT H. MOLLOHAN FAMILY CHARITABLE FOUNDATION, INC.

http://www.mollohanfoundation.org/

MARY OLIVE EDDY JONES ART SCHOLARSHIP
• See page 108

SAN FRANCISCO FOUNDATION

http://www.sff.org/

PHELAN AWARD IN PRINTMAKING

Award presented in every odd-numbered year to recognize achievement in printmaking for students. Must have been born in California, but need not be a current resident. Applicants must provide a copy of their birth certificate with their application. This award is not a scholarship.

Academic Fields/Career Goals: Graphics/Graphic Arts/Printing.

Award: Prize for use in freshman, sophomore, junior, senior, graduate, or postgraduate years; not renewable. *Number:* 2. *Amount:* up to $4000.

Eligibility Requirements: Applicant must be enrolled or expecting to enroll full- or part-time at a two-year or four-year institution or university. Available to U.S. citizens.

Application Requirements: Application, applicant must enter a contest, self-addressed stamped envelope. *Deadline:* May 4.

Contact: Art Awards Coordinator
San Francisco Foundation
225 Bush Street, Suite 500
San Francisco, CA 94104
Phone: 415-733-8500

SOUTH DAKOTA RETAILERS ASSOCIATION

http://www.sdra.org/

SOUTH DAKOTA RETAILERS ASSOCIATION SCHOLARSHIP PROGRAM
• See page 71

TAG AND LABEL MANUFACTURERS INSTITUTE INC.

http://www.tlmi.com/

TLMI FOUR-YEAR COLLEGES/FULL-TIME STUDENTS SCHOLARSHIP
• See page 273

TECHNICAL ASSOCIATION OF THE PULP & PAPER INDUSTRY (TAPPI)

http://www.tappi.org/

COATING AND GRAPHIC ARTS DIVISION SCHOLARSHIP

Scholarship to encourage talented science and engineering students to pursue careers in the paper industry and to utilize their capabilities in advancing the science and technology of coated paper and paperboard manufacturing and the graphic arts industry. The division may award up to four $1000 awards annually. Information can be found at http://www.tappi.org/s_tappi/sec.asp?CID=6101&DID=546695.

Academic Fields/Career Goals: Graphics/Graphic Arts/Printing; Paper and Pulp Engineering.

Award: Scholarship for use in freshman, sophomore, junior, or senior years; not renewable. *Number:* 1–4. *Amount:* $1000.

Eligibility Requirements: Applicant must be enrolled or expecting to enroll full-time at a four-year institution or university. Applicant must have 3.0 GPA or higher. Available to U.S. and non-U.S. citizens.

Application Requirements: Application, references, transcript. *Deadline:* February 15.

Contact: Mr. Charles Bohanan, Director of Standards and Awards
Technical Association of the Pulp & Paper Industry (TAPPI)
15 Technology Parkway South
Norcross, GA 30092
Phone: 770-209-7276
Fax: 770-446-6947
E-mail: standards@tappi.org

WORLDSTUDIO FOUNDATION

http://www.aiga.org/

WORLDSTUDIO AIGA SCHOLARSHIPS
• See page 117

HEALTH ADMINISTRATION

ALBERTA HERITAGE SCHOLARSHIP FUND

http://www.alis.alberta.ca/

ALBERTA HERITAGE SCHOLARSHIP FUND ABORIGINAL HEALTH CAREERS BURSARY
• See page 137

AMERICAN INDIAN SCIENCE AND ENGINEERING SOCIETY

http://www.aises.org/

BURLINGTON NORTHERN SANTA FE FOUNDATION SCHOLARSHIP
• *See page 93*

BETHESDA LUTHERAN COMMUNITIES

http://www.bethesdalutherancommunities.org/

DEVELOPMENTAL DISABILITIES SCHOLASTIC ACHIEVEMENT SCHOLARSHIP FOR COLLEGE STUDENTS WHO ARE LUTHERAN
• *See page 218*

CANADIAN SOCIETY FOR MEDICAL LABORATORY SCIENCE

http://www.csmls.org/

E.V. BOOTH SCHOLARSHIP AWARD
The fund was established to assist CSMLS members in fulfilling their vision of achieving university level education in the medical laboratory sciences. One-time award of CAN$500. Must be a Canadian citizen.

Academic Fields/Career Goals: Health Administration; Health and Medical Sciences; Health Information Management/Technology.

Award: Scholarship for use in freshman, sophomore, junior, or senior years; not renewable. *Number:* 2.

Eligibility Requirements: Applicant must be Canadian citizen and enrolled or expecting to enroll full- or part-time at a four-year institution or university. Applicant or parent of applicant must be member of Canadian Society for Medical Laboratory Science.

Application Requirements: Application, financial need analysis, self-addressed stamped envelope, transcript. *Deadline:* April 1.

Contact: Katherine Coles, Executive Assistant–Corporate Services
Canadian Society for Medical Laboratory Science
LCD 1, PO Box 2830
Hamilton, ON L8N 3N8
Phone: 905-528-8642 Ext. 8602
Fax: 905-528-4968
E-mail: lisal@csmls.org

CONGRESSIONAL BLACK CAUCUS FOUNDATION, INC.

http://www.cbcfinc.org/

CONGRESSIONAL BLACK CAUCUS SPOUSES CHEERIOS BRAND HEALTH INITIATIVE
• *See page 139*

GREATER KANAWHA VALLEY FOUNDATION

http://www.tgkvf.org/

WILLARD H. ERWIN JR. MEMORIAL SCHOLARSHIP FUND
• *See page 151*

HEALTHCARE INFORMATION AND MANAGEMENT SYSTEMS SOCIETY FOUNDATION

http://www.himss.org/

HIMSS FOUNDATION SCHOLARSHIP PROGRAM
The Foundation Scholarships can be awarded to undergraduate, Masters or PhD students enrolled in a program related to the healthcare information and management systems field. In addition to the $5000 scholarship award, the winner also receives an all-expense paid trip to the Annual HIMSS Conference and Exhibition. Applicants must be member in good standing of HIMS. Primary occupation must be that of student in an accredited program related to the healthcare information or management systems field. The specific degree program is not a critical factor, although it is expected that programs similar to those in industrial engineering, operations research, healthcare informatics, computer science and information systems, mathematics, and quantitative programs in business administration and hospital administration will predominate. Undergraduate applicants must be at least a first-term junior when the scholarship is awarded. Previous Foundation Scholarship winners are ineligible.

Academic Fields/Career Goals: Health Administration; Health and Medical Sciences; Health Information Management/Technology; Science, Technology, and Society.

Award: Scholarship for use in junior, senior, graduate, or postgraduate years; not renewable. *Number:* 4–12. *Amount:* $5000.

Eligibility Requirements: Applicant must be enrolled or expecting to enroll full-time at a four-year institution or university. Applicant or parent of applicant must be member of Healthcare Information and Management Systems Society. Available to U.S. and non-U.S. citizens.

Application Requirements: Application, essay, resume, references, transcript. *Deadline:* October 15.

Contact: Jessie Bird, Program Manager, Regional Affairs
Healthcare Information and Management Systems Society
Foundation
230 East Ohio, Suite 500
Chicago, IL 60611
Phone: 312-915-9269
Fax: 312-664-6143
E-mail: bsanders@himss.org

HEALTH RESEARCH COUNCIL OF NEW ZEALAND

http://www.hrc.govt.nz/

PACIFIC HEALTH WORKFORCE AWARD
Intended to support students studying towards a health or health-related qualification. The eligible courses of study are: health, health administration, or a recognized qualification aligned with the Pacific Island. Priority given to management training, medical, and nursing students. Applicants should be New Zealand citizens or hold residency in New Zealand at the time of application and be of Pacific Island descent. The value of the awards and dollar value will vary and for one year of study.

Academic Fields/Career Goals: Health Administration; Health and Medical Sciences; Health Information Management/Technology; Nursing.

Award: Scholarship for use in freshman, sophomore, junior, senior, graduate, or postgraduate years; not renewable. *Number:* varies. *Amount:* varies.

Eligibility Requirements: Applicant must be New Zealander citizen; Asian/Pacific Islander and enrolled or expecting to enroll full-time at a two-year or four-year institution or university. Available to citizens of countries other than the U.S. or Canada.

Application Requirements: Application, driver's license, essay, financial need analysis, references, transcript. *Deadline:* October 10.

Contact: Ngamau Wichman Tou, Manger, Pacific Health Research
Health Research Council of New Zealand
Wellesley Street
PO Box 5541
Auckland 1036
New Zealand
Phone: 64-3035255
Fax: 64-377 9988
E-mail: nwichmantou@hrc.govt.nz

PACIFIC MENTAL HEALTH WORK FORCE AWARD
Intended to provide one year of support for students studying towards a mental health or mental health-related qualification. Eligible courses of study include: nursing, psychology, health, health administration or a recognized qualification aligned with the Pacific Island mental health priority areas. Applicants should be New Zealand citizens or hold residency in New Zealand at the time of application and be of Pacific Island descent.

Academic Fields/Career Goals: Health Administration; Health and Medical Sciences; Health Information Management/Technology; Nursing; Psychology.

Award: Scholarship for use in freshman, sophomore, junior, senior, graduate, or postgraduate years; not renewable. *Number:* varies. *Amount:* varies.

Eligibility Requirements: Applicant must be New Zealander citizen; Asian/Pacific Islander and enrolled or expecting to enroll full-time at a two-year or four-year institution or university. Available to citizens of countries other than the U.S. or Canada.

Application Requirements: Application, essay, financial need analysis, resume, references, transcript. *Deadline:* October 10.

Contact: Ngamau Wichman Tou, Manger, Pacific Health Research
Health Research Council of New Zealand
Wellesley Street
PO Box 5541
Auckland 1036
New Zealand
Phone: 64-3035255
Fax: 64-377 9988
E-mail: nwichmantou@hrc.govt.nz

INDIAN HEALTH SERVICES, UNITED STATES DEPARTMENT OF HEALTH AND HUMAN SERVICES

http://www.ihs.gov/

HEALTH PROFESSIONS PREPARATORY SCHOLARSHIP PROGRAM

Renewable scholarship for undergraduate, graduate, or doctoral study in programs related to health professions and allied health professions. Minimum 2.0 GPA required. The dollar amount and number of awards varies annually.

Academic Fields/Career Goals: Health Administration; Health and Medical Sciences; Nursing; Pharmacy; Public Health.

Award: Scholarship for use in sophomore, junior, senior, or graduate years; renewable. *Number:* varies. *Amount:* varies.

Eligibility Requirements: Applicant must be American Indian/Alaska Native and enrolled or expecting to enroll full- or part-time at a two-year or four-year or technical institution or university. Available to U.S. citizens.

Application Requirements: Application, applicant must enter a contest, essay, references, transcript, proof of descent. *Deadline:* February 28.

Contact: Dawn Kelly, Branch Chief
Indian Health Services, United States Department of Health and Human Services
801 Thompson Avenue, Suite 120
Rockville, MD 20852
Phone: 301-443-6197
Fax: 301-443-6048
E-mail: dawn.kelly@ihs.gov

INDIAN HEALTH SERVICE HEALTH PROFESSIONS SCHOLARSHIP PROGRAM

Renewable scholarship for Native American students who are enrolled either part- or full-time in undergraduate programs relating to health professions or allied health professions. Minimum 2.0 GPA required. Service obligations are incurred upon acceptance of scholarship funding. Number of awards and the dollar value varies.

Academic Fields/Career Goals: Health Administration; Health and Medical Sciences; Nursing; Therapy/Rehabilitation.

Award: Scholarship for use in freshman, sophomore, junior, or senior years; renewable. *Number:* varies. *Amount:* varies.

Eligibility Requirements: Applicant must be American Indian/Alaska Native and enrolled or expecting to enroll full- or part-time at a two-year or four-year or technical institution or university. Available to U.S. citizens.

Application Requirements: Application, applicant must enter a contest, essay, references, transcript, proof of descent. *Deadline:* February 28.

Contact: Dawn Kelly, Branch Chief
Indian Health Services, United States Department of Health and Human Services
801 Thompson Avenue, Suite 120
Rockville, MD 20852
Phone: 301-443-6197
Fax: 301-443-6048
E-mail: dawn.kelly@ihs.gov

MINNESOTA COMMUNITY FOUNDATION

http://www.mncommunityfoundation.org/

TWO FEATHERS ENDOWMENT HEALTH INITIATIVE SCHOLARSHIP

Scholarship for students enrolled in a health-related field of study and intend to practice in Minnesota. Must be a Minnesota resident or have significant ties to a Minnesota Tribe.

Academic Fields/Career Goals: Health Administration.

Award: Scholarship for use in freshman, sophomore, junior, or senior years; not renewable. *Number:* varies. *Amount:* up to $5000.

Eligibility Requirements: Applicant must be enrolled or expecting to enroll full- or part-time at a four-year institution or university and resident of Minnesota. Available to U.S. citizens.

Application Requirements: Application, essay, resume, references. *Deadline:* July 1.

Contact: Dayonna Knutson, Program Assistant
Phone: 651-325-4252
E-mail: dlk@mncommunityfoundation.org

NATIONAL SOCIETY OF THE COLONIAL DAMES OF AMERICA

http://www.nscda.org/

AMERICAN INDIAN NURSE SCHOLARSHIP AWARDS

Renewable award of $500 to $1000. Currently able to fund between 10 and 15 students. Intended originally to benefit females only, the program has expanded to include males and the career goals now include not only nursing careers, but jobs in health care and health education, as well.

Academic Fields/Career Goals: Health Administration; Nursing.

Award: Scholarship for use in freshman, sophomore, junior, senior, graduate, or postgraduate years; renewable. *Number:* 10–15. *Amount:* $500–$1000.

Eligibility Requirements: Applicant must be American Indian/Alaska Native and enrolled or expecting to enroll full-time at a two-year or four-year or technical institution or university. Applicant must have 2.5 GPA or higher. Available to U.S. citizens.

Application Requirements: Application, driver's license, financial need analysis, photo, references, transcript. *Deadline:* continuous.

Contact: Mrs. Joe Calvin, Scholarship Awards Consultant
National Society of The Colonial Dames of America
Nine Cross Creek Drive
Birmingham, AL 35213
Phone: 205-871-4072
E-mail: info@nscda.org

NEW ENGLAND EMPLOYEE BENEFITS COUNCIL

http://www.neebc.org/

NEW ENGLAND EMPLOYEE BENEFITS COUNCIL SCHOLARSHIP PROGRAM

• *See page 68*

NORTH CAROLINA STATE EDUCATION ASSISTANCE AUTHORITY

http://www.ncseaa.edu/

NORTH CAROLINA STUDENT LOAN PROGRAM FOR HEALTH, SCIENCE, AND MATHEMATICS
• *See page 221*

STRAIGHTFORWARD MEDIA

http://www.straightforwardmedia.com/

STRAIGHTFORWARD MEDIA MEDICAL PROFESSIONS SCHOLARSHIP
• *See page 221*

HEALTH AND MEDICAL SCIENCES

ALBERTA HERITAGE SCHOLARSHIP FUND

http://www.alis.alberta.ca/

ALBERTA HERITAGE SCHOLARSHIP FUND ABORIGINAL HEALTH CAREERS BURSARY
• *See page 137*

JASON LANG SCHOLARSHIP
• *See page 213*

NORTHERN ALBERTA DEVELOPMENT COUNCIL BURSARY
• *See page 214*

NORTHERN ALBERTA DEVELOPMENT COUNCIL BURSARY FOR MEDICAL STUDENTS
Award to increase the number of trained professionals in Northern Alberta and to encourage students from Northern Alberta to obtain a postsecondary education. Must be residents of Alberta and enrolled in a medical program. Return-service bursary is valued at CAN$12,000 per year and available for four years of medical school. Students must live and work for one year in Northern Alberta for each year of funding received. For details, visit web site http://alis.alberta.ca.
Academic Fields/Career Goals: Health and Medical Sciences.
Award: Grant for use in freshman, sophomore, junior, or senior years; not renewable. *Number:* 1.
Eligibility Requirements: Applicant must be enrolled or expecting to enroll full-time at a two-year or four-year or technical institution or university; resident of Alberta and studying in Alberta. Available to Canadian citizens.
Application Requirements: Application, essay. *Deadline:* May 15.
Contact: Scholarship Committee
Alberta Heritage Scholarship Fund
9940 106th Street, Fourth Floor, Sterling Place
PO Box 28000, Station Main
Edmonton, AB T5J 4R4
Canada
Phone: 780-427-8640
E-mail: scholarships@gov.ab.ca

ALPENA REGIONAL MEDICAL CENTER

http://www.alpenaregionalmedicalcenter.org/

THELMA ORR MEMORIAL SCHOLARSHIP
Two $1500 scholarships for students pursuing a course of study related to human medicine at any state accredited Michigan college or university.

Academic Fields/Career Goals: Health and Medical Sciences.
Award: Scholarship for use in freshman, sophomore, junior, or senior years; not renewable. *Number:* 2. *Amount:* $1500.
Eligibility Requirements: Applicant must be enrolled or expecting to enroll full-time at a four-year institution or university; resident of Michigan and studying in Michigan. Available to U.S. citizens.
Application Requirements: Application. *Deadline:* April 15.
Contact: Marlene Pear, Director, Voluntary Services
Alpena Regional Medical Center
1501 West Chisholm Street
Alpena, MI 49707
Phone: 989-356-7351
E-mail: info@agh.org

ALPHA OMEGA ALPHA

http://www.alphaomegaalpha.org/

HELEN H. GLASER STUDENT ESSAY AWARDS
Award of $2000 first, $750 second, $500 third, and honorable mention awards of $250 each. Authors must be enrolled at medical schools with active Alpha Omega Alpha chapters. The essay may be on any nontechnical subject related to medicine, including ethics, history, education, philosophy, and policy. Well-referenced, scholarly fiction is an acceptable genre, as is creative narrative from personal experience.
Academic Fields/Career Goals: Health and Medical Sciences.
Award: Prize for use in freshman, sophomore, junior, or senior years; not renewable. *Number:* varies. *Amount:* $250–$2000.
Eligibility Requirements: Applicant must be enrolled or expecting to enroll full-time at a two-year or four-year or technical institution or university. Available to U.S. and non-U.S. citizens.
Application Requirements: Application, essay. *Deadline:* January 31.
Contact: Debbie Lancaster, Managing Editor
Alpha Omega Alpha
525 Middlefield Road, Suite 130
Menlo Park, CA 94025
Phone: 650-329-0291
Fax: 650-329-1618
E-mail: d.lancaster@alphaomegaalpha.org

PHAROS POETRY COMPETITION
Awards of $500, $250, $100 and $75; to encourage medical students to write poetry on medical subjects and to recognize and reward excellent and thoughtful compositions. Students must be enrolled at medical schools with active Alpha Omega Alpha chapters, but need not be members.
Academic Fields/Career Goals: Health and Medical Sciences.
Award: Prize for use in freshman, sophomore, junior, or senior years; not renewable. *Number:* 4. *Amount:* $75–$500.
Eligibility Requirements: Applicant must be enrolled or expecting to enroll full- or part-time at a two-year or four-year or technical institution or university and must have an interest in writing. Available to U.S. and non-U.S. citizens.
Application Requirements: Application, essay. *Deadline:* January 31.
Contact: Debbie Lancaster, Managing Editor
Alpha Omega Alpha
525 Middlefield Road, Suite 130
Menlo Park, CA 94025
Phone: 650-329-0291
E-mail: d.lancaster@alphaomegaalpha.org

AMERICAN INDIAN SCIENCE AND ENGINEERING SOCIETY

http://www.aises.org/

A.T. ANDERSON MEMORIAL SCHOLARSHIP PROGRAM
• *See page 93*

AMERICAN LEGION AUXILIARY DEPARTMENT OF ARIZONA

http://www.azlegion.org/majorp~2.htm

AMERICAN LEGION AUXILIARY DEPARTMENT OF ARIZONA HEALTH CARE OCCUPATION SCHOLARSHIPS

Award for Arizona residents enrolled at an institution in Arizona that awards degrees or certificates in health occupations. Preference given to an immediate family member of a veteran. Must be a U.S. citizen and Arizona resident for at least one year.

Academic Fields/Career Goals: Health and Medical Sciences.

Award: Scholarship for use in freshman, sophomore, junior, or senior years; not renewable. *Amount:* $500.

Eligibility Requirements: Applicant must be enrolled or expecting to enroll full- or part-time at a two-year or four-year or technical institution or university; resident of Arizona and studying in Arizona. Available to U.S. citizens.

Application Requirements: Application, essay, financial need analysis, photo, references, test scores, transcript. *Deadline:* May 15.

Contact: Department Secretary and Treasurer
American Legion Auxiliary Department of Arizona
4701 North 19th Avenue, Suite 100
Phoenix, AZ 85015-3727
Phone: 602-241-1080
Fax: 602-604-9640
E-mail: amlegauxaz@mcleodusa.net

AMERICAN LEGION AUXILIARY DEPARTMENT OF MAINE

http://www.mainelegion.org/

AMERICAN LEGION AUXILIARY DEPARTMENT OF MAINE PAST PRESIDENTS' PARLEY NURSES SCHOLARSHIP

One-time award for child, grandchild, sister, or brother of veteran. Must be resident of Maine and wishing to continue education at accredited school in medical field. Must submit photo, doctor's statement, and evidence of civic activity. Minimum 3.5 GPA required.

Academic Fields/Career Goals: Health and Medical Sciences; Nursing.

Award: Scholarship for use in freshman, sophomore, junior, or senior years; not renewable. *Number:* 1. *Amount:* $300.

Eligibility Requirements: Applicant must be age 18 and over; enrolled or expecting to enroll full-time at a two-year or four-year or technical institution or university and resident of Maine. Applicant or parent of applicant must have employment or volunteer experience in community service. Applicant must have 2.5 GPA or higher. Available to U.S. citizens. Applicant or parent must meet one or more of the following requirements: general military experience; retired from active duty; disabled or killed as a result of military service; prisoner of war; or missing in action.

Application Requirements: Application, photo, references, transcript, doctor's statement. *Deadline:* March 31.

Contact: Mary Wells, Education Chairman
American Legion Auxiliary Department of Maine
21 Limerock Street
PO Box 434
Rockland, ME 04841
Phone: 207-532-6007
E-mail: aladeptsecme@verizon.net

AMERICAN LEGION AUXILIARY DEPARTMENT OF MICHIGAN

http://www.michalaux.org/

AMERICAN LEGION AUXILIARY DEPARTMENT OF MICHIGAN MEDICAL CAREER SCHOLARSHIP

Award for training in Michigan as registered nurse, licensed practical nurse, physical therapist, respiratory therapist, or in any medical career. Must be child, grandchild, great-grandchild, wife, or widow of honorably discharged or deceased veteran who has served during the eligibility dates for American Legion membership. Must be Michigan resident attending a Michigan school.

Academic Fields/Career Goals: Health and Medical Sciences; Nursing; Therapy/Rehabilitation.

Award: Scholarship for use in freshman year; not renewable. *Number:* 10–20. *Amount:* $500.

Eligibility Requirements: Applicant must be high school student; planning to enroll or expecting to enroll full-time at a two-year or four-year or technical institution or university; resident of Michigan and studying in Michigan. Available to U.S. citizens. Applicant must have general military experience.

Application Requirements: Application, financial need analysis, references, transcript, veteran's discharge papers, copy of pages 1 and 2 of federal income tax return. *Deadline:* March 15.

Contact: Ms. LeAnn Knott, Scholarship Coordinator
American Legion Auxiliary Department of Michigan
212 North Verlinden Avenue, Suite B
Lansing, MI 48915
Phone: 517-267-8809 Ext. 22
Fax: 517-371-3698
E-mail: lknott@michalaux.org

AMERICAN LEGION AUXILIARY DEPARTMENT OF MINNESOTA

http://www.mnlegion.org/

AMERICAN LEGION AUXILIARY DEPARTMENT OF MINNESOTA PAST PRESIDENTS' PARLEY HEALTH CARE SCHOLARSHIP

One-time $1000 award for American Legion Auxiliary Department of Minnesota member for at least three years who is needy and deserving, to begin or continue education in any phase of the health care field. Must be a Minnesota resident, attend a vocational or postsecondary institution and maintain at least a C average in school.

Academic Fields/Career Goals: Health and Medical Sciences.

Award: Scholarship for use in freshman, sophomore, junior, or senior years; not renewable. *Number:* 1–10. *Amount:* $1000.

Eligibility Requirements: Applicant must be enrolled or expecting to enroll full-time at a two-year or four-year or technical institution or university; resident of Minnesota and studying in Minnesota. Applicant or parent of applicant must be member of American Legion or Auxiliary. Available to U.S. citizens.

Application Requirements: Application, financial need analysis. *Deadline:* March 15.

Contact: Eleanor Johnson, Executive Secretary
American Legion Auxiliary Department of Minnesota
State Veterans Service Building, 20 West 12th Street, Room 314
St. Paul, MN 55155
Phone: 651-224-7634
Fax: 651-224-5243

AMERICAN LEGION AUXILIARY DEPARTMENT OF TEXAS

http://www.alatexas.org/

AMERICAN LEGION AUXILIARY DEPARTMENT OF TEXAS PAST PRESIDENTS' PARLEY MEDICAL SCHOLARSHIP

Scholarships available for full-time students pursuing studies in human health care. Must be a resident of Texas. Must be a veteran or child, grandchild, great grandchild of a veteran who served in the Armed Forces during period of eligibility.

Academic Fields/Career Goals: Health and Medical Sciences.

Award: Scholarship for use in freshman, sophomore, junior, or senior years; not renewable. *Number:* 1–10. *Amount:* $1000.

Eligibility Requirements: Applicant must be enrolled or expecting to enroll full-time at a two-year or four-year or technical institution or university and resident of Texas. Available to U.S. citizens. Applicant must have general military experience.

Application Requirements: Application, financial need analysis, references, transcript, letter stating qualifications and intentions. *Deadline:* June 1.

Contact: Paula Raney, State Secretary
　　　　Phone: 512-476-7278
　　　　Fax: 512-482-8391
　　　　E-mail: alatexas@txlegion.org

AMERICAN LEGION AUXILIARY DEPARTMENT OF WYOMING

AMERICAN LEGION AUXILIARY DEPARTMENT OF WYOMING PAST PRESIDENTS' PARLEY HEALTH CARE SCHOLARSHIP
• *See page 218*

AMERICAN MEDICAL ASSOCIATION FOUNDATION

http://www.amafoundation.org/

AMA FOUNDATION MINORITY SCHOLARS AWARD

Awards $10,000 scholarships annually. Applicant must be a current first- or second-year medical student and a permanent resident or citizen of the United States. Eligible students of minority background include African American/Black, American Indian, Native Hawaiian, Alaska Native and Hispanic/Latino. Each medical school dean or dean's designate is invited to submit up to 2 nominees.

Academic Fields/Career Goals: Health and Medical Sciences.

Award: Scholarship for use in sophomore, junior, or senior years; not renewable. *Number:* 10. *Amount:* $10,000.

Eligibility Requirements: Applicant must be American Indian/Alaska Native, Black (non-Hispanic), or Hispanic and enrolled or expecting to enroll full-time at an institution or university. Available to U.S. citizens.

Application Requirements: Application, essay, financial need analysis, references, transcript, nomination from dean. *Deadline:* April 15.

Contact: Dina Lindenberg, Minority Scholars Award
　　　　American Medical Association Foundation
　　　　515 North State Street
　　　　Chicago, IL 60654
　　　　Phone: 312-464-4193
　　　　Fax: 312-464-4142
　　　　E-mail: scholarships@ama-assn.org

AMA FOUNDATION PHYSICIANS OF TOMORROW SCHOLARSHIP

Scholarship of $10,000 will be awarded to current third-year medical students, who are entering their fourth-year of study. Based on academic excellence and/or financial need. Awards four scholarships. Applicant must be nominated by medical school dean or dean's designate.

Academic Fields/Career Goals: Health and Medical Sciences.

Award: Scholarship for use in senior year; not renewable. *Number:* 1–12. *Amount:* $10,000.

Eligibility Requirements: Applicant must be enrolled or expecting to enroll full-time at an institution or university. Available to U.S. citizens.

Application Requirements: Application, essay, financial need analysis, references, nomination from dean. *Deadline:* May 31.

Contact: Dina Lindenberg, Program Officer
　　　　American Medical Association Foundation
　　　　515 North State Street
　　　　Chicago, IL 60654
　　　　Phone: 312-464-4193
　　　　Fax: 312-464-4142
　　　　E-mail: scholarships@ama-assn.org

AMERICAN MEDICAL TECHNOLOGISTS

http://www.amt1.com/

AMERICAN MEDICAL TECHNOLOGISTS STUDENT SCHOLARSHIP
• *See page 218*

AMERICAN OCCUPATIONAL THERAPY FOUNDATION INC.

http://www.aotf.org/

AMERICAN OCCUPATIONAL THERAPY FOUNDATION STATE ASSOCIATION SCHOLARSHIPS

Awards offered at the state association level by the Foundation, for study leading to associate and graduate degrees in occupational therapy. Must be a member of the American Occupational Therapy Association. Requirements vary by state. See web site at http://www.aotf.org for further details.

Academic Fields/Career Goals: Health and Medical Sciences; Therapy/Rehabilitation.

Award: Scholarship for use in sophomore, junior, senior, or graduate years; not renewable. *Number:* varies. *Amount:* $150–$5000.

Eligibility Requirements: Applicant must be enrolled or expecting to enroll full-time at a two-year or four-year institution or university. Applicant or parent of applicant must be member of American Occupational Therapy Association. Available to U.S. citizens.

Application Requirements: Application, essay, references, Curriculum Director's Statement. *Deadline:* March 1.

Contact: Jeanne Cooper, Scholarship Coordinator
　　　　American Occupational Therapy Foundation Inc.
　　　　4720 Montgomery Lane
　　　　PO Box 31220
　　　　Bethesda, MD 20824-1220
　　　　Phone: 301-652-6611 Ext. 2550
　　　　E-mail: jcooper@aotf.org

CARLOTTA WELLES SCHOLARSHIP

Award for study leading to an occupational therapy associate degree at an accredited institution. Must be a member of the American Occupational Therapy Association.

Academic Fields/Career Goals: Health and Medical Sciences; Therapy/Rehabilitation.

Award: Scholarship for use in sophomore year; not renewable. *Number:* varies. *Amount:* $500.

Eligibility Requirements: Applicant must be enrolled or expecting to enroll full-time at a two-year institution. Applicant or parent of applicant must be member of American Occupational Therapy Association. Available to U.S. citizens.

Application Requirements: Application, essay, references, Curriculum Director's Statement. *Deadline:* varies.

Contact: Ms. Jeanne Y. Cooper, Scholarship Coordinator
　　　　Phone: 301-652-6611 Ext. 2550
　　　　Fax: 301-656-3620
　　　　E-mail: jcooper@aotf.org

AMERICAN PHYSICAL THERAPY ASSOCIATION

http://www.apta.org/

MINORITY SCHOLARSHIP AWARD FOR ACADEMIC EXCELLENCE IN PHYSICAL THERAPY

Scholarships available to minority students enrolled in the final year of an accredited physical therapy program. Information is available on web site http://www.apta.org.

Academic Fields/Career Goals: Health and Medical Sciences.

Award: Scholarship for use in senior year; not renewable. *Number:* 8–10. *Amount:* $5000–$6000.

Eligibility Requirements: Applicant must be American Indian/Alaska Native, Asian/Pacific Islander, Black (non-Hispanic), or Hispanic and enrolled or expecting to enroll full-time at a four-year institution or university. Available to U.S. citizens.

Application Requirements: Application, essay, resume, references, transcript. *Deadline:* December 1.

Contact: Eva Jones, Assistant to the Director
American Physical Therapy Association
1111 North Fairfax Street
Alexandria, VA 22314-1488
Phone: 800-999-2782 Ext. 3144
Fax: 703-684-7343
E-mail: evajones@apta.org

MINORITY SCHOLARSHIP AWARD FOR ACADEMIC EXCELLENCE-PHYSICAL THERAPIST ASSISTANT

Scholarships available for minority students enrolled in the final year of an accredited physical therapist assistant program. Information and application is available on web site http://www.apta.org.

Academic Fields/Career Goals: Health and Medical Sciences; Therapy/Rehabilitation.

Award: Scholarship for use in senior year; not renewable. *Number:* 1. *Amount:* $2000–$2500.

Eligibility Requirements: Applicant must be American Indian/Alaska Native, Asian/Pacific Islander, Black (non-Hispanic), or Hispanic and enrolled or expecting to enroll full-time at a four-year institution or university. Available to U.S. citizens.

Application Requirements: Application, essay, resume, references, transcript. *Deadline:* December 1.

Contact: Eva Jones, Assistant to the Director
American Physical Therapy Association
1111 North Fairfax Street
Alexandria, VA 22314-1488
Phone: 800-999-2782 Ext. 3144
Fax: 703-684-7343
E-mail: evajones@apta.org

AMERICAN PHYSIOLOGICAL SOCIETY

http://www.the-aps.org/

DAVID S. BRUCE AWARDS FOR EXCELLENCE IN UNDERGRADUATE RESEARCH
• *See page 138*

AMERICAN RESPIRATORY CARE FOUNDATION

http://www.arcfoundation.org/

JIMMY A. YOUNG MEMORIAL EDUCATION RECOGNITION AWARD

Award available to students studying respiratory care at an American Medical Association-approved institution. Preference given to minority students. Must submit letters of recommendation and a paper on a respiratory care topic. Must have a minimum 3.0 GPA.

Academic Fields/Career Goals: Health and Medical Sciences; Therapy/Rehabilitation.

Award: Prize for use in freshman, sophomore, junior, or senior years; not renewable. *Number:* 1. *Amount:* up to $1000.

Eligibility Requirements: Applicant must be enrolled or expecting to enroll full- or part-time at a two-year or four-year institution or university. Applicant must have 3.0 GPA or higher. Available to U.S. citizens.

Application Requirements: Application, references, transcript, paper on respiratory care topic. *Deadline:* June 16.

Contact: Jill Nelson, Administrative Coordinator
American Respiratory Care Foundation
9425 North MacArthur Boulevard, Suite 100
Irving, TX 75063-4706
Phone: 972-243-2272
Fax: 972-484-2720
E-mail: info@arcfoundation.org

MORTON B. DUGGAN, JR. MEMORIAL EDUCATION RECOGNITION AWARD

Awards students with a minimum 3.0 GPA, enrolled in an American Medical Association-approved respiratory care program. Must be U.S. citizen or permanent resident. Need proof of college enrollment. Must submit an original referenced paper on respiratory care. Preference given

to Georgia and South Carolina residents. One-time merit-based award of up to $1000, and includes airfare, registration to AARC Congress, and one night's lodging.

Academic Fields/Career Goals: Health and Medical Sciences; Therapy/Rehabilitation.

Award: Scholarship for use in freshman, sophomore, junior, or senior years; not renewable. *Number:* 1. *Amount:* up to $1000.

Eligibility Requirements: Applicant must be enrolled or expecting to enroll full- or part-time at a two-year or four-year institution or university. Applicant must have 3.0 GPA or higher. Available to U.S. citizens.

Application Requirements: Application, references, transcript, paper on respiratory care. *Deadline:* June 16.

Contact: Jill Nelson, Administrative Coordinator
American Respiratory Care Foundation
9425 North MacArthur Boulevard, Suite 100
Irving, TX 75063-4706
Phone: 972-243-2272
Fax: 972-484-2720
E-mail: info@arcfoundation.org

NBRC/AMP ROBERT M. LAWRENCE, MD EDUCATION RECOGNITION AWARD

Merit-based award to a third- or fourth-year student with a minimum 3.0 GPA, enrolled in an accredited undergraduate respiratory therapy program leading to a baccalaureate degree.

Academic Fields/Career Goals: Health and Medical Sciences; Therapy/Rehabilitation.

Award: Scholarship for use in junior or senior years; not renewable. *Number:* 1. *Amount:* up to $2500.

Eligibility Requirements: Applicant must be enrolled or expecting to enroll full- or part-time at a four-year institution or university. Applicant must have 3.0 GPA or higher. Available to U.S. and non-U.S. citizens.

Application Requirements: Application, references, transcript, paper on respiratory care. *Deadline:* June 16.

Contact: Jill Nelson, Administrative Coordinator
American Respiratory Care Foundation
9425 North MacArthur Boulevard, Suite 100
Irving, TX 75063-4706
Phone: 972-243-2272
Fax: 972-484-2720
E-mail: info@arcfoundation.org

NBRC/AMP WILLIAM W. BURGIN, MD EDUCATION RECOGNITION AWARD

Merit-based award for second-year students enrolled in an accredited respiratory therapy program leading to an associate degree. Minimum GPA of 3.0 required. For more information visit web site http://www.arcfoundation.org/awards/undergraduate/burgin.cfm.

Academic Fields/Career Goals: Health and Medical Sciences; Therapy/Rehabilitation.

Award: Prize for use in sophomore year; not renewable. *Number:* 1. *Amount:* up to $2500.

Eligibility Requirements: Applicant must be enrolled or expecting to enroll full- or part-time at a two-year institution. Applicant must have 3.0 GPA or higher. Available to U.S. and non-U.S. citizens.

Application Requirements: Application, references, transcript, paper on respiratory care. *Deadline:* June 16.

Contact: Jill Nelson, Administrative Coordinator
American Respiratory Care Foundation
9425 North MacArthur Boulevard, Suite 100
Irving, TX 75063-4706
Phone: 972-243-2272
Fax: 972-484-2720
E-mail: info@arcfoundation.org

SEPRACOR ACHIEVEMENT AWARD FOR EXCELLENCE IN PULMONARY DISEASE STATE MANAGEMENT

Nominations may be made by anyone by submitting a paper of not more than 1000 words describing why a nominee should be considered for the award. Must be a member of the American Association for Respiratory Care. Must be a respiratory therapist or other healthcare professional, including physician. Nominees must have demonstrated the attainment of positive healthcare outcomes as a direct result of their disease-oriented practice of respiratory care, regardless of care setting.

Academic Fields/Career Goals: Health and Medical Sciences; Therapy/Rehabilitation.

Award: Prize for use in freshman, sophomore, junior, senior, graduate, or postgraduate years; not renewable. *Number;* 1. *Amount:* up to $2500.

Eligibility Requirements: Applicant must be enrolled or expecting to enroll full- or part-time at a four-year institution or university. Applicant or parent of applicant must have employment or volunteer experience in physical therapy/rehabilitation. Available to U.S. and non-U.S. citizens.

Application Requirements: Resume, references, paper describing why a nominee should be considered for the award. *Deadline:* June 1.

Contact: Jill Nelson, Administrative Coordinator
American Respiratory Care Foundation
9425 North MacArthur Boulevard, Suite 100
Irving, TX 75063-4706
Phone: 972-243-2272
Fax: 972-484-2720
E-mail: info@arcfoundation.org

ARIZONA PROFESSIONAL CHAPTER OF AISES

http://www.azpcofaises.org/

ARIZONA PROFESSIONAL CHAPTER OF AISES SCHOLARSHIP
• *See page 279*

ARNOLD AND MABEL BECKMAN FOUNDATION

http://www.beckman-foundation.com/

BECKMAN SCHOLARS PROGRAM
• *See page 138*

ARRL FOUNDATION INC.

http://www.arrl.org/

CAROLE J. STREETER, KB9JBR SCHOLARSHIP
• *See page 218*

WILLIAM R. GOLDFARB MEMORIAL SCHOLARSHIP
• *See page 146*

ASRT EDUCATION AND RESEARCH FOUNDATION

http://www.asrtfoundation.org/

ELEKTA RADIATION THERAPY EDUCATORS SCHOLARSHIP
• *See page 231*

JERMAN-CAHOON STUDENT SCHOLARSHIP

Merit scholarship for certificate or undergraduate students. Must have completed at least one semester in the radiological sciences to apply. Financial need is a factor. Requirements include 3.0 GPA, recommendation and several short answer essays.

Academic Fields/Career Goals: Health and Medical Sciences; Oncology; Radiology.

Award: Scholarship for use in freshman, sophomore, or junior years; not renewable. *Number:* 5–7. *Amount:* up to $2500.

Eligibility Requirements: Applicant must be enrolled or expecting to enroll full- or part-time at a two-year or four-year or technical institution or university. Applicant must have 3.0 GPA or higher. Available to U.S. citizens.

Application Requirements: Application, essay, financial need analysis, references, transcript. *Deadline:* February 1.

Contact: Debbie Freeman, Community and Program Manager
ASRT Education and Research Foundation
15000 Central Avenue, SE
Albuquerque, NM 87123-3909
Phone: 505-298-4500 Ext. 1307
E-mail: foundation@asrt.org

MEDICAL IMAGING EDUCATORS SCHOLARSHIP
• *See page 231*

PROFESSIONAL ADVANCEMENT SCHOLARSHIP

Open to ASRT members only who are certificate, undergraduate or graduate students pursuing any degree or certificate intended to further a career in the radiologic sciences profession. One of the following must also be true: applicant holds an unrestricted state license, is registered by the American Registry of Radiologic Technologists, or registered with an equivalent certifying body.

Academic Fields/Career Goals: Health and Medical Sciences; Oncology; Radiology.

Award: Scholarship for use in freshman, sophomore, junior, senior, or graduate years; not renewable. *Number:* 5–10. *Amount:* up to $1500.

Eligibility Requirements: Applicant must be enrolled or expecting to enroll full- or part-time at a two-year or four-year institution or university. Applicant or parent of applicant must be member of American Society of Radiologic Technologists. Available to U.S. and Canadian citizens.

Application Requirements: Application, essay, financial need analysis, resume, references. *Deadline:* February 1.

Contact: Debbie Freeman, Community and Program Manager
ASRT Education and Research Foundation
15000 Central Avenue, SE
Albuquerque, NM 87123-3909
Phone: 505-298-4500 Ext. 1307
E-mail: foundation@asrt.org

ROYCE OSBORN MINORITY STUDENT SCHOLARSHIP

Minority scholarship for certificate or undergraduate students. Must have completed at least one semester in the radiological sciences to apply. Financial need is a factor. Requirements include 3.0 GPA, recommendation and several short answer essays.

Academic Fields/Career Goals: Health and Medical Sciences; Radiology.

Award: Scholarship for use in freshman, sophomore, or junior years; not renewable. *Number:* 5–7. *Amount:* up to $4000.

Eligibility Requirements: Applicant must be American Indian/Alaska Native, Asian/Pacific Islander, Black (non-Hispanic), or Hispanic and enrolled or expecting to enroll full- or part-time at a two-year or four-year or technical institution or university. Applicant must have 3.0 GPA or higher. Available to U.S. citizens.

Application Requirements: Application, essay, financial need analysis, references, transcript. *Deadline:* February 1.

Contact: Debbie Freeman, Community and Program Manager
ASRT Education and Research Foundation
15000 Central Avenue, SE
Albuquerque, NM 87123-3909
Phone: 505-298-4500 Ext. 1307
E-mail: foundation@asrt.org

SIEMENS CLINICAL ADVANCEMENT SCHOLARSHIP

Open to ASRT members only who are pursuing a bachelor's or master's degree in the radiologic sciences to advance patient care skills or pursuing a certificate in a specialty discipline. One of the following must also be true: applicant holds an unrestricted state license, is registered by the American Registry of Radiologic Technologists, or registered with an equivalent certifying body.

Academic Fields/Career Goals: Health and Medical Sciences; Oncology; Radiology.

Award: Scholarship for use in freshman, sophomore, junior, senior, or graduate years; not renewable. *Number:* 4. *Amount:* $5000.

Eligibility Requirements: Applicant must be enrolled or expecting to enroll full- or part-time at a two-year or four-year or technical institution or university. Applicant or parent of applicant must be member of American Society of Radiologic Technologists. Available to U.S. and Canadian citizens.

Application Requirements: Application, essay, financial need analysis, resume, references. *Deadline:* February 1.

Contact: Debbie Freeman, Community and Program Manager
ASRT Education and Research Foundation
15000 Central Avenue, SE
Albuquerque, NM 87123-3909
Phone: 505-298-4500 Ext. 1307
E-mail: foundation@asrt.org

VARIAN RADIATION THERAPY STUDENT SCHOLARSHIP

Merit scholarship for undergraduate or certificate students enrolled in a radiation therapy program. Financial need is a factor. Requirements include 3.0 GPA, recommendation and several short answer essays.

Academic Fields/Career Goals: Health and Medical Sciences; Oncology.

Award: Scholarship for use in freshman, sophomore, or junior years; not renewable. *Number:* 19. *Amount:* $5000.

Eligibility Requirements: Applicant must be enrolled or expecting to enroll full- or part-time at a two-year or four-year or technical institution or university. Applicant must have 3.0 GPA or higher. Available to U.S. citizens.

Application Requirements: Application, essay, financial need analysis, references, transcript. *Deadline:* February 1.

Contact: Debbie Freeman, Community and Program Manager
ASRT Education and Research Foundation
15000 Central Avenue, SE
Albuquerque, NM 87123-3909
Phone: 505-298-4500 Ext. 1307
E-mail: foundation@asrt.org

ASSOCIATION OF SURGICAL TECHNOLOGISTS

http://www.ast.org/

DELMAR CENGAGE LEARNING SURGICAL TECHNOLOGY SCHOLARSHIP

Scholarship offers students in CAAHEP-accredited surgical technology programs the opportunity to apply for financial assistance. Must have a 2.5 GPA.

Academic Fields/Career Goals: Health and Medical Sciences.

Award: Scholarship for use in freshman, sophomore, junior, or senior years; not renewable. *Number:* 1. *Amount:* $1000.

Eligibility Requirements: Applicant must be enrolled or expecting to enroll full-time at a two-year or four-year institution or university. Applicant must have 2.5 GPA or higher. Available to U.S. citizens.

Application Requirements: Application, essay, references, self-addressed stamped envelope, transcript, course fee schedule. *Deadline:* April 1.

Contact: Karen Ludwig, Director of Publishing
Association of Surgical Technologists
Six West Dry Creek Circle, Suite 200
Littleton, CO 80120
Phone: 800-637-7433
Fax: 303-694-9169
E-mail: kludwig@ast.org

FOUNDATION STUDENT SCHOLARSHIP

Scholarship to encourage and reward educational excellence as well as to respond to the financial need demonstrated by the surgical technology student and offer assistance to those who seek a career in surgical technology. High school students also eligible to apply. Minimum GPA 3.2 is required.

Academic Fields/Career Goals: Health and Medical Sciences.

Award: Scholarship for use in freshman, sophomore, junior, or senior years; not renewable. *Number:* up to 12. *Amount:* $500–$2000.

Eligibility Requirements: Applicant must be enrolled or expecting to enroll full-time at a two-year or four-year institution or university. Available to U.S. citizens.

Application Requirements: Application, essay, financial need analysis, references, self-addressed stamped envelope, transcript. *Deadline:* April 1.

Contact: Karen Ludwig, Director of Publishing
Association of Surgical Technologists
Six West Dry Creek Circle, Suite 200
Littleton, CO 80120
Phone: 800-637-7433
Fax: 303-694-9169
E-mail: kludwig@ast.org

ASSOCIATION ON AMERICAN INDIAN AFFAIRS, INC.

http://www.indian-affairs.org/

ELIZABETH AND SHERMAN ASCHE MEMORIAL SCHOLARSHIP FUND
• See page 83

ATLANTIC HEALTH SYSTEM OVERLOOK HOSPITAL FOUNDATION

http://www.overlookhospitalfoundation.com/

OVERLOOK HOSPITAL FOUNDATION PROFESSIONAL DEVELOPMENT PROGRAM

Nursing and other allied health students who live in New Jersey are eligible to apply. Pays for one to two years of tuition in exchange for a commitment to work at Overlook Hospital upon graduation.

Academic Fields/Career Goals: Health and Medical Sciences; Nursing.

Award: Scholarship for use in freshman, sophomore, junior, or senior years; not renewable. *Number:* varies. *Amount:* varies.

Eligibility Requirements: Applicant must be enrolled or expecting to enroll full- or part-time at a two-year or four-year institution and resident of New Jersey. Available to U.S. citizens.

Application Requirements: Application. *Deadline:* varies.

Contact: Betsy Koehler, Scholarship Coordinator
Atlantic Health System Overlook Hospital Foundation
99 Beauvoir Avenue
Summit, NJ 07902
Phone: 908-522-2835
E-mail: betsy.koehler@ahsys.org

BETHESDA LUTHERAN COMMUNITIES

http://www.bethesdalutherancommunities.org/

DEVELOPMENTAL DISABILITIES AWARENESS AWARDS FOR HIGH SCHOOL STUDENTS WHO ARE LUTHERAN

Award available to high school seniors interested in the developmental disabilities field. Students must complete two activities from a suggested list, which, together with the application process, are designed to promote the student's knowledge of careers in the field of developmental disabilities services. Two $500 awards are given. For more information, visit web site at http://www.blhs.org.

Academic Fields/Career Goals: Health and Medical Sciences; Nursing; Social Services; Special Education; Therapy/Rehabilitation.

Award: Scholarship for use in freshman year; not renewable. *Number:* 2. *Amount:* up to $500.

Eligibility Requirements: Applicant must be Lutheran; high school student and planning to enroll or expecting to enroll full-time at a two-year or four-year or technical institution or university. Applicant must have 3.0 GPA or higher. Available to U.S. and Canadian citizens.

Application Requirements: Application, essay, resume, references, transcript. *Deadline:* April 15.

Contact: Pam Bergen, Executive Assistant for Mission Advancement
Bethesda Lutheran Communities
600 Hoffmann Drive
Watertown, WI 53094
Phone: 920-206-4410
Fax: 920-206-7706
E-mail: pam.bergen@mailblc.org

DEVELOPMENTAL DISABILITIES SCHOLASTIC ACHIEVEMENT SCHOLARSHIP FOR COLLEGE STUDENTS WHO ARE LUTHERAN
• *See page 218*

BOYS AND GIRLS CLUBS OF SAN DIEGO

http://www.sdyouth.org/

SPENCE REESE SCHOLARSHIP
• *See page 281*

CANADIAN SOCIETY FOR MEDICAL LABORATORY SCIENCE

http://www.csmls.org/

CANADIAN SOCIETY OF LABORATORY TECHNOLOGISTS STUDENT SCHOLARSHIP PROGRAM

Six one-time awards of CAN$500 available to students enrolled in their final year of general medical laboratory technology, cytotechnology, or clinical genetic studies. Must be student member of Canadian Society for Medical Laboratory Science, and Canadian citizen or permanent resident of Canada.

Academic Fields/Career Goals: Health and Medical Sciences.

Award: Scholarship for use in senior year; not renewable. *Number:* 6.

Eligibility Requirements: Applicant must be Canadian citizen and enrolled or expecting to enroll full-time at an institution or university. Applicant or parent of applicant must be member of Canadian Society for Medical Laboratory Science.

Application Requirements: Application, financial need analysis, references, self-addressed stamped envelope, transcript. *Deadline:* October 1.

Contact: Katherine Coles, Executive Assistant–Corporate Services
Canadian Society for Medical Laboratory Science
LCD 1, PO Box 2830
Hamilton, ON L8N 3N8
Phone: 905-528-8642 Ext. 8602
Fax: 905-528-4968
E-mail: lisal@csmls.org

E.V. BOOTH SCHOLARSHIP AWARD
• *See page 334*

CANFIT

http://www.canfit.org/

CANFIT NUTRITION, PHYSICAL EDUCATION AND CULINARY ARTS SCHOLARSHIP
• *See page 209*

CENTRAL SCHOLARSHIP BUREAU

http://www.centralsb.org/

CHESAPEAKE UROLOGY ASSOCIATES SCHOLARSHIP

Scholarship provides assistance to Maryland residents who are full-time undergraduate students pursuing a degree in pre-medicine, pre-nursing, and ancillary health fields. Recipients will be selected based on demonstrated commitment to the medical field, financial need, and academic achievement.

Academic Fields/Career Goals: Health and Medical Sciences; Nursing.

Award: Scholarship for use in sophomore, junior, or senior years; renewable. *Number:* 3. *Amount:* $1500–$5000.

Eligibility Requirements: Applicant must be enrolled or expecting to enroll full-time at a two-year or four-year institution or university and resident of Maryland. Applicant must have 3.0 GPA or higher. Available to U.S. citizens.

Application Requirements: Application, essay, financial need analysis, interview, resume, transcript. *Deadline:* May 1.

Contact: Roberta Goldman, Program Director
Central Scholarship Bureau
1700 Reisterstown Road, Suite 220
Baltimore, MD 21208-2903
Phone: 410-415-5558
Fax: 410-425-5501
E-mail: rgoldman@centralsb.org

CHRISTIANA CARE HEALTH SYSTEMS

http://www.christianacare.org/

RUTH SHAW JUNIOR BOARD SCHOLARSHIP

Offers financial assistance to students currently enrolled in nursing and selected allied health programs. Applicants are selected based on academic achievement and a proven commitment to quality patient care. Students receiving assistance are required to commit to a minimum of one year of employment with Christiana Care.

Academic Fields/Career Goals: Health and Medical Sciences; Nursing.

Award: Scholarship for use in freshman, sophomore, junior, or senior years; not renewable. *Number:* varies. *Amount:* varies.

Eligibility Requirements: Applicant must be enrolled or expecting to enroll full- or part-time at a four-year institution or university. Applicant or parent of applicant must have employment or volunteer experience in nursing. Available to U.S. citizens.

Application Requirements: Application, driver's license, resume, references, transcript. *Deadline:* April 30.

Contact: Wendy Gable, Scholarship Committee
Christiana Care Health Systems
200 Hygeia Drive, PO Box 6001
Newark, DE 19713
Phone: 302-428-5710
E-mail: wgable@christianacare.org

COLLEGE BOARD/ROBERT WOOD JOHNSON FOUNDATION YES PROGRAM

http://www.collegeboard.com/

YOUNG EPIDEMIOLOGY SCHOLARS COMPETITION
• *See page 304*

THE COMMUNITY FOUNDATION FOR GREATER ATLANTA, INC.

http://www.cfgreateratlanta.org/

STEVE DEARDUFF SCHOLARSHIP

Scholarship for undergraduate and graduate students pursuing degrees in medicine or social work. Legal resident of Georgia. Minimum 2.0 GPA. Previous recipients are encouraged to reapply, but are not guaranteed additional awards. For complete eligibility requirements or to submit an application, visit http://www.cfgreateratlanta.org.

Academic Fields/Career Goals: Health and Medical Sciences; Social Services.

Award: Scholarship for use in freshman, sophomore, junior, senior, or graduate years; not renewable. *Number:* 1–3. *Amount:* up to $2500.

Eligibility Requirements: Applicant must be enrolled or expecting to enroll full- or part-time at a four-year institution or university and resident of Georgia. Available to U.S. citizens.

Application Requirements: Application, driver's license, essay, financial need analysis, references, transcript. *Deadline:* March 15.

Contact: Kristina Morris, Program Associate
The Community Foundation for Greater Atlanta, Inc.
50 Hurt Plaza, Suite 449
Atlanta, GA 30303
Phone: 404-688-5525
E-mail: scholarships@cfgreateratlanta.org

CONGRESSIONAL BLACK CAUCUS FOUNDATION, INC.

http://www.cbcfinc.org/

CONGRESSIONAL BLACK CAUCUS SPOUSES CHEERIOS BRAND HEALTH INITIATIVE
• *See page 139*

CYNTHIA E. MORGAN SCHOLARSHIP FUND (CEMS)

http://www.cemsfund.com/

CYNTHIA E. MORGAN MEMORIAL SCHOLARSHIP FUND, INC.
• *See page 304*

FOUNDATION FOR SCIENCE AND DISABILITY

http://stemd.org/

GRANTS FOR DISABLED STUDENTS IN THE SCIENCES
• *See page 95*

FOUNDATION FOR SURGICAL TECHNOLOGY

http://www.ffst.org/

FOUNDATION FOR SURGICAL TECHNOLOGY SCHOLARSHIP FUND

Scholarships available for students who are currently enrolled in an accredited surgical technology program whose graduates are eligible to sit for the NBSTSA surgical technologist certifying examination. Must be preparing for a career as a surgical technologist. Minimum 3.0 GPA is required. One-time award. Amount varies from year to year. Applicant must be selected by sponsoring institution. Visit web site for more information.

Academic Fields/Career Goals: Health and Medical Sciences.

Award: Scholarship for use in freshman, sophomore, junior, or senior years; not renewable. *Number:* 10–20. *Amount:* $500–$2500.

Eligibility Requirements: Applicant must be enrolled or expecting to enroll full-time at a two-year or four-year or technical institution or university. Applicant must have 3.0 GPA or higher. Available to U.S. citizens.

Application Requirements: Application, financial need analysis, references, transcript. *Deadline:* March 1.

Contact: Karen Ludwig, Director of Publishing
Foundation for Surgical Technology
6 West Dry Creek Circle
Littleton, CO 80120
Phone: 303-694-9130
Fax: 303-694-9169

GARDEN CLUB OF AMERICA

http://www.gcamerica.org/

ZELLER SUMMER SCHOLARSHIP IN MEDICINAL BOTANY

Scholarship to students who show interest in medicinal botany, as evidenced by course work and/or professor recommendations. Established to encourage summer studies of medicinal botany at the undergraduate level for students enrolled in accredited U.S. colleges and universities.

Academic Fields/Career Goals: Health and Medical Sciences; Horticulture/Floriculture; Natural Sciences.

Award: Scholarship for use in freshman, sophomore, junior, or senior years; not renewable. *Number:* 1. *Amount:* $2000.

Eligibility Requirements: Applicant must be enrolled or expecting to enroll full-time at a four-year institution or university. Available to U.S. citizens.

Application Requirements: Application, essay, resume, references, transcript. *Deadline:* February 1.

Contact: Connie Yates, Scholarship Committee Administrator
Garden Club of America
14 East 60th Street, Third Floor
New York, NY 10022-1002
Phone: 212-753-8287
E-mail: cyates@gcamerica.org

GENERAL BOARD OF HIGHER EDUCATION AND MINISTRY

http://www.gbhem.org/

EDITH M. ALLEN SCHOLARSHIP
• *See page 236*

GREATER KANAWHA VALLEY FOUNDATION

http://www.tgkvf.org/

NICHOLAS AND MARY AGNES TRIVILLIAN MEMORIAL SCHOLARSHIP FUND

Renewable award for West Virginia residents pursuing medical or pharmacy programs. Must show financial need and academic merit. For information and on-line application go to http://www.tgkvf.org.

Academic Fields/Career Goals: Health and Medical Sciences; Pharmacy.

Award: Scholarship for use in freshman, sophomore, junior, or senior years; renewable. *Amount:* $1000.

Eligibility Requirements: Applicant must be enrolled or expecting to enroll full-time at a four-year institution or university and resident of West Virginia. Available to U.S. citizens.

Application Requirements: Application, essay, financial need analysis, references, self-addressed stamped envelope, test scores, transcript. *Deadline:* January 15.

Contact: Susan Hoover, Scholarship Coordinator
Greater Kanawha Valley Foundation
PO Box 3041
Charleston, WV 25331
Phone: 304-346-3620
Fax: 304-346-3640

HAWAIIAN LODGE, F&AM

http://www.glhawaii.org/

HAWAIIAN LODGE SCHOLARSHIPS
• *See page 106*

HEALTHCARE INFORMATION AND MANAGEMENT SYSTEMS SOCIETY FOUNDATION

http://www.himss.org/

HIMSS FOUNDATION SCHOLARSHIP PROGRAM
• *See page 334*

HEALTH PROFESSIONS EDUCATION FOUNDATION

http://www.healthprofessions.ca.gov/

KAISER PERMANENTE ALLIED HEALTHCARE SCHOLARSHIP

One-time award available to students enrolled in, or accepted to California accredited allied health education programs. Scholarship worth up to $4500. Deadlines: March 24 and September 11.

Academic Fields/Career Goals: Health and Medical Sciences; Social Services; Therapy/Rehabilitation.

Award: Scholarship for use in freshman, sophomore, junior, senior, graduate, or postgraduate years; not renewable. *Number:* up to 40. *Amount:* $3000–$4000.

Eligibility Requirements: Applicant must be enrolled or expecting to enroll full- or part-time at a two-year or four-year or technical institution or university; resident of California and studying in California. Available to U.S. citizens.

Application Requirements: Application, driver's license, financial need analysis, resume, references, transcript, Student Aid Report (SAR) or tax return with W2. *Deadline:* varies.

Contact: Margarita Miranda, Program Administrator
Health Professions Education Foundation
818 K Street, Suite 210
Sacramento, CA 95814
Phone: 916-326-3640
Fax: 916-324-6585

HEALTH RESEARCH COUNCIL OF NEW ZEALAND

http://www.hrc.govt.nz/

PACIFIC HEALTH WORKFORCE AWARD
• *See page 334*

PACIFIC MENTAL HEALTH WORK FORCE AWARD
• *See page 334*

HELLENIC UNIVERSITY CLUB OF PHILADELPHIA

http://www.hucphila.org/

DR. PETER A. THEODOS MEMORIAL GRADUATE SCHOLARSHIP

$2500 scholarship awarded to a senior undergraduate or graduate student with financial need pursuing studies leading to a Doctor of Medicine degree. Must be a U.S. citizen of Greek descent and a resident of particular counties in NJ or PA.

Academic Fields/Career Goals: Health and Medical Sciences.

Award: Scholarship for use in senior or graduate years; not renewable. *Number:* up to 1. *Amount:* up to $2500.

Eligibility Requirements: Applicant must be of Greek heritage; enrolled or expecting to enroll full-time at a four-year institution or university and resident of New Jersey or Pennsylvania. Available to U.S. citizens.

Application Requirements: Application, financial need analysis, transcript. *Deadline:* April 21.

Contact: Anna Hadgis, Scholarship Chairman
Hellenic University Club of Philadelphia
PO Box 42199
Philadelphia, PA 19101-2199
Phone: 610-613-4310
E-mail: hucphila@yahoo.com

INDEPENDENT COLLEGE FUND OF MARYLAND (I-FUND)

http://www.i-fundinfo.org/

HEALTH AND LIFE SCIENCES PROGRAM SCHOLARSHIPS
• *See page 140*

INDIAN HEALTH SERVICES, UNITED STATES DEPARTMENT OF HEALTH AND HUMAN SERVICES

http://www.ihs.gov/

HEALTH PROFESSIONS PREPARATORY SCHOLARSHIP PROGRAM
• *See page 335*

INDIAN HEALTH SERVICE HEALTH PROFESSIONS PRE-GRADUATE SCHOLARSHIPS
• *See page 219*

INDIAN HEALTH SERVICE HEALTH PROFESSIONS SCHOLARSHIP PROGRAM
• *See page 335*

INTERNATIONAL ORDER OF THE KING'S DAUGHTERS AND SONS

http://www.iokds.org/

HEALTH CAREERS SCHOLARSHIP
• *See page 219*

J.D. ARCHBOLD MEMORIAL HOSPITAL

http://www.archbold.org/

ARCHBOLD SCHOLARSHIP PROGRAM

Service cancelable loan awarded for a clinical degree. Awarded to residents of Southwest Georgia and North Florida. Specific clinical degree may vary, depending on need in area. Must agree to full-time employment for one to three years upon graduation.

Academic Fields/Career Goals: Health and Medical Sciences; Nursing.

Award: Forgivable loan for use in freshman, sophomore, junior, or senior years; not renewable. *Number:* 50. *Amount:* $600–$6000.

Eligibility Requirements: Applicant must be enrolled or expecting to enroll full- or part-time at a four-year institution or university and resident of Florida or Georgia. Available to U.S. citizens.

Application Requirements: Application, interview, references, transcript. *Deadline:* continuous.

Contact: Donna McMillan, Education Coordinator
J.D. Archbold Memorial Hospital
PO Box 1018
Thomasville, GA 31799
Phone: 229-228-2795
Fax: 229-228-8584

LADIES AUXILIARY TO THE VETERANS OF FOREIGN WARS, DEPARTMENT OF MAINE

http://mainevfw.org/

FRANCES L. BOOTH MEDICAL SCHOLARSHIP SPONSORED BY LAVFW DEPARTMENT OF MAINE

Award for an undergraduate student majoring in the field of medicine who has a parent or grandparent who is a member of the Maine VFW or VFW auxiliary.

Academic Fields/Career Goals: Health and Medical Sciences; Humanities; Nursing; Therapy/Rehabilitation.

Award: Scholarship for use in freshman, sophomore, junior, or senior years; renewable. *Number:* 2. *Amount:* $500–$1000.

Eligibility Requirements: Applicant must be enrolled or expecting to enroll full-time at a two-year or four-year institution or university and resident of Maine. Applicant or parent of applicant must be member of Veterans of Foreign Wars or Auxiliary. Applicant must have 3.0 GPA or higher. Available to U.S. citizens. Applicant or parent must meet one or more of the following requirements: general military experience; retired from active duty; disabled or killed as a result of military service; prisoner of war; or missing in action.

Application Requirements: Application, essay, financial need analysis, resume, references, transcript, personal letter. *Deadline:* March 31.

Contact: Sheila Webber, Chairman FBMS
Ladies Auxiliary to the Veterans of Foreign Wars, Department of Maine
PO Box 493
Old Orchard Beach, ME 04064
Phone: 207-934-2405
E-mail: swebber2@maine.rr.com

LINCOLN COMMUNITY FOUNDATION

http://www.lcf.org/

MEDICAL RESEARCH SCHOLARSHIP

Scholarship available to students who have completed appropriate undergraduate education and are currently pursuing an advanced degree in a medical related field with the exception of nurses who may apply as undergraduates. Preference will be given to females pursuing careers as physicians and nurses who demonstrate financial need.

Academic Fields/Career Goals: Health and Medical Sciences; Nursing.

Award: Scholarship for use in freshman, sophomore, junior, senior, graduate, or postgraduate years; renewable. *Number:* 1–5. *Amount:* $500–$1000.

Eligibility Requirements: Applicant must be enrolled or expecting to enroll full- or part-time at a two-year or four-year institution or university. Available to U.S. citizens.

Application Requirements: Application, essay, financial need analysis, test scores, transcript. *Deadline:* May 30.

Contact: Sonya Brakeman, Grants/Scholarships Coordinator
Lincoln Community Foundation
215 Centennial Mall South, Suite 100
Lincoln, NE 68508
Phone: 402-474-2345
Fax: 402-476-8532
E-mail: sonyab@lcf.org

MAINE OSTEOPATHIC ASSOCIATION MEMORIAL SCHOLARSHIP/MAINE OSTEOPATHIC ASSOCIATION

http://www.mainedo.org/

BEALE FAMILY MEMORIAL SCHOLARSHIP

One award of $1000 is made to a well qualified student in their second, third or fourth year of study at an osteopathic college, who has evidence of interest in returning to Maine to practice or in teaching in an osteopathic college in New England.

Academic Fields/Career Goals: Health and Medical Sciences; Osteopathy.

Award: Scholarship for use in sophomore, junior, or senior years; not renewable. *Number:* 1. *Amount:* $1000.

Eligibility Requirements: Applicant must be enrolled or expecting to enroll full- or part-time at a four-year institution or university. Available to U.S. citizens.

Application Requirements: Application, proof of residence. *Deadline:* May 1.

Contact: Dianne Jackson, Office Manager and Convention Coordinator
Maine Osteopathic Association Memorial Scholarship/Maine Osteopathic Association
693 Western Avenue, Suite 1
Manchester, ME 04351
Phone: 207-623-1101
Fax: 207-623-4228
E-mail: djackson@mainedo.org

MAINE OSTEOPATHIC ASSOCIATION MEMORIAL SCHOLARSHIP

One award of $1000 to a second, third, or fourth year student who is a resident of Maine. Must present proof of enrollment at an approved osteopathic college.

Academic Fields/Career Goals: Health and Medical Sciences; Osteopathy.

Award: Scholarship for use in sophomore, junior, or senior years; not renewable. *Number:* 1. *Amount:* $1000.

Eligibility Requirements: Applicant must be enrolled or expecting to enroll full- or part-time at a four-year institution or university and resident of Maine. Available to U.S. citizens.

Application Requirements: Application, proof of residence, proof of enrollment at an approved osteopathic college. *Deadline:* May 1.

Contact: Dianne Jackson, Office Manager and Convention Coordinator
Maine Osteopathic Association Memorial Scholarship/Maine Osteopathic Association
693 Western Avenue, Suite 1
Manchester, ME 04351
Phone: 207-623-1101
Fax: 207-623-4228
E-mail: djackson@mainedo.org

MAINE OSTEOPATHIC ASSOCIATION SCHOLARSHIP

One award of $1000 to a student who is a resident of Maine and able to present proof of enrollment at an approved osteopathic college.

Academic Fields/Career Goals: Health and Medical Sciences; Osteopathy.

Award: Scholarship for use in freshman year; not renewable. *Number:* 1. *Amount:* $1000.

Eligibility Requirements: Applicant must be high school student; planning to enroll or expecting to enroll full- or part-time at a two-year or four-year or technical institution or university and resident of Maine. Available to U.S. citizens.

Application Requirements: Application, transcript, proof of Maine residence. *Deadline:* May 1.

Contact: Dianne Jackson, Office Manager and Convention Coordinator
Maine Osteopathic Association Memorial Scholarship/Maine Osteopathic Association
693 Western Avenue, Suite 1
Manchester, ME 04351
Phone: 207-623-1101
Fax: 207-623-4228
E-mail: djackson@mainedo.org

MARYLAND STATE HIGHER EDUCATION COMMISSION

http://www.mhec.state.md.us/

CHARLES W. RILEY FIRE AND EMERGENCY MEDICAL SERVICES TUITION REIMBURSEMENT PROGRAM
• *See page 316*

GRADUATE AND PROFESSIONAL SCHOLARSHIP PROGRAM-MARYLAND
• *See page 220*

MISSISSIPPI OFFICE OF STUDENT FINANCIAL AID

http://www.mississippi.edu/

MISSISSIPPI HEALTH CARE PROFESSIONS LOAN/ SCHOLARSHIP PROGRAM

Renewable award for junior and senior undergraduates studying psychology or speech pathology, and graduate students studying physical therapy or occupational therapy. Must be Mississippi residents attending four-year colleges or universities in Mississippi. Must fulfill work obligation in Mississippi on the basis of one year's service for one year's loan received, or pay back as loan.

Academic Fields/Career Goals: Health and Medical Sciences; Psychology; Therapy/Rehabilitation.

Award: Forgivable loan for use in junior, senior, or graduate years; not renewable. *Number:* varies. *Amount:* $1500–$3000.

Eligibility Requirements: Applicant must be enrolled or expecting to enroll full-time at a four-year institution or university; resident of Mississippi and studying in Mississippi. Available to U.S. citizens.

Application Requirements: Application, transcript, letter of acceptance. *Deadline:* March 31.

Contact: Mrs. Jennifer Rogers, Director of Student Financial Aid
Mississippi Office of Student Financial Aid
3825 Ridgewood Road
Jackson, MS 39211-6453
Phone: 601-432-6997
E-mail: sfa@mississippi.edu

MISSOURI DEPARTMENT OF HEALTH AND SENIOR SERVICES

http://www.dhss.mo.gov/

PRIMARY CARE RESOURCE INITIATIVE FOR MISSOURI LOAN PROGRAM
• See page 136

NATIONAL ARAB AMERICAN MEDICAL ASSOCIATION

http://www.naama.com/

FOUNDATION SCHOLARSHIP
• See page 220

NATIONAL ASSOCIATION TO ADVANCE FAT ACCEPTANCE

http://www.naafa.org/

NATIONAL ASSOCIATION TO ADVANCE FAT ACCEPTANCE HAES SCHOLARSHIP

Undergraduate or graduate students from accredited academic institutions, which utilize Health at Every Size tenets in their studies and research are eligible to apply for the NAAFA HAES Scholarship. Students interested in being considered for this scholarship can find complete details and an application at: http://www.naafaonline.com/.

Academic Fields/Career Goals: Health and Medical Sciences.

Award: Scholarship for use in freshman or graduate years; not renewable. *Number:* 1–1. *Amount:* $1000.

Eligibility Requirements: Applicant must be enrolled or expecting to enroll full-time at an institution or university. Available to U.S. and Canadian citizens.

Application Requirements: Application, applicant must enter a contest, essay, references. *Deadline:* June 1.

Contact: Ms. Lisa Tealer, NAAFA Board Member and Director of Programs
National Association to Advance Fat Acceptance
PO Box 4662
Foster City, CA 94404-0662
Phone: 916-558-6880
E-mail: ltealer@naafa.org

NATIONAL ATHLETIC TRAINERS' ASSOCIATION RESEARCH AND EDUCATION FOUNDATION

http://www.natafoundation.org/

NATIONAL ATHLETIC TRAINERS' ASSOCIATION RESEARCH AND EDUCATION FOUNDATION SCHOLARSHIP PROGRAM

One-time award available to full-time students who are members of NATA. Minimum 3.2 GPA required. Open to undergraduate upperclassmen and graduate/postgraduate students.

Academic Fields/Career Goals: Health and Medical Sciences; Health Information Management/Technology; Sports-Related/Exercise Science; Therapy/Rehabilitation.

Award: Scholarship for use in junior, senior, graduate, or postgraduate years; not renewable. *Number:* 70. *Amount:* $2000.

Eligibility Requirements: Applicant must be enrolled or expecting to enroll full-time at a four-year institution or university. Applicant or parent of applicant must be member of National Athletic Trainers Association. Available to U.S. and non-U.S. citizens.

Application Requirements: Application, essay, references, transcript. *Deadline:* February 10.

Contact: Patsy Brown, Scholarship Coordinator
National Athletic Trainers' Association Research and Education Foundation
2952 Stemmons Freeway, Suite 200
Dallas, TX 75247
Phone: 214-637-6282 Ext. 151
Fax: 214-637-2206
E-mail: patsyb@nata.org

NATIONAL INSTITUTES OF HEALTH

https://ugsp.nih.gov/

NIH UNDERGRADUATE SCHOLARSHIP PROGRAM FOR STUDENTS FROM DISADVANTAGED BACKGROUNDS
• See page 142

NATIONAL INVENTORS HALL OF FAME

http://www.invent.org/

COLLEGIATE INVENTORS COMPETITION FOR UNDERGRADUATE STUDENTS
• See page 96

COLLEGIATE INVENTORS COMPETITION-GRAND PRIZE
• See page 97

NEW MEXICO COMMISSION ON HIGHER EDUCATION

http://www.hed.state.nm.us/

ALLIED HEALTH STUDENT LOAN PROGRAM-NEW MEXICO
• See page 220

NEW YORK STATE EDUCATION DEPARTMENT

http://www.highered.nysed.gov/

REGENTS PROFESSIONAL OPPORTUNITY SCHOLARSHIP
• See page 69

NORTH CAROLINA STATE EDUCATION ASSISTANCE AUTHORITY

http://www.ncseaa.edu/

NORTH CAROLINA STUDENT LOAN PROGRAM FOR HEALTH, SCIENCE, AND MATHEMATICS
• *See page 221*

OREGON COMMUNITY FOUNDATION

http://www.oregoncf.org/

FRANZ STENZEL M.D. AND KATHRYN STENZEL SCHOLARSHIP FUND

Scholarships for Oregon residents, with a focus on three types of students: (a) those pursuing any type of undergraduate degree, (b) those pursuing a nursing education through a two-year, four-year, or graduate program, and (c) medical students.

Academic Fields/Career Goals: Health and Medical Sciences; Nursing.

Award: Scholarship for use in freshman, sophomore, junior, or senior years; renewable. *Number:* up to 70. *Amount:* $2000–$5000.

Eligibility Requirements: Applicant must be enrolled or expecting to enroll full-time at a two-year or four-year institution or university and resident of Oregon. Available to U.S. citizens.

Application Requirements: Application, references. *Deadline:* March 1.

Contact: Dianne Causey, Program Associate for Scholarships and Grants
Oregon Community Foundation
1221 Yamhill, SW, Suite 100
Portland, OR 97205-2108
Phone: 503-227-6846 Ext. 1418
E-mail: dcausey@oregoncf.org

OREGON STUDENT ASSISTANCE COMMISSION

http://www.GetCollegeFunds.org/

CHESTER AND HELEN LUTHER SCHOLARSHIP

Award available to graduates of any high school in Oregon or Clark County, Washington. Applicants must also be residents of either Oregon or Clark County, Washington. Preference is given to first-generation college attendees. Recipients must attend a college or university in Oregon or Clark County, Washington, enroll at least half-time, and be at least 25 years old as of the March scholarship deadline.

Academic Fields/Career Goals: Health and Medical Sciences; Nursing.

Award: Scholarship for use in freshman, sophomore, junior, senior, or graduate years; not renewable.

Eligibility Requirements: Applicant must be age 25 and over; enrolled or expecting to enroll full- or part-time at a two-year or four-year institution or university; resident of Oregon or Washington and studying in Oregon or Washington. Applicant must have 3.0 GPA or higher.

Application Requirements: Application. *Deadline:* March 1.

Contact: Director of Grant Programs
Oregon Student Assistance Commission
1500 Valley River Drive, Suite 100
Eugene, OR 97401-7020
Phone: 800-452-8807

CLARK-PHELPS SCHOLARSHIP
• *See page 221*

HELEN HALL AND JOHN SEELY MEMORIAL SCHOLARSHIP

Award is open to graduates of Douglas County high schools. Minimum GPA of 3.0 is required. Preference for majors in medical, nursing, or other health-related fields. Evidence of healthcare and community-related activities will be taken into consideration. Must reapply annually for renewal.

Academic Fields/Career Goals: Health and Medical Sciences; Nursing.

Award: Scholarship for use in freshman, sophomore, junior, senior, or graduate years; not renewable.

Eligibility Requirements: Applicant must be enrolled or expecting to enroll full- or part-time at a four-year institution or university and resident of Oregon. Applicant must have 3.0 GPA or higher. Available to U.S. citizens.

Application Requirements: Application, test scores, transcript. *Deadline:* March 1.

Contact: Director of Grant Programs
Oregon Student Assistance Commission
1500 Valley River Drive, Suite 100
Eugene, OR 97401-7020
Phone: 800-452-8807

MARION A. LINDEMAN SCHOLARSHIP

Award for Willamette View Health Center or Willamette View Terrace employees who have completed one or more years of service. Must be pursuing a degree or certificate in nursing, speech, physical or occupational therapy, or other health-related fields. Must enroll at least half time in a U.S. college or university and reapply annually for award renewal. Oregon residency is not required.

Academic Fields/Career Goals: Health and Medical Sciences; Nursing; Therapy/Rehabilitation.

Award: Scholarship for use in freshman, sophomore, junior, or senior years; not renewable. *Number:* varies. *Amount:* varies.

Eligibility Requirements: Applicant must be enrolled or expecting to enroll full- or part-time at a two-year or four-year institution. Applicant or parent of applicant must be affiliated with Willamette View. Available to U.S. citizens.

Application Requirements: Application, essay, financial need analysis, references, transcript, activity chart. *Deadline:* March 1.

Contact: Director of Grant Programs
Oregon Student Assistance Commission
1500 Valley River Drive, Suite 100
Eugene, OR 97401-7020
Phone: 800-452-8807 Ext. 7395

PACERS FOUNDATION INC.

http://www.pacersfoundation.org/

LINDA CRAIG MEMORIAL SCHOLARSHIP PRESENTED BY ST. VINCENT SPORTS MEDICINE

Scholarship presented by St. Vincent Sports Medicine is for currently-enrolled juniors and seniors with declared majors of medicine, sports medicine, and/or physical therapy. Students must have completed at least 4 semesters and attend a school in Indiana. Minimum 3.0 GPA required.

Academic Fields/Career Goals: Health and Medical Sciences; Sports-Related/Exercise Science; Therapy/Rehabilitation.

Award: Scholarship for use in junior, senior, graduate, or postgraduate years; renewable. *Number:* 1–2. *Amount:* $2000.

Eligibility Requirements: Applicant must be enrolled or expecting to enroll full-time at a two-year or four-year institution or university and studying in Indiana. Applicant must have 3.0 GPA or higher. Available to U.S. citizens.

Application Requirements: Application, essay, references, transcript. *Deadline:* March 1.

Contact: Jami Marsh, Executive Director
Pacers Foundation Inc.
125 South Pennsylvania Street
Indianapolis, IN 46204
Phone: 317-917-2856
E-mail: foundation@pacers.com

PEARSON BENJAMIN CUMMINGS

http://www.pearsonhighered.com/

PEARSON BENJAMIN CUMMINGS ALLIED HEALTH STUDENT SCHOLARSHIP
• *See page 143*

PHYSICIAN ASSISTANT FOUNDATION

http://www.aapa.org/paf

PHYSICIAN ASSISTANT FOUNDATION ANNUAL SCHOLARSHIP

One-time award for student members of the American Academy of Physician Assistants enrolled in an ARC PA-accredited physician assistant program. Award based on financial need, academic achievement, and goals.

Academic Fields/Career Goals: Health and Medical Sciences.

Award: Scholarship for use in junior or senior years; not renewable. *Number:* up to 75. *Amount:* $2000.

Eligibility Requirements: Applicant must be enrolled or expecting to enroll full- or part-time at a four-year institution or university. Applicant or parent of applicant must be member of American Academy of Physicians Assistants. Available to U.S. and non-U.S. citizens.

Application Requirements: Application, essay, financial need analysis, photo, test scores, transcript. *Deadline:* January 15.

Contact: Tara Burnett, Scholarship Committee
Physician Assistant Foundation
950 North Washington Street
Alexandria, VA 22314-1552
Phone: 703-519-5686
Fax: 703-684-1924
E-mail: tburnett@aapa.org

PILOT INTERNATIONAL FOUNDATION

http://www.pilotinternational.org/

PILOT INTERNATIONAL FOUNDATION RUBY NEWHALL MEMORIAL SCHOLARSHIP

Scholarship available to international students for full-time study in the United States or Canada. Applicants must have visa or green card and must be majoring in a field related to human health and welfare. Minimum of one full academic semester in an accredited college in the United States or Canada must be completed before applying for the scholarship. Applicants must be sponsored by Pilot Club in their home town, or in the city in which their college or university is located.

Academic Fields/Career Goals: Health and Medical Sciences; Nursing; Psychology; Public Health; Social Services; Special Education; Therapy/Rehabilitation.

Award: Scholarship for use in freshman, sophomore, junior, or senior years; not renewable. *Number:* 8–10. *Amount:* up to $1500.

Eligibility Requirements: Applicant must be enrolled or expecting to enroll full- or part-time at a two-year or four-year or technical institution. Applicant must have 3.0 GPA or higher. Available to Canadian and non-U.S. citizens.

Application Requirements: Application, essay, financial need analysis, references, self-addressed stamped envelope, transcript, visa or F1 status. *Deadline:* March 1.

Contact: Jennifer Overbay, Foundation Services Director
Pilot International Foundation
PO Box 4844
Macon, GA 31208-5600
Phone: 478-743-7403
Fax: 478-474-7229
E-mail: pifinfo@pilothq.org

PILOT INTERNATIONAL FOUNDATION SCHOLARSHIP PROGRAM

Scholarship program for undergraduate students preparing for a career helping those with brain related disorders or disabilities. Applicant must have visa or green card. Minimum GPA Score to be 3.25.

Academic Fields/Career Goals: Health and Medical Sciences; Nursing; Psychology; Special Education; Therapy/Rehabilitation.

Award: Scholarship for use in freshman, sophomore, or junior years; not renewable. *Number:* 8–10. *Amount:* up to $2000.

Eligibility Requirements: Applicant must be enrolled or expecting to enroll full- or part-time at a two-year or four-year or technical institution. Available to U.S. and non-U.S. citizens.

Application Requirements: Application, essay, financial need analysis, references, self-addressed stamped envelope, transcript, visa or F1 status. *Deadline:* March 1.

Contact: Jennifer Overbay, Foundation Services Director
Pilot International Foundation
PO Box 4844
Macon, GA 31208-5600
Phone: 478-743-7403
Fax: 478-474-7229
E-mail: pifinfo@pilothq.org

PRESBYTERIAN CHURCH (USA)

http://www.pcusa.org/financialaid

STUDENT OPPORTUNITY SCHOLARSHIP
• *See page 246*

SIGMA XI, THE SCIENTIFIC RESEARCH SOCIETY

http://www.sigmaxi.org/

SIGMA XI GRANTS-IN-AID OF RESEARCH
• *See page 87*

SOCIETY FOR APPLIED ANTHROPOLOGY

http://www.sfaa.net/

PETER KONG-MING NEW STUDENT PRIZE
• *See page 137*

SOCIETY FOR THE SCIENTIFIC STUDY OF SEXUALITY

http://www.sexscience.org/

SOCIETY FOR THE SCIENTIFIC STUDY OF SEXUALITY STUDENT RESEARCH GRANT
• *See page 137*

SOCIETY OF NUCLEAR MEDICINE

http://www.snm.org/

PAUL COLE SCHOLARSHIP

Scholarship for students who are enrolled in or accepted for enrollment in associate, baccalaureate or certificate programs in nuclear medicine technology. Academic merit considered. Minimum 2.5 GPA required.

Academic Fields/Career Goals: Health and Medical Sciences; Nuclear Science; Radiology.

Award: Scholarship for use in freshman, sophomore, junior, or senior years; not renewable. *Number:* varies. *Amount:* $1000.

Eligibility Requirements: Applicant must be enrolled or expecting to enroll full- or part-time at a two-year or four-year institution or university. Applicant must have 2.5 GPA or higher. Available to U.S. citizens.

Application Requirements: Application, essay, references, transcript, acceptance letter. *Deadline:* October 15.

Contact: Development Office
Society of Nuclear Medicine
1850 Samuel Morse Drive
Reston, VA 20190
Phone: 703-708-9000 Ext. 1255
E-mail: grantinfo@snm.org

SOCIETY OF PEDIATRIC NURSES

http://www.pedsnurses.org/

SOCIETY OF PEDIATRIC NURSES EDUCATIONAL SCHOLARSHIP
• *See page 173*

STRAIGHTFORWARD MEDIA

http://www.straightforwardmedia.com/

STRAIGHTFORWARD MEDIA MEDICAL PROFESSIONS SCHOLARSHIP

• *See page 221*

UNITED NEGRO COLLEGE FUND

http://www.uncf.org/

ALTON HIGGINS, MD AND DOROTHY HIGGINS SCHOLARSHIP

Scholarship available for junior, senior, or pre-medicine graduate students attending a UNCF member college or university or Morehouse School of Medicine and Howard University Medical School. Minimum 3.0 GPA is required. Funds may be used for tuition, room and board, books, or to repay a federal student loan.

Academic Fields/Career Goals: Health and Medical Sciences.

Award: Scholarship for use in junior, senior, or graduate years; not renewable. *Number:* varies. *Amount:* $5000–$10,000.

Eligibility Requirements: Applicant must be Black (non-Hispanic) and enrolled or expecting to enroll full-time at a four-year institution or university. Applicant must have 3.0 GPA or higher. Available to U.S. and non-U.S. citizens.

Application Requirements: Application, essay, financial need analysis, references, transcript. *Deadline:* April 9.

Contact: Director, Program Services
United Negro College Fund
8260 Willow Oaks Corporate Drive
PO Box 10444
Fairfax, VA 22031-8044
Phone: 800-331-2244
E-mail: rebecca.bennett@uncf.org

CATHOLIC HEALTHCARE WEST CORPORATE SCHOLARS PROGRAM

• *See page 144*

CHARLES E. CULPEPPER SCHOLARSHIP

• *See page 144*

HARRY C. JAECKER SCHOLARSHIP

Award for pre-medical students attending a UNCF member college or university. Minimum 2.5 GPA required. For additional information go to web site http://www.uncf.org.

Academic Fields/Career Goals: Health and Medical Sciences.

Award: Scholarship for use in freshman, sophomore, junior, or senior years; not renewable. *Number:* varies. *Amount:* $2000–$5000.

Eligibility Requirements: Applicant must be Black (non-Hispanic) and enrolled or expecting to enroll full- or part-time at a four-year institution or university. Applicant must have 2.5 GPA or higher. Available to U.S. and non-U.S. citizens.

Application Requirements: Application, financial need analysis.

Contact: Director, Program Services
United Negro College Fund
8260 Willow Oaks Corporate Drive
PO Box 10444
Fairfax, VA 22031-8044
Phone: 800-331-2244
E-mail: rebecca.bennett@uncf.org

MEDTRONIC FOUNDATION SCHOLARSHIP

• *See page 145*

UNCF/MERCK SCIENCE INITIATIVE

• *See page 145*

U. S. DEPARTMENT OF HEALTH AND HUMAN SERVICES

http://www.hhs.gov/about/whatwedo.html/

U. S. PUBLIC HEALTH SERVICE-HEALTH RESOURCES AND SERVICES ADMINISTRATION, BUREAU OF HEALTH PROFESSIONS SCHOLARSHIPS FOR DISADVANTAGED STUDENTS

• *See page 221*

VESALIUS TRUST FOR VISUAL COMMUNICATION IN THE HEALTH SCIENCES

http://www.vesaliustrust.org/

STUDENT RESEARCH SCHOLARSHIP

Scholarships available to students currently enrolled in an undergraduate or graduate school program of bio-communications (medical illustration) who have completed one full year of the curriculum.

Academic Fields/Career Goals: Health and Medical Sciences.

Award: Scholarship for use in junior, senior, or graduate years; not renewable. *Number:* 10–15. *Amount:* $500.

Eligibility Requirements: Applicant must be enrolled or expecting to enroll full- or part-time at a four-year institution or university and must have an interest in art. Available to U.S. and non-U.S. citizens.

Application Requirements: Application, portfolio, resume, references, transcript. *Deadline:* November 7.

Contact: Wendy Hiller Gee, Student Grants and Scholarships
Vesalius Trust for Visual Communication in the Health Sciences
1100 Grundy Lane
San Bruno, CA 94066
Phone: 650-244-4320
E-mail: wendy.hillergee@krames.com

ZETA PHI BETA SORORITY INC. NATIONAL EDUCATIONAL FOUNDATION

http://www.zphib1920.org/

S. EVELYN LEWIS MEMORIAL SCHOLARSHIP IN MEDICAL HEALTH SCIENCES

Scholarships available for graduate or undergraduate women enrolled in a program leading to a degree in medicine or health sciences. Must be a full-time student. See web site for information and application http://www.zphib1920.org.

Academic Fields/Career Goals: Health and Medical Sciences.

Award: Scholarship for use in freshman, sophomore, junior, senior, or graduate years; not renewable. *Number:* 1. *Amount:* $500–$1000.

Eligibility Requirements: Applicant must be enrolled or expecting to enroll full-time at a four-year institution or university and female. Available to U.S. citizens.

Application Requirements: Application, essay, references, transcript, enrollment proof. *Deadline:* February 1.

Contact: Cheryl Williams, National Second Vice President
Zeta Phi Beta Sorority Inc. National Educational Foundation
1734 New Hampshire Avenue, NW
Washington, DC 20009-2595
Fax: 318-232-4593
E-mail: 2ndanti@zphib1920.org

HEALTH INFORMATION MANAGEMENT/ TECHNOLOGY

ALICE L. HALTOM EDUCATIONAL FUND

http://www.alhef.org/

ALICE L. HALTOM EDUCATIONAL FUND

Award for students pursuing a career in information and records management. Up to $1000 for those in an associate degree program, and up to $2000 for students in a baccalaureate or advanced degree program. Students must be citizens of the United States, Canada or Mexico.

Academic Fields/Career Goals: Health Information Management/Technology; Library and Information Sciences.

Award: Scholarship for use in freshman, sophomore, junior, senior, or graduate years; not renewable. *Number:* 5–25. *Amount:* $1000–$2000.

Eligibility Requirements: Applicant must be enrolled or expecting to enroll full- or part-time at a two-year or four-year institution or university. Available to U.S. and non-U.S. citizens.

Application Requirements: Application, essay, references, transcript. *Deadline:* May 1.

Contact: Executive Director
    E-mail: contact@alhef.org

BETHESDA LUTHERAN COMMUNITIES

http://www.bethesdalutherancommunities.org/

DEVELOPMENTAL DISABILITIES SCHOLASTIC ACHIEVEMENT SCHOLARSHIP FOR COLLEGE STUDENTS WHO ARE LUTHERAN
• *See page 218*

CANADIAN SOCIETY FOR MEDICAL LABORATORY SCIENCE

http://www.csmls.org/

E.V. BOOTH SCHOLARSHIP AWARD
• *See page 334*

CONGRESSIONAL BLACK CAUCUS FOUNDATION, INC.

http://www.cbcfinc.org/

CONGRESSIONAL BLACK CAUCUS SPOUSES CHEERIOS BRAND HEALTH INITIATIVE
• *See page 139*

CYNTHIA E. MORGAN SCHOLARSHIP FUND (CEMS)

http://www.cemsfund.com/

CYNTHIA E. MORGAN MEMORIAL SCHOLARSHIP FUND, INC.
• *See page 304*

HEALTHCARE INFORMATION AND MANAGEMENT SYSTEMS SOCIETY FOUNDATION

http://www.himss.org/

HIMSS FOUNDATION SCHOLARSHIP PROGRAM
• *See page 334*

HEALTH RESEARCH COUNCIL OF NEW ZEALAND

http://www.hrc.govt.nz/

PACIFIC HEALTH WORKFORCE AWARD
• *See page 334*

PACIFIC MENTAL HEALTH WORK FORCE AWARD
• *See page 334*

NATIONAL ATHLETIC TRAINERS' ASSOCIATION RESEARCH AND EDUCATION FOUNDATION

http://www.natafoundation.org/

NATIONAL ATHLETIC TRAINERS' ASSOCIATION RESEARCH AND EDUCATION FOUNDATION SCHOLARSHIP PROGRAM
• *See page 346*

STRAIGHTFORWARD MEDIA

http://www.straightforwardmedia.com/

STRAIGHTFORWARD MEDIA MEDICAL PROFESSIONS SCHOLARSHIP
• *See page 221*

HEATING, AIR-CONDITIONING, AND REFRIGERATION MECHANICS

AMERICAN SOCIETY OF HEATING, REFRIGERATING, AND AIR CONDITIONING ENGINEERS, INC.

http://www.ashrae.org/

ALWIN B. NEWTON SCHOLARSHIP FUND
• *See page 253*

ASHRAE GENERAL SCHOLARSHIP
• *See page 262*

ASHRAE MEMORIAL SCHOLARSHIP
• *See page 253*

DUANE HANSON SCHOLARSHIP
• *See page 253*

ENGINEERING TECHNOLOGY SCHOLARSHIP
• *See page 254*

FRANK M. CODA SCHOLARSHIP
• *See page 254*

HENRY ADAMS SCHOLARSHIP
• *See page 254*

REUBEN TRANE SCHOLARSHIP
• *See page 254*

WILLIS H. CARRIER SCHOLARSHIP
• *See page 254*

INTERNATIONAL SOCIETY OF AUTOMATION (ISA)

http://www.isa.org/

INTERNATIONAL SOCIETY OF AUTOMATION EDUCATION FOUNDATION SCHOLARSHIPS
• *See page 125*

PLUMBING-HEATING-COOLING CONTRACTORS EDUCATION FOUNDATION

http://www.foundation.phccweb.org/

BRADFORD WHITE CORPORATION SCHOLARSHIP

Scholarship for students enrolled in either an approved four-year PHCC apprenticeship program or at an accredited two-year community college, technical college, or trade school.

Academic Fields/Career Goals: Heating, Air-Conditioning, and Refrigeration Mechanics; Trade/Technical Specialties.

Award: Scholarship for use in freshman, sophomore, junior, or senior years; not renewable. *Number:* 3. *Amount:* $2500.

Eligibility Requirements: Applicant must be enrolled or expecting to enroll full-time at a two-year or technical institution. Available to U.S. and Canadian citizens.

Application Requirements: Application, references, test scores, transcript. *Deadline:* May 1.

Contact: John Zink, Scholarship Coordinator
Plumbing-Heating-Cooling Contractors Education Foundation
PO Box 6808
Falls Church, VA 22046
Phone: 800-533-7694
E-mail: naphcc@naphcc.org

DELTA FAUCET COMPANY SCHOLARSHIP PROGRAM
• *See page 103*

PHCC EDUCATIONAL FOUNDATION NEED-BASED SCHOLARSHIP
• *See page 155*

PHCC EDUCATIONAL FOUNDATION SCHOLARSHIP PROGRAM
• *See page 155*

PROFESSIONAL CONSTRUCTION ESTIMATORS ASSOCIATION

http://www.pcea.org/

TED WILSON MEMORIAL SCHOLARSHIP FOUNDATION
• *See page 179*

SOUTH CAROLINA ASSOCIATION OF HEATING AND AIR CONDITIONING CONTRACTORS

http://www.schvac.org/

SOUTH CAROLINA ASSOCIATION OF HEATING AND AIR CONDITIONING CONTRACTORS SCHOLARSHIP

Scholarship of $500 to pursue a career in the heating and air conditioning industry. Participating students must maintain an overall GPA of 2.5 and a GPA of 3.0 in all major topics. Deadline varies.

Academic Fields/Career Goals: Heating, Air-Conditioning, and Refrigeration Mechanics.

Award: Scholarship for use in freshman year; renewable. *Number:* varies. *Amount:* $500.

Eligibility Requirements: Applicant must be high school student and planning to enroll or expecting to enroll full- or part-time at a technical institution. Applicant must have 2.5 GPA or higher. Available to U.S. and non-U.S. citizens.

Application Requirements: Application, references. *Deadline:* varies.

Contact: Leigh Faircloth, Scholarship Committee
South Carolina Association of Heating and Air Conditioning Contractors
PO Box 11035
Columbia, SC 29211
Phone: 800-395-9276
Fax: 803-252-7799
E-mail: staff@schvac.org

STRAIGHTFORWARD MEDIA

http://www.straightforwardmedia.com/

STRAIGHTFORWARD MEDIA VOCATIONAL-TECHNICAL SCHOOL SCHOLARSHIP
• *See page 91*

HISTORIC PRESERVATION AND CONSERVATION

AMERICAN SCHOOL OF CLASSICAL STUDIES AT ATHENS

http://www.ascsa.edu.gr/

ASCSA SUMMER SESSIONS SCHOLARSHIPS
• *See page 92*

COSTUME SOCIETY OF AMERICA

http://www.costumesocietyamerica.com/

ADELE FILENE TRAVEL AWARD
• *See page 105*

STELLA BLUM RESEARCH GRANT
• *See page 105*

THE GEORGIA TRUST FOR HISTORIC PRESERVATION

http://www.georgiatrust.org/

B. PHINIZY SPALDING, HUBERT B. OWENS, AND THE NATIONAL SOCIETY OF THE COLONIAL DAMES OF AMERICA IN THE STATE OF GEORGIA ACADEMIC SCHOLARSHIPS
• *See page 89*

J. NEEL REID PRIZE
• *See page 101*

HISTORY

AMERICAN FEDERATION OF STATE, COUNTY, AND MUNICIPAL EMPLOYEES

http://www.afscme.org/

AFSCME/UNCF UNION SCHOLARS PROGRAM
• *See page 89*

AMERICAN PHILOLOGICAL ASSOCIATION

http://www.apaclassics.org/

MINORITY STUDENT SUMMER SCHOLARSHIP
• *See page 98*

AMERICAN SCHOOL OF CLASSICAL STUDIES AT ATHENS

http://www.ascsa.edu.gr/

ASCSA SUMMER SESSIONS SCHOLARSHIPS
• *See page 92*

ARRL FOUNDATION INC.

http://www.arrl.org/

FRANCIS WALTON MEMORIAL SCHOLARSHIP
• *See page 83*

ASSOCIATION OF FORMER INTELLIGENCE OFFICERS

http://www.afio.com/13_scholarships.htm

CIA UNDERGRADUATE SCHOLARSHIPS
• *See page 89*

CANADIAN INSTITUTE OF UKRAINIAN STUDIES

http://www.cius.ca/

LEO J. KRYSA UNDERGRADUATE SCHOLARSHIP
• *See page 104*

COLLEGEBOUND FOUNDATION

http://www.collegeboundfoundation.org/

DECATUR H. MILLER SCHOLARSHIP
You must: major in the field of political science, history, or pre-law; have a cumulative 3.0 GPA or better; and an SAT (CR+M) score of at least 1100.

Academic Fields/Career Goals: History; Law/Legal Services; Political Science.

Award: Scholarship for use in freshman, sophomore, junior, or senior years; renewable. *Number:* 1. *Amount:* $1500.

Eligibility Requirements: Applicant must be high school student; planning to enroll or expecting to enroll full-time at a four-year institution or university; resident of Maryland and studying in Maryland. Applicant must have 3.0 GPA or higher. Available to U.S. citizens.

Application Requirements: Application, financial need analysis, resume, references, test scores, transcript. *Deadline:* March 1.

Contact: Deana Carr-Davis, Associate Program Director, Scholarship Programs
CollegeBound Foundation
300 Water Street, Suite 300
Baltimore, MD 21202
Phone: 410-783-2905 Ext. 207
Fax: 410-727-5786
E-mail: dcarr-davis@collegeboundfoundation.org

CONCORD REVIEW

http://www.tcr.org/

RALPH WALDO EMERSON PRIZE
Prize awarded to high school students who have submitted an essay to the journal. Essay must be between 4000 to 6000 words with Turabian endnotes and bibliography. Pages must not be formatted. Essay may focus on any historical topic. Submission fee of $40. Please refer to web site for further details http://www.tcr.org.

Academic Fields/Career Goals: History.

Award: Prize for use in freshman year; not renewable. *Number:* up to 5. *Amount:* $800.

Eligibility Requirements: Applicant must be high school student; planning to enroll or expecting to enroll full- or part-time at a four-year institution or university and must have an interest in writing. Available to U.S. and non-U.S. citizens.

Application Requirements: Applicant must enter a contest, essay, self-addressed stamped envelope. *Fee:* $40. *Deadline:* continuous.

Contact: Will Fitzhugh, Founder and President
Concord Review
730 Boston Road, Suite 24
Sudbury, MA 01776
Phone: 978-443-0022
E-mail: fitzhugh@tcr.org

COSTUME SOCIETY OF AMERICA

http://www.costumesocietyamerica.com/

ADELE FILENE TRAVEL AWARD
• *See page 105*

STELLA BLUM RESEARCH GRANT
• *See page 105*

THE GEORGIA TRUST FOR HISTORIC PRESERVATION

http://www.georgiatrust.org/

B. PHINIZY SPALDING, HUBERT B. OWENS, AND THE NATIONAL SOCIETY OF THE COLONIAL DAMES OF AMERICA IN THE STATE OF GEORGIA ACADEMIC SCHOLARSHIPS
• *See page 89*

GREATER SALINA COMMUNITY FOUNDATION

http://www.gscf.org/

KANSAS FEDERATION OF REPUBLICAN WOMEN SCHOLARSHIP
Awards female students currently attending a Kansas college or university with declared major of political science, history, or public administration. Must be entering junior or senior year of undergraduate study, or attending graduate school. Must be Kansas residents and maintain cumulative GPA of 3.0 or better. Applicants must be registered members of the Republican Party. Must be involved in extracurricular activities.

Academic Fields/Career Goals: History; Political Science; Public Policy and Administration.

Award: Scholarship for use in junior, senior, or graduate years; renewable. *Number:* 1. *Amount:* up to $1000.

Eligibility Requirements: Applicant must be enrolled or expecting to enroll full-time at a two-year or four-year institution or university; female; resident of Kansas and studying in Kansas. Applicant must have 3.0 GPA or higher. Available to U.S. citizens.

Application Requirements: Application, essay. *Deadline:* March 31.

Contact: Michelle Griffin, Scholarship and Affiliate Coordinator
Greater Salina Community Foundation
PO Box 2876
Salina, KS 67402-2876
Phone: 785-823-1800
E-mail: michellegriffin@gscf.org

HARVARD TRAVELLERS CLUB

http://www.harvardtravellersclub.org/

HARVARD TRAVELLERS CLUB GRANTS
• See page 98

INSTITUTE FOR HUMANE STUDIES

http://www.theihs.org/

HUMANE STUDIES FELLOWSHIPS
• See page 185

KE ALI'I PAUAHI FOUNDATION

http://www.pauahi.org/

SARAH KELI'ILOLENA LUM KONIA NAKOA SCHOLARSHIP
• See page 327

LYNDON BAINES JOHNSON FOUNDATION

http://www.lbjfoundation.org/

LYNDON BAINES JOHNSON FOUNDATION GRANTS-IN-AID RESEARCH

Awards a limited number of grants in aid of research for the periods October 1 through March 31 and April 1 through September 30. October through March deadline is August 31. April through September deadline is February 28. Funds are to help defray costs while doing research at the LBJ Library. Must contact the Archives division of the Library prior to submitting proposal concerning material availability for the proposed topic. Grant applicants should have thoughtful and well-written proposals that state clearly and precisely how the holdings of the LBJ Library will contribute to historical research.

Academic Fields/Career Goals: History; Political Science.

Award: Grant for use in freshman, sophomore, junior, senior, graduate, or postgraduate years; not renewable. *Number:* 10–20. *Amount:* $500–$2500.

Eligibility Requirements: Applicant must be enrolled or expecting to enroll full- or part-time at a two-year or four-year or technical institution or university and studying in Texas. Available to U.S. and non-U.S. citizens.

Application Requirements: Application, references, research proposal. *Deadline:* varies.

Contact: Ms. Elizabeth Boone, Deputy Director
Lyndon Baines Johnson Foundation
2313 Red River Street
Austin, TX 78705
Phone: 512-232-2266 Ext. 2
E-mail: elizabeth@lbjfoundation.org

NATIONAL SOCIETY DAUGHTERS OF THE AMERICAN REVOLUTION

http://www.dar.org/

NATIONAL SOCIETY DAUGHTERS OF THE AMERICAN REVOLUTION DR. AURA-LEE A. PITTENGER AND

JAMES HOBBS PITTENGER AMERICAN HISTORY SCHOLARSHIP

Scholarship of $2000 each year for up to four consecutive years to a graduating high school senior who will have a concentrated study of a minimum of 24 credit hours in American history or American government while in college. United States citizens residing abroad may apply through a Units Overseas chapter.

Academic Fields/Career Goals: History; Political Science.

Award: Scholarship for use in freshman year; renewable. *Number:* 1. *Amount:* $2000.

Eligibility Requirements: Applicant must be high school student and planning to enroll or expecting to enroll full-time at a four-year institution or university. Available to U.S. citizens.

Application Requirements: Application, references, self-addressed stamped envelope, transcript, letter of sponsorship. *Deadline:* February 15.

Contact: Eric Weisz, Manager, Office of the Reporter General
National Society Daughters of the American Revolution
1776 D Street, NW
Washington, DC 20006-5303
Phone: 202-628-1776
Fax: 202-879-3348
E-mail: nsdarscholarships@dar.org

NATIONAL SOCIETY DAUGHTERS OF THE AMERICAN REVOLUTION ENID HALL GRISWOLD MEMORIAL SCHOLARSHIP
• See page 228

ORGANIZATION OF AMERICAN HISTORIANS

http://www.oah.org/

BINKLEY-STEPHENSON AWARD
• See page 89

PHI ALPHA THETA HISTORY HONOR SOCIETY, INC.

http://www.phialphatheta.org/

PHI ALPHA THETA PAPER PRIZES

Award for best graduate and undergraduate student papers. Grants $500 prize for best graduate student paper, $500 prize for best undergraduate paper, and four $350 prizes for either graduate or undergraduate papers. All applicants must be members of the association.

Academic Fields/Career Goals: History.

Award: Prize for use in freshman, sophomore, junior, senior, or graduate years; not renewable. *Number:* 6. *Amount:* $350–$500.

Eligibility Requirements: Applicant must be enrolled or expecting to enroll full-time at a four-year institution or university. Applicant or parent of applicant must be member of Phi Alpha Theta. Applicant must have 3.0 GPA or higher. Available to U.S. and non-U.S. citizens.

Application Requirements: Essay, references. *Deadline:* June 30.

Contact: Dr. Clayton Drees, Department of History
Phi Alpha Theta History Honor Society, Inc.
Virginia Wesleyan College, 1584 Wesleyan Drive
Norfolk, VA 23502-5599
E-mail: cdrees@vwc.edu

PHI ALPHA THETA UNDERGRADUATE STUDENT SCHOLARSHIP

Awards of $1000 available to exceptional juniors entering the senior year and majoring in modern European history (1815 to present). Must be Phi Alpha Theta members. Based on both financial need and merit.

Academic Fields/Career Goals: History.

Award: Scholarship for use in senior year; not renewable. *Number:* 1. *Amount:* $1000.

Eligibility Requirements: Applicant must be enrolled or expecting to enroll full-time at a four-year institution or university. Applicant or parent of applicant must be member of Phi Alpha Theta. Available to U.S. and non-U.S. citizens.

Application Requirements: Application, resume, references, transcript. *Deadline:* March 1.

Contact: Dr. Graydon A. Tunstall Jr., Executive Director
Phi Alpha Theta History Honor Society, Inc.
University of South Florida, 4202 East Fowler Avenue SOC 107
Tampa, FL 33620-8100
Phone: 800-394-8195
Fax: 813-974-8215
E-mail: info@phialphatheta.org

PHI ALPHA THETA/WESTERN FRONT ASSOCIATION PAPER PRIZE

Essay competition open to full-time undergraduate members of the association. The paper must be from 12 to 15 typed pages and must address the American experience in World War I, must be dealing with virtually any aspect of American involvement during the period from 1912 (second Moroccan crisis) to 1924 (Dawes plan). Primary source material must be used. For further details visit http://www.phialphatheta.org.

Academic Fields/Career Goals: History.

Award: Prize for use in freshman, sophomore, junior, or senior years; not renewable. *Number:* 1. *Amount:* $1000.

Eligibility Requirements: Applicant must be enrolled or expecting to enroll full-time at a four-year institution or university and must have an interest in writing. Applicant or parent of applicant must be member of Phi Alpha Theta. Applicant must have 3.0 GPA or higher. Available to U.S. and non-U.S. citizens.

Application Requirements: Application, essay, 5 copies of the paper, CD-ROM containing a file of the paper and cover letter. *Deadline:* January 31.

Contact: Dr. Graydon A. Tunstall Jr., Executive Director
Phi Alpha Theta History Honor Society, Inc.
University of South Florida, 4202 East Fowler Avenue, SOC107
Tampa, FL 33620-8100
Phone: 800-394-8195
Fax: 813-974-8215
E-mail: info@phialphatheta.org

PHI ALPHA THETA WORLD HISTORY ASSOCIATION PAPER PRIZE

Awards one undergraduate and one graduate-level prize for papers examining any historical issue with global implications such as: exchange or interchange of cultures, comparison of civilizations or cultures. This is a joint award with the World History Association. Must be a member of the World History Association or Phi Alpha Theta. Paper must have been composed while enrolled at an accredited college or university. Must send in four copies of paper along with professor's letter.

Academic Fields/Career Goals: History; Humanities; International Studies; Social Sciences.

Award: Prize for use in freshman, sophomore, junior, senior, or graduate years; not renewable. *Number:* 2. *Amount:* $400.

Eligibility Requirements: Applicant must be enrolled or expecting to enroll full-time at a four-year institution or university. Applicant or parent of applicant must be member of Phi Alpha Theta. Applicant must have 3.0 GPA or higher. Available to U.S. and non-U.S. citizens.

Application Requirements: References, 4 copies of paper, abstract, letter from faculty member or professor. *Deadline:* June 30.

Contact: Prof. Laura Wangerin
Phi Alpha Theta History Honor Society, Inc.
The Latin School of Chicago, 59 West North Boulevard
Chicago, IL 60610
E-mail: lwangerin@latinschool.org

SONS OF THE REPUBLIC OF TEXAS

http://www.srttexas.org/

PRESIDIO LA BAHIA AWARD
• *See page 89*

TEXAS HISTORY ESSAY CONTEST
• *See page 90*

STRAIGHTFORWARD MEDIA

http://www.straightforwardmedia.com/

STRAIGHTFORWARD MEDIA LIBERAL ARTS SCHOLARSHIP
• *See page 107*

TOPSFIELD HISTORICAL SOCIETY

http://www.topsfieldhistory.org/

JOHN KIMBALL MEMORIAL TRUST SCHOLARSHIP PROGRAM FOR THE STUDY OF HISTORY

Scholarship grants funds for tuition, books, and other educational and research expenses to undergraduate and graduate students; as well as college, university, and graduate school instructors and professors who have excelled in, and/or have a passion for the study of history and related disciplines; and who reside in, or have a substantial connection to Topsfield, Massachusetts.

Academic Fields/Career Goals: History.

Award: Grant for use in freshman, sophomore, junior, senior, graduate, or postgraduate years; not renewable. *Number:* 3–10. *Amount:* $300–$5000.

Eligibility Requirements: Applicant must be enrolled or expecting to enroll full- or part-time at a two-year or four-year institution or university and resident of Massachusetts. Available to U.S. and non-U.S. citizens.

Application Requirements: Application. *Deadline:* April 15.

Contact: Mr. Norman J. Isler, Trustee, John Kimball Scholarship Program
Topsfield Historical Society
PO Box 323
Topsfield, MA 01983
Phone: 978-887-9724
Fax: 978-887-0185
E-mail: normisler@comcast.net

UNITED DAUGHTERS OF THE CONFEDERACY

http://www.hqudc.org/

HELEN JAMES BREWER SCHOLARSHIP

Award for full-time undergraduate student who is a descendant of a Confederate soldier, sailor or marine. Must be from Alabama, Florida, Georgia, South Carolina, Tennessee or Virginia. Recipient must be enrolled in an accredited college or university and studying history and literature. Must be a member or former member of the Children of the Confederacy. Minimum 3.0 GPA required.

Academic Fields/Career Goals: History; Literature/English/Writing.

Award: Scholarship for use in freshman, sophomore, junior, or senior years; renewable. *Number:* 1–2. *Amount:* $800–$1000.

Eligibility Requirements: Applicant must be enrolled or expecting to enroll full-time at a four-year institution or university and resident of Alabama, Florida, Georgia, South Carolina, Tennessee, or Virginia. Applicant or parent of applicant must be member of Children of the Confederacy or United Daughters of the Confederacy. Applicant must have 3.0 GPA or higher. Available to U.S. citizens.

Application Requirements: Application, essay, financial need analysis, photo, references, self-addressed stamped envelope, transcript, copy of applicant's birth certificate, copy of confederate ancestor's proof of service. *Deadline:* March 15.

Contact: United Daughters of the Confederacy
328 North Boulevard
Richmond, VA 23220-4009
Phone: 804-355-1636
E-mail: hqudc@rcn.com

UNITED NEGRO COLLEGE FUND

http://www.uncf.org/

AFSCME/UNCF/HARVARD UNIVERSITY LWP UNION SCHOLARS PROGRAM
• *See page 90*

C-SPAN SCHOLARSHIP PROGRAM
• *See page 193*

TOYOTA/UNCF SCHOLARSHIP
• *See page 74*

HOME ECONOMICS

AMERICAN ASSOCIATION OF FAMILY & CONSUMER SERVICES

http://www.aafcs.org/

AMERICAN ASSOCIATION OF FAMILY & CONSUMER SCIENCES NATIONAL UNDERGRADUATE SCHOLARSHIP

The association awards scholarships to individuals who have exhibited the potential to make contributions to the family and consumer sciences profession.

Academic Fields/Career Goals: Home Economics.

Award: Scholarship for use in sophomore, junior, or senior years; not renewable. *Number:* up to 1. *Amount:* up to $5000.

Eligibility Requirements: Applicant must be enrolled or expecting to enroll full-time at a four-year institution or university. Available to U.S. citizens.

Application Requirements: Application, resume, references, transcript. *Deadline:* January 15.

Contact: American Association of Family & Consumer Services
Award, Grant, Fellowship, and Scholarship Programs
400 North Columbus Street, Suite 202
Alexandria, VA 22314
Phone: 703-706-4603
E-mail: awards@aafcs.org

COSTUME SOCIETY OF AMERICA

http://www.costumesocietyamerica.com/

ADELE FILENE TRAVEL AWARD
• *See page 105*

STELLA BLUM RESEARCH GRANT
• *See page 105*

FAMILY, CAREER AND COMMUNITY LEADERS OF AMERICA-TEXAS ASSOCIATION

http://www.texasfccla.org/

C.J. DAVIDSON SCHOLARSHIP FOR FCCLA

Renewable award for graduating high school seniors enrolled in full-time program in family and consumer sciences. Must be Texas resident and should study in Texas. Must have minimum GPA of 2.5.

Academic Fields/Career Goals: Home Economics.

Award: Scholarship for use in freshman year; renewable. *Number:* up to 10. *Amount:* up to $16,000.

Eligibility Requirements: Applicant must be high school student; planning to enroll or expecting to enroll full-time at a four-year institution or university; single; resident of Texas and studying in Texas. Applicant or parent of applicant must be member of Family, Career and Community Leaders of America. Applicant must have 2.5 GPA or higher. Available to U.S. citizens.

Application Requirements: Application, essay, references, test scores, transcript. *Deadline:* March 1.

Contact: Staff
Family, Career and Community Leaders of America-Texas Association
3530 Bee Caves Road, Suite 101
Austin, TX 78746-9616
Phone: 512-306-0099
Fax: 512-306-0041
E-mail: fccla@texasfccla.org

FCCLA HOUSTON LIVESTOCK SHOW AND RODEO SCHOLARSHIP
• *See page 149*

FCCLA REGIONAL SCHOLARSHIPS
• *See page 149*

FCCLA TEXAS FARM BUREAU SCHOLARSHIP
• *See page 149*

INTERNATIONAL EXECUTIVE HOUSEKEEPERS ASSOCIATION

http://www.ieha.org/

INTERNATIONAL EXECUTIVE HOUSEKEEPERS EDUCATIONAL FOUNDATION
• *See page 322*

MAINE SCHOOL FOOD SERVICE ASSOCIATION (MSFSA) CONTINUING EDUCATION SCHOLARSHIP

http://www.mainesfsa.org/

MAINE SCHOOL FOOD SERVICE ASSOCIATION CONTINUING EDUCATION SCHOLARSHIP
• *See page 213*

MARYLAND ASSOCIATION OF PRIVATE COLLEGES AND CAREER SCHOOLS

http://www.mapccs.org/

MARYLAND ASSOCIATION OF PRIVATE COLLEGES AND CAREER SCHOOLS SCHOLARSHIP
• *See page 153*

SAN DIEGO FOUNDATION

http://www.sdfoundation.org/

CALIFORNIA ASSOCIATION OF FAMILY AND CONSUMER SCIENCES-SAN DIEGO CHAPTER
• *See page 173*

UNITED DAUGHTERS OF THE CONFEDERACY

http://www.hqudc.org/

WALTER REED SMITH SCHOLARSHIP
• *See page 157*

HORTICULTURE/FLORICULTURE

ALABAMA GOLF COURSE SUPERINTENDENTS ASSOCIATION

http://www.agcsa.org/

ALABAMA GOLF COURSE SUPERINTENDENT'S ASSOCIATION'S DONNIE ARTHUR MEMORIAL SCHOLARSHIP
• *See page 81*

AMERICAN SOCIETY FOR ENOLOGY AND VITICULTURE

http://www.asev.org/

AMERICAN SOCIETY FOR ENOLOGY AND VITICULTURE SCHOLARSHIPS
• *See page 82*

AMERICAN SOCIETY FOR HORTICULTURAL SCIENCE

http://www.ashs.org/

ASHS SCHOLARS AWARD
Two annual scholarships of $1500 given to undergraduate students majoring in horticulture at a four-year institution. Applicants must be nominated by the chair/head of the department in which they are majoring, but only one applicant per department may be nominated.

Academic Fields/Career Goals: Horticulture/Floriculture.

Award: Scholarship for use in freshman, sophomore, junior, or senior years; not renewable. *Number:* 2. *Amount:* $1500.

Eligibility Requirements: Applicant must be enrolled or expecting to enroll full-time at a four-year institution or university and must have an interest in leadership. Applicant or parent of applicant must have employment or volunteer experience in community service. Available to U.S. and non-U.S. citizens.

Application Requirements: Application, essay, resume, references, transcript. *Deadline:* February 4.

Contact: Michael Neff, Executive Director
American Society for Horticultural Science
113 Southwest Street, Suite 200
Alexandria, VA 22314
Phone: 703-836-4606 Ext. 325
Fax: 703-836-2024
E-mail: mwneff@ashs.org

E. TED SIMS JR. MEMORIAL SCHOLARSHIP
A scholarship of $1000 for a full-time junior or senior class student standing beginning fall of award year and must show commitment to the horticulture profession. Applicants must be nominated by the chair/head of the department in which they are majoring, but only one applicant may be nominated per department.

Academic Fields/Career Goals: Horticulture/Floriculture.

Award: Scholarship for use in junior or senior years; not renewable. *Number:* 1. *Amount:* $1000.

Eligibility Requirements: Applicant must be enrolled or expecting to enroll full-time at a four-year institution or university. Available to U.S. citizens.

Application Requirements: Application, essay, resume, references, transcript. *Deadline:* February 4.

Contact: Michael Neff, Executive Director
American Society for Horticultural Science
113 Southwest Street, Suite 200
Alexandria, VA 22314
Phone: 703-836-4606 Ext. 325
Fax: 703-836-2024
E-mail: mwneff@ashs.org

ARIZONA NURSERY ASSOCIATION

http://www.azna.org/

ARIZONA NURSERY ASSOCIATION FOUNDATION SCHOLARSHIP
Provides research grants and scholarships for the Green Industry. Applicant must be an Arizona resident currently or planning to be enrolled in a horticultural related curriculum at an Arizona university, community college, or continuing education program. See web site for further details http://www.azna.org.

Academic Fields/Career Goals: Horticulture/Floriculture.

Award: Scholarship for use in freshman, sophomore, junior, or senior years; renewable. *Number:* 12–16. *Amount:* $500–$3000.

Eligibility Requirements: Applicant must be enrolled or expecting to enroll full- or part-time at a two-year or four-year or technical institution or university. Available to U.S. citizens.

Application Requirements: Application, references, transcript. *Deadline:* April 15.

Contact: Cheryl Goar, Executive Director
Arizona Nursery Association
1430 West Broadway Road, Suite 110
Tempe, AZ 85282
Phone: 480-966-1610
E-mail: cgoar@azna.org

CALIFORNIA ASSOCIATION OF NURSERYMEN ENDOWMENT FOR RESEARCH AND SCHOLARSHIPS

http://www.cangc.org/

CANERS FOUNDATION ENDOWMENT SCHOLARSHIP
Applicants must be college students who are currently enrolled in no fewer than six units within a program related to the nursery industry and who are entering or returning to college in a horticulture-related field in the fall.

Academic Fields/Career Goals: Horticulture/Floriculture.

Award: Scholarship for use in freshman, sophomore, junior, or senior years; not renewable. *Number:* varies. *Amount:* varies.

Eligibility Requirements: Applicant must be enrolled or expecting to enroll full-time at a four-year institution or university. Available to U.S. citizens.

Application Requirements: Application, transcript. *Deadline:* varies.

Contact: Darrelyn Adams, Membership Director
California Association of Nurserymen Endowment for
Research and Scholarships
3947 Lennane Drive, Suite 150
Sacramento, CA 95834
Phone: 916-928-3900 Ext. 13
Fax: 916-567-0505
E-mail: dadams@cangc.org

CHS FOUNDATION

http://www.chsfoundation.org/

CHS FOUNDATION HIGH SCHOOL SCHOLARSHIPS
• *See page 78*

CHS FOUNDATION TWO-YEAR COLLEGE SCHOLARSHIPS
• *See page 78*

FEDERATED GARDEN CLUBS OF CONNECTICUT

http://www.ctgardenclubs.org/

FEDERATED GARDEN CLUBS OF CONNECTICUT INC. SCHOLARSHIPS
• *See page 140*

FEDERATED GARDEN CLUBS OF MARYLAND

http://www.hometown.aol.com/fgcofmd

ROBERT LEWIS BAKER SCHOLARSHIP

Scholarship awards of up to $5000 to encourage the study of ornamental horticulture, and landscape design. Applicants must be high school graduates, current college and/or graduate students, and Maryland residents. Can attend any accredited college/university in the United States.

Academic Fields/Career Goals: Horticulture/Floriculture; Landscape Architecture.

Award: Scholarship for use in freshman, sophomore, junior, senior, or graduate years; not renewable. *Number:* 1. *Amount:* $5000.

Eligibility Requirements: Applicant must be enrolled or expecting to enroll full-time at a four-year institution or university and resident of Maryland. Available to U.S. citizens.

Application Requirements: Application. *Deadline:* June 30.

Contact: Marjorie Schiebel, Scholarship Chairman
Federated Garden Clubs of Maryland
1105 A Providence Road
Baltimore, MD 21286
Phone: 410-296-6961
E-mail: fgcofmd@aol.com

VIRGINIA P. HENRY SCHOLARSHIP

Scholarship of up to $1000 available to qualified undergraduate students enrolled in horticultural studies. For full-time study. Must be legal residents of Maryland.

Academic Fields/Career Goals: Horticulture/Floriculture.

Award: Scholarship for use in freshman, sophomore, junior, or senior years; not renewable. *Number:* 1. *Amount:* $1000.

Eligibility Requirements: Applicant must be enrolled or expecting to enroll full-time at a four-year institution or university and resident of Maryland. Available to U.S. citizens.

Application Requirements: Application. *Deadline:* May 1.

Contact: Marjorie Schiebel, Scholarship Chairman
Federated Garden Clubs of Maryland
1105 A Providence Road
Baltimore, MD 21286
Phone: 410-296-6961
E-mail: fgcofmd@aol.com

FRIENDS OF THE FRELINGHUYSEN ARBORETUM

http://www.arboretumfriends.org/

BENJAMIN C. BLACKBURN SCHOLARSHIP
• *See page 308*

GARDEN CLUB OF AMERICA

http://www.gcamerica.org/

GARDEN CLUB OF AMERICA SUMMER SCHOLARSHIP IN FIELD BOTANY

Scholarship of $2000 to undergraduate or graduate students up to master's level wishing to pursue summer field work in botany. All candidates must be enrolled in a U.S. college or university.

Academic Fields/Career Goals: Horticulture/Floriculture; Natural Sciences.

Award: Scholarship for use in freshman, sophomore, junior, senior, or graduate years; not renewable. *Number:* 1. *Amount:* $2000.

Eligibility Requirements: Applicant must be enrolled or expecting to enroll full-time at a four-year institution or university. Available to U.S. citizens.

Application Requirements: Application, essay, resume, references, transcript. *Deadline:* February 1.

Contact: Connie Yates, Scholarship Committee Administrator
Garden Club of America
14 East 60th Street, Third Floor
New York, NY 10022-1002
Phone: 212-753-8287
E-mail: cyates@gcamerica.org

GCA AWARD IN DESERT STUDIES
• *See page 101*

JOAN K. HUNT AND RACHEL M. HUNT SUMMER SCHOLARSHIP IN FIELD BOTANY

One or more scholarships of up to $2000 towards summer study in field botany. Purpose is to promote the awareness of the importance of botany to horticulture. For study within the U.S. only. Undergraduates and graduate students up to master's level may apply.

Academic Fields/Career Goals: Horticulture/Floriculture; Natural Sciences.

Award: Scholarship for use in freshman, sophomore, junior, or senior years; not renewable. *Number:* 1. *Amount:* up to $2000.

Eligibility Requirements: Applicant must be enrolled or expecting to enroll full-time at a four-year institution or university. Available to U.S. citizens.

Application Requirements: Application, essay, resume, references, transcript. *Deadline:* February 1.

Contact: Connie Yates, Scholarship Committee Administrator
Garden Club of America
14 East 60th Street, Third Floor
New York, NY 10022-1002
Phone: 212-753-8287
E-mail: cyates@gcamerica.org

KATHARINE M. GROSSCUP SCHOLARSHIP

Scholarships to encourage the study of horticulture and related fields by providing financial assistance to students who wish to pursue these academic endeavors. Preference is given to students from Ohio, Pennsylvania, West Virginia, Michigan, Indiana, and Kentucky.

Academic Fields/Career Goals: Horticulture/Floriculture; Landscape Architecture.

Award: Scholarship for use in junior, senior, or graduate years; not renewable. *Amount:* up to $3000.

Eligibility Requirements: Applicant must be enrolled or expecting to enroll full-time at a four-year institution or university and resident of Indiana, Kentucky, Michigan, Ohio, Pennsylvania, or West Virginia. Available to U.S. citizens.

Application Requirements: Application, interview, references, self-addressed stamped envelope, transcript. *Deadline:* January 15.

Contact: Grosscup Scholarship Committee
Garden Club of America
Cleveland Botanical Garden, 11030 East Boulevard
Cleveland, OH 44106
Fax: 216-721-2056

LOY MCCANDLESS MARKS SCHOLARSHIP IN TROPICAL ORNAMENTAL HORTICULTURE

Award of $4000 to graduate or advanced undergraduate student. Provides an opportunity to study at a leading foreign institution that specializes in the field of tropical plants. Awarded only in even numbered years.

Academic Fields/Career Goals: Horticulture/Floriculture.

Award: Scholarship for use in sophomore, junior, or senior years; not renewable. *Number:* 1. *Amount:* $4000.

Eligibility Requirements: Applicant must be enrolled or expecting to enroll full-time at a four-year institution or university. Available to U.S. citizens.

Application Requirements: Application, interview, references, self-addressed stamped envelope, transcript, budget. *Deadline:* January 15.

Contact: Connie Yates, Scholarship Committee Administrator
Garden Club of America
14 East 60th Street, Third Floor
New York, NY 10022-1002
Phone: 212-753-8287
E-mail: cyates@gcamerica.org

ZELLER SUMMER SCHOLARSHIP IN MEDICINAL BOTANY
• *See page 343*

GOLDEN STATE BONSAI FEDERATION

http://www.gsbf-bonsai.org/

HORTICULTURE SCHOLARSHIPS

Scholarship for study towards a certificate in ornamental horticulture from an accredited school. Applicant must be a current member of a GSBF member club and have a letter of recommendation from club president, or a responsible spokesperson from GSBF. Deadline varies.

Academic Fields/Career Goals: Horticulture/Floriculture.

Award: Scholarship for use in freshman, sophomore, junior, senior, graduate, or postgraduate years; not renewable. *Number:* 1–5. *Amount:* up to $400.

Eligibility Requirements: Applicant must be enrolled or expecting to enroll full-time at a two-year or four-year or technical institution or university. Applicant or parent of applicant must be member of Golden State Bonsai Federation. Available to U.S. citizens.

Application Requirements: Application, references. *Deadline:* varies.

Contact: Abe Far, Grants and Scholarship Committee
Golden State Bonsai Federation
2451 Galahad Road
San Diego, CA 92123
Phone: 619-234-3434
E-mail: abefar@cox.net

GOLF COURSE SUPERINTENDENTS ASSOCIATION OF AMERICA

http://www.eifg.org/

GCSAA SCHOLARS COMPETITION

Competition for outstanding students planning careers in golf course management. Must be full-time college undergraduates currently enrolled in a two-year or more accredited program related to golf course management and have completed one year of program. Must be member of GCSAA.

Academic Fields/Career Goals: Horticulture/Floriculture.

Award: Scholarship for use in sophomore, junior, or senior years; not renewable. *Number:* varies. *Amount:* $500–$6000.

Eligibility Requirements: Applicant must be enrolled or expecting to enroll full-time at a two-year or four-year institution or university. Applicant or parent of applicant must be member of Golf Course Superintendents Association of America. Available to U.S. and non-U.S. citizens.

Application Requirements: Application, applicant must enter a contest, essay, references, transcript, adviser's report, superintendent's report. *Deadline:* June 1.

Contact: Mischia Wright, Senior Manager, Development
Golf Course Superintendents Association of America
1421 Research Park Drive
Lawrence, KS 66049-3859
Phone: 800-472-7878 Ext. 4445
E-mail: mwright@gcsaa.org

GOLF COURSE SUPERINTENDENTS ASSOCIATION OF AMERICA STUDENT ESSAY CONTEST
• *See page 78*

SCOTTS COMPANY SCHOLARS PROGRAM

Applicant must be a graduating high school senior or freshman, sophomore, or junior in college. Applicants must be pursuing a career in the green industry.

Academic Fields/Career Goals: Horticulture/Floriculture.

Award: Scholarship for use in freshman, sophomore, or junior years; not renewable. *Number:* up to 5. *Amount:* $500–$2500.

Eligibility Requirements: Applicant must be enrolled or expecting to enroll full-time at a two-year or four-year institution or university. Available to U.S. and non-U.S. citizens.

Application Requirements: Application, essay, references, transcript. *Deadline:* March 1.

Contact: Mischia Wright, Senior Manager, Development
Golf Course Superintendents Association of America
1421 Research Park Drive
Lawrence, KS 66049-3859
Phone: 800-472-7878 Ext. 4445
E-mail: mwright@gcsaa.org

HERB SOCIETY OF AMERICA, WESTERN RESERVE UNIT

http://www.herbsociety.org/units/western-reserve.html

FRANCIS SYLVIA ZVERINA SCHOLARSHIP

Awards are given to needy students who plan a career in horticulture or related field. Preference will be given to applicants whose horticultural career goals involve teaching, research, or work in the public or nonprofit sector, such as public gardens, botanical gardens, parks, arboreta, city planning, public education, and awareness.

Academic Fields/Career Goals: Horticulture/Floriculture; Landscape Architecture.

Award: Scholarship for use in sophomore, junior, or senior years; not renewable. *Number:* 1. *Amount:* $5000.

Eligibility Requirements: Applicant must be enrolled or expecting to enroll full-time at a four-year institution or university. Available to U.S. citizens.

Application Requirements: Application, essay, references, transcript. *Deadline:* April 1.

Contact: Jewelann Stefanar, Committee Chair
Herb Society of America, Western Reserve Unit
4706 Bentwood Drive
Brooklyn, OH 44144
Phone: 216-741-0985
E-mail: jewelann1@roadrunner.com

WESTERN RESERVE HERB SOCIETY SCHOLARSHIP

Awards are given to needy students who plan a career in horticulture or related field. Preference will be given to applicants whose horticultural career goals involve teaching, research, or work in the public or nonprofit sector, such as public gardens, botanical gardens, parks, arboreta, city planning, public education and awareness.

Academic Fields/Career Goals: Horticulture/Floriculture; Landscape Architecture.

Award: Scholarship for use in sophomore, junior, senior, or graduate years; not renewable. *Number:* 1. *Amount:* $4000.

Eligibility Requirements: Applicant must be enrolled or expecting to enroll full-time at a four-year institution or university and resident of Ohio. Available to U.S. citizens.

Application Requirements: Application, essay, references, transcript. *Deadline:* April 1.

Contact: Jewelann Stefanar, Committee Chair
Herb Society of America, Western Reserve Unit
4706 Bentwood Drive
Brooklyn, OH 44144
Phone: 216-741-0985
E-mail: jewelann1@roadrunner.com

HORTICULTURAL RESEARCH INSTITUTE AND ENDOWMENT FUND

http://www.hriresearch.org/

CARVILLE M. AKEHURST MEMORIAL SCHOLARSHIP

Scholarship is available to resident of Maryland, Virginia, or West Virginia. Applicant must be enrolled in an accredited undergraduate or graduate landscape/ horticulture program or related discipline at a two- or four-year institution and must have minimum 3.0 GPA. Online application only. http//www.HRIresearch.org for complete information.

Academic Fields/Career Goals: Horticulture/Floriculture; Landscape Architecture.

Award: Scholarship for use in junior or senior years; not renewable. *Number:* 1–2. *Amount:* $1000.

Eligibility Requirements: Applicant must be enrolled or expecting to enroll full-time at a two-year or four-year or technical institution or university and resident of Maryland, Virginia, or West Virginia. Applicant must have 3.0 GPA or higher. Available to U.S. citizens.

Application Requirements: Application, essay, financial need analysis, resume, references, transcript. *Deadline:* May 31.

Contact: Ms. Teresa Jodon, Executive Director
Horticultural Research Institute and Endowment Fund
1000 Vermont Avenue, NW, Suite 300
Washington, DC 20005
Phone: 202-741-4852
Fax: 202-478-7288
E-mail: scholarships@hriresearch.org

MUGGETS SCHOLARSHIP

Annual scholarship available to students enrolled in an accredited undergraduate or graduate horticulture, landscape, or related discipline at a two- or four-year institution. Students in vocational agriculture programs will also be considered. High school seniors may apply for this scholarship. Minimum 2.5 GPA required. Online application submission. Visit http//www.HRIresearch.org for details.

Academic Fields/Career Goals: Horticulture/Floriculture; Landscape Architecture.

Award: Scholarship for use in sophomore, junior, senior, or graduate years; not renewable. *Number:* 1. *Amount:* $1000.

Eligibility Requirements: Applicant must be enrolled or expecting to enroll full-time at a two-year or four-year or technical institution or university. Applicant must have 2.5 GPA or higher. Available to U.S. and non-U.S. citizens.

Application Requirements: Application, essay, financial need analysis, resume, references, transcript. *Deadline:* May 31.

Contact: Ms. Teresa Jodon, Executive Director
Horticultural Research Institute and Endowment Fund
1000 Vermont Avenue, NW, Suite 300
Washington, DC 20005-4914
Phone: 202-741-4852
Fax: 202-478-7288
E-mail: scholarships@hriresearch.org

SPRING MEADOW NURSERY SCHOLARSHIP

Scholarship for the full-time study of horticulture or landscape architecture students in undergraduate or graduate horticulture program or related discipline at a two- or four-year institution. Applicant must have minimum 2.5 GPA. Spring Meadow Nursery's goal is to grant scholarships to students with an interest in woody plant production, woody plant propagation, woody plant breeding, horticultural sales and marketing. Undergraduate: Applicant must have at least a Sophomore standing in a four-year curriculum or Senior standing in a two-year curriculum as of the Fall semester of scholarship application year. Graduate: All applicants in graduate school regardless of year in school may apply. Online application only.

Academic Fields/Career Goals: Horticulture/Floriculture; Landscape Architecture.

Award: Scholarship for use in junior, senior, or graduate years; not renewable. *Number:* 1–1. *Amount:* $1500.

Eligibility Requirements: Applicant must be enrolled or expecting to enroll full-time at a two-year or four-year or technical institution or university. Applicant must have 2.5 GPA or higher. Available to U.S. and Canadian citizens.

Application Requirements: Application, essay, financial need analysis, resume, references, transcript. *Deadline:* May 31.

Contact: Ms. Teresa Jodon, Executive Director
Horticultural Research Institute and Endowment Fund
1000 Vermont Avenue, NW, Suite 300
Washington, DC 20005-4914
Phone: 202-741-4852
Fax: 202-478-7288
E-mail: scholarships@hriresearch.org

TIMOTHY AND PALMER W. BIGELOW JR, SCHOLARSHIP

Award for students who are enrolled in accredited undergraduate or graduate landscape/horticulture program. Must be resident of Connecticut, Maine, Massachusetts, New Hampshire, Rhode Island, or Vermont. Undergraduates must have a GPA of 2.25. Financial need,

desire to work in nursery industry are factors. For more information, visit web site http://www.hriresearch.org.

Academic Fields/Career Goals: Horticulture/Floriculture; Landscape Architecture.

Award: Scholarship for use in junior or senior years; not renewable. *Number:* 1. *Amount:* $2000.

Eligibility Requirements: Applicant must be enrolled or expecting to enroll full-time at a four-year institution or university and resident of Connecticut, Maine, Massachusetts, New Hampshire, Rhode Island, or Vermont. Available to U.S. citizens.

Application Requirements: Application, essay, financial need analysis, resume, references, transcript. *Deadline:* May 31.

Contact: Ms. Teresa Jodon, Executive Director
Horticultural Research Institute and Endowment Fund
1000 Vermont Avenue, NW, Suite 300
Washington, DC 20005
Phone: 202-741-4852
Fax: 202-789-1893
E-mail: scholarships@hriresearch.org

USREY FAMILY SCHOLARSHIP

Award for students accredited in undergraduate or graduate landscape horticulture program or related discipline at a two- or four-year institution. Preference given to applicants who plan to work within the industry. Must have a minimum 2.5 GPA. For more information, visit web site http://www.hriresearch.org.

Academic Fields/Career Goals: Horticulture/Floriculture; Landscape Architecture.

Award: Scholarship for use in sophomore, junior, senior, or graduate years; not renewable. *Amount:* $750–$2000.

Eligibility Requirements: Applicant must be enrolled or expecting to enroll full-time at a two-year or four-year or technical institution or university and studying in California. Applicant must have 2.5 GPA or higher. Available to U.S. and non-U.S. citizens.

Application Requirements: Application, essay, financial need analysis, resume, references, transcript. *Deadline:* May 31.

Contact: Teresa Jodon, Endowment Program Administrator
Horticultural Research Institute and Endowment Fund
1000 Vermont Avenue, NW, Suite 300
Washington, DC 20005
Phone: 202-789-2900 Ext. 3014
Fax: 202-789-1893
E-mail: scholarships@hriresearch.org

IDAHO NURSERY AND LANDSCAPE ASSOCIATION

http://www.inlagrow.org/

IDAHO NURSERY AND LANDSCAPE ASSOCIATION SCHOLARSHIPS

To encourage study of Horticulture, Floriculture, Plant Pathology, Landscape Design, Turfgrass Management, Botany and other allied subjects that pertain to the green industry. Applicant must be an Idaho resident.

Academic Fields/Career Goals: Horticulture/Floriculture.

Award: Scholarship for use in freshman, sophomore, junior, or senior years; not renewable. *Number:* 1–5. *Amount:* $750.

Eligibility Requirements: Applicant must be enrolled or expecting to enroll full- or part-time at a two-year or four-year or technical institution or university; resident of Idaho and studying in Idaho. Available to U.S. citizens.

Application Requirements: Application, essay, references, transcript. *Deadline:* November 1.

Contact: Ann Bates, Executive Director
Idaho Nursery and Landscape Association
PO Box 2065
Idaho Falls, ID 83403
Phone: 208-522-7307
Fax: 208-529-0832
E-mail: abates@inlagrow.org

JOSEPH SHINODA MEMORIAL SCHOLARSHIP FOUNDATION

http://www.shinodascholarship.org/

JOSEPH SHINODA MEMORIAL SCHOLARSHIP

One-time award for undergraduates in accredited colleges and universities. Must be furthering their education in the field of floriculture (production, distribution, research, or retail).

Academic Fields/Career Goals: Horticulture/Floriculture.

Award: Scholarship for use in sophomore, junior, or senior years; not renewable. *Number:* 8–15. *Amount:* $1000–$5000.

Eligibility Requirements: Applicant must be enrolled or expecting to enroll full-time at a four-year institution or university. Available to U.S. citizens.

Application Requirements: Application, essay, financial need analysis, references, transcript. *Deadline:* March 30.

Contact: Barbara A. McCaleb, Executive Secretary
Joseph Shinoda Memorial Scholarship Foundation
234 Via La Paz
San Luis Obispo, CA 93401
Phone: 805-544-0717

LAND CONSERVANCY OF NEW JERSEY

http://www.tlc-nj.org/

ROGERS FAMILY SCHOLARSHIP
• *See page 309*

RUSSELL W. MYERS SCHOLARSHIP
• *See page 309*

LANDSCAPE ARCHITECTURE FOUNDATION

http://www.lafoundation.org/

CLASS FUND ORNAMENTAL HORTICULTURE PROGRAM

Awards up to three $1000 scholarships to juniors and/or seniors enrolled in an ornamental horticulture curriculum.

Academic Fields/Career Goals: Horticulture/Floriculture.

Award: Grant for use in junior or senior years; not renewable. *Number:* up to 3. *Amount:* up to $1000.

Eligibility Requirements: Applicant must be enrolled or expecting to enroll full- or part-time at a four-year institution or university and studying in California. Available to U.S. citizens.

Application Requirements: Application, essay, references. *Deadline:* February 15.

Contact: Kathleen Le Dain, Communications Director
Landscape Architecture Foundation
818 18 Street, NW, Suite 810
Washington, DC 20006
Phone: 202-331-7070 Ext. 14
E-mail: rfigura@lafoundation.org

LANDSCAPE ARCHITECTURE FOUNDATION/ CALIFORNIA LANDSCAPE ARCHITECTURAL STUDENT FUND SCHOLARSHIPS PROGRAM

Nonrenewable scholarships designed to assist undergraduate or graduate students enrolled in landscape architecture and ornamental horticulture programs at eligible institutions in California. Based on financial need and commitment to profession.

Academic Fields/Career Goals: Horticulture/Floriculture; Landscape Architecture.

Award: Scholarship for use in freshman, sophomore, junior, or senior years; not renewable. *Number:* up to 15. *Amount:* $1000–$3000.

Eligibility Requirements: Applicant must be enrolled or expecting to enroll full-time at a four-year institution or university and studying in California. Available to U.S. and non-U.S. citizens.

Application Requirements: Application, financial need analysis, references, 300 word statement on profession. *Deadline:* February 15.

Contact: Kathleen Le Dain, Communications Director
Landscape Architecture Foundation
818 18 Street, NW, Suite 810
Washington, DC 20006
Phone: 202-331-7070 Ext. 14
E-mail: rfigura@lafoundation.org

LANDSCAPE ARCHITECTURE FOUNDATION/ CALIFORNIA LANDSCAPE ARCHITECTURE STUDENT FUND UNIVERSITY SCHOLARSHIP PROGRAM

Nonrenewable scholarships for juniors and/or seniors enrolled in landscape architecture curriculum in California. Based on financial need and commitment to profession.

Academic Fields/Career Goals: Horticulture/Floriculture; Landscape Architecture.

Award: Scholarship for use in junior or senior years; not renewable. *Number:* up to 6. *Amount:* up to $2000.

Eligibility Requirements: Applicant must be enrolled or expecting to enroll full- or part-time at a four-year institution or university and studying in California. Available to U.S. and non-U.S. citizens.

Application Requirements: Application, financial need analysis, references, 300-word statement on profession, 100-word statement on intended use of funds. *Deadline:* February 15.

Contact: Kathleen Le Dain, Communications Director
Landscape Architecture Foundation
818 18 Street, NW, Suite 810
Washington, DC 20006
Phone: 202-331-7070 Ext. 14
E-mail: rfigura@lafoundation.org

MONTANA FEDERATION OF GARDEN CLUBS

http://www.mtfgc.org/

LIFE MEMBER MONTANA FEDERATION OF GARDEN CLUBS SCHOLARSHIP
• *See page 225*

NATIONAL GARDEN CLUBS SCHOLARSHIP

Scholarship for a college student majoring in some branch of horticulture. Applicants must have sophomore or higher standing and be a legal resident of Montana.

Academic Fields/Career Goals: Horticulture/Floriculture.

Award: Scholarship for use in sophomore, junior, or senior years; not renewable. *Number:* 1. *Amount:* up to $3500.

Eligibility Requirements: Applicant must be enrolled or expecting to enroll full-time at a four-year institution or university and resident of Montana. Available to U.S. citizens.

Application Requirements: Application, financial need analysis. *Deadline:* February 28.

Contact: Margaret Yaw, Scholarship Committee, State Chairman
Montana Federation of Garden Clubs
2603 Spring Creek Drive
Bozeman, MT 59715-3621
Phone: 406-587-3621

NATIONAL COUNCIL OF STATE GARDEN CLUBS INC. SCHOLARSHIP

http://www.gardenclub.org/

NATIONAL COUNCIL OF STATE GARDEN CLUBS INC. SCHOLARSHIP
• *See page 85*

NATIONAL GARDEN CLUBS INC.

http://www.gardenclub.org/

NATIONAL GARDEN CLUBS INC. SCHOLARSHIP PROGRAM
• *See page 86*

NATIONAL POTATO COUNCIL WOMEN'S AUXILIARY

http://www.nationalpotatocouncil.org/

POTATO INDUSTRY SCHOLARSHIP
• *See page 80*

PENNSYLVANIA ASSOCIATION OF CONSERVATION DISTRICTS AUXILIARY

http://www.pacd.org/

PACD AUXILIARY SCHOLARSHIPS
• *See page 87*

PROFESSIONAL GROUNDS MANAGEMENT SOCIETY

http://www.pgms.org/

ANNE SEAMAN PROFESSIONAL GROUNDS MANAGEMENT SOCIETY MEMORIAL SCHOLARSHIP
• *See page 87*

SOIL AND WATER CONSERVATION SOCIETY-NEW JERSEY CHAPTER

http://www.geocities.com/njswcs

EDWARD R. HALL SCHOLARSHIP
• *See page 81*

SOUTHERN NURSERY ASSOCIATION

http://www.sna.org/

SIDNEY B. MEADOWS SCHOLARSHIP

Scholarship up to $2500 to students enrolled in an accredited undergraduate or graduate ornamental horticulture program or related discipline at a four-year institution. Student must be in a junior or senior standing at time of application. For undergraduate students minimum grade point average of 2.25 or 3.0 on a scale of 4.0 for graduate students.

Academic Fields/Career Goals: Horticulture/Floriculture.

Award: Scholarship for use in junior, senior, or graduate years; not renewable. *Number:* 10–15. *Amount:* $1500–$2500.

Eligibility Requirements: Applicant must be enrolled or expecting to enroll full-time at a four-year institution or university and resident of Arkansas, Florida, Georgia, Kentucky, Louisiana, Maryland, Mississippi, Missouri, North Carolina, Oklahoma, South Carolina, Tennessee, Texas, or Virginia. Available to U.S. and non-U.S. citizens.

Application Requirements: Application, resume, references, self-addressed stamped envelope, transcript. *Deadline:* May 31.

Contact: Program Director
Southern Nursery Association
1827 Powers Ferry Road, Building Four, Suite 100
Atlanta, GA 30339-8422
Phone: 770-953-3311
Fax: 770-953-4411
E-mail: mail@sna.org

TURF AND ORNAMENTAL COMMUNICATORS ASSOCIATION

http://www.toca.org/

TURF AND ORNAMENTAL COMMUNICATORS ASSOCIATION SCHOLARSHIP PROGRAM
• *See page 88*

WOMAN'S NATIONAL FARM AND GARDEN ASSOCIATION

http://www.wnfga.org/

WOMAN'S NATIONAL FARM AND GARDEN ASSOCIATION, INC. BURLINGAME/GERRITY HORTICULTURAL THERAPY SCHOLARSHIP

$500 scholarship for a student enrolled in a bachelor's degree program in horticultural therapy. The recipient is chosen by their college.

Academic Fields/Career Goals: Horticulture/Floriculture.

Award: Scholarship for use in freshman, sophomore, junior, or senior years; not renewable. *Number:* 1. *Amount:* $500.

Eligibility Requirements: Applicant must be enrolled or expecting to enroll full- or part-time at a four-year institution or university and female. Available to U.S. citizens.

Application Requirements: Application. *Deadline:* varies.

Contact: Mrs. EmmaJane Brice, Scholarship Coordinator
Woman's National Farm and Garden Association
Ninth Jenness Road
PO Box 1175
Midland, MI 48641-1175
Phone: 248-620-9281
E-mail: mgbertolini@aol.com

HOSPITALITY MANAGEMENT

AMERICAN HOTEL AND LODGING EDUCATIONAL FOUNDATION

http://www.ahlef.org/

AMERICAN EXPRESS SCHOLARSHIP PROGRAM

Award for full- and part-time students in undergraduate program leading to degree in hospitality management. Must be employed at hotel which is a member of AH&LA, and must work a minimum of 20 hours per week. Dependents of hotel employees may also apply.

Academic Fields/Career Goals: Hospitality Management.

Award: Scholarship for use in freshman, sophomore, junior, or senior years; not renewable. *Number:* varies. *Amount:* $500–$2000.

Eligibility Requirements: Applicant must be enrolled or expecting to enroll full- or part-time at a two-year or four-year institution or university. Available to U.S. and non-U.S. citizens.

Application Requirements: Application, essay, financial need analysis, resume, transcript. *Deadline:* May 1.

Contact: Christa Boatman, Foundation Manager
American Hotel and Lodging Educational Foundation
1201 New York Avenue NW, Suite 600
Washington, DC 20005-3931
Phone: 202-289-3139
Fax: 202-289-3199
E-mail: cboatman@ahlef.org

AMERICAN HOTEL & LODGING EDUCATIONAL FOUNDATION PEPSI SCHOLARSHIP
• *See page 207*

ANNUAL SCHOLARSHIP GRANT PROGRAM
• *See page 208*

ARTHUR J. PACKARD MEMORIAL SCHOLARSHIP
• *See page 208*

ECOLAB SCHOLARSHIP PROGRAM
• *See page 208*

HYATT HOTELS FUND FOR MINORITY LODGING MANAGEMENT
• *See page 208*

INCOMING FRESHMAN SCHOLARSHIPS
• *See page 208*

RAMA SCHOLARSHIP FOR THE AMERICAN DREAM
• *See page 208*

STEVEN HYMANS EXTENDED STAY SCHOLARSHIP
• *See page 209*

AMERICAN INSTITUTE OF WINE AND FOOD-PACIFIC NORTHWEST CHAPTER

http://www.aiwf.org/

CULINARY, VINIFERA, AND HOSPITALITY SCHOLARSHIP
• *See page 317*

CAREERS THROUGH CULINARY ARTS PROGRAM INC.

http://www.ccapinc.org/

CAREERS THROUGH CULINARY ARTS PROGRAM COOKING COMPETITION FOR SCHOLARSHIPS
• *See page 209*

CLUB FOUNDATION

http://www.clubfoundation.org/

JOE PERDUE SCHOLARSHIP PROGRAM

Awards for candidates seeking a managerial career in the private club industry and currently attending an accredited four year college or university. Must have completed freshman year and be enrolled full-time. Must have achieved and continue to maintain a GPA of at least 2.5. Minimum two awards of $2500 granted annually.

Academic Fields/Career Goals: Hospitality Management.

Award: Scholarship for use in sophomore, junior, or senior years; not renewable. *Number:* 2. *Amount:* $2500.

Eligibility Requirements: Applicant must be enrolled or expecting to enroll full-time at a four-year institution or university. Applicant must have 2.5 GPA or higher. Available to U.S. citizens.

Application Requirements: Application, essay, resume, references, self-addressed stamped envelope, transcript. *Deadline:* May 1.

Contact: Ashleigh Hill, Program Specialist
Club Foundation
1733 King Street
Alexandria, VA 22314
Phone: 703-299-4268 Ext. 268
Fax: 703-739-0124
E-mail: ashleigh.hill@cmaa.org

GOLDEN GATE RESTAURANT ASSOCIATION

http://www.ggra.org/

GOLDEN GATE RESTAURANT ASSOCIATION SCHOLARSHIP FOUNDATION
• *See page 322*

HAWAII HOTEL ASSOCIATION

http://www.hawaiihotels.org/

CLEM JUDD, JR. MEMORIAL SCHOLARSHIP

Scholarship for a Hawaii resident who must be able to prove Hawaiian ancestry. Applicant must be enrolled full-time at a U.S. accredited university/college majoring in hotel management. Must have a minimum 3.0 GPA.

Academic Fields/Career Goals: Hospitality Management.

Award: Scholarship for use in junior or senior years; not renewable. *Number:* 2. *Amount:* $1000–$2500.

Eligibility Requirements: Applicant must be Asian/Pacific Islander; enrolled or expecting to enroll full-time at a four-year institution and resident of Hawaii. Applicant must have 3.0 GPA or higher. Available to U.S. citizens.

Application Requirements: Application, essay, photo, resume, references. *Deadline:* July 1.

Contact: Scholarship Committee
Hawaii Hotel Association
2270 Kalakaua Avenue, Suite 1506
Honolulu, HI 96815
Phone: 808-923-0407
Fax: 808-924-3843
E-mail: hhla@hawaiihotels.org

R.W. BOB HOLDEN SCHOLARSHIP

One $1000 award for a student attending an accredited university or college in Hawaii, majoring in hotel management. Must be a Hawaii resident and a U.S. citizen. Must have a minimum 3.0 GPA.

Academic Fields/Career Goals: Hospitality Management; Travel/Tourism.

Award: Scholarship for use in junior or senior years; not renewable. *Number:* 1–5. *Amount:* $1000.

Eligibility Requirements: Applicant must be enrolled or expecting to enroll full-time at a two-year or four-year institution or university; resident of Hawaii and studying in Hawaii. Applicant must have 3.0 GPA or higher. Available to U.S. citizens.

Application Requirements: Application, essay, photo, resume, references, self-addressed stamped envelope, transcript. *Deadline:* July 1.

Contact: Naomi Kanna, Director of Membership Services
Hawaii Hotel Association
2270 Kalakaua Avenue, Suite 1506
Honolulu, HI 96815-2564
Phone: 808-923-0407
E-mail: hhla@hawaiihotels.org

ILLINOIS RESTAURANT ASSOCIATION EDUCATIONAL FOUNDATION

http://www.illinoisrestaurants.org/

ILLINOIS RESTAURANT ASSOCIATION EDUCATIONAL FOUNDATION SCHOLARSHIPS
• *See page 210*

INTERNATIONAL AIRLINES TRAVEL AGENT NETWORK

http://www.iatan.org/

INTERNATIONAL AIRLINES TRAVEL AGENT NETWORK FOUNDATION SCHOLARSHIP

Scholarships available annually to individuals who are interested in pursuing or enhancing their careers in travel. Must be U.S. citizens or permanent legal residents of the United States and not less than 17 years of age. Must have been employed for at least six months by an IATAN accredited travel agency or who are registered students at a recognized postsecondary educational/vocational institution having direct links with the travel industry.

Academic Fields/Career Goals: Hospitality Management; Travel/Tourism.

Award: Scholarship for use in freshman, sophomore, junior, senior, graduate, or postgraduate years; not renewable. *Number:* 10–15. *Amount:* $500–$3000.

Eligibility Requirements: Applicant must be age 17 and over and enrolled or expecting to enroll full- or part-time at a two-year or four-year or technical institution or university. Applicant or parent of applicant must have employment or volunteer experience in travel and tourism industry. Available to U.S. citizens.

Application Requirements: Application, essay, resume, references, transcript. *Deadline:* April 25.

Contact: Neil Scotten, Customer Service Representative
International Airlines Travel Agent Network
800 Place Victoria, Suite 800, PO Box 113
Montreal, QC H4Z 1M1
Phone: 514-868-8800 Ext. 4407
Fax: 514-868-8850
E-mail: scottenn@iata.org

JAMES BEARD FOUNDATION INC.

http://www.jamesbeard.org/

BERN LAXER MEMORIAL SCHOLARSHIP
• *See page 210*

MAINE RESTAURANT ASSOCIATION

http://www.mainerestaurant.com/

MAINE RESTAURANT ASSOCIATION EDUCATION FOUNDATION SCHOLARSHIP FUND
• *See page 212*

MISSOURI TRAVEL COUNCIL

http://www.missouritravel.com/

MISSOURI TRAVEL COUNCIL TOURISM SCHOLARSHIP
• *See page 323*

NATIONAL RESTAURANT ASSOCIATION EDUCATIONAL FOUNDATION

http://www.nraef.org/

NATIONAL RESTAURANT ASSOCIATION EDUCATIONAL FOUNDATION UNDERGRADUATE SCHOLARSHIPS FOR COLLEGE STUDENTS
• *See page 323*

NATIONAL RESTAURANT ASSOCIATION EDUCATIONAL FOUNDATION UNDERGRADUATE SCHOLARSHIPS FOR HIGH SCHOOL SENIORS AND GENERAL EDUCATION DIPLOMA (GED) GRADUATE S
• *See page 323*

NATIONAL TOURISM FOUNDATION

http://www.ntfonline.com/

ACADEMY OF TRAVEL AND TOURISM SCHOLARSHIPS

One $500 scholarship available for a graduating high school senior planning to attend accredited postsecondary education tourism-related program. Applicant must be completing senior year of high school at Academy of Travel and Tourism location. Each academy may submit most qualified student.

Academic Fields/Career Goals: Hospitality Management; Political Science; Travel/Tourism.

Award: Scholarship for use in freshman year; not renewable. *Number:* 1. *Amount:* $500.

Eligibility Requirements: Applicant must be high school student and planning to enroll or expecting to enroll full-time at a two-year or four-year institution or university. Applicant must have 3.0 GPA or higher. Available to U.S. citizens.

Application Requirements: Application, essay, resume, references. *Deadline:* May 10.

Contact: Michelle Gorin, Projects Coordinator
National Tourism Foundation
546 East Main Street
Lexington, KY 40508-3071
Phone: 800-682-8886
Fax: 859-226-4437

CLEVELAND LEGACY I AND II SCHOLARSHIP AWARDS
• *See page 324*

NEW HORIZONS KATHY LETARTE SCHOLARSHIP
• *See page 324*

PAT AND JIM HOST SCHOLARSHIP

Award for students who have a degree emphasis in a travel and tourism related field. Must maintain a 3.0 GPA for renewal.

Academic Fields/Career Goals: Hospitality Management; Travel/Tourism.

Award: Scholarship for use in freshman, sophomore, junior, or senior years; renewable. *Number:* 1. *Amount:* $2000–$8000.

Eligibility Requirements: Applicant must be enrolled or expecting to enroll full-time at a four-year institution or university. Applicant must have 3.0 GPA or higher. Available to U.S. citizens.

Application Requirements: Application, essay, resume, references, transcript. *Deadline:* May 10.

Contact: Michelle Gorin, Projects Coordinator
National Tourism Foundation
546 East Main Street
Lexington, KY 40508-3071
Phone: 800-682-8886
Fax: 859-226-4437

SOCIETIE DES CASINOS DU QUEBEC SCHOLARSHIP
• *See page 324*

TAMPA, HILLSBOROUGH LEGACY SCHOLARSHIP
• *See page 324*

TAUCK SCHOLARS SCHOLARSHIPS
• *See page 324*

TULSA SCHOLARSHIP AWARDS
• *See page 325*

YELLOW RIBBON SCHOLARSHIP
• *See page 325*

OHIO TRAVEL ASSOCIATION

http://www.ohiotravel.org/

BILL SCHWARTZ MEMORIAL SCHOLARSHIP

Scholarship will be granted to a qualified full-time, Ohio student after the completion of their freshman year. Must be studying hospitality management or travel/tourism with a minimum 2.5 GPA. As part of the scholarship program, the recipient will be invited to various OTA events throughout the year.

Academic Fields/Career Goals: Hospitality Management; Travel/Tourism.

Award: Scholarship for use in sophomore, junior, or senior years; not renewable. *Number:* 1. *Amount:* $1000.

Eligibility Requirements: Applicant must be enrolled or expecting to enroll full-time at a two-year or four-year or technical institution or university; resident of Ohio and studying in Ohio. Applicant must have 2.5 GPA or higher. Available to U.S. citizens.

Application Requirements: Application, financial need analysis, references, transcript. *Deadline:* June 15.

Contact: Ms. Betsy Decillis, Membership and Community Manager
Ohio Travel Association
130 East Chestnut Street, Suite 301
Columbus, OH 43215
Phone: 800-896-4682 Ext. 0#
E-mail: betsy@ohiotravel.org

UNITED NEGRO COLLEGE FUND

http://www.uncf.org/

AMERICAN HOTEL FOUNDATION SCHOLARSHIP

Scholarship available to hotel management majors attending UNCF member colleges and universities. Minimum 2.5 GPA required. Prospective applicants should complete the Student Profile found at web site http://www.uncf.org.

Academic Fields/Career Goals: Hospitality Management.

Award: Scholarship for use in freshman, sophomore, junior, or senior years; not renewable. *Number:* varies. *Amount:* $1500.

Eligibility Requirements: Applicant must be Black (non-Hispanic) and enrolled or expecting to enroll full-time at a four-year institution or university. Applicant must have 2.5 GPA or higher. Available to U.S. and non-U.S. citizens.

Application Requirements: Application. *Deadline:* May 1.

Contact: Director, Program Services
United Negro College Fund
8260 Willow Oaks Corporate Drive
PO Box 10444
Fairfax, VA 22031-8044
Phone: 800-331-2244
E-mail: rebecca.bennett@uncf.org

HUMAN RESOURCES

NEW ENGLAND EMPLOYEE BENEFITS COUNCIL

http://www.neebc.org/

NEW ENGLAND EMPLOYEE BENEFITS COUNCIL SCHOLARSHIP PROGRAM

• *See page 68*

SHRM FOUNDATION-SOCIETY FOR HUMAN RESOURCE MANAGEMENT

http://www.shrm.org/foundation

SHRM FOUNDATION STUDENT SCHOLARSHIPS

Applicants must be SHRM student members and must be pursuing a college degree in HR or a related field. Undergraduates must have a cumulative GPA of at least 3.0 on a 4.0 point scale, and graduate applicants must have at least a 3.5 GPA on a 4.0 scale. Course work in HR management is required. Awards are primarily merit-based. Scholarships are also available for students sitting for the Assurance of Learning Assessment.

Academic Fields/Career Goals: Human Resources.

Award: Scholarship for use in junior, senior, or graduate years; not renewable. *Number:* 40. *Amount:* $200–$5000.

Eligibility Requirements: Applicant must be enrolled or expecting to enroll full- or part-time at a four-year institution or university. Applicant or parent of applicant must be member of Society for Human Resource Management. Applicant must have 3.0 GPA or higher. Available to U.S. and non-U.S. citizens.

Application Requirements: Application, essay, resume, references. *Deadline:* December 1.

Contact: Beth McFarland, Manager, Special Projects
SHRM Foundation-Society for Human Resource Management
1800 Duke Street
Alexandria, VA 22314
Phone: 703-535-6371
E-mail: beth.mcfarland@shrm.org

UNITED NEGRO COLLEGE FUND

http://www.uncf.org/

GENERAL MILLS CORPORATE SCHOLARS AWARD

• *See page 73*

UNITED WATER CORPORATE SCHOLARS PROGRAM

• *See page 74*

UPS/UNCF CORPORATE SCHOLARS PROGRAM

• *See page 202*

VERIZON FOUNDATION SCHOLARSHIP

• *See page 74*

Y'S MEN INTERNATIONAL

http://www.ysmenusa.com/

ALEXANDER SCHOLARSHIP LOAN FUND

• *See page 159*

HUMANITIES

ALBERTA HERITAGE SCHOLARSHIP FUND

http://www.alis.alberta.ca/

LOIS HOLE HUMANITIES AND SOCIAL SCIENCES SCHOLARSHIP

Award of CAN$5000 available to Alberta residents who are students enrolled full time in the second or subsequent year of postsecondary study in the Faculty of Humanities or the Faculty of Social Sciences at University of Alberta, University of Calgary, University of Lethbridge, or Athabasca University. Awarded on the basis of academic merit, demonstrated leadership, and community service. For further information, see web site http://alis.alberta.ca.

Academic Fields/Career Goals: Humanities; Social Sciences.

Award: Scholarship for use in sophomore, junior, or senior years; not renewable. *Number:* 4.

Eligibility Requirements: Applicant must be Canadian citizen; enrolled or expecting to enroll full-time at a four-year institution or university; resident of Alberta; studying in Alberta and must have an interest in leadership.

Application Requirements: Application, transcript. *Deadline:* varies.

Contact: Scholarship Committee
Alberta Heritage Scholarship Fund
9940 106th Street, Fourth Floor, Sterling Place
PO Box 28000, Station Main
Edmonton, AB T5J 4R4
Canada
Phone: 780-427-8640
E-mail: scholarships@gov.ab.ca

AMERICAN CLASSICAL LEAGUE/ NATIONAL JUNIOR CLASSICAL LEAGUE

http://www.aclclassics.org/

NATIONAL JUNIOR CLASSICAL LEAGUE SCHOLARSHIP

• *See page 181*

AMERICAN SCHOOL OF CLASSICAL STUDIES AT ATHENS

http://www.ascsa.edu.gr/

ASCSA SUMMER SESSIONS SCHOLARSHIPS
• See page 92

BETHESDA LUTHERAN COMMUNITIES

http://www.bethesdalutherancommunities.org/

DEVELOPMENTAL DISABILITIES SCHOLASTIC ACHIEVEMENT SCHOLARSHIP FOR COLLEGE STUDENTS WHO ARE LUTHERAN
• See page 218

CANADIAN INSTITUTE OF UKRAINIAN STUDIES

http://www.cius.ca/

LEO J. KRYSA UNDERGRADUATE SCHOLARSHIP
• See page 104

CATCHING THE DREAM

http://www.catchingthedream.org/

MATH, ENGINEERING, SCIENCE, BUSINESS, EDUCATION, COMPUTERS SCHOLARSHIPS
• See page 147

NATIVE AMERICAN LEADERSHIP IN EDUCATION (NALE)
• See page 147

THE COMMUNITY FOUNDATION FOR GREATER ATLANTA, INC.

http://www.cfgreateratlanta.org/

JAMES M. AND VIRGINIA M. SMYTH SCHOLARSHIP
• See page 110

HARVARD TRAVELLERS CLUB

http://www.harvardtravellersclub.org/

HARVARD TRAVELLERS CLUB GRANTS
• See page 98

INSTITUTE FOR HUMANE STUDIES

http://www.theihs.org/

HUMANE STUDIES FELLOWSHIPS
• See page 185

JACK J. ISGUR FOUNDATION

JACK J. ISGUR FOUNDATION SCHOLARSHIP
• See page 112

LADIES AUXILIARY TO THE VETERANS OF FOREIGN WARS, DEPARTMENT OF MAINE

http://mainevfw.org/

FRANCES L. BOOTH MEDICAL SCHOLARSHIP SPONSORED BY LAVFW DEPARTMENT OF MAINE
• See page 344

METAVUE CORPORATION

http://www.metavue.com/

FW RAUSCH ARTS AND HUMANITIES PAPER CONTEST
• See page 113

PHI ALPHA THETA HISTORY HONOR SOCIETY, INC.

http://www.phialphatheta.org/

PHI ALPHA THETA WORLD HISTORY ASSOCIATION PAPER PRIZE
• See page 354

POLISH ARTS CLUB OF BUFFALO SCHOLARSHIP FOUNDATION

http://www.pacb.bfn.org/

POLISH ARTS CLUB OF BUFFALO SCHOLARSHIP FOUNDATION TRUST
• See page 114

POLISH HERITAGE ASSOCIATION OF MARYLAND

http://www.pha-md.org/

DR. JOSEPHINE WTULICH MEMORIAL SCHOLARSHIP
• See page 92

ROBERT P. PULA MEMORIAL SCHOLARSHIP

Scholarship will be awarded to a student whose major is in the humanities, social sciences, literature, or Polish studies. Must be of Polish descent (at least two Polish grandparents), a U.S. citizen, and a resident of Maryland. Scholarship value is $1500.

Academic Fields/Career Goals: Humanities; Literature/English/Writing; Social Sciences.

Award: Scholarship for use in freshman, sophomore, junior, or senior years; not renewable. *Number:* 1. *Amount:* up to $1500.

Eligibility Requirements: Applicant must be of Polish heritage; enrolled or expecting to enroll full-time at a four-year institution or university and resident of Maryland. Available to U.S. citizens.

Application Requirements: Application, essay, financial need analysis, interview, transcript. *Deadline:* March 31.

Contact: Thomas Hollowak, Scholarship Chair
Polish Heritage Association of Maryland
Seven Dendron Court
Baltimore, MD 21234
Phone: 410-837-4268
E-mail: thollowalk@ubmail.ubalt.edu

STRAIGHTFORWARD MEDIA

http://www.straightforwardmedia.com/

STRAIGHTFORWARD MEDIA LIBERAL ARTS SCHOLARSHIP
• See page 107

UNITED NEGRO COLLEGE FUND

http://www.uncf.org/

MCCLARE FAMILY TRUST SCHOLARSHIP

Scholarship for African American college freshmen majoring in the humanities with an interest in English literature. Must attend UNCF member institution and have a minimum 3.0 GPA. Amount of scholarship is based on need.

Academic Fields/Career Goals: Humanities; Literature/English/Writing.

Award: Scholarship for use in freshman year; not renewable. *Number:* varies. *Amount:* varies.

Eligibility Requirements: Applicant must be Black (non-Hispanic); enrolled or expecting to enroll full- or part-time at a four-year institution or university and must have an interest in English language. Applicant must have 3.0 GPA or higher. Available to U.S. citizens.

Application Requirements: Application, financial need analysis, FAFSA. *Deadline:* October 29.

Contact: Director, Program Services
United Negro College Fund
8260 Willow Oaks Corporate Drive
PO Box 10444
Fairfax, VA 22031-8044
Phone: 800-331-2244
E-mail: rebecca.bennett@uncf.org

OSSIE DAVIS ENDOWMENT SCHOLARSHIP
• *See page 116*

PRINCIPAL FINANCIAL GROUP SCHOLARSHIPS
• *See page 74*

HYDROLOGY

AMERICAN GEOLOGICAL INSTITUTE

http://www.agiweb.org/

AMERICAN GEOLOGICAL INSTITUTE MINORITY SCHOLARSHIP
• *See page 222*

AMERICAN GROUND WATER TRUST

http://www.agwt.org/

AMERICAN GROUND WATER TRUST-AMTROL INC. SCHOLARSHIP

Award for college/university entry-level students intending to pursue a career in ground water-related field. Must either have completed a science/environmental project involving ground water resources or have had vacation work experience related to the environment and natural resources. Must be U.S. citizen or legal resident with minimum 3.0 GPA. Submit two letters of recommendation and transcript.

Academic Fields/Career Goals: Hydrology; Natural Resources.

Award: Scholarship for use in freshman year; not renewable. *Number:* 2. *Amount:* up to $1500.

Eligibility Requirements: Applicant must be enrolled or expecting to enroll full-time at a four-year institution or university. Applicant must have 3.0 GPA or higher. Available to U.S. citizens.

Application Requirements: Application, essay, references, transcript. *Deadline:* June 1.

Contact: Garret Grasskamp, Ground Water Specialist
American Ground Water Trust
50 Pleasant Street, Suite 2
Concord, NH 03301-4073
Phone: 603-228-5444
Fax: 603-228-6557
E-mail: trustinfo@agwt.org

AMERICAN GROUND WATER TRUST-THOMAS STETSON SCHOLARSHIP
• *See page 174*

AMERICAN METEOROLOGICAL SOCIETY

http://www.ametsoc.org/

AMERICAN METEOROLOGICAL SOCIETY 75TH ANNIVERSARY SCHOLARSHIP

Award for full-time students entering their final year of undergraduate study majoring in atmospheric or related oceanic and hydrologic sciences. Must show clear intent to make the atmospheric or related sciences their career. Must be enrolled at a U.S. institution. Minimum GPA of 3.25 required. One-time award of $2000. Must be U.S. citizen or permanent resident to apply.

Academic Fields/Career Goals: Hydrology; Meteorology/Atmospheric Science; Oceanography.

Award: Scholarship for use in senior year; not renewable. *Number:* 7–10. *Amount:* $2000.

Eligibility Requirements: Applicant must be enrolled or expecting to enroll full-time at a four-year institution or university. Available to U.S. citizens.

Application Requirements: Application, essay, references, transcript. *Deadline:* February 20.

Contact: Donna Fernandez, Development Program Coordinator
American Meteorological Society
45 Beacon Street
Boston, MA 02108-3693
Phone: 617-227-2426 Ext. 246
Fax: 617-742-8718
E-mail: dfernand@ametsoc.org

AMERICAN METEOROLOGICAL SOCIETY DR. PEDRO GRAU UNDERGRADUATE SCHOLARSHIP

Award for full-time undergraduate students majoring in atmospheric or related oceanic and hydrologic sciences. Must be enrolled at a U.S. institution. Minimum GPA of 3.25 required. Must be U.S. citizen or permanent resident to apply. Award of $2500 annually for four years.

Academic Fields/Career Goals: Hydrology; Meteorology/Atmospheric Science; Oceanography.

Award: Scholarship for use in freshman, sophomore, junior, or senior years; not renewable. *Number:* 1. *Amount:* $2500.

Eligibility Requirements: Applicant must be enrolled or expecting to enroll full-time at a four-year institution or university. Available to U.S. citizens.

Application Requirements: Application, essay, references, transcript. *Deadline:* February 20.

Contact: Donna Fernandez, Development Program Coordinator
American Meteorological Society
45 Beacon Street
Boston, MA 02108-3693
Phone: 617-227-2426 Ext. 246
Fax: 617-742-8718
E-mail: dfernand@ametsoc.org

AMERICAN METEOROLOGICAL SOCIETY/INDUSTRY MINORITY SCHOLARSHIPS

Two-year scholarship of $3,000 per year for minority students entering their freshman year of college. Must plan to pursue careers in the atmospheric and related oceanic and hydrologic sciences. Must be U.S. citizen or permanent resident to apply.

Academic Fields/Career Goals: Hydrology; Meteorology/Atmospheric Science; Oceanography.

Award: Scholarship for use in freshman year; not renewable. *Number:* 6–13. *Amount:* $3000.

Eligibility Requirements: Applicant must be American Indian/Alaska Native, Asian/Pacific Islander, Black (non-Hispanic), or Hispanic; high school student and planning to enroll or expecting to enroll full-time at a four-year institution or university. Applicant must have 3.0 GPA or higher. Available to U.S. citizens.

Application Requirements: Application, references, test scores, transcript. *Deadline:* February 22.

Contact: Donna Sampson, Development and Student Program Manager
American Meteorological Society
45 Beacon Street
Boston, MA 02108-3693
Phone: 617-227-2426 Ext. 246
Fax: 617-742-8718
E-mail: dfernand@ametsoc.org

AMERICAN METEOROLOGICAL SOCIETY MARK J. SCHROEDER SCHOLARSHIP IN METEOROLOGY

Award for full-time students entering their final year of undergraduate study majoring in atmospheric or related oceanic and hydrologic sciences. Must be enrolled at a U.S. institution. Minimum GPA of 3.25 is required. Must be U.S. citizen or permanent resident to apply.

Academic Fields/Career Goals: Hydrology; Meteorology/Atmospheric Science; Oceanography.

Award: Scholarship for use in senior year; not renewable. *Number:* varies. *Amount:* varies.

Eligibility Requirements: Applicant must be enrolled or expecting to enroll full-time at a four-year institution or university. Available to U.S. citizens.

Application Requirements: Application, essay, financial need analysis, references, transcript. *Deadline:* February 20.

Contact: Donna Fernandez, Development Program Coordinator
American Meteorological Society
45 Beacon Street
Boston, MA 02108-3693
Phone: 617-227-2426 Ext. 246
Fax: 617-742-8718
E-mail: dfernand@ametsoc.org

AMERICAN METEOROLOGICAL SOCIETY RICHARD AND HELEN HAGEMEYER SCHOLARSHIP

Award for full-time students entering their final year of undergraduate study majoring in atmospheric or related oceanic and hydrologic sciences. Must be enrolled at a U.S. institution. Minimum GPA of 3.25 is required. One-time award of $3000. Must be U.S. citizen or permanent resident to apply.

Academic Fields/Career Goals: Hydrology; Meteorology/Atmospheric Science; Oceanography.

Award: Scholarship for use in junior or senior years; not renewable. *Number:* varies. *Amount:* $3000.

Eligibility Requirements: Applicant must be enrolled or expecting to enroll full-time at a two-year or four-year institution or university. Available to U.S. citizens.

Application Requirements: Application, essay, references, transcript. *Deadline:* February 20.

Contact: Donna Fernandez, Development Program Coordinator
American Meteorological Society
45 Beacon Street
Boston, MA 02108-3693
Phone: 617-227-2426 Ext. 246
Fax: 617-742-8718
E-mail: dfernand@ametsoc.org

AMERICAN METEOROLOGICAL SOCIETY WERNER A. BAUM UNDERGRADUATE SCHOLARSHIP

Award for full-time students entering final year of undergraduate study majoring in atmospheric or related oceanic or hydrologic science, and/or must show clear intent to make the atmospheric or related sciences their career. Must be enrolled at a U.S. institution. Minimum GPA of 3.25 is required. Must be U.S. citizen or permanent resident.

Academic Fields/Career Goals: Hydrology; Meteorology/Atmospheric Science; Oceanography.

Award: Scholarship for use in senior year; not renewable. *Number:* varies. *Amount:* $5000.

Eligibility Requirements: Applicant must be enrolled or expecting to enroll full-time at a four-year institution or university. Applicant must have 3.5 GPA or higher. Available to U.S. citizens.

Application Requirements: Application, essay, financial need analysis, references, transcript. *Deadline:* February 20.

Contact: Donna Fernandez, Development Program Coordinator
American Meteorological Society
45 Beacon Street
Boston, MA 02108-3693
Phone: 617-227-2426 Ext. 246
Fax: 617-742-8718
E-mail: dfernand@ametsoc.org

AMS FRESHMAN UNDERGRADUATE SCHOLARSHIP

• *See page 306*

CARL W. KREITZBERG ENDOWED SCHOLARSHIP

Scholarships of $2000 for full-time students entering their final year of undergraduate study, majoring in atmospheric or related oceanic/hydrologic science programs at accredited U.S. institutions. Minimum 3.25 GPA required. Must be U.S. citizen.

Academic Fields/Career Goals: Hydrology; Meteorology/Atmospheric Science; Oceanography.

Award: Scholarship for use in senior year; not renewable. *Number:* 1. *Amount:* up to $2000.

Eligibility Requirements: Applicant must be enrolled or expecting to enroll full-time at a four-year institution or university. Available to U.S. citizens.

Application Requirements: Application, essay, references, transcript. *Deadline:* February 20.

Contact: Donna Fernandez, Development Program Coordinator
American Meteorological Society
45 Beacon Street
Boston, MA 02108-3693
Phone: 617-227-2426 Ext. 246
Fax: 617-742-8718
E-mail: dfernand@ametsoc.org

ETHAN AND ALLAN MURPHY MEMORIAL SCHOLARSHIP

Award for entering their final year of undergraduate study majoring in atmospheric or related oceanic and hydrologic science. Must show clear intent to make the atmospheric or related sciences a career. Must be enrolled in an accredited U.S. institution. Minimum 3.25 GPA required. Must be a U.S. citizen.

Academic Fields/Career Goals: Hydrology; Meteorology/Atmospheric Science; Oceanography.

Award: Scholarship for use in senior year; not renewable. *Number:* varies. *Amount:* $2000.

Eligibility Requirements: Applicant must be enrolled or expecting to enroll full-time at a four-year institution or university. Available to U.S. citizens.

Application Requirements: Application, essay, references, transcript. *Deadline:* February 20.

Contact: Donna Fernandez, Development Program Coordinator
American Meteorological Society
45 Beacon Street
Boston, MA 02108-3693
Phone: 617-227-2426 Ext. 246
Fax: 617-742-8718
E-mail: dfernand@ametsoc.org

GEORGE S. BENTON SCHOLARSHIP

Scholarships are awarded to full-time students entering their final year of undergraduate study at accredited U.S. institutions for study in atmospheric sciences or related oceanic or hydrologic science. Minimum 3.25 GPA required. Must be U.S. citizen or permanent resident.

Academic Fields/Career Goals: Hydrology; Meteorology/Atmospheric Science; Oceanography.

Award: Scholarship for use in senior year; not renewable. *Number:* 1. *Amount:* up to $3500.

Eligibility Requirements: Applicant must be enrolled or expecting to enroll full-time at a four-year institution or university. Available to U.S. citizens.

Application Requirements: Application, financial need analysis, resume, transcript. *Deadline:* February 20.

Contact: Donna Fernandez, Development Program Coordinator
American Meteorological Society
45 Beacon Street
Boston, MA 02108-3693
Phone: 617-227-2426 Ext. 246
Fax: 617-742-8718
E-mail: dfernand@ametsoc.org

GUILLERMO SALAZAR RODRIGUES SCHOLARSHIP

Award for full-time undergraduate students majoring in atmospheric or related oceanic and hydrologic science. Must show clear intent to make the atmospheric or related sciences a career. Must be enrolled in an accredited U.S. institution. Minimum 3.25 GPA required. Must be a U.S. citizen. Award of $2,500 annually for four years.

Academic Fields/Career Goals: Hydrology; Meteorology/Atmospheric Science; Oceanography.

Award: Scholarship for use in freshman, sophomore, junior, or senior years; not renewable. *Number:* varies. *Amount:* $2500.

Eligibility Requirements: Applicant must be enrolled or expecting to enroll full-time at a four-year institution or university. Available to U.S. citizens.

Application Requirements: Application, essay, references, transcript. *Deadline:* February 20.

Contact: Donna Fernandez, Development Program Coordinator
American Meteorological Society
45 Beacon Street
Boston, MA 02108-3693
Phone: 617-227-2426 Ext. 246
Fax: 617-742-8718
E-mail: dfernand@ametsoc.org

JOHN R. HOPE SCHOLARSHIP

Award for students entering their final year of undergraduate study majoring in atmospheric or related oceanic and hydrological science. Must show clear intent to make the atmospheric or related science a career. Minimum 3.25 GPA required. Must be enrolled in an accredited U.S. institution. Must be a U.S. citizen to apply.

Academic Fields/Career Goals: Hydrology; Meteorology/Atmospheric Science; Oceanography.

Award: Scholarship for use in senior year; not renewable. *Number:* 1. *Amount:* up to $2500.

Eligibility Requirements: Applicant must be enrolled or expecting to enroll full-time at a four-year institution or university. Available to U.S. citizens.

Application Requirements: Application, essay, references, transcript. *Deadline:* February 20.

Contact: Donna Fernandez, Development Program Coordinator
American Meteorological Society
45 Beacon Street
Boston, MA 02108-3693
Phone: 617-227-2426 Ext. 246
Fax: 617-742-8718
E-mail: dfernand@ametsoc.org

LOREN W. CROW SCHOLARSHIP

One-time award for full-time students entering their final year of undergraduate study majoring in atmospheric or related oceanic and hydrologic sciences. Must be enrolled full-time at a U.S. institution with a 3.25 GPA. Must be U.S. citizen or permanent resident to apply.

Academic Fields/Career Goals: Hydrology; Meteorology/Atmospheric Science; Oceanography.

Award: Scholarship for use in senior year; not renewable. *Number:* varies. *Amount:* up to $2000.

Eligibility Requirements: Applicant must be enrolled or expecting to enroll full-time at a four-year institution or university. Available to U.S. citizens.

Application Requirements: Application, essay, references, transcript. *Deadline:* February 20.

Contact: Donna Fernandez, Development Program Coordinator
American Meteorological Society
45 Beacon Street
Boston, MA 02108-3693
Phone: 617-227-2426 Ext. 246
Fax: 617-742-8718
E-mail: dfernand@ametsoc.org

ARIZONA HYDROLOGICAL SOCIETY

http://www.azhydrosoc.org/

ARIZONA HYDROLOGICAL SOCIETY SCHOLARSHIP
• *See page 222*

ASSOCIATION FOR WOMEN GEOSCIENTISTS, PUGET SOUND CHAPTER

http://www.awg.org/

PUGET SOUND CHAPTER SCHOLARSHIP
• *See page 223*

ASSOCIATION OF CALIFORNIA WATER AGENCIES

http://www.acwa.com/

ASSOCIATION OF CALIFORNIA WATER AGENCIES SCHOLARSHIPS
• *See page 94*

CLAIR A. HILL SCHOLARSHIP
• *See page 94*

CALIFORNIA GROUNDWATER ASSOCIATION

http://www.groundh2o.org/

CALIFORNIA GROUNDWATER ASSOCIATION SCHOLARSHIP

Award for California residents who demonstrate an interest in some facet of groundwater technology. One to two $1000 awards. Must use for study in California. Submit letter of recommendation.

Academic Fields/Career Goals: Hydrology; Natural Resources.

Award: Scholarship for use in freshman, sophomore, junior, or senior years; not renewable. *Number:* 1–2. *Amount:* $1000.

Eligibility Requirements: Applicant must be enrolled or expecting to enroll full-time at a two-year or four-year or technical institution or university; resident of California and studying in California. Available to U.S. citizens.

Application Requirements: Application, essay, references, transcript. *Deadline:* April 1.

Contact: Mike Mortensson, Executive Director
California Groundwater Association
PO Box 14369
Santa Rosa, CA 95402
Phone: 707-578-4408
Fax: 707-546-4906
E-mail: wellguy@groundh2o.org

INTERNATIONAL ASSOCIATION OF GREAT LAKES RESEARCH

http://www.iaglr.org/

PAUL W. RODGERS SCHOLARSHIP
• *See page 224*

KENTUCKY ENERGY AND ENVIRONMENT CABINET

http://www.eec.ky.gov/

ENVIRONMENTAL PROTECTION SCHOLARSHIP
• *See page 141*

NATIONAL GROUND WATER RESEARCH AND EDUCATIONAL FOUNDATION

http://www.ngwa.org/

NATIONAL GROUND WATER RESEARCH AND EDUCATIONAL FOUNDATION'S LEN ASSANTE SCHOLARSHIP
• *See page 226*

INDUSTRIAL DESIGN

AMERICAN INSTITUTE OF CHEMICAL ENGINEERS

http://www.aiche.org/

SAFETY AND HEALTH NATIONAL STUDENT DESIGN COMPETITION AWARD FOR SAFETY
• *See page 163*

AMERICAN SOCIETY OF PLUMBING ENGINEERS

http://www.aspe.org/

ALFRED STEELE ENGINEERING SCHOLARSHIP
• *See page 278*

AUTOMOTIVE HALL OF FAME

http://www.automotivehalloffame.org/

AUTOMOTIVE HALL OF FAME EDUCATIONAL FUNDS
• *See page 164*

IFDA EDUCATIONAL FOUNDATION

http://www.ifdaef.org/

RUTH CLARK FURNITURE DESIGN SCHOLARSHIP
• *See page 112*

INDUSTRIAL DESIGNERS SOCIETY OF AMERICA

http://www.idsa.org/

INDUSTRIAL DESIGNERS SOCIETY OF AMERICA UNDERGRADUATE SCHOLARSHIP
One-time award to a U.S. citizen or permanent U.S. resident currently enrolled in an industrial design program. Must submit twenty visual examples of work and study full-time.
Academic Fields/Career Goals: Industrial Design.
Award: Scholarship for use in junior year; not renewable. *Number:* 2. *Amount:* $2500.
Eligibility Requirements: Applicant must be enrolled or expecting to enroll full-time at an institution or university. Applicant must have 3.0 GPA or higher. Available to U.S. citizens.
Application Requirements: Application, references, transcript, twenty visual examples of work. *Deadline:* May 18.
Contact: Max Taylor, Executive Assistant
Industrial Designers Society of America
45195 Business Court, Suite 250
Dulles, VA 20166
Phone: 703-707-6000
Fax: 703-787-8501
E-mail: maxt@idsa.org

MANUFACTURERS ASSOCIATION OF MAINE

http://www.mainemfg.com/

MAINE METAL PRODUCTS EDUCATION FUND SCHOLARSHIP PROGRAM
• *See page 127*

MIDWEST ROOFING CONTRACTORS ASSOCIATION

http://www.mrca.org/

MRCA FOUNDATION SCHOLARSHIP PROGRAM
• *See page 102*

NASA'S VIRGINIA SPACE GRANT CONSORTIUM

http://www.vsgc.odu.edu/

VIRGINIA STEM COMMUNITY COLLEGE SCHOLARSHIPS
• *See page 96*

RHODE ISLAND FOUNDATION

http://www.rifoundation.org/

JAMES J. BURNS AND C. A. HAYNES SCHOLARSHIP
Award of $1000 for students enrolled in a textile program at an educational institution offering this program, such as University of Massachusetts Dartmouth, Rhode Island School of Design, Philadelphia University, North Carolina State University, Clemson University, Georgia Tech and Auburn University. Preference given to children of members of National Association of Textile Supervisors. Must demonstrate financial need.
Academic Fields/Career Goals: Industrial Design.
Award: Scholarship for use in freshman, sophomore, junior, or senior years; not renewable. *Amount:* $1000.
Eligibility Requirements: Applicant must be enrolled or expecting to enroll full-time at a two-year or four-year institution or university. Available to U.S. citizens.
Application Requirements: Application, essay, financial need analysis, references, transcript. *Deadline:* June 1.
Contact: Libby Monahan, Funds Administrator
Rhode Island Foundation
One Union Station
Providence, RI 02903
Phone: 401-274-4564 Ext. 3117
E-mail: libbym@rifoundation.org

SIMPLEHUMAN

http://www.simplehuman.com/

SIMPLE SOLUTIONS DESIGN COMPETITION
• *See page 271*

SOCIETY OF MANUFACTURING ENGINEERS EDUCATION FOUNDATION

http://www.smeef.org/

CHAPTER 67-PHOENIX SCHOLARSHIP
• *See page 295*

CHAPTER 198-DOWNRIVER DETROIT SCHOLARSHIP
• *See page 295*

FORT WAYNE CHAPTER 56 SCHOLARSHIP
• *See page 297*

NORTH CENTRAL REGION 9 SCHOLARSHIP
• *See page 298*

WICHITA CHAPTER 52 SCHOLARSHIP
• *See page 298*

SOCIETY OF PLASTICS ENGINEERS (SPE) FOUNDATION

http://www.4spe.org/

FLEMING/BASZCAK SCHOLARSHIP
• *See page 169*

SOCIETY OF PLASTICS ENGINEERS SCHOLARSHIP PROGRAM
• *See page 170*

INSURANCE AND ACTUARIAL SCIENCE

THE ACTUARIAL FOUNDATION

http://www.actuarialfoundation.org/programs/actuarial/scholarships.shtml

ACTUARIAL DIVERSITY SCHOLARSHIP

This Scholarship promotes diversity through an annual scholarship program for Black/African American, Hispanic and Native North American students recognizing and encouraging academic achievements by awarding scholarships to full time undergraduate and graduate students pursuing a degree that may lead to a career in the actuarial profession.

Academic Fields/Career Goals: Insurance and Actuarial Science; Mathematics.

Award: Scholarship for use in freshman, sophomore, junior, senior, or graduate years; renewable. *Amount:* $1000–$3000.

Eligibility Requirements: Applicant must be American Indian/Alaska Native, Black (non-Hispanic), or Hispanic and enrolled or expecting to enroll full-time at a two-year or four-year institution or university. Applicant must have 3.0 GPA or higher. Available to U.S. and non-U.S. citizens.

Application Requirements: Application, essay, references, test scores, transcript. *Deadline:* May 4.

Contact: Debbie McCormac, Project Specialist
The Actuarial Foundation
475 North Martingale Road, Suite 600
Schaumburg, IL 60173-2226
Phone: 847-706-3535
Fax: 847-706-3599
E-mail: scholarships@actfnd.org

DADE COMMUNITY FOUNDATION

http://www.jackituckfield.org/

SEITLIN FRANKLIN E. WHEELER SCHOLARSHIP
• *See page 148*

D.W. SIMPSON & COMPANY

http://www.dwsimpson.com/

D.W. SIMPSON ACTUARIAL SCIENCE SCHOLARSHIP

One-time award for full-time actuarial science students. Must be entering senior year of undergraduate study in actuarial science. GPA of 3.2 or better in actuarial science and an overall GPA of 3.0 or better required.

Must have passed at least one actuarial exam and be eligible to work in the U.S. Deadlines: April 30 for fall and October 31 for spring.

Academic Fields/Career Goals: Insurance and Actuarial Science.

Award: Scholarship for use in senior year; not renewable. *Number:* up to 2. *Amount:* up to $1000.

Eligibility Requirements: Applicant must be enrolled or expecting to enroll full-time at a four-year institution or university. Applicant must have 3.0 GPA or higher. Available to U.S. citizens.

Application Requirements: Application, essay, resume, test scores. *Deadline:* varies.

Contact: Bethany Rave, Partner-Operations
D.W. Simpson & Company
1800 West Larchmont Avenue
Chicago, IL 60613
Phone: 312-867-2300
Fax: 312-951-8386
E-mail: scholarship@dwsimpson.com

MISSOURI INSURANCE EDUCATION FOUNDATION

http://www.mief.org/

MISSOURI INSURANCE EDUCATION FOUNDATION SCHOLARSHIP

One $2500 scholarship and five $2000 scholarships available to college and university students in their junior or senior year. Must be Missouri resident.

Academic Fields/Career Goals: Insurance and Actuarial Science.

Award: Scholarship for use in junior or senior years; renewable. *Number:* 6. *Amount:* $2000–$2500.

Eligibility Requirements: Applicant must be enrolled or expecting to enroll full-time at a four-year institution or university; resident of Missouri and studying in Missouri. Applicant must have 2.5 GPA or higher. Available to U.S. citizens.

Application Requirements: Application, financial need analysis, references, transcript. *Deadline:* March 31.

Contact: Amy Hamacher, Scholarship Chairman
Missouri Insurance Education Foundation
PO Box 1654
Jefferson City, MO 65102
Phone: 573-893-4234
Fax: 573-893-4996
E-mail: miis@midamerica.net

NEW ENGLAND EMPLOYEE BENEFITS COUNCIL

http://www.neebc.org/

NEW ENGLAND EMPLOYEE BENEFITS COUNCIL SCHOLARSHIP PROGRAM
• *See page 68*

SPENCER EDUCATIONAL FOUNDATION INC.

http://www.spencered.org/

SPENCER SCHOLARSHIP

Scholarship is available to outstanding applicants who are focused on a career in risk management, insurance, and related disciplines.

Academic Fields/Career Goals: Insurance and Actuarial Science.

Award: Scholarship for use in junior, senior, graduate, or postgraduate years; renewable. *Number:* 10–20. *Amount:* $5000–$10,000.

Eligibility Requirements: Applicant must be enrolled or expecting to enroll full-time at a two-year or four-year institution or university. Applicant must have 3.0 GPA or higher. Available to U.S. and non-U.S. citizens.

Application Requirements: Application, resume, references, transcript. *Deadline:* January 31.

Contact: Angela Sabatino, Secretary and Foundation Administrator
Spencer Educational Foundation Inc.
1065 Avenue of the Americas, 13th Floor
New York, NY 10018
Phone: 212-655-6223
Fax: 212-655-6044
E-mail: asabatino@rims.org

INTERIOR DESIGN

AMERICAN SOCIETY OF INTERIOR DESIGNERS (ASID) EDUCATION FOUNDATION INC.

http://www.asid.org/

ASID EDUCATIONAL FOUNDATION/YALE R. BURGE COMPETITION

Open to all students in their final years of undergraduate study enrolled in at least a three-year program of interior design. The competition is designed to encourage students to seriously plan their portfolios. Scholarship value is $750.

Academic Fields/Career Goals: Interior Design.

Award: Prize for use in senior year; not renewable. *Number:* 1. *Amount:* $750.

Eligibility Requirements: Applicant must be enrolled or expecting to enroll full-time at a four-year institution or university. Available to U.S. citizens.

Application Requirements: Application, applicant must enter a contest, portfolio. *Fee:* $10. *Deadline:* April 30.

Contact: Lisa Armstrong, Education Department
American Society of Interior Designers (ASID) Education Foundation Inc.
608 Massachusetts Avenue, NE
Washington, DC 20002-6006
Phone: 202-546-3480
Fax: 202-546-3240
E-mail: education@asid.org

ASSOCIATION FOR WOMEN IN ARCHITECTURE FOUNDATION

http://www.awa-la.org/

ASSOCIATION FOR WOMEN IN ARCHITECTURE SCHOLARSHIP
• See page 100

IFDA EDUCATIONAL FOUNDATION

http://www.ifdaef.org/

IFDA LEADERS COMMEMORATIVE SCHOLARSHIP

Scholarship available to students who have completed four courses related to the field of interior design. Award is made to a to full-time student. Applicant does not have to be IFDA student member. Applicant must submit 300 to 500 word essay explaining future plans and goals, indicating why they believe that they are deserving of this award. Decision based upon student's academic achievement, awards and accomplishments, future plans and goals, and letter of recommendation. Documents sent along with the application should be sent individually to the four judges (4 copies).

Academic Fields/Career Goals: Interior Design; Trade/Technical Specialties.

Award: Scholarship for use in sophomore or junior years; not renewable. *Number:* 1. *Amount:* $1500.

Eligibility Requirements: Applicant must be enrolled or expecting to enroll full-time at a four-year institution or university. Available to U.S. and Canadian citizens.

Application Requirements: Application, essay, references, transcript, 2 digital pictures of design work done in class. *Deadline:* March 31.

Contact: Merry Mabbett Dean, Director of Scholarships and Grants
IFDA Educational Foundation
10765 SW Canterbury Lane, #101
Tigard, OR 97224
Phone: 503-367-0151
Fax: 866-362-9107
E-mail: merrymabbettinc@comcast.net

IFDA STUDENT SCHOLARSHIP

Scholarship available to students who have completed four courses related to the field of interior design. Award of $2000 to full-time student. Applicant must be IFDA student member. Applicant must submit 300 to 500 word essay explaining why they joined IFDA, discuss future plans and goals, and indicate why they are deserving of this award. Decision based upon student's academic achievement, awards and accomplishments, future plans and goals, and letter of recommendation. Documents sent along with the application should be sent individually to the four judges (4 copies).

Academic Fields/Career Goals: Interior Design; Trade/Technical Specialties.

Award: Scholarship for use in sophomore or junior years; not renewable. *Number:* 1. *Amount:* $2000.

Eligibility Requirements: Applicant must be enrolled or expecting to enroll full-time at a four-year institution or university. Available to U.S. and non-U.S. citizens.

Application Requirements: Application, essay, references, transcript, 2 digital copies of the design work done in class. *Deadline:* March 31.

Contact: Merry Mabbett Dean, Director of Scholarships and Grants
IFDA Educational Foundation
10765 SW Canterbury Lane, #101
Tigard, OR 97224
Phone: 503-367-0151
Fax: 866-362-9107
E-mail: merrymabbettinc@comcast.net

ILLUMINATING ENGINEERING SOCIETY OF NORTH AMERICA

http://www.iesna.org/

ROBERT W. THUNEN MEMORIAL SCHOLARSHIPS
• See page 101

ILLUMINATING ENGINEERING SOCIETY OF NORTH AMERICA–GOLDEN GATE SECTION

http://www.iesgg.org/

ALAN LUCAS MEMORIAL EDUCATIONAL SCHOLARSHIP
• See page 102

INTERNATIONAL FACILITY MANAGEMENT ASSOCIATION FOUNDATION

http://www.ifmafoundation.org/

IFMA FOUNDATION SCHOLARSHIPS
• See page 102

INTERNATIONAL INTERIOR DESIGN ASSOCIATION (IIDA) FOUNDATION

http://www.iida.org/

KIMBALL OFFICE SCHOLARSHIP FUND

Three-year program that will award $5000 to a senior year student pursuing a degree in interior design. Deadline varies.

Academic Fields/Career Goals: Interior Design.

Award: Scholarship for use in senior year; not renewable. *Number:* 1. *Amount:* $5000.

Eligibility Requirements: Applicant must be enrolled or expecting to enroll full- or part-time at a four-year institution or university. Available to U.S. citizens.

Application Requirements: Application, resume. *Deadline:* varies.

Contact: Jocelyn Pysarchuk, Senior Director, Communications and Marketing
International Interior Design Association (IIDA) Foundation
222 Merchandise Mart Plaza
Chicago, IL 60654-1104
Phone: 312-467-1950
Fax: 312-467-0779
E-mail: jpysarchuk@iida.org

MINNESOTA COMMUNITY FOUNDATION

http://www.mncommunityfoundation.org/

ASID MINNESOTA CHAPTER SCHOLARSHIP FUND

Scholarship to students enrolled full-time or part-time in the upper division (junior or senior year) of a four year Interior Design program at: University of Minnesota, South Dakota State University, North Dakota State University or University of Wisconsin during the upcoming academic year.

Academic Fields/Career Goals: Interior Design.

Award: Scholarship for use in junior or senior years; renewable. *Number:* 1. *Amount:* $2000.

Eligibility Requirements: Applicant must be enrolled or expecting to enroll full- or part-time at a four-year institution or university and studying in Minnesota, North Dakota, South Dakota, or Wisconsin. Applicant must have 3.0 GPA or higher. Available to U.S. citizens.

Application Requirements: Application, portfolio, references, transcript. *Deadline:* April 18.

Contact: Donna Paulson, Administrative Assistant
Minnesota Community Foundation
55 Fifth Street East, Suite 600
St. Paul, MN 55101-1797
Phone: 651-325-4212
Fax: 651-224-9502
E-mail: dkp@mncommunityfoundation.org

NATIONAL ASSOCIATION OF WOMEN IN CONSTRUCTION

http://www.nawic.org/

NAWIC UNDERGRADUATE SCHOLARSHIPS
• *See page 102*

NEW YORK STATE EDUCATION DEPARTMENT

http://www.highered.nysed.gov/

REGENTS PROFESSIONAL OPPORTUNITY SCHOLARSHIP
• *See page 69*

SOUTH DAKOTA RETAILERS ASSOCIATION

http://www.sdra.org/

SOUTH DAKOTA RETAILERS ASSOCIATION SCHOLARSHIP PROGRAM
• *See page 71*

TURNER CONSTRUCTION COMPANY

http://www.turnerconstruction.com/

YOUTHFORCE 2020 SCHOLARSHIP PROGRAM
• *See page 103*

INTERNATIONAL STUDIES

ARMED FORCES COMMUNICATIONS AND ELECTRONICS ASSOCIATION, EDUCATIONAL FOUNDATION

http://www.afcea.org/education/scholarships

ARMED FORCES COMMUNICATIONS AND ELECTRONICS ASSOCIATION GENERAL EMMETT PAIGE SCHOLARSHIP
• *See page 122*

ARMED FORCES COMMUNICATIONS AND ELECTRONICS ASSOCIATION GENERAL JOHN A. WICKHAM SCHOLARSHIP
• *See page 164*

ARMED FORCES COMMUNICATIONS AND ELECTRONICS ASSOCIATION ROTC SCHOLARSHIP PROGRAM
• *See page 122*

ARRL FOUNDATION INC.

http://www.arrl.org/

DONALD RIEBHOFF MEMORIAL SCHOLARSHIP

One $1000 award available to students with a technician or higher class license for radio operation. Must be pursuing a baccalaureate or higher degree in international studies at any accredited institution above the high school level. Must be an ARRL member.

Academic Fields/Career Goals: International Studies.

Award: Scholarship for use in freshman, sophomore, junior, senior, or graduate years; not renewable. *Number:* 1. *Amount:* $1000.

Eligibility Requirements: Applicant must be enrolled or expecting to enroll full-time at a four-year institution or university and must have an interest in amateur radio. Applicant or parent of applicant must be member of American Radio Relay League. Available to U.S. citizens.

Application Requirements: Application, transcript. *Deadline:* February 1.

Contact: Ms. Mary Hobart, Secretary
ARRL Foundation Inc.
225 Main Street
Newington, CT 06111-1494
Phone: 860-594-0397
E-mail: k1mmh@arrl.org

CENTRAL INTELLIGENCE AGENCY

http://www.cia.gov/

CENTRAL INTELLIGENCE AGENCY UNDERGRADUATE SCHOLARSHIP PROGRAM
• *See page 58*

CONNECTICUT COMMUNITY FOUNDATION

http://www.conncf.org/

MALCOLM BALDRIGE SCHOLARSHIP

• *See page 148*

JORGE MAS CANOSA FREEDOM FOUNDATION

http://www.jorgemascanosa.org/

MAS FAMILY SCHOLARSHIP AWARD

• *See page 152*

NATIONAL SECURITY EDUCATION PROGRAM

http://www.iie.org/

NATIONAL SECURITY EDUCATION PROGRAM (NSEP) DAVID L. BOREN UNDERGRADUATE SCHOLARSHIPS

• *See page 154*

PHI ALPHA THETA HISTORY HONOR SOCIETY, INC.

http://www.phialphatheta.org/

PHI ALPHA THETA WORLD HISTORY ASSOCIATION PAPER PRIZE

• *See page 354*

UNITED STATES INSTITUTE OF PEACE

http://www.usip.org/

NATIONAL PEACE ESSAY CONTEST

Essay contest designed to have students research and write about international peace and conflict resolution. Topic changes yearly. State winners are awarded $1000 and invited to Washington, D.C. for the national awards program. Must be enrolled in a U.S. high school, home school, or be a U.S. citizen enrolled in a high school abroad.

Academic Fields/Career Goals: International Studies; Peace and Conflict Studies.

Award: Scholarship for use in freshman year; not renewable. *Number:* 50–53. *Amount:* $1000–$10,000.

Eligibility Requirements: Applicant must be high school student; planning to enroll or expecting to enroll full-time at a two-year or four-year institution or university and must have an interest in writing. Available to U.S. citizens.

Application Requirements: Application, essay, bibliography. *Deadline:* February 1.

Contact: Contest Coordinator
United States Institute of Peace
2301 Constitution Avenue NW
Washington, DC 20037
Phone: 202-429-7178
Fax: 202-833-2108
E-mail: essaycontest@usip.org

JOURNALISM

ADC RESEARCH INSTITUTE

http://www.adc.org/

JACK SHAHEEN MASS COMMUNICATIONS SCHOLARSHIP AWARD

• *See page 181*

AMERICAN COPY EDITORS SOCIETY

http://www.copydesk.org/

ACES COPY EDITING SCHOLARSHIP

Several $2500 scholarships awarded each year. Students not chosen as an Aubespin scholar are automatically eligible for ACES' other awards of $1000 each. Open to undergraduate students entering their junior or senior year, graduate students, and graduating students who will take full-time copy editing jobs or internships.

Academic Fields/Career Goals: Journalism.

Award: Scholarship for use in junior, senior, or graduate years; not renewable. *Number:* varies. *Amount:* $1000–$2500.

Eligibility Requirements: Applicant must be enrolled or expecting to enroll full-time at a four-year institution or university and must have an interest in writing. Applicant must have 2.5 GPA or higher. Available to U.S. citizens.

Application Requirements: Application, applicant must enter a contest, essay, references, list of course work relevant to copy editing, copy of a story edited by the applicant, copies of five to ten headlines. *Deadline:* November 15.

Contact: Kathy Schenck, Assistant Managing Editor
American Copy Editors Society
Milwaukee Journal Sentinel, 333 West State Street
Milwaukee, WI 53203
Phone: 414-224-2237

AMERICAN INSTITUTE OF POLISH CULTURE INC.

http://www.ampolinstitute.org/

HARRIET IRSAY SCHOLARSHIP GRANT

• *See page 109*

AMERICAN LEGION PRESS CLUB OF NEW JERSEY

http://www.alpcnj.org/

AMERICAN LEGION PRESS CLUB OF NEW JERSEY AND POST 170 ARTHUR DEHARDT MEMORIAL SCHOLARSHIP

• *See page 182*

AMERICAN QUARTER HORSE FOUNDATION (AQHF)

http://www.aqha.com/foundation

AQHF JOURNALISM OR COMMUNICATIONS SCHOLARSHIP

• *See page 182*

ARAB AMERICAN INSTITUTE FOUNDATION

http://www.aaiusa.org/

AL-MUAMMAR SCHOLARSHIP FOR JOURNALISM

Four scholarship grants of $5000 each to eligible Arab American college students who are majoring in journalism, as well as college seniors who have been accepted to a graduate journalism school.

Academic Fields/Career Goals: Journalism.

Award: Scholarship for use in sophomore, junior, senior, graduate, or postgraduate years; not renewable. *Number:* 1–4. *Amount:* $5000.

Eligibility Requirements: Applicant must be of Arab heritage and enrolled or expecting to enroll full- or part-time at a two-year or four-year institution or university. Available to U.S. citizens.

Application Requirements: Application, essay, portfolio, resume, transcript. *Deadline:* March 14.

Contact: Sabeen Altaf, Program Manager
Arab American Institute Foundation
1600 K Street NW, Suite 601
Washington, DC 20006
Phone: 202-429-9210
Fax: 202-429-9214
E-mail: saltaf@aaiusa.org

ARRL FOUNDATION INC.

http://www.arrl.org/

FRANCIS WALTON MEMORIAL SCHOLARSHIP
• *See page 83*

PHD ARA SCHOLARSHIP
• *See page 196*

ASIAN AMERICAN JOURNALISTS ASSOCIATION

http://www.aaja.org/

AAJA/COX FOUNDATION SCHOLARSHIP

Award of up to $1250 to full-time students pursuing careers in print, broadcast, or photo journalism. Must maintain an minimum GPA of 2.5.

Academic Fields/Career Goals: Journalism; TV/Radio Broadcasting.

Award: Scholarship for use in freshman, sophomore, junior, senior, or graduate years; not renewable. *Number:* varies. *Amount:* $1250.

Eligibility Requirements: Applicant must be Asian/Pacific Islander and enrolled or expecting to enroll full-time at a two-year or four-year or technical institution or university. Applicant must have 2.5 GPA or higher. Available to U.S. and non-U.S. citizens.

Application Requirements: Application, essay, financial need analysis, resume, references, transcript. *Deadline:* March 28.

Contact: Kim Mizuhara, Program Coordinator
Asian American Journalists Association
1182 Market Street, Suite 320
San Francisco, CA 94102
Phone: 415-346-2051 Ext. 102
Fax: 415-346-6343
E-mail: programs@aaja.org

ASIAN-AMERICAN JOURNALISTS ASSOCIATION SCHOLARSHIP
• *See page 183*

MARY MOY QUAN ING MEMORIAL SCHOLARSHIP AWARD

One-time award of up to $2000 for a deserving high school senior for undergraduate study. Must intend to pursue a journalism career and must show a commitment to the Asian-American community. Visit web site http://www.aaja.org for application and details.

Academic Fields/Career Goals: Journalism.

Award: Scholarship for use in freshman year; not renewable. *Number:* 1. *Amount:* up to $2000.

Eligibility Requirements: Applicant must be Asian/Pacific Islander; high school student and planning to enroll or expecting to enroll full-time at a two-year or four-year institution. Available to U.S. and non-U.S. citizens.

Application Requirements: Application, essay, financial need analysis, resume, references, transcript. *Deadline:* March 28.

Contact: Kim Mizuhara, Programs Coordinator
Asian American Journalists Association
1182 Market Street, Suite 320
San Francisco, CA 94102
Phone: 415-346-2051 Ext. 102
Fax: 415-346-6343
E-mail: programs@aaja.org

MINORU YASUI MEMORIAL SCHOLARSHIP AWARD

One-time award of $2000 for a promising Asian undergraduate male who will pursue a broadcasting career. For use at an accredited two- or four-year institution. Visit web site http://www.aaja.org for application and details.

Academic Fields/Career Goals: Journalism; TV/Radio Broadcasting.

Award: Scholarship for use in freshman, sophomore, junior, or senior years; not renewable. *Number:* 1. *Amount:* $2000.

Eligibility Requirements: Applicant must be Asian/Pacific Islander; enrolled or expecting to enroll full-time at a two-year or four-year institution or university and male. Available to U.S. and non-U.S. citizens.

Application Requirements: Application, essay, financial need analysis, resume, references, transcript. *Deadline:* March 28.

Contact: Kim Mizuhara, Programs Coordinator
Asian American Journalists Association
1182 Market Street, Suite 320
San Francisco, CA 94102
Phone: 415-346-2051 Ext. 102
Fax: 415-346-6343
E-mail: programs@aaja.org

NATIONAL ASIAN-AMERICAN JOURNALISTS ASSOCIATION NEWHOUSE SCHOLARSHIP

Awards up to $5000 for high school seniors and college students who plan to or are currently enrolled in a journalism program at any two- or four-year postsecondary institution. Scholarship awardees will be eligible for summer internships with a Newhouse publication. Applicants from underrepresented Asian Pacific American groups including Vietnamese, Hmong, Cambodians, and other Southeast Asians, South Asians, and Pacific Islanders are especially encouraged. Visit web site http://www.aaja.org for application and details.

Academic Fields/Career Goals: Journalism.

Award: Scholarship for use in freshman, sophomore, junior, or senior years; not renewable. *Number:* 5. *Amount:* $1000–$5000.

Eligibility Requirements: Applicant must be enrolled or expecting to enroll full-time at a two-year or four-year institution or university. Applicant must have 2.5 GPA or higher. Available to U.S. and non-U.S. citizens.

Application Requirements: Application, essay, financial need analysis, resume, references, transcript. *Deadline:* March 28.

Contact: Kim Mizuhara, Programs Coordinator
Asian American Journalists Association
1182 Market Street, Suite 320
San Francisco, CA 94102
Phone: 415-346-2051 Ext. 102
Fax: 415-346-6343
E-mail: programs@aaja.org

VINCENT CHIN MEMORIAL SCHOLARSHIP

$5000 award to a journalism student committed to keeping Vincent Chin's memory alive. Minimum GPA of 2.5.

Academic Fields/Career Goals: Journalism.

Award: Scholarship for use in freshman, sophomore, junior, senior, or graduate years; not renewable. *Number:* 1. *Amount:* up to $5000.

Eligibility Requirements: Applicant must be Asian/Pacific Islander and enrolled or expecting to enroll full-time at a two-year or four-year or technical institution or university. Applicant must have 2.5 GPA or higher. Available to U.S. and non-U.S. citizens.

Application Requirements: Application, essay, financial need analysis, resume, references, transcript, work samples. *Deadline:* March 28.

Contact: Kim Mizuhara, Program Coordinator
Asian American Journalists Association
1182 Market Street, Suite 320
San Francisco, CA 94102
Phone: 415-346-2051 Ext. 102
Fax: 415-346-6343
E-mail: programs@aaja.org

ASIAN AMERICAN JOURNALISTS ASSOCIATION (SEATTLE CHAPTER)

http://www.aajaseattle.org/

NORTHWEST JOURNALISTS OF COLOR SCHOLARSHIP

One-time award for Washington state high school and college students seeking careers in journalism. Must be an undergraduate enrolled in an accredited college or university or a senior in high school. Must be Asian-American, African-American, Native-American, or Latino.

Academic Fields/Career Goals: Journalism.

Award: Scholarship for use in freshman, sophomore, junior, or senior years; not renewable. *Number:* 1–4. *Amount:* $500–$2500.

Eligibility Requirements: Applicant must be American Indian/Alaska Native, Asian/Pacific Islander, Black (non-Hispanic), or Hispanic; enrolled or expecting to enroll full-time at a two-year or four-year or technical institution or university and resident of Washington. Available to U.S. citizens.

Application Requirements: Application, essay, financial need analysis, references, transcript, work samples. *Deadline:* May 1.

Contact: Ms. Mai Hoang, AAJA Chapter Treasurer
Asian American Journalists Association (Seattle chapter)
Yakima Herald&-Republic, 114 North Fourth Street
Yakima, WA 98909
Phone: 509-577-7724
E-mail: mhoang@yakimaherald.com

ASSOCIATED PRESS

http://www.aptra.org/

ASSOCIATED PRESS TELEVISION/RADIO ASSOCIATION-CLETE ROBERTS JOURNALISM SCHOLARSHIP AWARDS

Award for college undergraduates and graduate students studying in California, Nevada or Hawaii and pursuing careers in broadcast journalism. Submit application, references, and examples of broadcast-related work.

Academic Fields/Career Goals: Journalism; TV/Radio Broadcasting.

Award: Scholarship for use in freshman, sophomore, junior, or senior years; not renewable. *Number:* 3. *Amount:* $1500.

Eligibility Requirements: Applicant must be enrolled or expecting to enroll full-time at a two-year or four-year institution or university and studying in California, Hawaii, or Nevada. Available to U.S. citizens.

Application Requirements: Application, references. *Deadline:* December 14.

Contact: Roberta Gonzales, Scholarship Committee
Associated Press
CBS 5 TV, 855 Battery Street
San Francisco, CA 94111

KATHRYN DETTMAN MEMORIAL JOURNALISM SCHOLARSHIP

One-time award of $1500 for broadcast journalism students, enrolled at a California, Hawaii or Nevada college or university. Must submit entry form and examples of broadcast-related work.

Academic Fields/Career Goals: Journalism; TV/Radio Broadcasting.

Award: Scholarship for use in freshman, sophomore, junior, or senior years; renewable. *Number:* 1–4. *Amount:* $1500.

Eligibility Requirements: Applicant must be enrolled or expecting to enroll full-time at a two-year or four-year institution or university and studying in California, Hawaii, or Nevada. Available to U.S. citizens.

Application Requirements: Application, examples of broadcast-related work. *Deadline:* December 14.

Contact: Roberta Gonzales, Scholarship Committee
Associated Press
CBS 5 TV, 855 Battery Street
San Francisco, CA 94111

ASSOCIATION FOR WOMEN IN COMMUNICATIONS-SEATTLE PROFESSIONAL CHAPTER

http://www.seattleawc.org/

SEATTLE PROFESSIONAL CHAPTER OF THE ASSOCIATION FOR WOMEN IN COMMUNICATIONS

Scholarship of $3000 for women pursuing journalism in the state of Washington. For more details on eligibility criteria or selection procedure, refer to web site http://www.seattleawc.org/scholarships.html.

Academic Fields/Career Goals: Journalism.

Award: Scholarship for use in sophomore, junior, or senior years; not renewable. *Number:* 2. *Amount:* $3000.

Eligibility Requirements: Applicant must be enrolled or expecting to enroll full-time at a two-year or four-year or technical institution or university; female; resident of Washington and studying in Washington. Available to U.S. citizens.

Application Requirements: Application, resume, transcript, sample of work, cover letter. *Deadline:* March 16.

Contact: Jaron Snow, Office Administrator
Association for Women in Communications-Seattle
Professional Chapter
PO Box 472
Mountlake Terrace, WA 98043
Phone: 425-771-4189
E-mail: awcseattle@verizon.net

ATLANTA PRESS CLUB INC.

http://www.atlantapressclub.org/

ATLANTA PRESS CLUB JOURNALISM SCHOLARSHIP PROGRAM

Awards outstanding Georgia college or university sophomores, juniors, and seniors who are pursuing careers in journalism. Must attend an interview with the selection committee. Must be a U.S. citizen.

Academic Fields/Career Goals: Journalism; TV/Radio Broadcasting.

Award: Scholarship for use in sophomore, junior, or senior years; not renewable. *Number:* 4. *Amount:* $1500.

Eligibility Requirements: Applicant must be enrolled or expecting to enroll full- or part-time at a four-year institution or university; resident of Georgia; studying in Georgia and must have an interest in writing. Available to U.S. citizens.

Application Requirements: Application, essay, interview, portfolio, transcript, clips/tapes/CD. *Deadline:* February 15.

Contact: Elaine Hudson, Assistant Director, Scholarship Committee
Atlanta Press Club Inc.
34 Broad Street, 18th Floor
Atlanta, GA 30303
Phone: 404-577-7377
Fax: 404-223-3706
E-mail: ehudson@atlpressclub.org

BAY AREA BLACK JOURNALISTS ASSOCIATION SCHOLARSHIP CONTEST

http://www.babja.org/

YOUNG JOURNALISTS SCHOLARSHIP

Nonrenewable scholarship of $2500 open to photojournalism students. Applicant must be enrolled in any college or university nationwide. Must be studying journalism (television, radio, print, online).

Academic Fields/Career Goals: Journalism; Photojournalism/Photography.

Award: Scholarship for use in freshman, sophomore, junior, senior, or graduate years; not renewable. *Number:* varies. *Amount:* $2500.

Eligibility Requirements: Applicant must be enrolled or expecting to enroll full- or part-time at a four-year institution or university. Available to U.S. citizens.

Application Requirements: Application, essay, resume, references, transcript, work samples. *Deadline:* October 2.

Contact: Scholarship Committee
Bay Area Black Journalists Association Scholarship Contest
1714 Franklin Street, Suite 100-260
Oakland, CA 94612
Phone: 510-986-9390
Fax: 510-382-1980
E-mail: info@babja.org

CANADIAN PRESS

http://www.thecanadianpress.com/

GIL PURCELL MEMORIAL JOURNALISM SCHOLARSHIP FOR NATIVE CANADIANS

Scholarship is designed to encourage native Canadian students to enter the field of journalism in Canada. Awards aboriginal Canadians (status or non-status Indian, Metis, or Inuit) who are pursuing postsecondary studies and intend to work in the field of journalism.

Academic Fields/Career Goals: Journalism.

Award: Scholarship for use in freshman, sophomore, junior, or senior years; not renewable. *Number:* 1. *Amount:* $4000.

Eligibility Requirements: Applicant must be of Canadian heritage and Canadian citizen; American Indian/Alaska Native and enrolled or expecting to enroll full- or part-time at a four-year institution or university.

Application Requirements: Application, resume. *Deadline:* November 15.

Contact: Marissa D'Mello, Human Resources Coordinator
Canadian Press
36 King Street East
Toronto, ON M5C 2L9

CCNMA: LATINO JOURNALISTS OF CALIFORNIA

http://www.ccnma.org/

CCNMA SCHOLARSHIPS

Scholarships for Latinos interested in pursuing a career in journalism. Awards based on scholastic achievement, financial need, and community awareness. Submit sample of work. Award limited to California residents or those attending school in California.

Academic Fields/Career Goals: Journalism; Photojournalism/Photography; TV/Radio Broadcasting.

Award: Scholarship for use in freshman, sophomore, junior, senior, or graduate years; not renewable. *Number:* 5–10. *Amount:* $500–$1000.

Eligibility Requirements: Applicant must be of Latin American/Caribbean heritage; Hispanic; enrolled or expecting to enroll full-time at a two-year or four-year or technical institution or university and resident of California. Available to U.S. citizens.

Application Requirements: Application, applicant must enter a contest, essay, financial need analysis, interview, portfolio, resume, references, transcript. *Deadline:* April 1.

Contact: Julio Moran, Executive Director
CCNMA: Latino Journalists of California
727 W. 27th Street, Room 201
Los Angeles, CA 90007-3212
Phone: 213-821-0075
Fax: 213-743-1838
E-mail: ccnmainfo@ccnma.org

CIRI FOUNDATION (TCF)

http://www.thecirifoundation.org/

CAP LATHROP SCHOLARSHIP PROGRAM
• *See page 147*

CLEVELAND SCHOLARSHIP PROGRAMS

http://www.cspohio.org/

CSP MANAGED FUNDS-CLEVELAND BROWNS MARION MOTLEY SCHOLARSHIP
• *See page 58*

CONNECTICUT CHAPTER OF SOCIETY OF PROFESSIONAL JOURNALISTS

http://www.ctspj.org/

CONNECTICUT SPJ BOB EDDY SCHOLARSHIP PROGRAM
• *See page 184*

CUBAN AMERICAN NATIONAL FOUNDATION

http://www.masscholarships.org/

MAS FAMILY SCHOLARSHIPS
• *See page 148*

DADE COMMUNITY FOUNDATION

http://www.jackituckfield.org/

LEO SUAREZ SCHOLARSHIP
• *See page 184*

DAIRY MANAGEMENT

http://www.dairyinfo.com/

NATIONAL DAIRY PROMOTION AND RESEARCH BOARD SCHOLARSHIP
• *See page 84*

DOW JONES NEWS FUND, INC.

https://www.newsfund.org/

DOW JONES NEWS FUND HIGH SCHOOL JOURNALISM WORKSHOPS WRITING, PHOTOGRAPHY AND MULTIMEDIA COMPETITION

Participants in DJNF summer workshops are nominated for writing, multimedia and photography awards based on their published work. Scholarships are presented to the best writers, digital producers and photographers to pursue media careers.

Academic Fields/Career Goals: Journalism.

Award: Scholarship for use in freshman year; not renewable. *Number:* 8. *Amount:* up to $1000.

Eligibility Requirements: Applicant must be high school student and planning to enroll or expecting to enroll full-time at a four-year institution or university. Available to U.S. and non-U.S. citizens.

Application Requirements: Application, applicant must enter a contest, essay, portfolio, references. *Deadline:* October 1.

Contact: Mrs. Linda Shockley, Deputy Director
Dow Jones News Fund, Inc.
PO Box 300
Princeton, NJ 08543-0300
Phone: 609-452-2820
Fax: 609-520-5804
E-mail: djnf@dowjones.com

FISHER BROADCASTING COMPANY

http://www.fsci.com/

FISHER BROADCASTING INC. SCHOLARSHIP FOR MINORITIES
• *See page 150*

FLORIDA SOCIETY OF NEWSPAPER EDITORS-SCHOLARSHIP COMMITTEE

http://www.fsne.org/minorityscholar.html

FLORIDA SOCIETY OF NEWSPAPER EDITORS MINORITY SCHOLARSHIP PROGRAM
• *See page 185*

FLORIDA SOCIETY OF NEWSPAPER EDITORS MULTIMEDIA SCHOLARSHIP
• *See page 185*

FREEDOM FORUM

http://www.freedomforum.org/

AL NEUHARTH FREE SPIRIT SCHOLARSHIP AND JOURNALISM CONFERENCE PROGRAM

One-time award for high school seniors interested in pursuing a career in journalism. Must be actively involved in high school journalism and demonstrate qualities such as being a visionary, an innovative leader, an entrepreneur or a courageous achiever. Scholars come to Washington D.C. to receive their awards and participate in an all-expense paid journalism conference. See web site at http://www.freedomforum.org/free-spirit for further information.

Academic Fields/Career Goals: Journalism.

Award: Scholarship for use in freshman year; not renewable. *Number:* up to 102. *Amount:* $1000.

Eligibility Requirements: Applicant must be high school student; planning to enroll or expecting to enroll full-time at a four-year institution and must have an interest in entrepreneurship, leadership, or writing. Available to U.S. citizens.

Application Requirements: Application, essay, photo, references, transcript, sample of journalistic work. *Deadline:* October 15.

Contact: Diana Leckie, Program Manager/Free Spirit
Freedom Forum
555 Pennsylvania Avenue, NW
Washington, DC 20001
Phone: 202-292-6100
Fax: 202-292-6265
E-mail: freespirit@freedomforum.org

CHIPS QUINN SCHOLARS PROGRAM

One-time award for college juniors, seniors or recent graduates. Open to students with an interest in print/online journalism as a career. Award provides paid internship. Applicants may be nominated by their schools, by newspaper editors or by direct application with supporting letters of endorsement. See web site at http://www.freedomforumdiversity.org or http://www.chipsquinn.org for further information.

Academic Fields/Career Goals: Journalism.

Award: Scholarship for use in junior or senior years; not renewable. *Number:* 30–40. *Amount:* $500.

Eligibility Requirements: Applicant must be American Indian/Alaska Native, Asian/Pacific Islander, Black (non-Hispanic), or Hispanic and enrolled or expecting to enroll full-time at a four-year institution or university. Available to U.S. citizens.

Application Requirements: Application, essay, photo, portfolio, resume, references, transcript. *Deadline:* October 15.

Contact: Karen Catone, Director
Freedom Forum
555 Pennsylvania Avenue, NW
Washington, DC 20001
Phone: 202-292-6271
Fax: 202-292-6275
E-mail: kcatone@freedomforum.org

GEORGIA PRESS EDUCATIONAL FOUNDATION INC.

http://www.gapress.org/

DURWOOD MCALISTER SCHOLARSHIP

Scholarship awarded annually to an outstanding student majoring in print journalism at a Georgia college or university.

Academic Fields/Career Goals: Journalism.

Award: Scholarship for use in freshman, sophomore, junior, senior, graduate, or postgraduate years; not renewable. *Number:* 1. *Amount:* $500–$1500.

Eligibility Requirements: Applicant must be enrolled or expecting to enroll full-time at a two-year or four-year or technical institution or university; resident of Georgia and must have an interest in writing. Available to U.S. citizens.

Application Requirements: Application, essay, photo, references, transcript. *Deadline:* February 1.

Contact: Jenifer Farmer, Manager
Georgia Press Educational Foundation Inc.
3066 Mercer University Drive, Suite 200
Atlanta, GA 30341-4137
Phone: 770-454-6776
Fax: 770-454-6778

GEORGIA PRESS EDUCATIONAL FOUNDATION SCHOLARSHIPS

One-time awards to Georgia high school seniors and college undergraduates. Based on prior interest in newspaper journalism. Must be recommended by high school counselor, professor, and/or Georgia Press Educational Foundation member. Must reside and attend school in Georgia.

Academic Fields/Career Goals: Journalism.

Award: Scholarship for use in freshman, sophomore, junior, or senior years; not renewable. *Number:* 16. *Amount:* $500–$1500.

Eligibility Requirements: Applicant must be enrolled or expecting to enroll full-time at a two-year or four-year institution or university; resident of Georgia; studying in Georgia and must have an interest in writing. Available to U.S. citizens.

Application Requirements: Application, financial need analysis, photo, references, test scores, transcript. *Deadline:* February 1.

Contact: Jenifer Farmer, Manager
Georgia Press Educational Foundation Inc.
3066 Mercer University Drive, Suite 200
Atlanta, GA 30341-4137
Phone: 770-454-6776
Fax: 770-454-6778

KIRK SUTLIVE SCHOLARSHIP

Scholarship awarded annually to a junior or senior majoring in either the news-editorial or public relations sequence.

Academic Fields/Career Goals: Journalism.

Award: Scholarship for use in junior or senior years; not renewable. *Number:* 1. *Amount:* $500–$1500.

Eligibility Requirements: Applicant must be enrolled or expecting to enroll full-time at a four-year institution or university. Available to U.S. citizens.

Application Requirements: Application, essay, financial need analysis, photo, transcript. *Deadline:* February 1.

Contact: Jenifer Farmer, Manager
Georgia Press Educational Foundation Inc.
3066 Mercer University Drive, Suite 200
Atlanta, GA 30341-4137
Phone: 770-454-6776
Fax: 770-454-6778

MORRIS NEWSPAPER CORPORATION SCHOLARSHIP

Scholarship awarded annually to an outstanding print journalism student. Applications are submitted through newspapers in the Morris Newspaper Corporation chain and recipients are named by the Foundation.

Academic Fields/Career Goals: Journalism.

Award: Scholarship for use in freshman, sophomore, junior, or senior years; not renewable. *Number:* 1. *Amount:* $500–$1500.

Eligibility Requirements: Applicant must be enrolled or expecting to enroll full-time at a four-year or technical institution or university; resident of Georgia and must have an interest in writing. Available to U.S. citizens.

Application Requirements: Application, essay, photo, references, transcript. *Deadline:* February 1.

Contact: Jenifer Farmer, Manager
Georgia Press Educational Foundation Inc.
3066 Mercer University Drive, Suite 200
Atlanta, GA 30341-4137
Phone: 770-454-6776
Fax: 770-454-6778

WILLIAM C. ROGERS SCHOLARSHIP

Scholarship awarded to a junior or senior majoring in the news-editorial sequence. For full-time study only. Must be a resident of Georgia.

Academic Fields/Career Goals: Journalism.

Award: Scholarship for use in junior or senior years; not renewable. *Number:* 1. *Amount:* $500–$1500.

Eligibility Requirements: Applicant must be enrolled or expecting to enroll full-time at a four-year institution or university; resident of Georgia and must have an interest in writing. Available to U.S. citizens.

Application Requirements: Application, essay, photo, references, transcript. *Deadline:* February 1.

Contact: Jenifer Farmer, Manager
Georgia Press Educational Foundation Inc.
3066 Mercer University Drive, Suite 200
Atlanta, GA 30341-4137
Phone: 770-454-6776
Fax: 770-454-6778

GREAT LAKES COMMISSION

http://www.glc.org/

CAROL A. RATZA MEMORIAL SCHOLARSHIP
• *See page 185*

IDAHO STATE BROADCASTERS ASSOCIATION

http://www.idahobroadcasters.org/

WAYNE C. CORNILS MEMORIAL SCHOLARSHIP
• *See page 151*

INDIANA BROADCASTERS ASSOCIATION

http://www.indianabroadcasters.org/

INDIANA BROADCASTERS FOUNDATION SCHOLARSHIP

Awards a student majoring in broadcasting, electronic media, or journalism. Must maintain a 3.0 GPA and be a resident of Indiana. One-time award for full-time undergraduate study in Indiana.

Academic Fields/Career Goals: Journalism; TV/Radio Broadcasting.

Award: Scholarship for use in freshman, sophomore, junior, or senior years; not renewable. *Number:* up to 10. *Amount:* $500–$2000.

Eligibility Requirements: Applicant must be enrolled or expecting to enroll full-time at a two-year or four-year or technical institution or university; resident of Indiana and studying in Indiana. Applicant must have 3.0 GPA or higher. Available to U.S. citizens.

Application Requirements: Application, essay, references, transcript. *Deadline:* March 4.

Contact: Gwen C. Piening, Scholarship Administrator
Indiana Broadcasters Association
3003 East 98th Street, Suite 161
Indianapolis, IN 46280
Phone: 317-573-0119
Fax: 317-573-0895
E-mail: indba@aol.com

INTERNATIONAL FOODSERVICE EDITORIAL COUNCIL

http://www.ifeconline.com/

INTERNATIONAL FOODSERVICE EDITORIAL COUNCIL COMMUNICATIONS SCHOLARSHIP
• *See page 77*

JAPANESE AMERICAN CITIZENS LEAGUE (JACL)

http://www.jacl.org/

NATIONAL JACL HEADQUARTERS SCHOLARSHIP
• *See page 84*

JOHN BAYLISS BROADCAST FOUNDATION

http://www.baylissfoundation.org/

JOHN BAYLISS BROADCAST RADIO SCHOLARSHIP
• *See page 186*

JORGE MAS CANOSA FREEDOM FOUNDATION

http://www.jorgemascanosa.org/

MAS FAMILY SCHOLARSHIP AWARD
• *See page 152*

JOURNALISM EDUCATION ASSOCIATION

http://www.jea.org/

NATIONAL HIGH SCHOOL JOURNALIST OF THE YEAR/ SISTER RITA JEANNE SCHOLARSHIPS
• *See page 186*

KATU THOMAS R. DARGAN MINORITY SCHOLARSHIP

http://www.katu.com/

THOMAS R. DARGAN MINORITY SCHOLARSHIP
• *See page 186*

LIN TELEVISION CORPORATION

http://www.lintv.com/

LINTV MINORITY SCHOLARSHIP

Scholarship to help educate and train outstanding minority candidates who seek to enter the television broadcast field. Minimum 3.0 cumulative GPA required. Must have declared major in journalism or related broadcast field at an accredited university or college. Must be a sophomore or have completed sufficient semester hours or similar educational units to be within two years of receiving a bachelor's degree.

Academic Fields/Career Goals: Journalism; TV/Radio Broadcasting.

Award: Scholarship for use in sophomore year; not renewable. *Number:* 1. *Amount:* varies.

Eligibility Requirements: Applicant must be American Indian/Alaska Native, Asian/Pacific Islander, Black (non-Hispanic), or Hispanic and enrolled or expecting to enroll full-time at a two-year or four-year institution or university. Applicant must have 3.0 GPA or higher. Available to U.S. citizens.

Application Requirements: Application, transcript. *Deadline:* March 15.

Contact: Don Donohue, Director, Human Resources
Lin Television Corporation
One Richmond Square, Suite 230E
Providence, RI 02906
Phone: 401-457-9402
E-mail: dan.donohue@lintv.com

MARYLAND/DELAWARE/DISTRICT OF COLUMBIA PRESS FOUNDATION

http://www.mddcpress.com/

MICHAEL J. POWELL HIGH SCHOOL JOURNALIST OF THE YEAR

Scholarship of $1500 to an outstanding high school student. Applicant must submit five samples of work, mounted on unlined paper, a letter of recommendation from the nominee's advisor, an autobiography geared to the publication activities in which the nominee participated, and the nominee should write a paragraph or two on the most important aspect of scholastic journalism.

Academic Fields/Career Goals: Journalism.

Award: Scholarship for use in freshman year; not renewable. *Number:* 1. *Amount:* $1500.

Eligibility Requirements: Applicant must be high school student; planning to enroll or expecting to enroll full- or part-time at a four-year institution or university and must have an interest in writing. Available to U.S. citizens.

Application Requirements: Application, applicant must enter a contest, driver's license, references, five sample articles. *Deadline:* January 31.

Contact: Jennifer Thornberry, Administration Associate Coordinator
Maryland/Delaware/District of Columbia Press Foundation
2191 Defense Highway, Suite 300
Crofton, MD 21114-2487
Phone: 410-721-4000 Ext. 20
Fax: 410-721-4557
E-mail: info@mddcpress.com

MISSISSIPPI ASSOCIATION OF BROADCASTERS

http://www.msbroadcasters.org/

MISSISSIPPI ASSOCIATION OF BROADCASTERS SCHOLARSHIP

Scholarship available to a student enrolled in a fully accredited broadcast curriculum at a Mississippi two- or four-year college.

Academic Fields/Career Goals: Journalism; TV/Radio Broadcasting.

Award: Scholarship for use in freshman, sophomore, junior, or senior years; not renewable. *Number:* up to 8. *Amount:* $2000.

Eligibility Requirements: Applicant must be enrolled or expecting to enroll full-time at a two-year or four-year institution or university; resident of Mississippi and studying in Mississippi. Available to U.S. citizens.

Application Requirements: Application, financial need analysis, references, extracurricular activities and community involvement also considered. *Deadline:* May 1.

Contact: Jackie Lett, Scholarship Coordinator
Mississippi Association of Broadcasters
855 South Pear Orchard Road, Suite 403
Ridgeland, MS 39157
Phone: 601-957-9121
Fax: 601-957-9175
E-mail: jackie@msbroadcasters.org

MISSISSIPPI PRESS ASSOCIATION EDUCATION FOUNDATION

http://www.mspress.org/foundation/

MISSISSIPPI PRESS ASSOCIATION EDUCATION FOUNDATION SCHOLARSHIP

The foundation annually offers $1000 ($500 per semester) scholarships to qualified students enrolled in print journalism, and who are residents of Mississippi. The recipient who maintains a 3.0 GPA. Total value of the scholarship can be as much as $4000 when awarded to an incoming freshman who remains qualified throughout their four years of print journalism education.

Academic Fields/Career Goals: Journalism.

Award: Scholarship for use in freshman, sophomore, junior, or senior years; renewable. *Number:* 1. *Amount:* $1000–$4000.

Eligibility Requirements: Applicant must be enrolled or expecting to enroll full-time at a two-year or four-year institution or university and resident of Mississippi. Applicant must have 3.0 GPA or higher. Available to U.S. citizens.

Application Requirements: Application, resume, references, sample of work. *Deadline:* April 1.

Contact: Beth Boone, Scholarship Coordinator
Mississippi Press Association Education Foundation
371 Edgewood Terrace
Jackson, MS 39206
Phone: 601-981-3060
Fax: 601-981-3676
E-mail: bboone@mspress.org

NATIONAL ACADEMY OF TELEVISION ARTS AND SCIENCES-NATIONAL CAPITAL/CHESAPEAKE BAY CHAPTER

http://www.natasdc.org/

BETTY ENDICOTT/NTA-NCCB STUDENT SCHOLARSHIP

Scholarship for a full-time sophomore, junior or non-graduating senior student pursuing a career in communication, television or broadcast journalism. Must be enrolled in an accredited four-year college or university in Maryland, Virginia or Washington, D.C. Minimum GPA of 3.0 required. Must demonstrate an aptitude or interest in communication, television or broadcast journalism. Application URL http://capitalemmys.tv/betty_endicott.htm.

Academic Fields/Career Goals: Journalism; TV/Radio Broadcasting.

Award: Scholarship for use in sophomore, junior, or senior years; not renewable. *Number:* 1. *Amount:* $5000.

Eligibility Requirements: Applicant must be enrolled or expecting to enroll full-time at a four-year institution or university and studying in District of Columbia, Maryland, or Virginia. Applicant must have 3.0 GPA or higher. Available to U.S. citizens.

Application Requirements: Application, essay, resume, references, transcript, work samples (resume tape in VHS format and radio or television broadcast scripts). *Deadline:* April 22.

Contact: Diane Bruno, Student Affairs Committee
National Academy of Television Arts and Sciences-National Capital/Chesapeake Bay Chapter
9405 Russell Road
Silver Spring, MD 20910
Phone: 301-587-3993
E-mail: capitalemmys@aol.com

NATIONAL ASSOCIATION OF BLACK JOURNALISTS

http://www.nabj.org/

ALLISON FISHER SCHOLARSHIP

Scholarship for students currently attending an accredited college or university. Must be majoring in print journalism and maintain a 3.0 GPA. Recipient will attend NABJ convention and participate in the mentor program. Scholarship value and the number of awards granted varies.

Academic Fields/Career Goals: Journalism.

Award: Scholarship for use in freshman, sophomore, junior, senior, or graduate years; not renewable. *Number:* varies. *Amount:* varies.

Eligibility Requirements: Applicant must be enrolled or expecting to enroll full-time at a four-year institution or university. Applicant must have 3.0 GPA or higher. Available to U.S. and non-U.S. citizens.

Application Requirements: Driver's license, references, proof of enrollment. *Deadline:* March 17.

Contact: Irving Washington, Manager
National Association of Black Journalists
8701-A Adelphi Road
Adelphi, MD 20783-1716
Phone: 301-445-7100
Fax: 301-445-7101
E-mail: iwashington@nabj.org

GERALD BOYD/ROBIN STONE NON-SUSTAINING SCHOLARSHIP

One-time scholarship for students enrolled in an accredited four-year institution. Must be enrolled as an undergraduate or graduate student and maintain a 3.0 GPA. Must major in print journalism. Must be a member of NABJ. Scholarship value and the number of awards granted annually varies.

Academic Fields/Career Goals: Journalism.

Award: Scholarship for use in freshman, sophomore, junior, senior, or graduate years; not renewable. *Number:* varies. *Amount:* varies.

Eligibility Requirements: Applicant must be enrolled or expecting to enroll full-time at a four-year institution or university. Applicant must have 3.0 GPA or higher. Available to U.S. and non-U.S. citizens.

Application Requirements: Application, essay, photo, references, transcript, 6 samples of work. *Deadline:* March 17.

Contact: Irving Washington, Manager
National Association of Black Journalists
8701-A Adelphi Road
Adelphi, MD 20783-1716
Phone: 301-445-7100
Fax: 301-445-7101
E-mail: iwashington@nabj.org

NABJ SCHOLARSHIP
• *See page 187*

NATIONAL ASSOCIATION OF BLACK JOURNALISTS AND NEWHOUSE FOUNDATION SCHOLARSHIP

Award for high school seniors planning to attend an accredited four-year college or university and major in journalism. Minimum 3.0 GPA required. Must be a member of NABJ. The scholarship value and the number of awards granted varies.

Academic Fields/Career Goals: Journalism.

Award: Scholarship for use in freshman, sophomore, junior, or senior years; not renewable. *Number:* varies. *Amount:* varies.

Eligibility Requirements: Applicant must be enrolled or expecting to enroll full-time at a four-year institution or university and must have an interest in writing. Applicant must have 3.0 GPA or higher. Available to U.S. and non-U.S. citizens.

Application Requirements: Application, driver's license, essay, interview, references, transcript. *Deadline:* March 17.

Contact: Irving Washington, Manager
National Association of Black Journalists
8701-A Adelphi Road
Adelphi, MD 20783-1716
Phone: 301-445-7100
Fax: 301-445-7101
E-mail: iwashington@nabj.org

NATIONAL ASSOCIATION OF BLACK JOURNALISTS NON-SUSTAINING SCHOLARSHIP AWARDS

One-time award for college students attending a four-year institution and majoring in journalism. Minimum 2.5 GPA required. Must be a member of NABJ. Scholarship value and the number of awards varies annually.

Academic Fields/Career Goals: Journalism; Photojournalism/Photography; TV/Radio Broadcasting.

Award: Scholarship for use in freshman, sophomore, junior, or senior years; not renewable. *Number:* varies. *Amount:* varies.

Eligibility Requirements: Applicant must be enrolled or expecting to enroll full-time at a four-year institution or university and must have an interest in writing. Applicant must have 2.5 GPA or higher. Available to U.S. and non-U.S. citizens.

Application Requirements: Application, driver's license, photo, references, transcript, proof of enrollment. *Deadline:* March 17.

Contact: Irving Washington, Manager
National Association of Black Journalists
8701-A Adelphi Road
Adelphi, MD 20783-1716
Phone: 301-445-7100
Fax: 301-445-7101-
E-mail: iwashington@nabj.org

NATIONAL ASSOCIATION OF BROADCASTERS

http://www.nab.org/

NATIONAL ASSOCIATION OF BROADCASTERS GRANTS FOR RESEARCH IN BROADCASTING
• *See page 187*

NATIONAL ASSOCIATION OF HISPANIC JOURNALISTS (NAHJ)

http://www.nahj.org/

GERALDO RIVERA SCHOLARSHIP

Awards available to college undergraduates and graduate students pursuing careers in English- or Spanish-language TV broadcast journalism. Applications available on web site http://www.nahj.org.

Academic Fields/Career Goals: Journalism; TV/Radio Broadcasting.

Award: Scholarship for use in senior or graduate years; not renewable. *Number:* varies. *Amount:* $1000–$5000.

Eligibility Requirements: Applicant must be enrolled or expecting to enroll full-time at a four-year institution or university. Available to U.S. citizens.

Application Requirements: Application, financial need analysis, resume, references, transcript. *Deadline:* March 31.

Contact: Virginia Galindo, Program Assistant
National Association of Hispanic Journalists (NAHJ)
1000 National Press Building, 529 14th Street, NW, Suite 1000
Washington, DC 20045-2001
Phone: 202-662-7145
E-mail: vgalindo@nahj.org

MARIA ELENA SALINAS SCHOLARSHIP
• *See page 328*

NATIONAL ASSOCIATION OF HISPANIC JOURNALISTS SCHOLARSHIP
• *See page 188*

NEWHOUSE SCHOLARSHIP PROGRAM
• *See page 332*

WASHINGTON POST YOUNG JOURNALISTS SCHOLARSHIP

Four-year award of $10,000 for high school seniors in D.C. metropolitan area. Contact educational programs manager for application and information.

Academic Fields/Career Goals: Journalism.

Award: Scholarship for use in freshman year; not renewable. *Number:* varies. *Amount:* $10,000.

Eligibility Requirements: Applicant must be high school student; planning to enroll or expecting to enroll full-time at a four-year institution or university and resident of District of Columbia, Maryland, or Virginia. Available to U.S. citizens.

Application Requirements: Application, references, transcript. *Deadline:* March 31.

Contact: Virginia Galindo, Program Assistant
National Association of Hispanic Journalists (NAHJ)
1000 National Press Building, 529 14th Street, NW, Suite 1000
Washington, DC 20045-2001
Phone: 202-662-7145
E-mail: vgalindo@nahj.org

NATIONAL ASSOCIATION OF NEGRO BUSINESS AND PROFESSIONAL WOMEN'S CLUBS INC.

http://www.nanbpwc.org/

JULIANNE MALVEAUX SCHOLARSHIP
• *See page 227*

NATIONAL DAIRY SHRINE

http://www.dairyshrine.org/

MARSHALL E. MCCULLOUGH-NATIONAL DAIRY SHRINE SCHOLARSHIPS
• *See page 85*

NATIONAL INSTITUTE FOR LABOR RELATIONS RESEARCH

http://www.nilrr.org/

NATIONAL INSTITUTE FOR LABOR RELATIONS RESEARCH WILLIAM B. RUGGLES JOURNALISM SCHOLARSHIP
• *See page 188*

NATIONAL PRESS CLUB

http://www.npc.press.org/

NATIONAL PRESS CLUB SCHOLARSHIP FOR JOURNALISM DIVERSITY

Scholarship of $2500 per year awarded to a talented minority student planning to pursue a career in journalism. Applicant must be a high school senior. Must have applied to or been accepted by a college or university for the upcoming year.

Academic Fields/Career Goals: Journalism.

Award: Scholarship for use in freshman year; not renewable. *Number:* 1. *Amount:* $2500.

Eligibility Requirements: Applicant must be high school student and planning to enroll or expecting to enroll full-time at a four-year institution or university. Available to U.S. and non-U.S. citizens.

Application Requirements: Application, essay, financial need analysis, references, transcript, work samples demonstrating an ongoing interest in journalism. *Deadline:* March 1.

Contact: Joann Booze, Scholarship Coordinator
Phone: 202-662-7532
E-mail: jbooze@press.org

NATIONAL PRESS FOUNDATION

http://www.nationalpress.org/

EVERT CLARK/SETH PAYNE AWARD

Award to recognize outstanding reporting and writing in any field of science. Limited to non-technical, print journalism only. Articles published in newspapers (including college newspapers), magazines, and newsletters are eligible. Both freelancers and staff writers are eligible.

Academic Fields/Career Goals: Journalism; Literature/English/Writing.

Award: Prize for use in freshman, sophomore, junior, senior, graduate, or postgraduate years; not renewable. *Number:* 1000. *Amount:* varies.

Eligibility Requirements: Applicant must be age 30 or under; enrolled or expecting to enroll full- or part-time at a two-year or four-year or technical institution or university and must have an interest in writing. Available to U.S. citizens.

Application Requirements: Application, applicant must enter a contest, five photocopies of each article. *Deadline:* June 30.

Contact: John Carey, Scholarship Committee
National Press Foundation
1211 Connecticut Avenue, Suite 310
Washington, DC 20036
Phone: 202-383-2100

NATIONAL SCHOLASTIC PRESS ASSOCIATION

http://www.studentpress.org/

NSPA JOURNALISM HONOR ROLL SCHOLARSHIP

Scholarship to student journalists who have achieved a 3.75 or higher GPA and have worked in student media for two or more years.

Academic Fields/Career Goals: Journalism.

Award: Scholarship for use in freshman year; not renewable. *Number:* 1–3. *Amount:* $1000.

Eligibility Requirements: Applicant must be high school student and planning to enroll or expecting to enroll full-time at a four-year institution or university. Applicant or parent of applicant must have employment or volunteer experience in journalism/broadcasting. Available to U.S. and non-U.S. citizens.

Application Requirements: Application, essay, resume, references, transcript, proof of NSPA membership required. *Deadline:* February 15.

Contact: Marisa Dobson, Sponsorship Contest Coordinator
National Scholastic Press Association
2221 University Avenue, SE, Suite 121
Minneapolis, MN 55414
Phone: 612-625-6519
Fax: 612-626-0720
E-mail: marisa@studentpress.org

NATIONAL WRITERS ASSOCIATION FOUNDATION

http://www.nationalwriters.com/

NATIONAL WRITERS ASSOCIATION FOUNDATION SCHOLARSHIPS

Scholarships available to talented young writers with serious interest in any writing field.

Academic Fields/Career Goals: Journalism; Literature/English/Writing.

Award: Scholarship for use in freshman, sophomore, junior, senior, graduate, or postgraduate years; not renewable. *Number:* 1–4. *Amount:* $1000.

Eligibility Requirements: Applicant must be enrolled or expecting to enroll full- or part-time at a two-year or four-year or technical institution or university and must have an interest in writing. Available to U.S. and non-U.S. citizens.

Application Requirements: Application, transcript, writing samples. *Deadline:* January 15.

Contact: Sandy Welchel, Executive Director
National Writers Association Foundation
10940 South Parker Road, Suite 508
Parker, CO 80134
Phone: 303-841-0246
Fax: 303-841-2607
E-mail: natlwritersassn@hotmail.com

NATIVE AMERICAN JOURNALISTS ASSOCIATION

http://www.naja.com/

NATIVE AMERICAN JOURNALISTS ASSOCIATION SCHOLARSHIPS

One-time award for undergraduate study leading to journalism career at accredited colleges and universities. Applicants must be current members of Native-American Journalists Association or may join at time of application. Applicants must have proof of tribal association. Send cover letter, letters of reference, and work samples with application. Financial need considered.

Academic Fields/Career Goals: Journalism.

Award: Scholarship for use in freshman, sophomore, junior, or senior years; not renewable. *Number:* 10. *Amount:* $500–$5000.

Eligibility Requirements: Applicant must be American Indian/Alaska Native; enrolled or expecting to enroll full-time at a two-year or four-year institution or university and must have an interest in writing. Applicant or parent of applicant must be member of Native American Journalists Association. Applicant must have 2.5 GPA or higher. Available to U.S. and Canadian citizens.

Application Requirements: Application, essay, financial need analysis, interview, photo, portfolio, resume, references, test scores, transcript. *Deadline:* April 1.

Contact: Jeffrey Palmer, Education Director
Native American Journalists Association
University of Oklahoma, Gaylord School of Journalism
395 West Linsey Street
Norman, OK 73019
Phone: 405-325-9008
Fax: 866-325-7565
E-mail: jeffrey.p.palmer@ou.edu

NEBRASKA PRESS ASSOCIATION

http://www.nebpress.com/

NEBRASKA PRESS ASSOCIATION FOUNDATION INC. SCHOLARSHIP

Award for graduates of Nebraska high schools who have a minimum GPA of 2.5 and are enrolled or planning to enroll in programs in Nebraska colleges or universities leading to careers in print journalism.

Academic Fields/Career Goals: Journalism; Photojournalism/Photography.

Award: Scholarship for use in freshman, sophomore, or junior years; not renewable. *Number:* 2–4. *Amount:* $2000.

Eligibility Requirements: Applicant must be enrolled or expecting to enroll full-time at a four-year institution or university; resident of Nebraska and studying in Nebraska. Applicant must have 2.5 GPA or higher. Available to U.S. citizens.

Application Requirements: Application, references. *Deadline:* March 1.

Contact: Allen Beermann, Executive Director
Nebraska Press Association
845 South Street
Lincoln, NE 68508-1226
Phone: 402-476-2851
Fax: 402-476-2942
E-mail: abeermann@nebpress.com

NEW JERSEY BROADCASTERS ASSOCIATION

http://www.njba.com/

MICHAEL S. LIBRETTI SCHOLARSHIP
• *See page 188*

NEW JERSEY PRESS FOUNDATION

http://www.njpressfoundation.org/

BERNARD KILGORE MEMORIAL SCHOLARSHIP FOR THE NJ HIGH SCHOOL JOURNALIST OF THE YEAR

Program co-sponsored with the Garden State Scholastic Press Association. Winning student is nominated to the Journalism Education Association for the National High School Journalist of the Year Competition. Must be in high school with plans of entering a four-year college or university on a full-time basis. Minimum 3.0 GPA required.

Academic Fields/Career Goals: Journalism.

Award: Scholarship for use in freshman year; not renewable. *Number:* 1. *Amount:* $5000.

Eligibility Requirements: Applicant must be high school student; planning to enroll or expecting to enroll full-time at a four-year institution or university; resident of New Jersey and must have an interest in writing. Applicant must have 3.0 GPA or higher. Available to U.S. citizens.

Application Requirements: Application, applicant must enter a contest, essay, portfolio, resume, references, transcript. *Deadline:* February 15.

Contact: Thomas Engleman, Program Director
New Jersey Press Foundation
840 Bear Tavern Road, Suite 305
West Trenton, NJ 08628-1019
Phone: 609-406-0600 Ext. 19
E-mail: programs@njpressfoundation.org

NEWSPAPER GUILD-CWA

http://www.newsguild.org/

DAVID S. BARR AWARD

Award for high school seniors and college students for their journalistic achievements and to encourage young journalists to focus on issues of social justice. One $500 award will be given to a graduating high school senior and one $1500 award will be given to a college student.

Academic Fields/Career Goals: Journalism.

Award: Scholarship for use in freshman, sophomore, junior, senior, graduate, or postgraduate years; not renewable. *Number:* up to 2. *Amount:* $500–$1500.

Eligibility Requirements: Applicant must be enrolled or expecting to enroll full- or part-time at a two-year or four-year or technical institution or university. Available to U.S. and Canadian citizens.

Application Requirements: Application, applicant must enter a contest. *Deadline:* January 31.

Contact: Collective Bargaining Secretary
Newspaper Guild-CWA
501 Third Street, NW, Sixth Floor
Washington, DC 20001
Phone: 202-434-0675
Fax: 202-434-1472
E-mail: kdeneau@cwa-union.org

OHIO NEWSPAPERS FOUNDATION

http://www.ohionews.org/foundation.html

OHIO NEWSPAPERS FOUNDATION MINORITY SCHOLARSHIP

Three scholarships for minority high school seniors who plan to pursue a newspaper journalism career. Applicants must be enrolled in an accredited Ohio college or university. Must be African-American, Hispanic, Asian-American or American-Indian. A minimum high school GPA of 2.5 required.

Academic Fields/Career Goals: Journalism.

Award: Scholarship for use in freshman year; not renewable. *Number:* 3. *Amount:* $1000.

Eligibility Requirements: Applicant must be American Indian/Alaska Native, Asian/Pacific Islander, Black (non-Hispanic), or Hispanic; high school student; planning to enroll or expecting to enroll full-time at a four-year institution or university; resident of Ohio and studying in Ohio. Applicant must have 2.5 GPA or higher. Available to U.S. citizens.

Application Requirements: Application, driver's license, essay, transcript. *Deadline:* March 31.

Contact: Kathleen Pouliot, Secretary
Ohio Newspapers Foundation
1335 Dublin Road, Suite 216-B
Columbus, OH 43215-7038
Phone: 614-486-6677
Fax: 614-486-4940
E-mail: kpouliot@ohionews.org

OHIO NEWSPAPERS FOUNDATION UNIVERSITY JOURNALISM SCHOLARSHIP

One-time $1500 scholarship for a student who is enrolled in an Ohio college or university, majoring in journalism or equivalent degree program. Preference will be given to students demonstrating a career commitment to newspaper journalism. A minimum GPA of 2.5 required.

Academic Fields/Career Goals: Journalism.

Award: Scholarship for use in freshman, sophomore, junior, or senior years; not renewable. *Number:* 1. *Amount:* $1500.

Eligibility Requirements: Applicant must be enrolled or expecting to enroll full-time at a four-year institution or university; resident of Ohio and studying in Ohio. Applicant must have 2.5 GPA or higher. Available to U.S. citizens.

Application Requirements: Application, driver's license, essay, references, transcript. *Deadline:* March 31.

Contact: Kathleen Pouliot, Secretary
Ohio Newspapers Foundation
1335 Dublin Road, Suite 216-B
Columbus, OH 43215-7038
Phone: 614-486-6677
Fax: 614-486-4940
E-mail: kpouliot@ohionews.org

OHIO NEWSPAPER WOMEN'S SCHOLARSHIP

One-time scholarship for female student who is enrolled as a junior or senior in an Ohio college or university, majoring in journalism or an equivalent degree program. Must be U.S. citizen.

Academic Fields/Career Goals: Journalism.

Award: Scholarship for use in junior or senior years; not renewable. *Number:* 1. *Amount:* $1000.

Eligibility Requirements: Applicant must be enrolled or expecting to enroll full-time at a four-year institution or university; female and studying in Ohio. Available to U.S. citizens.

Application Requirements: Application, references, test scores, transcript. *Deadline:* March 31.

Contact: Kathleen Pouliot, Secretary
Ohio Newspapers Foundation
1335 Dublin Road, Suite 216-B
Columbus, OH 43215-7038
Phone: 614-486-6677
Fax: 614-486-4940
E-mail: kpouliot@ohionews.org

OREGON ASSOCIATION OF BROADCASTERS

http://www.theoab.org/

OAB FOUNDATION SCHOLARSHIP
• See page 188

OREGON COMMUNITY FOUNDATION

http://www.oregoncf.org/

JACKSON FOUNDATION JOURNALISM SCHOLARSHIP FUND

Scholarship for students attending an Oregon college or university and majoring in, or with emphasis on, journalism. For both full time and part time. Must be a resident of Oregon.

Academic Fields/Career Goals: Journalism.

Award: Scholarship for use in freshman, sophomore, junior, or senior years; renewable. *Number:* 5. *Amount:* $1500–$2000.

Eligibility Requirements: Applicant must be enrolled or expecting to enroll full-time at a four-year institution or university; resident of Oregon and studying in Oregon. Available to U.S. citizens.

Application Requirements: Application. *Deadline:* March 1.

Contact: Dianne Causey, Program Associate for Scholarships and Grants
Oregon Community Foundation
1221 Yamhill, SW, Suite 100
Portland, OR 97205-2108
Phone: 503-227-6846 Ext. 1418
E-mail: dcausey@oregoncf.org

OREGON STUDENT ASSISTANCE COMMISSION

http://www.GetCollegeFunds.org/

BUERKLE SCHOLARSHIP

Award available to graduates of Clackamas, Linn, and Washington County high schools (including GED recipients and home-schooled graduates). Preference for older, nontraditional students or students who are returning to college after a long absence. Must be intending to major in English, journalism, math, music or physical education and have at least a 3.6 GPA. Prior recipients may reapply regardless of high school counties where school was attended.

Academic Fields/Career Goals: Journalism; Literature/English/Writing; Mathematics; Music.

Award: Scholarship for use in freshman year; not renewable.

Eligibility Requirements: Applicant must be enrolled or expecting to enroll at a two-year or four-year institution or university.

Application Requirements: Application. *Deadline:* March 1.

Contact: Director of Grant Programs
Oregon Student Assistance Commission
1500 Valley River Drive, Suite 100
Eugene, OR 97401-7020
Phone: 800-452-8807

JACKSON FOUNDATION JOURNALISM SCHOLARSHIP

Renewable award for students at Oregon public and nonprofit schools who are journalism majors or whose course of study emphasizes journalism. Preference given to students who have taken the SAT and have received good scores.

Academic Fields/Career Goals: Journalism.

Award: Scholarship for use in freshman, sophomore, junior, or senior years; not renewable. *Number:* varies. *Amount:* varies.

Eligibility Requirements: Applicant must be enrolled or expecting to enroll full-time at a two-year or four-year institution; resident of Oregon and studying in Oregon. Available to U.S. citizens.

Application Requirements: Application, essay, financial need analysis, references, test scores, transcript, activity chart, SAT scores. *Deadline:* March 1.

Contact: Director of Grant Programs
Oregon Student Assistance Commission
1500 Valley River Drive, Suite 100
Eugene, OR 97401-7020
Phone: 800-452-8807 Ext. 7395

OUTDOOR WRITERS ASSOCIATION OF AMERICA

http://www.owaa.org/

OUTDOOR WRITERS ASSOCIATION OF AMERICA BODIE MCDOWELL SCHOLARSHIP AWARD
• See page 189

OVERSEAS PRESS CLUB FOUNDATION

http://www.overseaspressclubfoundation.org/

OVERSEAS PRESS CLUB FOUNDATION SCHOLARSHIPS

Students aspiring to become foreign correspondents can apply. Must write an essay of no more than 500 words concentrating on an area of the world or an international issue that is in keeping with the applicant's interest. Must be studying at an American college or university or be an American student studying abroad.

Academic Fields/Career Goals: Journalism.

Award: Scholarship for use in freshman, sophomore, junior, or senior years; not renewable. *Number:* 12. *Amount:* $2000.

Eligibility Requirements: Applicant must be enrolled or expecting to enroll full- or part-time at a two-year or four-year institution or university and must have an interest in writing. Available to U.S. and non-U.S. citizens.

Application Requirements: Application, applicant must enter a contest, essay, resume, cover letter. *Deadline:* December 1.

Contact: William J. Holstein, President
Overseas Press Club Foundation
40 West 45th Street
New York, NY 10036
Phone: 201-493-9087
Fax: 201-612-9915
E-mail: foundation@opcofamerica.org

PALM BEACH ASSOCIATION OF BLACK JOURNALISTS

http://www.pbabj.org/

PALM BEACH ASSOCIATION OF BLACK JOURNALISTS SCHOLARSHIP

Scholarship of $1000 are awarded to African-American graduating high school seniors plan to pursue a degree in journalism-print, television, radio broadcasting or photography industries. Have a GPA of 2.7 or better.

Academic Fields/Career Goals: Journalism; Photojournalism/Photography; TV/Radio Broadcasting.

Award: Scholarship for use in freshman year; not renewable. *Number:* 1. *Amount:* $1000.

Eligibility Requirements: Applicant must be Black (non-Hispanic); high school student and planning to enroll or expecting to enroll full- or part-time at a four-year institution or university. Available to U.S. and non-U.S. citizens.

Application Requirements: Application, driver's license, transcript, college acceptance proof. *Deadline:* March 30.

Contact: Christopher Smith, Scholarship Chair
Palm Beach Association of Black Journalists
PO Box 19533
West Palm Beach, FL 33416

PHILADELPHIA ASSOCIATION OF BLACK JOURNALISTS

http://www.pabj.org/

PHILADELPHIA ASSOCIATION OF BLACK JOURNALISTS SCHOLARSHIP

One-time award available to deserving high school students in the Delaware Valley who are interested in becoming journalists. Must have a 2.5 GPA. All applicants must state their intention to pursue journalism careers.

Academic Fields/Career Goals: Journalism.

Award: Scholarship for use in freshman, sophomore, junior, or senior years; not renewable. *Number:* 2. *Amount:* up to $1000.

Eligibility Requirements: Applicant must be Black (non-Hispanic); enrolled or expecting to enroll full-time at a four-year institution or university; resident of Pennsylvania and must have an interest in writing. Applicant must have 2.5 GPA or higher. Available to U.S. citizens.

Application Requirements: Application, driver's license, essay, references, transcript. *Deadline:* May 1.

Contact: Manny Smith, Scholarship Committee
Philadelphia Association of Black Journalists
PO Box 8232
Philadelphia, PA 19101
E-mail: manuelsmith@gmail.com

PRINTING INDUSTRY OF MINNESOTA EDUCATION FOUNDATION

http://www.pimn.org/

PRINTING INDUSTRY OF MINNESOTA EDUCATION FOUNDATION SCHOLARSHIP FUND

• See page 333

QUILL AND SCROLL FOUNDATION

http://www.uiowa.edu/~quill-sc

EDWARD J. NELL MEMORIAL SCHOLARSHIP IN JOURNALISM

Merit-based award for high school seniors planning to major in journalism. Must have won a National Quill and Scroll Writing Award or a Photography or Yearbook Excellence contest. Entry forms available from journalism adviser or Quill and Scroll. Must rank in upper third of class or have a minimum 3.0 GPA.

Academic Fields/Career Goals: Journalism.

Award: Scholarship for use in freshman year; not renewable. *Number:* 1-6. *Amount:* $500–$1500.

Eligibility Requirements: Applicant must be high school student; planning to enroll or expecting to enroll full-time at a four-year institution or university and must have an interest in photography/photogrammetry/filmmaking or writing. Applicant must have 3.0 GPA or higher. Available to U.S. citizens.

Application Requirements: Application, applicant must enter a contest, essay, photo, references, test scores, transcript. *Deadline:* May 10.

Contact: Vanessa Shelton, Executive Director
Quill and Scroll Foundation
School of Journalism, E346AJB
Iowa City, IA 52242-1528
Phone: 319-335-3457
Fax: 319-335-3989
E-mail: quill-scroll@uiowa.edu

RADIO & TELEVISION NEWS DIRECTORS FOUNDATION

http://www.rtndf.org/

CAROLE SIMPSON SCHOLARSHIP
• See page 189

ED BRADLEY SCHOLARSHIP

One-time, $10,000 award for minority sophomore, junior, or senior undergraduate student enrolled in an electronic journalism program. Submit examples of reporting or producing skills on CD or DVD, totaling 15 minutes or less, with scripts, resume and application form available at RTNDA.org.

Academic Fields/Career Goals: Journalism; TV/Radio Broadcasting.

Award: Scholarship for use in sophomore, junior, or senior years; not renewable. *Number:* 1. *Amount:* $10,000.

Eligibility Requirements: Applicant must be American Indian/Alaska Native, Asian/Pacific Islander, Black (non-Hispanic), or Hispanic and enrolled or expecting to enroll full-time at a four-year institution or university. Available to U.S. and non-U.S. citizens.

Application Requirements: Application, essay, resume, references, DVD or CD with work samples. *Deadline:* May 11.

Contact: Stacey Staniak, Project Manager
Radio & Television News Directors Foundation
4121 Plank Road 512
Fredericksburg, VA 22407-2838
Phone: 202-467-5214
E-mail: staceys@rtnda.org

KEN KASHIWAHARA SCHOLARSHIP
• See page 189

LOU AND CAROLE PRATO SPORTS REPORTING SCHOLARSHIP
• See page 189

PRESIDENTS SCHOLARSHIP
• See page 190

ST. PETERSBURG TIMES FUND INC.

http://www.sptimes.com/

ST. PETERSBURG TIMES JOURNALISM SCHOLARSHIPS

Scholarship to high school seniors in the Times' circulation area who have a demonstrated interest in pursuing journalism major in college and career after graduation.

Academic Fields/Career Goals: Journalism.

Award: Scholarship for use in freshman year; renewable. *Number:* 1. *Amount:* $2500.

Eligibility Requirements: Applicant must be high school student; planning to enroll or expecting to enroll full-time at a four-year institution or university and resident of Florida. Available to U.S. citizens.

Application Requirements: Application, essay, portfolio, resume, references. *Deadline:* January 5.

Contact: Nancy Waclawek, Director
St. Petersburg Times Fund Inc.
PO Box 1121
St. Petersburg, FL 33731
Phone: 727-893-8780
Fax: 727-892-2257
E-mail: waclawek@sptimes.com

SEATTLE POST-INTELLIGENCER

http://www.seattlepi.com/

BOBBI MCCALLUM MEMORIAL SCHOLARSHIP

Scholarship for female college juniors and seniors who are Washington residents studying in Washington and have an interest in print journalism. Minimum 3.0 GPA required. Must submit clips of published stories with transcripts, financial need analysis, application, and two letters of recommendation.

Academic Fields/Career Goals: Journalism.

Award: Scholarship for use in junior or senior years; not renewable. *Number:* 1. *Amount:* $1000.

Eligibility Requirements: Applicant must be enrolled or expecting to enroll full- or part-time at a four-year institution or university; female; resident of Washington and studying in Washington. Applicant must have 3.0 GPA or higher. Available to U.S. citizens.

Application Requirements: Application, financial need analysis, portfolio, resume, references, transcript. *Deadline:* April 1.

Contact: Janet Grimley, Assistant Managing Editor
Seattle Post-Intelligencer
101 Elliot Avenue West
Seattle, WA 98119
Phone: 206-448-8316
Fax: 206-448-8305
E-mail: janetgrimley@seattlep-i.com

SIGMA DELTA CHI FOUNDATION OF WASHINGTON D.C.

http://www.spj.org/washdcpro

SIGMA DELTA CHI SCHOLARSHIPS

One-time award to help pay tuition for full-time students in their junior or senior year demonstrating a clear intention to become journalists. Must demonstrate financial need. Grades and skills are also considered. Must be enrolled in a college or university in the Washington, D.C., metropolitan area. Sponsored by the Society of Professional Journalists.

Academic Fields/Career Goals: Journalism.

Award: Scholarship for use in sophomore or junior years; not renewable. *Number:* 5. *Amount:* $4000.

Eligibility Requirements: Applicant must be enrolled or expecting to enroll full-time at a four-year institution or university and studying in District of Columbia, Maryland, or Virginia. Applicant must have 3.0 GPA or higher. Available to U.S. and non-U.S. citizens.

Application Requirements: Application, essay, financial need analysis, interview, portfolio, references, transcript. *Deadline:* March 1.

Contact: Scholarship Committee
Sigma Delta Chi Foundation of Washington D.C.
PO Box 19555
Washington, DC 20036-0555
Phone: 301-405-5292
Fax: 301-314-9166

SOCIETY OF PROFESSIONAL JOURNALISTS, LOS ANGELES CHAPTER

http://www.spj.org/losangeles

BILL FARR SCHOLARSHIP

Award available to a student who is either a resident of Los Angeles, Ventura or Orange counties or is enrolled at a university in one of those counties. Must have completed sophomore year and be enrolled in or accepted to a journalism program.

Academic Fields/Career Goals: Journalism.

Award: Scholarship for use in junior, senior, or graduate years; not renewable. *Number:* 1. *Amount:* $500–$1000.

Eligibility Requirements: Applicant must be enrolled or expecting to enroll full-time at a four-year institution or university; resident of California and studying in California. Available to U.S. citizens.

Application Requirements: Application, essay, financial need analysis, resume, references, work samples. *Deadline:* April 15.

Contact: Daniel Garvey, Scholarship Chairman
Society of Professional Journalists, Los Angeles Chapter
1250 Bellflower
Long Beach, CA 90840
Phone: 562-985-5779

CARL GREENBERG SCHOLARSHIP

Award for a student who is either a resident of Los Angeles, Ventura or Orange counties or is enrolled at a university in one of those three California counties. Must have completed sophomore year and be enrolled in or accepted to an investigative or political journalism program.

Academic Fields/Career Goals: Journalism.

Award: Scholarship for use in junior, senior, or graduate years; not renewable. *Number:* 1. *Amount:* $1000.

Eligibility Requirements: Applicant must be enrolled or expecting to enroll full-time at a four-year institution or university; resident of California and studying in California. Available to U.S. citizens.

Application Requirements: Application, essay, financial need analysis, resume, references, work samples. *Deadline:* April 15.

Contact: Daniel Garvey, Scholarship Chairman
Society of Professional Journalists, Los Angeles Chapter
1250 Bellflower
Long Beach, CA 90840
Phone: 562-985-5779

HELEN JOHNSON SCHOLARSHIP

Awards are available to a student who is a resident of Los Angeles, Ventura or Orange counties or is enrolled at a university in one of those three California counties. Must have completed sophomore year and be enrolled in or accepted to a broadcast journalism program.

Academic Fields/Career Goals: Journalism; TV/Radio Broadcasting.

Award: Scholarship for use in junior, senior, or graduate years; not renewable. *Number:* 1. *Amount:* $500–$1000.

Eligibility Requirements: Applicant must be enrolled or expecting to enroll full-time at a four-year institution or university; resident of California and studying in California. Available to U.S. citizens.

Application Requirements: Application, essay, financial need analysis, resume, references, work samples. *Deadline:* April 15.

Contact: Daniel Garvey, Scholarship Chairman
Society of Professional Journalists, Los Angeles Chapter
1250 Bellflower
Long Beach, CA 90840
Phone: 562-985-5779

KEN INOUYE SCHOLARSHIP

Awards are available to a minority student who is either a resident of Los Angeles, Ventura or Orange counties or is enrolled at a university in one of those three California counties. Must have completed sophomore year and be enrolled in or accepted to a journalism program.

Academic Fields/Career Goals: Journalism.

Award: Scholarship for use in junior, senior, or graduate years; renewable. *Number:* 1. *Amount:* $500–$1000.

Eligibility Requirements: Applicant must be American Indian/Alaska Native, Asian/Pacific Islander, Black (non-Hispanic), or Hispanic; enrolled or expecting to enroll full-time at a four-year institution or university; resident of California and studying in California. Available to U.S. citizens.

Application Requirements: Application, essay, financial need analysis, resume, references, work samples. *Deadline:* April 15.

Contact: Daniel Garvey, Scholarship Chairman
Society of Professional Journalists, Los Angeles Chapter
1250 Bellflower
Long Beach, CA 90840
Phone: 562-985-5779

SOCIETY OF PROFESSIONAL JOURNALISTS MARYLAND PRO CHAPTER

http://www.spj.org/mdpro

MARYLAND SPJ PRO CHAPTER COLLEGE SCHOLARSHIP

Scholarships for journalism students whose regular home residence is in Maryland. May attend colleges or universities in Virginia, Washington D.C., or Pennsylvania.

Academic Fields/Career Goals: Journalism.

Award: Scholarship for use in freshman, sophomore, junior, or senior years; not renewable. *Number:* varies. *Amount:* varies.

Eligibility Requirements: Applicant must be enrolled or expecting to enroll full- or part-time at a four-year institution or university; resident of Maryland and studying in District of Columbia, Maryland, Pennsylvania, or Virginia. Available to U.S. citizens.

Application Requirements: Application, essay, financial need analysis, references, transcript, awards or honors received. *Deadline:* May 9.

Contact: Sue Kopen Katcef, Scholarship Chair
Society of Professional Journalists Maryland Pro Chapter
402 Fox Hollow Lane
Annapolis, MD 21403
Phone: 301-405-7526
E-mail: susiekk@aol.com

SOCIETY OF PROFESSIONAL JOURNALISTS-SOUTH FLORIDA CHAPTER

http://www.spjsofla.net/

GARTH REEVES, JR. MEMORIAL SCHOLARSHIPS
• *See page 190*

SOUTH ASIAN JOURNALISTS ASSOCIATION (SAJA)

http://www.saja.org/

SAJA JOURNALISM SCHOLARSHIP

Scholarships for students in North America who are of South Asian descent (includes Bangladesh, Bhutan, India, Maldives, Nepal, Pakistan and Sri Lanka, Indo-Caribbean) or those with a demonstrated interest in South Asia or South Asian issues. Must be interested in pursuing journalism. Applicant must be a high school senior, undergraduate student or graduate-level student.

Academic Fields/Career Goals: Journalism.

Award: Scholarship for use in freshman, sophomore, junior, senior, graduate, or postgraduate years; not renewable. *Number:* 1–4. *Amount:* $1000–$2000.

Eligibility Requirements: Applicant must be Asian/Pacific Islander and enrolled or expecting to enroll full-time at a two-year or four-year institution or university. Available to U.S. and non-U.S. citizens.

Application Requirements: Application, essay, financial need analysis, portfolio, resume, references, journalism clips or work samples. *Deadline:* February 15.

Contact: Sudeep Reddy, Student Committee and Scholarships
South Asian Journalists Association (SAJA)
Columbia Graduate School of Journalism
2950 Broadway
New York, NY 10027
Phone: 212-854-0191
E-mail: sudeepreddysaja@gmail.com

SOUTH CAROLINA PRESS ASSOCIATION FOUNDATION

http://www.scpress.org/

SOUTH CAROLINA PRESS ASSOCIATION FOUNDATION NEWSPAPER SCHOLARSHIPS

Renewable award for students entering junior year at a South Carolina institution. Based on grades, journalistic activities in college, and recommendations. Must agree to work in the newspaper field for two years after graduation or repay as loan.

Academic Fields/Career Goals: Journalism.

Award: Scholarship for use in junior year; renewable. *Number:* up to 3. *Amount:* $500–$1375.

Eligibility Requirements: Applicant must be enrolled or expecting to enroll full-time at a four-year institution or university and studying in South Carolina. Available to U.S. and non-U.S. citizens.

Application Requirements: Application, essay, financial need analysis, portfolio, resume, references, transcript. *Deadline:* January 20.

Contact: William C. Rogers, Secretary
South Carolina Press Association Foundation
PO Box 11429
Columbia, SC 29211-1429
Phone: 803-750-9561
Fax: 803-551-0903
E-mail: brogers@scpress.org

STRAIGHTFORWARD MEDIA

http://www.straightforwardmedia.com/

STRAIGHTFORWARD MEDIA MEDIA & COMMUNICATIONS SCHOLARSHIP
• *See page 77*

TEXAS GRIDIRON CLUB INC.

http://www.spjfw.org/

TEXAS GRIDIRON CLUB SCHOLARSHIPS
• *See page 192*

UNITED METHODIST COMMUNICATIONS

http://www.umcom.org/

LEONARD M. PERRYMAN COMMUNICATIONS SCHOLARSHIP FOR ETHNIC MINORITY STUDENTS
• *See page 192*

UNITED NEGRO COLLEGE FUND

http://www.uncf.org/

C-SPAN SCHOLARSHIP PROGRAM
• *See page 193*

READER'S DIGEST FOUNDATION SCHOLARSHIP
• *See page 193*

STAN SCOTT SCHOLARSHIP
• *See page 193*

VALLEY PRESS CLUB, SPRINGFIELD NEWSPAPERS

http://www.valleypressclub.com/

VALLEY PRESS CLUB SCHOLARSHIPS, THE REPUBLICAN SCHOLARSHIP, CHANNEL 22 SCHOLARSHIP
• *See page 194*

WASHINGTON NEWS COUNCIL

http://www.wanewscouncil.org/

DICK LARSEN SCHOLARSHIP PROGRAM
• *See page 194*

HERB ROBINSON SCHOLARSHIP PROGRAM
• *See page 194*

WMTW-TV 8-AUBURN, MAINE

http://www.wmtw.com/

BOB ELLIOT-WMTW-TV 8 JOURNALISM SCHOLARSHIP
• *See page 194*

WOMEN'S BASKETBALL COACHES ASSOCIATION

http://www.wbca.org/

ROBIN ROBERTS/WBCA SPORTS COMMUNICATIONS SCHOLARSHIP AWARD
• *See page 195*

LANDSCAPE ARCHITECTURE

AMERICAN INSTITUTE OF ARCHITECTS, NEW YORK CHAPTER

http://www.aiany.org/

DOUGLAS HASKELL AWARD FOR STUDENT JOURNALISM
• *See page 99*

ASSOCIATION FOR WOMEN IN ARCHITECTURE FOUNDATION

http://www.awa-la.org/

ASSOCIATION FOR WOMEN IN ARCHITECTURE SCHOLARSHIP
• *See page 100*

THE DALLAS FOUNDATION

http://www.dallasfoundation.org/

WHITLEY PLACE SCHOLARSHIP
• *See page 100*

FEDERATED GARDEN CLUBS OF CONNECTICUT

http://www.ctgardenclubs.org/

FEDERATED GARDEN CLUBS OF CONNECTICUT INC. SCHOLARSHIPS
• *See page 140*

FEDERATED GARDEN CLUBS OF MARYLAND

http://www.hometown.aol.com/fgcofmd

ROBERT LEWIS BAKER SCHOLARSHIP
• *See page 357*

FRIENDS OF THE FRELINGHUYSEN ARBORETUM

http://www.arboretumfriends.org/

BENJAMIN C. BLACKBURN SCHOLARSHIP
• *See page 308*

GARDEN CLUB OF AMERICA

http://www.gcamerica.org/

GCA AWARD IN DESERT STUDIES
• *See page 101*

KATHARINE M. GROSSCUP SCHOLARSHIP
• *See page 357*

THE GEORGIA TRUST FOR HISTORIC PRESERVATION

http://www.georgiatrust.org/

B. PHINIZY SPALDING, HUBERT B. OWENS, AND THE NATIONAL SOCIETY OF THE COLONIAL DAMES OF AMERICA IN THE STATE OF GEORGIA ACADEMIC SCHOLARSHIPS
• *See page 89*

J. NEEL REID PRIZE
• *See page 101*

HERB SOCIETY OF AMERICA, WESTERN RESERVE UNIT

http://www.herbsociety.org/units/western-reserve.html

FRANCIS SYLVIA ZVERINA SCHOLARSHIP
• *See page 358*

WESTERN RESERVE HERB SOCIETY SCHOLARSHIP
• *See page 358*

HORTICULTURAL RESEARCH INSTITUTE AND ENDOWMENT FUND

http://www.hriresearch.org/

CARVILLE M. AKEHURST MEMORIAL SCHOLARSHIP
• *See page 358*

MUGGETS SCHOLARSHIP
• *See page 359*

SPRING MEADOW NURSERY SCHOLARSHIP
• *See page 359*

TIMOTHY AND PALMER W. BIGELOW JR, SCHOLARSHIP
• *See page 359*

USREY FAMILY SCHOLARSHIP
• *See page 359*

LANDSCAPE ARCHITECTURE FOUNDATION

http://www.lafoundation.org/

ASLA COUNCIL OF FELLOWS SCHOLARSHIP

Scholarship to aid promising students with unmet financial need. Eligible applicants must be permanent U.S. citizens or permanent resident aliens who are third-, fourth-, or fifth-year undergraduates at landscape architecture accreditation board accredited programs.

Academic Fields/Career Goals: Landscape Architecture.

Award: Scholarship for use in junior or senior years; not renewable. *Number:* up to 2. *Amount:* up to $4000.

Eligibility Requirements: Applicant must be enrolled or expecting to enroll full- or part-time at a four-year institution or university. Available to U.S. citizens.

Application Requirements: Application, essay, financial need analysis, references. *Deadline:* February 15.

Contact: Kathleen Le Dain, Communications Director
Landscape Architecture Foundation
818 18 Street, NW, Suite 810
Washington, DC 20006
Phone: 202-331-7070 Ext. 14
E-mail: rfigura@lafoundation.org

COURTLAND PAUL SCHOLARSHIP

Scholarship for undergraduate students in the final two years of study in landscape architecture accreditation board accredited schools. Applicants must demonstrate financial need, must be U.S. citizens, and have a minimum GPA of C.

Academic Fields/Career Goals: Landscape Architecture.

Award: Scholarship for use in junior or senior years; not renewable. *Number:* 1. *Amount:* up to $5000.

Eligibility Requirements: Applicant must be enrolled or expecting to enroll full- or part-time at a four-year institution or university. Applicant must have 3.0 GPA or higher. Available to U.S. citizens.

Application Requirements: Application, essay, financial need analysis, references. *Deadline:* February 15.

Contact: Kathleen Le Dain, Communications Director
Landscape Architecture Foundation
818 18 Street, NW, Suite 810
Washington, DC 20006
Phone: 202-331-7070 Ext. 14
E-mail: rfigura@lafoundation.org

EDSA MINORITY SCHOLARSHIP

Scholarship established to help African American, Hispanic, Native American and minority students of other cultural and ethnic backgrounds to continue their landscape architecture education as they enter into their final two years of undergraduate study.

Academic Fields/Career Goals: Landscape Architecture.

Award: Scholarship for use in junior or senior years; not renewable. *Number:* up to 1. *Amount:* up to $5000.

Eligibility Requirements: Applicant must be American Indian/Alaska Native, Asian/Pacific Islander, Black (non-Hispanic), or Hispanic and enrolled or expecting to enroll full- or part-time at a four-year institution or university. Available to U.S. and non-U.S. citizens.

Application Requirements: Application, essay, references, photos of work samples. *Deadline:* February 15.

Contact: Kathleen Le Dain, Communications Director
Landscape Architecture Foundation
818 18 Street, NW, Suite 810
Washington, DC 20006
Phone: 202-331-7070 Ext. 14
E-mail: rfigura@lafoundation.org

HAWAII CHAPTER/DAVID T. WOOLSEY SCHOLARSHIP

One-time award for a third-, fourth-, or fifth-year undergraduate, or graduate student of landscape architecture. Must be permanent resident of Hawaii.

Academic Fields/Career Goals: Landscape Architecture.

Award: Scholarship for use in junior or senior years; not renewable. *Number:* 1. *Amount:* $2000.

Eligibility Requirements: Applicant must be enrolled or expecting to enroll full- or part-time at a four-year institution and resident of Hawaii. Available to U.S. citizens.

Application Requirements: Application, essay, financial need analysis, references, photos of work, proof of Hawaii residency. *Deadline:* February 15.

Contact: Kathleen Le Dain, Communications Director
Landscape Architecture Foundation
818 18 Street, NW, Suite 810
Washington, DC 20006
Phone: 202-331-7070 Ext. 14
E-mail: rfigura@lafoundation.org

LANDSCAPE ARCHITECTURE FOUNDATION/ CALIFORNIA LANDSCAPE ARCHITECTURAL STUDENT FUND SCHOLARSHIPS PROGRAM

• See page 360

LANDSCAPE ARCHITECTURE FOUNDATION/ CALIFORNIA LANDSCAPE ARCHITECTURE STUDENT FUND UNIVERSITY SCHOLARSHIP PROGRAM

• See page 360

RAIN BIRD INTELLIGENT USE OF WATER SCHOLARSHIP

One-time need-based award for students in the final two years of undergraduate study in landscape architecture.

Academic Fields/Career Goals: Landscape Architecture.

Award: Scholarship for use in junior or senior years; not renewable. *Number:* 1. *Amount:* $2500.

Eligibility Requirements: Applicant must be enrolled or expecting to enroll full- or part-time at a four-year institution or university. Available to U.S. and non-U.S. citizens.

Application Requirements: Application, essay, references, cover letter. *Deadline:* February 16.

Contact: Kathleen Le Dain, Communications Director
Landscape Architecture Foundation
818 18 Street, NW, Suite 810
Washington, DC 20006
Phone: 202-331-7070 Ext. 14
E-mail: rfigura@lafoundation.org

MONTANA FEDERATION OF GARDEN CLUBS

http://www.mtfgc.org/

LIFE MEMBER MONTANA FEDERATION OF GARDEN CLUBS SCHOLARSHIP

• See page 225

NATIONAL ASSOCIATION OF WOMEN IN CONSTRUCTION

http://www.nawic.org/

NAWIC UNDERGRADUATE SCHOLARSHIPS

• See page 102

NATIONAL GARDEN CLUBS INC.

http://www.gardenclub.org/

NATIONAL GARDEN CLUBS INC. SCHOLARSHIP PROGRAM

• See page 86

NEW YORK STATE EDUCATION DEPARTMENT

http://www.highered.nysed.gov/

REGENTS PROFESSIONAL OPPORTUNITY SCHOLARSHIP
• *See page 69*

PROFESSIONAL CONSTRUCTION ESTIMATORS ASSOCIATION

http://www.pcea.org/

TED WILSON MEMORIAL SCHOLARSHIP FOUNDATION
• *See page 179*

PROFESSIONAL GROUNDS MANAGEMENT SOCIETY

http://www.pgms.org/

ANNE SEAMAN PROFESSIONAL GROUNDS MANAGEMENT SOCIETY MEMORIAL SCHOLARSHIP
• *See page 87*

TURNER CONSTRUCTION COMPANY

http://www.turnerconstruction.com/

YOUTHFORCE 2020 SCHOLARSHIP PROGRAM
• *See page 103*

LAW ENFORCEMENT/ POLICE ADMINISTRATION

ALBERTA HERITAGE SCHOLARSHIP FUND

http://www.alis.alberta.ca/

ROBERT C. CARSON MEMORIAL BURSARY
• *See page 205*

AMERICAN SOCIETY OF CRIMINOLOGY

http://www.asc41.com/

AMERICAN SOCIETY OF CRIMINOLOGY GENE CARTE STUDENT PAPER COMPETITION
• *See page 206*

ASSOCIATION OF FORMER INTELLIGENCE OFFICERS

http://www.afio.com/13_scholarships.htm

CIA UNDERGRADUATE SCHOLARSHIPS
• *See page 89*

BOY SCOUTS OF AMERICA-MUSKINGUM VALLEY COUNCIL

http://www.learning-for-life.org/

SHERYL A. HORAK MEMORIAL SCHOLARSHIP
$1000 one-time scholarship for students enrolled either for full- or part-time study in a law enforcement field. Must be participant of the Learning for Life Exploring program.

Academic Fields/Career Goals: Law Enforcement/Police Administration.

Award: Scholarship for use in freshman, sophomore, junior, or senior years; not renewable. *Number:* 1. *Amount:* $1000.

Eligibility Requirements: Applicant must be enrolled or expecting to enroll full- or part-time at a two-year or four-year or technical institution or university. Available to U.S. and non-U.S. citizens.

Application Requirements: Application, essay, photo, references, transcript. *Deadline:* March 31.

Contact: Scholarship Committee
Boy Scouts of America-Muskingum Valley Council
1325 West Walnut Hill Lane, PO Box 152079
Irving, TX 75015-2079

CONNECTICUT ASSOCIATION OF WOMEN POLICE

http://www.cawp.net/

CONNECTICUT ASSOCIATION OF WOMEN POLICE SCHOLARSHIP
• *See page 206*

INDIANA SHERIFFS' ASSOCIATION

http://www.indianasheriffs.org/

INDIANA SHERIFFS' ASSOCIATION SCHOLARSHIP PROGRAM
• *See page 206*

INTERNATIONAL ASSOCIATION OF ARSON INVESTIGATORS EDUCATIONAL FOUNDATION INC.

http://www.firearson.com/

JOHN CHARLES WILSON SCHOLARSHIP & ROBERT DORAN SCHOLARSHIP
• *See page 316*

LEARNING FOR LIFE

http://www.learning-for-life.org/

CAPTAIN JAMES J. REGAN SCHOLARSHIP
Two one-time $500 scholarships are presented annually to Law Enforcement Explorers graduating from high school or from an accredited college program. Evaluation will be based on academic record.

Academic Fields/Career Goals: Law Enforcement/Police Administration.

Award: Scholarship for use in freshman, sophomore, junior, or senior years; not renewable. *Number:* 2. *Amount:* $500.

Eligibility Requirements: Applicant must be age 20 or under and enrolled or expecting to enroll full-time at a two-year or four-year or technical institution or university. Applicant or parent of applicant must be member of Explorer Program/Learning for Life. Available to U.S. citizens.

Application Requirements: Application, essay, photo, references, transcript. *Deadline:* March 31.

Contact: William Taylor, Scholarships and Awards Coordinator
Learning for Life
1329 West Walnut Hill Lane, PO Box 152225
Irving, TX 75015-2225
Phone: 972-580-2241
E-mail: btaylor@lflmail.org

DEA DRUG ABUSE PREVENTION SERVICE AWARDS

The award recognizes a Law Enforcement Explorer for outstanding service in drug abuse prevention.

Academic Fields/Career Goals: Law Enforcement/Police Administration.

Award: Prize for use in freshman, sophomore, junior, or senior years; not renewable. *Number:* 1. *Amount:* $1000.

Eligibility Requirements: Applicant must be enrolled or expecting to enroll full-time at a two-year or four-year institution or university. Applicant or parent of applicant must be member of Explorer Program/Learning for Life. Applicant or parent of applicant must have employment or volunteer experience in alcohol or drug abuse counseling/treatment/prevention. Available to U.S. citizens.

Application Requirements: Application, photo. *Deadline:* March 31.

Contact: William Taylor, Scholarships and Awards Coordinator
E-mail: btaylor@lflmail.org

FEDERAL CRIMINAL INVESTIGATORS SERVICE AWARD

The award recognizes Law Enforcement Explorers who render outstanding service to law enforcement agencies.

Academic Fields/Career Goals: Law Enforcement/Police Administration.

Award: Prize for use in freshman, sophomore, junior, or senior years; not renewable. *Number:* 1. *Amount:* $500.

Eligibility Requirements: Applicant must be enrolled or expecting to enroll full- or part-time at a two-year or four-year institution or university. Applicant or parent of applicant must be member of Explorer Program/Learning for Life. Available to U.S. citizens.

Application Requirements: Application, essay, photo, references. *Deadline:* March 31.

Contact: William Taylor, Scholarships and Awards Coordinator
E-mail: btaylor@lflmail.org

SHERYL A. HORAK MEMORIAL SCHOLARSHIP

Award for graduating high school students who are Law Enforcement Explorers joining a program in law enforcement in accredited college or university. Provides a one-time scholarship of $1000.

Academic Fields/Career Goals: Law Enforcement/Police Administration.

Award: Scholarship for use in freshman year; not renewable. *Number:* 1. *Amount:* $1000.

Eligibility Requirements: Applicant must be enrolled or expecting to enroll full-time at a two-year or four-year institution or university. Applicant or parent of applicant must be member of Explorer Program/Learning for Life. Available to U.S. citizens.

Application Requirements: Application, essay, photo, references, transcript. *Deadline:* March 31.

Contact: William Taylor, Scholarships and Awards Coordinator
E-mail: btaylor@lflmail.org

NATIONAL BLACK POLICE ASSOCIATION

http://www.blackpolice.org/

ALPHONSO DEAL SCHOLARSHIP AWARD
• *See page 206*

NORTH CAROLINA STATE EDUCATION ASSISTANCE AUTHORITY

http://www.ncseaa.edu/

NORTH CAROLINA SHERIFFS' ASSOCIATION UNDERGRADUATE CRIMINAL JUSTICE SCHOLARSHIPS
• *See page 207*

SOUTH CAROLINA POLICE CORPS

http://www.citadel.edu/

SOUTH CAROLINA POLICE CORPS SCHOLARSHIP

Tuition reimbursement scholarship available to a full-time student of an U.S. accredited college. Must agree to serve for four years on community patrol with a participating South Carolina police or sheriff's department. Up to $7500 per academic year with a limit of $30,000 per student.

Academic Fields/Career Goals: Law Enforcement/Police Administration.

Award: Scholarship for use in freshman, sophomore, junior, senior, or graduate years; renewable. *Number:* 20. *Amount:* $7500–$30,000.

Eligibility Requirements: Applicant must be enrolled or expecting to enroll full-time at a four-year institution or university. Available to U.S. citizens.

Application Requirements: Application, driver's license, essay, interview, references, test scores, transcript. *Deadline:* varies.

Contact: Bryan C. Jones, Community Action Team
South Carolina Police Corps
5623 Two Notch Road
Columbia, SC 29223
Phone: 803-865-4486
E-mail: bryan.jones@hcahealthcare.com

WIFLE FOUNDATION, INC.

http://www.wifle.org/

WIFLE SCHOLARSHIP PROGRAM
• *See page 202*

LAW/LEGAL SERVICES

ALBERTA HERITAGE SCHOLARSHIP FUND

http://www.alis.alberta.ca/

JASON LANG SCHOLARSHIP
• *See page 213*

ROBERT C. CARSON MEMORIAL BURSARY
• *See page 205*

AMERICAN ASSOCIATION OF LAW LIBRARIES

http://www.aallnet.org/

AALL LIBRARY SCHOOL SCHOLARSHIPS FOR NON-LAW SCHOOL GRADUATES

One-time award for college graduate with meaningful law library experience who is a degree candidate in an accredited library school with the intention of having a career as a law librarian. Preference given to AALL members. Scholarship amount and the number granted varies. Must submit evidence of financial need.

Academic Fields/Career Goals: Law/Legal Services.

Award: Scholarship for use in freshman, sophomore, junior, senior, or graduate years; not renewable. *Number:* varies. *Amount:* varies.

Eligibility Requirements: Applicant must be enrolled or expecting to enroll full- or part-time at a four-year institution or university. Applicant or parent of applicant must be member of American Association of Law Librarians. Available to U.S. and non-U.S. citizens.

Application Requirements: Application, essay, financial need analysis, references, self-addressed stamped envelope, transcript. *Deadline:* April 1.

Contact: Chair, Scholarships Committee
American Association of Law Libraries
105 West Adams Street, Suite 3300
Chicago, IL 60603
Phone: 312-939-4764
Fax: 312-431-1097
E-mail: scholarships@aall.org

AMERICAN CRIMINAL JUSTICE ASSOCIATION-LAMBDA ALPHA EPSILON

http://www.acjalae.org/

AMERICAN CRIMINAL JUSTICE ASSOCIATION-LAMBDA ALPHA EPSILON NATIONAL SCHOLARSHIP
• See page 205

AMERICAN SOCIETY OF CRIMINOLOGY

http://www.asc41.com/

AMERICAN SOCIETY OF CRIMINOLOGY GENE CARTE STUDENT PAPER COMPETITION
• See page 206

ARRL FOUNDATION INC.

http://www.arrl.org/

FRANCIS WALTON MEMORIAL SCHOLARSHIP
• See page 83

BLACK ENTERTAINMENT AND SPORTS LAWYERS ASSOCIATION INC.

http://www.besla.org/

BESLA SCHOLARSHIP LEGAL WRITING COMPETITION

$1500 award for the best 1000-word, or two-page essay on a compelling legal issue facing the entertainment or sports industry. Essay must be written by law school student who has completed at least one full year at an accredited law school. Minimum GPA of 2.8 required.

Academic Fields/Career Goals: Law/Legal Services.

Award: Scholarship for use in freshman, sophomore, junior, senior, or graduate years; not renewable. *Number:* 2. *Amount:* $1500.

Eligibility Requirements: Applicant must be enrolled or expecting to enroll full-time at a four-year institution or university. Available to U.S. and non-U.S. citizens.

Application Requirements: Application, essay, resume, transcript. *Deadline:* varies.

Contact: Rev. Phyllicia Hatton, Executive Administrator
Black Entertainment and Sports Lawyers Association Inc.
PO Box 441485
Fort Washington, MD 20749-1485
Phone: 301-248-1818
Fax: 301-248-0700
E-mail: beslamailbox@aol.com

BOYS AND GIRLS CLUBS OF SAN DIEGO

http://www.sdyouth.org/

SPENCE REESE SCHOLARSHIP
• See page 281

COLLEGEBOUND FOUNDATION

http://www.collegeboundfoundation.org/

DECATUR H. MILLER SCHOLARSHIP
• See page 352

JEANETTE R. WOLMAN SCHOLARSHIP
• See page 172

GRAND RAPIDS COMMUNITY FOUNDATION

http://www.grfoundation.org/

WARNER NORCROSS AND JUDD LLP SCHOLARSHIP FOR MINORITY STUDENTS

Financial assistance to students who are residents of Michigan, or attend a college/university/vocational school in Michigan, and are of racial and ethnic minority heritage pursuing a career in law, paralegal, or a legal secretarial program. Law school scholarship ($5000), paralegal scholarship ($2000), legal secretary scholarship ($1000).

Academic Fields/Career Goals: Law/Legal Services.

Award: Scholarship for use in freshman, sophomore, junior, senior, or graduate years; not renewable. *Number:* up to 3. *Amount:* $1000–$5000.

Eligibility Requirements: Applicant must be American Indian/Alaska Native, Asian/Pacific Islander, Black (non-Hispanic), or Hispanic; enrolled or expecting to enroll full-time at a two-year or four-year institution or university; resident of Michigan and studying in Michigan. Applicant must have 2.5 GPA or higher. Available to U.S. citizens.

Application Requirements: Application, essay, financial need analysis, references, transcript. *Deadline:* April 15.

Contact: Ruth Bishop, Education Program Officer
Grand Rapids Community Foundation
161 Ottawa Avenue, NW, 209 C
Grand Rapids, MI 49503-2757
Phone: 616-454-1751 Ext. 103
Fax: 616-454-6455
E-mail: rbishop@grfoundation.org

GREATER KANAWHA VALLEY FOUNDATION

http://www.tgkvf.org/

BERNICE PICKINS PARSONS FUND

Renewable award of $1000 open to students pursuing education or training in the fields of library science, nursing and paraprofessional training in the legal field. Grant based on financial need. Must be a resident of West Virginia; with preference given to Jackson county residents.

Academic Fields/Career Goals: Law/Legal Services; Library and Information Sciences; Nursing.

Award: Grant for use in freshman, sophomore, junior, or senior years; renewable. *Number:* 7. *Amount:* $1000.

Eligibility Requirements: Applicant must be enrolled or expecting to enroll full-time at a two-year or four-year institution or university and resident of West Virginia. Available to U.S. citizens.

Application Requirements: Application, essay, financial need analysis, references, self-addressed stamped envelope, test scores, transcript. *Deadline:* January 15.

Contact: Susan Hoover, Scholarship Program Officer
Greater Kanawha Valley Foundation
1600 Huntington Square, 900 Lee Street, East
PO Box 3041
Charleston, WV 25301
Phone: 304-346-3620
E-mail: shoover@tgkvf.org

INSTITUTE FOR HUMANE STUDIES

http://www.theihs.org/

HUMANE STUDIES FELLOWSHIPS
• *See page 185*

JAPANESE AMERICAN CITIZENS LEAGUE (JACL)

http://www.jacl.org/

NATIONAL JACL HEADQUARTERS SCHOLARSHIP
• *See page 84*

KE ALI'I PAUAHI FOUNDATION

http://www.pauahi.org/

WILLIAM S. RICHARDSON COMMEMORATIVE SCHOLARSHIP

This scholarship was established to honor William S. Richardson, retired Trustee of the Kamehameha Schools Bishop Estate and provides support for students of character and exceptional ability pursuing law degrees from the University of Hawai'i-Manoa William S. Richardson School of Law. Applicants must be a resident of the State of Hawai'i and preference will be given to applicants demonstrating financial need and commitment to contributing to the greater community.

Academic Fields/Career Goals: Law/Legal Services.

Award: Scholarship for use in freshman, sophomore, junior, senior, or graduate years; not renewable. *Number:* 5. *Amount:* up to $1000.

Eligibility Requirements: Applicant must be enrolled or expecting to enroll full-time at a four-year institution or university and resident of Hawaii. Available to U.S. citizens.

Application Requirements: Application, financial need analysis, references, transcript, college acceptance letter for first-year students. *Deadline:* April 1.

Contact: Mavis Shiraisji-Nagao, Scholarship Coordinator
    Phone: 808-534-3966
    E-mail: scholarships@pauahi.org

LINCOLN COMMUNITY FOUNDATION

http://www.lcf.org/

LAWRENCE "LARRY" FRAZIER MEMORIAL SCHOLARSHIP
• *See page 127*

MARYLAND STATE HIGHER EDUCATION COMMISSION

http://www.mhec.state.md.us/

GRADUATE AND PROFESSIONAL SCHOLARSHIP PROGRAM-MARYLAND
• *See page 220*

JANET L. HOFFMANN LOAN ASSISTANCE REPAYMENT PROGRAM
• *See page 241*

NATIONAL ASSOCIATION OF WATER COMPANIES-NEW JERSEY CHAPTER

http://www.nawc.org/

NATIONAL ASSOCIATION OF WATER COMPANIES-NEW JERSEY CHAPTER SCHOLARSHIP
• *See page 142*

NATIONAL BLACK POLICE ASSOCIATION

http://www.blackpolice.org/

ALPHONSO DEAL SCHOLARSHIP AWARD
• *See page 206*

NATIONAL COURT REPORTERS ASSOCIATION

http://www.ncraonline.org/

COUNCIL ON APPROVED STUDENT EDUCATION'S SCHOLARSHIP FUND

Applicant must have a writing speed of 140 to 180 words/min, and must be in an NCRA-approved court reporting program. Must write a two-page essay on topic chosen for the year and is also required to enter the competition.

Academic Fields/Career Goals: Law/Legal Services.

Award: Scholarship for use in sophomore year; not renewable. *Number:* 3. *Amount:* $500–$1500.

Eligibility Requirements: Applicant must be enrolled or expecting to enroll full- or part-time at a two-year or four-year or technical institution. Applicant must have 3.0 GPA or higher. Available to U.S. and Canadian citizens.

Application Requirements: Application, applicant must enter a contest, essay, references, transcript. *Deadline:* April 1.

Contact: Donna M. Gaede, Approval Program Manager
    National Court Reporters Association
    8224 Old Courthouse Road
    Vienna, VA 22182
    Phone: 703-556-6272 Ext. 171
    Fax: 703-556-6291
    E-mail: dgaede@ncrahq.org

FRANK SARLI MEMORIAL SCHOLARSHIP

One-time award to a student who is nearing graduation from a trade/technical school or four-year college. Must be enrolled in a court reporting program. Minimum 3.5 GPA required.

Academic Fields/Career Goals: Law/Legal Services.

Award: Scholarship for use in senior year; not renewable. *Number:* 1. *Amount:* $2000.

Eligibility Requirements: Applicant must be enrolled or expecting to enroll full- or part-time at a four-year or technical institution or university. Applicant or parent of applicant must be member of National Federation of Press Women. Applicant must have 3.5 GPA or higher. Available to U.S. and non-U.S. citizens.

Application Requirements: Application. *Deadline:* February 28.

Contact: B J. Shorak, Deputy Executive Director
    National Court Reporters Association
    8224 Old Courthouse Road
    Vienna, VA 22182-3808
    Phone: 703-556-6272 Ext. 126
    Fax: 703-556-6291
    E-mail: bjshorak@ncrahq.org

STUDENT MEMBER TUITION GRANT

Four $500 awards for students in good academic standing in a court reporting program. Students are required to write 120 to 200 words/min.

Academic Fields/Career Goals: Law/Legal Services.

Award: Grant for use in freshman, sophomore, junior, or senior years; not renewable. *Number:* 4. *Amount:* $500.

Eligibility Requirements: Applicant must be enrolled or expecting to enroll full- or part-time at a four-year or technical institution or university. Available to U.S. and non-U.S. citizens.

Application Requirements: Application. *Deadline:* May 31.

Contact: Amy Davidson, Assistant Director of Membership
    National Court Reporters Association
    8224 Old Courthouse Road
    Vienna, VA 22182
    Phone: 703-556-6272 Ext. 123
    E-mail: adavidson@ncrahq.org

NATIONAL FEDERATION OF PARALEGAL ASSOCIATIONS INC. (NFPA)

http://www.paralegals.org/

NATIONAL FEDERATION OF PARALEGAL ASSOCIATES INC. THOMSON REUTERS SCHOLARSHIP

Applicants must be full- or part-time students enrolled in an accredited paralegal education program or college-level program with emphasis in paralegal studies. Minimum GPA of 3.0 required. NFPA membership is not required. Travel stipend to annual convention, where recipients will receive awards, also provided.

Academic Fields/Career Goals: Law/Legal Services.

Award: Scholarship for use in freshman, sophomore, junior, senior, graduate, or postgraduate years; not renewable. *Number:* 2. *Amount:* $2000–$3000.

Eligibility Requirements: Applicant must be enrolled or expecting to enroll full- or part-time at a two-year or four-year or technical institution or university. Applicant must have 3.0 GPA or higher. Available to U.S. and non-U.S. citizens.

Application Requirements: Application, essay, references, transcript. *Deadline:* July 31.

Contact: Cindy Byfield, Managing Director
National Federation of Paralegal Associations Inc. (NFPA)
PO Box 2016
Edmonds, WA 98020
Phone: 425-967-0045
E-mail: info@paralegals.org

NEW ENGLAND EMPLOYEE BENEFITS COUNCIL

http://www.neebc.org/

NEW ENGLAND EMPLOYEE BENEFITS COUNCIL SCHOLARSHIP PROGRAM
• *See page 68*

NEW MEXICO COMMISSION ON HIGHER EDUCATION

http://www.hed.state.nm.us/

PUBLIC SERVICE LAW LOAN REPAYMENT ASSISTANCE PROGRAM

Program to provide legal educational loan repayment assistance to individuals providing public service in state or local government or the nonprofit sector in New Mexico to low income or underserved residents.

Academic Fields/Career Goals: Law/Legal Services.

Award: Forgivable loan for use in freshman, sophomore, junior, or senior years; renewable. *Number:* 1–16. *Amount:* up to $7200.

Eligibility Requirements: Applicant must be enrolled or expecting to enroll full-time at a four-year institution or university; resident of New Mexico and studying in New Mexico. Available to U.S. citizens.

Application Requirements: Application. *Deadline:* February 28.

Contact: Theresa Acker, Financial Aid Division
New Mexico Commission on Higher Education
1068 Cerrillos Road
Santa Fe, NM 87505
Phone: 505-476-6506
Fax: 505-475-6511
E-mail: theresa.acker@state.nm.us

NEW YORK STATE EDUCATION DEPARTMENT

http://www.highered.nysed.gov/

REGENTS PROFESSIONAL OPPORTUNITY SCHOLARSHIP
• *See page 69*

OKLAHOMA PARALEGAL ASSOCIATION

http://www.okparalegal.org/

JAMIE BOWIE MEMORIAL SCHOLARSHIP

Applicant must be currently enrolled in a legal assistant program at an ABA-approved institution and have successfully completed at least six credit hours. The director of the legal assistant program must provide verification of current enrollment. Recipient must be present at the presentation of the scholarship on the date to be announced.

Academic Fields/Career Goals: Law/Legal Services.

Award: Scholarship for use in freshman, sophomore, junior, or senior years; not renewable. *Number:* 1. *Amount:* $250.

Eligibility Requirements: Applicant must be enrolled or expecting to enroll full- or part-time at a four-year institution or university. Available to U.S. citizens.

Application Requirements: Application, financial need analysis, transcript. *Deadline:* April 15.

Contact: Emily Buckmaster, Student Director
Oklahoma Paralegal Association
714 Maple Drive
Weatherford, OK 73096
Phone: 405-235-7000
E-mail: ebuckmaster@hartzoglaw.com

RICHARD V. CRUZ MEMORIAL FOUNDATION

http://www.rvcruzfoundation.2givenow.org/

RICHARD V. CRUZ MEMORIAL FOUNDATION SCHOLARSHIP

$2000 scholarships to students from underserved populations enrolled in a California ABA-accredited law school. Applicants must have begun or completed their first year of law school and must be in good academic standing.

Academic Fields/Career Goals: Law/Legal Services.

Award: Scholarship for use in sophomore, junior, senior, or graduate years; not renewable. *Number:* varies. *Amount:* $2000.

Eligibility Requirements: Applicant must be Hispanic; enrolled or expecting to enroll full-time at a four-year institution or university and studying in California. Available to U.S. citizens.

Application Requirements: Application, financial need analysis, interview, resume, references, personal statement. *Deadline:* April 17.

Contact: Scholarship Committee
Richard V. Cruz Memorial Foundation
1605 Hope Street, Suite 210
South Pasadena, CA 91030
Phone: 626-799-7880
Fax: 626-799-0449

SOCIETY OF SATELLITE PROFESSIONALS INTERNATIONAL

http://www.sspi.org/

SSPI INTERNATIONAL SCHOLARSHIPS
• *See page 133*

TKE EDUCATIONAL FOUNDATION

http://www.tke.org/

HARRY J. DONNELLY MEMORIAL SCHOLARSHIP
• *See page 71*

UNITARIAN UNIVERSALIST ASSOCIATION

http://www.uua.org/

STANFIELD AND D'ORLANDO ART SCHOLARSHIP
• *See page 116*

UNITED NEGRO COLLEGE FUND

http://www.uncf.org/

ALFRED CHISHOLM/BASF MEMORIAL SCHOLARSHIP FUND
• *See page 72*

RAYMOND W. CANNON MEMORIAL SCHOLARSHIP PROGRAM

Annual scholarship awarded to undergraduate juniors majoring in pharmacy or pre-law, who have demonstrated leadership in high school and college. Minimum 2.5 GPA required. Must be enrolled in a UNCF member institution or a HBCU. Additional information and application on http://www.uncf.org.

Academic Fields/Career Goals: Law/Legal Services; Pharmacy.

Award: Scholarship for use in junior year; not renewable. *Number:* varies. *Amount:* $2000–$5000.

Eligibility Requirements: Applicant must be Black (non-Hispanic) and enrolled or expecting to enroll full- or part-time at a four-year institution or university. Applicant must have 2.5 GPA or higher. Available to U.S. and non-U.S. citizens.

Application Requirements: Application, financial need analysis. *Deadline:* continuous.

Contact: Director, Program Services
United Negro College Fund
8260 Willow Oaks Corporate Drive
PO Box 10444
Fairfax, VA 22031-8044
Phone: 800-331-2244
E-mail: rebecca.bennett@uncf.org

VIRGINIA STATE BAR

http://www.vsb.org/

LAW IN SOCIETY AWARD COMPETITION

Participants write an essay in response to a hypothetical situation dealing with legal issues. Awards are based on superior understanding of the value of law in everyday life. The top thirty essays are awarded prizes of a plaque and dictionary/thesaurus set. First place receives $2000 U.S. Savings Bond or $1000 cash; second place, $1,500 bond or $750 cash; third place, $1,000 bond or $500 cash; honorable mentions, $200 bond or $100 cash.

Academic Fields/Career Goals: Law/Legal Services.

Award: Prize for use in freshman year; not renewable. *Number:* up to 10. *Amount:* $100–$1000.

Eligibility Requirements: Applicant must be high school student; age 19 or under; planning to enroll or expecting to enroll full- or part-time at a four-year institution or university; resident of Virginia and must have an interest in writing. Available to U.S. citizens.

Application Requirements: Application, applicant must enter a contest, essay. *Deadline:* February 1.

Contact: Sandy Adkins, Public Relations Assistant
Virginia State Bar
707 East Main Street, Suite 1500
Richmond, VA 23219-2800
Phone: 804-775-0594
Fax: 804-775-0582
E-mail: adkins@vsb.org

WASHINGTON STATE TRIAL LAWYERS ASSOCIATION

http://www.wstla.org/

WSTLA AMERICAN JUSTICE ESSAY SCHOLARSHIP CONTEST

The purpose of the scholarship is to foster an awareness and understanding of the American justice system. The essay contest deals with advocacy in the American justice system and related topics. Three scholarships are available to students who are attending high school in Washington state.

Academic Fields/Career Goals: Law/Legal Services.

Award: Scholarship for use in freshman year; not renewable. *Number:* 3. *Amount:* $2000–$3000.

Eligibility Requirements: Applicant must be high school student; planning to enroll or expecting to enroll full- or part-time at a two-year or four-year institution or university and studying in Washington. Available to U.S. and non-U.S. citizens.

Application Requirements: Application, applicant must enter a contest, essay. *Deadline:* March 21.

Contact: Adrianne Williams, Scholarship Coordinator
Washington State Trial Lawyers Association
1511 State Avenue NW
Olympia, WA 98506

WHOMENTORS.COM, INC.

http://www.WHOmentors.com/

ACCREDITED REPRESENTATIVE (FULL)
• *See page 56*

LIBRARY AND INFORMATION SCIENCES

ALICE L. HALTOM EDUCATIONAL FUND

http://www.alhef.org/

ALICE L. HALTOM EDUCATIONAL FUND
• *See page 350*

AMERICAN SOCIETY FOR INFORMATION SCIENCE AND TECHNOLOGY

http://www.asis.org/

JOHN WILEY & SONS BEST JASIST PAPER AWARD
• *See page 195*

BIBLIOGRAPHICAL SOCIETY OF AMERICA

http://www.bibsocamer.org/

JUSTIN G. SCHILLER PRIZE FOR BIBLIOGRAPHICAL WORK IN PRE-20TH-CENTURY CHILDREN'S BOOKS

Award for bibliographic work in the field of pre-20th century children's books. Winner will receive a cash award of $2000 and a year's membership in the Society.

Academic Fields/Career Goals: Library and Information Sciences; Literature/English/Writing.

Award: Prize for use in freshman, sophomore, junior, or senior years; not renewable. *Number:* 1. *Amount:* $2000.

Eligibility Requirements: Applicant must be enrolled or expecting to enroll full- or part-time at a four-year institution or university. Available to U.S. and non-U.S. citizens.

Application Requirements: Application, applicant must enter a contest, resume, documentation regarding the approval of a thesis or dissertation or confirming the date of publication. *Deadline:* September 1.

Contact: Michele Randall, Executive Secretary
Bibliographical Society of America
PO Box 1537, Lenox Hill Station
New York, NY 10021
Phone: 212-452-2710
Fax: 212-452-2710
E-mail: bsa@bibsocamer.org

CALIFORNIA SCHOOL LIBRARY ASSOCIATION

http://www.csla.net/

JOHN BLANCHARD MEMORIAL FUND SCHOLARSHIP

Provides assistance to school library paraprofessional in obtaining preparation needed to qualify and serve as a school library media teacher in California. Applicant must be a member of the California School Library Association.

Academic Fields/Career Goals: Library and Information Sciences.

Award: Scholarship for use in freshman, sophomore, junior, or senior years; not renewable. *Number:* 1. *Amount:* $1000.

Eligibility Requirements: Applicant must be enrolled or expecting to enroll full- or part-time at an institution or university; resident of California and studying in California. Applicant or parent of applicant must have employment or volunteer experience in library work. Available to U.S. citizens.

Application Requirements: Application, references. *Deadline:* April 30.

Contact: Deidre Bryant, Executive Director
California School Library Association
950 Glenn Drive, Suite 150
Folsom, CA 95630
Phone: 916-447-2684
E-mail: info@csla.net

FLORIDA ASSOCIATION FOR MEDIA IN EDUCATION

http://www.floridamedia.org/

FAME/SANDY ULM SCHOLARSHIP

Scholarship for students studying to be school library media specialists. The scholarship awards at least $1000 to one or more students each year. Deadlines: September 15 and February 15.

Academic Fields/Career Goals: Library and Information Sciences.

Award: Scholarship for use in freshman year; not renewable. *Number:* varies. *Amount:* $1000.

Eligibility Requirements: Applicant must be high school student; planning to enroll or expecting to enroll full-time at a two-year or four-year or technical institution or university and studying in Florida. Available to U.S. citizens.

Application Requirements: Application. *Deadline:* varies.

Contact: Larry Bodkin, Executive Director
Florida Association for Media in Education
2563 Capital Medical Boulevard
Tallahassee, FL 32308
Phone: 850-531-8350
Fax: 850-531-8344
E-mail: lbodkin@floridamedia.org

FLORIDA LIBRARY ASSOCIATION

http://www.flalib.org/

FLORIDA LIBRARY ASSOCIATION-BACHELOR'S DEGREE SCHOLARSHIP

Scholarship will be awarded to a Florida resident with library experience who is pursuing a bachelor's degree. Applicants must be members of Florida Library Association. For further details, visit web site http://www.flalib.org.

Academic Fields/Career Goals: Library and Information Sciences.

Award: Scholarship for use in junior or senior years; not renewable. *Number:* 1. *Amount:* $1000.

Eligibility Requirements: Applicant must be enrolled or expecting to enroll at a four-year institution or university; resident of Florida and studying in Florida. Applicant or parent of applicant must have employment or volunteer experience in library work. Available to U.S. and non-U.S. citizens.

Application Requirements: Application, essay, resume, references. *Deadline:* February 1.

Contact: Faye Roberts, Executive Director
Florida Library Association
PO Box 1571
Lake City, FL 32056-1571
Phone: 386-438-5795

GREATER KANAWHA VALLEY FOUNDATION

http://www.tgkvf.org/

BERNICE PICKINS PARSONS FUND
• See page 391

IDAHO LIBRARY ASSOCIATION

http://www.idaholibraries.org/

IDAHO LIBRARY ASSOCIATION GARDNER HANKS SCHOLARSHIP

Scholarship for students who are beginning or continuing formal library education, pursuing a Master's of Library Science degree or Media Generalist certification. Must be an ILA member.

Academic Fields/Career Goals: Library and Information Sciences.

Award: Scholarship for use in freshman, sophomore, junior, or senior years; not renewable. *Number:* 1. *Amount:* $100–$500.

Eligibility Requirements: Applicant must be enrolled or expecting to enroll full-time at a four-year institution or university. Applicant or parent of applicant must be member of Idaho Library Association. Available to U.S. citizens.

Application Requirements: Application, financial need analysis, references. *Deadline:* September 1.

Contact: Suzy Ricks, Scholarships & Awards Committee Chair
Idaho Library Association
5210 Stuart Avenue
Chubbuck, ID 83202
Phone: 208-237-2192
Fax: 208-237-2194

IDAHO LIBRARY ASSOCIATION LIBRARY SCIENCE SCHOLARSHIPS

One-time award for students studying library science. Must be a member of the Idaho Library Association. Must be a resident of Idaho.

Academic Fields/Career Goals: Library and Information Sciences.

Award: Scholarship for use in freshman, sophomore, junior, senior, or graduate years; not renewable. *Number:* 2–6. *Amount:* $100–$500.

Eligibility Requirements: Applicant must be enrolled or expecting to enroll full- or part-time at a two-year or four-year institution or university and resident of Idaho. Applicant or parent of applicant must be member of Idaho Library Association. Available to U.S. and non-U.S. citizens.

Application Requirements: Application, essay, resume, references. *Deadline:* September 1.

Contact: Suzy Ricks, Scholarship Committee
Idaho Library Association
Eastern Idaho Technical College Library, 1600 South 2500 East
Idaho Falls, ID 83404
Phone: 208-524-3000 Ext. 3312
E-mail: sricks@eitc.edu

INDIANA LIBRARY FEDERATION

http://www.ilfonline.org/

AISLE SCHOLARSHIP FUND

Scholarships are provided for undergraduate or graduate students entering or currently enrolled in a program to receive educational certification in the field of school library media services. For more details, visit http//www.ilfonline.org.

Academic Fields/Career Goals: Library and Information Sciences.

Award: Scholarship for use in freshman, sophomore, junior, senior, or graduate years; not renewable. *Number:* varies. *Amount:* varies.

Eligibility Requirements: Applicant must be enrolled or expecting to enroll full-time at a four-year institution or university and resident of Indiana. Available to U.S. citizens.

Application Requirements: Application, references, transcript. *Deadline:* June 30.

Contact: Amanda Turney, Communications
Indiana Library Federation
941 East 86th Street, Suite 260
Indianapolis, IN 46240
Phone: 317-257-2040
Fax: 317-257-1389
E-mail: aturney@ilfonline.org

SPECIAL LIBRARIES ASSOCIATION

http://www.sla.org/

SPECIAL LIBRARIES ASSOCIATION AFFIRMATIVE ACTION SCHOLARSHIP

One $6000 scholarship for graduate study in librarianship leading to a master's degree. Must be U.S. citizen either by birth or naturalization or permanent resident alien and a member of a minority group. Must have an interest in special librarianship and submit evidence of financial need.

Academic Fields/Career Goals: Library and Information Sciences.

Award: Scholarship for use in senior or graduate years; not renewable. *Number:* 1. *Amount:* $6000.

Eligibility Requirements: Applicant must be American Indian/Alaska Native, Asian/Pacific Islander, Black (non-Hispanic), or Hispanic and enrolled or expecting to enroll full-time at a four-year institution or university. Available to U.S. citizens.

Application Requirements: Application, essay, financial need analysis, interview, references, test scores, transcript, statement of provisional acceptance. *Deadline:* September 30.

Contact: Teniakka Greene, Membership Services Associate
Special Libraries Association
331 South Patrick Street
Alexandria, VA 22314-3501
Phone: 703-647-4900
Fax: 703-647-4901
E-mail: tgreene@sla.org

SPECIAL LIBRARIES ASSOCIATION SCHOLARSHIP

Up to three $6000 awards for graduate study in librarianship leading to a master's degree at a recognized school of library or information science. Must be college graduate or college senior with an interest in special librarianship.

Academic Fields/Career Goals: Library and Information Sciences.

Award: Scholarship for use in senior or graduate years; not renewable. *Number:* up to 3. *Amount:* $6000.

Eligibility Requirements: Applicant must be enrolled or expecting to enroll full-time at a four-year institution or university. Available to U.S. citizens.

Application Requirements: Application, essay, financial need analysis, interview, references, test scores, transcript, statement of provisional acceptance. *Deadline:* September 30.

Contact: Teniakka Greene, Membership Services Associate
Special Libraries Association
331 South Patrick Street
Alexandria, VA 22314-3501
Phone: 703-647-4900
Fax: 703-647-4901
E-mail: tgreene@sla.org

WISCONSIN LIBRARY ASSOCIATION

http://www.wla.lib.wi.us/

SCHOLARSHIP FOR THE EDUCATION OF RURAL LIBRARIANS GLORIA HOEGH MEMORIAL FUND

Scholarship awarded to librarians planning to attend a workshop, conference, and/or a continuing education program within or outside Wisconsin. Applicant must be a library employee working in a Wisconsin community with a current population of 5000 or less or who works with library employees in those communities.

Academic Fields/Career Goals: Library and Information Sciences.

Award: Scholarship for use in freshman, sophomore, junior, senior, or graduate years; not renewable. *Number:* 1. *Amount:* $1000.

Eligibility Requirements: Applicant must be enrolled or expecting to enroll full- or part-time at a four-year institution or university and resident of Wisconsin. Available to U.S. citizens.

Application Requirements: Application, essay, financial need analysis. *Deadline:* August 1.

Contact: Brigitte Rupp Vacha, Member Services Coordinator
Wisconsin Library Association
4610 South Biltmore Lane, Suite 100
Madison, WI 53718-2153
Phone: 608-245-3640
E-mail: ruppvacha@scls.lib.wi.us

WLA CONTINUING EDUCATION SCHOLARSHIP

Scholarship awarded to employee who is planning to attend a continuing education program within or outside of Wisconsin. Applicant must be able to communicate the knowledge gained from the continuing education program to fellow librarians and information professionals in Wisconsin, employed in a library and information agency in Wisconsin.

Academic Fields/Career Goals: Library and Information Sciences.

Award: Scholarship for use in freshman, sophomore, junior, senior, graduate, or postgraduate years; not renewable. *Number:* 1. *Amount:* varies.

Eligibility Requirements: Applicant must be enrolled or expecting to enroll full- or part-time at a four-year institution or university and resident of Wisconsin. Available to U.S. citizens.

Application Requirements: Application, copy of the continuing education program. *Deadline:* June 1.

Contact: Brigitte Rupp Vacha, Member Services Coordinator
Wisconsin Library Association
4610 South Biltmore Lane, Suite 100
Madison, WI 53718-2153
Phone: 608-245-3640
E-mail: ruppvacha@scls.lib.wi.us

LITERATURE/ENGLISH/ WRITING

AIM MAGAZINE SHORT STORY CONTEST

http://www.aimmagazine.org/

AMERICA'S INTERCULTURAL MAGAZINE (AIM) SHORT STORY CONTEST

Short fiction award for a previously unpublished story that embodies the magazine's goal of furthering the brotherhood of man through the written word. Must provide proof that people from different racial/ethnic backgrounds are more alike than they are different. Maximum length 4000 words. Story should not moralize.

Academic Fields/Career Goals: Literature/English/Writing.

Award: Prize for use in freshman, sophomore, junior, senior, or graduate years; not renewable. *Number:* 1–2. *Amount:* $75–$100.

Eligibility Requirements: Applicant must be enrolled or expecting to enroll full- or part-time at a two-year or four-year or technical institution or university and must have an interest in writing. Available to U.S. and Canadian citizens.

Application Requirements: Application, applicant must enter a contest, essay. *Deadline:* August 15.

Contact: Mark Boone, Fiction Editor
Aim Magazine Short Story Contest
PO Box 1174
Maywood, IL 60153
Phone: 708-344-4414
E-mail: apiladoone@aol.com

ALLIANCE FOR YOUNG ARTISTS AND WRITERS INC.

http://www.artandwriting.org/

SCHOLASTIC ART AND WRITING AWARDS-ART SECTION
• *See page 108*

SCHOLASTIC ART AND WRITING AWARDS-WRITING SECTION SCHOLARSHIP
• *See page 109*

AMERICAN FOUNDATION FOR THE BLIND

http://www.afb.org/

R.L. GILLETTE SCHOLARSHIP

Two scholarships of $1000 each to women who are enrolled in a four-year undergraduate degree program in literature or music. In addition to the general requirements, applicants must submit a performance tape not to exceed 30 minutes, or a creative writing sample. Must submit proof of legal blindness. For additional information and application requirements, refer to web site http://www.afb.org/scholarships.asp.

Academic Fields/Career Goals: Literature/English/Writing; Music.

Award: Scholarship for use in freshman, sophomore, junior, or senior years; not renewable. *Number:* up to 2. *Amount:* $1000.

Eligibility Requirements: Applicant must be enrolled or expecting to enroll full-time at a four-year institution or university and female. Applicant must be visually impaired. Available to U.S. citizens.

Application Requirements: Application, essay, financial need analysis, references, transcript, performance tape (not to exceed 30 minutes) or creative writing sample, proof of legal blindness, acceptance letter. *Deadline:* April 30.

Contact: Dawn Bodrogi, Information Center and Library Coordinator
American Foundation for the Blind
11 Penn Plaza, Suite 300
New York, NY 10001
Phone: 212-502-7661
Fax: 212-502-7771
E-mail: afbinfo@afb.net

AMERICAN LEGION AUXILIARY DEPARTMENT OF WASHINGTON

http://www.walegion-aux.org/

FLORENCE LEMCKE MEMORIAL SCHOLARSHIP IN FINE ARTS
• *See page 107*

AMERICAN-SCANDINAVIAN FOUNDATION

http://www.amscan.org/

AMERICAN-SCANDINAVIAN FOUNDATION TRANSLATION PRIZE

Two prizes are awarded for outstanding English translations of poetry, fiction, drama or literary prose originally written in Danish, Finnish, Icelandic, Norwegian or Swedish. One-time award of $2000.

Academic Fields/Career Goals: Literature/English/Writing.

Award: Prize for use in freshman, sophomore, junior, or senior years; not renewable. *Number:* 2. *Amount:* $1000–$2000.

Eligibility Requirements: Applicant must be enrolled or expecting to enroll full- or part-time at a two-year or four-year or technical institution or university and must have an interest in Scandinavian language. Available to U.S. and non-U.S. citizens.

Application Requirements: Application, applicant must enter a contest, resume, translation sample. *Deadline:* June 1.

Contact: Director of Fellowships and Grants
American-Scandinavian Foundation
58 Park Avenue
New York, NY 10016
Phone: 212-879-9779
Fax: 212-686-2115
E-mail: info@amscan.org

AMY LOWELL POETRY TRAVELLING SCHOLARSHIP TRUST

http://www.amylowell.org/

AMY LOWELL POETRY TRAVELING SCHOLARSHIP

Scholarship to a poet of American birth. Upon acceptance, the recipient agrees to spend one year outside the continent of North America in a place deemed by the recipient suitable to advance the art of poetry. At the end of the year, the recipient shall submit at least three poems for consideration by the trust's committee. For additional information visit web site http://www.amylowell.org.

Academic Fields/Career Goals: Literature/English/Writing.

Award: Scholarship for use in freshman, sophomore, junior, or senior years; not renewable. *Number:* 1. *Amount:* up to $50,000.

Eligibility Requirements: Applicant must be enrolled or expecting to enroll full- or part-time at a two-year or four-year or technical institution or university and must have an interest in writing. Available to U.S. citizens.

Application Requirements: Application, applicant must enter a contest, poetry sample. *Deadline:* October 15.

Contact: Cathleen Croft, Trustee
Amy Lowell Poetry Travelling Scholarship Trust
Two International Place
Boston, MA 02110
Phone: 617-248-4855
E-mail: amylowell@choate.com

BIBLIOGRAPHICAL SOCIETY OF AMERICA

http://www.bibsocamer.org/

JUSTIN G. SCHILLER PRIZE FOR BIBLIOGRAPHICAL WORK IN PRE-20TH-CENTURY CHILDREN'S BOOKS
• *See page 394*

CENTER FOR LESBIAN AND GAY STUDIES (C.L.A.G.S.)

http://www.clags.org/

CENTER FOR GAY AND LESBIAN STUDIES UNDERGRADUATE PAPER AWARDS

A cash prize of $250 awarded to the best paper written in a California University of New York or State University of New York undergraduate class on a topic related to gay, lesbian, bisexual, queer, or transgender experiences. Essays should be between 12 and 30 pages.

Academic Fields/Career Goals: Literature/English/Writing.

Award: Prize for use in freshman, sophomore, junior, or senior years; not renewable. *Number:* 1. *Amount:* $250.

Eligibility Requirements: Applicant must be enrolled or expecting to enroll full- or part-time at a four-year institution or university and must have an interest in LGBT issues. Available to U.S. and non-U.S. citizens.

Application Requirements: Applicant must enter a contest, essay. *Deadline:* June 1.

Contact: Naz Qazi, Fellowship Membership Coordinator
Center for Lesbian and Gay Studies (C.L.A.G.S.)
365 Fifth Avenue, Room 7115
New York, NY 10016
Phone: 212-817-1955
Fax: 212-817-1567
E-mail: clags@gc.cuny.edu

CIRI FOUNDATION (TCF)

http://www.thecirifoundation.org/

CIRI FOUNDATION SUSIE QIMMIQSAK BEVINS ENDOWMENT SCHOLARSHIP FUND
• *See page 110*

DAVIDSON INSTITUTE FOR TALENT DEVELOPMENT

http://www.davidsongifted.org/

DAVIDSON FELLOWS SCHOLARSHIP PROGRAM

One-time award to recognize outstanding achievements of young people. Must be 18 or younger as of October 10, 2012. Must have completed a significant piece of work in one of the following areas: science, technology, mathematics, humanities (music, literature or philosophy) or outside the box. Must be a U.S. citizen or a permanent resident.

Academic Fields/Career Goals: Literature/English/Writing; Mathematics; Music; Philosophy; Science, Technology, and Society.

Award: Scholarship for use in freshman, sophomore, junior, senior, or graduate years; not renewable. *Number:* 15–20. *Amount:* $10,000–$50,000.

Eligibility Requirements: Applicant must be age 18 or under and enrolled or expecting to enroll full- or part-time at a two-year or four-year or technical institution or university. Available to U.S. citizens.

Application Requirements: Application, essay, portfolio, references. *Deadline:* February 1.

Contact: Tacie Moessner, Davidson Fellows Program Manager
Davidson Institute for Talent Development
9665 Gateway Drive, Suite B
Reno, NV 89521
Phone: 775-852-3483 Ext. 423
Fax: 775-852-2184
E-mail: davidsonfellows@davidsongifted.org

GOLDEN KEY INTERNATIONAL HONOUR SOCIETY

http://www.goldenkey.org/

LITERARY ACHIEVEMENT AWARDS

Award of $1000 will be given to winners in each of the following four categories: fiction, non-fiction, poetry, and feature writing. Eligible applicants are undergraduate, graduate and postgraduate members who are currently enrolled in classes at a degree-granting program.

Academic Fields/Career Goals: Literature/English/Writing.

Award: Prize for use in freshman, sophomore, junior, senior, graduate, or postgraduate years; not renewable. *Number:* 4. *Amount:* $1000.

Eligibility Requirements: Applicant must be enrolled or expecting to enroll full- or part-time at a four-year institution or university and must have an interest in writing. Available to U.S. and non-U.S. citizens.

Application Requirements: Application, applicant must enter a contest, essay, original composition. *Deadline:* April 1.

Contact: Scholarship Program Administrators
Golden Key International Honour Society
PO Box 23737
Nashville, TN 37202-3737
Phone: 800-377-2401
E-mail: scholarships@goldenkey.org

INSTITUTE FOR HUMANE STUDIES

http://www.theihs.org/

HUMANE STUDIES FELLOWSHIPS
• *See page 185*

INTERNATIONAL FOODSERVICE EDITORIAL COUNCIL

http://www.ifeconline.com/

INTERNATIONAL FOODSERVICE EDITORIAL COUNCIL COMMUNICATIONS SCHOLARSHIP
• *See page 77*

JACK J. ISGUR FOUNDATION

JACK J. ISGUR FOUNDATION SCHOLARSHIP
• *See page 112*

JAPANESE AMERICAN CITIZENS LEAGUE (JACL)

http://www.jacl.org/

NATIONAL JACL HEADQUARTERS SCHOLARSHIP
• *See page 84*

JOHN F. KENNEDY LIBRARY FOUNDATION

http://www.jfklibrary.org/

PROFILE IN COURAGE ESSAY CONTEST

Essay contest open to all high school students, grades nine to twelve. Students in U.S. territories and U.S. citizens attending schools overseas may also apply. All essays will be judged on the overall originality of topic and the clear communication of ideas through language. Winner and their nominating teacher are invited to Kennedy Library to accept award. Winner receives $3000, nomination teacher receives grant of $500; second place receives $1000 and five finalists receive $500.

Academic Fields/Career Goals: Literature/English/Writing.

Award: Prize for use in freshman year; not renewable. *Number:* 7. *Amount:* $500–$3000.

Eligibility Requirements: Applicant must be high school student; age 19 or under; planning to enroll or expecting to enroll full-time at a four-year institution and must have an interest in writing. Available to U.S. citizens.

Application Requirements: Application, applicant must enter a contest, essay, bibliography. *Deadline:* January 7.

Contact: Esther Kohn, Essay Contest Coordinator
John F. Kennedy Library Foundation
Columbia Point
Boston, MA 02125
Phone: 617-514-1649
Fax: 617-514-1641
E-mail: profiles@nara.gov

KAPLAN/NEWSWEEK

http://www.kaptest.com/

"MY TURN" ESSAY COMPETITION

Essay contest open to high school students entering college or university. Contestants can win up to $5000. Must be U.S. citizen. To enter, a student must submit 500- to 1000-word essay expressing their opinion, experience, or personal feelings on a topic of their own choice. First prize: $5000; second prize: $2000; and 8 finalists are awarded $1000.

Academic Fields/Career Goals: Literature/English/Writing.

Award: Scholarship for use in freshman year; not renewable. *Number:* up to 10. *Amount:* $1000–$5000.

Eligibility Requirements: Applicant must be high school student; planning to enroll or expecting to enroll full- or part-time at a two-year or four-year institution or university and must have an interest in writing. Available to U.S. and non-U.S. citizens.

Application Requirements: Application, applicant must enter a contest, essay. *Deadline:* March 1.

Contact: Scholarship Committee
Kaplan/Newsweek
1440 Broadway, Ninth Floor
New York, NY 10018
Phone: 212-997-5886

LAMBDA IOTA TAU, COLLEGE LITERATURE HONOR SOCIETY

http://www.bsu.edu/english/undergraduate/lit

LAMBDA IOTA TAU LITERATURE SCHOLARSHIP

Scholarships for members of Lambda Iota Tau who are pursuing the study of literature. Must be nominated by chapter sponsor and have 3.5 GPA.

Academic Fields/Career Goals: Literature/English/Writing.

Award: Scholarship for use in sophomore, junior, senior, or graduate years; not renewable. *Number:* 2–4. *Amount:* $1000.

Eligibility Requirements: Applicant must be enrolled or expecting to enroll full-time at a two-year or four-year institution or university. Applicant or parent of applicant must be member of Lambda Iota Tau Literature Honor Society. Applicant must have 3.5 GPA or higher. Available to U.S. citizens.

Application Requirements: Application, essay, references, transcript, nomination letter from chapter sponsor. *Deadline:* May 31.

Contact: Mrs. Mary Clark-Upchurch, Executive Secretary and Treasurer
Lambda Iota Tau, College Literature Honor Society
Ball State University, Department of English
2000 West University Avenue
Muncie, IN 47306-0460
Phone: 765-285-8382
E-mail: mcupchurchi@bsu.edu

NATIONAL PRESS FOUNDATION

http://www.nationalpress.org/

EVERT CLARK/SETH PAYNE AWARD
• *See page 381*

NATIONAL WRITERS ASSOCIATION FOUNDATION

http://www.nationalwriters.com/

NATIONAL WRITERS ASSOCIATION FOUNDATION SCHOLARSHIPS
• *See page 381*

OREGON STUDENT ASSISTANCE COMMISSION

http://www.GetCollegeFunds.org/

BUERKLE SCHOLARSHIP
• *See page 383*

SEHAR SALEHA AHMAD AND ABRAHIM EKRAMULLAH ZAFAR FOUNDATION SCHOLARSHIP

Scholarship available to Oregon residents who are graduating seniors from Oregon high schools (including GED recipients and home schooled students). Minimum 3.8 GPA required. Preference given to females. Must be an English major at a 4-year public or nonprofit college or university in Oregon.

Academic Fields/Career Goals: Literature/English/Writing.

Award: Scholarship for use in freshman year; renewable. *Number:* varies. *Amount:* varies.

Eligibility Requirements: Applicant must be high school student; planning to enroll or expecting to enroll full-time at a four-year institution or university; resident of Oregon and studying in Oregon. Available to U.S. citizens.

Application Requirements: Application, essay, financial need analysis, references, transcript, activity chart. *Deadline:* March 1.

Contact: Director of Grant Programs
Oregon Student Assistance Commission
1500 Valley River Drive, Suite 100
Eugene, OR 97401-7020
Phone: 800-452-8807 Ext. 7395

OUTDOOR WRITERS ASSOCIATION OF AMERICA

http://www.owaa.org/

OUTDOOR WRITERS ASSOCIATION OF AMERICA BODIE MCDOWELL SCHOLARSHIP AWARD
• *See page 189*

POLISH HERITAGE ASSOCIATION OF MARYLAND

http://www.pha-md.org/

ROBERT P. PULA MEMORIAL SCHOLARSHIP
• *See page 365*

SIGMA TAU DELTA

http://www.english.org/

HENRY REGNERY ENDOWED SCHOLARSHIP

One-time award of up to $2500 given to sophomore, junior, senior or graduates who has registered as full-time students in an English degree program or as full-time students with coursework in one or more English-related fields. Applicant should be a member of Sigma Tau Delta.

Academic Fields/Career Goals: Literature/English/Writing.

Award: Scholarship for use in sophomore, junior, senior, or graduate years; not renewable. *Number:* varies. *Amount:* up to $2500.

Eligibility Requirements: Applicant must be enrolled or expecting to enroll full-time at a four-year institution or university. Applicant or parent of applicant must be member of Supreme Council of Sociedade Do Espirito Santo. Applicant must have 3.0 GPA or higher. Available to U.S. and non-U.S. citizens.

Application Requirements: Application, essay, references, transcript, sample paper, professional goals. *Deadline:* October 30.

Contact: Sidney Watson, Scholarship Committee Chair
Sigma Tau Delta
Department of English, Northern Illinois University
DeKalb, IL 60115
Phone: 405-878-2201
E-mail: sidney.watson@okbu.edu

SIGMA TAU DELTA JUNIOR SCHOLARSHIP

One-time scholarship of up to $3000 given to juniors in college level who have registered as full-time students in an English degree program or as full-time students with coursework in one or more English-related fields. Applicant should be a member of Sigma Tau Delta.

Academic Fields/Career Goals: Literature/English/Writing.

Award: Scholarship for use in junior year; not renewable. *Number:* varies. *Amount:* up to $3000.

Eligibility Requirements: Applicant must be enrolled or expecting to enroll full-time at a four-year institution or university. Applicant or parent of applicant must be member of Supreme Council of Sociedade Do Espirito Santo. Applicant must have 3.0 GPA or higher. Available to U.S. and non-U.S. citizens.

Application Requirements: Application, essay, references, transcript, professional goals. *Deadline:* October 30.

Contact: Sidney Watson, Scholarship Committee Chair
Sigma Tau Delta
Oklahoma Baptist University, 500 West University
Shawnee, OK 74804-2558
Phone: 405-878-2210
E-mail: sidney.watson@okbu.edu

SIGMA TAU DELTA SCHOLARSHIP

One-time scholarship of up to $4000 given to sophomore, junior, senior, or graduates who have registered as full-time students in an English degree program or as full-time students with coursework in one or more English related fields. Applicant should be a member of Sigma Tau Delta.

Academic Fields/Career Goals: Literature/English/Writing.

Award: Scholarship for use in sophomore, junior, senior, or graduate years; not renewable. *Number:* varies. *Amount:* up to $4000.

Eligibility Requirements: Applicant must be enrolled or expecting to enroll full-time at a four-year institution or university. Applicant or parent of applicant must be member of Supreme Council of Sociedade Do Espirito Santo. Applicant must have 3.0 GPA or higher. Available to U.S. and non-U.S. citizens.

Application Requirements: Application, essay, references, transcript, sample paper, professional goals. *Deadline:* October 30.

Contact: Sidney Watson, Scholarship Committee Chair
Sigma Tau Delta
Department of English, Northern Illinois University
DeKalb, IL 60115
Phone: 405-878-2201
E-mail: sidney.watson@okbu.edu

SIGMA TAU DELTA SENIOR SCHOLARSHIP

One-time scholarship of up to $3000 given to seniors in college level who have registered as full-time students in an English degree program or as full-time students with coursework in one or more English related fields. Applicant should be a member of Sigma Tau Delta.

Academic Fields/Career Goals: Literature/English/Writing.

Award: Scholarship for use in senior year; not renewable. *Number:* varies. *Amount:* up to $3000.

Eligibility Requirements: Applicant must be enrolled or expecting to enroll full-time at a four-year institution or university. Applicant or parent of applicant must be member of Supreme Council of Sociedade Do Espirito Santo. Applicant must have 3.0 GPA or higher. Available to U.S. and non-U.S. citizens.

Application Requirements: Application, essay, references, transcript, summary of professional goals. *Deadline:* October 30.

Contact: Sidney Watson, Scholarship Committee Chair
Sigma Tau Delta
Oklahoma Baptist University, 500 West University
Shawnee, OK 74804-2558
Phone: 405-878-2210
E-mail: sidney.watson@okbu.edu

SIGMA TAU DELTA STUDY ABROAD SCHOLARSHIP

One-time scholarship of up to $3000 given to sophomore, junior, senior, or graduates who have registered as full-time students in an English degree program or as full-time students with coursework in one or more English related fields. Applicant should be a member of Sigma Tau Delta. Deadlines: March 30 and October 30.

Academic Fields/Career Goals: Literature/English/Writing.

Award: Scholarship for use in sophomore, junior, or senior years; not renewable. *Number:* varies. *Amount:* up to $3000.

Eligibility Requirements: Applicant must be enrolled or expecting to enroll full-time at a four-year institution or university. Applicant or parent of applicant must be member of Supreme Council of Sociedade Do Espirito Santo. Applicant must have 3.0 GPA or higher. Available to U.S. and non-U.S. citizens.

Application Requirements: Application, essay, references, transcript, sample paper, professional goals. *Deadline:* varies.

Contact: Sidney Watson, Scholarship Committee Chair
Sigma Tau Delta
Department of English, Northern Illinois University
DeKalb, IL 60115
Phone: 405-878-2201
E-mail: sidney.watson@okbu.edu

STRAIGHTFORWARD MEDIA

http://www.straightforwardmedia.com/

STRAIGHTFORWARD MEDIA LIBERAL ARTS SCHOLARSHIP

• *See page 107*

UNITED DAUGHTERS OF THE CONFEDERACY

http://www.hqudc.org/

HELEN JAMES BREWER SCHOLARSHIP

• *See page 354*

UNITED NEGRO COLLEGE FUND

http://www.uncf.org/

AFSCME/UNCF/HARVARD UNIVERSITY LWP UNION SCHOLARS PROGRAM

• *See page 90*

C-SPAN SCHOLARSHIP PROGRAM

• *See page 193*

MAE MAXEY MEMORIAL SCHOLARSHIP

• *See page 116*

MCCLARE FAMILY TRUST SCHOLARSHIP

• *See page 366*

READER'S DIGEST FOUNDATION SCHOLARSHIP

• *See page 193*

TOYOTA/UNCF SCHOLARSHIP

• *See page 74*

WILLA CATHER FOUNDATION

http://www.willacather.org/

NORMA ROSS WALTER SCHOLARSHIP

The award is to provide scholarship support to female Nebraska high school graduates who continue their higher education as English majors in accredited colleges or universities.

Academic Fields/Career Goals: Literature/English/Writing.

Award: Scholarship for use in freshman year; not renewable. *Number:* 1. *Amount:* $1000.

Eligibility Requirements: Applicant must be high school student; planning to enroll or expecting to enroll full-time at a four-year institution or university; female and resident of Nebraska. Applicant must have 3.0 GPA or higher. Available to U.S. citizens.

Application Requirements: Application, essay, references, test scores, transcript. *Deadline:* January 31.

Contact: Ashley M Olson, Associate Executive Director
Willa Cather Foundation
413 North Webster St.
Red Cloud, NE 68970
Phone: 402-746-2653
Fax: 402-746-2652
E-mail: info@willacather.org

MARINE BIOLOGY

ASSOCIATION ON AMERICAN INDIAN AFFAIRS, INC.

http://www.indian-affairs.org/

ELIZABETH AND SHERMAN ASCHE MEMORIAL SCHOLARSHIP FUND

• *See page 83*

CUSHMAN FOUNDATION FOR FORAMINIFERAL RESEARCH

http://www.cushmanfoundation.org/

LOEBLICH AND TAPPAN STUDENT RESEARCH AWARD
• *See page 140*

INTERNATIONAL ASSOCIATION OF GREAT LAKES RESEARCH

http://www.iaglr.org/

PAUL W. RODGERS SCHOLARSHIP
• *See page 224*

JUST WITHIN REACH FOUNDATION

ENVIRONMENTAL SCIENCES AND MARINE STUDIES SCHOLARSHIP
• *See page 309*

LOUISIANA OFFICE OF STUDENT FINANCIAL ASSISTANCE

http://www.osfa.la.gov/

ROCKEFELLER STATE WILDLIFE SCHOLARSHIP
• *See page 141*

MARINE TECHNOLOGY SOCIETY

http://www.mtsociety.org/

CHARLES H. BUSSMAN UNDERGRADUATE SCHOLARSHIP

Scholarship for undergraduate students enrolled full-time in a marine-related field. Must be a member of Marine Technology Society.

Academic Fields/Career Goals: Marine Biology; Marine/Ocean Engineering; Oceanography.

Award: Scholarship for use in freshman, sophomore, junior, or senior years; not renewable. *Number:* varies. *Amount:* up to $2500.

Eligibility Requirements: Applicant must be enrolled or expecting to enroll full-time at a four-year institution or university. Applicant or parent of applicant must be member of Marine Technology Society. Available to U.S. and non-U.S. citizens.

Application Requirements: Application, driver's license, references, transcript, proof of acceptance for an undergraduate course. *Deadline:* April 15.

Contact: Suzanne Voelker, Operations Administrator
Marine Technology Society
5565 Sterrett Place, Suite 108
Columbia, MD 21044
Phone: 410-884-5330
Fax: 410-884-9060
E-mail: suzanne.voelker@mtsociety.org

JOHN C. BAJUS SCHOLARSHIP

Scholarship available to undergraduate and graduate students enrolled full-time in a marine-related field. Must be a MTS student member with demonstrated commitment to community service/volunteer activities.

Academic Fields/Career Goals: Marine Biology; Marine/Ocean Engineering; Oceanography.

Award: Scholarship for use in freshman, sophomore, junior, senior, or graduate years; not renewable. *Number:* varies. *Amount:* up to $1000.

Eligibility Requirements: Applicant must be enrolled or expecting to enroll full-time at a four-year institution or university. Applicant or parent of applicant must be member of Marine Technology Society. Available to U.S. and non-U.S. citizens.

Application Requirements: Application, driver's license, references, transcript. *Deadline:* April 15.

Contact: Suzanne Voelker, Operations Administrator
Marine Technology Society
5565 Sterrett Place, Suite 108
Columbia, MD 21044
Phone: 410-884-5330
Fax: 410-884-9060
E-mail: suzanne.voelker@mtsociety.org

MTS STUDENT SCHOLARSHIP

Scholarships available to both Marine Technology Society members and non-members, undergraduates and graduate students, enrolled full-time in a marine-related field.

Academic Fields/Career Goals: Marine Biology; Marine/Ocean Engineering; Oceanography.

Award: Scholarship for use in freshman, sophomore, junior, senior, or graduate years; not renewable. *Number:* varies. *Amount:* up to $2000.

Eligibility Requirements: Applicant must be enrolled or expecting to enroll full-time at a four-year institution or university. Available to U.S. and non-U.S. citizens.

Application Requirements: Application, driver's license, references, transcript. *Deadline:* April 15.

Contact: Suzanne Voelker, Operations Administrator
Marine Technology Society
5565 Sterrett Place, Suite 108
Columbia, MD 21044
Phone: 410-884-5330
Fax: 410-884-9060
E-mail: suzanne.voelker@mtsociety.org

MTS STUDENT SCHOLARSHIP FOR GRADUATE AND UNDERGRADUATE STUDENTS

Scholarship of $2000 available to undergraduate students who are enrolled full-time in a marine-related field.

Academic Fields/Career Goals: Marine Biology; Marine/Ocean Engineering.

Award: Scholarship for use in freshman, sophomore, junior, senior, or graduate years; not renewable. *Number:* varies. *Amount:* $2000.

Eligibility Requirements: Applicant must be enrolled or expecting to enroll full-time at a four-year institution or university. Available to U.S. and non-U.S. citizens.

Application Requirements: Application, essay, references, transcript. *Deadline:* April 15.

Contact: Suzanne Voelker, Operations Administrator
Marine Technology Society
5565 Sterrett Place, Suite 108
Columbia, MD 21044
Phone: 410-884-5330
E-mail: suzanne.voelker@mtsociety.org

MTS STUDENT SCHOLARSHIP FOR TWO-YEAR TECHNICAL, ENGINEERING AND COMMUNITY COLLEGE STUDENTS

Scholarship of $2000 available to students enrolled in a two-year technical, engineering, or community college in a marine-related field.

Academic Fields/Career Goals: Marine Biology; Marine/Ocean Engineering.

Award: Scholarship for use in freshman or sophomore years; not renewable. *Number:* varies. *Amount:* $2000.

Eligibility Requirements: Applicant must be enrolled or expecting to enroll full-time at a two-year institution. Available to U.S. and non-U.S. citizens.

Application Requirements: Application, essay, references, transcript. *Deadline:* April 15.

Contact: Suzanne Voelker, Operations Administrator
Marine Technology Society
5565 Sterrett Place, Suite 108
Columbia, MD 21044
Phone: 410-884-5330
E-mail: suzanne.voelker@mtsociety.org

PAROS-DIGIQUARTZ SCHOLARSHIP

Scholarships available to both MTS members and non-members, undergraduates and graduate students, enrolled full-time in a marine-related field with an interest in marine instrumentation. High school seniors who have been accepted into a full-time undergraduate program in a marine-related field are also eligible to apply.

Academic Fields/Career Goals: Marine Biology; Marine/Ocean Engineering; Oceanography.

Award: Scholarship for use in freshman, sophomore, junior, senior, or graduate years; not renewable. *Number:* varies. *Amount:* up to $2000.

Eligibility Requirements: Applicant must be enrolled or expecting to enroll full-time at a four-year institution or university. Available to U.S. and non-U.S. citizens.

Application Requirements: Application, driver's license, references, transcript. *Deadline:* April 15.

Contact: Suzanne Voelker, Operations Administrator
Marine Technology Society
5565 Sterrett Place, Suite 108
Columbia, MD 21044
Phone: 410-884-5330
Fax: 410-884-9060
E-mail: suzanne.voelker@mtsociety.org

ROV SCHOLARSHIP

Scholarships for undergraduate and graduate students interested in remotely operated vehicles or underwater work that furthers the use of ROVs. Open to MTS student members and non-MTS members.

Academic Fields/Career Goals: Marine Biology; Marine/Ocean Engineering; Oceanography.

Award: Scholarship for use in freshman, sophomore, junior, senior, or graduate years; not renewable. *Number:* varies. *Amount:* up to $10,000.

Eligibility Requirements: Applicant must be enrolled or expecting to enroll full-time at a four-year institution or university. Available to U.S. and non-U.S. citizens.

Application Requirements: Application, driver's license, essay, references, transcript. *Deadline:* April 15.

Contact: Chuck Richards, Chair, Scholarship Committee
Marine Technology Society
c/o C.A. Richards and Associates Inc., 777 North Eldridge Parkway, Suite 280
Houston, TX 77079

NASA'S VIRGINIA SPACE GRANT CONSORTIUM

http://www.vsgc.odu.edu/

TEACHER EDUCATION STEM SCHOLARSHIP PROGRAM
• *See page 96*

SEASPACE INC.

http://www.seaspace.org/

SEASPACE SCHOLARSHIP PROGRAM

One-time award open to college junior/senior or graduate students pursuing degrees in the marine/aquatic sciences. Must be enrolled full-time with a minimum overall GPA of 3.3. Must be enrolled in an accredited U.S. institution. Must demonstrate financial need.

Academic Fields/Career Goals: Marine Biology; Oceanography.

Award: Scholarship for use in junior, senior, or graduate years; not renewable. *Number:* 10–15. *Amount:* $500–$3000.

Eligibility Requirements: Applicant must be enrolled or expecting to enroll full-time at a four-year institution or university. Available to U.S. and non-U.S. citizens.

Application Requirements: Application, financial need analysis, self-addressed stamped envelope, transcript. *Deadline:* December 1.

Contact: Jesse Cancelmo, Scholarship Committee Chairman
Seaspace Inc.
PO Box 3753
Houston, TX 77253-3753
Phone: 713-302-7920
E-mail: jesse@cancelmophoto.com

SOCIETY FOR INTEGRATIVE AND COMPARATIVE BIOLOGY

http://www.sicb.org/

LIBBIE H. HYMAN MEMORIAL SCHOLARSHIP
• *See page 143*

WOMAN'S SEAMEN'S FRIEND SOCIETY OF CONNECTICUT INC.

FINANCIAL SUPPORT FOR MARINE OR MARITIME STUDIES

Applicant must be full-time student. High school students not considered. Award available to U.S. citizens. Must be majoring in marine sciences at any college or university.

Academic Fields/Career Goals: Marine Biology; Oceanography.

Award: Scholarship for use in freshman, sophomore, junior, or senior years; not renewable. *Number:* varies. *Amount:* varies.

Eligibility Requirements: Applicant must be enrolled or expecting to enroll full-time at a four-year institution or university. Available to U.S. citizens.

Application Requirements: Application, financial need analysis, resume, references, test scores, transcript. *Deadline:* varies.

Contact: Marshall Davidson, Executive Director
Woman's Seamen's Friend Society of Connecticut Inc.
291 Whitney Avenue Suite 403
New Haven, CT 06511
Phone: 203-777-2165
Fax: 203-777-5774
E-mail: wsfsofct@earthlink.net

MARINE/OCEAN ENGINEERING

AMERICAN METEOROLOGICAL SOCIETY

http://www.ametsoc.org/

AMS FRESHMAN UNDERGRADUATE SCHOLARSHIP
• *See page 306*

AMERICAN SOCIETY OF NAVAL ENGINEERS

http://www.navalengineers.org/

AMERICAN SOCIETY OF NAVAL ENGINEERS SCHOLARSHIP
• *See page 93*

LOUISIANA OFFICE OF STUDENT FINANCIAL ASSISTANCE

http://www.osfa.la.gov/

ROCKEFELLER STATE WILDLIFE SCHOLARSHIP
• *See page 141*

MANUFACTURERS ASSOCIATION OF MAINE

http://www.mainemfg.com/

MAINE METAL PRODUCTS EDUCATION FUND SCHOLARSHIP PROGRAM
• *See page 127*

MARINE TECHNOLOGY SOCIETY

http://www.mtsociety.org/

CHARLES H. BUSSMAN UNDERGRADUATE SCHOLARSHIP
• See page 401

JOHN C. BAJUS SCHOLARSHIP
• See page 401

MTS STUDENT SCHOLARSHIP
• See page 401

MTS STUDENT SCHOLARSHIP FOR GRADUATE AND UNDERGRADUATE STUDENTS
• See page 401

MTS STUDENT SCHOLARSHIP FOR GRADUATING HIGH SCHOOL SENIORS
• See page 289

MTS STUDENT SCHOLARSHIP FOR TWO-YEAR TECHNICAL, ENGINEERING AND COMMUNITY COLLEGE STUDENTS
• See page 401

PAROS-DIGIQUARTZ SCHOLARSHIP
• See page 402

ROV SCHOLARSHIP
• See page 402

UTAH SOCIETY OF PROFESSIONAL ENGINEERS

http://www.uspeonline.com/

UTAH SOCIETY OF PROFESSIONAL ENGINEERS JOE RHOADS SCHOLARSHIP
• See page 171

MARKETING

AUTOMOTIVE HALL OF FAME

http://www.automotivehalloffame.org/

AUTOMOTIVE HALL OF FAME EDUCATIONAL FUNDS
• See page 164

BALTIMORE CHAPTER OF THE AMERICAN MARKETING ASSOCIATION

http://www.amabaltimore.org/

UNDERGRADUATE MARKETING EDUCATION MERIT SCHOLARSHIPS
• See page 147

CLEVELAND SCHOLARSHIP PROGRAMS

http://www.cspohio.org/

CSP MANAGED FUNDS-CLEVELAND BROWNS MARION MOTLEY SCHOLARSHIP
• See page 58

DECA (DISTRIBUTIVE EDUCATION CLUBS OF AMERICA)

http://www.deca.org/

HARRY A. APPLEGATE SCHOLARSHIP
• See page 149

ELECTRONIC DOCUMENT SYSTEMS FOUNDATION

http://www.edsf.org/

ELECTRONIC DOCUMENT SYSTEMS FOUNDATION SCHOLARSHIP AWARDS
• See page 197

GREATER KANAWHA VALLEY FOUNDATION

http://www.tgkvf.org/

CHARLESTON ROTARY CLUB SCHOLARSHIP
• See page 63

GREAT FALLS ADVERTISING FEDERATION

http://www.gfaf.com/

GREAT FALLS ADVERTISING FEDERATION COLLEGE SCHOLARSHIP
• See page 76

HIGH SCHOOL MARKETING/COMMUNICATIONS SCHOLARSHIP
• See page 76

NATIONAL DAIRY SHRINE

http://www.dairyshrine.org/

NATIONAL DAIRY SHRINE/DAIRY MARKETING INC. MILK MARKETING SCHOLARSHIPS
• See page 85

RHODE ISLAND FOUNDATION

http://www.rifoundation.org/

J. D. EDSAL ADVERTISING SCHOLARSHIP
• See page 77

STRAIGHTFORWARD MEDIA

http://www.straightforwardmedia.com/

STRAIGHTFORWARD MEDIA BUSINESS SCHOOL SCHOLARSHIP
• See page 77

STRAIGHTFORWARD MEDIA MEDIA & COMMUNICATIONS SCHOLARSHIP
• See page 77

UNITED NEGRO COLLEGE FUND

http://www.uncf.org/

AVON WOMEN IN SEARCH OF EXCELLENCE SCHOLARSHIP
• *See page 72*

BANK OF AMERICA SCHOLARSHIP
• *See page 157*

FLOWERS INDUSTRIES SCHOLARSHIP
• *See page 157*

FORD/UNCF CORPORATE SCHOLARS PROGRAM
• *See page 73*

GENERAL MILLS CORPORATE SCHOLARS AWARD
• *See page 73*

NASCAR/WENDELL SCOTT, SR. SCHOLARSHIP
• *See page 73*

UBS/PAINEWEBBER SCHOLARSHIP
• *See page 74*

UNITED WATER CORPORATE SCHOLARS PROGRAM
• *See page 74*

UPS/UNCF CORPORATE SCHOLARS PROGRAM
• *See page 202*

VERIZON FOUNDATION SCHOLARSHIP
• *See page 74*

WYOMING TRUCKING ASSOCIATION SCHOLARSHIP FUND TRUST

http://www.wytruck.org/

WYOMING TRUCKING ASSOCIATION SCHOLARSHIP TRUST FUND
• *See page 76*

MATERIALS SCIENCE, ENGINEERING, AND METALLURGY

AIST FOUNDATION

http://www.aistfoundation.org/

AISI/AIST FOUNDATION PREMIER SCHOLARSHIPS
• *See page 252*

AIST ALFRED B. GLOSSBRENNER AND JOHN KLUSCH SCHOLARSHIPS
• *See page 274*

AIST WILLIAM E. SCHWABE MEMORIAL SCHOLARSHIP
• *See page 252*

ASSOCIATION FOR IRON AND STEEL TECHNOLOGY BALTIMORE CHAPTER SCHOLARSHIP
• *See page 261*

ASSOCIATION FOR IRON AND STEEL TECHNOLOGY BENJAMIN F. FAIRLESS SCHOLARSHIP (AIME)
• *See page 160*

ASSOCIATION FOR IRON AND STEEL TECHNOLOGY DAVID H. SAMSON CANADIAN SCHOLARSHIP
• *See page 160*

ASSOCIATION FOR IRON AND STEEL TECHNOLOGY NORTHWEST MEMBER CHAPTER SCHOLARSHIP
• *See page 275*

ASSOCIATION FOR IRON AND STEEL TECHNOLOGY OHIO VALLEY CHAPTER SCHOLARSHIP
• *See page 137*

ASSOCIATION FOR IRON AND STEEL TECHNOLOGY PITTSBURGH CHAPTER SCHOLARSHIP
• *See page 275*

ASSOCIATION FOR IRON AND STEEL TECHNOLOGY RONALD E. LINCOLN SCHOLARSHIP
• *See page 252*

ASSOCIATION FOR IRON AND STEEL TECHNOLOGY SOUTHEAST MEMBER CHAPTER SCHOLARSHIP
• *See page 275*

ASSOCIATION FOR IRON AND STEEL TECHNOLOGY WILLY KORF MEMORIAL SCHOLARSHIP
• *See page 252*

FERROUS METALLURGY EDUCATION TODAY (FEMET)
Scholarship of US$5,000 toward tuition for the junior year of study, a paid summer internship with a North American steel company between junior and senior year. An additional US$5,000 toward tuition for the senior year of study provided the student maintains a 3.0 or higher QPA and receives a satisfactory report on the summer internship. Must be enrolled full-time in metallurgy or materials science program at an accredited North American university.

Academic Fields/Career Goals: Materials Science, Engineering, and Metallurgy.

Award: Scholarship for use in junior or senior years; renewable. *Number:* 10. *Amount:* $5000.

Eligibility Requirements: Applicant must be enrolled or expecting to enroll full-time at a four-year institution or university. Applicant or parent of applicant must be member of Association for Iron and Steel Technology. Applicant must have 3.0 GPA or higher. Available to U.S. and non-U.S. citizens.

Application Requirements: Application, essay, resume, references, transcript, list of source and amount of any other grants and scholarships being applied. *Deadline:* March 2.

Contact: Lori Wharrey, Board Administrator
AIST Foundation
186 Thorn Hill Road
Warrendale, PA 15086-7528
Phone: 724-814-3044
E-mail: lwharrey@aist.org

STEEL ENGINEERING EDUCATION LINK (STEEL) SCHOLARSHIPS
• *See page 252*

AMERICAN CHEMICAL SOCIETY

http://www.acs.org/

AMERICAN CHEMICAL SOCIETY SCHOLARS PROGRAM
• *See page 160*

AMERICAN CHEMICAL SOCIETY, RUBBER DIVISION

http://www.rubber.org/

AMERICAN CHEMICAL SOCIETY, RUBBER DIVISION UNDERGRADUATE SCHOLARSHIP
• See page 160

AMERICAN COUNCIL OF ENGINEERING COMPANIES OF PENNSYLVANIA (ACEC/PA)

http://www.acecpa.org/

ENGINEERING SCHOLARSHIP
• See page 161

AMERICAN INDIAN SCIENCE AND ENGINEERING SOCIETY

http://www.aises.org/

A.T. ANDERSON MEMORIAL SCHOLARSHIP PROGRAM
• See page 93

AMERICAN INSTITUTE OF AERONAUTICS AND ASTRONAUTICS

http://www.aiaa.org/

AIAA FOUNDATION UNDERGRADUATE SCHOLARSHIP
• See page 93

AMERICAN SOCIETY OF NAVAL ENGINEERS

http://www.navalengineers.org/

AMERICAN SOCIETY OF NAVAL ENGINEERS SCHOLARSHIP
• See page 93

AMERICAN WELDING SOCIETY

http://www.aws.org/

AIRGAS-JERRY BAKER SCHOLARSHIP
• See page 263

AIRGAS-TERRY JARVIS MEMORIAL SCHOLARSHIP
• See page 263

AMERICAN WELDING SOCIETY INTERNATIONAL SCHOLARSHIP
• See page 263

ARSHAM AMIRIKIAN ENGINEERING SCHOLARSHIP
• See page 175

DONALD AND SHIRLEY HASTINGS SCHOLARSHIP
• See page 278

JOHN C. LINCOLN MEMORIAL SCHOLARSHIP
• See page 264

MATSUO BRIDGE COMPANY LTD. OF JAPAN SCHOLARSHIP
• See page 176

MILLER ELECTRIC INTERNATIONAL WORLD SKILLS COMPETITION SCHOLARSHIP
• See page 264

MILLER ELECTRIC MFG. CO. SCHOLARSHIP
• See page 264

PRAXAIR INTERNATIONAL SCHOLARSHIP
• See page 264

RESISTANCE WELDER MANUFACTURERS' ASSOCIATION SCHOLARSHIP
• See page 279

ROBERT L. PEASLEE DETROIT BRAZING AND SOLDERING DIVISION SCHOLARSHIP
• See page 279

WILLIAM A. AND ANN M. BROTHERS SCHOLARSHIP
• See page 265

WILLIAM B. HOWELL MEMORIAL SCHOLARSHIP
• See page 265

ARRL FOUNDATION INC.

http://www.arrl.org/

GARY WAGNER, K3OMI SCHOLARSHIP
• See page 164

ASM MATERIALS EDUCATION FOUNDATION

http://www.asmfoundation.org/

ASM OUTSTANDING SCHOLARS AWARDS
• See page 280

EDWARD J. DULIS SCHOLARSHIP
• See page 280

GEORGE A. ROBERTS SCHOLARSHIP
• See page 280

JOHN M. HANIAK SCHOLARSHIP
• See page 280

WILLIAM P. WOODSIDE FOUNDER'S SCHOLARSHIP
• See page 280

ASTRONAUT SCHOLARSHIP FOUNDATION

http://www.astronautscholarship.org/

ASTRONAUT SCHOLARSHIP FOUNDATION
• See page 95

BARRY M. GOLDWATER SCHOLARSHIP AND EXCELLENCE IN EDUCATION FOUNDATION

http://www.act.org/goldwater

BARRY M. GOLDWATER SCHOLARSHIP AND EXCELLENCE IN EDUCATION PROGRAM
• See page 95

HISPANIC ENGINEER NATIONAL ACHIEVEMENT AWARDS CORPORATION (HENAAC)

http://www.henaac.org/

HISPANIC ENGINEER NATIONAL ACHIEVEMENT AWARDS CORPORATION SCHOLARSHIP PROGRAM
• See page 125

INDEPENDENT LABORATORIES INSTITUTE SCHOLARSHIP ALLIANCE

http://www.acil.org/

INDEPENDENT LABORATORIES INSTITUTE SCHOLARSHIP ALLIANCE
• See page 141

INTERNATIONAL SOCIETY FOR OPTICAL ENGINEERING-SPIE

http://www.spie.org/scholarships

SPIE EDUCATIONAL SCHOLARSHIPS IN OPTICAL SCIENCE AND ENGINEERING
• See page 96

INTERNATIONAL SOCIETY OF AUTOMATION (ISA)

http://www.isa.org/

INTERNATIONAL SOCIETY OF AUTOMATION EDUCATION FOUNDATION SCHOLARSHIPS
• See page 125

JORGE MAS CANOSA FREEDOM FOUNDATION

http://www.jorgemascanosa.org/

MAS FAMILY SCHOLARSHIP AWARD
• See page 152

LOS ANGELES COUNCIL OF BLACK PROFESSIONAL ENGINEERS

http://www.lablackengineers.org/

AL-BEN SCHOLARSHIP FOR ACADEMIC INCENTIVE
• See page 166

AL-BEN SCHOLARSHIP FOR PROFESSIONAL MERIT
• See page 166

AL-BEN SCHOLARSHIP FOR SCHOLASTIC ACHIEVEMENT
• See page 166

MANUFACTURERS ASSOCIATION OF MAINE

http://www.mainemfg.com/

MAINE METAL PRODUCTS EDUCATION FUND SCHOLARSHIP PROGRAM
• See page 127

MIDWEST ROOFING CONTRACTORS ASSOCIATION

http://www.mrca.org/

MRCA FOUNDATION SCHOLARSHIP PROGRAM
• See page 102

MINERALS, METALS, AND MATERIALS SOCIETY (TMS)

http://www.tms.org/

TMS/EMPMD GILBERT CHIN SCHOLARSHIP
• See page 268

TMS/EPD SCHOLARSHIP
• See page 268

TMS/INTERNATIONAL SYMPOSIUM ON SUPERALLOYS SCHOLARSHIP PROGRAM
• See page 268

TMS J. KEITH BRIMACOMBE PRESIDENTIAL SCHOLARSHIP
• See page 268

TMS/LMD SCHOLARSHIP PROGRAM
• See page 268

TMS OUTSTANDING STUDENT PAPER CONTEST-UNDERGRADUATE
• See page 269

TMS/STRUCTURAL MATERIALS DIVISION SCHOLARSHIP
• See page 269

NASA IDAHO SPACE GRANT CONSORTIUM

http://www.id.spacegrant.org/

NASA IDAHO SPACE GRANT CONSORTIUM SCHOLARSHIP PROGRAM
• See page 141

NASA/MARYLAND SPACE GRANT CONSORTIUM

http://www.mdspacegrant.org/

NASA MARYLAND SPACE GRANT CONSORTIUM UNDERGRADUATE SCHOLARSHIPS
• See page 127

NASA SOUTH CAROLINA SPACE GRANT CONSORTIUM

http://www.cofc.edu/~scsgrant

PRE-SERVICE TEACHER SCHOLARSHIP
• See page 129

NASA SOUTH DAKOTA SPACE GRANT CONSORTIUM

http://www.sdspacegrant.sdsmt.edu/

SOUTH DAKOTA SPACE GRANT CONSORTIUM UNDERGRADUATE AND GRADUATE STUDENT SCHOLARSHIPS
• See page 129

NASA'S VIRGINIA SPACE GRANT CONSORTIUM

http://www.vsgc.odu.edu/

UNDERGRADUATE RESEARCH STEM SCHOLARSHIPS

• See page 96

VIRGINIA STEM COMMUNITY COLLEGE SCHOLARSHIPS

• See page 96

NATIONAL INVENTORS HALL OF FAME

http://www.invent.org/

COLLEGIATE INVENTORS COMPETITION FOR UNDERGRADUATE STUDENTS

• See page 96

COLLEGIATE INVENTORS COMPETITION-GRAND PRIZE

• See page 97

NATIONAL SOCIETY OF PROFESSIONAL ENGINEERS

http://www.nspe.org/

MAUREEN L. AND HOWARD N. BLITMAN, PE SCHOLARSHIP TO PROMOTE DIVERSITY IN ENGINEERING

• See page 167

PAUL H. ROBBINS HONORARY SCHOLARSHIP

• See page 168

PROFESSIONAL ENGINEERS IN INDUSTRY SCHOLARSHIP

• See page 168

NATIONAL STONE, SAND AND GRAVEL ASSOCIATION (NSSGA)

http://www.nssga.org/

BARRY K. WENDT MEMORIAL SCHOLARSHIP

• See page 270

PLASTICS INSTITUTE OF AMERICA

http://www.plasticsinstitute.org/

PLASTICS PIONEERS SCHOLARSHIPS

• See page 168

ROCKY MOUNTAIN COAL MINING INSTITUTE

http://www.rmcmi.org/

ROCKY MOUNTAIN COAL MINING INSTITUTE SCHOLARSHIP

• See page 179

SEMICONDUCTOR RESEARCH CORPORATION (SRC)

http://www.src.org/

MASTER'S SCHOLARSHIP PROGRAM

• See page 169

SOCIETY OF AUTOMOTIVE ENGINEERS

http://www.sae.org/

TMC/SAE DONALD D. DAWSON TECHNICAL SCHOLARSHIP

• See page 133

YANMAR/SAE SCHOLARSHIP

• See page 271

SOCIETY OF HISPANIC PROFESSIONAL ENGINEERS FOUNDATION

http://www.henaac.org/

HENAAC SCHOLARS PROGRAM

• See page 199

SOCIETY OF HISPANIC PROFESSIONAL ENGINEERS FOUNDATION

• See page 169

SOCIETY OF PLASTICS ENGINEERS (SPE) FOUNDATION

http://www.4spe.org/

FLEMING/BASZCAK SCHOLARSHIP

• See page 169

SOCIETY OF PLASTICS ENGINEERS SCHOLARSHIP PROGRAM

• See page 170

STRAIGHTFORWARD MEDIA

http://www.straightforwardmedia.com/

STRAIGHTFORWARD MEDIA ENGINEERING SCHOLARSHIP

• See page 170

UNIVERSITIES SPACE RESEARCH ASSOCIATION

http://www.usra.edu/

UNIVERSITIES SPACE RESEARCH ASSOCIATION SCHOLARSHIP PROGRAM

• See page 97

VERMONT SPACE GRANT CONSORTIUM

http://www.cems.uvm.edu/vsgc

VERMONT SPACE GRANT CONSORTIUM SCHOLARSHIP PROGRAM

• See page 98

XEROX

http://www.xerox.com//

TECHNICAL MINORITY SCHOLARSHIP
• *See page 171*

MATHEMATICS

THE ACTUARIAL FOUNDATION

http://www.actuarialfoundation.org/programs/actuarial/ scholarships.shtml

ACTUARIAL DIVERSITY SCHOLARSHIP
• *See page 370*

AMERICAN LEGION DEPARTMENT OF MARYLAND

http://www.mdlegion.org/

AMERICAN LEGION DEPARTMENT OF MARYLAND MATH-SCIENCE SCHOLARSHIP

Scholarship for study in math or the sciences. Must be a Maryland resident and the dependent child of a veteran. Must submit essay, financial need analysis, and transcript with application. Nonrenewable award for freshman. Application available on web site http://mdlegion.org.

Academic Fields/Career Goals: Mathematics; Physical Sciences.

Award: Scholarship for use in freshman year; not renewable. *Number:* up to 3. *Amount:* up to $500.

Eligibility Requirements: Applicant must be high school student; planning to enroll or expecting to enroll full-time at a two-year or four-year institution or university and resident of Maryland. Available to U.S. citizens. Applicant or parent must meet one or more of the following requirements: general military experience; retired from active duty; disabled or killed as a result of military service; prisoner of war; or missing in action.

Application Requirements: Application, essay, financial need analysis, transcript. *Deadline:* April 1.

Contact: Thomas Davis, Department Adjutant
American Legion Department of Maryland
101 North Gay, Room E
Baltimore, MD 21202
Phone: 410-752-1405
Fax: 410-752-3822
E-mail: tom@mdlegion.org

AMERICAN MATHEMATICAL ASSOCIATION OF TWO YEAR COLLEGES

http://www.amatyc.org/

CHARLES MILLER SCHOLARSHIP

A grand prize of $3000 for the qualified individual with the highest total score of the student mathematics league exam. Funds to continue education at an accredited four-year institution. In the case of a tie for the grand prize, the scholarship will be evenly divided.

Academic Fields/Career Goals: Mathematics.

Award: Scholarship for use in freshman or sophomore years; not renewable. *Number:* 1. *Amount:* $3000.

Eligibility Requirements: Applicant must be enrolled or expecting to enroll full-time at a two-year institution. Available to U.S. citizens.

Application Requirements: Applicant must enter a contest, test scores. *Deadline:* September 30.

Contact: Cheryl Cleaves, Executive Director of Office Operations
American Mathematical Association of Two Year Colleges
c/o Southwest Tennessee Community College, 5983 Macon Cove
Memphis, TN 38134
Phone: 901-333-4643
Fax: 901-333-4651
E-mail: amatyc@amatyc.org

AMERICAN SOCIETY FOR ENGINEERING EDUCATION

http://www.asee.org/

SCIENCE, MATHEMATICS, AND RESEARCH FOR TRANSFORMATION DEFENSE SCHOLARSHIP FOR SERVICE PROGRAM
• *See page 93*

ARMED FORCES COMMUNICATIONS AND ELECTRONICS ASSOCIATION, EDUCATIONAL FOUNDATION

http://www.afcea.org/education/scholarships

AFCEA YOUNG ENTREPRENEUR SCHOLARSHIP
• *See page 163*

ARMED FORCES COMMUNICATIONS AND ELECTRONICS ASSOCIATION GENERAL EMMETT PAIGE SCHOLARSHIP
• *See page 122*

ARMED FORCES COMMUNICATIONS AND ELECTRONICS ASSOCIATION GENERAL JOHN A. WICKHAM SCHOLARSHIP
• *See page 164*

ARMED FORCES COMMUNICATIONS AND ELECTRONICS ASSOCIATION ROTC SCHOLARSHIP PROGRAM
• *See page 122*

DISABLED WAR VETERANS SCHOLARSHIP
• *See page 122*

LTG DOUGLAS D. BUCHHOLZ MEMORIAL SCHOLARSHIP
• *See page 122*

WILLIAM E. "BUCK" BRAGUNIER SCHOLARSHIP FOR OUTSTANDING LEADERSHIP
• *See page 123*

ASSOCIATION FOR WOMEN IN MATHEMATICS

http://www.awm-math.org/

ALICE T. SCHAFER MATHEMATICS PRIZE FOR EXCELLENCE IN MATHEMATICS BY AN UNDERGRADUATE WOMAN

One-time merit award for women undergraduates in the math field. Based on quality of performance in math courses and special programs, ability to work independently, interest in math, and performance in competitions. Must be nominated by a professor or an adviser.

Academic Fields/Career Goals: Mathematics.

Award: Prize for use in freshman, sophomore, junior, or senior years; not renewable. *Number:* 1. *Amount:* $250–$1000.

Eligibility Requirements: Applicant must be enrolled or expecting to enroll full-time at a four-year institution or university and female. Available to U.S. citizens.

Application Requirements: Application, applicant must enter a contest, references, transcript, 5 complete copies of nominations. *Deadline:* October 1.

Contact: Jennifer Lewis, Managing Director
Association for Women in Mathematics
11240 Waples Mill Road, Suite 200
Fairfax, VA 22030-2461
Phone: 703-934-0163 Ext. 213
Fax: 703-359-7562
E-mail: jennifer@awm-math.org

BRITISH COLUMBIA INNOVATION COUNCIL

http://www.bcic.ca/

BCIC YOUNG INNOVATOR SCHOLARSHIP COMPETITION (IDEA MASH UP)
• *See page 95*

CALIFORNIA MATHEMATICS COUNCIL-SOUTH

http://www.cmc-math.org/

CALIFORNIA MATHEMATICS COUNCIL-SOUTH SECONDARY EDUCATION SCHOLARSHIPS

Scholarships for students enrolled in accredited Southern California secondary education credential programs with math as a major. Applicants must be members of the California Math Council-South.

Academic Fields/Career Goals: Mathematics.

Award: Scholarship for use in freshman, sophomore, junior, or senior years; renewable. *Number:* 2–5. *Amount:* $100–$2000.

Eligibility Requirements: Applicant must be enrolled or expecting to enroll full- or part-time at a four-year institution or university; resident of California and studying in California. Available to U.S. and non-U.S. citizens.

Application Requirements: Application, essay, references, transcript. *Deadline:* January 31.

Contact: Dr. Sid Kolpas, Professor of Mathematics
California Mathematics Council-South
CMC-S Scholarship Committee, 1500 North Verdugo Road
Glendale, CA 91208-2894
Phone: 818-240-1000 Ext. 5378
E-mail: sjkolpas@sprintmail.com

COLLEGEBOUND FOUNDATION

http://www.collegeboundfoundation.org/

DR. FREEMAN A. HRABOWSKI, III SCHOLARSHIP
• *See page 282*

THE COMMUNITY FOUNDATION FOR GREATER ATLANTA, INC.

http://www.cfgreateratlanta.org/

TECH HIGH SCHOOL ALUMNI ASSOCIATION/W.O. CHENEY MERIT SCHOLARSHIP FUND
• *See page 282*

THE DALLAS FOUNDATION

http://www.dallasfoundation.org/

WHITLEY PLACE SCHOLARSHIP
• *See page 100*

DAVIDSON INSTITUTE FOR TALENT DEVELOPMENT

http://www.davidsongifted.org/

DAVIDSON FELLOWS SCHOLARSHIP PROGRAM
• *See page 398*

DAYTON FOUNDATION

http://www.daytonfoundation.org/

THRYSA FRAZIER SVAGER SCHOLARSHIP

Scholarship for African-American female students majoring in mathematics and attending Central State University, Wilberforce University, Wright State University, University of Dayton, Howard University or Spelman College. Must maintain average grade of "B" or better.

Academic Fields/Career Goals: Mathematics.

Award: Scholarship for use in sophomore, junior, or senior years; renewable. *Number:* 1–2. *Amount:* $2000.

Eligibility Requirements: Applicant must be Black (non-Hispanic); enrolled or expecting to enroll full-time at a four-year institution or university; female and studying in District of Columbia, Georgia, or Ohio. Applicant must have 3.0 GPA or higher. Available to U.S. citizens.

Application Requirements: Application, essay, references, transcript. *Deadline:* March 26.

Contact: Elizabeth Horner, Scholarship Program Officer
Dayton Foundation
500 Kettering Tower
Dayton, OH 45423
Phone: 937-222-9955
Fax: 937-222-0636
E-mail: ehorner@daytonfoundation.org

GREATER KANAWHA VALLEY FOUNDATION

http://www.tgkvf.org/

MATH AND SCIENCE SCHOLARSHIP
• *See page 140*

HEMOPHILIA HEALTH SERVICES

http://www.hemophiliahealth.com/

SCOTT TARBELL SCHOLARSHIP
• *See page 197*

MICHIGAN COUNCIL OF TEACHERS OF MATHEMATICS

http://www.mictm.org/

MIRIAM SCHAEFER SCHOLARSHIP

A scholarship of $1500 is given to a senior or a junior enrolled full-time in undergraduate degree with mathematics specialty. Applicants should be a resident of Michigan but citizenship does not matter.

Academic Fields/Career Goals: Mathematics.

Award: Scholarship for use in junior or senior years; not renewable. *Number:* 3–5. *Amount:* $1500.

Eligibility Requirements: Applicant must be enrolled or expecting to enroll full-time at a four-year institution or university and resident of Michigan. Applicant must have 3.0 GPA or higher. Available to U.S. and non-U.S. citizens.

Application Requirements: Application, essay, references, transcript. *Deadline:* April 1.

Contact: Mr. Chris Berry, Executive Director
Michigan Council of Teachers of Mathematics
4767 Stadler Road
Monroe, MI 48162
Phone: 734-477-0421
Fax: 734-241-4128
E-mail: info@mictm.org

MISSISSIPPI OFFICE OF STUDENT FINANCIAL AID

http://www.mississippi.edu/

CRITICAL NEEDS TEACHER LOAN/SCHOLARSHIP
• *See page 241*

NASA IDAHO SPACE GRANT CONSORTIUM

http://www.id.spacegrant.org/

NASA IDAHO SPACE GRANT CONSORTIUM SCHOLARSHIP PROGRAM
• *See page 141*

NASA/MARYLAND SPACE GRANT CONSORTIUM

http://www.mdspacegrant.org/

NASA MARYLAND SPACE GRANT CONSORTIUM UNDERGRADUATE SCHOLARSHIPS
• *See page 127*

NASA MINNESOTA SPACE GRANT CONSORTIUM

http://www.aem.umn.edu/mnsgc

MINNESOTA SPACE GRANT CONSORTIUM SCHOLARSHIP PROGRAM
• *See page 127*

NASA MISSISSIPPI SPACE GRANT CONSORTIUM

http://www.olemiss.edu/programs/nasa

MISSISSIPPI SPACE GRANT CONSORTIUM SCHOLARSHIP
• *See page 127*

NASA MONTANA SPACE GRANT CONSORTIUM

http://www.spacegrant.montana.edu/

MONTANA SPACE GRANT SCHOLARSHIP PROGRAM
• *See page 128*

NASA RHODE ISLAND SPACE GRANT CONSORTIUM

http://ri.spacegrant.org/

NASA RHODE ISLAND SPACE GRANT CONSORTIUM OUTREACH SCHOLARSHIP FOR UNDERGRADUATE STUDENTS
• *See page 269*

NASA RISGC SCIENCE EN ESPANOL SCHOLARSHIP FOR UNDERGRADUATE STUDENTS
• *See page 128*

NASA SOUTH DAKOTA SPACE GRANT CONSORTIUM

http://www.sdspacegrant.sdsmt.edu/

SOUTH DAKOTA SPACE GRANT CONSORTIUM UNDERGRADUATE AND GRADUATE STUDENT SCHOLARSHIPS
• *See page 129*

NASA'S VIRGINIA SPACE GRANT CONSORTIUM

http://www.vsgc.odu.edu/

UNDERGRADUATE RESEARCH STEM SCHOLARSHIPS
• *See page 96*

VIRGINIA STEM COMMUNITY COLLEGE SCHOLARSHIPS
• *See page 96*

NATIONAL COUNCIL OF TEACHERS OF MATHEMATICS

http://www.nctm.org/

PROSPECTIVE SECONDARY TEACHER COURSE WORK SCHOLARSHIPS
• *See page 242*

NATIONAL SECURITY AGENCY

http://www.nsa.gov/

NATIONAL SECURITY AGENCY STOKES EDUCATIONAL SCHOLARSHIP PROGRAM
• *See page 198*

NEVADA NASA SPACE GRANT CONSORTIUM

http://www.nvspacegrant.org/

NATIONAL SPACE GRANT COLLEGE AND FELLOWSHIP PROGRAM
• *See page 97*

NEW MEXICO COMMISSION ON HIGHER EDUCATION

http://www.hed.state.nm.us/

MINORITY DOCTORAL ASSISTANCE LOAN-FOR-SERVICE PROGRAM
• *See page 168*

OREGON STUDENT ASSISTANCE COMMISSION

http://www.GetCollegeFunds.org/

BUERKLE SCHOLARSHIP
• *See page 383*

SAN DIEGO FOUNDATION

http://www.sdfoundation.org/

QUALCOMM SAN DIEGO SCIENCE, TECHNOLOGY, ENGINEERING, AND MATHEMATICS SCHOLARSHIP
• *See page 292*

SOCIETY OF HISPANIC PROFESSIONAL ENGINEERS

http://www.shpe.org/

AHETEMS SCHOLARSHIPS
• *See page 293*

SOCIETY OF HISPANIC PROFESSIONAL ENGINEERS FOUNDATION

http://www.henaac.org/

HENAAC SCHOLARS PROGRAM
• *See page 199*

TKE EDUCATIONAL FOUNDATION

http://www.tke.org/

FRANCIS J. FLYNN MEMORIAL SCHOLARSHIP
• *See page 249*

UNITED NEGRO COLLEGE FUND

http://www.uncf.org/

ALFRED CHISHOLM/BASF MEMORIAL SCHOLARSHIP FUND
• *See page 72*

ARLENE BENTON NOLAN AND JOHN NOLAN SCHOLARSHIP
• *See page 144*

CARMEN ROSARIO BATTLE SCHOLARSHIP
• *See page 328*

GEORGE REID WILLIAMS SCHOLARSHIP
• *See page 158*

GILBANE SCHOLARSHIP PROGRAM
• *See page 103*

WISCONSIN MATHEMATICS COUNCIL, INC.

http://www.wismath.org/

ARNE ENGEBRETSEN WISCONSIN MATHEMATICS COUNCIL SCHOLARSHIP
• *See page 250*

ETHEL A. NEIJAHR WISCONSIN MATHEMATICS COUNCIL SCHOLARSHIP
• *See page 251*

SISTER MARY PETRONIA VAN STRATEN WISCONSIN MATHEMATICS COUNCIL SCHOLARSHIP
• *See page 251*

MECHANICAL ENGINEERING

AACE INTERNATIONAL

http://www.aacei.org/

AACE INTERNATIONAL COMPETITIVE SCHOLARSHIP
• *See page 99*

AHS INTERNATIONAL—THE VERTICAL FLIGHT SOCIETY

http://www.vtol.org/

VERTICAL FLIGHT FOUNDATION SCHOLARSHIP
• *See page 118*

AIST FOUNDATION

http://www.aistfoundation.org/

AISI/AIST FOUNDATION PREMIER SCHOLARSHIPS
• *See page 252*

AIST WILLIAM E. SCHWABE MEMORIAL SCHOLARSHIP
• *See page 252*

ASSOCIATION FOR IRON AND STEEL TECHNOLOGY BENJAMIN F. FAIRLESS SCHOLARSHIP (AIME)
• *See page 160*

ASSOCIATION FOR IRON AND STEEL TECHNOLOGY RONALD E. LINCOLN SCHOLARSHIP
• *See page 252*

ASSOCIATION FOR IRON AND STEEL TECHNOLOGY WILLY KORF MEMORIAL SCHOLARSHIP
• *See page 252*

STEEL ENGINEERING EDUCATION LINK (STEEL) SCHOLARSHIPS
• *See page 252*

AMERICAN CHEMICAL SOCIETY, RUBBER DIVISION

http://www.rubber.org/

AMERICAN CHEMICAL SOCIETY, RUBBER DIVISION UNDERGRADUATE SCHOLARSHIP
• *See page 160*

AMERICAN COUNCIL OF ENGINEERING COMPANIES OF PENNSYLVANIA (ACEC/PA)

http://www.acecpa.org/

ENGINEERING SCHOLARSHIP
• *See page 161*

AMERICAN INSTITUTE OF AERONAUTICS AND ASTRONAUTICS

http://www.aiaa.org/

AIAA FOUNDATION UNDERGRADUATE SCHOLARSHIP
• *See page 93*

AMERICAN PUBLIC TRANSPORTATION FOUNDATION

http://www.apta.com/

LOUIS T. KLAUDER SCHOLARSHIP
• *See page 253*

TRANSIT HALL OF FAME SCHOLARSHIP AWARD PROGRAM
• *See page 174*

AMERICAN SOCIETY OF HEATING, REFRIGERATING, AND AIR CONDITIONING ENGINEERS, INC.

http://www.ashrae.org/

ALWIN B. NEWTON SCHOLARSHIP FUND
• *See page 253*

FRANK M. CODA SCHOLARSHIP
• *See page 254*

REUBEN TRANE SCHOLARSHIP
• *See page 254*

AMERICAN SOCIETY OF MECHANICAL ENGINEERS (ASME)

http://www.asme.org/

KENNETH ANDREW ROE SCHOLARSHIP

Award of $10,000 for college juniors and seniors who are student members of ASME. Must be U.S. citizens and North American residents. Must be enrolled in an ABET-accredited, or substantially equivalent, mechanical engineering baccalaureate program in the United States.

Academic Fields/Career Goals: Mechanical Engineering.

Award: Scholarship for use in junior or senior years; not renewable. *Number:* 1. *Amount:* $10,000.

Eligibility Requirements: Applicant must be enrolled or expecting to enroll full-time at a four-year institution or university. Applicant must have 3.0 GPA or higher. Available to U.S. citizens.

Application Requirements: Application, essay, financial need analysis, references, transcript. *Deadline:* March 15.

Contact: Ms. Beth Lefever, Administrator, Centers Programs
American Society of Mechanical Engineers (ASME)
ASME, Three Park Avenue, 22nd Floor
New York, NY 10016-5990
Phone: 212-591-7790
Fax: 212-591-7856
E-mail: lefeverb@asme.org

AMERICAN SOCIETY OF MECHANICAL ENGINEERS AUXILIARY INC.

http://www.asme.org/

AGNES MALAKATE KEZIOS SCHOLARSHIP

Scholarship to college juniors for use in final year at a four year college. Must be majoring in mechanical engineering, be member of ASME (if available), and exhibit leadership values. Must be U.S. citizen enrolled in a college/university in the United States that has ABET accreditation. Scholarship value is $2000 and the number of awards granted varies.

Academic Fields/Career Goals: Mechanical Engineering.

Award: Scholarship for use in junior or senior years; not renewable. *Number:* varies. *Amount:* $2000.

Eligibility Requirements: Applicant must be enrolled or expecting to enroll full-time at a four-year institution or university. Available to U.S. citizens.

Application Requirements: Application, driver's license, references, self-addressed stamped envelope, transcript. *Deadline:* March 15.

Contact: Alverta Cover, Undergraduate Scholarships
American Society of Mechanical Engineers Auxiliary Inc.
5425 Caldwell Mill Road
Birmingham, AL 35242
Phone: 205-991-6109
E-mail: covera@asme.org

ALLEN J. BALDWIN SCHOLARSHIP

Scholarship available to college juniors for use in final year at a four year college. Must be majoring in mechanical engineering, be member of ASME (if available), and exhibit leadership values. Must be U.S. citizen enrolled in a college/university in the United States that has ABET accreditation. Scholarship value is $2000 and the number of awards granted varies.

Academic Fields/Career Goals: Mechanical Engineering.

Award: Scholarship for use in junior or senior years; not renewable. *Number:* varies. *Amount:* $2000.

Eligibility Requirements: Applicant must be enrolled or expecting to enroll full-time at a four-year institution or university. Available to U.S. citizens.

Application Requirements: Application, driver's license, financial need analysis, references, self-addressed stamped envelope, transcript. *Deadline:* March 15.

Contact: Alverta Cover, Undergraduate Scholarships
American Society of Mechanical Engineers Auxiliary Inc.
5425 Caldwell Mill Road
Birmingham, AL 35242
Phone: 205-991-6109
E-mail: covera@asme.org

ASME AUXILIARY UNDERGRADUATE SCHOLARSHIP CHARLES B. SHARP

Award of $2000 available only to ASME student members to be used in final year of undergraduate study in mechanical engineering. Must be a U.S. citizen.

Academic Fields/Career Goals: Mechanical Engineering.

Award: Scholarship for use in senior year; not renewable. *Number:* up to 4. *Amount:* $2000.

Eligibility Requirements: Applicant must be enrolled or expecting to enroll full-time at a four-year institution or university. Applicant or parent of applicant must be member of American Society of Mechanical Engineers. Available to U.S. citizens.

Application Requirements: Application, financial need analysis, references, transcript. *Deadline:* March 15.

Contact: Alverta Cover, Undergraduate Scholarship Chairman
American Society of Mechanical Engineers Auxiliary Inc.
5425 Caldwell Mill Road
Birmingham, AL 35242
Phone: 205-991-6109
E-mail: covera@asme.org

BERNA LOU CARTWRIGHT SCHOLARSHIP

Scholarship for college juniors for use in final year at a four year college. Must be majoring in mechanical engineering. Must be a U.S. citizen, enrolled in a college/university in the United States that has ABET accreditation. Number of awards varies.

Academic Fields/Career Goals: Mechanical Engineering.

Award: Scholarship for use in junior or senior years; not renewable. *Number:* varies. *Amount:* $2000.

Eligibility Requirements: Applicant must be enrolled or expecting to enroll full-time at a four-year institution or university and must have an interest in leadership. Available to U.S. citizens.

Application Requirements: Application, driver's license, references, self-addressed stamped envelope, transcript. *Deadline:* March 15.

Contact: Alverta Cover, Undergraduate Scholarships
American Society of Mechanical Engineers Auxiliary Inc.
5425 Caldwell Mill Road
Birmingham, AL 35242
Phone: 205-991-6109
E-mail: covera@asme.org

SYLVIA W. FARNY SCHOLARSHIP

One-time awards of $2000 to ASME student members for the final year of undergraduate study in mechanical engineering. Must be a U.S. citizen, enrolled in a college/university in the United States that has ABET accreditation. Number of scholarships granted varies.

Academic Fields/Career Goals: Mechanical Engineering.

Award: Scholarship for use in junior or senior years; not renewable. *Number:* varies. *Amount:* $2000.

Eligibility Requirements: Applicant must be enrolled or expecting to enroll full-time at a four-year institution or university. Available to U.S. citizens.

Application Requirements: Application, references, transcript. *Deadline:* March 15.

Contact: Alverta Cover, Undergraduate Scholarships
American Society of Mechanical Engineers Auxiliary Inc.
5425 Caldwell Mill Road
Birmingham, AL 35242
Phone: 205-991-6109
E-mail: covera@asme.org

AMERICAN SOCIETY OF NAVAL ENGINEERS

http://www.navalengineers.org/

AMERICAN SOCIETY OF NAVAL ENGINEERS SCHOLARSHIP
• *See page 93*

AMERICAN WELDING SOCIETY

http://www.aws.org/

PAST PRESIDENTS' SCHOLARSHIP
• *See page 278*

ARRL FOUNDATION INC.

http://www.arrl.org/

GARY WAGNER, K3OMI SCHOLARSHIP
• *See page 164*

ASTRONAUT SCHOLARSHIP FOUNDATION

http://www.astronautscholarship.org/

ASTRONAUT SCHOLARSHIP FOUNDATION
• *See page 95*

AUTOMOTIVE HALL OF FAME

http://www.automotivehalloffame.org/

AUTOMOTIVE HALL OF FAME EDUCATIONAL FUNDS
• *See page 164*

BARRY M. GOLDWATER SCHOLARSHIP AND EXCELLENCE IN EDUCATION FOUNDATION

http://www.act.org/goldwater

BARRY M. GOLDWATER SCHOLARSHIP AND EXCELLENCE IN EDUCATION PROGRAM
• *See page 95*

CUBAN AMERICAN NATIONAL FOUNDATION

http://www.masscholarships.org/

MAS FAMILY SCHOLARSHIPS
• *See page 148*

THE DALLAS FOUNDATION

http://www.dallasfoundation.org/

WHITLEY PLACE SCHOLARSHIP
• *See page 100*

ENGINEERS' SOCIETY OF WESTERN PENNSYLVANIA

http://www.eswp.com/

JOSEPH A. LEVENDUSKY MEMORIAL SCHOLARSHIP
• *See page 165*

FOUNDATION FOR SCIENCE AND DISABILITY

http://stemd.org/

GRANTS FOR DISABLED STUDENTS IN THE SCIENCES
• *See page 95*

HISPANIC ENGINEER NATIONAL ACHIEVEMENT AWARDS CORPORATION (HENAAC)

http://www.henaac.org/

HISPANIC ENGINEER NATIONAL ACHIEVEMENT AWARDS CORPORATION SCHOLARSHIP PROGRAM
• *See page 125*

INDEPENDENT LABORATORIES INSTITUTE SCHOLARSHIP ALLIANCE

http://www.acil.org/

INDEPENDENT LABORATORIES INSTITUTE SCHOLARSHIP ALLIANCE
• *See page 141*

INTERNATIONAL SOCIETY FOR OPTICAL ENGINEERING-SPIE

http://www.spie.org/scholarships

SPIE EDUCATIONAL SCHOLARSHIPS IN OPTICAL SCIENCE AND ENGINEERING
• *See page 96*

INTERNATIONAL SOCIETY OF AUTOMATION (ISA)

http://www.isa.org/

INTERNATIONAL SOCIETY OF AUTOMATION EDUCATION FOUNDATION SCHOLARSHIPS
• *See page 125*

JORGE MAS CANOSA FREEDOM FOUNDATION

http://www.jorgemascanosa.org/

MAS FAMILY SCHOLARSHIP AWARD
• *See page 152*

KENTUCKY ENERGY AND ENVIRONMENT CABINET

http://www.eec.ky.gov/

ENVIRONMENTAL PROTECTION SCHOLARSHIP
• *See page 141*

LOS ANGELES COUNCIL OF BLACK PROFESSIONAL ENGINEERS

http://www.lablackengineers.org/

AL-BEN SCHOLARSHIP FOR ACADEMIC INCENTIVE
• *See page 166*

AL-BEN SCHOLARSHIP FOR PROFESSIONAL MERIT
• *See page 166*

AL-BEN SCHOLARSHIP FOR SCHOLASTIC ACHIEVEMENT
• *See page 166*

MAINE EDUCATION SERVICES

http://www.mesfoundation.com/

MAINE METAL PRODUCTS ASSOCIATION SCHOLARSHIP

Awards available for individuals demonstrating an outstanding record and overall potential to attend an institution of higher learning majoring in: mechanical engineering, machine tool technician, sheet metal fabrication, welding, CAD/CAM for metals industry. Restricted to the study of metal working trades. The award value and the number of awards granted varies annually.

Academic Fields/Career Goals: Mechanical Engineering; Trade/Technical Specialties.

Award: Scholarship for use in freshman, sophomore, junior, or senior years; not renewable. *Number:* varies. *Amount:* varies.

Eligibility Requirements: Applicant must be enrolled or expecting to enroll full- or part-time at a two-year or four-year or technical institution or university; resident of Maine and studying in Maine. Available to U.S. citizens.

Application Requirements: Application, references, transcript. *Deadline:* April 18.

Contact: Kim Benjamin, Vice President of Operations
Maine Education Services
131 Presumpscot Street
Portland, ME 04103
Phone: 207-791-3600

MANUFACTURERS ASSOCIATION OF MAINE

http://www.mainemfg.com/

MAINE METAL PRODUCTS EDUCATION FUND SCHOLARSHIP PROGRAM
• *See page 127*

MICHIGAN SOCIETY OF PROFESSIONAL ENGINEERS

http://www.michiganspe.org/

MICHIGAN SOCIETY OF PROFESSIONAL ENGINEERS HARRY R. BALL, P.E. GRANT
• *See page 166*

MICHIGAN SOCIETY OF PROFESSIONAL ENGINEERS KENNETH B. FISHBECK, P.E. MEMORIAL GRANT
• *See page 166*

NASA IDAHO SPACE GRANT CONSORTIUM

http://www.id.spacegrant.org/

NASA IDAHO SPACE GRANT CONSORTIUM SCHOLARSHIP PROGRAM
• *See page 141*

NASA MONTANA SPACE GRANT CONSORTIUM

http://www.spacegrant.montana.edu/

MONTANA SPACE GRANT SCHOLARSHIP PROGRAM
• *See page 128*

NASA SOUTH CAROLINA SPACE GRANT CONSORTIUM

http://www.cofc.edu/~scsgrant

PRE-SERVICE TEACHER SCHOLARSHIP
• *See page 129*

NASA'S VIRGINIA SPACE GRANT CONSORTIUM

http://www.vsgc.odu.edu/

UNDERGRADUATE RESEARCH STEM SCHOLARSHIPS
• *See page 96*

VIRGINIA STEM COMMUNITY COLLEGE SCHOLARSHIPS
• *See page 96*

NATIONAL ASSOCIATION OF WOMEN IN CONSTRUCTION

http://www.nawic.org/

NAWIC UNDERGRADUATE SCHOLARSHIPS
• *See page 102*

NATIONAL BOARD OF BOILER AND PRESSURE VESSEL INSPECTORS

http://www.nationalboard.org/

NATIONAL BOARD TECHNICAL SCHOLARSHIP
• *See page 167*

NATIONAL SOCIETY OF PROFESSIONAL ENGINEERS

http://www.nspe.org/

MAUREEN L. AND HOWARD N. BLITMAN, PE SCHOLARSHIP TO PROMOTE DIVERSITY IN ENGINEERING
• *See page 167*

PAUL H. ROBBINS HONORARY SCHOLARSHIP
• *See page 168*

PROFESSIONAL ENGINEERS IN INDUSTRY SCHOLARSHIP
• *See page 168*

NEVADA NASA SPACE GRANT CONSORTIUM

http://www.nvspacegrant.org/

NATIONAL SPACE GRANT COLLEGE AND FELLOWSHIP PROGRAM
• *See page 97*

NEW MEXICO COMMISSION ON HIGHER EDUCATION

http://www.hed.state.nm.us/

MINORITY DOCTORAL ASSISTANCE LOAN-FOR-SERVICE PROGRAM
• *See page 168*

OREGON STUDENT ASSISTANCE COMMISSION

http://www.GetCollegeFunds.org/

AMERICAN COUNCIL OF ENGINEERING COMPANIES OF OREGON SCHOLARSHIP
• *See page 168*

PLUMBING-HEATING-COOLING CONTRACTORS EDUCATION FOUNDATION

http://www.foundation.phccweb.org/

DELTA FAUCET COMPANY SCHOLARSHIP PROGRAM
• *See page 103*

PHCC EDUCATIONAL FOUNDATION NEED-BASED SCHOLARSHIP
• *See page 155*

PHCC EDUCATIONAL FOUNDATION SCHOLARSHIP PROGRAM
• *See page 155*

PROFESSIONAL CONSTRUCTION ESTIMATORS ASSOCIATION

http://www.pcea.org/

TED WILSON MEMORIAL SCHOLARSHIP FOUNDATION
• *See page 179*

ROBERT H. MOLLOHAN FAMILY CHARITABLE FOUNDATION, INC.

http://www.mollohanfoundation.org/

HIGH TECHNOLOGY SCHOLARS PROGRAM
• *See page 143*

SIGMA XI, THE SCIENTIFIC RESEARCH SOCIETY

http://www.sigmaxi.org/

SIGMA XI GRANTS-IN-AID OF RESEARCH
• *See page 87*

SOCIETY OF AUTOMOTIVE ENGINEERS

http://www.sae.org/

BMW/SAE ENGINEERING SCHOLARSHIP
• *See page 132*

DETROIT SECTION SAE TECHNICAL SCHOLARSHIP
• *See page 271*

EDWARD D. HENDRICKSON/SAE ENGINEERING SCHOLARSHIP
• *See page 132*

RALPH K. HILLQUIST HONORARY SAE SCHOLARSHIP
• *See page 271*

TMC/SAE DONALD D. DAWSON TECHNICAL SCHOLARSHIP
• *See page 133*

YANMAR/SAE SCHOLARSHIP
• *See page 271*

SOCIETY OF HISPANIC PROFESSIONAL ENGINEERS FOUNDATION

http://www.henaac.org/

SOCIETY OF HISPANIC PROFESSIONAL ENGINEERS FOUNDATION
• *See page 169*

SOCIETY OF MANUFACTURING ENGINEERS EDUCATION FOUNDATION

http://www.smeef.org/

CHAPTER 4-LAWRENCE A. WACKER MEMORIAL SCHOLARSHIP
• *See page 294*

CHAPTER 67-PHOENIX SCHOLARSHIP
• *See page 295*

CHAPTER 198-DOWNRIVER DETROIT SCHOLARSHIP
• See page 295

FORT WAYNE CHAPTER 56 SCHOLARSHIP
• See page 297

MYRTLE AND EARL WALKER SCHOLARSHIP FUND
• See page 272

NORTH CENTRAL REGION 9 SCHOLARSHIP
• See page 298

WICHITA CHAPTER 52 SCHOLARSHIP
• See page 298

WILLIAM E. WEISEL SCHOLARSHIP FUND
• See page 258

SOCIETY OF WOMEN ENGINEERS-ROCKY MOUNTAIN SECTION

http://www.swe-rms.org/

SOCIETY OF WOMEN ENGINEERS-ROCKY MOUNTAIN SECTION SCHOLARSHIP PROGRAM
• See page 170

SONS OF NORWAY FOUNDATION

http://www.sonsofnorway.com/

NANCY LORRAINE JENSEN MEMORIAL SCHOLARSHIP
• See page 170

STRAIGHTFORWARD MEDIA

http://www.straightforwardmedia.com/

STRAIGHTFORWARD MEDIA ENGINEERING SCHOLARSHIP
• See page 170

TURNER CONSTRUCTION COMPANY

http://www.turnerconstruction.com/

YOUTHFORCE 2020 SCHOLARSHIP PROGRAM
• See page 103

UNITED NEGRO COLLEGE FUND

http://www.uncf.org/

ALFRED CHISHOLM/BASF MEMORIAL SCHOLARSHIP FUND
• See page 72

CARDINAL HEALTH SCHOLARSHIP
• See page 72

CARGILL SCHOLARSHIP PROGRAM
• See page 72

EMERSON PROCESS MANAGEMENT SCHOLARSHIP
• See page 170

FORD/UNCF CORPORATE SCHOLARS PROGRAM
• See page 73

GENERAL MILLS TECHNOLOGY SCHOLARS AWARD
• See page 171

LOCKHEED MARTIN/UNCF SCHOLARSHIP
• See page 73

MEDTRONIC FOUNDATION SCHOLARSHIP
• See page 145

NASCAR/WENDELL SCOTT, SR. SCHOLARSHIP
• See page 73

TOYOTA/UNCF SCHOLARSHIP
• See page 74

UNITED WATER CORPORATE SCHOLARS PROGRAM
• See page 74

UPS/UNCF CORPORATE SCHOLARS PROGRAM
• See page 202

UNIVERSITIES SPACE RESEARCH ASSOCIATION

http://www.usra.edu/

UNIVERSITIES SPACE RESEARCH ASSOCIATION SCHOLARSHIP PROGRAM
• See page 97

UTAH SOCIETY OF PROFESSIONAL ENGINEERS

http://www.uspeonline.com/

UTAH SOCIETY OF PROFESSIONAL ENGINEERS JOE RHOADS SCHOLARSHIP
• See page 171

WOMEN IN AVIATION, INTERNATIONAL

http://www.wai.org/

DELTA AIR LINES ENGINEERING SCHOLARSHIP
• See page 135

XEROX

http://www.xerox.com//

TECHNICAL MINORITY SCHOLARSHIP
• See page 171

METEOROLOGY/ ATMOSPHERIC SCIENCE

AMERICAN GEOLOGICAL INSTITUTE

http://www.agiweb.org/

AMERICAN GEOLOGICAL INSTITUTE MINORITY SCHOLARSHIP
• See page 222

AMERICAN INDIAN SCIENCE AND ENGINEERING SOCIETY

http://www.aises.org/

A.T. ANDERSON MEMORIAL SCHOLARSHIP PROGRAM
• *See page 93*

BURLINGTON NORTHERN SANTA FE FOUNDATION SCHOLARSHIP
• *See page 93*

AMERICAN METEOROLOGICAL SOCIETY

http://www.ametsoc.org/

AMERICAN METEOROLOGICAL SOCIETY 75TH ANNIVERSARY SCHOLARSHIP
• *See page 366*

AMERICAN METEOROLOGICAL SOCIETY DR. PEDRO GRAU UNDERGRADUATE SCHOLARSHIP
• *See page 366*

AMERICAN METEOROLOGICAL SOCIETY HOWARD H. HANKS, JR. METEOROLOGICAL SCHOLARSHIP

Scholarship of $700 available for college or university student entering final year in undergraduate study. Applicant must be a major in a meteorology department or other department actively engaged in work on some aspect of the atmospheric sciences, and must intend to make atmospheric science his or her career. Must be enrolled full-time at a U.S. institution with a 3.25 minimum GPA. U.S. citizenship required.

Academic Fields/Career Goals: Meteorology/Atmospheric Science.

Award: Scholarship for use in senior year; not renewable. *Number:* 1. *Amount:* $700.

Eligibility Requirements: Applicant must be enrolled or expecting to enroll full-time at a four-year institution or university. Available to U.S. citizens.

Application Requirements: Application, essay, references, transcript. *Deadline:* varies.

Contact: Donna Fernandez, Development Program Coordinator
American Meteorological Society
45 Beacon Street
Boston, MA 02108-3693
Phone: 617-227-2426 Ext. 246
Fax: 617-742-8718
E-mail: dfernand@ametsoc.org

AMERICAN METEOROLOGICAL SOCIETY HOWARD T. ORVILLE METEOROLOGY SCHOLARSHIP

One-time award for full-time students entering their final year of undergraduate study. Must major in a meteorology department or other department actively engaged in work on some aspect of the atmospheric sciences, and must intend to make atmospheric science his or her career. Must be enrolled full-time at a U.S. institution with a minimum of 3.25 GPA. Must be U.S. citizen or permanent resident to apply.

Academic Fields/Career Goals: Meteorology/Atmospheric Science.

Award: Scholarship for use in senior year; not renewable. *Number:* varies. *Amount:* up to $5000.

Eligibility Requirements: Applicant must be enrolled or expecting to enroll full-time at a four-year institution or university. Applicant must have 3.5 GPA or higher. Available to U.S. citizens.

Application Requirements: Application, essay, references, transcript. *Deadline:* February 20.

Contact: Donna Fernandez, Development Program Coordinator
American Meteorological Society
45 Beacon Street
Boston, MA 02108-3693
Phone: 617-227-2426 Ext. 246
Fax: 617-742-8718
E-mail: dfernand@ametsoc.org

AMERICAN METEOROLOGICAL SOCIETY/INDUSTRY MINORITY SCHOLARSHIPS
• *See page 366*

AMERICAN METEOROLOGICAL SOCIETY MARK J. SCHROEDER SCHOLARSHIP IN METEOROLOGY
• *See page 367*

AMERICAN METEOROLOGICAL SOCIETY RICHARD AND HELEN HAGEMEYER SCHOLARSHIP
• *See page 367*

AMERICAN METEOROLOGICAL SOCIETY WERNER A. BAUM UNDERGRADUATE SCHOLARSHIP
• *See page 367*

AMS FRESHMAN UNDERGRADUATE SCHOLARSHIP
• *See page 306*

CARL W. KREITZBERG ENDOWED SCHOLARSHIP
• *See page 367*

ETHAN AND ALLAN MURPHY MEMORIAL SCHOLARSHIP
• *See page 367*

FATHER JAMES B. MACELWANE ANNUAL AWARDS

Available to enrolled undergraduates who submit a paper on a phase of atmospheric sciences with a statement from a supervisor on the student's original contribution to the work. Minimum 3.0 GPA required. No more than two students from any one institution may enter papers in one contest. Must submit letter from department head or faculty member confirming applicant's undergraduate status and paper's originality. Must be a U.S. citizen.

Academic Fields/Career Goals: Meteorology/Atmospheric Science.

Award: Prize for use in sophomore, junior, or senior years; not renewable. *Number:* 1. *Amount:* $1000.

Eligibility Requirements: Applicant must be enrolled or expecting to enroll full-time at a four-year institution or university. Applicant must have 3.0 GPA or higher. Available to U.S. citizens.

Application Requirements: Applicant must enter a contest, references, original copy of paper, letter of application from the author, letter from the department head, abstract of no more than 250 words. *Deadline:* June 13.

Contact: Donna Sampson, Development and Student Program Manager
American Meteorological Society
45 Beacon Street
Boston, MA 02108-3693
Phone: 617-227-2426 Ext. 246
Fax: 617-742-8718
E-mail: dfernand@ametsoc.org

GEORGE S. BENTON SCHOLARSHIP
• *See page 367*

GUILLERMO SALAZAR RODRIGUES SCHOLARSHIP
• *See page 368*

JOHN R. HOPE SCHOLARSHIP
• *See page 368*

LOREN W. CROW SCHOLARSHIP
• *See page 368*

OM AND SARASWATI BAHETHI SCHOLARSHIP

Assists full-time students pursuing degrees in the atmospheric and related sciences. Minimum GPA of 3.25 required.

Academic Fields/Career Goals: Meteorology/Atmospheric Science.

Award: Scholarship for use in junior or senior years; not renewable. *Number:* 1. *Amount:* up to $2000.

Eligibility Requirements: Applicant must be enrolled or expecting to enroll full-time at a two-year or four-year institution or university. Available to U.S. citizens.

Application Requirements: Application, essay, references, transcript. *Deadline:* February 10.

Contact: Donna Fernandez, Development Program Coordinator
American Meteorological Society
45 Beacon Street
Boston, MA 02108-3693
Phone: 617-227-2426 Ext. 246
Fax: 617-742-8718
E-mail: dfernand@ametsoc.org

ASTRONAUT SCHOLARSHIP FOUNDATION

http://www.astronautscholarship.org/

ASTRONAUT SCHOLARSHIP FOUNDATION
• *See page 95*

BRITISH COLUMBIA INNOVATION COUNCIL

http://www.bcic.ca/

PAUL AND HELEN TRUSSELL SCIENCE AND TECHNOLOGY SCHOLARSHIP
• *See page 95*

NASA RHODE ISLAND SPACE GRANT CONSORTIUM

http://ri.spacegrant.org/

NASA RHODE ISLAND SPACE GRANT CONSORTIUM UNDERGRADUATE RESEARCH SCHOLARSHIP
• *See page 128*

NASA WEST VIRGINIA SPACE GRANT CONSORTIUM

http://www.nasa.wvu.edu/

WEST VIRGINIA SPACE GRANT CONSORTIUM UNDERGRADUATE FELLOWSHIP PROGRAM
• *See page 129*

SIGMA XI, THE SCIENTIFIC RESEARCH SOCIETY

http://www.sigmaxi.org/

SIGMA XI GRANTS-IN-AID OF RESEARCH
• *See page 87*

SOCIETY OF SATELLITE PROFESSIONALS INTERNATIONAL

http://www.sspi.org/

SSPI INTERNATIONAL SCHOLARSHIPS
• *See page 133*

TKE EDUCATIONAL FOUNDATION

http://www.tke.org/

CARROL C. HALL MEMORIAL SCHOLARSHIP
• *See page 97*

VERMONT SPACE GRANT CONSORTIUM

http://www.cems.uvm.edu/vsgc

VERMONT SPACE GRANT CONSORTIUM SCHOLARSHIP PROGRAM
• *See page 98*

MILITARY AND DEFENSE STUDIES

ASSOCIATION OF FORMER INTELLIGENCE OFFICERS

http://www.afio.com/13_scholarships.htm

CIA UNDERGRADUATE SCHOLARSHIPS
• *See page 89*

DEPARTMENT OF THE ARMY

http://www.goarmy.com/rotc

U.S. ARMY ROTC MILITARY JUNIOR COLLEGE (MJC) SCHOLARSHIP

One-time award for high school graduates who wish to attend a two-year military junior college. Must serve simultaneously in the Army National Guard or Reserve and qualify for the ROTC Advanced Course. Must have a minimum GPA of 2.5. Must be a U.S. citizen/national at time of award. Must also be eighteen years of age by October 1 and under twenty-seven years of age on June 30 in the year of graduation. On-line application available. Must be used at one of five military junior colleges. See Professor of Military Science at college for application.

Academic Fields/Career Goals: Military and Defense Studies.

Award: Scholarship for use in freshman year; renewable. *Number:* 110–150. *Amount:* $2705–$25,000.

Eligibility Requirements: Applicant must be age 18-26 and enrolled or expecting to enroll full-time at a two-year institution. Applicant must be physically disabled. Applicant must have 2.5 GPA or higher. Available to U.S. citizens. Applicant must have served in the Army or Army National Guard.

Application Requirements: Application, essay, interview, test scores, transcript, physical, physical fitness test, height/weight. *Deadline:* August 25.

Contact: Mr. Mike Sutton, Program Manager
Department of the Army
U.S. Army Cadet Command, 55 Patch Road, Building 56
Fort Monroe, VA 23651-1052
Phone: 757-788-7282
Fax: 757-788-4643
E-mail: michael.sutton@usacc.army.mil

INDEPENDENT COLLEGE FUND OF MARYLAND (I-FUND)

http://www.i-fundinfo.org/

NATIONAL SECURITY SCHOLARS PROGRAM

Program offers $15,000, assistance with national security clearance processing, paid summer internships with government and private industry plus the opportunity for job placement following graduation. Program is open to students with outstanding academic records.

Academic Fields/Career Goals: Military and Defense Studies.

Award: Scholarship for use in freshman, sophomore, junior, or senior years; not renewable. *Number:* 1. *Amount:* $15,000.

Eligibility Requirements: Applicant must be enrolled or expecting to enroll full-time at a four-year institution or university. Available to U.S. citizens.

Application Requirements: Application, test scores, transcript. *Deadline:* October 1.

Contact: Lori Subotich, Director of Programs and Scholarships
Independent College Fund of Maryland (I-Fund)
3225 Ellerslie Avenue, Suite C160
Baltimore, MD 21218-3519
Phone: 443-997-5700
Fax: 443-997-2740
E-mail: lsubot@jhmi.edu

NATIONAL MILITARY INTELLIGENCE ASSOCIATION

http://www.nmia.org/

NATIONAL MILITARY INTELLIGENCE ASSOCIATION SCHOLARSHIP

Scholarships to support the growth of professional studies in the field of military intelligence and to recognize and reward excellence in the development and transfer of knowledge about military and associated intelligence disciplines.

Academic Fields/Career Goals: Military and Defense Studies.

Award: Scholarship for use in freshman, sophomore, junior, or senior years; not renewable. *Number:* 3. *Amount:* $1000.

Eligibility Requirements: Applicant must be enrolled or expecting to enroll full-time at a four-year institution or university. Applicant or parent of applicant must be member of National Military Intelligence Association. Applicant must have 3.0 GPA or higher. Available to U.S. citizens.

Application Requirements: Application, test scores. *Deadline:* August 1.

Contact: Debra Davis, Director of Business development
National Military Intelligence Association
PO Box 479
Hamilton, VA 20159
Phone: 540-338-1143
Fax: 703-738-7487
E-mail: nmiassoc@comcast.net

SOCIETY OF SATELLITE PROFESSIONALS INTERNATIONAL

http://www.sspi.org/

SSPI INTERNATIONAL SCHOLARSHIPS
• *See page 133*

WOMEN IN DEFENSE (WID), A NATIONAL SECURITY ORGANIZATION

http://wid.ndia.org/

HORIZONS SCHOLARSHIP

Scholarships awarded to provide financial assistance to further educational objectives of women either currently employed in, or planning careers in, defense or national security arenas (not law enforcement or criminal justice). Must be U.S. citizen. Minimum 3.5 GPA required.

Academic Fields/Career Goals: Military and Defense Studies.

Award: Scholarship for use in junior, senior, graduate, or postgraduate years; renewable. *Number:* 5–6. *Amount:* $500–$10,000.

Eligibility Requirements: Applicant must be enrolled or expecting to enroll full- or part-time at a four-year institution or university and female. Applicant must have 3.5 GPA or higher. Available to U.S. citizens.

Application Requirements: Application, essay, financial need analysis, references, transcript, proof of citizenship. *Deadline:* July 1.

Contact: Trina Dickey
Women In Defense (WID), A National Security Organization
2111 Wilson Boulevard, Suite 400
Arlington, VA 22201-3061
Phone: 703-247-2589
Fax: 703-522-1885
E-mail: tdickey@ndia.org

MUSEUM STUDIES

AMERICAN SCHOOL OF CLASSICAL STUDIES AT ATHENS

http://www.ascsa.edu.gr/

ASCSA SUMMER SESSIONS SCHOLARSHIPS
• *See page 92*

COSTUME SOCIETY OF AMERICA

http://www.costumesocietyamerica.com/

ADELE FILENE TRAVEL AWARD
• *See page 105*

STELLA BLUM RESEARCH GRANT
• *See page 105*

MUSIC

AMERICAN COLLEGE OF MUSICIANS/ NATIONAL GUILD OF PIANO TEACHERS

http://www.pianoguild.com/

AMERICAN COLLEGE OF MUSICIANS/NATIONAL GUILD OF PIANO TEACHERS $200 SCHOLARSHIPS

Award available only to student affiliate members who have participated in National Guild of Piano Teachers auditions over a ten-year period. Must be Paderewski Medal winner and be sponsored by Guild member. Contact American College of Musicians for more information.

Academic Fields/Career Goals: Music.

Award: Scholarship for use in freshman, sophomore, junior, or senior years; not renewable. *Number:* up to 150. *Amount:* $200.

Eligibility Requirements: Applicant must be enrolled or expecting to enroll full-time at a two-year or four-year or technical institution or university and must have an interest in music. Applicant or parent of applicant must be member of American College of Musicians. Available to U.S. and non-U.S. citizens.

Application Requirements: Application, test scores. *Deadline:* September 15.

Contact: Scholarship Committee
American College of Musicians/National Guild of Piano Teachers
PO Box 1807
Austin, TX 78767-1807

AMERICAN COUNCIL FOR POLISH CULTURE

http://www.polishcultureacpc.org/

MARCELLA KOCHANSKA SEMBRICH VOCAL COMPETITION

Prize of $1500 given to high school graduates, male or female up to the age of 35 years who have pursued or are currently pursuing higher education study in voice or in the early stage of their vocal career. Contestant must be a U.S. citizen of Polish descent.

Academic Fields/Career Goals: Music.

Award: Prize for use in freshman, sophomore, junior, senior, graduate, or postgraduate years; not renewable. *Number:* 1. *Amount:* $1500.

Eligibility Requirements: Applicant must be of Polish heritage; age 35 or under; enrolled or expecting to enroll full- or part-time at a two-year or four-year institution or university and must have an interest in music/singing. Available to U.S. citizens.

Application Requirements: Application, applicant must enter a contest, references, 3 copies of a cassette or CD containing applicant's operatic vocal performance. *Deadline:* April 1.

Contact: Mrs. Alicia L. Dutka, ACPC Music Committee Chair
American Council for Polish Culture
1991 Selkirk Court
Inverness, IL 60010
Phone: 847-382-6339
Fax: 847-382-6338
E-mail: aldutka@comcast.net

AMERICAN FOUNDATION FOR THE BLIND

http://www.afb.org/

GLADYS C. ANDERSON MEMORIAL SCHOLARSHIP

Non-renewable award available to a legally-blind female undergraduate or graduate student studying religious or classical music. Must submit a letter from a post-secondary institution as proof of enrollment in a program in music. For online application and more information, visit web site http://www.afb.org.

Academic Fields/Career Goals: Music.

Award: Scholarship for use in freshman, sophomore, junior, or senior years; not renewable. *Number:* 1. *Amount:* $1000.

Eligibility Requirements: Applicant must be enrolled or expecting to enroll full-time at a four-year institution or university and female. Applicant must be visually impaired. Available to U.S. citizens.

Application Requirements: Application, essay, references, transcript, proof of enrollment letter from post secondary institution, proof of blindness letter from agency or medical doctor. *Deadline:* April 30.

Contact: Dawn Bodrogi, Information Center and Library Coordinator
American Foundation for the Blind
11 Penn Plaza, Suite 300
New York, NY 10001
Phone: 212-502-7661
E-mail: dbodrogi@afb.net

R.L. GILLETTE SCHOLARSHIP
• *See page 397*

AMERICAN LEGION DEPARTMENT OF KANSAS

http://www.ksamlegion.org/

MUSIC COMMITTEE SCHOLARSHIP

One-time award open to a high school senior or college freshman or sophomore. Must be a Kansas resident. Must have distinguished background in the field of music at an approved Kansas junior college, college or university. Award of $1000, with the disbursement as $500 award for each of the two semesters.

Academic Fields/Career Goals: Music; Performing Arts.

Award: Scholarship for use in freshman or sophomore years; not renewable. *Number:* 1. *Amount:* $1000.

Eligibility Requirements: Applicant must be enrolled or expecting to enroll full-time at a two-year or four-year or technical institution or university; resident of Kansas; studying in Kansas and must have an interest in music/singing. Available to U.S. citizens.

Application Requirements: Application, financial need analysis, photo, references, transcript, latest 1040 income statement of supporting parents. *Deadline:* February 15.

Contact: Jim Gravenstein, Chairman, Scholarship Committee
American Legion Department of Kansas
1314 Topeka Boulevard, SW
Topeka, KS 66612
Phone: 785-232-9315
Fax: 782-232-1399

BMI FOUNDATION INC.

http://www.bmifoundation.org/

BMI STUDENT COMPOSER AWARDS
• *See page 109*

JOHN LENNON SCHOLARSHIP PROGRAM

Scholarships available to songwriters and composers from music schools, universities, and youth orchestras. Also submissions from the Music Educators National Conference are solicited. The submitted work must be an original song with lyrics accompanied by whatever instrumentation is chosen by the applicant.

Academic Fields/Career Goals: Music.

Award: Scholarship for use in freshman, sophomore, junior, senior, graduate, or postgraduate years; not renewable. *Number:* up to 3. *Amount:* $5000–$10,000.

Eligibility Requirements: Applicant must be age 15-24; enrolled or expecting to enroll full- or part-time at a two-year or four-year or technical institution or university and must have an interest in music. Available to U.S. citizens.

Application Requirements: Application, applicant must enter a contest, CD or audio tape of a song written by the applicant with original words and music, three typed copies of the lyric. *Deadline:* January 26.

Contact: Mr. Ralph N. Jackson, President
BMI Foundation Inc.
320 West 57th Street
New York, NY 10019
Phone: 212-586-2000
Fax: 212-245-8986
E-mail: info@bmifoundation.org

PEERMUSIC LATIN SCHOLARSHIP

Award for the best song or instrumental work in any Latin genre. The competition is open to songwriters and composers between the ages of 16 and 24 who are current students at colleges and universities. Must submit an original work. Applicants must not have had any musical work commercially recorded or distributed.

Academic Fields/Career Goals: Music.

Award: Scholarship for use in freshman, sophomore, junior, senior, graduate, or postgraduate years; not renewable. *Number:* 1. *Amount:* up to $5000.

Eligibility Requirements: Applicant must be age 16-24; enrolled or expecting to enroll full-time at a two-year or four-year or technical institution or university and must have an interest in music. Available to U.S. citizens.

Application Requirements: Application, applicant must enter a contest, CD of original song or instrumental work, three typed lyric sheets. *Deadline:* varies.

Contact: Mr. Ralph N. Jackson, President
BMI Foundation Inc.
320 West 57th Street
New York, NY 10019
Phone: 212-586-2000
Fax: 212-245-8986
E-mail: rjackson@bmi.com

BNY MELLON, N.A.

http://www.bnymellon.com/

SUSAN GLOVER HITCHCOCK SCHOLARSHIP

Award for women who are majoring in music. Must be a Massachusetts resident. Eligible applicant must be recommended by educational institution. Not for graduate study programs.

Academic Fields/Career Goals: Music.

Award: Scholarship for use in freshman, sophomore, junior, or senior years; not renewable. *Number:* varies. *Amount:* up to $2000.

Eligibility Requirements: Applicant must be enrolled or expecting to enroll full-time at a two-year or four-year or technical institution or university; female and resident of Massachusetts. Available to U.S. citizens.

Application Requirements: Application, essay, transcript. *Deadline:* April 15.

Contact: June Kfoury McNeil, Vice President
BNY Mellon, N.A.
201 Washington Street, 024-0092
Boston, MA 02108
Phone: 617-722-3891

THE CHOPIN FOUNDATION OF THE UNITED STATES

http://www.chopin.org/

SCHOLARSHIP PROGRAM FOR YOUNG AMERICAN PIANISTS

Program aimed to help young American pianists to continue their piano education. Award(s) are available to students between ages 14 and 17 whose field of study is music and whose major is piano. Renewable for up to four years. Students will be assisted in preparing to qualify for the National Chopin Piano Competition. Must be U.S. citizen or legal resident. For more information, see web site http://www.chopin.org.

Academic Fields/Career Goals: Music; Performing Arts.

Award: Scholarship for use in freshman, sophomore, junior, or senior years; renewable. *Number:* 1–10. *Amount:* $1000.

Eligibility Requirements: Applicant must be age 14-17; enrolled or expecting to enroll full- or part-time at a four-year institution or university and must have an interest in music. Available to U.S. citizens.

Application Requirements: Application, applicant must enter a contest, references, unedited video recording of applicant playing specific required pieces. *Fee:* $25. *Deadline:* April 15.

Contact: Jadwiga Gewert, Executive Director
The Chopin Foundation of the United States
1440 79th Street Causeway, Suite 117
Miami, FL 33141
Phone: 305-868-0624
Fax: 305-865-5150
E-mail: info@chopin.org

COLLEGEBOUND FOUNDATION

http://www.collegeboundfoundation.org/

JANET B. SONDHEIM SCHOLARSHIP
• *See page 110*

THE COMMUNITY FOUNDATION FOR GREATER ATLANTA, INC.

http://www.cfgreateratlanta.org/

JAMES M. AND VIRGINIA M. SMYTH SCHOLARSHIP
• *See page 110*

DAVIDSON INSTITUTE FOR TALENT DEVELOPMENT

http://www.davidsongifted.org/

DAVIDSON FELLOWS SCHOLARSHIP PROGRAM
• *See page 398*

DAYTON FOUNDATION

http://www.daytonfoundation.org/

MU PHI EPSILON SCHOLARSHIP FUND

Scholarship to assist individuals in furthering their music studies. Should be enrolled full-time at Wright State University, University of Dayton, Central State University, Sinclair Community College, Wilberforce University or Cedarville University.

Academic Fields/Career Goals: Music.

Award: Scholarship for use in sophomore, junior, or senior years; not renewable. *Number:* 1. *Amount:* up to $1000.

Eligibility Requirements: Applicant must be enrolled or expecting to enroll full-time at a two-year or four-year institution or university and studying in Ohio. Applicant must have 3.0 GPA or higher. Available to U.S. citizens.

Application Requirements: Application, essay, references, transcript. *Deadline:* March 6.

Contact: Elizabeth Horner, Scholarship Program Officer
Dayton Foundation
500 Kettering Tower
Dayton, OH 45423
Phone: 937-225-9955
E-mail: ehorner@daytonfoundation.org

DELTA OMICRON FOUNDATION

http://www.delta-omicron.org/

DELTA OMICRON FOUNDATION EDUCATIONAL GRANTS IN MUSIC

Grants available to those studying music at a four-year college or university. Must have a minimum 2.5 GPA. Must be a member of Delta Omicron International Music Fraternity. For more information, visit web site http://www.dofoundation.org.

Academic Fields/Career Goals: Music.

Award: Grant for use in freshman, sophomore, junior, or senior years; not renewable. *Number:* 10–20. *Amount:* $500.

Eligibility Requirements: Applicant must be enrolled or expecting to enroll full- or part-time at a four-year institution or university and must have an interest in music. Applicant must have 3.5 GPA or higher. Available to U.S. and non-U.S. citizens.

Application Requirements: Application, resume, references. *Deadline:* April 30.

Contact: Kay C. Wideman, President
Delta Omicron Foundation
503 Greystone Lane
Douglasville, GA 30134
Phone: 770-920-2417
Fax: 770-577-5863
E-mail: widemans@bellsouth.net

DELTA OMICRON SUMMER SCHOLARSHIPS

Scholarships awarded to assist with summer study in the area of music for summer workshops, seminars and study abroad. Award cannot be used for college tuition. Recipients must be members of Delta Omicron International Music Fraternity.

Academic Fields/Career Goals: Music.

Award: Scholarship for use in freshman, sophomore, junior, or senior years; not renewable. *Number:* 8. *Amount:* $400–$500.

Eligibility Requirements: Applicant must be enrolled or expecting to enroll part-time at a four-year institution or university and must have an interest in music. Available to U.S. and non-U.S. citizens.

Application Requirements: Application. *Deadline:* April 2.

Contact: Ms. Michelle A. May, Chair, Summer Scholarships
Delta Omicron Foundation
1635 West Boston Boulevard
Detroit, MI 48206
Phone: 313-865-1149
E-mail: maybiz@aol.com

DOMENIC TROIANO GUITAR SCHOLARSHIP

http://www.domenictroiano.com/

DOMENIC TROIANO GUITAR SCHOLARSHIP

Scholarship of $3000 is presented annually to a Canadian guitarist who will be pursuing postsecondary guitar education in Canada or elsewhere. Any university, college or private institution guitar program will be funded. Funds will be forwarded directly to the chosen institution of the winner. Must submit a one-page letter outlining background and reasons why applicant should be considered for the scholarship.

Academic Fields/Career Goals: Music.

Award: Scholarship for use in freshman, sophomore, junior, or senior years; not renewable. *Number:* up to 2. *Amount:* $3000.

Eligibility Requirements: Applicant must be Canadian citizen; enrolled or expecting to enroll full-time at a four-year institution or university and must have an interest in music.

Application Requirements: References, two-song demo of the applicant playing guitar. *Deadline:* October 31.

Contact: Clinton Somerton, Administrator
Domenic Troiano Guitar Scholarship
18 Sherbourne Street
Toronto, ON M5A 2R2
Phone: 416-367-0178
Fax: 416-367-0178
E-mail: clinton@domenictroiano.com

GENERAL FEDERATION OF WOMEN'S CLUBS OF MASSACHUSETTS

http://www.gfwcma.org/

DORCHESTER WOMEN'S CLUB MUSIC SCHOLARSHIP

Scholarship for undergraduate major in voice. Applicant must be a Massachusetts resident and an undergraduate currently enrolled in a four-year accredited college, university or school of music, majoring in voice.

Academic Fields/Career Goals: Music; Performing Arts.

Award: Scholarship for use in freshman, sophomore, junior, or senior years; not renewable. *Number:* 1. *Amount:* $500.

Eligibility Requirements: Applicant must be enrolled or expecting to enroll full-time at a four-year institution or university; resident of Massachusetts and must have an interest in music/singing. Available to U.S. and Canadian citizens.

Application Requirements: Application, applicant must enter a contest, driver's license, interview, references, self-addressed stamped envelope, transcript. *Deadline:* March 1.

Contact: Joan Korslund, Music Chairman
General Federation of Women's Clubs of Massachusetts
25 Apple Lane
Wrentham, MA 02093
E-mail: nonnalda@aol.com

GENERAL FEDERATION OF WOMEN'S CLUBS OF MASSACHUSETTS NICKEL FOR NOTES MUSIC SCHOLARSHIP

Scholarship for high school seniors majoring in piano, instrument, music education, music therapy or voice. Applicant must be a senior in a Massachusetts High School.

Academic Fields/Career Goals: Music; Performing Arts.

Award: Scholarship for use in freshman year; not renewable. *Number:* varies. *Amount:* up to $800.

Eligibility Requirements: Applicant must be high school student; planning to enroll or expecting to enroll full-time at a four-year institution or university; resident of Massachusetts and must have an interest in music/singing. Available to U.S. citizens.

Application Requirements: Application, essay, interview, references, self-addressed stamped envelope, transcript. *Deadline:* March 1.

Contact: Joan Korslund, Music Chairman
General Federation of Women's Clubs of Massachusetts
25 Apple Lane
Wrentham, MA 02093
E-mail: nonnalda@aol.com

GLENN MILLER BIRTHPLACE SOCIETY

http://www.glennmiller.org/

GMBS-3RD PLACE INSTRUMENTAL SCHOLARSHIP

One scholarship for a male or female instrumentalist will be awarded as a competition prize to be used for any education-related expenses. Must submit 10-minute, high-quality audio tape of pieces selected for competition or those of similar style. Applicant is responsible for travel to and lodging during the competition. One-time award for high school seniors and college freshmen.

Academic Fields/Career Goals: Music.

Award: Scholarship for use in freshman year; not renewable. *Number:* 1–1. *Amount:* up to $1000.

Eligibility Requirements: Applicant must be enrolled or expecting to enroll full-time at a four-year institution or university. Available to U.S. and non-U.S. citizens.

Application Requirements: Application, essay, performance tape or CD. *Deadline:* March 10.

Contact: Arlene Leonard, Secretary
Glenn Miller Birthplace Society
PO Box 61
Clarinda, IA 51632
Phone: 712-542-2461
Fax: 712-542-2461
E-mail: gmbs@heartland.net

GMBS-BILL BAKER/HANS STARREVELD SCHOLARSHIP

One scholarship for a male or female instrumentalist will be awarded as a competition prize to be used for any education-related expenses. Must submit 10-minute, high-quality audio tape of pieces selected for competition or those of similar style. Applicant is responsible for travel to and lodging during the competition. One-time award for high school seniors and college freshmen.

Academic Fields/Career Goals: Music.

Award: Scholarship for use in freshman year; not renewable. *Number:* 1–1. *Amount:* up to $2000.

Eligibility Requirements: Applicant must be enrolled or expecting to enroll full-time at a four-year institution or university. Available to U.S. and non-U.S. citizens.

Application Requirements: Application, essay, performance tape or CD. *Deadline:* March 10.

Contact: Arlene Leonard, Secretary
Glenn Miller Birthplace Society
PO Box 61
Clarinda, IA 51632
Phone: 712-542-2461
Fax: 712-542-2461
E-mail: gmbs@heartland.net

GMBS-RAY EBERLE VOCAL SCHOLARSHIP

One scholarship for a male or female vocalist will be awarded as a competition prize to be used for any education-related expenses. Must submit 10-minute, high-quality audio tape of pieces selected for competition or those of similar style. Applicant is responsible for travel to and lodging during the competition. One-time award for high school seniors and college freshmen.

Academic Fields/Career Goals: Music.

Award: Scholarship for use in freshman year; not renewable. *Number:* 1–1. *Amount:* up to $4000.

Eligibility Requirements: Applicant must be enrolled or expecting to enroll full-time at a four-year institution. Available to U.S. and non-U.S. citizens.

Application Requirements: Application, essay, performance tape or CD. *Deadline:* March 10.

Contact: Arlene Leonard, Secretary
Glenn Miller Birthplace Society
PO Box 61
Clarinda, IA 51632
Phone: 712-542-2461
Fax: 712-542-2461
E-mail: gmbs@heartland.net

GRAND RAPIDS COMMUNITY FOUNDATION

http://www.grfoundation.org/

LLEWELLYN L. CAYVAN STRING INSTRUMENT SCHOLARSHIP

Scholarship for undergraduate students studying the violin, the viola, the violoncello, and/or the bass viol. High school students not considered. To apply, submit required application form, transcript, essay, reference.

Academic Fields/Career Goals: Music.

Award: Scholarship for use in freshman, sophomore, junior, or senior years; not renewable. *Number:* 6. *Amount:* $1000.

Eligibility Requirements: Applicant must be enrolled or expecting to enroll full-time at a four-year institution or university and must have an interest in music. Available to U.S. citizens.

Application Requirements: Application, references, transcript. *Deadline:* April 1.

Contact: Ruth Bishop, Education Program Officer
Grand Rapids Community Foundation
161 Ottawa Avenue, NW, 209 C
Grand Rapids, MI 49503-2757
Phone: 616-454-1751 Ext. 103
Fax: 616-454-6455
E-mail: rbishop@grfoundation.org

HAPCO MUSIC FOUNDATION INC.

http://www.hapcopromo.org/

TRADITIONAL MARCHING BAND EXTRAVAGANZA SCHOLARSHIP AWARD

Scholarship is offered to deserving students who will continue their participation in any college music program. Minimum 3.0 GPA required. Applicant should have best composite score of 970 SAT or 20 ACT.

Academic Fields/Career Goals: Music.

Award: Scholarship for use in freshman year; not renewable. *Number:* varies. *Amount:* $250–$1000.

Eligibility Requirements: Applicant must be enrolled or expecting to enroll full-time at a two-year or four-year institution or university and must have an interest in music. Applicant must have 3.0 GPA or higher. Available to U.S. citizens.

Application Requirements: Application, essay, photo, references, test scores, transcript. *Deadline:* varies.

Contact: Joseph McMullen, President
HapCo Music Foundation Inc.
PO Box 784581
Winter Garden, FL 34778-4581
Phone: 407-877-2262
Fax: 407-654-0308
E-mail: hapcopromo@aol.com

HARTFORD JAZZ SOCIETY INC.

http://www.hartfordjazzsociety.com/

HARTFORD JAZZ SOCIETY SCHOLARSHIPS

Scholarship of up to $3000 is awarded to graduating high school senior attending a four-year college or university. Must be a Connecticut resident. Music major with interest in jazz required.

Academic Fields/Career Goals: Music.

Award: Scholarship for use in freshman year; not renewable. *Number:* 2–3. *Amount:* up to $3000.

Eligibility Requirements: Applicant must be high school student; planning to enroll or expecting to enroll full- or part-time at a four-year institution or university; resident of Connecticut and must have an interest in music. Available to U.S. and Canadian citizens.

Application Requirements: Application, references, cassette tape or CD. *Deadline:* May 1.

Contact: Scholarship Committee Chair
Hartford Jazz Society Inc.
116 Cottage Grove Road
Bloomfield, CT 06002
Phone: 860-242-6688
Fax: 860-243-8871
E-mail: hartjazzsocinc@aol.com

HOUSTON SYMPHONY

http://www.houstonsymphony.org/

HOUSTON SYMPHONY IMA HOGG COMPETITION

Competition for musicians ages 16 to 29 who play standard instruments of the symphony orchestra. Goal is to offer a review by panel of music professionals and further career of an advanced student or a professional musician. Participants must be U.S. citizens or studying in the United States. Application fee is $30.

Academic Fields/Career Goals: Music.

Award: Prize for use in freshman, sophomore, junior, senior, graduate, or postgraduate years; not renewable. *Number:* 5. *Amount:* $300–$5000.

Eligibility Requirements: Applicant must be age 16-29; enrolled or expecting to enroll full- or part-time at a two-year or four-year or technical institution or university and must have an interest in music. Available to U.S. and non-U.S. citizens.

Application Requirements: Application, applicant must enter a contest, CD with required repertoire. *Fee:* $30. *Deadline:* February 13.

Contact: Carol Wilson, Manager, Music Matters!
Houston Symphony
615 Louisiana Street, Suite 102
Houston, TX 77002
Phone: 713-238-1447
Fax: 713-224-0453
E-mail: e&o@houstonsymphony.org

HOUSTON SYMPHONY LEAGUE CONCERTO COMPETITION

Competition is open to student musicians 18 years of age or younger who have not yet graduated from high school and who play any standard orchestral instrument or piano. Must live within a 200-mile radius of Houston and submit a screening CD of one movement of their concerto.

Academic Fields/Career Goals: Music.

Award: Prize for use in freshman year; not renewable. *Number:* up to 3. *Amount:* $250–$1000.

Eligibility Requirements: Applicant must be high school student; age 18 or under; planning to enroll or expecting to enroll full-time at a two-year or four-year institution; resident of Texas and must have an interest in music. Available to U.S. citizens.

Application Requirements: Application, applicant must enter a contest, CD. *Fee:* $25. *Deadline:* November 18.

Contact: Carol Wilson, Manager, Music Matters!
Houston Symphony
615 Louisiana Street, Suite 102
Houston, TX 77002
Phone: 713-238-1449
Fax: 713-224-0453
E-mail: e&o@houstonsymphony.org

JACK J. ISGUR FOUNDATION

JACK J. ISGUR FOUNDATION SCHOLARSHIP
• *See page 112*

KE ALI'I PAUAHI FOUNDATION

http://www.pauahi.org/

EDWIN MAHIAI COPP BEAMER SCHOLARSHIP

Award supports a post-secondary student pursuing a career in music, specifically piano and/or voice, with emphasis on Hawaiian music, opera or musical theatre. Must demonstrate a serious commitment to music training, a career in music and dedication to artistic excellence, and demonstrate financial need. Submit two letter of recommendations from teachers (piano, voice), counselor or music professionals. One-page essay describing the applicant's music background/education to-date, including any awards or special recognitions. Finalist may be asked to conduct an informal musical performance or provide a video of their performance.

Academic Fields/Career Goals: Music; Performing Arts.

Award: Scholarship for use in freshman, sophomore, junior, senior, graduate, or postgraduate years; not renewable. *Number:* up to 1. *Amount:* up to $1000.

Eligibility Requirements: Applicant must be enrolled or expecting to enroll full-time at a two-year or four-year or technical institution or university and must have an interest in Hawaiian language/culture, music, or music/singing. Available to U.S. citizens.

Application Requirements: Application, essay, financial need analysis, references, transcript, college acceptance letter, copy of completed SAR. *Deadline:* April 1.

Contact: Mavis Shiraishi-Nagao, Scholarship Administrator
Phone: 808-534-3966
E-mail: scholarships@pauahi.org

KOSCIUSZKO FOUNDATION

http://www.kosciuszkofoundation.org/

KOSCIUSZKO FOUNDATION CHOPIN PIANO COMPETITION

Three awards for students majoring or planning to major in piano studies, who are between the ages of 16 and 22. Application fee: $50. Must be U.S. citizen or full-time international student in the United States with valid visa.

Academic Fields/Career Goals: Music; Performing Arts.

Award: Prize for use in freshman, sophomore, junior, or senior years; not renewable. *Number:* 3. *Amount:* $1500–$5000.

Eligibility Requirements: Applicant must be age 16-22; enrolled or expecting to enroll full- or part-time at a four-year institution or university and must have an interest in music/singing. Available to U.S. and non-U.S. citizens.

Application Requirements: Application, applicant must enter a contest, photo, resume, references, proof of age. *Fee:* $50. *Deadline:* March 7.

Contact: Tom Pniewski, Director of Cultural Programs
Kosciuszko Foundation
15 East 65th Street
New York, NY 10021-6595
Phone: 212-734-2130
Fax: 212-628-4552
E-mail: tompkf@aol.com

NATIONAL ASSOCIATION OF PASTORAL MUSICIANS

http://www.npm.org/

DAN SCHUTTE SCHOLARSHIP

Scholarship for NPM members enrolled full-or part-time in an undergraduate or graduate pastoral music program. Applicant must intend to work at least two years in the field of pastoral music following graduation/program completion.

Academic Fields/Career Goals: Music.

Award: Scholarship for use in freshman, sophomore, junior, senior, or graduate years; not renewable. *Number:* 1. *Amount:* $1000.

Eligibility Requirements: Applicant must be enrolled or expecting to enroll full- or part-time at a two-year or four-year institution or university and must have an interest in music/singing. Applicant or parent of applicant must be member of National Association of Pastoral Musicians. Available to U.S. and non-U.S. citizens.

Application Requirements: Application, essay, financial need analysis, resume, references, CD of performance. *Deadline:* March 5.

Contact: Kathleen Haley, Director of Membership Services
National Association of Pastoral Musicians
962 Wayne Avenue, Suite 210
Silver Spring, MD 20910-4461
Phone: 240-247-3000
E-mail: haley@npm.org

ELAINE RENDLER-RENE DOSOGNE-GEORGETOWN CHORALE SCHOLARSHIP

Awards NPM members enrolled full-time or part-time in a graduate or undergraduate degree program of studies related to the field of pastoral music. Applicant must intend to work at least two years in the field of pastoral music following graduation or program completion.

Academic Fields/Career Goals: Music; Religion/Theology.

Award: Scholarship for use in freshman, sophomore, junior, senior, or graduate years; not renewable. *Number:* 1. *Amount:* $1000.

Eligibility Requirements: Applicant must be enrolled or expecting to enroll full- or part-time at a two-year or four-year institution or university and must have an interest in music/singing. Applicant or parent of applicant must be member of National Association of Pastoral Musicians. Available to U.S. and non-U.S. citizens.

Application Requirements: Application, essay, financial need analysis, resume, references, CD of performance. *Deadline:* March 5.

Contact: Kathleen Haley, Director of Membership Services
National Association of Pastoral Musicians
962 Wayne Avenue, Suite 210
Silver Spring, MD 20910-4461
Phone: 240-247-3000
E-mail: haley@npm.org

FUNK FAMILY MEMORIAL SCHOLARSHIP

Awards NPM members enrolled full-time or part-time in a graduate or undergraduate degree program of studies related to the field of pastoral music. Applicant must intend to work at least two years in the field of pastoral music following graduation or program completion.

Academic Fields/Career Goals: Music; Religion/Theology.

Award: Scholarship for use in freshman, sophomore, junior, senior, or graduate years; not renewable. *Number:* 1. *Amount:* $1000.

Eligibility Requirements: Applicant must be enrolled or expecting to enroll full- or part-time at a two-year or four-year or technical institution or university and must have an interest in music/singing. Applicant or parent of applicant must be member of National Association of Pastoral Musicians. Available to U.S. and non-U.S. citizens.

Application Requirements: Application, essay, financial need analysis, resume, references, CD of performance. *Deadline:* March 5.

Contact: Kathleen Haley, Director of Membership Services
National Association of Pastoral Musicians
962 Wayne Avenue, Suite 210
Silver Spring, MD 20910-4461
Phone: 240-247-3000
E-mail: haley@npm.org

GIA PUBLICATION PASTORAL MUSICIAN SCHOLARSHIP

Awards NPM members enrolled full-time or part-time in a graduate or undergraduate degree program of studies related to the field of pastoral music. Applicant must intend to work at least two years in the field of pastoral music following graduation or program completion.

Academic Fields/Career Goals: Music; Religion/Theology.

Award: Scholarship for use in freshman, sophomore, junior, senior, or graduate years; not renewable. *Number:* 1. *Amount:* $2000.

Eligibility Requirements: Applicant must be enrolled or expecting to enroll full- or part-time at a two-year or four-year institution or university and must have an interest in music/singing. Applicant or parent of applicant must be member of National Association of Pastoral Musicians. Available to U.S. and non-U.S. citizens.

Application Requirements: Application, essay, financial need analysis, resume, references, CD of performance. *Deadline:* March 5.

Contact: Kathleen Haley, Director of Membership Services
National Association of Pastoral Musicians
962 Wayne Avenue, Suite 210
Silver Spring, MD 20910-4461
Phone: 240-247-3000
E-mail: haley@npm.org

MUSONICS SCHOLARSHIP

Awards NPM members enrolled full-time or part-time in a graduate or undergraduate degree program of studies related to the field of pastoral music. Applicant must intend to work at least two years in the field of pastoral music following graduation or program completion. One award available for graduate study and one award available for undergraduate study.

Academic Fields/Career Goals: Music; Religion/Theology.

Award: Scholarship for use in freshman, sophomore, junior, senior, or graduate years; not renewable. *Number:* 2. *Amount:* $2000.

Eligibility Requirements: Applicant must be enrolled or expecting to enroll full- or part-time at a two-year or four-year institution or university and must have an interest in music/singing. Applicant or parent of applicant must be member of National Association of Pastoral Musicians. Available to U.S. and non-U.S. citizens.

Application Requirements: Application, essay, financial need analysis, resume, references, CD of performance. *Deadline:* March 5.

Contact: Kathleen Haley, Director of Membership Services
National Association of Pastoral Musicians
962 Wayne Avenue, Suite 210
Silver Spring, MD 20910-4461
Phone: 240-247-3000
E-mail: haley@npm.org

Contact: Kathleen Haley, Director of Membership Services
National Association of Pastoral Musicians
962 Wayne Avenue, Suite 210
Silver Spring, MD 20910-4461
Phone: 240-247-3000
E-mail: haley@npm.org

NATIONAL ASSOCIATION OF PASTORAL MUSICIANS MEMBERS' SCHOLARSHIP

Awards NPM members enrolled full-time or part-time in a graduate or undergraduate degree program of studies related to the field of pastoral music. Applicant must intend to work at least two years in the field of pastoral music following graduation or program completion.

Academic Fields/Career Goals: Music; Religion/Theology.

Award: Scholarship for use in freshman, sophomore, junior, senior, or graduate years; not renewable. *Number:* 1. *Amount:* $3000.

Eligibility Requirements: Applicant must be enrolled or expecting to enroll full- or part-time at a two-year or four-year or technical institution or university and must have an interest in music/singing. Applicant or parent of applicant must be member of National Association of Pastoral Musicians. Available to U.S. and non-U.S. citizens.

Application Requirements: Application, essay, financial need analysis, resume, references, CD of performance. *Deadline:* March 5.

Contact: Kathleen Haley, Director of Membership Services
National Association of Pastoral Musicians
962 Wayne Avenue, Suite 210
Silver Spring, MD 20910-4461
Phone: 240-247-3000
E-mail: haley@npm.org

NPM BOARD OF DIRECTORS SCHOLARSHIP

Scholarship for NPM members enrolled full- or part-time in an undergraduate or graduate pastoral music program. Must intend to work at least two years in the field of pastoral music following graduation/program completion.

Academic Fields/Career Goals: Music.

Award: Scholarship for use in freshman, sophomore, junior, senior, or graduate years; not renewable. *Number:* 1. *Amount:* $2000.

Eligibility Requirements: Applicant must be enrolled or expecting to enroll full- or part-time at a two-year or four-year institution or university and must have an interest in music/singing. Applicant or parent of applicant must be member of National Association of Pastoral Musicians. Available to U.S. and non-U.S. citizens.

Application Requirements: Application, essay, financial need analysis, resume, references, CD of performance. *Deadline:* March 5.

Contact: Kathleen Haley, Director of Membership Services
National Association of Pastoral Musicians
962 Wayne Avenue, Suite 210
Silver Spring, MD 20910-4461
Phone: 240-247-3000
E-mail: haley@npm.org

NPM KOINONIA/BOARD OF DIRECTORS SCHOLARSHIP

Awards NPM members enrolled full-time or part-time in a graduate or undergraduate degree program of studies related to the field of pastoral music. Applicant must intend to work at least two years in the field of pastoral music following graduation or program completion.

Academic Fields/Career Goals: Music; Religion/Theology.

Award: Scholarship for use in freshman, sophomore, junior, senior, or graduate years; not renewable. *Number:* 1. *Amount:* $2000.

Eligibility Requirements: Applicant must be enrolled or expecting to enroll full- or part-time at a two-year or four-year institution or university and must have an interest in music/singing. Applicant or parent of applicant must be member of National Association of Pastoral Musicians. Available to U.S. and non-U.S. citizens.

Application Requirements: Application, essay, financial need analysis, resume, references, CD of performance. *Deadline:* March 5.

Contact: Kathleen Haley, Director of Membership Services
National Association of Pastoral Musicians
962 Wayne Avenue, Suite 210
Silver Spring, MD 20910-4461
Phone: 240-247-3000
E-mail: haley@npm.org

NPM PERROT SCHOLARSHIP

Awards NPM members enrolled full-time or part-time in a graduate or undergraduate degree program of studies related to the field of pastoral music. Applicant must intend to work at least two years in the field of pastoral music following graduation or program completion.

Academic Fields/Career Goals: Music.

Award: Scholarship for use in freshman, sophomore, junior, senior, or graduate years; not renewable. *Number:* 1. *Amount:* $3000.

Eligibility Requirements: Applicant must be enrolled or expecting to enroll full- or part-time at a two-year or four-year institution or university. Applicant or parent of applicant must be member of National Association of Pastoral Musicians. Available to U.S. and non-U.S. citizens.

Application Requirements: Application, essay, financial need analysis, resume, references, CD of performance. *Deadline:* March 5.

Contact: Kathleen Haley, Director of Membership Services
National Association of Pastoral Musicians
962 Wayne Avenue, Suite 210
Silver Spring, MD 20910-4461
Phone: 240-247-3000
E-mail: haley@npm.org

OREGON CATHOLIC PRESS SCHOLARSHIP

Awards NPM members enrolled full-time or part-time in a graduate or undergraduate degree program of studies related to the field of pastoral music. Applicant must intend to work at least two years in the field of pastoral music following graduation or program completion.

Academic Fields/Career Goals: Music; Religion/Theology.

Award: Scholarship for use in freshman, sophomore, junior, senior, or graduate years; not renewable. *Number:* 1. *Amount:* up to $2500.

Eligibility Requirements: Applicant must be enrolled or expecting to enroll full- or part-time at a two-year or four-year institution or university and must have an interest in music/singing. Available to U.S. and non-U.S. citizens.

Application Requirements: Application, essay, financial need analysis, resume, references, CD of performance. *Deadline:* March 5.

Contact: Kathleen Haley, Director of Membership Services
National Association of Pastoral Musicians
962 Wayne Avenue, Suite 210
Silver Spring, MD 20910-4461
Phone: 240-247-3000
E-mail: haley@npm.org

PALUCH FAMILY FOUNDATION/WORLD LIBRARY PUBLICATIONS SCHOLARSHIP

Awards NPM members enrolled full-time or part-time in a graduate or undergraduate degree program of studies related to the field of pastoral music. Applicant must intend to work at least two years in the field of pastoral music following graduation or program completion.

Academic Fields/Career Goals: Music; Religion/Theology.

Award: Scholarship for use in freshman, sophomore, junior, senior, or graduate years; not renewable. *Number:* 1. *Amount:* up to $2500.

Eligibility Requirements: Applicant must be enrolled or expecting to enroll full- or part-time at a two-year or four-year institution or university and must have an interest in music/singing. Available to U.S. and non-U.S. citizens.

Application Requirements: Application, essay, financial need analysis, resume, references, CD of performance. *Deadline:* March 5.

Contact: Kathleen Haley, Director of Membership Services
National Association of Pastoral Musicians
962 Wayne Avenue, Suite 210
Silver Spring, MD 20910-4461
Phone: 240-247-3000
E-mail: haley@npm.org

STEVEN C. WARNER SCHOLARSHIP

Scholarship for NPM members enrolled full-or part-time in an undergraduate or graduate pastoral music program. Applicant must intend to work at least two years in the field of pastoral music following graduation/program completion.

Academic Fields/Career Goals: Music.

Award: Scholarship for use in freshman, sophomore, junior, senior, or graduate years; not renewable. *Number:* 1. *Amount:* $1000.

Eligibility Requirements: Applicant must be enrolled or expecting to enroll full- or part-time at a two-year or four-year institution or university and must have an interest in music/singing. Applicant or parent of applicant must be member of National Association of Pastoral Musicians. Available to U.S. and non-U.S. citizens.

Application Requirements: Application, essay, financial need analysis, resume, references, CD of performance. *Deadline:* March 5.

Contact: Kathleen Haley, Director of Membership Services
National Association of Pastoral Musicians
962 Wayne Avenue, Suite 210
Silver Spring, MD 20910-4461
Phone: 240-247-3000
E-mail: haley@npm.org

OREGON STUDENT ASSISTANCE COMMISSION

http://www.GetCollegeFunds.org/

BUERKLE SCHOLARSHIP
• *See page 383*

NICHOLAS DIERMANN MEMORIAL SCHOLARSHIP
• *See page 69*

PI LAMBDA THETA INC.

http://www.pilambda.org/

NADEEN BURKEHOLDER WILLIAMS MUSIC SCHOLARSHIP
• *See page 245*

POLISH ARTS CLUB OF BUFFALO SCHOLARSHIP FOUNDATION

http://www.pacb.bfn.org/

POLISH ARTS CLUB OF BUFFALO SCHOLARSHIP FOUNDATION TRUST
• *See page 114*

QUEEN ELISABETH INTERNATIONAL MUSIC COMPETITION OF BELGIUM

http://www.qeimc.be/

QUEEN ELISABETH COMPETITION
Competition is open to musicians who have already completed their training and who are ready to launch their international careers. The competition covers the following musical disciplines: piano, voice, violin and composition.

Academic Fields/Career Goals: Music.

Award: Prize for use in freshman, sophomore, junior, senior, or graduate years; not renewable. *Number:* varies. *Amount:* $1337–$26,749.

Eligibility Requirements: Applicant must be age 17-27; enrolled or expecting to enroll full- or part-time at a two-year or four-year or technical institution or university and must have an interest in music or music/singing. Available to U.S. and non-U.S. citizens.

Application Requirements: Application, applicant must enter a contest, photo, CD/DVD recording. *Deadline:* January 15.

Contact: Michel-Etienne Van Neste, Secretary General
Queen Elisabeth International Music Competition of Belgium
Rue Aux Laines 20
Brussels 1000
Belgium
Phone: 32 - 213 40 50
Fax: 32 - 514 32 97
E-mail: info@qeimc.be

RHODE ISLAND FOUNDATION

http://www.rifoundation.org/

BACH ORGAN AND KEYBOARD MUSIC SCHOLARSHIP
Scholarship for Rhode Island residents attending college as a music major or a church organist who is a Rhode Island resident and an ABO member. Applicants must demonstrate good grades and financial need. Must include music tape.

Academic Fields/Career Goals: Music.

Award: Scholarship for use in freshman, sophomore, junior, or senior years; not renewable. *Amount:* $800–$1000.

Eligibility Requirements: Applicant must be enrolled or expecting to enroll full-time at a two-year or four-year institution or university; resident of Rhode Island and must have an interest in music/singing. Available to U.S. citizens.

Application Requirements: Application, financial need analysis, references, self-addressed stamped envelope, transcript. *Deadline:* June 1.

Contact: Libby Monahan, Funds Administrator
Rhode Island Foundation
One Union Station
Providence, RI 02903
Phone: 401-274-4564 Ext. 3117
E-mail: libbym@rifoundation.org

CONSTANT MEMORIAL SCHOLARSHIP FOR AQUIDNECK ISLAND RESIDENTS
• *See page 114*

SAN ANGELO SYMPHONY SOCIETY

http://www.sanangelosymphony.org/

SORANTIN YOUNG ARTIST AWARD
Prizes awarded to full-time or part-time students in the field of music (pianists and string instrumentalists), who are under 28 years of age. Award amount ranges from $1000 to $3000. Overall winner will appear with the San Angelo Symphony Orchestra. Application fee of $75 is required. Deadline varies, usually sometime in October.

Academic Fields/Career Goals: Music; Performing Arts.

Award: Prize for use in freshman, sophomore, junior, senior, graduate, or postgraduate years; not renewable. *Number:* 5–12. *Amount:* $1000–$3000.

Eligibility Requirements: Applicant must be age 28 or under; enrolled or expecting to enroll full- or part-time at a two-year or four-year institution or university and must have an interest in music. Available to U.S. and non-U.S. citizens.

Application Requirements: Application, applicant must enter a contest, driver's license, photo, photocopy of a birth certificate. *Fee:* $75.

Contact: Jennifer Odom, Executive Director
San Angelo Symphony Society
PO Box 5922
San Angelo, TX 76902-5922
Phone: 325-658-5877
Fax: 325-653-1045
E-mail: director@sanangelosymphony.org

SAN DIEGO FOUNDATION

http://www.sdfoundation.org/

DR. BARTA-LEHMAN MUSICAL SCHOLARSHIP
Scholarship to graduating high school seniors, or current undergraduate or graduate students. Applicants must be serious and talented musicians who are planning to pursue a career in music and/or play professionally (string instruments preferred). Applicants must have a minimum 3.0 GPA and plan to attend an accredited four-year university or music academy in the U.S. Scholarship may be used for tuition, books and fees.

Academic Fields/Career Goals: Music.

Award: Scholarship for use in freshman, sophomore, junior, senior, or graduate years; not renewable. *Number:* 4. *Amount:* $2000.

Eligibility Requirements: Applicant must be enrolled or expecting to enroll full-time at a four-year institution or university; resident of California and must have an interest in music. Applicant must have 3.0 GPA or higher. Available to U.S. citizens.

Application Requirements: Application, references, transcript, personal statement, CD or video of applicant's music, copy of tax return. *Deadline:* January 26.

Contact: Shryl Helvie, Scholarship Coordinator
San Diego Foundation
2508 Historic Decatur Road, Suite 200
San Diego, CA 92106
Phone: 619-814-1307
Fax: 619-239-1710
E-mail: shryl@sdfoundation.org

SIGMA ALPHA IOTA PHILANTHROPIES, INC.

http://www.sai-national.org/

SIGMA ALPHA IOTA JAZZ PERFORMANCE AWARDS

Award for a college-initiated member of Sigma Alpha Iota who is enrolled in an undergraduate or graduate program in jazz studies or jazz performance at the time of application. Applicant must be no older than age 32.

Academic Fields/Career Goals: Music.

Award: Prize for use in freshman, sophomore, junior, senior, or graduate years; not renewable. *Number:* 2. *Amount:* $1500–$2000.

Eligibility Requirements: Applicant must be age 32 or under; enrolled or expecting to enroll full- or part-time at a four-year institution or university; female and must have an interest in music/singing. Applicant or parent of applicant must be member of Sigma Alpha Iota. Available to U.S. and non-U.S. citizens.

Application Requirements: Application, essay, references, CD recording. *Fee:* $25. *Deadline:* March 15.

Contact: Jaide Fried Massin, Project Director
Sigma Alpha Iota Philanthropies, Inc.
One Tunnel Road
Asheville, NC 28805
Phone: 828-251-0606
Fax: 828-251-0644
E-mail: toffuti@hotmail.com

SIGMA ALPHA IOTA JAZZ STUDIES SCHOLARSHIP

Award for an initiated member of Sigma Alpha Iota in good financial standing with the Fraternity. Scholarship must be applied toward study leading to a music degree with an emphasis in jazz studies.

Academic Fields/Career Goals: Music.

Award: Scholarship for use in freshman, sophomore, junior, or senior years; not renewable. *Number:* 1. *Amount:* $1500.

Eligibility Requirements: Applicant must be enrolled or expecting to enroll full- or part-time at a four-year institution or university; female and must have an interest in music/singing. Applicant or parent of applicant must be member of Sigma Alpha Iota. Available to U.S. and non-U.S. citizens.

Application Requirements: Application, financial need analysis, references, transcript. *Deadline:* March 15.

Contact: Jaide Fried Massen, Project Director
Sigma Alpha Iota Philanthropies, Inc.
One Tunnel Road
Asheville, NC 28805
Phone: 828-251-0606
Fax: 828-251-0644
E-mail: toffuti@hotmail.com

SIGMA ALPHA IOTA MUSIC BUSINESS/TECHNOLOGY SCHOLARSHIP

Tuition scholarship for an initiated member of Sigma Alpha Iota in good financial standing with the Fraternity. Must be enrolled full-time in a bachelor's degree program and entering the junior or senior year of study in fall semester. Minimum GPA of 3.0 required.

Academic Fields/Career Goals: Music.

Award: Scholarship for use in junior or senior years; not renewable. *Number:* varies. *Amount:* $2000.

Eligibility Requirements: Applicant must be enrolled or expecting to enroll full-time at a four-year institution or university; female and must have an interest in music/singing. Applicant or parent of applicant must be member of Sigma Alpha Iota. Applicant must have 3.0 GPA or higher. Available to U.S. and non-U.S. citizens.

Application Requirements: Application, references, transcript, statement of purpose, including career goals. *Deadline:* March 15.

Contact: Kim L. Wangler, Director
Sigma Alpha Iota Philanthropies, Inc.
One Tunnel Road
Asheville, NC 28805
Phone: 828-251-0606
Fax: 828-251-0644
E-mail: wanglerkl@appstate.edu

SIGMA ALPHA IOTA MUSICIANS WITH SPECIAL NEEDS SCHOLARSHIP

• *See page 246*

SIGMA ALPHA IOTA MUSIC THERAPY SCHOLARSHIP

One-time award offered yearly for female undergraduate and graduate members of SAI who have completed two years in music therapy training at a university approved by the American Music Therapy Association. Contact local chapter for further information.

Academic Fields/Career Goals: Music; Therapy/Rehabilitation.

Award: Scholarship for use in junior or senior years; not renewable. *Number:* 1. *Amount:* $1500.

Eligibility Requirements: Applicant must be enrolled or expecting to enroll full-time at a four-year institution or university; female and must have an interest in music/singing. Applicant or parent of applicant must be member of Sigma Alpha Iota. Available to U.S. and non-U.S. citizens.

Application Requirements: Application, essay, financial need analysis, references, transcript. *Deadline:* March 15.

Contact: Ruth Johnson, Director
Sigma Alpha Iota Philanthropies, Inc.
One Tunnel Road
Asheville, NC 28805
Phone: 828-251-0606
Fax: 828-251-0644
E-mail: nh@sai-national.org

SIGMA ALPHA IOTA SUMMER MUSIC SCHOLARSHIPS IN THE U.S. OR ABROAD

One-time award for use at summer music programs in the United States or abroad. Must be a female member of SAI and accepted by the summer music program. Contact local chapter for details.

Academic Fields/Career Goals: Music; Performing Arts.

Award: Scholarship for use in freshman, sophomore, junior, or senior years; not renewable. *Number:* 10. *Amount:* $1000.

Eligibility Requirements: Applicant must be enrolled or expecting to enroll full-time at a four-year institution or university; female and must have an interest in music/singing. Applicant or parent of applicant must be member of Sigma Alpha Iota. Available to U.S. and non-U.S. citizens.

Application Requirements: Application, essay, resume, references, transcript, acceptance letter. *Deadline:* March 15.

Contact: Mary Jennings, Director
Sigma Alpha Iota Philanthropies, Inc.
One Tunnel Road
Asheville, NC 28805
Phone: 828-251-0606
Fax: 828-251-0644
E-mail: maryj10101@aol.com

SIGMA ALPHA IOTA UNDERGRADUATE PERFORMANCE SCHOLARSHIPS

$1500 awards offered triennially for female SAI members in freshman, sophomore or junior year studying voice; keyboard and percussion; strings; or winds and brass. Must be younger than 25 years of age. Winners perform at national convention. Must submit tape with required repertoire. Consult local chapter for details. Application fee: $25.

Academic Fields/Career Goals: Music; Performing Arts.

Award: Scholarship for use in freshman, sophomore, or junior years; not renewable. *Number:* 4. *Amount:* $1500.

Eligibility Requirements: Applicant must be age 25 or under; enrolled or expecting to enroll full-time at a four-year institution or university; female and must have an interest in music/singing. Applicant or parent of applicant must be member of Sigma Alpha Iota. Available to U.S. and non-U.S. citizens.

Application Requirements: Application, applicant must enter a contest, essay, references, self-addressed stamped envelope, transcript, CD recording. *Deadline:* March 15.

Contact: Dr. Emily White, Director
Sigma Alpha Iota Philanthropies, Inc.
One Tunnel Road
Asheville, NC 28805
Phone: 828-251-0606
Fax: 828-251-0644
E-mail: hornstein1@aol.com

UNICO NATIONAL INC.

http://www.unico.org/

THEODORE MAZZA SCHOLARSHIP
• *See page 103*

UNITED NEGRO COLLEGE FUND

http://www.uncf.org/

ELLA FITZGERALD CHARITABLE FOUNDATION SCHOLARSHIP

Scholarship available to students at UNCF member colleges and universities who are studying music. Minimum 2.5 GPA required. For more information please see Web site http://www.uncf.org/forstudents/scholarship.asp.

Academic Fields/Career Goals: Music.

Award: Scholarship for use in freshman year; not renewable.

Eligibility Requirements: Applicant must be Black (non-Hispanic) and enrolled or expecting to enroll at a four-year institution or university. Applicant must have 2.5 GPA or higher. Available to U.S. citizens.

Application Requirements: *Deadline:* continuous.

Contact: Director, Program Services
United Negro College Fund
8260 Willow Oaks Corporate Drive
PO Box 10444
Fairfax, VA 22031-8044
Phone: 800-331-2244
E-mail: rebecca.bennett@uncf.org

JIMI HENDRIX ENDOWMENT FUND SCHOLARSHIP

Scholarship supports undergraduate students majoring in music and attending a UNCF member college or university. Minimum 2.5 GPA required. The scholarship value ranges from $2000 to $5000.

Academic Fields/Career Goals: Music.

Award: Scholarship for use in sophomore, junior, or senior years; not renewable. *Number:* varies. *Amount:* $2000–$5000.

Eligibility Requirements: Applicant must be Black (non-Hispanic) and enrolled or expecting to enroll full- or part-time at a four-year institution or university. Applicant must have 2.5 GPA or higher. Available to U.S. and non-U.S. citizens.

Application Requirements: Application, financial need analysis.

Contact: Director, Program Services
United Negro College Fund
8260 Willow Oaks Corporate Drive
PO Box 10444
Fairfax, VA 22031-8044
Phone: 800-331-2244
E-mail: rebecca.bennett@uncf.org

JOHN LENNON SCHOLARSHIP
• *See page 193*

WOMEN BAND DIRECTORS INTERNATIONAL

http://www.womenbanddirectors.org/

CHARLOTTE PLUMMER OWEN MEMORIAL SCHOLARSHIP
• *See page 251*

MARTHA ANN STARK MEMORIAL SCHOLARSHIP
• *See page 251*

VOLKWEIN MEMORIAL SCHOLARSHIP
• *See page 251*

NATURAL RESOURCES

AMERICAN GROUND WATER TRUST

http://www.agwt.org/

AMERICAN GROUND WATER TRUST-AMTROL INC. SCHOLARSHIP
• *See page 366*

AMERICAN GROUND WATER TRUST-BAROID SCHOLARSHIP

Award for entry-level students intending to pursue a career in ground water-related field. Must either have completed a science/environmental project involving ground water resources or have had vacation work experience related to the environment and natural resources. Must be a U.S. citizen or legal resident with minimum 3.0 GPA. Submit two letters of recommendation and transcript.

Academic Fields/Career Goals: Natural Resources.

Award: Scholarship for use in freshman year; not renewable. *Number:* 1. *Amount:* up to $2000.

Eligibility Requirements: Applicant must be enrolled or expecting to enroll full-time at a four-year institution or university. Applicant must have 3.0 GPA or higher. Available to U.S. citizens.

Application Requirements: Application, essay, references, transcript. *Deadline:* June 1.

Contact: Garret Grasskamp, Ground Water Specialist
American Ground Water Trust
50 Pleasant Street, Suite 2
Concord, NH 03301-4073
Phone: 603-228-5444
Fax: 603-228-6557
E-mail: ggraaskamp@agwt.org

AMERICAN GROUND WATER TRUST-THOMAS STETSON SCHOLARSHIP
• *See page 174*

AMERICAN INDIAN SCIENCE AND ENGINEERING SOCIETY

http://www.aises.org/

A.T. ANDERSON MEMORIAL SCHOLARSHIP PROGRAM
• *See page 93*

AMERICAN WATER RESOURCES ASSOCIATION

http://www.awra.org/

AWRA RICHARD A. HERBERT MEMORIAL SCHOLARSHIP

Two scholarships are available: one for full-time undergraduate student and one for a full-time graduate student, each working toward a degree in water resources. All applicants must be national AWRA members.

Academic Fields/Career Goals: Natural Resources.

Award: Scholarship for use in freshman, sophomore, junior, senior, or graduate years; not renewable. *Number:* 2. *Amount:* $2000.

Eligibility Requirements: Applicant must be enrolled or expecting to enroll full-time at a four-year institution or university. Available to U.S. and non-U.S. citizens.

Application Requirements: Application, essay, resume, references, transcript. *Deadline:* April 22.

Contact: Terry Meyer, Marketing Director
American Water Resources Association
4 West Federal Street, PO Box 1626
Middleburg, VA 20118-1626
Phone: 540-687-8390
Fax: 540-687-8395
E-mail: info@awra.org

ARCTIC INSTITUTE OF NORTH AMERICA

http://www.arctic.ucalgary.ca/

JIM BOURQUE SCHOLARSHIP
• See page 230

ARIZONA HYDROLOGICAL SOCIETY

http://www.azhydrosoc.org/

ARIZONA HYDROLOGICAL SOCIETY SCHOLARSHIP
• See page 222

ARIZONA PROFESSIONAL CHAPTER OF AISES

http://www.azpcofaises.org/

ARIZONA PROFESSIONAL CHAPTER OF AISES SCHOLARSHIP
• See page 279

ASSOCIATION OF CALIFORNIA WATER AGENCIES

http://www.acwa.com/

ASSOCIATION OF CALIFORNIA WATER AGENCIES SCHOLARSHIPS
• See page 94

CLAIR A. HILL SCHOLARSHIP
• See page 94

BRITISH COLUMBIA INNOVATION COUNCIL

http://www.bcic.ca/

PAUL AND HELEN TRUSSELL SCIENCE AND TECHNOLOGY SCHOLARSHIP
• See page 95

CALIFORNIA GROUNDWATER ASSOCIATION

http://www.groundh2o.org/

CALIFORNIA GROUNDWATER ASSOCIATION SCHOLARSHIP
• See page 368

CANADIAN RECREATIONAL CANOEING ASSOCIATION

http://www.paddlingcanada.com/

BILL MASON MEMORIAL SCHOLARSHIP FUND
• See page 232

CONNECTICUT FOREST AND PARK ASSOCIATION

http://www.ctwoodlands.org/

JAMES L. AND GENEVIEVE H. GOODWIN MEMORIAL SCHOLARSHIP
Scholarship to support Connecticut residents enrolled in a curriculum of silviculture or forest resource management.

Academic Fields/Career Goals: Natural Resources.
Award: Scholarship for use in freshman, sophomore, junior, or senior years; not renewable. *Number:* up to 10. *Amount:* $1000–$5000.
Eligibility Requirements: Applicant must be enrolled or expecting to enroll full-time at a two-year or four-year institution or university and resident of Connecticut. Available to U.S. citizens.
Application Requirements: Application, essay, financial need analysis, transcript. *Deadline:* March 15.
Contact: Eric Hammerling, Executive Director
Connecticut Forest and Park Association
16 Meriden Road
Rockfall, CT 06481-2961
Phone: 860-346-2372
Fax: 860-347-7463
E-mail: info@ctwoodlands.org

CONSERVATION FEDERATION OF MISSOURI

http://www.confedmo.org/

CHARLES P. BELL CONSERVATION SCHOLARSHIP
• See page 307

FRIENDS OF THE FRELINGHUYSEN ARBORETUM

http://www.arboretumfriends.org/

BENJAMIN C. BLACKBURN SCHOLARSHIP
• See page 308

GARDEN CLUB OF AMERICA

http://www.gcamerica.org/

THE ELIZABETH GARDNER NORWEB SUMMER ENVIRONMENTAL STUDIES SCHOLARSHIP
• See page 84

GREAT LAKES COMMISSION

http://www.glc.org/

CAROL A. RATZA MEMORIAL SCHOLARSHIP
• See page 185

INDIANA WILDLIFE FEDERATION ENDOWMENT

http://www.indianawildlife.org/

CHARLES A. HOLT INDIANA WILDLIFE FEDERATION ENDOWMENT SCHOLARSHIP
• See page 308

INTERNATIONAL ASSOCIATION OF GREAT LAKES RESEARCH

http://www.iaglr.org/

PAUL W. RODGERS SCHOLARSHIP
• See page 224

INTERTRIBAL TIMBER COUNCIL

http://www.itcnet.org/

TRUMAN D. PICARD SCHOLARSHIP
• See page 79

LAND CONSERVANCY OF NEW JERSEY

http://www.tlc-nj.org/

ROGERS FAMILY SCHOLARSHIP
• *See page 309*

RUSSELL W. MYERS SCHOLARSHIP
• *See page 309*

LOUISIANA OFFICE OF STUDENT FINANCIAL ASSISTANCE

http://www.osfa.la.gov/

ROCKEFELLER STATE WILDLIFE SCHOLARSHIP
• *See page 141*

MANITOBA FORESTRY ASSOCIATION

http://www.thinktrees.org/

DR. ALAN BEAVEN FORESTRY SCHOLARSHIP
• *See page 309*

MINERALOGICAL SOCIETY OF AMERICA

http://www.minsocam.org/

MINERALOGICAL SOCIETY OF AMERICA-GRANT FOR STUDENT RESEARCH IN MINERALOGY AND PETROLOGY
• *See page 225*

MONTANA FEDERATION OF GARDEN CLUBS

http://www.mtfgc.org/

LIFE MEMBER MONTANA FEDERATION OF GARDEN CLUBS SCHOLARSHIP
• *See page 225*

NATIONAL ASSOCIATION OF WATER COMPANIES-NEW JERSEY CHAPTER

http://www.nawc.org/

NATIONAL ASSOCIATION OF WATER COMPANIES-NEW JERSEY CHAPTER SCHOLARSHIP
• *See page 142*

OHIO FORESTRY ASSOCIATION

http://www.ohioforest.org/

OHIO FORESTRY ASSOCIATION MEMORIAL SCHOLARSHIP

Minimum of one scholarship will be awarded to provide assistance toward forest resource education to quality college students. Preference given to students attending Ohio colleges and universities.

Academic Fields/Career Goals: Natural Resources.

Award: Scholarship for use in freshman, sophomore, junior, or senior years; not renewable. *Number:* 1. *Amount:* $1000.

Eligibility Requirements: Applicant must be enrolled or expecting to enroll full-time at a two-year or four-year or technical institution or university and resident of Ohio. Available to U.S. citizens.

Application Requirements: Application, essay, test scores. *Deadline:* April 15.

Contact: John Dorka, Executive Director
Ohio Forestry Association
1100-H Brandywine Blvd.
Zanesville, OH 43701
Phone: 614-497-9580
Fax: 614-497-9581
E-mail: johnd@ohioforest.org

OREGON STUDENT ASSISTANCE COMMISSION

http://www.GetCollegeFunds.org/

OREGON FOUNDATION FOR BLACKTAIL DEER SCHOLARSHIP
• *See page 142*

ROYDEN M. BODLEY SCHOLARSHIP
• *See page 311*

RAILWAY TIE ASSOCIATION

http://www.rta.org/

JOHN MABRY FORESTRY SCHOLARSHIP

One-time award to potential forestry industry leaders. Open to junior and senior undergraduates who will be enrolled in accredited forestry schools. One scholarship is also available to second-year students in a two-year college. Applications reviewed with emphasis on leadership qualities, career objectives, scholastic achievement, and financial need.

Academic Fields/Career Goals: Natural Resources.

Award: Scholarship for use in sophomore, junior, or senior years; not renewable. *Number:* 2. *Amount:* $1500.

Eligibility Requirements: Applicant must be enrolled or expecting to enroll full-time at a two-year or four-year institution or university. Available to U.S. and Canadian citizens.

Application Requirements: Application, driver's license, essay, references, transcript. *Deadline:* June 30.

Contact: Debbie Corallo, Administrator
Railway Tie Association
115 Commerce Drive, Suite C
Fayetteville, GA 30214
Phone: 770-460-5553
E-mail: ties@rta.org

ROCKY MOUNTAIN ELK FOUNDATION

http://www.elkfoundation.org/

WILDLIFE LEADERSHIP AWARDS

Program established to recognize, encourage and promote leadership among future wildlife management professionals. Candidates must be an undergraduate in a recognized wildlife program, have at least a junior standing (completed a minimum of 56 semester hours or 108 quarter hours), and have at least one semester or two quarters remaining in their degree program.

Academic Fields/Career Goals: Natural Resources; Natural Sciences.

Award: Scholarship for use in junior or senior years; not renewable. *Number:* 1–10. *Amount:* $2000.

Eligibility Requirements: Applicant must be enrolled or expecting to enroll full- or part-time at a four-year institution or university and must have an interest in wildlife conservation/animal rescue. Available to U.S. and Canadian citizens.

Application Requirements: Application, letters of recommendation from faculty. *Deadline:* March 1.

Contact: Becky Bennett, Director of Human Resources
Rocky Mountain Elk Foundation
5705 Grant Creek
PO Box 8249
Missoula, MT 59808
Phone: 800-225-5355 Ext. 555
E-mail: bbennett@rmef.org

SAEMS-SOUTHERN ARIZONA ENVIRONMENTAL MANAGEMENT SOCIETY

http://www.saems.org/

ENVIRONMENTAL SCHOLARSHIPS
• *See page 305*

SOCIETY FOR RANGE MANAGEMENT

http://www.rangelands.org/

MASONIC RANGE SCIENCE SCHOLARSHIP
• *See page 80*

SOIL AND WATER CONSERVATION SOCIETY

http://www.swcs.org/

DONALD A. WILLIAMS SCHOLARSHIP SOIL CONSERVATION SCHOLARSHIP
• *See page 226*

SOIL AND WATER CONSERVATION SOCIETY-NEW JERSEY CHAPTER

http://www.geocities.com/njswcs

EDWARD R. HALL SCHOLARSHIP
• *See page 81*

SOUTH DAKOTA BOARD OF REGENTS

http://www.sdbor.edu/

SOUTH DAKOTA BOARD OF REGENTS BJUGSTAD SCHOLARSHIP
• *See page 81*

TECHNICAL ASSOCIATION OF THE PULP & PAPER INDUSTRY (TAPPI)

http://www.tappi.org/

WILLIAM L. CULLISON SCHOLARSHIP

Scholarship provides incentive for students to pursue an academic path related to the pulp and paper industry. Eligible students must meet all criteria and will have completed two years of undergraduate school with two years (or three years in a five-year program) remaining. For details, refer to web site http://www.tappi.org/s_tappi/doc.asp?CID=6101&DID=561682.

Academic Fields/Career Goals: Natural Resources; Paper and Pulp Engineering.

Award: Scholarship for use in junior or senior years; renewable. *Number:* 1. *Amount:* $2000–$4000.

Eligibility Requirements: Applicant must be enrolled or expecting to enroll full-time at a four-year institution or university. Available to U.S. and non-U.S. citizens.

Application Requirements: Application, references, transcript. *Deadline:* May 1.

Contact: Mr. Charles Bohanan, Director of Standards and Awards
Technical Association of the Pulp & Paper Industry (TAPPI)
15 Technology Parkway South
Norcross, GA 30092
Phone: 770-209-7276
Fax: 770-446-6947
E-mail: standards@tappi.org

TEXAS OUTDOOR WRITERS ASSOCIATION

http://www.towa.org/

TEXAS OUTDOOR WRITERS ASSOCIATION SCHOLARSHIP
• *See page 192*

TKE EDUCATIONAL FOUNDATION

http://www.tke.org/

TIMOTHY L. TASCHWER SCHOLARSHIP
• *See page 144*

UNITED STATES ENVIRONMENTAL PROTECTION AGENCY

http://www.epa.gov/enviroed

NATIONAL NETWORK FOR ENVIRONMENTAL MANAGEMENT STUDIES FELLOWSHIP
• *See page 312*

VIRGINIA ASSOCIATION OF SOIL AND WATER CONSERVATION DISTRICTS EDUCATIONAL FOUNDATION INC.

http://www.vaswcd.org/

VASWCD EDUCATIONAL FOUNDATION INC. SCHOLARSHIP AWARDS PROGRAM
• *See page 312*

WILSON ORNITHOLOGICAL SOCIETY

http://www.wilsonsociety.org/

GEORGE A. HALL/HAROLD F. MAYFIELD AWARD
• *See page 92*

PAUL A. STEWART AWARDS
• *See page 92*

NATURAL SCIENCES

AMERICAN CHEMICAL SOCIETY

http://www.acs.org/

AMERICAN CHEMICAL SOCIETY SCHOLARS PROGRAM
• *See page 160*

AMERICAN FOUNDATION FOR THE BLIND

http://www.afb.org/

PAUL W. RUCKES SCHOLARSHIP
• *See page 195*

AMERICAN INDIAN SCIENCE AND ENGINEERING SOCIETY

http://www.aises.org/

A.T. ANDERSON MEMORIAL SCHOLARSHIP PROGRAM
• *See page 93*

BURLINGTON NORTHERN SANTA FE FOUNDATION SCHOLARSHIP
• See page 93

ARCTIC INSTITUTE OF NORTH AMERICA

http://www.arctic.ucalgary.ca/

JIM BOURQUE SCHOLARSHIP
• See page 230

ARRL FOUNDATION INC.

http://www.arrl.org/

WILLIAM R. GOLDFARB MEMORIAL SCHOLARSHIP
• See page 146

YASME FOUNDATION SCHOLARSHIP
• See page 139

ASSOCIATION OF CALIFORNIA WATER AGENCIES

http://www.acwa.com/

ASSOCIATION OF CALIFORNIA WATER AGENCIES SCHOLARSHIPS
• See page 94

CLAIR A. HILL SCHOLARSHIP
• See page 94

ASSOCIATION OF FORMER INTELLIGENCE OFFICERS

http://www.afio.com/13_scholarships.htm

CIA UNDERGRADUATE SCHOLARSHIPS
• See page 89

ASSOCIATION ON AMERICAN INDIAN AFFAIRS, INC.

http://www.indian-affairs.org/

ELIZABETH AND SHERMAN ASCHE MEMORIAL SCHOLARSHIP FUND
• See page 83

AUDUBON SOCIETY OF WESTERN PENNSYLVANIA

http://www.aswp.org/

BEULAH FREY ENVIRONMENTAL SCHOLARSHIP
• See page 307

BARRY M. GOLDWATER SCHOLARSHIP AND EXCELLENCE IN EDUCATION FOUNDATION

http://www.act.org/goldwater

BARRY M. GOLDWATER SCHOLARSHIP AND EXCELLENCE IN EDUCATION PROGRAM
• See page 95

BRITISH COLUMBIA INNOVATION COUNCIL

http://www.bcic.ca/

BCIC YOUNG INNOVATOR SCHOLARSHIP COMPETITION (IDEA MASH UP)
• See page 95

PAUL AND HELEN TRUSSELL SCIENCE AND TECHNOLOGY SCHOLARSHIP
• See page 95

CANADIAN RECREATIONAL CANOEING ASSOCIATION

http://www.paddlingcanada.com/

BILL MASON MEMORIAL SCHOLARSHIP FUND
• See page 232

THE COMMUNITY FOUNDATION FOR GREATER ATLANTA, INC.

http://www.cfgreateratlanta.org/

JAMES M. AND VIRGINIA M. SMYTH SCHOLARSHIP
• See page 110

CONSERVATION FEDERATION OF MISSOURI

http://www.confedmo.org/

CHARLES P. BELL CONSERVATION SCHOLARSHIP
• See page 307

EXPLORERS CLUB

http://www.explorers.org/

YOUTH ACTIVITY FUND

Award given to college students or high school students pursuing a research project in the field of science. Applicants must have two letter of recommendation, one-page description of project, a budget or plan, and proof of student enrollment with dates.

Academic Fields/Career Goals: Natural Sciences; Science, Technology, and Society.

Award: Grant for use in freshman, sophomore, junior, or senior years; not renewable. *Number:* 10–30. *Amount:* $500–$5000.

Eligibility Requirements: Applicant must be enrolled or expecting to enroll full-time at a four-year institution or university. Available to U.S. and non-U.S. citizens.

Application Requirements: Application, essay, financial need analysis, references. *Deadline:* varies.

Contact: Annie Lee, Member Services
Explorers Club
46 East 70th Street
New York, NY 10021
Fax: 212-288-4449
E-mail: alee@explorers.org

GARDEN CLUB OF AMERICA

http://www.gcamerica.org/

FRANCES M. PEACOCK SCHOLARSHIP FOR NATIVE BIRD HABITAT

Offers scholars the opportunity to pursue habitat-related issues that will benefit bird species and lend useful information for land management decisions. To apply contact http://www.birds.cornell.edu/about/jobs.html.

Academic Fields/Career Goals: Natural Sciences.

Award: Scholarship for use in senior year; not renewable. *Number:* 1. *Amount:* $4000.

Eligibility Requirements: Applicant must be enrolled or expecting to enroll full- or part-time at a four-year institution or university. Available to U.S. citizens.

Application Requirements: Application, essay, resume, references, self-addressed stamped envelope, transcript, budget. *Deadline:* January 15.

Contact: Scott Sutcliffe, Scholarship Committee
Garden Club of America
Cornell Lab of Ornithology, 159 Sapsucker Woods Road
Ithaca, NY 14850
Fax: 607-254-2415
E-mail: sas10@cornell.edu

GARDEN CLUB OF AMERICA SUMMER SCHOLARSHIP IN FIELD BOTANY
• *See page 357*

GCA AWARD IN DESERT STUDIES
• *See page 101*

JOAN K. HUNT AND RACHEL M. HUNT SUMMER SCHOLARSHIP IN FIELD BOTANY
• *See page 357*

ZELLER SUMMER SCHOLARSHIP IN MEDICINAL BOTANY
• *See page 343*

GREAT LAKES COMMISSION

http://www.glc.org/

CAROL A. RATZA MEMORIAL SCHOLARSHIP
• *See page 185*

HARVARD TRAVELLERS CLUB

http://www.harvardtravellersclub.org/

HARVARD TRAVELLERS CLUB GRANTS
• *See page 98*

INTERNATIONAL ASSOCIATION OF GREAT LAKES RESEARCH

http://www.iaglr.org/

PAUL W. RODGERS SCHOLARSHIP
• *See page 224*

KENTUCKY ENERGY AND ENVIRONMENT CABINET

http://www.eec.ky.gov/

ENVIRONMENTAL PROTECTION SCHOLARSHIP
• *See page 141*

MINERALOGICAL SOCIETY OF AMERICA

http://www.minsocam.org/

MINERALOGICAL SOCIETY OF AMERICA-GRANT FOR STUDENT RESEARCH IN MINERALOGY AND PETROLOGY
• *See page 225*

NASA IDAHO SPACE GRANT CONSORTIUM

http://www.id.spacegrant.org/

NASA IDAHO SPACE GRANT CONSORTIUM SCHOLARSHIP PROGRAM
• *See page 141*

NASA SOUTH DAKOTA SPACE GRANT CONSORTIUM

http://www.sdspacegrant.sdsmt.edu/

SOUTH DAKOTA SPACE GRANT CONSORTIUM UNDERGRADUATE AND GRADUATE STUDENT SCHOLARSHIPS
• *See page 129*

NASA'S VIRGINIA SPACE GRANT CONSORTIUM

http://www.vsgc.odu.edu/

TEACHER EDUCATION STEM SCHOLARSHIP PROGRAM
• *See page 96*

NASA WEST VIRGINIA SPACE GRANT CONSORTIUM

http://www.nasa.wvu.edu/

WEST VIRGINIA SPACE GRANT CONSORTIUM UNDERGRADUATE FELLOWSHIP PROGRAM
• *See page 129*

NEVADA NASA SPACE GRANT CONSORTIUM

http://www.nvspacegrant.org/

NATIONAL SPACE GRANT COLLEGE AND FELLOWSHIP PROGRAM
• *See page 97*

NEW MEXICO COMMISSION ON HIGHER EDUCATION

http://www.hed.state.nm.us/

MINORITY DOCTORAL ASSISTANCE LOAN-FOR-SERVICE PROGRAM
• *See page 168*

OREGON STUDENT ASSISTANCE COMMISSION

http://www.GetCollegeFunds.org/

ROYDEN M. BODLEY SCHOLARSHIP
• *See page 311*

PENNSYLVANIA HIGHER EDUCATION ASSISTANCE AGENCY

http://www.pheaa.org/

NEW ECONOMY TECHNOLOGY AND SCITECH SCHOLARSHIPS
• *See page 270*

ROCKY MOUNTAIN ELK FOUNDATION

http://www.elkfoundation.org/

WILDLIFE LEADERSHIP AWARDS
• *See page 430*

SOCIETY OF HISPANIC PROFESSIONAL ENGINEERS FOUNDATION

http://www.henaac.org/

SOCIETY OF HISPANIC PROFESSIONAL ENGINEERS FOUNDATION
• *See page 169*

SOIL AND WATER CONSERVATION SOCIETY

http://www.swcs.org/

DONALD A. WILLIAMS SCHOLARSHIP SOIL CONSERVATION SCHOLARSHIP
• *See page 226*

SOIL AND WATER CONSERVATION SOCIETY-NEW JERSEY CHAPTER

http://www.geocities.com/njswcs

EDWARD R. HALL SCHOLARSHIP
• *See page 81*

UNITED NEGRO COLLEGE FUND

http://www.uncf.org/

CHARLES E. CULPEPPER SCHOLARSHIP
• *See page 144*

DIBNER FUND SCHOLARSHIP
Scholarship for students majoring in natural and physical sciences who are enrolled at UNCF member colleges and universities. Minimum 2.5 GPA required.

Academic Fields/Career Goals: Natural Sciences; Physical Sciences.

Award: Scholarship for use in freshman year; not renewable. *Amount:* up to $4000.

Eligibility Requirements: Applicant must be Black (non-Hispanic) and enrolled or expecting to enroll at a four-year institution or university. Applicant must have 2.5 GPA or higher. Available to U.S. citizens.

Application Requirements: *Deadline:* continuous.

Contact: Director, Program Services
United Negro College Fund
8260 Willow Oaks Corporate Drive
PO Box 10444
Fairfax, VA 22031-8044
Phone: 800-331-2244
E-mail: rebecca.bennett@uncf.org

UNCF/MERCK SCIENCE INITIATIVE
• *See page 145*

NEAR AND MIDDLE EAST STUDIES

ASSOCIATION OF FORMER INTELLIGENCE OFFICERS

http://www.afio.com/13_scholarships.htm

CIA UNDERGRADUATE SCHOLARSHIPS
• *See page 89*

NEUROBIOLOGY

AMERICAN PHYSIOLOGICAL SOCIETY

http://www.the-aps.org/

DAVID S. BRUCE AWARDS FOR EXCELLENCE IN UNDERGRADUATE RESEARCH
• *See page 138*

ARNOLD AND MABEL BECKMAN FOUNDATION

http://www.beckman-foundation.com/

BECKMAN SCHOLARS PROGRAM
• *See page 138*

CYNTHIA E. MORGAN SCHOLARSHIP FUND (CEMS)

http://www.cemsfund.com/

CYNTHIA E. MORGAN MEMORIAL SCHOLARSHIP FUND, INC.
• *See page 304*

UNITED NEGRO COLLEGE FUND

http://www.uncf.org/

UNCF/MERCK SCIENCE INITIATIVE
• *See page 145*

NUCLEAR SCIENCE

AMERICAN INDIAN SCIENCE AND ENGINEERING SOCIETY

http://www.aises.org/

A.T. ANDERSON MEMORIAL SCHOLARSHIP PROGRAM
• *See page 93*

BURLINGTON NORTHERN SANTA FE FOUNDATION SCHOLARSHIP
• *See page 93*

AMERICAN NUCLEAR SOCIETY

http://www.ans.org/

AMERICAN NUCLEAR SOCIETY OPERATIONS AND POWER SCHOLARSHIP

Undergraduate scholarship for students who have completed two or more years in a course of study leading to a degree in nuclear science, nuclear engineering, or a nuclear-related field.

Academic Fields/Career Goals: Nuclear Science.

Award: Scholarship for use in junior or senior years; not renewable. *Number:* 1. *Amount:* $2500.

Eligibility Requirements: Applicant must be enrolled or expecting to enroll full- or part-time at a four-year institution or university. Available to U.S. citizens.

Application Requirements: Application, references, transcript. *Deadline:* February 1.

Contact: Scholarship Coordinator
American Nuclear Society
555 North Kensington Avenue
La Grange Park, IL 60526
Phone: 708-352-6611
Fax: 708-352-0499
E-mail: outreach@ans.org

AMERICAN NUCLEAR SOCIETY UNDERGRADUATE SCHOLARSHIPS

Maximum of four scholarships for students who have completed one year in a course of study leading to a degree in nuclear science, nuclear engineering, or a nuclear-related field and who will be sophomores in the upcoming academic year; and a maximum of twenty one scholarships for students who have completed two or more years and will be entering as juniors or seniors. Must be sponsored by ANS member or branch. Must be U.S. citizen or permanent resident.

Academic Fields/Career Goals: Nuclear Science.

Award: Scholarship for use in junior or senior years; not renewable. *Number:* 4–21. *Amount:* $2000.

Eligibility Requirements: Applicant must be enrolled or expecting to enroll full-time at a four-year institution or university. Available to U.S. citizens.

Application Requirements: Application, references, transcript. *Deadline:* February 1.

Contact: Scholarship Coordinator
American Nuclear Society
555 North Kensington Avenue
La Grange Park, IL 60526
Phone: 708-352-6611
Fax: 708-352-0499
E-mail: outreach@ans.org

AMERICAN NUCLEAR SOCIETY VOGT RADIOCHEMISTRY SCHOLARSHIP

• *See page 276*

ANS INCOMING FRESHMAN SCHOLARSHIP

Scholarship for graduating high school seniors who have enrolled or plan to enroll full-time in a nuclear engineering degree program. Scholarships will be awarded based on an applicant's high school academic achievement and course of undergraduate study.

Academic Fields/Career Goals: Nuclear Science.

Award: Scholarship for use in freshman year; not renewable. *Number:* 1–4. *Amount:* $1000.

Eligibility Requirements: Applicant must be high school student and planning to enroll or expecting to enroll full-time at a four-year institution or university. Available to U.S. and non-U.S. citizens.

Application Requirements: Application, essay, references, transcript. *Deadline:* April 1.

Contact: Scholarship Committee
American Nuclear Society
555 North Kensington Avenue
La Grange Park, IL 60526
Phone: 708-352-6611
Fax: 708-352-0499

CHARLES (TOMMY) THOMAS MEMORIAL SCHOLARSHIP DIVISION SCHOLARSHIP

Undergraduate scholarship for students who have completed two or more years in a course of study leading to a degree in nuclear science, nuclear engineering, or a nuclear-related field.

Academic Fields/Career Goals: Nuclear Science.

Award: Scholarship for use in junior or senior years; not renewable. *Number:* 1. *Amount:* $3000.

Eligibility Requirements: Applicant must be enrolled or expecting to enroll full-time at a four-year institution or university. Available to U.S. citizens.

Application Requirements: Application, references, transcript. *Deadline:* February 1.

Contact: Scholarship Coordinator
American Nuclear Society
555 North Kensington Avenue
La Grange Park, IL 60526
Phone: 708-352-6611
Fax: 708-352-0499
E-mail: outreach@ans.org

DECOMMISSIONING, DECONTAMINATION, AND REUTILIZATION UNDERGRADUATE SCHOLARSHIP

• *See page 260*

DELAYED EDUCATION FOR WOMEN SCHOLARSHIPS

One-time award given to enable mature women whose formal studies in nuclear science, nuclear engineering, or related fields have been delayed or interrupted at least one year. Must be U.S. citizen or permanent resident. Minimum GPA of 2.5 required.

Academic Fields/Career Goals: Nuclear Science.

Award: Scholarship for use in freshman, sophomore, junior, or senior years; not renewable. *Number:* 1. *Amount:* $5000.

Eligibility Requirements: Applicant must be enrolled or expecting to enroll full-time at a four-year institution or university and female. Applicant must have 2.5 GPA or higher. Available to U.S. citizens.

Application Requirements: Application, financial need analysis, references, transcript. *Deadline:* February 1.

Contact: Scholarship Coordinator
American Nuclear Society
555 North Kensington Avenue
La Grange Park, IL 60526
Phone: 708-352-6611
Fax: 708-352-0499
E-mail: outreach@ans.org

JOHN AND MURIEL LANDIS SCHOLARSHIP AWARDS

Maximum of eight scholarships are awarded to undergraduate and graduate students who have greater than average financial need. Applicants should be planning a career in nuclear science, nuclear engineering, or a nuclear related field and be enrolled or planning to enroll in a college or university located in the United States, but need not be U.S. citizens.

Academic Fields/Career Goals: Nuclear Science.

Award: Scholarship for use in freshman, sophomore, junior, senior, or graduate years; not renewable. *Number:* 1–8. *Amount:* $5000.

Eligibility Requirements: Applicant must be enrolled or expecting to enroll full-time at a four-year institution or university. Available to U.S. and non-U.S. citizens.

Application Requirements: Application, financial need analysis, references, transcript. *Deadline:* February 1.

Contact: Scholarship Coordinator
American Nuclear Society
555 North Kensington Avenue
La Grange Park, IL 60526
Phone: 708-352-6611
Fax: 708-352-0469
E-mail: outreach@ans.org

JOHN R. LAMARSH SCHOLARSHIP

Undergraduate scholarship for students who have completed two or more years in a course of study leading to a degree in nuclear science, nuclear engineering, or a nuclear-related field.

Academic Fields/Career Goals: Nuclear Science.

Award: Scholarship for use in junior or senior years; not renewable. *Number:* 1. *Amount:* $2000.

Eligibility Requirements: Applicant must be enrolled or expecting to enroll full- or part-time at a four-year institution or university. Available to U.S. citizens.

Application Requirements: Application, references, transcript. *Deadline:* February 1.

Contact: Scholarship Coordinator
American Nuclear Society
555 North Kensington Avenue
La Grange Park, IL 60526
Phone: 708-352-6611
Fax: 708-352-0499
E-mail: outreach@ans.org

JOSEPH R. DIETRICH SCHOLARSHIP

Undergraduate scholarship for students who have completed two or more years in a course of study leading to a degree in nuclear science, nuclear engineering, or a nuclear-related field.

Academic Fields/Career Goals: Nuclear Science.

Award: Scholarship for use in junior or senior years; not renewable. *Number:* 1. *Amount:* $2000.

Eligibility Requirements: Applicant must be enrolled or expecting to enroll full- or part-time at a four-year institution or university. Available to U.S. citizens.

Application Requirements: Application, references, transcript. *Deadline:* February 1.

Contact: Scholarship Coordinator
American Nuclear Society
555 North Kensington Avenue
La Grange Park, IL 60526
Phone: 708-352-6611
Fax: 708-352-0499
E-mail: outreach@ans.org

RAYMOND DISALVO SCHOLARSHIP

Undergraduate scholarship for students who have completed two or more years in a course of study leading to a degree in nuclear science, nuclear engineering, or a nuclear-related field.

Academic Fields/Career Goals: Nuclear Science.

Award: Scholarship for use in junior or senior years; not renewable. *Number:* 1–21. *Amount:* $2000.

Eligibility Requirements: Applicant must be enrolled or expecting to enroll full-time at a four-year institution or university. Available to U.S. and non-U.S. citizens.

Application Requirements: Application, references, transcript, sponsorship letter from ANS organization. *Deadline:* February 1.

Contact: Scholarship Coordinator
American Nuclear Society
555 North Kensington Avenue
La Grange Park, IL 60526
Phone: 708-352-6611
Fax: 708-352-0499
E-mail: outreach@ans.org

ROBERT G. LACY SCHOLARSHIP

Undergraduate scholarship for students who have completed two or more years in a course of study leading to a degree in nuclear science, nuclear engineering, or a nuclear-related field.

Academic Fields/Career Goals: Nuclear Science.

Award: Scholarship for use in junior or senior years; not renewable. *Number:* 1. *Amount:* $2000.

Eligibility Requirements: Applicant must be enrolled or expecting to enroll full-time at a four-year institution or university. Available to U.S. and non-U.S. citizens.

Application Requirements: Application, references, transcript, sponsorship letter from ANS organization. *Deadline:* February 1.

Contact: Scholarship Coordinator
American Nuclear Society
555 North Kensington Avenue
La Grange Park, IL 60526
Phone: 708-352-6611
Fax: 708-352-0499
E-mail: outreach@ans.org

ROBERT T. "BOB" LINER SCHOLARSHIP

Undergraduate scholarship for students who have completed two or more years in a course of study leading to a degree in nuclear science, nuclear engineering, or a nuclear-related field.

Academic Fields/Career Goals: Nuclear Science.

Award: Scholarship for use in junior or senior years; not renewable. *Number:* 1. *Amount:* $2000.

Eligibility Requirements: Applicant must be enrolled or expecting to enroll full-time at a·four-year institution or university. Available to U.S. and non-U.S. citizens.

Application Requirements: Application, references, transcript, sponsorship letter from ANS organization. *Deadline:* February 1.

Contact: Scholarship Coordinator
American Nuclear Society
555 North Kensington Avenue
La Grange Park, IL 60526
Phone: 708-352-6611
Fax: 708-352-0499
E-mail: outreach@ans.org

ARIZONA HYDROLOGICAL SOCIETY

http://www.azhydrosoc.org/

ARIZONA HYDROLOGICAL SOCIETY SCHOLARSHIP
• *See page 222*

BARRY M. GOLDWATER SCHOLARSHIP AND EXCELLENCE IN EDUCATION FOUNDATION

http://www.act.org/goldwater

BARRY M. GOLDWATER SCHOLARSHIP AND EXCELLENCE IN EDUCATION PROGRAM
• *See page 95*

BRITISH COLUMBIA INNOVATION COUNCIL

http://www.bcic.ca/

PAUL AND HELEN TRUSSELL SCIENCE AND TECHNOLOGY SCHOLARSHIP
• *See page 95*

HISPANIC ENGINEER NATIONAL ACHIEVEMENT AWARDS CORPORATION (HENAAC)

http://www.henaac.org/

HISPANIC ENGINEER NATIONAL ACHIEVEMENT AWARDS CORPORATION SCHOLARSHIP PROGRAM
• *See page 125*

NASA WEST VIRGINIA SPACE GRANT CONSORTIUM

http://www.nasa.wvu.edu/

WEST VIRGINIA SPACE GRANT CONSORTIUM UNDERGRADUATE FELLOWSHIP PROGRAM
• *See page 129*

NATIONAL SCIENCE TEACHERS ASSOCIATION

http://www.nsta.org/

TOSHIBA/NSTA EXPLORAVISION AWARDS PROGRAM
• *See page 198*

SOCIETY OF NUCLEAR MEDICINE

http://www.snm.org/

PAUL COLE SCHOLARSHIP
• *See page 348*

UNIVERSITIES SPACE RESEARCH ASSOCIATION

http://www.usra.edu/

UNIVERSITIES SPACE RESEARCH ASSOCIATION SCHOLARSHIP PROGRAM
• *See page 97*

NURSING

AIR FORCE RESERVE OFFICER TRAINING CORPS

http://www.afrotc.com/

AIR FORCE ROTC FOUR-YEAR NURSING SCHOLARSHIP
Scholarship offers qualified individuals the chance to compete for scholarships of up to $15,000 per academic year. Nursing students can compete for scholarships through the In-College Scholarship Program, or may qualify for a nursing scholarship.

Academic Fields/Career Goals: Nursing.

Award: Scholarship for use in sophomore, junior, or senior years; not renewable. *Number:* varies. *Amount:* up to $15,000.

Eligibility Requirements: Applicant must be enrolled or expecting to enroll full-time at a four-year institution or university. Available to U.S. citizens.

Application Requirements: Application. *Deadline:* varies.

Contact: Capt. Elmarko Magee, Chief of Advertising
Air Force Reserve Officer Training Corps
551 East Maxwell Boulevard
Maxwell AFB, AL 36112-6106
Phone: 866-423-7682

ALBERTA HERITAGE SCHOLARSHIP FUND

http://www.alis.alberta.ca/

ALBERTA HERITAGE SCHOLARSHIP FUND ABORIGINAL HEALTH CAREERS BURSARY
• *See page 137*

AMARILLO AREA FOUNDATION

http://www.amarilloareafoundation.org/

E. EUGENE WAIDE, MD MEMORIAL SCHOLARSHIP
Scholarship for graduating senior from Ochiltree, Hansford, Lipscomb, Hutchinson, Roberts or Hemphill counties. Applicant must pursue a career as LVN, BSN (junior or senior), MSN.

Academic Fields/Career Goals: Nursing.

Award: Scholarship for use in freshman, sophomore, junior, senior, or graduate years; not renewable. *Number:* varies. *Amount:* varies.

Eligibility Requirements: Applicant must be enrolled or expecting to enroll full- or part-time at a two-year or four-year or technical institution or university and resident of Texas. Available to U.S. citizens.

Application Requirements: Application, photo. *Deadline:* February 1.

Contact: Scholarship Screening Committee
Amarillo Area Foundation
801 South Fillmore Street, Suite 700
Amarillo, TX 79101
Phone: 806-376-4521
Fax: 806-373-3656

NANCY GERALD MEMORIAL NURSING SCHOLARSHIP
Scholarship of $500 for graduating senior from one of the 26 counties in Texas. Applicant must be majoring in the field of nursing at Amarillo College or West Texas A & M University pursuing AAS, BSN or MSN degree.

Academic Fields/Career Goals: Nursing.

Award: Scholarship for use in freshman, sophomore, junior, senior, or graduate years; not renewable. *Number:* varies. *Amount:* $500.

Eligibility Requirements: Applicant must be enrolled or expecting to enroll full- or part-time at a two-year or four-year institution or university; resident of Texas and studying in Texas. Applicant must have 2.5 GPA or higher. Available to U.S. citizens.

Application Requirements: Application, photo. *Deadline:* February 1.

Contact: Scholarship Screening Committee
Amarillo Area Foundation
801 South Fillmore Street, Suite 700
Amarillo, TX 79101
Phone: 806-376-4521
Fax: 806-373-3656

AMERICAN ASSOCIATION OF NEUROSCIENCE NURSES

http://www.aann.org/

NEUROSCIENCE NURSING FOUNDATION SCHOLARSHIP
Scholarship available for registered nurse to attend an NLN accredited school. Submit letter of school acceptance along with application, transcript, and copy of current RN license. Applicants should have diploma or AD.

Academic Fields/Career Goals: Nursing.

Award: Scholarship for use in freshman, sophomore, junior, senior, or graduate years; not renewable. *Number:* varies. *Amount:* $1500.

Eligibility Requirements: Applicant must be enrolled or expecting to enroll full- or part-time at a two-year or four-year institution or university. Applicant must have 3.0 GPA or higher. Available to U.S. citizens.

Application Requirements: Application, transcript, letter of acceptance. *Deadline:* January 15.

Contact: Scholarship Programs Coordinator
American Association of Neuroscience Nurses
4700 West Lake Avenue
Glenview, IL 60025-1485
Phone: 888-557-2266
E-mail: info@aann.org

AMERICAN LEGION AUXILIARY DEPARTMENT OF ARIZONA

http://www.azlegion.org/majorp~2.htm

AMERICAN LEGION AUXILIARY DEPARTMENT OF ARIZONA NURSES' SCHOLARSHIPS
Award for Arizona residents enrolled in their second year at an institution in Arizona awarding degrees as a registered nurse. Preference given to immediate family member of a veteran. Must be a U.S. citizen and resident of Arizona for one year.

Academic Fields/Career Goals: Nursing.

Award: Scholarship for use in sophomore, junior, or senior years; not renewable. *Number:* 4. *Amount:* $600.

Eligibility Requirements: Applicant must be enrolled or expecting to enroll full-time at a two-year or four-year institution or university; resident of Arizona and studying in Arizona. Available to U.S. citizens.

Application Requirements: Application, essay, financial need analysis, photo, references, test scores, transcript. *Deadline:* May 15.

Contact: Department Secretary and Treasurer
American Legion Auxiliary Department of Arizona
4701 North 19th Avenue, Suite 100
Phoenix, AZ 85015-3727
Phone: 602-241-1080
Fax: 602-604-9640
E-mail: amlegauxaz@mcleodusa.net

AMERICAN LEGION AUXILIARY DEPARTMENT OF CALIFORNIA

http://www.calegionaux.org/

AMERICAN LEGION AUXILIARY DEPARTMENT OF CALIFORNIA PAST PRESIDENTS' PARLEY NURSING SCHOLARSHIPS

Award for student entering into or continuing studies in a nursing program.

Academic Fields/Career Goals: Nursing.

Award: Scholarship for use in freshman, sophomore, junior, or senior years; not renewable. *Number:* varies. *Amount:* $500–$1000.

Eligibility Requirements: Applicant must be enrolled or expecting to enroll full- or part-time at a four-year institution or university. Available to U.S. citizens. Applicant or parent must meet one or more of the following requirements: Army experience; retired from active duty; disabled or killed as a result of military service; prisoner of war; or missing in action.

Application Requirements: Application, references, transcript. *Deadline:* April 4.

Contact: Theresa Jacob, Secretary/Treasurer
American Legion Auxiliary Department of California
401 Van Ness Avenue, Room 113
San Francisco, CA 94102
Phone: 415-862-5092
Fax: 415-861-8365
E-mail: calegionaux@calegionaux.org

AMERICAN LEGION AUXILIARY DEPARTMENT OF COLORADO

http://www.coloradolegion.org/

AMERICAN LEGION AUXILIARY DEPARTMENT OF COLORADO PAST PRESIDENTS' PARLEY NURSES SCHOLARSHIP

Open to children, spouses, grandchildren, and great-grandchildren of American Legion veterans, and veterans who served in the armed forces during eligibility dates for membership in the American Legion. Must be Colorado residents who have been accepted by an accredited school of nursing in Colorado.

Academic Fields/Career Goals: Nursing.

Award: Scholarship for use in freshman, sophomore, junior, senior, or graduate years; not renewable. *Number:* 3–5. *Amount:* up to $500.

Eligibility Requirements: Applicant must be enrolled or expecting to enroll full- or part-time at a four-year institution or university; resident of Colorado and studying in Colorado. Applicant or parent of applicant must be member of American Legion or Auxiliary. Available to U.S. citizens. Applicant or parent must meet one or more of the following requirements: general military experience; retired from active duty; disabled or killed as a result of military service; prisoner of war; or missing in action.

Application Requirements: Application, essay, financial need analysis, references. *Deadline:* April 1.

Contact: American Legion Auxiliary Department of Colorado
7465 East First Avenue, Suite D
Denver, CO 80230
Phone: 303-367-5388
E-mail: ala@coloradolegion.org

AMERICAN LEGION AUXILIARY DEPARTMENT OF IDAHO

http://www.idahoala.org/

AMERICAN LEGION AUXILIARY DEPARTMENT OF IDAHO NURSING SCHOLARSHIP

Scholarship available to veterans or the children of veterans who are majoring in nursing. Applicants must be 17 to 35 years of age and residents of Idaho for five years prior to applying. One-time award of $1000.

Academic Fields/Career Goals: Nursing.

Award: Scholarship for use in freshman, sophomore, junior, or senior years; not renewable. *Number:* 1. *Amount:* $1000.

Eligibility Requirements: Applicant must be age 17-35; enrolled or expecting to enroll full-time at a four-year institution or university and resident of Idaho. Available to U.S. citizens. Applicant or parent must meet one or more of the following requirements: general military experience; retired from active duty; disabled or killed as a result of military service; prisoner of war; or missing in action.

Application Requirements: Application, financial need analysis, photo, references, self-addressed stamped envelope, transcript. *Deadline:* May 15.

Contact: Mary Sue Chase, Secretary
American Legion Auxiliary Department of Idaho
905 Warren Street
Boise, ID 83706-3825
Phone: 208-342-7066
Fax: 208-342-7066
E-mail: idalegionaux@msn.com

AMERICAN LEGION AUXILIARY DEPARTMENT OF IOWA

http://www.ialegion.org/ala

AMERICAN LEGION AUXILIARY DEPARTMENT OF IOWA M.V. MCCRAE MEMORIAL NURSES MERIT AWARD

One-time award available to the child of an Iowa American Legion Post member or Iowa American Legion Auxiliary Unit member. Award is for full-time study in an accredited nursing program. Must be U.S. citizen and Iowa resident. Must attend an Iowa institution.

Academic Fields/Career Goals: Nursing.

Award: Scholarship for use in freshman, sophomore, junior, or senior years; not renewable. *Number:* 1. *Amount:* $400.

Eligibility Requirements: Applicant must be enrolled or expecting to enroll full-time at a two-year or four-year or technical institution or university; resident of Iowa and studying in Iowa. Applicant or parent of applicant must be member of American Legion or Auxiliary. Available to U.S. citizens. Applicant or parent must meet one or more of the following requirements: general military experience; retired from active duty; disabled or killed as a result of military service; prisoner of war; or missing in action.

Application Requirements: Application, essay, financial need analysis, photo, references, self-addressed stamped envelope, test scores, transcript. *Deadline:* June 1.

Contact: Marlene Valentine, Secretary and Treasurer
American Legion Auxiliary Department of Iowa
720 Lyon Street
Des Moines, IA 50309
Phone: 515-282-7987
Fax: 515-282-7583
E-mail: alasectreas@ialegion.org

AMERICAN LEGION AUXILIARY DEPARTMENT OF MAINE

http://www.mainelegion.org/

AMERICAN LEGION AUXILIARY DEPARTMENT OF MAINE PAST PRESIDENTS' PARLEY NURSES SCHOLARSHIP

• *See page 337*

AMERICAN LEGION AUXILIARY DEPARTMENT OF MARYLAND

http://www.alamd.org/

AMERICAN LEGION AUXILIARY DEPARTMENT OF MARYLAND PAST PRESIDENTS' PARLEY NURSES SCHOLARSHIP

One scholarship of $2000 for undergraduate students enrolled full-time in nursing study at accredited colleges or universities. Must be U.S. citizen and a descendant of an ex-service veteran.

Academic Fields/Career Goals: Nursing.

Award: Scholarship for use in freshman, sophomore, junior, or senior years; renewable. *Number:* 1. *Amount:* $2000.

Eligibility Requirements: Applicant must be enrolled or expecting to enroll full-time at a four-year institution or university. Available to U.S. citizens. Applicant or parent must meet one or more of the following requirements: general military experience; retired from active duty; disabled or killed as a result of military service; prisoner of war; or missing in action.

Application Requirements: Application, financial need analysis, references, transcript. *Deadline:* May 1.

Contact: Meredith Beeg, President
American Legion Auxiliary Department of Maryland
1589 Sulphur Spring Road, Suite 105
Baltimore, MD 21227
Phone: 410-242-9519
E-mail: hq@alamd.org

AMERICAN LEGION AUXILIARY DEPARTMENT OF MICHIGAN

http://www.michalaux.org/

AMERICAN LEGION AUXILIARY DEPARTMENT OF MICHIGAN MEDICAL CAREER SCHOLARSHIP

• *See page 337*

AMERICAN LEGION AUXILIARY DEPARTMENT OF MISSOURI

http://www.missourilegion.org/

AMERICAN LEGION AUXILIARY DEPARTMENT OF MISSOURI PAST PRESIDENTS' PARLEY SCHOLARSHIP

Scholarship of $500 is awarded to high school graduate who has chosen to study nursing. $500 will be awarded upon receipt of verification from the college that student is enrolled. The applicant must be a resident of Missouri and a member of a veteran's family. The applicant must be validated by the sponsoring unit. Check with sponsoring unit for details on required recommendation letters.

Academic Fields/Career Goals: Nursing.

Award: Scholarship for use in freshman year; not renewable. *Number:* 2. *Amount:* $500.

Eligibility Requirements: Applicant must be high school student; planning to enroll or expecting to enroll full-time at a two-year or four-year or technical institution or university and resident of Missouri. Applicant or parent of applicant must be member of American Legion or Auxiliary. Available to U.S. citizens. Applicant or parent must meet one or more of the following requirements: general military experience; retired from active duty; disabled or killed as a result of military service; prisoner of war; or missing in action.

Application Requirements: Application, photo, resume. *Deadline:* March 1.

Contact: Mary Doerhoff, Department Secretary/Treasurer
American Legion Auxiliary Department of Missouri
600 Ellis Boulevard
Jefferson City, MO 65101-1615
Phone: 573-636-9133
E-mail: dptmoala@embarqmail.com

AMERICAN LEGION AUXILIARY DEPARTMENT OF NEW MEXICO

http://www.nmlegion.org/

AMERICAN LEGION AUXILIARY DEPARTMENT OF NEW MEXICO PAST PRESIDENTS' PARLEY NURSES SCHOLARSHIP

One-time award of $250 available to children of veterans who served in the Armed Forces during the eligibility dates for American Legion membership. Must be New Mexico resident, high school senior, and in pursuit of a nursing degree full-time at an accredited institution.

Academic Fields/Career Goals: Nursing.

Award: Scholarship for use in freshman year; not renewable. *Number:* 1. *Amount:* $250.

Eligibility Requirements: Applicant must be high school student; planning to enroll or expecting to enroll full-time at a two-year or four-year institution or university and resident of New Mexico. Available to U.S. citizens. Applicant or parent must meet one or more of the following requirements: general military experience; retired from active duty; disabled or killed as a result of military service; prisoner of war; or missing in action.

Application Requirements: Application, essay, references, self-addressed stamped envelope, transcript. *Deadline:* April 4.

Contact: Loreen Jorgensen, Treasurer
American Legion Auxiliary Department of New Mexico
1215 Mountain Road, NE
Albuquerque, NM 87102
Phone: 505-242-9918
Fax: 505-247-0478

AMERICAN LEGION AUXILIARY DEPARTMENT OF NORTH DAKOTA

http://www.ndlegion.org/

AMERICAN LEGION AUXILIARY DEPARTMENT OF NORTH DAKOTA PAST PRESIDENTS' PARLEY NURSES SCHOLARSHIP

One-time award for North Dakota resident who is the child, grandchild, or great-grandchild of a member of the American Legion or Auxiliary. Must be a graduate of a North Dakota high school and attending a nursing program in North Dakota. A minimum 2.5 GPA is required.

Academic Fields/Career Goals: Nursing.

Award: Scholarship for use in freshman year; not renewable. *Number:* 5. *Amount:* $500.

Eligibility Requirements: Applicant must be enrolled or expecting to enroll full- or part-time at a four-year institution or university; resident of North Dakota and studying in North Dakota. Applicant or parent of applicant must be member of American Legion or Auxiliary. Applicant must have 2.5 GPA or higher. Available to U.S. citizens. Applicant or parent must meet one or more of the following requirements: general military experience; retired from active duty; disabled or killed as a result of military service; prisoner of war; or missing in action.

Application Requirements: Application, driver's license, essay, financial need analysis, self-addressed stamped envelope, test scores, transcript. *Deadline:* May 15.

Contact: Myrna Ronholm, Department Secretary
American Legion Auxiliary Department of North Dakota
PO Box 1060
Jamestown, ND 58402-1060
Phone: 701-253-5992
E-mail: ala-hq@ndlegion.org

AMERICAN LEGION AUXILIARY DEPARTMENT OF OHIO

http://www.alaohio.org/

AMERICAN LEGION AUXILIARY DEPARTMENT OF OHIO PAST PRESIDENTS' PARLEY NURSES SCHOLARSHIP

One-time award worth $300 to $500 for Ohio residents who are the children or grandchildren of a veteran, living or deceased. Must enroll or be enrolled in a nursing program. Application requests must be received by May 1.

Academic Fields/Career Goals: Nursing.

Award: Scholarship for use in freshman, sophomore, junior, or senior years; not renewable. *Number:* 15–20. *Amount:* $300–$500.

Eligibility Requirements: Applicant must be enrolled or expecting to enroll full-time at a two-year or four-year institution or university and resident of Ohio. Available to U.S. citizens. Applicant or parent must meet one or more of the following requirements: general military experience; retired from active duty; disabled or killed as a result of military service; prisoner of war; or missing in action.

Application Requirements: Application, references. *Deadline:* May 1.

Contact: Heather Amspaugh, Scholarship Coordinator
American Legion Auxiliary Department of Ohio
PO Box 2760
Zanesville, OH 43702-2760
Phone: 740-452-8245
Fax: 740-452-2620
E-mail: hamspaugh@rrohio.com

AMERICAN LEGION AUXILIARY DEPARTMENT OF OREGON

http://www.alaoregon.org/

AMERICAN LEGION AUXILIARY DEPARTMENT OF OREGON NURSES SCHOLARSHIP

One-time award for Oregon residents who are in their senior year of High School, who are the children of veterans who served during eligibility dates for American Legion membership. Must enroll in a nursing program. Contact local units for application.

Academic Fields/Career Goals: Nursing.

Award: Scholarship for use in freshman year; not renewable. *Number:* 1. *Amount:* $1500.

Eligibility Requirements: Applicant must be high school student; planning to enroll or expecting to enroll full- or part-time at a four-year institution or university and resident of Oregon. Available to U.S. citizens. Applicant or parent must meet one or more of the following requirements: general military experience; retired from active duty; disabled or killed as a result of military service; prisoner of war; or missing in action.

Application Requirements: Application, essay, financial need analysis, interview, transcript. *Deadline:* May 15.

Contact: Virginia Biddle, Secretary/Treasurer
American Legion Auxiliary Department of Oregon
PO Box 1730
Wilsonville, OR 97070
Phone: 503-682-3162
Fax: 503-685-5008
E-mail: alaor@pcez.com

AMERICAN LEGION AUXILIARY DEPARTMENT OF WASHINGTON

http://www.walegion-aux.org/

MARGUERITE MCALPIN NURSE'S SCHOLARSHIP

One award for a child or grandchild of a veteran pursuing an education in nursing or have served in the Armed Forces. May be a high school senior or an enrolled nursing student. Submit a brief statement of military service of veteran parent or grandparent. Must be Washington State residents.

Academic Fields/Career Goals: Nursing.

Award: Scholarship for use in freshman, sophomore, junior, or senior years; not renewable. *Number:* 1. *Amount:* $300.

Eligibility Requirements: Applicant must be enrolled or expecting to enroll full- or part-time at a two-year or four-year or technical institution or university and resident of Washington. Available to U.S. citizens. Applicant or parent must meet one or more of the following requirements: general military experience; retired from active duty; disabled or killed as a result of military service; prisoner of war; or missing in action.

Application Requirements: Application, essay, financial need analysis, references, transcript. *Deadline:* March 1.

Contact: Nicole Ross, Department Secretary
American Legion Auxiliary Department of Washington
3600 Ruddell Road
Lacey, WA 98503
Phone: 360-456-5995
Fax: 360-491-7442
E-mail: secretary@walegion-aux.org

AMERICAN LEGION AUXILIARY DEPARTMENT OF WISCONSIN

http://www.amlegionauxwi.org/

AMERICAN LEGION AUXILIARY DEPARTMENT OF WISCONSIN PAST PRESIDENTS' PARLEY REGISTERED NURSE SCHOLARSHIP

One-time award of $1000. Applicant must be in nursing school or have positive acceptance to an accredited hospital or university registered nursing program. Applicant must be a daughter, son, wife, or widow of a veteran. Granddaughters and great-granddaughters of veterans who are auxiliary members may also apply. Must submit certification of an American Legion Auxiliary unit president, copy of proof that veteran was in service (i.e. discharge papers), letters of recommendation, transcripts, and essay. Must have minimum 3.5 GPA, show financial need, and be a resident of Wisconsin. Applications available on web site http://www.legion-aux.org.

Academic Fields/Career Goals: Nursing.

Award: Scholarship for use in freshman, sophomore, junior, or senior years; not renewable. *Number:* 3. *Amount:* $1000.

Eligibility Requirements: Applicant must be enrolled or expecting to enroll full- or part-time at an institution or university and resident of Wisconsin. Applicant or parent of applicant must be member of American Legion or Auxiliary. Applicant must have 3.5 GPA or higher. Available to U.S. citizens. Applicant or parent must meet one or more of the following requirements: general military experience; retired from active duty; disabled or killed as a result of military service; prisoner of war; or missing in action.

Application Requirements: Application, essay, financial need analysis, references, transcript. *Deadline:* March 15.

Contact: Kim Henderson, Scholarship Information
American Legion Auxiliary Department of Wisconsin
PO Box 140
Portage, WI 53901-0140
Phone: 608-745-0124
Fax: 608-745-1947

AMERICAN LEGION AUXILIARY DEPARTMENT OF WYOMING

AMERICAN LEGION AUXILIARY DEPARTMENT OF WYOMING PAST PRESIDENTS' PARLEY HEALTH CARE SCHOLARSHIP
• See page 218

AMERICAN LEGION DEPARTMENT OF KANSAS

http://www.ksamlegion.org/

HOBBLE (LPN) NURSING SCHOLARSHIP

Award of $300, payable one-time at the start of the first semester. Awarded only upon acceptance and verification of enrollment by the scholarship winner in an accredited Kansas school which awards a diploma for Licensed Practical Nursing (LPN). Must pursue this profession in a health related institution such as a nursing home or hospital in Kansas. Must have attained the age of 18 prior to taking the Kansas state board examination. Must be a Kansas resident.

Academic Fields/Career Goals: Nursing.

Award: Scholarship for use in freshman year; not renewable. *Number:* 1. *Amount:* $300.

Eligibility Requirements: Applicant must be age 18 and over; enrolled or expecting to enroll full-time at a two-year institution; resident of Kansas and studying in Kansas. Available to U.S. citizens.

Application Requirements: Application, financial need analysis. *Deadline:* February 15.

Contact: Jim Gravenstein, Chairman, Scholarship Committee
American Legion Department of Kansas
1314 SW Topeka Boulevard
Topeka, MD 66612
Phone: 785-232-9513
Fax: 785-232-1399

AMERICAN LEGION DEPARTMENT OF MISSOURI

http://www.missourilegion.org/

M.D. "JACK" MURPHY MEMORIAL SCHOLARSHIP

One $750 award for two successive semesters will be given to a Missouri resident who is a RN and under the age of 21. Applicant must be unmarried and a descendant of a veteran with at least ninety days active service in the U.S. Army, Navy, Air Force, Marines or Coast Guard receiving a Honorable Discharge for service. Applicant must have graduated in the top forty percent of their high school class or have a "C" or equivalent.

Academic Fields/Career Goals: Nursing.

Award: Scholarship for use in freshman year; not renewable. *Number:* 1. *Amount:* $750.

Eligibility Requirements: Applicant must be high school student; age 21 or under; planning to enroll or expecting to enroll full-time at a two-year or four-year institution or university; single female and resident of Missouri. Available to U.S. citizens. Applicant or parent must meet one or more of the following requirements: general military experience; retired from active duty; disabled or killed as a result of military service; prisoner of war; or missing in action.

Application Requirements: Application, financial need analysis, test scores, copy of the veteran's discharge or separation notice. *Deadline:* April 20.

Contact: John Doane, Chairman
American Legion Department of Missouri
PO Box 179
Jefferson City, MO 65102-0179
Phone: 417-924-8186
Fax: 573-893-2980

AMERICAN LEGION NATIONAL HEADQUARTERS

http://www.legion.org/

EIGHT AND FORTY LUNG AND RESPIRATORY NURSING SCHOLARSHIP FUND

The fund was established to assist registered nurses with advanced preparation for positions in supervision, administration, or teaching. Students are to have prospects of being employed in specific positions in hospitals, clinics, or health departments on completion of their education and the position must have a full-time and direct relationship to lung and respiratory control. Scholarship value is $3000.

Academic Fields/Career Goals: Nursing.

Award: Scholarship for use in junior or senior years; not renewable. *Number:* 1–22. *Amount:* up to $3000.

Eligibility Requirements: Applicant must be enrolled or expecting to enroll full-time at an institution or university. Available to U.S. citizens.

Application Requirements: Application. *Deadline:* May 15.

Contact: Jason Kees, Program Coordinator
American Legion National Headquarters
The American Legion, PO Box 1055
Indianapolis, IN 46206
Phone: 317-630-1323
Fax: 317-630-1369
E-mail: jkees@legion.org

AMERICAN MOBILE HEALTHCARE

http://www.americanmobile.com/

AMERICAN MOBILE HEALTHCARE ANNUAL SCHOLARSHIP

Scholarship of $2000 awarded to students enrolled in a bachelor's degree in nursing or master's degree in nursing program. Applicant must be enrolled in full time study.

Academic Fields/Career Goals: Nursing.

Award: Scholarship for use in freshman, sophomore, junior, senior, or graduate years; not renewable. *Number:* 1. *Amount:* up to $2000.

Eligibility Requirements: Applicant must be enrolled or expecting to enroll full-time at a four-year institution or university. Available to U.S. citizens.

Application Requirements: Application. *Deadline:* June 1.

Contact: Scholarship Committee
American Mobile Healthcare
12400 High Bluff Drive
San Diego, CA 92130
Phone: 800-282-0300
Fax: 800-282-0328
E-mail: contact@americanmobile.com

AMERICAN NEPHROLOGY NURSES' ASSOCIATION

http://www.annanurse.org/

ABBOTT/PAMELA BALZER CAREER MOBILITY SCHOLARSHIP

Scholarships available to support qualified ANNA members, who have been members for a minimum of two years, in the pursuit of either a BSN or advanced degree in nursing that will enhance their nephrology nursing practice. Details on web site http://www.annanurse.org.

Academic Fields/Career Goals: Nursing.

Award: Scholarship for use in freshman, sophomore, junior, senior, graduate, or postgraduate years; not renewable. *Number:* 1. *Amount:* $2500.

Eligibility Requirements: Applicant must be enrolled or expecting to enroll full- or part-time at a four-year institution or university. Applicant or parent of applicant must be member of American Nephrology Nurses' Association. Applicant or parent of applicant must have employment or volunteer experience in nursing. Available to U.S. citizens.

Application Requirements: Application, essay, references, transcript. *Deadline:* October 15.

Contact: Sharon Longton, Awards, Scholarships, and Grants Chairperson
American Nephrology Nurses' Association
200 East Holly Avenue, PO Box 56
Pitman, NJ 08071-0056
Phone: 313-966-2674
E-mail: slongton@dmc.org

AMERICAN NEPHROLOGY NURSES' ASSOCIATION CAREER MOBILITY SCHOLARSHIP

Scholarships available to support qualified ANNA members, who have been a member for a minimum two years, in the pursuit of either BSN or advanced degrees in nursing that will enhance their nephrology nursing practice. Must be accepted or enrolled in baccalaureate or higher degree program in nursing. Must be actively involved in nephrology nursing related health care services. Details on web site http://www.annanurse.org.

Academic Fields/Career Goals: Nursing.

Award: Scholarship for use in freshman, sophomore, junior, senior, graduate, or postgraduate years; not renewable. *Number:* 5. *Amount:* $2000.

Eligibility Requirements: Applicant must be enrolled or expecting to enroll full- or part-time at a four-year institution or university. Applicant or parent of applicant must be member of American Nephrology Nurses' Association. Applicant or parent of applicant must have employment or volunteer experience in nursing. Available to U.S. citizens.

Application Requirements: Application, essay, references, transcript, acceptance letter. *Deadline:* October 15.

Contact: Sharon Longton, Awards, Scholarships and Grants Chairperson
American Nephrology Nurses' Association
200 East Holly Avenue, PO Box 56
Pitman, NJ 08071-0056
Phone: 313-966-2674
E-mail: slongton@dmc.org

AMERICAN NEPHROLOGY NURSES' ASSOCIATION NNCC CAREER MOBILITY SCHOLARSHIP

Applicants must be current full member of ANNA, having been a member for a minimum of two years. Must have been accepted or enrolled in a baccalaureate or higher degree program in nursing. Must be actively involved in nephrology nursing related health care services. The applicant must hold a current credential as a certified nephrology nurse (CNN) or certified dialysis nurse (CDN) administered by the Nephrology Nursing Certification Commission (NNCC).

Academic Fields/Career Goals: Nursing.

Award: Scholarship for use in freshman, sophomore, junior, senior, graduate, or postgraduate years; not renewable. *Number:* 3. *Amount:* $2000.

Eligibility Requirements: Applicant must be enrolled or expecting to enroll full- or part-time at a four-year institution or university. Applicant or parent of applicant must be member of American Nephrology Nurses' Association. Applicant or parent of applicant must have employment or volunteer experience in nursing. Available to U.S. citizens.

Application Requirements: Application, essay, references, transcript. *Deadline:* October 15.

Contact: Sharon Longton, Awards, Scholarships and Grants Chairperson
American Nephrology Nurses' Association
200 East Holly Avenue, PO Box 56
Pitman, NJ 08071-0056
Phone: 313-966-2674
E-mail: slongton@dmc.org

AMERICAN NEPHROLOGY NURSES' ASSOCIATION WATSON PHARMA INC. CAREER MOBILITY SCHOLARSHIP

Applicants must be current full member of ANNA, having been a member for a minimum of two years. Must have been accepted or enrolled in a baccalaureate or higher degree program in nursing. Must be actively involved in nephrology nursing related health care services. For details visit the web site http://www.annanurse.org.

Academic Fields/Career Goals: Nursing.

Award: Scholarship for use in freshman, sophomore, junior, senior, graduate, or postgraduate years; not renewable. *Number:* 1. *Amount:* $2500.

Eligibility Requirements: Applicant must be enrolled or expecting to enroll full- or part-time at a four-year institution or university. Applicant or parent of applicant must be member of American Nephrology Nurses' Association. Applicant or parent of applicant must have employment or volunteer experience in nursing. Available to U.S. citizens.

Application Requirements: Application, essay, references, transcript. *Deadline:* October 15.

Contact: Sharon Longton, Awards, Scholarships and Grants Chairperson
American Nephrology Nurses' Association
200 East Holly Avenue, PO Box 56
Pitman, NJ 08071-0056
Phone: 313-966-2674
E-mail: slongton@dmc.org

ANNA ALCAVIS INTERNATIONAL, INC. CAREER MOBILITY SCHOLARSHIP

Scholarship to students accepted or enrolled in a baccalaureate or higher degree program in nursing. Applicant must hold a current credential as a Certified Nephrology Nurse (CNN) or Certified Dialysis Nurse (CDN) administered by the Nephrology Nursing Certification Commission (NNCC).

Academic Fields/Career Goals: Nursing.

Award: Forgivable loan for use in freshman, sophomore, junior, senior, or graduate years; renewable. *Number:* 5. *Amount:* $2000.

Eligibility Requirements: Applicant must be enrolled or expecting to enroll full-time at a four-year institution or university. Applicant or parent of applicant must be member of American Nephrology Nurses' Association. Applicant or parent of applicant must have employment or volunteer experience in nursing. Available to U.S. and non-Canadian citizens.

Application Requirements: Application, essay, financial need analysis, transcript. *Deadline:* October 15.

Contact: Sharon Longton, Awards, Scholarships, and Grants Chairperson
American Nephrology Nurses' Association
East Holly Avenue
PO Box 56
Pitman, NJ 08071-0056
Phone: 313-966-2674
E-mail: slongton@dmc.org

JANEL PARKER CAREER MOBILITY SCHOLARSHIP

Applicants must be current full member of ANNA, having been a member for a minimum of two years. Must have been accepted or enrolled in a baccalaureate or higher degree program in nursing. Must be actively involved in nephrology nursing related health care services. For details visit the web site http://www.annanurse.org.

Academic Fields/Career Goals: Nursing.

Award: Scholarship for use in freshman, sophomore, junior, senior, or postgraduate years; not renewable. *Number:* 1. *Amount:* up to $2500.

Eligibility Requirements: Applicant must be enrolled or expecting to enroll full- or part-time at a two-year or four-year institution or university. Applicant or parent of applicant must be member of American Nephrology Nurses' Association. Applicant or parent of applicant must have employment or volunteer experience in nursing. Available to U.S. citizens.

Application Requirements: Application, essay, references, transcript. *Deadline:* October 15.

Contact: Sharon Longton, Awards, Scholarships, and Grants Chairperson
American Nephrology Nurses' Association
200 East Holly Avenue, PO Box 56
Pitman, NJ 08071-0056
Phone: 313-966-2674
E-mail: slongton@dmc.org

ARRL FOUNDATION INC.

http://www.arrl.org/

CAROLE J. STREETER, KB9JBR SCHOLARSHIP
• *See page 218*

WILLIAM R. GOLDFARB MEMORIAL SCHOLARSHIP
• *See page 146*

ASSOCIATION ON AMERICAN INDIAN AFFAIRS, INC.

http://www.indian-affairs.org/

ELIZABETH AND SHERMAN ASCHE MEMORIAL SCHOLARSHIP FUND
• *See page 83*

ATLANTIC HEALTH SYSTEM OVERLOOK HOSPITAL FOUNDATION

http://www.overlookhospitalfoundation.com/

OVERLOOK HOSPITAL FOUNDATION PROFESSIONAL DEVELOPMENT PROGRAM
• *See page 341*

BETHESDA LUTHERAN COMMUNITIES

http://www.bethesdalutherancommunities.org/

DEVELOPMENTAL DISABILITIES AWARENESS AWARDS FOR HIGH SCHOOL STUDENTS WHO ARE LUTHERAN
• *See page 341*

CAMBRIDGE HOME HEALTH CARE

http://www.cambridgehomehealth.com/

CAMBRIDGE HOME HEALTH CARE NURSING EXCELLENCE SCHOLARSHIPS

Scholarships available for study towards LPN or RN degree. Must be a home health aide/nurse's aide or LPN who has worked for two of the past three years in that position. Two scholarships awarded to Cambridge employees, and two scholarships awarded to residents of the counties where Cambridge Home Health Care offices are located.

Academic Fields/Career Goals: Nursing.

Award: Scholarship for use in freshman, sophomore, junior, or senior years; not renewable. *Number:* up to 4. *Amount:* up to $1000.

Eligibility Requirements: Applicant must be enrolled or expecting to enroll full-time at a four-year institution or university. Applicant or parent of applicant must have employment or volunteer experience in nursing. Available to U.S. citizens.

Application Requirements: Application, essay, references. *Deadline:* May 15.

Contact: Elizabeth Bever, Director of Community Relations
Cambridge Home Health Care
4085 Embassy Parkway
Akron, OH 44333
Phone: 330-668-1922 Ext. 105
Fax: 330-668-1311
E-mail: lbever@cambridgehomehealth.com

CANADIAN NURSES FOUNDATION

http://www.cnf-fiic.ca/

CANADIAN NURSES FOUNDATION SCHOLARSHIPS

Study awards are granted annually to Canadian nurses wishing to pursue education and research. Must be a Canadian citizen or permanent resident and provide proof of citizenship. Current CNF membership required. Must be studying in Canada. Baccalaureate students must be full-time, masters and doctoral students may be full- or part-time (enrolled in a minimum of 2 courses per semester). Additional restrictions vary by specific scholarship.

Academic Fields/Career Goals: Nursing.

Award: Scholarship for use in sophomore, junior, senior, graduate, or postgraduate years; not renewable. *Number:* up to 30. *Amount:* varies.

Eligibility Requirements: Applicant must be Canadian citizen and enrolled or expecting to enroll full- or part-time at a four-year institution or university. Applicant or parent of applicant must be member of Canadian Nurses Foundation. Applicant or parent of applicant must have employment or volunteer experience in nursing.

Application Requirements: Application, references, transcript. *Fee:* $35. *Deadline:* March 31.

Contact: Jacqueline Sol? Foundation Coordinator
Canadian Nurses Foundation
50 Driveway
Ottawa, ON K2P IE2
Phone: 613-237-2159 Ext. 242
Fax: 613-237-3520
E-mail: jsolis@cna-aiic.ca

CENTRAL SCHOLARSHIP BUREAU

http://www.centralsb.org/

CHESAPEAKE UROLOGY ASSOCIATES SCHOLARSHIP
• *See page 342*

CHILDREN'S HEALTHCARE OF ATLANTA

http://www.choa.org/

CHANCES-CHILDREN'S HEALTHCARE OF ATLANTA NURSING COMMITMENT TO EMPLOYMENT AND STUDY PROGRAM (CHANCES)

Applicants will receive tuition equivalent assistance up to $16,000. Must be accepted into a nursing program. Minimum 3.0 GPA required.

Academic Fields/Career Goals: Nursing.

Award: Scholarship for use in freshman, sophomore, junior, senior, graduate, or postgraduate years; renewable. *Number:* varies. *Amount:* up to $16,000.

Eligibility Requirements: Applicant must be enrolled or expecting to enroll full-time at a four-year institution or university. Applicant must have 3.0 GPA or higher. Available to U.S. citizens.

Application Requirements: Essay, resume, references, online application. *Deadline:* May 1.

Contact: Shannon Dunlap, Program Coordinator
Children's Healthcare of Atlanta
1600 Tullie Circle NE
Atlanta, GA 30329-2321
Phone: 404-785-7211
E-mail: shannon.dunlap@choa.org

OPPORTUNITIES-CHILDREN'S HEALTHCARE OF ATLANTA BILINGUAL SCHOLARSHIP

Nursing scholarship to bilingual students interested in a pediatric nursing career. Open to students or individuals looking for a career change. Minimum 3.0 GPA required.

Academic Fields/Career Goals: Nursing.

Award: Scholarship for use in freshman, sophomore, junior, senior, graduate, or postgraduate years; renewable. *Number:* varies. *Amount:* $10,000.

Eligibility Requirements: Applicant must be enrolled or expecting to enroll full-time at a four-year institution or university. Applicant must have 3.0 GPA or higher. Available to U.S. citizens.

Application Requirements: Essay, interview, resume, references, online application. *Deadline:* May 1.

Contact: Shannon Dunlap, Program Coordinator
Children's Healthcare of Atlanta
1600 Tullie Circle NE
Atlanta, GA 30329-2321
Phone: 404-785-7211
E-mail: shannon.dunlap@choa.org

CHRISTIANA CARE HEALTH SYSTEMS

http://www.christianacare.org/

RUTH SHAW JUNIOR BOARD SCHOLARSHIP
• *See page 342*

CYNTHIA E. MORGAN SCHOLARSHIP FUND (CEMS)

http://www.cemsfund.com/

CYNTHIA E. MORGAN MEMORIAL SCHOLARSHIP FUND, INC.
• *See page 304*

DADE COMMUNITY FOUNDATION

http://www.jackituckfield.org/

JENNET COLLIFLOWER SCHOLARSHIP

Award for Florida residents enrolled full-time in the junior or senior year of an undergraduate nursing program at a public or private Florida college or university. For additional information and application, go to web site http://www.dadecommunityfoundation.org.

Academic Fields/Career Goals: Nursing.

Award: Scholarship for use in junior or senior years; not renewable. *Number:* 2. *Amount:* $1000.

Eligibility Requirements: Applicant must be enrolled or expecting to enroll full-time at a four-year institution or university; resident of Florida and studying in Florida. Available to U.S. citizens.

Application Requirements: Application, financial need analysis, references, transcript, personal statement. *Deadline:* May 1.

Contact: Ted Seijo, Scholarship Coordinator
Dade Community Foundation
1160 Northwest 87 Street
Miami, FL 33150-2544
Phone: 305-371-2711
E-mail: ted.seijo@dadecommunityfoundation.org

DELAWARE HIGHER EDUCATION OFFICE

http://www.doe.k12.de.us

DELAWARE NURSING INCENTIVE SCHOLARSHIP LOAN

Award for legal residents of Delaware who are U.S. citizens or eligible non-citizens. Must be full-time student enrolled in an accredited program leading to certification as an RN or LPN. High school seniors must rank in upper half of class with at least a 2.5 cumulative GPA.

Academic Fields/Career Goals: Nursing.

Award: Forgivable loan for use in freshman, sophomore, junior, or senior years; renewable. *Number:* 1–40. *Amount:* $1000–$5000.

Eligibility Requirements: Applicant must be enrolled or expecting to enroll full- or part-time at a two-year or four-year institution and resident of Delaware. Applicant must have 2.5 GPA or higher. Available to U.S. citizens.

Application Requirements: Application, essay, test scores, transcript. *Deadline:* March 28.

Contact: Carylin Brinkley, Program Administrator
Delaware Higher Education Office
Carvel State Office Building, 820 North French Street, Fifth Floor
Wilmington, DE 19801-3509
Phone: 302-577-5240
Fax: 302-577-6765
E-mail: cbrinkley@doe.k12.de.us

DEPARTMENT OF THE ARMY

http://www.goarmy.com/rotc

U.S. ARMY ROTC FOUR-YEAR NURSING SCHOLARSHIP

One-time award for freshman interested in nursing and accepted into an accredited nursing program. Must join ROTC program at the institution, pass physical evaluation, and have minimum GPA of 2.5. Applicant must be a U.S. citizen, have a qualifying SAT or ACT score, and be at least 17 years of age by college enrollment and under 31 years of age at time of graduation. Online application available.

Academic Fields/Career Goals: Nursing.

Award: Scholarship for use in freshman year; not renewable. *Number:* 250. *Amount:* $5000–$50,000.

Eligibility Requirements: Applicant must be age 17-26 and enrolled or expecting to enroll full-time at a four-year institution or university. Applicant must have 2.5 GPA or higher. Available to U.S. citizens. Applicant must have served in the Army or Army National Guard.

Application Requirements: Application, essay, interview, test scores, transcript. *Deadline:* January 10.

Contact: Mr. Larry Waller, Program Manager
Department of the Army
U.S. Army Cadet Command, 55 Patch Road, Building 56
Fort Monroe, VA 23651-1052
Phone: 757-788-5966
Fax: 757-788-4643
E-mail: larry.waller@usacc.army.mil

DERMATOLOGY NURSES' ASSOCIATION

http://www.dnanurse.org/

DERMIK LABORATORIES CAREER MOBILITY SCHOLARSHIP

Provides financial assistance to members of the Dermatology Nurses' Association (DNA) who are pursuing an undergraduate or graduate degree. The candidate must be a DNA member for two years, and be employed in the specialty of dermatology.

Academic Fields/Career Goals: Nursing.

Award: Scholarship for use in freshman, sophomore, junior, senior, or graduate years; not renewable. *Number:* 2. *Amount:* $2500.

Eligibility Requirements: Applicant must be enrolled or expecting to enroll full- or part-time at a four-year or technical institution or university. Applicant or parent of applicant must be member of Dermatology Nurses' Association. Applicant or parent of applicant must have employment or volunteer experience in nursing. Available to U.S. and non-U.S. citizens.

Application Requirements: Application, essay, financial need analysis, references, transcript. *Deadline:* October 1.

Contact: Program Coordinator
Dermatology Nurses' Association
East Holly Avenue, PO Box 56
Pitman, NJ 08071
Phone: 800-454-4362
Fax: 856-589-7463
E-mail: dna@mail.ajj.com

GALDERMA LABORATORIES CAREER MOBILITY SCHOLARSHIP

Applicants must be Dermatology Nurses' Association (DNA) members for at least two years, be employed in the specialty of dermatology, and be pursuing a degree in nursing or advanced degree in nursing.

Academic Fields/Career Goals: Nursing.

Award: Scholarship for use in freshman, sophomore, junior, senior, or graduate years; not renewable. *Number:* varies. *Amount:* varies.

Eligibility Requirements: Applicant must be enrolled or expecting to enroll full- or part-time at a four-year or technical institution or university. Applicant or parent of applicant must be member of Dermatology Nurses' Association. Applicant or parent of applicant must have employment or volunteer experience in nursing. Available to U.S. and non-U.S. citizens.

Application Requirements: Application, financial need analysis, references, transcript. *Deadline:* October 1.

Contact: Program Coordinator
Dermatology Nurses' Association
East Holly Avenue, PO Box 56
Pitman, NJ 08071
Phone: 800-454-4362
Fax: 856-589-7463
E-mail: dna@mail.ajj.com

EXCEPTIONALNURSE.COM

http://www.exceptionalnurse.com/

ANNA MAY ROLANDO SCHOLARSHIP AWARD

Scholarship of $500 awarded to a nursing student with a disability. Preference will be given to a graduate student who has demonstrated a commitment to working with people with disabilities.

Academic Fields/Career Goals: Nursing.

Award: Scholarship for use in freshman, sophomore, junior, senior, graduate, or postgraduate years; not renewable. *Number:* 1. *Amount:* $500.

Eligibility Requirements: Applicant must be enrolled or expecting to enroll full-time at a four-year institution or university. Applicant must be hearing impaired, learning disabled, physically disabled, or visually impaired. Available to U.S. citizens.

Application Requirements: Application, essay, references, transcript, medical verification of disability form. *Deadline:* June 1.

Contact: Donna Maheady, Founder
ExceptionalNurse.com
13019 Coastal Circle
Palm Beach Gardens, FL 33410
Phone: 561-627-9872
Fax: 561-776-9254
E-mail: exceptionalnurse@aol.com

BRUNO ROLANDO SCHOLARSHIP AWARD

Scholarship of $250 awarded to a nursing student with a disability. Preference will be given to a nursing student who is employed at a Veteran's Hospital.

Academic Fields/Career Goals: Nursing.

Award: Scholarship for use in freshman, sophomore, junior, senior, graduate, or postgraduate years; not renewable. *Number:* 1. *Amount:* $250.

Eligibility Requirements: Applicant must be enrolled or expecting to enroll full-time at a four-year institution or university. Applicant or parent of applicant must have employment or volunteer experience in nursing. Applicant must be hearing impaired, learning disabled, physically disabled, or visually impaired. Available to U.S. citizens.

Application Requirements: Application, essay, references, transcript, medical verification of disability form. *Deadline:* June 1.

Contact: Donna Maheady, Founder
ExceptionalNurse.com
13019 Coastal Circle
Palm Beach Gardens, FL 33410
Phone: 561-627-9872
Fax: 561-776-9254
E-mail: exceptionalnurse@aol.com

CAROLINE SIMPSON MAHEADY SCHOLARSHIP AWARD

Scholarship of $250 awarded to a nursing student with a disability. Preference will be given to an undergraduate student, of Scottish descent, who has demonstrated a commitment to working with people with disabilities.

Academic Fields/Career Goals: Nursing.

Award: Scholarship for use in freshman, sophomore, junior, senior, graduate, or postgraduate years; not renewable. *Number:* 1. *Amount:* $250.

Eligibility Requirements: Applicant must be enrolled or expecting to enroll full-time at a four-year institution or university. Applicant must be hearing impaired, learning disabled, physically disabled, or visually impaired. Available to U.S. citizens.

Application Requirements: Application, essay, references, transcript, medical verification of disability form. *Deadline:* June 1.

Contact: Donna Maheady, Founder
ExceptionalNurse.com
13019 Coastal Circle
Palm Beach Gardens, FL 33410
Phone: 561-627-9872
Fax: 561-776-9254
E-mail: exceptionalnurse@aol.com

GENEVIEVE SARAN RICHMOND AWARD

Scholarship of $500 awarded to a nursing student with a disability.

Academic Fields/Career Goals: Nursing.

Award: Scholarship for use in freshman, sophomore, junior, senior, graduate, or postgraduate years; not renewable. *Number:* 1. *Amount:* $500.

Eligibility Requirements: Applicant must be enrolled or expecting to enroll full-time at a four-year institution or university. Applicant must be hearing impaired, learning disabled, physically disabled, or visually impaired. Available to U.S. citizens.

Application Requirements: Application, essay, references, transcript, medical verification of disability form. *Deadline:* June 1.

Contact: Donna Maheady, Founder
ExceptionalNurse.com
13019 Coastal Circle
Palm Beach Gardens, FL 33410
Phone: 561-627-9872
Fax: 561-776-9254
E-mail: exceptionalnurse@aol.com

JILL LAURA CREEDON SCHOLARSHIP AWARD

Scholarship of $500 awarded to a nursing student with a disability or medical challenge.

Academic Fields/Career Goals: Nursing.

Award: Scholarship for use in freshman, sophomore, junior, senior, graduate, or postgraduate years; not renewable. *Number:* 1. *Amount:* $500.

Eligibility Requirements: Applicant must be enrolled or expecting to enroll full-time at a four-year institution or university. Applicant must be hearing impaired, learning disabled, physically disabled, or visually impaired. Available to U.S. citizens.

Application Requirements: Application, essay, references, transcript, medical verification of disability form. *Deadline:* June 1.

Contact: Donna Maheady, Founder
ExceptionalNurse.com
13019 Coastal Circle
Palm Beach Gardens, FL 33410
Phone: 561-627-9872
Fax: 561-776-9254
E-mail: exceptionalnurse@aol.com

MARY SERRA GILI SCHOLARSHIP AWARD

Scholarship of $250 awarded to a nursing student with a disability.

Academic Fields/Career Goals: Nursing.

Award: Scholarship for use in freshman, sophomore, junior, senior, graduate, or postgraduate years; not renewable. *Number:* 1. *Amount:* $250.

Eligibility Requirements: Applicant must be enrolled or expecting to enroll full-time at a four-year institution or university. Applicant must be hearing impaired, learning disabled, physically disabled, or visually impaired. Available to U.S. citizens.

Application Requirements: Application, essay, references, transcript, medical verification of disability form. *Deadline:* June 1.

Contact: Donna Maheady, Founder
ExceptionalNurse.com
13019 Coastal Circle
Palm Beach Gardens, FL 33410
Phone: 561-627-9872
Fax: 561-776-9254
E-mail: exceptionalnurse@aol.com

PETER GILI SCHOLARSHIP AWARD

Scholarship of $500 awarded to a nursing student with a disability.

Academic Fields/Career Goals: Nursing.

Award: Scholarship for use in freshman, sophomore, junior, senior, graduate, or postgraduate years; not renewable. *Number:* 1. *Amount:* $500.

Eligibility Requirements: Applicant must be enrolled or expecting to enroll full-time at a four-year institution or university. Applicant must be hearing impaired, learning disabled, physically disabled, or visually impaired. Available to U.S. citizens.

Application Requirements: Application, essay, references, transcript, medical verification of disability form. *Deadline:* June 1.

Contact: Donna Maheady, Founder
ExceptionalNurse.com
13019 Coastal Circle
Palm Beach Gardens, FL 33410
Phone: 561-627-9872
Fax: 561-776-9254
E-mail: exceptionalnurse@aol.com

FLORIDA NURSES ASSOCIATION

http://www.floridanurse.org/

AGNES NAUGHTON RN-BSN FUND

This fund is established to honor Agnes Naughton who was a lifelong FNA member and the mother of FNA Executive Director Paula Massey. She valued education and this scholarship will assist a RN who is continuing his or her education.

Academic Fields/Career Goals: Nursing.

Award: Scholarship for use in freshman, sophomore, junior, or senior years.

Eligibility Requirements: Applicant must be enrolled or expecting to enroll at a four-year institution; resident of Florida and studying in Florida.

Application Requirements: Application, essay, references, transcript, validation of Florida residency.

Contact: Leah Nash, Scholarship Committee
Florida Nurses Association
1235 East Concord Street
PO Box 536985
Orlando, FL 32853-6985
Phone: 407-896-3261 Ext. 303
E-mail: foundation@floridanurse.org

EDNA HICKS FUND SCHOLARSHIP

Applicant should be enrolled in a nationally accredited nursing program. Must be in associate, baccalaureate, or master's degree nursing programs or doctoral programs. Preference given to nurse researchers from South Florida.

Academic Fields/Career Goals: Nursing.

Award: Scholarship for use in freshman, sophomore, junior, or senior years; not renewable. *Number:* varies. *Amount:* varies.

Eligibility Requirements: Applicant must be enrolled or expecting to enroll full- or part-time at a two-year or four-year institution or university; resident of Florida and studying in Florida. Available to U.S. citizens.

Application Requirements: Application, references, transcript. *Deadline:* June 1.

Contact: Leah Nash, Scholarship Committee
Florida Nurses Association
1235 East Concord Street
PO Box 536985
Orlando, FL 32853-6985
Phone: 407-896-3261 Ext. 303
E-mail: foundation@floridanurse.org

RUTH FINAMORE SCHOLARSHIP FUND

The Ruth Finamore Scholarship Fund is available to all levels of Florida nursing students.

Academic Fields/Career Goals: Nursing.

Award: Scholarship for use in freshman, sophomore, junior, senior, or graduate years.

Eligibility Requirements: Applicant must be enrolled or expecting to enroll at a two-year or four-year or technical institution or university; resident of Florida and studying in Florida.

Application Requirements: Application, essay, references, transcript, validation of Florida residency.

Contact: Leah Nash, Scholarship Committee
Florida Nurses Association
1235 East Concord Street
PO Box 536985
Orlando, FL 32853-6985
Phone: 407-896-3261 Ext. 303
E-mail: foundation@floridanurse.org

FOUNDATION FOR NEONATAL RESEARCH AND EDUCATION (FNRE)

http://www.inurse.com/fnre/

FNRE BSN SCHOLARSHIP

Scholarship for students admitted into a bachelor's degree program in nursing. Applicant should have a minimum GPA of 3.0. Candidate must be a professionally active neonatal nurse. Application deadline May 1.

Academic Fields/Career Goals: Nursing.

Award: Scholarship for use in freshman, sophomore, junior, or senior years; not renewable. *Number:* varies. *Amount:* varies.

Eligibility Requirements: Applicant must be enrolled or expecting to enroll full- or part-time at a four-year institution or university. Applicant or parent of applicant must have employment or volunteer experience in nursing. Applicant must have 3.0 GPA or higher. Available to U.S. citizens.

Application Requirements: Application, resume, acceptance letter. *Deadline:* May 1.

Contact: Coordinator
Foundation for Neonatal Research and Education (FNRE)
c/o Anthony J. Jannetti, Inc.
East Holly Avenue, PO Box 56
Pitman, NJ 08071-0056
Phone: 856-256-2343
E-mail: fnre@ajj.com

FOUNDATION OF THE NATIONAL STUDENT NURSES' ASSOCIATION

http://www.nsna.org/

BREAKTHROUGH TO NURSING SCHOLARSHIPS FOR RACIAL/ETHNIC MINORITIES

Available to minority students enrolled in nursing or pre-nursing programs. Awards based on need, scholarship, and health-related activities. Application fee of $10. Send self-addressed stamped envelope with two stamps along with application request. Number of awards varies based on donors.

Academic Fields/Career Goals: Nursing.

Award: Scholarship for use in freshman, sophomore, junior, or senior years; not renewable. *Number:* varies. *Amount:* $1000–$2500.

Eligibility Requirements: Applicant must be American Indian/Alaska Native, Asian/Pacific Islander, Black (non-Hispanic), or Hispanic and enrolled or expecting to enroll full- or part-time at a two-year or four-year institution or university. Available to U.S. citizens.

Application Requirements: Application, financial need analysis, self-addressed stamped envelope, transcript. *Fee:* $10. *Deadline:* January 11.

Contact: Lauren Sperle, Scholarship Chairperson
Foundation of the National Student Nurses' Association
45 Main Street, Suite 606
Brooklyn, NY 11201
Phone: 718-210-0705
Fax: 718-210-0710
E-mail: lauren@nsna.org

FOUNDATION OF THE NATIONAL STUDENT NURSES' ASSOCIATION CAREER MOBILITY SCHOLARSHIP

One-time award open to registered nurses enrolled in nursing or licensed practical or vocational nurses enrolled in a program leading to licensure as a registered nurse. The award value is $1000 to $2500 and the number of awards varies. Submit copy of license. Application fee: $10. Send self-addressed stamped envelope.

Academic Fields/Career Goals: Nursing.

Award: Scholarship for use in freshman, sophomore, junior, or senior years; not renewable. *Number:* varies. *Amount:* $1000–$2500.

Eligibility Requirements: Applicant must be enrolled or expecting to enroll full- or part-time at a two-year or four-year institution or university. Available to U.S. citizens.

Application Requirements: Application, financial need analysis, self-addressed stamped envelope, transcript. *Fee:* $10. *Deadline:* January 11.

Contact: Lauren Sperle, Scholarship Chairperson
Foundation of the National Student Nurses' Association
45 Main Street, Suite 606
Brooklyn, NY 11201
Phone: 718-210-0705
Fax: 718-210-0710
E-mail: lauren@nsna.org

FOUNDATION OF THE NATIONAL STUDENT NURSES' ASSOCIATION GENERAL SCHOLARSHIPS

One-time award for National Student Nurses' Association members and nonmembers enrolled in nursing programs. Graduating high school seniors are not eligible. Send self-addressed stamped envelope with two stamps for application.

Academic Fields/Career Goals: Nursing.

Award: Scholarship for use in freshman, sophomore, junior, or senior years; not renewable. *Number:* varies. *Amount:* $1000–$2500.

Eligibility Requirements: Applicant must be enrolled or expecting to enroll full- or part-time at a two-year or four-year institution or university. Available to U.S. citizens.

Application Requirements: Application, financial need analysis, self-addressed stamped envelope, transcript. *Fee:* $10. *Deadline:* January 11.

Contact: Lauren Sperle, Scholarship Chairperson
Foundation of the National Student Nurses' Association
45 Main Street, Suite 606
Brooklyn, NY 11201
Phone: 718-210-0705
Fax: 718-210-0710
E-mail: lauren@nsna.org

FOUNDATION OF THE NATIONAL STUDENT NURSES' ASSOCIATION SPECIALTY SCHOLARSHIP

One-time award available to students currently enrolled in a state-approved school of nursing or prenursing. Must have interest in a specialty area of nursing. The award value is $1000 to $2500 and the number of awards granted varies.

Academic Fields/Career Goals: Nursing.

Award: Scholarship for use in freshman, sophomore, junior, or senior years; not renewable. *Number:* varies. *Amount:* $1000–$2500.

Eligibility Requirements: Applicant must be enrolled or expecting to enroll full- or part-time at a two-year or four-year institution or university. Available to U.S. citizens.

Application Requirements: Application, financial need analysis, self-addressed stamped envelope, transcript. *Fee:* $10. *Deadline:* January 11.

Contact: Lauren Sperle, Scholarship Chairperson
Foundation of the National Student Nurses' Association
45 Main Street, Suite 606
Brooklyn, NY 11201
Phone: 718-210-0705
Fax: 718-210-0710
E-mail: lauren@nsna.org

PROMISE OF NURSING SCHOLARSHIP

Applicants attending nursing school in California, South Florida, Georgia, Illinois, Massachusetts, Michigan, New Jersey, Tennessee, or Dallas/Fort Worth, Texas are eligible. Number of awards granted varies.

Academic Fields/Career Goals: Nursing.

Award: Scholarship for use in freshman, sophomore, junior, or senior years; renewable. *Number:* varies. *Amount:* $1000–$5000.

Eligibility Requirements: Applicant must be enrolled or expecting to enroll full- or part-time at a two-year or four-year institution or university and studying in California, Florida, Georgia, Illinois, Massachusetts, Michigan, New Jersey, Tennessee, or Texas. Available to U.S. citizens.

Application Requirements: Application, financial need analysis, self-addressed stamped envelope, transcript. *Fee:* $10. *Deadline:* January 11.

Contact: Lauren Sperle, Scholarship Chairperson
Foundation of the National Student Nurses' Association
45 Main Street, Suite 606
Brooklyn, NY 11201
Phone: 718-210-0705
Fax: 718-210-0710
E-mail: lauren@nsna.org

GENESIS HEALTH SERVICES FOUNDATION

http://www.genesishealth.com/

GALA NURSING SCHOLARSHIPS

Scholarships of $6000 for up to five recipients who are seeking admission to, or have been accepted into, an undergraduate baccalaureate program in nursing.

Academic Fields/Career Goals: Nursing.

Award: Scholarship for use in freshman, sophomore, junior, or senior years; not renewable. *Number:* up to 5. *Amount:* $6000.

Eligibility Requirements: Applicant must be enrolled or expecting to enroll full-time at a four-year institution or university; resident of Illinois or Iowa and studying in Illinois or Iowa. Available to U.S. citizens.

Application Requirements: Application, transcript. *Deadline:* March 8.

Contact: Melinda Gowey, Executive Director
Genesis Health Services Foundation
1227 East Rusholme Street
Davenport, IA 52803
Phone: 563-421-6865
Fax: 563-421-6869
E-mail: goweym@genesishealth.com

GOOD SAMARITAN FOUNDATION

http://www.gsftx.org/

GOOD SAMARITAN FOUNDATION SCHOLARSHIP

Scholarship for nursing students in their clinical level of education. Must be a resident of Texas and plan to work in a U.S. health-care system.

Academic Fields/Career Goals: Nursing.

Award: Scholarship for use in freshman, sophomore, junior, senior, graduate, or postgraduate years; renewable. *Number:* varies. *Amount:* $1000.

Eligibility Requirements: Applicant must be enrolled or expecting to enroll full-time at a four-year institution or university and resident of Texas. Available to U.S. and non-U.S. citizens.

Application Requirements: Application. *Deadline:* varies.

Contact: Kay Crawford, Scholarship Director
Good Samaritan Foundation
5615 Kirby Drive, Suite 610
Houston, TX 77005
Phone: 713-529-4646
Fax: 713-521-1169
E-mail: kcrawford@gsftx.org

GREATER KANAWHA VALLEY FOUNDATION

http://www.tgkvf.org/

BERNICE PICKINS PARSONS FUND
• *See page 391*

GERALDINE GEE NURSING SCHOLARSHIP

Award for resident of Boone County, West Virginia, who has successfully completed the freshman year at a college or university with an accredited nursing program. Must begin work toward a nursing degree in sophomore year and maintain a 3.0 GPA in order to renew the scholarship for the following year. For more information and application visit http://www.tgkvf.org.

Academic Fields/Career Goals: Nursing.

Award: Scholarship for use in sophomore, junior, or senior years; renewable. *Number:* 1. *Amount:* $500.

Eligibility Requirements: Applicant must be enrolled or expecting to enroll full-time at a four-year institution or university and resident of West Virginia. Applicant must have 3.0 GPA or higher. Available to U.S. citizens.

Application Requirements: Application, test scores, transcript. *Deadline:* January 15.

Contact: Susan Hoover, Scholarship Program Officer
Greater Kanawha Valley Foundation
1600 Huntington Square, 900 Lee Street, East
PO Box 3041
Charleston, WV 25301
Phone: 304-346-3620
E-mail: shoover@tgkvf.org

GUSTAVUS B. CAPITO FUND

Scholarships awarded to students who show financial need and are seeking education in nursing at any accredited college or university with a nursing program in West Virginia. Scholarships are awarded for one or more years. Must be a resident of West Virginia.

Academic Fields/Career Goals: Nursing.

Award: Scholarship for use in freshman, sophomore, junior, or senior years; renewable. *Number:* 4. *Amount:* $1000.

Eligibility Requirements: Applicant must be enrolled or expecting to enroll full-time at a four-year institution or university; resident of West Virginia and studying in West Virginia. Available to U.S. citizens.

Application Requirements: Application, essay, financial need analysis, references, transcript. *Deadline:* January 15.

Contact: Susan Hoover, Scholarship Coordinator
Greater Kanawha Valley Foundation
PO Box 3041
Charleston, WV 25331
Phone: 304-346-3620
Fax: 304-346-3640
E-mail: shoover@tgkvf.org

HAVANA NATIONAL BANK, TRUSTEE

http://www.havanabank.com/

MCFARLAND CHARITABLE NURSING SCHOLARSHIP

Scholarship for registered nursing students only. Must sign contract obliging to work in Havana, Illinois for two years for each year of funding or repay award with interest and liquidated damages. Must submit test scores, essay, transcripts, references, financial need analysis, and autobiography with application. Preference given to local residents. GPA is an important consideration in selection.

Academic Fields/Career Goals: Nursing.

Award: Forgivable loan for use in freshman, sophomore, junior, senior, graduate, or postgraduate years; renewable. *Number:* 3–5. *Amount:* $1000–$15,000.

Eligibility Requirements: Applicant must be enrolled or expecting to enroll full-time at a two-year or four-year institution or university. Available to U.S. and non-U.S. citizens.

Application Requirements: Application, driver's license, essay, financial need analysis, interview, photo, references, test scores, transcript. *Deadline:* April 1.

Contact: Trust Officer
Havana National Bank, Trustee
PO Box 200
Havana, IL 62644
Phone: 309-543-3361
Fax: 309-543-3441
E-mail: info@havanabank.com

HEALTH PROFESSIONS EDUCATION FOUNDATION

http://www.healthprofessions.ca.gov/

ASSOCIATE DEGREE NURSING SCHOLARSHIP PROGRAM

One-time award to nursing students accepted to or enrolled in associate degree nursing programs. Eligible applicants may receive up to $8000 per year in financial assistance. Deadlines: March 24 and September 11. Must be a resident of California. Minimum 2.0 GPA.

Academic Fields/Career Goals: Nursing.

Award: Scholarship for use in freshman, sophomore, junior, senior, graduate, or postgraduate years; not renewable. *Number:* up to 30. *Amount:* up to $8000.

Eligibility Requirements: Applicant must be enrolled or expecting to enroll full- or part-time at a two-year or four-year institution or university; resident of California and studying in California. Available to U.S. citizens.

Application Requirements: Application, essay, financial need analysis, references, transcript, graduation date verification form, verification of language fluency. *Deadline:* varies.

Contact: James Hall, Program Administrator
Health Professions Education Foundation
400 R street
Sacramento, CA 95811
Phone: 916-326-3640
Fax: 916-324-6585

HEALTH PROFESSIONS EDUCATION FOUNDATION BACHELOR OF SCIENCE NURSING SCHOLARSHIP PROGRAM

Scholarship of up to $10,000 for students pursuing bachelor's degree in nursing. Available for both full- and part-time students. Must be U.S. citizen.

Academic Fields/Career Goals: Nursing.

Award: Scholarship for use in freshman, sophomore, junior, senior, graduate, or postgraduate years; not renewable. *Number:* up to 40. *Amount:* up to $10,000.

Eligibility Requirements: Applicant must be enrolled or expecting to enroll full- or part-time at a two-year or four-year institution or university. Available to U.S. citizens.

Application Requirements: Application, references, transcript, personal statement, Student Aid Report (SAR) or tax return with W2, certification of enrollment. *Deadline:* varies.

Contact: Margarita Miranda, Program Administrator
Health Professions Education Foundation
400 R street
Sacramento, CA 95811
Phone: 916-326-3640

REGISTERED NURSE EDUCATION LOAN REPAYMENT PROGRAM

Repays governmental and commercial loans that were obtained for tuition expenses, books, equipment, and reasonable living expenses associated with attending college. In return for the repayment of educational debt, loan repayment recipients are required to practice full-time in direct patient care in a medically underserved area or county health facility. Deadlines: March 24 and September 11. Must be resident of California.

Academic Fields/Career Goals: Nursing.

Award: Grant for use in senior, graduate, or postgraduate years; not renewable. *Number:* 50–70. *Amount:* up to $10,000.

Eligibility Requirements: Applicant must be enrolled or expecting to enroll full- or part-time at a four-year institution or university; resident of California and studying in California. Available to U.S. citizens.

Application Requirements: Application, financial need analysis, references, transcript. *Deadline:* varies.

Contact: Monique Scott, Program Director
Health Professions Education Foundation
818 K Street, Suite 210
Sacramento, CA 95814
Phone: 916-324-6500
Fax: 916-324-6585
E-mail: mvoss@oshpd.state.ca.us

RN EDUCATION SCHOLARSHIP PROGRAM

One-time award to nursing students accepted to or enrolled in baccalaureate degree nursing programs in California. Eligible applicants may receive up to $10,000 per year in financial assistance. Deadlines: March 24 and September 11. Must be resident of California and a U.S. citizen. Minimum 2.0 GPA.

Academic Fields/Career Goals: Nursing.

Award: Scholarship for use in freshman, sophomore, junior, or senior years; not renewable. *Number:* 50–70. *Amount:* up to $10,000.

Eligibility Requirements: Applicant must be enrolled or expecting to enroll full- or part-time at a two-year or four-year institution or university; resident of California and studying in California. Available to U.S. citizens.

Application Requirements: Application, essay, financial need analysis, references, transcript, employment verification form, proof of RN license, verification of language fluency. *Deadline:* varies.

Contact: Monique Scott, Program Director
Health Professions Education Foundation
818 K Street, Suite 210
Sacramento, CA 95814
Phone: 916-324-6500
Fax: 916-324-6585
E-mail: mvoss@oshpd.state.ca.us

VOCATIONAL NURSE SCHOLARSHIP PROGRAM

Scholarships are available to students who are enrolled or accepted in an accredited Vocational Nurse program. Awardees must sign a contract with the Office of Statewide Health Planning and Development. Minimum 2.0 GPA required. Deadlines: March 24 and September 11.

Academic Fields/Career Goals: Nursing.

Award: Scholarship for use in freshman or sophomore years; not renewable. *Number:* varies. *Amount:* $4000–$8000.

Eligibility Requirements: Applicant must be enrolled or expecting to enroll full- or part-time at a two-year or technical institution and resident of California. Available to U.S. citizens.

Application Requirements: Application, references, transcript, Student Aid Report (SAR), personal statement, educational debt reporting form. *Deadline:* varies.

Contact: Scholarship Committee
Health Professions Education Foundation
400 R Street
Sacramento, CA 95811
Phone: 916-326-3640

HEALTH RESEARCH COUNCIL OF NEW ZEALAND

http://www.hrc.govt.nz/

PACIFIC HEALTH WORKFORCE AWARD
• *See page 334*

PACIFIC MENTAL HEALTH WORK FORCE AWARD
• *See page 334*

ILLINOIS NURSES ASSOCIATION

http://www.illinoisnurses.com/

SONNE SCHOLARSHIP

One-time award of up to $3000 available to nursing students. Funds may be used to cover tuition, fees, or any other cost encountered by students enrolled in Illinois state-approved nursing program. Award limited to U.S. citizens who are residents of Illinois. Recipients will receive a year's free membership in INA upon graduation.

Academic Fields/Career Goals: Nursing.

Award: Scholarship for use in freshman, sophomore, junior, or senior years; not renewable. *Number:* 2–4. *Amount:* $1000–$3000.

Eligibility Requirements: Applicant must be enrolled or expecting to enroll full-time at a four-year institution or university; resident of Illinois and studying in Illinois. Applicant must have 3.5 GPA or higher. Available to U.S. citizens.

Application Requirements: Application, essay, financial need analysis, references, transcript. *Deadline:* March 15.

Contact: Melinda Sweeney, Sonne Scholarship Committee
Illinois Nurses Association
105 West Adams Street, Suite 2101
Chicago, IL 60603
Phone: 312-419-2900 Ext. 222
Fax: 312-419-2920
E-mail: msweeney@illinoisnurses.com

INDEPENDENT COLLEGE FUND OF NEW JERSEY

http://www.njcolleges.org/

C.R. BARD FOUNDATION, INC. NURSING SCHOLARSHIP

Applicant must be entering at least the second semester of their sophomore year or the second semester of the second year of their nursing program and be enrolled full time at an ICFNJ member college or university. Must maintain a minimum GPA of 3.0.

Academic Fields/Career Goals: Nursing.

Award: Scholarship for use in junior or senior years; not renewable. *Number:* 8. *Amount:* $2500.

Eligibility Requirements: Applicant must be enrolled or expecting to enroll full-time at a four-year institution or university and studying in New Jersey. Applicant must have 3.0 GPA or higher. Available to U.S. citizens.

Application Requirements: Application, essay, financial need analysis, resume, references, transcript. *Deadline:* March 31.

Contact: Ms. Stacy Fischer, Development Officer
Independent College Fund of New Jersey
797 Springfield Avenue
Summit, NJ 07901
Phone: 908-277-3424
Fax: 908-277-0851
E-mail: scholarships@njcolleges.org

INDIANA HEALTH CARE POLICY INSTITUTE

http://www.ihca.org/

INDIANA HEALTH CARE POLICY INSTITUTE NURSING SCHOLARSHIP

Scholarship is for students pursuing a career in long-term care. One-time award of up to $5000 for Indiana residents studying nursing at an institution in Indiana, Ohio, Kentucky, Illinois or Michigan. Minimum 2.5 GPA required. Total number of awards varies.

Academic Fields/Career Goals: Nursing.

Award: Scholarship for use in freshman, sophomore, junior, or senior years; not renewable. *Number:* 1–5. *Amount:* $750–$5000.

Eligibility Requirements: Applicant must be high school student; planning to enroll or expecting to enroll full- or part-time at a two-year or four-year or technical institution or university; resident of Indiana and studying in Illinois, Indiana, Kentucky, Michigan, or Ohio. Applicant must have 2.5 GPA or higher. Available to U.S. citizens.

Application Requirements: Application, essay, interview, references, transcript. *Deadline:* May 13.

Contact: Dorothy Henry, Executive Director
Indiana Health Care Policy Institute
One North Capitol Avenue, Suite 100
Indianapolis, IN 46204
Phone: 317-616-9028
Fax: 877-298-3749
E-mail: dhenry@ihca.org

INDIAN HEALTH SERVICES, UNITED STATES DEPARTMENT OF HEALTH AND HUMAN SERVICES

http://www.ihs.gov/

HEALTH PROFESSIONS PREPARATORY SCHOLARSHIP PROGRAM
• *See page 335*

INDIAN HEALTH SERVICE HEALTH PROFESSIONS SCHOLARSHIP PROGRAM
• *See page 335*

INOVA HEALTH SYSTEM, EDELMAN NURSING CAREER DEVELOPMENT

http://www.inova.org/

EDELMAN NURSING EXCELLENCE SCHOLARSHIP PROGRAM

Scholarships will be awarded to high potential Inova employees, academically recognized college seniors, students enrolled in specially designated nursing programs, and Inova nurses working on an advanced degree. Must be entering senior year or final semester at an accredited nursing program. Must maintain a minimum of a 3.0 GPA.

Academic Fields/Career Goals: Nursing.

Award: Scholarship for use in senior, graduate, or postgraduate years; not renewable. *Number:* 20–30. *Amount:* $2000–$5000.

Eligibility Requirements: Applicant must be enrolled or expecting to enroll full-time at a four-year institution or university. Applicant or parent of applicant must be affiliated with Inova Health System. Applicant must have 3.0 GPA or higher. Available to U.S. citizens.

Application Requirements: Application, essay, interview, resume, references, transcript, proof of U.S. employment eligibility. *Deadline:* May 6.

Contact: Scholarship Coordinator
Inova Health System, Edelman Nursing Career Development
8110 Gatehouse Road, 200W
Falls Church, VA 22042
E-mail: edelmancareercenter@inova.org

INTERNATIONAL ORDER OF THE KING'S DAUGHTERS AND SONS

http://www.iokds.org/

HEALTH CAREERS SCHOLARSHIP
• *See page 219*

INTERNATIONAL UNION OF ELECTRONIC, ELECTRICAL, SALARIED, MACHINE, AND FURNITURE WORKERS-CWA

http://www.iue-cwa.org/

JAMES B. CAREY SCHOLARSHIP AWARD

Awards for students who are children or grandchildren of IUE-CWA members who are undergraduate students at accredited two-year, four-year, nursing, and technical schools.

Academic Fields/Career Goals: Nursing; Trade/Technical Specialties.

Award: Scholarship for use in freshman, sophomore, junior, or senior years; not renewable. *Number:* 1–9. *Amount:* $1000.

Eligibility Requirements: Applicant must be enrolled or expecting to enroll full-time at a two-year or four-year or technical institution or university. Applicant or parent of applicant must be member of International Union of Electronic, Electrical, Salaries, Machine and Furniture Workers. Available to U.S. and Canadian citizens.

Application Requirements: Application, essay, financial need analysis, references, test scores, transcript. *Deadline:* March 31.

Contact: Sue McElroy, Scholarship Committee
International Union of Electronic, Electrical, Salaried,
Machine, and Furniture Workers-CWA
501 Third Street, NW
Washington, DC 20001
Phone: 202-434-0676
Fax: 202-434-1250

J.D. ARCHBOLD MEMORIAL HOSPITAL

http://www.archbold.org/

ARCHBOLD SCHOLARSHIP PROGRAM
• *See page 344*

KAISER PERMANENTE

http://kpapan.org/

DELORAS JONES RN EXCELLENCE IN BACHELOR'S DEGREE NURSING SCHOLARSHIP

Merit-based scholarships of $5000 are awarded to Kaiser Permanente employees who are pursuing a bachelor's degree in nursing. Minimum 3.0 GPA required.

Academic Fields/Career Goals: Nursing.

Award: Scholarship for use in freshman, sophomore, junior, or senior years; not renewable. *Number:* varies. *Amount:* $5000.

Eligibility Requirements: Applicant must be enrolled or expecting to enroll full-time at a four-year institution or university and resident of California. Applicant or parent of applicant must be affiliated with Kaiser Permanente. Applicant must have 3.0 GPA or higher. Available to U.S. citizens.

Application Requirements: Application, transcript. *Deadline:* varies.

Contact: Dr. Michael Tran, KPAPAN Scholarship Committee Chairman
Kaiser Permanente
PO Box 950
Pasadena, CA 91102-0950
E-mail: michael.j.tran@kp.org

DELORAS JONES RN NURSING AS A SECOND CAREER SCHOLARSHIP

Need-based scholarships of $1000 to $2500 are offered to students enrolled in approved nursing degree programs in California. Applicants must be pursuing nursing as a second career. Minimum 2.5 GPA required.

Academic Fields/Career Goals: Nursing.

Award: Scholarship for use in freshman, sophomore, junior, senior, or graduate years; not renewable. *Number:* varies. *Amount:* $1000–$2500.

Eligibility Requirements: Applicant must be enrolled or expecting to enroll full-time at a four-year institution or university; resident of California and studying in California. Applicant must have 2.5 GPA or higher. Available to U.S. citizens.

Application Requirements: Application, transcript. *Deadline:* varies.

Contact: Dr. Michael Tran, KPAPAN Scholarship Committee Chairman
Kaiser Permanente
PO Box 950
Pasadena, CA 91102-0950
E-mail: michael.j.tran@kp.org

DELORAS JONES RN SCHOLARSHIP PROGRAM

Scholarship of up to $2500 awarded to nursing students in California having completed at least one academic term with minimum GPA of 2.5.

Academic Fields/Career Goals: Nursing.

Award: Scholarship for use in sophomore, junior, or senior years; not renewable. *Number:* varies. *Amount:* $1000–$2500.

Eligibility Requirements: Applicant must be enrolled or expecting to enroll full-time at a four-year institution or university; resident of California and studying in California. Applicant must have 2.5 GPA or higher. Available to U.S. citizens.

Application Requirements: Application, financial need analysis, references, transcript, copy of federal income tax return. *Deadline:* March 15.

Contact: *Phone:* 866-232-2934

DELORAS JONES RN UNDERREPRESENTED GROUPS IN NURSING SCHOLARSHIP

Need-based scholarships of $1000 to $2500 are offered to minority and male students enrolled in approved nursing degree programs in California.

Academic Fields/Career Goals: Nursing.

Award: Scholarship for use in freshman, sophomore, junior, senior, or graduate years; not renewable. *Number:* varies. *Amount:* $1000–$2500.

Eligibility Requirements: Applicant must be American Indian/Alaska Native, Asian/Pacific Islander, Black (non-Hispanic), or Hispanic; enrolled or expecting to enroll full- or part-time at a four-year institution or university; resident of California and studying in California. Available to U.S. citizens.

Application Requirements: Application. *Deadline:* varies.

Contact: Dr. Michael Tran, KPAPAN Scholarship Committee Chairman
Kaiser Permanente
PO Box 950
Pasadena, CA 91102-0950
E-mail: michael.j.tran@kp.org

KAISER PERMANENTE FORGIVABLE STUDENT LOAN PROGRAM

Forgivable loan of $2500 to $3750 available to students in their final one to three years of study. Graduate students may also apply. Following graduation, loans may be forgiven through qualifying employment with a Kaiser Permanente facility in Northern or Southern California. Minimum 3.0 GPA required.

Academic Fields/Career Goals: Nursing.

Award: Forgivable loan for use in sophomore, junior, senior, or graduate years; not renewable. *Number:* varies. *Amount:* $2500–$3750.

Eligibility Requirements: Applicant must be enrolled or expecting to enroll full-time at a four-year institution or university; resident of California and studying in California. Applicant or parent of applicant must be affiliated with Kaiser Permanente. Applicant must have 3.0 GPA or higher. Available to U.S. citizens.

Application Requirements: Application, applicant must enter a contest, references. *Deadline:* varies.

Contact: Dr. Michael Tran, KPAPAN Scholarship Committee Chairman
Kaiser Permanente
PO Box 950
Pasadena, CA 91102-0950
E-mail: michael.j.tran@kp.org

KANSAS BOARD OF REGENTS

http://www.kansasregents.org/

KANSAS NURSING SERVICE SCHOLARSHIP PROGRAM

This is a service scholarship loan program available to students attending two-year or four-year public and private postsecondary institutions as well as vocational technical schools with nursing education programs. Students can be pursuing either LPN or RN licensure. This is a service obligation scholarship, therefore students must agree to work in the field of nursing one year for each year they have received the scholarship or must repay the amount of the scholarship award that they received plus interest. Students must be Kansas residents attending a postsecondary institution in Kansas.

Academic Fields/Career Goals: Nursing.

Award: Scholarship for use in freshman, sophomore, junior, or senior years; renewable. *Number:* varies. *Amount:* $2500–$3500.

Eligibility Requirements: Applicant must be enrolled or expecting to enroll full-time at a two-year or four-year or technical institution or university. Available to U.S. citizens.

Application Requirements: Application, financial need analysis, test scores, transcript. *Fee:* $12. *Deadline:* May 1.

Contact: Diane Lindeman, Director of Student Financial Assistance
Kansas Board of Regents
1000 Jackson, SW, Suite 520
Topeka, KS 66612-1368
Phone: 785-296-3517
Fax: 785-296-0983
E-mail: dlindeman@ksbor.org

LADIES AUXILIARY TO THE VETERANS OF FOREIGN WARS, DEPARTMENT OF MAINE

http://mainevfw.org/

FRANCES L. BOOTH MEDICAL SCHOLARSHIP SPONSORED BY LAVFW DEPARTMENT OF MAINE
• *See page 344*

LINCOLN COMMUNITY FOUNDATION

http://www.lcf.org/

MEDICAL RESEARCH SCHOLARSHIP
• *See page 345*

MARION D. AND EVA S. PEEPLES FOUNDATION TRUST SCHOLARSHIP PROGRAM

http://www.jccf.org/

MARION A. AND EVA S. PEEPLES SCHOLARSHIPS
• *See page 240*

MARSHA'S ANGELS SCHOLARSHIP FUND

http://www.marshasangels.org/

MARSHA'S ANGELS SCHOLARSHIP FUND

Scholarship for students who have completed all prerequisites to enter their first year of an accredited nursing program. Applicants who are residents of Sedgwick County, Kansas or one of the surrounding counties may attend an accredited nursing program anywhere in the U.S.; applicants from any other state in the U.S. may use the scholarship to attend a qualified program in Sedgwick County, Kansas, one of the surrounding counties, or St. Luke's College in Kansas City, Missouri.

Academic Fields/Career Goals: Nursing.

Award: Scholarship for use in freshman year; renewable. *Number:* 1–1. *Amount:* $2000.

Eligibility Requirements: Applicant must be enrolled or expecting to enroll full-time at a two-year or four-year institution or university. Available to U.S. citizens.

Application Requirements: Application, essay, references. *Deadline:* June 30.

Contact: Scholarship Committee
Marsha's Angels Scholarship Fund
PO Box 401
Valley Center, KS 67147-0401
E-mail: marshasangels@gmail.com

MARYLAND STATE HIGHER EDUCATION COMMISSION

http://www.mhec.state.md.us/

GRADUATE AND PROFESSIONAL SCHOLARSHIP PROGRAM-MARYLAND
• *See page 220*

JANET L. HOFFMANN LOAN ASSISTANCE REPAYMENT PROGRAM
• *See page 241*

TUITION REDUCTION FOR NON-RESIDENT NURSING STUDENTS

Available to nonresidents of Maryland who attend a two-year or four-year public institution in Maryland. It is renewable provided student maintains academic requirements designated by institution attended. Recipient must agree to serve as a full-time nurse in a hospital or related institution for two to four years.

Academic Fields/Career Goals: Nursing.

Award: Scholarship for use in freshman, sophomore, junior, or senior years; renewable. *Number:* varies. *Amount:* varies.

Eligibility Requirements: Applicant must be enrolled or expecting to enroll full- or part-time at a two-year or four-year institution and studying in Maryland. Available to U.S. citizens.

Application Requirements: Application. *Deadline:* varies.

Contact: Robert Parker, Director
Maryland State Higher Education Commission
839 Bestgate Road, Suite 400
Annapolis, MD 21401-3013
Phone: 410-260-4558
E-mail: rparker@mhec.state.md.us

MICHIGAN LEAGUE FOR NURSING

http://www.michleaguenursing.org/

NURSING STUDENT SCHOLARSHIP

Four $500 scholarships will be awarded to students currently enrolled in a licensed practical nurse, associate degree, or bachelors degree nursing education program. Must have successfully completed at least one nursing course with a clinical component. For Michigan residents to use at colleges and universities within the state of Michigan.

Academic Fields/Career Goals: Nursing.

Award: Scholarship for use in sophomore, junior, or senior years; not renewable. *Number:* 4. *Amount:* $500.

Eligibility Requirements: Applicant must be enrolled or expecting to enroll full-time at a two-year or four-year institution; resident of Michigan and studying in Michigan. Available to U.S. and non-U.S. citizens.

Application Requirements: Application, essay, references, transcript, letters of endorsement. *Deadline:* January 1.

Contact: Carole Stacy, Director
Michigan League for Nursing
2410 Woodlake Drive
Okemos, MI 48864
Phone: 517-347-8091
Fax: 517-347-4096
E-mail: cstacy@mhc.org

MINORITY NURSE MAGAZINE

http://www.minoritynurse.com/

MINORITY NURSE MAGAZINE SCHOLARSHIP PROGRAM

Scholarships to help academically excellent, financially needy racial and ethnic minority nursing students complete a BSN degree.

Academic Fields/Career Goals: Nursing.

Award: Scholarship for use in junior or senior years; not renewable. *Number:* 3. *Amount:* $1000–$3000.

Eligibility Requirements: Applicant must be American Indian/Alaska Native, Asian/Pacific Islander, Black (non-Hispanic), or Hispanic and enrolled or expecting to enroll full- or part-time at a four-year institution or university. Applicant must have 3.0 GPA or higher. Available to U.S. citizens.

Application Requirements: Application, essay, references, transcript. *Deadline:* February 1.

Contact: Ms. Pam Chwedyk, Senior Editor and Editorial Manager
Minority Nurse Magazine
211 West Wacker Drive, Suite 900
Chicago, IL 60606
Phone: 312-525-3095
E-mail: pchwedyk@alloyeducation.com

MISSISSIPPI NURSES' ASSOCIATION (MNA)

http://www.msnurses.org/

MISSISSIPPI NURSES' ASSOCIATION FOUNDATION SCHOLARSHIP

Scholarship of $1000 to a Mississippi resident. Applicant should major in nursing and be a member of MASN.

Academic Fields/Career Goals: Nursing.

Award: Scholarship for use in freshman, sophomore, junior, or senior years; not renewable. *Number:* 1. *Amount:* $1000.

Eligibility Requirements: Applicant must be enrolled or expecting to enroll full- or part-time at a four-year institution or university and resident of Mississippi. Available to U.S. citizens.

Application Requirements: Application, essay, references, transcript. *Deadline:* October 1.

Contact: Scholarship Committee
Mississippi Nurses' Association (MNA)
31 Woodgreen Place
Madison, MS 39110
Phone: 601-898-0850
E-mail: foundation@msnurses.org

MISSISSIPPI OFFICE OF STUDENT FINANCIAL AID

http://www.mississippi.edu/

NURSING EDUCATION LOAN/SCHOLARSHIP-BSN

Award available to junior and senior students pursuing a baccalaureate degree in nursing as well as to the licensed registered nurse who wishes to continue education to the baccalaureate degree. Include transcript and references with application. Minimum 2.5 GPA required. Must be a Mississippi resident and agree to employment in professional nursing (patient care) in Mississippi.

Academic Fields/Career Goals: Nursing.

Award: Forgivable loan for use in junior or senior years; not renewable. *Number:* varies. *Amount:* $4000.

Eligibility Requirements: Applicant must be enrolled or expecting to enroll full- or part-time at a four-year institution or university; resident of Mississippi and studying in Mississippi. Applicant must have 2.5 GPA or higher. Available to U.S. citizens.

Application Requirements: Application, transcript, letter of acceptance. *Deadline:* March 31.

Contact: Mrs. Jennifer Rogers, Director of Student Financial Aid
Mississippi Office of Student Financial Aid
3825 Ridgewood Road
Jackson, MS 39211-6453
Phone: 601-432-6997
E-mail: sfa@mississippi.edu

NURSING EDUCATION LOAN/SCHOLARSHIP–RN TO BSN

Provides education opportunities to students who wish to upgrade their nursing degree and address Mississippi's nursing shortage by providing a constant source of qualified nurses. NELR awards will be made available, to the extent of appropriated funds, to persons seeking a bachelor's degree in nursing at one Mississippi institution of higher learning in exchange for employment in professional nursing in the State of Mississippi up to $4,000 per year academic year not to exceed two calendar years or $8,000. Those pursuing the NELR program part-time are eligible to receive a maximum of $8,000 prorated over three calendar years.

Academic Fields/Career Goals: Nursing.

Award: Forgivable loan for use in junior or senior years. *Amount:* up to $4000.

Eligibility Requirements: Applicant must be enrolled or expecting to enroll full- or part-time at a four-year institution or university; resident of Mississippi and studying in Mississippi. Available to U.S. citizens.

Application Requirements: Application, driver's license. *Deadline:* March 30.

Contact: Mrs. Jennifer Rogers, Director of Student Financial Aid
Mississippi Office of Student Financial Aid
3825 Ridgewood Road
Jackson, MS 39211-6453
Phone: 601-432-6997
E-mail: sfa@mississippi.edu

MISSOURI DEPARTMENT OF HEALTH AND SENIOR SERVICES

http://www.dhss.mo.gov/

MISSOURI PROFESSIONAL AND PRACTICAL NURSING STUDENT LOAN PROGRAM

Scholarship for Missouri residents enrolled or accepted into a nursing program at institutions in Missouri. Forgivable loan for nursing student attending a college or university with an 80% pass rate. Upon graduation, the student must work at a facility in a Health Professional Shortage Area in Missouri or any Hospital in Missouri. Minimum 2.5 GPA required for applicants.

Academic Fields/Career Goals: Nursing.

Award: Forgivable loan for use in freshman, sophomore, junior, senior, or graduate years; not renewable. *Number:* 60–70. *Amount:* $2500–$5000.

Eligibility Requirements: Applicant must be enrolled or expecting to enroll full-time at a two-year or four-year or technical institution or university; resident of Missouri and studying in Missouri. Applicant must have 2.5 GPA or higher.

Application Requirements: Application, proof of Missouri residency. *Deadline:* June 30.

Contact: L. Gail Ponder, Health Program Representative III
Missouri Department of Health and Senior Services
PO Box 570
Jefferson City, MO 65102-0570
Phone: 800-891-7415
Fax: 573-522-8146
E-mail: gail.ponder@dhss.mo.gov

PRIMARY CARE RESOURCE INITIATIVE FOR MISSOURI LOAN PROGRAM
• *See page 136*

MOUNT SINAI HOSPITAL DEPARTMENT OF NURSING

http://www.mountsinai.org/

BSN STUDENT SCHOLARSHIP/WORK REPAYMENT PROGRAM

Award for senior nursing student or in the last semester/year of the program. Minimum GPA is 3.25. Award value is $3000.

Academic Fields/Career Goals: Nursing.

Award: Scholarship for use in senior year; not renewable. *Number:* varies. *Amount:* $3000.

Eligibility Requirements: Applicant must be enrolled or expecting to enroll full-time at a four-year institution or university. Available to U.S. citizens.

Application Requirements: Application, resume, references, transcript. *Deadline:* October 1.

Contact: Maria L. Vezina, Director, Nursing Education and Recruitment
Mount Sinai Hospital Department of Nursing
One Gustave Levy Place, PO Box 1144
New York, NY 10029

NATIONAL ASSOCIATION DIRECTORS OF NURSING ADMINISTRATION

http://www.nadona.org/

NADONA/LTC STEPHANIE CARROLL MEMORIAL SCHOLARSHIP

Scholarship is for nursing student enrolled in an accredited nursing program or nursing students in an undergraduate or graduate program. Also for employees in the long term care continuum achieving an LPN/LVN.

Academic Fields/Career Goals: Nursing.

Award: Scholarship for use in freshman, sophomore, junior, or senior years; not renewable. *Number:* 1–5. *Amount:* varies.

Eligibility Requirements: Applicant must be enrolled or expecting to enroll full- or part-time at a two-year or four-year or technical institution or university. Available to U.S. citizens.

Application Requirements: Application, essay, financial need analysis, photo, transcript. *Deadline:* May 1.

Contact: Regina Kaurich, Executive Director
National Association Directors of Nursing Administration
11353 Reed Hartman Highway, Suite 210, Reed Hartman Tower
Cincinnati, OH 45241
Phone: 800-222-0539
Fax: 513-791-3699
E-mail: sherrie@nadona.org

NATIONAL ASSOCIATION OF HISPANIC NURSES

http://www.thehispanicnurses.org/

KAISER PERMANENTE AND NAHN SCHOLARSHIPS

Awards are presented to NAHN members enrolled in associate, diploma, baccalaureate, graduate or practical/vocational nursing programs.

Selection based on current academic standing. Scholarship award recipients are a select group of Hispanic students who demonstrate promise of future professional contributions to the nursing profession and who have the potential to act as role models for other aspiring nursing students.

Academic Fields/Career Goals: Nursing.

Award: Scholarship for use in freshman, sophomore, junior, senior, or graduate years; not renewable. *Number:* up to 10. *Amount:* up to $1000.

Eligibility Requirements: Applicant must be Hispanic and enrolled or expecting to enroll full-time at a four-year or technical institution or university. Available to U.S. citizens.

Application Requirements: Application, essay, references, transcript. *Deadline:* varies.

Contact: Carmen Ramirez, Awards and Scholarships Committee Chair
National Association of Hispanic Nurses
1501 16th Street, NW
Washington, DC 20036
Phone: 202-387-2477
Fax: 202-483-7183
E-mail: info@thehispanicnurses.org

NATIONAL BLACK NURSES ASSOCIATION INC.

http://www.nbna.org/

DR. HILDA RICHARDS SCHOLARSHIP

Scholarship for nurses currently enrolled in a nursing program who are members of NBNA. Applicant must have at least one full year of school remaining.

Academic Fields/Career Goals: Nursing.

Award: Scholarship for use in freshman, sophomore, junior, senior, graduate, or postgraduate years; not renewable. *Number:* 1. *Amount:* $1000–$2000.

Eligibility Requirements: Applicant must be enrolled or expecting to enroll full-time at a two-year or four-year institution or university. Applicant or parent of applicant must be member of National Black Nurses' Association. Applicant or parent of applicant must have employment or volunteer experience in community service. Available to U.S. and non-U.S. citizens.

Application Requirements: Application, essay, photo, references, self-addressed stamped envelope, transcript. *Deadline:* April 15.

Contact: Scholarship Committee
National Black Nurses Association Inc.
8630 Fenton Street, Suite 330
Silver Spring, MD 20910-3803
Phone: 301-589-3200
Fax: 301-589-3223
E-mail: nbna@erols.com

DR. LAURANNE SAMS SCHOLARSHIP

Award available for NBNA member who is currently enrolled full-time in a nursing program. Applicant must have at least one full year of school remaining. Scholarships will range from $1000 to $2000.

Academic Fields/Career Goals: Nursing.

Award: Scholarship for use in freshman, sophomore, junior, senior, graduate, or postgraduate years; not renewable. *Number:* up to 5. *Amount:* $1000–$2000.

Eligibility Requirements: Applicant must be enrolled or expecting to enroll full-time at a two-year or four-year institution or university. Applicant or parent of applicant must be member of National Black Nurses' Association. Available to U.S. and non-U.S. citizens.

Application Requirements: Application, essay, references, self-addressed stamped envelope, transcript. *Deadline:* April 15.

Contact: Scholarship Committee
National Black Nurses Association Inc.
8630 Fenton Street, Suite 330
Silver Spring, MD 20910-3803
Phone: 301-589-3200
Fax: 301-589-3223
E-mail: nbna@erols.com

KAISER PERMANENTE SCHOOL OF ANESTHESIA SCHOLARSHIP

Scholarship for nurses currently enrolled in a nursing program who are active members of NBNA. Must have at least one full year of school remaining.

Academic Fields/Career Goals: Nursing.

Award: Scholarship for use in freshman, sophomore, junior, senior, graduate, or postgraduate years; not renewable. *Number:* 1. *Amount:* $1000–$2000.

Eligibility Requirements: Applicant must be enrolled or expecting to enroll full-time at a two-year or four-year institution or university. Applicant or parent of applicant must be member of National Black Nurses' Association. Available to U.S. and non-U.S. citizens.

Application Requirements: Application, essay, references, self-addressed stamped envelope, transcript. *Deadline:* April 15.

Contact: Scholarship Committee
National Black Nurses Association Inc.
8630 Fenton Street, Suite 330
Silver Spring, MD 20910-3803
Phone: 301-589-3200
Fax: 301-589-3223
E-mail: nbna@erols.com

MARTHA R. DUDLEY LVN/LPN SCHOLARSHIP

Scholarship available for nurses currently enrolled full-time in a nursing program and must be a member of NBNA. Applicant must have at least one full year of school remaining. Scholarships will range from $1000 to $2000.

Academic Fields/Career Goals: Nursing.

Award: Scholarship for use in freshman, sophomore, junior, senior, graduate, or postgraduate years; not renewable. *Number:* 1. *Amount:* $1000–$2000.

Eligibility Requirements: Applicant must be Black (non-Hispanic) and enrolled or expecting to enroll full-time at a two-year or four-year institution or university. Applicant or parent of applicant must be member of National Black Nurses' Association. Applicant or parent of applicant must have employment or volunteer experience in community service. Available to U.S. and non-U.S. citizens.

Application Requirements: Application, essay, photo, references, self-addressed stamped envelope, transcript. *Deadline:* April 15.

Contact: Scholarship Committee
National Black Nurses Association Inc.
8630 Fenton Street, Suite 330
Silver Spring, MD 20910-3803
Phone: 301-589-3200
Fax: 301-589-3223
E-mail: nbna@erols.com

MAYO FOUNDATIONS SCHOLARSHIP

Scholarship for nurses currently enrolled full-time in a nursing program who are members of NBNA. Applicant must have at least one full year of school remaining.

Academic Fields/Career Goals: Nursing.

Award: Scholarship for use in freshman, sophomore, junior, senior, graduate, or postgraduate years; not renewable. *Number:* 1. *Amount:* $1000–$2000.

Eligibility Requirements: Applicant must be enrolled or expecting to enroll full-time at a two-year or four-year institution or university. Applicant or parent of applicant must be member of National Black Nurses' Association. Available to U.S. and non-U.S. citizens.

Application Requirements: Application, essay, photo, references, self-addressed stamped envelope, transcript. *Deadline:* April 15.

Contact: Scholarship Committee
National Black Nurses Association Inc.
8630 Fenton Street, Suite 330
Silver Spring, MD 20910-3803
Phone: 301-589-3200
Fax: 301-589-3223
E-mail: nbna@erols.com

NBNA BOARD OF DIRECTORS SCHOLARSHIP

The scholarship enables nurses to grow and better contribute their talents to the health and healthcare of communities. Candidate must be currently enrolled in a nursing program with at least one full year of school remaining and must be a member of NBNA.

Academic Fields/Career Goals: Nursing.

Award: Scholarship for use in freshman, sophomore, junior, senior, graduate, or postgraduate years; not renewable. *Number:* up to 2. *Amount:* $1000–$2000.

Eligibility Requirements: Applicant must be enrolled or expecting to enroll full-time at a two-year or four-year institution or university. Applicant or parent of applicant must be member of National Black Nurses' Association. Applicant or parent of applicant must have employment or volunteer experience in community service. Available to U.S. and non-U.S. citizens.

Application Requirements: Application, essay, photo, references, self-addressed stamped envelope, transcript. *Deadline:* April 15.

Contact: Scholarship Committee
National Black Nurses Association Inc.
8630 Fenton Street, Suite 330
Silver Spring, MD 20910-3803
Phone: 301-589-3200
Fax: 301-589-3223
E-mail: nbna@erols.com

NURSING SPECTRUM SCHOLARSHIP

Scholarship enables nurses to grow and better contribute their talents to the health and healthcare of communities. Candidate must be currently enrolled in a nursing program and be a member of NBNA. Applicant must have at least one full year of school remaining.

Academic Fields/Career Goals: Nursing.

Award: Scholarship for use in freshman, sophomore, junior, senior, graduate, or postgraduate years; not renewable. *Number:* 1. *Amount:* $1000–$2000.

Eligibility Requirements: Applicant must be enrolled or expecting to enroll full-time at a two-year or four-year institution or university. Applicant or parent of applicant must be member of National Black Nurses' Association. Available to U.S. and non-U.S. citizens.

Application Requirements: Application, essay, references, self-addressed stamped envelope, transcript. *Deadline:* April 15.

Contact: Scholarship Committee
National Black Nurses Association Inc.
8630 Fenton Street, Suite 330
Silver Spring, MD 20910-3803
Phone: 301-589-3200
Fax: 301-589-3223
E-mail: nbna@erols.com

NATIONAL SOCIETY DAUGHTERS OF THE AMERICAN REVOLUTION

http://www.dar.org/

NATIONAL SOCIETY DAUGHTERS OF THE AMERICAN REVOLUTION CAROLINE E. HOLT NURSING SCHOLARSHIPS

One-time award of $1000 for students who are in financial need and have been accepted or are enrolled in an accredited school of nursing. A letter of acceptance into the nursing program or the transcript stating that the applicant is enrolled in the nursing program must be included with the application.

Academic Fields/Career Goals: Nursing.

Award: Scholarship for use in freshman, sophomore, junior, or senior years; not renewable. *Number:* varies. *Amount:* $1000.

Eligibility Requirements: Applicant must be enrolled or expecting to enroll full-time at a two-year or four-year institution or university. Available to U.S. citizens.

Application Requirements: Application, financial need analysis, self-addressed stamped envelope, transcript, letter of sponsorship. *Deadline:* February 15.

Contact: Eric Weisz, Manager, Office of the Reporter General
National Society Daughters of the American Revolution
1776 D Street, NW
Washington, DC 20006-5303
Phone: 202-628-1776
Fax: 202-879-3348
E-mail: nsdarscholarships@dar.org

NATIONAL SOCIETY DAUGHTERS OF THE AMERICAN REVOLUTION MADELINE PICKETT (HALBERT) COGSWELL NURSING SCHOLARSHIP

Scholarship available to students who have been accepted or are currently enrolled in an accredited school of nursing, who are members of NSDAR, descendants of members of NSDAR, or are eligible to be members of NSDAR. A letter of acceptance into the nursing program or transcript showing enrollment in nursing program must be included with the application. DAR member number must be on the application.

Academic Fields/Career Goals: Nursing.

Award: Scholarship for use in freshman, sophomore, junior, or senior years; not renewable. *Number:* varies. *Amount:* $1000.

Eligibility Requirements: Applicant must be enrolled or expecting to enroll full-time at a two-year or four-year institution or university. Applicant or parent of applicant must be member of Daughters of the American Revolution. Available to U.S. and non-U.S. citizens.

Application Requirements: Application, references, self-addressed stamped envelope, letter of sponsorship. *Deadline:* February 15.

Contact: Eric Weisz, Manager, Office of the Reporter General
National Society Daughters of the American Revolution
1776 D Street, NW
Washington, DC 20006-5303
Phone: 202-628-1776
Fax: 202-879-3348
E-mail: nsdarscholarships@dar.org

NATIONAL SOCIETY DAUGHTERS OF THE AMERICAN REVOLUTION MILDRED NUTTING NURSING SCHOLARSHIP

A one-time $1000 scholarship for students who are in financial need and who have been accepted or are currently enrolled in an accredited school of nursing. A letter of acceptance into the nursing program or the transcript stating that the applicant is in the nursing program must be enclosed with the application. Preference will be given to candidates from the Lowell, Massachusetts area.

Academic Fields/Career Goals: Nursing.

Award: Scholarship for use in freshman, sophomore, junior, or senior years; not renewable. *Number:* varies. *Amount:* $1000.

Eligibility Requirements: Applicant must be enrolled or expecting to enroll full-time at a two-year or four-year institution or university. Available to U.S. citizens.

Application Requirements: Application, essay, financial need analysis, references, self-addressed stamped envelope, test scores, transcript, letter of sponsorship. *Deadline:* February 15.

Contact: Eric Weisz, Manager, Office of the Reporter General
National Society Daughters of the American Revolution
1776 D Street, NW
Washington, DC 20006-5303
Phone: 202-628-1776
Fax: 202-879-3348
E-mail: nsdarscholarships@dar.org

NATIONAL SOCIETY OF THE COLONIAL DAMES OF AMERICA

http://www.nscda.org/

AMERICAN INDIAN NURSE SCHOLARSHIP AWARDS
• See page 335

NEW HAMPSHIRE POSTSECONDARY EDUCATION COMMISSION

http://www.nh.gov/postsecondary

WORKFORCE INCENTIVE PROGRAM
• See page 243

NEW JERSEY STATE NURSES ASSOCIATION

http://www.njsna.org/

INSTITUTE FOR NURSING SCHOLARSHIP

Applicants must be New Jersey residents currently enrolled in a diploma, associate, baccalaureate, master's, or doctoral program in nursing or a related field. The amount awarded in each scholarship will be $1000 per recipient.

Academic Fields/Career Goals: Nursing.

Award: Scholarship for use in freshman, sophomore, junior, senior, or graduate years; not renewable. *Number:* 14. *Amount:* $1000.

Eligibility Requirements: Applicant must be enrolled or expecting to enroll full-time at a two-year or four-year institution or university and resident of New Jersey. Available to U.S. citizens.

Application Requirements: Application, references, transcript, tax form. *Deadline:* varies.

Contact: Sandy Kerr, Executive Assistant
New Jersey State Nurses Association
1479 Pennington Road
Trenton, NJ 08618-2661
Phone: 609-883-5335
Fax: 609-883-5343
E-mail: sandy@njsna.org

NEW MEXICO COMMISSION ON HIGHER EDUCATION

http://www.hed.state.nm.us/

ALLIED HEALTH STUDENT LOAN PROGRAM-NEW MEXICO
• See page 220

NURSE EDUCATOR LOAN-FOR-SERVICE

Forgivable loan of up to $5000 for New Mexico nursing majors to obtain an undergraduate, graduate, or post graduate degree in the state of New Mexico. Each loan has a service agreement wherein the student declares his/her intent to serve in a nurse faculty position in a New Mexico public, post-secondary institution. For every academic year of service, a portion of the loan is forgiven and if the entire service agreement is fulfilled, the entire loan is eligible for forgiveness. Must be a U.S. citizen.

Academic Fields/Career Goals: Nursing.

Award: Forgivable loan for use in senior year; renewable. *Number:* 1. *Amount:* up to $5000.

Eligibility Requirements: Applicant must be enrolled or expecting to enroll full- or part-time at a four-year institution or university; resident of New Mexico and studying in New Mexico. Available to U.S. citizens.

Application Requirements: Application, essay, transcript. *Deadline:* July 1.

Contact: Theresa Acker, Financial Aid Division
New Mexico Commission on Higher Education
1068 Cerrillos Road
Santa Fe, NM 85705-1650
Phone: 505-476-6506
Fax: 505-476-6511
E-mail: theresa.acker@state.nm.us

NURSING STUDENT LOAN-FOR-SERVICE PROGRAM

Award to increase the number of nurses in areas of New Mexico which have experienced shortages by making educational loans to students entering nursing programs. As a condition of each loan, the student shall declare his/her intent to practice as a health professional in a designated shortage area. For every year of service, a portion of the loan will be forgiven.

Academic Fields/Career Goals: Nursing.

Award: Forgivable loan for use in freshman, sophomore, junior, or senior years; renewable. *Number:* 1. *Amount:* up to $12,000.

Eligibility Requirements: Applicant must be enrolled or expecting to enroll full- or part-time at a four-year institution or university; resident of New Mexico and studying in New Mexico. Available to U.S. citizens.

Application Requirements: Application, financial need analysis, transcript, FAFSA. *Deadline:* July 1.

Contact: Theresa Acker, Financial Aid Division
New Mexico Commission on Higher Education
1068 Cerrillos Road
Santa Fe, NM 87505-1650
Phone: 505-476-6506
Fax: 505-476-6511
E-mail: theresa.acker@state.nm.us

NEW YORK STATE EDUCATION DEPARTMENT

http://www.highered.nysed.gov/

REGENTS PROFESSIONAL OPPORTUNITY SCHOLARSHIP
• *See page 69*

NEW YORK STATE EMERGENCY NURSES ASSOCIATION (ENA)

http://www.ena.org/

NEW YORK STATE ENA SEPTEMBER 11 SCHOLARSHIP FUND

Scholarships to rescue workers who are going to school to obtain their undergraduate nursing degree. Eligible rescue workers include prehospital care providers, fire fighters, and police officers. The scholarship is not limited geographically. The scholarship winner will also be awarded a complimentary one year ENA membership.

Academic Fields/Career Goals: Nursing.

Award: Scholarship for use in freshman, sophomore, junior, senior, graduate, or postgraduate years; not renewable. *Number:* 1. *Amount:* $2000.

Eligibility Requirements: Applicant must be enrolled or expecting to enroll full- or part-time at a four-year institution or university. Available to U.S. citizens.

Application Requirements: Application. *Deadline:* varies.

Contact: Educational Services
New York State Emergency Nurses Association (ENA)
915 Lee Street
Des Plaines, IL 60016-6569
Phone: 847-460-4123
Fax: 847-460-4005
E-mail: education@ena.org

NEW YORK STATE GRANGE

http://www.nysgrange.com/

JUNE GILL NURSING SCHOLARSHIP

One annual scholarship award to verified NYS Grange member pursuing a career in nursing. Selection based on verification of NYS Grange membership and enrollment in a nursing program, as well as applicant's career statement, academic records, and financial need. Payment made after successful completion of one term.

Academic Fields/Career Goals: Nursing.

Award: Scholarship for use in freshman, sophomore, junior, or senior years; not renewable. *Number:* 1. *Amount:* varies.

Eligibility Requirements: Applicant must be enrolled or expecting to enroll full-time at a two-year or four-year institution and resident of New York. Applicant or parent of applicant must be member of Grange Association. Available to U.S. citizens.

Application Requirements: Application, financial need analysis, transcript, nursing program enrollment letter, career statement. *Deadline:* April 15.

Contact: Scholarship Committee
New York State Grange
100 Grange Place
Cortland, NY 13045
Phone: 607-756-7553
Fax: 607-756-7757
E-mail: nysgrange@nysgrange.com

NIGHTINGALE AWARDS OF PENNSYLVANIA

http://www.nightingaleawards.org/

NIGHTINGALE AWARDS OF PENNSYLVANIA NURSING SCHOLARSHIP

Scholarships for students who are studying nursing at the basic or advanced level and intend to practice in Pennsylvania. Regardless of the type of nursing program, all candidates accepted into or presently enrolled in accredited nursing programs in Pennsylvania may apply. Scholarships are awarded to students who enter professional nursing programs, practical nursing programs, and advanced degree programs.

Academic Fields/Career Goals: Nursing.

Award: Scholarship for use in freshman, sophomore, junior, senior, or graduate years; not renewable. *Number:* up to 6. *Amount:* $6000–$10,000.

Eligibility Requirements: Applicant must be enrolled or expecting to enroll full-time at a four-year institution or university and studying in Pennsylvania. Available to U.S. citizens.

Application Requirements: Application, references, test scores, transcript. *Deadline:* January 31.

Contact: Christine Filipovich, President
Nightingale Awards of Pennsylvania
2090 Linglestown Road, Suite 107
Harrisburg, PA 17110
Phone: 717-909-0350
Fax: 717-234-6798
E-mail: nightingale@pronursingresources.com

NORTH CAROLINA STATE EDUCATION ASSISTANCE AUTHORITY

http://www.ncseaa.edu/

NORTH CAROLINA STUDENT LOAN PROGRAM FOR HEALTH, SCIENCE, AND MATHEMATICS
• *See page 221*

NURSE EDUCATION SCHOLARSHIP LOAN PROGRAM (NESLP)

Must be U.S. citizen and North Carolina resident. Award available through financial aid offices of North Carolina colleges and universities that offer programs to prepare students for licensure in the state as LPN or RN. Recipients enter contract with the State of North Carolina to work full time as a licensed nurse. Loans not repaid through service must be repaid in cash. Award based upon financial need. Maximum award for students enrolled in Associate Degree Nursing and Practical Nurse Education programs is $5000. Maximum award for students enrolled in a baccalaureate program is $400.

Academic Fields/Career Goals: Nursing.

Award: Forgivable loan for use in freshman, sophomore, junior, or senior years; renewable. *Number:* varies. *Amount:* $400–$5000.

Eligibility Requirements: Applicant must be enrolled or expecting to enroll full- or part-time at a four-year institution or university; resident of North Carolina and studying in North Carolina. Available to U.S. citizens.

Application Requirements: Application, financial need analysis. *Deadline:* continuous.

Contact: Bill Carswell, Manager of Scholarship and Grant Division
North Carolina State Education Assistance Authority
PO Box 14103
Research Triangle Park, NC 27709
Phone: 919-549-8614
Fax: 919-248-4687
E-mail: carswellb@ncseaa.edu

NURSE SCHOLARS PROGRAM-UNDERGRADUATE (NORTH CAROLINA)

Forgivable loans to residents of North Carolina who have been accepted to a North Carolina institution of higher education that offers a nursing program. Must apply to the North Carolina State Education and Welfare division. Must serve as a registered nurse in North Carolina for one year for each year of funding. Minimum 3.0 GPA required. Amount of award is based upon type of nursing education sought. Deadline varies.

Academic Fields/Career Goals: Nursing.

Award: Forgivable loan for use in freshman, sophomore, junior, or senior years; renewable. *Number:* up to 450. *Amount:* $3000–$5000.

Eligibility Requirements: Applicant must be enrolled or expecting to enroll full-time at a two-year or four-year institution or university; resident of North Carolina and studying in North Carolina. Applicant must have 3.0 GPA or higher. Available to U.S. citizens.

Application Requirements: Application, essay, references, test scores, transcript. *Deadline:* varies.

Contact: Terrence Scarborough, Manager, Merit-Based Scholarship
          Loan Programs
          North Carolina State Education Assistance Authority
          PO Box 13663
          Research Triangle Park, NC 27709
          Phone: 919-549-8614
          Fax: 919-248-4687
          E-mail: terrence@ncseaa.edu

ODD FELLOWS AND REBEKAHS

http://www.ioofme.org/

ODD FELLOWS AND REBEKAHS ELLEN F. WASHBURN NURSES TRAINING AWARD

Award for high school seniors and college undergraduates to attend an accredited Maine institution and pursue a registered nursing degree. Must have a minimum 2.5 GPA. Can reapply for award for up to four years.

Academic Fields/Career Goals: Nursing.

Award: Scholarship for use in freshman, sophomore, junior, or senior years; renewable. *Number:* up to 30. *Amount:* $150–$400.

Eligibility Requirements: Applicant must be enrolled or expecting to enroll full- or part-time at a two-year or four-year institution or university and studying in Maine. Applicant must have 2.5 GPA or higher. Available to U.S. citizens.

Application Requirements: Application, financial need analysis, photo, references. *Deadline:* April 15.

Contact: Joyce Young, Chairman
          Odd Fellows and Rebekahs
          131 Queen Street Extension
          Gorham, ME 04038
          Phone: 207-839-4723

OHIO BOARD OF REGENTS

http://www.uso.edu/

NURSE EDUCATION ASSISTANCE LOAN PROGRAM

The Nurse Education Assistance Loan Program (NEALP) provides financial assistance to Ohio students enrolled for at least half-time study (or accepted for enrollment) in an approved Ohio nurse education program. NEALP provides funding for nurses who intend to serve as instructors or students who intend to serve as nurses after graduation.

Academic Fields/Career Goals: Nursing.

Award: Forgivable loan for use in freshman, sophomore, junior, or senior years; not renewable. *Amount:* $1500–$5000.

Eligibility Requirements: Applicant must be enrolled or expecting to enroll full- or part-time at a two-year or four-year institution or university; resident of Ohio and studying in Ohio. Available to U.S. citizens.

Application Requirements: Application, FAFSA. *Deadline:* July 15.

Contact: *Phone:* 888-833-1133
          E-mail: nealp_admin@regents.state.oh.us

ONS FOUNDATION

http://www.ons.org/

ONS FOUNDATION ETHNIC MINORITY BACHELOR'S SCHOLARSHIP

Three one-time scholarships of $2000 available to registered nurses with a demonstrated interest in oncology nursing. Must be currently enrolled in an undergraduate program at an NLN-accredited school, and must currently hold a license to practice as a registered nurse. Must be minority student who has not received any BA grants previously from ONF.

Academic Fields/Career Goals: Nursing.

Award: Scholarship for use in freshman, sophomore, junior, or senior years; not renewable. *Amount:* $2000.

Eligibility Requirements: Applicant must be American Indian/Alaska Native, Asian/Pacific Islander, Black (non-Hispanic), or Hispanic and enrolled or expecting to enroll full- or part-time at a four-year institution or university. Available to U.S. citizens.

Application Requirements: Application, transcript. *Fee:* $5. *Deadline:* February 1.

Contact: Bonny Revo, Executive Assistant
          ONS Foundation
          125 Enterprise Drive
          Pittsburgh, PA 15275
          Phone: 412-859-6100
          E-mail: brevo@ons.org

ONS FOUNDATION JOSH GOTTHEIL MEMORIAL BONE MARROW TRANSPLANT CAREER DEVELOPMENT AWARDS

Awards available to any professional registered nurse in field of bone marrow transplant nursing for further study in a bachelor's or master's program. Submit examples of contributions to BMT nursing.

Academic Fields/Career Goals: Nursing.

Award: Scholarship for use in junior, senior, or graduate years; not renewable. *Number:* 4. *Amount:* $2000.

Eligibility Requirements: Applicant must be enrolled or expecting to enroll full- or part-time at a four-year institution or university. Available to U.S. and non-U.S. citizens.

Application Requirements: Application, essay, resume, references. *Deadline:* December 1.

Contact: Bonny Revo, Executive Assistant
          ONS Foundation
          125 Enterprise Drive
          Pittsburgh, PA 15275
          Phone: 412-859-6100
          E-mail: brevo@ons.org

ONS FOUNDATION/ONCOLOGY NURSING CERTIFICATION CORPORATION BACHELOR'S SCHOLARSHIPS

One-time awards to improve oncology nursing by assisting registered nurses in furthering their education. Applicants must hold a current license to practice and be enrolled in an undergraduate nursing degree program at an NLN-accredited school.

Academic Fields/Career Goals: Nursing; Oncology.

Award: Scholarship for use in freshman, sophomore, junior, or senior years; not renewable. *Amount:* $2000.

Eligibility Requirements: Applicant must be enrolled or expecting to enroll full- or part-time at a four-year institution or university. Available to U.S. and non-U.S. citizens.

Application Requirements: Application, transcript. *Fee:* $5. *Deadline:* February 1.

Contact: Bonny Revo, Executive Assistant
          ONS Foundation
          125 Enterprise Drive
          Pittsburgh, PA 15275
          Phone: 412-859-6100
          E-mail: brevo@ons.org

ONS FOUNDATION/PEARL MOORE CAREER DEVELOPMENT AWARDS

Awards to practicing staff nurses who possess or are pursuing a BSN and have two years oncology practice experience.

Academic Fields/Career Goals: Nursing; Oncology.

Award: Prize for use in junior, senior, or graduate years; not renewable. *Number:* 3. *Amount:* $3000.

Eligibility Requirements: Applicant must be enrolled or expecting to enroll full- or part-time at a four-year institution or university. Available to U.S. citizens.

Application Requirements: Application, references. *Deadline:* December 1.

Contact: Bonny Revo, Executive Assistant
ONS Foundation
125 Enterprise Drive
Pittsburgh, PA 15275
Phone: 412-859-6100
E-mail: brevo@ons.org

OREGON COMMUNITY FOUNDATION

http://www.oregoncf.org/

FRANZ STENZEL M.D. AND KATHRYN STENZEL SCHOLARSHIP FUND
• *See page 347*

NLN ELLA MCKINNEY SCHOLARSHIP FUND

Award for Oregon high school graduates (or the equivalent) for use in the pursuit of an undergraduate or graduate nursing education. Must attend a nonprofit college or university in Oregon accredited by the NLN Accrediting Commission. For more information, see Web http://www.getcollegefunds.org.

Academic Fields/Career Goals: Nursing.

Award: Scholarship for use in freshman, sophomore, junior, or senior years; renewable. *Number:* up to 2. *Amount:* $1000–$2000.

Eligibility Requirements: Applicant must be enrolled or expecting to enroll full-time at a two-year or four-year institution or university; resident of Oregon and studying in Oregon. Available to U.S. citizens.

Application Requirements: Application, references. *Deadline:* March 1.

Contact: Dianne Causey, Program Associate for Scholarships and Grants
Oregon Community Foundation
1221 Yamhill, SW, Suite 100
Portland, OR 97205-2108
Phone: 503-227-6846 Ext. 1418
E-mail: dcausey@oregoncf.org

OREGON NURSES ASSOCIATION

http://www.oregonrn.org/

ONF CENTENNIAL EDUCATION SCHOLARSHIPS

Scholarship available to Oregon residents accepted into or enrolled in an accredited nursing program in Oregon. Minimum 3.0 GPA required.

Academic Fields/Career Goals: Nursing.

Award: Scholarship for use in freshman year; not renewable. *Number:* 1. *Amount:* $1000.

Eligibility Requirements: Applicant must be enrolled or expecting to enroll full-time at a two-year or four-year institution or university; resident of Oregon and studying in Oregon. Applicant must have 3.0 GPA or higher. Available to U.S. citizens.

Application Requirements: Application, transcript, letter of acceptance from the nursing program. *Deadline:* varies.

Contact: Melissa Tangedal, Program Assistant
Oregon Nurses Association
18765 SW Boones Ferry Road, Suite 200
Tualatin, OR 97062
Phone: 503-293-0011
Fax: 503-293-0013
E-mail: tangedal@oregonrn.org

ONF-SMITH EDUCATION SCHOLARSHIP

Award for nursing students enrolled in an undergraduate or graduate program in Oregon. RN recipients must be current ONA members. Non-RN recipients of the baccalaureate scholarship must join the nurses association in their state of residence upon graduation.

Academic Fields/Career Goals: Nursing.

Award: Scholarship for use in freshman, sophomore, junior, senior, or graduate years; not renewable. *Number:* 3. *Amount:* $1000.

Eligibility Requirements: Applicant must be enrolled or expecting to enroll full-time at a two-year or four-year institution or university and studying in Oregon. Applicant must have 3.0 GPA or higher. Available to U.S. citizens.

Application Requirements: Application, references, letter of acceptance from nursing program. *Deadline:* February 1.

Contact: Melissa Tangedal, Program Assistant
Oregon Nurses Association
18765 SW Boones Ferry Road, Suite 200
Tualatin, OR 97062
Phone: 503-293-0011
Fax: 503-293-0013
E-mail: tangedal@oregonrn.org

OREGON STUDENT ASSISTANCE COMMISSION

http://www.GetCollegeFunds.org/

BERTHA P. SINGER NURSES SCHOLARSHIP

Renewable award for Oregon residents pursuing a nursing career. Must attend a college or university in Oregon. Minimum GPA of 3.0 required. Proof of enrollment in third year of four-year nursing degree program or second year of a two-year associate degree nursing program is required. Transcripts alone are not sufficient proof, must obtain a form or letter from department. U.S. Bank employees, their children, or close relatives are not eligible.

Academic Fields/Career Goals: Nursing.

Award: Scholarship for use in sophomore, junior, or senior years; renewable. *Amount:* varies.

Eligibility Requirements: Applicant must be enrolled or expecting to enroll full-time at a two-year or four-year institution or university; resident of Oregon and studying in Oregon. Applicant must have 3.0 GPA or higher. Available to U.S. citizens.

Application Requirements: Application, essay, transcript, form or letter from department. *Deadline:* March 1.

Contact: Scholarship Coordinator
Oregon Student Assistance Commission
1500 Valley River Drive, Suite 100
Eugene, OR 97401-7020
Phone: 800-452-8807 Ext. 7466

CHESTER AND HELEN LUTHER SCHOLARSHIP
• *See page 347*

CLARK-PHELPS SCHOLARSHIP
• *See page 221*

FRANKS FOUNDATION SCHOLARSHIP

Awards to students who are nursing or theology majors and residents of Crook, Deschutes, or Jefferson County (first preference) or residents of Grant, Harney, Klamath, or Lake County (second preference). High school seniors must have a minimum GPA of 2.5, college students must have a minimum GPA of 2.0. Must reapply annually for renewal. U.S. Bank employees, their children, and near relatives are not eligible.

Academic Fields/Career Goals: Nursing; Religion/Theology.

Award: Scholarship for use in freshman, sophomore, junior, senior, or graduate years; not renewable.

Eligibility Requirements: Applicant must be enrolled or expecting to enroll full- or part-time at a four-year institution or university and resident of Oregon. Available to U.S. citizens.

Application Requirements: Application, test scores, transcript. *Deadline:* March 1.

Contact: Director of Grant Programs
Oregon Student Assistance Commission
1500 Valley River Drive, Suite 100
Eugene, OR 97401-7020
Phone: 800-452-8807

HELEN HALL AND JOHN SEELY MEMORIAL SCHOLARSHIP
• *See page 347*

MARION A. LINDEMAN SCHOLARSHIP
• *See page 347*

WALTER C. AND MARIE C. SCHMIDT SCHOLARSHIP

Scholarship available to Oregon students enrolling in programs to become registered nurses and intending to pursue careers in geriatric health care. Applicants must submit an additional essay describing their desire to pursue a nursing career in geriatrics. U.S. Bank employees, their children, or near relatives are not eligible. Preference to students attending Lane County Community College, but students may attend any other two-year college nursing program. Essay describing desire to pursue nursing career in geriatric health care required.

Academic Fields/Career Goals: Nursing.

Award: Scholarship for use in freshman or sophomore years; renewable. *Number:* varies. *Amount:* varies.

Eligibility Requirements: Applicant must be enrolled or expecting to enroll full- or part-time at a two-year institution and resident of Oregon. Available to U.S. citizens.

Application Requirements: Application, essay, financial need analysis, references, transcript, activity chart. *Deadline:* March 1.

Contact: Director of Grant Programs
Oregon Student Assistance Commission
1500 Valley River Drive, Suite 100
Eugene, OR 97401-7020
Phone: 800-452-8807 Ext. 7395

PILOT INTERNATIONAL FOUNDATION

http://www.pilotinternational.org/

PILOT INTERNATIONAL FOUNDATION RUBY NEWHALL MEMORIAL SCHOLARSHIP
• See page 348

PILOT INTERNATIONAL FOUNDATION SCHOLARSHIP PROGRAM
• See page 348

RHODE ISLAND FOUNDATION

http://www.rifoundation.org/

ALBERT E. AND FLORENCE W. NEWTON NURSE SCHOLARSHIP

Applicant must be studying nursing on a full- or part-time basis. Preference will be given to Rhode Island residents committed to practicing in Rhode Island. Must be able to demonstrate financial need. Must be in one of the following categories: A registered nurse enrolled in a nursing baccalaureate degree program; student enrolled in a baccalaureate nursing program; student in a diploma nursing program; student in a two-year associate degree nursing program.

Academic Fields/Career Goals: Nursing.

Award: Scholarship for use in freshman, sophomore, junior, or senior years; renewable. *Number:* varies. *Amount:* $500–$2000.

Eligibility Requirements: Applicant must be enrolled or expecting to enroll full- or part-time at a two-year or four-year institution or university. Available to U.S. citizens.

Application Requirements: Application, essay, financial need analysis, self-addressed stamped envelope, transcript, copy of college acceptance letter, copy of most recent income tax return. *Deadline:* April 16.

Contact: Libby Monahan, Funds Administrator
Rhode Island Foundation
One Union Station
Providence, RI 02903
Phone: 401-274-4564 Ext. 3117
E-mail: libbym@rifoundation.org

EDWARD J. AND VIRGINIA M. ROUTHIER NURSING SCHOLARSHIP

Award is for licensed RNs seeking baccalaureate or graduate nursing degree in Rhode Island. Must demonstrate financial need. Award is renewable.

Academic Fields/Career Goals: Nursing.

Award: Scholarship for use in freshman, sophomore, junior, senior, or graduate years; renewable. *Amount:* $500–$3000.

Eligibility Requirements: Applicant must be enrolled or expecting to enroll at a four-year institution or university and studying in Rhode Island.

Contact: Libby Monahan, Funds Administrator
Rhode Island Foundation
One Union Station
Providence, RI 02903
Phone: 401-274-4564 Ext. 3117
E-mail: libbym@rifoundation.org

SOCIETY FOR THE SCIENTIFIC STUDY OF SEXUALITY

http://www.sexscience.org/

SOCIETY FOR THE SCIENTIFIC STUDY OF SEXUALITY STUDENT RESEARCH GRANT
• See page 137

SOCIETY OF PEDIATRIC NURSES

http://www.pedsnurses.org/

SOCIETY OF PEDIATRIC NURSES EDUCATIONAL SCHOLARSHIP
• See page 173

STATE STUDENT ASSISTANCE COMMISSION OF INDIANA (SSACI)

http://www.in.gov/ssaci

INDIANA NURSING SCHOLARSHIP FUND

Need-based tuition funding for nursing students enrolled full- or part-time at an eligible Indiana institution. Must be a U.S. citizen and an Indiana resident and have a minimum 2.0 GPA or meet the minimum requirements for the nursing program. Upon graduation, recipients must practice as a nurse in an Indiana health care setting for two years.

Academic Fields/Career Goals: Nursing.

Award: Scholarship for use in freshman, sophomore, junior, or senior years; not renewable. *Number:* 490–690. *Amount:* $200–$5000.

Eligibility Requirements: Applicant must be enrolled or expecting to enroll full- or part-time at a two-year or four-year institution or university; resident of Indiana and studying in Indiana. Available to U.S. citizens.

Application Requirements: Application, financial need analysis, FAFSA. *Deadline:* continuous.

Contact: Yvonne Heflin, Director, Special Programs
State Student Assistance Commission of Indiana (SSACI)
150 West Market Street, Suite 500
Indianapolis, IN 46204-2805
Phone: 317-232-2350
Fax: 317-232-3260

STRAIGHTFORWARD MEDIA

http://www.straightforwardmedia.com/

STRAIGHTFORWARD MEDIA MEDICAL PROFESSIONS SCHOLARSHIP
• See page 221

STRAIGHTFORWARD MEDIA NURSING SCHOOL SCHOLARSHIP

Scholarship of $500 available to students majoring in nursing. Awarded four times per year. Deadlines: April 14, July 14, October 14, and January 14. To apply, go to http://www.straightforwardmedia.com/nursing/form.php.

Academic Fields/Career Goals: Nursing.

Award: Scholarship for use in freshman, sophomore, junior, or senior years; not renewable. *Number:* 4. *Amount:* $500.

Eligibility Requirements: Applicant must be enrolled or expecting to enroll full- or part-time at a two-year or four-year or technical institution or university. Available to U.S. and non-U.S. citizens.

Application Requirements: Essay. *Deadline:* varies.

Contact: Scholarship Committee
StraightForward Media
508 7th Street
Suite 202
Rapid City, SD 57701
Phone: 605-348-3042

TAFFORD UNIFORMS

http://www.tafford.com/

TAFFORD UNIFORMS NURSING SCHOLARSHIP PROGRAM

Two scholarships of $1000 each awarded to nursing students enrolled in undergraduate and graduate study. Minimum 2.5 GPA required.

Academic Fields/Career Goals: Nursing.

Award: Scholarship for use in freshman, sophomore, junior, or senior years; not renewable. *Number:* 2. *Amount:* $1000.

Eligibility Requirements: Applicant must be enrolled or expecting to enroll full-time at a two-year or four-year institution or university. Applicant must have 2.5 GPA or higher. Available to U.S. citizens.

Application Requirements: Application. *Deadline:* continuous.

Contact: Scholarship Coordinator
Tafford Uniforms
1370 Welsh Road
North Wales, PA 19454
Phone: 215-643-9666

TEXAS HIGHER EDUCATION COORDINATING BOARD

http://www.collegefortexans.com/

TEXAS PROFESSIONAL NURSING SCHOLARSHIPS

Award to provide financial assistance to encourage students to become Professional Nurses. Only in-state (Texas) colleges or universities may participate in the program. Both public and private, non-profit colleges or universities with professional nursing programs may participate in the programs.

Academic Fields/Career Goals: Nursing.

Award: Scholarship for use in freshman, sophomore, junior, or senior years; not renewable. *Amount:* $2500.

Eligibility Requirements: Applicant must be enrolled or expecting to enroll at a two-year or four-year or technical institution; resident of Texas and studying in Texas.

Application Requirements: Application, financial need analysis.

Contact: Grants and Special Programs
Texas Higher Education Coordinating Board
PO Box 12788
Austin, TX 78711-2788
Phone: 512-427-6101
E-mail: grantinfo@thecb.state.tx.us

TOUCHMARK FOUNDATION

http://www.touchmarkfoundation.org/

TOUCHMARK FOUNDATION NURSING SCHOLARSHIP

Students pursuing nursing degrees at any level are encouraged to apply, including nurses interested pursuing advanced degrees in order to teach. Scholarship application deadlines are June 30 and December 30 of each year.

Academic Fields/Career Goals: Nursing.

Award: Scholarship for use in freshman, sophomore, junior, senior, graduate, or postgraduate years; not renewable. *Number:* varies. *Amount:* $500–$1000.

Eligibility Requirements: Applicant must be enrolled or expecting to enroll full-time at a four-year institution or university and studying in Alberta, Idaho, Minnesota, Montana, North Dakota, Oklahoma, Oregon, South Dakota, Washington, or Wisconsin. Available to U.S. citizens.

Application Requirements: Application, essay, references, transcript, FAFSA, copy of acceptance letter. *Deadline:* continuous.

Contact: Bret Cope, Chairman
Touchmark Foundation
5150 SW Griffith Drive
Beaverton, OR 97005
Phone: 800-796-8744
E-mail: bjc@touchmark.com

UNITED DAUGHTERS OF THE CONFEDERACY

http://www.hqudc.org/

PHOEBE PEMBER MEMORIAL SCHOLARSHIP

Award for full-time undergraduate students who are descendants of a Confederate soldier, enrolled in a school of nursing. Must be enrolled in an accredited college or university and have a minimum 3.0 GPA. Submit letter of endorsement from sponsoring Chapter of the United Daughters of the Confederacy.

Academic Fields/Career Goals: Nursing.

Award: Scholarship for use in freshman, sophomore, junior, or senior years; renewable. *Number:* 1–2. *Amount:* $800–$1000.

Eligibility Requirements: Applicant must be enrolled or expecting to enroll full-time at a four-year institution or university. Applicant or parent of applicant must be member of United Daughters of the Confederacy. Applicant must have 3.0 GPA or higher. Available to U.S. citizens.

Application Requirements: Application, essay, financial need analysis, photo, references, self-addressed stamped envelope, transcript, copy of applicant's birth certificate, copy of confederate ancestor's proof of service. *Deadline:* March 15.

Contact: United Daughters of the Confederacy
328 North Boulevard
Richmond, VA 23220-4009
Phone: 804-355-1636
E-mail: hqudc@rcn.com

WALTER REED SMITH SCHOLARSHIP
• *See page 157*

UNITED NEGRO COLLEGE FUND

http://www.uncf.org/

ARLENE BENTON NOLAN AND JOHN NOLAN SCHOLARSHIP
• *See page 144*

CATHOLIC HEALTHCARE WEST CORPORATE SCHOLARS PROGRAM
• *See page 144*

U. S. DEPARTMENT OF HEALTH AND HUMAN SERVICES

http://www.hhs.gov/about/whatwedo.html/

U. S. PUBLIC HEALTH SERVICE-HEALTH RESOURCES AND SERVICES ADMINISTRATION, BUREAU OF HEALTH PROFESSIONS SCHOLARSHIPS FOR DISADVANTAGED STUDENTS
• *See page 221*

VIRGINIA DEPARTMENT OF HEALTH, OFFICE OF MINORITY HEALTH AND PUBLIC HEALTH POLICY

http://www.vdh.virginia.gov/

MARY MARSHALL PRACTICAL NURSING SCHOLARSHIPS

Award for practical nursing students who are Virginia residents. Must attend a nursing program in Virginia. Recipient must agree to work in Virginia after graduation. Minimum 3.0 GPA required. Scholarship value and the number of scholarships granted varies annually.

Academic Fields/Career Goals: Nursing.

Award: Scholarship for use in freshman, sophomore, junior, or senior years; not renewable. *Number:* 50–150. *Amount:* $150–$500.

Eligibility Requirements: Applicant must be age 18 and over; enrolled or expecting to enroll full- or part-time at a four-year institution or university; resident of Virginia and studying in Virginia. Applicant must have 3.0 GPA or higher. Available to U.S. citizens.

Application Requirements: Application, financial need analysis, references, transcript. *Deadline:* June 30.

Contact: Mrs. Aileen Harris, Healthcare Workforce Manager
Virginia Department of Health, Office of Minority Health and Public Health Policy
PO Box 2448, 109 Governor Street, Suite 1016-E
Richmond, VA 23218-2448
Phone: 804-864-7435
Fax: 804-864-7440
E-mail: aileen.harris@vdh.virginia.gov

MARY MARSHALL REGISTERED NURSE SCHOLARSHIPS

Award for registered nursing students who are Virginia residents. Must attend a nursing program in Virginia. Recipient must agree to work in Virginia after graduation. Minimum 3.0 GPA required. The amount of each scholarship award is dependent upon the amount of money appropriated by the Virginia General Assembly and the number of qualified applicants.

Academic Fields/Career Goals: Nursing.

Award: Scholarship for use in freshman, sophomore, junior, or senior years; not renewable. *Amount:* $2000.

Eligibility Requirements: Applicant must be enrolled or expecting to enroll full- or part-time at a four-year institution or university; resident of Virginia and studying in Virginia. Applicant must have 3.0 GPA or higher. Available to U.S. citizens.

Application Requirements: Application, financial need analysis, references, transcript. *Deadline:* June 30.

Contact: Mrs. Aileen Harris, Healthcare Workforce Manager
Virginia Department of Health, Office of Minority Health and Public Health Policy
PO Box 2448, 109 Governor Street, Suite 1016-E
Richmond, VA 23218-2448
Phone: 804-864-7435
Fax: 804-864-7440
E-mail: aileen.harris@vdh.virginia.gov

NURSE PRACTITIONERS/NURSE MIDWIFE PROGRAM SCHOLARSHIPS

One-time award for nurse practitioner/nurse midwife students who have been residents of Virginia for at least one year. Must attend a nursing program in Virginia. Recipient must agree to work in an under-served community in Virginia following graduation. The amount of each scholarship award is dependent upon the amount of funds appropriated by the Virginia General Assembly. Minimum 3.0 GPA required.

Academic Fields/Career Goals: Nursing.

Award: Scholarship for use in freshman, sophomore, junior, or senior years; not renewable. *Number:* 5. *Amount:* $5000.

Eligibility Requirements: Applicant must be enrolled or expecting to enroll full- or part-time at a four-year institution or university; resident of Virginia and studying in Virginia. Applicant must have 3.0 GPA or higher. Available to U.S. citizens.

Application Requirements: Application, essay, references, transcript. *Deadline:* July 31.

Contact: Mrs. Aileen Harris, Healthcare Workforce Manager
Virginia Department of Health, Office of Minority Health and Public Health Policy
PO Box 2448, 109 Governor Street, Suite 1016-E
Richmond, VA 23218-2448
Phone: 804-864-7435
Fax: 804-864-7440
E-mail: aileen.harris@vdh.virginia.gov

WEST VIRGINIA NURSES ASSOCIATION

http://www.wvnurses.org/

BERNICE L. VANCE SCHOLARSHIP

Scholarship for native West Virginian students enrolled in an accredited full-time or part-time nursing program.

Academic Fields/Career Goals: Nursing.

Award: Scholarship for use in freshman, sophomore, junior, senior, graduate, or postgraduate years; not renewable. *Number:* 2. *Amount:* varies.

Eligibility Requirements: Applicant must be enrolled or expecting to enroll full- or part-time at a four-year institution or university and resident of West Virginia. Available to U.S. citizens.

Application Requirements: Application, financial need analysis, references, transcript. *Deadline:* July 1.

Contact: Monique Fortson, Scholarship Committee
West Virginia Nurses Association
PO Box 1946
Charleston, WV 25327
Phone: 304-342-1169
Fax: 304-414-3369
E-mail: centraloffice@wvnurses.org

WISCONSIN LEAGUE FOR NURSING, INC.

http://www.wisconsinwln.org/

NURSING SCHOLARSHIP FOR HIGH SCHOOL SENIORS

One scholarship for a Wisconsin high school senior who will be pursuing a professional nursing career. The senior must have been accepted by a Wisconsin NLN accredited school of nursing, have financial need, demonstrate scholastic excellence and leadership potential. Contact the WLN office by mail to request an application.

Academic Fields/Career Goals: Nursing.

Award: Scholarship for use in freshman year; not renewable. *Number:* 1. *Amount:* $500.

Eligibility Requirements: Applicant must be high school student; planning to enroll or expecting to enroll full-time at a two-year or four-year institution or university; resident of Wisconsin and studying in Wisconsin. Available to U.S. citizens.

Application Requirements: Application, financial need analysis. *Deadline:* March 1.

Contact: Mary Ann Tanner, Administrative Secretary
Wisconsin League for Nursing, Inc.
2121 East Newport Avenue
Milwaukee, WI 53211-2952
Phone: 888-755-3329
E-mail: wln@wisconsinwln.org

WISCONSIN LEAGUE FOR NURSING, INC. SCHOLARSHIP

One-time award for Wisconsin residents who have completed half of an accredited Wisconsin school of nursing program. Financial need of student must be demonstrated. Scholarship applications are mailed by WLN office ONLY to Wisconsin nursing schools in January for distribution to students. Students interested in obtaining an application must contact their nursing school and submit completed applications to their school. Applications sent directly to WLN office will be returned to applicant. For further information visit web site http://www.wisconsinwln.org/Scholarships.htm.

Academic Fields/Career Goals: Nursing.

Award: Scholarship for use in junior or senior years; not renewable. *Number:* 11–35. *Amount:* $500–$1000.

Eligibility Requirements: Applicant must be enrolled or expecting to enroll full-time at a two-year or four-year or technical institution or university; resident of Wisconsin and studying in Wisconsin. Available to U.S. citizens.

Application Requirements: Application, essay, financial need analysis. *Deadline:* March 1.

Contact: Mary Ann Tanner, Administrative Secretary
Wisconsin League for Nursing, Inc.
2121 East Newport Avenue
Milwaukee, WI 53211-2952
Phone: 888-755-3329
E-mail: wln@wisconsinwln.org

WOUND, OSTOMY AND CONTINENCE NURSES SOCIETY

http://www.wocn.org/

WOCN ACCREDITED NURSING EDUCATION PROGRAM SCHOLARSHIP

Scholarships are awarded to deserving individuals committed to working within the wound, ostomy and continence nursing specialty. Applicants must agree to support the WOCN Society philosophy and scope of practice. Number of scholarships and the dollar value varies annually. Deadlines: May 1 or November 1.

Academic Fields/Career Goals: Nursing.

Award: Scholarship for use in freshman, sophomore, junior, or senior years; not renewable. *Number:* varies. *Amount:* varies.

Eligibility Requirements: Applicant must be enrolled or expecting to enroll full-time at a two-year or four-year or technical institution or university. Available to U.S. and non-U.S. citizens.

Application Requirements: Application, references, acceptance letter, proof of current enrollment or certificate of completion from a WOCN accredited education program. *Deadline:* varies.

Contact: Scholarship Committee
Wound, Ostomy and Continence Nurses Society
15000 Commerce Parkway, Suite C
Mt. Laurel, NJ 08054
Phone: 888-224-9626
Fax: 856-439-0525

OCCUPATIONAL SAFETY AND HEALTH

AMERICAN SOCIETY OF SAFETY ENGINEERS (ASSE) FOUNDATION

http://www.asse.org/

AMERICA RESPONDS MEMORIAL SCHOLARSHIP

Scholarship of $1000 will be awarded to a student pursuing an undergraduate degree in occupational safety and health or a closely related field. Must have completed 60 semester hours and maintain at least a 3.0 GPA. Applicant must be a member of ASSE. Must be a U.S. citizen.

Academic Fields/Career Goals: Occupational Safety and Health.

Award: Scholarship for use in sophomore, junior, or senior years; not renewable. *Number:* 1. *Amount:* up to $1000.

Eligibility Requirements: Applicant must be enrolled or expecting to enroll full-time at a four-year institution or university. Applicant or parent of applicant must be member of American Society of Safety Engineers. Applicant must have 3.0 GPA or higher. Available to U.S. citizens.

Application Requirements: Application, essay, financial need analysis, references, transcript. *Deadline:* December 1.

Contact: Mary Goranson, Scholarship Coordinator
American Society of Safety Engineers (ASSE) Foundation
1800 East Oakton Street
Des Plaines, IL 60018
Phone: 847-768-3412
E-mail: mgoranson@asse.org

ASSE-EDWIN P. GRANBERRY JR. DISTINGUISHED SERVICE AWARD SCHOLARSHIP

Scholarships for students pursuing an undergraduate degree in occupational safety and health. Completion of at least 60 current semester hours and minimum GPA of 3.0 required. ASSE student membership is required.

Academic Fields/Career Goals: Occupational Safety and Health.

Award: Scholarship for use in sophomore, junior, or senior years; not renewable. *Number:* 1. *Amount:* up to $1000.

Eligibility Requirements: Applicant must be enrolled or expecting to enroll full-time at a four-year institution or university. Applicant or parent of applicant must be member of American Society of Safety Engineers. Applicant must have 3.0 GPA or higher. Available to U.S. citizens.

Application Requirements: Application, essay, references, transcript. *Deadline:* December 1.

Contact: Mary Goranson, Scholarship Coordinator
American Society of Safety Engineers (ASSE) Foundation
1800 East Oakton Street
Des Plaines, IL 60018
Phone: 847-768-3435
E-mail: mgoranson@asse.org

ASSE-GULF COAST PAST PRESIDENTS SCHOLARSHIP

Scholarship of $1000 will be awarded to a part- or full-time student pursuing an undergraduate degree in occupational safety and health or a closely related field. Must have completed 60 semester hours and maintain at least a 3.0 GPA. ASSE general or professional membership required if applicant is a part-time student. If applicant is a full-time student, must be student member of ASSE.

Academic Fields/Career Goals: Occupational Safety and Health.

Award: Scholarship for use in sophomore, junior, or senior years; not renewable. *Number:* 2. *Amount:* $1000.

Eligibility Requirements: Applicant must be enrolled or expecting to enroll full- or part-time at a four-year institution or university. Applicant or parent of applicant must be member of American Society of Safety Engineers. Applicant must have 3.0 GPA or higher. Available to U.S. citizens.

Application Requirements: Application, essay, financial need analysis, references, transcript. *Deadline:* December 1.

Contact: Mary Goranson, Scholarship Coordinator
American Society of Safety Engineers (ASSE) Foundation
1800 East Oakton Street
Des Plaines, IL 60018
Phone: 847-768-3412
E-mail: mgoranson@asse.org

ASSE-MARSH RISK CONSULTING SCHOLARSHIP

Scholarship for students pursuing an undergraduate degree in occupational safety. Completion of at least 60 credit hours and minimum GPA of 3.0 required. Must be a student member of ASSE.

Academic Fields/Career Goals: Occupational Safety and Health.

Award: Scholarship for use in sophomore, junior, or senior years; not renewable. *Number:* 1. *Amount:* up to $5000.

Eligibility Requirements: Applicant must be enrolled or expecting to enroll full-time at a four-year institution or university. Applicant or parent of applicant must be member of American Society of Safety Engineers. Applicant must have 3.0 GPA or higher. Available to U.S. and non-U.S. citizens.

Application Requirements: Application, essay, references, transcript. *Deadline:* December 1.

Contact: Mary Goranson, Scholarship Coordinator
American Society of Safety Engineers (ASSE) Foundation
1800 East Oakton Street
Des Plaines, IL 60018
Phone: 847-768-3435
E-mail: mgoranson@asse.org

ASSE-REGION IV/EDWIN P. GRANBERRY SCHOLARSHIP

Scholarship of $1000 will be awarded to a student pursuing an undergraduate degree in occupational safety and health or a closely related field. Must reside in the ASSE Region IV area (Louisiana, Alabama, Mississippi, Georgia, Florida, Puerto Rico or United States Virgin Islands). Natives of Region IV attending school elsewhere are also eligible. Must have completed 60 semester hours and maintain at least a 3.2 GPA. Eligible applicants will be members of American Society of Safety Engineers.

Academic Fields/Career Goals: Occupational Safety and Health.

Award: Scholarship for use in freshman, sophomore, junior, or senior years; not renewable. *Number:* 1. *Amount:* up to $1000.

Eligibility Requirements: Applicant must be enrolled or expecting to enroll full-time at a two-year or four-year institution or university and resident of Alabama, Florida, Georgia, Louisiana, Mississippi, or Puerto Rico. Applicant or parent of applicant must be member of American Society of Safety Engineers. Available to U.S. citizens.

Application Requirements: Application, essay, financial need analysis, references, transcript. *Deadline:* December 1.

Contact: Mary Goranson, Scholarship Coordinator
American Society of Safety Engineers (ASSE) Foundation
1800 East Oakton Street
Des Plaines, IL 60018
Phone: 847-768-3412

ASSE-UNITED PARCEL SERVICE SCHOLARSHIP

Scholarships for students pursuing a four-year BS or BA degree in occupational safety and health or related area. Completion of at least 60 current semester hours and a minimum 3.0 GPA is required. Must be a student member of ASSE.

Academic Fields/Career Goals: Occupational Safety and Health.

Award: Scholarship for use in sophomore, junior, or senior years; not renewable. *Number:* varies. *Amount:* $4000–$5300.

Eligibility Requirements: Applicant must be enrolled or expecting to enroll full-time at a four-year institution or university. Applicant or parent of applicant must be member of American Society of Safety Engineers. Applicant must have 3.0 GPA or higher. Available to U.S. and non-U.S. citizens.

Application Requirements: Application, essay, references, transcript. *Deadline:* December 1.

Contact: Mary Goranson, Scholarship Coordinator
American Society of Safety Engineers (ASSE) Foundation
1800 East Oakton Street
Des Plaines, IL 60018
Phone: 847-768-3412
E-mail: mgoranson@asse.org

BECHTEL FOUNDATION SCHOLARSHIP PROGRAM FOR SAFETY AND HEALTH

Scholarship of $5000 for students pursuing an undergraduate degree in occupational safety and health, with an emphasis on construction safety. ASSE student membership required. Must have a minimum GPA of 3.0. Must have completed at least 60 semester hours in the undergraduate study program.

Academic Fields/Career Goals: Occupational Safety and Health.

Award: Scholarship for use in sophomore, junior, or senior years; not renewable. *Number:* 1. *Amount:* $5000.

Eligibility Requirements: Applicant must be enrolled or expecting to enroll full-time at a four-year institution or university. Applicant or parent of applicant must be member of American Society of Safety Engineers. Applicant must have 3.0 GPA or higher. Available to U.S. and non-U.S. citizens.

Application Requirements: Application, essay, references, transcript. *Deadline:* December 1.

Contact: Mary Goranson, Scholarship Coordinator
American Society of Safety Engineers (ASSE) Foundation
1800 East Oakton Street
Des Plaines, IL 60018
Phone: 847-768-3435
Fax: Ext. 9220
E-mail: agabanski@asse.org

FORD MOTOR COMPANY SCHOLARSHIP-UNDERGRADUATE

Scholarship for women pursuing an undergraduate degree in occupational safety. Completion of at least 60 current semester hours and minimum GPA of 3.0 required. Applicant must be a member of ASSE.

Academic Fields/Career Goals: Occupational Safety and Health.

Award: Scholarship for use in sophomore, junior, or senior years; not renewable. *Number:* 2. *Amount:* up to $3450.

Eligibility Requirements: Applicant must be enrolled or expecting to enroll full-time at a four-year institution or university and female. Applicant or parent of applicant must be member of American Society of Safety Engineers. Applicant must have 3.0 GPA or higher. Available to U.S. and non-U.S. citizens.

Application Requirements: Application, essay, references, transcript. *Deadline:* December 1.

Contact: Mary Goranson, Scholarship Coordinator
American Society of Safety Engineers (ASSE) Foundation
1800 East Oakton Street
Des Plaines, IL 60018
Phone: 847-768-3435
E-mail: mgoranson@asse.org

GEORGIA CHAPTER OF ASSE ANNUAL SCHOLARSHIP

Scholarship of $1000 will be awarded to a student pursuing an undergraduate degree in occupational safety and health or a closely related field. Applicant must be a Georgia resident. Must have completed 60 semester hours and maintain at least a 3.0 GPA. Must be a member of American Society of Safety Engineers.

Academic Fields/Career Goals: Occupational Safety and Health.

Award: Scholarship for use in sophomore, junior, or senior years; not renewable. *Number:* 1. *Amount:* $1000.

Eligibility Requirements: Applicant must be enrolled or expecting to enroll full-time at a four-year institution or university; resident of Georgia and studying in Georgia. Applicant or parent of applicant must be member of American Society of Safety Engineers. Applicant must have 3.0 GPA or higher. Available to U.S. and non-U.S. citizens.

Application Requirements: Application, essay, financial need analysis, references, transcript. *Deadline:* December 1.

Contact: Mary Goranson, Scholarship Coordinator
American Society of Safety Engineers (ASSE) Foundation
1800 East Oakton Street
Des Plaines, IL 60018
Phone: 847-768-3412
E-mail: mgoranson@asse.org

GOLD COUNTRY SECTION AND REGION II SCHOLARSHIP

Scholarship of $1000 for students pursuing an undergraduate or graduate degree in occupational safety and health or a closely related field. Student residing within region II (MT, ID, WY, CO, UT, NV, AZ, NM) area will have priority on this award. ASSE student membership required. Must have completed at least 60 semester hours in the study program for undergraduate students. Minimum GPA is 3.0 for undergraduates and 3.5 for graduates.

Academic Fields/Career Goals: Occupational Safety and Health.

Award: Scholarship for use in sophomore, junior, senior, or graduate years; not renewable. *Number:* 1. *Amount:* up to $1000.

Eligibility Requirements: Applicant must be enrolled or expecting to enroll full-time at a four-year institution or university and resident of Arizona, Colorado, Idaho, Montana, Nevada, New Mexico, Utah, or Wyoming. Applicant or parent of applicant must be member of American Society of Safety Engineers. Available to U.S. and non-U.S. citizens.

Application Requirements: Application, financial need analysis, transcript. *Deadline:* December 1.

Contact: Mary Goranson, Scholarship Coordinator
American Society of Safety Engineers (ASSE) Foundation
1800 East Oakton Street
Des Plaines, IL 60018
Phone: 847-768-3412
E-mail: mgoranson@asse.org

HAROLD F. POLSTON SCHOLARSHIP

Scholarship of $2000 for students pursuing undergraduate or graduate degree in occupational safety and health or a closely related field. Priority will be given to students that belong to the Middle Tennessee Chapter, attending Middle Tennessee State University in Murfreesboro, TN, Murray State University in Murray, KY and those that live in the Region VII. Must have a minimum GPA of 3.0 for undergraduate study and 3.5 for graduate study. Must be a student member of ASSE.

Academic Fields/Career Goals: Occupational Safety and Health.

Award: Scholarship for use in sophomore, junior, senior, or graduate years; not renewable. *Number:* 1. *Amount:* $2000.

Eligibility Requirements: Applicant must be enrolled or expecting to enroll full-time at a four-year institution or university. Applicant or parent of applicant must be member of American Society of Safety Engineers. Available to U.S. and non-U.S. citizens.

Application Requirements: Application, essay, financial need analysis, references, transcript. *Deadline:* December 1.

Contact: Mary Goranson, Scholarship Coordinator
American Society of Safety Engineers (ASSE) Foundation
1800 East Oakton Street
Des Plaines, IL 60018
Phone: 847-768-3412
E-mail: mgoranson@asse.org

HARRY TABACK 9/11 MEMORIAL SCHOLARSHIP

Scholarship for students pursuing an undergraduate or graduate degree in occupational safety and health or a closely related field. Student must be a natural born United States citizen. Minimum GPA is 3.0 for undergraduates and 3.5 for graduates. Must be a student member of ASSE.

Academic Fields/Career Goals: Occupational Safety and Health.

Award: Scholarship for use in sophomore, junior, senior, or graduate years; not renewable. *Number:* 1. *Amount:* $1000.

Eligibility Requirements: Applicant must be enrolled or expecting to enroll full-time at a four-year institution or university. Applicant or parent of applicant must be member of American Society of Safety Engineers. Available to U.S. citizens.

Application Requirements: Application, financial need analysis, references, transcript. *Deadline:* December 1.

Contact: Mary Goranson, Scholarship Coordinator
American Society of Safety Engineers (ASSE) Foundation
1800 East Oakton Street
Des Plaines, IL 60018
Phone: 847-768-3412
E-mail: mgoranson@asse.org

LIBERTY MUTUAL SCHOLARSHIP

Scholarship of $3000 for students pursuing an undergraduate degree in occupational safety and health or a closely related field. ASSE student membership required. Minimum 3.0 GPA required. Must have completed 60 semester hours in the study program.

Academic Fields/Career Goals: Occupational Safety and Health.

Award: Scholarship for use in sophomore, junior, or senior years; not renewable. *Number:* 1. *Amount:* up to $3000.

Eligibility Requirements: Applicant must be enrolled or expecting to enroll full-time at a four-year institution or university. Applicant or parent of applicant must be member of American Society of Safety Engineers. Applicant must have 3.0 GPA or higher. Available to U.S. and non-U.S. citizens.

Application Requirements: Application, financial need analysis, transcript. *Deadline:* December 1.

Contact: Mary Goranson, Scholarship Coordinator
American Society of Safety Engineers (ASSE) Foundation
1800 East Oakton Street
Des Plaines, IL 60018
Phone: 847-768-3412
E-mail: mgoranson@asse.org

NORTHEASTERN ILLINOIS CHAPTER SCHOLARSHIP

Scholarship of $2500 for students pursuing an undergraduate or graduate degree in occupational safety and health or a closely related field. Students attending school in the Northeastern Illinois region, including Illinois and Wisconsin have priority on this award. ASSE student membership required. Undergraduate students must have completed at least 60 semester hours. Minimum GPA is 3.0 for undergraduates and 3.5 for graduates.

Academic Fields/Career Goals: Occupational Safety and Health.

Award: Scholarship for use in sophomore, junior, senior, graduate, or postgraduate years; not renewable. *Number:* 1. *Amount:* up to $2500.

Eligibility Requirements: Applicant must be enrolled or expecting to enroll full-time at a four-year institution or university and resident of Illinois or Wisconsin. Applicant or parent of applicant must be member of American Society of Safety Engineers. Available to U.S. citizens.

Application Requirements: Application, financial need analysis, transcript. *Deadline:* December 1.

Contact: Mary Goranson, Scholarship Coordinator
American Society of Safety Engineers (ASSE) Foundation
1800 East Oakton Street
Des Plaines, IL 60018
Phone: 847-768-3412
E-mail: mgoranson@asse.org

SCOTT DOMINGUEZ-CRATERS OF THE MOON SCHOLARSHIP

Scholarship for part-or full-time students pursuing an undergraduate or graduate degree in occupational safety and health or a closely related field. Students residing within the Craters of the Moon Chapter, Idaho, and Region II (MT, ID, WY, CO, UT, NV, AZ, NM) will have priority. ASSE student membership required for full-time student. ASSE general or professional membership required for part-time students. Minimum GPA is 3.0 for undergraduates and 3.5 for graduates.

Academic Fields/Career Goals: Occupational Safety and Health.

Award: Scholarship for use in sophomore, junior, senior, or graduate years; not renewable. *Number:* 1. *Amount:* up to $1000.

Eligibility Requirements: Applicant must be enrolled or expecting to enroll full- or part-time at a four-year institution or university and resident of Arizona, Colorado, Idaho, Montana, Nevada, New Mexico, Utah, or Wyoming. Applicant or parent of applicant must be member of American Society of Safety Engineers. Available to U.S. citizens.

Application Requirements: Application, financial need analysis, transcript. *Deadline:* December 1.

Contact: Mary Goranson, Scholarship Coordinator
American Society of Safety Engineers (ASSE) Foundation
1800 East Oakton Street
Des Plaines, IL 60018
Phone: 847-768-3412
E-mail: mgoranson@asse.org

UNITED PARCEL SERVICE DIVERSITY SCHOLARSHIP PROGRAM

Scholarship for students pursuing an undergraduate degree in occupational safety and health or a closely related field. Student must be of a minority ethnic or racial group and must be a United States citizen. Must be an ASSE member, and have a minimum 3.0 GPA.

Academic Fields/Career Goals: Occupational Safety and Health.

Award: Scholarship for use in sophomore, junior, or senior years; not renewable. *Number:* varies. *Amount:* $4000–$5250.

Eligibility Requirements: Applicant must be American Indian/Alaska Native, Asian/Pacific Islander, Black (non-Hispanic), or Hispanic and enrolled or expecting to enroll full-time at a four-year institution or university. Applicant or parent of applicant must be member of American Society of Safety Engineers. Applicant must have 3.0 GPA or higher. Available to U.S. citizens.

Application Requirements: Application, essay, financial need analysis, references, transcript. *Deadline:* December 1.

Contact: Mary Goranson, Scholarship Coordinator
American Society of Safety Engineers (ASSE) Foundation
1800 East Oakton Street
Des Plaines, IL 60018
Phone: 847-768-3412

CYNTHIA E. MORGAN SCHOLARSHIP FUND (CEMS)

http://www.cemsfund.com/

CYNTHIA E. MORGAN MEMORIAL SCHOLARSHIP FUND, INC.
• *See page 304*

NATIONAL SAFETY COUNCIL

http://www.cshema.org/

CAMPUS SAFETY, HEALTH AND ENVIRONMENTAL MANAGEMENT ASSOCIATION SCHOLARSHIP AWARD PROGRAM
• *See page 310*

STRAIGHTFORWARD MEDIA

http://www.straightforwardmedia.com/

STRAIGHTFORWARD MEDIA MEDICAL PROFESSIONS SCHOLARSHIP
• *See page 221*

TEXAS DEPARTMENT OF TRANSPORTATION

http://www.txdot.gov/

CONDITIONAL GRANT PROGRAM
• *See page 180*

OCEANOGRAPHY

AMERICAN GEOLOGICAL INSTITUTE

http://www.agiweb.org/

AMERICAN GEOLOGICAL INSTITUTE MINORITY SCHOLARSHIP
• *See page 222*

AMERICAN METEOROLOGICAL SOCIETY

http://www.ametsoc.org/

AMERICAN METEOROLOGICAL SOCIETY 75TH ANNIVERSARY SCHOLARSHIP
• *See page 366*

AMERICAN METEOROLOGICAL SOCIETY DR. PEDRO GRAU UNDERGRADUATE SCHOLARSHIP
• *See page 366*

AMERICAN METEOROLOGICAL SOCIETY/INDUSTRY MINORITY SCHOLARSHIPS
• *See page 366*

AMERICAN METEOROLOGICAL SOCIETY MARK J. SCHROEDER SCHOLARSHIP IN METEOROLOGY
• *See page 367*

AMERICAN METEOROLOGICAL SOCIETY RICHARD AND HELEN HAGEMEYER SCHOLARSHIP
• *See page 367*

AMERICAN METEOROLOGICAL SOCIETY WERNER A. BAUM UNDERGRADUATE SCHOLARSHIP
• *See page 367*

CARL W. KREITZBERG ENDOWED SCHOLARSHIP
• *See page 367*

ETHAN AND ALLAN MURPHY MEMORIAL SCHOLARSHIP
• *See page 367*

GEORGE S. BENTON SCHOLARSHIP
• *See page 367*

GUILLERMO SALAZAR RODRIGUES SCHOLARSHIP
• *See page 368*

JOHN R. HOPE SCHOLARSHIP
• *See page 368*

LOREN W. CROW SCHOLARSHIP
• *See page 368*

LOUISIANA OFFICE OF STUDENT FINANCIAL ASSISTANCE

http://www.osfa.la.gov/

ROCKEFELLER STATE WILDLIFE SCHOLARSHIP
• *See page 141*

MARINE TECHNOLOGY SOCIETY

http://www.mtsociety.org/

CHARLES H. BUSSMAN UNDERGRADUATE SCHOLARSHIP
• *See page 401*

JOHN C. BAJUS SCHOLARSHIP
• *See page 401*

MTS STUDENT SCHOLARSHIP
• *See page 401*

PAROS-DIGIQUARTZ SCHOLARSHIP
• *See page 402*

ROV SCHOLARSHIP
• *See page 402*

NASA'S VIRGINIA SPACE GRANT CONSORTIUM

http://www.vsgc.odu.edu/

TEACHER EDUCATION STEM SCHOLARSHIP PROGRAM
• *See page 96*

SEASPACE INC.

http://www.seaspace.org/

SEASPACE SCHOLARSHIP PROGRAM
• *See page 402*

WOMAN'S NATIONAL FARM AND GARDEN ASSOCIATION

http://www.wnfga.org/

WARREN, SANDERS, MCNAUGHTON OCEANOGRAPHIC SCHOLARSHIP

Upon receiving this award the student agrees to follow and complete the program of study or research as outlined in the application, and to communicate with the Scholarship Chair any changes in the program, as well as periodic progress reports. For further information visit web site http://www.wnfga.org/code/scholarships.htm.

Academic Fields/Career Goals: Oceanography.

Award: Scholarship for use in freshman, sophomore, junior, senior, graduate, or postgraduate years; not renewable. *Number:* 1. *Amount:* $1500.

Eligibility Requirements: Applicant must be enrolled or expecting to enroll full- or part-time at a four-year institution or university. Available to U.S. citizens.

Application Requirements: Resume, references, transcript. *Deadline:* May 25.

Contact: Mrs. EmmaJane Brice, Scholarship Coordinator
    Woman's National Farm and Garden Association
    Ninth Jenness Road
    PO Box 1175
    Midland, MI 48641-1175
    Phone: 248-620-9281
    E-mail: mgbertolini@aol.com

WOMAN'S SEAMEN'S FRIEND SOCIETY OF CONNECTICUT INC.

FINANCIAL SUPPORT FOR MARINE OR MARITIME STUDIES
• *See page 402*

ONCOLOGY

ARRL FOUNDATION INC.

http://www.arrl.org/

CAROLE J. STREETER, KB9JBR SCHOLARSHIP
• *See page 218*

ASRT EDUCATION AND RESEARCH FOUNDATION

http://www.asrtfoundation.org/

ELEKTA RADIATION THERAPY EDUCATORS SCHOLARSHIP
• *See page 231*

JERMAN-CAHOON STUDENT SCHOLARSHIP
• *See page 340*

PROFESSIONAL ADVANCEMENT SCHOLARSHIP
• *See page 340*

SIEMENS CLINICAL ADVANCEMENT SCHOLARSHIP
• *See page 340*

VARIAN RADIATION THERAPY STUDENT SCHOLARSHIP
• *See page 341*

CYNTHIA E. MORGAN SCHOLARSHIP FUND (CEMS)

http://www.cemsfund.com/

CYNTHIA E. MORGAN MEMORIAL SCHOLARSHIP FUND, INC.
• *See page 304*

ONS FOUNDATION

http://www.ons.org/

ONS FOUNDATION/ONCOLOGY NURSING CERTIFICATION CORPORATION BACHELOR'S SCHOLARSHIPS
• *See page 457*

ONS FOUNDATION/PEARL MOORE CAREER DEVELOPMENT AWARDS
• *See page 457*

STRAIGHTFORWARD MEDIA

http://www.straightforwardmedia.com/

STRAIGHTFORWARD MEDIA MEDICAL PROFESSIONS SCHOLARSHIP
• *See page 221*

OPTOMETRY

AMERICAN OPTOMETRIC FOUNDATION

http://www.aaopt.org/

VISTAKON AWARD OF EXCELLENCE IN CONTACT LENS PATIENT CARE

Open to any fourth-year student attending any school or college of optometry. Must have 3.0 GPA. Student's knowledge of subject matter and skillful, professional clinical contact lens patient care are considered. School makes selection and sends application to AOF.

Academic Fields/Career Goals: Optometry.

Award: Scholarship for use in senior or graduate years; not renewable. *Number:* 19. *Amount:* $1000.

Eligibility Requirements: Applicant must be enrolled or expecting to enroll full-time at a four-year institution or university. Applicant must have 3.0 GPA or higher. Available to U.S. and non-U.S. citizens.

Application Requirements: Application, references. *Deadline:* September 1.

Contact: Alisa Moore, Program Administrator
American Optometric Foundation
6110 Executive Boulevard, Suite 506
Rockville, MD 20852
Phone: 240-880-3084
Fax: 301-984-4737
E-mail: alisam@aaopt.org

ARRL FOUNDATION INC.

http://www.arrl.org/

CAROLE J. STREETER, KB9JBR SCHOLARSHIP
• *See page 218*

STRAIGHTFORWARD MEDIA

http://www.straightforwardmedia.com/

STRAIGHTFORWARD MEDIA MEDICAL PROFESSIONS SCHOLARSHIP
• *See page 221*

OSTEOPATHY

ARRL FOUNDATION INC.

http://www.arrl.org/

CAROLE J. STREETER, KB9JBR SCHOLARSHIP
• *See page 218*

CYNTHIA E. MORGAN SCHOLARSHIP FUND (CEMS)

http://www.cemsfund.com/

CYNTHIA E. MORGAN MEMORIAL SCHOLARSHIP FUND, INC.
• *See page 304*

MAINE OSTEOPATHIC ASSOCIATION MEMORIAL SCHOLARSHIP/MAINE OSTEOPATHIC ASSOCIATION

http://www.mainedo.org/

BEALE FAMILY MEMORIAL SCHOLARSHIP

• *See page 345*

MAINE OSTEOPATHIC ASSOCIATION MEMORIAL SCHOLARSHIP

• *See page 345*

MAINE OSTEOPATHIC ASSOCIATION SCHOLARSHIP

• *See page 345*

NATIONAL ARAB AMERICAN MEDICAL ASSOCIATION

http://www.naama.com/

FOUNDATION SCHOLARSHIP

• *See page 220*

STRAIGHTFORWARD MEDIA

http://www.straightforwardmedia.com/

STRAIGHTFORWARD MEDIA MEDICAL PROFESSIONS SCHOLARSHIP

• *See page 221*

PAPER AND PULP ENGINEERING

AMERICAN CHEMICAL SOCIETY

http://www.acs.org/

AMERICAN CHEMICAL SOCIETY SCHOLARS PROGRAM

• *See page 160*

INTERNATIONAL SOCIETY OF AUTOMATION (ISA)

http://www.isa.org/

INTERNATIONAL SOCIETY OF AUTOMATION EDUCATION FOUNDATION SCHOLARSHIPS

• *See page 125*

STRAIGHTFORWARD MEDIA

http://www.straightforwardmedia.com/

STRAIGHTFORWARD MEDIA ENGINEERING SCHOLARSHIP

• *See page 170*

TECHNICAL ASSOCIATION OF THE PULP & PAPER INDUSTRY (TAPPI)

http://www.tappi.org/

COATING AND GRAPHIC ARTS DIVISION SCHOLARSHIP

• *See page 333*

CORRUGATED PACKAGING DIVISION SCHOLARSHIPS

• *See page 273*

ENGINEERING DIVISION SCHOLARSHIP

Up to two $1500 scholarships offered. One may be awarded to a student who will be in his or her junior year, and the other will be offered to a student who will be in his or her senior year at the beginning of the next academic year. Information can be found at http://www.tappi.org/s_tappi/ sec.asp?CID=6101&DID=546695.

Academic Fields/Career Goals: Paper and Pulp Engineering.

Award: Scholarship for use in junior or senior years; not renewable. *Number:* 1–2. *Amount:* up to $1500.

Eligibility Requirements: Applicant must be enrolled or expecting to enroll full-time at a four-year institution or university. Applicant must have 3.0 GPA or higher. Available to U.S. and non-U.S. citizens.

Application Requirements: Application, references, transcript. *Deadline:* February 15.

Contact: Mr. Charles Bohanan, Director of Standards and Awards
Technical Association of the Pulp & Paper Industry (TAPPI)
15 Technology Parkway South
Norcross, GA 30092
Phone: 770-209-7276
Fax: 770-446-6947
E-mail: standards@tappi.org

ENVIRONMENTAL WORKING GROUP SCHOLARSHIP

• *See page 311*

NONWOVENS DIVISION SCHOLARSHIP

• *See page 301*

PAPER AND BOARD DIVISION SCHOLARSHIPS

• *See page 301*

PLACE DIVISION RALPH A. KLUCKEN SCHOLARSHIP AWARD

Award to high school seniors or college undergraduate or graduate students attending college full time. Part-time students working full time and attending night school are eligible to apply. Information can be found at http://www.tappi.org/s_tappi/sec.asp?CID=6101&DID=546695. Scholarship given in even-numbered years only.

Academic Fields/Career Goals: Paper and Pulp Engineering.

Award: Scholarship for use in freshman, sophomore, junior, senior, or graduate years; not renewable. *Number:* 1. *Amount:* $1000.

Eligibility Requirements: Applicant must be enrolled or expecting to enroll full- or part-time at a four-year institution or university. Available to U.S. and non-U.S. citizens.

Application Requirements: Application, references, transcript. *Deadline:* February 15.

Contact: Mr. Charles Bohanan, Director of Standards and Awards
Technical Association of the Pulp & Paper Industry (TAPPI)
15 Technology Parkway, South
Norcross, GA 30092
Phone: 770-209-7276
Fax: 770-446-6947
E-mail: standards@tappi.org

WILLIAM L. CULLISON SCHOLARSHIP

• *See page 431*

UNITED NEGRO COLLEGE FUND

http://www.uncf.org/

ALFRED CHISHOLM/BASF MEMORIAL SCHOLARSHIP FUND
• *See page 72*

PEACE AND CONFLICT STUDIES

ASSOCIATION OF FORMER INTELLIGENCE OFFICERS

http://www.afio.com/13_scholarships.htm

CIA UNDERGRADUATE SCHOLARSHIPS
• *See page 89*

EARTH ISLAND INSTITUTE

http://www.earthisland.org/

BROWER YOUTH AWARDS
• *See page 308*

UNITED STATES INSTITUTE OF PEACE

http://www.usip.org/

NATIONAL PEACE ESSAY CONTEST
• *See page 373*

PERFORMING ARTS

AMERICAN LEGION DEPARTMENT OF KANSAS

http://www.ksamlegion.org/

MUSIC COMMITTEE SCHOLARSHIP
• *See page 420*

THE CHOPIN FOUNDATION OF THE UNITED STATES

http://www.chopin.org/

SCHOLARSHIP PROGRAM FOR YOUNG AMERICAN PIANISTS
• *See page 421*

CIRI FOUNDATION (TCF)

http://www.thecirifoundation.org/

CIRI FOUNDATION SUSIE QIMMIQSAK BEVINS ENDOWMENT SCHOLARSHIP FUND
• *See page 110*

CONGRESSIONAL BLACK CAUCUS FOUNDATION, INC.

http://www.cbcfinc.org/

CONGRESSIONAL BLACK CAUCUS SPOUSES HEINEKEN USA PERFORMING ARTS SCHOLARSHIP

Award for minority students pursuing a career in the performing arts. Must be a full-time student enrolled in a performing arts program. Minimum 2.5 GPA required. Applicants must submit a video performance.

Academic Fields/Career Goals: Performing Arts.

Award: Scholarship for use in freshman, sophomore, junior, or senior years; not renewable. *Number:* 10–20. *Amount:* $3000.

Eligibility Requirements: Applicant must be enrolled or expecting to enroll full-time at a two-year or four-year or technical institution or university. Applicant must have 2.5 GPA or higher. Available to U.S. citizens.

Application Requirements: Application, essay, financial need analysis, photo, references, transcript, visual recording of performance. *Deadline:* April 29.

Contact: Ms. Janet J. Carter, Scholarships Coordinator
Congressional Black Caucus Foundation, Inc.
1720 Massachusetts Avenue, NW
Washington, DC 20036
Phone: 202-263-2800
Fax: 202-263-0845
E-mail: scholarships@cbcfinc.org

COSTUME SOCIETY OF AMERICA

http://www.costumesocietyamerica.com/

ADELE FILENE TRAVEL AWARD
• *See page 105*

STELLA BLUM RESEARCH GRANT
• *See page 105*

GENERAL FEDERATION OF WOMEN'S CLUBS OF MASSACHUSETTS

http://www.gfwcma.org/

DORCHESTER WOMEN'S CLUB MUSIC SCHOLARSHIP
• *See page 422*

GENERAL FEDERATION OF WOMEN'S CLUBS OF MASSACHUSETTS NICKEL FOR NOTES MUSIC SCHOLARSHIP
• *See page 422*

HOSTESS COMMITTEE SCHOLARSHIPS/ MISS AMERICA PAGEANT

http://www.missamerica.org/

EUGENIA VELLNER FISCHER AWARD FOR PERFORMING ARTS

Scholarship for Miss America contestants pursuing degree in performing arts. Award available to women who have competed within the Miss America system on the local, state, or national level from 1993 to the present, regardless of whether title was won. One or more scholarships are awarded annually, depending on qualifications of applicants. Applications must be received by June 30. Late or incomplete applications are not accepted.

Academic Fields/Career Goals: Performing Arts.

Award: Scholarship for use in freshman, sophomore, junior, senior, or graduate years; not renewable. *Number:* varies. *Amount:* varies.

Eligibility Requirements: Applicant must be enrolled or expecting to enroll full- or part-time at a four-year institution or university; female and must have an interest in beauty pageant. Available to U.S. citizens.

Application Requirements: Application, essay, financial need analysis, references, transcript. *Deadline:* June 30.

Contact: Doreen Lindell Gordon, Controller and Scholarship
Administrator
Hostess Committee Scholarships/Miss America Pageant
Two Miss America Way, Suite 1000
Atlantic City, NJ 08401
Phone: 609-345-7571 Ext. 27
Fax: 609-347-6079
E-mail: doreen@missamerica.org

ILLUMINATING ENGINEERING SOCIETY OF NORTH AMERICA

http://www.iesna.org/

ROBERT W. THUNEN MEMORIAL SCHOLARSHIPS
• *See page 101*

JACK J. ISGUR FOUNDATION

JACK J. ISGUR FOUNDATION SCHOLARSHIP
• *See page 112*

KE ALI'I PAUAHI FOUNDATION

http://www.pauahi.org/

EDWIN MAHIAI COPP BEAMER SCHOLARSHIP
• *See page 423*

KOSCIUSZKO FOUNDATION

http://www.kosciuszkofoundation.org/

KOSCIUSZKO FOUNDATION CHOPIN PIANO COMPETITION
• *See page 424*

NATIONAL OPERA ASSOCIATION

http://www.noa.org/

NOA VOCAL COMPETITION/LEGACY AWARD PROGRAM
• *See page 113*

OREGON STUDENT ASSISTANCE COMMISSION

http://www.GetCollegeFunds.org/

NICHOLAS DIERMANN MEMORIAL SCHOLARSHIP
• *See page 69*

POLISH ARTS CLUB OF BUFFALO SCHOLARSHIP FOUNDATION

http://www.pacb.bfn.org/

POLISH ARTS CLUB OF BUFFALO SCHOLARSHIP FOUNDATION TRUST
• *See page 114*

PRINCESS GRACE FOUNDATION-USA

http://www.pgfusa.org/

PRINCESS GRACE AWARDS IN DANCE, THEATER, AND FILM
• *See page 314*

SAN ANGELO SYMPHONY SOCIETY

http://www.sanangelosymphony.org/

SORANTIN YOUNG ARTIST AWARD
• *See page 426*

SERVICE EMPLOYEES INTERNATIONAL UNION (SEIU)

http://www.seiu.org/

SEIU MOE FONER SCHOLARSHIP PROGRAM FOR VISUAL AND PERFORMING ARTS
• *See page 115*

SIGMA ALPHA IOTA PHILANTHROPIES, INC.

http://www.sai-national.org/

SIGMA ALPHA IOTA MUSICIANS WITH SPECIAL NEEDS SCHOLARSHIP
• *See page 246*

SIGMA ALPHA IOTA SUMMER MUSIC SCHOLARSHIPS IN THE U.S. OR ABROAD
• *See page 427*

SIGMA ALPHA IOTA UNDERGRADUATE PERFORMANCE SCHOLARSHIPS
• *See page 427*

SIGMA ALPHA IOTA UNDERGRADUATE SCHOLARSHIPS
• *See page 247*

UNITED NEGRO COLLEGE FUND

http://www.uncf.org/

JOHN LENNON SCHOLARSHIP
• *See page 193*

OSSIE DAVIS ENDOWMENT SCHOLARSHIP
• *See page 116*

VSA

http://www.vsarts.org/

VSA INTERNATIONAL YOUNG SOLOISTS AWARD
Musical performance competition for persons with disabilities. Age limit for U.S residents is 25 or below and for international applicants is 30 or below. One-time award of $5000. Submit audio or video recording of performance. Contact VSA for information and application materials.

Academic Fields/Career Goals: Performing Arts.

Award: Scholarship for use in freshman, sophomore, junior, or senior years; not renewable. *Number:* 4. *Amount:* $5000.

Eligibility Requirements: Applicant must be age 30 or under; enrolled or expecting to enroll full- or part-time at a four-year institution or university and must have an interest in music/singing. Applicant must be hearing impaired, learning disabled, physically disabled, or visually impaired. Available to U.S. citizens.

Application Requirements: Application, applicant must enter a contest, driver's license, audition recording. *Deadline:* November 15.

Contact: Michelle Hoffmann, Performing Arts Manager
VSA
818 Connecticut Avenue, NW, Suite 600
Washington, DC 20006
Phone: 800-933-8721
Fax: 202-429-0868
E-mail: info@vsarts.org

WAMSO-MINNESOTA ORCHESTRA VOLUNTEER ASSOCIATION

http://www.wamso.org/

YOUNG ARTIST COMPETITION

Scholarship of $500 to $5000 for graduates and undergraduates. Applicant should be Canadian/ U.S citizens.

Academic Fields/Career Goals: Performing Arts.

Award: Prize for use in freshman, sophomore, junior, senior, graduate, or postgraduate years; not renewable. *Number:* 8. *Amount:* $500–$5000.

Eligibility Requirements: Applicant must be age 15-26; enrolled or expecting to enroll full- or part-time at a two-year or four-year or technical institution or university; resident of Illinois, Indiana, Iowa, Kansas, Manitoba, Michigan, Minnesota, Missouri, Nebraska, North Dakota, Ontario, South Dakota, or Wisconsin and must have an interest in music. Available to U.S. and Canadian citizens.

Application Requirements: Application, applicant must enter a contest, taped performance of specific repertoire. *Fee:* $75. *Deadline:* varies.

Contact: Eloise Breikjern, Executive Director
WAMSO-Minnesota Orchestra Volunteer Association
1111 Nicollet Mall, Orchestra Hall
Minneapolis, MN 55403-2477
Phone: 612-371-5654
E-mail: wamso@mnorch.org

WOMEN BAND DIRECTORS INTERNATIONAL

http://www.womenbanddirectors.org/

CHARLOTTE PLUMMER OWEN MEMORIAL SCHOLARSHIP
• *See page 251*

MARTHA ANN STARK MEMORIAL SCHOLARSHIP
• *See page 251*

VOLKWEIN MEMORIAL SCHOLARSHIP
• *See page 251*

PHARMACY

ALBERTA HERITAGE SCHOLARSHIP FUND

http://www.alis.alberta.ca/

JASON LANG SCHOLARSHIP
• *See page 213*

NORTHERN ALBERTA DEVELOPMENT COUNCIL BURSARY FOR PHARMACY STUDENTS

Award of CAN$6000 per year for up to four years to increase the number of trained pharmacy professionals in Northern Alberta and to encourage students from Northern Alberta to obtain a postsecondary education. Must be a resident of Alberta, must be enrolled in a four-year pharmacy degree program (years one to four) leading to a BSc in pharmacy, and must plan to live and work in Northern Alberta upon completion of studies. For further information, visit web site http://alis.alberta.ca.

Academic Fields/Career Goals: Pharmacy.

Award: Scholarship for use in freshman, sophomore, junior, or senior years; not renewable. *Number:* 125.

Eligibility Requirements: Applicant must be enrolled or expecting to enroll full-time at a four-year institution or university; resident of Alberta and studying in Alberta. Available to Canadian citizens.

Application Requirements: Application, essay. *Deadline:* May 15.

Contact: Scholarship Committee
Alberta Heritage Scholarship Fund
9940 106th Street, Fourth Floor, Sterling Place
PO Box 28000, Station Main
Edmonton, AB T5J 4R4
Canada
Phone: 780-427-8640
E-mail: scholarships@gov.ab.ca

AMERICAN FOUNDATION FOR PHARMACEUTICAL EDUCATION

http://www.afpenet.org/

AFPE GATEWAY TO RESEARCH SCHOLARSHIP PROGRAM

Scholarship for baccalaureate degree science students at any college and professional degree pharmacy students to undertake a faculty-mentored research program. Student applicants must be nominated by a faculty member.

Academic Fields/Career Goals: Pharmacy.

Award: Scholarship for use in sophomore, junior, senior, or graduate years; not renewable. *Number:* 10–15. *Amount:* up to $5000.

Eligibility Requirements: Applicant must be enrolled or expecting to enroll full-time at a four-year institution or university. Available to U.S. and non-U.S. citizens.

Application Requirements: Application, essay, references, transcript, faculty sponsor's curriculum vitae. *Deadline:* January 26.

Contact: Asinia Crawford, Grants Manager
American Foundation for Pharmaceutical Education
One Church Street, Suite 202
Rockville, MD 20850
Phone: 301-738-2160
Fax: 301-738-2161
E-mail: asinia.crawford@afpenet.org

KAPPA EPSILON-NELLIE WAKEMAN-AFPE FIRST YEAR GRADUATE SCHOOL SCHOLARSHIP

Applicant must be in final year of a pharmacy college BS or PharmD program or have completed a pharmacy degree. At time of application, the Kappa Epsilon member must be in good financial standing with the Fraternity and planning to pursue a PhD, master's degree, or combined Residency/master's degree program at an accredited U.S. College or School of Pharmacy.

Academic Fields/Career Goals: Pharmacy.

Award: Scholarship for use in senior year; not renewable. *Number:* 1. *Amount:* $7500.

Eligibility Requirements: Applicant must be enrolled or expecting to enroll full-time at a four-year institution or university. Available to U.S. citizens.

Application Requirements: Application, resume, references, transcript, student statement of interest in graduate school. *Deadline:* February 1.

Contact: Ms. Nancy Stankiewicz, Executive Director, Kappa Epsilon
American Foundation for Pharmaceutical Education
7700 Shawnee Mission Parkway
Overland Park, KS 66202
Phone: 913-262-2749
Fax: 913-432-9040
E-mail: kefrat@aol.com

PHI LAMBDA SIGMA-GLAXOSMITHKLINE-AFPE FIRST YEAR GRADUATE SCHOOL SCHOLARSHIP

Applicant must be in final year of pharmacy college BS or PharmD program and be a member of Phi Lambda Sigma.

Academic Fields/Career Goals: Pharmacy.

Award: Scholarship for use in senior year; not renewable. *Number:* 1. *Amount:* $7500.

Eligibility Requirements: Applicant must be enrolled or expecting to enroll full-time at an institution or university. Available to U.S. citizens.

Application Requirements: Application, essay, resume, references, test scores, transcript, statement of interest in graduate school. *Deadline:* February 1.

Contact: Mary Euler, Executive Director, Phi Lambda Sigma
American Foundation for Pharmaceutical Education
5005 Rockhill Road
Kansas City, MO 64110
Phone: 816-235-1738
Fax: 816-235-5190
E-mail: eulerm@umkc.edu

CYNTHIA E. MORGAN SCHOLARSHIP FUND (CEMS)

http://www.cemsfund.com/

CYNTHIA E. MORGAN MEMORIAL SCHOLARSHIP FUND, INC.

• *See page 304*

GREATER KANAWHA VALLEY FOUNDATION

http://www.tgkvf.org/

NICHOLAS AND MARY AGNES TRIVILLIAN MEMORIAL SCHOLARSHIP FUND

• *See page 343*

INDIAN HEALTH SERVICES, UNITED STATES DEPARTMENT OF HEALTH AND HUMAN SERVICES

http://www.ihs.gov/

HEALTH PROFESSIONS PREPARATORY SCHOLARSHIP PROGRAM

• *See page 335*

INTERNATIONAL SOCIETY OF AUTOMATION (ISA)

http://www.isa.org/

INTERNATIONAL SOCIETY OF AUTOMATION EDUCATION FOUNDATION SCHOLARSHIPS

• *See page 125*

NATIONAL COMMUNITY PHARMACIST ASSOCIATION (NCPA) FOUNDATION

http://www.ncpanet.org/

NATIONAL COMMUNITY PHARMACIST ASSOCIATION FOUNDATION PRESIDENTIAL SCHOLARSHIP

One-time award to student members of NCPA. Must be enrolled in an accredited U.S. school or college of pharmacy on a full-time basis. Award based on leadership qualities and accomplishments with a demonstrated interest in independent pharmacy, as well as involvement in extracurricular activities.

Academic Fields/Career Goals: Pharmacy.

Award: Scholarship for use in freshman, sophomore, junior, or senior years; not renewable. *Number:* up to 15. *Amount:* up to $2000.

Eligibility Requirements: Applicant must be enrolled or expecting to enroll full-time at a four-year institution or university and must have an interest in leadership. Applicant must have 2.5 GPA or higher. Available to U.S. citizens.

Application Requirements: Application, essay, resume, references, transcript. *Deadline:* March 15.

Contact: Jackie Lopez, Administrative Assistant
National Community Pharmacist Association (NCPA) Foundation
100 Daingerfield Road
Alexandria, VA 22314
Phone: 703-683-8200
Fax: 703-683-3619
E-mail: jackie.lopez@ncpanet.org

NEW YORK STATE EDUCATION DEPARTMENT

http://www.highered.nysed.gov/

REGENTS PROFESSIONAL OPPORTUNITY SCHOLARSHIP

• *See page 69*

STRAIGHTFORWARD MEDIA

http://www.straightforwardmedia.com/

STRAIGHTFORWARD MEDIA MEDICAL PROFESSIONS SCHOLARSHIP

• *See page 221*

STRAIGHTFORWARD MEDIA VOCATIONAL-TECHNICAL SCHOOL SCHOLARSHIP

• *See page 91*

UNITED NEGRO COLLEGE FUND

http://www.uncf.org/

CARDINAL HEALTH SCHOLARSHIP

• *See page 72*

CATHOLIC HEALTHCARE WEST CORPORATE SCHOLARS PROGRAM

• *See page 144*

CVS/PHARMACY SCHOLARSHIP

$2000 scholarship awarded to African American third and fourth year pharmacy majors from the Washington, D.C. area or Detroit, Michigan. Must have minimum 2.8 GPA.

Academic Fields/Career Goals: Pharmacy.

Award: Scholarship for use in junior or senior years; not renewable. *Number:* varies. *Amount:* $2000.

Eligibility Requirements: Applicant must be Black (non-Hispanic); enrolled or expecting to enroll full-time at a four-year institution or university and resident of District of Columbia or Michigan. Available to U.S. citizens.

Application Requirements: Application, financial need analysis, FAFSA, Student Aid Report (SAR).

Contact: Director, Program Services
United Negro College Fund
8260 Willow Oaks Corporate Drive
PO Box 10444
Fairfax, VA 22031-8044
Phone: 800-331-2244
E-mail: rebecca.bennett@uncf.org

RAYMOND W. CANNON MEMORIAL SCHOLARSHIP PROGRAM

• *See page 394*

PHILOSOPHY

AMERICAN SCHOOL OF CLASSICAL STUDIES AT ATHENS

http://www.ascsa.edu.gr/

ASCSA SUMMER SESSIONS SCHOLARSHIPS
• *See page 92*

DAVIDSON INSTITUTE FOR TALENT DEVELOPMENT

http://www.davidsongifted.org/

DAVIDSON FELLOWS SCHOLARSHIP PROGRAM
• *See page 398*

STRAIGHTFORWARD MEDIA

http://www.straightforwardmedia.com/

STRAIGHTFORWARD MEDIA LIBERAL ARTS SCHOLARSHIP
• *See page 107*

PHOTOJOURNALISM/ PHOTOGRAPHY

AMERICAN LEGION PRESS CLUB OF NEW JERSEY

http://www.alpcnj.org/

AMERICAN LEGION PRESS CLUB OF NEW JERSEY AND POST 170 ARTHUR DEHARDT MEMORIAL SCHOLARSHIP
• *See page 182*

ASIAN AMERICAN JOURNALISTS ASSOCIATION

http://www.aaja.org/

ASIAN-AMERICAN JOURNALISTS ASSOCIATION SCHOLARSHIP
• *See page 183*

BAY AREA BLACK JOURNALISTS ASSOCIATION SCHOLARSHIP CONTEST

http://www.babja.org/

LUCI S. WILLIAMS HOUSTON MEMORIAL SCHOLARSHIP

Nonrenewable scholarship of $2500 to photojournalism students. Applicant must be enrolled in any college or university nationwide. Must be studying photojournalism (including print, television, and online).

Academic Fields/Career Goals: Photojournalism/Photography.

Award: Scholarship for use in freshman, sophomore, junior, senior, or graduate years; not renewable. *Number:* varies. *Amount:* $2500.

Eligibility Requirements: Applicant must be enrolled or expecting to enroll full- or part-time at a four-year institution or university. Available to U.S. citizens.

Application Requirements: Application, essay, resume, references, transcript, work samples. *Deadline:* October 2.

Contact: Scholarship Committee
Bay Area Black Journalists Association Scholarship Contest
1714 Franklin Street, Suite 100-260
Oakland, CA 94612
Phone: 510-986-9390
Fax: 510-382-1980
E-mail: info@babja.org

YOUNG JOURNALISTS SCHOLARSHIP
• *See page 375*

CCNMA: LATINO JOURNALISTS OF CALIFORNIA

http://www.ccnma.org/

CCNMA SCHOLARSHIPS
• *See page 376*

COLLEGE PHOTOGRAPHER OF THE YEAR

http://www.cpoy.org/

COLLEGE PHOTOGRAPHER OF THE YEAR COMPETITION

Awards undergraduate and graduate students for juried contest of individual photographs, picture stories and photographic essay and multimedia presentations. Two awards in the dollar value of $500 and $1000 are granted. Deadline varies.

Academic Fields/Career Goals: Photojournalism/Photography.

Award: Prize for use in freshman, sophomore, junior, senior, or graduate years; not renewable. *Number:* up to 2. *Amount:* $500–$1000.

Eligibility Requirements: Applicant must be enrolled or expecting to enroll full- or part-time at a four-year institution or university. Available to U.S. and non-U.S. citizens.

Application Requirements: Application, applicant must enter a contest, essay, photo, portfolio. *Deadline:* varies.

Contact: Rita Ann Reed, Program Director
College Photographer of the Year
University of Missouri, School of Journalism, 107 Lee Hills Hall
Columbia, MO 65211
Phone: 573-882-2198
Fax: 573-884-4999
E-mail: info@cpoy.org

CONNECTICUT CHAPTER OF SOCIETY OF PROFESSIONAL JOURNALISTS

http://www.ctspj.org/

CONNECTICUT SPJ BOB EDDY SCHOLARSHIP PROGRAM
• *See page 184*

DAYTON FOUNDATION

http://www.daytonfoundation.org/

LARRY FULLERTON PHOTOJOURNALISM SCHOLARSHIP

One-time scholarship for Ohio residents pursuing careers in photojournalism. Must have experience and submit examples of work. Award for use in sophomore, junior or senior year at an Ohio two- or four-year college or university. High school students are ineligible. Minimum 2.5 GPA required. Must be U.S. citizen.

Academic Fields/Career Goals: Photojournalism/Photography.

Award: Scholarship for use in sophomore, junior, or senior years; not renewable. *Number:* 1–2. *Amount:* $500–$2500.

Eligibility Requirements: Applicant must be enrolled or expecting to enroll full-time at a two-year or four-year institution or university; resident of Ohio; studying in Ohio and must have an interest in photography/

photogrammetry/filmmaking. Applicant must have 2.5 GPA or higher. Available to U.S. citizens.

Application Requirements: Application, financial need analysis, portfolio, transcript, slide portfolio. *Deadline:* January 31.

Contact: Elizabeth Horner, Scholarship Program Officer
Dayton Foundation
2300 Kettering Tower
Dayton, OH 45423
Phone: 937-222-9955
Fax: 937-222-0636
E-mail: ehorner@daytonfoundation.org

INTERNATIONAL FOODSERVICE EDITORIAL COUNCIL

http://www.ifeconline.com/

INTERNATIONAL FOODSERVICE EDITORIAL COUNCIL COMMUNICATIONS SCHOLARSHIP
• *See page 77*

JOURNALISM EDUCATION ASSOCIATION

http://www.jea.org/

NATIONAL HIGH SCHOOL JOURNALIST OF THE YEAR/ SISTER RITA JEANNE SCHOLARSHIPS
• *See page 186*

KE ALI'I PAUAHI FOUNDATION

http://www.pauahi.org/

BRUCE T. AND JACKIE MAHI ERICKSON GRANT
• *See page 112*

NATIONAL ASSOCIATION OF BLACK JOURNALISTS

http://www.nabj.org/

NATIONAL ASSOCIATION OF BLACK JOURNALISTS NON-SUSTAINING SCHOLARSHIP AWARDS
• *See page 380*

VISUAL TASK FORCE SCHOLARSHIP

Scholarship for students attending an accredited four-year college or university and majoring in visual journalism. Minimum 3.0 GPA required. Must be a member of NABJ. Scholarship value and the number of scholarships granted varies annually.

Academic Fields/Career Goals: Photojournalism/Photography.

Award: Scholarship for use in freshman, sophomore, junior, senior, or graduate years; not renewable. *Number:* varies. *Amount:* varies.

Eligibility Requirements: Applicant must be enrolled or expecting to enroll full-time at a four-year institution or university. Applicant must have 3.0 GPA or higher. Available to U.S. and non-U.S. citizens.

Application Requirements: Application, driver's license, essay, interview, references, transcript. *Deadline:* March 17.

Contact: Irving Washington, Manager
National Association of Black Journalists
8701-A Adelphi Road
Adelphi, MD 20783-1716
Phone: 301-445-7100
Fax: 301-445-7101
E-mail: iwashington@nabj.org

NATIONAL ASSOCIATION OF HISPANIC JOURNALISTS (NAHJ)

http://www.nahj.org/

NATIONAL ASSOCIATION OF HISPANIC JOURNALISTS SCHOLARSHIP
• *See page 188*

NEWHOUSE SCHOLARSHIP PROGRAM
• *See page 332*

NATIONAL PRESS PHOTOGRAPHERS FOUNDATION INC.

http://www.nppa.org/

BOB EAST SCHOLARSHIP

Award of $2000 for applicant who is either an undergraduate in the first three and one-half years of college or is planning to pursue postgraduate work and offers indication of acceptance in such a program. Award is chosen primarily on portfolio quality.

Academic Fields/Career Goals: Photojournalism/Photography.

Award: Scholarship for use in freshman, sophomore, junior, senior, graduate, or postgraduate years; not renewable. *Number:* 1. *Amount:* $2000.

Eligibility Requirements: Applicant must be enrolled or expecting to enroll full-time at a four-year institution or university. Available to U.S. citizens.

Application Requirements: Application, applicant must enter a contest, essay, financial need analysis, portfolio, self-addressed stamped envelope, transcript. *Deadline:* March 1.

Contact: Chuck Fadely, Scholarship Committee
National Press Photographers Foundation Inc.
The Miami Herald, One Herald Plaza
Miami, FL 33132
Phone: 305-376-2015

NATIONAL PRESS PHOTOGRAPHERS FOUNDATION STILL PHOTOGRAPHER SCHOLARSHIP

Award of $2000 for students who have completed one year at a four-year college or university having photojournalism courses. Applicant must be pursuing a bachelor's degree and must have at least one-half year of undergraduate schooling remaining at the time of award.

Academic Fields/Career Goals: Photojournalism/Photography.

Award: Scholarship for use in sophomore, junior, or senior years; not renewable. *Number:* 1. *Amount:* $2000.

Eligibility Requirements: Applicant must be enrolled or expecting to enroll full-time at a four-year institution or university. Available to U.S. citizens.

Application Requirements: Application, applicant must enter a contest, financial need analysis, portfolio, self-addressed stamped envelope, transcript. *Deadline:* March 1.

Contact: Bill Sanders, Photo Editor
National Press Photographers Foundation Inc.
Asheville Citizen-Times, PO Box 2090
Asheville, NC 28802
E-mail: wsanders@citizen-times.com

NATIONAL PRESS PHOTOGRAPHERS FOUNDATION TELEVISION NEWS SCHOLARSHIP

Award of $1000 for student enrolled in a four-year college or university having courses in TV news photojournalism. Applicant must be pursuing a bachelor's degree and be in his/her junior or senior year at the time of award.

Academic Fields/Career Goals: Photojournalism/Photography; TV/ Radio Broadcasting.

Award: Scholarship for use in junior or senior years; not renewable. *Number:* 1. *Amount:* $1000.

Eligibility Requirements: Applicant must be enrolled or expecting to enroll full-time at a four-year institution or university. Available to U.S. citizens.

Application Requirements: Application, applicant must enter a contest, driver's license, essay, financial need analysis, portfolio, references, self-addressed stamped envelope, transcript. *Deadline:* March 1.

Contact: Ed Dooks, Scholarship Committee
National Press Photographers Foundation Inc.
Five Mohawk Drive
Lexington, MA 02421-6217
Phone: 781-861-6062
E-mail: dooks@verizon.net

REID BLACKBURN SCHOLARSHIP

Award of $2000 for a student who has completed one year of a photojournalism program at a four-year college or university in preparation for a bachelor's degree. Must have at least one-half year of undergraduate schooling remaining at time of award. The philosophy and goals statement is particularly important in this selection.

Academic Fields/Career Goals: Photojournalism/Photography.

Award: Scholarship for use in sophomore, junior, or senior years; not renewable. *Number:* 1. *Amount:* $2000.

Eligibility Requirements: Applicant must be enrolled or expecting to enroll full-time at a four-year institution or university. Available to U.S. citizens.

Application Requirements: Application, applicant must enter a contest, essay, financial need analysis, portfolio, self-addressed stamped envelope, transcript. *Deadline:* March 1.

Contact: Fay Blackburn, Manager
National Press Photographers Foundation Inc.
The Columbian, PO Box 180
Vancouver, WA 98666
Phone: 360-759-8027
E-mail: fay.blackburn@columbian.com

NEBRASKA PRESS ASSOCIATION

http://www.nebpress.com/

NEBRASKA PRESS ASSOCIATION FOUNDATION INC. SCHOLARSHIP

• *See page 382*

OUTDOOR WRITERS ASSOCIATION OF AMERICA

http://www.owaa.org/

OUTDOOR WRITERS ASSOCIATION OF AMERICA BODIE MCDOWELL SCHOLARSHIP AWARD

• *See page 189*

PALM BEACH ASSOCIATION OF BLACK JOURNALISTS

http://www.pbabj.org/

PALM BEACH ASSOCIATION OF BLACK JOURNALISTS SCHOLARSHIP

• *See page 384*

SAN FRANCISCO FOUNDATION

http://www.sff.org/

PHELAN AWARD IN PHOTOGRAPHY

Award presented in every odd-numbered year to recognize achievement in photography. Applicants must provide a copy of their birth certificate with their application.

Academic Fields/Career Goals: Photojournalism/Photography.

Award: Prize for use in freshman, sophomore, junior, senior, graduate, or postgraduate years; not renewable. *Number:* 3. *Amount:* $2500.

Eligibility Requirements: Applicant must be enrolled or expecting to enroll full- or part-time at a two-year or four-year institution or university. Available to U.S. citizens.

Application Requirements: Application, applicant must enter a contest, self-addressed stamped envelope. *Deadline:* May 4.

Contact: Art Awards Coordinator
San Francisco Foundation
225 Bush Street, Suite 500
San Francisco, CA 94104
Phone: 415-733-8500

STRAIGHTFORWARD MEDIA

http://www.straightforwardmedia.com/

STRAIGHTFORWARD MEDIA MEDIA & COMMUNICATIONS SCHOLARSHIP

• *See page 77*

TEXAS GRIDIRON CLUB INC.

http://www.spjfw.org/

TEXAS GRIDIRON CLUB SCHOLARSHIPS

• *See page 192*

UNITARIAN UNIVERSALIST ASSOCIATION

http://www.uua.org/

MARION BARR STANFIELD ART SCHOLARSHIP

• *See page 115*

PAULY D'ORLANDO MEMORIAL ART SCHOLARSHIP

• *See page 116*

UNITED METHODIST COMMUNICATIONS

http://www.umcom.org/

LEONARD M. PERRYMAN COMMUNICATIONS SCHOLARSHIP FOR ETHNIC MINORITY STUDENTS

• *See page 192*

VALLEY PRESS CLUB, SPRINGFIELD NEWSPAPERS

http://www.valleypressclub.com/

VALLEY PRESS CLUB SCHOLARSHIPS, THE REPUBLICAN SCHOLARSHIP, CHANNEL 22 SCHOLARSHIP

• *See page 194*

PHYSICAL SCIENCES

AIR & WASTE MANAGEMENT ASSOCIATION–COASTAL PLAINS CHAPTER

http://www.awmacoastalplains.org/

COASTAL PLAINS CHAPTER OF THE AIR AND WASTE MANAGEMENT ASSOCIATION ENVIRONMENTAL STEWARD SCHOLARSHIP

• *See page 306*

AIST FOUNDATION

http://www.aistfoundation.org/

ASSOCIATION FOR IRON AND STEEL TECHNOLOGY OHIO VALLEY CHAPTER SCHOLARSHIP
• *See page 137*

AMERICAN FOUNDATION FOR THE BLIND

http://www.afb.org/

PAUL W. RUCKES SCHOLARSHIP
• *See page 195*

AMERICAN INDIAN SCIENCE AND ENGINEERING SOCIETY

http://www.aises.org/

A.T. ANDERSON MEMORIAL SCHOLARSHIP PROGRAM
• *See page 93*

BURLINGTON NORTHERN SANTA FE FOUNDATION SCHOLARSHIP
• *See page 93*

AMERICAN INSTITUTE OF AERONAUTICS AND ASTRONAUTICS

http://www.aiaa.org/

AIAA FOUNDATION UNDERGRADUATE SCHOLARSHIP
• *See page 93*

AMERICAN LEGION DEPARTMENT OF MARYLAND

http://www.mdlegion.org/

AMERICAN LEGION DEPARTMENT OF MARYLAND MATH-SCIENCE SCHOLARSHIP
• *See page 408*

AMERICAN PHYSICAL SOCIETY

http://www.aps.org/

AMERICAN PHYSICAL SOCIETY SCHOLARSHIP FOR MINORITY UNDERGRADUATE PHYSICS MAJORS

One-time renewable award for high school seniors, college freshmen and sophomores planning to major in physics. Must be African-American, Hispanic, or Native American. Must be a U.S. citizen or a legal resident. For legal residents, a copy of alien registration card is required.

Academic Fields/Career Goals: Physical Sciences.

Award: Scholarship for use in freshman or sophomore years; not renewable. *Number:* 25–30. *Amount:* $2000–$3000.

Eligibility Requirements: Applicant must be American Indian/Alaska Native, Black (non-Hispanic), or Hispanic and enrolled or expecting to enroll full-time at a four-year institution or university. Available to U.S. citizens.

Application Requirements: Application, essay, references, test scores, transcript, copy of alien registration card, if applicable. *Deadline:* February 4.

Contact: Arlene Modeste Knowles, Scholarship Administrator
American Physical Society
One Physics Ellipse
College Park, MD 20740
Phone: 301-209-3232
E-mail: knowles@aps.org

AMERICAN SOCIETY FOR ENGINEERING EDUCATION

http://www.asee.org/

SCIENCE, MATHEMATICS, AND RESEARCH FOR TRANSFORMATION DEFENSE SCHOLARSHIP FOR SERVICE PROGRAM
• *See page 93*

AMERICAN SOCIETY OF NAVAL ENGINEERS

http://www.navalengineers.org/

AMERICAN SOCIETY OF NAVAL ENGINEERS SCHOLARSHIP
• *See page 93*

ARIZONA PROFESSIONAL CHAPTER OF AISES

http://www.azpcofaises.org/

ARIZONA PROFESSIONAL CHAPTER OF AISES SCHOLARSHIP
• *See page 279*

ARMED FORCES COMMUNICATIONS AND ELECTRONICS ASSOCIATION, EDUCATIONAL FOUNDATION

http://www.afcea.org/education/scholarships

AFCEA YOUNG ENTREPRENEUR SCHOLARSHIP
• *See page 163*

ARMED FORCES COMMUNICATIONS AND ELECTRONICS ASSOCIATION GENERAL EMMETT PAIGE SCHOLARSHIP
• *See page 122*

ARMED FORCES COMMUNICATIONS AND ELECTRONICS ASSOCIATION GENERAL JOHN A. WICKHAM SCHOLARSHIP
• *See page 164*

ARMED FORCES COMMUNICATIONS AND ELECTRONICS ASSOCIATION ROTC SCHOLARSHIP PROGRAM
• *See page 122*

DISABLED WAR VETERANS SCHOLARSHIP
• *See page 122*

LTG DOUGLAS D. BUCHHOLZ MEMORIAL SCHOLARSHIP
• *See page 122*

WILLIAM E. "BUCK" BRAGUNIER SCHOLARSHIP FOR OUTSTANDING LEADERSHIP
• *See page 123*

ARNOLD AND MABEL BECKMAN FOUNDATION

http://www.beckman-foundation.com/

BECKMAN SCHOLARS PROGRAM
• *See page 138*

ARRL FOUNDATION INC.

http://www.arrl.org/

WILLIAM R. GOLDFARB MEMORIAL SCHOLARSHIP
• See page 146

ASSOCIATION FOR WOMEN GEOSCIENTISTS, PUGET SOUND CHAPTER

http://www.awg.org/

PUGET SOUND CHAPTER SCHOLARSHIP
• See page 223

ASSOCIATION ON AMERICAN INDIAN AFFAIRS, INC.

http://www.indian-affairs.org/

ELIZABETH AND SHERMAN ASCHE MEMORIAL SCHOLARSHIP FUND
• See page 83

BARRY M. GOLDWATER SCHOLARSHIP AND EXCELLENCE IN EDUCATION FOUNDATION

http://www.act.org/goldwater

BARRY M. GOLDWATER SCHOLARSHIP AND EXCELLENCE IN EDUCATION PROGRAM
• See page 95

BRITISH COLUMBIA INNOVATION COUNCIL

http://www.bcic.ca/

BCIC YOUNG INNOVATOR SCHOLARSHIP COMPETITION (IDEA MASH UP)
• See page 95

PAUL AND HELEN TRUSSELL SCIENCE AND TECHNOLOGY SCHOLARSHIP
• See page 95

CATCHING THE DREAM

http://www.catchingthedream.org/

MATH, ENGINEERING, SCIENCE, BUSINESS, EDUCATION, COMPUTERS SCHOLARSHIPS
• See page 147

NATIVE AMERICAN LEADERSHIP IN EDUCATION (NALE)
• See page 147

CHEMICAL INSTITUTE OF CANADA

http://www.cheminst.ca/

ALFRED BADER SCHOLARSHIP
• See page 139

THE COMMUNITY FOUNDATION FOR GREATER ATLANTA, INC.

http://www.cfgreateratlanta.org/

JAMES M. AND VIRGINIA M. SMYTH SCHOLARSHIP
• See page 110

TECH HIGH SCHOOL ALUMNI ASSOCIATION/W.O. CHENEY MERIT SCHOLARSHIP FUND
• See page 282

THE DALLAS FOUNDATION

http://www.dallasfoundation.org/

WHITLEY PLACE SCHOLARSHIP
• See page 100

EAA AVIATION FOUNDATION, INC.

http://www.eaa.org/

PAYZER SCHOLARSHIP
• See page 124

FOUNDATION FOR SCIENCE AND DISABILITY

http://stemd.org/

GRANTS FOR DISABLED STUDENTS IN THE SCIENCES
• See page 95

GREATER KANAWHA VALLEY FOUNDATION

http://www.tgkvf.org/

MATH AND SCIENCE SCHOLARSHIP
• See page 140

INDEPENDENT LABORATORIES INSTITUTE SCHOLARSHIP ALLIANCE

http://www.acil.org/

INDEPENDENT LABORATORIES INSTITUTE SCHOLARSHIP ALLIANCE
• See page 141

LOS ANGELES COUNCIL OF BLACK PROFESSIONAL ENGINEERS

http://www.lablackengineers.org/

AL-BEN SCHOLARSHIP FOR ACADEMIC INCENTIVE
• See page 166

AL-BEN SCHOLARSHIP FOR PROFESSIONAL MERIT
• See page 166

AL-BEN SCHOLARSHIP FOR SCHOLASTIC ACHIEVEMENT
• See page 166

MINERALOGICAL SOCIETY OF AMERICA

http://www.minsocam.org/

MINERALOGICAL SOCIETY OF AMERICA-GRANT FOR STUDENT RESEARCH IN MINERALOGY AND PETROLOGY
• See page 225

NASA IDAHO SPACE GRANT CONSORTIUM

http://www.id.spacegrant.org/

NASA IDAHO SPACE GRANT CONSORTIUM SCHOLARSHIP PROGRAM
• See page 141

NASA/MARYLAND SPACE GRANT CONSORTIUM

http://www.mdspacegrant.org/

NASA MARYLAND SPACE GRANT CONSORTIUM UNDERGRADUATE SCHOLARSHIPS
• See page 127

NASA MINNESOTA SPACE GRANT CONSORTIUM

http://www.aem.umn.edu/mnsgc

MINNESOTA SPACE GRANT CONSORTIUM SCHOLARSHIP PROGRAM
• See page 127

NASA MISSISSIPPI SPACE GRANT CONSORTIUM

http://www.olemiss.edu/programs/nasa

MISSISSIPPI SPACE GRANT CONSORTIUM SCHOLARSHIP
• See page 127

NASA SOUTH CAROLINA SPACE GRANT CONSORTIUM

http://www.cofc.edu/~scsgrant

PRE-SERVICE TEACHER SCHOLARSHIP
• See page 129

NASA SOUTH DAKOTA SPACE GRANT CONSORTIUM

http://www.sdspacegrant.sdsmt.edu/

SOUTH DAKOTA SPACE GRANT CONSORTIUM UNDERGRADUATE AND GRADUATE STUDENT SCHOLARSHIPS
• See page 129

NASA'S VIRGINIA SPACE GRANT CONSORTIUM

http://www.vsgc.odu.edu/

TEACHER EDUCATION STEM SCHOLARSHIP PROGRAM
• See page 96

UNDERGRADUATE RESEARCH STEM SCHOLARSHIPS
• See page 96

NASA WEST VIRGINIA SPACE GRANT CONSORTIUM

http://www.nasa.wvu.edu/

WEST VIRGINIA SPACE GRANT CONSORTIUM UNDERGRADUATE FELLOWSHIP PROGRAM
• See page 129

NATIONAL ASSOCIATION FOR THE ADVANCEMENT OF COLORED PEOPLE

http://www.naacp.org/

HUBERTUS W.V. WELLEMS SCHOLARSHIP FOR MALE STUDENTS
• See page 167

NATIONAL ASSOCIATION OF WATER COMPANIES-NEW JERSEY CHAPTER

http://www.nawc.org/

NATIONAL ASSOCIATION OF WATER COMPANIES-NEW JERSEY CHAPTER SCHOLARSHIP
• See page 142

NATIONAL INVENTORS HALL OF FAME

http://www.invent.org/

COLLEGIATE INVENTORS COMPETITION FOR UNDERGRADUATE STUDENTS
• See page 96

COLLEGIATE INVENTORS COMPETITION-GRAND PRIZE
• See page 97

NATIONAL SCIENCE TEACHERS ASSOCIATION

http://www.nsta.org/

TOSHIBA/NSTA EXPLORAVISION AWARDS PROGRAM
• See page 198

NATIONAL SOCIETY OF BLACK PHYSICISTS

http://www.nsbp.org/

AMERICAN PHYSICAL SOCIETY CORPORATE-SPONSORED SCHOLARSHIP FOR MINORITY UNDERGRADUATE STUDENTS WHO MAJOR IN PHYSICS

Scholarship available for minority undergraduate students majoring in physics. Award of $2000 per year for new corporate scholars, and $3000 per year for renewal students. In addition, each physics department that hosts one or more APS minority undergraduate scholars and assigns a mentor for their students will receive a $500 award for programs to encourage minority students.

Academic Fields/Career Goals: Physical Sciences.

Award: Scholarship for use in freshman, sophomore, junior, or senior years; not renewable. *Number:* varies. *Amount:* $2000–$3000.

Eligibility Requirements: Applicant must be American Indian/Alaska Native, Asian/Pacific Islander, Black (non-Hispanic), or Hispanic and enrolled or expecting to enroll full- or part-time at a two-year or four-year institution or university. Available to U.S. citizens.

Application Requirements: Application, references, transcript. *Deadline:* December 1.

Contact: Dr. Kennedy Reed, Scholarship Chairman
National Society of Black Physicists
6704G Lee Highway
Arlington, VA 22205
Phone: 703-536-4207
Fax: 703-536-4203
E-mail: scholarships@nsbp.org

CHARLES S. BROWN SCHOLARSHIP IN PHYSICS

Scholarship providing and African-American student with financial assistance while enrolled in a physics degree program. Number of awards and dollar value varies.

Academic Fields/Career Goals: Physical Sciences.

Award: Scholarship for use in freshman, sophomore, junior, senior, or graduate years; not renewable. *Number:* varies. *Amount:* varies.

Eligibility Requirements: Applicant must be Black (non-Hispanic) and enrolled or expecting to enroll full- or part-time at a four-year institution or university. Available to U.S. and non-U.S. citizens.

Application Requirements: Application, financial need analysis, self-addressed stamped envelope. *Deadline:* January 12.

Contact: Scholarship Committee Chair
National Society of Black Physicists
6704G Lee Highway
Arlington, VA 22205
Phone: 703-536-4207
Fax: 703-536-4203
E-mail: scholarship@nsbp.org

ELMER S. IMES SCHOLARSHIP IN PHYSICS

Graduating high school seniors and undergraduate students already enrolled in college as physics majors may apply for the scholarship. U.S citizenship is required.

Academic Fields/Career Goals: Physical Sciences.

Award: Scholarship for use in freshman, sophomore, junior, or senior years; not renewable. *Number:* 1. *Amount:* $1000.

Eligibility Requirements: Applicant must be enrolled or expecting to enroll full-time at a two-year or four-year institution or university. Available to U.S. citizens.

Application Requirements: Application, driver's license, essay, resume, references, transcript. *Deadline:* January 12.

Contact: Scholarship Committee Chair
National Society of Black Physicists
6704G Lee Highway
Arlington, VA 22205
Phone: 703-536-4207
Fax: 703-536-4203
E-mail: scholarship@nsbp.org

HARVEY WASHINGTON BANKS SCHOLARSHIP IN ASTRONOMY

One-time award for an African American student pursuing an undergraduate degree in astronomy/physics.

Academic Fields/Career Goals: Physical Sciences.

Award: Scholarship for use in freshman, sophomore, junior, or senior years; not renewable. *Number:* 1. *Amount:* $1000.

Eligibility Requirements: Applicant must be Black (non-Hispanic) and enrolled or expecting to enroll full-time at a two-year or four-year institution or university. Available to U.S. citizens.

Application Requirements: Application, essay, references, transcript. *Deadline:* January 12.

Contact: Dr. Kennedy Reed, Scholarship Chairman
National Society of Black Physicists
6704G Lee Highway
Arlington, VA 22205
Phone: 703-536-4207
Fax: 703-536-4203
E-mail: scholarships@nsbp.org

MICHAEL P. ANDERSON SCHOLARSHIP IN SPACE SCIENCE

One-time award for an African American undergraduate student majoring in space science/physics.

Academic Fields/Career Goals: Physical Sciences.

Award: Scholarship for use in freshman, sophomore, junior, or senior years; not renewable. *Number:* 1. *Amount:* $1000.

Eligibility Requirements: Applicant must be Black (non-Hispanic) and enrolled or expecting to enroll full-time at a two-year or four-year institution or university. Available to U.S. citizens.

Application Requirements: Application, essay, references, transcript. *Deadline:* January 12.

Contact: Dr. Kennedy Reed, Scholarship Chairman
National Society of Black Physicists
6704G Lee Highway
Arlington, VA 22205
Phone: 703-536-4207
Fax: 703-536-4203
E-mail: scholarships@nsbp.org

NATIONAL SOCIETY OF BLACK PHYSICISTS AND LAWRENCE LIVERMORE NATIONAL LIBRARY UNDERGRADUATE SCHOLARSHIP

Scholarship for a graduating high school senior or undergraduate student enrolled in a physics major. Scholarship renewable up to four years if student maintains a 3.0 GPA and remains a physics major.

Academic Fields/Career Goals: Physical Sciences.

Award: Scholarship for use in freshman, sophomore, junior, or senior years; renewable. *Number:* 1. *Amount:* $5000.

Eligibility Requirements: Applicant must be Black (non-Hispanic) and enrolled or expecting to enroll full-time at a two-year or four-year institution or university. Applicant must have 3.0 GPA or higher. Available to U.S. citizens.

Application Requirements: Application, essay, references, transcript. *Deadline:* December 1.

Contact: Dr. Kennedy Reed, Scholarship Chairman
National Society of Black Physicists
6704G Lee Highway
Arlington, VA 22205
Phone: 703-536-4207
Fax: 703-536-4203
E-mail: scholarships@nsbp.org

RONALD E. MCNAIR SCHOLARSHIP IN SPACE AND OPTICAL PHYSICS

One-time award for African American undergraduate student majoring in physics. Must be U.S. citizen.

Academic Fields/Career Goals: Physical Sciences.

Award: Scholarship for use in freshman, sophomore, junior, or senior years; not renewable. *Number:* 1. *Amount:* $1000.

Eligibility Requirements: Applicant must be Black (non-Hispanic) and enrolled or expecting to enroll full-time at a two-year or four-year institution or university. Available to U.S. citizens.

Application Requirements: Application, essay, references, transcript. *Deadline:* January 12.

Contact: Dr. Kennedy Reed, Scholarship Chairman
National Society of Black Physicists
6704G Lee Highway
Arlington, VA 22205
Phone: 703-536-4207
Fax: 703-536-4203
E-mail: scholarships@nsbp.org

WALTER SAMUEL MCAFEE SCHOLARSHIP IN SPACE PHYSICS

One-time scholarship for African American full-time undergraduate student majoring in physics. Must be U.S. citizen.

Academic Fields/Career Goals: Physical Sciences.

Award: Scholarship for use in freshman, sophomore, junior, or senior years; not renewable. *Number:* 1. *Amount:* $1000.

Eligibility Requirements: Applicant must be Black (non-Hispanic) and enrolled or expecting to enroll full-time at a two-year or four-year institution or university. Available to U.S. citizens.

Application Requirements: Application, essay, references, transcript. *Deadline:* January 12.

Contact: Dr. Kennedy Reed, Scholarship Chairman
National Society of Black Physicists
6704G Lee Highway
Arlington, VA 22205
Phone: 703-536-4207
Fax: 703-536-4203
E-mail: scholarships@nsbp.org

WILLIE HOBBS MOORE, HARRY L. MORRISON, AND ARTHUR B.C. WALKER PHYSICS SCHOLARSHIPS

Scholarships are intended for African American undergraduate physics majors. Applicants should be either sophomores or juniors. Award for use in junior or senior year of study.

Academic Fields/Career Goals: Physical Sciences.

Award: Scholarship for use in sophomore, junior, or senior years; not renewable. *Number:* 3. *Amount:* $1000.

Eligibility Requirements: Applicant must be Black (non-Hispanic) and enrolled or expecting to enroll full-time at a two-year or four-year institution or university. Available to U.S. citizens.

Application Requirements: Application, essay, references, transcript. *Deadline:* January 12.

Contact: Dr. Kennedy Reed, Scholarship Chairman
National Society of Black Physicists
6704G Lee Highway
Arlington, VA 22205
Phone: 703-536-4207
Fax: 703-536-4203
E-mail: scholarships@nsbp.org

NEVADA NASA SPACE GRANT CONSORTIUM

http://www.nvspacegrant.org/

NATIONAL SPACE GRANT COLLEGE AND FELLOWSHIP PROGRAM
• *See page 97*

NEW MEXICO COMMISSION ON HIGHER EDUCATION

http://www.hed.state.nm.us/

MINORITY DOCTORAL ASSISTANCE LOAN-FOR-SERVICE PROGRAM
• *See page 168*

NORTH CAROLINA STATE EDUCATION ASSISTANCE AUTHORITY

http://www.ncseaa.edu/

NORTH CAROLINA STUDENT LOAN PROGRAM FOR HEALTH, SCIENCE, AND MATHEMATICS
• *See page 221*

PENNSYLVANIA HIGHER EDUCATION ASSISTANCE AGENCY

http://www.pheaa.org/

NEW ECONOMY TECHNOLOGY AND SCITECH SCHOLARSHIPS
• *See page 270*

ROBERT H. MOLLOHAN FAMILY CHARITABLE FOUNDATION, INC.

http://www.mollohanfoundation.org/

HIGH TECHNOLOGY SCHOLARS PROGRAM
• *See page 143*

SAN DIEGO FOUNDATION

http://www.sdfoundation.org/

BIOCOM SCHOLARSHIP
• *See page 143*

SIGMA XI, THE SCIENTIFIC RESEARCH SOCIETY

http://www.sigmaxi.org/

SIGMA XI GRANTS-IN-AID OF RESEARCH
• *See page 87*

SOCIETY FOR IMAGING SCIENCE AND TECHNOLOGY

http://www.imaging.org/

RAYMOND DAVIS SCHOLARSHIP
• *See page 292*

SOCIETY OF HISPANIC PROFESSIONAL ENGINEERS FOUNDATION

http://www.henaac.org/

SOCIETY OF HISPANIC PROFESSIONAL ENGINEERS FOUNDATION
• *See page 169*

SOCIETY OF PHYSICS STUDENTS

http://www.spsnational.org/

SOCIETY OF PHYSICS STUDENTS LEADERSHIP SCHOLARSHIPS

Scholarships of $2000 to $5000 are awarded to members of Society of Physics Students (SPS) for undergraduate study. The number of awards granted ranges from 17 to 22.

Academic Fields/Career Goals: Physical Sciences.

Award: Scholarship for use in sophomore, junior, or senior years; not renewable. *Number:* 17–22. *Amount:* $2000–$5000.

Eligibility Requirements: Applicant must be enrolled or expecting to enroll full-time at a two-year or four-year institution or university. Applicant or parent of applicant must be member of Society of Physics Students. Available to U.S. and non-U.S. citizens.

Application Requirements: Application, references, transcript. *Deadline:* February 15.

Contact: Scholarship Committee
Society of Physics Students
One Physics Ellipse
College Park, MD 20740
Phone: 301-209-3007
Fax: 301-209-0839
E-mail: sps@aip.org

SOCIETY OF PHYSICS STUDENTS OUTSTANDING STUDENT IN RESEARCH

Available to members of the Society of Physics Students. Winners will receive a $500 honorarium and a $500 award for their SPS Chapter. In addition, expenses for transportation, room, board, and registration for the ICPS will by paid by SPS.

Academic Fields/Career Goals: Physical Sciences.

Award: Prize for use in freshman, sophomore, junior, or senior years; not renewable. *Number:* 1–2. *Amount:* $500–$2500.

Eligibility Requirements: Applicant must be enrolled or expecting to enroll full-time at a two-year or four-year institution or university. Applicant or parent of applicant must be member of Society of Physics Students. Available to U.S. and non-U.S. citizens.

Application Requirements: Application, references, abstract. *Deadline:* April 15.

Contact: Secretary
Society of Physics Students
One Physics Ellipse
College Park, MD 20740
Phone: 301-209-3007
Fax: 301-209-0839
E-mail: sps@aip.org

SOCIETY OF PHYSICS STUDENTS PEGGY DIXON TWO-YEAR COLLEGE SCHOLARSHIP

Scholarship available to Society of Physics Students (SPS) members. Award based on performance both in physics and overall studies, and SPS participation. Must have completed at least one semester or quarter of the introductory physics sequence, and be currently registered in the appropriate subsequent physics courses.

Academic Fields/Career Goals: Physical Sciences.

Award: Scholarship for use in freshman or sophomore years; not renewable. *Number:* 1. *Amount:* $2000.

Eligibility Requirements: Applicant must be enrolled or expecting to enroll full-time at a two-year or four-year institution or university. Applicant or parent of applicant must be member of Society of Physics Students. Available to U.S. and non-U.S. citizens.

Application Requirements: Application, financial need analysis, transcript, letters from at least two faculty members. *Deadline:* February 15.

Contact: Sacha Purnell, Administrative Assistant
Society of Physics Students
One Physics Ellipse
College Park, MD 20740-3843
Phone: 301-209-3007
E-mail: sps@aip.org

SOCIETY OF WOMEN ENGINEERS

http://www.swe.org/

SWE CALIFORNIA GOLDEN GATE SECTION SCHOLARSHIPS
• *See page 199*

SWE CONNECTICUT SECTION JEAN R. BEERS SCHOLARSHIP
• *See page 199*

TKE EDUCATIONAL FOUNDATION

http://www.tke.org/

CARROL C. HALL MEMORIAL SCHOLARSHIP
• *See page 97*

UNITED NEGRO COLLEGE FUND

http://www.uncf.org/

ARLENE BENTON NOLAN AND JOHN NOLAN SCHOLARSHIP
• *See page 144*

CATHOLIC HEALTHCARE WEST CORPORATE SCHOLARS PROGRAM
• *See page 144*

DIBNER FUND SCHOLARSHIP
• *See page 434*

MEDTRONIC FOUNDATION SCHOLARSHIP
• *See page 145*

UNCF/MERCK SCIENCE INITIATIVE
• *See page 145*

UNIVERSITIES SPACE RESEARCH ASSOCIATION

http://www.usra.edu/

UNIVERSITIES SPACE RESEARCH ASSOCIATION SCHOLARSHIP PROGRAM
• *See page 97*

VERMONT SPACE GRANT CONSORTIUM

http://www.cems.uvm.edu/vsgc

VERMONT SPACE GRANT CONSORTIUM SCHOLARSHIP PROGRAM
• *See page 98*

WIFLE FOUNDATION, INC.

http://www.wifle.org/

WIFLE SCHOLARSHIP PROGRAM
• *See page 202*

XEROX

http://www.xerox.com//

TECHNICAL MINORITY SCHOLARSHIP
• *See page 171*

POLITICAL SCIENCE

AMERICAN FEDERATION OF STATE, COUNTY, AND MUNICIPAL EMPLOYEES

http://www.afscme.org/

AFSCME/UNCF UNION SCHOLARS PROGRAM
• *See page 89*

JERRY CLARK MEMORIAL SCHOLARSHIP

Renewable award for a student majoring in political science for his or her junior and senior years of study. Must be a child of an AFSCME member. Minimum 2.5 GPA required. Once awarded, the scholarship will be renewed for the senior year provided the student remains enrolled full-time as a political science major.

Academic Fields/Career Goals: Political Science.

Award: Scholarship for use in junior or senior years; renewable. *Number:* 2. *Amount:* $5000.

Eligibility Requirements: Applicant must be enrolled or expecting to enroll full-time at a four-year institution or university. Applicant or parent of applicant must be member of American Federation of State, County, and Municipal Employees. Applicant must have 2.5 GPA or higher. Available to U.S. citizens.

Application Requirements: Application, transcript, proof of parent. *Deadline:* July 1.

Contact: Philip Allen, Scholarship Coordinator
American Federation of State, County, and Municipal
Employees
1625 L Street, NW
Washington, DC 20036-5687
Phone: 202-429-1250
Fax: 202-429-1293
E-mail: pallen@asscme.org

AMERICAN LEGION AUXILIARY DEPARTMENT OF ARIZONA

http://www.azlegion.org/majorp~2.htm

AMERICAN LEGION AUXILIARY DEPARTMENT OF ARIZONA WILMA HOYAL-MAXINE CHILTON MEMORIAL SCHOLARSHIP

Annual scholarship to a student in second year or higher in one of the three state universities in Arizona. Must be enrolled in a program of study in political science, public programs, or special education. Must be a citizen of United States and of Arizona for at least one year. Honorably discharged veterans or immediate family members are given preference.

Academic Fields/Career Goals: Political Science; Public Policy and Administration; Social Services; Special Education.

Award: Scholarship for use in sophomore, junior, or senior years; not renewable. *Number:* 3. *Amount:* $1000.

Eligibility Requirements: Applicant must be enrolled or expecting to enroll full- or part-time at a two-year or four-year institution or university; resident of Arizona and studying in Arizona. Available to U.S. citizens.

Application Requirements: Application, essay, financial need analysis, photo, references, test scores, transcript. *Deadline:* May 15.

Contact: Department Secretary and Treasurer
American Legion Auxiliary Department of Arizona
4701 North 19th Avenue, Suite 100
Phoenix, AZ 85015-3727
Phone: 602-241-1080
E-mail: amlegauxaz@mcleodusa.net

ARAB AMERICAN SCHOLARSHIP FOUNDATION

http://www.lahc.org/

LEBANESE AMERICAN HERITAGE CLUB'S SCHOLARSHIP FUND

• *See page 182*

ASSOCIATION OF FORMER INTELLIGENCE OFFICERS

http://www.afio.com/13_scholarships.htm

CIA UNDERGRADUATE SCHOLARSHIPS

• *See page 89*

BOYS AND GIRLS CLUBS OF SAN DIEGO

http://www.sdyouth.org/

SPENCE REESE SCHOLARSHIP

• *See page 281*

CENTRAL INTELLIGENCE AGENCY

http://www.cia.gov/

CENTRAL INTELLIGENCE AGENCY UNDERGRADUATE SCHOLARSHIP PROGRAM

• *See page 58*

COLLEGEBOUND FOUNDATION

http://www.collegeboundfoundation.org/

DECATUR H. MILLER SCHOLARSHIP

• *See page 352*

CUBAN AMERICAN NATIONAL FOUNDATION

http://www.masscholarships.org/

MAS FAMILY SCHOLARSHIPS

• *See page 148*

GOVERNMENT FINANCE OFFICERS ASSOCIATION

http://www.gfoa.org/

MINORITIES IN GOVERNMENT FINANCE SCHOLARSHIP

• *See page 63*

GREATER SALINA COMMUNITY FOUNDATION

http://www.gscf.org/

KANSAS FEDERATION OF REPUBLICAN WOMEN SCHOLARSHIP

• *See page 352*

HARRY S. TRUMAN SCHOLARSHIP FOUNDATION

http://www.truman.gov/

HARRY S. TRUMAN SCHOLARSHIP

Scholarships for U.S. citizens or U.S. nationals who are college or university students with junior-level academic standing and who wish to attend professional or graduate school to prepare for careers in government or the nonprofit and advocacy sectors. Candidates must be nominated by their institution. Public service and leadership record considered. Visit web site http://www.truman.gov for further information and application.

Academic Fields/Career Goals: Political Science; Public Policy and Administration.

Award: Scholarship for use in junior year; renewable. *Number:* 65. *Amount:* $30,000.

Eligibility Requirements: Applicant must be enrolled or expecting to enroll full-time at a four-year institution or university and must have an interest in leadership. Available to U.S. citizens.

Application Requirements: Application, interview, references, policy proposal. *Deadline:* February 5.

Contact: Tonji Wade, Program Officer
Harry S. Truman Scholarship Foundation
712 Jackson Place, NW
Washington, DC 20006
Phone: 202-395-4831
Fax: 202-395-6995
E-mail: office@truman.gov

INSTITUTE FOR HUMANE STUDIES

http://www.theihs.org/

HUMANE STUDIES FELLOWSHIPS

• *See page 185*

LYNDON BAINES JOHNSON FOUNDATION

http://www.lbjfoundation.org/

LYNDON BAINES JOHNSON FOUNDATION GRANTS-IN-AID RESEARCH
• *See page 353*

NATIONAL SOCIETY DAUGHTERS OF THE AMERICAN REVOLUTION

http://www.dar.org/

NATIONAL SOCIETY DAUGHTERS OF THE AMERICAN REVOLUTION DR. AURA-LEE A. PITTENGER AND JAMES HOBBS PITTENGER AMERICAN HISTORY SCHOLARSHIP
• *See page 353*

NATIONAL SOCIETY DAUGHTERS OF THE AMERICAN REVOLUTION ENID HALL GRISWOLD MEMORIAL SCHOLARSHIP
• *See page 228*

NATIONAL TOURISM FOUNDATION

http://www.ntfonline.com/

ACADEMY OF TRAVEL AND TOURISM SCHOLARSHIPS
• *See page 363*

STRAIGHTFORWARD MEDIA

http://www.straightforwardmedia.com/

STRAIGHTFORWARD MEDIA LIBERAL ARTS SCHOLARSHIP
• *See page 107*

TKE EDUCATIONAL FOUNDATION

http://www.tke.org/

BRUCE B. MELCHERT SCHOLARSHIP
One-time award of $500 given to an undergraduate member of Tau Kappa Epsilon with sophomore, junior, or senior standing. Must be pursuing a degree in political science or government and have a record of leadership within his fraternity and other campus organizations. Should have as a goal to serve in a political or government position. Recent head and shoulders photograph must be submitted with application. Minimum 3.0 GPA required.

Academic Fields/Career Goals: Political Science.

Award: Scholarship for use in sophomore, junior, or senior years; not renewable. *Number:* 1. *Amount:* $500.

Eligibility Requirements: Applicant must be enrolled or expecting to enroll full-time at a four-year institution or university and must have an interest in leadership. Applicant or parent of applicant must be member of Tau Kappa Epsilon. Applicant must have 3.0 GPA or higher. Available to U.S. and non-U.S. citizens.

Application Requirements: Application, essay, photo, transcript, narrative summary of how TKE membership has benefited applicant. *Deadline:* February 29.

Contact: Gary A. Reed, President and Chief Executive Officer
TKE Educational Foundation
8645 Founders Road
Indianapolis, IN 46268-1393
Phone: 317-872-6533
Fax: 317-875-8353
E-mail: reedga@tke.org

UNITED NEGRO COLLEGE FUND

http://www.uncf.org/

AFSCME/UNCF/HARVARD UNIVERSITY LWP UNION SCHOLARS PROGRAM
• *See page 90*

C-SPAN SCHOLARSHIP PROGRAM
• *See page 193*

OSSIE DAVIS ENDOWMENT SCHOLARSHIP
• *See page 116*

TOYOTA/UNCF SCHOLARSHIP
• *See page 74*

WASHINGTON CROSSING FOUNDATION

http://www.gwcf.org/

WASHINGTON CROSSING FOUNDATION SCHOLARSHIP
Renewable, merit-based awards available to high school seniors who are planning a career in government service. Must write an essay stating reason for deciding on a career in public service. Minimum 3.0 GPA required.

Academic Fields/Career Goals: Political Science; Public Policy and Administration.

Award: Scholarship for use in freshman year; renewable. *Number:* 5–10. *Amount:* $1000–$20,000.

Eligibility Requirements: Applicant must be high school student and planning to enroll or expecting to enroll full-time at a four-year institution or university. Applicant must have 3.0 GPA or higher. Available to U.S. citizens.

Application Requirements: Application, essay, interview, photo, references, test scores, transcript. *Deadline:* January 15.

Contact: Eugene C. Fish, Vice Chairman
Washington Crossing Foundation
PO Box 503
Levittown, PA 19058-0503
Phone: 215-949-8841
Fax: 215-949-8843
E-mail: info@gwcf.org

WASHINGTON NEWS COUNCIL

http://www.wanewscouncil.org/

DICK LARSEN SCHOLARSHIP PROGRAM
• *See page 194*

HERB ROBINSON SCHOLARSHIP PROGRAM
• *See page 194*

PSYCHOLOGY

AMERICAN FEDERATION OF STATE, COUNTY, AND MUNICIPAL EMPLOYEES

http://www.afscme.org/

AFSCME/UNCF UNION SCHOLARS PROGRAM
• *See page 89*

AMERICAN PSYCHOLOGICAL ASSOCIATION

http://www.apa.org/

AMERICAN PSYCHOLOGICAL ASSOCIATION TEACHERS OF PSYCHOLOGY IN SECONDARY SCHOOLS SCHOLARS ESSAY COMPETITION

Three prizes of $500 each for essays of 3000 words with an abstract of 120 words. Applicants must have completed or be presently enrolled in a psychology course.

Academic Fields/Career Goals: Psychology.

Award: Prize for use in freshman year; not renewable. *Number;* 3. *Amount:* $500.

Eligibility Requirements: Applicant must be high school student; planning to enroll or expecting to enroll full- or part-time at a two-year or four-year institution or university and must have an interest in writing. Available to U.S. and non-U.S. citizens.

Application Requirements: Applicant must enter a contest, essay, cover letter. *Deadline:* March 3.

Contact: Jewel Beamon, Special Projects Associate
American Psychological Association
750 First Street, NE
Washington, DC 20002-4242
Phone: 202-336-6076
Fax: 202-336-5962
E-mail: jbeamon@apa.org

CYNTHIA E. MORGAN SCHOLARSHIP FUND (CEMS)

http://www.cemsfund.com/

CYNTHIA E. MORGAN MEMORIAL SCHOLARSHIP FUND, INC.
• *See page 304*

HEALTH RESEARCH COUNCIL OF NEW ZEALAND

http://www.hrc.govt.nz/

PACIFIC MENTAL HEALTH WORK FORCE AWARD
• *See page 334*

MISSISSIPPI OFFICE OF STUDENT FINANCIAL AID

http://www.mississippi.edu/

MISSISSIPPI HEALTH CARE PROFESSIONS LOAN/ SCHOLARSHIP PROGRAM
• *See page 346*

MISSOURI DEPARTMENT OF HEALTH AND SENIOR SERVICES

http://www.dhss.mo.gov/

PRIMARY CARE RESOURCE INITIATIVE FOR MISSOURI LOAN PROGRAM
• *See page 136*

NEW YORK STATE EDUCATION DEPARTMENT

http://www.highered.nysed.gov/

REGENTS PROFESSIONAL OPPORTUNITY SCHOLARSHIP
• *See page 69*

PILOT INTERNATIONAL FOUNDATION

http://www.pilotinternational.org/

PILOT INTERNATIONAL FOUNDATION RUBY NEWHALL MEMORIAL SCHOLARSHIP
• *See page 348*

PILOT INTERNATIONAL FOUNDATION SCHOLARSHIP PROGRAM
• *See page 348*

SOCIETY FOR THE SCIENTIFIC STUDY OF SEXUALITY

http://www.sexscience.org/

SOCIETY FOR THE SCIENTIFIC STUDY OF SEXUALITY STUDENT RESEARCH GRANT
• *See page 137*

STRAIGHTFORWARD MEDIA

http://www.straightforwardmedia.com/

STRAIGHTFORWARD MEDIA LIBERAL ARTS SCHOLARSHIP
• *See page 107*

UNITED NEGRO COLLEGE FUND

http://www.uncf.org/

TOYOTA/UNCF SCHOLARSHIP
• *See page 74*

WOMEN'S INDEPENDENCE SCHOLARSHIP PROGRAM, INC.

http://www.wispinc.org/

COUNSELOR, ADVOCATE, AND SUPPORT STAFF SCHOLARSHIP PROGRAM
• *See page 76*

ZETA PHI BETA SORORITY INC. NATIONAL EDUCATIONAL FOUNDATION

http://www.zphib1920.org/

LULLELIA W. HARRISON SCHOLARSHIP IN COUNSELING
• *See page 173*

PUBLIC HEALTH

AMERICAN DENTAL HYGIENISTS' ASSOCIATION (ADHA) INSTITUTE

http://www.adha.org/institute

IRENE E. NEWMAN SCHOLARSHIP
• *See page 217*

ASSOCIATION ON AMERICAN INDIAN AFFAIRS, INC.

http://www.indian-affairs.org/

ELIZABETH AND SHERMAN ASCHE MEMORIAL SCHOLARSHIP FUND
• *See page 83*

COLLEGE BOARD/ROBERT WOOD JOHNSON FOUNDATION YES PROGRAM

http://www.collegeboard.com/

YOUNG EPIDEMIOLOGY SCHOLARS COMPETITION
• *See page 304*

FLORIDA ENVIRONMENTAL HEALTH ASSOCIATION

http://www.feha.org/

FLORIDA ENVIRONMENTAL HEALTH ASSOCIATION EDUCATIONAL SCHOLARSHIP AWARDS
• *See page 304*

GENERAL FEDERATION OF WOMEN'S CLUBS OF MASSACHUSETTS

http://www.gfwcma.org/

CATHERINE E. PHILBIN SCHOLARSHIP
One scholarship of $500 will be awarded to a graduate or undergraduate student studying public health. Eligible applicants will be residents of Massachusetts. Along with the application, students must send a personal statement of no more than 500 words addressing professional goals and financial need.

Academic Fields/Career Goals: Public Health.

Award: Scholarship for use in freshman, sophomore, junior, senior, or graduate years; not renewable. *Number:* 1. *Amount:* $500.

Eligibility Requirements: Applicant must be enrolled or expecting to enroll full-time at a four-year institution or university and resident of Massachusetts. Available to U.S. citizens.

Application Requirements: Application, essay, references, transcript. *Deadline:* March 1.

Contact: Jane Howard, Scholarship Chairman
General Federation of Women's Clubs of Massachusetts
PO Box 679
Sudbury, MA 01776-0679
E-mail: jhoward@mountida.edu

INDIAN HEALTH SERVICES, UNITED STATES DEPARTMENT OF HEALTH AND HUMAN SERVICES

http://www.ihs.gov/

HEALTH PROFESSIONS PREPARATORY SCHOLARSHIP PROGRAM
• *See page 335*

NATIONAL ENVIRONMENTAL HEALTH ASSOCIATION/AMERICAN ACADEMY OF SANITARIANS

http://www.neha.org/

NATIONAL ENVIRONMENTAL HEALTH ASSOCIATION/AMERICAN ACADEMY OF SANITARIANS SCHOLARSHIP
• *See page 305*

NEW ENGLAND EMPLOYEE BENEFITS COUNCIL

http://www.neebc.org/

NEW ENGLAND EMPLOYEE BENEFITS COUNCIL SCHOLARSHIP PROGRAM
• *See page 68*

OREGON STUDENT ASSISTANCE COMMISSION

http://www.GetCollegeFunds.org/

LAURENCE R. FOSTER MEMORIAL SCHOLARSHIP
One-time award to students enrolled or planning to enroll in a public health degree program. First preference given to those working in the public health field and those pursuing a graduate degree in public health. Undergraduates entering junior or senior year health programs may apply if seeking a public health career, and not private practice. Prefer applicants from diverse cultures. Additional essays required.

Academic Fields/Career Goals: Public Health.

Award: Scholarship for use in freshman, sophomore, junior, or senior years; renewable. *Number:* varies. *Amount:* varies.

Eligibility Requirements: Applicant must be enrolled or expecting to enroll full- or part-time at a four-year institution. Available to U.S. citizens.

Application Requirements: Application, essay, financial need analysis, references, transcript, activity chart. *Deadline:* March 1.

Contact: Scholarship Coordinator
Oregon Student Assistance Commission
1500 Valley River Drive, Suite 100
Eugene, OR 97401-7020
Phone: 800-452-8807 Ext. 7395

PILOT INTERNATIONAL FOUNDATION

http://www.pilotinternational.org/

PILOT INTERNATIONAL FOUNDATION RUBY NEWHALL MEMORIAL SCHOLARSHIP
• *See page 348*

SOCIETY FOR THE SCIENTIFIC STUDY OF SEXUALITY

http://www.sexscience.org/

SOCIETY FOR THE SCIENTIFIC STUDY OF SEXUALITY STUDENT RESEARCH GRANT
• *See page 137*

SOUTH CAROLINA PUBLIC HEALTH ASSOCIATION

http://www.scpha.com/

SOUTH CAROLINA PUBLIC HEALTH ASSOCIATION PUBLIC HEALTH SCHOLARSHIPS
Current member of the SCPHA with more than 6 hours remaining and enrolled in a accredited higher education program for public health or related field. Dantzler- exhibit significant commitment to the public health profession through volunteer and/or professional activity as indicated on the application. Public Health Scholarship- exhibit significant commitment to the public health profession through volunteer and/or professional activity as indicated on the application.

Academic Fields/Career Goals: Public Health.

Award: Scholarship for use in freshman, sophomore, junior, senior, graduate, or postgraduate years; not renewable. *Number:* 2. *Amount:* $500–$750.

Eligibility Requirements: Applicant must be enrolled or expecting to enroll full- or part-time at a four-year institution or university. Applicant must have 3.5 GPA or higher. Available to U.S. citizens.

Application Requirements: Application, transcript, proof of number of hours remaining. *Deadline:* March 31.

Contact: Mr. Larry White, Scholarship Committee Chair
South Carolina Public Health Association
PO Box 11061
Columbia, SC 29211
Phone: 843-488-1329 Ext. 225
Fax: 843-488-1330
E-mail: larry@smokefreehorry.org

PUBLIC POLICY AND ADMINISTRATION

AMERICAN INSTITUTE OF POLISH CULTURE INC.

http://www.ampolinstitute.org/

HARRIET IRSAY SCHOLARSHIP GRANT
• *See page 109*

AMERICAN LEGION AUXILIARY DEPARTMENT OF ARIZONA

http://www.azlegion.org/majorp~2.htm

AMERICAN LEGION AUXILIARY DEPARTMENT OF ARIZONA WILMA HOYAL-MAXINE CHILTON MEMORIAL SCHOLARSHIP
• *See page 481*

THE DALLAS FOUNDATION

http://www.dallasfoundation.org/

WHITLEY PLACE SCHOLARSHIP
• *See page 100*

GOVERNMENT FINANCE OFFICERS ASSOCIATION

http://www.gfoa.org/

FRANK L. GREATHOUSE GOVERNMENT ACCOUNTING SCHOLARSHIP
• *See page 151*

MINORITIES IN GOVERNMENT FINANCE SCHOLARSHIP
• *See page 63*

GREATER SALINA COMMUNITY FOUNDATION

http://www.gscf.org/

KANSAS FEDERATION OF REPUBLICAN WOMEN SCHOLARSHIP
• *See page 352*

HARRY S. TRUMAN SCHOLARSHIP FOUNDATION

http://www.truman.gov/

HARRY S. TRUMAN SCHOLARSHIP
• *See page 481*

JAPANESE AMERICAN CITIZENS LEAGUE (JACL)

http://www.jacl.org/

NATIONAL JACL HEADQUARTERS SCHOLARSHIP
• *See page 84*

NATIONAL STONE, SAND AND GRAVEL ASSOCIATION (NSSGA)

http://www.nssga.org/

JENNIFER CURTIS BYLER SCHOLARSHIP FOR THE STUDY OF PUBLIC AFFAIRS
• *See page 188*

NEW ENGLAND EMPLOYEE BENEFITS COUNCIL

http://www.neebc.org/

NEW ENGLAND EMPLOYEE BENEFITS COUNCIL SCHOLARSHIP PROGRAM
• *See page 68*

UNITED NEGRO COLLEGE FUND

http://www.uncf.org/

AFSCME/UNCF/HARVARD UNIVERSITY LWP UNION SCHOLARS PROGRAM
• *See page 90*

TOYOTA/UNCF SCHOLARSHIP
• *See page 74*

WASHINGTON CROSSING FOUNDATION

http://www.gwcf.org/

WASHINGTON CROSSING FOUNDATION SCHOLARSHIP
• *See page 482*

WHOMENTORS.COM, INC.

http://www.WHOmentors.com/

ACCREDITED REPRESENTATIVE (FULL)
• *See page 56*

WIFLE FOUNDATION, INC.

http://www.wifle.org/

WIFLE SCHOLARSHIP PROGRAM
• *See page 202*

RADIOLOGY

ASRT EDUCATION AND RESEARCH FOUNDATION

http://www.asrtfoundation.org/

JERMAN-CAHOON STUDENT SCHOLARSHIP
• *See page 340*

MEDICAL IMAGING EDUCATORS SCHOLARSHIP
• *See page 231*

PROFESSIONAL ADVANCEMENT SCHOLARSHIP
• *See page 340*

ROYCE OSBORN MINORITY STUDENT SCHOLARSHIP
• *See page 340*

SIEMENS CLINICAL ADVANCEMENT SCHOLARSHIP
• *See page 340*

CYNTHIA E. MORGAN SCHOLARSHIP FUND (CEMS)

http://www.cemsfund.com/

CYNTHIA E. MORGAN MEMORIAL SCHOLARSHIP FUND, INC.
• *See page 304*

SOCIETY OF NUCLEAR MEDICINE

http://www.snm.org/

PAUL COLE SCHOLARSHIP
• *See page 348*

REAL ESTATE

APPRAISAL INSTITUTE EDUCATION TRUST

http://www.aiedtrust.org/

AIET MINORITIES AND WOMEN EDUCATIONAL SCHOLARSHIP

Awarded to minorities and women undergraduate students pursuing academic degrees in real estate appraisal or related fields.

Academic Fields/Career Goals: Real Estate.

Award: Scholarship for use in freshman, sophomore, junior, or senior years; not renewable. *Number:* varies. *Amount:* $1000.

Eligibility Requirements: Applicant must be American Indian/Alaska Native, Asian/Pacific Islander, Black (non-Hispanic), or Hispanic; enrolled or expecting to enroll full- or part-time at a four-year institution or university and female. Applicant must have 2.5 GPA or higher. Available to U.S. citizens.

Application Requirements: Application, essay, financial need analysis, photo, resume, references, transcript. *Deadline:* April 15.

Contact: Appraisal Institute Education Trust
550 West Van Buren Street, Suite 1000
Chicago, IL 60607
Phone: 312-335-4133
Fax: 312-335-4134
E-mail: educationtrust@appraisalinstitute.org

APPRAISAL INSTITUTE EDUCATION TRUST EDUCATION SCHOLARSHIPS

Awarded on the basis of academic excellence, this scholarship helps finance the educational endeavors of undergraduate and graduate students concentrating in real estate appraisal, land economics, real estate or allied fields.

Academic Fields/Career Goals: Real Estate.

Award: Scholarship for use in sophomore, junior, senior, or graduate years; not renewable. *Amount:* $1000–$2000.

Eligibility Requirements: Applicant must be enrolled or expecting to enroll full-time at a four-year institution or university. Available to U.S. citizens.

Application Requirements: Application, essay, resume, references, transcript. *Deadline:* March 15:

Contact: Hillary Richmond, Diversity Committee Staff Liaison
Appraisal Institute Education Trust
550 West Van Buren Street, Suite 1000
Chicago, IL 60607
Phone: 312-335-4133
Fax: 312-335-4134
E-mail: educationtrust@appraisalinstitute.orghrichmond@
appraisalinstitute.org

CALIFORNIA ASSOCIATION OF REALTORS

http://www.car.org/

C.A.R. SCHOLARSHIP FOUNDATION AWARD

Scholarships to students enrolled at a California College or University for professions which are centered on, or support a career in real estate transactional activity. Must have maintained a cumulative GPA of 2.6 or higher.

Academic Fields/Career Goals: Real Estate.

Award: Scholarship for use in sophomore, junior, or senior years; not renewable. *Number:* varies. *Amount:* $2000–$4000.

Eligibility Requirements: Applicant must be enrolled or expecting to enroll full-time at a two-year or four-year institution or university; resident of California and studying in California. Available to U.S. citizens.

Application Requirements: Application, essay, references, transcript. *Deadline:* May 11.

Contact: Mary Martinez, Scholarship Coordinator
California Association of Realtors
525 South Virgil Avenue
Los Angeles, CA 90020
Phone: 213-739-8200
Fax: 213-480-7724
E-mail: scholarship@car.org

ILLINOIS REAL ESTATE EDUCATIONAL FOUNDATION

http://www.ilreef.org/

ILLINOIS REAL ESTATE EDUCATIONAL FOUNDATION ACADEMIC SCHOLARSHIPS

Awards for Illinois residents attending an accredited two-or four-year junior college, college or university in Illinois. Must have completed 30 college credit hours and be pursuing a degree with an emphasis in real estate. Must be a U.S. citizen.

Academic Fields/Career Goals: Real Estate.

Award: Scholarship for use in freshman, sophomore, junior, or senior years; not renewable. *Number:* varies. *Amount:* $1000.

Eligibility Requirements: Applicant must be enrolled or expecting to enroll full-time at a two-year or four-year institution or university; resident of Illinois and studying in Illinois. Available to U.S. citizens.

Application Requirements: Application, essay, resume, references, transcript. *Deadline:* April 1.

Contact: Stephen Sundquist, Foundation Manager
Illinois Real Estate Educational Foundation
522 South 5th Street, PO Box 2607
Springfield, IL 62708
Phone: 866-854-7333
Fax: 217-241-9935
E-mail: ssundquist@ilreef.org

THOMAS F. SEAY SCHOLARSHIP

Award of $2000 to students pursuing a degree with an emphasis in real estate. Must be a U.S. citizen and attending any accredited U.S. college or university full-time. Must have completed at least 30 college credit hours. Minimum 3.5 GPA required.

Academic Fields/Career Goals: Real Estate.

Award: Scholarship for use in junior or senior years; not renewable. *Number:* varies. *Amount:* $2000.

Eligibility Requirements: Applicant must be enrolled or expecting to enroll full-time at a four-year institution or university; resident of Illinois and studying in Illinois. Applicant must have 3.5 GPA or higher. Available to U.S. citizens.

Application Requirements: Application, essay, resume, references, transcript. *Deadline:* April 1.

Contact: Stephen Sundquist, Foundation Manager
Illinois Real Estate Educational Foundation
522 South 5th Street, PO Box 2607
Springfield, IL 62708
Phone: 866-854-7333
Fax: 217-241-9935
E-mail: ssundquist@ilreef.org

INTERNATIONAL COUNCIL OF SHOPPING CENTERS FOUNDATION

http://www.icscfoundation.org/

JOHN T. RIORDAN SCHOOL FOR PROFESSIONAL DEVELOPMENT

Award for higher education for shopping center professionals. Must be a official ICSC member in good standing, actively employed in the shopping center industry for a minimum of one year, or recent graduate of college/university with coursework emphasis in real estate; or a graduate of REAP or Inroads programs within the past eighteen months prior to year end when the application is submitted.

Academic Fields/Career Goals: Real Estate.

Award: Scholarship for use in freshman, sophomore, junior, senior, graduate, or postgraduate years; not renewable. *Number:* 10–15. *Amount:* up to $3000.

Eligibility Requirements: Applicant must be enrolled or expecting to enroll full- or part-time at a technical institution. Available to U.S. and non-U.S. citizens.

Application Requirements: Application, essay, resume, references. *Deadline:* March 14.

Contact: Valerie Cammiso, Executive Director
International Council of Shopping Centers Foundation
1221 Avenue of the Americas, 41st Floor
New York, NY 10020-5370
Phone: 646-728-3559
E-mail: vcammiso@icsc.org

NEW JERSEY ASSOCIATION OF REALTORS

http://www.njar.com/

NEW JERSEY ASSOCIATION OF REALTORS EDUCATIONAL FOUNDATION SCHOLARSHIP PROGRAM

One-time awards for New Jersey residents who are high school seniors pursuing studies in real estate or allied fields. Preference to students considering a career in real estate. Must be member of NJAR or relative of a member. Selected candidates are interviewed in June. Must be a U.S. citizen.

Academic Fields/Career Goals: Real Estate.

Award: Scholarship for use in freshman year; not renewable. *Number:* 20–32. *Amount:* $1000–$2500.

Eligibility Requirements: Applicant must be high school student; planning to enroll or expecting to enroll full-time at a four-year institution or university and resident of New Jersey. Applicant or parent of applicant must be member of New Jersey Association of Realtors. Available to U.S. citizens.

Application Requirements: Application, essay, financial need analysis, interview, transcript, letter of verification of realtor/realtor associate/association staff. *Deadline:* April 9.

Contact: Diane Hatley, Educational Foundation
New Jersey Association of Realtors
PO Box 2098
Edison, NJ 08818
Phone: 732-494-5616
Fax: 732-494-4723

STRAIGHTFORWARD MEDIA

http://www.straightforwardmedia.com/

STRAIGHTFORWARD MEDIA VOCATIONAL-TECHNICAL SCHOOL SCHOLARSHIP
• *See page 91*

RECREATION, PARKS, LEISURE STUDIES

AMERICAN ALLIANCE FOR HEALTH, PHYSICAL EDUCATION, RECREATION AND DANCE

http://www.aahperd.org/

ROBERT W. CRAWFORD STUDENT LITERARY AWARD

Annual award recognizing writing excellence among graduate and undergraduate students. Any student enrolled in an HPERD professional track (health, physical education, recreation or dance) is eligible to submit. Applicants must submit manuscripts with a focus on leisure and recreation. Students must have a faculty sponsor to submit a paper for this award.

Academic Fields/Career Goals: Recreation, Parks, Leisure Studies.

Award: Scholarship for use in freshman, sophomore, junior, senior, or graduate years; not renewable. *Number:* 2. *Amount:* $500.

Eligibility Requirements: Applicant must be enrolled or expecting to enroll full- or part-time at a four-year institution or university. Available to U.S. and non-U.S. citizens.

Application Requirements: Application, applicant must enter a contest, essay, resume, faculty sponsor, sample evaluation sheets. *Deadline:* January 1.

Contact: Chris Neumann, Senior Program Manager
American Alliance for Health, Physical Education, Recreation and Dance
1900 Association Drive
Reston, VA 20191
Phone: 703-476-3432
Fax: 703-476-9527
E-mail: aapar@aahperd.org

RUTH ABERNATHY PRESIDENTIAL SCHOLARSHIP

Three award for undergraduate students and two for graduate students in January of each year. Must be majoring in the field of health, physical education, recreation or dance. Undergraduate awards are in the amount of $1,250 each and graduate awards are in the amount of $1,750 each. Recipients also receive a complimentary three-year AAHPERD membership. Applicant must be current member of AAHPERD.

Academic Fields/Career Goals: Recreation, Parks, Leisure Studies; Sports-Related/Exercise Science.

Award: Scholarship for use in junior, senior, or graduate years; not renewable. *Number:* 5. *Amount:* $1250–$1750.

Eligibility Requirements: Applicant must be enrolled or expecting to enroll full-time at a four-year institution or university and must have an interest in leadership. Applicant must have 3.5 GPA or higher. Available to U.S. and non-U.S. citizens.

Application Requirements: Application, references, transcript, letter from the school's dean/registrar indicating full-time status. *Deadline:* October 15.

Contact: Deb Callis, Secretary to Chief Executive Officer
American Alliance for Health, Physical Education, Recreation and Dance
1900 Association Drive
Reston, VA 20191
Phone: 703-476-3405
Fax: 703-476-9537
E-mail: dcallis@aahperd.org

AMERICAN HOTEL AND LODGING EDUCATIONAL FOUNDATION

http://www.ahlef.org/

AMERICAN HOTEL & LODGING EDUCATIONAL FOUNDATION PEPSI SCHOLARSHIP
• *See page 207*

ANNUAL SCHOLARSHIP GRANT PROGRAM
• *See page 208*

ARTHUR J. PACKARD MEMORIAL SCHOLARSHIP
• *See page 208*

ECOLAB SCHOLARSHIP PROGRAM
• *See page 208*

HYATT HOTELS FUND FOR MINORITY LODGING MANAGEMENT
• *See page 208*

INCOMING FRESHMAN SCHOLARSHIPS
• *See page 208*

RAMA SCHOLARSHIP FOR THE AMERICAN DREAM
• *See page 208*

STEVEN HYMANS EXTENDED STAY SCHOLARSHIP
• *See page 209*

AMERICAN QUARTER HORSE FOUNDATION (AQHF)

http://www.aqha.com/foundation

ARIZONA QUARTER HORSE YOUTH RACING SCHOLARSHIP
• *See page 90*

CANADIAN RECREATIONAL CANOEING ASSOCIATION

http://www.paddlingcanada.com/

BILL MASON MEMORIAL SCHOLARSHIP FUND
• *See page 232*

GOLF COURSE SUPERINTENDENTS ASSOCIATION OF AMERICA

http://www.eifg.org/

GOLF COURSE SUPERINTENDENTS ASSOCIATION OF AMERICA STUDENT ESSAY CONTEST
• *See page 78*

LAND CONSERVANCY OF NEW JERSEY

http://www.tlc-nj.org/

ROGERS FAMILY SCHOLARSHIP
• *See page 309*

RUSSELL W. MYERS SCHOLARSHIP
• *See page 309*

MAINE CAMPGROUND OWNERS ASSOCIATION

http://www.campmaine.com/home.php

MAINE CAMPGROUND OWNERS ASSOCIATION SCHOLARSHIP

One-time award of $500 to a Maine resident pursuing a career in outdoor recreation. Must have completed one year of study and have a minimum GPA of 2.5.

Academic Fields/Career Goals: Recreation, Parks, Leisure Studies.

Award: Scholarship for use in sophomore, junior, senior, graduate, or postgraduate years; not renewable. *Number:* 1. *Amount:* $500.

Eligibility Requirements: Applicant must be enrolled or expecting to enroll full-time at a two-year or four-year or technical institution or university and resident of Maine. Applicant must have 2.5 GPA or higher. Available to U.S. and non-U.S. citizens.

Application Requirements: Application, essay, financial need analysis, transcript. *Deadline:* March 31.

Contact: Richard Abare, Executive Director
Maine Campground Owners Association
10 Falcon Road, Suite 1
Lewiston, ME 04240
Phone: 207-782-5874
Fax: 207-782-4497
E-mail: info@campmaine.com

NATIONAL RECREATION AND PARK ASSOCIATION

http://www.nrpa.org/

AFRS STUDENT SCHOLARSHIP

Applicant must be currently enrolled in a NRPA accredited recreation/parks curriculum or related field. Number of awards varies.

Academic Fields/Career Goals: Recreation, Parks, Leisure Studies.

Award: Scholarship for use in freshman or sophomore years; not renewable. *Number:* varies. *Amount:* $500.

Eligibility Requirements: Applicant must be enrolled or expecting to enroll full- or part-time at a four-year institution or university. Applicant must have 3.0 GPA or higher. Available to U.S. citizens.

Application Requirements: Application, essay, references, test scores, transcript. *Deadline:* June 1.

Contact: Jessica Lytle, Senior Manager
National Recreation and Park Association
Director of Professional Services, 22377 Belmont Ridge Road
Ashburn, VA 20148
Phone: 703-858-2150
Fax: 703-858-0974
E-mail: jlytle@nrpa.org

RELIGION/THEOLOGY

AMERICAN SCHOOL OF CLASSICAL STUDIES AT ATHENS

http://www.ascsa.edu.gr/

ASCSA SUMMER SESSIONS SCHOLARSHIPS
• *See page 92*

BETHESDA LUTHERAN COMMUNITIES

http://www.bethesdalutherancommunities.org/

DEVELOPMENTAL DISABILITIES SCHOLASTIC ACHIEVEMENT SCHOLARSHIP FOR COLLEGE STUDENTS WHO ARE LUTHERAN
• *See page 218*

THE COMMUNITY FOUNDATION FOR GREATER ATLANTA, INC.

http://www.cfgreateratlanta.org/

JAMES M. AND VIRGINIA M. SMYTH SCHOLARSHIP
• *See page 110*

DISCIPLES OF CHRIST HOMELAND MINISTRIES

http://www.discipleshomemissions.org/

DAVID TAMOTSU KAGIWADA MEMORIAL SCHOLARSHIP

Scholarship of $2000 is available to Asian-American ministerial students. Must be a member of the Christian Church (Disciples of Christ), demonstrate financial need, have a C+ average, be a full-time student, and be under care of a regional Commission on the Ministry. Application may be submitted electronically.

Academic Fields/Career Goals: Religion/Theology.

Award: Scholarship for use in freshman, sophomore, junior, or senior years; not renewable. *Number:* varies. *Amount:* $2000.

Eligibility Requirements: Applicant must be Disciple of Christ; Asian/Pacific Islander and enrolled or expecting to enroll full-time at a two-year or four-year institution or university. Applicant must have 3.5 GPA or higher. Available to U.S. and Canadian citizens.

Application Requirements: Application, financial need analysis, references, transcript. *Deadline:* March 15.

Contact: Lorna Hernandez, Administrative Assistant
Disciples of Christ Homeland Ministries
PO Box 1986
Indianapolis, IN 46204-1986
Phone: 317-713-2666
E-mail: amoyars@dhm.disciples.org

DISCIPLE CHAPLAINS SCHOLARSHIP

Scholarship of $2000 is available to first year seminarians. Must be a member of the Christian Church (Disciples of Christ), demonstrate financial need, have a C+ average, be a full-time student, and be under the care of a regional Commission on the Ministry. Application may be submitted electronically.

Academic Fields/Career Goals: Religion/Theology.

Award: Scholarship for use in freshman year; not renewable. *Number:* varies. *Amount:* $2000.

Eligibility Requirements: Applicant must be Disciple of Christ; high school student and planning to enroll or expecting to enroll full-time at a four-year institution or university. Applicant must have 3.5 GPA or higher. Available to U.S. citizens.

Application Requirements: Application, financial need analysis, references, transcript. *Deadline:* March 15.

Contact: Lorna Hernandez, Administrative Assistant
Disciples of Christ Homeland Ministries
PO Box 1986
Indianapolis, IN 46204-1986
Phone: 317-713-2666
E-mail: amoyars@dhm.disciples.org

EDWIN G. AND LAURETTA M. MICHAEL SCHOLARSHIP

Scholarship of $2000 available to ministers wives. Must be a member of the Christian Church (Disciples of Christ), demonstrate financial need, have a C+ average, be a full-time student, and be under the care of a regional Commission on the Ministry. Application may be submitted electronically.

Academic Fields/Career Goals: Religion/Theology.

Award: Scholarship for use in freshman, sophomore, junior, or senior years; not renewable. *Number:* varies. *Amount:* $2000.

Eligibility Requirements: Applicant must be Disciple of Christ; enrolled or expecting to enroll full-time at a two-year or four-year institution or

university and married female. Applicant must have 2.5 GPA or higher. Available to U.S. and non-U.S. citizens.

Application Requirements: Application, financial need analysis, references, transcript. *Deadline:* March 15.

Contact: Lorna Hernandez, Administrative Assistant
Disciples of Christ Homeland Ministries
PO Box 1986
Indianapolis, IN 46204-1986
Phone: 317-713-2666
E-mail: amoyars@dhm.disciples.org

KATHERINE J. SHUTZE MEMORIAL SCHOLARSHIP

Scholarship of $2000 is available to female seminary students. Must be a member of the Christian Church (Disciples of Christ), demonstrate financial need, have a C+ average, be a full-time student, and be under the care of a regional Commission on the Ministry. Application may be submitted electronically.

Academic Fields/Career Goals: Religion/Theology.

Award: Scholarship for use in freshman, sophomore, junior, senior, or graduate years; not renewable. *Number:* varies. *Amount:* $2000.

Eligibility Requirements: Applicant must be Disciple of Christ; enrolled or expecting to enroll full-time at a four-year institution or university and female. Applicant must have 3.5 GPA or higher. Available to U.S. and non-U.S. citizens.

Application Requirements: Application, financial need analysis, references, transcript. *Deadline:* March 15.

Contact: Lorna Hernandez, Administrative Assistant
Disciples of Christ Homeland Ministries
PO Box 1986
Indianapolis, IN 46204-1986
Phone: 317-713-2666
E-mail: amoyars@dhm.disciples.org

ROWLEY/MINISTERIAL EDUCATION SCHOLARSHIP

Scholarship of $2000 is available to seminary students preparing for the ministry. Must be a member of the Christian Church (Disciples of Christ), demonstrate financial need, have a C+ average, be a full-time student and be under the care of a regional Commission on the Ministry. Application may be submitted electronically.

Academic Fields/Career Goals: Religion/Theology.

Award: Scholarship for use in freshman, sophomore, junior, senior, or graduate years; not renewable. *Number:* varies. *Amount:* $2000.

Eligibility Requirements: Applicant must be Disciple of Christ and enrolled or expecting to enroll full-time at a two-year or four-year institution or university. Applicant must have 3.5 GPA or higher. Available to U.S. and non-U.S. citizens.

Application Requirements: Application, financial need analysis, references, transcript. *Deadline:* March 15.

Contact: Lorna Hernandez, Administrative Assistant
Disciples of Christ Homeland Ministries
PO Box 1986
Indianapolis, IN 46204-1986
Phone: 317-713-2666
E-mail: amoyars@dhm.disciples.org

STAR SUPPORTER SCHOLARSHIP/LOAN

Scholarships in the form of forgivable loans are available to Black/African-Americans preparing for ministry. One year of full-time professional ministry reduces loan by one third. Three years of service repays loan. Must be member of the Christian Church (Disciples of Christ), have a C+ average, demonstrate financial need, be a full-time student in an accredited school or seminary and be under the care of a regional Commission on the Ministry. Application may be submitted electronically.

Academic Fields/Career Goals: Religion/Theology.

Award: Forgivable loan for use in freshman, sophomore, junior, or senior years; not renewable. *Number:* varies. *Amount:* $2000.

Eligibility Requirements: Applicant must be Disciple of Christ; Black (non-Hispanic) and enrolled or expecting to enroll full-time at a two-year or four-year institution or university. Applicant must have 3.5 GPA or higher. Available to U.S. citizens.

Application Requirements: Application, financial need analysis, references, transcript. *Deadline:* March 15.

Contact: Lorna Hernandez, Administrative Assistant
Disciples of Christ Homeland Ministries
PO Box 1986
Indianapolis, IN 46204-1986
Phone: 317-713-2666
E-mail: amoyars@dhm.disciples.org

EASTERN STAR-GRAND CHAPTER OF CALIFORNIA

http://www.oescal.org/

SCHOLARSHIPS FOR EDUCATION, BUSINESS AND RELIGION
• *See page 149*

ED E. AND GLADYS HURLEY FOUNDATION

ED E. AND GLADYS HURLEY FOUNDATION SCHOLARSHIP

Provides scholarships up to $1000 per year per student. Applicant must be Protestant enrolled or expecting to enroll full or part-time at a two-year or four-year institution or university and studying in Texas. Available to U.S. citizens.

Academic Fields/Career Goals: Religion/Theology.

Award: Scholarship for use in freshman, sophomore, junior, senior, graduate, or postgraduate years; not renewable. *Number:* 100–150. *Amount:* up to $1000.

Eligibility Requirements: Applicant must be Protestant; enrolled or expecting to enroll full- or part-time at a two-year or four-year institution or university; resident of Arkansas, Louisiana, or Texas and studying in Texas. Available to U.S. citizens.

Application Requirements: Application, financial need analysis, references. *Deadline:* April 30.

Contact: Rose Davis, Financial Aid Coordinator
Ed E. and Gladys Hurley Foundation
Houston Graduate School-Theology, 2501 Central Parkway, Suite A19
Houston, TX 77092
Phone: 713-942-9505
E-mail: rdavis@hgst.edu

FIRST PRESBYTERIAN CHURCH

http://www.firstchurchtulsa.org/

FIRST PRESBYTERIAN CHURCH SCHOLARSHIP PROGRAM

Awards to students pursuing full-time study at an accredited college, university or seminary. Preference given to church members in Tulsa, East Oklahoma, Synod of Sun, and at-large. Minimum 2.0 GPA. Must be a communicant member of the Presbyterian Church (U.S.A.).

Academic Fields/Career Goals: Religion/Theology.

Award: Scholarship for use in freshman, sophomore, junior, or senior years; not renewable. *Number:* 3–5. *Amount:* $500–$2000.

Eligibility Requirements: Applicant must be Presbyterian and enrolled or expecting to enroll full-time at a four-year institution or university. Available to U.S. citizens.

Application Requirements: Application, financial need analysis, interview, references, transcript. *Deadline:* April 15.

Contact: Tonye Briscoe, Administrative Assistant
First Presbyterian Church
709 South Boston Avenue
Tulsa, OK 74119-1629
Phone: 918-584-4701 Ext. 240
Fax: 918-584-5233
E-mail: tbriscoe@firstchurchtulsa.org

ULLERY CHARITABLE TRUST FUND

This fund was formed in 1972 from the estate of Miss Jimmie Ullery, a member of First Presbyterian Church in Tulsa, Oklahoma. Interest from the original corpus of the trust is used to assist students pursuing full-time Christian work with the Presbyterian Church (U.S.A.).

Academic Fields/Career Goals: Religion/Theology.

Award: Scholarship for use in freshman, sophomore, junior, or senior years; not renewable. *Number:* 5–7. *Amount:* $500–$2000.

Eligibility Requirements: Applicant must be Presbyterian and enrolled or expecting to enroll at a four-year institution or university. Available to U.S. and non-U.S. citizens.

Application Requirements: Application, financial need analysis, interview, references, transcript. *Deadline:* April 15.

Contact: Tonye Briscoe, Facilities and Benefits Coordinator
First Presbyterian Church
706 South Boston Avenue
Tulsa, OK 74119-1629
Phone: 918-584-4701
E-mail: tbriscoe@firstchurchtulsa.org

LINCOLN COMMUNITY FOUNDATION

http://www.lcf.org/

GEORGE AND LYNNA GENE COOK SCHOLARSHIP
• *See page 240*

MEMORIAL FOUNDATION FOR JEWISH CULTURE

http://www.mfjc.org/

MEMORIAL FOUNDATION FOR JEWISH CULTURE INTERNATIONAL SCHOLARSHIP PROGRAM FOR COMMUNITY SERVICE
• *See page 106*

MEMORIAL FOUNDATION FOR JEWISH CULTURE, SCHOLARSHIPS FOR POST-RABBINICAL STUDENTS
• *See page 241*

NATIONAL ASSOCIATION OF PASTORAL MUSICIANS

http://www.npm.org/

ELAINE RENDLER-RENE DOSOGNE-GEORGETOWN CHORALE SCHOLARSHIP
• *See page 424*

FUNK FAMILY MEMORIAL SCHOLARSHIP
• *See page 424*

GIA PUBLICATION PASTORAL MUSICIAN SCHOLARSHIP
• *See page 424*

MUSONICS SCHOLARSHIP
• *See page 424*

NATIONAL ASSOCIATION OF PASTORAL MUSICIANS MEMBERS' SCHOLARSHIP
• *See page 425*

NPM KOINONIA/BOARD OF DIRECTORS SCHOLARSHIP
• *See page 425*

OREGON CATHOLIC PRESS SCHOLARSHIP
• *See page 425*

PALUCH FAMILY FOUNDATION/WORLD LIBRARY PUBLICATIONS SCHOLARSHIP
• *See page 425*

OREGON STUDENT ASSISTANCE COMMISSION

http://www.GetCollegeFunds.org/

FRANKS FOUNDATION SCHOLARSHIP
• *See page 458*

PRESBYTERIAN CHURCH (USA)

http://www.pcusa.org/financialaid

STUDENT OPPORTUNITY SCHOLARSHIP
• *See page 246*

SOCIETY FOR THE SCIENTIFIC STUDY OF SEXUALITY

http://www.sexscience.org/

SOCIETY FOR THE SCIENTIFIC STUDY OF SEXUALITY STUDENT RESEARCH GRANT
• *See page 137*

UNITARIAN UNIVERSALIST ASSOCIATION

http://www.uua.org/

ROY H. POLLACK SCHOLARSHIP

Scholarship given to a junior or senior student with academic excellence and good character, studying for ordained ministry who actively participates in extracurricular activities at their theological school. Applicant must be pursuing in Divinity degree.

Academic Fields/Career Goals: Religion/Theology.

Award: Scholarship for use in junior or senior years; not renewable. *Number:* varies. *Amount:* varies.

Eligibility Requirements: Applicant must be Unitarian Universalist and enrolled or expecting to enroll full- or part-time at a four-year institution or university. Available to U.S. citizens.

Application Requirements: Application, financial need analysis. *Deadline:* April 15.

Contact: Ms. Hillary Goodridge, Program Director
Unitarian Universalist Association
PO Box 301149
Boston, MA 02130
Phone: 617-971-9600
Fax: 617-971-0029
E-mail: uufp@aol.com

UNITED METHODIST COMMUNICATIONS

http://www.umcom.org/

LEONARD M. PERRYMAN COMMUNICATIONS SCHOLARSHIP FOR ETHNIC MINORITY STUDENTS
• *See page 192*

UNITED NEGRO COLLEGE FUND

http://www.uncf.org/

DR. JOE RATLIFF CHALLENGE SCHOLARSHIP

Award for students at UNCF member colleges and universities pursing majors in religious study. Minimum 2.5 GPA required.

Academic Fields/Career Goals: Religion/Theology.

Award: Scholarship for use in freshman year; not renewable.

Eligibility Requirements: Applicant must be Black (non-Hispanic) and enrolled or expecting to enroll at a four-year institution or university. Applicant must have 2.5 GPA or higher. Available to U.S. citizens.

Application Requirements: *Deadline:* continuous.

Contact: Director, Program Services
United Negro College Fund
8260 Willow Oaks Corporate Drive
PO Box 10444
Fairfax, VA 22031-8044
Phone: 800-331-2244
E-mail: rebecca.bennett@uncf.org

SCIENCE, TECHNOLOGY, AND SOCIETY

AMERICAN CHEMICAL SOCIETY, RUBBER DIVISION

http://www.rubber.org/

AMERICAN CHEMICAL SOCIETY, RUBBER DIVISION UNDERGRADUATE SCHOLARSHIP
• *See page 160*

AMERICAN INSTITUTE OF AERONAUTICS AND ASTRONAUTICS

http://www.aiaa.org/

AIAA FOUNDATION UNDERGRADUATE SCHOLARSHIP
• *See page 93*

ARIZONA HYDROLOGICAL SOCIETY

http://www.azhydrosoc.org/

ARIZONA HYDROLOGICAL SOCIETY SCHOLARSHIP
• *See page 222*

ARMED FORCES COMMUNICATIONS AND ELECTRONICS ASSOCIATION, EDUCATIONAL FOUNDATION

http://www.afcea.org/education/scholarships

VICE ADMIRAL JERRY O. TUTTLE, USN (RET.) AND MRS. BARBARA A. TUTTLE SCIENCE AND TECHNOLOGY SCHOLARSHIP
• *See page 265*

ARRL FOUNDATION INC.

http://www.arrl.org/

YASME FOUNDATION SCHOLARSHIP
• *See page 139*

BRITISH COLUMBIA INNOVATION COUNCIL

http://www.bcic.ca/

PAUL AND HELEN TRUSSELL SCIENCE AND TECHNOLOGY SCHOLARSHIP
• *See page 95*

CATCHING THE DREAM

http://www.catchingthedream.org/

MATH, ENGINEERING, SCIENCE, BUSINESS, EDUCATION, COMPUTERS SCHOLARSHIPS
• *See page 147*

NATIVE AMERICAN LEADERSHIP IN EDUCATION (NALE)
• *See page 147*

COLLEGEBOUND FOUNDATION

http://www.collegeboundfoundation.org/

DR. FREEMAN A. HRABOWSKI, III SCHOLARSHIP
• *See page 282*

CONGRESSIONAL BLACK CAUCUS FOUNDATION, INC.

http://www.cbcfinc.org/

CONGRESSIONAL BLACK CAUCUS SPOUSES CHEERIOS BRAND HEALTH INITIATIVE
• *See page 139*

DAVIDSON INSTITUTE FOR TALENT DEVELOPMENT

http://www.davidsongifted.org/

DAVIDSON FELLOWS SCHOLARSHIP PROGRAM
• *See page 398*

DENVER FOUNDATION

http://www.denverfoundation.org/

RBC DAIN RAUSCHER COLORADO SCHOLARSHIP FUND
• *See page 282*

EXPLORERS CLUB

http://www.explorers.org/

YOUTH ACTIVITY FUND
• *See page 432*

GREAT LAKES COMMISSION

http://www.glc.org/

CAROL A. RATZA MEMORIAL SCHOLARSHIP
• *See page 185*

HEALTHCARE INFORMATION AND MANAGEMENT SYSTEMS SOCIETY FOUNDATION

http://www.himss.org/

HIMSS FOUNDATION SCHOLARSHIP PROGRAM
• *See page 334*

INTERNATIONAL TECHNOLOGY EDUCATION ASSOCIATION

http://www.iteaconnect.org/

INTERNATIONAL TECHNOLOGY EDUCATION ASSOCIATION UNDERGRADUATE SCHOLARSHIP IN TECHNOLOGY EDUCATION
• *See page 238*

KOREAN-AMERICAN SCIENTISTS AND ENGINEERS ASSOCIATION

http://www.ksea.org/

KSEA SCHOLARSHIPS
• *See page 257*

MONSANTO AGRIBUSINESS SCHOLARSHIP

http://www.monsanto.ca/

MONSANTO CANADA OPPORTUNITY SCHOLARSHIP PROGRAM
• *See page 79*

NASA RHODE ISLAND SPACE GRANT CONSORTIUM

http://ri.spacegrant.org/

NASA RHODE ISLAND SPACE GRANT CONSORTIUM OUTREACH SCHOLARSHIP FOR UNDERGRADUATE STUDENTS
• *See page 269*

NASA SOUTH DAKOTA SPACE GRANT CONSORTIUM

http://www.sdspacegrant.sdsmt.edu/

SOUTH DAKOTA SPACE GRANT CONSORTIUM UNDERGRADUATE AND GRADUATE STUDENT SCHOLARSHIPS
• *See page 129*

NASA'S VIRGINIA SPACE GRANT CONSORTIUM

http://www.vsgc.odu.edu/

TEACHER EDUCATION STEM SCHOLARSHIP PROGRAM
• *See page 96*

UNDERGRADUATE RESEARCH STEM SCHOLARSHIPS
• *See page 96*

SAN DIEGO FOUNDATION

http://www.sdfoundation.org/

BIOCOM SCHOLARSHIP
• *See page 143*

QUALCOMM SAN DIEGO SCIENCE, TECHNOLOGY, ENGINEERING, AND MATHEMATICS SCHOLARSHIP
• *See page 292*

SIEMENS FOUNDATION/SIEMENS-WESTINGHOUSE SCHOLARSHIP

http://www.siemens-foundation.org/

SIEMENS COMPETITION IN MATH, SCIENCE AND TECHNOLOGY

$1000 to $3000 scholarships for high school students willing to challenge themselves through science research. Students may enter as individuals or as part of a team.

Academic Fields/Career Goals: Science, Technology, and Society.

Award: Scholarship for use in freshman year; not renewable. *Number:* varies. *Amount:* $1000–$3000.

Eligibility Requirements: Applicant must be high school student and planning to enroll or expecting to enroll full-time at a four-year institution or university. Available to U.S. citizens.

Application Requirements: Application, applicant must enter a contest. *Deadline:* October 2.

Contact: Scholarship Committee
Siemens Foundation/Siemens-Westinghouse Scholarship
170 Wood Avenue South
Iselin, NJ 08830
Phone: 877-822-5233
Fax: 732-603-5890
E-mail: foundation.us@siemens.com

SIGMA XI, THE SCIENTIFIC RESEARCH SOCIETY

http://www.sigmaxi.org/

SIGMA XI GRANTS-IN-AID OF RESEARCH
• *See page 87*

SOCIETY FOR TECHNICAL COMMUNICATION

http://www.stc.org/

SOCIETY FOR TECHNICAL COMMUNICATION SCHOLARSHIP PROGRAM
• *See page 190*

SOCIETY OF HISPANIC PROFESSIONAL ENGINEERS

http://www.shpe.org/

AHETEMS SCHOLARSHIPS
• *See page 293*

SOCIETY OF HISPANIC PROFESSIONAL ENGINEERS FOUNDATION

http://www.henaac.org/

SOCIETY OF HISPANIC PROFESSIONAL ENGINEERS FOUNDATION
• *See page 169*

UNIVERSITIES SPACE RESEARCH ASSOCIATION

http://www.usra.edu/

UNIVERSITIES SPACE RESEARCH ASSOCIATION SCHOLARSHIP PROGRAM
• *See page 97*

WEST VIRGINIA HIGHER EDUCATION POLICY COMMISSION-STUDENT SERVICES

http://www.wvhepcnew.wvnet.edu/

WEST VIRGINIA ENGINEERING, SCIENCE AND TECHNOLOGY SCHOLARSHIP PROGRAM
• *See page 259*

SOCIAL SCIENCES

ALBERTA HERITAGE SCHOLARSHIP FUND

http://www.alis.alberta.ca/

LOIS HOLE HUMANITIES AND SOCIAL SCIENCES SCHOLARSHIP
• *See page 364*

AMERICAN CRIMINAL JUSTICE ASSOCIATION-LAMBDA ALPHA EPSILON

http://www.acjalae.org/

AMERICAN CRIMINAL JUSTICE ASSOCIATION-LAMBDA ALPHA EPSILON NATIONAL SCHOLARSHIP
• *See page 205*

AMERICAN FEDERATION OF STATE, COUNTY, AND MUNICIPAL EMPLOYEES

http://www.afscme.org/

AFSCME/UNCF UNION SCHOLARS PROGRAM
• *See page 89*

AMERICAN SOCIETY OF CRIMINOLOGY

http://www.asc41.com/

AMERICAN SOCIETY OF CRIMINOLOGY GENE CARTE STUDENT PAPER COMPETITION
• *See page 206*

CANADIAN INSTITUTE OF UKRAINIAN STUDIES

http://www.cius.ca/

LEO J. KRYSA UNDERGRADUATE SCHOLARSHIP
• *See page 104*

CATCHING THE DREAM

http://www.catchingthedream.org/

MATH, ENGINEERING, SCIENCE, BUSINESS, EDUCATION, COMPUTERS SCHOLARSHIPS
• *See page 147*

INSTITUTE FOR HUMANE STUDIES

http://www.theihs.org/

HUMANE STUDIES FELLOWSHIPS
• *See page 185*

NATIONAL BLACK POLICE ASSOCIATION

http://www.blackpolice.org/

ALPHONSO DEAL SCHOLARSHIP AWARD
• *See page 206*

NATIONAL INSTITUTES OF HEALTH

https://ugsp.nih.gov/

NIH UNDERGRADUATE SCHOLARSHIP PROGRAM FOR STUDENTS FROM DISADVANTAGED BACKGROUNDS
• *See page 142*

OFFICE AND PROFESSIONAL EMPLOYEES INTERNATIONAL UNION

http://www.opeiu.org/

JOHN KELLY LABOR STUDIES SCHOLARSHIP FUND
• *See page 228*

ORGONE BIOPHYSICAL RESEARCH LABORATORY

http://www.org/onelab.org/

LOU HOCHBERG-HIGH SCHOOL ESSAY AWARDS

One-time award of up to $500 will be given for the best high school student essay paper addressing Wilhlem Reich's sociological discoveries. Maximum length of 25 pages.

Academic Fields/Career Goals: Social Sciences.

Award: Prize for use in freshman year; not renewable. *Number:* 1. *Amount:* up to $500.

Eligibility Requirements: Applicant must be high school student and planning to enroll or expecting to enroll full- or part-time at a four-year institution or university. Available to U.S. and non-U.S. citizens.

Application Requirements: Applicant must enter a contest, essay, transcript, photocopy of student ID. *Deadline:* continuous.

Contact: Director
Orgone Biophysical Research Laboratory
PO Box 1148
Ashland, OR 97520
Phone: 541-552-0118
Fax: 541-552-0118
E-mail: info@orgonelab.org

PARAPSYCHOLOGY FOUNDATION

http://www.parapsychology.org/

CHARLES T. AND JUDITH A. TART STUDENT INCENTIVE

An annual incentive is awarded to promote the research of an undergraduate or graduate student, who shows dedication to work within parapsychology. For more details see web site http://www.parapsychology.org.

Academic Fields/Career Goals: Social Sciences.

Award: Scholarship for use in freshman, sophomore, junior, senior, graduate, or postgraduate years; not renewable. *Number:* 1. *Amount:* $500.

Eligibility Requirements: Applicant must be enrolled or expecting to enroll full-time at a two-year or four-year institution or university. Available to U.S. citizens.

Application Requirements: Application, essay, references, transcript. *Deadline:* October 15.

Contact: Lisette Coly, Vice President
Parapsychology Foundation
PO Box 1562
New York, NY 10021-0043
Phone: 212-628-1550
Fax: 212-628-1559
E-mail: office@parapsychology.org

EILEEN J. GARRETT SCHOLARSHIP FOR PARAPSYCHOLOGICAL RESEARCH

Scholarship requires applicants to demonstrate academic interest in the science of parapsychology through completed research, term papers, and courses for which credit was received. Those with only a general interest will not be considered. Visit web site for additional information.

Academic Fields/Career Goals: Social Sciences.

Award: Scholarship for use in freshman, sophomore, junior, senior, graduate, or postgraduate years; not renewable. *Number:* 1. *Amount:* $3000.

Eligibility Requirements: Applicant must be enrolled or expecting to enroll full-time at a two-year or four-year institution or university. Available to U.S. citizens.

Application Requirements: Application, essay, references, transcript. *Deadline:* July 15.

Contact: Lisette Coly, Vice President
Parapsychology Foundation
PO Box 1562
New York, NY 10021-0043
Phone: 212-628-1550
Fax: 212-628-1559
E-mail: office@parapsychology.org

PHI ALPHA THETA HISTORY HONOR SOCIETY, INC.

http://www.phialphatheta.org/

PHI ALPHA THETA WORLD HISTORY ASSOCIATION PAPER PRIZE
• *See page 354*

POLISH HERITAGE ASSOCIATION OF MARYLAND

http://www.pha-md.org/

DR. JOSEPHINE WTULICH MEMORIAL SCHOLARSHIP
• *See page 92*

ROBERT P. PULA MEMORIAL SCHOLARSHIP
• *See page 365*

PRESBYTERIAN CHURCH (USA)

http://www.pcusa.org/financialaid

STUDENT OPPORTUNITY SCHOLARSHIP
• *See page 246*

SIGMA XI, THE SCIENTIFIC RESEARCH SOCIETY

http://www.sigmaxi.org/

SIGMA XI GRANTS-IN-AID OF RESEARCH
• *See page 87*

SOCIETY FOR APPLIED ANTHROPOLOGY

http://www.sfaa.net/

PETER KONG-MING NEW STUDENT PRIZE
• *See page 137*

SOCIETY FOR THE SCIENTIFIC STUDY OF SEXUALITY

http://www.sexscience.org/

SOCIETY FOR THE SCIENTIFIC STUDY OF SEXUALITY STUDENT RESEARCH GRANT
• *See page 137*

STRAIGHTFORWARD MEDIA

http://www.straightforwardmedia.com/

STRAIGHTFORWARD MEDIA LIBERAL ARTS SCHOLARSHIP
• *See page 107*

UNITED NEGRO COLLEGE FUND

http://www.uncf.org/

AFSCME/UNCF/HARVARD UNIVERSITY LWP UNION SCHOLARS PROGRAM
• *See page 90*

OSSIE DAVIS ENDOWMENT SCHOLARSHIP
• *See page 116*

PRINCIPAL FINANCIAL GROUP SCHOLARSHIPS
• *See page 74*

WIFLE FOUNDATION, INC.

http://www.wifle.org/

WIFLE SCHOLARSHIP PROGRAM
• *See page 202*

WOMEN'S INDEPENDENCE SCHOLARSHIP PROGRAM, INC.

http://www.wispinc.org/

COUNSELOR, ADVOCATE, AND SUPPORT STAFF SCHOLARSHIP PROGRAM
• *See page 76*

Y'S MEN INTERNATIONAL

http://www.ysmenusa.com/

ALEXANDER SCHOLARSHIP LOAN FUND
• *See page 159*

ZETA PHI BETA SORORITY INC. NATIONAL EDUCATIONAL FOUNDATION

http://www.zphib1920.org/

LULLELIA W. HARRISON SCHOLARSHIP IN COUNSELING
• *See page 173*

SOCIAL SERVICES

ALBERTA HERITAGE SCHOLARSHIP FUND

http://www.alis.alberta.ca/

NORTHERN ALBERTA DEVELOPMENT COUNCIL BURSARY
• *See page 214*

AMERICAN FEDERATION OF STATE, COUNTY, AND MUNICIPAL EMPLOYEES

http://www.afscme.org/

AFSCME/UNCF UNION SCHOLARS PROGRAM
• *See page 89*

AMERICAN LEGION AUXILIARY DEPARTMENT OF ARIZONA

http://www.azlegion.org/majorp~2.htm

AMERICAN LEGION AUXILIARY DEPARTMENT OF ARIZONA WILMA HOYAL-MAXINE CHILTON MEMORIAL SCHOLARSHIP
• *See page 481*

BETHESDA LUTHERAN COMMUNITIES

http://www.bethesdalutherancommunities.org/

DEVELOPMENTAL DISABILITIES AWARENESS AWARDS FOR HIGH SCHOOL STUDENTS WHO ARE LUTHERAN
• *See page 341*

DEVELOPMENTAL DISABILITIES SCHOLASTIC ACHIEVEMENT SCHOLARSHIP FOR COLLEGE STUDENTS WHO ARE LUTHERAN
• *See page 218*

COLLEGEBOUND FOUNDATION

http://www.collegeboundfoundation.org/

JEANETTE R. WOLMAN SCHOLARSHIP
• *See page 172*

THE COMMUNITY FOUNDATION FOR GREATER ATLANTA, INC.

http://www.cfgreateratlanta.org/

STEVE DEARDUFF SCHOLARSHIP
• *See page 342*

CONTINENTAL SOCIETY, DAUGHTERS OF INDIAN WARS

http://www.csdiw.org/

CONTINENTAL SOCIETY, DAUGHTERS OF INDIAN WARS SCHOLARSHIP
• *See page 235*

GENERAL BOARD OF HIGHER EDUCATION AND MINISTRY

http://www.gbhem.org/

EDITH M. ALLEN SCHOLARSHIP
• *See page 236*

HEALTH PROFESSIONS EDUCATION FOUNDATION

http://www.healthprofessions.ca.gov/

KAISER PERMANENTE ALLIED HEALTHCARE SCHOLARSHIP
• *See page 344*

JEWISH VOCATIONAL SERVICE–CHICAGO

http://www.jvschicago.org/

JEWISH FEDERATION ACADEMIC SCHOLARSHIP PROGRAM

Scholarship for Jewish students who are born or raised in Chicago metropolitan area or Northwest Indiana or one continuous year of full-time employment in Chicago metropolitan area prior to starting professional education. Must intend to remain in the Chicago metropolitan area after completing school. For more details visit web site http://www.jvschicago.org/scholarship.

Academic Fields/Career Goals: Social Services.

Award: Scholarship for use in junior, senior, or graduate years; renewable. *Number:* up to 100. *Amount:* varies.

Eligibility Requirements: Applicant must be of Jewish heritage; enrolled or expecting to enroll full-time at a four-year institution or university and resident of Illinois or Indiana. Available to U.S. citizens.

Application Requirements: Application, financial need analysis, references. *Deadline:* February 15.

Contact: Scholarship Secretary
Jewish Vocational Service–Chicago
216 West Jackson Boulevard, Suite 700
Chicago, IL 60606
Phone: 312-673-3457
Fax: 312-553-5544
E-mail: jvsscholarship@jvschicago.org

MARGARET MCNAMARA MEMORIAL FUND

http://www.wbfn.org/

MARGARET MCNAMARA MEMORIAL FUND FELLOWSHIPS
• *See page 172*

MARYLAND STATE HIGHER EDUCATION COMMISSION

http://www.mhec.state.md.us/

GRADUATE AND PROFESSIONAL SCHOLARSHIP PROGRAM-MARYLAND
• *See page 220*

JANET L. HOFFMANN LOAN ASSISTANCE REPAYMENT PROGRAM
• *See page 241*

MEMORIAL FOUNDATION FOR JEWISH CULTURE

http://www.mfjc.org/

MEMORIAL FOUNDATION FOR JEWISH CULTURE INTERNATIONAL SCHOLARSHIP PROGRAM FOR COMMUNITY SERVICE
• *See page 106*

MEMORIAL FOUNDATION FOR JEWISH CULTURE, SCHOLARSHIPS FOR POST-RABBINICAL STUDENTS
• *See page 241*

NATIONAL BLACK POLICE ASSOCIATION

http://www.blackpolice.org/

ALPHONSO DEAL SCHOLARSHIP AWARD
• *See page 206*

NEW YORK STATE EDUCATION DEPARTMENT

http://www.highered.nysed.gov/

REGENTS PROFESSIONAL OPPORTUNITY SCHOLARSHIP
• *See page 69*

PILOT INTERNATIONAL FOUNDATION

http://www.pilotinternational.org/

PILOT INTERNATIONAL FOUNDATION RUBY NEWHALL MEMORIAL SCHOLARSHIP
• *See page 348*

PRESBYTERIAN CHURCH (USA)

http://www.pcusa.org/financialaid

STUDENT OPPORTUNITY SCHOLARSHIP
• *See page 246*

UNITED COMMUNITY SERVICES FOR WORKING FAMILIES

http://www.unitedcommunityservices.net/

TED BRICKER SCHOLARSHIP

One-time award available to child of a union member who is a parent or guardian. Must be a resident of Pennsylvania. Must submit essay that is clear, concise, persuasive, and shows a commitment to the community.

Academic Fields/Career Goals: Social Services.

Award: Scholarship for use in freshman year; not renewable. *Number:* 1. *Amount:* up to $500.

Eligibility Requirements: Applicant must be high school student; planning to enroll or expecting to enroll full-time at a four-year institution or university and resident of Pennsylvania. Applicant or parent of applicant must be member of AFL-CIO. Available to U.S. citizens.

Application Requirements: Application, essay, financial need analysis, transcript. *Deadline:* July 22.

Contact: Ruth Mathews, Executive Director
United Community Services for Working Families
601 HiestersLane'
Reading, PA 19605
Phone: 610-374-3319
E-mail: ruth.mathews@comcast.net

UNITED NEGRO COLLEGE FUND

http://www.uncf.org/

AFSCME/UNCF/HARVARD UNIVERSITY LWP UNION SCHOLARS PROGRAM
• *See page 90*

WOMEN'S INDEPENDENCE SCHOLARSHIP PROGRAM, INC.

http://www.wispinc.org/

COUNSELOR, ADVOCATE, AND SUPPORT STAFF SCHOLARSHIP PROGRAM
• *See page 76*

Y'S MEN INTERNATIONAL

http://www.ysmenusa.com/

ALEXANDER SCHOLARSHIP LOAN FUND
• *See page 159*

ZETA PHI BETA SORORITY INC. NATIONAL EDUCATIONAL FOUNDATION

http://www.zphib1920.org/

LULLELIA W. HARRISON SCHOLARSHIP IN COUNSELING
• *See page 173*

SPECIAL EDUCATION

ALBERTA HERITAGE SCHOLARSHIP FUND

http://www.alis.alberta.ca/

ANNA AND JOHN KOLESAR MEMORIAL SCHOLARSHIPS
• *See page 228*

AMERICAN LEGION AUXILIARY DEPARTMENT OF ARIZONA

http://www.azlegion.org/majorp~2.htm

AMERICAN LEGION AUXILIARY DEPARTMENT OF ARIZONA WILMA HOYAL-MAXINE CHILTON MEMORIAL SCHOLARSHIP
• *See page 481*

ARC OF WASHINGTON TRUST FUND

http://www.arcwa.org/

ARC OF WASHINGTON TRUST FUND STIPEND PROGRAM

Stipends of up to $5000 will be awarded to upper division or graduate students in schools in the states of Washington, Alaska, Oregon or Idaho. Applicants must have a demonstrated interest in the field of mental retardation. The application can be downloaded from the web site http://www.arcwa.org.

Academic Fields/Career Goals: Special Education.

Award: Scholarship for use in junior, senior, graduate, or postgraduate years; not renewable. *Number:* 1–8. *Amount:* up to $5000.

Eligibility Requirements: Applicant must be enrolled or expecting to enroll full- or part-time at a four-year institution or university and studying in Alaska, Idaho, Oregon, or Washington. Available to U.S. citizens.

Application Requirements: Application, driver's license, essay, references, transcript. *Deadline:* February 29.

Contact: Neal Lessenger, Secretary
ARC of Washington Trust Fund
PO Box 27028
Seattle, WA 98165-1428
Phone: 206-363-2206
E-mail: arcwatrust@charter.net

BETHESDA LUTHERAN COMMUNITIES

http://www.bethesdalutherancommunities.org/

DEVELOPMENTAL DISABILITIES AWARENESS AWARDS FOR HIGH SCHOOL STUDENTS WHO ARE LUTHERAN
• *See page 341*

DEVELOPMENTAL DISABILITIES SCHOLASTIC ACHIEVEMENT SCHOLARSHIP FOR COLLEGE STUDENTS WHO ARE LUTHERAN
• *See page 218*

COLLEGEBOUND FOUNDATION

http://www.collegeboundfoundation.org/

JANET B. SONDHEIM SCHOLARSHIP
• *See page 110*

ILLINOIS STUDENT ASSISTANCE COMMISSION (ISAC)

http://www.collegezone.org/

ILLINOIS SPECIAL EDUCATION TEACHER TUITION WAIVER

Teachers or students who are pursuing a career in special education as public, private or parochial preschool, elementary or secondary school teachers in Illinois may be eligible for this program. This program will exempt such individuals from paying tuition and mandatory fees at an eligible institution, for up to four years. The individual dollar amount awarded are subject to sufficient annual appropriations by the Illinois General Assembly.

Academic Fields/Career Goals: Special Education.

Award: Scholarship for use in freshman, sophomore, junior, senior, or graduate years; renewable. *Amount:* varies.

Eligibility Requirements: Applicant must be enrolled or expecting to enroll full- or part-time at a four-year institution or university; resident of Illinois and studying in Illinois. Available to U.S. citizens.

Application Requirements: Application. *Deadline:* March 1.

Contact: College Zone Counselor
Illinois Student Assistance Commission (ISAC)
1755 Lake Cook Road
Deerfield, IL 60015-5209
Phone: 800-899-4722
Fax: 847-831-8549
E-mail: collegezone@isac.org

MINORITY TEACHERS OF ILLINOIS SCHOLARSHIP PROGRAM
• *See page 238*

KENTUCKY HIGHER EDUCATION ASSISTANCE AUTHORITY (KHEAA)

http://www.kheaa.com/

MINORITY EDUCATOR RECRUITMENT AND RETENTION SCHOLARSHIP
• *See page 240*

MISSISSIPPI OFFICE OF STUDENT FINANCIAL AID

http://www.mississippi.edu/

CRITICAL NEEDS TEACHER LOAN/SCHOLARSHIP
• *See page 241*

NATIONAL FEDERATION OF THE BLIND OF CONNECTICUT

http://www.nfbct.org/

BRIAN CUMMINS MEMORIAL SCHOLARSHIP
• *See page 242*

NATIONAL INSTITUTE FOR LABOR RELATIONS RESEARCH

http://www.nilrr.org/

APPLEGATE/JACKSON/PARKS FUTURE TEACHER SCHOLARSHIP
• *See page 243*

NEW HAMPSHIRE POSTSECONDARY EDUCATION COMMISSION

http://www.nh.gov/postsecondary

WORKFORCE INCENTIVE PROGRAM
• *See page 243*

OREGON STUDENT ASSISTANCE COMMISSION

http://www.GetCollegeFunds.org/

JAMES CARLSON MEMORIAL SCHOLARSHIP
• *See page 245*

PILOT INTERNATIONAL FOUNDATION

http://www.pilotinternational.org/

PILOT INTERNATIONAL FOUNDATION RUBY NEWHALL MEMORIAL SCHOLARSHIP
• *See page 348*

PILOT INTERNATIONAL FOUNDATION SCHOLARSHIP PROGRAM
• *See page 348*

SOUTH CAROLINA STUDENT LOAN CORPORATION

http://www.scstudentloan.org/

SOUTH CAROLINA TEACHER LOAN PROGRAM
• *See page 247*

STRAIGHTFORWARD MEDIA

http://www.straightforwardmedia.com/

STRAIGHTFORWARD MEDIA TEACHER SCHOLARSHIP
• *See page 248*

TENNESSEE STUDENT ASSISTANCE CORPORATION

http://www.tn.gov/collegepays

MINORITY TEACHING FELLOWS PROGRAM/ TENNESSEE
• *See page 248*

WISCONSIN CONGRESS OF PARENTS AND TEACHERS INC.

http://www.wisconsinpta.org/

BROOKMIRE-HASTINGS SCHOLARSHIPS
• *See page 250*

SPORTS-RELATED/ EXERCISE SCIENCE

AMERICAN ALLIANCE FOR HEALTH, PHYSICAL EDUCATION, RECREATION AND DANCE

http://www.aahperd.org/

RUTH ABERNATHY PRESIDENTIAL SCHOLARSHIP
• *See page 487*

CANADIAN RECREATIONAL CANOEING ASSOCIATION

http://www.paddlingcanada.com/

BILL MASON MEMORIAL SCHOLARSHIP FUND
• *See page 232*

CANFIT

http://www.canfit.org/

CANFIT NUTRITION, PHYSICAL EDUCATION AND CULINARY ARTS SCHOLARSHIP
• *See page 209*

CLEVELAND SCHOLARSHIP PROGRAMS

http://www.cspohio.org/

CSP MANAGED FUNDS-CLEVELAND BROWNS MARION MOTLEY SCHOLARSHIP
• *See page 58*

CONNECTICUT ASSOCIATION FOR HEALTH, PHYSICAL EDUCATION, RECREATION & DANCE

http://www.ctahperd.org/

GIBSON-LAEMEL CTAHPERD SCHOLARSHIP

• *See page 234*

MARY BENEVENTO CTAHPERD SCHOLARSHIP

• *See page 234*

NATIONAL ATHLETIC TRAINERS' ASSOCIATION RESEARCH AND EDUCATION FOUNDATION

http://www.natafoundation.org/

NATIONAL ATHLETIC TRAINERS' ASSOCIATION RESEARCH AND EDUCATION FOUNDATION SCHOLARSHIP PROGRAM

• *See page 346*

PACERS FOUNDATION INC.

http://www.pacersfoundation.org/

LINDA CRAIG MEMORIAL SCHOLARSHIP PRESENTED BY ST. VINCENT SPORTS MEDICINE

• *See page 347*

PI LAMBDA THETA INC.

http://www.pilambda.org/

TOBIN SORENSON PHYSICAL EDUCATION SCHOLARSHIP

• *See page 246*

STRAIGHTFORWARD MEDIA

http://www.straightforwardmedia.com/

STRAIGHTFORWARD MEDIA VOCATIONAL-TECHNICAL SCHOOL SCHOLARSHIP

• *See page 91*

Y'S MEN INTERNATIONAL

http://www.ysmenusa.com/

ALEXANDER SCHOLARSHIP LOAN FUND

• *See page 159*

SURVEYING, SURVEYING TECHNOLOGY, CARTOGRAPHY, OR GEOGRAPHIC INFORMATION SCIENCE

AMERICAN CONGRESS ON SURVEYING AND MAPPING

http://www.acsm.net/

ACSM FELLOWS SCHOLARSHIP

One-time award available to a student with a junior or higher standing in any ACSM discipline (surveying, mapping, geographic information systems, and geodetic science). Must be ACSM member.

Academic Fields/Career Goals: Surveying, Surveying Technology, Cartography, or Geographic Information Science.

Award: Scholarship for use in freshman, sophomore, junior, or senior years; not renewable. *Number:* 1. *Amount:* $2000.

Eligibility Requirements: Applicant must be enrolled or expecting to enroll full- or part-time at a four-year institution or university. Applicant or parent of applicant must be member of American Congress on Surveying and Mapping. Available to U.S. citizens.

Application Requirements: Application, essay, references, transcript, membership proof. *Deadline:* October 1.

Contact: Dawn James, ACSM Member Organizations Administrator
American Congress on Surveying and Mapping
6 Montgomery Village Avenue, Suite 403
Gaithersburg, MD 20879
Phone: 240-632-9716 Ext. 113
Fax: 240-632-1321
E-mail: dawn.james@acsm.net

ACSM LOWELL H. AND DOROTHY LOVING UNDERGRADUATE SCHOLARSHIP

Scholarship available for a junior or senior in a college or university in the U.S. studying surveying. Program of study must include courses in two of the following areas: land surveying, geometric geodesy, photogrammetry/remote sensing, or analysis and design of spatial measurement systems.

Academic Fields/Career Goals: Surveying, Surveying Technology, Cartography, or Geographic Information Science.

Award: Scholarship for use in freshman, sophomore, junior, or senior years; not renewable. *Number:* 1. *Amount:* $2500.

Eligibility Requirements: Applicant must be enrolled or expecting to enroll full- or part-time at a four-year institution or university. Applicant or parent of applicant must be member of American Congress on Surveying and Mapping. Available to U.S. citizens.

Application Requirements: Application, essay, references, transcript, membership proof. *Deadline:* October 1.

Contact: Dawn James, ACSM Member Organizations Administrator
American Congress on Surveying and Mapping
6 Montgomery Village Avenue, Suite 403
Gaithersbutg, MD 20879
Phone: 240-632-9716
Fax: 240-632-1321
E-mail: dawn.james@acsm.net

AMERICAN ASSOCIATION FOR GEODETIC SURVEYING JOSEPH F. DRACUP SCHOLARSHIP AWARD

Award for students enrolled in a four-year degree program in surveying (or in closely-related degree programs such as geomatics or surveying engineering). Preference given to applicants from programs with significant focus on geodetic surveying. Must be ACSM member.

Academic Fields/Career Goals: Surveying, Surveying Technology, Cartography, or Geographic Information Science.

Award: Scholarship for use in freshman, sophomore, junior, or senior years; not renewable. *Number:* 1. *Amount:* $2000.

Eligibility Requirements: Applicant must be enrolled or expecting to enroll full- or part-time at a four-year institution or university. Applicant or parent of applicant must be member of American Congress on Surveying and Mapping. Available to U.S. and non-Canadian citizens.

Application Requirements: Application, essay, references, transcript. *Deadline:* October 1.

Contact: Dawn James, ACSM Member Organizations Administrator
American Congress on Surveying and Mapping
6 Montgomery Village Avenue, Suite 403
Gaithersburg, MD 20879
Phone: 240-632-9716 Ext. 113
Fax: 240-632-1321
E-mail: dawn.james@acsm.net

BERNTSEN INTERNATIONAL SCHOLARSHIP IN SURVEYING

Award of $1500 for full-time students enrolled in a four-year degree program in surveying or in a closely-related degree program, such as geomatics or surveying engineering. Must be ACSM member.

Academic Fields/Career Goals: Surveying, Surveying Technology, Cartography, or Geographic Information Science.

Award: Scholarship for use in freshman, sophomore, junior, or senior years; not renewable. *Number:* 1. *Amount:* $1500.

Eligibility Requirements: Applicant must be enrolled or expecting to enroll full-time at a four-year institution or university. Applicant or parent of applicant must be member of American Congress on Surveying and Mapping. Available to U.S. citizens.

Application Requirements: Application, essay, references, transcript. *Deadline:* October 1.

Contact: Dawn James, ACSM Member Organizations Administrator
American Congress on Surveying and Mapping
6 Montgomery Village Avenue, Suite 403
Gaithersburg, MD 20879
Phone: 240-632-9716 Ext. 113
Fax: 240-632-1321
E-mail: dawn.james@acsm.net

BERNTSEN INTERNATIONAL SCHOLARSHIP IN SURVEYING TECHNOLOGY

Award for full-time undergraduate students enrolled in a two-year degree program in surveying technology. For U.S. study only. Must be a member of the American Congress on Surveying and Mapping. See web site for application and more details http://www.acsm.net/scholar.html.

Academic Fields/Career Goals: Surveying, Surveying Technology, Cartography, or Geographic Information Science.

Award: Scholarship for use in freshman or sophomore years; not renewable. *Number:* 1. *Amount:* $500.

Eligibility Requirements: Applicant must be enrolled or expecting to enroll full-time at a two-year or four-year institution. Applicant or parent of applicant must be member of American Congress on Surveying and Mapping. Available to U.S. and non-Canadian citizens.

Application Requirements: Application, essay, references, transcript, proof of membership in ACSM. *Deadline:* October 1.

Contact: Dawn James, ACSM Member Organizations Administrator
American Congress on Surveying and Mapping
6 Montgomery Village Avenue, Suite 403
Gaithersburg, MD 20879
Phone: 240-632-9716 Ext. 113
Fax: 240-632-1321
E-mail: dawn.james@acsm.net

CADY MCDONNELL MEMORIAL SCHOLARSHIP

Award of $1000 for female surveying student. Must be a resident of one of the following western states: Alaska, Arizona, California, Colorado, Hawaii, Idaho, Montana, Nevada, New Mexico, Oregon, Utah, Washington, and Wyoming. Must provide proof of legal home residence and be a member of the American Congress on Surveying and Mapping.

Academic Fields/Career Goals: Surveying, Surveying Technology, Cartography, or Geographic Information Science.

Award: Scholarship for use in freshman, sophomore, junior, or senior years; not renewable. *Number:* 1. *Amount:* $1000.

Eligibility Requirements: Applicant must be enrolled or expecting to enroll full- or part-time at a two-year or four-year institution or uni-

versity; female and resident of Alaska, Arizona, California, Colorado, Hawaii, Idaho, Montana, Nevada, New Mexico, Oregon, Utah, Washington, or Wyoming. Applicant or parent of applicant must be member of American Congress on Surveying and Mapping. Available to U.S. citizens.

Application Requirements: Application, essay, financial need analysis, references, transcript, proof of residence, membership proof, personal statement. *Deadline:* October 1.

Contact: Dawn James, ACSM Member Organizations Administrator
American Congress on Surveying and Mapping
6 Montgomery Village Avenue, Suite 403
Gaithersburg, MD 20879
Phone: 240-632-9716 Ext. 113
Fax: 240-632-1321
E-mail: dawn.james@acsm.net

NATIONAL SOCIETY OF PROFESSIONAL SURVEYORS BOARD OF GOVERNORS SCHOLARSHIP

Award available to students enrolled in surveying program entering junior year of study at four-year institution. Minimum 3.0 GPA required. Must be ACSM member.

Academic Fields/Career Goals: Surveying, Surveying Technology, Cartography, or Geographic Information Science.

Award: Scholarship for use in junior year; not renewable. *Number:* 1. *Amount:* up to $1000.

Eligibility Requirements: Applicant must be enrolled or expecting to enroll full- or part-time at a four-year institution or university. Applicant or parent of applicant must be member of American Congress on Surveying and Mapping. Applicant must have 3.0 GPA or higher. Available to U.S. citizens.

Application Requirements: Application, essay, financial need analysis, references, transcript, membership proof. *Deadline:* October 1.

Contact: Dawn James, ACSM Member Organizations Administrator
American Congress on Surveying and Mapping
6 Montgomery Village Avenue, Suite 403
Gaithersburg, MD 20879
Phone: 240-632-9716 Ext. 113
Fax: 240-632-1321
E-mail: dawn.james@acsm.net

NATIONAL SOCIETY OF PROFESSIONAL SURVEYORS SCHOLARSHIPS

Two awards of $1000 each to students enrolled full-time in a four-year undergraduate surveying program. Must be ACSM member.

Academic Fields/Career Goals: Surveying, Surveying Technology, Cartography, or Geographic Information Science.

Award: Scholarship for use in freshman, sophomore, junior, or senior years; not renewable. *Number:* 2. *Amount:* $1000.

Eligibility Requirements: Applicant must be enrolled or expecting to enroll full-time at a four-year institution or university. Applicant or parent of applicant must be member of American Congress on Surveying and Mapping. Available to U.S. and non-Canadian citizens.

Application Requirements: Application, essay, references, transcript, ACSM membership. *Deadline:* October 1.

Contact: Dawn James, ACSM Member Organizations Administrator
American Congress on Surveying and Mapping
6 Montgomery Village Avenue, Suite 403
Gaithersburg, MD 20879
Phone: 240-632-9716 Ext. 113
Fax: 240-632-1321
E-mail: dawn.james@acsm.net

NETTIE DRACUP MEMORIAL SCHOLARSHIP

Award for undergraduate student enrolled in a four-year geodetic surveying program at an accredited college or university. Must be U.S. citizen. Must be ACSM member.

Academic Fields/Career Goals: Surveying, Surveying Technology, Cartography, or Geographic Information Science.

Award: Scholarship for use in freshman, sophomore, junior, or senior years; not renewable. *Number:* 2. *Amount:* $2000.

Eligibility Requirements: Applicant must be enrolled or expecting to enroll full-time at a four-year institution or university. Applicant or parent of applicant must be member of American Congress on Surveying and Mapping. Available to U.S. citizens.

Application Requirements: Application, essay, financial need analysis, references, transcript, ACSM membership proof. *Deadline:* October 1.

Contact: Dawn James, Member Organizations Administrator
American Congress on Surveying and Mapping
6 Montgomery Village Avenue, Suite 403
Gaithersburg, MD 20879
Phone: 240-632-9716 Ext. 113
Fax: 240-632-1321
E-mail: dawn.james@acsm.net

SCHONSTEDT SCHOLARSHIP IN SURVEYING

Award preference given to applicants with junior or senior standing in a four-year program in surveying. Schonstedt donates magnetic locator to surveying program at each recipient's school. Must be ACSM member.

Academic Fields/Career Goals: Surveying, Surveying Technology, Cartography, or Geographic Information Science.

Award: Scholarship for use in junior or senior years; not renewable. *Number:* 2. *Amount:* $1500.

Eligibility Requirements: Applicant must be enrolled or expecting to enroll full-time at a four-year institution or university. Applicant or parent of applicant must be member of American Congress on Surveying and Mapping. Available to U.S. citizens.

Application Requirements: Application, essay, references, transcript, ACSM membership proof. *Deadline:* October 1.

Contact: Dawn James, ACSM Member Organizations Administrator
American Congress on Surveying and Mapping
6 Montgomery Village Avenue, Suite 403
Gaithersburg, MD 20879
Phone: 240-632-9716 Ext. 113
Fax: 240-632-1321
E-mail: dawn.james@acsm.net

TRI-STATE SURVEYING AND PHOTOGRAMMETRY KRIS M. KUNZE MEMORIAL SCHOLARSHIP
• *See page 145*

ASPRS, THE IMAGING AND GEOSPATIAL INFORMATION SOCIETY

http://www.asprs.org/

ABRAHAM ANSON MEMORIAL SCHOLARSHIP
• *See page 280*

FRANCIS H. MOFFITT MEMORIAL SCHOLARSHIP
• *See page 280*

JOHN O. BEHRENS INSTITUTE FOR LAND INFORMATION MEMORIAL SCHOLARSHIP
• *See page 281*

KENNETH J. OSBORN MEMORIAL SCHOLARSHIP
• *See page 281*

ROBERT E. ALTENHOFEN MEMORIAL SCHOLARSHIP
• *See page 281*

ASSOCIATED GENERAL CONTRACTORS OF NEW YORK STATE, LLC

http://www.agcnys.org/

ASSOCIATED GENERAL CONTRACTORS NYS SCHOLARSHIP
• *See page 176*

ASSOCIATION OF CALIFORNIA WATER AGENCIES

http://www.acwa.com/

ASSOCIATION OF CALIFORNIA WATER AGENCIES SCHOLARSHIPS
• *See page 94*

CLAIR A. HILL SCHOLARSHIP
• *See page 94*

CENTRAL INTELLIGENCE AGENCY

http://www.cia.gov/

CENTRAL INTELLIGENCE AGENCY UNDERGRADUATE SCHOLARSHIP PROGRAM
• *See page 58*

FLORIDA ENGINEERING SOCIETY

http://www.fleng.org/

ACEC/FLORIDA SCHOLARSHIP
• *See page 283*

OREGON STUDENT ASSISTANCE COMMISSION

http://www.GetCollegeFunds.org/

PROFESSIONAL LAND SURVEYORS OF OREGON SCHOLARSHIPS

Award for sophomores or above enrolled in Oregon public and nonprofit colleges and engaged in a course of study leading to land-surveying career. Community college applicants must intend to transfer to four-year college. Oregon residency not required. Must intend to take Fundamentals of Land Surveying exam. Additional essay stating education/career goals and their relation to land surveying is required. FAFSA and two references also required.

Academic Fields/Career Goals: Surveying, Surveying Technology, Cartography, or Geographic Information Science.

Award: Scholarship for use in sophomore, junior, or senior years; renewable.

Eligibility Requirements: Applicant must be enrolled or expecting to enroll full-time at a four-year institution or university and studying in Oregon. Available to U.S. citizens.

Application Requirements: Application, essay, financial need analysis, references, transcript, activity chart. *Deadline:* March 1.

Contact: Director of Grant Programs
Oregon Student Assistance Commission
1500 Valley River Drive, Suite 100
Eugene, OR 97401-7020
Phone: 800-452-8807 Ext. 7395

PROFESSIONAL CONSTRUCTION ESTIMATORS ASSOCIATION

http://www.pcea.org/

TED WILSON MEMORIAL SCHOLARSHIP FOUNDATION
• *See page 179*

RHODE ISLAND SOCIETY OF PROFESSIONAL LAND SURVEYORS

http://www.rispls.org/

PIERRE H. GUILLEMETTE SCHOLARSHIP

Scholarship available to any Rhode Island resident enrolled in a certificate or degree program in land surveying at a qualified institution of higher learning.

Academic Fields/Career Goals: Surveying, Surveying Technology, Cartography, or Geographic Information Science.

Award: Scholarship for use in freshman, sophomore, junior, or senior years; not renewable. *Number:* varies. *Amount:* varies.

Eligibility Requirements: Applicant must be enrolled or expecting to enroll full- or part-time at a four-year institution or university and resident of Rhode Island. Available to U.S. citizens.

Application Requirements: Application, resume, transcript. *Deadline:* October 30.

Contact: Scholarship Coordinator
Rhode Island Society of Professional Land Surveyors
PO Box 544
East Greenwich, RI 02818
Phone: 401-294-1262
E-mail: info@rispls.org

THERAPY/ REHABILITATION

ALBERTA HERITAGE SCHOLARSHIP FUND

http://www.alis.alberta.ca/

ALBERTA HERITAGE SCHOLARSHIP FUND ABORIGINAL HEALTH CAREERS BURSARY
• *See page 137*

AMERICAN FOUNDATION FOR THE BLIND

http://www.afb.org/

DELTA GAMMA FOUNDATION FLORENCE MARGARET HARVEY MEMORIAL SCHOLARSHIP
• *See page 229*

RUDOLPH DILLMAN MEMORIAL SCHOLARSHIP
• *See page 230*

AMERICAN LEGION AUXILIARY DEPARTMENT OF MICHIGAN

http://www.michalaux.org/

AMERICAN LEGION AUXILIARY DEPARTMENT OF MICHIGAN MEDICAL CAREER SCHOLARSHIP
• *See page 337*

AMERICAN LEGION AUXILIARY DEPARTMENT OF WYOMING

AMERICAN LEGION AUXILIARY DEPARTMENT OF WYOMING PAST PRESIDENTS' PARLEY HEALTH CARE SCHOLARSHIP
• *See page 218*

AMERICAN OCCUPATIONAL THERAPY FOUNDATION INC.

http://www.aotf.org/

AMERICAN OCCUPATIONAL THERAPY FOUNDATION STATE ASSOCIATION SCHOLARSHIPS
• *See page 338*

CARLOTTA WELLES SCHOLARSHIP
• *See page 338*

AMERICAN PHYSICAL THERAPY ASSOCIATION

http://www.apta.org/

MINORITY SCHOLARSHIP AWARD FOR ACADEMIC EXCELLENCE-PHYSICAL THERAPIST ASSISTANT
• *See page 339*

AMERICAN RESPIRATORY CARE FOUNDATION

http://www.arcfoundation.org/

JIMMY A. YOUNG MEMORIAL EDUCATION RECOGNITION AWARD
• *See page 339*

MORTON B. DUGGAN, JR. MEMORIAL EDUCATION RECOGNITION AWARD
• *See page 339*

NBRC/AMP ROBERT M. LAWRENCE, MD EDUCATION RECOGNITION AWARD
• *See page 339*

NBRC/AMP WILLIAM W. BURGIN, MD EDUCATION RECOGNITION AWARD
• *See page 339*

SEPRACOR ACHIEVEMENT AWARD FOR EXCELLENCE IN PULMONARY DISEASE STATE MANAGEMENT
• *See page 339*

ARRL FOUNDATION INC.

http://www.arrl.org/

CAROLE J. STREETER, KB9JBR SCHOLARSHIP
• *See page 218*

BETHESDA LUTHERAN COMMUNITIES

http://www.bethesdalutherancommunities.org/

DEVELOPMENTAL DISABILITIES AWARENESS AWARDS FOR HIGH SCHOOL STUDENTS WHO ARE LUTHERAN
• *See page 341*

DEVELOPMENTAL DISABILITIES SCHOLASTIC ACHIEVEMENT SCHOLARSHIP FOR COLLEGE STUDENTS WHO ARE LUTHERAN
• *See page 218*

CLEVELAND SCHOLARSHIP PROGRAMS

http://www.cspohio.org/

CSP MANAGED FUNDS-CLEVELAND BROWNS MARION MOTLEY SCHOLARSHIP
• *See page 58*

CYNTHIA E. MORGAN SCHOLARSHIP FUND (CEMS)

http://www.cemsfund.com/

CYNTHIA E. MORGAN MEMORIAL SCHOLARSHIP FUND, INC.
• *See page 304*

HEALTH PROFESSIONS EDUCATION FOUNDATION

http://www.healthprofessions.ca.gov/

KAISER PERMANENTE ALLIED HEALTHCARE SCHOLARSHIP
• *See page 344*

INDIAN HEALTH SERVICES, UNITED STATES DEPARTMENT OF HEALTH AND HUMAN SERVICES

http://www.ihs.gov/

INDIAN HEALTH SERVICE HEALTH PROFESSIONS SCHOLARSHIP PROGRAM
• *See page 335*

INTERNATIONAL ORDER OF THE KING'S DAUGHTERS AND SONS

http://www.iokds.org/

HEALTH CAREERS SCHOLARSHIP
• *See page 219*

LADIES AUXILIARY TO THE VETERANS OF FOREIGN WARS, DEPARTMENT OF MAINE

http://mainevfw.org/

FRANCES L. BOOTH MEDICAL SCHOLARSHIP SPONSORED BY LAVFW DEPARTMENT OF MAINE
• *See page 344*

MARYLAND STATE HIGHER EDUCATION COMMISSION

http://www.mhec.state.md.us/

JANET L. HOFFMANN LOAN ASSISTANCE REPAYMENT PROGRAM
• *See page 241*

MISSISSIPPI OFFICE OF STUDENT FINANCIAL AID

http://www.mississippi.edu/

MISSISSIPPI HEALTH CARE PROFESSIONS LOAN/ SCHOLARSHIP PROGRAM
• *See page 346*

NATIONAL AMBUCS INC.

http://www.ambucs.org/

AMBUCS SCHOLARS-SCHOLARSHIPS FOR THERAPISTS
• *See page 118*

NATIONAL ATHLETIC TRAINERS' ASSOCIATION RESEARCH AND EDUCATION FOUNDATION

http://www.natafoundation.org/

NATIONAL ATHLETIC TRAINERS' ASSOCIATION RESEARCH AND EDUCATION FOUNDATION SCHOLARSHIP PROGRAM
• *See page 346*

NATIONAL SOCIETY DAUGHTERS OF THE AMERICAN REVOLUTION

http://www.dar.org/

NATIONAL SOCIETY DAUGHTERS OF THE AMERICAN REVOLUTION OCCUPATIONAL THERAPY SCHOLARSHIP

Scholarship of $1000 for students who are in financial need and have been accepted or are attending an accredited school of occupational therapy including art, music or physical therapy. A letter of acceptance into the occupational therapy program or the transcript stating the applicant is in the occupational therapy program must be included with the application.

Academic Fields/Career Goals: Therapy/Rehabilitation.

Award: Scholarship for use in freshman, sophomore, junior, senior, or graduate years; not renewable. *Number:* varies. *Amount:* $1000.

Eligibility Requirements: Applicant must be enrolled or expecting to enroll full- or part-time at a two-year or four-year institution or university. Available to U.S. citizens.

Application Requirements: Application, essay, financial need analysis, references, self-addressed stamped envelope, transcript, letter of sponsorship. *Deadline:* February 15.

Contact: Eric Weisz, Manager, Office of the Reporter General
National Society Daughters of the American Revolution
1776 D Street, NW
Washington, DC 20006-5303
Phone: 202-628-1776
Fax: 202-879-3348
E-mail: nsdarscholarships@dar.org

NEW MEXICO COMMISSION ON HIGHER EDUCATION

http://www.hed.state.nm.us/

ALLIED HEALTH STUDENT LOAN PROGRAM-NEW MEXICO
• *See page 220*

NORTH CAROLINA STATE EDUCATION ASSISTANCE AUTHORITY

http://www.ncseaa.edu/

NORTH CAROLINA STUDENT LOAN PROGRAM FOR HEALTH, SCIENCE, AND MATHEMATICS
• *See page 221*

OREGON STUDENT ASSISTANCE COMMISSION

http://www.GetCollegeFunds.org/

MARION A. LINDEMAN SCHOLARSHIP
• *See page 347*

PACERS FOUNDATION INC.

http://www.pacersfoundation.org/

LINDA CRAIG MEMORIAL SCHOLARSHIP PRESENTED BY ST. VINCENT SPORTS MEDICINE
• *See page 347*

PI LAMBDA THETA INC.

http://www.pilambda.org/

TOBIN SORENSON PHYSICAL EDUCATION SCHOLARSHIP
• *See page 246*

PILOT INTERNATIONAL FOUNDATION

http://www.pilotinternational.org/

PILOT INTERNATIONAL FOUNDATION RUBY NEWHALL MEMORIAL SCHOLARSHIP
• *See page 348*

PILOT INTERNATIONAL FOUNDATION SCHOLARSHIP PROGRAM
• *See page 348*

SIGMA ALPHA IOTA PHILANTHROPIES, INC.

http://www.sai-national.org/

SIGMA ALPHA IOTA MUSIC THERAPY SCHOLARSHIP
• *See page 427*

STRAIGHTFORWARD MEDIA

http://www.straightforwardmedia.com/

STRAIGHTFORWARD MEDIA MEDICAL PROFESSIONS SCHOLARSHIP
• *See page 221*

U. S. DEPARTMENT OF HEALTH AND HUMAN SERVICES

http://www.hhs.gov/about/whatwedo.html/

U. S. PUBLIC HEALTH SERVICE-HEALTH RESOURCES AND SERVICES ADMINISTRATION, BUREAU OF HEALTH PROFESSIONS SCHOLARSHIPS FOR DISADVANTAGED STUDENTS
• *See page 221*

WOMEN'S INDEPENDENCE SCHOLARSHIP PROGRAM, INC.

http://www.wispinc.org/

COUNSELOR, ADVOCATE, AND SUPPORT STAFF SCHOLARSHIP PROGRAM
• *See page 76*

TRADE/TECHNICAL SPECIALTIES

AIRCRAFT ELECTRONICS ASSOCIATION EDUCATIONAL FOUNDATION

http://www.aea.net/

BUD GLOVER MEMORIAL SCHOLARSHIP
• *See page 118*

DUTCH AND GINGER ARVER SCHOLARSHIP
• *See page 119*

GARMIN-JERRY SMITH MEMORIAL SCHOLARSHIP
• *See page 119*

GARMIN SCHOLARSHIP
• *See page 119*

LEE TARBOX MEMORIAL SCHOLARSHIP
• *See page 120*

LOWELL GAYLOR MEMORIAL SCHOLARSHIP
• *See page 120*

MID-CONTINENT INSTRUMENT SCHOLARSHIP
• *See page 120*

ALBERTA HERITAGE SCHOLARSHIP FUND

http://www.alis.alberta.ca/

REGISTERED APPRENTICESHIP PROGRAM (RAP) SCHOLARSHIPS
Scholarships of CAN$1000 available for high school graduates who are registered as apprentices in a trade while in high school to encourage recipients to continue their apprenticeship or occupational training programs after graduation. Must be a Canadian citizen or landed immigrant and Alberta resident. For more details see web site http://alis.alberta.ca.

Academic Fields/Career Goals: Trade/Technical Specialties.

Award: Scholarship for use in freshman year; not renewable.

Eligibility Requirements: Applicant must be enrolled or expecting to enroll full-time at a technical institution and resident of Alberta. Available to Canadian citizens.

Application Requirements: Application, essay. *Deadline:* July 31.

Contact: Scholarship Committee
Alberta Heritage Scholarship Fund
9940 106th Street, Fourth Floor, Sterling Place
PO Box 28000, Station Main
Edmonton, AB T5J 4R4
Canada
Phone: 780-427-8640
E-mail: scholarships@gov.ab.ca

AMERICAN LEGION DEPARTMENT OF PENNSYLVANIA

http://www.pa-legion.com/

ROBERT W. VALIMONT ENDOWMENT FUND SCHOLARSHIP (PART II)
Scholarships for any Pennsylvania high school senior seeking admission to a two-year college, post-high school trade/technical school, or training program. Must attend school in Pennsylvania. Continuation of award is based on grades. Renewable award of $600. Number of awards varies from year to year. Membership in an American Legion post in Pennsylvania is not required, but it must be documented if it does apply.

Academic Fields/Career Goals: Trade/Technical Specialties.

Award: Scholarship for use in freshman year; renewable. *Number:* varies. *Amount:* $600.

Eligibility Requirements: Applicant must be high school student; planning to enroll or expecting to enroll full-time at a two-year or technical institution; resident of Pennsylvania and studying in Pennsylvania. Applicant must have 2.5 GPA or higher. Available to U.S. citizens.

Application Requirements: Application, financial need analysis, test scores, transcript. *Deadline:* May 30.

Contact: Debbie Watson, Emblem Sales Supervisor
American Legion Department of Pennsylvania
PO Box 2324
Harrisburg, PA 17105-2324
Phone: 717-730-9100
Fax: 717-975-2836
E-mail: hq@pa-legion.com

AMERICAN SOCIETY OF HEATING, REFRIGERATING, AND AIR CONDITIONING ENGINEERS, INC.

http://www.ashrae.org/

ALWIN B. NEWTON SCHOLARSHIP FUND
• *See page 253*

ASHRAE GENERAL SCHOLARSHIP
• *See page 262*

ASHRAE MEMORIAL SCHOLARSHIP
• *See page 253*

DUANE HANSON SCHOLARSHIP
• *See page 253*

FRANK M. CODA SCHOLARSHIP
• *See page 254*

HENRY ADAMS SCHOLARSHIP
• *See page 254*

REUBEN TRANE SCHOLARSHIP
• *See page 254*

AMERICAN WELDING SOCIETY

http://www.aws.org/

AMERICAN WELDING SOCIETY DISTRICT SCHOLARSHIP PROGRAM
• *See page 263*

AMERICAN WELDING SOCIETY INTERNATIONAL SCHOLARSHIP
• *See page 263*

ARSHAM AMIRIKIAN ENGINEERING SCHOLARSHIP
• *See page 175*

DONALD F. HASTINGS SCHOLARSHIP
• *See page 263*

EDWARD J. BRADY MEMORIAL SCHOLARSHIP
• *See page 264*

HOWARD E. AND WILMA J. ADKINS MEMORIAL SCHOLARSHIP
• *See page 264*

MILLER ELECTRIC INTERNATIONAL WORLD SKILLS COMPETITION SCHOLARSHIP
• *See page 264*

MILLER ELECTRIC MFG. CO. SCHOLARSHIP
• *See page 264*

ASSOCIATED GENERAL CONTRACTORS OF NEW YORK STATE, LLC

http://www.agcnys.org/

ASSOCIATED GENERAL CONTRACTORS NYS SCHOLARSHIP
• *See page 176*

AUTOMOTIVE HALL OF FAME

http://www.automotivehalloffame.org/

AUTOMOTIVE HALL OF FAME EDUCATIONAL FUNDS
• *See page 164*

BOY SCOUTS OF AMERICA-MUSKINGUM VALLEY COUNCIL

http://www.learning-for-life.org/

AFL-CIO SKILL TRADES SCHOLARSHIP

Two $1000 scholarships awarded annually to skilled trade explorers to help them support their education. Must be a graduating high school senior in May or June of the year the application is made. School selected by the applicant must be an accredited public or proprietary institution or union apprentice program.

Academic Fields/Career Goals: Trade/Technical Specialties.

Award: Scholarship for use in freshman year; not renewable. *Number:* 2. *Amount:* $1000.

Eligibility Requirements: Applicant must be high school student and planning to enroll or expecting to enroll full- or part-time at a technical institution. Available to U.S. and non-U.S. citizens.

Application Requirements: Application, essay, photo, references, transcript. *Deadline:* April 30.

Contact: Bill Rogers, Associate Director
Boy Scouts of America-Muskingum Valley Council
1325 West Walnut Hill Lane
PO Box 152079
Irving, TX 75015-2079
Phone: 972-580-2433
Fax: 972-580-2137
E-mail: brogers@lflmail.org

GLOBAL AUTOMOTIVE AFTERMARKET SYMPOSIUM

http://www.automotivescholarships.com/

GAAS SCHOLARSHIP
• *See page 266*

IFDA EDUCATIONAL FOUNDATION

http://www.ifdaef.org/

IFDA LEADERS COMMEMORATIVE SCHOLARSHIP
• *See page 371*

IFDA STUDENT SCHOLARSHIP
• *See page 371*

INTERNATIONAL EXECUTIVE HOUSEKEEPERS ASSOCIATION

http://www.ieha.org/

INTERNATIONAL EXECUTIVE HOUSEKEEPERS EDUCATIONAL FOUNDATION
• *See page 322*

INTERNATIONAL UNION OF ELECTRONIC, ELECTRICAL, SALARIED, MACHINE, AND FURNITURE WORKERS-CWA

http://www.iue-cwa.org/

JAMES B. CAREY SCHOLARSHIP AWARD
• *See page 450*

LEARNING FOR LIFE

http://www.learning-for-life.org/

AFL-CIO SKILLED TRADES EXPLORING SCHOLARSHIPS

Two $1000 scholarships awarded annually to Explorers to help them support their education toward a career in skilled trades. Applicant must be a graduating high school senior in May or June of the year the application is issued. The school selected by the applicant must be an accredited public or proprietary institution or a union apprentice program.

Academic Fields/Career Goals: Trade/Technical Specialties.

Award: Scholarship for use in freshman year; not renewable. *Number:* up to 2. *Amount:* $1000.

Eligibility Requirements: Applicant must be high school student and planning to enroll or expecting to enroll full- or part-time at a technical institution. Applicant or parent of applicant must be member of Explorer Program/Learning for Life. Available to U.S. citizens.

Application Requirements: Application, essay, photo, references, transcript. *Deadline:* April 30.

Contact: Peggy Chestnutt
   Phone: 972-580-2428
   E-mail: pchestnu@lflmail.org

MAINE EDUCATION SERVICES

http://www.mesfoundation.com/

MAINE METAL PRODUCTS ASSOCIATION SCHOLARSHIP
• *See page 414*

MANUFACTURERS ASSOCIATION OF MAINE

http://www.mainemfg.com/

MAINE METAL PRODUCTS EDUCATION FUND SCHOLARSHIP PROGRAM
• *See page 127*

MARION D. AND EVA S. PEEPLES FOUNDATION TRUST SCHOLARSHIP PROGRAM

http://www.jccf.org/

MARION A. AND EVA S. PEEPLES SCHOLARSHIPS
• *See page 240*

MARYLAND ASSOCIATION OF PRIVATE COLLEGES AND CAREER SCHOOLS

http://www.mapccs.org/

MARYLAND ASSOCIATION OF PRIVATE COLLEGES AND CAREER SCHOOLS SCHOLARSHIP
• *See page 153*

MARYLAND STATE HIGHER EDUCATION COMMISSION

http://www.mhec.state.md.us/

CHARLES W. RILEY FIRE AND EMERGENCY MEDICAL SERVICES TUITION REIMBURSEMENT PROGRAM
• *See page 316*

MIDWEST ROOFING CONTRACTORS ASSOCIATION

http://www.mrca.org/

MRCA FOUNDATION SCHOLARSHIP PROGRAM
• *See page 102*

NASA'S VIRGINIA SPACE GRANT CONSORTIUM

http://www.vsgc.odu.edu/

TEACHER EDUCATION STEM SCHOLARSHIP PROGRAM
• *See page 96*

NATIONAL ASSOCIATION OF WATER COMPANIES-NEW JERSEY CHAPTER

http://www.nawc.org/

NATIONAL ASSOCIATION OF WATER COMPANIES-NEW JERSEY CHAPTER SCHOLARSHIP
• *See page 142*

NATIONAL ASSOCIATION OF WOMEN IN CONSTRUCTION

http://www.nawic.org/

NAWIC CONSTRUCTION TRADES SCHOLARSHIP

Scholarship for women pursuing a trade apprenticeship program. Only for students attending school in the United States or Canada.

Academic Fields/Career Goals: Trade/Technical Specialties.

Award: Scholarship for use in sophomore or junior years; not renewable. *Number:* 1. *Amount:* $1000–$2000.

Eligibility Requirements: Applicant must be enrolled or expecting to enroll full-time at a technical institution. Available to U.S. and Canadian citizens.

Application Requirements: Application, essay, transcript. *Deadline:* March 15.

Contact: Scholarship Committee
   National Association of Women in Construction
   327 South Adams Street
   Fort Worth, TX 76104
   Phone: 817-877-5551
   Fax: 817-877-0324

NAWIC UNDERGRADUATE SCHOLARSHIPS
• *See page 102*

NORTH CAROLINA COMMUNITY COLLEGE SYSTEM-STUDENT DEVELOPMENT SERVICES

http://www.ncccs.cc.nc.us/

WACHOVIA TECHNICAL SCHOLARSHIP PROGRAM

One scholarship per college valued at $500 each. These scholarships are distributed among the 58 colleges in the community college system, which may be distributed in two payments: fall semester, $250; and spring semester, $250. To qualify as a candidate for these scholarships, a person must meet the following criteria: 1. Is a full-time student enrolled in the second year of a two-year educational/technical program. 2. Demonstrate financial need. 3. Demonstrate scholastic promise. 4. Use the scholarship to pay for tuition, books, and transportation. The recipients of the scholarships will be selected each year from applicants meeting the above criteria at local colleges.

Academic Fields/Career Goals: Trade/Technical Specialties.

Award: Scholarship for use in freshman or sophomore years; not renewable. *Amount:* $500.

Eligibility Requirements: Applicant must be enrolled or expecting to enroll full-time at a two-year or technical institution; resident of North Carolina and studying in North Carolina. Available to U.S. citizens.

Application Requirements: Application, essay. *Deadline:* continuous.

Contact: Charletta Sims Evans, Associate Director of Student
        Development Services
      North Carolina Community College System-Student
        Development Services
      5016 Mail Service Center
      Raleigh, NC 27699-5016
      Phone: 919-807-7106
      E-mail: simsc@nccommunitycolleges.edu

PLASTICS INSTITUTE OF AMERICA

http://www.plasticsinstitute.org/

PLASTICS PIONEERS SCHOLARSHIPS
• *See page 168*

PLUMBING-HEATING-COOLING CONTRACTORS EDUCATION FOUNDATION

http://www.foundation.phccweb.org/

BRADFORD WHITE CORPORATION SCHOLARSHIP
• *See page 351*

DELTA FAUCET COMPANY SCHOLARSHIP PROGRAM
• *See page 103*

PHCC EDUCATIONAL FOUNDATION NEED-BASED SCHOLARSHIP
• *See page 155*

PHCC EDUCATIONAL FOUNDATION SCHOLARSHIP PROGRAM
• *See page 155*

PROFESSIONAL AVIATION MAINTENANCE FOUNDATION

http://www.pama.org/

PROFESSIONAL AVIATION MAINTENANCE FOUNDATION STUDENT SCHOLARSHIP PROGRAM
• *See page 132*

PROFESSIONAL CONSTRUCTION ESTIMATORS ASSOCIATION

http://www.pcea.org/

TED WILSON MEMORIAL SCHOLARSHIP FOUNDATION
• *See page 179*

ROCKY MOUNTAIN COAL MINING INSTITUTE

http://www.rmcmi.org/

ROCKY MOUNTAIN COAL MINING INSTITUTE TECHNICAL SCHOLARSHIP

Scholarship for a first or second year student at a two-year technical/trade school in good standing at the time of selection. The student must be in a discipline related to potential use in the coal mining industry. Must be U.S. citizen and a legal resident of one of the Rocky Mountain Coal Mining Institute member states.

Academic Fields/Career Goals: Trade/Technical Specialties.

Award: Scholarship for use in freshman or sophomore years; not renewable. *Number:* 8. *Amount:* $1000.

Eligibility Requirements: Applicant must be enrolled or expecting to enroll full-time at a technical institution and resident of Arizona, Colorado, Montana, New Mexico, North Dakota, Texas, Utah, or Wyoming. Available to U.S. citizens.

Application Requirements: Application, essay, interview. *Deadline:* February 1.

Contact: Shahreen Salam, Executive Assistant
      Rocky Mountain Coal Mining Institute
      8057 South Yukon Way
      Littleton, CO 80128-5510
      Phone: 303-948-3300
      Fax: 303-948-1132
      E-mail: mail@rmcmi.org

SOCIETY OF MANUFACTURING ENGINEERS EDUCATION FOUNDATION

http://www.smeef.org/

CHAPTER 67-PHOENIX SCHOLARSHIP
• *See page 295*

CHAPTER 198-DOWNRIVER DETROIT SCHOLARSHIP
• *See page 295*

CLINTON J. HELTON MANUFACTURING SCHOLARSHIP AWARD FUND
• *See page 296*

E. WAYNE KAY COMMUNITY COLLEGE SCHOLARSHIP AWARD
• *See page 297*

E. WAYNE KAY SCHOLARSHIP
• *See page 297*

FORT WAYNE CHAPTER 56 SCHOLARSHIP
• *See page 297*

NORTH CENTRAL REGION 9 SCHOLARSHIP
• *See page 298*

WICHITA CHAPTER 52 SCHOLARSHIP
• *See page 298*

WILLIAM E. WEISEL SCHOLARSHIP FUND
• *See page 258*

SOCIETY OF PLASTICS ENGINEERS (SPE) FOUNDATION

http://www.4spe.org/

FLEMING/BASZCAK SCHOLARSHIP
• *See page 169*

SOCIETY OF PLASTICS ENGINEERS SCHOLARSHIP PROGRAM
• *See page 170*

SPECIALTY EQUIPMENT MARKET ASSOCIATION

http://www.sema.org/

SPECIALTY EQUIPMENT MARKET ASSOCIATION MEMORIAL SCHOLARSHIP FUND
• *See page 301*

STRAIGHTFORWARD MEDIA

http://www.straightforwardmedia.com/

STRAIGHTFORWARD MEDIA VOCATIONAL-TECHNICAL SCHOOL SCHOLARSHIP
• *See page 91*

UNITED COMMUNITY SERVICES FOR WORKING FAMILIES

http://www.unitedcommunityservices.net/

RONALD LORAH MEMORIAL SCHOLARSHIP

One-time award available to a union member, spouse of a union member, or child of a union member. Must be a resident of Pennsylvania. Must submit essay that is clear, concise, persuasive and show an understanding of unions.

Academic Fields/Career Goals: Trade/Technical Specialties.

Award: Scholarship for use in freshman, sophomore, junior, or senior years; not renewable. *Number:* 2. *Amount:* $750–$1000.

Eligibility Requirements: Applicant must be enrolled or expecting to enroll full-time at a two-year or four-year or technical institution or university and resident of Pennsylvania. Applicant or parent of applicant must be member of AFL-CIO. Available to U.S. citizens.

Application Requirements: Application, essay, financial need analysis. *Deadline:* July 22.

Contact: Ruth Mathews, Executive Director
United Community Services for Working Families
601 HiestersLane'
Reading, PA 19605
Phone: 610-374-3319
E-mail: ruth.mathews@comcast.net

WOMEN IN LOGISTICS, NORTHERN CALIFORNIA

http://www.womeninlogistics.org/

WOMEN IN LOGISTICS SCHOLARSHIP
• *See page 159*

WOMEN'S JEWELRY ASSOCIATION

http://www.womensjewelry.org/

WJA SCHOLARSHIP PROGRAM
• *See page 117*

WYOMING TRUCKING ASSOCIATION SCHOLARSHIP FUND TRUST

http://www.wytruck.org/

WYOMING TRUCKING ASSOCIATION SCHOLARSHIP TRUST FUND
• *See page 76*

TRANSPORTATION

AMERICAN PUBLIC TRANSPORTATION FOUNDATION

http://www.apta.com/

DAN REICHARD JR. SCHOLARSHIP
• *See page 146*

DR. GEORGE M. SMERK SCHOLARSHIP

Scholarship for study towards a career in career in public transit management. Must be sponsored by APTA member organization. Minimum GPA of 3.0 required. College sophomores (30 hours or more satisfactorily completed), juniors, seniors, or those seeking advanced degrees may apply.

Academic Fields/Career Goals: Transportation.

Award: Scholarship for use in sophomore, junior, senior, or graduate years; not renewable. *Number:* 1. *Amount:* $2500.

Eligibility Requirements: Applicant must be enrolled or expecting to enroll full-time at a two-year or four-year institution or university. Applicant must have 3.0 GPA or higher. Available to U.S. citizens.

Application Requirements: Application, essay, financial need analysis, references, test scores, transcript, verification of enrollment for the fall semester, copy of fee schedule from the college/university. *Deadline:* June 16.

Contact: Pamela Boswell, Vice President of Program Management
American Public Transportation Foundation
1666 K Street, NW
Washington, DC 20006-1215
Phone: 202-496-4803
Fax: 202-496-2323
E-mail: pboswell@apta.com

DONALD C. HYDE ESSAY PROGRAM

Award of $500 for the best response to the required essay component of the program.

Academic Fields/Career Goals: Transportation.

Award: Prize for use in sophomore, junior, senior, or graduate years; not renewable. *Number:* 1. *Amount:* $500.

Eligibility Requirements: Applicant must be enrolled or expecting to enroll full-time at a two-year or four-year institution or university. Applicant must have 3.0 GPA or higher. Available to U.S. and Canadian citizens.

Application Requirements: Application, applicant must enter a contest, essay, financial need analysis, references, transcript. *Deadline:* June 16.

Contact: Pamela Boswell, Vice President of Program Management
American Public Transportation Foundation
1666 K Street, NW
Washington, DC 20006-1215
Phone: 202-496-4803
Fax: 202-496-2323
E-mail: pboswell@apta.com

JACK GILSTRAP SCHOLARSHIP
• *See page 276*

PARSONS BRINCKERHOFF-JIM LAMMIE SCHOLARSHIP

Scholarship for study in public transportation engineering field. Must be sponsored by APTA member organization and complete internship with APTA member organization. Minimum GPA of 3.0 required.

Academic Fields/Career Goals: Transportation.

Award: Scholarship for use in sophomore, junior, senior, or graduate years; renewable. *Number:* 1. *Amount:* $2500.

Eligibility Requirements: Applicant must be enrolled or expecting to enroll full-time at a two-year or four-year institution or university. Applicant must have 3.0 GPA or higher. Available to U.S. and Canadian citizens.

Application Requirements: Application, essay, financial need analysis, references, transcript, verification of enrollment for the current year and copy of fee schedule from the college/university. *Deadline:* June 16.

Contact: Pamela Boswell, Vice President of Program Management
American Public Transportation Foundation
1666 K Street, NW
Washington, DC 20006-1215
Phone: 202-496-4803
Fax: 202-496-2323
E-mail: pboswell@apta.com

TRANSIT HALL OF FAME SCHOLARSHIP AWARD PROGRAM
• *See page 174*

AMERICAN RAILWAY ENGINEERING AND MAINTENANCE OF WAY ASSOCIATION

http://www.arema.org/

JOHN J. CUNNINGHAM MEMORIAL SCHOLARSHIP (SPONSORED JOINTLY BY COMMITTEES 11 AND 17)
• *See page 276*

ASSOCIATED GENERAL CONTRACTORS OF NEW YORK STATE, LLC

http://www.agcnys.org/

ASSOCIATED GENERAL CONTRACTORS NYS SCHOLARSHIP
• *See page 176*

AUTOMOTIVE HALL OF FAME

http://www.automotivehalloffame.org/

AUTOMOTIVE HALL OF FAME EDUCATIONAL FUNDS
• *See page 164*

COMMERCIAL DRIVER TRAINING FOUNDATION

http://www.cdtfi.org/

MILITARY SCHOLARSHIP ASSISTANCE PROGRAM

More than 2200 scholarships in the amount of $500 for active duty, retired, or honorably discharged veterans of the U.S. armed services and the National Guard and Reserve Forces of the United States to defray a portion of the cost of attending truck driver training programs. Applicants must meet the requirements for commercial drivers that have been established by the Federal Motor Carrier Safety Administration, as well as enrollment criteria of the particular institution. Scholarships are only valid and available for new admissions.

Academic Fields/Career Goals: Transportation.

Award: Scholarship for use in freshman year; not renewable. *Number:* 2200. *Amount:* $500.

Eligibility Requirements: Applicant must be enrolled or expecting to enroll full-time at a technical institution. Available to U.S. citizens. Applicant or parent must meet one or more of the following requirements: general military experience; retired from active duty; disabled or killed as a result of military service; prisoner of war; or missing in action.

Application Requirements: Application, copy of discharge order (form DD214). *Deadline:* varies.

Contact: Michael O'Connell, Executive Director
Commercial Driver Training Foundation
PO Box 5310
Springfield, VA 22150
Phone: 703-642-9444
E-mail: ccatwood@cdta.org

DAVID EVANS AND ASSOCIATES, INC.

http://www.deainc.com/

DAVID EVANS AND ASSOCIATES, INC. SCHOLARSHIP

The goal of the DEA scholarship is to assist the recipient in pursuing a bachelor?s degree in a course of study related to transportation engineering. One scholarship will be awarded to a student attending college in the Northwest (Idaho, Oregon, Montana, or Washington) and the second scholarship will be awarded to a student attending college within Arizona, California, or Colorado. Applicant must be a woman and/or a minority.

Academic Fields/Career Goals: Transportation.

Award: Scholarship for use in freshman, sophomore, junior, or senior years; not renewable. *Number:* 2. *Amount:* $3000.

Eligibility Requirements: Applicant must be enrolled or expecting to enroll at a four-year institution and studying in Arizona, California, Colorado, Idaho, Montana, Oregon, or Washington. Applicant must have 3.0 GPA or higher. Available to U.S. citizens.

Application Requirements: Application, essay, resume, transcript.

Contact: Kim Holcombe, HR Specialist
David Evans and Associates, Inc.
2100 SW River Parkway
Portland, OR 97201
Phone: 503-499-0414
E-mail: kxho@deainc.com

NATIONAL CUSTOMS BROKERS AND FORWARDERS ASSOCIATION OF AMERICA

http://www.ncbfaa.org/

NATIONAL CUSTOMS BROKERS AND FORWARDERS ASSOCIATION OF AMERICA SCHOLARSHIP AWARD

One-time award for employees of National Customs Broker & Forwarders Association of America, Inc. (NCBFAA) regular member organizations and their children. Must be studying transportation logistics or international trade full time. Require minimum 2.0 GPA.

Academic Fields/Career Goals: Transportation.

Award: Scholarship for use in freshman, sophomore, junior, or senior years; not renewable. *Number:* 1. *Amount:* $5000.

Eligibility Requirements: Applicant must be enrolled or expecting to enroll full-time at a four-year institution or university. Available to U.S. citizens.

Application Requirements: Essay, employment verification letter from NCBFAA regular member firm, proof of acceptance to or current enrollment in an accredited college or university. *Deadline:* February 1.

Contact: Mr. Tom Mathers, Director Communications
National Customs Brokers and Forwarders Association of America
1200 18th Street, NW, Suite 901
Washington, DC 20036
Phone: 202-466-0222
Fax: 202-466-0226
E-mail: tom@ncbfaa.org

TRANSPORTATION ASSOCIATION OF CANADA

http://www.tac-foundation.ca/

TRANSPORTATION ASSOCIATION OF CANADA/ CEMENT ASSOCIATION OF CANADA SCHOLARSHIP

Scholarship for full-time undergraduate and postgraduate students enrolled in transportation-related disciplines. Must be Canadian citizen.

Academic Fields/Career Goals: Transportation.

Award: Scholarship for use in junior, senior, graduate, or postgraduate years; not renewable. *Number:* varies. *Amount:* $5000.

Eligibility Requirements: Applicant must be enrolled or expecting to enroll full-time at a four-year institution or university. Available to Canadian citizens.

Application Requirements: Application, references, transcript. *Deadline:* March 3.

Contact: Sylvie Rozon, Coordinator, Member Services & Meetings
Transportation Association of Canada
2323 Street Laurent Boulevard
Ottawa, ON K1G 4J8
Canada
Phone: 613-736-1350 Ext. 236
Fax: 613-736-1395
E-mail: srozon@tac-atc.ca

TRANSPORTATION ASSOCIATION OF CANADA FOUNDATION/3M CANADA COMPANY SCHOLARSHIP

Scholarship for undergraduate and postgraduate students enrolled full-time in the transportation field. Must be Canadian citizen enrolled in a Canadian University.

Academic Fields/Career Goals: Transportation.

Award: Scholarship for use in junior, senior, graduate, or postgraduate years; not renewable. *Number:* 1. *Amount:* $5000.

Eligibility Requirements: Applicant must be enrolled or expecting to enroll full-time at a four-year institution or university. Available to Canadian citizens.

Application Requirements: Application, references, transcript. *Deadline:* March 3.

Contact: Sylvie Rozon, Coordinator, Member Services & Meetings
Transportation Association of Canada
2323 Street Laurent Boulevard
Ottawa, ON K1G 4J8
Canada
Phone: 613-736-1350 Ext. 236
Fax: 613-736-1395
E-mail: srozon@tac-atc.ca

TRANSPORTATION ASSOCIATION OF CANADA FOUNDATION/BA GROUP SCHOLARSHIP

Scholarship for full-time undergraduate and postgraduate study in transportation planning or transportation engineering. Must be Canadian citizens.

Academic Fields/Career Goals: Transportation.

Award: Scholarship for use in junior, senior, graduate, or postgraduate years; not renewable. *Number:* varies. *Amount:* $5000.

Eligibility Requirements: Applicant must be enrolled or expecting to enroll full-time at a four-year institution or university. Available to Canadian citizens.

Application Requirements: Application, references, transcript. *Deadline:* March 3.

Contact: Sylvie Rozon, Coordinator, Member Services & Meetings
Transportation Association of Canada
2323 Street Laurent Boulevard
Ottawa, ON K1G 4J8
Canada
Phone: 613-736-1350 Ext. 236
Fax: 613-736-1395
E-mail: srozon@tac-atc.ca

TRANSPORTATION ASSOCIATION OF CANADA FOUNDATION/DELCAN CORPORATION SCHOLARSHIP

Scholarship for full-time undergraduate and postgraduate students enrolled in transportation-related disciplines. Must be Canadian citizen.

Academic Fields/Career Goals: Transportation.

Award: Scholarship for use in junior, senior, graduate, or postgraduate years; not renewable. *Number:* varies. *Amount:* $5000.

Eligibility Requirements: Applicant must be enrolled or expecting to enroll full-time at a four-year institution or university. Available to Canadian citizens.

Application Requirements: Application, references, transcript. *Deadline:* March 3.

Contact: Sylvie Rozon, Coordinator, Member Services & Meetings
Transportation Association of Canada
2323 Street Laurent Boulevard
Ottawa, ON K1G 4J8
Canada
Phone: 613-736-1350 Ext. 236
Fax: 613-736-1395
E-mail: srozon@tac-atc.ca

TRANSPORTATION ASSOCIATION OF CANADA FOUNDATION/EBA ENGINEERING CONSULTANTS LTD. SCHOLARSHIP

Scholarship provided for graduate and postgraduate research in transportation infrastructure and systems. Preference is given for research in the areas of design, construction, maintenance and operation of roadway transportation systems in rural and urban environments. Must be Canadian citizen.

Academic Fields/Career Goals: Transportation.

Award: Scholarship for use in junior, senior, graduate, or postgraduate years; not renewable. *Number:* varies. *Amount:* $5000.

Eligibility Requirements: Applicant must be enrolled or expecting to enroll full-time at a four-year institution or university. Available to Canadian citizens.

Application Requirements: Application, references, transcript. *Deadline:* March 3.

Contact: Sylvie Rozon, Coordinator, Member Services & Meetings
Transportation Association of Canada
2323 Street Laurent Boulevard
Ottawa, ON K1G 4J8
Canada
Phone: 613-736-1350 Ext. 236
Fax: 613-736-1395
E-mail: srozon@tac-atc.ca

TRANSPORTATION ASSOCIATION OF CANADA FOUNDATION/IBI GROUP SCHOLARSHIP

Scholarship for full-time undergraduate and postgraduate students enrolled in transportation-related disciplines. Must be Canadian citizen.

Academic Fields/Career Goals: Transportation.

Award: Scholarship for use in junior, senior, graduate, or postgraduate years; not renewable. *Number:* varies. *Amount:* $5000.

Eligibility Requirements: Applicant must be enrolled or expecting to enroll full-time at a four-year institution or university. Available to Canadian citizens.

Application Requirements: Application, references, transcript. *Deadline:* March 3.

Contact: Sylvie Rozon, Coordinator, Member Services & Meetings
Transportation Association of Canada
2323 Street Laurent Boulevard
Ottawa, ON K1G 4J8
Canada
Phone: 613-736-1350 Ext. 236
Fax: 613-736-1395
E-mail: srozon@tac-atc.ca

TRANSPORTATION CLUBS INTERNATIONAL

http://www.transportationclubsinternational.com/

ALICE GLAISYER WARFIELD MEMORIAL SCHOLARSHIP

Award is available to currently enrolled students majoring in transportation, logistics, traffic management, or related fields. Available to citizens of the United States, Canada, and Mexico. See web site for application http://www.transportationclubsinternational.com/.

Academic Fields/Career Goals: Transportation.

Award: Scholarship for use in freshman, sophomore, junior, or senior years; not renewable. *Number:* 1. *Amount:* $1500.

Eligibility Requirements: Applicant must be enrolled or expecting to enroll full- or part-time at a two-year or four-year or technical institution or university. Applicant or parent of applicant must be member of Transportation Club International. Available to U.S. and non-U.S. citizens.

Application Requirements: Application, essay, photo, references, transcript. *Deadline:* April 30.

Contact: Bill Blair, Scholarships Trustee
Transportation Clubs International
c/o Zimmer Worldwide Logistics
15710 JFK Boulevard, Suite 575
Houston, TX 77032
Phone: 832-300-5905
E-mail: bblair@zimmerworldwide.com

DENNY LYDIC SCHOLARSHIP

Award is available to currently enrolled college students majoring in transportation, logistics, traffic management, or related fields. Available to citizens of the United States, Canada, and Mexico. See web site for application http://www.transportationclubsinternational.com/.

Academic Fields/Career Goals: Transportation.

Award: Scholarship for use in freshman, sophomore, junior, or senior years; not renewable. *Number:* 1. *Amount:* $1000.

Eligibility Requirements: Applicant must be enrolled or expecting to enroll full- or part-time at a two-year or four-year or technical institution or university. Applicant or parent of applicant must be member of Transportation Club International. Available to U.S. and non-U.S. citizens.

Application Requirements: Application, essay, photo, references, transcript. *Deadline:* April 30.

Contact: Bill Blair, Scholarships Trustee
Transportation Clubs International
c/o Zimmer Worldwide Logistics
15710 JFK Boulevard, Suite 575
Houston, TX 77032
Phone: 832-300-5905
E-mail: bblair@zimmerworldwide.com

TEXAS TRANSPORTATION SCHOLARSHIP

Merit-based award for a student who is at least a sophomore studying transportation, traffic management, and related fields. Must have been enrolled in a school in Texas during some phase of education (elementary, secondary, high school). Must include photo and submit three references. One-time scholarship of $1000. See web site for application http://www.transportationclubinternational.com/.

Academic Fields/Career Goals: Transportation.

Award: Scholarship for use in sophomore, junior, or senior years; not renewable. *Number:* 1. *Amount:* $1000.

Eligibility Requirements: Applicant must be enrolled or expecting to enroll full- or part-time at a two-year or four-year or technical institution or university. Applicant or parent of applicant must be member of Transportation Club International. Available to U.S. citizens.

Application Requirements: Application, essay, photo, references, transcript. *Deadline:* April 30.

Contact: Bill Blair, Scholarships Trustee
Transportation Clubs International
c/o Zimmer Worldwide Logistics
15710 JFK Boulevard, Suite 575
Houston, TX 77032
Phone: 832-300-5905
E-mail: bblair@zimmerworldwide.com

TRANSPORTATION CLUBS INTERNATIONAL CHARLOTTE WOODS SCHOLARSHIP

Award available to an enrolled college student majoring in transportation or traffic management. Must be a member or a dependant of a member of Transportation Clubs International. Must have completed at least one year of post-high school education. One-time award of $1000. See web site for application http://www.transportationclubsinternational.com/.

Academic Fields/Career Goals: Transportation.

Award: Scholarship for use in freshman, sophomore, junior, or senior years; not renewable. *Number:* 1. *Amount:* $1000.

Eligibility Requirements: Applicant must be enrolled or expecting to enroll full- or part-time at a two-year or four-year or technical institution or university. Applicant or parent of applicant must be member of Transportation Club International. Available to U.S. and non-U.S. citizens.

Application Requirements: Application, essay, photo, references, transcript. *Deadline:* April 30.

Contact: Bill Blair, Scholarships Trustee
Transportation Clubs International
c/o Zimmer Worldwide Logistics
15710 JFK Boulevard, Suite 575
Houston, TX 77032
Phone: 832-300-5905
E-mail: bblair@zimmerworldwide.com

TRANSPORTATION CLUBS INTERNATIONAL FRED A. HOOPER MEMORIAL SCHOLARSHIP

• *See page 273*

TRANSPORTATION CLUBS INTERNATIONAL GINGER AND FRED DEINES CANADA SCHOLARSHIP

One-time award for a student of Canadian heritage, who is attending college or university in Canada or the United States and majoring in transportation, traffic management, logistics, or a related field. Academic merit is considered. See web site for application http://www.transportationclubsinternational.com/.

Academic Fields/Career Goals: Transportation.

Award: Scholarship for use in freshman, sophomore, junior, or senior years; not renewable. *Number:* 1. *Amount:* $1500.

Eligibility Requirements: Applicant must be of Canadian heritage and Canadian citizen and enrolled or expecting to enroll full- or part-time at a two-year or four-year or technical institution or university. Applicant or parent of applicant must be member of Transportation Club International.

Application Requirements: Application, essay, photo, references, transcript. *Deadline:* April 30.

Contact: Bill Blair, Scholarships Trustee
Transportation Clubs International
c/o Zimmer Worldwide Logistics
15710 JFK Boulevard, Suite 575
Houston, TX 77032
Phone: 832-300-5905
E-mail: bblair@zimmerworldwide.com

TRANSPORTATION CLUBS INTERNATIONAL GINGER AND FRED DEINES MEXICO SCHOLARSHIP

Scholarship of $2000 for a Canadian student who is enrolled in an accredited institution of higher learning in a vocational or degree program in the fields of transportation, logistics or traffic management, or related fields. May be enrolled in a U.S. or Canadian institution. See web site for application http://www.transportationclubsinternational.com/.

Academic Fields/Career Goals: Transportation.

Award: Scholarship for use in freshman, sophomore, junior, or senior years; not renewable. *Number:* 1. *Amount:* $2000.

Eligibility Requirements: Applicant must be Mexican citizen and enrolled or expecting to enroll full- or part-time at a two-year or four-year or technical institution or university. Applicant or parent of applicant must be member of Transportation Club International. Available to Canadian and non-U.S. citizens.

Application Requirements: Application, essay, photo, references, transcript. *Deadline:* April 30.

Contact: Bill Blair, Scholarships Trustee
Transportation Clubs International
c/o Zimmer Worldwide Logistics
15710 JFK Boulevard, Suite 575
Houston, TX 77032
Phone: 832-300-5905
E-mail: bblair@zimmerworldwide.com

TRUCKLOAD CARRIERS ASSOCIATION

http://www.truckload.org/

TRUCKLOAD CARRIERS ASSOCIATION SCHOLARSHIP FUND

• *See page 156*

WOMEN IN LOGISTICS, NORTHERN CALIFORNIA

http://www.womeninlogistics.org/

WOMEN IN LOGISTICS SCHOLARSHIP
• *See page 159*

WYOMING TRUCKING ASSOCIATION SCHOLARSHIP FUND TRUST

http://www.wytruck.org/

WYOMING TRUCKING ASSOCIATION SCHOLARSHIP TRUST FUND
• *See page 76*

TRAVEL/TOURISM

AMERICAN HOTEL AND LODGING EDUCATIONAL FOUNDATION

http://www.ahlef.org/

AMERICAN HOTEL & LODGING EDUCATIONAL FOUNDATION PEPSI SCHOLARSHIP
• *See page 207*

ANNUAL SCHOLARSHIP GRANT PROGRAM
• *See page 208*

ARTHUR J. PACKARD MEMORIAL SCHOLARSHIP
• *See page 208*

ECOLAB SCHOLARSHIP PROGRAM
• *See page 208*

HYATT HOTELS FUND FOR MINORITY LODGING MANAGEMENT
• *See page 208*

INCOMING FRESHMAN SCHOLARSHIPS
• *See page 208*

RAMA SCHOLARSHIP FOR THE AMERICAN DREAM
• *See page 208*

STEVEN HYMANS EXTENDED STAY SCHOLARSHIP
• *See page 209*

AMERICAN SOCIETY OF TRAVEL AGENTS (ASTA) FOUNDATION

http://www.astanet.com/

AMERICAN EXPRESS TRAVEL SCHOLARSHIP

Candidate must be enrolled in a travel or tourism program in either a two- or four-year college or university or proprietary travel school. Must write 500-word essay on student's view of travel industry's future. Minimum 2.5 GPA required.

Academic Fields/Career Goals: Travel/Tourism.

Award: Scholarship for use in freshman, sophomore, junior, or senior years; not renewable. *Number:* varies. *Amount:* varies.

Eligibility Requirements: Applicant must be enrolled or expecting to enroll full- or part-time at a two-year or four-year institution or university. Applicant must have 2.5 GPA or higher. Available to U.S. and Canadian citizens.

Application Requirements: Application, resume, references, transcript, 500-word paper detailing the student's plans in travel. *Deadline:* July 31.

Contact: Verlette Mitchell, Manager
American Society of Travel Agents (ASTA) Foundation
1101 King Street
Alexandria, VA 22314-2187
Phone: 703-739-8721
Fax: 703-684-8319
E-mail: scholarship@astahq.com

ARIZONA CHAPTER DEPENDENT/EMPLOYEE MEMBERSHIP SCHOLARSHIP

Candidate must be a dependent of an ASTA Arizona Chapter Active, Active Associate or Travel Professional member, or an employee of an Arizona ASTA member agency for a minimum of six months whose ASTA membership dues are current. One award of $1500 will be given. Must attend Arizona institution. Must be enrolled in their final year in a two year college, or as a junior or senior in a four-year college/university. Minimum 2.5 GPA required.

Academic Fields/Career Goals: Travel/Tourism.

Award: Scholarship for use in sophomore, junior, or senior years; not renewable. *Number:* 1. *Amount:* $1500.

Eligibility Requirements: Applicant must be enrolled or expecting to enroll full- or part-time at a two-year or four-year institution or university; resident of Arizona and studying in Arizona. Applicant or parent of applicant must be member of American Society of Travel Agents. Applicant must have 2.5 GPA or higher. Available to U.S. and Canadian citizens.

Application Requirements: Application, references, transcript, 500-word paper entitled "My Career Goals". *Deadline:* July 31.

Contact: Verlette Mitchell, Manager
American Society of Travel Agents (ASTA) Foundation
1101 King Street
Alexandria, VA 22314-2187
Phone: 703-739-8721
Fax: 703-684-8319
E-mail: scholarship@astahq.com

ARIZONA CHAPTER GOLD SCHOLARSHIP

One-time award for college undergraduates who are Arizona residents pursuing a travel or tourism degree at a four-year Arizona institution. Freshmen are not eligible. Must submit essay on career plans and interests. Minimum 2.5 GPA required. Must be a U.S. citizen or Canadian citizen.

Academic Fields/Career Goals: Travel/Tourism.

Award: Scholarship for use in sophomore, junior, or senior years; not renewable. *Number:* 1. *Amount:* $3000.

Eligibility Requirements: Applicant must be enrolled or expecting to enroll full- or part-time at a four-year institution or university; resident of Arizona and studying in Arizona. Applicant must have 2.5 GPA or higher. Available to U.S. and Canadian citizens.

Application Requirements: Application, references, transcript. *Deadline:* July 31.

Contact: Verlette Mitchell, Manager
American Society of Travel Agents (ASTA) Foundation
1101 King Street
Alexandria, VA 22314-2187
Phone: 703-739-8721
Fax: 703-684-8319
E-mail: scholarship@astahq.com

AVIS SCHOLARSHIP

Scholarship of $2000 for individuals who have already gained experience and/or training in the travel industry. Candidate must have a minimum of two years of full-time travel industry experience or an undergraduate degree in travel/tourism and must currently be employed in the travel industry. Must be enrolled in a minimum of two courses per semester in an accredited undergraduate or graduate level degree program in business, or equivalent degree program. Minimum GPA of 3.0 required.

Academic Fields/Career Goals: Travel/Tourism.

Award: Scholarship for use in freshman, sophomore, junior, senior, or graduate years; renewable. *Number:* 1. *Amount:* $2000.

Eligibility Requirements: Applicant must be enrolled or expecting to enroll full- or part-time at a four-year institution or university. Applicant must have 3.0 GPA or higher. Available to U.S. and Canadian citizens.

Application Requirements: Application, references, transcript, proof of current employment in the travel industry. *Deadline:* July 31.

Contact: Verlette Mitchell, Manager
American Society of Travel Agents (ASTA) Foundation
1101 King Street
Alexandria, VA 22314-2187
Phone: 703-739-8721
Fax: 703-684-8319
E-mail: scholarship@astahq.com

DONALD ESTEY SCHOLARSHIP FUND-ROCKY MOUNTAIN CHAPTER

Applicants must be enrolled in a licensed preparatory travel program or must be participating in either an ASTA sponsored training program, The Travel Institute Destination Specialist, or other industry training programs. Must have letter of recommendation from ASTA Rocky Mountain Chapter. Must be Colorado, Utah, or Wyoming resident. Must have a minimum of 2.5 GPA. Must be a U.S. citizen or Canadian citizen.

Academic Fields/Career Goals: Travel/Tourism.

Award: Scholarship for use in freshman or sophomore years; not renewable. *Number:* 3. *Amount:* $1000.

Eligibility Requirements: Applicant must be enrolled or expecting to enroll full- or part-time at a two-year or technical institution; resident of Colorado, Utah, or Wyoming and studying in Colorado, Utah, or Wyoming. Applicant or parent of applicant must be member of American Society of Travel Agents. Applicant or parent of applicant must have employment or volunteer experience in travel and tourism industry. Applicant must have 2.5 GPA or higher. Available to U.S. and Canadian citizens.

Application Requirements: Application, financial need analysis, references, test scores, transcript, statement indicating the program's expected benefit. *Deadline:* varies.

Contact: Verlette Mitchell, Manager
American Society of Travel Agents (ASTA) Foundation
1101 King Street
Alexandria, VA 22314-2187
Phone: 703-739-8721
Fax: 703-684-8319
E-mail: scholarship@astahq.com

GEORGE REINKE SCHOLARSHIPS

Applicant must write a 500-word essay on career goals in the travel or tourism industry. Must be a U.S. citizen living and studying in the United States and enrolled in a travel agent studies program in a junior college or travel school. Must have a minimum GPA of 2.5.

Academic Fields/Career Goals: Travel/Tourism.

Award: Scholarship for use in freshman or sophomore years; not renewable. *Number:* up to 6. *Amount:* $2000.

Eligibility Requirements: Applicant must be enrolled or expecting to enroll full- or part-time at a two-year institution. Applicant must have 2.5 GPA or higher. Available to U.S. citizens.

Application Requirements: Application, references, transcript, 500-word paper entitled "My Objectives in the Travel Agency Industry". *Deadline:* July 31.

Contact: Verlette Mitchell, Manager
American Society of Travel Agents (ASTA) Foundation
1101 King Street
Alexandria, VA 22314-2187
Phone: 703-739-8721
Fax: 703-684-8319
E-mail: scholarship@astahq.com

HEALY SCHOLARSHIP

One-time award of $2000 for a college undergraduate pursuing a travel or tourism degree. Must submit essay suggesting improvements for the travel industry. Must be a citizen of United States or Canada. Minimum 2.5 GPA required.

Academic Fields/Career Goals: Travel/Tourism.

Award: Scholarship for use in freshman, sophomore, junior, or senior years; not renewable. *Number:* 1. *Amount:* $2000.

Eligibility Requirements: Applicant must be enrolled or expecting to enroll full- or part-time at a four-year institution or university. Applicant must have 2.5 GPA or higher. Available to U.S. and Canadian citizens.

Application Requirements: Application, references, self-addressed stamped envelope, transcript, 500-word paper suggesting improvements in the travel industry. *Deadline:* July 31.

Contact: Cathy Clifton, Scholarship Committee
American Society of Travel Agents (ASTA) Foundation
1101 King Street, Suite 200
Alexandria, VA 22314-2187
Phone: 703-739-8721
Fax: 703-684-8319
E-mail: scholarship@astahq.com

HOLLAND-AMERICA LINE WESTOURS SCHOLARSHIPS

Students must write 500-word essay on the future of the cruise industry and must be enrolled in travel or tourism program at a two- or four-year college or proprietary travel school. Minimum 2.5 GPA required. Must be a U.S. or Canadian citizen.

Academic Fields/Career Goals: Travel/Tourism.

Award: Scholarship for use in freshman, sophomore, junior, or senior years; not renewable. *Number:* 2. *Amount:* $3000.

Eligibility Requirements: Applicant must be enrolled or expecting to enroll full- or part-time at a two-year or four-year institution or university. Applicant must have 2.5 GPA or higher. Available to U.S. and Canadian citizens.

Application Requirements: Application, financial need analysis, resume, references, transcript, 500-word paper on the future of the cruise industry. *Deadline:* July 31.

Contact: Verlette Mitchell, Manager
American Society of Travel Agents (ASTA) Foundation
1101 King Street
Alexandria, VA 22314-2187
Phone: 703-739-8721
Fax: 703-684-8319
E-mail: scholarship@astahq.com

JOHN HJORTH SCHOLARSHIP FUND-SAN DIEGO CHAPTER

Any employee of a San Diego ASTA Chapter member pursuing one of the Travel Institute certification programs, The Travel Institute Destination Specialists programs, or any ASTA Educational program is eligible to apply. Must have a minimum of two years travel industry experience. Must be a U.S. citizen or Canadian citizen.

Academic Fields/Career Goals: Travel/Tourism.

Award: Scholarship for use in freshman or sophomore years; not renewable. *Number:* 3. *Amount:* up to $250.

Eligibility Requirements: Applicant must be enrolled or expecting to enroll full- or part-time at a technical institution and resident of California. Applicant or parent of applicant must be member of American Society of Travel Agents. Applicant or parent of applicant must have employment or volunteer experience in travel and tourism industry. Applicant must have 2.5 GPA or higher. Available to U.S. and Canadian citizens.

Application Requirements: Application, essay, references, letter of interest and/or need. *Deadline:* July 31.

Contact: Verlette Mitchell, Manager
American Society of Travel Agents (ASTA) Foundation
1101 King Street
Alexandria, VA 22314-2187
Phone: 703-739-8721
Fax: 703-684-8319
E-mail: scholarship@astahq.com

JOSEPH R. STONE SCHOLARSHIPS

One-time award for high school senior or college undergraduate pursuing a travel or tourism degree. Must have a parent in the industry and proof of employment. Must submit a 500-word essay explaining career goals. Minimum 2.5 GPA required. Must be a citizen of United States or Canada.

Academic Fields/Career Goals: Travel/Tourism.

Award: Scholarship for use in freshman, sophomore, junior, or senior years; not renewable. *Number:* 3. *Amount:* $2400.

Eligibility Requirements: Applicant must be enrolled or expecting to enroll full- or part-time at a four-year institution or university. Applicant must have 2.5 GPA or higher. Available to U.S. and Canadian citizens.

Application Requirements: Application, references, transcript, 500-word paper on applicant's goals. *Deadline:* July 31.

Contact: Verlette Mitchell, Manager
American Society of Travel Agents (ASTA) Foundation
1101 King Street
Alexandria, VA 22314-2187
Phone: 703-739-8721
Fax: 703-684-8319
E-mail: scholarship@astahq.com

NANCY STEWART SCHOLARSHIP FUND-ALLEGHENY CHAPTER

One-time award for travel professionals working for an agency that is a member of American Society of Travel Agents' Allegheny Chapter. Must be pursuing one of The Travel Institute's four certification programs: CTC accreditation, Destination Specialist, Travel Career Development, Professional Management; or an ASTA educational program. Must be Pennsylvania resident. Must also have at least three years of travel industry experience. Must have a minimum of 2.5 GPA.

Academic Fields/Career Goals: Travel/Tourism.

Award: Scholarship for use in freshman or sophomore years; not renewable. *Number:* 3. *Amount:* $400.

Eligibility Requirements: Applicant must be enrolled or expecting to enroll part-time at a technical institution and resident of Pennsylvania. Applicant or parent of applicant must be member of American Society of Travel Agents. Applicant or parent of applicant must have employment or volunteer experience in travel and tourism industry. Applicant must have 2.5 GPA or higher. Available to U.S. and Canadian citizens.

Application Requirements: Application, essay, references, letter of intent. *Deadline:* July 31.

Contact: Verlette Mitchell, Manager
American Society of Travel Agents (ASTA) Foundation
1101 King Street
Alexandria, VA 22314-2187
Phone: 703-739-8721
Fax: 703-684-8319
E-mail: scholarship@astahq.com

NORTHERN CALIFORNIA CHAPTER RICHARD EPPING SCHOLARSHIP

Scholarship of $2000. Applicant must be currently enrolled in a travel and tourism curriculum at a college, university, or proprietary travel and tourism school in Northern California or Northern Nevada. Minimum 2.5 GPA required. Must be a U.S. or Canadian citizen.

Academic Fields/Career Goals: Travel/Tourism.

Award: Scholarship for use in freshman, sophomore, junior, or senior years; not renewable. *Number:* 1. *Amount:* $2000.

Eligibility Requirements: Applicant must be enrolled or expecting to enroll full- or part-time at a two-year or four-year institution or university and studying in California or Nevada. Applicant must have 2.5 GPA or higher. Available to U.S. and Canadian citizens.

Application Requirements: Application, essay, references, transcript. *Deadline:* July 31.

Contact: Verlette Mitchell, Manager
American Society of Travel Agents (ASTA) Foundation
1101 King Street
Alexandria, VA 22314-2187
Phone: 703-739-8721
Fax: 703-684-8319
E-mail: scholarship@astahq.com

ORANGE COUNTY CHAPTER/HARRY JACKSON SCHOLARSHIP FUND

Awards are available to any Active or Associate member of the Orange County ASTA office pursuing one of the following programs: ASTA Educational Programs, The Travel Institute certification programs, CTC, Destination Specialist, The Travel Institute Educational Programs, and The Travel Institute forums. The applicant must also have at least two years of travel industry experience. Must have a minimum of 2.5 GPA.

Academic Fields/Career Goals: Travel/Tourism.

Award: Scholarship for use in freshman or sophomore years; not renewable. *Number:* varies. *Amount:* $250.

Eligibility Requirements: Applicant must be enrolled or expecting to enroll full- or part-time at a technical institution and resident of California. Applicant or parent of applicant must be member of American Society of Travel Agents. Applicant must have 2.5 GPA or higher. Available to U.S. and Canadian citizens.

Application Requirements: Application, financial need analysis, resume, references, transcript, letter of interest. *Deadline:* July 31.

Contact: Verlette Mitchell, Manager
American Society of Travel Agents (ASTA) Foundation
1101 King Street
Alexandria, VA 22314-2187
Phone: 703-739-8721
Fax: 703-684-8319
E-mail: scholarship@astahq.com

PACIFIC NORTHWEST CHAPTER-WILLIAM HUNT SCHOLARSHIP FUND

One-time award for travel professionals. Applicant must be employed in the travel industry in an ASTA office or enrolled in a travel and tourism program in either a two- or four-year college, university or proprietary travel school. Must be a resident of and studying in one of the following states: Alaska, Idaho, Montana, Oregon, or Washington. Must be a U.S. or Canadian citizen. Must have a minimum of 2.5 GPA.

Academic Fields/Career Goals: Travel/Tourism.

Award: Scholarship for use in freshman, sophomore, junior, or senior years; not renewable. *Number:* up to 3. *Amount:* up to $1000.

Eligibility Requirements: Applicant must be enrolled or expecting to enroll full- or part-time at a two-year or four-year or technical institution or university; resident of Alaska, Idaho, Montana, Oregon, or Washington and studying in Alaska, Idaho, Montana, Oregon, or Washington. Applicant or parent of applicant must be member of American Society of Travel Agents. Applicant must have 2.5 GPA or higher. Available to U.S. and Canadian citizens.

Application Requirements: Application, essay, references, transcript, 300-word letter explaining reasons for interest in further training in travel. *Deadline:* July 31.

Contact: Verlette Mitchell, Manager
American Society of Travel Agents (ASTA) Foundation
1101 King Street
Alexandria, VA 22314-2187
Phone: 703-739-8721
Fax: 703-684-8319
E-mail: scholarship@astahq.com

PRINCESS CRUISES AND PRINCESS TOURS SCHOLARSHIP

Merit-based award for student accepted or enrolled as an undergraduate in a travel or tourism program. Submit 300-word essay on two features cruise ships will need to offer passengers in the next ten years. Minimum 2.5 GPA required. Must be a U.S. citizen or Canadian citizen.

Academic Fields/Career Goals: Travel/Tourism.

Award: Scholarship for use in freshman, sophomore, junior, or senior years; not renewable. *Number:* 2. *Amount:* $2000.

Eligibility Requirements: Applicant must be enrolled or expecting to enroll full- or part-time at a two-year or four-year institution or university. Applicant must have 2.5 GPA or higher. Available to U.S. and Canadian citizens.

Application Requirements: Application, references, transcript, 300-word paper on the two features cruise ships will need to offer passengers in the next ten years. *Deadline:* July 31.

Contact: Verlette Mitchell, Manager
American Society of Travel Agents (ASTA) Foundation
1101 King Street
Alexandria, VA 22314-2187
Phone: 703-739-8721
Fax: 703-684-8319
E-mail: scholarship@astahq.com

SOUTHEAST AMERICAN SOCIETY OF TRAVEL AGENTS CHAPTER SCHOLARSHIP

Applicants must be Active Associate members in good standing of the SEASTA chapter, and have at least two years of travel industry experience. Applicants must be pursuing any of the ASTA Specialist certification programs, ASTA educational conferences, The Travel Institute CTA, The Travel Institute CTC, or The Travel Institute Destination certification programs. Applicant must apply for scholarship within one year of receiving certification.

Academic Fields/Career Goals: Travel/Tourism.

Award: Scholarship for use in freshman year; not renewable. *Number:* up to 6. *Amount:* $350.

Eligibility Requirements: Applicant must be enrolled or expecting to enroll part-time at a technical institution; resident of Alabama, Georgia, Kentucky, Louisiana, Mississippi, North Carolina, South Carolina, or Tennessee and studying in Alabama, Georgia, Kentucky, Louisiana, Mississippi, North Carolina, South Carolina, or Tennessee. Applicant or parent of applicant must be member of American Society of Travel Agents. Applicant or parent of applicant must have employment or volunteer experience in travel and tourism industry. Applicant must have 2.5 GPA or higher. Available to U.S. and Canadian citizens.

Application Requirements: Application, references, letter of interest or need, proof of course certification. *Deadline:* July 31.

Contact: Verlette Mitchell, Manager
American Society of Travel Agents (ASTA) Foundation
1101 King Street
Alexandria, VA 22314-2187
Phone: 703-739-8721
Fax: 703-684-8319
E-mail: scholarship@astahq.com

SOUTHERN CALIFORNIA CHAPTER/PLEASANT HAWAIIAN HOLIDAYS SCHOLARSHIP

Two awards for students pursuing travel or tourism degrees. One award given to student attending college in southern California, and one award given to a student attending school anywhere in the United States. Applicant must be U.S. citizens. Minimum 2.5 GPA required.

Academic Fields/Career Goals: Travel/Tourism.

Award: Scholarship for use in freshman, sophomore, junior, or senior years; not renewable. *Number:* 2. *Amount:* $2500.

Eligibility Requirements: Applicant must be enrolled or expecting to enroll full- or part-time at a four-year institution or university. Applicant must have 2.5 GPA or higher. Available to U.S. citizens.

Application Requirements: Application, references, transcript, 500-word paper entitled "My Goals in the Travel Industry". *Deadline:* July 31.

Contact: Verlette Mitchell, Manager
American Society of Travel Agents (ASTA) Foundation
1101 King Street
Alexandria, VA 22314-2187
Phone: 703-739-8721
Fax: 703-684-8319
E-mail: scholarship@astahq.com

STAN AND LEONE POLLARD SCHOLARSHIPS

Candidate must be re-entering the job market by being enrolled in a travel and tourism curriculum in either a recognized proprietary travel school or a two-year junior college. Two awards of $2000 each will be given. Must have a minimum GPA of 2.5 and be a U.S. or Canadian citizen.

Academic Fields/Career Goals: Travel/Tourism.

Award: Scholarship for use in freshman or sophomore years; not renewable. *Number:* 2. *Amount:* $2000.

Eligibility Requirements: Applicant must be enrolled or expecting to enroll full- or part-time at a two-year or technical institution. Applicant must have 2.5 GPA or higher. Available to U.S. and Canadian citizens.

Application Requirements: Application, references, transcript, 500-word paper on the student's objectives in the travel and tourism industry. *Deadline:* July 31.

Contact: Verlette Mitchell, Manager
American Society of Travel Agents (ASTA) Foundation
1101 King Street
Alexandria, VA 22314-2187
Phone: 703-739-8721
Fax: 703-684-8319
E-mail: scholarship@astahq.com

HAWAII HOTEL ASSOCIATION

http://www.hawaiihotels.org/

R.W. BOB HOLDEN SCHOLARSHIP
• *See page 362*

INTERNATIONAL AIRLINES TRAVEL AGENT NETWORK

http://www.iatan.org/

INTERNATIONAL AIRLINES TRAVEL AGENT NETWORK FOUNDATION SCHOLARSHIP
• *See page 362*

MISSOURI TRAVEL COUNCIL

http://www.missouritravel.com/

MISSOURI TRAVEL COUNCIL TOURISM SCHOLARSHIP
• *See page 323*

NATIONAL TOURISM FOUNDATION

http://www.ntfonline.com/

ACADEMY OF TRAVEL AND TOURISM SCHOLARSHIPS
• *See page 363*

CLEVELAND LEGACY I AND II SCHOLARSHIP AWARDS
• *See page 324*

NEW HORIZONS KATHY LETARTE SCHOLARSHIP
• *See page 324*

PAT AND JIM HOST SCHOLARSHIP
• *See page 363*

SOCIETIE DES CASINOS DU QUEBEC SCHOLARSHIP
• *See page 324*

TAMPA, HILLSBOROUGH LEGACY SCHOLARSHIP
• *See page 324*

TAUCK SCHOLARS SCHOLARSHIPS
• *See page 324*

TULSA SCHOLARSHIP AWARDS
• *See page 325*

YELLOW RIBBON SCHOLARSHIP
• *See page 325*

OHIO TRAVEL ASSOCIATION

http://www.ohiotravel.org/

BILL SCHWARTZ MEMORIAL SCHOLARSHIP
• *See page 363*

TV/RADIO BROADCASTING

ADC RESEARCH INSTITUTE

http://www.adc.org/

JACK SHAHEEN MASS COMMUNICATIONS SCHOLARSHIP AWARD
• *See page 181*

ALABAMA BROADCASTERS ASSOCIATION

http://www.al-ba.com/

ALABAMA BROADCASTERS ASSOCIATION SCHOLARSHIP

Scholarship available to Alabama residents studying broadcasting at any accredited Alabama technical school, 2- or 4-year college, or university.

Academic Fields/Career Goals: TV/Radio Broadcasting.

Award: Scholarship for use in junior or senior years; not renewable. *Number:* up to 4. *Amount:* up to $2500.

Eligibility Requirements: Applicant must be enrolled or expecting to enroll full-time at a two-year or four-year or technical institution or university; resident of Alabama and studying in Alabama. Available to U.S. citizens.

Application Requirements: Application, references. *Deadline:* April 30.

Contact: Sharon Tinsley, President
Alabama Broadcasters Association
2180 Parkway Lake Drive
Hoover, AL 35244
Phone: 205-982-5001
Fax: 205-982-0015
E-mail: stinsley@al-ba.com

AMERICAN LEGION PRESS CLUB OF NEW JERSEY

http://www.alpcnj.org/

AMERICAN LEGION PRESS CLUB OF NEW JERSEY AND POST 170 ARTHUR DEHARDT MEMORIAL SCHOLARSHIP
• *See page 182*

ARRL FOUNDATION INC.

http://www.arrl.org/

FRANCIS WALTON MEMORIAL SCHOLARSHIP
• *See page 83*

ASIAN AMERICAN JOURNALISTS ASSOCIATION

http://www.aaja.org/

AAJA/COX FOUNDATION SCHOLARSHIP
• *See page 374*

ASIAN-AMERICAN JOURNALISTS ASSOCIATION SCHOLARSHIP
• *See page 183*

MINORU YASUI MEMORIAL SCHOLARSHIP AWARD
• *See page 374*

ASSOCIATED PRESS

http://www.aptra.org/

ASSOCIATED PRESS TELEVISION/RADIO ASSOCIATION-CLETE ROBERTS JOURNALISM SCHOLARSHIP AWARDS
• *See page 375*

KATHRYN DETTMAN MEMORIAL JOURNALISM SCHOLARSHIP
• *See page 375*

ATLANTA PRESS CLUB INC.

http://www.atlantapressclub.org/

ATLANTA PRESS CLUB JOURNALISM SCHOLARSHIP PROGRAM
• *See page 375*

CALIFORNIA BROADCASTERS FOUNDATION

http://www.cabroadcasters.org/

CALIFORNIA BROADCASTERS FOUNDATION INTERN SCHOLARSHIP

Two $500 scholarships awarded to radio interns and two $500 scholarships awarded to television interns each semester. Any enrolled college student working as an intern at any California Broadcasters Foundation or Association member radio or television station is eligible. No minimum number of hours per week required. Immediate family of current Foundation Board Members are not eligible. Deadlines: June 18 for fall and December 10 for spring.

Academic Fields/Career Goals: TV/Radio Broadcasting.

Award: Scholarship for use in freshman, sophomore, junior, senior, graduate, or postgraduate years; not renewable. *Number:* up to 4. *Amount:* $500.

Eligibility Requirements: Applicant must be enrolled or expecting to enroll full- or part-time at a two-year or four-year or technical institution or university and resident of California. Available to U.S. citizens.

Application Requirements: Application, essay, references. *Deadline:* varies.

Contact: Mark Powers, Government Affairs
California Broadcasters Foundation
915 L Street, Suite 1150
Sacramento, CA 95814
Phone: 916-444-2237
E-mail: cbapowers@cabroadcasters.org

CCNMA: LATINO JOURNALISTS OF CALIFORNIA

http://www.ccnma.org/

CCNMA SCHOLARSHIPS
• *See page 376*

CHARLES AND LUCILLE KING FAMILY FOUNDATION, INC.

http://www.kingfoundation.org/

CHARLES AND LUCILLE KING FAMILY FOUNDATION SCHOLARSHIPS
• *See page 184*

CIRI FOUNDATION (TCF)

http://www.thecirifoundation.org/

CAP LATHROP SCHOLARSHIP PROGRAM
• *See page 147*

DADE COMMUNITY FOUNDATION

http://www.jackituckfield.org/

LEO SUAREZ SCHOLARSHIP
• *See page 184*

FISHER BROADCASTING COMPANY

http://www.fsci.com/

FISHER BROADCASTING INC. SCHOLARSHIP FOR MINORITIES
• *See page 150*

GREAT LAKES COMMISSION

http://www.glc.org/

CAROL A. RATZA MEMORIAL SCHOLARSHIP
• *See page 185*

HAWAII ASSOCIATION OF BROADCASTERS INC.

http://www.hawaiibroadcasters.com/

HAWAII ASSOCIATION OF BROADCASTERS SCHOLARSHIP

Renewable scholarship for full-time college students with the career goal of working in the broadcast industry in Hawaii upon graduation. Minimum GPA of 2.75 required. Number of awards granted ranges between twenty and thirty. For more information, visit web site http://www.hawaiibroadcasters.com.

Academic Fields/Career Goals: TV/Radio Broadcasting.

Award: Scholarship for use in freshman, sophomore, junior, or senior years; renewable. *Number:* 20–30. *Amount:* $500–$4500.

Eligibility Requirements: Applicant must be enrolled or expecting to enroll full-time at a two-year or four-year institution or university. Applicant must have 2.5 GPA or higher. Available to U.S. and non-U.S. citizens.

Application Requirements: Application, references, transcript. *Deadline:* April 30.

Contact: Scholarship Committee
Hawaii Association of Broadcasters Inc.
PO Box 61562
Honolulu, HI 96839
Phone: 808-599-1455
Fax: 808-599-7784

IDAHO STATE BROADCASTERS ASSOCIATION

http://www.idahobroadcasters.org/

WAYNE C. CORNILS MEMORIAL SCHOLARSHIP
• *See page 151*

ILLUMINATING ENGINEERING SOCIETY OF NORTH AMERICA

http://www.iesna.org/

ROBERT W. THUNEN MEMORIAL SCHOLARSHIPS
• *See page 101*

INDIANA BROADCASTERS ASSOCIATION

http://www.indianabroadcasters.org/

INDIANA BROADCASTERS FOUNDATION SCHOLARSHIP
• *See page 378*

JOHN BAYLISS BROADCAST FOUNDATION

http://www.baylissfoundation.org/

JOHN BAYLISS BROADCAST RADIO SCHOLARSHIP
• *See page 186*

JOURNALISM EDUCATION ASSOCIATION

http://www.jea.org/

NATIONAL HIGH SCHOOL JOURNALIST OF THE YEAR/ SISTER RITA JEANNE SCHOLARSHIPS
• *See page 186*

KATU THOMAS R. DARGAN MINORITY SCHOLARSHIP

http://www.katu.com/

THOMAS R. DARGAN MINORITY SCHOLARSHIP
• *See page 186*

LIN TELEVISION CORPORATION

http://www.lintv.com/

LINTV MINORITY SCHOLARSHIP
• *See page 378*

LOUISIANA ASSOCIATION OF BROADCASTERS

http://www.broadcasters.org/

BROADCAST SCHOLARSHIP PROGRAM

Scholarship to students enrolled and attending classes, full-time, in a fully accredited broadcast curriculum at a Louisiana four-year college. Must be a Louisiana resident and maintain a minimum 2.5 GPA. Previous LAB Scholarship Award winners are eligible.

Academic Fields/Career Goals: TV/Radio Broadcasting.

Award: Scholarship for use in junior or senior years; not renewable. *Number:* 2. *Amount:* $2000.

Eligibility Requirements: Applicant must be enrolled or expecting to enroll full-time at a four-year institution or university; resident of Louisiana and studying in Louisiana. Applicant must have 2.5 GPA or higher. Available to U.S. citizens.

Application Requirements: Application, essay, references, transcript. *Deadline:* February 1.

Contact: Louise L. Munson, Scholarship Coordinator
Louisiana Association of Broadcasters
660 Florida Boulevard
Baton Rouge, LA 70801
Phone: 225-267-4522
Fax: 225-267-4329
E-mail: lmunson@broadcasters.org

MARYLAND ASSOCIATION OF PRIVATE COLLEGES AND CAREER SCHOOLS

http://www.mapccs.org/

MARYLAND ASSOCIATION OF PRIVATE COLLEGES AND CAREER SCHOOLS SCHOLARSHIP
• *See page 153*

MASSACHUSETTS BROADCASTERS ASSOCIATION

http://www.massbroadcasters.org/

MBA STUDENT BROADCASTER SCHOLARSHIP

Scholarship available to permanent residents of Massachusetts who will be enrolling or are currently enrolled at an accredited vocational school, two- or four-year college or university in the United States. Must be full-time students pursuing studies in radio and television broadcasting.

Academic Fields/Career Goals: TV/Radio Broadcasting.

Award: Scholarship for use in freshman, sophomore, junior, or senior years; not renewable. *Number:* varies. *Amount:* $2000.

Eligibility Requirements: Applicant must be enrolled or expecting to enroll full-time at a two-year or four-year or technical institution or university and resident of Massachusetts. Available to U.S. citizens.

Application Requirements: Application, financial need analysis, references, transcript. *Deadline:* April 4.

Contact: B. Sprague, President
Massachusetts Broadcasters Association
43 Riverside Avenue
PO Box 401
Medford, MA 02155
Phone: 800-471-1875
Fax: 800-471-1876
E-mail: als@massbroadcasters.org

MEDIA ACTION NETWORK FOR ASIAN AMERICANS

http://www.manaa.org/

MANAA MEDIA SCHOLARSHIPS FOR ASIAN AMERICAN STUDENTS
• *See page 113*

MICHIGAN ASSOCIATION OF BROADCASTERS FOUNDATION

http://www.michmab.com/

WXYZ-TV BROADCASTING SCHOLARSHIP

One-time $1000 scholarship to assist students who are actively pursuing a career in a broadcast-related field. No limit on the number of awards within the program. Interested applicants should send a cover letter, resume, letters of recommendation, and an essay (200 to 300 words). The scholarship is open to Michigan residents currently attending college in Michigan.

Academic Fields/Career Goals: TV/Radio Broadcasting.

Award: Scholarship for use in freshman year; not renewable. *Number:* 1. *Amount:* $1000.

Eligibility Requirements: Applicant must be high school student; planning to enroll or expecting to enroll full-time at a two-year or four-year institution or university; resident of Michigan and studying in Michigan. Available to U.S. citizens.

Application Requirements: Application, driver's license, essay, references. *Deadline:* January 15.

Contact: Julie Sochay, Executive Vice President
Michigan Association of Broadcasters Foundation
819 North Washington Avenue
Lansing, MI 48906
Phone: 517-484-7444
Fax: 517-484-5810
E-mail: mabf@michmab.com

MINNESOTA BROADCASTERS ASSOCIATION

http://www.minnesotabroadcasters.com/

JAMES J. WYCHOR SCHOLARSHIP

One-time scholarships to Minnesota residents interested in broadcasting who are planning to enter the broadcasting field or other electronic media. Minimum 3.0 GPA is required. Submit proof of enrollment at an accredited postsecondary institution.

Academic Fields/Career Goals: TV/Radio Broadcasting.

Award: Scholarship for use in freshman, sophomore, junior, senior, or graduate years; not renewable. *Number:* 10. *Amount:* $1500.

Eligibility Requirements: Applicant must be enrolled or expecting to enroll full-time at a two-year or four-year or technical institution or university and resident of Minnesota. Applicant must have 3.0 GPA or higher. Available to U.S. citizens.

Application Requirements: Application, essay, references, transcript. *Deadline:* May 31.

Contact: Linda Lasere, Administrative Assistant
Minnesota Broadcasters Association
3033 Excelsior Boulevard, Suite 440
Minneapolis, MN 55416-4675
Phone: 612-926-8123
Fax: 612-926-9761
E-mail: llasere@minnesotabroadcasters.com

MISSISSIPPI ASSOCIATION OF BROADCASTERS

http://www.msbroadcasters.org/

MISSISSIPPI ASSOCIATION OF BROADCASTERS SCHOLARSHIP
• *See page 379*

MISSOURI BROADCASTERS ASSOCIATION SCHOLARSHIP PROGRAM

http://www.mbaweb.org/

MISSOURI BROADCASTERS ASSOCIATION SCHOLARSHIP

Scholarship for a Missouri resident enrolled or planning to enroll in a broadcast or related curriculum which provides training and expertise applicable to a broadcast operation. Must maintain a GPA of at least 3.0 or equivalent. Multiple awards may be assigned each year and the amount of the scholarship will vary.

Academic Fields/Career Goals: TV/Radio Broadcasting.

Award: Scholarship for use in freshman, sophomore, junior, or senior years; not renewable. *Number:* 3. *Amount:* $1000–$2500.

Eligibility Requirements: Applicant must be enrolled or expecting to enroll full-time at a two-year or four-year institution or university; resident of Missouri and studying in Missouri. Applicant must have 3.0 GPA or higher. Available to U.S. citizens.

Application Requirements: Application, financial need analysis, references. *Deadline:* March 31.

Contact: Conny Heiland, Executive Assistant
Missouri Broadcasters Association Scholarship Program
PO Box 104445
Jefferson City, MO 65110-4445
Phone: 573-636-6692
Fax: 573-634-8258
E-mail: cheiland@mbaweb.org

MONTANA BROADCASTERS ASSOCIATION

http://www.mtbroadcasters.org/

GREAT FALLS BROADCASTERS ASSOCIATION SCHOLARSHIP

Scholarship available to a student who has graduated from a north-central Montana high school (Cascade, Meagher, Judith Basin, Fergus, Choteau, Teton, Pondera, Glacier, Toole, Liberty, Hill, Blaine, Phillips, and Valley counties) and is enrolled as at least a second year student in radio-TV at any public or private Montana college or university.

Academic Fields/Career Goals: TV/Radio Broadcasting.

Award: Scholarship for use in sophomore year; not renewable. *Number:* 1. *Amount:* $2000–$5000.

Eligibility Requirements: Applicant must be enrolled or expecting to enroll full-time at a two-year or four-year institution or university; resident of Montana and studying in Montana. Available to U.S. citizens.

Application Requirements: Application, essay, references, transcript. *Deadline:* March 15.

Contact: Gregory McDonald, Scholarship Coordinator
Montana Broadcasters Association
HC 70 PO Box 98
Bonner, MT 59823
Phone: 406-244-4622
Fax: 406-244-5518
E-mail: mba@mtbroadcasters.org

NATIONAL ACADEMY OF TELEVISION ARTS AND SCIENCES

http://www.emmyonline.tv/

NATIONAL ACADEMY OF TELEVISION ARTS AND SCIENCES JOHN CANNON MEMORIAL SCHOLARSHIP
• *See page 187*

NATIONAL ACADEMY OF TELEVISION ARTS AND SCIENCES-NATIONAL CAPITAL/CHESAPEAKE BAY CHAPTER

http://www.natasdc.org/

BETTY ENDICOTT/NTA-NCCB STUDENT SCHOLARSHIP
• *See page 379*

NATIONAL ASSOCIATION OF BLACK JOURNALISTS

http://www.nabj.org/

NABJ SCHOLARSHIP
• *See page 187*

NATIONAL ASSOCIATION OF BLACK JOURNALISTS NON-SUSTAINING SCHOLARSHIP AWARDS
• *See page 380*

NATIONAL ASSOCIATION OF BROADCASTERS

http://www.nab.org/

NATIONAL ASSOCIATION OF BROADCASTERS GRANTS FOR RESEARCH IN BROADCASTING
• *See page 187*

NATIONAL ASSOCIATION OF HISPANIC JOURNALISTS (NAHJ)

http://www.nahj.org/

GERALDO RIVERA SCHOLARSHIP
• *See page 380*

MARIA ELENA SALINAS SCHOLARSHIP
• *See page 328*

NATIONAL ASSOCIATION OF HISPANIC JOURNALISTS SCHOLARSHIP
• *See page 188*

NATIONAL PRESS PHOTOGRAPHERS FOUNDATION INC.

http://www.nppa.org/

NATIONAL PRESS PHOTOGRAPHERS FOUNDATION TELEVISION NEWS SCHOLARSHIP
• *See page 473*

NEW JERSEY BROADCASTERS ASSOCIATION

http://www.njba.com/

MICHAEL S. LIBRETTI SCHOLARSHIP
• *See page 188*

NORTH CAROLINA ASSOCIATION OF BROADCASTERS

http://www.ncbroadcast.com/

NCAB SCHOLARSHIP
One-time scholarship for high school seniors enrolled as full-time students in a North Carolina college or university with an interest in broadcasting. Must be between ages 17 and 20.

Academic Fields/Career Goals: TV/Radio Broadcasting.

Award: Scholarship for use in freshman year; not renewable. *Number:* 2. Amount: $10,000.

Eligibility Requirements: Applicant must be high school student; age 17-20; planning to enroll or expecting to enroll full-time at a two-year or four-year institution or university and studying in North Carolina. Available to U.S. citizens.

Application Requirements: Application, essay, references, transcript. *Deadline:* April 15.

Contact: Lisa Reynolds, Executive Manager
North Carolina Association of Broadcasters
PO Box 627
Raleigh, NC 27602
Phone: 919-821-7300
Fax: 919-839-0304

OREGON ASSOCIATION OF BROADCASTERS

http://www.theoab.org/

OAB FOUNDATION SCHOLARSHIP
• *See page 188*

OUTDOOR WRITERS ASSOCIATION OF AMERICA

http://www.owaa.org/

OUTDOOR WRITERS ASSOCIATION OF AMERICA BODIE MCDOWELL SCHOLARSHIP AWARD
• *See page 189*

PALM BEACH ASSOCIATION OF BLACK JOURNALISTS

http://www.pbabj.org/

PALM BEACH ASSOCIATION OF BLACK JOURNALISTS SCHOLARSHIP
• *See page 384*

RADIO & TELEVISION NEWS DIRECTORS FOUNDATION

http://www.rtndf.org/

CAROLE SIMPSON SCHOLARSHIP
• *See page 189*

ED BRADLEY SCHOLARSHIP
• *See page 384*

KEN KASHIWAHARA SCHOLARSHIP
• *See page 189*

LOU AND CAROLE PRATO SPORTS REPORTING SCHOLARSHIP
• *See page 189*

PRESIDENTS SCHOLARSHIP
• *See page 190*

RHODE ISLAND FOUNDATION

http://www.rifoundation.org/

J. D. EDSAL ADVERTISING SCHOLARSHIP
• *See page 77*

SOCIETY OF BROADCAST ENGINEERS INC.

http://www.sbe.org/

ROBERT GREENBERG/HAROLD E. ENNES SCHOLARSHIP FUND AND ENNES EDUCATIONAL FOUNDATION BROADCAST TECHNOLOGY SCHOLARSHIP
• *See page 258*

YOUTH SCHOLARSHIP

Award available to senior in high school with a serious interest in pursuing studies leading to a career in broadcast engineering or closely related field.

Academic Fields/Career Goals: TV/Radio Broadcasting.

Award: Scholarship for use in freshman year; renewable. *Number:* 1. *Amount:* $1000–$1500.

Eligibility Requirements: Applicant must be high school student and planning to enroll or expecting to enroll full-time at a four-year institution. Applicant must have 3.0 GPA or higher. Available to U.S. citizens.

Application Requirements: Application, transcript, written statement of education plans after high school. *Deadline:* July 1.

Contact: Debbie Hennessey, Executive Secretary
Society of Broadcast Engineers Inc.
9102 North Meridian Street, Suite 150
Indianapolis, IN 46260
Phone: 317-846-9000
Fax: 317-846-9120
E-mail: dhennessey@sbe.org

SOCIETY OF MOTION PICTURE AND TELEVISION ENGINEERS

http://www.smpte.org/

LOU WOLF MEMORIAL SCHOLARSHIP
• *See page 259*

STUDENT PAPER AWARD
• *See page 272*

SOCIETY OF PROFESSIONAL JOURNALISTS, LOS ANGELES CHAPTER

http://www.spj.org/losangeles

HELEN JOHNSON SCHOLARSHIP
• *See page 385*

STRAIGHTFORWARD MEDIA

http://www.straightforwardmedia.com/

STRAIGHTFORWARD MEDIA MEDIA & COMMUNICATIONS SCHOLARSHIP
• *See page 77*

TEXAS ASSOCIATION OF BROADCASTERS

http://www.tab.org/

BELO TEXAS BROADCAST EDUCATION FOUNDATION SCHOLARSHIP
• *See page 191*

BONNER MCLANE TEXAS BROADCAST EDUCATION FOUNDATION SCHOLARSHIP
• *See page 191*

STUDENT TEXAS BROADCAST EDUCATION FOUNDATION SCHOLARSHIP
• *See page 191*

TOM REIFF TEXAS BROADCAST EDUCATION FOUNDATION SCHOLARSHIP
• *See page 191*

UNDERGRADUATE TEXAS BROADCAST EDUCATION FOUNDATION SCHOLARSHIP
• *See page 191*

VANN KENNEDY TEXAS BROADCAST EDUCATION FOUNDATION SCHOLARSHIP
• *See page 192*

TEXAS GRIDIRON CLUB INC.

http://www.spjfw.org/

TEXAS GRIDIRON CLUB SCHOLARSHIPS
• *See page 192*

UNITED METHODIST COMMUNICATIONS

http://www.umcom.org/

LEONARD M. PERRYMAN COMMUNICATIONS SCHOLARSHIP FOR ETHNIC MINORITY STUDENTS
• *See page 192*

UNITED NEGRO COLLEGE FUND

http://www.uncf.org/

C-SPAN SCHOLARSHIP PROGRAM
• *See page 193*

VALLEY PRESS CLUB, SPRINGFIELD NEWSPAPERS

http://www.valleypressclub.com/

VALLEY PRESS CLUB SCHOLARSHIPS, THE REPUBLICAN SCHOLARSHIP, CHANNEL 22 SCHOLARSHIP
• *See page 194*

WISCONSIN BROADCASTERS ASSOCIATION FOUNDATION

http://www.wi-broadcasters.org/

WISCONSIN BROADCASTERS ASSOCIATION FOUNDATION SCHOLARSHIP
• *See page 194*

WMTW-TV 8-AUBURN, MAINE

http://www.wmtw.com/

BOB ELLIOT-WMTW-TV 8 JOURNALISM SCHOLARSHIP
• *See page 194*

WOWT-TV–OMAHA, NEBRASKA

http://www.wowt.com/

WOWT-TV BROADCASTING SCHOLARSHIP PROGRAM

Two annual scholarships of $1000 for high school graduates in the Channel 6 viewing area of Nebraska. Must be pursuing a full-time career in broadcasting and have a minimum GPA of 3.0.

Academic Fields/Career Goals: TV/Radio Broadcasting.

Award: Scholarship for use in freshman year; not renewable. *Number:* up to 2. *Amount:* up to $1000.

Eligibility Requirements: Applicant must be high school student; planning to enroll or expecting to enroll full-time at a two-year or four-year institution or university and resident of Nebraska. Applicant must have 3.0 GPA or higher. Available to U.S. citizens.

Application Requirements: Application, essay, interview, references, test scores, transcript. *Deadline:* March 15.

Contact: Gail Backer, Scholarship Committee
WOWT-TV–Omaha, Nebraska
3501 Farnam Street
Omaha, NE 68131
Phone: 402-346-6666
Fax: 402-233-7880

YOUNG AMERICAN BROADCASTERS SCHOLARSHIP

http://www.youngamericanbroadcasters.org/

YOUNG AMERICAN BROADCASTERS SCHOLARSHIP

Scholarship for ethnically diverse college population to encourage pursuit of studies in radio and Internet broadcasting. One-time scholarship for part-time students who have completed at least one year of study.

Academic Fields/Career Goals: TV/Radio Broadcasting.

Award: Scholarship for use in sophomore, junior, or senior years; not renewable. *Number:* varies. *Amount:* up to $5000.

Eligibility Requirements: Applicant must be enrolled or expecting to enroll part-time at a four-year institution or university. Available to U.S. and non-U.S. citizens.

Application Requirements: Application, applicant must enter a contest, transcript. *Deadline:* varies.

Contact: Scholarship Committee
Young American Broadcasters Scholarship
1030 15th Street, NW, Suite 1028
Washington, DC 20005
Phone: 202-408-8255
Fax: 202-408-5188

URBAN AND REGIONAL PLANNING

AMERICAN PLANNING ASSOCIATION

http://www.planning.org/

JUDITH MCMANUS PRICE SCHOLARSHIP

Scholarship available to women and underrepresented minority students enrolled in an approved Planning Accreditation Board (PAB) planning program who are U.S. citizens and intend to pursue careers as practicing planners in the public sector. Must demonstrate financial need. For further information visit http://www.planning.org/institutions/scholarship.htm.

Academic Fields/Career Goals: Urban and Regional Planning.

Award: Scholarship for use in freshman, sophomore, junior, or senior years; not renewable. *Number:* varies. *Amount:* $2000–$5000.

Eligibility Requirements: Applicant must be American Indian/Alaska Native, Black (non-Hispanic), or Hispanic and enrolled or expecting to enroll full-time at a four-year institution or university. Available to U.S. citizens.

Application Requirements: Application, financial need analysis, resume, transcript, 2- to 5-page personal and background statement written by the school, 2 letters of recommendation, acceptance letter. *Deadline:* April 30.

Contact: Kriss Blank, Leadership Affairs Associate
American Planning Association
122 South Michigan Avenue, Suite 1600
Chicago, IL 60603
Phone: 312-786-6722
Fax: 312-786-6727
E-mail: kblank@planning.org

CONNECTICUT CHAPTER OF THE AMERICAN PLANNING ASSOCIATION

http://www.ccapa.org/

DIANA DONALD SCHOLARSHIP

One-time award of $2500 for full-time students enrolled in a graduate or undergraduate program in city planning or a closely related field. Must be resident of Connecticut and study in Connecticut. Deadline varies.

Academic Fields/Career Goals: Urban and Regional Planning.

Award: Scholarship for use in freshman, sophomore, junior, senior, or graduate years; not renewable. *Number:* up to 1. *Amount:* up to $2500.

Eligibility Requirements: Applicant must be enrolled or expecting to enroll full-time at a four-year institution or university; resident of Connecticut and studying in Connecticut. Available to U.S. and non-U.S. citizens.

Application Requirements: Application, essay, financial need analysis, references, transcript. *Deadline:* varies.

Contact: Mary Savage-Dunham, Town Planner
Connecticut Chapter of the American Planning Association
Town of Southington, 75 Main St
Southington, CT 06489
Phone: 860-276-6248
E-mail: savagem@southington.org

INTERNATIONAL FACILITY MANAGEMENT ASSOCIATION FOUNDATION

http://www.ifmafoundation.org/

IFMA FOUNDATION SCHOLARSHIPS
• *See page 102*

WOMEN'S STUDIES

AMERICAN FEDERATION OF STATE, COUNTY, AND MUNICIPAL EMPLOYEES

http://www.afscme.org/

AFSCME/UNCF UNION SCHOLARS PROGRAM
• *See page 89*

MARGARET MCNAMARA MEMORIAL FUND

http://www.wbfn.org/

MARGARET MCNAMARA MEMORIAL FUND FELLOWSHIPS
• *See page 172*

SOCIETY FOR THE SCIENTIFIC STUDY OF SEXUALITY

http://www.sexscience.org/

SOCIETY FOR THE SCIENTIFIC STUDY OF SEXUALITY STUDENT RESEARCH GRANT
• *See page 137*

UNITED NEGRO COLLEGE FUND

http://www.uncf.org/

AFSCME/UNCF/HARVARD UNIVERSITY LWP UNION SCHOLARS PROGRAM
• *See page 90*

WHOMENTORS.COM, INC.

http://www.WHOmentors.com/

ACCREDITED REPRESENTATIVE (FULL)
• *See page 56*

WOMEN'S INDEPENDENCE SCHOLARSHIP PROGRAM, INC.

http://www.wispinc.org/

COUNSELOR, ADVOCATE, AND SUPPORT STAFF SCHOLARSHIP PROGRAM
• *See page 76*

Nonacademic/Noncareer Criteria

CIVIC, PROFESSIONAL, SOCIAL, OR UNION AFFILIATION

AIR LINE PILOTS ASSOCIATION, INTERNATIONAL

http://www.alpa.org/

AIRLINE PILOTS ASSOCIATION SCHOLARSHIP PROGRAM

Scholarship for children of medically retired, long-term disabled, or deceased pilot members of the Air Line Pilots Association. The total monetary value is $12,000 with $3000 disbursed annually to the recipient for four consecutive years, provided that a GPA of 3.0 is maintained. An additional $2000 per year is available which may be awarded to one or two additional applicants as a one-year special award, which is not renewable.

Award: Scholarship for use in freshman, sophomore, junior, or senior years; renewable. *Number:* 1–3. *Amount:* $1000–$12,000.

Eligibility Requirements: Applicant must be enrolled or expecting to enroll full-time at a four-year institution or university. Applicant or parent of applicant must be member of Airline Pilots Association. Applicant must have 3.0 GPA or higher. Available to U.S. and Canadian citizens.

Application Requirements: Application, financial need analysis, references, test scores, transcript. *Deadline:* April 1.

Contact: Maggie Erzen, Coordinator
Air Line Pilots Association, International
1625 Massachusetts Avenue, NW
Washington, DC 20036
Phone: 202-797-4059
Fax: 202-797-4014
E-mail: maggie.erzen@alpa.org

ALBERTA AGRICULTURE FOOD AND RURAL DEVELOPMENT 4-H BRANCH

http://www.4h.ab.ca/

ALBERTA AGRICULTURE FOOD AND RURAL DEVELOPMENT 4-H SCHOLARSHIP PROGRAM

Awards will be given to current and incoming students attending any institute of higher learning. Must have been a member of the Alberta 4-H Program and be a Canadian citizen. Must be a resident of Alberta.

Award: Scholarship for use in freshman, sophomore, junior, senior, or graduate years; not renewable. *Number:* 115–120. *Amount:* $200–$1500.

Eligibility Requirements: Applicant must be enrolled or expecting to enroll full-time at a two-year or four-year or technical institution or university and resident of Alberta. Applicant or parent of applicant must be member of National 4-H. Available to Canadian citizens.

Application Requirements: Application, essay, references, transcript. *Deadline:* May 5.

Contact: Susann Stone, Scholarship Coordinator
Alberta Agriculture Food and Rural Development 4-H Branch
RR1 West Rose
Edmonton, AB T0C 2V0
Canada
Phone: 780-682-2153
Fax: 780-682-3784
E-mail: foundation@4hab.com

ALPHA KAPPA ALPHA

http://www.akaeaf.org/

AKA EDUCATIONAL ADVANCEMENT FOUNDATION YOUTH PARTNERS ACCESSING CAPITAL SCHOLARSHIP

Scholarship for a member of the society. Must be an undergraduate of at least sophomore status. Must have a minimum GPA of 3.0 and participate in leadership, volunteer, civic, or campus activities. Must demonstrate academic achievement or financial need.

Award: Scholarship for use in sophomore, junior, or senior years; not renewable. *Number:* varies. *Amount:* $1000–$3000.

Eligibility Requirements: Applicant must be enrolled or expecting to enroll full-time at a four-year institution or university. Applicant or parent of applicant must be member of Alpha Kappa Alpha. Applicant must have 3.0 GPA or higher. Available to U.S. and non-U.S. citizens.

Application Requirements: Application, references, transcript. *Deadline:* April 15.

Contact: Andrea Kerr, Program Coordinator
Alpha Kappa Alpha
5656 South Stony Island Avenue
Chicago, IL 60637
Phone: 773-947-0026 Ext. 8
E-mail: akaeaf@akaeaf.net

AMERICAN BOWLING CONGRESS

http://www.bowl.com/

CHUCK HALL STAR OF TOMORROW SCHOLARSHIP

$1500 scholarship, renewable for up to three years, available to male high school seniors or college students who hold an average bowling score of 175 or greater. Minimum 2.5 GPA required. Must be a current USBC Youth or USBC member in good standing and currently compete in certified events.

Award: Scholarship for use in freshman, sophomore, junior, or senior years; renewable. *Number:* 1. *Amount:* $1500.

Eligibility Requirements: Applicant must be age 22 or under; enrolled or expecting to enroll full- or part-time at a two-year or four-year or technical institution or university; male and must have an interest in bowling. Applicant or parent of applicant must be member of Young American Bowling Alliance. Applicant must have 2.5 GPA or higher. Available to U.S. and Canadian citizens.

Application Requirements: Application, essay, references, self-addressed stamped envelope, transcript. *Deadline:* October 1.

Contact: Ed Gocha, Scholarship Administrator
American Bowling Congress
5301 South 76th Street
Greendale, WI 53129-1192
Phone: 800-514-2695 Ext. 3343
Fax: 414-423-3014
E-mail: smart@bowl.com

AMERICAN FEDERATION OF STATE, COUNTY, AND MUNICIPAL EMPLOYEES

http://www.afscme.org/

AMERICAN FEDERATION OF STATE, COUNTY, AND MUNICIPAL EMPLOYEES SCHOLARSHIP PROGRAM

Scholarship for family dependents of American Federation of State, County, and Municipal Employees members. Must be a graduating high school senior planning to pursue postsecondary education at a four-year institution. Submit proof of parent's membership. Renewable award of $2000.

Award: Scholarship for use in freshman, sophomore, junior, or senior years; renewable. *Number:* 13. *Amount:* $2000.

Eligibility Requirements: Applicant must be high school student and planning to enroll or expecting to enroll full-time at a four-year institution or university. Applicant or parent of applicant must be member of American Federation of State, County, and Municipal Employees. Available to U.S. citizens.

Application Requirements: Application, essay, references, test scores, transcript. *Deadline:* December 31.

Contact: Philip Allen, Scholarship Coordinator
American Federation of State, County, and Municipal
Employees
1625 L Street, NW
Washington, DC 20036-5687
Phone: 202-429-1250
Fax: 202-429-1293
E-mail: pallen@asscme.org

UNION PLUS CREDIT CARD SCHOLARSHIP PROGRAM

One-time award for AFSCME members, their spouses and dependent children. Graduate students and grandchildren are not eligible.

Award: Scholarship for use in freshman, sophomore, junior, or senior years; not renewable. *Number:* varies. *Amount:* $500–$4000.

Eligibility Requirements: Applicant must be enrolled or expecting to enroll full-time at a two-year or four-year or technical institution or university. Applicant or parent of applicant must be member of American Federation of State, County, and Municipal Employees. Available to U.S. citizens.

Application Requirements: Application, driver's license, essay, references, transcript. *Deadline:* January 31.

Contact: Philip Allen, Scholarship Coordinator
American Federation of State, County, and Municipal
Employees
1625 L Street, NW
Washington, DC 20036-5687
Phone: 202-429-1250
Fax: 202-429-1293
E-mail: pallen@asscme.org

AMERICAN FEDERATION OF TEACHERS

http://www.aft.org/

ROBERT G. PORTER SCHOLARS PROGRAM-AMERICAN FEDERATION OF TEACHERS DEPENDENTS

Scholarship of up to $8000 for high school seniors who are dependents of AFT members. Must submit transcript, test scores, essay, and recommendations with application. Must be U.S. citizen.

Award: Scholarship for use in freshman year; renewable. *Number:* 4. *Amount:* $8000.

Eligibility Requirements: Applicant must be high school student and planning to enroll or expecting to enroll full-time at a four-year institution or university. Applicant or parent of applicant must be member of American Federation of Teachers. Applicant or parent of applicant must have employment or volunteer experience in nursing or teaching/education. Available to U.S. citizens.

Application Requirements: Application, essay, references, test scores, transcript. *Deadline:* March 31.

Contact: Ms. Bernadette Bailey, Scholarship Coordinator
American Federation of Teachers
555 New Jersey Avenue, NW
Washington, DC 20001-2079
Phone: 202-879-4481
E-mail: bbailey@aft.org

AMERICAN FOREIGN SERVICE ASSOCIATION

http://www.afsa.org/

AMERICAN FOREIGN SERVICE ASSOCIATION (AFSA) FINANCIAL AID AWARD PROGRAM

Need-based financial aid scholarship program open only to students whose parents are in the us government foreign service, a special branch of the US Government. A parent who is in the Civil Service or in the Military, will not qualify the student. Must attend or will be attending full-time as an undergraduate at a two- or four-year accredited college, university, community college, art school, or conservatory. Must maintain a 2.0 GPA and demonstrate financial need.

Award: Scholarship for use in freshman, sophomore, junior, or senior years; not renewable. *Number:* 50–60. *Amount:* $1000–$3500.

Eligibility Requirements: Applicant must be enrolled or expecting to enroll full-time at a two-year or four-year institution or university and single. Applicant or parent of applicant must be member of American Foreign Service Association. Available to U.S. citizens.

Application Requirements: Application, financial need analysis, transcript, CSS profile. *Deadline:* February 6.

Contact: Lori Dec, Scholarship Director
American Foreign Service Association
2101 E Street, NW
Washington, DC 20037
Phone: 202-944-5504
Fax: 202-338-6820
E-mail: dec@afsa.org

AMERICAN FOREIGN SERVICE ASSOCIATION (AFSA) MERIT AWARD PROGRAM

One-time award for a high school seniors. It is open only to students whose parents are in the us government foreign service, a special branch of the US Government. A parent who is in the Civil Service or in the Military, will not qualify the student. The parent also needs to be a member of AFSA or AAFSW. Must maintain a satisfactory academic record of 2.0 GPA. Again, children of military parents or international students are not eligible. Award based upon academic and artistic achievements of the applicant.

Award: Prize for use in freshman year; not renewable. *Number:* 6–15. *Amount:* $1800.

Eligibility Requirements: Applicant must be high school student; planning to enroll or expecting to enroll full-time at a four-year institution or university; single and must have an interest in art. Applicant or parent of applicant must be member of American Foreign Service Association. Available to U.S. citizens.

Application Requirements: Application, essay, references, self-addressed stamped envelope, test scores, transcript. *Deadline:* February 6.

Contact: Lori Dec, Scholarship Director
American Foreign Service Association
2101 East Street NW
Washington, DC 20037
Phone: 202-944-5504
Fax: 202-338-6820
E-mail: dec@afsa.org

AMERICAN LEGION AUXILIARY DEPARTMENT OF CALIFORNIA

http://www.calegionaux.org/

AMERICAN LEGION AUXILIARY DEPARTMENT OF CALIFORNIA JUNIOR SCHOLARSHIP

Award for undergraduate students. Must be a California resident. Must have consecutive membership as a Junior for three years and be current with membership in the American Legion Auxiliary.

Award: Scholarship for use in freshman year; not renewable. *Number:* 1. *Amount:* $300–$1000.

Eligibility Requirements: Applicant must be high school student; age 17 and over; planning to enroll or expecting to enroll full- or part-time at a four-year institution or university and resident of California. Applicant or parent of applicant must be member of American Legion or Auxiliary. Available to U.S. citizens. Applicant or parent must meet one or more of the following requirements: Army experience; retired from active duty; disabled or killed as a result of military service; prisoner of war; or missing in action.

Application Requirements: Application. *Deadline:* April 13.

Contact: Theresa Jacob, Secretary/Treasurer
American Legion Auxiliary Department of California
401 Van Ness Avenue, Room 113
San Francisco, CA 94102
Phone: 415-862-5092
Fax: 415-861-8365
E-mail: calegionaux@calegionaux.org

AMERICAN LEGION AUXILIARY DEPARTMENT OF CONNECTICUT

http://www.ct.legion.org/

AMERICAN LEGION AUXILIARY DEPARTMENT OF CONNECTICUT MEMORIAL EDUCATIONAL GRANT

Half the number of available grants are awarded to children of veterans who are also residents of CT. Remaining grants awarded to child or grandchild of a member (or member at time of death) of the CT Departments of the American Legion/American Legion Auxiliary, regardless of residency; or are members of the CT Departments of the American Legion Auxiliary/Sons of the American Legion, regardless of residency. Contact local unit President. Must include list of community service activities.

Award: Grant for use in freshman, sophomore, junior, or senior years; not renewable. *Number:* 4. *Amount:* $500.

Eligibility Requirements: Applicant must be age 16-23 and enrolled or expecting to enroll full-time at a two-year or four-year or technical institution or university. Applicant or parent of applicant must be member of American Legion or Auxiliary. Available to U.S. citizens. Applicant must have general military experience.

Application Requirements: Application, essay, financial need analysis, references, self-addressed stamped envelope, transcript. *Deadline:* March 10.

Contact: Rita Barylski, State Secretary
American Legion Auxiliary Department of Connecticut
287 West Street
PO Box 266
Rocky Hill, CT 06067
Phone: 860-721-5945
E-mail: ctalahq@juno.com

AMERICAN LEGION AUXILIARY DEPARTMENT OF CONNECTICUT PAST PRESIDENTS' PARLEY MEMORIAL EDUCATION GRANT

The program gives preference a child or grandchild of an ex-service woman, who was or is a member of the CT departments of the American Legion/American Legion Auxiliary. In the event of a deficiency of preferred applicants, award may be granted to child or grandchild of a member of the CT Departments of the American Legion/American Legion Auxiliary or Sons of the American Legion. Minimum three-year membership required, or three years prior to death. Contact local unit President. Must include list of community service activities.

Award: Grant for use in freshman, sophomore, junior, or senior years; not renewable. *Number:* 4. *Amount:* up to $500.

Eligibility Requirements: Applicant must be age 16-23; enrolled or expecting to enroll full-time at a two-year or four-year or technical institution or university and resident of Connecticut. Applicant or parent of applicant must be member of American Legion or Auxiliary. Available to U.S. citizens. Applicant must have general military experience.

Application Requirements: Application, financial need analysis, references, test scores, transcript, list of school and community activities. *Deadline:* March 10.

Contact: Rita Barylski, State Secretary
American Legion Auxiliary Department of Connecticut
287 West Street
PO Box 266
Rocky Hill, CT 06067
Phone: 860-721-5945
E-mail: ctalahq@juno.com

AMERICAN LEGION AUXILIARY DEPARTMENT OF FLORIDA

http://www.alafl.org/

AMERICAN LEGION AUXILIARY DEPARTMENT OF FLORIDA MEMORIAL SCHOLARSHIP

Scholarship for a member, daughter, or granddaughter of a member of Florida American Legion Auxiliary with a minimum three-year membership. Award for Florida resident for undergraduate study in Florida school. Minimum 2.5 GPA required.

Award: Scholarship for use in freshman, sophomore, junior, or senior years; renewable. *Number:* 1–6. *Amount:* $500–$1000.

Eligibility Requirements: Applicant must be enrolled or expecting to enroll full-time at a two-year or four-year or technical institution or university; female; resident of Florida and studying in Florida. Applicant or parent of applicant must be member of American Legion or Auxiliary. Applicant must have 2.5 GPA or higher. Available to U.S. citizens. Applicant or parent must meet one or more of the following requirements: general military experience; retired from active duty; disabled or killed as a result of military service; prisoner of war; or missing in action.

Application Requirements: Application, financial need analysis, references, transcript. *Deadline:* March 1.

Contact: Robin Briere, Department Secretary and Treasurer
American Legion Auxiliary Department of Florida
PO Box 547917
Orlando, FL 32854-7917
Phone: 407-293-7411
Fax: 407-299-6522
E-mail: contact@alafl.org

AMERICAN LEGION AUXILIARY DEPARTMENT OF MARYLAND

http://www.alamd.org/

AMERICAN LEGION AUXILIARY DEPARTMENT OF MARYLAND GIRL SCOUT ACHIEVEMENT AWARD

Scholarship available to a Girl Scout who has received the Girl Scout Gold Award. Must be a senior in high school, an active member of her religious institution, and must have received the appropriate religious emblem, Cadette or Senior Scout level. Number of awards and the deadline vary annually.

Award: Scholarship for use in freshman year; not renewable. *Number:* 1. *Amount:* $1000.

Eligibility Requirements: Applicant must be high school student; planning to enroll or expecting to enroll full-time at a four-year institution or university and female. Applicant or parent of applicant must be member of Girl Scouts. Available to U.S. citizens.

Application Requirements: Application, references, transcript. *Deadline:* varies.

Contact: Meredith Beeg, President
American Legion Auxiliary Department of Maryland
1589 Sulphur Spring Road, Suite 105
Baltimore, MD 21227
Phone: 410-242-9519
E-mail: hq@alamd.org

AMERICAN LEGION AUXILIARY DEPARTMENT OF MISSOURI

http://www.missourilegion.org/

AMERICAN LEGION AUXILIARY DEPARTMENT OF MISSOURI LELA MURPHY SCHOLARSHIP

Scholarship of $500 for high school graduate. $250 will be awarded each semester. Applicant must be Missouri resident and the granddaughter or great-granddaughter of a living or deceased Auxiliary member. Sponsoring unit and department must validate application.

Award: Scholarship for use in freshman year; not renewable. *Number:* 1. *Amount:* $500.

Eligibility Requirements: Applicant must be high school student; planning to enroll or expecting to enroll full-time at a two-year or four-year or technical institution or university; female and resident of Missouri. Applicant or parent of applicant must be member of American Legion or Auxiliary. Available to U.S. citizens. Applicant or parent must meet one or more of the following requirements: general military experience; retired from active duty; disabled or killed as a result of military service; prisoner of war; or missing in action.

Application Requirements: Application. *Deadline:* March 1.

Contact: Mary Doerhoff, Department Secretary/Treasurer
American Legion Auxiliary Department of Missouri
600 Ellis Boulevard
Jefferson City, MO 65101-1615
Phone: 573-636-9133
E-mail: dptmoala@embarqmail.com

AMERICAN LEGION AUXILIARY DEPARTMENT OF MISSOURI NATIONAL PRESIDENT'S SCHOLARSHIP

State-level award. Offers one $500 scholarship. Applicant must complete 50 hours of community service during their high school years. Sponsoring unit and department must validate application. Applicant must be a Missouri resident.

Award: Scholarship for use in freshman year; not renewable. *Number:* 1. *Amount:* $500.

Eligibility Requirements: Applicant must be high school student; planning to enroll or expecting to enroll full-time at a two-year or four-year or technical institution or university and resident of Missouri. Applicant or parent of applicant must be member of American Legion or Auxiliary. Available to U.S. citizens. Applicant or parent must meet one or more of the following requirements: general military experience; retired from active duty; disabled or killed as a result of military service; prisoner of war; or missing in action.

Application Requirements: Application, resume. *Deadline:* March 1.

Contact: Mary Doerhoff, Department Secretary/Treasurer
American Legion Auxiliary Department of Missouri
600 Ellis Boulevard
Jefferson City, MO 65101-1615
Phone: 573-636-9133
E-mail: dptmoala@embarqmail.com

AMERICAN LEGION AUXILIARY DEPARTMENT OF NEBRASKA

http://www.nebraskalegionaux.net/

AMERICAN LEGION AUXILIARY DEPARTMENT OF NEBRASKA RUBY PAUL CAMPAIGN FUND SCHOLARSHIP

One-time award for Nebraska residents who are children, grandchildren, or great-grandchildren of an American Legion Auxiliary member, or who have been members of the American Legion, American Legion Auxiliary, or Sons of the American Legion or Auxiliary for two years prior to issuing the application. Must rank in upper third of class or have minimum 3.0 GPA.

Award: Scholarship for use in freshman year; not renewable. *Number:* 1–3. *Amount:* $100–$300.

Eligibility Requirements: Applicant must be high school student; planning to enroll or expecting to enroll full-time at a four-year institution or university and resident of Nebraska. Applicant or parent of applicant must be member of American Legion or Auxiliary. Applicant must have 3.0 GPA or higher. Available to U.S. citizens. Applicant or parent must meet one or more of the following requirements: general military experience; retired from active duty; disabled or killed as a result of military service; prisoner of war; or missing in action.

Application Requirements: Application, essay, financial need analysis, references, test scores, transcript, letter of acceptance, proof of enrollment. *Deadline:* March 15.

Contact: Jacki O'Neill, Department Secretary
American Legion Auxiliary Department of Nebraska
PO Box 5227
Lincoln, NE 68505-0227
Phone: 402-466-1808
E-mail: neaux@alltel.net

AMERICAN LEGION AUXILIARY DEPARTMENT OF OREGON

http://www.alaoregon.org/

AMERICAN LEGION AUXILIARY DEPARTMENT OF OREGON SPIRIT OF YOUTH SCHOLARSHIP

One-time award available to Oregon high school seniors. Must be a current female junior member of the American Legion Auxiliary with a three-year membership history. Apply through local units.

Award: Scholarship for use in freshman year; not renewable. *Number:* 1. *Amount:* $1000.

Eligibility Requirements: Applicant must be high school student; planning to enroll or expecting to enroll full- or part-time at a four-year institution or university; female and resident of Oregon. Applicant or parent of applicant must be member of American Legion or Auxiliary. Available to U.S. citizens. Applicant or parent must meet one or more of the following requirements: general military experience; retired from active duty; disabled or killed as a result of military service; prisoner of war; or missing in action.

Application Requirements: Application, essay, financial need analysis, interview, references, transcript. *Deadline:* March 1.

Contact: Virginia Biddle, Secretary/Treasurer
American Legion Auxiliary Department of Oregon
PO Box 1730
Wilsonville, OR 97070
Phone: 503-682-3162
Fax: 503-685-5008
E-mail: alaor@pcez.com

AMERICAN LEGION AUXILIARY DEPARTMENT OF SOUTH DAKOTA

http://www.sdlegion.org/

AMERICAN LEGION AUXILIARY DEPARTMENT OF SOUTH DAKOTA COLLEGE SCHOLARSHIPS

One-time award of $500 to assist veterans children or auxiliary members' children from South Dakota ages 16 to 22 to secure an education at a four-year school. Write for more information.

Award: Scholarship for use in freshman, sophomore, junior, or senior years; not renewable. *Number:* 2. *Amount:* $500.

Eligibility Requirements: Applicant must be age 16-22; enrolled or expecting to enroll full-time at a four-year institution or university and resident of South Dakota. Applicant or parent of applicant must be member of American Legion or Auxiliary. Available to U.S. and non-U.S. citizens. Applicant or parent must meet one or more of the following requirements: general military experience; retired from active duty; disabled or killed as a result of military service; prisoner of war; or missing in action.

Application Requirements: Application, essay, financial need analysis, references. *Deadline:* March 1.

Contact: Patricia Coyle, Executive Secretary
American Legion Auxiliary Department of South Dakota
PO Box 117
Huron, SD 57350
Phone: 605-353-1793
Fax: 605-352-0336
E-mail: sdlegionaux@msn.com

AMERICAN LEGION AUXILIARY DEPARTMENT OF SOUTH DAKOTA SENIOR SCHOLARSHIP

Award of $400 for current senior member of South Dakota American Legion Auxiliary who has been a member for three years. Based on financial need.

Award: Scholarship for use in freshman year; not renewable. *Number:* 1. *Amount:* $400.

Eligibility Requirements: Applicant must be high school student; planning to enroll or expecting to enroll full-time at a two-year or four-year or technical institution; female and resident of South Dakota. Applicant or parent of applicant must be member of American Legion or Auxiliary. Available to U.S. and non-U.S. citizens. Applicant or parent must meet one or more of the following requirements: general military experience; retired from active duty; disabled or killed as a result of military service; prisoner of war; or missing in action.

Application Requirements: Application, essay, financial need analysis, references, transcript. *Deadline:* March 1.

Contact: Patricia Coyle, Executive Secretary
American Legion Auxiliary Department of South Dakota
PO Box 117
Huron, SD 57350
Phone: 605-353-1793
Fax: 605-352-0336
E-mail: sdlegionaux@msn.com

AMERICAN LEGION AUXILIARY DEPARTMENT OF SOUTH DAKOTA THELMA FOSTER SCHOLARSHIP FOR SENIOR AUXILIARY MEMBERS

One-time award of $300 must be used within twelve months for a current senior member of the South Dakota American Legion Auxiliary who has been a member for three years. Applicant may be a high school senior or older and must be female.

Award: Scholarship for use in freshman year; not renewable. *Number:* 1. *Amount:* $300.

Eligibility Requirements: Applicant must be enrolled or expecting to enroll full-time at a four-year institution or university and female. Applicant or parent of applicant must be member of American Legion or Auxiliary. Available to U.S. and non-U.S. citizens. Applicant or parent must meet one or more of the following requirements: general military experience; retired from active duty; disabled or killed as a result of military service; prisoner of war; or missing in action.

Application Requirements: Application, essay, financial need analysis, references. *Deadline:* March 1.

Contact: Patricia Coyle, Executive Secretary
American Legion Auxiliary Department of South Dakota
PO Box 117
Huron, SD 57350
Phone: 605-353-1793
Fax: 605-352-0336
E-mail: sdlegionaux@msn.com

AMERICAN LEGION AUXILIARY DEPARTMENT OF SOUTH DAKOTA THELMA FOSTER SCHOLARSHIPS FOR JUNIOR AUXILIARY MEMBERS

One-time award of $300 for junior member of the South Dakota American Legion Auxiliary who has held membership for the past three years and holds a membership card for the current year. Must be a senior in high school.

Award: Scholarship for use in freshman year; not renewable. *Number:* 1. *Amount:* $300.

Eligibility Requirements: Applicant must be high school student; planning to enroll or expecting to enroll full-time at a four-year institution or university and female. Applicant or parent of applicant must be member of American Legion or Auxiliary. Available to U.S. and non-U.S. citizens. Applicant or parent must meet one or more of the following requirements: general military experience; retired from active duty; disabled or killed as a result of military service; prisoner of war; or missing in action.

Application Requirements: Application, essay, financial need analysis, references, transcript. *Deadline:* March 1.

Contact: Patricia Coyle, Executive Secretary
American Legion Auxiliary Department of South Dakota
PO Box 117
Huron, SD 57350
Phone: 605-353-1793
Fax: 605-352-0336
E-mail: sdlegionaux@msn.com

AMERICAN LEGION AUXILIARY DEPARTMENT OF SOUTH DAKOTA VOCATIONAL SCHOLARSHIP

One-time award of $500 to assist veterans children or auxiliary members children from South Dakota ages 16 to 22, secure a vocational education beyond the high school level. Write for more information.

Award: Scholarship for use in freshman or sophomore years; not renewable. *Number:* 2. *Amount:* $500.

Eligibility Requirements: Applicant must be age 16-22; enrolled or expecting to enroll full-time at a technical institution; resident of South Dakota and studying in South Dakota. Applicant or parent of applicant must be member of American Legion or Auxiliary. Available to U.S. and non-U.S. citizens. Applicant or parent must meet one or more of the following requirements: general military experience; retired from active duty; disabled or killed as a result of military service; prisoner of war; or missing in action.

Application Requirements: Application, essay, financial need analysis, references. *Deadline:* March 1.

Contact: Patricia Coyle, Executive Secretary
American Legion Auxiliary Department of South Dakota
PO Box 117
Huron, SD 57350
Phone: 605-353-1793
Fax: 605-352-0336
E-mail: sdlegionaux@msn.com

AMERICAN LEGION AUXILIARY DEPARTMENT OF UTAH

http://www.legion-aux.org/

AMERICAN LEGION AUXILIARY DEPARTMENT OF UTAH NATIONAL PRESIDENT'S SCHOLARSHIP

Scholarships available for graduating high school seniors. Must be a resident of Utah, a U.S. citizen, and the direct descendant of a veteran.

Award: Scholarship for use in freshman year; not renewable. *Number:* 15. *Amount:* $1000–$2500.

Eligibility Requirements: Applicant must be high school student; planning to enroll or expecting to enroll full-time at a two-year or four-year or technical institution or university; single and resident of Utah. Applicant or parent of applicant must be member of American Legion or Auxiliary. Available to U.S. citizens. Applicant or parent must meet one or more of the following requirements: general military experience; retired from active duty; disabled or killed as a result of military service; prisoner of war; or missing in action.

Application Requirements: Application, essay, references, test scores, transcript, statement of parent's military service. *Deadline:* March 1.

Contact: Lucia Anderson, Public Relations Manager and Associate Editor
American Legion Auxiliary Department of Utah
455 East 400 South, Suite 50
Salt Lake City, UT 84111
Phone: 801-539-1015
Fax: 801-521-9191
E-mail: landerson@legion-aux.org

AMERICAN LEGION AUXILIARY DEPARTMENT OF WISCONSIN

http://www.amlegionauxwi.org/

AMERICAN LEGION AUXILIARY DEPARTMENT OF WISCONSIN DELLA VAN DEUREN MEMORIAL SCHOLARSHIP

One-time award of $1000 for Wisconsin residents. Applicant or mother of applicant must be a member of an Auxiliary unit. Must submit certification of an American Legion Auxiliary unit president, copy of proof that veteran was in service (i.e. discharge papers), letters of recommendation, transcripts, and essay. Minimum 3.5 GPA required. Must demonstrate financial need. Applications available on web site http://www.legion-aux.org.

Award: Scholarship for use in freshman, sophomore, junior, or senior years; not renewable. *Number:* 2. *Amount:* $1000.

Eligibility Requirements: Applicant must be enrolled or expecting to enroll full- or part-time at a four-year institution or university and resident of Wisconsin. Applicant or parent of applicant must be member of American Legion or Auxiliary. Applicant must have 3.5 GPA or higher. Available to U.S. citizens. Applicant or parent must meet one or more of the following requirements: general military experience; retired from active duty; disabled or killed as a result of military service; prisoner of war; or missing in action.

Application Requirements: Application, essay, financial need analysis, references, transcript. *Deadline:* March 15.

Contact: Kim Henderson, Scholarship Information
American Legion Auxiliary Department of Wisconsin
PO Box 140
Portage, WI 53901-0140
Phone: 608-745-0124
Fax: 608-745-1947

AMERICAN LEGION AUXILIARY DEPARTMENT OF WISCONSIN H.S. AND ANGELINE LEWIS SCHOLARSHIPS

One-time award of $1000. Applicant must be a daughter, son, wife, or widow of a veteran. Granddaughters and great-granddaughters of veterans who are auxiliary members may also apply. Must submit certification of an American Legion Auxiliary unit president, copy of proof that veteran was in service (i.e. discharge papers), letters of recommendation, transcripts and essay. Must have minimum 3.5 GPA, show financial need, and be a resident of Wisconsin. Applications available on web site http://www.legion-aux.org.

Award: Scholarship for use in freshman, sophomore, junior, senior, or graduate years; not renewable. *Number:* 6. *Amount:* $1000.

Eligibility Requirements: Applicant must be enrolled or expecting to enroll full- or part-time at a two-year or four-year institution or university and resident of Wisconsin. Applicant or parent of applicant must be member of American Legion or Auxiliary. Applicant must have 3.5 GPA or higher. Available to U.S. citizens. Applicant or parent must meet one or more of the following requirements: general military experience; retired from active duty; disabled or killed as a result of military service; prisoner of war; or missing in action.

Application Requirements: Application, essay, financial need analysis, references, transcript. *Deadline:* March 15.

Contact: Katherine Ardnt, Education Chairman
American Legion Auxiliary Department of Wisconsin
2930 American Legion Drive
PO Box 140
Portage, WI 53901-0140
Phone: 715-453-1613
Fax: 608-745-1947
E-mail: katyann@newnorth.net

AMERICAN LEGION AUXILIARY DEPARTMENT OF WISCONSIN MERIT AND MEMORIAL SCHOLARSHIPS

One-time award of $1000. Applicant must be a daughter, son, wife, or widow of a veteran. Granddaughters and great-granddaughters of veterans who are auxiliary members may also apply. Must submit certification of an American Legion Auxiliary unit president, copy of proof that veteran was in service (i.e. discharge papers), letters of recommendation, transcripts, and essay. Must have minimum 3.5 GPA, show financial need, and be a resident of Wisconsin. Applications available on web site http://www.legion-aux.org.

Award: Scholarship for use in freshman, sophomore, junior, or senior years; not renewable. *Number:* 6. *Amount:* $1000.

Eligibility Requirements: Applicant must be enrolled or expecting to enroll full- or part-time at a four-year institution or university and resident of Wisconsin. Applicant or parent of applicant must be member of American Legion or Auxiliary. Applicant must have 3.5 GPA or higher. Available to U.S. citizens. Applicant or parent must meet one or more of

the following requirements: general military experience; retired from active duty; disabled or killed as a result of military service; prisoner of war; or missing in action.

Application Requirements: Application, essay, financial need analysis, references, transcript. *Deadline:* March 15.

Contact: Kim Henderson, Scholarship Information
American Legion Auxiliary Department of Wisconsin
PO Box 140
Portage, WI 53901-0140
Phone: 608-745-0124
Fax: 608-745-1947

AMERICAN LEGION AUXILIARY DEPARTMENT OF WISCONSIN PAST PRESIDENTS' PARLEY HEALTH CAREER SCHOLARSHIPS

One-time award of $1000. Course of study need not be a four-year program. A hospital, university, or technical school program is also acceptable. Applicant must be a daughter, son, wife, or widow of a veteran. Granddaughters and great-granddaughters of veterans who are auxiliary members may also apply. Must submit certification of an American Legion Auxiliary unit president, copy of proof that veteran was in service (i.e. discharge papers), letters of recommendation, transcripts, and essay. Must have minimum 3.5 GPA, show financial need, and be a resident of Wisconsin. Applications available on web site http://www.legion-aux.org.

Award: Scholarship for use in freshman, sophomore, junior, or senior years; not renewable. *Number:* 2. *Amount:* $1000.

Eligibility Requirements: Applicant must be enrolled or expecting to enroll full- or part-time at a two-year or four-year or technical institution or university and resident of Wisconsin. Applicant or parent of applicant must be member of American Legion or Auxiliary. Applicant must have 3.5 GPA or higher. Available to U.S. citizens. Applicant or parent must meet one or more of the following requirements: general military experience; retired from active duty; disabled or killed as a result of military service; prisoner of war; or missing in action.

Application Requirements: Application, essay, financial need analysis, references, transcript. *Deadline:* March 15.

Contact: Kim Henderson, Scholarship Information
American Legion Auxiliary Department of Wisconsin
PO Box 140
Portage, WI 53901-0140
Phone: 608-745-0124
Fax: 608-745-1947

AMERICAN LEGION AUXILIARY DEPARTMENT OF WISCONSIN PRESIDENT'S SCHOLARSHIPS

One-time award of $1000. The mother of the applicant or the applicant must be a member of an Auxiliary unit. Must submit certification of an American Legion Auxiliary unit president, copy of proof that veteran was in service (i.e. discharge papers), letters of recommendation, transcripts, and essay. Must have minimum 3.5 GPA, show financial need, and be a resident of Wisconsin. Applications available on web site http://www.legion-aux.org.

Award: Scholarship for use in freshman, sophomore, junior, or senior years; not renewable. *Number:* 3. *Amount:* $1000.

Eligibility Requirements: Applicant must be enrolled or expecting to enroll full- or part-time at a four-year institution or university and resident of Wisconsin. Applicant or parent of applicant must be member of American Legion or Auxiliary. Applicant must have 3.5 GPA or higher. Available to U.S. citizens. Applicant or parent must meet one or more of the following requirements: general military experience; retired from active duty; disabled or killed as a result of military service; prisoner of war; or missing in action.

Application Requirements: Application, essay, financial need analysis, references, transcript. *Deadline:* March 15.

Contact: Kim Henderson, Scholarship Information
American Legion Auxiliary Department of Wisconsin
PO Box 140
Portage, WI 53901-0140
Phone: 608-745-0124
Fax: 608-745-1947

AMERICAN LEGION AUXILIARY NATIONAL HEADQUARTERS

http://www.legion-aux.org/

AMERICAN LEGION AUXILIARY GIRL SCOUT ACHIEVEMENT AWARD

One scholarship available to recipients of Girl Scout Gold Award. Must be active in a religious institution and have received appropriate religious emblem at the Cadette or Senior Scout level. Must show practical citizenship in the religious institution, community, and school, and Girl Scouting.

Award: Scholarship for use in freshman year; not renewable. *Number:* 1. *Amount:* $1000.

Eligibility Requirements: Applicant must be high school student; planning to enroll or expecting to enroll full-time at a four-year institution or university and female. Applicant or parent of applicant must be member of Girl Scouts. Available to U.S. citizens.

Application Requirements: Application, applicant must enter a contest, essay, references, self-addressed stamped envelope, test scores, transcript. *Deadline:* April 1.

Contact: Maria Potts, Program Coordinator
American Legion Auxiliary National Headquarters
8945 North Meridian Street
Indianapolis, IN 46260
Phone: 317-955-3845
E-mail: mpotts@legion-aux.org

AMERICAN LEGION AUXILIARY NON-TRADITIONAL STUDENTS SCHOLARSHIPS

One-time award for students returning to the classroom after some period of time in which his/her formal schooling was interrupted or a student who has had at least one year of college and is in need of financial assistance to pursue an undergraduate degree. Must be a member of the American Legion, American Legion Auxiliary or Sons of the American Legion.

Award: Scholarship for use in freshman, sophomore, junior, or senior years; not renewable. *Number:* 5. *Amount:* $1000.

Eligibility Requirements: Applicant must be enrolled or expecting to enroll full-time at a two-year or four-year or technical institution or university. Applicant or parent of applicant must be member of American Legion or Auxiliary. Available to U.S. citizens. Applicant or parent must meet one or more of the following requirements: general military experience; retired from active duty; disabled or killed as a result of military service; prisoner of war; or missing in action.

Application Requirements: Application, essay, financial need analysis, references, test scores, transcript, statement of the military service of parents. *Deadline:* March 1.

Contact: Maria Potts, Program Coordinator
American Legion Auxiliary National Headquarters
8945 North Meridian Street
Indianapolis, IN 46260
Phone: 317-955-3845
E-mail: mpotts@legion-aux.org

AMERICAN LEGION AUXILIARY SPIRIT OF YOUTH SCHOLARSHIPS FOR JUNIOR MEMBERS

Renewable scholarship for graduating high school seniors. Must be women and current junior members of the American Legion Auxiliary, with a three-year membership history.

Award: Scholarship for use in freshman, sophomore, junior, or senior years; renewable. *Number:* 5. *Amount:* $1000.

Eligibility Requirements: Applicant must be high school student; planning to enroll or expecting to enroll full-time at a four-year institution or university and female. Applicant or parent of applicant must be member of American Legion or Auxiliary. Available to U.S. citizens.

Application Requirements: Application, essay, references, self-addressed stamped envelope, test scores, transcript. *Deadline:* March 1.

Contact: Maria Potts, Program Coordinator
American Legion Auxiliary National Headquarters
8945 North Meridian Street
Indianapolis, IN 46260
Phone: 317-955-3845
E-mail: mpotts@legion-aux.org

AMERICAN LEGION DEPARTMENT OF ARKANSAS

http://www.arklegion.homestead.com/

AMERICAN LEGION DEPARTMENT OF ARKANSAS COUDRET SCHOLARSHIP AWARD

Awards child, grandchild, or great-grandchild of American Legionnaire in good standing for two years. Two-year requirement is waived for Desert Storm and deceased veterans. One-time award for graduating Arkansas high school seniors.

Award: Scholarship for use in freshman year; not renewable. *Number:* 4. *Amount:* $1000.

Eligibility Requirements: Applicant must be high school student; age 16-24; planning to enroll or expecting to enroll full-time at a two-year or four-year or technical institution or university and resident of Arkansas. Applicant or parent of applicant must be member of American Legion or Auxiliary. Applicant must have 2.5 GPA or higher. Available to U.S. citizens. Applicant or parent must meet one or more of the following requirements: general military experience; retired from active duty; disabled or killed as a result of military service; prisoner of war; or missing in action.

Application Requirements: Application, driver's license, essay, financial need analysis, photo, references, transcript. *Deadline:* April 15.

Contact: William Winchell, Department Adjutant
American Legion Department of Arkansas
PO Box 3280
Little Rock, AR 72203-3280
Phone: 501-375-1104
Fax: 501-375-4236
E-mail: alegion@swbell.net

AMERICAN LEGION DEPARTMENT OF IDAHO

http://www.idlegion.home.mindspring.com/

AMERICAN LEGION DEPARTMENT OF IDAHO SCHOLARSHIP

One-time award of $500 to $750 for residents of Idaho studying at an Idaho institution. Must be related to a Idaho American Member.

Award: Scholarship for use in freshman year; not renewable. *Number:* 1–7. *Amount:* $500–$750.

Eligibility Requirements: Applicant must be high school student; planning to enroll or expecting to enroll full-time at a four-year institution or university; resident of Idaho and studying in Idaho. Applicant or parent of applicant must be member of American Legion or Auxiliary. Available to U.S. citizens. Applicant or parent must meet one or more of the following requirements: general military experience; retired from active duty; disabled or killed as a result of military service; prisoner of war; or missing in action.

Application Requirements: Application, financial need analysis, resume, references, self-addressed stamped envelope, test scores, transcript. *Deadline:* June 1.

Contact: Rickey L. Helsley, Adjutant
American Legion Department of Idaho
901 Warren St
Boise, ID 83706-3825
Phone: 208-342-7061
Fax: 208-342-1964
E-mail: idlegion@mindspring.com

AMERICAN LEGION DEPARTMENT OF ILLINOIS

http://www.illegion.org/

AMERICAN ESSAY CONTEST SCHOLARSHIP

Scholarship for students in 7th to 12th grades of any accredited Illinois high school. Must write a 500-word essay on selected topic.

Award: Prize for use in freshman year; not renewable. *Number:* up to 60. *Amount:* $50–$75.

Eligibility Requirements: Applicant must be high school student; planning to enroll or expecting to enroll full-time at a four-year institution or university; resident of Illinois and must have an interest in writing. Applicant or parent of applicant must be member of American Legion or Auxiliary. Available to U.S. citizens.

Application Requirements: Application, applicant must enter a contest, essay. *Deadline:* February 3.

Contact: Bill Bechtel, Assistant Adjutant
American Legion Department of Illinois
PO Box 2910
Bloomington, IL 61702
Phone: 309-663-0361
Fax: 309-663-5783

AMERICAN LEGION DEPARTMENT OF ILLINOIS BOY SCOUT/EXPLORER SCHOLARSHIP

Scholarship for a graduating high school senior who is a qualified Boy Scout or Explorer and a resident of Illinois. Must write a 500-word essay on Legion's Americanism and Boy Scout programs.

Award: Scholarship for use in freshman year; not renewable. *Number:* up to 5. *Amount:* $200–$1000.

Eligibility Requirements: Applicant must be high school student; planning to enroll or expecting to enroll full- or part-time at a four-year institution or university; male and resident of Illinois. Applicant or parent of applicant must be member of Boy Scouts. Available to U.S. citizens.

Application Requirements: Application, applicant must enter a contest, essay. *Deadline:* April 30.

Contact: Bill Bechtel, Assistant Adjutant
American Legion Department of Illinois
PO Box 2910
Bloomington, IL 61702
Phone: 309-663-0361
Fax: 309-663-5783

AMERICAN LEGION DEPARTMENT OF ILLINOIS SCHOLARSHIPS

Awards twenty $1000 scholarships for graduating students of Illinois high schools. May be used at any accredited college, university, trade or technical school. Applicant must be a child or grandchild of members of the American Legion-Illinois. Awards will be based on academic merit and financial need.

Award: Scholarship for use in freshman year; not renewable. *Number:* up to 25. *Amount:* $1000.

Eligibility Requirements: Applicant must be high school student; planning to enroll or expecting to enroll full- or part-time at a two-year or four-year or technical institution or university and resident of Illinois. Applicant or parent of applicant must be member of American Legion or Auxiliary. Available to U.S. citizens.

Application Requirements: Application, financial need analysis, test scores, transcript. *Deadline:* March 15.

Contact: Bill Bechtel, Assistant Adjutant
American Legion Department of Illinois
PO Box 2910
Bloomington, IL 61702
Phone: 309-663-0361
Fax: 309-663-5783

AMERICAN LEGION DEPARTMENT OF INDIANA

http://www.indlegion.org/

AMERICAN LEGION FAMILY SCHOLARSHIP

Scholarship open to children and grandchildren of current members of The American Legion, American Legion Auxiliary, and The Sons of the American Legion. Also open to the children and grandchildren of deceased members who were current paid members of the above organizations at the time of their death. Applicants must be attending or planning to attend an Indiana institution of higher education.

Award: Scholarship for use in freshman, sophomore, junior, or senior years; not renewable. *Number:* up to 3. *Amount:* $700–$1000.

Eligibility Requirements: Applicant must be enrolled or expecting to enroll full- or part-time at a two-year or four-year or technical institution or university; resident of Indiana and studying in Indiana. Applicant or parent of applicant must be member of American Legion or Auxiliary. Applicant must have 3.5 GPA or higher. Available to U.S. citizens.

Application Requirements: Application, essay, transcript. *Deadline:* April 1.

Contact: Susan Long, Program Coordinator
American Legion Department of Indiana
777 North Meridan Street, Room 104
Indianapolis, IN 46204
Phone: 317-630-1264
Fax: 317-237-9891
E-mail: slong@indlegion.org

AMERICAN LEGION DEPARTMENT OF IOWA

http://www.ialegion.org/

AMERICAN LEGION DEPARTMENT OF IOWA EAGLE SCOUT OF THE YEAR SCHOLARSHIP

Three one-time award for Eagle Scouts who are residents of Iowa. For full-time study only.

Award: Scholarship for use in freshman year; not renewable. *Number:* up to 3. *Amount:* $250–$1000.

Eligibility Requirements: Applicant must be high school student; planning to enroll or expecting to enroll full-time at a two-year or four-year institution or university; male and resident of Iowa. Applicant or parent of applicant must be member of Boy Scouts. Available to U.S. citizens.

Application Requirements: Application, applicant must enter a contest, references. *Deadline:* March 1.

Contact: Program Director
American Legion Department of Iowa
720 Lyon Street
Des Moines, IA 50309
Phone: 515-282-5068

AMERICAN LEGION DEPARTMENT OF KANSAS

http://www.ksamlegion.org/

ALBERT M. LAPPIN SCHOLARSHIP

Scholarship for children of the members of Kansas American Legion or its auxiliary. Membership must have been active for the past three years. The children of deceased members are also eligible if parents' dues were paid at the time of death. Applicant must be a son/daughter of a veteran. Must be high school senior or college freshman or sophomore. Must use award at a Kansas college, university, or trade school.

Award: Scholarship for use in freshman or sophomore years; not renewable. *Number:* 1. *Amount:* $1000.

Eligibility Requirements: Applicant must be enrolled or expecting to enroll full-time at a two-year or four-year or technical institution or university and studying in Kansas. Applicant or parent of applicant must be member of American Legion or Auxiliary. Available to U.S. citizens. Applicant or parent must meet one or more of the following requirements: general military experience; retired from active duty; disabled or killed as a result of military service; prisoner of war; or missing in action.

Application Requirements: Application, essay, financial need analysis, photo, transcript. *Deadline:* February 15.

Contact: Jim Gravenstein, Chairman, Scholarship Committee
American Legion Department of Kansas
1314 Topeka Boulevard, SW
Topeka, KS 66612
Phone: 785-232-9513
Fax: 785-232-1399

CHARLES W. AND ANNETTE HILL SCHOLARSHIP

Scholarship of $1000 to the descendants of veterans who are American Legion members or American Legion Auxiliary members holding membership for the past three consecutive years. Descendants of deceased members can also apply. Must be high school seniors or college freshmen or sophomores in a Kansas institution. Scholarship for use at an approved college, university, or trade school in Kansas. Must maintain a 3.0 GPA. Disbursement: $500 at beginning each semester for one year.

Award: Scholarship for use in freshman or sophomore years; not renewable. *Number:* 1. *Amount:* $1000.

Eligibility Requirements: Applicant must be enrolled or expecting to enroll full-time at a two-year or four-year or technical institution or university; resident of Kansas and studying in Kansas. Applicant or parent of applicant must be member of American Legion or Auxiliary. Applicant must have 3.0 GPA or higher. Available to U.S. citizens. Applicant or parent must meet one or more of the following requirements: general military experience; retired from active duty; disabled or killed as a result of military service; prisoner of war; or missing in action.

Application Requirements: Application, essay, references, transcript, latest 1040 income statement of supporting parents. *Deadline:* February 15.

Contact: Jim Gravenstein, Chairman, Scholarship Committee
American Legion Department of Kansas
1314 Topeka Boulevard, SW
Topeka, KS 66612
Phone: 785-232-9513
Fax: 785-232-1399

HUGH A. SMITH SCHOLARSHIP FUND

One-year scholarship of $500 to the children of American Legion/Auxiliary members holding membership for the past three consecutive years. Children of a deceased member can also apply. Parent of the applicant must be a veteran. Must be high school seniors or college freshmen or sophomores in a Kansas institution. Scholarship for use at an approved college, university, or trade school in Kansas. Must maintain a C average in college.

Award: Scholarship for use in freshman or sophomore years; not renewable. *Number:* 1. *Amount:* $500.

Eligibility Requirements: Applicant must be enrolled or expecting to enroll full-time at a two-year or four-year or technical institution or university; resident of Kansas and studying in Kansas. Applicant or parent of applicant must be member of American Legion or Auxiliary. Available to U.S. citizens. Applicant or parent must meet one or more of the following requirements: general military experience; retired from active duty; disabled or killed as a result of military service; prisoner of war; or missing in action.

Application Requirements: Application, financial need analysis, photo, references, transcript, latest 1040 income statement of supporting parents. *Deadline:* February 15.

Contact: Jim Gravenstein, Chairman, Scholarship Committee
American Legion Department of Kansas
1314 Topeka Boulevard, SW
Topeka, KS 66612
Phone: 785-232-9513
Fax: 785-232-1399

ROSEDALE POST 346 SCHOLARSHIP

Two scholarships of $1500 each awarded to the children of American Legion members or of American Legion Auxiliary members holding membership for the past three consecutive years. Children of a deceased member can also apply. Parent of the applicant must be a veteran. Must be high school seniors or college freshmen or sophomores in a Kansas institution. Scholarship for use at an approved college, university, or trade school in Kansas. Must maintain a C average in college.

Award: Scholarship for use in freshman or sophomore years; not renewable. *Number:* 2. *Amount:* $1500.

Eligibility Requirements: Applicant must be enrolled or expecting to enroll full-time at a two-year or four-year or technical institution or university; resident of Kansas and studying in Kansas. Applicant or parent of applicant must be member of American Legion or Auxiliary. Available to U.S. citizens. Applicant or parent must meet one or more of the following requirements: general military experience; retired from active duty; disabled or killed as a result of military service; prisoner of war; or missing in action.

Application Requirements: Application, essay, financial need analysis, photo, references, transcript, latest 1040 income statement of supporting parents). *Deadline:* February 15.

Contact: Jim Gravenstein, Chairman, Scholarship Committee
American Legion Department of Kansas
1314 Topeka Boulevard, SW
Topeka, KS 66612
Phone: 785-232-9513
Fax: 785-232-1399

TED AND NORA ANDERSON SCHOLARSHIPS

Scholarship of $250 for each semester (one year only) given to the children of American Legion members or Auxiliary members who are holding membership for the past three consecutive years. Children of a deceased member can also apply. Parent of the applicant must be a veteran. Must be high school seniors or college freshmen or sophomores in a Kansas institution. Scholarship for use at an approved college, university, or trade school in Kansas. Must maintain a C average in college.

Award: Scholarship for use in freshman or sophomore years; not renewable. *Number:* 4. *Amount:* $250–$500.

Eligibility Requirements: Applicant must be enrolled or expecting to enroll full-time at a two-year or four-year or technical institution or university; resident of Kansas and studying in Kansas. Applicant or parent of applicant must be member of American Legion or Auxiliary. Available to U.S. citizens. Applicant or parent must meet one or more of the following requirements: general military experience; retired from active duty; disabled or killed as a result of military service; prisoner of war; or missing in action.

Application Requirements: Application, essay, financial need analysis, photo, references, transcript. *Deadline:* February 15.

Contact: Jim Gravenstein, Chairman, Scholarship Committee
American Legion Department of Kansas
1314 Topeka Boulevard, SW
Topeka, KS 66612
Phone: 785-232-9315
Fax: 785-232-1399

AMERICAN LEGION DEPARTMENT OF MAINE

http://www.mainelegion.org/

JAMES V. DAY SCHOLARSHIP

One-time $500 award for a Maine resident whose parent is a member of the American Legion or Auxiliary in Maine, or is a member of Sons of the American Legion in Maine. Must be a U.S. citizen. Based on character and financial need.

Award: Scholarship for use in freshman, sophomore, junior, or senior years; not renewable. *Number:* 1–2. *Amount:* up to $500.

Eligibility Requirements: Applicant must be enrolled or expecting to enroll full-time at a two-year or four-year or technical institution or university and resident of Maine. Applicant or parent of applicant must be member of American Legion or Auxiliary. Available to U.S. citizens. Applicant or parent must meet one or more of the following requirements: general military experience; retired from active duty; disabled or killed as a result of military service; prisoner of war; or missing in action.

Application Requirements: Application, references, transcript. *Deadline:* May 1.

Contact: Mr. Lloyd Woods, Department Adjutant
American Legion Department of Maine
21 College Avenue
PO Box 900
Waterville, ME 04903-0900
Phone: 207-873-3229
Fax: 207-872-0501
E-mail: legionme@mainelegion.org

AMERICAN LEGION DEPARTMENT OF MINNESOTA

http://www.mnlegion.org/

AMERICAN LEGION DEPARTMENT OF MINNESOTA MEMORIAL SCHOLARSHIP

Scholarship available to Minnesota residents who are dependents of members of the Minnesota American Legion or auxiliary. One-time award of $500 for study at a Minnesota institution or neighboring state with reciprocating agreement. See web site for application information http://www.mnlegion.org.

Award: Scholarship for use in freshman, sophomore, junior, or senior years; not renewable. *Number:* 6. *Amount:* $500.

Eligibility Requirements: Applicant must be enrolled or expecting to enroll full- or part-time at a two-year or four-year or technical institution or university; resident of Minnesota and studying in Iowa, Minnesota,

North Dakota, South Dakota, or Wisconsin. Applicant or parent of applicant must be member of American Legion or Auxiliary. Available to U.S. citizens. Applicant or parent must meet one or more of the following requirements: general military experience; retired from active duty; disabled or killed as a result of military service; prisoner of war; or missing in action.

Application Requirements: Application, essay, financial need analysis, references, transcript. *Deadline:* April 1.

Contact: Jennifer Kelley, Program Coordinator
American Legion Department of Minnesota
20 West 12th Street, Room 300-A
St. Paul, MN 55155
Phone: 651-291-1800
Fax: 651-291-1057
E-mail: department@mnlegion.org

MINNESOTA LEGIONNAIRES INSURANCE TRUST SCHOLARSHIP

Scholarship for Minnesota residents who are veterans or dependents of veterans. One-time award of $500 for study at a Minnesota institution or neighboring state with reciprocating agreement. All applications must be approved and recommended by a post of the American Legion. See web site for application information http://www.mnlegion.org.

Award: Scholarship for use in freshman, sophomore, junior, or senior years; not renewable. *Number:* 3. *Amount:* $500.

Eligibility Requirements: Applicant must be enrolled or expecting to enroll full- or part-time at a two-year or four-year or technical institution or university; resident of Minnesota and studying in Iowa, Minnesota, North Dakota, South Dakota, or Wisconsin. Applicant or parent of applicant must be member of American Legion or Auxiliary. Available to U.S. citizens. Applicant or parent must meet one or more of the following requirements: general military experience; retired from active duty; disabled or killed as a result of military service; prisoner of war; or missing in action.

Application Requirements: Application, essay, financial need analysis, references, transcript. *Deadline:* April 1.

Contact: Jennifer Kelley, Program Coordinator
American Legion Department of Minnesota
20 West 12th Street, Room 300-A
St. Paul, MN 55155
Phone: 651-291-1800
Fax: 651-291-1057
E-mail: department@mnlegion.org

AMERICAN LEGION DEPARTMENT OF MISSOURI

http://www.missourilegion.org/

CHARLES L. BACON MEMORIAL SCHOLARSHIP

Two awards of $500 are given. Applicant must be a member of The American Legion, the American Legion Auxiliary, or the Sons of The American Legion, or a descendant of a member of any thereof. Applicants must be unmarried Missouri resident below age 21, and must use the scholarship as a full-time student in an accredited college or university in Missouri. Must submit proof of American Legion membership.

Award: Scholarship for use in freshman year; not renewable. *Number:* 2. *Amount:* $500.

Eligibility Requirements: Applicant must be high school student; age 21 or under; planning to enroll or expecting to enroll full-time at a two-year or four-year institution or university; single and resident of Missouri. Applicant or parent of applicant must be member of American Legion or Auxiliary. Available to U.S. citizens. Applicant or parent must meet one or more of the following requirements: general military experience; retired from active duty; disabled or killed as a result of military service; prisoner of war; or missing in action.

Application Requirements: Application, financial need analysis, test scores, discharge certificate. *Deadline:* April 20.

Contact: John Doane, Chairman
American Legion Department of Missouri
PO Box 179
Jefferson City, MO 65102
Phone: 417-924-8596
Fax: 573-225-1406
E-mail: info@missourilegion.org

AMERICAN LEGION DEPARTMENT OF NEBRASKA

http://www.nebraskalegion.net/

EAGLE SCOUT OF THE YEAR SCHOLARSHIP

Scholarship of $1000 is awarded to one recipient each year by The American Legion, Department of Nebraska. The Department recipient is then entered into The American Legion National Eagle Scout of the Year and is eligible to receive a $10,000 scholarship, or one of three second place scholarships of $2500.

Award: Scholarship for use in freshman, sophomore, junior, or senior years; not renewable. *Number:* 1. *Amount:* $1000–$10,000.

Eligibility Requirements: Applicant must be age 18 or under; enrolled or expecting to enroll full- or part-time at a two-year or four-year or technical institution or university; male and resident of Nebraska. Applicant or parent of applicant must be member of Boy Scouts. Available to U.S. citizens.

Application Requirements: Application, photo, references, transcript. *Deadline:* March 1.

Contact: Mr. Jody Moeller, Activities Director
American Legion Department of Nebraska
PO Box 5205
Lincoln, NE 68505-0205
Phone: 402-464-6338
Fax: 402-464-6330
E-mail: actdirlegion@alltel.net

MAYNARD JENSEN AMERICAN LEGION MEMORIAL SCHOLARSHIP

Scholarship for dependents or grandchildren of members, prisoner-of-war, missing-in-action veterans, killed-in-action veterans, or any deceased veterans of the American Legion. One-time award is based on academic achievement and financial need for Nebraska residents attending Nebraska institutions. Several scholarships of $500 each. Must have minimum 2.5 GPA and must submit school certification of GPA.

Award: Scholarship for use in freshman, sophomore, junior, or senior years; not renewable. *Number:* 1–10. *Amount:* $500.

Eligibility Requirements: Applicant must be enrolled or expecting to enroll full-time at a two-year or four-year or technical institution or university; resident of Nebraska and studying in Nebraska. Applicant or parent of applicant must be member of American Legion or Auxiliary. Applicant must have 2.5 GPA or higher. Available to U.S. citizens. Applicant or parent must meet one or more of the following requirements: general military experience; retired from active duty; disabled or killed as a result of military service; prisoner of war; or missing in action.

Application Requirements: Application, financial need analysis, test scores. *Deadline:* March 1.

Contact: Burdette Burkhart, Adjutant
American Legion Department of Nebraska
PO Box 5205
Lincoln, NE 68505-0205
Phone: 402-464-6338
Fax: 402-464-6330
E-mail: nebraska@legion.org

AMERICAN LEGION DEPARTMENT OF NEW JERSEY

http://www.njamericanlegion.org/

LUTERMAN SCHOLARSHIP

Applicant must be a natural or adopted descendant of a member of American Legion, Department of New Jersey. Applicant must be a member of the graduating class of high school including Vo-tech.

Award: Scholarship for use in freshman year; not renewable. *Number:* 7. *Amount:* $1000–$4000.

Eligibility Requirements: Applicant must be high school student and planning to enroll or expecting to enroll full-time at a two-year or four-year or technical institution or university. Applicant or parent of applicant must be member of American Legion or Auxiliary. Available to U.S. citizens. Applicant or parent must meet one or more of the following requirements: Army experience; retired from active duty; disabled or killed as a result of military service; prisoner of war; or missing in action.

Application Requirements: Application. *Deadline:* February 15.

Contact: Raymond Zawacki, Department Adjutant
American Legion Department of New Jersey
135 West Hanover Street
Trenton, NJ 08618
Phone: 609-695-5418
Fax: 609-394-1532
E-mail: ray@njamericanlegion.org

STUTZ SCHOLARSHIP

Award to natural or adopted son or daughter of a member of The American Legion, Department of New Jersey. Applicant must be a member of the graduating class of high school including Vo-tech.

Award: Scholarship for use in freshman year; not renewable. *Number:* 1. *Amount:* $4000.

Eligibility Requirements: Applicant must be high school student and planning to enroll or expecting to enroll full-time at a two-year or four-year or technical institution or university. Applicant or parent of applicant must be member of American Legion or Auxiliary. Available to U.S. citizens. Applicant or parent must meet one or more of the following requirements: Army experience; retired from active duty; disabled or killed as a result of military service; prisoner of war; or missing in action.

Application Requirements: Application. *Deadline:* February 15.

Contact: Raymond Zawacki, Department Adjutant
American Legion Department of New Jersey
135 West Hanover Street
Trenton, NJ 08618
Phone: 609-695-5418
Fax: 609-394-1532
E-mail: ray@njamericanlegion.org

AMERICAN LEGION DEPARTMENT OF OHIO

http://www.ohiolegion.com/

OHIO AMERICAN LEGION SCHOLARSHIPS

One-time award for full-time students attending an accredited institution. Open to students of any postsecondary academic year. Must have minimum 3.0 GPA. Must be a member of the American Legion, a direct descendent of a Legionnaire (living or deceased), or surviving spouse or child of a deceased U.S. military person who died on active duty or of injuries received on active duty.

Award: Scholarship for use in freshman, sophomore, junior, or senior years; not renewable. *Number:* 15–18. *Amount:* $2000–$3000.

Eligibility Requirements: Applicant must be enrolled or expecting to enroll full-time at a two-year or four-year or technical institution or university. Applicant or parent of applicant must be member of American Legion or Auxiliary. Applicant must have 3.0 GPA or higher. Available to U.S. and non-U.S. citizens. Applicant or parent must meet one or more of the following requirements: general military experience; retired from active duty; disabled or killed as a result of military service; prisoner of war; or missing in action.

Application Requirements: Application, resume, transcript. *Deadline:* April 15.

Contact: Donald Lanthorn, Service Director
American Legion Department of Ohio
60 Big Run Road, PO Box 8007
Delaware, OH 43015
Phone: 740-362-7478
Fax: 740-362-1429
E-mail: dlanthorn@iwaynet.net

AMERICAN LEGION DEPARTMENT OF PENNSYLVANIA

http://www.pa-legion.com/

JOSEPH P. GAVENONIS COLLEGE SCHOLARSHIP (PLAN I)

Scholarships for Pennsylvania residents seeking a four-year degree from a Pennsylvania college or university. Must be the child of a member of a Pennsylvania American Legion post. Must be a graduating high school senior. Award amount and number of awards determined annually. Renewable award. Must maintain 2.5 GPA in college. Total number of awards varies.

Award: Scholarship for use in freshman year; renewable. *Number:* varies. *Amount:* $500–$1000.

Eligibility Requirements: Applicant must be high school student; planning to enroll or expecting to enroll full-time at a four-year institution or university; resident of Pennsylvania and studying in Pennsylvania. Applicant or parent of applicant must be member of American Legion or Auxiliary. Applicant must have 2.5 GPA or higher. Available to U.S. citizens.

Application Requirements: Application, financial need analysis, test scores, transcript. *Deadline:* May 30.

Contact: Debbie Watson, Emblem Sales Supervisor
American Legion Department of Pennsylvania
PO Box 2324
Harrisburg, PA 17105-2324
Phone: 717-730-9100
Fax: 717-975-2836
E-mail: hq@pa-legion.com

AMERICAN LEGION DEPARTMENT OF TENNESSEE

http://www.tennesseelegion.org/

AMERICAN LEGION DEPARTMENT OF TENNESSEE EAGLE SCOUT OF THE YEAR

Scholarship for graduating high school seniors who are Eagle Scouts, enrolled either part-time or full-time for study in accredited colleges or universities. Scholarship value is $1500. Deadline varies.

Award: Scholarship for use in freshman year; renewable. *Number:* 1. *Amount:* $1500.

Eligibility Requirements: Applicant must be high school student; planning to enroll or expecting to enroll full- or part-time at a four-year institution or university and resident of Tennessee. Applicant or parent of applicant must be member of Boy Scouts. Available to U.S. citizens.

Application Requirements: Application, financial need analysis, transcript. *Deadline:* varies.

Contact: Darlene Burgess, Executive Assistant
American Legion Department of Tennessee
215 Eighth Avenue, North
Nashville, TN 37203
Phone: 615-254-0568
E-mail: tnleg1@bellsouth.net

AMERICAN LEGION DEPARTMENT OF VERMONT

http://www.legionvthq.com/

AMERICAN LEGION EAGLE SCOUT OF THE YEAR

Awarded to the Boy Scout chosen for outstanding service to his religious institution, school, and community. Must receive the award and reside in Vermont.

Award: Scholarship for use in freshman year; not renewable. *Number:* 1. *Amount:* $1000.

Eligibility Requirements: Applicant must be high school student; age 18 or under; planning to enroll or expecting to enroll full-time at a four-year institution or university and resident of Vermont. Applicant or parent of applicant must be member of Boy Scouts. Applicant or parent of applicant must have employment or volunteer experience in community service. Available to U.S. citizens.

Application Requirements: Application, photo. *Deadline:* March 1.

Contact: Frank Killay, Chairman
American Legion Department of Vermont
PO Box 396
Montpelier, VT 05601-0396
Phone: 802-223-7131
Fax: 802-223-0318
E-mail: alvthq@verizon.net

AMERICAN LEGION DEPARTMENT OF WASHINGTON

http://www.walegion.org/

AMERICAN LEGION DEPARTMENT OF WASHINGTON CHILDREN AND YOUTH SCHOLARSHIPS

One-time award for the son or daughter of a Washington American Legion or Auxiliary member, living or deceased. Must be high school senior and Washington resident planning to attend an accredited institution of higher education in Washington. Award based on need.

Award: Scholarship for use in freshman year; not renewable. *Number:* 2. *Amount:* $1500–$2500.

Eligibility Requirements: Applicant must be high school student; planning to enroll or expecting to enroll full- or part-time at a four-year institution or university; resident of Washington and studying in Washington. Applicant or parent of applicant must be member of American Legion or Auxiliary. Available to U.S. citizens. Applicant or parent must meet one or more of the following requirements: general military experience; retired from active duty; disabled or killed as a result of military service; prisoner of war; or missing in action.

Application Requirements: Application, financial need analysis, transcript. *Deadline:* April 1.

Contact: Marc O'Connor, Chairman, Children and Youth Commission
American Legion Department of Washington
3600 Ruddell Road, SE
PO Box 3917
Lacey, WA 98509-3917
Phone: 360-423-9542
E-mail: oconnorred@comcast.net

AMERICAN LEGION DEPARTMENT OF WEST VIRGINIA

http://www.wvlegion.org/

SONS OF THE AMERICAN LEGION WILLIAM F. "BILL" JOHNSON MEMORIAL SCHOLARSHIP

Applicant is required to write an essay based on a different question each year. Award is given during the second semester of college provided the winner has passing grades in the first semester. Must submit a copy of passing GPA of their first semester of college. Must be a resident of West Virginia and the child or grandchild of a member of The American Legion.

Award: Scholarship for use in freshman year; not renewable. *Number:* up to 2. *Amount:* up to $1500.

Eligibility Requirements: Applicant must be high school student; planning to enroll or expecting to enroll full-time at a two-year or four-year institution or university and resident of West Virginia. Applicant or parent of applicant must be member of American Legion or Auxiliary. Available to U.S. citizens. Applicant or parent must meet one or more of the following requirements: general military experience; retired from active duty; disabled or killed as a result of military service; prisoner of war; or missing in action.

Application Requirements: Application, essay, transcript. *Deadline:* May 15.

Contact: Ms. Lois E. Moles, State Adjutant
American Legion Department of West Virginia
2016 Kanawha Boulevard East, PO Box 3191
Charleston, WV 25332-3191
Phone: 304-343-7591
Fax: 304-343-7592
E-mail: wvlegion@suddenlinkmail.com

AMERICAN POSTAL WORKERS UNION

http://www.apwu.org/

E.C. HALLBECK SCHOLARSHIP FUND

Scholarship for children of American Postal Workers Union members. Applicant must be a child, grandchild, stepchild, or legally adopted child of an active member, Retirees Department member, or deceased member of American Postal Workers Union. Must be a senior attending high school or other corresponding secondary school. Must be 18 years or older. Recipient must attend accredited community college or university as a full-time student. Scholarship will be $1000 for each year of four consecutive years of college. Scholarship will provide five area winners. For additional information and to download applications go to web site http://www.apwu.org.

Award: Scholarship for use in freshman year; renewable. *Number:* 5. *Amount:* $1000.

Eligibility Requirements: Applicant must be high school student; age 18 and over and planning to enroll or expecting to enroll full-time at a two-year or four-year or technical institution or university. Applicant or parent of applicant must be member of American Postal Workers Union. Applicant or parent of applicant must have employment or volunteer experience in federal/postal service. Available to U.S. citizens.

Application Requirements: Application, essay, references, test scores, transcript. *Deadline:* March 15.

Contact: Terry Stapleton, Secretary and Treasurer
American Postal Workers Union
1300 L Street, NW
Washington, DC 20005
Phone: 202-842-4215
Fax: 202-842-8530

VOCATIONAL SCHOLARSHIP PROGRAM

A scholarship for a child, grandchild, stepchild, or legally adopted child of an active member, Retiree's Department member, or deceased member of the American Postal Workers Union. Applicant must be a senior attending high school who plans on attending an accredited vocational school or community college vocational program as a full-time student. The award is $1000 per year consecutively or until completion of the course. For additional information see web site http://www.apwu.org.

Award: Scholarship for use in freshman year; renewable. *Number:* 5. *Amount:* $1000.

Eligibility Requirements: Applicant must be high school student and planning to enroll or expecting to enroll full-time at a four-year institution or university. Applicant or parent of applicant must be member of American Postal Workers Union. Applicant or parent of applicant must have employment or volunteer experience in federal/postal service. Available to U.S. citizens.

Application Requirements: Application, essay, references, test scores, transcript. *Deadline:* March 15.

Contact: Terry Stapleton, Secretary and Treasurer
American Postal Workers Union
1300 L Street, NW
Washington, DC 20005
Phone: 202-842-4215
Fax: 202-842-8530

AMERICAN QUARTER HORSE FOUNDATION (AQHF)

http://www.aqha.com/foundation

AMERICAN QUARTER HORSE FOUNDATION YOUTH SCHOLARSHIPS

Scholarship to the members of AQHA/AQHYA who have completed a minimum of three years cumulative membership. Members must apply during their senior year of high school or home school equivalency. Students currently enrolled as a first-year college freshman are not eligible for consideration. Minimum 2.5 GPA required.

Award: Scholarship for use in sophomore, junior, or senior years; renewable. *Number:* 27. *Amount:* $8000.

Eligibility Requirements: Applicant must be enrolled or expecting to enroll full-time at a two-year or four-year or technical institution or university. Applicant or parent of applicant must be member of American Quarter Horse Association. Applicant must have 3.5 GPA or higher. Available to U.S. and Canadian citizens.

Application Requirements: Application, financial need analysis, references, transcript. *Deadline:* January 2.

Contact: Scholarship Office
American Quarter Horse Foundation (AQHF)
2601 East Interstate 40
Amarillo, TX 79104
Phone: 806-378-5029
Fax: 806-376-1005
E-mail: foundation@aqha.org

DR. GERALD O'CONNOR MICHIGAN SCHOLARSHIP

Scholarships for AQHA/AQHYA members from Michigan. Members may apply during their senior year of high school or while enrolled at an accredited college, university or vocational school. Minimum 2.5 GPA required. Renewable up to four years.

Award: Scholarship for use in freshman, sophomore, junior, or senior years; renewable. *Number:* 1. *Amount:* $2000.

Eligibility Requirements: Applicant must be enrolled or expecting to enroll full-time at a two-year or four-year or technical institution or university; resident of Michigan and must have an interest in animal/agricultural competition. Applicant or parent of applicant must be member of American Quarter Horse Association. Applicant must have 2.5 GPA or higher. Available to U.S. and Canadian citizens.

Application Requirements: Application, essay, financial need analysis, photo, references, transcript. *Deadline:* January 2.

Contact: Laura Owens, Scholarship Office
American Quarter Horse Foundation (AQHF)
2601 East Interstate 40
Amarillo, TX 79104
Phone: 806-378-5029
Fax: 806-376-1005
E-mail: foundation@aqha.org

EXCELLENCE IN EQUINE/AGRICULTURAL INVOLVEMENT SCHOLARSHIP

Scholarship to an AQHA/AQHYA member who exemplifies the characteristics of leadership and excellence acquired through participation in equine and or agriculture activities. Members may apply during their senior year of high school or while enrolled at an accredited college, university or vocational school. Renewable up to four years. Minimum GPA 3.5 required.

Award: Scholarship for use in freshman, sophomore, junior, or senior years; renewable. *Number:* 1. *Amount:* $25,000.

Eligibility Requirements: Applicant must be enrolled or expecting to enroll full-time at a two-year or four-year or technical institution or university. Applicant or parent of applicant must be member of American Quarter Horse Association. Applicant or parent of applicant must have employment or volunteer experience in agriculture. Applicant must have 3.5 GPA or higher. Available to U.S. and Canadian citizens.

Application Requirements: Application, financial need analysis, photo, references, transcript, telephone interview. *Deadline:* January 2.

Contact: Scholarship Office
American Quarter Horse Foundation (AQHF)
2601 East Interstate 40
Amarillo, TX 79104
Phone: 806-378-5029
Fax: 806-376-1005
E-mail: foundation@aqha.org

FARM AND RANCH HERITAGE SCHOLARSHIP

Scholarships to AQHA/AQHYA members from farming and or ranching backgrounds. Members may apply during their senior year of high school or while enrolled at an accredited college, university or vocational school. Minimum GPA 3.0 required.

Award: Scholarship for use in freshman, sophomore, junior, or senior years; renewable. *Number:* 4. *Amount:* $12,500.

Eligibility Requirements: Applicant must be enrolled or expecting to enroll full-time at a two-year or four-year or technical institution or university. Applicant or parent of applicant must be member of American Quarter Horse Association. Applicant or parent of applicant must have employment or volunteer experience in farming. Applicant must have 3.0 GPA or higher. Available to U.S. and Canadian citizens.

Application Requirements: Application, essay, financial need analysis, photo, references, transcript. *Deadline:* January 2.

Contact: Scholarship Office
American Quarter Horse Foundation (AQHF)
2601 East Interstate 40
Amarillo, TX 79104
Phone: 806-378-5029
Fax: 806-376-1005
E-mail: foundation@aqha.org

GUY STOOPS MEMORIAL PROFESSIONAL HORSEMEN'S FAMILY SCHOLARSHIP

Two scholarships of $500 to AQHA members whose parent is an AQHA Professional Horseman in good standing for three or more years. Members may apply during their senior year of high school or while enrolled at an accredited college, university or vocational school. Minimum GPA 2.5 required.

Award: Scholarship for use in freshman, sophomore, junior, or senior years; not renewable. *Number:* 2. *Amount:* $500.

Eligibility Requirements: Applicant must be enrolled or expecting to enroll full-time at a two-year or four-year or technical institution or university. Applicant or parent of applicant must be member of American Quarter Horse Association or Professional Horsemen Association. Applicant must have 2.5 GPA or higher. Available to U.S. and Canadian citizens.

Application Requirements: Application, financial need analysis, photo, references, transcript. *Deadline:* January 2.

Contact: Scholarship Office
American Quarter Horse Foundation (AQHF)
2601 East Interstate 40
Amarillo, TX 79104
Phone: 806-378-5029
Fax: 806-376-1005
E-mail: foundation@aqha.org

INDIANA QUARTER HORSE YOUTH SCHOLARSHIP

Scholarships of $1000 for AQHA/AQHYA members from Indiana. Applicants must also be a current member of the Indiana Quarter Horse Association and must have maintained two or more years of membership. Members may apply during their senior year of high school or while enrolled at an accredited college, university or vocational school. Minimum 2.5 GPA required.

Award: Scholarship for use in freshman, sophomore, junior, or senior years; not renewable. *Number:* 1. *Amount:* $1000.

Eligibility Requirements: Applicant must be enrolled or expecting to enroll full-time at a two-year or four-year or technical institution or university and resident of Indiana. Applicant or parent of applicant must be member of American Quarter Horse Association. Applicant must have 2.5 GPA or higher. Available to U.S. and Canadian citizens.

Application Requirements: Application, essay, financial need analysis, photo, references, transcript. *Deadline:* January 2.

Contact: Scholarship Office
American Quarter Horse Foundation (AQHF)
2601 East Interstate 40
Amarillo, TX 79104
Phone: 806-378-5029
Fax: 806-376-1005
E-mail: foundation@aqha.org

JOAN CAIN FLORIDA QUARTER HORSE YOUTH SCHOLARSHIP

Scholarship to an AQHA/AQHYA member from Florida. Applicants must also be a current member of the Florida Quarter Horse Youth Association and maintained two or more years of membership. Members may apply during their senior year of high school or while enrolled at an accredited college, university or vocational school. Minimum GPA 2.5 required.

Award: Scholarship for use in freshman, sophomore, junior, or senior years; not renewable. *Number:* 1. *Amount:* $1000.

Eligibility Requirements: Applicant must be enrolled or expecting to enroll full-time at a two-year or four-year or technical institution or university and resident of Florida. Applicant or parent of applicant must be member of American Quarter Horse Association. Applicant must have 2.5 GPA or higher. Available to U.S. and Canadian citizens.

Application Requirements: Application, photo, references, transcript, proof of residency. *Deadline:* January 2.

Contact: Scholarship Office
American Quarter Horse Foundation (AQHF)
2601 East Interstate 40
Amarillo, TX 79104
Phone: 806-378-5029
Fax: 806-376-1005
E-mail: foundation@aqha.org

NEBRASKA QUARTER HORSE YOUTH SCHOLARSHIP

Scholarship to an AQHA/AQHYA member from Nebraska. Members may apply during their senior year of high school or while enrolled at an accredited college, university or vocational school. Renewable up to four years. Minimum GPA 2.5 required.

Award: Scholarship for use in freshman, sophomore, junior, or senior years; renewable. *Number:* 1. *Amount:* $2000.

Eligibility Requirements: Applicant must be enrolled or expecting to enroll full-time at a two-year or four-year or technical institution or university and resident of Nebraska. Applicant or parent of applicant must be member of American Quarter Horse Association. Applicant or parent of applicant must have employment or volunteer experience in agriculture. Applicant must have 2.5 GPA or higher. Available to U.S. and Canadian citizens.

Application Requirements: Application, financial need analysis, photo, references, transcript, proof of residency. *Deadline:* January 2.

Contact: Scholarship Office
American Quarter Horse Foundation (AQHF)
2601 East Interstate 40
Amarillo, TX 79104
Phone: 806-378-5029
Fax: 806-376-1005
E-mail: foundation@aqha.org

RAY MELTON MEMORIAL VIRGINIA QUARTER HORSE YOUTH SCHOLARSHIP

Scholarship to an AQHA/AQHYA member from Virginia. Members may apply during their senior year of high school or while enrolled at an accredited college, university or vocational school. Minimum GPA 2.5 required.

Award: Scholarship for use in freshman, sophomore, junior, or senior years; not renewable. *Number:* 1. *Amount:* $500.

Eligibility Requirements: Applicant must be enrolled or expecting to enroll full-time at a two-year or four-year or technical institution or university and resident of Virginia. Applicant or parent of applicant must be member of American Quarter Horse Association. Applicant must have 2.5 GPA or higher. Available to U.S. and Canadian citizens.

Application Requirements: Application, financial need analysis, photo, references, transcript, proof of residency. *Deadline:* January 2.

Contact: Scholarship Office
American Quarter Horse Foundation (AQHF)
2601 East Interstate 40
Amarillo, TX 79104
Phone: 806-378-5029
Fax: 806-376-1005
E-mail: foundation@aqha.org

SWAYZE WOODRUFF MEMORIAL MID-SOUTH SCHOLARSHIP

Scholarships for AQHA/AQHYA members from Alabama, Arkansas, Louisiana, Mississippi or Tennessee. Applicants must compete in AQHA or AQHYA-approved shows. Members may apply during their senior year of high school or while enrolled at an accredited college, university or vocational school. Minimum 2.5 GPA required. Recipient receives $2000 per year for four-year degree plan. Must be renewed annually.

Award: Scholarship for use in freshman, sophomore, junior, or senior years; renewable. *Number:* 1. *Amount:* $2000.

Eligibility Requirements: Applicant must be enrolled or expecting to enroll full-time at a two-year or four-year or technical institution or university; resident of Alabama, Arkansas, Louisiana, Mississippi, or Tennessee and must have an interest in animal/agricultural competition. Applicant or parent of applicant must be member of American Quarter Horse Association. Applicant must have 2.5 GPA or higher. Available to U.S. and Canadian citizens.

Application Requirements: Application, essay, financial need analysis, photo, references, transcript. *Deadline:* January 2.

Contact: Laura Owens, Scholarship Office
American Quarter Horse Foundation (AQHF)
2601 East Interstate 40
Amarillo, TX 79104
Phone: 806-378-5029
Fax: 806-376-1005
E-mail: foundation@aqha.org

AMERICAN WATER SKI EDUCATIONAL FOUNDATION

http://www.waterskihalloffame.com/

AMERICAN WATER SKI EDUCATIONAL FOUNDATION SCHOLARSHIP

Awards for incoming college sophomores through incoming seniors who are members of U.S.A. Water Ski. Awards are based upon academics, leadership, extracurricular activities, recommendations, and financial need.

Award: Scholarship for use in sophomore, junior, or senior years; renewable. *Number:* 5. *Amount:* $1500–$3000.

Eligibility Requirements: Applicant must be enrolled or expecting to enroll full-time at a two-year or four-year institution or university and must have an interest in leadership. Applicant or parent of applicant must be member of USA Water Ski. Available to U.S. citizens.

Application Requirements: Application, essay, financial need analysis, references, self-addressed stamped envelope, transcript. *Deadline:* April 1.

Contact: Carole Lowe, Scholarship Director
American Water Ski Educational Foundation
1251 Holy Cow Road
Polk City, FL 33868-8200
Phone: 863-324-2472 Ext. 127
Fax: 863-324-3996
E-mail: info@waterskihalloffame.com

AMVETS AUXILIARY

http://www.amvetsaux.org/

AMVETS NATIONAL LADIES AUXILIARY SCHOLARSHIP

One-time award of up to $1000 for a member of AMVETS or the Auxiliary. Applicant may also be the family member of a member. Award for full-time study at any accredited U.S. institution. Minimum 2.5 GPA required.

Award: Scholarship for use in sophomore, junior, or senior years; not renewable. *Number:* up to 7. *Amount:* $750–$1000.

Eligibility Requirements: Applicant must be enrolled or expecting to enroll full-time at a two-year or four-year or technical institution. Applicant or parent of applicant must be member of AMVETS Auxiliary. Applicant must have 2.5 GPA or higher. Available to U.S. citizens. Applicant or parent must meet one or more of the following requirements: general military experience; retired from active duty; disabled or killed as a result of military service; prisoner of war; or missing in action.

Application Requirements: Application, essay, references, transcript. *Deadline:* June 1.

Contact: Kellie Haggerty, Executive Administrator
AMVETS Auxiliary
4647 Forbes Boulevard
Lanham, MD 20706-4380
Phone: 301-459-6255
Fax: 301-459-5403
E-mail: auxhdqs@amvets.org

APPALOOSA HORSE CLUB-APPALOOSA YOUTH PROGRAM

http://www.appaloosayouth.com/

APPALOOSA YOUTH EDUCATIONAL SCHOLARSHIPS

Scholarship of up to $1000 available for members or dependents of members of the Appaloosa Youth Association or Appaloosa Horse Club. Based on academics, leadership, sportsmanship, and horsemanship. Printable application is available http://www.appaloosayouth.com.

Award: Scholarship for use in freshman, sophomore, junior, or senior years; not renewable. *Number:* 6–8. *Amount:* $100–$1000.

Eligibility Requirements: Applicant must be enrolled or expecting to enroll full-time at a two-year or four-year institution or university and must have an interest in animal/agricultural competition or leadership. Applicant or parent of applicant must be member of Appaloosa Horse Club/Appaloosa Youth Association. Applicant must have 3.5 GPA or higher. Available to U.S. citizens.

Application Requirements: Application, applicant must enter a contest, essay, photo, references, test scores, transcript. *Deadline:* June 1.

Contact: Anna Brown, AYF Coordinator
Appaloosa Horse Club-Appaloosa Youth Program
2720 West Pullman Road
Moscow, ID 83843
Phone: 208-882-5578 Ext. 264
Fax: 208-882-8150
E-mail: youth@appaloosa.com

ARRL FOUNDATION INC.

http://www.arrl.org/

YOU'VE GOT A FRIEND IN PENNSYLVANIA SCHOLARSHIP

One-time award available to licensed general amateur radio operators. Must be a member of American Radio Relay League. Residents of the Commonwealth of Pennsylvania preferred.

Award: Scholarship for use in freshman, sophomore, junior, senior, graduate, or postgraduate years; not renewable. *Number:* 2. *Amount:* $2000.

Eligibility Requirements: Applicant must be enrolled or expecting to enroll full-time at a two-year or four-year or technical institution or university; resident of Pennsylvania and must have an interest in amateur radio. Applicant or parent of applicant must be member of American Radio Relay League. Applicant must have 3.5 GPA or higher. Available to U.S. citizens.

Application Requirements: Application, transcript. *Deadline:* February 1.

Contact: Ms. Mary Hobart, Secretary
ARRL Foundation Inc.
225 Main Street
Newington, CT 06111-1494
Phone: 860-594-0397
E-mail: k1mmh@arrl.org

AUTOMOTIVE RECYCLERS ASSOCIATION SCHOLARSHIP FOUNDATION

http://www.a-r-a.org/

AUTOMOTIVE RECYCLERS ASSOCIATION SCHOLARSHIP FOUNDATION SCHOLARSHIP

Scholarships are available for the post-high school educational pursuits of the children of employees of direct ARA member companies.

Award: Scholarship for use in freshman, sophomore, junior, or senior years; not renewable. *Number:* varies. *Amount:* varies.

Eligibility Requirements: Applicant must be enrolled or expecting to enroll full-time at a two-year or four-year institution or university. Applicant or parent of applicant must be member of Automotive Recyclers Association. Applicant must have 3.0 GPA or higher. Available to U.S. and non-U.S. citizens.

Application Requirements: Application, photo, transcript, letter verifying parents' employment. *Deadline:* March 15.

Contact: Kelly Badillo, Director Member Services
Automotive Recyclers Association Scholarship Foundation
3975 Fair Ridge Drive, Suite 20-North
Fairfax, VA 22033
Phone: 703-385-1001 Ext. 26
Fax: 703-385-1494
E-mail: kelly@a-r-a.org

BOYS & GIRLS CLUBS OF AMERICA

http://www.bgca.org/

BOYS AND GIRLS CLUBS OF AMERICA NATIONAL YOUTH OF THE YEAR AWARD

Nonrenewable award available to youths 14 to 18 years old who have been active members of their Boys Club or Girls Club for at least two years. Contact local club for nomination form. Minimum 3.0 GPA required. Must be a member and nominated by local Club.

Award: Scholarship for use in freshman, sophomore, junior, or senior years; not renewable. *Number:* 5. *Amount:* up to $10,000.

Eligibility Requirements: Applicant must be age 14-18; enrolled or expecting to enroll full- or part-time at a two-year or four-year or technical institution; single and must have an interest in leadership. Applicant or parent of applicant must be member of Boys or Girls Club. Applicant must have 3.0 GPA or higher. Available to U.S. citizens.

Application Requirements: Application, essay, interview, resume, references. *Deadline:* varies.

Contact: Kelvin Davis, Senior Director Character and Citizenship
Boys & Girls Clubs of America
1275 West Peachtree Street, NW
Atlanta, GA 30309-3506
Phone: 404-815-5700
Fax: 404-815-5789

BOYS AND GIRLS CLUBS OF CHICAGO

http://www.bgcc.org/

BOYS AND GIRLS CLUBS OF CHICAGO SCHOLARSHIPS

Scholarships are awarded to graduating high school seniors who are local Club members. Scholarships are based upon academic achievement, club involvement, financial need, and personal interviews. Students are asked to maintain their grades, seek internships and job opportunities, and lend guidance to younger children.

Award: Scholarship for use in freshman year; renewable. *Number:* varies. *Amount:* $3000–$5000.

Eligibility Requirements: Applicant must be high school student; planning to enroll or expecting to enroll full- or part-time at a two-year or four-year or technical institution or university and resident of Illinois. Applicant or parent of applicant must be member of Boys or Girls Club. Applicant must have 3.5 GPA or higher. Available to U.S. citizens.

Application Requirements: Application, essay, financial need analysis, interview, references, test scores, transcript. *Deadline:* varies.

Contact: Katie Huckaby, Project Director
Boys and Girls Clubs of Chicago
550 West Van Buren Street, Suite 350
Chicago, IL 60607
Phone: 312-235-8000 Ext. 8008
E-mail: khuckaby@bgcc.org

BUFFALO AFL-CIO COUNCIL

http://www.wnyalf.org/

AFL-CIO COUNCIL OF BUFFALO SCHOLARSHIP WNY ALF SCHOLARSHIP

One-time award of up to $1000 for a high school senior who is a son or daughter of a member of a local union affiliated with the Buffalo AFL-CIO Council. Must be a New York resident and use the award for study in New York.

Award: Scholarship for use in freshman year; not renewable. *Number:* up to 3. *Amount:* up to $1000.

Eligibility Requirements: Applicant must be high school student; planning to enroll or expecting to enroll full-time at a two-year or four-year institution or university; resident of New York and studying in New York. Applicant or parent of applicant must be member of AFL-CIO. Available to U.S. and Canadian citizens.

Application Requirements: Application, essay, references, transcript. *Deadline:* March 31.

Contact: Mike Hoffert, President
Buffalo AFL-CIO Council
2495 Main Street, Suite 440
Buffalo, NY 14214
Phone: 716-852-0375
Fax: 716-855-1802
E-mail: mhoffert@wnyalf.org

CALIFORNIA GRANGE FOUNDATION

http://www.californiagrange.org/

CALIFORNIA GRANGE FOUNDATION SCHOLARSHIP

Scholarship program available for Grange members residing in California who wish to attend a higher institution of learning of their choice.

Award: Scholarship for use in freshman, sophomore, junior, or senior years; renewable. *Number:* 5–8. *Amount:* $250–$1000.

Eligibility Requirements: Applicant must be enrolled or expecting to enroll full- or part-time at a two-year or four-year or technical institution or university and resident of California. Applicant or parent of applicant must be member of Grange Association. Available to U.S. citizens.

Application Requirements: Application, essay, financial need analysis, references, transcript. *Deadline:* April 1.

Contact: Mrs. Leslie Parker, Executive Assistant
California Grange Foundation
3830 U Street
Sacramento, CA 95817-1336
Phone: 916-454-5805 Ext. 21
Fax: 916-739-8189
E-mail: info@californiagrange.org

CALIFORNIA STATE PARENT-TEACHER ASSOCIATION

http://www.capta.org/

CONTINUING EDUCATION-PTA VOLUNTEERS SCHOLARSHIP

Scholarships are available annually from the California State PTA to be used for continuing education at accredited colleges, universities, trade or technical schools. These scholarships recognize volunteer service in PTA and enable PTA volunteers to continue their education.

Award: Scholarship for use in freshman, sophomore, junior, senior, or graduate years; not renewable. *Number:* varies. *Amount:* $500.

Eligibility Requirements: Applicant must be enrolled or expecting to enroll full- or part-time at a two-year or four-year or technical institution or university and resident of California. Applicant or parent of applicant must be member of Parent-Teacher Association/Organization. Applicant or parent of applicant must have employment or volunteer experience in community service. Available to U.S. citizens.

Application Requirements: Application, essay, references, transcript, copy of membership card. *Deadline:* November 15.

Contact: Becky Reece, Scholarship and Award Chairman
California State Parent-Teacher Association
930 Georgia Street
Los Angeles, CA 90015-1322
Phone: 213-620-1100
Fax: 213-620-1141

CALIFORNIA TEACHERS ASSOCIATION (CTA)

http://www.cta.org/

CALIFORNIA TEACHERS ASSOCIATION SCHOLARSHIP FOR DEPENDENT CHILDREN

Awards scholarships annually for dependant children of active, retired, or deceased members of California Teachers Association. Minimum 3.5 GPA required.

Award: Scholarship for use in freshman, sophomore, junior, senior, or graduate years; not renewable. *Number:* up to 25. *Amount:* $2500.

Eligibility Requirements: Applicant must be enrolled or expecting to enroll full-time at a two-year or four-year or technical institution or university. Applicant or parent of applicant must be member of California Teachers Association. Applicant must have 3.5 GPA or higher. Available to U.S. citizens.

Application Requirements: Application, essay, references, transcript. *Deadline:* February 8.

Contact: Janeya Collins, Scholarship Coordinator
California Teachers Association (CTA)
PO Box 921
Burlingame, CA 94011-0921
Phone: 650-552-5468
Fax: 650-552-5001
E-mail: scholarships@cta.org

CALIFORNIA TEACHERS ASSOCIATION SCHOLARSHIP FOR MEMBERS

Must be an active member of California Teachers Association (including members working on an emergency credential). Available for study in a degree, credential, or graduate program.

Award: Scholarship for use in freshman, sophomore, junior, senior, or graduate years; not renewable. *Number:* 5. *Amount:* $2500.

Eligibility Requirements: Applicant must be enrolled or expecting to enroll full-time at a two-year or four-year institution or university and resident of California. Applicant or parent of applicant must be member of California Teachers Association. Applicant or parent of applicant must have employment or volunteer experience in teaching/education. Applicant must have 3.0 GPA or higher. Available to U.S. citizens.

Application Requirements: Application, essay, references, transcript. *Deadline:* February 8.

Contact: Janeya Collins, Scholarship Coordinator
California Teachers Association (CTA)
PO Box 921
Burlingame, CA 94011-0921
Phone: 650-552-5468
E-mail: scholarships@cta.org

CATHOLIC WORKMAN

http://www.fcsla.com/

FIRST CATHOLIC SLOVAK LADIES ASSOCIATION COLLEGE SCHOLARSHIP

$1250 scholarship for young member of FCSLA. Must be a member in good standing for at least three years prior to date of application.

Award: Scholarship for use in freshman, sophomore, junior, or senior years; not renewable. *Number:* 15–55. *Amount:* $1250.

Eligibility Requirements: Applicant must be enrolled or expecting to enroll full-time at a two-year or four-year institution or university. Applicant or parent of applicant must be member of First Catholic Slovak Ladies Association. Available to U.S. and non-U.S. citizens.

Application Requirements: Application, driver's license, transcript, letter of acceptance. *Deadline:* March 1.

Contact: Lenore Krava, Executive Secretary
Catholic Workman
24950 Chagrin Boulevard
Beachwood, OH 44122-5634
Phone: 216-464-8015
Fax: 216-464-9260
E-mail: info@fcsla.com

THERESA SAJAN SCHOLARSHIP FOR GRADUATE STUDENTS

Scholarship for graduate study available to a member in good standing of the First Catholic Slovak Ladies Association. Must be member of the association for at least three years prior to date of application. For more information check the web site http://www.fcsla.com/scholarship.shtml.

Award: Scholarship for use in freshman, sophomore, junior, or senior years; renewable. *Number:* 15–55. *Amount:* $1250–$1750.

Eligibility Requirements: Applicant must be enrolled or expecting to enroll full-time at a four-year institution. Applicant or parent of applicant must be member of First Catholic Slovak Ladies Association. Available to U.S. and non-U.S. citizens.

Application Requirements: Application, driver's license, test scores, transcript, document of acceptance. *Deadline:* varies.

Contact: Lenore Krava, Executive Secretary
Catholic Workman
24950 Chagrin Boulevard
Beachwood, OH 44122-5634
Phone: 216-464-8015
Fax: 216-464-9260
E-mail: info@fcsla.com

CIVIL AIR PATROL, USAF AUXILIARY

http://www.capnhq.gov/

CIVIL AIR PATROL ACADEMIC SCHOLARSHIPS

One-time award for active members of the Civil Air Patrol to pursue undergraduate, graduate, or trade or technical education. Must be a current CAP member. Significant restrictions apply. Not open to the general public.

Award: Scholarship for use in freshman, sophomore, junior, senior, or graduate years; not renewable. *Number:* up to 40. *Amount:* $1000–$7500.

Eligibility Requirements: Applicant must be enrolled or expecting to enroll full-time at a two-year or four-year or technical institution or university. Applicant or parent of applicant must be member of Civil Air Patrol. Available to U.S. citizens.

Application Requirements: Application, essay, photo, resume, references, test scores, transcript. *Deadline:* January 31.

Contact: Kelly Easterly, Assistant Program Manager
Civil Air Patrol, USAF Auxiliary
105 South Hansell Street, Building 714
Maxwell Air Force Base, AL 36112-6332
Phone: 334-953-8640
Fax: 334-953-6699
E-mail: cpr@capnhq.gov

CLEVELAND SCHOLARSHIP PROGRAMS

http://www.cspohio.org/

CSP MANAGED FUNDS-LABORERS' INTERNATIONAL UNION OF NORTH AMERICA, AFL-CIO LOCAL NO. 84 SCHOLARSHIP

Scholarship to assist graduating high school seniors and current college students, who are sons or daughters of members of LIUNA Local 894 and who meet specific criteria. Minimum 2.5 GPA required. Students selected for this scholarship should follow a full-time college course of study or major in a four-year college.

Award: Scholarship for use in freshman, sophomore, junior, or senior years; not renewable. *Number:* 1–10. *Amount:* $1000.

Eligibility Requirements: Applicant must be enrolled or expecting to enroll full-time at a four-year institution or university. Applicant or parent of applicant must be member of AFL-CIO. Applicant must have 2.5 GPA or higher. Available to U.S. citizens.

Application Requirements: Application, resume, references, test scores, transcript. *Deadline:* May 1.

Contact: Bridget Vaughn, Manager of Special Projects
Cleveland Scholarship Programs
200 Public Square, Suite 3820
Cleveland, OH 44114
Phone: 216-241-5587 Ext. 113
Fax: 216-241-6184
E-mail: bvaughn@cspohio.org

COMMUNITY BANKER ASSOCIATION OF ILLINOIS

http://www.cbai.com/

COMMUNITY BANKER ASSOCIATION OF ILLINOIS CHILDREN OF COMMUNITY BANKING SCHOLARSHIP WILLIAM C. HARRIS MEMORIAL SCHOLARSHIP

Eligible Illinois community banks can submit one name for each $1000 they have donated to the CBAI Foundation. Children of eligible community bankers and part-time bank employees entering freshman year of higher education are eligible. Winner determined by drawing. Must be Illinois resident.

Award: Scholarship for use in freshman year; renewable. *Number:* 1. *Amount:* $1000–$4000.

Eligibility Requirements: Applicant must be high school student; planning to enroll or expecting to enroll full-time at a two-year or four-year or technical institution or university and resident of Illinois. Applicant or parent of applicant must be member of Community Banker Association of Illinois. Applicant or parent of applicant must have employment or volunteer experience in banking. Available to U.S. citizens.

Application Requirements: Application. *Deadline:* August 1.

Contact: Ms. Andrea Cusick, Senior Vice President of Communications
Community Banker Association of Illinois
901 Community Drive
Springfield, IL 62703-5184
Phone: 217-529-2265
E-mail: cbaicom@cbai.com

COMMUNITY FOUNDATION OF WESTERN MASSACHUSETTS

http://www.communityfoundation.org/

HORACE HILL SCHOLARSHIP

Scholarships are given to children or grandchildren of a member of the Springfield Newspapers 25-Year Club. For more information or application visit http://www.communityfoundation.org.

Award: Scholarship for use in freshman, sophomore, junior, senior, or graduate years; not renewable. *Number:* 2. *Amount:* up to $1000.

Eligibility Requirements: Applicant must be enrolled or expecting to enroll full- or part-time at a two-year or four-year institution or university. Applicant or parent of applicant must be member of Springfield Newspaper 25-Year Club. Available to U.S. citizens.

Application Requirements: Application, financial need analysis, transcript, Student Aid Report (SAR). *Deadline:* March 31.

Contact: Dorothy Theriaque, Education Associate
Community Foundation of Western Massachusetts
1500 Main Street, PO Box 15769
Springfield, MA 01115
Phone: 413-732-2858
Fax: 413-733-8565
E-mail: scholar@communityfoundation.org

DAUGHTERS OF PENELOPE FOUNDATION

http://daughtersofpenelope.org/

ALEXANDRA APOSTOLIDES SONENFELD SCHOLARSHIP

Annual award for female graduating high school seniors or undergraduate students who are members of the Daughters of Penelope or the Maids of Athena, or have a member of the immediate family in the Daughters of Penelope, or the Order of AHEPA. Membership must be for a minimum of two years in good standing.

Award: Scholarship for use in freshman, sophomore, junior, or senior years; not renewable. *Number:* 1. *Amount:* up to $1500.

Eligibility Requirements: Applicant must be of Greek heritage; enrolled or expecting to enroll full-time at a two-year or four-year or technical institution or university and female. Applicant or parent of applicant must be member of Daughters of Penelope/Maids of Athena/Order of Ahepa. Available to U.S. citizens.

Application Requirements: Application, essay, references, test scores, transcript, IRS forms. *Deadline:* June 1.

Contact: Helen Santire, National Scholarship Chairman
Daughters of Penelope Foundation
PO Box 19709
Houston, TX 77024
Phone: 713-468-6531
E-mail: helen.santire@duchesne.org

JOANNE V. HOLOGGITAS, PHD SCHOLARSHIP

Annual award for female graduating high school seniors or undergraduate students who are related to an AHEPAN or a Daughter of Penelope, or must be members of the Maids of Athens. Membership must be for a minimum of two years in good standing.

Award: Scholarship for use in freshman, sophomore, junior, or senior years; not renewable. *Number:* 1. *Amount:* up to $1500.

Eligibility Requirements: Applicant must be of Greek heritage; enrolled or expecting to enroll full-time at a two-year or four-year or technical institution or university and female. Applicant or parent of applicant must be member of Daughters of Penelope/Maids of Athena/Order of Ahepa. Available to U.S. and Canadian citizens.

Application Requirements: Application, essay, references, test scores, transcript, IRS forms. *Deadline:* June 1.

Contact: Helen Santire, National Scholarship Chairman
Daughters of Penelope Foundation
PO Box 19709
Houston, TX 77024
Phone: 713-468-6531
E-mail: helen.santire@duchesne.org

KOTTIS FAMILY SCHOLARSHIP

Annual award for female graduating high school seniors or undergraduate students who are related to an AHEPAN or a Daughter of Penelope, or a member of the Maids of Athens. Membership must be for a minimum of two years in good standing.

Award: Scholarship for use in freshman, sophomore, junior, or senior years; not renewable. *Number:* 1. *Amount:* up to $1500.

Eligibility Requirements: Applicant must be of Greek heritage; enrolled or expecting to enroll full-time at a two-year or four-year or technical institution or university and female. Applicant or parent of applicant must be member of Daughters of Penelope/Maids of Athena/Order of Ahepa. Available to U.S. and Canadian citizens.

Application Requirements: Application, essay, references, test scores, transcript, IRS forms. *Deadline:* June 1.

Contact: Helen Santire, National Scholarship Chairman
Daughters of Penelope Foundation
PO Box 19709
Houston, TX 77024
Phone: 713-468-6531
E-mail: helen.santire@duchesne.org

MARY M. VERGES SCHOLARSHIP

Annual award for female graduating high school seniors or undergraduate students who are members of the Daughters of Penelope or the Maids of Athena, or have a member of the immediate family in the Daughters of Penelope, or the Order of AHEPA. Membership must be for a minimum of two years in good standing.

Award: Scholarship for use in freshman, sophomore, junior, or senior years; not renewable. *Number:* 1. *Amount:* up to $1500.

Eligibility Requirements: Applicant must be of Greek heritage; enrolled or expecting to enroll full-time at a two-year or four-year or technical institution or university and female. Applicant or parent of applicant must be member of Daughters of Penelope/Maids of Athena/Order of Ahepa. Available to U.S. and Canadian citizens.

Application Requirements: Application, essay, references, test scores, transcript, IRS forms. *Deadline:* June 1.

Contact: Helen Santire, National Scholarship Chairman
Daughters of Penelope Foundation
PO Box 19709
Houston, TX 77024
Phone: 713-468-6531
E-mail: helen.santire@duchesne.org

PAST GRAND PRESIDENTS SCHOLARSHIP

Scholarship for female students of Greek descent. Must be a graduating high school senior or an undergraduate student who is related to an AHEPAN or a Daughter of Penelope, or must be a member of the Maids of Athens. Must be a citizen of the United States, Canada, Greece, or any country in which there is an established Daughters of Penelope chapter.

Award: Scholarship for use in freshman, sophomore, junior, or senior years; not renewable. *Number:* 1. *Amount:* up to $1500.

Eligibility Requirements: Applicant must be of Greek heritage; enrolled or expecting to enroll full-time at a two-year or four-year or technical institution or university and female. Applicant or parent of applicant must be member of Daughters of Penelope/Maids of Athena/Order of Ahepa. Available to U.S. and Canadian citizens.

Application Requirements: Application, essay, references, test scores, transcript, IRS forms. *Deadline:* June 1.

Contact: Helen Santire, National Scholarship Chairman
Daughters of Penelope Foundation
PO Box 19709
Houston, TX 77024
Phone: 713-468-6531
E-mail: helen.santire@duchesne.org·

DELTA DELTA DELTA FOUNDATION

http://www.tridelta.org/

DELTA DELTA DELTA UNDERGRADUATE SCHOLARSHIP

One-time award to any initiated sophomore or junior member in good-standing of Delta Delta Delta based on academic achievement, campus, chapter, and community involvement. Application and information available at web site http://www.tridelta.org.

Award: Scholarship for use in sophomore or junior years; not renewable. *Number:* 48–50. *Amount:* $500–$1500.

Eligibility Requirements: Applicant must be enrolled or expecting to enroll full-time at a four-year institution or university and single female. Applicant or parent of applicant must have employment or volunteer experience in community service. Available to U.S. and Canadian citizens.

Application Requirements: Application, references, transcript, alumna adviser check-off, personal statement. *Deadline:* March 15.

Contact: Laura Allen, Foundation Manager of Scholarships and
Financial Services
Delta Delta Delta Foundation
PO Box 5987
Arlington, TX 76005
Phone: 817-633-8001
Fax: 817-652-0212
E-mail: lallen@trideltaeo.org

DELTA PHI EPSILON EDUCATIONAL FOUNDATION

http://www.dphie.org/

DELTA PHI EPSILON EDUCATIONAL FOUNDATION GRANT

Scholarships are awarded based on three criteria: service and involvement, academics, and need. Applications may be submitted for undergraduate only. Applicants must be members of Delta Phi Epsilon or the sons/daughters of members. Refer to web site http://www.dphie.org/foundation/apply.shtml for details.

Award: Grant for use in freshman, sophomore, junior, or senior years; not renewable. *Number:* 6–8. *Amount:* $1000.

Eligibility Requirements: Applicant must be enrolled or expecting to enroll full-time at a four-year institution or university. Available to U.S. and non-U.S. citizens.

Application Requirements: Application, driver's license, essay, financial need analysis, photo, references, transcript. *Deadline:* April 15.

Contact: Nicole DeFeo, Executive Director
Delta Phi Epsilon Educational Foundation
251 South Camac Street
Philadelphia, PA 19107
Phone: 215-732-5901
Fax: 215-275-2655
E-mail: info@dphie.org

EASTERN ORTHODOX COMMITTEE ON SCOUTING

http://www.eocs.org/

EASTERN ORTHODOX COMMITTEE ON SCOUTING SCHOLARSHIPS

One-time award for high school seniors planning to attend a four-year institution. Must be a registered member of a Boy or Girl Scout unit, an Eagle Scout or Gold Award recipient, active member of an Eastern Orthodox Church, and recipient of the Alpha Omega religious award.

Award: Scholarship for use in freshman year; not renewable. *Number:* 2. *Amount:* $500–$1000.

Eligibility Requirements: Applicant must be Eastern Orthodox; high school student; planning to enroll or expecting to enroll full-time at a four-year institution or university and single. Applicant or parent of applicant must be member of Boy Scouts or Girl Scouts. Available to U.S. citizens.

Application Requirements: Application, references, self-addressed stamped envelope, test scores, transcript. *Deadline:* May 1.

Contact: George Boulukos, Scholarship Chairman
Eastern Orthodox Committee on Scouting
862 Guy Lombardo Avenue
Freeport, NY 11520
Phone: 516-868-4050
E-mail: geobou03@aol.com

EASTERN SURFING ASSOCIATION (ESA)

http://www.surfesa.org/

ESA MARSH SCHOLARSHIP PROGRAM

Grants are awarded to ESA current members in good standing on the basis of academics and U.S. citizenship rather than athletic ability.

Award: Scholarship for use in freshman, sophomore, junior, or senior years; not renewable. *Number:* 2. *Amount:* up to $8000.

Eligibility Requirements: Applicant must be enrolled or expecting to enroll full-time at a four-year institution or university. Applicant or parent of applicant must be member of Eastern Surfing Association. Available to U.S. citizens.

Application Requirements: Application, essay, references, transcript. *Deadline:* May 15.

Contact: Debbie Hodges, Scholarship Committee
Eastern Surfing Association (ESA)
PO Box 625
Virginia Beach, VA 23451
Phone: 757-233-1790
E-mail: centralhq@surfesa.org

ELKS NATIONAL FOUNDATION

http://www.elks.org/enf

ELKS EMERGENCY EDUCATIONAL GRANTS

Grant available to children of Elks who are deceased or totally incapacitated. Applicants for the one-year renewable awards must be unmarried, under the age of 23, be a full-time undergraduate student, and demonstrate financial need.

Award: Scholarship for use in freshman, sophomore, junior, or senior years; not renewable. *Number:* varies. *Amount:* $1000–$4000.

Eligibility Requirements: Applicant must be age 23 or under; enrolled or expecting to enroll full-time at a two-year or four-year institution or university and single. Applicant or parent of applicant must be member of Elks Club. Available to U.S. citizens.

Application Requirements: Application, applicant must enter a contest, essay, financial need analysis, references, self-addressed stamped envelope, test scores, transcript. *Deadline:* December 31.

Contact: Scholarship Office
Elks National Foundation
2750 North Lakeview Avenue
Chicago, IL 60614-2256
Phone: 773-755-4732
Fax: 773-755-4733
E-mail: scholarship@elks.org

ELKS NATIONAL FOUNDATION LEGACY AWARDS

$4000 four-year scholarships available for children and grandchildren of Elks in good standing. Parent or grandparent must have been an Elk for two years. Must be high school senior and apply through the related member's Elks Lodge. Applications available after September 1 online only http://www.elks.org/enf/scholars/legacy.cfm.

Award: Scholarship for use in freshman, sophomore, junior, or senior years; renewable. *Number:* 250. *Amount:* $4000.

Eligibility Requirements: Applicant must be high school student and planning to enroll or expecting to enroll full-time at a two-year or four-year institution or university. Applicant or parent of applicant must be member of Elks Club. Available to U.S. citizens.

Application Requirements: Application, essay, test scores, transcript. *Deadline:* February 1.

Contact: Scholarship Office
Elks National Foundation
2750 North Lakeview Avenue
Chicago, IL 60614-2256
Phone: 773-755-4732
Fax: 773-755-4733
E-mail: scholarship@elks.org

FEDERATION OF AMERICAN CONSUMERS AND TRAVELERS

http://www.usafact.org/

FEDERATION OF AMERICAN CONSUMERS AND TRAVELERS GRADUATING HIGH SCHOOL SENIOR SCHOLARSHIP

One $10,000 scholarship and one $2500 scholarship are given to graduating high school seniors per year. Eligible applicants must be a member or the child or grandchild of a member of FACT. Awards are designed for the average student: the young man or woman who may never have made the honor roll or who did not excel on the athletic field and wants to obtain a higher education, but is all too often overlooked by other scholarship sources.

Award: Scholarship for use in freshman year; not renewable. *Number:* 2. *Amount:* $2500–$10,000.

Eligibility Requirements: Applicant must be high school student and planning to enroll or expecting to enroll full-time at a two-year or four-year institution or university. Applicant or parent of applicant must be member of Federation of American Consumers and Travelers. Available to U.S. citizens.

Application Requirements: Application, essay, references, test scores, transcript. *Deadline:* January 15.

Contact: Vicki Rolens, Managing Director
Federation of American Consumers and Travelers
PO Box 104
Edwardsville, IL 62025
Phone: 800-872-3228
Fax: 618-656-5369
E-mail: vrolens@usafact.org

FEDERATION OF AMERICAN CONSUMERS AND TRAVELERS TRADE/TECHNICAL SCHOOL SCHOLARSHIP

Scholarships offered in four categories: current high school seniors, persons who graduated from high school four or more years ago and now plan to go to a university or college, students currently enrolled in a college or university, and trade or technical school aspirants. Members of FACT, their children and grandchildren are eligible to apply.

Award: Scholarship for use in freshman, sophomore, junior, or senior years; not renewable. *Number:* 1–3. *Amount:* $1000–$5000.

Eligibility Requirements: Applicant must be enrolled or expecting to enroll full- or part-time at a technical institution. Applicant or parent of applicant must be member of Federation of American Consumers and Travelers. Available to U.S. citizens.

Application Requirements: Application, essay, resume, references, test scores, transcript. *Deadline:* January 15.

Contact: Vicki Rolens, Managing Director
Federation of American Consumers and Travelers
PO Box 104
Edwardsville, IL 62025
Phone: 800-872-3228
Fax: 618-656-5369
E-mail: vrolens@usafact.org

FIRST CATHOLIC SLOVAK LADIES ASSOCIATION

http://www.fcsla.org/

FIRST CATHOLIC SLOVAK LADIES ASSOCIATION HIGH SCHOOL SCHOLARSHIPS

Scholarship for high school students. A written report of approximately 250 words on "What This High School Scholarship Will Do for Me" must be submitted with application. Candidate must have been a beneficial member of the Association for at least three years prior to date of application.

Award: Scholarship for use in freshman year; renewable. *Number:* up to 32. *Amount:* $1000.

Eligibility Requirements: Applicant must be high school student and planning to enroll or expecting to enroll full-time at a four-year institution or university. Applicant or parent of applicant must be member of First Catholic Slovak Ladies Association. Available to U.S. and Canadian citizens.

Application Requirements: Application, essay, photo, transcript. *Deadline:* March 1.

Contact: Director of Fraternal Scholarships
First Catholic Slovak Ladies Association
24950 Chagrin Boulevard
Beachwood, OH 44122
Phone: 800-464-4642
E-mail: info@fcsla.com

FLEET RESERVE ASSOCIATION EDUCATION FOUNDATION

http://www.fra.org/

COLONEL HAZEL ELIZABETH BENN U.S.M.C. SCHOLARSHIP

Scholarship available to a student who will attend freshman or sophomore undergraduate education and is an unmarried dependent child of a Fleet Reserve Association member in good standing who served or is now serving in the United States Navy as an enlisted medical rating serving with the United States Marine Corps.

Award: Scholarship for use in freshman or sophomore years; not renewable. *Number:* 1–6. *Amount:* up to $2000.

Eligibility Requirements: Applicant must be enrolled or expecting to enroll full-time at a four-year institution or university and single. Applicant or parent of applicant must be member of Fleet Reserve Association/Auxiliary. Available to U.S. citizens. Applicant must have served in the Navy.

Application Requirements: Application, essay, financial need analysis, references, test scores, transcript, SAT/ACT. *Deadline:* April 15.

Contact: Vince Cuthie, FRA Education Foundation
Fleet Reserve Association Education Foundation
125 North West Street
Alexandria, VA 22314-2754
Phone: 703-683-1400 Ext. 107
E-mail: scholars@fra.org

STANLEY A. DORAN MEMORIAL SCHOLARSHIP

Award for dependent children of members in good standing of the Fleet Reserve Association or of a member in good standing at time of death. Minimum 3.0 GPA required. Applications available on Web at http://www.fra.org/foundation. Applications located at the bottom of the page in PDF format. Download both part 1 and part 2.

Award: Scholarship for use in freshman, sophomore, junior, or senior years; not renewable. *Number:* 1. *Amount:* $2000–$5000.

Eligibility Requirements: Applicant must be enrolled or expecting to enroll full-time at a two-year or four-year institution or university. Applicant or parent of applicant must be member of Fleet Reserve Association/Auxiliary. Applicant must have 3.0 GPA or higher. Available to U.S. citizens. Applicant must have served in the Coast Guard, Marine Corps, or Navy.

Application Requirements: Application, essay, financial need analysis, references, test scores, transcript, sat/act. *Deadline:* April 15.

Contact: Scholarship Administrator
Fleet Reserve Association Education Foundation
125 North West Street
Alexandria, VA 22314-2754

GEOLOGICAL SOCIETY OF AMERICA

http://www.geosociety.org/

NORTHEASTERN SECTION UNDERGRADUATE STUDENT RESEARCH GRANTS

Grants to support individual research by sophomore or junior undergraduates attending universities within geographic boundaries of the Northeastern Section. Must be a student associate or a member of GSA.

Award: Grant for use in sophomore or junior years; not renewable. *Number:* varies. *Amount:* varies.

Eligibility Requirements: Applicant must be enrolled or expecting to enroll full- or part-time at a four-year institution or university. Applicant or parent of applicant must be member of Geological Society of America. Available to U.S. citizens.

Application Requirements: Application, financial need analysis, proposal text, endorsement form. *Deadline:* February 28.

Contact: Stephen Pollock, Secretary
Geological Society of America
37 College Avenue
Gorham, ME 04038
Phone: 207-780-5353
Fax: 207-228-8361
E-mail: pollock@usm.maine.edu

GIRL SCOUTS OF CONNECTICUT

http://www.gsofct.org/

EMILY CHAISON GOLD AWARD SCHOLARSHIP

An annual scholarship of $750 is awarded each year to one Gold Award recipient from the state of Connecticut during her senior year.

Award: Scholarship for use in freshman year; not renewable. *Number:* 1. *Amount:* $750.

Eligibility Requirements: Applicant must be high school student; planning to enroll or expecting to enroll full-time at a four-year institution or university; female and resident of Connecticut. Applicant or parent of applicant must be member of Girl Scouts. Available to U.S. citizens.

Application Requirements: Application, essay, references. *Deadline:* April 1.

Contact: Nancy Bussman, Scholarship Committee
Girl Scouts of Connecticut
340 Washington Street
Hartford, CT 06106
Phone: 203-239-2922
E-mail: nbussman@gsofct.org

GLASS, MOLDERS, POTTERY, PLASTICS AND ALLIED WORKERS INTERNATIONAL UNION

http://www.gmpiu.org/

GMP MEMORIAL SCHOLARSHIP PROGRAM

Six college scholarships of $4000 per year available to the sons and daughters of members of the union. Renewable each year for a full four-year college program if adequate academic standards are maintained. Four vocational/technical/two-year associate degree scholarships of $2000 also available (not to exceed the cost of the program).

Award: Scholarship for use in freshman year; renewable. *Number:* 10. *Amount:* $2000–$4000.

Eligibility Requirements: Applicant must be high school student and planning to enroll or expecting to enroll full-time at a two-year or four-year or technical institution or university. Applicant or parent of applicant must be member of Glass, Molders, Pottery, Plastics and Allied Workers International Union. Available to U.S. and Canadian citizens.

Application Requirements: Application, test scores. *Deadline:* November 1.

Contact: Bruce R. Smith, International Secretary and Treasurer
Glass, Molders, Pottery, Plastics and Allied Workers
International Union
608 East Baltimore Pike, PO Box 607
Media, PA 19063
Phone: 610-565-5051 Ext. 220
Fax: 610-565-0983

GOLDEN KEY INTERNATIONAL HONOUR SOCIETY

http://www.goldenkey.org/

GEICO LIFE SCHOLARSHIP

Ten $1000 awards will be given to outstanding students while balancing additional responsibilities. Must have completed at least 12 undergraduate credit hours in the previous year. Must be enrolled at the time of application and must be working toward a baccalaureate degree.

Award: Scholarship for use in freshman, sophomore, junior, or senior years; not renewable. *Number:* 10. *Amount:* $1000.

Eligibility Requirements: Applicant must be enrolled or expecting to enroll full- or part-time at a four-year institution or university. Applicant or parent of applicant must be member of Golden Key National Honor Society. Available to U.S. and non-U.S. citizens.

Application Requirements: Application, essay, references, transcript. *Deadline:* April 1.

Contact: Scholarship Program Administrators
Golden Key International Honour Society
PO Box 23737
Nashville, TN 37202
Phone: 800-377-2401

GOLDEN KEY STUDY ABROAD SCHOLARSHIPS

Ten $1000 scholarships will be awarded each year to assist students in the pursuit of a study abroad program. Eligible members are undergraduate members who are currently enrolled in a study abroad program or will be enrolled in the academic year immediately following the granting of the award. Deadlines: April 15 and October 20.

Award: Scholarship for use in freshman, sophomore, junior, or senior years; not renewable. *Number:* 10. *Amount:* $1000.

Eligibility Requirements: Applicant must be enrolled or expecting to enroll full-time at a four-year institution or university. Applicant or parent of applicant must be member of Golden Key National Honor Society. Available to U.S. and non-U.S. citizens.

Application Requirements: Application, essay, transcript, description of the planned academic program. *Deadline:* varies.

Contact: Scholarship Program Administrators
Golden Key International Honour Society
PO Box 23737
Nashville, TN 37202-3737
Phone: 800-377-2401
E-mail: scholarships@goldenkey.org

GOLF COURSE SUPERINTENDENTS ASSOCIATION OF AMERICA

http://www.eifg.org/

GOLF COURSE SUPERINTENDENTS ASSOCIATION OF AMERICA LEGACY AWARD

Awards of $1500 for the children or grandchildren of Golf Course Superintendents Association of America members. Applicants must be enrolled full-time at an accredited institution of higher learning, or for high school seniors, they must have been accepted at such an institution for the next academic year.

Award: Scholarship for use in freshman, sophomore, junior, or senior years; not renewable. *Number:* 20. *Amount:* $1500.

Eligibility Requirements: Applicant must be enrolled or expecting to enroll full-time at a two-year or four-year or technical institution or university. Applicant or parent of applicant must be member of Golf Course Superintendents Association of America. Available to U.S. and non-U.S. citizens.

Application Requirements: Application, essay, references, transcript. *Deadline:* April 15.

Contact: Mischia Wright, Senior Manager, Development
Golf Course Superintendents Association of America
1421 Research Park Drive
Lawrence, KS 66049-3859
Phone: 800-472-7878 Ext. 4445
E-mail: mwright@gcsaa.org

JOSEPH S. GARSKE COLLEGIATE GRANT PROGRAM

Renewable award available to children/step children of GCSAA members who have been active members for five or more consecutive years for use at an accredited college or trade school. Applicant must be a graduating high school senior and be accepted at an institution of higher learning for the upcoming year.

Award: Scholarship for use in freshman year; not renewable. *Number:* 1–4. *Amount:* $1500–$2500.

Eligibility Requirements: Applicant must be high school student and planning to enroll or expecting to enroll full-time at a two-year or four-year or technical institution or university. Applicant or parent of applicant must be member of Golf Course Superintendents Association of America. Available to U.S. and non-U.S. citizens.

Application Requirements: Application, essay, transcript, letter of acceptance. *Deadline:* March 15.

Contact: Mischia Wright, Senior Manager, Development
Golf Course Superintendents Association of America
1421 Research Park Drive
Lawrence, KS 66049-3859
Phone: 800-472-7878 Ext. 4445
E-mail: mwright@gcsaa.org

HAWAII EDUCATION ASSOCIATION

http://www.heaed.com/

HAWAII EDUCATION ASSOCIATION HIGH SCHOOL STUDENT SCHOLARSHIP

Scholarship available to high school seniors planning on attending four-year college/university. Must be children or grandchildren of HEA members. Membership must be for at least one year.

Award: Scholarship for use in freshman year; not renewable. *Number:* up to 5. *Amount:* up to $1000.

Eligibility Requirements: Applicant must be high school student; planning to enroll or expecting to enroll full-time at a four-year institution or university and resident of Hawaii. Applicant or parent of applicant must be member of Hawaii Education Association. Available to U.S. citizens.

Application Requirements: Application, driver's license, financial need analysis, photo, references, transcript. *Deadline:* April 1.

Contact: Scholarship Committee
Hawaii Education Association
1953 South Beretania Street, Suite 3C
Honolulu, HI 96826-1304
Phone: 808-949-6657
Fax: 808-944-2032
E-mail: hea.office@heaed.com

HAWAII EDUCATION ASSOCIATION UNDERGRADUATE COLLEGE STUDENT SCHOLARSHIP

Scholarships to children and grandchildren of HEA members. To qualify, the HEA member should have at least one year membership in HEA. Four scholarships of $1000 each are offered to deserving continuing, full-time undergraduate college students in any two- or four-year accredited institution of higher learning.

Award: Scholarship for use in freshman, sophomore, junior, or senior years; not renewable. *Number:* up to 4. *Amount:* up to $1000.

Eligibility Requirements: Applicant must be enrolled or expecting to enroll full-time at a two-year or four-year institution or university. Applicant or parent of applicant must be member of Hawaii Education Association. Available to U.S. citizens.

Application Requirements: Application, financial need analysis, references, transcript, personal statement. *Deadline:* April 1.

Contact: Carol Yoneshige, Executive Director
Hawaii Education Association
1953 South Beretania Street, Suite 3C
Honolulu, HI 96826-1304
Phone: 808-949-6657
Fax: 808-944-2032

HEBREW IMMIGRANT AID SOCIETY

http://www.hias.org/

HEBREW IMMIGRANT AID SOCIETY SCHOLARSHIP AWARDS COMPETITION

Contestants must be Hebrew Immigrant Aid Society-assisted refugee who came to the United States after January 1, 1992. Must have completed two semesters at a U.S. high school, college, or graduate school. Application and information are available at web site http://www.hias.org. Applications will be accepted only if submitted online.

Award: Scholarship for use in freshman, sophomore, junior, senior, or graduate years; not renewable. *Number:* 75–150. *Amount:* $2000.

Eligibility Requirements: Applicant must be of Jewish heritage and enrolled or expecting to enroll full-time at a two-year or four-year or technical institution or university. Applicant or parent of applicant must be member of Hebrew Immigrant Aid Society. Available to U.S. citizens.

Application Requirements: Application, essay, financial need analysis, test scores, transcript. *Deadline:* March 1.

Contact: Miriam Ignatoff, Scholarship Committee
Hebrew Immigrant Aid Society
333 Seventh Avenue, 16th Floor
New York, NY 10001-5004
Phone: 212-613-1358
E-mail: scholarship@hias.org

HELLENIC UNIVERSITY CLUB OF PHILADELPHIA

http://www.hucphila.org/

PAIDEIA SCHOLARSHIP

$3000 merit scholarship awarded to the child of a Hellenic University Club of Philadelphia member. Must be a U.S. citizen of Greek descent and a resident of particular counties in NJ or PA.

Award: Scholarship for use in freshman, sophomore, junior, or senior years; not renewable. *Number:* 1. *Amount:* up to $3000.

Eligibility Requirements: Applicant must be of Greek heritage; enrolled or expecting to enroll full-time at a four-year institution or university and resident of New Jersey or Pennsylvania. Applicant or parent of applicant must be member of Hellenic University Club of Pennsylvania. Available to U.S. citizens.

Application Requirements: Application, financial need analysis, transcript. *Deadline:* April 21.

Contact: Anna Hadgis, Scholarship Chairman
Hellenic University Club of Philadelphia
PO Box 42199
Philadelphia, PA 19101-2199
Phone: 610-613-4310
E-mail: hucphila@yahoo.com

HONOR SOCIETY OF PHI KAPPA PHI

http://www.phikappaphi.org/

LITERACY GRANT COMPETITION

Grants up to $2500 are awarded to Phi Kappa Phi members for projects relating to a broad definition of literacy (math, science, music, art, reading, health, etc.). These projects should fulfill the spirit of volunteerism and community.

Award: Grant for use in freshman, sophomore, junior, senior, graduate, or postgraduate years; not renewable. *Number:* up to 18. *Amount:* $300–$2500.

Eligibility Requirements: Applicant must be enrolled or expecting to enroll full- or part-time at a two-year or four-year or technical institution or university. Applicant or parent of applicant must be member of Phi Kappa Phi. Available to U.S. and non-U.S. citizens.

Application Requirements: Application, Itemized Budget. *Deadline:* February 3.

Contact: Mrs. Maria C. Davis, National Marketing Development Manager
Honor Society of Phi Kappa Phi
7576 Goodwood Boulevard
Baton Rouge, LA 70806
Phone: 225-388-4917 Ext. 35
Fax: 225-388-4900
E-mail: mdavis@phikappaphi.org

INDEPENDENT OFFICE PRODUCTS AND FURNITURE DEALERS ASSOCIATION

http://www.iopfda.org/

NOPA AND OFDA SCHOLARSHIP AWARD

Candidates must have graduated from high school or its equivalent before July 1 of the year in which they would use the scholarship. Must have an academic record sufficient to be accepted by an accredited college, junior college or technical institute. Must be a relative of a member of NOPA or OFDA.

Award: Scholarship for use in freshman, sophomore, junior, or senior years; not renewable. *Number:* up to 25. *Amount:* $2000.

Eligibility Requirements: Applicant must be enrolled or expecting to enroll full- or part-time at a two-year or four-year or technical institution or university. Applicant or parent of applicant must be member of Independent Office Products and Furniture Dealers Association. Available to U.S. and non-U.S. citizens.

Application Requirements: Application, references, transcript. *Deadline:* March 16.

Contact: Billie Zidek, Scholarship Administrator
Independent Office Products and Furniture Dealers Association
301 North Fairfax Street, Suite 200
Alexandria, VA 22314-2696
Phone: 703-549-9040 Ext. 121
E-mail: bzidek@iopfda.org

INTERNATIONAL BROTHERHOOD OF TEAMSTERS SCHOLARSHIP FUND

http://www.teamster.org/

JAMES R. HOFFA MEMORIAL SCHOLARSHIP FUND

Scholarships available to children and grandchildren of members of the International Brotherhood of Teamsters (in good standing). Thirty-one of the awards are renewed on an annual basis. Sixty-nine of the awards are a one-time award (non-renewable). The recipient plan to attend a four-year institution and must maintain 3.0 GPA.

Award: Scholarship for use in freshman, sophomore, junior, or senior years; renewable. *Number:* 1–100. *Amount:* $1000–$10,000.

Eligibility Requirements: Applicant must be high school student and planning to enroll or expecting to enroll full-time at a four-year institution or university. Applicant or parent of applicant must be member of International Brotherhood of Teamsters. Applicant must have 3.0 GPA or higher. Available to U.S. and Canadian citizens.

Application Requirements: Application, applicant must enter a contest, references, test scores, transcript, list of activities. *Deadline:* March 31.

Contact: Mrs. Traci Jacobs, Administrative Manager
International Brotherhood of Teamsters Scholarship Fund
25 Louisiana Avenue, NW
Washington, DC 20001
Phone: 202-624-8735
Fax: 202-624-7457
E-mail: scholarship@teamster.org

INTERNATIONAL CHEMICAL WORKERS UNION

http://www.icwuc.org/

WALTER L. MITCHELL MEMORIAL AWARDS

Award available to children of International Chemical Workers Union members. Applicants must be starting their freshman year of college.

Award: Scholarship for use in freshman year; not renewable. *Number:* 12. *Amount:* $1500.

Eligibility Requirements: Applicant must be high school student and planning to enroll or expecting to enroll full-time at a two-year or four-year or technical institution or university. Applicant or parent of applicant must be member of International Chemical Workers Union. Available to U.S. citizens.

Application Requirements: Application, test scores, transcript, biographical questionnaire. *Deadline:* April 23.

Contact: Sue Everhart, Secretary for Research and Education
International Chemical Workers Union
1799 Akron-Peninsula Road
Akron, OH 44313
Phone: 330-926-1444 Ext. 134
Fax: 330-926-0816
E-mail: severhart@icwuc.org

INTERNATIONAL EXECUTIVE HOUSEKEEPERS ASSOCIATION

http://www.ieha.org/

INTERNATIONAL EXECUTIVE HOUSEKEEPERS ASSOCIATION EDUCATIONAL FOUNDATION SPARTAN SCHOLARSHIP

Award available to IEHA members and their immediate families. Scholarship will be awarded to the best qualified candidate as determined by IEHA's education committee.

Award: Scholarship for use in freshman, sophomore, junior, or senior years; not renewable. *Number:* 1. *Amount:* $1500.

Eligibility Requirements: Applicant must be enrolled or expecting to enroll full- or part-time at a four-year institution or university. Applicant or parent of applicant must be member of International Executive Housekeepers Association. Available to U.S. and non-U.S. citizens.

Application Requirements: Application, financial need analysis. *Deadline:* September 10.

Contact: Scholarship Selection Committee
International Executive Housekeepers Association
1001 Eastwind Drive, Suite 301
Westerville, OH 43081-3361
Phone: 800-200-6342
Fax: 614-895-1248

INTERNATIONAL FEDERATION OF PROFESSIONAL AND TECHNICAL ENGINEERS

http://www.ifpte.org/

INTERNATIONAL FEDERATION OF PROFESSIONAL AND TECHNICAL ENGINEERS ANNUAL SCHOLARSHIP

Scholarship for high school seniors who have demonstrated academic achievement and service to their school and community. Only children or grandchildren of IFPTE members are eligible. Must be a U.S. or Canadian citizen. Three scholarships of $1500 are granted.

Award: Scholarship for use in freshman year; not renewable. *Number:* 3. *Amount:* $1500.

Eligibility Requirements: Applicant must be high school student and planning to enroll or expecting to enroll full-time at a four-year institution or university. Applicant or parent of applicant must be member of International Federation of Professional and Technical Engineers. Applicant or parent of applicant must have employment or volunteer experience in community service. Available to U.S. and Canadian citizens.

Application Requirements: Application, essay, references, transcript. *Deadline:* March 15.

Contact: Candace M. Rhett, Communications Representative
International Federation of Professional and Technical Engineers
8630 Fenton Street, Suite 400
Silver Spring, MD 20910
Phone: 301-565-9016
Fax: 301-565-0018
E-mail: crhett@ifpte.org

INTERNATIONAL UNION OF BRICKLAYERS AND ALLIED CRAFTSMEN

http://www.bacweb.org/

CANADIAN BATES SCHOLARSHIP PROGRAM

Renewable scholarship for high school seniors for their undergraduate study. Two scholarships are granted annually and the award value is CAN$1200 or CAN$1500. Must be the son or daughter of a Canadian BAC member in good standing of a Canadian BAC local, and a high school senior planning to attend college in the fall.

Award: Scholarship for use in freshman year; renewable. *Number:* 2.

Eligibility Requirements: Applicant must be Canadian citizen; high school student and planning to enroll or expecting to enroll full- or part-time at a four-year institution or university. Applicant or parent of applicant must be member of International Union of Bricklayers and Allied Craftworkers.

Application Requirements: Application. *Deadline:* March 1.

Contact: Constance Lambert, Director of Education
International Union of Bricklayers and Allied Craftsmen
620 F Street, NW
Washington, DC 20004
Phone: 202-383-3110
E-mail: mmccarthy@bacweb.org

U.S. BATES SCHOLARSHIP PROGRAM

Scholarship awards a stipend of $2500 per year for up to four years to two students annually. The program is open to sons and daughters of U.S. BAC members in good standing of U.S. BAC locals who are in their junior year of high school, and who either have taken or plan to take the standardized PSAT exam.

Award: Scholarship for use in freshman year; renewable. *Number:* 2. *Amount:* $2500.

Eligibility Requirements: Applicant must be high school student and planning to enroll or expecting to enroll full- or part-time at a four-year institution or university. Applicant or parent of applicant must be member of International Union of Bricklayers and Allied Craftworkers. Available to U.S. citizens.

Application Requirements: Application. *Deadline:* March 1.

Contact: Constance Lambert, Director of Education
International Union of Bricklayers and Allied Craftsmen
620 F Street, NW
Washington, DC 20004
Phone: 202-383-3110
E-mail: mmccarthy@bacweb.org

INTERNATIONAL UNION OF ELECTRONIC, ELECTRICAL, SALARIED, MACHINE, AND FURNITURE WORKERS-CWA

http://www.iue-cwa.org/

CWA JOE BEIRNE FOUNDATION SCHOLARSHIP PROGRAM

Scholarships of $3000 annually to Communication Workers of America members, their spouses, children, and grandchildren (including dependents of laid-off, retired or deceased CWA members). A second-year award is contingent on academic accomplishment of the first year. No specific studies are required. Scholarship winners may pursue whatever courses they wish. Winner chosen by lottery drawing.

Award: Scholarship for use in freshman, sophomore, junior, senior, or graduate years; not renewable. *Number:* up to 30. *Amount:* $3000.

Eligibility Requirements: Applicant must be enrolled or expecting to enroll full-time at a two-year or four-year institution or university. Applicant or parent of applicant must be member of AFL-CIO. Available to U.S. and Canadian citizens.

Application Requirements: Application, essay. *Deadline:* April 30.

Contact: Sue McElroy, Scholarship Committee
International Union of Electronic, Electrical, Salaried,
Machine, and Furniture Workers-CWA
501 Third Street, NW
Washington, DC 20001
Phone: 202-434-0676
Fax: 202-434-1250

IUE-CWA INTERNATIONAL BRUCE VAN ESS SCHOLARSHIP

Scholarship of $2500 to all IUE-CWA members and employees and their children and grandchildren. Applicant must be accepted for admission or already enrolled as a full-time student at an accredited college or university, nursing, or technical school offering college credit courses. All study must be completed at the undergraduate level.

Award: Scholarship for use in freshman, sophomore, junior, or senior years; not renewable. *Number:* 1. *Amount:* $2500.

Eligibility Requirements: Applicant must be enrolled or expecting to enroll full-time at a four-year institution or university. Applicant or parent of applicant must be member of International Union of Electronic, Electrical, Salaries, Machine and Furniture Workers. Available to U.S. and Canadian citizens.

Application Requirements: Application, essay, financial need analysis, references, test scores, transcript. *Deadline:* March 31.

Contact: Sue McElroy, Scholarship Committee
International Union of Electronic, Electrical, Salaried,
Machine, and Furniture Workers-CWA
501 Third Street, NW
Washington, DC 20001
Phone: 202-434-0676
Fax: 202-434-1250

IUE-CWA ROBERT L. LIVINGSTON SCHOLARSHIPS

Scholarships of $1500 to a child of an IUE-CWA Automotive Conference Board member (or the child of a deceased or retired IUE-CWA Conference Board member). Applicant must be accepted for admission or already enrolled as a full-time student at an accredited college or university, nursing or technical school offering college credit courses. All study must be completed at the undergraduate level.

Award: Scholarship for use in freshman, sophomore, junior, or senior years; not renewable. *Number:* 2. *Amount:* $1500.

Eligibility Requirements: Applicant must be enrolled or expecting to enroll full-time at a four-year institution or university. Applicant or parent of applicant must be member of International Union of Electronic, Electrical, Salaries, Machine and Furniture Workers. Available to U.S. and Canadian citizens.

Application Requirements: Application, essay, financial need analysis, references, transcript, career objectives, documentation of civic commitment and extracurricular activities. *Deadline:* March 31.

Contact: Sue McElroy, Scholarship Committee
International Union of Electronic, Electrical, Salaried,
Machine, and Furniture Workers-CWA
501 Third Street, NW
Washington, DC 20001
Phone: 202-434-0676
Fax: 202-434-1250

PAUL JENNINGS SCHOLARSHIP AWARD

One award for a student whose parent or grandparent is or has been a local union elected official. Families of full-time international union officers are not eligible. Submit family financial status form with application.

Award: Scholarship for use in freshman, sophomore, junior, senior, or graduate years; not renewable. *Number:* 1. *Amount:* $3000.

Eligibility Requirements: Applicant must be enrolled or expecting to enroll full-time at a two-year or four-year or technical institution or university. Applicant or parent of applicant must be member of International Union of Electronic, Electrical, Salaries, Machine and Furniture Workers. Available to U.S. and Canadian citizens.

Application Requirements: Application, essay, financial need analysis, references, test scores, transcript. *Deadline:* March 31.

Contact: Sue McElroy, Scholarship Committee
International Union of Electronic, Electrical, Salaried,
Machine, and Furniture Workers-CWA
501 Third Street, NW
Washington, DC 20001
Phone: 202-434-0676
Fax: 202-434-1250

WILLIE RUDD SCHOLARSHIP

One-time award available to all IUE-CWA members and employees and their children and grandchildren. Applicant must be accepted for admission or already enrolled as a full-time student at an accredited college or university, nursing, or technical school offering college credit courses. All study must be completed at the undergraduate level.

Award: Scholarship for use in freshman, sophomore, junior, or senior years; not renewable. *Number:* 1. *Amount:* $1000.

Eligibility Requirements: Applicant must be enrolled or expecting to enroll full-time at a four-year or technical institution or university. Applicant or parent of applicant must be member of International Union of Electronic, Electrical, Salaries, Machine and Furniture Workers. Available to U.S. and Canadian citizens.

Application Requirements: Application, essay, financial need analysis, references, test scores, transcript. *Deadline:* March 31.

Contact: Sue McElroy, Scholarship Committee
International Union of Electronic, Electrical, Salaried,
Machine, and Furniture Workers-CWA
501 Third Street, NW
Washington, DC 20001
Phone: 202-434-0676
Fax: 202-434-1250

ITALIAN CATHOLIC FEDERATION INC.

http://www.icf.org/

ITALIAN CATHOLIC FEDERATION FIRST YEAR SCHOLARSHIP

Scholarship for undergraduate students of the Catholic faith and of Italian heritage (or children or grand children of non-Italian ICF members). Must have minimum 3.2 GPA.

Award: Scholarship for use in freshman year; not renewable. *Number:* 180–200. *Amount:* varies.

Eligibility Requirements: Applicant must be Roman Catholic; high school student; planning to enroll or expecting to enroll full-time at a four-year institution or university and resident of Arizona, California, Illinois, or Nevada. Applicant or parent of applicant must be member of Italian Catholic Federation. Available to U.S. citizens.

Application Requirements: Application, essay, financial need analysis, references, test scores, transcript. *Deadline:* March 15.

Contact: Scholarship Committee
Italian Catholic Federation Inc.
ICF Central Council Office, 675 Hegenberger Road, Suite 230
Oakland, CA 94621
Phone: 510-633-9058
Fax: 510-633-9758

JUNIOR ACHIEVEMENT

http://www.ja.org/

HUGH B. SWEENY ACHIEVEMENT AWARD

Award recognizes graduating seniors who demonstrate extraordinary impact on a community through entrepreneurship and similar initiatives. Must have completed JA Company Program or JA Economics.

Award: Scholarship for use in freshman year; not renewable. *Number:* 1. *Amount:* up to $5000.

Eligibility Requirements: Applicant must be high school student; planning to enroll or expecting to enroll full-time at a four-year institution or university and must have an interest in entrepreneurship or leadership. Applicant or parent of applicant must be member of Junior Achievement. Applicant must have 3.0 GPA or higher. Available to U.S. citizens.

Application Requirements: Application, essay, financial need analysis, references. *Deadline:* February 1.

Contact: Gwen Rose, Scholarship Coordinator
Junior Achievement
One Education Way
Colorado Springs, CO 80906-4477
Phone: 719-540-6134
E-mail: dterry@ja.org

JOE FRANCOMANO SCHOLARSHIP

Renewable award to high school seniors who have demonstrated academic achievement, leadership skills, and financial need. May be used at any accredited post secondary educational institution for any field of study resulting in a baccalaureate degree. Must have completed JA Company Program or JA Economics.

Award: Scholarship for use in freshman year; renewable. *Number:* 1. *Amount:* $5000.

Eligibility Requirements: Applicant must be high school student; planning to enroll or expecting to enroll full-time at a four-year institution or university and must have an interest in leadership. Applicant or parent of applicant must be member of Junior Achievement. Applicant must have 3.0 GPA or higher. Available to U.S. citizens.

Application Requirements: Application, essay, financial need analysis, references, transcript. *Deadline:* February 1.

Contact: Gwen Rose, Scholarship Coordinator
Junior Achievement
One Education Way
Colorado Springs, CO 80906-4477
Phone: 719-540-6134
E-mail: dterry@ja.org

KAPPA ALPHA THETA FOUNDATION

http://www.kappaalphathetafoundation.org/

KAPPA ALPHA THETA FOUNDATION MERIT BASED SCHOLARSHIP PROGRAM

Kappa Alpha Theta Foundation awards scholarships to graduate and undergraduate members of Kappa Alpha Theta Fraternity. The merit-based scholarships are awarded based upon academic performance, fraternity activities, campus and/or community activities, and references.

Award: Scholarship for use in sophomore, junior, senior, graduate, or postgraduate years; not renewable. *Number:* 200–230. *Amount:* $1000–$12,000.

Eligibility Requirements: Applicant must be enrolled or expecting to enroll full- or part-time at a two-year or four-year institution or university and female. Available to U.S. and non-U.S. citizens.

Application Requirements: Application, essay, references, transcript. *Deadline:* February 1.

Contact: Ms. Nicole Fritz, Manager of Programs and Communication
Kappa Alpha Theta Foundation
8740 Founders Road
Indianapolis, IN 46268
Phone: 317-876-1870 Ext. 147
E-mail: nfritz@kappaalphatheta.org

KAPPA ALPHA THETA FOUNDATION NAMED ENDOWMENT GRANT PROGRAM

Kappa Alpha Theta Foundation grants provide funds for undergraduate and alumna members of Kappa Alpha Theta Fraternity for leadership training and non-degree educational opportunities. Individual Thetas, collegiate or alumna, and college and alumnae chapters are eligible to apply.

Award: Grant for use in freshman, sophomore, junior, senior, graduate, or postgraduate years; not renewable. *Number:* 1–50. *Amount:* $100–$5000.

Eligibility Requirements: Applicant must be enrolled or expecting to enroll full- or part-time at a four-year institution and female. Available to U.S. and non-U.S. citizens.

Application Requirements: Application, resume, references, budget, proposal, narrative. *Deadline:* continuous.

Contact: Ms. Nicole Fritz, Manager of Programs and Communication
Kappa Alpha Theta Foundation
8740 Founders Road
Indianapolis, IN 46268
Phone: 317-876-1870 Ext. 147
E-mail: nfritz@kappaalphatheta.org

KNIGHTS OF COLUMBUS

http://www.kofc.org/

FOURTH DEGREE PRO DEO AND PRO PATRIA (CANADA)

Renewable scholarships for members of Canadian Knights of Columbus councils and their children who are entering first year of study for baccalaureate degree. Based on academic excellence. Award not limited to Fourth Degree members.

Award: Scholarship for use in freshman year; renewable. *Number:* varies. *Amount:* $1500.

Eligibility Requirements: Applicant must be Roman Catholic; Canadian citizen and enrolled or expecting to enroll full-time at a four-year institution or university. Applicant or parent of applicant must be member of Knights of Columbus. Applicant must have 3.0 GPA or higher.

Application Requirements: Application, references, test scores, transcript. *Deadline:* May 1.

Contact: Knights of Columbus
Department of Scholarships, PO Box 1670
New Haven, CT 06507-0901
Phone: 203-752-4332
Fax: 203-752-4103
E-mail: info@kofc.org

FOURTH DEGREE PRO DEO AND PRO PATRIA SCHOLARSHIPS

Award available to students entering freshman year at a Catholic university or college in United States. Applicant must be a member or child of a member of Knights of Columbus or Columbian Squires. Scholarships are awarded on the basis of academic excellence. Minimum 3.0 GPA required. See web site for additional information http://www.kofc.org.

Award: Scholarship for use in freshman, sophomore, junior, or senior years; renewable. *Number:* varies. *Amount:* $1500.

Eligibility Requirements: Applicant must be Roman Catholic and enrolled or expecting to enroll full-time at a four-year institution or university. Applicant or parent of applicant must be member of Columbian Squires or Knights of Columbus. Applicant must have 3.0 GPA or higher. Available to U.S. citizens.

Application Requirements: Application, essay, references, test scores, transcript. *Deadline:* March 1.

Contact: Knights of Columbus
Department of Scholarships
PO Box 1670
New Haven, CT 06507-0901
Phone: 203-752-4332
E-mail: info@kofc.org

FRANCIS P. MATTHEWS AND JOHN E. SWIFT EDUCATIONAL TRUST SCHOLARSHIPS

Available to dependent children of Knights of Columbus who died or became permanently disabled while in military service during a time of conflict, from a cause connected with military service, or who died as the result of criminal violence while in the performance of their duties as full-time law enforcement officers or firemen. The scholarship is awarded at a Catholic college in the amount not covered by other financial aid for tuition up to $25,000 annually.

Award: Scholarship for use in freshman, sophomore, junior, or senior years; renewable. *Number:* varies. *Amount:* up to $25,000.

Eligibility Requirements: Applicant must be Roman Catholic and enrolled or expecting to enroll full-time at a four-year institution or university. Applicant or parent of applicant must be member of Knights of Columbus. Available to U.S. citizens. Applicant or parent must meet one or more of the following requirements: general military experience; retired from active duty; disabled or killed as a result of military service; prisoner of war; or missing in action.

Application Requirements: Application, proof of parent's military service or employment in law enforcement services. *Deadline:* March 1.

Contact: Knights of Columbus
Department of Scholarships, PO Box 1670
New Haven, CT 06507-0901
Phone: 203-752-4332
Fax: 203-752-4103

JOHN W. MCDEVITT (FOURTH DEGREE) SCHOLARSHIPS

Scholarship for students entering freshman year at a Catholic college or university in United States. Applicant must submit Pro Deo and Pro Patria Scholarship application. Must be a member or wife, son, or daughter of a member of the Knights of Columbus. Minimum 3.0 GPA required. See web site for additional information http://www.fofc.org.

Award: Scholarship for use in freshman year; renewable. *Number:* varies. *Amount:* $1500.

Eligibility Requirements: Applicant must be Roman Catholic and enrolled or expecting to enroll full-time at a four-year institution or university. Applicant or parent of applicant must be member of Knights of Columbus. Applicant must have 3.0 GPA or higher. Available to U.S. citizens.

Application Requirements: Application, references, test scores, transcript. *Deadline:* March 1.

Contact: Knights of Columbus
Department of Scholarships, PO Box 1670
New Haven, CT 06507-0901
Phone: 203-752-4332
Fax: 203-752-4103

PERCY J. JOHNSON ENDOWED SCHOLARSHIPS

Renewable scholarship for young men entering freshman year at a Catholic college or university. Applicants must submit Pro Deo and Pro Patria Scholarship application and a copy of Student Aid Report (SAR). Must be a member or a son of a member of the Knights of Columbus. Must also rank in upper third of class or have 3.0 GPA. See web site for additional information http://www.kofc.org.

Award: Scholarship for use in freshman year; renewable. *Number:* varies. *Amount:* $1500.

Eligibility Requirements: Applicant must be Roman Catholic; enrolled or expecting to enroll full-time at a four-year institution or university and male. Applicant or parent of applicant must be member of Knights of Columbus. Applicant must have 3.0 GPA or higher. Available to U.S. citizens.

Application Requirements: Application, financial need analysis, references, test scores, transcript. *Deadline:* March 1.

Contact: Knights of Columbus
Department of Scholarships, PO Box 1670
New Haven, CT 06507-0901
Phone: 203-752-4332
Fax: 203-752-4103
E-mail: info@kofc.org

LADIES AUXILIARY OF THE FLEET RESERVE ASSOCIATION

http://www.fra.org/

ALLIE MAE ODEN MEMORIAL SCHOLARSHIP

Scholarships are given to the children/grandchildren of members of the FRA or LA FRA. Selections are based on financial need, academic standing, character, and leadership qualities. Must be sponsored by a FRA member in good standing.

Award: Scholarship for use in freshman, sophomore, junior, senior, graduate, or postgraduate years; not renewable. *Number:* varies. *Amount:* $1500.

Eligibility Requirements: Applicant must be enrolled or expecting to enroll full-time at a two-year or four-year institution or university. Applicant or parent of applicant must be member of Fleet Reserve Association/Auxiliary. Available to U.S. citizens. Applicant or parent must meet one or more of the following requirements: Coast Guard, Marine Corps, or Navy experience; retired from active duty; disabled or killed as a result of military service; prisoner of war; or missing in action.

Application Requirements: Application, essay, references, transcript. *Deadline:* April 15.

Contact: Ruth Boggs, Scholarship Chairman
Ladies Auxiliary of the Fleet Reserve Association
125 North West Street
Alexandria, VA 22314-2754
Phone: 209-295-4567

LADIES AUXILIARY OF THE FLEET RESERVE ASSOCIATION-NATIONAL PRESIDENT'S SCHOLARSHIP

Scholarships are given to children/grandchildren of U.S. Navy, Marine Corps and Coast Guard personnel active Fleet Reserve, Fleet Marine Corps Reserve and Coast Guard Reserve, retired with pay or deceased. Selections are based on financial need, academic standing, character, and leadership qualities. Must be sponsored by a FRA member in good standing.

Award: Scholarship for use in freshman, sophomore, junior, or senior years; not renewable. *Number:* 1. *Amount:* $1500.

Eligibility Requirements: Applicant must be enrolled or expecting to enroll full-time at a four-year institution or university. Applicant or parent of applicant must be member of Fleet Reserve Association/Auxiliary. Available to U.S. citizens. Applicant or parent must meet one or more of the following requirements: Coast Guard, Marine Corps, or Navy experience; retired from active duty; disabled or killed as a result of military service; prisoner of war; or missing in action.

Application Requirements: Application, essay, references, transcript. *Deadline:* April 15.

Contact: Ruth Boggs, National Scholarship Chair
Ladies Auxiliary of the Fleet Reserve Association
PO Box 3459
Pahrump, NV 89041-3459
Phone: 775-751-3309

LADIES AUXILIARY OF THE FLEET RESERVE ASSOCIATION SCHOLARSHIP

Scholarships are given to the daughters/granddaughters of U.S. Navy, Marine Corps, and Coast Guard personnel, active Fleet Reserve, Fleet Marine Corps Reserve, and Coast Guard Reserve, retired with pay or deceased. Selections are based on financial need, academic standing, character, and leadership qualities. Must be sponsored by a FRA member in good standing.

Award: Scholarship for use in freshman, sophomore, junior, or senior years; not renewable. *Number:* varies. *Amount:* $1500.

Eligibility Requirements: Applicant must be enrolled or expecting to enroll full-time at a four-year institution or university and female. Applicant or parent of applicant must be member of Fleet Reserve Association/Auxiliary. Available to U.S. citizens. Applicant or parent must meet one or more of the following requirements: Coast Guard, Marine Corps, or Navy experience; retired from active duty; disabled or killed as a result of military service; prisoner of war; or missing in action.

Application Requirements: Application, essay, references, transcript. *Deadline:* April 15.

Contact: Ruth Boggs, National Scholarship Chair
Ladies Auxiliary of the Fleet Reserve Association
PO Box 3459
Pahrump, NV 89041-3459
Phone: 775-751-3309

SAM ROSE MEMORIAL SCHOLARSHIP

Scholarships are given to the child/grandchild of a deceased FRA member or persons who were eligible to be FRA members at the time of death. Selections are based on financial need, academic standing, character, and leadership qualities. Must be sponsored by a FRA member in good standing.

Award: Scholarship for use in freshman, sophomore, junior, or senior years; not renewable. *Number:* varies. *Amount:* $1500.

Eligibility Requirements: Applicant must be enrolled or expecting to enroll full-time at a four-year institution or university. Applicant or parent of applicant must be member of Fleet Reserve Association/Auxiliary. Available to U.S. citizens. Applicant or parent must meet one or more of the following requirements: Coast Guard, Marine Corps, or Navy experience; retired from active duty; disabled or killed as a result of military service; prisoner of war; or missing in action.

Application Requirements: Application, essay, references, transcript. *Deadline:* April 15.

Contact: Ruth Boggs, National Scholarship Chair
Ladies Auxiliary of the Fleet Reserve Association
PO Box 3459
Pahrump, NV 89041-3459
Phone: 775-751-3309

LADIES AUXILIARY TO THE VETERANS OF FOREIGN WARS

http://www.ladiesauxvfw.org/

JUNIOR GIRLS SCHOLARSHIP PROGRAM

One-time awards available to female high school students under age 17 who have been members of Junior Girls Unit of Ladies Auxiliary for one year. Awards based on scholastic aptitude, participation in Junior Girls Unit, and school activities.

Award: Scholarship for use in freshman year; not renewable. *Number:* 1. *Amount:* $7500.

Eligibility Requirements: Applicant must be high school student; age 13-16; planning to enroll or expecting to enroll full-time at a two-year or four-year or technical institution; single female and must have an interest in leadership. Applicant or parent of applicant must be member of Veterans of Foreign Wars or Auxiliary. Available to U.S. citizens.

Application Requirements: Application, applicant must enter a contest, references, transcript. *Deadline:* March 11.

Contact: Judith Millick, Administrator of Programs
Ladies Auxiliary to the Veterans of Foreign Wars
406 West 34th Street, 10th Floor
Kansas City, MO 64111
Phone: 816-561-8655 Ext. 19
Fax: 816-931-4753
E-mail: jmillick@ladiesauxvfw.org

LINCOLN COMMUNITY FOUNDATION

http://www.lcf.org/

P.G. RICHARDSON MASONIC MEMORIAL SCHOLARSHIP

Scholarship for graduating high school seniors who have a family member belonging to Custer Lodge Number 148 A.F. & A.M. Must be Nebraska resident.

Award: Scholarship for use in freshman year; not renewable. *Number:* 1. *Amount:* $500–$2000.

Eligibility Requirements: Applicant must be enrolled or expecting to enroll full-time at a two-year or four-year or technical institution or university and resident of Nebraska. Applicant or parent of applicant must be member of Freemasons. Applicant must have 2.5 GPA or higher. Available to U.S. citizens.

Application Requirements: Application, references, test scores, transcript. *Deadline:* March 6.

Contact: Doug Sadler, Masonic Scholarship Chairman
Lincoln Community Foundation
611 South N Street
Broken Bow, NE 68822

MINNESOTA AFL-CIO

http://www.mnaflcio.org/

BILL PETERSON SCHOLARSHIP

Scholarship available to an union member, spouse, or dependent to attend a postsecondary institution. Must have participated in, or made a donation to the Bill Peterson Golf Tournament. See web site for additional information http://www.mnaflcio.org.

Award: Scholarship for use in freshman, sophomore, junior, or senior years; not renewable. *Number:* 20. *Amount:* $1000.

Eligibility Requirements: Applicant must be enrolled or expecting to enroll full-time at a four-year institution or university; resident of Minnesota; studying in Minnesota and must have an interest in golf. Applicant or parent of applicant must be member of AFL-CIO. Available to U.S. citizens.

Application Requirements: Application, essay. *Deadline:* April 30.

Contact: Computer Information Specialist
Minnesota AFL-CIO
175 Aurora Avenue
St. Paul, MN 55103
Phone: 651-227-7647
Fax: 651-227-3801

MARTIN DUFFY ADULT LEARNER SCHOLARSHIP AWARD

Scholarship available for union members affiliated with the Minnesota AFL-CIO or the Minnesota Joint Council 32. May be used at any postsecondary institution in Minnesota. Information available on web site at http://www.mnaflcio.org.

Award: Scholarship for use in freshman, sophomore, junior, or senior years; not renewable. *Number:* 4. *Amount:* $500.

Eligibility Requirements: Applicant must be enrolled or expecting to enroll full-time at a four-year institution or university; resident of Minnesota and studying in Minnesota. Applicant or parent of applicant must be member of AFL-CIO. Available to U.S. citizens.

Application Requirements: Application. *Deadline:* April 30.

Contact: Computer Information Specialist
Minnesota AFL-CIO
175 Aurora Avenue
St. Paul, MN 55103
Phone: 651-227-7647
Fax: 651-227-3801

MINNESOTA AFL-CIO SCHOLARSHIPS

Applicant must be attending a college or university located in Minnesota. Must have a parent or legal guardian, who has held a one year membership in a local union which is an affiliate of the Minnesota AFL-CIO. Winners are selected by lot. Academic eligibility based on a straight "B" average or better. See web site http://www.mnaflcio.org for information and application.

Award: Scholarship for use in freshman year; not renewable. *Number:* up to 5. *Amount:* $1000.

Eligibility Requirements: Applicant must be high school student; planning to enroll or expecting to enroll full-time at a two-year or four-year or technical institution or university and studying in Minnesota. Applicant or parent of applicant must be member of AFL-CIO. Applicant must have 3.0 GPA or higher. Available to U.S. citizens.

Application Requirements: Application, transcript. *Deadline:* April 30.

Contact: Computer Information Specialist
Minnesota AFL-CIO
175 Aurora Avenue
St. Paul, MN 55103
Phone: 651-227-7647
Fax: 651-227-3801

MINNESOTA COMMUNITY FOUNDATION

http://www.mncommunityfoundation.org/

JOSIP AND AGNETE TEMALI SCHOLARSHIP (BIG BROTHERS/BIG SISTERS)

Scholarship intended to help finance the postsecondary education of a graduating high school senior who: has been an active program participant or volunteer in Big Brothers Big Sisters of the Greater Twin Cities during the two years immediately preceding application; is a United States citizen; and expects to attend an accredited public college, university or technical college in Minnesota as a full-time student upon graduation from high school.

Award: Scholarship for use in freshman year; renewable. *Number:* varies. *Amount:* $4000.

Eligibility Requirements: Applicant must be high school student; planning to enroll or expecting to enroll full- or part-time at a two-year or four-year or technical institution or university; resident of Minnesota and studying in Minnesota. Applicant or parent of applicant must be member of Big Brothers/Big Sisters. Applicant must have 2.5 GPA or higher. Available to U.S. citizens.

Application Requirements: Application, references, transcript. *Deadline:* April 16.

Contact: Donna Paulson, Administrative Assistant
Minnesota Community Foundation
55 Fifth Street East, Suite 600
St. Paul, MN 55101-1797
Phone: 651-325-4212
Fax: 651-224-9502
E-mail: dkp@mncommunityfoundation.org

NATIONAL ACADEMY OF AMERICAN SCHOLARS

http://www.naas.org/

NAAS AWARDS

Merit-based scholarships available for tuition, room, board, books, and academically-related supplies. Applicants must be high school seniors or equivalent home-school seniors. Application periods are September 15 to May 1. Required 2.0 GPA. Electronic applications available to NAAS Subscribers; no fees for NAAS Subscribers.

Award: Scholarship for use in freshman year; renewable. *Number:* 10–14. *Amount:* $200–$10,000.

Eligibility Requirements: Applicant must be high school student and planning to enroll or expecting to enroll full-time at a four-year institution or university. Applicant or parent of applicant must be member of National Academy of American Scholars. Available to U.S. and non-U.S. citizens.

Application Requirements: Application, self-addressed stamped envelope. *Fee:* $3. *Deadline:* May 1.

Contact: K. France, Program Director
National Academy of American Scholars
2248 Meridian Boulevard, Suite H
Minden, NV 89423
Phone: 702-233-5049
E-mail: staff@naas.org

NATIONAL AGRICULTURAL AVIATION ASSOCIATION

http://www.agaviation.org/

WNAAA ANNUAL SCHOLARSHIP ESSAY CONTEST

Awards two prizes of $1000 and $2000 to entrants who are members of NAAA or to children, grandchildren, sons-in-law, daughters-in-law, or spouse of any NAAA operator. Must be high school graduate and enrolled in continuing education during the year of entry. Essays judged on content, theme development, clarity, originality, and proper grammar.

Award: Prize for use in freshman, sophomore, junior, senior, graduate, or postgraduate years; not renewable. *Number:* 2. *Amount:* $1000–$2000.

Eligibility Requirements: Applicant must be enrolled or expecting to enroll full- or part-time at a two-year or four-year or technical institution or university. Applicant or parent of applicant must be member of National Agricultural Aviation Association. Available to U.S. citizens.

Application Requirements: Application, applicant must enter a contest, driver's license, essay, photo, one copy of the manuscript. *Deadline:* August 15.

Contact: Scholarship Chairman
National Agricultural Aviation Association
4142 57th Avenue, SE
Medina, ND 58467
Phone: 701-486-3414
E-mail: medfly@daktel.com

NATIONAL ALLIANCE OF POSTAL AND FEDERAL EMPLOYEES (NAPFE)

http://www.napfe.com/

ASHBY B. CARTER MEMORIAL SCHOLARSHIP FUND FOUNDERS AWARD

Scholarships available to high school seniors. Must be a U.S. citizen. Applicant must be a dependent of NAPFE Labor Union member with a minimum three year membership. Applicant must take the SAT on or before March 1 of the year they apply for award.

Award: Scholarship for use in freshman year; not renewable. *Number:* 3. *Amount:* $2000–$5000.

Eligibility Requirements: Applicant must be high school student and planning to enroll or expecting to enroll full-time at a four-year institution or university. Applicant or parent of applicant must be member of National Alliance of Postal and Federal Employees. Available to U.S. citizens.

Application Requirements: Application, photo, references, self-addressed stamped envelope, test scores, transcript. *Deadline:* April 1.

Contact: Melissa Jeffries-Stewart, Director
National Alliance of Postal and Federal Employees (NAPFE)
1628 11th Street, NW
Washington, DC 20001
Phone: 202-939-6325 Ext. 239
Fax: 202-939-6389
E-mail: headquarters@napfe.org

NATIONAL ASSOCIATION FOR THE ADVANCEMENT OF COLORED PEOPLE

http://www.naacp.org/

AGNES JONES JACKSON SCHOLARSHIP

Scholarship for undergraduate and graduate students who have been members of the NAACP for at least one year, or fully paid life members. Undergraduates must have 2.5 GPA and graduate students must have 3.0 GPA.

Award: Scholarship for use in freshman, sophomore, junior, senior, or graduate years; not renewable. *Number:* 1. *Amount:* $1500–$2500.

Eligibility Requirements: Applicant must be American Indian/Alaska Native, Asian/Pacific Islander, Black (non-Hispanic), or Hispanic; age 24 or under and enrolled or expecting to enroll full- or part-time at a two-year or four-year institution or university. Applicant or parent of applicant must be member of National Association for the Advancement of Colored People. Available to U.S. citizens.

Application Requirements: Application, financial need analysis, references, transcript, evidence of NAACP membership. *Deadline:* March 7.

Contact: Victor Goode, Attorney
National Association for the Advancement of Colored People
4805 Mount Hope Drive
Baltimore, MD 21215-3297
Phone: 410-580-5760
E-mail: info@naacp.org

ROY WILKINS SCHOLARSHIP

One-time award for a freshman enrolled full-time in an accredited U.S. college. Must be U.S. citizen and have minimum 2.5 GPA. NAACP membership and participation is preferable.

Award: Scholarship for use in freshman year; not renewable. *Number:* 1. *Amount:* up to $1000.

Eligibility Requirements: Applicant must be American Indian/Alaska Native, Asian/Pacific Islander, Black (non-Hispanic), or Hispanic; high school student and planning to enroll or expecting to enroll full-time at a two-year or four-year institution or university. Applicant or parent of applicant must be member of National Association for the Advancement of Colored People. Applicant must have 2.5 GPA or higher. Available to U.S. citizens.

Application Requirements: Application, financial need analysis, references, transcript. *Deadline:* March 7.

Contact: Victor Goode, Attorney
National Association for the Advancement of Colored People
4805 Mount Hope Drive
Baltimore, MD 21215-3297
Phone: 410-580-5760
E-mail: info@naacp.org

NATIONAL ASSOCIATION FOR THE SELF-EMPLOYED

http://www.nase.org/

NASE FUTURE ENTREPRENEUR SCHOLARSHIP

Scholarship of $12,000 given to undergraduate and young micro-business owner in any field of study. May renew for a $4,000 scholarship each additional year for up to three consecutive years of undergraduate work for a maximum award of $24,000. Applicant must be child or dependent of an NASE Member.

Award: Scholarship for use in freshman, sophomore, junior, or senior years; not renewable. *Number:* 1. *Amount:* up to $12,000.

Eligibility Requirements: Applicant must be enrolled or expecting to enroll full-time at a four-year institution or university and must have an interest in entrepreneurship. Applicant or parent of applicant must be member of National Association for the Self-Employed. Available to U.S. citizens.

Application Requirements: Application, essay, financial need analysis, references. *Deadline:* April 1.

Contact: Molly Nelson, Communications Associate
National Association for the Self-Employed
P.O. Box 241
Annapolis Junction, MD 20701-0241
Phone: 202-466-2100
Fax: 202-466-2123
E-mail: mnelson@naseadmin.org

NASE SCHOLARSHIPS

Scholarship of $4,000 for high school students or college undergraduates enrolled in full-time program of study. Total number of available awards varies. Applicants must be children or dependents of NASE Members and between the ages of 16 and 24.

Award: Scholarship for use in freshman, sophomore, junior, or senior years; not renewable. *Number:* varies. *Amount:* $4000.

Eligibility Requirements: Applicant must be age 16-24; enrolled or expecting to enroll full-time at a four-year institution or university and must have an interest in leadership. Applicant or parent of applicant must be member of National Association for the Self-Employed. Available to U.S. citizens.

Application Requirements: Application, financial need analysis, resume, references. *Deadline:* April 1.

Contact: Molly Nelson, Communications Associate
National Association for the Self-Employed
P.O. Box 241
Annapolis Junction, MD 20701-0241
Phone: 202-466-2100
Fax: 202-466-2123
E-mail: mnelson@naseadmin.org

NATIONAL ASSOCIATION OF ENERGY SERVICE COMPANIES

http://www.aesc.net/

ASSOCIATION OF ENERGY SERVICE COMPANIES SCHOLARSHIP PROGRAM

Applicant must be the legal dependent of an employee of an AESC member company, or an employee. Dependents of company officers are not eligible. Must submit application to local AESC chapter chairman. Application must include ACT or SAT test scores.

Award: Scholarship for use in freshman, sophomore, junior, senior, or graduate years; renewable. *Number:* 150–200. *Amount:* $1000.

Eligibility Requirements: Applicant must be enrolled or expecting to enroll full-time at a two-year or four-year or technical institution or university. Applicant or parent of applicant must be member of Association of Energy Service Companies. Available to U.S. and non-U.S. citizens.

Application Requirements: Application, essay, test scores, transcript. *Deadline:* March 14.

Contact: Nikki James, Administrative Assistant
National Association of Energy Service Companies
10200 Richmond Avenue, Suite 275
Houston, TX 77042
Phone: 800-692-0771
Fax: 713-781-7542
E-mail: njames@aesc.net

NATIONAL ASSOCIATION OF LETTER CARRIERS

http://www.nalc.org/

COSTAS G. LEMONOPOULOS SCHOLARSHIP

Scholarships to children of NALC members attending public, four-year colleges or universities supported by the state of Florida or St. Petersburg Junior College. Scholarships are renewable one time.

Award: Scholarship for use in freshman, sophomore, junior, or senior years; renewable. *Number:* 1–20. *Amount:* varies.

Eligibility Requirements: Applicant must be enrolled or expecting to enroll full-time at a two-year or four-year institution or university and studying in Florida. Applicant or parent of applicant must be member of National Association of Letter Carriers. Available to U.S. citizens.

Application Requirements: Application, references, transcript. *Deadline:* June 1.

Contact: Ann Porch, Membership Committee
National Association of Letter Carriers
100 Indiana Avenue, NW
Washington, DC 20001-2144
Phone: 202-393-4695
E-mail: nalcinf@nalc.org

JOHN T. DONELON SCHOLARSHIP

Scholarship for sons and daughters of NALC members who are high school seniors when making application. The $1000 scholarship will be renewable for four years.

Award: Scholarship for use in freshman year; renewable. *Number:* 5. *Amount:* $1000.

Eligibility Requirements: Applicant must be high school student and planning to enroll or expecting to enroll full-time at a four-year institution or university. Applicant or parent of applicant must be member of National Association of Letter Carriers. Available to U.S. citizens.

Application Requirements: Application, references, transcript. *Deadline:* December 31.

Contact: Ann Porch, Membership Committee
National Association of Letter Carriers
100 Indiana Avenue, NW
Washington, DC 20001-2144
Phone: 202-393-4695
E-mail: nalcinf@nalc.org

UNION PLUS SCHOLARSHIP PROGRAM

One-time cash award available for undergraduate and graduate study programs. Scholarship ranges from $500 to $4000. Three awards are granted. Must be children of members of NALC.

Award: Scholarship for use in freshman year; not renewable. *Number:* 3. *Amount:* $500–$4000.

Eligibility Requirements: Applicant must be high school student and planning to enroll or expecting to enroll full-time at a four-year institution or university. Applicant or parent of applicant must be member of National Association of Letter Carriers. Available to U.S. citizens.

Application Requirements: Application, references, transcript. *Deadline:* January 31.

Contact: Ann Porch, Membership Committee
National Association of Letter Carriers
100 Indiana Avenue, NW
Washington, DC 20001-2144
Phone: 202-393-4695
E-mail: nalcinf@nalc.org

WILLIAM C. DOHERTY SCHOLARSHIP FUND

Five scholarships of $4000 each are awarded to children of members in NALC. Renewable for three consecutive years thereafter providing the winner maintains satisfactory grades. Applicant must be a high school senior when making application.

Award: Scholarship for use in freshman year; renewable. *Number:* 5. *Amount:* $4000.

Eligibility Requirements: Applicant must be high school student and planning to enroll or expecting to enroll full-time at a four-year institution or university. Applicant or parent of applicant must be member of National Association of Letter Carriers. Available to U.S. citizens.

Application Requirements: Application, test scores, transcript. *Deadline:* December 31.

Contact: Ann Porch, Membership Committee
National Association of Letter Carriers
100 Indiana Avenue, NW
Washington, DC 20001-2144
Phone: 202-393-4695
E-mail: nalcinf@nalc.org

NATIONAL ASSOCIATION OF SECONDARY SCHOOL PRINCIPALS

http://www.nhs.us/

NATIONAL HONOR SOCIETY SCHOLARSHIPS

One-time award to high school seniors who are National Honor Society members for use at an accredited two- or four-year college or university in the U.S. Application fee $6. Contact school counselor or NHS chapter adviser as they must nominate seniors in good standing for the award. Minimum 3.0 GPA.

Award: Scholarship for use in freshman year; not renewable. *Number:* 200. *Amount:* $1000–$13,000.

Eligibility Requirements: Applicant must be high school student and planning to enroll or expecting to enroll full-time at a two-year or four-year institution or university. Applicant or parent of applicant must be member of National Honor Society. Applicant must have 3.0 GPA or higher. Available to U.S. and non-U.S. citizens.

Application Requirements: Application, essay, references, test scores, transcript, nomination by NHS adviser. *Fee:* $6. *Deadline:* January 23.

Contact: Wanda Carroll, Program Manager
National Association of Secondary School Principals
1904 Association Drive
Reston, VA 20191-1537
Phone: 703-860-0200
E-mail: carrollw@principals.org

NATIONAL BETA CLUB

http://www.betaclub.org/

NATIONAL BETA CLUB SCHOLARSHIP

Applicant must be in twelfth grade and a member of the National Beta Club. Must be nominated by school chapter of the National Beta Club, therefore, applications will not be sent to the individual students. Renewable and nonrenewable awards available. Contact school Beta Club sponsor for more information.

Award: Scholarship for use in freshman year; renewable. *Number:* 213. *Amount:* $1000–$15,000.

Eligibility Requirements: Applicant must be high school student and planning to enroll or expecting to enroll full-time at a two-year or four-year institution or university. Applicant or parent of applicant must be member of National Beta Club. Available to U.S. citizens.

Application Requirements: Application, essay, references, test scores, transcript. *Fee:* $10. *Deadline:* December 10.

Contact: Mrs. Joan Burnett, Scholarship Coordinator
National Beta Club
151 Beta Club Way
Spartanburg, SC 29306-3012
Phone: 864-583-4553
Fax: 864-542-9300
E-mail: jburnett@betaclub.org

NATIONAL BICYCLE LEAGUE (NBL)

http://www.nbl.org/

BOB WARNICKE MEMORIAL SCHOLARSHIP PROGRAM

Scholarship assists students and their families in meeting the costs of undergraduate or trade school education. Applicant must be a high school senior, graduate or attending a postsecondary school at the time of application, or accepted and plan to attend an accredited postsecondary school as a full-time or part-time student for the complete award year. Must be an active member or official of the National Bicycle League.

Award: Scholarship for use in freshman year; not renewable. *Number:* varies. *Amount:* varies.

Eligibility Requirements: Applicant must be enrolled or expecting to enroll full- or part-time at a two-year or four-year or technical institution or university. Applicant or parent of applicant must be member of National Bicycle League. Available to U.S. citizens.

Application Requirements: Application, photo, references, transcript, acceptance letter from the school. *Deadline:* December 15.

Contact: Alyson Willett, Scholarship Committee
National Bicycle League (NBL)
3958 Brown Park Drive, Suite D
Hilliard, OH 43026
Phone: 800-886-2691
Fax: 614-777-1680
E-mail: awillett@nbl.org

NATIONAL FFA ORGANIZATION

http://www.ffa.org/

NATIONAL FFA COLLEGIATE SCHOLARSHIP PROGRAM

Scholarships to high school seniors planning to enroll in a full-time course of study at an accredited vocational/technical school, college or university. A smaller number of awards are available to currently enrolled undergraduates. Most awards require the applicant be an FFA member. Some awards are available to non-members.

Award: Scholarship for use in freshman, sophomore, junior, or senior years; not renewable. *Number:* 1500–1600. *Amount:* $1000–$22,000.

Eligibility Requirements: Applicant must be age 17-23 and enrolled or expecting to enroll full-time at a two-year or four-year or technical institution or university. Applicant or parent of applicant must be member of Future Farmers of America. Available to U.S. citizens.

Application Requirements: Application, signature page mailed by deadline. *Deadline:* February 15.

Contact: Scholarship Program Manager
National FFA Organization
PO Box 68960
Indianapolis, IN 46268-0960
Phone: 317-802-6099
E-mail: scholarships@ffa.org

NATIONAL FOSTER PARENT ASSOCIATION

http://www.nfpaonline.org/

NATIONAL FOSTER PARENT ASSOCIATION YOUTH SCHOLARSHIP

Award for high school senior who will be entering first year of college, comparable education, or training program. Six $1000 awards, three for foster children currently in foster care with an NFPA member family, and one each for birth and adopted children of foster parents. NFPA family membership required ($35 membership fee).

Award: Scholarship for use in freshman year; not renewable. *Number:* 6. *Amount:* $1000.

Eligibility Requirements: Applicant must be high school student and planning to enroll or expecting to enroll full- or part-time at a two-year or four-year or technical institution or university. Applicant or parent of applicant must be member of National Foster Parent Association. Available to U.S. citizens.

Application Requirements: Application, driver's license, essay, references, test scores, transcript. *Deadline:* March 31.

Contact: Karen Jorgenson, Executive Director
National Foster Parent Association
7512 Stanich Avenue, Suite 6
Gig Harbor, WA 98335
Phone: 253-853-4000
Fax: 253-853-4001
E-mail: info@nfpaonline.org

NATIONAL FRATERNAL SOCIETY OF THE DEAF

http://www.nfsd.com/

NATIONAL FRATERNAL SOCIETY OF THE DEAF SCHOLARSHIPS

Provides scholarship to cover room and board, tuition and/or fees. Applicant or parent must be member of the NFSD for one full year. Applicant must be in a postsecondary program or ready to enter one as a full-time student.

Award: Scholarship for use in freshman, sophomore, junior, senior, graduate, or postgraduate years; not renewable. *Number:* 5–10. *Amount:* $1000.

Eligibility Requirements: Applicant must be enrolled or expecting to enroll full-time at a two-year or four-year institution or university. Applicant or parent of applicant must be member of National Fraternal Society of the Deaf. Available to U.S. citizens.

Application Requirements: Application, photo, references, transcript. *Deadline:* July 1.

Contact: Scholarship Information
National Fraternal Society of the Deaf
1118 South Sixth Street
Springfield, IL 62703
Phone: 217-789-7429
Fax: 217-789-7489
E-mail: thefrat@nfsd.com

NATIONAL JUNIOR ANGUS ASSOCIATION

http://www.angus.org/njaa/

ANGUS FOUNDATION SCHOLARSHIPS

Applicants must have at one time been a National Junior Angus Association member and currently be a junior, regular or life member of the association. Must have applied to undergraduate studies in any field. Applicants must have a minimum 2.0 GPA. See web site for further information and to download application.

Award: Scholarship for use in freshman, sophomore, junior, senior, or graduate years; not renewable. *Number:* 75–90. *Amount:* $250–$5000.

Eligibility Requirements: Applicant must be age 25 or under and enrolled or expecting to enroll full-time at a two-year or four-year or technical institution or university. Applicant or parent of applicant must be member of American Angus Association. Available to U.S. and Canadian citizens.

Application Requirements: Application, references, transcript. *Deadline:* May 1.

Contact: Mr. Milford Jenkins, Angus Foundation President
National Junior Angus Association
3201 Frederick Avenue
St. Joseph, MO 64506
Phone: 816-383-5100 Ext. 163
Fax: 816-383-5146
E-mail: mjenkins@angusfoundation.org

NATIONAL ORDER OF OMEGA

http://www.orderofomega.org/

FOUNDERS SCHOLARSHIP

Scholarship of $1000 available to juniors or seniors displaying leadership and service to their Order of Omega chapter.

Award: Scholarship for use in junior or senior years; not renewable. *Number:* 1. *Amount:* $1000.

Eligibility Requirements: Applicant must be enrolled or expecting to enroll full-time at a four-year institution or university and must have an interest in leadership. Applicant or parent of applicant must be member of Order of Omega. Available to U.S. and Canadian citizens.

Application Requirements: Application, essay, photo, references, transcript. *Deadline:* November 16.

Contact: Scholarship Committee
National Order of Omega
300 East Border Street
Arlington, TX 76010-1656

NATIONAL RIFLE ASSOCIATION

http://www.nrafoundation.org/

JEANNE E. BRAY MEMORIAL SCHOLARSHIP PROGRAM

Renewable scholarship of $2000 for a maximum of four years for undergraduate students enrolled full-time in accredited colleges or universities. Must have a minimum GPA of 2.5.

Award: Scholarship for use in freshman, sophomore, junior, or senior years; renewable. *Number:* 1. *Amount:* $2000.

Eligibility Requirements: Applicant must be enrolled or expecting to enroll full-time at a two-year or four-year institution or university. Applicant or parent of applicant must be member of National Rifle Association. Applicant must have 2.5 GPA or higher. Available to U.S. citizens.

Application Requirements: Application, essay, references, test scores, transcript, proof of acceptance to college or university, referral on letterhead signed by agency official documenting qualifying parent. *Deadline:* November 15.

Contact: Sandy Elkin, Grants Manager
National Rifle Association
11250 Waples Mill Road
Fairfax, VA 22030
Phone: 703-267-1131
Fax: 703-267-1083
E-mail: selkin@nrahqn.org

NATIONAL SOCIETY DAUGHTERS OF THE AMERICAN REVOLUTION

http://www.dar.org/

NATIONAL SOCIETY DAUGHTERS OF THE AMERICAN REVOLUTION LILLIAN AND ARTHUR DUNN SCHOLARSHIP

A $2000 scholarship awarded for up to four years to well-qualified, deserving sons and daughters of members of the NSDAR. Outstanding recipients will be considered for an additional period of up to four years of study. Must include DAR member number.

Award: Scholarship for use in freshman, sophomore, junior, or senior years; renewable. *Number:* varies. *Amount:* $2000.

Eligibility Requirements: Applicant must be enrolled or expecting to enroll full-time at a four-year institution or university. Applicant or parent of applicant must be member of Daughters of the American Revolution. Available to U.S. citizens.

Application Requirements: Application, financial need analysis, references, self-addressed stamped envelope, transcript, letter of sponsorship. *Deadline:* February 15.

Contact: Eric Weisz, Manager, Office of the Reporter General
National Society Daughters of the American Revolution
1776 D Street, NW
Washington, DC 20006-5303
Phone: 202-628-1776
Fax: 202-879-3348
E-mail: nsdarscholarships@dar.org

NATIONAL SOCIETY OF COLLEGIATE SCHOLARS (NSCS)

http://www.nscs.org/

NSCS EXEMPLARY SCHOLAR AWARD

Scholarship of $1000 available to outstanding undergraduates among the NSCS members for their high academic achievement as well as additional scholarly pursuits outside of the classroom. They should exemplify the NSCS mission: "Honoring and inspiring academic excellence and engaged citizenship for a lifetime" and show integrity in everything they do. Must have a completed profile and resume in NSCS database. Apply on web site http://www.nscs.org/exemplary_scholar_award.

Award: Scholarship for use in freshman, sophomore, junior, or senior years; not renewable. *Number:* 3. *Amount:* $1000.

Eligibility Requirements: Applicant must be enrolled or expecting to enroll full- or part-time at a four-year institution or university and must have an interest in leadership. Applicant or parent of applicant must be member of National Society of Collegiate Scholars. Available to U.S. and non-U.S. citizens.

Application Requirements: Application. *Deadline:* April 30.

Contact: Stephen Loflin, Executive Director
National Society of Collegiate Scholars (NSCS)
11 Dupont Circle, NW, Suite 650
Washington, DC 20036
Phone: 202-965-9000
E-mail: nscs@nscs.org

NSCS INTEGRITY SCHOLARSHIP

Award of $1000 to ten NSCS members who demonstrate a true commitment to integrity through a series of short answer questions describing a time when their integrity has been challenged. Must be working towards an undergraduate or graduate degree at an accredited university. Must have minimum GPA of 3.4 and have their resume in the NSCS database. Apply on web site http://www.nscs.org/integrity-scholarship.

Award: Scholarship for use in freshman, sophomore, junior, senior, or graduate years; not renewable. *Number:* 10. *Amount:* $1000.

Eligibility Requirements: Applicant must be enrolled or expecting to enroll full- or part-time at a four-year institution or university. Applicant or parent of applicant must be member of National Society of Collegiate Scholars. Available to U.S. and non-U.S. citizens.

Application Requirements: Application, resume. *Deadline:* January 13.

Contact: Stephen Loflin, Executive Director
National Society of Collegiate Scholars (NSCS)
11 Dupont Circle, NW, Suite 650
Washington, DC 20036
Phone: 202-965-9000
E-mail: nscs@nscs.org

NSCS MERIT AWARD

Fifty merit awards to outstanding new NSCS members around the country. Student is chosen based upon how they exemplify the mission of NSCS. Must have a resume in the NSCS database and be a member who has joined between August of the previous year and July of the present year. Must have a minimum GPA of 3.4 and be enrolled in an accredited institution. For additional information, see web site http://www.nscs.org.

Award: Scholarship for use in freshman, sophomore, junior, or senior years; not renewable. *Number:* 50. *Amount:* $1000.

Eligibility Requirements: Applicant must be enrolled or expecting to enroll full- or part-time at a two-year or four-year or technical institution or university. Applicant or parent of applicant must be member of National Society of Collegiate Scholars. Available to U.S. and non-U.S. citizens.

Application Requirements: Application, resume, references, transcript. *Deadline:* July 31.

Contact: Stephen Loflin, Executive Director
National Society of Collegiate Scholars (NSCS)
11 Dupont Circle, NW, Suite 650
Washington, DC 20036
Phone: 202-965-9000
E-mail: nscs@nscs.org

NSCS SCHOLAR ABROAD SCHOLARSHIP

Scholarship for an active NSCS member who has been accepted to and enrolled in an accredited study abroad program. One $5000 scholarship is awarded each fall and spring semester and one $2500 scholarship is awarded for the summer term. Must have profile and resume in NSCS database and have a minimum 3.4 GPA. Apply at web site http://www.nscs.org/scholar-abroad-scholarship.

Award: Scholarship for use in freshman, sophomore, junior, or senior years; not renewable. *Number:* 3. *Amount:* $2500–$5000.

Eligibility Requirements: Applicant must be enrolled or expecting to enroll full-time at a two-year or four-year institution or university. Applicant or parent of applicant must be member of National Society of Collegiate Scholars. Available to U.S. and non-U.S. citizens.

Application Requirements: Application, resume. *Deadline:* April 15.

Contact: Stephen Loflin, Executive Director
National Society of Collegiate Scholars (NSCS)
11 Dupont Circle, NW, Suite 650
Washington, DC 20036
Phone: 202-965-9000
E-mail: nscs@nscs.org

NATIONAL SOCIETY OF HIGH SCHOOL SCHOLARS

http://www.nshss.org/

ABERCROMBIE & FITCH GLOBAL DIVERSITY & LEADERSHIP SCHOLAR AWARDS

Ten scholarships of $1000 to high school seniors who are members of NSHSS. Must submit written response to the question posed by A&F regarding diversity and inclusion.

Award: Scholarship for use in freshman year; not renewable. *Number:* 10. *Amount:* $1000.

Eligibility Requirements: Applicant must be high school student and planning to enroll or expecting to enroll full-time at a four-year institution or university. Applicant or parent of applicant must be member of National Society of High School Scholars. Applicant must have 3.5 GPA or higher. Available to U.S. and non-U.S. citizens.

Application Requirements: Application, essay, photo, references, transcript. *Deadline:* April 1.

Contact: Dr. Susan Thurman, Scholarship Director
National Society of High School Scholars
1936 North Druid Hills Road
Atlanta, GA 30319
Phone: 866-343-1800
Fax: 404-235-5510
E-mail: susan.thurman@nshss.org

CLAES NOBEL ACADEMIC SCHOLARSHIPS FOR NSHSS MEMBERS

Scholarship of $5000 to current high school seniors who are members of NSHSS. Award is based upon community service, leadership, academic performance, and school and extracurricular activities. Must complete an online application form. Deadline varies.

Award: Scholarship for use in freshman year; not renewable. *Number:* 5–10. *Amount:* $5000.

Eligibility Requirements: Applicant must be high school student; planning to enroll or expecting to enroll full- or part-time at a four-year institution or university and must have an interest in leadership. Applicant or parent of applicant must be member of National Society of High School Scholars. Applicant must have 3.5 GPA or higher. Available to U.S. and non-U.S. citizens.

Application Requirements: Application, essay, photo, references, transcript. *Deadline:* November 30.

Contact: Dr. Susan Thurman, Scholarship Director
National Society of High School Scholars
1936 North Druid Hills Road
Atlanta, GA 30319
Phone: 404-235-5500
Fax: 404-235-5510

GRIFFITH COLLEGE SCHOLARS SCHOLARSHIPS FOR NSHSS MEMBERS

Five $1000 scholarships awarded to NSHSS members who are part- and full-time students. May be used at any college or university.

Award: Scholarship for use in freshman year; not renewable. *Number:* 5. *Amount:* $1000.

Eligibility Requirements: Applicant must be high school student and planning to enroll or expecting to enroll full- or part-time at a four-year institution or university. Applicant or parent of applicant must be member of National Society of High School Scholars. Applicant must have 3.5 GPA or higher. Available to U.S. and non-U.S. citizens.

Application Requirements: Application, essay, photo, resume, references, transcript. *Deadline:* May 15.

Contact: Dr. Susan Thurman, Scholarship Director
National Society of High School Scholars
1936 North Druid Hills Road
Atlanta, GA 30319
Phone: 404-235-5500
Fax: 404-235-5510
E-mail: information@nshss.org

NATIONAL SCHOLAR AWARDS FOR NSHSS MEMBERS

Scholarship of $1000 for undergraduate study. Applicant must be a member of NSHSS.

Award: Scholarship for use in freshman year; not renewable. *Number:* 10–30. *Amount:* $1000.

Eligibility Requirements: Applicant must be high school student and planning to enroll or expecting to enroll full- or part-time at a two-year or four-year or technical institution or university. Applicant or parent of applicant must be member of National Society of High School Scholars. Available to U.S. and non-U.S. citizens.

Application Requirements: Application, photo, resume, references, transcript. *Deadline:* November 30.

Contact: Dr. Susan Thurman, Scholarship Director
National Society of High School Scholars
1936 North Druid Hills Road
Atlanta, GA 30319
Phone: 866-343-1800
E-mail: information@nshss.org

NATIONAL UNION OF PUBLIC AND GENERAL EMPLOYEES

http://www.nupge.ca/

SCHOLARSHIP FOR ABORIGINAL CANADIANS

Award for aboriginal Canadian students who plan to enter the first year of a Canadian college or university and who are children or foster children of a member of the NUPGE. Must write a 750 to 1000 words essay on: "The importance of quality public services in enhancing the quality of life of Aboriginal Canadians."

Award: Scholarship for use in freshman year; not renewable. *Number:* 1. *Amount:* $1500.

Eligibility Requirements: Applicant must be of Canadian heritage and Canadian citizen; American Indian/Alaska Native; high school student; planning to enroll or expecting to enroll full-time at a four-year institution or university and studying in Alberta, British Columbia, Manitoba, New Brunswick, Newfoundland, North West Territories, Nova Scotia, Ontario, Prince Edward Island, Saskatchewan, or Yukon. Applicant or parent of applicant must be member of National Union of Public and General Employees.

Application Requirements: Application, applicant must enter a contest, essay. *Deadline:* June 30.

Contact: Ms. Lisa Bullee, Administrative Representative
National Union of Public and General Employees
15 Auriga Drive
Nepean, ON K2E 1B7
Phone: 613-228-9800
Fax: 613-228-9801
E-mail: lbullee@nupge.ca

SCHOLARSHIP FOR VISIBLE MINORITIES

Award for first year Canadian students who are, by race or color, in a visible minority and who are children or foster children of a member of the NUPGE. Must write a 750 to 1000 words essay on: "The importance of quality public services in enhancing the quality of life of visible minorities".

Award: Scholarship for use in freshman year; not renewable. *Number:* 1. *Amount:* $1500.

Eligibility Requirements: Applicant must be Canadian citizen; American Indian/Alaska Native, Asian/Pacific Islander, Black (non-Hispanic), or Hispanic; high school student; planning to enroll or expecting to enroll full-time at a four-year institution or university and studying in Alberta, British Columbia, Manitoba, New Brunswick, Newfoundland, North West Territories, Nova Scotia, Ontario, Prince Edward Island, Saskatchewan, or Yukon. Applicant or parent of applicant must be member of National Union of Public and General Employees.

Application Requirements: Application, applicant must enter a contest, essay. *Deadline:* June 30.

Contact: Ms. Lisa Bullee, Administrative Representative
National Union of Public and General Employees
15 Auriga Drive
Nepean, ON K2E 1B7
Phone: 613-228-9800
Fax: 613-228-9801
E-mail: lbullee@nupge.ca

TERRY FOX MEMORIAL SCHOLARSHIP

Award for Canadian students with disabilities who plan to enter the first year of a Canadian college or university and who are the children or foster children of a member of the NUPGE. Must write a 750 to 1000 words essay on: "The importance of quality public services in enhancing the quality of life of people with disabilities".

Award: Scholarship for use in freshman year; not renewable. *Number:* 1. *Amount:* $1500.

Eligibility Requirements: Applicant must be Canadian citizen; high school student; planning to enroll or expecting to enroll full-time at a four-year institution or university and studying in Alberta, British

Columbia, Manitoba, New Brunswick, Newfoundland, North West Territories, Nova Scotia, Ontario, Prince Edward Island, Saskatchewan, or Yukon. Applicant or parent of applicant must be member of National Union of Public and General Employees. Applicant must be hearing impaired, learning disabled, physically disabled, or visually impaired.

Application Requirements: Application, applicant must enter a contest, essay. *Deadline:* June 30.

Contact: Ms. Lisa Bullee, Administrative Representative
National Union of Public and General Employees
15 Auriga Drive
Nepean, ON K2G 6G5
Phone: 613-228-9800
Fax: 613-228-9801
E-mail: lbullee@nupge.ca

TOMMY DOUGLAS SCHOLARSHIP

Award for first year students at a Canadian college or university who are children or foster children of members of NUPGE. Must write an essay on the topic: "How Tommy Douglas contributed to making Canada a more just and equitable society".

Award: Scholarship for use in freshman year; not renewable. *Number:* 1. *Amount:* $1500.

Eligibility Requirements: Applicant must be Canadian citizen; high school student; planning to enroll or expecting to enroll full-time at a four-year institution or university and studying in Alberta, British Columbia, Manitoba, New Brunswick, Newfoundland, North West Territories, Nova Scotia, Ontario, Prince Edward Island, Saskatchewan, or Yukon. Applicant or parent of applicant must be member of National Union of Public and General Employees.

Application Requirements: Application, applicant must enter a contest, essay. *Deadline:* June 30.

Contact: Ms. Lisa Bullee, Administrative Representative
National Union of Public and General Employees
15 Auriga Drive
Nepean, ON K2E 1B7
Phone: 613-228-9800
E-mail: lbullee@nupge.ca

NEW YORK STATE GRANGE

http://www.nysgrange.com/

CAROLINE KARK AWARD

Award available to a Grange member who is preparing for a career working with the deaf, or a deaf individual who is furthering his or her education beyond high school. The recipient must be a New York State resident. The award is based on funds available.

Award: Scholarship for use in freshman year; not renewable. *Number:* varies. *Amount:* varies.

Eligibility Requirements: Applicant must be high school student; planning to enroll or expecting to enroll full- or part-time at a four-year institution or university and resident of New York. Applicant or parent of applicant must be member of Grange Association. Applicant must be hearing impaired. Available to U.S. citizens.

Application Requirements: Application. *Deadline:* April 15.

Contact: Program Manager
New York State Grange
100 Grange Place
Cortland, NY 13045
Phone: 607-756-7553
Fax: 607-756-7757
E-mail: nysgrange@nysgrange.com

SUSAN W. FREESTONE EDUCATION AWARD

Grants for members of Junior Grange and Subordinate Grange in New York State. Students must enroll in an approved two or four-year college in New York State. Second grants available with reapplication.

Award: Scholarship for use in freshman year; renewable. *Number:* 1. *Amount:* $1000.

Eligibility Requirements: Applicant must be high school student; planning to enroll or expecting to enroll full-time at a two-year or four-year institution; resident of New York and studying in New York. Applicant or parent of applicant must be member of Grange Association. Applicant must have 2.5 GPA or higher. Available to U.S. citizens.

Application Requirements: Application, financial need analysis, references, self-addressed stamped envelope, transcript. *Deadline:* April 15.

Contact: Scholarship Committee
New York State Grange
100 Grange Place
Cortland, NY 13045
Phone: 607-756-7553
Fax: 607-756-7757
E-mail: nysgrange@nysgrange.com

NORTHEASTERN LOGGERS' ASSOCIATION INC.

http://www.northernlogger.com/

NORTHEASTERN LOGGERS' ASSOCIATION SCHOLARSHIPS

Scholarships available to those whose family belongs to the Northeastern Loggers' Association or whose family member is an employee of the Industrial and Associate Members of the Northeastern Loggers' Association. Must submit paper on topic of "What it means to grow up in the forest industry."

Award: Scholarship for use in freshman, sophomore, junior, or senior years; not renewable. *Number:* 8. *Amount:* $500–$1000.

Eligibility Requirements: Applicant must be enrolled or expecting to enroll full-time at a two-year or four-year or technical institution or university. Applicant or parent of applicant must be member of Northeastern Loggers Association. Available to U.S. and non-U.S. citizens.

Application Requirements: Application, applicant must enter a contest, essay, transcript. *Deadline:* March 31.

Contact: Mona Lincoln, Director, Training and Safety
Northeastern Loggers' Association Inc.
PO Box 69
Old Forge, NY 13420-0069
Phone: 315-369-3078
Fax: 315-369-3736
E-mail: mona@northernlogger.com

NORTH EAST ROOFING EDUCATIONAL FOUNDATION

http://www.nerca.org/

NORTH EAST ROOFING EDUCATIONAL FOUNDATION SCHOLARSHIP

Applicants must be a member of NERCA, their employees, or their respective immediate family. Immediate family is defined as self, spouse, or child. The child may be natural, legally adopted, or a stepchild. Also must be a high school senior or graduate who plans to enroll in a full-time undergraduate course of study at an accredited two-year or four-year college, university, or vocational-technical school.

Award: Scholarship for use in freshman, sophomore, junior, or senior years; not renewable. *Number:* 11. *Amount:* up to $2000.

Eligibility Requirements: Applicant must be enrolled or expecting to enroll full-time at a two-year or four-year or technical institution or university. Applicant or parent of applicant must be member of North East Roofing Contractors Association. Available to U.S. and Canadian citizens.

Application Requirements: Application, references, self-addressed stamped envelope, transcript. *Deadline:* May 1.

Contact: Patsy Sweeney, Clerk
North East Roofing Educational Foundation
150 Grossman Drive Street, Suite 313
Braintree, MA 02184
Phone: 781-849-0555
Fax: 781-849-3223
E-mail: info@nerca.org

OFFICE AND PROFESSIONAL EMPLOYEES INTERNATIONAL UNION

http://www.opeiu.org/

OFFICE AND PROFESSIONAL EMPLOYEES INTERNATIONAL UNION HOWARD COUGHLIN MEMORIAL SCHOLARSHIP FUND

Scholarship of twelve full-time awards of $6000 and six part-time awards of $2400 is given to undergraduate students. Applicants should be a member or associate member of the Union.

Award: Scholarship for use in freshman, sophomore, junior, or senior years; not renewable. *Number:* 18. *Amount:* $2400–$6000.

Eligibility Requirements: Applicant must be enrolled or expecting to enroll full- or part-time at a two-year or four-year or technical institution or university. Applicant or parent of applicant must be member of Office and Professional Employees International Union. Available to U.S. citizens.

Application Requirements: Application, transcript, SAT/CAT scores. *Deadline:* March 31.

Contact: Mary Mahoney, Secretary-Treasurer
Office and Professional Employees International Union
80 Eighth Avenue, 6th Floor
New York, NY 10011
Phone: 202-393-4464
Fax: 202-887-0910
E-mail: mmahoney@opeiudc.org

OHIO CIVIL SERVICE EMPLOYEES ASSOCIATION

http://www.ocsea.org/

LES BEST SCHOLARSHIP

Scholarships will be awarded to eligible union members, spouses and their dependent children. For more details see web site http://www.ocsea.org.

Award: Scholarship for use in freshman, sophomore, junior, or senior years; not renewable. *Number:* 8–10. *Amount:* $500–$2000.

Eligibility Requirements: Applicant must be enrolled or expecting to enroll full- or part-time at a two-year or four-year or technical institution or university and resident of Ohio. Applicant or parent of applicant must be member of Ohio Civil Service Employee Association. Available to U.S. citizens.

Application Requirements: Application, essay, references, transcript, proof of enrollment. *Deadline:* April 30.

Contact: Customer Service Representative
Ohio Civil Service Employees Association
390 Worthington Road, Suite A
Westerville, OH 43082-8331
Phone: 614-865-4700
Fax: 614-865-4777

OKLAHOMA ALUMNI & ASSOCIATES OF FHA, HERO AND FCCLA INC.

http://www.okfccla.net/

OKLAHOMA ALUMNI & ASSOCIATES OF FHA, HERO AND FCCLA INC. SCHOLARSHIP

One-time award for FCCLA members who will be pursuing a postsecondary education. Must be a resident of Oklahoma. Scholarship value is $1000. Two scholarships are granted.

Award: Scholarship for use in freshman year; not renewable. *Number:* 2. *Amount:* $1000.

Eligibility Requirements: Applicant must be high school student; planning to enroll or expecting to enroll full-time at a two-year or four-year or technical institution or university and resident of Oklahoma. Applicant or parent of applicant must be member of Family, Career and Community Leaders of America. Applicant must have 3.0 GPA or higher. Available to U.S. citizens.

Application Requirements: Application, essay, references, transcript. *Deadline:* March 1.

Contact: Denise Morris, State FCCLA Adviser
Oklahoma Alumni & Associates of FHA, HERO and FCCLA Inc.
1500 West Seventh Avenue
Stillwater, OK 74074
Phone: 405-743-5467
Fax: 405-743-6809
E-mail: dmorr@okcareertech.org

OREGON STUDENT ASSISTANCE COMMISSION

http://www.GetCollegeFunds.org/

AFSCME: AMERICAN FEDERATION OF STATE, COUNTY, AND MUNICIPAL EMPLOYEES COUNCIL # 75 SCHOLARSHIP

Renewable award for active, laid-off, retired, or disabled members in good standing or spouses (including life partners and their children), natural children, or grandchildren of active, laid-off, retired, disabled, or deceased members in good standing. Qualifying members must have been active in AFSCME Council # 75 one year or more as of the March 1 scholarship deadline or have been a member one year or more preceding the date of layoff, death, disability, or retirement. Enrollment of at least half-time is required. FAFSA and essay required. Financial need may or may not be considered.

Award: Scholarship for use in freshman, sophomore, junior, or senior years; renewable. *Number:* varies. *Amount:* varies.

Eligibility Requirements: Applicant must be enrolled or expecting to enroll full- or part-time at a two-year or four-year institution or university. Applicant or parent of applicant must be member of American Federation of State, County, and Municipal Employees. Available to U.S. citizens.

Application Requirements: Application, essay, financial need analysis, transcript, activity chart. *Deadline:* March 1.

Contact: Director of Grant Programs
Oregon Student Assistance Commission
1500 Valley River Drive, Suite 100
Eugene, OR 97401-7020
Phone: 800-452-8807 Ext. 7395

AFSCME: AMERICAN FEDERATION OF STATE, COUNTY, AND MUNICIPAL EMPLOYEES LOCAL 2067 SCHOLARSHIP

Award for active members in good standing or spouses, children, or grandchildren of active members in good standing of Oregon AFSCME Local 2067. Qualifying members must have been active in AFSCME Local 2067 one+ year as of the March scholarship deadline. Oregon residency is not required. FAFSA and essay required. Financial need is not a requirement, but may or may not be considered.

Award: Scholarship for use in freshman, sophomore, junior, or senior years; not renewable. *Number:* varies. *Amount:* varies.

Eligibility Requirements: Applicant must be enrolled or expecting to enroll full- or part-time at a four-year institution or university and resident of Oregon. Applicant or parent of applicant must be member of American Federation of State, County, and Municipal Employees. Applicant must have 2.5 GPA or higher. Available to U.S. citizens.

Application Requirements: Application, essay, financial need analysis, references, transcript, activity chart. *Deadline:* March 1.

Contact: Director of Grant Programs
Oregon Student Assistance Commission
1500 Valley River Drive, Suite 100
Eugene, OR 97401-7020
Phone: 800-452-8807 Ext. 7395

INTERNATIONAL BROTHERHOOD OF ELECTRICAL WORKERS LOCAL 280 SCHOLARSHIP

One-time award available for children or grandchildren of active or retired members of IBEW Local 280. Must be graduating high school seniors enrolling as first-time freshman in any college or university in the U.S. Oregon residency not required. Not based on financial need.

Award: Scholarship for use in freshman year; not renewable. *Amount:* varies.

Eligibility Requirements: Applicant must be enrolled or expecting to enroll full-time at a four-year institution or university. Applicant or parent of applicant must be member of International Brotherhood of Electrical Workers. Available to U.S. citizens.

Application Requirements: Application, essay, transcript. *Deadline:* March 1.

Contact: Director of Grant Programs
Oregon Student Assistance Commission
1500 Valley River Drive, Suite 100
Eugene, OR 97401-7020
Phone: 800-452-8807 Ext. 7395

INTERNATIONAL UNION OF OPERATING ENGINEERS LOCAL 701 SCHOLARSHIP

One-time award available for graduating high school seniors who are children of International Union of Operating Engineers Local 701 members. Not based on financial need. Oregon residency is not required.

Award: Scholarship for use in freshman year; not renewable. *Amount:* varies.

Eligibility Requirements: Applicant must be enrolled or expecting to enroll full-time at a four-year institution or university. Applicant or parent of applicant must be member of International Union of Operating Engineers. Available to U.S. citizens.

Application Requirements: Application, essay, transcript, activities chart. *Deadline:* March 1.

Contact: Director of Grant Programs
Oregon Student Assistance Commission
1500 Valley River Drive, Suite 100
Eugene, OR 97401-7020
Phone: 800-452-8807 Ext. 7395

NORTHWEST AUTOMATIC VENDING ASSOCIATION SCHOLARSHIP

One-time award to recent high school graduates who are first-time freshmen and either children (natural, adopted, or stepchildren) or grandchildren of members or associate members of Northwest Automatic Vending Association. Oregon residency not required.

Award: Scholarship for use in freshman year; not renewable. *Number:* varies. *Amount:* varies.

Eligibility Requirements: Applicant must be high school student and planning to enroll or expecting to enroll full-time at a four-year institution or university. Applicant or parent of applicant must be member of Northwest Automatic Vending Association. Available to U.S. citizens.

Application Requirements: Application, essay, financial need analysis, transcript, activities chart. *Deadline:* March 1.

Contact: Director of Grant Programs
Oregon Student Assistance Commission
1500 Valley River Drive, Suite 100
Eugene, OR 97401-7020
Phone: 800-452-8807 Ext. 7395

OREGON STATE FISCAL ASSOCIATION SCHOLARSHIP

One-time award for OSFA members or their children. Members must enroll in an Oregon public or nonprofit institution at least half-time and must study public administration, finance, economics, or related fields. Children of members must enroll full-time in an Oregon institution and may enter any program of study. Must reapply annually.

Award: Scholarship for use in freshman, sophomore, junior, or senior years; not renewable. *Number:* varies. *Amount:* varies.

Eligibility Requirements: Applicant must be enrolled or expecting to enroll full- or part-time at a two-year or four-year institution; resident of Oregon and studying in Oregon. Applicant or parent of applicant must be member of Oregon State Fiscal Association. Available to U.S. citizens.

Application Requirements: Application, essay, financial need analysis, references, transcript, activity chart. *Deadline:* March 1.

Contact: Director of Grant Programs
Oregon Student Assistance Commission
1500 Valley River Drive, Suite 100
Eugene, OR 97401-7020
Phone: 800-452-8807 Ext. 7395

TEAMSTERS CLYDE C. CROSBY/JOSEPH M. EDGAR MEMORIAL SCHOLARSHIP

Renewable scholarship available for Oregon resident who is a graduating high school senior with a minimum 3.0 cumulative GPA and is a child, or dependent stepchild of an active, retired, disabled, or deceased member of local union affiliated with Teamsters 37. Member must have been active for at least one year. Award may be received for a maximum of twelve quarters. For additional information and application, see web site http://secure.osac.state.or.us.

Award: Scholarship for use in freshman, sophomore, junior, or senior years; renewable. *Number:* varies. *Amount:* varies.

Eligibility Requirements: Applicant must be high school student; planning to enroll or expecting to enroll full-time at a four-year institution and resident of Oregon. Applicant or parent of applicant must be member of Teamsters. Applicant must have 3.0 GPA or higher. Available to U.S. citizens.

Application Requirements: Application, essay, financial need analysis, transcript, activity chart. *Deadline:* March 1.

Contact: Director of Grant Programs
Oregon Student Assistance Commission
1500 Valley River Drive, Suite 100
Eugene, OR 97401-7020
Phone: 800-452-8807 Ext. 7395

TEAMSTERS COUNCIL 37 FEDERAL CREDIT UNION SCHOLARSHIP

One-time award for members (or dependents of members) of Council 37 Federal Credit Union who are active for one year as of the March 1 deadline, in a local that is affiliated with the Joint Council of Teamsters 37. Applicant must have a minimum GPA between 2.0 and 3.0, and be enrolled at least half-time in a two- or four-year college or university in the U.S.

Award: Scholarship for use in freshman, sophomore, junior, or senior years; not renewable. *Number:* varies. *Amount:* varies.

Eligibility Requirements: Applicant must be enrolled or expecting to enroll full- or part-time at a two-year or four-year institution or university. Applicant or parent of applicant must be member of Teamsters. Available to U.S. citizens.

Application Requirements: Application, financial need analysis, references, transcript. *Deadline:* March 1.

Contact: Director of Grant Programs
Oregon Student Assistance Commission
1500 Valley River Drive, Suite 100
Eugene, OR 97401-7020
Phone: 800-452-8807 Ext. 7395

TEAMSTERS LOCAL 305 SCHOLARSHIP

Renewable award for graduating Oregon high school seniors who are children or dependent stepchildren of active, retired, disabled, or deceased members of Local 305 of the Joint Council of Teamsters #37. Members must have been active for at least one year. Not based on financial need. Oregon state residency is not required.

Award: Scholarship for use in freshman, sophomore, junior, or senior years; renewable. *Amount:* varies.

Eligibility Requirements: Applicant must be enrolled or expecting to enroll full-time at a four-year institution or university. Applicant or parent of applicant must be member of Teamsters. Available to U.S. citizens.

Application Requirements: Application, essay, transcript. *Deadline:* March 1.

Contact: Director of Grant Programs
Oregon Student Assistance Commission
1500 Valley River Drive, Suite 100
Eugene, OR 97401-7020
Phone: 800-452-8807 Ext. 7395

PENNSYLVANIA AFL-CIO

http://www.paaflcio.org/

PA AFL-CIO UNIONISM IN AMERICA ESSAY CONTEST

Contest consists of three categories: high school seniors, students currently attending an accredited postsecondary institution, and affiliated members attending an accredited postsecondary institution. Must be a U.S. citizen.

Award: Prize for use in freshman, sophomore, junior, or senior years; not renewable. *Number:* 9. *Amount:* $500–$2000.

Eligibility Requirements: Applicant must be enrolled or expecting to enroll full-time at a two-year or four-year or technical institution or university. Applicant or parent of applicant must be member of AFL-CIO. Available to U.S. citizens.

Application Requirements: Application, applicant must enter a contest, references, hard copy, CD copy of essay. *Deadline:* January 31.

Contact: Carl Dillinger, Education Director
Pennsylvania AFL-CIO
231 State Street
Harrisburg, PA 17101-1110
Phone: 717-231-2843
Fax: 717-238-8541
E-mail: cdillinger@paaflcio.org

PENNSYLVANIA FEDERATION OF DEMOCRATIC WOMEN INC.

http://www.pfdw.org/

PENNSYLVANIA FEDERATION OF DEMOCRATIC WOMEN INC. ANNUAL SCHOLARSHIP AWARDS

Award of $1000 for any female resident of Pennsylvania who is a junior at an accredited college or university and is a registered Democrat. Applicants must possess a Democratic Party family background and be an active participant in activities of the Democratic Party.

Award: Scholarship for use in senior year; not renewable. *Number:* 2–6. *Amount:* $1000.

Eligibility Requirements: Applicant must be enrolled or expecting to enroll full-time at a four-year institution or university; female and resident of Pennsylvania. Applicant or parent of applicant must be member of Democratic Party. Available to U.S. citizens.

Application Requirements: Application, essay, references, transcript. *Deadline:* May 1.

Contact: Bonita Hannis, Scholarship Chair
Pennsylvania Federation of Democratic Women Inc.
36 Betts Lane
Lock Haven, PA 17745
Phone: 570-769-7175
E-mail: behannis@kcnet.org

PENNSYLVANIA YOUTH FOUNDATION

http://www.pmyf.org/

PENNSYLVANIA MASONIC YOUTH FOUNDATION EDUCATIONAL ENDOWMENT FUND SCHOLARSHIPS

Grants for children, stepchildren, grandchildren, siblings, or dependents of members in good standing of a Pennsylvania Masonic Lodge, or members in good standing of a PA Masonic-sponsored youth group. Applicants must be high school graduates or high school seniors pursuing a college education. Minimum GPA 3.0.

Award: Grant for use in freshman, sophomore, junior, or senior years; not renewable. *Number:* varies. *Amount:* $1000–$3000.

Eligibility Requirements: Applicant must be enrolled or expecting to enroll full-time at a two-year or four-year or technical institution or university. Applicant or parent of applicant must be member of Freemasons. Applicant must have 3.0 GPA or higher. Available to U.S. and non-U.S. citizens.

Application Requirements: Application, essay, financial need analysis, test scores, transcript, proof of relationship to a Pennsylvania Masonic or membership in a Pennsylvania Masonic-sponsored youth group. *Deadline:* March 15.

Contact: Amy Nace, Executive Assistant
Pennsylvania Youth Foundation
1244 Bainbridge Road
Elizabethtown, PA 17022-9423
Phone: 717-367-1536 Ext. 2
E-mail: pmyf@pagrandlodge.org

PHILIPINO-AMERICAN ASSOCIATION OF NEW ENGLAND

http://www.pamas.org/

PAMAS RESTRICTED SCHOLARSHIP AWARD

Award of $500 for any sons or daughters of PAMAS members who are currently active in PAMAS projects and activities. Must be of Filipino descent, a resident of New England, a high school senior at the time of award, and have college acceptance letter from accredited institution.

Minimum of 3.3 GPA required. For application details visit http://www.pamas.org.

Award: Scholarship for use in freshman year; not renewable. *Number:* 1. *Amount:* $500.

Eligibility Requirements: Applicant must be Asian/Pacific Islander; high school student; planning to enroll or expecting to enroll full-time at a four-year institution or university and resident of Connecticut, Maine, Massachusetts, New Hampshire, Rhode Island, or Vermont. Applicant or parent of applicant must be member of Philipino-American Association. Available to U.S. citizens.

Application Requirements: Application, essay, references, transcript, college acceptance letter. *Deadline:* May 31.

Contact: Amanda Kalb, First Vice President
Philipino-American Association of New England
Quincy Post Office
PO Box 690372
Quincy, MA 02269-0372
Phone: 617-471-3513
E-mail: balic2ss@comcast.net

PHI SIGMA KAPPA INTERNATIONAL HEADQUARTERS

http://www.phisigmakappa.org/

WENDEROTH UNDERGRADUATE SCHOLARSHIP

Available to sophomores and juniors on the basis of academic criteria. Must submit an essay and letter of recommendation along with the application.

Award: Scholarship for use in sophomore or junior years; not renewable. *Number:* 1–4. *Amount:* $1750–$4000.

Eligibility Requirements: Applicant must be enrolled or expecting to enroll full-time at a four-year institution or university. Applicant or parent of applicant must be member of Phi Sigma Kappa. Available to U.S. and non-U.S. citizens.

Application Requirements: Application, essay, photo, resume, references, transcript. *Deadline:* January 31.

Contact: Michael Carey, Executive Director
Phi Sigma Kappa International Headquarters
2925 East 96th Street
Indianapolis, IN 46240
Phone: 317-573-5420
Fax: 317-573-5430
E-mail: michael@phisigmakappa.org

ZETA SCHOLARSHIP

Scholarships are available following a generous gift to the Phi Sigma Kappa Foundation from the Zeta Alumni Association. Phi Sig or a child of a Phi Sig having minimum 3.0 GPA are eligible to apply.

Award: Scholarship for use in freshman, sophomore, junior, senior, or graduate years; not renewable. *Number:* 2. *Amount:* $2500.

Eligibility Requirements: Applicant must be enrolled or expecting to enroll full-time at a four-year institution or university. Applicant or parent of applicant must be member of Phi Sigma Kappa. Applicant must have 3.0 GPA or higher. Available to U.S. citizens.

Application Requirements: Application, photo, resume, references, test scores, transcript. *Deadline:* January 31.

Contact: Scholarship Program Coordinator
Phi Sigma Kappa International Headquarters
2925 East 96th Street
Indianapolis, IN 46240
Phone: 317-573-5420
Fax: 317-573-5430

PHI SIGMA PI NATIONAL HONOR FRATERNITY

http://www.phisigmapi.org/

RICHARD CECIL TODD AND CLAUDA PENNOCK TODD TRIPOD SCHOLARSHIP

Scholarship to promote the future academic opportunity of brothers (members) of the fraternity, who have excelled in embodying the ideals of scholarship, leadership, and fellowship. One-time award for full-time student, sophomore level or higher, with minimum 3.0 GPA.

Award: Scholarship for use in sophomore, junior, or senior years; not renewable. *Number:* 1. *Amount:* up to $1500.

Eligibility Requirements: Applicant must be enrolled or expecting to enroll full-time at a two-year or four-year or technical institution or university and must have an interest in leadership. Applicant must have 3.0 GPA or higher. Available to U.S. and non-U.S. citizens.

Application Requirements: Application, driver's license, essay, references, transcript. *Deadline:* April 15.

Contact: Suzanne Schaffer, Executive Director
Phi Sigma Pi National Honor Fraternity
2119 Ambassador Circle
Lancaster, PA 17603
Phone: 717-299-4710
Fax: 717-390-3054
E-mail: schaffer@phisigmapi.org

PONY OF THE AMERICAS CLUB

http://www.poac.org/

PONY OF THE AMERICAS SCHOLARSHIP

Two to four renewable awards that may be used for any year or any institution but must be for full-time undergraduate study. Application and transcript required. Award restricted to those who have interest in animal or agricultural competition and active involvement in Pony of the Americas.

Award: Scholarship for use in freshman, sophomore, junior, or senior years; not renewable. *Number:* 2–4. *Amount:* $500–$1000.

Eligibility Requirements: Applicant must be enrolled or expecting to enroll full- or part-time at a two-year or four-year or technical institution or university and must have an interest in animal/agricultural competition. Applicant or parent of applicant must be member of Pony of the Americas Club. Available to U.S. and non-U.S. citizens.

Application Requirements: Application, applicant must enter a contest, driver's license, essay, references, transcript. *Deadline:* March 1.

Contact: Lynda Corn, Scholarship Administrator
Pony of the Americas Club
3828 South Emerson Avenue
Indianapolis, IN 46203
Phone: 317-788-0107 Ext. 2
Fax: 317-788-8974
E-mail: poac@poac.org

PROFESSIONAL BOWLERS ASSOCIATION

http://www.pba.com/

PROFESSIONAL BOWLERS ASSOCIATION BILLY WELU MEMORIAL SCHOLARSHIP

One-time award available to a currently enrolled student who demonstrates outstanding academic and bowling achievement. Must be a member of USBC. Must have minimum 2.5 GPA.

Award: Scholarship for use in freshman, sophomore, junior, or senior years; not renewable. *Number:* 1. *Amount:* $1000.

Eligibility Requirements: Applicant must be enrolled or expecting to enroll full- or part-time at a four-year institution or university and must have an interest in bowling. Applicant or parent of applicant must be member of Young American Bowling Alliance. Applicant must have 2.5 GPA or higher. Available to U.S. citizens.

Application Requirements: Application, essay, references, transcript. *Deadline:* May 31.

Contact: Scholarship Administrator
Professional Bowlers Association
719 Second Avenue, Suite 701
Seattle, WA 98104
Phone: 206-332-9688
Fax: 206-332-9722

PROFESSIONAL HORSEMEN'S SCHOLARSHIP FUND INC.

http://www.nationalpha.com/

PROFESSIONAL HORSEMEN'S SCHOLARSHIP FUND

Scholarship provides financial assistance from a fund established for children of professional members or professional members of more than two years who are enrolled in an approved school for the advancement of their education beyond the secondary level.

Award: Scholarship for use in freshman, sophomore, junior, senior, graduate, or postgraduate years; not renewable. *Number:* 10–20. *Amount:* $500–$1000.

Eligibility Requirements: Applicant must be enrolled or expecting to enroll full-time at a two-year or four-year or technical institution or university. Applicant or parent of applicant must be member of Professional Horsemen Association. Available to U.S. citizens.

Application Requirements: Application, essay, financial need analysis, references, transcript. *Deadline:* May 1.

Contact: Mrs. Ann Grenci, Chairman, Scholarship Committee
    Phone: 561-707-9094
    Fax: 914-206-4574
    E-mail: foxhill33@aol.com

PROJECT BEST SCHOLARSHIP FUND

http://www.projectbest.com/

PROJECT BEST SCHOLARSHIP

One-time award of $1000 to $2000 for employees or children or spouses of employees working for a company or labor union in the construction industry that is affiliated with Project BEST. Must be residents of West Virginia, Pennsylvania, or Ohio and attend a West Virginia or Ohio postsecondary institution. Must be U.S. citizens.

Award: Scholarship for use in freshman, sophomore, junior, senior, or graduate years; renewable. *Number:* 11–22. *Amount:* $1000–$2000.

Eligibility Requirements: Applicant must be enrolled or expecting to enroll full-time at a two-year or four-year institution or university; resident of Ohio, Pennsylvania, or West Virginia and studying in Ohio or West Virginia. Applicant or parent of applicant must be member of AFL-CIO. Applicant or parent of applicant must have employment or volunteer experience in construction. Available to U.S. citizens.

Application Requirements: Application. *Deadline:* continuous.

Contact: Mary Jo Klempa, Director
    Project BEST Scholarship Fund
    21 Armory Drive
    Wheeling, WV 26003
    Phone: 304-242-0520
    Fax: 304-242-7261
    E-mail: best2003@swave.net

PUEBLO OF ISLETA, DEPARTMENT OF EDUCATION

http://www.isletapueblo.com/

HIGHER EDUCATION SUPPLEMENTAL SCHOLARSHIP ISLETA PUEBLO HIGHER EDUCATION DEPARTMENT

Applicants must be students seeking a postsecondary degree. The degree granting institution must be a nationally accredited vocational or postsecondary institution offering a certificate, associate, bachelors, master's or doctorate degree. Enrolled tribal members of the Isleta Pueblo may apply for this scholarship if they also apply for additional scholarships from different sources. Deadlines: April 1 for summer, November 1 for spring and July 1 for fall.

Award: Scholarship for use in freshman, sophomore, junior, senior, graduate, or postgraduate years; renewable. *Number:* varies. *Amount:* varies.

Eligibility Requirements: Applicant must be American Indian/Alaska Native and enrolled or expecting to enroll full- or part-time at a two-year or four-year or technical institution or university. Applicant or parent of applicant must be member of Ice Skating Institute. Available to U.S. citizens.

Application Requirements: Application, financial need analysis, transcript, certificate of Indian blood, class schedule. *Deadline:* varies.

Contact: Higher Education Director
    Pueblo of Isleta, Department of Education
    PO Box 1270
    Isleta, NM 87022
    Phone: 505-869-2680
    Fax: 505-869-7690
    E-mail: isletahighered@yahoo.com

RAILWAY SUPPLY INSTITUTE

http://www.rsiweb.org/

RSI UNDERGRADUATE SCHOLARSHIP PROGRAM

Scholarship available to a full-time student enrolled in a four- or five-year program leading to a bachelor's degree. Applicants must be 22 years old or under and be the dependant son, daughter, grandson or granddaughter of a railroad employee, who is a member of one of the mechanical associations listed in the web site. For application and association list go to http://www.rsiweb.org/scholarship.

Award: Scholarship for use in sophomore, junior, or senior years; not renewable. *Number:* 4. *Amount:* $3000.

Eligibility Requirements: Applicant must be age 22 or under and enrolled or expecting to enroll full-time at a four-year institution or university. Applicant or parent of applicant must be member of Mutual Benefit Society. Available to U.S. and Canadian citizens.

Application Requirements: Application, essay, resume, references, transcript. *Deadline:* April 2.

Contact: Thomas Simpson, Executive Director
    Railway Supply Institute
    50 F Street NW, Suite 7030
    Washington, DC 20001
    Phone: 202-347-4664
    E-mail: rsi@railwaysupply.org

RECORDING FOR THE BLIND & DYSLEXIC

http://www.rfbd.org/

MARION HUBER LEARNING THROUGH LISTENING AWARDS

Awards presented to RFB&D members who are high school seniors with learning disabilities, in recognition of extraordinary leadership, scholarship, enterprise and service to others. Must have minimum 3.0 GPA.

Award: Prize for use in freshman year; not renewable. *Number:* 6. *Amount:* $2000–$6000.

Eligibility Requirements: Applicant must be high school student; planning to enroll or expecting to enroll full-time at a two-year or four-year institution and must have an interest in leadership. Applicant or parent of applicant must be member of Recording for the Blind and Dyslexic. Applicant or parent of applicant must have employment or volunteer experience in community service. Applicant must be learning disabled. Applicant must have 3.0 GPA or higher. Available to U.S. citizens.

Application Requirements: Application, essay, references, transcript. *Deadline:* March 3.

Contact: Julie Haggith, Strategic Communications Department
    Recording for the Blind & Dyslexic
    20 Roszel Road
    Princeton, NJ 08540
    Phone: 609-520-8044
    Fax: 609-520-7990
    E-mail: jhaggith@rfbd.org

MARY P. OENSLAGER SCHOLASTIC ACHIEVEMENT AWARDS

Award presented to RFB&D members who are college seniors and blind or visually impaired, in recognition of extraordinary leadership, scholarship, enterprise, and service to others.

Award: Prize for use in senior or graduate years; not renewable. *Number:* up to 9. *Amount:* $1000–$6000.

Eligibility Requirements: Applicant must be enrolled or expecting to enroll full-time at a four-year institution or university and must have an interest in leadership. Applicant or parent of applicant must be member of Recording for the Blind and Dyslexic. Applicant or parent of applicant must have employment or volunteer experience in community service.

Applicant must be visually impaired. Applicant must have 3.0 GPA or higher. Available to U.S. citizens.

Application Requirements: Application, essay, references, transcript. *Deadline:* April 14.

Contact: Julie Haggith, Strategic Communications Department
Recording for the Blind & Dyslexic
20 Roszel Road
Princeton, NJ 08540
Phone: 609-520-8044
Fax: 609-520-7990
E-mail: jhaggith@rfbd.org

RED ANGUS ASSOCIATION OF AMERICA

http://www.redangus.org/

4 RAAA/JUNIOR RED ANGUS SCHOLARSHIP

Scholarship of $500 given to active members of the National Junior Red Angus Association. Must be high school seniors or college underclassmen.

Award: Scholarship for use in freshman or sophomore years; not renewable. *Number:* 2. *Amount:* $500.

Eligibility Requirements: Applicant must be enrolled or expecting to enroll full-time at a two-year or four-year institution or university. Applicant or parent of applicant must be member of National Junior Red Angus Association. Available to U.S. citizens.

Application Requirements: Application, photo, references, transcript. *Deadline:* March 31.

Contact: Betty Grimshaw, Association Administrative Director
Red Angus Association of America
4201 North Interstate 35
Denton, TX 76207-3415
Phone: 940-387-3502
Fax: 940-383-4036
E-mail: betty@redangus.org

DEE SONSTEGARD MEMORIAL SCHOLARSHIP

Scholarship of $500 given to active members of the National Junior Red Angus Association. Must be high school seniors or college underclassmen.

Award: Scholarship for use in freshman or sophomore years; not renewable. *Number:* 2. *Amount:* $500.

Eligibility Requirements: Applicant must be enrolled or expecting to enroll full-time at a two-year or four-year institution or university. Applicant or parent of applicant must be member of National Junior Red Angus Association. Available to U.S. citizens.

Application Requirements: Application, photo, references, transcript. *Deadline:* March 31.

Contact: Betty Grimshaw, Association Administrative Director
Red Angus Association of America
4201 North Interstate 35
Denton, TX 76207-3415
Phone: 940-387-3502
Fax: 940-383-4036
E-mail: betty@redangus.org

FARM AND RANCH CONNECTION SCHOLARSHIP

Scholarship of $500 given to active members of the National Junior Red Angus Association. Must be high school seniors or college underclassmen.

Award: Scholarship for use in freshman or sophomore years; not renewable. *Number:* 1. *Amount:* $500.

Eligibility Requirements: Applicant must be enrolled or expecting to enroll full-time at a two-year or four-year institution or university. Applicant or parent of applicant must be member of National Junior Red Angus Association. Available to U.S. citizens.

Application Requirements: Application, photo, references, transcript. *Deadline:* March 31.

Contact: Betty Grimshaw, Association Administrative Director
Red Angus Association of America
4201 North Interstate 35
Denton, TX 76207-3415
Phone: 940-387-3502
Fax: 940-383-4036
E-mail: betty@redangus.org

LEONARD A. LORENZEN MEMORIAL SCHOLARSHIP

Scholarship of $500 given to active members of the National Junior Red Angus Association. Must be high school seniors or college underclassmen.

Award: Scholarship for use in freshman or sophomore years; not renewable. *Number:* 2. *Amount:* $500.

Eligibility Requirements: Applicant must be enrolled or expecting to enroll full-time at a two-year or four-year institution or university. Applicant or parent of applicant must be member of National Junior Red Angus Association. Available to U.S. citizens.

Application Requirements: Application, photo, references, transcript. *Deadline:* March 31.

Contact: Betty Grimshaw, Association Administrative Director
Red Angus Association of America
4201 North Interstate 35
Denton, TX 76207-3415
Phone: 940-387-3502
Fax: 940-383-4036
E-mail: betty@redangus.org

THE RESERVE OFFICERS ASSOCIATION

http://www.roa.org/

HENRY J. REILLY MEMORIAL SCHOLARSHIP-HIGH SCHOOL SENIORS AND FIRST YEAR FRESHMEN

One-time award for high school seniors or college freshmen who are U.S. citizens and children or grandchildren of active members of the Reserve Officers Association. Must demonstrate leadership, have minimum 3.0 GPA and 1250 on the SAT. Must submit sponsor verification. College freshmen must submit college transcript.

Award: Scholarship for use in freshman year; not renewable. *Number:* 25–30. *Amount:* $1000.

Eligibility Requirements: Applicant must be enrolled or expecting to enroll full-time at a four-year institution or university and must have an interest in leadership. Applicant or parent of applicant must be member of Reserve Officers Association. Applicant must have 3.0 GPA or higher. Available to U.S. citizens. Applicant or parent must meet one or more of the following requirements: general military experience; retired from active duty; disabled or killed as a result of military service; prisoner of war; or missing in action.

Application Requirements: Application, essay, test scores, transcript. *Deadline:* May 15.

Contact: Keith Weller, Executive Administrator
The Reserve Officers Association
One Constitution Avenue, NE
Washington, DC 20002-5655
Phone: 202-646-7718
E-mail: scholarship@roa.org

HENRY J. REILLY MEMORIAL UNDERGRADUATE SCHOLARSHIP PROGRAM FOR COLLEGE ATTENDEES

One-time award of $1,000 for members and children or grandchildren of members of the Reserve Officers Association or its Auxiliary. Must be a U.S. citizen, 26 years old or younger, and enrolled at an accredited four-year institution. Must submit sponsor verification. Minimum 3.0 GPA required. Submit SAT or ACT scores; contact for score requirements.

Award: Scholarship for use in freshman, sophomore, junior, or senior years; not renewable. *Number:* 25–30. *Amount:* $1000.

Eligibility Requirements: Applicant must be age 26 or under and enrolled or expecting to enroll full-time at a two-year or four-year institution or university. Applicant or parent of applicant must be member of Reserve Officers Association. Applicant must have 3.0 GPA or higher. Available to U.S. citizens. Applicant or parent must meet one or more of the following requirements: general military experience; retired from active duty; disabled or killed as a result of military service; prisoner of war; or missing in action.

Application Requirements: Application, essay, test scores, transcript, sponsor verification. *Deadline:* May 15.

Contact: Keith Weller, Executive Administrator
The Reserve Officers Association
One Constitution Avenue, NE
Washington, DC 20002-5655
Phone: 202-646-7718
E-mail: scholarship@roa.org

RETAIL, WHOLESALE AND DEPARTMENT STORE UNION

http://www.rwdsu.org/

ALVIN E. HEAPS MEMORIAL SCHOLARSHIP

Scholarship for RWDSU members or members of an RWDSU family. Applicant must submit 500-word essay on the benefits of union membership. See web site for application http://www.rwdsu.info/heapss-cholar.htm.

Award: Scholarship for use in freshman, sophomore, junior, or senior years; not renewable. *Number:* varies. *Amount:* varies.

Eligibility Requirements: Applicant must be enrolled or expecting to enroll full- or part-time at a two-year or four-year institution or university. Applicant or parent of applicant must be member of Retail, Wholesale and Department Store Union. Available to U.S. citizens.

Application Requirements: Application, essay, transcript. *Deadline:* varies.

Contact: Scholarship Committee
Retail, Wholesale and Department Store Union
30 East 29th Street
New York, NY 10016
Phone: 212-684-5300
Fax: 212-779-2809

RHODE ISLAND FOUNDATION

http://www.rifoundation.org/

EDWARD LEON DUHAMEL FREEMASONS SCHOLARSHIP

Applicants must be descendants of members of Franklin Lodge or descendants of other Freemasons in Rhode Island. Must be accepted into an accredited postsecondary institution. Must demonstrate scholastic achievement, financial need and good citizenship.

Award: Scholarship for use in freshman, sophomore, junior, or senior years; renewable. *Amount:* $500–$1000.

Eligibility Requirements: Applicant must be enrolled or expecting to enroll full-time at a four-year institution or university. Applicant or parent of applicant must be member of Freemasons. Available to U.S. citizens.

Application Requirements: Application, essay, financial need analysis, self-addressed stamped envelope, transcript. *Deadline:* varies.

Contact: Libby Monahan, Funds Administrator
Rhode Island Foundation
One Union Station
Providence, RI 02903
Phone: 401-274-4564 Ext. 3117
E-mail: libbym@rifoundation.org

SCREEN ACTORS' GUILD FOUNDATION

http://www.sagfoundation.org/

JOHN L. DALES SCHOLARSHIP PROGRAM

Applicant must have ten vested years of pension credits with the Screen Actors Guild or lifetime earnings of $150,000. Must be U.S. citizen. Scholarship amount ranges between $3000 and $5000. Consult office or web site for more information.

Award: Scholarship for use in freshman, sophomore, junior, senior, graduate, or postgraduate years; not renewable. *Number:* 1–16. *Amount:* $3000–$4000.

Eligibility Requirements: Applicant must be high school student and planning to enroll or expecting to enroll full-time at a two-year or four-year institution or university. Applicant or parent of applicant must be member of Screen Actors' Guild. Available to U.S. citizens.

Application Requirements: Application, essay, financial need analysis, resume, references, test scores, transcript. *Deadline:* March 15.

Contact: Davidson Lloyd, Managing Director
Screen Actors' Guild Foundation
5757 Wilshire Boulevard, Suite 124
Los Angeles, CA 90036-3600
Phone: 323-549-6649
E-mail: dlloyd@sag.org

SCREEN ACTORS GUILD FOUNDATION/JOHN L. DALES SCHOLARSHIP FUND (STANDARD)

Applicant must be a member of the Screen Actors Guild or the child of a member of SAG. Member under the age of twenty-one must have been a member of SAG for five years and have a lifetime earnings of $30,000. Parent of an applicant must have ten vested years of pension credits OR lifetime earnings of $150,000. Consult office or web site for more information. Number and amount of awards vary.

Award: Scholarship for use in freshman, sophomore, junior, senior, graduate, or postgraduate years; not renewable. *Number:* 100–125. *Amount:* $3000–$5000.

Eligibility Requirements: Applicant must be enrolled or expecting to enroll full-time at a two-year or four-year or technical institution or university. Applicant or parent of applicant must be member of Screen Actors' Guild. Available to U.S. citizens.

Application Requirements: Application, essay, financial need analysis, resume, references, test scores, transcript. *Deadline:* March 15.

Contact: Davidson Lloyd, Managing Director
Screen Actors' Guild Foundation
5757 Wilshire Boulevard, Suite 124
Los Angeles, CA 90036-3600
Phone: 323-549-6649
E-mail: dlloyd@sag.org

SEMINOLE TRIBE OF FLORIDA

http://www.seminoletribe.com/

SEMINOLE TRIBE OF FLORIDA BILLY L. CYPRESS SCHOLARSHIP PROGRAM

Awards full scholarships to applicants who meet membership requirements (must have a membership number). Applicant must belong to Seminole tribe of Florida to be eligible. Must maintain a 2.0 GPA with 12 semester credit hours earned each semester.

Award: Scholarship for use in freshman, sophomore, junior, senior, graduate, or postgraduate years; renewable. *Number:* 75. *Amount:* varies.

Eligibility Requirements: Applicant must be American Indian/Alaska Native and enrolled or expecting to enroll full- or part-time at a two-year or four-year institution or university. Applicant or parent of applicant must be member of Teamsters. Available to U.S. citizens.

Application Requirements: Application, transcript, acceptance letter from university. *Deadline:* varies.

Contact: Linda Iley, Higher Education Adviser
Seminole Tribe of Florida
6300 Stirling Road
Hollywood, FL 33024-2153
Phone: 954-989-6840 Ext. 10540
Fax: 954-233-9545
E-mail: eiley@semtribe.com

SERVICE EMPLOYEES INTERNATIONAL UNION-CALIFORNIA STATE COUNCIL OF SERVICE EMPLOYEES

http://www.seiuca.org/

CHARLES HARDY MEMORIAL SCHOLARSHIP AWARDS

Renewable $1000 award for California residents. For full-time study only. Must be SEIU members or children of members. For recent affiliates to SEIU, you must have been a member of the association for three years.

Award: Scholarship for use in freshman year; renewable. *Number:* 1–4. *Amount:* $1000.

Eligibility Requirements: Applicant must be high school student; planning to enroll or expecting to enroll full-time at a two-year or four-

year institution or university and resident of California. Applicant or parent of applicant must be member of Service Employees International Union. Available to U.S. citizens.

Application Requirements: Application, online test. *Deadline:* April 1.

Contact: Scholarship Committee
Service Employees International Union-California State
Council of Service Employees
1313 L Street, NW
Washington, DC 20005
Phone: 800-846-1561

SERVICE EMPLOYEES INTERNATIONAL UNION (SEIU)

http://www.seiu.org/

SEIU JESSE JACKSON SCHOLARSHIP PROGRAM

Renewable scholarship of $5000 given to a student whose work and aspirations for economic and social justice reflect the values and accomplishments of the Rev. Jackson.

Award: Scholarship for use in freshman, sophomore, junior, or senior years; renewable. *Number:* 1. *Amount:* $5000.

Eligibility Requirements: Applicant must be enrolled or expecting to enroll full-time at a four-year institution or university. Applicant or parent of applicant must be member of Service Employees International Union. Available to U.S. citizens.

Application Requirements: Application, essay. *Deadline:* March 1.

Contact: c/o Scholarship Program Administrators, Inc.
Service Employees International Union (SEIU)
PO Box 23737
Nashville, TN 37202-3737
Phone: 615-320-3149
Fax: 615-320-3151
E-mail: info@spaprog.com

SEIU JOHN GEAGAN SCHOLARSHIP

Scholarship to SEIU members or their children or SEIU local union staff. Priority will be given to those applicants who are not served by traditional education institutions-typically adults who have been in the workforce and have decided to go, or return to, college.

Award: Scholarship for use in freshman, sophomore, junior, or senior years; not renewable. *Number:* 1. *Amount:* $2500.

Eligibility Requirements: Applicant must be enrolled or expecting to enroll full-time at a two-year or four-year or technical institution or university. Applicant or parent of applicant must be member of Service Employees International Union. Available to U.S. citizens.

Application Requirements: Application, essay. *Deadline:* March 1.

Contact: c/o Scholarship Program Administrators, Inc.
Service Employees International Union (SEIU)
PO Box 23737
Nashville, TN 37202-3737
Phone: 615-320-3149
Fax: 615-320-3151
E-mail: info@spaprog.com

SEIU NORA PIORE SCHOLARSHIP PROGRAM

Renewable award of $4375 to SEIU members enrolled full-time in an undergraduate study. Applicant's financial need will be considered during the selection process.

Award: Scholarship for use in freshman, sophomore, junior, or senior years; renewable. *Number:* 1. *Amount:* $4375.

Eligibility Requirements: Applicant must be enrolled or expecting to enroll full-time at a four-year institution or university. Applicant or parent of applicant must be member of Service Employees International Union. Available to U.S. citizens.

Application Requirements: Application. *Deadline:* March 1.

Contact: c/o Scholarship Program Administrators, Inc.
Service Employees International Union (SEIU)
PO Box 23737
Nashville, TN 37202-3737
Phone: 615-320-3149
Fax: 615-320-3151
E-mail: info@spaprog.com

SEIU SCHOLARSHIP PROGRAM

Fifteen $1000 scholarships available in annual installments for up to four years. Applicants must graduate from a high school or GED program by August. Must be enrolled as a full-time college freshman by the fall semester at an accredited, four-year college or university.

Award: Scholarship for use in freshman year; renewable. *Number:* 15. *Amount:* $1000.

Eligibility Requirements: Applicant must be high school student and planning to enroll or expecting to enroll full-time at a four-year institution or university. Applicant or parent of applicant must be member of Service Employees International Union. Available to U.S. citizens.

Application Requirements: Application. *Deadline:* March 1.

Contact: c/o Scholarship Program Administrators, Inc.
Service Employees International Union (SEIU)
PO Box 23737
Nashville, TN 37202-3737
Phone: 615-320-3149
Fax: 615-320-3151
E-mail: info@spaprog.com

SIGMA ALPHA MU

http://www.sam.org/default.asp/

UNDERGRADUATE ACHIEVEMENT AWARDS

Scholarship for seniors or juniors of undergraduate students enrolled full-time study. Must be member of Sigma Alpha Mu Foundation. Scholarship value varies.

Award: Scholarship for use in junior or senior years; not renewable. *Number:* 2. *Amount:* varies.

Eligibility Requirements: Applicant must be enrolled or expecting to enroll full-time at a four-year institution or university. Applicant or parent of applicant must be member of Sigma Alpha Mu Foundation. Available to U.S. citizens.

Application Requirements: Application, transcript. *Deadline:* March 1.

Contact: Bill Schwartz, Executive Director
Sigma Alpha Mu
9245 North Meridian, Suite 105
Indianapolis, IN 46260
Phone: 317-846-0600
Fax: 317-846-9462
E-mail: bill@sam.org

YOUNG SCHOLARS PROGRAM

Scholarship for candidates achieving a 3.75 GPA (or equivalent) for courses taken in the academic term of the undergraduate study. Must be member of Sigma Alpha Mu Foundation. Deadline varies.

Award: Scholarship for use in freshman, sophomore, junior, or senior years; not renewable. *Number:* varies. *Amount:* $200.

Eligibility Requirements: Applicant must be enrolled or expecting to enroll full-time at a four-year institution or university. Applicant or parent of applicant must be member of Sigma Alpha Mu Foundation. Applicant must have 3.5 GPA or higher. Available to U.S. citizens.

Application Requirements: Application, transcript. *Deadline:* varies.

Contact: Bill Schwartz, Executive Director
Sigma Alpha Mu
9245 North Meridian, Suite 105
Indianapolis, IN 46260
Phone: 317-846-0600
Fax: 317-846-9462
E-mail: bill@sam.org

SIGMA CHI FOUNDATION

http://www.sigmachi.org/

GENERAL SCHOLARSHIP GRANTS

Applicants must have completed three semesters (or four quarters) of undergraduate study to be considered for current year awards. Funds are available for tuition/fees payments only.

Award: Scholarship for use in sophomore, junior, or senior years; not renewable. *Number:* varies. *Amount:* varies.

Eligibility Requirements: Applicant must be enrolled or expecting to enroll full-time at a four-year institution or university and male.

Applicant or parent of applicant must be member of Sigma Chi Fraternity. Available to U.S. and non-U.S. citizens.

Application Requirements: Application, financial need analysis, references, transcript. *Deadline:* April 13.

Contact: Chadd Montgomery, Associate Director Accountability
Sigma Chi Foundation
1714 Hinman Avenue
PO Box 469
Evanston, IL 60201-0469
Phone: 847-869-3655
Fax: 847-869-4906
E-mail: chadd.montgomery@sigmachi.org

ORDER OF THE SCROLL AWARD

Awarded to undergraduates who have been nominated by fellow chapter members for the outstanding direction of the chapter's educational program. Must be member of Sigma Chi.

Award: Scholarship for use in sophomore, junior, or senior years; not renewable. *Number:* varies. *Amount:* $1000.

Eligibility Requirements: Applicant must be enrolled or expecting to enroll full-time at a four-year institution or university and male. Applicant or parent of applicant must be member of Sigma Chi Fraternity. Available to U.S. and non-U.S. citizens.

Application Requirements: Application, financial need analysis, references, transcript. *Deadline:* April 13.

Contact: Chadd Montgomery, Associate Director Accountability
Sigma Chi Foundation
1714 Hinman Avenue
PO Box 469
Evanston, IL 60201-0469
Phone: 847-869-3655
Fax: 847-869-4906
E-mail: chadd.montgomery@sigmachi.org

SLOVAK GYMNASTIC UNION SOKOL, USA

http://www.sokolusa.org/

SLOVAK GYMNASTIC UNION SOKOL, USA/MILAN GETTING SCHOLARSHIP

Available to members of SOKOL, U.S.A who have been in good standing for at least three years. Must have plans to attend college. Renewable for a maximum of four years, based upon academic achievement. Minimum GPA 2.5 required.

Award: Scholarship for use in freshman, sophomore, junior, or senior years; renewable. *Number:* 4–8. *Amount:* $500.

Eligibility Requirements: Applicant must be enrolled or expecting to enroll full-time at a four-year institution or university. Applicant or parent of applicant must be member of SOKOL, USA. Available to U.S. citizens.

Application Requirements: Application, references, transcript, must be a member of the Slovak Gymnastic Union Sokol of the U.S.A. for at least 3 years. *Deadline:* April 15.

Contact: Milan Kovac, Supreme Secretary
Slovak Gymnastic Union SOKOL, USA
276 Prospect Street, PO Box 189
East Orange, NJ 07019
Phone: 973-676-0280
Fax: 973-676-3348
E-mail: sokolusahqs@aol.com

SLOVENIAN WOMEN'S UNION SCHOLARSHIP FOUNDATION

http://www.swua.org/

CONTINUING EDUCATION AWARD

Award of $500 given to 2 applicants to continue or update their education. Applicant must be an active participant of the Slovenian Women's Union for the three years prior to applying for an award. Visit http://www.swua.org for additional information and an application.

Award: Scholarship for use in freshman, sophomore, junior, or senior years; not renewable. *Number:* 2. *Amount:* $500.

Eligibility Requirements: Applicant must be enrolled or expecting to enroll full- or part-time at a two-year or four-year or technical institution

or university. Applicant or parent of applicant must be member of Slovenian Women's Union of America. Available to U.S. citizens.

Application Requirements: Application, autobiography, essay, financial need analysis, photo, resume, references, test scores, transcript. *Deadline:* March 1.

Contact: Mary H. Turvey, Director
Slovenian Women's Union Scholarship Foundation
4 Lawrence Drive
Marquette, MI 49855
Phone: 906-249-4288
E-mail: mturvey@aol.com

SLOVENIAN WOMEN'S UNION OF AMERICA SCHOLARSHIP FOUNDATION

One-time award for full-time study only. Applicant must have been an active participant or member of Slovenian Women's Union for the past three years. Essay, transcripts, letters of recommendation from principal/teacher and SWU branch officer, financial need form, photo, civic and church activities information required. Open to high school seniors.

Award: Scholarship for use in freshman, sophomore, junior, or senior years; not renewable. *Number:* 5–6. *Amount:* $1000–$2000.

Eligibility Requirements: Applicant must be enrolled or expecting to enroll full-time at a two-year or four-year or technical institution or university. Applicant or parent of applicant must be member of Slovenian Women's Union of America. Available to U.S. citizens.

Application Requirements: Application, autobiography, essay, financial need analysis, photo, resume, references, self-addressed stamped envelope, test scores, transcript. *Deadline:* March 1.

Contact: Mary Turvey, Director
Slovenian Women's Union Scholarship Foundation
4 Lawrence Drive
Marquette, MI 49855
Phone: 906-249-4288
E-mail: mturvey@aol.com

SONS OF NORWAY FOUNDATION

http://www.sonsofnorway.com/

ASTRID G. CATES AND MYRTLE BEINHAUER SCHOLARSHIP FUNDS

Merit and need-based award available to students ages 17 to 22 who are members, children, or grandchildren of members of the Sons of Norway. School transcript required. Academic potential and clarity of study plan is key criterion for award. Minimum 3.0 GPA required.

Award: Scholarship for use in freshman, sophomore, junior, or senior years; not renewable. *Number:* 2–7. *Amount:* $1000–$3000.

Eligibility Requirements: Applicant must be age 17-22; enrolled or expecting to enroll full-time at a two-year or four-year institution or university and resident of Yukon. Applicant or parent of applicant must be member of Mutual Benefit Society. Applicant must have 3.0 GPA or higher. Available to U.S. citizens.

Application Requirements: Application, essay, financial need analysis, photo, references, test scores, transcript. *Deadline:* March 1.

Contact: Scholarship Coordinator
Sons of Norway Foundation
1455 West Lake Street
Minneapolis, MN 55408-2666
Phone: 612-827-3611
Fax: 612-827-0658
E-mail: foundation@sofn.com

SOUTH CAROLINA STATE EMPLOYEES ASSOCIATION

http://www.scsea.com/

ANNE A. AGNEW SCHOLARSHIP

Nonrenewable scholarship for full-time study only. Must be a sophomore, junior, senior, graduate or postgraduate student. Application forms are available after January 1 of each year.

Award: Scholarship for use in sophomore, junior, senior, graduate, or postgraduate years; not renewable. *Number:* 3. *Amount:* $1000.

Eligibility Requirements: Applicant must be enrolled or expecting to enroll full-time at a four-year institution or university and resident of

South Carolina. Applicant or parent of applicant must be member of South Carolina State Employees Association. Available to U.S. and non-U.S. citizens.

Application Requirements: Application, essay, financial need analysis, transcript. *Deadline:* March 12.

Contact: Broadus Jamerson, Executive Director
South Carolina State Employees Association
PO Box 8447
Columbia, SC 29202
Phone: 803-765-0680
Fax: 803-779-6558
E-mail: scsea@scsea.com

RICHLAND/LEXINGTON SCSEA SCHOLARSHIP

Scholarships available to SCSEA members or their relatives, with priority given to Richland-Lexington Chapter members, spouses and/or children of Chapter members. The awardees must be currently enrolled at a recognized and accredited college, university, trade school or other institution of higher learning and must have completed at least one academic semester/quarter.

Award: Scholarship for use in sophomore, junior, senior, graduate, or postgraduate years; not renewable. *Number:* 3. *Amount:* $750.

Eligibility Requirements: Applicant must be enrolled or expecting to enroll full-time at a two-year or four-year institution or university and resident of South Carolina. Applicant or parent of applicant must be member of Society of Architectural Historians. Available to U.S. citizens.

Application Requirements: Application, essay, transcript. *Deadline:* March 12.

Contact: Broadus Jamerson, Executive Director
South Carolina State Employees Association
PO Box 8447
Columbia, SC 29202
Phone: 803-765-0680
Fax: 803-779-6558
E-mail: scsea@scsea.com

SUPREME COUNCIL OF SES

http://www.seslife.org/

SUPREME COUNCIL OF SOCIEDADE DO ESPIRITO SANTO SCHOLARSHIP PROGRAM

Applicant must be a member of the SES for a minimum of two years prior to filling date of scholarship and have insurance premiums paid to date. Must be graduating seniors at time of application or have graduated from high school during the current year. Minimum of 3.0 GPA required.

Award: Scholarship for use in freshman year; not renewable. *Number:* 35. *Amount:* $500–$1200.

Eligibility Requirements: Applicant must be enrolled or expecting to enroll full-time at a four-year institution or university. Applicant or parent of applicant must be member of Supreme Council of Sociedade Do Espirito Santo. Applicant must have 3.0 GPA or higher. Available to U.S. citizens.

Application Requirements: Application, essay, resume, references, transcript. *Deadline:* February 15.

Contact: Scholarship Committee
Supreme Council of SES
PO Box 247
Santa Clara, CA 95052-0247

SUPREME GUARDIAN COUNCIL, INTERNATIONAL ORDER OF JOB'S DAUGHTERS

http://www.iojd.org/

SUPREME GUARDIAN COUNCIL SCHOLARSHIP

Scholarships of $750 to aid Job's Daughters students of outstanding ability whom have a sincerity of purpose. High school seniors, or graduates, junior college, technical school, or college students who are in early graduation programs, are eligible to apply.

Award: Scholarship for use in freshman, sophomore, junior, senior, graduate, or postgraduate years; not renewable. *Number:* 5–10. *Amount:* $750.

Eligibility Requirements: Applicant must be age 18-30; enrolled or expecting to enroll full- or part-time at a two-year or four-year or technical institution or university and single female. Applicant or parent of applicant must be member of Jobs Daughters. Available to U.S. and non-U.S. citizens.

Application Requirements: Application, essay, financial need analysis, references, recommendation from Executive Bethel Guardian Council, achievements outside of Job's Daughters. *Deadline:* April 30.

Contact: Christal M. Bindrich, Scholarship Committee Chairman
Supreme Guardian Council, International Order of Job's Daughters
5351 South Butterfield Way
Greenfield, WI 53221
Phone: 414-423-0016
E-mail: christalbindrich@wi.rr.com

SUSIE HOLMES MEMORIAL SCHOLARSHIP

Scholarships of $1000 awarded to Job's Daughters high school students with a minimum of 2.5 GPA.

Award: Scholarship for use in freshman, sophomore, junior, senior, graduate, or postgraduate years; not renewable. *Number:* 1. *Amount:* $1000.

Eligibility Requirements: Applicant must be age 18-30; enrolled or expecting to enroll full-time at a two-year or four-year or technical institution or university and single female. Applicant or parent of applicant must be member of Jobs Daughters. Applicant must have 2.5 GPA or higher. Available to U.S. and non-U.S. citizens.

Application Requirements: Application, essay, references, test scores, transcript. *Deadline:* April 30.

Contact: Christal Bindrich, Scholarship Committee Chairman
Supreme Guardian Council, International Order of Job's Daughters
5351 South Butterfield Way
Greenfield, WI 53221
Phone: 414-423-0016
E-mail: christalbindrich@wi.rr.com

TENNESSEE EDUCATION ASSOCIATION

http://www.teateachers.org/

TEA DON SAHLI-KATHY WOODALL SONS AND DAUGHTERS SCHOLARSHIP

Scholarship is available to a TEA member's child who is a high school senior, undergraduate or graduate student, and is planning to enroll, or is already enrolled, in a Tennessee college.

Award: Scholarship for use in freshman, sophomore, junior, senior, or graduate years; not renewable. *Number:* 1. *Amount:* $1000.

Eligibility Requirements: Applicant must be enrolled or expecting to enroll full-time at a four-year institution or university; resident of Tennessee and studying in Tennessee. Applicant or parent of applicant must be member of Tennessee Education Association. Applicant must have 3.0 GPA or higher. Available to U.S. citizens.

Application Requirements: Application, applicant must enter a contest, essay, financial need analysis, references, transcript, statement of income. *Deadline:* March 1.

Contact: Stephanie Faulkner, Manager of Business Affairs
Tennessee Education Association
801 Second Avenue North
Nashville, TN 37201-1099
Phone: 615-242-8392
Fax: 615-259-4581
E-mail: sfaulkner@tea.nea.org

TEXAS AFL-CIO

http://www.texasaflcio.org/

TEXAS AFL-CIO SCHOLARSHIP PROGRAM

Award for sons or daughters of affiliated union members. Selection by testing or interview process. One-time awards of $1000. Applicant must be a graduating high school senior and Texas resident.

Award: Scholarship for use in freshman year; not renewable. *Number:* 20–35. *Amount:* $1000.

Eligibility Requirements: Applicant must be high school student; planning to enroll or expecting to enroll full-time at a two-year or four-year institution or university and resident of Texas. Applicant or parent of applicant must be member of AFL-CIO. Available to U.S. citizens.

Application Requirements: Application, essay, financial need analysis, interview, photo, test scores, transcript. *Deadline:* January 31.

Contact: Mr. Edward Sills, Director of Communications
Texas AFL-CIO
PO Box 12727
Austin, TX 78711 ·
Phone: 512-477-6195
E-mail: ed@texasaflcio.org

TEXAS WOMEN IN LAW ENFORCEMENT

http://www.twle.com/

VANESSA RUDLOFF SCHOLARSHIP PROGRAM

Scholarships of $1000 awarded to qualified TWLE members and their dependents who are entering or continuing students at an accredited college or university. For details refer to web site http://www.twle.net/.

Award: Scholarship for use in freshman, sophomore, junior, senior, graduate, or postgraduate years; not renewable. *Number:* 4. *Amount:* $1000.

Eligibility Requirements: Applicant must be enrolled or expecting to enroll full- or part-time at a two-year or four-year or technical institution or university. Applicant or parent of applicant must be member of Texas Women in Law Enforcement. Applicant must have 3.0 GPA or higher. Available to U.S. and non-U.S. citizens.

Application Requirements: Application, essay, references. *Deadline:* April 15.

Contact: Glenda Baker, Scholarship Awards Chairperson
Texas Women in Law Enforcement
12605 Rhea Court
Austin, TX 78727
E-mail: gbakerab@aol.com

TKE EDUCATIONAL FOUNDATION

http://www.tke.org/

ALL-TKE ACADEMIC TEAM RECOGNITION AND JOHN A. COURSON TOP SCHOLAR AWARD

One-time award given to full-time students who are active members of Tau Kappa Epsilon with junior or senior standing. Candidates should be able to maintain excellent academic standing while making positive contributions to chapter, campus, and community. Must have a minimum of 3.0 GPA.

Award: Scholarship for use in junior or senior years; not renewable. *Number:* 10. *Amount:* up to $3250.

Eligibility Requirements: Applicant must be enrolled or expecting to enroll full-time at a four-year institution or university and must have an interest in leadership. Applicant or parent of applicant must be member of Tau Kappa Epsilon. Applicant must have 3.0 GPA or higher. Available to U.S. and Canadian citizens.

Application Requirements: Application, photo, transcript. *Deadline:* February 29.

Contact: Gary A. Reed, President and Chief Executive Officer
TKE Educational Foundation
8645 Founders Road
Indianapolis, IN 46268-1393
Phone: 317-872-6533
Fax: 317-875-8353
E-mail: reedga@tke.org

CANADIAN TKE SCHOLARSHIP

Scholarship available to an undergraduate who has been initiated into a Canadian TKE chapter and has demonstrated leadership qualities within the fraternity and the campus community, while maintaining a good academic record.

Award: Scholarship for use in freshman, sophomore, junior, or senior years; not renewable. *Number:* 1. *Amount:* $250.

Eligibility Requirements: Applicant must be enrolled or expecting to enroll full-time at a four-year institution or university; male and must have an interest in leadership. Applicant or parent of applicant must be

member of Tau Kappa Epsilon. Applicant must have 2.5 GPA or higher. Available to U.S. and non-U.S. citizens.

Application Requirements: Application, essay, photo, transcript. · *Deadline:* February 28.

Contact: Gary Reed, President and Chief Executive Officer
TKE Educational Foundation
8645 Founders Road
Indianapolis, IN 46268
Phone: 317-872-6533
Fax: 317-875-8353
E-mail: reedga@tke.org

CHARLES WALGREEN JR. SCHOLARSHIP

Award given in recognition of outstanding leadership, as demonstrated by the activities and accomplishments of an individual within the chapter, on campus and in the community, while maintaining a good academic record. All initiated undergraduate members of TKE, in good standing with a cumulative GPA of 3.0 or higher, are eligible to apply.

Award: Scholarship for use in freshman, sophomore, junior, or senior years; not renewable. *Number:* 1. *Amount:* $2500.

Eligibility Requirements: Applicant must be enrolled or expecting to enroll full-time at a four-year institution or university; male and must have an interest in leadership. Applicant or parent of applicant must be member of Tau Kappa Epsilon. Applicant must have 3.0 GPA or higher. Available to U.S. and non-U.S. citizens.

Application Requirements: Application, essay, photo, transcript, narrative summary of how TKE membership has benefited applicant. *Deadline:* February 29.

Contact: Scholarship Committee
TKE Educational Foundation
8645 Founders Road
Indianapolis, IN 46268-1336
Phone: 317-872-6533
Fax: 317-875-8353
E-mail: tef@tke.org

DONALD A. AND JOHN R. FISHER MEMORIAL SCHOLARSHIP

One-time award of $1400 given to an undergraduate member of Tau Kappa Epsilon, who has demonstrated leadership ability within his chapter, campus, or community. Must be a full-time student in good standing with a GPA of 3.0 or higher.

Award: Scholarship for use in freshman, sophomore, junior, or senior years; not renewable. *Number:* 1. *Amount:* $1400.

Eligibility Requirements: Applicant must be enrolled or expecting to enroll full-time at a four-year institution or university and must have an interest in leadership. Applicant or parent of applicant must be member of Tau Kappa Epsilon. Applicant must have 3.0 GPA or higher. Available to U.S. and non-U.S. citizens.

Application Requirements: Application, essay, photo, transcript. *Deadline:* February 29.

Contact: Gary A. Reed, President and Chief Executive Officer
TKE Educational Foundation
8645 Founders Road
Indianapolis, IN 46268-1393
Phone: 317-872-6533
Fax: 317-875-8353
E-mail: reedga@tke.org

DWAYNE R. WOERPEL MEMORIAL LEADERSHIP AWARD

Award available to an undergraduate Tau Kappa Epsilon member who is a full-time student and graduate of the TKE Leadership Academy. Applicants should have demonstrated leadership qualities in service to the Fraternity and to the civic and religious community while maintaining a 3.0 GPA or higher.

Award: Scholarship for use in freshman, sophomore, junior, or senior years; not renewable. *Number:* 1. *Amount:* $700.

Eligibility Requirements: Applicant must be enrolled or expecting to enroll full-time at a four-year institution or university; male and must have an interest in leadership. Applicant or parent of applicant must be member of Tau Kappa Epsilon. Applicant must have 3.0 GPA or higher. Available to U.S. and non-U.S. citizens.

Application Requirements: Application, essay, photo, transcript. *Deadline:* February 29.

Contact: Scholarship Committee
TKE Educational Foundation
8645 Founders Road
Indianapolis, IN 46268-1336
Phone: 317-872-6533
Fax: 317-875-8353
E-mail: tef@tke.org

ELMER AND DORIS SCHMITZ SR. MEMORIAL SCHOLARSHIP

One-time award of $500 given to an undergraduate member of Tau Kappa Epsilon from Wisconsin who has demonstrated leadership ability within his chapter, campus, or community. Must be a full-time student in good standing with a GPA of 2.5 or higher.

Award: Scholarship for use in freshman, sophomore, junior, or senior years; not renewable. *Number:* 1. *Amount:* $500.

Eligibility Requirements: Applicant must be enrolled or expecting to enroll full-time at a four-year institution or university; resident of Wisconsin and must have an interest in leadership. Applicant or parent of applicant must be member of Tau Kappa Epsilon. Applicant must have 2.5 GPA or higher. Available to U.S. and non-U.S. citizens.

Application Requirements: Application, essay, photo, transcript, narrative summary of how TKE membership has benefited applicant. *Deadline:* February 29.

Contact: Gary A. Reed, President and Chief Executive Officer
TKE Educational Foundation
8645 Founders Road
Indianapolis, IN 46268-1393
Phone: 317-872-6533
Fax: 317-875-8353
E-mail: reedga@tke.org

EUGENE C. BEACH MEMORIAL SCHOLARSHIP

One-time award of $400 given to an undergraduate member of Tau Kappa Epsilon who has demonstrated leadership ability within chapter, campus, or community. Must be a full-time student in good standing with a GPA of 3.0 or higher.

Award: Scholarship for use in freshman, sophomore, junior, or senior years; not renewable. *Number:* 1. *Amount:* $400.

Eligibility Requirements: Applicant must be enrolled or expecting to enroll full-time at a four-year institution or university and must have an interest in leadership. Applicant or parent of applicant must be member of Tau Kappa Epsilon. Applicant must have 3.0 GPA or higher. Available to U.S. and non-U.S. citizens.

Application Requirements: Application, essay, photo, transcript, narrative summary of how TKE membership has benefited applicant. *Deadline:* February 29.

Contact: Gary A. Reed, President and Chief Executive Officer
TKE Educational Foundation
8645 Founders Road
Indianapolis, IN 46268-1393
Phone: 317-872-6533
Fax: 317-875-8353
E-mail: reedga@tke.org

J. RUSSEL SALSBURY MEMORIAL SCHOLARSHIP

One-time award of $300 given to an undergraduate member of Tau Kappa Epsilon who has demonstrated leadership ability within his chapter, campus, or community. Must be a full-time student in good standing with a GPA of 3.0 or higher.

Award: Scholarship for use in freshman, sophomore, junior, or senior years; not renewable. *Number:* 1. *Amount:* $300.

Eligibility Requirements: Applicant must be enrolled or expecting to enroll full-time at a four-year institution or university and must have an interest in leadership. Applicant or parent of applicant must be member of Tau Kappa Epsilon. Applicant must have 3.0 GPA or higher. Available to U.S. and non-U.S. citizens.

Application Requirements: Application, essay, photo, transcript. *Deadline:* February 29.

Contact: Gary A. Reed, President and Chief Executive Officer
TKE Educational Foundation
8645 Founders Road
Indianapolis, IN 46268-1393
Phone: 317-872-6533
Fax: 317-875-8353
E-mail: reedga@tke.org

MICHAEL J. MORIN MEMORIAL SCHOLARSHIP

One-time award for any undergraduate member of Tau Kappa Epsilon who has demonstrated leadership capacity within his chapter, on campus or the community. Must have a cumulative GPA of 3.0 or higher and be a full-time student in good standing.

Award: Scholarship for use in freshman, sophomore, junior, or senior years; not renewable. *Number:* 1. *Amount:* $400.

Eligibility Requirements: Applicant must be enrolled or expecting to enroll full-time at a four-year institution or university and must have an interest in leadership. Applicant or parent of applicant must be member of Tau Kappa Epsilon. Applicant must have 3.0 GPA or higher. Available to U.S. and non-U.S. citizens.

Application Requirements: Application, essay, photo, transcript, narrative summary of how TKE membership has benefited applicant. *Deadline:* February 29.

Contact: Scholarship Committee
TKE Educational Foundation
8645 Founders Road
Indianapolis, IN 46268-1336
Phone: 317-872-6553
Fax: 317-875-8353
E-mail: tef@tke.org

MILES GRAY MEMORIAL SCHOLARSHIP

One-time award of $400 given to an undergraduate member of Tau Kappa Epsilon who has demonstrated leadership ability within his chapter, campus, or community. Must be a full-time student in good standing with a GPA of 3.0 or higher.

Award: Scholarship for use in freshman, sophomore, junior, or senior years; not renewable. *Number:* 1. *Amount:* $400.

Eligibility Requirements: Applicant must be enrolled or expecting to enroll full-time at a four-year institution or university and must have an interest in leadership. Applicant or parent of applicant must be member of Tau Kappa Epsilon. Applicant must have 3.0 GPA or higher. Available to U.S. and non-U.S. citizens.

Application Requirements: Application, essay, photo, transcript. *Deadline:* February 29.

Contact: Gary A. Reed, President and Chief Executive Officer
TKE Educational Foundation
8645 Founders Road
Indianapolis, IN 46268-1393
Phone: 317-872-6533
Fax: 317-875-8353
E-mail: reedga@tke.org

RONALD REAGAN LEADERSHIP AWARD

One-time award of $2000 for initiated undergraduate member of Tau Kappa Epsilon, given in recognition of outstanding leadership, as demonstrated by activities and accomplishments within chapter, on campus, and in community. Recipient should attend official fraternity function to accept award.

Award: Scholarship for use in freshman, sophomore, junior, or senior years; not renewable. *Number:* 1. *Amount:* $2000.

Eligibility Requirements: Applicant must be enrolled or expecting to enroll full-time at a four-year institution or university and must have an interest in leadership. Applicant or parent of applicant must be member of Tau Kappa Epsilon. Applicant must have 3.0 GPA or higher. Available to U.S. and non-U.S. citizens.

Application Requirements: Application, essay, photo, transcript, narrative summary of how TKE membership has benefited applicant. *Deadline:* February 29.

Contact: Gary A. Reed, President and Chief Executive Officer
TKE Educational Foundation
8645 Founders Road
Indianapolis, IN 46268-1393
Phone: 317-872-6533
Fax: 317-875-8353
E-mail: reedga@tke.org

T.J. SCHMITZ SCHOLARSHIP

Award for an initiated undergraduate member of TKE. Must be a full-time student in good standing with a minimum cumulative GPA of 3.0. Must have demonstrated leadership capability within chapter, campus, or community.

Award: Scholarship for use in freshman, sophomore, junior, or senior years; not renewable. *Number:* 1. *Amount:* $800.

Eligibility Requirements: Applicant must be enrolled or expecting to enroll full-time at a four-year institution or university; male and must have an interest in leadership. Applicant or parent of applicant must be member of Tau Kappa Epsilon. Applicant must have 3.0 GPA or higher. Available to U.S. and non-U.S. citizens.

Application Requirements: Application, essay, photo, transcript, narrative summary of how TKE membership has benefited applicant. *Deadline:* February 29.

Contact: Gary A. Reed, President and Chief Executive Officer
TKE Educational Foundation
8645 Founders Road
Indianapolis, IN 46268-1393
Phone: 317-872-6533
Fax: 317-875-8353
E-mail: reedga@tke.org

WALLACE MCCAULEY MEMORIAL SCHOLARSHIP

One-time award to undergraduate member of Tau Kappa Epsilon with junior or senior standing. Must have demonstrated understanding of the importance of good alumni relations. Must have excelled in the development, promotion, and execution of programs which increase alumni contact, awareness, and participation in fraternity activities.

Award: Scholarship for use in junior or senior years; not renewable. *Number:* 1. *Amount:* $500.

Eligibility Requirements: Applicant must be enrolled or expecting to enroll full-time at a four-year institution or university and must have an interest in leadership. Applicant or parent of applicant must be member of Tau Kappa Epsilon. Applicant must have 3.0 GPA or higher. Available to U.S. and non-U.S. citizens.

Application Requirements: Application, essay, photo, transcript, narrative summary of how TKE membership has benefited applicant. *Deadline:* February 29.

Contact: Gary A. Reed, President and Chief Executive Officer
TKE Educational Foundation
8645 Founders Road
Indianapolis, IN 46268-1393
Phone: 317-872-6533
Fax: 317-875-8353
E-mail: reedga@tke.org

WILLIAM V. MUSE SCHOLARSHIP

Award of $700 given to an undergraduate member of Tau Kappa Epsilon who has completed at least 30 semester hours of course work. Applicant should demonstrate leadership within chapter and maintain 3.0 GPA. Preference given to members of Epsilon-Upsilon Chapter.

Award: Scholarship for use in freshman, sophomore, junior, or senior years; not renewable. *Number:* 1. *Amount:* $700.

Eligibility Requirements: Applicant must be enrolled or expecting to enroll full-time at a four-year institution or university and must have an interest in leadership. Applicant or parent of applicant must be member of Tau Kappa Epsilon. Applicant must have 3.0 GPA or higher. Available to U.S. and non-U.S. citizens.

Application Requirements: Application, essay, photo, transcript, narrative summary of how TKE membership has benefited applicant. *Deadline:* February 29.

Contact: Gary A. Reed, President and Chief Executive Officer
TKE Educational Foundation
8645 Founders Road
Indianapolis, IN 46268-1393
Phone: 317-872-6533
Fax: 317-875-8353
E-mail: reedga@tke.org

WILLIAM WILSON MEMORIAL SCHOLARSHIP

One-time award given to undergraduate member of Tau Kappa Epsilon with junior or senior standing. Must have demonstrated understanding of the importance of good alumni relations. Must have excelled in the development, promotion, and execution of programs which increase alumni contact, awareness, and participation in fraternity activities.

Award: Scholarship for use in junior or senior years; not renewable. *Number:* 1. *Amount:* $500.

Eligibility Requirements: Applicant must be enrolled or expecting to enroll full-time at a four-year institution or university and must have an interest in leadership. Applicant or parent of applicant must be member of Tau Kappa Epsilon. Applicant must have 3.0 GPA or higher. Available to U.S. and non-U.S. citizens.

Application Requirements: Application, essay, photo, transcript, narrative summary of how TKE membership has benefited applicant. *Deadline:* February 29.

Contact: Gary A. Reed, President and Chief Executive Officer
TKE Educational Foundation
8645 Founders Road
Indianapolis, IN 46268-1393
Phone: 317-872-6533
Fax: 317-875-8353
E-mail: reedga@tke.org

UNION PLUS SCHOLARSHIP PROGRAM

http://www.unionplus.org/

UNION PLUS EDUCATION FOUNDATION SCHOLARSHIP PROGRAM

One-time cash award for current or retired union members affiliated with the AFL-CIO, their spouses, and dependent children. Based upon academic achievement, character, leadership, career goals, social awareness and financial need. Must be from Canada or U.S., including Puerto Rico and the Virgin Islands. Members must download application from web site: http://www.unionplus.org/scholarships.

Award: Scholarship for use in freshman, sophomore, junior, or senior years; not renewable. *Number:* 100–120. *Amount:* $500–$4000.

Eligibility Requirements: Applicant must be enrolled or expecting to enroll full- or part-time at a two-year or four-year or technical institution or university. Applicant or parent of applicant must be member of AFL-CIO. Available to U.S. and non-U.S. citizens.

Application Requirements: Application, essay, financial need analysis, references, test scores. *Deadline:* January 31.

Contact: Mrs. Shana E. Higgins, Union Plus Education Foundation
Union Plus Scholarship Program
c/o Union Privilege, PO Box 34800
Washington, DC 20043-4800
E-mail: shiggins@unionprivilege.org

UNITED DAUGHTERS OF THE CONFEDERACY

http://www.hqudc.org/

BARBARA JACKSON SICHEL MEMORIAL SCHOLARSHIP

Renewable award for undergraduate students who are descendant of a Confederate soldier, sailor or marine. Must be enrolled in an accredited college or university. Minimum of 3.0 GPA required. Submit a letter of endorsement from sponsoring Chapter of the United Daughters of the Confederacy.

Award: Scholarship for use in freshman, sophomore, junior, or senior years; renewable. *Number:* 1–2. *Amount:* $800–$1000.

Eligibility Requirements: Applicant must be enrolled or expecting to enroll full-time at a four-year institution or university. Applicant or parent of applicant must be member of United Daughters of the Confederacy. Applicant must have 3.0 GPA or higher. Available to U.S. citizens.

Application Requirements: Application, essay, financial need analysis, photo, references, self-addressed stamped envelope, transcript, proof of confederate ancestor's service, copy of applicant's birth certificate. *Deadline:* March 15.

Contact: United Daughters of the Confederacy
328 North Boulevard
Richmond, VA 23220-4009
Phone: 804-355-1636
E-mail: hqudc@rcn.com

CHARLOTTE M. F. BENTLEY/NEW YORK CHAPTER 103 SCHOLARSHIP

Renewable award for undergraduate students who are descendant of a Confederate soldier, sailor or marine. Must be enrolled in an accredited college or university. Minimum of 3.0 GPA required. Must be members of United Daughters of the Confederacy and Children of the Confederacy from New York.

Award: Scholarship for use in freshman, sophomore, junior, or senior years; renewable. *Number:* 1–2. *Amount:* $800–$1000.

Eligibility Requirements: Applicant must be enrolled or expecting to enroll full-time at a four-year institution or university and resident of New York. Applicant or parent of applicant must be member of Children of the Confederacy or United Daughters of the Confederacy. Applicant must have 3.0 GPA or higher. Available to U.S. citizens.

Application Requirements: Application, essay, financial need analysis, photo, references, self-addressed stamped envelope, transcript, proof of confederate ancestor's service, copy of applicant's birth certificate. *Deadline:* March 15.

Contact: United Daughters of the Confederacy
328 North Boulevard
Richmond, VA 23220-4009
Phone: 804-355-1636
E-mail: hqudc@rcn.com

ELIZABETH AND WALLACE KINGSBURY SCHOLARSHIP

Award for full-time undergraduate students who are descendants of a Confederate soldier, studying at an accredited college or university. Must have been a member of the Children of the Confederacy for a minimum of three years. Minimum 3.0 GPA required.

Award: Scholarship for use in freshman, sophomore, junior, or senior years; renewable. *Number:* 1–2. *Amount:* $800–$1000.

Eligibility Requirements: Applicant must be enrolled or expecting to enroll full-time at a four-year institution or university. Applicant or parent of applicant must be member of Children of the Confederacy. Applicant must have 3.0 GPA or higher. Available to U.S. citizens.

Application Requirements: Application, essay, financial need analysis, photo, references, self-addressed stamped envelope, transcript, copy of applicant's birth certificate, copy of confederate ancestor's proof of service. *Deadline:* March 15.

Contact: United Daughters of the Confederacy
328 North Boulevard
Richmond, VA 23220-4009
Phone: 804-355-1636
E-mail: hqudc@rcn.com

GERTRUDE BOTTS-SAUCIER SCHOLARSHIP

Award for full-time undergraduate students who are descendants of a Confederate soldier, sailor or marine. Must be from Texas, Mississippi or Louisiana. Must be enrolled in an accredited college or university and have a minimum 3.0 GPA. Submit application and letter of endorsement from sponsoring chapter of the United Daughters of the Confederacy.

Award: Scholarship for use in freshman, sophomore, junior, or senior years; renewable. *Number:* 1–2. *Amount:* $800–$1000.

Eligibility Requirements: Applicant must be enrolled or expecting to enroll full-time at a four-year institution or university and resident of Louisiana, Mississippi, or Texas. Applicant or parent of applicant must be member of United Daughters of the Confederacy. Applicant must have 3.0 GPA or higher. Available to U.S. citizens.

Application Requirements: Application, essay, financial need analysis, photo, references, self-addressed stamped envelope, transcript, copy of

applicant's birth certificate, copy of confederate ancestor's proof of service. *Deadline:* March 15.

Contact: United Daughters of the Confederacy
328 North Boulevard
Richmond, VA 23220-4009
Phone: 804-355-1636
E-mail: hqudc@rcn.com

LOLA B. CURRY SCHOLARSHIP

Award for full-time undergraduate students from Alabama who are descendants of a Confederate soldier. Must be enrolled in an accredited college or university in Alabama. Minimum 3.0 GPA required. Submit letter of endorsement from sponsoring chapter of the United Daughters of the Confederacy.

Award: Scholarship for use in freshman, sophomore, junior, or senior years; renewable. *Number:* 1–2. *Amount:* $800–$1000.

Eligibility Requirements: Applicant must be enrolled or expecting to enroll full-time at a four-year institution or university; resident of Alabama and studying in Alabama. Applicant or parent of applicant must be member of United Daughters of the Confederacy. Applicant must have 3.0 GPA or higher. Available to U.S. citizens.

Application Requirements: Application, essay, financial need analysis, photo, references, self-addressed stamped envelope, transcript, copy of applicant's birth certificate, copy of confederate ancestor's proof of service. *Deadline:* March 15.

Contact: United Daughters of the Confederacy
328 North Boulevard
Richmond, VA 23220-4009
Phone: 804-355-1636
E-mail: hqudc@rcn.com

UNITED DAUGHTERS OF THE CONFEDERACY UNDERGRADUATE SCHOLARSHIPS

Renewable award for undergraduate students who are descendants of an eligible Confederate soldier. Must be enrolled in an accredited college or university. Minimum 3.0 GPA required. Applicants must be endorsed by the President and the Second Vice President/Education Chairman of Chapter and Division, and by the Second Vice President General. Applications are submitted through local chapters.

Award: Scholarship for use in freshman, sophomore, junior, or senior years; renewable. *Number:* 18–30. *Amount:* $800–$1000.

Eligibility Requirements: Applicant must be enrolled or expecting to enroll full-time at a two-year or four-year institution or university. Applicant or parent of applicant must be member of United Daughters of the Confederacy. Applicant must have 3.0 GPA or higher. Available to U.S. citizens.

Application Requirements: Application, essay, financial need analysis, photo, references, self-addressed stamped envelope, transcript, copy of applicant's birth certificate, copy of confederate ancestor's proof of service. *Deadline:* March 15.

Contact: United Daughters of the Confederacy
328 North Boulevard
Richmond, VA 23220-4009
Phone: 804-355-1636
E-mail: hqudc@rcn.com

WINNIE DAVIS-CHILDREN OF THE CONFEDERACY SCHOLARSHIP

Award for full-time undergraduate students who are descendants of a Confederate soldier, enrolled in an accredited college or university. Recipient must be, or have been until age of 18, a participating member of the Children of the Confederacy and approved by the Third Vice President General. Minimum 3.0 GPA required.

Award: Scholarship for use in freshman, sophomore, junior, or senior years; renewable. *Number:* 1–2. *Amount:* $800–$1000.

Eligibility Requirements: Applicant must be age 18 and over and enrolled or expecting to enroll full-time at a four-year institution or university. Applicant or parent of applicant must be member of Children of the Confederacy. Applicant must have 3.0 GPA or higher. Available to U.S. citizens.

Application Requirements: Application, essay, financial need analysis, photo, references, self-addressed stamped envelope, transcript, copy of applicant's birth certificate, copy of confederate ancestor's proof of service. *Deadline:* March 15.

Contact: United Daughters of the Confederacy
328 North Boulevard
Richmond, VA 23220-4009
Phone: 804-355-1636
E-mail: hqudc@rcn.com

UNITED FOOD AND COMMERCIAL WORKERS INTERNATIONAL UNION

http://www.ufcw.org/

JAMES A. SUFFRIDGE UNITED FOOD AND COMMERCIAL WORKERS SCHOLARSHIP PROGRAM

Scholarships available to graduating high school seniors and college students during the specific program year. Must be an active member of UFCW or unmarried dependent under age 20 of a UFCW member. Scholarship is disbursed over a four-year period.

Award: Scholarship for use in freshman, sophomore, junior, or senior years; renewable. *Number:* 14–20. *Amount:* up to $8000.

Eligibility Requirements: Applicant must be age 20 or under and enrolled or expecting to enroll full- or part-time at a two-year or four-year or technical institution or university. Applicant or parent of applicant must be member of United Food and Commercial Workers. Available to U.S. and Canadian citizens.

Application Requirements: Application, essay, transcript. *Deadline:* April 15.

Contact: Field Assistant
United Food and Commercial Workers International Union
1775 K Street NW
Washington, DC 20006
Phone: 202-223-3111
Fax: 202-721-8008
E-mail: scholarship@ufcw.org

UNITED STATES JUNIOR CHAMBER OF COMMERCE

http://www.usjaycees.org/

CHARLES R. FORD SCHOLARSHIP

One-time award of $3000 available to active members of Jaycee wishing to return to college to complete his/her formal education. Must be U.S. citizen, possess academic potential and leadership qualities and show financial need. To receive an application, send $10 application fee and self-addressed stamped envelope by February 1.

Award: Scholarship for use in freshman, sophomore, junior, senior, graduate, or postgraduate years; not renewable. *Number:* 1. *Amount:* $3000.

Eligibility Requirements: Applicant must be age 18-40 and enrolled or expecting to enroll full- or part-time at a two-year or four-year institution or university. Applicant or parent of applicant must be member of Jaycees. Available to U.S. citizens.

Application Requirements: Application, financial need analysis, self-addressed stamped envelope, transcript. *Fee:* $10. *Deadline:* February 1.

Contact: Karen Fitzgerald, Customer Service and Data Processing
United States Junior Chamber of Commerce
7447 South Lewis Avenue
Tulsa, OK 74102-0007
Phone: 918-584-2481
E-mail: customerservice@usjaycees.org

THOMAS WOOD BALDRIDGE SCHOLARSHIP

One-time award of $3000 available to a Jaycee immediate family member or a descendant of a Jaycee member. Must be U.S. citizen, possess academic potential and leadership qualities and show financial need. To receive an application, send $10 application fee and self-addressed stamped envelope by February 1.

Award: Scholarship for use in freshman, sophomore, junior, senior, graduate, or postgraduate years; not renewable. *Number:* 1. *Amount:* $3000.

Eligibility Requirements: Applicant must be age 18-40 and enrolled or expecting to enroll full- or part-time at a two-year or four-year or technical institution or university. Applicant or parent of applicant must be member of Jaycees. Available to U.S. citizens.

Application Requirements: Application, financial need analysis, self-addressed stamped envelope, transcript. *Fee:* $10. *Deadline:* February 1.

Contact: Karen Fitzgerald, Customer Service and Data Processing
United States Junior Chamber of Commerce
7447 South Lewis Avenue
Tulsa, OK 74102-0007
Phone: 918-584-2481
E-mail: customerservice@usjaycees.org

UNITED STATES MARINE CORPS SCHOLARSHIP FOUNDATION, INC.

http://www.mcsf.org/

MARINE CORPS SCHOLARSHIP FOUNDATION

Available to the sons and daughters of active duty Marines and to the children of former and deceased Marines whose family income does not exceed $82,000. Must submit proof of parent's service. Apply online at mcsf.org and call for further information 1-800-292-7777.

Award: Scholarship for use in freshman, sophomore, junior, or senior years; not renewable. *Number:* 1000–1500. *Amount:* $500–$10,000.

Eligibility Requirements: Applicant must be enrolled or expecting to enroll full- or part-time at a two-year or four-year or technical institution or university. Applicant or parent of applicant must be member of American Legion or Auxiliary or Boy Scouts. Available to U.S. citizens. Applicant must have served in the Marine Corps.

Application Requirements: Application, essay, financial need analysis, transcript, Marine parent DD-214 or active duty statement of service, pages 1 & 2 of Federal Income Tax Return. *Deadline:* April 1.

Contact: June Hering, Scholarship Program Director
United States Marine Corps Scholarship Foundation, Inc.
PO Box 3008
Princeton, NJ 08543-3008
Phone: 800-292-7777
Fax: 609-452-2259
E-mail: mcsf@marine-scholars.org

UNITED STATES NAVAL SEA CADET CORPS

http://www.seacadets.org/

HARRY AND ROSE HOWELL SCHOLARSHIP

Renewable award for Sea Cadets only. Two Howell Scholarships of $2500 each and one scholarship of $2000. Applicants must be U.S. citizens with a minimum 3.0 GPA.

Award: Scholarship for use in freshman, sophomore, junior, or senior years; renewable. *Number:* 3. *Amount:* $2000–$2500.

Eligibility Requirements: Applicant must be enrolled or expecting to enroll full-time at a two-year or four-year institution or university. Applicant or parent of applicant must be member of Naval Sea Cadet Corps. Applicant must have 3.0 GPA or higher. Available to U.S. citizens.

Application Requirements: Application, financial need analysis, references, test scores, transcript. *Deadline:* May 1.

Contact: M. Ford, Executive Director
United States Naval Sea Cadet Corps
2300 Wilson Boulevard
Arlington, VA 22201-3308
Phone: 703-243-6910
Fax: 703-243-3985
E-mail: mford@navyleague.org

KINGSLEY FOUNDATION AWARDS

One-time award to assist Cadets in continuing their education at an accredited four-year college or university. Must be a member of NSCC for at least two years. Minimum 3.0 GPA required.

Award: Scholarship for use in freshman, sophomore, junior, or senior years; not renewable. *Number:* 5. *Amount:* $1000.

Eligibility Requirements: Applicant must be enrolled or expecting to enroll full-time at a four-year institution or university. Applicant or parent of applicant must be member of Naval Sea Cadet Corps. Applicant must have 3.0 GPA or higher. Available to U.S. citizens.

Application Requirements: Application, financial need analysis, references, test scores, transcript. *Deadline:* May 1.

Contact: M. Ford, Executive Director
United States Naval Sea Cadet Corps
2300 Wilson Boulevard
Arlington, VA 22201-3308
Phone: 703-243-6910
Fax: 703-243-3985
E-mail: mford@navyleague.org

NAVAL SEA CADET CORPS BOARD OF DIRECTORS SCHOLARSHIP

Renewable award up to $1400 is available for Sea Cadets. Award available to U.S. citizens and minimum GPA of 3.0 is required.

Award: Scholarship for use in freshman, sophomore, junior, or senior years; renewable. *Number:* 1. *Amount:* $1200–$1400.

Eligibility Requirements: Applicant must be enrolled or expecting to enroll full-time at a two-year or four-year institution. Applicant or parent of applicant must be member of Naval Sea Cadet Corps. Applicant must have 3.0 GPA or higher. Available to U.S. citizens.

Application Requirements: Application, financial need analysis, references, test scores, transcript. *Deadline:* May 1.

Contact: M. Ford, Executive Director
United States Naval Sea Cadet Corps
2300 Wilson Boulevard
Arlington, VA 22201-3308
Phone: 703-243-6910
Fax: 703-243-3985
E-mail: mford@navyleague.org

NAVAL SEA CADET CORPS SCHOLARSHIP PROGRAM

One-time award to assist Cadets in continuing their education at an accredited four-year college or university. Must be a member of NSCC for at least two years. Minimum 3.0 GPA required.

Award: Scholarship for use in freshman, sophomore, junior, or senior years; not renewable. *Number:* up to 5. *Amount:* $1000.

Eligibility Requirements: Applicant must be enrolled or expecting to enroll full-time at a four-year institution or university. Applicant or parent of applicant must be member of Naval Sea Cadet Corps. Applicant must have 3.0 GPA or higher. Available to U.S. citizens.

Application Requirements: Application, financial need analysis, references, test scores, transcript. *Deadline:* May 1.

Contact: M. Ford, Executive Director
United States Naval Sea Cadet Corps
2300 Wilson Boulevard
Arlington, VA 22201-3308
Phone: 703-243-6910
Fax: 703-243-3985
E-mail: mford@navyleague.org

ROBERT AND HELEN HUTTON SCHOLARSHIP

One renewable award of $1000 is available for Sea Cadets to assist them in continuing their education at an accredited four-year college or university. Minimum 3.0 GPA required.

Award: Scholarship for use in freshman, sophomore, junior, or senior years; renewable. *Number:* 1. *Amount:* $1000.

Eligibility Requirements: Applicant must be enrolled or expecting to enroll full-time at a two-year or four-year institution or university. Applicant or parent of applicant must be member of Naval Sea Cadet Corps. Applicant must have 3.0 GPA or higher. Available to U.S. citizens.

Application Requirements: Application, financial need analysis, references, test scores, transcript. *Deadline:* May 1.

Contact: M. Ford, Executive Director
United States Naval Sea Cadet Corps
2300 Wilson Boulevard
Arlington, VA 22201-3308
Phone: 703-243-6910
Fax: 703-243-3985
E-mail: mford@navyleague.org

STOCKHOLM SCHOLARSHIP PROGRAM

Renewable award for a selected Cadet, to be designated a Stockholm Scholar. Must be a member of NSCC for at least two years. Assistance provided for no more than four consecutive years at an accredited college or university. Minimum 3.0 GPA required.

Award: Scholarship for use in freshman, sophomore, junior, or senior years; renewable. *Number:* 1. *Amount:* $2000–$2500.

Eligibility Requirements: Applicant must be enrolled or expecting to enroll full-time at a four-year institution or university. Applicant or parent of applicant must be member of Naval Sea Cadet Corps. Applicant must have 3.0 GPA or higher. Available to U.S. citizens.

Application Requirements: Application, financial need analysis, references, test scores, transcript. *Deadline:* May 1.

Contact: M. Ford, Executive Director
United States Naval Sea Cadet Corps
2300 Wilson Boulevard
Arlington, VA 22201-3308
Phone: 703-243-6910
Fax: 703-243-3985
E-mail: mford@navyleague.org

UNITED STATES SUBMARINE VETERANS

http://www.ussvcf.org/

UNITED STATES SUBMARINE VETERANS INC. NATIONAL SCHOLARSHIP PROGRAM

Program requires the sponsor to be a qualified Base Member or Member-at-Large in good standing. Must demonstrate financial need, have a minimum 2.5 GPA, and submit an essay. Open to children, stepchildren, and grandchildren of qualified members. Applicants must be between the ages of 17 to 23 and must be unmarried.

Award: Scholarship for use in freshman, sophomore, junior, or senior years; not renewable. *Number:* 2–18. *Amount:* $950–$1500.

Eligibility Requirements: Applicant must be age 17-23; enrolled or expecting to enroll full-time at a two-year or four-year or technical institution or university and single. Applicant or parent of applicant must be member of Veterans of Foreign Wars or Auxiliary. Applicant or parent of applicant must have employment or volunteer experience in seafaring/fishing industry. Applicant must have 3.5 GPA or higher. Available to U.S. citizens. Applicant or parent must meet one or more of the following requirements: Navy experience; retired from active duty; disabled or killed as a result of military service; prisoner of war; or missing in action.

Application Requirements: Application, essay, financial need analysis, references, test scores, transcript. *Deadline:* April 15.

Contact: Paul William Orstad, National Scholarship Chairman
United States Submarine Veterans
30 Surrey Lane
Norwich, CT 06369-6541
Phone: 860-889-4750
Fax: 860-334-6457
E-mail: hogan343@aol.com

UTILITY WORKERS UNION OF AMERICA

http://www.uwua.net/

UTILITY WORKERS UNION OF AMERICA SCHOLARSHIP AWARDS PROGRAM

Renewable award for high school juniors who are children of active members of the Utility Workers Union of America. Must take the PSAT National Merit Scholarship Qualifying Test in junior year and plan to enter college in the fall after high school graduation.

Award: Scholarship for use in freshman, sophomore, junior, or senior years; renewable. *Number:* 2. *Amount:* $500–$2000.

Eligibility Requirements: Applicant must be high school student and planning to enroll or expecting to enroll full-time at a four-year institution or university. Applicant or parent of applicant must be member of Utility Workers Union of America. Available to U.S. citizens.

Application Requirements: Application, test scores. *Deadline:* December 31.

Contact: Rosanna Farley, Office Manager
Utility Workers Union of America
815 16th Street, NW
Washington, DC 20006
Phone: 202-974-8200
E-mail: rfarley@aflcio.org

VIETNOW NATIONAL HEADQUARTERS

http://www.vietnow.com/

VIETNOW NATIONAL SCHOLARSHIP

One-time award available to dependants of members of VietNow only. Applicants' academic achievements, abilities and extracurricular activities will be reviewed. Must be U.S. citizen and under the age of 35.

Award: Scholarship for use in freshman, sophomore, junior, senior, or graduate years; not renewable. *Number:* varies. *Amount:* $500–$1000.

Eligibility Requirements: Applicant must be age 35 or under and enrolled or expecting to enroll full-time at a four-year institution or university. Applicant or parent of applicant must be member of VietNow. Available to U.S. citizens.

Application Requirements: Application, driver's license, essay, test scores, transcript. *Deadline:* April 1.

Contact: Eileen Shoemaker, Executive Assistant
VietNow National Headquarters
1835 Broadway
Rockford, IL 61104
Phone: 815-227-5100
Fax: 815-227-5127
E-mail: vnnatl@inwave.com

WESTERN FRATERNAL LIFE ASSOCIATION

http://www.wflains.org/

WESTERN FRATERNAL LIFE ASSOCIATION NATIONAL SCHOLARSHIP

Ten national scholarships will be awarded annually for up to $1000 to qualified members attending college or vocational programs. Traditional and non-traditional students are eligible. Must be a WFLA member in good standing for two years prior to the application deadline. A member is an individual who has life insurance or an annuity with WFLA. High school seniors may apply. Members who are qualified for the National Scholarship may also qualify for 3 state scholarships.

Award: Scholarship for use in freshman, sophomore, junior, senior, or graduate years; renewable. *Number:* 10. *Amount:* $1000.

Eligibility Requirements: Applicant must be enrolled or expecting to enroll full-time at a two-year or four-year or technical institution or university. Applicant or parent of applicant must be member of Western Fraternal Life Association. Available to U.S. citizens.

Application Requirements: Application, essay, references, test scores, transcript. *Deadline:* March 1.

Contact: Linda Grove, Publication Coordinator
Western Fraternal Life Association
1900 First Avenue, NE
Cedar Rapids, IA 52402-5372
Phone: 877-935-2467
Fax: 319-363-8806
E-mail: wflains@wflains.org

WISCONSIN ASSOCIATION FOR FOOD PROTECTION

http://www.wafp-wi.org/

WAFP MEMORIAL SCHOLARSHIP

Scholarship for a child or dependent of a current or deceased association member, or the applicant may be a WAFP student member. Must have been accepted into an accredited degree program in a university, college, or technical institute.

Award: Scholarship for use in freshman, sophomore, junior, or senior years; not renewable. *Number:* 1. *Amount:* $1000.

Eligibility Requirements: Applicant must be enrolled or expecting to enroll full-time at a two-year or four-year or technical institution or university. Applicant or parent of applicant must be member of Wisconsin Association for Food Protection. Available to U.S. and non-U.S. citizens.

Application Requirements: Application, references, transcript. *Deadline:* July 1.

Contact: Mr. Jim Wickert, Scholarship Committee Chairman
Wisconsin Association for Food Protection
3834 Ridgeway Ave.
Madison, WI 53704
Phone: 608-241-2438
E-mail: jwick16060@tds.net

WOMEN'S INTERNATIONAL NETWORK OF UTILITY PROFESSIONALS

http://www.winup.org/

WINUP MEMBERSHIP SCHOLARSHIP

Scholarship of $500 annually given to a member of WiNUP who desires to further education in any field that is applicable to the energy industry. For more information, visit web site http://www.winup.org.

Award: Scholarship for use in freshman, sophomore, junior, senior, graduate, or postgraduate years; not renewable. *Number:* 1. *Amount:* $500.

Eligibility Requirements: Applicant must be enrolled or expecting to enroll full- or part-time at a two-year or four-year or technical institution or university. Applicant or parent of applicant must be member of Women's International Network of Utility Professionals. Available to U.S. and non-U.S. citizens.

Application Requirements: Application, references, transcript. *Deadline:* March 31.

Contact: Theresa Drexler, Executive Director
Women's International Network of Utility Professionals
PO Box 817
Fergus Falls, MN 56538-0817
Phone: 218-731-1659
E-mail: drexler@runestone.net

WOODMEN OF THE WORLD AND/OR ASSURED LIFE ASSOCIATION

http://www.denverwoodmen.com/

WOODMEN OF THE WORLD AND/OR ASSURED LIFE ASSOCIATION ENDOWMENT SCHOLARSHIP PROGRAM

Award for full-time study at a trade/technical school, two-year college, four-year college or university. Applicant must be a benefit member, or a child or grandchild of a benefit member of Woodmen the World and/or Assured Life Association of Colorado. Applicant may reapply each year he/she is a full-time student.

Award: Scholarship for use in freshman, sophomore, junior, senior, or graduate years; not renewable. *Number:* 60–70. *Amount:* $500–$1500.

Eligibility Requirements: Applicant must be enrolled or expecting to enroll full-time at a two-year or four-year or technical institution or university. Applicant or parent of applicant must be member of Woodmen of the World. Available to U.S. and Canadian citizens.

Application Requirements: Application, essay, photo, transcript. *Deadline:* March 15.

Contact: Mr. Jerome L. Christensen, Vice President of Fraternal Affairs
Woodmen of the World and/or Assured Life Association
8000 East Maplewood Avenue, Suite 105
Greenwood Village, CO 80111
Phone: 303-468-3773
Fax: 303-792-9793
E-mail: jlc@denverwoodmen.com

WYOMING FARM BUREAU FEDERATION

http://www.wyfb.org/

KING-LIVINGSTON SCHOLARSHIP

One-time award given to graduates of Wyoming high schools. Must attend a Wyoming junior college or the University of Wyoming. Minimum 2.5 GPA required. Applicant's family must be a current member of the Wyoming Farm Bureau.

Award: Scholarship for use in freshman, sophomore, junior, senior, or graduate years; not renewable. *Number:* 1. *Amount:* $1000.

Eligibility Requirements: Applicant must be enrolled or expecting to enroll full-time at a two-year or four-year institution or university; resident of Wyoming and studying in Wyoming. Applicant or parent of applicant must be member of Wyoming Farm Bureau. Applicant must have 2.5 GPA or higher. Available to U.S. and non-U.S. citizens.

Application Requirements: Application, financial need analysis, photo, resume, references, transcript. *Deadline:* March 1.

Contact: Ellen Westbrook, Executive Secretary
Wyoming Farm Bureau Federation
931 Boulder Drive
Laramie, WY 82070
Phone: 307-721-7719
E-mail: ewestbrook@wyfb.org

WYOMING FARM BUREAU CONTINUING EDUCATION SCHOLARSHIPS

Award to students attending a two-year college in Wyoming or the University of Wyoming. Must be a resident of Wyoming and applicant's family must be a current member of the Wyoming Farm Bureau. Must submit at least two semesters of college grade transcripts. Freshmen must submit first semester grades and proof of enrollment in second semester. Minimum 2.5 GPA.

Award: Scholarship for use in freshman, sophomore, junior, senior, or graduate years; not renewable. *Number:* 3. *Amount:* $500.

Eligibility Requirements: Applicant must be enrolled or expecting to enroll full-time at a two-year or four-year institution or university; resident of Wyoming and studying in Wyoming. Applicant or parent of applicant must be member of Wyoming Farm Bureau. Applicant must have 2.5 GPA or higher. Available to U.S. and non-U.S. citizens.

Application Requirements: Application, financial need analysis, photo, resume, references, test scores, transcript. *Deadline:* March 1.

Contact: Ellen Westbrook, Executive Secretary
Wyoming Farm Bureau Federation
931 Boulder Drive
Laramie, WY 82070
Phone: 307-721-7719
E-mail: ewestbrook@wyfb.org

WYOMING FARM BUREAU FEDERATION SCHOLARSHIPS

Five $500 scholarships will be given to graduates of Wyoming high schools. Eligible candidates must be enrolled in a two-year college in Wyoming or the University of Wyoming and must have a minimum 2.5 GPA. Applicant's family should be current member of the Wyoming Farm Bureau Federation.

Award: Scholarship for use in freshman, sophomore, junior, senior, or graduate years; not renewable. *Number:* 5. *Amount:* $500.

Eligibility Requirements: Applicant must be enrolled or expecting to enroll full-time at a two-year or four-year institution or university; resident of Wyoming and studying in Wyoming. Applicant or parent of applicant must be member of Wyoming Farm Bureau. Applicant must have 2.5 GPA or higher. Available to U.S. and non-U.S. citizens.

Application Requirements: Application, financial need analysis, photo, resume, references, transcript. *Deadline:* March 1.

Contact: Ellen Westbrook, Executive Secretary
Wyoming Farm Bureau Federation
931 Boulder Drive
Laramie, WY 82070
Phone: 307-721-7719
E-mail: ewestbrook@wyfb.org

YOUNG AMERICAN BOWLING ALLIANCE (YABA)

http://www.bowl.com/

GIFT FOR LIFE SCHOLARSHIP

One-time award for high school students who compete in the sport of bowling. Minimum 2.0 GPA required. Must demonstrate financial need. Must be a member in good standing of YABA.

Award: Scholarship for use in freshman year; not renewable. *Number:* 12. *Amount:* $1000.

Eligibility Requirements: Applicant must be high school student; planning to enroll or expecting to enroll full- or part-time at a four-year institution or university and must have an interest in bowling. Applicant or parent of applicant must be member of Young American Bowling Alliance. Available to U.S. citizens.

Application Requirements: Application, references, transcript. *Deadline:* April 1.

Contact: Scholarship Programs Manager
Young American Bowling Alliance (YABA)
5301 South 76th Street
Greendale, WI 53129
Phone: 800-514-2695 Ext. 3318
E-mail: egocha@bowlinginc.com

PEPSI-COLA YOUTH BOWLING CHAMPIONSHIPS

Awarded to members of the Young American Bowling Alliance. Must win state or provincial tournaments to be eligible for international championships. U.S. citizens abroad may participate through military affiliate. Application fee varies by state. Contact Youth Director at local bowling center.

Award: Scholarship for use in freshman, sophomore, junior, or senior years; not renewable. *Number:* 292. *Amount:* $500–$2000.

Eligibility Requirements: Applicant must be enrolled or expecting to enroll full- or part-time at a two-year or four-year institution or university and must have an interest in bowling. Applicant or parent of applicant must be member of Young American Bowling Alliance. Available to U.S. citizens.

Application Requirements: Application, applicant must enter a contest, references, transcript. *Deadline:* February 28.

Contact: Ed Gocha, Scholarship Programs Manager
Young American Bowling Alliance (YABA)
5301 South 76th Street
Greendale, WI 53129-1192
Phone: 800-514-2695
Fax: 414-423-3014
E-mail: smart@bowlinginc.com

CORPORATE AFFILIATION

BUTLER MANUFACTURING COMPANY

http://www.butlermfg.com/

BUTLER MANUFACTURING COMPANY FOUNDATION SCHOLARSHIP PROGRAM

Award for high school seniors who are the children of full-time employees of Butler Manufacturing Company and its subsidiaries. Award is renewable for up to four years. Must enroll full-time and stay in upper half of class.

Award: Scholarship for use in freshman year; renewable. *Number:* 8. *Amount:* $3000.

Eligibility Requirements: Applicant must be high school student and planning to enroll or expecting to enroll full-time at a four-year institution or university. Applicant or parent of applicant must be affiliated with Butler Manufacturing Company. Available to U.S. and Canadian citizens.

Application Requirements: Application, essay, financial need analysis, references, test scores, transcript. *Deadline:* February 15.

Contact: Jill Harmon, Foundation Administrator
Butler Manufacturing Company
1540 Genessee Street
PO Box 419917
Kansas City, MO 64102
Phone: 816-968-3208
Fax: 816-968-6501
E-mail: jcharmon@butlermfg.org

CARGILL

http://www.cargill.com/

CARGILL NATIONAL MERIT SCHOLARSHIP PROGRAM FOR SONS AND DAUGHTERS

Scholarships of $1000 for children of Cargill Inc. and Cargill joint venture employees in the United States.

Award: Scholarship for use in freshman year; renewable. *Number:* 10. *Amount:* $1000.

Eligibility Requirements: Applicant must be high school student and planning to enroll or expecting to enroll full-time at a four-year institution or university. Applicant or parent of applicant must be affiliated with Cargill, Inc. Available to U.S. citizens.

Application Requirements: Application. *Deadline:* February 15.

Contact: Rebecca Oswald, Community Relations Associate
Cargill
PO Box 9300
Minneapolis, MN 55440-9300
Phone: 952-742-6247
Fax: 952-742-7224
E-mail: cargill_scholarships@cargill.com

CARGILL SCHOLARSHIP PROGRAM FOR SONS AND DAUGHTERS

Scholarships of $3000 to high school seniors who are the children of Cargill Inc. and Cargill joint venture employees in the United States.

Award: Scholarship for use in freshman year; not renewable. *Number:* 40. *Amount:* $3000.

Eligibility Requirements: Applicant must be high school student and planning to enroll or expecting to enroll full-time at a four-year institution or university. Applicant or parent of applicant must be affiliated with Cargill, Inc. Available to U.S. citizens.

Application Requirements: Application, transcript. *Deadline:* February 15.

Contact: Rebecca Oswald, Community Relations Associate
Cargill
PO Box 9300
Minneapolis, MN 55440-9300
Phone: 952-742-6247
Fax: 952-742-7224
E-mail: cargill_scholarships@cargill.com

CHICK-FIL-A INC.

http://www.chick-fil-a.com/

CHICK-FIL-A LEADERSHIP SCHOLARSHIP

Scholarships available to current employees of Chick-fil-A restaurants. Must show proof of enrollment in technical school, two- or four-year college or university. Must demonstrate solid work ethic, be actively involved in school or community activities, and possess strong leadership abilities. Must apply with approval of a Unit Operator accompanied by their letter of recommendation. Letter of recommendation from non-work-related individual also required.

Award: Scholarship for use in freshman, sophomore, junior, or senior years; not renewable. *Number:* up to 1400. *Amount:* $1000.

Eligibility Requirements: Applicant must be enrolled or expecting to enroll full- or part-time at a two-year or four-year or technical institution or university. Applicant or parent of applicant must be affiliated with Chick-Fil-A, Inc. Applicant or parent of applicant must have employment or volunteer experience in food service. Available to U.S. citizens.

Application Requirements: Application, references, transcript, letter of acceptance. *Deadline:* continuous.

Contact: Scholarship Coordinator
Chick-fil-A Inc.
5200 Buffington Road
Atlanta, GA 30349-2998
Phone: 404-765-8038

S. TRUETT CATHY SCHOLAR AWARDS

This award is given to the top twenty-five Chick-fil-A Leadership Scholarship recipients each year. Scholarship amount is $1000.

Award: Scholarship for use in freshman, sophomore, junior, or senior years; not renewable. *Number:* up to 25. *Amount:* up to $1000.

Eligibility Requirements: Applicant must be enrolled or expecting to enroll full- or part-time at a two-year or four-year or technical institution or university. Applicant or parent of applicant must be affiliated with Chick-Fil-A, Inc. Available to U.S. citizens.

Application Requirements: Application, references, transcript, unit operator approval, proof of enrollment. *Deadline:* continuous.

Contact: Scholarship Coordinator
Chick-fil-A Inc.
5200 Buffington Road
Atlanta, GA 30349-2998
Phone: 404-765-8038

CLEVELAND SCHOLARSHIP PROGRAMS

http://www.cspohio.org/

CSP MANAGED FUNDS-OGLEBAY NORTON COMPANY EMPLOYEE SCHOLARSHIP

Award to assist graduating high school seniors or current college students who are sons and daughters of full-time employees of Oglebay Norton Company and its subsidiaries. Must have at least 3.0 GPA.

Award: Scholarship for use in freshman, sophomore, junior, or senior years; renewable. *Number:* 1. *Amount:* $1000.

Eligibility Requirements: Applicant must be high school student and planning to enroll or expecting to enroll full-time at a two-year or four-year institution or university. Applicant or parent of applicant must be affiliated with Oglebay Norton Company. Applicant must have 3.0 GPA or higher. Available to U.S. citizens.

Application Requirements: Application, test scores, transcript. *Deadline:* April 21.

Contact: Bridget Vaughn, Special Projects Manager
Cleveland Scholarship Programs
200 Public Square, Suite 3820
Cleveland, OH 44114
E-mail: bvaughn@cspohio.org

COMMUNITY FOUNDATION OF WESTERN MASSACHUSETTS

http://www.communityfoundation.org/

DEERFIELD PLASTICS/BARKER FAMILY SCHOLARSHIP

Children, step-children, and grandchildren of employees of the former Deerfield Plastics Company, Inc. as of October 1996. Seventeen awards totaling $40,000 were made in 2010.

Award: Scholarship for use in freshman, sophomore, junior, senior, or graduate years; not renewable. *Number:* 1. *Amount:* $1500–$3000.

Eligibility Requirements: Applicant must be enrolled or expecting to enroll full- or part-time at a two-year or four-year institution or university and resident of Kentucky or Massachusetts. Applicant or parent of applicant must be affiliated with Deerfield Plastics. Available to U.S. citizens.

Application Requirements: Application, financial need analysis, transcript, Student Aid Report (SAR). *Deadline:* March 31.

Contact: Dorothy Theriaque, Education Associate
Community Foundation of Western Massachusetts
1500 Main Street, PO Box 15769
Springfield, MA 01115
Phone: 413-732-2858
Fax: 413-733-8565
E-mail: scholar@communityfoundation.org

DEMOLAY FOUNDATION INCORPORATED

http://www.demolay.org/

FRANK S. LAND SCHOLARSHIP

Scholarship awarded to members of DeMolay International only, who have not yet reached the age of 21, to assist in financing their education. Must be U.S. resident.

Award: Scholarship for use in freshman, sophomore, junior, or senior years; not renewable. *Number:* 10–15. *Amount:* $1000.

Eligibility Requirements: Applicant must be age 21 or under; enrolled or expecting to enroll full-time at a two-year or four-year institution or university and male. Applicant or parent of applicant must be affiliated with DeMolay. Available to U.S. citizens.

Application Requirements: Application, references, self-addressed stamped envelope, transcript. *Deadline:* April 1.

Contact: Jeffrey C. Kitsmiller Sr., Executive Director
DeMolay Foundation Incorporated
10200 Northwest Ambassador Drive
Kansas City, MO 64153
Phone: 800-336-6529
Fax: 816-891-9062
E-mail: admin@demolay.org

DONALDSON COMPANY

http://www.donaldson.com/

DONALDSON COMPANY INC. SCHOLARSHIP PROGRAM

Scholarships for children of U.S. employees of Donaldson Company Inc. Any form of accredited postsecondary education is eligible. The amount of the award can range from $1000 to $3000 for each year of full-time study and may be renewed for up to a total of four years. The number of scholarships awarded is limited to a maximum of 25 percent of the number of applicants.

Award: Scholarship for use in freshman, sophomore, junior, or senior years; renewable. *Number:* varies. *Amount:* $1000–$3000.

Eligibility Requirements: Applicant must be enrolled or expecting to enroll full-time at a two-year or four-year institution or university. Applicant or parent of applicant must be affiliated with Donaldson Company. Available to U.S. citizens.

Application Requirements: Application, essay, financial need analysis, references, transcript. *Deadline:* March 15.

Contact: Norm Linnell, Vice President, General Counsel and Secretary
Donaldson Company
PO Box 1299
Minneapolis, MN 55440
Phone: 952-887-3631
Fax: 952-887-3005
E-mail: norm.linnell@donaldson.com

DUKE ENERGY CORPORATION

http://www.duke-energy.com/

DUKE ENERGY SCHOLARS PROGRAM

The scholarship is for undergraduate study at accredited, two-year technical schools or community colleges and/or four-year colleges or universities in the United States and Canada who are children of eligible employees and retirees of Duke Energy and its subsidiaries. Recipients selected by five-member outside committee.

Award: Scholarship for use in freshman, sophomore, junior, or senior years; renewable. *Number:* 15. *Amount:* $1000–$5000.

Eligibility Requirements: Applicant must be enrolled or expecting to enroll full-time at a two-year or four-year or technical institution or university. Applicant or parent of applicant must be affiliated with Duke Energy Corporation. Available to U.S. and Canadian citizens.

Application Requirements: Application, driver's license, essay, financial need analysis, references, test scores, transcript. *Deadline:* December 1.

Contact: Celia Beam, Scholarship Administrator
Duke Energy Corporation
526 South Church Street
PO Box 1244
Charlotte, NC 28202-1904
Phone: 704-382-5544
Fax: 704-382-3553
E-mail: chbeam@duke-energy.com

GANNETT FOUNDATION

http://www.gannettfoundation.org/

GANNETT FOUNDATION/MADELYN P. JENNINGS SCHOLARSHIP AWARD

One-time awards for high school students whose parents are current full-time Gannett Company employees. Must be planning to attend a 4-year college or university for full-time study in the fall after graduation. Students must meet all requirements for participation in the National Merit Scholarship Program and take the PSAT/NMSQT in their junior year of high school. For more information, visit web site: https://programentry.nationalmerit.org/HKRCDTRG.

Award: Scholarship for use in freshman year; not renewable. *Number:* 12. *Amount:* $3000.

Eligibility Requirements: Applicant must be high school student and planning to enroll or expecting to enroll full-time at a four-year institution or university. Applicant or parent of applicant must be affiliated with Gannett Company, Inc. Available to U.S. citizens.

Application Requirements: Application. *Deadline:* March 1.

Contact: Collette Horton, Benefits Representative
Gannett Foundation
7950 Jones Branch Drive
McLean, VA 22107
Phone: 703-854-6254
E-mail: cnhorton@gannett.com

GATEWAY PRESS INC. OF LOUISVILLE

http://www.gatewaypressinc.com/

GATEWAY PRESS SCHOLARSHIP

Scholarship for graduating high school seniors whose parents have been employees of Gateway Press Inc. for a minimum of 5 years. Applicant must be accepted at a college or university and maintain a minimum GPA of 2.25.

Award: Scholarship for use in freshman year; renewable. *Number:* varies. *Amount:* up to $3000.

Eligibility Requirements: Applicant must be high school student and planning to enroll or expecting to enroll full-time at a four-year institution or university. Applicant or parent of applicant must be affiliated with Gateway Press Inc. Available to U.S. citizens.

Application Requirements: Application, references, transcript. *Deadline:* January 1.

Contact: Chris Georgehead, Human Resources Manager
Gateway Press Inc. of Louisville
4500 Robards Lane
Louisville, KY 40218
Phone: 502-454-0431
Fax: 502-459-7930
E-mail: kit@gatewaypressinc.com

GRACO INC.

http://www.graco.com/

GRACO EXCELLENCE SCHOLARSHIP

Three awards of $7500 (one for athletic achievement) for children of Graco employees with at least one year of company service. Award based on academics, financial need, and tuition costs. Must be under 25 years of age.

Award: Scholarship for use in freshman, sophomore, junior, senior, or graduate years; renewable. *Number:* 3. *Amount:* $7500.

Eligibility Requirements: Applicant must be age 25 or under; enrolled or expecting to enroll full-time at a two-year or four-year or technical institution or university and must have an interest in athletics/sports. Applicant or parent of applicant must be affiliated with Graco, Inc. Available to U.S. and non-U.S. citizens.

Application Requirements: Application, financial need analysis, test scores, transcript. *Deadline:* March 15.

Contact: Kristin Ridley, Grants Administration Manager
Graco Inc.
PO Box 1441
Minneapolis, MN 55440-1441
Phone: 612-623-6684
Fax: 612-623-6944

GRACO INC. SCHOLARSHIP PROGRAM

Renewable award for children of Graco employees under 26 years of age pursuing undergraduate or graduate education. Awards are based upon academics, financial need, and tuition costs. Submit transcripts, test scores, and financial need analysis with application.

Award: Scholarship for use in freshman, sophomore, junior, senior, or graduate years; renewable. *Number:* varies. *Amount:* $3500–$5000.

Eligibility Requirements: Applicant must be age 26 or under and enrolled or expecting to enroll full-time at a two-year or four-year or technical institution or university. Applicant or parent of applicant must be affiliated with Graco, Inc. Available to U.S. and non-U.S. citizens.

Application Requirements: Application, financial need analysis, test scores, transcript. *Deadline:* March 15.

Contact: Kristin Ridley, Grants Administration Manager
Graco Inc.
PO Box 1441
Minneapolis, MN 55440-1441
Phone: 612-623-6684
Fax: 612-623-6944

HERMAN O. WEST FOUNDATION

http://www.westpharma.com/

HERMAN O. WEST FOUNDATION SCHOLARSHIP PROGRAM

Awards up to seven scholarships per year to high school seniors who will be attending college in the fall after graduation. The scholarship may only be applied toward tuition cost up to $2500 per year for up to four years. Available only to children of active employees of West Pharmaceutical Services, Inc.

Award: Scholarship for use in freshman, sophomore, junior, or senior years; renewable. *Number:* 1–7. *Amount:* $2500–$10,000.

Eligibility Requirements: Applicant must be high school student and planning to enroll or expecting to enroll full-time at a two-year or four-year institution or university. Applicant or parent of applicant must be affiliated with West Pharmaceuticals. Available to U.S. citizens.

Application Requirements: Application, essay, references, test scores, transcript. *Deadline:* February 28.

Contact: Maureen Goebel, Administrator
Herman O. West Foundation
101 Gordon Drive
Lionville, PA 19341
Phone: 610-594-2945
Fax: 610-594-3011
E-mail: maureen.goebel@westpharma.com

JOHNSON CONTROLS INC.

http://www.johnsoncontrols.com/

JOHNSON CONTROLS FOUNDATION SCHOLARSHIP PROGRAM

Available to high school seniors who are children of Johnson Controls, Inc. employees. 20 one-time awards of $2000 and 25 renewable scholarships of $2000 a year for up to four years.

Award: Scholarship for use in freshman year; renewable. *Number:* up to 45. *Amount:* $2000.

Eligibility Requirements: Applicant must be high school student and planning to enroll or expecting to enroll full-time at a four-year institution or university. Applicant or parent of applicant must be affiliated with Johnson Controls, Inc. Applicant must have 3.0 GPA or higher. Available to U.S. citizens.

Application Requirements: Application, transcript. *Deadline:* March 3.

Contact: Marlene Griffith, Human Resources Administration Coordinator
Johnson Controls Inc.
5757 North Green Bay Avenue, X-34
Milwaukee, WI 53209
Phone: 414-524-2425
Fax: 414-524-2299
E-mail: marlene.f.griffith@jci.com

LINCOLN COMMUNITY FOUNDATION

http://www.lcf.org/

GEORGE L. WATTERS/NEBRASKA PETROLEUM MARKETERS ASSOCIATION SCHOLARSHIP

Multiple scholarships are available to current high school seniors who are the sons, daughters or grandchildren of any Nebraska Petroleum Marketer and Convenience Store Association member or of a full- or part-time employee. Must demonstrate academic achievement, leadership qualities, and have expressed a desire and intent to continue education leading to a degree.

Award: Scholarship for use in freshman year; not renewable. *Number:* varies. *Amount:* $1000.

Eligibility Requirements: Applicant must be high school student; planning to enroll or expecting to enroll full-time at a four-year institution or university; resident of Nebraska; studying in Nebraska and must have an interest in leadership. Applicant or parent of applicant must be affiliated with Nebraska Petroleum Marketers Association. Applicant must have 3.0 GPA or higher. Available to U.S. citizens.

Application Requirements: Application, references, transcript. *Deadline:* March 1.

Contact: Grafton and Associates Certified Public Accountants
Lincoln Community Foundation
8101 O Street, Suite 200
Lincoln, NE 68510

THOMAS C. WOODS, JR. MEMORIAL SCHOLARSHIP

Scholarships for graduating seniors or former graduates of any high school in the following counties in Nebraska: Adams, Butler, Cass, Clay, Fillmore, Gage, Hamilton, Jefferson, Johnson, Lancaster, Nemaha, Nucholls, Otoe, Pawnee, Polk, Richardson, Saline, Saunders, Seward, Thayer, Webster, and York. Applicants must be qualified dependents of current ALLTEL employees. Minimum 2.5 GPA required.

Award: Scholarship for use in freshman, sophomore, junior, or senior years; renewable. *Number:* varies. *Amount:* $500–$2000.

Eligibility Requirements: Applicant must be enrolled or expecting to enroll full-time at a two-year or four-year institution or university; resident of Nebraska and studying in Nebraska. Applicant or parent of applicant must be affiliated with ALLTEL. Applicant must have 2.5 GPA or higher. Available to U.S. citizens.

Application Requirements: Application, essay, financial need analysis, test scores. *Deadline:* April 17.

Contact: Sonya Brakeman, Grants/Scholarships Coordinator
Lincoln Community Foundation
215 Centennial Mall South, Suite 100
Lincoln, NE 68508
Phone: 402-474-2345
Fax: 402-476-8532
E-mail: sonyab@lcf.org

MINNESOTA COMMUNITY FOUNDATION

http://www.mncommunityfoundation.org/

CEMSTONE COMPANIES SCHOLARSHIP

Scholarship to full-time employees of Cemstone Company and their dependents. Two or more awards of at least $2000 are awarded.

Award: Scholarship for use in freshman, sophomore, junior, senior, or graduate years; not renewable. *Number:* 2. *Amount:* $2000.

Eligibility Requirements: Applicant must be enrolled or expecting to enroll full- or part-time at a two-year or four-year or technical institution or university. Applicant or parent of applicant must be affiliated with Cemstone Company. Available to U.S. citizens.

Application Requirements: Application, transcript. *Deadline:* May 1.

Contact: Donna Paulson, Administrative Assistant
Minnesota Community Foundation
55 Fifth Street East, Suite 600
St. Paul, MN 55101-1797
Phone: 651-325-4212
Fax: 651-224-9502
E-mail: dkp@mncommunityfoundation.org

J.C. AND L.A. DUKE SCHOLARSHIP

Awards 50 or more renewable scholarships ranging from $1500 to $2000 each year to legal dependents of active, disabled, retired or deceased persons employed by 3M for a minimum of two years prior to January 1 of the year in which the student graduates from high school.

Award: Scholarship for use in freshman year; renewable. *Number:* 50. *Amount:* $1500–$2000.

Eligibility Requirements: Applicant must be high school student and planning to enroll or expecting to enroll full- or part-time at a four-year institution or university. Applicant or parent of applicant must be affiliated with 3M Corporation. Available to U.S. citizens.

Application Requirements: Application, transcript, income of parents, IRS Form 1040. *Deadline:* March 1.

Contact: Donna Paulson, Administrative Assistant
Minnesota Community Foundation
55 Fifth Street East, Suite 600
St. Paul, MN 55101-1797
Phone: 651-325-4212
Fax: 651-224-9502
E-mail: dkp@mncommunityfoundation.org

PAUL AND FERN YOCUM SCHOLARSHIP

Scholarship to dependent children of full-time Yocum Oil employees.

Award: Scholarship for use in freshman, sophomore, junior, senior, or graduate years; not renewable. *Number:* 3. *Amount:* $1000.

Eligibility Requirements: Applicant must be enrolled or expecting to enroll full- or part-time at a four-year institution or university. Applicant or parent of applicant must be affiliated with Yocum Oil Company. Available to U.S. and non-Canadian citizens.

Application Requirements: Application. *Deadline:* April 15.

Contact: Donna Paulson, Administrative Assistant
Minnesota Community Foundation
55 Fifth Street East, Suite 600
St. Paul, MN 55101-1797
Phone: 651-325-4212
Fax: 651-224-9502
E-mail: dkp@mncommunityfoundation.org

YOUNG AMERICA CORPORATION SCHOLARSHIP

Scholarship to employees or dependent children or grandchildren of active Young America employees with a minimum of one year of active employment as of the application deadline, enrolling in an undergraduate course of study. Five awards of $1000 are awarded annually.

Award: Scholarship for use in freshman, sophomore, junior, or senior years; not renewable. *Number:* 5. *Amount:* $1000.

Eligibility Requirements: Applicant must be enrolled or expecting to enroll full- or part-time at a four-year institution or university. Applicant or parent of applicant must be affiliated with Young America Corporation. Available to U.S. citizens.

Application Requirements: Application, resume, references, transcript. *Deadline:* June 15.

Contact: Donna Paulson, Administrative Assistant
Minnesota Community Foundation
55 Fifth Street East, Suite 600
St. Paul, MN 55101-1797
Phone: 651-325-4212
Fax: 651-224-9502
E-mail: dkp@mncommunityfoundation.org

NEW HAMPSHIRE FOOD INDUSTRIES EDUCATION FOUNDATION

http://www.grocers.org/

NEW HAMPSHIRE FOOD INDUSTRY SCHOLARSHIPS

Awards are $1000 each. The purpose is to assist students who are employees or children of employees working for New Hampshire Grocers Association member firms (either retailer or supplier).

Award: Scholarship for use in freshman, sophomore, junior, or senior years; renewable. *Number:* up to 35. *Amount:* $1000.

Eligibility Requirements: Applicant must be enrolled or expecting to enroll full- or part-time at a two-year or four-year or technical institution or university and resident of New Hampshire. Applicant or parent of applicant must be affiliated with New Hampshire Grocers Association member companies. Available to U.S. citizens.

Application Requirements: Application, essay, references, test scores, transcript. *Deadline:* April 1.

Contact: Mr. John M. Dumais, Secretary and Treasurer
New Hampshire Food Industries Education Foundation
110 Stark Street
Manchester, NH 03101-1977
Phone: 603-669-9333 Ext. 110
Fax: 603-623-1137
E-mail: scholarships@grocers.org

OREGON STUDENT ASSISTANCE COMMISSION

http://www.GetCollegeFunds.org/

ALBINA FUEL COMPANY SCHOLARSHIP

Scholarship available to a dependent child of a current Albina Fuel Company employee. The employee must have been employed for at least one full year as of October 1 prior to the scholarship deadline. Must reapply annually. Oregon residency not required. For additional information, see web site: https://secure.osac.state.or.us/.

Award: Scholarship for use in freshman, sophomore, junior, or senior years; not renewable. *Number:* varies. *Amount:* varies.

Eligibility Requirements: Applicant must be enrolled or expecting to enroll full-time at a four-year institution. Applicant or parent of applicant must be affiliated with Albina Fuel Company. Available to U.S. citizens.

Application Requirements: Application, essay, transcript, activity chart. *Deadline:* March 1.

Contact: Director of Grant Programs
Oregon Student Assistance Commission
1500 Valley River Drive, Suite 100
Eugene, OR 97401-7020
Phone: 800-452-8807 Ext. 7395

A. VICTOR ROSENFELD SCHOLARSHIP

Award for dependents of employees of Calbag Metals of Portland, Oregon who have worked for that company for three or more years prior to the March 1 scholarship deadline. Applicants must be enrolled at any public or nonprofit U.S. college or university. Must reapply annually for award renewal.

Award: Scholarship for use in freshman, sophomore, junior, or senior years; not renewable. *Number:* varies. *Amount:* varies.

Eligibility Requirements: Applicant must be enrolled or expecting to enroll full-time at a four-year institution or university and resident of Oregon. Applicant or parent of applicant must be affiliated with Calbag Metals. Available to U.S. citizens.

Application Requirements: Application, essay, financial need analysis, references, transcript. *Deadline:* March 1.

Contact: Director of Grant Programs
Oregon Student Assistance Commission
1500 Valley River Drive, Suite 100
Eugene, OR 97401-7020
Phone: 800-452-8807 Ext. 7395

ESSEX GENERAL CONSTRUCTION SCHOLARSHIP

Award for an employee, or dependent of a current employee of Essex General Construction. Employee must have been continuously employed at Essex for one year or more at no fewer than 20 hours per week as of the

March 1 application deadline. Applicant must be a high school graduate, Oregon residency not required. Must be enrolling as an undergraduate in a college or university in the U.S. Must reapply each year to renew award for up to four years.

Award: Scholarship for use in freshman, sophomore, junior, or senior years; not renewable.

Eligibility Requirements: Applicant must be enrolled or expecting to enroll full- or part-time at a four-year institution and resident of Oregon. Applicant or parent of applicant must be affiliated with Essex General Construction. Available to U.S. citizens.

Application Requirements: Application, essay, financial need analysis, transcript, activities chart. *Deadline:* March 1.

Contact: Director of Grant Programs
Oregon Student Assistance Commission
1500 Valley River Drive, Suite 100
Eugene, OR 97401-7020
Phone: 800-452-8807 Ext. 7395

GLENN JACKSON SCHOLARS SCHOLARSHIPS

Renewable award for Oregon graduating high school seniors who are dependents of employees or retirees of Oregon Department of Transportation or Parks and Recreation Department. Employees must have worked in their department at least three years as of the March 1 scholarship deadline.

Award: Scholarship for use in freshman, sophomore, junior, or senior years; renewable. *Number:* varies. *Amount:* varies.

Eligibility Requirements: Applicant must be high school student; planning to enroll or expecting to enroll full- or part-time at a two-year or four-year institution or university and resident of Oregon. Applicant or parent of applicant must be affiliated with Oregon Department of Transportation Parks and Recreation. Available to U.S. citizens.

Application Requirements: Application, essay, financial need analysis, references, transcript, activity chart. *Deadline:* March 1.

Contact: Director of Grant Programs
Oregon Student Assistance Commission
1500 Valley River Drive, Suite 100
Eugene, OR 97401-7020
Phone: 800-452-8807 Ext. 7395

KONNIE MEMORIAL DEPENDENTS SCHOLARSHIP

Renewable award for graduating high school seniors who are children of Swanson Brothers Lumber Co. employees. Must be an Oregon resident and enrolled in an Oregon public college.

Award: Scholarship for use in freshman year; renewable. *Number:* varies. *Amount:* varies.

Eligibility Requirements: Applicant must be high school student; planning to enroll or expecting to enroll full-time at a four-year institution; resident of Oregon and studying in Oregon. Applicant or parent of applicant must be affiliated with Swanson Brothers Lumber Company. Available to U.S. citizens.

Application Requirements: Application, essay, references, transcript, activity chart. *Deadline:* March 1.

Contact: Director of Grant Programs
Oregon Student Assistance Commission
1500 Valley River Drive, Suite 100
Eugene, OR 97401-7020
Phone: 800-452-8807 Ext. 7395

OREGON TRUCKING ASSOCIATION SAFETY MANAGEMENT COUNCIL SCHOLARSHIP

One-time award available to a child of an Oregon Trucking Association member, or child of an employee of OTA member. Applicants must be graduating high school seniors from an Oregon high school planning to attend a public or nonprofit college or university. Oregon residency is not required.

Award: Scholarship for use in freshman year; not renewable. *Amount:* varies.

Eligibility Requirements: Applicant must be high school student and planning to enroll or expecting to enroll full-time at a four-year institution. Applicant or parent of applicant must be affiliated with Oregon Trucking Association. Available to U.S. citizens.

Application Requirements: Application, essay, financial need analysis, references, transcript, activity chart. *Deadline:* March 1.

Contact: Director of Grant Programs
Oregon Student Assistance Commission
1500 Valley River Drive, Suite 100
Eugene, OR 97401-7020
Phone: 800-452-8807 Ext. 7395

PACIFICSOURCE HEALTH PLANS SCHOLARSHIP

Award for high school graduates or GED recipients who are the dependents of PacificSource Health Plans employees. Employee must have been continuously employed at PacificSource for at least two years at no fewer than 20 hours per week as of the March 1 application deadline. Dependents of company officers are not eligible. Award is to be used for undergraduate study at a U.S. college or university. Oregon residency is not required.

Award: Scholarship for use in freshman, sophomore, junior, or senior years; not renewable. *Number:* varies. *Amount:* varies.

Eligibility Requirements: Applicant must be enrolled or expecting to enroll full-time at a four-year institution or university. Applicant or parent of applicant must be affiliated with PacificSource. Applicant must have 3.0 GPA or higher. Available to U.S. citizens.

Application Requirements: Application, essay, transcript, activities chart. *Deadline:* March 1.

Contact: Director of Grant Programs
Oregon Student Assistance Commission
1500 Valley River Drive, Suite 100
Eugene, OR 97401-7020
Phone: 800-452-8807 Ext. 7395

REED'S FUEL AND TRUCKING COMPANY SCHOLARSHIP

Award for employees and dependents of Reed's Fuel and Trucking Company. Eligible employees will have been employed one year as of the March 1 scholarship deadline. Minimum cumulative 2.5 GPA required. Employees may be enrolled as part-time students; dependents must be enrolled full-time.

Award: Scholarship for use in freshman, sophomore, junior, or senior years; renewable. *Number:* varies. *Amount:* varies.

Eligibility Requirements: Applicant must be enrolled or expecting to enroll full- or part-time at a two-year or four-year institution or university. Applicant or parent of applicant must be affiliated with Reeds Fuel and Trucking Company. Applicant must have 2.5 GPA or higher. Available to U.S. citizens.

Application Requirements: Application, essay, references, transcript. *Deadline:* March 1.

Contact: Director of Grant Programs
Oregon Student Assistance Commission
1500 Valley River Drive, Suite 100
Eugene, OR 97401-7020
Phone: 800-452-8807 Ext. 7395

RICHARD F. BRENTANO MEMORIAL SCHOLARSHIP

One-time award for legal dependents of eligible employees of Waste Control Systems Inc., and subsidiaries. Employees must be employed at least one year as of the March 1 scholarship deadline. Oregon residency is not required. Must reapply annually to renew award.

Award: Scholarship for use in freshman, sophomore, junior, or senior years; not renewable. *Number:* varies. *Amount:* varies.

Eligibility Requirements: Applicant must be enrolled or expecting to enroll full-time at a four-year institution. Applicant or parent of applicant must be affiliated with Waste Control Systems, Inc. Available to U.S. citizens.

Application Requirements: Application, essay, references, transcript, activity chart. *Deadline:* March 1.

Contact: Director of Grant Programs
Oregon Student Assistance Commission
1500 Valley River Drive, Suite 100
Eugene, OR 97401-7020
Phone: 800-452-8807 Ext. 7395

ROBERT D. FORSTER SCHOLARSHIP

One scholarship available to an employee of Walsh Construction Co. or a dependent child of an employee. Oregon residency not required. Award may be renewed for a maximum of twelve quarters of undergraduate study if renewal criteria are met, and may be used at any four-year college or university in the U.S.

Award: Scholarship for use in freshman, sophomore, junior, or senior years; renewable. *Number:* varies. *Amount:* varies.

Eligibility Requirements: Applicant must be enrolled or expecting to enroll full-time at a four-year institution. Applicant or parent of applicant must be affiliated with Walsh Construction Company. Available to U.S. citizens.

Application Requirements: Application, essay, financial need analysis, references, transcript, activity chart. *Deadline:* March 1.

Contact: Director of Grant Programs
Oregon Student Assistance Commission
1500 Valley River Drive, Suite 100
Eugene, OR 97401-7020
Phone: 800-452-8807 Ext. 7395

ROGER W. EMMONS MEMORIAL SCHOLARSHIP

Scholarship available to a graduating Oregon high school senior who is a child or grandchild of an employee (for at least three years) of member of the Oregon Refuse and Recycling Association. Oregon residency is not required; award may be used at any accredited U.S. public or nonprofit college or university. See web site for additional information https://secure.osac.state.or.us.

Award: Scholarship for use in freshman year; renewable. *Number:* varies. *Amount:* varies.

Eligibility Requirements: Applicant must be high school student and planning to enroll or expecting to enroll full-time at a four-year institution. Applicant or parent of applicant must be affiliated with Oregon Refuse and Recycling Association. Available to U.S. citizens.

Application Requirements: Application, essay, references, transcript, activity chart. *Deadline:* March 1.

Contact: Director of Grant Programs
Oregon Student Assistance Commission
1500 Valley River Drive, Suite 100
Eugene, OR 97401-7020
Phone: 800-452-8807 Ext. 7395

SP NEWSPRINT COMPANY, NEWBERG MILL, EMPLOYEE DEPENDENTS SCHOLARSHIP

One-time award available to dependents of active employees of SP Newsprint Company. Eligible employees must have been employed by the company one year as of the March 1 scholarship deadline. Students must be enrolled as undergraduates in a U.S. college or university, and reapply annually for award renewal. Oregon residency is not required.

Award: Scholarship for use in freshman, sophomore, junior, or senior years; not renewable. *Number:* varies. *Amount:* varies.

Eligibility Requirements: Applicant must be enrolled or expecting to enroll full-time at a two-year or four-year institution. Applicant or parent of applicant must be affiliated with SP Newsprint Company. Available to U.S. citizens.

Application Requirements: Application, essay, financial need analysis, references, transcript, activity chart. *Deadline:* March 1.

Contact: Director of Grant Programs
Oregon Student Assistance Commission
1500 Valley River Drive, Suite 100
Eugene, OR 97401-7020
Phone: 800-452-8807 Ext. 7395

STIMSON LUMBER COMPANY SCHOLARSHIP

Award for dependents of Stimson Lumber Company employees who are graduating seniors that have a minimum 3.0 GPA. Oregon residency is not required. One-year-only scholarships available for students attending two- or four-year public or nonprofit colleges. Renewable scholarships are for students enrolled in four-year public or nonprofit colleges who meet renewal criteria and maintain 2.7 GPA.

Award: Scholarship for use in freshman year; not renewable. *Number:* varies. *Amount:* varies.

Eligibility Requirements: Applicant must be enrolled or expecting to enroll full-time at a two-year or four-year institution. Applicant or parent of applicant must be affiliated with Stimson Lumber Company. Applicant must have 3.0 GPA or higher. Available to U.S. citizens.

Application Requirements: Application, essay, financial need analysis, references, transcript, activity chart. *Deadline:* March 1.

TAYLOR MADE LABELS SCHOLARSHIP

Award available to dependents of active employees of Taylor Made Label Company. Employee must have been employed by Taylor Made for a minimum of one year as of the March 1 scholarship deadline. Oregon residency is not required. Applicant must be enrolled as an undergraduate in a U.S. college or university and must reapply annually for award renewal.

Award: Scholarship for use in freshman, sophomore, junior, or senior years; not renewable. *Number:* varies. *Amount:* varies.

Eligibility Requirements: Applicant must be enrolled or expecting to enroll full- or part-time at a four-year institution. Applicant or parent of applicant must be affiliated with Taylor Made Label Company. Available to U.S. citizens.

Application Requirements: Application, essay, financial need analysis, references, transcript, activity chart, FAFSA. *Deadline:* March 1.

Contact: Director of Grant Programs
Oregon Student Assistance Commission
1500 Valley River Drive, Suite 100
Eugene, OR 97401-7020
Phone: 800-452-8807 Ext. 7395

WALTER DAVIES SCHOLARSHIP

Award for current U.S. Bank employees or employees' natural or adopted children. Must be Oregon high school graduate. Oregon residency is not required; must re-apply annually. Financial need will be considered.

Award: Scholarship for use in freshman, sophomore, junior, or senior years; not renewable. *Number:* varies. *Amount:* varies.

Eligibility Requirements: Applicant must be enrolled or expecting to enroll full-time at a four-year institution. Applicant or parent of applicant must be affiliated with U.S. Bancorp. Available to U.S. citizens.

Application Requirements: Application, essay, financial need analysis, references, transcript, activity chart, FAFSA. *Deadline:* March 1.

Contact: Director of Grant Programs
Oregon Student Assistance Commission
1500 Valley River Drive, Suite 100
Eugene, OR 97401-7020
Phone: 800-452-8807 Ext. 7395

WILLETT AND MARGUERITE LAKE SCHOLARSHIP

Scholarship awards for children, stepchildren, and grandchildren of current employees of Bonita Pioneer Packaging Company who have been employed by the company for two years. Open to high school seniors and undergraduates who are Oregon residents. Reapply annually.

Award: Scholarship for use in freshman, sophomore, junior, or senior years; not renewable. *Number:* varies. *Amount:* varies.

Eligibility Requirements: Applicant must be enrolled or expecting to enroll full-time at a four-year institution or university and resident of Oregon. Applicant or parent of applicant must be affiliated with Bonita Pioneer Packaging Company. Available to U.S. citizens.

Application Requirements: Application, essay, financial need analysis, transcript, activity chart. *Deadline:* March 1.

Contact: Director of Grant Programs
Oregon Student Assistance Commission
1500 Valley River Drive, Suite 100
Eugene, OR 97401-7020
Phone: 800-452-8807 Ext. 7395

WOODARD FAMILY SCHOLARSHIP

Scholarships are available to employees and dependents of eligible employees of Kimwood Corporation. Awards may be used at Oregon public and nonprofit colleges only. FAFSA required. May reapply annually for award.

Award: Scholarship for use in freshman, sophomore, junior, or senior years; renewable. *Number:* varies. *Amount:* varies.

Eligibility Requirements: Applicant must be enrolled or expecting to enroll full-time at a two-year or four-year institution; resident of Oregon and studying in Oregon. Applicant or parent of applicant must be affiliated with Kimwood Corporation or Middlefield Village. Available to U.S. citizens.

Application Requirements: Application, essay, financial need analysis, references, transcript. *Deadline:* March 1.

Contact: Director of Grant Programs
Oregon Student Assistance Commission
1500 Valley River Drive, Suite 100
Eugene, OR 97401-7020
Phone: 800-452-8807 Ext. 7395

RHODE ISLAND FOUNDATION

http://www.rifoundation.org/

A.T. CROSS SCHOLARSHIP

Scholarships ranging from $1000 to $3000 for new applicants and from $300 to $2000 for renewals are available to children of full-time employees of A.T. Cross Company. Must be Rhode Island residents.

Award: Scholarship for use in freshman, sophomore, junior, or senior years; renewable. *Number:* varies. *Amount:* $1000–$3000.

Eligibility Requirements: Applicant must be enrolled or expecting to enroll full-time at a four-year institution or university and resident of Rhode Island. Applicant or parent of applicant must be affiliated with A.T. Cross. Available to U.S. citizens.

Application Requirements: Application, essay, financial need analysis, references, self-addressed stamped envelope, transcript. *Deadline:* May 14.

Contact: Libby Monahan, Funds Administrator
Rhode Island Foundation
One Union Station
Providence, RI 02903
Phone: 401-274-4564 Ext. 3117
E-mail: libbym@rifoundation.org

SAN DIEGO FOUNDATION

http://www.sdfoundation.org/

CLUB AT MORNINGSIDE SCHOLARSHIP

Scholarships to employees, full or part-time, employed by The Club at Morningside for a minimum of two consecutive years on a seasonal or year-round basis. Open to graduating high school seniors, students already in school, or those planning to attend an accredited two- or four-year college or university, graduate school, or licensed trade/vocational school in the United States. Minimum 2.5 GPA required.

Award: Scholarship for use in freshman, sophomore, junior, or senior years; not renewable. *Number:* varies. *Amount:* varies.

Eligibility Requirements: Applicant must be enrolled or expecting to enroll full-time at a two-year or four-year or technical institution or university and resident of California. Applicant or parent of applicant must be affiliated with Club at Morningside. Applicant must have 2.5 GPA or higher. Available to U.S. citizens.

Application Requirements: Application, financial need analysis, references, transcript. *Deadline:* January 26.

Contact: Shryl Helvie, Scholarship Coordinator
San Diego Foundation
2508 Historic Decatur Road, Suite 200
San Diego, CA 92106
Phone: 619-814-1307
Fax: 619-239-1710
E-mail: shryl@sdfoundation.org

REMINGTON CLUB SCHOLARSHIP

Scholarship to employees and the children of employees at The Remington Club. Applicants must plan to attend an accredited two- or four-year college or university, or licensed trade/vocational school in the United States. Must have a commitment to their community as demonstrated by their involvement in extracurricular activities, community service, sports, or work experience. May be renewable for up to four years provided the recipient maintains positive academic and citizenship standing.

Award: Scholarship for use in freshman year; renewable. *Number:* varies. *Amount:* $1000–$4000.

Eligibility Requirements: Applicant must be high school student; planning to enroll or expecting to enroll full-time at a two-year or four-year or technical institution or university and resident of California.

Applicant or parent of applicant must be affiliated with Remington Club. Applicant must have 2.5 GPA or higher. Available to U.S. citizens.

Application Requirements: Application, references, transcript, personal statement, copy of tax return. *Deadline:* January 26.

Contact: Shryl Helvie, Scholarship Coordinator
San Diego Foundation
2508 Historic Decatur Road, Suite 200
San Diego, CA 92106
Phone: 619-814-1307
Fax: 619-239-1710
E-mail: shryl@sdfoundation.org

THEODORE R. AND VIVIAN M. JOHNSON SCHOLARSHIP FOUNDATION INC.

http://www.jsf.bz/

THEODORE R. AND VIVIAN M. JOHNSON SCHOLARSHIP PROGRAM FOR CHILDREN OF UPS EMPLOYEES OR UPS RETIREES

The children of United Parcel Service employees or retirees who live in Florida are eligible for scholarship funds to attend college or vocational school in Florida. Awards are for undergraduate study only and ranges from $1000 to $10,000. Community college students and vocational school students may receive a maximum of $5000 per year.

Award: Scholarship for use in freshman year; renewable. *Number:* 1–50. *Amount:* $1000–$10,000.

Eligibility Requirements: Applicant must be high school student; planning to enroll or expecting to enroll full-time at a two-year or four-year institution or university; resident of Florida and studying in Florida. Applicant or parent of applicant must be affiliated with UPS-United Parcel Service. Available to U.S. and non-U.S. citizens.

Application Requirements: Application, financial need analysis, transcript. *Deadline:* April 15.

Contact: Sharon Wood, Office and Grants Administrator
Theodore R. and Vivian M. Johnson Scholarship Foundation Inc.
505 South Flagler Drive, Suite 1460
West Palm Beach, FL 33401
Phone: 561-659-2005
Fax: 561-659-1054
E-mail: wood@jsf.bz

UNITED NEGRO COLLEGE FUND

http://www.uncf.org/

CHURCH'S CHICKEN OPPORTUNITY SCHOLARSHIP

Scholarship available to children of Church's Chicken employees who attend UNCF member colleges or universities. Minimum 3.0 GPA required.

Award: Scholarship for use in freshman year; not renewable. *Amount:* $2000–$4000.

Eligibility Requirements: Applicant must be Black (non-Hispanic) and enrolled or expecting to enroll at a four-year institution or university. Applicant or parent of applicant must be affiliated with Church's Chicken. Applicant must have 3.0 GPA or higher. Available to U.S. citizens.

Application Requirements: *Deadline:* continuous.

Contact: Director, Program Services
United Negro College Fund
8260 Willow Oaks Corporate Drive
PO Box 10444
Fairfax, VA 22031-8044
Phone: 800-331-2244
E-mail: rebecca.bennett@uncf.org

KFC SCHOLARS PROGRAM

Award for KFC corporate or franchise African American employee who has at least one year of work experience with KFC and who wishes to pursue a bachelor's degree in business management, computer sciences, restaurant management, retail sales, or liberal arts at a UNCF member institution. Amount of scholarship is based on proven unmet need. Must have a 2.5 GPA and be an employee in good standing.

Award: Scholarship for use in freshman year; renewable. *Number:* 1. *Amount:* varies.

Eligibility Requirements: Applicant must be Black (non-Hispanic) and enrolled or expecting to enroll full- or part-time at a four-year institution or university. Applicant or parent of applicant must be affiliated with Kentucky Fried Chicken. Applicant must have 2.5 GPA or higher. Available to U.S. citizens.

Application Requirements: Application, essay, transcript. *Deadline:* June 30.

Contact: Director, Program Services
United Negro College Fund
8260 Willow Oaks Corporate Drive
PO Box 10444
Fairfax, VA 22031-8044
Phone: 800-331-2244
E-mail: rebecca.bennett@uncf.org

VERIZON FOUNDATION

http://www.foundation.verizon.com/

VERIZON FOUNDATION SCHOLARSHIP

Award up to 250 four-year scholarships to high school seniors who are children of Verizon employees in the United States, and are planning to attend a four-year college or university. Deadline varies.

Award: Scholarship for use in freshman year; renewable. *Number:* up to 250. *Amount:* $5000–$20,000.

Eligibility Requirements: Applicant must be high school student and planning to enroll or expecting to enroll full- or part-time at a four-year institution or university. Applicant or parent of applicant must be affiliated with Verizon. Available to U.S. citizens.

Application Requirements: Application. *Deadline:* varies.

Contact: Scholarship Committee
Verizon Foundation
One Verizon Way
Basking Ridge, NJ 07920
Phone: 800-360-7955
Fax: 908-630-2660
E-mail: veriizon.foundation@verizon.com

WAL-MART FOUNDATION

http://www.walmartfoundation.org/

WAL-MART ASSOCIATE SCHOLARSHIPS

Awards for college-bound graduating high school seniors, those receiving a home-school diploma, or receiving a GED equivalency who work for Wal-Mart at least six months. Based on minimum 2.5 cumulative high school GPA and can prove financial need by required documents. One-time award of up to $3000. For use at an accredited two- or four-year U.S. institution. Apply online at https//www.applyists.net, Access Key: WMAS.

Award: Scholarship for use in freshman year; not renewable. *Amount:* up to $3000.

Eligibility Requirements: Applicant must be high school student and planning to enroll or expecting to enroll full-time at a two-year or four-year institution or university. Applicant or parent of applicant must be affiliated with Wal-Mart Foundation. Applicant must have 2.5 GPA or higher. Available to U.S. citizens.

Application Requirements: Application, test scores, transcript, federal income tax return. *Deadline:* January 31.

Contact: International Scholarship and Tuition Services, Inc.
Wal-Mart Foundation
PO Box 22492
Nashville, TN 37202
Phone: 866-524-7385
Fax: 615-523-7100

WAL-MART HIGHER REACH SCHOLARSHIP

Applicant must be full-time or part-time Wal-Mart Associate. Must have been employed by Wal-Mart Stores for at least six months. Must have been out of high school for at least one year or have equivalent home school or GED. Award is based on financial need and community involvement. Applications available online https://www.applyists.net. Access key: WALMT.

Award: Scholarship for use in freshman, sophomore, junior, or senior years; not renewable. *Number:* varies. *Amount:* $250–$3000.

Eligibility Requirements: Applicant must be enrolled or expecting to enroll full- or part-time at a two-year or four-year institution or university. Applicant or parent of applicant must be affiliated with Wal-Mart Foundation. Available to U.S. citizens.

Application Requirements: Application, test scores, federal tax form. *Deadline:* January 31.

Contact: International Scholarship and Tuition Services, Inc.
Wal-Mart Foundation
PO Box 22492
Nashville, TN 37202
Phone: 866-524-7385
Fax: 615-523-7100

WALTON FAMILY FOUNDATION SCHOLARSHIP

Award for high-school seniors, or those receiving a home-school diploma, or receiving a GED-equivalency who are children of a Wal-Mart associate who has been employed as a full-time associate for at least one year. A $13,000 undergraduate scholarship is payable over four years. Minimum of 22 (ACT) or 1030 (SAT) score and can prove financial need by required documents. Application available online at https://www.applyists.net. Access key: WFFS.

Award: Scholarship for use in freshman year; renewable. *Number:* 175–175. *Amount:* $13,000.

Eligibility Requirements: Applicant must be high school student and planning to enroll or expecting to enroll full-time at a two-year or four-year institution or university. Applicant or parent of applicant must be affiliated with Wal-Mart Foundation. Available to U.S. citizens.

Application Requirements: Application, test scores, transcript, federal income tax return. *Deadline:* January 31.

Contact: International Scholarship and Tuition Services, Inc.
Wal-Mart Foundation
PO Box 22492
Nashville, TN 37202
Phone: 866-524-7385
Fax: 615-523-7100

WEYERHAEUSER COMPANY FOUNDATION

http://www.weyerhaeuser.com/

WEYERHAEUSER COMPANY FOUNDATION SCHOLARSHIPS

Renewable awards for children of Weyerhaeuser Company employees. Must be in senior year in high school. Thirty scholarships to four-year institutions and 20 scholarships to community colleges or vocational/technical schools are awarded each year.

Award: Scholarship for use in freshman year; renewable. *Number:* 50. *Amount:* $1000–$4000.

Eligibility Requirements: Applicant must be high school student and planning to enroll or expecting to enroll full-time at a two-year or four-year or technical institution. Applicant or parent of applicant must be affiliated with Weyerhauser Company. Available to U.S. and Canadian citizens.

Application Requirements: Application. *Deadline:* January 15.

Contact: Program Manager
Weyerhaeuser Company Foundation
CH 1K36, PO Box 9777
Federal Way, WA 98063-9777
Phone: 253-924-3159
Fax: 253-924-3658

WILLITS FOUNDATION

WILLITS FOUNDATION SCHOLARSHIP PROGRAM

Renewable awards for children of full-time employees of C. R. Bard Inc. Children of Bard officers are not eligible. Must be pursuing, or planning to pursue, full-time postsecondary studies in the year in which the application is made.

Award: Scholarship for use in freshman, sophomore, junior, or senior years; renewable. *Number:* 10–15. *Amount:* $5000.

Eligibility Requirements: Applicant must be enrolled or expecting to enroll full-time at a four-year institution or university. Applicant or parent of applicant must be affiliated with C.R. Bard, Inc. Available to U.S. and Canadian citizens.

Application Requirements: Application, essay, photo, references, test scores, transcript. *Deadline:* March 1.

Contact: Linda Hrevnack, Program Manager
Willits Foundation
730 Central Avenue
Murray Hill, NJ 07974
Phone: 908-277-8182
Fax: 908-277-8098

EMPLOYMENT/ VOLUNTEER EXPERIENCE

AIR TRAFFIC CONTROL ASSOCIATION INC.

http://www.atca.org/

BUCKINGHAM MEMORIAL SCHOLARSHIP

Scholarships granted to children of air traffic control specialists pursuing a bachelor's degree or higher in any course of study. Must be the child, natural or by adoption, of a person serving, or having served as an air traffic control specialist, be it with the U.S. government, U.S. military, or in a private facility in the United States.

Award: Scholarship for use in freshman, sophomore, junior, senior, or graduate years; not renewable. *Number:* 2–4. *Amount:* $1000–$2500.

Eligibility Requirements: Applicant must be enrolled or expecting to enroll full- or part-time at a four-year institution or university. Applicant or parent of applicant must have employment or volunteer experience in air traffic control. Available to U.S. citizens.

Application Requirements: Application, driver's license, essay, financial need analysis, references, transcript. *Deadline:* May 1.

Contact: Miguel Vazquez, Director
Air Traffic Control Association Inc.
1101 King Street, Suite 300
Alexandria, VA 22201
Phone: 703-522-5717
Fax: 703-527-7251
E-mail: info@atca.org

AMERICAN FEDERATION OF TEACHERS

http://www.aft.org/

ROBERT G. PORTER SCHOLARS PROGRAM-AMERICAN FEDERATION OF TEACHERS DEPENDENTS
• See page 524

AMERICAN LEGION AUXILIARY DEPARTMENT OF MAINE

http://www.mainelegion.org/

AMERICAN LEGION AUXILIARY DEPARTMENT OF MAINE NATIONAL PRESIDENT'S SCHOLARSHIP

Scholarships to children of veterans who served in the Armed Forces during the eligibility dates for The American Legion. One $2500, one $2000, and one $1000 scholarship will be awarded. Applicant must complete 50 hours of community service during his/her high school years.

Award: Scholarship for use in freshman year; not renewable. *Number:* 3. *Amount:* $1000–$2500.

Eligibility Requirements: Applicant must be high school student; planning to enroll or expecting to enroll full-time at a four-year institution or university and resident of Maine. Applicant or parent of applicant must have employment or volunteer experience in community service. Available to U.S. citizens. Applicant or parent must meet one or more of the following requirements: general military experience; retired

from active duty; disabled or killed as a result of military service; prisoner of war; or missing in action.

Application Requirements: Application, essay, references, test scores, transcript. *Deadline:* March 1.

Contact: Mary Wells, Education Chairman
American Legion Auxiliary Department of Maine
21 Limerock Street
P.O. Box 434
Rockland, ME 04841
Phone: 207-532-6007
E-mail: aladeptsecme@verizon.net

AMERICAN LEGION AUXILIARY DEPARTMENT OF MASSACHUSETTS

http://www.masslegion-aux.org/

AMERICAN LEGION AUXILIARY DEPARTMENT OF MASSACHUSETTS DEPARTMENT PRESIDENT'S SCHOLARSHIP

Awarded to children of veterans who served in the armed forces during the eligibility dates specified by the legion. The applicant must complete 50 hours of community service during high school years to be eligible for this scholarship.

Award: Scholarship for use in freshman, sophomore, junior, or senior years; not renewable. *Number:* 12. *Amount:* $200–$750.

Eligibility Requirements: Applicant must be age 16-22; enrolled or expecting to enroll full-time at a two-year or four-year institution or university; resident of Massachusetts and studying in Massachusetts. Applicant or parent of applicant must have employment or volunteer experience in community service. Available to U.S. citizens. Applicant or parent must meet one or more of the following requirements: general military experience; retired from active duty; disabled or killed as a result of military service; prisoner of war; or missing in action.

Application Requirements: Application. *Deadline:* March 1.

Contact: Beverly Monaco, Secretary and Treasurer
American Legion Auxiliary Department of Massachusetts
546-2 State House
Boston, MA 02133-1044
Phone: 617-727-2958
Fax: 617-727-0741

AMERICAN LEGION AUXILIARY DEPARTMENT OF NORTH DAKOTA

http://www.ndlegion.org/

AMERICAN LEGION AUXILIARY DEPARTMENT OF NORTH DAKOTA NATIONAL PRESIDENT'S SCHOLARSHIP

Three division scholarships for children of veterans who served in the Armed Forces during eligible dates for American Legion membership. Must be U.S. citizen and a high school senior with a minimum 2.5 GPA. Must be entered by local American Legion Auxiliary Unit.

Award: Scholarship for use in freshman year; not renewable. *Number:* 3. *Amount:* $1000–$2500.

Eligibility Requirements: Applicant must be high school student; planning to enroll or expecting to enroll full-time at a four-year institution or university; resident of North Dakota and studying in North Dakota. Applicant or parent of applicant must have employment or volunteer experience in community service. Applicant must have 2.5 GPA or higher. Available to U.S. citizens. Applicant or parent must meet one or more of the following requirements: general military experience; retired from active duty; disabled or killed as a result of military service; prisoner of war; or missing in action.

Application Requirements: Application, essay, financial need analysis, references, test scores, transcript, proof of 50 hours voluntary service. *Deadline:* March 1.

Contact: Myrna Runholm, Department Secretary
American Legion Auxiliary Department of North Dakota
PO Box 1060
Jamestown, ND 58402-1060
Phone: 701-253-5992
Fax: 701-952-5993
E-mail: ala-hq@ndlegion.org

AMERICAN LEGION DEPARTMENT OF VERMONT

http://www.legionvthq.com/

AMERICAN LEGION EAGLE SCOUT OF THE YEAR
• *See page 533*

AMERICAN LEGION NATIONAL HEADQUARTERS

http://www.legion.org/

AMERICAN LEGION NATIONAL HEADQUARTERS EAGLE SCOUT OF THE YEAR

The winner of the competition receives a $10,000 scholarship and 3 runners-up are each awarded $2500 scholarships. May be used to attend any state accredited postsecondary institution in the U.S.

Award: Scholarship for use in freshman, sophomore, junior, or senior years; not renewable. *Number:* 4. *Amount:* $2500–$10,000.

Eligibility Requirements: Applicant must be high school student; age 15-18; planning to enroll or expecting to enroll full-time at a two-year or four-year institution or university and male. Applicant or parent of applicant must have employment or volunteer experience in community service. Available to U.S. citizens.

Application Requirements: Application, essay, references, transcript. *Deadline:* March 1.

Contact: Michael Buss, Assistant Director
American Legion National Headquarters
The American Legion, PO Box 1055
Indianapolis, IN 46206
Phone: 317-630-1249
Fax: 317-630-1369
E-mail: mbuss@legion.org

AMERICAN POSTAL WORKERS UNION

http://www.apwu.org/

E.C. HALLBECK SCHOLARSHIP FUND
• *See page 534*

VOCATIONAL SCHOLARSHIP PROGRAM
• *See page 534*

AMERICAN QUARTER HORSE FOUNDATION (AQHF)

http://www.aqha.com/foundation

EXCELLENCE IN EQUINE/AGRICULTURAL INVOLVEMENT SCHOLARSHIP
• *See page 535*

FARM AND RANCH HERITAGE SCHOLARSHIP
• *See page 535*

NEBRASKA QUARTER HORSE YOUTH SCHOLARSHIP
• *See page 536*

AMERICAN ROAD & TRANSPORTATION BUILDERS ASSOCIATION-TRANSPORTATION DEVELOPMENT FOUNDATION (ARTBA-TDF)

http://www.artba.org/

ARTBA-TDF LANFORD FAMILY HIGHWAY WORKERS MEMORIAL SCHOLARSHIP PROGRAM

The ARTBA-TDF Highway Worker Memorial Scholarship Program provides financial assistance to help the sons, daughters or legally adopted children of highway workers killed or permanently disabled in the line of duty pursue post-high school education. Minimum 2.5 GPA required.

Award: Scholarship for use in freshman, sophomore, junior, or senior years; not renewable. *Number:* varies. *Amount:* $1000–$5000.

Eligibility Requirements: Applicant must be enrolled or expecting to enroll full- or part-time at a two-year or four-year or technical institution or university. Applicant or parent of applicant must have employment or volunteer experience in construction or roadway work. Applicant must have 2.5 GPA or higher. Available to U.S. citizens.

Application Requirements: Application, essay, financial need analysis, photo, references, transcript, copy of current year's federal tax return, copy of parent's current year federal tax return. *Deadline:* April 22.

Contact: Holly Bolton, Scholarship and Awards Manager
American Road & Transportation Builders Association-Transportation Development Foundation (ARTBA-TDF)
1219 28th Street, NW
Washington, DC 20007
Phone: 202-289-4434 Ext. 411
E-mail: hbolton@artba.org

A.W. BODINE-SUNKIST GROWERS INC.

http://www.sunkist.com/

A.W. BODINE-SUNKIST MEMORIAL SCHOLARSHIP

Renewable award for undergraduate study for applicants whose family derives most of its income from the agriculture industry in Arizona or California. Award is based on minimum 2.7 GPA and financial need.

Award: Scholarship for use in freshman, sophomore, junior, or senior years; renewable. *Number:* 20. *Amount:* $2000.

Eligibility Requirements: Applicant must be enrolled or expecting to enroll full-time at a two-year or four-year institution or university and resident of Arizona or California. Applicant or parent of applicant must have employment or volunteer experience in agriculture. Available to U.S. citizens.

Application Requirements: Application, essay, financial need analysis, resume, references, test scores, transcript. *Deadline:* April 30.

Contact: Claire Smith, Scholarship Administrator
A.W. Bodine-Sunkist Growers Inc.
PO Box 7888
Van Nuys, CA 91409-7888
Phone: 818-986-4800
Fax: 818-986-7511

BOY SCOUTS OF AMERICA-MUSKINGUM VALLEY COUNCIL

http://www.learning-for-life.org/

YOUNG AMERICAN AWARD

Award for young adults between the ages of 15 and 25, who have achieved excellence in the fields of art, athletics, business, education, government, humanities, literature, music, religion, science, or service. Applicant must have been involved in service to their community, state, or country that adds to the quality of life. Must be participant of the Learning for Life Exploring program.

Award: Prize for use in freshman year; not renewable. *Number:* 5. *Amount:* $7500.

Eligibility Requirements: Applicant must be high school student; age 15-25 and planning to enroll or expecting to enroll full-time at a four-year institution or university. Applicant or parent of applicant must have employment or volunteer experience in community service. Available to U.S. and non-U.S. citizens.

Application Requirements: Application, applicant must enter a contest, references, transcript. *Deadline:* December 1.

Contact: Bill Rogers, Associate Director
Boy Scouts of America-Muskingum Valley Council
1325 West Walnut Hill Lane
PO Box 152079
Irving, TX 75015-2079
Phone: 972-580-2433
Fax: 972-580-2137
E-mail: brogers@lflmail.org

CALIFORNIA CORRECTIONAL PEACE OFFICERS ASSOCIATION

http://www.ccpoa.org/

CALIFORNIA CORRECTIONAL PEACE OFFICERS ASSOCIATION JOE HARPER SCHOLARSHIP

Scholarship program for immediate relatives of current, retired, or deceased correctional peace officers working the toughest beat in the state. Must be or must have been members in good standing of CCPOA. Applicant must be a high school senior with minimum 3.0 GPA or currently enrolled college student.

Award: Scholarship for use in freshman, sophomore, junior, senior, or graduate years; not renewable. *Number:* 100–200. *Amount:* $500–$1000.

Eligibility Requirements: Applicant must be enrolled or expecting to enroll full- or part-time at a two-year or four-year or technical institution or university and resident of California. Applicant or parent of applicant must have employment or volunteer experience in police/firefighting. Applicant must have 3.0 GPA or higher. Available to U.S. citizens.

Application Requirements: Application, essay, financial need analysis, photo, references, test scores, transcript, copies of federal income tax return from the previous year. *Deadline:* April 30.

Contact: Marcia Bartlett, CCPOA Membership Committee
California Correctional Peace Officers Association
755 Riverpoint Drive, Suite 200
West Sacramento, CA 95605-1634
Phone: 916-372-6060
Fax: 916-372-6623
E-mail: marcia.bartlett@ccpoa.org

CALIFORNIA STATE PARENT-TEACHER ASSOCIATION

http://www.capta.org/

CONTINUING EDUCATION-PTA VOLUNTEERS SCHOLARSHIP
• *See page 538*

GRADUATING HIGH SCHOOL SENIOR SCHOLARSHIP

Available to high school seniors graduating between January 1 and June 30 of the current academic year from high schools in California with a PTA/PTSA unit in good standing. Must be a California resident. Must have volunteered in the school and community volunteer service.

Award: Scholarship for use in freshman year; renewable. *Number:* varies. *Amount:* $500.

Eligibility Requirements: Applicant must be high school student; planning to enroll or expecting to enroll full-time at a two-year or four-year or technical institution or university and resident of California. Applicant or parent of applicant must have employment or volunteer experience in community service. Available to U.S. citizens.

Application Requirements: Application, essay, references, transcript, copy of current PTA/PTSA membership card. *Deadline:* February 1.

Contact: Becky Reece, Scholarship and Award Chairman
California State Parent-Teacher Association
930 Georgia Street
Los Angeles, CA 90015-1322
Phone: 213-620-1100
Fax: 213-620-1411
E-mail: info@capta.org

CALIFORNIA STUDENT AID COMMISSION

http://www.csac.ca.gov/

LAW ENFORCEMENT PERSONNEL DEPENDENTS SCHOLARSHIP

Provides college grants to needy dependents of California law enforcement officers, officers and employees of the Department of Corrections and Department of Youth Authority, and firefighters killed or disabled in the line of duty.

Award: Grant for use in freshman, sophomore, junior, or senior years; renewable. *Number:* varies. *Amount:* $100–$11,853.

Eligibility Requirements: Applicant must be enrolled or expecting to enroll full- or part-time at a two-year or four-year institution or university; resident of California and studying in California. Applicant or parent of applicant must have employment or volunteer experience in police/firefighting. Available to U.S. citizens.

Application Requirements: Application, financial need analysis, transcript, birth certificate, death certificate of parents or spouse, police report. *Deadline:* continuous.

Contact: Catalina Mistler, Chief, Program Administration & Services Division
California Student Aid Commission
PO Box 419026
Rancho Cordova, CA 95741-9026
Phone: 916-526-7268
Fax: 916-526-8002
E-mail: studentsupport@csac.ca.gov

CALIFORNIA TABLE GRAPE COMMISSION

http://www.freshcaliforniagrapes.com/

CALIFORNIA TABLE GRAPE FARM WORKERS SCHOLARSHIP PROGRAM

Applicants must be high school graduates who plan to attend any college or university in California. The applicant, a parent, or a legal guardian must have worked in the California table grape harvest during the last season. School activities, personal references, and financial need are considered. Must be a U.S. citizen.

Award: Scholarship for use in freshman year; not renewable. *Number:* 3. *Amount:* $16,000.

Eligibility Requirements: Applicant must be enrolled or expecting to enroll full-time at a four-year institution or university and studying in California. Applicant or parent of applicant must have employment or volunteer experience in agriculture. Available to U.S. citizens.

Application Requirements: Application, essay, references, test scores, transcript. *Deadline:* March 19.

Contact: Scholarship Coordinator
California Table Grape Commission
392 West Fallbrook, Suite 101
Fresno, CA 93711-6150
Phone: 559-447-8350
Fax: 559-447-9184

CALIFORNIA TEACHERS ASSOCIATION (CTA)

http://www.cta.org/

CALIFORNIA TEACHERS ASSOCIATION SCHOLARSHIP FOR MEMBERS
• *See page 538*

CHICK-FIL-A INC.

http://www.chick-fil-a.com/

CHICK-FIL-A LEADERSHIP SCHOLARSHIP
• *See page 574*

COCA-COLA SCHOLARS FOUNDATION INC.

http://www.coca-colascholars.org/

COCA-COLA TWO-YEAR COLLEGES SCHOLARSHIP

Nonrenewable awards based on community involvement, leadership, and academic performance. Must pursue a two-year degree. Each institution may nominate up to two applicants. Minimum 2.5 GPA is required.

Award: Scholarship for use in freshman or sophomore years; not renewable. *Number:* 350. *Amount:* $1000.

Eligibility Requirements: Applicant must be enrolled or expecting to enroll full- or part-time at a two-year institution and must have an interest in leadership. Applicant or parent of applicant must have employment or volunteer experience in community service. Applicant must have 2.5 GPA or higher. Available to U.S. citizens.

Application Requirements: Application, essay, nomination from institution. *Deadline:* May 31.

Contact: Ryan Rodriguez, Program Facilitator
Coca-Cola Scholars Foundation Inc.
PO Box 442
Atlanta, GA 30301-0442
Phone: 800-306-2653
Fax: 404-733-5439
E-mail: scholars@na.ko.com

COLLEGEBOUND FOUNDATION

http://www.collegeboundfoundation.org/

BALTIMORE ROTARY SERVICE ABOVE SELF AWARD PROGRAM

One time scholarship awards ranging from $1000 to $1500 for high school graduates who possess a minimum GPA of 2.5. Must have verifiable community service. For more information visit web site http://www.collegeboundfoundation.org.

Award: Scholarship for use in freshman year; not renewable. *Number:* 1–4. *Amount:* $1000–$1500.

Eligibility Requirements: Applicant must be high school student and planning to enroll or expecting to enroll full-time at a two-year or four-year institution or university. Applicant or parent of applicant must have employment or volunteer experience in community service. Applicant must have 2.5 GPA or higher. Available to U.S. citizens.

Application Requirements: Application, essay, financial need analysis, references, transcript, financial aid award letters, Student Aid Report (SAR). *Deadline:* March 1.

Contact: Deana Carr-Davis, Associate Program Director, Scholarship Programs
CollegeBound Foundation
300 Water Street, Suite 300
Baltimore, MD 21202
Phone: 410-783-2905 Ext. 207
Fax: 410-727-5786
E-mail: dcarr-davis@collegeboundfoundation.org

COMCAST LEADERS AND ACHIEVERS SCHOLARSHIP PROGRAM

http://www.com/cast.com/

COMCAST LEADERS AND ACHIEVERS SCHOLARSHIP

Nominees must be full-time high school seniors, must demonstrate a strong commitment to community service and display leadership abilities. Minimum 2.8 GPA required. Must be nominated by their high school principal. Employees of Comcast, its subsidiaries and affiliates, and their families, are not eligible. E-mail for nomination form: comcast@spaprog.com.

Award: Scholarship for use in freshman year; not renewable. *Number:* varies. *Amount:* $1000.

Eligibility Requirements: Applicant must be high school student and planning to enroll or expecting to enroll full-time at a two-year or four-year institution or university. Applicant or parent of applicant must have employment or volunteer experience in community service. Applicant must have 3.0 GPA or higher. Available to U.S. and non-U.S. citizens.

Application Requirements: *Deadline:* January 29.

Contact: Executive Director
Comcast Leaders and Achievers Scholarship Program
1500 Market Street, East Tower, 33rd Floor
Philadelphia, PA 19102
Phone: 866-851-4274
E-mail: comcast@spaprog.com

COMMERCE BANK

http://www.com/merceonline.com/

AMERICAN DREAM SCHOLARSHIPS

Nonrenewable scholarships awarded to graduating high school seniors who reside in a county served by Commerce Bank. Must be planning to enroll in full-time programs at accredited 2- or 4-year colleges or vocational-technical schools in the United States. Recipients are selected on the basis of demonstrated academic achievement and community service. Financial need is not a factor. See web site for eligible counties and application http://www.commerceonline.com/americandream.

Award: Scholarship for use in freshman year; not renewable. *Number:* 225. *Amount:* $1000.

Eligibility Requirements: Applicant must be high school student; planning to enroll or expecting to enroll full-time at a two-year or four-year or technical institution or university; resident of Connecticut, Delaware, District of Columbia, Florida, Maryland, New Jersey, New York, Pennsylvania, or Virginia and must have an interest in leadership. Applicant or parent of applicant must have employment or volunteer experience in community service. Applicant must have 3.0 GPA or higher. Available to U.S. citizens.

Application Requirements: Application. *Deadline:* December 15.

Contact: Scholarship Management Services, Division of Scholarship America
Commerce Bank
1 Scholarship Way, PO Box 297
St. Peter, MN 56082
Phone: 800-537-4180

COMMUNITY BANKER ASSOCIATION OF ILLINOIS

http://www.cbai.com/

COMMUNITY BANKER ASSOCIATION OF ILLINOIS CHILDREN OF COMMUNITY BANKING SCHOLARSHIP WILLIAM C. HARRIS MEMORIAL SCHOLARSHIP
• *See page 539*

DELAWARE HIGHER EDUCATION OFFICE

http://www.doe.k12.de.us

AGENDA FOR DELAWARE WOMEN TRAILBLAZER SCHOLARSHIP

Award for women legal residents of Delaware who are U.S. citizens or eligible non-citizens. Must enroll in a public or private nonprofit college in Delaware as an undergraduate student. Must have a cumulative GPA of 2.5 or higher. Award based 50 percent on financial need, 50 percent on community and school activities, vision, participation, and leadership.

Award: Scholarship for use in freshman, sophomore, junior, or senior years; renewable. *Number:* 2. *Amount:* $2500.

Eligibility Requirements: Applicant must be enrolled or expecting to enroll full-time at a four-year institution or university; female; resident of Delaware; studying in Delaware and must have an interest in leadership. Applicant or parent of applicant must have employment or volunteer experience in community service. Applicant must have 2.5 GPA or higher. Available to U.S. citizens.

Application Requirements: Application, financial need analysis, FAFSA, Student Aid Report (SAR). *Deadline:* April 11.

Contact: Carylin Brinkley, Program Administrator
Delaware Higher Education Office
Carvel State Office Building, 820 North French Street, Fifth Floor
Wilmington, DE 19801-3509
Phone: 302-577-5240
Fax: 302-577-6765
E-mail: cbrinkley@doe.k12.de.us

EDUCATIONAL BENEFITS FOR CHILDREN OF DECEASED VETERANS

Award for children between the ages of 16 and 24 of deceased/MIA/POW veterans or state police officers. Must have been a resident of Delaware for 3 or more years prior to the date of application. If the applicant's parent is a member of the armed forces, the parent must have been a resident of Delaware at the time of death or declaration of missing in action or prisoner of war status. Award will not exceed tuition and fees at a Delaware public college.

Award: Grant for use in freshman, sophomore, junior, or senior years; renewable. *Number:* varies. *Amount:* varies.

Eligibility Requirements: Applicant must be age 16-24; enrolled or expecting to enroll full-time at a two-year or four-year institution or university and resident of Delaware. Applicant or parent of applicant must have employment or volunteer experience in police/firefighting. Available to U.S. citizens. Applicant or parent must meet one or more of the following requirements: general military experience; retired from active duty; disabled or killed as a result of military service; prisoner of war; or missing in action.

Application Requirements: Application, verification of service-related death. *Deadline:* continuous.

Contact: *Phone:* 302-577-5240
Fax: 302-577-6765

DELTA DELTA DELTA FOUNDATION

http://www.tridelta.org/

DELTA DELTA DELTA UNDERGRADUATE SCHOLARSHIP

• *See page 540*

DIAMANTE, INC.

http://www.diamanteinc.org/

LATINO DIAMANTE SCHOLARSHIP FUND

Awards for Hispanic high school seniors recognizing their contributions to the community and their leadership qualities. Graduating high school seniors in North Carolina who plan to enroll at North Carolina institutions of higher education, and first-year undergraduates can apply for this scholarship. Must maintain a GPA of at least 2.5.

Award: Scholarship for use in freshman year; not renewable. *Number:* 2. *Amount:* $500.

Eligibility Requirements: Applicant must be Hispanic; enrolled or expecting to enroll full- or part-time at a two-year or four-year institution or university; resident of North Carolina; studying in North Carolina and must have an interest in leadership. Applicant or parent of applicant must have employment or volunteer experience in community service. Applicant must have 2.5 GPA or higher. Available to U.S. citizens.

Application Requirements: Application, essay, references, transcript.

Contact: Diamante, Inc.
315 North Academy Street, Suite 256
Cary, NC 27513
Phone: 919-852-0075
E-mail: latinodiamanteawards@diamanteinc.org

DISABLED AMERICAN VETERANS

http://www.dav.org/

JESSE BROWN MEMORIAL YOUTH SCHOLARSHIP PROGRAM

Scholarship awarded annually to outstanding youth volunteers who are active in Department of Veterans Affairs Voluntary Services (VAVS) programs and activities.

Award: Scholarship for use in freshman, sophomore, junior, senior, graduate, or postgraduate years; renewable. *Number:* 12. *Amount:* $5000–$15,000.

Eligibility Requirements: Applicant must be age 21 or under and enrolled or expecting to enroll full-time at a two-year or four-year or technical institution or university. Applicant or parent of applicant must have employment or volunteer experience in community service or helping handicapped. Available to U.S. citizens.

Application Requirements: Application, essay. *Deadline:* varies.

Contact: Edward Hartman, National Director of Voluntary Services
Disabled American Veterans
807 Maine Avenue, SW
Washington, DC 20024
Phone: 202-554-3501
Fax: 202-354-3581
E-mail: ehartman@davmail.org

DISCOVER FINANCIAL SERVICES

http://www.discoverfinancial.com/

DISCOVER SCHOLARSHIP PROGRAM

Applicants should be current high school juniors with minimum 2.75 GPA. Must plan to further education beyond high school in any accredited certification, licensing, or training program or institution of higher education. Must demonstrate accomplishments in community service and leadership and obstacle(s) overcome. Application and information at https://www.applyists.net/emailrequestform.asp. Access key is DISC.

Award: Scholarship for use in freshman year; not renewable. *Number:* up to 10. *Amount:* up to $30,000.

Eligibility Requirements: Applicant must be high school student; planning to enroll or expecting to enroll full- or part-time at a two-year or four-year or technical institution or university and must have an interest in leadership. Applicant or parent of applicant must have employment or volunteer experience in community service. Available to U.S. citizens.

Application Requirements: Application, essay, references, transcript. *Deadline:* January 31.

Contact: ISTS Program Coordinator
Phone: 866-756-7932

EXPLOSIVE ORDNANCE DISPOSAL MEMORIAL COMMITTEE

http://www.eodmemorial.org/

EXPLOSIVE ORDNANCE DISPOSAL MEMORIAL SCHOLARSHIP

Award based on academic merit, community involvement, and financial need for the children and spouses of military Explosive Ordnance Disposal technicians. This scholarship is for students enrolled or planning to enroll full-time as an undergraduate in a U.S. accredited two year, four year, or vocational school. Applications are only available on the web site at http://www.eodmemorial.org.

Award: Scholarship for use in freshman, sophomore, junior, or senior years; not renewable. *Number:* 25–75. *Amount:* $1900–$2500.

Eligibility Requirements: Applicant must be enrolled or expecting to enroll full-time at a two-year or four-year or technical institution or university. Applicant or parent of applicant must have employment or volunteer experience in explosive ordnance disposal. Available to U.S. citizens. Applicant or parent must meet one or more of the following requirements: general military experience; retired from active duty; disabled or killed as a result of military service; prisoner of war; or missing in action.

Application Requirements: Application, financial need analysis, transcript. *Deadline:* March 1.

Contact: Mary McKinley, Administrator
Explosive Ordnance Disposal Memorial Committee
PO Box 594
Niceville, FL 32588
Phone: 850-729-2401
Fax: 850-729-2401
E-mail: admin@eodmemorial.org

FINANCE AUTHORITY OF MAINE

http://www.famemaine.com/

TUITION WAIVER PROGRAMS

Provides tuition waivers for children and spouses of EMS personnel, firefighters, and law enforcement officers who have been killed in the line of duty and for students who were foster children under the custody of the Department of Human Services when they graduated from high school. Waivers valid at the University of Maine System, the Maine Technical

College System, and Maine Maritime Academy. Applicant must reside and study in Maine.

Award: Grant for use in freshman, sophomore, junior, or senior years; renewable. *Number:* up to 30. *Amount:* varies.

Eligibility Requirements: Applicant must be enrolled or expecting to enroll full- or part-time at a four-year institution or university; resident of Maine and studying in Maine. Applicant or parent of applicant must have employment or volunteer experience in police/firefighting. Available to U.S. citizens.

Application Requirements: Application, letter from the Department of Human Services documenting that applicant is in their custody and residing in foster care at the time of graduation from high school or its equivalent. *Deadline:* continuous.

Contact: Claude Roy, Manager, Operations
Finance Authority of Maine
Five Community Drive
PO Box 949
Augusta, ME 04332-0949
Phone: 207-620-3507
E-mail: education@famemaine.com

FLORIDA LIBRARY ASSOCIATION

http://www.flalib.org/

FLORIDA LIBRARY ASSOCIATION-ASSOCIATE'S DEGREE SCHOLARSHIP

Scholarship will be awarded to a Florida resident with library experience who is pursuing an associate degree. Applicants must be members of the Florida Library Association. For further details, visit web site http://www.flalib.org.

Award: Scholarship for use in freshman or sophomore years; not renewable. *Number:* 1. *Amount:* $500.

Eligibility Requirements: Applicant must be enrolled or expecting to enroll full- or part-time at a two-year or four-year institution or university; resident of Florida and studying in Florida. Applicant or parent of applicant must have employment or volunteer experience in library work. Available to U.S. and non-U.S. citizens.

Application Requirements: Application, essay, resume, references. *Deadline:* February 1.

Contact: Faye Roberts, Executive Director
Florida Library Association
PO Box 1571
Lake City, FL 32056-1571
Phone: 386-438-5795

FRATERNAL ORDER OF POLICE ASSOCIATES OF OHIO INC.

http://www.fopaohio.org/

FRATERNAL ORDER OF POLICE ASSOCIATES, STATE LODGE OF OHIO INC., SCHOLARSHIP FUND

Scholarship available to a graduating high school senior whose parent or guardian is a member in good standing of the Fraternal Order of Police, State Lodge of Ohio Inc. The amount of each scholarship will be up to $4000 payable over a four-year period. A one-time award of $500 will be given to the first runner-up. Scholarships will be awarded on the basis of scholastic merit, economic need and goals in life.

Award: Scholarship for use in freshman year; renewable. *Number:* 1–4. *Amount:* $500–$1000.

Eligibility Requirements: Applicant must be high school student; planning to enroll or expecting to enroll full-time at a four-year institution or university and resident of Ohio. Applicant or parent of applicant must have employment or volunteer experience in police/firefighting. Available to U.S. citizens.

Application Requirements: Application, essay, financial need analysis, photo, references, test scores, transcript, proof of guardianship. *Deadline:* May 1.

Contact: Mr. Michael J. Esposito, FOPA Scholarship Assistance Program
Fraternal Order of Police Associates of Ohio Inc.
PO Box 14564
Cincinnati, OH 45250-0564
Phone: 513-684-4755
E-mail: mje@fopaohio.org

GREATER WASHINGTON URBAN LEAGUE

http://www.gwul.org/

SAFEWAY/GREATER WASHINGTON URBAN LEAGUE SCHOLARSHIP

Award to graduating high school students who reside in the service area of the League. Applicants must complete an essay on a subject selected by the sponsors and must have completed 90 percent of their school district's community service requirement. Minimum GPA of 2.7 required.

Award: Scholarship for use in freshman year; not renewable. *Number:* 6. *Amount:* $3000.

Eligibility Requirements: Applicant must be high school student; planning to enroll or expecting to enroll full-time at a four-year institution or university and resident of District of Columbia. Applicant or parent of applicant must have employment or volunteer experience in community service. Available to U.S. citizens.

Application Requirements: Application, applicant must enter a contest, essay, test scores. *Deadline:* February 12.

Contact: Audrey Epperson, Director of Education
Greater Washington Urban League
2901 14th Street, NW
Washington, DC 20009
Phone: 202-265-8200
Fax: 202-387-7019
E-mail: epperson@gwulparentcenter.org

HARNESS HORSE YOUTH FOUNDATION

http://www.hhyf.org/

CHARLES BRADLEY MEMORIAL SCHOLARSHIP

One-time award for full-time undergraduates between the ages of 18 and 24. Open to children of licensed pari-mutuel harness racing officials. Minimum 2.5 GPA required. Must be U.S. or Canadian citizens.

Award: Scholarship for use in freshman, sophomore, junior, or senior years; not renewable. *Number:* 1–3. *Amount:* $250–$500.

Eligibility Requirements: Applicant must be age 18-24 and enrolled or expecting to enroll full-time at a two-year or four-year or technical institution or university. Applicant or parent of applicant must have employment or volunteer experience in harness racing. Applicant must have 3.5 GPA or higher. Available to U.S. and Canadian citizens.

Application Requirements: Application, essay, references, transcript, page 1 of parent's IRS form. *Deadline:* April 30.

Contact: Ellen Taylor, Executive Director
Harness Horse Youth Foundation
16575 Carey Road
Westfield, IN 46074
Phone: 317-867-5877
Fax: 317-867-5896
E-mail: ellen@hhyf.org

CURT GREENE MEMORIAL SCHOLARSHIP

One-time award with preference given to those under age 24 who have a passion for harness racing. Based on merit, need, and horsemanship or racing experience. Minimum 2.5 GPA required. Available for study in any field. May reapply.

Award: Scholarship for use in freshman, sophomore, junior, or senior years; not renewable. *Number:* 1–2. *Amount:* $2500.

Eligibility Requirements: Applicant must be age 18-24; enrolled or expecting to enroll full-time at a two-year or four-year or technical institution or university and must have an interest in animal/agricultural competition. Applicant or parent of applicant must have employment or volunteer experience in harness racing. Applicant must have 3.5 GPA or higher. Available to U.S. and Canadian citizens.

Application Requirements: Application, essay, references, transcript, page 1 of parent's IRS form. *Deadline:* April 30.

Contact: Ellen Taylor, Executive Director
Harness Horse Youth Foundation
16575 Carey Road
Westfield, IN 46074
Phone: 317-867-5877
Fax: 317-867-5896
E-mail: ellen@hhyf.org

HARNESS TRACKS OF AMERICA

http://www.harnesstracks.com/

HARNESS TRACKS OF AMERICA SCHOLARSHIP

One-time, merit-based award of $5000 for students actively involved in harness racing or the children of licensed drivers, trainers, breeders, or caretakers, living or deceased. Based on financial need, academic merit, and active harness racing involvement by applicant or family member. High school seniors may apply for the following school year award.

Award: Scholarship for use in freshman, sophomore, junior, senior, or graduate years; not renewable. *Number:* 5. *Amount:* $5000.

Eligibility Requirements: Applicant must be enrolled or expecting to enroll full-time at a two-year or four-year or technical institution or university. Applicant or parent of applicant must have employment or volunteer experience in harness racing. Available to U.S. and Canadian citizens.

Application Requirements: Application, essay, financial need analysis, transcript, IRS 1040 of parents and/or applicant. *Deadline:* May 15.

Contact: Jennifer Foley, Manager of Web Development and Information Services
Harness Tracks of America
12025 E Dry Gulch Place
Tucson, AZ 85749
Phone: 520-529-2525
Fax: 520-529-3235
E-mail: jen@harnesstracks.com

HEART OF A MARINE FOUNDATION

http://www.heartofamarine.org/

LANCE CORPORAL PHILLIP E. FRANK MEMORIAL SCHOLARSHIP

Scholarships available nationally to graduating high school seniors who will be enrolling at an accredited college or trade school within one year of receiving the award. Applicants should exemplify the spirit of "The Heart of a Marine" ideal, which is honor, patriotism, loyalty, respect and concern for others and are required to submit an essay on how they demonstrate these qualities. There is no GPA requirement; character is what counts the most. Discharged military personnel continuing their education are also encouraged to apply.

Award: Scholarship for use in freshman year; not renewable. *Number:* 2. *Amount:* $1000.

Eligibility Requirements: Applicant must be enrolled or expecting to enroll full-time at a two-year or four-year or technical institution or university. Applicant or parent of applicant must have employment or volunteer experience in community service. Available to U.S. citizens.

Application Requirements: Application, driver's license, essay, photo, letter of recommendation from a school official. *Deadline:* March 15.

Contact: Georgette Frank, Executive Director
Heart of a Marine Foundation
PO Box 1732
Elk Grove Village, IL 60007
E-mail: theheartofamarine@comcast.net

HERB KOHL EDUCATIONAL FOUNDATION INC.

http://www.kohleducation.org/

HERB KOHL EXCELLENCE SCHOLARSHIP PROGRAM

Scholarships of $1000 to Wisconsin high school graduates awarded annually. Applicants must be Wisconsin residents. Recipients are chosen for their demonstrated academic potential, outstanding leadership, citizenship, community service, integrity and other special talents.

Award: Scholarship for use in freshman year; not renewable. *Number:* 100. *Amount:* $1000.

Eligibility Requirements: Applicant must be high school student; planning to enroll or expecting to enroll full-time at a two-year or four-year or technical institution or university; resident of Wisconsin and must have an interest in leadership. Applicant or parent of applicant must have employment or volunteer experience in community service. Available to U.S. citizens.

Application Requirements: Application, essay, references, transcript. *Deadline:* November 16.

Contact: Scholarship Committee
Herb Kohl Educational Foundation Inc.
PO Box 877
Sheboygan, WI 53802-0877
Phone: 608-283-3131

HISPANIC ANNUAL SALUTE

http://www.hispanicannualsalute.org/

HISPANIC ANNUAL SALUTE SCHOLARSHIP

Scholarships of $2000 are awarded to graduating high school seniors. Program is intended to help foster a strong Hispanic presence within colleges and universities that will ultimately lead to active community leadership and volunteerism. Applicant must maintain a minimum GPA of 2.5.

Award: Scholarship for use in freshman year; not renewable. *Number:* 10. *Amount:* $2000.

Eligibility Requirements: Applicant must be Hispanic; high school student and planning to enroll or expecting to enroll full-time at a four-year institution or university. Applicant or parent of applicant must have employment or volunteer experience in community service. Applicant must have 2.5 GPA or higher. Available to U.S. citizens.

Application Requirements: Application, essay, references, test scores. *Deadline:* December 4.

Contact: Dan Sandos, President
Hispanic Annual Salute
PO Box 40720
Denver, CO 80204
Phone: 303-699-0715
Fax: 303-627-4205
E-mail: dcsandos@aol.com

HOSPITAL CENTRAL SERVICES INC.

http://www.giveapint.org/

HOSPITAL CENTRAL SERVICES STUDENT VOLUNTEER SCHOLARSHIP

Award to a graduating high school senior. Must have completed a minimum of 135 hours of volunteer service to the Blood Center in no less than a two calendar year period. Minimum 2.5 GPA required. Children of employees of Hospital Central Services or its affiliates are not eligible.

Award: Scholarship for use in freshman year; not renewable. *Number:* up to 2. *Amount:* $1000.

Eligibility Requirements: Applicant must be high school student and planning to enroll or expecting to enroll full- or part-time at a two-year or four-year institution or university. Applicant or parent of applicant must have employment or volunteer experience in community service. Applicant must have 2.5 GPA or higher. Available to U.S. citizens.

Application Requirements: Application, references, test scores, transcript. *Deadline:* March 31.

Contact: Sandra D. Thomas, Director of Development and Customer Service
Hospital Central Services Inc.
1465 Valley Center Parkway
Bethlehem, PA 18017
Phone: 610-691-5850 Ext. 292

IDAHO STATE BOARD OF EDUCATION

http://www.boardofed.idaho.gov/

IDAHO GOVERNOR'S CUP SCHOLARSHIP

Renewable scholarship available to Idaho residents enrolled full-time in an undergraduate academic or vocational-technical program at an eligible Idaho public or private college or university. Minimum GPA of 2.8 required. Must demonstrate commitment to public service and submit forms documenting service. Must be a high school senior and U.S. citizen to apply. For additional information and application, see web site http://www.boardofed.idaho.gov/scholarships.

Award: Scholarship for use in freshman year; renewable. *Number:* up to 12. *Amount:* $3000.

Eligibility Requirements: Applicant must be high school student; planning to enroll or expecting to enroll full-time at a two-year or four-year or technical institution or university; resident of Idaho and studying in Idaho. Applicant or parent of applicant must have employment or volunteer experience in community service. Available to U.S. citizens.

Application Requirements: Application, essay, portfolio, references, test scores, transcript. *Deadline:* January 15.

Contact: Dana Kelly, Program Manager, Student Affairs
Idaho State Board of Education
PO Box 83720
Boise, ID 83720-0037
Phone: 208-332-1574
Fax: 208-334-2632
E-mail: dana.kelly@osbe.idaho.gov

PUBLIC SAFETY OFFICER DEPENDENT SCHOLARSHIP

Scholarship for dependents of full-time Idaho public safety officers who were killed or disabled in the line of duty. Recipients will attend an Idaho postsecondary institution with a full waiver of fees, including tuition, on-campus housing and campus meal plan, and up to $500 per semester for books and supplies. For complete information, see web site http://www.boardofed.idaho.gov/scholarships/.

Award: Scholarship for use in freshman year; renewable. *Number:* varies.

Eligibility Requirements: Applicant must be enrolled or expecting to enroll full- or part-time at a two-year or four-year institution or university; resident of Idaho and studying in Idaho. Applicant or parent of applicant must have employment or volunteer experience in police/firefighting. Available to U.S. citizens.

Application Requirements: Application. *Deadline:* January 15.

Contact: Dana Kelly, Program Manager
Idaho State Board of Education
PO Box 83720
Boise, ID 83720-0037
Phone: 208-332-1574
E-mail: dana.kelly@osbe.idaho.gov

INDEPENDENT COLLEGE FUND OF MARYLAND (I-FUND)

http://www.i-fundinfo.org/

MARYLAND SCHOLARS

Scholarship awarded to permanent residents of Maryland. Must have at least 3.0 GPA. Preference given to students with a history of volunteerism and/or community involvement.

Award: Scholarship for use in freshman, sophomore, junior, or senior years; renewable. *Number:* 1. *Amount:* $1000.

Eligibility Requirements: Applicant must be enrolled or expecting to enroll full- or part-time at a four-year institution or university and resident of Maryland. Applicant or parent of applicant must have employment or volunteer experience in community service. Applicant must have 3.0 GPA or higher. Available to U.S. citizens.

Application Requirements: Application, financial need analysis, thank you letters. *Deadline:* varies.

Contact: Lori Subotich, Director of Programs and Scholarships
Independent College Fund of Maryland (I-Fund)
3225 Ellerslie Avenue, Suite C160
Baltimore, MD 21218-3519
Phone: 443-997-5700
Fax: 443-997-2740
E-mail: lsubot@jhmi.edu

INTERNATIONAL ASSOCIATION OF FIRE FIGHTERS

http://www.iaff.org/

W. H. "HOWIE" MCCLENNAN SCHOLARSHIP

Sons, daughters, or legally adopted children of IAFF members killed in the line of duty who are planning to attend an institution of higher learning can apply. Award of $2500 for each year. Renewable up to four years. Applicant must have a GPA of 2.0.

Award: Scholarship for use in freshman year; renewable. *Number:* 20–25. *Amount:* $2500.

Eligibility Requirements: Applicant must be enrolled or expecting to enroll full- or part-time at a two-year or four-year or technical institution. Applicant or parent of applicant must have employment or volunteer experience in police/firefighting. Available to U.S. citizens.

Application Requirements: Application, essay, financial need analysis, references, transcript. *Deadline:* February 1.

Contact: Office of the McClennan Scholarship General President
International Association of Fire Fighters
1750 New York Avenue, NW
Washington, DC 20006-5395
Phone: 202-737-8484
Fax: 202-737-8418

INTERNATIONAL FEDERATION OF PROFESSIONAL AND TECHNICAL ENGINEERS

http://www.ifpte.org/

INTERNATIONAL FEDERATION OF PROFESSIONAL AND TECHNICAL ENGINEERS ANNUAL SCHOLARSHIP
• *See page 545*

INTERNATIONAL ORGANIZATION OF MASTERS, MATES AND PILOTS HEALTH AND BENEFIT PLAN

http://www.bridgedeck.org/

M.M. & P. HEALTH AND BENEFIT PLAN SCHOLARSHIP PROGRAM

Scholarships available to dependent children (under 23 years of age) of parents who meet the eligibility requirements set forth by the MM&P Health and Benefit Plan. Selection of winners will be based on test scores, high school record, extracurricular activities, leadership qualities, recommendations, and students' own statements.

Award: Scholarship for use in freshman, sophomore, junior, or senior years; renewable. *Number:* 6. *Amount:* up to $5000.

Eligibility Requirements: Applicant must be age 23 or under; enrolled or expecting to enroll full-time at a four-year institution or university and single. Applicant or parent of applicant must have employment or volunteer experience in seafaring/fishing industry. Available to U.S. citizens.

Application Requirements: Application, test scores. *Deadline:* November 30.

Contact: Mary Ellen Beach, Scholarship Committee
International Organization of Masters, Mates and Pilots Health and Benefit Plan
700 Maritime Boulevard, Suite B
Linthicum Heights, MD 21090-1941
Phone: 410-850-8624
Fax: 410-871-8747
E-mail: communications@bridgedeck.org

JACKIE ROBINSON FOUNDATION

http://www.jackierobinson.org/

JACKIE ROBINSON SCHOLARSHIP

Scholarship for graduating high school seniors accepted to accredited four-year colleges or universities. Must be a minority student, United States citizen, and demonstrate leadership potential and financial need. See web site for additional details.

Award: Scholarship for use in freshman, sophomore, junior, senior, or graduate years; renewable. *Number:* 200–250. *Amount:* up to $7500.

Eligibility Requirements: Applicant must be American Indian/Alaska Native, Asian/Pacific Islander, Black (non-Hispanic), or Hispanic; high school student; planning to enroll or expecting to enroll full-time at a four-year institution or university and must have an interest in leadership. Applicant or parent of applicant must have employment or volunteer experience in community service. Available to U.S. citizens.

Application Requirements: Application, essay, financial need analysis, references, test scores, transcript. *Deadline:* March 31.

Contact: Scholarship Application
Jackie Robinson Foundation
75 Varick Street, 2nd Floor
New York, NY 10013
Phone: 212-290-8600
Fax: 212-290-8081
E-mail: scholarships@jackierobinson.org

KE ALI'I PAUAHI FOUNDATION

http://www.pauahi.org/

DANIEL KAHIKINA AND MILLIE AKAKA SCHOLARSHIP

Educational scholarships for undergraduate or graduate students demonstrating financial need. Minimum GPA of 3.2 required. Recipients are strongly encouraged to provide a minimum of 10 hours of community service to the Council for Native Hawaiian Advancement. Submit two letters of recommendation.

Award: Scholarship for use in freshman, sophomore, junior, senior, or graduate years; not renewable. *Number:* up to 2. *Amount:* up to $900.

Eligibility Requirements: Applicant must be enrolled or expecting to enroll full-time at a two-year or four-year institution or university and resident of Hawaii. Applicant or parent of applicant must have employment or volunteer experience in community service. Available to U.S. citizens.

Application Requirements: Application, essay, financial need analysis, references, transcript, college acceptance letter, copy of SAR. *Deadline:* April 1.

Contact: Mavis Shiraishi-Nagao
Phone: 808-534-3966
E-mail: scholarships@ pauahi.org

KAMEHAMEHA SCHOOLS ALUMNI ASSOCIATION-MAUI REGION SCHOLARSHIP

Scholarship available to assist students who are residents of the island of Maui and did not graduate from Kamehameha Schools in pursuing a postsecondary education. Applicants must demonstrate academic achievement or excellence, service to the community, financial need. Submit two letters of recommendation from school, employer or community organization.

Award: Scholarship for use in freshman, sophomore, junior, senior, or graduate years; not renewable. *Number:* 1. *Amount:* $500.

Eligibility Requirements: Applicant must be enrolled or expecting to enroll full-time at a four-year institution or university and resident of Hawaii. Applicant or parent of applicant must have employment or volunteer experience in community service. Available to U.S. citizens.

Application Requirements: Application, financial need analysis, references, transcript, Student Aid Report (SAR), college acceptance letter. *Deadline:* April 1.

Contact: Mavis Shiraishi-Nagao, Scholarship Administrator
Phone: 808-534-3966
E-mail: scholarships@pauahi.org

KAMEHAMEHA SCHOOLS CLASS OF 1960 GRANT

Grant recognizes a Hawaii resident who has demonstrated scholastic excellence, provided service to the community, demonstrated good character, and demonstrated an intent to utilize special skills in order to benefit the Hawaiian community.

Award: Grant for use in freshman, sophomore, junior, senior, or graduate years; not renewable. *Number:* 1. *Amount:* $1200.

Eligibility Requirements: Applicant must be enrolled or expecting to enroll full-time at a four-year institution or university. Applicant or parent of applicant must have employment or volunteer experience in community service. Available to U.S. citizens.

Application Requirements: Application, financial need analysis, transcript, Student Aid Report (SAR), college acceptance letter. *Deadline:* April 1.

Contact: Mavis Shiraishi-Nagao, Scholarship Administrator
Phone: 808-534-3966
E-mail: scholarships@pauahi.org

KAMEHAMEHA SCHOOLS CLASS OF 1970 SCHOLARSHIP

Scholarship recognizes a student who has a minimum GPA of 2.0. Submit essay describing involvement in community service (beyond what required through their school)including organizations, numbers or hours/length of volunteer service and how applicant intends to continue to serve the Hawaiian community.

Award: Scholarship for use in freshman, sophomore, junior, senior, or graduate years; not renewable. *Number:* 2. *Amount:* $1300.

Eligibility Requirements: Applicant must be enrolled or expecting to enroll full-time at a four-year institution or university. Applicant or parent of applicant must have employment or volunteer experience in community service. Available to U.S. citizens.

Application Requirements: Application, essay, financial need analysis, transcript, Student Aid Report (SAR), college acceptance letter. *Deadline:* April 1.

Contact: Mavis Shiraishi-Nagao, Scholarship Administrator
Phone: 808-534-3966
E-mail: scholarships@pauahi.org

LOWE'S COMPANIES INC.

http://www.lowes.com/

LOWE'S EDUCATIONAL SCHOLARSHIP

$1000-$15,000 scholarships available to all high school seniors who plan to attend any accredited 2-year or 4-year college or university within the United States. Selection based upon leadership skills, community service, and academic achievement.

Award: Scholarship for use in freshman year; not renewable. *Number:* up to 375. *Amount:* $1000–$15,000.

Eligibility Requirements: Applicant must be high school student; planning to enroll or expecting to enroll full- or part-time at a two-year or four-year or technical institution or university and must have an interest in leadership. Applicant or parent of applicant must have employment or volunteer experience in community service. Available to U.S. citizens.

Application Requirements: Application, resume. *Deadline:* March 15.

Contact: Scholarship Committee
Lowe's Companies Inc.
1000 Lowes Boulevard
Mooresville, NC 28117
Phone: 704-758-1000
Fax: 336-658-6937

MAGIC JOHNSON FOUNDATION INC.

http://www.magicjohnson.org/

TAYLOR MICHAELS SCHOLARSHIP FUND

Scholarship to provide support for deserving minority high school students who exemplify a strong potential for academic achievement but face social-economic conditions that hinder them from reaching their full potential. Must have strong community service involvement.

Award: Scholarship for use in freshman year; renewable. *Number:* varies. *Amount:* $1000–$5000.

Eligibility Requirements: Applicant must be American Indian/Alaska Native, Asian/Pacific Islander, Black (non-Hispanic), or Hispanic; high school student and planning to enroll or expecting to enroll full-time at a four-year institution or university. Applicant or parent of applicant must have employment or volunteer experience in community service.

Applicant must have 2.5 GPA or higher. Available to U.S. and non-U.S. citizens.

Application Requirements: Application, essay, references, transcript. *Deadline:* February 5.

Contact: Scholarship Coordinator
Magic Johnson Foundation Inc.
9100 Wilshire Boulevard, Suite 700, East Tower
Beverly Hills, CA 90212
Phone: 310-246-4400

MANA DE SAN DIEGO

http://www.sdmana.org/

MANA DE SAN DIEGO SYLVIA CHAVEZ MEMORIAL SCHOLARSHIP

Scholarship for Latinas with permanent residence in San Diego County who are enrolled or about to enroll in a two-year, four-year, or graduate program. Must have a minimum 2.75 GPA and demonstrate financial need. For an application and additional information visit http://www.sdmana.org.

Award: Scholarship for use in freshman, sophomore, junior, or senior years; not renewable. *Amount:* $500–$2000.

Eligibility Requirements: Applicant must be Hispanic; enrolled or expecting to enroll full- or part-time at a two-year or four-year institution or university; female; resident of California and must have an interest in leadership. Applicant or parent of applicant must have employment or volunteer experience in community service. Available to U.S. citizens.

Application Requirements: Application, essay, references, transcript. *Deadline:* February 13.

Contact: Lucy Hernandez, Scholarship Director
MANA de San Diego
PO Box 81364
San Diego, CA 92138-1364
Phone: 619-225-9594
Fax: 619-225-0500
E-mail: scholarships@sdmana.org

MARYLAND STATE HIGHER EDUCATION COMMISSION

http://www.mhec.state.md.us/

EDWARD T. CONROY MEMORIAL SCHOLARSHIP PROGRAM

Scholarship for dependents of deceased or 100 percent disabled U.S. Armed Forces personnel; the son, daughter, or surviving spouse of a victim of the September 11, 2001 terrorist attacks who died as a result of the attacks on the World Trade Center in New York City, the attack on the Pentagon in Virginia, or the crash of United Airlines Flight 93 in Pennsylvania; a POW/MIA of the Vietnam Conflict or his/her son or daughter; the son, daughter or surviving spouse (who has not remarried) of a state or local public safety employee or volunteer who died in the line of duty; or a state or local public safety employee or volunteer who was 100 percent disabled in the line of duty. Must be Maryland resident at time of disability. Submit applicable VA certification. Must be at least 16 years of age and attend Maryland institution.

Award: Scholarship for use in freshman, sophomore, junior, or senior years; renewable. *Number:* up to 121. *Amount:* $7200–$9000.

Eligibility Requirements: Applicant must be age 16-24; enrolled or expecting to enroll full- or part-time at a two-year or four-year institution or university; resident of Maryland and studying in Maryland. Applicant or parent of applicant must have employment or volunteer experience in police/firefighting. Available to U.S. citizens. Applicant or parent must meet one or more of the following requirements: general military experience; retired from active duty; disabled or killed as a result of military service; prisoner of war; or missing in action.

Application Requirements: Application, birth and death certificate, disability papers. *Deadline:* July 15.

Contact: Linda Asplin, Office of Student Financial Assistance
Maryland State Higher Education Commission
839 Bestgate Road, Suite 400
Annapolis, MD 21401-3013
Phone: 410-260-4563
Fax: 410-260-3203
E-mail: lasplin@mhec.state.md.us

MASSACHUSETTS OFFICE OF STUDENT FINANCIAL ASSISTANCE

http://www.osfa.mass.edu/

MASSACHUSETTS PUBLIC SERVICE GRANT PROGRAM

Scholarships for children and/or spouses of deceased members of fire, police, and corrections departments, who were killed in the line of duty. Awards Massachusetts residents attending Massachusetts institutions. Applicant should have not received a prior bachelor's degree or its equivalent.

Award: Grant for use in freshman, sophomore, junior, or senior years; not renewable. *Number:* varies. *Amount:* varies.

Eligibility Requirements: Applicant must be enrolled or expecting to enroll full-time at a four-year institution or university and resident of Massachusetts. Applicant or parent of applicant must have employment or volunteer experience in police/firefighting. Available to U.S. and non-U.S. citizens. Applicant or parent must meet one or more of the following requirements: general military experience; retired from active duty; disabled or killed as a result of military service; prisoner of war; or missing in action.

Application Requirements: Application, financial need analysis, copy of birth certificate, copy of veteran's death certificate. *Deadline:* May 1.

Contact: Alison Leary, Director of Scholarships and Grants
Massachusetts Office of Student Financial Assistance
454 Broadway, Suite 200
Revere, MA 02151
Phone: 617-727-9420
Fax: 617-727-0667
E-mail: osfa@osfa.mass.edu

MINNESOTA DEPARTMENT OF MILITARY AFFAIRS

http://www.minnesotanationalguard.org/

LEADERSHIP, EXCELLENCE AND DEDICATED SERVICE SCHOLARSHIP

Scholarship provides a maximum of thirty $1000 to selected high school seniors who become a member of the Minnesota National Guard and complete the application process. The award recognizes demonstrated leadership, community services and potential for success in the Minnesota National Guard.

Award: Scholarship for use in freshman year; not renewable. *Number:* up to 30. *Amount:* $1000.

Eligibility Requirements: Applicant must be high school student; planning to enroll or expecting to enroll full- or part-time at a two-year or four-year or technical institution or university; resident of Minnesota and must have an interest in leadership. Applicant or parent of applicant must have employment or volunteer experience in community service. Available to U.S. citizens. Applicant or parent must meet one or more of the following requirements: Air Force National Guard or Army National Guard experience; retired from active duty; disabled or killed as a result of military service; prisoner of war; or missing in action.

Application Requirements: Essay, resume, references, transcript. *Deadline:* March 15.

Contact: Barbara O'Reilly, Education Services Officer
Minnesota Department of Military Affairs
20 West 12th Street, Veterans Services Building
St. Paul, MN 55155-2098
Phone: 651-282-4508
E-mail: barbara.oreilly@mn.ngb.army.mil

MINNESOTA OFFICE OF HIGHER EDUCATION

http://www.getreadyforcollege.org/

SAFETY OFFICERS' SURVIVOR GRANT PROGRAM

Grant for eligible survivors of Minnesota public safety officers killed in the line of duty. Safety officers who have been permanently or totally disabled in the line of duty are also eligible. Must be used at a Minnesota institution participating in State Grant Program. Write for details. Must submit proof of death or disability and Public Safety Officers Benefit Fund Certificate. Must apply for renewal each year for four years.

Award: Grant for use in freshman, sophomore, junior, or senior years; not renewable. *Number:* 1. *Amount:* up to $10,488.

Eligibility Requirements: Applicant must be age 23 or under; enrolled or expecting to enroll full- or part-time at a two-year or four-year or technical institution or university; resident of Minnesota and studying in Minnesota. Applicant or parent of applicant must have employment or volunteer experience in police/firefighting. Available to U.S. citizens.

Application Requirements: Application, proof of death or disability. *Deadline:* continuous.

Contact: Brenda Larter, Program Administrator
Phone: 651-355-0612
Fax: 651-642-0675
E-mail: brenda.larter@state.mn.us

MISSISSIPPI OFFICE OF STUDENT FINANCIAL AID

http://www.mississippi.edu/

LAW ENFORCEMENT OFFICERS/FIREMEN SCHOLARSHIP

Financial assistance to dependent children and spouses of any Mississippi law enforcement officer, full-time fire fighter or volunteer fire fighter who has suffered fatal injuries or wounds or become permanently and totally disabled as a result of injuries or wounds which occurred in the performance of the official and appointed duties of his or her office. This financial assistance is offered as an eight semester tuition and room scholarship at any state-supported college or university in Mississippi.

Award: Scholarship for use in freshman, sophomore, junior, or senior years; not renewable.

Eligibility Requirements: Applicant must be enrolled or expecting to enroll full-time at a four-year institution or university; resident of Mississippi and studying in Mississippi. Applicant or parent of applicant must have employment or volunteer experience in police/firefighting.

Application Requirements: Application. *Deadline:* continuous.

Contact: Stephanie Green, Program Administrator
Phone: 800-327-2980 Ext. 4
E-mail: sgreen@mississippi.edu

NATIONAL ASSOCIATION FOR CAMPUS ACTIVITIES

http://www.naca.org/

LORI RHETT MEMORIAL SCHOLARSHIP

Scholarships will be given to undergraduate or graduate students with a cumulative GPA of 2.5 or better at the time of the application and during the academic term in which the scholarship is awarded. Must demonstrate significant leadership skill and ability while holding a significant leadership position on campus. Applicants must have made contributions via volunteer involvement, either on or off campus.

Award: Scholarship for use in freshman, sophomore, junior, senior, or graduate years; not renewable. *Number:* 1. *Amount:* $250–$300.

Eligibility Requirements: Applicant must be enrolled or expecting to enroll full- or part-time at a two-year or four-year institution or university; studying in Alaska, Idaho, Montana, Oregon, or Washington and must have an interest in leadership. Applicant or parent of applicant must have employment or volunteer experience in community service. Applicant must have 2.5 GPA or higher. Available to U.S. citizens.

Application Requirements: Application, resume, references, transcript. *Deadline:* June 30.

Contact: Dionne Ellison, Administrative Assistant
National Association for Campus Activities
13 Harbison Way
Columbia, SC 29212-3401
Phone: 803-732-6222 Ext. 131
Fax: 803-749-1047
E-mail: dionnee@naca.org

NATIONAL ASSOCIATION FOR CAMPUS ACTIVITIES EAST COAST UNDERGRADUATE SCHOLARSHIP FOR STUDENT LEADERS

Scholarship for undergraduate students who are in good standing at the time of the application and during the academic term in which the scholarship is awarded. Applicants must maintain a 2.5 GPA, demonstrate leadership skills and abilities while holding a significant leadership position on campus or in community, and have made significant contributions via volunteer involvement. Eligible students must be attending a college or university within the NACA East Coast Region.

Award: Scholarship for use in freshman, sophomore, junior, or senior years; not renewable. *Number:* up to 2. *Amount:* $250–$300.

Eligibility Requirements: Applicant must be enrolled or expecting to enroll full- or part-time at a two-year or four-year institution or university; studying in Delaware, District of Columbia, Maryland, New Jersey, New York, or Pennsylvania and must have an interest in leadership. Applicant or parent of applicant must have employment or volunteer experience in community service. Applicant must have 2.5 GPA or higher. Available to U.S. citizens.

Application Requirements: Application, essay, resume, references, transcript, current enrollment form. *Deadline:* March 31.

Contact: Dionne Ellison, Administrative Assistant
National Association for Campus Activities
13 Harbison Way
Columbia, SC 29212-3401
Phone: 803-732-6222 Ext. 131
Fax: 803-749-1047
E-mail: dionnee@naca.org

NATIONAL ASSOCIATION FOR CAMPUS ACTIVITIES SOUTHEAST REGION STUDENT LEADERSHIP SCHOLARSHIP

Scholarships will be given to full-time undergraduate students in good standing at the time of the application and during the academic term in which the scholarship is awarded. Must demonstrate significant leadership skill and ability while holding a significant leadership position on campus. Applicants must have made contributions via volunteer involvement, either on or off campus. Must be enrolled in a college/university in the NACA Southeast Region.

Award: Scholarship for use in freshman, sophomore, junior, or senior years; not renewable. *Number:* up to 4. *Amount:* $250–$300.

Eligibility Requirements: Applicant must be enrolled or expecting to enroll full-time at a two-year or four-year institution or university; studying in Alabama, Florida, Georgia, Mississippi, North Carolina, Puerto Rico, South Carolina, Tennessee, or Virginia and must have an interest in leadership. Applicant or parent of applicant must have employment or volunteer experience in community service. Available to U.S. citizens.

Application Requirements: Application, essay, resume, references, transcript, enrollment form. *Deadline:* March 31.

Contact: Dionne Ellison, Administrative Assistant
National Association for Campus Activities
13 Harbison Way
Columbia, SC 29212-3401
Phone: 803-732-6222 Ext. 131
Fax: 803-749-1047
E-mail: dionnee@naca.org

NATIONAL ASSOCIATION FOR CAMPUS ACTIVITIES WISCONSIN REGION STUDENT LEADERSHIP SCHOLARSHIP

Scholarships will be awarded to undergraduate or graduate students in good standing and enrolled in the equivalent of at least six academic credits at the time of the application and during the academic term in which the scholarship is awarded. Must be currently enrolled in or received a degree from a college or university within the NACA Wisconsin Region or Michigan (area code 906) and demonstrated leadership skill and significant service to their campus community.

Award: Scholarship for use in freshman, sophomore, junior, senior, or graduate years; not renewable. *Number:* 1. *Amount:* $250–$300.

Eligibility Requirements: Applicant must be enrolled or expecting to enroll full- or part-time at a two-year or four-year institution or university; studying in Michigan or Wisconsin and must have an interest in leadership. Applicant or parent of applicant must have employment or volunteer experience in community service. Available to U.S. citizens.

Application Requirements: Application, essay, resume, references, transcript. *Deadline:* January 15.

Contact: Dionne Ellison, Administrative Assistant
National Association for Campus Activities
13 Harbison Way
Columbia, SC 29212-3401
Phone: 803-732-6222 Ext. 131
Fax: 803-749-1047
E-mail: dionnee@naca.org

SCHOLARSHIPS FOR STUDENT LEADERS

Scholarships will be awarded to undergraduate students in good standing at the time of the application and who, during the academic term in which the scholarship is awarded, hold a significant leadership position on their campus. Must make significant contributions to their campus communities and demonstrate leadership skills and abilities.

Award: Scholarship for use in freshman, sophomore, junior, or senior years; not renewable. *Number:* up to 6. *Amount:* $250–$300.

Eligibility Requirements: Applicant must be enrolled or expecting to enroll full- or part-time at a two-year or four-year institution or university and must have an interest in leadership. Applicant or parent of applicant must have employment or volunteer experience in community service. Available to U.S. and non-U.S. citizens.

Application Requirements: Application, resume, references, transcript, current enrollment form. *Deadline:* November 1.

Contact: Dionne Ellison, Administrative Assistant
National Association for Campus Activities
13 Harbison Way
Columbia, SC 29212-3401
Phone: 803-732-6222 Ext. 131
Fax: 803-749-1047
E-mail: dionnee@naca.org

NATIONAL BURGLAR AND FIRE ALARM ASSOCIATION

http://www.alarm.org/

NBFAA YOUTH SCHOLARSHIP PROGRAM

One-time award for high school seniors entering postsecondary education, who are deserving sons or daughters of police and fire officials. The number of awards granted varies annually.

Award: Scholarship for use in freshman year; not renewable. *Number:* varies. *Amount:* $500–$10,000.

Eligibility Requirements: Applicant must be high school student; age 15–20; planning to enroll or expecting to enroll full-time at a four-year institution or university and resident of California, Connecticut, Georgia, Indiana, Kentucky, Louisiana, Maryland, Minnesota, New Jersey, New York, North Carolina, Pennsylvania, Tennessee, Virginia, or Washington. Applicant or parent of applicant must have employment or volunteer experience in police/firefighting. Available to U.S. citizens.

Application Requirements: Application, essay, test scores, transcript. *Deadline:* March 30.

Contact: Georjia Calaway, Marketing Coordinator
National Burglar and Fire Alarm Association
8380 Colesville Road, Suite 750
Silver Spring, MD 20910
Phone: 301-585-1855 Ext. 133
Fax: 301-585-1866
E-mail: georjiac@alarm.org

NATSO FOUNDATION

http://www.natso.com/

BILL MOON SCHOLARSHIP

Available to employees or dependents of NATSO-affiliated truck stops/travel plazas. Visit web site at http://www.natsofoundation.org for additional information.

Award: Scholarship for use in freshman, sophomore, junior, senior, or graduate years; not renewable. *Number:* 13. *Amount:* $2500.

Eligibility Requirements: Applicant must be enrolled or expecting to enroll full- or part-time at a two-year or four-year institution or university. Applicant or parent of applicant must have employment or volunteer experience in transportation industry. Available to U.S. and non-U.S. citizens.

Application Requirements: Application, essay, financial need analysis, references, transcript, signature from employer. *Deadline:* April 14.

Contact: Sharon Corigliano, Executive Director
NATSO Foundation
1737 King Street, Suite 200
Alexandria, VA 22314
Phone: 703-549-2100 Ext. 8561
Fax: 703-684-9667
E-mail: scorigliano@natso.com

NETAID FOUNDATION/MERCY CORPS

http://www.globalactionawards.org/

GLOBAL ACTION AWARDS

Awards honor high school students who have taken outstanding actions to fight global poverty. Honorees receive $5000 for their education or a charity of their choice. College freshman who completed their project while in a U.S. high school may apply.

Award: Scholarship for use in freshman year; not renewable. *Number:* 5. *Amount:* $5000.

Eligibility Requirements: Applicant must be high school student; planning to enroll or expecting to enroll full-time at a four-year institution and must have an interest in leadership. Applicant or parent of applicant must have employment or volunteer experience in community service. Available to U.S. citizens.

Application Requirements: Application, references, projects. *Deadline:* varies.

Contact: Suzanne Guthrie, Manager, Education and Youth Programs
NetAid Foundation/Mercy Corps
75 Broad Street, Suite 2410
New York, NY 10004
Phone: 212-537-0518
Fax: 212-537-0501
E-mail: gaa@nyc.mercycorps.org

NEW JERSEY HIGHER EDUCATION STUDENT ASSISTANCE AUTHORITY

http://www.hesaa.org/

LAW ENFORCEMENT OFFICER MEMORIAL SCHOLARSHIP

Scholarships for full-time undergraduate study at approved New Jersey institutions for the dependent children of New Jersey law enforcement officers killed in the line of duty. Value of scholarship will be established annually. Deadline varies.

Award: Scholarship for use in freshman, sophomore, junior, or senior years; renewable. *Number:* varies. *Amount:* varies.

Eligibility Requirements: Applicant must be enrolled or expecting to enroll full-time at a four-year institution or university; resident of New Jersey and studying in New Jersey. Applicant or parent of applicant must have employment or volunteer experience in police/firefighting. Available to U.S. citizens.

Application Requirements: Application. *Deadline:* varies.

Contact: Carol Muka, Assistant Director of Grants and Scholarships
New Jersey Higher Education Student Assistance Authority
PO Box 540
Trenton, NJ 08625
Phone: 800-792-8670 Ext. 3266
Fax: 609-588-2228
E-mail: cmuka@hesaa.org

SURVIVOR TUITION BENEFITS PROGRAM

The scholarship provides tuition fees for spouses and dependents of law enforcement officers, fire, or emergency services personnel killed in the line of duty. Eligible recipients may attend any independent institution in the state; however, the annual value of the grant cannot exceed the highest tuition charged at a New Jersey public institution.

Award: Scholarship for use in freshman, sophomore, junior, or senior years; renewable. *Number:* varies. *Amount:* varies.

Eligibility Requirements: Applicant must be enrolled or expecting to enroll full- or part-time at a two-year or four-year institution or university; resident of New Jersey and studying in New Jersey. Applicant or parent of applicant must have employment or volunteer experience in police/firefighting. Available to U.S. citizens.

Application Requirements: Application. *Deadline:* varies.

Contact: Carol Muka, Scholarship Coordinator
New Jersey Higher Education Student Assistance Authority
PO Box 540
Trenton, NJ 08625
Phone: 800-792-8670 Ext. 3266
Fax: 609-588-2228
E-mail: cmuka@hesaa.org

PACERS FOUNDATION INC.

http://www.pacersfoundation.org/

PACERS TEAMUP SCHOLARSHIP

Scholarship is awarded to Indiana high school seniors for their first year of undergraduate study at any accredited four-year college or university or two-year college or junior college. Primary selection criteria is student involvement in community service.

Award: Scholarship for use in freshman year; not renewable. *Number:* 5. *Amount:* $2000.

Eligibility Requirements: Applicant must be enrolled or expecting to enroll full-time at a two-year or four-year institution or university and resident of Indiana. Applicant or parent of applicant must have employment or volunteer experience in community service. Available to U.S. citizens.

Application Requirements: Application, essay, references, transcript. *Deadline:* March 1.

Contact: Jami Marsh, Executive Director
Pacers Foundation Inc.
125 South Pennsylvania Street
Indianapolis, IN 46204
Phone: 317-917-2856
E-mail: foundation@pacers.com

PENNSYLVANIA BURGLAR AND FIRE ALARM ASSOCIATION

http://www.pbfaa.com/

PENNSYLVANIA BURGLAR AND FIRE ALARM ASSOCIATION YOUTH SCHOLARSHIP PROGRAM

Non-renewable scholarships available to sons and daughters of active Pennsylvania police and fire personnel, and volunteer fire department personnel for full-time study at a two- or four-year college, or university. Must be a senior attending a Pennsylvania high school. Scholarship amount in the range of $500 to $6500.

Award: Scholarship for use in freshman year; not renewable. *Number:* 6–8. *Amount:* $500–$6500.

Eligibility Requirements: Applicant must be high school student; planning to enroll or expecting to enroll full-time at a two-year or four-year institution or university and resident of Pennsylvania. Applicant or parent of applicant must have employment or volunteer experience in police/firefighting. Available to U.S. citizens.

Application Requirements: Application, essay, resume, test scores, transcript. *Deadline:* March 1.

Contact: Dale Eller, Executive Director
Pennsylvania Burglar and Fire Alarm Association
3718 West Lake Road
Erie, PA 16505
Phone: 814-838-3093
Fax: 814-838-5127
E-mail: info@pbfaa.com

PENNSYLVANIA COMMERCE BANCORP, INC.

http://www.com/mercepc.com/

"CASH FOR COLLEGE" SCHOLARSHIP

Award available to graduating high school seniors who have demonstrated exceptional community service and plan to enroll in a full-time course of study at an accredited two- or four-year college or university or vocational-technical school in the United States. Must reside within Commerce Bank's service area in one of the following Pennsylvania counties: Berks, Cumberland, Dauphin, Lebanon, Lancaster, or York. Submission of two essays is required. See web site for details and application http://www.commercepc.com/inside_commerce/scholarship.cfm.

Award: Scholarship for use in freshman year; not renewable. *Number:* 1. *Amount:* $2500.

Eligibility Requirements: Applicant must be high school student; planning to enroll or expecting to enroll full-time at a two-year or four-year or technical institution or university and resident of Pennsylvania. Applicant or parent of applicant must have employment or volunteer experience in community service. Available to U.S. citizens.

Application Requirements: Application, essay, transcript. *Deadline:* March 7.

Contact: Scholarship Committee
Pennsylvania Commerce Bancorp, Inc.
3801 Paxton Street
Harrisburg, PA 17111

PHOENIX SUNS CHARITIES/SUN STUDENTS SCHOLARSHIP

http://www.suns.com/

SUN STUDENT COLLEGE SCHOLARSHIP PROGRAM

Applicants must be seniors preparing to graduate from a high school in Arizona. Eligible applicants must have a minimum 2.5 GPA. Must provide evidence of regular involvement in charitable activities or volunteer service in school, church, or community organizations. Fifteen $2000 scholarships and one $5000 scholarship will be awarded.

Award: Scholarship for use in freshman year; not renewable. *Number:* 1–16. *Amount:* $2000–$5000.

Eligibility Requirements: Applicant must be high school student; planning to enroll or expecting to enroll full- or part-time at a two-year or four-year institution or university and resident of Arizona. Applicant or parent of applicant must have employment or volunteer experience in community service. Applicant must have 2.5 GPA or higher. Available to U.S. citizens.

Application Requirements: Application, essay, references, transcript. *Deadline:* February 15.

Contact: Janell Jakubowski, Administrative Assistant
Phoenix Suns Charities/Sun Students Scholarship
PO Box 1369
Phoenix, AZ 85001
Phone: 602-379-7767
Fax: 602-379-7922
E-mail: jornelas@suns.com

PROJECT BEST SCHOLARSHIP FUND

http://www.projectbest.com/

PROJECT BEST SCHOLARSHIP
• *See page 560*

PUEBLO OF SAN JUAN, DEPARTMENT OF EDUCATION

http://www.sanjuaned.org/

OHKAY OWINGEH TRIBAL SCHOLARSHIP OF THE PUEBLO OF SAN JUAN

Scholarship for residents of New Mexico enrolled either full-time or part-time in accredited colleges or universities. Minimum GPA of 2.0 required. Must complete required number of hours of community service in the San Juan Pueblo. Up to thirty scholarships are granted and the value of the award ranges from $300 to $600. Deadline varies.

Award: Scholarship for use in freshman, sophomore, junior, or senior years; renewable. *Number:* 1–30. *Amount:* $300–$600.

Eligibility Requirements: Applicant must be American Indian/Alaska Native; enrolled or expecting to enroll full- or part-time at a two-year or four-year or technical institution or university and resident of New Mexico. Applicant or parent of applicant must have employment or volunteer experience in community service. Available to U.S. citizens.

Application Requirements: Application, transcript, letter of acceptance. *Deadline:* varies.

Contact: Adam Garcia, Education Coordinator
Pueblo of San Juan, Department of Education
State Highway 74, Day School Street
PO Box 1269
Ohkay Owingeh, NM 87566
Phone: 505-852-3477
Fax: 505-852-3030
E-mail: wevog68@valornet.com

POP'AY SCHOLARSHIP

Scholarship for members of Pueblo of San Juan tribe pursuing their first associate or baccalaureate degree. Must complete a minimum of 20 hours of community service within the San Juan Pueblo. Scholarship value is $2500. Seventeen awards are granted. Deadlines: December 30 for spring, April 30 for summer, and June 30 for fall.

Award: Scholarship for use in freshman, sophomore, junior, or senior years; renewable. *Number:* up to 17. *Amount:* $2500.

Eligibility Requirements: Applicant must be American Indian/Alaska Native; enrolled or expecting to enroll full-time at a two-year or four-year institution or university and resident of New Mexico. Applicant or parent of applicant must have employment or volunteer experience in community service. Available to U.S. citizens.

Application Requirements: Application, transcript, letter of acceptance. *Deadline:* varies.

Contact: Adam Garcia, Education Coordinator
Pueblo of San Juan, Department of Education
State Highway 74, Day School Street
PO Box 1269
Ohkay Owingeh, NM 87566
Phone: 505-852-3477
Fax: 505-852-3030
E-mail: wevog68@valornet.com

RAISE THE NATION FOUNDATION

http://www.raisethenation.org/

RAISE THE NATION STUDENT LOAN GRANT

Grant is awarded to professional single parent women with outstanding student loan debt who contribute to their community through volunteer work. Community service hours will be determined/decided when you receive an award.

Award: Grant for use in freshman, sophomore, junior, senior, graduate, or postgraduate years; renewable. *Number:* 1–50. *Amount:* $100–$5000.

Eligibility Requirements: Applicant must be age 18-99; enrolled or expecting to enroll full- or part-time at a two-year or four-year or technical institution or university and single female. Applicant or parent of applicant must have employment or volunteer experience in community service. Available to U.S. citizens.

Application Requirements: Application, driver's license, essay, financial need analysis, transcript. *Fee:* $20. *Deadline:* varies.

Contact: Michelle McMullen, Executive Director
Raise the Nation Foundation
PO Box 8058
Albuquerque, NM 87198
Phone: 505-265-1201
E-mail: suppoetdesk@raisethenation.org

RECORDING FOR THE BLIND & DYSLEXIC

http://www.rfbd.org/

MARION HUBER LEARNING THROUGH LISTENING AWARDS
• *See page 560*

MARY P. OENSLAGER SCHOLASTIC ACHIEVEMENT AWARDS
• *See page 560*

ST. CLAIRE REGIONAL MEDICAL CENTER

http://www.st-claire.org/

SR. MARY JEANNETTE WESS, S.N.D. SCHOLARSHIP

Scholarships available for undergraduates in their junior or senior year of study, or graduate students. Must have graduated from an eastern Kentucky high school in one of the following counties: Bath, Carter, Elliott, Fleming, Lewis, Magoffin, Menifee, Montgomery, Morgan, Rowan, or Wolfe. Must demonstrate academic achievement, leadership, service, and financial need.

Award: Scholarship for use in junior, senior, or graduate years; renewable. *Number:* 2. *Amount:* $750.

Eligibility Requirements: Applicant must be enrolled or expecting to enroll full-time at a four-year institution or university; resident of Kentucky and must have an interest in leadership. Applicant or parent of applicant must have employment or volunteer experience in community service. Available to U.S. and non-U.S. citizens.

Application Requirements: Application, financial need analysis, references, self-addressed stamped envelope, transcript. *Deadline:* varies.

Contact: Tom Lewis, Director of Development
St. Claire Regional Medical Center
222 Medical Circle
Morehead, KY 40351
Phone: 606-783-6511
Fax: 606-783-6795
E-mail: telewis@st-claire.org

SAN DIEGO FOUNDATION

http://www.sdfoundation.org/

DRINKWATER FAMILY SCHOLARSHIP

Scholarship to graduating high school seniors who will be the first in their family to attend an accredited four-year university in the United States. Must have minimum GPA of 3.25, a demonstrated financial need, and be actively involved in serving their community as shown by their participation in extracurricular or church activities, or community service. Scholarship may be used for tuition, books and fees.

Award: Scholarship for use in freshman year; not renewable. *Number:* varies. *Amount:* varies.

Eligibility Requirements: Applicant must be high school student; planning to enroll or expecting to enroll full-time at an institution or university and resident of California. Applicant or parent of applicant must have employment or volunteer experience in community service. Available to U.S. citizens.

Application Requirements: Application, references, transcript, personal statement, copy of tax return. *Deadline:* January 26.

Contact: Shryl Helvie, Scholarship Coordinator
San Diego Foundation
2508 Historic Decatur Road, Suite 200
San Diego, CA 92106
Phone: 619-814-1307
Fax: 619-239-1710
E-mail: shryl@sdfoundation.org

HARVEY L. SIMMONS MEMORIAL SCHOLARSHIP

Scholarship to graduating high school seniors who will attend an accredited two-year college or four-year university in the United States. Applicants must demonstrate financial need, and a commitment to serving their community through their involvement in community service, church or extracurricular activities. Preference given to applicants who have participated in high school sports for at least three years, two at the varsity level, and are intending to play at the college level.

Award: Scholarship for use in freshman year; not renewable. *Number:* 2. *Amount:* $500.

Eligibility Requirements: Applicant must be high school student; planning to enroll or expecting to enroll full-time at a two-year or four-year institution or university and resident of California. Applicant or parent of applicant must have employment or volunteer experience in community service. Available to U.S. citizens.

Application Requirements: Application, references, transcript, personal statement, copy of tax return. *Deadline:* January 26.

Contact: Shryl Helvie, Scholarship Coordinator
San Diego Foundation
2508 Historic Decatur Road, Suite 200
San Diego, CA 92106
Phone: 619-814-1307
Fax: 619-239-1710
E-mail: shryl@sdfoundation.org

LESLIE JANE HAHN MEMORIAL SCHOLARSHIP

Scholarship to graduating high school senior girls from a public school who will be attending an accredited four-year college or university in the United States. Applicants must have at least a 3.75 GPA and a demonstrated financial need. Must also have a history of active involvement in athletics, other extracurricular activities, community service or work experience.

Award: Scholarship for use in freshman, sophomore, junior, or senior years; renewable. *Number:* 1. *Amount:* $3000.

Eligibility Requirements: Applicant must be enrolled or expecting to enroll full-time at a four-year institution or university; female; resident of California and must have an interest in athletics/sports. Applicant or parent of applicant must have employment or volunteer experience in community service. Available to U.S. citizens.

Application Requirements: Application, financial need analysis, references, transcript, personal statement, copy of tax return. *Deadline:* January 26.

Contact: Shryl Helvie, Scholarship Coordinator
San Diego Foundation
2508 Historic Decatur Road, Suite 200
San Diego, CA 92106
Phone: 619-814-1307
Fax: 619-239-1710
E-mail: shryl@sdfoundation.org

SAN DIEGO PATHWAYS TO COLLEGE SCHOLARSHIP

Scholarship to graduating high school seniors who are attending a four-year university in the state of California. Must be legal residents of San Diego County. Applicants must have a minimum 3.0 GPA and a demonstrated financial need. Also, students must be actively involved in extracurricular activities, community service, religious activities, work experience, or athletics.

Award: Scholarship for use in freshman year; not renewable. *Number:* 25. *Amount:* $1000–$10,000.

Eligibility Requirements: Applicant must be high school student; planning to enroll or expecting to enroll full-time at a four-year institution or university; resident of California and studying in California. Applicant or parent of applicant must have employment or volunteer experience in community service. Applicant must have 3.0 GPA or higher. Available to U.S. citizens.

Application Requirements: Application, financial need analysis, references, transcript, personal statement, copy of tax return. *Deadline:* January 26.

Contact: Shryl Helvie, Scholarship Coordinator
San Diego Foundation
2508 Historic Decatur Road, Suite 200
San Diego, CA 92106
Phone: 619-814-1307
Fax: 619-239-1710
E-mail: shryl@sdfoundation.org

USA FREESTYLE MARTIAL ARTS SCHOLARSHIP

Scholarship to students who are currently attending or have attended USA Freestyle Martial Arts for at least two years. Applicants must have a minimum 2.5 GPA and either be graduating high school seniors or current college students who plan to attend an accredited two- or four-year college or university, or licensed trade/vocational school in the United States. Applicants must be committed to their communities as demonstrated by their involvement in community service.

Award: Scholarship for use in freshman, sophomore, junior, or senior years; not renewable. *Number:* 2. *Amount:* $1000–$3000.

Eligibility Requirements: Applicant must be enrolled or expecting to enroll full-time at a two-year or four-year or technical institution or university; resident of California and must have an interest in athletics/sports. Applicant or parent of applicant must have employment or volunteer experience in community service. Applicant must have 2.5 GPA or higher. Available to U.S. citizens.

Application Requirements: Application, financial need analysis, references, transcript, personal statement, copy of tax return. *Deadline:* January 26.

Contact: Shryl Helvie, Scholarship Coordinator
San Diego Foundation
2508 Historic Decatur Road, Suite 200
San Diego, CA 92106
Phone: 619-814-1307
Fax: 619-239-1710
E-mail: shryl@sdfoundation.org

SKILLSUSA

http://www.skillsusa.org/

SKILLSUSA ALUMNI AND FRIENDS MERIT SCHOLARSHIP

Scholarship of up to $1000 recognizes qualities of leadership, commitment to community service, improving the image of career and technical education, and improving the image of his/her chosen occupation.

Award: Scholarship for use in freshman, sophomore, junior, senior, graduate, or postgraduate years; not renewable. *Number:* 1. *Amount:* $500–$1000.

Eligibility Requirements: Applicant must be enrolled or expecting to enroll full-time at a two-year or four-year or technical institution or university and must have an interest in leadership. Applicant or parent of applicant must have employment or volunteer experience in community service. Available to U.S. citizens.

Application Requirements: Application, references. *Deadline:* May 15.

Contact: Karen Perrino, Associate Director
SkillsUSA
PO Box 3000
Leesburg, VA 20177-0300
Phone: 703-737-0610
Fax: 703-777-8999
E-mail: kperrino@skillsusa.org

STATE FARM COMPANIES/YOUTH SERVICE AMERICA

http://www.ysa.org/

HARRIS WOFFORD AWARDS

Awards recognize extraordinary achievements in three categories: youth (ages 12 to 25), organization (nonprofit, corporate, foundation), and media (organization or individual) for actively contributing towards, "Making service and service-learning the common expectation and common experience of every young person."

Award: Grant for use in freshman, sophomore, junior, senior, graduate, or postgraduate years; not renewable. *Number:* up to 3. *Amount:* $500–$1000.

Eligibility Requirements: Applicant must be age 12-25 and enrolled or expecting to enroll full- or part-time at a two-year or four-year or technical institution or university. Applicant or parent of applicant must have employment or volunteer experience in community service. Available to U.S. citizens.

Application Requirements: Application. *Deadline:* October 19.

Contact: Julie Mancuso, Grant Manager
State Farm Companies/Youth Service America
1101 15th Street, NW, Suite 200
Washington, DC 20005
Phone: 202-296-2992 Ext. 111
Fax: 202-296-4030
E-mail: jmancuso@ysa.org

STONEWALL COMMUNITY FOUNDATION

http://www.stonewallfoundation.org/

HARRY BARTEL MEMORIAL SCHOLARSHIP FUND

Gay male students who are 23 years or younger with a record of community service can apply for this scholarship. Deadline varies.

Award: Scholarship for use in freshman, sophomore, junior, senior, graduate, or postgraduate years; not renewable. *Number:* varies. *Amount:* varies.

Eligibility Requirements: Applicant must be age 23 or under; enrolled or expecting to enroll full-time at a two-year or four-year or technical institution or university; male and must have an interest in LGBT issues. Applicant or parent of applicant must have employment or volunteer experience in community service. Available to U.S. citizens.

Application Requirements: Application. *Deadline:* varies.

Contact: Roz Lee, Program Director
Stonewall Community Foundation
119 West 24th Street, Seventh Floor
New York, NY 10011
Phone: 212-367-1155
Fax: 212-367-1157
E-mail: stonewall@stonewallfoundation.org

TERRY FOX HUMANITARIAN AWARD PROGRAM

http://www.terryfox.org/

TERRY FOX HUMANITARIAN AWARD

Award granted to Canadian students entering postsecondary education. Criteria includes commitment to voluntary humanitarian work, courage in overcoming obstacles, excellence in academics, fitness and amateur sports. Value of award is CAN$7000 awarded annually for maximum of four years. Must be no older than age 25.

Award: Scholarship for use in freshman, sophomore, junior, or senior years; renewable. *Number:* up to 20.

Eligibility Requirements: Applicant must be Canadian citizen; age 25 or under; enrolled or expecting to enroll full-time at a two-year or four-year institution or university and must have an interest in athletics/sports. Applicant or parent of applicant must have employment or volunteer experience in community service.

Application Requirements: Application, references, self-addressed stamped envelope, transcript. *Deadline:* February 1.

Contact: W. Davis, Executive Director
Terry Fox Humanitarian Award Program
Simon Fraser University, 8888 University Drive
Burnaby, BC V5A 1S6
Canada
Phone: 604-291-3057
Fax: 604-291-3311
E-mail: terryfox@sfu.ca

TEXAS RESTAURANT ASSOCIATION

http://www.restaurantville.com/

W. PRICE JR. MEMORIAL SCHOLARSHIP

Scholarships of $5000 for recipients attending a four-year university, culinary academy, or graduate program, and $2000 for recipients attending a two-year college. Applicant must be employed by an ARA member in good standing, must have an overall B grade average, and must submit an essay summarizing how their experience in the food service industry has affected their career goals.

Award: Scholarship for use in freshman, sophomore, junior, or senior years; not renewable. *Number:* 4. *Amount:* $2000–$5000.

Eligibility Requirements: Applicant must be enrolled or expecting to enroll full-time at a two-year or four-year institution or university. Applicant or parent of applicant must have employment or volunteer experience in food service. Available to U.S. citizens.

Application Requirements: Application, references, transcript. *Deadline:* February 1.

Contact: Susan Petty, Scholarship Coordinator
Texas Restaurant Association
PO Box 1429
Austin, TX 78767-1429
Phone: 512-457-4100
Fax: 512-472-2777
E-mail: spetty@tramail.org

TUITION EXCHANGE INC.

http://www.tuitionexchange.org/

TUITION EXCHANGE SCHOLARSHIPS

The Tuition Exchange is an association of over 600 colleges and universities awarding over 5700 full or substantial scholarships each year for children and other family members of faculty and staff employed at participating institutions. Students must maintain satisfactory academic progress and a cumulative GPA as established by each institution. Application procedures and deadlines vary by school. Contact Tuition Exchange Liaison Officer at home institution for details.

Award: Scholarship for use in freshman, sophomore, junior, senior, graduate, or postgraduate years; renewable. *Number:* 5000–7000. *Amount:* $4000–$41,000.

Eligibility Requirements: Applicant must be enrolled or expecting to enroll full- or part-time at a two-year or four-year institution or university. Applicant or parent of applicant must have employment or volunteer experience in teaching/education. Available to U.S. and non-U.S. citizens.

Application Requirements: Application. *Deadline:* continuous.

Contact: Mr. Robert D. Shorb, Executive Director/CEO
Tuition Exchange Inc.
1743 Connecticut Avenue, NW
Washington, DC 20009-1108
Phone: 202-518-0135
Fax: 202-518-0137
E-mail: rshorb@tuitionexchange.org

TWO TEN FOOTWEAR FOUNDATION

http://www.twoten.org/

TWO TEN FOOTWEAR FOUNDATION SCHOLARSHIP

Renewable, merit and need-based award available to students who have 500 hours work experience in footwear, leather, or allied industries during year of application, or have a parent employed in one of these fields for at least two years. Must have proof of employment and maintain 2.5 GPA.

Award: Scholarship for use in freshman, sophomore, junior, or senior years; renewable. *Number:* 200–300. *Amount:* $500–$3000.

Eligibility Requirements: Applicant must be enrolled or expecting to enroll full- or part-time at a two-year or four-year institution or university. Applicant or parent of applicant must have employment or volunteer experience in leather/footwear industry. Available to U.S. citizens.

Application Requirements: Application, essay, financial need analysis, references, transcript. *Deadline:* February 16.

Contact: Phyllis Molta, Director of Scholarship
Two Ten Footwear Foundation
1466 Main Street
Waltham, MA 02451-1623
Phone: 781-736-1510
E-mail: scholarship@twoten.org

UNITED NEGRO COLLEGE FUND

http://www.uncf.org/

GIANT FOODS SCHOLARSHIP

Scholarship available to students who have demonstrated a minimum of 8 hours of community service. Students from the Washington, DC metro area attending Bowie State, Coppin State, University of Maryland-Eastern Shore, Morgan State, or a UNCF member school. Minimum 2.5 GPA required.

Award: Scholarship for use in freshman year; not renewable. *Amount:* $1000.

Eligibility Requirements: Applicant must be Black (non-Hispanic); enrolled or expecting to enroll at a four-year institution or university and resident of District of Columbia. Applicant or parent of applicant must have employment or volunteer experience in community service. Applicant must have 2.5 GPA or higher. Available to U.S. citizens.

Application Requirements: *Deadline:* continuous.

Contact: Director, Program Services
United Negro College Fund
8260 Willow Oaks Corporate Drive
PO Box 10444
Fairfax, VA 22031-8044
Phone: 800-331-2244
E-mail: rebecca.bennett@uncf.org

RYAN HOWARD FAMILY FOUNDATION SCHOLARSHIP-ST. LOUIS/PHILADELPHIA

Scholarship for graduating high school students who are residents of Philadelphia, PA or St. Louis, MO. Students should have a minimum GPA 2.5, possess leadership qualities, have performed no less than 20 hours of community service, have the potential for success in college, and be involved in school and the community. For more information see Website: http://www.uncf.org/forstudents/scholarship.asp.

Award: Scholarship for use in freshman year. *Amount:* $1000.

Eligibility Requirements: Applicant must be Black (non-Hispanic); high school student; planning to enroll or expecting to enroll at a four-year institution or university and resident of Missouri or Pennsylvania. Applicant or parent of applicant must have employment or volunteer experience in community service. Applicant must have 2.5 GPA or higher.

Contact: Director, Program Services
United Negro College Fund
8260 Willow Oaks Corporate Drive
PO Box 10444
Fairfax, VA 22031-8044
Phone: 800-331-2244
E-mail: rebecca.bennett@uncf.org

UNITED STATES SUBMARINE VETERANS

http://www.ussvcf.org/

UNITED STATES SUBMARINE VETERANS INC. NATIONAL SCHOLARSHIP PROGRAM

• See page 571

WESTERN GOLF ASSOCIATION-EVANS SCHOLARS FOUNDATION

http://www.evansscholarsfoundation.com/

CHICK EVANS CADDIE SCHOLARSHIP

Full tuition and housing awards renewable up to four years available to high school seniors who have worked at least two years as a caddy at a Western Golf Association member club. Must demonstrate need, outstanding character, and at least a B average in college preparatory courses. Limited to use at universities where Evans Foundation maintains a Scholarship House, where recipients are required to reside. See web site for complete list.

Award: Scholarship for use in freshman year; renewable. *Number:* up to 200. *Amount:* varies.

Eligibility Requirements: Applicant must be high school student; planning to enroll or expecting to enroll full-time at a four-year institution or university and studying in Colorado, Illinois, Indiana, Kansas, Michigan, Minnesota, Missouri, Ohio, Oregon, Pennsylvania, Washington, or Wisconsin. Applicant or parent of applicant must have employment or volunteer experience in private club/caddying. Available to U.S. and non-U.S. citizens.

Application Requirements: Application, essay, financial need analysis, interview, references, test scores, transcript. *Deadline:* September 30.

Contact: Scholarship Committee
Western Golf Association-Evans Scholars Foundation
One Briar Road
Golf, IL 60029
Phone: 847-724-4600
E-mail: evansscholars@wgaesf

YOUNG AMERICAN BOWLING ALLIANCE (YABA)

http://www.bowl.com/

USBC ANNUAL ZEB SCHOLARSHIP

Scholarship awarded to a USBC Youth member who achieves academic success and gives back to the community through service. Candidates must have a current GPA of 2.0 or better.

Award: Scholarship for use in freshman year; not renewable. *Number:* 1. *Amount:* $2500.

Eligibility Requirements: Applicant must be high school student; planning to enroll or expecting to enroll full- or part-time at a four-year institution or university and must have an interest in bowling. Applicant or parent of applicant must have employment or volunteer experience in community service. Available to U.S. citizens.

Application Requirements: Application, references, transcript. *Deadline:* April 1.

Contact: Ed Gocha, Scholarship Programs Manager
Young American Bowling Alliance (YABA)
5301 South 76th Street
Greendale, WI 53129-1192
Phone: 800-514-2695
Fax: 414-423-3014
E-mail: smart@bowlinginc.com

YOUTH FOUNDATION INC.

http://www.foundationcenter.org/grantmaker/youthfdn/index.html

ALEXANDER AND MAUDE HADDEN SCHOLARSHIP

Youth Foundation offers exceptional students with financial need an award of $2500 to $4000 per year which is renewable for four years at the foundation's discretion. Minimum GPA of 3.5 required, community service and extra curricular activities expected. Must write Foundation for information and application request form.

Award: Scholarship for use in freshman, sophomore, junior, or senior years; renewable. *Number:* varies. *Amount:* $2500–$4000.

Eligibility Requirements: Applicant must be enrolled or expecting to enroll full- or part-time at a four-year institution or university. Applicant or parent of applicant must have employment or volunteer experience in community service. Applicant must have 3.5 GPA or higher. Available to U.S. citizens.

Application Requirements: Application, essay, test scores, transcript. *Deadline:* February 29.

Contact: Scholarship Committee
Youth Foundation Inc.
36 West 44th Street
New York, NY 10036
Phone: 212-840-6291

IMPAIRMENT

ALEXANDER GRAHAM BELL ASSOCIATION FOR THE DEAF AND HARD OF HEARING

http://www.agbell.org/

AG BELL COLLEGE SCHOLARSHIP PROGRAM

Available to students with pre-lingual hearing loss who attend a mainstream and accredited college or university on a full-time basis. Specific eligibility criteria, submission guidelines, deadline and application available on AG Bell web site at http://www.agbell.org.

Award: Scholarship for use in freshman, sophomore, junior, senior, graduate, or postgraduate years; not renewable. *Number:* 10–25. *Amount:* $1000–$10,000.

Eligibility Requirements: Applicant must be enrolled or expecting to enroll full-time at a four-year institution or university. Applicant must be hearing impaired. Applicant must have 3.5 GPA or higher. Available to U.S. and non-U.S. citizens.

Application Requirements: Application, essay, references, transcript, unaided audiogram or CI programming report.

Contact: Wendy Will, Youth & Family Programs Manager
　　　Alexander Graham Bell Association for the Deaf and Hard of
　　　　Hearing
　　　3417 Volta Place, NW
　　　Washington, DC 20007
　　　Phone: 202-337-5220
　　　E-mail: financialaid@agbell.org

AMERICAN CANCER SOCIETY

http://www.cancer.org/

AMERICAN CANCER SOCIETY, FLORIDA DIVISION R.O.C.K. COLLEGE SCHOLARSHIP PROGRAM

Applicants must have had a personal diagnosis of cancer, be a Florida resident between the ages of 18 and 21, and plan to attend college in Florida. Minimum 2.5 GPA required. Awards will be based on financial need, scholarship, community service, cancer diagnosis, type and length of treatment.

Award: Scholarship for use in freshman, sophomore, junior, or senior years; renewable. *Number:* 200–225. *Amount:* $300–$3300.

Eligibility Requirements: Applicant must be age 18-21; enrolled or expecting to enroll full- or part-time at a two-year or four-year or technical institution or university; resident of Florida; studying in Florida and must have an interest in leadership. Applicant must be physically disabled. Applicant must have 2.5 GPA or higher. Available to U.S. citizens.

Application Requirements: Application, essay, financial need analysis, interview, photo, resume, references, test scores, transcript, letter from physician. *Deadline:* April 10.

Contact: Susan Bellomy, Director of Childhood Cancer Programs
　　　American Cancer Society
　　　3709 West Jetton Avenue
　　　Tampa, FL 33629
　　　Phone: 800-444-1410 Ext. 4405
　　　Fax: 813-254-5857
　　　E-mail: susan.bellomy@cancer.org

AMERICAN COUNCIL OF THE BLIND

http://www.acb.org/

AMERICAN COUNCIL OF THE BLIND SCHOLARSHIPS

Merit-based award available to undergraduate students who are legally blind in both eyes. Submit certificate of legal blindness and proof of acceptance at an accredited postsecondary institution.

Award: Scholarship for use in freshman, sophomore, junior, or senior years; renewable. *Number:* 16–20. *Amount:* $1000–$2500.

Eligibility Requirements: Applicant must be enrolled or expecting to enroll full- or part-time at a four-year institution or university. Applicant must be visually impaired. Applicant must have 3.5 GPA or higher. Available to U.S. citizens.

Application Requirements: Application, driver's license, essay, references, transcript, evidence of legal blindness, proof of post-secondary school acceptance. *Deadline:* March 1.

Contact: Tatricia Castillo, Scholarship Coordinator
　　　American Council of the Blind
　　　1155 15th Street, NW, Suite 1004
　　　Washington, DC 20005
　　　Phone: 202-467-5081
　　　Fax: 202-467-5085
　　　E-mail: tcastillo@acp.org

AMERICAN FOUNDATION FOR THE BLIND

http://www.afb.org/

FERDINAND TORRES SCHOLARSHIP

Awards one scholarship of $2500 to a full-time undergraduate or graduate student who presents evidence of economic need. To be eligible the applicant must reside in the U.S., but need not be a citizen of the U.S. Preference will be given to applicants residing in the New York City metropolitan area and new immigrants to the U.S. Must submit proof of legal blindness. For additional information and application requirements, visit http://www.afb.org/scholarships.asp.

Award: Scholarship for use in freshman, sophomore, junior, senior, or graduate years; not renewable. *Number:* 1. *Amount:* $2500.

Eligibility Requirements: Applicant must be enrolled or expecting to enroll full-time at a two-year or four-year institution or university. Applicant must be visually impaired. Available to U.S. and non-U.S. citizens.

Application Requirements: Application, essay, financial need analysis, references, transcript, proof of acceptance in an accredited full-time undergraduate or graduate program, proof of legal blindness. *Deadline:* April 30.

Contact: Dawn Bodrogi, Information Center and Library Coordinator
　　　American Foundation for the Blind
　　　11 Penn Plaza, Suite 300
　　　New York, NY 10001
　　　Phone: 212-502-7661
　　　Fax: 212-502-7771
　　　E-mail: dbodrogi@afb.net

ARRL FOUNDATION INC.

http://www.arrl.org/

CHALLENGE MET SCHOLARSHIP

Multiple $500 awards are available to students with any active amateur radio license who are studying at a two- or four-year college, university or technical school. Preference to applicants with documented learning disabilities (by physician or school) and indications that applicant is putting forth substantial effort regardless of resulting academic grades.

Award: Scholarship for use in freshman, sophomore, junior, or senior years; not renewable. *Amount:* $500.

Eligibility Requirements: Applicant must be enrolled or expecting to enroll at a two-year or four-year or technical institution or university and must have an interest in amateur radio. Applicant must be hearing impaired, learning disabled, physically disabled, or visually impaired.

Application Requirements: Application, documentation of learning disability. *Deadline:* February 1.

Contact: Ms. Mary Hobart, Secretary
　　　ARRL Foundation Inc.
　　　225 Main Street
　　　Newington, CT 06111-1494
　　　Phone: 860-594-0397
　　　E-mail: k1mmh@arrl.org

ASHLEY FOUNDATION

http://www.theashleyfoundation.org/

ASHLEY TAMBURRI SCHOLARSHIP

Scholarship for a cancer survivor or individual currently diagnosed with cancer. An active cancer patient does not have to be receiving treatment to qualify. The cancer may be in remission or deemed cured. Applicant must be a senior, attending a high school in a county served by the Foundation as of the beginning of that current academic year. Students attending a high school in Carroll, Frederick, Howard, Montgomery, or Washington County, Maryland are eligible to apply.

Award: Scholarship for use in freshman year; renewable. *Number:* varies. *Amount:* up to $1000.

Eligibility Requirements: Applicant must be high school student; planning to enroll or expecting to enroll full-time at a four-year institution or university and resident of Maryland. Applicant must be physically disabled. Available to U.S. citizens.

Application Requirements: Application, essay, references. *Deadline:* March 31.

Contact: Lori Maze, Community Liaison
Ashley Foundation
22 South Market Street, Suite 17
PO Box 672
New Market, MD 21774
Phone: 301-694-6414
E-mail: info@theashleyfoundation.org

ASSOCIATION FOR EDUCATION AND REHABILITATION OF THE BLIND AND VISUALLY IMPAIRED

http://www.aerbvi.org/

WILLIAM AND DOROTHY FERREL SCHOLARSHIP

Nonrenewable scholarship given in even years for postsecondary education leading to career in services for blind or visually impaired. Applicant must submit proof of legal blindness or visual field impairment of 20 percent or less.

Award: Scholarship for use in freshman, sophomore, junior, or senior years; not renewable. *Number:* 2. *Amount:* $1000.

Eligibility Requirements: Applicant must be enrolled or expecting to enroll full- or part-time at a two-year or four-year or technical institution or university. Applicant must be visually impaired. Available to U.S. and non-U.S. citizens.

Application Requirements: Application, proof of legal blindness. *Deadline:* February 15.

Contact: Scholarship Coordinator
Association for Education and Rehabilitation of the Blind and Visually Impaired
1703 North Beauregard Street, Suite 440
Alexandria, VA 22311-1717
Phone: 703-671-4500 Ext. 201
E-mail: bsherr@aerbvi.org

ASSOCIATION OF BLIND CITIZENS

http://www.blindcitizens.org/

REGGIE JOHNSON MEMORIAL SCHOLARSHIP

Award for high school or college student who is legally blind. High school or college transcript, certificate of legal blindness, or a letter from ophthalmologist required. Must submit two letters of reference and a CD copy of your biographical sketch.

Award: Scholarship for use in freshman, sophomore, junior, senior, graduate, or postgraduate years; not renewable. *Number:* 1–4. *Amount:* $1000–$2000.

Eligibility Requirements: Applicant must be enrolled or expecting to enroll full-time at a two-year or four-year institution or university and resident of California, Connecticut, Florida, Maine, Massachusetts, New Hampshire, Rhode Island, or Vermont. Applicant must be visually impaired. Available to U.S. citizens.

Application Requirements: Application, essay, references, transcript, certificate of legal blindness or a letter from an ophthalmologist. *Deadline:* April 15.

Contact: John Oliveira, President
Association of Blind Citizens
PO Box 246
Holbrook, MA 02343
Phone: 781-961-1023
Fax: 781-961-0004
E-mail: president@blindcitizens.org

CALIFORNIA COUNCIL OF THE BLIND

http://www.ccbnet.org/

CALIFORNIA COUNCIL OF THE BLIND SCHOLARSHIPS

Scholarships available to blind student applicants who are California residents entering or continuing studies at an accredited California college, university, or vocational training school. Must be a full-time student registered for at least twelve units for the entire academic year. Applications must be typed and all blanks must be filled to be considered for scholarship. Applications available at web site http://www.ccbnet.org.

Award: Scholarship for use in freshman, sophomore, junior, or senior years; renewable. *Number:* up to 20. *Amount:* $375–$2500.

Eligibility Requirements: Applicant must be enrolled or expecting to enroll full-time at a two-year or four-year or technical institution or university; resident of California and studying in California. Applicant must be visually impaired. Available to U.S. and non-U.S. citizens.

Application Requirements: Application, interview, references, transcript, proof of blindness. *Deadline:* June 15.

Contact: Colette Davis, Scholarship Chair, CA Council of the Blind
California Council of the Blind
1510 J Street, Suite 125
Sacramento, CA 95814-2098
Phone: 916-441-2100
Fax: 916-441-2188
E-mail: ccotb@ccbnet.org

CHAIRSCHOLARS FOUNDATION INC.

http://www.chairscholars.org/

NATIONAL SCHOLARSHIP PROGRAM

Award for students who are severely physically challenged. Applicants may be high school seniors or college freshmen. Must be outstanding citizen with history of public service. Minimum 3.5 GPA required. Ten to twelve renewable awards of $5000 are granted. Must be under 21 years of age.

Award: Scholarship for use in freshman year; renewable. *Number:* 10–20. *Amount:* $1000–$5000.

Eligibility Requirements: Applicant must be age 21 or under and enrolled or expecting to enroll full-time at a two-year or four-year institution or university. Applicant must be hearing impaired, physically disabled, or visually impaired. Applicant must have 3.5 GPA or higher. Available to U.S. citizens.

Application Requirements: Application, essay, photo, resume, references, test scores, transcript, parent's tax return from previous year. *Deadline:* February 28.

Contact: Caroll Vick, Program Director
Chairscholars Foundation Inc.
16101 Carencia Lane
Odessa, FL 33556
Phone: 866-926-0544
Fax: 813-920-7661
E-mail: chairscholars@tampabay.rr.com

CHRISTIAN RECORD SERVICES INC.

http://www.christianrecord.org/

CHRISTIAN RECORD SERVICES INC. SCHOLARSHIPS

One-time award for legally blind or blind college undergraduates. Submit application, essay-autobiography, photo, references, and financial information by April 1.

Award: Scholarship for use in freshman, sophomore, junior, or senior years; renewable. *Number:* 7–10. *Amount:* $250–$500.

Eligibility Requirements: Applicant must be enrolled or expecting to enroll full-time at a four-year institution or university. Applicant must be visually impaired. Available to U.S. citizens.

Application Requirements: Application, driver's license, essay, financial need analysis, photo, references. *Deadline:* April 1.

Contact: Shelly Kittleson, Assistant to Treasurer

Christian Record Services Inc.

4444 South 52nd Street

Lincoln, NE 68516-1302

Phone: 402-488-0981 Ext. 213

Fax: 402-488-7582

E-mail: info@christianrecord.org

CIEE: COUNCIL ON INTERNATIONAL EDUCATIONAL EXCHANGE

http://www.ciee.org/

ROBERT B. BAILEY SCHOLARSHIP

One-time award for students from underrepresented groups in study abroad participating in CIEE-administered study abroad programs ONLY. Deadlines: April 1 and November 1. Applicant must be self-identified as belonging to an underrepresented group in study abroad.

Award: Scholarship for use in freshman, sophomore, junior, or senior years; not renewable. *Number:* 24. *Amount:* $500–$1500.

Eligibility Requirements: Applicant must be American Indian/Alaska Native, Asian/Pacific Islander, Black (non-Hispanic), or Hispanic and enrolled or expecting to enroll full-time at a four-year institution or university. Applicant must be hearing impaired, learning disabled, physically disabled, or visually impaired. Available to U.S. and non-U.S. citizens.

Application Requirements: Application, essay, financial need analysis, references, transcript. *Deadline:* varies.

Contact: CIEE Scholarship Committee

CIEE: Council on International Educational Exchange

300 Fore Street

Portland, ME 04101

Phone: 800-407-8839

E-mail: studyinfo@ciee.org

COALITION OF TEXANS WITH DISABILITIES

http://www.cotwd.org/

KENNY MURGIA MEMORIAL SCHOLARSHIP

Awarded annually to a high school senior who has demonstrated activism on disability issues. This program also provides for a part-time paid internship for a college student with disabilities at CTD's Austin office.

Award: Scholarship for use in freshman year; not renewable. *Number:* 1. *Amount:* $1000.

Eligibility Requirements: Applicant must be high school student; planning to enroll or expecting to enroll full-time at a four-year institution or university and resident of Texas. Applicant must be hearing impaired, learning disabled, physically disabled, or visually impaired. Available to U.S. citizens.

Application Requirements: Application, references, transcript. *Deadline:* May 31.

Contact: Jodi Park, Director of Projects and Communications

Coalition of Texans with Disabilities

316 West 12th Street, Suite 405

Austin, TX 78701

Phone: 512-478-3366

Fax: 512-478-3370

E-mail: cotwd@cotwd.org

COLLEGE WOMEN'S ASSOCIATION OF JAPAN

http://www.cwaj.org/

SCHOLARSHIP FOR THE VISUALLY IMPAIRED TO STUDY ABROAD

Scholarship for visually impaired Japanese nationals or permanent residents of Japan who have been accepted into an undergraduate or graduate degree program at an accredited English-speaking university or research institution. Former recipients of CWAJ awards and members of CWAJ are ineligible. Award value is JPY3 million. Deadline on or between November 1 and November 30.

Award: Scholarship for use in junior or senior years; not renewable. *Number:* 1.

Eligibility Requirements: Applicant must be of Japanese heritage and Japanese citizen and enrolled or expecting to enroll full-time at a four-year institution or university. Applicant must be visually impaired. Available to citizens of countries other than the U.S. or Canada.

Application Requirements: Application, essay, references, test scores, transcript, certificate of disability. *Fee:* $10. *Deadline:* varies.

Contact: Scholarship Committee

College Women's Association of Japan

2-24-13-1202 Kami-Osaki

Shinagawa-ku

Tokyo 141-0021

Japan

E-mail: scholarship@cwaj.org

SCHOLARSHIP FOR THE VISUALLY IMPAIRED TO STUDY IN JAPAN

Scholarship for visually impaired Japanese or permanent resident students for graduate or undergraduate study in Japan. Former recipients of CWAJ awards and members of CWAJ are ineligible. Award Value is JPY2.0 million. Deadline on or between November 1 and November 30.

Award: Scholarship for use in junior or senior years; not renewable. *Number:* 1–2.

Eligibility Requirements: Applicant must be of Japanese heritage and Japanese citizen and enrolled or expecting to enroll full-time at a four-year institution or university. Applicant must be visually impaired. Available to citizens of countries other than the U.S. or Canada.

Application Requirements: Application, essay, references, self-addressed stamped envelope, transcript, certificate of disability. *Fee:* $10. *Deadline:* varies.

Contact: Scholarship Committee

College Women's Association of Japan

2-24-13-1202 Kami-Osaki

Shinagawa-ku

Tokyo 141-0021

Japan

E-mail: scholarship@cwaj.org

COMMITTEE OF TEN THOUSAND

http://www.cott1.org/

RACHEL WARNER SCHOLARSHIP

Scholarship for persons with any bleeding disorder. For educational use, both undergraduate and graduate studies. Scholarship amount and the number of available awards varies.

Award: Scholarship for use in freshman, sophomore, junior, senior, or graduate years; not renewable. *Number:* varies. *Amount:* up to $1000.

Eligibility Requirements: Applicant must be enrolled or expecting to enroll full- or part-time at a two-year or four-year or technical institution or university. Applicant must be physically disabled. Available to U.S. citizens.

Application Requirements: Application, essay, references. *Deadline:* May 1.

Contact: Scholarship Coordinator

Committee of Ten Thousand

236 Massachusetts Avenue, NE, Suite 609

Washington, DC 20002

Phone: 800-488-2688

E-mail: cott-dc@earthlink.net

CYSTIC FIBROSIS SCHOLARSHIP FOUNDATION

http://www.cfscholarship.org/

CYSTIC FIBROSIS SCHOLARSHIP

One-time $1000 to $10,000 scholarships for young adults with cystic fibrosis to be used to further their education after high school. Awards may be used for tuition, books, and fees. Students may reapply in subsequent years.

Award: Scholarship for use in freshman, sophomore, junior, or senior years; not renewable. *Number:* 40–50. *Amount:* $1000–$10,000.

Eligibility Requirements: Applicant must be enrolled or expecting to enroll full-time at a two-year or four-year or technical institution or university. Applicant must be physically disabled. Available to U.S. citizens.

Application Requirements: Application, essay, financial need analysis, references, test scores, transcript. *Deadline:* March 21.

Contact: Mary K. Bottorff, President
Cystic Fibrosis Scholarship Foundation
2814 Grant Street
Evanston, IL 60201
Phone: 847-328-0127
Fax: 847-328-0127
E-mail: mkbcfsf@aol.com

DEPARTMENT OF THE ARMY

http://www.goarmy.com/rotc

ARMY (ROTC) RESERVE OFFICERS TRAINING CORPS TWO-, THREE-, FOUR-YEAR CAMPUS-BASED SCHOLARSHIPS

One-time award for college freshmen, sophomores, or juniors or students with BA who need two years to obtain graduate degree. Must be a member of school's ROTC program. Must pass physical. Minimum 2.5 GPA required. Professor of military science must submit application. Applicant must be at least 17 when enrolled in college and under thirty-one years of age in the year of graduation. Must be U.S. citizen/national at time of award. Open year-round.

Award: Scholarship for use in freshman, sophomore, junior, or graduate years; not renewable. *Number:* 1400–2000. *Amount:* $10,000.

Eligibility Requirements: Applicant must be age 17-30 and enrolled or expecting to enroll full-time at a four-year institution or university. Applicant must be physically disabled. Applicant must have 2.5 GPA or higher. Available to U.S. citizens. Applicant or parent must meet one or more of the following requirements: Army or Army National Guard experience; retired from active duty; disabled or killed as a result of military service; prisoner of war; or missing in action.

Application Requirements: Application, interview, test scores, transcript. *Deadline:* continuous.

Contact: Mr. Joseph O'Donnell, Scholarship Management Branch
Department of the Army
U.S. Army Cadet Command, 55 Patch Road, Building 56
Fort Monroe, VA 23651-1052
Phone: 757-788-2994
Fax: 757-788-4643
E-mail: joseph.odonnell@usacc.army.mil

U.S. ARMY ROTC FOUR-YEAR HISTORICALLY BLACK COLLEGE/UNIVERSITY SCHOLARSHIP

One-time award for students attending college for the first time Must attend a historically black college or university and must join school's ROTC program. Must pass physical. Must have a qualifying SAT or ACT score and minimum GPA of 2.5. Applicant must be at least 17 by college enrollment and under thirty-one years of age in the year of graduation. Must be a U.S. citizen/national at time of award. Application available online.

Award: Scholarship for use in freshman year; not renewable. *Number:* 20–200. *Amount:* $9000–$40,000.

Eligibility Requirements: Applicant must be age 17-26 and enrolled or expecting to enroll full-time at a four-year institution or university. Applicant must be physically disabled. Applicant must have 2.5 GPA or higher. Available to U.S. citizens. Applicant must have served in the Army or Army National Guard.

Application Requirements: Application, essay, interview, test scores, transcript. *Deadline:* January 10.

Contact: Ms. Kathleen Stafford, Supervisor, Human Resources Specialist
Department of the Army
U.S. Army Cadet Command, 55 Patch Road, Building 56
Fort Monroe, VA 23651-1052
Phone: 502-624-7371
Fax: 757-788-5781
E-mail: kathleen.stafford@usacc.army.mil

U.S. ARMY ROTC GUARANTEED RESERVE FORCES DUTY (GRFD), (ARNG/USAR) AND DEDICATED ARNG SCHOLARSHIPS

One-time award for college sophomores and juniors, or two-year graduate degree students. Must be a member of school's ROTC program. Must pass physical. Minimum 2.5 GPA required. Applicant must be at least seventeen years of age when enrolled in college and under thirty-one years of age in the year of graduation. Must be a U.S. citizen/national at the time of award.

Award: Scholarship for use in sophomore, junior, or graduate years; renewable. *Number:* 800–1000. *Amount:* $10,000–$12,000.

Eligibility Requirements: Applicant must be age 17-30 and enrolled or expecting to enroll full-time at a two-year or four-year institution or university. Applicant must be physically disabled. Applicant must have 2.5 GPA or higher. Available to U.S. citizens. Applicant must have served in the Army National Guard.

Application Requirements: Application, interview, test scores, transcript. *Deadline:* June 15.

Contact: Capt. Edward Wharton, Program Manager
Department of the Army
U.S. Army Cadet Command, 55 Patch Road, Building 56
Fort Monroe, VA 23651-1052
Phone: 757-788-4551
Fax: 757-788-4643
E-mail: edward.wharton@usacc.army.mil

DISABLEDPERSON INC. COLLEGE SCHOLARSHIP

http://www.disabledperson.com/

DISABLEDPERSON INC. NATIONAL COLLEGE SCHOLARSHIP AWARD

Essay contest for disabled persons who are enrolled as full-time students in a two- or four-year accredited college or university. Length of the essay must not exceed 1000 words.

Award: Prize for use in freshman, sophomore, junior, senior, graduate, or postgraduate years; not renewable. *Number:* up to 1. *Amount:* up to $1000.

Eligibility Requirements: Applicant must be enrolled or expecting to enroll full-time at a two-year or four-year or technical institution or university and must have an interest in writing. Applicant must be hearing impaired, learning disabled, physically disabled, or visually impaired. Available to U.S. citizens.

Application Requirements: Application, applicant must enter a contest, essay, transcript, proof of disability.

Contact: Diana Corso, Executive Director
disABLEDperson Inc. College Scholarship
PO Box 230636
Encinitas, CA 92023
E-mail: scholarships@disabledperson.com

EASTERN AMPUTEE GOLF ASSOCIATION

http://www.eaga.org/

EASTERN AMPUTEE GOLF ASSOCIATION SCHOLARSHIP FUND

Six $1000 college scholarships are available to any EAGA amputee member and/or a member of his or her family. Award recipients do not need to be in attendance. Award covers each of the four school years depending on when applications are accepted. Award recipient must maintain a 2.0 GPA.

Award: Scholarship for use in freshman, sophomore, junior, or senior years; renewable. *Number:* 6. *Amount:* $1000.

Eligibility Requirements: Applicant must be enrolled or expecting to enroll full-time at a four-year institution or university. Applicant must be physically disabled. Available to U.S. and Canadian citizens.

Application Requirements: Application, essay, financial need analysis, resume, transcript, Student Aid Report (SAR). *Deadline:* June 25.

Contact: Bob Buck, Secretary
Eastern Amputee Golf Association
2015 Amherst Drive
Bethlehem, PA 18015-5606
Phone: 888-868-0992
E-mail: info@eaga.org

ELAINE CHAPIN MEMORIAL SCHOLARSHIP FUND

http://www.elainememorial.com/

ELAINE CHAPIN MEMORIAL SCHOLARSHIP FUND

Scholarship program that benefits students whose lives are impacted by multiple sclerosis.

Award: Scholarship for use in freshman, sophomore, junior, or senior years; not renewable. *Number:* 7. *Amount:* $1000.

Eligibility Requirements: Applicant must be enrolled or expecting to enroll full-time at a two-year or four-year or technical institution or university. Applicant must be physically disabled. Available to U.S. citizens.

Application Requirements: Application, essay, references, transcript. *Deadline:* April 30.

Contact: Joseph Chapin, Chairman
Elaine Chapin Memorial Scholarship Fund
4367 Humber Circle
Saint Louis, MO 63129
Phone: 314-487-1708
E-mail: elainememorial@sbcglobal.net

EPILEPSY FOUNDATION OF IDAHO

http://www.epilepsyidaho.org/

GREGORY W. GILE MEMORIAL SCHOLARSHIP PROGRAM

Scholarship of $1000 to $1500 awarded to a graduate of an Idaho high school who is entering or continuing school and pursuing an academic or vocational undergraduate degree or certificate. Must be a resident of Idaho.

Award: Scholarship for use in freshman, sophomore, junior, or senior years; not renewable. *Number:* 1. *Amount:* $1000–$1500.

Eligibility Requirements: Applicant must be enrolled or expecting to enroll full-time at a two-year or four-year or technical institution or university and resident of Idaho. Applicant must be physically disabled. Available to U.S. citizens.

Application Requirements: Application, essay, references, doctor's statement. *Deadline:* March 15.

Contact: Marcia L. Karakas, Executive Director
Epilepsy Foundation of Idaho
310 West Idaho Street
Boise, ID 83702
Phone: 208-344-4340 Ext. 12
Fax: 208-343-0093
E-mail: efid@epilepsyidaho.org

MARK MUSIC MEMORIAL SCHOLARSHIP

One-time award of $500 to promote educational opportunities for Idaho residents with epilepsy. Applicant must be a high school graduate or hold an equivalent certificate, and be either entering or continuing school and pursuing an academic or vocational undergraduate degree or certificate.

Award: Scholarship for use in freshman, sophomore, junior, or senior years; not renewable. *Number:* 1. *Amount:* $500.

Eligibility Requirements: Applicant must be enrolled or expecting to enroll full-time at a two-year or four-year or technical institution or university and resident of Idaho. Applicant must be physically disabled. Available to U.S. citizens.

Application Requirements: Application, essay, references, doctor's statement. *Deadline:* March 15.

Contact: Marcia L. Karakas, Executive Director
Epilepsy Foundation of Idaho
310 West Idaho Street
Boise, ID 83702

FACTOR SUPPORT NETWORK

http://www.factorsupport.com/

MIKE HYLTON AND RON NIEDERMAN MEMORIAL SCHOLARSHIPS

One-time scholarship for men with hemophilia or von Willebrand Disease and their immediate family members. Must be attending or entering a college, university, trade or technical school, either full-time or part-time. Only U.S. residents are eligible.

Award: Scholarship for use in freshman, sophomore, junior, or senior years; not renewable. *Number:* 5. *Amount:* $1000.

Eligibility Requirements: Applicant must be enrolled or expecting to enroll full- or part-time at a two-year or four-year or technical institution or university and male. Applicant must be physically disabled. Available to U.S. citizens.

Application Requirements: Application, essay, references, proof of diagnosis from physician. *Deadline:* April 30.

Contact: Scholarship Committee
Factor Support Network
900 Avenida Acaso, Suite A
Camarillo, CA 93012-8749
E-mail: scholarships@factorsupport.com

MILLIE GONZALEZ MEMORIAL SCHOLARSHIP

Scholarship for women with hemophilia or von Willebrand Disease who are attending or entering a college, university, trade or technical school, either full-time or part-time. Must be U.S. resident.

Award: Scholarship for use in freshman, sophomore, junior, senior, or graduate years; not renewable. *Number:* 2. *Amount:* $1000.

Eligibility Requirements: Applicant must be enrolled or expecting to enroll full- or part-time at a two-year or four-year or technical institution or university and female. Applicant must be physically disabled. Available to U.S. citizens.

Application Requirements: Application, essay, references, proof of diagnosis from physician. *Deadline:* April 30.

Contact: Scholarship Committee
Factor Support Network
900 Avenida Acaso, Suite A
Camarillo, CA 93012-8749
E-mail: scholarships@factorsupport.com

GEORGIA STUDENT FINANCE COMMISSION

http://www.GAcollege411.org/

GEORGIA TUITION EQUALIZATION GRANT (GTEG)

Award for Georgia residents pursuing undergraduate study at an accredited two- or four-year Georgia private postsecondary institution.

Award: Grant for use in freshman, sophomore, junior, or senior years; not renewable. *Number:* 1–35,000.

Eligibility Requirements: Applicant must be Hispanic; enrolled or expecting to enroll full-time at a two-year or four-year institution or university; resident of Georgia and studying in Georgia. Applicant must be learning disabled. Available to U.S. citizens.

Application Requirements: Application, social security number.

Contact: GA 30084
Phone: 800-505-4732

GREAT LAKES HEMOPHILIA FOUNDATION

http://www.glhf.org/

GLHF INDIVIDUAL CLASS SCHOLARSHIP

Scholarship available to members of the Wisconsin bleeding disorder community, individuals with a bleeding disorder and their immediate families. Provides funding assistance for tuition and enrollment fees relevant to continuing education in a non-traditional or non-degree format.

Award: Scholarship for use in freshman, sophomore, junior, or senior years; not renewable. *Number:* 1. *Amount:* up to $500.

Eligibility Requirements: Applicant must be enrolled or expecting to enroll full- or part-time at a two-year or four-year or technical institution or university and resident of Wisconsin. Applicant must be physically disabled. Available to U.S. citizens.

Application Requirements: Application, essay, references, transcript. *Deadline:* varies.

Contact: Karin Koppen, Program Services Coordinator
Great Lakes Hemophilia Foundation
638 North 18 Street, Suite 108
Milwaukee, WI 53233
Phone: 414-257-0200
Fax: 414-257-1225
E-mail: kkoppen@glhf.org

GREAT LAKES HEMOPHILIA FOUNDATION EDUCATION SCHOLARSHIP

This scholarship not only targets the traditional college and vocational students, but also looks at retraining adults with bleeding disorders who are finding it difficult to function in their chosen field because of health complications. It also targets parents of children with bleeding disorders who through career advancement can better meet the financial needs of caring for their child.

Award: Scholarship for use in freshman, sophomore, junior, senior, graduate, or postgraduate years; not renewable. *Number:* 5–6. *Amount:* $500–$2000.

Eligibility Requirements: Applicant must be enrolled or expecting to enroll full- or part-time at a two-year or four-year or technical institution or university and resident of Wisconsin. Applicant must be physically disabled. Available to U.S. citizens.

Application Requirements: Application, essay, references, transcript. *Deadline:* May 1.

Contact: Karin Koppen, Program Services Coordinator
Great Lakes Hemophilia Foundation
638 North 18 Street, Suite 108
Milwaukee, WI 53233
Phone: 414-257-0200
Fax: 414-257-1225
E-mail: kkoppen@glhf.org

HEARING BRIDGES (FORMERLY LEAGUE FOR THE DEAF AND HARD OF HEARING AND EAR FOUNDATION)

http://www.hearingbridges.org/

LINDA COWDEN MEMORIAL SCHOLARSHIP

Non-renewable award offered to deaf and hard of hearing individuals who are attending or planning to attend a trade school, junior college, college, or university and individuals in a program leading to a profession serving the deaf or hard of hearing community. Applicants must live in one of 16 Tennessee counties served by Hearing Bridges (formerly the League for the Deaf and Hard of Hearing and EAR Foundation).

Award: Scholarship for use in freshman, sophomore, junior or senior years; not renewable. *Number:* 1. *Amount:* $1000.

Eligibility Requirements: Applicant must be enrolled or expecting to enroll full- or part-time at a two-year or four-year or technical institution or university and resident of Tennessee. Applicant must be hearing impaired. Available to U.S. citizens.

Application Requirements: Application, essay, interview, photo, references, transcript, audiology repor. *Deadline:* March 12.

Contact: Nikki Ringenberg, Director, Marketing & Special Projects
Hearing Bridges (formerly League for the Deaf and Hard of Hearing and EAR Foundation)
415 Fourth Avenue South
Nashville, TN 37201
Phone: 615-248-8828
E-mail: nr@hearingbridges.org

MINNIE PEARL SCHOLARSHIP

Renewable scholarship for full-time college students with a severe to profound bilateral hearing loss. Initially, recipients must be mainstreamed high school seniors with at least a 3.0 GPA. Renewals based upon maintenance of 3.0 GPA, with a $500 bonus per year for a cumulative GPA of at least 3.5. The scholarship is available for up to four years of undergraduate study at schools in the United States.

Award: Scholarship for use in freshman, sophomore, junior, or senior years; renewable. *Number:* 1. *Amount:* up to $10,000.

Eligibility Requirements: Applicant must be high school student and planning to enroll or expecting to enroll full-time at a two-year or four-year or technical institution or university. Applicant must be hearing impaired. Applicant must have 3.0 GPA or higher. Available to U.S. citizens.

Application Requirements: Application, essay, photo, references, transcript, audiology report. *Deadline:* March 12.

Contact: Nikki Ringenberg, Director, Marketing & Special Projects
Hearing Bridges (formerly League for the Deaf and Hard of Hearing and EAR Foundation)
415 Fourth Avenue South
Nashville, TN 37201
Phone: 615-248-8828
E-mail: nr@hearingbridges.org

HEMOPHILIA FEDERATION OF AMERICA

http://www.hemophiliaed.org/

ARTISTIC ENCOURAGEMENT GRANT

Grant available for an individual with hemophilia or von Willebrand (VWD). Award may be used for mounting an exhibition of applicant's artistic work, publishing a story/ book or animation, writing a play, holding a recital, or any kind of creative endeavor.

Award: Grant for use in freshman, sophomore, junior, senior, graduate, or postgraduate years; not renewable. *Number:* 1. *Amount:* $1500.

Eligibility Requirements: Applicant must be enrolled or expecting to enroll full- or part-time at a two-year or four-year or technical institution or university and must have an interest in art, theater, or writing. Applicant must be physically disabled. Available to U.S. citizens.

Application Requirements: Application, essay, financial need analysis, portfolio, references, brief summary of project, timeline. *Deadline:* April 30.

Contact: Scholarship Committee
Hemophilia Federation of America
1405 West Pinhook Road, Suite 101
Lafayette, LA 70503
Phone: 337-261-9787
Fax: 337-261-1787
E-mail: info@hemophiliafed.org

HEMOPHILIA FEDERATION OF AMERICA EDUCATIONAL SCHOLARSHIP

One-time scholarship for persons with hemophilia, attending either full-time or part-time in any accredited two- or four-year college, university, or vocation/technical school in the United States.

Award: Scholarship for use in freshman, sophomore, junior, or senior years; not renewable. *Number:* 1–3. *Amount:* $1500.

Eligibility Requirements: Applicant must be enrolled or expecting to enroll full- or part-time at a two-year or four-year or technical institution or university. Applicant must be physically disabled. Available to U.S. citizens.

Application Requirements: Application, essay, financial need analysis, references. *Deadline:* April 30.

Contact: Scholarship Committee
Hemophilia Federation of America
1405 West Pinhook Road, Suite 101
Lafayette, LA 70503
Phone: 337-261-9787
Fax: 337-261-1787
E-mail: info@hemophiliafed.org

HEMOPHILIA FOUNDATION OF MICHIGAN

http://www.hfmich.org/

BILL MCADAM SCHOLARSHIP FUND

Scholarship for a person with hemophilia, including their spouse, partner, child or sibling, planning to attend an accredited college, university, trade, or technical school.

Award: Scholarship for use in freshman, sophomore, junior, senior, graduate, or postgraduate years; not renewable. *Number:* 1. *Amount:* $2000.

Eligibility Requirements: Applicant must be enrolled or expecting to enroll full- or part-time at a two-year or four-year or technical institution or university. Applicant must be physically disabled. Available to U.S. citizens.

Application Requirements: Application. *Deadline:* May 15.

Contact: Academic Scholarship Committee
Hemophilia Foundation of Michigan
1921 West Michigan
Ypsilanti, MI 48197
Phone: 734-544-0015
E-mail: hfm@hfmich.org

HEMOPHILIA FOUNDATION OF MICHIGAN ACADEMIC SCHOLARSHIP

Scholarship for individuals or immediate family members, with hemophilia or other inherited bleeding disorder and residing in Michigan. Must be pursuing education in accredited colleges or universities in the United States.

Award: Scholarship for use in freshman, sophomore, junior, or senior years; not renewable. *Number:* 3. *Amount:* $1500–$2000.

Eligibility Requirements: Applicant must be enrolled or expecting to enroll full- or part-time at a two-year or four-year or technical institution or university. Applicant must be physically disabled. Available to U.S. citizens.

Application Requirements: Application. *Deadline:* March 14.

Contact: Academic Scholarship Committee
Hemophilia Foundation of Michigan
1921 West Michigan
Ypsilanti, MI 48197
Phone: 734-544-0015
E-mail: hfm@hfmich.org

HEMOPHILIA FOUNDATION OF SOUTHERN CALIFORNIA

http://www.hemosocal.org/

CHRISTOPHER MARK PITKIN MEMORIAL SCHOLARSHIP

Scholarship open to all members of the hemophilia community, including spouses and siblings. Applicants must be pursuing a college or technical/trade school education.

Award: Scholarship for use in freshman, sophomore, junior, or senior years; not renewable. *Number:* 2. *Amount:* $500–$1000.

Eligibility Requirements: Applicant must be enrolled or expecting to enroll full- or part-time at a two-year or four-year or technical institution or university. Applicant must be physically disabled. Available to U.S. citizens.

Application Requirements: Application, references. *Deadline:* July 25.

Contact: Scholarship Coordinator
Hemophilia Foundation of Southern California
6720 Melrose Avenue
Hollywood, CA 90038
Phone: 323-525-0440
E-mail: ofcmgr@hemosocal.org

HEMOPHILIA HEALTH SERVICES

http://www.hemophiliahealth.com/

HEMOPHILIA HEALTH SERVICES MEMORIAL SCHOLARSHIP

Award to U.S. citizens with hemophilia and related bleeding disorders. Applicants must be high school seniors, college freshmen, sophomores, or juniors. Also eligible to apply are college seniors who are planning to attend graduate school, or students who are already enrolled in graduate school.

Award: Scholarship for use in freshman, sophomore, junior, senior, graduate, or postgraduate years; not renewable. *Number:* 7–10. *Amount:* $1500–$2000.

Eligibility Requirements: Applicant must be enrolled or expecting to enroll full-time at a four-year institution or university. Applicant must be physically disabled. Available to U.S. citizens.

Application Requirements: Application, essay, financial need analysis, references, test scores, transcript, physician certification form. *Deadline:* May 1.

Contact: Sally Johnson, Manager Operations Support
Hemophilia Health Services
c/o Scholarship Program Administrators, Inc.
PO Box 23737
Nashville, TN 37202-3737
Phone: 615-850-5175
Fax: 615-352-2588
E-mail: scholarship@hemophiliahealth.com

IDAHO STATE BOARD OF EDUCATION

http://www.boardofed.idaho.gov/

IDAHO MINORITY AND "AT RISK" STUDENT SCHOLARSHIP

Renewable award for Idaho residents who are disabled or members of a minority group and have financial need. Must attend one of eight postsecondary institutions in the state for undergraduate study. Deadlines vary by institution. Must be a U.S. citizen and be a graduate of an Idaho high school. Contact college financial aid office. The awards range up to $3000 a year for a maximum of four years. For additional information, go to web site http://www.boardofed.idaho.gov/scholarships/.

Award: Scholarship for use in freshman, sophomore, junior, or senior years; renewable. *Number:* 35–40. *Amount:* up to $3000.

Eligibility Requirements: Applicant must be American Indian/Alaska Native, Black (non-Hispanic), or Hispanic; enrolled or expecting to enroll full-time at a two-year or four-year or technical institution or university; resident of Idaho and studying in Idaho. Applicant must be hearing impaired, physically disabled, or visually impaired. Available to U.S. citizens.

Application Requirements: Application, financial need analysis, transcript. *Deadline:* varies.

Contact: Dana Kelly, Program Manager
Idaho State Board of Education
PO Box 83720
Boise, ID 83720-0037
Phone: 208-332-1574
E-mail: dana.kelly@osbe.idaho.gov

ILLINOIS COUNCIL OF THE BLIND

http://www.icbonline.org/

FLOYD R. CARGILL SCHOLARSHIP

Award for a visually impaired Illinois resident attending or planning to attend an Illinois college. One-time award of $1000.

Award: Scholarship for use in freshman, sophomore, junior, or senior years; not renewable. *Number:* 1. *Amount:* $1000.

Eligibility Requirements: Applicant must be enrolled or expecting to enroll full-time at a two-year or four-year or technical institution or university; resident of Illinois and studying in Illinois. Applicant must be visually impaired. Applicant must have 3.5 GPA or higher. Available to U.S. citizens.

Application Requirements: Application, references, test scores, transcript. *Deadline:* July 15.

Contact: Maggie Ulrich, Office Manager
Illinois Council of the Blind
522 East Monroe, Suite 200
PO Box 1336
Springfield, IL 62705
Phone: 217-523-4967
E-mail: icb@icbonline.org

IMMUNE DEFICIENCY FOUNDATION

http://www.primaryimmune.org/

IMMUNE DEFICIENCY FOUNDATION SCHOLARSHIP

One-time award available to individuals diagnosed with a primary immune deficiency disease. Must submit medical verification of diagnosis. Available for study at the undergraduate level at any postsecondary institution. Must be U.S. citizen.

Award: Scholarship for use in freshman, sophomore, junior, or senior years; not renewable. *Number:* 30–40. *Amount:* $750–$2000.

Eligibility Requirements: Applicant must be enrolled or expecting to enroll full- or part-time at a two-year or four-year or technical institution or university. Applicant must be physically disabled. Available to U.S. citizens.

Application Requirements: Application, driver's license, essay, financial need analysis, references, medical verification of diagnosis. *Deadline:* March 31.

Contact: Diana Gill, Director of Patient Programs
Immune Deficiency Foundation
40 West Chesapeake Avenue, Suite 308
Towson, MD 21204
Phone: 800-296-4433 Ext. 2545
Fax: 410-321-9165
E-mail: dgill@primaryimmune.org

JAY'S WORLD CHILDHOOD CANCER FOUNDATION

http://www.jaysworld.org/

JAY'S WORLD CHILDHOOD CANCER FOUNDATION SCHOLARSHIP

Scholarship for a student either cured of cancer, in remission, or able to attend college while undergoing treatment. Must be a graduating high school senior and a New York State resident.

Award: Scholarship for use in freshman year; not renewable. *Number:* varies. *Amount:* varies.

Eligibility Requirements: Applicant must be high school student; planning to enroll or expecting to enroll full- or part-time at a four-year institution or university and resident of New York. Applicant must be physically disabled. Available to U.S. citizens.

Application Requirements: Application, references, transcript, current 1040 tax form, letter from the oncologist. *Deadline:* April 15.

Contact: Jason Napolitano, President
Jay's World Childhood Cancer Foundation
825 East Gate Boulevard, Suite 100
PO Box 173
Garden City, NY 11530
Phone: 516-297-5328
E-mail: info@jaysworld.org

JEWISH GUILD FOR THE BLIND

http://www.jgb.org/

GUILDSCHOLAR AWARD

Annual scholarship program for college-bound high school students who are legally blind. Applications will be accepted from students at the beginning of the senior year (September. 15th). For more information, visit web site http://www.jgb.org/guildscholar.asp.

Award: Scholarship for use in freshman year; not renewable. *Number:* up to 16. *Amount:* $10,000–$15,000.

Eligibility Requirements: Applicant must be high school student and planning to enroll or expecting to enroll full-time at a four-year institution or university. Applicant must be visually impaired. Applicant must have 3.0 GPA or higher. Available to U.S. citizens.

Application Requirements: Application, autobiography, essay, references, test scores, transcript, leadership, extracurricular activities. *Deadline:* September 15.

Contact: Mr. Gordon Rovins, Director of Special Programs
Jewish Guild for the Blind
15 West 65th Street
New York, NY 10023
Phone: 212-769-7801
Fax: 212-579-3251
E-mail: guildscholar@jgb.org

LAWRENCE MADEIROS MEMORIAL SCHOLARSHIP

http://www.adirondackspintacular.com/

LAWRENCE MADEIROS MEMORIAL SCHOLARSHIP

Award to a high school student with bleeding disorder or other chronic disorder. Applicant must have applied to and been accepted at an accredited college or university and must be graduating high school in the year of the scholarship award.

Award: Scholarship for use in freshman year; not renewable. *Number:* 1. *Amount:* $1000.

Eligibility Requirements: Applicant must be high school student and planning to enroll or expecting to enroll full- or part-time at a two-year or four-year institution or university. Applicant must be physically disabled. Available to U.S. citizens.

Application Requirements: Application, interview. *Deadline:* June 1.

Contact: Carol Madeiros, Scholarship Committee
Lawrence Madeiros Memorial Scholarship
PO Box 11
Mayfield, NY 12117
Phone: 518-661-6005
Fax: 518-863-6126
E-mail: carol@adirondackspintacular.com

LIGHTHOUSE INTERNATIONAL

http://www.lighthouse.org/

SCHOLARSHIP AND CAREER AWARDS

One-time award designed to reward excellence, recognize accomplishments, and to help students who are blind or visually impaired achieve their academic and career goals. There are 3 categories: college bound, undergraduate, and graduate. Students must be legally blind, U.S. citizens, enrolled in an accredited college or university.

Award: Scholarship for use in freshman, sophomore, junior, senior, or graduate years; not renewable. *Number:* 6. *Amount:* $10,000.

Eligibility Requirements: Applicant must be enrolled or expecting to enroll full-time at a two-year or four-year institution or university. Applicant must be visually impaired. Available to U.S. citizens.

Application Requirements: Application, essay, photo, references, transcript, proof of U.S. citizenship, visual status statement (proof of legal blindness). *Deadline:* March 14.

Contact: Danielle Penabad
111 E. 59th Street, NY 10022
Phone: 212-821-9688
Fax: 212-821-9687
E-mail: sca@Lighthouse.org

LILLY REINTEGRATION PROGRAMS

http://www.reintegration.com/

LILLY REINTEGRATION SCHOLARSHIP

Scholarships available to students diagnosed with schizophrenia, bipolar, schizophreniform, or a schizoaffective disorder. Must be currently receiving medical treatment for the disease, including medications and psychiatric follow-up. Must also be U.S. citizen and actively involved in rehabilitative or reintegration efforts. Applicants must be at least 18 years of age.

Award: Scholarship for use in freshman, sophomore, junior, senior, graduate, or postgraduate years; not renewable. *Number:* 70–100. *Amount:* $2500–$5000.

Eligibility Requirements: Applicant must be age 18 and over and enrolled or expecting to enroll full- or part-time at a two-year or four-year or technical institution or university. Applicant must be physically disabled. Available to U.S. citizens.

Application Requirements: Application, essay, references, transcript. *Deadline:* January 25.

Contact: Lilly Secretariat
Lilly Reintegration Programs
310 Busse Highway, PO Box 327
Park Ridge, IL 60068-3251
Phone: 800-809-8202
E-mail: lillyscholarships@reintegration.com

NATIONAL CENTER FOR LEARNING DISABILITIES, INC.

http://www.ld.org/

ANNE FORD & ALLEGRA FORD SCHOLARSHIP

Award of $10,000 given to two high school seniors of high merit with an identified learning disability who is pursuing a college degree. The ideal candidate is a person who has faced the challenges of having a learning disability and who, through perseverance and academic endeavor, has created a life of purpose and achievement.

Award: Scholarship for use in freshman, sophomore, junior, or senior years; not renewable. *Number:* 2. *Amount:* $10,000.

Eligibility Requirements: Applicant must be high school student and planning to enroll or expecting to enroll full-time at a four-year institution or university. Applicant must be learning disabled. Applicant must have 3.0 GPA or higher. Available to U.S. citizens.

Application Requirements: Application, essay, financial need analysis, references, test scores, transcript. *Deadline:* December 31.

Contact: Catherine Boswell, Coordinator
National Center for Learning Disabilities, Inc.
381 Park Avenue South, Suite 1401
New York, NY 10016-8806
Phone: 646-616-1233
Fax: 212-545-9665
E-mail: afscholarship@ncld.org

NATIONAL COUNCIL OF JEWISH WOMEN NEW YORK SECTION

http://www.ncjwny.org/

JACKSON-STRICKS SCHOLARSHIP

Scholarship provides financial aid to a physically challenged person for academic study or vocational training that leads to independent living.

Award: Scholarship for use in sophomore, junior, senior, graduate, or postgraduate years; not renewable. *Number:* 1–7. *Amount:* $1500–$2500.

Eligibility Requirements: Applicant must be enrolled or expecting to enroll full- or part-time at a two-year or four-year institution or university; resident of New York and studying in New York. Applicant must be physically disabled. Available to U.S. citizens.

Application Requirements: Application, essay, references, transcript. *Deadline:* April 15.

Contact: Jackson-Stricks Scholarship Committee
National Council of Jewish Women New York Section
820 Second Avenue, 2nd Floor
New York, NY 10017
Phone: 212-687-5030 Ext. 14
Fax: 212-687-5032
E-mail: sdrazen@ncjwny.org

NATIONAL FEDERATION OF BLIND OF MISSOURI

http://www.nfbmo.org/

NATIONAL FEDERATION OF THE BLIND OF MISSOURI SCHOLARSHIPS TO LEGALLY BLIND STUDENTS

Awards are based on achievement, commitment to community, and financial need. Recipients must be legally blind. Amount of money each year available for program will vary.

Award: Scholarship for use in freshman, sophomore, junior, senior, or graduate years; not renewable. *Number:* 1–3. *Amount:* $500–$1500.

Eligibility Requirements: Applicant must be enrolled or expecting to enroll full- or part-time at a two-year or four-year or technical institution or university; resident of Missouri and studying in Missouri. Applicant must be visually impaired. Available to U.S. citizens.

Application Requirements: Application, essay, financial need analysis, interview, references, transcript. *Deadline:* February 1.

Contact: Ms. Shelia Wright, Chair, NFB of Missouri Scholarship Program
National Federation of Blind of Missouri
3910 Tropical Lane
Columbia, MO 65202-6205
Phone: 816-741-6402
Fax: 816-746-1748
E-mail: firstvice.president@nfbmo.org

NATIONAL FEDERATION OF THE BLIND (NFB)

http://www.nfb.org/scholarships

CHARLES AND MELVA T. OWEN MEMORIAL SCHOLARSHIP FOR $3,000

Merit-based scholarship requires academic excellence and leadership; permanent residency in United States/Puerto Rico; accredited institution's degree program (in US/PR) directed toward financial independence (excludes degrees in religious studies or solely for cultural education). Winner assisted to attend NFB annual convention to receive this award; membership not required.

Award: Scholarship for use in freshman, sophomore, junior, senior, graduate, or postgraduate years; not renewable. *Number:* 1. *Amount:* $3000.

Eligibility Requirements: Applicant must be enrolled or expecting to enroll full- or part-time at a two-year or four-year institution or university. Applicant must be visually impaired. Available to U.S. and non-U.S. citizens.

Application Requirements: Application, essay, interview, references, test scores, transcript, proof of legal blindness in both eyes. *Deadline:* March 31.

Contact: Ms. Patti Chang Esq., Chairperson, NFB Scholarship Committee
National Federation of the Blind (NFB)
200 East Wells Street
Baltimore, MD 21230
Phone: 410-659-9314 Ext. 2415
E-mail: scholarships@nfb.org

CHARLES AND MELVA T. OWEN SCHOLARSHIP FOR $10,000

Merit-based scholarship requires academic excellence and leadership; permanent residency in United States/Puerto Rico; accredited institution's degree program (in US/PR) directed toward financial independence (excludes degrees in religious studies or solely for cultural education). Winner assisted to attend NFB annual convention to receive this award; membership not required.

Award: Scholarship for use in freshman, sophomore, junior, senior, graduate, or postgraduate years; not renewable. *Number:* 1. *Amount:* $10,000.

Eligibility Requirements: Applicant must be enrolled or expecting to enroll full- or part-time at a two-year or four-year institution or university. Applicant must be visually impaired. Available to U.S. and non-U.S. citizens.

Application Requirements: Application, essay, interview, references, test scores, transcript, proof of legal blindness in both eyes. *Deadline:* March 31.

Contact: Ms. Patti Chang Esq., Chairperson, NFB Scholarship
Committee
National Federation of the Blind (NFB)
200 East Wells Street
Baltimore, MD 21230
Phone: 410-659-9314 Ext. 2415
E-mail: scholarships@nfb.org

KENNETH JERNIGAN SCHOLARSHIP FOR $12,000

The American Action Fund for Blind Children & Adults $12,000 award to honor the top blind college student residing in and attending an accredited institution in the US/Puerto Rico is the most prestigious in the NFB Scholarship Program. Winner receives financial assistance to attend NFB convention to receive scholarship.

Award: Scholarship for use in freshman, sophomore, junior, senior, graduate, or postgraduate years; not renewable. *Number:* 1. *Amount:* $12,000.

Eligibility Requirements: Applicant must be enrolled or expecting to enroll full- or part-time at a two-year or four-year institution or university. Applicant must be visually impaired. Available to U.S. and non-U.S. citizens.

Application Requirements: Application, essay, interview, references, test scores, transcript, proof of legal blindness. *Deadline:* March 31.

Contact: Ms. Patti Chang Esq., Chairperson
National Federation of the Blind (NFB)
NFB Scholarship Committee, 200 East Wells Street
Baltimore, MD 21230
Phone: 410-659-9314 Ext. 2415
E-mail: scholarships@nfb.org

NATIONAL FEDERATION OF THE BLIND SCHOLARSHIP FOR $3,000

Applicants must be legally blind, permanent residents of the USA or Puerto Rico, pursuing a postsecondary degree at an accredited institution in USA/PR. Selection is merit-based on academic excellence and leadership. With NFB assistance, winner attends NFB annual convention to receive award; membership in NFB is not required.

Award: Scholarship for use in freshman, sophomore, junior, senior, graduate, or postgraduate years; not renewable. *Number:* 21. *Amount:* $3000.

Eligibility Requirements: Applicant must be enrolled or expecting to enroll full- or part-time at a two-year or four-year institution or university. Applicant must be visually impaired. Available to U.S. and non-U.S. citizens.

Application Requirements: Application, essay, interview, references, test scores, transcript, proof of legal blindness in both eyes. *Deadline:* March 31.

Contact: Ms. Patti Chang Esq., Chairperson, Scholarship Committee
National Federation of the Blind (NFB)
200 East Wells Street
Baltimore, MD 21230
Phone: 410-659-9314 Ext. 2415
E-mail: scholarships@nfb.org

NATIONAL FEDERATION OF THE BLIND SCHOLARSHIP FOR $7,000

Applicants must be legally blind, permanent residents of the USA or Puerto Rico, pursuing a postsecondary degree at an accredited institution in USA/PR. Selection is merit-based on academic excellence and leadership. With NFB assistance, winner attends NFB annual convention to receive award; membership in NFB is not required.

Award: Scholarship for use in freshman, sophomore, junior, senior, graduate, or postgraduate years; not renewable. *Number:* 2. *Amount:* $7000.

Eligibility Requirements: Applicant must be enrolled or expecting to enroll full- or part-time at a two-year or four-year institution or university. Applicant must be visually impaired. Available to U.S. and non-U.S. citizens.

Application Requirements: Application, essay, interview, references, test scores, transcript, proof of legal blindness in both eyes. *Deadline:* March 31.

Contact: Ms. Patti Chang Esq., Chairperson, NFB Scholarship
Committee
National Federation of the Blind (NFB)
200 East Wells Street
Baltimore, MD 21230
Phone: 410-659-9314 Ext. 2415
E-mail: scholarships@nfb.org

NFB SCHOLARSHIP FOR $5000

Applicants must be legally blind, permanent residents of the USA or Puerto Rico, pursuing a postsecondary degree at an accredited institution in USA/PR. Selection is merit-based on academic excellence and leadership. With NFB assistance, winner attends NFB annual convention to receive award; membership in NFB is not required.

Award: Scholarship for use in freshman, sophomore, junior, senior, graduate, or postgraduate years; not renewable. *Number:* 4. *Amount:* $5000.

Eligibility Requirements: Applicant must be enrolled or expecting to enroll full- or part-time at a two-year or four-year institution or university. Applicant must be visually impaired. Available to U.S. and non-U.S. citizens.

Application Requirements: Application, essay, interview, references, test scores, transcript, proof of legal blindness in both eyes. *Deadline:* March 31.

Contact: Ms. Patti Chang Esq., Chairperson, NFB Scholarship Program
National Federation of the Blind (NFB)
200 East Wells Street
Baltimore, MD 21230
Phone: 410-659-9314 Ext. 2415
E-mail: scholarships@nfb.org

NATIONAL FEDERATION OF THE BLIND OF CALIFORNIA

http://www.nfbcal.org/

GERALD DRAKE MEMORIAL SCHOLARSHIP

One-time award for legally blind students pursuing an undergraduate or graduate degree. Must be a California resident and full-time student.

Award: Scholarship for use in freshman, sophomore, junior, senior, or graduate years; not renewable. *Number:* up to 5. *Amount:* $1500.

Eligibility Requirements: Applicant must be enrolled or expecting to enroll full-time at a four-year institution or university and resident of California. Applicant must be visually impaired. Available to U.S. and non-U.S. citizens.

Application Requirements: Application. *Deadline:* March 31.

Contact: Robert Stigile, President
National Federation of the Blind of California
5530 Corbin Avenue, Suite 313
Tarzana, CA 91356
Phone: 818-342-6524
Fax: 818-344-7930
E-mail: nfbcal@yahoo.com

JULIE LANDUCCI SCHOLARSHIP

Award for legally blind students pursuing an undergraduate or graduate degree. Must be a California resident and full-time student. Award available to U.S. citizens.

Award: Scholarship for use in freshman, sophomore, junior, senior, or graduate years; renewable. *Number:* 1. *Amount:* up to $2000.

Eligibility Requirements: Applicant must be enrolled or expecting to enroll full-time at a four-year institution or university and resident of California. Applicant must be visually impaired. Available to U.S. citizens.

Application Requirements: Application. *Deadline:* March 31.

Contact: Robert Stigile, President
* National Federation of the Blind of California
5530 Corbin Avenue, Suite 313
Tarzana, CA 91356
Phone: 818-342-6524
Fax: 818-344-7930
E-mail: nfbcal@yahoo.com

LA VYRL "PINKY" JOHNSON MEMORIAL SCHOLARSHIP

One-time award up to $2000 for legally blind students pursuing an undergraduate or graduate degree. Must be a California resident and full-time student.

Award: Scholarship for use in freshman, sophomore, junior, senior, or graduate years; renewable. *Number:* 1. *Amount:* $2000.

Eligibility Requirements: Applicant must be enrolled or expecting to enroll full-time at a four-year institution or university and resident of California. Applicant must be visually impaired. Available to U.S. citizens.

Application Requirements: Application. *Deadline:* March 31.

Contact: Robert Stigile, President
National Federation of the Blind of California
5530 Corbin Avenue, Suite 313
Tarzana, CA 91356
Phone: 818-342-6524
Fax: 818-344-7930
E-mail: nfbcal@yahoo.com

LAWRENCE "MUZZY" MARCELINO MEMORIAL SCHOLARSHIP

Scholarship provides financial assistance for graduate or undergraduate education to blind students in California. Any legally blind student may apply for a scholarship but must attend the convention of the National Federation of the Blind of California. Selection is based first on academic merit and second on financial need.

Award: Scholarship for use in freshman, sophomore, junior, senior, or graduate years; renewable. *Number:* up to 4. *Amount:* $1500.

Eligibility Requirements: Applicant must be enrolled or expecting to enroll full-time at a four-year institution or university and resident of California. Applicant must be visually impaired. Available to U.S. citizens.

Application Requirements: Application. *Deadline:* March 15.

Contact: Robert Stigile, President
National Federation of the Blind of California
5530 Corbin Avenue, Suite 313
Tarzana, CA 91356
Phone: 818-342-6524
Fax: 818-344-7930
E-mail: nfbcal@yahoo.com

NATIONAL FEDERATION OF THE BLIND OF CALIFORNIA MERIT SCHOLARSHIPS

Scholarships to qualified blind students pursuing undergraduate or graduate studies in order to achieve an academic degree. This opportunity is also available to high school seniors preparing to enter undergraduate programs.

Award: Scholarship for use in freshman, sophomore, junior, senior, or graduate years; renewable. *Number:* up to 5. *Amount:* $1000.

Eligibility Requirements: Applicant must be enrolled or expecting to enroll full-time at a four-year institution or university and resident of California. Applicant must be visually impaired. Available to U.S. citizens.

Application Requirements: Application. *Deadline:* March 15.

Contact: Robert Stigile, President
National Federation of the Blind of California
5530 Corbin Avenue, Suite 313
Tarzana, CA 91356
Phone: 818-342-6524
Fax: 818-344-7930
E-mail: nfbcal@yahoo.com

NATIONAL FEDERATION OF THE BLIND OF CONNECTICUT

http://www.nfbct.org/

C. RODNEY DEMAREST MEMORIAL SCHOLARSHIP

Scholarship of $3000 awarded for graduating high school senior or college student residing or attending school full-time in Connecticut. Applicant must be legally blind.

Award: Scholarship for use in freshman, sophomore, junior, or senior years; not renewable. *Number:* 1. *Amount:* $3000.

Eligibility Requirements: Applicant must be enrolled or expecting to enroll full-time at a two-year or four-year or technical institution or university; resident of Connecticut and studying in Connecticut. Applicant must be visually impaired. Available to U.S. citizens.

Application Requirements: Application, references, transcript, state officer letter. *Deadline:* September 15.

Contact: Scholarship Committee
National Federation of the Blind of Connecticut
477 Connecticut Boulevard, Suite 217
East Hartford, CT 06108
Phone: 860-289-1971
Fax: 860-291-2795
E-mail: info@nfbct.org

DORIS E. HIGLEY MEMORIAL SCHOLARSHIP

Scholarship of $6000 awarded for graduating high school senior or college student residing or attending school full-time in Connecticut. Applicant must be legally blind.

Award: Scholarship for use in freshman, sophomore, junior, or senior years; not renewable. *Number:* 1. *Amount:* $6000.

Eligibility Requirements: Applicant must be enrolled or expecting to enroll full-time at a two-year or four-year or technical institution or university; resident of Connecticut and studying in Connecticut. Applicant must be visually impaired. Available to U.S. citizens.

Application Requirements: Application, references, transcript, state officer letter. *Deadline:* September 15.

Contact: Scholarship Committee
National Federation of the Blind of Connecticut
477 Connecticut Boulevard, Suite 217
East Hartford, CT 06108
Phone: 860-289-1971
Fax: 860-291-2795
E-mail: info@nfbct.org

HOWARD E. MAY MEMORIAL SCHOLARSHIP

Scholarship of $6000 awarded for graduating high school senior or college student residing or attending school full-time in Connecticut. Applicant must be legally blind.

Award: Scholarship for use in freshman, sophomore, junior, or senior years; not renewable. *Number:* 1. *Amount:* $6000.

Eligibility Requirements: Applicant must be enrolled or expecting to enroll full-time at a two-year or four-year or technical institution or university; resident of Connecticut and studying in Connecticut. Applicant must be visually impaired. Available to U.S. citizens.

Application Requirements: Application, references, transcript, state officer letter. *Deadline:* September 15.

Contact: Scholarship Committee
National Federation of the Blind of Connecticut
477 Connecticut Boulevard, Suite 217
East Hartford, CT 06108
Phone: 860-289-1971
Fax: 860-291-2795
E-mail: info@nfbct.org

MARY MAIN MEMORIAL SCHOLARSHIP

Scholarship of $4000 awarded for graduating high school senior or college student residing or attending school full-time in Connecticut. Applicant must be legally blind.

Award: Scholarship for use in freshman, sophomore, junior, or senior years; not renewable. *Number:* 1. *Amount:* $4000.

Eligibility Requirements: Applicant must be enrolled or expecting to enroll full-time at a two-year or four-year or technical institution or university; resident of Connecticut and studying in Connecticut. Applicant must be visually impaired. Available to U.S. citizens.

Application Requirements: Application, references, transcript, state officer letter. *Deadline:* September 15.

Contact: Scholarship Committee
National Federation of the Blind of Connecticut
477 Connecticut Boulevard, Suite 217
East Hartford, CT 06108
Phone: 860-289-1971
Fax: 860-291-2795
E-mail: info@nfbct.org

NATIONAL HEMOPHILIA FOUNDATION

http://www.hemophilia.org/

KEVIN CHILD SCHOLARSHIP

Scholarship for a person with hemophilia or von Willebrand disease. Must be a high school senior planning to attend college, university, or vocational school, or a college student already pursuing postsecondary education.

Award: Scholarship for use in freshman year; not renewable. *Number:* 1. *Amount:* $500–$1000.

Eligibility Requirements: Applicant must be high school student and planning to enroll or expecting to enroll full- or part-time at a two-year or four-year or technical institution or university. Applicant must be physically disabled. Available to U.S. citizens.

Application Requirements: Application. *Deadline:* June 27.

Contact: Renee LaBrew, Department of Finance, Administration and MIS
National Hemophilia Foundation
116 West 32nd Street, 11th Floor
New York, NY 10001-3212
Phone: 212-328-3700

NATIONAL KIDNEY FOUNDATION OF INDIANA INC.

http://www.kidneyindiana.org/

LARRY SMOCK SCHOLARSHIP

Scholarship provides financial assistance for kidney dialysis and transplant patients to pursue post-secondary education. Applicant must be resident of Indiana over the age of 18. Must have a high school diploma or its equivalent.

Award: Scholarship for use in freshman, sophomore, junior, or senior years; renewable. *Number:* 2–6. *Amount:* $500–$1000.

Eligibility Requirements: Applicant must be age 18 and over; enrolled or expecting to enroll full- or part-time at a two-year or four-year or technical institution or university and resident of Indiana. Applicant must be physically disabled. Available to U.S. citizens.

Application Requirements: Application, references, transcript.

Contact: Nicki Howard, Public Health Coordinator
National Kidney Foundation of Indiana Inc.
911 E. 86th Street, Suite 100
Indianapolis, IN 46240-1840
Phone: 317-722-5640
Fax: 317-722-5650
E-mail: nhoward@kidneyindiana.org

NATIONAL MULTIPLE SCLEROSIS SOCIETY–MID AMERICA CHAPTER

http://www.msmidamerica.org/

NATIONAL MULTIPLE SCLEROSIS SOCIETY MID AMERICA CHAPTER SCHOLARSHIP

Scholarships available from $1000 to $3000 to high school seniors and graduates (or GED) with MS, or who are children of people with MS. Must be attending a postsecondary school for the first time.

Award: Scholarship for use in freshman, sophomore, junior, or senior years; not renewable. *Number:* 100. *Amount:* $1000–$3000.

Eligibility Requirements: Applicant must be enrolled or expecting to enroll full- or part-time at a two-year or four-year or technical institution

or university. Applicant must be physically disabled. Available to U.S. citizens.

Application Requirements: Application, driver's license, essay, financial need analysis, references, test scores, transcript. *Deadline:* January 15.

Contact: Director of Programs
National Multiple Sclerosis Society–Mid America Chapter
5442 Martway
Mission, KS 66205
Phone: 913-432-3926
E-mail: info@nmsskc.org

NATIONAL PKU NEWS

http://www.pkunews.org/

ROBERT GUTHRIE PKU SCHOLARSHIP AND AWARDS

Scholarship for persons with phenylketonuria (PKU) who are on a special diet for PKU treatment. Award is for full-time or part-time study at any accredited U.S. institution. Up to 8 scholarships of between $500 and $3500 are granted.

Award: Scholarship for use in freshman, sophomore, junior, or senior years; not renewable. *Number:* 4–8. *Amount:* $500–$3500.

Eligibility Requirements: Applicant must be enrolled or expecting to enroll full- or part-time at a two-year or four-year or technical institution or university. Applicant must be physically disabled. Available to U.S. and non-U.S. citizens.

Application Requirements: Application, essay, photo, resume, references, test scores, transcript. *Deadline:* October 15.

Contact: Virginia Schuett, Director
National PKU News
6869 Woodlawn Avenue, NE, Suite 116
Seattle, WA 98115-5469
Phone: 206-525-8140
E-mail: schuett@pkunews.org

NATIONAL UNION OF PUBLIC AND GENERAL EMPLOYEES

http://www.nupge.ca/

TERRY FOX MEMORIAL SCHOLARSHIP
• *See page 555*

NEW YORK STATE GRANGE

http://www.nysgrange.com/

CAROLINE KARK AWARD
• *See page 555*

NORTH CAROLINA DIVISION OF SERVICES FOR THE BLIND

http://www.ncdhhs.gov/

NORTH CAROLINA DIVISION OF SERVICES FOR THE BLIND REHABILITATION SERVICES

Financial assistance is available for North Carolina residents who are blind or visually impaired and who require vocational rehabilitation to help find employment. Tuition and other assistance provided based on need. Open to U.S. citizens and legal residents of United States. Applicants goal must be to work after receiving vocational services. To apply, contact the local DSB office and apply for vocational rehabilitation services.

Award: Scholarship for use in freshman, sophomore, junior, or senior years; renewable. *Number:* varies. *Amount:* varies.

Eligibility Requirements: Applicant must be enrolled or expecting to enroll full-time at a two-year or four-year or technical institution or university and resident of North Carolina. Applicant must be visually impaired. Available to U.S. citizens.

Application Requirements: Application, financial need analysis, interview, proof of eligibility. *Deadline:* continuous.

Contact: JoAnn Strader, Chief of Rehabilitation Field Services
North Carolina Division of Services for the Blind
2601 Mail Service Center
Raleigh, NC 27699-2601
Phone: 919-733-9700
Fax: 919-715-8771
E-mail: joann.strader@ncmail.net

NORTH CAROLINA DIVISION OF VOCATIONAL REHABILITATION SERVICES

http://www.dhhs.state.nc.us/

TRAINING SUPPORT FOR YOUTH WITH DISABILITIES

Public service program that helps persons with disabilities obtain competitive employment. To qualify: student must have a mental, physical or learning disability that is an impediment to employment. A Rehabilitation Counselor along with the eligible student individually develops a rehabilitation program to achieve an employment outcome. Assistance is based on financial need and type of program in which the student enrolls.

Award: Grant for use in freshman, sophomore, junior, or senior years; renewable. *Number:* varies. *Amount:* $2400.

Eligibility Requirements: Applicant must be enrolled or expecting to enroll full- or part-time at a two-year or four-year or technical institution or university and resident of North Carolina. Applicant must be hearing impaired, learning disabled, physically disabled, or visually impaired. Available to U.S. citizens.

Application Requirements: Application, financial need analysis, interview, test scores, transcript, medical and psychological records. *Deadline:* continuous.

Contact: Alma Taylor, Program Specialist for Transition
North Carolina Division of Vocational Rehabilitation Services
2801 Mail Service Center
Raleigh, NC 27699-2801
Phone: 919-855-3572
E-mail: alma.taylor@ncmail.net

NUFACTOR

http://www.nufactor.com/

ERIC DOSTIE MEMORIAL COLLEGE SCHOLARSHIP

Scholarship for persons or family members with hemophilia or other bleeding disorder, enrolled full-time in an accredited college. Must be a U.S. citizen.

Award: Scholarship for use in freshman, sophomore, junior, senior, or graduate years; not renewable. *Number:* 10. *Amount:* $1000.

Eligibility Requirements: Applicant must be enrolled or expecting to enroll full-time at a two-year or four-year institution or university. Applicant must be physically disabled. Applicant must have 2.5 GPA or higher. Available to U.S. citizens.

Application Requirements: Application, essay, photo, references, test scores, transcript, request application after November 1. *Deadline:* March 1.

Contact: Scholarship Coordinator
NuFACTOR
41093 County Center Drive, Suite B
Temecula, CA 92591
Phone: 800-323-6832
Fax: 951-432-6258

OPTIMIST INTERNATIONAL FOUNDATION

http://www.optimist.org/

COMMUNICATION CONTEST FOR THE DEAF AND HARD OF HEARING

College scholarship (district level) for young people through grade twelve in the U.S. and Canada, to CEGEP in Quebec and grade thirteen in the Caribbean. Students interested in participating must submit the results of an audiogram conducted no longer than twenty four months prior to the date of the contest from a qualified audiologist. Students must be certified to have a hearing loss of forty decibels or more and supported by the audiogram to be eligible to compete. Students attending either public school or schools providing special services are eligible to enter if criteria are met.

Award: Scholarship for use in freshman, sophomore, junior, or senior years; not renewable. *Number:* 1–30. *Amount:* up to $2500.

Eligibility Requirements: Applicant must be enrolled or expecting to enroll full- or part-time at a two-year or four-year or technical institution or university. Applicant must be hearing impaired. Available to U.S. and Canadian citizens.

Application Requirements: Application, applicant must enter a contest, self-addressed stamped envelope, speech/presentation, audiogram. *Deadline:* varies.

Contact: Danielle Baugher, Director of International Programs
Optimist International Foundation
4494 Lindell Boulevard
St. Louis, MO 63108
Phone: 800-500-8130
Fax: 314-371-6006
E-mail: programs@optimist.org

OREGON COMMUNITY FOUNDATION

http://www.oregoncf.org/

HARRY LUDWIG SCHOLARSHIP FUND

Scholarship for visually impaired students for use in the pursuit of a post-secondary education at a college or university. For full-time students only.

Award: Scholarship for use in freshman, sophomore, junior, or senior years; renewable. *Number:* 1–3. *Amount:* $500–$5000.

Eligibility Requirements: Applicant must be enrolled or expecting to enroll full-time at a four-year institution or university. Applicant must be visually impaired. Available to U.S. citizens.

Application Requirements: Application, references. *Deadline:* March 1.

Contact: Dianne Causey, Program Associate for Scholarships and Grants
Oregon Community Foundation
1221 Yamhill, SW, Suite 100
Portland, OR 97205-2108
Phone: 503-227-6846 Ext. 1418
E-mail: dcausey@oregoncf.org

OREGON STUDENT ASSISTANCE COMMISSION

http://www.GetCollegeFunds.org/

HARRY LUDWIG MEMORIAL SCHOLARSHIP

Award for visually-impaired Oregon residents planning to enroll full-time in undergraduate or graduate studies at an Oregon college or university. Must document visual impairment with a letter from a physician. Must reapply for award annually.

Award: Scholarship for use in freshman, sophomore, junior, senior, or graduate years; not renewable. *Number:* varies. *Amount:* varies.

Eligibility Requirements: Applicant must be enrolled or expecting to enroll full-time at a two-year or four-year institution or university; resident of Oregon and studying in Oregon. Applicant must be visually impaired. Available to U.S. citizens.

Application Requirements: Application, essay, financial need analysis, references, transcript, documentation of visual impairment. *Deadline:* March 1.

Contact: Director of Grant Programs
Oregon Student Assistance Commission
1500 Valley River Drive, Suite 100
Eugene, OR 97401-7020
Phone: 800-452-8807 Ext. 7395

SALEM FOUNDATION ANSEL & MARIE SOLIE SCHOLARSHIP

Award is available to visually impaired Oregon residents planning to enroll in full-time undergraduate studies. Must be a U.S. citizen. Award may be used only at a four-year, nonprofit Oregon college or university.

Award: Scholarship for use in freshman year; not renewable.

Eligibility Requirements: Applicant must be enrolled or expecting to enroll full-time at a four-year institution or university; resident of Oregon and studying in Oregon. Applicant must be visually impaired. Available to U.S. citizens.

Application Requirements: Application, proof of visual impairment. *Deadline:* March 1.

Contact: Director of Grant Programs
Oregon Student Assistance Commission
1500 Valley River Drive, Suite 100
Eugene, OR 97401-7020
Phone: 800-452-8807

P. BUCKLEY MOSS FOUNDATION

http://www.mossfoundation.org/

ANNE AND MATT HARBISON SCHOLARSHIP

Scholarship of $1500 to one high school senior with a certified language-related learning difference who is pursuing postsecondary education.

Award: Scholarship for use in freshman, sophomore, junior, or senior years; renewable. *Number:* 1. *Amount:* $1500.

Eligibility Requirements: Applicant must be high school student and planning to enroll or expecting to enroll full- or part-time at a four-year institution or university. Applicant must be learning disabled. Applicant must have 2.5 GPA or higher. Available to U.S. citizens.

Application Requirements: Application, essay, transcript. *Deadline:* March 31.

Contact: P. Buckley Moss Foundation Scholarship Committee
P. Buckley Moss Foundation
152 P. Buckley Moss Drive
Waynesboro, VA 22980
Phone: 540-932-1728
E-mail: Foundation@mossfoundation.org

PFIZER

http://www.epilepsy-scholarship.com/

PFIZER EPILEPSY SCHOLARSHIP AWARD

Award for students with epilepsy who excel academically and in extra-curricular activities. Must be pursuing an undergraduate degree or be a college senior entering first year of graduate school. Must be under the care of a physician for epilepsy to qualify.

Award: Scholarship for use in freshman, sophomore, junior, senior, or graduate years; not renewable. *Number:* 40. *Amount:* up to $2000.

Eligibility Requirements: Applicant must be enrolled or expecting to enroll full- or part-time at a two-year or four-year or technical institution or university. Applicant must be physically disabled. Available to U.S. citizens.

Application Requirements: Application, essay, references, test scores, transcript. *Deadline:* June 15.

Contact: Love Vieira, Coordinator
Pfizer
Pfizer Epilepsy Scholarship Award c/o AdelphiEden Health
Communications, 30 Irvi
New York, NY 10003
Phone: 800-292-7373

PFIZER, INC.–US PHARMACEUTICALS GROUP

http://www.promisingminds.com/

SOOZIE COURTER "SHARING A BRIGHTER TOMORROW" HEMOPHILIA SCHOLARSHIP PROGRAM

Scholarship for students with hemophilia A or B. Must be a high school senior, or recipient of a GED, or currently enrolled in an accredited junior college, college (undergraduate or graduate) or vocational school. Fund includes sixteen $5000 undergraduate scholarships, two $7500 graduate scholarships, and two $2500 vocational scholarships. See web site for details and application http://www.hemophiliavillage.com.

Award: Scholarship for use in freshman, sophomore, junior, senior, or graduate years; not renewable. *Number:* 20. *Amount:* $2500–$7500.

Eligibility Requirements: Applicant must be enrolled or expecting to enroll full-time at a two-year or four-year or technical institution or university. Applicant must be physically disabled. Available to U.S. citizens.

Application Requirements: Application. *Deadline:* April 4.

Contact: MedPoint
Pfizer, Inc.–US Pharmaceuticals Group
235 East 42nd Street
685/14/67
New York, NY 10017-5755
Phone: 800-382-7075
E-mail: mapinfo@medpt.com

RECORDING FOR THE BLIND & DYSLEXIC

http://www.rfbd.org/

MARION HUBER LEARNING THROUGH LISTENING AWARDS
• *See page 560*

MARY P. OENSLAGER SCHOLASTIC ACHIEVEMENT AWARDS
• *See page 560*

SAN DIEGO FOUNDATION

http://www.sdfoundation.org/

RUBINSTEIN CROHN'S AND COLITIS SCHOLARSHIP

Scholarship provides financial assistance to graduating high school seniors or students already enrolled at an institution of higher education who have been diagnosed with Crohn's and Colitis. Applicants must have a minimum 3.0 GPA and plan to attend an accredited two-year college or four-year university in the U.S. Scholarship may be renewable for up to four years provided recipients maintain full-time enrollment, a 3.0 cumulative GPA and positive record of citizenship.

Award: Scholarship for use in freshman year; renewable. *Number:* 1. *Amount:* $1000.

Eligibility Requirements: Applicant must be enrolled or expecting to enroll full-time at a two-year or four-year institution or university and resident of California. Applicant must be physically disabled. Applicant must have 3.0 GPA or higher. Available to U.S. citizens.

Application Requirements: Application, essay, references, transcript, personal statement, copy of tax return. *Deadline:* January 26.

Contact: Shryl Helvie, Scholarship Coordinator
San Diego Foundation
2508 Historic Decatur Road, Suite 200
San Diego, CA 92106
Phone: 619-814-1307
Fax: 619-239-1710
E-mail: shryl@sdfoundation.org

SERTOMA, INC.

http://www.sertoma.org/

SERTOMA SCHOLARSHIP FOR STUDENTS WHO ARE DEAF OR HARD OF HEARING

Applicants must have a minimum 40dB bilateral hearing loss as evidenced on audiogram by a SRT of 40dB or greater in both ears. Must have a minimum 3.2 unweighted GPA or be at least 85 percent in all courses.

Award: Scholarship for use in freshman, sophomore, junior, or senior years; not renewable. *Number:* 45. *Amount:* $1000.

Eligibility Requirements: Applicant must be enrolled or expecting to enroll full-time at a four-year institution or university. Applicant must be hearing impaired. Available to U.S. citizens.

Application Requirements: Application, essay, references, transcript, proof of hearing loss. *Deadline:* May 1.

Contact: Amy Ellington, Director of Finance
Sertoma, Inc.
1912 East Meyer Boulevard
Kansas City, MO 64132-1174
Phone: 816-333-8300
E-mail: aellington@sertomahq.org

SEVENSECURE

http://www.changingpossibilities-us.com/SupportPrograms/ SevenSecure.aspx

SEVENSECURE ADULT EDUCATION GRANTS

Provides grants to adults aged 23 and over with either hemophilia with inhibitors or FVII deficiency who would like to take courses or get more training to help improve their career or transition to a new one. Applications are accepted throughout the year. One award per eligible patient per year.

Award: Grant for use in freshman, sophomore, junior, senior, or graduate years; not renewable. *Number:* varies. *Amount:* up to $2500.

Eligibility Requirements: Applicant must be age 23 and over and enrolled or expecting to enroll full-time at a four-year institution or university. Applicant must be physically disabled. Available to U.S. citizens.

Application Requirements: Application. *Deadline:* continuous.

Contact: SevenSECURE
PO Box 18648
Louisville, KY 40261
Phone: 877-668-6777

SICKLE CELL DISEASE ASSOCIATION OF AMERICA/CONNECTICUT CHAPTER INC.

http://www.sicklecellct.org/

I. H. MCLENDON MEMORIAL SCHOLARSHIP

One-time scholarship to graduating high school seniors with sickle cell disease in Connecticut who will enter collége, university, or technical training. Minimum 3.0 GPA required.

Award: Scholarship for use in freshman year; not renewable. *Number:* 1. *Amount:* $1000.

Eligibility Requirements: Applicant must be high school student; planning to enroll or expecting to enroll full- or part-time at a two-year or four-year or technical institution or university and resident of Connecticut. Applicant must be physically disabled. Applicant must have 3.0 GPA or higher. Available to U.S. citizens.

Application Requirements: Application, driver's license, interview, references, self-addressed stamped envelope, transcript, letter from physician attesting to existence of sickle cell disease. *Deadline:* April 30.

Contact: Samuel Byrd, Program Assistant
Sickle Cell Disease Association of America/Connecticut Chapter Inc.
Gengras Ambulatory Center, 114 Woodland Street, Suite 2101
Hartford, CT 06105-1299
Phone: 860-714-5540
Fax: 860-714-8007
E-mail: scdaa@iconn.net

SICKLE CELL DISEASE ASSOCIATION OF AMERICA INC.

http://www.sicklecelldisease.org/

KERMIT B. NASH, JR. ACADEMIC SCHOLARSHIP

One award for a total of $5000 per academic year for up to four years. Award will be disbursed per semester based on academic status. Must be graduating high school seniors with Sickle Cell Disease attending four-year accredited college. Minimum of 3.0 GPA required. Must be a U.S. citizen or permanent resident.

Award: Scholarship for use in freshman year; renewable. *Number:* 1. *Amount:* $5000–$20,000.

Eligibility Requirements: Applicant must be high school student and planning to enroll or expecting to enroll full-time at a four-year institution. Applicant must be physically disabled. Applicant must have 3.0 GPA or higher. Available to U.S. citizens.

Application Requirements: Application, essay, interview, photo, references, self-addressed stamped envelope, test scores, transcript. *Deadline:* May 31.

Contact: Lawrence Manning, Office Manager
Sickle Cell Disease Association of America Inc.
231 East Baltimore Street, Suite 800
Baltimore, MD 21202
Phone: 410-528-1555
Fax: 410-528-1495
E-mail: scdaa@sicklecelldisease.org

SISTER KENNY REHABILITATION INSTITUTE

http://www.allina.com/ahs/ski.nsf

INTERNATIONAL ART SHOW FOR ARTISTS WITH DISABILITIES

One-time award for artwork submitted by artists of any age with visual, hearing, physical, or learning impairment. Contact Sister Kenny Rehabilitation Institute for show information. This is a one-time prize, not an academic scholarship.

Award: Prize for use in freshman, sophomore, junior, senior, or graduate years; not renewable. *Number:* 25–70. *Amount:* $25–$500.

Eligibility Requirements: Applicant must be enrolled or expecting to enroll full- or part-time at a four-year institution or university and must have an interest in art. Applicant must be hearing impaired, learning disabled, physically disabled, or visually impaired. Available to U.S. and non-U.S. citizens.

Application Requirements: Application, applicant must enter a contest. *Deadline:* March 17.

Contact: Laura Swift, Administrative Assistant
Sister Kenny Rehabilitation Institute
800 East 28th Street
Minneapolis, MN 55407-3799
Phone: 612-863-4466
Fax: 612-863-8942
E-mail: laura.swift@allina.com

SPINA BIFIDA ASSOCIATION OF AMERICA

http://www.sbaa.org/

SBAA ONE-YEAR SCHOLARSHIP

Scholarship available for a student with spina bifida who has applied for, enrolled in, or accepted by a junior college, approved trade, vocational or business school. Applicant must be high school graduate or possess a GED.

Award: Scholarship for use in freshman year; not renewable. *Number:* up to 5. *Amount:* $2000.

Eligibility Requirements: Applicant must be enrolled or expecting to enroll full-time at a four-year or technical institution or university. Applicant must be physically disabled. Available to U.S. citizens.

Application Requirements: Application, transcript, physician's statement of disability. *Deadline:* March 2.

Contact: Caroline Alston, Director of Programs
Spina Bifida Association of America
4590 MacArthur Boulevard, Suite 250
Washington, DC 20007-4226
Phone: 202-944-3285
Fax: 202-944-3295
E-mail: sbaa@sbaa.org

SPINA BIFIDA ASSOCIATION OF AMERICA EDUCATIONAL SCHOLARSHIP

One-time award to enhance opportunities for persons born with spina bifida to achieve their full potential through higher education. Minimum 2.5 GPA required. Must submit doctor's statement of disability and acceptance letter from college/university/school.

Award: Scholarship for use in freshman, sophomore, junior, or senior years; not renewable. *Number:* varies. *Amount:* $1000.

Eligibility Requirements: Applicant must be enrolled or expecting to enroll full-time at a four-year or technical institution or university. Applicant must be physically disabled. Applicant must have 2.5 GPA or higher. Available to U.S. citizens.

Application Requirements: Application, essay, financial need analysis, references, test scores, transcript, statement of disability. *Deadline:* March 2.

Contact: Caroline Alston, Director of Programs
Spina Bifida Association of America
4590 MacArthur Boulevard, Suite 250
Washington, DC 20007-4226
Phone: 202-944-3285
Fax: 202-944-3295
E-mail: sbaa@sbaa.org

SPINA BIFIDA ASSOCIATION OF AMERICA FOUR-YEAR SCHOLARSHIP FUND

Renewable award for a young person born with spina bifida to achieve full potential through higher education, and attend a four-year college otherwise outside of their family's financial reach. Open to U.S. citizens.

Award: Scholarship for use in freshman, sophomore, junior, or senior years; renewable. *Number:* 1. *Amount:* $5000.

Eligibility Requirements: Applicant must be enrolled or expecting to enroll full-time at a four-year institution or university. Applicant must be physically disabled. Available to U.S. citizens.

Application Requirements: Application, essay, financial need analysis, references, test scores, transcript, physician's statement of disability. *Deadline:* March 2.

Contact: Caroline Alston, Director of Programs
Spina Bifida Association of America
4590 MacArthur Boulevard, Suite 250
Washington, DC 20007-4226
Phone: 202-944-3285
Fax: 202-944-3295
E-mail: sbaa@sbaa.org

TPA SCHOLARSHIP TRUST FOR THE DEAF AND NEAR DEAF

http://www.tpahq.org/

TRAVELERS PROTECTIVE ASSOCIATION SCHOLARSHIP TRUST FOR THE HEARING IMPAIRED

Scholarships are awarded to deaf or hearing-impaired persons of any age, race, or religion for specialized education, mechanical devices, or medical or specialized treatment. Based on financial need.

Award: Scholarship for use in freshman, sophomore, junior, or senior years; not renewable. *Number:* varies. *Amount:* $200–$600.

Eligibility Requirements: Applicant must be enrolled or expecting to enroll full- or part-time at a two-year or four-year or technical institution or university. Applicant must be hearing impaired. Available to U.S. citizens.

Application Requirements: Application, financial need analysis, photo. *Deadline:* March 1.

Contact: Brian K. Schulte, Chief Administrative Officer
TPA Scholarship Trust for the Deaf and Near Deaf
3755 Lindell Boulevard
St. Louis, MO 63108
Phone: 314-371-0533
Fax: 314-371-0537

UCB INC.

http://www.ucb.com/

UCB CROHN'S SCHOLARSHIP PROGRAM

Awards thirty one-time scholarships of up to $10,000 each to people diagnosed with Crohn's disease who are entering college or are currently enrolled in college or to adults of any age returning to school. Students of all ages are welcome to apply, and the scholarship can be used for a two-year, four-year, trade or specialty school.

Award: Scholarship for use in freshman, sophomore, junior, senior, or graduate years; not renewable. *Number:* up to 30. *Amount:* up to $10,000.

Eligibility Requirements: Applicant must be enrolled or expecting to enroll full- or part-time at a two-year or four-year or technical institution or university. Applicant must be physically disabled. Available to U.S. citizens.

Application Requirements: Application, essay, photo, references, self-addressed stamped envelope, test scores, transcript, medical certificate. *Deadline:* February 12.

Contact: UCB Inc.
c/o Summit Medical Communications, 1421 East Broad Street, Suite 340
Fuquay Varina, NC 27526
Phone: 866-757-4440
E-mail: ucbcrohnsscholarship@summitmedcomm.com

UCB FAMILY RA SCHOLARSHIP

Awards thirty one-time scholarships of up to $10,000 each to people diagnosed with rheumatoid arthritis and their immediate family members (parent, child, spouse, or sibling) who are entering college or are currently enrolled in college or to adults of any age returning to school. Students of all ages are welcome to apply and the scholarship can be used for a two-year, four-year, trade or specialty school.

Award: Scholarship for use in freshman, sophomore, junior, senior, or graduate years; not renewable. *Number:* up to 30. *Amount:* up to $10,000.

Eligibility Requirements: Applicant must be enrolled or expecting to enroll full- or part-time at a two-year or four-year or technical institution or university. Applicant must be physically disabled. Available to U.S. citizens.

Application Requirements: Application, essay, photo, references, test scores, transcript, physician's letter. *Deadline:* March 19.

Contact: UCB Family RA Scholarship Program
UCB Inc.
c/o Summit Medical Communications, 1421 East Broad Street, Suite 340
Fuguay-Varina, NC 27526
Phone: 888-854-4996
E-mail: ucbrascholarship@summitmedcomm.com

ULMAN CANCER FUND FOR YOUNG ADULTS

http://www.ulmanfund.org/

MARYLAND COMMUNITY CANCER SCHOLARSHIP AWARD

Scholarship for college students who were diagnosed with cancer or who have lost a parent to cancer, or whose parent is currently fighting cancer. The diagnosis must have occurred when the applicant was between the ages of 15 and 35, and the applicant must be age 35 or younger at the time of the application. Must be a resident of Maryland, Virginia, or Washington, D.C., or enrolled in, or attending a 2- or 4-year college/university or vocational school in Maryland, Virginia, or Washington, D.C. Visit http://www.ulmancancerfund.org in mid-January to download scholarship applications.

Award: Scholarship for use in freshman, sophomore, junior, or senior years; not renewable. *Number:* 1. *Amount:* $2500.

Eligibility Requirements: Applicant must be age 15-35; enrolled or expecting to enroll full- or part-time at a two-year or four-year or technical institution or university; resident of District of Columbia, Maryland, or Virginia and studying in District of Columbia, Maryland, or Virginia. Applicant must be physically disabled. Available to U.S. and non-U.S. citizens.

Application Requirements: Application, essay, financial need analysis, references, pertinent medical history. *Deadline:* May 1.

Contact: Fay Baker, Scholarship Coordinator
Ulman Cancer Fund for Young Adults
4725 Dorsey Hall Drive, Suite A
PO Box 505
Ellicott City, MD 21042
Phone: 410-964-0202
E-mail: scholarship@ulmanfund.org

SEAN SILVER MEMORIAL SCHOLARSHIP AWARD

The Sean Silver Memorial Award is available to young adults, aged 30 or younger, currently undergoing treatment for cancer and seeking a 4-year degree.

Award: Scholarship for use in freshman, sophomore, junior, or senior years; not renewable. *Number:* 1. *Amount:* $2500.

Eligibility Requirements: Applicant must be age 17-30 and enrolled or expecting to enroll full- or part-time at a four-year institution. Applicant must be physically disabled. Available to U.S. citizens.

Application Requirements: Application, essay, financial need analysis, references. *Deadline:* May 1.

Contact: Ulman Cancer Fund–Scholarship Program Coordinator
Ulman Cancer Fund for Young Adults
10440 Little Patuxent Parkway, Suite 1G
Columbia, MD 21044
Phone: 888-393-3863
Fax: 410-964-0202
E-mail: scholarship@ulmanfund.org

VERA YIP MEMORIAL SCHOLARSHIP

Scholarships for college students who were diagnosed with cancer between the ages of 15 and 35, or who have lost a parent to cancer, or whose parent is currently fighting cancer. Applicants must be age 35 or younger at the time of application and be currently attending or accepted into a 4-year college/university, seeking a bachelor's degree or higher. Must have commitment to community service and using their cancer experience to influence the lives of other young adults confronted by cancer. Must be a resident of Maryland, Virginia, or Washington, D.C., or enrolled in a college/university in Maryland, Virginia, or Washington, D.C. Visit http://www.ulmancancerfund for more information and application.

Award: Scholarship for use in freshman, sophomore, junior, or senior years; not renewable. *Number:* 1. *Amount:* $2500.

Eligibility Requirements: Applicant must be age 35 or under; enrolled or expecting to enroll full- or part-time at a four-year institution or university; resident of District of Columbia, Maryland, or Virginia and studying in District of Columbia, Maryland, or Virginia. Applicant must be physically disabled. Available to U.S. and non-U.S. citizens.

Application Requirements: Application, essay, references, pertinent medical history. *Deadline:* May 1.

Contact: Fay Baker, Scholarship Coordinator
Ulman Cancer Fund for Young Adults
4725 Dorsey Hall Drive, Suite A
PO Box 505
Ellicott City, MD 21042
Phone: 410-964-0202
E-mail: scholarship@ulmanfund.org

UNITED NEGRO COLLEGE FUND

http://www.uncf.org/

ROBERT DOLE SCHOLARSHIP FOR DISABLED STUDENTS

Scholarship for students with a physical or mental disability who are attending UNCF member colleges and universities and demonstrate financial need. Minimum GPA 2.5. For more information see Website: http://www.uncf.org/forstudents/scholarship.asp.

Award: Scholarship for use in freshman year. *Amount:* up to $3500.

Eligibility Requirements: Applicant must be Black (non-Hispanic) and enrolled or expecting to enroll at a four-year institution or university. Applicant must be physically disabled. Applicant must have 2.5 GPA or higher.

Contact: Director, Program Services
United Negro College Fund
8260 Willow Oaks Corporate Drive
PO Box 10444
Fairfax, VA 22031-8044
Phone: 800-331-2244
E-mail: rebecca.bennett@uncf.org

UNITED STATES ASSOCIATION FOR BLIND ATHLETES

http://www.usaba.org/

ARTHUR E. AND HELEN COPELAND SCHOLARSHIPS

Scholarship for a full-time college student who is blind or visually impaired. All applicants must be current members of USABA.

Award: Scholarship for use in freshman, sophomore, junior, or senior years; not renewable. *Number:* 1–2. *Amount:* $500.

Eligibility Requirements: Applicant must be enrolled or expecting to enroll full-time at a four-year institution or university. Applicant must be visually impaired. Available to U.S. citizens.

Application Requirements: Application, driver's license, references, transcript, proof of acceptance. *Deadline:* October 1.

Contact: Mark Lucas, Executive Director
United States Association for Blind Athletes
33 North Institute Street
Colorado Springs, CO 80903
Phone: 719-630-0422 Ext. 13
Fax: 719-630-0616
E-mail: mlucas@usaba.org

WISCONSIN HIGHER EDUCATIONAL AID BOARD

http://www.heab.wi.gov/

HANDICAPPED STUDENT GRANT-WISCONSIN

One-time award available to residents of Wisconsin who have severe or profound hearing or visual impairment. Must be enrolled at least half-time at a nonprofit institution. If the handicap prevents the student from attending a Wisconsin school, the award may be used out-of-state in a specialized college. Refer to web site for further details http://www.heab.state.wi.us.

Award: Grant for use in freshman, sophomore, junior, or senior years; not renewable. *Number:* varies. *Amount:* $250–$1800.

Eligibility Requirements: Applicant must be enrolled or expecting to enroll full- or part-time at a four-year institution or university and resident of Wisconsin. Applicant must be hearing impaired or visually impaired. Available to U.S. citizens.

Application Requirements: Application, financial need analysis. *Deadline:* continuous.

Contact: Sandy Thomas, Program Coordinator
Wisconsin Higher Educational Aid Board
PO Box 7885
Madison, WI 53707-7885
Phone: 608-266-0888
Fax: 608-267-2808
E-mail: sandy.thomas@wi.gov

MILITARY SERVICE: AIR FORCE

AIR FORCE AID SOCIETY

http://www.afas.org/

GENERAL HENRY H. ARNOLD EDUCATION GRANT PROGRAM

Need-based grants awarded to dependent sons and daughters of active duty, Title 10 AGR/Reserve, Title 32 AGR performing full-time active duty, retired, retired reserve and deceased Air Force members; spouses (stateside) of active members and Title 10 AGR/Reservist; and surviving spouses of deceased personnel for their undergraduate studies. Dependent children must be unmarried and under the age of 23. High school seniors may apply. Minimum 2.0 GPA is required. Students must reapply and compete each year. Full-time enrollment status required.

Award: Grant for use in freshman, sophomore, junior, or senior years; not renewable. *Number:* 3000. *Amount:* $2000.

Eligibility Requirements: Applicant must be enrolled or expecting to enroll full-time at a two-year or four-year or technical institution or university. Available to U.S. citizens. Applicant or parent must meet one or more of the following requirements: Air Force or Air Force National Guard experience; retired from active duty; disabled or killed as a result of military service; prisoner of war; or missing in action.

Application Requirements: Application, financial need analysis, transcript, program's own financial forms, USAF military orders (member/parent), ID cards (applicant and member parent). *Deadline:* March 11.

Contact: Education Assistance Department
Air Force Aid Society
241 18th Street South, Suite 202
Arlington, VA 22202-3409
Phone: 800-429-9475
E-mail: AFAS.ED@afas-hq.org

AIR FORCE RESERVE OFFICER TRAINING CORPS

http://www.afrotc.com/

AFROTC HBCU SCHOLARSHIP PROGRAM

Up to $15,000 awarded to student studying at a historically black college or university (HBCU). Please refer to web site for more information http://www.afrotc.com/scholarships/incolschol/minority/hbcu.php.

Award: Scholarship for use in freshman, sophomore, junior, or senior years; not renewable. *Number:* up to 15. *Amount:* up to $15,000.

Eligibility Requirements: Applicant must be enrolled or expecting to enroll full-time at a four-year institution or university. Available to U.S. citizens. Applicant must have served in the Air Force or Air Force National Guard.

Application Requirements: Application. *Deadline:* varies.

Contact: Elmarko Magee, Chief of Advertising
Air Force Reserve Officer Training Corps
551 East Maxwell Boulevard
Maxwell AFB, AL 36112
Phone: 866-423-7682

AFROTC HSI SCHOLARSHIP PROGRAM

$15,000 scholarships to students at colleges and universities defined as Hispanic Serving Institutions by the United States Department of Education. Student must already be enrolled in school to receive award.

Award: Scholarship for use in freshman, sophomore, junior, or senior years; not renewable. *Number:* up to 15. *Amount:* $15,000.

Eligibility Requirements: Applicant must be enrolled or expecting to enroll full-time at a four-year institution or university. Available to U.S. citizens. Applicant must have served in the Air Force or Air Force National Guard.

Application Requirements: Application. *Deadline:* varies.

Contact: Capt. Elmarko Magee, Chief of Advertising
Air Force Reserve Officer Training Corps
551 East Maxwell Boulevard
Maxwell Air Force Base, AL 36112-6106
Phone: 334-953-2278
E-mail: elmarko.magee@maxwell.af.mil

AIR FORCE ROTC COLLEGE SCHOLARSHIP

Scholarship program provides three- and four-year scholarships in three different types to high school seniors. All scholarship cadets receive a nontaxable monthly allowance (stipend) during the academic year. For more details refer to web site http://www.afrotc.com/scholarships/hsschol/types.php.

Award: Scholarship for use in freshman, sophomore, junior, or senior years; renewable. *Number:* 2000–4000. *Amount:* $9000–$15,000.

Eligibility Requirements: Applicant must be age 17-30 and enrolled or expecting to enroll full-time at a two-year or four-year institution or university. Applicant must have 3.0 GPA or higher. Available to U.S. citizens. Applicant or parent must meet one or more of the following requirements: Air Force experience; retired from active duty; disabled or killed as a result of military service; prisoner of war; or missing in action.

Application Requirements: Application, interview, test scores, transcript. *Deadline:* December 1.

Contact: Ty Christian, Chief Air Force ROTC Advertising Manager
Air Force Reserve Officer Training Corps
551 East Maxwell Boulevard
Maxwell Air Force Base, AL 36112-6106
Phone: 334-953-2278
Fax: 334-953-4384
E-mail: ty.christian@maxwell.af.mil

AIRMEN MEMORIAL FOUNDATION/AIR FORCE SERGEANTS ASSOCIATION

http://www.afsahq.org/

AIR FORCE SERGEANTS ASSOCIATION SCHOLARSHIP

Scholarships awarded to dependent youth of Air Force Sergeants Association/Auxiliary members. Must be under the age of 23, be enrolled or accepted as an undergraduate in an accredited college or university, have minimum combined score of 1650 on SAT or 24 on ACT, and a minimum GPA of 3.5.

Award: Scholarship for use in freshman, sophomore, junior, or senior years; not renewable. *Number:* up to 30. *Amount:* $500–$3000.

Eligibility Requirements: Applicant must be age 23 or under and enrolled or expecting to enroll full-time at a four-year institution or university. Applicant must have 3.5 GPA or higher. Available to U.S. and non-U.S. citizens. Applicant or parent must meet one or more of the following requirements: Air Force or Air Force National Guard experience; retired from active duty; disabled or killed as a result of military service; prisoner of war; or missing in action.

Application Requirements: Application, essay, references, transcript. *Deadline:* March 31.

Contact: Melanie Shirley, Scholarship Coordinator
Airmen Memorial Foundation/Air Force Sergeants Association
5211 Auth Road
Suitland, MD 20746
Phone: 301-899-3500
Fax: 301-899-8136
E-mail: staff@afsahq.org

AIRMEN MEMORIAL FOUNDATION SCHOLARSHIP

Scholarship for full-time undergraduate studies of dependent children of Air Force, Air Force Reserve Command and Air National Guard members in active duty, retired or veteran status. Must be under age of 23, have minimum combined score of 1650 on SAT or 24 on ACT, and a minimum GPA of 3.5.

Award: Scholarship for use in freshman, sophomore, junior, or senior years; not renewable. *Number:* 20. *Amount:* $500–$2000.

Eligibility Requirements: Applicant must be age 23 or under and enrolled or expecting to enroll full-time at a four-year institution or university. Applicant must have 3.5 GPA or higher. Available to U.S. and non-U.S. citizens. Applicant or parent must meet one or more of the following requirements: Air Force or Air Force National Guard experience; retired from active duty; disabled or killed as a result of military service; prisoner of war; or missing in action.

Application Requirements: Application, essay, references, transcript. *Deadline:* March 31.

Contact: Melanie Shirley, Scholarship Coordinator
Airmen Memorial Foundation/Air Force Sergeants Association
5211 Auth Road
Suitland, MD 20746
Phone: 301-899-3500
Fax: 301-899-8136
E-mail: staff@afsahq.org

CHIEF MASTER SERGEANTS OF THE AIR FORCE SCHOLARSHIP PROGRAM

Scholarship to financially assist the full-time undergraduate studies of dependent children of Air Force, Air Force Reserve Command and Air National Guard enlisted members in active duty, retired or veteran status. Must be under age twenty-three, and participate in the Airmen Memorial Foundation Scholarship Program. Must have minimum combined score of 1650 on SAT or 24 on ACT, and a minimum GPA of 3.5.

Award: Scholarship for use in freshman, sophomore, junior, or senior years; not renewable. *Number:* up to 30. *Amount:* $500–$3000.

Eligibility Requirements: Applicant must be age 23 or under and enrolled or expecting to enroll full-time at a four-year institution or university. Applicant must have 3.5 GPA or higher. Available to U.S. and non-U.S. citizens. Applicant or parent must meet one or more of the following requirements: Air Force or Air Force National Guard experience; retired from active duty; disabled or killed as a result of military service; prisoner of war; or missing in action.

Application Requirements: Application, essay, references, transcript. *Deadline:* March 31.

Contact: Melanie Shirley, Scholarship Coordinator
Airmen Memorial Foundation/Air Force Sergeants Association
5211 Auth Road
Suitland, MD 20746
Phone: 301-899-3500
Fax: 301-899-8136
E-mail: staff@afsahq.org

DAUGHTERS OF THE CINCINNATI

http://www.daughters1894.org/

DAUGHTERS OF THE CINCINNATI SCHOLARSHIP

Need and merit-based award available to graduating high school seniors. Minimum GPA of 3.0 required. Must be daughter of commissioned officer in regular Army, Navy, Coast Guard, Air Force, Marines (active, retired, or deceased). Must submit parent's rank and branch of service. Application can be completed and downloaded from web site http://www.daughters1894.org.

Award: Scholarship for use in freshman year; renewable. *Number:* 4–5. *Amount:* $3000–$5000.

Eligibility Requirements: Applicant must be high school student; planning to enroll or expecting to enroll full-time at a four-year institution or university and female. Applicant must have 3.0 GPA or higher. Available to U.S. citizens. Applicant or parent must meet one or more of the following requirements: Air Force, Army, Coast Guard, Marine Corps, or Navy experience; retired from active duty; disabled or killed as a result of military service; prisoner of war; or missing in action.

Application Requirements: Application, essay, financial need analysis, references, test scores, transcript. *Deadline:* March 15.

Contact: Mrs. Jane Gonzalez, Scholarship Administrator
Daughters of the Cincinnati
20 West 44th Street, Room 508
New York, NY 10036
Phone: 212-991-9945
E-mail: scholarships@daughters1894.org

DEPARTMENT OF VETERANS AFFAIRS (VA)

http://www.gibill.va.gov/

MONTGOMERY GI BILL (SELECTED RESERVE)

Educational assistance program for members of the selected reserve of the Army, Navy, Air Force, Marine Corps and Coast Guard, as well as the Army and Air National Guard. Available to all reservists and National Guard personnel who commit to a six-year obligation, and remain in the Reserve or Guard during the six years. Award is renewable. Monthly benefit is $309 for up to thirty-six months for full-time.

Award: Scholarship for use in freshman, sophomore, junior, senior, or postgraduate years; renewable. *Number:* varies.

Eligibility Requirements: Applicant must be enrolled or expecting to enroll full- or part-time at a two-year or four-year or technical institution or university. Available to U.S. citizens. Applicant or parent must meet one or more of the following requirements: general military experience; retired from active duty; disabled or killed as a result of military service; prisoner of war; or missing in action.

Application Requirements: Application, proof of military service of six years in the reserve or guard. *Deadline:* continuous.

Contact: Keith Wilson, Director, Education Service
Department of Veterans Affairs (VA)
810 Vermont Avenue, NW
Washington, DC 20420
Phone: 888-442-4551

FOUNDATION OF THE 1ST CAVALRY DIVISION ASSOCIATION

http://www.1cda.org/

FOUNDATION OF THE 1ST CAVALRY DIVISION ASSOCIATION (IA DRANG) SCHOLARSHIP

Award for children and grandchildren of soldiers of 1st Cavalry Division, U.S. Air Force Forward Air Controllers and A1E pilots, and war corre-spondents who served in designated qualifying units which were involved in battles of the Ia Drang Valley during the period of November 3–19, 1965. Include self-addressed stamped envelope. More information on http://www.1cda.org.

Award: Scholarship for use in freshman, sophomore, junior, or senior years; renewable. *Number:* varies. *Amount:* up to $1200.

Eligibility Requirements: Applicant must be enrolled or expecting to enroll full-time at a two-year or four-year institution or university. Available to U.S. citizens. Applicant or parent must meet one or more of the following requirements: Air Force or Army experience; retired from active duty; disabled or killed as a result of military service; prisoner of war; or missing in action.

Application Requirements: Application, self-addressed stamped envelope, birth certificate, proof of father or grandfather's participation in specified units and battles, proof of registration for Selective Service for males. *Deadline:* continuous.

Contact: Dennis Webster, Executive Director
Foundation of the 1st Cavalry Division Association
302 North Main Street
Copperas Cove, TX 76522-1703
Phone: 254-547-6537
Fax: 254-547-8853
E-mail: firstcav@1cda.org

INDIANA DEPARTMENT OF VETERANS AFFAIRS

http://www.in.gov/dva

RESIDENT TUITION FOR ACTIVE DUTY MILITARY PERSONNEL

Applicant must be a nonresident of Indiana serving on active duty and stationed in Indiana and attending any state-supported college or university. Dependents remain eligible for the duration of their enrollment, even if the active duty person is no longer in Indiana. Entitlement is to the resident tuition rate.

Award: Grant for use in freshman, sophomore, junior, senior, graduate, or postgraduate years; renewable. *Number:* varies. *Amount:* varies.

Eligibility Requirements: Applicant must be enrolled or expecting to enroll full- or part-time at a two-year or four-year or technical institution or university and studying in Indiana. Available to U.S. citizens. Applicant or parent must meet one or more of the following requirements: Air Force, Army, Marine Corps, or Navy experience; retired from active duty; disabled or killed as a result of military service; prisoner of war; or missing in action.

Application Requirements: Application. *Deadline:* continuous.

Contact: Jon Brinkley, State Service Officer
Indiana Department of Veterans Affairs
302 West Washington Street, Room E-120
Indianapolis, IN 46204-2738
Phone: 317-232-3910
Fax: 317-232-7721
E-mail: jbrinkley@dva.in.gov

WISCONSIN DEPARTMENT OF VETERANS AFFAIRS (WDVA)

http://www.dva.state.wi.us/

VETERANS EDUCATION (VETED) REIMBURSEMENT GRANT

The grant is for eligible Wisconsin veterans enrolled at approved schools who have not yet earned a BS/BA. Reimburses up to 120 credits or eight semesters at the UW Madison rate for the same number of credits taken in one semester or term. The number of credits or semesters is based on length of time serving on active duty in the armed forces (active duty for training does not apply). Application is due no later than 60 days after the course start date. The student must earn a 2.0 or better for the semester. An eligible veteran will have entered active duty as a Wisconsin resident or lived in state for twelve consecutive months since entering active duty.

Award: Grant for use in freshman, sophomore, junior, or senior years; renewable. *Number:* up to 350. *Amount:* up to $4000.

Eligibility Requirements: Applicant must be enrolled or expecting to enroll full- or part-time at a two-year or four-year or technical institution or university; resident of Wisconsin and studying in Minnesota or Wisconsin. Available to U.S. citizens. Applicant must have served in the Air Force, Army, Coast Guard, Marine Corps, or Navy.

Application Requirements: Application, certified Wisconsin veteran. *Deadline:* continuous.

Contact: Ms. Leslie Ann Busby-Amegashie, Analyst
Wisconsin Department of Veterans Affairs (WDVA)
PO Box 7843
Madison, WI 53707-7843
Phone: 800-947-8387
E-mail: leslie.busby-amegashie@dva.state.wi.us

MILITARY SERVICE: AIR FORCE NATIONAL GUARD

AIR FORCE AID SOCIETY

http://www.afas.org/

GENERAL HENRY H. ARNOLD EDUCATION GRANT PROGRAM
• *See page 615*

AIR FORCE RESERVE OFFICER TRAINING CORPS

http://www.afrotc.com/

AFROTC HBCU SCHOLARSHIP PROGRAM
• *See page 616*

AFROTC HSI SCHOLARSHIP PROGRAM
• *See page 616*

AIRMEN MEMORIAL FOUNDATION/AIR FORCE SERGEANTS ASSOCIATION

http://www.afsahq.org/

AIR FORCE SERGEANTS ASSOCIATION SCHOLARSHIP
• *See page 616*

AIRMEN MEMORIAL FOUNDATION SCHOLARSHIP
• *See page 616*

CHIEF MASTER SERGEANTS OF THE AIR FORCE SCHOLARSHIP PROGRAM
• *See page 616*

ALABAMA COMMISSION ON HIGHER EDUCATION

http://www.ache.alabama.gov/

ALABAMA NATIONAL GUARD EDUCATIONAL ASSISTANCE PROGRAM

Renewable award aids Alabama residents who are members of the Alabama National Guard and are enrolled in an accredited college in Alabama. Forms must be signed by a representative of the Alabama Military Department and financial aid officer. Recipient must be in a degree-seeking program.

Award: Scholarship for use in freshman, sophomore, junior, senior, or graduate years; renewable. *Number:* up to 575. *Amount:* $25–$1000.

Eligibility Requirements: Applicant must be age 17 and over; enrolled or expecting to enroll full- or part-time at a two-year or four-year or technical institution or university; resident of Alabama and studying in Alabama. Available to U.S. citizens. Applicant must have served in the Air Force National Guard or Army National Guard.

Application Requirements: Application. *Deadline:* continuous.

Contact: Cheryl Newton, Grants Coordinator
Alabama Commission on Higher Education
100 North Union Street
PO Box 302000
Montgomery, AL 36130-2000
Phone: 334-242-2273
E-mail: cheryl.newton@ache.alabama.gov

AMERICAN LEGION DEPARTMENT OF TENNESSEE

http://www.tennesseelegion.org/

JROTC SCHOLARSHIP

One scholarship of $2000 available to a Tennessee JROTC cadet who has been awarded either The American Legion General Military Excellence, or The American Legion Scholastic Award Medal. JROTC Senior Instructor must provide the recommendation for the award. Information and recommendation forms are provided each JROTC Unit in Tennessee. Must be U.S. citizen.

Award: Scholarship for use in freshman year; not renewable. *Number:* 1. *Amount:* $2000.

Eligibility Requirements: Applicant must be high school student; planning to enroll or expecting to enroll full- or part-time at a four-year institution or university; resident of Tennessee and studying in Tennessee. Available to U.S. citizens. Applicant must have served in the Air Force National Guard or Army National Guard.

Application Requirements: Application. *Deadline:* May 15.

Contact: Darlene Burgess, Executive Assistant
American Legion Department of Tennessee
215 Eighth Avenue, North
Nashville, TN 37203
Phone: 615-254-0568
E-mail: tnleg1@bellsouth.net

DELAWARE NATIONAL GUARD

http://www.delawarenationalguard.com/

STATE TUITION ASSISTANCE

You must enlist in the Delaware National Guard to be eligible for this scholarship award. Award providing tuition assistance for any member of the Air or Army National Guard attending a Delaware two-year or four-year college. Awards are renewable. Applicant's minimum GPA must be 2.0.

Award: Scholarship for use in freshman, sophomore, junior, or senior years; renewable. *Number:* 1–300. *Amount:* up to $10,000.

Eligibility Requirements: Applicant must be enrolled or expecting to enroll full- or part-time at a two-year or four-year institution or university and studying in Delaware. Available to U.S. citizens. Applicant or parent must meet one or more of the following requirements: Air Force National Guard or Army National Guard experience; retired from active duty; disabled or killed as a result of military service; prisoner of war; or missing in action.

Application Requirements: Application, transcript.

Contact: Robert Csizmadia, State Tuition Assistance Manager
Delaware National Guard
1st Regiment Road
Wilmington, DE 19808-2191
Phone: 302-326-7012
Fax: 302-326-7029
E-mail: robert.csizmadia@us.army.mil

DEPARTMENT OF VETERANS AFFAIRS (VA)

http://www.gibill.va.gov/

MONTGOMERY GI BILL (SELECTED RESERVE)
• *See page 617*

RESERVE EDUCATION ASSISTANCE PROGRAM

The program provides educational assistance to members of National Guard and reserve components. Selected Reserve and Individual Ready Reserve (IRR) who are called or ordered to active duty service in response to a war or national emergency as declared by the president or Congress are eligible. For further information see web site http://www.GIBILL.va.gov.

Award: Scholarship for use in freshman, sophomore, junior, senior, graduate, or postgraduate years; renewable.

Eligibility Requirements: Applicant must be enrolled or expecting to enroll full- or part-time at a two-year or four-year or technical institution or university. Available to U.S. citizens. Applicant or parent must meet one or more of the following requirements: general military experience; retired from active duty; disabled or killed as a result of military service; prisoner of war; or missing in action.

Application Requirements: Application. *Deadline:* continuous.

Contact: Keith Wilson, Director, Education Service
Department of Veterans Affairs (VA)
810 Vermont Avenue, NW
Washington, DC 20420
Phone: 888-442-4551

EDUCATION FOUNDATION. INC. NATIONAL GUARD ASSOCIATION OF COLORADO

http://www.ngaco.org/

EDUCATION FOUNDATION, INC. NATIONAL GUARD ASSOCIATION OF COLORADO SCHOLARSHIPS

Scholarships for current members of the Colorado National Guard. Applicants must be enrolled as full or part-time at a college, university, trade or business school. Deadlines: August 1st for the fall semester and December 1st for the spring semester.

Award: Scholarship for use in freshman, sophomore, junior, senior, graduate, or postgraduate years; not renewable. *Number:* 20–30. *Amount:* $500–$2500.

Eligibility Requirements: Applicant must be enrolled or expecting to enroll full- or part-time at a two-year or four-year or technical institution or university and resident of Colorado. Available to U.S. citizens. Applicant must have served in the Air Force National Guard or Army National Guard.

Application Requirements: Application, essay, financial need analysis, references, transcript. *Deadline:* varies.

Contact: Mr. Bernie Rogoff, Executive Director
Education Foundation. Inc. National Guard Association of Colorado
PO Box 440889
Aurora, CO 80044-8889
Phone: 303-909-6369
Fax: 720-535-5925
E-mail: BernieRogoff@Comcast.net

ENLISTED ASSOCIATION OF THE NATIONAL GUARD OF NEW JERSEY

http://www.eang-nj.org/

CSM VINCENT BALDASSARI MEMORIAL SCHOLARSHIP PROGRAM

Scholarships open to the legal children of New Jersey National Guard Members who are also members of the Enlisted Association. Also open to any drilling guardsperson who is a member of the Enlisted Association. Along with application, submit proof of parent's membership and a letter stating the reason for applying and future intents.

Award: Scholarship for use in freshman, sophomore, junior, senior, graduate, or postgraduate years; not renewable. *Number:* 5. *Amount:* $1000.

Eligibility Requirements: Applicant must be enrolled or expecting to enroll full- or part-time at a two-year or four-year or technical institution or university and resident of New Jersey. Available to U.S. and non-U.S. citizens. Applicant must meet one or more of the following requirements: Air Force National Guard or Army National Guard experience; retired from active duty; disabled or killed as a result of military service; prisoner of war; or missing in action.

Application Requirements: Application, essay, photo, references, transcript. *Deadline:* May 15.

Contact: Michael Amoroso, Scholarship Committee Chairman
Enlisted Association of the National Guard of New Jersey
3650 Saylors Pond Road
Fort Dix, NJ 08640
Phone: 609-562-0754
Fax: 609-562-0731
E-mail: michael.c@us.army.mil

USAA SCHOLARSHIP

Scholarship of $1000 open to any drilling guardsperson (need not be a member of the EANGNJ).

Award: Scholarship for use in freshman, sophomore, junior, senior, graduate, or postgraduate years; not renewable. *Number:* 1. *Amount:* $1000.

Eligibility Requirements: Applicant must be enrolled or expecting to enroll full- or part-time at a two-year or four-year or technical institution or university. Available to U.S. and non-U.S. citizens. Applicant or parent must meet one or more of the following requirements: Air Force National Guard or Army National Guard experience; retired from active duty; disabled or killed as a result of military service; prisoner of war; or missing in action.

Application Requirements: Application, essay, photo, transcript. *Deadline:* May 15.

Contact: Michael Amoroso, Scholarship Committee Chairman
Enlisted Association of the National Guard of New Jersey
3650 Saylors Pond Road
Fort Dix, NJ 08640
Phone: 609-562-0754
Fax: 609-562-0731
E-mail: michael.c@us.army.mil

ILLINOIS STUDENT ASSISTANCE COMMISSION (ISAC)

http://www.collegezone.org/

ILLINOIS NATIONAL GUARD GRANT PROGRAM

Active duty members of the Illinois National Guard, or who are within 12 months of discharge, and who have completed one full year of service are eligible. May be used for study at Illinois two- or four-year public colleges for a maximum of the equivalent of four academic years of full-time enrollment. Deadlines: October 1 of the academic year for full year, March 1 for second/third term, or June 15 for the summer term.

Award: Grant for use in freshman, sophomore, junior, senior, or graduate years; renewable. *Number:* varies. *Amount:* varies.

Eligibility Requirements: Applicant must be enrolled or expecting to enroll full- or part-time at a two-year or four-year institution or university; resident of Illinois and studying in Illinois. Available to U.S. citizens. Applicant or parent must meet one or more of the following requirements: Air Force National Guard or Army National Guard experience; retired from active duty; disabled or killed as a result of military service; prisoner of war; or missing in action.

Application Requirements: Application, documentation of service. *Deadline:* varies.

Contact: College Zone Counselor
Illinois Student Assistance Commission (ISAC)
1755 Lake Cook Road
Deerfield, IL 60015-5209
Phone: 800-899-4722
Fax: 847-831-8549
E-mail: collegezone@isac.org

INDIANA DEPARTMENT OF VETERANS AFFAIRS

http://www.in.gov/dva

NATIONAL GUARD SCHOLARSHIP EXTENSION PROGRAM

A scholarship extension applicant is eligible for a tuition scholarship under Indiana Code 21-13-5-4 for a period not to exceed the period of scholarship extension the applicant served on active duty as a member of the National Guard (mobilized and deployed). Must apply not later than one (1) year after the applicant ceases to be a member of the Indiana National Guard. Applicant should apply through the education officer of their last unit of assignment.

Award: Grant for use in freshman, sophomore, junior, or senior years; renewable. *Number:* varies. *Amount:* varies.

Eligibility Requirements: Applicant must be enrolled or expecting to enroll full- or part-time at a two-year or four-year or technical institution or university and studying in Indiana. Available to U.S. citizens. Applicant must have served in the Air Force National Guard or Army National Guard.

Application Requirements: Application. *Deadline:* continuous.

Contact: Pamela Moody, National Guard Education Officer
Indiana Department of Veterans Affairs
302 West Washington Street, Suite E120
Indianapolis, IN 46204
Phone: 317-964-7017
Fax: 317-232-7721
E-mail: pamela.moody@in.ngb.army.mil

NATIONAL GUARD TUITION SUPPLEMENT PROGRAM

Applicant must be a member of the Indiana National Guard, in active drilling status, who has not been AWOL during the last 12 months, does not possess a bachelor's degree, possesses the requisite academic qualifications, meets the requirements of the state-supported college or university, and meets all National Guard requirements.

Award: Grant for use in freshman, sophomore, junior, or senior years; renewable. *Number:* varies. *Amount:* varies.

Eligibility Requirements: Applicant must be enrolled or expecting to enroll full- or part-time at a two-year or four-year or technical institution or university and studying in Indiana. Available to U.S. citizens. Applicant must have served in the Air Force National Guard or Army National Guard.

Application Requirements: Application, FAFSA. *Deadline:* continuous.

Contact: Jon Brinkley, State Service Officer
Indiana Department of Veterans Affairs
302 West Washington Street, Room E-120
Indianapolis, IN 46204-2738
Phone: 317-232-3910
Fax: 317-232-7721
E-mail: jbrinkley@dva.in.gov

TUITION AND FEE REMISSION FOR CHILDREN AND SPOUSES OF NATIONAL GUARD MEMBERS

Award to an individual whose father, mother or spouse was a member of the Indiana National Guard and suffered a service-connected death while serving on state active duty (which includes mobilized and deployed for federal active duty). The student must be eligible to pay the resident tuition rate at the state-supported college or university and must possess the requisite academic qualifications.

Award: Grant for use in freshman, sophomore, junior, or senior years; renewable. *Number:* varies. *Amount:* varies.

Eligibility Requirements: Applicant must be enrolled or expecting to enroll full- or part-time at a two-year or four-year or technical institution or university and studying in Indiana. Available to U.S. citizens. Applicant or parent must meet one or more of the following requirements: Air Force National Guard or Army National Guard experience; retired from active duty; disabled or killed as a result of military service; prisoner of war; or missing in action.

Application Requirements: Application, FAFSA. *Deadline:* continuous.

Contact: R. Martin Umbarger, Adjutant General
Indiana Department of Veterans Affairs
2002 South Holt Road
Indianapolis, IN 46241
Phone: 317-247-3559
Fax: 317-247-3540
E-mail: r.martin.umbarger@in.ngb.army.mil

IOWA COLLEGE STUDENT AID COMMISSION

http://www.iowacollegeaid.gov/

IOWA NATIONAL GUARD EDUCATION ASSISTANCE PROGRAM

Program provides postsecondary tuition assistance to members of Iowa National Guard Units. Must study at a postsecondary institution in Iowa. Contact the office for additional information.

Award: Grant for use in freshman, sophomore, junior, or senior years; not renewable. *Number:* 700–1500.

Eligibility Requirements: Applicant must be enrolled or expecting to enroll full- or part-time at a two-year or four-year or technical institution or university; resident of Iowa and studying in Iowa. Available to U.S. citizens. Applicant must have served in the Air Force National Guard or Army National Guard.

Application Requirements: Application. *Deadline:* continuous.

Contact: Todd Brown, Director, Scholarships, Grants, and Loan Forgiveness
Iowa College Student Aid Commission
603 E 12th Street, 5th FL
Des Moines, IA 50319
Phone: 515-725-3405
Fax: 515-725-3401
E-mail: todd.brown@iowa.gov

LOUISIANA NATIONAL GUARD, JOINT TASK FORCE LA

http://www.la.ngb.army.mil/

LOUISIANA NATIONAL GUARD STATE TUITION EXEMPTION PROGRAM

Renewable award for college undergraduates to receive tuition exemption upon satisfactory performance in the Louisiana National Guard. Applicant must attend a state-funded institution in Louisiana, be a resident and registered voter in Louisiana, meet the academic and residency requirements of the university attended, and provide documentation of Louisiana National Guard enlistment. The exemption can be used for up to 15 semesters. Minimum 2.5 GPA required.

Award: Scholarship for use in freshman, sophomore, junior, or senior years; renewable. *Number:* varies. *Amount:* varies.

Eligibility Requirements: Applicant must be enrolled or expecting to enroll full- or part-time at a two-year or four-year or technical institution or university; resident of Louisiana and studying in Louisiana. Applicant must have 2.5 GPA or higher. Available to U.S. citizens. Applicant or parent must meet one or more of the following requirements: Air Force National Guard or Army National Guard experience; retired from active duty; disabled or killed as a result of military service; prisoner of war; or missing in action.

Application Requirements: Application, test scores, transcript. *Deadline:* continuous.

Contact: Jona M. Hughes, Education Services Officer
Louisiana National Guard, Joint Task Force LA
Building 35, Jackson Barracks, JI-PD
New Orleans, LA 70146-0330
Phone: 504-278-8531 Ext. 8304
Fax: 504-278-8025
E-mail: hughesj@la-arng.ngb.army.mil

MINNESOTA DEPARTMENT OF MILITARY AFFAIRS

http://www.minnesotanationalguard.org/

LEADERSHIP, EXCELLENCE AND DEDICATED SERVICE SCHOLARSHIP
• *See page 591*

NORTH CAROLINA NATIONAL GUARD

http://www.nc.ngb.army.mil/

NORTH CAROLINA NATIONAL GUARD TUITION ASSISTANCE PROGRAM

Scholarship for members of the North Carolina Air and Army National Guard who will remain in the service for two years following the period for which assistance is provided. Must reapply for each academic period. For use at approved North Carolina institutions.

Award: Grant for use in freshman, sophomore, junior, senior, or graduate years; not renewable. *Number:* varies. *Amount:* up to $2000.

Eligibility Requirements: Applicant must be enrolled or expecting to enroll full- or part-time at a two-year or four-year or technical institution or university; resident of North Carolina and studying in North Carolina. Available to U.S. citizens. Applicant or parent must meet one or more of the following requirements: Air Force National Guard or Army National Guard experience; retired from active duty; disabled or killed as a result of military service; prisoner of war; or missing in action.

Application Requirements: Application. *Deadline:* varies.

Contact: Anne Gildhouse, Education Services Officer
North Carolina National Guard
Claude T. Bowers Military Center, 4105 Reedy Creek Road
Raleigh, NC 27607-6410
Phone: 919-664-6000
Fax: 919-664-6520
E-mail: anne.gildhouse@nc.ngb.army.mil

OHIO NATIONAL GUARD

http://www.ongsp.org/

OHIO NATIONAL GUARD SCHOLARSHIP PROGRAM

Scholarships are for undergraduate studies at an approved Ohio post-secondary institution. Applicants must enlist for six or three years of Selective Service Reserve Duty in the Ohio National Guard. Scholarship pays 100% instructional and general fees for public institutions and an average of cost of public universities is available for private schools. May reapply up to four years of studies (12 quarters or 8 semesters) for six year enlistment and two years of studies (6 quarters or 4 semesters) for three year enlistment. Deadlines: July 1 (fall), November 1 (winter quarter/spring semester), February 1 (spring quarter), April 1 (summer).

Award: Scholarship for use in freshman, sophomore, junior, or senior years; not renewable. *Number:* up to 3500. *Amount:* up to $4006.

Eligibility Requirements: Applicant must be enrolled or expecting to enroll full- or part-time at a two-year or four-year or technical institution or university; resident of Ohio and studying in Ohio. Available to U.S. citizens. Applicant must have served in the Air Force National Guard or Army National Guard.

Application Requirements: Application. *Deadline:* varies.

Contact: Mrs. Toni E. Davis, Grants Administrator
Ohio National Guard
2825 West Dublin Granville Road, ONGSP
Columbus, OH 43235-2789
Phone: 614-336-7143
Fax: 614-336-7318
E-mail: toni.davis7@us.army.mil

PENNSYLVANIA HIGHER EDUCATION ASSISTANCE AGENCY

http://www.pheaa.org/

POSTSECONDARY EDUCATION GRATUITY PROGRAM

The program offers waiver of tuition and fees for children of Pennsylvania police officers, firefighters, rescue or ambulance squad members, corrections facility employees, or National Guard members who died in line of duty after January 1, 1976.

Award: Grant for use in freshman, sophomore, junior, or senior years; renewable. *Number:* varies. *Amount:* varies.

Eligibility Requirements: Applicant must be age 25 or under; enrolled or expecting to enroll full-time at a two-year or four-year institution or university; resident of Pennsylvania and studying in Pennsylvania. Available to U.S. citizens. Applicant or parent must meet one or more of the following requirements: Air Force National Guard or Army National Guard experience; retired from active duty; disabled or killed as a result of military service; prisoner of war; or missing in action.

Application Requirements: Application. *Deadline:* August 1.

Contact: Keith New, Director of Public Relations
Pennsylvania Higher Education Assistance Agency
1200 North Seventh Street
Harrisburg, PA 17102-1444
Phone: 717-720-2509
E-mail: knew@pheaa.org

STATE STUDENT ASSISTANCE COMMISSION OF INDIANA (SSACI)

http://www.in.gov/ssaci

INDIANA NATIONAL GUARD SUPPLEMENTAL GRANT

The award is a supplement to the Indiana Higher Education Grant program. Applicants must be members of the Indiana National Guard. All Guard paperwork must be completed prior to the start of each semester. The FAFSA must be received by March 10. Award covers certain tuition and fees at select public colleges.

Award: Grant for use in freshman, sophomore, junior, or senior years; not renewable. *Number:* 503–925. *Amount:* $20–$7110.

Eligibility Requirements: Applicant must be enrolled or expecting to enroll full- or part-time at a two-year or four-year institution or university; resident of Indiana and studying in Indiana. Available to U.S. citizens. Applicant or parent must meet one or more of the following requirements: Air Force National Guard or Army National Guard experience; retired from active duty; disabled or killed as a result of military service; prisoner of war; or missing in action.

Application Requirements: Application. *Deadline:* March 10.

Contact: Kathryn Moore, Grants Counselor
State Student Assistance Commission of Indiana (SSACI)
150 West Market Street, Suite 500
Indianapolis, IN 46204-2805
Phone: 317-232-2350
Fax: 317-232-2360
E-mail: kmoore@ssaci.in.gov

TEXAS HIGHER EDUCATION COORDINATING BOARD

http://www.collegefortexans.com/

TEXAS NATIONAL GUARD TUITION ASSISTANCE PROGRAM

Provides exemption from the payment of tuition to certain members of the Texas National Guard, Texas Air Guard or the State Guard. Must be Texas resident and attend school in Texas. Deadline varies.

Award: Scholarship for use in freshman, sophomore, junior, or senior years; renewable. *Number:* varies. *Amount:* varies.

Eligibility Requirements: Applicant must be enrolled or expecting to enroll full- or part-time at a four-year institution or university; resident of Texas and studying in Texas. Available to U.S. citizens. Applicant or parent must meet one or more of the following requirements: Air Force National Guard or Army National Guard experience; retired from active duty; disabled or killed as a result of military service; prisoner of war; or missing in action.

Application Requirements: Application. *Deadline:* varies.

Contact: State Adjutant General's Office
Texas Higher Education Coordinating Board
PO Box 5218
Austin, TX 78763-5218
Phone: 512-465-5515
E-mail: education.office@tx.ngb.army.mil

MILITARY SERVICE: ARMY

1ST INFANTRY DIVISION FOUNDATION

http://www.bigredone.org/

LIEUTENANT GENERAL CLARENCE R. HUEBNER SCHOLARSHIP PROGRAM

Award for undergraduate study for children and grandchildren of veterans of the First Infantry Division, U.S. Army. Essay, letter of acceptance, high school transcript, test scores, letters of recommendation, proof of registration with selective service (if male), and proof of parent's or grandparent's service required. Must be high school senior to apply. Send self-addressed stamped envelope for essay topic and details or send request for application to Fdn1ID@aol.com.

Award: Scholarship for use in freshman, sophomore, junior, or senior years; renewable. *Number:* 5. *Amount:* $10,000.

Eligibility Requirements: Applicant must be high school student and planning to enroll or expecting to enroll full-time at a four-year institution or university. Available to U.S. citizens. Applicant or parent must meet one or more of the following requirements: Army experience; retired from active duty; disabled or killed as a result of military service; prisoner of war; or missing in action.

Application Requirements: Application, essay, references, test scores, transcript, letter of acceptance, proof of parent's or grandparent's service with the First Infantry Division. *Deadline:* June 1.

Contact: Rosemary Wirs, Secretary-Treasurer
1st Infantry Division Foundation
1933 Morris Road
Blue Bell, PA 19422

AMERICAN LEGION AUXILIARY DEPARTMENT OF CALIFORNIA

http://www.calegionaux.org/

AMERICAN LEGION AUXILIARY DEPARTMENT OF CALIFORNIA JUNIOR SCHOLARSHIP
• See page 524

AMERICAN LEGION AUXILIARY DEPARTMENT OF KENTUCKY

http://www.kylegion.org/

AMERICAN LEGION AUXILIARY DEPARTMENT OF KENTUCKY LAURA BLACKBURN MEMORIAL SCHOLARSHIP

Scholarship to the child, grandchild, or great grandchild of a veteran who served in the Armed Forces. Applicant must be a Kentucky resident.

Award: Scholarship for use in freshman year; not renewable. *Number:* 1. *Amount:* $1000.

Eligibility Requirements: Applicant must be high school student; planning to enroll or expecting to enroll full-time at a four-year institution or university and resident of Kentucky. Available to U.S. citizens. Applicant or parent must meet one or more of the following requirements: Army experience; retired from active duty; disabled or killed as a result of military service; prisoner of war; or missing in action.

Application Requirements: Application, financial need analysis, transcript. *Deadline:* March 31.

Contact: Betty Cook, Secretary and Treasurer
American Legion Auxiliary Department of Kentucky
PO Box 189
Greensburg, KY 42743
Phone: 270-932-7533
Fax: 270-932-7672
E-mail: secretarykyala@aol.com

AMERICAN LEGION DEPARTMENT OF NEW JERSEY

http://www.njamericanlegion.org/

LUTERMAN SCHOLARSHIP
• See page 532

STUTZ SCHOLARSHIP
• See page 533

ARMY OFFICERS' WIVES CLUB OF GREATER WASHINGTON AREA

http://www.fmthriftshop.org/

ARMY OFFICERS WIVES CLUB OF THE GREATER WASHINGTON AREA SCHOLARSHIP

Scholarship for high school seniors, college students or children or spouses of U.S. Army personnel. Scholarship awards are based on scholastic merit and community involvement.

Award: Scholarship for use in freshman, sophomore, junior, or senior years; not renewable. *Number:* 1–3. *Amount:* $100–$500.

Eligibility Requirements: Applicant must be age 22 or under and enrolled or expecting to enroll full-time at a four-year institution or university. Available to U.S. citizens. Applicant or parent must meet one or more of the following requirements: Army experience; retired from active duty; disabled or killed as a result of military service; prisoner of war; or missing in action.

Application Requirements: Application, essay, references, self-addressed stamped envelope, transcript, military dependent ID card. *Deadline:* March 31.

Contact: Janis Waller, Scholarship Committee Chair
Army Officers' Wives Club of Greater Washington Area
12025 William & Mary Circle
Woodbridge, VA 22192-1634

DAUGHTERS OF THE CINCINNATI

http://www.daughters1894.org/

DAUGHTERS OF THE CINCINNATI SCHOLARSHIP
• See page 617

DEPARTMENT OF THE ARMY

http://www.goarmy.com/rotc

ARMY ROTC GREEN TO GOLD SCHOLARSHIP PROGRAM FOR TWO-YEAR, THREE-YEAR AND FOUR-YEAR SCHOLARSHIPS, ACTIVE DUTY ENLISTED PERSONNEL

Award for freshman, sophomore, and junior year for use at a four-year institution for Army enlisted personnel. Merit considered. Must also be member of the school's ROTC program. Must pass physical and have completed two years of active duty. Applicant must be at least seventeen years of age by college enrollment and under thirty-one years of age in the year of graduation. Submit recommendations from Commanding Officer and Field Grade Commander. Include DODMERB Physical Forms and DA Form 2A.

Award: Scholarship for use in freshman, sophomore, junior, senior, or graduate years; not renewable. *Number:* 300–400. *Amount:* $10,000–$130,000.

Eligibility Requirements: Applicant must be age 17-30 and enrolled or expecting to enroll full-time at a four-year institution or university.

Applicant must have 2.5 GPA or higher. Available to U.S. citizens. Applicant must have served in the Army.

Application Requirements: Application, essay, photo, references, test scores, transcript, Enlisted Record Brief, DODMERB physical, APFT, GT. *Deadline:* April 1.

Contact: Mr. Joseph FX O'Donnell, Scholarship Management Branch
Department of the Army
U.S. Army Cadet Command, 55 Patch Road, Building 56
Fort Monroe, VA 23651-1052
Phone: 757-788-4559
Fax: 757-788-4643
E-mail: joseph.odonnell@usacc.army.mil

ARMY (ROTC) RESERVE OFFICERS TRAINING CORPS TWO-, THREE-, FOUR-YEAR CAMPUS-BASED SCHOLARSHIPS
• *See page 602*

U.S. ARMY ROTC FOUR-YEAR COLLEGE SCHOLARSHIP

One-time award for students entering college for the first time, or freshmen in a documented five-year degree program. Must join school's ROTC program, pass physical, and submit teacher evaluations. Must be a U.S. citizen and have a qualifying SAT or ACT score. Applicant must be at least seventeen years of age by college enrollment and under thirty-one years of age in the year of graduation. Online application available.

Award: Scholarship for use in freshman or sophomore years; not renewable. *Number:* 1000–2000. *Amount:* $9000–$40,000.

Eligibility Requirements: Applicant must be age 17-26 and enrolled or expecting to enroll full-time at a four-year institution or university. Applicant must have 2.5 GPA or higher. Available to U.S. citizens. Applicant must have served in the Army or Army National Guard.

Application Requirements: Application, essay, interview, test scores, transcript. *Deadline:* January 10.

Contact: Ms. Kathleen Stafford, Supervisor, Human Resources
Specialist
Department of the Army
U.S. Army Cadet Command, 55 Patch Road, Building 56
Fort Monroe, VA 23651-1052
Phone: 502-624-7371
Fax: 757-788-5781
E-mail: kathleen.stafford@usacc.army.mil

U.S. ARMY ROTC FOUR-YEAR HISTORICALLY BLACK COLLEGE/UNIVERSITY SCHOLARSHIP
• *See page 602*

DEPARTMENT OF VETERANS AFFAIRS (VA)

http://www.gibill.va.gov/

MONTGOMERY GI BILL (SELECTED RESERVE)
• *See page 617*

FOUNDATION OF THE 1ST CAVALRY DIVISION ASSOCIATION

http://www.1cda.org/

FOUNDATION OF THE 1ST CAVALRY DIVISION ASSOCIATION (IA DRANG) SCHOLARSHIP
• *See page 617*

INDIANA DEPARTMENT OF VETERANS AFFAIRS

http://www.in.gov/dva

RESIDENT TUITION FOR ACTIVE DUTY MILITARY PERSONNEL
• *See page 617*

SOCIETY OF DAUGHTERS OF THE UNITED STATES ARMY

SOCIETY OF DAUGHTERS OF THE UNITED STATES ARMY SCHOLARSHIPS

Scholarship for daughters or granddaughters of career warrant or commissioned officer in the U.S. who is: on active duty, retired from active duty after 20 years of service, medically retired before 20 years of active service, died while on active duty or died after retiring from active duty. Please contact for application and further eligibility requirements.

Award: Scholarship for use in freshman, sophomore, junior, or senior years; renewable. *Number:* 10–15. *Amount:* $1000.

Eligibility Requirements: Applicant must be enrolled or expecting to enroll full-time at a two-year or four-year or technical institution or university; female and must have an interest in leadership. Applicant must have 3.0 GPA or higher. Available to U.S. citizens. Applicant or parent must meet one or more of the following requirements: Army or Army National Guard experience; retired from active duty; disabled or killed as a result of military service; prisoner of war; or missing in action.

Application Requirements: Application, applicant must enter a contest, essay, resume, references, self-addressed stamped envelope, test scores, transcript, proof of service of qualifying service member (state relationship to member), SASE. *Deadline:* March 1.

Contact: Mary Maroney, Chairperson, Memorial and Scholarship Funds
Society of Daughters of the United States Army
11804 Grey Birch Place
Reston, VA 20191

WISCONSIN DEPARTMENT OF VETERANS AFFAIRS (WDVA)

http://www.dva.state.wi.us/

VETERANS EDUCATION (VETED) REIMBURSEMENT GRANT
• *See page 617*

WOMEN'S ARMY CORPS VETERANS ASSOCIATION

http://www.armywomen.org/

WOMEN'S ARMY CORPS VETERANS' ASSOCIATION SCHOLARSHIP

Scholarship to graduating high school senior showing academic promise. Must be a child, grandchild, niece or nephew of an Army servicewoman. Minimum cumulative GPA of 3.5 required. Applicants must plan to enroll in a degree program as a full-time student at an accredited college or university in the United States.

Award: Scholarship for use in freshman year; not renewable. *Number:* 1. *Amount:* $1500.

Eligibility Requirements: Applicant must be high school student and planning to enroll or expecting to enroll full-time at a four-year institution or university. Applicant must have 3.5 GPA or higher. Available to U.S. citizens. Applicant or parent must meet one or more of the following requirements: Army experience; retired from active duty; disabled or killed as a result of military service; prisoner of war; or missing in action.

Application Requirements: Application, references, transcript, documentation of sponsor's military service. *Deadline:* May 1.

Contact: Eldora Engebretson, Scholarship Committee
Women's Army Corps Veterans Association
PO Box 5577
Fort McClellan, AL 36205-5577
Phone: 623-566-9299
E-mail: info@armywomen.org

MILITARY SERVICE: ARMY NATIONAL GUARD

ALABAMA COMMISSION ON HIGHER EDUCATION

http://www.ache.alabama.gov/

ALABAMA NATIONAL GUARD EDUCATIONAL ASSISTANCE PROGRAM
• *See page 618*

AMERICAN LEGION DEPARTMENT OF TENNESSEE

http://www.tennesseelegion.org/

JROTC SCHOLARSHIP
• *See page 618*

CONNECTICUT ARMY NATIONAL GUARD

http://www.ct.ngb.army.mil/

CONNECTICUT ARMY NATIONAL GUARD 100% TUITION WAIVER
Program is for any active member of the Connecticut Army National Guard in good standing. Must be a resident of Connecticut attending any Connecticut state (public) university, community-technical college or regional vocational-technical school. The total number of available awards is unlimited.

Award: Scholarship for use in freshman, sophomore, junior, or senior years; not renewable. *Number:* varies. *Amount:* $16,000.

Eligibility Requirements: Applicant must be age 17-65; enrolled or expecting to enroll full- or part-time at a two-year or four-year or technical institution or university; resident of Connecticut and studying in Connecticut. Available to U.S. and non-U.S. citizens. Applicant or parent must meet one or more of the following requirements: Army National Guard experience; retired from active duty; disabled or killed as a result of military service; prisoner of war; or missing in action.

Application Requirements: Application. *Deadline:* July 1.

Contact: Capt. Jeremy Lingenfelser, Education Services Officer
Connecticut Army National Guard
360 Broad Street
Hartford, CT 06105-3795
Phone: 860-524-4816
Fax: 860-524-4904
E-mail: education@ct.ngb.army.mil

DELAWARE NATIONAL GUARD

http://www.delawarenationalguard.com/

STATE TUITION ASSISTANCE
• *See page 618*

DEPARTMENT OF THE ARMY

http://www.goarmy.com/rotc

ARMY (ROTC) RESERVE OFFICERS TRAINING CORPS TWO-, THREE-, FOUR-YEAR CAMPUS-BASED SCHOLARSHIPS
• *See page 602*

U.S. ARMY ROTC FOUR-YEAR COLLEGE SCHOLARSHIP
• *See page 623*

U.S. ARMY ROTC FOUR-YEAR HISTORICALLY BLACK COLLEGE/UNIVERSITY SCHOLARSHIP
• *See page 602*

U.S. ARMY ROTC GUARANTEED RESERVE FORCES DUTY (GRFD), (ARNG/USAR) AND DEDICATED ARNG SCHOLARSHIPS
• *See page 602*

DEPARTMENT OF VETERANS AFFAIRS (VA)

http://www.gibill.va.gov/

MONTGOMERY GI BILL (SELECTED RESERVE)
• *See page 617*

RESERVE EDUCATION ASSISTANCE PROGRAM
• *See page 619*

EDUCATION FOUNDATION. INC. NATIONAL GUARD ASSOCIATION OF COLORADO

http://www.ngaco.org/

EDUCATION FOUNDATION, INC. NATIONAL GUARD ASSOCIATION OF COLORADO SCHOLARSHIPS
• *See page 619*

ENLISTED ASSOCIATION OF THE NATIONAL GUARD OF NEW JERSEY

http://www.eang-nj.org/

CSM VINCENT BALDASSARI MEMORIAL SCHOLARSHIP PROGRAM
• *See page 619*

USAA SCHOLARSHIP
• *See page 619*

ILLINOIS STUDENT ASSISTANCE COMMISSION (ISAC)

http://www.collegezone.org/

ILLINOIS NATIONAL GUARD GRANT PROGRAM
• *See page 619*

INDIANA DEPARTMENT OF VETERANS AFFAIRS

http://www.in.gov/dva

NATIONAL GUARD SCHOLARSHIP EXTENSION PROGRAM
• *See page 620*

NATIONAL GUARD TUITION SUPPLEMENT PROGRAM
• *See page 620*

TUITION AND FEE REMISSION FOR CHILDREN AND SPOUSES OF NATIONAL GUARD MEMBERS
• *See page 620*

IOWA COLLEGE STUDENT AID COMMISSION

http://www.iowacollegeaid.gov/

IOWA NATIONAL GUARD EDUCATION ASSISTANCE PROGRAM
• *See page 620*

LOUISIANA NATIONAL GUARD, JOINT TASK FORCE LA

http://www.la.ngb.army.mil/

LOUISIANA NATIONAL GUARD STATE TUITION EXEMPTION PROGRAM
• *See page 620*

MINNESOTA DEPARTMENT OF MILITARY AFFAIRS

http://www.minnesotanationalguard.org/

LEADERSHIP, EXCELLENCE AND DEDICATED SERVICE SCHOLARSHIP
• *See page 591*

NORTH CAROLINA NATIONAL GUARD

http://www.nc.ngb.army.mil/

NORTH CAROLINA NATIONAL GUARD TUITION ASSISTANCE PROGRAM
• *See page 621*

OHIO NATIONAL GUARD

http://www.ongsp.org/

OHIO NATIONAL GUARD SCHOLARSHIP PROGRAM
• *See page 621*

PENNSYLVANIA HIGHER EDUCATION ASSISTANCE AGENCY

http://www.pheaa.org/

POSTSECONDARY EDUCATION GRATUITY PROGRAM
• *See page 621*

SOCIETY OF DAUGHTERS OF THE UNITED STATES ARMY

SOCIETY OF DAUGHTERS OF THE UNITED STATES ARMY SCHOLARSHIPS
• *See page 623*

STATE STUDENT ASSISTANCE COMMISSION OF INDIANA (SSACI)

http://www.in.gov/ssaci

INDIANA NATIONAL GUARD SUPPLEMENTAL GRANT
• *See page 621*

TEXAS HIGHER EDUCATION COORDINATING BOARD

http://www.collegefortexans.com/

TEXAS NATIONAL GUARD TUITION ASSISTANCE PROGRAM
• *See page 621*

MILITARY SERVICE: COAST GUARD

DAUGHTERS OF THE CINCINNATI

http://www.daughters1894.org/

DAUGHTERS OF THE CINCINNATI SCHOLARSHIP
• *See page 617*

DEPARTMENT OF VETERANS AFFAIRS (VA)

http://www.gibill.va.gov/

MONTGOMERY GI BILL (SELECTED RESERVE)
• *See page 617*

FLEET RESERVE ASSOCIATION EDUCATION FOUNDATION

http://www.fra.org/

FLEET RESERVE ASSOCIATION EDUCATION FOUNDATION SCHOLARSHIPS

The FRA Education Foundation makes scholarships available to Navy, Marine Corps and Coast Guard personnel and their families who are U.S. citizens attending accredited colleges and universities as full-time students in the United States. You may apply for FRA Education Foundation Scholarships if 1. The sponsor is a member in good standing of the FRA, currently or at time of death. Applicant must be an FRA member or be the spouse; biological, step, or adoptive child; or biological, step, or adoptive grandchild of the FRA member or 2. The sponsor is an FRA non-member (living) on active duty, Reserve, or retired of the Navy, Marine Corps, or Coast Guard. Applicant must be an FRA non-member or be the spouse; biological or adoptive child; or biological or adoptive grandchild of the FRA non-member.

Award: Scholarship for use in freshman, sophomore, junior, senior, graduate, or postgraduate years; not renewable. *Number:* 1–25. *Amount:* $1000–$5000.

Eligibility Requirements: Applicant must be enrolled or expecting to enroll full-time at a two-year or four-year institution or university. Applicant must have 3.0 GPA or higher. Available to U.S. citizens. Applicant must have served in the Coast Guard, Marine Corps, or Navy.

Application Requirements: Application, essay, financial need analysis, references, test scores, transcript, SAT/ACT. *Deadline:* April 15.

Contact: Scholarship Administrator
Fleet Reserve Association Education Foundation
125 North West Street
Alexandria, VA 22314-2754
Phone: 800-372-1924
E-mail: scholars@fra.org

STANLEY A. DORAN MEMORIAL SCHOLARSHIP
• *See page 542*

LADIES AUXILIARY OF THE FLEET RESERVE ASSOCIATION

http://www.fra.org/

ALLIE MAE ODEN MEMORIAL SCHOLARSHIP
• *See page 548*

LADIES AUXILIARY OF THE FLEET RESERVE ASSOCIATION-NATIONAL PRESIDENT'S SCHOLARSHIP
• *See page 548*

LADIES AUXILIARY OF THE FLEET RESERVE ASSOCIATION SCHOLARSHIP
• *See page 548*

SAM ROSE MEMORIAL SCHOLARSHIP
• *See page 548*

TAILHOOK EDUCATIONAL FOUNDATION

http://www.tailhook.org/

TAILHOOK EDUCATIONAL FOUNDATION SCHOLARSHIP

Applicant must be a high school graduate and the natural, step or adopted son or daughter of a current or former Naval Aviator, Naval Flight Officer or Naval Air-crewman. Individuals or children of individuals serving or having served on board a U.S. Navy Aircraft Carrier in ship's company or the Air Wing also eligible.

Award: Scholarship for use in freshman, sophomore, junior, or senior years; renewable. *Number:* 50. *Amount:* $2000–$10,000.

Eligibility Requirements: Applicant must be enrolled or expecting to enroll full-time at a two-year or four-year institution or university. Applicant must have 3.0 GPA or higher. Available to U.S. citizens. Applicant or parent must meet one or more of the following requirements: Coast Guard, Marine Corps, or Navy experience; retired from active duty; disabled or killed as a result of military service; prisoner of war; or missing in action.

Application Requirements: Application, essay, references, self-addressed stamped envelope, test scores, transcript, proof of eligibility. *Deadline:* March 15.

Contact: Marc Ostertag, Executive Director of Education
Tailhook Educational Foundation
PO Box 26626
San Diego, CA 92196
Phone: 800-269-8267
Fax: 858-578-8839
E-mail: tag@tailhook.net

WISCONSIN DEPARTMENT OF VETERANS AFFAIRS (WDVA)

http://www.dva.state.wi.us/

VETERANS EDUCATION (VETED) REIMBURSEMENT GRANT
• *See page 617*

MILITARY SERVICE: GENERAL

37TH DIVISION VETERANS ASSOCIATION

http://www.37thdva.org/

37TH DIVISION VETERANS ASSOCIATION SCHOLARSHIP

Scholarships are awarded annually to a son or a daughter of a 37th Division veteran who served in World War I, World War II, or the Korean War. Applicants must display financial need and academic excellence.

Award: Scholarship for use in freshman, sophomore, junior, senior, or graduate years; not renewable. *Number:* varies. *Amount:* varies.

Eligibility Requirements: Applicant must be enrolled or expecting to enroll full- or part-time at a two-year or four-year institution or university. Available to U.S. citizens. Applicant or parent must meet one or more of the following requirements: general military experience; retired from active duty; disabled or killed as a result of military service; prisoner of war; or missing in action.

Application Requirements: Application, financial need analysis, references. *Deadline:* April 1.

Contact: Cyril Sedlacko, Secretary and Treasurer
37th Division Veterans Association
35 East Chestnut Street
Suite 425
Columbus, OH 43215
Phone: 614-228-3788
Fax: 614-228-3793
E-mail: ops@37thdva.org

ALABAMA DEPARTMENT OF VETERANS AFFAIRS

http://www.va.alabama.gov/

ALABAMA G.I. DEPENDENTS SCHOLARSHIP PROGRAM

Full scholarship for dependents of Alabama disabled, prisoner-of-war, or missing-in-action veterans. Child or stepchild must initiate training before 26th birthday; age 30 deadline may apply in certain situations. No age deadline for spouses or widows.

Award: Scholarship for use in freshman, sophomore, junior, or senior years; renewable. *Number:* varies. *Amount:* varies.

Eligibility Requirements: Applicant must be age 30 or under; enrolled or expecting to enroll full- or part-time at a four-year institution or university; resident of Alabama and studying in Alabama. Available to U.S. and non-U.S. citizens. Applicant or parent must meet one or more of the following requirements: general military experience; retired from active duty; disabled or killed as a result of military service; prisoner of war; or missing in action.

Application Requirements: Application. *Deadline:* varies.

Contact: Willie E. Moore, Scholarship Administrator
Alabama Department of Veterans Affairs
PO Box 1509
Montgomery, AL 36102-1509
Phone: 334-242-5077
Fax: 334-242-5102
E-mail: wmoore@va.state.al.us

AMERICAN LEGION AUXILIARY DEPARTMENT OF ALABAMA

http://americanlegionalabama.org/

AMERICAN LEGION AUXILIARY DEPARTMENT OF ALABAMA SCHOLARSHIP PROGRAM

Merit-based scholarships for Alabama residents, preferably ages 17 to 25, who are children or grandchildren of veterans of World War I, World War II, Korea, Vietnam, Operation Desert Storm, Beirut, Grenada, or Panama. Submit proof of relationship and service record. Renewable awards of $850 each. Must send self-addressed stamped envelope for application.

Award: Scholarship for use in freshman, sophomore, junior, or senior years; renewable. *Number:* up to 40. *Amount:* $850.

Eligibility Requirements: Applicant must be age 17-25; enrolled or expecting to enroll full-time at a four-year institution or university and resident of Alabama. Applicant must have 3.5 GPA or higher. Available to U.S. citizens. Applicant or parent must meet one or more of the following requirements: general military experience; retired from active duty; disabled or killed as a result of military service; prisoner of war; or missing in action.

Application Requirements: Application, financial need analysis, photo, references, self-addressed stamped envelope, test scores, transcript, birth certificate, service record. *Deadline:* April 1.

Contact: Education and Scholarship Chairperson
American Legion Auxiliary Department of Alabama
120 North Jackson Street
Montgomery, AL 36104-3811
Phone: 334-262-1176
Fax: 334-262-1176
E-mail: americanlegionaux1@juno.com

AMERICAN LEGION AUXILIARY DEPARTMENT OF COLORADO

http://www.coloradolegion.org/

AMERICAN LEGION AUXILIARY DEPARTMENT OF COLORADO DEPARTMENT PRESIDENT'S SCHOLARSHIP FOR JUNIOR MEMBER

Open to children, spouses, grandchildren, and great-grandchildren of veterans, and veterans who served in the Armed Forces during eligibility dates for membership in the American Legion. Applicants must be Colorado residents who have been accepted by an accredited school in Colorado.

Award: Scholarship for use in freshman year; not renewable. *Number:* 1–2. *Amount:* up to $500.

Eligibility Requirements: Applicant must be high school student; planning to enroll or expecting to enroll full- or part-time at a four-year institution or university; resident of Colorado and studying in Colorado. Available to U.S. citizens. Applicant or parent must meet one or more of the following requirements: general military experience; retired from active duty; disabled or killed as a result of military service; prisoner of war; or missing in action.

Application Requirements: Application, essay, references, transcript. *Deadline:* April 15.

Contact: Jean Lennie, Department Secretary and Treasurer
American Legion Auxiliary Department of Colorado
7465 East First Avenue, Suite D
Denver, CO 80230
Phone: 303-367-5388
Fax: 303-367-0688
E-mail: ala@coloradolegion.org

AMERICAN LEGION AUXILIARY DEPARTMENT OF CONNECTICUT

http://www.ct.legion.org/

AMERICAN LEGION AUXILIARY DEPARTMENT OF CONNECTICUT MEMORIAL EDUCATIONAL GRANT

• *See page 525*

AMERICAN LEGION AUXILIARY DEPARTMENT OF CONNECTICUT PAST PRESIDENTS' PARLEY MEMORIAL EDUCATION GRANT

• *See page 525*

AMERICAN LEGION AUXILIARY DEPARTMENT OF FLORIDA

http://www.alafl.org/

AMERICAN LEGION AUXILIARY DEPARTMENT OF FLORIDA DEPARTMENT SCHOLARSHIPS

Scholarship for children of veterans who were honorably discharged. Must be Florida resident attending an institution within Florida for full-time undergraduate study. Minimum 2.5 GPA. Must submit copy of parent's military discharge.

Award: Scholarship for use in freshman, sophomore, junior, or senior years; renewable. *Number:* 16–22. *Amount:* $500–$1000.

Eligibility Requirements: Applicant must be enrolled or expecting to enroll full-time at a two-year or four-year or technical institution or university; resident of Florida and studying in Florida. Applicant must have 2.5 GPA or higher. Available to U.S. citizens. Applicant or parent must meet one or more of the following requirements: general military experience; retired from active duty; disabled or killed as a result of military service; prisoner of war; or missing in action.

Application Requirements: Application, financial need analysis, references, transcript, proof of discharge from armed services. *Deadline:* March 1.

Contact: Robin Briere, Department Secretary and Treasurer
American Legion Auxiliary Department of Florida
PO Box 547917
Orlando, FL 32854-7917
Phone: 407-293-7411
Fax: 407-299-6522
E-mail: contact@alafl.org

AMERICAN LEGION AUXILIARY DEPARTMENT OF FLORIDA MEMORIAL SCHOLARSHIP

• *See page 525*

AMERICAN LEGION AUXILIARY DEPARTMENT OF FLORIDA NATIONAL PRESIDENTS' SCHOLARSHIP

Nonrenewable scholarship for children of veterans who served in the Armed Forces during eligibility dates for American Legion membership. Must be a high school senior and have completed 50 hours of community service.

Award: Scholarship for use in freshman year; not renewable. *Number:* 3–15. *Amount:* $500–$2500.

Eligibility Requirements: Applicant must be high school student and planning to enroll or expecting to enroll full-time at a four-year institution or university. Available to U.S. citizens. Applicant or parent must meet one or more of the following requirements: general military experience; retired from active duty; disabled or killed as a result of military service; prisoner of war; or missing in action.

Application Requirements: Application, essay, references. *Deadline:* March 15.

Contact: Robin Briere, Department Secretary and Treasurer
American Legion Auxiliary Department of Florida
PO Box 547917
Orlando, FL 32854-7917
Phone: 407-293-7411
Fax: 407-299-6522
E-mail: contact@alafl.org

AMERICAN LEGION AUXILIARY DEPARTMENT OF INDIANA

http://www.amlegauxin.org/

AMERICAN LEGION AUXILIARY DEPARTMENT OF INDIANA EDNA M. BURCUS/HOOSIER SCHOOLHOUSE MEMORIAL SCHOLARSHIP

One-time award for child, grandchild, or great-grandchild of veteran who served during American Legion eligibility dates. Must be Indiana resident and graduating high school senior enrolled as full-time undergraduate at an accredited Indiana institution.

Award: Scholarship for use in freshman year; not renewable. *Number:* 3. *Amount:* $500.

Eligibility Requirements: Applicant must be high school student; planning to enroll or expecting to enroll full-time at a two-year or four-year institution or university; resident of Indiana and studying in Indiana. Available to U.S. citizens. Applicant or parent must meet one or more of the following requirements: general military experience; retired from active duty; disabled or killed as a result of military service; prisoner of war; or missing in action.

Application Requirements: Application, essay, financial need analysis, self-addressed stamped envelope. *Deadline:* April 1.

Contact: Judy Otey, Department Secretary and Treasurer
American Legion Auxiliary Department of Indiana
777 North Meridian, Room 107
Indianapolis, IN 46204
Phone: 317-630-1390
Fax: 317-630-1277
E-mail: ala777@sbcglobal.net

AMERICAN LEGION AUXILIARY DEPARTMENT OF IOWA

http://www.ialegion.org/ala

AMERICAN LEGION AUXILIARY DEPARTMENT OF IOWA CHILDREN OF VETERANS MERIT AWARD

One-time award available to a high school senior, child of a veteran who served in the armed forces during eligibility dates for American Legion membership. Must be U.S. citizen and Iowa resident enrolled at an Iowa institution.

Award: Scholarship for use in freshman year; not renewable. *Number:* 10. *Amount:* $300.

Eligibility Requirements: Applicant must be high school student; planning to enroll or expecting to enroll full- or part-time at a four-year institution or university; resident of Iowa and studying in Iowa. Available to U.S. citizens. Applicant or parent must meet one or more of the following requirements: general military experience; retired from active duty; disabled or killed as a result of military service; prisoner of war; or missing in action.

Application Requirements: Application, essay, financial need analysis, photo, references, self-addressed stamped envelope, test scores, transcript. *Deadline:* June 1.

Contact: Marlene Valentine, Secretary and Treasurer
American Legion Auxiliary Department of Iowa
720 Lyon Street
Des Moines, IA 50309
Phone: 515-282-7987
Fax: 515-282-7583
E-mail: alasectreas@ialegion.org

AMERICAN LEGION AUXILIARY DEPARTMENT OF KENTUCKY

http://www.kylegion.org/

AMERICAN LEGION AUXILIARY DEPARTMENT OF KENTUCKY MARY BARRETT MARSHALL SCHOLARSHIP

Scholarship to the daughter or grand daughter of a veteran in The American Legion. Applicant must attend a Kentucky college, and demonstrate financial need.

Award: Scholarship for use in freshman year; not renewable. *Number:* 1. *Amount:* $1000.

Eligibility Requirements: Applicant must be high school student; planning to enroll or expecting to enroll full-time at a four-year institution or university; female and studying in Kentucky. Available to U.S. citizens. Applicant or parent must meet one or more of the following requirements: general military experience; retired from active duty; disabled or killed as a result of military service; prisoner of war; or missing in action.

Application Requirements: Application, financial need analysis, transcript. *Deadline:* April 1.

Contact: Betty Cook, Secretary and Treasurer
American Legion Auxiliary Department of Kentucky
PO Box 189
Greensburg, KY 42743
Phone: 270-932-7533
Fax: 270-932-7672
E-mail: secretarykyala@aol.com

AMERICAN LEGION AUXILIARY DEPARTMENT OF MAINE

http://www.mainelegion.org/

AMERICAN LEGION AUXILIARY DEPARTMENT OF MAINE DANIEL E. LAMBERT MEMORIAL SCHOLARSHIP

Scholarships to assist young men and women in continuing their education beyond high school. Must demonstrate financial need, must be a resident of the State of Maine, U.S. citizen, and parent must be a veteran.

Award: Scholarship for use in freshman year; not renewable. *Number:* up to 2. *Amount:* $1000.

Eligibility Requirements: Applicant must be high school student; planning to enroll or expecting to enroll full-time at a four-year institution or university and resident of Maine. Available to U.S. citizens. Applicant or parent must meet one or more of the following requirements: general military experience; retired from active duty; disabled or killed as a result of military service; prisoner of war; or missing in action.

Application Requirements: Application, financial need analysis. *Deadline:* May 1.

Contact: Mary Wells, Education Chairman
American Legion Auxiliary Department of Maine
21 Limerock Street
PO Box 434
Rockland, ME 04841
Phone: 207-532-6007
E-mail: aladeptsecme@verizon.net

AMERICAN LEGION AUXILIARY DEPARTMENT OF MAINE NATIONAL PRESIDENT'S SCHOLARSHIP
• *See page 582*

AMERICAN LEGION AUXILIARY DEPARTMENT OF MARYLAND

http://www.alamd.org/

AMERICAN LEGION AUXILIARY DEPARTMENT OF MARYLAND CHILDREN AND YOUTH SCHOLARSHIPS

One scholarship of $2000 for undergraduate student enrolled in full-time study at an accredited college or university. Must be U.S. citizen, Maryland resident, and child of a military veteran.

Award: Scholarship for use in freshman, sophomore, junior, or senior years; renewable. *Number:* 1. *Amount:* $2000.

Eligibility Requirements: Applicant must be enrolled or expecting to enroll full-time at a four-year institution or university and resident of Maryland. Available to U.S. citizens. Applicant or parent must meet one or more of the following requirements: general military experience; retired from active duty; disabled or killed as a result of military service; prisoner of war; or missing in action.

Application Requirements: Application, financial need analysis, references, transcript. *Deadline:* May 1.

Contact: Meredith Beeg, President
American Legion Auxiliary Department of Maryland
1589 Sulphur Spring Road, Suite 105
Baltimore, MD 21227
Phone: 410-242-9519
E-mail: hq@alamd.org

AMERICAN LEGION AUXILIARY DEPARTMENT OF MASSACHUSETTS

http://www.masslegion-aux.org/

AMERICAN LEGION AUXILIARY DEPARTMENT OF MASSACHUSETTS DEPARTMENT PRESIDENT'S SCHOLARSHIP
• *See page 582*

AMERICAN LEGION AUXILIARY DEPARTMENT OF MASSACHUSETTS PAST PRESIDENTS' PARLEY SCHOLARSHIP

One-time awards of $200 to $750 for residents of Massachusetts who are children of living or deceased veterans. Must be between the ages of 16 to 22 years and enrolled full-time at a Massachusetts institution.

Award: Scholarship for use in freshman, sophomore, junior, or senior years; not renewable. *Number:* 1. *Amount:* $200–$750.

Eligibility Requirements: Applicant must be age 16-22; enrolled or expecting to enroll full-time at a two-year or four-year institution or university; resident of Massachusetts and studying in Massachusetts. Available to U.S. citizens. Applicant or parent must meet one or more of the following requirements: general military experience; retired from active duty; disabled or killed as a result of military service; prisoner of war; or missing in action.

Application Requirements: Application. *Deadline:* March 1.

Contact: Beverly Monaco, Secretary and Treasurer
American Legion Auxiliary Department of Massachusetts
546-2 State House
Boston, MA 02133-1044
Phone: 617-727-2958
Fax: 617-727-0741

AMERICAN LEGION AUXILIARY DEPARTMENT OF MICHIGAN

http://www.michalaux.org/

AMERICAN LEGION AUXILIARY DEPARTMENT OF MICHIGAN MEMORIAL SCHOLARSHIP

Scholarship for daughter, granddaughter, and great-granddaughter of any honorably discharged or deceased veteran of U.S. wars or conflicts. Must be Michigan resident for minimum of one year, female between 16 and 21 years, and attend college in Michigan. Must include copy of military discharge and copy of parent or guardian's IRS 1040 form.

Award: Scholarship for use in freshman or sophomore years; not renewable. *Number:* 10–20. *Amount:* $500.

Eligibility Requirements: Applicant must be age 16-21; enrolled or expecting to enroll full-time at a two-year or four-year or technical institution or university; female; resident of Michigan and studying in Michigan. Available to U.S. citizens. Applicant must have general military experience.

Application Requirements: Application, financial need analysis, references, transcript, discharge papers. *Deadline:* March 15.

Contact: LeAnn Knott, Scholarship Coordinator
American Legion Auxiliary Department of Michigan
212 North Verlinden Avenue, Suite B
Lansing, MI 48915
Phone: 517-267-8809 Ext. 22
Fax: 517-371-3698
E-mail: lknott@michalaux.org

AMERICAN LEGION AUXILIARY DEPARTMENT OF MICHIGAN SCHOLARSHIP FOR NON-TRADITIONAL STUDENT

Applicant must be a dependent of a veteran. Must be one of the following: nontraditional student returning to classroom after some period of time in which their education was interrupted, student over the age of 22 attending college for the first time to pursue a degree, or student over the age of 22 attending a trade or vocational school. Applicants must be Michigan residents only and attend Michigan institution. Judging based on: need-25 points, character/leadership-25 points, scholastic standing-25 points, initiative/goal-25 points.

Award: Scholarship for use in freshman, sophomore, junior, or senior years; renewable. *Number:* 1–1. *Amount:* $500.

Eligibility Requirements: Applicant must be age 23-99; enrolled or expecting to enroll full- or part-time at a two-year or four-year or technical institution or university; resident of Michigan and studying in Michigan. Available to U.S. citizens. Applicant must have general military experience.

Application Requirements: Application, financial need analysis, transcript, copy of veteran's discharge papers. *Deadline:* March 15.

Contact: LeAnn Knott, Scholarship Coordinator
American Legion Auxiliary Department of Michigan
212 North Verlinden Avenue, Suite B
Lansing, MI 48915
Phone: 517-267-8809 Ext. 22
Fax: 517-371-3698
E-mail: lknott@michalaux.org

AMERICAN LEGION AUXILIARY NATIONAL PRESIDENT'S SCHOLARSHIP

One-time scholarship for son or daughter of veterans, who were in armed forces during the eligibility dates for American Legion membership. Must be high school senior. Only one candidate per Auxiliary Unit. Applicant must complete 50 hours of volunteer service in the community. Must submit essay of no more than 1000 words on a specified topic.

Award: Scholarship for use in freshman year; not renewable. *Number:* 10–15. *Amount:* $1500–$2500.

Eligibility Requirements: Applicant must be high school student and planning to enroll or expecting to enroll full-time at a two-year or four-year institution or university. Available to U.S. citizens. Applicant must have general military experience.

Application Requirements: Application, applicant must enter a contest, essay, financial need analysis, references, test scores, transcript, original article (1000-word maximum). *Deadline:* March 1.

Contact: LeAnn Knott, Scholarship Coordinator
American Legion Auxiliary Department of Michigan
212 North Verlinden Avenue, Suite B
Lansing, MI 48915
Phone: 517-267-8809 Ext. 22
Fax: 517-371-3698
E-mail: lknott@michalaux.org

AMERICAN LEGION AUXILIARY SPIRIT OF YOUTH SCHOLARSHIP

Scholarship valued at $1000 per year for four years is available to one Junior American Legion Auxiliary member in each division. The applicant must have held membership in the American Legion Auxiliary for the past three years, must hold a current membership card, and must continue to maintain their membership throughout the four-year scholarship period.

Award: Scholarship for use in freshman, sophomore, junior, or senior years; renewable. *Number:* 5–5. *Amount:* $1000–$4000.

Eligibility Requirements: Applicant must be high school student; planning to enroll or expecting to enroll full-time at a two-year or four-year or technical institution or university and female. Applicant must have 3.0 GPA or higher. Available to U.S. citizens. Applicant must have general military experience.

Application Requirements: Application, applicant must enter a contest, essay, financial need analysis, references, transcript, original article (1000-word maximum, typed and double-spaced). *Deadline:* March 1.

Contact: LeAnn Knott, Scholarship Coordinator
American Legion Auxiliary Department of Michigan
212 North Verlinden Avenue, Suite B
Lansing, MI 48915
Phone: 517-267-8809 Ext. 22
Fax: 517-371-3698
E-mail: lknott@michalaux.org

AMERICAN LEGION AUXILIARY DEPARTMENT OF MINNESOTA

http://www.mnlegion.org/

AMERICAN LEGION AUXILIARY DEPARTMENT OF MINNESOTA SCHOLARSHIPS

Seven $1000 awards for the sons, daughters, grandsons, or granddaughters of veterans who served in the Armed Forces during specific eligibility dates. Must be a Minnesota resident, a high school senior or graduate, in need of financial assistance, of good character, having a good scholastic record and at least a C average. Must be planning to attend a Minnesota post secondary institution.

Award: Scholarship for use in freshman, sophomore, junior, or senior years; not renewable. *Number:* up to 7. *Amount:* $1000.

Eligibility Requirements: Applicant must be enrolled or expecting to enroll full-time at a two-year or four-year or technical institution or university; resident of Minnesota and studying in Minnesota. Available to U.S. citizens. Applicant or parent must meet one or more of the following requirements: general military experience; retired from active duty; disabled or killed as a result of military service; prisoner of war; or missing in action.

Application Requirements: Application, essay, financial need analysis, references, transcript. *Deadline:* March 15.

Contact: Eleanor Johnson, Executive Secretary
American Legion Auxiliary Department of Minnesota
State Veterans Service Building, 20 West 12th Street, Room 314
St. Paul, MN 55155
Phone: 651-224-7634
Fax: 651-224-5243

AMERICAN LEGION AUXILIARY DEPARTMENT OF MISSOURI

http://www.missourilegion.org/

AMERICAN LEGION AUXILIARY DEPARTMENT OF MISSOURI LELA MURPHY SCHOLARSHIP
• *See page 526*

AMERICAN LEGION AUXILIARY DEPARTMENT OF MISSOURI NATIONAL PRESIDENT'S SCHOLARSHIP
• *See page 526*

AMERICAN LEGION AUXILIARY DEPARTMENT OF NEBRASKA

http://www.nebraskalegionaux.net/

AMERICAN LEGION AUXILIARY DEPARTMENT OF NEBRASKA RUBY PAUL CAMPAIGN FUND SCHOLARSHIP
• *See page 526*

AMERICAN LEGION AUXILIARY DEPARTMENT OF NORTH DAKOTA

http://www.ndlegion.org/

AMERICAN LEGION AUXILIARY DEPARTMENT OF NORTH DAKOTA NATIONAL PRESIDENT'S SCHOLARSHIP
• *See page 582*

AMERICAN LEGION AUXILIARY DEPARTMENT OF OHIO

http://www.alaohio.org/

AMERICAN LEGION AUXILIARY DEPARTMENT OF OHIO CONTINUING EDUCATION FUND

One-time award for Ohio residents who are the children or grandchildren of veterans, living or deceased, honorably discharged during eligibility dates for American Legion membership. Awards are for undergraduate use, based on need. Freshmen not eligible. Application must be signed by a unit representative.

Award: Scholarship for use in sophomore, junior, or senior years; not renewable. *Number:* 15. *Amount:* $200.

Eligibility Requirements: Applicant must be enrolled or expecting to enroll full-time at a two-year or four-year institution or university and resident of Ohio. Available to U.S. citizens. Applicant or parent must meet one or more of the following requirements: general military experience; retired from active duty; disabled or killed as a result of military service; prisoner of war; or missing in action.

Application Requirements: Application, financial need analysis, transcript. *Deadline:* November 1.

Contact: Heather Amspaugh, Scholarship Coordinator
American Legion Auxiliary Department of Ohio
PO Box 2760
Zanesville, OH 43702-2760
Phone: 740-452-8245
Fax: 740-452-2620
E-mail: hamspaugh@rrohio.com

AMERICAN LEGION AUXILIARY DEPARTMENT OF OHIO DEPARTMENT PRESIDENT'S SCHOLARSHIP

Scholarship for children or grandchildren of veterans who served in Armed Forces during eligibility dates for American Legion membership. Must be high school senior, ages 16 to 18, Ohio resident, and U.S. citizen. Award for full-time undergraduate study. One-time award of $1000 to $1500.

Award: Scholarship for use in freshman year; not renewable. *Number:* 2. *Amount:* $1000–$1500.

Eligibility Requirements: Applicant must be high school student; age 16-18; planning to enroll or expecting to enroll full-time at a two-year or four-year institution or university and resident of Ohio. Available to U.S. citizens. Applicant or parent must meet one or more of the following requirements: general military experience; retired from active duty; disabled or killed as a result of military service; prisoner of war; or missing in action.

Application Requirements: Application, essay, financial need analysis, references, transcript. *Deadline:* March 1.

Contact: Department Scholarship Coordinator
American Legion Auxiliary Department of Ohio
PO Box 2760
Zanesville, OH 43702-2760
Phone: 740-452-8245
Fax: 740-452-2620

AMERICAN LEGION AUXILIARY DEPARTMENT OF OREGON

http://www.alaoregon.org/

AMERICAN LEGION AUXILIARY DEPARTMENT OF OREGON DEPARTMENT GRANTS

One-time award for educational use in the state of Oregon. Must be a resident of Oregon who is the child or widow of a veteran or the wife of a disabled veteran.

Award: Grant for use in freshman, sophomore, junior, or senior years; not renewable. *Number:* 2. *Amount:* $1000.

Eligibility Requirements: Applicant must be enrolled or expecting to enroll full- or part-time at a two-year or four-year or technical institution or university and resident of Oregon. Available to U.S. citizens. Applicant or parent must meet one or more of the following requirements: general military experience; retired from active duty; disabled or killed as a result of military service; prisoner of war; or missing in action.

Application Requirements: Application, essay, financial need analysis, interview, references, test scores, transcript. *Deadline:* March 10.

Contact: Virginia Biddle, Secretary/Treasurer
American Legion Auxiliary Department of Oregon
PO Box 1730
Wilsonville, OR 97070
Phone: 503-682-3162
Fax: 503-685-5008
E-mail: alaor@pcez.com

AMERICAN LEGION AUXILIARY DEPARTMENT OF OREGON NATIONAL PRESIDENT'S SCHOLARSHIP

One-time award for children of veterans who served in the Armed Forces during eligibility dates for American Legion membership. Must be high school senior and Oregon resident. Must be entered by a local American Legion auxiliary unit. Three scholarships of varying amounts.

Award: Scholarship for use in freshman year; not renewable. *Number:* 3. *Amount:* $1000–$2500.

Eligibility Requirements: Applicant must be high school student; planning to enroll or expecting to enroll full-time at a four-year institution or university and resident of Oregon. Available to U.S. citizens. Applicant or parent must meet one or more of the following requirements: general military experience; retired from active duty; disabled or killed as a result of military service; prisoner of war; or missing in action.

Application Requirements: Application, essay, financial need analysis, interview, references, transcript. *Deadline:* March 1.

Contact: Virginia Biddle, Secretary/Treasurer
American Legion Auxiliary Department of Oregon
PO Box 1730
Wilsonville, OR 97070
Phone: 503-682-3162
Fax: 503-685-5008
E-mail: alaor@pcez.com

AMERICAN LEGION AUXILIARY DEPARTMENT OF OREGON SPIRIT OF YOUTH SCHOLARSHIP
• *See page 526*

AMERICAN LEGION AUXILIARY DEPARTMENT OF SOUTH DAKOTA

http://www.sdlegion.org/

AMERICAN LEGION AUXILIARY DEPARTMENT OF SOUTH DAKOTA COLLEGE SCHOLARSHIPS
• *See page 526*

AMERICAN LEGION AUXILIARY DEPARTMENT OF SOUTH DAKOTA SENIOR SCHOLARSHIP
• *See page 527*

AMERICAN LEGION AUXILIARY DEPARTMENT OF SOUTH DAKOTA THELMA FOSTER SCHOLARSHIP FOR SENIOR AUXILIARY MEMBERS
• *See page 527*

AMERICAN LEGION AUXILIARY DEPARTMENT OF SOUTH DAKOTA THELMA FOSTER SCHOLARSHIPS FOR JUNIOR AUXILIARY MEMBERS
• *See page 527*

AMERICAN LEGION AUXILIARY DEPARTMENT OF SOUTH DAKOTA VOCATIONAL SCHOLARSHIP
• *See page 527*

AMERICAN LEGION AUXILIARY DEPARTMENT OF TENNESSEE

http://www.legion-aux.org/

AMERICAN LEGION AUXILIARY DEPARTMENT OF TENNESSEE VARA GRAY SCHOLARSHIP-GENERAL

One-time award for high school senior who is the child of a veteran (Verification of veteran eligibility is required.) Must be Tennessee resident and single. Must have completed 50 hours of voluntary community service. Award must be used within one year. A written essay is required covering a topic determined by the Auxiliary yearly.

Award: Scholarship for use in freshman year; not renewable. *Number:* 3. *Amount:* $500.

Eligibility Requirements: Applicant must be high school student; planning to enroll or expecting to enroll full-time at a two-year or four-year institution or university; single and resident of Tennessee. Available to U.S. citizens. Applicant or parent must meet one or more of the following requirements: general military experience; retired from active duty; disabled or killed as a result of military service; prisoner of war; or missing in action.

Application Requirements: Application, essay, financial need analysis, references, test scores, transcript. *Deadline:* March 15.

Contact: Mrs. Sue Milliken, Department Secretary and Treasurer
American Legion Auxiliary Department of Tennessee
104 Point East Drive
Nashville, TN 37216
Phone: 615-226-8648
Fax: 615-226-8649
E-mail: alatn@bellsouth.net

AMERICAN LEGION AUXILIARY DEPARTMENT OF TEXAS

http://www.alatexas.org/

AMERICAN LEGION AUXILIARY DEPARTMENT OF TEXAS GENERAL EDUCATION SCHOLARSHIP

Scholarships available for Texas residents. Must be a child of a veteran who served in the Armed Forces during eligibility dates. Some additional criteria used for selection are recommendations, academics, and finances.

Award: Scholarship for use in freshman, sophomore, junior, or senior years; not renewable. *Number:* 1–10. *Amount:* $500.

Eligibility Requirements: Applicant must be enrolled or expecting to enroll full-time at a two-year or four-year or technical institution or university and resident of Texas. Available to U.S. citizens. Applicant must have general military experience.

Application Requirements: Application, financial need analysis, resume, references, transcript, letter stating qualifications and intentions. *Deadline:* June 1.

Contact: Paula Raney, State Secretary
American Legion Auxiliary Department of Texas
PO Box 140407
Austin, TX 78714
Phone: 512-476-7278
Fax: 512-482-8391
E-mail: alatexas@txlegion.org

AMERICAN LEGION AUXILIARY DEPARTMENT OF UTAH

http://www.legion-aux.org/

AMERICAN LEGION AUXILIARY DEPARTMENT OF UTAH NATIONAL PRESIDENT'S SCHOLARSHIP
• *See page 527*

AMERICAN LEGION AUXILIARY DEPARTMENT OF WASHINGTON

http://www.walegion-aux.org/

AMERICAN LEGION AUXILIARY DEPARTMENT OF WASHINGTON GIFT SCHOLARSHIPS

Scholarship for a child of an incapacitated or deceased veteran. Award is for high school seniors and should be used within twelve months of receipt. Submit statement of military service of veteran parent through which applicant is eligible. One-time award of $400 for residents of Washington.

Award: Scholarship for use in freshman year; not renewable. *Number:* 2. *Amount:* $400.

Eligibility Requirements: Applicant must be high school student; age 20 or under; planning to enroll or expecting to enroll full- or part-time at a two-year or four-year or technical institution or university and resident of Washington. Available to U.S. citizens. Applicant or parent must meet one or more of the following requirements: general military experience; retired from active duty; disabled or killed as a result of military service; prisoner of war; or missing in action.

Application Requirements: Application, essay, references, transcript. *Deadline:* March 1.

Contact: Nicole Ross, Department Secretary
American Legion Auxiliary Department of Washington
3600 Ruddell Road
Lacey, WA 98503
Phone: 360-456-5995
Fax: 360-491-7442
E-mail: secretary@walegion-aux.org

AMERICAN LEGION AUXILIARY DEPARTMENT OF WISCONSIN

http://www.amlegionauxwi.org/

AMERICAN LEGION AUXILIARY DEPARTMENT OF WISCONSIN DELLA VAN DEUREN MEMORIAL SCHOLARSHIP
• *See page 527*

AMERICAN LEGION AUXILIARY DEPARTMENT OF WISCONSIN H.S. AND ANGELINE LEWIS SCHOLARSHIPS
• *See page 528*

AMERICAN LEGION AUXILIARY DEPARTMENT OF WISCONSIN MERIT AND MEMORIAL SCHOLARSHIPS
• *See page 528*

AMERICAN LEGION AUXILIARY DEPARTMENT OF WISCONSIN PAST PRESIDENTS' PARLEY HEALTH CAREER SCHOLARSHIPS
• *See page 528*

AMERICAN LEGION AUXILIARY DEPARTMENT OF WISCONSIN PRESIDENT'S SCHOLARSHIPS
• *See page 528*

AMERICAN LEGION AUXILIARY NATIONAL HEADQUARTERS

http://www.legion-aux.org/

AMERICAN LEGION AUXILIARY NATIONAL PRESIDENT'S SCHOLARSHIPS

One-time scholarship for high school children of veterans who served in the Armed Forces during the eligibility dates for The American Legion. The applicant must complete 50 hours of community service during his/her high school years to be eligible for one of these scholarships.

Award: Scholarship for use in freshman year; not renewable. *Number:* 15. *Amount:* $1000–$2500.

Eligibility Requirements: Applicant must be high school student and planning to enroll or expecting to enroll full-time at a four-year institution or university. Available to U.S. citizens. Applicant or parent must meet one or more of the following requirements: general military experience; retired from active duty; disabled or killed as a result of military service; prisoner of war; or missing in action.

Application Requirements: Application, essay, references, self-addressed stamped envelope, test scores, transcript. *Deadline:* March 1.

Contact: Maria Potts, Program Coordinator
American Legion Auxiliary National Headquarters
8945 North Meridian Street
Indianapolis, IN 46260
Phone: 317-955-3845
E-mail: mpotts@legion-aux.org

AMERICAN LEGION AUXILIARY NON-TRADITIONAL STUDENTS SCHOLARSHIPS
• *See page 529*

AMERICAN LEGION DEPARTMENT OF ARKANSAS

http://www.arklegion.homestead.com/

AMERICAN LEGION DEPARTMENT OF ARKANSAS COUDRET SCHOLARSHIP AWARD
• *See page 529*

AMERICAN LEGION DEPARTMENT OF IDAHO

http://www.idlegion.home.mindspring.com/

AMERICAN LEGION DEPARTMENT OF IDAHO SCHOLARSHIP
• *See page 529*

AMERICAN LEGION DEPARTMENT OF KANSAS

http://www.ksamlegion.org/

ALBERT M. LAPPIN SCHOLARSHIP
• *See page 530*

CHARLES W. AND ANNETTE HILL SCHOLARSHIP
• *See page 530*

HUGH A. SMITH SCHOLARSHIP FUND
• *See page 531*

ROSEDALE POST 346 SCHOLARSHIP
• *See page 531*

TED AND NORA ANDERSON SCHOLARSHIPS
• *See page 531*

AMERICAN LEGION DEPARTMENT OF MAINE

http://www.mainelegion.org/

AMERICAN LEGION DEPARTMENT OF MAINE CHILDREN AND YOUTH SCHOLARSHIP

Scholarships available to high school seniors, college students, and veterans who are residents of Maine. Must be in upper half of high school class. One-time award of $500.

Award: Scholarship for use in freshman, sophomore, junior, or senior years; not renewable. *Number:* 7. *Amount:* $500.

Eligibility Requirements: Applicant must be enrolled or expecting to enroll full-time at a two-year or four-year or technical institution or university and resident of Maine. Available to U.S. citizens. Applicant or parent must meet one or more of the following requirements: general military experience; retired from active duty; disabled or killed as a result of military service; prisoner of war; or missing in action.

Application Requirements: Application, essay, financial need analysis, references, transcript. *Deadline:* May 1.

Contact: *Phone:* 207-873-3229
Fax: 207-872-0501

DANIEL E. LAMBERT MEMORIAL SCHOLARSHIP

One-time award for undergraduate and graduate student whose parents are veterans. Award is based on financial need and good character. Must be U.S. citizen. Applicant must show evidence of being enrolled, or attending accredited college or vocational technical school. Scholarship value is from $500 to $1000.

Award: Scholarship for use in freshman, sophomore, junior, or senior years; not renewable. *Number:* 1–2. *Amount:* $500–$1000.

Eligibility Requirements: Applicant must be enrolled or expecting to enroll full-time at a two-year or four-year or technical institution or university and resident of Maine. Available to U.S. citizens. Applicant or parent must meet one or more of the following requirements: general military experience; retired from active duty; disabled or killed as a result of military service; prisoner of war; or missing in action.

Application Requirements: Application, references. *Deadline:* May 1.

Contact: Mr. Lloyd Woods, Department Adjutant
American Legion Department of Maine
21 College Avenue
PO Box 900
Waterville, ME 04903-0900
Phone: 207-873-3229
Fax: 207-872-0501
E-mail: legionme@mainelegion.org

JAMES V. DAY SCHOLARSHIP
• *See page 531*

AMERICAN LEGION DEPARTMENT OF MARYLAND

http://www.mdlegion.org/

AMERICAN LEGION DEPARTMENT OF MARYLAND GENERAL SCHOLARSHIP FUND

Nonrenewable scholarship for veterans or children of veterans who served in the Armed Forces during dates of eligibility for American Legion membership. Merit-based award. Application available on web site http://mdlegion.org.

Award: Scholarship for use in freshman, sophomore, junior, or senior years; not renewable. *Number:* up to 3. *Amount:* up to $500.

Eligibility Requirements: Applicant must be enrolled or expecting to enroll full-time at a four-year institution or university and resident of Maryland. Available to U.S. citizens. Applicant or parent must meet one or more of the following requirements: general military experience;

retired from active duty; disabled or killed as a result of military service; prisoner of war; or missing in action.

Application Requirements: Application, essay, financial need analysis, transcript. *Deadline:* April 1.

Contact: Thomas Davis, Department Adjutant
American Legion Department of Maryland
101 North Gay, Room E
Baltimore, MD 21202
Phone: 410-752-1405
Fax: 410-752-3822
E-mail: tom@mdlegion.org

AMERICAN LEGION DEPARTMENT OF MICHIGAN

http://www.michiganlegion.org/

GUY M. WILSON SCHOLARSHIPS

Scholarship for undergraduate use at a Michigan college. Must be resident of Michigan and the son, daughter, grandchild, or great grandchild of a veteran, living or deceased. Must submit copy of veteran's honorable discharge. Must have minimum 2.5 GPA. Total number of awards given vary each year depending upon the number of applications received. Applicants have to refer the web site for the deadline.

Award: Scholarship for use in freshman year; not renewable. *Number:* 11. *Amount:* $500.

Eligibility Requirements: Applicant must be high school student; planning to enroll or expecting to enroll full- or part-time at a two-year or four-year institution or university; resident of Michigan and studying in Michigan. Applicant must have 2.5 GPA or higher. Available to U.S. citizens. Applicant or parent must meet one or more of the following requirements: general military experience; retired from active duty; disabled or killed as a result of military service; prisoner of war; or missing in action.

Application Requirements: Application, essay, financial need analysis, test scores, transcript.

Contact: Deanna Clark, Department Administrative Assistant for
Programs
American Legion Department of Michigan
212 North Verlinden Avenue, Suite A
Lansing, MI 48915
Phone: 517-371-4720 Ext. 11
Fax: 517-371-2401
E-mail: programs@michiganlegion.org

WILLIAM D. AND JEWELL W. BREWER SCHOLARSHIP TRUSTS

One-time award for residents of Michigan who are the son, daughter, grandchild, or great grandchild of veterans, living or deceased. Must submit copy of veteran's honorable discharge. Several scholarships of $500 each. Must have minimum 2.5 GPA. Scholarship can be applied to any college or university within the United States.

Award: Scholarship for use in freshman, sophomore, junior, or senior years; not renewable. *Number:* 4. *Amount:* $500.

Eligibility Requirements: Applicant must be enrolled or expecting to enroll full- or part-time at a two-year or four-year institution or university and resident of Michigan. Applicant must have 2.5 GPA or higher. Available to U.S. citizens. Applicant or parent must meet one or more of the following requirements: general military experience; retired from active duty; disabled or killed as a result of military service; prisoner of war; or missing in action.

Application Requirements: Application, essay, financial need analysis, test scores, transcript.

Contact: Deanna Clark, Department Administrative Assistant for
Programs
American Legion Department of Michigan
212 North Verlinden Avenue, Suite A
Lansing, MI 48915
Phone: 517-371-4720 Ext. 11
Fax: 517-371-2401
E-mail: programs@michiganlegion.org

AMERICAN LEGION DEPARTMENT OF MINNESOTA

http://www.mnlegion.org/

AMERICAN LEGION DEPARTMENT OF MINNESOTA MEMORIAL SCHOLARSHIP
• *See page 531*

MINNESOTA LEGIONNAIRES INSURANCE TRUST SCHOLARSHIP
• *See page 532*

AMERICAN LEGION DEPARTMENT OF MISSOURI

http://www.missourilegion.org/

CHARLES L. BACON MEMORIAL SCHOLARSHIP
• *See page 532*

LILLIE LOIS FORD SCHOLARSHIP FUND

Two awards of $1000 each are given each year to one boy and one girl. Applicant must have attended a full session of Missouri Boys/Girls State or Missouri Cadet Patrol Academy. Must be a Missouri resident below age 21, attending an accredited college/university as a full-time student. Must be an unmarried descendant of a veteran having served at least 90 days on active duty in the Army, Air Force, Navy, Marine Corps or Coast Guard of the United States.

Award: Scholarship for use in freshman year; not renewable. *Number:* 2. *Amount:* $1000.

Eligibility Requirements: Applicant must be high school student; age 21 or under; planning to enroll or expecting to enroll full-time at a two-year or four-year institution or university; single and resident of Missouri. Available to U.S. citizens. Applicant or parent must meet one or more of the following requirements: general military experience; retired from active duty; disabled or killed as a result of military service; prisoner of war; or missing in action.

Application Requirements: Application, financial need analysis, test scores, copy of the veteran's discharge certificate. *Deadline:* April 20.

Contact: John Doane, Chairman, Education and Scholarship Committee
American Legion Department of Missouri
PO Box 179
Jefferson City, MO 65102-0179
Phone: 417-924-8186

AMERICAN LEGION DEPARTMENT OF NEBRASKA

http://www.nebraskalegion.net/

MAYNARD JENSEN AMERICAN LEGION MEMORIAL SCHOLARSHIP
• *See page 532*

AMERICAN LEGION DEPARTMENT OF NORTH DAKOTA

http://www.ndlegion.org/

HATTIE TEDROW MEMORIAL FUND SCHOLARSHIP

Applicants must be legal residents of North Dakota, high school seniors, and direct descendents of a veteran with honorable service in the U.S. military. The student will have two years from the date of graduation from high school to use his/her award.

Award: Scholarship for use in freshman, sophomore, junior, or senior years; not renewable. *Number:* varies. *Amount:* $200–$500.

Eligibility Requirements: Applicant must be American Indian/Alaska Native, Asian/Pacific Islander, Black (non-Hispanic), or Hispanic; high school student; age 17-18; planning to enroll or expecting to enroll full-time at a two-year or four-year or technical institution or university and resident of North Dakota. Available to U.S. citizens. Applicant or parent must meet one or more of the following requirements: general military experience; retired from active duty; disabled or killed as a result of military service; prisoner of war; or missing in action.

Application Requirements: Application, self-addressed stamped envelope, test scores. *Deadline:* April 15.

Contact: Teri Bryant, Programs/Membership Coordinator
American Legion Department of North Dakota
405 West Main Avenue
PO Box 5057
West Fargo, ND 58078
Phone: 701-293-3120
Fax: 701-293-9951
E-mail: programs@ndlegion.org

AMERICAN LEGION DEPARTMENT OF OHIO

http://www.ohiolegion.com/

OHIO AMERICAN LEGION SCHOLARSHIPS
• *See page 533*

AMERICAN LEGION DEPARTMENT OF VERMONT

http://www.legionvthq.com/

AMERICAN LEGION DEPARTMENT OF VERMONT HIGH SCHOOL ORATORICAL CONTEST

Students in grades 9 to 12 are eligible to compete. Must attend an accredited Vermont high school. Must be a U.S. citizen. Selection based on oration.

Award: Prize for use in freshman year; not renewable. *Number:* 1. *Amount:* $2000.

Eligibility Requirements: Applicant must be high school student; planning to enroll or expecting to enroll full- or part-time at a two-year or four-year or technical institution or university; resident of Vermont and must have an interest in public speaking. Available to U.S. citizens. Applicant or parent must meet one or more of the following requirements: general military experience; retired from active duty; disabled or killed as a result of military service; prisoner of war; or missing in action.

Application Requirements: Applicant must enter a contest. *Deadline:* January 1.

Contact: Ronald Aldrich, Chairman
American Legion Department of Vermont
126 State Street
Montpelier, VT 05601
E-mail: alvthq@verizon.net

AMERICAN LEGION DEPARTMENT OF WASHINGTON

http://www.walegion.org/

AMERICAN LEGION DEPARTMENT OF WASHINGTON CHILDREN AND YOUTH SCHOLARSHIPS
• *See page 534*

AMERICAN LEGION DEPARTMENT OF WEST VIRGINIA

http://www.wvlegion.org/

SONS OF THE AMERICAN LEGION WILLIAM F. "BILL" JOHNSON MEMORIAL SCHOLARSHIP
• *See page 534*

AMERICAN LEGION NATIONAL HEADQUARTERS

http://www.legion.org/

AMERICAN LEGION LEGACY SCHOLARSHIP

Scholarship for child/children or legally adopted child/children of active duty U.S. military, National Guard, and Reserve personnel who were federalized and died on active duty on or after September 11, 2001. Must be a high school senior or high school graduate. For undergraduate study at a U.S. school of higher education.

Award: Scholarship for use in freshman, sophomore, junior, or senior years; not renewable. *Number:* varies. *Amount:* $2000–$5000.

Eligibility Requirements: Applicant must be enrolled or expecting to enroll full-time at a two-year or four-year or technical institution or university. Available to U.S. citizens. Applicant or parent must meet one or more of the following requirements: general military experience; retired from active duty; disabled or killed as a result of military service; prisoner of war; or missing in action.

Application Requirements: Application, financial need analysis, test scores, transcript, photocopy of veteran's certificate of death. *Deadline:* April 15.

Contact: Michael Novak, Assistant Director
American Legion National Headquarters
The American Legion, PO Box 1055
Indianapolis, IN 46206
Phone: 317-630-1212
Fax: 317-630-1369
E-mail: mnovak@legion.org

SAMSUNG AMERICAN LEGION SCHOLARSHIP

Scholarship for high school juniors who participate in and complete either an American Legion Boys State or American Legion Auxiliary Girls State program and are a direct descendant or a legally adopted child of a U.S. wartime veteran. For undergraduate study only and may be used for tuition, books, fees, and room and board.

Award: Scholarship for use in freshman, sophomore, junior, or senior years; not renewable. *Number:* 98. *Amount:* $1000–$20,000.

Eligibility Requirements: Applicant must be high school student and planning to enroll or expecting to enroll full-time at a four-year institution or university. Available to U.S. citizens. Applicant or parent must meet one or more of the following requirements: general military experience; retired from active duty; disabled or killed as a result of military service; prisoner of war; or missing in action.

Application Requirements: Application, financial need analysis, test scores, transcript, grandparent's Military Discharge Papers. *Deadline:* May 1.

Contact: Michael Novak, Assistant Director
American Legion National Headquarters
The American Legion, PO Box 1055
Indianapolis, IN 46206
Phone: 317-630-1212
Fax: 317-630-1369
E-mail: mnovak@legion.org

AMERICAN MILITARY RETIREES ASSOCIATION

http://www.amra1973.org/

SERGEANT MAJOR DOUGLAS R. DRUM MEMORIAL SCHOLARSHIP

Applicant's sponsor must be a current member of our association.

Award: Scholarship for use in freshman, sophomore, junior, or senior years; not renewable. *Number:* 1–24. *Amount:* $1000–$5000.

Eligibility Requirements: Applicant must be enrolled or expecting to enroll full-time at a two-year or four-year institution or university. Available to U.S. citizens. Applicant must have general military experience.

Application Requirements: Application, essay, references, test scores, transcript. *Deadline:* March 1.

Contact: Ms. Crystal Maine, Office Manager
American Military Retirees Association
5436 Peru Street, Suite 1
Plattsburgh, NY 12901
Phone: 518-563-9479
E-mail: info@amra1973.org

AMVETS AUXILIARY

http://www.amvetsaux.org/

AMVETS NATIONAL LADIES AUXILIARY SCHOLARSHIP
• *See page 536*

ARKANSAS DEPARTMENT OF HIGHER EDUCATION

http://www.adhe.edu/

MILITARY DEPENDENT'S SCHOLARSHIP PROGRAM

Renewable waiver of tuition, fees, room and board undergraduate students seeking a bachelor's degree or certificate of completion at any public college, university or technical school in Arkansas who qualify as a spouse or dependent child of an Arkansas resident who has been declared to be missing in action, killed in action, a POW, or killed on ordnance delivery, or a veteran who has been declared to be 100 percent totally and permanently disabled during, or as a result of, active military service.

Award: Scholarship for use in freshman, sophomore, junior, or senior years; renewable. *Number:* 1–60.

Eligibility Requirements: Applicant must be enrolled or expecting to enroll full-time at a two-year or four-year or technical institution or university; resident of Arkansas and studying in Arkansas. Available to U.S. citizens. Applicant or parent must meet one or more of the following requirements: general military experience; retired from active duty; disabled or killed as a result of military service; prisoner of war; or missing in action.

Application Requirements: Application, references, report of casualty. *Deadline:* June 1.

Contact: Tara Smith, Director of Financial Aid
Arkansas Department of Higher Education
114 East Capitol Avenue
Little Rock, AR 72201-3818
Phone: 501-371-2000
Fax: 501-371-2001
E-mail: taras@adhe.edu

BLINDED VETERANS ASSOCIATION

http://www.bva.org/

KATHERN F. GRUBER SCHOLARSHIP

Award for undergraduate or graduate study is available to dependent children and spouses of legally blind veterans to include Active Duty Armed Forces members. The veteran's blindness may be either service or non-service connected. High school seniors may apply. Applicant must be enrolled or accepted for admission as a full-time student in an accredited institution of higher learning, business, secretarial, or vocational school. Six awards of $2000 each are given.

Award: Scholarship for use in freshman, sophomore, junior, senior, or graduate years; not renewable. *Number:* 6. *Amount:* $2000.

Eligibility Requirements: Applicant must be enrolled or expecting to enroll full-time at a two-year or four-year or technical institution or university. Available to U.S. citizens. Applicant or parent must meet one or more of the following requirements: general military experience; retired from active duty; disabled or killed as a result of military service; prisoner of war; or missing in action.

Application Requirements: Application, essay, references, transcript. *Deadline:* April 16.

Contact: Keleeba Scott, Scholarship Coordinator
Blinded Veterans Association
477 H Street, NW
Washington, DC 20001-2694
Phone: 202-371-8880
E-mail: kscott@bva.org

DATATEL INC.

http://www.datatelscholars.org/

ANGELFIRE SCHOLARSHIP

For any student who is a 1964 to 1975 Vietnam veteran, or spouse or child of same. Available to refugees from Cambodia, Laos, or Vietnam. Also available to military personnel who have served or are serving in Operations Desert Storm, Enduring Freedom, and Iraqi Freedom. Applicant must attend a Datatel client institution. School list can be found at http://www.datatel.com/dsf. Completed on-line applications and 2 letters of recommendation must be submitted electronically by January 31.

Award: Scholarship for use in freshman, sophomore, junior, senior, graduate, or postgraduate years; not renewable. *Number:* 15–30. *Amount:* $1700.

Eligibility Requirements: Applicant must be enrolled or expecting to enroll full- or part-time at a two-year or four-year or technical institution or university. Available to U.S. and non-U.S. citizens. Applicant or parent must meet one or more of the following requirements: general military experience; retired from active duty; disabled or killed as a result of military service; prisoner of war; or missing in action.

Application Requirements: Application, essay, references, transcript. *Deadline:* January 30.

Contact: Stacey Fessler, Project Leader
Datatel Inc.
4375 Fair Lakes Court
Fairfax, VA 22033
Phone: 800-486-4332
E-mail: scholars@datatel.com

DEFENSE COMMISSARY AGENCY

http://www.militaryscholar.org/

SCHOLARSHIPS FOR MILITARY CHILDREN

One-time award to unmarried dependants of military personnel for full-time undergraduate study at a four-year institution. Must be 23 years of age. Minimum 3.0 GPA required. Further information and applications available at web site http://www.militaryscholar.org.

Award: Scholarship for use in freshman, sophomore, or junior years; not renewable. *Number:* 500. *Amount:* $1500.

Eligibility Requirements: Applicant must be age 23 or under; enrolled or expecting to enroll full-time at a four-year institution or university and single. Applicant must have 3.0 GPA or higher. Available to U.S. citizens. Applicant or parent must meet one or more of the following requirements: general military experience; retired from active duty; disabled or killed as a result of military service; prisoner of war; or missing in action.

Application Requirements: Application, essay, transcript. *Deadline:* February 20.

Contact: Mr. Bernard Cote, Scholarship Coordinator
Defense Commissary Agency
307 Provincetown Road
Cherry Hill, NJ 08134
Phone: 856-573-9400
E-mail: militaryscholar@scholarshipmanagers.com

DELAWARE HIGHER EDUCATION OFFICE

http://www.doe.k12.de.us

EDUCATIONAL BENEFITS FOR CHILDREN OF DECEASED VETERANS
• *See page 585*

DEPARTMENT OF VETERANS AFFAIRS (VA)

http://www.gibill.va.gov/

MONTGOMERY GI BILL (ACTIVE DUTY) CHAPTER 30

Award provides up to thirty-six months of education benefits to eligible veterans for college, business school, technical courses, vocational courses, correspondence courses, apprenticeships/job training, or flight training. Must be an eligible veteran with an Honorable Discharge and have high school diploma or GED before applying for benefits.

Award: Scholarship for use in freshman, sophomore, junior, senior, or graduate years; renewable. *Number:* varies.

Eligibility Requirements: Applicant must be enrolled or expecting to enroll full- or part-time at a two-year or four-year or technical institution or university. Available to U.S. citizens. Applicant or parent must meet one or more of the following requirements: general military experience; retired from active duty; disabled or killed as a result of military service; prisoner of war; or missing in action.

Application Requirements: Application, proof of active military service of at least 2 years. *Deadline:* continuous.

Contact: Keith Wilson, Director, Education Service
Department of Veterans Affairs (VA)
810 Vermont Avenue, NW
Washington, DC 20420
Phone: 888-442-4551

MONTGOMERY GI BILL (SELECTED RESERVE)
• *See page 617*

RESERVE EDUCATION ASSISTANCE PROGRAM
• *See page 619*

SURVIVORS AND DEPENDENTS EDUCATIONAL ASSISTANCE (CHAPTER 35)-VA

Monthly $860 benefits for up to 45 months. Must be spouses or children under age 26 of current veterans missing in action or of deceased or totally and permanently disabled (service-related) service persons. For more information visit the following web site http://www.gibill.va.gov.

Award: Scholarship for use in freshman, sophomore, junior, or senior years; renewable.

Eligibility Requirements: Applicant must be age 25 or under and enrolled or expecting to enroll full- or part-time at a two-year or four-year or technical institution or university. Available to U.S. and non-U.S. citizens. Applicant or parent must meet one or more of the following requirements: general military experience; retired from active duty; disabled or killed as a result of military service; prisoner of war; or missing in action.

Application Requirements: Application, proof of parent or spouse's qualifying service. *Deadline:* continuous.

Contact: Keith Wilson, Director, Education Service
Department of Veterans Affairs (VA)
810 Vermont Avenue, NW
Washington, DC 20420
Phone: 888-442-4551

DEVRY, INC.

http://www.devry.edu/

DEVRY/KELLER MILITARY SERVICE GRANT

Grant is available to students called to active duty at a time which necessitates the interruption of studies during a term. The grant is available only to those students who resume their studies following their active duty service. Upon resuming their studies, students must provide written documentation of active duty service. The grant is to be used during the first term the student resumes. For details visit http://finance.devry.edu/devrygrants_scholarships.html#military.

Award: Grant for use in freshman, sophomore, junior, senior, or graduate years; not renewable. *Number:* varies. *Amount:* $1000–$4500.

Eligibility Requirements: Applicant must be enrolled or expecting to enroll full- or part-time at an institution or university. Available to U.S. citizens. Applicant or parent must meet one or more of the following requirements: general military experience; retired from active duty; dis-

abled or killed as a result of military service; prisoner of war; or missing in action.

Application Requirements: Documentation of active duty service. *Deadline:* varies.

Contact: Thonie Simpson, National High School Program Manager
DeVry, Inc.
One Tower Lane
Oak Brook Terrace, IL 60181-4624
Phone: 630-706-3122
E-mail: scholarships@devry.edu

EXPLOSIVE ORDNANCE DISPOSAL MEMORIAL COMMITTEE

http://www.eodmemorial.org/

EXPLOSIVE ORDNANCE DISPOSAL MEMORIAL SCHOLARSHIP
• *See page 586*

FLORIDA STATE DEPARTMENT OF EDUCATION

http://www.floridastudentfinancialaid.org/

SCHOLARSHIPS FOR CHILDREN & SPOUSES OF DECEASED OR DISABLED VETERANS OR SERVICEMEMBERS

Renewable scholarships for children and spouses of deceased or disabled veterans and service members. Children must be between the ages of 16 and 22, and attend an eligible Florida postsecondary institution and enrolled at least part-time. Must ensure that the Florida Department of Veterans Affairs certifies the applicant's eligibility. Must maintain GPA of 2.0.

Award: Scholarship for use in freshman, sophomore, junior, or senior years; renewable. *Number:* varies. *Amount:* varies.

Eligibility Requirements: Applicant must be age 16-22; enrolled or expecting to enroll full- or part-time at a two-year or four-year or technical institution or university; resident of Florida and studying in Florida. Available to U.S. citizens. Applicant or parent must meet one or more of the following requirements: general military experience; retired from active duty; disabled or killed as a result of military service; prisoner of war; or missing in action.

Application Requirements: Application. *Deadline:* April 1.

Contact: Florida Department of Education, Office of Student Financial Assistance, Customer Service
Florida State Department of Education
325 West Gaines Street
Tallahassee, FL 32399
Phone: 888-827-2004
E-mail: osfa@fldoe.org

FOUNDATION OF THE 1ST CAVALRY DIVISION ASSOCIATION

http://www.1cda.org/

FOUNDATION OF THE 1ST CAVALRY DIVISION ASSOCIATION SCHOLARSHIP

Several scholarships for children of the 1st Cavalry Division soldiers who died or have been declared permanently and totally (100%) disabled from combat with the 1st Cavalry Division. Show proof of relationship, death or disability of parent, and acceptance at higher education institution. Include self-addressed stamped envelope.

Award: Scholarship for use in freshman, sophomore, junior, or senior years; not renewable. *Number:* varies. *Amount:* up to $1200.

Eligibility Requirements: Applicant must be enrolled or expecting to enroll full- or part-time at a two-year or four-year institution or university. Available to U.S. citizens. Applicant or parent must meet one or more of the following requirements: general military experience; retired from active duty; disabled or killed as a result of military service; prisoner of war; or missing in action.

Application Requirements: Application, self-addressed stamped envelope, birth certificate, proof of service with the division, proof of disability or death of parent due to service with the 1st Cavalry Division in combat. *Deadline:* continuous.

Contact: Dennis Webster, Executive Director
Foundation of the 1st Cavalry Division Association
302 North Main Street
Copperas Cove, TX 76522-1703
Phone: 254-547-6537
Fax: 254-547-8853
E-mail: firstcav@1cda.org

IDAHO STATE BOARD OF EDUCATION

http://www.boardofed.idaho.gov/

FREEDOM SCHOLARSHIP

Full tuition, room and board scholarship and up to $500 for books per semester for children of Idaho citizens determined by the federal government to have been prisoners of war, missing in action, or killed in action or died of injuries or wounds sustained in action in southeast Asia, including Korea, or who shall become so hereafter, in any area of armed conflicts. Applicant must attend an Idaho public college or university and meet all requirements for regular admission. The award value and the number of awards granted varies. For additional information, see web site http://www.boardofed.idaho.gov/scholarships/.

Award: Scholarship for use in freshman, sophomore, junior, or senior years; not renewable. *Number:* varies. *Amount:* varies.

Eligibility Requirements: Applicant must be enrolled or expecting to enroll full- or part-time at a two-year or four-year or technical institution or university; resident of Idaho and studying in Idaho. Available to U.S. citizens. Applicant or parent must meet one or more of the following requirements: general military experience; retired from active duty; disabled or killed as a result of military service; prisoner of war; or missing in action.

Application Requirements: Application. *Deadline:* January 15.

Contact: Dana Kelly, Program Manager
Idaho State Board of Education
PO Box 83720
Boise, ID 83720-0037
Phone: 208-332-1574
E-mail: dana.kelly@osbe.idaho.gov

ILLINOIS AMVETS

http://www.ilamvets.org/

ILLINOIS AMVETS LADIES AUXILIARY MEMORIAL SCHOLARSHIP

Applicant must be an Illinois student and a child of an honorably discharged veteran who served after September 15, 1940. Must submit ACT scores, IRS 1040 form, high school rank and grades.

Award: Scholarship for use in freshman year; not renewable. *Number:* 1–3. *Amount:* $500.

Eligibility Requirements: Applicant must be high school student; planning to enroll or expecting to enroll full-time at a two-year or four-year or technical institution or university and resident of Illinois. Available to U.S. citizens. Applicant or parent must meet one or more of the following requirements: general military experience; retired from active duty; disabled or killed as a result of military service; prisoner of war; or missing in action.

Application Requirements: Application, financial need analysis, test scores, transcript, IRS 1040 form. *Deadline:* March 1.

Contact: Sara Van Dyke, Scholarship Director
Illinois AMVETS
2200 South Sixth Street
Springfield, IL 62703-3496
Phone: 217-528-4713
Fax: 217-528-9896
E-mail: scholarship@amvetsillinois.com

ILLINOIS AMVETS LADIES AUXILIARY WORCHID SCHOLARSHIPS

Applicant must be an Illinois student and the child of an honorably discharged, deceased veteran who served after September 15, 1940. Must submit ACT score and IRS 1040 form.

Award: Scholarship for use in freshman year; not renewable. *Number:* 1–3. *Amount:* $500.

Eligibility Requirements: Applicant must be high school student; age 17-18; planning to enroll or expecting to enroll full-time at a two-year or four-year or technical institution or university and resident of Illinois. Available to U.S. citizens. Applicant or parent must meet one or more of the following requirements: general military experience; retired from active duty; disabled or killed as a result of military service; prisoner of war; or missing in action.

Application Requirements: Application, financial need analysis, test scores, transcript, IRS 1040 form. *Deadline:* March 1.

Contact: Sara Van Dyke, Scholarship Director
Illinois AMVETS
2200 South Sixth Street
Springfield, IL 62703-3496
Phone: 217-528-4713
Fax: 217-528-9896
E-mail: scholarship@amvetsillinois.com

ILLINOIS AMVETS SERVICE FOUNDATION

Applicant must be a resident of Illinois and accepted for training at an approved school. Preference given to child of deceased veteran and/or student nurse in training in the order: third, second, first-year student. Must submit IRS 1040 form.

Award: Scholarship for use in freshman year; not renewable. *Number:* 10–30. *Amount:* $1000.

Eligibility Requirements: Applicant must be high school student; age 17-19; planning to enroll or expecting to enroll full-time at a two-year or four-year institution or university; resident of Illinois and studying in Illinois. Applicant must have 2.5 GPA or higher. Available to U.S. citizens. Applicant must have general military experience.

Application Requirements: Application, financial need analysis, references, test scores, transcript, IRS 1040 form, acceptance letter. *Deadline:* March 1.

Contact: Sara Van Dyke, Scholarship Director
Illinois AMVETS
2200 South Sixth Street
Springfield, IL 62703-3496
Phone: 217-528-4713
Fax: 217-528-9896
E-mail: Crystal@ilamvets.org

ILLINOIS AMVETS TRADE SCHOOL SCHOLARSHIP

Applicant must be an Illinois student who has been accepted in a pre-approved trade school program. Must be a child or grandchild of a veteran who served after September 15th, 1940 and was honorably discharged or is presently serving in the military.

Award: Scholarship for use in freshman year; not renewable. *Number:* 1–2. *Amount:* $1000.

Eligibility Requirements: Applicant must be age 17-18; enrolled or expecting to enroll full-time at a technical institution and resident of Illinois. Available to U.S. citizens. Applicant or parent must meet one or more of the following requirements: general military experience; retired from active duty; disabled or killed as a result of military service; prisoner of war; or missing in action.

Application Requirements: Application, acceptance letter. *Deadline:* March 1.

Contact: Crystal Blakeman, Scholarship Director
Illinois AMVETS
2200 South Sixth Street
Springfield, IL 62703-3496
Phone: 217-528-4713
Fax: 217-528-9896
E-mail: Crystal@ilamvets.org

ILLINOIS DEPARTMENT OF VETERANS' AFFAIRS

http://www.state.il.us/agency/dva

MIA/POW SCHOLARSHIPS

One-time award for spouse, child, or step-child of veterans who are missing in action or were a prisoner of war. Must be enrolled at a state-supported school in Illinois. Candidate must be U.S. citizen. Must apply and be accepted before beginning of school. Also for children and spouses of veterans who are determined to be 100 percent disabled as established by the Veterans Administration. Scholarship value and the number of awards granted varies.

Award: Scholarship for use in freshman, sophomore, junior, or senior years; renewable. *Number:* varies. *Amount:* varies.

Eligibility Requirements: Applicant must be enrolled or expecting to enroll full- or part-time at a two-year or four-year institution or university; resident of Illinois and studying in Illinois. Available to U.S. citizens. Applicant or parent must meet one or more of the following requirements: general military experience; retired from active duty; disabled or killed as a result of military service; prisoner of war; or missing in action.

Application Requirements: Application. *Deadline:* continuous.

Contact: Ms. Tracy Smith, Grants Section
Illinois Department of Veterans' Affairs
833 South Spring Street
Springfield, IL 62794-9432
Phone: 217-782-3564
Fax: 217-782-4161

VETERANS' CHILDREN EDUCATIONAL OPPORTUNITIES

$250 award for each child aged 10 to 18 of a veteran who died or became totally disabled as a result of service during World War I, World War II, Korean, or Vietnam War. Must be Illinois resident studying in Illinois. Death must be service-connected. Disability must be rated 100 percent for two or more years.

Award: Grant for use in freshman year; not renewable. *Number:* varies. *Amount:* $250.

Eligibility Requirements: Applicant must be age 10-18; enrolled or expecting to enroll full- or part-time at a two-year or four-year institution or university; resident of Illinois and studying in Illinois. Available to U.S. citizens. Applicant or parent must meet one or more of the following requirements: general military experience; retired from active duty; disabled or killed as a result of military service; prisoner of war; or missing in action.

Application Requirements: Application. *Deadline:* June 30.

Contact: Tracy Smith, Grants Section
Illinois Department of Veterans' Affairs
833 South Spring Street
Springfield, IL 62794-9432
Phone: 217-782-3564
Fax: 217-782-4161

ILLINOIS STUDENT ASSISTANCE COMMISSION (ISAC)

http://www.collegezone.org/

ILLINOIS VETERAN GRANT PROGRAM-IVG

Awards qualified veterans and pays eligible tuition and fees for study in Illinois public universities or community colleges. Program eligibility units are based on the enrolled hours for a particular term, not the dollar amount of the benefits paid. Applications are available at college financial aid office and can be submitted any time during the academic year for which assistance is being requested.

Award: Grant for use in freshman, sophomore, junior, senior, or graduate years; renewable.

Eligibility Requirements: Applicant must be enrolled or expecting to enroll full- or part-time at a two-year or four-year institution or university; resident of Illinois and studying in Illinois. Available to U.S. citizens. Applicant or parent must meet one or more of the following requirements: general military experience; retired from active duty; disabled or killed as a result of military service; prisoner of war; or missing in action.

Application Requirements: Application. *Deadline:* continuous.

Contact: College Zone Counselor
Illinois Student Assistance Commission (ISAC)
1755 Lake Cook Road
Deerfield, IL 60015-5209
Phone: 800-899-4722
Fax: 847-831-8549
E-mail: collegezone@isac.org

INDIANA DEPARTMENT OF VETERANS AFFAIRS

http://www.in.gov/dva

CHILD OF DISABLED VETERAN GRANT OR PURPLE HEART RECIPIENT GRANT

Free tuition at Indiana state-supported colleges or universities for children of disabled veterans or Purple Heart recipients. Must submit form DD214 or service record. Covers tuition and mandatory fees.

Award: Grant for use in freshman, sophomore, junior, senior, graduate, or postgraduate years; renewable. *Number:* varies. *Amount:* varies.

Eligibility Requirements: Applicant must be enrolled or expecting to enroll full- or part-time at a two-year or four-year institution or university; resident of Indiana and studying in Indiana. Available to U.S. citizens. Applicant or parent must meet one or more of the following requirements: general military experience; retired from active duty; disabled or killed as a result of military service; prisoner of war; or missing in action.

Application Requirements: Application, FAFSA. *Deadline:* continuous.

Contact: Jon Brinkley, State Service Officer
Indiana Department of Veterans Affairs
302 West Washington Street, Room E-120
Indianapolis, IN 46204-2738
Phone: 317-232-3910
Fax: 317-232-7721
E-mail: jbrinkley@dva.in.gov

DEPARTMENT OF VETERANS AFFAIRS FREE TUITION FOR CHILDREN OF POW/MIA'S IN VIETNAM

Renewable award for residents of Indiana who are the children of veterans declared missing in action or prisoner-of-war after January 1, 1960. Provides tuition at Indiana state-supported institutions for undergraduate study.

Award: Grant for use in freshman, sophomore, junior, senior, graduate, or postgraduate years; renewable. *Number:* varies. *Amount:* varies.

Eligibility Requirements: Applicant must be age 24 or under; enrolled or expecting to enroll full- or part-time at a two-year or four-year institution or university; resident of Indiana and studying in Indiana. Available to U.S. citizens. Applicant or parent must meet one or more of the following requirements: general military experience; retired from active duty; disabled or killed as a result of military service; prisoner of war; or missing in action.

Application Requirements: Application. *Deadline:* continuous.

Contact: Jon Brinkley, State Service Officer
Indiana Department of Veterans Affairs
302 West Washington Street, Room E-120
Indianapolis, IN 46204-2738
Phone: 317-232-3910
Fax: 317-232-7721
E-mail: jbrinkley@dva.in.gov

KANSAS COMMISSION ON VETERANS AFFAIRS

http://www.kcva.org/

KANSAS EDUCATIONAL BENEFITS FOR CHILDREN OF MIA, POW, AND DECEASED VETERANS OF THE VIETNAM WAR

Scholarship awarded to students who are children of veterans. Must show proof of parent's status as missing in action, prisoner-of-war, or killed in action in the Vietnam War. Kansas residence required of veteran at time of entry to service. Must attend a state-supported postsecondary school.

Award: Scholarship for use in freshman, sophomore, junior, or senior years; not renewable. *Number:* 1. *Amount:* varies.

Eligibility Requirements: Applicant must be enrolled or expecting to enroll full-time at a two-year or four-year or technical institution or university and studying in Kansas. Available to U.S. citizens. Applicant or parent must meet one or more of the following requirements: general military experience; retired from active duty; disabled or killed as a result of military service; prisoner of war; or missing in action.

Application Requirements: Application, birth certificate, school acceptance letter, military discharge of veteran. *Deadline:* varies.

Contact: Wayne Bollig, Program Director
Kansas Commission on Veterans Affairs
700 Jackson, SW, Suite 701
Topeka, KS 66603-3743
Phone: 785-296-3976
Fax: 785-296-1462
E-mail: wbollig@kcva.org

KNIGHTS OF COLUMBUS

http://www.kofc.org/

FRANCIS P. MATTHEWS AND JOHN E. SWIFT EDUCATIONAL TRUST SCHOLARSHIPS
• *See page 547*

LOUISIANA DEPARTMENT OF VETERAN AFFAIRS

http://www.vetaffairs.com/

LOUISIANA DEPARTMENT OF VETERANS AFFAIRS STATE AID PROGRAM

Tuition exemption at any state-supported college, university, or technical institute in Louisiana for children (dependents between the ages of 18–25) of veterans that are rated 90 percent or above service connected disabled by the U.S. Department of Veterans Affairs. Tuition exemption also available for the surviving spouse and children (dependents between the ages of 18–25) of veterans who died on active duty, in line of duty, or where death was the result of a disability incurred in or aggravated by military service. For residents of Louisiana.

Award: Scholarship for use in freshman, sophomore, junior, or senior years; not renewable. *Number:* varies. *Amount:* varies.

Eligibility Requirements: Applicant must be age 18-25; enrolled or expecting to enroll full-time at a two-year or four-year or technical institution or university; resident of Louisiana and studying in Louisiana. Available to U.S. citizens. Applicant or parent must meet one or more of the following requirements: general military experience; retired from active duty; disabled or killed as a result of military service; prisoner of war; or missing in action.

Application Requirements: Application. *Deadline:* continuous.

Contact: Mr. Richard Blackwell, Veterans Affairs Deputy Assistant
Secretary
Louisiana Department of Veteran Affairs
PO Box 94095
Capitol Station
Baton Rouge, LA 70804-4095
Phone: 225-922-0500 Ext. 203
E-mail: richard.blackwell@vetaffairs.la.gov

MAINE DIVISION OF VETERANS SERVICES

http://www.maine.gov/dvem/bvs

VETERANS DEPENDENTS EDUCATIONAL BENEFITS-MAINE

Tuition waiver award for dependent children or spouses of veterans permanently and totally disabled resulting from service-connected disability; died from a service-connected disability; at time of death was totally and permanently disabled due to service-connected disability, but whose death was not related to the service-connected disability; or member of the Armed Forces on active duty who has been listed for more than 90 days as missing in action, captured or forcibly detained or interned in the line of duty. Benefits apply only to the University of Maine System, Maine community colleges and Maine Maritime Academy. Must be high school graduate. Must submit with application proof of veteran's VA disability along with dependent verification paperwork such as birth, marriage, or adoption certificate and proof of enrollment in degree program.

Award: Scholarship for use in freshman, sophomore, junior, or senior years; not renewable. *Number:* varies. *Amount:* varies.

Eligibility Requirements: Applicant must be enrolled or expecting to enroll full- or part-time at a two-year or four-year institution or university; resident of Maine and studying in Maine. Available to U.S. citizens. Applicant or parent must meet one or more of the following requirements: general military experience; retired from active duty; disabled or killed as a result of military service; prisoner of war; or missing in action.

Application Requirements: Application.

Contact: Mrs. Paula Gagnon, Office Associate II
Maine Division of Veterans Services
State House Station 117
Augusta, ME 04333-0117
Phone: 207-626-4464
Fax: 207-626-4471
E-mail: mainebvs@maine.gov

MARYLAND STATE HIGHER EDUCATION COMMISSION

http://www.mhec.state.md.us/

EDWARD T. CONROY MEMORIAL SCHOLARSHIP PROGRAM
• *See page 591*

VETERANS OF THE AFGHANISTAN AND IRAQ CONFLICTS SCHOLARSHIP PROGRAM

Provides financial assistance to Maryland resident U.S. Armed Forces personnel who served in Afghanistan or Iraq Conflicts and their children or spouses who are attending Maryland institutions.

Award: Scholarship for use in freshman, sophomore, junior, or senior years; renewable. *Number:* 123. *Amount:* $8850.

Eligibility Requirements: Applicant must be enrolled or expecting to enroll full- or part-time at a two-year or four-year institution or university; resident of Maryland and studying in Maryland. Available to U.S. citizens. Applicant or parent must meet one or more of the following requirements: general military experience; retired from active duty; disabled or killed as a result of military service; prisoner of war; or missing in action.

Application Requirements: Application, financial need analysis, birth certificate/marriage certificate, documentation of military order. *Deadline:* March 1.

Contact: Linda Asplin, Program Administrator
Maryland State Higher Education Commission
839 Bestgate Road, Suite 400
Annapolis, MD 21401-3013
Phone: 410-260-4563
Fax: 410-260-3203
E-mail: lasplin@mhec.state.md.us

MASSACHUSETTS OFFICE OF STUDENT FINANCIAL ASSISTANCE

http://www.osfa.mass.edu/

MASSACHUSETTS PUBLIC SERVICE GRANT PROGRAM
• *See page 591*

MILITARY OFFICERS ASSOCIATION OF AMERICA (MOAA)

http://www.moaa.org/

GENERAL JOHN RATAY EDUCATIONAL FUND GRANTS

Grants available to the children of the surviving spouse of retired officers. Must be under 24 years old and the child of a deceased retired officer who was a member of MOAA. For more details and an application go to web site http://www.moaa.org/education.

Award: Grant for use in freshman, sophomore, junior, or senior years; renewable. *Number:* 1–5. *Amount:* $4000–$5000.

Eligibility Requirements: Applicant must be age 24 or under and enrolled or expecting to enroll full-time at a two-year or four-year institution or university. Applicant must have 3.0 GPA or higher. Available to U.S. citizens. Applicant or parent must meet one or more of the following requirements: general military experience; retired from active duty; disabled or killed as a result of military service; prisoner of war; or missing in action.

Application Requirements: Application, financial need analysis, test scores, transcript, extracurricular activities. *Deadline:* March 1.

Contact: Laurie Wavering, Program Director
Military Officers Association of America (MOAA)
201 North Washington Street
Alexandria, VA 22314
Phone: 800-234-6622 Ext. 163
Fax: 703-838-5819

MOAA AMERICAN PATRIOT SCHOLARSHIP

Scholarships are available to a student under the age of 24 and who are children of MOAA members and children of active-duty, reserve, National Guard, or enlisted personnel whose military parent has died on active service are eligible to apply. For more information and to access the online application go to web site http://www.moaa.org/education.

Award: Grant for use in freshman, sophomore, junior, or senior years; renewable. *Number:* up to 65. *Amount:* $2500–$5500.

Eligibility Requirements: Applicant must be age 24 or under and enrolled or expecting to enroll full-time at a two-year or four-year institution or university. Applicant must have 3.0 GPA or higher. Available to U.S. citizens. Applicant or parent must meet one or more of the following requirements: general military experience; retired from active duty; disabled or killed as a result of military service; prisoner of war; or missing in action.

Application Requirements: Application, test scores, transcript, extracurricular activities, death certificate. *Deadline:* March 1.

Contact: Laurie Wavering, Program Director
Military Officers Association of America (MOAA)
201 North Washington Street
Alexandria, VA 22314
Phone: 800-234-6622 Ext. 163
Fax: 703-838-5819
E-mail: edassist@moaa.org

MILITARY ORDER OF THE PURPLE HEART

http://www.purpleheart.org/

MILITARY ORDER OF THE PURPLE HEART SCHOLARSHIP

Scholarship for Military Order of the Purple Heart (MOPH) Members/spouses or children, stepchildren, adopted children or grandchildren, veterans killed-in-action or veterans who died of wounds and did not have the opportunity to join the MOPH. Must submit $10 application fee, essay, high school/college transcript, and letters of recommendation. Must be U.S. citizen and high school graduate with minimum GPA of 2.75 and accepted or enrolled as a full-time student at a U.S. college, university of trade school at the time the scholarship is awarded.

Award: Scholarship for use in freshman, sophomore, junior, or senior years; not renewable. *Number:* up to 83. *Amount:* $3000.

Eligibility Requirements: Applicant must be enrolled or expecting to enroll full-time at a two-year or four-year or technical institution or university. Applicant must have 3.0 GPA or higher. Available to U.S. citizens. Applicant or parent must meet one or more of the following requirements: general military experience; retired from active duty; disabled or killed as a result of military service; prisoner of war; or missing in action.

Application Requirements: Application, essay, references, transcript, MOPH membership proof. *Fee:* $10. *Deadline:* February 17.

Contact: Mr. Stewart Mckeown, Scholarship Coordinator
Military Order of the Purple Heart
5413-B Backlick Road
Springfield, VA 22151-3960
Phone: 703-642-5360
Fax: 703-642-2054
E-mail: info@purpleheart.org

MINNESOTA OFFICE OF HIGHER EDUCATION

http://www.getreadyforcollege.org/

MINNESOTA GI BILL PROGRAM

Provides financial assistance to eligible Minnesota veterans and non-veterans who have served 5 or more years cumulatively as a member of the National Guard or Reserves, and served on or after September 11, 2001. Surviving spouses and children of service members who have died or have a total and permanent disability and who served on or after September 11, 2001, may also be eligible. Full-time students may receive up to $1000 per term, and part-time students up to $500 per term up to $3,000 per year. Maximum lifetime benefit is $10,000.

Award: Scholarship for use in freshman, sophomore, junior, senior, graduate, or postgraduate years; not renewable. *Number:* varies. *Amount:* up to $3000.

Eligibility Requirements: Applicant must be enrolled or expecting to enroll full- or part-time at a two-year or four-year or technical institution or university; resident of Minnesota and studying in Minnesota. Available to U.S. citizens. Applicant or parent must meet one or more of the following requirements: general military experience; retired from active duty; disabled or killed as a result of military service; prisoner of war; or missing in action.

Application Requirements: Application, financial need analysis, military records. *Deadline:* continuous.

Contact: Scholarship Staff
Minnesota Office of Higher Education
1450 Energy Park Drive
St. Paul, MN 55108
Phone: 651-642-0567 Ext. 1
Fax: 651-642-0675

MINNESOTA STATE VETERANS' DEPENDENTS ASSISTANCE PROGRAM

Tuition assistance to dependents of persons considered to be prisoner-of-war or missing in action after August 1, 1958. Must be Minnesota resident attending Minnesota two- or four-year school.

Award: Scholarship for use in freshman, sophomore, junior, or senior years; renewable. *Number:* varies. *Amount:* varies.

Eligibility Requirements: Applicant must be enrolled or expecting to enroll full- or part-time at a two-year or four-year institution; resident of Minnesota and studying in Minnesota. Available to U.S. citizens. Applicant or parent must meet one or more of the following requirements: general military experience; retired from active duty; disabled or killed as a result of military service; prisoner of war; or missing in action.

Application Requirements: Application. *Deadline:* continuous.

Contact: Ginny Dodds, Manager
Minnesota Office of Higher Education
1450 Energy Park Drive, Suite 350
St. Paul, MN 55108-5227
Phone: 651-355-0610
E-mail: ginny.dodds@state.mn.us

NATIONAL MILITARY FAMILY ASSOCIATION

http://www.nmfa.org/

NMFA JOANNE HOLBROOK PATTON MILITARY SPOUSE SCHOLARSHIPS

Scholarships ranging from $500 to $1000 are awarded to spouses of Uniformed Services members (active duty, National Guard and Reserve, retirees, and survivors) to obtain professional certification or to attend postsecondary or graduate school. Award number varies.

Award: Scholarship for use in freshman, sophomore, junior, or senior years; not renewable. *Number:* varies. *Amount:* $500–$1000.

Eligibility Requirements: Applicant must be enrolled or expecting to enroll full- or part-time at a two-year or four-year or technical institution or university and married. Available to U.S. citizens. Applicant or parent must meet one or more of the following requirements: general military experience; retired from active duty; disabled or killed as a result of military service; prisoner of war; or missing in action.

Application Requirements: Application, essay, copy of current United States Uniformed Services ID card/ DEERS card (back and front). *Deadline:* February 1.

Contact: Ms. Sharon L. Jankosky, Deputy Director, Development and Membership
National Military Family Association
2500 N. Van Dorn Street, Suite 102
Alexandria, VA 22302
Phone: 703-931-6632
Fax: 703-931-4600
E-mail: scholarships@nmfa.org

NEW HAMPSHIRE POSTSECONDARY EDUCATION COMMISSION

http://www.nh.gov/postsecondary

SCHOLARSHIPS FOR ORPHANS OF VETERANS-NEW HAMPSHIRE

Scholarship to provide financial assistance (room, board, books and supplies) to children of parents) who served in World War II, Korean Conflict, Vietnam (Southeast Asian Conflict) or the Gulf Wars, or any other operation for which the armed forces expeditionary medal or theater of operations service medal was awarded to the veteran.

Award: Scholarship for use in freshman, sophomore, junior, or senior years; renewable. *Number:* 1–10. *Amount:* up to $2500.

Eligibility Requirements: Applicant must be age 16-25; enrolled or expecting to enroll full-time at a two-year or four-year institution or university; resident of New Hampshire and studying in New Hampshire. Available to U.S. citizens. Applicant or parent must meet one or more of the following requirements: general military experience; retired from active duty; disabled or killed as a result of military service; prisoner of war; or missing in action.

Application Requirements: Application. *Deadline:* varies.

Contact: Ms. Cynthia Capodestria, Student Financial Aid Administrator
New Hampshire Postsecondary Education Commission
Three Barrell Court, Suite 300
Concord, NH 03301-8543
Phone: 603-271-2555 Ext. 360
E-mail: cynthia.capodestria@pec.state.nh.us

NEW JERSEY DEPARTMENT OF MILITARY AND VETERANS AFFAIRS

http://www.state.nj.us/military

NEW JERSEY WAR ORPHANS TUITION ASSISTANCE

$500 scholarship to children of those service personnel who died while in the military or due to service-connected disabilities, or who are officially listed as missing in action by the U.S. Department of Defense. Must be a resident of New Jersey for at least one year immediately preceding the filing of the application and be between the ages of 16 and 21 at the time of application.

Award: Scholarship for use in freshman, sophomore, junior, or senior years; renewable. *Number:* varies. *Amount:* $500.

Eligibility Requirements: Applicant must be age 16-21; enrolled or expecting to enroll full-time at a four-year institution or university and resident of New Jersey. Available to U.S. citizens. Applicant or parent must meet one or more of the following requirements: general military experience; retired from active duty; disabled or killed as a result of military service; prisoner of war; or missing in action.

Application Requirements: Application, transcript. *Deadline:* varies.

Contact: Patricia Richter, Grants Manager
New Jersey Department of Military and Veterans Affairs
PO Box 340
Trenton, NJ 08625-0340
Phone: 609-530-6854
Fax: 609-530-6970
E-mail: patricia.richter@njdmava.state.nj.us

POW-MIA TUITION BENEFIT PROGRAM

Free undergraduate college tuition provided to any child born or adopted before or during the period of time his or her parent was officially declared a prisoner of war or person missing in action after January 1,

1960. The POW-MIA must have been a New Jersey resident at the time he or she entered the service. Child of veteran must attend either a public or private institution in New Jersey. A copy of DD 1300 must be furnished with the application. Minimum 2.5 GPA required.

Award: Scholarship for use in freshman, sophomore, junior, or senior years; renewable. *Number:* varies. *Amount:* varies.

Eligibility Requirements: Applicant must be enrolled or expecting to enroll full-time at a two-year or four-year or technical institution or university; resident of New Jersey and studying in New Jersey. Applicant must have 2.5 GPA or higher. Available to U.S. citizens. Applicant or parent must meet one or more of the following requirements: general military experience; retired from active duty; disabled or killed as a result of military service; prisoner of war; or missing in action.

Application Requirements: Application, transcript, copy of DD 1300. *Deadline:* varies.

Contact: Patricia Richter, Grants Manager
New Jersey Department of Military and Veterans Affairs
PO Box 340
Trenton, NJ 08625-0340
Phone: 609-530-6854
Fax: 609-530-6970
E-mail: patricia.richter@njdmava.state.nj.us

VETERANS TUITION CREDIT PROGRAM-NEW JERSEY

Award for New Jersey resident veterans who served in the armed forces between December 31, 1960, and May 7, 1975. Must have been a New Jersey resident at time of induction or discharge or for two years immediately prior to application.

Award: Scholarship for use in freshman, sophomore, junior, or senior years; renewable. *Number:* varies. *Amount:* $200–$400.

Eligibility Requirements: Applicant must be enrolled or expecting to enroll full- or part-time at a two-year or four-year or technical institution or university and resident of New Jersey. Available to U.S. citizens. Applicant or parent must meet one or more of the following requirements: general military experience; retired from active duty; disabled or killed as a result of military service; prisoner of war; or missing in action.

Application Requirements: Application. *Deadline:* varies.

Contact: Patricia Richter, Grants Manager
New Jersey Department of Military and Veterans Affairs
PO Box 340
Trenton, NJ 08625-0340
Phone: 609-530-6854
Fax: 609-530-6970
E-mail: patricia.richter@njdmava.state.nj.us

NEW MEXICO COMMISSION ON HIGHER EDUCATION

http://www.hed.state.nm.us/

VIETNAM VETERANS' SCHOLARSHIP PROGRAM

Renewable scholarship program created to provide aid for Vietnam veterans who are undergraduate and graduate students attending public postsecondary institutions or select private colleges in New Mexico. Private colleges include: College of Santa Fe, St. John's College and College of the Southwest.

Award: Scholarship for use in freshman, sophomore, junior, or senior years; renewable. *Number:* 1. *Amount:* varies.

Eligibility Requirements: Applicant must be enrolled or expecting to enroll full-time at a two-year or four-year institution; resident of New Mexico and studying in New Mexico. Available to U.S. citizens. Applicant or parent must meet one or more of the following requirements: general military experience; retired from active duty; disabled or killed as a result of military service; prisoner of war; or missing in action.

Application Requirements: Application, certification by the NM Veteran's commission. *Deadline:* varies.

Contact: Tashina Banks Moore, Director of Financial Aid
New Mexico Commission on Higher Education
1068 Cerrillos Road
Santa Fe, NM 87505-1650
Phone: 505-476-6549
Fax: 505-476-6511
E-mail: tashina.banks-moore@state.nm.us

NEW MEXICO DEPARTMENT OF VETERANS' SERVICES

http://www.dvs.state.nm.us/

CHILDREN OF DECEASED VETERANS SCHOLARSHIP-NEW MEXICO

Award for New Mexico residents who are children of veterans killed or disabled as a result of service, prisoner of war, or veterans missing in action. Must be between ages 16 and 26. For use at New Mexico schools for undergraduate study. Must submit parent's death certificate and DD form 214.

Award: Scholarship for use in freshman, sophomore, junior, or senior years; renewable. *Number:* varies. *Amount:* $300.

Eligibility Requirements: Applicant must be age 16-26; enrolled or expecting to enroll full- or part-time at a two-year or four-year institution or university; resident of New Mexico and studying in New Mexico. Available to U.S. citizens. Applicant or parent must meet one or more of the following requirements: general military experience; retired from active duty; disabled or killed as a result of military service; prisoner of war; or missing in action.

Application Requirements: Application, transcript, death certificate or notice of casualty, DD form 214. *Deadline:* continuous.

Contact: Alan Martinez, Deputy Secretary
New Mexico Department of Veterans' Services
Bataan Memorial Building
PO BOX 2324
Santa Fe, NM 87504
Phone: 505-827-6300
E-mail: alan.martinez@state.nm.us

NEW MEXICO VIETNAM VETERAN SCHOLARSHIP

Award for Vietnam veterans who have been New Mexico residents for a minimum of ten years and are attending state-funded postsecondary schools. Must have been awarded the Vietnam Campaign medal. Must submit DD 214 and discharge papers.

Award: Scholarship for use in freshman, sophomore, junior, or senior years; renewable. *Number:* 100. *Amount:* $3500–$4000.

Eligibility Requirements: Applicant must be enrolled or expecting to enroll full- or part-time at a two-year or four-year or technical institution or university; resident of New Mexico and studying in New Mexico. Available to U.S. citizens. Applicant or parent must meet one or more of the following requirements: general military experience; retired from active duty; disabled or killed as a result of military service; prisoner of war; or missing in action.

Application Requirements: Application, copy of DD Form 214. *Deadline:* continuous.

Contact: Alan Martinez, Deputy Secretary
New Mexico Department of Veterans' Services
Bataan Memorial Building
PO BOX 2324
Santa Fe, NM 87504
Phone: 505-827-6300
E-mail: alan.martinez@state.nm.us

NEW YORK STATE HIGHER EDUCATION SERVICES CORPORATION

http://www.hesc.com/

NEW YORK VIETNAM/PERSIAN GULF/AFGHANISTAN VETERANS TUITION AWARDS

Scholarship for veterans who served in Vietnam, the Persian Gulf, or Afghanistan. Must be a New York resident attending a New York institution. Must establish eligibility by September 1.

Award: Scholarship for use in freshman, sophomore, junior, or senior years; renewable. *Number:* varies.

Eligibility Requirements: Applicant must be enrolled or expecting to enroll full- or part-time at a two-year or four-year or technical institution or university; resident of New York and studying in New York. Available to U.S. citizens. Applicant or parent must meet one or more of the following requirements: general military experience; retired from active duty; disabled or killed as a result of military service; prisoner of war; or missing in action.

Application Requirements: Application, financial need analysis. *Deadline:* May 1.

Contact: Associate HESC Information Representative
New York State Higher Education Services Corporation
99 Washington Avenue
Grants & Scholarships Unit
Albany, NY 12255
Phone: 888-NYS-HESC
E-mail: scholarship@hesc.com

REGENTS AWARD FOR CHILD OF VETERAN

Award for students whose parent, as a result of service in U.S. Armed Forces during war or national emergency, died; suffered a 40 percent or more disability; or is classified as missing in action or a prisoner of war. Veteran must be current New York State resident or have been so at time of death. Student must be a New York resident, attending, or planning to attend, college in New York State. Must establish eligibility before applying for payment.

Award: Scholarship for use in freshman, sophomore, junior, or senior years; not renewable. *Number:* varies. *Amount:* up to $450.

Eligibility Requirements: Applicant must be enrolled or expecting to enroll full-time at a two-year or four-year institution or university; resident of New York and studying in New York. Available to U.S. citizens. Applicant or parent must meet one or more of the following requirements: general military experience; retired from active duty; disabled or killed as a result of military service; prisoner of war; or missing in action.

Application Requirements: Application, proof of eligibility. *Deadline:* May 1.

Contact: Rita McGivern, Student Information
New York State Higher Education Services Corporation
99 Washington Avenue, Room 1320
Albany, NY 12255
E-mail: rmcgivern@hesc.com

NORTH CAROLINA DIVISION OF VETERANS AFFAIRS

http://www.doa.state.nc.us/vets/va.htm

NORTH CAROLINA VETERANS SCHOLARSHIPS CLASS I-A

Scholarships for children of certain deceased, disabled or POW/MIA veterans. Award value is $4500 per nine-month academic year in private colleges and junior colleges. No limit on number awarded each year.

Award: Scholarship for use in freshman, sophomore, junior, or senior years; renewable. *Number:* varies. *Amount:* $4500.

Eligibility Requirements: Applicant must be enrolled or expecting to enroll full-time at a two-year or four-year or technical institution or university; resident of North Carolina and studying in North Carolina. Available to U.S. citizens. Applicant or parent must meet one or more of the following requirements: general military experience; retired from active duty; disabled or killed as a result of military service; prisoner of war; or missing in action.

Application Requirements: Application, financial need analysis, interview, transcript. *Deadline:* continuous.

Contact: Charles Smith, Assistant Secretary
North Carolina Division of Veterans Affairs
325 North Salisbury Street
Raleigh, NC 27603
Phone: 919-733-3851
Fax: 919-733-2834
E-mail: charlie.smith@ncmail.net

NORTH CAROLINA VETERANS SCHOLARSHIPS CLASS I-B

Awards for children of veterans rated by USDVA as 100 percent disabled due to wartime service as defined in the law, and currently or at time of death drawing compensation for such disability. Parent must have been a North Carolina resident at time of entry into service. Duration of the scholarship is four academic years (8 semesters) if used within 8 years. No limit on number awarded each year.

Award: Scholarship for use in freshman, sophomore, junior, or senior years; renewable. *Number:* varies. *Amount:* $1500.

Eligibility Requirements: Applicant must be enrolled or expecting to enroll full- or part-time at a two-year or four-year or technical institution or university; resident of North Carolina and studying in North Carolina. Available to U.S. citizens. Applicant or parent must meet one or more of the following requirements: general military experience; retired from active duty; disabled or killed as a result of military service; prisoner of war; or missing in action.

Application Requirements: Application, financial need analysis, interview, transcript. *Deadline:* continuous.

Contact: Charles Smith, Assistant Secretary
North Carolina Division of Veterans Affairs
325 North Salisbury Street
Raleigh, NC 27603
Phone: 919-733-3851
Fax: 919-733-2834
E-mail: charlie.smith@ncmail.net

NORTH CAROLINA VETERANS SCHOLARSHIPS CLASS II

Awards for children of veterans rated by USDVA as much as 20 percent but less than 100 percent disabled due to wartime service as defined in the law, or awarded Purple Heart Medal for wounds received. Parent must have been a North Carolina resident at time of entry into service. Duration of the scholarship is four academic years (8 semesters) if used within 8 years. Free tuition and exemption from certain mandatory fees as set forth in the law in Public, Community and Technical Colleges.

Award: Scholarship for use in freshman, sophomore, junior, or senior years; renewable. *Number:* up to 100. *Amount:* $4500.

Eligibility Requirements: Applicant must be enrolled or expecting to enroll full- or part-time at a two-year or four-year or technical institution or university; resident of North Carolina and studying in North Carolina. Available to U.S. citizens. Applicant or parent must meet one or more of the following requirements: general military experience; retired from active duty; disabled or killed as a result of military service; prisoner of war; or missing in action.

Application Requirements: Application, financial need analysis, interview, transcript. *Deadline:* March 1.

Contact: Charles Smith, Assistant Secretary
North Carolina Division of Veterans Affairs
325 North Salisbury Street
Raleigh, NC 27603
Phone: 919-733-3851
Fax: 919-733-2834
E-mail: charlie.smith@ncmail.net

NORTH CAROLINA VETERANS SCHOLARSHIPS CLASS III

Awards for children of a deceased war veteran, who was honorably discharged and who does not qualify under any other provision within this synopsis or veteran who served in a combat zone or waters adjacent to a combat zone and received a campaign badge or medal and who does not qualify under any other provision within this synopsis. Duration of the scholarship is four academic years (8 semesters) if used within 8 years.

Award: Scholarship for use in freshman, sophomore, junior, or senior years; renewable. *Number:* up to 100. *Amount:* $4500.

Eligibility Requirements: Applicant must be enrolled or expecting to enroll full- or part-time at a two-year or four-year or technical institution or university; resident of North Carolina and studying in North Carolina. Available to U.S. citizens. Applicant or parent must meet one or more of the following requirements: general military experience; retired from active duty; disabled or killed as a result of military service; prisoner of war; or missing in action.

Application Requirements: Application, financial need analysis, interview, transcript. *Deadline:* March 1.

Contact: Charles Smith, Assistant Secretary
North Carolina Division of Veterans Affairs
325 North Salisbury Street
Raleigh, NC 27603
Phone: 919-733-3851
Fax: 919-733-2834
E-mail: charlie.smith@ncmail.net

NORTH CAROLINA VETERANS SCHOLARSHIPS CLASS IV

Awards for children of veterans, who were prisoner of war or missing in action. Duration of the scholarship is four academic years (8 semesters) if

used within 8 years. No limit on number awarded each year. Award value is $4500 per nine-month academic year in private colleges and junior colleges.

Award: Scholarship for use in freshman, sophomore, junior, or senior years; renewable. *Number:* varies. *Amount:* $4500.

Eligibility Requirements: Applicant must be enrolled or expecting to enroll full- or part-time at a two-year or four-year or technical institution or university; resident of North Carolina and studying in North Carolina. Available to U.S. citizens. Applicant or parent must meet one or more of the following requirements: general military experience; retired from active duty; disabled or killed as a result of military service; prisoner of war; or missing in action.

Application Requirements: Application, financial need analysis, interview, transcript. *Deadline:* continuous.

Contact: Charles Smith, Assistant Secretary
North Carolina Division of Veterans Affairs
325 North Salisbury Street
Raleigh, NC 27603
Phone: 919-733-3851
Fax: 919-733-2834
E-mail: charlie.smith@ncmail.net

OHIO BOARD OF REGENTS

http://www.uso.edu/

OHIO WAR ORPHANS SCHOLARSHIP

Aids Ohio residents attending an eligible college in Ohio. Must be between the ages of 16 and 25, the child of a disabled or deceased veteran, and enrolled full-time. Renewable up to five years. Amount of award varies. Must include Form DD214.

Award: Scholarship for use in freshman, sophomore, junior, or senior years; renewable. *Amount:* varies.

Eligibility Requirements: Applicant must be age 16-25; enrolled or expecting to enroll full-time at a two-year or four-year institution or university; resident of Ohio and studying in Ohio. Available to U.S. citizens. Applicant or parent must meet one or more of the following requirements: general military experience; retired from active duty; disabled or killed as a result of military service; prisoner of war; or missing in action.

Application Requirements: Application, Form DD214. *Deadline:* July 1.

Contact: Jathiya Abdullah-Simmons, Program Manager
Ohio Board of Regents
30 East Broad Street, 36th Floor
Columbus, OH 43215-3414
Phone: 614-752-9528
Fax: 614-752-5903
E-mail: jabdullah-simmons@regents.state.oh.us

OREGON DEPARTMENT OF VETERANS' AFFAIRS

http://www.oregon.gov/odva

OREGON VETERANS' EDUCATION AID

To be eligible, veteran must have actively served in U.S. armed forces 90 days and been discharged under honorable conditions. Must be U.S. citizen and Oregon resident. Korean War veteran or received campaign or expeditionary medal or ribbon awarded by U.S. armed forces for services after June 30, 1958. Full-time students receive up to $150 per month, and part-time students receive up to $100 per month for a maximum of 36 months. Length of benefits depend on length of service. Payments contingent upon available funding.

Award: Grant for use in freshman, sophomore, junior, senior, graduate, or postgraduate years; not renewable. *Number:* 1–200. *Amount:* $3600–$5400.

Eligibility Requirements: Applicant must be enrolled or expecting to enroll full- or part-time at a two-year or four-year or technical institution or university; resident of Oregon and studying in Oregon. Available to U.S. citizens. Applicant must have general military experience.

Application Requirements: Application, certified copy of DD Form 214. *Deadline:* continuous.

Contact: Loriann Sheridan, Veterans Programs Consultant
Oregon Department of Veterans' Affairs
700 Summer Street, NE
Salem, OR 97301-1289
Phone: 503-373-2264
Fax: 503-373-2393
E-mail: sheridl@odva.state.or.us

OREGON STUDENT ASSISTANCE COMMISSION

http://www.GetCollegeFunds.org/

DARLENE HOOLEY FOR OREGON VETERANS SCHOLARSHIP

Applicants must have served during the Global War on Terror; no minimum length of service required. Recipients must enroll at least half-time in an Oregon college or university. If you are selected as a semifinalist for this scholarship, you will be required to submit a copy of your DD214 showing service during the correct time frame.

Award: Scholarship for use in freshman year; not renewable.

Eligibility Requirements: Applicant must be enrolled or expecting to enroll full- or part-time at a two-year or four-year institution or university and studying in Oregon. Available to U.S. citizens. Applicant must have general military experience.

Application Requirements: Application, proof of military service. *Deadline:* March 1.

Contact: Director of Grant Programs
Oregon Student Assistance Commission
1500 Valley River Drive; Suite 100
Eugene, OR 97401-7020
Phone: 800-452-8807

MARIA C. JACKSON/GENERAL GEORGE A. WHITE SCHOLARSHIP

Available to Oregon residents who served or whose parents serve or have served in the U.S. Armed Forces and resided in Oregon at time of enlistment. Must have at least 3.75 GPA and submit documentation of service. (No GPA requirement for graduate-level students and students attending a technical school). For use at Oregon colleges only. U.S. Bank employees, their children, and near relatives are not eligible.

Award: Scholarship for use in freshman, sophomore, junior, or senior years; not renewable. *Amount:* varies.

Eligibility Requirements: Applicant must be enrolled or expecting to enroll full-time at a two-year or four-year or technical institution or university; resident of Oregon and studying in Oregon. Available to U.S. citizens. Applicant or parent must meet one or more of the following requirements: general military experience; retired from active duty; disabled or killed as a result of military service; prisoner of war; or missing in action.

Application Requirements: Application, essay, transcript, proof of service (DD93, DD214, or discharge papers). *Deadline:* March 1.

Contact: Scholarship Coordinator
Oregon Student Assistance Commission
1500 Valley River Drive, Suite 100
Eugene, OR 97401-7020
Phone: 800-452-8807 Ext. 7466

PETER CONNACHER MEMORIAL SCHOLARSHIP

Renewable award for American prisoners-of-war and their descendants. Written proof of prisoner-of-war status and discharge papers from the U.S. Armed Forces must accompany application. Statement of relationship between applicant and former prisoner-of-war is required. Oregon residency preferred but not required. See web site at http://www.osac.state.or.us for details.

Award: Scholarship for use in freshman, sophomore, junior, or senior years; renewable. *Number:* varies. *Amount:* varies.

Eligibility Requirements: Applicant must be enrolled or expecting to enroll full-time at a two-year or four-year institution. Available to U.S. citizens. Applicant or parent must meet one or more of the following requirements: general military experience; retired from active duty; disabled or killed as a result of military service; prisoner of war; or missing in action.

Application Requirements: Application, essay, financial need analysis, transcript, military discharge papers, documentation of POW status. *Deadline:* March 1.

Contact: Director of Grant Programs
Oregon Student Assistance Commission
1500 Valley River Drive, Suite 100
Eugene, OR 97401-7020
Phone: 800-452-8807 Ext. 7395

PARALYZED VETERANS OF AMERICA-SPINAL CORD RESEARCH FOUNDATION

http://www.pva.org/

PARALYZED VETERANS OF AMERICA EDUCATIONAL SCHOLARSHIP PROGRAM

Open to PVA members, their spouses and unmarried children, under 24 years of age, to obtain a postsecondary education. Applicants must be U.S. citizens accepted or enrolled as full-time students in a degree program. For details and application visit web site http://www.pva.org.

Award: Scholarship for use in freshman, sophomore, junior, or senior years; renewable. *Number:* 10–20. *Amount:* $500–$1000.

Eligibility Requirements: Applicant must be age 24 or under and enrolled or expecting to enroll full- or part-time at a four-year institution or university. Available to U.S. citizens. Applicant or parent must meet one or more of the following requirements: general military experience; retired from active duty; disabled or killed as a result of military service; prisoner of war; or missing in action.

Application Requirements: Application, references, transcript, personal statement, verification of enrollment. *Deadline:* June 30.

Contact: Patricia Rollins, Member Services Coordinator
Paralyzed Veterans of America-Spinal Cord Research Foundation
801 Eighteenth Street, NW
Washington, DC 20006-3517
Phone: 800-424-8200 Ext. 619
E-mail: trishr@pva.org

PENNSYLVANIA HIGHER EDUCATION ASSISTANCE AGENCY

http://www.pheaa.org/

ARMED FORCES LOAN FORGIVENESS PROGRAM

Loan forgiveness for non-residents of Pennsylvania who served in Armed Forces in an active duty status after September 11, 2001. Must be a student who either left a PA approved institution of postsecondary education due to call to active duty, or was living in PA at time of enlistment, or enlisted in military immediately after attending a PA approved institution of postsecondary education. Number of loans forgiven varies.

Award: Forgivable loan for use in freshman, sophomore, junior, or senior years; not renewable. *Number:* varies. *Amount:* up to $2500.

Eligibility Requirements: Applicant must be enrolled or expecting to enroll full- or part-time at a two-year or four-year or technical institution or university. Available to U.S. citizens. Applicant or parent must meet one or more of the following requirements: general military experience; retired from active duty; disabled or killed as a result of military service; prisoner of war; or missing in action.

Application Requirements: Application. *Deadline:* December 31.

Contact: Keith New, Director of Public Relations
Pennsylvania Higher Education Assistance Agency
1200 North Seventh Street
Harrisburg, PA 17102-1444
Phone: 717-720-2509
E-mail: knew@pheaa.org

THE RESERVE OFFICERS ASSOCIATION

http://www.roa.org/

HENRY J. REILLY MEMORIAL SCHOLARSHIP-HIGH SCHOOL SENIORS AND FIRST YEAR FRESHMEN

• *See page 561*

HENRY J. REILLY MEMORIAL UNDERGRADUATE SCHOLARSHIP PROGRAM FOR COLLEGE ATTENDEES

• *See page 561*

RETIRED ENLISTED ASSOCIATION

http://www.trea.org/

RETIRED ENLISTED ASSOCIATION SCHOLARSHIP

One-time award for dependent children or grandchildren of a TREA member or TREA auxiliary member in good standing.

Award: Scholarship for use in freshman, sophomore, junior, senior, graduate, or postgraduate years; not renewable. *Number:* varies. *Amount:* $1000–$1500.

Eligibility Requirements: Applicant must be enrolled or expecting to enroll full-time at a two-year or four-year or technical institution or university. Available to U.S. citizens. Applicant or parent must meet one or more of the following requirements: general military experience; retired from active duty; disabled or killed as a result of military service; prisoner of war; or missing in action.

Application Requirements: Application, essay, financial need analysis, photo, references, test scores, transcript, copy of IRS tax forms. *Deadline:* April 30.

Contact: Donnell Minnis, Executive Assistant
Retired Enlisted Association
c/o National Scholarship Committee, 1111 South Abilene Court
Aurora, CO 80012-4909
Phone: 303-752-0660
Fax: 303-752-0835
E-mail: execasst@trea.org

SOUTH CAROLINA DIVISION OF VETERANS AFFAIRS

http://www.govoepp.state.sc.us/vetaff.htm

EDUCATIONAL ASSISTANCE FOR CERTAIN WAR VETERANS DEPENDENTS SCHOLARSHIP-SOUTH CAROLINA

Free tuition for South Carolina residents whose parent is a resident, wartime veteran, and meets one of these criteria; awarded Purple Heart or Congressional Medal of Honor; permanently and totally disabled or killed as a result of military service; prisoner of war; or missing in action. Must be age 18–26 and enrolled or expecting to enroll full or part-time at a two-year or four-year technical institution or university in South Carolina. Complete information and qualifications for this award are on web site http://www.govoepp.state.sc.us.

Award: Scholarship for use in freshman, sophomore, junior, or senior years; not renewable. *Number:* varies. *Amount:* varies.

Eligibility Requirements: Applicant must be age 18-26; enrolled or expecting to enroll full- or part-time at a two-year or four-year or technical institution or university; resident of South Carolina and studying in South Carolina. Available to U.S. citizens. Applicant or parent must meet one or more of the following requirements: general military experience; retired from active duty; disabled or killed as a result of military service; prisoner of war; or missing in action.

Application Requirements: Application, transcript, proof of qualification of veteran. *Deadline:* continuous.

Contact: Dianne Coley, Free Tuition Program Assistant
South Carolina Division of Veterans Affairs
South Carolina
GovernorsOffice,1205PendletonStreet,Suite369'
Columbia, SC 29201
Phone: 803-255-4317
E-mail: va@oepp.sc.gov

STATE OF WYOMING, ADMINISTERED BY UNIVERSITY OF WYOMING

http://www.uwyo.edu/scholarships

VIETNAM VETERANS AWARD-WYOMING

Scholarship available to Wyoming residents who served in the armed forces between August 5, 1964 and May 7, 1975, and received a Vietnam service medal.

Award: Scholarship for use in freshman, sophomore, junior, or senior years; renewable. *Number:* varies. *Amount:* varies.

Eligibility Requirements: Applicant must be enrolled or expecting to enroll full- or part-time at a two-year or four-year institution or university and resident of Wyoming. Available to U.S. citizens. Applicant or parent must meet one or more of the following requirements: general military experience; retired from active duty; disabled or killed as a result of military service; prisoner of war; or missing in action.

Application Requirements: Application. *Deadline:* continuous.

Contact: Tammy Mack, Assistant Director, Scholarships
State of Wyoming, Administered by University of Wyoming
Student Financial Aid Department 3335, 1000 East University Avenue
Laramie, WY 82071-3335
Phone: 307-766-2412
E-mail: westmack@uwyo.edu

VA MORTGAGE CENTER.COM

http://www.vamortgagecenter.com/

MILITARY EDUCATION SCHOLARSHIP

Scholarships for all ROTC program students or active duty military looking to return to college. To compete, applicants must submit a two to three page essay on "Why I Choose to Serve". For more information, please see web site http://www.vamortgagecenter.com/guidelines.html.

Award: Scholarship for use in freshman, sophomore, junior, senior, graduate, or postgraduate years; not renewable. *Number:* 5. *Amount:* $1500.

Eligibility Requirements: Applicant must be enrolled or expecting to enroll full- or part-time at a two-year or four-year or technical institution or university. Available to U.S. citizens. Applicant or parent must meet one or more of the following requirements: general military experience; retired from active duty; disabled or killed as a result of military service; prisoner of war; or missing in action.

Application Requirements: Application, essay. *Deadline:* May 12.

Contact: Mr. Nathan Long, Chief Executive Officer
VA Mortgage Center.com
2101 Chapel Plaza Court, Suite 107
Columbia, MO 65203
Phone: 800-405-6682
E-mail: customer_service@vamortgagecenter.com

VIRGINIA DEPARTMENT OF VETERANS SERVICES

http://www.dvs.virginia.gov/

VIRGINIA MILITARY SURVIVORS AND DEPENDENTS EDUCATION PROGRAM

Scholarships for post-secondary students between ages 16 and 19 to attend Virginia state-supported institutions. Must be child or surviving child of veteran who has either been permanently or totally disabled due to war or other armed conflict; died as a result of war or other armed conflict; or been listed as a POW or MIA. Parent must also meet Virginia residency requirements.

Award: Scholarship for use in freshman, sophomore, junior, senior, or graduate years; renewable. *Number:* varies. *Amount:* varies.

Eligibility Requirements: Applicant must be age 16-19; enrolled or expecting to enroll full-time at a two-year or four-year or technical institution or university; resident of Virginia and studying in Virginia. Available to U.S. citizens. Applicant or parent must meet one or more of the following requirements: general military experience; retired from active duty; disabled or killed as a result of military service; prisoner of war; or missing in action.

Application Requirements: Application, references. *Deadline:* varies.

Contact: Doris Sullivan, Coordinator
Virginia Department of Veterans Services
Poff Federal Building, 270 Franklin Road, SW, Room 503
Roanoke, VA 24011-2215
Phone: 540-857-7101 Ext. 213
Fax: 540-857-7573

MILITARY SERVICE: MARINES

DAUGHTERS OF THE CINCINNATI

http://www.daughters1894.org/

DAUGHTERS OF THE CINCINNATI SCHOLARSHIP
• *See page 617*

DEPARTMENT OF VETERANS AFFAIRS (VA)

http://www.gibill.va.gov/

MONTGOMERY GI BILL (SELECTED RESERVE)
• *See page 617*

FIRST MARINE DIVISION ASSOCIATION

http://www.1stmarinedivisionassociation.org/

FIRST MARINE DIVISION ASSOCIATION SCHOLARSHIP FUND

Scholarship to assist dependents of deceased or 100 percent permanently disabled veterans of service with the 1st Marine Division in furthering their education towards a bachelor's degree. Awarded to full-time, undergraduate students who are attending an accredited college, university, or higher technical trade school, up to a maximum of four years.

Award: Scholarship for use in freshman, sophomore, junior, or senior years; not renewable. *Number:* varies. *Amount:* up to $1750.

Eligibility Requirements: Applicant must be age 22 or under; enrolled or expecting to enroll full-time at a four-year or technical institution or university and single. Available to U.S. citizens. Applicant or parent must meet one or more of the following requirements: Marine Corps experience; retired from active duty; disabled or killed as a result of military service; prisoner of war; or missing in action.

Application Requirements: Application, essay, photo, transcript, social security number, birth certificate, proof of parent's death. *Deadline:* continuous.

Contact: Col. Len Hayes, Executive Director
First Marine Division Association
410 Pier View Way
Oceanside, CA 92054
Phone: 760-967-8561
Fax: 760-967-8567
E-mail: oldbreed@sbcglobal.net

FLEET RESERVE ASSOCIATION EDUCATION FOUNDATION

http://www.fra.org/

FLEET RESERVE ASSOCIATION EDUCATION FOUNDATION SCHOLARSHIPS
• *See page 625*

STANLEY A. DORAN MEMORIAL SCHOLARSHIP
• *See page 542*

INDIANA DEPARTMENT OF VETERANS AFFAIRS

http://www.in.gov/dva

RESIDENT TUITION FOR ACTIVE DUTY MILITARY PERSONNEL
• *See page 617*

LADIES AUXILIARY OF THE FLEET RESERVE ASSOCIATION

http://www.fra.org/

ALLIE MAE ODEN MEMORIAL SCHOLARSHIP
• *See page 548*

LADIES AUXILIARY OF THE FLEET RESERVE ASSOCIATION-NATIONAL PRESIDENT'S SCHOLARSHIP
• *See page 548*

LADIES AUXILIARY OF THE FLEET RESERVE ASSOCIATION SCHOLARSHIP
• *See page 548*

SAM ROSE MEMORIAL SCHOLARSHIP
• *See page 548*

MARINE CORPS TANKERS ASSOCIATION INC.

http://www.USMarinetankers.org/

MARINE CORPS TANKERS ASSOCIATION, JOHN CORNELIUS/MAX ENGLISH SCHOLARSHIP

Award for Marine tankers or former Marine tankers, or dependents of Marines who served in a tank unit and are on active duty, retired, reserve or have been honorably discharged. Applicant must be a high school graduate or planning to graduate in June. May be enrolled in college, undergraduate or graduate or have previously attended college. Must be a member of MCTA or intends to join in the future.

Award: Scholarship for use in freshman, sophomore, junior, senior, or graduate years; not renewable. *Number:* 10. *Amount:* up to $2000.

Eligibility Requirements: Applicant must be enrolled or expecting to enroll full-time at a two-year or four-year or technical institution or university. Available to U.S. citizens. Applicant or parent must meet one or more of the following requirements: Marine Corps experience; retired from active duty; disabled or killed as a result of military service; prisoner of war; or missing in action.

Application Requirements: Application, essay, photo, references, test scores, transcript. *Deadline:* March 15.

Contact: Phil Morell, Scholarship Chair
Marine Corps Tankers Association Inc.
1112 Alpine Heights Road
Alpine, CA 91901-2814
Phone: 619-445-8423
Fax: 619-445-8423
E-mail: mpmorell@cox.net

NAVY-MARINE CORPS RELIEF SOCIETY

http://www.nmcrs.org/education

ADMIRAL MIKE BOORDA LOAN PROGRAM

Scholarship for undergraduate students enrolled full-time in accredited colleges or universities. Must be serving in Navy or Marine Corps and chosen for enrollment in one of the following: Marine Enlisted Commissioning Education Program (MECEP), Medical Enlisted Commissioning Program (MECP), or Meritorious Commissioning Program (MCP). Repayment to begin within three months of commissioning into Navy or Marine Corps.

Award: Forgivable loan for use in freshman, sophomore, junior, or senior years; not renewable. *Number:* 1–100. *Amount:* $500–$3000.

Eligibility Requirements: Applicant must be enrolled or expecting to enroll full-time at a two-year or four-year or technical institution or university. Available to U.S. citizens. Applicant or parent must meet one or more of the following requirements: Marine Corps or Navy experience; retired from active duty; disabled or killed as a result of military service; prisoner of war; or missing in action.

Application Requirements: Application, financial need analysis, copy of military ID/orders. *Deadline:* May 1.

Contact: Mrs. Beverly Langdon, Education, Program Manager
Navy-Marine Corps Relief Society
875 North Randolph Street, Suite 225
Arlington, VA 22203
Phone: 703-696-4960
E-mail: education@nmcrs.org

JOSEPH A. MCALINDEN DIVERS SCHOLARSHIP

Navy-Marine Corps Divers: active duty/retired and dependents pursuing study in the area of ocean agriculture, Oceanography, Aquaculture. Or advanced diver training, certifications and recertifications.

Award: Scholarship for use in freshman, sophomore, junior, or senior years; not renewable. *Amount:* $500–$3000.

Eligibility Requirements: Applicant must be enrolled or expecting to enroll full- or part-time at a two-year or four-year or technical institution or university. Available to U.S. citizens. Applicant must have served in the Marine Corps or Navy.

Application Requirements: Application.

Contact: Mrs. Beverly Langdon, Education, Program Manager

NMCRS GOLD STAR SCHOLARSHIPS FOR CHILDREN OF DECEASED SERVICE MEMBERS

Scholarship for full-time undergraduate students enrolled in accredited colleges or universities. Must be 22 years of age or younger. Must have minimum 2.0 GPA.

Award: Scholarship for use in freshman, sophomore, junior, or senior years; not renewable. *Number:* 1–100. *Amount:* $500–$2500.

Eligibility Requirements: Applicant must be age 22 or under; enrolled or expecting to enroll full-time at a two-year or four-year or technical institution or university and single. Available to U.S. citizens. Applicant or parent must meet one or more of the following requirements: Marine Corps or Navy experience; retired from active duty; disabled or killed as a result of military service; prisoner of war; or missing in action.

Application Requirements: Application, financial need analysis. *Deadline:* March 1.

Contact: Mrs. Beverly Langdon, Education, Program Manager
Navy-Marine Corps Relief Society
875 North Randolph Street, Suite 225
Arlington, VA 22203
Phone: 703-696-4960
E-mail: education@nmcrs.org

SOCIETY OF SPONSORS OF THE UNITED STATES NAVY CENTENNIAL SCHOLARSHIP PROGRAM

The Centennial Scholarship is offered to Iraq-Afghanistan combat wounded veterans who are pursuing a degree that leads to license and certification as a teacher.

Award: Scholarship for use in freshman, sophomore, junior, or senior years; not renewable. *Number:* 1–5. *Amount:* $500–$3000.

Eligibility Requirements: Applicant must be enrolled or expecting to enroll full-time at a two-year or four-year or technical institution or university. Applicant must have 2.5 GPA or higher. Available to U.S. citizens. Applicant or parent must meet one or more of the following requirements: Marine Corps or Navy experience; retired from active duty; disabled or killed as a result of military service; prisoner of war; or missing in action.

Application Requirements: Application, essay.

Contact: Mrs. Beverly Langdon, Education, Program Manager

SECOND MARINE DIVISION ASSOCIATION

http://www.2dmardiv.com/

SECOND MARINE DIVISION ASSOCIATION MEMORIAL SCHOLARSHIP FUND

Renewable award for students who are unmarried, dependent sons, daughters or grandchildren of former or current members of Second Marine Division or attached units. Must submit proof of parent's or grandparent's service. Family adjusted gross income must not exceed $70,000. Award is merit-based. Minimum 2.5 GPA required.

Award: Scholarship for use in freshman, sophomore, junior, or senior years; not renewable. *Number:* 35–42. *Amount:* $1200.

Eligibility Requirements: Applicant must be enrolled or expecting to enroll full-time at a two-year or four-year or technical institution or university and single. Applicant must have 2.5 GPA or higher. Available to U.S. and non-U.S. citizens. Applicant must have served in the Marine Corps or Navy.

Application Requirements: Application, essay, financial need analysis, photo, references, self-addressed stamped envelope, transcript. *Deadline:* April 1.

Contact: Mr. Martin McNulty, Chairman, Board of Trustees, SMDA Memorial Scholarship Fund
Second Marine Division Association
280 Briarwood Road
Tyrone, GA 30290
Phone: 678-364-1328

TAILHOOK EDUCATIONAL FOUNDATION

http://www.tailhook.org/

TAILHOOK EDUCATIONAL FOUNDATION SCHOLARSHIP
• See page 626

THIRD MARINE DIVISION ASSOCIATION, INC.

http://www.caltrap.com/

THIRD MARINE DIVISION ASSOCIATION MEMORIAL SCHOLARSHIP FUND

Scholarship assistance for dependents of qualified Third Marine Division Association members (Marine or Navy), or qualified service-connected deceased 3d Marine Division veterans. For further details visit web site http://www.caltrap.com. Total number of awards varies.

Award: Scholarship for use in freshman, sophomore, junior, or senior years; renewable. *Number:* 5–25. *Amount:* $500–$1500.

Eligibility Requirements: Applicant must be age 16-23; enrolled or expecting to enroll full-time at a two-year or four-year or technical institution or university and single. Available to U.S. citizens. Applicant must have served in the Marine Corps or Navy.

Application Requirements: Application, financial need analysis, photo, transcript, birth certificate/adoption order (if applicable). *Deadline:* April 15.

Contact: James G. Kyser III, USMC-Retd., Secretary, Memorial Scholarship Fund
Third Marine Division Association, Inc.
15727 Vista Drive
Dumfries, VA 22025-1810
E-mail: supertop@aol.com

UNITED STATES MARINE CORPS SCHOLARSHIP FOUNDATION, INC.

http://www.mcsf.org/

MARINE CORPS SCHOLARSHIP FOUNDATION
• See page 570

WISCONSIN DEPARTMENT OF VETERANS AFFAIRS (WDVA)

http://www.dva.state.wi.us/

VETERANS EDUCATION (VETED) REIMBURSEMENT GRANT
• *See page 617*

MILITARY SERVICE: NAVY

ANCHOR SCHOLARSHIP FOUNDATION

http://www.anchorscholarship.com/

ANCHOR SCHOLARSHIP FOUNDATION PROGRAM

Must be dependent child or spouse of US Navy service member (active or retired) having served at least six years after 1975 under administrative control of US Naval Surface Forces, Atlantic or Pacific Fleets. To obtain application, must submit sponsor's full name, rank/rate, list of duty stations, home-ports, ship hull numbers and dates served aboard. Selection basis: academics, extracurricular activities, character, and financial need.

Award: Scholarship for use in freshman, sophomore, junior, or senior years; not renewable. *Number:* 35–43. *Amount:* $1000–$3500.

Eligibility Requirements: Applicant must be enrolled or expecting to enroll full-time at a four-year institution or university. Available to U.S. citizens. Applicant or parent must meet one or more of the following requirements: Navy experience; retired from active duty; disabled or killed as a result of military service; prisoner of war; or missing in action.

Application Requirements: Application, essay, financial need analysis, references, self-addressed stamped envelope, test scores, transcript, eligibility application (on-line). *Deadline:* March 15.

Contact: Danielle Dawley, Executive Director
Anchor Scholarship Foundation
PO Box 9535
Norfolk, VA 23505-0535
Phone: 757-374-3769
E-mail: admin@anchorscholarship.com

DAUGHTERS OF THE CINCINNATI

http://www.daughters1894.org/

DAUGHTERS OF THE CINCINNATI SCHOLARSHIP
• *See page 617*

DEPARTMENT OF VETERANS AFFAIRS (VA)

http://www.gibill.va.gov/

MONTGOMERY GI BILL (SELECTED RESERVE)
• *See page 617*

DOLPHIN SCHOLARSHIP FOUNDATION

http://www.dolphinscholarship.org/

DOLPHIN SCHOLARSHIPS

Renewable award for undergraduate students. Applicant's parent/stepparent must meet one of the following requirements: be current/former member of the U.S. Navy who qualified in submarines and served in the Submarine Force for at least eight years; current or former member of the Navy who served in submarine support activities for at least ten years; or Navy member who died while on active duty in the Submarine Force. Must be single, under age 24.

Award: Scholarship for use in freshman, sophomore, junior, or senior years; renewable. *Number:* 30–35. *Amount:* up to $3250.

Eligibility Requirements: Applicant must be age 24 or under; enrolled or expecting to enroll full-time at a four-year institution or university and single. Available to U.S. citizens. Applicant or parent must meet one or more of the following requirements: Navy experience; retired from active duty; disabled or killed as a result of military service; prisoner of war; or missing in action.

Application Requirements: Application, essay, financial need analysis, references, self-addressed stamped envelope, test scores, transcript. *Deadline:* March 15.

Contact: Tomi Roeske, Scholarship Administrator
Dolphin Scholarship Foundation
5040 Virginia Beach Boulevard, Suite 104A
Virginia Beach, VA 23462
Phone: 757-671-3200 Ext. 111
Fax: 757-671-3330
E-mail: scholars@dolphinscholarship.org

FLEET RESERVE ASSOCIATION EDUCATION FOUNDATION

http://www.fra.org/

COLONEL HAZEL ELIZABETH BENN U.S.M.C. SCHOLARSHIP
• *See page 542*

FLEET RESERVE ASSOCIATION EDUCATION FOUNDATION SCHOLARSHIPS
• *See page 625*

STANLEY A. DORAN MEMORIAL SCHOLARSHIP
• *See page 542*

GAMEWARDENS OF VIETNAM ASSOCIATION INC.

http://www.tf116.org/

GAMEWARDENS OF VIETNAM SCHOLARSHIP

Scholarship for entering freshman who is a descendant of a U.S. Navy man or woman who worked with TF-116 in Vietnam. One-time award, but applicant may reapply.

Award: Scholarship for use in freshman year; not renewable. *Number:* 1–3. *Amount:* $500.

Eligibility Requirements: Applicant must be high school student; age 16-21 and planning to enroll or expecting to enroll full-time at a two-year or four-year or technical institution or university. Applicant must have 2.5 GPA or higher. Available to U.S. and non-U.S. citizens. Applicant or parent must meet one or more of the following requirements: Navy experience; retired from active duty; disabled or killed as a result of military service; prisoner of war; or missing in action.

Application Requirements: Application, resume, references, test scores, transcript. *Deadline:* April 1.

Contact: David Ajax, Scholarship Coordinator
Gamewardens of Vietnam Association Inc.
6630 Perry Court
Arvada, CO 80003
Phone: 303-426-6385
Fax: 303-426-6186
E-mail: dpajax@comcast.net

INDIANA DEPARTMENT OF VETERANS AFFAIRS

http://www.in.gov/dva

RESIDENT TUITION FOR ACTIVE DUTY MILITARY PERSONNEL
• *See page 617*

LADIES AUXILIARY OF THE FLEET RESERVE ASSOCIATION

http://www.fra.org/

ALLIE MAE ODEN MEMORIAL SCHOLARSHIP
• *See page 548*

LADIES AUXILIARY OF THE FLEET RESERVE ASSOCIATION-NATIONAL PRESIDENT'S SCHOLARSHIP
• *See page 548*

LADIES AUXILIARY OF THE FLEET RESERVE ASSOCIATION SCHOLARSHIP
• *See page 548*

SAM ROSE MEMORIAL SCHOLARSHIP
• *See page 548*

NAVAL RESERVE ASSOCIATION

http://www.navy-reserve.org/

NAVAL RESERVE ASSOCIATION SCHOLARSHIP PROGRAM

Award is given to children of active members of the association. Must be U.S. citizens and under the age of 24. Must be enrolled in or accepted for full-time enrollment at an accredited college, university or a fully-accredited technical school.

Award: Scholarship for use in freshman, sophomore, junior, or senior years; not renewable. *Number:* varies. *Amount:* $1000–$5000.

Eligibility Requirements: Applicant must be age 24 or under and enrolled or expecting to enroll full-time at a two-year or four-year or technical institution or university. Available to U.S. citizens. Applicant or parent must meet one or more of the following requirements: Navy experience; retired from active duty; disabled or killed as a result of military service; prisoner of war; or missing in action.

Application Requirements: Application, driver's license, essay, financial need analysis, references, test scores, transcript. *Deadline:* May 1.

Contact: Mr. Bob Lyman, Chief Financial Officer
Naval Reserve Association
1619 King Street
Alexandria, VA 22314
Phone: 703-548-5800
Fax: 703-683-3647
E-mail: cfo@navy-reserve.org

NAVY-MARINE CORPS RELIEF SOCIETY

http://www.nmcrs.org/education

ADMIRAL MIKE BOORDA LOAN PROGRAM
• *See page 646*

JOSEPH A. MCALINDEN DIVERS SCHOLARSHIP
• *See page 647*

NMCRS GOLD STAR SCHOLARSHIPS FOR CHILDREN OF DECEASED SERVICE MEMBERS
• *See page 647*

SOCIETY OF SPONSORS OF THE UNITED STATES NAVY CENTENNIAL SCHOLARSHIP PROGRAM
• *See page 647*

SEABEE MEMORIAL SCHOLARSHIP ASSOCIATION, INC.

http://www.seabee.org/

SEABEE MEMORIAL ASSOCIATION SCHOLARSHIP

Award available to children or grandchildren of current or former members of the Naval Construction Force (Seabees) or Naval Civil Engineer Corps. Not available for graduate study or to great-grandchildren of Seabees.

Award: Scholarship for use in freshman, sophomore, junior, or senior years; renewable. *Number:* 99. *Amount:* $1800.

Eligibility Requirements: Applicant must be enrolled or expecting to enroll full-time at a four-year institution or university. Available to U.S. citizens. Applicant or parent must meet one or more of the following requirements: Navy experience; retired from active duty; disabled or killed as a result of military service; prisoner of war; or missing in action.

Application Requirements: Application, essay, financial need analysis, test scores, transcript, IRS Form 1040. *Deadline:* April 15.

Contact: Sheryl Chiogioji, Administrative Assistant
Seabee Memorial Scholarship Association, Inc.
PO Box 6574
Silver Spring, MD 20916
Phone: 301-570-2850
Fax: 301-570-2873
E-mail: smsa@erols.com

SECOND MARINE DIVISION ASSOCIATION

http://www.2dmardiv.com/

SECOND MARINE DIVISION ASSOCIATION MEMORIAL SCHOLARSHIP FUND
• *See page 647*

TAILHOOK EDUCATIONAL FOUNDATION

http://www.tailhook.org/

TAILHOOK EDUCATIONAL FOUNDATION SCHOLARSHIP
• *See page 626*

THIRD MARINE DIVISION ASSOCIATION, INC.

http://www.caltrap.com/

THIRD MARINE DIVISION ASSOCIATION MEMORIAL SCHOLARSHIP FUND
• *See page 647*

UDT-SEAL ASSOCIATION

http://www.nswfoundation.org/

HAD RICHARDS UDT-SEAL MEMORIAL SCHOLARSHIP

One-time award for dependent children of UDT-SEAL association members. Freshmen given priority. Applicant may not be older than 22 and not married. Must be U.S. citizen.

Award: Scholarship for use in freshman, sophomore, junior, or senior years; not renewable. *Number:* 1–2. *Amount:* varies.

Eligibility Requirements: Applicant must be age 22 or under; enrolled or expecting to enroll full-time at a two-year or four-year institution or university and single. Available to U.S. citizens. Applicant or parent must meet one or more of the following requirements: Navy experience; retired from active duty; disabled or killed as a result of military service; prisoner of war; or missing in action.

Application Requirements: Application, essay, photo, test scores, transcript, proof of active duty or parent/spouse's active duty. *Deadline:* varies.

Contact: Robert Rieve, President and CEO
UDT-Seal Association
PO Box 5965
Virginia Beach, VA 23471
Phone: 757-363-7490
E-mail: info@nswfoundation.org

NAVAL SPECIAL WARFARE SCHOLARSHIP

Awards given to active duty SEAL's, SWCC's, and other active duty military serving in a Naval Special Warfare command or their spouses and dependents.

Award: Scholarship for use in freshman, sophomore, junior, or senior years; not renewable. *Number:* 80–100. *Amount:* varies.

Eligibility Requirements: Applicant must be enrolled or expecting to enroll full- or part-time at a two-year or four-year institution or university. Available to U.S. citizens. Applicant or parent must meet one or more of the following requirements: Navy experience; retired from active duty; disabled or killed as a result of military service; prisoner of war; or missing in action.

Application Requirements: Application, essay, photo, transcript, proof of active duty or parent/spouse's active duty.

Contact: Robert Rieve, President and CEO
UDT-Seal Association
PO Box 5965
Virginia Beach, VA 23471
Phone: 757-363-7490
E-mail: info@nswfoundation.org

UDT-SEAL SCHOLARSHIP

Award for dependent children of UDT-SEAL association members. Freshmen given priority. Applicant may not be older than 22 and not married. Must be U.S. citizen.

Award: Scholarship for use in freshman, sophomore, junior, or senior years; not renewable. *Number:* 10–20. *Amount:* varies.

Eligibility Requirements: Applicant must be age 22 or under; enrolled or expecting to enroll full-time at a two-year or four-year or technical institution or university and single. Available to U.S. citizens. Applicant or parent must meet one or more of the following requirements: Navy experience; retired from active duty; disabled or killed as a result of military service; prisoner of war; or missing in action.

Application Requirements: Application, essay, photo, test scores, transcript, proof of active duty or parent/spouse's active duty. *Deadline:* varies.

Contact: Robert Rieve, President and CEO
UDT-Seal Association
PO Box 5965
Virginia Beach, VA 23471
Phone: 757-363-7490
E-mail: info@nswfoundation.org

UNITED STATES SUBMARINE VETERANS

http://www.ussvcf.org/

UNITED STATES SUBMARINE VETERANS INC. NATIONAL SCHOLARSHIP PROGRAM

• See page 571

WINGS OVER AMERICA SCHOLARSHIP FOUNDATION

http://www.wingsoveramerica.us/

WINGS OVER AMERICA SCHOLARSHIP

Applicant must be graduates of an accredited high school or the equivalent home school or institution and must plan to attend an accredited academic institution.

Award: Scholarship for use in freshman, sophomore, or junior years; not renewable. *Number:* 40. *Amount:* $1000–$3000.

Eligibility Requirements: Applicant must be enrolled or expecting to enroll full- or part-time at a two-year or four-year institution or university. Available to U.S. citizens. Applicant must have served in the Navy.

Application Requirements: Application, essay, references, transcript, pre-qualification form based on military service of sponsor. *Deadline:* March 1.

Contact: Susan Hunter, Scholarship Administrator
Wings Over America Scholarship Foundation
4966 Euclid Road Suite 109
Virginia Beach, VA 23462
Phone: 757-671-3200
E-mail: info@wingsoveramerica.us

WISCONSIN DEPARTMENT OF VETERANS AFFAIRS (WDVA)

http://www.dva.state.wi.us/

VETERANS EDUCATION (VETED) REIMBURSEMENT GRANT

• See page 617

NATIONALITY OR ETHNIC HERITAGE

ADELANTE! U.S. EDUCATION LEADERSHIP FUND

http://www.adelantefund.org/

ADELANTE FUND SCHOLARSHIPS

Awards are primarily created to enhance the leadership qualities of the recipients for transition into postgraduate education, business and/or corporate America. Financial need is a factor for these awards. Minimum 2.5 GPA is required on one of the awards but a 3.0 GPA is required on the rest. Awards are available for colleges located in the states of California, New Mexico, Arizona, Texas, Florida, Illinois, and New York. Applicants should view web site for all award criteria and for scholarship application forms.

Award: Scholarship for use in sophomore, junior, or senior years; renewable. *Number:* 30–45. *Amount:* $1000–$3000.

Eligibility Requirements: Applicant must be of Hispanic heritage; enrolled or expecting to enroll full-time at a two-year or four-year institution or university; studying in Arizona, California, Florida, Illinois, New Mexico, New York, or Texas and must have an interest in leadership. Applicant must have 3.0 GPA or higher. Available to U.S. citizens.

Application Requirements: Application, essay, financial need analysis, resume, references, transcript. *Deadline:* May 28.

Contact: Miss. Sarah Ramos, Program Coordinator
Adelante! U.S. Education Leadership Fund
8415 Datapoint Drive, Suite 400
San Antonio, TX 78229
Phone: 210-692-1971
Fax: 210-692-1951
E-mail: sramos@adelantefund.org

ALABAMA INDIAN AFFAIRS COMMISSION

http://www.aiac.alabama.gov/

AIAC SCHOLARSHIP

Must be a member of a state or federally recognized Indian tribe. Must have a tribal roll card. Must be a resident of the state of Alabama. Must attend a school in the state of Alabama, unless program is not offered in an Alabama school.

Award: Scholarship for use in freshman, sophomore, junior, senior, or graduate years; not renewable. *Number:* 25–55. *Amount:* $500.

Eligibility Requirements: Applicant must be American Indian/Alaska Native; enrolled or expecting to enroll full-time at a two-year or four-year or technical institution or university; resident of Alabama and studying in Alabama. Applicant must have 2.5 GPA or higher. Available to U.S. citizens.

Application Requirements: Application, essay, financial need analysis, references, test scores, transcript, tribal certification, letter of acceptance from school of choice. *Deadline:* March 7.

Contact: Mrs. Eloise Josey, Executive Director
Alabama Indian Affairs Commission
771 South Lawrence Street
Suite 106
Montgomery, AL 36104
Phone: 334-242-2831
Fax: 334-240-3408
E-mail: aiac@att.net

ALBERTA HERITAGE SCHOLARSHIP FUND

http://www.alis.alberta.ca/

ADULT HIGH SCHOOL EQUIVALENCY SCHOLARSHIPS

Awards of CAN$500 to recognize and reward the academic achievement of mature students in the attainment of high school equivalency and provide an incentive for students to continue their education at the postsecondary level. Applicants must be residents of Alberta, have been out of high school for a minimum of three years prior to commencing a high school equivalency program, and be enrolled full-time in a high school equivalency program. Must be nominated by high school. See web site for additional information and application http://alis.alberta.ca.

Award: Scholarship for use in freshman year; not renewable. *Number:* up to 200.

Eligibility Requirements: Applicant must be Canadian citizen; enrolled or expecting to enroll full-time at a two-year or four-year or technical institution or university; resident of Alberta and studying in Alberta. Applicant must have 3.0 GPA or higher.

Application Requirements: Application, nomination. *Deadline:* September 1.

Contact: Scholarship Committee
Alberta Heritage Scholarship Fund
9940 106th Street, Fourth Floor, PO Box 28000, Station Main
Edmonton, AB T5J 4R4
Phone: 780-427-8640
Fax: 780-422-4516
E-mail: scholarships@gov.ab.ca

ALBERTA CENTENNIAL PREMIER'S SCHOLARSHIPS-ALBERTA

Awards of CAN$2005 to commemorate the province of Alberta's centennial. Twenty-five awards have been established. Must be Canadian citizens or permanent residents of Canada and Alberta residents. Awards students entering any level of postsecondary study at any university, college, technical institute, or apprenticeship program in Canada. Each high school in Alberta nominates a recipient and all are considered for the 25 awards. For additional information and application form, visit web site http://alis.alberta.ca.

Award: Scholarship for use in freshman, sophomore, junior, or senior years; not renewable. *Number:* 25.

Eligibility Requirements: Applicant must be Canadian citizen; high school student; planning to enroll or expecting to enroll full-time at a two-year or four-year or technical institution or university and resident of Alberta.

Application Requirements: Nomination from high school counselors. *Deadline:* June 15.

Contact: Scholarship Committee
Alberta Heritage Scholarship Fund
9940 106th Street, Fourth Floor, Sterling Place
PO Box 28000, Station Main
Edmonton, AB T5J 4R4
Canada
Phone: 780-427-8640
E-mail: scholarships@gov.ab.ca

ALEXANDER RUTHERFORD SCHOLARSHIPS FOR HIGH SCHOOL ACHIEVEMENT

Award of up to CAN$2500 available to high school students who are residents of Alberta and plan to enroll or are enrolled in a full-time postsecondary program of at least one semester. Awarded on the basis of achieving an 75 percent average on seven designated subjects in grades 10, 11 and 12. For additional information, see web site http://alis.alberta.ca.

Award: Scholarship for use in freshman year; not renewable.

Eligibility Requirements: Applicant must be Canadian citizen; high school student; planning to enroll or expecting to enroll full-time at a two-year or four-year or technical institution or university and resident of Alberta.

Application Requirements: Application, transcript. *Deadline:* May 1.

Contact: Scholarship Committee
Alberta Heritage Scholarship Fund
9940 106th Street, Fourth Floor, Sterling Place
PO Box 28000, Station Main
Edmonton, AB T5J 4R4
Canada
Phone: 780-427-8640
E-mail: scholarships@gov.ab.ca

CHARLES S. NOBLE JUNIOR A HOCKEY SCHOLARSHIPS

Awards of CAN$2000 to reward the athletic and academic excellence of Junior A Hockey league players and to provide an incentive and means for these players to continue their postsecondary education. Must be Alberta residents and enrolled full-time at a postsecondary institution in Alberta. Interested applicants should contact their team coach or manager, as nominations must come from the participant's hockey team. For additional information, see web site http://alis.alberta.ca.

Award: Scholarship for use in freshman, sophomore, junior, or senior years; not renewable. *Number:* 10.

Eligibility Requirements: Applicant must be Canadian citizen; enrolled or expecting to enroll full-time at a two-year or four-year or technical institution or university; resident of Alberta; studying in Alberta and must have an interest in athletics/sports.

Application Requirements: Application, essay, transcript. *Deadline:* December 1.

Contact: Scholarship Committee
Alberta Heritage Scholarship Fund
9940 106th Street, Fourth Floor, Sterling Place
PO Box 28000, Station Main
Edmonton, AB T5J 4R4
Canada
Phone: 780-427-8640
E-mail: scholarships@gov.ab.ca

CHARLES S. NOBLE JUNIOR FOOTBALL SCHOLARSHIPS

Scholarships of up to CAN$1000 available to reward the athletic and academic excellence of junior football players at universities, colleges, and technical institutes in Alberta. Must be Alberta residents and enrolled full-time in an undergraduate, professional, or graduate program at a university, college, or technical institute in Alberta. Must be a playing member on an Alberta junior football team. Interested applicants should contact their team coach or manager as nominations must come from the football team. For additional information, visit web site http://alis.alberta.ca.

Award: Scholarship for use in freshman, sophomore, junior, or senior years; not renewable. *Number:* 30.

Eligibility Requirements: Applicant must be Canadian citizen; enrolled or expecting to enroll full-time at a two-year or four-year or technical institution or university; resident of Alberta; studying in Alberta and must have an interest in athletics/sports.

Application Requirements: Nomination from junior football team. *Deadline:* October 1.

Contact: Scholarship Committee
Alberta Heritage Scholarship Fund
9940 106th Street, Fourth Floor, Sterling Place
PO Box 28000, Station Main
Edmonton, AB T5J 4R4
Canada
Phone: 780-427-8640
E-mail: scholarships@gov.ab.ca

DR. ERNEST AND MINNIE MEHL SCHOLARSHIP

Award of CAN$3500 to encourage students to pursue a postsecondary education and to recognize and reward exceptional academic achievement at the senior high school level. Applicants must be Canadian citizens or landed immigrants who have completed their grade twelve in Alberta at a school that follows the Alberta Education Curriculum. Applicants must be continuing their studies at a degree granting postsecondary institution in Canada. University transfer programs are acceptable. For additional information and application, see web site http://alis.alberta.ca.

Award: Scholarship for use in freshman, sophomore, junior, or senior years; not renewable. *Number:* 1.

Eligibility Requirements: Applicant must be Canadian citizen; high school student; planning to enroll or expecting to enroll full-time at a two-year or four-year or technical institution or university; resident of Alberta and studying in Alberta, British Columbia, Manitoba, New Brunswick, Newfoundland, Nova Scotia, Ontario, Prince Edward Island, Quebec, or Saskatchewan.

Application Requirements: Application, financial need analysis, transcript. *Deadline:* June 1.

Contact: Scholarship Committee
Alberta Heritage Scholarship Fund
9940 106th Street, Fourth Floor, Sterling Place
PO Box 28000, Station Main
Edmonton, AB T5J 4R4
Canada
Phone: 780-427-8640
E-mail: scholarships@gov.ab.ca

EARL AND COUNTESS OF WESSEX-WORLD CHAMPIONSHIPS IN ATHLETICS SCHOLARSHIPS

Award of CAN$3000 to recognize the top male and female Alberta students who have excelled in track and field, have a strong academic record, and plan to continue their studies at the postsecondary level in Alberta. Must be Canadian citizens or landed immigrants and residents of Alberta. Must have completed grade twelve in Alberta in the same year they apply for the scholarship. Must be planning on continuing their studies at a postsecondary institution in Alberta. For additional information and application, go to web site http://alis.alberta.ca.

Award: Scholarship for use in freshman year; not renewable. *Number:* 2.

Eligibility Requirements: Applicant must be Canadian citizen; high school student; planning to enroll or expecting to enroll full-time at a two-year or four-year or technical institution or university; resident of Alberta; studying in Alberta and must have an interest in athletics/sports.

Application Requirements: Application, transcript. *Deadline:* October 1.

Contact: Scholarship Committee
Alberta Heritage Scholarship Fund
9940 106th Street, Fourth Floor, Sterling Place
PO Box 28000, Station Main
Edmonton, AB T5J 4R4
Canada
Phone: 780-427-8640
E-mail: scholarships@gov.ab.ca

GRANT MACEWAN UNITED WORLD COLLEGE SCHOLARSHIPS

Award to reward Alberta's best grade eleven students with a chance to complete their high school at one of the twelve United World Colleges located throughout the world. Applicants must be Alberta residents and be between the ages of 16 and 17 and a half. Applicants are normally in the process of completing their grade eleven. Scholarship is based on a student's academic record, breadth of study, personal accomplishments, community involvement, and interest in the goals of the United World Colleges. For additional information and application, see web site http://alis.alberta.ca.

Award: Scholarship for use in freshman year; renewable. *Amount:* varies.

Eligibility Requirements: Applicant must be Canadian citizen; high school student; age 16-17; planning to enroll or expecting to enroll full-time at a four-year institution or university and resident of Alberta.

Application Requirements: Application, essay, interview, references, transcript. *Deadline:* February 15.

Contact: Scholarship Committee
Alberta Heritage Scholarship Fund
9940 106th Street, Fourth Floor, Sterling Place
PO Box 28000, Station Main
Edmonton, AB T5J 4R4
Canada
Phone: 780-427-8640
E-mail: scholarships@gov.ab.ca

INTERNATIONAL EDUCATION AWARDS-UKRAINE

Awards of CAN$5000 to recognize the accomplishments of intern, co-op, practicum, apprenticeship, and research students. Must be a postsecondary student or an apprenticeship student taking a practicum, internship, co-op, apprenticeship program, or a student conducting research (one-term). Recipient will be selected based on demonstrated past accomplishments and potential for improving relations between Ukraine and Alberta. For additional information and application, see web site http://alis.alberta.ca.

Award: Scholarship for use in freshman, sophomore, junior, or senior years; not renewable. *Number:* 5.

Eligibility Requirements: Applicant must be Canadian or Ukrainian citizen; enrolled or expecting to enroll full-time at a two-year or four-year or technical institution or university and studying in Alberta. Available to Canadian and non-U.S. citizens.

Application Requirements: Application. *Deadline:* February 1.

Contact: Scholarship Committee
Alberta Heritage Scholarship Fund
9940 106th Street, Fourth Floor, Sterling Place
PO Box 28000, Station Main
Edmonton, AB T5J 4R4
Canada
Phone: 780-427-8640
E-mail: scholarships@gov.ab.ca

JIMMIE CONDON ATHLETIC SCHOLARSHIPS

Award of CAN$1800 available to Alberta residents enrolled full-time in an undergraduate, professional, or graduate program at a university, college, or technical institute in Alberta. Must be a member of a designated sports team or a Provincial Disabled Athletic Team recognized by the Alberta Athlete Development Program, and must be nominated by coach. For additional information, go to web site http://alis.alberta.ca.

Award: Scholarship for use in freshman, sophomore, junior, or senior years; not renewable.

Eligibility Requirements: Applicant must be Canadian citizen; enrolled or expecting to enroll full-time at a two-year or four-year or technical institution or university; resident of Alberta; studying in Alberta and must have an interest in athletics/sports.

Application Requirements: Application, nomination by athletic coach. *Deadline:* November 1.

Contact: Scholarship Committee
Alberta Heritage Scholarship Fund
9940 106th Street, Fourth Floor, Sterling Place
PO Box 28000, Station Main
Edmonton, AB T5J 4R4
Canada
Phone: 780-427-8640
E-mail: scholarships@gov.ab.ca

LAURENCE DECORE STUDENT LEADERSHIP AWARDS

Awards of CAN$500 for postsecondary students who have demonstrated outstanding dedication and leadership to fellow students and to their community. Must be Alberta residents who are currently enrolled in a minimum of three full courses at a designated Alberta postsecondary institution. Selected on the basis of involvement in either student government or student societies, clubs, or organizations. For additional information, visit web site http://alis.alberta.ca.

Award: Scholarship for use in freshman, sophomore, junior, or senior years; not renewable. *Number:* 100.

Eligibility Requirements: Applicant must be Canadian citizen; enrolled or expecting to enroll full- or part-time at a two-year or four-year or technical institution or university; resident of Alberta; studying in Alberta and must have an interest in leadership.

Application Requirements: Application, nomination from school. *Deadline:* March 1.

Contact: Scholarship Committee
Alberta Heritage Scholarship Fund
9940 106th Street, Fourth Floor, Sterling Place
PO Box 28000, Station Main
Edmonton, AB T5J 4R4
Canada
Phone: 780-427-8640
E-mail: scholarships@gov.ab.ca

LOUISE MCKINNEY POSTSECONDARY SCHOLARSHIPS

Student awards of up to CAN$2500 to residents of Alberta who are enrolled at a university, college, or technical institute in the second or subsequent year of full-time study. Alberta students studying out-of-province because their program of study is not offered in Alberta will be considered for a scholarship if their class standing is in the top two percent of their program. For additional information, go to web site http://alis.alberta.ca.

Award: Scholarship for use in sophomore, junior, or senior years; not renewable.

Eligibility Requirements: Applicant must be Canadian citizen; enrolled or expecting to enroll full-time at a two-year or four-year institution or university and resident of Alberta.

Application Requirements: Application, test scores, transcript. *Deadline:* varies.

Contact: Scholarship Committee
Alberta Heritage Scholarship Fund
9940 106th Street, Fourth Floor, Sterling Place
PO Box 28000, Station Main
Edmonton, AB T5J 4R4
Canada
Phone: 780-427-8640
E-mail: scholarships@gov.ab.ca

PERSONS CASE SCHOLARSHIPS

Awards of up to CAN$5000 to assist female students whose studies will ultimately contribute to the advancement of women, or who are studying in a field that is non-traditional for women. Applicants must be residents of Alberta and enrolled full-time at a postsecondary institution in Alberta. Students studying out-of-province may be considered for this award if their program of study is not available in Alberta. Selection is based on chosen program of study, financial need, and academic achievement. For additional information and application, visit web site http://alis.alberta.ca.

Award: Scholarship for use in freshman, sophomore, junior, or senior years; not renewable. *Number:* 5–10.

Eligibility Requirements: Applicant must be Canadian citizen; enrolled or expecting to enroll full-time at a two-year or four-year or technical institution or university; female; resident of Alberta and studying in Alberta. Applicant must have 3.0 GPA or higher.

Application Requirements: Application, essay, financial need analysis, resume, transcript. *Deadline:* September 30.

Contact: Scholarship Committee
Alberta Heritage Scholarship Fund
9940 106th Street, Fourth Floor, Sterling Place
PO Box 28000, Station Main
Edmonton, AB T5J 4R4
Canada
Phone: 780-427-8640
E-mail: scholarships@gov.ab.ca

QUEEN ELIZABETH II GOLDEN JUBILEE CITIZENSHIP MEDAL

Award of CAN$5000, a medal, and letter of commendation from the Lieutenant Governor to recognize the eight most outstanding high school students among those who received a Premier's Citizenship award in recognition of the Queen's Golden Jubilee. Premier's Citizenship Award is for each high school in Alberta to nominate one student for superior public service. For additional information, see web site http://alis.alberta.ca.

Award: Prize for use in freshman year; not renewable. *Number:* 8.

Eligibility Requirements: Applicant must be Canadian citizen; high school student; planning to enroll or expecting to enroll full-time at a four-year institution or university and resident of Alberta.

Application Requirements: Proof of winning the Premier's Citizenship Award. *Deadline:* June 15.

Contact: Scholarship Committee
Alberta Heritage Scholarship Fund
9940 106th Street, Fourth Floor, Sterling Place
PO Box 28000, Station Main
Edmonton, AB T5J 4R4
Canada
Phone: 780-427-8640
E-mail: scholarships@gov.ab.ca

RUTHERFORD SCHOLARS

Recipients are selected on the basis of results obtained on Diploma Examinations in English 30, or Francais 30, Social Studies 30 and three other subjects. Averages normally are in the 98.0 to 98.8 percent range. Only the first writing of the diploma exam will be considered. No application is required. Recipients are selected from all Alexander Rutherford Scholarship applications received before August 1. Amount of award is CAN$2500.

Award: Scholarship for use in freshman year; not renewable. *Number:* 10.

Eligibility Requirements: Applicant must be Canadian citizen; high school student; planning to enroll or expecting to enroll full-time at a four-year institution or university and resident of Alberta.

Application Requirements: Test scores, transcript. *Deadline:* August 1.

Contact: Scholarship Committee
Alberta Heritage Scholarship Fund
9940 106th Street, Fourth Floor, Sterling Place
PO Box 28000, Station Main
Edmonton, AB T5J 4R4
Canada
Phone: 780-427-8640
E-mail: scholarships@gov.ab.ca

ALBUQUERQUE COMMUNITY FOUNDATION

http://www.albuquerquefoundation.org/

NOTAH BEGAY III SCHOLARSHIP PROGRAM FOR NATIVE AMERICAN SCHOLAR ATHLETES

The program requires the applicant to attend an accredited, not-for-profit educational institution in the United States. Total number of awards and dollar value varies. Must have played in varsity level sports in high school and maintain a 3.0 GPA. Deadline varies.

Award: Scholarship for use in freshman, sophomore, junior, or senior years; not renewable. *Number:* 2. *Amount:* $2000.

Eligibility Requirements: Applicant must be American Indian/Alaska Native; high school student; planning to enroll or expecting to enroll full-time at a two-year or four-year institution or university; resident of New Mexico and must have an interest in athletics/sports. Applicant must have 3.0 GPA or higher. Available to U.S. citizens.

Application Requirements: Application, essay, financial need analysis, resume, references, test scores, transcript, proof of tribal enrollment or certificate of Indian blood (minimum 25 percent).

Contact: Nancy Johnson, Program Director
Albuquerque Community Foundation
PO Box 36960
Albuquerque, NM 87176-6960
Phone: 505-883-6240
E-mail: foundation@albuquerquefoundation.org

AMERICAN BAPTIST FINANCIAL AID PROGRAM

http://www.abc-usa.org/

AMERICAN BAPTIST FINANCIAL AID PROGRAM NATIVE AMERICAN GRANTS

Renewable award of $1000 to $2000 for Native Americans who are members of an American Baptist Church/USA congregation. Must be a U.S. citizen. Must be attending an accredited educational institution in the United States.

Award: Grant for use in freshman, sophomore, junior, senior, or graduate years; renewable. *Number:* 1–5. *Amount:* $1000–$2000.

Eligibility Requirements: Applicant must be Baptist; American Indian/Alaska Native and enrolled or expecting to enroll full-time at a four-year institution or university. Available to U.S. citizens.

Application Requirements: Application, financial need analysis, references. *Deadline:* May 31.

Contact: Lynne Eckman, Director of Financial Aid
American Baptist Financial Aid Program
PO Box 851
Valley Forge, PA 19482-0851
Phone: 610-768-2067
Fax: 610-768-2470
E-mail: lynne.eckman@abc-usa.org

AMERICAN INDIAN EDUCATION FOUNDATION

http://www.aiefprograms.org/

AMERICAN INDIAN EDUCATION FOUNDATION SCHOLARSHIP

AIEF provides tuition and books for American Indian students. 200 undergraduate, 25 graduate scholarships.

Award: Scholarship for use in freshman, sophomore, junior, senior, or graduate years; not renewable. *Number:* 200. *Amount:* $2000.

Eligibility Requirements: Applicant must be of Indian heritage; American Indian/Alaska Native and enrolled or expecting to enroll full- or part-time at a two-year or four-year or technical institution or university. Available to U.S. citizens.

Application Requirements: Application, essay, photo, transcript, Certificate of Tribal Enrollment. *Deadline:* April 4.

Contact: Murray Lee, Scholarship Specialist
American Indian Education Foundation
2401 Eglin Street
Rapid City, SD 57703
Phone: 605-342-9968
E-mail: mlee@nrc1.org

AMERICAN INDIAN GRADUATE CENTER

http://www.aigcs.org/

ACCENTURE AMERICAN INDIAN SCHOLARSHIP

Scholarships awarded to American Indian and Alaska Natives from U.S. federally recognized tribes. This program is for first year undergraduates and first year graduate students. Must have a cumulative GPA of a 3.0 on a 4.0 scale and demonstrate financial need. Areas of study: banking, resort management, gaming operations, management and administration, including accounting, finance, information technology and human resources.

Award: Scholarship for use in freshman or graduate years; renewable. *Number:* up to 10. *Amount:* $2000–$20,000.

Eligibility Requirements: Applicant must be American Indian/Alaska Native and enrolled or expecting to enroll full-time at a four-year institution or university. Applicant must have 3.0 GPA or higher. Available to U.S. citizens.

Application Requirements: Application, essay, financial need analysis, photo, resume, references, transcript, tribal eligibility certificate. *Deadline:* May 4.

Contact: Marveline Vallo Gabbard, Program Assistant
American Indian Graduate Center
4520 Montgomery Boulevard, NE Ste 1-B
Albuquerque, NM 87109
Phone: 505-881-4584
Fax: 505-884-0427
E-mail: marveline@aigcs.org

GATES MILLENNIUM SCHOLARS PROGRAM

Award enables American-Indian/Alaska native students to complete an undergraduate and graduate education. Must be entering a U.S. accredited college or university as a full-time student. Minimum 3.3 GPA required. Must demonstrate leadership abilities. Must meet federal Pell Grant eligibility criteria. Visit web site at http://www.gmsp.org.

Award: Scholarship for use in freshman, sophomore, junior, senior, or graduate years; renewable. *Number:* 150. *Amount:* $500–$20,000.

Eligibility Requirements: Applicant must be American Indian/Alaska Native; enrolled or expecting to enroll full-time at a two-year or four-year institution or university and must have an interest in leadership. Available to U.S. citizens.

Application Requirements: Application, financial need analysis, references, nomination packet. *Deadline:* January 16.

Contact: Christa Moya, GMS Representative
American Indian Graduate Center
4520 Montgomery Boulevard, NE, Suite 1B
Albuquerque, NM 87109
Phone: 866-884-7007
Fax: 505-884-8683
E-mail: christa@aigcs.org

WELLS FARGO SCHOLARSHIP AMERICAN INDIAN SCHOLARSHIP

Must be an enrolled member of a U.S. federally recognized American Indian or Alaska Native tribe. Be pursuing a degree in the banking, resort management, gaming operations, management and administration, including accounting, finance, information technology and human resources. Must have a cumulative GPA of a 3.0 on a 4.0 scale and demonstrate financial need.

Award: Scholarship for use in junior, senior, or graduate years; renewable. *Number:* up to 10.

Eligibility Requirements: Applicant must be American Indian/Alaska Native and enrolled or expecting to enroll full-time at a four-year institution or university. Applicant must have 3.0 GPA or higher. Available to U.S. citizens.

Application Requirements: Application, essay, financial need analysis, photo, resume, transcript, tribal eligibility certificate. *Deadline:* May 4.

Contact: Marveline Vallo Gabbard, Program Assistant
American Indian Graduate Center
4520 Montgomery Boulevard, NE Ste 1-B
Albuquerque, NM 87109
Phone: 505-881-4584
Fax: 505-884-0427
E-mail: marveline@aigcs.org

AMERICAN INSTITUTE FOR FOREIGN STUDY

http://www.aifsabroad.com/

AIFS DIVERSITYABROAD.COM SCHOLARSHIP

Scholarships are available for students studying abroad on any program offered by a DiversityAbroad.com member organization. African-American, Asian-American, Hispanic/Latino and Native-American students are strongly encouraged to apply. Visit http://www.aifsabroad.com/scholarships.asp for more information.

Award: Scholarship for use in freshman, sophomore, junior, or senior years; not renewable. *Number:* up to 20. *Amount:* up to $1000.

Eligibility Requirements: Applicant must be American Indian/Alaska Native, Asian/Pacific Islander, Black (non-Hispanic), or Hispanic; enrolled or expecting to enroll full-time at a two-year or four-year institution or university and must have an interest in international exchange. Applicant must have 3.5 GPA or higher. Available to U.S. citizens.

Application Requirements: Application, essay, photo, resume, references, transcript. *Fee:* $95. *Deadline:* varies.

Contact: David Mauro, Admissions Counselor
American Institute for Foreign Study
River Plaza, 9 West Broad Street
Stamford, CT 06902-3788
Phone: 800-727-2437 Ext. 5163
Fax: 203-399-5463
E-mail: dmauro@aifs.com

AIFS-HACU SCHOLARSHIPS

Scholarships to outstanding Hispanic students to study abroad with AIFS. Available to students attending HACU member schools. Students will receive scholarships of up to 50 percent of the full program fee. Students must meet all standard AIFS eligibility requirements. Deadlines: April 15 for fall, October 1 for spring, and March 15 for summer.

Award: Scholarship for use in freshman, sophomore, junior, or senior years; not renewable. *Number:* varies. *Amount:* $6000–$8000.

Eligibility Requirements: Applicant must be Hispanic; age 17 and over; enrolled or expecting to enroll full-time at a two-year or four-year institution or university and must have an interest in international exchange. Applicant must have 3.0 GPA or higher. Available to U.S. and non-U.S. citizens.

Application Requirements: Application, essay, photo, references, transcript. *Fee:* $95. *Deadline:* varies.

Contact: David Mauro, Admissions Counselor
American Institute for Foreign Study
River Plaza, 9 West Broad Street
Stamford, CT 06902-3788
Phone: 800-727-2437 Ext. 5163
Fax: 203-399-5463
E-mail: dmauro@aifs.com

AMERICAN LEGION DEPARTMENT OF NORTH DAKOTA

http://www.ndlegion.org/

HATTIE TEDROW MEMORIAL FUND SCHOLARSHIP
• *See page 633*

ARAB AMERICAN INSTITUTE FOUNDATION

http://www.aaiusa.org/

HELEN ABBOTT COMMUNITY SERVICE AWARDS

Maximum of two $1000 prizes for college students and one $500 grant to a high school student whose devotion to community service, selfless acts of care, and interest in improving the quality of life for others reflect the life of the Awards' namesake. Must be U.S. citizen and be of Arab descent.

Award: Prize for use in freshman, sophomore, junior, or senior years; not renewable. *Number:* up to 3. *Amount:* $500–$1000.

Eligibility Requirements: Applicant must be of Arab heritage and enrolled or expecting to enroll full- or part-time at a four-year institution or university. Available to U.S. citizens.

Application Requirements: Application, essay, resume, transcript. *Deadline:* March 14.

Contact: Sabeen Altaf, Program Manager
Arab American Institute Foundation
1600 K Street NW, Suite 601
Washington, DC 20006
Phone: 202-429-9210
Fax: 202-429-9214
E-mail: saltaf@aaiusa.org

RAYMOND JALLOW AWARDS FOR PUBLIC SERVICE

Two $500 grants are given annually to students and adults who are actively involved in, or plan to participate, in public service. Must be currently enrolled at a college or university, be a U.S. citizen under the age of 30, and be of Arab descent.

Award: Prize for use in freshman, sophomore, junior, senior, graduate, or postgraduate years; not renewable. *Number:* 2. *Amount:* $500.

Eligibility Requirements: Applicant must be of Arab heritage; age 30 or under and enrolled or expecting to enroll full- or part-time at a two-year or four-year or technical institution or university. Available to U.S. citizens.

Application Requirements: Application, essay, resume, references. *Deadline:* March 14.

Contact: Sabeen Altaf, Program Manager
Arab American Institute Foundation
1600 K Street NW, Suite 601
Washington, DC 20006
Phone: 202-429-9210
Fax: 202-429-9214
E-mail: saltaf@aaiusa.org

ARMENIAN RELIEF SOCIETY OF EASTERN USA INC.-REGIONAL OFFICE

http://www.arseastus.org/

ARMENIAN RELIEF SOCIETY UNDERGRADUATE SCHOLARSHIP

Applicant must be an undergraduate student of Armenian heritage attending an accredited four-year college or university in the United States. Award for full-time students only. Must be U.S. or Canadian citizen. High school students may not apply.

Award: Scholarship for use in freshman, sophomore, junior, or senior years; not renewable. *Number:* varies. *Amount:* $13,000–$15,000.

Eligibility Requirements: Applicant must be of Armenian heritage and enrolled or expecting to enroll full-time at a four-year institution or university. Available to U.S. and Canadian citizens.

Application Requirements: Application, financial need analysis, references, self-addressed stamped envelope, transcript. *Deadline:* April 1.

Contact: Scholarship Committee
Armenian Relief Society of Eastern USA Inc.-Regional Office
80 Bigelow Avenue, Suite 200
Watertown, MA 02472
Phone: 617-926-3801
Fax: 617-924-7238
E-mail: arseastus@aol.com

ARMENIAN STUDENTS ASSOCIATION OF AMERICA INC.

http://www.asainc.org/

ARMENIAN STUDENTS ASSOCIATION OF AMERICA INC. SCHOLARSHIPS

One-time award for students of Armenian descent. Must be an undergraduate in sophomore, junior, or senior years, or graduate student, attending an accredited U.S. institution. Award based on need, merit, and character. Application fee: $15.

Award: Scholarship for use in sophomore, junior, senior, or graduate years; not renewable. *Number:* 30. *Amount:* $1000–$3500.

Eligibility Requirements: Applicant must be of Armenian heritage and enrolled or expecting to enroll full-time at a four-year institution or university. Available to U.S. citizens.

Application Requirements: Application, essay, financial need analysis, references, transcript, proof of tuition costs and enrollment. *Fee:* $15. *Deadline:* March 15.

Contact: Nathalie Yaghoobian, ASA Scholarship Committee
Armenian Students Association of America Inc.
333 Atlantic Avenue
Warwick, RI 02888
Phone: 401-461-6114
Fax: 401-461-6112
E-mail: asa@asainc.org

ASIAN PROFESSIONAL EXTENSION INC.

http://www.apex-ny.org/

APEX SCHOLARSHIP

Scholarship to students based on academic excellence, personal essays, letters of recommendation, extracurricular activities/volunteer service, and financial need. Two winners will receive scholarships of $500 and $1000. Deadline varies.

Award: Scholarship for use in freshman, sophomore, junior, senior, or graduate years; not renewable. *Number:* 2. *Amount:* $500–$1000.

Eligibility Requirements: Applicant must be American Indian/Alaska Native or Asian/Pacific Islander and enrolled or expecting to enroll full- or part-time at a four-year institution or university. Available to U.S. citizens.

Application Requirements: Application, applicant must enter a contest, essay, financial need analysis, references, transcript. *Deadline:* varies.

Contact: Trang Le-Chan, Deputy Director of Programs
Asian Professional Extension Inc.
352 Seventh Avenue, Suite 201
New York, NY 10001
Phone: 212-748-1225 Ext. 101
Fax: 212-748-1250
E-mail: trang.le-chan@apex-ny.org

ASIAN REPORTER

http://www.arfoundation.net/

ASIAN REPORTER SCHOLARSHIP

Scholarship available to graduating high school student or currently enrolled college student of Asian descent. Must be a resident of Washington or Oregon and attend school full-time in either state. Minimum 3.5 GPA required. Must demonstrate financial need, and involvement in community or school-related activities.

Award: Scholarship for use in freshman, sophomore, junior, or senior years; renewable. *Number:* 4. *Amount:* $500–$2000.

Eligibility Requirements: Applicant must be Asian/Pacific Islander; enrolled or expecting to enroll full-time at a four-year institution or university; resident of Oregon or Washington and studying in Oregon or Washington. Applicant must have 3.5 GPA or higher. Available to U.S. citizens.

Application Requirements: Application, essay, financial need analysis, photo, references, transcript. *Deadline:* February 28.

Contact: Jason Lim, Program Director
Asian Reporter
922 North Killingsworth Street, Suite 1A
Portland, OR 97217
Phone: 503-283-0595
Fax: 503-283-4445
E-mail: arfoundation@asianreporter.com

ASSOCIATION ON AMERICAN INDIAN AFFAIRS, INC.

http://www.indian-affairs.org/

ADOLPH VAN PELT SPECIAL FUND FOR INDIAN SCHOLARSHIPS

Scholarship is open to undergraduate students pursuing a bachelor's degree in any curriculum. Must be an American Indian. See http://www.indian-affairs.org for specific details.

Award: Scholarship for use in freshman, sophomore, junior, or senior years; not renewable. *Number:* 16. *Amount:* up to $1500.

Eligibility Requirements: Applicant must be American Indian/Alaska Native and enrolled or expecting to enroll full-time at a two-year or four-year institution or university. Available to U.S. citizens.

Application Requirements: Application, essay, financial need analysis, references, transcript. *Deadline:* June 13.

Contact: Lisa Wyzlic, Director of Scholarship Programs
Association on American Indian Affairs, Inc.
966 Hungerford Drive, Suite 12-B
Rockville, MD 20850
Phone: 240-314-7155
Fax: 240-314-7155
E-mail: lw.aaia@verizon.net

ALLOGAN SLAGLE MEMORIAL SCHOLARSHIP

Scholarship available for American Indian undergraduate and graduate students who are members of tribes that are not federally recognized. Students must apply each year. See http://www.indian-affairs.org for specific details.

Award: Scholarship for use in freshman, sophomore, junior, senior, or graduate years; not renewable. *Number:* 7. *Amount:* $1500.

Eligibility Requirements: Applicant must be American Indian/Alaska Native and enrolled or expecting to enroll full-time at a two-year or four-year institution or university. Available to U.S. citizens.

Application Requirements: Application, essay, financial need analysis, references, transcript. *Deadline:* June 13.

Contact: Lisa Wyzlic, Director of Scholarship Programs
Association on American Indian Affairs, Inc.
966 Hungerford Drive, Suite 12-B
Rockville, MD 20850
Phone: 240-314-7155
Fax: 240-314-7159
E-mail: lw.aaia@verizon.net

DAVID RISLING EMERGENCY AID SCHOLARSHIP

Scholarship is for acute, temporary, unexpected emergencies that would keep undergraduate students from attending school. Tuition, books, com-

puters and other expected expenses are not considered emergencies. Must be Native American. See our web site at http://www.indian-affairs.org for details, including acceptance period. Call the Rockville office prior to submission to see if funding is available and if your situation qualifies as an emergency.

Award: Scholarship for use in freshman, sophomore, junior, senior, or graduate years; not renewable. *Number:* varies. *Amount:* $100–$400.

Eligibility Requirements: Applicant must be American Indian/Alaska Native and enrolled or expecting to enroll full-time at a two-year or four-year institution or university. Available to U.S. citizens.

Application Requirements: Application, essay, financial need analysis, references, transcript. *Deadline:* continuous.

Contact: Lisa Wyzlic, Director of Scholarship Programs
Association on American Indian Affairs, Inc.
966 Hungerford Drive, Suite 12-B
Rockville, MD 20850
Phone: 240-314-7155
Fax: 240-314-7159
E-mail: lw.aaia@verizon.net

DISPLACED HOMEMAKER SCHOLARSHIP

This undergraduate scholarship is for men and women who would not otherwise be able to complete their educational goals due to family responsibilities. Must be an American Indian. Applications will be accepted between April 4 and June 13, mailed to the Rockville, Maryland office only. For an application and complete information on necessary documentation, see web site http://www.indian-affairs.org.

Award: Scholarship for use in freshman, sophomore, junior, or senior years; not renewable. *Number:* 8. *Amount:* $1500.

Eligibility Requirements: Applicant must be American Indian/Alaska Native; age 30 and over and enrolled or expecting to enroll full-time at a two-year or four-year institution or university. Available to U.S. citizens.

Application Requirements: Application, essay, financial need analysis, references, transcript. *Deadline:* June 13.

Contact: Lisa Wyzlic, Director of Scholarship Programs
Association on American Indian Affairs, Inc.
966 Hungerford Drive, Suite 12-B
Rockville, MD 20850
Phone: 240-314-7155
Fax: 240-314-7159
E-mail: lw.aaia@verizon.net

BLACKFEET NATION HIGHER EDUCATION PROGRAM

http://www.blackfeetnation.com/

BLACKFEET NATION HIGHER EDUCATION GRANT

Grants of $2800-$3000 will be awarded to students who are enrolled members of the Blackfeet Tribe and actively pursuing an undergraduate degree. Must submit a certification of Blackfeet blood.

Award: Grant for use in freshman, sophomore, junior, or senior years; not renewable. *Number:* 180. *Amount:* $2800–$3000.

Eligibility Requirements: Applicant must be American Indian/Alaska Native and enrolled or expecting to enroll full-time at a two-year or four-year or technical institution or university. Available to U.S. citizens.

Application Requirements: Application, essay, financial need analysis, transcript, certification of Blackfeet blood. *Deadline:* March 1.

Contact: Conrad LaFromboise, Director
Blackfeet Nation Higher Education Program
PO Box 850
Browning, MT 59417
Phone: 406-338-7539
Fax: 406-338-7529
E-mail: bhep@3rivers.net

BUREAU OF INDIAN AFFAIRS OFFICE OF INDIAN EDUCATION PROGRAMS

http://www.oiep.bia.edu/

BUREAU OF INDIAN EDUCATION GRANT PROGRAM

Grants are provided to supplement financial assistance to eligible American Indian/Alaska Native students entering college seeking a baccalaureate degree. A student must be a member of, or at least one-quarter degree Indian blood descendent of a member of an American Indian tribe who are eligible for the special programs and services provided by the United States through the Bureau of Indian Affairs to Indians because of their status as Indians.

Award: Grant for use in freshman year; not renewable. *Number:* varies. *Amount:* varies.

Eligibility Requirements: Applicant must be American Indian/Alaska Native; high school student and planning to enroll or expecting to enroll full-time at a two-year or four-year institution or university. Available to U.S. citizens.

Application Requirements: Application, references, test scores, transcript. *Deadline:* varies.

Contact: Paulina Bell, Office Automation Assistant
Bureau of Indian Affairs Office of Indian Education Programs
1849 C Street, NW, MS 3609-MIB
Washington, DC 20240-0001
Phone: 202-208-6123
Fax: 202-208-3312

CABRILLO CIVIC CLUBS OF CALIFORNIA INC.

http://www.cabrillocivicclubs.org/

CABRILLO CIVIC CLUBS OF CALIFORNIA SCHOLARSHIP

Applicants must be graduating California high school seniors of Portuguese heritage and American citizenship, with an overall 3.5 GPA.

Award: Scholarship for use in freshman year; not renewable. *Number:* 75–100. *Amount:* $500.

Eligibility Requirements: Applicant must be of Portuguese heritage; high school student; planning to enroll or expecting to enroll full-time at a technical institution and resident of California. Applicant must have 3.5 GPA or higher. Available to U.S. citizens.

Application Requirements: Application, driver's license, photo, resume, references, self-addressed stamped envelope, transcript. *Deadline:* March 15.

Contact: Breck L. Austin, Scholarship Chairperson
Cabrillo Civic Clubs of California Inc.
2174 South Coast Highway
Oceanside, CA 92054
E-mail: shampoobla@sbcglobal.net

CENTRAL COUNCIL, TLINGIT AND HAIDA INDIAN TRIBES OF ALASKA

http://www.hied.org/

ALUMNI STUDENT ASSISTANCE PROGRAM

The program provides annual scholarship awards to all enrolled Tlingit or Haida tribal members regardless of service area, community affiliation, origination, residence, tribal compact, or signatory status.

Award: Scholarship for use in freshman, sophomore, junior, senior, graduate, or postgraduate years; not renewable. *Number:* 1–100. *Amount:* $300–$500.

Eligibility Requirements: Applicant must be American Indian/Alaska Native and enrolled or expecting to enroll full-time at a two-year or four-year institution or university. Applicant must have 2.5 GPA or higher. Available to U.S. citizens.

Application Requirements: Application, essay, financial need analysis, references, transcript, tribal enrollment certification form, letter of admission. *Deadline:* September 15.

Contact: Miss. Leslie Rae Isturis, Education Specialist
Central Council, Tlingit and Haida Indian Tribes of Alaska
3239 Hospital Drive
Juneau, AK 99801
Phone: 907-463-7375
Fax: 907-463-7173
E-mail: listuris@ccthita.org

COLLEGE STUDENT ASSISTANCE PROGRAM

A federally funded program which authorizes a program of assistance, by educational grants, to Indians seeking higher education. Awards available only to enrolled T&H members. Minimum 2.0 GPA required.

Award: Scholarship for use in freshman, sophomore, junior, senior, graduate, or postgraduate years; renewable. *Number:* 1–200. *Amount:* up to $2000.

Eligibility Requirements: Applicant must be American Indian/Alaska Native and enrolled or expecting to enroll full-time at a two-year or four-year institution or university. Available to U.S. citizens.

Application Requirements: Application, test scores, transcript, letter of admission. *Deadline:* May 15.

Contact: Miss. Leslie Rae Isturis, Education Specialist
Central Council, Tlingit and Haida Indian Tribes of Alaska
3239 Hospital Drive
Juneau, AK 99801
Phone: 907-463-7375
Fax: 907-463-7173
E-mail: listuris@ccthita.org

CENTRAL SCHOLARSHIP BUREAU

http://www.centralsb.org/

LESSANS FAMILY SCHOLARSHIP

Scholarship available for Jewish students from Maryland who attend undergraduate colleges, universities or vocational schools full-time. Students can attend any accredited U.S. college or university. Awards are based on need and merit. The scholarship committee award amounts. For more information, visit web site http://www.centralsb.org.

Award: Scholarship for use in freshman, sophomore, junior, or senior years; renewable. *Number:* 12–20. *Amount:* $1000–$2500.

Eligibility Requirements: Applicant must be Jewish; of Jewish heritage; enrolled or expecting to enroll full-time at a two-year or four-year institution or university and resident of Maryland. Applicant must have 3.0 GPA or higher. Available to U.S. citizens.

Application Requirements: Application, essay, financial need analysis, interview, resume, transcript. *Deadline:* May 1.

Contact: Roberta Goldman, Program Director
Central Scholarship Bureau
1700 Reisterstown Road, Suite 220
Baltimore, MD 21208-2903
Phone: 410-415-5558
Fax: 410-425-5501
E-mail: rgoldman@centralsb.org

CHEROKEE NATION OF OKLAHOMA

http://www.cherokee.org/

CHEROKEE NATION HIGHER EDUCATION SCHOLARSHIP

A supplementary program that provides financial assistance to Cherokee Nation Members only. It is a need-based program which provides assistance in seeking a bachelor's degree.

Award: Scholarship for use in freshman, sophomore, junior, or senior years; renewable. *Number:* up to 2800. *Amount:* $100–$1000.

Eligibility Requirements: Applicant must be American Indian/Alaska Native and enrolled or expecting to enroll full-time at a four-year institution or university. Applicant must have 2.5 GPA or higher. Available to U.S. citizens.

Application Requirements: Test scores, transcript, written request for application. *Deadline:* June 13.

Contact: Nita Wilson, Higher Education Specialist
Cherokee Nation of Oklahoma
PO Box 948
Tahlequah, OK 74465
Phone: 918-458-6195
E-mail: nwilson@cherokee.org

CHICANA/LATINA FOUNDATION

http://www.chicanalatina.org/

SCHOLARSHIPS FOR LATINA STUDENTS ENROLLED IN COLLEGES/UNIVERSITIES IN NORTHERN CALIFORNIA

Scholarships are awarded to female Latina students enrolled in two-year, four-year or graduate levels. Applicants must be from and/or attending colleges in the nine counties of Northern California listed on the application.

Award: Scholarship for use in freshman, sophomore, junior, or senior years; not renewable. *Number:* 25–30. *Amount:* $1500.

Eligibility Requirements: Applicant must be of Hispanic heritage; enrolled or expecting to enroll full-time at a two-year or four-year institution or university; female and resident of California. Available to U.S. citizens.

Application Requirements: Application, essay, interview, references, transcript, leadership qualities.

Contact: Claudia Leon, Program Coordinator
Chicana/Latina Foundation
1419 Burlingame Avenue, Suite N
Burlingame, CA 94010
Phone: 650-373-1085
Fax: 650-373-1090
E-mail: claudia@chicanalatina.org

CHINESE AMERICAN ASSOCIATION OF MINNESOTA

http://www.caam.org/

CHINESE AMERICAN ASSOCIATION OF MINNESOTA (CAAM) SCHOLARSHIPS

Merit and need scholarships of $1000 each are available for college and graduate students of Chinese descent and a resident of Minnesota. Applicants will be evaluated on their academic records, leadership qualities, and community service.

Award: Scholarship for use in freshman, sophomore, junior, senior, or graduate years; not renewable. *Number:* varies. *Amount:* $1000.

Eligibility Requirements: Applicant must be of Chinese heritage; Asian/Pacific Islander; enrolled or expecting to enroll full-time at a two-year or four-year or technical institution or university and resident of Minnesota. Available to U.S. citizens.

Application Requirements: Application, financial need analysis, references, SAT score. *Deadline:* November 15.

Contact: Scholarship Committee
Chinese American Association of Minnesota
PO Box 582584
Minneapolis, MN 55458-2584

CIEE: COUNCIL ON INTERNATIONAL EDUCATIONAL EXCHANGE

http://www.ciee.org/

ROBERT B. BAILEY SCHOLARSHIP
• See page 601

CIRI FOUNDATION (TCF)

http://www.thecirifoundation.org/

CAREER UPGRADE GRANTS

Original enrollees of CIRI and their direct lineal descendants. Should have a high school diploma or GED; should maintain at least a 2.5 grade point average (2.0 GPA for TNC applicants); must be prepared to demonstrate the availability of employment upon completion of the training.

Award: Grant for use in freshman, sophomore, junior, senior, graduate, or postgraduate years; not renewable. *Number:* varies. *Amount:* up to $4500.

Eligibility Requirements: Applicant must be American Indian/Alaska Native and enrolled or expecting to enroll part-time at a two-year or four-year institution or university. Applicant must have 2.5 GPA or higher. Available to U.S. and non-U.S. citizens.

Application Requirements: Application, essay, references, transcript, proof of eligibility, birth certificate or adoption decree. *Deadline:* varies.

Contact: Susan Anderson, President and Chief Executive Officer
CIRI Foundation (TCF)
3600 San Jeronimo Drive, Suite 256
Anchorage, AK 99508-2870
Phone: 907-793-3575
E-mail: tcf@thecirifoundation.org

CIRI FOUNDATION ACHIEVEMENT ANNUAL SCHOLARSHIPS

Merit scholarships for applicants with exceptional academic promise. Annual award includes two academic semesters. Must be an Alaska Native student. Original enrollees of CIRI and their direct lineal descendants only. Should have a cumulative 3.0 GPA or better.

Award: Scholarship for use in freshman, sophomore, junior, senior, or graduate years; not renewable. *Number:* varies. *Amount:* $8000.

Eligibility Requirements: Applicant must be American Indian/Alaska Native and enrolled or expecting to enroll full-time at a four-year institution or university. Applicant must have 3.0 GPA or higher. Available to U.S. and non-U.S. citizens.

Application Requirements: Application, essay, references, transcript, proof of eligibility, birth certificate or adoption decree. *Deadline:* June 1.

Contact: Susan Anderson, President and Chief Executive Officer
CIRI Foundation (TCF)
3600 San Jeronimo Drive, Suite 256
Anchorage, AK 99508-2870
Phone: 907-793-3575
E-mail: tcf@thecirifoundation.org

CIRI FOUNDATION EXCELLENCE ANNUAL SCHOLARSHIPS

Merit scholarships for outstanding academic and community services experience. Annual award includes two academic semesters. Must be an Alaska Native student. Original enrollees of CIRI and their direct lineal descendants only. Should have a cumulative 3.5 GPA or better. Must be accepted or enrolled full-time in a 4-year undergraduate degree or graduate degree program.

Award: Scholarship for use in freshman, sophomore, junior, senior, or graduate years; not renewable. *Number:* varies. *Amount:* up to $10,000.

Eligibility Requirements: Applicant must be American Indian/Alaska Native and enrolled or expecting to enroll full-time at a four-year institution or university. Applicant must have 3.5 GPA or higher. Available to U.S. and non-U.S. citizens.

Application Requirements: Application, essay, references, transcript, proof of eligibility, birth certificate or adoption decree. *Deadline:* June 1.

Contact: Susan Anderson, President and Chief Executive Officer
CIRI Foundation (TCF)
3600 San Jeronimo Drive, Suite 256
Anchorage, AK 99508-2870
Phone: 907-793-3575
E-mail: tcf@thecirifoundation.org

CIRI FOUNDATION GENERAL SEMESTER SCHOLARSHIP

Merit scholarships for applicants with academic promise. Award of $2500 maximum based on stated need. Must be an Alaska Native student. Original enrollees of CIRI and their direct lineal descendants only. Must be accepted or enrolled full-time in a 2-year or 4-year undergraduate degree or graduate degree program. Deadlines: June 1 and December 1.

Award: Scholarship for use in freshman, sophomore, junior, senior, or graduate years; not renewable. *Number:* varies. *Amount:* up to $2500.

Eligibility Requirements: Applicant must be American Indian/Alaska Native and enrolled or expecting to enroll full-time at a two-year or four-year institution or university. Available to U.S. and non-U.S. citizens.

Application Requirements: Application, essay, references, transcript, proof of eligibility, birth certificate or adoption decree. *Deadline:* varies.

Contact: Susan Anderson, President and Chief Executive Officer
CIRI Foundation (TCF)
3600 San Jeronimo Drive, Suite 256
Anchorage, AK 99508-2870
Phone: 907-793-3575
E-mail: tcf@thecirifoundation.org

CIRI FOUNDATION SPECIAL EXCELLENCE SCHOLARSHIP

Awards a scholarship of $20,000. Must be enrolled full-time in a four-year undergraduate or graduate degree program in the United States. Applicant must be Alaska Native original enrollees or descendants of Cook Inlet Region Inc. Must have a cumulative GPA of 3.7 or better. Preference given to study in fields of business, education, math, sciences, health services, and engineering. Special Excellence Scholarships may or may not be given at the discretion of the Education Awards Committee.

Award: Scholarship for use in freshman, sophomore, junior, senior, or graduate years; not renewable. *Number:* 1. *Amount:* $20,000.

Eligibility Requirements: Applicant must be American Indian/Alaska Native and enrolled or expecting to enroll full-time at a four-year institution or university. Available to U.S. and non-U.S. citizens.

Application Requirements: Application, essay, references, transcript, proof of eligibility, birth certificate or adoption decree. *Deadline:* June 1.

Contact: Susan Anderson, President and Chief Executive Officer
CIRI Foundation (TCF)
3600 San Jeronimo Drive, Suite 256
Anchorage, AK 99508-2870
Phone: 907-793-3575
E-mail: tcf@thecirifoundation.org

CULTURAL FELLOWSHIP GRANTS

Awards applicants who are accepted or enrolled in a seminar or conference that is accredited, authorized, or approved by the CIRI Foundation. May reapply each quarter until grant cap is reached and may reapply the following year. Must be Alaska Native student, CIRI original enrollee, or descendant. Must have studies in Alaska Native arts and cultures, including visual or performing arts, communications, languages, history. Must be at least 18 years of age; should have a high school diploma or GED. Should have a cumulative GPA of 2.5 or better. Deadlines: March 31, June 30, September 30, and December 1.

Award: Grant for use in freshman, sophomore, junior, senior, graduate, or postgraduate years; not renewable. *Number:* varies. *Amount:* $250.

Eligibility Requirements: Applicant must be American Indian/Alaska Native; enrolled or expecting to enroll full- or part-time at a two-year or four-year institution or university and resident of Alaska. Applicant must have 2.5 GPA or higher. Available to U.S. and non-U.S. citizens.

Application Requirements: Application, essay, references, transcript, proof of eligibility, birth certificate or adoption decree. *Deadline:* varies.

Contact: Susan Anderson, President and Chief Executive Officer
CIRI Foundation (TCF)
3600 San Jeronimo Drive, Suite 256
Anchorage, AK 99508-2870
Phone: 907-793-3575
E-mail: tcf@thecirifoundation.org

GENERAL FELLOWSHIP GRANTS

Original enrollees of CIRI and their direct lineal descendants (either natural-born or legally adopted). Must be at least 18 years of age; should have a high school diploma or GED. Should have a cumulative GPA of 2.5 or better. The applicant must be accepted or enrolled in a seminar or conference approved by The CIRI Foundation. Deadlines: March 31, June 30, September 30, and December 1.

Award: Grant for use in freshman, sophomore, junior, senior, graduate, or postgraduate years; not renewable. *Number:* varies. *Amount:* up to $250.

Eligibility Requirements: Applicant must be American Indian/Alaska Native; age 18 and over; enrolled or expecting to enroll full- or part-time at a two-year or four-year or technical institution or university and resident of Alaska. Applicant must have 2.5 GPA or higher. Available to U.S. and non-U.S. citizens.

Application Requirements: Application, essay, references, transcript, proof of eligibility, birth certificate or adoption decree. *Deadline:* varies.

Contact: Susan Anderson, President and Chief Executive Officer
CIRI Foundation (TCF)
3600 San Jeronimo Drive, Suite 256
Anchorage, AK 99508-2870
Phone: 907-793-3575
E-mail: tcf@thecirifoundation.org

HOWARD ROCK FOUNDATION SCHOLARSHIP PROGRAM

Scholarships are available to undergraduate and graduate students, who are Alaska Native original enrollees of an ANCSA regional and/or village corporation, a direct lineal descendant, or a member of a tribal or other organization. Preference is given to junior and senior standing students. Affiliated regional and/or village corporations must be current members of Alaska Village Initiatives. Must have a minimum GPA of 2.5 for undergraduates and 3.0 for graduates.

Award: Scholarship for use in freshman, sophomore, junior, senior, or graduate years; not renewable. *Number:* 3. *Amount:* $2500–$5000.

Eligibility Requirements: Applicant must be American Indian/Alaska Native and enrolled or expecting to enroll full-time at a four-year institution or university. Available to U.S. and Canadian citizens.

Application Requirements: Application, essay, financial need analysis, photo, references, transcript, proof of eligibility, statement of purpose. *Deadline:* March 31.

Contact: Susan Anderson, President and Chief Executive Officer
CIRI Foundation (TCF)
3600 San Jeronimo Drive, Suite 256
Anchorage, AK 99508-2870
Phone: 907-793-3575
E-mail: tcf@thecirifoundation.org

NINILCHIK NATIVE ASSOCIATION INC. SCHOLARSHIP AND GRANT PROGRAM

Original enrollees of NNAI and their direct lineal descendants. Must be accepted or enrolled full-time in an undergraduate or graduate degree program or technical skills training program. For tuition, required fees, books, on-campus-related room, and meal plan and for other direct school related costs. Should have a cumulative 2.5 grade point average or better. Deadline: June 1 and December 1.

Award: Scholarship for use in freshman, sophomore, junior, senior, or graduate years; renewable. *Amount:* $1000–$2000.

Eligibility Requirements: Applicant must be American Indian/Alaska Native and enrolled or expecting to enroll full-time at a two-year or four-year or technical institution or university. Applicant must have 2.5 GPA or higher. Available to U.S. citizens.

Application Requirements: Application, essay, photo, references, test scores, transcript. *Deadline:* varies.

Contact: Susan Anderson, President and Chief Executive Officer
CIRI Foundation (TCF)
3600 San Jeronimo Drive, Suite 256
Anchorage, AK 99508-2870
Phone: 907-793-3575
E-mail: tcf@thecirifoundation.org

SALAMATOF NATIVE ASSOCIATION INC. SCHOLARSHIP PROGRAM

Two annual scholarships or education grants are awarded to qualified applicants. Alaska Native original enrollees of SNAI and their lineal descendants and spouses may apply. Must be accepted or enrolled full-time in an undergraduate or graduate degree program or technical skills training program. For tuition, required fees, books, on-campus-related room, and meal plan and for other direct school related costs. Should have a cumulative 2.5 grade point average or better.

Award: Scholarship for use in freshman, sophomore, junior, senior, or graduate years; not renewable. *Number:* 2. *Amount:* varies.

Eligibility Requirements: Applicant must be American Indian/Alaska Native and enrolled or expecting to enroll full-time at a four-year institution or university. Applicant must have 2.5 GPA or higher. Available to U.S. and non-U.S. citizens.

Application Requirements: Application, essay, transcript, proof of eligibility, birth certificate or adoption degree. *Deadline:* June 1.

Contact: Susan Anderson, President and Chief Executive Officer
CIRI Foundation (TCF)
3600 San Jeronimo Drive, Suite 256
Anchorage, AK 99508-2870
Phone: 907-793-3575
E-mail: tcf@thecirifoundation.org

TYONEK NATIVE CORPORATION SCHOLARSHIP AND GRANT FUND

Award to encourage Alaska Native student to prepare for professional career after high school. Applicant must be accepted or enrolled full-time in an accredited or otherwise approved postsecondary college, university, or technical skills education program. Must be Alaska Native original enrollee to Tyonek Native Corporation or the Native Village of Tyonek, or lineal descendant. Must have a cumulative grade point average of 2.0 or better.

Award: Scholarship for use in freshman, sophomore, junior, senior, or graduate years; not renewable. *Number:* varies. *Amount:* varies.

Eligibility Requirements: Applicant must be American Indian/Alaska Native and enrolled or expecting to enroll full-time at a two-year or four-year or technical institution or university. Available to U.S. and non-U.S. citizens.

Application Requirements: Application, essay, references, transcript, proof of eligibility, birth certificate or adoption decree. *Deadline:* March 31.

Contact: Susan Anderson, President and Chief Executive Officer
CIRI Foundation (TCF)
3600 San Jeronimo Drive, Suite 256
Anchorage, AK 99508-2870
Phone: 907-793-3575
E-mail: tcf@thecirifoundation.org

VOCATIONAL TRAINING GRANTS

Original enrollees of CIRI and their direct lineal descendants. Should have a high school diploma or GED; should maintain at least a 2.5 grade point average. For applicants preparing to enter, re-enter, or upgrade in the job market upon completion of training; must be able to demonstrate the availability of employment.

Award: Grant for use in freshman, sophomore, junior, senior, graduate, or postgraduate years; not renewable. *Number:* varies. *Amount:* up to $4500.

Eligibility Requirements: Applicant must be American Indian/Alaska Native and enrolled or expecting to enroll full- or part-time at a two-year or four-year or technical institution or university. Applicant must have 2.5 GPA or higher. Available to U.S. and non-U.S. citizens.

Application Requirements: Application, essay, references, transcript, proof of eligibility, birth certificate or adoption decree. *Deadline:* varies.

Contact: Susan Anderson, President and Chief Executive Officer
CIRI Foundation (TCF)
3600 San Jeronimo Drive, Suite 256
Anchorage, AK 99508-2870
Phone: 907-793-3575
E-mail: tcf@thecirifoundation.org

CITIZEN POTAWATOMI NATION

http://www.potawatomi.org/

CITIZEN POTAWATOMI NATION TRIBAL SCHOLARSHIP

Provides financial assistance for payment of tuition for members of the Citizen Potawatomi Nation. Minimum 2.0 GPA required. Deadlines: December 1 for spring, August 1 for fall, June 1 for summer. Award amount varies from $750 to $1500.

Award: Scholarship for use in freshman, sophomore, junior, senior, or graduate years; renewable. *Number:* varies. *Amount:* $750–$1500.

Eligibility Requirements: Applicant must be American Indian/Alaska Native and enrolled or expecting to enroll full- or part-time at a two-year or four-year institution or university. Available to U.S. citizens.

Application Requirements: Application, financial need analysis, test scores, transcript. *Deadline:* varies.

Contact: Charles Clark, Director, Tribal Rolls
Citizen Potawatomi Nation
1601 South Gordon Cooper Drive
Shawnee, OK 74801-8699
Phone: 800-880-9880
Fax: 405-275-0198
E-mail: cclark@potawatomi.org

COLLEGE WOMEN'S ASSOCIATION OF JAPAN

http://www.cwaj.org/

SCHOLARSHIP FOR THE VISUALLY IMPAIRED TO STUDY ABROAD
• See page 601

SCHOLARSHIP FOR THE VISUALLY IMPAIRED TO STUDY IN JAPAN
• See page 601

CONFEDERATED TRIBES OF GRAND RONDE

http://www.grandronde.org/

ADULT VOCATIONAL TRAINING COMPETITIVE SCHOLARSHIP

Available to any enrolled member of the Confederated Tribes of Grand Ronde. Four $6000 full-time and one $3000 part-time awards are given each year. Intended for programs of study two years or less in length.

Award: Scholarship for use in freshman or sophomore years; renewable. *Number:* 5. *Amount:* $3000–$6000.

Eligibility Requirements: Applicant must be American Indian/Alaska Native and enrolled or expecting to enroll full- or part-time at a two-year or technical institution. Available to U.S. and non-U.S. citizens.

Application Requirements: Application, essay, references, transcript, verification of tribal enrollment. *Deadline:* April 30.

Contact: Tribal Scholarship Coordinator
Confederated Tribes of Grand Ronde
9615 Grand Ronde Road
Grand Ronde, OR 97347
Phone: 800-422-0232 Ext. 2275
Fax: 503-879-2286
E-mail: education@grandronde.org

UNDERGRADUATE COMPETITIVE SCHOLARSHIP

Available to any enrolled member of the Confederated Tribes of Grand Ronde. Ten $3000, two $4500, and three $6000 full-time awards, and two $3000 part-time awards are given each year. Renewable for twelve terms/eight semesters of continuous study. Scholarship may be used at community colleges for transfer credits.

Award: Scholarship for use in freshman, sophomore, junior, or senior years; renewable. *Number:* 17. *Amount:* $3000–$6000.

Eligibility Requirements: Applicant must be American Indian/Alaska Native and enrolled or expecting to enroll full- or part-time at a two-year or four-year institution or university. Available to U.S. and non-U.S. citizens.

Application Requirements: Application, essay, references, transcript, verification of tribal enrollment. *Deadline:* April 30.

Contact: Tribal Scholarship Coordinator
Confederated Tribes of Grand Ronde
9615 Grand Ronde Road
Grand Ronde, OR 97347
Phone: 800-422-0232 Ext. 2275
Fax: 503-879-2286
E-mail: education@grandronde.org

CONGRESSIONAL HISPANIC CAUCUS INSTITUTE

http://www.chci.org/

CONGRESSIONAL HISPANIC CAUCUS INSTITUTE SCHOLARSHIP AWARDS

Needs Based Scholarship award for Latino students who have a history of public service-oriented activities. Provides scholarships to students enrolled full time in school. Scholarship levels are: $1000 for community college, $2500 for four year academic institution, $5000 for graduate level institution. See web site at http://www.chci.org for further information.

Award: Scholarship for use in freshman, sophomore, junior, senior, or graduate years; renewable. *Number:* 100–150. *Amount:* $1000–$5000.

Eligibility Requirements: Applicant must be Hispanic and enrolled or expecting to enroll full-time at a two-year or four-year institution or university. Available to U.S. citizens.

Application Requirements: Application, essay, financial need analysis, resume, references, transcript. *Deadline:* April 16.

Contact: Anissa Perez, Scholarship Specialist
Congressional Hispanic Caucus Institute
911 2nd Street, NE
Washington, DC 20002
Phone: 202-543-1771
Fax: 202-546-2143
E-mail: aperez@chci.org

CROATIAN SCHOLARSHIP FUND

http://www.croatianscholarship.org/

CROATIAN SCHOLARSHIP FUND

Scholarship for students of Croatian heritage. Award based on academic achievement and financial need. Must demonstrate appropriate degree selection. Scholarships are awarded depending on availability of funds and number of applicants.

Award: Scholarship for use in freshman, sophomore, junior, or senior years; renewable. *Number:* varies. *Amount:* $1200–$1500.

Eligibility Requirements: Applicant must be of Croatian/Serbian heritage; age 18-25 and enrolled or expecting to enroll full-time at a four-year institution or university. Applicant must have 2.5 GPA or higher. Available to U.S. and non-U.S. citizens.

Application Requirements: Application, financial need analysis, photo, references, test scores, transcript. *Deadline:* May 15.

Contact: Vesna Brekalo, Scholarship Liaison
Croatian Scholarship Fund
31 Mesa Vista Court
San Ramon, CA 94583
Phone: 925-556-6263
Fax: 925-556-6263
E-mail: vbrekalo@msn.com

DADE COMMUNITY FOUNDATION

http://www.jackituckfield.org/

RODNEY THAXTON/MARTIN E. SEGAL SCHOLARSHIP

Award available to a graduating high school senior who is African American and a Miami-Dade county area resident. Must demonstrate a commitment to social justice and have financial need. For additional information and application, visit web site http://www.dadecommunity-foundation.org.

Award: Scholarship for use in freshman year; not renewable. *Number:* 11. *Amount:* $1000.

Eligibility Requirements: Applicant must be Black (non-Hispanic); high school student; planning to enroll or expecting to enroll full-time at a four-year institution or university and resident of Florida. Available to U.S. citizens.

Application Requirements: Application, resume, transcript. *Deadline:* April 17.

Contact: Ted Seijo, Scholarship Coordinator
Dade Community Foundation
1160 Northwest 87 Street
Miami, FL 33150-2544
Phone: 305-371-2711
E-mail: ted.seijo@dadecommunityfoundation.org

SIDNEY M. ARONOVITZ SCHOLARSHIP

Award available for minority students who are seniors at a Miami-Dade county public school or GED recipient from Miami-Dade area. Must be enrolled or planning to enroll in a college or university and plan to live and work in South Florida. Must have a minimum of 3.0 GPA. Additional information and application on web site http://www.dadecommunity-foundation.org.

Award: Scholarship for use in freshman year; not renewable. *Number:* 1. *Amount:* $500.

Eligibility Requirements: Applicant must be American Indian/Alaska Native, Black (non-Hispanic), or Hispanic; high school student; planning to enroll or expecting to enroll full-time at a four-year institution or university and resident of Florida. Applicant must have 3.0 GPA or higher. Available to U.S. citizens.

Application Requirements: Application, financial need analysis, transcript. *Deadline:* March 20.

Contact: Ted Seijo, Scholarship Coordinator
Dade Community Foundation
1160 Northwest 87 Street
Miami, FL 33150-2544
Phone: 305-371-2711
E-mail: ted.seijo@dadecommunityfoundation.org

THE DALLAS FOUNDATION

http://www.dallasfoundation.org/

DR. DAN J. AND PATRICIA S. PICKARD SCHOLARSHIP

The Dr. Dan J. and Patricia S. Pickard Scholarship Fund was established at the Dallas Foundation in 2004 to assist African-American male students in Dallas County. Dr. Pickard was an optometrist and founder of the Pickard eye clinic. He believed that if you did something nice for someone and they do something nice for someone else, you can affect the lives of many people. The Scholarship Fund is his way of "passing it on".

Award: Scholarship for use in freshman year; renewable. *Number:* 1–2. *Amount:* $1000–$2000.

Eligibility Requirements: Applicant must be Black (non-Hispanic); high school student; planning to enroll or expecting to enroll full-time at a two-year or four-year institution; male; resident of Texas and studying in Texas. Applicant must have 2.5 GPA or higher. Available to U.S. citizens.

Application Requirements: Application, essay, financial need analysis, references, transcript. *Deadline:* April 1.

Contact: Ms. Rachel Lasseter, Program Associate
The Dallas Foundation
900 Jackson Street, Suite 705
Dallas, TX 75202
Phone: 214-741-9898
Fax: 214-741-9848
E-mail: scholarships@dallasfoundation.org

DAUGHTERS OF PENELOPE FOUNDATION

http://daughtersofpenelope.org/

ALEXANDRA APOSTOLIDES SONENFELD SCHOLARSHIP
• *See page 539*

JOANNE V. HOLOGGITAS, PHD SCHOLARSHIP
• *See page 539*

KOTTIS FAMILY SCHOLARSHIP
• *See page 540*

MARY M. VERGES SCHOLARSHIP
• *See page 540*

PAST GRAND PRESIDENTS SCHOLARSHIP
• *See page 540*

DIAMANTE, INC.

http://www.diamanteinc.org/

LATINO DIAMANTE SCHOLARSHIP FUND
• *See page 586*

DIVERSITY CITY MEDIA

http://www.blacknews.com/

BLACKNEWS.COM SCHOLARSHIP ESSAY CONTEST

Scholarship of $500 awarded to an African-American student for the best essay submitted. Must be a U.S. citizen.

Award: Scholarship for use in freshman, sophomore, junior, or senior years; not renewable. *Number:* up to 4. *Amount:* $500.

Eligibility Requirements: Applicant must be Black (non-Hispanic); enrolled or expecting to enroll full- or part-time at a two-year or four-year or technical institution or university and must have an interest in writing. Available to U.S. citizens.

Application Requirements: Application, applicant must enter a contest, essay. *Deadline:* April 31.

Contact: Dante Lee, President and Chief Executive Officer
Diversity City Media
750-Q Cross Pointe Road, Suite 203
Columbus, OH 43230
Phone: 866-910-6277
E-mail: scholarship@blacknews.com

EDGAR ALLEN POE LITERARY SOCIETY

http://www.ravens.org/

DISTINGUISHED RAVEN FAC MEMORIAL SCHOLARSHIP

Scholarship provides educational assistance to the descendants of those Lao/Hmong who served alongside the Ravens in defense of their country.

Award: Scholarship for use in freshman, sophomore, junior, or senior years; not renewable. *Number:* 5–10. *Amount:* $500–$3000.

Eligibility Requirements: Applicant must be of Lao/Hmong heritage; Asian/Pacific Islander and enrolled or expecting to enroll full-time at a two-year or four-year or technical institution or university. Available to U.S. and non-U.S. citizens.

Application Requirements: Application, essay, references, transcript. *Deadline:* March 1.

Contact: Col. Jerry W. Milam, USAF-Retd, Scholarship Administrator
Edgar Allen Poe Literary Society
4320 Saddle Ridge Trail
Flower Mound, TX 75028
Phone: 972-691-2569
E-mail: spikemilam@verizon.net

EDMONTON COMMUNITY FOUNDATION

http://www.DollarsForLearners.com/

YOUTH FORMERLY IN CARE BURSARY

Scholarship funds awarded to disadvantaged young people to support their postsecondary education and training. Supports students who are residents of Alberta and who have spent a minimum of two years in the care and/or guardianship of Alberta Children's Services. Students considering part-time studies may be considered for an award.

Award: Grant for use in freshman, sophomore, junior, or senior years; renewable. *Number:* 1. *Amount:* $1000.

Eligibility Requirements: Applicant must be Canadian citizen; enrolled or expecting to enroll full- or part-time at a four-year institution or university and resident of Alberta.

Application Requirements: Application, financial need analysis, references, transcript, personal letter. *Deadline:* May 15.

Contact: Craig Stumpf-Allen, Associate Director, Scholarships
Edmonton Community Foundation
9910-103 Street, NW
Edmonton, AB T5K 2V7
Canada
Phone: 780-426-0015
Fax: 780-425-0121
E-mail: info@dollarsforlearners.com

EDSOUTH

http://www.edsouth.org/

ECAMPUSTOURS SCHOLARSHIP DRAWING

Two $1000 awards are available.

Award: Scholarship for use in freshman, sophomore, junior, senior, or graduate years; not renewable. *Number:* 2. *Amount:* $1000.

Eligibility Requirements: Applicant must be Hispanic and enrolled or expecting to enroll full- or part-time at a two-year or four-year or technical institution or university. Available to U.S. citizens.

Application Requirements: Applicant must enter a contest, online registration form. *Deadline:* March 31.

Contact: Application information at: http://www.ecampustou
Edsouth
298 North 7 Oaks Drive
Knoxville, TN 37922

EPSILON SIGMA ALPHA

http://www.esaintl.com/esaf

EPSILON SIGMA ALPHA FOUNDATION SCHOLARSHIPS

Awards for various fields of study. Required GPA vary with scholarship. Applications must be sent to the Epsilon Sigma Alpha designated state counselor. See web site at http://www.esaintl.com/esaf for further information, application forms and a list of state counselors.

Award: Scholarship for use in freshman, sophomore, junior, senior, graduate, or postgraduate years; not renewable. *Number:* 125–175. *Amount:* $350–$7500.

Eligibility Requirements: Applicant must be American Indian/Alaska Native, Asian/Pacific Islander, Black (non-Hispanic), or Hispanic and enrolled or expecting to enroll full- or part-time at a two-year or four-year or technical institution or university. Applicant must have 3.0 GPA or higher. Available to U.S. and non-U.S. citizens.

Application Requirements: Application, essay, references, test scores, transcript. *Fee:* $5. *Deadline:* February 1.

Contact: Kathy B. Loyd, Scholarship Chairman
Epsilon Sigma Alpha
1222 NW 651
Blairstown, MO 64726
Phone: 660-678-2611
Fax: 660-747-0807
E-mail: kloyd@knoxy.net

FIRST CATHOLIC SLOVAK LADIES ASSOCIATION

http://www.fcsla.org/

FIRST CATHOLIC SLOVAK LADIES ASSOCIATION FRATERNAL SCHOLARSHIP AWARD

Must be FCSLA member in good standing for at least three years. Must attend accredited college in the United States or Canada in undergraduate or graduate degree program. Must submit certified copy of college acceptance. Award value is $1250 for undergraduate and $1750 for graduate students.

Award: Scholarship for use in freshman, sophomore, junior, senior, or graduate years; not renewable. *Number:* 133. *Amount:* $1250–$1750.

Eligibility Requirements: Applicant must be of Slavic/Czech heritage and enrolled or expecting to enroll full-time at a two-year or four-year institution or university. Available to U.S. and Canadian citizens.

Application Requirements: Application, driver's license, essay, photo, references, test scores, transcript. *Deadline:* March 1.

Contact: Dorothy Szumski, Director of Fraternal Scholarships
First Catholic Slovak Ladies Association
24950 Chagrin Boulevard
Beachwood, OH 44122
Phone: 216-464-8015 Ext. 134
Fax: 216-464-9260
E-mail: info@fcsla.com

FLORIDA STATE DEPARTMENT OF EDUCATION

http://www.floridastudentfinancialaid.org/

JOSE MARTI SCHOLARSHIP CHALLENGE GRANT FUND

Award available to Hispanic-American students who were born in, or whose parent was born in a Hispanic country. Must be a Florida resident, be enrolled full-time in Florida at an eligible school, and have a GPA of 3.0 or above. Must be U.S. citizen or eligible non-citizen. FAFSA must be processed by May 15. For more information, visit web site http://www.floridastudentfinancialaid.org/ssfad/home/ProgramsOffered.htm. For more details, visit the web site at http://www.FloridaStudentFinancialAid.org/SSFAD/home/uamain.htm.

Award: Scholarship for use in freshman, sophomore, junior, or senior years; renewable. *Number:* varies. *Amount:* $2000.

Eligibility Requirements: Applicant must be of Hispanic heritage; high school student; planning to enroll or expecting to enroll full-time at a two-year or four-year institution or university; resident of Florida and studying in Florida. Applicant must have 3.0 GPA or higher. Available to U.S. citizens.

Application Requirements: Application, financial need analysis. *Deadline:* April 1.

Contact: Florida Department of Education, Office of Student Financial Assistance, Customer Service
Florida State Department of Education
325 West Gaines Street
Tallahassee, FL 32303
Phone: 888-827-2004
E-mail: osfa@fldoe.org

GENERAL BOARD OF GLOBAL MINISTRIES

http://www.gbgm-umc.org/

NATIONAL LEADERSHIP DEVELOPMENT GRANT

Award for racial and ethnic minority members of the United Methodist Church who are pursuing undergraduate study. Must be U.S. citizen, resident alien, or reside in U.S. as a refugee.

Award: Grant for use in freshman, sophomore, junior, or senior years; renewable. *Number:* 5–10. *Amount:* $1000–$5000.

Eligibility Requirements: Applicant must be Methodist; American Indian/Alaska Native, Asian/Pacific Islander, Black (non-Hispanic), or Hispanic and enrolled or expecting to enroll full-time at a two-year or four-year or technical institution or university. Available to U.S. citizens.

Application Requirements: Application, essay, financial need analysis, photo, references, transcript. *Deadline:* May 31.

Contact: Lisa Katzenstein Gomez, Administrator
General Board of Global Ministries
475 Riverside Drive, Room 333
New York, NY 10115
Phone: 212-870-3787
Fax: 212-870-3932
E-mail: scholars@gbgm-umc.org

GENERAL BOARD OF HIGHER EDUCATION AND MINISTRY

http://www.gbhem.org/

BISHOP JOSEPH B. BETHEA SCHOLARSHIP

Undergraduate scholarship for full-time African American students. Must be a member of the Southeastern Jurisdiction Black Methodists for Church Renewal (SEJBMCR) and an active, full member of a United Methodist Church for at least one year prior to applying. Must be U.S. citizen or permanent resident, maintain a GPA of 2.8, and demonstrate financial need.

Award: Scholarship for use in freshman, sophomore, junior, or senior years; not renewable. *Number:* varies. *Amount:* varies.

Eligibility Requirements: Applicant must be Methodist; Black (non-Hispanic) and enrolled or expecting to enroll full-time at a four-year institution or university. Available to U.S. citizens.

Application Requirements: Application, essay, references, transcript. *Deadline:* March 1.

Contact: Scholarship Committee
General Board of Higher Education and Ministry
The United Methodist Church, 1001 19th Avenue South
PO Box 340007
Nashville, TN 37202
Phone: 615-340-7344
E-mail: umscholar@gbhem.org

ETHNIC MINORITY SCHOLARSHIP

Undergraduate award for U.S. citizens who are Native American, Asian, African American, Hispanic or Pacific Islanders. Must maintain a GPA of 2.5 or higher, and be a full and active member of a United Methodist Church for at least one year.

Award: Scholarship for use in freshman, sophomore, junior, or senior years; not renewable. *Number:* varies. *Amount:* varies.

Eligibility Requirements: Applicant must be Methodist; American Indian/Alaska Native, Asian/Pacific Islander, Black (non-Hispanic), or Hispanic and enrolled or expecting to enroll full-time at a four-year institution or university. Applicant must have 2.5 GPA or higher. Available to U.S. and non-Canadian citizens.

Application Requirements: Application, essay, references, transcript. *Deadline:* March 1.

Contact: Scholarship Committee
General Board of Higher Education and Ministry
The United Methodist Church, 1001 19th Avenue South
PO Box 340007
Nashville, TN 37202
Phone: 615-340-7344
E-mail: umscholar@gbhem.org

HANA SCHOLARSHIP

Award for a full-time college junior, senior, or graduate student of Hispanic, Asian, Native American/Alaskan Indian, or Pacific Islander parentage. Must be an active, full member of the United Methodist Church for at least three years prior to application. Undergraduates must have GPA of 2.85, graduate students must have 3.0 GPA. Must demonstrate leadership ability within UMC.

Award: Scholarship for use in junior, senior, graduate, or postgraduate years; not renewable. *Number:* varies. *Amount:* $1500–$2500.

Eligibility Requirements: Applicant must be Methodist; American Indian/Alaska Native, Asian/Pacific Islander, or Hispanic; enrolled or expecting to enroll full-time at a four-year institution or university and must have an interest in leadership. Applicant must have 3.0 GPA or higher. Available to U.S. and non-Canadian citizens.

Application Requirements: Application, references, transcript, leadership development plan. *Deadline:* March 1.

Contact: Scholarship Committee
General Board of Higher Education and Ministry
The United Methodist Church, 1001 19th Avenue South
PO Box 340007
Nashville, TN 37202
Phone: 615-340-7344
E-mail: umscholar@gbhem.org

GEORGIA STUDENT FINANCE COMMISSION

http://www.GAcollege411.org/

GEORGIA TUITION EQUALIZATION GRANT (GTEG)
• *See page 603*

HBCUCONNECT.COM

http://www.hbcuconnect.com/

HBCUCONNECT.COM MINORITY SCHOLARSHIP PROGRAM

Scholarship to minorities attending a historically Black college or university. Must attend or be enrolled into an HBCU. Selection based on quality of content in the online registration, and financial need.

Award: Scholarship for use in freshman, sophomore, junior, senior, graduate, or postgraduate years; not renewable. *Number:* 1–12. *Amount:* $1000–$2500.

Eligibility Requirements: Applicant must be American Indian/Alaska Native, Asian/Pacific Islander, Black (non-Hispanic), or Hispanic and enrolled or expecting to enroll full- or part-time at a two-year or four-year institution or university. Available to U.S. citizens.

Application Requirements: Application, essay, resume. *Deadline:* continuous.

Contact: Mr. William Moss, III, CEO
HBCUConnect.com
750 Cross Pointe Road, Suite Q
Columbus, OH 43230
Phone: 614-416-5515
Fax: 614-864-8901
E-mail: wrmoss@hbcuconnect.com

HEBREW IMMIGRANT AID SOCIETY

http://www.hias.org/

HEBREW IMMIGRANT AID SOCIETY SCHOLARSHIP AWARDS COMPETITION
• *See page 544*

HELLENIC TIMES SCHOLARSHIP FUND

http://www.htsf.org/

HELLENIC TIMES SCHOLARSHIP FUND

One-time award to students of Greek/Hellenic descent. Must be between the ages of 17 and 25. For use in any year of undergraduate education. Employees of the Hellenic Times and their families are not eligible.

Award: Scholarship for use in freshman, sophomore, junior, or senior years; not renewable. *Number:* 30–40. *Amount:* $500–$10,000.

Eligibility Requirements: Applicant must be of Greek heritage; age 17-25 and enrolled or expecting to enroll full-time at a two-year or four-year or technical institution or university. Available to U.S. and non-U.S. citizens.

Application Requirements: Application, financial need analysis, resume, references, transcript. *Deadline:* February 19.

Contact: Nick Katsoris, President of Scholarship Fund
Hellenic Times Scholarship Fund
823 11th Avenue, Fifth Floor
New York, NY 10019-3535
Phone: 212-986-6881
Fax: 212-977-3662
E-mail: htsfund@aol.com

HELLENIC UNIVERSITY CLUB OF PHILADELPHIA

http://www.hucphila.org/

CHRISTOPHER DEMETRIS SCHOLARSHIP

$1200 scholarship for a full-time student enrolled in a degree program at an accredited four-year college or university. High school seniors accepted for enrollment in such a degree program may also apply. Must be a U.S. citizen of Greek descent and a resident of particular counties in NJ or PA.

Award: Scholarship for use in freshman, sophomore, junior, or senior years; not renewable. *Number:* varies. *Amount:* up to $1200.

Eligibility Requirements: Applicant must be of Greek heritage; enrolled or expecting to enroll full-time at a four-year institution or university and resident of New Jersey or Pennsylvania. Available to U.S. citizens.

Application Requirements: Application, financial need analysis, transcript. *Deadline:* April 21.

Contact: Anna Hadgis, Scholarship Chairman
Hellenic University Club of Philadelphia
PO Box 42199
Philadelphia, PA 19101-2199
Phone: 610-613-4310
E-mail: hucphila@yahoo.com

DR. NICHOLAS PADIS MEMORIAL GRADUATE SCHOLARSHIP

$5000 scholarship for a qualifying senior undergraduate or graduate student pursuing a full-time degree at an accredited university or professional school. Must be a U.S. citizen of Greek descent and a resident of particular counties in NJ or PA. Academic excellence is the primary consideration for this scholarship.

Award: Scholarship for use in senior or graduate years; not renewable. *Number:* up to 1. *Amount:* up to $5000.

Eligibility Requirements: Applicant must be of Greek heritage; enrolled or expecting to enroll full-time at a four-year institution or university and resident of New Jersey or Pennsylvania. Available to U.S. citizens.

Application Requirements: Application, financial need analysis, transcript. *Deadline:* April 21.

Contact: Anna Hadgis, Scholarship Chairman
Hellenic University Club of Philadelphia
PO Box 42199
Philadelphia, PA 19101-2199
Phone: 610-613-4310
E-mail: hucphila@yahoo.com

DORIZAS MEMORIAL SCHOLARSHIP

$3000 award for a full-time student enrolled in a degree program at an accredited four-year college or university. Must be a U.S. citizen of Greek descent and a resident of particular counties in NJ or PA.

Award: Scholarship for use in freshman, sophomore, junior, or senior years; not renewable. *Number:* varies. *Amount:* up to $3000.

Eligibility Requirements: Applicant must be of Greek heritage; enrolled or expecting to enroll full-time at a four-year institution or university and resident of New Jersey or Pennsylvania. Available to U.S. citizens.

Application Requirements: Application, financial need analysis, transcript. *Deadline:* April 21.

Contact: Anna Hadgis, Scholarship Chairman
Hellenic University Club of Philadelphia
PO Box 42199
Philadelphia, PA 19101-2199
Phone: 610-613-4310
E-mail: hucphila@yahoo.com

FOUNDERS SCHOLARSHIP

$3000 award for a full-time student enrolled in a degree program at an accredited four-year college or university. Must be a U.S. citizen of Greek descent and a resident of particular counties in NJ or PA.

Award: Scholarship for use in freshman, sophomore, junior, or senior years; not renewable. *Number:* varies. *Amount:* up to $3000.

Eligibility Requirements: Applicant must be of Greek heritage; enrolled or expecting to enroll full-time at a four-year institution or university and resident of New Jersey or Pennsylvania. Available to U.S. citizens.

Application Requirements: Application, financial need analysis, transcript. *Deadline:* April 21.

Contact: Anna Hadgis, Scholarship Chairman
Hellenic University Club of Philadelphia
PO Box 42199
Philadelphia, PA 19101-2199
Phone: 610-613-4310
E-mail: hucphila@yahoo.com

JAMES COSMOS MEMORIAL SCHOLARSHIP

Scholarship of up to $1000 for students enrolled full-time in a degree program at an accredited four-year college or university. High school seniors accepted for enrollment in such a degree program may also apply. Must be a U.S. citizen of Greek descent and a resident of particular counties in NJ or PA.

Award: Scholarship for use in freshman, sophomore, junior, or senior years; not renewable. *Number:* varies. *Amount:* $1000.

Eligibility Requirements: Applicant must be of Greek heritage; enrolled or expecting to enroll full-time at a four-year institution or university and resident of New Jersey or Pennsylvania. Available to U.S. citizens.

Application Requirements: Application, financial need analysis. *Deadline:* April 20.

Contact: Anna Hadgis, Scholarship Chairman
Hellenic University Club of Philadelphia
PO Box 42199
Philadelphia, PA 19101-2199
Phone: 610-613-4310
E-mail: hucphila@yahoo.com

PAIDEIA SCHOLARSHIP
• *See page 544*

HENRY SACHS FOUNDATION

http://www.sachsfoundation.org/

SACHS FOUNDATION SCHOLARSHIPS

Award to undergraduate students based on performance, financial need, and applicant's area of study and life goals. Must be African-American and a resident of Colorado. Minimum 3.5 GPA required.

Award: Scholarship for use in freshman year; renewable. *Number:* up to 50. *Amount:* up to $4000.

Eligibility Requirements: Applicant must be Black (non-Hispanic); high school student; planning to enroll or expecting to enroll full-time at a four-year institution or university and resident of Colorado. Applicant must have 3.5 GPA or higher. Available to U.S. citizens.

Application Requirements: Application, financial need analysis, photo. *Deadline:* March 1.

Contact: Lisa Harris, Secretary and Treasurer
Henry Sachs Foundation
90 South Cascade Avenue, Suite 1410
Colorado Springs, CO 80903
Phone: 719-633-2353
E-mail: info@sachsfoundation.org

HISPANIC ANNUAL SALUTE

http://www.hispanicannualsalute.org/

HISPANIC ANNUAL SALUTE SCHOLARSHIP
• *See page 588*

HISPANIC COLLEGE FUND

http://www.hispanicfund.org/

HISPANIC COLLEGE FUND SCHOLARSHIP PROGRAM

Scholarships to U.S. citizens or permanent residents who are Hispanic or of Hispanic descent. Must be studying at an accredited university in the United States or Puerto Rico and enrolled full-time as an undergraduate for the upcoming academic year. Must maintain GPA of 3.0.

Award: Scholarship for use in freshman, sophomore, junior, or senior years; renewable. *Number:* 500–600. *Amount:* $500–$10,000.

Eligibility Requirements: Applicant must be Hispanic and enrolled or expecting to enroll full-time at a two-year or four-year institution or university. Applicant must have 3.0 GPA or higher. Available to U.S. citizens.

Application Requirements: Application, essay, financial need analysis, resume, references, transcript, copy of tax return, Student Aid Report (SAR), proof of citizenship status. *Deadline:* March 15.

Contact: Tatiana Santiago, Scholarship Program Assistant
Hispanic College Fund
1301 K Street, NW, Suite 450-A West
Washington, DC 20005
Phone: 202-296-5400 Ext. 117
E-mail: tsantiago@hispanicfund.org

HISPANIC METROPOLITAN CHAMBER SCHOLARSHIPS

http://www.hmccoregon.com/

HISPANIC METROPOLITAN CHAMBER SCHOLARSHIPS

Scholarships to encourage Hispanics to pursue higher education. Applicant must have a minimum 3.00 GPA. For full-time study only. The award is available only to Hispanic students from Oregon and Southwest Washington.

Award: Scholarship for use in freshman, sophomore, junior, senior, graduate, or postgraduate years; renewable. *Number:* up to 40. *Amount:* $1000–$5000.

Eligibility Requirements: Applicant must be of Hispanic heritage; enrolled or expecting to enroll full- or part-time at a four-year institution or university and resident of Oregon or Washington. Applicant must have 3.0 GPA or higher. Available to U.S. citizens.

Application Requirements: Application, essay, references, transcript, extracurricular activities. *Deadline:* January 29.

Contact: Nicole Ferr? Scholarship Coordinator
E-mail: scholarship@hmccoregon.com

HISPANIC SCHOLARSHIP FUND

http://www.hsf.net/

GATES MILLENNIUM SCHOLARS PROGRAM

Award enables Hispanic-American students to complete an undergraduate or graduate education. Applicant may be pursuing undergraduate studies in any discipline; graduate studies limited to fields of mathematics, science, engineering, education, public health, or library science. Must be entering a U.S. accredited college or university as a full-time degree-seeking student. Minimum 3.3 GPA required. Must demonstrate leadership abilities and significant financial need. Information and application can be found at http://www.gmsp.org.

Award: Scholarship for use in freshman, sophomore, junior, senior, or graduate years; renewable. *Number:* 1000. *Amount:* varies.

Eligibility Requirements: Applicant must be American Indian/Alaska Native, Asian/Pacific Islander, Black (non-Hispanic), or Hispanic and enrolled or expecting to enroll full-time at a four-year institution or university. Applicant must have 3.5 GPA or higher. Available to U.S. and non-Canadian citizens.

Application Requirements: Application, financial need analysis. *Deadline:* January 10.

Contact: GMS Representative
Hispanic Scholarship Fund
55 Second Street, Suite 1500
San Francisco, CA 94105
Phone: 877-473-4636
Fax: 415-808-2302
E-mail: gmsinfo@hsf.net

HSF/GENERAL COLLEGE SCHOLARSHIP PROGRAM

Merit-based award for U.S. citizens or permanent residents of Hispanic heritage with plans to enroll full time in a degree-seeking program at a U.S. accredited institution in the upcoming academic year. Applicants must have a minimum 3.0 GPA. Must complete FAFSA. Must include official transcript and SAR. For additional information please go to http://www.hsf.net/innercontent.aspx?id=34.

Award: Scholarship for use in freshman, sophomore, junior, or senior years; not renewable. *Number:* 2900–3500. *Amount:* $1000–$10,000.

Eligibility Requirements: Applicant must be of Hispanic, Latin American/Caribbean, Mexican, or Spanish heritage and enrolled or expecting to enroll full-time at a two-year or four-year institution or university. Applicant must have 3.0 GPA or higher. Available to U.S. citizens.

Application Requirements: Application, essay, financial need analysis, references, transcript, Student Aid Report (SAR). *Deadline:* varies.

Contact: Scholarship Administrator
Hispanic Scholarship Fund
55 Second Street, Suite 1500
San Francisco, CA 94105
Phone: 877-473-4636
E-mail: scholar1@hsf.net

HOPI TRIBE

http://www.hopi-nsn.gov/

BIA HIGHER EDUCATION GRANT

Grant provides financial support for eligible Hopi individuals pursuing postsecondary education. Minimum 2.5 CGPA required. Deadlines: July 1 for fall, and December 1 for spring.

Award: Grant for use in freshman, sophomore, junior, or senior years; not renewable. *Number:* 1–150. *Amount:* $50–$2500.

Eligibility Requirements: Applicant must be American Indian/Alaska Native and enrolled or expecting to enroll full-time at a two-year or four-year institution or university. Applicant must have 2.5 GPA or higher. Available to U.S. citizens.

Application Requirements: Application, financial need analysis, test scores, transcript, verification of Hopi Indian blood. *Deadline:* varies.

Contact: Theresa Lomakema, Financial Aid Processor/Monitor
Hopi Tribe
PO Box 123
Kykotsmovi, AZ 86039-0123
Phone: 928-734-3533
E-mail: info@hopi.nsn.us

HOPI EDUCATION AWARD

Grant provides financial support for eligible Hopi individuals pursuing postsecondary education. Minimum 2.5 CGPA required. Deadlines: April 1 for summer, July 1 for fall, and December 1 for spring.

Award: Scholarship for use in freshman, sophomore, junior, or senior years; not renewable. *Number:* 1–400. *Amount:* $50–$2500.

Eligibility Requirements: Applicant must be American Indian/Alaska Native and enrolled or expecting to enroll full- or part-time at a two-year or four-year institution or university. Applicant must have 2.5 GPA or higher. Available to U.S. citizens.

Application Requirements: Application, financial need analysis, test scores, transcript, verification of Hopi Indian blood. *Deadline:* varies.

Contact: Theresa Lomakema, Financial Aid Processor/Monitor
Hopi Tribe
PO Box 123
Kykotsmovi, AZ 86039-0123
Phone: 928-734-3533
E-mail: info@hopi.nsn.us

TRIBAL PRIORITY AWARD

Scholarship provides financial support for eligible Hopi individuals pursuing postsecondary education. Minimum 3.0 GPA required.

Award: Scholarship for use in junior or senior years; not renewable. *Number:* 1–5. *Amount:* $2500–$15,000.

Eligibility Requirements: Applicant must be American Indian/Alaska Native and enrolled or expecting to enroll full-time at a two-year or four-year institution or university. Applicant must have 3.0 GPA or higher. Available to U.S. citizens.

Application Requirements: Application, financial need analysis, interview, references, test scores, transcript, verification of Hopi Indian blood. *Deadline:* July 1.

Contact: Theresa Lomakema, Financial Aid Processor/Monitor
Hopi Tribe
PO Box 123
Kykotsmovi, AZ 86039-0123
Phone: 928-734-3533
E-mail: info@hopi.nsn.us

HOUSTON COMMUNITY SERVICES

AZTECA SCHOLARSHIP

Scholarships are awarded annually to a male and a female high school senior planning to attend a university or a college as first-time, first-year students. Must be Texas resident.

Award: Scholarship for use in freshman year; not renewable. *Number:* 2. *Amount:* $500.

Eligibility Requirements: Applicant must be of Mexican heritage; Hispanic; high school student; planning to enroll or expecting to enroll full-time at a two-year or four-year institution or university and resident of Texas. Available to U.S. citizens.

Application Requirements: Application, essay, photo, transcript, income tax report, letter of acceptance. *Deadline:* March 28.

Contact: Edward Castillo, Coordinator
Houston Community Services
Centro Aztlan, 5115 Harrisburg Boulevard
Houston, TX 77011
Phone: 713-926-8771
E-mail: hcsaztlan@sbcglobal.net

HUGH FULTON BYAS MEMORIAL FUNDS INC.

HUGH FULTON BYAS MEMORIAL GRANT

Grant is awarded only to the U.K. citizens. Available only for college students. Dollar value of awards and number of available awards varies.

Award: Grant for use in sophomore, junior, senior, or graduate years; renewable. *Number:* varies. *Amount:* varies.

Eligibility Requirements: Applicant must be English, Scottish, or Welsh citizen and enrolled or expecting to enroll full-time at a four-year institution or university. Available to citizens of countries other than the U.S. or Canada.

Application Requirements: Application, document of U.K. passport. *Deadline:* varies.

Contact: Linda Maffei, Administrator
Hugh Fulton Byas Memorial Funds Inc.
261 Bradley Street
New Haven, CT 06511
Phone: 203-777-8356
Fax: 203-562-6288
E-mail: byasmfund@gmail.com

IDAHO STATE BOARD OF EDUCATION

http://www.boardofed.idaho.gov/

IDAHO MINORITY AND "AT RISK" STUDENT SCHOLARSHIP

• See page 605

INDIAN AMERICAN CULTURAL ASSOCIATION

http://www.iasf.org/

INDIAN AMERICAN SCHOLARSHIP FUND

Scholarships for descendents of families who are from modern-day India and are graduating from public or private high schools in Georgia. They must be enrolled in four-year colleges or universities. There are both academic and need-based awards available through this program.

Award: Scholarship for use in freshman year; renewable. *Number:* 3. *Amount:* $500–$5000.

Eligibility Requirements: Applicant must be of Indian heritage; Asian/Pacific Islander; high school student; planning to enroll or expecting to enroll full-time at a four-year institution or university and resident of Georgia. Applicant must have 3.0 GPA or higher. Available to U.S. citizens.

Application Requirements: Application, essay, financial need analysis, resume, test scores, transcript, IRS 1040 form. *Deadline:* varies.

Contact: Rajesh Kurup, Scholarship Coordinator
Indian American Cultural Association
2407 Waterford Cove
Decatur, GA 30126
E-mail: rajnina@mindspring.com

INTERNATIONAL ORDER OF THE KING'S DAUGHTERS AND SONS

http://www.iokds.org/

INTERNATIONAL ORDER OF THE KING'S DAUGHTERS AND SONS NORTH AMERICAN INDIAN SCHOLARSHIP

Scholarships available for Native American students. Proof of reservation registration, college acceptance letter, and financial aid office address required. Merit-based award. Send self-addressed stamped envelope. Must maintain minimum 2.5 GPA.

Award: Scholarship for use in freshman, sophomore, junior, or senior years; renewable. *Number:* 45–60. *Amount:* $500–$650.

Eligibility Requirements: Applicant must be American Indian/Alaska Native and enrolled or expecting to enroll full-time at a two-year or four-year or technical institution or university. Applicant must have 2.5 GPA or higher. Available to U.S. and Canadian citizens.

Application Requirements: Application, essay, financial need analysis, references, self-addressed stamped envelope, transcript, written documentation of reservation registration. *Deadline:* varies.

Contact: Chris White, Office Manager
International Order of the King's Daughters and Sons
PO Box 1017
Chautauqua, NY 14722-1017
Phone: 716-357-4951
Fax: 716-357-3762
E-mail: iokds5@alltel.net

INTERNATIONAL UNION OF BRICKLAYERS AND ALLIED CRAFTSMEN

http://www.bacweb.org/

CANADIAN BATES SCHOLARSHIP PROGRAM
• *See page 545*

INTERTRIBAL TIMBER COUNCIL

http://www.itcnet.org/

DICK FRENCH MEMORIAL SCHOLARSHIP PROGRAM

Program to assist Native American/Native Alaskan undergraduate or graduate student enrolled full-time at an accredited two- or four-year college or university.

Award: Scholarship for use in freshman, sophomore, junior, senior, or graduate years; not renewable. *Number:* 1. *Amount:* $500.

Eligibility Requirements: Applicant must be American Indian/Alaska Native and enrolled or expecting to enroll full-time at a two-year or four-year institution or university. Available to U.S. citizens.

Application Requirements: Application, references, transcript, federal tax records. *Deadline:* April 1.

Contact: Education Committee
Intertribal Timber Council
1112 21st Avenue, NE, Suite 4
Portland, OR 97232-2114
Phone: 503-282-4296
E-mail: itc1@teleport.com

ITALIAN-AMERICAN CHAMBER OF COMMERCE OF CHICAGO

http://www.italianchamber.us/

ITALIAN-AMERICAN CHAMBER OF COMMERCE OF CHICAGO SCHOLARSHIP

One-time awards for Illinois residents of Italian descent. Available to high school seniors and college students for use at a four-year institution. Applicants must have a 3.5 GPA. Must reside in Cook, Du Page, Kane, Lake, McHenry, or Will counties of Illinois. Must submit a letter including a biographical account of themselves and two letters of recommendation, one from a teacher and one from their counselor.

Award: Scholarship for use in freshman, sophomore, junior, or senior years; not renewable. *Number:* 1. *Amount:* up to $1000.

Eligibility Requirements: Applicant must be of Italian heritage; enrolled or expecting to enroll full-time at a four-year institution and resident of Illinois. Applicant must have 2.5 GPA or higher. Available to U.S. and non-U.S. citizens.

Application Requirements: Application, essay, photo, references, self-addressed stamped envelope, transcript. *Deadline:* May 31.

Contact: Frank Pugno, Scholarship Chairman
Italian-American Chamber of Commerce of Chicago
30 South Michigan Avenue, Suite 504
Chicago, IL 60603
Phone: 312-553-9137 Ext. 13
Fax: 312-553-9142
E-mail: info.chicago@italchambers.net

JACKIE ROBINSON FOUNDATION

http://www.jackierobinson.org/

JACKIE ROBINSON SCHOLARSHIP
• *See page 590*

JEWISH VOCATIONAL SERVICE LOS ANGELES

http://www.jvsla.org/

JEWISH VOCATIONAL SERVICE SCHOLARSHIP FUND

Need-based scholarships to support Jewish students from Los Angeles County in their pursuit of college, graduate, and vocational education. Applicants must be Jewish, permanent residents of Los Angeles, maintain a minimum 2.7 GPA, and demonstrate verifiable financial need.

Award: Scholarship for use in freshman, sophomore, junior, senior, or graduate years; not renewable. *Number:* 125–200. *Amount:* $1000–$5000.

Eligibility Requirements: Applicant must be Jewish; of Jewish heritage; enrolled or expecting to enroll full-time at a two-year or four-year or technical institution or university and resident of California. Applicant must have 3.0 GPA or higher. Available to U.S. citizens.

Application Requirements: Application, essay, financial need analysis, interview, resume, references, transcript, FAFSA, Student Aid Report (SAR). *Deadline:* March 12.

Contact: Cathy Kersh, Scholarship Program Manager
Jewish Vocational Service Los Angeles
6505 Wilshire Boulevard, Suite 200
Los Angeles, CA 90048
Phone: 323-761-8888 Ext. 8868
Fax: 323-761-8575
E-mail: scholarship@jvsla.org

KAISER PERMANENTE

http://kpapan.org/

KAISER PERMANENTE ASIAN PACIFIC AMERICAN NETWORK SCHOLARSHIP PROGRAM

Award for graduating high school senior planning to attend college, university, trade or technical school. Must reside in Southern California and be of Asian descent.

Award: Scholarship for use in freshman year; not renewable. *Number:* 6–8. *Amount:* $1000.

Eligibility Requirements: Applicant must be Asian/Pacific Islander; high school student; planning to enroll or expecting to enroll full- or part-time at a two-year or four-year or technical institution or university and resident of California. Applicant must have 3.0 GPA or higher. Available to U.S. citizens.

Application Requirements: Application, essay, references, self-addressed stamped envelope, transcript. *Deadline:* April 10.

Contact: Dr. Michael J. Tran, KPAPAN Scholarship Committee Chairman
Kaiser Permanente
PO Box 950
Pasadena, CA 91102-0950
E-mail: michael.j.tran@kp.org

KANSAS BOARD OF REGENTS

http://www.kansasregents.org/

KANSAS ETHNIC MINORITY SCHOLARSHIP

Scholarship program designed to assist financially needy, academically competitive students who are identified as members of any of the following ethnic/racial groups: African-American, American Indian or Alaskan Native, Asian or Pacific Islander, or Hispanic. Priority is given to applicants who are freshmen. Students must be Kansas residents attending postsecondary institutions in Kansas. For more details refer to web site http://www.kansasregents.org/financial_aid/minority.html.

Award: Scholarship for use in freshman, sophomore, junior, or senior years; renewable. *Number:* varies. *Amount:* up to $1850.

Eligibility Requirements: Applicant must be American Indian/Alaska Native, Asian/Pacific Islander, Black (non-Hispanic), or Hispanic; enrolled or expecting to enroll full-time at a two-year or four-year institution or university; resident of Kansas and studying in Kansas. Applicant must have 3.0 GPA or higher. Available to U.S. citizens.

Application Requirements: Application, financial need analysis, test scores. *Fee:* $12. *Deadline:* May 1.

Contact: Diane Lindeman, Director of Student Financial Assistance
Kansas Board of Regents
1000 Jackson, SW, Suite 520
Topeka, KS 66612-1368
Phone: 785-296-3517
Fax: 785-296-0983
E-mail: dlindeman@ksbor.org

KIMBO FOUNDATION

http://www.kimbofoundation.org/

KIMBO FOUNDATION SCHOLARSHIP

Scholarship available to Korean-American students only. Full time study only. Application deadline varies every year.

Award: Scholarship for use in freshman, sophomore, junior, senior, graduate, or postgraduate years; not renewable. *Number:* 30–50. *Amount:* $1500.

Eligibility Requirements: Applicant must be of Korean heritage; Asian/Pacific Islander and enrolled or expecting to enroll full-time at a two-year or four-year or technical institution or university. Available to citizens of countries other than the U.S. or Canada.

Application Requirements: Application, essay, references, transcript, copy of household income tax return. *Deadline:* varies.

Contact: Jennifer Chung, Program Coordinator
Kimbo Foundation
430 Shotwell Street
San Francisco, CA 94110
Phone: 415-285-4100
Fax: 415-285-4103
E-mail: info@kimbofoundation.org

KNIGHTS OF COLUMBUS

http://www.kofc.org/

FOURTH DEGREE PRO DEO AND PRO PATRIA (CANADA)
• *See page 547*

KONIAG EDUCATION FOUNDATION

http://www.koniageducation.org/

GLENN GODFREY MEMORIAL SCHOLARSHIP

Scholarship for sophomore, junior, or seniors in their undergraduate study. Applicants must be Alaska Native shareholders or descendants (may be adopted) of the Koniag Region. Must have and maintain a minimum cumulative GPA of 2.5.

Award: Scholarship for use in sophomore, junior, or senior years; not renewable. *Number:* 1. *Amount:* up to $5000.

Eligibility Requirements: Applicant must be American Indian/Alaska Native and enrolled or expecting to enroll full-time at a four-year institution or university. Applicant must have 2.5 GPA or higher. Available to U.S. citizens.

Application Requirements: Application, essay, interview, photo, resume, references, transcript, birth certificate (for descendants only). *Deadline:* varies.

Contact: Tyan Hayes, Executive Director
Koniag Education Foundation
6927 Old Seward Highway, Suite 103
Anchorage, AK 99518
Phone: 907-562-9093
Fax: 907-562-9023

KONIAG EDUCATION CAREER DEVELOPMENT GRANT

Applicants must be Alaska Native shareholders or descendents (may be adopted) of the Koniag Region. Applicants must be accepted or enrolled in a career development course and able to demonstrate how the training will assist the student in gaining employment or job security and/or advancement. Awards up to $1000.

Award: Grant for use in freshman year; not renewable. *Number:* 1. *Amount:* $1000.

Eligibility Requirements: Applicant must be American Indian/Alaska Native and enrolled or expecting to enroll part-time at a technical institution. Available to U.S. and non-Canadian citizens.

Application Requirements: Application, driver's license, resume. *Deadline:* varies.

Contact: Tyan Hayes, Executive Director
Koniag Education Foundation
6927 Old Seward Highway, Suite 103
Anchorage, AK 99518
Phone: 907-562-9093
Fax: 907-562-9023

KONIAG EDUCATION FOUNDATION ACADEMIC/GRADUATE SCHOLARSHIP

Scholarships to honor students who excel academically, and who show the potential to succeed in college studies. Applicants must be Alaska Native shareholders or descendents (may be adopted) of the Koniag Region. Deadlines: March 15 for summer term, June 1 for fall/spring terms.

Award: Scholarship for use in freshman, sophomore, junior, senior, graduate, or postgraduate years; not renewable. *Number:* 130–170. *Amount:* $500–$2500.

Eligibility Requirements: Applicant must be American Indian/Alaska Native and enrolled or expecting to enroll full- or part-time at a two-year or four-year or technical institution or university. Applicant must have 3.0 GPA or higher. Available to U.S. citizens.

Application Requirements: Application, driver's license, essay, financial need analysis, photo, references, transcript, proof of eligibility from Koniag Inc. *Deadline:* varies.

Contact: Tyan Hayes, Executive Director
Koniag Education Foundation
6927 Old Seward Highway, Suite 103
Anchorage, AK 99518
Phone: 907-562-9093
Fax: 907-562-9023

KONIAG EDUCATION FOUNDATION COLLEGE/UNIVERSITY BASIC SCHOLARSHIP

Scholarship to honor students who show the potential to succeed in college studies. Applicants must be Alaska Native shareholders or descendants (may be adopted) of the Koniag Region. Must maintain a minimum cumulative GPA of 2.0 or equivalent scores. Awarded up to $1000 a year. Deadlines: March 15 for summer term, June 1 for fall/spring terms.

Award: Scholarship for use in freshman, sophomore, junior, senior, graduate, or postgraduate years; not renewable. *Number:* varies. *Amount:* up to $1000.

Eligibility Requirements: Applicant must be American Indian/Alaska Native and enrolled or expecting to enroll full- or part-time at a two-year or four-year or technical institution or university. Available to U.S. citizens.

Application Requirements: Application, essay, references, transcript. *Deadline:* varies.

Contact: Tyan Hayes, Executive Director
Koniag Education Foundation
6927 Old Seward Highway, Suite 103
Anchorage, AK 99518
Phone: 907-562-9093
Fax: 907-562-9023

KOREAN AMERICAN SCHOLARSHIP FOUNDATION

http://www.kasf.org/

KOREAN-AMERICAN SCHOLARSHIP FOUNDATION EASTERN REGION SCHOLARSHIPS

Scholarships available to Korean-American and Korean students enrolled in a full-time undergraduate or graduate program in the United States. Selection based on financial need, academic achievement, school activities, and community services. Each applicant must submit an application to the respective KASF region. For more details and an application see web site http://www.kasf.org.

Award: Scholarship for use in freshman, sophomore, junior, senior, or graduate years; not renewable. *Number:* varies. *Amount:* $1000.

Eligibility Requirements: Applicant must be of Korean heritage; Asian/Pacific Islander; enrolled or expecting to enroll full-time at a four-year institution or university and studying in Delaware, District of Columbia, Kentucky, Maryland, North Carolina, Pennsylvania, Virginia, or West Virginia. Available to U.S. and non-U.S. citizens.

Application Requirements: Application, essay, financial need analysis, photo, references, self-addressed stamped envelope, transcript. *Deadline:* May 31.

Contact: Dr. Brandon Yi, Scholarship Committee
Korean American Scholarship Foundation
803 Russell Avenue, Suite 2C
Reston, VA 20879
E-mail: eastern@kasf.org

KOREAN-AMERICAN SCHOLARSHIP FOUNDATION NORTHEASTERN REGION SCHOLARSHIPS

Scholarships available to Korean-American and Korean students enrolled in a full-time undergraduate or graduate program in the United States. Selection based on financial need, academic achievement, school activities, and community services. Each applicant must submit an application to the respective KASF region. For more details and an application see web site http://www.kasf.org.

Award: Scholarship for use in freshman, sophomore, junior, senior, graduate, or postgraduate years; not renewable. *Number:* 60. *Amount:* $1000–$2500.

Eligibility Requirements: Applicant must be of Korean heritage; Asian/Pacific Islander; enrolled or expecting to enroll full-time at a four-year institution or university and studying in Connecticut, Maine, Massachusetts, New Hampshire, New Jersey, New York, Rhode Island, or Vermont. Available to U.S. citizens.

Application Requirements: Application, essay, financial need analysis, photo, references, transcript. *Deadline:* June 23.

Contact: Mr. William Y. Kim, Scholarship Committee Chairman
Korean American Scholarship Foundation
51 West Overlook
Port Washington, NY 11050
Phone: 516-883-1142
Fax: 516-883-1964
E-mail: kim.william@gmail.com

KOREAN-AMERICAN SCHOLARSHIP FOUNDATION SOUTHERN REGION SCHOLARSHIPS

Scholarships available to Korean-American and Korean students enrolled in a full-time undergraduate or graduate program in the United States. Selection based on financial need, academic achievement, school activities, and community services. Each applicant must submit an application to the respective KASF region. For more details and an application see web site http://www.kasf.org.

Award: Scholarship for use in freshman, sophomore, junior, senior, or graduate years; not renewable. *Number:* up to 45. *Amount:* $1000.

Eligibility Requirements: Applicant must be of Korean heritage; Asian/Pacific Islander; enrolled or expecting to enroll full-time at a four-year institution or university and studying in Alabama, Arkansas, Florida, Georgia, Louisiana, Mississippi, North Carolina, Oklahoma, South Carolina, Tennessee, or Texas. Available to U.S. citizens.

Application Requirements: Application, essay, financial need analysis, photo, references, transcript. *Deadline:* June 10.

Contact: Dr. Sam Sook Chung, Scholarship Committee
Korean American Scholarship Foundation
2989 Preston Drive
Rex, GA 30273
Phone: 770-968-6768
E-mail: samsookchung@hotmail.com

KOREAN-AMERICAN SCHOLARSHIP FOUNDATION WESTERN REGION SCHOLARSHIPS

Scholarships available to Korean-American and Korean students enrolled in a full-time undergraduate or graduate program in the United States. Selection based on financial need, academic achievement, school activities, and community services. Each applicant must submit an application to the respective KASF region. For more details and an application see web site http://www.kasf.org.

Award: Scholarship for use in freshman, sophomore, junior, senior, or graduate years; not renewable. *Number:* varies. *Amount:* $2000.

Eligibility Requirements: Applicant must be of Korean heritage; Asian/Pacific Islander; enrolled or expecting to enroll full-time at a four-year institution or university and studying in Alaska, Arizona, California, Colorado, Hawaii, Idaho, Montana, Nevada, New Mexico, Oregon, Utah, or Washington. Applicant must have 3.0 GPA or higher. Available to U.S. citizens.

Application Requirements: Application, essay, financial need analysis, photo, references, transcript. *Deadline:* May 31.

Contact: KASF Western Regional Chapter
Korean American Scholarship Foundation
3435 Wilshire Boulevard, Suite 2450B
Los Angeles, CA 90010
Phone: 213-380-5273
Fax: 213-380-5273
E-mail: western@kasf.org

KOSCIUSZKO FOUNDATION

http://www.kosciuszkofoundation.org/

MASSACHUSETTS FEDERATION OF POLISH WOMEN'S CLUBS SCHOLARSHIPS

Nonrenewable award for sophomores, juniors, and seniors attending an accredited four-year college or university. The scholarship is awarded to residents of Massachusetts. If no residents of Massachusetts apply the award is offered to residents of New England. Must submit proof of Polish ancestry. Minimum 3.0 GPA required.

Award: Scholarship for use in sophomore, junior, or senior years; not renewable. *Number:* 3. *Amount:* $1250.

Eligibility Requirements: Applicant must be of Polish heritage; enrolled or expecting to enroll full-time at a four-year institution or university and resident of Massachusetts. Applicant must have 3.0 GPA or higher. Available to U.S. and non-Canadian citizens.

Application Requirements: Application, essay, financial need analysis, photo, references, transcript, proof of Polish ancestry. *Fee:* $35. *Deadline:* January 5.

Contact: Ms. Addy Tymczyszyn, Scholarship and Grant Officer for Americans
Kosciuszko Foundation
15 East 65th Street
New York, NY 10065
Phone: 212-734-2130 Ext. 210
Fax: 212-628-4552
E-mail: Addy@thekf.org

POLISH AMERICAN CLUB OF NORTH JERSEY SCHOLARSHIPS

Scholarships of $500 to $2000 awarded to qualified students for full-time undergraduate and graduate studies at accredited colleges and universities in the United States. The scholarship is renewable. U.S. citizens of Polish descent and Polish citizens with permanent residency status in the United States with minimum GPA of 3.0 are eligible. Applicants must be members of the Polish American Club of North Jersey.

Award: Scholarship for use in freshman, sophomore, junior, senior, or graduate years; renewable. *Number:* varies. *Amount:* $500–$2000.

Eligibility Requirements: Applicant must be of Polish heritage and enrolled or expecting to enroll full-time at a four-year institution or university. Applicant must have 3.0 GPA or higher. Available to U.S. and non-Canadian citizens.

Application Requirements: Application, essay, photo, references, transcript, proof of Polish ancestry. *Fee:* $35. *Deadline:* January 5.

Contact: Ms. Addy Tymczyszyn, Scholarship and Grant Officer for Americans
E-mail: addy@thekf.org

POLISH NATIONAL ALLIANCE OF BROOKLYN USA INC. SCHOLARSHIPS

Scholarships of $2000 available to qualified undergraduate students for full-time studies at accredited colleges and universities in the United States. U.S. citizens of Polish descent and Polish citizens with permanent residency status in the United States with minimum GPA of 3.0 are eligible. Applicants must be members in good standing of the Polish National Alliance of Brooklyn Lodge#1903.

Award: Scholarship for use in freshman, sophomore, junior, or senior years; not renewable. *Number:* 1–3. *Amount:* $2000.

Eligibility Requirements: Applicant must be of Polish heritage; enrolled or expecting to enroll full-time at a four-year institution or university and resident of New York. Applicant must have 3.0 GPA or higher. Available to U.S. and non-Canadian citizens.

Application Requirements: Application, essay, photo, references, transcript, proof of Polish ancestry. *Fee:* $35. *Deadline:* January 5.

Contact: Ms. Addy Tymczyszyn
Kosciuszko Foundation
15 East 65th Street
New York, NY 10065
Phone: 212-734-2130 Ext. 210
Fax: 212-628-4552
E-mail: Addy@thekf.org

LATIN AMERICAN EDUCATIONAL FOUNDATION

http://www.laef.org/

LATIN AMERICAN EDUCATIONAL FOUNDATION SCHOLARSHIPS

Scholarship for Colorado residents of Hispanic heritage. Applicant should be accepted in an accredited college, university or vocational school. Must maintain a minimum GPA of 3.0.

Award: Scholarship for use in freshman, sophomore, junior, senior, or graduate years; not renewable. *Number:* varies. *Amount:* varies.

Eligibility Requirements: Applicant must be Hispanic and enrolled or expecting to enroll full-time at a four-year institution or university. Applicant must have 3.0 GPA or higher. Available to U.S. citizens.

Application Requirements: Application, essay, financial need analysis, interview, references, transcript. *Deadline:* March 1.

Contact: Scholarship Selection Committee
Latin American Educational Foundation
561 Santa Fe Drive
Denver, CO 80204

LEAGUE OF UNITED LATIN AMERICAN CITIZENS NATIONAL EDUCATIONAL SERVICE CENTERS INC.

http://www.lnesc.org/

LULAC NATIONAL SCHOLARSHIP FUND

Awards scholarships to Hispanic students who are enrolled or planning to enroll in accredited colleges or universities in the United States. Applicants must be U.S. citizens or legal residents. Scholarships may be used for the payment of tuition, academic fees, room, board and the purchase of required educational materials. For additional information visit web site http://www.lnesc.org to see a list of participating councils or send a self-addressed stamped envelope.

Award: Scholarship for use in freshman, sophomore, junior, or senior years; not renewable. *Number:* 1000. *Amount:* $250–$2000.

Eligibility Requirements: Applicant must be Hispanic and enrolled or expecting to enroll full-time at a two-year or four-year institution or university. Available to U.S. citizens.

Application Requirements: Application, driver's license, essay, financial need analysis, interview, references, self-addressed stamped envelope, test scores, transcript. *Deadline:* March 31.

Contact: Scholarship Coordinator
League of United Latin American Citizens National
Educational Service Centers Inc.
2000 L Street, NW, Suite 610
Washington, DC 20036
Phone: 202-835-9646
Fax: 202-835-9685

LOS PADRES FOUNDATION

http://www.lospadresfoundation.com/

COLLEGE TUITION ASSISTANCE PROGRAM

Program for eligible students who are the first family member to attend college. Must be a legal resident or citizen of the U.S. and a resident of New York or New Jersey. Must have a 3.0 GPA. For further information, refer to web site http://www.lospadresfoundation.com.

Award: Scholarship for use in freshman, sophomore, junior, or senior years; not renewable. *Number:* 25–30. *Amount:* $2000–$3000.

Eligibility Requirements: Applicant must be Hispanic; high school student; planning to enroll or expecting to enroll full-time at a two-year or four-year institution or university and resident of New Jersey or New York. Applicant must have 3.0 GPA or higher. Available to U.S. citizens.

Application Requirements: Application, essay, financial need analysis, interview, photo, references, transcript. *Deadline:* January 12.

Contact: Mrs. Andrea Betancourt, Office Manager
Los Padres Foundation
PO Box 8421
McLean, VA 22106-0421
Phone: 800-528-4105
Fax: 866-810-1361
E-mail: lpfadmin@lospadresfoundation.com

SECOND CHANCE SCHOLARSHIPS

Scholarships granted to Puerto Rican/Latinos students who wish to return to college, trade school or apprenticeship program. Must be a resident of New York or New Jersey. Must demonstrate financial need. For further information, refer to web site http://www.lospadresfoundation.com.

Award: Scholarship for use in freshman year; renewable. *Number:* 1–5. *Amount:* $2000.

Eligibility Requirements: Applicant must be of Hispanic or Latin American/Caribbean heritage; enrolled or expecting to enroll full-time at a two-year or four-year or technical institution or university and resident of New Jersey or New York. Available to U.S. citizens.

Application Requirements: Application, essay, financial need analysis, interview, photo, references, transcript. *Deadline:* January 20.

Contact: Mrs. Andrea Betancourt, Office Manager
Los Padres Foundation
PO Box 8421
McLean, VA 22106-0421
Phone: 800-528-4105
Fax: 866-810-1361
E-mail: lpfadmin@lospadresfoundation.com

MAGIC JOHNSON FOUNDATION INC.

http://www.magicjohnson.org/

TAYLOR MICHAELS SCHOLARSHIP FUND
• *See page 590*

MANA DE SAN DIEGO

http://www.sdmana.org/

MANA DE SAN DIEGO SYLVIA CHAVEZ MEMORIAL SCHOLARSHIP
• *See page 591*

MENOMINEE INDIAN TRIBE OF WISCONSIN

http://www.menominee-nsn.gov/

MENOMINEE INDIAN TRIBE ADULT VOCATIONAL TRAINING PROGRAM

Renewable award for enrolled Menominee tribal members to use at vocational or technical schools. Must be at least 1/4 Menominee and show proof of Indian blood. Must complete financial aid form. Deadlines: March 1 and November 1.

Award: Grant for use in freshman or sophomore years; renewable. *Number:* 50–70. *Amount:* $100–$2200.

Eligibility Requirements: Applicant must be American Indian/Alaska Native and enrolled or expecting to enroll full- or part-time at a technical institution. Available to U.S. citizens.

Application Requirements: Application, financial need analysis, proof of Indian blood. *Deadline:* varies.

Contact: Virginia Nuske, Education Director
Menominee Indian Tribe of Wisconsin
PO Box 910
Keshena, WI 54135
Phone: 715-799-5110
Fax: 715-799-5102
E-mail: vnuske@mitw.org

MENOMINEE INDIAN TRIBE OF WISCONSIN HIGHER EDUCATION GRANTS

Renewable award for only enrolled Menominee tribal members to use at a two- or four-year college or university. Must be at least 1/4 Menominee and show proof of Indian blood. Must complete the Free Application for Federal Student Aid (FAFSA)financial aid form and demonstrate financial need.

Award: Grant for use in freshman, sophomore, junior, or senior years; renewable. *Number:* 136. *Amount:* $100–$2200.

Eligibility Requirements: Applicant must be American Indian/Alaska Native and enrolled or expecting to enroll full- or part-time at a two-year or four-year institution or university. Available to U.S. citizens.

Application Requirements: Application, financial need analysis, proof of Indian blood. *Deadline:* continuous.

Contact: Virginia Nuske, Education Director
Menominee Indian Tribe of Wisconsin
PO Box 910
Keshena, WI 54135
Phone: 715-799-5110
Fax: 715-799-5102
E-mail: vnuske@mitw.org

MINNESOTA OFFICE OF HIGHER EDUCATION

http://www.getreadyforcollege.org/

MINNESOTA INDIAN SCHOLARSHIP

Scholarship for Minnesota residents who are one-fourth or more American Indian ancestry and attending an eligible Minnesota postsecondary institution. Maximum award is $4000 for undergraduate students and $6000 for graduate students. Scholarships are limited to 3 years for certificate or AA/AS programs, 5 years for bachelor's degree programs, and 5 years for graduate programs. Applicants must maintain satisfactory academic progress, not be in default on student loans, and be eligible to receive Pell or State Grant and have remaining need. Undergraduates must be enrolled on a least a 3/4-time basis.

Award: Scholarship for use in freshman, sophomore, junior, senior, graduate, or postgraduate years; not renewable. *Number:* 500–600. *Amount:* up to $6000.

Eligibility Requirements: Applicant must be American Indian/Alaska Native; enrolled or expecting to enroll full- or part-time at a two-year or four-year or technical institution or university; resident of Minnesota and studying in Minnesota. Available to U.S. citizens.

Application Requirements: Application, financial need analysis, American Indian ancestry documentation. *Deadline:* continuous.

Contact: Scholarship Staff
Minnesota Office of Higher Education
1450 Energy Park Drive, Suite 350
St. Paul, MN 55108
Phone: 651-642-0567 Ext. 1
Fax: 651-642-0675
E-mail: sandy.bowes@state.mn.us

MISSOURI DEPARTMENT OF ELEMENTARY AND SECONDARY EDUCATION

http://www.dese.mo.gov/

ROBERT C. BYRD HONORS SCHOLARSHIP-MISSOURI

Award for high school seniors who are residents of Missouri. Amount of the award each year depends on the amount the state is allotted by the U.S. Department of Education. Maximum amount awarded per student is $1500. Students must score above 10th percentile on ACT.

Award: Scholarship for use in freshman year; renewable. *Number:* 100–150. *Amount:* up to $1500.

Eligibility Requirements: Applicant must be American Indian/Alaska Native, Asian/Pacific Islander, Black (non-Hispanic), or Hispanic; high school student; planning to enroll or expecting to enroll full-time at a four-year institution or university and resident of Missouri. Available to U.S. citizens.

Application Requirements: Application, test scores, transcript. *Deadline:* April 15.

Contact: Laura Harrison, Administrative Assistant II
Missouri Department of Elementary and Secondary Education
PO Box 480
Jefferson City, MO 65102-0480
Phone: 573-751-1668
Fax: 573-526-3580
E-mail: laura.harrison@dese.mo.gov

MONGOLIA SOCIETY, INC.

http://www.mongoliasociety.org/

DR. GOMBOJAB HANGIN MEMORIAL SCHOLARSHIP

One-time award for students of Mongolian heritage only. Must have permanent residency in Mongolia, the People's Republic of China, or the former Soviet Union. Award is for tuition at U.S. institutions. Upon conclusion of award year, recipient must write a report of his or her activities. Application requests must be in English and the application must be filled out in English. Write for application.

Award: Scholarship for use in freshman, sophomore, junior, or senior years; not renewable. *Number:* 1. *Amount:* up to $1000.

Eligibility Requirements: Applicant must be of Mongolian heritage and Chinese or Russian citizen; Asian/Pacific Islander and enrolled or expecting to enroll full-time at a two-year or four-year or technical institution or university. Available to citizens of countries other than the U.S. or Canada.

Application Requirements: Application, photo, references, curriculum vitae, copy of ID card and passport. *Deadline:* January 1.

Contact: Mrs. Susie Drost, Executive Director
Mongolia Society, Inc.
Indiana University, 322 Goodbody Hall
1011 East Third Street
Bloomington, IN 47405-7005
Phone: 812-855-4078
E-mail: monsoc@indiana.edu

NAACP LEGAL DEFENSE AND EDUCATIONAL FUND INC.

http://www.naacpldf.org/

HERBERT LEHMAN SCHOLARSHIP PROGRAM

Renewable award for successful African-American high school seniors and freshmen to attend a four-year college on a full-time basis. Candidates are required to be U.S. citizens and must have outstanding potential as evidenced by their high school academic records, test scores, and personal essays.

Award: Scholarship for use in freshman, sophomore, junior, or senior years; renewable. *Number:* 25–30. *Amount:* $2000.

Eligibility Requirements: Applicant must be Black (non-Hispanic) and enrolled or expecting to enroll full-time at a four-year institution or university. Available to U.S. citizens.

Application Requirements: Application, essay, photo, references, test scores, transcript. *Deadline:* April 30.

Contact: Michael Bagley, Program Director
NAACP Legal Defense and Educational Fund Inc.
99 Hudson Street, Suite 1600
New York, NY 10013
Phone: 212-965-2225
Fax: 212-219-1595

NANA (NORTHWEST ALASKA NATIVE ASSOCIATION) REGIONAL CORPORATION

http://www.nana.com/

ROBERT AQQALUK NEWLIN SR. MEMORIAL TRUST SCHOLARSHIP

Scholarship for NANA shareholders, descendants of NANA shareholders, or dependents of NANA shareholders or their descendants. Applicant must be enrolled or accepted for admittance at a postsecondary educational institution or vocational school.

Award: Scholarship for use in freshman, sophomore, junior, or senior years; not renewable. *Number:* 250–400. *Amount:* $1000–$2000.

Eligibility Requirements: Applicant must be American Indian/Alaska Native and enrolled or expecting to enroll full- or part-time at a two-year or four-year or technical institution or university. Available to U.S. citizens.

Application Requirements: Application, financial need analysis, references, transcript, college acceptance letter, enrollment proof. *Deadline:* varies.

Contact: Erica Nelson, Education Director
NANA (Northwest Alaska Native Association) Regional Corporation
PO Box 509
Kotzebue, AK 99752
Phone: 907-442-1607
Fax: 907-442-2289
E-mail: erica.nelson@nana.org

NATIONAL ASSOCIATION FOR CAMPUS ACTIVITIES

http://www.naca.org/

MULTICULTURAL SCHOLARSHIP PROGRAM

Scholarships will be given to applicants identified as African-American, Latina/Latino, Native-American, Asian-American or Pacific Islander ethnic minorities. A letter of recommendation affirming his/her ethnic minority status, his/her financial need, and that he/she will be in the campus activity field at least one year following the program for which a scholarship is being sought, should accompany applications.

Award: Scholarship for use in freshman, sophomore, junior, senior, or graduate years; not renewable. *Number:* up to 4. *Amount:* $250–$300.

Eligibility Requirements: Applicant must be American Indian/Alaska Native, Asian/Pacific Islander, Black (non-Hispanic), or Hispanic; enrolled or expecting to enroll full- or part-time at a two-year or four-year institution or university and must have an interest in leadership. Available to U.S. and non-U.S. citizens.

Application Requirements: Application, essay, financial need analysis, references. *Deadline:* May 1.

Contact: Dionne Ellison, Administrative Assistant
National Association for Campus Activities
13 Harbison Way
Columbia, SC 29212-3401
Phone: 803-732-6222 Ext. 131
Fax: 803-749-1047
E-mail: dionnee@naca.org

NATIONAL ASSOCIATION FOR THE ADVANCEMENT OF COLORED PEOPLE

http://www.naacp.org/

AGNES JONES JACKSON SCHOLARSHIP
• *See page 550*

ROY WILKINS SCHOLARSHIP
• *See page 550*

NATIONAL ASSOCIATION OF COLORED WOMEN'S CLUBS

http://www.nacwc.org/

HALLIE Q. BROWN SCHOLARSHIP

One-time $1000–$2000 scholarship for high school graduates who have completed at least one semester in a postsecondary accredited institution with a minimum "C" average.

Award: Scholarship for use in freshman year; not renewable. *Number:* 4–6. *Amount:* $1000–$2000.

Eligibility Requirements: Applicant must be Black (non-Hispanic); high school student and planning to enroll or expecting to enroll full-time at a two-year or four-year institution or university. Available to U.S. citizens.

Application Requirements: Application, references, transcript. *Deadline:* March 30.

Contact: Dr. Gerldine Jenkins, Program Coordinator
National Association of Colored Women's Clubs
Program Coordinator
Washington, DC 20009
Phone: 202-667-4080
Fax: 202-667-2574

NATIONAL ASSOCIATION OF NEGRO BUSINESS AND PROFESSIONAL WOMEN'S CLUBS INC.

http://www.nanbpwc.org/

NATIONAL SCHOLARSHIP

Scholarship for African-American graduating high school seniors with a minimum 3.0 GPA. Must submit 300-word essay on the topic "Why Education is Important to Me".

Award: Scholarship for use in freshman year; not renewable. *Number:* 6–8. *Amount:* $500–$1000.

Eligibility Requirements: Applicant must be Black (non-Hispanic); high school student and planning to enroll or expecting to enroll full-time at a four-year institution or university. Applicant must have 3.0 GPA or higher. Available to U.S. citizens.

Application Requirements: Application, essay, references, test scores, transcript. *Deadline:* March 1.

Contact: Twyla Whitby, National Director of Education Scholarship Program
National Association of Negro Business and Professional Women's Clubs Inc.
1806 New Hampshire Avenue, NW
Washington, DC 20009-3298
Phone: 202-483-4206
E-mail: info@nanbpwc.org

NATIONAL BLACK MBA ASSOCIATION

http://www.nbmbaa.org/

NATIONAL BLACK MBA ASSOCIATION PHD SCHOLARSHIP PROGRAM

Program's mission is to identify and increase the pool of Black talent for business, public, private and non-profit sectors.

Award: Scholarship for use in freshman, sophomore, junior, or senior years; not renewable. *Number:* 1–2. *Amount:* $5000–$15,000.

Eligibility Requirements: Applicant must be Black (non-Hispanic) and enrolled or expecting to enroll full-time at an institution or university. Available to U.S. and non-U.S. citizens.

Application Requirements: Application, essay, interview, resume, transcript. *Deadline:* May 1.

Contact: Ms. Lori O. Johnson, Program Administrator, University Relations
National Black MBA Association
180 North Michigan Avenue, Suite 1400
Chicago, IL 60601
Phone: 312-580-8086
Fax: 312-580-8703
E-mail: scholarship@nbmbaa.org

NATIONAL ITALIAN AMERICAN FOUNDATION

http://www.niaf.org/

NATIONAL ITALIAN AMERICAN FOUNDATION CATEGORY I SCHOLARSHIP

Award available to Italian-American students who have outstanding potential and high academic achievements. Minimum 3.5 GPA required. Must be a U.S. citizen and be enrolled in an accredited institution of higher education. Application can only be submitted online. For further information, deadlines, and online application visit web site http://www.niaf.org/scholarships/index.asp.

Award: Scholarship for use in freshman, sophomore, junior, senior, or graduate years; not renewable. *Number:* varies. *Amount:* $2500–$12,000.

Eligibility Requirements: Applicant must be of Italian heritage and enrolled or expecting to enroll full-time at a two-year or four-year institution or university. Applicant must have 3.5 GPA or higher. Available to U.S. and non-Canadian citizens.

Application Requirements: Application, essay, references, transcript.

Contact: NIAF Education and Culture Department
National Italian American Foundation
1860 19th Street, NW
Washington, DC 20009
Phone: 202-387-0600

NATIONAL SOCIETY DAUGHTERS OF THE AMERICAN REVOLUTION

http://www.dar.org/

NATIONAL SOCIETY DAUGHTERS OF THE AMERICAN REVOLUTION AMERICAN INDIAN SCHOLARSHIP

One-time scholarship available to Native Americans. All awards are judged based on financial need and academic achievement. Undergraduate students are given preference. GPA of 2.75 or higher is required. Deadlines: April 1 for fall term and October 1 for spring term.

Award: Scholarship for use in freshman, sophomore, junior, senior, or graduate years; not renewable. *Number:* varies. *Amount:* $500.

Eligibility Requirements: Applicant must be American Indian/Alaska Native and enrolled or expecting to enroll full-time at a two-year or four-year or technical institution or university. Available to U.S. citizens.

Application Requirements: Application, self-addressed stamped envelope, proof of American Indian blood. *Deadline:* varies.

Contact: Eric Weisz, Manager, Office of the Reporter General
National Society Daughters of the American Revolution
1776 D Street, NW
Washington, DC 20006-5303
Phone: 202-628-1776
Fax: 202-879-3348
E-mail: nsdarscholarships@dar.org

NATIONAL SOCIETY DAUGHTERS OF THE AMERICAN REVOLUTION FRANCES CRAWFORD MARVIN AMERICAN INDIAN SCHOLARSHIP

Nonrenewable award available for a Native American to attend any two- or four-year college or university. Must demonstrate financial need, academic achievement, and have a 3.0 GPA or higher. Must submit a self-addressed stamped envelope to be considered.

Award: Scholarship for use in freshman, sophomore, junior, or senior years; not renewable. *Number:* 1. *Amount:* varies.

Eligibility Requirements: Applicant must be American Indian/Alaska Native and enrolled or expecting to enroll full-time at a two-year or four-year institution or university. Applicant must have 3.0 GPA or higher. Available to U.S. citizens.

Application Requirements: Application, financial need analysis, self-addressed stamped envelope, transcript, letter or proof papers. *Deadline:* February 1.

Contact: Eric Weisz, Manager, Office of the Reporter General
National Society Daughters of the American Revolution
1776 D Street, NW
Washington, DC 20006-5303
Phone: 202-628-1776
Fax: 202-879-3348
E-mail: nsdarscholarships@dar.org

NATIONAL UNION OF PUBLIC AND GENERAL EMPLOYEES

http://www.nupge.ca/

SCHOLARSHIP FOR ABORIGINAL CANADIANS
• *See page 555*

SCHOLARSHIP FOR VISIBLE MINORITIES
• *See page 555*

TERRY FOX MEMORIAL SCHOLARSHIP
• *See page 555*

TOMMY DOUGLAS SCHOLARSHIP
• *See page 555*

NATIONAL WELSH-AMERICAN FOUNDATION

http://www.wales-usa.org/

EXCHANGE SCHOLARSHIP

Limited to colleges/universities in Wales only. Applicant must have a Welsh background through birth and be willing to promote Welsh-American relations both here and abroad. Requested to consider becoming a member of NWAF upon completion of study. Required to complete four-year college study in United States. Applicant must be 21 years of age or older.

Award: Scholarship for use in freshman, sophomore, junior, senior, graduate, or postgraduate years; not renewable. *Number:* 1. *Amount:* $5000.

Eligibility Requirements: Applicant must be of Welsh heritage; age 21 and over and enrolled or expecting to enroll full-time at a four-year institution or university. Available to U.S. and Canadian citizens.

Application Requirements: Application, essay, references, test scores. *Deadline:* March 1.

Contact: Donna Lloyd-Kolkin, Scholarship Committee
National Welsh-American Foundation
143 Sunny Hillside Road
Benton, PA 17814-7822
Phone: 570-925-6923
E-mail: nwaf@epix.net

NATIVE VISION SCHOLARSHIP

http://www.nativevision.org/

NATIVE VISION

Scholarship available to any American Indian high school senior who has been accepted to college.

Award: Scholarship for use in freshman year; not renewable. *Number:* 2. *Amount:* $5000.

Eligibility Requirements: Applicant must be American Indian/Alaska Native; high school student and planning to enroll or expecting to enroll full-time at a four-year institution or university. Applicant must have 3.0 GPA or higher. Available to U.S. and non-U.S. citizens.

Application Requirements: Application, essay, references, transcript. *Deadline:* May 1.

Contact: Marlena Hammen, Scholarship Coordinator
Native Vision Scholarship
621 North Washington Street
Baltimore, MD 21205
Phone: 410-955-6931
Fax: 410-955-2010
E-mail: mhammen@jhsph.edu

NEED

http://www.needld.org/

UNMET NEED GRANT PROGRAM

The program provides "last dollar" funding to lower-income students that still have a need for aid after all federal, state, local and private scholarships and grants have been secured. Must be a U.S. citizen, high school graduate, resident of one of nine participating counties in Southwestern Pennsylvania (Allegheny, Armstrong, Beaver, Butler, Fayette, Greene, Lawrence, Washington or Westmoreland county), and have a minimum 2.0 GPA.

Award: Grant for use in freshman, sophomore, junior, or senior years; not renewable. *Number:* 10–500. *Amount:* $1000–$3500.

Eligibility Requirements: Applicant must be Black (non-Hispanic); enrolled or expecting to enroll full- or part-time at a two-year or four-year or technical institution or university and resident of Pennsylvania. Available to U.S. citizens.

Application Requirements: Application, essay, financial need analysis, photo, transcript. *Deadline:* May 31.

Contact: Arlene Holland, Student Services Manager
NEED
The Warner Centre
332 5th Avenue, First Floor
Pittsburgh, PA 15222
Phone: 412-566-2760
E-mail: atyler@needld.org

NEW YORK STATE HIGHER EDUCATION SERVICES CORPORATION

http://www.hesc.com/

NEW YORK STATE AID TO NATIVE AMERICANS

Award for enrolled members of a New York State tribe and their children who are attending or planning to attend a New York State college and who are New York State residents. Deadlines: July 15 for the fall semester, December 31 for the spring semester, and May 20 for summer session.

Award: Scholarship for use in freshman, sophomore, junior, or senior years; renewable. *Number:* varies. *Amount:* $85–$2000.

Eligibility Requirements: Applicant must be American Indian/Alaska Native; enrolled or expecting to enroll full- or part-time at a two-year or four-year or technical institution or university; resident of New York and studying in New York. Available to U.S. citizens.

Application Requirements: Application, financial need analysis, references, transcript. *Deadline:* varies.

Contact: Native American Education Unit
New York State Higher Education Services Corporation
EBA Room 475
Albany, NY 12234
Phone: 518-474-0537

NEXTGEN NETWORK INC.

http://www.nextgennetwork.com/

DONNA JAMISON LAGO MEMORIAL SCHOLARSHIP

Awards to assist with future educational expenses of African-American, U.S. citizens. The essay competition is open to those who would complete their studies in that current year. Applicants must be seeking acceptance to an accredited U.S. college or university. The essay competition encourages high school seniors to think critically about important issues that affect their lives.

Award: Scholarship for use in freshman year; not renewable. *Number:* 9. *Amount:* $500–$2500.

Eligibility Requirements: Applicant must be Black (non-Hispanic); high school student; planning to enroll or expecting to enroll full-time at a two-year or four-year institution or university and must have an interest in writing. Available to U.S. citizens.

Application Requirements: Application, applicant must enter a contest, driver's license, essay, photo, references. *Deadline:* May 30.

Contact: Mr. K.J. Mburu, Scholarship Committee
NextGen Network Inc.
1010 Wisconsin Avenue, NW, Suite 430
Washington, DC 20007
Phone: 202-686-9260 Ext. 101
Fax: 202-944-3322
E-mail: info@nextgennetwork.com

NISEI STUDENT RELOCATION COMMEMORATIVE FUND

http://www.nsrcfund.org/

NISEI STUDENT RELOCATION COMMEMORATIVE FUND

Eligibility: only high school seniors of Southeast Asian (Vietnamese, Cambodian, Laotian, Hmong) ancestry living in the U.S. awarded. Deadline to apply varies. Scholarships awarded in a different city each year.

Award: Scholarship for use in freshman year; not renewable. *Number:* up to 40. *Amount:* $1000–$2000.

Eligibility Requirements: Applicant must be of Lao/Hmong or Vietnamese heritage; Asian/Pacific Islander; high school student and planning to enroll or expecting to enroll full- or part-time at a two-year or four-year or technical institution or university. Available to U.S. citizens.

Application Requirements: Application, essay, financial need analysis, photo, references, test scores, transcript.

Contact: Jean Hibino, Executive Secretary
Nisei Student Relocation Commemorative Fund
19 Scenic Drive
Portland, CT 06480
E-mail: jeanhibino@aol.com

NORTH CAROLINA SOCIETY OF HISPANIC PROFESSIONALS

http://www.thencshp.org/

NORTH CAROLINA HISPANIC COLLEGE FUND SCHOLARSHIP

Four-year renewable scholarship for Hispanic students. Must have graduated from a North Carolina high school within the past 2 years, have a four-year cumulative GPA of 2.5, and be accepted into a two- or four-year college or university. Preference is given to full-time students but part-time students may apply. Preference will be given to foreign-born applicants or native-born children of foreign-born parents. Applications are available online at http://www.thencshp.org/.

Award: Scholarship for use in freshman, sophomore, junior, or senior years; renewable. *Number:* varies. *Amount:* $500–$2500.

Eligibility Requirements: Applicant must be Hispanic; enrolled or expecting to enroll full- or part-time at a two-year or four-year institution or university and resident of North Carolina. Applicant must have 2.5 GPA or higher. Available to U.S. and non-U.S. citizens.

Application Requirements: Application, transcript. *Deadline:* continuous.

Contact: North Carolina Society of Hispanic Professionals
8450 Chapel Hill Road, Suite 209
Cary, NC 27513
Phone: 919-467-8424
Fax: 919-469-1785
E-mail: mailbox@thencshp.org

NORTH DAKOTA UNIVERSITY SYSTEM

http://www.ndus.edu/

NORTH DAKOTA INDIAN SCHOLARSHIP PROGRAM

Award of $800 to $2000 per year to assist American Indian students who are North Dakota residents in obtaining a college education. Must have been accepted for admission at an institution of higher learning or state vocational education program within North Dakota. Based upon scholastic ability and unmet financial need. Minimum 2.0 GPA required.

Award: Scholarship for use in freshman, sophomore, junior, or senior years; renewable. *Number:* 175–230. *Amount:* $800–$2000.

Eligibility Requirements: Applicant must be American Indian/Alaska Native; enrolled or expecting to enroll full- or part-time at a two-year or four-year or technical institution or university; resident of North Dakota and studying in North Dakota. Available to U.S. citizens.

Application Requirements: Application, financial need analysis, transcript, proof of tribal enrollment, budget. *Deadline:* July 15.

Contact: Rhonda Schauer, Coordinator of American Indian Higher
    Education
    North Dakota University System
    BSC Horizon Building, Suite 202, 1815 Schafer Street
    Bismarck, ND 58501-1217
    Phone: 701-224-2497
    E-mail: rhonda.schauer@ndus.edu

NORTHERN CHEYENNE TRIBAL EDUCATION DEPARTMENT

http://www.cheyennenation.com/education.html

HIGHER EDUCATION SCHOLARSHIP PROGRAM

Scholarships will be provided for enrolled Northern Cheyenne Tribal members who meet the requirements listed in the higher education guidelines. Must be U.S. citizen enrolled in a postsecondary institution. Minimum 2.0 GPA required.

Award: Scholarship for use in freshman, sophomore, junior, or senior years; renewable. *Number:* 72. *Amount:* $50–$6000.

Eligibility Requirements: Applicant must be American Indian/Alaska Native and enrolled or expecting to enroll full- or part-time at a two-year or four-year institution or university. Available to U.S. citizens.

Application Requirements: Application, essay, financial need analysis, references, test scores, transcript. *Deadline:* March 1.

Contact: Norma Bixby, Director
    Northern Cheyenne Tribal Education Department
    PO Box 307
    Lame Deer, MT 59043
    Phone: 406-477-6602
    Fax: 406-477-8150
    E-mail: norma@rangeweb.net

OCA

http://www.ocanational.org/

OCA-AXA ACHIEVEMENT SCHOLARSHIP

A college achievement scholarship for Asian Pacific Americans entering their first year of college. For full-time study only. Must have an minimum GPA of 3.0.

Award: Scholarship for use in freshman year; not renewable. *Number:* 10. *Amount:* $2000.

Eligibility Requirements: Applicant must be Asian/Pacific Islander; high school student and planning to enroll or expecting to enroll full-time at a two-year or four-year institution or university. Applicant must have 3.0 GPA or higher. Available to U.S. citizens.

Application Requirements: Application, essay, financial need analysis, self-addressed stamped envelope, transcript. *Deadline:* April 18.

Contact: Scholarship Coordinator
    OCA
    1322 18th Street NW
    Washington, DC 20036
    Phone: 202-223-5500
    Fax: 202-296-0540
    E-mail: oca@ocanational.org

OCA/UPS FOUNDATION GOLD MOUNTAIN SCHOLARSHIP

Scholarships for Asian Pacific Americans who are the first person in their immediate family to attend college. Must be entering first year of college in the upcoming fall. Please check out http//www.ocanational.org for more information.

Award: Scholarship for use in freshman year; not renewable. *Amount:* $2000.

Eligibility Requirements: Applicant must be Asian/Pacific Islander; high school student and planning to enroll or expecting to enroll full-time at a two-year or four-year institution or university. Applicant must have 3.0 GPA or higher. Available to U.S. citizens.

Application Requirements: Application, essay, financial need analysis, resume, self-addressed stamped envelope, transcript. *Deadline:* April 18.

Contact: Scholarship Coordinator
    OCA
    1322 18th Street NW
    Washington, DC 20036
    Phone: 202-223-5500
    Fax: 202-296-0540
    E-mail: oca@ocanational.org

OCA-VERIZON COLLEGE SCHOLARSHIP

Please check out the OCA web site at http//www.ocanational.org for more information.

Award: Scholarship for use in sophomore, junior, or senior years; not renewable. *Amount:* up to $2000.

Eligibility Requirements: Applicant must be Asian/Pacific Islander and enrolled or expecting to enroll full-time at a two-year or four-year institution or university. Applicant must have 3.0 GPA or higher. Available to U.S. citizens.

Application Requirements: Application, essay, financial need analysis, self-addressed stamped envelope, transcript. *Deadline:* April 18.

Contact: Scholarship Coordinator
    OCA
    1322 18th Street NW
    Washington, DC 20036
    Phone: 202-223-5500
    E-mail: oca@ocanatl.org

OFFICE OF NAVAJO NATION SCHOLARSHIP AND FINANCIAL ASSISTANCE

http://www.onnsfa.org/

CHIEF MANUELITO SCHOLARSHIP PROGRAM

Award programs established to recognize and award undergraduate students with high test scores and GPA of 3.0. Priorities to Navajo Nation applicants. Must be enrolled as a full-time undergraduate and pursue a degree program leading to a baccalaureate. For further details visit web site http://www.onnsfa.org/docs/polproc.pdf.

Award: Scholarship for use in freshman, sophomore, junior, or senior years; not renewable. *Number:* 1. *Amount:* $7000.

Eligibility Requirements: Applicant must be American Indian/Alaska Native and enrolled or expecting to enroll full-time at a two-year or four-year institution or university. Applicant must have 3.0 GPA or higher. Available to U.S. citizens.

Application Requirements: Application, financial need analysis, test scores, transcript. *Deadline:* April 1.

Contact: Maxine Damon Sr., Financial Aid Counselor
    Office of Navajo Nation Scholarship and Financial Assistance
    PO Box 1870
    Window Rock, AZ 86515-1870
    Phone: 800-243-2956
    Fax: 928-871-6561
    E-mail: maxinedamon@navajo.org

ONEIDA TRIBE OF INDIANS OF WISCONSIN

http://www.oneidanation.org/highered

ONEIDA HIGHER EDUCATION GRANT PROGRAM

Renewable award available to enrolled members of the Oneida Tribe of Indians of Wisconsin, who are accepted into an accredited postsecondary institution within the United States. Have a high school diploma, HSED or GED.

Award: Grant for use in freshman, sophomore, junior, senior, graduate, or postgraduate years; renewable. *Number:* up to 1300. *Amount:* up to $20,000.

Eligibility Requirements: Applicant must be American Indian/Alaska Native and enrolled or expecting to enroll full- or part-time at a two-year or four-year or technical institution or university. Available to U.S. citizens.

Application Requirements: Application, financial need analysis, Oneida tribal enrollment. *Deadline:* April 15.

Contact: Higher Education Advisor
Oneida Tribe of Indians of Wisconsin
PO Box 365
Oneida, WI 54155
Phone: 920-869-4033
Fax: 920-869-4039
E-mail: highered@oneidanation.org

OREGON NATIVE AMERICAN CHAMBER OF COMMERCE SCHOLARSHIP

http://www.onacc.org/

OREGON NATIVE AMERICAN CHAMBER OF COMMERCE SCHOLARSHIP

Scholarships available to Native American students studying in Oregon. Must verify Native American status and be actively involved in the Native American community.

Award: Scholarship for use in freshman, sophomore, junior, or senior years; not renewable. *Number:* 1. *Amount:* $1000.

Eligibility Requirements: Applicant must be American Indian/Alaska Native; enrolled or expecting to enroll full- or part-time at a four-year institution or university and studying in Oregon. Available to U.S. and Canadian citizens.

Application Requirements: Application, transcript, proof of Native American descent. *Deadline:* varies.

Contact: Kelly Anne Ilagan, Secretary
Oregon Native American Chamber of Commerce Scholarship
PO Box 82068
Portland, OR 97282
Phone: 503-654-2138
E-mail: kellyanne@onacc.org

OSAGE TRIBAL EDUCATION COMMITTEE

http://www.osagetribe.com/education/

OSAGE TRIBAL EDUCATION COMMITTEE SCHOLARSHIP

Available for Osage Tribal members only. 150 to 250 renewable scholarship awards. Spring Deadline: December 31; Fall Deadline: July 1; Summer Deadline: May 1.

Award: Scholarship for use in freshman, sophomore, junior, or senior years; renewable. *Number:* 150–250. *Amount:* $200.

Eligibility Requirements: Applicant must be American Indian/Alaska Native and enrolled or expecting to enroll full- or part-time at a two-year or four-year or technical institution or university. Applicant must have 2.5 GPA or higher. Available to U.S. and non-U.S. citizens.

Application Requirements: Application, essay, photo, references, transcript. *Deadline:* varies.

Contact: Cheryl Lewis, Business Manager
Osage Tribal Education Committee
4149 Highline Boulevard, Suite 380
Oklahoma City, OK 73108
Phone: 405-605-6051 Ext. 304
Fax: 405-605-6057

OSAGE TRIBAL EDUCATION DEPARTMENT

http://www.osagetribe.com/education

OSAGE HIGHER EDUCATION SCHOLARSHIP

Award available only to those who have proof of Osage Indian descent. Must submit proof of financial need. Deadlines: July 1 for fall, December 31 for spring, May 1 for summer.

Award: Scholarship for use in freshman, sophomore, junior, senior, graduate, or postgraduate years; renewable. *Number:* up to 1000. *Amount:* $1200–$2100.

Eligibility Requirements: Applicant must be American Indian/Alaska Native and enrolled or expecting to enroll full- or part-time at a two-year or four-year institution or university. Available to U.S. citizens.

Application Requirements: Application, financial need analysis, transcript, verification of enrollment, Osage Indian descent proof, copy of CDIB card, copy of membership card. *Deadline:* varies.

Contact: Jennifer Holding, Scholarship Coordinator
Osage Tribal Education Department
HC 66, PO Box 900
Hominy, OK 74035
Phone: 800-390-6724
Fax: 918-287-5567
E-mail: jholding@osagetribe.org

PETER AND ALICE KOOMRUIAN FUND

PETER AND ALICE KOOMRUIAN ARMENIAN EDUCATION FUND

Award for students of Armenian descent to pursue postsecondary studies in any field at any accredited college or university in the U.S. Submit student identification and letter of enrollment. Must rank in upper third of class or have minimum GPA of 3.0.

Award: Scholarship for use in freshman, sophomore, junior, or senior years; not renewable. *Number:* 5–20. *Amount:* $1000–$2300.

Eligibility Requirements: Applicant must be of Armenian heritage and enrolled or expecting to enroll full-time at a two-year or four-year institution or university. Applicant must have 3.0 GPA or higher. Available to U.S. and non-U.S. citizens.

Application Requirements: Application, photo, references, self-addressed stamped envelope, transcript, school ID, current enrollment letter. *Deadline:* April 15.

Contact: Mr. Terenik Koujakian, Awards Committee Member
Peter and Alice Koomruian Fund
15915 Ventura Boulevard, Suite P-1
Encino, CA 91436
Phone: 818-990-7454
Fax: 818-990-7466
E-mail: terenikkoujakian@hotmail.com

PETER DOCTOR MEMORIAL INDIAN SCHOLARSHIP FOUNDATION INC.

PETER DOCTOR MEMORIAL IROQUOIS SCHOLARSHIP

One-time award available to enrolled New York state Iroquois Indian students. Must be a full-time student at the sophomore level or above.

Award: Scholarship for use in sophomore, junior, senior, or graduate years; not renewable. *Number:* varies. *Amount:* $700–$1500.

Eligibility Requirements: Applicant must be American Indian/Alaska Native; enrolled or expecting to enroll full-time at a two-year or four-year or technical institution or university and resident of New York. Available to U.S. citizens.

Application Requirements: Application, driver's license, financial need analysis, references, tribal certification. *Deadline:* May 31.

Contact: Clara Hill, Treasurer
Peter Doctor Memorial Indian Scholarship Foundation Inc.
PO Box 431
Basom, NY 14013
Phone: 716-542-2025
E-mail: cehill@wnynet.net

PHILIPINO-AMERICAN ASSOCIATION OF NEW ENGLAND

http://www.pamas.org/

BLESSED LEON OF OUR LADY OF THE ROSARY AWARD

Award for any Filipino-American high school student. Must be of Filipino descent, and have a minimum GPA of 3.3. Application details URL http://www.pamas.org.

Award: Scholarship for use in freshman year; not renewable. *Number:* 1. *Amount:* $250.

Eligibility Requirements: Applicant must be Asian/Pacific Islander; high school student; planning to enroll or expecting to enroll full-time at a two-year or four-year or technical institution or university and resident of Connecticut, Maine, Massachusetts, New Hampshire, Rhode Island, or Vermont. Available to U.S. citizens.

Application Requirements: Application, essay, references, transcript, college acceptance letter. *Deadline:* May 31.

Contact: Amanda Kalb, First Vice President
Philipino-American Association of New England
Quincy Post Office
PO Box 690372
Quincy, MA 02269-0372
Phone: 617-471-3513
E-mail: balic2ss@comcast.net

PAMAS RESTRICTED SCHOLARSHIP AWARD

• *See page 558*

RAVENSCROFT FAMILY AWARD

Award for any Filipino-American high school student, who is active in the Filipino community. Must be of Filipino descent, a resident of New England, and have a minimum GPA of 3.3. Application details URL http://www.pamas.org.

Award: Scholarship for use in freshman year; not renewable. *Number:* 1. *Amount:* $250.

Eligibility Requirements: Applicant must be Asian/Pacific Islander; high school student; planning to enroll or expecting to enroll full-time at a four-year institution or university and resident of Connecticut, Maine, Massachusetts, New Hampshire, Rhode Island, or Vermont. Available to U.S. citizens.

Application Requirements: Application, essay, references, transcript, college acceptance letter. *Deadline:* May 31.

Contact: Amanda Kalb, First Vice President
Philipino-American Association of New England
Quincy Post Office
PO Box 690372
Quincy, MA 02269-0372
Phone: 617-471-3513
E-mail: balic2ss@comcast.net

POLISH HERITAGE ASSOCIATION OF MARYLAND

http://www.pha-md.org/

DR KENNETH AND NANCY WILLIAMS SCHOLARSHIP

Scholarship available for study towards a baccalaureate degree in a college or university in the United States. Must be of Polish descent (at least two Polish grandparents), resident of Maryland, and a U.S. citizen.

Award: Scholarship for use in freshman, sophomore, junior, or senior years; not renewable. *Number:* 1. *Amount:* up to $1000.

Eligibility Requirements: Applicant must be of Polish heritage; enrolled or expecting to enroll full-time at a two-year or four-year institution or university and resident of Maryland. Available to U.S. citizens.

Application Requirements: Application, financial need analysis, references, transcript. *Deadline:* March 31.

Contact: Thomas Hollowak, Scholarship Committee Chair
Polish Heritage Association of Maryland
Seven Dendron Court
Parkville, MD 21234
Phone: 410-837-4268
E-mail: thollowak@ubalt.edu

POLISH HERITAGE SCHOLARSHIP

Scholarships given to individuals of Polish descent (at least two Polish grandparents) who demonstrates academic excellence, financial need, and promotes their Polish Heritage. Must be a legal Maryland resident. Scholarship value is $1500.

Award: Scholarship for use in freshman, sophomore, junior, or senior years; not renewable. *Number:* 1. *Amount:* up to $1500.

Eligibility Requirements: Applicant must be of Polish heritage; enrolled or expecting to enroll full-time at a two-year or four-year institution or university and resident of Maryland. Applicant must have 3.0 GPA or higher. Available to U.S. citizens.

Application Requirements: Application, essay, financial need analysis, interview, photo, references, transcript. *Deadline:* March 31.

Contact: Thomas Hollowak, Scholarship Chair
Polish Heritage Association of Maryland
Seven Dendron Court
Baltimore, MD 21234
Phone: 410-837-4268
E-mail: thollowalk@ubmail.ubalt.edu

POLISH WOMEN'S ALLIANCE

http://www.pwaa.org/

POLISH WOMEN'S ALLIANCE SCHOLARSHIP

Scholarships are given to members of the Polish Women's Alliance of America who have been in good standing for five years. Awards are given for the sophomore, junior, and senior year level of undergraduate study. For details visit web site http://www.pwaa.org.

Award: Scholarship for use in sophomore, junior, or senior years; renewable. *Number:* 5. *Amount:* $1000.

Eligibility Requirements: Applicant must be of Polish heritage and enrolled or expecting to enroll full-time at a four-year institution or university. Available to U.S. citizens.

Application Requirements: Application, essay, photo, transcript. *Deadline:* May 15.

Contact: Sharon Zago, Vice President and Scholarship Chairman
Polish Women's Alliance
6643 North Northwest Highway
Chicago, IL 60068
Phone: 847-384-1208
E-mail: vpres@pwaa.org

PORTUGUESE FOUNDATION INC.

http://www.pfict.org/

PORTUGUESE FOUNDATION SCHOLARSHIP PROGRAM

Scholarships of $4000 to four deserving students. Student must be of Portuguese ancestry, resident of Connecticut, U.S. citizen or a permanent resident, applying for, or currently in college, full-time student in an undergraduate degree conferring program or a part-time student in a master's or doctorate program.

Award: Scholarship for use in freshman, sophomore, junior, senior, or graduate years; not renewable. *Number:* 4. *Amount:* $4000.

Eligibility Requirements: Applicant must be of Portuguese heritage; enrolled or expecting to enroll full- or part-time at a four-year institution or university and resident of Connecticut. Applicant must have 2.5 GPA or higher. Available to U.S. citizens.

Application Requirements: Application, essay, financial need analysis, references, test scores, transcript, FAFSA, copy of recent federal income tax return. *Deadline:* March 15.

Contact: John Bairos, President
Portuguese Foundation Inc.
PO Box 331441
Hartford, CT 06133-1441
Phone: 860-614-8614
E-mail: info@pfict.org

PRESBYTERIAN CHURCH (USA)

http://www.pcusa.org/financialaid

NATIVE AMERICAN EDUCATION GRANT

Awarded to students seeking first undergraduate degree. Applicants are full-time students who are registered members of federally or state recognized Native American tribes.

Award: Grant for use in freshman, sophomore, junior, or senior years; renewable. *Number:* 34. *Amount:* $200–$1500.

Eligibility Requirements: Applicant must be American Indian/Alaska Native and enrolled or expecting to enroll full-time at a two-year or four-year or technical institution or university. Applicant must have 2.5 GPA or higher. Available to U.S. citizens.

Application Requirements: Application, essay, financial need analysis, references, transcript, copy of the tribal membership card. *Deadline:* June 1.

Contact: Laura Bryan, Associate, Financial Aid for Studies
Presbyterian Church (USA)
Financial Aid for Studies
100 Witherspoon Street
Louisville, KY 40202-1396
Phone: 888-728-7228 Ext. 5735
E-mail: finaid@pcusa.org

NATIVE AMERICAN EDUCATION GRANTS

Award to assist members of any tribe with their education. Students receive funding beginning with their postsecondary education and grants are awarded through a doctoral degree.

Award: Grant for use in freshman, sophomore, junior, senior, graduate, or postgraduate years; renewable. *Number:* 10–125. *Amount:* $500–$1500.

Eligibility Requirements: Applicant must be American Indian/Alaska Native and enrolled or expecting to enroll full-time at a two-year or four-year or technical institution or university. Applicant must have 2.5 GPA or higher. Available to U.S. citizens.

Application Requirements: Application, essay, financial need analysis, test scores, transcript, tribal membership. *Deadline:* June 15.

Contact: Frances Cook, Associate
Presbyterian Church (USA)
100 Witherspoon Street
Louisville, KY 40202-1396
Phone: 502-569-5776
Fax: 502-569-8766
E-mail: frances.cook@pcusa.org

PUEBLO OF ISLETA, DEPARTMENT OF EDUCATION

http://www.isletapueblo.com/

HIGHER EDUCATION SUPPLEMENTAL SCHOLARSHIP ISLETA PUEBLO HIGHER EDUCATION DEPARTMENT
• *See page 560*

PUEBLO OF SAN JUAN, DEPARTMENT OF EDUCATION

http://www.sanjuaned.org/

OHKAY OWINGEH TRIBAL SCHOLARSHIP OF THE PUEBLO OF SAN JUAN
• *See page 595*

POP'AY SCHOLARSHIP
• *See page 595*

ROMAN CATHOLIC DIOCESE OF TULSA

http://www.dioceseoftulsa.org/

MAE LASSLEY OSAGE SCHOLARSHIP

This scholarship fund gives the Catholic Church an opportunity to continue it's educational work with the Osage Tribe.

Award: Scholarship for use in freshman, sophomore, junior, or senior years; renewable. *Amount:* $500–$1000.

Eligibility Requirements: Applicant must be Roman Catholic; American Indian/Alaska Native and enrolled or expecting to enroll full-time at a two-year or four-year institution or university. Available to U.S. citizens.

Application Requirements: Application, financial need analysis, references, transcript, copy of CDIB card or Osage Tribal Membership card. *Deadline:* April 15.

Contact: Sarah Jameson, Administrative Assistant, Department of
Religious Formation
Roman Catholic Diocese of Tulsa
PO Box 690240
Tulsa, OK 74169-0240
Phone: 918-307-4928
Fax: 918-294-0920
E-mail: sarah.jameson@dioceseoftulsa.org

RON BROWN SCHOLAR FUND

http://www.ronbrown.org/

RON BROWN SCHOLAR PROGRAM

The program seeks to identify African-American high school seniors who will make significant contributions to the society. Applicants must excel academically, show exceptional leadership potential, participate in community service activities, and demonstrate financial need. Must be a U.S. citizen or hold permanent resident visa. Must plan to attend a four-year college or university. Deadlines: November 1 and January 9.

Award: Scholarship for use in freshman year; renewable. *Number:* 10–20. *Amount:* $10,000–$40,000.

Eligibility Requirements: Applicant must be Black (non-Hispanic); high school student; planning to enroll or expecting to enroll full-time at a four-year institution or university and must have an interest in leadership. Available to U.S. citizens.

Application Requirements: Application, essay, financial need analysis, interview, photo, references, test scores, transcript.

Contact: Ms. Vanessa M. Evans, Associate Director
Ron Brown Scholar Fund
1160 Pepsi Place, Suite 206
Charlottesville, VA 22901
Phone: 434-964-1588
Fax: 434-964-1589
E-mail: info@ronbrown.org

RYU FAMILY FOUNDATION, INC.

http://www.seolbong.org/

SEOL BONG SCHOLARSHIP

One-time award to support and advance education and research. Must be Korean residing in DE, PA, NJ, NY, CT, VT, RI, NH, MA or ME. Minimum 3.5 GPA required.

Award: Scholarship for use in freshman, sophomore, junior, senior, or graduate years; not renewable. *Number:* 23. *Amount:* $2000–$3000.

Eligibility Requirements: Applicant must be of Korean heritage; Asian/Pacific Islander; enrolled or expecting to enroll full-time at a four-year institution or university; resident of Connecticut, Delaware, Maine, Massachusetts, New Hampshire, New Jersey, New York, Pennsylvania, Rhode Island, or Vermont and studying in Connecticut, Delaware, Maine, Massachusetts, New Hampshire, New Jersey, New York, Pennsylvania, Rhode Island, or Vermont. Available to U.S. and non-Canadian citizens.

Application Requirements: Application, essay, financial need analysis, photo, portfolio, resume, references, test scores, transcript. *Deadline:* November 15.

Contact: Jenny Kang, Scholarship Secretary
Ryu Family Foundation, Inc.
186 Parish Drive
Wayne, NJ 07470
Phone: 973-692-9696 Ext. 20
E-mail: jennyk@toplineus.com

SAINT ANDREW'S SOCIETY OF THE STATE OF NEW YORK

http://www.standrewsny.org/

ST. ANDREWS SCHOLARSHIP

Scholarship for senior undergraduate students who will obtain a bachelor's degree from an accredited college or university in the spring and can demonstrate the significance of studying in Scotland. Proof of application to their selected school will be required for finalists. Applicant must be of Scottish descent.

Award: Scholarship for use in senior year; not renewable. *Number:* 2. *Amount:* up to $15,000.

Eligibility Requirements: Applicant must be of Scottish heritage and enrolled or expecting to enroll full-time at a four-year institution or university. Applicant must have 2.5 GPA or higher. Available to U.S. citizens.

Application Requirements: Application. *Deadline:* December 15.

Contact: Brigid Franklin, Office Manager
Saint Andrew's Society of the State of New York
150 East 55th Street
New York, NY 10022
Phone: 212-223-4248
Fax: 212-223-0748
E-mail: office@standrewsny.org

ST. ANDREW'S SOCIETY OF WASHINGTON, DC

http://www.saintandrewsociety.org/

DONALD MALCOLM MACARTHUR SCHOLARSHIP

One-time award is available for U.S. students to study in Scotland or students from Scotland to study in the United States. Special attention will be given to applicants whose work would demonstrably contribute to enhanced knowledge of Scottish history or culture. Must be a college junior, senior, or graduate student to apply. Need for financial assistance and academic record considered. Visit web site for details and application http://www.thecapitalscot.com/standrew/scholarships.html.

Award: Scholarship for use in junior, senior, or graduate years; not renewable. *Number:* 1. *Amount:* up to $2500.

Eligibility Requirements: Applicant must be of Scottish heritage; enrolled or expecting to enroll full-time at a four-year institution or university and resident of Delaware, District of Columbia, Maryland, New Jersey, North Carolina, Pennsylvania, Virginia, or Wisconsin. Available to U.S. and non-U.S. citizens.

Application Requirements: Application, essay, financial need analysis, interview, references, self-addressed stamped envelope. *Deadline:* April 30.

Contact: T J. Holland, Chairman, Scholarship Committee
St. Andrew's Society of Washington, DC
1443 Laurel Hill Road
Vienna, VA 22182-1711
E-mail: tjholland@wmalumni.com

SALVADORAN AMERICAN LEADERSHIP AND EDUCATIONAL FUND

http://www.salef.org/

FULFILLING OUR DREAMS SCHOLARSHIP FUND

Up to 60 scholarships ranging from $500 to $2500 will be awarded to students who come from a Latino heritage. Must have a 2.5 GPA. See web site for more details http://www.salef.org.

Award: Scholarship for use in freshman, sophomore, junior, senior, graduate, or postgraduate years; not renewable. *Number:* 50–60. *Amount:* $500–$2500.

Eligibility Requirements: Applicant must be of Hispanic or Latin American/Caribbean heritage; enrolled or expecting to enroll full- or part-time at a two-year or four-year institution or university; resident of California and studying in California. Applicant must have 2.5 GPA or higher. Available to U.S. and non-U.S. citizens.

Application Requirements: Application, essay, financial need analysis, interview, photo, resume, references, self-addressed stamped envelope, test scores, transcript. *Deadline:* June 30.

Contact: Mayra Soriano, Educational and Youth Programs Manager
Salvadoran American Leadership and Educational Fund
1625 West Olympic Boulevard, Suite 718
Los Angeles, CA 90015
Phone: 213-480-1052
Fax: 213-487-2530
E-mail: msoriano@salef.org

SAN DIEGO FOUNDATION

http://www.sdfoundation.org/

SAN DIEGO FIRE VICTIMS SCHOLARSHIP-LATINO FUND

Scholarship to graduating Latino high school seniors and current Latino college students who lost their homes in the 2003 wildfires and plan to attend an accredited two-year college, four-year university, or licensed trade or vocational school in the state of California. Must be legal residents of San Diego County. Minimum 2.0 GPA required. Preference will be given to students who are attending a public institution. Scholarship may be renewable for up to two years provided recipients continue to meet the terms of the scholarship. Deadline varies.

Award: Scholarship for use in freshman, sophomore, junior, or senior years; renewable. *Number:* 5. *Amount:* $500–$2500.

Eligibility Requirements: Applicant must be Hispanic; enrolled or expecting to enroll full-time at a two-year or four-year or technical institution or university; resident of California and studying in California. Available to U.S. citizens.

Application Requirements: Application, financial need analysis, references, transcript, personal statement, copy of tax return, formal documentation. *Deadline:* varies.

Contact: Shryl Helvie, Scholarship Coordinator
San Diego Foundation
2508 Historic Decatur Road, Suite 200
San Diego, CA 92106
Phone: 619-814-1307
Fax: 619-239-1710
E-mail: shryl@sdfoundation.org

SANTO DOMINGO SCHOLARSHIP PROGRAM

SANTO DOMINGO SCHOLARSHIP

An organization instituted for the welfare of the Santo Domingo Pueblo enrolled members. Santo Domingo Tribe—Education Offices offers scholarships in Higher Education and Adult Education. To be considered and applicant, you must fill out an application. Deadlines: Fall semester—March 1 and Spring semester—November 1.

Award: Scholarship for use in freshman, sophomore, junior, or senior years; renewable. *Number:* varies. *Amount:* $200–$1000.

Eligibility Requirements: Applicant must be American Indian/Alaska Native and enrolled or expecting to enroll full- or part-time at a two-year or four-year or technical institution or university. Applicant must have 2.5 GPA or higher. Available to U.S. citizens.

Application Requirements: Application, financial need analysis, references, transcript, certificate of Indian blood. *Deadline:* varies.

Contact: Charlene L. Reano, Education Director
Santo Domingo Scholarship Program
PO Box 160
Santo Domingo Pueblo, NM 87052
Phone: 505-465-2214 Ext. 227
Fax: 505-465-2542
E-mail: kewaeduc@yahoo.com

SEMINOLE TRIBE OF FLORIDA

http://www.seminoletribe.com/

SEMINOLE TRIBE OF FLORIDA BILLY L. CYPRESS SCHOLARSHIP PROGRAM
• *See page 562*

SENECA NATION OF INDIANS

http://www.sni.org/

SENECA NATION HIGHER EDUCATION PROGRAM
Renewable award for enrolled Senecas of the Cattaraugus and Allegany Indian reservations who are in need of financial assistance. Application deadlines: July 1 for fall; December 1 for spring; May 1 for summer. Must be degree seeking and enrolled in a two-year college, four-year college or university. Must have GPA of 2.0.

Award: Scholarship for use in freshman, sophomore, junior, senior, graduate, or postgraduate years; renewable. *Number:* varies. *Amount:* $6000–$11,000.

Eligibility Requirements: Applicant must be American Indian/Alaska Native and enrolled or expecting to enroll full- or part-time at a two-year or four-year institution or university. Available to U.S. citizens.

Application Requirements: Application, essay, financial need analysis, references, transcript, tribal certification. *Deadline:* varies.

Contact: Debra Hoag, Higher Education Coordinator
Seneca Nation of Indians
PO Box 231
Salamanca, NY 14779
Phone: 716-945-1790 Ext. 3103
E-mail: dhoag@sni.org

SONS OF ITALY FOUNDATION

http://www.osia.org/

SONS OF ITALY NATIONAL LEADERSHIP GRANTS COMPETITION GENERAL SCHOLARSHIPS
Scholarships for undergraduate or graduate students who are U.S. citizens of Italian descent. Must demonstrate academic excellence. For more details see web site http://www.osia.org.

Award: Scholarship for use in freshman, sophomore, junior, or senior years; not renewable. *Number:* 8–14. *Amount:* $5000–$25,000.

Eligibility Requirements: Applicant must be of Italian heritage and enrolled or expecting to enroll full-time at a four-year institution or university. Available to U.S. citizens.

Application Requirements: Application, essay, resume, references, self-addressed stamped envelope, test scores, transcript. *Fee:* $30. *Deadline:* February 27.

Contact: Ms. Amy Petrine
Phone: 202-547-2900
Fax: 202-546-8168
E-mail: scholarships@osia.org

SONS OF ITALY NATIONAL LEADERSHIP GRANTS COMPETITION HENRY SALVATORI SCHOLARSHIPS
Scholarships for college-bound high school seniors who demonstrate exceptional leadership, distinguished scholarship, and a deep understanding and respect for the principles upon which our nation was founded: liberty, freedom, and equality. Must be a U.S. citizen of Italian descent. For more details see web site http://www.osia.org.

Award: Scholarship for use in freshman year; not renewable. *Number:* up to 1. *Amount:* up to $5000.

Eligibility Requirements: Applicant must be of Italian heritage; high school student and planning to enroll or expecting to enroll full-time at a four-year institution or university. Available to U.S. citizens.

Application Requirements: Application, essay, resume, references, self-addressed stamped envelope, test scores, transcript. *Fee:* $30. *Deadline:* February 27.

Contact: Ms. Amy Petrine
Phone: 202-547-2900
Fax: 202-546-8168
E-mail: scholarships@osia.org

STEVEN KNEZEVICH TRUST

STEVEN KNEZEVICH GRANT
One-time grant for students of Serbian descent. Award not restricted to citizens of the United States. Amount of award varies. Applicants must be attending an accredited institution of higher learning. Grant will be applied toward student's spring semester. To receive additional information and the application itself, applicant must send SASE, along with proof of Serbian descent.

Award: Grant for use in freshman, sophomore, junior, senior, or graduate years; not renewable. *Number:* varies. *Amount:* varies.

Eligibility Requirements: Applicant must be of Croatian/Serbian heritage and enrolled or expecting to enroll full- or part-time at a two-year or four-year or technical institution or university. Available to U.S. and non-U.S. citizens.

Application Requirements: Application, self-addressed stamped envelope, transcript, proof of Serbian heritage. *Deadline:* November 30.

Contact: Jill Brodkey
Steven Knezevich Trust
7781 Ashwood Dr. SE
Ada, MI 49301
Phone: 616-682-5191
E-mail: jbrodkey@hotmail.com

STRAIGHTFORWARD MEDIA

http://www.straightforwardmedia.com/

STRAIGHTFORWARD MEDIA MINORITY SCHOLARSHIP
Four scholarships a year offered to students who are members of racial or ethnic minority groups and who are currently enrolled in or planning to enroll in postsecondary education. For more information, see Web http://www.straightforwardmedia.com/minority/form.php.

Award: Scholarship for use in freshman, sophomore, junior, or senior years; not renewable. *Number:* 4. *Amount:* $500.

Eligibility Requirements: Applicant must be American Indian/Alaska Native, Asian/Pacific Islander, Black (non-Hispanic), or Hispanic and enrolled or expecting to enroll full- or part-time at a two-year or four-year or technical institution or university. Available to U.S. and non-U.S. citizens.

Application Requirements: Essay. *Deadline:* varies.

Contact: Scholarship Committee
StraightForward Media
508 7th Street
Suite 202
Rapid City, SD 57701
Phone: 605-348-3042

SWEDISH INSTITUTE/SVENSKA INSTITUTET

http://www.si.se/

VISBY PROGRAM: HIGHER EDUCATION AND RESEARCH
Scholarships to pursue studies in Sweden are available to citizens of Belarus, Russia and Ukraine. For more details see web site http://www.studyinsweden.se.

Award: Scholarship for use in freshman, sophomore, junior, or senior years; not renewable. *Number:* varies. *Amount:* varies.

Eligibility Requirements: Applicant must be of Latvian, Lithuanian, Polish, Russian, or Ukrainian heritage and enrolled or expecting to enroll full-time at a four-year institution or university. Available to citizens of countries other than the U.S. or Canada.

Application Requirements: Application. *Deadline:* January 15.

Contact: Olle Wastberg, Director General
Swedish Institute/Svenska Institutet
Skeppsbron 2
PO Box 7434
Stockholm SE-103 91
Sweden
E-mail: grant@si.se

SWISS BENEVOLENT SOCIETY OF CHICAGO

http://www.sbschicago.org/

SWISS BENEVOLENT SOCIETY OF CHICAGO SCHOLARSHIPS

Scholarship for undergraduate college students of Swiss descent, having permanent residence in Illinois or Southern Wisconsin. Must have 3.3 GPA. High school students need a 26 on ACT or 1050 on SAT.

Award: Scholarship for use in freshman, sophomore, junior, or senior years; renewable. *Number:* 30. *Amount:* $750–$2500.

Eligibility Requirements: Applicant must be of Swiss heritage; enrolled or expecting to enroll full-time at a four-year institution or university and resident of Illinois or Wisconsin. Available to U.S. citizens.

Application Requirements: Application, essay, self-addressed stamped envelope, test scores, transcript. *Deadline:* April 1.

Contact: Franziska Lys, Chair
Swiss Benevolent Society of Chicago
PO Box 2137
Chicago, IL 60690-2137
Phone: 847-491-8298
E-mail: education@sbschicago.org

SWISS BENEVOLENT SOCIETY OF NEW YORK

http://www.sbsny.org/

MEDICUS STUDENT EXCHANGE

One-time award to students of Swiss nationality or parentage. Open to U.S. residents for study in Switzerland and to Swiss residents for study in the U.S. Must be proficient in foreign language of instruction.

Award: Grant for use in junior, senior, or graduate years; not renewable. *Number:* 1–10. *Amount:* $2000–$10,000.

Eligibility Requirements: Applicant must be of Swiss heritage; enrolled or expecting to enroll full-time at a four-year institution or university and must have an interest in foreign language. Applicant must have 3.5 GPA or higher. Available to U.S. and non-Canadian citizens.

Application Requirements: Application, references, test scores, transcript. *Deadline:* March 31.

Contact: Scholarship Committee
Swiss Benevolent Society of New York
500 Fifth Avenue, Room 1800
New York, NY 10110
Phone: 212-246-0655
Fax: 212-246-1366

PELLEGRINI SCHOLARSHIP GRANTS

Award to students who have a minimum 3.0 GPA and show financial need. Must submit proof of Swiss nationality or descent. Must be a permanent resident of Connecticut, Delaware, New Jersey, New York, or Pennsylvania.

Award: Scholarship for use in freshman, sophomore, junior, senior, or graduate years; renewable. *Number:* 50. *Amount:* $500–$5000.

Eligibility Requirements: Applicant must be of Swiss heritage; enrolled or expecting to enroll full-time at a two-year or four-year or technical institution or university and resident of Connecticut, Delaware, New Jersey, New York, or Pennsylvania. Applicant must have 3.0 GPA or higher. Available to U.S. citizens.

Application Requirements: Application, financial need analysis, references, test scores, transcript, copies of tax return. *Deadline:* March 31.

Contact: Scholarship Committee
Swiss Benevolent Society of New York
500 Fifth Avenue, Room 1800
New York, NY 10110
Phone: 212-246-0655
Fax: 212-246-1366

SYNOD OF THE TRINITY

http://www.syntrinity.org/index/

RACIAL ETHNIC EDUCATIONAL SCHOLARSHIP

The Racial Ethnic Educational Scholarship assists full-time undergraduate students who are African American, Asian, Hispanic, Latino, Middle Eastern, or Native American. The student must meet income criteria and reside within our boundaries: Pennsylvania and some counties in West Virginia and Ohio.

Award: Scholarship for use in freshman, sophomore, junior, or senior years; not renewable.

Eligibility Requirements: Applicant must be of African, Chinese, Hispanic, Indian, or Korean heritage; American Indian/Alaska Native, Asian/Pacific Islander, or Black (non-Hispanic); enrolled or expecting to enroll full-time at a two-year or four-year or technical institution or university and resident of Ohio, Pennsylvania, or West Virginia. Applicant must have 2.5 GPA or higher. Available to U.S. citizens.

Application Requirements: Application, essay, financial need analysis, references. *Deadline:* April 30.

Contact: Marcia Humer, Grants & Scholarships
Synod of the Trinity
3040 Market Street
Camp Hill, PA 17011
Phone: 800-242-0534 Ext. 233
E-mail: mhumer@syntrinity.org

TERRY FOX HUMANITARIAN AWARD PROGRAM

http://www.terryfox.org/

TERRY FOX HUMANITARIAN AWARD
• See page 597

TEXAS BLACK BAPTIST SCHOLARSHIP COMMITTEE

http://www.bgct.org/

TEXAS BLACK BAPTIST SCHOLARSHIP

Renewable award for Texas residents attending a Baptist educational institution in Texas. Must be of African-American descent with a minimum 2.0 GPA. Must be a member in good standing of a Baptist church.

Award: Scholarship for use in freshman, sophomore, junior, or senior years; renewable. *Number:* varies. *Amount:* $1600.

Eligibility Requirements: Applicant must be Baptist; Black (non-Hispanic); age 18 and over; enrolled or expecting to enroll full- or part-time at a two-year or four-year institution or university; resident of Texas and studying in Texas. Available to U.S. citizens.

Application Requirements: Application, driver's license, financial need analysis, interview, photo, portfolio, resume, references, test scores, transcript. *Deadline:* continuous.

Contact: Charlie Singleton, Director
Texas Black Baptist Scholarship Committee
African American Ministries, 333 North Washington, Suite 340
Dallas, TX 75246-1798
Phone: 214-828-5130
Fax: 214-828-5284
E-mail: charlie.singleton@bgct.org

TLICHO COMMUNITY SERVICES AGENCY

http://www.tlicho.ca/

BHP BILLITON UNIVERSITY SCHOLARSHIPS

Award for undergraduate, master's or PhD degree students of Tlicho ancestry. Applicants should be a member of Tlicho Citizens. Must be enrolled full-time in a Canadian university degree program and be interested and active in community affairs. Scholarship value is $5000.

Award: Scholarship for use in junior, senior, graduate, or postgraduate years; not renewable. *Number:* 4–4. *Amount:* $5000.

Eligibility Requirements: Applicant must be Canadian citizen; American Indian/Alaska Native and enrolled or expecting to enroll full-time at an institution or university. Applicant must have 2.5 GPA or higher.

Application Requirements: Application, references, transcript, Indian Status Card, Acceptance Letter. *Deadline:* July 15.

Contact: Mr. Joe Beaverho, Program Manager
Tlicho Community Services Agency
PO Box 5
Behchoko, NT X0E 0Y0
Canada
Phone: 867-392-3000 Ext. 269
E-mail: jbeaverho@tlicho.net

DIAVIK DIAMONDS INC. SCHOLARSHIPS FOR COLLEGE STUDENTS

Scholarship for students enrolled full-time in a Canadian college diploma program. Must be of Tlicho ancestry. Must be interested and active in community affairs. Applicants should be a member of Tilcho Citizens. Scholarship value is $3000.

Award: Scholarship for use in freshman, sophomore, junior, or senior years; not renewable. *Number:* 10. *Amount:* $3000.

Eligibility Requirements: Applicant must be Canadian citizen; American Indian/Alaska Native and enrolled or expecting to enroll full-time at a two-year or four-year or technical institution. Applicant must have 2.5 GPA or higher.

Application Requirements: Application, essay, references, transcript, personal letter, acceptance letter and Indian Status Card. *Deadline:* July 15.

Contact: Mr. Joe Beaverho, Program Manager
Tlicho Community Services Agency
PO Box 5
Behchoko, NT X0E 0Y0
Canada
Phone: 867-392-3000 Ext. 269
E-mail: jbeaverho@tlicho.net

UNICO NATIONAL INC.

http://www.unico.org/

ALPHONSE A. MIELE SCHOLARSHIP

Scholarship available to a graduating high school senior. Must reside and attend high school within the corporate limits or adjoining suburbs of a city wherein an active chapter of UNICO National is located. Application must be signed by student's principal and properly certified by sponsoring chapter president and chapter secretary. Must have letter of endorsement from president or scholarship chairperson of sponsoring chapter.

Award: Scholarship for use in freshman year; not renewable. *Number:* 1. *Amount:* up to $1500.

Eligibility Requirements: Applicant must be of Italian heritage; high school student and planning to enroll or expecting to enroll full-time at a four-year institution or university. Available to U.S. citizens.

Application Requirements: Application, financial need analysis, references, transcript. *Deadline:* varies.

Contact: Ann Tichenor, Secretary
UNICO National Inc.
271 U.S. Highway 46 West, Suite A-108
Fairfield, NJ 07004
Phone: 973-808-0035
Fax: 973-808-0043

MAJOR DON S. GENTILE SCHOLARSHIP

Annual awards for students of Italian origin who are enrolled at a post-secondary institution. Due date and number of awards varies.

Award: Scholarship for use in freshman year; not renewable. *Number:* varies. *Amount:* $1500.

Eligibility Requirements: Applicant must be of Italian heritage; high school student and planning to enroll or expecting to enroll full-time at a two-year or four-year or technical institution or university. Available to U.S. citizens.

Application Requirements: Application, financial need analysis, references, transcript. *Deadline:* varies.

Contact: Ann Tichenor, Secretary
UNICO National Inc.
271 U.S. Highway 46 West, Suite A-108
Fairfield, NJ 07004
Phone: 973-808-0035
Fax: 973-808-0043

WILLIAM C. DAVINI SCHOLARSHIP

Scholarship available to a graduating high school senior of Italian descent. Applicant must reside and attend high school within the corporate limits or adjoining suburbs of a city wherein an active chapter of UNICO National is located. Application must be signed by student's principal and properly certified by sponsoring chapter president and chapter secretary. Must have letter of endorsement from president or scholarship chairperson of sponsoring chapter.

Award: Scholarship for use in freshman year; not renewable. *Number:* 1. *Amount:* $1500.

Eligibility Requirements: Applicant must be of Italian heritage; high school student and planning to enroll or expecting to enroll full-time at a four-year institution or university. Available to U.S. citizens.

Application Requirements: Application, financial need analysis, references, transcript. *Deadline:* varies.

Contact: Ann Tichenor, Secretary
UNICO National Inc.
271 U.S. Highway 46 West, Suite A-108
Fairfield, NJ 07004
Phone: 973-808-0035
Fax: 973-808-0043

UNITED METHODIST CHURCH

http://www.gbhem.org/

UNITED METHODIST CHURCH ETHNIC SCHOLARSHIP

Awards for minority students pursuing undergraduate degree. Must have been certified members of the United Methodist Church for one year. Proof of membership and pastor's statement required. One-time award but applicant may re-apply each year. Minimum 2.5 GPA required.

Award: Scholarship for use in freshman, sophomore, junior, or senior years; not renewable. *Number:* varies. *Amount:* varies.

Eligibility Requirements: Applicant must be Methodist; American Indian/Alaska Native, Asian/Pacific Islander, Black (non-Hispanic), or Hispanic and enrolled or expecting to enroll full-time at a two-year or four-year institution or university. Applicant must have 2.5 GPA or higher. Available to U.S. citizens.

Application Requirements: Application, essay, references, transcript, membership proof, pastor's statement. *Deadline:* May 1.

Contact: Patti J. Zimmerman, Scholarships Administrator
United Methodist Church
PO Box 340007
Nashville, TN 37203-0007
Phone: 615-340-7344
E-mail: pzimmer@gbhem.org

UNITED METHODIST CHURCH HISPANIC, ASIAN, AND NATIVE AMERICAN SCHOLARSHIP

Award for members of United Methodist Church who are Hispanic, Asian, Native-American, or Pacific Islander college juniors, seniors, or graduate students. Proof of membership and pastor's letter required. Minimum 2.85 GPA.

Award: Scholarship for use in freshman, sophomore, junior, senior, or graduate years; not renewable. *Number:* varies. *Amount:* varies.

Eligibility Requirements: Applicant must be Methodist; American Indian/Alaska Native, Asian/Pacific Islander, or Hispanic and enrolled or expecting to enroll full-time at a four-year institution or university. Available to U.S. citizens.

Application Requirements: Application, essay, references, transcript, membership proof, pastor's letter. *Deadline:* April 1.

Contact: Patti J. Zimmerman, Scholarships Administrator
United Methodist Church
PO Box 340007
Nashville, TN 37203-0007
Phone: 615-340-7344
E-mail: pzimmer@gbhem.org

UNITED METHODIST YOUTH ORGANIZATION

http://www.gbod.org/youngpeople

RICHARD S. SMITH SCHOLARSHIP

Open to racial/ethnic minority youth only. Must be a United Methodist Youth who has been active in local church for at least one year prior to application. Must be a graduating senior in high school (who maintained at least a "C" average) entering the first year of undergraduate study and be pursuing a "church-related" career.

Award: Scholarship for use in freshman year; not renewable. *Number:* up to 2. *Amount:* up to $2500.

Eligibility Requirements: Applicant must be Methodist; American Indian/Alaska Native, Asian/Pacific Islander, Black (non-Hispanic), or Hispanic; high school student and planning to enroll or expecting to enroll full-time at a two-year or four-year or technical institution or university. Available to U.S. citizens.

Application Requirements: Application, essay, financial need analysis, references, transcript, certification of church membership by pastor. *Deadline:* June 1.

Contact: Grants Coordinator
United Methodist Youth Organization
PO Box 340003
Nashville, TN 37203-0003
Phone: 877-899-2780 Ext. 7184
Fax: 615-340-7063
E-mail: youngpeople@gbod.org

UNITED NEGRO COLLEGE FUND

http://www.uncf.org/

ABBINGTON, VALLANTEEN SCHOLARSHIP

Scholarship of $5000 to high school students who plan to attend a UNCF member college or university. Applicant must be a resident of the Greater St. Louis, Missouri, metropolitan area. Scholarship is renewed annually. Minimum 3.0 GPA in high school. GPA requirement increases to 3.3 after the sophomore year and 3.5 after the junior year. Visit web site for more information http://www.uncf.org.

Award: Scholarship for use in freshman year; renewable. *Number:* varies. *Amount:* $5000.

Eligibility Requirements: Applicant must be Black (non-Hispanic); high school student; planning to enroll or expecting to enroll full- or part-time at a four-year institution or university and resident of Missouri. Applicant must have 3.0 GPA or higher. Available to U.S. citizens.

Application Requirements: Application, financial need analysis, FAFSA, Student Aid Report (SAR).

Contact: Program Services
United Negro College Fund
8260 Willow Oaks Corporate Drive
Fairfax, VA 22031
Phone: 703-205-3486

ABBOTT LABORATORIES FUND

Award for students attending UNCF colleges and universities. Must have minimum 2.5 GPA. For more information, please see Web site http://www.uncf.org/forstudents/scholarship.asp.

Award: Scholarship for use in freshman, sophomore, junior, or senior years; not renewable.

Eligibility Requirements: Applicant must be Black (non-Hispanic) and enrolled or expecting to enroll full- or part-time at a four-year institution or university. Applicant must have 2.5 GPA or higher. Available to U.S. citizens.

Application Requirements: *Deadline:* continuous.

Contact: Director, Program Services
United Negro College Fund
8260 Willow Oaks Corporate Drive
PO Box 10444
Fairfax, VA 22031-8044
Phone: 800-331-2244
E-mail: rebecca.bennett@uncf.org

ALLEN AND JOAN BILDNER SCHOLARSHIP

Scholarship open to New Jersey residents attending a UNCF member college or university. Must have minimum 2.5 GPA. Prospective applicants should complete the Student Profile found at web site http://www.uncf.org.

Award: Scholarship for use in freshman, sophomore, junior, or senior years; not renewable. *Number:* varies. *Amount:* $2000–$2500.

Eligibility Requirements: Applicant must be Black (non-Hispanic); enrolled or expecting to enroll full- or part-time at a four-year institution or university and resident of New Jersey. Applicant must have 2.5 GPA or higher. Available to U.S. citizens.

Application Requirements: Application. *Deadline:* continuous.

Contact: Director, Program Services
United Negro College Fund
8260 Willow Oaks Corporate Drive
PO Box 10444
Fairfax, VA 22031-8044
Phone: 800-331-2244
E-mail: rebecca.bennett@uncf.org

ARTHUR ROSS FOUNDATION SCHOLARSHIP

Up to $3000 scholarship for students attending UNCF member schools and residing in the 5 boroughs of New York City or Kentucky, Georgia, Florida, Alabama, South Carolina, Tennessee, Louisiana, Mississippi, or North Carolina. Minimum 2.5 GPA required.

Award: Scholarship for use in freshman year; not renewable. *Amount:* $1000–$3000.

Eligibility Requirements: Applicant must be Black (non-Hispanic) and enrolled or expecting to enroll at a four-year institution or university. Applicant must have 2.5 GPA or higher. Available to U.S. citizens.

Application Requirements: *Deadline:* continuous.

Contact: Director, Program Services
United Negro College Fund
8260 Willow Oaks Corporate Drive
PO Box 10444
Fairfax, VA 22031-8044
Phone: 800-331-2244
E-mail: rebecca.bennett@uncf.org

BANK ONE ARIZONA CORPORATION SCHOLARSHIP

Up to $2500 scholarship providing funds for tuition, room/board, books, or to repay federal student loans. Must be resident of Arizona, attend a UNCF member college or university, and have minimum 2.5 GPA.

Award: Scholarship for use in freshman year; not renewable. *Amount:* up to $2500.

Eligibility Requirements: Applicant must be Black (non-Hispanic); enrolled or expecting to enroll at a four-year institution or university and resident of Arizona. Applicant must have 2.5 GPA or higher.

Application Requirements: *Deadline:* continuous.

Contact: Director, Program Services
United Negro College Fund
8260 Willow Oaks Corporate Drive
PO Box 10444
Fairfax, VA 22031-8044
Phone: 800-331-2244
E-mail: rebecca.bennett@uncf.org

BENDIX CORPORATION SCHOLARSHIP

Scholarships available to students at UNCF member colleges and universities who are residents of Georgia. Minimum 2.5 GPA required.

Award: Scholarship for use in freshman year; not renewable. *Amount:* $1000–$2000.

Eligibility Requirements: Applicant must be Black (non-Hispanic); enrolled or expecting to enroll at a four-year institution or university and resident of Georgia. Applicant must have 2.5 GPA or higher. Available to U.S. citizens.

Application Requirements: *Deadline:* continuous.

Contact: Director, Program Services
United Negro College Fund
8260 Willow Oaks Corporate Drive
PO Box 10444
Fairfax, VA 22031-8044
Phone: 800-331-2244
E-mail: rebecca.bennett@uncf.org

BESSIE IRENE SMITH TRUST SCHOLARSHIP

Scholarships available to students at UNCF member colleges and universities. Must have minimum GPA of 2.5.

Award: Scholarship for use in freshman year; not renewable.

Eligibility Requirements: Applicant must be Black (non-Hispanic) and enrolled or expecting to enroll at a four-year institution or university. Applicant must have 2.5 GPA or higher. Available to U.S. citizens.

Application Requirements: *Deadline:* continuous.

Contact: Director, Program Services
United Negro College Fund
8260 Willow Oaks Corporate Drive
PO Box 10444
Fairfax, VA 22031-8044
Phone: 800-331-2244
E-mail: rebecca.bennett@uncf.org

BORDEN SCHOLARSHIP FUND

Scholarships available to students attending UNCF member colleges and universities who are residents of Ohio. Must have minimum 2.5 GPA.

Award: Scholarship for use in freshman year; not renewable.

Eligibility Requirements: Applicant must be Black (non-Hispanic); enrolled or expecting to enroll at a four-year institution or university and resident of Ohio. Applicant must have 2.5 GPA or higher. Available to U.S. citizens.

Application Requirements: *Deadline:* continuous.

Contact: Director, Program Services
United Negro College Fund
8260 Willow Oaks Corporate Drive
PO Box 10444
Fairfax, VA 22031-8044
Phone: 800-331-2244
E-mail: rebecca.bennett@uncf.org

BRISTOL-MYERS SQUIBB SCHOLARSHIP

This scholarship is a ?Last Dollar? award directed to New Jersey residents. Must attend college or university within New Jersey or one of the UNCF member institutions and have minimum 2.5 GPA.

Award: Scholarship for use in freshman year; not renewable. *Amount:* $500–$650.

Eligibility Requirements: Applicant must be Black (non-Hispanic); enrolled or expecting to enroll at a four-year institution or university and resident of New Jersey. Applicant must have 2.5 GPA or higher. Available to U.S. citizens.

Application Requirements: *Deadline:* continuous.

Contact: Director, Program Services
United Negro College Fund
8260 Willow Oaks Corporate Drive
PO Box 10444
Fairfax, VA 22031-8044
Phone: 800-331-2244
E-mail: rebecca.bennett@uncf.org

BURTON G. BETTINGEN FOUNDATION SCHOLARSHIP

Awards available to students at UNCF member colleges and universities. Minimum 2.5 GPA required.

Award: Scholarship for use in freshman year; not renewable.

Eligibility Requirements: Applicant must be Black (non-Hispanic) and enrolled or expecting to enroll at a four-year institution or university. Applicant must have 2.5 GPA or higher. Available to U.S. citizens.

Application Requirements: *Deadline:* continuous.

Contact: Director, Program Services
United Negro College Fund
8260 Willow Oaks Corporate Drive
PO Box 10444
Fairfax, VA 22031-8044
Phone: 800-331-2244
E-mail: rebecca.bennett@uncf.org

CAREER AGENCY COMPANIES SCHOLARSHIP

$5000 scholarship offered only to existing policyholders of one of the Career Agency Companies (The Reliable Life Insurance Company, Old Reliable Casualty Company, Capitol County Mutual, United Insurance Company of America, United Casualty, Union National Life Insurance Company and Union National Fire Insurance Company). Students must attend UNCF member colleges and universities or HBCU schools. Must have minimum 2.5 GPA and reside in one of 27 states.

Award: Scholarship for use in freshman year; not renewable. *Amount:* $5000.

Eligibility Requirements: Applicant must be Black (non-Hispanic) and enrolled or expecting to enroll at a four-year institution or university. Applicant must have 2.5 GPA or higher. Available to U.S. citizens.

Application Requirements: *Deadline:* continuous.

Contact: Director, Program Services
United Negro College Fund
8260 Willow Oaks Corporate Drive
PO Box 10444
Fairfax, VA 22031-8044
Phone: 800-331-2244
E-mail: rebecca.bennett@uncf.org

CATHERINE ROBERTS BRIDGEMAN SCHOLARSHIP PROGRAM

Scholarship for students from Harlem, New York attending Historically Black Colleges and Universities and majoring in nursing or hospital administration. Consideration will also be given to students who reside in the boroughs of New York City. Applicants must be high school seniors or high school graduates at the time of application and planning to enroll full-time at Historically Black Colleges and Universities in the fall.

Award: Scholarship for use in freshman year; renewable. *Amount:* up to $2000.

Eligibility Requirements: Applicant must be Black (non-Hispanic) and enrolled or expecting to enroll full-time at a four-year institution or university. Applicant must have 3.0 GPA or higher.

Application Requirements: Application, essay, financial need analysis, references, transcript. *Deadline:* May 31.

Contact: Director, Program Services
United Negro College Fund
8260 Willow Oaks Corporate Drive
PO Box 10444
Fairfax, VA 22031-8044
Phone: 800-331-2244
E-mail: rebecca.bennett@uncf.org

CHICAGO INTER-ALUMNI COUNCIL SCHOLARSHIP

Scholarship for African American high school seniors residing in the greater Chicago area. The three candidates raising the most funds for the annual scholarship pageant receive scholarships to attend a UNCF member college or university. The scholarship value varies according to need. Minimum GPA of 2.5 required.

Award: Scholarship for use in freshman year; not renewable. *Number:* 3. *Amount:* varies.

Eligibility Requirements: Applicant must be Black (non-Hispanic); high school student; planning to enroll or expecting to enroll full-time at a four-year institution or university and resident of Illinois. Applicant must have 2.5 GPA or higher. Available to U.S. citizens.

Application Requirements: Application, applicant must enter a contest, financial need analysis, FAFSA, Student Aid Report (SAR).

Contact: Director, Program Services
United Negro College Fund
8260 Willow Oaks Corporate Drive
PO Box 10444
Fairfax, VA 22031-8044
Phone: 800-331-2244
E-mail: rebecca.bennett@uncf.org

CHICAGO PUBLIC SCHOOLS UNCF CAMPAIGN

Scholarship open to African American students who have attended Chicago public schools. Minimum 2.5 GPA required and must be accepted to a UNCF member college or university. The scholarship pays tuition and fees for four years; amount varies according to need. General scholarship application and additional information are at web site http://www.uncf.org.

Award: Scholarship for use in freshman, sophomore, junior, or senior years; renewable. *Number:* varies. *Amount:* up to $10,000.

Eligibility Requirements: Applicant must be Black (non-Hispanic); enrolled or expecting to enroll full-time at a four-year institution or university and resident of Illinois. Applicant must have 2.5 GPA or higher. Available to U.S. citizens.

Application Requirements: Application, financial need analysis, FAFSA, Student Aid Report (SAR).

Contact: Director, Program Services
United Negro College Fund
8260 Willow Oaks Corporate Drive
PO Box 10444
Fairfax, VA 22031-8044
Phone: 800-331-2244
E-mail: rebecca.bennett@uncf.org

CHRYSLER CORPORATION SCHOLARSHIP

10 scholarships available to students who attend UNCF member colleges and universities. Minimum 2.5 GPA required.

Award: Scholarship for use in freshman year; not renewable. *Number:* up to 10. *Amount:* $3900.

Eligibility Requirements: Applicant must be Black (non-Hispanic) and enrolled or expecting to enroll at a four-year institution or university. Applicant must have 2.5 GPA or higher. Available to U.S. citizens.

Application Requirements: *Deadline:* continuous.

Contact: Director, Program Services
United Negro College Fund
8260 Willow Oaks Corporate Drive
PO Box 10444
Fairfax, VA 22031-8044
Phone: 800-331-2244
E-mail: rebecca.bennett@uncf.org

CHURCH'S CHICKEN OPPORTUNITY SCHOLARSHIP

• *See page 580*

CITY OF CLEVELAND: MAYOR JACKSON SCHOLARSHIP FOR CLEVELAND METROPOLITAN SCHOOL DISTRICT

Scholarships awarded to African American residents of Cleveland, who are graduating seniors from a Cleveland Metropolitan School District high school with minimum GPA of 2.5. Must be accepted at any two- or four-year college or university. Apply online at web site http://www.uncf.org.

Award: Scholarship for use in freshman year; not renewable. *Amount:* up to $2000.

Eligibility Requirements: Applicant must be Black (non-Hispanic); high school student; planning to enroll or expecting to enroll full-time at a four-year institution or university and resident of Ohio. Applicant must have 2.5 GPA or higher. Available to U.S. citizens.

Application Requirements: Application, financial need analysis, FAFSA, Student Aid Report (SAR). *Deadline:* April 30.

Contact: Director, Program Services
United Negro College Fund
8260 Willow Oaks Corporate Drive
PO Box 10444
Fairfax, VA 22031-8044
Phone: 800-331-2244
E-mail: rebecca.bennett@uncf.org

CITY OF CLEVELAND: MAYOR JACKSON SCHOLARSHIP FOR HISTORICALLY BLACK COLLEGES AND UNIVERSITIES

Award available to graduating African American high school seniors who have been accepted for enrollment at a four-year historically black college or university and have a minimum GPA of 2.5. For complete list of HBCU schools and to apply online, go to web site http://www.uncf.org.

Award: Scholarship for use in freshman year; not renewable. *Amount:* up to $2000.

Eligibility Requirements: Applicant must be Black (non-Hispanic); high school student; planning to enroll or expecting to enroll full-time at a four-year institution or university and resident of Ohio. Applicant must have 2.5 GPA or higher. Available to U.S. citizens.

Application Requirements: Application. *Deadline:* April 29.

Contact: Director, Program Services
United Negro College Fund
8260 Willow Oaks Corporate Drive
PO Box 10444
Fairfax, VA 22031-8044
Phone: 800-331-2244
E-mail: rebecca.bennett@uncf.org

CITY OF CLEVELAND: MAYOR JACKSON SCHOLARSHIPS FOR CITY EMPLOYEES

Scholarship for students who have been accepted to a 4-year college or university (full or part-time) or working on earning their bachelor's degree, with at least a 2.5 cumulative GPA. Must be an employee of the City of Cleveland and attend a four year college/university. Apply online at web site: http://www.uncf.org.

Award: Scholarship for use in freshman, sophomore, junior, or senior years; not renewable. *Amount:* up to $1000.

Eligibility Requirements: Applicant must be Black (non-Hispanic); enrolled or expecting to enroll full- or part-time at a four-year institution or university and resident of Ohio. Applicant must have 2.5 GPA or higher. Available to U.S. citizens.

Application Requirements: Application, financial need analysis, transcript. *Deadline:* April 29.

Contact: Director, Program Services
United Negro College Fund
8260 Willow Oaks Corporate Drive
PO Box 10444
Fairfax, VA 22031-8044
Phone: 800-331-2244
E-mail: rebecca.bennett@uncf.org

CLEVELAND MAYOR JACKSON SCHOLARSHIP FOR RECREATION CENTERS

Award open to Cleveland residents who have maintained a cumulative 2.5 grade point average or higher and attended one of the Mayor's recreation centers. Must be accepted to any four-year college or university. Verification of recreation center attendance will be conducted.

Award: Scholarship for use in freshman year; not renewable. *Amount:* up to $2000.

Eligibility Requirements: Applicant must be Black (non-Hispanic); high school student; planning to enroll or expecting to enroll at a four-year institution and resident of Ohio. Applicant must have 2.5 GPA or higher. Available to U.S. citizens.

Application Requirements: *Deadline:* April 29.

Contact: Director, Program Services
United Negro College Fund
8260 Willow Oaks Corporate Drive
PO Box 10444
Fairfax, VA 22031-8044
Phone: 800-331-2244
E-mail: rebecca.bennett@uncf.org

CLOROX COMPANY FOUNDATION SCHOLARSHIP

Scholarship awarded each year to African American students from the San Francisco Bay area, attending UNCF member colleges or universities on a full-time basis. Must be a resident of California with minimum GPA of 2.5. General scholarship application and additional information on web site http://www.uncf.org.

Award: Scholarship for use in freshman, sophomore, junior, or senior years; not renewable. *Amount:* up to $2000.

Eligibility Requirements: Applicant must be Black (non-Hispanic); enrolled or expecting to enroll full-time at a four-year institution or university and resident of California. Applicant must have 2.5 GPA or higher. Available to U.S. citizens.

Application Requirements: Application, financial need analysis, FAFSA, Student Aid Report (SAR). *Deadline:* February 18.

Contact: Director, Program Services
United Negro College Fund
8260 Willow Oaks Corporate Drive
PO Box 10444
Fairfax, VA 22031-8044
Phone: 800-331-2244
E-mail: rebecca.bennett@uncf.org

CLOWES FUND SCHOLARSHIP

Scholarship of up to $3000 for Indiana resident attending UNCF member college or university. Minimum 2.5 GPA required.

Award: Scholarship for use in freshman year; not renewable. *Amount:* up to $3000.

Eligibility Requirements: Applicant must be Black (non-Hispanic); enrolled or expecting to enroll at a four-year institution or university and resident of Indiana. Applicant must have 2.5 GPA or higher.

Application Requirements: *Deadline:* continuous.

Contact: Director, Program Services
United Negro College Fund
8260 Willow Oaks Corporate Drive
PO Box 10444
Fairfax, VA 22031-8044
Phone: 800-331-2244
E-mail: rebecca.bennett@uncf.org

CONSUMER ENERGY FOUNDATION SCHOLARSHIP

Paid internship and scholarship for undergraduate juniors and seniors attending UNCF member colleges and universities. Internship will take place in Michigan. Minimum 3.0 GPA required.

Award: Scholarship for use in junior or senior years; not renewable.

Eligibility Requirements: Applicant must be Black (non-Hispanic); enrolled or expecting to enroll at a four-year institution and studying in Michigan. Applicant must have 3.0 GPA or higher. Available to U.S. citizens.

Application Requirements: *Deadline:* continuous.

Contact: Director, Program Services
United Negro College Fund
8260 Willow Oaks Corporate Drive
PO Box 10444
Fairfax, VA 22031-8044
Phone: 800-331-2244
E-mail: rebecca.bennett@uncf.org

COSTCO SCHOLARSHIP

Renewable scholarship of $5000 for students from Washington and Oregon attending UNCF member colleges and universities. Minimum 2.5 GPA required. To apply online go to: http://www.uncf.org.

Award: Scholarship for use in freshman, sophomore, junior, or senior years; renewable. *Number:* 1. *Amount:* $5000.

Eligibility Requirements: Applicant must be Black (non-Hispanic); enrolled or expecting to enroll full- or part-time at a four-year institution or university and resident of Oregon or Washington. Applicant must have 2.5 GPA or higher. Available to U.S. citizens.

Application Requirements: Application. *Deadline:* continuous.

Contact: Program Services
United Negro College Fund
8260 Willow Oaks Corporate Drive
Fairfax, VA 22031-4511
Phone: 703-205-3486

CRANE FUND FOR WIDOWS AND CHILDREN

Scholarship available for disadvantaged students with a deceased parent who attend UNCF member colleges and universities. Minimum 2.5 GPA required.

Award: Scholarship for use in freshman year; not renewable.

Eligibility Requirements: Applicant must be Black (non-Hispanic) and enrolled or expecting to enroll at a four-year institution or university. Applicant must have 2.5 GPA or higher. Available to U.S. citizens.

Application Requirements: *Deadline:* continuous.

Contact: Director, Program Services
United Negro College Fund
8260 Willow Oaks Corporate Drive
PO Box 10444
Fairfax, VA 22031-8044
Phone: 800-331-2244
E-mail: rebecca.bennett@uncf.org

DALLAS INDEPENDENT SCHOOL DISTRICT SCHOLARSHIP

Applicant must be a African American high school senior from the Dallas Independent School District with minimum GPA of 2.5. Must attend a UNCF member college/university or any other Historically Black College or University. Award based on financial need and academic potential. Apply online at http://www.uncf.org.

Award: Scholarship for use in freshman year; not renewable. *Number:* varies. *Amount:* up to $2500.

Eligibility Requirements: Applicant must be Black (non-Hispanic); high school student; planning to enroll or expecting to enroll full-time at a four-year institution or university and resident of Texas. Applicant must have 2.5 GPA or higher. Available to U.S. citizens.

Application Requirements: Application, essay, financial need analysis, FAFSA. *Deadline:* April 25.

Contact: Dr. Kendall Beck, Scholarship Coordinator
United Negro College Fund
2538 South Ervay
Dallas, TX 75215
Phone: 972-925-4893

DAVENPORT FORTE PEDESTAL FUND

Scholarship of $10,000 available for African American students who graduated from the Detroit Public School system. Applicant must be a first semester freshman attending a UNCF member college or university. Must have a minimum of 2.7 GPA. For additional information and to complete general scholarship application, visit web site: http://www.uncf.org.

Award: Scholarship for use in freshman or sophomore years; not renewable. *Number:* 1. *Amount:* $10,000.

Eligibility Requirements: Applicant must be Black (non-Hispanic); enrolled or expecting to enroll full-time at a four-year institution or university and resident of Michigan. Available to U.S. citizens.

Application Requirements: Application, financial need analysis, FAFSA, Student Aid Report (SAR).

Contact: Director, Program Services
United Negro College Fund
8260 Willow Oaks Corporate Drive
PO Box 10444
Fairfax, VA 22031-8044
Phone: 800-331-2244
E-mail: rebecca.bennett@uncf.org

DEBORAH L. VINCENT FAHRO EDUCATION SCHOLARSHIP AWARD

Award for residents of federally assisted housing or a recipient of assistance through the Community Development Block Grant program in Florida. Must be a high school senior and meet income requirements as defined by HUD for public/assisted housing and Community Development Block Grant targeted area recipients. Must have a sponsor that is an active member of FAHRO as a housing authority/agency or community development agency that is willing to support travel expenses to attend Annual Convention awards banquet to receive scholarship if selected. Minimum 2.5 GPA required.

Award: Scholarship for use in freshman year; not renewable. *Amount:* up to $2500.

Eligibility Requirements: Applicant must be Black (non-Hispanic); high school student and planning to enroll or expecting to enroll at a two-year or four-year institution. Applicant must have 2.5 GPA or higher. Available to U.S. citizens.

Application Requirements: *Deadline:* May 31.

Contact: Director, Program Services
United Negro College Fund
8260 Willow Oaks Corporate Drive
PO Box 10444
Fairfax, VA 22031-8044
Phone: 800-331-2244
E-mail: rebecca.bennett@uncf.org

DENIS D'AMORE SCHOLARSHIP

Scholarship is open to African American students from the Boston metropolitan area. Must have a minimum GPA of 2.5 and be enrolled at a UNCF member college or university. For additional information and to fill out a general scholarship application, go to web site http://www.uncf.org.

Award: Scholarship for use in freshman, sophomore, junior, or senior years; not renewable. *Number:* varies. *Amount:* $2000.

Eligibility Requirements: Applicant must be Black (non-Hispanic); enrolled or expecting to enroll full- or part-time at a four-year institution or university and resident of Massachusetts. Applicant must have 2.5 GPA or higher. Available to U.S. citizens.

Application Requirements: Application, financial need analysis, FAFSA, Student Aid Report (SAR).

Contact: Director, Program Services
United Negro College Fund
8260 Willow Oaks Corporate Drive
PO Box 10444
Fairfax, VA 22031-8044
Phone: 800-331-2244
E-mail: rebecca.bennett@uncf.org

DR. SCHOLL FOUNDATION SCHOLARSHIP

Scholarships for students at UNCF member colleges and universities. Minimum 2.5 GPA required.

Award: Scholarship for use in freshman year; not renewable.

Eligibility Requirements: Applicant must be Black (non-Hispanic) and enrolled or expecting to enroll at a four-year institution or university. Applicant must have 2.5 GPA or higher. Available to U.S. citizens.

Application Requirements: *Deadline:* continuous.

Contact: Director, Program Services
United Negro College Fund
8260 Willow Oaks Corporate Drive
PO Box 10444
Fairfax, VA 22031-8044
Phone: 800-331-2244
E-mail: rebecca.bennett@uncf.org

DOMINIQUE AND JACQUES CASIMIR SCHOLARSHIP

Scholarship is available for two male and two female African American undergraduate sophomores or juniors from the state of Texas. Minimum GPA of 2.5 is required. For additional information and a general scholarship application online, visit http://www.uncf.org.

Award: Scholarship for use in sophomore or junior years; renewable. *Number:* 4. *Amount:* $1500.

Eligibility Requirements: Applicant must be Black (non-Hispanic); enrolled or expecting to enroll full-time at a four-year institution or university and resident of Texas. Applicant must have 2.5 GPA or higher. Available to U.S. citizens.

Application Requirements: Application, financial need analysis, FAFSA, Student Aid Report (SAR).

Contact: Director, Program Services
United Negro College Fund
8260 Willow Oaks Corporate Drive
PO Box 10444
Fairfax, VA 22031-8044
Phone: 800-331-2244
E-mail: rebecca.bennett@uncf.org

DORIS AND JOHN CARPENTER SCHOLARSHIP

Award for undergraduate freshmen showing great financial need and attending UNCF member colleges and universities. Minimum 2.5 GPA required.

Award: Scholarship for use in freshman year; not renewable. *Amount:* $2000–$5000.

Eligibility Requirements: Applicant must be Black (non-Hispanic) and enrolled or expecting to enroll at a four-year institution. Applicant must have 2.5 GPA or higher. Available to U.S. citizens.

Application Requirements: Financial need analysis. *Deadline:* continuous.

Contact: Director, Program Services
United Negro College Fund
8260 Willow Oaks Corporate Drive
PO Box 10444
Fairfax, VA 22031-8044
Phone: 800-331-2244
E-mail: rebecca.bennett@uncf.org

DOROTHY N. MCNEAL SCHOLARSHIP

Award for students at UNCF member colleges and universities pursuing careers in community service. Minimum 2.5 GPA required.

Award: Scholarship for use in freshman year; not renewable.

Eligibility Requirements: Applicant must be Black (non-Hispanic) and enrolled or expecting to enroll at a four-year institution or university. Applicant must have 2.5 GPA or higher. Available to U.S. citizens.

Application Requirements: *Deadline:* continuous.

Contact: Director, Program Services
United Negro College Fund
8260 Willow Oaks Corporate Drive
PO Box 10444
Fairfax, VA 22031-8044
Phone: 800-331-2244
E-mail: rebecca.bennett@uncf.org

EDNA F. BLUM FOUNDATION SCHOLARSHIP

Scholarship available to students at UNCF member colleges and universities who are residents of New York. Minimum 2.5 GPA required.

Award: Scholarship for use in freshman year; not renewable. *Amount:* $1000–$3000.

Eligibility Requirements: Applicant must be Black (non-Hispanic); enrolled or expecting to enroll at a four-year institution or university and resident of New York. Applicant must have 2.5 GPA or higher. Available to U.S. citizens.

Application Requirements: *Deadline:* continuous.

Contact: Director, Program Services
United Negro College Fund
8260 Willow Oaks Corporate Drive
PO Box 10444
Fairfax, VA 22031-8044
Phone: 800-331-2244
E-mail: rebecca.bennett@uncf.org

EDWARD & HAZEL STEPHENSON SCHOLARSHIP

Scholarship available to senior undergraduate students attending UNCF member colleges and universities. Minimum 2.5 GPA required.

Award: Scholarship for use in senior year; not renewable. *Amount:* $1000–$3000.

Eligibility Requirements: Applicant must be Black (non-Hispanic) and enrolled or expecting to enroll at a four-year institution. Applicant must have 2.5 GPA or higher. Available to U.S. citizens.

Application Requirements: *Deadline:* continuous.

Contact: Director, Program Services
United Negro College Fund
8260 Willow Oaks Corporate Drive
PO Box 10444
Fairfax, VA 22031-8044
Phone: 800-331-2244
E-mail: rebecca.bennett@uncf.org

EDWARD D. GRIGG SCHOLARSHIP

Scholarship available at UNCF member colleges and schools. Must have minimum 2.5 GPA. For more information please see Web site at http://www.uncf.org/forstudents/scholarship.asp.

Award: Scholarship for use in freshman year; not renewable.

Eligibility Requirements: Applicant must be Black (non-Hispanic) and enrolled or expecting to enroll at a four-year institution. Applicant must have 2.5 GPA or higher. Available to U.S. citizens.

Application Requirements: *Deadline:* continuous.

Contact: Director, Program Services
United Negro College Fund
8260 Willow Oaks Corporate Drive
PO Box 10444
Fairfax, VA 22031-8044
Phone: 800-331-2244
E-mail: rebecca.bennett@uncf.org

EDWARD FITTERMAN FOUNDATION SCHOLARSHIP

Awards for students at UNCF member colleges and universities. Minimum 2.5 GPA required. For more information, please go to Web site http://www.uncf.org/forstudents/scholarship.asp.

Award: Scholarship for use in freshman year; not renewable.

Eligibility Requirements: Applicant must be Black (non-Hispanic) and enrolled or expecting to enroll at a four-year institution or university. Applicant must have 2.5 GPA or higher. Available to U.S. citizens.

Application Requirements: *Deadline:* continuous.

Contact: Director, Program Services
United Negro College Fund
8260 Willow Oaks Corporate Drive
PO Box 10444
Fairfax, VA 22031-8044
Phone: 800-331-2244
E-mail: rebecca.bennett@uncf.org

EDWARD N. NEY SCHOLARSHIP

Scholarships for students attending UNCF member colleges and schools. Minimum 3.5 GPA required. For more information, please see Web site at http://www.uncf.org/forstudents/scholarship.asp.

Award: Scholarship for use in freshman year.

Eligibility Requirements: Applicant must be Black (non-Hispanic) and enrolled or expecting to enroll at a four-year institution. Applicant must have 3.5 GPA or higher. Available to U.S. citizens.

Application Requirements: *Deadline:* continuous.

Contact: Director, Program Services
United Negro College Fund
8260 Willow Oaks Corporate Drive
PO Box 10444
Fairfax, VA 22031-8044
Phone: 800-331-2244
E-mail: rebecca.bennett@uncf.org

ELMER ROE DEAVER FOUNDATION SCHOLARSHIP

$4000 scholarships available to students attending UNCF member colleges and universities who are residents of Pennsylvania, New Jersey, or Delaware. Minimum 2.5 GPA required.

Award: Scholarship for use in freshman year; not renewable. *Amount:* $4000.

Eligibility Requirements: Applicant must be Black (non-Hispanic); enrolled or expecting to enroll at a four-year institution or university and resident of Delaware, New Jersey, or Pennsylvania. Applicant must have 2.5 GPA or higher. Available to U.S. citizens.

Application Requirements: *Deadline:* continuous.

Contact: Director, Program Services
United Negro College Fund
8260 Willow Oaks Corporate Drive
PO Box 10444
Fairfax, VA 22031-8044
Phone: 800-331-2244
E-mail: rebecca.bennett@uncf.org

ELSIE L. WILDUNG SCHOLARSHIP

Scholarships available for students at UNCF member colleges and universities. Minimum 2.5 GPA required. For more information please see Web site http://www.uncf.org/forstudents/scholarship.asp.

Award: Scholarship for use in freshman year; not renewable.

Eligibility Requirements: Applicant must be Black (non-Hispanic) and enrolled or expecting to enroll at a four-year institution or university. Applicant must have 2.5 GPA or higher. Available to U.S. citizens.

Application Requirements: *Deadline:* continuous.

Contact: Director, Program Services
United Negro College Fund
8260 Willow Oaks Corporate Drive
PO Box 10444
Fairfax, VA 22031-8044
Phone: 800-331-2244
E-mail: rebecca.bennett@uncf.org

ESSENCE SCHOLARS PROGRAM

$10,000 scholarship for African American women attending one of the UNCF member institutions, Hampton University, or Howard University. Must be undergraduate sophomore or junior. Minimum 3.0 GPA required.

Award: Scholarship for use in sophomore or junior years. *Amount:* $10,000.

Eligibility Requirements: Applicant must be Black (non-Hispanic); enrolled or expecting to enroll at a four-year institution and female. Applicant must have 3.0 GPA or higher. Available to U.S. citizens.

Application Requirements: *Deadline:* continuous.

Contact: Director, Program Services
United Negro College Fund
8260 Willow Oaks Corporate Drive
PO Box 10444
Fairfax, VA 22031-8044
Phone: 800-331-2244
E-mail: rebecca.bennett@uncf.org

EUNICE WALKER JOHNSON ENDOWED SCHOLARSHIP

Award of up to $5000 available to African American students who attend UNCF member colleges and universities. Must have a 3.0 GPA. For additional information and to apply online, go to web site http://www.uncf.org.

Award: Scholarship for use in freshman, sophomore, junior, or senior years; renewable. *Number:* varies. *Amount:* up to $5000.

Eligibility Requirements: Applicant must be Black (non-Hispanic) and enrolled or expecting to enroll full- or part-time at a four-year institution or university. Applicant must have 3.0 GPA or higher. Available to U.S. and non-U.S. citizens.

Application Requirements: Application, financial need analysis, FAFSA. *Deadline:* December 1.

Contact: Director, Program Services
United Negro College Fund
8260 Willow Oaks Corporate Drive
PO Box 10444
Fairfax, VA 22031-8044
Phone: 800-331-2244
E-mail: rebecca.bennett@uncf.org

EVELYN LEVINA WRIGHT SCHOLARSHIP

Scholarship of $3500 is available to an African American resident of the Philadelphia, Pennsylvania; Wilmington, Delaware; or Camden, New Jersey, area who is enrolled at a UNCF member college or university. Must have a minimum GPA of 2.5. For information and general scholarship application, visit web site http://www.uncf.org.

Award: Scholarship for use in freshman, sophomore, junior, or senior years; renewable. *Number:* 1. *Amount:* $3500.

Eligibility Requirements: Applicant must be Black (non-Hispanic); enrolled or expecting to enroll full- or part-time at a four-year institution or university and resident of Delaware, New Jersey, or Pennsylvania. Applicant must have 2.5 GPA or higher. Available to U.S. citizens.

Application Requirements: Application, financial need analysis, FAFSA.

Contact: Director, Program Services
United Negro College Fund
8260 Willow Oaks Corporate Drive
PO Box 10444
Fairfax, VA 22031-8044
Phone: 800-331-2244
E-mail: rebecca.bennett@uncf.org

FIFTH/THIRD SCHOLARS PROGRAM

Scholarship awards available to African American students who are residents of Dayton, Columbus, or Cincinnati, Ohio. Student must attend a UNCF member college or university. Must have a minimum GPA of 2.5 and the scholarship value varies based on need. Scholarship may be used for tuition, books, room and board, or to repay student loans.

Award: Scholarship for use in freshman, sophomore, junior, or senior years; renewable. *Number:* varies. *Amount:* varies.

Eligibility Requirements: Applicant must be Black (non-Hispanic); enrolled or expecting to enroll full- or part-time at a four-year institution or university and resident of Ohio. Applicant must have 2.5 GPA or higher. Available to U.S. citizens.

Application Requirements: Application, financial need analysis, FAFSA, Student Aid Report (SAR).

Contact: Director, Program Services
United Negro College Fund
8260 Willow Oaks Corporate Drive
PO Box 10444
Fairfax, VA 22031-8044
Phone: 800-331-2244
E-mail: rebecca.bennett@uncf.org

FORT WORTH INDEPENDENT SCHOOL DISTRICT SCHOLARSHIP

Scholarship awarded to graduating African American high school senior from the Fort Worth Independent School District. Applicants must be enrolled full-time at a UNCF member institution or Historically Black College or University (HBCU). Special consideration given to students who will be attending or attend a UNCF school in the state of Texas which include, Paul Quinn College, Texas College, Jarvis Christian College, Wiley College, or Huston-Tillotson University. Scholarship award amount is up to $5000 and will be awarded to students who demonstrate financial need and academic potential. Apply online at web site http://www.uncf.org.

Award: Scholarship for use in freshman, sophomore, junior, or senior years; not renewable. *Number:* varies. *Amount:* up to $5000.

Eligibility Requirements: Applicant must be Black (non-Hispanic); high school student; planning to enroll or expecting to enroll full- or part-time at a four-year institution or university and resident of Texas. Applicant must have 3.0 GPA or higher. Available to U.S. citizens.

Application Requirements: Application, financial need analysis, FAFSA, Student Aid Report (SAR). *Deadline:* April 15.

Contact: Director, Program Services
United Negro College Fund
8260 Willow Oaks Corporate Drive
PO Box 10444
Fairfax, VA 22031-8044
Phone: 800-331-2244
E-mail: rebecca.bennett@uncf.org

FREDERICK D. PATTERSON SCHOLARSHIP

Scholarship available to students at UNCF member colleges and universities. Minimum 2.5 GPA required. For more information, see Web site http://www.uncf.org/forstudents/scholarship.asp.

Award: Scholarship for use in freshman year.

Eligibility Requirements: Applicant must be Black (non-Hispanic) and enrolled or expecting to enroll at a four-year institution or university. Applicant must have 2.5 GPA or higher. Available to U.S. citizens.

Application Requirements: *Deadline:* continuous.

Contact: Director, Program Services
United Negro College Fund
8260 Willow Oaks Corporate Drive
PO Box 10444
Fairfax, VA 22031-8044
Phone: 800-331-2244
E-mail: rebecca.bennett@uncf.org

GAP FOUNDATION SCHOLARSHIP

Awards of up to $5,000 available to undergraduate sophomores and juniors attending UNCF member colleges and universities. Must be majoring in business, retail, or fashion design. Minimum 3.0 GPA required.

Award: Scholarship for use in sophomore or junior years. *Amount:* up to $5000.

Eligibility Requirements: Applicant must be Black (non-Hispanic) and enrolled or expecting to enroll at a four-year institution. Applicant must have 3.0 GPA or higher. Available to U.S. citizens.

Application Requirements: *Deadline:* continuous.

Contact: Director, Program Services
United Negro College Fund
8260 Willow Oaks Corporate Drive
PO Box 10444
Fairfax, VA 22031-8044
Phone: 800-331-2244
E-mail: rebecca.bennett@uncf.org

GARY PAYTON FOUNDATION ENDOWED SCHOLARSHIP

Scholarship for student entering their freshman year who is a permanent resident of Washington. Must also demonstrate a commitment to community through volunteer work and attend a UNCF member college or university. Minimum 2.5 GPA required.

Award: Scholarship for use in freshman year; not renewable.

Eligibility Requirements: Applicant must be Black (non-Hispanic); enrolled or expecting to enroll at a four-year institution and resident of Washington. Applicant must have 2.5 GPA or higher. Available to U.S. citizens.

Application Requirements: *Deadline:* continuous.

Contact: Director, Program Services
United Negro College Fund
8260 Willow Oaks Corporate Drive
PO Box 10444
Fairfax, VA 22031-8044
Phone: 800-331-2244
E-mail: rebecca.bennett@uncf.org

GATES MILLENNIUM SCHOLARS PROGRAM (GATES FOUNDATION)

Award enables African-American students to complete an undergraduate and graduate education in targeted disciplines. Must be entering a U.S. accredited college or university as full-time degree-seeking student. Minimum 3.0 GPA required. Must demonstrate leadership abilities. Must meet federal Pell Grant eligibility criteria. For additional information visit web site http://www.uncf.org.

Award: Scholarship for use in freshman, sophomore, junior, or senior years; renewable. *Number:* varies.

Eligibility Requirements: Applicant must be Black (non-Hispanic) and enrolled or expecting to enroll full-time at a four-year institution or university. Applicant must have 3.0 GPA or higher. Available to U.S. citizens.

Application Requirements: Application, financial need analysis, nomination packet. *Deadline:* January 10.

Contact: Director, Program Services
United Negro College Fund
8260 Willow Oaks Corporate Drive
PO Box 10444
Fairfax, VA 22031-8044
Phone: 800-331-2244
E-mail: rebecca.bennett@uncf.org

GENA WRIGHT MEMORIAL SCHOLARSHIP

Two scholarships available to students attending UNCF member colleges and universities and having an expressed career interest in working with children. Minimum 3.0 GPA required.

Award: Scholarship for use in freshman year; not renewable. *Number:* 2.

Eligibility Requirements: Applicant must be Black (non-Hispanic) and enrolled or expecting to enroll at a four-year institution or university. Applicant must have 3.0 GPA or higher. Available to U.S. citizens.

Application Requirements: *Deadline:* continuous.

Contact: Director, Program Services
United Negro College Fund
8260 Willow Oaks Corporate Drive
PO Box 10444
Fairfax, VA 22031-8044
Phone: 800-331-2244
E-mail: rebecca.bennett@uncf.org

GEORGE AND FRANCIS BALL FOUNDATION SCHOLARSHIP

Scholarship for students attending UNCF member colleges and universities who are residents of Indiana. Minimum 2.5 GPA required. For more information, see Web site http://www.uncf.org/forstudents/scholarship.asp.

Award: Scholarship for use in freshman year; not renewable.

Eligibility Requirements: Applicant must be Black (non-Hispanic); enrolled or expecting to enroll at a four-year institution or university and resident of Indiana. Applicant must have 2.5 GPA or higher. Available to U.S. citizens.

Application Requirements: *Deadline:* continuous.

Contact: Director, Program Services
United Negro College Fund
8260 Willow Oaks Corporate Drive
PO Box 10444
Fairfax, VA 22031-8044
Phone: 800-331-2244
E-mail: rebecca.bennett@uncf.org

GEORGE BUNKER SCHOLARSHIP

Scholarship available for students attending UNCF member colleges and universities. Minimum 2.5 GPA required. For more information, see Web site http://www.uncf.org/forstudents/scholarship.asp.

Award: Scholarship for use in freshman year; not renewable.

Eligibility Requirements: Applicant must be Black (non-Hispanic) and enrolled or expecting to enroll at a four-year institution or university. Applicant must have 2.5 GPA or higher. Available to U.S. citizens.

Application Requirements: *Deadline:* continuous.

Contact: Director, Program Services
United Negro College Fund
8260 Willow Oaks Corporate Drive
PO Box 10444
Fairfax, VA 22031-8044
Phone: 800-331-2244
E-mail: rebecca.bennett@uncf.org

GERALD W. & JEAN PURMAL ENDOWED SCHOLARSHIP

Awards of $1,000-$4,000 available to students attending UNCF member colleges and universities. Minimum 2.5 GPA required. For additional information, see Web site http://www.uncf.org/forstudents/scholarship.asp.

Award: Scholarship for use in freshman year. *Amount:* $1000–$4000.

Eligibility Requirements: Applicant must be Black (non-Hispanic) and enrolled or expecting to enroll at a four-year institution or university. Applicant must have 2.5 GPA or higher. Available to U.S. citizens.

Application Requirements: *Deadline:* continuous.

Contact: Director, Program Services
United Negro College Fund
8260 Willow Oaks Corporate Drive
PO Box 10444
Fairfax, VA 22031-8044
Phone: 800-331-2244
E-mail: rebecca.bennett@uncf.org

GHEENS FOUNDATION SCHOLARSHIP

Scholarship supports African American students from Louisville, KY. For use in one of the following universities: Clark Atlanta University, Morehouse College, Spelman College, Tuskegee University, Howard University. Apply online at http://www.uncf.org.

Award: Scholarship for use in freshman, sophomore, junior, or senior years; not renewable. *Number:* varies. *Amount:* up to $2000.

Eligibility Requirements: Applicant must be Black (non-Hispanic); enrolled or expecting to enroll full- or part-time at a four-year institution or university; resident of Kentucky and studying in Alabama, District of Columbia, or Georgia. Applicant must have 2.5 GPA or higher. Available to U.S. citizens.

Application Requirements: Application, financial need analysis, transcript.

Contact: Director, Program Services
United Negro College Fund
8260 Willow Oaks Corporate Drive
PO Box 10444
Fairfax, VA 22031-8044
Phone: 800-331-2244
E-mail: rebecca.bennett@uncf.org

GIANT FOODS SCHOLARSHIP
• *See page 598*

JOHN W. ANDERSON FOUNDATION SCHOLARSHIP

Need-based scholarship for students from Indiana attending UNCF member colleges and universities. Prospective applicants should complete the Student Profile found at web site http://www.uncf.org.

Award: Scholarship for use in freshman, sophomore, junior, or senior years; not renewable. *Number:* 1. *Amount:* up to $3000.

Eligibility Requirements: Applicant must be Black (non-Hispanic); enrolled or expecting to enroll full- or part-time at a four-year institution or university and resident of Indiana. Applicant must have 2.5 GPA or higher. Available to U.S. citizens.

Application Requirements: Application, financial need analysis. *Deadline:* continuous.

Contact: Director, Program Services
United Negro College Fund
8260 Willow Oaks Corporate Drive
PO Box 10444
Fairfax, VA 22031-8044
Phone: 800-331-2244
E-mail: rebecca.bennett@uncf.org

JOSEPH A. TOWLES AFRICAN STUDY ABROAD SCHOLARSHIP

Scholarship enabling black Americans, conscious of their African descent, to have an opportunity to experience the richness of African cultures. Available to UNCF students who have been accepted into a study abroad program in Africa and have a minimum 3.0 GPA.

Award: Scholarship for use in sophomore or junior years; not renewable. *Amount:* up to $15,000.

Eligibility Requirements: Applicant must be Black (non-Hispanic) and enrolled or expecting to enroll full-time at a four-year institution or university. Applicant must have 3.0 GPA or higher.

Application Requirements: *Deadline:* April 15.

Contact: Director, Program Services
United Negro College Fund
8260 Willow Oaks Corporate Drive
PO Box 10444
Fairfax, VA 22031-8044
Phone: 800-331-2244
E-mail: rebecca.bennett@uncf.org

KANAWHA COUNTY, WV PEER LEADERS SCHOLARSHIP

This scholarship is established for graduating seniors in Kanawha County, WV who demonstrates the skills of a peer leader. Eligible students have the opportunity to receive up to $1,500 for four years. Students must also have a financial need established by the financial aid office at the school the student is enrolled. Minimum 2.5 GPA required.

Award: Scholarship for use in freshman, sophomore, junior, or senior years; renewable. *Amount:* up to $6000.

Eligibility Requirements: Applicant must be Black (non-Hispanic); high school student; planning to enroll or expecting to enroll full-time at a two-year or four-year institution or university and must have an interest in leadership. Applicant must have 2.5 GPA or higher.

Application Requirements: *Deadline:* February 7.

Contact: Director, Program Services
United Negro College Fund
8260 Willow Oaks Corporate Drive
PO Box 10444
Fairfax, VA 22031-8044
Phone: 800-331-2244
E-mail: rebecca.bennett@uncf.org

KANSAS CITY INITIATIVE SCHOLARSHIP

Award for an African American student in the Kansas City metropolitan area, who is enrolled at a UNCF member college or university or the University of Missouri at Kansas City. The entering freshman must have a GPA of at least a 3.0 and the upperclassman must have a GPA of 2.5. For additional information and general scholarship application, go to web site http://www.uncf.org.

Award: Scholarship for use in freshman, sophomore, junior, or senior years; renewable. *Number:* varies. *Amount:* $2500–$5000.

Eligibility Requirements: Applicant must be Black (non-Hispanic); enrolled or expecting to enroll full- or part-time at a four-year institution or university and resident of Kansas. Applicant must have 3.0 GPA or higher. Available to U.S. citizens.

Application Requirements: Application, financial need analysis, FAFSA, Student Aid Report (SAR).

Contact: Director, Program Services
United Negro College Fund
8260 Willow Oaks Corporate Drive
PO Box 10444
Fairfax, VA 22031-8044
Phone: 800-331-2244
E-mail: rebecca.bennett@uncf.org

KECK FOUNDATION SCHOLARSHIP

Scholarship is available to African American students attending UNCF colleges and universities whose families have suffered a financial hardship as a result of the September 11 tragedy. For additional information and general scholarship application, visit web site http://www.uncf.org.

Award: Scholarship for use in freshman, sophomore, junior, or senior years; renewable. *Number:* varies. *Amount:* $2000–$5000.

Eligibility Requirements: Applicant must be Black (non-Hispanic) and enrolled or expecting to enroll full- or part-time at a four-year institution or university. Applicant must have 2.5 GPA or higher. Available to U.S. citizens.

Application Requirements: Application.

Contact: Director, Program Services
United Negro College Fund
8260 Willow Oaks Corporate Drive
PO Box 10444
Fairfax, VA 22031-8044
Phone: 800-331-2244
E-mail: rebecca.bennett@uncf.org

KFC SCHOLARS PROGRAM
• *See page 580*

KROGER SCHOLARSHIP

Award available for African American high school senior residing in targeted Kroger retail store locations (GA, AL, SC, TN) who will be attending a UNCF participating college or university. Additional information and online application at http://www.uncf.org.

Award: Scholarship for use in freshman year; not renewable. *Number:* varies. *Amount:* up to $5000.

Eligibility Requirements: Applicant must be Black (non-Hispanic); high school student; planning to enroll or expecting to enroll full- or part-time at a four-year institution or university and resident of Alabama, Georgia, South Carolina, or Tennessee. Applicant must have 2.5 GPA or higher. Available to U.S. citizens.

Application Requirements: Application, financial need analysis, FAFSA, Student Aid Report (SAR). *Deadline:* April 5.

Contact: Director, Program Services
United Negro College Fund
8260 Willow Oaks Corporate Drive
PO Box 10444
Fairfax, VA 22031-8044
Phone: 800-331-2244
E-mail: rebecca.bennett@uncf.org

MASTERCARD WORLDWIDE SPECIAL SUPPORT PROGRAM

Scholarship designed to award students attending an UNCF member institution with a "last dollar" scholarship ranging between $2,000-$3,000. Minimum GPA of 2.5 required. Apply online at web site http://www.uncf.org.

Award: Scholarship for use in freshman, sophomore, junior, or senior years; not renewable. *Number:* 1. *Amount:* $2000–$3000.

Eligibility Requirements: Applicant must be Black (non-Hispanic) and enrolled or expecting to enroll full-time at a four-year institution or university. Applicant must have 2.5 GPA or higher. Available to U.S. and Canadian citizens.

Application Requirements: Application, financial need analysis.

Contact: Director, Program Services
United Negro College Fund
8260 Willow Oaks Corporate Drive
PO Box 10444
Fairfax, VA 22031-8044
Phone: 800-331-2244
E-mail: rebecca.bennett@uncf.org

NEW JERSEY MAYOR'S TASK FORCE SCHOLARSHIP

Awards available for African American students who live in one of these New Jersey Task Force participating cities: Atlantic City, Bayonne, Elizabeth, Newark, Patterson and Trenton. Must attend a historically black college or university or a UNCF member institution and maintain a 2.5 GPA. Funds may be used toward tuition, room/board, books, or to repay federal student loans. Check web site for details. http://www.uncf.org.

Award: Scholarship for use in freshman, sophomore, junior, or senior years; renewable. *Number:* varies. *Amount:* $1350.

Eligibility Requirements: Applicant must be American Indian/Alaska Native or Black (non-Hispanic); enrolled or expecting to enroll full- or part-time at a four-year institution or university and resident of New Jersey. Applicant must have 2.5 GPA or higher. Available to U.S. citizens.

Application Requirements: Application, essay, financial need analysis, photo, references, transcript, FAFSA, Student Aid Report (SAR). *Deadline:* December 10.

Contact: Director, Program Services
United Negro College Fund
8260 Willow Oaks Corporate Drive
PO Box 10444
Fairfax, VA 22031-8044
Phone: 800-331-2244
E-mail: rebecca.bennett@uncf.org

ORACLE COMMUNITY IMPACT SCHOLARSHIP

Award for deserving but financially challenged African American students from East Palo Alto, Bay View, Hunter's Point, Richmond, Marin City, and Oakland, California, who are attending UNCF colleges and universities. Minimum GPA of 2.5 required. Apply online at web site http://www.uncf.org.

Award: Grant for use in freshman, sophomore, junior, or senior years; not renewable. *Amount:* $5000–$10,000.

Eligibility Requirements: Applicant must be Black (non-Hispanic); enrolled or expecting to enroll full-time at a four-year institution or university and resident of California. Applicant must have 2.5 GPA or higher. Available to U.S. citizens.

Application Requirements: Application, transcript. *Deadline:* April 5.

Contact: Director, Program Services
United Negro College Fund
8260 Willow Oaks Corporate Drive
PO Box 10444
Fairfax, VA 22031-8044
Phone: 800-331-2244
E-mail: rebecca.bennett@uncf.org

PENNSYLVANIA STATE EMPLOYEES SCHOLARSHIP (SECA)

Scholarships for UNCF students from Pennsylvania. Funds may be used for tuition, room and board, books, or to repay federal student loans. Minimum 2.5 GPA required. Prospective applicants should complete the Student Profile found at web site http://www.uncf.org.

Award: Scholarship for use in freshman, sophomore, junior, or senior years; not renewable. *Amount:* up to $4000.

Eligibility Requirements: Applicant must be Black (non-Hispanic); enrolled or expecting to enroll full-time at a four-year institution or university and resident of Pennsylvania. Applicant must have 2.5 GPA or higher. Available to U.S. citizens.

Application Requirements: Application, financial need analysis, student profile. *Deadline:* July 14.

Contact: Director, Program Services
United Negro College Fund
8260 Willow Oaks Corporate Drive
PO Box 10444
Fairfax, VA 22031-8044
Phone: 800-331-2244
E-mail: rebecca.bennett@uncf.org

ROBERT DOLE SCHOLARSHIP FOR DISABLED STUDENTS
• *See page 615*

RONALD MCDONALD'S CHICAGOLAND AND NORTHWEST INDIANA SCHOLARSHIP

Scholarships awarded to students attending a UNCF member college or university who are residents of the following counties in Illinois and Indiana: Cook, Lake, Will, DuPage, Kankakee, Kendall, Jasper, Kane, La Salle, Livingston, McHenry, Iroquois, Boone, Bureau, Decal, Ford, and Grundy in IL; Lake, La Porte, and Porter in Indiana. Scholarship value is $3000. Must maintain minimum GPA of 2.5 and is applicable for four years of study.

Award: Scholarship for use in freshman, sophomore, junior, or senior years; renewable. *Number:* varies. *Amount:* $3000.

Eligibility Requirements: Applicant must be Black (non-Hispanic); enrolled or expecting to enroll full-time at a four-year institution or university and resident of Illinois or Indiana. Applicant must have 2.5 GPA or higher. Available to U.S. citizens.

Application Requirements: Application, financial need analysis. *Deadline:* continuous.

Contact: Director, Program Services
United Negro College Fund
8260 Willow Oaks Corporate Drive
PO Box 10444
Fairfax, VA 22031-8044
Phone: 800-331-2244
E-mail: rebecca.bennett@uncf.org

RONALD MCDONALD'S HOUSE CHARITIES SCHOLARSHIP-OHIO

Scholarships available for African American students residing in Ohio. Must attend a UNCF member college or university and have a minimum 2.5 GPA. Information on web site at http://www.uncf.org.

Award: Scholarship for use in freshman, sophomore, junior, or senior years; renewable. *Number:* varies. *Amount:* varies.

Eligibility Requirements: Applicant must be Black (non-Hispanic); enrolled or expecting to enroll full- or part-time at a two-year or four-year institution or university and resident of Ohio. Applicant must have 2.5 GPA or higher. Available to U.S. citizens.

Application Requirements: Application, financial need analysis, FAFSA, Student Aid Report (SAR).

Contact: Director, Program Services
ⁱUnited Negro College Fund
8260 Willow Oaks Corporate Drive
PO Box 10444
Fairfax, VA 22031-8044
Phone: 800-331-2244
E-mail: rebecca.bennett@uncf.org

RYAN HOWARD FAMILY FOUNDATION SCHOLARSHIP-ST. LOUIS/PHILADELPHIA
• *See page 598*

ST. PETERSBURG GOLF CLASSIC SCHOLARSHIP

Scholarship available for African American undergraduate students from Florida who are enrolled at a UNCF member colleges or universities, and have a minimum 2.5 GPA. Visit web site for more information http://www.uncf.org.

Award: Scholarship for use in freshman, sophomore, junior, or senior years; renewable. *Amount:* up to $6000.

Eligibility Requirements: Applicant must be Black (non-Hispanic); enrolled or expecting to enroll full- or part-time at a four-year institution or university and resident of Florida. Applicant must have 2.5 GPA or higher. Available to U.S. citizens.

Application Requirements: Application, financial need analysis, FAFSA, Student Aid Report (SAR). *Deadline:* May 31.

Contact: Director, Program Services
United Negro College Fund
8260 Willow Oaks Corporate Drive
PO Box 10444
Fairfax, VA 22031-8044
Phone: 800-331-2244
E-mail: rebecca.bennett@uncf.org

SHELL/EQUILON UNCF CLEVELAND SCHOLARSHIP FUND

Scholarship available to African American undergraduate students who are residents of Cuyahoga County, Ohio, and attending a UNCF member college or university. Award is renewable for three years if eligibility is maintained. Must have minimum 2.5 GPA. For additional information and general scholarship application, visit web site http://www.uncf.org.

Award: Scholarship for use in freshman, sophomore, junior, or senior years; renewable. *Number:* varies. *Amount:* $3000.

Eligibility Requirements: Applicant must be Black (non-Hispanic); enrolled or expecting to enroll full- or part-time at a four-year institution or university and resident of Ohio. Applicant must have 2.5 GPA or higher. Available to U.S. citizens.

Application Requirements: Application, financial need analysis, FAFSA, Student Aid Report (SAR).

Contact: Director, Program Services
United Negro College Fund
8260 Willow Oaks Corporate Drive
PO Box 10444
Fairfax, VA 22031-8044
Phone: 800-331-2244
E-mail: rebecca.bennett@uncf.org

SIDNEY STONEMAN SCHOLARSHIP

Scholarship for students who are residents of Florida and attending UNCF member colleges and universities. Minimum GPA of 2.5. For more information see Website: http://www.uncf.org/forstudents/scholarship.asp.

Award: Scholarship for use in freshman year. *Amount:* $3500.

Eligibility Requirements: Applicant must be Black (non-Hispanic); enrolled or expecting to enroll at a four-year institution or university and resident of Florida. Applicant must have 2.5 GPA or higher.

Contact: Director, Program Services
United Negro College Fund
8260 Willow Oaks Corporate Drive
PO Box 10444
Fairfax, VA 22031-8044
Phone: 800-331-2244
E-mail: rebecca.bennett@uncf.org

SIRAGUSA FOUNDATION SCHOLARSHIP

Scholarships available to students attending a UNCF member college or university. Minimum 2.5 GPA required. Apply online at web site http://www.uncf.org.

Award: Scholarship for use in freshman, sophomore, junior, or senior years; not renewable. *Number:* 1. *Amount:* $2000.

Eligibility Requirements: Applicant must be Black (non-Hispanic) and enrolled or expecting to enroll full-time at a four-year institution or university. Applicant must have 2.5 GPA or higher. Available to U.S. and non-U.S. citizens.

Application Requirements: Application, financial need analysis. *Deadline:* continuous.

Contact: Director, Program Services
United Negro College Fund
8260 Willow Oaks Corporate Drive
PO Box 10444
Fairfax, VA 22031-8044
Phone: 800-331-2244
E-mail: rebecca.bennett@uncf.org

TJX FOUNDATION SCHOLARSHIP

Award available to African American students who are Massachusetts residents who live near TJ Maxx stores. Must be enrolled at a UNCF member college or university and have 2.5 GPA. Please visit web site for more information http://www.uncf.org.

Award: Scholarship for use in freshman, sophomore, junior, or senior years; renewable. *Number:* varies. *Amount:* $1000.

Eligibility Requirements: Applicant must be Black (non-Hispanic); enrolled or expecting to enroll full- or part-time at a four-year institution or university and resident of Massachusetts. Applicant must have 2.5 GPA or higher. Available to U.S. citizens.

Application Requirements: Application, financial need analysis, FAFSA, Student Aid Report (SAR).

Contact: Director, Program Services
United Negro College Fund
8260 Willow Oaks Corporate Drive
PO Box 10444
Fairfax, VA 22031-8044
Phone: 800-331-2244
E-mail: rebecca.bennett@uncf.org

UNCF/FOOT LOCKER FOUNDATION, INC. SCHOLARSHIP

Scholarship for African American high school seniors or students attending or planning to attend a UNCF member college or university. Minimum GPA of 2.5 required. Scholarship is renewable if student continues to be eligible. For additional information and general scholarship application, go to web site http://www.uncf.org.

Award: Scholarship for use in freshman, sophomore, junior, or senior years; renewable. *Amount:* up to $5000.

Eligibility Requirements: Applicant must be Black (non-Hispanic) and enrolled or expecting to enroll full-time at a four-year institution or university. Applicant must have 2.5 GPA or higher. Available to U.S. citizens.

Application Requirements: Application, financial need analysis, transcript. *Deadline:* April 15.

Contact: Director, Program Services
United Negro College Fund
8260 Willow Oaks Corporate Drive
PO Box 10444
Fairfax, VA 22031-8044
Phone: 800-331-2244
E-mail: rebecca.bennett@uncf.org

UNION BANK OF CALIFORNIA

Scholarship available to all California students who attend a UNCF member college or university. Minimum 2.5 GPA required. Prospective applicants should complete the Student Profile found at web site http://www.uncf.org.

Award: Scholarship for use in freshman, sophomore, junior, or senior years; not renewable. *Number:* 1. *Amount:* varies.

Eligibility Requirements: Applicant must be Black (non-Hispanic); enrolled or expecting to enroll full- or part-time at a four-year institution or university and resident of California. Applicant must have 2.5 GPA or higher. Available to U.S. citizens.

Application Requirements: Application, financial need analysis. *Deadline:* continuous.

Contact: Director, Program Services
United Negro College Fund
8260 Willow Oaks Corporate Drive
PO Box 10444
Fairfax, VA 22031-8044
Phone: 800-331-2244
E-mail: rebecca.bennett@uncf.org

UNITED PARCEL SERVICE FOUNDATION SCHOLARSHIP

Award available to provide African American undergraduate students with financial support for tuition and other education costs. Applicants must be enrolled at UNCF member colleges and universities and have a minimum 2.5 GPA. Amount of scholarship varies based on need. Please visit web site for more information and general scholarship application http://www.uncf.org.

Award: Scholarship for use in freshman, sophomore, junior, or senior years; renewable. *Number:* varies. *Amount:* varies.

Eligibility Requirements: Applicant must be Black (non-Hispanic) and enrolled or expecting to enroll full-time at a four-year institution or university. Applicant must have 2.5 GPA or higher. Available to U.S. citizens.

Application Requirements: Application, financial need analysis, FAFSA, Student Aid Report (SAR).

Contact: Director, Program Services
United Negro College Fund
8260 Willow Oaks Corporate Drive
PO Box 10444
Fairfax, VA 22031-8044
Phone: 800-331-2244
E-mail: rebecca.bennett@uncf.org

UNITED WAY OF NEW ORLEANS EMERGENCY ASSISTANCE FUND

Award providing emergency assistance for African American students at Dillard University and Xavier University in Louisiana. Assistance for demonstrated financial need due to family emergency, job loss, low income, death of income provider. For both full-time and part-time students with minimum 2.5 GPA. See web site for more information and application http://www.uncf.org.

Award: Scholarship for use in freshman, sophomore, junior, or senior years; renewable. *Number:* varies. *Amount:* up to $2500.

Eligibility Requirements: Applicant must be Black (non-Hispanic); enrolled or expecting to enroll full- or part-time at a four-year institution or university; resident of Louisiana and studying in Louisiana. Applicant must have 2.5 GPA or higher. Available to U.S. citizens.

Application Requirements: Application, financial need analysis, FAFSA, Student Aid Report (SAR).

Contact: Director, Program Services
United Negro College Fund
8260 Willow Oaks Corporate Drive
PO Box 10444
Fairfax, VA 22031-8044
Phone: 800-331-2244
E-mail: rebecca.bennett@uncf.org

UNITED WAY OF WESTCHESTER & PUTNAM INC./ UNCF EMERGENCY ASSISTANCE FUND

Award providing emergency assistance for African American and Hispanic American students from the Westchester/Putnam, NY area. A 2.0 GPA is required if attending a UNCF school, or 2.0 if attending Mercy College or Westchester Community College. Students are only eligible to receive emergency assistance for two consecutive semesters. Visit web site for more information http://www.uncf.org.

Award: Scholarship for use in freshman, sophomore, junior, or senior years; not renewable. *Number:* varies. *Amount:* up to $5000.

Eligibility Requirements: Applicant must be Black (non-Hispanic) or Hispanic; enrolled or expecting to enroll full- or part-time at a four-year institution or university and resident of New York. Available to U.S. citizens.

Application Requirements: Application, financial need analysis, FAFSA, Student Aid Report (SAR).

Contact: Director, Program Services
United Negro College Fund
8260 Willow Oaks Corporate Drive
PO Box 10444
Fairfax, VA 22031-8044
Phone: 800-331-2244
E-mail: rebecca.bennett@uncf.org

UNITRIN CAREER AGENCY COMPANIES SCHOLARSHIP

Scholarship for students attending or planning to attend HBCU member colleges and universities and are residents of selected states. The basic qualification is that a parent or legal guardian of the student must be a current Reliable, United, Union National, or Mutual Savings policyholder or one of their affiliated fire companies. Minimum 2.5 GPA required. For more information see Website: http://www.uncf.org/forstudents/scholarship.asp.

Award: Scholarship for use in freshman year. *Amount:* $5000.

Eligibility Requirements: Applicant must be Black (non-Hispanic) and enrolled or expecting to enroll at a four-year institution or university. Applicant must have 2.5 GPA or higher.

Contact: Director, Program Services
United Negro College Fund
8260 Willow Oaks Corporate Drive
PO Box 10444
Fairfax, VA 22031-8044
Phone: 800-331-2244
E-mail: rebecca.bennett@uncf.org

V103/WAOK UNCF EMERGENCY ASSISTANCE SCHOLARSHIP FUND

Scholarship is open to graduating seniors in their final semester at Clark Atlanta University, Morehouse College, Spelman College or Interdenominational Theological Center. Must be enrolled full-time with at least 2.5 GPA. Apply online at web site http://www.uncf.org.

Award: Scholarship for use in senior year; not renewable. *Number:* varies. *Amount:* varies.

Eligibility Requirements: Applicant must be Black (non-Hispanic); enrolled or expecting to enroll full-time at a four-year institution or university and studying in Georgia. Applicant must have 2.5 GPA or higher. Available to U.S. citizens.

Application Requirements: Application, financial need analysis. *Deadline:* April 8.

Contact: Director, Program Services
United Negro College Fund
8260 Willow Oaks Corporate Drive
PO Box 10444
Fairfax, VA 22031-8044
Phone: 800-331-2244
E-mail: rebecca.bennett@uncf.org

VIAD/DIAL CORPORATION SCHOLARSHIP

Scholarship for students who are residents of Arizona and attending UNCF member colleges and universities. For more information see Website: http://www.uncf.org/forstudents/scholarship.asp.

Award: Scholarship for use in freshman year.

Eligibility Requirements: Applicant must be Black (non-Hispanic); enrolled or expecting to enroll at a four-year institution or university and resident of Arizona.

Contact: Director, Program Services
United Negro College Fund
8260 Willow Oaks Corporate Drive
PO Box 10444
Fairfax, VA 22031-8044
Phone: 800-331-2244
E-mail: rebecca.bennett@uncf.org

WHIRLPOOL FOUNDATION SCHOLARSHIP

Renewable award for African American students participating in Whirlpool's INROADS program in LaPorte, IN; Benton Harbor, MI; and LaVerne, TN. Must have 3.0 GPA and be enrolled in a UNCF member college or university. For additional information see web site http://www.uncf.org.

Award: Scholarship for use in freshman, sophomore, junior, or senior years; renewable. *Number:* varies. *Amount:* $2500.

Eligibility Requirements: Applicant must be Black (non-Hispanic); enrolled or expecting to enroll full-time at a four-year institution or university and resident of Indiana, Michigan, or Tennessee. Applicant must have 3.0 GPA or higher. Available to U.S. citizens.

Application Requirements: Application, financial need analysis, FAFSA, Student Aid Report (SAR).

Contact: Director, Program Services
United Negro College Fund
8260 Willow Oaks Corporate Drive
PO Box 10444
Fairfax, VA 22031-8044
Phone: 800-331-2244
E-mail: rebecca.bennett@uncf.org

WISCONSIN STUDENT AID

Award for African American Wisconsin residents who are enrolled full- or part-time in a UNCF member college or university. Must have 2.5 GPA. Please visit web site for more information http://www.uncf.org.

Award: Scholarship for use in freshman, sophomore, junior, or senior years; renewable. *Number:* varies. *Amount:* up to $2500.

Eligibility Requirements: Applicant must be Black (non-Hispanic); enrolled or expecting to enroll full- or part-time at a four-year institution or university and resident of Wisconsin. Applicant must have 2.5 GPA or higher. Available to U.S. citizens.

Application Requirements: Application, financial need analysis, FAFSA, Student Aid Report (SAR).

Contact: Director, Program Services
United Negro College Fund
8260 Willow Oaks Corporate Drive
PO Box 10444
Fairfax, VA 22031-8044
Phone: 800-331-2244
E-mail: rebecca.bennett@uncf.org

YOUTH EMPOWERMENT SCHOLARSHIP

This scholarship is open to freshmen attending UNCF schools, Lincoln, Cheyney, or Temple Universities, and residing in Bucks, Montgomery, Chester, Philadelphia or Delaware County in Pennsylvania; Gloucester, Camden, Burlington or Mercer County in New Jersey; or New Castle County in Delaware. Student must come from a single-parent household and have a minimum 3.0 GPA. For application and information, visit http://www.uncf.org.

Award: Scholarship for use in freshman year; not renewable. *Number:* 1. *Amount:* $4000.

Eligibility Requirements: Applicant must be Black (non-Hispanic); enrolled or expecting to enroll full- or part-time at a four-year institution or university and resident of Delaware, New Jersey, or Pennsylvania. Applicant must have 3.0 GPA or higher. Available to U.S. citizens.

Application Requirements: Application, financial need analysis. *Deadline:* October 30.

Contact: Director, Program Services
United Negro College Fund
8260 Willow Oaks Corporate Drive
PO Box 10444
Fairfax, VA 22031-8044
Phone: 800-331-2244
E-mail: rebecca.bennett@uncf.org

YOUTH GALA SCHOLARSHIP

Scholarship for incoming freshmen who attended the 2011 UNCF Youth Gala in Houston. Students must plan to enrolled at a four year college/university and be resident of the greater Houston, TX community. Student will be required to verify their attendance and residency. Minimum 2.5 GPA required.

Award: Scholarship for use in freshman year; not renewable. *Amount:* up to $2600.

Eligibility Requirements: Applicant must be Black (non-Hispanic); high school student; planning to enroll or expecting to enroll full-time at a four-year institution or university and resident of Texas. Applicant must have 2.5 GPA or higher.

Application Requirements: *Deadline:* May 30.

Contact: Director, Program Services
United Negro College Fund
8260 Willow Oaks Corporate Drive
PO Box 10444
Fairfax, VA 22031-8044
Phone: 800-331-2244
E-mail: rebecca.bennett@uncf.org

UNITED SOUTH AND EASTERN TRIBES INC.

http://www.usetinc.org/

UNITED SOUTH AND EASTERN TRIBES SCHOLARSHIP FUND

One-time scholarship for Native American students who are members of United South and Eastern Tribes, enrolled or accepted in a postsecondary educational institution.

Award: Scholarship for use in freshman, sophomore, junior, or senior years; not renewable. *Number:* 4–8. *Amount:* $500.

Eligibility Requirements: Applicant must be Indian citizen; American Indian/Alaska Native and enrolled or expecting to enroll full- or part-time at a four-year institution or university.

Application Requirements: Application, essay, financial need analysis, transcript, proof of tribal enrollment. *Deadline:* April 30.

Contact: Theresa Embry, Executive Assistant to Director
United South and Eastern Tribes Inc.
711 Stewarts Ferry Pike, Suite 100
Nashville, TN 37214-2634
Phone: 615-872-7900
Fax: 615-872-7417

UNITED STATES HISPANIC LEADERSHIP INSTITUTE

http://www.ushli.org/

DR. JUAN ANDRADE, JR. SCHOLARSHIP

Scholarship for young Hispanic leaders. Applicants must be enrolled or accepted for enrollment as a full-time student in a four-year institution in the United States or U.S. territories, and demonstrate a verifiable need for financial support. At least one parent must be of Hispanic ancestry.

Award: Scholarship for use in freshman, sophomore, junior, or senior years; not renewable. *Number:* 30. *Amount:* $500–$1000.

Eligibility Requirements: Applicant must be Hispanic and enrolled or expecting to enroll full-time at a two-year or four-year institution or university. Available to U.S. citizens.

Application Requirements: Application, driver's license, essay, photo, resume, references, transcript. *Deadline:* January 11.

Contact: Isabel Reyes, Scholarship Coordinator
United States Hispanic Leadership Institute
431 South Dearborn Street, Suite 1203
Chicago, IL 60605
Phone: 312-427-8683
Fax: 312-427-5183
E-mail: ireyes@ushli.org

URBAN LEAGUE OF RHODE ISLAND INC.

http://www.ulri.org/

URBAN LEAGUE OF RHODE ISLAND SCHOLARSHIP

Scholarship offered to minority students who are Rhode Island residents seeking postsecondary education. Priority is given to recent high school graduates.

Award: Scholarship for use in freshman, sophomore, junior, or senior years; not renewable. *Number:* varies. *Amount:* varies.

Eligibility Requirements: Applicant must be American Indian/Alaska Native, Asian/Pacific Islander, Black (non-Hispanic), or Hispanic; enrolled or expecting to enroll full-time at a two-year or four-year or technical institution or university and resident of Rhode Island. Available to U.S. citizens.

Application Requirements: Application, financial need analysis, interview, references, transcript. *Deadline:* April 30.

Contact: Marcia Ranglin-Vassell, Associate Director
Urban League of Rhode Island Inc.
246 Prairie Avenue
Providence, RI 02905
Phone: 401-351-5000
Fax: 401-454-1946
E-mail: education@ulri.org

VIKKI CARR SCHOLARSHIP FOUNDATION

http://www.vikkicarrfoundation.com/

VIKKI CARR SCHOLARSHIPS

Scholarship awarded for high school senior entering the first year of college. Applicant must be of Mexican-American descent and Texas resident.

Award: Scholarship for use in freshman year; not renewable. *Number:* varies. *Amount:* varies.

Eligibility Requirements: Applicant must be Hispanic; high school student; planning to enroll or expecting to enroll full- or part-time at a two-year or four-year institution and resident of Texas. Available to U.S. citizens.

Application Requirements: Application, essay, financial need analysis, photo, test scores, transcript. *Deadline:* March 1.

Contact: Scholarship Committee
Vikki Carr Scholarship Foundation
PO Box 780968
San Antonio, TX 78278
E-mail: vicarent@aol.com

WASHINGTON HIGHER EDUCATION COORDINATING BOARD

http://www.hecb.wa.gov/

AMERICAN INDIAN ENDOWED SCHOLARSHIP

Awarded to financially needy undergraduate and graduate students with close social and cultural ties with a Native-American community. Must be Washington resident and enrolled full-time at Washington public or private school. Must be committed to use education to return service to the state's American Indian community.

Award: Scholarship for use in freshman, sophomore, junior, senior, graduate, or postgraduate years; not renewable. *Number:* 11–20. *Amount:* $500–$2000.

Eligibility Requirements: Applicant must be American Indian/Alaska Native; enrolled or expecting to enroll full-time at a two-year or four-year or technical institution or university; resident of Washington and studying in Washington. Available to U.S. citizens.

Application Requirements: Application, essay, references, transcript. *Deadline:* February 1.

Contact: Ann Voyles, Program Manager
Washington Higher Education Coordinating Board
917 Lakeridge Way, PO Box 43430
Olympia, WA 98504-3430
Phone: 360-753-7843
Fax: 360-704-6243
E-mail: annv@hecb.wa.gov

WHITE EARTH TRIBAL COUNCIL

http://www.whiteearth.com/

WHITE EARTH SCHOLARSHIP PROGRAM

Renewable scholarship for students who are enrolled in postsecondary institutions. Must have a GPA of 2.5. Must be U.S. citizen.

Award: Scholarship for use in freshman, sophomore, junior, senior, graduate, or postgraduate years; renewable. *Number:* 200. *Amount:* $3000.

Eligibility Requirements: Applicant must be American Indian/Alaska Native and enrolled or expecting to enroll full- or part-time at a two-year or four-year or technical institution or university. Applicant must have 2.5 GPA or higher. Available to U.S. citizens.

Application Requirements: Application, financial need analysis, transcript. *Deadline:* May 31.

Contact: Leslie Nessman, Scholarship Manager
White Earth Tribal Council
PO Box 418
White Earth, MN 56591-0418
Phone: 218-983-3285
Fax: 218-983-4299

WILLIAM E. DOCTER EDUCATIONAL FUND/ST. MARY ARMENIAN CHURCH

http://www.wedfund.org/

WILLIAM ERVANT DOCTER EDUCATIONAL FUND

Grant up to $2000 available to worthy students regardless of age, gender, or level of education or training. Funds given to American citizens of Armenian ancestry to pursue studies and training in the United States or Canada.

Award: Grant for use in freshman, sophomore, junior, senior, graduate, or postgraduate years; not renewable. *Number:* 20. *Amount:* $1000–$2000.

Eligibility Requirements: Applicant must be of Armenian heritage and enrolled or expecting to enroll full- or part-time at a two-year or four-year or technical institution or university. Available to U.S. citizens.

Application Requirements: Application, essay, financial need analysis, test scores, transcript, proof of U.S. citizenship. *Deadline:* June 30.

Contact: Edward Alexander, Scholarship Committee Chairman
William E. Docter Educational Fund/St. Mary Armenian Church
PO Box 39224
Washington, DC 20016
Fax: 202-364-1441
E-mail: wedfund@aol.com

WISCONSIN HIGHER EDUCATIONAL AID BOARD

http://www.heab.wi.gov/

MINORITY UNDERGRADUATE RETENTION GRANT-WISCONSIN

The grant provides financial assistance to African-American, Native-American, Hispanic, and former citizens of Laos, Vietnam, and Cambodia, for study in Wisconsin. Must be Wisconsin resident, enrolled at least half-time in Wisconsin Technical College System schools, non-profit independent colleges and universities, and tribal colleges. Refer to web site for further details http://www.heab.state.wi.us.

Award: Grant for use in sophomore, junior, or senior years; not renewable. *Number:* varies. *Amount:* $250–$2500.

Eligibility Requirements: Applicant must be American Indian/Alaska Native, Asian/Pacific Islander, Black (non-Hispanic), or Hispanic; enrolled or expecting to enroll full- or part-time at a two-year or four-year or technical institution or university; resident of Wisconsin and studying in Wisconsin. Available to U.S. and non-U.S. citizens.

Application Requirements: Application, financial need analysis. *Deadline:* continuous.

Contact: Mary Lou Kuzdas, Program Coordinator
Wisconsin Higher Educational Aid Board
PO Box 7885
Madison, WI 53707-7885
Phone: 608-267-2212
Fax: 608-267-2808
E-mail: mary.kuzdas@wi.gov

WISCONSIN NATIVE AMERICAN/INDIAN STUDENT ASSISTANCE GRANT

Grants for Wisconsin residents who are at least one-quarter American Indian. Must be attending a college or university within the state. Refer to web site for further details http://www.heab.state.wi.us.

Award: Grant for use in freshman, sophomore, junior, or senior years; not renewable. *Number:* varies. *Amount:* $250–$1100.

Eligibility Requirements: Applicant must be American Indian/Alaska Native; enrolled or expecting to enroll full- or part-time at a two-year or four-year or technical institution or university; resident of Wisconsin and studying in Wisconsin. Available to U.S. citizens.

Application Requirements: Application, financial need analysis. *Deadline:* continuous.

Contact: Sandra Thomas, Program Coordinator
Wisconsin Higher Educational Aid Board
PO Box 7885
Madison, WI 53707-7885
Phone: 608-266-0888
Fax: 608-267-2808
E-mail: sandy.thomas@wi.gov

WOMEN OF THE EVANGELICAL LUTHERAN CHURCH IN AMERICA

http://www.womenoftheelca.org/

AMELIA KEMP SCHOLARSHIP

Scholarship for ELCA women who are of an ethnic minority in undergraduate, graduate, professional, or vocational courses of study. Must be at least 21 years old and hold membership in the ELCA. Must have experienced an interruption of two or more years in education since the completion of high school.

Award: Scholarship for use in freshman, sophomore, junior, senior, or graduate years; not renewable. *Number:* 1. *Amount:* up to $1000.

Eligibility Requirements: Applicant must be Lutheran; American Indian/Alaska Native, Asian/Pacific Islander, Black (non-Hispanic), or Hispanic; age 21 and over; enrolled or expecting to enroll full- or part-time at a two-year or four-year or technical institution or university and female. Available to U.S. citizens.

Application Requirements: Application, resume, references, transcript. *Deadline:* February 15.

Contact: Emily Hansen, Scholarship Committee
Women of the Evangelical Lutheran Church in America
8765 West Higgins Road
Chicago, IL 60631-4189
Phone: 800-638-3522 Ext. 2736
Fax: 773-380-2419
E-mail: womenelca@elca.org

YMCA BLACK ACHIEVERS SCHOLARSHIP

http://www.ymcaofcentralky.org/

YMCA BLACK ACHIEVERS SCHOLARSHIP

Need-based scholarships awarded to deserving African-American students. Dollar value and number of available awards varies, and application deadline varies.

Award: Scholarship for use in freshman, sophomore, junior, or senior years; not renewable. *Number:* varies. *Amount:* varies.

Eligibility Requirements: Applicant must be Black (non-Hispanic) and enrolled or expecting to enroll full- or part-time at a two-year or four-year or technical institution or university. Available to U.S. citizens.

Application Requirements: Application, financial need analysis. *Deadline:* varies.

Contact: Jill Wilson, Director, Black Achievers
YMCA Black Achievers Scholarship
Central Kentucky YMCA, 644 Georgetown Street
Lexington, KY 40508
Phone: 859-226-0393 Ext. 15
Fax: 859-226-0385
E-mail: jwilson@ymcaofcentralky.org

RELIGIOUS AFFILIATION

AMERICAN BAPTIST FINANCIAL AID PROGRAM

http://www.abc-usa.org/

AMERICAN BAPTIST FINANCIAL AID PROGRAM NATIVE AMERICAN GRANTS
• *See page 653*

AMERICAN BAPTIST SCHOLARSHIPS

One-time award for undergraduates who are members of an American Baptist Church. Must be attending an accredited college or university in the United States or Puerto Rico. If attending an ABC-related school, the scholarship amount is $2000 for the year. If not ABC-related, the amount is $1000. Minimum GPA of 2.75 required.

Award: Scholarship for use in freshman, sophomore, junior, or senior years; not renewable. *Number:* 1–5. *Amount:* $1000–$2000.

Eligibility Requirements: Applicant must be Baptist and enrolled or expecting to enroll full-time at a four-year institution or university. Available to U.S. citizens.

Application Requirements: Application, financial need analysis, references. *Deadline:* May 31.

Contact: Lynne Eckman, Director of Financial Aid
American Baptist Financial Aid Program
PO Box 851
Valley Forge, PA 19482-0851
Phone: 610-768-2067
Fax: 610-768-2470
E-mail: lynne.eckman@abc-usa.org

AMERICAN SEPHARDI FOUNDATION

http://www.americansephardifederation.org/

BROOME AND ALLEN BOYS CAMP AND SCHOLARSHIP FUND

The Broome and Allen Scholarship is awarded to students of Sephardic origin or those working in Sephardic studies. Both graduate and undergraduate degree candidates as well as those doing research projects will be considered. It is awarded for one year and must be renewed for successive years. Enclose copy of tax returns with application.

Award: Scholarship for use in freshman, sophomore, junior, senior, graduate, or postgraduate years; not renewable. *Number:* 20–60. *Amount:* $500–$2000.

Eligibility Requirements: Applicant must be Jewish and enrolled or expecting to enroll full- or part-time at a two-year or four-year or technical institution or university. Available to U.S. and non-U.S. citizens.

Application Requirements: Application, essay, financial need analysis, references, transcript, copy of tax returns. *Deadline:* May 15.

Contact: Ms. Ellen Cohen, Membership and Outreach Coordinator
American Sephardi Foundation
15 West 16th Street
New York, NY 10011
Phone: 212-294-8350 Ext. 4
Fax: 212-294-8348
E-mail: ecohen@asf.cjh.org

BNY MELLON, N.A.

http://www.bnymellon.com/

HENRY FRANCIS BARROWS SCHOLARSHIP

Award for Protestant males only. Must be a resident of Massachusetts and applying to a non-Catholic U.S. institution of higher learning. Eligible applicant must be recommended by educational institution. Not for graduate study programs.

Award: Scholarship for use in freshman, sophomore, junior, or senior years; not renewable. *Number:* varies. *Amount:* up to $2000.

Eligibility Requirements: Applicant must be Protestant; enrolled or expecting to enroll full-time at a two-year or four-year or technical institution or university; male and resident of Massachusetts. Available to U.S. citizens.

Application Requirements: Application, essay, transcript. *Deadline:* April 15.

Contact: June Kfoury McNeil, Vice President
BNY Mellon, N.A.
201 Washington Street, 024-0092
Boston, MA 02108
Phone: 617-722-3891

CENTRAL SCHOLARSHIP BUREAU

http://www.centralsb.org/

LESSANS FAMILY SCHOLARSHIP
• *See page 657*

EASTERN ORTHODOX COMMITTEE ON SCOUTING

http://www.eocs.org/

EASTERN ORTHODOX COMMITTEE ON SCOUTING SCHOLARSHIPS
• *See page 540*

FADEL EDUCATIONAL FOUNDATION, INC.

http://www.fadelfoundation.org/

ANNUAL AWARD PROGRAM

Grants of $800 to $3000 awarded on the basis of merit, financial need, and the potential of an applicant to positively impact Muslims' lives in the United States.

Award: Grant for use in freshman, sophomore, junior, senior, or graduate years; renewable. *Number:* 20–45. *Amount:* $800–$3000.

Eligibility Requirements: Applicant must be Muslim faith and enrolled or expecting to enroll full- or part-time at a two-year or four-year or technical institution or university. Available to U.S. citizens.

Application Requirements: Application, essay, financial need analysis, references, test scores, transcript. *Deadline:* May 28.

Contact: Mr. Ayman Fadel, Secretary
Fadel Educational Foundation, Inc.
PO Box 212135
Augusta, GA 30917-2135
Phone: 484-694-1783
E-mail: secretary@fadelfoundation.org

FOUNDATION FOR CHRISTIAN COLLEGE LEADERS

http://www.collegechristianleader.com/

FOUNDATION FOR COLLEGE CHRISTIAN LEADERS SCHOLARSHIP

Applicant must be accepted to or currently enrolled in an undergraduate degree program. Candidate must demonstrate Christian leadership. Combined income of parents and student must be less than $60,000. Minimum 3.0 GPA required.

Award: Scholarship for use in freshman, sophomore, junior, senior, or graduate years; not renewable. *Number:* varies. *Amount:* varies.

Eligibility Requirements: Applicant must be Christian; enrolled or expecting to enroll full- or part-time at a four-year institution or university and must have an interest in leadership. Applicant must have 3.0 GPA or higher. Available to U.S. citizens.

Application Requirements: Application, financial need analysis, interview, references, leadership assessment form, cover sheet. *Deadline:* May 7.

Contact: Scholarship Committee
Foundation for Christian College Leaders
2658 Del Mar Heights Road
PO Box 266
Del Mar, CA 92014
Phone: 858-481-0848
Fax: 858-481-0848
E-mail: lmhays@aol.com

GENERAL BOARD OF GLOBAL MINISTRIES

http://www.gbgm-umc.org/

NATIONAL LEADERSHIP DEVELOPMENT GRANT
• *See page 663*

GENERAL BOARD OF HIGHER EDUCATION AND MINISTRY

http://www.gbhem.org/

BISHOP JOSEPH B. BETHEA SCHOLARSHIP
• *See page 663*

E. CRAIG BRANDENBURG GRADUATE AWARD

Scholarship for students 35 years of age or older, desiring to continue their education or to go into a second career. Must be enrolled full time at an accredited institution, and be active, full-time members of the United Methodist Church for at least one year.

Award: Scholarship for use in freshman, sophomore, junior, senior, or graduate years; not renewable. *Number:* varies. *Amount:* varies.

Eligibility Requirements: Applicant must be Methodist; age 35 and over and enrolled or expecting to enroll full-time at a four-year institution or university. Available to U.S. citizens.

Application Requirements: Application, essay, resume, references, transcript. *Deadline:* March 1.

Contact: Scholarship Committee
General Board of Higher Education and Ministry
The United Methodist Church, 1001 19th Avenue South
PO Box 340007
Nashville, TN 37202
Phone: 615-340-7344
E-mail: umscholar@gbhem.org

ETHNIC MINORITY SCHOLARSHIP
• *See page 663*

HANA SCHOLARSHIP
• *See page 663*

HELEN AND ALLEN BROWN SCHOLARSHIP

Scholarship for outstanding high school graduates and undergraduate college students who are members of the Nashville District of the Tennessee Annual Conference of UMC or members of the New Orleans District of the Louisiana Annual Conference of UMC. Must have been full and active members of The United Methodist Church for at least three years and maintain a GPA of 3.0.

Award: Scholarship for use in freshman, sophomore, junior, or senior years; not renewable. *Number:* varies. *Amount:* varies.

Eligibility Requirements: Applicant must be Methodist and enrolled or expecting to enroll full-time at a four-year institution or university. Applicant must have 3.0 GPA or higher. Available to U.S. citizens.

Application Requirements: Application, essay, references, transcript. *Deadline:* March 1.

Contact: Scholarship Committee
General Board of Higher Education and Ministry
The United Methodist Church, 1001 19th Avenue South
PO Box 340007
Nashville, TN 37202
Phone: 615-340-7344
E-mail: umscholar@gbhem.org

THE REV. DR. KAREN LAYMAN GIFT OF HOPE: 21ST CENTURY SCHOLARS PROGRAM

$1000 scholarship to United Methodist undergraduate students who are full-time, active members of UMC for at least three years prior to applying. Must demonstrate leadership in the United Methodist Church and be enrolled in a full-time degree program at a regionally accredited U.S. institution. Cumulative GPA of 3.0 or higher required.

Award: Scholarship for use in freshman, sophomore, junior, or senior years; not renewable. *Number:* varies. *Amount:* $1000.

Eligibility Requirements: Applicant must be Methodist; enrolled or expecting to enroll full-time at a two-year or four-year institution or university and must have an interest in leadership. Applicant must have 3.0 GPA or higher. Available to U.S. and non-Canadian citizens.

Application Requirements: Application, essay, references, transcript. *Deadline:* March 1.

Contact: Scholarship Committee
General Board of Higher Education and Ministry
The United Methodist Church, 1001 19th Avenue South
PO Box 340007
Nashville, TN 37202
Phone: 615-340-7344
E-mail: umscholar@gbhem.org

ITALIAN CATHOLIC FEDERATION INC.

http://www.icf.org/

ITALIAN CATHOLIC FEDERATION FIRST YEAR SCHOLARSHIP
• *See page 546*

JEWISH VOCATIONAL SERVICE LOS ANGELES

http://www.jvsla.org/

JEWISH VOCATIONAL SERVICE SCHOLARSHIP FUND
• *See page 667*

KNIGHTS OF COLUMBUS

http://www.kofc.org/

FOURTH DEGREE PRO DEO AND PRO PATRIA (CANADA)
• *See page 547*

FOURTH DEGREE PRO DEO AND PRO PATRIA SCHOLARSHIPS
• *See page 547*

FRANCIS P. MATTHEWS AND JOHN E. SWIFT EDUCATIONAL TRUST SCHOLARSHIPS
• *See page 547*

JOHN W. MCDEVITT (FOURTH DEGREE) SCHOLARSHIPS
• *See page 548*

PERCY J. JOHNSON ENDOWED SCHOLARSHIPS
• *See page 548*

LINCOLN COMMUNITY FOUNDATION

http://www.lcf.org/

WILLIAM B. AND VIRGINIA S. ROLOFSON SCHOLARSHIP

Applicants must be a current graduating senior or a first year college student and be a member of St. Luke United Methodist Church in Lincoln, Nebraska. Applicants must attend a two- or four-year college or university in Nebraska, must be first year college students. Preference will be given to those applicants under the age of 25 but all students are welcome to apply.

Award: Scholarship for use in freshman year; renewable. *Number:* 1. *Amount:* $500.

Eligibility Requirements: Applicant must be Methodist; enrolled or expecting to enroll full-time at a two-year or four-year institution or university; resident of Nebraska and studying in Nebraska. Available to U.S. citizens.

Application Requirements: Application, financial need analysis, references, test scores, transcript. *Deadline:* April 30.

Contact: Sonya Brakeman, Grants/Scholarships Coordinator
Lincoln Community Foundation
215 Centennial Mall South, Suite 100
Lincoln, NE 68508
Phone: 402-474-2345
Fax: 402-476-8532
E-mail: sonyab@lcf.org

MORRIS J. AND BETTY KAPLUN FOUNDATION

http://www.kaplunfoundation.org/

MORRIS J. AND BETTY KAPLUN FOUNDATION ANNUAL ESSAY CONTEST

Prize up to $1800 will be awarded to the first place contest winner for essay on a topic related to Jewish heritage, culture, or values. Additional awards for five finalists. Essay must be between 250–1000 words. Open to students in grades 7–12. See web site for specific essay questions and additional details http://www.kaplunfoundation.org/.

Award: Prize for use in freshman year; not renewable. *Number:* 12–18. *Amount:* $750–$1800.

Eligibility Requirements: Applicant must be Jewish; high school student; planning to enroll or expecting to enroll full- or part-time at a four-year institution or university and must have an interest in Jewish culture or writing. Available to U.S. and non-U.S. citizens.

Application Requirements: Applicant must enter a contest, essay. *Deadline:* March 17.

Contact: Eve Seligson, Essay Contest Committee
Morris J. and Betty Kaplun Foundation
PO Box 234428
Great Neck, NY 11023
Phone: 212-966-5020
Fax: 212-966-6205

PRESBYTERIAN CHURCH (USA)

http://www.pcusa.org/financialaid

NATIONAL PRESBYTERIAN COLLEGE SCHOLARSHIP

Scholarships between $200 and $1400 available to incoming undergraduate enrolled in full-time programs in colleges associated with the Presbyterian Church (U.S.A.). Applicants must have a minimum GPA of 3.0 and demonstrate financial need.

Award: Scholarship for use in freshman, sophomore, junior, or senior years; renewable. *Number:* 250. *Amount:* $200–$1400.

Eligibility Requirements: Applicant must be Presbyterian; high school student and planning to enroll or expecting to enroll full-time at a four-year institution or university. Applicant must have 3.0 GPA or higher. Available to U.S. and non-Canadian citizens.

Application Requirements: Application, essay, financial need analysis, resume, references, test scores, transcript. *Deadline:* January 31.

Contact: Ms. Laura Bryan, Associate, Financial Aid for Studies
Presbyterian Church (USA)
100 Witherspoon Street
Louisville, KY 40202-1396
Phone: 888-728-7228 Ext. 5735
Fax: 502-569-8776
E-mail: finaid@pcusa.org

SAMUEL ROBINSON AWARD

Prize granted to full-time junior and senior students attending a Presbyterian related college or university who successfully recite answers to the Westminster Shorter Catechism and write an essay on an assigned topic.

Award: Prize for use in junior or senior years; not renewable. *Number:* 16. *Amount:* $250–$5000.

Eligibility Requirements: Applicant must be Presbyterian and enrolled or expecting to enroll full-time at a four-year institution or university. Available to U.S. citizens.

Application Requirements: Application, applicant must enter a contest, essay. *Deadline:* April 1.

Contact: Laura Bryan, Associate, Financial Aid for Studies
Presbyterian Church (USA)
Financial Aid for Studies
100 Witherspoon Street
Louisville, KY 40202-1396
Phone: 888-728-7228 Ext. 5735
E-mail: finaid@pcusa.org

ROMAN CATHOLIC DIOCESE OF TULSA

http://www.dioceseoftulsa.org/

MAE LASSLEY OSAGE SCHOLARSHIP
• *See page 678*

SYNOD OF THE COVENANT

http://www.synodofthecovenant.org/

CECA ETHNIC SCHOLARSHIP

Scholarship will be awarded for full- or part-time study toward baccalaureate degree or certification at colleges, universities, and vocational schools. Award also available for full-time students enrolled in master's degree programs for church vocations at approved Presbyterian theological institutions. Priority will be given to Presbyterian applicants from the states of Michigan and Ohio. Applicants must maintain a minimum 2.0 GPA. Deadlines: February 1 and September 1.

Award: Scholarship for use in freshman, sophomore, junior, senior, or graduate years; not renewable. *Number:* 30. *Amount:* $400–$800.

Eligibility Requirements: Applicant must be Presbyterian; enrolled or expecting to enroll full- or part-time at a four-year institution or university and resident of Michigan or Ohio. Available to U.S. and non-U.S. citizens.

Application Requirements: Application, financial need analysis, test scores, transcript, verification enrollment letter. *Deadline:* varies.

Contact: Ms. Janet Chapman, Executive Assistant
Synod of the Covenant
Attn: CECA Ethnic Scholarship Committee
1911 Indian Wood Circle, Suite B
Maumee, OH 43537
Phone: 419-754-4050
Fax: 419-754-4051
E-mail: j.chapman@synodofthecovenant.org

SYNOD OF THE TRINITY

http://www.syntrinity.org/index/

SYNOD OF THE TRINITY EDUCATIONAL SCHOLARSHIP

The Synod of the Trinity Educational Scholarship assists full-time undergraduate students who are members of or are actively involved in a Presbyterian Church (USA) within the Synod. The student must meet income criteria and reside within our boundaries of Pennsylvania and some counties in West Virginia and Ohio.

Award: Scholarship for use in freshman, sophomore, junior, or senior years; not renewable.

Eligibility Requirements: Applicant must be Presbyterian; enrolled or expecting to enroll full-time at a two-year or four-year or technical institution or university and resident of Ohio, Pennsylvania, or West Virginia. Applicant must have 2.5 GPA or higher. Available to U.S. citizens.

Application Requirements: Application, essay, financial need analysis, references, verification by pastor of membership or involvement in your PC(USA) church. *Deadline:* April 30.

Contact: Marcia Humer, Grants & Scholarships
Synod of the Trinity
3040 Market Street
Camp Hill, PA 17011
Phone: 800-242-0534 Ext. 233
E-mail: mhumer@syntrinity.org

TEXAS BLACK BAPTIST SCHOLARSHIP COMMITTEE

http://www.bgct.org/

TEXAS BLACK BAPTIST SCHOLARSHIP
• *See page 681*

UNITARIAN UNIVERSALIST ASSOCIATION

http://www.uua.org/

CHILDREN OF UNITARIAN UNIVERSALIST MINISTERS

Non-renewable scholarship available to children of Unitarian Universalist Ministers to defray undergraduate college expenses. Dollar value and number of awards varies. Priority is given to applicants whose family income does not exceed $50,000.

Award: Scholarship for use in freshman, sophomore, junior, or senior years; not renewable. *Number:* varies. *Amount:* varies.

Eligibility Requirements: Applicant must be Unitarian Universalist and enrolled or expecting to enroll full- or part-time at a four-year institution or university. Available to U.S. citizens.

Application Requirements: Application. *Deadline:* July 31.

Contact: Ms. Hillary Goodridge, Program Director
Unitarian Universalist Association
PO Box 301149
Boston, MA 02130
Phone: 617-971-9600
Fax: 617-971-0029
E-mail: uufp@aol.com

JOSEPH SUMNER SMITH SCHOLARSHIP

Funds are available for Unitarian Universalist (UU) students attending Anitoch (including satellite and nonresidential campuses) and Harvard. While there is no restriction on the course of studies the student may elect to pursue, nor any restrictions on choice of career, student interested in pursuing the ministry after graduation are especially urged to apply.

Award: Scholarship for use in freshman, sophomore, junior, senior, or graduate years; not renewable. *Number:* varies. *Amount:* $500–$1000.

Eligibility Requirements: Applicant must be Unitarian Universalist and enrolled or expecting to enroll full- or part-time at a two-year or four-year or technical institution or university. Available to U.S. citizens.

Application Requirements: Application. *Deadline:* April 30.

Contact: Ms. Hillary Goodridge, Program Director
Unitarian Universalist Association
PO Box 301149
Boston, MA 02130
Phone: 617-971-9600
Fax: 617-971-0029
E-mail: uufp@aol.com

UNITED METHODIST CHURCH

http://www.gbhem.org/

J. A. KNOWLES MEMORIAL SCHOLARSHIP

One-time award for Texas residents attending a United Methodist institution in Texas. Must have been United Methodist Church member for at least one year. Must be U.S. citizens or permanent residents. Minimum 2.5 GPA required.

Award: Scholarship for use in freshman, sophomore, junior, senior, or graduate years; not renewable. *Number:* varies. *Amount:* varies.

Eligibility Requirements: Applicant must be Methodist; enrolled or expecting to enroll full-time at a two-year or four-year institution or university; resident of Texas and studying in Texas. Applicant must have 2.5 GPA or higher. Available to U.S. citizens.

Application Requirements: Application, essay, references, transcript. *Deadline:* May 15.

Contact: Scholarships Administrator
United Methodist Church
PO Box 340007
Nashville, TN 37203-0007
Phone: 615-340-7344
E-mail: pzimmer@gbhem.org

UNITED METHODIST CHURCH ETHNIC SCHOLARSHIP
• *See page 682*

UNITED METHODIST CHURCH HISPANIC, ASIAN, AND NATIVE AMERICAN SCHOLARSHIP
• *See page 682*

UNITED METHODIST YOUTH ORGANIZATION

http://www.gbod.org/youngpeople

DAVID W. SELF SCHOLARSHIP

Must be a United Methodist Youth who has been active in local church for at least one year prior to application. Must be a graduating senior in high school (who maintained at least a "C" average) entering the first year of undergraduate study. Must be pursuing a "church-related" career and should have maintained at least a "C" average throughout high school.

Award: Scholarship for use in freshman year; not renewable. *Number:* up to 5. *Amount:* up to $2800.

Eligibility Requirements: Applicant must be Methodist; high school student and planning to enroll or expecting to enroll full-time at a four-year institution or university. Available to U.S. citizens.

Application Requirements: Application, essay, financial need analysis, transcript, certification of church membership. *Deadline:* June 1.

Contact: Grants & Scholarships Coordinator
United Methodist Youth Organization
PO Box 340003
Nashville, TN 37203-0003
Phone: 877-899-2780 Ext. 7184
Fax: 615-340-7063
E-mail: youngpeople@gbod.org

RICHARD S. SMITH SCHOLARSHIP
• *See page 683*

WOMAN'S MISSIONARY UNION FOUNDATION

http://www.wmufoundation.com/

WOMAN'S MISSIONARY UNION SCHOLARSHIP PROGRAM

The program is primarily for Baptist young women with high scholastic accomplishments and service through Baptist organizations. Must have an interest in Christian women's leadership development or missionary service. Preference is given for WMU/Acteen membership in a Baptist church. The total number of available awards and dollar amount varies. For more information, see web site http://www.wmufoundation.com.

Award: Scholarship for use in freshman, sophomore, junior, or senior years; renewable. *Number:* 5–10. *Amount:* $500–$1500.

Eligibility Requirements: Applicant must be Baptist; enrolled or expecting to enroll full-time at a two-year or four-year institution or university and female. Available to U.S. and non-U.S. citizens.

Application Requirements: Application, references, transcript. *Deadline:* March 1.

Contact: Mrs. Linda Lucas, Administrative Assistant
Woman's Missionary Union Foundation
100 Missionary Ridge
Birmingham, AL 35242
Phone: 205-408-5525
E-mail: llucas@wmu.org

WOMEN OF THE EVANGELICAL LUTHERAN CHURCH IN AMERICA

http://www.womenoftheelca.org/

AMELIA KEMP SCHOLARSHIP
• *See page 696*

BELMER/FLORA PRINCE SCHOLARSHIP

Scholarship for women who have experienced an interruption of two or more years in education since the completion of high school. Must be member of ELCA and be at least 21 years old.

Award: Scholarship for use in freshman, sophomore, junior, senior, or graduate years; not renewable. *Number:* 2. *Amount:* up to $1000.

Eligibility Requirements: Applicant must be Lutheran; age 21 and over; enrolled or expecting to enroll full- or part-time at a two-year or four-year or technical institution or university and female. Available to U.S. citizens.

Application Requirements: Application, resume, references, transcript. *Deadline:* February 15.

Contact: Emily Hansen, Scholarship Committee
Women of the Evangelical Lutheran Church in America
8765 West Higgins Road
Chicago, IL 60631-4189
Phone: 800-638-3522 Ext. 2736
Fax: 773-380-2419
E-mail: womenelca@elca.org

RESIDENCE

ABBIE SARGENT MEMORIAL SCHOLARSHIP INC.

http://www.nhfarmbureau.org/

ABBIE SARGENT MEMORIAL SCHOLARSHIP

Up to three awards between $400 and $500 will be provided to deserving New Hampshire residents, planning to attend an institution of higher learning. Must be a U.S. citizen.

Award: Scholarship for use in freshman, sophomore, junior, senior, graduate, or postgraduate years; not renewable. *Number:* 1–3. *Amount:* $400–$500.

Eligibility Requirements: Applicant must be enrolled or expecting to enroll full- or part-time at a two-year or four-year or technical institution or university and resident of New Hampshire. Available to U.S. citizens.

Application Requirements: Application, driver's license, financial need analysis, photo, references, transcript. *Deadline:* March 15.

Contact: Melanie Phelps, Treasurer
Abbie Sargent Memorial Scholarship Inc.
295 Sheep Davis Road
Concord, NH 03301
Phone: 603-224-1934
Fax: 603-228-8432
E-mail: melaniep@nhfarmbureau.org

ADELANTE! U.S. EDUCATION LEADERSHIP FUND

http://www.adelantefund.org/

ADELANTE FUND SCHOLARSHIPS
• *See page 650*

AIKEN ELECTRIC COOPERATIVE INC.

http://www.aikenco-op.org/

TRUSTEE SCHOLARSHIP

Scholarship awarded to high school graduating senior in the cooperative service area. Award based on need and academic performance. The primary residence of the applicant must have an account with either Aiken Electric Cooperative Inc. or Aikenelectric.net.

Award: Scholarship for use in freshman year; not renewable. *Number:* 1. *Amount:* up to $1000.

Eligibility Requirements: Applicant must be high school student; planning to enroll or expecting to enroll full-time at a two-year or four-year institution or university and resident of South Carolina. Available to U.S. citizens.

Application Requirements: Application, essay, financial need analysis. *Deadline:* January 12.

Contact: Marilyn Gerrity, Manager, Marketing and Strategic Services
Aiken Electric Cooperative Inc.
2790 Wagener Road
PO Box 417
Aiken, SC 29802
Phone: 803-649-6245
Fax: 803-641-8310
E-mail: aec@aikenco-op.org

ALABAMA COMMISSION ON HIGHER EDUCATION

http://www.ache.alabama.gov/

ALABAMA NATIONAL GUARD EDUCATIONAL ASSISTANCE PROGRAM

• *See page 618*

ALABAMA STUDENT ASSISTANCE PROGRAM

Scholarship award of $300 to $5000 per academic year given to undergraduate students residing in the state of Alabama and attending a college or university in Alabama.

Award: Grant for use in freshman, sophomore, junior, or senior years; not renewable. *Number:* varies. *Amount:* $300–$5000.

Eligibility Requirements: Applicant must be enrolled or expecting to enroll full- or part-time at a two-year or four-year or technical institution or university; resident of Alabama and studying in Alabama. Available to U.S. citizens.

Application Requirements: Application. *Deadline:* continuous.

Contact: Cheryl Newton, Grants Coordinator
Alabama Commission on Higher Education
100 North Union Street
PO Box 302000
Montgomery, AL 36130-2000
Phone: 334-242-2273
E-mail: cheryl.newton@ache.alabama.gov

ALABAMA STUDENT GRANT PROGRAM

Nonrenewable awards available to Alabama residents for undergraduate study at certain independent colleges within the state. Both full and half-time students are eligible. Deadlines: September 15, January 15, and February 15.

Award: Grant for use in freshman, sophomore, junior, or senior years; not renewable. *Number:* up to 1200. *Amount:* up to $1200.

Eligibility Requirements: Applicant must be enrolled or expecting to enroll full- or part-time at a four-year institution or university; resident of Alabama and studying in Alabama. Available to U.S. citizens.

Application Requirements: Application.

Contact: Cheryl Newton, Grants Coordinator
Alabama Commission on Higher Education
100 North Union Street
PO Box 302000
Montgomery, AL 36130-2000
Phone: 334-242-2273
E-mail: cheryl.newton@ache.alabama.gov

POLICE OFFICERS AND FIREFIGHTERS SURVIVORS EDUCATION ASSISTANCE PROGRAM-ALABAMA

Provides tuition, fees, books, and supplies to dependents of full-time police officers and firefighters killed in the line of duty. Must attend any Alabama public college as an undergraduate. Must be Alabama resident.

Award: Scholarship for use in freshman, sophomore, junior, or senior years; renewable. *Number:* 15–30. *Amount:* $2000–$5000.

Eligibility Requirements: Applicant must be age 21 or under; enrolled or expecting to enroll full- or part-time at a two-year or four-year or technical institution or university; single; resident of Alabama and studying in Alabama. Available to U.S. citizens.

Application Requirements: Application, transcript, birth certificate, marriage license, death certificate, letter from medical doctor. *Deadline:* continuous.

Contact: Cheryl Newton, Grants Coordinator
Alabama Commission on Higher Education
100 North Union Street
PO Box 302000
Montgomery, AL 36130-2000
Phone: 334-242-2273
E-mail: cheryl.newton@ache.alabama.gov

ALABAMA DEPARTMENT OF VETERANS AFFAIRS

http://www.va.alabama.gov/

ALABAMA G.I. DEPENDENTS SCHOLARSHIP PROGRAM

• *See page 626*

ALABAMA INDIAN AFFAIRS COMMISSION

http://www.aiac.alabama.gov/

AIAC SCHOLARSHIP

• *See page 650*

ALASKA STATE DEPARTMENT OF EDUCATION

http://www.eed.state.ak.us/

GEAR UP ALASKA SCHOLARSHIP

Scholarship provides up to $7000 each year for up to four years of undergraduate study (up to $3500 each year for half-time study) for students who participated in the GEAR UP Programs in 6th, 7th, and 8th grade and have met the academic milestones established by their district. Must reapply each year and application must be signed by GEAR UP program director. Must be an Alaska high school senior or have an Alaska diploma or GED. Must submit FAFSA and have financial need. Must be under age 22.

Award: Scholarship for use in freshman, sophomore, junior, or senior years; not renewable. *Number:* varies. *Amount:* $3500–$7000.

Eligibility Requirements: Applicant must be age 22 or under; enrolled or expecting to enroll full- or part-time at a two-year or four-year institution or university and resident of Alaska. Available to U.S. citizens.

Application Requirements: Application, financial need analysis, references, transcript, FAFSA, Student Aid Report (SAR). *Deadline:* May 31.

Contact: Adam Weed, Special Projects Coordinator
Alaska State Department of Education
801 West 10th Street, Suite 200, PO Box 110500
Juneau, AK 99811-0500
Phone: 907-465-6685
E-mail: adam.weed@alaska.gov

ALBERTA AGRICULTURE FOOD AND RURAL DEVELOPMENT 4-H BRANCH

http://www.4h.ab.ca/

ALBERTA AGRICULTURE FOOD AND RURAL DEVELOPMENT 4-H SCHOLARSHIP PROGRAM
• *See page 523*

ALBERTA HERITAGE SCHOLARSHIP FUND

http://www.alis.alberta.ca/

ADULT HIGH SCHOOL EQUIVALENCY SCHOLARSHIPS
• *See page 651*

ALBERTA APPRENTICESHIP AND INDUSTRY TRAINING SCHOLARSHIPS

Awards of CAN$1000 to recognize the accomplishments of Alberta high school students taking the registered apprenticeship program and to encourage recipients to continue their apprenticeship training after completing high school. Must be a Canadian citizen or landed immigrant and a resident of Alberta, must have completed the requirements for high school graduation between August 1 and July 31 of the current year and must be registered as an Alberta apprentice in a trade while still attending high school. For additional information, please visit web site http://alis.alberta.ca.

Award: Scholarship for use in freshman year; not renewable.

Eligibility Requirements: Applicant must be enrolled or expecting to enroll full-time at a two-year or four-year or technical institution or university and resident of Alberta. Available to Canadian citizens.

Application Requirements: Application, essay, references. *Deadline:* July 17.

Contact: Scholarship Committee
Alberta Heritage Scholarship Fund
9940 106th Street, Fourth Floor, Sterling Place
PO Box 28000, Station Main
Edmonton, AB T5J 4R4
Canada
Phone: 780-427-8640
E-mail: scholarships@gov.ab.ca

ALBERTA CENTENNIAL PREMIER'S SCHOLARSHIPS-ALBERTA
• *See page 651*

ALEXANDER RUTHERFORD SCHOLARSHIPS FOR HIGH SCHOOL ACHIEVEMENT
• *See page 651*

CHARLES S. NOBLE JUNIOR A HOCKEY SCHOLARSHIPS
• *See page 651*

CHARLES S. NOBLE JUNIOR FOOTBALL SCHOLARSHIPS
• *See page 651*

DR. ERNEST AND MINNIE MEHL SCHOLARSHIP
• *See page 651*

EARL AND COUNTESS OF WESSEX-WORLD CHAMPIONSHIPS IN ATHLETICS SCHOLARSHIPS
• *See page 652*

GRANT MACEWAN UNITED WORLD COLLEGE SCHOLARSHIPS
• *See page 652*

INTERNATIONAL EDUCATION AWARDS-UKRAINE
• *See page 652*

JIMMIE CONDON ATHLETIC SCHOLARSHIPS
• *See page 652*

LAURENCE DECORE STUDENT LEADERSHIP AWARDS
• *See page 652*

LOUISE MCKINNEY POSTSECONDARY SCHOLARSHIPS
• *See page 653*

NORTHERN ALBERTA DEVELOPMENT COUNCIL BURSARY PARTNERSHIP PROGRAM

Award of CAN$1750 is intended to attract graduates to live and work in Northern Alberta. Bursary recipients must live and work in Northern Alberta within six months of graduation. The return service obligation is one year of work for every year of bursary funds received. Students who do not work in the North will be required to repay the bursary. Must be Alberta resident, enrolled full-time in a postsecondary program at an institution recognized by Alberta Advanced Education and demonstrate financial need. For additional information and application, see web site http://alis.alberta.ca.

Award: Forgivable loan for use in freshman, sophomore, junior, or senior years; not renewable. *Number:* varies.

Eligibility Requirements: Applicant must be enrolled or expecting to enroll full-time at a two-year or four-year or technical institution or university; resident of Alberta and studying in Alberta. Available to Canadian citizens.

Application Requirements: Application, financial need analysis. *Deadline:* February 1.

Contact: Scholarship Committee
Alberta Heritage Scholarship Fund
9940 106th Street, Fourth Floor, Sterling Place
PO Box 28000, Station Main
Edmonton, AB T5J 4R4
Canada
Phone: 780-427-8640
E-mail: scholarships@gov.ab.ca

PERSONS CASE SCHOLARSHIPS
• *See page 653*

PRAIRIE BASEBALL ACADEMY SCHOLARSHIPS

Scholarships of between CAN$500 and CAN$2500 reward athletic and academic excellence of Alberta baseball players, and provides an incentive and means for these players to continue with their postsecondary education. Must be Alberta residents and enrolled full-time at a postsecondary institution in Alberta. Applicants must be a participant in the Prairie Baseball Academy and must have achieved a minimum GPA of 2.0 in their previous semester. For additional information, visit web site http://alis.alberta.ca.

Award: Scholarship for use in freshman, sophomore, junior, or senior years; not renewable.

Eligibility Requirements: Applicant must be enrolled or expecting to enroll full-time at a two-year or four-year or technical institution or university; resident of Alberta; studying in Alberta and must have an interest in athletics/sports. Available to Canadian citizens.

Application Requirements: Application, references. *Deadline:* October 15.

Contact: Scholarship Committee
Alberta Heritage Scholarship Fund
9940 106th Street, Fourth Floor, Sterling Place
PO Box 28000, Station Main
Edmonton, AB T5J 4R4
Canada
Phone: 780-427-8640
E-mail: scholarships@gov.ab.ca

QUEEN ELIZABETH II GOLDEN JUBILEE CITIZENSHIP MEDAL
• *See page 653*

RUTHERFORD SCHOLARS
• *See page 653*

ALBUQUERQUE COMMUNITY FOUNDATION

http://www.albuquerquefoundation.org/

NEW MEXICO MANUFACTURED HOUSING SCHOLARSHIP PROGRAM

The scholarship is to be used for study in a four-year college or university. The total number of available awards and the dollar value of each award varies. Deadline varies. Refer to web site for details and application http://www.albuquerquefoundation.org.

Award: Scholarship for use in freshman year; not renewable. *Number:* 1–2. *Amount:* $1000.

Eligibility Requirements: Applicant must be high school student; planning to enroll or expecting to enroll full-time at a four-year institution or university; resident of New Mexico and studying in New Mexico. Applicant must have 3.0 GPA or higher. Available to U.S. citizens.

Application Requirements: Application, financial need analysis, resume, references, test scores, transcript.

Contact: Nancy Johnson, Program Director
Albuquerque Community Foundation
PO Box 36960
Albuquerque, NM 87176-6960
Phone: 505-883-6240
E-mail: foundation@albuquerquefoundation.org

NOTAH BEGAY III SCHOLARSHIP PROGRAM FOR NATIVE AMERICAN SCHOLAR ATHLETES

• *See page 653*

SUSSMAN-MILLER EDUCATIONAL ASSISTANCE FUND

The program provides financial aid to enable students to continue with an undergraduate program. This is a gap program based on financial need. Must be resident of New Mexico. Minimum 3.0 GPA required. Deadline varies. The fund requests not to write or call for information. Please visit web site http://www.albuquerquefoundation.org for complete information.

Award: Scholarship for use in freshman, sophomore, junior, or senior years; renewable. *Number:* 29. *Amount:* $500–$3100.

Eligibility Requirements: Applicant must be enrolled or expecting to enroll full-time at a four-year institution or university and resident of New Mexico. Applicant must have 3.0 GPA or higher. Available to U.S. citizens.

Application Requirements: Application, essay, financial need analysis, resume, references, test scores, transcript.

Contact: Nancy Johnson, Program Director
Albuquerque Community Foundation
PO Box 36960
Albuquerque, NM 87176-6960
Phone: 505-883-6240
E-mail: foundation@albuquerquefoundation.org

YOUTH IN FOSTER CARE SCHOLARSHIP PROGRAM

This award is designed to support youth who have been in the New Mexico foster care system.

Award: Scholarship for use in freshman, sophomore, junior, or senior years; not renewable. *Number:* 1–4. *Amount:* $500–$1000.

Eligibility Requirements: Applicant must be age 17-21; enrolled or expecting to enroll full- or part-time at a two-year or four-year or technical institution or university and resident of New Mexico. Available to U.S. citizens.

Application Requirements: Application, essay, resume, references, transcript. *Deadline:* June 2.

Contact: Nancy Johnson, Program Director
Albuquerque Community Foundation
3301 Mcnaul NE, PO Box 36960
Albuquerque, NM 87176
Phone: 505-883-6240
Fax: 505-883-3629
E-mail: njohnson@albuquerquefoundation.org

ALERT SCHOLARSHIP

http://www.alertmagazine.org/

ALERT SCHOLARSHIP

$500 scholarship for the best essay on drug and alcohol abuse. Applicant must be a current high school senior living in Washington, Idaho, Montana, Minnesota, Wyoming, Colorado, North Dakota, or South Dakota. Minimum 2.5 GPA required. For more information visit: http://www.alertmagazine.org/scholarship.php.

Award: Scholarship for use in freshman year; not renewable. *Number:* 16. *Amount:* $500.

Eligibility Requirements: Applicant must be high school student; planning to enroll or expecting to enroll full- or part-time at a four-year institution or university; resident of Colorado, Idaho, Minnesota, Montana, North Dakota, South Dakota, Washington, or Wyoming and must have an interest in writing. Applicant must have 2.5 GPA or higher. Available to U.S. citizens.

Application Requirements: Applicant must enter a contest, essay, photo, transcript. *Deadline:* continuous.

Contact: Editor
Alert Scholarship
3085 North Cole, Suite 105
PO Box 4833
Boise, ID 83711
Phone: 208-375-7911
Fax: 208-376-0770
E-mail: alertmagazine@aol.com

THE ALEXANDER FOUNDATION

http://www.thealexanderfoundation.org/

THE ALEXANDER FOUNDATION SCHOLARSHIP PROGRAM

Alexander scholarships provide financial assistance to undergraduate or graduate students accepted or enrolled in Colorado institutions of higher education. Applicants must be gay, lesbian, bisexual, or transgendered and reside in Colorado, must demonstrate financial need, and should be active/supporting/contributing members of the community.

Award: Scholarship for use in freshman, sophomore, junior, senior, graduate, or postgraduate years; not renewable. *Number:* 6–35. *Amount:* $300–$3000.

Eligibility Requirements: Applicant must be enrolled or expecting to enroll full- or part-time at a two-year or four-year or technical institution or university; resident of Colorado; studying in Colorado and must have an interest in LGBT issues. Available to U.S. citizens.

Application Requirements: Application, essay, financial need analysis, references, transcript. *Deadline:* April 15.

Contact: Scholarship Committee
The Alexander Foundation
PO Box 1995
Denver, CO 80201-1995
Phone: 303-331-7733
Fax: 303-331-1953
E-mail: infoalexander@thealexanderfoundation.org

AMERICAN CANCER SOCIETY

http://www.cancer.org/

AMERICAN CANCER SOCIETY, FLORIDA DIVISION R.O.C.K. COLLEGE SCHOLARSHIP PROGRAM

• *See page 599*

AMERICAN LEGION AUXILIARY DEPARTMENT OF ALABAMA

http://americanlegionalabama.org/

AMERICAN LEGION AUXILIARY DEPARTMENT OF ALABAMA SCHOLARSHIP PROGRAM

• *See page 626*

AMERICAN LEGION AUXILIARY DEPARTMENT OF CALIFORNIA

http://www.calegionaux.org/

AMERICAN LEGION AUXILIARY DEPARTMENT OF CALIFORNIA CONTINUING/RE-ENTRY STUDENT SCHOLARSHIP

Awarded to undergraduate students. Must be a continuing or re-entry college student and attend a California college or university.

Award: Scholarship for use in freshman, sophomore, junior, or senior years; not renewable. *Number:* 2–3. *Amount:* $500–$1000.

Eligibility Requirements: Applicant must be enrolled or expecting to enroll full- or part-time at a two-year or four-year institution or university; resident of California and studying in California. Available to U.S. citizens.

Application Requirements: Application. *Deadline:* March 16.

Contact: Theresa Jacob, Secretary/Treasurer
American Legion Auxiliary Department of California
401 Van Ness Avenue, Room 113
San Francisco, CA 94102
Phone: 415-862-5092
Fax: 415-861-8365
E-mail: calegionaux@calegionaux.org

AMERICAN LEGION AUXILIARY DEPARTMENT OF CALIFORNIA GENERAL SCHOLARSHIP

Award ranges from $500 to $1000 for high school senior or graduate of an accredited high school who has not been able to begin college due to circumstances of illness or finance. Student must attend a California college or university. Deadline March 16.

Award: Scholarship for use in freshman, sophomore, junior, or senior years; not renewable. *Number:* varies. *Amount:* $500–$1000.

Eligibility Requirements: Applicant must be enrolled or expecting to enroll full- or part-time at a two-year or four-year institution or university; resident of California and studying in California. Available to U.S. citizens.

Application Requirements: Application. *Deadline:* March 16.

Contact: Theresa Jacob, Secretary/Treasurer
American Legion Auxiliary Department of California
401 Van Ness Avenue, Room 113
San Francisco, CA 94102
Phone: 415-862-5092
Fax: 415-861-8365
E-mail: calegionaux@calegionaux.org

AMERICAN LEGION AUXILIARY DEPARTMENT OF CALIFORNIA JUNIOR SCHOLARSHIP

• *See page 524*

AMERICAN LEGION AUXILIARY DEPARTMENT OF COLORADO

http://www.coloradolegion.org/

AMERICAN LEGION AUXILIARY DEPARTMENT OF COLORADO DEPARTMENT PRESIDENT'S SCHOLARSHIP FOR JUNIOR MEMBER

• *See page 627*

AMERICAN LEGION AUXILIARY DEPARTMENT OF CONNECTICUT

http://www.ct.legion.org/

AMERICAN LEGION AUXILIARY DEPARTMENT OF CONNECTICUT PAST PRESIDENTS' PARLEY MEMORIAL EDUCATION GRANT

• *See page 525*

AMERICAN LEGION AUXILIARY DEPARTMENT OF FLORIDA

http://www.alafl.org/

AMERICAN LEGION AUXILIARY DEPARTMENT OF FLORIDA DEPARTMENT SCHOLARSHIPS

• *See page 627*

AMERICAN LEGION AUXILIARY DEPARTMENT OF FLORIDA MEMORIAL SCHOLARSHIP

• *See page 525*

AMERICAN LEGION AUXILIARY DEPARTMENT OF INDIANA

http://www.amlegauxin.org/

AMERICAN LEGION AUXILIARY DEPARTMENT OF INDIANA EDNA M. BURCUS/HOOSIER SCHOOLHOUSE MEMORIAL SCHOLARSHIP

• *See page 627*

AMERICAN LEGION AUXILIARY DEPARTMENT OF IOWA

http://www.ialegion.org/ala

AMERICAN LEGION AUXILIARY DEPARTMENT OF IOWA CHILDREN OF VETERANS MERIT AWARD

• *See page 628*

AMERICAN LEGION AUXILIARY DEPARTMENT OF KENTUCKY

http://www.kylegion.org/

AMERICAN LEGION AUXILIARY DEPARTMENT OF KENTUCKY LAURA BLACKBURN MEMORIAL SCHOLARSHIP

• *See page 622*

AMERICAN LEGION AUXILIARY DEPARTMENT OF KENTUCKY MARY BARRETT MARSHALL SCHOLARSHIP

• *See page 628*

AMERICAN LEGION AUXILIARY DEPARTMENT OF MAINE

http://www.mainelegion.org/

AMERICAN LEGION AUXILIARY DEPARTMENT OF MAINE DANIEL E. LAMBERT MEMORIAL SCHOLARSHIP

• *See page 628*

AMERICAN LEGION AUXILIARY DEPARTMENT OF MAINE NATIONAL PRESIDENT'S SCHOLARSHIP

• *See page 582*

AMERICAN LEGION AUXILIARY DEPARTMENT OF MARYLAND

http://www.alamd.org/

AMERICAN LEGION AUXILIARY DEPARTMENT OF MARYLAND CHILDREN AND YOUTH SCHOLARSHIPS

• *See page 628*

AMERICAN LEGION AUXILIARY DEPARTMENT OF MASSACHUSETTS

http://www.masslegion-aux.org/

AMERICAN LEGION AUXILIARY DEPARTMENT OF MASSACHUSETTS DEPARTMENT PRESIDENT'S SCHOLARSHIP
• *See page 582*

AMERICAN LEGION AUXILIARY DEPARTMENT OF MASSACHUSETTS PAST PRESIDENTS' PARLEY SCHOLARSHIP
• *See page 628*

AMERICAN LEGION AUXILIARY DEPARTMENT OF MICHIGAN

http://www.michalaux.org/

AMERICAN LEGION AUXILIARY DEPARTMENT OF MICHIGAN MEMORIAL SCHOLARSHIP
• *See page 629*

AMERICAN LEGION AUXILIARY DEPARTMENT OF MICHIGAN SCHOLARSHIP FOR NON-TRADITIONAL STUDENT
• *See page 629*

AMERICAN LEGION AUXILIARY DEPARTMENT OF MINNESOTA

http://www.mnlegion.org/

AMERICAN LEGION AUXILIARY DEPARTMENT OF MINNESOTA SCHOLARSHIPS
• *See page 629*

AMERICAN LEGION AUXILIARY DEPARTMENT OF MISSOURI

http://www.missourilegion.org/

AMERICAN LEGION AUXILIARY DEPARTMENT OF MISSOURI LELA MURPHY SCHOLARSHIP
• *See page 526*

AMERICAN LEGION AUXILIARY DEPARTMENT OF MISSOURI NATIONAL PRESIDENT'S SCHOLARSHIP
• *See page 526*

AMERICAN LEGION AUXILIARY DEPARTMENT OF NEBRASKA

http://www.nebraskalegionaux.net/

AMERICAN LEGION AUXILIARY DEPARTMENT OF NEBRASKA RUBY PAUL CAMPAIGN FUND SCHOLARSHIP
• *See page 526*

AMERICAN LEGION AUXILIARY DEPARTMENT OF NORTH DAKOTA

http://www.ndlegion.org/

AMERICAN LEGION AUXILIARY DEPARTMENT OF NORTH DAKOTA NATIONAL PRESIDENT'S SCHOLARSHIP
• *See page 582*

AMERICAN LEGION AUXILIARY DEPARTMENT OF NORTH DAKOTA SCHOLARSHIPS

One-time award for North Dakota residents who are already attending a North Dakota institution of higher learning. Contact local or nearest American Legion Auxiliary Unit for more information. Must be a U.S. citizen.

Award: Scholarship for use in sophomore, junior, senior, or graduate years; not renewable. *Number:* 3. *Amount:* $400.

Eligibility Requirements: Applicant must be enrolled or expecting to enroll full-time at a two-year or four-year or technical institution or university; resident of North Dakota and studying in North Dakota. Available to U.S. citizens.

Application Requirements: Application, driver's license, essay, financial need analysis, references, self-addressed stamped envelope, test scores, transcript. *Deadline:* January 15.

Contact: Myrna Runholm, Department Secretary
American Legion Auxiliary Department of North Dakota
PO Box 1060
Jamestown, ND 58402-1060
Phone: 701-253-5992
E-mail: ala-hq@ndlegion.org

AMERICAN LEGION AUXILIARY DEPARTMENT OF OHIO

http://www.alaohio.org/

AMERICAN LEGION AUXILIARY DEPARTMENT OF OHIO CONTINUING EDUCATION FUND
• *See page 630*

AMERICAN LEGION AUXILIARY DEPARTMENT OF OHIO DEPARTMENT PRESIDENT'S SCHOLARSHIP
• *See page 630*

AMERICAN LEGION AUXILIARY DEPARTMENT OF OREGON

http://www.alaoregon.org/

AMERICAN LEGION AUXILIARY DEPARTMENT OF OREGON DEPARTMENT GRANTS
• *See page 630*

AMERICAN LEGION AUXILIARY DEPARTMENT OF OREGON NATIONAL PRESIDENT'S SCHOLARSHIP
• *See page 630*

AMERICAN LEGION AUXILIARY DEPARTMENT OF OREGON SPIRIT OF YOUTH SCHOLARSHIP
• *See page 526*

AMERICAN LEGION AUXILIARY DEPARTMENT OF PENNSYLVANIA

http://www.pa-legion.com/

AMERICAN LEGION AUXILIARY DEPARTMENT OF PENNSYLVANIA PAST DEPARTMENT PRESIDENTS' MEMORIAL SCHOLARSHIP

Renewable award of $400 given each year to high school seniors. Must be residents of Pennsylvania.

Award: Scholarship for use in freshman year; renewable. *Number:* 1. *Amount:* $400.

Eligibility Requirements: Applicant must be high school student; planning to enroll or expecting to enroll full-time at a four-year institution or university and resident of Pennsylvania. Available to U.S. citizens.

Application Requirements: Application. *Deadline:* March 15.

Contact: Colleen Watson, Executive Secretary and Treasurer
American Legion Auxiliary Department of Pennsylvania
PO Box 1285
Camp Hill, PA 17001-1285
Phone: 717-763-7545
Fax: 717-763-0617
E-mail: paalad@hotmail.com

AMERICAN LEGION AUXILIARY DEPARTMENT OF PENNSYLVANIA SCHOLARSHIP FOR DEPENDENTS OF DISABLED OR DECEASED VETERANS

Renewable award of $600 to high school seniors who are residents of Pennsylvania. Applicants must enroll in full-time studies.

Award: Scholarship for use in freshman year; renewable. *Number:* 1. *Amount:* $600.

Eligibility Requirements: Applicant must be high school student; planning to enroll or expecting to enroll full-time at a four-year institution or university and resident of Pennsylvania. Available to U.S. citizens.

Application Requirements: Application. *Deadline:* March 15.

Contact: Colleen Watson, Executive Secretary and Treasurer
American Legion Auxiliary Department of Pennsylvania
PO Box 1285
Camp Hill, PA 17001-1285
Phone: 717-763-7545
Fax: 717-763-0617
E-mail: paalad@hotmail.com

AMERICAN LEGION AUXILIARY DEPARTMENT OF PENNSYLVANIA SCHOLARSHIP FOR DEPENDENTS OF LIVING VETERANS

Renewable award of $600 for high school seniors who are residents of Pennsylvania. Applicants must enroll in a program of full-time study.

Award: Scholarship for use in freshman year; renewable. *Number:* 1. *Amount:* $600.

Eligibility Requirements: Applicant must be high school student; planning to enroll or expecting to enroll full-time at a four-year institution or university and resident of Pennsylvania. Available to U.S. citizens.

Application Requirements: Application. *Deadline:* March 15.

Contact: Colleen Watson, Executive Secretary and Treasurer
American Legion Auxiliary Department of Pennsylvania
PO Box 1285
Camp Hill, PA 17001-1285
Phone: 717-763-7545
Fax: 717-763-0617
E-mail: paalad@hotmail.com

AMERICAN LEGION AUXILIARY DEPARTMENT OF SOUTH DAKOTA

http://www.sdlegion.org/

AMERICAN LEGION AUXILIARY DEPARTMENT OF SOUTH DAKOTA COLLEGE SCHOLARSHIPS
• See page 526

AMERICAN LEGION AUXILIARY DEPARTMENT OF SOUTH DAKOTA SENIOR SCHOLARSHIP
• See page 527

AMERICAN LEGION AUXILIARY DEPARTMENT OF SOUTH DAKOTA VOCATIONAL SCHOLARSHIP
• See page 527

AMERICAN LEGION AUXILIARY DEPARTMENT OF TENNESSEE

http://www.legion-aux.org/

AMERICAN LEGION AUXILIARY DEPARTMENT OF TENNESSEE VARA GRAY SCHOLARSHIP-GENERAL
• See page 631

AMERICAN LEGION AUXILIARY DEPARTMENT OF TEXAS

http://www.alatexas.org/

AMERICAN LEGION AUXILIARY DEPARTMENT OF TEXAS GENERAL EDUCATION SCHOLARSHIP
• See page 631

AMERICAN LEGION AUXILIARY DEPARTMENT OF UTAH

http://www.legion-aux.org/

AMERICAN LEGION AUXILIARY DEPARTMENT OF UTAH NATIONAL PRESIDENT'S SCHOLARSHIP
• See page 527

AMERICAN LEGION AUXILIARY DEPARTMENT OF WASHINGTON

http://www.walegion-aux.org/

AMERICAN LEGION AUXILIARY DEPARTMENT OF WASHINGTON GIFT SCHOLARSHIPS
• See page 631

SUSAN BURDETT SCHOLARSHIP

The American Legion Auxiliary, Department of Washington will award one Scholarship of $300 to a former citizen of Evergreen Girls State. Must be a Washington State resident and a child or grandchild of deceased or incapacitated Veteran.

Award: Scholarship for use in freshman, sophomore, junior, or senior years; not renewable. *Number:* 1. *Amount:* $300.

Eligibility Requirements: Applicant must be enrolled or expecting to enroll full- or part-time at a two-year or four-year or technical institution or university; female and resident of Washington. Available to U.S. citizens.

Application Requirements: Application, essay, references, transcript. *Deadline:* March 1.

Contact: Nicole Ross, Department Secretary
American Legion Auxiliary Department of Washington
3600 Ruddell Road
Lacey, WA 98503
Phone: 360-456-5995
Fax: 360-491-7442
E-mail: secretary@walegion-aux.org

AMERICAN LEGION AUXILIARY DEPARTMENT OF WISCONSIN

http://www.amlegionauxwi.org/

AMERICAN LEGION AUXILIARY DEPARTMENT OF WISCONSIN DELLA VAN DEUREN MEMORIAL SCHOLARSHIP
• See page 527

AMERICAN LEGION AUXILIARY DEPARTMENT OF WISCONSIN H.S. AND ANGELINE LEWIS SCHOLARSHIPS
• See page 528

AMERICAN LEGION AUXILIARY DEPARTMENT OF WISCONSIN MERIT AND MEMORIAL SCHOLARSHIPS
• See page 528

AMERICAN LEGION AUXILIARY DEPARTMENT OF WISCONSIN PAST PRESIDENTS' PARLEY HEALTH CAREER SCHOLARSHIPS
• See page 528

AMERICAN LEGION AUXILIARY DEPARTMENT OF WISCONSIN PRESIDENT'S SCHOLARSHIPS

• *See page 528*

AMERICAN LEGION DEPARTMENT OF ARIZONA

http://www.azlegion.org/

AMERICAN LEGION DEPARTMENT OF ARIZONA HIGH SCHOOL ORATORICAL CONTEST

Each student must present an 8 to 10 minute prepared oration on any part of the U.S. Constitution without any notes, podiums, or coaching. The student will then be asked to do a 3 to 5 minute oration on one of four possible topics. Which one of the four topics will not be known in advance, so students must be prepared to respond to any of the four. Open to students in grades 9 to 12.

Award: Scholarship for use in freshman year; not renewable. *Number:* 10–20. *Amount:* $50–$1500.

Eligibility Requirements: Applicant must be high school student; age 20 or under; planning to enroll or expecting to enroll full-time at a two-year or four-year institution or university; resident of Arizona and must have an interest in public speaking. Available to U.S. citizens.

Application Requirements: Application, applicant must enter a contest. *Deadline:* January 15.

Contact: Roger Munchbach, Department Oratorical Chairman
American Legion Department of Arizona
4701 North 19th Avenue, Suite 200
Phoenix, AZ 85015-3799
Phone: 602-264-7706
Fax: 602-264-0029
E-mail: legionoratoricalcontest@msn.com

AMERICAN LEGION DEPARTMENT OF ARKANSAS

http://www.arklegion.homestead.com/

AMERICAN LEGION DEPARTMENT OF ARKANSAS COUDRET SCHOLARSHIP AWARD

• *See page 529*

AMERICAN LEGION DEPARTMENT OF ARKANSAS HIGH SCHOOL ORATORICAL CONTEST

Oratorical contest open to students in ninth to twelfth grades of any accredited Arkansas high school. Begins with finalists at the post level and proceeds through area and district levels to national contest.

Award: Prize for use in freshman year; not renewable. *Number:* 4. *Amount:* $1250–$3500.

Eligibility Requirements: Applicant must be high school student; age 19 or under; planning to enroll or expecting to enroll full-time at a four-year institution or university; resident of Arkansas and must have an interest in public speaking. Applicant must have 2.5 GPA or higher. Available to U.S. citizens.

Application Requirements: Application, applicant must enter a contest, photo, references. *Deadline:* December 15.

Contact: William Winchell, Department Adjutant
American Legion Department of Arkansas
PO Box 3280
Little Rock, AR 72203-3280
Phone: 501-375-1104
Fax: 501-375-4236
E-mail: alegion@swbell.net

AMERICAN LEGION DEPARTMENT OF HAWAII

http://www.legion.org/

AMERICAN LEGION DEPARTMENT OF HAWAII HIGH SCHOOL ORATORICAL CONTEST

Oratorical contest open to students in ninth to twelfth grades of any accredited Hawaii high school. Must be under 20 years of age. Speech contests begin in January at post level and continue on to the national competition. Contact local American Legion Post or department for deadlines and application details.

Award: Prize for use in freshman year; not renewable. *Number:* 1–3. *Amount:* $50–$1500.

Eligibility Requirements: Applicant must be high school student; age 14-20; planning to enroll or expecting to enroll full-time at a four-year institution or university and resident of Hawaii. Available to U.S. citizens.

Application Requirements: Application, applicant must enter a contest. *Deadline:* January 1.

Contact: Adm. Bernard Lee, Department Adjutant
American Legion Department of Hawaii
612 McCully Street
Honolulu, HI 96826-3935
Phone: 808-946-6383
Fax: 808-947-3957
E-mail: aldepthi@hawaii.rr.com

AMERICAN LEGION DEPARTMENT OF IDAHO

http://www.idlegion.home.mindspring.com/

AMERICAN LEGION DEPARTMENT OF IDAHO SCHOLARSHIP

• *See page 529*

AMERICAN LEGION DEPARTMENT OF ILLINOIS

http://www.illegion.org/

AMERICAN ESSAY CONTEST SCHOLARSHIP

• *See page 529*

AMERICAN LEGION DEPARTMENT OF ILLINOIS BOY SCOUT/EXPLORER SCHOLARSHIP

• *See page 530*

AMERICAN LEGION DEPARTMENT OF ILLINOIS HIGH SCHOOL ORATORICAL CONTEST

Single oratorical contest with winners advancing to the next level. Open to students in 9th to 12th grades of any accredited Illinois high school. Seniors must be in attendance as of January 1. Must contact local American Legion post or department headquarters for complete information and applications, which will be available in the fall.

Award: Prize for use in freshman year; not renewable. *Number:* up to 25. *Amount:* $100–$2000.

Eligibility Requirements: Applicant must be high school student; planning to enroll or expecting to enroll full- or part-time at a four-year institution or university; resident of Illinois and must have an interest in public speaking. Available to U.S. citizens.

Application Requirements: Application, applicant must enter a contest. *Deadline:* varies.

Contact: Bill Bechtel, Assistant Adjutant
American Legion Department of Illinois
PO Box 2910
Bloomington, IL 61702
Phone: 309-663-0361
Fax: 309-663-5783

AMERICAN LEGION DEPARTMENT OF ILLINOIS SCHOLARSHIPS

• *See page 530*

AMERICAN LEGION DEPARTMENT OF INDIANA

http://www.indlegion.org/

AMERICAN LEGION DEPARTMENT OF INDIANA, AMERICANISM AND GOVERNMENT TEST

Study guides are provided to high schools. Students take a test and write an essay. Two students from each grade (10 to 12) are selected as state winners.

Award: Scholarship for use in freshman, sophomore, junior, or senior years; not renewable. *Number:* 6. *Amount:* $1000.

Eligibility Requirements: Applicant must be high school student; planning to enroll or expecting to enroll full- or part-time at a two-year or four-year or technical institution or university and resident of Indiana. Available to U.S. citizens.

Application Requirements: Applicant must enter a contest, essay, test scores. *Deadline:* December 1.

Contact: Susan Long, Program Coordinator
American Legion Department of Indiana
777 North Meridan Street, Room 104
Indianapolis, IN 46204
Phone: 317-630-1264
Fax: 317-237-9891
E-mail: slong@indlegion.org

AMERICAN LEGION DEPARTMENT OF INDIANA HIGH SCHOOL ORATORICAL CONTEST

Oratorical contest open to students in grades nine to twelve of any accredited Indiana high school or home schooled students in an equivalent grade. Speech contests begin in November at post level and continue on to national competition. Contact local American Legion post for application details or visit our web site at http//www.indlegion.org.

Award: Scholarship for use in freshman, sophomore, junior, or senior years; not renewable. *Number:* 4–8. *Amount:* $200–$4200.

Eligibility Requirements: Applicant must be high school student; age 19 or under; planning to enroll or expecting to enroll full- or part-time at a two-year or four-year or technical institution or university; resident of Indiana and must have an interest in public speaking. Available to U.S. citizens.

Application Requirements: Application, applicant must enter a contest, assigned and prepared speech contest. *Deadline:* December 15.

Contact: Susan Long, Program Coordinator
American Legion Department of Indiana
777 North Meridan Street, Room 104
Indianapolis, IN 46204
Phone: 317-630-1264
Fax: 317-237-9891
E-mail: slong@indlegion.org

AMERICAN LEGION FAMILY SCHOLARSHIP
• *See page 530*

FRANK W. MCHALE MEMORIAL SCHOLARSHIPS

One-time award for Indiana high school juniors who recently participated in The American Legion Hoosier Boys State Program. Must be nominated by Boys State official. Write for more information and deadline.

Award: Scholarship for use in freshman, sophomore, junior, or senior years; not renewable. *Number:* 3. *Amount:* $1000–$1500.

Eligibility Requirements: Applicant must be high school student; planning to enroll or expecting to enroll full- or part-time at a four-year institution or university; male; resident of Indiana and must have an interest in leadership. Available to U.S. citizens.

Application Requirements: Application, essay, participation in the Boys State Program, nomination from Boys State official. *Deadline:* June 13.

Contact: Susan Long, Program Coordinator
American Legion Department of Indiana
777 North Meridan Street, Room 104
Indianapolis, IN 46204-1189
Phone: 317-630-1264
Fax: 317-237-9891
E-mail: slong@indlegion.org

AMERICAN LEGION DEPARTMENT OF IOWA

http://www.ialegion.org/

AMERICAN LEGION DEPARTMENT OF IOWA EAGLE SCOUT OF THE YEAR SCHOLARSHIP
• *See page 530*

AMERICAN LEGION DEPARTMENT OF IOWA HIGH SCHOOL ORATORICAL CONTEST

All contestants in the department of Iowa American Legion High School Oratorical Contest shall be citizens or lawful permanent residents of the United States. The department of Iowa American Legion High School Oratorical Contest shall consist of one contestant from each of the three area contests. The area contest shall consist of one contestant from each district in the designated Area.

Award: Prize for use in freshman year; not renewable. *Number:* up to 3. *Amount:* $1000–$2000.

Eligibility Requirements: Applicant must be high school student; planning to enroll or expecting to enroll full-time at a two-year or four-year institution or university; resident of Iowa and must have an interest in public speaking. Available to U.S. citizens.

Application Requirements: Application, applicant must enter a contest. *Deadline:* varies.

Contact: Kathy Nees, Program Director, Youth Programs
American Legion Department of Iowa
720 Lyon Street
Des Moines, IA 50309
Phone: 515-282-5068
Fax: 515-282-7583
E-mail: knees@ialegion.org

AMERICAN LEGION DEPARTMENT OF IOWA OUTSTANDING SENIOR BASEBALL PLAYER

One-time award for Iowa residents who participated in the American Legion Senior Baseball Program and display outstanding sportsmanship, athletic ability, and proven academic achievements. Must be recommended by Baseball Committee.

Award: Scholarship for use in freshman year; not renewable. *Number:* 1. *Amount:* $750–$1500.

Eligibility Requirements: Applicant must be high school student; age 15-18; planning to enroll or expecting to enroll full-time at a two-year or four-year institution or university; resident of Iowa and must have an interest in athletics/sports. Available to U.S. citizens.

Application Requirements: Application, applicant must enter a contest, references. *Deadline:* July 15.

Contact: Kathy Nees, Program Director, Youth Programs
American Legion Department of Iowa
720 Lyon Street
Des Moines, IA 50309
Phone: 515-282-5068
Fax: 515-282-7583
E-mail: knees@ialegion.org

AMERICAN LEGION DEPARTMENT OF KANSAS

http://www.ksamlegion.org/

ALBERT M. LAPPIN SCHOLARSHIP
• *See page 530*

CHARLES W. AND ANNETTE HILL SCHOLARSHIP
• *See page 530*

DR. CLICK COWGER BASEBALL SCHOLARSHIP

Scholarship available to a high school senior or college freshman or sophomore enrolled in a Kansas institution. Applicant may intend to enroll in a junior college, university or trade school in Kansas only. Must be a male and should play or has played Kansas American Legion baseball. Must be an average or a better student scholastically.

Award: Scholarship for use in freshman or sophomore years; not renewable. *Number:* 1. *Amount:* $500.

Eligibility Requirements: Applicant must be enrolled or expecting to enroll full-time at a two-year or four-year or technical institution or university; male; resident of Kansas; studying in Kansas and must have an interest in athletics/sports. Available to U.S. citizens.

Application Requirements: Application, financial need analysis, photo, references, transcript. *Deadline:* July 15.

Contact: Jim Gravenstein, Chairman, Scholarship Committee
American Legion Department of Kansas
1314 Topeka Boulevard, SW
Topeka, KS 66612
Phone: 785-232-9315
Fax: 785-232-1399

HUGH A. SMITH SCHOLARSHIP FUND
• *See page 531*

PAUL FLAHERTY ATHLETIC SCHOLARSHIP

Scholarship available to high school seniors, college level freshmen or sophomores enrolled or intending to enroll in an approved junior college, college, university, or trade school. Must have participated in any form of high school athletics. Must be an average or a better student scholastically.

Award: Scholarship for use in freshman or sophomore years; not renewable. *Number:* 1. *Amount:* $250.

Eligibility Requirements: Applicant must be enrolled or expecting to enroll full-time at a two-year or four-year or technical institution or university; studying in Kansas and must have an interest in athletics/sports. Available to U.S. citizens.

Application Requirements: Application, financial need analysis, photo, references, transcript, latest 1040 income statement of supporting parents. *Deadline:* July 15.

Contact: Jim Gravenstein, Chairman, Scholarship Committee
American Legion Department of Kansas
1314 Topeka Boulevard, SW
Topeka, KS 66612
Phone: 785-232-9513
Fax: 785-232-1399

ROSEDALE POST 346 SCHOLARSHIP
• *See page 531*

TED AND NORA ANDERSON SCHOLARSHIPS
• *See page 531*

AMERICAN LEGION DEPARTMENT OF MAINE

http://www.mainelegion.org/

AMERICAN LEGION DEPARTMENT OF MAINE CHILDREN AND YOUTH SCHOLARSHIP
• *See page 632*

DANIEL E. LAMBERT MEMORIAL SCHOLARSHIP
• *See page 632*

JAMES V. DAY SCHOLARSHIP
• *See page 531*

AMERICAN LEGION DEPARTMENT OF MARYLAND

http://www.mdlegion.org/

AMERICAN LEGION DEPARTMENT OF MARYLAND GENERAL SCHOLARSHIP

Scholarship of $500 for Maryland high school students. Must plan on attending a two-year or four-year college or university in the state of Maryland. Nonrenewable award. Based on financial need and citizenship. Applications available on web site http://mdlegion.org.

Award: Scholarship for use in freshman year; not renewable. *Number:* up to 3. *Amount:* up to $500.

Eligibility Requirements: Applicant must be high school student; age 19 or under; planning to enroll or expecting to enroll full-time at a two-year or four-year institution or university; resident of Maryland and studying in Maryland. Available to U.S. citizens.

Application Requirements: Application, essay, financial need analysis, transcript. *Deadline:* April 1.

Contact: Thomas Davis, Department Adjutant
American Legion Department of Maryland
101 North Gay, Room E
Baltimore, MD 21202
Phone: 410-752-1405
Fax: 410-752-3822
E-mail: tom@mdlegion.org

AMERICAN LEGION DEPARTMENT OF MARYLAND GENERAL SCHOLARSHIP FUND
• *See page 632*

AMERICAN LEGION DEPARTMENT OF MICHIGAN

http://www.michiganlegion.org/

AMERICAN LEGION DEPARTMENT OF MICHIGAN ORATORICAL SCHOLARSHIP PROGRAM

Oratorical contest open to students in ninth to twelfth grades of any accredited Michigan high school or state accredited home school. Five one-time awards of varying amounts. State winner advances to National Competition for scholarship money ranging from $14,000 to $18,000.

Award: Scholarship for use in freshman year; not renewable. *Number:* 5. *Amount:* $800–$1500.

Eligibility Requirements: Applicant must be high school student; age 20 or under; planning to enroll or expecting to enroll full- or part-time at a two-year or four-year institution or university; resident of Michigan and must have an interest in public speaking. Available to U.S. citizens.

Application Requirements: Application, applicant must enter a contest, essay. *Deadline:* January 2.

Contact: Deanna Clark, Department Administrative Assistant for Programs
American Legion Department of Michigan
212 North Verlinden Avenue, Suite A
Lansing, MI 48915
Phone: 517-371-4720 Ext. 11
Fax: 517-371-2401
E-mail: programs@michiganlegion.org

GUY M. WILSON SCHOLARSHIPS
• *See page 633*

WILLIAM D. AND JEWELL W. BREWER SCHOLARSHIP TRUSTS
• *See page 633*

AMERICAN LEGION DEPARTMENT OF MINNESOTA

http://www.mnlegion.org/

AMERICAN LEGION DEPARTMENT OF MINNESOTA HIGH SCHOOL ORATORICAL CONTEST

Oratorical contest open to students in ninth to twelfth grades of any accredited Minnesota high school or home-schooled students. Must be Minnesota resident. Speech must be student's original work on the general subject of the Constitution. Speech contests begin in December at local Legion post level and continue on to the national competition. See web site for specific topic and application details http://www.mnlegion.org.

Award: Prize for use in freshman year; not renewable. *Number:* 4. *Amount:* $500–$1500.

Eligibility Requirements: Applicant must be high school student; planning to enroll or expecting to enroll full- or part-time at a two-year or four-year or technical institution or university; resident of Minnesota and must have an interest in public speaking. Available to U.S. citizens.

Application Requirements: Application, applicant must enter a contest. *Deadline:* November 30.

Contact: Jennifer Kelley, Program Coordinator
American Legion Department of Minnesota
20 West 12th Street, Room 300-A
St. Paul, MN 55155
Phone: 651-291-1800
Fax: 651-291-1057
E-mail: department@mnlegion.org

AMERICAN LEGION DEPARTMENT OF MINNESOTA MEMORIAL SCHOLARSHIP
• *See page 531*

MINNESOTA LEGIONNAIRES INSURANCE TRUST SCHOLARSHIP
• *See page 532*

AMERICAN LEGION DEPARTMENT OF MISSOURI

http://www.missourilegion.org/

CHARLES L. BACON MEMORIAL SCHOLARSHIP
• *See page 532*

LILLIE LOIS FORD SCHOLARSHIP FUND
• *See page 633*

AMERICAN LEGION DEPARTMENT OF MONTANA

http://www.mtlegion.org/

AMERICAN LEGION DEPARTMENT OF MONTANA HIGH SCHOOL ORATORICAL CONTEST

Applicants participate in a statewide memorized oratorical contest on the U.S. Constitution. Four places are awarded. Must be a Montana high school student. Contact state adjutant American Legion Department of Montana for further details. Each state winner who competes in the first round of the national contest will receive a $1000 scholarship. Participants in the second round who do not advance to the national final round will receive an additional $1000 scholarship.

Award: Scholarship for use in freshman year; not renewable. *Number:* 1–4. *Amount:* $300–$2000.

Eligibility Requirements: Applicant must be high school student; planning to enroll or expecting to enroll full-time at a two-year or four-year or technical institution or university; resident of Montana and must have an interest in public speaking. Available to U.S. citizens.

Application Requirements: Application, applicant must enter a contest. *Deadline:* continuous.

Contact: Gary White, State Adjutant
American Legion Department of Montana
PO Box 6075
Helena, MT 59604
Phone: 406-324-3989
Fax: 406-324-3991
E-mail: amlegmt@in-tch.com

AMERICAN LEGION DEPARTMENT OF NEBRASKA

http://www.nebraskalegion.net/

AMERICAN LEGION BASEBALL SCHOLARSHIP-NEBRASKA AMERICAN LEGION BASEBALL PLAYER OF THE YEAR

Any Team Manager or Head Coach of an American Legion Post-affiliated team may nominate one player for consideration for this award. Application, letters of recommendation, and certification form must be completed, postmarked, and mailed to the state's Department Head-

quarters no later than July 15. Three letters of testimony must be attached to the nomination form.

Award: Scholarship for use in freshman year; not renewable. *Number:* 1. *Amount:* $600–$750.

Eligibility Requirements: Applicant must be high school student; planning to enroll or expecting to enroll full- or part-time at a two-year or four-year or technical institution or university; resident of Nebraska and must have an interest in athletics/sports. Available to U.S. citizens.

Application Requirements: Application, photo, references. *Deadline:* July 15.

Contact: Mr. Jody Moeller, Activities Director
American Legion Department of Nebraska
PO Box 5205
Lincoln, NE 68505-0205
Phone: 402-464-6338
Fax: 402-464-6330
E-mail: actdirlegion@alltel.net

AMERICAN LEGION DEPARTMENT OF NEBRASKA HIGH SCHOOL ORATORICAL CONTEST

Local high school winners advance to District. Fifteen District Winners advance to Area contest. Area contestants awarded $100. Four Area winners advance to State contest. State prizes range from $200 to $1000. State winner advances to National contest. National prizes range from $14,000 to $18,000.

Award: Prize for use in freshman year; not renewable. *Number:* 4–19. *Amount:* $100–$1000.

Eligibility Requirements: Applicant must be high school student; planning to enroll or expecting to enroll full- or part-time at a two-year or four-year or technical institution or university; resident of Nebraska and must have an interest in public speaking. Available to U.S. citizens.

Application Requirements: Applicant must enter a contest, 8- to 10-minute prepared oration on some aspect the U.S. Constitution, a discourse on an assigned topic lasting 3 to 5 minutes. *Deadline:* varies.

Contact: Jody Moeller, Activities Director
American Legion Department of Nebraska
PO Box 5205
Lincoln, NE 68505-0205
Phone: 402-464-6338
Fax: 402-464-6880
E-mail: actdirlegion@alltel.net

AMERICAN LEGION DEPARTMENT OF NEBRASKA JIM HURLBERT MEMORIAL BASEBALL SCHOLARSHIP

Award to a Nebraska American Legion Baseball player in last year of eligibility and/or graduating senior. One applicant nominated by each Senior American Legion Baseball team. Student must attend a postsecondary educational institution within the state of Nebraska, and must have maintained a GPA in the upper half of his/her graduating class.

Award: Scholarship for use in freshman year; not renewable. *Number:* up to 4. *Amount:* up to $500.

Eligibility Requirements: Applicant must be high school student; planning to enroll or expecting to enroll full- or part-time at a two-year or four-year or technical institution or university; resident of Nebraska; studying in Nebraska and must have an interest in athletics/sports. Applicant must have 2.5 GPA or higher. Available to U.S. citizens.

Application Requirements: Application, financial need analysis, references, transcript. *Deadline:* June 15.

Contact: Mr. Jody Moeller, Activities Director
American Legion Department of Nebraska
PO Box 5205
Lincoln, NE 68505-0205
Phone: 402-464-6338
Fax: 402-464-6330
E-mail: actdirlegion@alltel.net

EAGLE SCOUT OF THE YEAR SCHOLARSHIP
• *See page 532*

MAYNARD JENSEN AMERICAN LEGION MEMORIAL SCHOLARSHIP
• *See page 532*

AMERICAN LEGION DEPARTMENT OF NEW YORK

http://www.ny.legion.org/

AMERICAN LEGION DEPARTMENT OF NEW YORK HIGH SCHOOL ORATORICAL CONTEST

Oratorical contest open to students under 20 years in 9th-12th grades of any accredited New York high school. Speech contests begin in November at post levels and continue to national competition. Must be U.S. citizen or permanent resident. Payments are made directly to college and are awarded over a four-year period. Deadline varies.

Award: Scholarship for use in freshman year; not renewable. *Number:* varies. *Amount:* $2000–$6000.

Eligibility Requirements: Applicant must be high school student; age 20 or under; planning to enroll or expecting to enroll full-time at a four-year institution or university; resident of New York and must have an interest in public speaking. Available to U.S. citizens.

Application Requirements: Application, applicant must enter a contest. *Deadline:* varies.

Contact: Richard Pedro, Department Adjutant
American Legion Department of New York
112 State Street, Suite 400
Albany, NY 12207
Phone: 518-463-2215
Fax: 518-427-8443
E-mail: newyork@legion.org

AMERICAN LEGION DEPARTMENT OF NORTH CAROLINA

http://www.nclegion.org/

AMERICAN LEGION DEPARTMENT OF NORTH CAROLINA HIGH SCHOOL ORATORICAL CONTEST

Objective of the contest is to develop a deeper knowledge and appreciation of the U.S. Constitution, develop leadership qualities, the ability to think and speak clearly and intelligently, and prepare for acceptance of duties, responsibilities, rights, and privileges of American citizenship. Open to North Carolina high school students. Must be U.S. citizen or lawful permanent resident. The contestant must have a prepared eight to ten minute oration on some aspect of the Constitution of the United States, as well as 4 three to five minute discourses on specific assigned topics to test the speaker's knowledge of the subject.

Award: Scholarship for use in freshman year; not renewable. *Number:* 5. *Amount:* $500–$2000.

Eligibility Requirements: Applicant must be high school student; age 20 or under; planning to enroll or expecting to enroll full- or part-time at a two-year or four-year or technical institution or university; resident of North Carolina and must have an interest in public speaking. Available to U.S. citizens.

Application Requirements: Applicant must enter a contest. *Deadline:* varies.

Contact: Deborah Rose, Department Executive Secretary
American Legion Department of North Carolina
4 North Blount Street, PO Box 26657
Raleigh, NC 27611-6657
Phone: 919-832-7506
Fax: 919-832-6428
E-mail: drose-nclegion@nc.rr.com

AMERICAN LEGION DEPARTMENT OF NORTH DAKOTA

http://www.ndlegion.org/

AMERICAN LEGION DEPARTMENT OF NORTH DAKOTA NATIONAL HIGH SCHOOL ORATORICAL CONTEST

Oratorical contest for high school students in grades nine to twelve. Contestants must prepare to speak on the topic of the U.S. Constitution. Must graduate from an accredited North Dakota high school. Contest begins at the local level and continues to the national level. Several one-time awards of $100 to $2000.

Award: Prize for use in freshman, sophomore, junior, or senior years; not renewable. *Number:* 38. *Amount:* $100–$2000.

Eligibility Requirements: Applicant must be high school student; planning to enroll or expecting to enroll full-time at a four-year institution or university; resident of North Dakota and must have an interest in public speaking. Available to U.S. citizens.

Application Requirements: Application, applicant must enter a contest. *Deadline:* November 30.

Contact: Teri Bryant, Programs/Membership Coordinator
American Legion Department of North Dakota
405 West Main Avenue
PO Box 5057
West Fargo, ND 58078
Phone: 701-293-3120
Fax: 701-293-9951
E-mail: programs@ndlegion.org

HATTIE TEDROW MEMORIAL FUND SCHOLARSHIP
• *See page 633*

NORTH DAKOTA CARING CITIZEN SCHOLARSHIP

One-time award for North Dakota high school juniors who participated in the Boys State Program. Must be nominated by Boys State official. Must demonstrate care and concern for fellow students.

Award: Scholarship for use in freshman year; not renewable. *Number:* varies. *Amount:* varies.

Eligibility Requirements: Applicant must be high school student; planning to enroll or expecting to enroll full-time at a two-year or four-year or technical institution or university; male and resident of North Dakota. Available to U.S. citizens.

Application Requirements: Application, references, nomination. *Deadline:* varies.

Contact: Teri Bryant, Programs/Membership Coordinator
American Legion Department of North Dakota
405 West Main Avenue
PO Box 5057
West Fargo, ND 58078
Phone: 701-293-3120
Fax: 701-293-9951
E-mail: programs@ndlegion.org

AMERICAN LEGION DEPARTMENT OF OREGON

http://www.orlegion.org/

AMERICAN LEGION DEPARTMENT OF OREGON HIGH SCHOOL ORATORICAL CONTEST

Students give two orations, one prepared and one extemporaneous on an assigned topic pertaining to the Constitution of the United States of America. Awards are given at Post, District, and State level with the state winner advancing to the National level contest. Open to students enrolled in high schools within the state of Oregon.

Award: Scholarship for use in freshman year; not renewable. *Number:* up to 4. *Amount:* $200–$500.

Eligibility Requirements: Applicant must be high school student; planning to enroll or expecting to enroll full-time at a four-year institution or university; resident of Oregon and must have an interest in public speaking. Available to U.S. citizens.

Application Requirements: Application, applicant must enter a contest. *Deadline:* December 1.

Contact: Barry Snyder, Adjutant
American Legion Department of Oregon
PO Box 1730
Wilsonville, OR 97070-1730
Phone: 503-685-5006
Fax: 503-968-5432
E-mail: orlegion@aol.com

AMERICAN LEGION DEPARTMENT OF PENNSYLVANIA

http://www.pa-legion.com/

AMERICAN LEGION DEPARTMENT OF PENNSYLVANIA HIGH SCHOOL ORATORICAL CONTEST

Oratorical contest open to students in 9th-12th grades of any accredited Pennsylvania high school. Speech contests begin in January at post level and continue on to national competition. Contact local American Legion post for deadlines and application details. Three one-time awards ranging from $7500 for first place, second place $5000, and third place $4000.

Award: Prize for use in freshman year; not renewable. *Number:* 3. *Amount:* $4000–$7500.

Eligibility Requirements: Applicant must be high school student; planning to enroll or expecting to enroll full-time at a two-year or four-year or technical institution or university; resident of Pennsylvania and must have an interest in public speaking. Available to U.S. citizens.

Application Requirements: Application, applicant must enter a contest. *Deadline:* varies.

Contact: Colleen Washinger, Executive Secretary
American Legion Department of Pennsylvania
PO Box 2324
Harrisburg, PA 17105-2324
Phone: 717-730-9100
Fax: 717-975-2836
E-mail: hq@pa-legion.com

JOSEPH P. GAVENONIS COLLEGE SCHOLARSHIP (PLAN I)
• *See page 533*

AMERICAN LEGION DEPARTMENT OF SOUTH DAKOTA

http://www.sdlegion.org/

AMERICAN LEGION DEPARTMENT OF SOUTH DAKOTA HIGH SCHOOL ORATORICAL CONTEST

Provide an 8 to 10 minute oration on some phase of the U.S. Constitution. Be prepared to speak extemporaneously for 3 to 5 minutes on specified articles or amendments. Compete at Local, District, and State levels. State winner goes on to National Contest and opportunity to win $18,000 in scholarships. Contact local American Legion post for contest dates.

Award: Prize for use in freshman, sophomore, junior, or senior years; not renewable. *Number:* 1–4. *Amount:* $200–$1000.

Eligibility Requirements: Applicant must be enrolled or expecting to enroll full-time at a two-year or four-year or technical institution or university; resident of South Dakota and must have an interest in public speaking. Available to U.S. citizens.

Application Requirements: Applicant must enter a contest, oration. *Deadline:* varies.

Contact: Dennis Brendan, Department Adjutant
American Legion Department of South Dakota
PO Box 67
Watertown, SD 57201-0067
Phone: 605-886-3604
Fax: 605-886-2870
E-mail: sdlegion@dailypost.com

AMERICAN LEGION DEPARTMENT OF TENNESSEE

http://www.tennesseelegion.org/

AMERICAN LEGION DEPARTMENT OF TENNESSEE EAGLE SCOUT OF THE YEAR
• *See page 533*

AMERICAN LEGION DEPARTMENT OF TENNESSEE HIGH SCHOOL ORATORICAL CONTEST

Scholarship for graduating Tennessee high school seniors enrolled either part-time or full-time in accredited colleges or universities.

Award: Scholarship for use in freshman year; not renewable. *Number:* 1–3. *Amount:* $1000–$4000.

Eligibility Requirements: Applicant must be high school student; planning to enroll or expecting to enroll full- or part-time at a two-year or four-year institution or university; resident of Tennessee and must have an interest in public speaking. Available to U.S. citizens.

Application Requirements: Applicant must enter a contest. *Deadline:* varies.

Contact: Darlene Burgess, Executive Assistant
American Legion Department of Tennessee
215 Eighth Avenue, North
Nashville, TN 37203
Phone: 615-254-0568
E-mail: tnleg1@bellsouth.net

JROTC SCHOLARSHIP
• *See page 618*

AMERICAN LEGION DEPARTMENT OF TEXAS

http://www.txlegion.org/

AMERICAN LEGION DEPARTMENT OF TEXAS HIGH SCHOOL ORATORICAL CONTEST

Scholarships will be given to the winners of oratorical contests. Contestants must be in high school with plans to further their education in a postsecondary institution. The winner of first place will be certified to national headquarters as the Texas representative in the quarter finals and the department will award a $2000 scholarship to the college of the applicant's choice. The department champion will receive additional scholarships each time he/she advances to the next level.

Award: Prize for use in freshman year; not renewable. *Number:* up to 20. *Amount:* $500–$2000.

Eligibility Requirements: Applicant must be high school student; age 20 or under; planning to enroll or expecting to enroll full-time at a two-year or four-year or technical institution or university; resident of Texas and must have an interest in public speaking. Available to U.S. citizens.

Application Requirements: Application, applicant must enter a contest, essay, interview, copy of prepared oration. *Deadline:* varies.

Contact: Robert Squyres, Director of Internal Affairs
American Legion Department of Texas
3401 Ed Bluestein Boulevard
Austin, TX 78721-2902
Phone: 512-472-4138
Fax: 512-472-0603
E-mail: programs@txlegion.org

AMERICAN LEGION DEPARTMENT OF VERMONT

http://www.legionvthq.com/

AMERICAN LEGION DEPARTMENT OF VERMONT DEPARTMENT SCHOLARSHIPS

Awards for high school seniors who attend a Vermont high school or similar school in an adjoining state whose parents are legal residents of Vermont, or reside in an adjoining state and attend a Vermont secondary school.

Award: Scholarship for use in freshman year; not renewable. *Number:* up to 12. *Amount:* $500–$1500.

Eligibility Requirements: Applicant must be high school student; planning to enroll or expecting to enroll full- or part-time at a two-year or four-year or technical institution or university and resident of New Hampshire, New York, or Vermont. Available to U.S. citizens.

Application Requirements: Application, essay, financial need analysis, references, transcript. *Deadline:* April 1.

Contact: Huzon "Jerry" Stewart, Chairman
American Legion Department of Vermont
PO Box 396
Montpelier, VT 05601-0396
Phone: 802-223-7131
Fax: 802-223-0318
E-mail: alvthq@myfairpoint.net

AMERICAN LEGION DEPARTMENT OF VERMONT HIGH SCHOOL ORATORICAL CONTEST

• *See page 634*

AMERICAN LEGION EAGLE SCOUT OF THE YEAR

• *See page 533*

AMERICAN LEGION DEPARTMENT OF VIRGINIA

http://www.valegion.org/

AMERICAN LEGION DEPARTMENT OF VIRGINIA HIGH SCHOOL ORATORICAL CONTEST

Three one-time awards of up to $1100. Oratorical contest open to applicants who are winners of the Virginia department oratorical contest and who attend high school in Virginia. Competitors must demonstrate their knowledge of the U.S. Constitution. Must be students in ninth to twelfth grades at accredited Virginia high schools.

Award: Prize for use in freshman year; not renewable. *Number:* 3. *Amount:* $600–$1100.

Eligibility Requirements: Applicant must be high school student; age 20 or under; planning to enroll or expecting to enroll full-time at a four-year institution or university and resident of Virginia. Available to U.S. citizens.

Application Requirements: Application, applicant must enter a contest. *Deadline:* December 1.

Contact: Dale Chapman, Adjutant
American Legion Department of Virginia
1708 Commonwealth Avenue
Richmond, VA 23230
Phone: 804-353-6606
Fax: 804-358-1940
E-mail: eeccleston@valegion.org

AMERICAN LEGION DEPARTMENT OF WASHINGTON

http://www.walegion.org/

AMERICAN LEGION DEPARTMENT OF WASHINGTON CHILDREN AND YOUTH SCHOLARSHIPS

• *See page 534*

AMERICAN LEGION DEPARTMENT OF WEST VIRGINIA

http://www.wvlegion.org/

AMERICAN LEGION DEPARTMENT OF WEST VIRGINIA BOARD OF REGENTS SCHOLARSHIP

One-time prize awarded annually to the winner of the West Virginia American Legion State Oratorical Scholarship Program Contest. Must be in ninth to twelfth grade of an accredited West Virginia high school to compete. For use at a West Virginia institution only.

Award: Scholarship for use in freshman year; not renewable. *Number:* 1. *Amount:* up to $1500.

Eligibility Requirements: Applicant must be high school student; planning to enroll or expecting to enroll full-time at a four-year institution or university; resident of West Virginia; studying in West Virginia and must have an interest in public speaking. Available to U.S. citizens.

Application Requirements: Application, applicant must enter a contest. *Deadline:* January 1.

Contact: Mr. Miles Epling, State Adjutant
American Legion Department of West Virginia
2016 Kanawha Boulevard East, PO Box 3191
Charleston, WV 25332-3191
Phone: 304-343-7591
Fax: 304-343-7592
E-mail: wvlegion@suddenlinkmail.com

AMERICAN LEGION DEPARTMENT OF WEST VIRGINIA HIGH SCHOOL ORATORICAL CONTEST

Oratorical Scholarship Program Contest open to students in ninth to twelfth grades of any accredited West Virginia high school. Speech contests begin in January at post level and continue on to national competition. Contact local American Legion Post for deadlines and application details, or American Legion State Headquarters 304-343-7591.

Award: Scholarship for use in freshman year; not renewable. *Number:* 25–39. *Amount:* $150–$500.

Eligibility Requirements: Applicant must be high school student; planning to enroll or expecting to enroll full-time at a four-year institution or university; resident of West Virginia and must have an interest in public speaking. Available to U.S. citizens.

Application Requirements: Application, applicant must enter a contest. *Deadline:* January 1.

Contact: Ms. Lois E. Moles, State Adjutant
American Legion Department of West Virginia
2016 Kanawha Boulevard East, PO Box 3191
Charleston, WV 25332-3191
Phone: 304-343-7591
Fax: 304-343-7592
E-mail: wvlegion@suddenlinkmail.com

SONS OF THE AMERICAN LEGION WILLIAM F. "BILL" JOHNSON MEMORIAL SCHOLARSHIP

• *See page 534*

AMERICAN QUARTER HORSE FOUNDATION (AQHF)

http://www.aqha.com/foundation

DR. GERALD O'CONNOR MICHIGAN SCHOLARSHIP

• *See page 535*

INDIANA QUARTER HORSE YOUTH SCHOLARSHIP

• *See page 535*

JOAN CAIN FLORIDA QUARTER HORSE YOUTH SCHOLARSHIP

• *See page 535*

NEBRASKA QUARTER HORSE YOUTH SCHOLARSHIP

• *See page 536*

RAY MELTON MEMORIAL VIRGINIA QUARTER HORSE YOUTH SCHOLARSHIP

• *See page 536*

SWAYZE WOODRUFF MEMORIAL MID-SOUTH SCHOLARSHIP

• *See page 536*

AMERICAN SAVINGS FOUNDATION

http://www.asfdn.org/

AMERICAN SAVINGS FOUNDATION SCHOLARSHIPS

Scholarship awards range from $500 to $3000 for students entering any year of a two- or four-year undergraduate program or technical/vocational program at an accredited institution. Applicant must be a Connecticut resident. Minimum 2.5 GPA required.

Award: Scholarship for use in freshman, sophomore, junior, or senior years; renewable. *Number:* varies. *Amount:* $500–$3000.

Eligibility Requirements: Applicant must be enrolled or expecting to enroll full- or part-time at a two-year or four-year or technical institution or university and resident of Connecticut. Applicant must have 2.5 GPA or higher. Available to U.S. citizens.

Application Requirements: Application, financial need analysis, references, transcript. *Deadline:* March 31.

Contact: Maria Falvo, Senior Program Officer, Scholarships
American Savings Foundation
185 Main Street
New Britain, CT 06051
Phone: 860-827-2572
Fax: 860-832-4582
E-mail: mfalvo@asfdn.org

AMERICAN SWEDISH INSTITUTE

http://www.americanswedishinst.org/

LILLY LORENZEN SCHOLARSHIP

One-time award for a Minnesota resident, or a student attending a school in Minnesota. Must have working knowledge of Swedish and present a creditable plan for study in Sweden. Must be a U.S. citizen.

Award: Scholarship for use in freshman, sophomore, junior, senior, graduate, or postgraduate years; not renewable. *Number:* 1. *Amount:* $1000.

Eligibility Requirements: Applicant must be age 18 and over; enrolled or expecting to enroll full- or part-time at a two-year or four-year or technical institution or university; resident of Minnesota and must have an interest in Scandinavian language. Available to U.S. citizens.

Application Requirements: Application, interview, transcript. *Deadline:* May 1.

Contact: Karin Krull, Adult Programs Coordinator
American Swedish Institute
2600 Park Avenue
Minneapolis, MN 55407-1090
Phone: 612-870-3355
Fax: 612-871-8682
E-mail: karink@americanswedishinst.org

ARIZONA COMMISSION FOR POSTSECONDARY EDUCATION

http://www.azhighered.gov/

ARIZONA PRIVATE POSTSECONDARY EDUCATION STUDENT FINANCIAL ASSISTANCE PROGRAM

Provides grants to financially needy Arizona Community College graduates, to attend a private postsecondary baccalaureate degree-granting institution.

Award: Forgivable loan for use in junior or senior years; renewable. *Number:* varies. *Amount:* $1000–$2000.

Eligibility Requirements: Applicant must be enrolled or expecting to enroll full-time at a four-year institution or university; resident of Arizona and studying in Arizona. Applicant must have 2.5 GPA or higher. Available to U.S. citizens.

Application Requirements: Application, financial need analysis, transcript, promissory note. *Deadline:* June 30.

Contact: Mila Zaporteza, Business Manager
Arizona Commission for Postsecondary Education
2020 North Central Avenue, Suite 650
Phoenix, AZ 85004-4503
Phone: 602-258-2435 Ext. 102
Fax: 602-258-2483
E-mail: mila@azhighered.gov

LEVERAGING EDUCATIONAL ASSISTANCE PARTNERSHIP

Grants to financially needy students, who enroll in and attend postsecondary education or training in Arizona schools. Program was formerly known as the State Student Incentive Grant or SSIG Program.

Award: Grant for use in freshman, sophomore, junior, senior, or graduate years; not renewable. *Number:* varies. *Amount:* $100–$2500.

Eligibility Requirements: Applicant must be enrolled or expecting to enroll full- or part-time at a two-year or four-year or technical institution or university; resident of Arizona and studying in Arizona. Available to U.S. citizens.

Application Requirements: Application, financial need analysis, transcript. *Deadline:* April 30.

Contact: Mila A. Zaporteza, Business Manager and LEAP Financial Aid Manager
Arizona Commission for Postsecondary Education
2020 North Central Avenue, Suite 650
Phoenix, AZ 85004-4503
Phone: 602-258-2435 Ext. 102
Fax: 602-258-2483
E-mail: mila@azhighered.gov

POSTSECONDARY EDUCATION GRANT PROGRAM

Awards of up to $2000 to Arizona residents studying in Arizona. May be renewed annually for a maximum of four calendar years. Minimum 2.5 GPA required. Deadline June 30.

Award: Forgivable loan for use in freshman, sophomore, junior, or senior years; renewable. *Number:* varies. *Amount:* $1000–$2000.

Eligibility Requirements: Applicant must be enrolled or expecting to enroll full- or part-time at a four-year institution or university; resident of Arizona and studying in Arizona. Applicant must have 2.5 GPA or higher. Available to U.S. citizens.

Application Requirements: Application, transcript, promissory note. *Deadline:* June 30.

Contact: Dr. April Osborn, Executive Director
Arizona Commission for Postsecondary Education
2020 North Central Avenue, Suite 650
Phoenix, AZ 85004-4503
Phone: 602-258-2435
Fax: 602-258-2483
E-mail: aosborn@azhighered.gov

ARIZONA PRIVATE SCHOOL ASSOCIATION

http://www.arizonapsa.org/

ARIZONA PRIVATE SCHOOL ASSOCIATION SCHOLARSHIP

Scholarships are for graduating students from Arizona and the high school determines the recipients of the awards. Each spring the Arizona Private School Association awards two $1000 Scholarships to every private high school in Arizona.

Award: Scholarship for use in freshman year; not renewable. *Number:* 600. *Amount:* $1000.

Eligibility Requirements: Applicant must be high school student; planning to enroll or expecting to enroll full-time at a four-year institution or university and resident of Arizona. Available to U.S. citizens.

Application Requirements: Application, essay. *Deadline:* April 30.

Contact: Fred Lockhart, Executive Director
Arizona Private School Association
202 East McDowell Road, Suite 273
Phoenix, AZ 85004
Phone: 602-254-5199
Fax: 602-254-5073
E-mail: apsa@eschelon.com

ARIZONA STATE DEPARTMENT OF EDUCATION

http://www.ade.az.gov/

ROBERT C. BYRD HONORS SCHOLARSHIP-ARIZONA

A program for high school graduates who show academic excellence and the promise of continued success in postsecondary education. A Byrd Scholar receives $1500 for each academic year for a maximum of four years to be applied toward undergraduate study at any accredited college or university in the United States. The number of scholarships awarded each year is subject to change due to funding.

Award: Scholarship for use in freshman year; renewable. *Number:* 50–150. *Amount:* $1500.

Eligibility Requirements: Applicant must be high school student; planning to enroll or expecting to enroll full-time at a four-year institution or university and resident of Arizona. Available to U.S. citizens.

Application Requirements: Application, transcript. *Deadline:* March 25.

Contact: Karla Bravo, Program and Project Coordinator
Arizona State Department of Education
1535 West Jefferson
Phoenix, AZ 85007
Phone: 602-542-3710
Fax: 602-364-1532
E-mail: byrd@azed.gov

ARKANSAS DEPARTMENT OF HIGHER EDUCATION

http://www.adhe.edu/

ARKANSAS ACADEMIC CHALLENGE SCHOLARSHIP PROGRAM

Awards for Arkansas residents who are graduating high school seniors, currently enrolled college students and nontraditional students to study at an approved Arkansas institution. Must have at least a 2.5 GPA or 19 ACT composite score (or the equivalent). Renewable up to three additional years.

Award: Scholarship for use in freshman, sophomore, junior, or senior years; renewable. *Number:* 25,000–30,000. *Amount:* $1250–$5000.

Eligibility Requirements: Applicant must be enrolled or expecting to enroll full-time at a two-year or four-year institution or university; resident of Arkansas and studying in Arkansas. Applicant must have 2.5 GPA or higher. Available to U.S. citizens.

Application Requirements: Application, test scores, transcript. *Deadline:* June 1.

Contact: Tara Smith, Director of Financial Aid
Arkansas Department of Higher Education
114 East Capitol Avenue
Little Rock, AR 72201-3818
Phone: 501-371-2000
Fax: 501-371-2001
E-mail: finaid@adhe.arknet.edu

ARKANSAS GOVERNOR'S SCHOLARS PROGRAM

Awards for outstanding Arkansas high school seniors. Must be an Arkansas resident and have a high school GPA of at least 3.5 or have scored at least 27 on the ACT. Award is $4000 per year for four years of full-time undergraduate study. Applicants who attain 32 or above on ACT, 1410 or above on SAT and have an academic 3.5 GPA, or are selected as National Merit or National Achievement finalists may receive an award equal to tuition, mandatory fees, room, and board up to $10,000 per year at any Arkansas institution.

Award: Scholarship for use in freshman, sophomore, junior, or senior years; renewable. *Number:* up to 375. *Amount:* $4000–$10,000.

Eligibility Requirements: Applicant must be enrolled or expecting to enroll full-time at a two-year or four-year institution or university; resident of Arkansas and studying in Arkansas. Applicant must have 3.5 GPA or higher. Available to U.S. citizens.

Application Requirements: Application, test scores, transcript. *Deadline:* February 1.

Contact: Tara Smith, Director of Financial Aid
Arkansas Department of Higher Education
114 East Capitol Avenue
Little Rock, AR 72201-3818
Phone: 501-371-2000
Fax: 501-371-2001
E-mail: taras@adhe.edu

LAW ENFORCEMENT OFFICERS' DEPENDENTS SCHOLARSHIP–ARKANSAS

Scholarship for dependents, under 23 years old, of Arkansas law-enforcement officers killed or permanently disabled in the line of duty. Renewable award is a waiver of tuition, fees, and room at two- or four-year Arkansas institution. Submit birth certificate, death certificate, and claims commission report of findings of fact. Proof of disability from State Claims Commission may also be submitted.

Award: Scholarship for use in freshman, sophomore, junior, or senior years; renewable. *Number:* 27–32.

Eligibility Requirements: Applicant must be age 23 or under; enrolled or expecting to enroll full- or part-time at a two-year or four-year or technical institution or university; resident of Arkansas and studying in Arkansas. Available to U.S. citizens.

Application Requirements: Application. *Deadline:* continuous.

Contact: Tara Smith, Director of Financial Aid
Arkansas Department of Higher Education
114 East Capitol Avenue
Little Rock, AR 72201-3818
Phone: 501-371-2000
Fax: 501-371-2001
E-mail: taras@adhe.edu

MILITARY DEPENDENT'S SCHOLARSHIP PROGRAM
• *See page 635*

SECOND EFFORT SCHOLARSHIP

Awarded to those scholars who achieved one of the 10 highest scores on the Arkansas High School Diploma Test (GED). Must be at least age 18 and not have graduated from high school. Students do not apply for this award, they are contacted by the Arkansas Department of Higher Education.

Award: Scholarship for use in freshman year; renewable. *Number:* 10. *Amount:* up to $1000.

Eligibility Requirements: Applicant must be high school student; planning to enroll or expecting to enroll full- or part-time at a two-year or four-year institution or university; resident of Arkansas and studying in Arkansas. Available to U.S. citizens.

Application Requirements: Application. *Deadline:* varies.

Contact: Tara Smith, Director of Financial Aid
Arkansas Department of Higher Education
114 East Capitol Avenue
Little Rock, AR 72201-3818
Phone: 501-371-2000
Fax: 501-371-2001
E-mail: taras@adhe.edu

ARKANSAS SINGLE PARENT SCHOLARSHIP FUND

http://www.aspsf.org/

ARKANSAS SINGLE PARENT SCHOLARSHIP

Scholarships are awarded to economically disadvantaged single parents who reside in Arkansas who have custodial care of at least one minor child and have not already received a baccalaureate degree. Award values, application deadlines, and other criteria vary by county. Visit http://www.aspsf.org for more information.

Award: Scholarship for use in freshman, sophomore, junior, or senior years; not renewable. *Number:* up to 2600. *Amount:* $200–$1800.

Eligibility Requirements: Applicant must be enrolled or expecting to enroll full- or part-time at a two-year or four-year or technical institution or university; single; resident of Arkansas and must have an interest in designated field specified by sponsor. Available to U.S. citizens.

Application Requirements: Application, financial need analysis, interview, references, transcript, statement of goals, FAFSA Student Aid Report (SAR). *Deadline:* varies.

Contact: Ralph Nesson, Executive Director
Arkansas Single Parent Scholarship Fund
614 East Emma Avenue, Suite 119
Springdale, AR 72764
Phone: 479-927-1402 Ext. 11
E-mail: rnesson@jtlshop.jonesnet.org

ARKANSAS STATE DEPARTMENT OF EDUCATION

http://www.arkansased.org/

ROBERT C. BYRD HONORS SCHOLARSHIP-ARKANSAS

Applicant must be a graduate of a public or private school or receive a recognized equivalent of a high school diploma. Must be a resident of Arkansas. Must be admitted to an institution of higher education, demonstrate outstanding academic achievement and show promise of continued academic achievement. Award is $1500 for each academic year for a maximum of four years.

Award: Scholarship for use in freshman year; renewable. *Number:* 60–68. *Amount:* $1500.

Eligibility Requirements: Applicant must be high school student; planning to enroll or expecting to enroll full-time at a two-year or four-year or technical institution or university and resident of Arkansas. Available to U.S. citizens.

Application Requirements: Application, essay, references, test scores, transcript. *Deadline:* February 16.

Contact: Mr. Thomas Charles Coy, Public School Program Manager
Arkansas State Department of Education
4 Capitol Mall Room 107-A
Little Rock, AR 72201
Phone: 501-682-4250
E-mail: thomas.coy@arkansas.gov

ARKANSAS STUDENT LOAN AUTHORITY

http://www.asla.info/

R. PRESTON WOODRUFF JR. SCHOLARSHIP

Twenty $1,000 scholarships awarded annually. Online entries only and only one entry per applicant. Eligible entries will be drawn at random to select the scholarship winners. Winners must submit a 500-word essay. One renewable scholarship (up to 4 years) will be awarded to the student with the most outstanding essay.

Award: Scholarship for use in freshman, sophomore, junior, senior, or graduate years; renewable. *Number:* 20. *Amount:* $1000.

Eligibility Requirements: Applicant must be enrolled or expecting to enroll full- or part-time at a two-year or four-year or technical institution or university and resident of Arkansas. Available to U.S. citizens.

Application Requirements: Application. *Deadline:* April 1.

Contact: Nancy Smith, Federal Contracts & Compliance Manager
Arkansas Student Loan Authority
3801 Woodland Heights
Suite 200
Little Rock, AR 72212
Phone: 800-443-6030
E-mail: nsmith@asla.info

ARRL FOUNDATION INC.

http://www.arrl.org/

ALBERT H. HIX W8AH MEMORIAL SCHOLARSHIP

One-time award available to general class or higher class amateur radio operators. Preference is given to the residents of the West Virginia section, or those attending postsecondary school in the West Virginia section.

Award: Scholarship for use in freshman, sophomore, junior, or senior years; not renewable. *Number:* 1. *Amount:* $500.

Eligibility Requirements: Applicant must be enrolled or expecting to enroll full-time at a two-year or four-year or technical institution or university; resident of West Virginia; studying in West Virginia and must have an interest in amateur radio. Applicant must have 3.0 GPA or higher. Available to U.S. citizens.

Application Requirements: Application, test scores, transcript. *Deadline:* February 1.

Contact: Ms. Mary Hobart, Secretary
ARRL Foundation Inc.
225 Main Street
Newington, CT 06111-1494
Phone: 860-594-0397
E-mail: k1mmh@arrl.org

ALBUQUERQUE AMATEUR RADIO CLUB/TOBY CROSS SCHOLARSHIP

Scholarship of $500 for students working on undergraduate degree. Must be a licensed amateur radio operator. Residents of New Mexico preferred. Must supply one-page essay on role of amateur radio in their life.

Award: Scholarship for use in freshman, sophomore, junior, or senior years; not renewable. *Number:* 1. *Amount:* $500.

Eligibility Requirements: Applicant must be enrolled or expecting to enroll full-time at a four-year institution or university; resident of New Mexico and must have an interest in amateur radio. Available to U.S. citizens.

Application Requirements: Application, essay, transcript. *Deadline:* February 1.

Contact: Ms. Mary Hobart, Secretary
ARRL Foundation Inc.
225 Main Street
Newington, CT 06111-1494
Phone: 860-594-0397
E-mail: k1mmh@arrl.org

CENTRAL ARIZONA DX ASSOCIATION SCHOLARSHIP

Award available to amateur radio operators with a technician license. Preference given to residents of Arizona. Graduating high school students will be considered before current college students. Must have 3.2 GPA or above.

Award: Scholarship for use in freshman year; not renewable. *Number:* 1. *Amount:* $1000.

Eligibility Requirements: Applicant must be high school student; planning to enroll or expecting to enroll full-time at a two-year or four-year institution or university; resident of Arizona and must have an interest in amateur radio.

Application Requirements: Application, transcript. *Deadline:* February 1.

Contact: Ms. Mary Hobart, Secretary
ARRL Foundation Inc.
225 Main Street
Newington, CT 06111-1494
Phone: 860-594-0397
E-mail: k1mmh@arrl.org

CENTRAL ARIZONA DX ASSOCIATION SCHOLARSHIP

One $1000 award is a available to a student who is an Arizona resident and who a possesses a Technician class or higher radio license. Graduating high school students will be considered before current college students.

Award: Scholarship for use in freshman, sophomore, junior, or senior years; not renewable. *Number:* 1. *Amount:* $1000.

Eligibility Requirements: Applicant must be enrolled or expecting to enroll at a two-year or four-year institution or university; resident of Arizona and must have an interest in amateur radio. Applicant must have 3.0 GPA or higher.

Application Requirements: Application, transcript. *Deadline:* February 1.

Contact: Ms. Mary Hobart, Secretary
ARRL Foundation Inc.
225 Main Street
Newington, CT 06111-1494
Phone: 860-594-0397
E-mail: k1mmh@arrl.org

CHARLES CLARKE CORDLE MEMORIAL SCHOLARSHIP

One-time award for licensed amateur radio operators. Must have minimum GPA of 2.5. Preference to students studying electronics, communications or related fields.

Award: Scholarship for use in freshman, sophomore, junior, or senior years; not renewable. *Number:* 1. *Amount:* $1000.

Eligibility Requirements: Applicant must be enrolled or expecting to enroll full-time at a four-year institution or university; resident of Alabama or Georgia; studying in Alabama or Georgia and must have an interest in amateur radio. Applicant must have 2.5 GPA or higher. Available to U.S. citizens.

Application Requirements: Application, transcript. *Deadline:* February 1.

Contact: Ms. Mary Hobart, Secretary
ARRL Foundation Inc.
225 Main Street
Newington, CT 06111-1494
Phone: 860-594-0397
E-mail: k1mmh@arrl.org

CHICAGO FM CLUB SCHOLARSHIPS

Multiple awards available to amateur radio operators with technician license. Preference given to residents of FCC Ninth Call District (Indiana, Illinois, Wisconsin). Student in post-secondary course of study at accredited 2- or 4-year college or trade school is eligible. Must be U.S. citizen or within 3 months of citizenship.

Award: Scholarship for use in freshman, sophomore, junior, or senior years; not renewable. *Number:* varies. *Amount:* $500.

Eligibility Requirements: Applicant must be enrolled or expecting to enroll full-time at a two-year or four-year or technical institution or university; resident of Illinois, Indiana, or Wisconsin and must have an interest in amateur radio. Available to U.S. citizens.

Application Requirements: Application, transcript. *Deadline:* February 1.

Contact: Ms. Mary Hobart, Secretary
ARRL Foundation Inc.
225 Main Street
Newington, CT 06111-1494
Phone: 860-594-0397
E-mail: k1mmh@arrl.org

GWINNETT AMATEUR RADIO SOCIETY SCHOLARSHIP

One $500 award is a available to a Georgia resident majoring in a technology-related field. Applicant must possess an active amateur radio license. Preference is given to electrical engineer majors and students from Gwinnett County, GA.

Award: Scholarship for use in freshman, sophomore, junior, senior, or graduate years; not renewable. *Number:* 1. *Amount:* $500.

Eligibility Requirements: Applicant must be enrolled or expecting to enroll at a four-year institution or university; resident of Georgia and must have an interest in amateur radio.

Application Requirements: Application, transcript. *Deadline:* February 1.

Contact: Ms. Mary Hobart, Secretary
ARRL Foundation Inc.
225 Main Street
Newington, CT 06111-1494
Phone: 860-594-0397
E-mail: k1mmh@arrl.org

LOUISIANA MEMORIAL SCHOLARSHIP

One $750 award is available to a resident of Louisiana or a student studying in Louisiana who possesses a Technician class or higher amateur radio license.

Award: Scholarship for use in freshman, sophomore, junior, or senior years; not renewable. *Number:* 1. *Amount:* $750.

Eligibility Requirements: Applicant must be enrolled or expecting to enroll at a four-year institution or university; resident of Louisiana; studying in Louisiana and must have an interest in amateur radio. Applicant must have 3.0 GPA or higher.

Application Requirements: Application, transcript. *Deadline:* February 1.

Contact: Ms. Mary Hobart, Secretary
ARRL Foundation Inc.
225 Main Street
Newington, CT 06111-1494
Phone: 860-594-0397
E-mail: k1mmh@arrl.org

MARY LOU BROWN SCHOLARSHIP

Multiple awards available to amateur radio operators with general license. Preference given to residents of Alaska, Idaho, Montana, Oregon, and Washington pursuing baccalaureate or higher course of study. GPA of 3.0 or higher required. Must demonstrate interest in promoting Amateur Radio Service.

Award: Scholarship for use in freshman, sophomore, junior, senior, or graduate years; not renewable. *Number:* varies. *Amount:* $2500.

Eligibility Requirements: Applicant must be enrolled or expecting to enroll full-time at a four-year institution or university; resident of Alaska, Idaho, Montana, Oregon, or Washington and must have an interest in amateur radio. Applicant must have 3.0 GPA or higher. Available to U.S. citizens.

Application Requirements: Application, transcript. *Deadline:* February 1.

Contact: Ms. Mary Hobart, Secretary
ARRL Foundation Inc.
225 Main Street
Newington, CT 06111-1494
Phone: 860-594-0397
E-mail: k1mmh@arrl.org

NEW ENGLAND FEMARA SCHOLARSHIPS

One-time award of $1000 available to students licensed as amateur radio operator technicians. Multiple Awards per year. Preference is given to the residents of Vermont, Maine, New Hampshire, Rhode Island, Massachusetts, or Connecticut.

Award: Scholarship for use in freshman, sophomore, junior, or senior years; not renewable. *Number:* varies. *Amount:* $1000.

Eligibility Requirements: Applicant must be enrolled or expecting to enroll full-time at a four-year institution or university; resident of Connecticut, Maine, New Hampshire, Rhode Island, or Vermont and must have an interest in amateur radio. Available to U.S. citizens.

Application Requirements: Application, transcript. *Deadline:* February 1.

Contact: Ms. Mary Hobart, Secretary
ARRL Foundation Inc.
225 Main Street
Newington, CT 06111-1494
Phone: 860-594-0397
E-mail: k1mmh@arrl.org

NORMAN E. STROHMEIER, W2VRS MEMORIAL SCHOLARSHIP

One $500 award is available to students who are residents of Western New York and who possess Technician class or higher amateur radio licenses. A 3.2 GPA on a 4.0 scale is required for application. Preference is given to graduating high school seniors.

Award: Scholarship for use in freshman, sophomore, junior, senior, or graduate years; not renewable. *Number:* 1. *Amount:* $500.

Eligibility Requirements: Applicant must be enrolled or expecting to enroll at a two-year or four-year or technical institution or university; resident of New York and must have an interest in amateur radio. Applicant must have 3.0 GPA or higher.

Application Requirements: Application, transcript. *Deadline:* February 1.

Contact: Ms. Mary Hobart, Secretary
ARRL Foundation Inc.
225 Main Street
Newington, CT 06111-1494
Phone: 860-594-0397
E-mail: k1mmh@arrl.org

PEORIA AREA AMATEUR RADIO CLUB SCHOLARSHIP

One $500 award is available to residents of the Central Illinois counties of: Peoria, Tazewell, Woodford, Knox, McLean, Fulton, Logan, Marshall and Stark. Applicants must possess a Technician class or higher amateur radio license.

Award: Scholarship for use in freshman, sophomore, junior, or senior years; not renewable. *Number:* 1. *Amount:* $500.

Eligibility Requirements: Applicant must be enrolled or expecting to enroll at a two-year or four-year institution or university; resident of Illinois and must have an interest in amateur radio.

Application Requirements: Application, transcript. *Deadline:* February 1.

Contact: Ms. Mary Hobart, Secretary
ARRL Foundation Inc.
225 Main Street
Newington, CT 06111-1494
Phone: 860-594-0397
E-mail: k1mmh@arrl.org

SIX METER CLUB OF CHICAGO SCHOLARSHIP

For licensed amateur radio operators. Award must be used at an institution of higher education in Illinois.

Award: Scholarship for use in freshman, sophomore, junior, or senior years; not renewable. *Number:* 1. *Amount:* $500.

Eligibility Requirements: Applicant must be enrolled or expecting to enroll full- or part-time at a two-year or four-year or technical institution or university; resident of Illinois, Indiana, or Wisconsin and must have an interest in amateur radio. Applicant must have 2.5 GPA or higher. Available to U.S. citizens.

Application Requirements: Application, transcript. *Deadline:* February 1.

Contact: Ms. Mary Hobart, Secretary
ARRL Foundation Inc.
225 Main Street
Newington, CT 06111-1494
Phone: 860-594-0397
E-mail: k1mmh@arrl.org

THOMAS W. PORTER SCHOLARSHIP

One $1000 award is available to a student with a Technician class or higher amateur radio license. Preference will be given to applicants from Ohio or West Virginia.

Award: Scholarship for use in freshman, sophomore, junior, or senior years; not renewable. *Number:* 1. *Amount:* $1000.

Eligibility Requirements: Applicant must be enrolled or expecting to enroll at a two-year or four-year or technical institution or university; resident of Ohio or West Virginia and must have an interest in amateur radio.

Application Requirements: Application, transcript. *Deadline:* February 1.

Contact: Ms. Mary Hobart, Secretary
ARRL Foundation Inc.
225 Main Street
Newington, CT 06111-1494
Phone: 860-594-0397
E-mail: k1mmh@arrl.org

TOM AND JUDITH COMSTOCK SCHOLARSHIP

One-time award of $2000 for high school seniors. Preference given to residents of Texas and Oklahoma. Must be licensed amateur radio operator. Must be accepted at a two- or four-year institution.

Award: Scholarship for use in freshman year; not renewable. *Number:* 1. *Amount:* $2000.

Eligibility Requirements: Applicant must be high school student; planning to enroll or expecting to enroll full-time at a two-year or four-year institution or university; resident of Oklahoma or Texas and must have an interest in amateur radio. Available to U.S. citizens.

Application Requirements: Application, transcript. *Deadline:* February 1.

Contact: Ms. Mary Hobart, Secretary
ARRL Foundation Inc.
225 Main Street
Newington, CT 06111-1494
Phone: 860-594-0397
E-mail: k1mmh@arrl.org

WILLIAM BENNETT W7PHO MEMORIAL SCHOLARSHIP

One $500 award is available to residents of ARRL's Northwest, Pacific and Southwest divisions. Applicants should have a General class or higher amateur radio license.

Award: Scholarship for use in freshman, sophomore, junior, or senior years; not renewable. *Number:* 1. *Amount:* $500.

Eligibility Requirements: Applicant must be enrolled or expecting to enroll at a four-year institution or university and resident of Arizona, California, Colorado, Idaho, Montana, Nevada, New Mexico, Oregon, Utah, Washington, or Wyoming. Applicant must have 3.0 GPA or higher.

Application Requirements: Application. *Deadline:* February 1.

Contact: Ms. Mary Hobart, Secretary
ARRL Foundation Inc.
225 Main Street
Newington, CT 06111-1494
Phone: 860-594-0397
E-mail: k1mmh@arrl.org

YANKEE CLIPPER CONTEST CLUB INC. YOUTH SCHOLARSHIP

One-time award available to general class or higher licensed amateur radio operators. Must reside or attend college within the 175-mile radius of YCCC Center in Erving, MA.

Award: Scholarship for use in freshman, sophomore, junior, or senior years; not renewable. *Number:* 1. *Amount:* $1200.

Eligibility Requirements: Applicant must be enrolled or expecting to enroll full-time at a two-year or four-year institution or university; resident of Connecticut, Maine, Massachusetts, New Hampshire, New Jersey, New York, Pennsylvania, Rhode Island, or Vermont and must have an interest in amateur radio. Available to U.S. citizens.

Application Requirements: Application, transcript. *Deadline:* February 1.

Contact: Ms. Mary Hobart, Secretary
ARRL Foundation Inc.
225 Main Street
Newington, CT 06111-1494
Phone: 860-594-0397
E-mail: k1mmh@arrl.org

YOU'VE GOT A FRIEND IN PENNSYLVANIA SCHOLARSHIP
• *See page 537*

ZACHARY TAYLOR STEVENS MEMORIAL SCHOLARSHIP

One $750 award is available to students who possess a Technician class or higher amateur radio license. Preference will be given to residents of Michigan, Ohio and West Virginia.

Award: Scholarship for use in freshman, sophomore, junior, or senior years; not renewable. *Number:* 1. *Amount:* $750.

Eligibility Requirements: Applicant must be enrolled or expecting to enroll at a two-year or four-year or technical institution or university; resident of Michigan, Ohio, or West Virginia and must have an interest in amateur radio.

Application Requirements: Application, transcript. *Deadline:* February 1.

Contact: Ms. Mary Hobart, Secretary
ARRL Foundation Inc.
225 Main Street
Newington, CT 06111-1494
Phone: 860-594-0397
E-mail: k1mmh@arrl.org

ASHLEY FOUNDATION

http://www.theashleyfoundation.org/

ASHLEY TAMBURRI SCHOLARSHIP
• *See page 600*

ASIAN REPORTER

http://www.arfoundation.net/

ASIAN REPORTER SCHOLARSHIP
• *See page 656*

ASSOCIATION OF BLIND CITIZENS

http://www.blindcitizens.org/

REGGIE JOHNSON MEMORIAL SCHOLARSHIP
• *See page 600*

A.W. BODINE-SUNKIST GROWERS INC.

http://www.sunkist.com/

A.W. BODINE-SUNKIST MEMORIAL SCHOLARSHIP
• *See page 583*

BARKING FOUNDATION

http://www.barkingfoundation.org/

BARKING FOUNDATION GRANTS

One-time award of $3000 available to Maine residents. Minimum GPA of 3.5 is desirable. Only first 300 completed applications will be accepted. Essay, financial information, and transcripts required. Available to full- and part-time students. Scholarships vary in number from year to year.

Award: Grant for use in freshman, sophomore, junior, senior, graduate, or postgraduate years; not renewable. *Number:* up to 25. *Amount:* $3000.

Eligibility Requirements: Applicant must be enrolled or expecting to enroll full- or part-time at a four-year institution or university and resident of Maine. Applicant must have 3.5 GPA or higher. Available to U.S. citizens.

Application Requirements: Application, essay, financial need analysis, references, transcript, copy of SAR. *Deadline:* February 15.

Contact: Stephanie Leonard, Administrator
Barking Foundation
PO Box 855
Bangor, ME 04402
Phone: 207-990-2910
Fax: 207-990-2975
E-mail: info@barkingfoundation.org

BIG Y FOODS INC.

http://www.bigy.com/

BIG Y SCHOLARSHIPS

Awards for customers or dependents of customers of Big Y Foods. Big Y trade area covers Norfolk county, western and central Massachusetts, and Connecticut. Also awards for Big Y employees and dependents of employees. Awards are based on academic excellence. Grades, board scores and two letters of recommendation required.

Award: Scholarship for use in freshman, sophomore, junior, senior, or graduate years; not renewable. *Number:* 300–350. *Amount:* $500–$2000.

Eligibility Requirements: Applicant must be enrolled or expecting to enroll full- or part-time at a two-year or four-year or technical institution or university; resident of Connecticut or Massachusetts and studying in Connecticut or Massachusetts. Available to U.S. and non-U.S. citizens.

Application Requirements: Application, resume, references, test scores, transcript. *Deadline:* February 1.

Contact: Missy Lajoie, Scholarship Committee
Big Y Foods Inc.
PO Box 7840
Springfield, MA 01102-7840
Phone: 413-504-4047
Fax: 413-504-6509
E-mail: wecare@bigy.com

BLUE GRASS ENERGY

http://www.bgenergy.com/

BLUE GRASS ENERGY ACADEMIC SCHOLARSHIP

Scholarships for Kentucky high school seniors living with parents or guardians who are members of Blue Grass Energy. Must have minimum GPA of 3.0 and have demonstrated academic achievement, extracurricular involvement and financial need. For application and information, visit web site http://www.bgenergy.com/forStudents.aspx.

Award: Scholarship for use in freshman year; not renewable. *Number:* 10. *Amount:* $1000.

Eligibility Requirements: Applicant must be high school student; planning to enroll or expecting to enroll full-time at a two-year or four-year or technical institution or university and resident of Kentucky. Applicant must have 3.0 GPA or higher. Available to U.S. citizens.

Application Requirements: Application, essay, financial need analysis, resume, test scores, transcript, explanation of how scholarship is necessary to further education. *Deadline:* April 1.

Contact: Ms. Magen Howard, Communications Adviser
Blue Grass Energy
PO Box 990
1201 Lexington Road
Nicholasville, KY 40340-0990
Phone: 859-885-2104
E-mail: magenh@bgenergy.com

BNY MELLON, N.A.

http://www.bnymellon.com/

CHARLES C. ELY EDUCATIONAL FUND

Award for men who are residents of Massachusetts. Academic performance, character and financial need will be considered. Eligible applicant must be recommended by educational institution. Not for graduate study programs.

Award: Scholarship for use in freshman, sophomore, junior, or senior years; not renewable. *Number:* varies. *Amount:* up to $2000.

Eligibility Requirements: Applicant must be enrolled or expecting to enroll full-time at a two-year or four-year or technical institution or university; male and resident of Massachusetts. Available to U.S. citizens.

Application Requirements: Application, essay, transcript. *Deadline:* April 15.

Contact: June Kfoury McNeil, Vice President
BNY Mellon, N.A.
201 Washington Street, 024-0092
Boston, MA 02108
Phone: 617-722-3891
E-mail: brown-mcmullen.s@mellon.com

HENRY FRANCIS BARROWS SCHOLARSHIP
• *See page 697*

BOETTCHER FOUNDATION

http://www.boettcherfoundation.org/

BOETTCHER FOUNDATION SCHOLARSHIPS

Merit-based scholarship available to graduating seniors in the state of Colorado. Selection based on class rank (top 5 percent), test scores, leadership, service and character. Renewable for four years and can be used at any Colorado university or college. Includes full tuition and fees, living stipend of $2800 per year, and a stipend for books.

Award: Scholarship for use in freshman, sophomore, junior, or senior years; renewable. *Number:* 40. *Amount:* $13,000–$40,000.

Eligibility Requirements: Applicant must be high school student; planning to enroll or expecting to enroll full-time at a four-year institution or university; resident of Colorado; studying in Colorado and must have an interest in leadership. Applicant must have 3.5 GPA or higher. Available to U.S. citizens.

Application Requirements: Application, essay, interview, references, test scores, transcript. *Deadline:* November 1.

Contact: Stephanie Panion, Scholarship Program Coordinator
Boettcher Foundation
600 17th Street, Suite 2210 S
Denver, CO 80202-5422
Phone: 303-285-6207
Fax: 303-534-1943
E-mail: scholarships@boettcherfoundation.org

BOYS AND GIRLS CLUBS OF CHICAGO

http://www.bgcc.org/

BOYS AND GIRLS CLUBS OF CHICAGO SCHOLARSHIPS
• *See page 537*

BRITISH COLUMBIA MINISTRY OF ADVANCED EDUCATION

http://www.studentaidbc.ca/

IRVING K. BARBER BRITISH COLUMBIA SCHOLARSHIP PROGRAM (FOR STUDY IN BRITISH COLUMBIA)

Scholarship to students who, after completing two years at a British Columbia public community college, university college or institute, must transfer to another public postsecondary institution in British Columbia to complete their degree. Students must demonstrate merit as well as exceptional involvement in their institution and community. Must have a GPA of at least 3.5. For more details, visit http://www.aved.gov.bc.ca/studentaidbc/specialprograms/irvingkbarber/bc_scholarship.htm.

Award: Scholarship for use in junior or senior years; not renewable. *Number:* up to 150. *Amount:* up to $5000.

Eligibility Requirements: Applicant must be enrolled or expecting to enroll full-time at a four-year institution or university and studying in British Columbia. Applicant must have 3.5 GPA or higher. Available to Canadian citizens.

Application Requirements: Application, essay, references, test scores, transcript. *Deadline:* March 31.

Contact: Victoria Thibeau, Loan Remission and Management Unit
British Columbia Ministry of Advanced Education
Station Prov Government, First Floor
PO Box 9173
Victoria, BC V8W 9H7
Canada
Phone: 250-387-6100
E-mail: victoria.thibeau@gov.bc.ca

BUFFALO AFL-CIO COUNCIL

http://www.wnyalf.org/

AFL-CIO COUNCIL OF BUFFALO SCHOLARSHIP WNY ALF SCHOLARSHIP

• *See page 537*

CABRILLO CIVIC CLUBS OF CALIFORNIA INC.

http://www.cabrillocivicclubs.org/

CABRILLO CIVIC CLUBS OF CALIFORNIA SCHOLARSHIP

• *See page 657*

CALIFORNIA COMMUNITY COLLEGES

http://www.ccco.edu/

COOPERATIVE AGENCIES RESOURCES FOR EDUCATION PROGRAM

Renewable award available to California resident enrolled as a full-time student at a two-year California community college. Must currently receive CalWORKs/TANF and have at least one child under fourteen years of age at time of acceptance into CARE program. Must be in EOPS, a single head of household, and age 18 or older. Contact local college EOPS-CARE office for application and more information. To locate nearest campus, see http://www.icanaffordcollege.com/applications/homepage2.cfm.

Award: Grant for use in freshman or sophomore years; renewable. *Number:* 10,000–11,000. *Amount:* varies.

Eligibility Requirements: Applicant must be age 18 and over; enrolled or expecting to enroll full-time at a two-year institution; single; resident of California and studying in California. Available to U.S. citizens.

Application Requirements: Application, financial need analysis, test scores, transcript. *Deadline:* continuous.

Contact: Contact local community college EOPS/CARE program

CALIFORNIA CORRECTIONAL PEACE OFFICERS ASSOCIATION

http://www.ccpoa.org/

CALIFORNIA CORRECTIONAL PEACE OFFICERS ASSOCIATION JOE HARPER SCHOLARSHIP

• *See page 584*

CALIFORNIA COUNCIL OF THE BLIND

http://www.ccbnet.org/

CALIFORNIA COUNCIL OF THE BLIND SCHOLARSHIPS

• *See page 600*

CALIFORNIA GRANGE FOUNDATION

http://www.californiagrange.org/

CALIFORNIA GRANGE FOUNDATION SCHOLARSHIP

• *See page 538*

CALIFORNIA JUNIOR MISS SCHOLARSHIP PROGRAM

http://www.ajm.org/

CALIFORNIA JUNIOR MISS SCHOLARSHIP PROGRAM

Scholarship program to recognize and reward outstanding high school junior females in the areas of academics, leadership, athletics, public speaking, and the performing arts. Must be single, U.S. citizen, and resident of California. Minimum 3.0 GPA required.

Award: Scholarship for use in freshman year; not renewable. *Number:* 25. *Amount:* $500–$10,000.

Eligibility Requirements: Applicant must be high school student; age 15-17; planning to enroll or expecting to enroll full-time at a four-year institution or university; single female; resident of California and must have an interest in beauty pageant, leadership, or public speaking. Applicant must have 3.0 GPA or higher. Available to U.S. citizens.

Application Requirements: Application, essay, interview, test scores, transcript. *Deadline:* varies.

Contact: Joan McDonald, Chairman
California Junior Miss Scholarship Program
385 Via Montanosa
Encinitas, CA 92024
Phone: 760-420-4177
E-mail: jmcdonald@bellmicro.com

CALIFORNIA MASONIC FOUNDATION

http://www.freemason.org/index.php

CALIFORNIA MASONIC FOUNDATION SCHOLARSHIP AWARDS

Scholarships range from $1000 to $10,000 each and are granted to high school seniors demonstrating high academic achievement, financial need and the greatest potential for using education to improve their lives. Most are also renewable annually if the student has maintained at least a 3.0 cumulative GPA and attends a four-year accredited institution (or a two-year institution with plans to transfer) as a full-time student. Applicants must be a U.S. citizen and a resident of California for at least one year to be considered.

Award: Scholarship for use in freshman, sophomore, junior, or senior years; renewable. *Number:* 50–60. *Amount:* $1000–$10,000.

Eligibility Requirements: Applicant must be high school student; planning to enroll or expecting to enroll full-time at a two-year or four-year institution or university and resident of California. Applicant must have 3.0 GPA or higher. Available to U.S. citizens.

Application Requirements: Application, essay, financial need analysis, interview, references, self-addressed stamped envelope, test scores, transcript. *Deadline:* February 15.

Contact: Ms. Joyce K. Hahn, Foundation Programs Coordinator
California Masonic Foundation
1111 California Street
San Francisco, CA 94108-2284
Phone: 415-292-9139
Fax: 415-776-7170
E-mail: foundation@freemason.org

CALIFORNIA STATE PARENT-TEACHER ASSOCIATION

http://www.capta.org/

CONTINUING EDUCATION-PTA VOLUNTEERS SCHOLARSHIP

• *See page 538*

GRADUATING HIGH SCHOOL SENIOR SCHOLARSHIP
• *See page 584*

CALIFORNIA STUDENT AID COMMISSION

http://www.csac.ca.gov/

CAL GRANT C

Award for California residents who are enrolled in a short-term vocational training program. Program must lead to a recognized degree or certificate. Course length must be a minimum of 4 months and no longer than 24 months. Students must be attending an approved California institution and show financial need.

Award: Grant for use in freshman or sophomore years; renewable. *Number:* up to 7761. *Amount:* $576–$3168.

Eligibility Requirements: Applicant must be enrolled or expecting to enroll full- or part-time at a two-year or technical institution; resident of California and studying in California. Available to U.S. citizens.

Application Requirements: Application, financial need analysis, GPA verification. *Deadline:* March 2.

Contact: Catalina Mistler, Chief, Program Administration & Services Division
California Student Aid Commission
PO Box 419026
Rancho Cordova, CA 95741-9026
Phone: 916-526-7268
Fax: 916-526-8002
E-mail: studentsupport@csac.ca.gov

COMPETITIVE CAL GRANT A

Award for California residents who are not recent high school graduates attending an approved college or university within the state. Must show financial need and meet minimum 3.0 GPA requirement.

Award: Grant for use in freshman, sophomore, junior, or senior years; renewable. *Number:* 1000–2000. *Amount:* $4370–$10,302.

Eligibility Requirements: Applicant must be enrolled or expecting to enroll full- or part-time at a two-year or four-year institution or university; resident of California and studying in California. Applicant must have 3.0 GPA or higher. Available to U.S. citizens.

Application Requirements: Application, financial need analysis, GPA verification. *Deadline:* March 2.

Contact: Catalina Mistler, Chief, Program Administration & Services Division
California Student Aid Commission
PO Box 419026
Rancho Cordova, CA 95741-9026
Phone: 916-526-7268
Fax: 916-526-8002
E-mail: studentsupport@csac.ca.gov

ENTITLEMENT CAL GRANT B

Provide grant funds for access costs for low-income students in an amount not to exceed $1551 and tuition/fee expenses of up to $10302. Must be California residents and enroll in an undergraduate academic program of not less than one academic year at a qualifying postsecondary institution. Must show financial need and meet the minimum 2.00 GPA requirement.

Award: Grant for use in freshman, sophomore, junior, or senior years; renewable. *Number:* 56,200. *Amount:* $700–$11,853.

Eligibility Requirements: Applicant must be enrolled or expecting to enroll full- or part-time at a two-year or four-year or technical institution or university; resident of California and studying in California. Available to U.S. citizens.

Application Requirements: Application, financial need analysis. *Deadline:* March 2.

Contact: Catalina Mistler, Chief, Program Administration & Services Division
California Student Aid Commission
PO Box 419026
Rancho Cordova, CA 95741-9026
Phone: 916-526-7268
Fax: 916-526-8002
E-mail: studentsupport@csac.ca.gov

LAW ENFORCEMENT PERSONNEL DEPENDENTS SCHOLARSHIP
• *See page 584*

ROBERT C. BYRD HONORS SCHOLARSHIP-CALIFORNIA

Federally funded award is available to California high school seniors. Students are awarded based on outstanding academic merit. Students must be nominated by their high school. Recipients must maintain satisfactory academic progress.

Award: Scholarship for use in freshman year; renewable. *Number:* 700–800. *Amount:* up to $1500.

Eligibility Requirements: Applicant must be high school student; planning to enroll or expecting to enroll full-time at a two-year or four-year institution or university and resident of California. Applicant must have 3.5 GPA or higher. Available to U.S. citizens.

Application Requirements: Application, financial need analysis, test scores, GPA/test score verification form. *Deadline:* April 30.

Contact: Catalina Mistler, Chief, Program Administration & Services Division
California Student Aid Commission
PO Box 419026
Rancho Cordova, CA 95741-9026
Phone: 916-526-7268
Fax: 916-526-8002
E-mail: studentsupport@csac.ca.gov

CALIFORNIA TABLE GRAPE COMMISSION

http://www.freshcaliforniagrapes.com/

CALIFORNIA TABLE GRAPE FARM WORKERS SCHOLARSHIP PROGRAM
• *See page 584*

CALIFORNIA TEACHERS ASSOCIATION (CTA)

http://www.cta.org/

CALIFORNIA TEACHERS ASSOCIATION SCHOLARSHIP FOR MEMBERS
• *See page 538*

CALIFORNIA WINE GRAPE GROWERS FOUNDATION

http://www.cwggf.org/

CALIFORNIA WINE GRAPE GROWERS FOUNDATION SCHOLARSHIP

Scholarship for high school seniors whose parents or legal guardians are vineyard employees of wine grape growers. Recipients may study the subject of their choice at any campus of the University of California system, the California State University system, or the California Community College system.

Award: Scholarship for use in freshman year; not renewable. *Number:* 1–6. *Amount:* $1000–$4000.

Eligibility Requirements: Applicant must be high school student; planning to enroll or expecting to enroll full-time at a two-year or four-year institution or university; resident of California and studying in California. Available to U.S. citizens.

Application Requirements: Application, essay, references, test scores, transcript. *Deadline:* April 2.

Contact: Carolee Williams, Assistant Executive Director
California Wine Grape Growers Foundation
1325 J Street, #1560
Sacramento, CA 95814
Phone: 800-241-1800
Fax: 916-379-8999
E-mail: carolee@cawg.org

CANADA ICELAND FOUNDATION INC. SCHOLARSHIPS

http://www.logberg.com/

CANADA ICELAND FOUNDATION SCHOLARSHIP PROGRAM

One scholarship of $500, to be awarded annually. To be offered to a university student studying towards a degree in any Canadian university.

Award: Scholarship for use in freshman, sophomore, junior, senior, or graduate years; not renewable. *Number:* 1. *Amount:* $500.

Eligibility Requirements: Applicant must be enrolled or expecting to enroll full-time at an institution or university; studying in Alberta, British Columbia, Manitoba, New Brunswick, Newfoundland, Nova Scotia, Ontario, Quebec, or Saskatchewan and must have an interest in leadership. Available to Canadian citizens.

Application Requirements: Application, references, test scores, transcript. *Deadline:* varies.

Contact: Karen Bowman, Administrative Assistant
Canada Iceland Foundation Inc. Scholarships
100-283 Portage Avenue, The Sterling Building
Winnipeg, MB R3B 2B5
Canada
Phone: 204-284-5686
Fax: 204-284-7099
E-mail: karen@lh-inc.ca

CAREER COLLEGES AND SCHOOLS OF TEXAS

http://www.ccst.org/

CAREER COLLEGES AND SCHOOLS OF TEXAS SCHOLARSHIP PROGRAM

One-time award available to graduating high school seniors who plan to attend a Texas trade or technical institution. Must be a Texas resident. Criteria selection, which is determined independently by each school's guidance counselors, may be based on academic excellence, financial need, or student leadership. Must be U.S. citizen. Deadline: continuous.

Award: Scholarship for use in freshman year; not renewable. *Number:* up to 27,770. *Amount:* $1000.

Eligibility Requirements: Applicant must be high school student; planning to enroll or expecting to enroll full- or part-time at a technical institution; resident of Texas and studying in Texas. Available to U.S. citizens.

Application Requirements: Application, references. *Deadline:* continuous.

Contact: Jennifer George, Association Manager
Career Colleges and Schools of Texas
823 Congress Avenue, Suite 230
Austin, TX 78701
Phone: 512-479-0425 Ext. 17
Fax: 512-495-9031
E-mail: jgeorge@eami.com

CASUALTY ACTUARIES OF THE SOUTHEAST

http://www.casact.org/

CASUALTY ACTUARIES OF THE SOUTHEAST SCHOLARSHIP PROGRAM

Scholarships available for undergraduate students in the southeastern states for the study of actuarial science. Must be studying in: Alabama, Arkansas, Florida, Georgia, Kentucky, Louisiana, Mississippi, North Carolina, South Carolina, Tennessee, or Virginia. Incoming freshmen/first-year students are not eligible for the scholarship.

Award: Scholarship for use in sophomore, junior, or senior years; not renewable. *Number:* 2. *Amount:* $1500.

Eligibility Requirements: Applicant must be enrolled or expecting to enroll full-time at a four-year institution or university and studying in Alabama, Arkansas, Florida, Georgia, Kentucky, Louisiana, Mississippi, North Carolina, South Carolina, Tennessee, or Virginia. Available to U.S. and Canadian citizens.

Application Requirements: Application, references. *Deadline:* May 1.

Contact: Vice President of College Relations
Casualty Actuaries of the Southeast
3500 Lenox Road, Suite 900
Atlanta, GA 30326-4238
Phone: 404-365-1549
Fax: 404-365-1663
E-mail: michael.miller@towersperrin.com

CENTRAL NATIONAL BANK & TRUST COMPANY OF ENID TRUSTEE

http://www.onecentralsource.us/trust_services.html

MAY T. HENRY SCHOLARSHIP FOUNDATION

A $1000 scholarship renewed annually for four years. Awarded to any student enrolled in an Oklahoma state-supported college, university or tech school. Based on need, scholastic performance and personal traits valued by May T. Henry. Minimum 3.0 GPA required.

Award: Scholarship for use in freshman, sophomore, junior, senior, graduate, or postgraduate years; renewable. *Number:* varies. *Amount:* $1000.

Eligibility Requirements: Applicant must be enrolled or expecting to enroll full-time at a two-year or four-year or technical institution or university and studying in Oklahoma. Applicant must have 3.0 GPA or higher. Available to U.S. and non-U.S. citizens.

Application Requirements: Application, essay, financial need analysis, references, test scores, transcript. *Deadline:* April 1.

Contact: Trust Department
Central National Bank & Trust Company of Enid Trustee
PO Box 3448
Enid, OK 73702-3448
Phone: 580-213-1612
Fax: 580-249-5926
E-mail: waholt@cnb-enid.com

CENTRAL SCHOLARSHIP BUREAU

http://www.centralsb.org/

CENTRAL SCHOLARSHIP BUREAU GRANTS

A limited number of grants are available each year on a competitive basis. Selection criteria is a combination of merit and demonstrated need.

Award: Grant for use in freshman, sophomore, junior, senior, or graduate years; renewable. *Number:* 20–30. *Amount:* $1000–$5000.

Eligibility Requirements: Applicant must be enrolled or expecting to enroll full-time at a two-year or four-year or technical institution or university and resident of Maryland. Applicant must have 3.0 GPA or higher. Available to U.S. citizens.

Application Requirements: Application, essay, financial need analysis, interview, resume, transcript, CSB online application. *Deadline:* May 1.

Contact: Roberta Goldman, Program Director
Central Scholarship Bureau
1700 Reisterstown Road, Suite 220
Baltimore, MD 21208-2903
Phone: 410-415-5558
Fax: 410-425-5501
E-mail: rgoldman@centralsb.org

LESSANS FAMILY SCHOLARSHIP
• *See page 657*

MARY RUBIN AND BENJAMIN M. RUBIN SCHOLARSHIP FUND

Renewable scholarship for tuition only to women who are attending a college, university, or other institution of higher learning. Must be a resident of Maryland. Have a GPA of 3.0 or better and meet the financial requirements. Contact for application or download from web site http://www.centralsb.org.

Award: Scholarship for use in sophomore, junior, senior, or graduate years; renewable. *Number:* 20–35. *Amount:* $1000–$2500.

Eligibility Requirements: Applicant must be enrolled or expecting to enroll full- or part-time at a two-year or four-year or technical institution or university; female and resident of Maryland. Applicant must have 3.0 GPA or higher. Available to U.S. citizens.

Application Requirements: Application, essay, financial need analysis, references, transcript. *Deadline:* May 1.

Contact: Roberta Goldman, Program Director
Central Scholarship Bureau
1700 Reisterstown Road, Suite 220
Baltimore, MD 21208-2903
Phone: 410-415-5558
Fax: 410-425-5501
E-mail: rgoldman@centralsb.org

SHOE CITY-WB54/WB50 SCHOLARSHIP

Scholarship for high school seniors who are permanent residents of Maryland or Washington D.C. Four $1500 awards are granted annually. For more information, visit web site http://www.centralsb.org.

Award: Scholarship for use in freshman year; not renewable. *Number:* 4. *Amount:* up to $1500.

Eligibility Requirements: Applicant must be high school student; planning to enroll or expecting to enroll full-time at a four-year institution or university and resident of District of Columbia or Maryland. Available to U.S. citizens.

Application Requirements: Application, essay, financial need analysis, interview, resume, references, test scores, transcript. *Deadline:* May 1.

Contact: Roberta Goldman, Program Director
Central Scholarship Bureau
1700 Reisterstown Road, Suite 220
Baltimore, MD 21208-2903
Phone: 410-415-5558
Fax: 410-425-5501
E-mail: rgoldman@centralsb.org

STRAUS SCHOLARSHIP PROGRAM FOR UNDERGRADUATE EDUCATION

Scholarship provides assistance to Maryland residents who are full-time undergraduate students in their sophomore, junior, or senior years at an accredited college or university. Renewable grants of up to $5000 each per year will be awarded. If the recipient graduates within four years with a cumulative GPA of 3.0 or higher, an additional $5000 grant will be awarded to apply toward student loan debt.

Award: Scholarship for use in sophomore, junior, or senior years; renewable. *Number:* 5–8. *Amount:* up to $5000.

Eligibility Requirements: Applicant must be enrolled or expecting to enroll full-time at a four-year institution or university and resident of Maryland. Applicant must have 3.0 GPA or higher. Available to U.S. citizens.

Application Requirements: Application, essay, financial need analysis, interview, resume, transcript, CSB online application. *Deadline:* May 1.

Contact: Roberta Goldman, Program Director
Central Scholarship Bureau
1700 Reisterstown Road, Suite 220
Baltimore, MD 21208-2903
Phone: 410-415-5558
Fax: 410-425-5501
E-mail: rgoldman@centralsb.org

CHICANA/LATINA FOUNDATION

http://www.chicanalatina.org/

SCHOLARSHIPS FOR LATINA STUDENTS ENROLLED IN COLLEGES/UNIVERSITIES IN NORTHERN CALIFORNIA
• *See page 658*

CHINESE AMERICAN ASSOCIATION OF MINNESOTA

http://www.caam.org/

CHINESE AMERICAN ASSOCIATION OF MINNESOTA (CAAM) SCHOLARSHIPS
• *See page 658*

CIRI FOUNDATION (TCF)

http://www.thecirifoundation.org/

CULTURAL FELLOWSHIP GRANTS
• *See page 659*

GENERAL FELLOWSHIP GRANTS
• *See page 659*

CIVIL SERVICE EMPLOYEES INSURANCE COMPANY

http://www.cseinsurance.com/

YOUTH AUTOMOBILE SAFETY SCHOLARSHIP ESSAY COMPETITION FOR CHILDREN OF PUBLIC EMPLOYEES

Applicants must be residents of California, Arizona, Utah, or Nevada with minimum 3.0 GPA. Awards are for children of full-time or retired public employees. Letter of acceptance required.

Award: Scholarship for use in freshman year; not renewable. *Number:* 15. *Amount:* $500–$1500.

Eligibility Requirements: Applicant must be high school student; planning to enroll or expecting to enroll full-time at a two-year or four-year or technical institution or university and resident of Arizona, California, Nevada, or Utah. Applicant must have 3.0 GPA or higher. Available to U.S. citizens.

Application Requirements: Application, applicant must enter a contest, essay, references, transcript. *Deadline:* May 13.

Contact: Mr. Jerry Wilson, Social and Creative Media Specialist
Civil Service Employees Insurance Company
2121 N. California Blvd., Ste. 555, P.O. Box 8041
Walnut Creek, CA 94956-8041
Phone: 925-817-6373
Fax: 925-817-6489
E-mail: jwilson@cseinsurance.com

CLEVELAND SCHOLARSHIP PROGRAMS

http://www.cspohio.org/

CLEVELAND SCHOLARSHIP PROGRAMS ADULT LEARNER PROGRAM SCHOLARSHIP

Scholarship for students pursuing first associate or bachelor's degree in an eligible two- or four-year program. Individuals already having a bachelor's degree are not eligible. Students must be 19 years old or older and must have interrupted the education for at least one year. Applicants must be a resident of Ashtabula, Cuyahoga, Geauga, Lake, Lorain, Mahoning, Medina, Portage, Stark, Summit or Trumbull County. Student must meet income guidelines and maintain a 2.5 GPA. Student must be attending a public or private not for profit institution.

Award: Scholarship for use in freshman, sophomore, junior, or senior years; renewable. *Number:* 350–450. *Amount:* $500–$1250.

Eligibility Requirements: Applicant must be age 19 and over; enrolled or expecting to enroll full- or part-time at a two-year or four-year or technical institution or university and resident of Ohio. Applicant must have 2.5 GPA or higher. Available to U.S. citizens.

Application Requirements: Application, essay, financial need analysis, transcript. *Deadline:* April 15.

Contact: Mr. Robert Durham, Manager of Financial Aid
Cleveland Scholarship Programs
BP Tower, 200 Public Square, Suite 3820
Cleveland, OH 44114
Phone: 216-241-5587 Ext. 146
Fax: 216-241-6184
E-mail: rdurham@cspohio.org

CSP FINALIST SCHOLARSHIPS FOR HIGH SCHOOL SENIORS

Scholarship to students attending a high school serviced by a CSP Advisor. Winners are selected based on recommendations by the CSP advisor and students must also meet CSP criteria for academic performance (high school grades, SAT/ACT test scores and financial need) to receive the grant.

Award: Scholarship for use in freshman, sophomore, junior, or senior years; renewable. *Number:* 300–400. *Amount:* $500–$5000.

Eligibility Requirements: Applicant must be high school student; planning to enroll or expecting to enroll full-time at a two-year or four-year or technical institution or university and resident of Ohio. Applicant must have 2.5 GPA or higher. Available to U.S. citizens.

Application Requirements: Application, financial need analysis, interview, test scores, transcript.

Contact: Mr. Robert Durham, Manager of Financial Aid
Cleveland Scholarship Programs
200 Public Square, Suite 3820
Cleveland, OH 44114
E-mail: rdurham@cspohio.org

CSP MANAGED FUNDS-OHIO TRANSFER COUNCIL DAVID GALL MEMORIAL SCHOLARSHIP

Five one-year, non-renewable $2000 scholarships to students presently enrolled with a minimum overall cumulative GPA of 3.0 during their undergraduate course work.

Award: Scholarship for use in sophomore, junior, or senior years; not renewable. *Number:* 5. *Amount:* $2000.

Eligibility Requirements: Applicant must be enrolled or expecting to enroll full- or part-time at a four-year institution or university and studying in Ohio. Applicant must have 3.0 GPA or higher. Available to U.S. citizens.

Application Requirements: Application, essay, references, transcript, copy of class schedule, financial aid award letter. *Deadline:* June 30.

Contact: Bridget Vaughn, Special Projects Manager
Cleveland Scholarship Programs
200 Public Square, Suite 3820
Cleveland, OH 44114
E-mail: bvaughn@cspohio.org

COALITION OF TEXANS WITH DISABILITIES

http://www.cotwd.org/

KENNY MURGIA MEMORIAL SCHOLARSHIP
• See page 601

COLLEGEBOUND FOUNDATION

http://www.collegeboundfoundation.org/

BALTIMORE JUNIOR ASSOCIATION OF COMMERCE (BJAC) SCHOLARSHIP

You must: have a cumulative 3.0 GPA or better; have at least 200 hours of verifiable community service; and submit a one-page essay describing in detail the community service activities in which you have been involved (specify the amount of time you have committed and describe your involvement—focusing on the importance of these activities to you).

Award: Scholarship for use in freshman year; not renewable. *Number:* 1. *Amount:* $1000.

Eligibility Requirements: Applicant must be high school student; planning to enroll or expecting to enroll full-time at a two-year or four-year institution or university and resident of Maryland. Applicant must have 3.0 GPA or higher. Available to U.S. citizens.

Application Requirements: Application, essay, resume, references, transcript. *Deadline:* March 1.

Contact: Deana Carr-Davis, Associate Program Director, Scholarship
Programs
CollegeBound Foundation
300 Water Street, Suite 300
Baltimore, MD 21202
Phone: 410-783-2905 Ext. 207
Fax: 410-727-5786
E-mail: dcarr-davis@collegeboundfoundation.org

CARMEN V. D'ANNA MEMORIAL SCHOLARSHIP OF THE MARS SUPERMARKET EDUCATIONAL FUND

Must be a senior in a Baltimore City public high school entering a Maryland college or university for the first time. Must demonstrate financial need and exhibit a strong desire to achieve. Submit a typed one-page essay describing why a college education is important to you.

Award: Scholarship for use in freshman, sophomore, junior, or senior years; renewable. *Number:* 1. *Amount:* up to $10,000.

Eligibility Requirements: Applicant must be high school student; planning to enroll or expecting to enroll full-time at a two-year or four-year institution or university; resident of Maryland and studying in Maryland. Available to U.S. citizens.

Application Requirements: Application, essay, financial need analysis, resume, references, transcript. *Deadline:* March 1.

Contact: Deana Carr-Davis, Associate Program Director, Scholarship
Programs
CollegeBound Foundation
300 Water Street, Suite 300
Baltimore, MD 21202
Phone: 410-783-2905 Ext. 207
Fax: 410-727-5786
E-mail: dcarr-davis@collegeboundfoundation.org

COLLEGEBOUND FOUNDATION LAST DOLLAR GRANT

A need-based award for Baltimore City public high school graduates whose expected family contribution and financial aid package total less than the cost to attend college. Grant value is up to $3,000 per year, renewable for up to five years of college or the maximum amount of $15,000.

Award: Grant for use in freshman, sophomore, junior, or senior years; renewable. *Number:* 45–60. *Amount:* $500–$3000.

Eligibility Requirements: Applicant must be high school student; planning to enroll or expecting to enroll full-time at a four-year institution or university; resident of Maryland and studying in Maryland. Available to U.S. citizens.

Application Requirements: Application, financial need analysis, transcript, acceptance letter. *Deadline:* March 1.

Contact: Deana Carr-Davis, Associate Program Director, Scholarship
Programs
CollegeBound Foundation
300 Water Street, Suite 300
Baltimore, MD 21202
Phone: 410-783-2905 Ext. 207
Fax: 410-727-5786
E-mail: dcarr-davis@collegeboundfoundation.org

COX EDUCATION FUND

Award for Baltimore City public high school graduates. Applicant should be a valedictorian in high school graduating class, or be ranked in the top ten of class while applying for award, and attend two- or four-year college or university.

Award: Scholarship for use in freshman year; not renewable. *Number:* 4. *Amount:* $300.

Eligibility Requirements: Applicant must be high school student; planning to enroll or expecting to enroll full-time at a two-year or four-year institution or university and resident of Maryland. Applicant must have 3.5 GPA or higher. Available to U.S. citizens.

Application Requirements: Application, resume, references, transcript. *Deadline:* March 1.

Contact: Deana Carr-Davis, Associate Program Director, Scholarship
Programs
CollegeBound Foundation
300 Water Street, Suite 300
Baltimore, MD 21202
Phone: 410-783-2905 Ext. 207
Fax: 410-727-5786
E-mail: dcarr-davis@collegeboundfoundation.org

EXCHANGE CLUB OF BALTIMORE SCHOLARSHIP

Award for Baltimore City public high school graduates. Minimum GPA of 3.0 and SAT score of 1000 is required. Must have verifiable community service. Submit a typed one-page essay describing your personal and professional goals and your expectations for college.

Award: Scholarship for use in freshman year; not renewable. *Number:* 1–5. *Amount:* $1000–$2000.

Eligibility Requirements: Applicant must be high school student; planning to enroll or expecting to enroll full-time at a two-year or four-year institution or university and resident of Maryland. Applicant must have 3.0 GPA or higher. Available to U.S. citizens.

Application Requirements: Application, essay, financial need analysis, references, test scores, transcript, financial aid award letters, Student Aid Report (SAR). *Deadline:* March 1.

Contact: Deana Carr-Davis, Associate Program Director, Scholarship Programs
CollegeBound Foundation
300 Water Street, Suite 300
Baltimore, MD 21202
Phone: 410-783-2905 Ext. 207
Fax: 410-727-5786
E-mail: dcarr-davis@collegeboundfoundation.org

GREEN FAMILY BOOK AWARD

One-time award of $800 for a high school graduate who possess a minimum GPA of 3.0. Must have verifiable community service and demonstrate financial need. Must submit an essay (250–500 words) describing a significant experience, achievement or risk that you have taken and its impact on you.

Award: Scholarship for use in freshman year; not renewable. *Number:* 1. *Amount:* $800.

Eligibility Requirements: Applicant must be high school student; planning to enroll or expecting to enroll full-time at a two-year or four-year institution or university and resident of Maryland. Applicant must have 3.0 GPA or higher. Available to U.S. citizens.

Application Requirements: Application, essay, financial need analysis, resume, references, transcript. *Deadline:* March 1.

Contact: Deana Carr-Davis, Associate Program Director, Scholarship Programs
CollegeBound Foundation
300 Water Street, Suite 300
Baltimore, MD 21202
Phone: 410-783-2905 Ext. 207
Fax: 410-727-5786
E-mail: dcarr-davis@collegeboundfoundation.org

HY ZOLET STUDENT ATHLETE SCHOLARSHIP

Scholarship available to a high school athlete with a minimum cumulative GPA of 2.5. Must furnish at least two letters verifying participation in high school athletics. Must submit SAT (critical reading and math) scores, and a one-page essay indicating why you should receive this award.

Award: Scholarship for use in freshman, sophomore, junior, or senior years; renewable. *Number:* 4. *Amount:* $1000.

Eligibility Requirements: Applicant must be high school student; planning to enroll or expecting to enroll full-time at a four-year institution or university; resident of Maryland and must have an interest in athletics/sports. Applicant must have 2.5 GPA or higher. Available to U.S. citizens.

Application Requirements: Application, essay, references, test scores, transcript. *Deadline:* March 1.

Contact: Deana Carr-Davis, Associate Program Director, Scholarship Programs
CollegeBound Foundation
300 Water Street, Suite 300
Baltimore, MD 21202
Phone: 410-783-2905 Ext. 207
Fax: 410-727-5786
E-mail: dcarr-davis@collegeboundfoundation.org

JANE AND CLARENCE SPILMAN SCHOLARSHIP

You must: have a cumulative 3.0 GPA or better; verifiable community service; and an SAT (CR+M) score of at least 1000.

Award: Scholarship for use in freshman, sophomore, junior, or senior years; renewable. *Number:* 1. *Amount:* $1500.

Eligibility Requirements: Applicant must be high school student; planning to enroll or expecting to enroll full-time at a two-year or four-year institution or university; resident of Maryland and studying in Maryland. Applicant must have 3.0 GPA or higher. Available to U.S. citizens.

Application Requirements: Application, financial need analysis, resume, references, test scores, transcript. *Deadline:* March 1.

Contact: Deana Carr-Davis, Associate Program Director, Scholarship Programs
CollegeBound Foundation
300 Water Street, Suite 300
Baltimore, MD 21202
Phone: 410-783-2905 Ext. 207
Fax: 410-727-5786
E-mail: dcarr-davis@collegeboundfoundation.org

KENNETH HOFFMAN SCHOLARSHIP

You must: have a cumulative 3.0 GPA or better; verifiable community service; and an SAT (CR+M) score of at least 1000.

Award: Scholarship for use in freshman, sophomore, junior, or senior years; renewable. *Number:* 1. *Amount:* $1500.

Eligibility Requirements: Applicant must be high school student; planning to enroll or expecting to enroll full-time at a four-year institution or university; resident of Maryland and studying in Maryland. Applicant must have 3.0 GPA or higher. Available to U.S. citizens.

Application Requirements: Application, financial need analysis, resume, references, test scores, transcript. *Deadline:* March 1.

Contact: Deana Carr-Davis, Associate Program Director, Scholarship Programs
CollegeBound Foundation
300 Water Street, Suite 300
Baltimore, MD 21202
Phone: 410-783-2905 Ext. 207
Fax: 410-727-5786
E-mail: dcarr-davis@collegeboundfoundation.org

LESLIE MOORE FOUNDATION SCHOLARSHIP

Three awards for students from Baltimore City public high schools and two from other county schools. Must have GPA of at least 2.0 and verifiable community service. See web site for application http://www.collegeboundfoundation.org.

Award: Scholarship for use in freshman, sophomore, junior, or senior years; renewable. *Number:* 5. *Amount:* $2500.

Eligibility Requirements: Applicant must be high school student; planning to enroll or expecting to enroll full-time at a two-year or four-year institution and resident of Maryland. Available to U.S. citizens.

Application Requirements: Application, essay, financial need analysis, interview, references, transcript. *Deadline:* March 1.

Contact: Deana Carr-Davis, Associate Program Director, Scholarship Programs
CollegeBound Foundation
300 Water Street, Suite 300
Baltimore, MD 21202
Phone: 410-783-2905 Ext. 207
Fax: 410-727-5786
E-mail: dcarr-davis@collegeboundfoundation.org

SCARBOROUGH-SCHEELER SCHOLARSHIP

Scholarship for students with a cumulative high school GPA of at least 2.5. Must demonstrate financial need. Submit an essay (500–1000 words) describing your college expectations. Must plan on attending Goucher College, McDaniel College, Towson University or University of Maryland College Park.

Award: Scholarship for use in freshman, sophomore, junior, or senior years; renewable. *Number:* 1. *Amount:* $1000.

Eligibility Requirements: Applicant must be high school student; planning to enroll or expecting to enroll full-time at a four-year institution or university; resident of Maryland and studying in Maryland. Applicant must have 2.5 GPA or higher. Available to U.S. citizens.

Application Requirements: Application, essay, financial need analysis, references, transcript. *Deadline:* March 1.

Contact: Deana Carr-Davis, Associate Program Director, Scholarship Programs
CollegeBound Foundation
300 Water Street, Suite 300
Baltimore, MD 21202
Phone: 410-783-2905 Ext. 207
Fax: 410-727-5786
E-mail: dcarr-davis@collegeboundfoundation.org

COLLEGE FOUNDATION OF NORTH CAROLINA

http://www.cfnc.org/

CRUMLEY AND ASSOCIATES-CRIB TO COLLEGE SCHOLARSHIP

Scholarship will provide financial assistance and laptop computers to five outstanding North Carolina high school seniors. Applicants must be a graduating senior at a North Carolina high school and enroll at an accredited four-year college or university or an accredited two-year technical school or community college. Must maintain a minimum GPA of 3.0. Application is available only on the company web site at http://www.crumleyandassociates.com/crib-to-college.php and must be completed online only.

Award: Scholarship for use in freshman year; not renewable. *Number:* 5. *Amount:* $1000.

Eligibility Requirements: Applicant must be high school student; planning to enroll or expecting to enroll full-time at a two-year or four-year or technical institution or university and resident of North Carolina. Applicant must have 3.0 GPA or higher. Available to U.S. citizens.

Application Requirements: Application, essay, references, test scores, transcript. *Deadline:* March 15.

Contact: Stephen Keaney, Scholarship Committee
College Foundation of North Carolina
Crumley and Associates, 2400 Freeman Mill Road, Suite 300
Greensboro, NC 27406
Phone: 336-333-0044
E-mail: smkeaney@crumleyandassociates.com

FEDERAL SUPPLEMENTAL EDUCATIONAL OPPORTUNITY GRANT PROGRAM

Applicant must have exceptional financial need to qualify for this award. Amount of financial need is determined by the educational institution the student attends. Available only to undergraduate students. Recipient must be a U.S. citizen or permanent resident. Priority is given to a students who receive Federal Pell Grants.

Award: Grant for use in freshman, sophomore, junior, or senior years; not renewable. *Number:* varies. *Amount:* $100–$4400.

Eligibility Requirements: Applicant must be enrolled or expecting to enroll full-time at a four-year institution or university and resident of North Carolina. Available to U.S. citizens.

Application Requirements: Application, financial need analysis, transcript. *Deadline:* continuous.

Contact: Federal Student Aid Information Center
College Foundation of North Carolina
PO Box 84
Washington, DC 20044
Phone: 800-433-3243

GOLDEN LEAF SCHOLARSHIP (PUBLIC UNIVERSITY AND PRIVATE COLLEGE AND UNIVERSITY PROGRAM)

Scholarship for current high school seniors and current community college students planning to enter a North Carolina public, four-year university and for currently enrolled students at NC public, four-year universities. Must be a permanent resident of a rural NC county that is economically distressed and/or tobacco crop-dependent. Must demonstrate financial need. For this program, the real value of farm property is not considered when determining need.

Award: Grant for use in freshman, sophomore, junior, or senior years; renewable. *Number:* 215. *Amount:* $3000.

Eligibility Requirements: Applicant must be enrolled or expecting to enroll full-time at a four-year institution or university; resident of North Carolina and studying in North Carolina. Available to U.S. citizens.

Application Requirements: Application, essay, financial need analysis, transcript. *Deadline:* March 1.

Contact: Robbie Schultz, Outreach Manager, North Carolina State
Education Assistance Authority
College Foundation of North Carolina
PO Box 13663
RTP, NC 27709-3663
Phone: 866-866-CFNC
Fax: 919-248-6686
E-mail: programinformation@cfnc.org

GOLDEN LEAF SCHOLARS PROGRAM-TWO-YEAR COLLEGES

Need- and merit-based scholarships of up to $750 per semester, including summer session for curriculum students, and up to $250 per semester for occupational education students. Student must be a permanent resident of one of the seventy-three eligible counties and be enrolled at one of the fifty-eight member institutions of the North Carolina community college system. Must demonstrate a need under federal TRIO formula.

Award: Scholarship for use in freshman or sophomore years; not renewable. *Number:* varies. *Amount:* $500–$1500.

Eligibility Requirements: Applicant must be enrolled or expecting to enroll part-time at a two-year institution; resident of North Carolina and studying in North Carolina. Available to U.S. citizens.

Application Requirements: Application, financial need analysis, transcript, waiver form. *Deadline:* varies.

Contact: Scholarship Coordinator
College Foundation of North Carolina
2917 Highwoods Boulevard
PO Box 41966
Raleigh, NC 27604
Phone: 866-866-2362
E-mail: programinformation@cfnc.org

UNIVERSITY OF NORTH CAROLINA NEED-BASED GRANT

Grants available for eligible students attending one of the 16 campuses of the University of North Carolina. Students must be enrolled in at least 6 credit hours at one of the 16 constituent institutions of The University of North Carolina. Award amounts vary based on legislative appropriations.

Award: Grant for use in freshman, sophomore, junior, or senior years; not renewable. *Number:* varies. *Amount:* varies.

Eligibility Requirements: Applicant must be enrolled or expecting to enroll full- or part-time at a four-year institution or university; resident of North Carolina and studying in North Carolina. Available to U.S. citizens.

Application Requirements: Financial need analysis. *Deadline:* continuous.

Contact: *Phone:* 866-866-CFNC
Fax: 919-248-4687
E-mail: programinformation@cfnc.org

COLLEGE SUCCESS FOUNDATION

http://www.collegesuccessfoundation.org/

GOVERNORS SCHOLARSHIP PROGRAM

Scholarship award amounts range from $1000 to $5000 depending on each student's financial need. Scholarships can be used up to five years until completion of the student's program of study. Students must be enroll full time and maintain satisfactory academic progress in order to renew scholarships each year. Minimum 2.0 GPA required.

Award: Scholarship for use in freshman year; renewable. *Number:* 30. *Amount:* $1000–$5000.

Eligibility Requirements: Applicant must be high school student; planning to enroll or expecting to enroll full-time at a four-year institution or university; resident of Washington and studying in Washington. Available to U.S. citizens.

Application Requirements: Application, references, FAFSA. *Deadline:* March 4.

Contact: Erica Meier, Director, Human Resources and Operations
College Success Foundation
1605 NW Sammamish Road, Suite 100
Issaquah, WA 98027
Phone: 425-416-2000
Fax: 425-416-2001
E-mail: info@collegesuccessfoundation.org

WASHINGTON STATE ACHIEVERS PROGRAM SCHOLARSHIP

Scholarship amounts will be established annually for students attending public community colleges, public four-year and independent institutions. Scholarships averages approximately between $5000 to $10,000.

Award: Scholarship for use in freshman year; not renewable. *Number:* 600. *Amount:* $5000–$10,000.

Eligibility Requirements: Applicant must be high school student; planning to enroll or expecting to enroll full-time at a two-year or four-year or technical institution or university; resident of Washington and studying in Washington. Available to U.S. citizens.

Application Requirements: Application, financial need analysis. *Deadline:* varies.

Contact: Erica Meier, Director, Human Resources and Operations
College Success Foundation
1605 NW Sammamish Road, Suite 100
Issaquah, WA 98027
Phone: 425-416-2000
Fax: 425-416-2001
E-mail: info@collegesuccessfoundation.org

COLLEGE SUCCESS NETWORK

http://www.collegesuccessnetwork.org/

NEW MEXICO FINISH LINE SCHOLARSHIP

Awards range from $300 to $1000. Scholarship is for the academically proven New Mexico college student who has completed at least one semester of undergraduate coursework. Must have at least 3.0 GPA.

Award: Scholarship for use in freshman, sophomore, junior, or senior years; renewable. *Number:* 1. *Amount:* $300–$1000.

Eligibility Requirements: Applicant must be enrolled or expecting to enroll full- or part-time at a four-year institution or university; resident of New Mexico and studying in New Mexico. Applicant must have 3.0 GPA or higher. Available to U.S. citizens.

Application Requirements: Application, essay, self-addressed stamped envelope, transcript, financial aid award letter. *Deadline:* October 15.

Contact: Robert W. Paton, Business Development and Outreach
Director
College Success Network
414 Alvarado Square, SW
Albuquerque, NM 87158
Phone: 505-241-4483
Fax: 505-241-4484
E-mail: bpaton@collegesuccessnetwork.org

COLORADO COMMISSION ON HIGHER EDUCATION

http://www.highered.colorado.gov/dhedefault.html

COLORADO LEVERAGING EDUCATIONAL ASSISTANCE PARTNERSHIP (CLEAP)

Scholarship of up to $5000 awarded for an undergraduate student enrolled at least half time. Applicant must be a U.S citizen and Colorado resident.

Award: Scholarship for use in freshman, sophomore, junior, or senior years; not renewable. *Number:* varies. *Amount:* up to $5000.

Eligibility Requirements: Applicant must be enrolled or expecting to enroll full- or part-time at a two-year or four-year or technical institution or university and resident of Colorado. Available to U.S. citizens.

Application Requirements: Application.

Contact: Celina Duran, Financial Aid Administrator
Colorado Commission on Higher Education
1560 Broadway, Suite 1600
Denver, CO 80202
Phone: 303-866-2723
E-mail: celina.duran@dhe.state.co.us

COLORADO STUDENT GRANT

Grants for Colorado residents attending eligible public, private, or vocational institutions within the state. Students must complete a Free Application for Federal Student Aid (FAFSA) and qualify at 150% of Pell eligibility. Application deadlines vary by institution. Renewable award for undergraduates. Contact the financial aid office at the college/institution for application and more information.

Award: Grant for use in freshman, sophomore, junior, or senior years; renewable. *Number:* 60,307. *Amount:* $850–$5000.

Eligibility Requirements: Applicant must be enrolled or expecting to enroll full- or part-time at a two-year or four-year or technical institution

or university; resident of Colorado and studying in Colorado. Available to U.S. citizens.

Application Requirements: Application, financial need analysis, student must have an active FAFSA on file at the institution.

Contact: Celina Duran, Financial Aid Administrator
Colorado Commission on Higher Education
1560 Broadway, Suite 1600
Denver, CO 80202
Phone: 303-866-2723
E-mail: celina.duran@dhe.state.co.us

GOVERNOR'S OPPORTUNITY SCHOLARSHIP

Scholarship was awarded to the most needy first-time freshman whose parents' adjusted gross income is less than $26,000. The program is in phase out and not accepting new applicants. Continuing students must be U.S. citizen or permanent legal resident. Work-study is part of the program. This program is in phase out and will sunset in 2012.

Award: Scholarship for use in freshman, sophomore, junior, or senior years; renewable. *Number:* 265. *Amount:* up to $10,700.

Eligibility Requirements: Applicant must be enrolled or expecting to enroll full-time at a two-year or four-year or technical institution or university; resident of Colorado and studying in Colorado.

Application Requirements: Application, financial need analysis, test scores, transcript. *Deadline:* continuous.

Contact: Celina Duran, Financial Aid Administrator
Colorado Commission on Higher Education
1560 Broadway, Suite 1600
Denver, CO 80202
Phone: 303-866-2723
E-mail: celina.duran@dhe.state.co.us

COLORADO COUNCIL ON HIGH SCHOOL/ COLLEGE RELATIONS

http://www.coloradocouncil.org/

COLORADO COUNCIL VOLUNTEERISM/COMMUNITY SERVICE SCHOLARSHIP

Awarded to a graduating high school senior, who will attend a Colorado College that is a member of the Colorado Council for High School/College Relations. The application is on the web site http://www.coloradocouncil.org. Applicant must have a minimum GPA 2.5. Award value is $1250.

Award: Scholarship for use in freshman year; not renewable. *Number:* 16. *Amount:* $1250.

Eligibility Requirements: Applicant must be high school student; planning to enroll or expecting to enroll full-time at a two-year or four-year institution or university; resident of Colorado and studying in Colorado. Applicant must have 2.5 GPA or higher. Available to U.S. citizens.

Application Requirements: Application, essay, references, transcript. *Deadline:* January 31.

Contact: Mark Thompson, Counselor
Colorado Council on High School/College Relations
600 17th Street, Suite 2210 South
Denver, CO 80202
Phone: 970-264-2231 Ext. 226
E-mail: mthompson@pagosa.k12.co.us

COLORADO EDUCATIONAL SERVICES AND DEVELOPMENT ASSOCIATION

http://www.cesda.org/

CESDA DIVERSITY SCHOLARSHIPS

Award for underrepresented, economically, and disadvantaged high school seniors planning to pursue undergraduate studies at a Colorado college or university. Must be Colorado resident. Applicant must be a first generation student, or member of an underrepresented ethnic or racial minority, and/or show financial need. Minimum 2.8 GPA required.

Award: Scholarship for use in freshman, sophomore, junior, or senior years; not renewable. *Number:* 6. *Amount:* $1000.

Eligibility Requirements: Applicant must be enrolled or expecting to enroll full- or part-time at a two-year or four-year institution or university; resident of Colorado and studying in Colorado. Available to U.S. citizens.

Application Requirements: Application, financial need analysis, transcript. *Deadline:* March 31.

Contact: Ximena Quintana, Scholarship Committee
Colorado Educational Services and Development Association
2960 North Speer Boulevard
Denver, CO 80211
Phone: 720-423-2907
E-mail: xquintana@denverscholarship.org

COLORADO MASONS BENEVOLENT FUND ASSOCIATION

http://www.coloradofreemasons.org/

COLORADO MASONS BENEVOLENT FUND SCHOLARSHIPS

Applicants must be graduating seniors from a Colorado public high school accepted at a Colorado postsecondary institution. The maximum grant is $7000 renewable over four years. Obtain scholarship materials and specific requirements from high school counselor.

Award: Scholarship for use in freshman, sophomore, junior, or senior years; renewable. *Number:* 10–14. *Amount:* up to $7000.

Eligibility Requirements: Applicant must be high school student; planning to enroll or expecting to enroll full-time at a two-year or four-year or technical institution or university; resident of Colorado and studying in Colorado. Available to U.S. citizens.

Application Requirements: Application, essay, financial need analysis, interview, references, test scores, transcript. *Deadline:* March 7.

Contact: Ron Kadera, Scholarship Administrator
Colorado Masons Benevolent Fund Association
1130 Panorama Drive
Colorado Springs, CO 80904
Phone: 719-471-9587
Fax: 719-471-9157
E-mail: scholarships@coloradofreemasons.org

COMMERCE BANK

http://www.com/merceonline.com/

AMERICAN DREAM SCHOLARSHIPS
• *See page 585*

COMMUNITY BANKER ASSOCIATION OF ILLINOIS

http://www.cbai.com/

COMMUNITY BANKER ASSOCIATION OF ILLINOIS ANNUAL SCHOLARSHIP PROGRAM

Open to Illinois high school seniors who are sponsored by a CBAI member bank. Student bank employees, immediate families of bank employees, board members, stockholders, CBAI employees, and judges are ineligible. For more details see web site http://www.cbai.com.

Award: Scholarship for use in freshman year; not renewable. *Number:* up to 13. *Amount:* $1000–$4000.

Eligibility Requirements: Applicant must be high school student; planning to enroll or expecting to enroll full-time at a two-year or four-year or technical institution or university and resident of Illinois. Available to U.S. citizens.

Application Requirements: Application, applicant must enter a contest, essay. *Deadline:* February 11.

Contact: Ms. Andrea Cusick, Senior Vice President of Communications
Community Banker Association of Illinois
901 Community Drive
Springfield, IL 62703-5184
Phone: 217-529-2265
E-mail: cbaicom@cbai.com

COMMUNITY BANKER ASSOCIATION OF ILLINOIS CHILDREN OF COMMUNITY BANKING SCHOLARSHIP WILLIAM C. HARRIS MEMORIAL SCHOLARSHIP
• *See page 539*

COMMUNITY BANKERS ASSOCIATION OF GEORGIA

http://www.cbaofga.com/

JULIAN AND JAN HESTER MEMORIAL SCHOLARSHIP

Scholarship available to Georgia high school seniors who will be entering a Georgia two- or four-year college or university, or a program at a technical institution. Recipients will be named on the basis of merit, and family financial need is not considered. Application must be sponsored by a local community bank, and must include an essay on community banking and what it represents.

Award: Scholarship for use in freshman year; not renewable. *Number:* 4. *Amount:* $1000.

Eligibility Requirements: Applicant must be high school student; planning to enroll or expecting to enroll full-time at a two-year or four-year or technical institution or university; resident of Georgia and studying in Georgia. Available to U.S. citizens.

Application Requirements: Application, references, test scores, transcript. *Deadline:* March 30.

Contact: Lauren Dismuke, Public Relations and Marketing Coordinator
Community Bankers Association of Georgia
1900 The Exchange, Suite 600
Atlanta, GA 30339
Phone: 770-541-4490
Fax: 770-541-4496
E-mail: lauren@cbaofga.com

THE COMMUNITY FOUNDATION FOR GREATER ATLANTA, INC.

http://www.cfgreateratlanta.org/

GEORGE AND PEARL STRICKLAND SCHOLARSHIP

For undergraduate or graduate students with financial need pursuing degrees at Atlanta University Center Colleges. For complete eligibility requirements and for an application, please visit http://www.cfgreateratlanta.org.

Award: Scholarship for use in freshman, sophomore, junior, senior, or graduate years; not renewable. *Number:* up to 30. *Amount:* $1000–$2000.

Eligibility Requirements: Applicant must be enrolled or expecting to enroll full- or part-time at a four-year institution or university; resident of Georgia and studying in Georgia. Available to U.S. citizens.

Application Requirements: Application, driver's license, essay, financial need analysis, references, transcript. *Deadline:* March 15.

Contact: Kristina Morris, Program Associate
The Community Foundation for Greater Atlanta, Inc.
50 Hurt Plaza, Suite 449
Atlanta, GA 30303
Phone: 404-688-5525
E-mail: scholarships@cfgreateratlanta.org

NANCY PENN LYONS SCHOLARSHIP FUND

Award for graduating high school seniors with financial need living in Georgia who have been accepted for enrollment at prestigious or out-of-state universities. Please visit the web site (www.cfgreateratlanta.org) for complete eligibility requirements.

Award: Scholarship for use in freshman, sophomore, junior, or senior years; renewable. *Number:* 1–5. *Amount:* $5000.

Eligibility Requirements: Applicant must be high school student; planning to enroll or expecting to enroll full-time at a four-year institution or university and resident of Georgia. Applicant must have 3.0 GPA or higher. Available to U.S. citizens.

Application Requirements: Application, driver's license, essay, financial need analysis, interview, references, test scores, transcript. *Deadline:* March 15.

Contact: Kristina Morris, Program Associate
The Community Foundation for Greater Atlanta, Inc.
50 Hurt Plaza, Suite 449
Atlanta, GA 30303
Phone: 404-688-5525
E-mail: scholarships@cfgreateratlanta.org

COMMUNITY FOUNDATION FOR PALM BEACH AND MARTIN COUNTIES

http://www.yourcommunityfoundation.org/

COMMUNITY FOUNDATION SCHOLARSHIP PROGRAM

Awards range between $1,000 and $15,000 per year. Applicant must be a full-time student and graduating high school senior from a public or independent high school located in Palm Beach County or Martin County, Florida.

Award: Scholarship for use in freshman, sophomore, junior, senior, or graduate years; renewable. *Number:* 100–150. *Amount:* $1000–$15,000.

Eligibility Requirements: Applicant must be high school student; planning to enroll or expecting to enroll full-time at a two-year or four-year or technical institution or university and resident of Florida. Applicant must have 2.5 GPA or higher. Available to U.S. citizens.

Application Requirements: Application, essay, financial need analysis, interview, references, test scores, transcript, proof of citizenship/legal resident. *Deadline:* February 1.

Contact: Ms. Patricia Rowan, Fund Distributions Manager
Community Foundation for Palm Beach and Martin Counties
700 South Dixie Highway, Suite 200
West Palm Beach, FL 33401
Phone: 561-659-6800
Fax: 561-832-6542
E-mail: prowan@cfpbmc.org

COMMUNITY FOUNDATION OF WESTERN MASSACHUSETTS

http://www.communityfoundation.org/

DEERFIELD PLASTICS/BARKER FAMILY SCHOLARSHIP
• *See page 574*

MASSMUTUAL CAREER PATHWAYS SCHOLARS PROGRAM

Graduating high school seniors with a strong interest in pursuing careers in business, financial services, or information technology.

Award: Scholarship for use in freshman year; renewable. *Number:* 10. *Amount:* $5000.

Eligibility Requirements: Applicant must be enrolled or expecting to enroll full-time at a two-year or four-year institution or university and resident of Connecticut or Massachusetts. Applicant must have 3.0 GPA or higher. Available to U.S. citizens.

Application Requirements: Application, essay, financial need analysis, transcript. *Deadline:* March 31.

Contact: Dorothy Theriaque, Education Associate
Community Foundation of Western Massachusetts
1500 Main Street, Tower Square, Suite 2300
PO Box 15769
Springfield, MA 01115
Phone: 413-732-2858
Fax: 413-733-8565
E-mail: scholar@communityfoundation.org

CONNECTICUT ARMY NATIONAL GUARD

http://www.ct.ngb.army.mil/

CONNECTICUT ARMY NATIONAL GUARD 100% TUITION WAIVER
• *See page 624*

CONNECTICUT COMMUNITY FOUNDATION

http://www.conncf.org/

REGIONAL AND RESTRICTED SCHOLARSHIP AWARD PROGRAM

Supports accredited college or university study for residents of the Connecticut community twenty-one town service area. In addition, a variety of restricted award programs are based on specific fund criteria (residency, school, course of study, etc). Scholarships are awarded on a competitive basis with consideration given to academic record, extracurricular activities, work experience, financial need, reference letter, and an essay.

Award: Scholarship for use in freshman, sophomore, junior, or senior years; renewable. *Number:* 200–300. *Amount:* $250–$5000.

Eligibility Requirements: Applicant must be enrolled or expecting to enroll full-time at a two-year or four-year institution or university and resident of Connecticut. Applicant must have 3.0 GPA or higher. Available to U.S. citizens.

Application Requirements: Application, essay, financial need analysis, references, transcript. *Deadline:* March 15.

Contact: Josh Carey, Program Officer
Connecticut Community Foundation
43 Field Street
Waterbury, CT 06702-1216
Phone: 203-753-1315
E-mail: jcarey@conncf.org

CONNECTICUT DEPARTMENT OF HIGHER EDUCATION

http://www.ctdhe.org/

CAPITOL SCHOLARSHIP PROGRAM

Award for Connecticut residents attending eligible institutions in Connecticut or in a state with reciprocity with Connecticut (Massachusetts, Maine, New Hampshire, Pennsylvania, Rhode Island, Vermont, or Washington, D.C). Must be U.S. citizen or permanent resident alien who is a high school senior or graduate. Must rank in top 20% of class or score at least 1800 on SAT or score at least 27 on the ACT. Students must also demonstrate financial need as a result of filing the FAFSA.

Award: Scholarship for use in freshman, sophomore, junior, or senior years; renewable. *Number:* 4500–5500. *Amount:* $500–$3000.

Eligibility Requirements: Applicant must be enrolled or expecting to enroll full- or part-time at a two-year or four-year or technical institution or university; resident of Connecticut and studying in Connecticut, District of Columbia, Maine, Massachusetts, New Hampshire, Pennsylvania, Rhode Island, or Vermont. Available to U.S. citizens.

Application Requirements: Application, financial need analysis, test scores, FAFSA. *Deadline:* February 15.

Contact: Mrs. Linda Diamond, Senior Associate
Connecticut Department of Higher Education
61 Woodland Street
Hartford, CT 06105
Phone: 860-947-1855
Fax: 860-947-1313
E-mail: csp@ctdhe.org

CONNECTICUT AID TO PUBLIC COLLEGE STUDENTS GRANT

Award for Connecticut residents attending public colleges or universities within the state. Renewable awards based on financial need. Application deadline varies by institution. Apply at college financial aid office.

Award: Grant for use in freshman, sophomore, junior, or senior years; renewable. *Number:* varies. *Amount:* varies.

Eligibility Requirements: Applicant must be enrolled or expecting to enroll full- or part-time at a two-year or four-year institution or university; resident of Connecticut and studying in Connecticut. Available to U.S. citizens.

Application Requirements: Financial need analysis, FAFSA. *Deadline:* continuous.

Contact: Ms. Lynne Little, Executive Assistant
Connecticut Department of Higher Education
61 Woodland Street
Hartford, CT 06105
Phone: 860-947-1855
Fax: 860-947-1838
E-mail: caps@ctdhe.org

CONNECTICUT INDEPENDENT COLLEGE STUDENT GRANTS

Award for Connecticut residents attending an independent college or university within the state on at least a half-time basis. Renewable awards based on financial need. Application deadline varies by institution. Apply at college financial aid office.

Award: Grant for use in freshman, sophomore, junior, or senior years; renewable. *Number:* varies. *Amount:* $250–$8700.

Eligibility Requirements: Applicant must be enrolled or expecting to enroll full- or part-time at a two-year or four-year institution or university; resident of Connecticut and studying in Connecticut. Available to U.S. citizens.

Application Requirements: Financial need analysis, FAFSA. *Deadline:* continuous.

Contact: Ms. Lynne Little, Executive Assistant
Connecticut Department of Higher Education
61 Woodland Street
Hartford, CT 06105
Phone: 860-947-1855
Fax: 860-947-1838
E-mail: cics@ctdhe.org

ROBERT C. BYRD HONORS SCHOLARSHIP-CONNECTICUT

Renewable scholarship for Connecticut high school seniors and home-schooled students in the top 2% of their class or scoring 2100 or above on the SAT or 32 or above on the ACT. Acceptance letter from college required. File applications through high school guidance office.

Award: Scholarship for use in freshman, sophomore, junior, or senior years; renewable. *Number:* 322. *Amount:* $1500.

Eligibility Requirements: Applicant must be high school student; planning to enroll or expecting to enroll full-time at a two-year or four-year institution or university and resident of Connecticut. Available to U.S. citizens.

Application Requirements: Application, test scores. *Deadline:* April 1.

Contact: Ms. Judy-Ann Staple, Associate
Connecticut Department of Higher Education
61 Woodland Street
Hartford, CT 06105
Phone: 860-947-1855
Fax: 860-947-1838
E-mail: byrd@ctdhe.org

CONNECTICUT STUDENT LOAN FOUNDATION

http://www.cslf.com/

VINCENT J. MAIOCCO SCHOLARSHIP

Award to provide access to postsecondary education. Must have received a Federal Stafford Loan guaranteed by CSLF, must be a United States citizen and Connecticut resident since the time of high school graduation, and must have successfully completed his or her first year of study at a four-year degree granting institution within the United States.

Award: Scholarship for use in sophomore, junior, or senior years; not renewable. *Number:* varies. *Amount:* varies.

Eligibility Requirements: Applicant must be enrolled or expecting to enroll full-time at a four-year institution or university and resident of Connecticut. Available to U.S. citizens.

Application Requirements: Application, essay, transcript, financial aid award letter. *Deadline:* varies.

Contact: Melissa Trombley, Executive Manager
Connecticut Student Loan Foundation
525 Brook Street, PO Box 1009
Rocky Hill, CT 06067
Phone: 800-237-9721 Ext. 204
Fax: 860-257-1743
E-mail: mtrombl@mail.cslf.org

CORPORATION FOR OHIO APPALACHIAN DEVELOPMENT (COAD)

http://www.coadinc.org/

DAVID V. STIVISON APPALACHIAN SCHOLARSHIP FUND

Provides financial assistance to students who are residents in the Corporation for Ohio Appalachian Development's (COAD) service area and want to attend college but lack the required resources. Individual income must not exceed 200 percent of Federal Poverty Level. See web site for application information http://www.coadinc.org/Main.php?page=scholarships-info.

Award: Scholarship for use in freshman, sophomore, junior, or senior years; not renewable. *Number:* 17. *Amount:* $500–$1500.

Eligibility Requirements: Applicant must be enrolled or expecting to enroll full-time at a two-year or four-year institution or university and resident of Ohio. Available to U.S. citizens.

Application Requirements: Application, financial need analysis, photo, transcript. *Deadline:* March 1.

Contact: Allyssa Mefford, Operations Manager
Corporation for Ohio Appalachian Development (COAD)
1 Pinchot Lane
PO Box 787
Athens, OH 45701-0787
Phone: 740-594-8499 Ext. 213
E-mail: amefford@coadinc.org

COURAGE CENTER, VOCATIONAL SERVICES DEPARTMENT

http://www.couragecenter.org/

SCHOLARSHIP FOR PEOPLE WITH DISABILITIES

Award provides financial assistance to students with sensory or physical disabilities. May reapply each year. Applicant must be pursuing educational goals or technical expertise beyond high school. Must be U.S. citizen and resident of Minnesota, or participate in Courage Center Services. Indication of extracurricular work and volunteer history must be submitted along with application form.

Award: Scholarship for use in freshman, sophomore, junior, or senior years; not renewable. *Number:* 15–19. *Amount:* $500–$1000.

Eligibility Requirements: Applicant must be enrolled or expecting to enroll full-time at a two-year or four-year or technical institution or university and resident of Minnesota. Available to U.S. citizens.

Application Requirements: Application, essay, financial need analysis, interview. *Deadline:* May 31.

Contact: Ms. Nancy Robinow, Administrative Assistant
Courage Center, Vocational Services Department
3915 Golden Valley Road
Golden Valley, MN 55422-4298
Phone: 763-520-0553
Fax: 763-520-0861
E-mail: nrobinow@couragecenter.org

DADE COMMUNITY FOUNDATION

http://www.jackituckfield.org/

ALAN R. EPSTEIN SCHOLARSHIP

Award available for a high school senior who is a Dade county resident. Must have a 3.0 GPA and attach a copy of acceptance letter to two- or four-year college or university. For additional information and application, visit web site http://www.dadecommunityfoundation.org.

Award: Scholarship for use in freshman year; not renewable.

Eligibility Requirements: Applicant must be high school student; planning to enroll or expecting to enroll full-time at a two-year or four-year institution or university and resident of Florida. Applicant must have 3.0 GPA or higher. Available to U.S. citizens.

Application Requirements: Application, financial need analysis, references, transcript, acceptance letter, personal statement. *Deadline:* April 10.

Contact: Ted Seijo, Scholarship Coordinator
Dade Community Foundation
1160 Northwest 87 Street
Miami, FL 33150-2544
Phone: 305-371-2711
E-mail: ted.seijo@dadecommunityfoundation.org

CONTINENTAL GROUP SCHOLARSHIP

Renewable award for the children of current full-time employees of Continental Group and its subsidiaries. Must be a high school senior planning to enroll in a college or university in the U.S. Minimum 3.0 GPA required. Award may be available up to four years. For additional information and application, visit web site http://www.dadecommunityfoundation.org.

Award: Scholarship for use in freshman, sophomore, junior, or senior years; renewable. *Number:* 4. *Amount:* $1000.

Eligibility Requirements: Applicant must be high school student; planning to enroll or expecting to enroll full-time at a four-year institution or university and resident of Florida. Applicant must have 3.0 GPA or higher. Available to U.S. citizens.

Application Requirements: Application, references, transcript. *Deadline:* March 27.

Contact: Ted Seijo, Scholarship Coordinator
Dade Community Foundation
1160 Northwest 87 Street
Miami, FL 33150-2544
Phone: 305-371-2711
E-mail: ted.seijo@dadecommunityfoundation.org

RODNEY THAXTON/MARTIN E. SEGAL SCHOLARSHIP
• *See page 661*

SIDNEY M. ARONOVITZ SCHOLARSHIP
• *See page 661*

THE DALLAS FOUNDATION

http://www.dallasfoundation.org/

THE AKIN AYODELE SCHOLARSHIP IN MEMORY OF MICHAEL TILMON

Michael Tilmon was a best friend and teammate of Dallas Cowboy Akin Ayodele while at MacArthur High School. Sadly, he passed away in a car accident in March of 1997. This scholarship program is intended to honor those who demonstrate the type of character and integrity that Michael possessed.

Award: Scholarship for use in freshman year; not renewable. *Amount:* $10,000.

Eligibility Requirements: Applicant must be high school student; planning to enroll or expecting to enroll full-time at a two-year or four-year institution or university and resident of Texas.

Application Requirements: Application, transcript. *Deadline:* April 15.

Contact: Rachel Lasseter, Program Associate
The Dallas Foundation
900 Jackson Street, Suite 705
Dallas, TX 75202
Phone: 214-741-9898
E-mail: scholarships@dallasfoundation.org

DR. DAN J. AND PATRICIA S. PICKARD SCHOLARSHIP
• *See page 661*

DR. DON AND ROSE MARIE BENTON SCHOLARSHIP

Award is available to students, parents of students and volunteers who have been affiliated with Trinity River Mission in Dallas, Texas. Must be enrolled in a graduate or undergraduate program in a regionally accredited college or university. Scholarship is renewable for two years if the student maintains a specified grade point average and fulfills all reporting requirements as determined by the Scholarship Committee.

Award: Scholarship for use in freshman, sophomore, junior, senior, graduate, or postgraduate years; renewable. *Number:* 1–3. *Amount:* $1500.

Eligibility Requirements: Applicant must be enrolled or expecting to enroll full-time at a two-year or four-year institution or university and resident of Texas.

Application Requirements: Application, transcript. *Deadline:* April 1.

Contact: Ms. Dolores Sosa Green, Trinity River Mission
The Dallas Foundation
2060 Singleton Boulevard, Suite 104
Dallas, TX 75212
Phone: 214-744-5648

THE LANDON RUSNAK SCHOLARSHIP

The Landon Rusnak Scholarship Fund was established at The Dallas Foundation in 2007. This scholarship is established by the employees of LEAM Drilling Systems, Inc. and Conroe Machine, LLC in memory of Landon Rusnak, son of David and Janet Rusnak and brother of Cady Rusnak. Landon's sister Cady is an active member of the Mexia High School Black Cat Band.

Award: Scholarship for use in freshman year; not renewable. *Number:* 1. *Amount:* $3000.

Eligibility Requirements: Applicant must be high school student; planning to enroll or expecting to enroll full-time at a two-year or four-year institution or university; resident of Texas and must have an interest in music.

Application Requirements: Application, financial need analysis, transcript. *Deadline:* February 28.

Contact: Rachel Lasseter, Program Associate
The Dallas Foundation
900 Jackson Street, Suite 705
Dallas, TX 75202
Phone: 214-741-9898
E-mail: scholarships@dallasfoundation.org

THE MAYOR'S CHESAPEAKE ENERGY SCHOLARSHIP

The Mayor's Chesapeake Energy Scholarship was established at The Dallas Foundation by Chesapeake Energy Corporation. The goal of the Fund is to make a college degree or vocational certification possible for minority and socially disadvantaged youth. Graduating students in the Dallas ISD are eligible to apply. Applicants should be female or a member of a minority group. Applicants must have participated in the Education is Freedom program.

Award: Scholarship for use in freshman, sophomore, junior, or senior years; renewable. *Amount:* $20,000.

Eligibility Requirements: Applicant must be high school student; planning to enroll or expecting to enroll full-time at a two-year or four-year or technical institution or university and resident of Texas. Applicant must have 3.0 GPA or higher. Available to U.S. citizens.

Application Requirements: Application, financial need analysis, test scores, transcript. *Deadline:* April 15.

Contact: Rachel Lasseter, Program Associate
The Dallas Foundation
900 Jackson Street, Suite 705
Dallas, TX 75202
Phone: 214-741-9898
E-mail: scholarships@dallasfoundation.org

TOMMY TRANCHIN AWARD

Established at The Dallas Foundation to support students with physical, emotional or intellectual disabilities who have excelled or shown promise in a chosen field of interest. Tommy's family wants to recognize his creativity and his refusal to allow his disability to limit his personal growth by helping others to develop their own talents. Applicants should be residents of North Texas.

Award: Scholarship for use in freshman year; not renewable. *Amount:* $1500.

Eligibility Requirements: Applicant must be high school student; planning to enroll or expecting to enroll full-time at a two-year or four-year or technical institution or university and resident of Texas.

Application Requirements: Application, physical, proof of physical, emotional or intellectual disability. *Deadline:* March 5.

Contact: Rachel Lasseter, Program Associate
The Dallas Foundation
900 Jackson Street, Suite 705
Dallas, TX 75202
Phone: 214-741-9898
E-mail: scholarships@dallasfoundation.org

DAYTON FOUNDATION

http://www.daytonfoundation.org/

BRIGHTWELL FAMILY MEMORIAL SCHOLARSHIP

Scholarship awarded to a high school senior who is a child or grandchild of current or retired full-time Dayton firefighter. Must be an Ohio resident.

Award: Scholarship for use in freshman, sophomore, junior, or senior years; not renewable. *Number:* 1–2. *Amount:* up to $1000.

Eligibility Requirements: Applicant must be enrolled or expecting to enroll full-time at a four-year institution or university and resident of Ohio. Applicant must have 3.0 GPA or higher. Available to U.S. citizens.

Application Requirements: Application, essay, financial need analysis, references, transcript. *Deadline:* March 26.

Contact: Elizabeth Horner, Scholarship Program Officer
Dayton Foundation
500 Kettering Tower
Dayton, OH 45423
Phone: 937-225-9955
E-mail: ehorner@daytonfoundation.org

DELAWARE HIGHER EDUCATION OFFICE

http://www.doe.k12.de.us

AGENDA FOR DELAWARE WOMEN TRAILBLAZER SCHOLARSHIP
• *See page 585*

DIAMOND STATE SCHOLARSHIP

Award for legal residents of Delaware who are U.S. citizens or eligible non-citizens. Must be enrolled as a full-time student in a degree program at a nonprofit, regionally accredited institution. Minimum 3.0 GPA required. High school seniors should rank in upper quarter of class and have a combined score of at least 1800 on the SAT.

Award: Scholarship for use in freshman year; renewable. *Number:* 50. *Amount:* $1250.

Eligibility Requirements: Applicant must be high school student; planning to enroll or expecting to enroll full-time at a four-year institution or university and resident of Delaware. Applicant must have 3.0 GPA or higher. Available to U.S. citizens.

Application Requirements: Application, essay, test scores, transcript. *Deadline:* March 28.

Contact: Carylin Brinkley, Program Administrator
Delaware Higher Education Office
Carvel State Office Building, 820 North French Street, Fifth Floor
Wilmington, DE 19801-3509
Phone: 302-577-5240
Fax: 302-577-6765
E-mail: cbrinkley@doe.k12.de.us

EDUCATIONAL BENEFITS FOR CHILDREN OF DECEASED VETERANS
• *See page 585*

FIRST STATE MANUFACTURED HOUSING ASSOCIATION SCHOLARSHIP

Award for legal residents of Delaware who are high school seniors or former graduates seeking to further their education. Must have been a resident of a manufactured home for at least one year prior to the application. Evaluated on scholastic record, financial need, essay, and recommendations. Award for any type of accredited two- or four-year degree program, or for any accredited training, licensing, or certification program.

Award: Scholarship for use in freshman, sophomore, junior, or senior years; renewable. *Number:* up to 2. *Amount:* up to $2000.

Eligibility Requirements: Applicant must be enrolled or expecting to enroll full- or part-time at a two-year or four-year or technical institution or university and resident of Delaware. Available to U.S. citizens.

Application Requirements: Application, essay, financial need analysis, references, transcript, FAFSA. *Deadline:* March 7.

Contact: Carylin Brinkley, Program Administrator
Delaware Higher Education Office
Carvel State Office Building, 820 North French Street, Fifth Floor
Wilmington, DE 19801-3509
Phone: 302-577-5240
Fax: 302-577-6765
E-mail: cbrinkley@doe.k12.de.us

GOVERNOR'S WORKFORCE DEVELOPMENT GRANT

Grants for part-time undergraduate students attending Delaware College of Art and Design, Delaware State University, Delaware Technical and Community College, Goldey-Beacom College, University of Delaware, Wesley College, Widener University (Delaware Campus), or Wilmington College. Must be at least 18 years old, a resident of Delaware, and employed by a company in Delaware that contributes to the Blue Collar Training Fund Program.

Award: Grant for use in freshman, sophomore, junior, or senior years; renewable. *Number:* 40. *Amount:* $2000.

Eligibility Requirements: Applicant must be age 18 and over; enrolled or expecting to enroll full- or part-time at a two-year or four-year institution or university; resident of Delaware and studying in Delaware. Available to U.S. and non-U.S. citizens.

Application Requirements: Application. *Deadline:* varies.

Contact: Carylin Brinkley, Program Administrator
Delaware Higher Education Office
Carvel State Office Building, 820 North French Street, Fifth Floor
Wilmington, DE 19801-3509
Phone: 302-577-5240
Fax: 302-577-6765
E-mail: cbrinkley@doe.k12.de.us

LEGISLATIVE ESSAY SCHOLARSHIP

Award for legal residents of Delaware who are U.S. citizens or eligible non-citizens. Must be high school seniors in public or private schools or in home school programs who plans to enroll full-time at a nonprofit, regionally accredited college. Must submit an essay on topic: "Pluribus Unum: Is this motto adopted in 1782 relevant to our country today?".

Award: Prize for use in freshman year; not renewable. *Number:* up to 62. *Amount:* $1000–$10,000.

Eligibility Requirements: Applicant must be high school student; planning to enroll or expecting to enroll full- or part-time at a two-year or four-year or technical institution or university and resident of Delaware. Available to U.S. citizens.

Application Requirements: Application, applicant must enter a contest, essay. *Deadline:* November 30.

Contact: Carylin Brinkley, Program Administrator
Delaware Higher Education Office
Carvel State Office Building, 820 North French Street, Fifth Floor
Wilmington, DE 19801-3509
Phone: 302-577-5240
Fax: 302-577-6765
E-mail: cbrinkley@doe.k12.de.us

ROBERT C. BYRD HONORS SCHOLARSHIP-DELAWARE

Award for legal residents of Delaware who are U.S. citizens or eligible non-citizens. For high school seniors who rank in upper quarter of class or GED recipients with a minimum score of 300 and a combined score of at least 1800 on the SAT. Minimum 3.5 GPA required. Must be enrolled at least half-time at a nonprofit, regionally accredited institution.

Award: Scholarship for use in freshman year; renewable. *Number:* 20. *Amount:* $1500.

Eligibility Requirements: Applicant must be high school student; planning to enroll or expecting to enroll full-time at a two-year or four-year institution or university and resident of Delaware. Applicant must have 3.5 GPA or higher. Available to U.S. citizens.

Application Requirements: Application, essay, test scores, transcript. *Deadline:* March 28.

Contact: Carylin Brinkley, Program Administrator
Delaware Higher Education Office
Carvel State Office Building, 820 North French Street, Fifth Floor
Wilmington, DE 19801-3509
Phone: 302-577-5240
Fax: 302-577-6765
E-mail: cbrinkley@doe.k12.de.us

SCHOLARSHIP INCENTIVE PROGRAM (SCIP)

Award for legal residents of Delaware who are U.S. citizens or eligible non-citizens. Must demonstrate substantial financial need and enroll full-time in an undergraduate degree program at a nonprofit, regionally accredited institution in Delaware or Pennsylvania. Minimum 2.5 GPA required.

Award: Grant for use in freshman, sophomore, junior, senior, or graduate years; not renewable. *Number:* 1000–1253. *Amount:* $700–$2200.

Eligibility Requirements: Applicant must be enrolled or expecting to enroll full-time at a two-year or four-year institution or university; resident of Delaware and studying in Delaware or Pennsylvania. Applicant must have 2.5 GPA or higher. Available to U.S. citizens.

Application Requirements: Application, financial need analysis, transcript, FAFSA. *Deadline:* April 15.

Contact: Carylin Brinkley, Program Administrator
Delaware Higher Education Office
Carvel State Office Building, 820 North French Street, Fifth Floor
Wilmington, DE 19801-3509
Phone: 302-577-5240
Fax: 302-577-6765
E-mail: cbrinkley@doe.k12.de.us

DELAWARE NATIONAL GUARD

http://www.delawarenationalguard.com/

STATE TUITION ASSISTANCE
• See page 618

DEMOCRATIC WOMEN'S CLUB OF FLORIDA INC.

http://www.democratic-women.org/

DEMOCRATIC WOMEN'S CLUB OF FLORIDA SCHOLARSHIP

Scholarship to high school seniors attending schools in Florida. Award value is $1000. Minimum 3.0 GPA required.

Award: Scholarship for use in freshman year; not renewable. *Number:* 1. *Amount:* $1000.

Eligibility Requirements: Applicant must be high school student; age 18 and over; planning to enroll or expecting to enroll full-time at a four-year institution or university; resident of Florida and studying in Florida. Applicant must have 3.0 GPA or higher. Available to U.S. citizens.

Application Requirements: Application, essay, financial need analysis, references, transcript, copy of voter registration card. *Deadline:* varies.

Contact: Janie Holman, President
Democratic Women's Club of Florida Inc.
117 NE Surfside Avenue
Port St. Lucie, FL 34983
Phone: 321-639-4717
E-mail: president@democratic-women.org

DENVER FOUNDATION

http://www.denverfoundation.org/

REISHER FAMILY SCHOLARSHIP FUND

Scholarships awarded to Colorado residents who attend Metropolitan State College, the University of Northern Colorado, and the University of Colorado at Denver. Sophomores or transferring juniors who do not have sufficient funding to otherwise complete their degrees are eligible to apply. Must have at least a 3.0 GPA.

Award: Scholarship for use in sophomore or junior years; not renewable. *Number:* varies. *Amount:* varies.

Eligibility Requirements: Applicant must be enrolled or expecting to enroll full-time at a four-year institution or university; resident of Colorado and studying in Colorado. Applicant must have 3.0 GPA or higher. Available to U.S. citizens.

Application Requirements: Application. *Deadline:* varies.

Contact: Karla Bieniulis, Scholarship Committee
Denver Foundation
55 Madison Street, Eighth Floor
Denver, CO 80206
Phone: 303-300-1790 Ext. 103
Fax: 303-300-6547
E-mail: info@denverfoundation.org

DIAMANTE, INC.

http://www.diamanteinc.org/

LATINO DIAMANTE SCHOLARSHIP FUND
• See page 586

DISTRICT OF COLUMBIA OFFICE OF THE STATE SUPERINTENDENT

http://www.osse.dc.gov/

DC LEVERAGING EDUCATIONAL ASSISTANCE PARTNERSHIP PROGRAM (LEAP)

$250 to $1500 grants available to District of Columbia residents, who qualify for federal need-based aid and are enrolled in undergraduate programs, and pursuing a first baccalaureate degree. Must attend a Title IV eligible college or university at least half-time.

Award: Grant for use in freshman, sophomore, junior, or senior years; renewable. *Number:* up to 3200. *Amount:* $250–$1500.

Eligibility Requirements: Applicant must be enrolled or expecting to enroll full- or part-time at a two-year or four-year institution or university and resident of District of Columbia. Available to U.S. citizens.

Application Requirements: Application, financial need analysis, transcript, Student Aid Report (SAR), FAFSA. *Deadline:* June 30.

Contact: Ms. Rehva D. Jones, Director, Higher Education Financial Services and Preparatory Programs
District of Columbia Office of the State Superintendent
810 First Street, NW
Washington, DC 20002
Phone: 202-481-3948
Fax: 202-741-6491
E-mail: rehva.jones@dc.gov

DC TUITION ASSISTANCE GRANT PROGRAM

Grant pays the difference between in-state and out-of-state tuition and fees at any public college or university in the United States, Guam, Puerto Rico or U.S. Virgin Islands, up to $10,000 per year. It also pays up to $2500 per year of tuition and fees at private colleges and universities in the Washington metropolitan area and at historically black colleges and universities throughout the United States. Students must be enrolled in a degree-granting program at an eligible institution, and live in the District of Columbia.

Award: Grant for use in freshman, sophomore, junior, or senior years; renewable. *Number:* up to 7000. *Amount:* $2500–$10,000.

Eligibility Requirements: Applicant must be age 24 or under; enrolled or expecting to enroll full- or part-time at a two-year or four-year institution or university and resident of District of Columbia. Available to U.S. citizens.

Application Requirements: Application, transcript, Student Aid Report (SAR), current utility bill, D-40 tax return. *Deadline:* June 30.

Contact: Ms. Rehva D. Jones, Director, Higher Education Financial Services and Preparatory Programs
District of Columbia Office of the State Superintendent
810 First Street, NE
Washington, DC 20002
Phone: 202-481-3948
Fax: 202-741-6491
E-mail: rehva.jones@dc.gov

DISTRICT OF COLUMBIA ADOPTION SCHOLARSHIP

Scholarship assists District of Columbia students who were adopted from the DC Child and Family Services agency after October 1, 2001, and students who lost one or both parents as a result of the events of September 11, 2001. The DC Adoption Scholarship awards up to $10,000 toward the total cost of attendance at Title IV eligible colleges and universities throughout the United States, Guam, Puerto Rico and U.S. Virgin Islands. This scholarship is neither need nor merit based.

Award: Grant for use in freshman, sophomore, junior, or senior years; not renewable. *Number:* varies. *Amount:* up to $10,000.

Eligibility Requirements: Applicant must be age 24 or under; enrolled or expecting to enroll full-time at a two-year or four-year institution or university and resident of District of Columbia. Available to U.S. citizens.

Application Requirements: Application, proof of adoption, enrollment verification. *Deadline:* June 30.

Contact: Ms. Rehva D. Jones, Director, Higher Education Financial
    Services and Preparatory Programs
    District of Columbia Office of the State Superintendent
    810 First Street, NE
    Washington, DC 20002
    Phone: 202-481-3948
    Fax: 202-741-6491
    E-mail: rehva.jones@dc.gov

DIXIE BOYS BASEBALL

http://www.dixie.org/boys

DIXIE BOYS BASEBALL BERNIE VARNADORE SCHOLARSHIP PROGRAM

Eleven scholarships presented annually to deserving high school seniors who have participated in the Dixie Boys Baseball Program. Citizenship, scholarship, residency in a state with Dixie Baseball Programs and financial need are considered in determining the awards.

Award: Scholarship for use in freshman year; not renewable. *Number:* 11. *Amount:* $1250.

Eligibility Requirements: Applicant must be high school student; planning to enroll or expecting to enroll full-time at a two-year or four-year institution or university; resident of Alabama, Arkansas, Florida, Georgia, Louisiana, Mississippi, North Carolina, South Carolina, Tennessee, Texas, or Virginia and must have an interest in athletics/sports. Available to U.S. citizens.

Application Requirements: Application, financial need analysis, photo, references. *Deadline:* April 1.

Contact: James Jones, Commissioner/CEO
    Dixie Boys Baseball
    PO Box 8263
    Dothan, AL 36305
    Phone: 334-793-3331
    E-mail: jjones29@sw.rr.com

DIXIE YOUTH SCHOLARSHIP PROGRAM

Scholarships are presented annually to deserving high school seniors who participated in the Dixie Youth Baseball program while age 12 and under. Financial need is considered. Scholarship value is $2000.

Award: Scholarship for use in freshman year; not renewable. *Number:* up to 70. *Amount:* $2000.

Eligibility Requirements: Applicant must be high school student; planning to enroll or expecting to enroll full-time at a two-year or four-year or technical institution or university; resident of Alabama, Arkansas, Florida, Georgia, Louisiana, Mississippi, North Carolina, South Carolina, Tennessee, Texas, or Virginia and must have an interest in athletics/sports. Available to U.S. citizens.

Application Requirements: Application, essay, financial need analysis, photo, references, transcript, 1040 form. *Deadline:* March 1.

Contact: Scholarship Chairman
    Dixie Boys Baseball
    PO Box 877
    Marshall, TX 75671-0877
    E-mail: dyb@dixie.org

DOC HURLEY SCHOLARSHIP FOUNDATION INC.

http://www.docscholar.org/

DOC HURLEY SCHOLARSHIP

Scholarship of $2000 to $10,000 awarded for graduating senior from eligible Greater Hartford area high school. Number of awards varies.

Award: Scholarship for use in freshman year; not renewable. *Number:* varies. *Amount:* $2000–$10,000.

Eligibility Requirements: Applicant must be high school student; planning to enroll or expecting to enroll full-time at a four-year institution or university and resident of Connecticut. Available to U.S. citizens.

Application Requirements: Application, essay, financial need analysis, references, test scores, transcript, Student Aid Report (SAR). *Deadline:* March 21.

Contact: Scholarship Committee
    Doc Hurley Scholarship Foundation Inc.
    103 Woodland Street
    Hartford, CT 06105
    Phone: 860-549-5012
    Fax: 860-549-5955
    E-mail: dhsf@docscholar.org

DON'T MESS WITH TEXAS

http://www.dontmesswithtexas.org/

DON'T MESS WITH TEXAS SCHOLARSHIP PROGRAM

Scholarship for Texas graduating high school seniors who plan to attend accredited two- or four-year colleges or public or private universities in Texas.

Award: Scholarship for use in freshman year; not renewable. *Number:* 2–3. *Amount:* $1000–$3000.

Eligibility Requirements: Applicant must be high school student; planning to enroll or expecting to enroll full- or part-time at a two-year or four-year institution or university; resident of Texas and studying in Texas. Available to U.S. and non-U.S. citizens.

Application Requirements: Application, essay, references. *Deadline:* April 4.

Contact: Michael Roberts, Scholarship Committee
    Don't Mess With Texas
    1717 West Sixth Street, Suite 400
    Austin, TX 78703
    Phone: 512-476-4368
    Fax: 512-476-4392
    E-mail: scholarship@dontmesswithtexas.org

EAST BAY COLLEGE FUND

http://www.eastbaycollegefund.org/

GREAT EXPECTATIONS AWARD

Program provides renewable scholarships, mentoring, college counseling, and life skills training. Must have at least 3.0 cumulative GPA. Restricted to graduating seniors of Oakland, California public high schools.

Award: Scholarship for use in freshman, sophomore, junior, or senior years; renewable. *Number:* 20. *Amount:* $16,000.

Eligibility Requirements: Applicant must be enrolled or expecting to enroll full-time at a four-year institution or university and resident of California. Applicant must have 3.0 GPA or higher. Available to U.S. and non-U.S. citizens.

Application Requirements: Application, essay, financial need analysis, interview, references, transcript.

Contact: Program Assistant
    East Bay College Fund
    6114 LaSalle Avenue, Suite 314
    Oakland, CA 94611
    Phone: 510-836-8900
    E-mail: info@eastbaycollegefund.org

EAST BAY FOOTBALL OFFICIALS ASSOCIATION

http://www.ebfoa.org/

EAST BAY FOOTBALL OFFICIALS ASSOCIATION COLLEGE SCHOLARSHIP

Scholarship for high school seniors who currently participate in one of the football programs served by the East Bay Football Officials Association. Must be a resident of California, achieve at least a 3.0 GPA and have plans to attend any accredited two- or four-year institution.

Award: Scholarship for use in freshman year; renewable. *Number:* 3–4. *Amount:* up to $1000.

Eligibility Requirements: Applicant must be high school student; planning to enroll or expecting to enroll full-time at a two-year or four-year institution or university; resident of California and must have an interest in athletics/sports. Applicant must have 3.0 GPA or higher. Available to U.S. citizens.

Application Requirements: Application, essay, references, transcript. *Deadline:* October 31.

Contact: Sam Moriana, Program Coordinator
East Bay Football Officials Association
21 Chatham Pointe
Alameda, CA 94502
Phone: 510-521-4121
E-mail: smoriana@comcast.net

EAST LOS ANGELES COMMUNITY UNION (TELACU) SCHOLARSHIP PROGRAM

http://www.telacu.com/

TELACU EDUCATION FOUNDATION

Applicant must be a first-generation college student from a low-income family and have a minimum GPA of 2.5. Must attend partnering colleges and universities and be enrolled full-time for the entire academic year. California applicants: Must be permanent resident of unincorporated East Los Angeles, Bell Gardens, Commerce, Huntington Park, City of Los Angeles, Montebello, Monterey Park, Pico Rivera, Pomona and the Inland Empire, Santa Ana, South Gate, or other communities selected by foundation. Texas applicants: Must be permanent resident of San Antonio or Austin. Illinois Applicants: Must be permanent resident of Greater Chicagoland Area. New York applicants: Must be permanent resident of the state of New York.

Award: Scholarship for use in freshman, sophomore, junior, or senior years; not renewable. *Number:* 350–600. *Amount:* $500–$7500.

Eligibility Requirements: Applicant must be enrolled or expecting to enroll full-time at a two-year or four-year institution or university and resident of California, Illinois, New York, or Texas. Applicant must have 2.5 GPA or higher. Available to U.S. citizens.

Application Requirements: Application, essay, financial need analysis, interview, resume, references, test scores, transcript. *Deadline:* March 14.

Contact: Mr. Daniel Garcia, Associate Director
East Los Angeles Community Union (TELACU) Scholarship Program
5400 East Olympic Blvd
Los Angeles, CA 90022
Phone: 323-721-1655 Ext. 486
E-mail: dgarcia@TELACU.com

EDMONTON COMMUNITY FOUNDATION

http://www.DollarsForLearners.com/

YOUTH FORMERLY IN CARE BURSARY
• *See page 662*

EDMUND F. MAXWELL FOUNDATION

http://www.maxwell.org/

EDMUND F. MAXWELL FOUNDATION SCHOLARSHIP

Scholarships awarded to residents of Western Washington to attend accredited independent colleges or universities. Awards up to $5000 per year based on need, merit, citizenship, and activities. Renewable for up to four years if academic progress is suitable and financial need is unchanged.

Award: Scholarship for use in freshman year; renewable. *Number:* 110. *Amount:* up to $5000.

Eligibility Requirements: Applicant must be enrolled or expecting to enroll full-time at a four-year institution or university and resident of Washington. Available to U.S. and non-U.S. citizens.

Application Requirements: Application, essay, financial need analysis, test scores, transcript, employment history. *Deadline:* April 30.

Contact: Jane Thomas, Administrator
Edmund F. Maxwell Foundation
PO Box 22537
Seattle, WA 98122
Phone: 206-303-4402
Fax: 206-303-4419
E-mail: admin@maxwell.org

EDUCATION FOUNDATION. INC. NATIONAL GUARD ASSOCIATION OF COLORADO

http://www.ngaco.org/

EDUCATION FOUNDATION, INC. NATIONAL GUARD ASSOCIATION OF COLORADO SCHOLARSHIPS
• *See page 619*

ENLISTED ASSOCIATION OF THE NATIONAL GUARD OF NEW JERSEY

http://www.eang-nj.org/

CSM VINCENT BALDASSARI MEMORIAL SCHOLARSHIP PROGRAM
• *See page 619*

EPILEPSY FOUNDATION OF IDAHO

http://www.epilepsyidaho.org/

GREGORY W. GILE MEMORIAL SCHOLARSHIP PROGRAM
• *See page 603*

MARK MUSIC MEMORIAL SCHOLARSHIP
• *See page 603*

EQUALITYMAINE FOUNDATION

http://www.equalitymaine.org/

JOEL ABROMSON MEMORIAL FOUNDATION

One-time award for full-time postsecondary study available to winner of essay contest. Open to Maine residents only. Contact for essay topic and complete information. SASE.

Award: Scholarship for use in freshman year; not renewable. *Number:* 3. *Amount:* $500–$1000.

Eligibility Requirements: Applicant must be high school student; planning to enroll or expecting to enroll full-time at a two-year or four-year or technical institution or university and resident of Maine. Available to U.S. citizens.

Application Requirements: Application, applicant must enter a contest, essay, references, self-addressed stamped envelope, copy of acceptance letter to institution of higher learning. *Deadline:* April 15.

Contact: Betsy Smith, Executive Director
EqualityMaine Foundation
PO Box 1951
Portland, ME 04104
Phone: 207-761-3732
Fax: 207-761-3752
E-mail: info@equalitymaine.org

ESSAYJOLT.COM

http://www.essayjolt.com/

ESSAYJOLT SCHOLARSHIP

Essay contest open to high school juniors and seniors who may be citizens of any country, but must live in New Jersey. Essays are judged on originality, insight, and quality of writing by an independent panel of writers and editors. Only one winner is selected. See web site for current essay question and guidelines http://www.essayjolt.com.

Award: Prize for use in freshman year; not renewable. *Number:* 1. *Amount:* $500.

Eligibility Requirements: Applicant must be high school student; planning to enroll or expecting to enroll full- or part-time at a two-year or four-year or technical institution or university; resident of New Jersey and must have an interest in writing. Available to U.S. and non-U.S. citizens.

Application Requirements: Applicant must enter a contest, essay. *Deadline:* varies.

Contact: Meg Hartmann, Director
EssayJolt.com
1308 Centennial Avenue, Suite 243
Piscataway, NJ 08854
Phone: 917-575-3165
E-mail: scholarship@essayjolt.com

EVERLY SCHOLARSHIP FUND INC.

EVERLY SCHOLARSHIP

Renewable award for undergraduates attending an accredited institution full-time. Must be New Jersey residents. Minimum 3.0 GPA required and minimum SAT score of 1100.

Award: Scholarship for use in senior year; renewable. *Number:* varies. *Amount:* $2500.

Eligibility Requirements: Applicant must be enrolled or expecting to enroll full-time at a four-year institution or university and resident of New Jersey. Applicant must have 3.0 GPA or higher. Available to U.S. citizens.

Application Requirements: Application, driver's license, essay, financial need analysis, interview, references, test scores, transcript. *Deadline:* May 1.

Contact: John R. Lolio Jr., President
Everly Scholarship Fund Inc.
4300 Haddonfield Road, Suite 311
Pennsauken, NJ 08109
Phone: 856-661-2094
Fax: 856-662-0165
E-mail: jlolio@sskrplaw.com

FINANCE AUTHORITY OF MAINE

http://www.famemaine.com/

ROBERT C. BYRD HONORS SCHOLARSHIP-MAINE

Merit-based, renewable scholarship of up to $1500 annually for graduating high school seniors. Must have a minimum of 3.0 GPA. Must be a resident of Maine. Superior academic performance is the primary criterion. For application, see web site http://www.famemaine.com.

Award: Scholarship for use in freshman year; renewable. *Number:* up to 30. *Amount:* up to $1500.

Eligibility Requirements: Applicant must be high school student; planning to enroll or expecting to enroll full-time at a two-year or four-year or technical institution or university and resident of Maine. Applicant must have 3.0 GPA or higher. Available to U.S. citizens.

Application Requirements: Application, essay, transcript, high school profile. *Deadline:* May 1.

Contact: Claude Roy, Manager, Operations
Finance Authority of Maine
Five Community Drive
PO Box 949
Augusta, ME 04332-0949
Phone: 207-620-3507
E-mail: education@famemaine.com

STATE OF MAINE GRANT PROGRAM

Scholarship for residents of Maine, attending an eligible school in Connecticut, Maine, Massachusetts, New Hampshire, Pennsylvania, Rhode Island, Washington, D.C., or Vermont. Award based on need. Must apply annually. Complete free application for Federal Student Aid to apply. One-time award for undergraduate study. For further information see web site http://www.famemaine.com.

Award: Grant for use in freshman, sophomore, junior, or senior years; not renewable. *Number:* up to 18,000. *Amount:* $500–$1250.

Eligibility Requirements: Applicant must be enrolled or expecting to enroll full- or part-time at a two-year or four-year or technical institution or university; resident of Maine and studying in Connecticut, District of Columbia, Maine, Massachusetts, New Hampshire, Pennsylvania, Rhode Island, or Vermont. Available to U.S. citizens.

Application Requirements: Application, financial need analysis, FAFSA. *Deadline:* May 1.

Contact: Claude Roy, Manager, Operations
Finance Authority of Maine
Five Community Drive
PO Box 949
Augusta, ME 04332-0949
Phone: 207-620-3507
E-mail: education@famemaine.com

TUITION WAIVER PROGRAMS
• *See page 586*

FLORIDA ASSOCIATION FOR MEDIA IN EDUCATION

http://www.floridamedia.org/

INTELLECTUAL FREEDOM STUDENT SCHOLARSHIP

Scholarship in the amount of $1000 is awarded annually to a graduating senior from a high school in Florida. Only students whose library media specialists are members of FAME are eligible. Essays written by senior students will be submitted to the FAME Intellectual Freedom Committee.

Award: Scholarship for use in freshman year; not renewable. *Number:* 1. *Amount:* $1000.

Eligibility Requirements: Applicant must be high school student; planning to enroll or expecting to enroll full-time at a two-year or four-year or technical institution or university and resident of Florida. Available to U.S. citizens.

Application Requirements: Application, essay. *Deadline:* March 15.

Contact: Larry Bodkin, Executive Director
Florida Association for Media in Education
2563 Capital Medical Boulevard
Tallahassee, FL 32308
Phone: 850-531-8350
Fax: 850-531-8344
E-mail: lbodkin@floridamedia.org

FLORIDA ASSOCIATION OF POSTSECONDARY SCHOOLS AND COLLEGES

http://www.FAPSC.org/

FLORIDA ASSOCIATION OF POST-SECONDARY SCHOOLS AND COLLEGES SCHOLARSHIP PROGRAM

The scholarship program is open to eligible Florida high school seniors graduating during the 2010–2011 school year or anyone awarded a GED between March 1, 2010 and February 28, 2011. Application must meet all eligibility requirements of the institution, complete the application personally, and enclose your official transcript confirming a cumulative unweighted GPA of 2.0 or higher and a 300 minimum word essay.

Award: Scholarship for use in freshman year; not renewable. *Number:* 1–400. *Amount:* $1000–$30,000.

Eligibility Requirements: Applicant must be high school student; planning to enroll or expecting to enroll full-time at a two-year or four-year or technical institution or university; resident of Florida and studying in Florida. Applicant must have 2.5 GPA or higher. Available to U.S. citizens.

Application Requirements: Application, essay, transcript. *Deadline:* May 15.

Contact: Wanda G. Minick, Deputy Executive Director of Membership Services
Florida Association of Postsecondary Schools and Colleges
150 South Monroe Street, Suite 303
Tallahassee, FL 32301
Phone: 850-577-3139
Fax: 850-577-3133
E-mail: scholarship@fapsc.org

FLORIDA LIBRARY ASSOCIATION

http://www.flalib.org/

FLORIDA LIBRARY ASSOCIATION-ASSOCIATE'S DEGREE SCHOLARSHIP
• See page 587

FLORIDA PTA/PTSA

http://www.floridapta.org/

FLORIDA PTA/PTSA ANNUAL SCHOLARSHIP
Renewable scholarship of $1000 awarded to students enrolled full-time in their undergraduate study. Must maintain minimum 3.0 GPA.

Award: Scholarship for use in freshman, sophomore, junior, or senior years; renewable. *Number:* 2–3. *Amount:* $1000.

Eligibility Requirements: Applicant must be enrolled or expecting to enroll full-time at a four-year institution or university and resident of Florida. Applicant must have 3.0 GPA or higher. Available to U.S. citizens.

Application Requirements: Application, essay, references. *Deadline:* March 1.

Contact: Janice Bailey, Executive Director
Florida PTA/PTSA
1747 Orlando Central Parkway
Orlando, FL 32809
Phone: 407-855-7604
Fax: 407-240-9577
E-mail: janice@floridapta.org

FLORIDA PTA/PTSA COMMUNITY/JUNIOR COLLEGE SCHOLARSHIP
One time award of $1000 to high school students who enrolled in a community or junior college. Must be a resident of Florida for at least 2 years. Must be a U.S. citizen and have at least a two-year attendance in a Florida PTA/PTSA high school. Minimum 2.5 GPA or higher.

Award: Scholarship for use in freshman year; not renewable. *Number:* 1–2. *Amount:* $1000.

Eligibility Requirements: Applicant must be enrolled or expecting to enroll full-time at a two-year institution and resident of Florida. Applicant must have 2.5 GPA or higher. Available to U.S. citizens.

Application Requirements: Application, essay, references, proof of enrollment. *Deadline:* March 1.

Contact: Janice Bailey, Executive Director
Florida PTA/PTSA
1747 Orlando Central Parkway
Orlando, FL 32809
Phone: 407-855-7604
Fax: 407-240-9577
E-mail: janice@floridapta.org

FLORIDA PTA/PTSA VOCATIONAL/TECHNICAL SCHOLARSHIP
Scholarship of $1000 is awarded to graduating senior enrolled full time in a vocational/technical institution within the state of Florida. Must have at least a two-year attendance in a Florida PTA/PTSA high school. Minimum GPA is 2.0.

Award: Scholarship for use in freshman year; not renewable. *Number:* 3. *Amount:* $1000.

Eligibility Requirements: Applicant must be high school student; planning to enroll or expecting to enroll full-time at a two-year or tech-

nical institution; resident of Florida and studying in Florida. Available to U.S. citizens.

Application Requirements: Application, essay, references, proof of enrollment. *Deadline:* March 1.

Contact: Janice Bailey, Executive Director
Florida PTA/PTSA
1747 Orlando Central Parkway
Orlando, FL 32809
Phone: 407-855-7604
Fax: 407-240-9577
E-mail: janice@floridapta.org

FLORIDA SOCIETY, SONS OF THE AMERICAN REVOLUTION

http://www.flssar.org/

GEORGE S. AND STELLA M. KNIGHT ESSAY CONTEST
Award for the best essay about an event, person, philosophy, or ideal associated with the American Revolution, the Declaration of Independence, or the framing of the U.S. Constitution. Must be a resident of Florida and U.S. citizen or legal resident. State winner may enter the national contest. For more information, see web site http://www.patriot-web.com/essay/.

Award: Prize for use in sophomore, junior, or senior years; not renewable. *Number:* up to 3. *Amount:* up to $500.

Eligibility Requirements: Applicant must be high school student; planning to enroll or expecting to enroll full- or part-time at a two-year or four-year or technical institution or university and resident of Florida. Available to U.S. citizens.

Application Requirements: Applicant must enter a contest, essay. *Deadline:* January 31.

Contact: Robert Yarnell
Florida Society, Sons of the American Revolution
7401 Cypress Dr.
New Port Richey, FL 34653
E-mail: knight.essay@gmail.com

FLORIDA STATE DEPARTMENT OF EDUCATION

http://www.floridastudentfinancialaid.org/

ACCESS TO BETTER LEARNING AND EDUCATION GRANT
Grant program provides tuition assistance to Florida undergraduate students enrolled in degree programs at eligible private Florida colleges or universities. Must be a U.S. citizen or eligible non-citizen and must meet Florida residency requirements. The participating institution determines application procedures, deadlines, and student eligibility. For more details, visit the web site at http//www.FloridaStudentFinancialAid.org/SSFAD/home/uamain.htm.

Award: Grant for use in freshman, sophomore, junior, or senior years; renewable. *Number:* varies. *Amount:* up to $945.

Eligibility Requirements: Applicant must be enrolled or expecting to enroll full-time at a four-year institution or university; resident of Florida and studying in Florida. Available to U.S. citizens.

Contact: Florida Department of Education, Office of Student Financial Assistance, Customer Service
Florida State Department of Education
325 West Gaines Street
Tallahassee, FL 32399
Phone: 888-827-2007
E-mail: osfa@fldoe.org

FIRST GENERATION MATCHING GRANT PROGRAM
Need-based grants to Florida resident undergraduate students who are enrolled in state universities and community colleges in Florida and whose parents have not earned baccalaureate degrees. Available state funds are contingent upon matching contributions from private sources on a dollar-for-dollar basis. Institutions determine application procedures, deadlines, and student eligibility. For more details, visit the web site at http//www.FloridaStudentFinancialAid.org/SSFAD/home/uamain.htm.

Award: Grant for use in freshman, sophomore, junior, or senior years; renewable. *Number:* varies. *Amount:* varies.

Eligibility Requirements: Applicant must be enrolled or expecting to enroll full- or part-time at a two-year or four-year institution or university; resident of Florida and studying in Florida. Available to U.S. citizens.

Contact: Florida Department of Education, Office of Student Financial
Assistance, Customer Service
Florida State Department of Education
325 West Gaines Street
Tallahassee, FL 32399
Phone: 888-828-2004
E-mail: osfa@fldoe.org

FLORIDA BRIGHT FUTURES SCHOLARSHIP PROGRAM

Three lottery-funded scholarships reward Florida high school graduates for high academic achievement. Program is comprised of the following three awards: Florida Academic Scholars Award, Florida Medallion Scholars Award and Florida Gold Seal Vocational Scholars Award. For more details, visit the web site at http//www.FloridaStudentFinancialAid.org/SSFAD/home/uamain.htm.

Award: Scholarship for use in freshman, sophomore, junior, or senior years; renewable.

Eligibility Requirements: Applicant must be high school student; planning to enroll or expecting to enroll full- or part-time at a two-year or four-year or technical institution or university; resident of Florida and studying in Florida. Applicant must have 3.0 GPA or higher. Available to U.S. citizens.

Application Requirements: Application, test scores, transcript.

Contact: Florida Department of Education, Office of Student Financial
Assistance, Customer Service
Florida State Department of Education
325 West Gaines Street
Tallahassee, FL 32399
Phone: 888-827-2004
E-mail: osfa@fldoe.org

FLORIDA POSTSECONDARY STUDENT ASSISTANCE GRANT

Scholarships to degree-seeking, resident, undergraduate students who demonstrate substantial financial need and are enrolled in eligible degree-granting private colleges and universities not eligible under the Florida Private Student Assistance Grant. FSAG is a decentralized program, and each participating institution determines application procedures, deadlines and student eligibility. Number of awards varies. For more details, visit the web site at http//www.FloridaStudentFinancialAid.org/SSFAD/home/uamain.htm.

Award: Grant for use in freshman, sophomore, junior, or senior years; renewable. *Number:* varies. *Amount:* $200–$2235.

Eligibility Requirements: Applicant must be enrolled or expecting to enroll full-time at a two-year or four-year institution or university; resident of Florida and studying in Florida. Available to U.S. citizens.

Application Requirements: Application, financial need analysis.

Contact: Florida Department of Education, Office of Student Financial
Assistance, Customer Service
Florida State Department of Education
325 West Gaines Street
Tallahassee, FL 32399
Phone: 888-827-2004
E-mail: osfa@fldoe.org

FLORIDA PRIVATE STUDENT ASSISTANCE GRANT

Grants for Florida residents who are U.S. citizens or eligible non-citizens attending eligible private, nonprofit, four-year colleges and universities in Florida. Must be a full-time student and demonstrate substantial financial need. For renewal, must have earned a minimum cumulative GPA of 2.0 at the last institution attended. For more details, visit the web site at http://www.FloridaStudentFinancialAid.org/SSFAD/home/uamain.htm.

Award: Grant for use in freshman, sophomore, junior, or senior years; renewable. *Number:* varies. *Amount:* $200–$2235.

Eligibility Requirements: Applicant must be enrolled or expecting to enroll full-time at a four-year institution or university; resident of Florida and studying in Florida. Available to U.S. citizens.

Application Requirements: Application, financial need analysis.

Contact: Florida Department of Education, Office of Student Financial
Assistance, Customer Service
Florida State Department of Education
325 West Gaines Street
Tallahassee, FL 32399
Phone: 888-827-2004
E-mail: osfa@fldoe.org

FLORIDA PUBLIC STUDENT ASSISTANCE GRANT

Grants for Florida residents, U.S. citizens or eligible non-citizens who attend state universities and public community colleges and demonstrate substantial financial need. For renewal, must have earned a minimum cumulative GPA of 2.0 at the last institution attended.

Award: Grant for use in freshman, sophomore, junior, or senior years; renewable. *Number:* varies. *Amount:* $200–$2235.

Eligibility Requirements: Applicant must be enrolled or expecting to enroll full- or part-time at a two-year or four-year institution or university; resident of Florida and studying in Florida. Available to U.S. citizens.

Application Requirements: Application, financial need analysis.

Contact: Florida Department of Education, Office of Student Financial
Assistance, Customer Service
Florida State Department of Education
325 West Gaines Street
Tallahassee, FL 32399
Phone: 888-827-2004
E-mail: osfa@fldoe.org

FLORIDA STUDENT ASSISTANCE GRANT-CAREER EDUCATION

Need-based grant program available to Florida residents enrolled in certificate programs of 450 or more clock hours at participating community colleges or career centers operated by district school boards. FSAG-CE is a decentralized state of Florida program, which means that each participating institution determines application procedures, deadlines, student eligibility, and award amounts. For more details, visit the web site at http//www.FloridaStudentFinancialAid.org/SSFAD/home/uamain.htm.

Award: Grant for use in freshman, sophomore, junior, or senior years; renewable. *Amount:* $200–$2235.

Eligibility Requirements: Applicant must be enrolled or expecting to enroll full- or part-time at a two-year or technical institution; resident of Florida and studying in Florida. Available to U.S. citizens.

Application Requirements: Application, financial need analysis.

Contact: Florida Department of Education, Office of Student Financial
Assistance, Customer Service
Florida State Department of Education
325 West Gaines Street
Tallahassee, FL 32399
Phone: 888-847-2004
E-mail: osfa@fldoe.org

FLORIDA WORK EXPERIENCE PROGRAM

Need-based program providing eligible Florida residents work experiences that will complement and reinforce their educational and career goals. Must maintain GPA of 2.0. Postsecondary institution will determine applicant's eligibility, number of hours to be worked per week, and the award amount. For more details, visit the web site at http//www.FloridaStudentFinancialAid.org/SSFAD/home/uamain.htm.

Award: Grant for use in freshman, sophomore, junior, or senior years; renewable. *Number:* varies. *Amount:* varies.

Eligibility Requirements: Applicant must be enrolled or expecting to enroll full- or part-time at a two-year or four-year institution or university; resident of Florida and studying in Florida. Available to U.S. citizens.

Application Requirements: Application, financial need analysis.

Contact: Florida Department of Education, Office of Student Financial
Assistance, Customer Service
Florida State Department of Education
325 West Gaines Street
Tallahassee, FL 32399
Phone: 888-827-2004
E-mail: osfa@fldoe.com

JOSE MARTI SCHOLARSHIP CHALLENGE GRANT FUND
• *See page 662*

MARY MCLEOD BETHUNE SCHOLARSHIP

Renewable award to Florida residents with a GPA of 3.0 or above, who will attend Bethune-Cookman University, Edward Waters College, Florida A&M University, or Florida Memorial University. Must not have previously received a baccalaureate degree. Must demonstrate financial need as specified by the institution. For more details, visit the web site at http://www.FloridaStudentFinancialAid.org/SSFAD/home/uamain.htm.

Award: Scholarship for use in freshman, sophomore, junior, or senior years; renewable. *Number:* varies. *Amount:* $3000.

Eligibility Requirements: Applicant must be enrolled or expecting to enroll full-time at a four-year institution or university; resident of Florida and studying in Florida. Applicant must have 3.0 GPA or higher. Available to U.S. citizens.

Application Requirements: Application, financial need analysis.

Contact: Florida Department of Education, Office of Student Financial Assistance, Customer Service
Florida State Department of Education
325 West Gaines Street
Tallahassee, FL 32399
Phone: 888-827-2004
E-mail: osfa@fldoe.org

ROBERT C. BYRD HONORS SCHOLARSHIP-FLORIDA

One applicant per Florida high school may be nominated by the high school principal or designee by May 15. Must be U.S. citizen or eligible non-citizen and Florida resident. Application must be submitted in the same year as graduation. Must meet selective service system registration requirements. May attend any postsecondary accredited institution. For more details, visit the web site at FloridaStudentFinancialAid.org/SSFAD/home/uamain.htm.

Award: Scholarship for use in freshman, sophomore, junior, or senior years; renewable. *Amount:* $1500.

Eligibility Requirements: Applicant must be high school student; planning to enroll or expecting to enroll full-time at a two-year or four-year or technical institution or university and resident of Florida. Applicant must have 3.5 GPA or higher. Available to U.S. citizens.

Application Requirements: Application, references, test scores, transcript. *Deadline:* April 15.

Contact: Florida Department of Education, Office of Student Financial Assistance, Customer Service
Florida State Department of Education
325 West Gaines Street
Tallahassee, FL 32399
Phone: 888-827-2004
E-mail: osfa@fldoe.org

ROSEWOOD FAMILY SCHOLARSHIP FUND

Renewable award for eligible direct descendants of African-American Rosewood families affected by the incident of January 1923. Must not have previously received a baccalaureate degree. For more details, visit the web site at http//www.FloridaStudentFinancialAid.org/SSFAD/home/uamain.htm.

Award: Scholarship for use in freshman, sophomore, junior, or senior years; renewable. *Number:* up to 25. *Amount:* up to $4000.

Eligibility Requirements: Applicant must be enrolled or expecting to enroll full-time at a two-year or four-year or technical institution or university and studying in Florida. Available to U.S. citizens.

Application Requirements: Application, financial need analysis, documentation of Rosewood ancestry. *Deadline:* April 1.

Contact: Florida Department of Education, Office of Student Financial Assistance, Customer Service
Florida State Department of Education
325 West Gaines Street
Tallahassee, FL 32399
Phone: 888-827-2004
E-mail: osfa@fldoe.org

SCHOLARSHIPS FOR CHILDREN & SPOUSES OF DECEASED OR DISABLED VETERANS OR SERVICEMEMBERS
• *See page 636*

WILLIAM L. BOYD IV FLORIDA RESIDENT ACCESS GRANT

Renewable awards to Florida undergraduate residents attending an eligible private, nonprofit Florida college or university. Postsecondary institution will determine applicant's eligibility. Renewal applicant must have earned a minimum institutional GPA of 2.0. For more details, visit the web site at http//www.FloridaStudentFinancialAid.org/SSFAD/home/uamain.htm.

Award: Grant for use in freshman, sophomore, junior, or senior years; renewable. *Number:* varies. *Amount:* up to $2425.

Eligibility Requirements: Applicant must be enrolled or expecting to enroll full-time at a four-year institution or university; resident of Florida and studying in Florida. Available to U.S. citizens.

Application Requirements: Application.

Contact: Florida Department of Education, Office of Student Financial Assistance, Customer Service
Florida State Department of Education
325 West Gaines Street
Tallahassee, FL 32399
Phone: 888-827-2004
E-mail: osfa@fldoe.org

FLORIDA WOMEN'S STATE GOLF ASSOCIATION

http://www.fwsga.org/

FLORIDA WOMEN'S STATE GOLF ASSOCIATION JUNIOR GIRLS' SCHOLARSHIP FUND

The FWSGA Scholarship Fund assists in paying for the education of young women to whom golf is meaningful. Applicants must be Florida residents, play golf, maintain a 3.0 GPA, attend a Florida college or university, and have a need for financial assistance.

Award: Scholarship for use in freshman year; renewable. *Number:* 1. *Amount:* $5000.

Eligibility Requirements: Applicant must be high school student; planning to enroll or expecting to enroll full-time at a two-year or four-year institution or university; female; resident of Florida; studying in Florida and must have an interest in golf. Applicant must have 3.0 GPA or higher. Available to U.S. citizens.

Application Requirements: Application, financial need analysis, interview, references, test scores, transcript. *Deadline:* April 1.

Contact: Kelly Thormahlen, Executive Director
Florida Women's State Golf Association
8875 Hidden River Parkway, Suite 110
Tampa, FL 33637
Phone: 813-864-2130
Fax: 813-864-2129
E-mail: info@fwsga.org

FRATERNAL ORDER OF POLICE ASSOCIATES OF OHIO INC.

http://www.fopaohio.org/

FRATERNAL ORDER OF POLICE ASSOCIATES, STATE LODGE OF OHIO INC., SCHOLARSHIP FUND
• *See page 587*

FRIENDS OF 440 SCHOLARSHIP FUND INC.

http://www.440scholarship.org/

FRIENDS OF 440 SCHOLARSHIP FUND, INC.

Scholarships to students who are dependents of workers who were injured or killed in the course and scope of their employment and who are eligible to receive benefits under the Florida Workers' Compensation system, or are dependents of those primarily engaged in the administration of the Florida Workers' Compensation Law.

Award: Scholarship for use in freshman, sophomore, junior, or senior years; renewable. *Number:* 1–60. *Amount:* $500–$6000.

Eligibility Requirements: Applicant must be enrolled or expecting to enroll full-time at a two-year or four-year or technical institution or university and resident of Florida. Available to U.S. and non-U.S. citizens.

Application Requirements: Application, transcript, copy of tax return. *Deadline:* February 28.

Contact: Ms. Sharon McMorris, Executive Director
Friends of 440 Scholarship Fund Inc.
9100 South Dadeland Blvd.
Suite 1010
Miami, FL 33156
Phone: 305-423-8710
Fax: 305-670-0716
E-mail: info@440scholarship.org

FULFILLMENT FUND

http://www.fulfillment.org/

FULFILLMENT FUND SCHOLARSHIPS

Award is for undergraduates. Serving students in seven partner high schools, Fremont, Hamilton, Locke, Los Angeles, Manual Arts, Crenshaw and Wilson. Only students who participated in the Fulfillment Fund High School Program for at least two years are eligible to apply for the scholarship.

Award: Scholarship for use in freshman, sophomore, junior, or senior years; not renewable. *Number:* varies. *Amount:* $1000–$1500.

Eligibility Requirements: Applicant must be enrolled or expecting to enroll full- or part-time at a four-year institution or university and resident of California. Available to U.S. citizens.

Application Requirements: Application. *Deadline:* varies.

Contact: Darcine Thomas, Community Outreach Manager
Fulfillment Fund
6100 Wilshire Boulevard, Suite 600
Los Angeles, CA 90048
Phone: 323-900-8753
Fax: 525-3095

GENERAL FEDERATION OF WOMEN'S CLUBS OF MASSACHUSETTS

http://www.gfwcma.org/

GENERAL FEDERATION OF WOMEN'S CLUBS OF MASSACHUSETTS STUDY ABROAD SCHOLARSHIP

Scholarship for undergraduate or graduate students to study abroad. Applicant must submit personal statement and letter of endorsement from the president of the sponsoring General Federation of Women's Clubs of Massachusetts. Must be resident of Massachusetts.

Award: Scholarship for use in freshman, sophomore, junior, senior, or graduate years; not renewable. *Number:* 1. *Amount:* $800.

Eligibility Requirements: Applicant must be enrolled or expecting to enroll full-time at a four-year institution or university and resident of Massachusetts. Available to U.S. citizens.

Application Requirements: Application, essay, interview, references, self-addressed stamped envelope, transcript. *Deadline:* March 1.

Contact: Marta DiBenedetto, Scholarship Chairperson
General Federation of Women's Clubs of Massachusetts
PO Box 679, 245 Dutton Road
Sudbury, MA 01776-0679
Phone: 978-444-9105
E-mail: marta_dibenedetto@nylim.com

GENERAL FEDERATION OF WOMEN'S CLUBS OF VERMONT

BARBARA JEAN BARKER MEMORIAL SCHOLARSHIP FOR A DISPLACED HOMEMAKER

Applicants must be Vermont residents who have been homemakers (primarily) for at least fifteen years and have lost their main means of support through death, divorce, separation, spouse's long-time illness, or spouse's long-time unemployment. Provides one to three scholarships ranging from $500 to $1500.

Award: Grant for use in freshman, sophomore, junior, senior, or graduate years; not renewable. *Number:* 1–3. *Amount:* $500–$1500.

Eligibility Requirements: Applicant must be age 35 and over; enrolled or expecting to enroll full- or part-time at a two-year or four-year or technical institution or university; female and resident of Vermont. Available to U.S. citizens.

Application Requirements: Application, driver's license, financial need analysis, interview, references. *Deadline:* March 15.

Contact: Betty Haggerty, Chairman
General Federation of Women's Clubs of Vermont
16 Taylor Street
Bellows Falls, VT 05101
Phone: 802-463-4159
E-mail: hubett@hotmail.com

GEORGE SNOW SCHOLARSHIP FUND

http://www.snow.accrisoft.com/

GEORGE SNOW SCHOLARSHIP FUND/FEMINIST SCHOLARSHIP

Scholarships available to graduating Florida high school seniors entering their first year of college. Students applying for this scholarship can attend any accredited college, university, vocational/technical school they wish, anywhere in the country and major in any subject.

Award: Scholarship for use in freshman year; not renewable. *Number:* varies. *Amount:* varies.

Eligibility Requirements: Applicant must be high school student; planning to enroll or expecting to enroll full- or part-time at a two-year or four-year or technical institution or university and resident of Florida. Available to U.S. and non-U.S. citizens.

Application Requirements: Application, interview, transcript, IRS 1040 forms, FAFSA. *Deadline:* February 1.

Contact: Scholarship Coordinator
George Snow Scholarship Fund
Citibank Building, 998 South Federal Highway, Suite 203
Boca Raton, FL 33432
Phone: 561-347-6799
E-mail: info@scholarship.org

GEORGIA STUDENT FINANCE COMMISSION

http://www.GAcollege411.org/

GEORGIA PUBLIC SAFETY MEMORIAL GRANT

Award for children of Georgia Public Safety Officers, prison guards, fire fighters, law enforcement officers or emergency medical technicians killed or permanently disabled in the line of duty. Must attend an accredited postsecondary Georgia school. Complete the Public Safety Memorial Grant application.

Award: Grant for use in freshman, sophomore, junior, or senior years; not renewable. *Number:* 20–40. *Amount:* $2000.

Eligibility Requirements: Applicant must be enrolled or expecting to enroll full-time at a two-year or four-year or technical institution or university; resident of Georgia and studying in Georgia. Available to U.S. citizens.

Application Requirements: Application, selective service registration. *Deadline:* continuous.

Contact: Caylee B French, Division Director
Georgia Student Finance Commission
2082 East Exchange Place, Suite 100
Tucker, GA 30084
Phone: 770-724-9244
E-mail: cayleef@gsfc.org

GEORGIA TUITION EQUALIZATION GRANT (GTEG)

• *See page 603*

ROBERT C. BYRD HONORS SCHOLARSHIP-GEORGIA

Complete the application provided by the Georgia Department of Education. Renewable awards for outstanding graduating Georgia high school seniors to be used for full-time undergraduate study at eligible U.S. institution. Must a legal resident of Georgia and a U.S. citizen.

Award: Scholarship for use in freshman, sophomore, junior, or senior years; renewable. *Number:* 600–720. *Amount:* up to $1500.

Eligibility Requirements: Applicant must be high school student; planning to enroll or expecting to enroll full-time at a two-year or four-year institution or university and resident of Georgia. Applicant must have 3.0 GPA or higher. Available to U.S. citizens.

Application Requirements: Application, transcript. *Deadline:* February 1.

Contact: Caylee B French, Division Director
Georgia Student Finance Commission
2082 East Exchange Place, Suite 100
Tucker, GA 30084
Phone: 770-724-9244
E-mail: cayleef@gsfc.org

GIRL SCOUTS OF CONNECTICUT

http://www.gsofct.org/

EMILY CHAISON GOLD AWARD SCHOLARSHIP
• *See page 542*

GRANGE INSURANCE ASSOCIATION

http://www.grange.com/

GRANGE INSURANCE GROUP SCHOLARSHIP

Scholarships to current GIG policyholder/ member (or children or grandchildren of GIG policyholder) in California, Colorado, Idaho, Oregon, Washington or Wyoming. See web site at http://www.grange.com for further details.

Award: Scholarship for use in freshman, sophomore, junior, senior, graduate, or postgraduate years; renewable. *Number:* 25–28. *Amount:* $1000–$1500.

Eligibility Requirements: Applicant must be enrolled or expecting to enroll full- or part-time at a two-year or four-year or technical institution or university and resident of California, Colorado, Idaho, Oregon, Washington, or Wyoming. Available to U.S. citizens.

Application Requirements: Application, driver's license, essay, financial need analysis, references, transcript. *Deadline:* April 15.

Contact: Scholarship Committee
Grange Insurance Association
PO Box 21089
Seattle, WA 98111-3089
Phone: 800-247-2643 Ext. 2200

GREATER KANAWHA VALLEY FOUNDATION

http://www.tgkvf.org/

EVANS MEMORIAL SCHOLARSHIP

Renewable award available to West Virginia resident who is enrolling or has enrolled in a two-year or four-year college/university in West Virginia. Must demonstrate financial need. Information and application available at http://www.tgkvf.org.

Award: Scholarship for use in freshman, sophomore, junior, or senior years; renewable. *Number:* up to 24. *Amount:* $1000.

Eligibility Requirements: Applicant must be enrolled or expecting to enroll full-time at a two-year or four-year institution or university; resident of West Virginia and studying in West Virginia. Available to U.S. citizens.

Application Requirements: Application, financial need analysis, test scores, transcript. *Deadline:* January 15.

Contact: Susan Hoover, Scholarship Program Officer
Greater Kanawha Valley Foundation
1600 Huntington Square, 900 Lee Street, East
PO Box 3041
Charleston, WV 25301
Phone: 304-346-3620
E-mail: shoover@tgkvf.org

HENRY E. KING SCHOLARSHIP FUND

Award available for immediate family members of owners, or employees, of companies that are current members of the Home Builders Association of Greater Charleston, West Virginia. Award to be used for full-time study in a two- or four-year college/university. Must be a resident of West Virginia and demonstrate financial need. For additional information and application, please visit http://www.tgkvf.org.

Award: Scholarship for use in freshman, sophomore, junior, or senior years; renewable. *Number:* 1. *Amount:* $1000.

Eligibility Requirements: Applicant must be enrolled or expecting to enroll full-time at a two-year or four-year institution or university and resident of West Virginia. Available to U.S. citizens.

Application Requirements: Application, financial need analysis, transcript. *Deadline:* January 15.

Contact: Susan Hoover, Scholarship Program Officer
Greater Kanawha Valley Foundation
1600 Huntington Square, 900 Lee Street, East
PO Box 3041
Charleston, WV 25301
Phone: 304-346-3620
E-mail: shoover@tgkvf.org

JUNIOR LEAGUE OF CHARLESTON REBECCA DICKSON GOLDSMITH SCHOLARSHIP

Non-renewable scholarship available for a student who is a resident of Kanawha County, West Virginia, and demonstrates outstanding community service. Must submit detailed list of volunteer activities beginning with the ninth grade, and reference letters from adults directly associated with the volunteer activities are requested. Children of Junior League members, past members or sustainers are not eligible. Additional information and application available at http://www.tgkvf.org.

Award: Scholarship for use in freshman year; not renewable. *Number:* 2. *Amount:* $1000.

Eligibility Requirements: Applicant must be high school student; planning to enroll or expecting to enroll full-time at a two-year or four-year institution or university and resident of West Virginia. Available to U.S. citizens.

Application Requirements: Application, references, transcript. *Deadline:* January 15.

Contact: Susan Hoover, Scholarship Program Officer
Greater Kanawha Valley Foundation
1600 Huntington Square, 900 Lee Street, East
PO Box 3041
Charleston, WV 25301
Phone: 304-346-3620
E-mail: shoover@tgkvf.org

KID'S CHANCE OF WEST VIRGINIA SCHOLARSHIP

Award of $1000 awarded to children (between the ages of 16 and 25) of a parent injured in a WV work-related accident. Preference shall be given to students with financial need, academic performance, leadership abilities, demonstrated and potential contributions to school and community who are pursuing any field of study in any accredited trade, vocational school, college, or university. Must attach a copy of the order or letter from the worker's compensation carrier granting a permanent total disability award or dependent's benefits.

Award: Scholarship for use in freshman, sophomore, junior, or senior years; renewable. *Number:* up to 8. *Amount:* $1000.

Eligibility Requirements: Applicant must be age 16-25; enrolled or expecting to enroll full-time at a two-year or four-year or technical institution or university; resident of West Virginia and must have an interest in leadership. Available to U.S. citizens.

Application Requirements: Application, essay, financial need analysis, references, transcript, worker's compensation order/letter. *Deadline:* January 15.

Contact: Susan Hoover, Scholarship Coordinator
Greater Kanawha Valley Foundation
PO Box 3041
Charleston, WV 25331
Phone: 304-346-3620
Fax: 304-346-3640

NORMAN S. AND BETTY M. FITZHUGH FUND

Award available to West Virginia residents who demonstrate academic excellence and financial need to attend any accredited college or university. Scholarships are awarded for full-time study for one or more years. For information and online application go to http://www.tgkvf.org.

Award: Scholarship for use in freshman, sophomore, junior, or senior years; renewable. *Number:* 1. *Amount:* $850.

Eligibility Requirements: Applicant must be enrolled or expecting to enroll full-time at a two-year or four-year or technical institution or university and resident of West Virginia. Available to U.S. citizens.

Application Requirements: Application, essay, financial need analysis, references, transcript. *Deadline:* January 15.

Contact: Susan Hoover, Scholarship Coordinator
Greater Kanawha Valley Foundation
PO Box 3041
Charleston, WV 25331
Phone: 304-346-3620
Fax: 304-346-3640

R. RAY SINGLETON FUND

Renewable award available for undergraduate or graduate study in a West Virginia two- or four-year college/university. Applicant must be resident of Kanawha, Boone, Clay, Putnam, Lincoln, or Fayette counties, and demonstrate financial need and academic excellence. For additional information and application, visit http://www.tgkvf.org.

Award: Scholarship for use in freshman, sophomore, junior, or senior years; renewable. *Amount:* $1000.

Eligibility Requirements: Applicant must be enrolled or expecting to enroll full-time at a four-year institution or university; resident of West Virginia and studying in West Virginia. Available to U.S. citizens.

Application Requirements: Application, financial need analysis, transcript. *Deadline:* January 15.

Contact: Susan Hoover, Scholarship Program Officer
Greater Kanawha Valley Foundation
1600 Huntington Square, 900 Lee Street, East
PO Box 3041
Charleston, WV 25301
Phone: 304-346-3620
E-mail: shoover@tgkvf.org

SCPA SCHOLARSHIP FUND

Renewable award for West Virginia residents who are full-time students with minimum 2.5 GPA. Applicant must have parent who is employed or has been previously employed by the coal industry in southern West Virginia (list of eligible counties on web site http://www.tgkvf.org). Scholarships are awarded on a financial need basis and may be awarded for one or more years.

Award: Scholarship for use in freshman, sophomore, junior, or senior years; renewable. *Number:* up to 10. *Amount:* $945–$1000.

Eligibility Requirements: Applicant must be enrolled or expecting to enroll full-time at a four-year institution or university and resident of West Virginia. Applicant must have 3.5 GPA or higher. Available to U.S. citizens.

Application Requirements: Application, essay, financial need analysis, references, self-addressed stamped envelope, test scores, transcript. *Deadline:* January 15.

Contact: Susan Hoover, Scholarship Coordinator
Greater Kanawha Valley Foundation
PO Box 3041
Charleston, WV 25331
Phone: 304-346-3620
Fax: 304-346-3640
E-mail: tgkvf@tgkvf.org

THALHEIMER FAMILY SUPPLEMENTAL SCHOLARSHIP

Award available to West Virginia students who are current scholarship winners to provide supplemental funds for goods and services necessary for the student to attend college. Must be a resident of Kanawha, Putnam, Boone, Clay, Fayette, or Lincoln counties and submit a written request for additional aid, listing all financial aid that has been awarded and reason for request. For additional information and application, visit http://www.tgkvf.org.

Award: Scholarship for use in freshman, sophomore, junior, or senior years; not renewable. *Number:* 1. *Amount:* $1000.

Eligibility Requirements: Applicant must be enrolled or expecting to enroll full-time at a two-year or four-year institution or university and resident of West Virginia. Available to U.S. citizens.

Application Requirements: Application, financial need analysis, transcript, letter requesting aid. *Deadline:* January 15.

Contact: Susan Hoover, Scholarship Program Officer
Greater Kanawha Valley Foundation
1600 Huntington Square, 900 Lee Street, East
PO Box 3041
Charleston, WV 25301
Phone: 304-346-3620
E-mail: shoover@tgkvf.org

WEST VIRGINIA GOLF ASSOCIATION FUND

Award of $1000 available to students at any accredited West Virginia college or university. This fund is open to individuals who meet the following criteria:(1) have played golf in WV as an amateur for recreation or competition or(2) have been or are presently employed in WV as a caddie, groundskeeper, bag boy, etc. Must also include a reference by a coach, golf professional or employer and an essay explaining how the game of golf has made an impact in applicant's life. Scholarships are awarded with a commitment of one year.

Award: Scholarship for use in freshman, sophomore, junior, or senior years; not renewable. *Number:* 2. *Amount:* $1000.

Eligibility Requirements: Applicant must be enrolled or expecting to enroll full-time at a two-year or four-year or technical institution or university; resident of West Virginia and studying in West Virginia. Available to U.S. citizens.

Application Requirements: Application, essay, references, transcript. *Deadline:* January 15.

Contact: Susan Hoover, Scholarship Coordinator
Greater Kanawha Valley Foundation
PO Box 3041
Charleston, WV 25331
Phone: 304-346-3620
Fax: 304-346-3640
E-mail: shoover@tgkvf.org

WILLIAM GIACOMO FIREFIGHTER SCHOLARSHIP

Non-renewable scholarship available for West Virginia resident for study in sophomore year at a West Virginia two- or four-year college or university unless student is studying for a fire safety degree in an accredited program outside of West Virginia. Must be an active firefighter, or a spouse, child, or grandchild of an active firefighter on a department that is a member of and in good standing with Fayette County Firefighters Association. Applicants must submit with application a notarized statement affirming firefighter status and relationship. Minimum 2.75 GPA required. For additional information visit http://www.tgkvf.org.

Award: Scholarship for use in sophomore, junior, or senior years; not renewable. *Number:* 1. *Amount:* $650.

Eligibility Requirements: Applicant must be enrolled or expecting to enroll full-time at a two-year or four-year institution or university and resident of West Virginia. Available to U.S. citizens.

Application Requirements: Application, transcript, notarized statement of firefighter status. *Deadline:* January 15.

Contact: Susan Hoover, Scholarship Program Officer
Greater Kanawha Valley Foundation
1600 Huntington Square, 900 Lee Street, East
PO Box 3041
Charleston, WV 25301
Phone: 304-346-3620
E-mail: shoover@tgkvf.org

W. P. BLACK SCHOLARSHIP FUND

Renewable award for West Virginia residents who demonstrate academic excellence and financial need and who are enrolled in an undergraduate program in any accredited college or university.

Award: Scholarship for use in freshman, sophomore, junior, or senior years; renewable. *Number:* 68. *Amount:* $1000.

Eligibility Requirements: Applicant must be enrolled or expecting to enroll full-time at a four-year institution or university and resident of West Virginia. Available to U.S. citizens.

Application Requirements: Application, essay, financial need analysis, references, self-addressed stamped envelope, test scores, transcript. *Deadline:* January 15.

Contact: Susan Hoover, Scholarship Coordinator
Greater Kanawha Valley Foundation
PO Box 3041
Charleston, WV 25331
Phone: 304-346-3620
Fax: 304-346-3640
E-mail: tgkvf@tgkvf.org

GREATER WASHINGTON URBAN LEAGUE

http://www.gwul.org/

SAFEWAY/GREATER WASHINGTON URBAN LEAGUE SCHOLARSHIP
• *See page 587*

GREAT LAKES HEMOPHILIA FOUNDATION

http://www.glhf.org/

GLHF INDIVIDUAL CLASS SCHOLARSHIP
• *See page 604*

GREAT LAKES HEMOPHILIA FOUNDATION EDUCATION SCHOLARSHIP
• *See page 604*

GREENHOUSE SCHOLARS

http://www.greenhousescholars.org/

GREENHOUSE SCHOLARS

Greenhouse Scholars provides comprehensive personal and financial support to high-performing, under-resourced college students. Using our unique Whole Person approach, which offers intellectual, academic, professional, and financial support, we are cultivating the next generation of community leaders. The day our Scholars leave college they'll be prepared to succeed in their professional endeavors and make significant contributions in their communities. Applicants shoould be able to demonstrate a strong interest and commitment to the community; demonstrate an ability to persevere through difficult circumstances; possess excellent leadership skills; and demonstrate financial need [annual household income no greater than $70,000].

Award: Scholarship for use in freshman, sophomore, junior, or senior years; renewable. *Number:* 8–20. *Amount:* $500–$20,000.

Eligibility Requirements: Applicant must be high school student; planning to enroll or expecting to enroll full-time at a four-year institution or university; resident of Colorado and must have an interest in leadership. Applicant must have 3.5 GPA or higher. Available to U.S. citizens.

Application Requirements: Application, essay, financial need analysis, interview, references, test scores, transcript. *Deadline:* January 20.

Contact: Bess Moodie, Associate
Greenhouse Scholars
1011 Walnut Street, 3rd Floor
Boulder, CO 80121
Phone: 303-460-1735
E-mail: scholars@greenhousescholars.org

HARTFORD WHALERS BOOSTER CLUB

http://www.whalerwatch.com/

HARTFORD WHALERS BOOSTER CLUB SCHOLARSHIP

Scholarship for graduating high-school seniors who have played high school hockey and intend to play collegiate hockey. Must be a Connecticut resident.

Award: Scholarship for use in freshman year; not renewable. *Number:* 1. *Amount:* up to $1000.

Eligibility Requirements: Applicant must be high school student; planning to enroll or expecting to enroll full- or part-time at a four-year institution or university; resident of Connecticut and must have an interest in athletics/sports. Available to U.S. citizens.

Application Requirements: Application, resume, references, transcript, brief description of career goals. *Deadline:* March 20.

Contact: Alan Victor, President
Hartford Whalers Booster Club
PO Box 273
Hartford, CT 06141
Phone: 860-225-0265
Fax: 860-257-8331
E-mail: alan_m_victor@sbcglobal.net

HAWAII DEPARTMENT OF EDUCATION

http://www.doe.k12.hi.us/

ROBERT C. BYRD HONORS SCHOLARSHIP-HAWAII

Scholarship is available to students planning to attend college. The scholarship is federally funded, state-administered and recognizes exceptional high school seniors who show promise of continued excellence in the post-secondary educational system. Must have a minimum GPA of 3.3 and 1270 SAT. Applicant must be a legal resident of the State of Hawaii. Hawaii residents who are attending high school in another state are eligible to apply.

Award: Scholarship for use in freshman year; renewable. *Number:* 28. *Amount:* $1500.

Eligibility Requirements: Applicant must be high school student; planning to enroll or expecting to enroll full-time at a four-year institution or university and resident of Hawaii. Available to U.S. citizens.

Application Requirements: Application, transcript. *Deadline:* March 13.

Contact: Education Specialist
Hawaii Department of Education
Student Support Section, 641 18th Avenue, Building V, Room 201
Honolulu, HI 96816-4444
Phone: 808-735-6222

HAWAII EDUCATION ASSOCIATION

http://www.heaed.com/

HAWAII EDUCATION ASSOCIATION HIGH SCHOOL STUDENT SCHOLARSHIP
• *See page 543*

HAWAII SCHOOLS FEDERAL CREDIT UNION

http://www.hawaiischoolsfcu.org/

EDWIN KUNIYUKI MEMORIAL SCHOLARSHIP

Annual scholarship for an incoming college freshman in recognition of academic excellence. Applicant must be Hawaii Schools Federal Credit Union member for one year prior to scholarship application.

Award: Scholarship for use in freshman year; not renewable. *Number:* 1. *Amount:* $1000.

Eligibility Requirements: Applicant must be high school student; planning to enroll or expecting to enroll full-time at a two-year or four-year or technical institution or university and resident of Hawaii. Applicant must have 3.0 GPA or higher. Available to U.S. citizens.

Application Requirements: Application, essay, references, transcript. *Deadline:* February 28.

Contact: Kristy Garan, Administrative Assistant
Hawaii Schools Federal Credit Union
233 Vineyard Street
Honolulu, HI 96813
Phone: 808-521-0302
Fax: 808-791-6229
E-mail: kgaran@hawaiischoolsfcu.org

HAWAII STATE POSTSECONDARY EDUCATION COMMISSION

HAWAII STATE STUDENT INCENTIVE GRANT

Grants are given to residents of Hawaii who are enrolled in a participating Hawaiian state school. Funds are for undergraduate tuition only. Applicants must submit a financial need analysis.

Award: Grant for use in freshman, sophomore, junior, or senior years; renewable. *Number:* 470. *Amount:* $200–$2000.

Eligibility Requirements: Applicant must be enrolled or expecting to enroll full- or part-time at a two-year or four-year or technical institution or university; resident of Hawaii and studying in Hawaii. Available to U.S. citizens.

Application Requirements: Application, financial need analysis. *Deadline:* continuous.

Contact: Janine Oyama, Financial Aid Specialist
Hawaii State Postsecondary Education Commission
University of Hawaii
Honolulu, HI 96822
Phone: 808-956-6066

HEARING BRIDGES (FORMERLY LEAGUE FOR THE DEAF AND HARD OF HEARING AND EAR FOUNDATION)

http://www.hearingbridges.org/

LINDA COWDEN MEMORIAL SCHOLARSHIP
• *See page 604*

HELLENIC UNIVERSITY CLUB OF PHILADELPHIA

http://www.hucphila.org/

CHRISTOPHER DEMETRIS SCHOLARSHIP
• *See page 664*

DR. NICHOLAS PADIS MEMORIAL GRADUATE SCHOLARSHIP
• *See page 664*

DORIZAS MEMORIAL SCHOLARSHIP
• *See page 664*

FOUNDERS SCHOLARSHIP
• *See page 664*

JAMES COSMOS MEMORIAL SCHOLARSHIP
• *See page 664*

PAIDEIA SCHOLARSHIP
• *See page 544*

HENRY SACHS FOUNDATION

http://www.sachsfoundation.org/

SACHS FOUNDATION SCHOLARSHIPS
• *See page 664*

HERBERT HOOVER PRESIDENTIAL LIBRARY ASSOCIATION

http://www.hooverassociation.org/

HERBERT HOOVER UNCOMMON STUDENT AWARD

Award for juniors in an Iowa high school or home school program only. Grades and test scores are not evaluated. Applicants are chosen on the basis of submitted project proposals. Those chosen to complete their project and make a presentation receive $1000. Three are chosen for $5000 award.

Award: Scholarship for use in freshman or sophomore years; not renewable. *Number:* 15. *Amount:* $1000–$5000.

Eligibility Requirements: Applicant must be high school student; planning to enroll or expecting to enroll full-time at a four-year institution or university and resident of Iowa. Available to U.S. citizens.

Application Requirements: Application, references, project proposal. *Deadline:* March 31.

Contact: Ms. Delene McConnaha, Academic Program Manager
Herbert Hoover Presidential Library Association
302 Parkside Drive, P.O. Box 696
West Branch, IA 52358
Phone: 319-643-5327
Fax: 319-643-2391
E-mail: scholarship@hooverassociation.org

HERB KOHL EDUCATIONAL FOUNDATION INC.

http://www.kohleducation.org/

HERB KOHL EXCELLENCE SCHOLARSHIP PROGRAM
• *See page 588*

HISPANIC METROPOLITAN CHAMBER SCHOLARSHIPS

http://www.hmccoregon.com/

HISPANIC METROPOLITAN CHAMBER SCHOLARSHIPS
• *See page 665*

HORIZONS FOUNDATION

http://www.horizonsfoundation.org/

MARKOWSKI-LEACH SCHOLARSHIP

Scholarship of $1250 awarded to a student who attends San Francisco State University, Stanford University, or University of California, and self-identifies as lesbian, gay, bisexual, transgender, or queer. Recipient is chosen based on demonstrated promise for becoming a positive role model for other LGBTQ people. All prospective undergraduate and graduate students may apply. Students transferring to one of these universities are also encouraged to apply.

Award: Scholarship for use in freshman, sophomore, junior, or senior years; renewable. *Number:* 1. *Amount:* $1250.

Eligibility Requirements: Applicant must be enrolled or expecting to enroll full-time at a two-year or four-year or technical institution or university; studying in California and must have an interest in LGBT issues. Applicant must have 2.5 GPA or higher. Available to U.S. and Canadian citizens.

Application Requirements: Application, essay, references. *Deadline:* April 1.

Contact: The Markowski-Leach Scholarship Committee
Horizons Foundation
PO Box 13315, PMB #206
Oakland, CA 94661-0315
E-mail: MLScholarships@gmail.com

HOUSTON COMMUNITY SERVICES

AZTECA SCHOLARSHIP
• *See page 666*

HUMANE SOCIETY OF THE UNITED STATES

http://www.hsus.org/

SHAW-WORTH MEMORIAL SCHOLARSHIP

Scholarship for a New England high school senior, who has made a meaningful contribution to animal protection over a significant amount of time. Passive liking of animals or the desire to enter an animal care field does not justify the award.

Award: Scholarship for use in freshman year; not renewable. *Number:* 1. *Amount:* $2000.

Eligibility Requirements: Applicant must be high school student; planning to enroll or expecting to enroll full-time at a four-year institution or university and resident of Connecticut, Maine, Massachusetts, New Hampshire, Rhode Island, or Vermont. Available to U.S. citizens.

Application Requirements: Essay, references. *Deadline:* March 17.

Contact: Administrator
Humane Society of the United States
PO Box 619
Jacksonville, VT 05342-0619
Phone: 802-368-2790
Fax: 802-368-2756

IDAHO POWER COMPANY

http://www.idahopower.com/

IDAHO POWER SCHOLARSHIP FOR ACADEMIC EXCELLENCE

Scholarship of $1000 for graduating high school students of Idaho. Applicants must have a minimum 3.75 unweighted GPA. Must be enrolled at an accredited Idaho or Oregon college, university or vocational-technical school. Recipients may renew their scholarship annually, up to three times.

Award: Scholarship for use in freshman year; renewable. *Number:* 5. *Amount:* $1000.

Eligibility Requirements: Applicant must be high school student; planning to enroll or expecting to enroll full-time at a two-year or four-year or technical institution or university; resident of Idaho and studying in Idaho or Oregon. Available to U.S. citizens.

Application Requirements: Application, essay, resume, references, test scores, transcript. *Deadline:* June 15.

Contact: Scholarship Program Administrator
Idaho Power Company
PO Box 1000
Pocatello, ID 83204

IDAHO STATE BOARD OF EDUCATION

http://www.boardofed.idaho.gov/

FREEDOM SCHOLARSHIP
• *See page 637*

IDAHO GOVERNOR'S CUP SCHOLARSHIP
• *See page 589*

IDAHO MINORITY AND "AT RISK" STUDENT SCHOLARSHIP
• *See page 605*

IDAHO PROMISE CATEGORY A SCHOLARSHIP PROGRAM

Renewable award available to Idaho residents who are graduating high school seniors. Must attend an approved Idaho institution of higher education on full-time basis and be enrolled in an eligible program. Must have a minimum GPA of 3.5 and an ACT score of 28 or above if enrolling in an academic program, and a GPA of 2.8 and must take the COMPASS test if enrolling in a professional-technical program. For additional information, list of eligible programs, and application, go to web site http://www.boardofed.idaho.gov/scholarships/.

Award: Scholarship for use in freshman year; renewable. *Number:* 25. *Amount:* $3000.

Eligibility Requirements: Applicant must be high school student; planning to enroll or expecting to enroll full-time at a two-year or four-year or technical institution or university; resident of Idaho and studying in Idaho. Available to U.S. citizens.

Application Requirements: Application, applicant must enter a contest, test scores. *Deadline:* January 15.

Contact: Dana Kelly, Program Manager, Student Affairs
Idaho State Board of Education
PO Box 83720
Boise, ID 83720-0037
Phone: 208-332-1574
E-mail: dana.kelly@osbe.idaho.gov

IDAHO PROMISE CATEGORY B SCHOLARSHIP PROGRAM

Available to Idaho residents entering college for the first time prior to the age of 22. Must have completed high school or its equivalent in Idaho and have a minimum GPA of 3.0 or an ACT score of 20 or higher. Scholarship limited to four semesters. Please go to web site for complete information http://www.boardofed.idaho.gov/scholarships/.

Award: Scholarship for use in freshman year; renewable. *Number:* varies. *Amount:* up to $600.

Eligibility Requirements: Applicant must be high school student; age 22 or under; planning to enroll or expecting to enroll full-time at a two-year or four-year or technical institution or university; resident of Idaho and studying in Idaho. Applicant must have 3.0 GPA or higher. Available to U.S. citizens.

Application Requirements: Application, transcript. *Deadline:* continuous.

Contact: Dana Kelly, Program Manager
Idaho State Board of Education
PO Box 83720
Boise, ID 83720-0037
Phone: 208-332-1574
Fax: 208-334-2632
E-mail: dana.kelly@osbe.idaho.gov

LEVERAGING EDUCATIONAL ASSISTANCE STATE PARTNERSHIP PROGRAM (LEAP)

One-time award assists students from any state, attending participating Idaho trade schools, colleges, and universities, and majoring in any field except theology or divinity. Must be enrolled for at least six credits and show financial need. Must be U.S. citizen or permanent resident. Deadlines vary by institution. For a list of eligible institutions, go to web site http://www.boardofed.idaho.gov/scholarships/.

Award: Grant for use in freshman, sophomore, junior, or senior years; not renewable. *Number:* varies. *Amount:* $400–$5000.

Eligibility Requirements: Applicant must be enrolled or expecting to enroll full- or part-time at a two-year or four-year or technical institution or university and studying in Idaho. Available to U.S. citizens.

Application Requirements: Application, financial need analysis, self-addressed stamped envelope. *Deadline:* varies.

Contact: Dana Kelly, Student Affairs
Idaho State Board of Education
PO Box 83720
Boise, ID 83720-0037
Phone: 208-332-1574
Fax: 208-334-2632

PUBLIC SAFETY OFFICER DEPENDENT SCHOLARSHIP
• *See page 589*

ROBERT C. BYRD HONORS SCHOLARSHIP-IDAHO

Renewable scholarships available to Idaho residents based on outstanding academic achievement. Students must apply as high school seniors and be enrolled or planning to attend a college or university as a full-time student. For additional information, please see web site http://www.boardofed.idaho.gov.

Award: Scholarship for use in freshman year; renewable. *Number:* 90. *Amount:* up to $1500.

Eligibility Requirements: Applicant must be high school student; planning to enroll or expecting to enroll full-time at a four-year institution or university and resident of Idaho. Available to U.S. citizens.

Application Requirements: Application, references, test scores, transcript. *Deadline:* January 15.

Contact: Dana Kelly, Manager, Student Affairs Programs
Idaho State Board of Education
PO Box 83720
Boise, ID 83720-0037
Phone: 208-332-1574
Fax: 208-334-2632
E-mail: dana.kelly@osbe.idaho.gov

ILLINOIS AMVETS

http://www.ilamvets.org/

ILLINOIS AMVETS JUNIOR ROTC SCHOLARSHIPS

One year non-renewal $1000 per year for students who have taken the ACT or SAT tests. Preference will be given to children or grandchildren of veterans.

Award: Scholarship for use in freshman, sophomore, junior, or senior years; not renewable. *Number:* varies. *Amount:* $1000.

Eligibility Requirements: Applicant must be high school student; age 17-19; planning to enroll or expecting to enroll full-time at a four-year institution or university and resident of Illinois. Available to U.S. citizens.

Application Requirements: Application, test scores. *Deadline:* March 1.

Contact: Crystal Blakeman, Program Director
Illinois AMVETS
State Headquarters, 2200 South Sixth Street
Springfield, IL 62703
Phone: 217-528-4713 Ext. 207
E-mail: crystal@ilamvets.org

ILLINOIS AMVETS LADIES AUXILIARY MEMORIAL SCHOLARSHIP
• *See page 637*

ILLINOIS AMVETS LADIES AUXILIARY WORCHID SCHOLARSHIPS
• *See page 637*

ILLINOIS AMVETS SERVICE FOUNDATION
• *See page 637*

ILLINOIS AMVETS TRADE SCHOOL SCHOLARSHIP
• *See page 637*

ILLINOIS COUNCIL OF THE BLIND

http://www.icbonline.org/

FLOYD R. CARGILL SCHOLARSHIP
• *See page 605*

ILLINOIS DEPARTMENT OF VETERANS' AFFAIRS

http://www.state.il.us/agency/dva

MIA/POW SCHOLARSHIPS
• *See page 637*

VETERANS' CHILDREN EDUCATIONAL OPPORTUNITIES
• *See page 638*

ILLINOIS EDUCATION FOUNDATION

http://www.iledfoundation.org/

ILLINOIS EDUCATION FOUNDATION SIGNATURE FUND SCHOLARSHIP

The Illinois Education Foundation (IEF) is a public/private partnership that broadens opportunities to low-income, high-potential community college students by providing a comprehensive scholarship program. IEF scholarships combine last dollar financial assistance along with a full set of academic support services including mentoring, tutoring and academic advising to empower more Illinois college students to achieve their degrees and reach their full potential.

Award: Scholarship for use in freshman, sophomore, junior, or senior years; renewable. *Number:* up to 30. *Amount:* $800–$3000.

Eligibility Requirements: Applicant must be enrolled or expecting to enroll full-time at a two-year or technical institution; resident of Illinois and studying in Illinois. Available to U.S. citizens.

Application Requirements: Application, essay, financial need analysis, interview, resume, references, test scores, transcript, completion of FAFSA. *Deadline:* June 1.

Contact: Ms. Nina Sanchez, Program Manager
Illinois Education Foundation
226 West Jackson Boulevard, Suite 426
Chicago, IL 60606
Phone: 312-920-9605
E-mail: info@iledfoundation.org

ILLINOIS STUDENT ASSISTANCE COMMISSION (ISAC)

http://www.collegezone.org/

GRANT PROGRAM FOR DEPENDENTS OF POLICE, FIRE, OR CORRECTIONAL OFFICERS

Awards available to Illinois residents who are dependents of police, fire, and correctional officers killed or disabled in line of duty. Provides for tuition and fees at approved Illinois institutions. Number of grants and individual dollar amount awarded vary.

Award: Grant for use in freshman, sophomore, junior, senior, graduate, or postgraduate years; renewable. *Number:* varies. *Amount:* varies.

Eligibility Requirements: Applicant must be enrolled or expecting to enroll full- or part-time at a two-year or four-year or technical institution or university; resident of Illinois and studying in Illinois. Available to U.S. citizens.

Application Requirements: Application, proof of status. *Deadline:* varies.

Contact: College Zone Counselor
Illinois Student Assistance Commission (ISAC)
1755 Lake Cook Road
Deerfield, IL 60015-5209
Phone: 800-899-4722
Fax: 847-831-8549
E-mail: collegezone@isac.org

HIGHER EDUCATION LICENSE PLATE PROGRAM-HELP

Grants for students who attend Illinois colleges for which the special collegiate license plates are available. The Illinois Secretary of State issues the license plates, and part of the proceeds are used for grants for undergraduate students attending these colleges, to pay tuition and mandatory fees.

Award: Grant for use in freshman, sophomore, junior, or senior years; not renewable. *Number:* varies. *Amount:* varies.

Eligibility Requirements: Applicant must be enrolled or expecting to enroll full- or part-time at a two-year or four-year institution or university; resident of Illinois and studying in Illinois. Available to U.S. citizens.

Application Requirements: Application, financial need analysis. *Deadline:* varies.

Contact: College Zone Counselor
Illinois Student Assistance Commission (ISAC)
1755 Lake Cook Road
Deerfield, IL 60015-5209
Phone: 800-899-4722
Fax: 847-831-8549
E-mail: collegezone@isac.org

ILLINOIS COLLEGE SAVINGS BOND BONUS INCENTIVE GRANT PROGRAM

Program offers Illinois college savings bond holders a grant for each year of bond maturity payable upon bond redemption if at least 70 percent of proceeds are used to attend college in Illinois. The amount of grant will depend on the amount of the bond, ranging from a $40 to $440 grant per $5000 of the bond. Applications are accepted between August 1 and May 30 of the academic year in which the bonds matured, or in the academic year immediately following maturity.

Award: Grant for use in freshman, sophomore, junior, senior, graduate, or postgraduate years; not renewable. *Number:* varies.

Eligibility Requirements: Applicant must be enrolled or expecting to enroll full- or part-time at a two-year or four-year or technical institution or university and studying in Illinois. Available to U.S. citizens.

Application Requirements: Application. *Deadline:* varies.

Contact: College Zone Counselor
Illinois Student Assistance Commission (ISAC)
1755 Lake Cook Road
Deerfield, IL 60015-5209
Phone: 800-899-4722
Fax: 847-831-8549
E-mail: collegezone@isac.org

ILLINOIS GENERAL ASSEMBLY SCHOLARSHIP

Scholarships available for Illinois students enrolled at an Illinois four-year state-supported college. Must contact the general assembly member for eligibility criteria. Deadline varies.

Award: Scholarship for use in freshman, sophomore, junior, or senior years; not renewable. *Number:* varies. *Amount:* varies.

Eligibility Requirements: Applicant must be enrolled or expecting to enroll full- or part-time at a four-year institution or university; resident of Illinois and studying in Illinois. Available to U.S. citizens.

Application Requirements: Application. *Deadline:* varies.

Contact: College Zone Counselor
Illinois Student Assistance Commission (ISAC)
1755 Lake Cook Road
Deerfield, IL 60015-5209
Phone: 800-899-4722
Fax: 847-831-8549
E-mail: collegezone@isac.org

ILLINOIS MONETARY AWARD PROGRAM

Awards to Illinois residents enrolled in a minimum of 3 hours per term in a degree program at an approved Illinois institution. See web site for complete list of participating schools. Must demonstrate financial need, based on the information provided on the Free Application for Federal Student Aid. Number of grants and the individual dollar amount awarded vary. Deadline: As soon as possible after January 1 of the year in which the student will enter college.

Award: Grant for use in freshman, sophomore, junior, or senior years; renewable. *Amount:* $2637.

Eligibility Requirements: Applicant must be enrolled or expecting to enroll full- or part-time at a two-year or four-year or technical institution or university; resident of Illinois and studying in Illinois. Available to U.S. citizens.

Application Requirements: Financial need analysis, FAFSA online. *Deadline:* varies.

Contact: College Zone Counselor
Illinois Student Assistance Commission (ISAC)
1755 Lake Cook Road
Deerfield, IL 60015-5209
Phone: 800-899-4722
Fax: 847-831-8549
E-mail: collegezone@isac.org

ILLINOIS NATIONAL GUARD GRANT PROGRAM

• *See page 619*

ILLINOIS STUDENT-TO-STUDENT PROGRAM OF MATCHING GRANTS

Matching grant is available to undergraduates at participating state-supported colleges. Number of grants and the individual dollar amount awarded vary. Contact financial aid office at institution.

Award: Grant for use in freshman, sophomore, junior, or senior years; not renewable. *Number:* varies. *Amount:* $300–$1000.

Eligibility Requirements: Applicant must be enrolled or expecting to enroll full- or part-time at a two-year or four-year institution or university; resident of Illinois and studying in Illinois. Available to U.S. citizens.

Application Requirements: Application, financial need analysis. *Deadline:* varies.

Contact: College Zone Counselor
Illinois Student Assistance Commission (ISAC)
1755 Lake Cook Road
Deerfield, IL 60015-5209
Phone: 800-899-4722
Fax: 847-831-8549
E-mail: collegezone@isac.org

ILLINOIS VETERAN GRANT PROGRAM-IVG

• *See page 638*

MERIT RECOGNITION SCHOLARSHIP (MRS) PROGRAM

One-time awards available to Illinois residents for use at Illinois institutions. Must be ranked in the top 5 percent of high school class or have scored among the top 5 percent on the ACT, SAT, or Prairie State Achievement Exam. Number of scholarships granted varies. Program not currently funded.

Award: Scholarship for use in freshman year; not renewable. *Number:* varies. *Amount:* up to $1000.

Eligibility Requirements: Applicant must be high school student; planning to enroll or expecting to enroll full- or part-time at a two-year or four-year institution or university; resident of Illinois and studying in Illinois. Available to U.S. citizens.

Application Requirements: Application, transcript. *Deadline:* June 15.

Contact: College Zone Counselor
Illinois Student Assistance Commission (ISAC)
1755 Lake Cook Road
Deerfield, IL 60015-5209
Phone: 800-899-4722
Fax: 847-831-8549
E-mail: collegezone@isac.org

ROBERT C. BYRD HONORS SCHOLARSHIP-ILLINOIS

Scholarship for Illinois residents and graduating high school seniors accepted on a full-time basis as an undergraduate student at an Illinois college or university. The award is up to $1500 per year, for a maximum of four years. Minimum 3.5 GPA required. Students are automatically considered for this scholarship if they meet the eligibility requirements. High school counselors submit information to selection process.

Award: Scholarship for use in freshman, sophomore, junior, or senior years; renewable. *Number:* varies. *Amount:* up to $1500.

Eligibility Requirements: Applicant must be high school student; planning to enroll or expecting to enroll full-time at a two-year or four-year institution or university; resident of Illinois and studying in Illinois. Available to U.S. citizens.

Application Requirements: Application, test scores, transcript. *Deadline:* July 15.

Contact: College Zone Counselor
Illinois Student Assistance Commission (ISAC)
1755 Lake Cook Road
Deerfield, IL 60015-5209
Phone: 800-899-4722
E-mail: collegezone@isac.org

SILAS PURNELL ILLINOIS INCENTIVE FOR ACCESS PROGRAM

Students whose information provided on the FAFSA results in a calculated zero expected family contribution when they are college freshmen may be eligible to receive a grant of up to $500. Must be a U.S. citizen and an Illinois resident studying at a participating Illinois institution. See web site for complete list of schools and additional requirements.

Award: Grant for use in freshman year; not renewable. *Number:* varies. *Amount:* up to $500.

Eligibility Requirements: Applicant must be high school student; planning to enroll or expecting to enroll full- or part-time at a two-year or four-year or technical institution or university; resident of Illinois and studying in Illinois. Available to U.S. citizens.

Application Requirements: Financial need analysis, FAFSA. *Deadline:* July 1.

Contact: College Zone Counselor
Illinois Student Assistance Commission (ISAC)
1755 Lake Cook Road
Deerfield, IL 60015-5209
Phone: 800-899-4722
Fax: 847-831-8549
E-mail: collegezone@isac.org

INDEPENDENT COLLEGE FUND OF MARYLAND (I-FUND)

http://www.i-fundinfo.org/

LEADERSHIP SCHOLARSHIPS

Annual scholarship available to an outstanding student for study at one of the Independent Colleges of Maryland. A $25,000 Challenge Grant from UPS is matched dollar for dollar, with the goal of providing one $5000 scholarship for each independent college in Maryland.

Award: Scholarship for use in junior or senior years; not renewable. *Number:* 1. *Amount:* $5000.

Eligibility Requirements: Applicant must be enrolled or expecting to enroll full- or part-time at a four-year institution or university; studying in Maryland and must have an interest in leadership. Available to U.S. citizens.

Application Requirements: Application. *Deadline:* varies.

Contact: Lori Subotich, Director of Programs and Scholarships
Independent College Fund of Maryland (I-Fund)
3225 Ellerslie Avenue, Suite C160
Baltimore, MD 21218-3519
Phone: 443-997-5700
Fax: 443-997-2740
E-mail: lsubot@jhmi.edu

MARYLAND SCHOLARS
• *See page 589*

T. ROWE PRICE FOUNDATION SCHOLARSHIPS

Award of $3000 to students who exhibit outstanding leadership qualities on campus and/or in the community. Must be permanent residents of Maryland and have at least 3.0 GPA.

Award: Scholarship for use in freshman, sophomore, junior, or senior years; not renewable. *Number:* 1. *Amount:* $3000.

Eligibility Requirements: Applicant must be enrolled or expecting to enroll full-time at a four-year institution or university; resident of Maryland and must have an interest in leadership. Applicant must have 3.0 GPA or higher. Available to U.S. citizens.

Application Requirements: Application, financial need analysis, thank you letters. *Deadline:* varies.

Contact: Lori Subotich, Director of Programs and Scholarships
Independent College Fund of Maryland (I-Fund)
3225 Ellerslie Avenue, Suite C160
Baltimore, MD 21218-3519
Phone: 443-997-5700
Fax: 443-997-2740
E-mail: lsubot@jhmi.edu

INDIANA DEPARTMENT OF VETERANS AFFAIRS

http://www.in.gov/dva

CHILD OF DISABLED VETERAN GRANT OR PURPLE HEART RECIPIENT GRANT
• *See page 638*

DEPARTMENT OF VETERANS AFFAIRS FREE TUITION FOR CHILDREN OF POW/MIA'S IN VIETNAM
• *See page 638*

NATIONAL GUARD SCHOLARSHIP EXTENSION PROGRAM
• *See page 620*

NATIONAL GUARD TUITION SUPPLEMENT PROGRAM
• *See page 620*

RESIDENT TUITION FOR ACTIVE DUTY MILITARY PERSONNEL
• *See page 617*

TUITION AND FEE REMISSION FOR CHILDREN AND SPOUSES OF NATIONAL GUARD MEMBERS
• *See page 620*

INDIAN AMERICAN CULTURAL ASSOCIATION

http://www.iasf.org/

INDIAN AMERICAN SCHOLARSHIP FUND
• *See page 666*

INTER-COUNTY ENERGY

http://www.intercountyenergy.net/

INTER-COUNTY ENERGY SCHOLARSHIP

One $1,000 scholarship given to a high school senior in each of Inter-County Energy's six directorial districts: Boyle, Lincoln, Mercer, Garrard, Casey and Marion. Applicant's parent or legal guardian must be a member of Inter-County Energy with the primary residence being on the cooperative lines.

Award: Scholarship for use in freshman year; not renewable. *Number:* 6. *Amount:* up to $1000.

Eligibility Requirements: Applicant must be high school student; planning to enroll or expecting to enroll full-time at a four-year institution or university and resident of Kentucky. Available to U.S. citizens.

Application Requirements: Application, financial need analysis, references, transcript. *Deadline:* March 25.

Contact: Farrah Coleman, Communications Specialist
Inter-County Energy
PO Box 87
Danville, KY 40423-0087
Phone: 859-236-4561 Ext. 7821
Fax: 859-236-5012
E-mail: farrah@intercountyenergy.net

IOWA COLLEGE STUDENT AID COMMISSION

http://www.iowacollegeaid.gov/

ALL IOWA OPPORTUNITY SCHOLARSHIP

Students attending eligible Iowa colleges and universities may receive awards of up to $6420. Minimum 2.5 GPA. Priority will be given to students who participated in the Federal TRIO Programs, graduated from alternative high schools, and to homeless youth. Applicant must enroll within two academic years of graduating from high school. Maximum individual awards cannot exceed more than the resident tuition rate at Iowa Regent Universities.

Award: Scholarship for use in freshman or sophomore years; not renewable. *Number:* 200–800.

Eligibility Requirements: Applicant must be enrolled or expecting to enroll full- or part-time at a two-year or four-year or technical institution or university; resident of Iowa and studying in Iowa. Applicant must have 2.5 GPA or higher. Available to U.S. citizens.

Application Requirements: Application, financial need analysis. *Deadline:* March 1.

Contact: Todd Brown, Director, Scholarships, Grants, and Loan Forgiveness
Iowa College Student Aid Commission
603 E 12th Street, 5th FL
Des Moines, IA 50319
Phone: 877-272-4456
Fax: 515-725-3401
E-mail: grants@iowacollegeaid.gov

IOWA GRANTS

Statewide need-based program to assist high-need Iowa residents. Recipients must demonstrate a high level of financial need to receive awards ranging from $100 to $1000. Awards are prorated for students enrolled for less than full-time. Awards must be used at Iowa postsecondary institutions.

Award: Grant for use in freshman, sophomore, junior, or senior years; not renewable. *Number:* 2000–3000. *Amount:* $100–$1000.

Eligibility Requirements: Applicant must be enrolled or expecting to enroll full- or part-time at a two-year or four-year or technical institution or university; resident of Iowa and studying in Iowa. Available to U.S. citizens.

Application Requirements: Application, financial need analysis. *Deadline:* continuous.

Contact: Todd Brown, Director, Scholarships, Grants, and Loan Forgiveness
Iowa College Student Aid Commission
603 E 12th Street, 5th FL
Des Moines, IA 50319
Phone: 877-272-4456
Fax: 515-725-3401
E-mail: grants@iowacollegeaid.gov

IOWA NATIONAL GUARD EDUCATION ASSISTANCE PROGRAM

• See page 620

IOWA TUITION GRANT PROGRAM

Program assists students who attend independent postsecondary institutions in Iowa. Iowa residents currently enrolled, or planning to enroll, for at least 3 semester hours at one of the eligible Iowa postsecondary institutions may apply. Awards currently range from $100 to $4000. Grants may not exceed the difference between independent college and university tuition fees and the average tuition fees at the three public Regent universities.

Award: Grant for use in freshman, sophomore, junior, or senior years; renewable. *Number:* 16,000–17,500. *Amount:* $100–$4000.

Eligibility Requirements: Applicant must be enrolled or expecting to enroll full- or part-time at a four-year institution or university; resident of Iowa and studying in Iowa. Available to U.S. citizens.

Application Requirements: Application, financial need analysis. *Deadline:* July 1.

Contact: Todd Brown, Director, Scholarships, Grants, and Loan Forgiveness
Iowa College Student Aid Commission
603 E 12th Street, 5th FL
Des Moines, IA 50319
Phone: 515-725-3420
Fax: 515-725-3401
E-mail: todd.brown@iowa.gov

IOWA VOCATIONAL-TECHNICAL TUITION GRANT PROGRAM

Program provides need-based financial assistance to Iowa residents enrolled in career education (vocational-technical), and career option programs at Iowa area community colleges. Grants range from $150 to $1200, depending on the length of the program, financial need, and available funds.

Award: Grant for use in freshman or sophomore years; not renewable. *Number:* 2500–3500. *Amount:* $150–$1200.

Eligibility Requirements: Applicant must be enrolled or expecting to enroll full- or part-time at a two-year or technical institution; resident of Iowa and studying in Iowa. Available to U.S. citizens.

Application Requirements: Application, financial need analysis. *Deadline:* July 1.

Contact: Todd Brown, Director, Program Administration
Iowa College Student Aid Commission
603 E 12th Street, 5th FL
Des Moines, IA 50319
Phone: 515-725-3405
Fax: 515-725-3401
E-mail: todd.brown@iowa.gov

ITALIAN-AMERICAN CHAMBER OF COMMERCE OF CHICAGO

http://www.italianchamber.us/

ITALIAN-AMERICAN CHAMBER OF COMMERCE OF CHICAGO SCHOLARSHIP

• See page 667

ITALIAN CATHOLIC FEDERATION INC.

http://www.icf.org/

ITALIAN CATHOLIC FEDERATION FIRST YEAR SCHOLARSHIP

• See page 546

JACKSON ENERGY COOPERATIVE

http://www.jacksonenergy.com/

JACKSON ENERGY SCHOLARSHIP

Scholarships are awarded to winners in an essay contest. Must be at least a senior in a Kentucky high school and no more than 21 years of age. Parents or legal guardian must be a cooperative member, but not an employee of Jackson Energy.

Award: Scholarship for use in freshman, sophomore, junior, or senior years; not renewable. *Number:* 8. *Amount:* $1000.

Eligibility Requirements: Applicant must be age 21 or under; enrolled or expecting to enroll full-time at a two-year or four-year or technical institution or university and resident of Kentucky. Available to U.S. citizens.

Application Requirements: Application, applicant must enter a contest, essay. *Deadline:* March 1.

Contact: Karen Combs, Director of Public Relations
Jackson Energy Cooperative
115 Jackson Energy lane
McKee, KY 40447
Phone: 606-364-9223
Fax: 606-364-1011
E-mail: karencombs@jacksonenergy.com

JAMES F. BYRNES FOUNDATION

http://www.byrnesscholars.org/

JAMES F. BYRNES SCHOLARSHIP

Renewable award for residents of South Carolina ages 17–22 with one or both parents deceased. Must show financial need; a satisfactory scholastic record; and qualities of character, ability, and enterprise. Award is for undergraduate study. Results of SAT must be provided. Information available on web site http://www.byrnesscholars.org.

Award: Scholarship for use in freshman year; renewable. *Number:* 6–10. *Amount:* up to $13,000.

Eligibility Requirements: Applicant must be high school student; age 17-19; planning to enroll or expecting to enroll full-time at a four-year institution and resident of South Carolina. Available to U.S. citizens.

Application Requirements: Application, essay, financial need analysis, interview, photo, references, test scores, transcript. *Deadline:* February 15.

Contact: Kenya White, Executive Secretary
James F. Byrnes Foundation
PO Box 6781
Columbia, SC 29260-6781
Phone: 803-254-9325
Fax: 803-254-9354
E-mail: info@byrnesscholars.org

JAY'S WORLD CHILDHOOD CANCER FOUNDATION

http://www.jaysworld.org/

JAY'S WORLD CHILDHOOD CANCER FOUNDATION SCHOLARSHIP
• *See page 606*

J. CRAIG AND PAGE T. SMITH SCHOLARSHIP FOUNDATION

http://www.jcraigsmithfoundation.org/

FIRST IN FAMILY SCHOLARSHIP

Scholarships are available for graduating Alabama high school seniors. Must be planning to enroll in an Alabama institution in fall and pursue a four-year degree. Students who apply must want to give back to their community by volunteer and civic work. Special consideration will be given to applicants who would be the first in either their mother's or father's family (or both) to attend college.

Award: Scholarship for use in freshman year; renewable. *Number:* 10. *Amount:* $12,500–$15,000.

Eligibility Requirements: Applicant must be high school student; planning to enroll or expecting to enroll full-time at a four-year institution or university; resident of Alabama and studying in Alabama. Applicant must have 2.5 GPA or higher. Available to U.S. citizens.

Application Requirements: Application, essay, financial need analysis, references, test scores, transcript. *Deadline:* January 15.

Contact: Ahrian Tyler, Administrator/Chairman of the Board
    J. Craig and Page T. Smith Scholarship Foundation
    505 20th Street North, Suite 1800
    Birmingham, AL 35203
    Phone: 205-250-6669
    Fax: 205-328-7234
    E-mail: ahrian@jcraigsmithfoundation.org

JEWISH VOCATIONAL SERVICE LOS ANGELES

http://www.jvsla.org/

JEWISH VOCATIONAL SERVICE SCHOLARSHIP FUND
• *See page 667*

KAISER PERMANENTE

http://kpapan.org/

KAISER PERMANENTE ASIAN PACIFIC AMERICAN NETWORK SCHOLARSHIP PROGRAM
• *See page 667*

KANSAS BOARD OF REGENTS

http://www.kansasregents.org/

KANSAS ETHNIC MINORITY SCHOLARSHIP
• *See page 667*

KANSAS COMMISSION ON VETERANS AFFAIRS

http://www.kcva.org/

KANSAS EDUCATIONAL BENEFITS FOR CHILDREN OF MIA, POW, AND DECEASED VETERANS OF THE VIETNAM WAR
• *See page 638*

KE ALI'I PAUAHI FOUNDATION

http://www.pauahi.org/

DANIEL KAHIKINA AND MILLIE AKAKA SCHOLARSHIP
• *See page 590*

JALENE KANANI BELL 'OHANA SCHOLARSHIP

Scholarship open to part-time or full-time undergraduate or graduate students who is a Hawaii residents with a GPA of 2.5 or above. Demonstrate characteristics of a well-rounded, community minded student of good moral character with a "can-do" attitude. Submit two letters of recommendation one from a teacher or counselor and one from a community organization. Submit essay that explains where you draw inspiration and strength from.

Award: Scholarship for use in freshman, sophomore, junior, senior, or graduate years; not renewable. *Number:* 1. *Amount:* $700.

Eligibility Requirements: Applicant must be enrolled or expecting to enroll full- or part-time at a two-year or four-year institution or university and resident of Hawaii. Applicant must have 2.5 GPA or higher. Available to U.S. citizens.

Application Requirements: Application, essay, references, transcript, Student Aid Report (SAR), college acceptance letter. *Deadline:* April 1.

Contact: Mavis Shiraishi-Nagao, Scholarship Administrator
    Phone: 808-534-3966
    E-mail: scholarships@pauahi.org

KAMEHAMEHA SCHOOLS ALUMNI ASSOCIATION-MAUI REGION SCHOLARSHIP
• *See page 590*

KAMEHAMEHA SCHOOLS CLASS OF 1956 GRANT

Grant to assist at least one male and one female student who demonstrate financial need and have a minimum 2.5 GPA. Applicants must show an interest in Hawaiian language, culture and history, and demonstrate a commitment to contribute to the greater community. Submit two letters of recommendation from a teacher, counselor, employer or community organization.

Award: Grant for use in freshman, sophomore, junior, senior, or graduate years; not renewable. *Number:* 2. *Amount:* $500.

Eligibility Requirements: Applicant must be enrolled or expecting to enroll full-time at a four-year institution or university; resident of Hawaii and must have an interest in Hawaiian language/culture. Applicant must have 2.5 GPA or higher. Available to U.S. citizens.

Application Requirements: Application, financial need analysis, references, transcript, Student Aid Report (SAR), college acceptance letter. *Deadline:* April 1.

Contact: Mavis Shiraishi-Nagao, Scholarship Administrator
    Phone: 808-534-3966
    E-mail: scholarships@pauahi.org

KAMEHAMEHA SCHOOLS CLASS OF 1972 SCHOLARSHIP

Scholarship to assist Kamehameha Schools Class of 1972 graduates, and their children and grandchildren with a minimum GPA of 2.8, to earn an undergraduate or graduate degree. May also be awarded to assist individuals whose lives have been impacted by challenging circumstances, such as death of a significant family member, domestic violence, sexual abuse, poverty, or major illness.

Award: Scholarship for use in freshman, sophomore, junior, senior, or graduate years; not renewable. *Number:* varies. *Amount:* $1100.

Eligibility Requirements: Applicant must be enrolled or expecting to enroll full-time at a four-year institution or university and resident of Hawaii. Available to U.S. citizens.

Application Requirements: Application, financial need analysis, references, transcript, Student Aid Report (SAR), college acceptance letter. *Deadline:* May 2.

Contact: Mavis Shiraishi-Nagao, Scholarship Administrator
    Ke Ali'i Pauahi Foundation
    567 South King Street, Suite 160
    Honolulu, HI 96813
    Phone: 808-534-3966
    E-mail: scholarships@pauahi.org

KAMEHAMEHA SCHOOLS CLASS OF 1973 "PROUD TO BE 73" SCHOLARSHIP

Provides scholarships to students who graduated from a Hawaiian Focused Charter School in the state of Hawaii. Part-time students is acceptable.

Award: Scholarship for use in freshman, sophomore, junior, senior, or graduate years; not renewable. *Number:* 2. *Amount:* $700.

Eligibility Requirements: Applicant must be enrolled or expecting to enroll full- or part-time at a two-year or four-year or technical institution or university and resident of Hawaii. Available to U.S. citizens.

Application Requirements: Application, transcript, Student Aid Report (SAR), college acceptance letter. *Deadline:* April 1.

Contact: Mavis Shiraishi-Nagao, Scholarship Administrator
Phone: 808-534-3966
E-mail: scholarships@pauahi.org

KAMEHAMEHA SCHOOLS CLASS OF 1974 SCHOLARSHIP

Scholarship will provide support to students enrolled at a postsecondary institution, including non-traditional programs such as Hawaiian culture or self-improvement seminars. Applicants must have a minimum GPA of 2.8 and demonstrate financial need. Preference will be given to family members of Kamehameha Schools Class of 1974.

Award: Scholarship for use in freshman, sophomore, junior, senior, or graduate years; not renewable. *Number:* varies. *Amount:* $1200.

Eligibility Requirements: Applicant must be enrolled or expecting to enroll full-time at a two-year or four-year institution or university; resident of Hawaii and must have an interest in Hawaiian language/culture. Available to U.S. citizens.

Application Requirements: Application, financial need analysis, references, transcript, Student Aid Report (SAR), college acceptance letter. *Deadline:* May 2.

Contact: Mavis Shiraishi-Nagao, Scholarship Administrator
Ke Ali'i Pauahi Foundation
567 South King Street, Suite 160
Honolulu, HI 96813
Phone: 808-534-3966
E-mail: scholarships@pauahi.org

KENERGY CORPORATION

http://www.kenergycorp.com/

KENERGY SCHOLARSHIP

Student must be a member owner of Kenergy, or must have his/her primary residence with a parent or legal guardian who receives electric service from Kenergy. Must be accompanied by his/her parent(s) or legal guardians to the Kenergy Annual Membership Meeting in Henderson, Kentucky where the student may register for scholarship drawings.

Award: Scholarship for use in freshman, sophomore, junior, senior, or graduate years; not renewable. *Number:* up to 20. *Amount:* $500.

Eligibility Requirements: Applicant must be enrolled or expecting to enroll full-time at a two-year or four-year or technical institution or university and resident of Kentucky. Available to U.S. and non-U.S. citizens.

Application Requirements: Application, transcript. *Deadline:* varies.

Contact: Beverly Hooper, Scholarship Coordinator
Kenergy Corporation
6402 Old Corydon Road, PO Box 18
Henderson, KY 42420
Phone: 270-826-3991 Ext. 3811
Fax: 270-826-3999
E-mail: bhooper@kenergycorp.com

KENTUCKY ASSOCIATION OF ELECTRIC COOPERATIVES, INC.

http://www.kaec.com/

WIRE SCHOLARSHIPS

Scholarship available to Kentucky students who are juniors or seniors in a Kentucky college or university and have 60 credit hours by fall semester. Immediate family of student must be served by one of the state's 24 rural electric distribution cooperatives. Awards based on academic achievement, extracurricular activities, career goals, recommendations.

Award: Scholarship for use in junior or senior years; not renewable. *Number:* 3–5. *Amount:* $1000.

Eligibility Requirements: Applicant must be enrolled or expecting to enroll full-time at a two-year or four-year or technical institution or university; resident of Kentucky and studying in Kentucky. Available to U.S. citizens.

Application Requirements: Application, transcript, letter explaining how this scholarship would enhance your academic goals. *Deadline:* June 17.

Contact: Ellie Hobgood, Scholarship Coordinator
Kentucky Association of Electric Cooperatives, Inc.
PO Box 32170
Louisville, KY 40232
Phone: 800-595-4846
E-mail: ehobgood@kentuckyliving.com

KENTUCKY DEPARTMENT OF VETERANS AFFAIRS

http://www.veterans.ky.gov/

DEPARTMENT OF VETERANS AFFAIRS TUITION WAIVER-KY KRS 164-507

Scholarship available to college students who are residents of Kentucky under the age of 26.

Award: Scholarship for use in freshman, sophomore, junior, or senior years; not renewable. *Number:* 400. *Amount:* varies.

Eligibility Requirements: Applicant must be age 26 or under; enrolled or expecting to enroll full- or part-time at a two-year or four-year institution or university and resident of Kentucky. Available to U.S. citizens.

Application Requirements: Application. *Deadline:* varies.

Contact: Barbara Sipek, Tuition Waiver Coordinator
Kentucky Department of Veterans Affairs
321 West Main Street, Suite 390
Louisville, KY 40213-9095
Phone: 502-595-4447
E-mail: barbaraa.sipek@ky.gov

KENTUCKY HIGHER EDUCATION ASSISTANCE AUTHORITY (KHEAA)

http://www.kheaa.com/

COLLEGE ACCESS PROGRAM (CAP) GRANT

Award for U.S. citizens and Kentucky residents seeking their first undergraduate degree. Applicants enrolled in sectarian institutions are not eligible. Must submit Free Application for Federal Student Aid to demonstrate financial need. Funding is limited. Awards are made on a first-come, first-serve basis.

Award: Grant for use in freshman, sophomore, junior, or senior years; not renewable. *Number:* 35,000–45,000. *Amount:* up to $1900.

Eligibility Requirements: Applicant must be enrolled or expecting to enroll full- or part-time at a two-year or four-year or technical institution or university; resident of Kentucky and studying in Kentucky. Available to U.S. citizens.

Application Requirements: FAFSA. *Deadline:* continuous.

Contact: Sheila Roe, Program Coordinator
Kentucky Higher Education Assistance Authority (KHEAA)
PO Box 798
Frankfort, KY 40602-0798
Phone: 800-928-8926 Ext. 67393
Fax: 502-696-7373
E-mail: sroe@kheaa.com

GO HIGHER GRANT

Need-based grant for adult students pursuing their first undergraduate degree. Completion of the FAFSA is required.

Award: Grant for use in freshman, sophomore, junior, or senior years; not renewable. *Number:* 100–300. *Amount:* up to $1000.

Eligibility Requirements: Applicant must be age 24 and over; enrolled or expecting to enroll full- or part-time at a two-year or four-year or technical institution or university; resident of Kentucky and studying in Kentucky. Available to U.S. citizens.

Application Requirements: Application, FAFSA. *Deadline:* continuous.

Contact: Sheila Roe, Grant Program Coordinator
Kentucky Higher Education Assistance Authority (KHEAA)
PO Box 798
Frankfort, KY 40206-0798
Phone: 800-928-8926 Ext. 67393
E-mail: sroe@kheaa.com

KENTUCKY EDUCATIONAL EXCELLENCE SCHOLARSHIP (KEES)

Annual award based on yearly high school GPA and highest ACT or SAT score received by high school graduation. Awards are renewable, if required cumulative GPA is maintained at a Kentucky postsecondary school. Must be a Kentucky resident, and a graduate of a Kentucky high school.

Award: Scholarship for use in freshman, sophomore, junior, or senior years; renewable. *Number:* 65,000–68,000. *Amount:* $125–$2500.

Eligibility Requirements: Applicant must be high school student; planning to enroll or expecting to enroll full- or part-time at a two-year or four-year or technical institution or university; resident of Kentucky and studying in Kentucky. Applicant must have 2.5 GPA or higher. Available to U.S. citizens.

Application Requirements: Test scores, data submitted by KY high schools. *Deadline:* continuous.

Contact: Megan Cummins, KEES Coordinator
Kentucky Higher Education Assistance Authority (KHEAA)
PO Box 798
Frankfort, KY 40602
Phone: 800-928-8926 Ext. 67397
Fax: 502-696-7373
E-mail: mcummins@kheaa.com

KENTUCKY TUITION GRANT (KTG)

Grants available to Kentucky residents who are full-time undergraduates at an independent college within the state. Based on financial need. Must submit FAFSA.

Award: Grant for use in freshman, sophomore, junior, or senior years; not renewable. *Number:* 12,000–13,000. *Amount:* $200–$3000.

Eligibility Requirements: Applicant must be enrolled or expecting to enroll full-time at a two-year or four-year institution or university; resident of Kentucky and studying in Kentucky. Available to U.S. citizens.

Application Requirements: FAFSA. *Deadline:* continuous.

Contact: Sheila Roe, Grant Program Coordinator
Kentucky Higher Education Assistance Authority (KHEAA)
PO Box 798
Frankfort, KY 40602-0798
Phone: 800-928-8926 Ext. 67393
Fax: 502-696-7373
E-mail: sroe@kheaa.com

KENTUCKY TOUCHSTONE ENERGY COOPERATIVES

http://www.ekpc.coop

TOUCHSTONE ENERGY ALL "A" CLASSIC SCHOLARSHIP

Award of $1000 for senior student in good standing at a Kentucky high school which is a member of the All Classic. Applicant must be a U.S. citizen and must plan to attend a postsecondary institution in Kentucky in the upcoming year as a full-time student and be drug free.

Award: Scholarship for use in freshman year; not renewable. *Number:* 12. *Amount:* $1000.

Eligibility Requirements: Applicant must be high school student; planning to enroll or expecting to enroll full-time at a two-year or four-year or technical institution or university; resident of Kentucky and studying in Kentucky. Available to U.S. citizens.

Application Requirements: Application, essay, photo, references, transcript. *Deadline:* December 3.

Contact: David Cowden, Chairperson, Scholarship Committee
Kentucky Touchstone Energy Cooperatives
1320 Lincoln Road
Lewisport, KY 42351
Phone: 859-744-4812
E-mail: allaclassic@alltel.net

KOREAN AMERICAN SCHOLARSHIP FOUNDATION

http://www.kasf.org/

KOREAN-AMERICAN SCHOLARSHIP FOUNDATION EASTERN REGION SCHOLARSHIPS
• *See page 668*

KOREAN-AMERICAN SCHOLARSHIP FOUNDATION NORTHEASTERN REGION SCHOLARSHIPS
• *See page 669*

KOREAN-AMERICAN SCHOLARSHIP FOUNDATION SOUTHERN REGION SCHOLARSHIPS
• *See page 669*

KOREAN-AMERICAN SCHOLARSHIP FOUNDATION WESTERN REGION SCHOLARSHIPS
• *See page 669*

KOSCIUSZKO FOUNDATION

http://www.kosciuszkofoundation.org/

MASSACHUSETTS FEDERATION OF POLISH WOMEN'S CLUBS SCHOLARSHIPS
• *See page 669*

POLISH NATIONAL ALLIANCE OF BROOKLYN USA INC. SCHOLARSHIPS
• *See page 669*

LEE-JACKSON EDUCATIONAL FOUNDATION

http://www.lee-jackson.org/

LEE-JACKSON EDUCATIONAL FOUNDATION SCHOLARSHIP COMPETITION

Essay contest for junior and senior Virginia high school students. Must demonstrate appreciation for the exemplary character and soldierly virtues of Generals Robert E. Lee and Thomas J. "Stonewall" Jackson. Three one-time awards of $1000 in each of Virginia's eight regions. A bonus scholarship of $1000 will be awarded to the author of the best essay in each of the eight regions. An additional award of $8000 will go to the essay judged the best in the state.

Award: Scholarship for use in freshman, sophomore, junior, or senior years; not renewable. *Number:* 27. *Amount:* $1000–$10,000.

Eligibility Requirements: Applicant must be high school student; planning to enroll or expecting to enroll full-time at a four-year institution or university; resident of Virginia and must have an interest in writing. Available to U.S. citizens.

Application Requirements: Application, applicant must enter a contest, essay, transcript. *Deadline:* December 21.

Contact: Stephanie Leech, Administrator
Lee-Jackson Educational Foundation
PO Box 8121
Charlottesville, VA 22906
Phone: 434-977-1861
E-mail: salp_leech@yahoo.com

LIBERTY GRAPHICS INC.

http://www.lgtees.com/

ANNUAL LIBERTY GRAPHICS ART CONTEST

One-time scholarship to the successful student who submits the winning artwork depicting appreciation of the natural environment of Maine. Applicants must be residents of Maine and be a high school senior. Original works in traditional flat media are the required format. Photography, sculpture and computer-generated work will not be considered. Multiple submissions are allowed.

Award: Prize for use in freshman year; not renewable. *Number:* 1. *Amount:* $1000.

Eligibility Requirements: Applicant must be high school student; planning to enroll or expecting to enroll full- or part-time at a two-year or four-year or technical institution or university and resident of Maine. Available to U.S. citizens.

Application Requirements: Application, applicant must enter a contest, self-addressed stamped envelope, artwork in keeping with the contest theme. *Deadline:* March 21.

Contact: Mr. Jay Sproul, Scholarship Coordinator
Liberty Graphics Inc.
44 Main Street, PO Box 5
Liberty, ME 04949
Phone: 207-589-4596
Fax: 207-589-4415
E-mail: jay@lgtees.com

LINCOLN COMMUNITY FOUNDATION

http://www.lcf.org/

BRENDA BROWN DESATNICK MEMORIAL SCHOLARSHIP

Applicants must be a former graduate of any high school in the United States. Must plan to attend any qualified, regionally accredited two- or four-year college or university. Preference will be given to women over the age of 25 who reside in Lincoln/Lancaster County in Nebraska. Applicants must show interest in becoming self-supporting and independent and demonstrate financial need. No criteria related to field of study.

Award: Scholarship for use in freshman, sophomore, junior, senior, graduate, or postgraduate years; not renewable. *Number:* 1. *Amount:* $500–$800.

Eligibility Requirements: Applicant must be enrolled or expecting to enroll full-time at a two-year or four-year institution or university; female and resident of Nebraska. Available to U.S. citizens.

Application Requirements: Application, essay, financial need analysis, references. *Deadline:* June 1.

Contact: Sonya Brakeman, Grants/Scholarships Coordinator
Lincoln Community Foundation
215 Centennial Mall South, Suite 100
Lincoln, NE 68508
Phone: 402-474-2345
Fax: 402-476-8532
E-mail: sonyab@lcf.org

GEORGE L. WATTERS/NEBRASKA PETROLEUM MARKETERS ASSOCIATION SCHOLARSHIP

• See page 576

HARRY RICHARDSON-CEDARS SCHOLARSHIP

Scholarship for individuals with a GED or have been a recipient of any service offered by Cedars Youth Services in Lincoln, Nebraska. Applicants must demonstrate financial need and ability to complete coursework. Recipients must be high school graduating seniors or first year college students.

Award: Scholarship for use in freshman, sophomore, junior, or senior years; not renewable. *Number:* 1. *Amount:* $1000.

Eligibility Requirements: Applicant must be enrolled or expecting to enroll full-time at a two-year or four-year institution or university and resident of Nebraska. Available to U.S. citizens.

Application Requirements: Application, essay, references. *Deadline:* April 1.

Contact: Sonya Brakeman, Grants/Scholarships Coordinator
Lincoln Community Foundation
215 Centennial Mall South, Suite 100
Lincoln, NE 68508
Phone: 402-474-2345
Fax: 402-476-8532
E-mail: sonyab@lcf.org

JENNINGS AND BEULAH HAGGERTY SCHOLARSHIP

Scholarship for graduating seniors from public or private high schools in Lincoln, NE area. Must be in the top third of graduating class, and enroll in a two- or four-year institution in Nebraska. Must demonstrate financial need and academic achievement.

Award: Scholarship for use in freshman year; not renewable. *Number:* 10–20. *Amount:* $500–$1000.

Eligibility Requirements: Applicant must be high school student; planning to enroll or expecting to enroll full-time at a two-year or four-year or technical institution or university; resident of Nebraska and studying in Nebraska. Applicant must have 3.0 GPA or higher. Available to U.S. citizens.

Application Requirements: Application, essay, financial need analysis, interview, references, test scores, transcript. *Deadline:* July 1.

Contact: Sonya Brakeman, Grants/Scholarships Coordinator
Lincoln Community Foundation
215 Centennial Mall South, Suite 100
Lincoln, NE 68508
Phone: 402-474-2345
Fax: 402-476-8532
E-mail: sonyab@lcf.org

NEBRASKA RURAL SCHOOLS SCHOLARSHIP

Multi-scholarships available to current high school seniors or graduates of a rural high school in Nebraska who rank in the top ten percent of their high school graduating class, or are college students with a 3.5 GPA or better. Applicants attending a university, college or community college in Nebraska are eligible to apply. See web site for application http://www.lcf.org.

Award: Scholarship for use in freshman, sophomore, junior, or senior years; renewable. *Number:* 4. *Amount:* $500–$2000.

Eligibility Requirements: Applicant must be enrolled or expecting to enroll full-time at a four-year institution or university; resident of Nebraska and studying in Nebraska. Applicant must have 3.5 GPA or higher. Available to U.S. citizens.

Application Requirements: Application, essay, financial need analysis, test scores, transcript. *Deadline:* August 1.

Contact: Sonya Brakeman, Grants/Scholarships Coordinator
Lincoln Community Foundation
215 Centennial Mall South, Suite 100
Lincoln, NE 68508
Phone: 402-474-2345
Fax: 402-476-8532
E-mail: sonyab@lcf.org

NORMAN AND RUTH GOOD EDUCATIONAL ENDOWMENT

Multi-scholarships available to current college students attending private colleges in Nebraska with junior or senior standing. Must have a 3.5 GPA or better. See web site for application http://www.lcf.org.

Award: Scholarship for use in junior or senior years; renewable. *Number:* 10–15. *Amount:* $500–$2000.

Eligibility Requirements: Applicant must be enrolled or expecting to enroll full-time at a four-year institution or university and studying in Nebraska. Applicant must have 3.5 GPA or higher. Available to U.S. citizens.

Application Requirements: Application, test scores, transcript. *Deadline:* April 15.

Contact: Sonya Brakeman, Grants/Scholarships Coordinator
Lincoln Community Foundation
215 Centennial Mall South, Suite 100
Lincoln, NE 68508
Phone: 402-474-2345
Fax: 402-476-8532
E-mail: sonyab@lcf.org

RESIDENCE

P.G. RICHARDSON MASONIC MEMORIAL SCHOLARSHIP
• *See page 549*

THOMAS C. WOODS, JR. MEMORIAL SCHOLARSHIP
• *See page 576*

WHITE MEMORIAL SCHOLARSHIP

Applicants must be current graduating seniors or former graduates of any high school in Nebraska. Preference will be given to those students graduating from high schools in Lincoln, Lyons or Fairbury high schools in Nebraska. Applicants must demonstrate financial need. Preference will be given to first year college students. Scholarship may be renewed for a period of up to four years provided the applicant continues to meet the criteria.

Award: Scholarship for use in freshman year; renewable. *Number:* 3. *Amount:* $500–$1000.

Eligibility Requirements: Applicant must be high school student; planning to enroll or expecting to enroll full-time at a two-year or four-year institution or university and resident of Nebraska. Available to U.S. citizens.

Application Requirements: Application, essay, financial need analysis, test scores, transcript. *Deadline:* March 15.

Contact: Sonya Brakeman, Grants/Scholarships Coordinator
Lincoln Community Foundation
215 Centennial Mall South, Suite 100
Lincoln, NE 68508
Phone: 402-474-2345
Fax: 402-476-8532
E-mail: sonyab@lcf.org

WILLIAM B. AND VIRGINIA S. ROLOFSON SCHOLARSHIP
• *See page 698*

LOS ALAMOS NATIONAL LABORATORY FOUNDATION

http://www.lanlfoundation.org/

LOS ALAMOS EMPLOYEES' SCHOLARSHIP

Scholarship supports students in Northern New Mexico who are pursuing undergraduate degrees in fields that will serve the region. Financial need, diversity, and regional representation are integral components of the selections process. Applicant should be a permanent resident of Northern New Mexico with at least a 3.25 cumulative GPA and 19 ACT or 930 SAT score.

Award: Scholarship for use in freshman, sophomore, junior, or senior years; renewable. *Number:* 50. *Amount:* $1000–$30,000.

Eligibility Requirements: Applicant must be enrolled or expecting to enroll full- or part-time at a two-year or four-year institution or university and resident of New Mexico. Available to U.S. and non-U.S. citizens.

Application Requirements: Application, essay, photo, references, test scores, transcript. *Deadline:* January 22.

Contact: Tony Fox, Program Officer
Los Alamos National Laboratory Foundation
1302 Calle de la Merced, Suite A
Espanola, NM 87532
Phone: 505-753-8890 Ext. 16
Fax: 505-753-8915
E-mail: tfox@lanlfoundation.org

LOS PADRES FOUNDATION

http://www.lospadresfoundation.com/

COLLEGE TUITION ASSISTANCE PROGRAM
• *See page 670*

SECOND CHANCE SCHOLARSHIPS
• *See page 670*

LOUISIANA DEPARTMENT OF VETERAN AFFAIRS

http://www.vetaffairs.com/

LOUISIANA DEPARTMENT OF VETERANS AFFAIRS STATE AID PROGRAM
• *See page 639*

LOUISIANA NATIONAL GUARD, JOINT TASK FORCE LA

http://www.la.ngb.army.mil/

LOUISIANA NATIONAL GUARD STATE TUITION EXEMPTION PROGRAM
• *See page 620*

LOUISIANA OFFICE OF STUDENT FINANCIAL ASSISTANCE

http://www.osfa.la.gov/

LEVERAGING EDUCATIONAL ASSISTANCE PROGRAM (LEAP)/SPECIAL LEVERAGING EDUCATIONAL ASSISTANCE PROGRAM (SLEAP)

Apply by completing the FAFSA each year. Must be a resident of Louisiana and must be attending an institution in Louisiana. Institution the student plans to attend must recommend student for award. When you submit the FAFSA, you have automatically applied for all four levels of TOPS, for the LA LEAP/SLEAP Grant, for Louisiana Guaranteed Loans, and for Federal Pell Grants and Go Grants. Please do not send separate letters of application to the TOPS office.

Award: Grant for use in freshman, sophomore, junior, or senior years; renewable. *Number:* 4810. *Amount:* $200–$2000.

Eligibility Requirements: Applicant must be enrolled or expecting to enroll full-time at a two-year or four-year or technical institution or university; resident of Louisiana and studying in Louisiana. Available to U.S. citizens.

Application Requirements: Application, financial need analysis, FAFSA. *Deadline:* July 1.

Contact: Bonnie Lavergne, Public Information
Louisiana Office of Student Financial Assistance
PO Box 91202
Baton Rouge, LA 70821-9202
Phone: 800-259-5626 Ext. 1012
Fax: 225-612-6508
E-mail: custserv@osfa.la.gov

TAYLOR OPPORTUNITY PROGRAM FOR STUDENTS–HONORS LEVEL

Program awards 8 semesters or 12 terms of tuition to any Louisiana State postsecondary institution plus $400 stipend per semester. Program awards 8 semesters or 12 terms of an amount equal to the weighted average public tuition to students attending a LAICU (Louisiana Association of Independent Colleges and Universities) institution plus $400 stipend per semester. Program awards 8 semesters or 12 terms of an amount equal to the weighted average public tuition to two out-of-state Institutions for Hearing Impaired Students: Gallaudet University and Rochester Institute of Technology plus $400 stipend per semester. Program awards $1120 per year to Approved Proprietary and Cosmetology schools. When you submit the FAFSA, you have automatically applied for all four levels of TOPS, for the LA LEAP/SLEAP Grant, for Louisiana Guaranteed Loans, and for Federal Pell Grants and Go Grants. Please do not send separate letters of application to the TOPS office.

Award: Scholarship for use in freshman, sophomore, junior, or senior years; renewable. *Number:* 7522. *Amount:* $680–$5106.

Eligibility Requirements: Applicant must be enrolled or expecting to enroll full-time at a two-year or four-year or technical institution or university; resident of Louisiana and studying in Louisiana. Applicant must have 3.0 GPA or higher. Available to U.S. citizens.

Application Requirements: Application, test scores, transcript. *Deadline:* July 1.

754   www.facebook.com/pay4undergrad

Contact: Public Information
Louisiana Office of Student Financial Assistance
PO Box 91202
Baton Rouge, LA 70821-9202
Phone: 800-259-5626 Ext. 1012
Fax: 225-208-1496
E-mail: custserv@osfa.la.gov

TAYLOR OPPORTUNITY PROGRAM FOR STUDENTS–OPPORTUNITY LEVEL

Program awards 8 semesters or 12 terms of tuition to any Louisiana State postsecondary institution. Program awards 8 semesters or 12 terms of an amount equal to the weighted average public tuition to students attending a LAICU (Louisiana Association of Independent Colleges and Universities) institution. Program awards 8 semesters or 12 terms of an amount equal to the weighted average public tuition to two out-of-state Institutions for Hearing Impaired Students: Gallaudet University and Rochester Institute of Technology. Program awards $1120 per year to Approved Proprietary and Cosmetology schools. When you submit the FAFSA, you have automatically applied for all four levels of TOPS, for the LA LEAP/SLEAP Grant, for Louisiana Guaranteed Loans, and for Federal Pell Grants and Go Grants. Please do not send separate letters of application to the TOPS office.

Award: Scholarship for use in freshman, sophomore, junior, or senior years; renewable. *Number:* 23,645. *Amount:* $280–$4306.

Eligibility Requirements: Applicant must be enrolled or expecting to enroll full-time at a two-year or four-year or technical institution or university; resident of Louisiana and studying in Louisiana. Applicant must have 2.5 GPA or higher. Available to U.S. citizens.

Application Requirements: Application, test scores, transcript. *Deadline:* July 1.

Contact: Public Information
Louisiana Office of Student Financial Assistance
PO Box 91202
Baton Rouge, LA 70821-9202
Phone: 800-259-5626 Ext. 1012
Fax: 225-208-1496
E-mail: custserv@osfa.la.gov

TAYLOR OPPORTUNITY PROGRAM FOR STUDENTS–PERFORMANCE LEVEL

Program awards 8 semesters or 12 terms of tuition to any Louisiana State postsecondary institution plus $200 stipend per semester. Program awards 8 semesters or 12 terms of an amount equal to the weighted average public tuition to students attending a LAICU (Louisiana Association of Independent Colleges and Universities) institution plus $200 stipend per semester. Program awards 8 semesters or 12 terms of an amount equal to the weighted average public tuition to two out-of-state Institutions for Hearing Impaired Students: Gallaudet University and Rochester Institute of Technology plus $200 stipend per semester. Program awards $1120 per year to Approved Proprietary and Cosmetology schools. When you submit the FAFSA, you have automatically applied for all four levels of TOPS, for the LA LEAP/SLEAP Grant, for Louisiana Guaranteed Loans, and for Federal Pell Grants and Go Grants. Please do not send separate letters of application to the TOPS office.

Award: Scholarship for use in freshman, sophomore, junior, or senior years; renewable. *Number:* 9621. *Amount:* $480–$4706.

Eligibility Requirements: Applicant must be enrolled or expecting to enroll full-time at a two-year or four-year or technical institution or university; resident of Louisiana and studying in Louisiana. Applicant must have 3.0 GPA or higher. Available to U.S. citizens.

Application Requirements: Application, test scores, transcript. *Deadline:* July 1.

Contact: Public Information
Louisiana Office of Student Financial Assistance
PO Box 91202
Baton Rouge, LA 70821-9202
Phone: 800-259-5626 Ext. 1012
Fax: 225-208-1496
E-mail: custserv@osfa.la.gov

TAYLOR OPPORTUNITY PROGRAM FOR STUDENTS–TECH LEVEL

Program awards an amount equal to tuition for up to 4 semesters and two summers of technical training at a Louisiana postsecondary institution that offers a vocational or technical education certificate or diploma program, or a non-academic degree program; or up to $1120 to an approved Proprietary or Cosmetology school. Must have completed the TOPS Opportunity core curriculum or the TOPS Tech core curriculum, must have achieved a 2.50 grade point average over the core curriculum only, and must have achieved an ACT score of 17 or an SAT score of 810. Program awards an amount equal to the weighted average public tuition for technical programs to students attending a LAICU private institution for technical training. When you submit the FAFSA, you have automatically applied for all four levels of TOPS, for the LA LEAP/SLEAP Grant, for Louisiana Guaranteed Loans, and for Federal Pell Grants and Go Grants. Please do not send separate letters of application to the TOPS office.

Award: Scholarship for use in freshman or sophomore years; renewable. *Number:* 1785. *Amount:* $280–$3021.

Eligibility Requirements: Applicant must be enrolled or expecting to enroll full-time at a technical institution; resident of Louisiana and studying in Louisiana. Applicant must have 2.5 GPA or higher. Available to U.S. citizens.

Application Requirements: Application, test scores, transcript, ACT of 17 OR SAT of 810. *Deadline:* July 1.

Contact: Public Information
Louisiana Office of Student Financial Assistance
PO Box 91202
Baton Rouge, LA 70821-9202
Phone: 800-259-5626 Ext. 1012
Fax: 225-208-1496
E-mail: custserv@osfa.la.gov

LOUISIANA STATE DEPARTMENT OF EDUCATION

http://www.doe.state.la.us/

ROBERT C. BYRD HONORS SCHOLARSHIP-LOUISIANA

Applicant must have earned a high school diploma or equivalent (GED) in Louisiana in the same academic year in which the scholarship is to be awarded. Minimum 3.5 GPA and an ACT composite score of 23 or SAT critical reading and math score of 970. Must be a U.S. citizen and legal resident of Louisiana. Total number of awards vary each year.

Award: Scholarship for use in freshman, sophomore, junior, or senior years; renewable.

Eligibility Requirements: Applicant must be enrolled or expecting to enroll full-time at a four-year institution or university and resident of Louisiana. Applicant must have 3.5 GPA or higher. Available to U.S. citizens.

Application Requirements: Application, essay, test scores, transcript, selective service form. *Deadline:* March 10.

Contact: Shan Davis, Scholarship Coordinator
Louisiana State Department of Education
PO Box 94064
Baton Rouge, LA 70804-9064
Phone: 225-342-5849
E-mail: shan.davis@la.gov

MAINE COMMUNITY COLLEGE SYSTEM

http://www.mccs.me.edu/

EARLY COLLEGE FOR ME

Scholarship for high school students who have not made plans for college but are academically capable of success in college. Recipients are selected by their school principal or Guidance Director. Students must be entering a Maine Community College. Refer to web site http://www.mccs.me.edu/scholarships.html.

Award: Scholarship for use in freshman or sophomore years; renewable. *Number:* 250–500. *Amount:* $2000.

Eligibility Requirements: Applicant must be high school student; planning to enroll or expecting to enroll full-time at a two-year institution; resident of Maine and studying in Maine. Available to U.S. citizens.

Application Requirements: Application, financial need analysis, references, transcript. *Deadline:* varies.

Contact: Charles P. Collins, State Director, Center for Career
Development
Maine Community College System
2 Fort Road
South Portland, ME 04106
Phone: 207-767-5210 Ext. 4115
Fax: 207-767-2542
E-mail: ccollins@mccs.me.edu

OSHER SCHOLARSHIP

Scholarships to students who are Maine residents not currently enrolled in a program at any college or university, have accumulated no more than 24 college credits and qualify for and are accepted into the Associate in Arts in liberal/general studies program.

Award: Scholarship for use in freshman year; not renewable. *Number:* varies. *Amount:* up to $504.

Eligibility Requirements: Applicant must be enrolled or expecting to enroll full-time at a two-year or technical institution; resident of Maine and studying in Maine. Available to U.S. citizens.

Application Requirements: Application. *Deadline:* varies.

Contact: Scholarship Committee
Maine Community College System
323 State Street
Augusta, ME 04330
Phone: 207-629-4000
E-mail: info@mccs.me.edu

MAINE COMMUNITY FOUNDATION, INC.

http://www.mainecf.org/

MAINE COMMUNITY FOUNDATION SCHOLARSHIP PROGRAMS

Various scholarships available for Maine residents attending secondary, post-secondary, and graduate programs. Restrictions and application requirements vary based on specific scholarship. See web site for details http://www.mainecf.org. Deadline varies.

Award: Scholarship for use in freshman, sophomore, junior, or senior years; not renewable. *Number:* 150–700. *Amount:* $500–$5000.

Eligibility Requirements: Applicant must be enrolled or expecting to enroll full- or part-time at a two-year or four-year or technical institution or university and resident of Maine. Available to U.S. citizens.

Application Requirements: Application. *Deadline:* continuous.

Contact: Ms. Amy Pollien, Grants Administration
Maine Community Foundation, Inc.
245 Main Street
Ellsworth, ME 04605
Phone: 207-667-9735
Fax: 207-667-0447
E-mail: apollien@mainecf.org

MAINE DIVISION OF VETERANS SERVICES

http://www.maine.gov/dvem/bvs

VETERANS DEPENDENTS EDUCATIONAL BENEFITS-MAINE

• See page 639

MAINE EDUCATION SERVICES

http://www.mesfoundation.com/

MAINE LEGISLATIVE MEMORIAL SCHOLARSHIP

One-time awards for students going to a two- or four-year degree-granting Maine school. Scholarships are available to graduating high school seniors or full/part-time postsecondary students accepted or enrolled in a Maine college. Graduate students are also eligible.

Award: Scholarship for use in freshman, sophomore, junior, senior, graduate, or postgraduate years; not renewable. *Number:* up to 16. *Amount:* up to $1000.

Eligibility Requirements: Applicant must be enrolled or expecting to enroll full- or part-time at a two-year or four-year or technical institution or university; resident of Maine and studying in Maine. Available to U.S. citizens.

Application Requirements: Application, essay, financial need analysis, references, transcript. *Deadline:* April 16.

Contact: Kim Benjamin, Vice President of Operations
Maine Education Services
131 Presumpscot Street
Portland, ME 04103
Phone: 207-791-3600

MAINE STATE CHAMBER OF COMMERCE SCHOLARSHIP-ADULT LEARNER

One $1500 scholarship is given to an adult learner planning to pursue an education at a two-year, four-year degree granting college. Preference may be to a student attending a Maine college and seeking a degree in a business- or education-related field. Awards are based on an adult being 23 years or older and having legal dependents other than a spouse.

Award: Scholarship for use in freshman, sophomore, junior, or senior years; not renewable. *Number:* up to 1. *Amount:* up to $1500.

Eligibility Requirements: Applicant must be age 23 and over; enrolled or expecting to enroll full- or part-time at a two-year or four-year or technical institution or university and resident of Maine. Available to U.S. citizens.

Application Requirements: Application, essay, financial need analysis, references, transcript. *Deadline:* April 18.

Contact: Kim Benjamin, Vice President of Operations
Maine Education Services
131 Presumpscot Street
Portland, ME 04103
Phone: 207-791-3600

MAINE STATE SOCIETY FOUNDATION OF WASHINGTON, DC INC.

http://www.mainestatesociety.org/

MAINE STATE SOCIETY FOUNDATION SCHOLARSHIP

Scholarship(s) awarded to full-time students enrolled in undergraduate courses at a four-year degree-granting, nonprofit institution in Maine. Must be Maine resident. All inquiries must be accompanied by a self-addressed stamped envelope. Applicant must be 25 or younger.

Award: Scholarship for use in sophomore, junior, or senior years; not renewable. *Number:* 5–10. *Amount:* $1000–$2500.

Eligibility Requirements: Applicant must be age 25 or under; enrolled or expecting to enroll full-time at a four-year institution; resident of Maine and studying in Maine. Applicant must have 3.0 GPA or higher. Available to U.S. citizens.

Application Requirements: Application, essay, self-addressed stamped envelope, transcript. *Deadline:* April 15.

Contact: Hugh Dwelley, Director
Maine State Society Foundation of Washington, DC Inc.
3508 Wilson Street
Fairfax, VA 22030
Phone: 703-352-0846
E-mail: hldwelley@aol.com

MANA DE SAN DIEGO

http://www.sdmana.org/

MANA DE SAN DIEGO SYLVIA CHAVEZ MEMORIAL SCHOLARSHIP

• See page 591

MARYLAND STATE DEPARTMENT OF EDUCATION

http://www.marylandpublicschools.org/

ROBERT C. BYRD HONORS SCHOLARSHIP-MARYLAND

Scholarship amount varies each year, ranging from $1000 to $1500. Amount received is based on the total cost of attendance at each institution of higher education. Awarded on merit basis. Students in the top 1 percent of their graduating class may be nominated by the principal or headmaster. Home schooled students are also encouraged to apply. Must be admitted to an institution of higher education as a full-time student and be a Maryland resident. Nominated students receive the award through a random selection process.

Award: Scholarship for use in freshman, sophomore, junior, or senior years; renewable. *Number:* 114–130. *Amount:* $1000–$1500.

Eligibility Requirements: Applicant must be high school student; planning to enroll or expecting to enroll full-time at a two-year or four-year or technical institution or university and resident of Maryland. Available to U.S. citizens.

Application Requirements: Application, nomination from school principal/headmaster. *Deadline:* April 5.

Contact: William Cappe, Robert C. Byrd Honors Scholarship
Coordinator
Maryland State Department of Education
200 West Baltimore Street
Baltimore, MD 21201
Phone: 410-767-0483
E-mail: wcappe@msde.state.md.us

MARYLAND STATE HIGHER EDUCATION COMMISSION

http://www.mhec.state.md.us/

DELEGATE SCHOLARSHIP PROGRAM-MARYLAND

Delegate scholarships help Maryland residents attending Maryland degree-granting institutions, certain career schools, or nursing diploma schools. May attend out-of-state institution if Maryland Higher Education Commission deems major to be unique and not offered at a Maryland institution. Free Application for Federal Student Aid may be required. Students interested in this program should apply by contacting their legislative district delegate.

Award: Scholarship for use in freshman, sophomore, junior, or senior years; not renewable. *Number:* up to 3500. *Amount:* $200–$8650.

Eligibility Requirements: Applicant must be enrolled or expecting to enroll full- or part-time at a two-year or four-year or technical institution or university; resident of Maryland and studying in Maryland. Available to U.S. citizens.

Application Requirements: Application, FAFSA. *Deadline:* continuous.

Contact: Monica Wheatley, Office of Student Financial Assistance
Maryland State Higher Education Commission
839 Bestgate Road, Suite 400
Annapolis, MD 21401-3013
Phone: 800-974-1024
Fax: 410-260-3200
E-mail: osfamail@mhec.state.md.us

DISTINGUISHED SCHOLAR AWARD-MARYLAND

Renewable award for Maryland students enrolled full-time at Maryland institutions. National Merit Scholar Finalists automatically offered award. Others may qualify for the award in satisfying criteria of a minimum 3.7 GPA or in combination with high test scores, or for Talent in Arts competition in categories of music, drama, dance, or visual arts. Must maintain annual 3.0 GPA in college for award to be renewed.

Award: Scholarship for use in freshman, sophomore, junior, or senior years; renewable. *Number:* up to 1400. *Amount:* up to $3000.

Eligibility Requirements: Applicant must be high school student; planning to enroll or expecting to enroll full-time at a two-year or four-year institution or university; resident of Maryland and studying in Maryland. Available to U.S. citizens.

Application Requirements: Application, test scores, transcript.

Contact: Tamika McKelvin, Program Administrator
Maryland State Higher Education Commission
839 Bestgate Road, Suite 400
Annapolis, MD 21401-3013
Phone: 410-260-4546
Fax: 410-260-3200
E-mail: tmckelvi@mhec.state.md.us

DISTINGUISHED SCHOLAR COMMUNITY COLLEGE TRANSFER PROGRAM

Scholarship available for Maryland residents who have completed 60 credit hours or an associate degree at a Maryland community college and are transferring to a Maryland four-year institution.

Award: Scholarship for use in freshman or sophomore years; renewable. *Number:* 127. *Amount:* $3000.

Eligibility Requirements: Applicant must be enrolled or expecting to enroll full-time at a two-year institution; resident of Maryland and studying in Maryland. Available to U.S. citizens.

Application Requirements: Application, transcript. *Deadline:* March 1.

Contact: Maura Sappington, Program Manager
Maryland State Higher Education Commission
839 Bestgate Road, Suite 400
Annapolis, MD 21401-3013
Phone: 410-260-4569
Fax: 410-260-3203
E-mail: msapping@mhec.state.md.us

EDWARD T. CONROY MEMORIAL SCHOLARSHIP PROGRAM

• *See page 591*

HOWARD P. RAWLINGS EDUCATIONAL EXCELLENCE AWARDS EDUCATIONAL ASSISTANCE GRANT

Award for Maryland residents accepted or enrolled in a full-time undergraduate degree or certificate program at a Maryland institution or hospital nursing school. Must submit financial aid form by March 1. Must earn 2.0 GPA in college to maintain award.

Award: Grant for use in freshman, sophomore, junior, or senior years; renewable. *Number:* 15,000–30,000. *Amount:* $400–$2700.

Eligibility Requirements: Applicant must be enrolled or expecting to enroll full-time at a two-year or four-year institution or university; resident of Maryland and studying in Maryland. Available to U.S. citizens.

Application Requirements: Application, financial need analysis. *Deadline:* March 1.

Contact: Office of Student Financial Assistance
Maryland State Higher Education Commission
839 Bestgate Road, Suite 400
Annapolis, MD 21401-3013
Phone: 800-974-1024
Fax: 410-260-3200
E-mail: osfamail@mhec.state.md.us

HOWARD P. RAWLINGS EDUCATIONAL EXCELLENCE AWARDS GUARANTEED ACCESS GRANT

Award for Maryland resident enrolling full-time in an undergraduate program at a Maryland institution. Must be under 21 at time of first award and begin college within one year of completing high school in Maryland with a minimum 2.5 GPA. Must have an annual family income less than 130 percent of the federal poverty level guideline.

Award: Grant for use in freshman, sophomore, junior, or senior years; renewable. *Number:* up to 1000. *Amount:* $400–$14,800.

Eligibility Requirements: Applicant must be age 21 or under; enrolled or expecting to enroll full-time at a two-year or four-year institution or university; resident of Maryland and studying in Maryland. Applicant must have 3.5 GPA or higher. Available to U.S. citizens.

Application Requirements: Application, financial need analysis, transcript. *Deadline:* March 1.

Contact: Theresa Lowe, Office of Student Financial Assistance
Maryland State Higher Education Commission
839 Bestgate Road, Suite 400
Annapolis, MD 21401-3013
Phone: 410-260-4555
Fax: 410-260-3200
E-mail: osfamail@mhec.state.md.us

J.F. TOLBERT MEMORIAL STUDENT GRANT PROGRAM

Awards of $500 granted to Maryland residents attending a private career school in Maryland. The scholarship deadline continues.

Award: Grant for use in freshman or sophomore years; not renewable. *Number:* 522. *Amount:* $500.

Eligibility Requirements: Applicant must be enrolled or expecting to enroll full-time at a technical institution; resident of Maryland and studying in Maryland. Available to U.S. citizens.

Application Requirements: Application, financial need analysis. *Deadline:* continuous.

PART-TIME GRANT PROGRAM-MARYLAND

Funds provided to Maryland colleges and universities. Eligible students must be enrolled on a part-time basis (6 to 11 credits) in an undergraduate degree program. Must demonstrate financial need and also be Maryland resident. Contact financial aid office at institution for more information.

Award: Grant for use in freshman, sophomore, junior, or senior years; renewable. *Number:* 1800–9000. *Amount:* $200–$1500.

Eligibility Requirements: Applicant must be enrolled or expecting to enroll part-time at a two-year or four-year institution or university; resident of Maryland and studying in Maryland. Available to U.S. citizens.

Application Requirements: Application, financial need analysis. *Deadline:* March 1.

Contact: Monica Wheatley, Program Manager
Maryland State Higher Education Commission
839 Bestgate Road, Suite 400
Annapolis, MD 21401
Phone: 410-260-4560
Fax: 410-260-3202
E-mail: mwheatle@mhec.state.md.us

SENATORIAL SCHOLARSHIPS-MARYLAND

Renewable award for Maryland residents attending a Maryland degree-granting institution, nursing diploma school, or certain private career schools. May be used out-of-state only if Maryland Higher Education Commission deems major to be unique and not offered at Maryland institution. The scholarship value is $400 to $7000.

Award: Scholarship for use in freshman, sophomore, junior, or senior years; renewable. *Number:* up to 7000. *Amount:* $400–$7000.

Eligibility Requirements: Applicant must be enrolled or expecting to enroll full- or part-time at a two-year or four-year or technical institution or university; resident of Maryland and studying in Maryland. Available to U.S. citizens.

Application Requirements: Application, financial need analysis, test scores. *Deadline:* March 1.

Contact: Monica Wheatley, Office of Student Financial Assistance
Maryland State Higher Education Commission
839 Bestgate Road, Suite 400
Annapolis, MD 21401-3013
Phone: 800-974-1024
Fax: 410-260-3200
E-mail: osfamail@mhec.state.md.us

TUITION WAIVER FOR FOSTER CARE RECIPIENTS

Applicant must be a high school graduate or GED recipient and under the age of 21. Must either have resided in a foster care home in Maryland at the time of high school graduation or GED reception, or until 14th birthday, and been adopted after 14th birthday. Applicant, if status approved, will be exempt from paying tuition and mandatory fees at a public college in Maryland.

Award: Grant for use in freshman, sophomore, junior, senior, or graduate years; renewable. *Number:* varies. *Amount:* varies.

Eligibility Requirements: Applicant must be age 21 or under; enrolled or expecting to enroll full- or part-time at a two-year or four-year institution or university; resident of Maryland and studying in Maryland. Available to U.S. citizens.

Application Requirements: Application, financial need analysis, must inquire at financial aid office of schools. *Deadline:* March 1.

Contact: Robert Parker, Director
Maryland State Higher Education Commission
839 Bestgate Road, Suite 400
Annapolis, MD 21401-3013
Phone: 410-260-4558
E-mail: rparker@mhec.state.md.us

VETERANS OF THE AFGHANISTAN AND IRAQ CONFLICTS SCHOLARSHIP PROGRAM

• *See page 639*

WORKFORCE SHORTAGE STUDENT ASSISTANCE GRANT PROGRAM

Scholarship of $4000 available to students who will be required to major in specific areas and will be obligated to serve in the state of Maryland after completion of degree.

Award: Scholarship for use in freshman, sophomore, junior, or senior years; renewable. *Number:* 1300. *Amount:* $4000.

Eligibility Requirements: Applicant must be enrolled or expecting to enroll full- or part-time at a two-year or four-year institution or university; resident of Maryland and studying in Maryland. Available to U.S. citizens.

Application Requirements: Application, essay, financial need analysis, resume, references, transcript, certain majors require additional documentation. *Deadline:* July 1.

Contact: Maura Sappington, Program Manager
Maryland State Higher Education Commission
839 Bestgate Road, Suite 400
Annapolis, MD 21401-3013
Phone: 410-260-4569
Fax: 410-260-3203
E-mail: msapping@mhec.state.md.us

MASSACHUSETTS AFL-CIO

http://www.massaflcio.org/

MASSACHUSETTS AFL-CIO SCHOLARSHIP

Scholarships to union members, their children/stepchildren, grandchildren, nieces, nephews, and non-union Massachusetts high school seniors.

Award: Scholarship for use in freshman year; not renewable. *Number:* 100–150. *Amount:* $250–$12,000.

Eligibility Requirements: Applicant must be high school student; planning to enroll or expecting to enroll full-time at a four-year institution or university; resident of Massachusetts and studying in Massachusetts. Available to U.S. citizens.

Application Requirements: Application. *Deadline:* December 21.

Contact: Jackie Bergantino, Scholarship Administrator
Massachusetts AFL-CIO
389 Main Street, Suite 101
Malden, MA 02148
Phone: 781-324-8230
Fax: 781-324-8225
E-mail: jbergantino@massaflcio.org

MASSACHUSETTS DEPARTMENT OF EDUCATION

http://www.doe.mass.edu/

ROBERT C. BYRD HONORS SCHOLARSHIP-MASSACHUSETTS

Scholarship for high school senior who is a resident of Massachusetts for at least one year prior to the beginning of the academic year he/she will enter college. Must have applied or been accepted to an accredited institution of higher education and be a U.S. citizen, national or permanent resident.

Award: Scholarship for use in freshman year; renewable. *Number:* varies. *Amount:* $1500.

Eligibility Requirements: Applicant must be high school student; planning to enroll or expecting to enroll full-time at a four-year institution or university and resident of Massachusetts. Applicant must have 3.5 GPA or higher. Available to U.S. citizens.

Application Requirements: Application, transcript. *Deadline:* June 1.

Contact: Sally Teixeira, Scholarship Coordinator
Massachusetts Department of Education
350 Main Street
Malden, MA 02148-5023
Phone: 781-338-6304
E-mail: steixeira@doe.mass.edu

MASSACHUSETTS OFFICE OF STUDENT FINANCIAL ASSISTANCE

http://www.osfa.mass.edu/

AGNES M. LINDSAY SCHOLARSHIP

Scholarships for students with demonstrated financial need who are from rural areas of Massachusetts and attend public institutions of higher education in Massachusetts. Deadline varies.

Award: Scholarship for use in freshman, sophomore, junior, or senior years; not renewable. *Number:* varies. *Amount:* varies.

Eligibility Requirements: Applicant must be enrolled or expecting to enroll full-time at a two-year or four-year institution or university; resident of Massachusetts and studying in Massachusetts. Available to U.S. citizens.

Application Requirements: Application, financial need analysis. *Deadline:* varies.

Contact: Robert Brun, Director of Scholarships and Grants
Massachusetts Office of Student Financial Assistance
454 Broadway, Suite 200
Revere, MA 02151
Phone: 617-727-9420
Fax: 617-727-0667
E-mail: osfa@osfa.mass.edu

CHRISTIAN A. HERTER MEMORIAL SCHOLARSHIP

Renewable award for Massachusetts residents who are in the tenth and eleventh grades, and whose socio-economic backgrounds and environment may inhibit their ability to attain educational goals. Must exhibit severe personal or family-related difficulties, medical problems, or have overcome a personal obstacle. Provides up to 50 percent of the student's calculated need, as determined by federal methodology, at the college of their choice within the continental United States.

Award: Scholarship for use in freshman year; renewable. *Number:* 25. *Amount:* up to $15,000.

Eligibility Requirements: Applicant must be high school student; planning to enroll or expecting to enroll full-time at a two-year or four-year or technical institution or university and resident of Massachusetts. Applicant must have 2.5 GPA or higher. Available to U.S. citizens.

Application Requirements: Application, driver's license, financial need analysis, interview, references. *Deadline:* March 14.

Contact: Robert Brun, Director of Scholarships and Grants
Massachusetts Office of Student Financial Assistance
454 Broadway, Suite 200
Revere, MA 02151
Phone: 617-727-9420
Fax: 617-727-0667
E-mail: osfa@osfa.mass.edu

DSS ADOPTED CHILDREN TUITION WAIVER

Need-based tuition waiver for Massachusetts residents who are full-time undergraduate students. Must attend a Massachusetts public institution of higher education and be under 24 years of age. File the FAFSA after January 1. Contact school financial aid office for more information.

Award: Scholarship for use in freshman, sophomore, junior, or senior years; renewable. *Number:* varies. *Amount:* varies.

Eligibility Requirements: Applicant must be age 24 or under; enrolled or expecting to enroll full-time at a two-year or four-year institution and resident of Massachusetts. Available to U.S. and non-Canadian citizens.

Application Requirements: Application, financial need analysis, FAFSA. *Deadline:* varies.

Contact: Robert Brun, Director of Scholarships and Grants
Massachusetts Office of Student Financial Assistance
454 Broadway, Suite 200
Revere, MA 02151
Phone: 617-727-9420
Fax: 617-727-0667
E-mail: osfa@osfa.mass.edu

JOHN AND ABIGAIL ADAMS SCHOLARSHIP

Scholarship to reward and inspire student achievement, attract more high-performing students to Massachusetts public higher education, and provide families of college-bound students with financial assistance. Must be a U.S. citizen or an eligible non-citizen. There is no application

process for the scholarship. Students who are eligible will be notified in the fall of their senior year in high school.

Award: Scholarship for use in freshman year; not renewable. *Number:* varies. *Amount:* varies.

Eligibility Requirements: Applicant must be high school student; planning to enroll or expecting to enroll full-time at a two-year or four-year institution or university; resident of Massachusetts and studying in Massachusetts. Applicant must have 3.0 GPA or higher. Available to U.S. citizens.

Application Requirements: *Deadline:* varies.

Contact: Robert Brun, Director of Scholarships and Grants
Massachusetts Office of Student Financial Assistance
454 Broadway, Suite 200
Revere, MA 02151
Phone: 617-727-9420
Fax: 617-727-0667
E-mail: osfa@osfa.mass.edu

MASSACHUSETTS ASSISTANCE FOR STUDENT SUCCESS PROGRAM

Provides need-based financial assistance to Massachusetts residents to attend undergraduate postsecondary institutions in Connecticut, Maine, Massachusetts, New Hampshire, Pennsylvania, Rhode Island, Vermont, and District of Columbia. High school seniors may apply. Expected Family Contribution (EFC) should be $3850. Timely filing of FAFSA required.

Award: Grant for use in freshman, sophomore, junior, or senior years; not renewable. *Number:* 25,000–30,000. *Amount:* $300–$2400.

Eligibility Requirements: Applicant must be enrolled or expecting to enroll full-time at a two-year or four-year or technical institution or university; resident of Massachusetts and studying in Connecticut, District of Columbia, Maine, Massachusetts, New Hampshire, Pennsylvania, Rhode Island, or Vermont. Available to U.S. citizens.

Application Requirements: Financial need analysis, FAFSA. *Deadline:* May 1.

Contact: Robert Brun, Director of Scholarships and Grants
Massachusetts Office of Student Financial Assistance
454 Broadway, Suite 200
Revere, MA 02151
Phone: 617-727-9420
Fax: 617-727-0667
E-mail: osfa@osfa.mass.edu

MASSACHUSETTS CASH GRANT PROGRAM

A need-based grant to assist with mandatory fees and non-state supported tuition. This supplemental award is available to Massachusetts residents, who are undergraduates at public two-year, four-year colleges and universities in Massachusetts. Must file FAFSA before May 1. Contact college financial aid office for information.

Award: Grant for use in freshman, sophomore, junior, or senior years; not renewable. *Number:* varies. *Amount:* varies.

Eligibility Requirements: Applicant must be enrolled or expecting to enroll full-time at a two-year or four-year institution or university and resident of Massachusetts. Available to U.S. citizens.

Application Requirements: Application, financial need analysis, FAFSA. *Deadline:* continuous.

Contact: Robert Brun, Director of Scholarships and Grants
Massachusetts Office of Student Financial Assistance
454 Broadway, Suite 200
Revere, MA 02151
Phone: 617-727-9420
Fax: 617-727-0667
E-mail: osfa@osfa.mass.edu

MASSACHUSETTS GILBERT MATCHING STUDENT GRANT PROGRAM

Grants for permanent Massachusetts residents attending an independent, regionally accredited Massachusetts school or school of nursing full time. Must be U.S. citizen and permanent legal resident of Massachusetts. File the Free Application for Federal Student Aid after January 1. Contact college financial aid office for complete details and deadlines.

Award: Grant for use in freshman, sophomore, junior, or senior years; not renewable. *Number:* varies. *Amount:* $200–$2500.

Eligibility Requirements: Applicant must be enrolled or expecting to enroll full-time at a four-year institution or university; resident of Massachusetts and studying in Massachusetts. Available to U.S. citizens.

Application Requirements: Financial need analysis, FAFSA. *Deadline:* varies.

Contact: Robert Brun, Director of Scholarships and Grants
Massachusetts Office of Student Financial Assistance
454 Broadway, Suite 200
Revere, MA 02151
Phone: 617-727-9420
Fax: 617-727-0667
E-mail: rbrun@osfa.mass.edu

MASSACHUSETTS PART-TIME GRANT PROGRAM

Award for permanent Massachusetts residents who have enrolled part-time for at least one year in a state-approved postsecondary school. The recipient must not have a bachelor's degree. FAFSA must be filed before May 1. Contact college financial aid office for further information.

Award: Grant for use in freshman, sophomore, junior, or senior years; not renewable. *Number:* 200. *Amount:* $200–$1150.

Eligibility Requirements: Applicant must be enrolled or expecting to enroll part-time at a two-year or four-year or technical institution or university and resident of Massachusetts. Available to U.S. citizens.

Application Requirements: Application, financial need analysis, FAFSA. *Deadline:* varies.

Contact: Robert Brun, Director of Scholarships and Grants
Massachusetts Office of Student Financial Assistance
454 Broadway, Suite 200
Revere, MA 02151
Phone: 617-727-9420
Fax: 617-727-0667
E-mail: osfa@osfa.mass.edu

MASSACHUSETTS PUBLIC SERVICE GRANT PROGRAM
• *See page 591*

PAUL TSONGAS SCHOLARSHIP PROGRAM

Scholarship to recognize achievement and reward Massachusetts students, who have graduated from high school within three years with a GPA of 3.75 and a SAT score of at least 1200, and who also meet the one year residency requirement for tuition classification at the state colleges.

Award: Scholarship for use in freshman, sophomore, junior, or senior years; renewable. *Number:* varies. *Amount:* varies.

Eligibility Requirements: Applicant must be enrolled or expecting to enroll full-time at a two-year or four-year institution or university; resident of Massachusetts and studying in Massachusetts. Available to U.S. citizens.

Application Requirements: Application, test scores. *Deadline:* varies.

Contact: Robert Brun, Director of Scholarships and Grants
Massachusetts Office of Student Financial Assistance
454 Broadway, Suite 200
Revere, MA 02151
Phone: 617-727-9420
Fax: 617-727-0667
E-mail: osfa@osfa.mass.edu

MCCURRY FOUNDATION INC.

http://www.mccurryfoundation.org/

MCCURRY FOUNDATION SCHOLARSHIP

Scholarship open to all public high school seniors, with preference given to applicants from Clay, Duval, Nassau, and St. Johns Counties, Florida and from Glynn County, Georgia. Scholarship emphasizes leadership, work ethic, and academic excellence. A minimum GPA of 3.0 is required and family income cannot exceed a maximum of $75,000 (AGI).

Award: Scholarship for use in freshman year; renewable. *Number:* varies. *Amount:* varies.

Eligibility Requirements: Applicant must be high school student; planning to enroll or expecting to enroll full-time at a two-year or four-year or technical institution or university; resident of Florida or Georgia and must have an interest in leadership. Applicant must have 3.0 GPA or higher. Available to U.S. and non-U.S. citizens.

Application Requirements: Application, essay, financial need analysis, interview, resume, references, transcript, report card, tax return. *Deadline:* February 15.

Contact: Scholarship Selection Committee
McCurry Foundation Inc.
4417 Beach Boulevard, Suite 200
Jacksonville, FL 32207
Phone: 904-389-6036
E-mail: mccurryfndn@bellsouth.net

MICHIGAN HIGHER EDUCATION ASSISTANCE AUTHORITY

http://www.michigan.gov/studentaid

MICHIGAN COMPETITIVE SCHOLARSHIP

Renewable awards for Michigan resident to pursue undergraduate study at a Michigan institution. Awards limited to tuition. Must maintain at least a 2.0 grade point average and meet the college's academic progress requirements. Must file Free Application for Federal Student Aid.

Award: Scholarship for use in freshman, sophomore, junior, or senior years; renewable. *Number:* varies. *Amount:* $510–$1610.

Eligibility Requirements: Applicant must be enrolled or expecting to enroll full- or part-time at a two-year or four-year institution or university; resident of Michigan and studying in Michigan. Available to U.S. citizens.

Application Requirements: Application, financial need analysis, test scores. *Deadline:* March 1.

Contact: Scholarship and Grant Director
Michigan Higher Education Assistance Authority
PO Box 30466
Lansing, MI 48909-7962
Phone: 888-447-2687
E-mail: osg@michigan.gov

MICHIGAN TUITION GRANT

Need-based program. Students must be Michigan residents and attend a Michigan private, nonprofit, degree-granting college. Must file the Free Application for Federal Student Aid and meet the college's academic progress requirements.

Award: Grant for use in freshman, sophomore, junior, or senior years; renewable. *Number:* varies. *Amount:* up to $1610.

Eligibility Requirements: Applicant must be enrolled or expecting to enroll full- or part-time at a four-year institution or university; resident of Michigan and studying in Michigan. Available to U.S. citizens.

Application Requirements: Financial need analysis. *Deadline:* July 1.

Contact: Scholarship and Grant Director
Michigan Higher Education Assistance Authority
PO Box 30462
Lansing, MI 48909-7962
Phone: 888-447-2687
E-mail: osg@michigan.gov

TUITION INCENTIVE PROGRAM

Award for Michigan residents who receive or have received Medicaid for required period of time through the Department of Human Services. Scholarship provides two years tuition towards an associate degree at a Michigan college or university and $2000 total assistance for third and fourth years. Must apply before graduating from high school or earning a general education development diploma.

Award: Grant for use in freshman, sophomore, junior, or senior years; renewable. *Number:* varies. *Amount:* varies.

Eligibility Requirements: Applicant must be high school student; planning to enroll or expecting to enroll full- or part-time at a two-year or four-year institution or university; resident of Michigan and studying in Michigan. Available to U.S. citizens.

Application Requirements: Application, Medicaid eligibility for specified period of time. *Deadline:* continuous.

Contact: Scholarship and Grant Director
Michigan Higher Education Assistance Authority
PO Box 30462
Lansing, MI 48909-7962
Phone: 888-447-2687
E-mail: osg@michigan.gov

MIDWESTERN HIGHER EDUCATION COMPACT

http://www.mhec.org/

MIDWEST STUDENT EXCHANGE PROGRAM

Over 140 colleges and universities in Illinois, Indiana, Kansas, Michigan, Minnesota, Missouri, Nebraska, North Dakota, and Wisconsin participate in the MSEP tuition reciprocity program. It is not a scholarship, but for qualified students, provides a discount on out-of-state tuition. Requirements vary by institution. See web site for details http://msep.mhec.org.

Award: Grant for use in freshman, sophomore, junior, senior, graduate, or postgraduate years; renewable. *Number:* varies. *Amount:* varies.

Eligibility Requirements: Applicant must be enrolled or expecting to enroll full- or part-time at a two-year or four-year or technical institution or university; resident of Illinois, Indiana, Kansas, Michigan, Minnesota, Missouri, Nebraska, North Dakota, or Wisconsin and studying in Illinois, Indiana, Kansas, Michigan, Minnesota, Missouri, Nebraska, North Dakota, or Wisconsin. Available to U.S. citizens.

Application Requirements: Application.

Contact: Ms. Amber Cameron, Research Associate
Midwestern Higher Education Compact
1300 South Second Street, Suite 130
Minneapolis, MN 55454-1079
Phone: 612-625-4368
Fax: 612-626-8290
E-mail: amberc@mhec.org

MINNESOTA AFL-CIO

http://www.mnaflcio.org/

BILL PETERSON SCHOLARSHIP
• *See page 549*

MARTIN DUFFY ADULT LEARNER SCHOLARSHIP AWARD
• *See page 549*

MINNESOTA AFL-CIO SCHOLARSHIPS
• *See page 549*

MINNESOTA COMMUNITY FOUNDATION

http://www.mncommunityfoundation.org/

COSS FAMILY FOUNDATION SCHOLARSHIP

Scholarship for graduating high school seniors located in Ramsey or Dakota counties in Minnesota and Meade, Pennington, Hyde, Hand or Buffalo counties in South Dakota. Must demonstrate financial need.

Award: Scholarship for use in freshman year; renewable. *Number:* 20. *Amount:* $3000.

Eligibility Requirements: Applicant must be high school student; planning to enroll or expecting to enroll full- or part-time at a four-year institution or university and resident of Minnesota or South Dakota. Available to U.S. citizens.

Application Requirements: Application, transcript. *Deadline:* March 1.

Contact: Donna Paulson, Administrative Assistant
Minnesota Community Foundation
55 Fifth Street East, Suite 600
St. Paul, MN 55101-1797
Phone: 651-325-4212
Fax: 651-224-9502
E-mail: dkp@mncommunityfoundation.org

JANE RING AND SUE RING-JARVI GIRLS'/WOMEN'S HOCKEY FUND

Two non-renewable scholarships of $2000 awarded to students who have demonstrated leadership ability together with athletic and academic achievement. Applicant must be a senior female student graduating from a high school in Minnesota.

Award: Scholarship for use in freshman year; not renewable. *Number:* 2. *Amount:* $2000.

Eligibility Requirements: Applicant must be high school student; planning to enroll or expecting to enroll full- or part-time at a four-year institution or university; female; resident of Minnesota and must have an interest in athletics/sports or leadership. Applicant must have 3.0 GPA or higher. Available to U.S. citizens.

Application Requirements: Application, references, transcript. *Deadline:* April 20.

Contact: Donna Paulson, Administrative Assistant
Minnesota Community Foundation
55 Fifth Street East, Suite 600
St. Paul, MN 55101-1797
Phone: 651-325-4212
Fax: 651-224-9502
E-mail: dkp@mncommunityfoundation.org

JOSIP AND AGNETE TEMALI SCHOLARSHIP (BIG BROTHERS/BIG SISTERS)
• *See page 549*

RICHARD W. TANNER SCHOLARSHIP

Scholarship for students in junior or senior year in college. Must be a Minnesota resident or have significant ties to a Minnesota Tribe.

Award: Scholarship for use in junior or senior years; not renewable. *Number:* 1. *Amount:* $1000.

Eligibility Requirements: Applicant must be enrolled or expecting to enroll full- or part-time at a four-year institution or university and resident of Minnesota. Available to U.S. citizens.

Application Requirements: Application, essay, financial need analysis, references, transcript, proof of tribal enrollment. *Deadline:* July 1.

Contact: Donna Paulson, Administrative Assistant
Minnesota Community Foundation
55 Fifth Street East, Suite 600
St. Paul, MN 55101-1797
Phone: 651-325-4212
Fax: 651-224-9502
E-mail: dkp@mncommunityfoundation.org

TWO FEATHERS ENDOWMENT SCHOLARSHIP

Scholarship of $1000 to a Minnesota resident or students with significant ties to a Minnesota Tribe.

Award: Scholarship for use in freshman, sophomore, junior, or senior years; not renewable. *Number:* varies. *Amount:* $1000.

Eligibility Requirements: Applicant must be enrolled or expecting to enroll full- or part-time at a four-year institution or university and resident of Minnesota. Available to U.S. citizens.

Application Requirements: Application, essay, resume, references, transcript. *Deadline:* July 1.

Contact: Dayonna Knutson, Program Assistant
Phone: 651-325-4252
E-mail: dlk@mncommunityfoundation.org

WILLIAM C. AND CORINNE J. DIETRICH AWARD

Scholarship for a graduating senior at a Minnesota public high school. Available for both full- or part-time study.

Award: Scholarship for use in freshman year; not renewable. *Number:* 1. *Amount:* $20,000.

Eligibility Requirements: Applicant must be high school student; planning to enroll or expecting to enroll full- or part-time at a four-year institution or university and resident of Minnesota. Available to U.S. and non-Canadian citizens.

Application Requirements: Application, transcript. *Deadline:* April 1.

Contact: Donna Paulson, Administrative Assistant
Minnesota Community Foundation
55 Fifth Street East, Suite 600
St. Paul, MN 55101-1797
Phone: 651-325-4212
Fax: 651-224-9502
E-mail: dkp@mncommunityfoundation.org

MINNESOTA DEPARTMENT OF MILITARY AFFAIRS

http://www.minnesotanationalguard.org/

LEADERSHIP, EXCELLENCE AND DEDICATED SERVICE SCHOLARSHIP
• *See page 591*

MINNESOTA OFFICE OF HIGHER EDUCATION

http://www.getreadyforcollege.org/

MINNESOTA ACADEMIC EXCELLENCE SCHOLARSHIP

Students must demonstrate outstanding ability, achievement, and potential in one of the following subjects: English or creative writing, fine arts, foreign language, math, science, or social science. Implementation depends on the availability of funds, which are to come from the sale of special collegiate license plates. Apply directly to college. Must be a Minnesota resident and study in Minnesota. At public institutions, the scholarship may cover up to the full price of tuition and fees for one academic year. At private institutions, the scholarship may cover either the actual tuition and fees charged by that school, or the tuition and fees in comparable public institutions whichever is less.

Award: Scholarship for use in freshman, sophomore, junior, or senior years; renewable. *Number:* varies. *Amount:* varies.

Eligibility Requirements: Applicant must be enrolled or expecting to enroll full-time at a four-year institution or university; resident of Minnesota; studying in Minnesota and must have an interest in art, English language, foreign language, or writing. Available to U.S. citizens.

Application Requirements: Application, transcript. *Deadline:* continuous.

Contact: Ginny Dodds, Manager
Minnesota Office of Higher Education
1450 Energy Park Drive, Suite 350
St. Paul, MN 55108-5227
Phone: 651-355-0610
E-mail: ginny.dodds@state.mn.us

MINNESOTA ACHIEVE SCHOLARSHIP

Eligible Minnesota high school graduates who complete any one of four sets of courses defined as rigorous earn a one-time scholarship to help pay for college at a public or private university or college in Minnesota. Eligible students who graduated between January 1, 2008 and December 31, 2008 can receive a one-time scholarship of $1,200 available for use within the four years immediately following their high school graduation. Eligible students who graduate after January 1, 2009 and enroll full time (15 credits) in an eligible college or university in the academic year immediately following their high school graduation can receive a one-time scholarship for use in their first academic year ranging from $1,200 to approximately $4,000 depending on financial need and funds availability.

Award: Scholarship for use in freshman year; not renewable. *Number:* varies. *Amount:* up to $1200.

Eligibility Requirements: Applicant must be high school student; planning to enroll or expecting to enroll full-time at a two-year or four-year or technical institution or university; resident of Minnesota and studying in Minnesota. Applicant must have 2.5 GPA or higher. Available to U.S. citizens.

Application Requirements: Application, financial need analysis, test scores, transcript. *Deadline:* continuous.

Contact: Scholarship Staff
Minnesota Office of Higher Education
1450 Energy Park Drive
St. Paul, MN 55108
Phone: 651-642-0567
Fax: 651-642-0675

MINNESOTA GI BILL PROGRAM
• *See page 640*

MINNESOTA INDIAN SCHOLARSHIP
• *See page 671*

MINNESOTA RECIPROCAL AGREEMENT

Renewable tuition waiver for Minnesota residents. Waives all or part of non-resident tuition surcharge at public institutions in Indiana, Iowa, Kansas, Michigan, Missouri, Nebraska, North Dakota, South Dakota, Wisconsin and Manitoba. Deadline: last day of academic term.

Award: Scholarship for use in freshman, sophomore, junior, senior, graduate, or postgraduate years; renewable. *Number:* varies. *Amount:* varies.

Eligibility Requirements: Applicant must be enrolled or expecting to enroll full- or part-time at a two-year or four-year or technical institution or university; resident of Minnesota and studying in Indiana, Iowa, Kansas, Manitoba, Michigan, Missouri, Nebraska, North Dakota, South Dakota, or Wisconsin. Available to U.S. citizens.

Application Requirements: Application. *Deadline:* continuous.

Contact: Jodi Rouland, Program Assistant
Phone: 651-355-0614
Fax: 651-642-0675
E-mail: jodi.rouland@state.mn.us

MINNESOTA STATE GRANT PROGRAM

Need-based grant program available for Minnesota residents attending Minnesota colleges. Student covers 46% of cost with remainder covered by Pell Grant, parent contribution and state grant. Students apply with FAFSA and college administers the program on campus.

Award: Grant for use in freshman, sophomore, junior, or senior years; not renewable. *Number:* 71,000–105,000. *Amount:* $100–$9444.

Eligibility Requirements: Applicant must be age 17 and over; enrolled or expecting to enroll full- or part-time at a two-year or four-year or technical institution or university; resident of Minnesota and studying in Minnesota. Available to U.S. citizens.

Application Requirements: Application, financial need analysis. *Deadline:* continuous.

Contact: Grant Staff
Minnesota Office of Higher Education
1450 Energy Park Drive, Suite 350
St. Paul, MN 55108
Phone: 651-642-0567 Ext. 1

MINNESOTA STATE VETERANS' DEPENDENTS ASSISTANCE PROGRAM
• *See page 640*

POSTSECONDARY CHILD CARE GRANT PROGRAM-MINNESOTA

Grant available for students not receiving MFIP. Based on financial need. Cannot exceed actual child care costs or maximum award chart (based on income). Must be Minnesota resident. For use at Minnesota two- or four-year school, including public technical colleges. Available until student has attended college for the equivalent of four full-time academic years.

Award: Grant for use in freshman, sophomore, junior, or senior years; not renewable. *Number:* varies. *Amount:* $100–$2600.

Eligibility Requirements: Applicant must be enrolled or expecting to enroll full- or part-time at a two-year or four-year or technical institution or university; resident of Minnesota and studying in Minnesota. Available to U.S. citizens.

Application Requirements: Application, financial need analysis. *Deadline:* continuous.

Contact: Brenda Larter, Program Administrator
Minnesota Office of Higher Education
1450 Energy Park Drive, Suite 350
St. Paul, MN 55108-5227
Phone: 651-355-0612
Fax: 651-642-0675
E-mail: brenda.larter@state.mn.us

SAFETY OFFICERS' SURVIVOR GRANT PROGRAM
• *See page 592*

MISSISSIPPI OFFICE OF STUDENT FINANCIAL AID

http://www.mississippi.edu/

HIGHER EDUCATION LEGISLATIVE PLAN (HELP)

Eligible applicant must be resident of Mississippi and be freshman and/or sophomore student who graduated from high school within the immediate past two years. Must demonstrate need as determined by the results of the FAFSA: documenting an average family adjusted gross income of $36,500 or less over the prior two years. Must be enrolled full-time at a Mississippi college or university, have a GPA of 2.5 and have scored 20 on the ACT.

Award: Scholarship for use in freshman, sophomore, junior, or senior years; not renewable. *Number:* varies. *Amount:* $830–$5151.

Eligibility Requirements: Applicant must be enrolled or expecting to enroll full-time at a two-year or four-year institution or university; resident of Mississippi and studying in Mississippi. Applicant must have 2.5 GPA or higher. Available to U.S. citizens.

Application Requirements: Application, financial need analysis, test scores, transcript, FAFSA, specific high school curriculum. *Deadline:* March 31.

Contact: Mrs. Jennifer Rogers, Director of Student Financial Aid
Mississippi Office of Student Financial Aid
3825 Ridgewood Road
Jackson, MS 39211-6453
Phone: 601-432-6997
E-mail: sfa@mississippi.edu

LAW ENFORCEMENT OFFICERS/FIREMEN SCHOLARSHIP

• *See page 592*

MISSISSIPPI EMINENT SCHOLARS GRANT

Award for an entering freshmen or as a renewal for sophomore, junior or senior. who are residents of Mississippi. Applicants must achieve a GPA of 3.5 and must have scored 29 on the ACT. Must enroll full-time at an eligible Mississippi college or university.

Award: Grant for use in freshman, sophomore, junior, or senior years; not renewable. *Number:* varies. *Amount:* up to $2500.

Eligibility Requirements: Applicant must be enrolled or expecting to enroll full-time at a two-year or four-year institution or university; resident of Mississippi and studying in Mississippi. Applicant must have 3.5 GPA or higher. Available to U.S. citizens.

Application Requirements: Application, test scores, transcript. *Deadline:* September 15.

Contact: Mrs. Jennifer Rogers, Director of Student Financial Aid
Mississippi Office of Student Financial Aid
3825 Ridgewood Road
Jackson, MS 39211-6453
Phone: 601-432-6997
E-mail: sfa@mississippi.edu

MISSISSIPPI LEVERAGING EDUCATIONAL ASSISTANCE PARTNERSHIP (LEAP)

Award for Mississippi residents enrolled for full-time study at a Mississippi college or university. Based on financial need. Contact college financial aid office. Award value and deadline varies.

Award: Grant for use in freshman, sophomore, junior, or senior years; not renewable. *Number:* varies. *Amount:* varies.

Eligibility Requirements: Applicant must be enrolled or expecting to enroll full-time at a two-year or four-year institution or university; resident of Mississippi and studying in Mississippi. Available to U.S. citizens.

Application Requirements: Application, financial need analysis, FAFSA. *Deadline:* varies.

Contact: Mrs. Jennifer Rogers, Director of Student Financial Aid
Mississippi Office of Student Financial Aid
3825 Ridgewood Road
Jackson, MS 39211-6453
Phone: 601-432-6997
E-mail: sfa@mississippi.edu

MISSISSIPPI RESIDENT TUITION ASSISTANCE GRANT

Must be a resident of Mississippi enrolled full-time at an eligible Mississippi college or university. Must maintain a minimum 2.5 GPA each semester. MTAG awards may be up to $500 per academic year for freshman and sophomores and $1000 per academic year for juniors and seniors.

Award: Grant for use in freshman, sophomore, junior, or senior years; not renewable. *Number:* varies. *Amount:* $10–$1000.

Eligibility Requirements: Applicant must be enrolled or expecting to enroll full-time at a two-year or four-year institution or university; resident of Mississippi and studying in Mississippi. Applicant must have 2.5 GPA or higher. Available to U.S. citizens.

Application Requirements: Application, test scores, transcript. *Deadline:* September 15.

Contact: Mrs. Jennifer Rogers, Director of Student Financial Aid
Mississippi Office of Student Financial Aid
3825 Ridgewood Road
Jackson, MS 39211-6453
Phone: 601-432-6997
E-mail: sfa@mississippi.edu

NISSAN SCHOLARSHIP

Renewable award for Mississippi residents attending a Mississippi institution. Must be graduating from a Mississippi high school in the current year. The scholarship will pay full tuition and a book allowance. Minimum GPA of 2.0 as well as an ACT composite of at least 20 or combined SAT scores of 940 or better. Must demonstrate financial need and leadership abilities.

Award: Scholarship for use in freshman, sophomore, junior, or senior years; renewable. *Number:* varies. *Amount:* $5596–$5652.

Eligibility Requirements: Applicant must be high school student; planning to enroll or expecting to enroll full-time at a two-year institution or university; resident of Mississippi and studying in Mississippi. Applicant must have 2.5 GPA or higher. Available to U.S. citizens.

Application Requirements: Application, essay, financial need analysis, resume, references, test scores, transcript. *Deadline:* March 1.

Contact: Mrs. Jennifer Rogers, Director of Student Financial Aid
Mississippi Office of Student Financial Aid
3825 Ridgewood Road
Jackson, MS 39211-6453
Phone: 601-432-6997
E-mail: sfa@mississippi.edu

MISSOURI CONSERVATION AGENTS ASSOCIATION SCHOLARSHIP

http://www.moagent.com/

MISSOURI CONSERVATION AGENTS ASSOCIATION SCHOLARSHIP

Scholarship of up to $500 per student per year for full-time undergraduate students who reside in the state of Missouri. The applicant must be a U.S. citizen.

Award: Scholarship for use in freshman, sophomore, junior, or senior years; not renewable. *Number:* varies. *Amount:* up to $500.

Eligibility Requirements: Applicant must be enrolled or expecting to enroll full-time at a four-year or technical institution or university and resident of Missouri. Applicant must have 2.5 GPA or higher. Available to U.S. citizens.

Application Requirements: Essay, transcript. *Deadline:* February 1.

Contact: Brian Ham, Scholarship Committee
Missouri Conservation Agents Association Scholarship
PO Box 1072
Kirksville, MO 63501
Phone: 573-896-8628

MISSOURI DEPARTMENT OF ELEMENTARY AND SECONDARY EDUCATION

http://www.dese.mo.gov/

ROBERT C. BYRD HONORS SCHOLARSHIP-MISSOURI
• See page 671

MISSOURI DEPARTMENT OF HIGHER EDUCATION

http://www.dhe.mo.gov/

ACCESS MISSOURI FINANCIAL ASSISTANCE PROGRAM

Need-based program that provides awards to students who are enrolled full time and have an expected family contribution (EFC) of $12,000 or less based on their Free Application for Federal Student Aid (FAFSA). Awards vary depending on EFC and the type of postsecondary school.

Award: Grant for use in freshman, sophomore, junior, or senior years; not renewable.

Eligibility Requirements: Applicant must be enrolled or expecting to enroll full-time at a two-year or four-year or technical institution or university; resident of Missouri and studying in Missouri. Applicant must have 2.5 GPA or higher. Available to U.S. citizens.

Application Requirements: FAFSA on file by April 1.

Contact: Information Center
Missouri Department of Higher Education
P.O. Box 1469
Jefferson City, MO 65102-1469
Phone: 800-473-6757 Ext. 4
Fax: 573-751-6635
E-mail: info@dhe.mo.gov

MARGUERITE ROSS BARNETT MEMORIAL SCHOLARSHIP

Scholarship was established for students who are employed while attending school part-time. Must be enrolled at least half-time but less than full-time at a participating Missouri postsecondary school, be employed and compensated for at least 20 hours per week, be 18 years of age, be a Missouri resident and a U.S. citizen or a permanent resident.

Award: Scholarship for use in freshman, sophomore, junior, or senior years; renewable. *Number:* varies. *Amount:* varies.

Eligibility Requirements: Applicant must be age 18 and over; enrolled or expecting to enroll part-time at a two-year or four-year or technical institution or university; resident of Missouri and studying in Missouri. Applicant must have 2.5 GPA or higher. Available to U.S. citizens.

Application Requirements: FAFSA on file by August 1. *Deadline:* August 1.

Contact: Information Center
Missouri Department of Higher Education
P.O. Box 1469
Jefferson City, MO 65102-1469
Phone: 800-473-6757 Ext. 4
Fax: 573-751-6635
E-mail: info@dhe.mo.gov

MISSOURI HIGHER EDUCATION ACADEMIC SCHOLARSHIP (BRIGHT FLIGHT)

Program encourages top-ranked high school seniors to attend approved Missouri postsecondary schools. Must be a Missouri resident and a U.S. citizen or permanent resident. Must have a composite score on the ACT or SAT in the top 5 percent of all Missouri students taking those tests. Students with scores in the top 3 percent are eligible for an annual award of up to $3000 (up to $1500 each semester). Students with scores in the top 4% and 5% are eligible for an annual award of up to $1000 (up to $500 each semester). Award amounts, and the availability of the award for students in the 4% and 5%, are subject to change based on the amount of funding allocated for the program in the legislative session.

Award: Scholarship for use in freshman, sophomore, junior, or senior years; renewable. *Number:* varies. *Amount:* $1000–$3000.

Eligibility Requirements: Applicant must be enrolled or expecting to enroll full-time at a two-year or four-year or technical institution or uni-versity; resident of Missouri and studying in Missouri. Applicant must have 2.5 GPA or higher. Available to U.S. citizens.

Application Requirements: Test scores. *Deadline:* June 11.

Contact: Information Center
Missouri Department of Higher Education
P.O. Box 1469
Jefferson City, MO 65102-1469
Phone: 800-473-6757 Ext. 4
Fax: 573-751-6635
E-mail: info@dhe.mo.gov

MITCHELL INSTITUTE

http://www.mitchellinstitute.org/

THE SENATOR GEORGE J. MITCHELL SCHOLARSHIP RESEARCH INSTITUTE

The Mitchell Institute awards scholarship to graduating senior from every public high school in Maine each year. The scholarship award is in the amount of up to $5000 ($1250 per year) for students who are pursuing a four-year degree and $2500 for students pursuing a two-year degree. One scholarship per county in the amount of $6000 ($1500 per year) is awarded with a preference to a first-generation college student.

Award: Scholarship for use in freshman, sophomore, junior, or senior years; renewable. *Number:* 130. *Amount:* $1250–$1500.

Eligibility Requirements: Applicant must be high school student; planning to enroll or expecting to enroll full- or part-time at a two-year or four-year or technical institution or university and resident of Maine. Available to U.S. citizens.

Application Requirements: Application, essay, financial need analysis, photo, references, transcript. *Deadline:* April 1.

Contact: Colleen Quint, Executive Director
Mitchell Institute
22 Monument Square, Suite 200
Portland, ME 04101
Phone: 207-773-7700
Fax: 207-773-1133
E-mail: cquint@mitchellinstitute.org

MONTANA STATE OFFICE OF PUBLIC INSTRUCTION

http://www.opi.mt.gov/

ROBERT C. BYRD HONORS SCHOLARSHIP-MONTANA

The scholarship is available to outstanding Montana seniors, graduates of GED programs and home school high school seniors who will be entering college as freshmen. Minimum 3.6 GPA in a college preparatory cur-riculum required. ACT or SAT scores are also required. Award restricted to Montana residents and U.S. citizens. Scholarship value is $1,500 for the first year of study, renewable for up to three additional years, as a full-time student at any public or private institution of higher education for students who remain in good standing. Proprietary institutions are not included and neither are nonprofit institutions that only provide training programs of less than one year.

Award: Scholarship for use in freshman, sophomore, junior, or senior years; renewable. *Number:* 20–32. *Amount:* $1500.

Eligibility Requirements: Applicant must be high school student; planning to enroll or expecting to enroll full-time at a four-year insti-tution or university and resident of Montana. Available to U.S. citizens.

Application Requirements: Application, essay, test scores, transcript. *Deadline:* March 4.

Contact: Mrs. Carol Gneckow, Program Specialist
Montana State Office of Public Instruction
PO Box 202501
Helena, MT 59620-2501
Phone: 406-444-2417
E-mail: cgneckow@mt.gov

UNITED STATES SENATE YOUTH PROGRAM-THE WILLIAM RANDOLPH HEARST FOUNDATION

Two high school juniors or seniors from Montana have a week long ori-entation in Washington, D.C. on the operation of the United States Senate and other components of the federal government. Potential awardees compete for the scholarship by taking an exam on current politics, then the top semi-finalists answer 5 to 7 questions in a video presentation. Must be currently serving in a high school government office. See web site for specific details.

Award: Scholarship for use in freshman year; not renewable. *Number:* 2. *Amount:* $5000.

Eligibility Requirements: Applicant must be high school student; planning to enroll or expecting to enroll full-time at a four-year institution or university and resident of Montana. Available to U.S. citizens.

Application Requirements: Application, applicant must enter a contest, interview, test scores, video presentation. *Deadline:* October 14.

Contact: Mrs. Carol Gneckow, Program Specialist
Montana State Office of Public Instruction
PO Box 202501
Helena, MT 59620-2501
Phone: 406-444-2417
E-mail: cgneckow@mt.gov

MONTANA UNIVERSITY SYSTEM, OFFICE OF COMMISSIONER OF HIGHER EDUCATION

http://www.scholarship.mt.gov/

MONTANA HIGHER EDUCATION OPPORTUNITY GRANT

This grant is awarded based on need to undergraduate students attending either part-time or full-time who are residents of Montana and attending participating Montana schools. Awards are limited to the most needy students. A specific major or program of study is not required. This grant does not need to be repaid, and students may apply each year. Apply by filing FAFSA by March 1 and contacting the financial aid office at the admitting college.

Award: Grant for use in freshman, sophomore, junior, or senior years; not renewable. *Number:* up to 800. *Amount:* $400–$600.

Eligibility Requirements: Applicant must be enrolled or expecting to enroll full- or part-time at a two-year or four-year institution or university; resident of Montana and studying in Montana. Available to U.S. citizens.

Application Requirements: Application, financial need analysis, resume, FAFSA. *Deadline:* March 1.

Contact: Jamie Dushin, Budget Analyst
Montana University System, Office of Commissioner of
Higher Education
PO Box 203101
Helena, MT 59620-3101
Phone: 406-444-0638
Fax: 406-444-1869
E-mail: jdushin@mgslp.state.mt.us

MONTANA TUITION ASSISTANCE PROGRAM-BAKER GRANT

Need-based grant for Montana residents attending participating Montana schools who have earned at least $2575 during the previous calendar year. Must be enrolled full time. Grant does not need to be repaid. Award covers the first undergraduate degree or certificate. Apply by filing FAFSA by March 1 and contacting the financial aid office at the admitting college.

Award: Grant for use in freshman, sophomore, junior, or senior years; not renewable. *Number:* 1000–3000. *Amount:* $100–$1000.

Eligibility Requirements: Applicant must be enrolled or expecting to enroll full-time at a two-year or four-year institution or university; resident of Montana and studying in Montana. Available to U.S. citizens.

Application Requirements: Application, financial need analysis, resume, FAFSA. *Deadline:* March 1.

Contact: Jamie Dushin, Budget Analyst
Montana University System, Office of Commissioner of
Higher Education
PO Box 203101
Helena, MT 59620-3101
Phone: 406-444-0638
Fax: 406-444-1869
E-mail: jdushin@mgslp.state.mt.us

MONTANA UNIVERSITY SYSTEM HONOR SCHOLARSHIP

Scholarship will be awarded annually to high school seniors graduating from accredited Montana high schools. The MUS Honor Scholarship is a four year renewable scholarship that waives the tuition and registration fee at one of the Montana University System campuses or one of the three community colleges (Flathead Valley in Kalispell, Miles in Miles City or Dawson in Glendive). The scholarship must be used within 9 months after high school graduation. Applicant must have a minimum GPA of 3.4.

Award: Scholarship for use in freshman year; renewable. *Number:* up to 200. *Amount:* $4000–$6000.

Eligibility Requirements: Applicant must be high school student; planning to enroll or expecting to enroll full-time at a two-year or four-year institution or university; resident of Montana and studying in Montana. Applicant must have 3.5 GPA or higher. Available to U.S. citizens.

Application Requirements: Application, test scores, transcript, college acceptance letter. *Deadline:* March 15.

Contact: Sheila Nelwun, Grants and Scholarship Coordinator
Montana University System, Office of Commissioner of
Higher Education
2500 Broadway
PO Box 203101
Helena, MT 59620-3101
Phone: 406-444-0638
Fax: 406-444-1869
E-mail: snewlun@montana.edu

MOUNT VERNON URBAN RENEWAL AGENCY

http://www.ci.mount-vernon.ny.us/

THOMAS E. SHARPE MEMORIAL EDUCATIONAL ASSISTANCE PROGRAM

Awards offered only to the low and moderate income residents of the city of Mount Vernon for the purpose of pursuing higher education at a vocational/technical school or college.

Award: Grant for use in freshman, sophomore, junior, or senior years; renewable. *Number:* up to 150. *Amount:* varies.

Eligibility Requirements: Applicant must be enrolled or expecting to enroll full-time at a two-year or four-year or technical institution or university and resident of New York. Applicant must have 2.5 GPA or higher. Available to U.S. citizens.

Application Requirements: Application, essay, financial need analysis, transcript, proof of residence. *Deadline:* July 1.

Contact: Mary E. Fleming, Director, Scholarship Programs
Mount Vernon Urban Renewal Agency
Department of Planning, One Roosevelt Square, City Hall
Mount Vernon, NY 10550
Phone: 914-699-7230 Ext. 110
Fax: 914-699-1435
E-mail: mfleming@ci.mount-vernon.ny.us

NATIONAL ASSOCIATION FOR CAMPUS ACTIVITIES

http://www.naca.org/

LORI RHETT MEMORIAL SCHOLARSHIP
• *See page 592*

NATIONAL ASSOCIATION FOR CAMPUS ACTIVITIES EAST COAST UNDERGRADUATE SCHOLARSHIP FOR STUDENT LEADERS
• *See page 592*

NATIONAL ASSOCIATION FOR CAMPUS ACTIVITIES SOUTHEAST REGION STUDENT LEADERSHIP SCHOLARSHIP
• *See page 592*

NATIONAL ASSOCIATION FOR CAMPUS ACTIVITIES WISCONSIN REGION STUDENT LEADERSHIP SCHOLARSHIP

• *See page 592*

TESS CALDARELLI MEMORIAL SCHOLARSHIP

Scholarship available to undergraduate or graduate students with a minimum 3.0 GPA. Must demonstrate significant leadership skills and hold a significant position on campus. Must attend school in the NACA Great Lakes Region. The scholarship is to be used for educational purposes, such as tuition, fees and books or for professional development purposes.

Award: Scholarship for use in freshman, sophomore, junior, senior, or graduate years; not renewable. *Number:* varies. *Amount:* $250–$300.

Eligibility Requirements: Applicant must be enrolled or expecting to enroll full- or part-time at a two-year or four-year institution or university; studying in Kentucky, Michigan, Ohio, Pennsylvania, or West Virginia and must have an interest in leadership. Applicant must have 3.0 GPA or higher. Available to U.S. citizens.

Application Requirements: Application, resume, references, transcript. *Deadline:* November 1.

Contact: Dionne Ellison, Administrative Assistant
National Association for Campus Activities
13 Harbison Way
Columbia, SC 29212-3401
Phone: 803-732-6222 Ext. 131
Fax: 803-749-1047
E-mail: dionnee@naca.org

ZAGUNIS STUDENT LEADERS SCHOLARSHIP

Scholarships will be awarded to undergraduate or graduate students maintaining a cumulative GPA of 3.0 or better at the time of the application and during the academic term in which the scholarship is awarded. Applicants should demonstrate leadership skills and abilities while holding a significant leadership position on campus. Applicants must submit two letters of recommendation and a description of the applicant's leadership activities, skills, abilities and accomplishments. Must be enrolled in a college/university in the NACA Great Lakes Region.

Award: Scholarship for use in freshman, sophomore, junior, senior, or graduate years; not renewable. *Number:* 1. *Amount:* $300.

Eligibility Requirements: Applicant must be enrolled or expecting to enroll full- or part-time at a two-year or four-year institution or university; studying in Kentucky, Michigan, Ohio, Pennsylvania, or West Virginia and must have an interest in leadership. Applicant must have 3.0 GPA or higher. Available to U.S. citizens.

Application Requirements: Application, resume, references, transcript, current enrollment form. *Deadline:* November 1.

Contact: Dionne Ellison, Administrative Assistant
National Association for Campus Activities
13 Harbison Way
Columbia, SC 29212-3401
Phone: 803-732-6222 Ext. 131
Fax: 803-749-1047
E-mail: dionnee@naca.org

NATIONAL ASSOCIATION OF LETTER CARRIERS

http://www.nalc.org/

COSTAS G. LEMONOPOULOS SCHOLARSHIP

• *See page 551*

NATIONAL BURGLAR AND FIRE ALARM ASSOCIATION

http://www.alarm.org/

NBFAA YOUTH SCHOLARSHIP PROGRAM

• *See page 593*

NATIONAL COUNCIL OF JEWISH WOMEN NEW YORK SECTION

http://www.ncjwny.org/

JACKSON-STRICKS SCHOLARSHIP

• *See page 607*

NATIONAL DEFENSE TRANSPORTATION ASSOCIATION-SCOTT ST. LOUIS CHAPTER

http://www.ndtascottstlouis.org/

NATIONAL DEFENSE TRANSPORTATION ASSOCIATION, SCOTT AIR FORCE BASE-ST. LOUIS AREA CHAPTER SCHOLARSHIP

The Scott/St. Louis Chapter of the NDTA intends to award a minimum of two (2) scholarships of $3,500 each and four (4) scholarships of $2,000 each. Additional awards may be granted pending availability of funds. Scholarships are open to any high school student that meets the eligibility criteria. High school students must be reside and go to school in Illinois or Missouri. College applicants must be a full-time student in the following states: CO, IA, IL, IN, KS, MI, MN, MO, MT, ND, NE, SD, WI, or WY.

Award: Scholarship for use in freshman, sophomore, junior, or senior years; not renewable. *Number:* 6. *Amount:* $2000–$3500.

Eligibility Requirements: Applicant must be enrolled or expecting to enroll full-time at a two-year or four-year institution or university; resident of Illinois or Missouri and studying in Colorado, Illinois, Indiana, Iowa, Kansas, Michigan, Minnesota, Missouri, Montana, Nebraska, North Dakota, or South Dakota. Applicant must have 3.0 GPA or higher. Available to U.S. citizens.

Application Requirements: Application, essay, references, test scores, transcript. *Deadline:* March 1.

Contact: Mr. Michael Carnes, Chairman, Professional Development Committee
National Defense Transportation Association-Scott St. Louis Chapter
PO Box 25486
Scott AFB, IL 62225
Phone: 618-229-4756
E-mail: michael.carnes.ctr@ustranscom.mil

NATIONAL FEDERATION OF BLIND OF MISSOURI

http://www.nfbmo.org/

NATIONAL FEDERATION OF THE BLIND OF MISSOURI SCHOLARSHIPS TO LEGALLY BLIND STUDENTS

• *See page 607*

NATIONAL FEDERATION OF THE BLIND OF CALIFORNIA

http://www.nfbcal.org/

GERALD DRAKE MEMORIAL SCHOLARSHIP

• *See page 608*

JULIE LANDUCCI SCHOLARSHIP

• *See page 608*

LA VYRL "PINKY" JOHNSON MEMORIAL SCHOLARSHIP

• *See page 609*

LAWRENCE "MUZZY" MARCELINO MEMORIAL SCHOLARSHIP

• *See page 609*

NATIONAL FEDERATION OF THE BLIND OF CALIFORNIA MERIT SCHOLARSHIPS
• *See page 609*

NATIONAL FEDERATION OF THE BLIND OF CONNECTICUT

http://www.nfbct.org/

C. RODNEY DEMAREST MEMORIAL SCHOLARSHIP
• *See page 609*

DORIS E. HIGLEY MEMORIAL SCHOLARSHIP
• *See page 609*

HOWARD E. MAY MEMORIAL SCHOLARSHIP
• *See page 609*

MARY MAIN MEMORIAL SCHOLARSHIP
• *See page 609*

NATIONAL KIDNEY FOUNDATION OF INDIANA INC.

http://www.kidneyindiana.org/

LARRY SMOCK SCHOLARSHIP
• *See page 610*

NATIONAL UNION OF PUBLIC AND GENERAL EMPLOYEES

http://www.nupge.ca/

SCHOLARSHIP FOR ABORIGINAL CANADIANS
• *See page 555*

SCHOLARSHIP FOR VISIBLE MINORITIES
• *See page 555*

TERRY FOX MEMORIAL SCHOLARSHIP
• *See page 555*

TOMMY DOUGLAS SCHOLARSHIP
• *See page 555*

NEBRASKA DEPARTMENT OF EDUCATION

http://www.education.ne.gov/

ROBERT C. BYRD HONORS SCHOLARSHIP-NEBRASKA

Federally funded award for high school seniors, renewable for up to four years. Must be U.S. citizen, a Nebraska resident, and have a minimum ACT composite score of 30. Awards designed to promote student excellence and achievement, and to recognize students who show promise of continued excellence. Funded scholars must submit renewal application each year. Renewal based on continuing eligibility requirements. Application available at online http//www.education.ne.gov/byrd.

Award: Scholarship for use in freshman, sophomore, junior, or senior years; renewable. *Number:* 40–45. *Amount:* $1500.

Eligibility Requirements: Applicant must be high school student; planning to enroll or expecting to enroll full-time at a two-year or four-year or technical institution or university and resident of Nebraska. Available to U.S. citizens.

Application Requirements: Application, test scores, transcript. *Deadline:* March 15.

Contact: Mardi North, Robert C. Byrd Scholarship Information
Nebraska Department of Education
301 Centennial Mall South, PO Box 94987
Lincoln, NE 68509-4987
Phone: 402-471-3962
Fax: 402-471-8850
E-mail: mardi.north@nebraska.gov

NEBRASKA'S COORDINATING COMMISSION FOR POSTSECONDARY EDUCATION

http://www.ccpe.state.ne.us/

NEBRASKA OPPORTUNITY GRANT

Available to undergraduates attending a participating postsecondary institution in Nebraska. Must demonstrate financial need. Nebraska residency required. Awards determined by each participating institution. Student must complete the Free Application for Federal Student Aid (FAFSA) to apply. Contact financial aid office at institution for additional information.

Award: Grant for use in freshman, sophomore, junior, or senior years; not renewable. *Number:* varies. *Amount:* $100–$3400.

Eligibility Requirements: Applicant must be enrolled or expecting to enroll full- or part-time at a two-year or four-year or technical institution or university; resident of Nebraska and studying in Nebraska. Available to U.S. citizens.

Application Requirements: Application, financial need analysis. *Deadline:* continuous.

Contact: Mr. J. Ritchie Morrow, Financial Aid Coordinator
Nebraska's Coordinating Commission for Postsecondary
   Education
140 North Eighth Street, Suite 300, PO Box 95005
Lincoln, NE 68509-5005
Phone: 402-471-2847
Fax: 402-471-2886
E-mail: Ritchie.Morrow@nebraska.gov

NEBRASKA SPORTS COUNCIL/THE GALLUP ORGANIZATION

http://www.cornhuskerstategames.com/

NEBRASKA SPORTS COUNCIL/GALLUP ORGANIZATION CORNHUSKER STATE GAMES SCHOLARSHIP PROGRAM

One-time award for Nebraska students who are participants in the Cornhusker State Games. For use at a Nebraska postsecondary institution.

Award: Scholarship for use in freshman, sophomore, junior, or senior years; not renewable. *Number:* 5. *Amount:* $1000.

Eligibility Requirements: Applicant must be enrolled or expecting to enroll full- or part-time at a two-year or four-year or technical institution or university; resident of Nebraska; studying in Nebraska and must have an interest in athletics/sports. Available to U.S. citizens.

Application Requirements: Application, essay, transcript. *Deadline:* June 1.

Contact: Dave Mlnarik, Executive Director
Nebraska Sports Council/The Gallup Organization
4903 North 57th Street
PO Box 29366
Lincoln, NE 68529
Phone: 402-471-2544
E-mail: info@nebraskasportscouncil.com

NEED

http://www.needld.org/

UNMET NEED GRANT PROGRAM
• *See page 674*

NEVADA DEPARTMENT OF EDUCATION

http://www.doe.nv.gov/

ROBERT C. BYRD HONORS SCHOLARSHIP-NEVADA

Award for senior graduating from public or private Nevada high school. Must be Nevada resident. Renewable award of $1500. No application necessary. Nevada scholars are chosen from a database supplied by ACT and SAT. SAT scores of 1100 and above qualify as initial application. ACT score is automatically submitted for a score of 25 or greater. GPA must be 3.5 or higher. Award is for undergraduate studies only.

Award: Scholarship for use in freshman, sophomore, junior, or senior years; renewable. *Number:* 40–40. *Amount:* $1500.

Eligibility Requirements: Applicant must be high school student; planning to enroll or expecting to enroll full-time at a two-year or four-year institution or university and resident of Nevada. Applicant must have 3.5 GPA or higher. Available to U.S. citizens.

Application Requirements: Test scores, transcript. *Deadline:* continuous.

Contact: Mrs. Stephanie Swanson, Scholarship Coordinator
Nevada Department of Education
700 E. Fifth Street
Carson City, NV 89701
Phone: 775-687-9150
Fax: 775-687-9250
E-mail: sswanson@doe.nv.gov

NEVADA OFFICE OF THE STATE TREASURER

http://www.nevadatreasurer.gov/

GOVERNOR GUINN MILLENNIUM SCHOLARSHIP

Scholarship for high school graduates with a diploma from a Nevada public or private high school in the graduating class of the year 2000 or later. Must complete high school with at least 3.25 GPA.

Award: Scholarship for use in freshman, sophomore, junior, or senior years; not renewable. *Number:* 1. *Amount:* $10,000.

Eligibility Requirements: Applicant must be enrolled or expecting to enroll full-time at a two-year or four-year institution or university and resident of Nevada. Available to U.S. citizens.

Application Requirements: Application. *Deadline:* varies.

Contact: Reba Coombs, Executive Director
Nevada Office of the State Treasurer
555 East Washington Avenue, Suite 4600
Las Vegas, NV 89101
Phone: 702-486-3383
Fax: 702-486-3246
E-mail: info@nevadatreasurer.gov

NEW ENGLAND BOARD OF HIGHER EDUCATION

http://www.nebhe.org/

NEW ENGLAND REGIONAL STUDENT PROGRAM-TUITION BREAK

Tuition discount for residents of six New England states (Connecticut, Maine, Massachusetts, New Hampshire, Rhode Island, Vermont). Students pay reduced out-of-state tuition at public colleges or universities in other New England states when enrolling in certain majors not offered at public institutions in home state. Details are available at http://www.nebhe.org/tuitionbreak.

Award: Scholarship for use in freshman, sophomore, junior, senior, or graduate years; renewable. *Amount:* varies.

Eligibility Requirements: Applicant must be enrolled or expecting to enroll full- or part-time at a two-year or four-year institution or university; resident of Connecticut, Maine, Massachusetts, New Hampshire, Rhode Island, or Vermont and studying in Connecticut, Maine, Massachusetts, New Hampshire, Rhode Island, or Vermont. Available to U.S. citizens.

Application Requirements: College application for admission. *Deadline:* continuous.

Contact: Wendy Lindsay, Senior Director of Regional Student Program
New England Board of Higher Education
45 Temple Place
Boston, MA 02111
Phone: 617-357-9620 Ext. 111
Fax: 617-338-1577
E-mail: tuitionbreak@nebhe.org

NEW HAMPSHIRE DEPARTMENT OF EDUCATION

http://www.state.nh.us/doe/

ROBERT C. BYRD HONORS SCHOLARSHIP-NEW HAMPSHIRE

Scholarships awarded to graduates of approved New Hampshire secondary schools based on academic achievement. Contact department for application deadlines. May be funded through four years of college if recipient maintains high academic achievement. Must be high school senior to apply and must submit letters of recommendation. Award is offered in senior year of high school. Minimum 3.0 GPA required.

Award: Scholarship for use in freshman, sophomore, junior, or senior years; renewable. *Number:* 22–26. *Amount:* $1500.

Eligibility Requirements: Applicant must be high school student; planning to enroll or expecting to enroll full- or part-time at a two-year or four-year institution or university and resident of New Hampshire. Applicant must have 3.0 GPA or higher. Available to U.S. citizens.

Application Requirements: Application, essay, portfolio, references, test scores, transcript.

Contact: Mrs. Patricia T. Butler, Administrative Assistant II
New Hampshire Department of Education
101 Pleasant Street
Concord, NH 03301
Phone: 603-271-3144
Fax: 603-271-3830
E-mail: pbutler@ed.state.nh.us

NEW HAMPSHIRE FOOD INDUSTRIES EDUCATION FOUNDATION

http://www.grocers.org/

NEW HAMPSHIRE FOOD INDUSTRY SCHOLARSHIPS
• See page 577

NEW HAMPSHIRE POSTSECONDARY EDUCATION COMMISSION

http://www.nh.gov/postsecondary

LEVERAGED INCENTIVE GRANT PROGRAM

Grants to provide assistance on the basis of merit and need to full-time undergraduate New Hampshire students at New Hampshire accredited institutions. Must be a New Hampshire resident, and demonstrate financial need as determined by the federal formula and by merit as determined by the institution. Must be a sophomore, junior or senior undergraduate student.

Award: Grant for use in sophomore, junior, or senior years; not renewable. *Number:* varies. *Amount:* $250–$7500.

Eligibility Requirements: Applicant must be enrolled or expecting to enroll full-time at a two-year or four-year or technical institution or university; resident of New Hampshire and studying in New Hampshire. Available to U.S. citizens.

Application Requirements: FAFSA. *Deadline:* varies.

Contact: Ms. Cynthia Capodestria, Student Financial Aid Administrator
New Hampshire Postsecondary Education Commission
Three Barrell Court, Suite 300
Concord, NH 03301-8543
Phone: 603-271-2555 Ext. 360
E-mail: cynthia.capodestria@pec.state.nh.us

NEW HAMPSHIRE INCENTIVE PROGRAM (NHIP)

Grants to provide financial assistance to New Hampshire students attending eligible institutions in New England. Must demonstrate financial need. May be a part- or full-time undergraduate student with no previous bachelor's degree.

Award: Grant for use in freshman, sophomore, junior, or senior years; renewable. *Number:* 4300–4500. *Amount:* $125–$1000.

Eligibility Requirements: Applicant must be enrolled or expecting to enroll full- or part-time at a two-year or four-year institution or university; resident of New Hampshire and studying in Connecticut, Maine, Massachusetts, New Hampshire, Rhode Island, or Vermont. Available to U.S. citizens.

Application Requirements: FAFSA. *Deadline:* May 1.

Contact: Ms. Cynthia Capodestria, Student Financial Aid Administrator
New Hampshire Postsecondary Education Commission
Three Barrell Court, Suite 300
Concord, NH 03301-8543
Phone: 603-271-2555 Ext. 360
E-mail: cynthia.capodestria@pec.state.nh.us

SCHOLARSHIPS FOR ORPHANS OF VETERANS-NEW HAMPSHIRE
• *See page 641*

UNIQUE SCHOLARSHIP

Grant available to New Hampshire residents enrolled at a New Hampshire institution of higher education. Must demonstrate financial need. Contact financial aid office for more information. High school students not considered.

Award: Grant for use in freshman, sophomore, junior, or senior years; renewable. *Amount:* $1300.

Eligibility Requirements: Applicant must be enrolled or expecting to enroll full-time at a two-year or four-year or technical institution or university; resident of New Hampshire and studying in New Hampshire. Available to U.S. citizens.

Application Requirements: FAFSA. *Deadline:* May 1.

Contact: Ms. Cynthia Capodestria, Student Financial Aid Administrator
New Hampshire Postsecondary Education Commission
Three Barrell Court, Suite 300
Concord, NH 03301-8543
Phone: 603-271-2555 Ext. 360
E-mail: cynthia.capodestria@pec.state.nh.us

NEW JERSEY DEPARTMENT OF EDUCATION

http://www.state.nj.us/

ROBERT C. BYRD HONORS SCHOLARSHIP-NEW JERSEY

Award for outstanding graduating high school seniors who have been accepted for full-time study at a U.S. college or university. Must have a minimum 3.5 GPA. Award is renewable for up to four years. Must be legal resident of New Jersey and U.S. citizen.

Award: Scholarship for use in freshman year; renewable. *Number:* varies. *Amount:* $1500.

Eligibility Requirements: Applicant must be high school student; planning to enroll or expecting to enroll full-time at a four-year institution or university and resident of New Jersey. Applicant must have 3.5 GPA or higher. Available to U.S. citizens.

Application Requirements: Application. *Deadline:* April 4.

Contact: Sue Sliker, Program Administrator
New Jersey Department of Education
PO Box 500
Trenton, NJ 08625-0500
Phone: 609-777-0800

NEW JERSEY DEPARTMENT OF MILITARY AND VETERANS AFFAIRS

http://www.state.nj.us/military

NEW JERSEY WAR ORPHANS TUITION ASSISTANCE
• *See page 641*

POW-MIA TUITION BENEFIT PROGRAM
• *See page 641*

VETERANS TUITION CREDIT PROGRAM-NEW JERSEY
• *See page 641*

NEW JERSEY HIGHER EDUCATION STUDENT ASSISTANCE AUTHORITY

http://www.hesaa.org/

DANA CHRISTMAS SCHOLARSHIP FOR HEROISM

Honors young New Jersey residents for acts of heroism. Scholarship is a nonrenewable award of up to $10,000 for 5 students. This scholarship may be used for undergraduate or graduate study. Deadline varies.

Award: Scholarship for use in freshman, sophomore, junior, senior, or graduate years; not renewable. *Number:* up to 5. *Amount:* up to $10,000.

Eligibility Requirements: Applicant must be age 21 or under; enrolled or expecting to enroll full- or part-time at a two-year or four-year or technical institution or university and resident of New Jersey. Available to U.S. citizens.

Application Requirements: Application. *Deadline:* varies.

Contact: Gisele Joachim, Director, Financial Aid Services
New Jersey Higher Education Student Assistance Authority
4 Quakerbridge Plaza, PO Box 540
Trenton, NJ 08625
Phone: 800-792-8670 Ext. 2349
Fax: 609-588-7389
E-mail: gjoachim@hesaa.org

EDWARD J. BLOUSTEIN DISTINGUISHED SCHOLARS

Renewable scholarship for students who are placed in top 10 percent of their classes and have a minimum combined SAT score of 1260, or ranked first, second or third in their classes as of end of junior year. Must be New Jersey resident and must attend a New Jersey two-year college, four-year college or university, or approved programs at proprietary institutions. Secondary schools must forward to HESAA, the names and class standings for all nominees. Award value up to $1000 and deadline varies.

Award: Scholarship for use in freshman, sophomore, junior, senior, or graduate years; renewable. *Number:* varies. *Amount:* up to $1000.

Eligibility Requirements: Applicant must be enrolled or expecting to enroll full-time at a two-year or four-year institution or university; resident of New Jersey and studying in New Jersey. Available to U.S. citizens.

Application Requirements: Application, test scores, nomination by high school. *Deadline:* varies.

Contact: Carol Muka, Assistant Director of Grants and Scholarships
New Jersey Higher Education Student Assistance Authority
PO Box 540
Trenton, NJ 08625
Phone: 800-792-8670 Ext. 3266
Fax: 609-588-2228
E-mail: cmuka@hesaa.org

LAW ENFORCEMENT OFFICER MEMORIAL SCHOLARSHIP
• *See page 593*

NEW JERSEY STUDENT TUITION ASSISTANCE REWARD SCHOLARSHIP II

Scholarship for high school graduates who plan to pursue a baccalaureate degree at a New Jersey four-year public institution. Scholarship will cover the cost of tuition and approved fees for up to 18 credits per semester when combined with other state, federal and institutional aid. Deadline varies.

Award: Scholarship for use in freshman year; renewable. *Number:* varies. *Amount:* $2000.

Eligibility Requirements: Applicant must be enrolled or expecting to enroll full-time at a four-year institution or university; resident of New Jersey and studying in New Jersey. Applicant must have 3.0 GPA or higher. Available to U.S. citizens.

Application Requirements: Application, FAFSA. *Deadline:* varies.

Contact: Cathleen Lewis, Assistant Director, Client Services
New Jersey Higher Education Student Assistance Authority
4 Quaker Bridge Plaza
PO Box 540
Trenton, NJ 08625-0540
Phone: 609-588-3280
Fax: 609-588-2228
E-mail: clewis@hesaa.org

NEW JERSEY WORLD TRADE CENTER SCHOLARSHIP

Scholarship was established by the legislature to aid the dependent children and surviving spouses of New Jersey residents who were killed in the terrorist attacks, or who are missing and officially presumed dead as a direct result of the attacks; applies to instate and out-of-state institutions for students seeking undergraduate degrees. Deadlines: March 1 for fall, October 1 for spring.

Award: Scholarship for use in freshman, sophomore, junior, or senior years; renewable. *Number:* varies. *Amount:* up to $6500.

Eligibility Requirements: Applicant must be enrolled or expecting to enroll full-time at a four-year institution or university and resident of New Jersey. Available to U.S. citizens.

Application Requirements: Application. *Deadline:* varies.

Contact: Giselle Joachim, Director of Financial Aid Services
New Jersey Higher Education Student Assistance Authority
PO Box 540
Trenton, NJ 08625
Phone: 800-792-8670 Ext. 2349
Fax: 609-588-7389
E-mail: gjoachim@hesaa.org

NJ STUDENT TUITION ASSISTANCE REWARD SCHOLARSHIP

Scholarship for students who graduate in the top 20 percent of their high school class. Recipients may be awarded up to five semesters of tuition (up to 15 credits per term) and approved fees at one of New Jersey's nineteen county colleges.

Award: Scholarship for use in freshman, sophomore, junior, or senior years; renewable. *Number:* varies. *Amount:* $2500–$7500.

Eligibility Requirements: Applicant must be enrolled or expecting to enroll full-time at a two-year or four-year institution or university; resident of New Jersey and studying in New Jersey. Applicant must have 3.0 GPA or higher. Available to U.S. citizens.

Application Requirements: Application, transcript. *Deadline:* varies.

Contact: Carol Muka, Assistant Director of Grants and Scholarships
New Jersey Higher Education Student Assistance Authority
PO Box 540
Trenton, NJ 08625
Phone: 800-792-8670 Ext. 3266
Fax: 609-588-2228
E-mail: cmuka@hessa.org

OUTSTANDING SCHOLAR RECRUITMENT PROGRAM

Awards students who meet the eligibility criteria and who are enrolled as first-time freshmen at participating New Jersey institutions receive annual scholarship awards of up to $7500.

Award: Scholarship for use in freshman, sophomore, junior, or senior years; renewable. *Number:* varies. *Amount:* $2500–$7500.

Eligibility Requirements: Applicant must be enrolled or expecting to enroll full-time at a four-year institution or university; resident of New Jersey and studying in New Jersey. Available to U.S. citizens.

Application Requirements: Application. *Deadline:* varies.

Contact: Carol Muka, Assistant Director of Grants and Scholarships
New Jersey Higher Education Student Assistance Authority
PO Box 540
Trenton, NJ 08625
Phone: 800-792-8670 Ext. 3266
Fax: 609-588-2228
E-mail: cmuka@hesaa.org

PART-TIME TUITION AID GRANT (TAG) FOR COUNTY COLLEGES

Provides financial aid to eligible part-time undergraduate students enrolled for 9 to 11 credits at participating New Jersey community colleges. Deadlines: March 1 for spring and October 1 for fall.

Award: Grant for use in freshman, sophomore, junior, or senior years; not renewable. *Number:* varies. *Amount:* $419–$628.

Eligibility Requirements: Applicant must be enrolled or expecting to enroll part-time at a two-year or four-year institution or university; resident of New Jersey and studying in New Jersey. Available to U.S. citizens.

Application Requirements: Application, financial need analysis. *Deadline:* varies.

Contact: Sherri Fox, Acting Director of Grants and Scholarships
New Jersey Higher Education Student Assistance Authority
PO Box 540
Trenton, NJ 08625
Phone: 800-792-8670
Fax: 609-588-2228

SURVIVOR TUITION BENEFITS PROGRAM
• See page 594

TUITION AID GRANT

The program provides tuition fees to eligible undergraduate students attending participating in-state institutions. Deadlines: March 1 for fall, October 1 for spring.

Award: Grant for use in freshman, sophomore, junior, or senior years; not renewable. *Number:* varies. *Amount:* $868–$7272.

Eligibility Requirements: Applicant must be enrolled or expecting to enroll full-time at a two-year or four-year institution or university; resident of New Jersey and studying in New Jersey. Available to U.S. citizens.

Application Requirements: Application, financial need analysis. *Deadline:* varies.

Contact: Sherri Fox, Acting Director of Grants and Scholarships
New Jersey Higher Education Student Assistance Authority
PO Box 540
Trenton, NJ 08625
Phone: 800-792-8670
Fax: 609-588-2228

URBAN SCHOLARS

Renewable scholarship to high achieving students attending public secondary schools in the urban and economically distressed areas of New Jersey. Students must rank in the top 10 percent of their class and have a GPA of at least 3.0 at the end of their junior year. Must be New Jersey resident and attend a New Jersey two-year college, four-year college or university, or approved programs at proprietary institutions. Students do not apply directly for scholarship consideration. Deadline varies.

Award: Scholarship for use in freshman, sophomore, junior, or senior years; renewable. *Number:* varies. *Amount:* up to $1000.

Eligibility Requirements: Applicant must be enrolled or expecting to enroll full-time at a two-year or four-year institution or university; resident of New Jersey and studying in New Jersey. Applicant must have 3.0 GPA or higher. Available to U.S. citizens.

Application Requirements: Application, test scores, nomination by school. *Deadline:* varies.

Contact: Carol Muka, Assistant Director of Grants and Scholarships
New Jersey Higher Education Student Assistance Authority
PO Box 540
Trenton, NJ 08625
Phone: 800-792-8670 Ext. 3266
Fax: 609-588-2228
E-mail: cmuka@hesaa.org

NEW JERSEY VIETNAM VETERANS' MEMORIAL FOUNDATION

http://www.njvvmf.org/

NEW JERSEY VIETNAM VETERANS' MEMORIAL FOUNDATION SCHOLARSHIP

One-time scholarship for graduating high school seniors of New Jersey. For full-time study only.

Award: Scholarship for use in freshman year; not renewable. *Number:* 2. *Amount:* $2500.

Eligibility Requirements: Applicant must be high school student; planning to enroll or expecting to enroll full-time at a two-year or four-

year or technical institution or university and resident of New Jersey. Available to U.S. citizens.

Application Requirements: Application, essay, college acceptance letter. *Deadline:* April 15.

Contact: Lynn Duane, Administrator
New Jersey Vietnam Veterans' Memorial Foundation
One Memorial Lane, PO Box 648
Holmdel, NJ 07733
Phone: 732-335-0033 Ext. 100
Fax: 732-335-1107
E-mail: lduane@njvvmf.org

NEW MEXICO COMMISSION ON HIGHER EDUCATION

http://www.hed.state.nm.us/

COLLEGE AFFORDABILITY GRANT

Grant available to New Mexico students with financial need who do not qualify for other state grants and scholarships to attend and complete educational programs at a New Mexico public college or university. Student must have unmet need after all other financial aid has been awarded. Student may not be receiving any other state grants or scholarships. Renewable upon satisfactory academic progress.

Award: Grant for use in freshman, sophomore, junior, or senior years; renewable. *Number:* 1. *Amount:* up to $1000.

Eligibility Requirements: Applicant must be enrolled or expecting to enroll full- or part-time at a two-year or four-year institution or university; resident of New Mexico and studying in New Mexico. Available to U.S. citizens.

Application Requirements: Application, financial need analysis, FAFSA. *Deadline:* continuous.

Contact: Tashina Banks Acker, Director of Financial Aid
New Mexico Commission on Higher Education
1068 Cerrillos Road
Santa Fe, NM 87505-1650
Phone: 505-476-6549
Fax: 505-476-6511
E-mail: tashina.banks-moore@state.nm.us

LEGISLATIVE ENDOWMENT SCHOLARSHIPS

Renewable scholarships to provide aid for undergraduate students with substantial financial need who are attending public postsecondary institutions in New Mexico. Four-year schools may award up to $2500 per academic year, two-year schools may award up to $1000 per academic year. Deadlines vary.

Award: Scholarship for use in freshman, sophomore, junior, or senior years; renewable. *Number:* 1. *Amount:* $1000–$2500.

Eligibility Requirements: Applicant must be enrolled or expecting to enroll full- or part-time at a two-year or four-year institution or university; resident of New Mexico and studying in New Mexico. Available to U.S. citizens.

Application Requirements: Application, financial need analysis, FAFSA. *Deadline:* varies.

Contact: Tashina Banks Moore, Director of Financial Aid
New Mexico Commission on Higher Education
1068 Cerrillos Road
Santa Fe, NM 87505-1650
Phone: 505-475-6549
Fax: 505-476-6511
E-mail: tashina.banks-moore@state.nm.us

LEGISLATIVE LOTTERY SCHOLARSHIP

Renewable Scholarship for New Mexico high school graduates or GED recipients who plan to attend an eligible New Mexico public college or university. Must be enrolled full-time and maintain 2.5 GPA.

Award: Scholarship for use in freshman year; renewable. *Number:* 1. *Amount:* varies.

Eligibility Requirements: Applicant must be high school student; planning to enroll or expecting to enroll full-time at a four-year institution or university; resident of New Mexico and studying in New Mexico. Applicant must have 3.5 GPA or higher. Available to U.S. citizens.

Application Requirements: Application, FAFSA. *Deadline:* varies.

Contact: Tashina Banks Moore, Director of Financial Aid
New Mexico Commission on Higher Education
1068 Cerrillos Road
Santa Fe, NM 87505
Phone: 505-476-6549
Fax: 505-476-6511
E-mail: tashina.banks-moore@state.nm.us

NEW MEXICO COMPETITIVE SCHOLARSHIP

Scholarships for non-residents or non-citizens of the United States to encourage out-of-state students who have demonstrated high academic achievement in high school to enroll in public four-year universities in New Mexico. Renewable for up to four years. For details visit http://fin.hed.state.nm.us.

Award: Scholarship for use in freshman year; renewable. *Number:* varies. *Amount:* varies.

Eligibility Requirements: Applicant must be high school student; planning to enroll or expecting to enroll full-time at a four-year institution or university and studying in New Mexico. Available to Canadian and non-U.S. citizens.

Application Requirements: Application, essay, references, test scores. *Deadline:* varies.

Contact: Tashina Banks Moore, Director of Financial Aid
New Mexico Commission on Higher Education
1068 Cerrillos Road
Santa Fe, NM 87505
Phone: 505-476-6549
Fax: 505-476-6511
E-mail: tashina.banks-moore@state.nm.us

NEW MEXICO SCHOLARS' PROGRAM

Renewable award program created to encourage New Mexico high school students to attend public postsecondary institutions or the following private colleges in New Mexico: College of Santa Fe, St. John's College, College of the Southwest. For details visit http://fin.hed.state.nm.us.

Award: Scholarship for use in freshman year; renewable. *Number:* 1. *Amount:* varies.

Eligibility Requirements: Applicant must be high school student; age 21 or under; planning to enroll or expecting to enroll full-time at a two-year or four-year institution; resident of New Mexico and studying in New Mexico. Available to U.S. citizens.

Application Requirements: Application, financial need analysis, test scores, FAFSA. *Deadline:* varies.

Contact: Tashina Banks Moore, Director of Financial Aid
New Mexico Commission on Higher Education
1068 Cerrillos Road
Santa Fe, NM 87505-1650
Phone: 505-476-6549
Fax: 505-476-6511
E-mail: tashina.banks-moore@state.nm.us

NEW MEXICO STUDENT INCENTIVE GRANT

Grant created to provide aid for undergraduate students with substantial financial need who are attending public colleges or universities or the following eligible colleges in New Mexico: College of Santa Fe, St. John's College, College of the Southwest, Institute of American Indian Art, Crownpoint Institute of Technology, Dine College and Southwestern Indian Polytechnic Institute. Part-time students are eligible for pro-rated awards.

Award: Grant for use in freshman, sophomore, junior, or senior years; not renewable. *Number:* 1. *Amount:* $200–$2500.

Eligibility Requirements: Applicant must be enrolled or expecting to enroll full- or part-time at a two-year or four-year or technical institution or university; resident of New Mexico and studying in New Mexico. Available to U.S. citizens.

Application Requirements: Application, financial need analysis, FAFSA. *Deadline:* varies.

Contact: Tashina Banks Moore, Director of Financial Aid
New Mexico Commission on Higher Education
1068 Cerrillos Road
Santa Fe, NM 87505-1650
Phone: 505-476-6549
Fax: 505-476-6511
E-mail: tashina.banks-moore@state.nm.us

VIETNAM VETERANS' SCHOLARSHIP PROGRAM
• See page 641

NEW MEXICO DEPARTMENT OF VETERANS' SERVICES

http://www.dvs.state.nm.us/

CHILDREN OF DECEASED VETERANS SCHOLARSHIP-NEW MEXICO
• See page 642

NEW MEXICO VIETNAM VETERAN SCHOLARSHIP
• See page 642

NEW YORK STATE EDUCATION DEPARTMENT

http://www.highered.nysed.gov/

ROBERT C. BYRD HONORS SCHOLARSHIP-NEW YORK

Award for outstanding high school seniors accepted to U.S. college or university. Based on SAT score and high school average. Minimum 1875 combined SAT score from one sitting. Must be legal resident of New York and a U.S. citizen. Renewable for up to four years.

Award: Scholarship for use in freshman year; renewable. *Number:* 400. *Amount:* $1500.

Eligibility Requirements: Applicant must be high school student; planning to enroll or expecting to enroll full-time at a two-year or four-year institution or university and resident of New York. Available to U.S. citizens.

Application Requirements: Application. *Deadline:* March 1.

Contact: Lewis Hall, Supervisor
New York State Education Department
89 Washington Avenue, Room 1078 EBA
Albany, NY 12234
Phone: 518-486-1319
Fax: 518-486-5346
E-mail: scholar@mail.nysed.gov

SCHOLARSHIP FOR ACADEMIC EXCELLENCE

Renewable award for New York residents. Scholarship winners must attend a college or university in New York. 2000 scholarships are for $1500 and 6000 are for $500. The selection criteria used are based on Regents test scores or rank in class or local exam. Must be U.S. citizen or permanent resident.

Award: Scholarship for use in freshman year; renewable. *Number:* up to 8000. *Amount:* $500–$1500.

Eligibility Requirements: Applicant must be high school student; planning to enroll or expecting to enroll full-time at a two-year or four-year institution or university; resident of New York and studying in New York. Available to U.S. citizens.

Application Requirements: Application. *Deadline:* December 19.

Contact: Lewis Hall, Supervisor
New York State Education Department
89 Washington Avenue, Room 1078 EBA
Albany, NY 12234
Phone: 518-486-1319
Fax: 518-486-5346
E-mail: scholar@mail.nysed.gov

NEW YORK STATE GRANGE

http://www.nysgrange.com/

CAROLINE KARK AWARD
• See page 555

SUSAN W. FREESTONE EDUCATION AWARD
• See page 555

NEW YORK STATE HIGHER EDUCATION SERVICES CORPORATION

http://www.hesc.com/

NEW YORK AID FOR PART-TIME STUDY (APTS)

Renewable scholarship provides tuition assistance to part-time undergraduate students who are New York residents, meet income eligibility requirements and are attending New York accredited institutions. Deadline varies. Must be U.S. citizen.

Award: Grant for use in freshman, sophomore, junior, or senior years; renewable. *Number:* varies. *Amount:* up to $2000.

Eligibility Requirements: Applicant must be enrolled or expecting to enroll part-time at a two-year or four-year institution or university; resident of New York and studying in New York. Available to U.S. citizens.

Application Requirements: Application, financial need analysis. *Deadline:* varies.

Contact: Student Information
New York State Higher Education Services Corporation
99 Washington Avenue, Room 1320
Albany, NY 12255
Phone: 518-473-3887
Fax: 518-474-2839

NEW YORK MEMORIAL SCHOLARSHIPS FOR FAMILIES OF DECEASED POLICE OFFICERS, FIRE FIGHTERS AND PEACE OFFICERS

Renewable scholarship for children, spouses and financial dependents of deceased fire fighters, volunteer firefighters, police officers, peace officers and emergency medical service workers who died in the line of duty. Provides up to the cost of SUNY educational expenses.

Award: Scholarship for use in freshman, sophomore, junior, or senior years; renewable. *Number:* varies. *Amount:* varies.

Eligibility Requirements: Applicant must be enrolled or expecting to enroll full-time at a four-year institution or university; resident of New York and studying in New York. Available to U.S. citizens.

Application Requirements: Application, financial need analysis, transcript. *Deadline:* May 1.

Contact: Scholarships
Phone: 888-697-4372

NEW YORK STATE AID TO NATIVE AMERICANS
• See page 674

NEW YORK STATE TUITION ASSISTANCE PROGRAM

Award for New York state residents attending a New York postsecondary institution. Must be full-time student in approved program with tuition over $200 per year. Must show financial need and not be in default in any other state program. Renewable award of $500 to $5000 dependent on family income and tuition charged.

Award: Grant for use in freshman, sophomore, junior, or senior years; renewable. *Number:* 350,000–360,000. *Amount:* $500–$5000.

Eligibility Requirements: Applicant must be enrolled or expecting to enroll full-time at a two-year or four-year institution or university; resident of New York and studying in New York. Available to U.S. citizens.

Application Requirements: Application, financial need analysis. *Deadline:* May 1.

Contact: Student Information
New York State Higher Education Services Corporation
99 Washington Avenue, Room 1400
Albany, NY 12255
Phone: 888-697-4372

NEW YORK VIETNAM/PERSIAN GULF/AFGHANISTAN VETERANS TUITION AWARDS
• See page 642

REGENTS AWARD FOR CHILD OF VETERAN
• See page 642

REGENTS PROFESSIONAL OPPORTUNITY SCHOLARSHIPS

Award for New York State residents pursuing career in certain licensed professions. Must attend New York State college. Priority given to economically disadvantaged members of minority group underrepresented in chosen profession and graduates of SEEK, College Discovery, EOP, and HEOP. Must work in New York State in chosen profession one year for each annual payment. Scholarships are awarded to undergraduate or graduate students, depending on the program.

Award: Scholarship for use in freshman, sophomore, junior, senior, graduate, or postgraduate years; not renewable. *Amount:* $1000–$5000.

Eligibility Requirements: Applicant must be enrolled or expecting to enroll full-time at a two-year or four-year institution or university; resident of New York and studying in New York. Available to U.S. citizens.

Application Requirements: Application. *Deadline:* May 3.

Contact: Scholarship Coordinator
New York State Higher Education Services Corporation
Education Building Addition Room 1071
Albany, NY 12234
Phone: 518-486-1319

SCHOLARSHIPS FOR ACADEMIC EXCELLENCE

Renewable awards of up to $1500 for academically outstanding New York State high school graduates planning to attend an approved postsecondary institution in New York State. For full-time study only. Contact high school guidance counselor to apply.

Award: Scholarship for use in freshman, sophomore, junior, or senior years; renewable. *Number:* up to 8000. *Amount:* $500–$1500.

Eligibility Requirements: Applicant must be high school student; planning to enroll or expecting to enroll full-time at a four-year institution or university; resident of New York and studying in New York. Available to U.S. citizens.

Application Requirements: Application. *Deadline:* varies.

Contact: Rita McGivern, Student Information
New York State Higher Education Services Corporation
99 Washington Avenue, Room 1320
Albany, NY 12255
E-mail: scholarship@hesc.com

WORLD TRADE CENTER MEMORIAL SCHOLARSHIP

Renewable awards of up to the cost of educational expenses at a State University of New York four-year college. Available to the children, spouses and financial dependents of victims who died or were severely disabled as a result of the September 11, 2001 terrorist attacks on the U.S. and the rescue and recovery efforts.

Award: Scholarship for use in freshman, sophomore, junior, or senior years; renewable. *Number:* varies. *Amount:* varies.

Eligibility Requirements: Applicant must be enrolled or expecting to enroll full-time at a four-year institution or university and studying in New York. Available to U.S. and non-U.S. citizens.

Application Requirements: Application, financial need analysis, references, transcript. *Deadline:* May 1.

Contact: Scholarship Unit
New York State Higher Education Services Corporation
99 Washington Avenue, Room 1320
Albany, NY 12255
Phone: 888-697-4372

NORTH CAROLINA 4-H

http://www.nc4h.org/

NORTH CAROLINA 4-H DEVELOPMENT FUND SCHOLARSHIPS

Scholarship for a resident of North Carolina, enrolling as an undergraduate in a four-year accredited North Carolina college or university or a junior or community college in the state, provided the program of study selected is transferable to a four-year college. Must demonstrate an aptitude for college work through SAT scores. For some of the awards, financial need is a prerequisite. Some awards have geographic restrictions to regions of the state. Some scholarships are renewable.

Award: Scholarship for use in freshman, sophomore, junior, or senior years; renewable. *Number:* varies. *Amount:* $500–$2500.

Eligibility Requirements: Applicant must be enrolled or expecting to enroll full-time at a two-year or four-year institution or university; resident of North Carolina and studying in North Carolina. Available to U.S. citizens.

Application Requirements: Application, financial need analysis, test scores, transcript. *Deadline:* January 15.

Contact: Shannon McCollum, Extension 4-H Associate
North Carolina 4-H
Box 7606
North Carolina State University
Raleigh, NC 27695-7606
E-mail: shannon_mccollum@ncsu.edu

NORTH CAROLINA ASSOCIATION OF EDUCATORS

http://www.ncae.org/

NORTH CAROLINA ASSOCIATION OF EDUCATORS MARTIN LUTHER KING JR. SCHOLARSHIP

One-time award for high school seniors who are North Carolina residents to attend a postsecondary institution. Must be a U.S. citizen. Based upon financial need, GPA, and essay. Must have a GPA of at least 4.0 on a 5.0 scale or a 3.0 on a 4.0 scale.

Award: Scholarship for use in freshman year; not renewable. *Number:* 3–4. *Amount:* $500–$1000.

Eligibility Requirements: Applicant must be high school student; planning to enroll or expecting to enroll full-time at a four-year institution or university and resident of North Carolina. Available to U.S. citizens.

Application Requirements: Application, essay, financial need analysis, references, transcript. *Deadline:* February 1.

Contact: Dee Leach, Scholarship Coordinator
North Carolina Association of Educators
PO Box 27347
Raleigh, NC 27611
Phone: 800-662-7924
E-mail: dee.leach@ncae.org

NORTH CAROLINA BAR ASSOCIATION

http://www.ncbar.org/

NORTH CAROLINA BAR ASSOCIATION YOUNG LAWYERS DIVISION SCHOLARSHIP

Renewable award for children of North Carolina Law Enforcement Officers killed or permanently disabled in the line of duty, studying full-time in accredited colleges or universities. Must be resident of North Carolina and under 26 years of age. The number of awards and the dollar value of the award varies annually.

Award: Scholarship for use in freshman, sophomore, junior, senior, graduate, or postgraduate years; renewable. *Number:* varies. *Amount:* varies.

Eligibility Requirements: Applicant must be age 26 or under; enrolled or expecting to enroll full-time at a two-year or four-year or technical institution or university and resident of North Carolina. Available to U.S. citizens.

Application Requirements: Application, essay, financial need analysis, photo, test scores, transcript, verification letter from law enforcement agency. *Deadline:* April 1.

Contact: Jacquelyn Terrell, Director of Sections/Divisions Activities, YLD Staff Liaison
North Carolina Bar Association
PO Box 3688
Cary, NC 27519
Phone: 919-677-0561 Ext. 331
Fax: 919-677-0761
E-mail: jterrell@ncbar.org

NORTH CAROLINA DIVISION OF SERVICES FOR THE BLIND

http://www.ncdhhs.gov/

NORTH CAROLINA DIVISION OF SERVICES FOR THE BLIND REHABILITATION SERVICES

• *See page 610*

NORTH CAROLINA DIVISION OF VETERANS AFFAIRS

http://www.doa.state.nc.us/vets/va.htm

NORTH CAROLINA VETERANS SCHOLARSHIPS CLASS I-A
• *See page 642*

NORTH CAROLINA VETERANS SCHOLARSHIPS CLASS I-B
• *See page 642*

NORTH CAROLINA VETERANS SCHOLARSHIPS CLASS II
• *See page 643*

NORTH CAROLINA VETERANS SCHOLARSHIPS CLASS III
• *See page 643*

NORTH CAROLINA VETERANS SCHOLARSHIPS CLASS IV
• *See page 643*

NORTH CAROLINA DIVISION OF VOCATIONAL REHABILITATION SERVICES

http://www.dhhs.state.nc.us/

TRAINING SUPPORT FOR YOUTH WITH DISABILITIES
• *See page 611*

NORTH CAROLINA NATIONAL GUARD

http://www.nc.ngb.army.mil/

NORTH CAROLINA NATIONAL GUARD TUITION ASSISTANCE PROGRAM
• *See page 621*

NORTH CAROLINA SOCIETY OF HISPANIC PROFESSIONALS

http://www.thencshp.org/

NORTH CAROLINA HISPANIC COLLEGE FUND SCHOLARSHIP
• *See page 674*

NORTH CAROLINA STATE EDUCATION ASSISTANCE AUTHORITY

http://www.ncseaa.edu/

AUBREY LEE BROOKS SCHOLARSHIPS

Renewable award for high school seniors who are residents of designated North Carolina counties and are planning to attend North Carolina State University, the University of North Carolina at Chapel Hill or the University of North Carolina at Greensboro. Scholarship is renewable, provided the recipient has continued financial need, remains enrolled full time at an eligible institution. Minimum GPA 2.75 required. Write for further details or visit web site http://www.cfnc.org.

Award: Scholarship for use in freshman year; renewable. *Number:* 17–19. *Amount:* up to $8000.

Eligibility Requirements: Applicant must be high school student; planning to enroll or expecting to enroll full-time at a four-year institution or university; resident of North Carolina and studying in North Carolina. Applicant must have 3.0 GPA or higher. Available to U.S. and non-Canadian citizens.

Application Requirements: Application, essay, financial need analysis, interview, photo, references, test scores, transcript. *Deadline:* February 1.

Contact: Bill Carswell, Manager of Scholarship and Grant Division
North Carolina State Education Assistance Authority
PO Box 14103
Research Triangle Park, NC 27709
Phone: 919-549-8614
Fax: 919-549-4687
E-mail: carswellb@ncseaa.edu

JAGANNATHAN SCHOLARSHIP

Available to graduating high school seniors who plan to enroll as college freshmen in a full-time degree program at one of the constituent institutions of The University of North Carolina. Applicant must be resident of North Carolina. Applicant must document financial need.

Award: Scholarship for use in freshman year; renewable. *Number:* varies. *Amount:* up to $3500.

Eligibility Requirements: Applicant must be enrolled or expecting to enroll full-time at a four-year institution or university; resident of North Carolina and studying in North Carolina. Applicant must have 3.0 GPA or higher. Available to U.S. citizens.

Application Requirements: Application, financial need analysis. *Deadline:* February 15.

Contact: Bill Carswell, Manager of Scholarship and Grant Division
North Carolina State Education Assistance Authority
PO Box 13663
Research Triangle Park, NC 27709
Phone: 919-549-8614
Fax: 919-248-4687
E-mail: carswellb@ncseaa.edu

NORTH CAROLINA COMMUNITY COLLEGE GRANT PROGRAM

Annual award for North Carolina residents enrolled at least part-time in a North Carolina community college curriculum program. Priority given to those enrolled in college transferable curriculum programs, persons seeking new job skills, women in non-traditional curricula, and those participating in an ABE, GED, or high school diploma program. Contact financial aid office of institution the student attends for information and deadline. Must complete Free Application for Federal Student Aid.

Award: Grant for use in freshman or sophomore years; renewable. *Number:* varies. *Amount:* $683.

Eligibility Requirements: Applicant must be enrolled or expecting to enroll full- or part-time at a two-year or technical institution; resident of North Carolina and studying in North Carolina. Available to U.S. citizens.

Application Requirements: Application, financial need analysis, FAFSA. *Deadline:* varies.

Contact: Bill Carswell, Manager, Scholarship and Grants Division
North Carolina State Education Assistance Authority
PO Box 14103
Research Triangle Park, NC 27709
Phone: 919-549-8614
Fax: 919-248-4687
E-mail: carswellb@ncseaa.edu

NORTH CAROLINA LEGISLATIVE TUITION GRANT PROGRAM (NCLTG)

Renewable aid for North Carolina residents attending approved private colleges or universities within the state. Must be enrolled full or part-time in an undergraduate program not leading to a religious vocation. Contact college financial aid office for deadlines.

Award: Grant for use in freshman, sophomore, junior, or senior years; renewable. *Number:* varies. *Amount:* $1950.

Eligibility Requirements: Applicant must be enrolled or expecting to enroll full- or part-time at a two-year or four-year institution or university; resident of North Carolina and studying in North Carolina. Available to U.S. citizens.

Application Requirements: Application. *Deadline:* varies.

Contact: Bill Carswell, Manager of Scholarship and Grant Division
North Carolina State Education Assistance Authority
PO Box 13663
Research Triangle Park, NC 27709
Phone: 919-549-8614
Fax: 919-248-4687
E-mail: carswellb@ncseaa.edu

STATE CONTRACTUAL SCHOLARSHIP FUND PROGRAM-NORTH CAROLINA

Renewable award for North Carolina residents already attending an approved private college or university in the state and pursuing an undergraduate degree. Must have financial need. Contact college financial aid office for deadline and information. May not be enrolled in a program leading to a religious vocation.

Award: Scholarship for use in freshman, sophomore, junior, or senior years; renewable. *Number:* varies. *Amount:* up to $1350.

Eligibility Requirements: Applicant must be enrolled or expecting to enroll full- or part-time at a four-year institution or university; resident of North Carolina and studying in North Carolina. Available to U.S. citizens.

Application Requirements: Application, financial need analysis. *Deadline:* varies.

Contact: Bill Carswell, Manager of Scholarship and Grant Division
North Carolina State Education Assistance Authority
PO Box 13663
Research Triangle Park, NC 27709
Phone: 919-549-8614
Fax: 919-248-4687
E-mail: carswellb@ncseaa.edu

UNIVERSITY OF NORTH CAROLINA NEED-BASED GRANT

Applicants must be enrolled in at least 6 credit hours at one of sixteen UNC system universities. Eligibility based on need; award varies, consideration for grant automatic when FAFSA is filed. Late applications may be denied due to insufficient funds.

Award: Grant for use in freshman, sophomore, junior, or senior years; renewable. *Number:* varies. *Amount:* varies.

Eligibility Requirements: Applicant must be enrolled or expecting to enroll full- or part-time at an institution or university; resident of North Carolina and studying in North Carolina. Available to U.S. citizens.

Application Requirements: Application, financial need analysis, FAFSA. *Deadline:* varies.

Contact: Bill Carswell, Manager of Scholarship and Grant Division
North Carolina State Education Assistance Authority
PO Box 13663
Research Triangle Park, NC 27709
Phone: 919-549-8614
Fax: 919-248-4687
E-mail: carswellb@ncseaa.edu

NORTH DAKOTA DEPARTMENT OF PUBLIC INSTRUCTION

http://www.dpi.state.nd.us/

ROBERT C. BYRD HONORS SCHOLARSHIP-NORTH DAKOTA

Awards to high school graduates who have been accepted for enrollment at institutions of higher education (IHEs), have demonstrated outstanding academic achievement, and show promise of continued academic excellence. For details refer to web site http://www.ed.gov/programs/iduesbyrd/eligibility.html.

Award: Scholarship for use in freshman, sophomore, junior, or senior years; renewable. *Number:* 10–16. *Amount:* $1500.

Eligibility Requirements: Applicant must be enrolled or expecting to enroll full-time at a two-year or four-year or technical institution or university and resident of North Dakota. Available to U.S. citizens.

Application Requirements: Application, essay, references, test scores, transcript, college acceptance letter. *Deadline:* April 30.

Contact: Pauline Iler, Scholarship Contact
North Dakota Department of Public Instruction
600 East Boulevard Avenue, Department 201
Bismarck, ND 58505-0440
Phone: 707-328-4518
Fax: 701-328-4770
E-mail: hbergland@state.nd.us

NORTH DAKOTA UNIVERSITY SYSTEM

http://www.ndus.edu/

NORTH DAKOTA INDIAN SCHOLARSHIP PROGRAM
• *See page 675*

NORTH DAKOTA SCHOLARS PROGRAM

Provides scholarships equal to cost of tuition at the public colleges in North Dakota for North Dakota residents. To be eligible for consideration for a ND Scholars scholarship, a high school junior must take the ACT Assessment between October and June of their junior year and score in the upper five percentile of all ND ACT test takers. The numeric sum of the English, Math, reading and science reasoning scores will be used as a second selection criteria. The numeric sum of a student's English and mathematics scores will be used as selection criteria if a tie-breaker is needed.

Award: Scholarship for use in freshman, sophomore, junior, or senior years; renewable. *Number:* 45–50. *Amount:* $4160–$5461.

Eligibility Requirements: Applicant must be high school student; planning to enroll or expecting to enroll full-time at a two-year or four-year institution or university; resident of North Dakota and studying in North Dakota. Available to U.S. citizens.

Application Requirements: References, test scores.

Contact: Peggy Wipf, Director of Financial Aid
North Dakota University System
600 East Boulevard Avenue, Department 215
Bismarck, ND 58505-0230
Phone: 701-328-4114
E-mail: peggy.wipf@ndus.nodak.edu

NORTH DAKOTA STATE STUDENT INCENTIVE GRANT PROGRAM

Aids North Dakota residents attending an approved college or university in North Dakota. Must be enrolled in a program of at least nine months in length. Must be a U.S. citizen. Must complete the FAFSAA. Needs-based.

Award: Grant for use in freshman, sophomore, junior, or senior years; not renewable. *Number:* 7500–8300. *Amount:* $1200.

Eligibility Requirements: Applicant must be enrolled or expecting to enroll full-time at a two-year or four-year institution or university; resident of North Dakota and studying in North Dakota. Available to U.S. citizens.

Application Requirements: Financial need analysis. *Deadline:* March 15.

Contact: Peggy Wipf, Director of Financial Aid
North Dakota University System
600 East Boulevard Avenue, Department 215
Bismarck, ND 58505-0230
Phone: 701-328-4114

OHIO ASSOCIATION FOR ADULT AND CONTINUING EDUCATION

http://www.oaace.org/

LIFELONG LEARNING SCHOLARSHIP

Scholarship available for a Ohio resident student with Ohio high school equivalence diploma or high school diploma, who is currently enrolled in any adult education program or has been enrolled within the last twelve months. Must enroll in postsecondary education or training within six months of receiving scholarship. Number of awards granted varies.

Award: Scholarship for use in freshman year; not renewable. *Number:* varies. *Amount:* $1500.

Eligibility Requirements: Applicant must be high school student; planning to enroll or expecting to enroll full-time at a four-year institution or university and resident of Ohio. Available to U.S. citizens.

Application Requirements: Application, references. *Deadline:* March 1.

Contact: Chairman, Scholarship Committee
Ohio Association for Adult and Continuing Education
1601 West Fifth Avenue
PO Box 103
Columbus, OH 43212-2310
Phone: 866-996-2223
Fax: 740-435-0212
E-mail: awards@oaace.org

LINDA LUCA MEMORIAL GED SCHOLARSHIP

Scholarship available for a Ohio resident student who scored in the top 100 of GED scores for the year. Must enroll in postsecondary education or training within six months of receiving scholarship. Scholarship value: $1500.

Award: Scholarship for use in freshman year; not renewable. *Number:* varies. *Amount:* $1500.

Eligibility Requirements: Applicant must be high school student; planning to enroll or expecting to enroll full-time at a four-year institution or university and resident of Ohio. Available to U.S. citizens.

Application Requirements: Application, references. *Deadline:* varies.

Contact: Chairman, Scholarship Committee
Ohio Association for Adult and Continuing Education
1601 West Fifth Avenue
PO Box 103
Columbus, OH 43212-2310
Phone: 866-996-2223
Fax: 740-435-0212
E-mail: awards@oaace.org

OAACE MEMBER SCHOLARSHIP

Scholarship for Ohio resident and member of OAACE. Should enroll in postsecondary education or professional development training within six months of receiving scholarship.

Award: Scholarship for use in freshman year; not renewable. *Number:* varies. *Amount:* $2000.

Eligibility Requirements: Applicant must be high school student; planning to enroll or expecting to enroll full-time at a four-year institution or university and resident of Ohio. Available to U.S. citizens.

Application Requirements: Application, references. *Deadline:* March 1.

Contact: Chairman, Scholarship Committee
Ohio Association for Adult and Continuing Education
1601 West Fifth Avenue
PO Box 103
Columbus, OH 43212-2310
Phone: 866-996-2223
Fax: 740-435-0212
E-mail: awards@oaace.org

OHIO ASSOCIATION OF CAREER COLLEGES AND SCHOOLS

http://www.ohiocareercolleges.org/

LEGISLATIVE SCHOLARSHIP

One-time scholarship for graduating high school seniors enrolling in a career college or school that is a participating member of OACCS. The applicant must be an Ohio high school student with a 2.0 GPA or better and does not have to demonstrate a financial need. The scholarship amount and the number of scholarships granted varies.

Award: Scholarship for use in freshman or sophomore years; not renewable. *Number:* 275. *Amount:* $2000–$12,995.

Eligibility Requirements: Applicant must be high school student; planning to enroll or expecting to enroll full-time at a two-year or four-year or technical institution or university; resident of Ohio and studying in Ohio. Available to U.S. and non-U.S. citizens.

Application Requirements: Application, essay, references, transcript. *Deadline:* April 1.

Contact: R. Rankin, Executive Director
Ohio Association of Career Colleges and Schools
1328 Dublin Rd
Columbus, OH 43215
Phone: 614-487-8180
E-mail: oaccs1@aol.com

OHIO BOARD OF REGENTS

http://www.uso.edu/

OHIO COLLEGE OPPORTUNITY GRANT

OCOG provides grant money to Ohio residents who demonstrate the highest levels of financial need (as determined by the results of FAFSA) who are enrolled at Ohio public university main campuses (not regional campuses or community colleges), Ohio private, non-profit colleges or universities (not private, for-profit institutions) or eligible Pennsylvania institutions.

Award: Grant for use in freshman, sophomore, junior, or senior years; not renewable. *Amount:* up to $1848.

Eligibility Requirements: Applicant must be enrolled or expecting to enroll full- or part-time at a four-year institution or university; resident of Ohio and studying in Ohio or Pennsylvania. Available to U.S. citizens.

Application Requirements: FAFSA. *Deadline:* October 1.

Contact: *Phone:* 888-833-1133
E-mail: ocog_admin@regents.state.oh.us

OHIO SAFETY OFFICERS COLLEGE MEMORIAL FUND

Renewable award covering up to full tuition is available to children and surviving spouses of peace officers, other safety officers and fire fighters killed in the line of duty in any state. Children must be under 26 years of age. Dollar value of each award varies. Must be an Ohio resident and enroll full-time or part-time at an Ohio college or university. Any spouse/child of a member of the armed services of the U.S., who has been killed in the line duty during Operation Enduring Freedom, Operation Iraqi Freedom or a combat zone designated by the President of the United States. Dollar value of each award varies.

Award: Scholarship for use in freshman, sophomore, junior, or senior years; renewable. *Amount:* varies.

Eligibility Requirements: Applicant must be age 26 or under; enrolled or expecting to enroll full- or part-time at a two-year or four-year institution or university; resident of Ohio and studying in Ohio. Available to U.S. citizens.

Application Requirements: *Deadline:* continuous.

Contact: Barbara Thoma, Assistant Director
Ohio Board of Regents
30 East Broad Street, 36th Floor
Columbus, OH 43215-3414
Phone: 614-752-9535
Fax: 614-752-5903
E-mail: bthoma@regents.state.oh.us

OHIO WAR ORPHANS SCHOLARSHIP
• See page 643

OHIO CIVIL SERVICE EMPLOYEES ASSOCIATION

http://www.ocsea.org/

LES BEST SCHOLARSHIP
• See page 556

OHIO DEPARTMENT OF EDUCATION

http://www.ode.state.oh.us/

ROBERT C. BYRD HONORS SCHOLARSHIP

Competitive, merit-based scholarship for which students may be nominated by their school. The award is made to outstanding high school graduates who show promise of continued excellence in an effort to recognize and promote students excellence and achievement. The scholarship is renewable for up to four yeas of academic undergraduate study.

Award: Scholarship for use in freshman, sophomore, junior, or senior years; not renewable. *Number:* 200–225. *Amount:* up to $1500.

Eligibility Requirements: Applicant must be high school student; planning to enroll or expecting to enroll full-time at a two-year or four-year or technical institution or university and resident of Ohio. Available to U.S. citizens.

Application Requirements: References, test scores, school nomination. *Deadline:* April 30.

Contact: Mr. Mark Lynskey, Program Administrator
Ohio Department of Education
25 South Front Street, Second Floor
Columbus, OH 43215
Phone: 614-466-2650
E-mail: mark.lynskey@ode.state.oh.us

OHIO NATIONAL GUARD

http://www.ongsp.org/

OHIO NATIONAL GUARD SCHOLARSHIP PROGRAM
• *See page 621*

OKLAHOMA ALUMNI & ASSOCIATES OF FHA, HERO AND FCCLA INC.

http://www.okfccla.net/

OKLAHOMA ALUMNI & ASSOCIATES OF FHA, HERO AND FCCLA INC. SCHOLARSHIP
• *See page 556*

OKLAHOMA STATE DEPARTMENT OF EDUCATION

http://www.sde.state.ok.us/

ROBERT C. BYRD HONORS SCHOLARSHIP-OKLAHOMA

Scholarships available to high school seniors. Applicants must be U.S. citizens or national, or be permanent residents of the United States. Must be legal residents of Oklahoma. Must have a minimum ACT composite score of 32 and/or a minimum SAT combined score of 1420 and/or 2130 or a minimum GED score of 700. Application URL http://www.sde.state.ok.us/pro/Byrd/application.pdf.

Award: Scholarship for use in freshman year; not renewable. *Number:* 10. *Amount:* $1500.

Eligibility Requirements: Applicant must be high school student; planning to enroll or expecting to enroll full-time at a four-year institution or university and resident of Oklahoma. Available to U.S. citizens.

Application Requirements: Application, essay, references, transcript. *Deadline:* April 11.

Contact: Certification Specialist
Oklahoma State Department of Education
2500 North Lincoln Boulevard, Suite 212
Oklahoma City, OK 73105-4599
Phone: 405-521-2808

OKLAHOMA STATE REGENTS FOR HIGHER EDUCATION

http://www.okhighered.org/

ACADEMIC SCHOLARS PROGRAM

Awards for students of high academic ability to attend institutions in Oklahoma. Renewable up to four years. ACT or SAT scores must fall between 99.5 and 100th percentiles, or applicant must be designated as a National Merit scholar or finalist. Oklahoma public institutions can also select institutional nominees.

Award: Scholarship for use in freshman, sophomore, junior, senior, or graduate years; renewable. *Number:* varies. *Amount:* $1800–$5500.

Eligibility Requirements: Applicant must be high school student; planning to enroll or expecting to enroll full-time at a two-year or four-year institution or university and studying in Oklahoma. Available to U.S. citizens.

Application Requirements: Application, test scores, transcript. *Deadline:* continuous.

Contact: Scholarship Programs Coordinator
Oklahoma State Regents for Higher Education
PO Box 108850
Oklahoma City, OK 73101-8850
Phone: 800-858-1840
Fax: 405-225-9230
E-mail: studentinfo@osrhe.edu

OKLAHOMA TUITION AID GRANT

Award for Oklahoma residents enrolled at an Oklahoma institution at least part time each semester in a degree program. May be enrolled in two- or four-year or approved vocational-technical institution. Award for students attending public institutions or private colleges. Application is made through FAFSA.

Award: Grant for use in freshman, sophomore, junior, or senior years; not renewable. *Number:* varies. *Amount:* $1000–$1300.

Eligibility Requirements: Applicant must be enrolled or expecting to enroll full- or part-time at a two-year or four-year or technical institution or university; resident of Oklahoma and studying in Oklahoma. Available to U.S. citizens.

Application Requirements: Application, financial need analysis, FAFSA. *Deadline:* varies.

Contact: Oklahoma State Regents for Higher Education
PO Box 108850
Oklahoma City, OK 73101-8850
Phone: 405-858-1840
Fax: 405-225-9230
E-mail: studentinfo@osrhe.edu

REGIONAL UNIVERSITY BACCALAUREATE SCHOLARSHIP

Renewable award for Oklahoma residents attending one of 11 participating Oklahoma public universities. Must have an ACT composite score of at least 30 or be a National Merit semifinalist or commended student. In addition to the award amount, each recipient will receive a resident tuition waiver from the institution. Must maintain a 3.25 GPA. Deadlines vary depending upon the institution attended.

Award: Scholarship for use in freshman, sophomore, junior, or senior years; renewable. *Number:* varies. *Amount:* $3000.

Eligibility Requirements: Applicant must be enrolled or expecting to enroll full-time at an institution or university; resident of Oklahoma and studying in Oklahoma. Available to U.S. citizens.

Application Requirements: Application. *Deadline:* varies.

Contact: Scholarship Programs Coordinator
Oklahoma State Regents for Higher Education
PO Box 108850
Oklahoma City, OK 73101-8850
Phone: 405-858-1840
Fax: 405-225-9230
E-mail: studentinfo@osrhe.edu

WILLIAM P. WILLIS SCHOLARSHIP

Renewable award for low-income Oklahoma residents attending an Oklahoma institution. Must be a full-time undergraduate. Deadline varies.

Award: Scholarship for use in freshman, sophomore, junior, or senior years; renewable. *Amount:* $2000–$3000.

Eligibility Requirements: Applicant must be enrolled or expecting to enroll full-time at a two-year or four-year institution or university; resident of Oklahoma and studying in Oklahoma. Available to U.S. citizens.

Application Requirements: Application. *Deadline:* varies.

Contact: Scholarship Programs Coordinator
Oklahoma State Regents for Higher Education
PO Box 108850
Oklahoma City, OK 73101-8850
Phone: 405-858-1840
Fax: 405-225-9230
E-mail: studentinfo@osrhe.edu

OREGON COMMUNITY FOUNDATION

http://www.oregoncf.org/

ERNEST ALAN AND BARBARA PARK MEYER SCHOLARSHIP FUND

Scholarship for Oregon high school graduates for use in the pursuit of a postsecondary education (undergraduate or graduate) at a nonprofit two- or four-year college or university.

Award: Scholarship for use in freshman, sophomore, junior, or senior years; renewable. *Number:* up to 5. *Amount:* $1000–$4500.

Eligibility Requirements: Applicant must be enrolled or expecting to enroll full-time at a two-year or four-year or technical institution or university and resident of Oregon. Available to U.S. citizens.

Application Requirements: Application, references. *Deadline:* March 1.

Contact: Dianne Causey, Program Associate for Scholarships and Grants
Oregon Community Foundation
1221 Yamhill, SW, Suite 100
Portland, OR 97205-2108
Phone: 503-227-6846 Ext. 1418
E-mail: dcausey@oregoncf.org

FRIENDS OF BILL RUTHERFORD EDUCATION FUND

Scholarship for Oregon high school graduates or GED recipients who are dependent children of individuals holding statewide elected office or currently serving in the Oregon State Legislature. Students must be enrolled full time in a two- or four-year college or university. For more information, see Web http://www.getcollegefunds.org.

Award: Scholarship for use in freshman, sophomore, junior, or senior years; renewable. *Number:* 1–2. *Amount:* $1000–$2500.

Eligibility Requirements: Applicant must be enrolled or expecting to enroll full-time at a two-year or four-year institution or university and resident of Oregon. Available to U.S. citizens.

Application Requirements: Application, references. *Deadline:* March 1.

Contact: Dianne Causey, Program Associate for Scholarships and Grants
Oregon Community Foundation
1221 Yamhill, SW, Suite 100
Portland, OR 97205-2108
Phone: 503-227-6846 Ext. 1418
E-mail: dcausey@oregoncf.org

MARY E. HORSTKOTTE SCHOLARSHIP FUND

Award available for academically talented and financially needy students for use in the pursuit of a postsecondary education. Must be an Oregon resident. For full-time study only.

Award: Scholarship for use in freshman, sophomore, junior, or senior years; not renewable. *Number:* 1–10. *Amount:* $2000.

Eligibility Requirements: Applicant must be enrolled or expecting to enroll full-time at a two-year or four-year or technical institution or university and resident of Oregon. Available to U.S. citizens.

Application Requirements: Application, references. *Deadline:* March 1.

Contact: Dianne Causey, Program Associate for Scholarships and Grants
Oregon Community Foundation
1221 Yamhill, SW, Suite 100
Portland, OR 97205-2108
Phone: 503-227-6846 Ext. 1418
E-mail: dcausey@oregoncf.org

RUBE AND MINAH LESLIE EDUCATIONAL FUND

Scholarship for Oregon residents for the pursuit of a postsecondary education. Selection is based on financial need.

Award: Scholarship for use in freshman, sophomore, junior, or senior years; renewable. *Number:* up to 50. *Amount:* $2000.

Eligibility Requirements: Applicant must be enrolled or expecting to enroll full-time at a two-year or four-year institution or university and resident of Oregon. Available to U.S. citizens.

Application Requirements: Application, financial need analysis. *Deadline:* March 1.

Contact: Dianne Causey, Program Associate for Scholarships and Grants
Oregon Community Foundation
1221 Yamhill, SW, Suite 100
Portland, OR 97205-2108
Phone: 503-227-6846 Ext. 1418
E-mail: dcausey@oregoncf.org

WILLIAM L. AND DELLA WAGGONER SCHOLARSHIP FUND

Scholarship for undergraduates of any Oregon high school who show academic potential and financial need for use in the pursuit of a postsecondary education. For more information, see Web http://www.getcollegefunds.org.

Award: Scholarship for use in freshman, sophomore, junior, or senior years; renewable. *Number:* up to 30. *Amount:* $2000.

Eligibility Requirements: Applicant must be enrolled or expecting to enroll full-time at a two-year or four-year institution or university and resident of Oregon. Available to U.S. citizens.

Application Requirements: Application. *Deadline:* March 1.

Contact: Dianne Causey, Program Associate for Scholarships and Grants
Oregon Community Foundation
1221 Yamhill, SW, Suite 100
Portland, OR 97205-2108
Phone: 503-227-6846 Ext. 1418
E-mail: dcausey@oregoncf.org

OREGON DEPARTMENT OF VETERANS' AFFAIRS

http://www.oregon.gov/odva

OREGON VETERANS' EDUCATION AID
• *See page 643*

OREGON NATIVE AMERICAN CHAMBER OF COMMERCE SCHOLARSHIP

http://www.onacc.org/

OREGON NATIVE AMERICAN CHAMBER OF COMMERCE SCHOLARSHIP
• *See page 676*

OREGON STUDENT ASSISTANCE COMMISSION

http://www.GetCollegeFunds.org/

AFSCME: AMERICAN FEDERATION OF STATE, COUNTY, AND MUNICIPAL EMPLOYEES LOCAL 2067 SCHOLARSHIP
• *See page 557*

A. VICTOR ROSENFELD SCHOLARSHIP
• *See page 577*

BANDON SUBMARINE CABLE COUNCIL SCHOLARSHIP

Award for members or dependent children of members of the Bandon Submarine Cable Council; any commercial fisherman who resides in Coos County or family member; any postsecondary student residing in Clatsop, Coos, Curry, Lane, Lincoln, or Tillamook County; or any postsecondary student in Oregon. Essay must be submitted. Award is automatically renewable if criteria is met.

Award: Scholarship for use in freshman, sophomore, junior, or senior years; renewable. *Number:* varies. *Amount:* varies.

Eligibility Requirements: Applicant must be enrolled or expecting to enroll full-time at a four-year institution and resident of Oregon. Available to U.S. citizens.

Application Requirements: Application, essay, financial need analysis, transcript, activities chart, FAFSA. *Deadline:* March 1.

Contact: Director of Grant Programs
Oregon Student Assistance Commission
1500 Valley River Drive, Suite 100
Eugene, OR 97401-7020
Phone: 800-452-8807 Ext. 7395

BENJAMIN FRANKLIN/EDITH GREEN SCHOLARSHIP

One-time award for graduating Oregon high school seniors to attend four-year public Oregon colleges. GPA of 3.45 to 3.55 required. Award is based on financial need.

Award: Scholarship for use in freshman year; not renewable. *Number:* varies. *Amount:* varies.

Eligibility Requirements: Applicant must be high school student; planning to enroll or expecting to enroll full- or part-time at a four-year institution; resident of Oregon and studying in Oregon. Available to U.S. citizens.

Application Requirements: Application, essay, financial need analysis, transcript, activity chart. *Deadline:* March 1.

Contact: Director of Grant Programs
Oregon Student Assistance Commission
1500 Valley River Drive, Suite 100
Eugene, OR 97401-7020
Phone: 800-452-8807 Ext. 7395

BEN SELLING SCHOLARSHIP

Award for Oregon residents enrolling as undergraduate sophomores, juniors, or seniors. College GPA 3.5 or higher required. Apply/compete annually.

Award: Scholarship for use in sophomore, junior, or senior years; not renewable. *Number:* varies. *Amount:* varies.

Eligibility Requirements: Applicant must be enrolled or expecting to enroll full-time at a two-year or four-year institution and resident of Oregon. Applicant must have 3.5 GPA or higher. Available to U.S. citizens.

Application Requirements: Application, essay, financial need analysis, references, transcript, activity chart. *Deadline:* March 1.

Contact: Director of Grant Programs
Oregon Student Assistance Commission
1500 Valley River Drive, Suite 100
Eugene, OR 97401-7020
Phone: 800-452-8807 Ext. 7395

CONGRESSMAN PETER DEFAZIO SCHOLARSHIP

Award is available to dislocated workers residing in Oregon's Fourth Congressional District, which includes parts of Benton, Coos, Curry, Douglas, Josephine, Lane, and Linn counties. Recipients must attend one of Lane, Linn-Benton, Rogue, Southwestern Oregon or Umpqua Community Colleges and enroll at least half-time. If selected as a semi-finalist for the scholarship, verification of status as a dislocated worker is required.

Award: Scholarship for use in freshman year; not renewable.

Eligibility Requirements: Applicant must be enrolled or expecting to enroll full- or part-time at a two-year institution; resident of Oregon and studying in Oregon.

Application Requirements: Application, proof of unemployment. *Deadline:* March 1.

Contact: Director of Grant Programs
Oregon Student Assistance Commission
1500 Valley River Drive, Suite 100
Eugene, OR 97401-7020
Phone: 800-452-8807

DARLENE HOOLEY FOR OREGON VETERANS SCHOLARSHIP
• *See page 644*

DOROTHY CAMPBELL MEMORIAL SCHOLARSHIP

Renewable award for female Oregon high school graduates with a minimum 2.75 GPA. Must submit essay describing strong, continuing interest in golf and the contribution that sport has made to applicant's development. Must have played on high school golf team (including intramural), if available.

Award: Scholarship for use in freshman, sophomore, junior, or senior years; renewable. *Number:* varies. *Amount:* varies.

Eligibility Requirements: Applicant must be enrolled or expecting to enroll full-time at a four-year institution; female; resident of Oregon; studying in Oregon and must have an interest in golf. Available to U.S. citizens.

Application Requirements: Application, essay, financial need analysis, transcript. *Deadline:* March 1.

Contact: Scholarship Coordinator
Oregon Student Assistance Commission
1500 Valley River Drive, Suite 100
Eugene, OR 97401-7020
Phone: 800-452-8807

ESSEX GENERAL CONSTRUCTION SCHOLARSHIP
• *See page 577*

FORD OPPORTUNITY PROGRAM

Renewable award for Oregon residents who are single heads of household with custody of a dependent child or children and without the support of a domestic partner. Must be planning to earn a bachelor's degree and study full-time at an Oregon college or university. Minimum cumulative GPA of 3.0 required. If minimum requirements are not met, special recommendation form required (see high school counselor or contact OSAC).

Award: Scholarship for use in freshman, sophomore, junior, or senior years; renewable. *Number:* varies. *Amount:* varies.

Eligibility Requirements: Applicant must be enrolled or expecting to enroll full-time at a four-year institution or university; single; resident of Oregon and studying in Oregon. Applicant must have 3.0 GPA or higher. Available to U.S. citizens.

Application Requirements: Application, essay, financial need analysis, interview, transcript, activities chart. *Deadline:* March 1.

Contact: Ford Family Foundation Scholarship Office
Oregon Student Assistance Commission
440 East Broadway, Suite 200
Eugene, OR 97401
Phone: 877-864-2872
E-mail: fordscholarships@tfff.org

FORD RESTART PROGRAM

Award to support nontraditional, full-time adult students who wish to begin or continue education at the postsecondary level in Oregon. Must be an Oregon resident and at least 25 years of age by March 1 of the application year. Must have a high school diploma or GED certificate and must not have previously earned a bachelors degree. A Restart Reference Form is required and must be submitted with the application. Strong preference given to applicants with little or no recent college experience.

Award: Scholarship for use in freshman, sophomore, junior, or senior years; renewable. *Number:* varies. *Amount:* varies.

Eligibility Requirements: Applicant must be age 25 and over; enrolled or expecting to enroll full-time at a two-year or four-year or technical institution or university; resident of Oregon and studying in Oregon. Available to U.S. citizens.

Application Requirements: Application, essay, financial need analysis, interview, transcript, activity chart, reference form. *Deadline:* March 1.

Contact: Scholarship Office
Oregon Student Assistance Commission
440 East Broadway, Suite 200
Eugene, OR 97401
Phone: 877-864-2872

FORD SCHOLARS PROGRAM

Renewable award for Oregon residents who are graduating high school seniors or students at the point of transferring from a community college to a four-year college. Must have minimum cumulative GPA of 3.0, be planning to earn a bachelor's degree, and be enrolled as a full-time student. If minimum requirements are not met, special recommendation form required (see high school counselor or contact OSAC).

Award: Scholarship for use in freshman, sophomore, junior, or senior years; renewable. *Number:* varies. *Amount:* varies.

Eligibility Requirements: Applicant must be enrolled or expecting to enroll full-time at a four-year institution or university; resident of Oregon and studying in Oregon. Applicant must have 3.0 GPA or higher. Available to U.S. citizens.

Application Requirements: Application, essay, financial need analysis, interview, test scores, transcript. *Deadline:* March 1.

Contact: Ford Family Foundation Scholarship Office
Oregon Student Assistance Commission
440 East Broadway, Suite 200
Eugene, OR 97401
Phone: 877-864-2872
E-mail: fordscholarships@tfff.org

GLENN JACKSON SCHOLARS SCHOLARSHIPS
• *See page 578*

HARRY LUDWIG MEMORIAL SCHOLARSHIP
• *See page 611*

IDA M. CRAWFORD SCHOLARSHIP

Scholarship available to graduates of accredited Oregon high schools. Minimum GPA of 3.5 required. Not available to applicants majoring in law, medicine, theology, teaching, or music. U.S. Bank employees, their children or near relatives, are not eligible. Reapply annually for award renewal.

Award: Scholarship for use in freshman year; not renewable. *Number:* varies. *Amount:* varies.

Eligibility Requirements: Applicant must be enrolled or expecting to enroll full-time at a four-year institution and resident of Oregon. Applicant must have 3.5 GPA or higher. Available to U.S. citizens.

Application Requirements: Application, essay, financial need analysis, transcript, activities chart, copy of birth certificate. *Deadline:* March 1.

Contact: Scholarship Coordinator
Oregon Student Assistance Commission
1500 Valley River Drive, Suite 100
Eugene, OR 97401-7020
Phone: 800-452-8807

JEROME B. STEINBACH SCHOLARSHIP

Award for Oregon residents enrolled in Oregon institution as sophomore or above with minimum 3.5 GPA. Award for undergraduate study only. U.S. Bank employees, their children, or near relatives are not eligible. Must submit proof of U.S. birth.

Award: Scholarship for use in sophomore, junior, or senior years; renewable. *Amount:* varies.

Eligibility Requirements: Applicant must be enrolled or expecting to enroll full-time at a four-year institution or university and resident of Oregon. Applicant must have 3.5 GPA or higher. Available to U.S. citizens.

Application Requirements: Application, essay, financial need analysis, transcript, proof of U.S. birth. *Deadline:* March 1.

Contact: Scholarship Administrator
Oregon Student Assistance Commission
1500 Valley River Drive, Suite 100
Eugene, OR 97401-7020
Phone: 800-452-8807

KONNIE MEMORIAL DEPENDENTS SCHOLARSHIP
• *See page 578*

MARIA C. JACKSON/GENERAL GEORGE A. WHITE SCHOLARSHIP
• *See page 644*

OREGON DUNGENESS CRAB COMMISSION SCHOLARSHIP

One-time scholarship available to children, stepchildren, or legal dependents of licensed Oregon Dungeness Crab fishermen or crew. If a high school senior, may be enrolled in any major; other students must be enrolled in marine biology, environmental science, wildlife science, or related major. Must be 23 years of age or under as of the March scholarship deadline.

Award: Scholarship for use in freshman, sophomore, junior, or senior years; not renewable. *Amount:* varies.

Eligibility Requirements: Applicant must be age 23 or under; enrolled or expecting to enroll full-time at a four-year institution and resident of Oregon. Available to U.S. citizens.

Application Requirements: Application, essay, financial need analysis, transcript, activity chart, name of vessel in place of work-site in membership section. *Deadline:* March 1.

Contact: Director of Grant Programs
Oregon Student Assistance Commission
1500 Valley River Drive, Suite 100
Eugene, OR 97401-7020
Phone: 800-452-8807 Ext. 7395

OREGON OCCUPATIONAL SAFETY AND HEALTH DIVISION WORKERS MEMORIAL SCHOLARSHIP

One-time award for Oregon high school graduates or GED recipients who are either dependents or spouses of an Oregon worker who has incurred permanent total disability or was fatally injured on the job while working for an Oregon employer. Must submit essay on how the injury or death of your parent or spouse affected or influenced your decision to further your education.

Award: Scholarship for use in freshman, sophomore, junior, or senior years; not renewable. *Number:* varies. *Amount:* varies.

Eligibility Requirements: Applicant must be enrolled or expecting to enroll full- or part-time at a four-year institution or university and resident of Oregon. Available to U.S. citizens.

Application Requirements: Application, essay, financial need analysis, test scores, transcript, activity chart, proof of death or disability. *Deadline:* March 1.

Contact: Director of Grant Programs
Oregon Student Assistance Commission
1500 Valley River Drive, Suite 100
Eugene, OR 97401-7020
Phone: 800-452-8807 Ext. 7395

OREGON SALMON COMMISSION SCOTT BOLEY MEMORIAL SCHOLARSHIP

Award for dependents of licensed Oregon troll salmon permit fishermen. Preference given to graduating high school seniors. To be used for full-time study at any U.S. college or university.

Award: Scholarship for use in freshman year; not renewable. *Number:* varies. *Amount:* varies.

Eligibility Requirements: Applicant must be enrolled or expecting to enroll full-time at a four-year institution or university and resident of Oregon. Available to U.S. citizens.

Application Requirements: Application, essay, financial need analysis, transcript, activity chart. *Deadline:* March 1.

Contact: Director of Grant Programs
Oregon Student Assistance Commission
1500 Valley River Drive, Suite 100
Eugene, OR 97401-7020
Phone: 800-452-8807 Ext. 7395

OREGON SCHOLARSHIP FUND COMMUNITY COLLEGE STUDENT AWARD

Scholarship open to students enrolled or planning to enroll at least half time in Oregon community college programs. Recipients may reapply for one additional year.

Award: Scholarship for use in freshman or sophomore years; not renewable. *Number:* varies. *Amount:* varies.

Eligibility Requirements: Applicant must be enrolled or expecting to enroll full- or part-time at a two-year institution and studying in Oregon. Available to U.S. citizens.

Application Requirements: Application, essay, financial need analysis, transcript, activity chart. *Deadline:* March 1.

Contact: Director of Grant Programs
Oregon Student Assistance Commission
1500 Valley River Drive, Suite 100
Eugene, OR 97401-7020
Phone: 800-452-8807 Ext. 7395

OREGON SCHOLARSHIP FUND TRANSFER STUDENT AWARD

Award open to Oregon residents who are currently enrolled in their second year at an Oregon community college and are planning to transfer to a four-year college in Oregon. Prior recipients may apply for one additional year. Must enroll at least half-time.

Award: Scholarship for use in junior or senior years; not renewable. *Number:* varies. *Amount:* varies.

Eligibility Requirements: Applicant must be enrolled or expecting to enroll full- or part-time at a four-year institution or university; resident of Oregon and studying in Oregon. Available to U.S. citizens.

Application Requirements: Application, essay, financial need analysis, transcript, activity chart. *Deadline:* March 1.

Contact: Director of Grant Programs
Oregon Student Assistance Commission
1500 Valley River Drive, Suite 100
Eugene, OR 97401-7020
Phone: 800-452-8807 Ext. 7395

OREGON STATE FISCAL ASSOCIATION SCHOLARSHIP
• *See page 557*

OREGON TRAWL COMMISSION SCHOLARSHIP

Award for graduating Oregon high school seniors and college students in any accredited U.S. college or university who are dependents of licensed Oregon Trawl fishermen or crew. Must reapply annually for renewal.

Award: Scholarship for use in freshman, sophomore, junior, or senior years; not renewable. *Number:* varies. *Amount:* varies.

Eligibility Requirements: Applicant must be enrolled or expecting to enroll full-time at a four-year institution or university and resident of Oregon. Available to U.S. citizens.

Application Requirements: Application, essay, financial need analysis, references, transcript, activity chart. *Deadline:* March 1.

Contact: Director of Grant Programs
Oregon Student Assistance Commission
1500 Valley River Drive, Suite 100
Eugene, OR 97401-7020
Phone: 800-452-8807 Ext. 7395

PACIFIC NW FEDERAL CREDIT UNION SCHOLARSHIP

Scholarship available to graduating high school senior who is a member of Pacific North West Federal Credit Union. Must submit an essay on "Why My Credit Union is an Important Consumer Option." Immediate family members of Pacific NW Federal Credit Union employees and credit union elected or appointed officials are not eligible. Oregon and Washington state residents eligible.

Award: Scholarship for use in freshman year; not renewable. *Amount:* varies.

Eligibility Requirements: Applicant must be high school student; planning to enroll or expecting to enroll full-time at a four-year institution or university and resident of Oregon or Washington. Available to U.S. citizens.

Application Requirements: Application, essay, references, transcript, document name of credit union. *Deadline:* March 1.

Contact: Director of Grant Programs
Oregon Student Assistance Commission
1500 Valley River Drive, Suite 100
Eugene, OR 97401-7020
Phone: 800-452-8807 Ext. 7395

P.E.O. JEAN FISH GIBBONS

Award is available to female graduates of high schools in Jackson, Josephine, or Klamath County who will be college juniors or seniors in the upcoming academic year. A minimum GPA of 3.5 is required to apply. Recipients may reapply for one additional year of funding.

Award: Scholarship for use in junior or senior years; not renewable.

Eligibility Requirements: Applicant must be enrolled or expecting to enroll at a four-year institution or university; female and resident of Oregon. Applicant must have 3.5 GPA or higher.

Application Requirements: Application. *Deadline:* March 1.

Contact: Director of Grant Programs
Oregon Student Assistance Commission
1500 Valley River Drive, Suite 100
Eugene, OR 97401-7020
Phone: 800-452-8807

PETER CROSSLEY MEMORIAL SCHOLARSHIP

Renewable award for graduating seniors of Oregon public alternative high schools. Must be highly motivated to succeed despite overcoming a severe personal obstacle or challenge during high school career. Must submit essay and plan to enroll at least half-time in an Oregon college or university.

Award: Scholarship for use in freshman, sophomore, junior, or senior years; renewable. *Number:* varies. *Amount:* varies.

Eligibility Requirements: Applicant must be high school student; planning to enroll or expecting to enroll full- or part-time at a four-year institution or university; resident of Oregon and studying in Oregon. Available to U.S. citizens.

Application Requirements: Application, essay, financial need analysis, transcript, activity chart. *Deadline:* March 1.

Contact: Director of Grant Programs
Oregon Student Assistance Commission
1500 Valley River Drive, Suite 100
Eugene, OR 97401-7020
Phone: 800-452-8807 Ext. 7395

ROBERT C. BYRD FEDERAL HONORS PROGRAM-OREGON

National merit program for outstanding students. Automatically renewable award available to Oregon high school seniors with a minimum GPA of 3.85 or minimum GED score of 3300, and ACT scores of at least 29 or SAT combined math and critical reading scores of 1300. 75 new awards each year, 15 per Congressional District. See OSAC web site: http://www.getcollegefunds.org for more information.

Award: Scholarship for use in freshman, sophomore, junior, or senior years; renewable. *Number:* 75. *Amount:* $1500.

Eligibility Requirements: Applicant must be high school student; planning to enroll or expecting to enroll full-time at a two-year or four-year or technical institution or university and resident of Oregon. Available to U.S. citizens.

Application Requirements: Application, essay, test scores, transcript, activities chart. *Deadline:* March 1.

Contact: Program Coordinator
Oregon Student Assistance Commission
1500 Valley River Drive, Suite 100
Eugene, OR 97401-2148
Phone: 541-687-7387

SALEM FOUNDATION ANSEL & MARIE SOLIE SCHOLARSHIP
• *See page 611*

TEAMSTERS CLYDE C. CROSBY/JOSEPH M. EDGAR MEMORIAL SCHOLARSHIP
• *See page 557*

TYKESON FAMILY CHARITABLE TRUST SCHOLARSHIP

Renewable award available to dependents of full-time employees of Bend Cable Communications LLC, Central Oregon Cable Advertising LLC, or Tykeson/Associates Enterprises. Eligible employees must have been employed by one of these companies two or more years as of the March scholarship deadline. Applicants must be enrolled or planning to enroll in an undergraduate program at an Oregon public college or university.

Award: Scholarship for use in freshman, sophomore, junior, or senior years; renewable. *Number:* varies. *Amount:* varies.

Eligibility Requirements: Applicant must be enrolled or expecting to enroll full-time at a four-year institution or university and studying in Oregon. Available to U.S. citizens.

Application Requirements: Application, essay, financial need analysis, references, transcript, activity chart. *Deadline:* March 1.

Contact: Director of Grant Programs
Oregon Student Assistance Commission
1500 Valley River Drive, Suite 100
Eugene, OR 97401-7020
Phone: 800-452-8807 Ext. 7395

WILLETT AND MARGUERITE LAKE SCHOLARSHIP
• *See page 579*

WOODARD FAMILY SCHOLARSHIP
• *See page 579*

OWEN ELECTRIC COOPERATIVE

http://www.owenelectric.com/

OWEN ELECTRIC COOPERATIVE SCHOLARSHIP PROGRAM

Scholarships available to college juniors and seniors who are enrolled full-time at a four-year college or university. Parents of applicant must have an active Owen Electric account in good standing. If applicant has not earned 60 hours at time of application, must provide additional transcript upon completion of 60 hours. Must submit 400- to 700-word essay. For essay topics, application, and additional information visit web site http://www.owenelectric.com.

Award: Scholarship for use in junior or senior years; not renewable. *Number:* 12. *Amount:* $2000.

Eligibility Requirements: Applicant must be enrolled or expecting to enroll full-time at a four-year institution or university and resident of Kentucky. Applicant must have 3.0 GPA or higher. Available to U.S. citizens.

Application Requirements: Application, applicant must enter a contest, essay, references, transcript. *Deadline:* February 1.

Contact: Brian Linder, Manager of Key Accounts
Owen Electric Cooperative
8205 Highway 127 North
PO Box 400
Owenton, KY 40359-0400
Phone: 502-484-3471 Ext. 3542
Fax: 502-484-2661
E-mail: blinder@owenelectric.com

PACERS FOUNDATION INC.

http://www.pacersfoundation.org/

PACERS TEAMUP SCHOLARSHIP
• *See page 594*

PACIFIC AND ASIAN AFFAIRS COUNCIL

http://www.paachawaii.org/

PAAC ACADEMIC SCHOLARSHIPS

PAAC's academic scholarships are available to college-bound seniors and underclassmen attending Hawaii public or private high school. Applicants must be active in PAAC's high school program.

Award: Scholarship for use in freshman year; not renewable. *Number:* 5. *Amount:* $100–$1000.

Eligibility Requirements: Applicant must be high school student; planning to enroll or expecting to enroll full-time at a two-year or four-year or technical institution or university and resident of Hawaii. Available to U.S. and non-U.S. citizens.

Application Requirements: Application. *Deadline:* April 30.

Contact: Natasha Chappel, High School Program Director
Pacific and Asian Affairs Council
1601 East-West Road, Fourth Floor
Honolulu, HI 96848-1601
Phone: 808-944-7759
E-mail: hs@paachawaii.org

PARENTS, FAMILIES, AND FRIENDS OF LESBIANS AND GAYS-ATLANTA

http://www.pflagatl.org/

PFLAG SCHOLARSHIP AWARDS PROGRAM

Scholarship to recognize outstanding lesbian, gay, bisexual, and transgender (LGBT) individuals; encourage continuing education for self-identified LGBT individuals; and foster a positive image of LGBT people in society. For more details on eligibility and terms, see web site http://www.pflagatl.org/scholarships.htm.

Award: Scholarship for use in freshman, sophomore, junior, or senior years; not renewable. *Number:* 5–10. *Amount:* $500–$3000.

Eligibility Requirements: Applicant must be age 16 and over; enrolled or expecting to enroll full- or part-time at a two-year or four-year or technical institution or university; resident of Georgia; studying in Georgia and must have an interest in LGBT issues. Available to U.S. and non-U.S. citizens.

Application Requirements: Application, driver's license, essay, financial need analysis, references, test scores, transcript. *Deadline:* March 31.

Contact: Scholarship Program Coordinator
Parents, Families, and Friends of Lesbians and Gays-Atlanta
PO Box 450393
Atlanta, GA 31145-0393
Phone: 770-662-6475
E-mail: pflagatlschols@netscape.net

PENNSYLVANIA BURGLAR AND FIRE ALARM ASSOCIATION

http://www.pbfaa.com/

PENNSYLVANIA BURGLAR AND FIRE ALARM ASSOCIATION YOUTH SCHOLARSHIP PROGRAM
• *See page 594*

PENNSYLVANIA COMMERCE BANCORP, INC.

http://www.com/mercepc.com/

"CASH FOR COLLEGE" SCHOLARSHIP
• *See page 594*

PENNSYLVANIA FEDERATION OF DEMOCRATIC WOMEN INC.

http://www.pfdw.org/

PENNSYLVANIA FEDERATION OF DEMOCRATIC WOMEN INC. ANNUAL SCHOLARSHIP AWARDS
• *See page 558*

PENNSYLVANIA HIGHER EDUCATION ASSISTANCE AGENCY

http://www.pheaa.org/

PENNSYLVANIA STATE GRANT

Award for Pennsylvania residents attending an approved postsecondary institution as undergraduates in a program of at least two years duration. Renewable for up to eight semesters if applicants show continued need and academic progress. Must submit FAFSA. Number of awards granted varies annually. Scholarship value is $200 to $4120. Deadlines: May 1 and August 1.

Award: Grant for use in freshman, sophomore, junior, or senior years; renewable. *Number:* varies. *Amount:* $200–$4120.

Eligibility Requirements: Applicant must be enrolled or expecting to enroll full- or part-time at a two-year or four-year or technical institution or university and resident of Pennsylvania. Available to U.S. citizens.

Application Requirements: Financial need analysis, FAFSA. *Deadline:* varies.

Contact: Keith New, Director of Public Relations
Pennsylvania Higher Education Assistance Agency
1200 North Seventh Street
Harrisburg, PA 17102-1444
Phone: 717-720-2509
Fax: 717-720-3903

POSTSECONDARY EDUCATION GRATUITY PROGRAM
• *See page 621*

ROBERT C. BYRD HONORS SCHOLARSHIP-PENNSYLVANIA

Awards Pennsylvania residents who are graduating high school seniors. Must rank in the top 5 percent of graduating class, have at least a 3.5 GPA and score 1150 or above on the SAT, 25 or above on the ACT, or 355 or above on the GED. Renewable award and the amount granted varies.

Applicants are expected to be a full-time freshman student enrolled at an eligible institution of higher education, following high school graduation.

Award: Scholarship for use in freshman year; renewable. *Number:* varies. *Amount:* $1500.

Eligibility Requirements: Applicant must be high school student; planning to enroll or expecting to enroll full-time at a four-year institution or university and resident of Pennsylvania. Available to U.S. citizens.

Application Requirements: Application, references, test scores, transcript, letter of acceptance. *Deadline:* April 1.

Contact: Keith R. New, Director of Public Relations
Pennsylvania Higher Education Assistance Agency
1200 North Seventh Street
Harrisburg, PA 17102
Phone: 717-720-2509
Fax: 717-720-3903

PETER DOCTOR MEMORIAL INDIAN SCHOLARSHIP FOUNDATION INC.

PETER DOCTOR MEMORIAL IROQUOIS SCHOLARSHIP
• *See page 676*

PFUND FOUNDATION

http://www.pfundonline.org/

PFUND FOUNDATION SCHOLARSHIP PROGRAM

Scholarship available for gay, lesbian, bisexual, transgender or allied student leaders. Must be a legal resident of the state of Minnesota or attending a qualified Minnesota academic institution. Former winners of this fund are not eligible. For more details, visit http://www.pfundonline.org/scholarships.html.

Award: Scholarship for use in freshman, sophomore, junior, or senior years; not renewable. *Number:* 18–20. *Amount:* $2000–$5000.

Eligibility Requirements: Applicant must be enrolled or expecting to enroll full- or part-time at a two-year or four-year or technical institution or university; resident of Minnesota; studying in Minnesota and must have an interest in LGBT issues. Available to U.S. and non-U.S. citizens.

Application Requirements: Application, essay, photo, references, transcript, confidentiality statement. *Deadline:* February 1.

Contact: Mr. Ryan Kroening, Programs and Development Associate
PFund Foundation
1409 Willow Street, Suite 210
Minneapolis, MN 55403
Phone: 612-870-1806
E-mail: rkroening@pfundonline.org

PHILIPINO-AMERICAN ASSOCIATION OF NEW ENGLAND

http://www.pamas.org/

BLESSED LEON OF OUR LADY OF THE ROSARY AWARD
• *See page 677*

PAMAS RESTRICTED SCHOLARSHIP AWARD
• *See page 558*

RAVENSCROFT FAMILY AWARD
• *See page 677*

PHOENIX SUNS CHARITIES/SUN STUDENTS SCHOLARSHIP

http://www.suns.com/

SUN STUDENT COLLEGE SCHOLARSHIP PROGRAM
• *See page 594*

PINE TREE STATE 4-H CLUB FOUNDATION/ 4-H POSTSECONDARY SCHOLARSHIP

http://www.umaine.edu/

PARKER-LOVEJOY SCHOLARSHIP

One-time scholarship of $1000 is available to a graduating high school senior. Applicants must be residents of Maine.

Award: Scholarship for use in freshman year; not renewable. *Number:* 1. *Amount:* $1000.

Eligibility Requirements: Applicant must be high school student; planning to enroll or expecting to enroll full-time at a two-year or four-year institution or university and resident of Maine. Available to U.S. citizens.

Application Requirements: Application. *Deadline:* March 14.

Contact: Angela Martin, Administrative Assistant
Pine Tree State 4-H Club Foundation/4-H Postsecondary Scholarship
c/o University of Maine, 5714 Libby Hall
Orono, ME 04469-5717
Phone: 207-581-3739
Fax: 207-581-1387
E-mail: amartin@umext.maine.edu

WAYNE S. RICH SCHOLARSHIP

Scholarship for an outstanding Maine or New Hampshire 4-H member for postsecondary study. Awarded to a Maine student in odd numbered years and a New Hampshire student in even numbered years.

Award: Scholarship for use in freshman year; not renewable. *Number:* 1. *Amount:* up to $1000.

Eligibility Requirements: Applicant must be high school student; planning to enroll or expecting to enroll full-time at a two-year or four-year institution or university and resident of Maine or New Hampshire. Available to U.S. citizens.

Application Requirements: Application. *Deadline:* March 14.

Contact: Angela Martin, Administrative Assistant
Pine Tree State 4-H Club Foundation/4-H Postsecondary Scholarship
c/o University of Maine, 5714 Libby Hall
Orono, ME 04469-5717
Phone: 207-581-3739
Fax: 207-581-1387
E-mail: amartin@umext.maine.edu

POLISH HERITAGE ASSOCIATION OF MARYLAND

http://www.pha-md.org/

DR KENNETH AND NANCY WILLIAMS SCHOLARSHIP
• *See page 677*

POLISH HERITAGE SCHOLARSHIP
• *See page 677*

PORTUGUESE FOUNDATION INC.

http://www.pfict.org/

PORTUGUESE FOUNDATION SCHOLARSHIP PROGRAM
• *See page 677*

PRIDE FOUNDATION

http://www.PrideFoundation.org/

PRIDE FOUNDATION SCHOLARSHIP PROGRAM

Pride Foundation provides scholarships to current and future lesbian, gay, bisexual, transgender and straight-ally student leaders from Alaska, Idaho, Montana, Oregon, and Washington. Our scholarships cover most accredited post-secondary schools, including community colleges; 4-year public or private colleges and universities; trade or certificate programs; and graduate, medical, or law school.

Award: Scholarship for use in freshman, sophomore, junior, senior, graduate, or postgraduate years; not renewable. *Number:* 90–130. *Amount:* $1000–$15,000.

Eligibility Requirements: Applicant must be enrolled or expecting to enroll full- or part-time at a two-year or four-year or technical institution or university; resident of Alaska, Idaho, Montana, Oregon, or Washington and must have an interest in LGBT issues. Available to U.S. and non-U.S. citizens.

Application Requirements: Application, essay, financial need analysis, interview, resume, references, transcript. *Deadline:* January 31.

Contact: Anthony Papini, Director of Scholarship Programs
Pride Foundation
1122 East Pike St.
PMB 1001
Seattle, WA 98122-3934
Phone: 206-323-3318 Ext. 110
E-mail: scholarships@pridefoundation.org

PROJECT BEST SCHOLARSHIP FUND

http://www.projectbest.com/

PROJECT BEST SCHOLARSHIP
• *See page 560*

PUEBLO OF SAN JUAN, DEPARTMENT OF EDUCATION

http://www.sanjuaned.org/

OHKAY OWINGEH TRIBAL SCHOLARSHIP OF THE PUEBLO OF SAN JUAN
• *See page 595*

POP'AY SCHOLARSHIP
• *See page 595*

RHODE ISLAND FOUNDATION

http://www.rifoundation.org/

ALDO FREDA LEGISLATIVE PAGES SCHOLARSHIP

One-time scholarship of $1000 awarded to support Rhode Island Legislative Pages to further the education in a college or university. Must show scholastic achievement and good citizenship. Must be accepted into a full-time accredited postsecondary institution or graduate program. Must be a Rhode Island resident and a citizen of the United States.

Award: Scholarship for use in freshman, sophomore, junior, senior, or graduate years; not renewable. *Number:* 2–3. *Amount:* $1000.

Eligibility Requirements: Applicant must be enrolled or expecting to enroll full- or part-time at a two-year or four-year institution or university and resident of Rhode Island. Available to U.S. citizens.

Application Requirements: Application, essay, financial need analysis, references, transcript. *Deadline:* June 1.

Contact: Libby Monahan, Funds Administrator
Rhode Island Foundation
One Union Station
Providence, RI 02903
Phone: 401-274-4564 Ext. 3117
E-mail: libbym@rifoundation.org

A.T. CROSS SCHOLARSHIP
• *See page 580*

BRUCE AND MARJORIE SUNDLUN SCHOLARSHIP

Scholarships for low-income single parents seeking to upgrade their career skills. Preference given to single parents previously receiving state support, and also for those previously incarcerated. Must be a Rhode Island resident and must attend school in the state.

Award: Scholarship for use in freshman, sophomore, junior, or senior years; not renewable. *Amount:* up to $1500.

Eligibility Requirements: Applicant must be enrolled or expecting to enroll full- or part-time at a two-year or four-year or technical institution or university; resident of Rhode Island and studying in Rhode Island. Available to U.S. and non-U.S. citizens.

Application Requirements: Application, essay, financial need analysis, references, self-addressed stamped envelope, transcript. *Deadline:* June 15.

Contact: Libby Monahan, Funds Administrator
Rhode Island Foundation
One Union Station
Providence, RI 02903
Phone: 401-274-4564 Ext. 3117
E-mail: libbym@rifoundation.org

DAVID M. GOLDEN MEMORIAL SCHOLARSHIP

Scholarship awarded to benefit college-bound Rhode Island high school graduates, whose parents did not have the benefit of attending college. Must be enrolled in an accredited nonprofit postsecondary institution offering either a two- or a four-year college degree. Must demonstrate financial need.

Award: Scholarship for use in freshman, sophomore, junior, or senior years; renewable. *Number:* varies. *Amount:* varies.

Eligibility Requirements: Applicant must be enrolled or expecting to enroll full-time at a two-year or four-year institution or university and resident of Rhode Island. Available to U.S. citizens.

Application Requirements: Application, essay, references, self-addressed stamped envelope, transcript. *Deadline:* varies.

Contact: Libby Monahan, Funds Administrator
Rhode Island Foundation
One Union Station
Providence, RI 02903
Phone: 401-274-4564 Ext. 3117
E-mail: libbym@rifoundation.org

LILY AND CATELLO SORRENTINO MEMORIAL SCHOLARSHIP

Scholarships for Rhode Island residents. Applicant must be 25 years or older wishing to attend college or university in Rhode Island (only students attending non-parochial schools). Must demonstrate financial need. Preference to first-time applicants. Financial need must be demonstrated.

Award: Scholarship for use in freshman, sophomore, junior, or senior years; not renewable. *Number:* varies. *Amount:* $500–$1000.

Eligibility Requirements: Applicant must be age 25 and over; enrolled or expecting to enroll full- or part-time at a four-year institution or university; resident of Rhode Island and studying in Rhode Island. Available to U.S. citizens.

Application Requirements: Application, financial need analysis, self-addressed stamped envelope, transcript. *Deadline:* May 14.

Contact: Libby Monahan, Funds Administrator
Rhode Island Foundation
One Union Station
Providence, RI 02903
Phone: 401-274-4564 Ext. 3117
E-mail: libbym@rifoundation.org

MICHAEL P. METCALF MEMORIAL SCHOLARSHIP

One-time award of up to $7500 awarded to encourage personal growth through travel, study, and public service programs for college sophomores and juniors. Must be a Rhode Island resident. The scholarship is for educational enrichment outside the classroom; therefore, the awards are not to be used for school tuition. Those selected must submit a final project in writing, perhaps another medium used to communicate the value of the experience in furthering their long-term goals.

Award: Scholarship for use in freshman, sophomore, or junior years; not renewable. *Number:* varies. *Amount:* up to $7500.

Eligibility Requirements: Applicant must be enrolled or expecting to enroll full-time at a four-year institution or university and resident of Rhode Island. Available to U.S. citizens.

Application Requirements: Application, financial need analysis, references, transcript, description of enrichment experience, supporting documentation concerning the proposed experience, 3 forms of proof of Rhode Island residency. *Deadline:* January 15.

Contact: Libby Monahan, Funds Administrator
Rhode Island Foundation
One Union Station
Providence, RI 02903
Phone: 401-274-4564 Ext. 3117
E-mail: libbym@rifoundation.org

RHODE ISLAND COMMISSION ON WOMEN/FREDA GOLDMAN EDUCATION AWARD

Applicant must meet the following criteria: either preparing for a nontraditional job or career through an educational program; or returning to the labor market in need of training to sharpen your skills; or be an ex-offender wishing to undertake vocational or career education and training; or be a displaced homemaker and/or single mother wishing to further their education. Must be enrolled or registered in an educational or job skills training program. Must be a woman living in Rhode Island.

Award: Scholarship for use in freshman, sophomore, junior, or senior years; renewable. *Number:* varies. *Amount:* $500–$1000.

Eligibility Requirements: Applicant must be enrolled or expecting to enroll full- or part-time at a four-year institution or university; female and resident of Rhode Island. Available to U.S. citizens.

Application Requirements: Application, essay, references, self-addressed stamped envelope, transcript. *Deadline:* June 15.

Contact: Libby Monahan, Funds Administrator
Rhode Island Foundation
One Union Station
Providence, RI 02903
Phone: 401-274-4564 Ext. 3117
E-mail: libbym@rifoundation.org

RHODE ISLAND FOUNDATION ASSOCIATION OF FORMER LEGISLATORS SCHOLARSHIP

One-time award of $1500 for graduating high school seniors who are Rhode Island residents. Must have a history of substantial voluntary involvement in community service. Must be accepted into an accredited post-secondary institution and should be able to demonstrate financial need.

Award: Scholarship for use in freshman year; not renewable. *Number:* 4–5. *Amount:* $1500.

Eligibility Requirements: Applicant must be high school student; planning to enroll or expecting to enroll full-time at a four-year institution or university and resident of Rhode Island. Available to U.S. citizens.

Application Requirements: Application, essay, financial need analysis, references, self-addressed stamped envelope, test scores, transcript. *Deadline:* May 3.

Contact: Libby Monahan, Funds Administrator
Rhode Island Foundation
One Union Station
Providence, RI 02903
Phone: 401-274-4564 Ext. 3117
E-mail: libbym@rifoundation.org

RHODE ISLAND HIGHER EDUCATION ASSISTANCE AUTHORITY

http://www.riheaa.org/

COLLEGE BOUND FUND ACADEMIC PROMISE SCHOLARSHIP

Award to graduating high school seniors. Eligibility based on financial need and SAT/ACT scores. Must maintain specified GPA each year for renewal. Must be Rhode Island resident and attend college full-time. Must complete the FAFSA. GPA required: first year is 2.5, second year is 2.62 and third year is 2.75.

Award: Scholarship for use in freshman, sophomore, junior, or senior years; renewable. *Number:* 100. *Amount:* $2500.

Eligibility Requirements: Applicant must be high school student; planning to enroll or expecting to enroll full-time at a two-year or four-year or technical institution or university and resident of Rhode Island. Available to U.S. citizens.

Application Requirements: Application, financial need analysis, test scores. *Deadline:* March 1.

Contact: Mr. Michael Joyce JD, Director of Program Administration
Rhode Island Higher Education Assistance Authority
560 Jefferson Boulevard, Suite 100
Warwick, RI 02886
Phone: 401-736-1170
Fax: 401-736-1178
E-mail: grants@riheaa.org

RHODE ISLAND STATE GRANT PROGRAM

Grants for residents of Rhode Island attending an approved school in United States. Based on need. Renewable for up to four years if in good academic standing and meet financial need requirements.

Award: Grant for use in freshman, sophomore, junior, or senior years; renewable. *Number:* 10,000–17,000. *Amount:* $250–$900.

Eligibility Requirements: Applicant must be enrolled or expecting to enroll full- or part-time at a two-year or four-year or technical institution or university and resident of Rhode Island. Available to U.S. citizens.

Application Requirements: Application, financial need analysis. *Deadline:* March 1.

Contact: Mr. Michael Joyce JD, Director of Program Administration
Rhode Island Higher Education Assistance Authority
560 Jefferson Boulevard, Suite 100
Warwick, RI 02886
Phone: 401-736-1170
Fax: 401-736-1178
E-mail: grants@riheaa.org

ROOTHBERT FUND INC.

http://www.roothbertfund.org/

ROOTHBERT FUND INC. SCHOLARSHIP

Scholarships are open to all in the United States regardless of sex, age, color, nationality or religious background. Provide SASE when requesting an application.

Award: Scholarship for use in freshman, sophomore, junior, senior, or graduate years; renewable. *Number:* 20. *Amount:* $2000–$3000.

Eligibility Requirements: Applicant must be enrolled or expecting to enroll full-time at a two-year or four-year or technical institution or university and studying in Connecticut, Delaware, District of Columbia, Maryland, Massachusetts, New Hampshire, New Jersey, New York, Ohio, Pennsylvania, Rhode Island, or Virginia. Available to U.S. citizens.

Application Requirements: Application, driver's license, essay, financial need analysis, interview, photo, references, self-addressed stamped envelope, test scores, transcript. *Deadline:* February 1.

Contact: Percy Preston Jr., Office Manager
Roothbert Fund Inc.
475 Riverside Drive, Room 252
New York, NY 10115
Phone: 212-870-3116

RYU FAMILY FOUNDATION, INC.

http://www.seolbong.org/

SEOL BONG SCHOLARSHIP
• *See page 678*

ST. ANDREW'S SOCIETY OF WASHINGTON, DC

http://www.saintandrewsociety.org/

DONALD MALCOLM MACARTHUR SCHOLARSHIP
• *See page 679*

ST. CLAIRE REGIONAL MEDICAL CENTER

http://www.st-claire.org/

SR. MARY JEANNETTE WESS, S.N.D. SCHOLARSHIP
• *See page 595*

ST. PETERSBURG TIMES FUND INC.

http://www.sptimes.com/

ST. PETERSBURG TIMES BARNES SCHOLARSHIP

Four high school seniors from the St. Petersburg Times' audience area are selected each year and each are awarded up to $15,000 annually for four years to attend any nationally accredited college or university. Criteria for scholarship include high academic achievement, financial need, evidence of having overcome significant obstacles in life, and community service.

Award: Scholarship for use in freshman year; renewable. *Number:* 4. *Amount:* up to $15,000.

Eligibility Requirements: Applicant must be high school student; planning to enroll or expecting to enroll full- or part-time at a four-year institution or university and resident of Florida. Available to U.S. citizens.

Application Requirements: Application, applicant must enter a contest, financial need analysis. *Deadline:* October 15.

Contact: Nancy Waclawek, Director
St. Petersburg Times Fund Inc.
PO Box 1121
St. Petersburg, FL 33731
Phone: 727-893-8780
Fax: 727-892-2257
E-mail: waclawek@sptimes.com

SALT RIVER ELECTRIC COOPERATIVE CORPORATION

http://www.srelectric.com/

SALT RIVER ELECTRIC SCHOLARSHIP PROGRAM

Scholarships available to Kentucky high school seniors who reside in Salt River Electric Service area or the primary residence of their parents/guardian is in the service area. Must be enrolled or plan to enroll in a postsecondary institution. Minimum GPA of 2.5 required. Must demonstrate financial need. Must submit a 500-word essay on a topic chosen from the list on the web site. Application and additional information available on web site http://www.srelectric.com.

Award: Scholarship for use in freshman year; not renewable. *Number:* 4. *Amount:* $1000.

Eligibility Requirements: Applicant must be high school student; planning to enroll or expecting to enroll full- or part-time at a two-year or four-year or technical institution or university and resident of Kentucky. Applicant must have 2.5 GPA or higher. Available to U.S. citizens.

Application Requirements: Application, essay, financial need analysis, photo, transcript. *Deadline:* April 4.

Contact: Nicky Rapier, Scholarship Coordinator
Salt River Electric Cooperative Corporation
111 West Brashear Avenue
Bardstown, KY 40004
Phone: 502-348-3931
Fax: 502-348-1993
E-mail: nickyr@srelectric.com

SALVADORAN AMERICAN LEADERSHIP AND EDUCATIONAL FUND

http://www.salef.org/

FULFILLING OUR DREAMS SCHOLARSHIP FUND
• *See page 679*

SAN DIEGO FOUNDATION

http://www.sdfoundation.org/

CLUB AT MORNINGSIDE SCHOLARSHIP
• *See page 580*

DRINKWATER FAMILY SCHOLARSHIP
• *See page 595*

HARVEY L. SIMMONS MEMORIAL SCHOLARSHIP
• *See page 596*

JOSEPH C. LARSON ENTREPRENEURIAL SCHOLARSHIP

Scholarship to graduating high school seniors who will attend an accredited four-year university or students who have successfully completed at least one full academic year toward their undergraduate degree at an accredited four-year university in the United States. Students who can demonstrate their interest in entrepreneurial endeavors through the creation of their own business or consulting venue, will be given special consideration.

Award: Scholarship for use in freshman, sophomore, junior, or senior years; not renewable. *Number:* 3. *Amount:* $2500.

Eligibility Requirements: Applicant must be enrolled or expecting to enroll full-time at an institution or university; resident of California and must have an interest in entrepreneurship. Applicant must have 3.0 GPA or higher. Available to U.S. citizens.

Application Requirements: Application, essay, financial need analysis, references, transcript, personal statement, copy of tax return. *Deadline:* January 26.

Contact: Shryl Helvie, Scholarship Coordinator
San Diego Foundation
2508 Historic Decatur Road, Suite 200
San Diego, CA 92106
Phone: 619-814-1307
Fax: 619-239-1710
E-mail: shryl@sdfoundation.org

JULIE ALLEN WORLD CLASSROOM SCHOLARSHIP

Scholarship to undergraduate students already enrolled at the University of San Diego, University of California, San Diego, or San Diego State University with a minimum 2.5 GPA and a demonstrated financial need. Applicants must be planning to study abroad for a minimum of one semester in a second- or third-world country whose culture, language and customs are different from their own. For more details visit http://www.sdfoundation.org/scholarships/allen.shtml.

Award: Scholarship for use in freshman, sophomore, junior, or senior years; not renewable. *Number:* 1. *Amount:* $1000.

Eligibility Requirements: Applicant must be enrolled or expecting to enroll full-time at an institution or university; resident of California and must have an interest in international exchange. Applicant must have 2.5 GPA or higher. Available to U.S. and non-U.S. citizens.

Application Requirements: Application, essay, references, transcript, personal statement, copy of tax return. *Deadline:* January 26.

Contact: Shryl Helvie, Scholarship Coordinator
San Diego Foundation
2508 Historic Decatur Road, Suite 200
San Diego, CA 92106
Phone: 619-814-1307
Fax: 619-239-1710
E-mail: shryl@sdfoundation.org

LESLIE JANE HAHN MEMORIAL SCHOLARSHIP
• *See page 596*

LOUISE A. BRODERICK SAN DIEGO COUNTY SCHOLARSHIP

Scholarship to single parents with dependent children who are re-entering college or are already enrolled in college. Applicants must have a minimum 2.0 GPA, demonstrated financial need, and plan to attend a two-year community college, four-year university, or trade and vocational school. This scholarship may be renewable for up to four years dependent upon the recipient maintaining a positive academic (minimum 2.0 GPA) and citizenship record.

Award: Scholarship for use in freshman, sophomore, junior, or senior years; renewable. *Number:* 2. *Amount:* $2000.

Eligibility Requirements: Applicant must be enrolled or expecting to enroll full-time at a two-year or four-year or technical institution or university and resident of California. Available to U.S. citizens.

Application Requirements: Application, financial need analysis, references, transcript, personal statement, copy of tax return. *Deadline:* January 26.

Contact: Shryl Helvie, Scholarship Coordinator
San Diego Foundation
2508 Historic Decatur Road, Suite 200
San Diego, CA 92106
Phone: 619-814-1307
Fax: 619-239-1710
E-mail: shryl@sdfoundation.org

RANDY WILLIAMS SCHOLARSHIP

Scholarship to graduating high school seniors who have participated in high school and/or club competitive swimming programs and plan to attend an accredited two-year college, four-year university or licensed trade/vocational school in the United States. Preference given to applicants planning to attend school outside of San Diego County. Minimum 2.5 GPA required. For more details visit http://www.sdfoundation.org/scholarships/randy.shtml.

Award: Scholarship for use in freshman year; renewable. *Number:* 1. *Amount:* $1000.

Eligibility Requirements: Applicant must be high school student; planning to enroll or expecting to enroll full-time at a two-year or four-year or technical institution or university; resident of California and must have an interest in athletics/sports. Applicant must have 2.5 GPA or higher. Available to U.S. citizens.

Application Requirements: Application, essay, references, transcript, personal statement. *Deadline:* January 26.

Contact: Shryl Helvie, Scholarship Coordinator
San Diego Foundation
2508 Historic Decatur Road, Suite 200
San Diego, CA 92106
Phone: 619-814-1307
Fax: 619-239-1710
E-mail: shryl@sdfoundation.org

REMINGTON CLUB SCHOLARSHIP
• *See page 580*

RUBINSTEIN CROHN'S AND COLITIS SCHOLARSHIP
• *See page 612*

SAN DIEGO FIRE VICTIMS SCHOLARSHIP-GENERAL FUND

Scholarship is open to graduating high school seniors and current college students who lost their homes in the 2003 wildfires and plan to attend an accredited two-year college, four-year university, or licensed trade or vocational school in the United States. Must be legal residents of San Diego County. Scholarship may be renewable for up to two years provided recipients continue to meet the terms of the scholarship and maintain a positive academic and citizenship record.

Award: Scholarship for use in freshman, sophomore, junior, or senior years; renewable. *Number:* 5. *Amount:* $500–$2500.

Eligibility Requirements: Applicant must be enrolled or expecting to enroll full-time at a two-year or four-year or technical institution or university and resident of California. Applicant must have 2.5 GPA or higher. Available to U.S. citizens.

Application Requirements: Application, references, transcript, personal statement, copy of tax return, formal documentation. *Deadline:* January 26.

Contact: Shryl Helvie, Scholarship Coordinator
San Diego Foundation
2508 Historic Decatur Road, Suite 200
San Diego, CA 92106
Phone: 619-814-1307
Fax: 619-239-1710
E-mail: shryl@sdfoundation.org

SAN DIEGO FIRE VICTIMS SCHOLARSHIP-LATINO FUND
• *See page 679*

SAN DIEGO PATHWAYS TO COLLEGE SCHOLARSHIP
• *See page 596*

USA FREESTYLE MARTIAL ARTS SCHOLARSHIP
• *See page 596*

WILLIAM AND LUCILLE ASH SCHOLARSHIP

Scholarship fund is to provide financial assistance to adult re-entry students. Applicants must have a minimum 3.0 GPA, demonstrated financial need, and be attending an accredited two- or 4-year college or university, or licensed trade/vocational school in the state of California. Students must be employed (minimum part-time). Scholarship may be renewable for up to four years provided recipients maintain a positive academic and citizenship record.

Award: Scholarship for use in freshman, sophomore, junior, or senior years; renewable. *Number:* 3. *Amount:* $1000–$5000.

Eligibility Requirements: Applicant must be enrolled or expecting to enroll full-time at a two-year or four-year or technical institution or university; resident of California and studying in California. Applicant must have 3.0 GPA or higher. Available to U.S. citizens.

Application Requirements: Application, financial need analysis, references, transcript, personal statement, copy of tax return. *Deadline:* January 26.

Contact: Shryl Helvie, Scholarship Coordinator
San Diego Foundation
2508 Historic Decatur Road, Suite 200
San Diego, CA 92106
Phone: 619-814-1307
Fax: 619-239-1710
E-mail: shryl@sdfoundation.org

SAN FRANCISCO FOUNDATION

http://www.sff.org/

JOSEPH HENRY JACKSON LITERARY AWARD

Award presented annually to an author of an unpublished work in progress: fiction, nonfiction, prose, or poetry. Must be residents of and currently living in northern California or the state of Nevada for three consecutive years and be between 20 to 35 years of age. Award values from $2000 to $3000. Submit manuscript.

Award: Prize for use in freshman, sophomore, junior, senior, graduate, or postgraduate years; not renewable. *Number:* 3. *Amount:* $2000–$3000.

Eligibility Requirements: Applicant must be age 20-35; enrolled or expecting to enroll full- or part-time at a two-year or four-year institution or university; resident of California or Nevada and must have an interest in writing. Available to U.S. citizens.

Application Requirements: Application, applicant must enter a contest, self-addressed stamped envelope, manuscript. *Deadline:* March 31.

Contact: Awards Coordinator
San Francisco Foundation
225 Bush Street, Suite 500
San Francisco, CA 94104-4224
Phone: 415-733-8500
E-mail: rec@sff.org

SERVICE EMPLOYEES INTERNATIONAL UNION-CALIFORNIA STATE COUNCIL OF SERVICE EMPLOYEES

http://www.seiuca.org/

CHARLES HARDY MEMORIAL SCHOLARSHIP AWARDS
• *See page 562*

SHELBY ENERGY COOPERATIVE

http://www.shelbyenergy.com/

SHELBY ENERGY COOPERATIVE SCHOLARSHIPS

Scholarships for high school seniors in Kentucky, whose parents or guardians are Shelby Energy members. Award based on financial need, academic excellence, community and school involvement, and essay.

Award: Scholarship for use in freshman year; not renewable. *Number:* 6. *Amount:* $1000.

Eligibility Requirements: Applicant must be high school student; planning to enroll or expecting to enroll full-time at a four-year institution or university and resident of Kentucky. Available to U.S. citizens.

Application Requirements: Application, financial need analysis. *Deadline:* April 5.

Contact: Teresa Atha, Marketing Department
Shelby Energy Cooperative
620 Old Finchville Road
Shelbyville, KY 40065
Phone: 502-633-4420
Fax: 502-633-2387
E-mail: shelbyenergy@shelbyenergy.com

SICKLE CELL DISEASE ASSOCIATION OF AMERICA/CONNECTICUT CHAPTER INC.

http://www.sicklecellct.org/

I. H. MCLENDON MEMORIAL SCHOLARSHIP
• *See page 613*

SYBIL FONG SAM SCHOLARSHIP ESSAY CONTEST

The program provides three scholarships to graduating high school seniors based upon submission of an essay on a pre-selected topic. Minimum 3.0 GPA required. Must be a Connecticut resident.

Award: Scholarship for use in freshman year; not renewable. *Number:* 3. *Amount:* $200–$500.

Eligibility Requirements: Applicant must be high school student; planning to enroll or expecting to enroll full- or part-time at a two-year or four-year or technical institution or university; resident of Connecticut and must have an interest in writing. Applicant must have 3.0 GPA or higher. Available to U.S. citizens.

Application Requirements: Application, applicant must enter a contest, essay, references, transcript. *Deadline:* April 30.

Contact: Samuel Byrd, Program Assistant
Sickle Cell Disease Association of America/Connecticut Chapter Inc.
Gengras Ambulatory Center, 114 Woodland Street, Suite 2101
Hartford, CT 06105-1299
Phone: 860-714-5540
Fax: 860-714-8007
E-mail: scdaa@iconn.net

SIMON FOUNDATION FOR EDUCATION AND HOUSING

http://www.sfeh.org/

SIMON SCHOLARS PROGRAM

Scholarships are given to high school seniors at qualified high schools in Atlanta, GA, Santa Fe and Albuquerque, NM, and Anaheim, Santa Ana, Oceanside, or Garden Grove, CA. Deadlines vary for each region. For more details visit web site http://www.simonscholars.org.

Award: Scholarship for use in freshman year; not renewable. *Number:* 100–100. *Amount:* $16,000.

Eligibility Requirements: Applicant must be high school student; planning to enroll or expecting to enroll full-time at a two-year or four-year institution or university and resident of California, Georgia, or New Mexico. Applicant must have 3.0 GPA or higher. Available to U.S. citizens.

Application Requirements: Application, essay, financial need analysis, interview, references, test scores, transcript. *Deadline:* varies.

Contact: Dr. Heather Huntley, Director of Partnerships and Development
Simon Foundation for Education and Housing
620 Newport Center Drive, 12th Floor
Newport Beach, CA 92660
Phone: 949-270-3622
Fax: 949-729-8072
E-mail: heatherh@simonscholars.org

SONS OF NORWAY FOUNDATION

http://www.sonsofnorway.com/

ASTRID G. CATES AND MYRTLE BEINHAUER SCHOLARSHIP FUNDS
• *See page 564*

SOUTH CAROLINA COMMISSION ON HIGHER EDUCATION

http://www.che.sc.gov/

PALMETTO FELLOWS SCHOLARSHIP PROGRAM

Renewable award for qualified high school seniors in South Carolina to attend a four-year South Carolina institution. The scholarship must be applied directly towards the cost of attendance, less any other gift aid received.

Award: Scholarship for use in freshman year; renewable. *Number:* 4846. *Amount:* $6700–$7500.

Eligibility Requirements: Applicant must be high school student; planning to enroll or expecting to enroll full-time at a four-year institution or university; resident of South Carolina and studying in South Carolina. Applicant must have 3.5 GPA or higher. Available to U.S. citizens.

Application Requirements: Application, test scores, transcript. *Deadline:* December 15.

Contact: Dr. Karen Woodfaulk, Director of Student Services
South Carolina Commission on Higher Education
1333 Main Street, Suite 200
Columbia, SC 29201
Phone: 803-737-2244
Fax: 803-737-3610
E-mail: kwoodfaulk@che.sc.gov

SOUTH CAROLINA HOPE SCHOLARSHIP

A merit-based scholarship for eligible first-time entering freshman attending a four-year South Carolina institution. Minimum GPA of 3.0 required. Must be a resident of South Carolina.

Award: Scholarship for use in freshman year; not renewable. *Number:* 2605. *Amount:* $2800.

Eligibility Requirements: Applicant must be high school student; planning to enroll or expecting to enroll full-time at a four-year institution or university; resident of South Carolina and studying in South Carolina. Applicant must have 3.0 GPA or higher. Available to U.S. citizens.

Application Requirements: Transcript. *Deadline:* continuous.

Contact: Gerrick Hampton, Scholarship Coordinator
South Carolina Commission on Higher Education
1333 Main Street, Suite 200
Columbia, SC 29201
Phone: 803-737-4544
Fax: 803-737-3610
E-mail: ghampton@che.sc.gov

SOUTH CAROLINA NEED-BASED GRANTS PROGRAM

Award based on FAFSA. A student may receive up to $2500 annually for full-time and up to $1250 annually for part-time study. The grant must be applied directly towards the cost of college attendance for a maximum of eight full-time equivalent terms.

Award: Grant for use in freshman, sophomore, junior, senior, or graduate years; renewable. *Number:* 1–26,730. *Amount:* $1250–$2500.

Eligibility Requirements: Applicant must be enrolled or expecting to enroll full- or part-time at a two-year or four-year or technical institution or university; resident of South Carolina and studying in South Carolina. Available to U.S. citizens.

Application Requirements: Application, financial need analysis. *Deadline:* continuous.

Contact: Dr. Karen Woodfaulk, Director of Student Service
South Carolina Commission on Higher Education
1333 Main Street, Suite 200
Columbia, SC 29201
Phone: 803-737-2244
Fax: 803-737-2297
E-mail: kwoodfaulk@che.sc.gov

SOUTH CAROLINA DEPARTMENT OF EDUCATION

http://www.ed.sc.gov/

ROBERT C. BYRD HONORS SCHOLARSHIP-SOUTH CAROLINA

Renewable award for a graduating high school senior from South Carolina, who will be attending a two- or four-year institution. Applicants should be superior students who demonstrate academic achievement and show promise of continued success at a postsecondary institution. Interested applicants should contact their high school counselors after the first week of December for an application.

Award: Scholarship for use in freshman year; renewable. *Number:* varies. *Amount:* varies.

Eligibility Requirements: Applicant must be high school student; planning to enroll or expecting to enroll full-time at a two-year or four-year institution or university and resident of South Carolina. Available to U.S. citizens.

Application Requirements: Application, test scores, ACT or SAT scores. *Deadline:* varies.

Contact: Beth Cope, Program Coordinator
South Carolina Department of Education
1424 Senate Street
Columbia, SC 29201
Phone: 803-734-8116
Fax: 803-734-4387
E-mail: bcope@sde.state.sc.us

SOUTH CAROLINA DIVISION OF VETERANS AFFAIRS

http://www.govoepp.state.sc.us/vetaff.htm

EDUCATIONAL ASSISTANCE FOR CERTAIN WAR VETERANS DEPENDENTS SCHOLARSHIP-SOUTH CAROLINA

• *See page 645*

SOUTH CAROLINA STATE EMPLOYEES ASSOCIATION

http://www.scsea.com/

ANNE A. AGNEW SCHOLARSHIP

• *See page 564*

RICHLAND/LEXINGTON SCSEA SCHOLARSHIP

• *See page 565*

SOUTH CAROLINA TUITION GRANTS COMMISSION

http://www.sctuitiongrants.com/

SOUTH CAROLINA TUITION GRANTS PROGRAM

Need-based grant set aside for 21 eligible independent colleges in South Carolina. Student must be a South Carolina resident. Must apply annually by submitting the Free Application for Federal Student Aid (FAFSA). Freshmen must graduate in top 75% of high school class OR score 900 on SAT/19 on ACT OR graduate with at least 2.0 on SC Uniform Grading Scale. Upperclassmen must pass a minimum of 24 credit hours annually.

Award: Grant for use in freshman, sophomore, junior, or senior years; not renewable. *Amount:* $100–$2600.

Eligibility Requirements: Applicant must be enrolled or expecting to enroll full-time at a two-year or four-year institution or university; resident of South Carolina and studying in South Carolina. Available to U.S. citizens.

Application Requirements: Application, FAFSA. *Deadline:* June 30.

Contact: Toni K. Cave, Financial Aid Counselor
South Carolina Tuition Grants Commission
800 Dutch Square Boulevard, Suite 260A
Columbia, SC 29210
Phone: 803-896-1120
Fax: 803-896-1126
E-mail: toni@sctuitiongrants.org

SOUTH DAKOTA BOARD OF REGENTS

http://www.sdbor.edu/

SOUTH DAKOTA BOARD OF REGENTS MARLIN R. SCARBOROUGH MEMORIAL SCHOLARSHIP

One-time merit-based award for a student who is a junior at a South Dakota university. Must be nominated by the university and must have community service and leadership experience. Minimum 3.5 GPA required. Application deadline varies.

Award: Scholarship for use in junior year; not renewable. *Number:* 1. *Amount:* $1000.

Eligibility Requirements: Applicant must be enrolled or expecting to enroll full-time at an institution or university; resident of South Dakota; studying in South Dakota and must have an interest in leadership. Applicant must have 3.5 GPA or higher. Available to U.S. citizens.

Application Requirements: Application, essay. *Deadline:* varies.

Contact: Dr. Paul Turman, Director of Academic Assessment
South Dakota Board of Regents
306 East Capitol Avenue, Suite 200
Pierre, SD 57501-2545
Phone: 605-773-3455
E-mail: pault@sdbor.edu

SOUTH DAKOTA OPPORTUNITY SCHOLARSHIP

Renewable scholarship may be worth up to $5000 over four years to students who take a rigorous college-prep curriculum while in high school and stay in the state for their postsecondary education.

Award: Scholarship for use in freshman, sophomore, junior, or senior years; renewable. *Number:* 1000. *Amount:* $1000.

Eligibility Requirements: Applicant must be high school student; planning to enroll or expecting to enroll full-time at a two-year or four-year or technical institution or university; resident of South Dakota and studying in South Dakota. Applicant must have 3.0 GPA or higher. Available to U.S. citizens.

Application Requirements: Application, test scores, transcript. *Deadline:* September 1.

Contact: Janelle Toman, Scholarship Committee
South Dakota Board of Regents
306 East Capitol, Suite 200
Pierre, SD 57501-2545
Phone: 605-773-3455
Fax: 605-773-2422
E-mail: info@sdbor.edu

SOUTH DAKOTA DEPARTMENT OF EDUCATION

http://www.doe.sd.gov/

ROBERT C. BYRD HONORS SCHOLARSHIP-SOUTH DAKOTA

For South Dakota residents in their senior year of high school. Must have a minimum 3.5 GPA and a minimum ACT score of 30 or above. Awards are renewable up to four years. Contact high school guidance office for more details.

Award: Scholarship for use in freshman, sophomore, junior, or senior years; renewable. *Number:* 15–25. *Amount:* $1500.

Eligibility Requirements: Applicant must be high school student; planning to enroll or expecting to enroll full-time at a two-year or four-year or technical institution or university and resident of South Dakota. Applicant must have 3.5 GPA or higher. Available to U.S. citizens.

Application Requirements: Application, references, test scores, transcript. *Deadline:* March 18.

Contact: Mr. Mark Gageby, Management Analyst
South Dakota Department of Education
Department of Education, 800 Governors Drive
Pierre, SD 57501-2291
Phone: 605-773-3248
Fax: 605-773-6139
E-mail: mark.gageby@state.sd.us

SOUTH FLORIDA FAIR AND PALM BEACH COUNTY EXPOSITIONS INC.

http://www.southfloridafair.com/

SOUTH FLORIDA FAIR COLLEGE SCHOLARSHIP

Renewable award of up to $4000 for students who might not otherwise have an opportunity to pursue a college education. Must be a permanent resident of Florida.

Award: Scholarship for use in freshman, sophomore, junior, or senior years; renewable. *Number:* 10. *Amount:* $1000–$4000.

Eligibility Requirements: Applicant must be enrolled or expecting to enroll full- or part-time at a four-year institution or university and resident of Florida. Available to U.S. and non-U.S. citizens.

Application Requirements: Application, essay, references, self-addressed stamped envelope, test scores, transcript. *Deadline:* October 15.

Contact: Scholarship Committee
South Florida Fair and Palm Beach County Expositions Inc.
PO Box 210367
West Palm Beach, FL 33421-0367
Phone: 561-790-5245

STATE EMPLOYEES ASSOCIATION OF NORTH CAROLINA (SEANC)

http://www.seanc.org/

STATE EMPLOYEES ASSOCIATION OF NORTH CAROLINA (SEANC) SCHOLARSHIPS

Scholarships available to SEANC members, their spouses and dependents seeking postsecondary education. Awarded in three categories: based on academic merit, financial need, and awards for SEANC members only. For application and more information visit http://www.seanc.org/.

Award: Scholarship for use in freshman, sophomore, junior, or senior years; not renewable. *Number:* 2. *Amount:* $500–$1000.

Eligibility Requirements: Applicant must be enrolled or expecting to enroll full-time at a two-year or four-year or technical institution or university and resident of North Carolina. Available to U.S. citizens.

Application Requirements: Application, financial need analysis, test scores, transcript. *Deadline:* April 15.

Contact: Renee Vaughan
State Employees Association of North Carolina (SEANC)
1621 Midtown Place
Raleigh, NC 27609
Phone: 919-833-6436
E-mail: rvaughan@seanc.org

STATE OF UTAH

http://www.utahsbr.edu/

NEW CENTURY SCHOLARSHIP

The New Century Scholarship is for Utah high school students who complete the requirements for an Associate's Degree by September 1st of the year they graduate from high school. Recipients receive an award of up to 75% of Bachelor Degree tuition at eligible institutions in Utah for up to 60 credit hours.

Award: Scholarship for use in junior or senior years; renewable. *Number:* 1. *Amount:* $457–$2682.

Eligibility Requirements: Applicant must be enrolled or expecting to enroll full-time at a four-year institution or university; resident of Utah and studying in Utah. Applicant must have 3.0 GPA or higher. Available to U.S. citizens.

Application Requirements: Application, transcript, GPA/copy of enrollment verification from an eligible Utah 4-year institution, verification from registrar of completion of requirements for associate's degree. *Deadline:* January 8.

Contact: David Hughes, Manager of Financial Aid
State of Utah
Board of Regents Building, The Gateway, 60 South 400 West
Salt Lake City, UT 84101-1284
Phone: 801-321-7221
E-mail: dhughes@utahsbr.edu

STATE OF WYOMING, ADMINISTERED BY UNIVERSITY OF WYOMING

http://www.uwyo.edu/scholarships

VIETNAM VETERANS AWARD-WYOMING
• *See page 645*

STATE STUDENT ASSISTANCE COMMISSION OF INDIANA (SSACI)

http://www.in.gov/ssaci

FRANK O'BANNON GRANT PROGRAM

A need-based, tuition-restricted program for students attending Indiana public, private, or proprietary institutions seeking a first undergraduate degree. Students (and parents of dependent students) who are U.S. citizens and Indiana residents must file the FAFSA yearly by the March 10 deadline.

Award: Grant for use in freshman, sophomore, junior, or senior years; not renewable. *Number:* 48,408–70,239. *Amount:* $200–$10,992.

Eligibility Requirements: Applicant must be enrolled or expecting to enroll full-time at a two-year or four-year or technical institution or university; resident of Indiana and studying in Indiana. Available to U.S. citizens.

Application Requirements: Application, financial need analysis, FAFSA. *Deadline:* March 10.

Contact: Grants Counselor
State Student Assistance Commission of Indiana (SSACI)
150 West Market Street, Suite 500
Indianapolis, IN 46204-2805
Phone: 317-232-2350
Fax: 317-232-3260
E-mail: grants@ssaci.state.in.us

HOOSIER SCHOLAR AWARD

A $500 nonrenewable award. Based on the size of the senior class, one to three scholars are selected by the guidance counselors of each accredited high school in Indiana. The award is based on academic merit and may be used for any educational expense at an eligible Indiana institution of higher education.

Award: Scholarship for use in freshman year; not renewable. *Number:* 666–840. *Amount:* $500.

Eligibility Requirements: Applicant must be high school student; planning to enroll or expecting to enroll full-time at a two-year or four-year institution or university; resident of Indiana and studying in Indiana. Applicant must have 3.5 GPA or higher. Available to U.S. citizens.

Application Requirements: Application, references. *Deadline:* March 10.

Contact: Ada Sparkman, Program Coordinator
State Student Assistance Commission of Indiana (SSACI)
150 West Market Street, Suite 500
Indianapolis, IN 46204-2805
Phone: 317-232-2350
Fax: 317-232-3260

INDIANA NATIONAL GUARD SUPPLEMENTAL GRANT
• *See page 621*

PART-TIME GRANT PROGRAM

Program is designed to encourage part-time undergraduates to start and complete their associate or baccalaureate degrees or certificates by subsidizing part-time tuition costs. It is a term-based award that is based on need. State residency requirements must be met and a FAFSA must be filed. Eligibility is determined at the institutional level subject to approval by SSACI.

Award: Grant for use in freshman, sophomore, junior, or senior years; not renewable. *Number:* 4680–6700. *Amount:* $20–$4000.

Eligibility Requirements: Applicant must be enrolled or expecting to enroll part-time at a two-year or four-year or technical institution or university; resident of Indiana and studying in Indiana. Available to U.S. citizens.

Application Requirements: Application, financial need analysis. *Deadline:* continuous.

Contact: Grants Counselor
State Student Assistance Commission of Indiana (SSACI)
150 West Market Street, Suite 500
Indianapolis, IN 46204-2805
Phone: 317-232-2350
Fax: 317-232-3260
E-mail: grants@ssaci.state.in.us

ROBERT C. BYRD HONORS SCHOLARSHIP-INDIANA

Scholarship is designed to recognize academic achievement and requires a minimum SAT score of 1300 or ACT score of 31, or recent GED score of 65. The scholarship is awarded equally among Indiana's congressional districts. The amount of the scholarship varies depending upon federal funding and is automatically renewed if the institution's satisfactory academic progress requirements are met.

Award: Scholarship for use in freshman, sophomore, junior, or senior years; renewable. *Number:* 550–570. *Amount:* $1500.

Eligibility Requirements: Applicant must be enrolled or expecting to enroll full-time at a two-year or four-year institution or university and resident of Indiana. Applicant must have 3.5 GPA or higher. Available to U.S. citizens.

Application Requirements: Application, test scores, transcript. *Deadline:* April 24.

Contact: Yvonne Heflin, Director, Special Programs
State Student Assistance Commission of Indiana (SSACI)
150 West Market Street, Suite 500
Indianapolis, IN 46204-2805
Phone: 317-232-2350
Fax: 317-232-3260

TWENTY-FIRST CENTURY SCHOLARS GEAR UP SUMMER SCHOLARSHIP

Grant of up to $3000 that pays for summer school tuition and regularly assessed course fees (does not cover other costs such as textbooks or room and board).

Award: Scholarship for use in freshman, sophomore, junior, or senior years; not renewable. *Number:* 1. *Amount:* up to $3000.

Eligibility Requirements: Applicant must be enrolled or expecting to enroll full-time at a two-year or four-year institution or university; resident of Indiana and studying in Indiana. Available to U.S. citizens.

Application Requirements: Application, must be in twenty-first century scholars program, high school diploma. *Deadline:* varies.

Contact: Coordinator, Office of Twenty-First Century Scholars
State Student Assistance Commission of Indiana (SSACI)
150 West Market Street, Suite 500
Indianapolis, IN 46204
Phone: 317-234-1394
E-mail: 21stscholars@ssaci.in.gov

STEPHEN PHILLIPS MEMORIAL SCHOLARSHIP FUND

http://www.phillips-scholarship.org/

STEPHEN PHILLIPS MEMORIAL SCHOLARSHIP FUND

Award open to full-time undergraduate students with financial need who display academic excellence, strong citizenship and character, and a desire to make a meaningful contribution to society. Only to students who are permanent residents of a New England state are eligible. Qualifying students may attend college anywhere in the U.S. For more details see web site http://www.phillips-scholarship.org.

Award: Scholarship for use in freshman, sophomore, junior, or senior years; renewable. *Number:* 150–200. *Amount:* $3000–$10,000.

Eligibility Requirements: Applicant must be enrolled or expecting to enroll full-time at a two-year or four-year institution or university and resident of Connecticut, Maine, Massachusetts, New Hampshire, Rhode Island, or Vermont. Applicant must have 3.0 GPA or higher. Available to U.S. citizens.

Application Requirements: Application, essay, financial need analysis, references, test scores, transcript. *Deadline:* May 1.

Contact: Karen Emery, Program Director
Stephen Phillips Memorial Scholarship Fund
PO Box 870
Salem, MA 01970
Phone: 978-744-2111
Fax: 978-744-0456
E-mail: kemery@spscholars.org

STEPHEN T. MARCHELLO SCHOLARSHIP FOUNDATION

http://www.stmfoundation.org/

A LEGACY OF HOPE SCHOLARSHIPS FOR SURVIVORS OF CHILDHOOD CANCER

Scholarship of up to $10,000 per year for four years of postsecondary undergraduate education. Applicant must be a survivor of childhood cancer. Must submit a letter from doctor, clinic, or hospital where cancer treatment was received. Residents of CO and MT are eligible. Must be U.S. citizen. Minimum 2.5 GPA required.

Award: Scholarship for use in freshman year; not renewable. *Number:* 1–6. *Amount:* $500–$10,000.

Eligibility Requirements: Applicant must be high school student; age 17-20; planning to enroll or expecting to enroll full- or part-time at a two-year or four-year or technical institution or university and resident of Colorado or Montana. Applicant must have 2.5 GPA or higher. Available to U.S. citizens.

Application Requirements: Application, essay, references, self-addressed stamped envelope, test scores, transcript. *Deadline:* March 15.

Contact: Mr. Mario Marchello, Secretary
Stephen T. Marchello Scholarship Foundation
1170 East Long Place
Centennial, CO 80122
Phone: 303-886-5018

SWISS BENEVOLENT SOCIETY OF CHICAGO

http://www.sbschicago.org/

SWISS BENEVOLENT SOCIETY OF CHICAGO SCHOLARSHIPS
• *See page 681*

SWISS BENEVOLENT SOCIETY OF NEW YORK

http://www.sbsny.org/

PELLEGRINI SCHOLARSHIP GRANTS
• *See page 681*

SYNOD OF THE COVENANT

http://www.synodofthecovenant.org/

CECA ETHNIC SCHOLARSHIP
• *See page 699*

SYNOD OF THE TRINITY

http://www.syntrinity.org/index/

RACIAL ETHNIC EDUCATIONAL SCHOLARSHIP
• *See page 681*

SYNOD OF THE TRINITY EDUCATIONAL SCHOLARSHIP
• *See page 699*

TENNESSEE EDUCATION ASSOCIATION

http://www.teateachers.org/

TEA DON SAHLI-KATHY WOODALL SONS AND DAUGHTERS SCHOLARSHIP
• *See page 565*

TENNESSEE STUDENT ASSISTANCE CORPORATION

http://www.tn.gov/collegepays

DEPENDENT CHILDREN SCHOLARSHIP PROGRAM

Scholarship for Tennessee residents who are dependent children of a Tennessee law enforcement officer, fireman, or an emergency medical service technician who has been killed or totally and permanently disabled while performing duties within the scope of such employment. The scholarship is awarded to full-time undergraduate students for a maximum of four academic years or the period required for the completion of the program of study.

Award: Scholarship for use in freshman, sophomore, junior, or senior years; renewable. *Amount:* varies.

Eligibility Requirements: Applicant must be enrolled or expecting to enroll full-time at a two-year or four-year institution or university; resident of Tennessee and studying in Tennessee. Available to U.S. citizens.

Application Requirements: Application, FAFSA. *Deadline:* July 15.

Contact: Ms. Naomi Derryberry, Director of Grant and Scholarship
Programs
Tennessee Student Assistance Corporation
Parkway Towers, 404 James Robertson Parkway, Suite 1510
Nashville, TN 37243-0820
Phone: 866-291-2675 Ext. 125
Fax: 615-741-6101
E-mail: naomi.derryberry@tn.gov

HOPE WITH ASPIRE

HOPE Scholarship of $4,000 (four-year institution) or $2,000 (two-year institution) with $1500 supplement. Must meet Tennessee HOPE Scholarship requirements and Adjusted Gross Income (AGI) attributable to the student must be $36,000 or less.

Award: Scholarship for use in freshman, sophomore, junior, or senior years; renewable. *Number:* varies. *Amount:* up to $5500.

Eligibility Requirements: Applicant must be enrolled or expecting to enroll full- or part-time at a two-year or four-year institution or university; resident of Tennessee and studying in Tennessee. Applicant must have 3.0 GPA or higher. Available to U.S. citizens.

Application Requirements: Application, financial need analysis. *Deadline:* September 1.

Contact: Mr. Robert Biggers, Director of Lottery Scholarship Programs
Tennessee Student Assistance Corporation
Parkway Towers, 404 James Robertson Parkway, Suite 1510
Nashville, TN 37243-0820
Phone: 866-291-2675 Ext. 106
Fax: 615-741-6101
E-mail: robert.biggers@tn.gov

NED MCWHERTER SCHOLARS PROGRAM

Award for Tennessee high school seniors with high academic ability. Must have minimum high school GPA of 3.5 and a score of 29 on the ACT or SAT equivalent. Must attend a college or university in Tennessee and be a permanent U.S. citizen. For more information, visit web site http://tn.gov/collegepays.

Award: Scholarship for use in freshman, sophomore, junior, or senior years; renewable. *Number:* up to 200. *Amount:* up to $3000.

Eligibility Requirements: Applicant must be enrolled or expecting to enroll full-time at a two-year or four-year or technical institution or university; resident of Tennessee and studying in Tennessee. Applicant must have 3.5 GPA or higher. Available to U.S. citizens.

Application Requirements: Application, test scores, transcript. *Deadline:* February 15.

Contact: Mrs. Kathy Stripling, Scholarship Administrator
Tennessee Student Assistance Corporation
404 James Robertson Parkway, Suite 1510, Parkway Towers
Nashville, TN 37243-0820
Phone: 866-291-2675 Ext. 155
Fax: 615-741-6101
E-mail: kathy.stripling@tn.gov

ROBERT C. BYRD HONORS SCHOLARSHIP-TENNESSEE

Award available to outstanding Tennessee residents graduating from high school. Minimum GPA of 3.5 required. May also qualify with a 3.0 GPA and 24 ACT or 1090 SAT. Renewable up to four years. Those with GED Test score of 570 or above may also apply.

Award: Scholarship for use in freshman, sophomore, junior, or senior years; renewable. *Number:* 500–550. *Amount:* up to $1500.

Eligibility Requirements: Applicant must be enrolled or expecting to enroll full-time at a two-year or four-year institution or university and resident of Tennessee. Applicant must have 3.0 GPA or higher. Available to U.S. citizens.

Application Requirements: Application, test scores, transcript. *Deadline:* March 1.

Contact: Mrs. Kathy Stripling, Scholarship Administrator
Tennessee Student Assistance Corporation
404 James Robertson Parkway, Suite 1510, Parkway Towers
Nashville, TN 37243-0820
Phone: 866-291-2675 Ext. 155
Fax: 615-741-6101
E-mail: kathy.stripling@tn.gov

TENNESSEE DUAL ENROLLMENT GRANT

Grant for study at an eligible Tennessee postsecondary institution awarded to juniors and seniors in a Tennessee high school who have been admitted to undergraduate study while still pursuing a high school diploma. For more information, visit web site http://www.tn.gov/collegepays.

Award: Grant for use in freshman year; renewable. *Amount:* up to $600.

Eligibility Requirements: Applicant must be high school student; planning to enroll or expecting to enroll part-time at a two-year or four-year or technical institution or university; resident of Tennessee and studying in Tennessee. Available to U.S. citizens.

Application Requirements: Application. *Deadline:* September 1.

Contact: Mr. Robert Biggers, Director of Lottery Scholarship Program
Tennessee Student Assistance Corporation
Parkway Towers, 404 James Robertson Parkway, Suite 1510
Nashville, TN 37243-0820
Phone: 866-291-2675 Ext. 106
Fax: 615-741-1601
E-mail: robert.biggers@tn.gov

TENNESSEE EDUCATION LOTTERY SCHOLARSHIP PROGRAM HOPE ACCESS GRANT

Non-renewable award of $2,750 for students at four-year colleges or $1,750 for students at two-year colleges. Entering freshmen must have a minimum GPA of 2.75, ACT score of 18–20 (or SAT equivalent), and adjusted gross income attributable to the student must be $36,000 or less. Recipients will become eligible for Tennessee HOPE Scholarship by meeting HOPE Scholarship renewal criteria.

Award: Scholarship for use in freshman, sophomore, junior, or senior years; not renewable. *Number:* varies. *Amount:* up to $2750.

Eligibility Requirements: Applicant must be enrolled or expecting to enroll full- or part-time at a two-year or four-year institution or university; resident of Tennessee and studying in Tennessee. Available to U.S. citizens.

Application Requirements: Application, financial need analysis. *Deadline:* September 1.

Contact: Mr. Robert Biggers, Director of Lottery Scholarship Programs
Tennessee Student Assistance Corporation
Parkway Towers, 404 James Robertson Parkway, Suite 1510
Nashville, TN 37243-0820
Phone: 866-291-2675 Ext. 106
Fax: 615-741-6101
E-mail: robert.biggers@tn.gov

TENNESSEE EDUCATION LOTTERY SCHOLARSHIP PROGRAM-HOPE WITH GENERAL ASSEMBLY MERIT SCHOLARSHIP (GAMS)

HOPE Scholarship of $4,000 (four-year institution) or $2,00 (two-year institution) with supplemental award of $1,000. Entering freshmen must have 3.75 GPA and 29 ACT (1280 SAT). Must be a U.S. citizen and a resident of Tennessee.

Award: Scholarship for use in freshman, sophomore, junior, or senior years; renewable. *Number:* varies. *Amount:* up to $5000.

Eligibility Requirements: Applicant must be enrolled or expecting to enroll full- or part-time at a two-year or four-year institution or university; resident of Tennessee and studying in Tennessee. Available to U.S. citizens.

Application Requirements: Application. *Deadline:* September 1.

Contact: Mr. Robert Biggers, Director of Lottery Scholarship Programs
Tennessee Student Assistance Corporation
Parkway Towers, 404 James Robertson Parkway, Suite 1510
Nashville, TN 37243-0820
Phone: 866-291-2675 Ext. 106
Fax: 615-741-6101
E-mail: robert.biggers@tn.gov

TENNESSEE EDUCATION LOTTERY SCHOLARSHIP PROGRAM TENNESSEE HOPE SCHOLARSHIP

Award amount is $4,000 for four-year institutions and $2,000 for two-year institutions. Must be a Tennessee resident attending an eligible post-secondary institution in Tennessee. For more information, visit http://www.TN.gov/CollegePays.

Award: Scholarship for use in freshman, sophomore, junior, or senior years; renewable. *Number:* varies. *Amount:* $2000–$4000.

Eligibility Requirements: Applicant must be enrolled or expecting to enroll full- or part-time at a two-year or four-year institution or university; resident of Tennessee and studying in Tennessee. Applicant must have 3.0 GPA or higher. Available to U.S. citizens.

Application Requirements: Application. *Deadline:* September 1.

Contact: Mr. Robert Biggers, Director of Lottery Scholarship Programs
Tennessee Student Assistance Corporation
Parkway Towers, 404 James Robertson Parkway, Suite 1510
Nashville, TN 37243-0820
Phone: 866-291-2675 Ext. 106
Fax: 615-741-6101
E-mail: robert.biggers@tn.gov

TENNESSEE EDUCATION LOTTERY SCHOLARSHIP PROGRAM WILDER-NAIFEH TECHNICAL SKILLS GRANT

Award up to $2,000 for students enrolled in a certificate or diploma program at a Tennessee Technology Center. Cannot be prior recipient of Tennessee HOPE Scholarship. For more information, visit http://www.TN.gov/CollegePays.

Award: Grant for use in freshman or sophomore years; renewable. *Number:* varies. *Amount:* up to $2000.

Eligibility Requirements: Applicant must be enrolled or expecting to enroll full- or part-time at a technical institution; resident of Tennessee and studying in Tennessee. Available to U.S. citizens.

Application Requirements: Application. *Deadline:* November 1.

Contact: Mr. Robert Biggers, Director of Lottery Scholarship Programs
Tennessee Student Assistance Corporation
Parkway Towers, 404 James Robertson Parkway, Suite 1510
Nashville, TN 37243-0820
Phone: 866-291-2675 Ext. 106
Fax: 615-741-6101
E-mail: robert.biggers@tn.gov

TENNESSEE HOPE FOSTER CHILD TUITION GRANT

Renewable tuition award available for recipients of the HOPE Scholarship or HOPE Access Grant. Student must have been in Tennessee state custody as a foster child for at least one year after reaching age 14. Award amount varies and shall not exceed the tuition and mandatory fees at an eligible Tennessee public postsecondary institution. For additional information, visit web site http://www.tn.gov/collegepays.

Award: Scholarship for use in freshman, sophomore, junior, or senior years; renewable.

Eligibility Requirements: Applicant must be enrolled or expecting to enroll full- or part-time at a two-year or four-year institution or university; resident of Tennessee and studying in Tennessee. Applicant must have 3.0 GPA or higher. Available to U.S. citizens.

Application Requirements: Application. *Deadline:* September 1.

Contact: Mr. Robert Biggers, Director of Lottery Scholarship Programs
Tennessee Student Assistance Corporation
Parkway Towers, 404 James Robertson Parkway, Suite 1510
Nashville, TN 37243-0820
Phone: 866-291-2675 Ext. 106
Fax: 615-741-6101
E-mail: robert.biggers@tn.gov

TENNESSEE STUDENT ASSISTANCE AWARD

Award to assist financially-needy Tennessee residents attending an approved college or university within the state. Complete a Free Application for Federal Student Aid form. FAFSA must be processed as soon as possible after January 1 for priority consideration. For more information, see http://www.fafsa.gov.

Award: Grant for use in freshman, sophomore, junior, or senior years; not renewable. *Number:* 25,000–35,000. *Amount:* $100–$4000.

Eligibility Requirements: Applicant must be enrolled or expecting to enroll full- or part-time at a two-year or four-year or technical institution or university; resident of Tennessee and studying in Tennessee. Available to U.S. citizens.

Application Requirements: Application, financial need analysis.

Contact: Ms. Naomi Derryberry, Director of Grants and Scholarship Programs
Tennessee Student Assistance Corporation
Parkway Towers, 404 James Robertson Parkway, Suite 1510
Nashville, TN 37243-0820
Phone: 866-291-2675 Ext. 125
Fax: 615-741-6101
E-mail: naomi.derryberry@tn.gov

TERRY FOUNDATION

http://www.terryfoundation.org/

TERRY FOUNDATION SCHOLARSHIP

Scholarships to Texas high school seniors who have been admitted to the universities affiliated with the foundation: University of Texas at Austin, Texas A&M University at College Station, University of Houston, Texas State University–San Marcos, University of Texas at San Antonio and University of Texas at Dallas.

Award: Scholarship for use in freshman year; renewable. *Number:* 208–650. *Amount:* $19,000–$76,000.

Eligibility Requirements: Applicant must be high school student; planning to enroll or expecting to enroll full-time at a four-year institution or university; resident of Texas; studying in Texas and must have an interest in leadership. Applicant must have 2.5 GPA or higher. Available to U.S. citizens.

Application Requirements: Application, essay, financial need analysis, interview, references, transcript. *Deadline:* January 12.

Contact: Ms. Beth Freeman, Scholarship Committee
Terry Foundation
3104 Edloe, Suite 205
Houston, TX 77027
Phone: 713-552-0002
Fax: 713-650-8729
E-mail: beth.freeman@terryfoundation.org

TEXAS 4-H YOUTH DEVELOPMENT FOUNDATION

http://www.texas4-h.tamu.edu/

TEXAS 4-H OPPORTUNITY SCHOLARSHIP

Renewable award for Texas 4-H members to attend a Texas college or university. Minimum GPA of 2.5 required. Must attend full-time.

Award: Scholarship for use in freshman, sophomore, junior, or senior years; renewable. *Number:* 225. *Amount:* $1500–$15,000.

Eligibility Requirements: Applicant must be enrolled or expecting to enroll full-time at a two-year or four-year or technical institution; resident of Texas; studying in Texas and must have an interest in animal/agricultural competition. Applicant must have 2.5 GPA or higher. Available to U.S. citizens.

Application Requirements: Application, essay, financial need analysis, interview, references, test scores, transcript. *Deadline:* varies.

Contact: Jim Reeves, Executive Director
Texas 4-H Youth Development Foundation
Texas A&M University
7607 Eastmark Drive, Suite 101
College Station, TX 77840-2473
Phone: 979-845-1213
Fax: 979-845-6495
E-mail: jereeves@ag.tamu.edu

TEXAS AFL-CIO

http://www.texasaflcio.org/

TEXAS AFL-CIO SCHOLARSHIP PROGRAM
• *See page 565*

TEXAS BLACK BAPTIST SCHOLARSHIP COMMITTEE

http://www.bgct.org/

TEXAS BLACK BAPTIST SCHOLARSHIP
• *See page 681*

TEXAS CHRISTIAN UNIVERSITY NEELY ENTREPRENEURSHIP CENTER

http://www.nec.tcu.edu/

TCU TEXAS YOUTH ENTREPRENEUR OF THE YEAR AWARDS

Award available to currently enrolled Texas high school students who started and managed a business while in high school. Must submit description of currently-operating business they founded. Finalists must attend TCU Young Entrepreneurs Days and individually participate in interviews. Award may be applied to any college, but is doubled if the student attends TCU. Information and application available on web site http://www.tcuyeya.org.

Award: Scholarship for use in freshman year; not renewable. *Number:* 6. *Amount:* $1000–$5000.

Eligibility Requirements: Applicant must be high school student; age 14-19; planning to enroll or expecting to enroll full- or part-time at a two-year or four-year or technical institution or university; resident of Texas and must have an interest in entrepreneurship. Available to U.S. citizens.

Application Requirements: Application, interview, marketing and promotional material encouraged. *Deadline:* November 1.

Contact: Sheryl Doll, Program Director, TCU Texas Youth Entrepreneur
Texas Christian University Neely Entrepreneurship Center
PO Box 298530
Fort Worth, TX 76129
Phone: 817-257-5078
E-mail: s.doll@tcu.edu

TEXAS HIGHER EDUCATION COORDINATING BOARD

http://www.collegefortexans.com/

TEXAS NATIONAL GUARD TUITION ASSISTANCE PROGRAM
• *See page 621*

TOWARD EXCELLENCE ACCESS AND SUCCESS (TEXAS GRANT)

Renewable aid for students enrolled in public colleges or universities in Texas. Must be a resident of Texas and have completed the Recommended High School Curriculum or Distinguished Achievement Curriculum in high school. For renewal awards, must maintain a minimum GPA of 2.5. Based on need. Amount of award is determined by the financial aid office of each school. Deadlines vary. Contact the college/university financial aid office for application information.

Award: Grant for use in freshman, sophomore, junior, or senior years; renewable. *Amount:* $2680–$6080.

Eligibility Requirements: Applicant must be enrolled or expecting to enroll full- or part-time at a two-year or four-year or technical institution or university; resident of Texas and studying in Texas. Available to U.S. citizens.

Application Requirements: Financial need analysis, transcript.

Contact: Financial Aid Office of relevant school

TUITION EQUALIZATION GRANT (TEG) PROGRAM

Renewable award for Texas residents enrolled full-time at an independent college or university within the state. Based on financial need. Renewal awards require the student to maintain an overall college GPA of at least 2.5. Deadlines vary by institution. Must not be receiving athletic scholarship. Contact college/university financial aid office for application information. Nonresidents who are National Merit Finalists may also receive awards.

Award: Grant for use in freshman, sophomore, junior, or senior years; renewable. *Amount:* $3808–$5712.

Eligibility Requirements: Applicant must be enrolled or expecting to enroll full-time at a two-year or four-year institution or university; resident of Texas and studying in Texas. Available to U.S. citizens.

Application Requirements: Financial need analysis, FAFSA.

Contact: Financial Aid Office of Relevant Institution

TEXAS TENNIS FOUNDATION

http://www.texastennisfoundation.com/

TEXAS TENNIS FOUNDATION SCHOLARSHIPS AND ENDOWMENTS

College scholarships for highly recommended students residing in Texas, with an interest in tennis. Financial need is considered. Must be between the ages of 17 and 19. Refer to web site for details http://www.texastennisfoundation.com/web90/scholarships/tenniscampsscholarships.asp.

Award: Scholarship for use in freshman, sophomore, junior, or senior years; not renewable. *Number:* 10. *Amount:* $1000.

Eligibility Requirements: Applicant must be age 17-19; enrolled or expecting to enroll full-time at a two-year or four-year or technical institution or university; resident of Texas and must have an interest in athletics/sports. Available to U.S. citizens.

Application Requirements: Application, essay, financial need analysis, photo, references, test scores, transcript, copy of parent or guardian's federal tax return. *Deadline:* April 15.

Contact: Ken McAllister, Executive Director
Texas Tennis Foundation
8105 Exchange Drive
Austin, TX 78754-4788
Phone: 512-443-1334 Ext. 201
Fax: 512-443-4748
E-mail: kmcallister@texas.usta.com

THEODORE R. AND VIVIAN M. JOHNSON SCHOLARSHIP FOUNDATION INC.

http://www.jsf.bz/

THEODORE R. AND VIVIAN M. JOHNSON SCHOLARSHIP PROGRAM FOR CHILDREN OF UPS EMPLOYEES OR UPS RETIREES
• *See page 580*

TIDEWATER SCHOLARSHIP FOUNDATION

http://www.accesscollege.org/

ACCESS SCHOLARSHIP/LAST DOLLAR AWARD

A renewable scholarship of $500 to $1000 for the undergraduates participating in Norfolk, Portsmouth, and Virginia Beach, Virginia secure scholarships and financial aid for college.

Award: Scholarship for use in freshman year; renewable. *Number:* varies. *Amount:* $500–$1000.

Eligibility Requirements: Applicant must be high school student; planning to enroll or expecting to enroll full-time at a two-year or four-year institution or university and resident of Virginia. Applicant must have 2.5 GPA or higher. Available to U.S. citizens.

Application Requirements: Application, financial need analysis. *Deadline:* May 1.

Contact: Bonnie Sutton, President and Chief Executive Officer
Tidewater Scholarship Foundation
7300 Newport Avenue, Suite 500
Norfolk, VA 23505
Phone: 757-962-6113
Fax: 757-962-7314
E-mail: bsutton@accesscollege.org

TIGER WOODS FOUNDATION

http://www.tigerwoodsfoundation.org/

ALFRED "TUP" HOLMES MEMORIAL SCHOLARSHIP

Given yearly to one worthy Atlanta metropolitan area graduating high school senior who has displayed high moral character while demonstrating leadership potential and academic excellence. Must be U.S. citizen. Minimum 3.0 GPA required.

Award: Scholarship for use in freshman year; not renewable. *Number:* 1. *Amount:* $2500.

Eligibility Requirements: Applicant must be high school student; planning to enroll or expecting to enroll full-time at a two-year or four-year institution or university and resident of Georgia. Applicant must have 3.0 GPA or higher. Available to U.S. citizens.

Application Requirements: Application, essay, references, test scores, transcript. *Deadline:* April 1.

Contact: Michelle Kim, Scholarship and Grant Coordinator
Tiger Woods Foundation
121 Innovation, Suite 150
Irvine, CA 92617
Phone: 949-725-3003
Fax: 949-725-3002
E-mail: grants@tigerwoodsfoundation.org

TKE EDUCATIONAL FOUNDATION

http://www.tke.org/

ELMER AND DORIS SCHMITZ SR. MEMORIAL SCHOLARSHIP
• *See page 567*

TOWNSHIP OFFICIALS OF ILLINOIS

http://www.toi.org/

TOWNSHIP OFFICIALS OF ILLINOIS SCHOLARSHIP FUND

The scholarships are awarded to graduating Illinois high school seniors who have a B average or above, have demonstrated an active interest in school activities, who have submitted an essay on "The Importance of Township Government", high school transcript, and letters of recommendation. Students must attend Illinois institutions, either four-year or junior colleges. Must be full-time student. Must complete an interview with a current township official.

Award: Scholarship for use in freshman year; not renewable. *Number:* 7. *Amount:* $2000.

Eligibility Requirements: Applicant must be high school student; planning to enroll or expecting to enroll full-time at a two-year or four-year institution or university; resident of Illinois and studying in Illinois. Applicant must have 3.0 GPA or higher. Available to U.S. citizens.

Application Requirements: Application, essay, interview, references, test scores, transcript. *Deadline:* March 1.

Contact: Bryan Smith, Editor and Executive Director
Township Officials of Illinois
408 South Fifth Street
Springfield, IL 62701-1804
Phone: 217-744-2212
Fax: 217-744-7419
E-mail: bryan@toi.org

TRIANGLE COMMUNITY FOUNDATION

http://www.trianglecf.org/

GLAXOSMITHKLINE OPPORTUNITY SCHOLARSHIP

Renewable award for any type of education or training program. Must be a legal resident of the United States with a permanent residence in Durham, Orange, Wake. No income limitations. The applicant must demonstrate the potential to succeed despite adversity as well as an exceptional desire to improve himself or herself through further education. For further information see web site at http://www.tranglecf.org.

Award: Scholarship for use in freshman, sophomore, junior, senior, or graduate years; renewable. *Number:* 1–10. *Amount:* $5000–$20,000.

Eligibility Requirements: Applicant must be enrolled or expecting to enroll full- or part-time at a two-year or four-year institution or university; resident of North Carolina and studying in North Carolina. Available to U.S. citizens.

Application Requirements: Application, essay, financial need analysis, references, test scores, transcript, proof of U.S. citizenship. *Deadline:* March 15.

Contact: Libby Richards, Scholarship and Special Projects Coordinator
Triangle Community Foundation
324 Blackwell St., Suite 1220
Durham, NC 27701
Phone: 919-474-8370 Ext. 134
Fax: 919-941-9208
E-mail: Scholarships@trianglecf.org

ULMAN CANCER FUND FOR YOUNG ADULTS

http://www.ulmanfund.org/

MARILYN YETSO MEMORIAL SCHOLARSHIP

Provides support for the financial needs of college students who have a parent with cancer or who have lost a parent to cancer. Currently attending, or accepted to, a two- or four-year college, university or vocational program (including graduate and professional schools). Must be a resident of, or attending or planning to attend an educational institution in: Maryland, Virginia, or Washington, D.C.

Award: Scholarship for use in freshman, sophomore, junior, or senior years; not renewable. *Number:* 1–2. *Amount:* $1000.

Eligibility Requirements: Applicant must be age 15-35; enrolled or expecting to enroll full- or part-time at a two-year or four-year or technical institution or university; resident of District of Columbia, Maryland, or Virginia and studying in District of Columbia, Maryland, or Virginia. Available to U.S. and non-U.S. citizens.

Application Requirements: Application, essay, financial need analysis, references, self-addressed stamped envelope, parent's medical history. *Deadline:* May 10.

Contact: Fay Baker, Scholarship Coordinator
Ulman Cancer Fund for Young Adults
4725 Dorsey Hall Drive, Suite A
PO Box 505
Ellicott City, MD 21042
Phone: 410-964-0202
E-mail: scholarship@ulmanfund.org

MARYLAND COMMUNITY CANCER SCHOLARSHIP AWARD
• *See page 614*

VERA YIP MEMORIAL SCHOLARSHIP
• *See page 615*

UNITED DAUGHTERS OF THE CONFEDERACY

http://www.hqudc.org/

CHARLOTTE M. F. BENTLEY/NEW YORK CHAPTER 103 SCHOLARSHIP
• *See page 569*

GERTRUDE BOTTS-SAUCIER SCHOLARSHIP
• *See page 569*

LOLA B. CURRY SCHOLARSHIP
• *See page 569*

UNITED METHODIST CHURCH

http://www.gbhem.org/

J. A. KNOWLES MEMORIAL SCHOLARSHIP
• *See page 699*

UNITED NEGRO COLLEGE FUND

http://www.uncf.org/

ABBINGTON, VALLANTEEN SCHOLARSHIP
• *See page 683*

ALLEN AND JOAN BILDNER SCHOLARSHIP
• *See page 683*

AMOS DEINARD FOUNDATION SCHOLARSHIP
Scholarship of up to $3000 available to a Minnesota student attending UNCF member college or university. Minimum 2.5 GPA required.

Award: Scholarship for use in freshman, sophomore, junior, or senior years; not renewable. *Amount:* up to $3000.

Eligibility Requirements: Applicant must be enrolled or expecting to enroll full- or part-time at a four-year institution or university and resident of Minnesota. Applicant must have 2.5 GPA or higher. Available to U.S. citizens.

Application Requirements: *Deadline:* continuous.

Contact: Director, Program Services
United Negro College Fund
8260 Willow Oaks Corporate Drive
PO Box 10444
Fairfax, VA 22031-8044
Phone: 800-331-2244
E-mail: rebecca.bennett@uncf.org

BANK ONE ARIZONA CORPORATION SCHOLARSHIP
• *See page 683*

BENDIX CORPORATION SCHOLARSHIP
• *See page 683*

BORDEN SCHOLARSHIP FUND
• *See page 684*

BRISTOL-MYERS SQUIBB SCHOLARSHIP
• *See page 684*

CHARLES & ELLORA ALLIS FOUNDATION SCHOLARSHIP
Award of up to $3000 for Minnesota residents attending a UNCF college or university. May be used for any year of undergraduate study. Must have minimum 2.5 GPA.

Award: Scholarship for use in freshman, sophomore, junior, or senior years; not renewable. *Amount:* up to $3000.

Eligibility Requirements: Applicant must be enrolled or expecting to enroll at a four-year institution and resident of Minnesota. Applicant must have 2.5 GPA or higher. Available to U.S. citizens.

Application Requirements: *Deadline:* continuous.

Contact: Director, Program Services
United Negro College Fund
8260 Willow Oaks Corporate Drive
PO Box 10444
Fairfax, VA 22031-8044
Phone: 800-331-2244
E-mail: rebecca.bennett@uncf.org

CHICAGO INTER-ALUMNI COUNCIL SCHOLARSHIP
• *See page 684*

CHICAGO PUBLIC SCHOOLS UNCF CAMPAIGN
• *See page 684*

CITY OF CLEVELAND: MAYOR JACKSON SCHOLARSHIP FOR CLEVELAND METROPOLITAN SCHOOL DISTRICT
• *See page 685*

CITY OF CLEVELAND: MAYOR JACKSON SCHOLARSHIP FOR HISTORICALLY BLACK COLLEGES AND UNIVERSITIES
• *See page 685*

CITY OF CLEVELAND: MAYOR JACKSON SCHOLARSHIPS FOR CITY EMPLOYEES
• *See page 685*

CLEVELAND MAYOR JACKSON SCHOLARSHIP FOR RECREATION CENTERS
• *See page 685*

CLOROX COMPANY FOUNDATION SCHOLARSHIP
• *See page 685*

CLOWES FUND SCHOLARSHIP
• *See page 686*

CONSUMER ENERGY FOUNDATION SCHOLARSHIP
• *See page 686*

COSTCO SCHOLARSHIP
• *See page 686*

DALLAS INDEPENDENT SCHOOL DISTRICT SCHOLARSHIP
• *See page 686*

DAVENPORT FORTE PEDESTAL FUND
• *See page 686*

DENIS D'AMORE SCHOLARSHIP
• *See page 686*

DOMINIQUE AND JACQUES CASIMIR SCHOLARSHIP
• *See page 687*

EDNA F. BLUM FOUNDATION SCHOLARSHIP
• *See page 687*

EDWARD & STELLA VANHOUTEN SCHOLARSHIP
One-time award for students attending UNCF member colleges and universities. Must be a resident of Massachusetts. For additional information, please see website http://www.uncf.org/forstudents/scholarship.asp.

Award: Scholarship for use in freshman year; not renewable.

Eligibility Requirements: Applicant must be enrolled or expecting to enroll at a four-year institution or university and resident of Massachusetts. Available to U.S. citizens.

Application Requirements: *Deadline:* continuous.

Contact: Director, Program Services
United Negro College Fund
8260 Willow Oaks Corporate Drive
PO Box 10444
Fairfax, VA 22031-8044
Phone: 800-331-2244
E-mail: rebecca.bennett@uncf.org

ELMER ROE DEAVER FOUNDATION SCHOLARSHIP
• *See page 688*

EVELYN LEVINA WRIGHT SCHOLARSHIP
• *See page 688*

FIFTH/THIRD SCHOLARS PROGRAM
• *See page 688*

FORT WORTH INDEPENDENT SCHOOL DISTRICT SCHOLARSHIP
• *See page 689*

GARY PAYTON FOUNDATION ENDOWED SCHOLARSHIP
• *See page 689*

GEORGE AND FRANCIS BALL FOUNDATION SCHOLARSHIP
• *See page 689*

GHEENS FOUNDATION SCHOLARSHIP
• *See page 690*

GIANT FOODS SCHOLARSHIP
• *See page 598*

JOHN W. ANDERSON FOUNDATION SCHOLARSHIP
• *See page 690*

KANSAS CITY INITIATIVE SCHOLARSHIP
• *See page 690*

KROGER SCHOLARSHIP
• *See page 691*

NEW JERSEY MAYOR'S TASK FORCE SCHOLARSHIP
• *See page 691*

ORACLE COMMUNITY IMPACT SCHOLARSHIP
• *See page 691*

PENNSYLVANIA STATE EMPLOYEES SCHOLARSHIP (SECA)
• *See page 691*

RONALD MCDONALD'S CHICAGOLAND AND NORTHWEST INDIANA SCHOLARSHIP
• *See page 691*

RONALD MCDONALD'S HOUSE CHARITIES SCHOLARSHIP-OHIO
• *See page 692*

ROSA E. BLACKWELL SCHOLARSHIP FUND

Scholarship encouraging exceptional youth to seek professional and technical careers. Must attend a Cincinnati public high school, show school and community leadership and service, and have good attendance and citizenship. Minimum 2.5 GPA required.

Award: Scholarship for use in freshman year; not renewable. *Number:* 3. *Amount:* up to $5000.

Eligibility Requirements: Applicant must be high school student; planning to enroll or expecting to enroll full-time at a four-year institution or university and resident of Ohio. Applicant must have 2.5 GPA or higher.

Application Requirements: *Deadline:* May 31.
Contact: Director, Program Services
United Negro College Fund
8260 Willow Oaks Corporate Drive
PO Box 10444
Fairfax, VA 22031-8044
Phone: 800-331-2244
E-mail: rebecca.bennett@uncf.org

RYAN HOWARD FAMILY FOUNDATION SCHOLARSHIP-ST. LOUIS/PHILADELPHIA
• *See page 598*

ST. PETERSBURG GOLF CLASSIC SCHOLARSHIP
• *See page 692*

SHELL/EQUILON UNCF CLEVELAND SCHOLARSHIP FUND
• *See page 692*

SIDNEY STONEMAN SCHOLARSHIP
• *See page 692*

SONYA WILLIAMS MEMORIAL SCHOLARSHIP

Scholarship for students who are residents of New York and attending UNCF member colleges and universities. Minimum GPA 2.5. For more information see web site: http://www.uncf.org/forstudents/scholarship.asp.

Award: Scholarship for use in freshman year.

Eligibility Requirements: Applicant must be enrolled or expecting to enroll at a four-year institution or university and resident of New York. Applicant must have 2.5 GPA or higher.

Contact: Director, Program Services
United Negro College Fund
8260 Willow Oaks Corporate Drive
PO Box 10444
Fairfax, VA 22031-8044
Phone: 800-331-2244
E-mail: rebecca.bennett@uncf.org

TJX FOUNDATION SCHOLARSHIP
• *See page 692*

UNION BANK OF CALIFORNIA
• *See page 693*

UNITED WAY OF NEW ORLEANS EMERGENCY ASSISTANCE FUND
• *See page 693*

UNITED WAY OF WESTCHESTER & PUTNAM INC./ UNCF EMERGENCY ASSISTANCE FUND
• *See page 693*

V103/WAOK UNCF EMERGENCY ASSISTANCE SCHOLARSHIP FUND
• *See page 693*

VIAD/DIAL CORPORATION SCHOLARSHIP
• *See page 694*

WHIRLPOOL FOUNDATION SCHOLARSHIP
• *See page 694*

WISCONSIN STUDENT AID
• *See page 694*

YOUTH EMPOWERMENT SCHOLARSHIP
• *See page 694*

YOUTH GALA SCHOLARSHIP
• *See page 694*

UNIVERSITY AVIATION ASSOCIATION

http://www.uaa.aero/

CHICAGO AREA BUSINESS AVIATION ASSOCIATION SCHOLARSHIP

One-time awards of $2500. Must be a U.S. citizen. Minimum GPA of 2.5. Priority given to Chicagoland residents followed by Illinois residents.

Award: Scholarship for use in freshman, sophomore, junior, senior, graduate, or postgraduate years; not renewable. *Number:* 6. *Amount:* $2500.

Eligibility Requirements: Applicant must be enrolled or expecting to enroll full-time at a two-year or four-year or technical institution or university and resident of Illinois. Applicant must have 2.5 GPA or higher. Available to U.S. citizens.

Application Requirements: Application, essay, references. *Deadline:* April 20.

Contact: David A. Newmyer, Department Chair, Aviation Management and Flight
University Aviation Association
Southern Illinois University at Carbondale, College of Applied Sciences and Arts
Carbondale, IL 62901-6623
Phone: 618-453-8898
Fax: 618-453-7286
E-mail: newmyer@siu.edu

UNIVERSITY OF NEW MEXICO

http://www.unm.edu/

BRIDGE TO SUCCESS SCHOLARSHIP

Scholarship to the students who reside in New Mexico and are U.S. citizens. Applicant must be a graduate from a New Mexico public (or accredited private) high school or be a GED recipient. Must have a minimum high school GPA of 2.5 or GED score 530. Deadline varies for fall it is June 30 and for spring it is November 30.

Award: Scholarship for use in freshman year; not renewable. *Number:* varies. *Amount:* varies.

Eligibility Requirements: Applicant must be high school student; planning to enroll or expecting to enroll full-time at a four-year institution or university and resident of New Mexico. Applicant must have 2.5 GPA or higher. Available to U.S. citizens.

Application Requirements: Application, transcript, proof of enrollment. *Deadline:* continuous.

Contact: Robert Romero, Financial Aid Adviser
University of New Mexico
Mesa Vista Hall, Room 3019
Albuquerque, NM 87131
Phone: 505-277-6090
Fax: 505-277-5275
E-mail: schol@unm.edu

NM LOTTERY SUCCESS SCHOLARSHIP

Scholarship to the residents of New Mexico. Applicant must be graduate from a New Mexico public (or accredited private) high school or receive a GED. Must enroll full-time in a baccalaureate degree program.

Award: Scholarship for use in freshman year; renewable. *Number:* varies. *Amount:* varies.

Eligibility Requirements: Applicant must be enrolled or expecting to enroll full-time at a four-year institution or university and resident of New Mexico. Applicant must have 2.5 GPA or higher. Available to U.S. citizens.

Application Requirements: Application, resume, transcript. *Deadline:* varies.

Contact: Robert Romero, Financial Aid Adviser
University of New Mexico
Mesa Vista Hall, Room 3019
Albuquerque, NM 87131
Phone: 505-277-6090
Fax: 505-277-5275
E-mail: schol@unm.edu

URBAN LEAGUE OF RHODE ISLAND INC.

http://www.ulri.org/

URBAN LEAGUE OF RHODE ISLAND SCHOLARSHIP
• *See page 695*

UTAH STATE BOARD OF REGENTS

http://www.uheaa.org/

UTAH CENTENNIAL OPPORTUNITY PROGRAM FOR EDUCATION

Award available to students with substantial financial need for use at any of the participating Utah institutions. The student must be a Utah resident. Contact the financial aid office of the participating institution for requirements and deadlines.

Award: Grant for use in freshman, sophomore, junior, or senior years; not renewable. *Number:* up to 2988. *Amount:* $300–$5000.

Eligibility Requirements: Applicant must be enrolled or expecting to enroll full- or part-time at a two-year or four-year or technical institution or university; resident of Utah and studying in Utah. Available to U.S. citizens.

Application Requirements: Financial need analysis, FAFSA. *Deadline:* continuous.

Contact: Mr. David Hughes, Manager of Financial Aid and Scholarships
Utah State Board of Regents
60 South 400 West
The Board of Regents Building, The Gateway
Salt Lake City, UT 84101-1284
Phone: 801-321-7220
Fax: 801-321-7168
E-mail: dhughes@utahsbr.edu

UTAH LEVERAGING EDUCATIONAL ASSISTANCE PARTNERSHIP

Award available to Utah resident students with substantial financial need for use at any of the participating Utah institutions. Contact the financial aid office of the participating institution for requirements and deadlines.

Award: Grant for use in freshman, sophomore, junior, or senior years; not renewable. *Number:* up to 3252. *Amount:* $300–$2500.

Eligibility Requirements: Applicant must be enrolled or expecting to enroll full- or part-time at a two-year or four-year or technical institution or university; resident of Utah and studying in Utah. Available to U.S. citizens.

Application Requirements: Financial need analysis, FAFSA. *Deadline:* continuous.

Contact: Mr. David Hughes, Manager of Financial Aid and Scholarships
Utah State Board of Regents
60 South 400 West
The Board of Regents Building, The Gateway
Salt Lake City, UT 84101-1284
Phone: 801-321-7220
Fax: 801-321-7168
E-mail: dhughes@utahsbr.edu

VERMONT STUDENT ASSISTANCE CORPORATION

http://www.vsac.org/

VERMONT INCENTIVE GRANTS

Renewable grants for Vermont residents based on financial need. Must meet needs test. Must be college undergraduate or graduate student enrolled full-time at an approved post secondary institution. Only available to Vermont residents.

Award: Grant for use in freshman, sophomore, junior, or senior years; renewable. *Number:* varies. *Amount:* $500–$10,800.

Eligibility Requirements: Applicant must be enrolled or expecting to enroll full-time at a two-year or four-year or technical institution or university and resident of Vermont. Available to U.S. citizens.

Application Requirements: Application, financial need analysis, FAFSA. *Deadline:* continuous.

Contact: Grant Program
Vermont Student Assistance Corporation
PO Box 2000
Winooski, VT 05404-2000
Phone: 802-655-9602
Fax: 802-654-3765

VERMONT NON-DEGREE STUDENT GRANT PROGRAM

Need-based, renewable grants for Vermont residents enrolled in non-degree programs in a college, vocational school, or high school adult program, that will improve employability or encourage further study. Award amounts vary.

Award: Grant for use in freshman, sophomore, junior, or senior years; renewable. *Number:* varies. *Amount:* varies.

Eligibility Requirements: Applicant must be enrolled or expecting to enroll full- or part-time at a two-year or four-year or technical institution or university and resident of Vermont. Available to U.S. citizens.

Application Requirements: Application, financial need analysis. *Deadline:* continuous.

Contact: Grant Program Department
Vermont Student Assistance Corporation
10 East Allen Street
PO Box 2000
Winooski, VT 05404-2000
Phone: 802-655-9602

VERMONT PART-TIME STUDENT GRANTS

For undergraduates carrying less than twelve credits per semester who have not received a bachelor's degree. Must be Vermont resident. Based on financial need. Complete Vermont Financial Aid Packet to apply. May be used at any approved post-secondary institution.

Award: Grant for use in freshman, sophomore, junior, or senior years; renewable. *Number:* varies. *Amount:* $250–$8100.

Eligibility Requirements: Applicant must be enrolled or expecting to enroll part-time at a four-year institution or university and resident of Vermont. Available to U.S. citizens.

Application Requirements: Application, financial need analysis. *Deadline:* continuous.

Contact: Grant Program
Vermont Student Assistance Corporation
PO Box 2000
Winooski, VT 05404-2000
Phone: 802-655-9602
Fax: 802-654-3765

VIKKI CARR SCHOLARSHIP FOUNDATION

http://www.vikkicarrfoundation.com/

VIKKI CARR SCHOLARSHIPS
• *See page 695*

VINCENT L. HAWKINSON FOUNDATION FOR PEACE AND JUSTICE

http://www.graceattheu.org/

VINCENT L. HAWKINSON SCHOLARSHIP FOR PEACE AND JUSTICE

Scholarships are awarded to students who have demonstrated a commitment to peace and justice through participation in a peace and justice project, leadership and participation in a peace organization, or serving as a role model. Candidates are screened based on submitted essays and reference letters, and recipients are selected based a personal interview which takes place in Minneapolis. Applicants must either reside or study in Iowa, Minnesota, North Dakota, South Dakota, or Wisconsin.

Award: Scholarship for use in freshman, sophomore, junior, senior, graduate, or postgraduate years; not renewable. *Number:* 1–10. *Amount:* $1000–$5000.

Eligibility Requirements: Applicant must be enrolled or expecting to enroll full- or part-time at a two-year or four-year institution or university; resident of Iowa, Minnesota, North Dakota, South Dakota, or Wisconsin; studying in Iowa, Minnesota, North Dakota, South Dakota, or Wisconsin and must have an interest in leadership. Available to U.S. and non-U.S. citizens.

Application Requirements: Application, essay, interview, references, transcript. *Deadline:* March 15.

Contact: Scholarship Committee
Vincent L. Hawkinson Foundation for Peace and Justice
Grace University Lutheran Church
324 Harvard Street, SE
Minneapolis, MN 55414
Phone: 612-331-8125
E-mail: info@graceattheu.org

VIRGINIA DEPARTMENT OF EDUCATION

http://www.pen.k12.va.us/

GRANVILLE P. MEADE SCHOLARSHIP

High school seniors only are eligible to apply for scholarship. Students are selected based upon GPA, standardized test scores, letters of recommendations, extra curricular activities, and financial need.

Award: Scholarship for use in freshman year; renewable. *Number:* 5. *Amount:* $2000.

Eligibility Requirements: Applicant must be high school student; planning to enroll or expecting to enroll full-time at a two-year or four-year institution or university and resident of Virginia. Available to U.S. citizens.

Application Requirements: Application, essay, financial need analysis, references, test scores, transcript. *Deadline:* March 16.

Contact: Joseph Wharff, School Counseling Connections Specialist
Virginia Department of Education
101 North 14th Street, James Monroe Building
PO Box 2120
Richmond, VA 23218-2120
Phone: 804-225-3370
E-mail: joseph.wharff@doe.virginia.gov

ROBERT C. BYRD HONORS SCHOLARSHIP-VIRGINIA

High school seniors are the only students eligible to apply for the scholarships. Students are selected based upon GPA, standardized test scores, letters of recommendation, extracurricular activities, and community involvement.

Award: Scholarship for use in freshman year; renewable. *Number:* 100–150. *Amount:* $750–$1500.

Eligibility Requirements: Applicant must be high school student; planning to enroll or expecting to enroll full-time at a two-year or four-year institution or university and resident of Virginia. Available to U.S. citizens.

Application Requirements: Application, references, test scores, transcript. *Deadline:* April 6.

Contact: Joseph Wharff, School Counseling Connections Specialist
Virginia Department of Education
101 North 14th Street, James Monroe Building
PO Box 2120
Richmond, VA 23218-2120
Phone: 804-225-3370
E-mail: joseph.wharff@doe.virginia.gov

VIRGINIA DEPARTMENT OF VETERANS SERVICES

http://www.dvs.virginia.gov/

VIRGINIA MILITARY SURVIVORS AND DEPENDENTS EDUCATION PROGRAM
• *See page 645*

VIRGINIA SOCIETY OF CERTIFIED PUBLIC ACCOUNTANTS EDUCATIONAL FOUNDATION

http://www.vscpa.com/

GOODMAN & COMPANY ANNUAL SCHOLARSHIP

Scholarship for student currently enrolled in an accredited Virginia college or university who has demonstrated academic excellence and financial need.

Award: Scholarship for use in freshman, sophomore, junior, or senior years; not renewable. *Number:* 1. *Amount:* $2500.

Eligibility Requirements: Applicant must be enrolled or expecting to enroll full- or part-time at a four-year institution or university and studying in Virginia. Applicant must have 3.0 GPA or higher. Available to U.S. citizens.

Application Requirements: Application, essay, resume, references, transcript. *Deadline:* April 1.

Contact: Tracey Zink, Community Relations Coordinator
Virginia Society of Certified Public Accountants Educational Foundation
4309 Cox Road
Glen Allen, VA 23060
Phone: 800-612-9427
E-mail: tzink@vscpa.com

VIRGINIA STATE COUNCIL OF HIGHER EDUCATION

http://www.schev.edu/

COLLEGE SCHOLARSHIP ASSISTANCE PROGRAM

Need-based scholarship for undergraduate study by a Virginia resident at a participating Virginia two- or four-year college, or university. Contact financial aid office at the participating Virginia public or nonprofit private institution. The program does not have its own application; institutions use results from the federal FAFSA form.

Award: Grant for use in freshman, sophomore, junior, or senior years; not renewable. *Number:* varies. *Amount:* $400–$5000.

Eligibility Requirements: Applicant must be enrolled or expecting to enroll full- or part-time at a two-year or four-year institution or university; resident of Virginia and studying in Virginia. Available to U.S. citizens.

Application Requirements: Financial need analysis.

Contact: Contact the financial aid office of participating Virginia college.

VIRGINIA COMMONWEALTH AWARD

Need-based award for undergraduate or graduate study at a Virginia public two- or four-year college, or university. Undergraduates must be Virginia residents. The application and awards process are administered by the financial aid office at the Virginia public institution where student is enrolled. Dollar value of each award varies. Contact financial aid office for application and deadlines.

Award: Grant for use in freshman, sophomore, junior, or senior years; not renewable. *Number:* varies. *Amount:* varies.

Eligibility Requirements: Applicant must be enrolled or expecting to enroll full- or part-time at a two-year or four-year institution or university; resident of Virginia and studying in Virginia. Available to U.S. citizens.

Application Requirements: Financial need analysis.

Contact: Contact the financial aid office of participating Virginia college.

VIRGINIA GUARANTEED ASSISTANCE PROGRAM

Awards to undergraduate students proportional to their need, up to full tuition, fees and book allowance. Must be a graduate of a Virginia high school. High school GPA of 2.5 required. Must be enrolled full-time in a Virginia two- or four-year institution and demonstrate financial need. Must maintain minimum college GPA of 2.0 for renewal awards.

Award: Grant for use in freshman, sophomore, junior, or senior years; not renewable. *Number:* varies. *Amount:* varies.

Eligibility Requirements: Applicant must be enrolled or expecting to enroll full-time at a two-year or four-year institution or university; resident of Virginia and studying in Virginia. Available to U.S. citizens.

Application Requirements: Financial need analysis, transcript.

Contact: Contact the financial aid office of participating Virginia college.

VIRGINIA TUITION ASSISTANCE GRANT PROGRAM (PRIVATE INSTITUTIONS)

Awards for undergraduate students. Also available to graduate and first professional degree students pursuing a health-related degree program. Not to be used for religious study. Must be US citizen or eligible noncitizen, Virginia domiciled, and enrolled full-time at an approved private, nonprofit college within Virginia. Information and application available from participating Virginia colleges financial aid office. Visit http://www.schev.edu and click on Financial Aid.

Award: Grant for use in freshman, sophomore, junior, senior, or graduate years; renewable. *Number:* 22,000. *Amount:* up to $2650.

Eligibility Requirements: Applicant must be enrolled or expecting to enroll full-time at a four-year institution or university; resident of Virginia and studying in Virginia. Available to U.S. citizens.

Application Requirements: Application. *Deadline:* July 31.

Contact: Contact the financial aid office of participating Virginia college.

WALLACE S. AND WILMA K. LAUGHLIN FOUNDATION TRUST

http://www.nefda.org/

SWANSON SCHOLARSHIP

Scholarship for a Nebraska student entering the mortuary science program at a Kansas City community college. Must be a US citizen, a high school graduate and have completed Nebraska pre-mortuary science hours. Scholarship value and number of awards varies annually.

Award: Scholarship for use in junior or senior years; not renewable. *Number:* 1–10. *Amount:* $1000–$10,000.

Eligibility Requirements: Applicant must be enrolled or expecting to enroll full-time at a two-year institution and resident of Nebraska. Available to U.S. citizens.

Application Requirements: Application, financial need analysis, interview, references, transcript. *Deadline:* June 30.

Contact: Craig Draucker, Chairman
Wallace S. and Wilma K. Laughlin Foundation Trust
1633 Normandy Court Suite A
Lincoln, NE 68516
Phone: 402-423-8900
Fax: 402-476-6547

WASHINGTON HIGHER EDUCATION COORDINATING BOARD

http://www.hecb.wa.gov/

AMERICAN INDIAN ENDOWED SCHOLARSHIP
• *See page 695*

PASSPORT TO COLLEGE PROMISE SCHOLARSHIP

Scholarship to encourage Washington residents who are former foster care youth to prepare for and succeed in college. Recipients must have spent at least one year in foster care after their 16th birthday and emancipated from care.

Award: Scholarship for use in freshman, sophomore, junior, or senior years; renewable. *Number:* 1–400. *Amount:* $1–$3000.

Eligibility Requirements: Applicant must be age 18-26; enrolled or expecting to enroll full- or part-time at a two-year or four-year or technical institution or university; resident of Washington and studying in Washington. Available to U.S. citizens.

Application Requirements: Application, financial need analysis, consent form. *Deadline:* continuous.

Contact: Ms. Dawn Cypriano-McAferty, Program Manager
Washington Higher Education Coordinating Board
917 Lakeridge Way SW, PO Box 43430
Olympia, WA 98504-3430
Phone: 888-535-0747 Ext. 5
Fax: 360-704-6246
E-mail: passporttocollege@hecb.wa.gov

WASHINGTON AWARD FOR VOCATIONAL EXCELLENCE (WAVE)

Award to honor vocational students from the legislative districts of Washington. Grants for up to two years of undergraduate resident tuition. Must be enrolled in Washington high school, skills center, or community or technical college at time of application. To be eligible to apply student must complete 360 hours in single vocational program in high school or one year at technical college. Contact principal, guidance counselor, or on-campus WAVE coordinator for more information.

Award: Scholarship for use in freshman, sophomore, junior, or senior years; renewable. *Number:* 147. *Amount:* $1–$8592.

Eligibility Requirements: Applicant must be enrolled or expecting to enroll full- or part-time at a two-year or four-year or technical institution or university; resident of Washington and studying in Washington. Available to U.S. citizens.

Application Requirements: Application, references.

Contact: Terri Colbert, Program Specialist
Washington Higher Education Coordinating Board
Workforce Training and Education Coordinating Board,
PO Box 43105
Olympia, WA 98504-3105
Phone: 360-753-5680
Fax: 360-586-5862
E-mail: tcolbert@wtb.wa.gov

WASHINGTON SCHOLARS PROGRAM

Awards high school students from the legislative districts of Washington. Must enroll in college or university in Washington. Scholarships up to four years of full-time resident undergraduate tuition and fees. Student must not pursue a degree in theology. Contact principal or guidance counselor for more information. Requires nomination by high school principal and be in the top 1 percent of his or her graduating senior class.

Award: Scholarship for use in freshman, sophomore, junior, or senior years; renewable. *Number:* 147. *Amount:* $1–$7733.

Eligibility Requirements: Applicant must be high school student; planning to enroll or expecting to enroll full- or part-time at a two-year or four-year institution or university; resident of Washington and studying in Washington. Available to U.S. citizens.

Application Requirements: Application, test scores, transcript. *Deadline:* January 17.

Contact: Ann Voyles, Program Manager
Washington Higher Education Coordinating Board
917 Lakeridge Way, PO Box 43430
Olympia, WA 98504-3430
Phone: 360-753-7843
Fax: 360-704-6243
E-mail: annv@hecb.wa.gov

WASHINGTON STATE NEED GRANT PROGRAM

The program helps Washington's lowest-income undergraduate students to pursue degrees, hone skills, or retrain for new careers. Students with family incomes equal to or less than 50 percent of the state median are eligible for up to 100 percent of the maximum grant. Students with incomes between 51–70% of the state median are prorated dependent on income. All grants are subject to funding.

Award: Grant for use in freshman, sophomore, junior, or senior years; not renewable. *Number:* 71,233. *Amount:* $103–$7717.

Eligibility Requirements: Applicant must be enrolled or expecting to enroll full- or part-time at a two-year or four-year or technical institution or university; resident of Washington and studying in Washington. Available to U.S. citizens.

Application Requirements: Application, financial need analysis, FAFSA. *Deadline:* continuous.

Contact: Program Manager
Washington Higher Education Coordinating Board
PO Box 43430
Olympia, WA 98504-3430
Phone: 360-753-7800
E-mail: finaid@hecb.wa.gov

WASHINGTON HOSPITAL HEALTHCARE SYSTEM

http://www.whhs.com/

WASHINGTON HOSPITAL EMPLOYEE ASSOCIATION SCHOLARSHIP

Scholarship for a dependent of a Washington Hospital Employee. Must be a graduating senior, community college student, transferring community college student, or a student attending a four-year institution.

Award: Scholarship for use in freshman, sophomore, junior, or senior years; not renewable. *Number:* 1. *Amount:* $2000.

Eligibility Requirements: Applicant must be enrolled or expecting to enroll full- or part-time at a two-year or four-year or technical institution or university and resident of California. Available to U.S. citizens.

Application Requirements: Application, driver's license, essay, references, test scores, transcript. *Deadline:* March 5.

Contact: Scholarship Chair, c/o Personnel Department
Washington Hospital Healthcare System
2500 Mowry Avenue
Fremont, CA 94538
Phone: 510-818-6220

WASHINGTON STATE PARENT TEACHER ASSOCIATION SCHOLARSHIP PROGRAM

http://www.wastatepta.org/

WASHINGTON STATE PARENT TEACHER ASSOCIATION SCHOLARSHIPS FOUNDATION

One-time scholarships for students who have graduated from a public high school in the state of Washington, and who greatly need financial help to begin full-time postsecondary education.

Award: Scholarship for use in freshman year; not renewable. *Number:* 60–80. *Amount:* $1000–$2000.

Eligibility Requirements: Applicant must be high school student; planning to enroll or expecting to enroll full-time at a four-year institution or university and resident of Washington. Available to U.S. citizens.

Application Requirements: Application, essay, financial need analysis, references, transcript. *Deadline:* March 31.

Contact: Mr. Bill Williams, Executive Director
Washington State Parent Teacher Association Scholarship Program
2003 65th Avenue West
Tacoma, WA 98466-6215
Phone: 253-565-2153
Fax: 253-565-7753
E-mail: jcarpenter@wastatepta.org

WATSON-BROWN FOUNDATION INC.

http://www.watson-brown.org/

WATSON-BROWN FOUNDATION SCHOLARSHIP

Scholarships are awarded based on academic merit and financial need. Students must be from designated counties in Georgia or South Carolina and may attend any four-year, accredited, non-profit U.S. college or university. Renewable scholarships are awarded on two levels: $3000 and $5000.

Award: Scholarship for use in freshman, sophomore, junior, or senior years; renewable. *Number:* 200–200. *Amount:* $3000–$5000.

Eligibility Requirements: Applicant must be enrolled or expecting to enroll full-time at a four-year institution or university and resident of Georgia or South Carolina. Applicant must have 3.0 GPA or higher. Available to U.S. citizens.

Application Requirements: Application, essay, financial need analysis, references, test scores, transcript, IRS Form 1040. *Deadline:* February 15.

Contact: Sarah Katherine McNeil, Director, Scholarships and Alumni Relations
Watson-Brown Foundation Inc.
310 Tom Watson Way
Thomson, GA 30824
Phone: 866-923-6863
E-mail: skmcneil@watson-brown.org

WESTERN GOLF ASSOCIATION-EVANS SCHOLARS FOUNDATION

http://www.evansscholarsfoundation.com/

CHICK EVANS CADDIE SCHOLARSHIP
• *See page 598*

WESTERN INTERSTATE COMMISSION FOR HIGHER EDUCATION

http://www.wiche.edu/

WICHE'S WESTERN UNDERGRADUATE EXCHANGE (WUE)

Students from designated states can enroll in two- and four-year undergraduate programs at 145 public institutions in participating Western states and pay 150 percent of resident tuition. Applicants apply directly to the admissions office at participating institution. Applicants must indicate that they want to be considered for the WUE tuition discount. Participating institutions and the majors available at the WUE rate are listed at http://wiche.edu/wue.

Award: Scholarship for use in freshman, sophomore, junior, or senior years; renewable. *Number:* varies. *Amount:* varies.

Eligibility Requirements: Applicant must be enrolled or expecting to enroll full-time at a two-year or four-year institution or university; resident of Alaska, Arizona, California, Colorado, Hawaii, Idaho, Montana, Nevada, New Mexico, North Dakota, Oregon, South Dakota, Utah, Washington, or Wyoming and studying in Alaska, Arizona, California, Colorado, Hawaii, Idaho, Montana, Nevada, New Mexico, North Dakota, Oregon, or South Dakota. Available to U.S. citizens.

Application Requirements: Application, test scores, transcript.

Contact: Ms. Laura Ewing, Administrative Assistant, Student Exchange
Western Interstate Commission for Higher Education
3035 Center Green Drive
Boulder, CO 80301
Phone: 303-541-0270
E-mail: info-sep@wiche.edu

WEST VIRGINIA HIGHER EDUCATION POLICY COMMISSION-STUDENT SERVICES

http://www.wvhepcnew.wvnet.edu/

ROBERT C. BYRD HONORS SCHOLARSHIP-WEST VIRGINIA

Award for West Virginia residents who have demonstrated outstanding academic achievement. Must be a graduating high school senior. May apply for renewal consideration for a total of four years of assistance. For full-time study only.

Award: Scholarship for use in freshman year; renewable. *Number:* 36. *Amount:* $1500.

Eligibility Requirements: Applicant must be high school student; planning to enroll or expecting to enroll full-time at a two-year or four-year or technical institution or university and resident of West Virginia. Applicant must have 3.0 GPA or higher. Available to U.S. citizens.

Application Requirements: Application, test scores, transcript, letter of acceptance from a college/university. *Deadline:* March 1.

Contact: Darlene Elmore, Scholarship Coordinator
West Virginia Higher Education Policy Commission-Student Services
1018 Kanawha Boulevard East, Suite 700
Charleston, WV 25301
Phone: 304-558-4618 Ext. 278
Fax: 304-558-4622
E-mail: elmore@hepc.wvnet.edu

WEST VIRGINIA HIGHER EDUCATION GRANT PROGRAM

Award available for West Virginia resident for one year immediately preceding the date of application, high school graduate or the equivalent, demonstrate financial need, and enroll as a full-time undergraduate at an approved university or college located in West Virginia or Pennsylvania.

Award: Grant for use in freshman, sophomore, junior, or senior years; not renewable. *Number:* 20,000–21,152. *Amount:* $375–$2100.

Eligibility Requirements: Applicant must be enrolled or expecting to enroll full-time at a two-year or four-year institution or university; resident of West Virginia and studying in Pennsylvania or West Virginia. Available to U.S. citizens.

Application Requirements: Financial need analysis, FAFSA. *Deadline:* April 15.

Contact: Judy Kee Smith, Senior Project Coordinator
West Virginia Higher Education Policy Commission-Student Services
1018 Kanawha Boulevard East, Suite 700
Charleston, WV 25301-2827
Phone: 304-558-4618
Fax: 304-558-4622
E-mail: kee@hepc.wvnet.edu

WILLIAM D. SQUIRES EDUCATIONAL FOUNDATION INC.

http://www.wmdsquiresfoundation.org/

WILLIAM D. SQUIRES SCHOLARSHIP

Applicants must be graduating high school seniors from Ohio that are planning to pursue a four year program. The William D. Squires Scholarship is primarily financial need based but students must also have a clear career goal and be highly motivated. Minimum 3.2 GPA is required.

Award: Scholarship for use in freshman, sophomore, junior, or senior years; renewable. *Number:* 12. *Amount:* $12,000.

Eligibility Requirements: Applicant must be high school student; planning to enroll or expecting to enroll full-time at a four-year institution or university and resident of Ohio. Available to U.S. citizens.

Application Requirements: Application, essay, financial need analysis, references, test scores, transcript. *Deadline:* April 5.

Contact: Cynthia Squires Gross, Scholarship Director
William D. Squires Educational Foundation Inc.
PO Box 2940
Jupiter, FL 33468
Phone: 561-741-7751
E-mail: info@wmdsquiresfoundation.org

WILLIAM F. COOPER SCHOLARSHIP TRUST

http://www.wachoviascholars.com/

WILLIAM F. COOPER SCHOLARSHIP

Scholarship to provide financial assistance to women living within the state of Georgia for undergraduate studies. Cannot be used for law, theology or medicine fields of study. Nursing is an approved area of study. For more details visit web site http://www.wachoviascholars.com.

Award: Scholarship for use in freshman, sophomore, junior, or senior years; renewable. *Number:* varies. *Amount:* $1000.

Eligibility Requirements: Applicant must be enrolled or expecting to enroll full- or part-time at a four-year institution or university; female and resident of Georgia. Available to U.S. citizens.

Application Requirements: Application, financial need analysis, references, test scores, transcript, federal tax form 1040, W-2 forms. *Deadline:* April 1.

Contact: Sally King, Program Coordinator
William F. Cooper Scholarship Trust
4320-G Wade Hampton Boulevard
Taylors, SC 29687
Phone: 800-576-5135
Fax: 864-268-7160
E-mail: sallyking@bellsouth.net

WILLIAM G. AND MARIE SELBY FOUNDATION

http://www.selbyfdn.org/

SELBY SCHOLAR PROGRAM

Must be a resident of Sarasota, Manatee, Charlotte, or Desoto counties in Florida. Scholarships awarded up to $7,000 annually, not to exceed 1/3 of individual's financial need. Renewable for four years if student is full-time undergraduate at accredited college or university and maintains 3.0 GPA. Must demonstrate financial need and values of leadership and service to the community.

Award: Scholarship for use in freshman, sophomore, junior, or senior years; renewable. *Number:* 40. *Amount:* up to $7000.

Eligibility Requirements: Applicant must be enrolled or expecting to enroll full-time at a four-year institution or university; resident of Florida and must have an interest in leadership. Applicant must have 3.0 GPA or higher. Available to U.S. citizens.

Application Requirements: Application, essay, financial need analysis, interview, references, test scores, transcript. *Deadline:* April 1.

Contact: Evan G. Jones, Grants Manager
William G. and Marie Selby Foundation
1800 Second Street, Suite 750
Sarasota, FL 34236
Phone: 941-957-0442
Fax: 941-957-3135
E-mail: ejones@selbyfdn.org

WILMINGTON WOMEN IN BUSINESS, INC.

http://www.wwb.org/freshstart.html

FRESH START SCHOLARSHIP

Must be entering an undergraduate program at a college or university in Delaware. Scholarship offering a fresh start to women who are returning to school after a hiatus of two years to better their life and opportunities.

Award: Scholarship for use in freshman, sophomore, junior, or senior years; not renewable. *Number:* 10–15. *Amount:* $750–$2000.

Eligibility Requirements: Applicant must be age 20 and over; enrolled or expecting to enroll full- or part-time at a two-year or four-year institution or university; female and studying in Delaware. Applicant must have 2.5 GPA or higher. Available to U.S. citizens.

Application Requirements: Application, essay, financial need analysis, references, transcript. *Deadline:* May 31.

Contact: Scholarship Chair
Wilmington Women in Business, Inc.
PO Box 7784
Wilmington, DE 19803
Phone: 302-656-4411
E-mail: fsscholar@comcast.net

WISCONSIN DEPARTMENT OF VETERANS AFFAIRS (WDVA)

http://www.dva.state.wi.us/

VETERANS EDUCATION (VETED) REIMBURSEMENT GRANT
• *See page 617*

WISCONSIN HIGHER EDUCATIONAL AID BOARD

http://www.heab.wi.gov/

HANDICAPPED STUDENT GRANT-WISCONSIN
• *See page 615*

MINORITY UNDERGRADUATE RETENTION GRANT-WISCONSIN
• *See page 695*

TALENT INCENTIVE PROGRAM GRANT

Grant assists residents of Wisconsin who are attending a nonprofit institution in Wisconsin, and who have substantial financial need. Must meet income criteria, be considered economically and educationally disadvantaged, and be enrolled at least half-time. Refer to web site for further details http://www.heab.state.wi.us.

Award: Grant for use in freshman, sophomore, junior, or senior years; renewable. *Number:* varies. *Amount:* $250–$1800.

Eligibility Requirements: Applicant must be enrolled or expecting to enroll full- or part-time at a two-year or four-year or technical institution or university; resident of Wisconsin and studying in Wisconsin. Available to U.S. citizens.

Application Requirements: Application, financial need analysis, nomination by financial aid office. *Deadline:* continuous.

Contact: Colette Brown, Program Coordinator
Wisconsin Higher Educational Aid Board
PO Box 7885
Madison, WI 53707-7885
Phone: 608-266-1665
Fax: 608-267-2808
E-mail: colette.brown@wi.gov

WISCONSIN ACADEMIC EXCELLENCE SCHOLARSHIP

Renewable award for high school seniors with the highest GPA in graduating class. Must be a Wisconsin resident attending a nonprofit Wisconsin institution full-time. Scholarship value is $2250 toward tuition each year for up to four years. Must maintain 3.0 GPA for renewal. Refer to your high school counselor for more details.

Award: Scholarship for use in freshman year; renewable. *Number:* varies. *Amount:* up to $2250.

Eligibility Requirements: Applicant must be high school student; planning to enroll or expecting to enroll full-time at a two-year or four-year or technical institution or university; resident of Wisconsin and studying in Wisconsin. Applicant must have 3.0 GPA or higher. Available to U.S. citizens.

Application Requirements: Application, test scores, transcript. *Deadline:* continuous.

Contact: Nancy Wilkison, Program Coordinator
Wisconsin Higher Educational Aid Board
PO Box 7885
Madison, WI 53707-7885
Phone: 608-267-2213
Fax: 608-267-2808
E-mail: nancy.wilkison@wi.gov

WISCONSIN HIGHER EDUCATION GRANTS (WHEG)

Grants for residents of Wisconsin enrolled at least half-time in degree or certificate programs at a University of Wisconsin Institution, Wisconsin Technical College or an approved Tribal College. Must show financial need. Refer to web site for further details http://www.heab.wi.gov.

Award: Grant for use in freshman, sophomore, junior, or senior years; not renewable. *Number:* varies. *Amount:* $250–$3000.

Eligibility Requirements: Applicant must be enrolled or expecting to enroll full- or part-time at a two-year or four-year or technical institution or university; resident of Wisconsin and studying in Wisconsin. Available to U.S. citizens.

Application Requirements: Application, financial need analysis. *Deadline:* continuous.

Contact: Sandra Thomas, Program Coordinator
Wisconsin Higher Educational Aid Board
PO Box 7885
Madison, WI 53707-7885
Phone: 608-266-0888
Fax: 608-267-2808
E-mail: sandy.thomas@heab.state.wi.us

WISCONSIN NATIVE AMERICAN/INDIAN STUDENT ASSISTANCE GRANT
• *See page 696*

WISCONSIN SCHOOL COUNSELOR ASSOCIATION

http://www.wscaweb.org/

WISCONSIN SCHOOL COUNSELOR ASSOCIATION HIGH SCHOOL SCHOLARSHIP

Scholarship is available to high school seniors in Wisconsin who plan to attend a two-year or four-year postsecondary institution in the fall. Students are asked to submit an essay that describes how a school counselor or school counseling program has impacted their life.

Award: Scholarship for use in freshman year; not renewable. *Number:* 2–4. *Amount:* $1000.

Eligibility Requirements: Applicant must be high school student; planning to enroll or expecting to enroll full-time at a two-year or four-year institution or university and resident of Wisconsin. Available to U.S. citizens.

Application Requirements: Application, applicant must enter a contest, essay. *Deadline:* December 1.

Contact: Allison Spencer, Professional Recognition and Scholarship Committee
Wisconsin School Counselor Association
2830 Agriculture Drive
Madison, WI 53718
Phone: 608-698-2467
E-mail: allicepo@hotmail.com

WYOMING DEPARTMENT OF EDUCATION

DOUVAS MEMORIAL SCHOLARSHIP

Available to Wyoming residents who are first-generation Americans. Must be between 18 and 22 years old. Must be used at any Wyoming public institution of higher education for study in freshman year.

Award: Scholarship for use in freshman year; not renewable. *Number:* 1. *Amount:* $500.

Eligibility Requirements: Applicant must be age 18-22; enrolled or expecting to enroll full- or part-time at a two-year or four-year institution or university; resident of Wyoming and studying in Wyoming. Available to U.S. citizens.

Application Requirements: Application. *Deadline:* March 24.

Contact: Gerry Maas, Director, Health and Safety
Wyoming Department of Education
2300 Capitol Avenue, Hathaway Building, 2nd Floor
Cheyenne, WY 82002-0050
Phone: 307-777-6282
Fax: 307-777-6234
E-mail: gmaas@educ.state.wy.us

HATHAWAY SCHOLARSHIP

Scholarship for Wyoming students to pursue postsecondary education within the state. Award ranges from $1000 to $1600. Deadline varies.

Award: Scholarship for use in freshman, sophomore, junior, or senior years; not renewable. *Number:* 1. *Amount:* $1000–$1600.

Eligibility Requirements: Applicant must be enrolled or expecting to enroll full-time at a two-year or four-year institution or university; resident of Wyoming and studying in Wyoming. Available to U.S. citizens.

Application Requirements: Application. *Deadline:* varies.

Contact: Kay Post, Director
Wyoming Department of Education
2020 Grand Avenue, Suite 500
Laramie, WY 82070
Phone: 307-777-5599
E-mail: kpost@educ.state.wy.us

ROBERT C. BYRD HONORS SCHOLARSHIP-WYOMING

Award available to Wyoming residents who show outstanding academic ability. Must attend an accredited postsecondary institution, have a minimum 3.8 GPA, and be a high school senior. Renewable award of $1500. Applications are mailed to all high school counselors in the spring.

Award: Scholarship for use in freshman year; renewable. *Number:* 11. *Amount:* $1500.

Eligibility Requirements: Applicant must be high school student; planning to enroll or expecting to enroll full-time at a two-year or four-year institution or university and resident of Wyoming. Applicant must have 3.5 GPA or higher. Available to U.S. citizens.

Application Requirements: Application, essay, test scores, transcript, nomination. *Deadline:* April 18.

Contact: D. Leeds Pickering, Scholarship Committee
Wyoming Department of Education
Hathaway Building, Second Floor
Cheyenne, WY 82002-0050

WYOMING FARM BUREAU FEDERATION

http://www.wyfb.org/

KING-LIVINGSTON SCHOLARSHIP
• *See page 572*

WYOMING FARM BUREAU CONTINUING EDUCATION SCHOLARSHIPS
• *See page 573*

WYOMING FARM BUREAU FEDERATION SCHOLARSHIPS
• *See page 573*

TALENT/INTEREST AREA

ACTORS THEATRE OF LOUISVILLE

http://www.actorstheatre.org/

NATIONAL TEN-MINUTE PLAY CONTEST

Writers submit short plays (10 pages or less) that have not received an equity production, which are considered for the annual Apprentice Showcase (to be eligible, characters in the play must be appropriate for actors aged 20 to 30), the Humana Festival of new American plays, and the $1000 Heideman Award. Must be U.S. citizen.

Award: Prize for use in freshman, sophomore, junior, senior, graduate, or postgraduate years; not renewable. *Number:* 1. *Amount:* $1000.

Eligibility Requirements: Applicant must be enrolled or expecting to enroll full- or part-time at a two-year or four-year or technical institution or university and must have an interest in theater or writing. Available to U.S. citizens.

Application Requirements: Application, applicant must enter a contest, 10-page play. *Deadline:* November 1.

Contact: Ms. Amy Wegener, Literary Manager
Actors Theatre of Louisville
316 West Main Street
Louisville, KY 40202-4218
Phone: 502-584-1265 Ext. 3031
Fax: 502-561-3300
E-mail: awegener@actorstheatre.org

ADELANTE! U.S. EDUCATION LEADERSHIP FUND

http://www.adelantefund.org/

ADELANTE FUND SCHOLARSHIPS
• *See page 650*

ALBERTA HERITAGE SCHOLARSHIP FUND

http://www.alis.alberta.ca/

CHARLES S. NOBLE JUNIOR A HOCKEY SCHOLARSHIPS
• *See page 651*

CHARLES S. NOBLE JUNIOR FOOTBALL SCHOLARSHIPS
• *See page 651*

EARL AND COUNTESS OF WESSEX-WORLD CHAMPIONSHIPS IN ATHLETICS SCHOLARSHIPS
• *See page 652*

JIMMIE CONDON ATHLETIC SCHOLARSHIPS
• *See page 652*

LAURENCE DECORE STUDENT LEADERSHIP AWARDS
• *See page 652*

PRAIRIE BASEBALL ACADEMY SCHOLARSHIPS
• *See page 702*

ALBUQUERQUE COMMUNITY FOUNDATION

http://www.albuquerquefoundation.org/

NOTAH BEGAY III SCHOLARSHIP PROGRAM FOR NATIVE AMERICAN SCHOLAR ATHLETES
• *See page 653*

ALERT SCHOLARSHIP

http://www.alertmagazine.org/

ALERT SCHOLARSHIP
• *See page 703*

THE ALEXANDER FOUNDATION

http://www.thealexanderfoundation.org/

THE ALEXANDER FOUNDATION SCHOLARSHIP PROGRAM
• *See page 703*

AMERICAN BOWLING CONGRESS

http://www.bowl.com/

CHUCK HALL STAR OF TOMORROW SCHOLARSHIP
• *See page 523*

AMERICAN CANCER SOCIETY

http://www.cancer.org/

AMERICAN CANCER SOCIETY, FLORIDA DIVISION R.O.C.K. COLLEGE SCHOLARSHIP PROGRAM
• *See page 599*

AMERICAN FOREIGN SERVICE ASSOCIATION

http://www.afsa.org/

AMERICAN FOREIGN SERVICE ASSOCIATION (AFSA) MERIT AWARD PROGRAM
• *See page 524*

AMERICAN INDIAN GRADUATE CENTER

http://www.aigcs.org/

GATES MILLENNIUM SCHOLARS PROGRAM
• *See page 654*

AMERICAN INSTITUTE FOR FOREIGN STUDY

http://www.aifsabroad.com/

AIFS AFFILIATE SCHOLARSHIPS

Students from colleges and universities that participate in the AIFS Affiliates program are eligible. Application fee: $95. For more details, visit http://www.aifsabroad.com/scholarships.asp.

Award: Scholarship for use in freshman, sophomore, junior, or senior years; not renewable. *Number:* varies. *Amount:* varies.

Eligibility Requirements: Applicant must be enrolled or expecting to enroll full-time at a two-year or four-year institution or university and must have an interest in international exchange. Available to U.S. and non-U.S. citizens.

Application Requirements: Application, essay, photo, references, transcript. *Fee:* $95. *Deadline:* varies.

Contact: David Mauro, Admissions Counselor
American Institute for Foreign Study
River Plaza, 9 West Broad Street
Stamford, CT 06902-3788
Phone: 800-727-2437 Ext. 5163
Fax: 203-399-5463
E-mail: dmauro@aifs.com

AIFS DIVERSITYABROAD.COM SCHOLARSHIP
• *See page 654*

AIFS GILMAN SCHOLARSHIP BONUS-$500 SCHOLARSHIPS

Award of $500 available to each undergraduate recipient for use toward an AIFS program. More information is available at http://www.iie.org/gilman.

Award: Scholarship for use in freshman, sophomore, junior, or senior years; not renewable. *Number:* varies. *Amount:* $500.

Eligibility Requirements: Applicant must be age 17 and over; enrolled or expecting to enroll full-time at a four-year institution or university and must have an interest in international exchange. Available to U.S. and non-U.S. citizens.

Application Requirements: Application, essay, photo, references, transcript. *Fee:* $95. *Deadline:* varies.

Contact: David Mauro, Admissions Counselor
American Institute for Foreign Study
River Plaza, 9 West Broad Street
Stamford, CT 06902-3788
Phone: 800-727-2437 Ext. 5163
Fax: 203-399-5463
E-mail: dmauro@aifs.com

AIFS-HACU SCHOLARSHIPS
• *See page 654*

AIFS INTERNATIONAL SCHOLARSHIPS

Awards available to undergraduates on an AIFS study abroad program. Applicants must demonstrate leadership potential, have a minimum 3.0 cumulative GPA, and meet program requirements. The program application fee is $95. Deadlines: April 15 for fall, October 1 for spring, and March 1 for summer.

Award: Scholarship for use in freshman, sophomore, junior, or senior years; not renewable. *Number:* up to 130. *Amount:* $500–$1000.

Eligibility Requirements: Applicant must be age 17 and over; enrolled or expecting to enroll full-time at a two-year or four-year institution or university and must have an interest in international exchange or leadership. Applicant must have 3.0 GPA or higher. Available to U.S. and non-U.S. citizens.

Application Requirements: Application, essay, photo, references, transcript. *Fee:* $95. *Deadline:* varies.

Contact: David Mauro, Admissions Counselor
American Institute for Foreign Study
River Plaza, 9 West Broad Street
Stamford, CT 06902-3788
Phone: 800-727-2437 Ext. 5163
Fax: 203-399-5463
E-mail: dmauro@aifs.com

AIFS STUDY AGAIN SCHOLARSHIPS

Students who studied abroad on an AIFS summer program will receive a $1000 scholarship to study abroad on an AIFS semester or academic year catalog program or a $500 scholarship toward a summer catalog program. Students who studied abroad on an AIFS semester or academic year program will receive a $500 scholarship toward a summer catalog program or a $1000 scholarship toward a semester program in a different academic year. Deadlines: April 15 for fall, October 15 for spring, and March 1 for summer.

Award: Scholarship for use in freshman, sophomore, junior, or senior years; not renewable. *Number:* varies. *Amount:* $500–$1000.

Eligibility Requirements: Applicant must be age 17 and over; enrolled or expecting to enroll full-time at a two-year or four-year institution or university and must have an interest in international exchange. Applicant must have 2.5 GPA or higher. Available to U.S. and non-U.S. citizens.

Application Requirements: Application, essay, photo, references, transcript. *Fee:* $95. *Deadline:* varies.

Contact: David Mauro, Admissions Counselor
American Institute for Foreign Study
River Plaza, 9 West Broad Street
Stamford, CT 06902-3788
Phone: 800-727-2437 Ext. 5163
Fax: 203-399-5463
E-mail: dmauro@aifs.com

AMERICAN JEWISH LEAGUE FOR ISRAEL

http://www.americanjewishleague.org/

AMERICAN JEWISH LEAGUE FOR ISRAEL SCHOLARSHIP PROGRAM

Scholarship provides support with tuition for a full year of study (September to May) at one of seven Israeli universities, Bar Ilan, Ben Gurion, Haifa, Hebrew, Tel Aviv, Technion, and Weizmann, Interdisciplinary Center at Herzliya. Additional information is available on web site http://www.americanjewishleague.org/ScholarshipInformation.html.

Award: Scholarship for use in freshman, sophomore, junior, or senior years; not renewable. *Number:* 3–15. *Amount:* $2000.

Eligibility Requirements: Applicant must be enrolled or expecting to enroll full-time at a four-year institution or university and must have an interest in Jewish culture. Available to U.S. citizens.

Application Requirements: Application, essay, references, transcript, personal and academic aspirations. *Deadline:* May 1.

Contact: Mr. Karl D. Zukerman, University Scholarship Fund
American Jewish League for Israel
4485 Hazleton Lane
Wellington, FL 33449
Fax: 561-963-2923
E-mail: kdzwork@aol.com

AMERICAN LEGION DEPARTMENT OF ARIZONA

http://www.azlegion.org/

AMERICAN LEGION DEPARTMENT OF ARIZONA HIGH SCHOOL ORATORICAL CONTEST
• *See page 707*

AMERICAN LEGION DEPARTMENT OF ARKANSAS

http://www.arklegion.homestead.com/

AMERICAN LEGION DEPARTMENT OF ARKANSAS HIGH SCHOOL ORATORICAL CONTEST
• *See page 707*

AMERICAN LEGION DEPARTMENT OF ILLINOIS

http://www.illegion.org/

AMERICAN ESSAY CONTEST SCHOLARSHIP
• *See page 529*

AMERICAN LEGION DEPARTMENT OF ILLINOIS HIGH SCHOOL ORATORICAL CONTEST
• *See page 707*

AMERICAN LEGION DEPARTMENT OF INDIANA

http://www.indlegion.org/

AMERICAN LEGION DEPARTMENT OF INDIANA HIGH SCHOOL ORATORICAL CONTEST
• *See page 708*

FRANK W. MCHALE MEMORIAL SCHOLARSHIPS
• *See page 708*

AMERICAN LEGION DEPARTMENT OF IOWA

http://www.ialegion.org/

AMERICAN LEGION DEPARTMENT OF IOWA HIGH SCHOOL ORATORICAL CONTEST
• *See page 708*

AMERICAN LEGION DEPARTMENT OF IOWA OUTSTANDING SENIOR BASEBALL PLAYER
• *See page 708*

AMERICAN LEGION DEPARTMENT OF KANSAS

http://www.ksamlegion.org/

AMERICAN LEGION DEPARTMENT OF KANSAS HIGH SCHOOL ORATORICAL CONTEST

Awards a total of $2400 ($1500, $500, $250, and $150) in scholarships to the top four winners in each state. The state winner's school receives $500. The top three contestants in the nation are awarded scholarships totaling $48,000 ($18,000, $16,000, and $14,000).

Award: Prize for use in freshman year; not renewable. *Number:* 4. *Amount:* $150–$18,000.

Eligibility Requirements: Applicant must be high school student; planning to enroll or expecting to enroll full-time at a four-year institution or university and must have an interest in public speaking. Available to U.S. citizens.

Application Requirements: Application, applicant must enter a contest. *Deadline:* varies.

Contact: Ralph Snyder, Oratorical Contest Committee
American Legion Department of Kansas
1314 Topeka Boulevard, SW
Topeka, KS 66612
Phone: 785-232-9315
Fax: 785-232-1399

DR. CLICK COWGER BASEBALL SCHOLARSHIP
• *See page 708*

PAUL FLAHERTY ATHLETIC SCHOLARSHIP
• *See page 709*

AMERICAN LEGION DEPARTMENT OF MICHIGAN

http://www.michiganlegion.org/

AMERICAN LEGION DEPARTMENT OF MICHIGAN ORATORICAL SCHOLARSHIP PROGRAM
• *See page 709*

AMERICAN LEGION DEPARTMENT OF MINNESOTA

http://www.mnlegion.org/

AMERICAN LEGION DEPARTMENT OF MINNESOTA HIGH SCHOOL ORATORICAL CONTEST
• *See page 709*

AMERICAN LEGION DEPARTMENT OF MONTANA

http://www.mtlegion.org/

AMERICAN LEGION DEPARTMENT OF MONTANA HIGH SCHOOL ORATORICAL CONTEST
• *See page 710*

AMERICAN LEGION DEPARTMENT OF NEBRASKA

http://www.nebraskalegion.net/

AMERICAN LEGION BASEBALL SCHOLARSHIP-NEBRASKA AMERICAN LEGION BASEBALL PLAYER OF THE YEAR
• *See page 710*

AMERICAN LEGION DEPARTMENT OF NEBRASKA HIGH SCHOOL ORATORICAL CONTEST
• *See page 710*

AMERICAN LEGION DEPARTMENT OF NEBRASKA JIM HURLBERT MEMORIAL BASEBALL SCHOLARSHIP
• *See page 710*

AMERICAN LEGION DEPARTMENT OF NEW JERSEY

http://www.njamericanlegion.org/

AMERICAN LEGION DEPARTMENT OF NEW JERSEY HIGH SCHOOL ORATORICAL CONTEST

Award to promote and coordinate the Oratorical Contest Program at the Department, District, County and Post Levels. High School Oratorical Contest is to develop a deeper knowledge and understanding of the constitution of the United States.

Award: Prize for use in freshman year; not renewable. *Number:* 5. *Amount:* $1000–$4000.

Eligibility Requirements: Applicant must be high school student; planning to enroll or expecting to enroll full-time at a four-year institution or university and must have an interest in public speaking. Available to U.S. citizens.

Application Requirements: Application, applicant must enter a contest. *Deadline:* March 8.

Contact: Raymond Zawacki, Department Adjutant
American Legion Department of New Jersey
135 West Hanover Street
Trenton, NJ 08618
Phone: 609-695-5418
Fax: 609-394-1532
E-mail: ray@njamericanlegion.org

AMERICAN LEGION DEPARTMENT OF NEW YORK

http://www.ny.legion.org/

AMERICAN LEGION DEPARTMENT OF NEW YORK HIGH SCHOOL ORATORICAL CONTEST
• *See page 711*

AMERICAN LEGION DEPARTMENT OF NORTH CAROLINA

http://www.nclegion.org/

AMERICAN LEGION DEPARTMENT OF NORTH CAROLINA HIGH SCHOOL ORATORICAL CONTEST
• *See page 711*

AMERICAN LEGION DEPARTMENT OF NORTH DAKOTA

http://www.ndlegion.org/

AMERICAN LEGION DEPARTMENT OF NORTH DAKOTA NATIONAL HIGH SCHOOL ORATORICAL CONTEST
• *See page 711*

AMERICAN LEGION DEPARTMENT OF OREGON

http://www.orlegion.org/

AMERICAN LEGION DEPARTMENT OF OREGON HIGH SCHOOL ORATORICAL CONTEST
• *See page 711*

AMERICAN LEGION DEPARTMENT OF PENNSYLVANIA

http://www.pa-legion.com/

AMERICAN LEGION DEPARTMENT OF PENNSYLVANIA HIGH SCHOOL ORATORICAL CONTEST
• *See page 712*

AMERICAN LEGION DEPARTMENT OF SOUTH DAKOTA

http://www.sdlegion.org/

AMERICAN LEGION DEPARTMENT OF SOUTH DAKOTA HIGH SCHOOL ORATORICAL CONTEST
• *See page 712*

AMERICAN LEGION DEPARTMENT OF TENNESSEE

http://www.tennesseelegion.org/

AMERICAN LEGION DEPARTMENT OF TENNESSEE HIGH SCHOOL ORATORICAL CONTEST

• *See page 712*

AMERICAN LEGION DEPARTMENT OF TEXAS

http://www.txlegion.org/

AMERICAN LEGION DEPARTMENT OF TEXAS HIGH SCHOOL ORATORICAL CONTEST

• *See page 712*

AMERICAN LEGION DEPARTMENT OF VERMONT

http://www.legionvthq.com/

AMERICAN LEGION DEPARTMENT OF VERMONT HIGH SCHOOL ORATORICAL CONTEST

• *See page 634*

AMERICAN LEGION DEPARTMENT OF WEST VIRGINIA

http://www.wvlegion.org/

AMERICAN LEGION DEPARTMENT OF WEST VIRGINIA BOARD OF REGENTS SCHOLARSHIP

• *See page 713*

AMERICAN LEGION DEPARTMENT OF WEST VIRGINIA HIGH SCHOOL ORATORICAL CONTEST

• *See page 713*

AMERICAN LEGION NATIONAL HEADQUARTERS

http://www.legion.org/

AMERICAN LEGION NATIONAL HIGH SCHOOL ORATORICAL CONTEST

Scholarship up to $18,000 will be presented to the 3 finalists in the final round of the national contest. Students currently in high school are eligible to apply for this contest.

Award: Scholarship for use in freshman, sophomore, junior, or senior years; not renewable. *Number:* 54. *Amount:* $1500–$18,000.

Eligibility Requirements: Applicant must be high school student; planning to enroll or expecting to enroll full-time at a two-year or four-year institution or university and must have an interest in public speaking. Available to U.S. citizens.

Application Requirements: Application, applicant must enter a contest. *Deadline:* December 1.

Contact: Michael Novak, Assistant Director
American Legion National Headquarters
PO Box 1055
Indianapolis, IN 46206-1055
Phone: 317-630-1200
Fax: 317-630-1369
E-mail: acy@legion.org

AMERICAN MORGAN HORSE INSTITUTE

http://www.morganhorse.com/

AMERICAN MORGAN HORSE INSTITUTE EDUCATIONAL SCHOLARSHIPS

Selection is based on the ability and aptitude for serious study, community service, leadership, and financial need. Must be actively involved with registered Morgan Horses Association. Application deadline varies every year. For information and application go to http://www.morgan-horse.com.

Award: Scholarship for use in freshman year; not renewable. *Number:* 5. *Amount:* $3000.

Eligibility Requirements: Applicant must be enrolled or expecting to enroll full- or part-time at a two-year or four-year or technical institution or university and must have an interest in animal/agricultural competition. Available to U.S. and non-U.S. citizens.

Application Requirements: Application, essay, photo, references, transcript. *Deadline:* varies.

Contact: Sally Wadhams, Development Officer
American Morgan Horse Institute
122 Bostwick Road
PO Box 837
Shelburne, VT 05482-0519
Phone: 802-985-8477
Fax: 802-985-8430
E-mail: amhioffice@aol.com

AMERICAN MORGAN HORSE INSTITUTE GRAND PRIX DRESSAGE AWARD

Award available to riders of registered Morgan horses who reach a certain proficiency at the Grand Prix dressage level. For information and application go to http://www.morganhorse.com. The application deadline varies every year.

Award: Scholarship for use in freshman, sophomore, junior, senior, graduate, or postgraduate years; not renewable. *Number:* 1. *Amount:* $2500.

Eligibility Requirements: Applicant must be enrolled or expecting to enroll full- or part-time at a two-year or four-year or technical institution or university and must have an interest in animal/agricultural competition. Available to U.S. and non-U.S. citizens.

Application Requirements: Application, essay, photo, references, transcript, copy of horse's USDF report. *Deadline:* varies.

Contact: Sally Wadhams, Development Officer
American Morgan Horse Institute
122 Bostwick Road
PO Box 837
Shelburne, VT 05482-0519
Phone: 802-985-8477
Fax: 802-985-8430
E-mail: amhioffice@aol.com

AMERICAN MORGAN HORSE INSTITUTE GRAYWOOD YOUTH HORSEMANSHIP GRANT

Provides a youth who is an active member of the American Morgan Horse Association (AMHA) or an AMHA youth group with the opportunity to further his/her practical study of Morgan horses. For information and application go to http://www.morganhorse.com.

Award: Grant for use in freshman year; not renewable. *Number:* up to 2. *Amount:* $250–$500.

Eligibility Requirements: Applicant must be age 13-21; enrolled or expecting to enroll full- or part-time at a two-year or four-year or technical institution or university and must have an interest in animal/agricultural competition. Available to U.S. and non-U.S. citizens.

Application Requirements: Application, essay, photo, references, transcript. *Deadline:* February 1.

Contact: Sally Wadhams, Development Officer
American Morgan Horse Institute
122 Bostwick Road
PO Box 837
Shelburne, VT 05482-0519
Phone: 802-985-8477
Fax: 802-985-8430
E-mail: amhioffice@aol.com

AMERICAN MORGAN HORSE INSTITUTE VAN SCHAIK DRESSAGE SCHOLARSHIP

Awarded to an individual wishing to further their proficiency in classically ridden dressage on a registered Morgan horse. For information and application go to http://www.morganhorse.com.

Award: Scholarship for use in freshman, sophomore, junior, senior, graduate, or postgraduate years; not renewable. *Number:* 1. *Amount:* $1000.

Eligibility Requirements: Applicant must be enrolled or expecting to enroll full- or part-time at a two-year or four-year or technical institution or university and must have an interest in animal/agricultural competition. Available to U.S. and non-U.S. citizens.

Application Requirements: Application, essay, photo, references, narrative. *Deadline:* February 1.

Contact: Sally Wadhams, Development Officer
American Morgan Horse Institute
122 Bostwick Road
PO Box 837
Shelburne, VT 05482-0519
Phone: 802-985-8477
Fax: 802-985-8430
E-mail: amhioffice@aol.com

AMERICAN MUSEUM OF NATURAL HISTORY

http://www.rggs.amnh.org/

YOUNG NATURALIST AWARDS

Essay contest open to students in grades 7–12 who are currently enrolled in a public, private, parochial, or home school in the United States, Canada, the U.S. territories, or a U.S.-sponsored school abroad. Essays must be based on an original scientific investigation conducted by the student. See web site for guidelines http://www.amnh.org/nationalcenter/youngnaturalistawards/read.html.

Award: Prize for use in freshman year; not renewable. *Number:* 1. *Amount:* varies.

Eligibility Requirements: Applicant must be high school student; planning to enroll or expecting to enroll part-time at a four-year institution or university and must have an interest in writing. Available to Canadian citizens.

Application Requirements: Application, essay, photo. *Deadline:* March 1.

Contact: Maria Rios-Dickson, Assistant Director, Fellowships and
Student Affair
American Museum of Natural History
Central Park West, 79th Street
New York, NY 10024-5192
Phone: 212-769-5017
E-mail: fellowships-rggs@amnh.org

AMERICAN QUARTER HORSE FOUNDATION (AQHF)

http://www.aqha.com/foundation

DR. GERALD O'CONNOR MICHIGAN SCHOLARSHIP
• *See page 535*

SWAYZE WOODRUFF MEMORIAL MID-SOUTH SCHOLARSHIP
• *See page 536*

AMERICAN SHEEP INDUSTRY ASSOCIATION

http://www.sheepusa.org/

NATIONAL MAKE IT WITH WOOL COMPETITION

Awards available for entrants ages 13 years & older. Must enter at state level with home-constructed garment of at least 60 percent wool. Applicant must model garment. Entry fee is $10.

Award: Prize for use in freshman, sophomore, junior, senior, or graduate years; not renewable. *Number:* 2–8. *Amount:* $25–$1000.

Eligibility Requirements: Applicant must be enrolled or expecting to enroll full- or part-time at a two-year or four-year or technical institution or university and must have an interest in sewing. Available to U.S. citizens.

Application Requirements: Application, applicant must enter a contest, self-addressed stamped envelope, sample of fabric (5x5). *Fee:* $10. *Deadline:* continuous.

Contact: Marie Lehfeldt, Coordinator
American Sheep Industry Association
PO Box 175
Lavina, MT 59046
Phone: 406-636-2731
Fax: 406-636-2731
E-mail: levi@midrivers.com

AMERICAN STRING TEACHERS ASSOCIATION

http://www.astaweb.com/

NATIONAL SOLO COMPETITION

Twenty-six individual awards. Instrument categories are violin, viola, cello, double bass, classical guitar, and harp. Applicants competing in Junior Division must be under age 19. Senior Division competitors must be ages 19 to 25. Application fee is $75. Visit web site for application forms. Applicant must be a member of ASTA.

Award: Prize for use in freshman, sophomore, junior, senior, or graduate years; not renewable. *Number:* 26. *Amount:* varies.

Eligibility Requirements: Applicant must be age 19-25; enrolled or expecting to enroll full- or part-time at a two-year or four-year or technical institution or university and must have an interest in music. Available to U.S. and Canadian citizens.

Application Requirements: Application, applicant must enter a contest, proof of age, proof of membership. *Fee:* $75. *Deadline:* varies.

Contact: Laura Kobayashi, Committee Chair
American String Teachers Association
4153 Chain Bridge Road
Fairfax, VA 22030
Phone: 703-279-2113
Fax: 703-279-2114
E-mail: lkobayas@myway.com

AMERICAN SWEDISH INSTITUTE

http://www.americanswedishinst.org/

LILLY LORENZEN SCHOLARSHIP
• *See page 714*

AMERICAN THEATRE ORGAN SOCIETY INC.

http://www.atos.org/

AMERICAN THEATRE ORGAN SOCIETY ORGAN PERFORMANCE SCHOLARSHIP

Renewable awards available to students between the ages of 13 to 27. Must have a talent in music and have an interest in theater organ performance studies (not for general music studies). There are two categories for this scholarship Category A: Organ students studying with professional theatre organ instructors. Category B: Theatre organ students furthering their musical education by working toward a college organ performance degree.

Award: Scholarship for use in freshman, sophomore, junior, or senior years; renewable. *Number:* 11. *Amount:* $500–$1000.

Eligibility Requirements: Applicant must be age 13-27; enrolled or expecting to enroll full- or part-time at a four-year institution or university and must have an interest in music. Available to U.S. and non-U.S. citizens.

Application Requirements: Application, essay. *Deadline:* April 15.

Contact: Carlton B. Smith, Chairperson, Scholarship Program
American Theatre Organ Society Inc.
2175 North Irwin Street
Indianapolis, IN 46219-2220
Phone: 317-356-1270
Fax: 317-322-9379
E-mail: smith@atos.org

AMERICAN WATER SKI EDUCATIONAL FOUNDATION

http://www.waterskihalloffame.com/

AMERICAN WATER SKI EDUCATIONAL FOUNDATION SCHOLARSHIP
• *See page 536*

AMERICA'S JUNIOR MISS SCHOLARSHIP PROGRAM

http://www.ajm.org/

AMERICA'S JUNIOR MISS SCHOLARSHIP PROGRAM
Awards are given to contestants in local, regional, and national levels of competition. Must be female, high school juniors or seniors, U.S. citizens, and legal residents of the county and state of competition. Contestants are evaluated on scholastic, interview, talent, fitness, and poise. The number of awards and their amount vary from year to year.

Award: Scholarship for use in freshman year; not renewable. *Number:* varies. *Amount:* varies.

Eligibility Requirements: Applicant must be high school student; age 16-18; planning to enroll or expecting to enroll full-time at a two-year or four-year institution or university; single female and must have an interest in beauty pageant. Available to U.S. citizens.

Application Requirements: Application, applicant must enter a contest, test scores, transcript, birth certificate, certificate of health. *Deadline:* varies.

Contact: National Field Director
America's Junior Miss Scholarship Program
751 Government Street
Mobile, AL 36602
Phone: 251-438-3621
Fax: 251-431-0063
E-mail: nicole@ajm.org

APPALACHIAN CENTER AND APPALACHIAN STUDIES ASSOCIATION

http://www.appalachianstudies.org/

WEATHERFORD AWARD
One-time award given to the best work of fiction, non-fiction, book, poetry, or short piece about the Appalachian South published in the most recent calendar year. Two awards will be given: one for non-fiction, one for fiction, and one for poetry. Seven copies of the nominated work must be sent to the chair of the award committee.

Award: Prize for use in freshman, sophomore, junior, or senior years; not renewable. *Number:* 3. *Amount:* up to $500.

Eligibility Requirements: Applicant must be enrolled or expecting to enroll full- or part-time at a two-year or four-year or technical institution or university and must have an interest in writing. Available to U.S. and non-U.S. citizens.

Application Requirements: Application, nomination, 7 copies of the book. *Deadline:* December 31.

Contact: Chad Berry, Chair, Award Committee
Appalachian Center and Appalachian Studies Association
Loyal Jones Appalachian Center, Berea College, 205 N. Main
St., CPO 2166
Berea, KY 40404

APPALOOSA HORSE CLUB-APPALOOSA YOUTH PROGRAM

http://www.appaloosayouth.com/

APPALOOSA YOUTH EDUCATIONAL SCHOLARSHIPS
• *See page 536*

ARKANSAS SINGLE PARENT SCHOLARSHIP FUND

http://www.aspsf.org/

ARKANSAS SINGLE PARENT SCHOLARSHIP
• *See page 715*

ARRL FOUNDATION INC.

http://www.arrl.org/

ALBERT H. HIX W8AH MEMORIAL SCHOLARSHIP
• *See page 716*

ALBUQUERQUE AMATEUR RADIO CLUB/TOBY CROSS SCHOLARSHIP
• *See page 716*

ARRL FOUNDATION GENERAL FUND SCHOLARSHIPS
Available to students who are amateur radio operators. Students can be licensed in any class of operators. Nonrenewable award for use in undergraduate years. Multiple awards per year.

Award: Scholarship for use in freshman, sophomore, junior, or senior years; not renewable. *Number:* varies. *Amount:* $2000.

Eligibility Requirements: Applicant must be enrolled or expecting to enroll full-time at a four-year institution or university and must have an interest in amateur radio. Available to U.S. citizens.

Application Requirements: Application, transcript. *Deadline:* February 1.

Contact: Ms. Mary Hobart, Secretary
ARRL Foundation Inc.
225 Main Street
Newington, CT 06111-1494
Phone: 860-594-0397
E-mail: k1mmh@arrl.org

ARRL SCHOLARSHIP HONORING BARRY GOLDWATER, K7UGA
One $5000 award is available to an undergraduate or graduate student with a Novice class or higher radio operator license.

Award: Scholarship for use in freshman, sophomore, junior, senior, or graduate years; not renewable. *Number:* 1. *Amount:* $5000.

Eligibility Requirements: Applicant must be enrolled or expecting to enroll at a four-year institution or university and must have an interest in amateur radio.

Application Requirements: Application, transcript. *Deadline:* February 1.

Contact: Ms. Mary Hobart, Secretary
ARRL Foundation Inc.
225 Main Street
Newington, CT 06111-1494
Phone: 860-594-0397
E-mail: k1mmh@arrl.org

BILL, W2ONV, AND ANN SALERNO MEMORIAL SCHOLARSHIP
Two $1000 awards are available to students who possess any amateur radio license. Applicants should have a 3.7 GPA or higher on a 4.0 scale. Aggregate annual income of the family household should not exceed $100,000. A recipient can only receive the scholarship once.

Award: Scholarship for use in freshman, sophomore, junior, senior, or graduate years; not renewable. *Number:* 2. *Amount:* $1000.

Eligibility Requirements: Applicant must be enrolled or expecting to enroll at a four-year institution or university and must have an interest in amateur radio. Applicant must have 3.5 GPA or higher.

Application Requirements: Application, transcript. *Deadline:* February 1.

Contact: Ms. Mary Hobart, Secretary
ARRL Foundation Inc.
225 Main Street
Newington, CT 06111-1494
Phone: 860-594-0397
E-mail: k1mmh@arrl.org

CEBIK MEMORIAL SCHOLARSHIP

One $1000 award is available to a student with a Technician class or higher radio license.

Award: Scholarship for use in freshman, sophomore, junior, or senior years; not renewable. *Number:* 1. *Amount:* $1000.

Eligibility Requirements: Applicant must be enrolled or expecting to enroll at a four-year institution or university and must have an interest in amateur radio.

Application Requirements: Application, transcript. *Deadline:* February 1.

Contact: Ms. Mary Hobart, Secretary
ARRL Foundation Inc.
225 Main Street
Newington, CT 06111-1494
Phone: 860-594-0397
E-mail: k1mmh@arrl.org

CENTRAL ARIZONA DX ASSOCIATION SCHOLARSHIP
• *See page 716*

CENTRAL ARIZONA DX ASSOCIATION SCHOLARSHIP
• *See page 716*

CHALLENGE MET SCHOLARSHIP
• *See page 599*

CHARLES CLARKE CORDLE MEMORIAL SCHOLARSHIP
• *See page 716*

CHICAGO FM CLUB SCHOLARSHIPS
• *See page 716*

DAYTON AMATEUR RADIO ASSOCIATION SCHOLARSHIP

Four $1000 awards are available to students with any active amateur radio license.

Award: Scholarship for use in freshman, sophomore, junior, or senior years; not renewable. *Number:* 4. *Amount:* $1000.

Eligibility Requirements: Applicant must be enrolled or expecting to enroll at a four-year institution or university and must have an interest in amateur radio.

Application Requirements: Application, transcript. *Deadline:* February 1.

Contact: Ms. Mary Hobart, Secretary
ARRL Foundation Inc.
225 Main Street
Newington, CT 06111-1494
Phone: 860-594-0397
E-mail: k1mmh@arrl.org

GWINNETT AMATEUR RADIO SOCIETY SCHOLARSHIP
• *See page 717*

K2TEO MARTIN J. GREEN SR. MEMORIAL SCHOLARSHIP

Available to students with a general amateur license for radio operation. Preference given to students from a ham family. Nonrenewable award for use in undergraduate years.

Award: Scholarship for use in freshman, sophomore, junior, or senior years; not renewable. *Number:* 1. *Amount:* $1000.

Eligibility Requirements: Applicant must be enrolled or expecting to enroll full-time at a four-year institution or university and must have an interest in amateur radio. Available to U.S. citizens.

LOUISIANA MEMORIAL SCHOLARSHIP
• *See page 717*

MARY LOU BROWN SCHOLARSHIP
• *See page 717*

NEW ENGLAND FEMARA SCHOLARSHIPS
• *See page 717*

NORMAN E. STROHMEIER, W2VRS MEMORIAL SCHOLARSHIP
• *See page 717*

NORTHERN CALIFORNIA DX FOUNDATION SCHOLARSHIP

Two $1500 awards are available to students with a Technician class or higher amateur radio license. Applicant must demonstrate interest and activity in Dxing.

Award: Scholarship for use in freshman, sophomore, junior, or senior years; not renewable. *Number:* 2. *Amount:* $1500.

Eligibility Requirements: Applicant must be enrolled or expecting to enroll at a two-year or four-year or technical institution or university and must have an interest in amateur radio.

Application Requirements: Application, transcript. *Deadline:* February 1.

Contact: Ms. Mary Hobart, Secretary
ARRL Foundation Inc.
225 Main Street
Newington, CT 06111-1494
Phone: 860-594-0397
E-mail: k1mmh@arrl.org

PEORIA AREA AMATEUR RADIO CLUB SCHOLARSHIP
• *See page 717*

SCHOLARSHIP OF THE MORRIS RADIO CLUB OF NEW JERSEY

One $1000 award is available to a student who possesses a Technician class or higher amateur radio license.

Award: Scholarship for use in freshman, sophomore, junior, or senior years; not renewable. *Number:* 1. *Amount:* $1000.

Eligibility Requirements: Applicant must be enrolled or expecting to enroll at a four-year institution or university and must have an interest in amateur radio.

Application Requirements: Application, transcript. *Deadline:* February 1.

Contact: Ms. Mary Hobart, Secretary
ARRL Foundation Inc.
225 Main Street
Newington, CT 06111-1494
Phone: 860-594-0397
E-mail: k1mmh@arrl.org

SIX METER CLUB OF CHICAGO SCHOLARSHIP
• *See page 717*

THOMAS W. PORTER SCHOLARSHIP
• *See page 718*

TOM AND JUDITH COMSTOCK SCHOLARSHIP
• *See page 718*

YANKEE CLIPPER CONTEST CLUB INC. YOUTH SCHOLARSHIP
• *See page 718*

YOU'VE GOT A FRIEND IN PENNSYLVANIA SCHOLARSHIP
• *See page 537*

ZACHARY TAYLOR STEVENS MEMORIAL SCHOLARSHIP
• *See page 718*

AUTHOR SERVICES, INC.
http://www.writersofthefuture.com/

L. RON HUBBARD'S ILLUSTRATORS OF THE FUTURE CONTEST

An ongoing competition for new and amateur artists judged by professional artists. Eligible submissions consist of three science fiction or fantasy illustrations. Prize amount ranges from $500 to $5000. Quarterly deadlines: December 31, March 31, June 30 and September 30. All entrants retain rights to artwork.

Award: Prize for use in freshman, sophomore, junior, senior, graduate, or postgraduate years; not renewable. *Number:* up to 12. *Amount:* $500–$5000.

Eligibility Requirements: Applicant must be enrolled or expecting to enroll full- or part-time at a two-year or four-year or technical institution or university and must have an interest in art. Available to U.S. and non-U.S. citizens.

Application Requirements: Applicant must enter a contest, self-addressed stamped envelope, 3 illustrations. *Deadline:* continuous.

Contact: Joni Labaqui, Contest Administrator
Author Services, Inc.
PO Box 3190
Los Angeles, CA 90078
Phone: 323-466-3310
Fax: 323-466-6474
E-mail: contests@authorservicesinc.com

L. RON HUBBARD'S WRITERS OF THE FUTURE CONTEST

An ongoing competition for new and amateur writers judged by professional writers. Eligible submissions are short stories and novelettes of science fiction or fantasy. Deadline varies and prize amount ranges from $500 to $5000.

Award: Prize for use in freshman, sophomore, junior, senior, graduate, or postgraduate years; not renewable. *Number:* up to 12. *Amount:* $500–$5000.

Eligibility Requirements: Applicant must be enrolled or expecting to enroll full- or part-time at a two-year or four-year or technical institution or university and must have an interest in writing. Available to U.S. and non-U.S. citizens.

Application Requirements: Applicant must enter a contest, self-addressed stamped envelope, copy of the manuscript. *Deadline:* continuous.

Contact: Joni Labaqui, Contest Administrator
Author Services, Inc.
PO Box 1630
Los Angeles, CA 90078
Phone: 323-466-3310
Fax: 323-466-6474
E-mail: contests@authorservicesinc.com

AYN RAND INSTITUTE
http://www.aynrandnovels.com/

"ANTHEM" ESSAY CONTEST

Entrant must be in the 8th, 9th, or 10th grade. Essays will be judged on both style and content. Winning essays must demonstrate an outstanding grasp of the philosophical meaning of Ayn Rand's novelette, "Anthem." For complete rules and guidelines visit web site http://www.aynrand.org/contests.

Award: Prize for use in freshman, sophomore, junior, senior, graduate, or postgraduate years; not renewable. *Number:* 236. *Amount:* $30–$2000.

Eligibility Requirements: Applicant must be high school student; planning to enroll or expecting to enroll full-time at a two-year or four-

year or technical institution or university and must have an interest in writing. Available to U.S. and non-U.S. citizens.

Application Requirements: Applicant must enter a contest, essay. *Deadline:* March 20.

Contact: Jason Eriksen, Essay Contest Coordinator
Ayn Rand Institute
2121 Alton Parkway, Suite 250
Irvine, CA 92606-4926
Phone: 949-222-6550
E-mail: essay@aynrand.org

BABE RUTH LEAGUE INC.
http://www.baberuthleague.org/

BABE RUTH SCHOLARSHIP PROGRAM

Program to provide assistance to individuals (former Babe Ruth Baseball, Cal Ripken Baseball or Babe Ruth Softball players) who plan on furthering their education beyond high school. Outstanding student athletes will receive $1000 each towards their college tuition.

Award: Scholarship for use in freshman year; not renewable. *Number:* 1–10. *Amount:* $1000.

Eligibility Requirements: Applicant must be high school student; planning to enroll or expecting to enroll full- or part-time at a two-year or four-year institution or university and must have an interest in athletics/sports. Available to U.S. citizens.

Application Requirements: Application, references, transcript. *Deadline:* September 1.

Contact: Mr. Joseph Smiegocki, Scholarship Committee
Phone: 800-880-3142
Fax: 609-695-2505
E-mail: info@baberuthleague.org

BILL DICKEY SCHOLARSHIP ASSOCIATION
http://www.nmjgsa.org/

BDSA SCHOLARSHIPS

One-time and renewable awards available. Awards are based on academic achievement, entrance exam scores, financial need, references, evidence of community service, and golfing ability. High school seniors or younger who are not already in the association's database may see web site to enter profile for eligibility and for application.

Award: Scholarship for use in freshman year; renewable. *Number:* varies. *Amount:* $1000–$3500.

Eligibility Requirements: Applicant must be high school student; planning to enroll or expecting to enroll full-time at a four-year institution or university and must have an interest in golf. Available to U.S. citizens.

Application Requirements: Application, financial need analysis, references. *Deadline:* April 20.

Contact: Andrea Bourdeaux, Executive Director
Bill Dickey Scholarship Association
1140 East Washington Street, Suite 103
Phoenix, AZ 85034
Phone: 602-258-7851
E-mail: andrea@bdscholar.org

BOETTCHER FOUNDATION
http://www.boettcherfoundation.org/

BOETTCHER FOUNDATION SCHOLARSHIPS
• *See page 719*

BOYS & GIRLS CLUBS OF AMERICA
http://www.bgca.org/

BOYS AND GIRLS CLUBS OF AMERICA NATIONAL YOUTH OF THE YEAR AWARD
• *See page 537*

CALIFORNIA JUNIOR MISS SCHOLARSHIP PROGRAM

http://www.ajm.org/

CALIFORNIA JUNIOR MISS SCHOLARSHIP PROGRAM
• *See page 720*

CANADA ICELAND FOUNDATION INC. SCHOLARSHIPS

http://www.logberg.com/

CANADA ICELAND FOUNDATION SCHOLARSHIP PROGRAM
• *See page 722*

CARGILL

http://www.cargill.com/

CARGILL COMMUNITY SCHOLARSHIP PROGRAM

One-time scholarships administered by the National FFA Organization. Each award is valued at $1000, and also enables the recipient's high school to become eligible for a $200 library grant. Award based upon academic performance and leadership in school and community activities. Applicants must be U.S. high school students who live in or near Cargill communities. Students are required to obtain a signature on their applications from a employee at a local Cargill facility or subsidiary.

Award: Scholarship for use in freshman year; not renewable. *Number:* 350. *Amount:* $1000.

Eligibility Requirements: Applicant must be high school student; planning to enroll or expecting to enroll full-time at a two-year or four-year institution or university and must have an interest in leadership. Available to U.S. citizens.

Application Requirements: Application. *Deadline:* February 15.

Contact: Rebecca Oswald, Community Relations Associate
Cargill
PO Box 9300
Minneapolis, MN 55440-9300
Phone: 952-742-6247
Fax: 952-742-7224
E-mail: cargill_scholarships@cargill.com

CENTER FOR LESBIAN AND GAY STUDIES (C.L.A.G.S.)

http://www.clags.org/

SYLVIA RIVERA AWARD IN TRANSGENDER STUDIES

Award given for the best book or article to appear on transgender studies during the current year. Applications may be submitted by the author or by nomination.

Award: Prize for use in freshman, sophomore, junior, senior, graduate, or postgraduate years; not renewable. *Number:* 1. *Amount:* $1000.

Eligibility Requirements: Applicant must be enrolled or expecting to enroll full- or part-time at a two-year or four-year institution or university and must have an interest in LGBT issues or writing. Available to U.S. and non-U.S. citizens.

Application Requirements: Application, 6 copies of the article or 6 copies of the first chapter or first 20 pages for books, cover sheet, details about the publication, contact details. *Deadline:* June 1.

Contact: Naz Qazi, Fellowship Membership Coordinator
Center for Lesbian and Gay Studies (C.L.A.G.S.)
365 Fifth Avenue, Room 7115
New York, NY 10016
Phone: 212-817-1955
Fax: 212-817-1567
E-mail: clags@gc.cuny.edu

CHRISTOPHERS

http://www.christophers.org/

POSTER CONTEST FOR HIGH SCHOOL STUDENTS

Contest invites students in grades nine through twelve to interpret the theme: "You can make a difference." Posters must include this statement and illustrate the idea that one person can change the world for the better. Judging is based on overall impact, content, originality and artistic merit. More information can be found at http://www.christophers.org.

Award: Prize for use in freshman year; not renewable. *Number:* up to 8. *Amount:* $100–$1000.

Eligibility Requirements: Applicant must be high school student; planning to enroll or expecting to enroll full- or part-time at a four-year institution or university and must have an interest in art. Available to U.S. and non-U.S. citizens.

Application Requirements: Application, applicant must enter a contest, poster. *Deadline:* January 8.

Contact: David Dicerto, Youth Coordinator
Christophers
5 Hanover Square, 11th Floor
New York, NY 10014
Phone: 212-759-4050
Fax: 212-838-5073
E-mail: youth@christophers.org

VIDEO CONTEST FOR COLLEGE STUDENTS

Contest requires college students to use any style or format to express the following theme: "One person can make a difference." Entries can be up to 5 minutes in length and must be submitted in standard, full-sized VHS format. Entries will be judged on content, artistic and technical proficiency, and adherence to contest rules. More information is available at http://www.christophers.org.

Award: Prize for use in freshman, sophomore, junior, senior, or graduate years; not renewable. *Number:* 8. *Amount:* $100–$3000.

Eligibility Requirements: Applicant must be enrolled or expecting to enroll full- or part-time at a two-year or four-year or technical institution or university and must have an interest in art. Available to U.S. and non-U.S. citizens.

Application Requirements: Application, applicant must enter a contest, VHS tape or DVD. *Deadline:* June 6.

Contact: David Dicerto, Youth Coordinator
Christophers
5 Hanover Square, 11th Floor
New York, NY 10014
Phone: 212-759-4050
Fax: 212-838-5073
E-mail: youth@christophers.org

COCA-COLA SCHOLARS FOUNDATION INC.

http://www.coca-colascholars.org/

COCA-COLA TWO-YEAR COLLEGES SCHOLARSHIP
• *See page 584*

COLAGE: PEOPLE WITH A LESBIAN, GAY, BISEXUAL, TRANSGENDER OR QUEER PARENT

http://www.colage.org/

COLAGE SCHOLARSHIP PROGRAM FOR STUDENTS WITH LESBIAN, GAY, BISEXUAL, TRANSGENDER AND/OR QUEER (LGBTQ) PARENT(S)

COLAGE will award four scholarships to children of LGBTQ parents. Each scholarship will provide $1,000 to post-secondary students who have one or more LGBTQ parent(s)/guardian(s) and have demonstrated ability and commitment to effecting change in the LGBTQ community and the community at large.

Award: Scholarship for use in freshman, sophomore, junior, or senior years; not renewable. *Number:* 3–5. *Amount:* $500–$1000.

Eligibility Requirements: Applicant must be enrolled or expecting to enroll full- or part-time at a two-year or four-year or technical institution or university and must have an interest in leadership or LGBT issues. Available to U.S. citizens.

Application Requirements: Application, essay, financial need analysis, transcript, proof of enrollment. *Deadline:* April 30.

Contact: Scholarship Committee
COLAGE: People with a Lesbian, Gay, Bisexual, Transgender or Queer Parent
1550 Bryant Street, Suite 830
San Francisco, CA 94103
Phone: 415-861-5437
E-mail: colage@colage.org

COLLEGEBOUND FOUNDATION

http://www.collegeboundfoundation.org/

HY ZOLET STUDENT ATHLETE SCHOLARSHIP
• *See page 725*

COLLEGEFINANCIALAIDINFORMATION. COM

http://www.easyaid.com/

FRANK O'NEILL MEMORIAL SCHOLARSHIP

One-time award available to applicants attending or aspiring to attend a university, college, trade school, technical institute, vocational training, or other postsecondary education program. Must submit essay explaining educational goals and financial need.

Award: Scholarship for use in freshman, sophomore, junior, senior, or graduate years; not renewable. *Number:* 2. *Amount:* $1000.

Eligibility Requirements: Applicant must be enrolled or expecting to enroll full- or part-time at a two-year or four-year or technical institution or university and must have an interest in writing. Available to U.S. and non-U.S. citizens.

Application Requirements: Application, essay. *Deadline:* December 31.

Contact: Geoff Anderla, Owner
CollegeFinancialAidInformation.com
11200 West Wisconsin Avenue, Suite 9
Youngtown, AZ 85363
Phone: 623-972-4282
E-mail: questions@easyaid.com

COLLEGEWEEKLIVE.COM

http://www.collegeweeklive.com/

COLLEGEWEEKLIVE.COM SCHOLARSHIP

$2500 scholarship to high school students demonstrating excellence in writing ability, creativity and originality. Students must submit an online application and participate in an online virtual college fair. For more information, see web site http://www.collegeweeklive.com/register.php?code=SE_D.

Award: Scholarship for use in freshman year; not renewable. *Number:* 1. *Amount:* $2500.

Eligibility Requirements: Applicant must be high school student; planning to enroll or expecting to enroll full- or part-time at a two-year or four-year or technical institution or university and must have an interest in writing. Available to U.S. citizens.

Application Requirements: Application, essay. *Deadline:* varies.

Contact: Lori Grandstaff, Scholarship Management Coordinator
CollegeWeekLive.com
3020 Hartley Road, Suite 220
Jacksonville, FL 32257
Phone: 904-854-6750 Ext. 11
Fax: 904-483-2934
E-mail: lori@scholarshipexperts.com

COLUMBIA 300

http://www.columbia300.com/

COLUMBIA 300 JOHN JOWDY SCHOLARSHIP

Renewable scholarship for graduating high school seniors who are actively involved in the sport of bowling. Must have minimum GPA of 3.0.

Award: Scholarship for use in freshman year; renewable. *Number:* 1. *Amount:* $500.

Eligibility Requirements: Applicant must be high school student; planning to enroll or expecting to enroll full- or part-time at a four-year institution or university and must have an interest in bowling. Applicant must have 3.0 GPA or higher. Available to U.S. citizens.

Application Requirements: Application. *Deadline:* April 1.

Contact: Dale Garner, Scholarship Committee
Columbia 300
PO Box 13430
San Antonio, TX 78213
Phone: 800-531-5920

COLUMBIA UNIVERSITY, DEPARTMENT OF MUSIC

http://www.music.columbia.edu/

JOSEPH H. BEARNS PRIZE IN MUSIC

This prize is open to U.S. citizens between 18 and 25 years of age on January 1st of the competition year, and offers prizes for both short form and long form works of music in order to encourage talented young composers.

Award: Prize for use in freshman, sophomore, junior, or senior years; renewable. *Number:* 2. *Amount:* $2000–$3000.

Eligibility Requirements: Applicant must be age 18-25; enrolled or expecting to enroll full- or part-time at a two-year or four-year or technical institution or university and must have an interest in music. Available to U.S. citizens.

Application Requirements: Applicant must enter a contest, self-addressed stamped envelope, music score, information regarding prior studies, social security number. *Deadline:* March 17.

Contact: Department of Music
Columbia University, Department of Music
621 Dodge Hall, MC No. 1813, 2960 Broadway
New York, NY 10027
Phone: 212-854-3825
Fax: 212-854-8191

COMMERCE BANK

http://www.com/merceonline.com/

AMERICAN DREAM SCHOLARSHIPS
• *See page 585*

CONTEMPORARY RECORD SOCIETY

http://www.crsnews.org/

CONTEMPORARY RECORD SOCIETY NATIONAL COMPETITION FOR PERFORMING ARTISTS

There are no age restrictions to participate. Applicant may submit one performance tape of varied length including music of any period of music with each application. The applicant may use any number of instrumentalists and voices. First prize is a commercial distribution of the winner's recording. Application fee is $50 for each recording submitted. The annual application deadline is April 10. Submit self-addressed stamped envelope with the application. The winning applicant will participate in a CD recording released by CRS. (This prize is not applicable toward tuition.)

Award: Prize for use in freshman, sophomore, junior, senior, graduate, or postgraduate years; not renewable. *Number:* 1. *Amount:* $2000–$6000.

Eligibility Requirements: Applicant must be enrolled or expecting to enroll full- or part-time at a two-year or four-year or technical institution or university and must have an interest in music/singing. Available to U.S. and non-U.S. citizens.

Application Requirements: Application, applicant must enter a contest, resume, references, self-addressed stamped envelope. *Fee:* $50. *Deadline:* April 10.

Contact: Mr. Jack Shusterman, Artist Representative
Contemporary Record Society
724 Winchester Road
Broomall, PA 19008
Phone: 610-544-5920
Fax: 915-808-4232
E-mail: crsnews@verizon.net

NATIONAL COMPETITION FOR COMPOSERS' RECORDINGS

Must submit a musical composition that is non-published and not commercially recorded. First prize is a CD recording grant (not tuition). there is no age restriction. It is limited to nine performers and twenty-five minutes duration. (Works with additional performers will be accepted provided there is a release of the original recorded master for CD reproduction!) Send self-addressed stamped envelope with $4 postage if applicant wants work returned. Application fee is $50. for each composition submitted. (There is a limit of 5 works per applicant!)

Award: Prize for use in freshman, sophomore, junior, senior, graduate, or postgraduate years; not renewable. *Number:* 1. *Amount:* $2000–$6000.

Eligibility Requirements: Applicant must be enrolled or expecting to enroll full- or part-time at a two-year or four-year or technical institution or university and must have an interest in music/singing. Available to U.S. and non-U.S. citizens.

Application Requirements: Application, applicant must enter a contest, resume, references, self-addressed stamped envelope. *Fee:* $50. *Deadline:* April 10.

Contact: Mr. Jack Shusterman, Artist Representative
Contemporary Record Society
724 Winchester Road
Broomall, PA 19008
Phone: 610-544-5920
Fax: 915-808-4232
E-mail: crsnews@verizon.net

CROSSLITES

http://www.crosslites.com/

CROSSLITES SCHOLARSHIP AWARD

Scholarship contest is open to high school, college and graduate school students. There are no minimum GPA, SAT, ACT, GMAT, GRE, or any other test score requirements.

Award: Prize for use in freshman, sophomore, junior, senior, or graduate years; not renewable. *Number:* 33. *Amount:* $100–$2500.

Eligibility Requirements: Applicant must be enrolled or expecting to enroll full- or part-time at a two-year or four-year or technical institution or university and must have an interest in writing. Available to U.S. and non-U.S. citizens.

Application Requirements: Application, applicant must enter a contest, essay. *Deadline:* December 15.

Contact: Samuel Certo, Scholarship Committee
CrossLites
1000 Holt Avenue
Winter Park, FL 32789

THE DALLAS FOUNDATION

http://www.dallasfoundation.org/

THE LANDON RUSNAK SCHOLARSHIP
• *See page 731*

DELAWARE HIGHER EDUCATION OFFICE

http://www.doe.k12.de.us

AGENDA FOR DELAWARE WOMEN TRAILBLAZER SCHOLARSHIP
• *See page 585*

DEVRY, INC.

http://www.devry.edu/

DEVRY UNIVERSITY FIRST SCHOLAR AWARD

Award to high school graduates and GED recipients. Must be a registered participant in any regional FIRST Robotics Competition. Must have an ACT composite score of 19 or SAT combined math and verbal/critical reading score of at least 900. Must submit letter of recommendation from FIRST team advisor. Deadline: one year from high school graduation to apply and start.

Award: Scholarship for use in freshman year; renewable. *Amount:* $3000–$9000.

Eligibility Requirements: Applicant must be high school student; planning to enroll or expecting to enroll full-time at an institution or university and must have an interest in science. Available to U.S. and Canadian citizens.

Application Requirements: Application, essay, references, test scores, transcript.

Contact: Thonie Simpson, National High School Program Manager
DeVry, Inc.
One Tower Lane
Oak Brook Terrace, IL 60181-4624
Phone: 630-706-3122
E-mail: scholarships@devry.edu

DIAMANTE, INC.

http://www.diamanteinc.org/

LATINO DIAMANTE SCHOLARSHIP FUND
• *See page 586*

DISABLEDPERSON INC. COLLEGE SCHOLARSHIP

http://www.disabledperson.com/

DISABLEDPERSON INC. NATIONAL COLLEGE SCHOLARSHIP AWARD
• *See page 602*

DISCOVER FINANCIAL SERVICES

http://www.discoverfinancial.com/

DISCOVER SCHOLARSHIP PROGRAM
• *See page 586*

DIVERSITY CITY MEDIA

http://www.blacknews.com/

BLACKNEWS.COM SCHOLARSHIP ESSAY CONTEST
• *See page 661*

DIXIE BOYS BASEBALL

http://www.dixie.org/boys

DIXIE BOYS BASEBALL BERNIE VARNADORE SCHOLARSHIP PROGRAM
• *See page 734*

DIXIE YOUTH SCHOLARSHIP PROGRAM
• *See page 734*

DUPONT IN COOPERATION WITH GENERAL LEARNING COMMUNICATIONS

http://www.thechallenge.dupont.com/

DUPONT CHALLENGE SCIENCE ESSAY AWARDS PROGRAM

Student science and technology prize program in the United States and Canada. Students must submit an essay of 700 to 1000 words discussing a scientific or technological development, event, or theory that has captured their interest. For students in grades 7–12. Must mail all entries in a 9x12 inch envelope. For more details go to web site http://www.thechallenge.dupont.com.

Award: Prize for use in freshman year; not renewable. *Number:* 100. *Amount:* $100–$3000.

Eligibility Requirements: Applicant must be high school student; age 12-19; planning to enroll or expecting to enroll full- or part-time at a four-year institution or university and must have an interest in writing. Available to U.S. and Canadian citizens.

Application Requirements: Applicant must enter a contest, essay, official entry form. *Deadline:* January 31.

Contact: Carole Rubenstein, Editorial Director
DuPont in Cooperation with General Learning
Communications
900 Skokie Boulevard, Suite 200
Northbrook, IL 60062-4028
Phone: 847-205-3000
Fax: 847-564-8197
E-mail: c.rubenstein@glcomm.com

EAST BAY FOOTBALL OFFICIALS ASSOCIATION

http://www.ebfoa.org/

EAST BAY FOOTBALL OFFICIALS ASSOCIATION COLLEGE SCHOLARSHIP

• *See page 735*

ELDER & LEEMAUR PUBLISHERS

http://www.elpublishers.com/

AUTHORS OF TOMORROW SCHOLARSHIP

Scholarship is available to current undergraduate students in any field of study and any student in either junior or senior high school.

Award: Scholarship for use in freshman, sophomore, junior, or senior years; not renewable. *Number:* varies. *Amount:* up to $10,000.

Eligibility Requirements: Applicant must be enrolled or expecting to enroll full- or part-time at a four-year institution or university and must have an interest in writing. Available to U.S. citizens.

Application Requirements: Application, essay. *Deadline:* December 1.

Contact: Joni Hara, Public Relations Assistant
Elder & Leemaur Publishers
115 Garfield Street, Suite 5432
Sumas, WA 98295
Phone: 604-263-3540
E-mail: joni@elpublishers.com

ELIE WIESEL FOUNDATION FOR HUMANITY

http://www.eliewieselfoundation.org/

ELIE WIESEL PRIZE IN ETHICS ESSAY CONTEST

Scholarship for full-time junior or senior at a four-year accredited college or university in the United States. Up to five awards are granted.

Award: Prize for use in junior or senior years; not renewable. *Number:* up to 5. *Amount:* $500–$5000.

Eligibility Requirements: Applicant must be enrolled or expecting to enroll full-time at a four-year institution or university and must have an interest in writing. Available to U.S. and non-U.S. citizens.

Application Requirements: Application, applicant must enter a contest, essay, self-addressed stamped envelope, student entry form, faculty sponsor form. *Deadline:* January 1.

Contact: Mr. Alexander S. Heit, Essay Contest Coordinator
Elie Wiesel Foundation for Humanity
555 Madison Avenue, 20th Floor
New York, NY 10022
Phone: 212-490-7788
Fax: 212-490-6006
E-mail: aheit@eliewieselfoundation.org

ELKS NATIONAL FOUNDATION

http://www.elks.org/enf

ELKS NATIONAL FOUNDATION MOST VALUABLE STUDENT SCHOLARSHIP CONTEST

Five hundred awards ranging from $1000 to $15,000 per year, renewable for four years, are allocated nationally by state quota for graduating high school seniors. Based on scholarship, leadership, and financial need. Must be a U.S. citizen pursuing a 4-year degree full-time at a U.S. college or university. For more information, visit http://www.elks.org/enf/scholars.

Award: Scholarship for use in freshman, sophomore, junior, or senior years; renewable. *Number:* 500. *Amount:* $4000–$60,000.

Eligibility Requirements: Applicant must be high school student; planning to enroll or expecting to enroll full-time at a four-year institution or university and must have an interest in leadership. Available to U.S. citizens.

Application Requirements: Application, applicant must enter a contest, essay, financial need analysis, self-addressed stamped envelope, test scores, transcript. *Deadline:* November 1.

Contact: Scholarship Office
Elks National Foundation
2750 North Lakeview Avenue
Chicago, IL 60614-2256
Phone: 773-755-4732
Fax: 773-755-4733
E-mail: scholarship@elks.org

ESSAYJOLT.COM

http://www.essayjolt.com/

ESSAYJOLT SCHOLARSHIP

• *See page 736*

FINANCIAL SERVICE CENTERS OF AMERICA INC.

http://www.fisca.org/

FINANCIAL SERVICE CENTERS OF AMERICA SCHOLARSHIP FUND

Cash grants of at least $2000 to two students from each of the 5 geographic regions across the country. Criteria is based on academic achievement, financial need, leadership skills in schools and the community, and an essay written expressly for the competition. Applicant must be single.

Award: Grant for use in freshman year; not renewable. *Number:* 10–22. *Amount:* $2000.

Eligibility Requirements: Applicant must be high school student; planning to enroll or expecting to enroll full-time at a two-year or four-year institution or university; single and must have an interest in leadership. Available to U.S. citizens.

Application Requirements: Application, applicant must enter a contest, essay, financial need analysis, photo, references, transcript. *Deadline:* April 8.

Contact: Henry Shyne, Executive Director
Financial Service Centers of America Inc.
21 Main Street, First Floor, Court Plaza South, East Wing
PO Box 647
Hackensack, NJ 07602
Phone: 201-487-0412
E-mail: hshyne@fisca.org

FLORIDA WOMEN'S STATE GOLF ASSOCIATION

http://www.fwsga.org/

FLORIDA WOMEN'S STATE GOLF ASSOCIATION JUNIOR GIRLS' SCHOLARSHIP FUND
• *See page 739*

FOREST ROBERTS THEATRE

http://www.nmu.edu/

MILDRED AND ALBERT PANOWSKI PLAYWRITING AWARD

Prize designed to encourage and stimulate artistic growth among playwrights. Winner receives a cash prize and a world premiere of their play.

Award: Prize for use in freshman, sophomore, junior, senior, graduate, or postgraduate years; not renewable. *Number:* 1. *Amount:* $2000.

Eligibility Requirements: Applicant must be enrolled or expecting to enroll full- or part-time at a two-year or four-year or technical institution or university and must have an interest in theater or writing. Available to U.S. and non-U.S. citizens.

Application Requirements: Application, applicant must enter a contest, self-addressed stamped envelope, manuscript in English. *Deadline:* October 31.

Contact: Matt Hudson, Playwriting Award Coordinator
Forest Roberts Theatre
Northern Michigan University, 1401 Presque Isle Avenue
Marquette, MI 49855-5364
Phone: 906-227-2559
Fax: 906-227-2567

FORT COLLINS SYMPHONY ASSOCIATION

http://www.fcsymphony.org/

ADELINE ROSENBERG MEMORIAL PRIZE

$4000 to $6000 prize for senior division (25 years or under) instrumental competitions held in odd-numbered years. Piano competitions held in even-numbered years. Auditions required. Must submit proof of age, perform a standard concerto, and be recommended by music teacher. Send self-addressed stamped envelope for application.

Award: Prize for use in freshman, sophomore, junior, senior, graduate, or postgraduate years; not renewable. *Number:* 2. *Amount:* $4000–$6000.

Eligibility Requirements: Applicant must be age 25 or under; enrolled or expecting to enroll full- or part-time at a four-year institution or university and must have an interest in music. Available to U.S. and non-U.S. citizens.

Application Requirements: Application, applicant must enter a contest, driver's license, references, self-addressed stamped envelope, proof of age. *Fee:* $50. *Deadline:* March 21.

Contact: Carol Kauffman, Office Manager
Fort Collins Symphony Association
214 South College Avenue
PO Box 1963
Fort Collins, CO 80524
Phone: 970-482-4823
Fax: 970-482-4858
E-mail: yac@fcsymphony.org

FORT COLLINS SYMPHONY ASSOCIATION YOUNG ARTIST COMPETITION, JUNIOR DIVISION

Junior division (between 12 and 18 years of age on day of competition) piano and instrumental competition held every year. Auditions required. Limited to the first twenty applicants and two alternates per division. Must submit verification of age. Applicant must perform one movement of a standard concerto and be recommended by music teacher. Send self-addressed stamped envelope for application. Fee of $35.

Award: Prize for use in freshman, sophomore, junior, or senior years; not renewable. *Number:* 4. *Amount:* $300–$500.

Eligibility Requirements: Applicant must be age 12-18; enrolled or expecting to enroll full- or part-time at a four-year institution or university and must have an interest in art. Available to U.S. and non-U.S. citizens.

Application Requirements: Application, applicant must enter a contest, driver's license, references, self-addressed stamped envelope, proof of age. *Fee:* $40. *Deadline:* March 21.

Contact: Carol Kauffman, Office Manager
Fort Collins Symphony Association
214 South College Avenue
PO Box 1963
Fort Collins, CO 80524
Phone: 970-482-4823
Fax: 970-482-4858
E-mail: yac@fcsymphony.org

FOUNDATION FOR CHRISTIAN COLLEGE LEADERS

http://www.collegechristianleader.com/

FOUNDATION FOR COLLEGE CHRISTIAN LEADERS SCHOLARSHIP
• *See page 697*

FREEDOM FROM RELIGION FOUNDATION

http://www.ffrf.org/

FREEDOM FROM RELIGION FOUNDATION COLLEGE ESSAY COMPETITION

Any currently enrolled college student may submit essay. Essays should be typed, double-spaced 4–5 pages with standard margins. Contestants must choose an original title for essay. 2010 topic: "Why I Reject Religion", "Why I am an Atheist/Agnostic/Unbeliever", or "Growing Up a Freethinker." Each contestant must include a paragraph biography giving campus and permanent addresses, phone numbers, and emails. The scholarship value varies. The essay topic and specific guidelines are posted in February.

Award: Scholarship for use in freshman, sophomore, junior, or senior years; not renewable. *Number:* 5–10. *Amount:* $200–$2000.

Eligibility Requirements: Applicant must be enrolled or expecting to enroll full-time at a four-year institution or university and must have an interest in writing. Available to U.S. and Canadian citizens.

Application Requirements: Applicant must enter a contest, essay, one-paragraph biography. *Deadline:* July 1.

Contact: College Essay Competition
Freedom From Religion Foundation
PO Box 750
Madison, WI 53701

FREEDOM FROM RELIGION FOUNDATION HIGH SCHOOL SENIOR ESSAY COMPETITION

High-school essay submitted must have an original title. 2010 topic: "The Harm of Religion" or "The Harm of Religion to Women." Each entrant must include a paragraph biography giving campus and permanent addresses, phone numbers and emails. First prize winner will receive $2000, second place $1000, third place $500, honorable mentions $200. The essay topic and specific guidelines are posted in February. For more information visit http://www.ffrf.org/.

Award: Scholarship for use in freshman year; not renewable. *Number:* 5–10. *Amount:* $200–$2000.

Eligibility Requirements: Applicant must be high school student; planning to enroll or expecting to enroll full-time at a two-year or four-year or technical institution or university and must have an interest in writing. Available to U.S. and Canadian citizens.

Application Requirements: Applicant must enter a contest, essay, one-paragraph biography. *Deadline:* June 1.

Contact: High School Essay Competition
Freedom From Religion Foundation
PO Box 750
Madison, WI 53701

GENERAL BOARD OF HIGHER EDUCATION AND MINISTRY

http://www.gbhem.org/

HANA SCHOLARSHIP
• *See page 663*

THE REV. DR. KAREN LAYMAN GIFT OF HOPE: 21ST CENTURY SCHOLARS PROGRAM
• *See page 698*

GEORGE T. WELCH TRUST

http://www.bakerboyer.com/

EDUCATION EXCHANGE COLLEGE GRANT PROGRAM

Awards range from four $1000 to thirty $5000 scholarships. Must be U.S. citizens and provide written acceptance to an accredited four-year college by May 15 of the award year.

Award: Grant for use in freshman year; not renewable. *Number:* 34. *Amount:* $1000–$5000.

Eligibility Requirements: Applicant must be high school student; planning to enroll or expecting to enroll full-time at a four-year institution or university and must have an interest in leadership. Available to U.S. citizens.

Application Requirements: Application, essay, references, transcript, acceptance letter to a four-year institution, copy of first two pages of parent or guardian's federal income tax return. *Deadline:* March 15.

Contact: Scholarship Committee
George T. Welch Trust
Education Exchange, PO Box 559
Morris Plains, NJ 07950

GERMAN ACADEMIC EXCHANGE SERVICE (DAAD)

http://www.daad.org/

DAAD STUDY SCHOLARSHIP

One of DAAD's flagship competitive scholarship awarded for study at all public universities in Germany. Open to students of all fields. Graduate study scholarships are granted for one academic year (10 months) with the possibility of a one-year extension for students completing a full degree program in Germany. Monthly stipends are approximately 750 euros. DAAD will cover health insurance and provide a flat rate subsidy for travel costs (US East: 750 euros/West: 800 euros; Canada East: 850 euros/West: 1,300 euros).

Award: Scholarship for use in senior, graduate, or postgraduate years; renewable. *Number:* varies. *Amount:* varies.

Eligibility Requirements: Applicant must be enrolled or expecting to enroll full-time at a four-year institution or university and must have an interest in German language/culture. Available to U.S. and non-U.S. citizens.

Application Requirements: Application, applicant must enter a contest, resume, transcript, proposal, DAAD German language certificate. *Deadline:* November 15.

Contact: Jane Fu, Information Officer
German Academic Exchange Service (DAAD)
871 United Nations Plaza
New York, NY 10017
Phone: 212-758-3223 Ext. 201
E-mail: daadny@daad.org

GLAMOUR

http://www.glamour.com/

TOP 10 COLLEGE WOMEN COMPETITION

Female students with leadership experience on and off campus, excellence in field of study, and inspiring goals can apply for this competition. Winners will be awarded $3000 along with a trip to New York City. Must be a junior studying full-time with a minimum GPA of 3.0. in either the United States or Canada. Non-U.S. citizens may apply if attending U.S. postsecondary institutions.

Award: Prize for use in junior year; not renewable. *Number:* 10. *Amount:* $3000.

Eligibility Requirements: Applicant must be enrolled or expecting to enroll full-time at a four-year institution or university; female and must have an interest in leadership. Applicant must have 3.0 GPA or higher. Available to U.S. and non-U.S. citizens.

Application Requirements: Application, essay, photo, references, transcript. *Deadline:* February 2.

Contact: Lynda Laux-Bachand, Reader Services Editor
Glamour
Four Times Square, 16th Floor
New York, NY 10036-6593
Phone: 212-286-6667
Fax: 212-286-6922

GLENN MILLER BIRTHPLACE SOCIETY

http://www.glennmiller.org/

GLENN MILLER INSTRUMENTAL SCHOLARSHIP

One-time awards for high school seniors and college freshmen. Scholarships are awarded as competition prizes and must be used for any education-related expenses. Must submit 10-minute, high-quality audio tape of pieces selected for competition or those of similar style. Applicant is responsible for travel to and lodging during the competition.

Award: Scholarship for use in freshman year; not renewable. *Number:* 3. *Amount:* $1000–$4500.

Eligibility Requirements: Applicant must be high school student; planning to enroll or expecting to enroll full-time at a four-year institution or university and must have an interest in music/singing. Available to U.S. and non-U.S. citizens.

Application Requirements: Application, applicant must enter a contest, essay, performance tape or CD. *Deadline:* March 15.

Contact: Arlene Leonard, Secretary
Glenn Miller Birthplace Society
107 East Main Street, PO Box 61
Clarinda, IA 51632-0061
Phone: 712-542-2461
Fax: 712-542-2461
E-mail: gmbs@heartland.net

JACK PULLAN MEMORIAL SCHOLARSHIP

One scholarship for a male or female vocalist, awarded as competition prize and, to be used for any education-related expenses. Must submit 10 minute, high-quality audio tape of pieces selected for competition or those of similar style. Applicant is responsible for travel to and lodging during the competition. One-time award for high school seniors and college freshmen. More information on http://www.glennmiller.org/scholar.htm.

Award: Scholarship for use in freshman year; not renewable. *Number:* 1. *Amount:* $1000.

Eligibility Requirements: Applicant must be high school student; planning to enroll or expecting to enroll full-time at a four-year institution or university and must have an interest in music/singing. Available to U.S. and non-U.S. citizens.

Application Requirements: Application, applicant must enter a contest, essay, performance tape or CD. *Deadline:* March 15.

Contact: Arlene Leonard, Secretary
Glenn Miller Birthplace Society
107 East Main Street, PO Box 61
Clarinda, IA 51632-0061
Phone: 712-542-2461
Fax: 712-542-2461
E-mail: gmbs@heartland.net

RALPH BREWSTER VOCAL SCHOLARSHIP

One scholarship for a male or female vocalist, awarded as competition prize and, to be used for any education-related expenses. Must submit 10 minute, high-quality audio tape of pieces selected for competition or those of similar style. Applicant is responsible for travel to and lodging during the competition. One-time award for high school seniors and college freshmen.

Award: Scholarship for use in freshman year; not renewable. *Number:* 1. *Amount:* $2000.

Eligibility Requirements: Applicant must be high school student; planning to enroll or expecting to enroll full-time at a four-year institution or university and must have an interest in music/singing. Available to U.S. and non-U.S. citizens.

Application Requirements: Application, applicant must enter a contest, essay, performance tape of competition or concert quality (up to 5 minutes duration). *Deadline:* March 15.

Contact: Arlene Leonard, Secretary
Glenn Miller Birthplace Society
107 East Main Street, PO Box 61
Clarinda, IA 51632-0061
Phone: 712-542-2461
Fax: 712-542-2461
E-mail: gmbs@heartland.net

GLORIA BARRON PRIZE FOR YOUNG HEROES

http://www.barronprize.org/

GLORIA BARRON PRIZE FOR YOUNG HEROES

Award honors young people ages 8 to 18 who have shown leadership and courage in public service to people or to the planet. Must be nominated by a responsible adult who is not a relative. Award is to be applied to higher education or a service project. For further information and nomination forms, see web site at http://www.barronprize.org.

Award: Prize for use in freshman year; not renewable. *Number:* 1–10. *Amount:* up to $2000.

Eligibility Requirements: Applicant must be age 8-18; enrolled or expecting to enroll full- or part-time at a two-year or four-year or technical institution or university and must have an interest in leadership. Available to U.S. and Canadian citizens.

Application Requirements: Application, essay, photo, nomination form, references form. *Deadline:* April 30.

Contact: Barbara Ann Richman, Executive Director
Gloria Barron Prize for Young Heroes
545 Pearl Street
Boulder, CO 80302
E-mail: ba_richman@barronprize.org

GRACO INC.

http://www.graco.com/

GRACO EXCELLENCE SCHOLARSHIP
• *See page 575*

GREATER KANAWHA VALLEY FOUNDATION

http://www.tgkvf.org/

KID'S CHANCE OF WEST VIRGINIA SCHOLARSHIP
• *See page 741*

GREENHOUSE SCHOLARS

http://www.greenhousescholars.org/

GREENHOUSE SCHOLARS
• *See page 743*

GUARDIAN LIFE INSURANCE COMPANY OF AMERICA

http://www.girlsgoingplaces.com/

GIRLS GOING PLACES ENTREPRENEURSHIP AWARD PROGRAM

Rewards enterprising female students between the ages of 12–18 and currently enrolled in middle school, high school, or home school, who demonstrate budding entrepreneurship, are taking the first steps toward financial independence, and making a difference in their school and community.

Award: Grant for use in freshman year; not renewable. *Number:* 15. *Amount:* $1000–$10,000.

Eligibility Requirements: Applicant must be high school student; age 12-18; planning to enroll or expecting to enroll full-time at a two-year or four-year or technical institution or university; female and must have an interest in entrepreneurship or leadership. Available to U.S. citizens.

Application Requirements: Application, applicant must enter a contest, essay, references, financial statements from business. *Deadline:* February 28.

Contact: Maureen Charles, Marketing Specialist
Guardian Life Insurance Company of America
7 Hanover Square, H26-J
New York, NY 10004
Phone: 212-598-1559
Fax: 212-919-4117
E-mail: maureen_charles@glic.com

HARNESS HORSE YOUTH FOUNDATION

http://www.hhyf.org/

CURT GREENE MEMORIAL SCHOLARSHIP
• *See page 587*

HARTFORD WHALERS BOOSTER CLUB

http://www.whalerwatch.com/

HARTFORD WHALERS BOOSTER CLUB SCHOLARSHIP
• *See page 743*

HEMOPHILIA FEDERATION OF AMERICA

http://www.hemophiliaed.org/

ARTISTIC ENCOURAGEMENT GRANT
• *See page 604*

HERB KOHL EDUCATIONAL FOUNDATION INC.

http://www.kohleducation.org/

HERB KOHL EXCELLENCE SCHOLARSHIP PROGRAM
• *See page 588*

HOLLAND & KNIGHT CHARITABLE FOUNDATION HOLOCAUST REMEMBRANCE PROJECT

http://www.foundation.hklaw.com/

HOLOCAUST REMEMBRANCE PROJECT ESSAY CONTEST

Contest open to all students age 19 and under who are currently enrolled as high school students, and are residents of either the United States or Mexico, or who are United States citizens living abroad. Submit essay on any aspect of the Holocaust using relevant research sources and addressing key points indicated in the instructions. Prizes for winning essays include scholarships. Essay must be submitted online. For information see web site http://holocaust.hklaw.com.

Award: Prize for use in freshman year; not renewable. *Number:* 30. *Amount:* $300–$10,000.

Eligibility Requirements: Applicant must be high school student; age 19 or under; planning to enroll or expecting to enroll full- or part-time at a four-year institution or university and must have an interest in writing. Available to U.S. citizens.

Application Requirements: Application, essay. *Deadline:* April 30.

Contact: Scholarship Committee
Holland & Knight Charitable Foundation Holocaust
Remembrance Project
PO Box 2877
Tampa, FL 33601-2877
Phone: 866-452-2737
E-mail: holocaust@hklaw.com

HORIZONS FOUNDATION

http://www.horizonsfoundation.org/

MARKOWSKI-LEACH SCHOLARSHIP
• *See page 744*

HOSTESS COMMITTEE SCHOLARSHIPS/ MISS AMERICA PAGEANT

http://www.missamerica.org/

MISS AMERICA ORGANIZATION COMPETITION SCHOLARSHIPS

Scholarship competition open to 70 contestants, each serving as state representative. Women will be judged in Private Interview, Swimsuit, Evening Wear and Talent competition. Other awards may be based on points assessed by judges during competitions. Upon reaching the National level, award values range from $2000 to $50,000. Additional awards not affecting the competition can be won with values from $1000 to $10,000.

Award: Prize for use in freshman, sophomore, junior, senior, or graduate years; not renewable. *Number:* 70. *Amount:* $2000–$50,000.

Eligibility Requirements: Applicant must be age 17-24; enrolled or expecting to enroll full- or part-time at a two-year or four-year or technical institution or university; female and must have an interest in beauty pageant. Available to U.S. citizens.

Application Requirements: Application, applicant must enter a contest. *Deadline:* varies.

Contact: Doreen Lindell Gordon, Controller and Scholarship
Administrator
Hostess Committee Scholarships/Miss America Pageant
Two Miss America Way, Suite 1000
Atlantic City, NJ 08401
Phone: 609-345-7571 Ext. 27
Fax: 609-347-6079
E-mail: doreen@missamerica.org

MISS STATE SCHOLAR

Award available only to pageant participants at the state level. Candidates evaluated strictly on academics.

Award: Scholarship for use in freshman, sophomore, junior, senior, or graduate years; not renewable. *Number:* up to 51. *Amount:* up to $1000.

Eligibility Requirements: Applicant must be enrolled or expecting to enroll full-time at a two-year or four-year institution or university; female and must have an interest in beauty pageant. Available to U.S. citizens.

Application Requirements: Application, transcript. *Deadline:* varies.

Contact: Doreen Lindell Gordon, Controller and Scholarship
Administrator
Hostess Committee Scholarships/Miss America Pageant
Two Miss America Way, Suite 1000
Atlantic City, NJ 08401
Phone: 609-345-7571 Ext. 27
Fax: 609-347-6079
E-mail: doreen@missamerica.org

HUMANIST MAGAZINE

http://www.thehumanist.org/

HUMANIST ESSAY CONTEST

Contest is open to students residing in the United States or Canada who are enrolled in grades 9–12. Essays should be 1,500 to 2,500 words, written in English, single-spaced, on a topic relevant to humanists.

Award: Prize for use in freshman year; not renewable. *Number:* 3. *Amount:* up to $1000.

Eligibility Requirements: Applicant must be high school student; planning to enroll or expecting to enroll full- or part-time at a two-year or four-year or technical institution or university and must have an interest in writing. Available to U.S. and Canadian citizens.

Application Requirements: Application, applicant must enter a contest, essay. *Deadline:* March 3.

Contact: Scholarship Committee
Humanist Magazine
1777 T Street, NW
Washington, DC 20009-7125
Phone: 800-837-3792
E-mail: contest@thehumanist.org

INDEPENDENT COLLEGE FUND OF MARYLAND (I-FUND)

http://www.i-fundinfo.org/

LEADERSHIP SCHOLARSHIPS
• *See page 748*

T. ROWE PRICE FOUNDATION SCHOLARSHIPS
• *See page 748*

JACKIE ROBINSON FOUNDATION

http://www.jackierobinson.org/

JACKIE ROBINSON SCHOLARSHIP
• *See page 590*

JAPANESE GOVERNMENT/THE MONBUSHO SCHOLARSHIP PROGRAM

http://www.la.us.emb-japan.go.jp/

VOCATIONAL SCHOOL STUDENT SCHOLARSHIPS

Award open to students enrolled in vocational schools in Japan. Study involves one year of language training and two years of vocational school. All vocational training will be in Japanese. Scholarship comprises transportation, accommodations, medical expenses, and monthly and arrival allowances.

Award: Scholarship for use in freshman or sophomore years; not renewable. *Number:* varies. *Amount:* varies.

Eligibility Requirements: Applicant must be age 17-20; enrolled or expecting to enroll full-time at a technical institution and must have an interest in Japanese language. Available to U.S. citizens.

Application Requirements: Application, essay, interview, photo, references, transcript, medical certificate, certificate of enrollment. *Deadline:* varies.

Contact: Jean Do, Scholarship Coordinator
Japanese Government/The Monbusho Scholarship Program
350 South Grand Avenue, Suite 1700
Los Angeles, CA 90071
Phone: 213-617-6700 Ext. 338
Fax: 213-617-6728
E-mail: info@la-cgjapan.org

JUNIOR ACHIEVEMENT

http://www.ja.org/

HUGH B. SWEENY ACHIEVEMENT AWARD
• *See page 546*

JOE FRANCOMANO SCHOLARSHIP
• *See page 547*

KARMEL SCHOLARSHIP

http://www.karenandmelody.com/

KARMEL SCHOLARSHIP

Scholarship to encourage students to write or create something that will express their views on a topic related to GLBT issues.

Award: Scholarship for use in freshman, sophomore, junior, senior, or graduate years; not renewable. *Number:* 2. *Amount:* $300–$400.

Eligibility Requirements: Applicant must be enrolled or expecting to enroll full- or part-time at a two-year or four-year or technical institution or university and must have an interest in art, LGBT issues, music/singing, or writing. Available to U.S. and non-U.S. citizens.

Application Requirements: Application, applicant must enter a contest, essay. *Deadline:* March 31.

Contact: Scholarship Committee
KarMel Scholarship
PO Box 70382
Sunnyvale, CA 94086
E-mail: karen@karenandmelody.com

KE ALI'I PAUAHI FOUNDATION

http://www.pauahi.org/

DWAYNE "NAKILA" STEELE SCHOLARSHIP

Scholarship supports students who demonstrate a desire to work in the area of perpetuating the Hawaiian language upon graduation. Requirements include demonstrated interest in the Hawaiian language, culture, and history, in addition to a commitment to contribute to the greater community and demonstrated financial need. Submit two letters of recommendation; one from a teacher or counselor and one from a community organization or other citing how the applicant is working toward perpetuating the Hawaiian Language.

Award: Scholarship for use in freshman, sophomore, junior, senior, or graduate years; not renewable. *Number:* 1. *Amount:* $800.

Eligibility Requirements: Applicant must be enrolled or expecting to enroll full-time at a two-year or four-year institution or university and must have an interest in Hawaiian language/culture. Available to U.S. citizens.

Application Requirements: Application, financial need analysis, references, transcript, Student Aid Report (SAR), college acceptance letter. *Deadline:* April 1.

Contact: Mavis Shiraishi-Nagao, Scholarship Administrator
Phone: 808-534-3966
E-mail: scholarships@pauahi.org

KAMEHAMEHA SCHOOLS CLASS OF 1956 GRANT
• *See page 750*

KAMEHAMEHA SCHOOLS CLASS OF 1974 SCHOLARSHIP
• *See page 751*

KNIGHTS OF PYTHIAS

http://www.pythias.org/

KNIGHTS OF PYTHIAS POSTER CONTEST

Poster contest open to all high school students in the U.S. and Canada. Contestants must submit an original drawing. Eight winners are chosen. The winners are not required to attend institution of higher education.

Award: Prize for use in freshman year; not renewable. *Number:* 8. *Amount:* $100–$1000.

Eligibility Requirements: Applicant must be high school student; planning to enroll or expecting to enroll full- or part-time at a four-year institution or university and must have an interest in art. Available to U.S. and Canadian citizens.

Application Requirements: Applicant must enter a contest. *Deadline:* April 30.

Contact: Alfred Saltzman, Supreme Secretary
Knights of Pythias
Office of Supreme Lodge
59 Coddington Street, Suite 202
Quincy, MA 02169-4150
Phone: 617-472-8800
Fax: 617-376-0363
E-mail: kop@earthlink.net

KOSCIUSZKO FOUNDATION

http://www.kosciuszkofoundation.org/

MARCELLA SEMBRICH VOICE COMPETITION

The competition encourages young singers to study the repertoire of Polish composers. Three prizes awarded: $2000, $1250 and $750. Open to all singers who are at least 18 years old and preparing for professional careers. Must be U.S. citizens or international full-time students with a valid student visa.

Award: Prize for use in freshman, sophomore, junior, senior, or graduate years; not renewable. *Number:* 3. *Amount:* $750–$2000.

Eligibility Requirements: Applicant must be age 18 and over; enrolled or expecting to enroll full- or part-time at a four-year institution or university and must have an interest in music/singing. Available to U.S. and non-Canadian citizens.

Application Requirements: Application, applicant must enter a contest, photo, references, 2 cassette tapes. *Fee:* $35. *Deadline:* January 18.

Contact: Mr. Thomas Pniewski, Director of Cultural Programs
Kosciuszko Foundation
15 East 65th Street
New York, NY 10021-6595
Phone: 212-734-2130
Fax: 212-628-4552
E-mail: tompkf@aol.com

KURT WEILL FOUNDATION FOR MUSIC

http://www.kwf.org/

LOTTE LENYA COMPETITION FOR SINGERS

The competition recognizes excellence in the performance of music for the theater, including opera, operetta, and American musical theater. Applicants should contact the foundation for more information.

Award: Prize for use in freshman, sophomore, junior, senior, or graduate years; not renewable. *Number:* varies. *Amount:* varies.

Eligibility Requirements: Applicant must be age 19-32; enrolled or expecting to enroll full- or part-time at a two-year or four-year institution or university and must have an interest in music/singing or theater. Available to U.S. and non-U.S. citizens.

Application Requirements: Application, applicant must enter a contest, audition.

Contact: Carolyn Weber, Director
Kurt Weill Foundation for Music
Seven East 20th Street
New York, NY 10003-1106
Phone: 212-505-5240
E-mail: cweber@kwf.org

LADIES AUXILIARY TO THE VETERANS OF FOREIGN WARS

http://www.ladiesauxvfw.org/

JUNIOR GIRLS SCHOLARSHIP PROGRAM
• *See page 549*

YOUNG AMERICAN CREATIVE PATRIOTIC ART AWARDS PROGRAM

One-time awards for high school students in grades 9 through 12. Must submit an original work of art expressing their patriotism. First place state-level winners go on to national competition. Eight awards of varying amounts. Must reside in same state as sponsoring organization.

Award: Scholarship for use in freshman year; not renewable. *Number:* up to 8. *Amount:* $500–$10,000.

Eligibility Requirements: Applicant must be high school student; planning to enroll or expecting to enroll full-time at a two-year or four-year or technical institution; single and must have an interest in art. Available to U.S. citizens.

Application Requirements: Application, applicant must enter a contest, references. *Deadline:* March 31.

Contact: Judith Millick, Administrator of Programs
Ladies Auxiliary to the Veterans of Foreign Wars
406 West 34th Street, 10th Floor
Kansas City, MO 64111
Phone: 816-561-8655
E-mail: jmillick@ladiesauxvfw.org

LEAGUE FOUNDATION

http://www.leaguefoundation.org/

LEAGUE FOUNDATION ACADEMIC SCHOLARSHIP

Every student has the right and the potential to excel. The LEAGUE Foundation provides financial resources for America's Gay, Lesbian, Bisexual, Transgender youth to attend institutions of higher learning to meet this mission. More information can be found on the LEAGUE Foundation web site: http://www.LEAGUEFoundation.org.

Award: Scholarship for use in freshman year; not renewable. *Number:* 4–8. *Amount:* $1500–$2500.

Eligibility Requirements: Applicant must be high school student; planning to enroll or expecting to enroll full-time at a two-year or four-year or technical institution or university and must have an interest in LGBT issues. Applicant must have 3.0 GPA or higher. Available to U.S. citizens.

Application Requirements: Application, essay, references, test scores, transcript, college or university acceptance letter. *Deadline:* April 30.

Contact: Charles Eader, Executive Director
LEAGUE Foundation
One AT&T Way, Room 4B214J
Bedminster, NJ 07921
Phone: 571-354-4525
E-mail: info@leaguefoundation.org

LEE-JACKSON EDUCATIONAL FOUNDATION

http://www.lee-jackson.org/

LEE-JACKSON EDUCATIONAL FOUNDATION SCHOLARSHIP COMPETITION
• *See page 752*

LIEDERKRANZ FOUNDATION

http://www.liederkranznycity.org/

LIEDERKRANZ FOUNDATION SCHOLARSHIP AWARD FOR VOICE

Nonrenewable awards for voice for both full-and part-time study. Those studying general voice must be between ages 18 to 45 years old while those studying Wagnerian voice must be between ages 25 to 45 years old. Application fee: $50. Applications not available before August and September.

Award: Prize for use in freshman, sophomore, junior, senior, or graduate years; not renewable. *Number:* 14–18. *Amount:* $1000–$8000.

Eligibility Requirements: Applicant must be age 18-45; enrolled or expecting to enroll full- or part-time at a four-year institution or university and must have an interest in music/singing. Available to U.S. and non-U.S. citizens.

Application Requirements: Application, applicant must enter a contest, self-addressed stamped envelope, proof of age. *Fee:* $50. *Deadline:* November 15.

Contact: Manager
Liederkranz Foundation
Six East 87th Street
New York, NY 10128
Phone: 212-534-0880
Fax: 212-828-5372
E-mail: contactus@liederkranznycity.org

LINCOLN COMMUNITY FOUNDATION

http://www.lcf.org/

GEORGE L. WATTERS/NEBRASKA PETROLEUM MARKETERS ASSOCIATION SCHOLARSHIP
• *See page 576*

THE LINCOLN FORUM

http://www.thelincolnforum.org/

PLATT FAMILY SCHOLARSHIP PRIZE ESSAY CONTEST

Scholarship essay contest is designed for students who are full-time students in an American college or university. For details, refer to web site http://www.thelincolnforum.org/essayContest.html.

Award: Prize for use in freshman, sophomore, junior, or senior years; not renewable. *Number:* 3. *Amount:* $250–$1000.

Eligibility Requirements: Applicant must be enrolled or expecting to enroll full-time at a two-year or four-year institution or university and must have an interest in writing. Available to U.S. citizens.

Application Requirements: Applicant must enter a contest, essay. *Deadline:* July 31.

Contact: Don McCue, Curator
The Lincoln Forum
125 West Vine Street
Redlands, CA 92373
Phone: 909-798-7632
E-mail: archives@akspl.org

LIVE POETS SOCIETY AND JUST POETRY!!! MAGAZINE

http://www.highschoolpoetrycontest.com/

NATIONAL HIGH SCHOOL POETRY CONTEST

Award to encourage the youth of America in the pursuit of literary exploration and excellence, and to help provide a venue in which American High School students may share their poetic works. All U.S. high school students are eligible to enter this contest.

Award: Scholarship for use in freshman year; not renewable. *Number:* 1–12. *Amount:* $100–$1000.

Eligibility Requirements: Applicant must be high school student; planning to enroll or expecting to enroll full-time at a two-year or four-year institution or university and must have an interest in English language or writing. Available to U.S. citizens.

Application Requirements: Applicant must enter a contest, self-addressed stamped envelope, poem of 20 lines or less. *Deadline:* continuous.

Contact: Mr. D. Edwards, Editor
Live Poets Society and JUST POETRY!!! magazine
PO Box 8841
Turnersville, NJ 08012
E-mail: lpsnj@comcast.net

LOWE'S COMPANIES INC.

http://www.lowes.com/

LOWE'S EDUCATIONAL SCHOLARSHIP
• *See page 590*

MANA DE SAN DIEGO

http://www.sdmana.org/

MANA DE SAN DIEGO SYLVIA CHAVEZ MEMORIAL SCHOLARSHIP
• *See page 591*

MARTIN D. ANDREWS SCHOLARSHIP

http://www.mdascholarship.tripod.com/

MARTIN D. ANDREWS MEMORIAL SCHOLARSHIP FUND

One-time award for student seeking undergraduate or graduate degree. Recipient must have been in a Drum Corp for at least three years. Must submit essay and two recommendations. Must be U.S. citizen.

Award: Scholarship for use in freshman, sophomore, junior, senior, or graduate years; not renewable. *Number:* 2–5. *Amount:* $300–$1000.

Eligibility Requirements: Applicant must be enrolled or expecting to enroll full- or part-time at a two-year or four-year institution or university and must have an interest in drum corps. Available to U.S. citizens.

Application Requirements: Application, essay, references. *Deadline:* April 1.

Contact: Peter D. Andrews, Scholarship Committee
Martin D. Andrews Scholarship
2069 Perkins Street
Bristol, CT 06010
Phone: 860-673-2929
E-mail: mdascholarship@musician.org

MCCURRY FOUNDATION INC.

http://www.mccurryfoundation.org/

MCCURRY FOUNDATION SCHOLARSHIP
• *See page 760*

METAVUE CORPORATION

http://www.metavue.com/

FAMOUS PEOPLE AND THEIR WORK

Scholarship contest is looking for good biographies dealing with a famous person who has made a contribution to our lives and society. Contest is most appropriate for upper high schools levels and undergraduate students pursuing a liberal arts education. Visit http://www.metavue.com for additional details.

Award: Prize for use in freshman, sophomore, junior, or senior years; not renewable. *Number:* 8–11. *Amount:* $15–$500.

Eligibility Requirements: Applicant must be enrolled or expecting to enroll full-time at a two-year or four-year institution or university and must have an interest in writing. Applicant must have 3.0 GPA or higher. Available to U.S. citizens.

Application Requirements: Application, applicant must enter a contest, essay. *Deadline:* March 1.

Contact: Teresa Rufflo
Phone: 608-577-0642
E-mail: scholarships@metavue.com

MINNESOTA AFL-CIO

http://www.mnaflcio.org/

BILL PETERSON SCHOLARSHIP
• *See page 549*

MINNESOTA COMMUNITY FOUNDATION

http://www.mncommunityfoundation.org/

JANE RING AND SUE RING-JARVI GIRLS'/WOMEN'S HOCKEY FUND
• *See page 761*

MINNESOTA DEPARTMENT OF MILITARY AFFAIRS

http://www.minnesotanationalguard.org/

LEADERSHIP, EXCELLENCE AND DEDICATED SERVICE SCHOLARSHIP
• *See page 591*

MINNESOTA OFFICE OF HIGHER EDUCATION

http://www.getreadyforcollege.org/

MINNESOTA ACADEMIC EXCELLENCE SCHOLARSHIP
• *See page 762*

MISS AMERICAN COED PAGEANTS INC.

http://www.gocoed.com/

MISS AMERICAN COED PAGEANT

Awards available for girls aged 3 to 22. Must be single and maintain a 3.0 GPA where applicable. Prizes are awarded by age groups. Winners of state competitions may compete at the national level. Application fee would vary for each state between $25 to $35 and will be refunded if not accepted into competition. Deadline varies each year.

Award: Prize for use in freshman year; not renewable. *Number:* up to 52. *Amount:* $150–$3000.

Eligibility Requirements: Applicant must be age 3-22; enrolled or expecting to enroll full- or part-time at a two-year or four-year institution; single female and must have an interest in beauty pageant. Applicant must have 3.0 GPA or higher. Available to U.S. citizens.

Application Requirements: Application, applicant must enter a contest, transcript. *Deadline:* varies.

Contact: George Scarborough, National Director
Miss American Coed Pageants Inc.
3695 Wimbledon Drive
Pensacola, FL 32504-4555
Phone: 850-432-0069
Fax: 850-469-8841
E-mail: amerteen@aol.com

MORRIS J. AND BETTY KAPLUN FOUNDATION

http://www.kaplunfoundation.org/

MORRIS J. AND BETTY KAPLUN FOUNDATION ANNUAL ESSAY CONTEST
• *See page 698*

NATIONAL AMATEUR BASEBALL FEDERATION (NABF)

http://www.nabf.com/

NATIONAL AMATEUR BASEBALL FEDERATION SCHOLARSHIP FUND

Scholarships are awarded to candidates who are enrolled in an accredited college or university. Applicant must be a bona fide participant in a federation event and be sponsored by an NABF-franchised member association. Self-nominated candidates are not eligible for this scholarship award.

Award: Scholarship for use in freshman, sophomore, junior, or senior years; not renewable. *Number:* varies. *Amount:* varies.

Eligibility Requirements: Applicant must be enrolled or expecting to enroll full-time at a two-year or four-year or technical institution or university and must have an interest in athletics/sports. Available to U.S. citizens.

Application Requirements: Application, essay, references, transcript, letter of acceptance. *Deadline:* November 15.

Contact: Awards Committee Chairman
National Amateur Baseball Federation (NABF)
PO Box 705
Bowie, MD 20718

NATIONAL ASSOCIATION FOR CAMPUS ACTIVITIES

http://www.naca.org/

LORI RHETT MEMORIAL SCHOLARSHIP
• *See page 592*

MULTICULTURAL SCHOLARSHIP PROGRAM
• *See page 672*

NATIONAL ASSOCIATION FOR CAMPUS ACTIVITIES EAST COAST UNDERGRADUATE SCHOLARSHIP FOR STUDENT LEADERS
• *See page 592*

NATIONAL ASSOCIATION FOR CAMPUS ACTIVITIES REGIONAL COUNCIL STUDENT LEADER SCHOLARSHIPS

Scholarships will be given to undergraduate students in good standing at the time of the application and during the academic term in which the scholarship is awarded. Must demonstrate significant leadership skill and ability while holding a significant leadership position on campus. The scholarship value and the number of awards granted varies.

Award: Scholarship for use in freshman, sophomore, junior, or senior years; not renewable. *Number:* up to 7. *Amount:* $250–$300.

Eligibility Requirements: Applicant must be enrolled or expecting to enroll full- or part-time at a four-year institution or university and must have an interest in leadership. Available to U.S. and non-U.S. citizens.

Application Requirements: Application, essay, resume, references, transcript. *Deadline:* May 1.

Contact: Dionne Ellison, Administrative Assistant
National Association for Campus Activities
13 Harbison Way
Columbia, SC 29212-3401
Phone: 803-732-6222 Ext. 131
Fax: 803-749-1047
E-mail: dionnee@naca.org

NATIONAL ASSOCIATION FOR CAMPUS ACTIVITIES SOUTHEAST REGION STUDENT LEADERSHIP SCHOLARSHIP
• *See page 592*

NATIONAL ASSOCIATION FOR CAMPUS ACTIVITIES WISCONSIN REGION STUDENT LEADERSHIP SCHOLARSHIP
• *See page 592*

SCHOLARSHIPS FOR STUDENT LEADERS
• *See page 593*

TESS CALDARELLI MEMORIAL SCHOLARSHIP
• *See page 766*

ZAGUNIS STUDENT LEADERS SCHOLARSHIP
• *See page 766*

NATIONAL ASSOCIATION FOR THE SELF-EMPLOYED

http://www.nase.org/

NASE FUTURE ENTREPRENEUR SCHOLARSHIP
• *See page 550*

NASE SCHOLARSHIPS
• *See page 551*

NATIONAL ASSOCIATION OF SECONDARY SCHOOL PRINCIPALS

http://www.nhs.us/

PRINCIPAL'S LEADERSHIP AWARD

One-time award available only to high school seniors for use at an accredited two- or four-year college or university. Selection based on leadership and school or community involvement. Contact school counselor or principal. Citizens of countries other than the U.S. may only apply if attending a United States overseas institution. Minimum 3.0 GPA. Application fee: $6.

Award: Scholarship for use in freshman year; not renewable. *Number:* 100. *Amount:* $1000–$12,000.

Eligibility Requirements: Applicant must be high school student; planning to enroll or expecting to enroll full-time at a two-year or four-year institution or university and must have an interest in leadership. Applicant must have 3.0 GPA or higher. Available to U.S. and non-U.S. citizens.

Application Requirements: Application, essay, references, test scores, transcript. *Fee:* $6. *Deadline:* December 5.

Contact: Wanda Carroll, Program Manager
National Association of Secondary School Principals
1904 Association Drive
Reston, VA 20191-1537
Phone: 703-860-0200
E-mail: carrollw@principals.org

NATIONAL FEDERATION OF STATE POETRY SOCIETIES (NFSPS)

http://www.nfsps.com/

NATIONAL FEDERATION OF STATE POETRY SOCIETIES SCHOLARSHIP AWARDS-COLLEGE/ UNIVERSITY LEVEL POETRY COMPETITION

Must submit application and ten original poems, forty-line per-poem limit. Manuscript must be titled. For more information, visit the web site.

Award: Scholarship for use in freshman, sophomore, junior, or senior years; not renewable. *Number:* 2. *Amount:* $500.

Eligibility Requirements: Applicant must be enrolled or expecting to enroll full-time at a two-year or four-year institution or university and must have an interest in writing. Available to U.S. citizens.

Application Requirements: Application, applicant must enter a contest, must be notarized. *Deadline:* February 1.

Contact: Colwell Snell, Chairman
National Federation of State Poetry Societies (NFSPS)
3444 South Dover Terrace, PO Box 520698
Salt Lake City, UT 84152-0698
Phone: 801-484-3113
E-mail: sbsenior@juno.com

NATIONAL ORDER OF OMEGA

http://www.orderofomega.org/

FOUNDERS SCHOLARSHIP
• *See page 553*

NATIONAL SOCIETY OF COLLEGIATE SCHOLARS (NSCS)

http://www.nscs.org/

NSCS EXEMPLARY SCHOLAR AWARD
• *See page 553*

NATIONAL SOCIETY OF HIGH SCHOOL SCHOLARS

http://www.nshss.org/

CLAES NOBEL ACADEMIC SCHOLARSHIPS FOR NSHSS MEMBERS
• *See page 554*

NATIONAL SOCIETY OF THE SONS OF THE AMERICAN REVOLUTION

http://www.sar.org/

JOSEPH S. RUMBAUGH HISTORICAL ORATION CONTEST

Prize ranging from $1000 to $3000 is awarded to a sophomore, junior, or senior. The oration must be original and not less than five minutes or more than six minutes in length.

Award: Prize for use in sophomore, junior, or senior years; not renewable. *Number:* 1–3. *Amount:* $1000–$3000.

Eligibility Requirements: Applicant must be enrolled or expecting to enroll full-time at a two-year or four-year or technical institution or university and must have an interest in public speaking. Available to U.S. and non-U.S. citizens.

Application Requirements: Application, applicant must enter a contest. *Deadline:* June 15.

Contact: Lawrence Mckinley, National Chairman
National Society of the Sons of the American Revolution
12158 Holly Knoll Circle
Great Fall, VA 22066
E-mail: dustoff@bellatlantic.net

NEBRASKA SPORTS COUNCIL/THE GALLUP ORGANIZATION

http://www.cornhuskerstategames.com/

NEBRASKA SPORTS COUNCIL/GALLUP ORGANIZATION CORNHUSKER STATE GAMES SCHOLARSHIP PROGRAM
• *See page 767*

NETAID FOUNDATION/MERCY CORPS

http://www.globalactionawards.org/

GLOBAL ACTION AWARDS
• *See page 593*

NEXTGEN NETWORK INC.

http://www.nextgennetwork.com/

DONNA JAMISON LAGO MEMORIAL SCHOLARSHIP
• *See page 674*

NIMROD INTERNATIONAL JOURNAL

http://www.utulsa.edu/nimrod

THE KATHERINE ANNE PORTER PRIZE FOR FICTION

The Katherine Ann Porter Prize is given for a single extraordinary short story of less than 7,500 words.

Award: Prize for use in freshman, sophomore, junior, senior, or postgraduate years; not renewable. *Number:* 2. *Amount:* $1000–$2000.

Eligibility Requirements: Applicant must be enrolled or expecting to enroll full- or part-time at a two-year or four-year or technical institution or university and must have an interest in writing. Available to U.S. citizens.

Application Requirements: Application, applicant must enter a contest, essay, short story. *Fee:* $20. *Deadline:* April 30.

Contact: Ellis O'Neal, Managing Editor
Nimrod International Journal
The University of Tulsa, 800 South Tucker Drive
Tulsa, OK 74112
Phone: 918-631-3080
Fax: 918-631-3033
E-mail: nimrod@utulsa.edu

THE PABLO NERUDA PRIZE FOR POETRY

The Pablo Neruda Prize is given for an extraordinary single long poem or group of poems.

Award: Prize for use in freshman, sophomore, junior, senior, graduate, or postgraduate years; not renewable. *Number:* 2. *Amount:* $1000–$2000.

Eligibility Requirements: Applicant must be enrolled or expecting to enroll full- or part-time at a two-year or four-year or technical institution or university and must have an interest in writing. Available to U.S. citizens.

Application Requirements: Application, applicant must enter a contest, essay, single long poem or group of poems. *Fee:* $20. *Deadline:* April 30.

Contact: Ellis O'Neal, Managing Editor
Nimrod International Journal
The University of Tulsa, 800 South Tucker Drive
Tulsa, OK 74104
Phone: 918-631-3080
Fax: 918-631-3033
E-mail: nimrod@utulsa.edu

OPTIMIST INTERNATIONAL FOUNDATION

http://www.optimist.org/

OPTIMIST INTERNATIONAL ESSAY CONTEST

Essay contest for youth under the age of 19 who have not graduated high school or its equivalent. US students attending school on a military installation outside the United States are eligible to enter in their last US home of record. Club winners advance to the District contest to compete for a college scholarship. District winners are entered into the International essay contest where one first place winner is awarded a plaque and recognition in "The Optimist" magazine.

Award: Scholarship for use in freshman, sophomore, junior, or senior years; not renewable. *Number:* 40–49. *Amount:* up to $2500.

Eligibility Requirements: Applicant must be age 19 or under; enrolled or expecting to enroll full- or part-time at a two-year or four-year or technical institution or university and must have an interest in writing. Available to U.S. and Canadian citizens.

Application Requirements: Application, applicant must enter a contest, essay, self-addressed stamped envelope, birth certificate. *Deadline:* varies.

Contact: Danielle Baugher, Director of International Programs
Optimist International Foundation
4494 Lindell Boulevard
St. Louis, MO 63108
Phone: 800-500-8130
Fax: 314-371-6006
E-mail: programs@optimist.org

OPTIMIST INTERNATIONAL ORATORICAL CONTEST

Contest for youth to gain experience in public speaking and to provide them with the opportunity to compete for college scholarships. The contest is open to youth under the age of 18 as of December 31 of the current school year, who have not yet graduated from high school or the equivalent.Students must first compete at the Club level. Club winners are then entered into the Zone/Regional contest and those winners compete in the District contest. District winners are awarded scholarships.

Award: Scholarship for use in freshman, sophomore, junior, or senior years; not renewable. *Number:* 90–115. *Amount:* $1000–$2500.

Eligibility Requirements: Applicant must be age 18 or under; enrolled or expecting to enroll full- or part-time at a two-year or four-year or technical institution or university and must have an interest in public speaking. Available to U.S. and Canadian citizens.

Application Requirements: Application, applicant must enter a contest, self-addressed stamped envelope, birth certificate, speech. *Deadline:* varies.

Contact: Danielle Baugher, Director of International Programs
Optimist International Foundation
4494 Lindell Boulevard
St. Louis, MO 63108
Phone: 800-500-8130
Fax: 314-371-6006
E-mail: programs@optimist.org

OREGON COMMUNITY FOUNDATION

http://www.oregoncf.org/

DOROTHY S. CAMPBELL MEMORIAL SCHOLARSHIP FUND

Scholarship for female graduates of Oregon high schools with a strong and continuing interest in the game of golf. For use in the pursuit of a postsecondary education at a four-year college or university in Oregon.

Award: Scholarship for use in freshman, sophomore, junior, or senior years; renewable. *Number:* 9. *Amount:* $1000.

Eligibility Requirements: Applicant must be enrolled or expecting to enroll full-time at a four-year institution or university; female and must have an interest in golf. Available to U.S. citizens.

Application Requirements: Application, references. *Deadline:* March 1.

Contact: Dianne Causey, Program Associate for Scholarships and Grants
Oregon Community Foundation
1221 Yamhill, SW, Suite 100
Portland, OR 97205-2108
Phone: 503-227-6846 Ext. 1418
E-mail: dcausey@oregoncf.org

OREGON STUDENT ASSISTANCE COMMISSION

http://www.GetCollegeFunds.org/

DOROTHY CAMPBELL MEMORIAL SCHOLARSHIP

• *See page 779*

OUR WORLD UNDERWATER SCHOLARSHIP SOCIETY

http://www.owuscholarship.org/

OUR WORLD UNDERWATER SCHOLARSHIPS

Annual award for individual planning to pursue a career in a water-related discipline through practical exposure to various fields and leaders of underwater endeavors. Scuba experience required. Must be at least 21 but not yet 26. Scholarship value is $20,000 for the North American Rolex Scholar, open to North American citizens only. The European Rolex Scholarship is open to European citizens and the Australasian Rolex Scholarship is open to citizens of the Australasian region.

Award: Scholarship for use in freshman, sophomore, junior, or senior years; not renewable. *Number:* 3. *Amount:* $20,000.

Eligibility Requirements: Applicant must be age 21-26; enrolled or expecting to enroll full- or part-time at a two-year or four-year or technical institution or university and must have an interest in scuba diving. Available to U.S. and non-U.S. citizens.

Application Requirements: Application, driver's license, essay, interview, resume, references, transcript, scuba diver certification. *Fee:* $25. *Deadline:* December 31.

Contact: Roberta Flanders, Scholarship Application Coordinator
Our World Underwater Scholarship Society
PO Box 4428
Chicago, IL 60680-4428
Phone: 800-969-6690
Fax: 630-969-6690
E-mail: info@owuscholarship.org

PARENTS, FAMILIES, AND FRIENDS OF LESBIANS AND GAYS-ATLANTA

http://www.pflagatl.org/

PFLAG SCHOLARSHIP AWARDS PROGRAM

• *See page 782*

PENGUIN GROUP

http://www.us.penguingroup.com/static/pages/services-academic/essayhome.html

SIGNET CLASSIC SCHOLARSHIP ESSAY CONTEST

Open to 11th and 12th grade full-time matriculated students who are attending high schools located in the fifty United States and the District of Columbia, or home-schooled students between the ages of 16–18 who are residents of the fifty United States and the District of Columbia. Students should submit four copies of a two- to three-page double-spaced essay answering one of three possible questions on a designated novel. Entries must be submitted by a high school English teacher.

Award: Scholarship for use in freshman year; not renewable. *Number:* 5. *Amount:* $1000.

Eligibility Requirements: Applicant must be high school student; planning to enroll or expecting to enroll full-time at a four-year institution or university and must have an interest in writing. Available to U.S. citizens.

Application Requirements: Applicant must enter a contest, essay, references. *Deadline:* April 15.

Contact: Kym Giacoppe, Academic Marketing Assistant
Penguin Group
375 Hudson Street
New York, NY 10014
Phone: 212-366-2377
E-mail: academic@penguin.com

PFUND FOUNDATION

http://www.pfundonline.org/

PFUND FOUNDATION SCHOLARSHIP PROGRAM

• *See page 783*

THE PHILLIPS FOUNDATION

http://www.thephillipsfoundation.org/

RONALD REAGAN COLLEGE LEADERS SCHOLARSHIP PROGRAM

The program offers renewable scholarships to college juniors and seniors who demonstrate leadership on behalf of freedom, American values, and constitutional principles. Winners will receive a scholarship for their junior year and may apply for renewal before their senior year.

Award: Scholarship for use in sophomore or junior years; not renewable. *Number:* up to 100. *Amount:* $1000–$10,000.

Eligibility Requirements: Applicant must be enrolled or expecting to enroll full-time at a four-year institution or university and must have an interest in leadership. Available to U.S. citizens.

Application Requirements: Application, essay, resume, references, proof of full-time enrollment in good standing. *Deadline:* January 15.

Contact: Jeff Hollingsworth, Assistant Secretary
The Phillips Foundation
One Massachusetts Avenue, NW, Suite 620
Washington, DC 20001
Phone: 202-250-3887
E-mail: jhollingsworth@thephillipsfoundation.org

PHI SIGMA PI NATIONAL HONOR FRATERNITY

http://www.phisigmapi.org/

RICHARD CECIL TODD AND CLAUDA PENNOCK TODD TRIPOD SCHOLARSHIP

• *See page 559*

PIRATE'S ALLEY FAULKNER SOCIETY

http://www.wordsandmusic.org/

WILLIAM FAULKNER-WILLIAM WISDOM CREATIVE WRITING COMPETITION

Prizes for unpublished manuscripts written in English. One prize awarded in each category: $7500, novel; $2500, novella; $2000 novel-in-progress; $1500, short story; $1000, essay; $750, poem; $750 high school short story-student author, $250 sponsoring teacher. Manuscripts will not be returned and must be mailed, not emailed or faxed, accompanied by entry fee ranging from $10 for high school category to $35 for novel.

Award: Prize for use in freshman, sophomore, junior, senior, or graduate years; not renewable. *Number:* 7. *Amount:* $250–$7500.

Eligibility Requirements: Applicant must be enrolled or expecting to enroll full- or part-time at a two-year or four-year institution or university and must have an interest in English language or writing. Available to U.S. and non-U.S. citizens.

Application Requirements: Application, applicant must enter a contest. *Deadline:* April 1.

Contact: Rosemary P. James, Director
Pirate's Alley Faulkner Society
624 PiratesAlley'
New Orleans, LA 70116
Phone: 504-586-1609
E-mail: faulkhouse@aol.com

PONY OF THE AMERICAS CLUB

http://www.poac.org/

PONY OF THE AMERICAS SCHOLARSHIP

• *See page 559*

PRIDE FOUNDATION

http://www.PrideFoundation.org/

PRIDE FOUNDATION SCHOLARSHIP PROGRAM

• *See page 783*

PRO BOWLERS ASSOCIATION

http://www.pba.com/

BILLY WELU BOWLING SCHOLARSHIP

Scholarship awarded annually, recognizing exemplary qualities in male and female college students who compete in the sport of bowling. Winner will receive $1000. Candidates must be amateur bowlers who are currently in college (preceding the application deadline) and maintain at least a 2.5 GPA or equivalent.

Award: Scholarship for use in freshman, sophomore, junior, or senior years; not renewable. *Number:* 1. *Amount:* $1000.

Eligibility Requirements: Applicant must be enrolled or expecting to enroll full-time at a two-year or four-year institution or university and must have an interest in bowling. Applicant must have 2.5 GPA or higher. Available to U.S. citizens.

Application Requirements: Application, essay, transcript. *Deadline:* May 31.

Contact: Karen Day, Controller
Pro Bowlers Association
719 Second Avenue, Suite 701
Seattle, WA 98104
Phone: 206-332-9688
Fax: 206-332-9722
E-mail: karen.day@pba.com

PROFESSIONAL BOWLERS ASSOCIATION

http://www.pba.com/

PROFESSIONAL BOWLERS ASSOCIATION BILLY WELU MEMORIAL SCHOLARSHIP

• *See page 559*

RECORDING FOR THE BLIND & DYSLEXIC

http://www.rfbd.org/

MARION HUBER LEARNING THROUGH LISTENING AWARDS

• *See page 560*

MARY P. OENSLAGER SCHOLASTIC ACHIEVEMENT AWARDS

• *See page 560*

THE RESERVE OFFICERS ASSOCIATION

http://www.roa.org/

HENRY J. REILLY MEMORIAL SCHOLARSHIP-HIGH SCHOOL SENIORS AND FIRST YEAR FRESHMEN

• *See page 561*

RON BROWN SCHOLAR FUND

http://www.ronbrown.org/

RON BROWN SCHOLAR PROGRAM

• *See page 678*

ROTARY FOUNDATION OF ROTARY INTERNATIONAL

http://www.rotary.org/

ROTARY FOUNDATION AMBASSADORIAL SCHOLARSHIPS

One-time award defrays costs associated with travel, tuition, and room and board for one academic year of study in a foreign country. Must have completed at least 2 years of university course work and be proficient in language of host country. Apply through local Rotary club; appearances before clubs required during award period. Deadlines vary between March and August.

Award: Scholarship for use in junior, senior, graduate, or postgraduate years; not renewable. *Number:* 400–500. *Amount:* $27,000.

Eligibility Requirements: Applicant must be enrolled or expecting to enroll full-time at a four-year or technical institution or university and must have an interest in foreign language or international exchange. Available to U.S. and non-U.S. citizens.

Application Requirements: Application, autobiography, essay, interview, resume, references, test scores, transcript. *Deadline:* varies.

Contact: The Rotary Foundation Contact Center
Phone: 866-976-8279
E-mail: contact.center@rotary.org

ST. CLAIRE REGIONAL MEDICAL CENTER

http://www.st-claire.org/

SR. MARY JEANNETTE WESS, S.N.D. SCHOLARSHIP
• *See page 595*

SAN DIEGO FOUNDATION

http://www.sdfoundation.org/

JOSEPH C. LARSON ENTREPRENEURIAL SCHOLARSHIP
• *See page 786*

JULIE ALLEN WORLD CLASSROOM SCHOLARSHIP
• *See page 786*

LESLIE JANE HAHN MEMORIAL SCHOLARSHIP
• *See page 596*

RANDY WILLIAMS SCHOLARSHIP
• *See page 787*

USA FREESTYLE MARTIAL ARTS SCHOLARSHIP
• *See page 596*

SAN FRANCISCO FOUNDATION

http://www.sff.org/

JAMES DUVAL PHELAN LITERARY AWARD

Award presented annually to an author of an unpublished work in progress: fiction, nonfiction, prose, poetry, or drama. Must have been born in California, but need not be a current resident. Must be between 20 to 35 years of age. Submit manuscript.

Award: Prize for use in freshman, sophomore, junior, senior, graduate, or postgraduate years; not renewable. *Number:* 3. *Amount:* $2000–$3000.

Eligibility Requirements: Applicant must be age 20-35; enrolled or expecting to enroll full- or part-time at a two-year or four-year institution or university and must have an interest in writing. Available to U.S. citizens.

Application Requirements: Application, applicant must enter a contest, self-addressed stamped envelope, manuscript. *Deadline:* March 31.

Contact: Awards Coordinator
San Francisco Foundation
225 Bush Street, Suite 500
San Francisco, CA 94104-4224
Phone: 415-733-8500
E-mail: rec@sff.org

JOSEPH HENRY JACKSON LITERARY AWARD
• *See page 787*

SCHOLARSHIP WORKSHOP LLC

http://www.scholarshipworkshop.com/

LEADING THE FUTURE II SCHOLARSHIP

Scholarship designed to elevate students' consciousness about their future and their role in helping others once they receive a college degree and become established in a community. It is open to U.S. residents who are high school seniors or college undergraduates at any level. Students must visit http://www.scholarshipworkshop.com to get additional information and to download an application.

Award: Scholarship for use in freshman, sophomore, junior, or senior years; not renewable. *Number:* 1–3. *Amount:* $100–$300.

Eligibility Requirements: Applicant must be enrolled or expecting to enroll full-time at a four-year institution or university and must have an interest in leadership. Available to U.S. citizens.

Application Requirements: Application, essay. *Deadline:* March 1.

Contact: Scholarship Coordinator
Scholarship Workshop LLC
PO Box 176
Centreville, VA 20122
Phone: 703-579-4245
E-mail: scholars@scholarshipworkshop.com

RAGINS/BRASWELL NATIONAL SCHOLARSHIP

Scholarship available to high school seniors, undergraduate, and graduate students who attend The Scholarship Workshop presentation or an online class given by Marianne Ragins. Award is based on application, essay, leadership, extracurricular activities, achievements, and community responsibility. See web site http://www.scholarshipworkshop.com. Scholarship amounts vary.

Award: Scholarship for use in freshman, sophomore, junior, or senior years; not renewable. *Number:* 1–3. *Amount:* $100–$500.

Eligibility Requirements: Applicant must be enrolled or expecting to enroll full-time at a four-year institution or university and must have an interest in leadership. Available to U.S. citizens.

Application Requirements: Application, essay. *Deadline:* April 30.

Contact: Scholarship Coordinator
Scholarship Workshop LLC
PO Box 176
Centreville, VA 20122
Phone: 703-579-4245
E-mail: scholars@scholarshipworkshop.com

SEVENTEEN MAGAZINE

http://www.seventeen.com/

SEVENTEEN MAGAZINE FICTION CONTEST

Enter by submitting an original short story of no longer than 2000 words. Submissions must be typed, double-spaced, on one side of each sheet of paper, and must not have been previously published in any form, with the exception of school publications. All entries must include the full name, age, home and e-mail addresses, telephone number, date of birth, and signature in the top right hand corner of each page of every story you send. Multiple entries are permitted.

Award: Prize for use in freshman, sophomore, junior, senior, graduate, or postgraduate years; not renewable. *Number:* 8. *Amount:* $100–$2500.

Eligibility Requirements: Applicant must be age 13-21; enrolled or expecting to enroll full- or part-time at a two-year or four-year or technical institution or university and must have an interest in writing. Available to U.S. citizens.

Application Requirements: Applicant must enter a contest, essay, photo, copy of story. *Deadline:* December 31.

Contact: Fiction Contest Coordinator
Seventeen Magazine
300 West 57th Street, 17th Floor
New York, NY 10019
Phone: 917-934-6500
Fax: 917-934-6574

SICKLE CELL DISEASE ASSOCIATION OF AMERICA/CONNECTICUT CHAPTER INC.

http://www.sicklecellct.org/

SYBIL FONG SAM SCHOLARSHIP ESSAY CONTEST
• *See page 788*

SISTER KENNY REHABILITATION INSTITUTE

http://www.allina.com/ahs/ski.nsf

INTERNATIONAL ART SHOW FOR ARTISTS WITH DISABILITIES
• *See page 613*

SKILLSUSA

http://www.skillsusa.org/

INTERNATIONAL SKILLSUSA DEGREE SCHOLARSHIP

Scholarship for students who successfully receive their degree. To qualify, all candidates must submit a letter of application for the scholarship within 45 days of receipt of the degree. The scholarship candidate must include with the application copies of receipts for lodging, meals, travel, and preparation of the presentation.

Award: Scholarship for use in senior year; not renewable. *Number:* 1. *Amount:* up to $1000.

Eligibility Requirements: Applicant must be enrolled or expecting to enroll full-time at a four-year institution or university and must have an interest in leadership. Available to U.S. citizens.

Application Requirements: Application, references, copies of receipts for lodging, meals, travel, and preparation of the presentation. *Deadline:* May 1.

Contact: Karen Perrino, Associate Director
SkillsUSA
PO Box 3000
Leesburg, VA 20177-0300
Phone: 703-737-0610
Fax: 703-777-8999
E-mail: kperrino@skillsusa.org

NTHS SKILLSUSA SCHOLARSHIP

NTHS will award two $1000 scholarships to SkillsUSA members at the SkillsUSA national leadership conference. One scholarship will be awarded to a high school member, and one scholarship will be awarded to a college/postsecondary member. Students must be active, dues-paying members of both SkillsUSA and NTHS.

Award: Scholarship for use in freshman, sophomore, junior, or senior years; not renewable. *Number:* 2. *Amount:* $1000.

Eligibility Requirements: Applicant must be enrolled or expecting to enroll full-time at a two-year or four-year or technical institution or university and must have an interest in leadership. Available to U.S. citizens.

Application Requirements: Application, references. *Deadline:* March 1.

Contact: Karen Perrino, Associate Director
SkillsUSA
PO Box 3000
Leesburg, VA 20177-0300
Phone: 703-737-0610
Fax: 703-777-8999
E-mail: kperrino@skillsusa.org

SKILLSUSA ALUMNI AND FRIENDS MERIT SCHOLARSHIP
• *See page 596*

SOCIETY OF DAUGHTERS OF THE UNITED STATES ARMY

SOCIETY OF DAUGHTERS OF THE UNITED STATES ARMY SCHOLARSHIPS
• *See page 623*

SOUTH DAKOTA BOARD OF REGENTS

http://www.sdbor.edu/

SOUTH DAKOTA BOARD OF REGENTS MARLIN R. SCARBOROUGH MEMORIAL SCHOLARSHIP
• *See page 789*

SOUTHERN TEXAS PGA

http://www.stpga.com/

DICK FORESTER COLLEGE SCHOLARSHIP

One-time award of $4000 to promote the attainment of higher education goals of youth who have demonstrated a high level of achievement during high school or college. Must demonstrate financial need, and have shown an interest in the game of golf.

Award: Scholarship for use in freshman, sophomore, junior, senior, graduate, or postgraduate years; not renewable. *Number:* 1. *Amount:* $4000.

Eligibility Requirements: Applicant must be enrolled or expecting to enroll full-time at a two-year or four-year institution or university and must have an interest in golf. Available to U.S. citizens.

Application Requirements: Application, financial need analysis, test scores, transcript. *Deadline:* April 4.

Contact: Steve Termeer, Scholarship Committee Chairperson
Southern Texas PGA
21604 Cypresswood Drive
Spring, TX 77373
Phone: 832-442-2404
Fax: 832-442-2403
E-mail: stexas@pgahq.com

STONEWALL COMMUNITY FOUNDATION

http://www.stonewallfoundation.org/

GENE AND JOHN ATHLETIC SCHOLARSHIP

Scholarship of $2500 to $5000 for LGBT student athletes looking to continue their education while pursuing athletics.

Award: Scholarship for use in freshman, sophomore, junior, senior, graduate, or postgraduate years; not renewable. *Number:* 1–3. *Amount:* $2500–$5000.

Eligibility Requirements: Applicant must be enrolled or expecting to enroll full-time at a two-year or four-year or technical institution or university and must have an interest in athletics/sports or LGBT issues. Available to U.S. and Canadian citizens.

Application Requirements: Application, essay, references. *Deadline:* July 31.

Contact: Roz Lee, Program Director
Stonewall Community Foundation
119 West 24th Street, Seventh Floor
New York, NY 10011
Phone: 212-367-1155
Fax: 212-367-1157
E-mail: stonewall@stonewallfoundation.org

HARRY BARTEL MEMORIAL SCHOLARSHIP FUND
• *See page 597*

TRAUB-DICKER RAINBOW SCHOLARSHIP

Non-renewable scholarships available to lesbian-identified students. Must be graduating high school seniors planning to attend a recognized college, or already matriculated college students in any year of study, including graduate school.

Award: Scholarship for use in freshman, sophomore, junior, senior, or graduate years; not renewable. *Number:* 3. *Amount:* $3000.

Eligibility Requirements: Applicant must be enrolled or expecting to enroll full- or part-time at a four-year institution or university; female and must have an interest in LGBT issues. Available to U.S. citizens.

Application Requirements: Application, essay, references. *Deadline:* April 15.

Contact: Roz Lee, Program Director
Stonewall Community Foundation
119 West 24th Street, Seventh Floor
New York, NY 10011
Phone: 212-367-1155
Fax: 212-367-1157
E-mail: stonewall@stonewallfoundation.org

SUPERCOLLEGE.COM

http://www.supercollege.com/

$1,500 SUPERCOLLEGE.COM SCHOLARSHIP

An award for outstanding high school, college or graduate students. Based on academic and extracurricular achievement, leadership, and integrity. May study any major and attend or plan to attend any accredited college or university in the United States. No paper applications accepted. Applications are only available online at http://www.super-college.com/scholarship/.

Award: Scholarship for use in freshman, sophomore, junior, senior, or graduate years; not renewable. *Number:* 1–5. *Amount:* $500–$1500.

Eligibility Requirements: Applicant must be enrolled or expecting to enroll full-time at a two-year or four-year or technical institution or university and must have an interest in leadership. Available to U.S. citizens.

Application Requirements: Application. *Deadline:* continuous.

Contact: Scholarship Coordinator
SuperCollege.com
3286 Oak Court
Belmont, CA 94002
Phone: 650-618-2221
E-mail: supercollege@supercollege.com

SWISS BENEVOLENT SOCIETY OF NEW YORK

http://www.sbsny.org/

MEDICUS STUDENT EXCHANGE
• *See page 681*

TERRY FOUNDATION

http://www.terryfoundation.org/

TERRY FOUNDATION SCHOLARSHIP
• *See page 793*

TERRY FOX HUMANITARIAN AWARD PROGRAM

http://www.terryfox.org/

TERRY FOX HUMANITARIAN AWARD
• *See page 597*

TEXAS 4-H YOUTH DEVELOPMENT FOUNDATION

http://www.texas4-h.tamu.edu/

TEXAS 4-H OPPORTUNITY SCHOLARSHIP
• *See page 793*

TEXAS CHRISTIAN UNIVERSITY NEELY ENTREPRENEURSHIP CENTER

http://www.nec.tcu.edu/

TCU TEXAS YOUTH ENTREPRENEUR OF THE YEAR AWARDS
• *See page 794*

TEXAS TENNIS FOUNDATION

http://www.texastennisfoundation.com/

TEXAS TENNIS FOUNDATION SCHOLARSHIPS AND ENDOWMENTS
• *See page 794*

TKE EDUCATIONAL FOUNDATION

http://www.tke.org/

ALL-TKE ACADEMIC TEAM RECOGNITION AND JOHN A. COURSON TOP SCHOLAR AWARD
• *See page 566*

CANADIAN TKE SCHOLARSHIP
• *See page 566*

CHARLES WALGREEN JR. SCHOLARSHIP
• *See page 566*

DONALD A. AND JOHN R. FISHER MEMORIAL SCHOLARSHIP
• *See page 566*

DWAYNE R. WOERPEL MEMORIAL LEADERSHIP AWARD
• *See page 566*

ELMER AND DORIS SCHMITZ SR. MEMORIAL SCHOLARSHIP
• *See page 567*

EUGENE C. BEACH MEMORIAL SCHOLARSHIP
• *See page 567*

J. RUSSEL SALSBURY MEMORIAL SCHOLARSHIP
• *See page 567*

MICHAEL J. MORIN MEMORIAL SCHOLARSHIP
• *See page 567*

MILES GRAY MEMORIAL SCHOLARSHIP
• *See page 567*

RONALD REAGAN LEADERSHIP AWARD
• *See page 567*

T.J. SCHMITZ SCHOLARSHIP
• *See page 568*

WALLACE MCCAULEY MEMORIAL SCHOLARSHIP
• *See page 568*

WILLIAM V. MUSE SCHOLARSHIP
• *See page 568*

WILLIAM WILSON MEMORIAL SCHOLARSHIP
• *See page 568*

TOSHIBA/NSTA

http://www.exploravision.org/

EXPLORAVISION SCIENCE COMPETITION

Competition for students in grades K–12 who enter as small teams by grade level and work on a science project. In each group, first place team members are each awarded a savings bond worth $10,000 at maturity, second place, a $5000 savings bond. Deadline varies.

Award: Prize for use in freshman year; not renewable. *Number:* varies. *Amount:* $5000–$10,000.

Eligibility Requirements: Applicant must be enrolled or expecting to enroll full- or part-time at a four-year institution or university and must have an interest in science. Available to U.S. citizens.

Application Requirements: Application, applicant must enter a contest. *Deadline:* varies.

Contact: Paloma Olbes, Media Contact
Toshiba/NSTA
c/o Dobbin/Bolgla Associates
156 Fifth Avenue, Fifth Floor
New York, NY 10010
Phone: 212-388-1400
E-mail: polbes@dba-pr.com

TOURO SYNAGOGUE FOUNDATION

http://www.tourosynagogue.org/

AARON AND RITA SLOM SCHOLARSHIP FUND FOR FREEDOM AND DIVERSITY

Scholarship available for high school seniors who plan to enroll in an institute of higher learning for a minimum of 6 credits. Entries should include an interpretative work focusing on the historic "George Washington Letter to the Congregation" in context with the present time. Text of the letter is available on the web site. Submissions may be in the form of an essay, story, poem, film, video, or computer presentation. Applications, guidelines, resource materials are available on web site http://www.touro.

Award: Scholarship for use in freshman year; not renewable. *Number:* 2. *Amount:* $1000.

Eligibility Requirements: Applicant must be high school student; planning to enroll or expecting to enroll full- or part-time at a four-year institution or university and must have an interest in writing. Available to U.S. citizens.

Application Requirements: Application, interpretative work based on historic George Washington letter. *Deadline:* March 30.

Contact: Scholarship Committee
Touro Synagogue Foundation
85 Touro Street
Newport, RI 02840
Phone: 401-847-4794 Ext. 31
Fax: 401-845-6790

UNITED NATIONS ASSOCIATION OF THE UNITED STATES OF AMERICA

http://www.unausa.org/

NATIONAL HIGH SCHOOL ESSAY CONTEST

Essay contest is open to all US students in grades 9–12. Essays should be no longer than 1500 words, typed and double-spaced.

Award: Prize for use in freshman year; not renewable. *Number:* 3. *Amount:* $750–$3000.

Eligibility Requirements: Applicant must be high school student; planning to enroll or expecting to enroll full- or part-time at a four-year institution or university and must have an interest in writing. Available to U.S. citizens.

Application Requirements: Application, applicant must enter a contest, essay. *Deadline:* January 3.

Contact: Scholarship Committee
United Nations Association of the United States of America
801 Second Avenue
New York, NY 10017
Phone: 212-907-1300
Fax: 212-682-9185
E-mail: unahq@unausa.org

UNITED NEGRO COLLEGE FUND

http://www.uncf.org/

KANAWHA COUNTY, WV PEER LEADERS SCHOLARSHIP

• See page 690

UNITED STATES JUNIOR CHAMBER OF COMMERCE

http://www.usjaycees.org/

JAYCEE WAR MEMORIAL FUND SCHOLARSHIP

$1000 scholarship for students who are U.S. citizens, possess academic potential and leadership qualities, and show financial need. Minimum 2.5 GPA required. To receive an application, send $10 application fee and stamped, self-addressed envelope by February 1.

Award: Scholarship for use in freshman, sophomore, junior, or senior years; not renewable. *Number:* 10. *Amount:* $1000.

Eligibility Requirements: Applicant must be enrolled or expecting to enroll full-time at a two-year or four-year or technical institution or university and must have an interest in leadership. Applicant must have 2.5 GPA or higher. Available to U.S. citizens.

Application Requirements: Application, financial need analysis, self-addressed stamped envelope, transcript. *Fee:* $10. *Deadline:* February 1.

Contact: Karen Fitzgerald, Customer Service and Data Processing
United States Junior Chamber of Commerce
7447 South Lewis Avenue
Tulsa, OK 74102-0007
Phone: 918-584-2481
E-mail: customerservice@usjaycees.org

USA BADMINTON REGION 1

http://www.northeastbadminton.net/

BADMINTON SCHOLARSHIP PROGRAM

Scholarship awarded to a collegiate varsity badminton player exhibiting outstanding achievement, participation, and performance during the badminton playing season. Award is restricted to residents of the northeast region of the United States.

Award: Scholarship for use in freshman, sophomore, junior, or senior years; renewable. *Number:* 1. *Amount:* $1000.

Eligibility Requirements: Applicant must be enrolled or expecting to enroll full-time at a four-year institution or university and must have an interest in athletics/sports. Available to U.S. citizens.

Application Requirements: Application, applicant must enter a contest, references, coaches letter, NCAA team verification. *Deadline:* continuous.

Contact: Eric Miller, Scholarship Program Coordinator
USA Badminton Region 1
125 Prospect Street
Phoenixville, PA 19460
Phone: 610-999-5960
E-mail: eric@usbadminton.net

USA TODAY/MILKPEP—GOT MILK?

http://www.bodybymilk.com/

SAMMY AWARDS (SCHOLAR ATHLETE MILK MUSTACHE OF THE YEAR)

One-time award for senior high school athletes who also achieve in academics, community service, and leadership. Open to legal residents of the 48 contiguous United States and District of Columbia. Residents of Hawaii, Alaska, and Puerto Rico are not eligible. Must submit essay of 75 words or less on how drinking milk has been a part of their life and training regimen. Application only through web site http//www.bodybymilk.com.

Award: Scholarship for use in freshman year; not renewable. *Number:* 25. *Amount:* $7500.

Eligibility Requirements: Applicant must be high school student; planning to enroll or expecting to enroll full-time at a four-year institution or university and must have an interest in athletics/sports. Available to U.S. citizens.

Application Requirements: Application, essay, photo, references, transcript. *Deadline:* March 7.

Contact: Debbie McMahon, Director, Marketing Programs
USA TODAY/MilkPEP—Got Milk?
7950 Jones Branch Drive
McLean, VA 22108
Phone: 703-854-5418
E-mail: dmcmahon@usatoday.com

VETERANS OF FOREIGN WARS OF THE UNITED STATES

http://www.vfw.org/

PATRIOT'S PEN

Nationwide essay contest that gives students in grades 6, 7 and 8 the opportunity to write essays expressing their views on democracy and win

US Savings Bonds. Participants must be permanent U.S. residents; U.S. Citizenship is not required.

Award: Prize for use in freshman, sophomore, junior, senior, graduate, or postgraduate years; not renewable. *Number:* up to 46. *Amount:* $1000–$10,000.

Eligibility Requirements: Applicant must be enrolled or expecting to enroll full- or part-time at a two-year or four-year or technical institution or university and must have an interest in writing. Available to U.S. citizens.

Application Requirements: Application, applicant must enter a contest, essay. *Deadline:* November 1.

Contact: Kris Harmer, Program Coordinator
Veterans of Foreign Wars of the United States
406 West 34th Street, VFW Building
Kansas City, MO 64111
Phone: 816-968-1117
E-mail: kharmer@vfw.org

VOICE OF DEMOCRACY PROGRAM

Student must be sponsored by a local VFW Post. Student submits a three to five minute audio essay on a contest theme (changes each year). Open to high school students (9th to 12th grade). Award available for all levels of postsecondary study in an American institution. Open to permanent U.S. residents only. Competition starts at local level. No entries are to be submitted to the National Headquarters. Visit web site http://www.vfw.org for more information.

Award: Scholarship for use in freshman, sophomore, junior, senior, graduate, or postgraduate years; not renewable. *Number:* 54. *Amount:* $1000–$30,000.

Eligibility Requirements: Applicant must be high school student; age 14-19; planning to enroll or expecting to enroll full- or part-time at a two-year or four-year or technical institution or university and must have an interest in public speaking or writing. Available to U.S. citizens.

Application Requirements: Application, applicant must enter a contest, essay, audio cassette tape or CD of essay. *Deadline:* November 1.

Contact: Kris Harmer, Program Coordinator
Veterans of Foreign Wars of the United States
406 West 34th Street, VFW Building
Kansas City, MO 64111
Phone: 816-968-1117
E-mail: kharmer@vfw.org

VINCENT L. HAWKINSON FOUNDATION FOR PEACE AND JUSTICE

http://www.graceattheu.org/

VINCENT L. HAWKINSON SCHOLARSHIP FOR PEACE AND JUSTICE
• *See page 799*

VSA

http://www.vsarts.org/

VSA PLAYWRIGHT DISCOVERY AWARD

One-time award for students in grades 6 to 12, with and without disabilities. One-act script must explore the experience of living with a disability. One script is selected for production at the John F. Kennedy Center for the Performing Arts. A jury of theater professionals selects the winning script, and award recipients receive monetary awards and a trip to Washington, D.C. to view the production.

Award: Scholarship for use in freshman year; not renewable. *Number:* 1. *Amount:* $2000.

Eligibility Requirements: Applicant must be high school student; age 12-18; planning to enroll or expecting to enroll full- or part-time at a four-year institution or university and must have an interest in theater or writing. Available to U.S. citizens.

Application Requirements: Application, applicant must enter a contest, driver's license, 2 copies of typed script. *Deadline:* April 11.

Contact: Michelle Hoffmann, Performing Arts Manager
VSA
818 Connecticut Avenue, NW, Suite 600
Washington, DC 20006
Phone: 800-933-8721
Fax: 202-429-0868
E-mail: info@vsarts.org

THE WALTER J. TRAVIS SOCIETY

http://www.buff-golf.com/travis.htm

THE WALTER J. TRAVIS MEMORIAL SCHOLARSHIP

This scholarship is awarded to students who are pursuing a career in one of the following professions: golf course architecture, golf course superintendent/turfgrass manager, sports journalism, or professional golf management. Also, any college student who is an outstanding amateur golfer is eligible. Awards based on academic record, extracurricular activities including volunteer service, work experience, and golf-related interests and accomplishments. Award may be used for any educational expenses.

Award: Scholarship for use in freshman, sophomore, junior, senior, or graduate years; not renewable. *Number:* 4–5. *Amount:* $700.

Eligibility Requirements: Applicant must be enrolled or expecting to enroll full-time at a two-year or four-year or technical institution or university and must have an interest in designated field specified by sponsor or golf. Applicant must have 2.5 GPA or higher. Available to U.S. and non-U.S. citizens.

Application Requirements: Application, references, transcript. *Deadline:* June 1.

Contact: Mr. Edward B Homsey, Scholarship Chairman
Phone: 585-663-6120
E-mail: TravisSociety@yahoo.com

WALTER W. NAUMBURG FOUNDATION

http://www.naumburg.org/

INTERNATIONAL VIOLONCELLO COMPETITION

Prizes of $2500 to $7500 awarded to violoncellists between the ages of 17 and 31. Application fee is $125.

Award: Prize for use in freshman, sophomore, junior, senior, graduate, or postgraduate years; not renewable. *Number:* 3. *Amount:* $2500–$7500.

Eligibility Requirements: Applicant must be age 17-31; enrolled or expecting to enroll full- or part-time at a two-year or four-year or technical institution or university and must have an interest in music. Available to U.S. and non-U.S. citizens.

Application Requirements: Application, applicant must enter a contest, references, self-addressed stamped envelope, applicant's audio track (CD) of no less than 30 minutes. *Fee:* $125. *Deadline:* March 1.

Contact: Lucy Mann, Executive Director
Walter W. Naumburg Foundation
120 Claremont Avenue
New York, NY 10027-4698
Phone: 212-362-9877
Fax: 212-362-9877
E-mail: luciamann@aol.com

WILLIAM G. AND MARIE SELBY FOUNDATION

http://www.selbyfdn.org/

SELBY SCHOLAR PROGRAM
• *See page 803*

WILLIAM RANDOLPH HEARST FOUNDATION

http://www.hearstfdn.org/

UNITED STATES SENATE YOUTH PROGRAM

Scholarship for high school juniors and seniors holding elected student offices. Two students selected from each state. Selection process will vary by state. Contact school principal or state department of education for information. Deadlines: early fall of each year for most states, but specific date will vary by state. Program is open to citizens and permanent residents of the United States Department of Defense schools overseas and the District of Columbia (not the territories).

Award: Scholarship for use in freshman, sophomore, junior, or senior years; not renewable. *Number:* 104. *Amount:* $5000.

Eligibility Requirements: Applicant must be high school student; planning to enroll or expecting to enroll full-time at a two-year or four-year institution or university; single and must have an interest in leadership. Applicant must have 3.5 GPA or higher. Available to U.S. citizens.

Application Requirements: Application, essay, interview, application procedures will vary by state. *Deadline:* varies.

Contact: Lynn DeSmet, Deputy Program Director
William Randolph Hearst Foundation
90 New Montgomery Street, Suite 1212
San Francisco, CA 94105-4504
Phone: 415-908-4540
Fax: 415-243-0760
E-mail: ussyp@hearstfdn.org

WOMEN'S BASKETBALL COACHES ASSOCIATION

http://www.wbca.org/

WBCA SCHOLARSHIP AWARD

One-time award for two women's basketball players who have demonstrated outstanding commitment to the sport of women's basketball and to academic excellence. Minimum 3.5 GPA required. Must be nominated by the head coach of women's basketball who is WBCA member.

Award: Scholarship for use in freshman, sophomore, junior, senior, or graduate years; not renewable. *Number:* up to 2. *Amount:* up to $1000.

Eligibility Requirements: Applicant must be enrolled or expecting to enroll full- or part-time at a four-year institution or university; female and must have an interest in athletics/sports. Applicant must have 3.5 GPA or higher. Available to U.S. and non-U.S. citizens.

Application Requirements: Application, references, statistics. *Deadline:* February 15.

Contact: Betty Jaynes, Consultant
Women's Basketball Coaches Association
4646 Lawrenceville Highway
Lilburn, GA 30047-3620
Phone: 770-279-8027 Ext. 102
Fax: 770-279-6290
E-mail: bettyj@wbca.org

WOMEN'S INTERNATIONAL BOWLING CONGRESS

http://www.bowl.com/

ALBERTA E. CROWE STAR OF TOMORROW AWARD

Nonrenewable award for a U.S. or Canadian female college student who competes in the sport of bowling. Must be a current USBC member in good standing, and under 21 years of age. Minimum 2.5 GPA required.

Award: Scholarship for use in sophomore, junior, or senior years; not renewable. *Number:* 1. *Amount:* $6000.

Eligibility Requirements: Applicant must be age 21 or under; enrolled or expecting to enroll full-time at a four-year institution or university; female and must have an interest in bowling. Applicant must have 2.5 GPA or higher. Available to U.S. and non-U.S. citizens.

Application Requirements: Application, essay, references, transcript. *Deadline:* October 1.

Contact: Ed Gocha, Manager
Women's International Bowling Congress
5301 South 76th Street
Greendale, WI 53129-1192
Phone: 800-514-2695 Ext. 3343
Fax: 414-423-3014
E-mail: readsmart@bowl.com

WOMEN'S WESTERN GOLF FOUNDATION

http://www.wwga.org/foundation.htm

WOMEN'S WESTERN GOLF FOUNDATION SCHOLARSHIP

Scholarships for female high school seniors for use at a four-year college or university. Based on academic record, financial need, character, and involvement in golf. Golf skill not a criteria. Must continue to have financial need. Award is $2000 per student per year. Must be 17 to 18 years of age.

Award: Scholarship for use in freshman year; renewable. *Number:* up to 70. *Amount:* $2000.

Eligibility Requirements: Applicant must be high school student; age 17-18; planning to enroll or expecting to enroll full-time at a four-year institution or university; female and must have an interest in golf. Applicant must have 3.0 GPA or higher. Available to U.S. citizens.

Application Requirements: Application, self-addressed stamped envelope. *Deadline:* March 1.

Contact: Richard Willis, Scholarship Chairman
Women's Western Golf Foundation
393 Ramsay Road
Deerfield, IL 60015
Phone: 847-945-0451
E-mail: wwgasfw@aol.com

WRITER'S DIGEST

http://www.writersdigest.com/

WRITER'S DIGEST ANNUAL WRITING COMPETITION

Annual writing competition. Only original, unpublished entries in any of the ten categories accepted. Send self-addressed stamped envelope for guidelines and entry form. Application fee: $15.

Award: Prize for use in freshman, sophomore, junior, senior, or graduate years; not renewable. *Number:* 100. *Amount:* $25–$3000.

Eligibility Requirements: Applicant must be enrolled or expecting to enroll full- or part-time at a two-year or four-year or technical institution or university and must have an interest in writing. Available to U.S. and non-U.S. citizens.

Application Requirements: Application, applicant must enter a contest, self-addressed stamped envelope. *Fee:* $15. *Deadline:* May 1.

Contact: Joan Gay, Customer Service Representative
Writer's Digest
4700 East Galbraith Road
Cincinnati, OH 45236
Phone: 513-531-2690
Fax: 513-531-0798
E-mail: competitions@fwpubs.com

WRITER'S DIGEST POPULAR FICTION AWARDS

Writing contest accepts as many manuscripts as the applicant likes in each of the following categories: romance, mystery/crime fiction, sci-fi/fantasy, thriller/suspense and horror. Manuscripts must not be more than 4,000 words.

Award: Prize for use in freshman, sophomore, junior, senior, graduate, or postgraduate years; not renewable. *Number:* 6. *Amount:* $500–$2500.

Eligibility Requirements: Applicant must be enrolled or expecting to enroll full- or part-time at a two-year or four-year or technical institution or university and must have an interest in writing. Available to U.S. and non-U.S. citizens.

Application Requirements: Application, applicant must enter a contest, self-addressed stamped envelope, manuscript. *Fee:* $12. *Deadline:* November 1.

Contact: Terri Boes, Customer Service Representative
Writer's Digest
4700 East Galbraith Road
Cincinnati, OH 45236
Phone: 513-531-2690 Ext. 1328
Fax: 513-531-0798
E-mail: competitions@fwpubs.com

WRITER'S DIGEST SELF-PUBLISHED BOOK AWARDS

Awards open to self-published books for which the author has paid full cost. Send self-addressed stamped envelope for guidelines and entry form. Application fee: $100.

Award: Prize for use in freshman, sophomore, junior, senior, graduate, or postgraduate years; not renewable. *Number:* 10. *Amount:* $1000–$3000.

Eligibility Requirements: Applicant must be enrolled or expecting to enroll full- or part-time at a two-year or four-year or technical institution or university and must have an interest in writing. Available to U.S. and non-U.S. citizens.

Application Requirements: Application, applicant must enter a contest, self-addressed stamped envelope. *Fee:* $100. *Deadline:* May 1.

Contact: Joan Gay, Customer Service Representative
Writer's Digest
4700 East Galbraith Road
Cincinnati, OH 45236
Phone: 513-531-2690 Ext. 1328
Fax: 513-531-0798
E-mail: competitions@fwpubs.com

YOUNG AMERICAN BOWLING ALLIANCE (YABA)

http://www.bowl.com/

GIFT FOR LIFE SCHOLARSHIP
• *See page 573*

PEPSI-COLA YOUTH BOWLING CHAMPIONSHIPS
• *See page 573*

USBC ALBERTA E. CROWE STAR OF TOMORROW AWARD

Award given to recognize star qualities in a female high school or college student who competes in the sport of bowling. Applicants must be current USBC Youth or USBC members in good standing and currently competing in certified events.

Award: Prize for use in freshman, sophomore, junior, or senior years; not renewable. *Number:* 1. *Amount:* $6000.

Eligibility Requirements: Applicant must be enrolled or expecting to enroll full-time at a two-year or four-year institution or university; female and must have an interest in bowling. Applicant must have 2.5 GPA or higher. Available to U.S. citizens.

Application Requirements: Application, applicant must enter a contest, references, transcript. *Deadline:* October 1.

Contact: Ed Gocha, Scholarship Programs Manager
Young American Bowling Alliance (YABA)
5301 South 76th Street
Greendale, WI 53129-1192
Phone: 800-514-2695
Fax: 414-423-3014
E-mail: smart@bowlinginc.com

USBC ANNUAL ZEB SCHOLARSHIP
• *See page 598*

USBC CHUCK HALL STAR OF TOMORROW SCHOLARSHIP

Scholarship is given to recognize star qualities in a male high school senior or college student who competes in the sport of bowling.

Applicant must be a current USBC Youth or USBC member in good standing and currently compete in certified events.

Award: Scholarship for use in freshman, sophomore, junior, or senior years; renewable. *Number:* 1. *Amount:* $6000.

Eligibility Requirements: Applicant must be enrolled or expecting to enroll full-time at a two-year or four-year institution or university; male and must have an interest in bowling. Applicant must have 2.5 GPA or higher. Available to U.S. citizens.

Application Requirements: Application, references, transcript. *Deadline:* October 1.

Contact: Ed Gocha, Scholarship Programs Manager
Young American Bowling Alliance (YABA)
5301 South 76th Street
Greendale, WI 53129-1192
Phone: 800-514-2695
Fax: 414-423-3014
E-mail: smart@bowlinginc.com

USBC EARL ANTHONY MEMORIAL SCHOLARSHIPS

Scholarship given to recognize male and/or female bowlers for their community involvement and academic achievements, both in high school and college. Candidates must be enrolled in their senior year of high school or presently attending college and be current members of USBC in good standing.

Award: Scholarship for use in freshman, sophomore, junior, or senior years; not renewable. *Number:* 5. *Amount:* $5000.

Eligibility Requirements: Applicant must be enrolled or expecting to enroll full- or part-time at a two-year or four-year institution or university and must have an interest in bowling. Applicant must have 2.5 GPA or higher. Available to U.S. citizens.

Application Requirements: Application, references, transcript. *Deadline:* May 1.

Contact: Ed Gocha, Scholarship Programs Manager
Young American Bowling Alliance (YABA)
5301 South 76th Street
Greendale, WI 53129-1192
Phone: 800-514-2695
Fax: 414-423-3014
E-mail: smart@bowlinginc.com

USBC MALE AND FEMALE YOUTH LEADERS OF THE YEAR SCHOLARSHIP

Scholarship presented to one male and one female Youth Leader who has demonstrated outstanding skills in organizing, administering and promoting youth bowling at the local and/or state level.

Award: Scholarship for use in freshman year; not renewable. *Number:* 2. *Amount:* $1500.

Eligibility Requirements: Applicant must be high school student; planning to enroll or expecting to enroll full- or part-time at a four-year institution or university and must have an interest in bowling. Available to U.S. citizens.

Application Requirements: Application, references, transcript. *Deadline:* November 1.

Contact: Ed Gocha, Scholarship Programs Manager
Young American Bowling Alliance (YABA)
5301 South 76th Street
Greendale, WI 53129-1192
Phone: 800-514-2695
Fax: 414-423-3014
E-mail: smart@bowlinginc.com

YOUNGARTS, NATIONAL FOUNDATION FOR ADVANCEMENT IN THE ARTS

http://www.youngarts.org//

YOUNGARTS, NATIONAL FOUNDATION FOR ADVANCEMENT IN THE ARTS

One-time award for high school seniors 17 to 18 years old who show talent in dance, film and video, jazz, music, photography, theater, visual arts, voice, and/or writing. Must submit portfolio, videotape or audiotape, along with application fee. Must be citizens or permanent residents of the U.S., except for the music/jazz discipline, which accepts international applicants.

Award: Prize for use in freshman year; not renewable. *Number:* up to 15. *Amount:* $100–$10,000.

Eligibility Requirements: Applicant must be high school student; age 17-18; planning to enroll or expecting to enroll full- or part-time at a two-year or four-year or technical institution or university and must have an interest in art, music/singing, photography/photogrammetry/filmmaking, theater, or writing. Available to U.S. citizens.

Application Requirements: Application, applicant must enter a contest, portfolio. *Fee:* $25. *Deadline:* October 1.

Contact: Carla Hill, Programs Department
YoungArts, National Foundation for Advancement in the Arts
777 Brickell Avenue, Suite 370
Miami, FL 33131
Phone: 305-377-1140
E-mail: hillc@youngArts.org

Miscellaneous Criteria

101ST AIRBORNE DIVISION ASSOCIATION

http://www.screamingeagle.org/

101ST AIRBORNE DIVISION ASSOCIATION CHAPPIE HALL SCHOLARSHIP PROGRAM

The major factors to be considered in the evaluation and rating of applicants are eligibility, career objectives, academic record, financial need, and insight gained from the letter and/or essay requesting consideration, and letters of recommendation. Applicant's parents, grandparents, or spouse, living or deceased must have/had regular membership with 101st Airborne Division. Dollar amount and total number of awards varies.

Award: Scholarship for use in freshman, sophomore, junior, or senior years; not renewable. *Number:* 15–25. *Amount:* $1000–$2000.

Eligibility Requirements: Applicant must be enrolled or expecting to enroll full-time at a two-year or four-year or technical institution or university. Available to U.S. and non-U.S. citizens.

Application Requirements: Application, essay, photo, references, test scores, transcript, proof of regular membership in 101st Airborne Division Association. *Deadline:* May 31.

Contact: Sam Bass, Executive Secretary-Treasurer
101st Airborne Division Association
PO Box 929
Fort Campbell, KY 42223-0929
Phone: 931-431-0199 Ext. 35
Fax: 931-431-0195
E-mail: 101exec@comcast.net

ACADEMY OF TELEVISION ARTS AND SCIENCES FOUNDATION

http://www.emmysfoundation.org/

ACADEMY OF TELEVISION ARTS AND SCIENCES COLLEGE TELEVISION AWARDS

A competition for excellence in college student video, digital, and film productions. Rules and guidelines are updated annually in the fall at emmysfoundation.org. Awards of up to $4000. Open to those students who have produced their video while enrolled in a community college, college, or university in the United States.

Award: Prize for use in freshman, sophomore, junior, or senior years; not renewable. *Number:* 25. *Amount:* $500–$4000.

Eligibility Requirements: Applicant must be enrolled or expecting to enroll full- or part-time at a two-year or four-year or technical institution or university. Available to U.S. and non-U.S. citizens.

Application Requirements: Application, online application and video submission. *Fee:* $25. *Deadline:* January 15.

Contact: Debbie Slavkin, Program Manager
Academy of Television Arts and Sciences Foundation
5220 Lankershim Boulevard
North Hollywood, CA 91601
Phone: 818-754-2820
Fax: 818-761-2827
E-mail: ctasupport@ermmys.org

THE ACTUARIAL FOUNDATION

http://www.actuarialfoundation.org/programs/actuarial/scholarships.shtml

ACTUARY OF TOMORROW—STUART A. ROBERTSON MEMORIAL SCHOLARSHIP

The Actuary of Tomorrow Scholarship recognizes and encourages the academic achievements of undergraduate students pursuing a career in actuarial science. The Actuarial Foundation will provide an award of $7,500 for education expenses at any accredited U.S. educational institution. This award will be forwarded to the college/university of the recipient?s choosing or other arrangements may be considered on an individual basis. Applicants must have successfully completed two actuarial exams.

Award: Scholarship for use in sophomore, junior, or senior years; not renewable. *Number:* 1. *Amount:* $7500.

Eligibility Requirements: Applicant must be enrolled or expecting to enroll full-time at a four-year institution. Applicant must have 3.0 GPA or higher.

Application Requirements: Application, essay, references, transcript. *Deadline:* June 1.

Contact: Debbie McCormac, Project Specialist
The Actuarial Foundation
475 North Martingale Road, Suite 600
Schaumburg, IL 60173-2226
Phone: 847-706-3535
Fax: 847-706-3599
E-mail: scholarships@actfnd.org

JOHN CULVER WOODDY SCHOLARSHIP

The John Culver Wooddy Scholarship was established in 1996 by the estate of John Culver Wooddy, a distinguished actuary who set aside funds to provide scholarships to encourage the academic achievement of students pursuing an actuarial career. Applicants must have successfully completed one actuarial examination. Preference will be given to candidates who have demonstrated leadership potential through extracurricular activities.

Award: Scholarship for use in freshman, sophomore, junior, or senior years. *Amount:* $2000.

Eligibility Requirements: Applicant must be enrolled or expecting to enroll at a four-year institution or university. Applicant must have 3.5 GPA or higher.

Application Requirements: Application, essay, references. *Deadline:* June 24.

Contact: Debbie McCormac, Project Specialist
The Actuarial Foundation
475 North Martingale Road, Suite 600
Schaumburg, IL 60173-2226
Phone: 847-706-3535
Fax: 847-706-3599
E-mail: scholarships@actfnd.org

ALFRED G. AND ELMA M. MILOTTE SCHOLARSHIP FUND

http://www.milotte.org/

ALFRED G. AND ELMA M. MILOTTE SCHOLARSHIP

Grant of up to $4000 to high school graduate or students holding the GED. Applicants must have been accepted at a trade school, art school, two-year or four-year college or university for undergraduate or graduate studies.

Award: Scholarship for use in freshman, sophomore, junior, senior, or graduate years; not renewable. *Number:* varies. *Amount:* up to $4000.

Eligibility Requirements: Applicant must be enrolled or expecting to enroll full- or part-time at a two-year or four-year or technical institution or university. Applicant must have 3.0 GPA or higher. Available to U.S. citizens.

Application Requirements: Application, references, transcript, samples of work expressing applicant's observations of the natural world. *Deadline:* March 1.

Contact: Sean Ferguson, Assistant Vice President
Alfred G. and Elma M. Milotte Scholarship Fund
Bank of America Trust Services
715 Peachtree Street, Eighth Floor
Atlanta, GA 30308
Phone: 800-832-9071
Fax: 800-552-3182
E-mail: info@milotte.org

ALL-INK.COM PRINTER SUPPLIES ONLINE

http://www.all-ink.com/

ALL-INK.COM COLLEGE SCHOLARSHIP PROGRAM

One-time award for any level of postsecondary education. Minimum 2.5 GPA. Must apply online only at web site http://www.all-ink.com. Recipients selected annually.

Award: Scholarship for use in freshman, sophomore, junior, senior, graduate, or postgraduate years; not renewable. *Number:* 5–10. *Amount:* $1000–$5000.

Eligibility Requirements: Applicant must be enrolled or expecting to enroll full-time at a two-year or four-year or technical institution or university. Applicant must have 2.5 GPA or higher. Available to U.S. and non-U.S. citizens.

Application Requirements: Application, applicant must enter a contest, essay. *Deadline:* December 31.

Contact: Aaron M. Gale, President
Eligibility Requirements: All-Ink.com Printer Supplies Online
1460 North Main Street, Suite 2
Spanish Fork, UT 84660
Phone: 801-794-0123
Fax: 801-794-0124
E-mail: scholarship@all-ink.com

ALPHA KAPPA ALPHA

http://www.akaeaf.org/

AKA EDUCATIONAL ADVANCEMENT FOUNDATION UNMET FINANCIAL NEED SCHOLARSHIP

Scholarship for students who have completed a minimum of one year in a degree-granting institution and need financial aid to continue their studies in such an institution. May also be a student in a non-institutional based program that may or may not grant degrees, and must submit a course of study outline. Must have a minimum GPA of 2.5.

Award: Scholarship for use in sophomore, junior, senior, or graduate years; not renewable. *Number:* varies. *Amount:* $750–$2000.

Eligibility Requirements: Applicant must be enrolled or expecting to enroll full-time at a four-year institution or university. Applicant must have 2.5 GPA or higher. Available to U.S. and non-U.S. citizens.

Application Requirements: Application, references. *Deadline:* varies.

Contact: Andrea Kerr, Program Coordinator
Alpha Kappa Alpha
5656 South Stony Island Avenue
Chicago, IL 60637
Phone: 773-947-0026 Ext. 8
E-mail: akaeaf@akaeaf.net

ALPHA LAMBDA DELTA

http://www.nationalald.org/

JO ANNE J. TROW SCHOLARSHIPS

One-time award for initiated members of Alpha Lambda Delta. Minimum 3.5 GPA required. Must be nominated by chapter.

Award: Scholarship for use in junior year; not renewable. *Number:* up to 35. *Amount:* $1000–$3000.

Eligibility Requirements: Applicant must be enrolled or expecting to enroll full-time at a four-year institution or university. Applicant must have 3.5 GPA or higher. Available to U.S. and non-U.S. citizens.

Application Requirements: Application, essay, references, transcript. *Deadline:* April 1.

Contact: Dr. Glenda Earwood, Executive Director
Alpha Lambda Delta
PO Box 4403
Macon, GA 31208-4403
Phone: 478-744-9595
E-mail: glenda@nationalald.org

AMERICAN FIRE SPRINKLER ASSOCIATION

http://www.afsascholarship.org/

AFSA SCHOLARSHIP CONTEST

One-time award for high school seniors. This scholarship essay contest requires applicants to go online to http://www.afsascholarship.org, and read a short essay about sprinklers and fire safety. After finishing, they complete a ten-question quiz on what they just read. Each correct answer gives the student a chance at winning one of ten $2,000 scholarships (maximum 10 chances per entrant).

Award: Scholarship for use in freshman year; not renewable. *Number:* 10. *Amount:* $2000.

Eligibility Requirements: Applicant must be high school student and planning to enroll or expecting to enroll full-time at a two-year or four-year or technical institution or university. Available to U.S. citizens.

Application Requirements: *Deadline:* May 3.

Contact: D'Arcy Montalvo, Public Relations Manager
American Fire Sprinkler Association
12750 Merit Drive, Suite 350
Dallas, TX 75251
Phone: 214-349-5965
Fax: 214-343-8898
E-mail: dmontalvo@firesprinkler.org

AMERICAN HOLISTIC NURSES' ASSOCIATION

http://www.ahna.org/

CHARLOTTE MCGUIRE SCHOLARSHIPS

The Charlotte McGuire Scholarship Program (CMGSP) was established in 1986 through a gracious gift to the American Holistic Nurses Association. Since 1987, AHNA nurses in pursuit of their professional education have been assisted by this program. These awards celebrate the commitment of nurses to a holistic path, and are presented at AHNA's annual conference held each year in June. Since 1997, more than $30,000 has been awarded.

Award: Scholarship for use in freshman, sophomore, junior, senior, or graduate years; not renewable. *Number:* 1. *Amount:* $1000.

Eligibility Requirements: Applicant must be enrolled or expecting to enroll full- or part-time at a two-year or four-year or technical institution or university. Available to U.S. citizens.

Contact: American Holistic Nurses' Association
323 North San Francisco Street
Flagstaff, AZ 86001-4660
Phone: 800-278-2462 Ext. 10
Fax: 928-526-2752
E-mail: info@ahna.org

AMERICAN INSTITUTE FOR FOREIGN STUDY

http://www.aifsabroad.com/

STUDY AGAIN SCHOLARSHIPS

Scholarships for AIFS alumni. AIFS summer program students will receive a $1000 scholarship to study abroad on an AIFS semester or academic year program. AIFS semester or academic year program students will receive a $500 scholarship toward a summer program.

Award: Scholarship for use in freshman, sophomore, junior, or senior years; not renewable. *Amount:* $500–$1000.

Eligibility Requirements: Applicant must be enrolled or expecting to enroll full-time at a two-year or four-year institution or university. Applicant must have 2.5 GPA or higher. Available to U.S. and non-U.S. citizens.

Application Requirements: Application, essay, photo, references, transcript. *Fee:* $95. *Deadline:* varies.

Contact: David Mauro, Admissions Counselor
American Institute for Foreign Study
9 West Broad Street, River Plaza
Stamford, CT 06902
Phone: 800-727-2437 Ext. 5163
Fax: 203-399-5597
E-mail: info@aifs.com

AMERICAN LEGION BASEBALL

http://www.legion.org/baseball

AMERICAN LEGION BASEBALL SCHOLARSHIP

Awarded to graduated seniors who were nominated by American Legion Baseball coach who demonstrate outstanding academics, citizenship, community spirit, leadership and financial need.

Award: Scholarship for use in freshman, sophomore, junior, senior, or graduate years; not renewable. *Number:* 1–51. *Amount:* $500–$600.

Eligibility Requirements: Applicant must be high school student and planning to enroll or expecting to enroll full-time at a two-year or four-year or technical institution or university. Applicant must have 2.5 GPA or higher. Available to U.S. and non-U.S. citizens.

Application Requirements: Application, photo, transcript. *Deadline:* June 15.

Contact: Mr. James Quinlan, National Program Coordinator
American Legion Baseball
PO Box 1055
Indianapolis, IN 46206
Phone: 317-630-1249
Fax: 317-360-1369
E-mail: baseball@legion.org

AMERICAN NATIONAL CATTLE WOMEN INC.

http://www.nationalbeefambassador.org/

NATIONAL BEEF AMBASSADOR PROGRAM

Award's purpose is to train young spokespersons in the beef industry. Applicant must be fully prepared to answer questions and debate focusing on topic related to beef consumption and distribution, as well as social factors related to the industry. The prize value is $1,000. Details and tools for preparation are available on the web site http://www.nationalbeefambassador.org.

Award: Scholarship for use in freshman, sophomore, junior, or senior years; not renewable. *Number:* 5. *Amount:* $1000.

Eligibility Requirements: Applicant must be age 17-20; enrolled or expecting to enroll full-time at a two-year or four-year institution or university and single. Applicant must have 2.5 GPA or higher. Available to U.S. citizens.

Application Requirements: Applicant must enter a contest, applicants must compete in and win their state beef ambassador competition. *Deadline:* varies.

Contact: Carol Abrahamzon
E-mail: cabrahamzon@beef.org

AMERICAN OCCUPATIONAL THERAPY FOUNDATION INC.

http://www.aotf.org/

AOTA'S ASSEMBLY OF STUDENT DELEGATES AWARD

Award for study leading to a degree as an occupational therapy assistant or a Master's in occupational therapy. Must be a member of the American Occupational Therapy Association.

Award: Scholarship for use in sophomore, junior, senior, or graduate years; not renewable. *Number:* 2. *Amount:* $600.

Eligibility Requirements: Applicant must be enrolled or expecting to enroll full-time at a two-year or four-year institution or university. Available to U.S. citizens.

Application Requirements: Application, essay, references, Curriculum Director's Statement. *Deadline:* varies.

Contact: Jeanne Cooper, Scholarship Coordinator
American Occupational Therapy Foundation Inc.
4720 Montgomery Lane
PO Box 31220
Bethesda, MD 20824-1220
Phone: 301-652-6611 Ext. 2550
E-mail: jcooper@aotf.org

AMERICAN SWEDISH INSTITUTE

http://www.americanswedishinst.org/

MALMBERG SCHOLARSHIP FOR STUDY IN SWEDEN

Award for a U.S. resident interested in Sweden and Swedish America. Applicant must be either a student enrolled in a degree-granting program at an accredited college or university or a qualified scholar engaged in study or research whose work can be enhanced by study in Sweden. Scholarships are usually granted for a full academic year term (nine months) but can be for study periods of shorter duration.

Award: Scholarship for use in senior, graduate, or postgraduate years; not renewable. *Number:* up to 1. *Amount:* up to $10,000.

Eligibility Requirements: Applicant must be age 18 and over and enrolled or expecting to enroll full- or part-time at a four-year institution or university. Available to U.S. citizens.

Application Requirements: Application, essay, resume, references, transcript, letter of invitation from host institution. *Deadline:* November 15.

Contact: Karin Krull, Adult Programs Coordinator
American Swedish Institute
2600 Park Avenue
Minneapolis, MN 55407
Phone: 612-870-3355
Fax: 612-871-8682
E-mail: karink@americanswedishinst.org

AMERICAN TRAFFIC SAFETY SERVICES FOUNDATION

http://www.atssa.com/cs/roadway-worker-scholarship

ROADWAY WORKER MEMORIAL SCHOLARSHIP PROGRAM

Scholarship will provide financial assistance for post-high school education to the children of roadway workers killed or permanently disabled in work zone accidents, including mobile operations and the installation of roadway safety features are eligible for the Foundation's annual scholarships in support of higher education (college or vocational). Parents with custody or legal guardianship of surviving children are also eligible.

Award: Scholarship for use in freshman, sophomore, junior, senior, graduate, or postgraduate years; not renewable. *Number:* 2–5. *Amount:* $2000–$3000.

Eligibility Requirements: Applicant must be enrolled or expecting to enroll full- or part-time at a two-year or four-year or technical institution or university. Available to U.S. citizens.

Application Requirements: Application, essay, financial need analysis, resume, references, test scores, transcript, 200-word statement. *Deadline:* February 15.

Contact: Melanie McKee, Foundation Director
American Traffic Safety Services Foundation
15 Riverside Parkway, Suite 100
Fredericksburg, VA 22406
Phone: 540-368-1701 Ext. 112
Fax: 540-368-1717
E-mail: melanie.mckee@atssa.com

ANYCOLLEGE.COM

http://www.anycollege.com/

ANYCOLLEGE.COM SCHOLARSHIP

Four $2000 scholarships awarded annually by random drawing. All students planning to attend an accredited college or university that they had not previously attended are eligible to apply. Deadlines: March 31, June 30, September 30, and December 31.

Award: Scholarship for use in freshman, sophomore, junior, or senior years; not renewable. *Number:* 4. *Amount:* $2000.

Eligibility Requirements: Applicant must be enrolled or expecting to enroll full-time at a two-year or four-year or technical institution or university. Available to U.S. and non-U.S. citizens.

Application Requirements: Application. *Deadline:* continuous.

Contact: Mr. Cory Klinnert, Director of Marketing
AnyCollege.com
403 Center Avenue, Seventh Floor
Moorhead, MN 56560
Phone: 218-284-9933
Fax: 218-284-3394
E-mail: cklinnert@anycollege.com

APPALACHIAN CENTER AND APPALACHIAN STUDIES ASSOCIATION

http://www.appalachianstudies.org/

CARL A. ROSS STUDENT PAPER AWARD

Middle/high school students should submit papers of 12–15 pages in length and undergraduate/graduate students should submit papers of 20–30 pages in length. Winners receive $100 each. Costs of attending the conference are the winners' responsibility. All papers must adhere to the guidelines for scholarly research. Must be enrolled in courses at the time of the conference. To verify their student status, students can submit one of the following: a copy of a schedule of classes for the term, transcripts, or letter from a faculty advisor stating their current student status.

Award: Prize for use in freshman, sophomore, junior, senior, or graduate years; not renewable. *Number:* 2. *Amount:* $100.

Eligibility Requirements: Applicant must be high school student and planning to enroll or expecting to enroll full- or part-time at a two-year or four-year or technical institution or university. Available to U.S. and non-U.S. citizens.

Application Requirements: Essay, resume. *Deadline:* December 9.

Contact: Joette Morris Gates
E-mail: kywoman102950@gmail.com

ARMED FORCES COMMUNICATIONS AND ELECTRONICS ASSOCIATION, EDUCATIONAL FOUNDATION

http://www.afcea.org/education/scholarships

AFCEA CYBER STUDIES SCHOLARSHIP

$5,000 scholarships will be awarded to undergraduate students majoring in a field directly related to the support of U.S. cyber enterprises with relevance to the mission of AFCEA such as cyber security, cyber attack, computer science, information technology, or electronic engineering.

Award: Scholarship for use in sophomore, junior, or senior years; not renewable. *Number:* 8–10. *Amount:* $5000.

Eligibility Requirements: Applicant must be enrolled or expecting to enroll at a two-year or four-year institution or university. Applicant must have 3.0 GPA or higher. Available to U.S. citizens.

Application Requirements: Application, references, transcript. *Deadline:* May 15.

Contact: Miss Norma Corrales, Director of AFCEA Educational Foundation Scholarship Program
Armed Forces Communications and Electronics Association, Educational Foundation
4400 Fair Lakes Court
Fairfax, VA 22033
Phone: 703-631-6149
E-mail: ncorrales@afcea.org

STEM TEACHERS SCHOLARSHIP

The AFCEA Educational Foundation will offer scholarships of $5,000 to students actively pursuing an undergraduate degree, graduate degree or credential/licensure for the purpose of teaching STEM (Science, Technology, Engineering or Mathematics) subjects at a U.S. middle or secondary school.

Award: Scholarship for use in junior, senior, or postgraduate years; not renewable. *Number:* 38. *Amount:* $5000.

Eligibility Requirements: Applicant must be enrolled or expecting to enroll full-time at a four-year institution or university. Applicant must have 3.0 GPA or higher. Available to U.S. citizens.

Application Requirements: Application, references, transcript. *Deadline:* May 1.

Contact: Miss. Norma Corrrales, Director of AFCEA Educational Scholarship Program
Armed Forces Communications and Electronics Association, Educational Foundation
4400 Fair Lakes Court
Fairfax, VA 22033
Phone: 703-631-7149
E-mail: ncorrales@afcea.org

ARRL FOUNDATION INC.

http://www.arrl.org/

DAVID W. MISEK, N8NPX MEMORIAL SCHOLARSHIP

Up to three $1500 awards are available to residents of the following nine Ohio counties: Greene, Montgomery, Champaign, Darke, Preble, Miami, Clark, Butler, Warren. Applicants must have a Technician class or higher amateur radio license.

Award: Scholarship for use in freshman, sophomore, junior, or senior years; not renewable. *Number:* 1–3. *Amount:* $1500.

Eligibility Requirements: Applicant must be enrolled or expecting to enroll at a four-year institution or university.

Application Requirements: *Deadline:* February 1.

Contact: Ms. Mary Hobart, Secretary
ARRL Foundation Inc.
225 Main Street
Newington, CT 06111-1494
Phone: 860-594-0397
E-mail: k1mmh@arrl.org

NEMAL ELECTRONICS SCHOLARSHIP

One $1000 award is available to students majoring in electronics, communications or related fields who possess a General class or higher amateur radio license. Financial need must be demonstrated. Preference is given to residents of the Southeastern United States.

Award: Scholarship for use in freshman, sophomore, junior, or senior years; not renewable. *Number:* 1. *Amount:* $1000.

Eligibility Requirements: Applicant must be enrolled or expecting to enroll at a four-year institution or university. Applicant must have 3.0 GPA or higher.

Application Requirements: *Deadline:* February 1.

Contact: Ms. Mary Hobart, Secretary
ARRL Foundation Inc.
225 Main Street
Newington, CT 06111-1494
Phone: 860-594-0397
E-mail: k1mmh@arrl.org

RICHARD W. BENDICKSEN MEMORIAL SCHOLARSHIP

One $2000 award is available to a student with any active amateur radio license.

Award: Scholarship for use in freshman, sophomore, junior, or senior years; not renewable. *Number:* 1. *Amount:* $2000.

Eligibility Requirements: Applicant must be enrolled or expecting to enroll at a four-year institution or university.

Application Requirements: Application. *Deadline:* February 1.

Contact: Ms. Mary Hobart, Secretary
ARRL Foundation Inc.
225 Main Street
Newington, CT 06111-1494
Phone: 860-594-0397
E-mail: k1mmh@arrl.org

SETH HOREN, K1LOM MEMORIAL SCHOLARSHIP

One $500 award for a student who possesses any active amateur radio license.

Award: Scholarship for use in freshman, sophomore, junior, or senior years; not renewable. *Number:* 1. *Amount:* $500.

MISCELLANEOUS CRITERIA

Eligibility Requirements: Applicant must be enrolled or expecting to enroll at a four-year institution or university.

Application Requirements: *Deadline:* February 1.

Contact: Ms. Mary Hobart, Secretary
ARRL Foundation Inc.
225 Main Street
Newington, CT 06111-1494
Phone: 860-594-0397
E-mail: k1mmh@arrl.org

AYN RAND INSTITUTE

http://www.aynrandnovels.com/

"ATLAS SHRUGGED" ESSAY CONTEST

Annual Essay Contest on Ayn Rand's novel, Atlas Shrugged, for college/university and 12th grade students. Essays will be judged on both style and content. Judges will look for writing that is clear, articulate and logically organized. Winning essays must demonstrate an outstanding grasp of the philosophic and psychological meaning of Atlas Shrugged. For complete rules and guidelines, visit web site http://www.aynrand.org/contests.

Award: Prize for use in freshman, sophomore, junior, senior, graduate, or postgraduate years; not renewable. *Number:* 84. *Amount:* $50–$10,000.

Eligibility Requirements: Applicant must be enrolled or expecting to enroll full- or part-time at a two-year or four-year or technical institution or university. Available to U.S. and non-U.S. citizens.

Application Requirements: Applicant must enter a contest, essay. *Deadline:* September 17.

Contact: Jason Eriksen, Essay Contest Coordinator
Ayn Rand Institute
2121 Alton Parkway, Suite 250
Irvine, CA 92606-4926
Phone: 949-222-6550
E-mail: essay@aynrand.org

"THE FOUNTAINHEAD" ESSAY CONTEST

Annual Essay Contest on Ayn Rand's novel, "The Fountainhead", for 11th and 12th graders. Essays will be judged on both style and content. Judges will look for writing that is clear, articulate and logically organized. Winning essays must demonstrate an outstanding grasp of the philosophic and psychological meaning of The Fountainhead. Essays should be between 800 and 1600 words. For complete rules and guidelines, refer to web site http://www.aynrand.org/contests.

Award: Prize for use in freshman, sophomore, junior, senior, graduate, or postgraduate years; not renewable. *Number:* 236. *Amount:* $50–$10,000.

Eligibility Requirements: Applicant must be high school student and planning to enroll or expecting to enroll full- or part-time at a two-year or four-year or technical institution or university. Available to U.S. and non-U.S. citizens.

Application Requirements: Applicant must enter a contest, essay. *Deadline:* April 26.

Contact: Jason Eriksen, Essay Contest Coordinator
Ayn Rand Institute
2121 Alton Parkway, Suite 250
Irvine, CA 92606-4926
Phone: 949-222-6550
E-mail: essay@aynrand.org

BAPTIST JOINT COMMITTEE FOR RELIGIOUS LIBERTY

http://www.BJConline.org/

RELIGIOUS LIBERTY ESSAY SCHOLARSHIP CONTEST

To enter, students submit an essay based on the year's topic. All high school juniors and seniors are eligible, and they must have a submission coordinator (a family friend, teacher, or church member) to verify that the student's work is his or her own. http://www.BJConline.org/contest.

Award: Scholarship for use in freshman year; not renewable. *Number:* up to 3. *Amount:* $100–$1000.

Eligibility Requirements: Applicant must be high school student and planning to enroll or expecting to enroll full- or part-time at a two-year or four-year institution or university. Available to U.S. citizens.

Application Requirements: Application, applicant must enter a contest, essay, submission coordinator form. *Deadline:* March 15.

Contact: Cherilyn Crowe, Associate Director of Communications
Baptist Joint Committee for Religious Liberty
200 Maryland Avenue NE
Washington, DC 20002
Phone: 202-544-4226
Fax: 202-544-2094
E-mail: ccrowe@BJConline.org

BARBIZON INTERNATIONAL LLC

http://www.barbizonscholarship.com/

BARBIZON COLLEGE TUITION SCHOLARSHIP

Scholarship for full college tuition is awarded every other year by random drawing. Entry forms are available at high schools throughout the United States. For more details, visit web site http://www.barbizon-scholarship.com.

Award: Scholarship for use in freshman, sophomore, junior, or senior years; not renewable. *Number:* 1. *Amount:* up to $100,000.

Eligibility Requirements: Applicant must be enrolled or expecting to enroll full-time at a four-year institution or university. Available to U.S. citizens.

Application Requirements: Application, applicant must enter a contest. *Deadline:* December 1.

Contact: Wendy Cleveland, Vice President of Marketing
Barbizon International LLC
3111 North University Drive, Suite 1002
Coral Springs, FL 33065
Phone: 954-345-4140
Fax: 954-345-8055
E-mail: wendy@barbizonmodeling.com

BENBELLA BOOKS, INC.

http://www.benbellabooks.com/

MENTOR APPRECIATION SCHOLARSHIP

Essay competition for adults who have been a mentor or were mentored by a remarkable individual. For the best true story of a mentorship experience submitted by July 15, the award is a $10,000 college scholarship for a young student of the winner's choice. Author, J.R. Parrish is offering the award through his publisher and entries become his property. Submit essays to web site: mentorscholarship.com or email to: hardwaybook@gmail.com. Scholarship recipient must be a high school senior or undergraduate student formally enrolled in an accredited four-year college or university and provide proof of enrollment.

Award: Scholarship for use in freshman, sophomore, junior, or senior years; not renewable. *Number:* 1. *Amount:* $10,000.

Eligibility Requirements: Applicant must be enrolled or expecting to enroll full-time at a four-year institution or university. Available to U.S. citizens.

Application Requirements: Application, applicant must enter a contest. *Deadline:* July 15.

Contact: Adrienne Lang, Marketing Associate
BenBella Books, Inc.
6440 North Central Expressway, Suite 503
Dallas, TX 75206
Phone: 214-750-3600
Fax: 214-750-3645

BEST BUY CHILDREN FOUNDATION

http://www.bestbuy-communityrelations.com/

BEST BUY @15 SCHOLARSHIP PROGRAM

$1000 scholarships available to students based on outstanding community service and academic achievement. Must be entering an accredited U.S. university, college, or technical school in the fall immediately following high school graduation. For additional information and application, go to web site http://www.bestbuy.com/communityrelations.

Award: Scholarship for use in freshman year; not renewable. *Number:* 1000. *Amount:* $1000.

Eligibility Requirements: Applicant must be high school student and planning to enroll or expecting to enroll full-time at a two-year or four-year or technical institution or university. Available to U.S. citizens.

Application Requirements: Application, references, transcript. *Deadline:* February 15.

Contact: Scholarship Committee
Best Buy Children Foundation
PO Box 9448
Minneapolis, MN 55440
Phone: 888-237-8289
E-mail: communityrelations@bestbuy.com

BRICKFISH

http://www.brickfish.com/

BRICKFISH SCHOLARSHIPS

Scholarships for Brickfish.com members who are at least 13 years of age or older.

Award: Scholarship for use in freshman, sophomore, junior, or senior years; not renewable. *Number:* 5–30. *Amount:* $50–$5000.

Eligibility Requirements: Applicant must be age 13 and over and enrolled or expecting to enroll full- or part-time at a two-year or four-year or technical institution or university. Available to U.S. and Canadian citizens.

Application Requirements: Application, Membership sign-up. *Deadline:* varies.

Contact: Robert Rushing, Social Media Specialist
Brickfish
5930 Cornerstone Court West, Suite 190
San Diego, CA 92121
Phone: 858-587-2530
E-mail: membersupport@brickfishemail.com

BRIDGESTONE FIRESTONE

http://www.bfor.com/

SAFETY SCHOLARS VIDEO CONTEST SCHOLARSHIP

Three $5000 college scholarships for the most compelling and effective videos that drive home life-saving messages on auto and tire safety. Must be between the ages of 16 and 21, possess a valid driver's license, and be enrolled as a full-time student in an accredited secondary, college level, or trade school.

Award: Scholarship for use in freshman, sophomore, junior, or senior years; not renewable. *Number:* 3. *Amount:* $5000.

Eligibility Requirements: Applicant must be age 16-21 and enrolled or expecting to enroll full-time at a four-year institution. Available to U.S. citizens.

Application Requirements: Applicant must enter a contest, 25- or 55-second video about auto safety. *Deadline:* June 24.

Contact: Miss. Ashley Charlton, Assistant Account Executive
Bridgestone Firestone
209 Seventh Avenue, North
Nashville, TN 37219
Phone: 615-780-3383
E-mail: ashley.charlton@dvl.com

BWDVM SCHOLARSHIP FOUNDATION

http://www.peacescholarships.org/

BARBARA WIEDNER AND DOROTHY VANDERCOOK MEMORIAL PEACE SCHOLARSHIP

Scholarships given to high school seniors or college freshmen with demonstrated leadership and personal initiative involving peace and social justice, nuclear disarmament issues, or conflict resolution. There are no GPA or age requirements, and students from any country may apply. Application and references required. Download application PDF from http://www.peacescholarships.org/ and follow the instructions for applying.

Award: Scholarship for use in freshman or sophomore years; not renewable. *Number:* 1–8. *Amount:* $250–$500.

Eligibility Requirements: Applicant must be enrolled or expecting to enroll full- or part-time at a two-year or four-year institution or university. Available to U.S. and non-U.S. citizens.

Application Requirements: Application, essay, references, self-addressed stamped envelope, transcript. *Deadline:* March 15.

Contact: Leal Portis, President, BWDVM Scholarship Foundation
BWDVM Scholarship Foundation
301 Redbud Way
Nevada City, CA 95959
Phone: 530-265-3887
E-mail: portis.leal@gmail.com

CAMPUSDISCOVERY.COM, A DIVISION OF WISECHOICE BRANDS, LLC

http://www.campusdiscovery.com/

CAMPUS DISCOVERY $2,500 "ADVICE TO YOUR HIGH SCHOOL SELF" SCHOLARSHIP

Applicant must submit a complete survey about their college campus and a short original response to the scholarship topic, "Assume you could go back in time and talk to yourself as a high school senior know what you know now about college life and making the transition, what advice would you give yourself?" Applicant must be a U.S. student enrolled at a college or university.

Award: Scholarship for use in freshman, sophomore, junior, senior, graduate, or postgraduate years; not renewable. *Number:* 1. *Amount:* $2500.

Eligibility Requirements: Applicant must be enrolled or expecting to enroll full- or part-time at a two-year or four-year or technical institution or university. Available to U.S. citizens.

Application Requirements: Application, essay. *Deadline:* July 31.

Contact: Scholarship Committee
CampusDiscovery.com, a division of WiseChoice Brands, LLC
1229 King Street
Suite 300
Alexandria, VA 22314
Phone: 904-483-2930
Fax: 904-483-2931
E-mail: info@campusdiscovery.com

CARPE DIEM FOUNDATION OF ILLINOIS

http://www.carpediemfoundation.org/

CARPE DIEM FOUNDATION OF ILLINOIS SCHOLARSHIP COMPETITION

Renewable awards for U.S. citizens studying full-time at accredited U.S. educational institutions, including music conservatories, schools of design, and academies of the arts. For undergraduate study only. Merit based. Priority is given to students whose parents are or have been employed in education; local, state, or federal government; social service or public health; the administration of justice; or the fine arts. Must maintain a B average and demonstrate commitment to public service.

Award: Scholarship for use in freshman, sophomore, junior, or senior years; renewable. *Number:* 10–20. *Amount:* $1500–$2500.

Eligibility Requirements: Applicant must be enrolled or expecting to enroll full-time at a four-year institution or university. Available to U.S. citizens.

Application Requirements: Application, essay, references, self-addressed stamped envelope, test scores, transcript, portfolio, CD, web site (if arts or music candidate). *Fee:* $10. *Deadline:* May 11.

Contact: Gordon V. Levine, Executive Director
Carpe Diem Foundation of Illinois
PO Box A3194
Chicago, IL 60690-3194
E-mail: glevine@carpediemfoundation.org

CHURCH HILL CLASSICS

http://www.diplomaframe.com/

"FRAME MY FUTURE" SCHOLARSHIP CONTEST

Students submit an original creation within a digital image (ex. photo, collage, art piece, poem, etc.), that expresses what they hope to achieve in their personal & professional life after college. 24 Finalists will be selected by Church Hill Classics & the public will vote to select 5 $1,000 scholarship winners. The recipient with the most votes will also receive a bonus matching $1,000 donation for their college or university. Full scholarship details & rules are available at http://www.framemy-future.com.

Award: Scholarship for use in freshman, sophomore, junior, senior, or graduate years; not renewable. *Number:* 5–5. *Amount:* $1000.

Eligibility Requirements: Applicant must be enrolled or expecting to enroll full-time at a two-year or four-year institution or university. Available to U.S. citizens.

Application Requirements: Applicant must enter a contest, submission of an original creation in an image format that shows how you frame your future by uploading it onto and completing an online entry form.

Contact: Church Hill Classics
594 Pepper Street
Monroe, CT 06468

CIEE: COUNCIL ON INTERNATIONAL EDUCATIONAL EXCHANGE

http://www.ciee.org/

JOHN E. BOWMAN TRAVEL GRANT

The applicant must attend a CIEE Member or CIEE Academic Consortium member institution (as listed at http://www.ciee.org/study). The applicant must plan to study at a CIEE Study Center in a non-traditional destination. Regions currently eligible include: Africa, Asia, Eastern Europe, and Latin America. Recipients receive awards to be used as partial reimbursement for travel costs to program destination. Deadlines: April 1 and November 1.

Award: Grant for use in freshman, sophomore, junior, or senior years; not renewable. *Number:* 20–30. *Amount:* $500–$1500.

Eligibility Requirements: Applicant must be enrolled or expecting to enroll full-time at a two-year or four-year or technical institution or university. Available to U.S. and non-U.S. citizens.

Application Requirements: Application, applicant must enter a contest, essay, financial need analysis, references, transcript. *Deadline:* varies.

Contact: CIEE Scholarship Committee
CIEE: Council on International Educational Exchange
300 Fore Street
Portland, ME 04101
Phone: 800-407-8839
E-mail: studyinfo@ciee.org

CLARICODE

http://www.claricode.com/

CLARICODE MEDICAL SOFTWARE SCHOLARSHIP ESSAY

Three awards from $500–$2500 available to full-time undergraduate or graduate students attending a U.S. accredited college or university. Must be at least 18 years old at time of entry and submit a 500–1000-word essay on the topic chosen by Claricode (and listed on the web site). All majors/concentrations are welcome to apply. For additional information visit web site http://www.claricode.com/scholarship.

Award: Scholarship for use in freshman, sophomore, junior, senior, graduate, or postgraduate years; not renewable. *Number:* 3. *Amount:* $500–$2500.

Eligibility Requirements: Applicant must be age 18 and over and enrolled or expecting to enroll full-time at a two-year or four-year or technical institution or university. Available to U.S. citizens.

Application Requirements: Application, applicant must enter a contest, essay. *Deadline:* October 31.

Contact: Jennifer Eagan, Office Manager
Claricode
716 Main Street, 2nd Floor
Waltham, MA 02451
Phone: 781-899-9190 Ext. 112
E-mail: scholarship@claricode.com

COCA-COLA SCHOLARS FOUNDATION INC.

http://www.coca-colascholars.org/

COCA-COLA SCHOLARS PROGRAM

Renewable scholarship for graduating high school seniors enrolled either full-time or part-time in accredited colleges or universities. Minimum 3.0 GPA required. 250 awards are granted annually.

Award: Scholarship for use in freshman year; renewable. *Number:* 250. *Amount:* $10,000–$20,000.

Eligibility Requirements: Applicant must be high school student and planning to enroll or expecting to enroll full- or part-time at a two-year or four-year or technical institution or university. Applicant must have 3.0 GPA or higher. Available to U.S. citizens.

Application Requirements: Application, essay, interview, references, test scores, transcript. *Deadline:* varies.

Contact: Mark Davis, President
Coca-Cola Scholars Foundation Inc.
PO Box 442
Atlanta, GA 30301-0442
Phone: 800-306-2653
Fax: 404-733-5439
E-mail: scholars@na.ko.com

CODA INTERNATIONAL

http://coda-international.org/blog/

MILLIE BROTHER SCHOLARSHIP FOR CHILDREN OF DEAF ADULTS

Scholarship awarded to any higher education student who is the hearing child of deaf parents. One-time award based on transcripts, letters of reference, and an essay.

Award: Scholarship for use in freshman, sophomore, junior, senior, or graduate years; not renewable. *Number:* 2–3. *Amount:* up to $3000.

Eligibility Requirements: Applicant must be enrolled or expecting to enroll full-time at a two-year or four-year institution or university. Available to U.S. and non-U.S. citizens.

Application Requirements: Application, essay, references, transcript, letter of agreement to publish essay. *Deadline:* April 1.

Contact: Dr. Jennie E. Pyers, Chair, CODA Scholarship Committee
CODA International
Wellesley College, 106 Central Street, SCI 480
Wellesley, MA 02481
Phone: 781-283-3736
Fax: 781-283-3730
E-mail: coda.scholarship@gmail.com

COLLEGE IN COLORADO

http://www.collegeincolorado.org/

GET SCHOOLED! SCHOLARSHIP

Entrants must be legal residents of the United States and a student between the ages of 13–18 residing in Colorado. Residency is subject to verification under Colorado law. One entry per student. Amount ranges from $400 to $850.

Award: Scholarship for use in freshman year; not renewable. *Number:* varies. *Amount:* $400–$850.

Eligibility Requirements: Applicant must be age 13-18 and enrolled or expecting to enroll full- or part-time at a four-year institution or university. Available to U.S. citizens.

Application Requirements: Application, essay. *Deadline:* varies.

Contact: Scholarship Committee
College in Colorado
1801 Broadway, Suite 360
Denver, CO 80202

COLLEGE INSIDER RESOURCES

http://www.ezcir.com/

COLLEGE INSIDER RADIO SCHOLARSHIP

Scholarship for both high school and college students in the U.S. as well as international students. High school students must have a 2.0 GPA, and college students must have 2.5 GPA. This is a need/merit based scholarship awarded monthly.

Award: Scholarship for use in freshman, sophomore, junior, senior, graduate, or postgraduate years; renewable. *Number:* 1–3. *Amount:* $500–$1000.

Eligibility Requirements: Applicant must be enrolled or expecting to enroll full-time at a two-year or four-year institution or university. Available to U.S. and non-U.S. citizens.

Application Requirements: Application, essay, financial need analysis. *Deadline:* continuous.

Contact: Mr. Cliff deQuilettes, CEO
Phone: 406-670-3866
E-mail: cliff@ezcir.com

COLLEGE INSIDER SCHOLARSHIP PROGRAM

Scholarship offered to undergraduate students with a minimum GPA of 2.5. International students attending college in the United States are also eligible. Refer to web site for additional information http://www.ezcir.com/college_request.asp.

Award: Scholarship for use in freshman, sophomore, junior, or senior years; renewable. *Number:* 1. *Amount:* $1000.

Eligibility Requirements: Applicant must be age 13 and over and enrolled or expecting to enroll full-time at a two-year or four-year or technical institution or university. Available to U.S. and non-U.S. citizens.

Application Requirements: Application. *Deadline:* varies.

Contact: Mr. Cliff deQuilettes, CEO
Phone: 406-652-8900
E-mail: cliff@ezcir.com

COLLEGE PROWLER INC.

http://www.collegeprowler.com/

$2,000 "NO ESSAY" SCHOLARSHIP

We know you're busy and we know that times are tough. That's why we decided to create the easiest possible scholarship to give something back to students. Students can use the money to help cover tuition, housing, meal plans, books, computers, or any education-related expenses.

Award: Scholarship for use in freshman, sophomore, junior, or senior years; not renewable. *Number:* 12. *Amount:* $2000.

Eligibility Requirements: Applicant must be enrolled or expecting to enroll full-time at a two-year or four-year or technical institution or university. Available to U.S. citizens.

Application Requirements: Application. *Deadline:* continuous.

Contact: Mark Tressler, Manager of Business Development
College Prowler Inc.
5001 Baum Boulevard
Suite 750
Pittsburgh, PA 15213
E-mail: scholarship@collegeprowler.com

COLLEGETOOLKIT.COM

http://www.collegetoolkit.com/

COLLEGE TOOLKIT SCHOLARSHIP CONTEST FOR COLLEGE STUDENTS

College Toolkit is giving away a $1,000 scholarship to a college student. We want you to hear your thoughts about the college you attend. The award is open to anyone who will be an undergraduate college student this upcoming fall. You must be attending an accredited 2-year or 4-year college and a U.S. resident to enter.

Award: Scholarship for use in sophomore, junior, or senior years; not renewable. *Number:* 1. *Amount:* $1000.

Eligibility Requirements: Applicant must be enrolled or expecting to enroll full- or part-time at a two-year or four-year institution or university. Available to U.S. citizens.

Application Requirements: Application. *Deadline:* September 30.

Contact: Scholarship Committee
CollegeToolkit.com
11 St. MarksAvenue'
Suite #2R
Brooklyn, NY 11217
Phone: 800-265-0179

COLLEGE TOOLKIT SCHOLARSHIP CONTEST FOR HIGH SCHOOL STUDENTS

College Toolkit is giving away a $1,000 scholarship to a high school student. We want you to share with us what colleges you are most interested in. The award is open to anyone who will be a high school student this upcoming fall. You must be 14 years of age or older and a U.S. resident to enter.

Award: Scholarship for use in freshman year; not renewable. *Number:* 1. *Amount:* $1000.

Eligibility Requirements: Applicant must be high school student and planning to enroll or expecting to enroll full- or part-time at a two-year or four-year institution. Available to U.S. citizens.

Application Requirements: Application.

Contact: Scholarship Committee
CollegeToolkit.com
11 St. MarksAvenue'
Suite #2R
Brooklyn, NY 11217
Phone: 800-265-0179

COMMON KNOWLEDGE SCHOLARSHIP FOUNDATION

http://www.cksf.org/

COMMON KNOWLEDGE SCHOLARSHIPS

The Common Knowledge Scholarship Foundation awards scholarships to students who score the highest on internet-based quizzes. Register once at http://www.cksf.org and all of the scholarship quizzes you are eligible to participate in will appear in y our account.

Award: Scholarship for use in freshman, sophomore, junior, senior, graduate, or postgraduate years; not renewable. *Number:* 20–50. *Amount:* $250–$1000.

Eligibility Requirements: Applicant must be enrolled or expecting to enroll full- or part-time at a two-year or four-year or technical institution or university. Available to U.S. and non-U.S. citizens.

Application Requirements: *Deadline:* continuous.

Contact: Mr. Daryl Hulce, President
Common Knowledge Scholarship Foundation
PO Box 290361
Davie, FL 33329-0361
E-mail: info@cksf.org

THE COMMUNITY FOUNDATION FOR GREATER ATLANTA, INC.

http://www.cfgreateratlanta.org/

DREAMS2 SCHOLARSHIP

Scholarship designed to provide scholarship opportunities for deserving students who want to pursue their education. Minimum 2.0 GPA, maximum 3.0 GPA required. For complete eligibility requirements or to submit an application, please visit http://www.cfgreateratlanta.org.

Award: Scholarship for use in freshman, sophomore, junior, or senior years; not renewable. *Number:* up to 6. *Amount:* $2000.

Eligibility Requirements: Applicant must be enrolled or expecting to enroll full-time at a two-year or four-year or technical institution or university. Available to U.S. citizens.

Application Requirements: Application, driver's license, essay, financial need analysis, references, transcript. *Deadline:* March 15.

Contact: Kristina Morris, Program Associate
The Community Foundation for Greater Atlanta, Inc.
50 Hurt Plaza, Suite 449
Atlanta, GA 30303
Phone: 404-688-5525
E-mail: scholarships@cfgreateratlanta.org

CONGRESSIONAL BLACK CAUCUS FOUNDATION, INC.

http://www.cbcfinc.org/

CONGRESSIONAL BLACK CAUCUS SPOUSES EDUCATION SCHOLARSHIP

The CBC Spouses Educational scholarship is a national program that awards scholarships to academically talented and highly motivated students who intend to pursue full-time undergraduate, graduate or doctoral degrees. Awards are made to students who reside or attend school in a congressional district represented by a member of the Congressional Black Caucus. Minimum 2.5 GPA required. Contact the Congressional office in the appropriate district for information and applications.

Award: Scholarship for use in freshman, sophomore, junior, senior, or graduate years; not renewable. *Number:* 250–400. *Amount:* $500–$5000.

Eligibility Requirements: Applicant must be enrolled or expecting to enroll full-time at a two-year or four-year or technical institution or university. Applicant must have 2.5 GPA or higher. Available to U.S. citizens.

Application Requirements: Application, essay, financial need analysis, photo, resume, references, transcript. *Deadline:* June 1.

Contact: Ms. Janet J. Carter, Scholarships Coordinator
Congressional Black Caucus Foundation, Inc.
1720 Massachusetts Avenue, NW
Washington, DC 20036
Phone: 202-263-2800
Fax: 202-263-0845
E-mail: scholarships@cbcfinc.org

COURAGE TO GROW SCHOLARSHIP PROGRAM

http://couragetogrowscholarship.com/

COURAGE TO GROW SCHOLARSHIP

High school seniors or college students with a minimum GPA of 2.0 or better are eligible. U.S. citizens only please. An essay of 250 words or less is required. One award of $500 will be given out per month. Applicants can reapply each month throughout the year.

Award: Scholarship for use in freshman, sophomore, junior, senior, graduate, or postgraduate years; not renewable. *Number:* 1–12. *Amount:* up to $500.

Eligibility Requirements: Applicant must be enrolled or expecting to enroll full- or part-time at a two-year or four-year or technical institution or university. Available to U.S. citizens.

Application Requirements: Application, essay. *Deadline:* continuous.

Contact: Kimberly Johnson, Founder
Courage to Grow Scholarship Program
PO Box 2507
Chelan, WA 98816
Phone: 509-731-3056
E-mail: support@couragetogrowscholarship.com

THE DALLAS FOUNDATION

http://www.dallasfoundation.org/

BROOK HOLLOW GOLF CLUB SCHOLARSHIP

Established in 2007 to benefit children or grandchildren of full- or part-time employees of Brook Hollow Golf Club. Applicants must be a child or grandchild of an active employee in good standing of Brook Hollow Golf Club and a graduating high school senior who has been accepted in, or a student already enrolled in, an undergraduate program of study in pursuit of a degree from a public or private, regionally accredited community college, college, university, or vocational or trade institute. Applicants must demonstrate financial need.

Award: Scholarship for use in freshman or sophomore years; renewable. *Amount:* $2000–$4500.

Eligibility Requirements: Applicant must be high school student and planning to enroll or expecting to enroll full-time at a two-year or four-year or technical institution or university.

Application Requirements: Application, financial need analysis, transcript. *Deadline:* April 1.

Contact: Rachel Lasseter, Program Associate
The Dallas Foundation
900 Jackson Street, Suite 705
Dallas, TX 75202
Phone: 214-741-9898
E-mail: scholarships@dallasfoundation.org

THE HIRSCH FAMILY SCHOLARSHIP

The Hirsch Family Scholarship was established as a scholarship fund in 2009 to benefit dependent children of active employees of Eagle Materials, Performance Chemicals and Ingredients, Martin Fletcher, Hadlock Plastics, Highlander Partners and any of their majority-owned subsidiaries.

Award: Scholarship for use in freshman, sophomore, junior, or senior years; not renewable. *Amount:* $2000–$10,000.

Eligibility Requirements: Applicant must be enrolled or expecting to enroll full-time at a two-year or four-year or technical institution or university.

Application Requirements: Application, transcript. *Deadline:* March 15.

Contact: Rachel Lasseter, Program Associate
The Dallas Foundation
900 Jackson Street, Suite 705
Dallas, TX 75202
Phone: 214-741-9898
E-mail: scholarships@dallasfoundation.org

KRISTOPHER KASPER MEMORIAL SCHOLARSHIP

The Kristopher Kasper Memorial Scholarship will be awarded to a child of a Centex Homes–Texas Region employee. Based on the eligibility criteria, one scholarship of at least $1,000 will be awarded annually. The scholarship may be used for tuition, fees, or books, and will be paid directly to the school. There will be an opportunity for renewal if renewal requirements are met.

Award: Scholarship for use in freshman, sophomore, junior, or senior years; renewable. *Number:* 1. *Amount:* $1000.

Eligibility Requirements: Applicant must be high school student and planning to enroll or expecting to enroll full-time at a two-year or four-year or technical institution or university. Applicant must have 2.5 GPA or higher.

Application Requirements: Application, resume, references, transcript. *Deadline:* April 15.

Contact: Rachel Lasseter, Program Associate
The Dallas Foundation
900 Jackson Street, Suite 705
Dallas, TX 75202
Phone: 214-741-9898
E-mail: scholarships@dallasfoundation.org

DATATEL INC.

http://www.datatelscholars.org/

DATATEL SCHOLARS FOUNDATION SCHOLARSHIP

One-time award for students attending institutions which use Datatel administrative software. Available for students currently attending at least 6 credits. Completed online applications, including two letters of recommendation must be submitted electronically.

Award: Scholarship for use in freshman, sophomore, junior, senior, graduate, or postgraduate years; not renewable. *Number:* up to 270. *Amount:* $1000–$2400.

Eligibility Requirements: Applicant must be enrolled or expecting to enroll full- or part-time at a two-year or four-year or technical institution or university. Available to U.S. and non-U.S. citizens.

Application Requirements: Application, essay, references, transcript. *Deadline:* January 30.

Contact: Stacey Fessler, Project Leader
Datatel Inc.
4375 Fair Lakes Court
Fairfax, VA 22033
Phone: 800-486-4332
E-mail: scholars@datatel.com

RUSS GRIFFITH MEMORIAL SCHOLARSHIP

For any student who has returned to higher education after an absence of five years or more. One-time award for students attending institutions which use Datatel administrative software. Must be currently enrolled in courses totaling at least 6 credits. Completed online applications, including two letters of recommendation must be submitted electronically.

Award: Scholarship for use in freshman, sophomore, junior, senior, graduate, or postgraduate years; not renewable. *Number:* 50. *Amount:* $2000.

Eligibility Requirements: Applicant must be enrolled or expecting to enroll full- or part-time at a two-year or four-year or technical institution or university. Available to U.S. and non-U.S. citizens.

Application Requirements: Application, essay, references, transcript. *Deadline:* January 30.

Contact: Stacey Fessler, Project Leader
Datatel Inc.
4375 Fair Lakes Court
Fairfax, VA 22033
Phone: 800-486-4332
E-mail: scholars@datatel.com

THE DAVID & DOVETTA WILSON SCHOLARSHIP FUND

http://www.wilsonfund.org/

THE DAVID & DOVETTA WILSON SCHOLARSHIP FUND

The purpose of The David and Dovetta Wilson Scholarship Fund (DDWSF) is to provide deserving high school seniors across the nation with financial assistance to pursue their academic goals.

Award: Scholarship for use in freshman year; not renewable. *Number:* up to 9. *Amount:* $300–$1000.

Eligibility Requirements: Applicant must be high school student and planning to enroll or expecting to enroll full-time at a two-year or four-year institution or university. Available to U.S. citizens.

Application Requirements: Application, financial need analysis, references, transcript, religious involvement. *Fee:* $20. *Deadline:* March 31.

Contact: Timothy M. Wilson, Treasurer
The David & Dovetta Wilson Scholarship Fund
115-67 237th Street
Elmont, NY 11003
Phone: 516-643-5762
E-mail: ddwsf4@aol.com

DEVRY, INC.

http://www.devry.edu/

DEVRY DEAN'S SCHOLARSHIPS

Awards to high school seniors or GED recipients who have SAT scores of 1100 or higher, or ACT scores of 24 or higher; Canada-Composite CPT of 430 or higher for Canadians. There is no separate scholarship application.

Award: Scholarship for use in freshman year; renewable. *Number:* varies. *Amount:* $1500–$13,500.

Eligibility Requirements: Applicant must be high school student and planning to enroll or expecting to enroll full-time at a four-year institution or university. Available to U.S. and Canadian citizens.

Application Requirements: Application, interview, test scores, transcript. *Deadline:* varies.

Contact: Thonie Simpson, National High School Program Manager
DeVry, Inc.
One Tower Lane
Oak Brook Terrace, IL 60181-4624
Phone: 630-706-3122
E-mail: scholarships@devry.edu

DEVRY HIGH SCHOOL SCHOLARSHIP

Award to high school graduates. Amount of $1000 per semester to students, valued up to $9000. Must be in top 50 percent of class or have a GPA of 2.7. Nominations must be received by July 1 and students have one year from high school graduation to apply and start.

Award: Scholarship for use in freshman year; renewable. *Number:* varies. *Amount:* $2000–$9000.

Eligibility Requirements: Applicant must be high school student and planning to enroll or expecting to enroll full-time at an institution or university. Available to U.S. and Canadian citizens.

Application Requirements: Application, interview, references, test scores, transcript. *Deadline:* July 1.

Contact: Thonie Simpson, National High School Program Manager
DeVry, Inc.
One Tower Lane
Oak Brook Terrace, IL 60181-4624
Phone: 630-706-3122
E-mail: scholarships@devry.edu

DEVRY TRANSFER SCHOLARSHIP

Award to community college graduates who earned an associate degree from a regionally accredited or public community or junior college with a minimum GPA of 3.2. Must apply and start with DeVry University within one year of the official college graduation date.

Award: Scholarship for use in junior or senior years; renewable. *Number:* varies. *Amount:* $2000.

Eligibility Requirements: Applicant must be enrolled or expecting to enroll full-time at a four-year institution or university. Available to U.S. citizens.

Application Requirements: Application, interview, transcript.

Contact: Thonie Simpson, National High School Program Manager
DeVry, Inc.
One Tower Lane
Oak Brook Terrace, IL 60181-4624
Phone: 630-706-3122
E-mail: scholarships@devry.edu

E-COLLEGEDEGREE.COM

http://www.e-collegedegree.com/

E-COLLEGEDEGREE.COM ONLINE EDUCATION SCHOLARSHIP AWARD

The award is to be used for online education. Application must be submitted online. Visit web site for more information and application http://www.e-collegedegree.com.

Award: Scholarship for use in freshman, sophomore, junior, senior, graduate, or postgraduate years; renewable. *Number:* 1. *Amount:* $1000.

Eligibility Requirements: Applicant must be age 18 and over and enrolled or expecting to enroll full- or part-time at a two-year or four-year or technical institution or university. Available to U.S. citizens.

Application Requirements: Application, applicant must enter a contest, essay. *Deadline:* December 31.

Contact: Chris Lee, Site Manager
e-CollegeDegree.com
9109 West 101st Terrace
Overland Park, KS 66212
Phone: 913-341-6949
E-mail: scholarship@e-collegedegree.com

EDUCAID, WACHOVIA CORPORATION

http://www.wachovia.com/

EDUCAID GIMME FIVE SCHOLARSHIP SWEEPSTAKES

Awards twelve high school seniors for their first year at an accredited college or trade school. The scholarships are not based on grades or financial need, so every eligible high school senior who enters has an equal chance of winning. Apply online at the following web site http://www.educaid.com.

Award: Prize for use in freshman year; not renewable. *Number:* 12. *Amount:* $5000.

Eligibility Requirements: Applicant must be enrolled or expecting to enroll full-time at a two-year or four-year or technical institution or university. Available to U.S. citizens.

Application Requirements: Application, self-addressed stamped envelope. *Deadline:* March 31.

Contact: Scholarship Committee
Educaid, Wachovia Corporation
PO Box 13667
Sacramento, CA 95853-3667
Phone: 877-689-0763

EDUCATION IS FREEDOM FOUNDATION

http://www.educationisfreedom.com/

EDUCATION IS FREEDOM NATIONAL SCHOLARSHIP

Applicants for this renewable scholarship must be high school seniors planning full-time undergraduate study at a two- or four-year college or university. Selection criteria are based on financial need, leadership and activities, work history, and candidate appraisal. Application available online at http://www.educationisfreedom.com.

Award: Scholarship for use in freshman year; renewable. *Number:* up to 225. *Amount:* $2000.

Eligibility Requirements: Applicant must be high school student and planning to enroll or expecting to enroll full-time at a two-year or four-year institution or university. Applicant must have 3.0 GPA or higher. Available to U.S. citizens.

Application Requirements: Application, financial need analysis, references, transcript. *Deadline:* April 15.

Contact: Barb Weber, Director of Operations
Education is Freedom Foundation
4711 North Haskell Avenue
Saint Peter, MN 56082

ELECTROCHEMICAL SOCIETY INC.

http://www.electrochem.org/

H.H. DOW MEMORIAL STUDENT ACHIEVEMENT AWARD OF THE INDUSTRIAL ELECTROLYSIS AND ELECTROCHEMICAL ENGINEERING DIVISION OF THE ELECTROCHEMICAL SOCIETY INC.

Award to recognize promising young engineers and scientists in the field of electrochemical engineering and applied electrochemistry. Applicant must be enrolled or accepted for enrollment in a college or university as a graduate student. Must submit description of proposed research project and how it relates to the field of electrochemistry, a letter of recommendation from research supervisor, and biography or resume.

Award: Scholarship for use in freshman, sophomore, junior, senior, or graduate years; not renewable. *Number:* 1. *Amount:* $1000.

Eligibility Requirements: Applicant must be enrolled or expecting to enroll full-time at a four-year institution or university. Available to U.S. and non-U.S. citizens.

Application Requirements: Application, resume, references, transcript, abstract of research project, statement of relationship of the project to the field of electrochemical engineering or applied electrochemistry. *Deadline:* September 15.

Contact: Mrs. Colleen Klepser, Executive Administrator
Electrochemical Society Inc.
65 South Main Street, Building D
Pennington, NJ 08534-2839
Phone: 609-737-1902 Ext. 111
Fax: 609-737-2743
E-mail: awards@electrochem.org

STUDENT ACHIEVEMENT AWARDS OF THE INDUSTRIAL ELECTROLYSIS AND ELECTROCHEMICAL

ENGINEERING DIVISION OF THE ELECTROCHEMICAL SOCIETY INC.

Award to recognize promising young engineers and scientists in the field of electrochemical engineering. Applicant must be enrolled in a college or university or accepted for enrollment in a graduate program. Application must include outline of research project to be engaged in during the next year and how it relates to the field of electrochemical engineering and a letter of recommendation from research supervisor is required.

Award: Scholarship for use in freshman, sophomore, junior, senior, or graduate years; not renewable. *Number:* 1. *Amount:* $1000.

Eligibility Requirements: Applicant must be enrolled or expecting to enroll full-time at a four-year institution or university. Available to U.S. and non-U.S. citizens.

Application Requirements: Application, resume, references, transcript, description of proposed research project. *Deadline:* September 15.

Contact: Mrs. Colleen Klepser, Executive Administrator
Electrochemical Society Inc.
65 South Main Street, Building D
Pennington, NJ 08534-2839
Phone: 609-737-1902 Ext. 111
Fax: 609-737-2743
E-mail: awards@electrochem.org

STUDENT RESEARCH AWARDS OF THE BATTERY DIVISION OF THE ELECTROCHEMICAL SOCIETY INC.

Award to recognize promising young engineers and scientists in the field of electrochemical power sources. Student must be enrolled or must have been accepted for enrollment at a college or university.

Award: Prize for use in freshman, sophomore, junior, senior, or graduate years; not renewable. *Number:* 1. *Amount:* $1000.

Eligibility Requirements: Applicant must be enrolled or expecting to enroll full-time at a four-year institution or university. Available to U.S. and non-U.S. citizens.

Application Requirements: Application, resume, references, transcript, written summary of research accomplished. *Deadline:* March 15.

Contact: Mrs. Colleen Klepser, Executive Administrator
Electrochemical Society Inc.
65 South Main Street, Building D
Pennington, NJ 08534-2839
Phone: 609-737-1902 Ext. 111
Fax: 609-737-2743
E-mail: awards@electrochem.org

EXECUTIVE WOMEN INTERNATIONAL

http://www.ewiconnect.com/

ADULT STUDENTS IN SCHOLASTIC TRANSITION

Scholarship for adult students at transitional points in their lives. Applicants may be single parents, individuals just entering the workforce, or displaced homemakers. Applications are available on the organization's web site http://www.ewiconnect.com.

Award: Scholarship for use in freshman, sophomore, junior, or senior years; not renewable. *Number:* 100–150. *Amount:* $250–$2500.

Eligibility Requirements: Applicant must be enrolled or expecting to enroll full-time at a two-year or four-year or technical institution or university. Available to U.S. and non-U.S. citizens.

Application Requirements: Application, essay, financial need analysis, interview, photo, references, self-addressed stamped envelope, transcript, tax information.

Contact: Executive Women International
515 South 700 East, Suite 2A
Salt Lake City, UT 84102
Phone: 801-355-2800
Fax: 801-355-2852
E-mail: ewi@ewiconnect.com

EXECUTIVE WOMEN INTERNATIONAL SCHOLARSHIP PROGRAM

Competitive award to high school juniors planning careers in any business or professional field of study which requires a four-year college degree. Award is renewable based on continuing eligibility. All awards are given through local Chapters of the EWI. Applicant must apply through nearest Chapter and live within the Chapter's boundaries.

Student must have a sponsoring teacher and school to be considered, and only one applicant per school. For more details visit http://www.ewic-onnect.com.

Award: Scholarship for use in freshman, sophomore, junior, or senior years; renewable. *Number:* 75–100. *Amount:* $1000–$10,000.

Eligibility Requirements: Applicant must be high school student; age 15-17 and planning to enroll or expecting to enroll full-time at a four-year institution or university. Available to U.S. and non-U.S. citizens.

Application Requirements: Application, essay, interview, photo, references, self-addressed stamped envelope, transcript.

Contact: Executive Women International
515 South 700 East, Suite 2A
Salt Lake City, UT 84102
Phone: 801-355-2800
E-mail: ewi@ewiconnect.com

FEDERAL EMPLOYEE EDUCATION AND ASSISTANCE FUND

http://www.feea.org/

FEDERAL EMPLOYEE EDUCATION AND ASSISTANCE FUND SCHOLARSHIP PROGRAM

The FEEA Scholarship Program is for current civilian federal employees and their dependent family members (spouse/child). The applicant or the applicant's sponsoring federal employee must have at least three (3) years of civilian federal service by August 31. The applicant must be at least a college freshman by the fall semester. All applicants must have at least a 3.0 cumulative grade point average (CGPA) unweighted on a 4.0 scale. Current college freshman must have a minimum 3.0 GPA for the fall semester. All applicants must be current high school seniors or college students working towards an accredited degree or enrolled in a two- or four-year undergraduate, graduate or postgraduate program.

Award: Scholarship for use in freshman, sophomore, junior, senior, graduate, or postgraduate years; not renewable. *Amount:* $500–$2000.

Eligibility Requirements: Applicant must be enrolled or expecting to enroll full- or part-time at a two-year or four-year or technical institution or university. Applicant must have 3.0 GPA or higher. Available to U.S. citizens.

Application Requirements: Application, essay, references, self-addressed stamped envelope, test scores, transcript. *Deadline:* varies.

Contact: Niki Gleason, Office Manager/Scholarship Coordinator
Federal Employee Education and Assistance Fund
3333 South Wadsworth Boulevard, Suite 300
Lakewood, CO 80227
Phone: 303-933-7580
E-mail: nlogan@feea.org

NATIONAL ACTIVE AND RETIRED FEDERAL EMPLOYEE SCHOLARSHIP PROGRAM

Children, grandchildren, great-grandchildren and step-children of all current NARFE members are eligible. Applicant must be a high school senior planning to attend college full time. Must have a GPA of at least 3.0 on an unweighted 4.0 scale.

Award: Scholarship for use in freshman year; not renewable. *Number:* 60. *Amount:* $1000.

Eligibility Requirements: Applicant must be high school student and planning to enroll or expecting to enroll full-time at a two-year or four-year institution or university. Applicant must have 3.0 GPA or higher. Available to U.S. citizens.

Application Requirements: Application, essay, references, self-addressed stamped envelope, test scores, transcript. *Deadline:* April 30.

Contact: Niki Gleason, Office Manager/Scholarship Coordinator
Federal Employee Education and Assistance Fund
3333 South Wadsworth Boulevard, Suite 300
Lakewood, CO 80227
Phone: 303-933-7580
E-mail: nlogan@feea.org

FEDERATION OF AMERICAN CONSUMERS AND TRAVELERS

http://www.usafact.org/

FEDERATION OF AMERICAN CONSUMERS AND TRAVELERS IN-SCHOOL SCHOLARSHIP

FACT scholarships are offered in four categories for current high school seniors, persons who graduated from high school, four or more years ago and now plan to go to a university or college, for students currently enrolled in a college or university, and for trade or technical school aspirants. Scholarships range in amount from $2500 to $10,000. Members of FACT, their children and grandchildren are eligible to apply.

Award: Scholarship for use in freshman, sophomore, junior, or senior years; not renewable. *Number:* 2. *Amount:* $2500–$10,000.

Eligibility Requirements: Applicant must be enrolled or expecting to enroll full-time at a two-year or four-year institution or university. Available to U.S. citizens.

Application Requirements: Application, essay, resume, references, test scores, transcript. *Deadline:* January 15.

Contact: Vicki Rolens, Managing Director
Federation of American Consumers and Travelers
PO Box 104
Edwardsville, IL 62025
Phone: 800-872-3228
E-mail: vrolens@usafact.org

FEDERATION OF AMERICAN CONSUMERS AND TRAVELERS SECOND CHANCE SCHOLARSHIP

FACT scholarships are offered in four categories: (1) for current high school seniors: (2) for persons who graduated from high school four or more years ago and now plan to go to a university or college; (3) for students currently enrolled in a college or university, and (4) for trade or technical school aspirants. Scholarships range in size from $2500 to $10,000. Members of FACT, their children and grandchildren are eligible to apply.

Award: Scholarship for use in freshman, sophomore, junior, or senior years; not renewable. *Number:* 2. *Amount:* $2500–$10,000.

Eligibility Requirements: Applicant must be enrolled or expecting to enroll full- or part-time at a two-year or four-year or technical institution or university. Available to U.S. citizens.

Application Requirements: Application, essay, resume, references, test scores, transcript. *Deadline:* January 15.

Contact: Vicki Rolens, Managing Director
Federation of American Consumers and Travelers
PO Box 104
Edwardsville, IL 62025
Phone: 800-872-3228
Fax: 618-656-5369
E-mail: vrolens@usafact.org

FIRST CHOICE COLLEGE PLACEMENT LLC

http://www.firstchoicecollege.com/

ADMISSIONHOOK.COM ESSAY CONTEST

This award is part of our ongoing mission to help students get into and pay for the college of their dreams. There are two ways to win the scholarship. First, you can create an account and submit your essay. If your essay is one of the top 5 vote recipients, your essay will be reviewed by a committee and the winner will be notified within 14 days of the close of the scholarship contest. Second, you can create an account and vote on other student's essays (you can also vote on your own). The registered user who votes on the most essays as of the scholarship deadline will receive a $500 scholarship.

Award: Prize for use in freshman year.

Eligibility Requirements: Applicant must be enrolled or expecting to enroll at a two-year or four-year institution.

Contact: James Maroney, Director of Educational Consulting
First Choice College Placement LLC
50 Cherry Street
50 Cherry Street
Milford, CT 06460
Phone: 203-878-7998
Fax: 203-878- Ext. 6087
E-mail: jmaroney@firstchoicecollege.com

FIRST COMMAND EDUCATIONAL FOUNDATION

http://www.fcef.com/

DONALDSON D. FRIZZELL SCHOLARSHIP

Scholarship awarded to students seeking associate, undergraduate, or graduate degrees. Also available to those seeking professional certification or attending vocational school. Details announced in February of each year.

Award: Scholarship for use in freshman, sophomore, junior, senior, or graduate years; not renewable. *Number:* up to 6. *Amount:* $2500–$5000.

Eligibility Requirements: Applicant must be enrolled or expecting to enroll full-time at a four-year or technical institution or university. Available to U.S. and non-U.S. citizens.

Application Requirements: Application, essay, resume, references, transcript. *Deadline:* March 31.

Contact: Adriane McManus, Scholarship Programs Manager
First Command Educational Foundation
One FirstComm Plaza
Ft Worth, TX 76109-4999
E-mail: Scholarships@fcef.com

FLORIDA NURSES ASSOCIATION

http://www.floridanurse.org/

MARY YORK SCHOLARSHIP FUND

Need criteria for the Mary York Scholarship Fund is not restricted at this time.

Award: Scholarship for use in freshman, sophomore, junior, or senior years.

Eligibility Requirements: Applicant must be enrolled or expecting to enroll at a two-year or four-year or technical institution or university.

Contact: Leah Nash, Scholarship Committee
Florida Nurses Association
1235 East Concord Street
PO Box 536985
Orlando, FL 32853-6985
Phone: 407-896-3261 Ext. 303
E-mail: foundation@floridanurse.org

UNDINE SAMS AND FRIENDS SCHOLARSHIP FUND

The Undine Sams and Friends Scholarship Fund is available statewide to all levels of Nursing students.

Award: Scholarship for use in freshman, sophomore, junior, senior, or graduate years.

Eligibility Requirements: Applicant must be enrolled or expecting to enroll at a two-year or four-year or technical institution or university.

Contact: Leah Nash, Scholarship Committee
Florida Nurses Association
1235 East Concord Street
PO Box 536985
Orlando, FL 32853-6985
Phone: 407-896-3261 Ext. 303
E-mail: foundation@floridanurse.org

FORECLOSURE.COM

http://www.foreclosure.com/

FORECLOSURE.COM SCHOLARSHIP PROGRAM

The Foreclosure.com Scholarship Program encourages students to offer innovative ideas and solutions to 'solve the foreclosure crisis' in the form of an essay. Essay submissions must be between 1,000 and 2,500 words and all accepted freshman and enrolled undergraduate and graduate-stu-

dents are eligible to apply. First place prize is $5,000 and second through fifth place will be awarded $1,000 each. Checks will be made out to the college or university attended in the form of a non-renewable scholarship grant. The best five plans will be sent to Congress and to President Barack Obama.

Award: Grant for use in freshman, sophomore, junior, senior, graduate, or postgraduate years; not renewable. *Number:* 5. *Amount:* $1000–$5000.

Eligibility Requirements: Applicant must be enrolled or expecting to enroll full- or part-time at a two-year or four-year or technical institution or university. Available to U.S. citizens.

Application Requirements: Application, applicant must enter a contest, essay. *Deadline:* continuous.

Contact: Mrs. Linda Yates, Director of Education
Foreclosure.com
1095 Broken Sound Parkway NW, Suite 200
Boca Raton, FL 33487
Phone: 561-988-9669 Ext. 7383
E-mail: lyates@foreclosure.com

FOUNDATION FOR INDEPENDENT HIGHER EDUCATION

http://www.fihe.org/

HSBC FIRST OPPORTUNITY PARTNERS SCHOLARSHIPS

Award targets the students with multiple at-risk factors as identified by financial aid officers in FIHE colleges. For undergraduate students with at least 2.4 GPA after the first semester of the freshman year. Deadline varies.

Award: Scholarship for use in sophomore or junior years; renewable. *Amount:* $5000.

Eligibility Requirements: Applicant must be enrolled or expecting to enroll full-time at a four-year institution or university. Available to U.S. citizens.

Application Requirements: Application, essay, financial need analysis, transcript. *Deadline:* varies.

Contact: Ms. Jacalyn Cox, Program Manager
E-mail: jcox@fihe.org

UPS SCHOLARSHIP PROGRAM

Scholarship program for undergraduate students attending FIHE-affiliated colleges. Deadline varies.

Award: Scholarship for use in freshman, sophomore, junior, or senior years; not renewable. *Amount:* $2700.

Eligibility Requirements: Applicant must be enrolled or expecting to enroll full- or part-time at a four-year institution or university. Available to U.S. and non-U.S. citizens.

Application Requirements: *Deadline:* varies.

Contact: Dr. Myrvin Christopherson, Acting President
Foundation for Independent Higher Education
1920 N Street, NW
Suite 210
Washington, DC 20036
Phone: 202-367-0333
E-mail: info@fihe.org

FOUNDATION FOR OUTDOOR ADVERTISING RESEARCH AND EDUCATION (FOARE)

http://www.oaaa.org/

FOARE SCHOLARSHIP PROGRAM

One-time award of $2000 for 6 students. High school seniors, undergraduates, and graduate students enrolled in or accepted to an accredited institution are eligible to apply. Selections are based on financial need, academic performance, and career goals.

Award: Scholarship for use in freshman, sophomore, junior, senior, or graduate years; not renewable. *Number:* 6. *Amount:* $2000.

Eligibility Requirements: Applicant must be enrolled or expecting to enroll full-time at a four-year institution or university. Available to U.S. citizens.

Application Requirements: Application, essay, financial need analysis, transcript. *Deadline:* June 15.

Contact: Scholarship Program
Foundation for Outdoor Advertising Research and Education (FOARE)
c/o Thomas M. Smith & Associates, 4601 Tilden Street, NW
Washington, DC 20016
Phone: 202-364-7130
E-mail: tmfsmith@starpower.net

THE FRANK M. AND GERTRUDE R. DOYLE FOUNDATION INC.

http://www.frankmdoyle.org/

THE FRANK M. AND GERTRUDE R. DOYLE FOUNDATION, INC.

Eligible applicants for this scholarship must be: Graduating seniors or graduates, (G.E.D. is acceptable), of the Huntington Beach Union High School District, Huntington Beach, California; Washoe County Unified High School District, Reno, Nevada; students or graduates of the Huntington Beach Adult High School; students or graduates of the Washoe County Adult High School; graduates or current/previous students of the following community colleges in Southern California: Orange Coast, Golden West, Coastline, Irvine Valley, Fullerton, Cypress, Santa Ana, Saddleback, or Santiago Canyon. Age is not a factor. Applications may be downloaded from the foundations web site, http//www.frankmdoyle.org anytime after 1 December. See web site for details.

Award: Scholarship for use in freshman, sophomore, junior, senior, graduate, or postgraduate years; not renewable. *Number:* varies. *Amount:* $500–$30,000.

Eligibility Requirements: Applicant must be age 17-99 and enrolled or expecting to enroll full- or part-time at a two-year or four-year or technical institution or university. Available to U.S. citizens.

Application Requirements: Application, essay, references, transcript, Student Aid Report (SAR). *Deadline:* March 1.

Contact: The Frank M. and Gertrude R. Doyle Foundation Inc.
3732 Lakeside Drive, Suite 202A
Reno, NV 89509-5238
Phone: 775-829-1972
Fax: 775-829-1974
E-mail: fmdfoundation@aol.com

GEN AND KELLY TANABE FOUNDATION

http://www.genkellyscholarship.com/

$1,000 GEN AND KELLY TANABE PARENT SCHOLARSHIP

Applicants must be the parents of current high school or college students. Only online applications are accepted. For more information, visit http://www.parentscholarship.com.

Award: Scholarship for use in freshman, sophomore, junior, or senior years; not renewable. *Amount:* $1000.

Eligibility Requirements: Applicant must be enrolled or expecting to enroll full- or part-time at a two-year or four-year or technical institution or university. Available to U.S. citizens.

Application Requirements: Application, essay. *Deadline:* December 31.

Contact: Scholarship Coordinator
Gen and Kelly Tanabe Foundation
3286 Oak Court
Belmont, CA 94002
Phone: 650-618-2221
E-mail: tanabe@gmail.com

GEN AND KELLY TANABE SCHOLARSHIP

The scholarship is open to 9th-12th grade high school students, college students or graduate students who are legal residents of the U.S. Applicants may study any major and attend any college in the U.S. Only online applications are accepted.

Award: Scholarship for use in freshman, sophomore, junior, senior, or graduate years; not renewable. *Amount:* $1000.

Eligibility Requirements: Applicant must be enrolled or expecting to enroll full- or part-time at a two-year or four-year or technical institution or university. Available to U.S. citizens.

Application Requirements: Application, essay. *Deadline:* July 31.

Contact: Scholarship Coordinator
Gen and Kelly Tanabe Foundation
3286 Oak Court
Belmont, CA 94002
Phone: 650-618-2221
E-mail: tanabe@gmail.com

GEORGE T. WELCH TRUST

http://www.bakerboyer.com/

JOHN O. HENDRICKS MEMORIAL SCHOLARSHIP

Grants payable to students after completion of first quarter or semester. Must be enrolled full-time. Must maintain a minimum GPA of 2.0. Must reapply. The budget form must be completed and cover the entire school year.

Award: Scholarship for use in freshman, sophomore, junior, or senior years; not renewable. *Number:* varies. *Amount:* varies.

Eligibility Requirements: Applicant must be enrolled or expecting to enroll full-time at a four-year institution or university. Available to U.S. citizens.

Application Requirements: Application, responsibility shown in one or more of the following areas: community, school, home, church. *Deadline:* April 13.

Contact: Ted Cohan, Trust Portfolio Manager
George T. Welch Trust
Baker Boyer Bank, Investment Management & Trust Services
7 West Main, PO Box 1796
Walla Walla, WA 99362
Phone: 509-526-1204
Fax: 509-522-3136
E-mail: cohant@bakerboyer.com

MILTON-FREEWATER AREA FOUNDATION SCHOLARSHIPS

Grants for all four years of undergraduate work. Entering freshman must maintain a GPA of 2.5, and all students must maintain a minimum GPA of 2.0. Must reapply. The budget form must be completed and cover the entire school year.

Award: Scholarship for use in freshman, sophomore, junior, senior, or graduate years; not renewable. *Number:* varies. *Amount:* varies.

Eligibility Requirements: Applicant must be enrolled or expecting to enroll full-time at a two-year or four-year institution or university. Available to U.S. citizens.

Application Requirements: Application. *Deadline:* April 13.

Contact: Scholarship Committee
George T. Welch Trust
Baker Boyer Bank, Wealth Management Services, PO Box 1796
Walla Walla, WA 99362

GETEDUCATED.COM

http://www.geteducated.com/

$1,000 EXCELLENCE IN ONLINE EDUCATION SCHOLARSHIP

Scholarships for distance education available only to U.S. citizens enrolled in a CHEA-accredited online degree program located in the USA with a minimum cumulative GPA of 3.0. Provide a copy of your most recent grade transcripts, completed application, a copy of your most recent FAFSA, and submit a 500-word essay: "What a College Degree Means to Me."

Award: Scholarship for use in freshman, sophomore, junior, senior, or graduate years; not renewable. *Number:* 3–7. *Amount:* $1000.

Eligibility Requirements: Applicant must be enrolled or expecting to enroll full- or part-time at a two-year or four-year institution or university. Applicant must have 3.0 GPA or higher. Available to U.S. citizens.

Application Requirements: Application, essay, financial need analysis, transcript. *Deadline:* October 15.

Contact: Online Education Scholarship Committee
GetEducated.com
4 Carmichael, #2160
Essex Junction, VT 05452
Phone: 802-899-4866

GOLDEN KEY INTERNATIONAL HONOUR SOCIETY

http://www.goldenkey.org/

GOLDEN KEY SERVICE AWARD

One award totaling $500, disbursed as $250 to the recipient and $250 to the charity of the recipient's choice. Undergraduate and graduate members who were enrolled as students during the previous academic year are eligible.

Award: Scholarship for use in sophomore, junior, senior, or graduate years; not renewable. *Number:* 1. *Amount:* $500.

Eligibility Requirements: Applicant must be enrolled or expecting to enroll full- or part-time at a four-year institution or university. Available to Canadian and non-U.S. citizens.

Application Requirements: Application, essay, references, cover page from the online registration, statement of project. *Deadline:* March 3.

Contact: Crystal Hunter, Program Manager
Golden Key International Honour Society
1040 Crown Pointe Parkway
Suite 900
Atlanta, GA 30338
Phone: 800-377-2401
E-mail: awards@goldenkey.org

GREEN CHEMISTRY INSTITUTE-AMERICAN CHEMICAL SOCIETY

http://www.acs.org/greenchemistry

JOSEPH BREEN MEMORIAL FELLOWSHIP IN GREEN CHEMISTRY

The award sponsors the participation of a young international Green Chemistry scholar in a Green Chemistry technical meeting, conference, or training program of their choice. International scholar is defined as undergraduate students and above, but below the level of assistant professor and within the first seven years of a professional career.

Award: Prize for use in freshman, sophomore, junior, senior, graduate, or postgraduate years; not renewable. *Number:* 1–2. *Amount:* $1–$2000.

Eligibility Requirements: Applicant must be enrolled or expecting to enroll full-time at a four-year institution or university. Available to U.S. and non-U.S. citizens.

Application Requirements: Application, applicant must enter a contest, essay, resume, references. *Deadline:* February 1.

Contact: Jennifer Young, Manager
Green Chemistry Institute-American Chemical Society
1155 16th Street NW
Washington, DC 20036
Phone: 202-872-6102
E-mail: gci@acs.org

KENNETH G. HANCOCK MEMORIAL AWARD IN GREEN CHEMISTRY

Award of $1000 for the students who have completed their education or research in green chemistry. The scholarship provides national recognition for outstanding student contributions to furthering the goals of green chemistry through research or education.

Award: Prize for use in freshman, sophomore, junior, senior, or graduate years; not renewable. *Number:* 1–2. *Amount:* $1000.

Eligibility Requirements: Applicant must be enrolled or expecting to enroll full-time at a four-year institution or university. Available to U.S. and non-U.S. citizens.

Application Requirements: Application, applicant must enter a contest, essay. *Deadline:* February 1.

Contact: Jennifer Young, Manager
Green Chemistry Institute-American Chemical Society
1155 16th Street, NW
Washington, DC 20036
Phone: 202-872-6102
E-mail: gci@acs.org

GUERNSEY-MUSKINGUM ELECTRIC COOPERATIVE INC.

http://www.gmenergy.com/

HIGH SCHOOL SENIOR SCHOLARSHIP

Two $1000 scholarships, two $500 scholarships, two $300 scholarships, and two $200 scholarships are available to a student graduating from high school whose parent or legal guardian receives electric service from Guernsey-Muskingum Electric Cooperative.

Award: Scholarship for use in freshman year; not renewable. *Number:* 8. *Amount:* $200–$1000.

Eligibility Requirements: Applicant must be high school student and planning to enroll or expecting to enroll full-time at a two-year or four-year institution or university. Applicant must have 3.0 GPA or higher. Available to U.S. citizens.

Application Requirements: Application, interview, references, transcript. *Deadline:* February 1.

Contact: Brian Bennett, Manager, Member Services
Guernsey-Muskingum Electric Cooperative Inc.
17 South Liberty Street
New Concord, OH 43762
Phone: 740-826-7661
Fax: 740-826-7171
E-mail: mailbox@gmenergy.com

HELPING HANDS FOUNDATION

http://www.helpinghandsbookscholarship.com/

HELPING HANDS BOOK SCHOLARSHIP PROGRAM

The grant assists students with the high cost of textbooks and study materials. Awards are open to individuals of ages 16 and up, planning to attend or currently attending a two- or four-year college or university or a technical/vocational institution. Application fee is $5. Scholarship value is from $100 to $1000. Deadline varies.

Award: Grant for use in freshman, sophomore, junior, senior, or graduate years; not renewable. *Number:* 20–50. *Amount:* $100–$1000.

Eligibility Requirements: Applicant must be age 16 and over and enrolled or expecting to enroll full- or part-time at a two-year or four-year or technical institution or university. Available to U.S. and non-U.S. citizens.

Application Requirements: Application, essay, self-addressed stamped envelope, transcript. *Fee:* $5. *Deadline:* varies.

Contact: Scholarship Director
Helping Hands Foundation
4480-H South Cobb Drive, PO Box 435
Smyrna, GA 30080

HEMOPHILIA FEDERATION OF AMERICA

http://www.hemophiliaed.org/

PARENT CONTINUING EDUCATION SCHOLARSHIP

Scholarship for a parent of a school-age child with a blood clotting disorder. For use in furthering the parent's own education. Previous scholarship recipients are encouraged to reapply.

Award: Scholarship for use in freshman or sophomore years; not renewable. *Number:* 2. *Amount:* $1500.

Eligibility Requirements: Applicant must be enrolled or expecting to enroll full- or part-time at a technical institution. Available to U.S. citizens.

Application Requirements: Application, essay, financial need analysis, references. *Deadline:* April 30.

Contact: Sandy Aultman, Scholarship Coordinator
Hemophilia Federation of America
1045 West Pinhook Road, Suite 101
Lafayette, LA 70503
Phone: 337-261-9787
Fax: 337-261-1787

SIBLING CONTINUING EDUCATION SCHOLARSHIP

Scholarship for the sibling of a school-age child with a blood clotting disorder. For use in furthering the sibling's own education. Previous scholarship recipients may reapply.

Award: Scholarship for use in freshman year; not renewable. *Number:* 3. *Amount:* $1500.

Eligibility Requirements: Applicant must be high school student and planning to enroll or expecting to enroll full- or part-time at a four-year institution or university. Available to U.S. citizens.

Application Requirements: Application, essay, financial need analysis, references. *Deadline:* April 30.

Contact: Scholarship Committee
Hemophilia Federation of America
1405 West Pinhook Road, Suite 101
Lafayette, LA 70503
Phone: 337-261-9787
Fax: 337-261-1787
E-mail: info@hemophiliafed.org

HENKEL CONSUMER ADHESIVES INC.

http://www.ducktapeclub.com/

DUCK BRAND DUCT TAPE "STUCK AT PROM" SCHOLARSHIP CONTEST

Contest is open to residents of the United States and Canada. Must be 14 years or older. First place winners receive a $3000 college scholarship each and $3000 for the high school hosting the winning couple's prom. The second place winners will each receive a $2000 college scholarship, with the high school receiving $2000. The third place couple will each win a $1000 college scholarship and the high school will receive $1000.

Award: Prize for use in freshman, sophomore, junior, or senior years; not renewable. *Number:* 3. *Amount:* $1000–$3000.

Eligibility Requirements: Applicant must be age 14 and over and enrolled or expecting to enroll full- or part-time at a two-year or four-year or technical institution or university. Available to U.S. and Canadian citizens.

Application Requirements: Application, applicant must enter a contest, photo, entry form, release form. *Deadline:* June 11.

Contact: Michelle Heffner, Digital Marketing Communications Manager
Henkel Consumer Adhesives Inc.
32150 Just Imagine Drive
Avon, OH 44011-1355
Phone: 440-937-7000

HISPANIC ASSOCIATION OF COLLEGES AND UNIVERSITIES (HACU)

http://www.hacu.net/

HISPANIC ASSOCIATION OF COLLEGES AND UNIVERSITIES SCHOLARSHIP PROGRAMS

The scholarship programs are sponsored by corporate organizations. To be eligible, students must attend a HACU member college or university and meet all additional criteria. Visit web site http//www.hacu.net for details.

Award: Scholarship for use in freshman, sophomore, junior, senior, or graduate years; not renewable. *Number:* up to 200. *Amount:* up to $2000.

Eligibility Requirements: Applicant must be enrolled or expecting to enroll full- or part-time at a two-year or four-year institution or uni-

versity. Applicant must have 3.0 GPA or higher. Available to U.S. citizens.

Application Requirements: Application, essay, financial need analysis, resume, transcript, enrollment certification form. *Deadline:* May 27.

Contact: Scholarship Department
Hispanic Association of Colleges and Universities (HACU)
High Point Tower, 8415 Datapoint Drive, Suite 400
San Antonio, TX 78229
Phone: 210-692-3805
Fax: 210-692-0823
E-mail: scholarship@hacu.net

HONOR SOCIETY OF PHI KAPPA PHI

http://www.phikappaphi.org/

STUDY ABROAD GRANT COMPETITION

Grants up to $1,000 awarded to undergraduate as support for seeking knowledge and experience by studying abroad. Must have 3.5 GPA or above and minimum of 30 semester hours but no more than 90. Travel cannot begin prior to May 1. Must attend a college/university with an active Phi Kappa Phi chapter.

Award: Grant for use in freshman, sophomore, junior, or senior years; not renewable. *Number:* 45. *Amount:* $1000.

Eligibility Requirements: Applicant must be enrolled or expecting to enroll full-time at a four-year institution or university. Applicant must have 3.5 GPA or higher. Available to U.S. and non-U.S. citizens.

Application Requirements: Application, essay, references, transcript, letter of acceptance into a study abroad program. *Deadline:* February 24.

Contact: Mrs. Maria C. Davis, National Marketing Development Manager
Honor Society of Phi Kappa Phi
7576 Goodwood Boulevard
Baton Rouge, LA 70806
Phone: 225-388-4917 Ext. 35
Fax: 225-388-4900
E-mail: mdavis@phikappaphi.org

HORATIO ALGER ASSOCIATION OF DISTINGUISHED AMERICANS

http://www.horatioalger.org/

HORATIO ALGER SCHOLARSHIP PROGRAMS

The Association provides financial assistance to high school seniors (U.S citizens only) who have faced adversity., have financial need and are pursuing higher education. Recipients must pursue a bachelor's degree however they may start their studies at a 2 year school and then transfer to a 4 year university. Minimum 2.0 GPA required.

Award: Scholarship for use in freshman, sophomore, junior, or senior years; renewable. *Number:* 784. *Amount:* $2500–$20,000.

Eligibility Requirements: Applicant must be high school student; age 19 or under and planning to enroll or expecting to enroll full-time at a four-year institution or university. Available to U.S. citizens.

Application Requirements: Application, essay, financial need analysis, references, test scores, transcript. *Deadline:* October 30.

Contact: Ms. Lindsay Paul, Educational Programs Coordinator
Horatio Alger Association of Distinguished Americans
99 Canal Center Plaza, Suite 320
Alexandria, VA 22314
Phone: 703-684-9444
Fax: 703-684-9445
E-mail: lpaul@horatioalger.com

HUGH FULTON BYAS MEMORIAL FUNDS INC.

HUGH FULTON BYAS MEMORIAL GRANT
• *See page 666*

HUMANA FOUNDATION

http://www.humanafoundation.org/

HUMANA FOUNDATION SCHOLARSHIP PROGRAM

Applicants must be under 25 years of age and a United States citizen. Must be a dependent of a Humana Inc. employee. For more information, visit web site http://www.humanafoundation.org.

Award: Scholarship for use in freshman, sophomore, junior, or senior years; renewable. *Number:* up to 75. *Amount:* $1500–$3000.

Eligibility Requirements: Applicant must be age 25 or under and enrolled or expecting to enroll full-time at a two-year or four-year institution or university. Available to U.S. citizens.

Application Requirements: Application, references, transcript. *Deadline:* January 15.

Contact: Charles Jackson, Program Manager
Humana Foundation
500 West Main Street, Room 208
Louisville, KY 40202
Phone: 502-580-1245
Fax: 502-580-1256
E-mail: cjackson@humana.com

IMAGINE AMERICA FOUNDATION

http://www.imagine-america.org/

IMAGINE AMERICA SCHOLARSHIP

Imagine America, sponsored by the Imagine America Foundation (IAF), is a $1,000 career education award that is available to recent high school graduates who are pursuing postsecondary education at participating career colleges across the United States. Only recent high school graduates who meet the following recommended guidelines should apply: likelihood of successful completion of postsecondary education; high school grade point average of 2.5 or greater; financial need; demonstrated voluntary community service during senior year.

Award: Scholarship for use in freshman year; not renewable. *Number:* up to 15,000. *Amount:* $1000.

Eligibility Requirements: Applicant must be high school student; age 17-18 and planning to enroll or expecting to enroll full- or part-time at a two-year or four-year or technical institution. Available to U.S. citizens.

Application Requirements: Financial need analysis, nomination. *Deadline:* December 31.

Contact: Torian Brown, Director of Operations
Imagine America Foundation
1101 Connecticut Avenue, NW, Suite 901
Washington, DC 20036
Phone: 202-336-6800
Fax: 202-408-8102
E-mail: torianb@imagine-america.org

INDEPENDENT INSTITUTE

http://www.independent.org/

SIR JOHN M. TEMPLETON FELLOWSHIPS ESSAY CONTEST

Essay contest for junior higher education faculty and students. Student applicants must be born on or after May 2, 1972. Student applicants may be pursuing any degree including associates, undergraduate, postgraduate or doctoral.

Award: Prize for use in freshman, sophomore, junior, senior, graduate, or postgraduate years; not renewable. *Number:* 6. *Amount:* $1000–$10,000.

Eligibility Requirements: Applicant must be age 35 or under and enrolled or expecting to enroll full- or part-time at a two-year or four-year institution or university. Available to U.S. and non-U.S. citizens.

Application Requirements: Application, applicant must enter a contest, essay. *Deadline:* May 1.

Contact: Carl Close, Academic Affairs Director
Independent Institute
100 Swan Way, Suite 200
Oakland, CA 94621-1428
Phone: 510-632-1366
Fax: 510-568-6040
E-mail: cclose@independent.org

INSTITUTE OF FOOD TECHNOLOGISTS

http://www.ift.org/

AMERICAN INSTITUTE OF BAKING SCHOLARSHIP

One $10,535 is available to juniors, seniors and graduate students in order to enable them to complete the American Institute of Baking's 16 week semester course at AIB located in Manhattan, Kansas.

Award: Scholarship for use in junior, senior, or graduate years; not renewable. *Number:* 1. *Amount:* $10,535.

Eligibility Requirements: Applicant must be enrolled or expecting to enroll full-time at a four-year institution or university.

Application Requirements: *Deadline:* varies.

Contact: Anna Proctor, IFT Foundation Coordinator
Institute of Food Technologists
525 West Van Buren Street, Suite 1000
Chicago, IL 60607
Phone: 312-782-8424
E-mail: akproctor@ift.org

INTEREXCHANGE FOUNDATION

http://www.interexchange.org/

CHRISTIANSON GRANT

A total of 8 scholarships awarded every year. Two $10,000, two $5000 and four $2500 scholarships are awarded to undergraduate students. Applicants should be between the ages of 18 and 28. Deadlines: March 15 and October 15.

Award: Grant for use in freshman, sophomore, junior, or senior years; not renewable. *Number:* 8. *Amount:* $2500–$10,000.

Eligibility Requirements: Applicant must be age 18-28 and enrolled or expecting to enroll full- or part-time at a two-year or four-year or technical institution or university. Available to U.S. citizens.

Application Requirements: Application, essay, interview, resume, references. *Fee:* $25. *Deadline:* varies.

Contact: Myisha Battle, Foundation Coordinator
InterExchange Foundation
161 Sixth Avenue
New York, NY 10013
Phone: 917-305-5471
Fax: 212-924-0575
E-mail: grants@interexchange.org

WORKING ABROAD GRANT

Grant open to applicants who have been accepted to an InterExchange Working Abroad program. Awards cover program fees plus up to $2000 toward transportation, insurance, and living expenses.

Award: Grant for use in freshman, sophomore, junior, or senior years; not renewable. *Number:* 5–8. *Amount:* $2000–$4000.

Eligibility Requirements: Applicant must be age 18-28 and enrolled or expecting to enroll full- or part-time at a two-year or four-year or technical institution or university. Available to U.S. citizens.

Application Requirements: Application, essay, interview, resume, references. *Fee:* $25. *Deadline:* continuous.

Contact: Myisha Battle, Foundation Coordinator
InterExchange Foundation
161 Sixth Avenue
New York, NY 10013
Phone: 917-305-5471
Fax: 212-924-0575
E-mail: grants@interexchange.org

JACK KENT COOKE FOUNDATION

http://www.jackkentcookefoundation.org/

JACK KENT COOKE FOUNDATION UNDERGRADUATE TRANSFER SCHOLARSHIP PROGRAM

Scholarships to students and recent alumni from community college to complete their bachelor's degrees at accredited four-year colleges or universities in the United States or abroad. Candidates must be nominated by a faculty representative from their community college.

Award: Scholarship for use in freshman, sophomore, junior, or senior years; renewable. *Number:* 50. *Amount:* $30,000.

Eligibility Requirements: Applicant must be enrolled or expecting to enroll full-time at a four-year institution or university. Applicant must have 3.5 GPA or higher. Available to U.S. and non-U.S. citizens.

Application Requirements: Application, essay, financial need analysis, references, transcript. *Deadline:* February 1.

Contact: Gaby Ruess, Scholarship Committee
Jack Kent Cooke Foundation
44325 Woodridge Parkway
Lansdowne, VA 20176
Phone: 800-498-6478
E-mail: jkc-u@act.org

JEANNETTE RANKIN FOUNDATION, INC.

http://www.rankinfoundation.org/

JEANNETTE RANKIN FOUNDATION AWARDS

Applicants must be low-income women, age 35 or older, who are U.S. citizens pursuing a technical/vocational education, an associate degree, or a first-time bachelor's degree at a regionally or ACICS accredited college. Applications may be printed from our web site from November through February.

Award: Scholarship for use in freshman, sophomore, junior, or senior years; renewable. *Number:* 80. *Amount:* $2000.

Eligibility Requirements: Applicant must be age 35 and over; enrolled or expecting to enroll full- or part-time at a two-year or four-year or technical institution or university and female. Available to U.S. citizens.

Application Requirements: Application, essay, financial need analysis, references, transcript. *Deadline:* March 1.

Contact: April Greene, Program Coordinator
Jeannette Rankin Foundation, Inc.
1 Huntington Road, #701
Athens, GA 30606
Phone: 706-208-1211
E-mail: info@rankinfoundation.org

JOHN GYLES EDUCATION CENTER

http://www.johngyleseducationcenter.com/

JOHN GYLES EDUCATION AWARDS

Financial assistance available to students enrolled full-time at (or accepted to) a college or university program as an undergraduate or graduate student in any area of postsecondary study. High school seniors, and others, may apply pending acceptance. Applicants must have a minimum GPA of 3.0 (or similar grade assessment) and must have U.S. or Canadian citizenship. For more information, visit web site http://www.johngyleseducationcenter.com.

Award: Scholarship for use in freshman, sophomore, junior, or senior years; not renewable. *Number:* 2–5.

Eligibility Requirements: Applicant must be enrolled or expecting to enroll full-time at a two-year or four-year institution or university. Applicant must have 3.0 GPA or higher. Available to U.S. and Canadian citizens.

Application Requirements: Application. *Deadline:* June 1.

Contact: R. James Cougle, Administrator
John Gyles Education Center
259-103 Brunswick Street, PO Box 4808
Fredericton, NB E3B 5G4
Phone: 506-459-7460

J. WOOD PLATT CADDIE SCHOLARSHIP TRUST

http://www.plattcaddiescholarship.org/

J. WOOD PLATT CADDIE SCHOLARSHIP TRUST

This is a need-based scholarship available to those employed as golf caddies at Golf Association of Philadelphia member clubs.

Award: Scholarship for use in freshman, sophomore, junior, or senior years; renewable.

Eligibility Requirements: Applicant must be enrolled or expecting to enroll full-time at a two-year or four-year institution or university. Available to U.S. and non-U.S. citizens.

Application Requirements: Application, essay, financial need analysis, interview, references, test scores, transcript. *Deadline:* April 25.

Contact: Barbara Scott, Director, Platt Caddie Scholarship
J. Wood Platt Caddie Scholarship Trust
1974 Sproul Road
Suite 400
Broomall, PA 19008
Phone: 610-687-2340 Ext. 21
Fax: 610-687-2082
E-mail: bscott@gapgolf.org

K2 PROGRESSIVE, LLC

http://www.admissionscholarship.com/aboutus/

ADMISSIONSCHOLARSHIP.COM SCHOLARSHIP

The AdmissionScholarship.com Scholarship Program is a program that awards (2) $1,000 scholarships per year to students who are currently enrolled or are planning on enrolling in a college or university. Scholarships are awarded through random drawings to give each student an equal chance of winning. Deadlines are June 30 and December 31 of each year.

Award: Scholarship for use in freshman, sophomore, junior, senior, graduate, or postgraduate years; not renewable. *Number:* 2. *Amount:* $1000.

Eligibility Requirements: Applicant must be age 13 and over and enrolled or expecting to enroll full- or part-time at a two-year or four-year or technical institution or university. Available to U.S. and non-U.S. citizens.

Application Requirements: Application. *Deadline:* continuous.

Contact: Mr. Cory M Klinnert, President
K2 Progressive, LLC
PO Box 23
Moorhead, MN 56561
Phone: 218-329-1308
E-mail: info@admissionscholarship.com

KE ALI'I PAUAHI FOUNDATION

http://www.pauahi.org/

CHOY-KEE 'OHANA SCHOLARSHIP

Scholarship recognizes the academic achievements and efforts of worthy students with a minimum GPA of 3.0 who are pursuing a postsecondary education. Must submit essay addressing what the biggest problem in Hawaii is and potential solutions. Submit two letters of recommendation; one from teacher or counselor and one from a community organization.

Award: Scholarship for use in freshman, sophomore, junior, senior, or graduate years; not renewable. *Number:* 2. *Amount:* $500.

Eligibility Requirements: Applicant must be enrolled or expecting to enroll full-time at a two-year or four-year institution or university. Applicant must have 3.0 GPA or higher. Available to U.S. citizens.

Application Requirements: Application, essay, references, transcript, Student Aid Report (SAR), college acceptance letter. *Deadline:* April 1.

Contact: Mavis Shiraishi-Nagao, Scholarship Administrator
Phone: 808-534-3966
E-mail: scholarships@pauahi.org

DENIS WONG & ASSOCIATES SCHOLARSHIP

Scholarship to recognize an outstanding student pursuing an undergraduate degree in liberal arts or science, or a graduate degree in a professional field from an accredited university. Recipient must have a well-rounded and balanced record of achievement in preparation for career objectives, demonstrate a commitment to contribute to the greater community. Minimum GPA of 3.5 required. Submit two letters of recommendation from teacher, counselors, coaches or employers citing applicant's credentials and potential for success.

Award: Scholarship for use in freshman, sophomore, junior, senior, or graduate years; not renewable. *Number:* up to 3. *Amount:* up to $1000.

Eligibility Requirements: Applicant must be enrolled or expecting to enroll full-time at a four-year institution or university. Applicant must have 3.5 GPA or higher. Available to U.S. citizens.

Application Requirements: Application, essay, references, transcript, college acceptance letter, copy of SAR. *Deadline:* April 1.

Contact: Mavis Shiraishi-Nagao, Scholarship Administrator
    Phone: 808-534-3966
    E-mail: scholarships@pauahi.org

KAMEHAMEHA SCHOOLS CLASS OF 1952 "NA HOALOHA O KAMEHAMEHA" SCHOLARSHIP

Scholarship to assist students pursuing a certificate or degree from an accredited vocational/business school or a two- or four-year post-secondary institution. Must demonstrate financial need. Minimum 2.0 GPA required.

Award: Scholarship for use in freshman, sophomore, junior, or senior years; not renewable. *Number:* 1–2. *Amount:* $1000.

Eligibility Requirements: Applicant must be enrolled or expecting to enroll full-time at a two-year or four-year or technical institution or university. Available to U.S. citizens.

Application Requirements: Application, financial need analysis, transcript, Student Aid Report (SAR), college acceptance letter. *Deadline:* April 1.

Contact: Mavis Shiraishi-Nagao, Scholarship Administrator
    Phone: 808-534-3966
    E-mail: scholarships@pauahi.org

KAMEHAMEHA SCHOOLS CLASS OF 1968 "KA POLI O KAIONA" SCHOLARSHIP

Scholarships for students pursuing a two-year, four-year, or graduate degree from an accredited post-secondary institution. Minimum 2.8 GPA required. Must demonstrate financial need. Submit two letters of recommendation from educator, employer or community organization. Submit essay on how this award would support and extend the legacy of Ke Ali`i Bernice Pauahi Bishop.

Award: Scholarship for use in freshman, sophomore, junior, senior, or graduate years; not renewable. *Number:* up to 2. *Amount:* up to $700.

Eligibility Requirements: Applicant must be enrolled or expecting to enroll full-time at a two-year or four-year institution or university. Applicant must have 2.5 GPA or higher. Available to U.S. citizens.

Application Requirements: Application, essay, financial need analysis, references, transcript, Student Aid Report (SAR), college acceptance letter. *Deadline:* April 1.

Contact: Mavis Shiraishi-Nagao, Scholarship Administrator
    Phone: 808-534-3966
    E-mail: scholarships@pauahi.org

KENNEDY FOUNDATION

http://www.columbinecorp.com/kennedyfoundation

KENNEDY FOUNDATION SCHOLARSHIPS

Renewable scholarships for current high school students for up to four years of undergraduate study. Renewal contingent upon academic performance. Must maintain a GPA of 2.5. Send self-addressed stamped envelope for application. See web site for details http://www.columbinecorp.com/kennedyfoundation to download an application.

Award: Scholarship for use in freshman year; renewable. *Number:* 8–14. *Amount:* $2000.

Eligibility Requirements: Applicant must be high school student and planning to enroll or expecting to enroll full-time at a two-year or four-year institution or university. Applicant must have 2.5 GPA or higher. Available to U.S. citizens.

Application Requirements: Application, self-addressed stamped envelope, test scores, transcript. *Deadline:* June 30.

Contact: Jonathan Kennedy, Vice President

KENTUCKY OFFICE OF VOCATIONAL REHABILITATION

http://www.ovr.ky.gov/

KENTUCKY OFFICE OF VOCATIONAL REHABILITATION

Grant provides services necessary to secure employment. Eligible individual must possess physical or mental impairment that results in a substantial impediment to employment; benefit from vocational rehabilitation services in terms of an employment outcome; and require vocational rehabilitation services to prepare for, enter, or retain employment.

Award: Grant for use in freshman, sophomore, junior, senior, graduate, or postgraduate years; renewable. *Number:* varies. *Amount:* varies.

Eligibility Requirements: Applicant must be enrolled or expecting to enroll full- or part-time at a two-year or four-year or technical institution or university. Available to U.S. citizens.

Application Requirements: Application, financial need analysis, interview, transcript, eligibility for OVR services and in proper priority category. *Deadline:* continuous.

Contact: Charles Puckett, Program Administrator
    Kentucky Office of Vocational Rehabilitation
    600 West Cedar Street, Suite 2E
    Louisville, KY 40202
    Phone: 502-595-4173
    Fax: 502-564-2358
    E-mail: marianu.spencer@mail.state.ky.us

LEOPOLD SCHEPP FOUNDATION

http://www.scheppfoundation.org/

LEOPOLD SCHEPP SCHOLARSHIP

Scholarship for undergraduates under 30 years of age and graduate students under 40 years of age at the time of application. Applicants must have a minimum GPA of 3.0. High school seniors are not eligible. All applicants must either be enrolled in college or have completed at least one year of college at the time of issuing the application. Must be citizens or permanent residents of the United States. Deadline varies.

Award: Scholarship for use in sophomore, junior, senior, or graduate years; renewable. *Number:* 1–30. *Amount:* up to $8500.

Eligibility Requirements: Applicant must be enrolled or expecting to enroll full-time at a four-year institution or university. Applicant must have 3.0 GPA or higher. Available to U.S. citizens.

Application Requirements: Application, financial need analysis, interview, references, transcript. *Deadline:* varies.

Contact: Scholarship Committee
    Leopold Schepp Foundation
    551 Fifth Avenue, Suite 3000
    New York, NY 10176
    Phone: 212-692-0191

LIFE AND HEALTH INSURANCE FOUNDATION FOR EDUCATION

http://www.naifa.org/consumer/life.cfm

LIFE LESSONS SCHOLARSHIPS PROGRAM

LIFE Lessons Scholarship Program is for college students and college-bound high school seniors who have experienced the death of a parent or legal guardian. To apply you must complete and submit an application, including an essay of no more than 500 words or a video entry of no more than 3 minutes.

Award: Scholarship for use in freshman, sophomore, junior, senior, or graduate years; not renewable. *Number:* 51. *Amount:* $1000–$10,000.

Eligibility Requirements: Applicant must be age 17-24 and enrolled or expecting to enroll full- or part-time at a two-year or four-year or technical institution or university. Available to U.S. citizens.

Application Requirements: Application, applicant must enter a contest, essay or video. *Deadline:* April 15.

Contact: Julie Lattanzi, Consumer Education Coordinator
    Phone: 202-464-5000 Ext. 4446
    Fax: 202-464-5011
    E-mail: scholarship@lifehappens.org

MENNONITE WOMEN

http://www.mennonitewomenusa.org/

INTERNATIONAL WOMEN'S FUND

Scholarship for women from developing countries for postsecondary studies. Must submit letter of recommendations or reference from the church.

Award: Scholarship for use in freshman, sophomore, junior, senior, graduate, or postgraduate years; renewable. *Number:* 12. *Amount:* $500–$1000.

Eligibility Requirements: Applicant must be enrolled or expecting to enroll full- or part-time at a two-year or four-year institution or university and female. Available to citizens of countries other than the U.S. or Canada.

Application Requirements: Application, references. *Deadline:* September 1.

Contact: Rhoda Keener, Program Director
    Mennonite Women
    722 Main Street
    PO Box 347
    Newton, KS 67114
    Phone: 717-532-9723
    Fax: 316-283-0454
    E-mail: office@mennonitewomenusa.org

METAVUE CORPORATION

http://www.metavue.com/

DR. ROBERT RUFFLO SCIENCES PAPER CONTEST

Scholarship contest grants awards to writers of exemplary work in a variety of applied and basic science fields. Work may focus on original research, a research review, or critical essay. Contest is most appropriate for upper high schools levels and undergraduate students pursuing a sciences-oriented education. Visit http://www.metavue.com for additional details.

Award: Scholarship for use in freshman, sophomore, junior, or senior years; not renewable. *Number:* 8–11. *Amount:* $15–$500.

Eligibility Requirements: Applicant must be enrolled or expecting to enroll full-time at a two-year or four-year institution or university. Applicant must have 3.0 GPA or higher. Available to U.S. citizens.

Application Requirements: Application, applicant must enter a contest, essay. *Deadline:* June 15.

Contact: Teresa Rufflo
    Phone: 608-577-0642
    E-mail: scholarships@metavue.com

MICHAEL AND SUSAN DELL FOUNDATION

http://www.msdf.org/

DELL SCHOLARS PROGRAM

250 scholarships offered annually to high school students participating in approved college readiness programs. Must have a minimum 2.4 GPA and should be participating in a MSDF-approved college readiness program for a minimum of two years prior to application.

Award: Scholarship for use in freshman year; not renewable. *Number:* 250. *Amount:* varies.

Eligibility Requirements: Applicant must be high school student and planning to enroll or expecting to enroll full- or part-time at a two-year or four-year or technical institution or university. Available to U.S. citizens.

Application Requirements: Application, references, transcript. *Deadline:* January 15.

Contact: Scholarship Committee
    Michael and Susan Dell Foundation
    PO Box 163867
    Austin, TX 78716
    Phone: 512-329-0799

MILITARY ORDER OF THE STARS AND BARS

http://www.mosbihq.org/

MILITARY ORDER OF THE STARS AND BARS SCHOLARSHIPS

Applicants must be accepted to a degree-granting junior college or four-year college or university. Awards shall be made annually, and the total amount of the scholarship money to be awarded each year to each recipient shall not exceed $1000. Applicants must be sponsored by a local MOS&B Chapter or MOS&B State Society. Applicants must be able to prove they are a descendant of a commissioned officer or civil servant of the Confederate States of America. Preference is given to relatives of currently active MOS&B members. All application information is found on the MOS&B web site.

Award: Scholarship for use in freshman, sophomore, junior, or senior years; not renewable. *Number:* 5. *Amount:* $1000.

Eligibility Requirements: Applicant must be enrolled or expecting to enroll full-time at a two-year or four-year institution or university. Applicant must have 3.0 GPA or higher. Available to U.S. and non-U.S. citizens.

Application Requirements: Application, resume, references, transcript, sponsor's letter and descendant proof. *Deadline:* March 1.

Contact: Dr. Gary Loudermilk, Scholarship Chairman
    Military Order of the Stars and Bars
    2801 14th Street
    Brownwood, TX 76801
    E-mail: gmldhl@harrisbb.com

NATIONAL ACADEMY OF AMERICAN SCHOLARS

http://www.naas.org/

NAAS II NATIONAL AWARDS

One renewable scholarship of $500 to $3000 available for tuition, room, board, books, and academic supplies. Applicant must be college freshman or sophomore attending an American college/university. U.S. citizenship is not required. Must be under the age of 25. Applicants that request an application by mail must enclose a $3 handling fee and a self-addressed stamped envelope. Electronic applications are available to NAAS Subscribers at http://www.naas.org; no fees for NAAS subscribers.

Award: Scholarship for use in freshman or sophomore years; renewable. *Number:* 1–5. *Amount:* $500–$3000.

Eligibility Requirements: Applicant must be age 25 or under and enrolled or expecting to enroll full-time at a four-year institution or university. Available to U.S. and non-U.S. citizens.

Application Requirements: Application, self-addressed stamped envelope. *Fee:* $3. *Deadline:* May 1.

Contact: K. France, Program Director
    National Academy of American Scholars
    2248 Meridian Boulevard, Suite H
    Minden, NV 89423
    Phone: 702-233-5049
    E-mail: staff@naas.org

NATIONAL ASSOCIATION OF RAILWAY BUSINESS WOMEN

http://www.narbw.org/

NARBW SCHOLARSHIP

Scholarship awarded to the members of NARBW and their relatives. The number of awards varies every year. Applications are judged on scholastic ability, ambition and potential, and financial need.

Award: Scholarship for use in freshman, sophomore, junior, or senior years; not renewable. *Number:* varies. *Amount:* $500–$1000.

Eligibility Requirements: Applicant must be enrolled or expecting to enroll full-time at a two-year or four-year or technical institution or university and female. Available to U.S. citizens.

Application Requirements: Application, financial need analysis. *Deadline:* varies.

Contact: Scholarship Chairman
National Association of Railway Business Women
2631 Daleton Boulevard NE
Roanoke, VA 24012
E-mail: narbwinfo@narbw.org

NATIONAL BLACK MBA ASSOCIATION

http://www.nbmbaa.org/

NATIONAL BLACK MBA ASSOCIATION GRADUATE SCHOLARSHIP PROGRAM

Program's mission is to identify and increase the pool of Black talent for business, public, private and non-profit sectors.

Award: Scholarship for use in freshman, sophomore, junior, or senior years; not renewable. *Number:* 10–25. *Amount:* $2500–$15,000.

Eligibility Requirements: Applicant must be enrolled or expecting to enroll full-time at a four-year institution or university. Available to U.S. and non-U.S. citizens.

Application Requirements: Application, essay, interview, resume, transcript. *Deadline:* April 17.

Contact: Ms. Lori O. Johnson, Program Administrator, University
Relations
National Black MBA Association
180 North Michigan Avenue, Suite 1400
Chicago, IL 60601
Phone: 312-580-8086
E-mail: scholarship@nbmbaa.org

NATIONAL DAIRY SHRINE

http://www.dairyshrine.org/

NATIONAL DAIRY SHRINE/MAURICE E. CORE SCHOLARSHIP

Available to college freshman who are majoring in a dairy/animal industry related field with interest in working in the dairy industry in the future. Scholarship is based on leadership abilities, volunteerism, activities and plans for the future.

Award: Scholarship for use in freshman year; not renewable. *Number:* 1. *Amount:* $1000.

Eligibility Requirements: Applicant must be enrolled or expecting to enroll at a two-year or four-year institution. Applicant must have 2.5 GPA or higher. Available to U.S. citizens.

Application Requirements: Application, references, transcript. *Deadline:* April 15.

Contact: Dr. David Selner, Executive Director
National Dairy Shrine
PO Box 725
Denmark, WI 54208
Phone: 920-863-6333
E-mail: info@dairyshrine.org

NATIONAL JUNIOR ANGUS ASSOCIATION

http://www.angus.org/njaa/

AMERICAN ANGUS AUXILIARY SCHOLARSHIP

Scholarship available to graduating high school senior. Can apply only in one state. Any unmarried girl or unmarried boy recommended by a state or regional Auxiliary is eligible.

Award: Scholarship for use in freshman year; not renewable. *Number:* 10. *Amount:* $1000–$14,000.

Eligibility Requirements: Applicant must be high school student; planning to enroll or expecting to enroll full-time at a two-year or four-year or technical institution or university and single. Available to U.S. and Canadian citizens.

Application Requirements: Application, applicant must enter a contest, photo, references, test scores, transcript. *Deadline:* May 1.

Contact: Mrs. Anne Lampe, American Angus Auxiliary Scholarship
Chairman
National Junior Angus Association
5201 E. Road 110
Scott City, KS 67871
Phone: 620-872-3915

NATIONAL RIFLE ASSOCIATION

http://www.nrafoundation.org/

NRA YOUTH EDUCATIONAL SUMMIT (YES) SCHOLARSHIPS

Awards for Youth Educational Summit participants based on the initial application, on-site debate, and degree of participation during the week-long event. Must be graduating high school seniors enrolled in undergraduate program. Must have a minimum GPA of 3.0.

Award: Scholarship for use in freshman year; not renewable. *Number:* 1–6. *Amount:* $1000–$10,000.

Eligibility Requirements: Applicant must be high school student and planning to enroll or expecting to enroll full- or part-time at a two-year or four-year or technical institution or university. Applicant must have 3.0 GPA or higher. Available to U.S. citizens.

Application Requirements: Application, applicant must enter a contest, essay, references, transcript. *Deadline:* March 1.

Contact: Event Services Manager
National Rifle Association
11250 Waples Mill Road
Fairfax, VA 22030
Phone: 703-267-1354
E-mail: fnra@nrahq.org

NATIONAL SCIENCE FOUNDATION

http://www.nsf.gov/

FEDERAL CYBER SERVICE: SCHOLARSHIP FOR SERVICE (SFS) PROGRAM

This program provides scholarships that generally fund books, tuition, room and board, and a stipend while attending a participating institution in an Information Assurance program. Participants must apply directly to participating institutions.

Award: Scholarship for use in junior, senior, graduate, or postgraduate years; not renewable.

Eligibility Requirements: Applicant must be enrolled or expecting to enroll full-time at a four-year institution or university. Available to U.S. citizens.

Application Requirements: Application.

Contact: Arden Bement, Jr., Director
National Science Foundation
4201 Wilson Boulevard
Arlington, VA 22230
Phone: 703-292-5111
E-mail: info@nsfgrfp.org

NATIONAL SOCIETY OF HIGH SCHOOL SCHOLARS

http://www.nshss.org/

ROBERT P. SHEPPARD LEADERSHIP AWARD FOR NSHSS MEMBERS

Scholarship of $1000 awarded to an NSHSS member demonstrating outstanding dedication to community service and initiative in volunteer activities. Runner up awards of $250 are given as well.

Award: Scholarship for use in freshman year; not renewable. *Number:* 1–5. *Amount:* $250–$1000.

Eligibility Requirements: Applicant must be high school student and planning to enroll or expecting to enroll full- or part-time at a four-year institution or university. Applicant must have 3.5 GPA or higher. Available to U.S. and non-U.S. citizens.

Application Requirements: Application, essay, photo, references, transcript. *Deadline:* February 15.

Contact: Dr. Susan Thurman, Scholarship Director
National Society of High School Scholars
1936 North Druid Hills Road
Atlanta, GA 30319
Phone: 404-235-5500
Fax: 404-235-5510
E-mail: information@nshss.org

NATIONAL SPEAKERS ASSOCIATION

http://www.nsaspeaker.org/

NATIONAL SPEAKERS ASSOCIATION SCHOLARSHIP

One-time award for junior, senior, or graduate students who have a burning desire to pursue professional speaking as a career. Must be full-time student at accredited four-year institution with above average academic record. Submit 500 word essay on goals. Application available only on web site http://www.nsafoundation.org.

Award: Scholarship for use in junior, senior, or graduate years; not renewable. *Number:* 4. *Amount:* $5000.

Eligibility Requirements: Applicant must be enrolled or expecting to enroll full-time at a four-year institution or university. Available to U.S. and non-U.S. citizens.

Application Requirements: Application, essay, references, transcript, link to URL of applicant speaking. *Deadline:* June 1.

Contact: Andrea DiMickele, Foundation Specialist
National Speakers Association
1500 South Priest Drive
Tempe, AZ 85281
Phone: 480-968-2552
Fax: 480-968-0911
E-mail: andrea@nsaspeaker.org

NAVAL SERVICE TRAINING COMMAND/NROTC

https://www.nrotc.navy.mil/

NROTC SCHOLARSHIP PROGRAM

Scholarships are based on merit and are awarded through a highly competitive national selection process. NROTC scholarships pay for college tuition, fees, uniforms, a book stipend, a monthly allowance and other financial benefits. Room and board expenses are not covered. Scholarship nominees must be medically qualified. Upon graduation scholarship recipients have an obligation of eight years commissioned service, five of which must be active duty. For more information, visit our web site at https://www.nrotc.navy.mil.

Award: Scholarship for use in freshman, sophomore, junior, or senior years; renewable. *Number:* 2400–2900. *Amount:* varies.

Eligibility Requirements: Applicant must be age 17-23 and enrolled or expecting to enroll full-time at a four-year institution or university. Available to U.S. citizens.

Application Requirements: Application, essay, interview, references, test scores, transcript. *Deadline:* January 31.

Contact: NROTC Scholarship Selection Office (OD2)
Naval Service Training Command/NROTC
OD2-Selection and Placement
250 Dallas Street, Suite A
Pensacola, FL 32508-5268
Phone: 800-628-7682
E-mail: pnsc_nrotc.scholarship@navy.mil

NAVY COUNSELORS ASSOCIATION

http://www.usnca.org/

NAVY COUNSELORS ASSOCIATION EDUCATIONAL SCHOLARSHIP

The program awards at least one scholarship to a deserving student who is currently enrolled in, or accepted to, an undergraduate-level college, university or vocational tech program. Scholarship nominations must be from immediate family members of NCA members.

Award: Scholarship for use in freshman, sophomore, junior, or senior years; not renewable. *Number:* 1–4. *Amount:* varies.

Eligibility Requirements: Applicant must be enrolled or expecting to enroll full- or part-time at a four-year institution or university. Applicant must have 3.0 GPA or higher. Available to U.S. citizens.

Application Requirements: Application, essay, references, transcript. *Deadline:* April 30.

Contact: Joseph Mack, President
Navy Counselors Association
National Headquarters
PO Box 15233
Norfolk, VA 23511-0233
Phone: 901-874-3194
Fax: 901-874-2055
E-mail: president@usnca.org

NEEDHAM AND COMPANY WTC SCHOLARSHIP FUND

http://www.needhamco.com/

NEEDHAM AND COMPANY SEPTEMBER 11TH SCHOLARSHIP FUND

Scholarship going to those individuals who had a pre-September 11th gross income of less than $125,000. Must be currently accepted or attending an accredited university or college. Recipients decided on a case-by-case basis. Fund designed to benefit the children of the victims who lost their lives at the World Trade Center.

Award: Scholarship for use in freshman, sophomore, junior, or senior years; not renewable. *Number:* 8–15. *Amount:* $7000–$10,000.

Eligibility Requirements: Applicant must be enrolled or expecting to enroll full-time at a four-year institution or university. Available to U.S. citizens.

Application Requirements: Application, financial need analysis. *Deadline:* continuous.

Contact: Joseph J. Turano, Secretary and Treasurer
Needham and Company WTC Scholarship Fund
445 Park Avenue
New York, NY 10022
Phone: 212-705-0314
E-mail: jturano@needhamco.com

NEXTSTEPU

http://www.nextstepu.com/

WIN FREE COLLEGE TUITION GIVEAWAY

NextStepU will award a year of free tuition, up to $10,000, to one randomly selected winner. Applicants must enter online at http://www.nextstepu.com/winfreetuition or see official rules for alternate method of entry. Winner must be enrolled in college within 3 years of when prize is awarded.

Award: Scholarship for use in freshman, sophomore, junior, or senior years; not renewable. *Number:* 1. *Amount:* $500–$10,000.

Eligibility Requirements: Applicant must be age 14 and over and enrolled or expecting to enroll full- or part-time at a two-year or four-year or technical institution or university. Available to U.S. and Canadian citizens.

Application Requirements: Application. *Deadline:* June 30.

Contact: Web Department
NextStepU
2 West Main Street
Suite 200
Victor, NY 14564
E-mail: webcopy@nextstepu.com

NICODEMUS WILDERNESS PROJECT

http://www.wildernessproject.org/

APPRENTICE ECOLOGIST SCHOLARSHIP

The Apprentice Ecologist Scholarship is open to students interested in protecting wildlife and the environment. This program elevates young people into leadership roles by engaging them in environmental stewardship and conservation projects that benefit native ecosystems and local communities. Applicants should demonstrate personal initiative, leadership, and dedication in their projects.

Award: Scholarship for use in freshman, sophomore, junior, or senior years; not renewable. *Number:* 3. *Amount:* $100–$500.

Eligibility Requirements: Applicant must be age 13-21 and enrolled or expecting to enroll full- or part-time at a two-year or four-year or technical institution or university. Available to U.S. and non-U.S. citizens.

Application Requirements: Essay. *Deadline:* December 31.

Contact: Dr. Robert Dudley, Director
Nicodemus Wilderness Project
PO Box 40712
Albuquerque, NM 87196
E-mail: mail@wildernessproject.org

NORTH CAROLINA STATE DEPARTMENT OF HEALTH AND HUMAN SERVICES/ DIVISION OF SOCIAL SERVICES

http://www.dhhs.state.nc.us/dss/

NORTH CAROLINA EDUCATION AND TRAINING VOUCHER PROGRAM

Four-year scholarship for foster youth and former foster youth. Must have been accepted into or be enrolled in a degree, certificate or other accredited program at a college, university, technical or vocational school and show progress towards a degree or certificate. Must be a U.S. citizen or qualified non-citizen. Applications available at: nc@statevoucher.org.

Award: Grant for use in freshman, sophomore, junior, or senior years; renewable. *Number:* varies. *Amount:* up to $5000.

Eligibility Requirements: Applicant must be age 18-20 and enrolled or expecting to enroll full- or part-time at a two-year or four-year or technical institution or university. Available to U.S. and non-U.S. citizens.

Application Requirements: Application, essay. *Deadline:* continuous.

Contact: Scholarship Committee
Phone: 919-733-9464
E-mail: dssweb@ncmail.net

OP LOFTBED COMPANY

http://www.oploftbed.com/

OP LOFTBED $500 SCHOLARSHIP AWARD

Scholarship is awarded to the student whose answers to the application questions on the OP Loftbed web site are the most creative and interesting. Must be a U.S. citizen who is enrolled in a college or university in the U.S. Deadline for summer award: 7/31. Deadline for winter award: 1/31. Submit entry on web site http://www.oploftbed.com.

Award: Scholarship for use in freshman, sophomore, junior, senior, graduate, or postgraduate years; not renewable. *Number:* 2. *Amount:* $500.

Eligibility Requirements: Applicant must be enrolled or expecting to enroll full- or part-time at a two-year or four-year or technical institution or university. Available to U.S. citizens.

Application Requirements: Application, essay.

Contact: Program Coordinator
OP Loftbed Company
7324 Farmbrook Place
Thomasville, NC 27360
Phone: 866-567-5638

OREGON POLICE CORPS

http://www.portlandonline.com/

OREGON POLICE CORPS SCHOLARSHIP

Scholarships available for undergraduate juniors and seniors and graduate students, or for reimbursement of educational expenses for college graduates. Must agree to commit to four years of employment at a participating law enforcement agency. Check web site for details http://www.oregonpolicecorps.com.

Award: Scholarship for use in junior, senior, or graduate years; not renewable. *Number:* 10. *Amount:* up to $30,000.

Eligibility Requirements: Applicant must be enrolled or expecting to enroll full-time at a four-year institution or university. Available to U.S. citizens.

Application Requirements: Application, essay, interview, resume, references. *Deadline:* continuous.

Contact: Tim Evans, Scholarship Coordinator
Oregon Police Corps
1120 Fifth Avenue, SW, Room 404
Portland, OR 97204
Phone: 888-735-4259
E-mail: tevans@police.ci.portland.or.us

OREGON STUDENT ASSISTANCE COMMISSION

http://www.GetCollegeFunds.org/

ALLCOTT/HUNT SHARE IT NOW II SCHOLARSHIP

Award for first or second generation immigrants to the United States. Eligible applicants must provide an answer to the citizenship status question in Item 4 of the Scholarship Application. Recipients must enroll at least half-time in college in the United States. FAFSA filing is strongly recommended. Essay and references are required.

Award: Scholarship for use in freshman year; not renewable.

Eligibility Requirements: Applicant must be high school student and planning to enroll or expecting to enroll full- or part-time at a two-year or four-year institution or university.

Application Requirements: Application, essay, references. *Deadline:* March 1.

Contact: Director of Grant Programs
Oregon Student Assistance Commission
1500 Valley River Drive, Suite 100
Eugene, OR 97401-7020
Phone: 800-452-8807

BARTOO/MOSHINSKY SCHOLARSHIP

Award is available to dependents of eligible employees of credit unions affiliated with, current clients of, or past clients of Merger Solution Group, The Watch Reports, and any other division of Bartoo Associates, LLC. Oregon residency is not required. Recipient must enroll at least half-time in a college or university in the United States.

Award: Scholarship for use in freshman year; not renewable.

Eligibility Requirements: Applicant must be high school student and planning to enroll or expecting to enroll full- or part-time at a two-year or four-year institution or university.

Application Requirements: Application. *Deadline:* March 1.

Contact: Director of Grant Programs
Oregon Student Assistance Commission
1500 Valley River Drive, Suite 100
Eugene, OR 97401-7020
Phone: 800-452-8807

BETTER A LIFE SCHOLARSHIP

Scholarship award available to single parents age 17–25. High schools seniors must have at least 3.0 GPA and college students must have at least a 2.5 GPA. Applicants may not already possess a bachelor's degree. Applicants may reapply for one additional year of funding.

Award: Scholarship for use in freshman or sophomore years; not renewable.

Eligibility Requirements: Applicant must be age 17-25; enrolled or expecting to enroll full- or part-time at a two-year or four-year institution or university and single.

Application Requirements: Application. *Deadline:* March 1.

Contact: Director of Grant Programs
Oregon Student Assistance Commission
1500 Valley River Drive, Suite 100
Eugene, OR 97401-7020
Phone: 800-452-8807

BRUCE AND KARIN BAILEY SCHOLARSHIP

Award is for dependents of eligible employees of Bend Garbage & Recycling, Deschutes Recycling, Deschutes Transfer, High Country Disposal, and Mid Oregon Recycling. Eligible employees must have been employed by one of these companies two or more years as of the March scholarship deadline. Applicant must have at least a 3.25 GPA.

Award: Scholarship for use in freshman year; not renewable.

Eligibility Requirements: Applicant must be high school student and planning to enroll or expecting to enroll at a two-year or four-year institution or university.

Application Requirements: Application. *Deadline:* March 1.

Contact: Director of Grant Programs
Oregon Student Assistance Commission
1500 Valley River Drive, Suite 100
Eugene, OR 97401-7020
Phone: 800-452-8807

CHILDREN OF INSITU SCHOLARSHIP

Award available to dependents of eligible employees or former employees of Insitu, Inc. Oregon residency is not required. Recipients must enroll at least half-time in a college or university in the United States.

Award: Scholarship for use in freshman year; not renewable.

Eligibility Requirements: Applicant must be enrolled or expecting to enroll full- or part-time at a two-year or four-year institution or university.

Application Requirements: Application. *Deadline:* March 1.

Contact: Director of Grant Programs
Oregon Student Assistance Commission
1500 Valley River Drive, Suite 100
Eugene, OR 97401-7020
Phone: 800-452-8807

FARROLD STEPHENS SCHOLARSHIP

Awards for students that have experience in vocal performance or music education. Must enroll at least half time as college junior or above for fall term. Oregon residency is not required. Semifinalists will be contacted by donor group and invited to submit a non-returnable CD of a musical performance.

Award: Scholarship for use in junior, senior, or graduate years; not renewable.

Eligibility Requirements: Applicant must be enrolled or expecting to enroll full- or part-time at a four-year institution or university.

Application Requirements: Application. *Deadline:* March 1.

Contact: Director of Grant Programs
Oregon Student Assistance Commission
1500 Valley River Drive, Suite 100
Eugene, OR 97401-7020
Phone: 800-452-8807

LYNDA PILGER SCHOLARSHIP

One-time award available to graduating seniors (including home-schooled seniors) of Clackamas, Multnomah, or Washington County high schools. Minimum GPA of 2.75 required. Award must be used at a four-year public college or university in the United States. Must submit an essay describing work in the area of animal rights or animal welfare and how a college education will enhance efforts in these areas.

Award: Scholarship for use in freshman year; not renewable.

Eligibility Requirements: Applicant must be high school student and planning to enroll or expecting to enroll at a four-year institution or university.

Application Requirements: Application, essay. *Deadline:* March 1.

Contact: Director of Grant Programs
Oregon Student Assistance Commission
1500 Valley River Drive, Suite 100
Eugene, OR 97401-7020
Phone: 800-452-8807

REGISTER-GUARD FEDERAL CREDIT UNION SCHOLARSHIP

Award is available to current members of the Register-Guard Federal Credit Union, or those eligible for membership, with preference in the following order: (1) current employees, independent contractors of The Register-Guard including members of their immediate families or households, (2) retired persons as pensioners or annuitants, (3) spouses of persons who died within membership, (4) organizations of such persons. Oregon residency is not required. Minimum 2.5 GPA and essay required.

Award: Scholarship for use in freshman year; not renewable.

Eligibility Requirements: Applicant must be enrolled or expecting to enroll at a two-year or four-year institution or university. Applicant must have 2.5 GPA or higher.

Application Requirements: Application, essay. *Deadline:* March 1.

Contact: Director of Grant Programs
Oregon Student Assistance Commission
1500 Valley River Drive, Suite 100
Eugene, OR 97401-7020
Phone: 800-452-8807

TECHNICAL TRAINING FUND SCHOLARSHIP

Award is available to graduates (including GED recipients and home-schooled graduates) of Oregon high schools. Preference will be given to graduate students. Applicants must demonstrate extraordinary technical or artistic potential in areas such as craftsmanship, manual skills, art, music, or culinary arts. Recipient must enroll at least half-time.

Award: Scholarship for use in freshman, sophomore, junior, senior, or graduate years; not renewable.

Eligibility Requirements: Applicant must be enrolled or expecting to enroll full- or part-time at a four-year institution or university.

Application Requirements: Application, essay, references. *Deadline:* March 1.

Contact: Director of Grant Programs
Oregon Student Assistance Commission
1500 Valley River Drive, Suite 100
Eugene, OR 97401-7020
Phone: 800-452-8807

UMATILLA ELECTRIC COOPERATIVE SCHOLARSHIP

Award for a high school graduate (including home-school graduate) or GED recipient enrolled or planning to enroll at a U.S. college or university. Applicant or applicant's parents/legal guardians must be active members of the Umatilla Electric Cooperative (UEC) and be receiving service from UEC at their primary residence. Must reapply for award annually.

Award: Scholarship for use in freshman, sophomore, junior, or senior years; not renewable. *Number:* varies. *Amount:* varies.

Eligibility Requirements: Applicant must be enrolled or expecting to enroll full- or part-time at a four-year institution or university. Available to U.S. citizens.

Application Requirements: Application, essay, financial need analysis, references, transcript, activity chart. *Deadline:* March 1.

Contact: Director of Grant Programs
Oregon Student Assistance Commission
1500 Valley River Drive, Suite 100
Eugene, OR 97401-7020
Phone: 800-452-8807 Ext. 7395

UNIVERSITY CLUB OF PORTLAND SCHOLARSHIP

Award is available to eligible employees and dependents of eligible employees of the University Club of Portland. Eligible employees be in good standing and must have been employed by University Club of Portland one or more years as of the March scholarship deadline. Oregon residency is not required.

Award: Scholarship for use in freshman, sophomore, junior, or senior years; not renewable.

Eligibility Requirements: Applicant must be enrolled or expecting to enroll full- or part-time at a four-year institution or university. Applicant must have 2.5 GPA or higher.

Application Requirements: Application. *Deadline:* March 1.

Contact: Director of Grant Programs
Oregon Student Assistance Commission
1500 Valley River Drive, Suite 100
Eugene, OR 97401-7020
Phone: 800-452-8807

ORPHAN FOUNDATION OF AMERICA

http://www.orphan.org/

OFA NATIONAL SCHOLARSHIP/CASEY FAMILY SCHOLARS

Award of up to $6000 to young people under the age of 25 who spent the 12 months prior to their 18th birthday in foster care or who were adopted or placed into legal guardianship from foster care after their 16th birthday. Scholarships are awarded for the pursuit of postsecondary education, including vocational/technical training, and are renewable for up to five years based on satisfactory progress and financial need.

Award: Scholarship for use in freshman, sophomore, junior, or senior years; not renewable. *Number:* 100. *Amount:* up to $6000.

Eligibility Requirements: Applicant must be age 25 or under and enrolled or expecting to enroll full- or part-time at a two-year or four-year or technical institution or university. Available to U.S. citizens.

Application Requirements: Application, essay, financial need analysis, references, transcript, foster care verification, parents'; death certificates. *Deadline:* March 31.

Contact: Tina Raheem, Scholarship Director
Orphan Foundation of America
21351 Gentry Drive, Suite 130
Sterling, VA 20166
Phone: 571-203-0270 Ext. 102
Fax: 571-203-0273
E-mail: tinar@orphan.org

OUTSTANDING STUDENTS OF AMERICA

http://www.outstandingstudentsofamerica.com/

OUTSTANDING STUDENTS OF AMERICA SCHOLARSHIP

Awards of $1000 each are payable to the college of the recipient's choice. Students must be high school seniors, participate in community/school activities, and maintain a minimum GPA of 3.0. For details refer to web site http://www.outstandingstudentsofamerica.com/.

Award: Scholarship for use in freshman year; not renewable. *Number:* varies. *Amount:* $1000.

Eligibility Requirements: Applicant must be high school student and planning to enroll or expecting to enroll full- or part-time at a four-year institution or university. Applicant must have 3.0 GPA or higher. Available to U.S. citizens.

Application Requirements: Application, self-addressed stamped envelope. *Deadline:* October 1.

Contact: Michael Layson, President
Outstanding Students of America
3047 Sagefield Road
Tuscaloosa, AL 35405
Phone: 205-344-6322
Fax: 205-344-6322
E-mail: info@outstandingstudentsofamerica.com

PADGETT BUSINESS SERVICES FOUNDATION

http://www.smallbizpros.com/

PADGETT BUSINESS SERVICES FOUNDATION SCHOLARSHIP PROGRAM

Scholarship awards to the dependents of small business owners throughout the United States and Canada. Must be a dependent of a business owner who employs fewer than 20 people, owns at least 10 percent of the stock or capital in the business, and is active in the day-to-day operations of the business. For more details, visit the web site http://www.smallbizpros.com.

Award: Scholarship for use in freshman year; not renewable. *Number:* 65–75. *Amount:* $500.

Eligibility Requirements: Applicant must be high school student and planning to enroll or expecting to enroll full-time at a two-year or four-year or technical institution or university. Available to U.S. and Canadian citizens.

Application Requirements: Application, essay, test scores, transcript, school activities. *Deadline:* March 1.

Contact: Heather Stokley, Administrator
Padgett Business Services Foundation
160 Hawthorne Park
Athens, GA 30606
Phone: 800-723-4388
Fax: 800-548-1040
E-mail: hstokley@smallbizpros.com

PAPERCHECK

http://www.papercheck.com/

PAPER-CHECK.COM, LLC. CHARLES SHAFAE' SCHOLARSHIP FUND

Awards two $500 scholarships each year to winners of the Papercheck essay contest. Must be enrolled at an accredited four-year college or university. Must maintain a cumulative GPA of at least 3.2. Scholarship guidelines available at http://http://www.papercheck.com/scholarship.asp.

Award: Scholarship for use in freshman, sophomore, junior, or senior years; not renewable. *Number:* 2. *Amount:* $500.

Eligibility Requirements: Applicant must be enrolled or expecting to enroll full-time at a four-year institution or university. Applicant must have 3.0 GPA or higher. Available to U.S. citizens.

Application Requirements: Application, essay, transcript. *Deadline:* continuous.

Contact: Mr. Darren M. Shafae, Scholarship Coordinator
Papercheck
12 Geary Street, Suite 808
San Francisco, CA 94108
Phone: 866-693-3348
E-mail: scholarships@papercheck.com

PATIENT ADVOCATE FOUNDATION

http://www.patientadvocate.org/

SCHOLARSHIPS FOR SURVIVORS

Scholarships to provide support to patients seeking to initiate or complete a course of study that has been interrupted or delayed by a diagnosis of cancer or another critical or life threatening illness. Up to ten awards of $3000 available to U.S. citizens. Minimum 3.0 GPA required.

Award: Scholarship for use in freshman, sophomore, junior, or senior years; renewable. *Number:* up to 10. *Amount:* up to $3000.

Eligibility Requirements: Applicant must be age 25 or under and enrolled or expecting to enroll full-time at a two-year or four-year institution or university. Applicant must have 3.0 GPA or higher. Available to U.S. citizens.

Application Requirements: Application, essay, financial need analysis, references, transcript, physician letter. *Deadline:* April 14.

Contact: Ruth Anne Reed, Vice President of Human Resource Programs
Patient Advocate Foundation
700 Thimble Shoals Boulevard, Suite 200
Newport News, VA 23606
Phone: 800-532-5274
Fax: 757-952-2475
E-mail: scholarship@patientadvocate.org

PATRICK KERR SKATEBOARD SCHOLARSHIP FUND

http://www.skateboardscholarship.org/

PATRICK KERR SKATEBOARD SCHOLARSHIP

Scholarship for high school senior accepted in a full-time undergraduate course of study at an accredited two- or four-year college/university. One individual will receive a $5000 scholarship and three individuals will receive a $1000 scholarship. Applicant must be a skateboarder and U.S. citizen. Minimum 2.5 GPA required.

Award: Scholarship for use in freshman year; not renewable. *Number:* 4. *Amount:* $1000–$5000.

Eligibility Requirements: Applicant must be high school student and planning to enroll or expecting to enroll full-time at a two-year or four-year institution or university. Applicant must have 2.5 GPA or higher. Available to U.S. citizens.

Application Requirements: Application, essay, references, transcript. *Deadline:* April 20.

Contact: Patrick Kerr, Scholarship Committee
Patrick Kerr Skateboard Scholarship Fund
PO Box 2054
Jenkintown, PA 19046
Phone: 215-663-9329
Fax: 215-663-5897
E-mail: info@skateboardscholarship.org

PHI BETA SIGMA FRATERNITY INC.

http://www.pbs1914.org/

PHI BETA SIGMA FRATERNITY NATIONAL PROGRAM OF EDUCATION

Scholarships are awarded to both graduate and undergraduate students. Applicants must have minimum 3.0 GPA.

Award: Scholarship for use in freshman, sophomore, junior, senior, or graduate years; not renewable. *Number:* varies. *Amount:* varies.

Eligibility Requirements: Applicant must be enrolled or expecting to enroll full-time at a four-year institution or university and male. Applicant must have 3.0 GPA or higher. Available to U.S. citizens.

Application Requirements: Application, essay, photo, resume, references, transcript. *Deadline:* June 15.

Contact: Emile Pitre, Chairman
Phi Beta Sigma Fraternity Inc.
2 Belmonte Circle, SW
Atlanta, GA 30311
Phone: 404-759-6827
E-mail: mikewhines@aol.com

PROOF-READING, INC.

http://www.proof-reading.com/

PROOF-READING, INC. SCHOLARSHIP PROGRAM

Applicants must write an essay that satisfies the question found on the organization web site. The minimum word count is 1,500 words. Focus will be on grammar and ability to present ideas clearly. Include a Works Cited page, with a minimum of three sources. The essay must follow MLA writing guidelines. For more information, visit web site http://www.proof-reading.com/proof-reading_scholarship_program.asp.

Award: Scholarship for use in freshman, sophomore, junior, or senior years; not renewable. *Number:* 1. *Amount:* $1500.

Eligibility Requirements: Applicant must be enrolled or expecting to enroll full-time at a four-year institution or university. Applicant must have 3.5 GPA or higher. Available to U.S. citizens.

Application Requirements: Application, essay, transcript. *Deadline:* continuous.

Contact: Mr. Mike Williams, Scholarship Coordinator
Proof-Reading, Inc.
12 Geary Street, Suite 806
San Francisco, CA 94108
Phone: 866-433-4867
E-mail: scholarships@proof-reading.com

PRUDENT PUBLISHING COMPANY INC.

http://www.gallerycollection.com/

4TH ANNUAL CREATE-A-GREETING-CARD $10,000 SCHOLARSHIP CONTEST

Students must submit an original photo, piece of artwork, or computer graphic for the front of a greeting card. The student with the best design will win a $10,000 scholarship and have his or her entry made into an actual greeting card to be sold in The Gallery Collection's line. The winning student's school will also receive a $1,000 prize for helping to promote the contest. For complete details visit http://www.gallerycollection.com/greeting-cards-scholarship.htm.

Award: Scholarship for use in freshman, sophomore, junior, senior, or graduate years; not renewable. *Number:* 1. *Amount:* $10,000.

Eligibility Requirements: Applicant must be age 14 and over and enrolled or expecting to enroll full- or part-time at a two-year or four-year or technical institution or university. Available to U.S. citizens.

Application Requirements: Application, applicant must enter a contest, greeting card design. *Deadline:* December 31.

Contact: Scholarship Administrator
Prudent Publishing Company Inc.
Prudent Publishing Company, 65 Challenger Road
Ridgefield Park, NJ 07660
Phone: 201-641-7900
E-mail: scholarshipadmin@gallerycollection.com

PUSH FOR EXCELLENCE

http://www.pushexcel.org/

ORA LEE SANDERS SCHOLARSHIP

U.S. Citizens who will be freshmen, sophomore, juniors or seniors are eligible. The scholarship is renewable up to 4 years based upon GPA. Full time study with minimum 2.5 GPA.

Award: Scholarship for use in freshman, sophomore, junior, or senior years; renewable. *Number:* varies. *Amount:* $1000.

Eligibility Requirements: Applicant must be enrolled or expecting to enroll full-time at a four-year institution or university. Applicant must have 2.5 GPA or higher. Available to U.S. citizens.

Application Requirements: Application, essay, references, self-addressed stamped envelope, transcript, proof of current enrollment or acceptance in a college or university. *Deadline:* April 30.

Contact: Scholarship Committee
Push for Excellence
930 East 50th Street
Chicago, IL 60615
Phone: 773-373-3366
E-mail: info@pushexcel.org

RAISE THE NATION FOUNDATION

http://www.raisethenation.org/

RAISE THE NATION CHILD OF A SINGLE PARENT SCHOLARSHIP

Scholarship to reduce the financial burden of paying for college faced by children of single parent women. Applicant must be claimed by their mother as a dependent child (under 24 years of age) and entering or currently enrolled in a postsecondary course of study.

Award: Scholarship for use in freshman, sophomore, junior, or senior years; renewable. *Number:* 1–50. *Amount:* $100–$5000.

Eligibility Requirements: Applicant must be age 17-23 and enrolled or expecting to enroll full- or part-time at a two-year or four-year or technical institution or university. Available to U.S. citizens.

Application Requirements: Application, driver's license, essay, financial need analysis, proof of single parent status (tax form 1040), proof of acceptance or enrollment into a postsecondary degree program. *Fee:* $20. *Deadline:* varies.

Contact: Michelle McMullen, Executive Director
Raise the Nation Foundation
PO Box 8058
Albuquerque, NM 87198
Phone: 505-265-1201
E-mail: suppoetdesk@raisethenation.org

RAISE THE NATION CONTINUING EDUCATION SCHOLARSHIP

Scholarship available to single parent women who would like to go to school or continue with their education, but have been denied sufficient resources. Applicant must be accepted or currently enrolled in a postsecondary course of study to qualify for this scholarship.

Award: Scholarship for use in freshman, sophomore, junior, or senior years; renewable. *Number:* 1–50. *Amount:* $100–$5000.

Eligibility Requirements: Applicant must be age 18-99; enrolled or expecting to enroll full- or part-time at a two-year or four-year or technical institution or university and single female. Available to U.S. citizens.

Application Requirements: Application, driver's license, essay, financial need analysis, proof of enrollment or acceptance into a postsecondary program, proof of single parent status (tax form 1040). *Fee:* $20. *Deadline:* varies.

Contact: Michelle McMullen, Executive Director
Raise the Nation Foundation
PO Box 8058
Albuquerque, NM 87198
Phone: 505-265-1201
E-mail: suppoetdesk@raisethenation.org

RENEE B. FISHER FOUNDATION

http://www.rbffoundation.org/

MILTON FISHER SCHOLARSHIP FOR INNOVATION AND CREATIVITY

The Milton Fisher Scholarship is a four-year scholarship of up to $20,000 awarded to exceptionally innovative and creative high school juniors, seniors, and college freshmen from the Connecticut and New York City Metropolitan Area, or those who plan to attend university in this area.

Award: Scholarship for use in freshman, sophomore, junior, or senior years; renewable. *Number:* 5–8. *Amount:* $1000–$20,000.

Eligibility Requirements: Applicant must be enrolled or expecting to enroll full-time at a four-year institution or university. Available to U.S. citizens.

Application Requirements: Application, essay, references, transcript. *Deadline:* April 18.

Contact: Ms. Gina Ackeifi, Philanthropic Officer
Renee B. Fisher Foundation
77 Audobon St.
New Haven, CT 06510
Phone: 203-777-2386

ROPAGE GROUP LLC

http://www.patricias-scholarship.org/

PATRICIA M. MCNAMARA MEMORIAL SCHOLARSHIP

Scholarship open to students who are already attending college or will be attending college within a year of the deadline. Students must utilize the online form to submit the scholarship application and essay. For more details, see web site http://www.patricias-scholarship.org.

Award: Scholarship for use in freshman, sophomore, junior, or senior years; not renewable. *Number:* 1. *Amount:* $1000.

Eligibility Requirements: Applicant must be enrolled or expecting to enroll full- or part-time at a two-year or four-year or technical institution or university. Available to U.S. and non-U.S. citizens.

Application Requirements: Application, essay. *Deadline:* varies.

Contact: Scholarship Committee
Ropage Group LLC
8877 North 107th Avenue, Suite 302, PO Box 287
Peoria, AZ 85345
E-mail: questions@patricias-scholarship.org

SABERTEC LLC/BLADE YOUR RIDE

http://www.bladeyourride.com/

BLADE YOUR RIDE SCHOLARSHIP PROGRAM

Scholarship for students enrolled in a full-time bachelor's degree program or master's degree program. Applicant should maintain a GPA of 3.0.

Award: Scholarship for use in freshman, sophomore, junior, senior, or graduate years; not renewable. *Number:* 3–5. *Amount:* $5000–$15,000.

Eligibility Requirements: Applicant must be enrolled or expecting to enroll full-time at a four-year institution or university. Applicant must have 3.0 GPA or higher. Available to U.S. and non-U.S. citizens.

Application Requirements: Application, resume, references, transcript, short video/webcast. *Deadline:* June 30.

Contact: Ashley Fontaine, Scholarship Committee
Sabertec LLC/Blade Your Ride
12357 Riata Trace Parkway
Building 7, Suite C-155
Austin, TX 78727
Phone: 512-358-6219
E-mail: ashley@bladeyourride.com

SALLIE MAE FUND

http://www.thesalliemaefund.org/

SALLIE MAE 911 EDUCATION FUND LOAN RELIEF

Funds individuals or spouses, same-sex partners, or co-borrowers of those killed or declared totally and permanently disabled in the 9/11 terrorist attacks, and who are borrowers of loan owned or serviced by Sallie Mae. Applicant can also be an estate administrator who has held an education loan.

Award: Forgivable loan for use in sophomore, junior, or senior years; not renewable. *Number:* varies. *Amount:* up to $5000.

Eligibility Requirements: Applicant must be enrolled or expecting to enroll full- or part-time at a two-year or four-year or technical institution or university. Available to U.S. citizens.

Application Requirements: Application, supporting documents. *Deadline:* continuous.

Contact: Laura Gemery, Scholarship Committee
Sallie Mae Fund
12061 Bluemont Way
Reston, VA 20190
Phone: 703-810-3000
Fax: 703-984-5042

SALLIE MAE 911 EDUCATION FUND SCHOLARSHIP PROGRAM

Scholarship program open to children of those who were killed or permanently disabled as a result of the 9/11 terrorist attacks who are enrolled as full-time undergraduate students at approved accredited institutions. May be renewed on an annual academic basis subject to satisfactory academic progress. Applications available at the following web site http://www.thesalliemaefund.org/smfnew/pdf/911application.pdf.

Award: Scholarship for use in freshman, sophomore, junior, or senior years; renewable. *Number:* up to 335. *Amount:* up to $2500.

Eligibility Requirements: Applicant must be enrolled or expecting to enroll full-time at a two-year or four-year institution or university. Available to U.S. citizens.

Application Requirements: Application, financial need analysis, proof of death or disability of parent. *Deadline:* May 15.

Contact: Laura Gemery, Scholarship Committee
Sallie Mae Fund
12061 Bluemont Way
Reston, VA 20190
Phone: 703-810-3000
Fax: 703-984-5042

SALLIE MAE FUND UNMET NEED SCHOLARSHIP PROGRAM

Open to families with a combined income of $30,000 or less, this program is intended to supplement financial aid packages that fall more than $1000 short of students' financial need. Open to U.S. citizens and permanent residents who are accepted or enrolled as full-time undergraduate students. Students must have minimum 2.5 GPA.

Award: Scholarship for use in freshman, sophomore, junior, or senior years; not renewable. *Number:* varies. *Amount:* $1000–$3800.

Eligibility Requirements: Applicant must be enrolled or expecting to enroll full-time at a four-year institution or university. Applicant must have 2.5 GPA or higher. Available to U.S. citizens.

Application Requirements: Application, test scores, transcript. *Deadline:* May 31.

Contact: Scholarship Committee
Sallie Mae Fund
One Scholarship Way, PO Box 297
Saint Peter, MN 56082
Phone: 507-931-1682

SAMUEL HUNTINGTON FUND

http://www.nationalgridus.com/huntington.asp

SAMUEL HUNTINGTON PUBLIC SERVICE AWARD

Award provides a $10,000 stipend to a graduating college senior to perform a one-year public service project anywhere in the world immediately following graduation. Written proposals of 1000 words or less are required with application. Project may encompass any activity that furthers the public good. Awards will be based on quality of proposal, academic record, and other personal achievements. Semi-finalists will be interviewed.

Award: Grant for use in senior year; not renewable. *Number:* 1–3. *Amount:* $10,000.

Eligibility Requirements: Applicant must be enrolled or expecting to enroll full-time at a four-year institution or university. Available to U.S. and non-U.S. citizens.

Application Requirements: Application, essay, financial need analysis, resume, references, transcript. *Deadline:* January 18.

Contact: Amy Stacy, Executive Assistant
Samuel Huntington Fund
National Grid, 40 Sylvan Road
Waltham, MA 02451
Phone: 781-907-3358
Fax: 781-907-5705
E-mail: amy.stacy@us.ngrid.com

SCHOLARSHIPEXPERTS.COM

http://www.scholarshipexperts.com/apply.htx

ALL ABOUT EDUCATION SCHOLARSHIP

Applicants must: Complete a profile on the scholarshipexperts.com web site. Be thirteen years of age or older at the time of application. Be legal residents of the fifty United States or the District of Columbia. Be currently enrolled (or enroll no later than the fall of 2017) in an accredited post-secondary institution of higher education. Submit an online short written response (250 words or less) for the topic: "Tell us what you think about the following statement: The key to fixing our nation is 'all about education.'"

Award: Scholarship for use in freshman, sophomore, junior, or senior years; not renewable. *Number:* 1. *Amount:* $3000.

Eligibility Requirements: Applicant must be age 13 and over and enrolled or expecting to enroll full- or part-time at a two-year or four-year or technical institution or university. Available to U.S. citizens.

Application Requirements: Application, essay. *Deadline:* April 30.

Contact: Scholarship Committee
ScholarshipExperts.com
3020 Hartley Road, Suite 220
Jacksonville, FL 32258
Phone: 904-483-2930
Fax: 904-483-2931
E-mail: info@scholarshipexperts.com

DO-OVER SCHOLARSHIP

Applicants must: Be thirteen years of age or older at the time of application. Be legal residents of the fifty United States or the District of Columbia. Be currently enrolled (or enroll no later than the fall of 2017) in an accredited post-secondary institution of higher education. Submit an online short written response (250 words or less) for the question: "If you could give any celebrity or famous person a 'do-over', who would you give it to and why?"

Award: Scholarship for use in freshman, sophomore, junior, or senior years; not renewable. *Number:* 3. *Amount:* $1000.

Eligibility Requirements: Applicant must be age 13 and over and enrolled or expecting to enroll full- or part-time at a two-year or four-year or technical institution or university. Available to U.S. citizens.

Application Requirements: Application, applicant must enter a contest, essay. *Deadline:* June 30.

Contact: Scholarship Committee
ScholarshipExperts.com
3020 Hartley Road, Suite 220
Jacksonville, FL 32258
Phone: 904-483-2930
Fax: 904-483-2931
E-mail: info@scholarshipexperts.com

EDUCATION MATTERS SCHOLARSHIP

Applicants must: Complete a profile on the scholarshipexperts.com web site. Be thirteen years of age or older at the time of application. Be legal residents of the fifty United States or the District of Columbia. Be currently enrolled (or enroll no later than the fall of 2017) in an accredited post-secondary institution of higher education. Submit an online short

written response (250 words or less) for the question: What would you say to someone who thinks education doesn't matter, or that college is a waste of time and money?

Award: Scholarship for use in freshman, sophomore, junior, or senior years; not renewable. *Number:* 1. *Amount:* $3000.

Eligibility Requirements: Applicant must be age 13 and over and enrolled or expecting to enroll full- or part-time at a two-year or four-year or technical institution or university. Available to U.S. citizens.

Application Requirements: Application, essay. *Deadline:* October 31.

Contact: Scholarship Committee
ScholarshipExperts.com
3020 Hartley Road, Suite 220
Jacksonville, FL 32258
Phone: 904-483-2930
Fax: 904-483-2931
E-mail: info@scholarshipexperts.com

I WAS BORN IN 1994 SCHOLARSHIP

Applicants must: Have been born in 1994; Be legal residents of the fifty United States or the District of Columbia; Plan to enroll no later than the fall of 2014 in an accredited post-secondary institution of higher education; submit an online short written response (250 words or less) for the topic: What is unique about students born in 1994? Explain.

Award: Scholarship for use in freshman year; not renewable. *Number:* 1. *Amount:* $1994.

Eligibility Requirements: Applicant must be high school student and planning to enroll or expecting to enroll full- or part-time at a two-year or four-year or technical institution or university. Available to U.S. citizens.

Application Requirements: Application, essay. *Deadline:* July 31.

Contact: Scholarship Committee
ScholarshipExperts.com
3020 Hartley Road, Suite 220
Jacksonville, FL 32258
Phone: 904-483-2930
Fax: 904-483-2931
E-mail: info@scholarshipexperts.com

I WAS BORN IN 1995 SCHOLARSHIP

Applicants must: Have been born in 1995. Be legal residents of the fifty United States or the District of Columbia. Plan to enroll no later than the fall of 2015 in an accredited post-secondary institution of higher education. Submit an online short written response (250 words or less) for the topic: Share something we might not know about students born in 1995.

Award: Scholarship for use in freshman year; not renewable. *Number:* 1. *Amount:* $1995.

Eligibility Requirements: Applicant must be high school student and planning to enroll or expecting to enroll full- or part-time at a two-year or four-year or technical institution or university. Available to U.S. citizens.

Application Requirements: Application, essay. *Deadline:* August 31.

Contact: Scholarship Committee
ScholarshipExperts.com
3020 Hartley Road, Suite 220
Jacksonville, FL 32258
Phone: 904-483-2930
Fax: 904-483-2931
E-mail: info@scholarshipexperts.com

I WAS BORN IN 1996 SCHOLARSHIP

Applicants must: Have been born in 1996. Be legal residents of the fifty United States or the District of Columbia. Plan to enroll no later than the fall of 2016 in an accredited post-secondary institution of higher education. Submit an online short written response (250 words or less) for the question: You were born in 1996. Tell us what will be going on in your life in 2026.

Award: Scholarship for use in freshman year; not renewable. *Number:* 1. *Amount:* $1996.

Eligibility Requirements: Applicant must be high school student and planning to enroll or expecting to enroll full- or part-time at a two-year or four-year or technical institution or university. Available to U.S. citizens.

Application Requirements: Application, applicant must enter a contest, essay. *Deadline:* November 30.

Contact: Scholarship Committee
ScholarshipExperts.com
3020 Hartley Road, Suite 220
Jacksonville, FL 32258
Phone: 904-483-2930
Fax: 904-483-2931
E-mail: info@scholarshipexperts.com

SUPERPOWER SCHOLARSHIP

Applicants must: Be thirteen years of age or older at the time of application. Be legal residents of the fifty United States or the District of Columbia. Be currently enrolled (or enroll no later than the fall of 2017) in an accredited post-secondary institution of higher education. Submit an online short written response (250 words or less) for the question: If you were granted a superpower for just one day, what would it be and how would you use it?

Award: Scholarship for use in freshman, sophomore, junior, or senior years; not renewable. *Number:* 3. *Amount:* $1000.

Eligibility Requirements: Applicant must be age 13 and over and enrolled or expecting to enroll full- or part-time at a two-year or four-year or technical institution or university. Available to U.S. citizens.

Application Requirements: Application, essay. *Deadline:* March 31.

Contact: Scholarship Committee
ScholarshipExperts.com
3020 Hartley Road, Suite 220
Jacksonville, FL 32258
Phone: 904-483-2930
Fax: 904-483-2931
E-mail: info@scholarshipexperts.com

TOP TEN LIST SCHOLARSHIP

Applicants must: Be thirteen years of age or older at the time of application. Be legal residents of the fifty United States or the District of Columbia. Be currently enrolled (or enroll no later than the fall of 2017) in an accredited post-secondary institution of higher education. Submit an online short written response (250 words or less) for the topic: Create a list of your 10 favorite books and what they have taught you.

Award: Scholarship for use in freshman, sophomore, junior, or senior years; not renewable. *Number:* 3. *Amount:* $1000.

Eligibility Requirements: Applicant must be age 13 and over and enrolled or expecting to enroll full- or part-time at a two-year or four-year or technical institution or university. Available to U.S. citizens.

Application Requirements: Application, essay. *Deadline:* December 31.

Contact: Scholarship Committee
ScholarshipExperts.com
3020 Hartley Road, Suite 220
Jacksonville, FL 32258
Phone: 904-483-2930
Fax: 904-483-2931
E-mail: info@scholarshipexperts.com

SIEMENS FOUNDATION/SIEMENS-WESTINGHOUSE SCHOLARSHIP

http://www.siemens-foundation.org/

SIEMENS AWARDS FOR ADVANCED PLACEMENT

$2000 scholarships for students from each state who have earned the greatest number of AP grades of 5 in eight exams. Each state potentially has two winners, one male and one female.

Award: Prize for use in freshman year; not renewable. *Number:* 102. *Amount:* $2000–$5000.

Eligibility Requirements: Applicant must be high school student and planning to enroll or expecting to enroll full-time at a four-year institution or university. Available to U.S. citizens.

Application Requirements: Application. *Deadline:* varies.

Contact: Scholarship Committee
Siemens Foundation/Siemens-Westinghouse Scholarship
170 Wood Avenue South
Iselin, NJ 08830
Phone: 877-822-5233
Fax: 732-603-5890
E-mail: foundation.us@siemens.com

SIMON YOUTH FOUNDATION

http://www.sms.scholarshipamerica.org/simonyouth

SIMON YOUTH FOUNDATION COMMUNITY SCHOLARSHIP PROGRAM

Scholarship available to any high school senior living in a community that hosts a Simon property. Must be planning to enroll in a full-time undergraduate course of study at an accredited two- or four-year college, university, or vocational/technical school.

Award: Scholarship for use in freshman year; not renewable. *Number:* 100–200. *Amount:* $1400–$2500.

Eligibility Requirements: Applicant must be high school student and planning to enroll or expecting to enroll full-time at a two-year or four-year or technical institution or university. Available to U.S. citizens.

Application Requirements: Application, financial need analysis, test scores, transcript, copy of page 1 of parents' tax Form 1040. *Deadline:* January 31.

Contact: Program Manager
Simon Youth Foundation
Scholarship Management Services, One Scholarship Way
Saint Peter, MN 56082
Phone: 800-537-4180

SOCIETY FOR SCIENCE & THE PUBLIC

http://www.societyforscience.org/

INTEL INTERNATIONAL SCIENCE AND ENGINEERING FAIR

Culminating event in a series of local, regional, and state science fairs. Students in ninth through twelfth grades must compete at local fairs in order to be nominated for international competition. Awards include scholarships. Visit web site for more information http://www.societyforscience.org.

Award: Prize for use in freshman year; not renewable. *Number:* 1. *Amount:* $500–$50,000.

Eligibility Requirements: Applicant must be high school student and planning to enroll or expecting to enroll full-time at a two-year or four-year institution or university. Available to U.S. and non-U.S. citizens.

Application Requirements: Application, applicant must enter a contest, essay, interview. *Deadline:* varies.

Contact: Michelle Glidden, Director, Science Education Programs
Society for Science & the Public
1719 North Street, NW
Washington, DC 20036
Phone: 202-785-2255
E-mail: mglidden@societyforscience.org

INTEL SCIENCE TALENT SEARCH

Science competition for high school seniors. Students must submit an individually researched project. Forty finalists will be chosen to attend Science Talent Institute in Washington, DC to exhibit their project and compete for $100,000 award. For more information, visit web site http://www.societyforscience.org/sts.

Award: Prize for use in freshman year; not renewable. *Number:* 40. *Amount:* $7500–$100,000.

Eligibility Requirements: Applicant must be high school student and planning to enroll or expecting to enroll full-time at a two-year or four-year institution or university. Available to U.S. citizens.

Application Requirements: Application, applicant must enter a contest, essay, references, test scores, transcript. *Deadline:* November 15.

Contact: Michelle Glidden, Director, Science Education Programs
Society for Science & the Public
1719 North Street, NW
Washington, DC 20036
Phone: 202-785-2255
E-mail: mglidden@societyforscience.org

SOROPTIMIST INTERNATIONAL OF THE AMERICAS

http://www.soroptimist.org/

SOROPTIMIST WOMEN'S OPPORTUNITY AWARD

Applicant must be a woman who is the head of household, be the primary financial provider for her family and pursuing a vocational or an undergraduate degree. Recipients are chosen on the basis of financial need as well as a statement of clear career goals. Applicants must apply on-line at http://www.soroptimist.org/awards/awards.html.

Award: Prize for use in freshman, sophomore, junior, or senior years; not renewable. *Number:* varies. *Amount:* $500–$10,000.

Eligibility Requirements: Applicant must be enrolled or expecting to enroll full- or part-time at a two-year or four-year or technical institution or university and female. Available to U.S. and non-U.S. citizens.

Application Requirements: Application, essay, financial need analysis, references. *Deadline:* December 1.

Contact: Dawn Walsh, Program Manager
Soroptimist International of the Americas
1709 Spruce Street
Philadelphia, PA 19103-6103
Phone: 215-893-9000 Ext. 113
Fax: 215-893-5200
E-mail: program@soroptimist.org

SPENDONLIFE.COM

http://www.students.spendonlife.com/

SPENDONLIFE COLLEGE SCHOLARSHIP

$500 to $5000 scholarship program offers financial assistance for college students who are unable to obtain student loans due to a negative credit history. Awards are based on financial need and participation in the application process.

Award: Scholarship for use in freshman, sophomore, junior, senior, graduate, or postgraduate years; not renewable. *Number:* 2–10. *Amount:* $500–$5000.

Eligibility Requirements: Applicant must be enrolled or expecting to enroll full-time at a two-year or four-year institution or university. Available to U.S. citizens.

Application Requirements: Application, essay. *Deadline:* May 15.

Contact: Keith Lauren, Scholarship Administrator
SPENDonLIFE.com
8144 Walnut Hill Lane, Suite 510
Dallas, TX 75231
Phone: 469-916-1700 Ext. 269
E-mail: scholarship@spendonlife.com

STATE DEPARTMENT FEDERAL CREDIT UNION ANNUAL SCHOLARSHIP PROGRAM

http://www.sdfcu.org/

STATE DEPARTMENT FEDERAL CREDIT UNION ANNUAL SCHOLARSHIP PROGRAM

Scholarships available to members who are currently enrolled in a degree program and have completed 12 credit hours of coursework at an accredited college or university. Must have own account in good standing with SDFCU, have a minimum 2.5 GPA, submit official cumulative transcripts, and describe need for financial assistance to continue their education. Scholarship only open to members of State Department Federal Credit Union.

Award: Scholarship for use in sophomore, junior, senior, or graduate years; not renewable. *Number:* varies. *Amount:* $2500.

Eligibility Requirements: Applicant must be enrolled or expecting to enroll full-time at a four-year institution or university. Applicant must have 2.5 GPA or higher. Available to U.S. and non-U.S. citizens.

Application Requirements: Application, applicant must enter a contest, financial need analysis, transcript, personal statement. *Deadline:* April 29.

Contact: Scholarship Coordinator
State Department Federal Credit Union Annual Scholarship Program
1630 King Street
Alexandria, VA 22314-2745
Phone: 703-706-5000
E-mail: sdfcu@sdfcu.org

STRAIGHTFORWARD MEDIA

http://www.straightforwardmedia.com/

DALE E. FRIDELL MEMORIAL SCHOLARSHIP

Scholarships are open to anyone aspiring to attend a university, college, trade school, technical institute, vocational training, or other postsecondary education program. Eligible students may not have already been awarded a full tuition scholarship or waiver from another source. International students are welcome to apply. For more information, visit web site http://www.straightforwardmedia.com/fridell/form.php.

Award: Scholarship for use in freshman, sophomore, junior, or senior years; not renewable. *Number:* 2. *Amount:* $1000.

Eligibility Requirements: Applicant must be enrolled or expecting to enroll full- or part-time at a two-year or four-year or technical institution or university. Available to U.S. and non-U.S. citizens.

Application Requirements: Essay. *Deadline:* varies.

Contact: Scholarship Committee
StraightForward Media
508 7th Street
Suite 202
Rapid City, SD 57701
Phone: 605-348-3042

HELPING HAND SCHOLARSHIP

Annual award to help students hampered by debt to continue their studies. Must be attending or planning to attend a college, trade school, technical institute, vocational program or other postsecondary education program. For more information, see Web http://www.straightforwardmedia.com/debt2/debt-apply.html.

Award: Scholarship for use in freshman, sophomore, junior, or senior years; not renewable. *Number:* 4. *Amount:* $500.

Eligibility Requirements: Applicant must be enrolled or expecting to enroll full- or part-time at a two-year or four-year or technical institution or university. Available to U.S. and non-U.S. citizens.

Application Requirements: Essay. *Deadline:* varies.

Contact: Scholarship Committee
StraightForward Media
508 7th Street
Suite 202
Rapid City, SD 57701
Phone: 605-348-3042

MESOTHELIOMA MEMORIAL SCHOLARSHIP

Open to all students attending or planning to attend a postsecondary educational program, including 2- or 4-year college or university, vocational school, continuing education, ministry training, and job skills training. Refer to web site for details http://www.straightforwardmedia.com/meso/

Award: Scholarship for use in freshman, sophomore, junior, or senior years; not renewable. *Number:* 4. *Amount:* $500.

Eligibility Requirements: Applicant must be enrolled or expecting to enroll full- or part-time at a two-year or four-year or technical institution or university. Available to U.S. and non-U.S. citizens.

Application Requirements: Essay. *Deadline:* varies.

Contact: Scholarship Committee
StraightForward Media
508 7th Street
Suite 202
Rapid City, SD 57701
Phone: 605-348-3042

STUDENT INSIGHTS

http://www.student-view.com/

STUDENT-VIEW SCHOLARSHIP PROGRAM

Scholarship available by random drawing from the pool of entrants who respond to an online survey from Student Insights marketing organization. Parental permission to participate required for applicants under age 18.

Award: Scholarship for use in freshman year; not renewable. *Number:* 11. *Amount:* $500–$4000.

Eligibility Requirements: Applicant must be high school student and planning to enroll or expecting to enroll full-time at a two-year or four-year or technical institution or university. Available to U.S. citizens.

Application Requirements: Application. *Deadline:* April 22.

Contact: Mr. John Becker, Program Coordinator
Student Insights
136 Justice Drive
Valencia, PA 16059
Phone: 724-612-3685
E-mail: contact@studentinsights.com

SUNTRUST BANK

http://www.suntrusteducation.com/

OFF TO COLLEGE SCHOLARSHIP SWEEPSTAKES AWARD

Award of $1,000 to a high school senior planning to attend college in the fall. Must complete an online entry form by accessing the web site http://www.offtocollege.info. Scholarship sweepstakes drawings are random and occur every other week from October 31 to May 15.

Award: Scholarship for use in freshman year; not renewable. *Number:* 15. *Amount:* $1000.

Eligibility Requirements: Applicant must be high school student; age 13 and over and planning to enroll or expecting to enroll full- or part-time at a two-year or four-year or technical institution or university. Available to U.S. citizens.

Application Requirements: Application. *Deadline:* continuous.

Contact: Joy Blauvelt, Scholarship Coordinator
SunTrust Bank
1001 Semmes Avenue
PO Box 27172
Richmond, VA 23224
Phone: 800-552-3006

TAG AND LABEL MANUFACTURERS INSTITUTE INC.

http://www.tlmi.com/

TLMI SCHOLARSHIP GRANT FOR STUDENTS OF TWO-YEAR COLLEGES

Scholarship program for students enrolled at a two-year college or in a degree technical program whose major course work includes courses appropriate for future work in the tag and label manufacturing industry. Must submit statements including personal information, financial circumstances, career and/or educational goals, employment experience, and reasons applicant should be selected for this award.

Award: Scholarship for use in freshman or sophomore years; renewable. *Number:* up to 4. *Amount:* $1000.

Eligibility Requirements: Applicant must be enrolled or expecting to enroll full- or part-time at a two-year or technical institution. Applicant must have 3.0 GPA or higher. Available to U.S. and Canadian citizens.

Application Requirements: Application, portfolio, references, transcript. *Deadline:* March 31.

Contact: Scholarship Committee
Tag and Label Manufacturers Institute Inc.
Once Blackburn Center
Gloucester, MA 01930
Phone: 978-282-1400
E-mail: office@tlmi.com

TALBOTS CHARITABLE FOUNDATION

http://www.talbots.com/

TALBOTS WOMEN'S SCHOLARSHIP FUND

One-time scholarship for women who earned their high school diploma or GED at least 10 years ago, and who are now seeking an undergraduate college degree.

Award: Scholarship for use in freshman, sophomore, junior, or senior years; not renewable. *Number:* 5–50. *Amount:* $1000–$10,000.

Eligibility Requirements: Applicant must be enrolled or expecting to enroll full- or part-time at a two-year or four-year or technical institution or university and female. Available to U.S. citizens.

Application Requirements: Application, essay, financial need analysis, references, transcript. *Deadline:* January 3.

Contact: Genny Miller, Program Manager, Scholarship America
Talbots Charitable Foundation
1 Scholarship Way, PO Box 297
Saint Peter, MN 56082
Phone: 507-931-0452
Fax: 507-931-9278
E-mail: gmiller@scholarshipamerica.org

TALL CLUBS INTERNATIONAL FOUNDATION, INC.

http://www.tall.org/

KAE SUMNER EINFELDT SCHOLARSHIP

Females 5'10", or males 6'2" (minimum heights), are eligible to apply for the scholarship. Interested individuals should contact their local Tall Clubs Chapter. Canadian and U.S. winners are selected from finalists submitted by each local chapter.

Award: Scholarship for use in freshman year; not renewable. *Number:* 2–6. *Amount:* $1000.

Eligibility Requirements: Applicant must be age 17-21 and enrolled or expecting to enroll full- or part-time at a four-year institution or university. Available to U.S. and Canadian citizens.

Application Requirements: Application, essay, photo, references, transcript, verification of height. *Deadline:* March 1.

Contact: Sheila Koster, TCI Foundation Scholarship Contact
E-mail: bskoster@aol.com

TENNESSEE STUDENT ASSISTANCE CORPORATION

http://www.tn.gov/collegepays

HELPING HEROES GRANT

Provides assistance to Tennessee veterans who have been awarded the Iraq Campaign Medal, Afghanistan Campaign Medal, or Global War on Terrorism Expeditionary Medal (on or after 9/11/01) and who meet eligibility requirements for the program. Award is up to $2000 per year. For more information, visit http://www.TN.gov/collegepays.

Award: Grant for use in freshman, sophomore, junior, or senior years; not renewable. *Amount:* up to $2000.

Eligibility Requirements: Applicant must be enrolled or expecting to enroll full- or part-time at a two-year or four-year institution or university. Available to U.S. citizens.

Application Requirements: Application, DD-214. *Deadline:* September 1.

Contact: Mr. Robert Biggers, Director of Lottery Programs
Tennessee Student Assistance Corporation
Parkway Towers, Suite 1510, 404 James Robertson Parkway
Nashville, TN 37243
Phone: 866-291-2675 Ext. 106
Fax: 615-741-6101
E-mail: robert.biggers@tn.gov

TEXAS FEDERATION OF BUSINESS AND PROFESSIONAL WOMEN'S FOUNDATION

http://www.bpwtx.org/foundation.asp

GILDA MURRAY SCHOLARSHIP

Scholarship of $500 awarded to members of BPW/Texas, age 25 or older, to obtain education or training at an accredited college or university, technology institution, or training center. The number of awards varies.

Award: Scholarship for use in freshman, sophomore, junior, or senior years; not renewable. *Number:* varies. *Amount:* $500.

Eligibility Requirements: Applicant must be age 25 and over and enrolled or expecting to enroll full- or part-time at a four-year or technical institution or university. Available to U.S. citizens.

Application Requirements: Application, essay, references, regular attendance at LO meetings, active participation on at least one BPW committee. *Deadline:* May 1.

Contact: Nancy Jackson, Chair
Texas Federation of Business and Professional Women's Foundation
803 Forest Ridge Drive, Suite 104
Bedford, TX 76022
Phone: 817-283-0862
E-mail: bpwtx@sbcglobal.net

TEXAS MUTUAL INSURANCE COMPANY

http://www.texasmutual.com/

TEXAS MUTUAL INSURANCE COMPANY SCHOLARSHIP PROGRAM

A scholarship program open to qualified family members of policyholder employees who died from on-the-job injuries or accidents, policyholder employees who qualify for lifetime income benefits pursuant to the Texas Workers Compensation Act, and family members of injured employees who qualify for lifetime income benefits.

Award: Scholarship for use in freshman, sophomore, junior, or senior years; renewable. *Number:* 11. *Amount:* up to $4000.

Eligibility Requirements: Applicant must be age 17 and over and enrolled or expecting to enroll full- or part-time at a two-year or four-year or technical institution. Available to U.S. and non-U.S. citizens.

Application Requirements: Application, financial need analysis, references, test scores, transcript, fee bill, death certificate of family member, acceptance letter for freshmen. *Deadline:* varies.

Contact: Doris Limon, Administrative Assistant
Texas Mutual Insurance Company
6210 East Highway 290
PO Box 12058
Austin, TX 78723-1098
Phone: 800-859-5995 Ext. 3820
E-mail: dlimon@texasmutual.com

TG

http://www.tgslc.org/

CHARLEY WOOTAN GRANT PROGRAM

Grants available to high school seniors or graduates, including GED recipients, who plan to enroll or are already enrolled at least half-time in an undergraduate course of study. Must be a U.S. citizen or permanent resident, demonstrate financial need, and be eligible to receive Title IV federal financial aid funding. Only the first 6,000 applications submitted will be considered. See web site for details http://www.aie.org/wootan.

Award: Grant for use in freshman, sophomore, junior, or senior years; not renewable. *Number:* varies. *Amount:* $1000–$4394.

Eligibility Requirements: Applicant must be enrolled or expecting to enroll full- or part-time at a two-year or four-year or technical institution or university. Available to U.S. citizens.

Application Requirements: Application, financial need analysis, transcript. *Deadline:* May 22.

Contact: Grant Program Manager
TG
301 Sundance Parkway
PO Box 83100
Round Rock, TX 78683-3100
Phone: 800-537-4180
E-mail: wootan@scholarshipamerica.org

THETA DELTA CHI EDUCATIONAL FOUNDATION INC.

http://www.tdx.org/

THETA DELTA CHI EDUCATIONAL FOUNDATION INC. SCHOLARSHIP

Scholarships for undergraduate or graduate students enrolled in an accredited institution. Awards are based on candidate's history of service to the fraternity, scholastic achievement, and need. See web site for application and additional information http://www.tdx.org/scholarship/scholarship.html.

Award: Scholarship for use in freshman, sophomore, junior, senior, or graduate years; renewable. *Number:* 15. *Amount:* $1000–$5000.

Eligibility Requirements: Applicant must be enrolled or expecting to enroll full-time at a four-year institution or university. Available to U.S. and non-U.S. citizens.

Application Requirements: Application, financial need analysis, references, transcript. *Deadline:* May 15.

Contact: William McClung, Executive Director
Theta Delta Chi Educational Foundation Inc.
214 Lewis Wharf
Boston, MA 02110-3927
Phone: 617-742-8886
Fax: 617-742-8868
E-mail: execdir@tdx.org

THURGOOD MARSHALL SCHOLARSHIP FUND

http://www.thurgoodmarshallfund.org/

THURGOOD MARSHALL SCHOLARSHIP

Merit scholarships for students attending one of 45 member HBCUs (historically black colleges, universities) including 5 member law schools. Must maintain an average GPA of 3.0 to renew, demonstrate financial need, and be a U.S. citizen. Apply through member HBCU's campus scholarship coordinator. For further details refer to web site http://www.thurgoodmarshallfund.org.

Award: Scholarship for use in freshman, sophomore, junior, senior, or graduate years; renewable. *Number:* varies. *Amount:* up to $4400.

Eligibility Requirements: Applicant must be enrolled or expecting to enroll full-time at a four-year institution or university. Applicant must have 3.0 GPA or higher. Available to U.S. citizens.

Application Requirements: Application, essay, financial need analysis, interview, photo, resume, references, test scores, transcript. *Deadline:* July 15.

Contact: Sophia Rogers, Scholarship Manager
Thurgood Marshall Scholarship Fund
80 Maiden Lane, Suite 2204
New York, NY 10038
Phone: 212-573-8888
E-mail: srogers@tmcfund.org

TRIANGLE EDUCATION FOUNDATION

http://www.triangle.org/

MORTIN SCHOLARSHIP

One-time award of $2500 annually for an active member of the Triangle Fraternity. Awarded based on a combination of need, grades and participation in campus and Triangle Activities. Minimum 3.0 GPA. Further information available at web site http://www.triangle.org.

Award: Scholarship for use in freshman, sophomore, junior, or senior years; not renewable. *Number:* 1. *Amount:* up to $2500.

MISCELLANEOUS CRITERIA

Eligibility Requirements: Applicant must be enrolled or expecting to enroll full-time at a four-year institution or university and male. Applicant must have 3.0 GPA or higher. Available to U.S. and non-U.S. citizens.

Application Requirements: Application, essay, financial need analysis, references, self-addressed stamped envelope, transcript. *Deadline:* February 15.

Contact: Scott Bova, President
Triangle Education Foundation
120 South Center Street
Plainfield, IN 46168-1214
Phone: 317-705-9803
Fax: 317-837-9642
E-mail: sbova@triangle.org

PETER AND BARBARA BYE SCHOLARSHIP

Scholarship for a Triangle Fraternity member for undergraduate study. Preference given to applicants from Cornell University Triangle chapter. Applicant must have a minimum GPA of 2.7. Additional information on web site http://www.triangle.org.

Award: Scholarship for use in freshman, sophomore, junior, or senior years; not renewable. *Number:* 1. *Amount:* up to $2000.

Eligibility Requirements: Applicant must be enrolled or expecting to enroll full- or part-time at a four-year institution or university and male. Available to U.S. and non-U.S. citizens.

Application Requirements: Application, financial need analysis, references, transcript. *Deadline:* February 15.

Contact: Scott Bova, President
Triangle Education Foundation
120 South Center Street
Plainfield, IN 46168-1214
Phone: 317-705-9803
Fax: 317-837-9642
E-mail: sbova@triangle.org

TWIN TOWERS ORPHAN FUND

http://www.ttof.org/

TWIN TOWERS ORPHAN FUND

Fund offers assistance to children who lost one or both parents in the terrorist attacks on September 11, 2001. Long-term education program established to provide higher education needs to children until they complete their uninterrupted studies, or reach age of majority. Visit web site for additional information http://www.ttof.org.

Award: Scholarship for use in freshman, sophomore, junior, senior, or graduate years; not renewable. *Number:* varies. *Amount:* $5000–$7000.

Eligibility Requirements: Applicant must be age 22 or under and enrolled or expecting to enroll full- or part-time at a two-year or four-year or technical institution or university. Available to U.S. and non-U.S. citizens.

Application Requirements: Application, financial need analysis, birth certificate, parent's death certificate, marriage license. *Deadline:* varies.

Contact: Karlene Boss, Case Manager
Twin Towers Orphan Fund
7004 Outingdale Drive
Bakersfield, CA 93309
Phone: 661-633-9076
E-mail: ttof2@ttof.org

THE UDALL FOUNDATION

http://www.udall.gov/

THE UDALL SCHOLARSHIP

Eighty one-time scholarships and fifty one-time honorable mention awards to full-time college sophomores or juniors with demonstrated commitment to careers related to the environment, tribal public policy (Native American/Alaska Native students only), or Native American health care (Native American/Alaska Native students only). Students from all fields and disciplines are encouraged to apply. Students must be nominated by their college or university. Visit http://www.udall.gov for additional information.

Award: Scholarship for use in sophomore or junior years; not renewable. *Number:* 80. *Amount:* up to $5000.

Eligibility Requirements: Applicant must be enrolled or expecting to enroll full-time at a two-year or four-year or technical institution or university. Applicant must have 3.0 GPA or higher. Available to U.S. citizens.

Application Requirements: Application, essay, references, transcript, nomination by campus faculty representative. *Deadline:* March 2.

Contact: Mia Ibarra, Scholarship Program Manager
The Udall Foundation
130 South Scott Avenue
Tucson, AZ 85701
Phone: 520-901-8564
Fax: 520-901-8570
E-mail: ibarra@udall.gov

UNITED NEGRO COLLEGE FUND

http://www.uncf.org/

AMERICAN AIRLINES SCHOLARSHIP

20 scholarships available to full-time undergraduate students enrolled at an UNCF institution. Students must have a financial need due to the negative impact from Hurricane Katrina.

Award: Scholarship for use in freshman, sophomore, junior, or senior years; not renewable. *Number:* 20. *Amount:* $1677.

Eligibility Requirements: Applicant must be enrolled or expecting to enroll full-time at a four-year institution. Applicant must have 2.5 GPA or higher. Available to U.S. citizens.

Application Requirements: *Deadline:* continuous.

Contact: Director, Program Services
United Negro College Fund
8260 Willow Oaks Corporate Drive
PO Box 10444
Fairfax, VA 22031-8044
Phone: 800-331-2244
E-mail: rebecca.bennett@uncf.org

CARNIVAL/MIAMI HEAT SCHOLARSHIP

Scholarships for students who have demonstrated a capacity to succeed and completed the Carnival or Miami HEAT School to Work Mentoring Program. Must be a U.S. citizen or permanent resident, enrolled full-time, and have an unmet financial need. Minimum 2.8 GPA required.

Award: Scholarship for use in freshman, sophomore, junior, or senior years; not renewable. *Amount:* up to $5000.

Eligibility Requirements: Applicant must be enrolled or expecting to enroll full-time at a two-year or four-year institution or university.

Application Requirements: Application, essay, references, transcript. *Deadline:* May 13.

Contact: Director, Program Services
United Negro College Fund
8260 Willow Oaks Corporate Drive
PO Box 10444
Fairfax, VA 22031-8044
Phone: 800-331-2244
E-mail: rebecca.bennett@uncf.org

TIME WARNER SCHOLARS PROGRAM

Scholarship for students who attend a college or university from a selected list. Minimum GPA 3.0. For more information see Website: http://www.uncf.org/forstudents/scholarship.asp.

Award: Scholarship for use in sophomore year. *Amount:* $2500.

Eligibility Requirements: Applicant must be enrolled or expecting to enroll at a four-year institution or university. Applicant must have 3.0 GPA or higher.

Contact: Director, Program Services
United Negro College Fund
8260 Willow Oaks Corporate Drive
PO Box 10444
Fairfax, VA 22031-8044
Phone: 800-331-2244
E-mail: rebecca.bennett@uncf.org

UNCF GENERAL SCHOLARSHIP

Scholarship for students attending UNCF Institutes. Minimum 2.5 GPA required. This application information will be used to match students to specific programs administered by UNCF. For more information see Website: http://www.uncf.org/forstudents/scholarship.asp.

Award: Scholarship for use in freshman, sophomore, junior, senior, or graduate years. *Amount:* up to $5000.

Eligibility Requirements: Applicant must be enrolled or expecting to enroll at a four-year institution or university. Applicant must have 2.5 GPA or higher.

Application Requirements: *Deadline:* May 15.

Contact: Director, Program Services
United Negro College Fund
8260 Willow Oaks Corporate Drive
PO Box 10444
Fairfax, VA 22031-8044
Phone: 800-331-2244
E-mail: rebecca.bennett@uncf.org

UNITED STATES ACHIEVEMENT ACADEMY

http://www.usaa-academy.com/

DR. GEORGE A. STEVENS FOUNDER'S AWARD

One $10,000 scholarship cash grant to enhance the intellectual and personal growth of students who demonstrate a genuine interest in learning. Award must be used for educational purposes. Must maintain a minimum GPA of 3.0.

Award: Grant for use in freshman year; not renewable. *Number:* 1. *Amount:* $10,000.

Eligibility Requirements: Applicant must be high school student and planning to enroll or expecting to enroll full-time at a four-year institution or university. Applicant must have 3.0 GPA or higher. Available to U.S. and non-U.S. citizens.

Application Requirements: Application.

Contact: Scholarship Committee
United States Achievement Academy
2528 Palumbo Drive
Lexington, KY 40509
Phone: 859-269-5674
Fax: 859-268-9068
E-mail: usaa@usaa-academy.com

NATIONAL SCHOLARSHIP CASH GRANT

The Foundation awards 400 national scholarship cash grants of $1500. All scholarship winners are determined by an independent selection committee. Winners are selected based on GPA, school activities, SAT scores (if applicable), honors and awards. All students in grades 6–12 are eligible.

Award: Grant for use in freshman year; not renewable. *Number:* 400. *Amount:* $1500.

Eligibility Requirements: Applicant must be high school student and planning to enroll or expecting to enroll full-time at a four-year institution or university. Applicant must have 3.0 GPA or higher. Available to U.S. and non-U.S. citizens.

Application Requirements: Application. *Deadline:* June 1.

Contact: Scholarship Committee
United States Achievement Academy
2528 Palumbo Drive
Lexington, KY 40509
Phone: 859-269-5674
Fax: 859-268-9068
E-mail: usaa@usaa-academy.com

UNITED STATES-INDONESIA SOCIETY

http://www.usindo.org/

UNITED STATES-INDONESIA SOCIETY TRAVEL GRANTS

Grants are provided to fund travel to Indonesia or the United States for American and Indonesian students and professors to conduct research, language training or other independent study/research. Must have a minimum 3.0 GPA.

Award: Grant for use in freshman, sophomore, junior, senior, graduate, or postgraduate years; not renewable. *Number:* 1–15. *Amount:* $1000–$2000.

Eligibility Requirements: Applicant must be enrolled or expecting to enroll full- or part-time at a four-year institution or university. Applicant must have 3.0 GPA or higher. Available to U.S. and non-Canadian citizens.

Application Requirements: Application, resume, references, transcript, basic budget. *Deadline:* continuous.

Contact: Thomas Spooner, Educational Officer
United States-Indonesia Society
1625 Massachusetts Avenue, NW, Suite 550
Washington, DC 20036-2260
Phone: 202-232-1400
Fax: 202-232-7300
E-mail: tspooner@usindo.org

UNITED TRANSPORTATION UNION INSURANCE ASSOCIATION

http://www.utuia.org/

UTUIA SCHOLARSHIP

Scholarships of $500 awarded to undergraduate students. Applicant must be at least a high school senior or equivalent, age 25 or under, be a UTU or UTUIA insured member, the child or grandchild of a UTU or UTUIA insured member, or the child of a deceased UTU or UTUIA-insured member.

Award: Scholarship for use in freshman, sophomore, junior, or senior years; renewable. *Number:* 50. *Amount:* $500.

Eligibility Requirements: Applicant must be age 25 or under and enrolled or expecting to enroll full-time at a four-year institution or university. Available to U.S. citizens.

Application Requirements: Application. *Deadline:* March 31.

Contact: Scholarship Committee
United Transportation Union Insurance Association
14600 Detroit Avenue
Cleveland, OH 44107-4250
Phone: 216-228-9400

U.S. BANK INTERNET SCHOLARSHIP PROGRAM

http://www.usbank.com/

U.S. BANK INTERNET SCHOLARSHIP PROGRAM

A high school senior planning to enroll or a current college freshmen, sophomore or junior at an eligible four-year college or university participating in the U.S. Bank No Fee Education Loan Program. Apply online at usbank.com/studentbanking from October through March. No paper applications accepted.

Award: Scholarship for use in freshman, sophomore, or junior years; not renewable. *Number:* up to 40. *Amount:* up to $1000.

Eligibility Requirements: Applicant must be enrolled or expecting to enroll full- or part-time at a four-year institution or university. Available to U.S. and non-U.S. citizens.

Application Requirements: Application. *Deadline:* March 31.

Contact: Mary Ennis, Scholarship Coordinator
U.S. Bank Internet Scholarship Program
2322 East Sprague Avenue
Spokane, WA 99202
Phone: 800-242-1200
E-mail: mary.ennis@usbank.com

THE VEGETARIAN RESOURCE GROUP

http://www.vrg.org/

VEGETARIAN RESOURCE GROUP SCHOLARSHIP

Two scholarships will be awarded to graduating U.S. high school students who have promoted vegetarianism in their schools and/or communities. Vegetarians do not eat meat, fish, or fowl. Applicants will be judged on having shown compassion, courage, and a strong commitment to promoting a peaceful world through a vegetarian diet/lifestyle.

Award: Scholarship for use in freshman year; not renewable. *Number:* up to 2. *Amount:* up to $5000.

Eligibility Requirements: Applicant must be high school student and planning to enroll or expecting to enroll full- or part-time at a two-year or four-year or technical institution or university. Available to U.S. citizens.

Application Requirements: Application, essay, references, transcript. *Deadline:* February 20.

Contact: Sonja Helman, Scholarship Coordinator
The Vegetarian Resource Group
PO Box 1463
Baltimore, MD 21203
Phone: 410-366-8343
Fax: 410-366-8804
E-mail: sonjah@vrg.org

VHMNETWORK LLC

http://www.vhmnetwork.com/

ONLINE-DEGREE-SCHOLARSHIPS

Advertising-based scholarship available twice a year to students age 18 and older for tuition, books, rent, or additional expenses. See web site for details http://www.Online-Degree-Scholarships.com.

Award: Scholarship for use in freshman, sophomore, junior, or senior years; not renewable. *Number:* 2. *Amount:* $2000.

Eligibility Requirements: Applicant must be age 18 and over and enrolled or expecting to enroll full- or part-time at a two-year or four-year or technical institution or university. Available to U.S. citizens.

Application Requirements: Application.

Contact: Michael Derikrava, President
VHMnetwork LLC
419 Lafayette Street, 2nd Floor
New York, NY 10003
Phone: 646-723-4353 Ext. 4444
E-mail: michael@vhmnetwork.com

WAL-MART FOUNDATION

http://www.walmartfoundation.org/

SAM WALTON COMMUNITY SCHOLARSHIP

Award for high school seniors not affiliated with Wal-Mart stores. Based on financial need, academic merit, and school or community work activities. Must be a permanent legal resident of the United States. For use at an accredited two- or four-year U.S. institution. Applications available online at https://www.applyists.net, Access key: SWCS. Applicants may apply beginning November 1.

Award: Scholarship for use in freshman year; not renewable. *Number:* 2,695. *Amount:* $3000.

Eligibility Requirements: Applicant must be high school student and planning to enroll or expecting to enroll full-time at a two-year or four-year institution or university. Applicant must have 2.5 GPA or higher. Available to U.S. citizens.

Application Requirements: Application, financial need analysis, test scores, transcript. *Deadline:* January 31.

Contact: International Scholarship and Tuition Services, Inc.
Wal-Mart Foundation
PO Box 22117
Nashville, TN 37202-2117
Phone: 866-524-7385
Fax: 615-523-7100

WISECHOICE BRANDS, LLC

http://www.wisechoice.com/

WISECHOICE $2,500 "FIND THE RIGHT COLLEGE" SCHOLARSHIP

This scholarship program was designed to assist students in the college planning process, and to help them to really investigate their options when it comes to choosing a college for the right reasons. Applicants must register at WiseChoice.com.

Award: Scholarship for use in freshman year; not renewable. *Number:* 1. *Amount:* $2500.

Eligibility Requirements: Applicant must be high school student and planning to enroll or expecting to enroll at a four-year institution. Available to U.S. citizens.

Application Requirements: Application, essay. *Deadline:* May 31.

Contact: Information at: http://www.wisechoice.com/scholars
WiseChoice Brands, LLC
3020 Hartley Road, Suite 220
Jacksonville, FL 32257

WOMEN'S INDEPENDENCE SCHOLARSHIP PROGRAM, INC.

http://www.wispinc.org/

WOMEN'S INDEPENDENCE SCHOLARSHIP PROGRAM

Scholarship of $250 to $5000 to enable female survivors of domestic violence (partner abuse) to return to school to gain skills necessary to become independent and self-sufficient. Requires sponsorship by nonprofit domestic violence service agency. First priority candidates are single mothers with young children. Must be U.S. citizens or permanent legal residents with critical financial need. Deadline varies.

Award: Scholarship for use in freshman, sophomore, junior, senior, or graduate years; renewable. *Number:* 500–600. *Amount:* $250–$5000.

Eligibility Requirements: Applicant must be enrolled or expecting to enroll full- or part-time at a two-year or four-year or technical institution or university and female. Available to U.S. citizens.

Application Requirements: Application, essay, financial need analysis, references. *Deadline:* continuous.

Contact: Nancy Soward, Executive Director
Women's Independence Scholarship Program, Inc.
4900 Randall Parkway, Suite H
Wilmington, NC 28403
Phone: 910-397-7742 Ext. 101
Fax: 910-397-0023
E-mail: nancy@wispinc.org

WOMEN'S JEWELRY ASSOCIATION

http://www.womensjewelry.org/

WJA MEMBER GRANT

Grants are generally up to $500 and can be used by members to pay for any aspect of further education during the year. For more information please visit web site http://www.womensjewelry.org/.

Award: Grant for use in freshman, sophomore, junior, senior, graduate, or postgraduate years; not renewable. *Number:* 1. *Amount:* up to $500.

Eligibility Requirements: Applicant must be enrolled or expecting to enroll full- or part-time at a two-year or four-year or technical institution or university and female. Available to U.S. and non-U.S. citizens.

Application Requirements: Application, essay. *Deadline:* January 1.

Contact: Scholarship Committee
Women's Jewelry Association
7000 West Southwest Highway, Suite 202
Chicago Ridge, IL 60415
Phone: 708-361-6266
Fax: 708-361-6166
E-mail: info@womensjewelry.org

WOMEN'S OVERSEAS SERVICE LEAGUE

http://www.wosl.org/

WOMEN'S OVERSEAS SERVICE LEAGUE SCHOLARSHIPS FOR WOMEN

Awarded to women committed to careers in public service who have completed 12 semester or 18 quarter units in any higher education institution with a 2.5 GPA, are admitted to an institution in a program leading to an Associate's Degree or higher and enrolled for a minimum of 6 semester or 9 quarter hours.

Award: Scholarship for use in sophomore, junior, senior, graduate, or postgraduate years; renewable. *Number:* 10–20. *Amount:* $1000–$2000.

Eligibility Requirements: Applicant must be enrolled or expecting to enroll full- or part-time at a two-year or four-year or technical institution or university and female. Applicant must have 2.5 GPA or higher. Available to U.S. citizens.

Application Requirements: Application, essay, financial need analysis, resume, references, transcript. *Deadline:* March 1.

Contact: Ms. Ann L. Kelsey, Scholarship Committee Chair
E-mail: kelsey@openix.com

YOUTH MARITIME TRAINING ASSOCIATION

http://www.ymta.net/

NORM MANLY—YMTA MARITIME EDUCATIONAL SCHOLARSHIPS

The scholarships may be used by students pursuing maritime training and education in community colleges, technical and vocational programs, colleges, universities, maritime academies or other educational institutions. Scholarships will be awarded in the amounts of one $5,000, one $3,000, and two $1,000. In addition, Pacific Maritime Magazine will award a $500 scholarship to one of the finalists planning to pursue a sea-going maritime career.

Award: Scholarship for use in freshman, sophomore, junior, or senior years; not renewable. *Amount:* $1000–$5000.

Eligibility Requirements: Applicant must be enrolled or expecting to enroll at a two-year or four-year or technical institution or university.

Contact: Dr. Gary Stauffer, President
Youth Maritime Training Association
PO Box 70425
Seattle, WA 98127
Phone: 206-300-5559
E-mail: garystauffer47@msn.com

ZETA PHI BETA SORORITY INC. NATIONAL EDUCATIONAL FOUNDATION

http://www.zphib1920.org/

GENERAL UNDERGRADUATE SCHOLARSHIP

Scholarships available for undergraduate students. Awarded for full-time study for one academic year. Check web site for information and application http://www.zphib1920.org.

Award: Scholarship for use in freshman, sophomore, junior, or senior years; not renewable. *Number:* 1. *Amount:* $500–$1000.

Eligibility Requirements: Applicant must be enrolled or expecting to enroll full-time at a four-year institution or university. Available to U.S. citizens.

Application Requirements: Application, essay, references, transcript, enrollment proof. *Deadline:* February 1.

Contact: Cheryl Williams, National Second Vice President
Zeta Phi Beta Sorority Inc. National Educational Foundation
1734 New Hampshire Avenue, NW
Washington, DC 20009-2595
Fax: 318-232-4593
E-mail: 2ndanti@zphib1920.org

ZINCH

http://www.zinch.com/

MARCH MADNEZZ

If you are new to Zinch, this is our longest running and most prestigious scholarship award. Each year semi-finalists are selected for this scholarship based on their Zinch profile. The semi-finalists then compete, March Madnezz style, in a bracket of 64 students. Students go head-to-head, with the best Zinch profile advancing, until only one student remains claiming the $20,000 scholarship.

Award: Scholarship for use in freshman, sophomore, junior, or senior years; renewable. *Number:* 1. *Amount:* $20,000.

Eligibility Requirements: Applicant must be age 16 and over and enrolled or expecting to enroll full- or part-time at a two-year or four-year institution or university. Applicant must have 2.5 GPA or higher. Available to U.S. and non-U.S. citizens.

Application Requirements: Application, Zinch profile. *Deadline:* May 25.

Contact: Sean Castillo, Scholarship Manager
Zinch
600 Townsend Street E, 4th Floor
San Francisco, CA 94103
Phone: 888-229-4624

ZONTA INTERNATIONAL FOUNDATION

http://www.zonta.org/

YOUNG WOMEN IN PUBLIC AFFAIRS AWARD

One-time award for pre-college women with a commitment to the volunteer sector and evidence of volunteer leadership achievements. Must be 16 to 19 years of age with a career interest in public affairs, public policy and community organizations. Further information and application available at web site http://www.zonta.org.

Award: Scholarship for use in freshman, sophomore, or junior years; not renewable. *Number:* up to 5. *Amount:* $1000–$4000.

Eligibility Requirements: Applicant must be high school student; age 16-19; planning to enroll or expecting to enroll full-time at a four-year institution and female. Available to U.S. and non-U.S. citizens.

Application Requirements: Application, references. *Deadline:* varies.

Contact: Ana Ubides, Programs Manager
Zonta International Foundation
1211 West 22nd Street, Suite 900
Oak Brook, IL 60523
Fax: 630-928-1559
E-mail: progrmas@zonta.org

INDEXES

Award Name

American Morgan Horse Institute Graywood Youth Horsemanship Grant *808*

American Morgan Horse Institute van Schaik Dressage Scholarship *809*

American Nephrology Nurses' Association Career Mobility Scholarship *441*

American Nephrology Nurses' Association NNCC Career Mobility Scholarship *442*

American Nephrology Nurses' Association Watson Pharma Inc. Career Mobility Scholarship *442*

American Nuclear Society Operations and Power Scholarship *435*

American Nuclear Society Undergraduate Scholarships *435*

American Nuclear Society Vogt Radiochemistry Scholarship *276*

American Occupational Therapy Foundation State Association Scholarships *338*

American Philological Association/ Archaeological Institute of America Minority Scholarship *98*

American Physical Society Corporate-Sponsored Scholarship for Minority Undergraduate Students Who Major in Physics *477*

American Physical Society Scholarship for Minority Undergraduate Physics Majors *475*

American Psychological Association Teachers of Psychology in Secondary Schools Scholars Essay Competition *483*

American Quarter Horse Foundation Youth Scholarships *534*

American Restaurant Scholarship *210*

American Savings Foundation Scholarships *713*

American-Scandinavian Foundation Translation Prize *397*

American Society for Enology and Viticulture Scholarships *82*

American Society of Agricultural and Biological Engineers Foundation Scholarship *82*

American Society of Civil Engineers-Maine High School Scholarship *175*

American Society of Criminology Gene Carte Student Paper Competition *206*

American Society of Naval Engineers Scholarship *93*

American Society of Women Accountants Two-Year College Scholarship *57*

American Society of Women Accountants Undergraduate Scholarship *57*

American Theatre Organ Society Organ Performance Scholarship *809*

American Water Ski Educational Foundation Scholarship *536*

American Welding Society District Scholarship Program *263*

American Welding Society International Scholarship *263*

America Responds Memorial Scholarship *462*

America's Intercultural Magazine (AIM) Short Story Contest *396*

America's Junior Miss Scholarship Program *810*

Amos Deinard Foundation Scholarship *796*

AMS Freshman Undergraduate Scholarship *306*

AMVETS National Ladies Auxiliary Scholarship *536*

Amy Lowell Poetry Traveling Scholarship *397*

Anchor Scholarship Foundation Program *648*

Angelfire Scholarship *635*

Angus Foundation Scholarships *553*

ANNA Alcavis International, Inc. Career Mobility Scholarship *442*

Anna and John Kolesar Memorial Scholarships *228*

Anna May Rolando Scholarship Award *445*

Anne A. Agnew Scholarship *564*

Anne and Matt Harbison Scholarship *612*

Anne Ford & Allegra Ford Scholarship *607*

Anne Seaman Professional Grounds Management Society Memorial Scholarship *87*

Annual Award Program *697*

Annual Liberty Graphics Art Contest *753*

Annual Scholarship Grant Program *208*

ANS Incoming Freshman Scholarship *435*

"Anthem" Essay Contest *812*

AnyCollege.com Scholarship *838*

AOCS Biotechnology Student Excellence Award *82*

AOCS Health and Nutrition Division Student Excellence Award *318*

AOPA Air Safety Foundation/Donald Burnside Memorial Scholarship *121*

AOPA Air Safety Foundation/McAllister Memorial Scholarship *122*

A.O. Putnam Memorial Scholarship *285*

AOTA'S Assembly of Student Delegates Award *838*

APEX Scholarship *655*

Appaloosa Youth Educational Scholarships *536*

Applegate/Jackson/Parks Future Teacher Scholarship *243*

Appraisal Institute Education Trust Education Scholarships *486*

Apprentice Ecologist Scholarship *857*

AQHF Journalism or Communications Scholarship *182*

AQHF Racing Scholarships *90*

AQHF Telephony Equine Veterinary Scholarship *90*

Archbold Scholarship Program *344*

ARC of Washington Trust Fund Stipend Program *497*

AREMA Michael R. Garcia Scholarship *174*

AREMA Presidential Spouse Scholarship *174*

AREMA Undergraduate Scholarships *174*

Arizona Chapter Dependent/Employee Membership Scholarship *512*

Arizona Chapter Gold Scholarship *512*

Arizona Hydrological Society Scholarship *222*

Arizona Nursery Association Foundation Scholarship *356*

Arizona Private Postsecondary Education Student Financial Assistance Program *714*

Arizona Private School Association Scholarship *714*

Arizona Professional Chapter of AISES Scholarship *279*

Arizona Quarter Horse Youth Racing Scholarship *90*

Arkansas Academic Challenge Scholarship Program *715*

Arkansas Governor's Scholars Program *715*

Arkansas Single Parent Scholarship *715*

Arlene Benton Nolan and John Nolan Scholarship *144*

Armed Forces Communications and Electronics Association General Emmett Paige Scholarship *122*

Armed Forces Communications and Electronics Association General John A. Wickham Scholarship *164*

Armed Forces Communications and Electronics Association ROTC Scholarship Program *122*

Armed Forces Loan Forgiveness Program *644*

Armenian Relief Society Undergraduate Scholarship *655*

Armenian Students Association of America Inc. Scholarships *655*

Army Officers Wives Club of the Greater Washington Area Scholarship *622*

Army ROTC Green to Gold Scholarship Program for Two-Year, Three-Year and Four-Year Scholarships, Active Duty Enlisted Personnel *622*

Army (ROTC) Reserve Officers Training Corps Two-, Three-, Four-Year Campus-Based Scholarships *602*

Arne Engebretsen Wisconsin Mathematics Council Scholarship *250*

ARRL Foundation General Fund Scholarships *810*

ARRL Scholarship Honoring Barry Goldwater, K7UGA *810*

Arsham Amirikian Engineering Scholarship *175*

ARTBA-TDF Lanford Family Highway Workers Memorial Scholarship Program *583*

ARTC Glen Moon Scholarship *231*

Art Directors Club National Scholarships *109*

Arthur and Gladys Cervenka Scholarship Award *294*

Arthur E. and Helen Copeland Scholarships *615*

Arthur J. Packard Memorial Scholarship *208*

Arthur Ross Foundation Scholarship *683*

Artistic Encouragement Grant *604*

ASABE Foundation Scholarship *277*

ASCPA Educational Foundation Scholarship *56*

ASCSA Summer Sessions Scholarships *92*

Asea Brown Boveri Scholarship *302*

Ashby B. Carter Memorial Scholarship Fund Founders Award *550*

Ashley Tamburri Scholarship *600*

ASHRAE General Scholarship *262*

ASHRAE Memorial Scholarship *253*

ASHRAE Region IV Benny Bootle Scholarship *100*

ASHRAE Region VIII Scholarship *262*

ASHS Scholars Award *356*

Asian-American Journalists Association Scholarship *183*

Asian Reporter Scholarship *656*

ASID Educational Foundation/Yale R. Burge Competition *371*

ASID Minnesota Chapter Scholarship Fund *372*

ASLA Council of Fellows Scholarship *388*

ASME Auxiliary Undergraduate Scholarship Charles B. Sharp *412*

ASM Outstanding Scholars Awards *280*

ASSE-Edwin P. Granberry Jr. Distinguished Service Award Scholarship *462*

ASSE-Gulf Coast Past Presidents Scholarship *462*

ASSE-Marsh Risk Consulting Scholarship *462*

ASSE-Region IV/Edwin P. Granberry Scholarship *462*

ASSE-United Parcel Service Scholarship *463*

Associate Degree Nursing Scholarship Program *448*

Associated General Contractors NYS Scholarship *176*

Associated Press Television/Radio Association-Clete Roberts Journalism Scholarship Awards *375*

Association for Food and Drug Officials Scholarship Fund *146*

Association for Iron and Steel Technology Baltimore Chapter Scholarship *261*

Association for Iron and Steel Technology Benjamin F. Fairless Scholarship (AIME) *160*

Association for Iron and Steel Technology David H. Samson Canadian Scholarship *160*

Association for Iron and Steel Technology Midwest Chapter Betty McKern Scholarship *274*

Library Research Grants *108*

Liederkranz Foundation Scholarship Award for Voice *822*

Lieutenant General Clarence R. Huebner Scholarship Program *622*

LIFE Lessons Scholarships Program *854*

Lifelong Learning Scholarship *775*

Life Member Montana Federation of Garden Clubs Scholarship *225*

Lillie Lois Ford Scholarship Fund *633*

Lilly Lorenzen Scholarship *714*

Lilly Reintegration Scholarship *607*

Lily and Catello Sorrentino Memorial Scholarship *784*

Linda Cowden Memorial Scholarship *604*

Linda Craig Memorial Scholarship presented by St. Vincent Sports Medicine *347*

Linda Luca Memorial GED Scholarship *776*

LinTV Minority Scholarship *378*

Lisa Zaken Award For Excellence *287*

Literacy Grant Competition *544*

Literary Achievement Awards *398*

Llewellyn L. Cayvan String Instrument Scholarship *422*

Lloyd A. Chacey, PE-Ohio Society of Professional Engineers Memorial Scholarship *283*

Lockheed Martin/UNCF Scholarship *73*

Loeblich and Tappan Student Research Award *140*

Lois Hole Humanities and Social Sciences Scholarship *364*

Lois McMillen Memorial Scholarship Fund *110*

Lola B. Curry Scholarship *569*

Lone Star Community Scholarships *190*

Loren W. Crow Scholarship *368*

Lori Rhett Memorial Scholarship *592*

Los Alamos Employees' Scholarship *754*

Lotte Lenya Competition for Singers *821*

Lou and Carole Prato Sports Reporting Scholarship *189*

Lou Hochberg-High School Essay Awards *494*

Louise A. Broderick San Diego County Scholarship *786*

Louise McKinney Postsecondary Scholarships *653*

Louisiana Department of Veterans Affairs State Aid Program *639*

Louisiana Memorial Scholarship *717*

Louisiana National Guard State Tuition Exemption Program *620*

Louis T. Klauder Scholarship *253*

Lou Wolf Memorial Scholarship *259*

Lowell Gaylor Memorial Scholarship *120*

Lowe's Educational Scholarship *590*

Loy McCandless Marks Scholarship in Tropical Ornamental Horticulture *357*

L. Phil Wicker Scholarship *183*

L. Ron Hubbard's Illustrators of the Future Contest *812*

L. Ron Hubbard's Writers of the Future Contest *812*

LTG Douglas D. Buchholz Memorial Scholarship *122*

Lucile B. Kaufman Women's Scholarship *297*

Luci S. Williams Houston Memorial Scholarship *472*

LULAC National Scholarship Fund *670*

Lullelia W. Harrison Scholarship in Counseling *173*

Luterman Scholarship *532*

Lynda Pilger Scholarship *859*

Lyndon Baines Johnson Foundation Grants-in-Aid Research *353*

Mae Lassley Osage Scholarship *678*

Mae Maxey Memorial Scholarship *116*

Magnolia DX Association Scholarship *183*

Maine Campground Owners Association Scholarship *488*

Maine Community Foundation Scholarship Programs *756*

Maine Graphics Art Association *332*

Maine Legislative Memorial Scholarship *756*

Maine Metal Products Association Scholarship *414*

Maine Metal Products Education Fund Scholarship Program *127*

Maine Osteopathic Association Memorial Scholarship *345*

Maine Osteopathic Association Scholarship *345*

Maine Restaurant Association Education Foundation Scholarship Fund *212*

Maine Rural Rehabilitation Fund Scholarship Program *79*

Maine School Food Service Association Continuing Education Scholarship *213*

Maine Society of Professional Engineers Vernon T. Swaine-Robert E. Chute Scholarship *267*

Maine State Chamber of Commerce Scholarship-Adult Learner *756*

Maine State Chamber of Commerce Scholarship-High School Senior *153*

Maine State Society Foundation Scholarship *756*

Major Don S. Gentile Scholarship *682*

Major General Lucas V. Beau Flight Scholarships Sponsored by the Order of Daedalians *124*

Malcolm Baldrige Scholarship *148*

Malcolm Pirnie Corporate Scholars Program *171*

Malmberg Scholarship for Study in Sweden *838*

MANAA Media Scholarships for Asian American Students *113*

MANA de San Diego Sylvia Chavez Memorial Scholarship *591*

Marcella Kochanska Sembrich Vocal Competition *419*

Marcella Sembrich Voice Competition *821*

March Madnezz *871*

Margaret E. Swanson Scholarship *217*

Margaret McNamara Memorial Fund Fellowships *172*

Marguerite McAlpin Nurse's Scholarship *440*

Marguerite Ross Barnett Memorial Scholarship *764*

Maria C. Jackson/General George A. White Scholarship *644*

Maria Elena Salinas Scholarship *328*

Marilyn Yetso Memorial Scholarship *795*

Marine Corps Scholarship Foundation *570*

Marine Corps Tankers Association, John Cornelius/Max English Scholarship *646*

Marion A. and Eva S. Peeples Scholarships *240*

Marion A. Lindeman Scholarship *347*

Marion Barr Stanfield Art Scholarship *115*

Marion Huber Learning Through Listening Awards *560*

Markley Scholarship *159*

Mark Music Memorial Scholarship *603*

Markowski-Leach Scholarship *744*

Marliave Fund *224*

Marsh Affinity Group Services Scholarship *217*

Marshall E. McCullough-National Dairy Shrine Scholarships *85*

Marsha's Angels Scholarship Fund *451*

Martha Ann Stark Memorial Scholarship *251*

Martha R. Dudley LVN/LPN Scholarship *454*

Martin D. Andrews Memorial Scholarship Fund *823*

Martin Duffy Adult Learner Scholarship Award *549*

Martin Luther King, Jr. Memorial Scholarship *232*

Marvin Mundel Memorial Scholarship *287*

Mary Benevento CTAHPERD Scholarship *234*

Mary E. Horstkotte Scholarship Fund *778*

Maryland Association of Private Colleges and Career Schools Scholarship *153*

Maryland Community Cancer Scholarship Award *614*

Maryland Scholars *589*

Maryland SPJ Pro Chapter College Scholarship *386*

Mary Lou Brown Scholarship *717*

Mary Macey Scholarship *88*

Mary Main Memorial Scholarship *609*

Mary Marshall Practical Nursing Scholarships *460*

Mary Marshall Registered Nurse Scholarships *461*

Mary McLeod Bethune Scholarship *739*

Mary Morrow-Edna Richards Scholarship *243*

Mary Moy Quan Ing Memorial Scholarship Award *374*

Mary M. Verges Scholarship *540*

Mary Olive Eddy Jones Art Scholarship *108*

Mary P. Oenslager Scholastic Achievement Awards *560*

Mary Rubin and Benjamin M. Rubin Scholarship Fund *722*

Mary Serra Gili Scholarship Award *445*

Mary York Scholarship Fund *848*

Mas Family Scholarship Award *152*

Mas Family Scholarships *148*

Masonic Range Science Scholarship *80*

Massachusetts AFL-CIO Scholarship *758*

Massachusetts Assistance for Student Success Program *759*

Massachusetts Cash Grant Program *759*

Massachusetts Federation of Polish Women's Clubs Scholarships *669*

Massachusetts Gilbert Matching Student Grant Program *759*

Massachusetts Part-Time Grant Program *760*

Massachusetts Public Service Grant Program *591*

MassMutual Career Pathways Scholars Program *729*

MasterCard Worldwide Special Support Program *691*

Master's Scholarship Program *169*

Math and Science Scholarship *140*

Math, Engineering, Science, Business, Education, Computers Scholarships *147*

Matsuo Bridge Company Ltd. of Japan Scholarship *176*

Maureen L. and Howard N. Blitman, PE Scholarship to Promote Diversity in Engineering *167*

Maynard Jensen American Legion Memorial Scholarship *532*

Mayo Foundations Scholarship *454*

The Mayor's Chesapeake Energy Scholarship *731*

May T. Henry Scholarship Foundation *722*

MBA Student Broadcaster Scholarship *518*

MBIA/William O. Bailey Scholars Program *73*

McClare Family Trust Scholarship *366*

McCurry Foundation Scholarship *760*

McFarland Charitable Nursing Scholarship *448*

M.D. "Jack" Murphy Memorial Scholarship *441*

Medical Imaging Educators Scholarship *231*

Medical Research Scholarship *345*

Medicus Student Exchange *681*

Medtronic Foundation Scholarship *145*

Memorial Foundation for Jewish Culture International Scholarship Program for Community Service *106*

Sponsor

American Legion Auxiliary Department of Nebraska   526, 630, 705

American Legion Auxiliary Department of New Mexico   439

American Legion Auxiliary Department of North Dakota   439, 582, 630, 705

American Legion Auxiliary Department of Ohio   440, 630, 705

American Legion Auxiliary Department of Oregon   440, 526, 630, 705

American Legion Auxiliary Department of Pennsylvania   705

American Legion Auxiliary Department of South Dakota   526, 631, 706

American Legion Auxiliary Department of Tennessee   631, 706

American Legion Auxiliary Department of Texas   337, 631, 706

American Legion Auxiliary Department of Utah   527, 631, 706

American Legion Auxiliary Department of Washington   107, 109, 397, 440, 631, 706

American Legion Auxiliary Department of Wisconsin   440, 527, 631, 706

American Legion Auxiliary Department of Wyoming   218, 338, 440, 502

American Legion Auxiliary National Headquarters   529, 632

American Legion Baseball   838

American Legion Department of Arizona   707, 806

American Legion Department of Arkansas   529, 632, 707, 806

American Legion Department of Hawaii   707

American Legion Department of Idaho   529, 632, 707

American Legion Department of Illinois   529, 707, 806

American Legion Department of Indiana   530, 708, 806

American Legion Department of Iowa   530, 708, 806

American Legion Department of Kansas   420, 440, 468, 530, 632, 708, 806

American Legion Department of Maine   531, 632, 709

American Legion Department of Maryland   408, 475, 632, 709

American Legion Department of Michigan   633, 709, 807

American Legion Department of Minnesota   531, 633, 709, 807

American Legion Department of Missouri   230, 441, 532, 633, 710

American Legion Department of Montana   710, 807

American Legion Department of Nebraska   532, 633, 710, 807

American Legion Department of New Jersey   532, 622, 807

American Legion Department of New York   181, 711, 807

American Legion Department of North Carolina   711, 807

American Legion Department of North Dakota   633, 655, 711, 807

American Legion Department of Ohio   533, 634

American Legion Department of Oregon   711, 807

American Legion Department of Pennsylvania   504, 533, 712, 807

American Legion Department of South Dakota   712, 807

American Legion Department of Tennessee   533, 618, 624, 712, 808

American Legion Department of Texas   712, 808

American Legion Department of Vermont   533, 583, 634, 712, 808

American Legion Department of Virginia   713

American Legion Department of Washington   534, 634, 713

American Legion Department of West Virginia   534, 634, 713, 808

American Legion National Headquarters   441, 583, 634, 808

American Legion Press Club of New Jersey   182, 373, 472, 516

American Mathematical Association of Two Year Colleges   408

American Medical Association Foundation   338

American Medical Technologists   218, 338

American Meteorological Society   306, 366, 402, 417, 465

American Military Retirees Association   634

American Mobile Healthcare   441

American Montessori Society   230

American Morgan Horse Institute   808

American Museum of Natural History   809

American National Cattle Women Inc.   838

American Nephrology Nurses' Association   441

American Nuclear Society   260, 276, 435

American Occupational Therapy Foundation Inc.   338, 502, 838

American Oil Chemists' Society   82, 163, 318

American Optometric Foundation   466

American Philological Association   98, 109, 181, 326, 352

American Physical Society   475

American Physical Therapy Association   338, 502

American Physiological Society   138, 339, 434

American Planning Association   521

American Postal Workers Union   534, 583

American Psychological Association   483

American Public Transportation Foundation   146, 174, 253, 261, 276, 412, 508

American Quarter Horse Foundation (AQHF)   90, 182, 373, 488, 534, 583, 713, 809

American Railway Engineering and Maintenance of Way Association   174, 203, 253, 261, 276, 509

American Research Institute in Turkey (ARIT)   326

American Respiratory Care Foundation   339, 502

American Road & Transportation Builders Association-Transportation Development Foundation (ARTBA-TDF)   583

American Savings Foundation   713

American-Scandinavian Foundation   397

American School of Classical Studies at Athens   92, 98, 100, 108, 109, 181, 351, 352, 365, 419, 472, 488

American Sephardi Foundation   696

American Sheep Industry Association   809

American Society for Engineering Education   93, 262, 277, 408, 475

American Society for Enology and Viticulture   82, 163, 318, 356

American Society for Horticultural Science   356

American Society for Information Science and Technology   195, 394

American Society of Agricultural and Biological Engineers   82, 138, 277

American Society of Agronomy, Crop Science Society of America, Soil Science Society of America   82

American Society of Certified Engineering Technicians   277

American Society of Civil Engineers   175, 203

American Society of Civil Engineers-Maine Section   175

American Society of Criminology   206, 389, 391, 493

American Society of Heating, Refrigerating, and Air Conditioning Engineers, Inc.   100, 253, 260, 262, 277, 350, 412, 505

American Society of Ichthyologists and Herpetologists   138

American Society of Interior Designers (ASID) Education Foundation Inc.   371

American Society of Mechanical Engineers (ASME)   412

American Society of Mechanical Engineers Auxiliary Inc.   412

American Society of Naval Engineers   93, 121, 175, 255, 260, 277, 402, 405, 413, 475

American Society of Plumbing Engineers   278, 369

American Society of Safety Engineers (ASSE) Foundation   462

American Society of Travel Agents (ASTA) Foundation   512

American Society of Women Accountants   57

American String Teachers Association   809

American Swedish Institute   714, 809, 838

American Theatre Organ Society Inc.   809

American Traffic Safety Services Foundation   838

American Water Resources Association   428

American Water Ski Educational Foundation   536, 810

American Welding Society   146, 175, 263, 278, 405, 413, 505

American Wholesale Marketers Association   146

America's Junior Miss Scholarship Program   810

AMVETS Auxiliary   536, 635

Amy Lowell Poetry Travelling Scholarship Trust   397

Anchor Scholarship Foundation   648

AnyCollege.com   838

AOPA Air Safety Foundation   121

Appalachian Center and Appalachian Studies Association   810, 839

Appaloosa Horse Club-Appaloosa Youth Program   91, 536, 810

Appraisal Institute Education Trust   486

Arab American Institute Foundation   374, 655

Arab American Scholarship Foundation   182, 481

Archaeological Institute of America   98, 181

ARC of Washington Trust Fund   497

Arctic Institute of North America   230, 307, 429, 432

Arizona Business Education Association   231

Arizona Commission for Postsecondary Education   714

Arizona Hydrological Society   222, 368, 429, 436, 491

Arizona Nursery Association   356

Arizona Private School Association   714

Arizona Professional Chapter of AISES   279, 340, 429, 475

Arizona State Department of Education   714

Arkansas Department of Higher Education   635, 715

Arkansas Single Parent Scholarship Fund   715, 810

Arkansas State Department of Education   715

Arkansas Student Loan Authority   716

Armed Forces Communications and Electronics Association, Educational Foundation   122, 163, 182, 195, 231, 255, 265, 279, 326, 372, 408, 475, 491, 839

Armenian Relief Society of Eastern USA Inc.-Regional Office   655

Armenian Students Association of America Inc.   655

Academic Fields/Career Goals

Behavioral Science

Biology

Business/Consumer Services

Campus Activities

Canadian Studies

Chemical Engineering

Child and Family Studies

Civil Engineering

Classics

Energy and Power Engineering

Engineering-Related Technologies

Engineering/Technology

Entomology

Environmental Health

Environmental Science

Health Information Management/Technology

Heating, Air-Conditioning, and Refrigeration Mechanics

Historic Preservation and Conservation

Landscape Architecture

Law Enforcement/Police Administration

Law/Legal Services

Library and Information Sciences

Pharmacy

AFPE Gateway to Research Scholarship Program 470

Cardinal Health Scholarship 72

Catholic Healthcare West Corporate Scholars Program 144

CVS/Pharmacy Scholarship 471

Cynthia E. Morgan Memorial Scholarship Fund, Inc. 304

Health Professions Preparatory Scholarship Program 335

International Society of Automation Education Foundation Scholarships 125

Jason Lang Scholarship 213

Kappa Epsilon-Nellie Wakeman-AFPE First Year Graduate School Scholarship 470

National Community Pharmacist Association Foundation Presidential Scholarship 471

Nicholas and Mary Agnes Trivillian Memorial Scholarship Fund 343

Northern Alberta Development Council Bursary for Pharmacy Students 470

Phi Lambda Sigma-GlaxoSmithKline-AFPE First Year Graduate School Scholarship 470

Raymond W. Cannon Memorial Scholarship Program 394

Regents Professional Opportunity Scholarship 69

StraightForward Media Medical Professions Scholarship 221

StraightForward Media Vocational-Technical School Scholarship 91

Philosophy

ASCSA Summer Sessions Scholarships 92

Davidson Fellows Scholarship Program 398

StraightForward Media Liberal Arts Scholarship 107

Photojournalism/Photography

American Legion Press Club of New Jersey and Post 170 Arthur Dehardt Memorial Scholarship 182

Asian-American Journalists Association Scholarship 183

Bob East Scholarship 473

Bruce T. and Jackie Mahi Erickson Grant 112

CCNMA Scholarships 376

College Photographer of the Year Competition 472

Connecticut SPJ Bob Eddy Scholarship Program 184

International Foodservice Editorial Council Communications Scholarship 77

Larry Fullerton Photojournalism Scholarship 472

Leonard M. Perryman Communications Scholarship for Ethnic Minority Students 192

Luci S. Williams Houston Memorial Scholarship 472

Marion Barr Stanfield Art Scholarship 115

National Association of Black Journalists Non-Sustaining Scholarship Awards 380

National Association of Hispanic Journalists Scholarship 188

National High School Journalist of the Year/Sister Rita Jeanne Scholarships 186

National Press Photographers Foundation Still Photographer Scholarship 473

National Press Photographers Foundation Television News Scholarship 473

Nebraska Press Association Foundation Inc. Scholarship 382

Newhouse Scholarship Program 332

Outdoor Writers Association of America Bodie McDowell Scholarship Award 189

Palm Beach Association of Black Journalists Scholarship 384

Pauly D'Orlando Memorial Art Scholarship 116

Phelan Award in Photography 474

Reid Blackburn Scholarship 474

StraightForward Media Media & Communications Scholarship 77

Texas Gridiron Club Scholarships 192

Valley Press Club Scholarships, The Republican Scholarship, Channel 22 Scholarship 194

Visual Task Force Scholarship 473

Young Journalists Scholarship 375

Physical Sciences

AFCEA Young Entrepreneur Scholarship 163

AIAA Foundation Undergraduate Scholarship 93

Al-Ben Scholarship for Academic Incentive 166

Al-Ben Scholarship for Professional Merit 166

Al-Ben Scholarship for Scholastic Achievement 166

Alfred Bader Scholarship 139

American Legion Department of Maryland Math-Science Scholarship 408

American Physical Society Corporate-Sponsored Scholarship for Minority Undergraduate Students Who Major in Physics 477

American Physical Society Scholarship for Minority Undergraduate Physics Majors 475

American Society of Naval Engineers Scholarship 93

Arizona Professional Chapter of AISES Scholarship 279

Arlene Benton Nolan and John Nolan Scholarship 144

Armed Forces Communications and Electronics Association General Emmett Paige Scholarship 122

Armed Forces Communications and Electronics Association General John A. Wickham Scholarship 164

Armed Forces Communications and Electronics Association ROTC Scholarship Program 122

Association for Iron and Steel Technology Ohio Valley Chapter Scholarship 137

A.T. Anderson Memorial Scholarship Program 93

Barry M. Goldwater Scholarship and Excellence in Education Program 95

BCIC Young Innovator Scholarship Competition (Idea Mash Up) 95

Beckman Scholars Program 138

BIOCOM Scholarship 143

Burlington Northern Santa Fe Foundation Scholarship 93

Carrol C. Hall Memorial Scholarship 97

Catholic Healthcare West Corporate Scholars Program 144

Charles S. Brown Scholarship in Physics 478

Coastal Plains Chapter of the Air and Waste Management Association Environmental Steward Scholarship 306

Collegiate Inventors Competition for Undergraduate Students 96

Collegiate Inventors Competition-Grand Prize 97

Dibner Fund Scholarship 434

Disabled War Veterans Scholarship 122

Elizabeth and Sherman Asche Memorial Scholarship Fund 83

Elmer S. Imes Scholarship in Physics 478

Grants for Disabled Students in the Sciences 95

Harvey Washington Banks Scholarship in Astronomy 478

High Technology Scholars Program 143

Hubertus W.V. Wellems Scholarship for Male Students 167

Independent Laboratories Institute Scholarship Alliance 141

James M. and Virginia M. Smyth Scholarship 110

LTG Douglas D. Buchholz Memorial Scholarship 122

Math and Science Scholarship 140

Math, Engineering, Science, Business, Education, Computers Scholarships 147

Medtronic Foundation Scholarship 145

Michael P. Anderson Scholarship in Space Science 478

Mineralogical Society of America-Grant for Student Research in Mineralogy and Petrology 225

Minnesota Space Grant Consortium Scholarship Program 127

Minority Doctoral Assistance Loan-For-Service Program 168

Mississippi Space Grant Consortium Scholarship 127

NASA Idaho Space Grant Consortium Scholarship Program 141

NASA Maryland Space Grant Consortium Undergraduate Scholarships 127

National Association of Water Companies-New Jersey Chapter Scholarship 142

National Society of Black Physicists and Lawrence Livermore National Library Undergraduate Scholarship 478

National Space Grant College and Fellowship Program 97

Native American Leadership in Education (NALE) 147

New Economy Technology and SciTech Scholarships 270

North Carolina Student Loan Program for Health, Science, and Mathematics 221

Paul and Helen Trussell Science and Technology Scholarship 95

Paul W. Ruckes Scholarship 195

Payzer Scholarship 124

Pre-Service Teacher Scholarship 129

Puget Sound Chapter Scholarship 223

Raymond Davis Scholarship 292

Ronald E. McNair Scholarship in Space and Optical Physics 478

Science, Mathematics, and Research for Transformation Defense Scholarship for Service Program 93

Sigma Xi Grants-In-Aid of Research 87

Society of Hispanic Professional Engineers Foundation 169

Society of Physics Students Leadership Scholarships 479

Society of Physics Students Outstanding Student in Research 479

Society of Physics Students Peggy Dixon Two-Year College Scholarship 480

South Dakota Space Grant Consortium Undergraduate and Graduate Student Scholarships 129

SWE California Golden Gate Section Scholarships 199

SWE Connecticut Section Jean R. Beers Scholarship 199

Teacher Education STEM Scholarship Program 96

Tech High School Alumni Association/W.O. Cheney Merit Scholarship Fund 282

Technical Minority Scholarship 171

Toshiba/NSTA ExploraVision Awards Program 198

Civic, Professional, Social, or Union Affiliation

AFL-CIO
AFL-CIO Council of Buffalo Scholarship WNY ALF Scholarship *537*
Bill Peterson Scholarship *549*
CSP Managed Funds-Laborers' International Union of North America, AFL-CIO Local No. 84 Scholarship *539*
CWA Joe Beirne Foundation Scholarship Program *545*
Martin Duffy Adult Learner Scholarship Award *549*
Minnesota AFL-CIO Scholarships *549*
PA AFL-CIO Unionism in America Essay Contest *558*
Project BEST Scholarship *560*
Ronald Lorah Memorial Scholarship *508*
Ted Bricker Scholarship *496*
Texas AFL-CIO Scholarship Program *565*
Union Plus Education Foundation Scholarship Program *568*

Airline Pilots Association
Airline Pilots Association Scholarship Program *523*

Alpha Kappa Alpha
AKA Educational Advancement Foundation Youth Partners Accessing Capital Scholarship *523*

Alpha Mu Gamma
National Alpha Mu Gamma Scholarships *325*

American Academy of Physicians Assistants
Physician Assistant Foundation Annual Scholarship *348*

American Angus Association
Angus Foundation Scholarships *553*

American Association of Law Librarians
AALL Library School Scholarships for Non-Law School Graduates *390*

American College of Musicians
American College of Musicians/National Guild of Piano Teachers $200 Scholarships *419*

American Congress on Surveying and Mapping
ACSM Fellows Scholarship *499*
ACSM Lowell H. and Dorothy Loving Undergraduate Scholarship *499*
American Association for Geodetic Surveying Joseph F. Dracup Scholarship Award *499*
Berntsen International Scholarship in Surveying *500*
Berntsen International Scholarship in Surveying Technology *500*
Cady McDonnell Memorial Scholarship *500*
National Society of Professional Surveyors Board of Governors Scholarship *500*
National Society of Professional Surveyors Scholarships *500*
Nettie Dracup Memorial Scholarship *500*
Schonstedt Scholarship in Surveying *501*

Tri-State Surveying and Photogrammetry Kris M. Kunze Memorial Scholarship *145*

American Criminal Justice Association
American Criminal Justice Association-Lambda Alpha Epsilon National Scholarship *205*

American Dental Assistants Association
Juliette A. Southard/Oral B Laboratories Scholarship *214*

American Dental Hygienist's Association
ADHA Institute General Scholarships *215*
American Dental Hygienists' Association Institute Minority Scholarship *215*
American Dental Hygienists' Association Institute Research Grant *216*
American Dental Hygienists' Association Part-Time Scholarship *216*
Colgate "Bright Smiles, Bright Futures" Minority Scholarship *216*
Crest Oral-B Laboratories Dental Hygiene Scholarship *216*
Dr. Alfred C. Fones Scholarship *216*
Dr. Harold Hillenbrand Scholarship *216*
Irene E. Newman Scholarship *217*
Margaret E. Swanson Scholarship *217*
Marsh Affinity Group Services Scholarship *217*
Sigma Phi Alpha Undergraduate Scholarship *217*
Wilma Motley California Merit Scholarship *217*

American Dietetic Association
American Dietetic Association Foundation Scholarship Program *317*

American Federation of State, County, and Municipal Employees
AFSCME: American Federation of State, County, and Municipal Employees Council # 75 Scholarship *557*
AFSCME: American Federation of State, County, and Municipal Employees Local 2067 Scholarship *557*
AFSCME/UNCF/Harvard University LWP Union Scholars Program *90*
American Federation of State, County, and Municipal Employees Scholarship Program *524*
Jerry Clark Memorial Scholarship *480*
Union Plus Credit Card Scholarship Program *524*

American Federation of Teachers
Robert G. Porter Scholars Program-American Federation of Teachers Dependents *524*

American Foreign Service Association
American Foreign Service Association (AFSA) Financial Aid Award Program *524*
American Foreign Service Association (AFSA) Merit Award Program *524*

American Institute of Aeronautics and Astronautics
AIAA Foundation Undergraduate Scholarship *93*

American Legion or Auxiliary
Albert M. Lappin Scholarship *530*
American Essay Contest Scholarship *529*
American Legion Auxiliary Department of California Junior Scholarship *524*
American Legion Auxiliary Department of Colorado Past Presidents' Parley Nurses Scholarship *438*
American Legion Auxiliary Department of Connecticut Memorial Educational Grant *525*
American Legion Auxiliary Department of Connecticut Past Presidents' Parley Memorial Education Grant *525*
American Legion Auxiliary Department of Florida Memorial Scholarship *525*
American Legion Auxiliary Department of Iowa M.V. McCrae Memorial Nurses Merit Award *438*
American Legion Auxiliary Department of Minnesota Past Presidents' Parley Health Care Scholarship *337*
American Legion Auxiliary Department of Missouri Lela Murphy Scholarship *526*
American Legion Auxiliary Department of Missouri National President's Scholarship *526*
American Legion Auxiliary Department of Missouri Past Presidents' Parley Scholarship *439*
American Legion Auxiliary Department of Nebraska Ruby Paul Campaign Fund Scholarship *526*
American Legion Auxiliary Department of North Dakota Past Presidents' Parley Nurses Scholarship *439*
American Legion Auxiliary Department of Oregon Spirit of Youth Scholarship *526*
American Legion Auxiliary Department of South Dakota College Scholarships *526*
American Legion Auxiliary Department of South Dakota Senior Scholarship *527*
American Legion Auxiliary Department of South Dakota Thelma Foster Scholarship for Senior Auxiliary Members *527*
American Legion Auxiliary Department of South Dakota Thelma Foster Scholarships for Junior Auxiliary Members *527*
American Legion Auxiliary Department of South Dakota Vocational Scholarship *527*
American Legion Auxiliary Department of Utah National President's Scholarship *527*
American Legion Auxiliary Department of Wisconsin Della Van Deuren Memorial Scholarship *527*
American Legion Auxiliary Department of Wisconsin H.S. and Angeline Lewis Scholarships *528*
American Legion Auxiliary Department of Wisconsin Merit and Memorial Scholarships *528*
American Legion Auxiliary Department of Wisconsin Past Presidents' Parley Health Career Scholarships *528*

Association for Iron and Steel Technology Pittsburgh Chapter Scholarship *275*
Association for Iron and Steel Technology Southeast Member Chapter Scholarship *275*
Ferrous Metallurgy Education Today (FeMET) *404*

Association of Energy Service Companies
Association of Energy Service Companies Scholarship Program *551*

Association of Engineering Geologists
Tilford Fund *224*

Automotive Recyclers Association
Automotive Recyclers Association Scholarship Foundation Scholarship *537*

Big Brothers/Big Sisters
Josip and Agnete Temali Scholarship (Big Brothers/Big Sisters) *549*

Boy Scouts
American Legion Department of Illinois Boy Scout/Explorer Scholarship *530*
American Legion Department of Iowa Eagle Scout of the Year Scholarship *530*
American Legion Department of Tennessee Eagle Scout of the Year *533*
American Legion Eagle Scout of the Year *533*
Eagle Scout of the Year Scholarship *532*
Eastern Orthodox Committee on Scouting Scholarships *540*
Lawrence "Larry" Frazier Memorial Scholarship *127*
Marine Corps Scholarship Foundation *570*
Royden M. Bodley Scholarship *311*

Boys or Girls Club
Boys and Girls Clubs of America National Youth of the Year Award *537*
Boys and Girls Clubs of Chicago Scholarships *537*

California Teachers Association
California Teachers Association Scholarship for Dependent Children *538*
California Teachers Association Scholarship for Members *538*
L. Gordon Bittle Memorial Scholarship *232*
Martin Luther King, Jr. Memorial Scholarship *232*

Canadian Nurses Foundation
Canadian Nurses Foundation Scholarships *443*

Canadian Society for Chemical Engineering
CSChE Chemical Engineering Local Section Scholarships *165*

Canadian Society for Chemistry
Alfred Bader Scholarship *139*

Canadian Society for Medical Laboratory Science
Canadian Society of Laboratory Technologists Student Scholarship Program *342*
E.V. Booth Scholarship Award *334*

Children of the Confederacy
Charlotte M. F. Bentley/New York Chapter 103 Scholarship *569*
Elizabeth and Wallace Kingsbury Scholarship *569*
Helen James Brewer Scholarship *354*
Winnie Davis-Children of the Confederacy Scholarship *569*

Civil Air Patrol
Civil Air Patrol Academic Scholarships *539*
Major General Lucas V. Beau Flight Scholarships Sponsored by the Order of Daedalians *124*

Columbian Squires
Fourth Degree Pro Deo and Pro Patria Scholarships *547*

Community Banker Association of Illinois
Community Banker Association of Illinois Children of Community Banking Scholarship William C. Harris Memorial Scholarship *539*

Costume Society of America
Adele Filene Travel Award *105*
Stella Blum Research Grant *105*

Daughters of Penelope/Maids of Athena/ Order of Ahepa
Alexandra Apostolides Sonenfeld Scholarship *539*
Joanne V. Hologgitas, PhD Scholarship *539*
Kottis Family Scholarship *540*
Mary M. Verges Scholarship *540*
Past Grand Presidents Scholarship *540*

Daughters of the American Revolution
National Society Daughters of the American Revolution Lillian and Arthur Dunn Scholarship *553*
National Society Daughters of the American Revolution Madeline Pickett (Halbert) Cogswell Nursing Scholarship *455*

Democratic Party
Pennsylvania Federation of Democratic Women Inc. Annual Scholarship Awards *558*

Dermatology Nurses' Association
Dermik Laboratories Career Mobility Scholarship *444*
Galderma Laboratories Career Mobility Scholarship *444*

Distribution Ed Club or Future Business Leaders of America
Harry A. Applegate Scholarship *149*
Nebraska DECA Leadership Scholarship *154*

Eastern Surfing Association
ESA Marsh Scholarship Program *541*

Elks Club
Elks Emergency Educational Grants *541*
Elks National Foundation Legacy Awards *541*

Experimental Aircraft Association
Hansen Scholarship *124*
Payzer Scholarship *124*

Explorer Program/Learning for Life
AFL-CIO Skilled Trades Exploring Scholarships *506*
Captain James J. Regan Scholarship *389*
DEA Drug Abuse Prevention Service Awards *390*
Federal Criminal Investigators Service Award *390*
International Associations of Fire Chiefs Foundation Scholarship *316*
Sheryl A. Horak Memorial Scholarship *390*

Family, Career and Community Leaders of America
C.J. Davidson Scholarship for FCCLA *355*
FCCLA Houston Livestock Show and Rodeo Scholarship *149*
FCCLA Regional Scholarships *149*

FCCLA Texas Farm Bureau Scholarship *149*
Oklahoma Alumni & Associates of FHA, HERO and FCCLA Inc. Scholarship *556*

Federation of American Consumers and Travelers
Federation of American Consumers and Travelers Graduating High School Senior Scholarship *541*
Federation of American Consumers and Travelers Trade/Technical School Scholarship *541*

First Catholic Slovak Ladies Association
First Catholic Slovak Ladies Association College Scholarship *538*
First Catholic Slovak Ladies Association High School Scholarships *541*
Theresa Sajan Scholarship for Graduate Students *538*

Fleet Reserve Association/Auxiliary
Allie Mae Oden Memorial Scholarship *548*
Colonel Hazel Elizabeth Benn U.S.M.C. Scholarship *542*
Ladies Auxiliary of the Fleet Reserve Association-National President's Scholarship *548*
Ladies Auxiliary of the Fleet Reserve Association Scholarship *548*
Sam Rose Memorial Scholarship *548*
Stanley A. Doran Memorial Scholarship *542*

Florida Environmental Health Association
Florida Environmental Health Association Educational Scholarship Awards *304*

Freemasons
Edward Leon Duhamel Freemasons Scholarship *562*
Pennsylvania Masonic Youth Foundation Educational Endowment Fund Scholarships *558*
P.G. Richardson Masonic Memorial Scholarship *549*

Future Farmers of America
National FFA Collegiate Scholarship Program *552*

Gamma Theta Upsilon
Buzzard-Maxfield-Richason and Rechlin Scholarship *330*

Geological Society of America
Northeastern Section Undergraduate Student Research Grants *542*

Girl Scouts
American Legion Auxiliary Department of Maryland Girl Scout Achievement Award *525*
American Legion Auxiliary Girl Scout Achievement Award *529*
Eastern Orthodox Committee on Scouting Scholarships *540*
Emily Chaison Gold Award Scholarship *542*
Lawrence "Larry" Frazier Memorial Scholarship *127*

Glass, Molders, Pottery, Plastics and Allied Workers International Union
GMP Memorial Scholarship Program *542*

Golden Key National Honor Society
GEICO Life Scholarship *543*
Golden Key Study Abroad Scholarships *543*

Golden State Bonsai Federation
Horticulture Scholarships *358*

National Bicycle League
Bob Warnicke Memorial Scholarship Program   *552*

National Black Nurses' Association
Dr. Hilda Richards Scholarship   *453*
Dr. Lauranne Sams Scholarship   *453*
Kaiser Permanente School of Anesthesia Scholarship   *454*
Martha R. Dudley LVN/LPN Scholarship   *454*
Mayo Foundations Scholarship   *454*
NBNA Board of Directors Scholarship   *454*
Nursing Spectrum Scholarship   *454*

National Board of Boiler and Pressure Vessel Inspectors
National Board Technical Scholarship   *167*

National Federation of Press Women
Frank Sarli Memorial Scholarship   *392*

National Foster Parent Association
National Foster Parent Association Youth Scholarship   *552*

National Fraternal Society of the Deaf
National Fraternal Society of the Deaf Scholarships   *552*

National Honor Society
National Honor Society Scholarships   *552*

National Junior Red Angus Association
4 RAAA/Junior Red Angus Scholarship   *561*
Dee Sonstegard Memorial Scholarship   *561*
Farm and Ranch Connection Scholarship   *561*
Leonard A. Lorenzen Memorial Scholarship   *561*

National Military Intelligence Association
National Military Intelligence Association Scholarship   *419*

National Rifle Association
Jeanne E. Bray Memorial Scholarship Program   *553*

National Society of Accountants
Stanley H. Stearman Scholarship   *67*

National Society of Collegiate Scholars
NSCS Exemplary Scholar Award   *553*
NSCS Integrity Scholarship   *554*
NSCS Merit Award   *554*
NSCS Scholar Abroad Scholarship   *554*

National Society of High School Scholars
Abercrombie & Fitch Global Diversity & Leadership Scholar Awards   *554*
Claes Nobel Academic Scholarships for NSHSS Members   *554*
Griffith College Scholars Scholarships for NSHSS Members   *554*
National Scholar Awards for NSHSS Members   *554*

National Society of Professional Engineers
Paul H. Robbins Honorary Scholarship   *168*

National Union of Public and General Employees
Scholarship for Aboriginal Canadians   *555*
Scholarship for Visible Minorities   *555*
Terry Fox Memorial Scholarship   *555*
Tommy Douglas Scholarship   *555*

Native American Journalists Association
Native American Journalists Association Scholarships   *381*

Naval Sea Cadet Corps
Harry and Rose Howell Scholarship   *570*

Kingsley Foundation Awards   *570*
Naval Sea Cadet Corps Board of Directors Scholarship   *571*
Naval Sea Cadet Corps Scholarship Program   *571*
Robert and Helen Hutton Scholarship   *571*
Stockholm Scholarship Program   *571*

New England Water Works Association
Elson T. Killam Memorial Scholarship   *179*
Francis X. Crowley Scholarship   *155*
Joseph Murphy Scholarship   *179*

New Jersey Association of Realtors
New Jersey Association of Realtors Educational Foundation Scholarship Program   *487*

Northeastern Loggers Association
Northeastern Loggers' Association Scholarships   *556*

North East Roofing Contractors Association
North East Roofing Educational Foundation Scholarship   *556*

Northwest Automatic Vending Association
Northwest Automatic Vending Association Scholarship   *557*

Office and Professional Employees International Union
Office and Professional Employees International Union Howard Coughlin memorial scholarship fund   *556*

Ohio Civil Service Employee Association
Les Best Scholarship   *556*

Ohio Farmers Union
Joseph Fitcher Scholarship Contest   *86*
Virgil Thompson Memorial Scholarship Contest   *80*

Order of Omega
Founders Scholarship   *553*

Oregon Education Association
James Carlson Memorial Scholarship   *245*

Oregon State Fiscal Association
Oregon State Fiscal Association Scholarship   *557*

Other Student Academic Clubs
American Society of Agricultural and Biological Engineers Foundation Scholarship   *82*
ASABE Foundation Scholarship   *277*
Berna Lou Cartwright Scholarship   *412*
Mary Morrow-Edna Richards Scholarship   *243*
Phi Alpha Theta World History Association Paper Prize   *354*
Sylvia W. Farny Scholarship   *413*
William J. Adams, Jr. and Marijane E. Adams Scholarship   *82*

Parent-Teacher Association/Organization
Continuing Education-PTA Volunteers Scholarship   *538*
Frieda L. Koontz Scholarship   *250*
General (unnamed) Scholarships   *250*
S. John Davis Scholarship   *250*

Phi Alpha Theta
Phi Alpha Theta Paper Prizes   *353*
Phi Alpha Theta Undergraduate Student Scholarship   *353*
Phi Alpha Theta/Western Front Association Paper Prize   *354*
Phi Alpha Theta World History Association Paper Prize   *354*

Phi Kappa Phi
Literacy Grant Competition   *544*

Philipino-American Association
PAMAS Restricted Scholarship Award   *558*

Phi Sigma Kappa
Wenderoth Undergraduate Scholarship   *559*
Zeta Scholarship   *559*

Pony of the Americas Club
Pony of the Americas Scholarship   *559*

Professional Horsemen Association
Guy Stoops Memorial Professional Horsemen's Family Scholarship   *535*
Professional Horsemen's Scholarship Fund   *560*

Recording for the Blind and Dyslexic
Marion Huber Learning Through Listening Awards   *560*
Mary P. Oenslager Scholastic Achievement Awards   *560*

Reserve Officers Association
Henry J. Reilly Memorial Scholarship-High School Seniors and First Year Freshmen   *561*
Henry J. Reilly Memorial Undergraduate Scholarship Program for College Attendees   *561*

Retail, Wholesale and Department Store Union
Alvin E. Heaps Memorial Scholarship   *562*

Screen Actors' Guild
John L. Dales Scholarship Program   *562*
Screen Actors Guild Foundation/John L. Dales Scholarship Fund (Standard)   *562*

Service Employees International Union
Charles Hardy Memorial Scholarship Awards   *562*
SEIU Jesse Jackson Scholarship Program   *563*
SEIU John Geagan Scholarship   *563*
SEIU Moe Foner Scholarship Program for Visual and Performing Arts   *115*
SEIU Nora Piore Scholarship Program   *563*
SEIU Scholarship Program   *563*

Sigma Alpha Iota
Sigma Alpha Iota Jazz Performance Awards   *427*
Sigma Alpha Iota Jazz Studies Scholarship   *427*
Sigma Alpha Iota Music Business/Technology Scholarship   *427*
Sigma Alpha Iota Musicians with Special Needs Scholarship   *246*
Sigma Alpha Iota Music Therapy Scholarship   *427*
Sigma Alpha Iota Summer Music Scholarships in the U.S. or Abroad   *427*
Sigma Alpha Iota Undergraduate Performance Scholarships   *427*
Sigma Alpha Iota Undergraduate Scholarships   *247*

Sigma Alpha Mu Foundation
Undergraduate Achievement Awards   *563*
Young Scholars Program   *563*

Sigma Chi Fraternity
General Scholarship Grants   *563*
Order of the Scroll Award   *564*

Slovenian Women's Union of America
Continuing Education Award   *564*
Slovenian Women's Union of America Scholarship Foundation   *564*

Society for Human Resource Management
SHRM Foundation Student Scholarships *364*

Society of Architectural Historians
Richland/Lexington SCSEA Scholarship *565*

Society of Automotive Engineers
Detroit Section SAE Technical Scholarship *271*
Ralph K. Hillquist Honorary SAE
  Scholarship *271*
SAE Baltimore Section Bill Brubaker
  Scholarship *293*
SAE Long Term Member Sponsored
  Scholarship *293*

Society of Motion Picture and Television Engineers
Lou Wolf Memorial Scholarship *259*
Student Paper Award *272*

Society of Pediatric Nurses
Society of Pediatric Nurses Educational
  Scholarship *173*

Society of Physics Students
Society of Physics Students Leadership
  Scholarships *479*
Society of Physics Students Outstanding Student in
  Research *479*
Society of Physics Students Peggy Dixon Two-
  Year College Scholarship *480*

Society of Women Engineers
SWE St. Louis Scholarship *300*

Soil and Water Conservation Society
Donald A. Williams Scholarship Soil Conservation
  Scholarship *226*
Walt Bartram Memorial Education Award *298*

SOKOL, USA
Slovak Gymnastic Union SOKOL, USA/Milan
  Getting Scholarship *564*

South Carolina State Employees Association
Anne A. Agnew Scholarship *564*

Springfield Newspaper 25-Year Club
Horace Hill Scholarship *539*

Supreme Council of Sociedade Do Espirito Santo
Henry Regnery Endowed Scholarship *399*
Sigma Tau Delta Junior Scholarship *399*
Sigma Tau Delta Scholarship *400*
Sigma Tau Delta Senior Scholarship *400*
Sigma Tau Delta Study Abroad Scholarship *400*
Supreme Council of Sociedade Do Espirito Santo
  Scholarship Program *565*

Tau Beta Pi Association
Tau Beta Pi Scholarship Program *301*

Tau Kappa Epsilon
All-TKE Academic Team Recognition and John A.
  Courson Top Scholar Award *566*
Bruce B. Melchert Scholarship *482*
Canadian TKE Scholarship *566*
Carrol C. Hall Memorial Scholarship *97*
Charles Walgreen Jr. Scholarship *566*
Donald A. and John R. Fisher Memorial
  Scholarship *566*
Dwayne R. Woerpel Memorial Leadership
  Award *566*
Elmer and Doris Schmitz Sr. Memorial
  Scholarship *567*
Eugene C. Beach Memorial Scholarship *567*
Francis J. Flynn Memorial Scholarship *249*
George W. Woolery Memorial Scholarship *192*

Harry J. Donnelly Memorial Scholarship *71*
J. Russel Salsbury Memorial Scholarship *567*
Michael J. Morin Memorial Scholarship *567*
Miles Gray Memorial Scholarship *567*
Ronald Reagan Leadership Award *567*
Timothy L. Taschwer Scholarship *144*
T.J. Schmitz Scholarship *568*
Wallace McCauley Memorial Scholarship *568*
W. Allan Herzog Scholarship *71*
William V. Muse Scholarship *568*
William Wilson Memorial Scholarship *568*

Teamsters
Seminole Tribe of Florida Billy L. Cypress
  Scholarship Program *562*
Teamsters Clyde C. Crosby/Joseph M. Edgar
  Memorial Scholarship *557*
Teamsters Council 37 Federal Credit Union
  Scholarship *558*
Teamsters Local 305 Scholarship *558*

Tennessee Education Association
TEA Don Sahli-Kathy Woodall Sons and
  Daughters Scholarship *565*
TEA Don Sahli-Kathy Woodall Undergraduate
  Scholarship *248*

Texas Association of Broadcasters
Belo Texas Broadcast Education Foundation
  Scholarship *191*
Bonner McLane Texas Broadcast Education
  Foundation Scholarship *191*
Student Texas Broadcast Education Foundation
  Scholarship *191*
Tom Reiff Texas Broadcast Education Foundation
  Scholarship *191*
Undergraduate Texas Broadcast Education
  Foundation Scholarship *191*
Vann Kennedy Texas Broadcast Education
  Foundation Scholarship *192*

Texas Women in Law Enforcement
Vanessa Rudloff Scholarship Program *566*

Transportation Club International
Alice Glaisyer Warfield Memorial
  Scholarship *510*
Denny Lydic Scholarship *511*
Texas Transportation Scholarship *511*
Transportation Clubs International Charlotte
  Woods Scholarship *511*
Transportation Clubs International Ginger and
  Fred Deines Canada Scholarship *511*
Transportation Clubs International Ginger and
  Fred Deines Mexico Scholarship *511*

United Daughters of the Confederacy
Barbara Jackson Sichel Memorial
  Scholarship *569*
Charlotte M. F. Bentley/New York Chapter 103
  Scholarship *569*
Gertrude Botts-Saucier Scholarship *569*
Helen James Brewer Scholarship *354*
Lola B. Curry Scholarship *569*
Phoebe Pember Memorial Scholarship *460*
United Daughters of the Confederacy
  Undergraduate Scholarships *569*
Walter Reed Smith Scholarship *157*

United Food and Commercial Workers
James A. Suffridge United Food and Commercial
  Workers Scholarship Program *570*

USA Water Ski
American Water Ski Educational Foundation
  Scholarship *536*

Utility Workers Union of America
Utility Workers Union of America Scholarship
  Awards Program *571*

Vermont-NEA
Vermont-NEA/Maida F. Townsend
  Scholarship *249*

Veterans of Foreign Wars or Auxiliary
Frances L. Booth Medical Scholarship sponsored
  by LAVFW Department of Maine *344*
Junior Girls Scholarship Program *549*
United States Submarine Veterans Inc. National
  Scholarship Program *571*

VietNow
VietNow National Scholarship *572*

Western Fraternal Life Association
Western Fraternal Life Association National
  Scholarship *572*

Wisconsin Association for Food Protection
WAFP Memorial Scholarship *572*

Women in Aviation, International
Airbus Leadership Grant *134*
Boeing Company Career Enhancement
  Scholarship *134*
Dassault Falcon Jet Corporation Scholarship *135*
Delta Air Lines Aircraft Maintenance Technology
  Scholarship *135*
Delta Air Lines Engineering Scholarship *135*
Delta Air Lines Maintenance Management/
  Aviation Business Management
  Scholarship *135*
GAT Wings to the Future Management
  Scholarship *135*
Keep Flying Scholarship *135*
Women in Aviation, International Achievement
  Awards *136*
Women in Aviation, International Management
  Scholarships *136*
Women in Corporate Aviation Career
  Scholarships *136*
Women Military Aviators Inc. Dream of Flight
  Scholarship *136*
Wright Chapter, Women in Aviation, International,
  Elisha Hall Memorial Scholarship *136*

Women in Logistics
Women in Logistics Scholarship *159*

Women's International Network of Utility Professionals
WiNUP Membership Scholarship *572*

Woodmen of the World
Woodmen of the World and/or Assured Life
  Association Endowment Scholarship
  Program *572*

Wyoming Farm Bureau
King-Livingston Scholarship *572*
Wyoming Farm Bureau Continuing Education
  Scholarships *573*
Wyoming Farm Bureau Federation
  Scholarships *573*

Young American Bowling Alliance
Chuck Hall Star of Tomorrow Scholarship *523*
Gift for Life Scholarship *573*
Pepsi-Cola Youth Bowling Championships *573*
Professional Bowlers Association Billy Welu
  Memorial Scholarship *559*

Zeta Phi Beta
Lullelia W. Harrison Scholarship in
  Counseling *173*

Corporate Affiliation

Employment/Volunteer Experience

Impairment

Military Service

Air Force

AFROTC HBCU Scholarship Program *616*
AFROTC HSI Scholarship Program *616*
Air Force ROTC College Scholarship *616*
Air Force Sergeants Association
  Scholarship *616*
Airmen Memorial Foundation Scholarship *616*
Armed Forces Communications and Electronics
  Association ROTC Scholarship
  Program *122*
Chief Master Sergeants of the Air Force
  Scholarship Program *616*
Daughters of the Cincinnati Scholarship *617*
Foundation of the 1st Cavalry Division
  Association (Ia Drang) Scholarship *617*
General Henry H. Arnold Education Grant
  Program *615*
Montgomery GI Bill (Selected Reserve) *617*
Resident Tuition for Active Duty Military
  Personnel *617*
Veterans Education (VetEd) Reimbursement
  Grant *617*

Air Force National Guard

AFROTC HBCU Scholarship Program *616*
AFROTC HSI Scholarship Program *616*
Air Force Sergeants Association
  Scholarship *616*
Airmen Memorial Foundation Scholarship *616*
Alabama National Guard Educational Assistance
  Program *618*
Chief Master Sergeants of the Air Force
  Scholarship Program *616*
CSM Vincent Baldassari Memorial Scholarship
  Program *619*
Education Foundation, Inc. National Guard
  Association of Colorado Scholarships *619*
General Henry H. Arnold Education Grant
  Program *615*
Illinois National Guard Grant Program *619*
Indiana National Guard Supplemental Grant *621*
Iowa National Guard Education Assistance
  Program *620*
JROTC Scholarship *618*
Leadership, Excellence and Dedicated Service
  Scholarship *591*
Louisiana National Guard State Tuition
  Exemption Program *620*
Montgomery GI Bill (Selected Reserve) *617*
National Guard Scholarship Extension
  Program *620*
National Guard Tuition Supplement
  Program *620*
North Carolina National Guard Tuition Assistance
  Program *621*
Ohio National Guard Scholarship Program *621*
Postsecondary Education Gratuity Program *621*
Reserve Education Assistance Program *619*
State Tuition Assistance *618*
Texas National Guard Tuition Assistance
  Program *621*
Tuition and Fee Remission for Children and
  Spouses of National Guard Members *620*
USAA Scholarship *619*

Army

American Legion Auxiliary Department of
  California Junior Scholarship *524*
American Legion Auxiliary Department of
  California Past Presidents' Parley Nursing
  Scholarships *438*

American Legion Auxiliary Department of
  Kentucky Laura Blackburn Memorial
  Scholarship *622*
Armed Forces Communications and Electronics
  Association ROTC Scholarship
  Program *122*
Army Officers Wives Club of the Greater
  Washington Area Scholarship *622*
Army ROTC Green to Gold Scholarship Program
  for Two-Year, Three-Year and Four-Year
  Scholarships, Active Duty Enlisted
  Personnel *622*
Army (ROTC) Reserve Officers Training Corps
  Two-, Three-, Four-Year Campus-Based
  Scholarships *602*
Daughters of the Cincinnati Scholarship *617*
Foundation of the 1st Cavalry Division
  Association (Ia Drang) Scholarship *617*
Lieutenant General Clarence R. Huebner
  Scholarship Program *622*
Luterman Scholarship *532*
Montgomery GI Bill (Selected Reserve) *617*
Resident Tuition for Active Duty Military
  Personnel *617*
Society of Daughters of the United States Army
  Scholarships *623*
Stutz Scholarship *533*
U.S. Army ROTC Four-Year College
  Scholarship *623*
U.S. Army ROTC Four-Year Historically Black
  College/University Scholarship *602*
U.S. Army ROTC Four-Year Nursing
  Scholarship *444*
U.S. Army ROTC Military Junior College (MJC)
  Scholarship *418*
Veterans Education (VetEd) Reimbursement
  Grant *617*
Women's Army Corps Veterans' Association
  Scholarship *623*

Army National Guard

Alabama National Guard Educational Assistance
  Program *618*
Army (ROTC) Reserve Officers Training Corps
  Two-, Three-, Four-Year Campus-Based
  Scholarships *602*
Connecticut Army National Guard 100% Tuition
  Waiver *624*
CSM Vincent Baldassari Memorial Scholarship
  Program *619*
Education Foundation, Inc. National Guard
  Association of Colorado Scholarships *619*
Illinois National Guard Grant Program *619*
Indiana National Guard Supplemental Grant *621*
Iowa National Guard Education Assistance
  Program *620*
JROTC Scholarship *618*
Leadership, Excellence and Dedicated Service
  Scholarship *591*
Louisiana National Guard State Tuition
  Exemption Program *620*
Montgomery GI Bill (Selected Reserve) *617*
National Guard Scholarship Extension
  Program *620*
National Guard Tuition Supplement
  Program *620*
North Carolina National Guard Tuition Assistance
  Program *621*
Ohio National Guard Scholarship Program *621*
Postsecondary Education Gratuity Program *621*

Reserve Education Assistance Program *619*
Society of Daughters of the United States Army
  Scholarships *623*
State Tuition Assistance *618*
Texas National Guard Tuition Assistance
  Program *621*
Tuition and Fee Remission for Children and
  Spouses of National Guard Members *620*
USAA Scholarship *619*
U.S. Army ROTC Four-Year College
  Scholarship *623*
U.S. Army ROTC Four-Year Historically Black
  College/University Scholarship *602*
U.S. Army ROTC Four-Year Nursing
  Scholarship *444*
U.S. Army ROTC Guaranteed Reserve Forces
  Duty (GRFD), (ARNG/USAR) and Dedicated
  ARNG Scholarships *602*
U.S. Army ROTC Military Junior College (MJC)
  Scholarship *418*

Coast Guard

Allie Mae Oden Memorial Scholarship *548*
Daughters of the Cincinnati Scholarship *617*
Fleet Reserve Association Education Foundation
  Scholarships *625*
Ladies Auxiliary of the Fleet Reserve Association-
  National President's Scholarship *548*
Ladies Auxiliary of the Fleet Reserve Association
  Scholarship *548*
Montgomery GI Bill (Selected Reserve) *617*
Sam Rose Memorial Scholarship *548*
Stanley A. Doran Memorial Scholarship *542*
Tailhook Educational Foundation
  Scholarship *626*
Veterans Education (VetEd) Reimbursement
  Grant *617*

General

37th Division Veterans Association
  Scholarship *626*
Alabama G.I. Dependents Scholarship
  Program *626*
Albert M. Lappin Scholarship *530*
American Legion Auxiliary Department of
  Alabama Scholarship Program *626*
American Legion Auxiliary Department of
  Colorado Department President's Scholarship
  for Junior Member *627*
American Legion Auxiliary Department of
  Colorado Past Presidents' Parley Nurses
  Scholarship *438*
American Legion Auxiliary Department of
  Connecticut Memorial Educational
  Grant *525*
American Legion Auxiliary Department of
  Connecticut Past Presidents' Parley Memorial
  Education Grant *525*
American Legion Auxiliary Department of Florida
  Department Scholarships *627*
American Legion Auxiliary Department of Florida
  Memorial Scholarship *525*
American Legion Auxiliary Department of Florida
  National Presidents' Scholarship *627*
American Legion Auxiliary Department of Idaho
  Nursing Scholarship *438*
American Legion Auxiliary Department of
  Indiana Edna M. Burcus/Hoosier Schoolhouse
  Memorial Scholarship *627*
American Legion Auxiliary Department of Iowa
  Children of Veterans Merit Award *628*

Nationality or Ethnic Heritage

African

CANFIT Nutrition, Physical Education and Culinary Arts Scholarship *209*

Racial Ethnic Educational Scholarship *681*

American Indian/Alaska Native

Accenture American Indian Scholarship *654*

Actuarial Diversity Scholarship *370*

Adolph Van Pelt Special Fund for Indian Scholarships *656*

Adult Vocational Training Competitive Scholarship *660*

AFSCME/UNCF Union Scholars Program *89*

Agnes Jones Jackson Scholarship *550*

AIA/AAF Minority/Disadvantaged Scholarship *99*

AIAC Scholarship *650*

AIET Minorities and Women Educational Scholarship *486*

AIFS DiversityAbroad.com Scholarship *654*

Al-Ben Scholarship for Academic Incentive *166*

Al-Ben Scholarship for Professional Merit *166*

Al-Ben Scholarship for Scholastic Achievement *166*

Alberta Heritage Scholarship Fund Aboriginal Health Careers Bursary *137*

Allogan Slagle Memorial Scholarship *656*

Alumni Student Assistance Program *657*

AMA Foundation Minority Scholars Award *338*

Amelia Kemp Scholarship *696*

American Baptist Financial Aid Program Native American Grants *653*

American Chemical Society Scholars Program *160*

American Dental Association Foundation Underrepresented Minority Dental Student Scholarship Program *215*

American Dental Hygienists' Association Institute Minority Scholarship *215*

American Geological Institute Minority Scholarship *222*

American Indian Education Foundation Scholarship *654*

American Indian Endowed Scholarship *695*

American Indian Nurse Scholarship Awards *335*

American Meteorological Society/Industry Minority Scholarships *366*

American Philological Association/ Archaeological Institute of America Minority Scholarship *98*

American Physical Society Corporate-Sponsored Scholarship for Minority Undergraduate Students Who Major in Physics *477*

American Physical Society Scholarship for Minority Undergraduate Physics Majors *475*

APEX Scholarship *655*

Arizona Professional Chapter of AISES Scholarship *279*

A.T. Anderson Memorial Scholarship Program *93*

AWG Minority Scholarship *223*

BHP Billiton University Scholarships *681*

BIA Higher Education Grant *665*

Blackfeet Nation Higher Education Grant *656*

Breakthrough to Nursing Scholarships for Racial/ Ethnic Minorities *446*

Bureau of Indian Education Grant Program *656*

Burlington Northern Santa Fe Foundation Scholarship *93*

CANFIT Nutrition, Physical Education and Culinary Arts Scholarship *209*

Cap Lathrop Scholarship Program *147*

Career Upgrade Grants *658*

Carl H. Marrs Scholarship Fund *58*

Carole Simpson Scholarship *189*

Cherokee Nation Higher Education Scholarship *657*

Chief Manuelito Scholarship Program *675*

Chips Quinn Scholars Program *377*

CIRI Foundation Achievement Annual Scholarships *658*

CIRI Foundation Excellence Annual Scholarships *658*

CIRI Foundation General Semester Scholarship *658*

CIRI Foundation Special Excellence Scholarship *659*

CIRI Foundation Susie Qimmiqsak Bevins Endowment Scholarship Fund *110*

Citizen Potawatomi Nation Tribal Scholarship *660*

Colgate "Bright Smiles, Bright Futures" Minority Scholarship *216*

College Student Assistance Program *657*

Continental Society, Daughters of Indian Wars Scholarship *235*

Cultural Fellowship Grants *659*

David Risling Emergency Aid Scholarship *656*

Deloras Jones RN Underrepresented Groups in Nursing Scholarship *450*

Diavik Diamonds Inc. Scholarships for College Students *682*

Dick French Memorial Scholarship Program *667*

Displaced Homemaker Scholarship *656*

Earl G. Graves NAACP Scholarship *154*

Ed Bradley Scholarship *384*

EDSA Minority Scholarship *388*

Elizabeth and Sherman Asche Memorial Scholarship Fund *83*

Emilie Hesemeyer Memorial Scholarship *232*

Environmental Education Scholarship Program (EESP) *309*

Epsilon Sigma Alpha Foundation Scholarships *662*

Ethnic Minority Scholarship *663*

Eula Petite Memorial Competitive Scholarship *233*

Fisher Broadcasting Inc. Scholarship for Minorities *150*

Florida Society of Newspaper Editors Minority Scholarship Program *185*

Garth Reeves, Jr. Memorial Scholarships *190*

Gates Millennium Scholars Program *654, 665*

GE/LULAC Scholarship *153*

General Fellowship Grants *659*

Gil Purcell Memorial Journalism Scholarship for Native Canadians *376*

Glenn Godfrey Memorial Scholarship *668*

GM/LULAC Scholarship *288*

HANA Scholarship *663*

Hattie Tedrow Memorial Fund Scholarship *633*

HBCUConnect.com Minority Scholarship Program *663*

Health Professions Preparatory Scholarship Program *335*

Higher Education Scholarship Program *675*

Higher Education Supplemental Scholarship Isleta Pueblo Higher Education Department *560*

Hopi Education Award *666*

Howard Rock Foundation Scholarship Program *659*

Hubertus W.V. Wellems Scholarship for Male Students *167*

Hyatt Hotels Fund for Minority Lodging Management *208*

Idaho Minority and "At Risk" Student Scholarship *605*

Indian Health Service Health Professions Pre-graduate Scholarships *219*

Indian Health Service Health Professions Scholarship Program *335*

International Order of the King's Daughters and Sons North American Indian Scholarship *666*

Jackie Robinson Scholarship *590*

Jim Bourque Scholarship *230*

Judith McManus Price Scholarship *521*

Kansas Ethnic Minority Scholarship *667*

Ken Inouye Scholarship *385*

Ken Kashiwahara Scholarship *189*

Kentucky Minority Educator Recruitment and Retention (KMERR) Scholarship *239*

Koniag Education Career Development Grant *668*

Koniag Education Foundation Academic/ Graduate Scholarship *668*

Koniag Education Foundation College/University Basic Scholarship *668*

Lagrant Foundation Scholarship for Graduates *152*

Lagrant Foundation Scholarship for Undergraduates *153*

Leonard M. Perryman Communications Scholarship for Ethnic Minority Students *192*

LinTV Minority Scholarship *378*

Mae Lassley Osage Scholarship *678*

Martin Luther King, Jr. Memorial Scholarship *232*

Master's Scholarship Program *169*

Math, Engineering, Science, Business, Education, Computers Scholarships *147*

Maureen L. and Howard N. Blitman, PE Scholarship to Promote Diversity in Engineering *167*

Menominee Indian Tribe Adult Vocational Training Program *670*

Menominee Indian Tribe of Wisconsin Higher Education Grants *671*

Minnesota Indian Scholarship *671*

Minorities in Government Finance Scholarship *63*

Minority Affairs Committee Award for Outstanding Scholastic Achievement *161*

Minority Doctoral Assistance Loan-For-Service Program *168*

Minority Educator Recruitment and Retention Scholarship *240*

Minority Nurse Magazine Scholarship Program *452*

Minority Scholarship Award for Academic Excellence in Physical Therapy *338*

Minority Scholarship Award for Academic Excellence-Physical Therapist Assistant *339*

Minority Scholarship Awards for College Students *162*

Minority Scholarship Awards for Incoming College Freshmen *162*

Religious Affiliation

Residence

RESIDENCE

Location of Study

LOCATION OF STUDY

Talent/Interest Area

SPECIAL ADVERTISING SECTION

Saint Louis University

St. Mary's University

Thomas Jefferson University School of Population Health

University of Medicine & Dentistry of New Jersey

The Winston Preparatory Schools

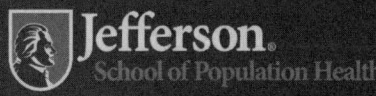

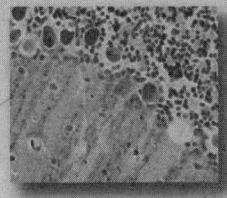
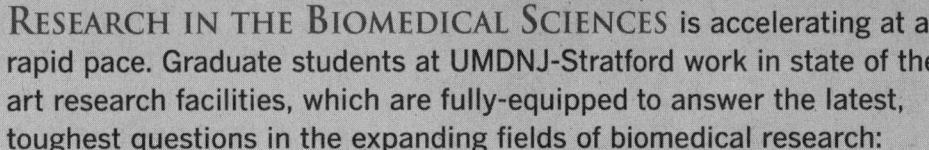
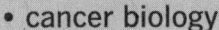

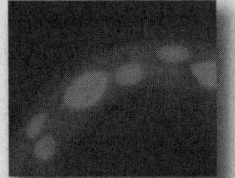

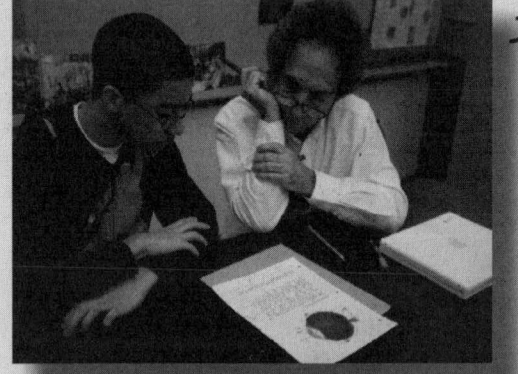

NOTES

NOTES

NOTES

NOTES

NOTES

NOTES

NOTES